Holidays, Festivals, and Celebrations of the World Dictionary

Detailing More Than 3,300 Observances from All 50 States and More Than 100 Nations

5th Edition

A Compendious Reference Guide to Popular, Ethnic, Religious, National, and Ancient Holidays, Festivals, Celebrations, Commemorations, Holy Days, Feasts, and Fasts, Including Contact Information and Websites. Supplemented by Special Sections on Words Relating to Time, Calendar Systems, Phases of the Moon, the World's Major Living Religions, Facts about the U.S. States and Territories, Legal Holidays by State, Facts about the U.S. Presidents, Facts about Countries around the World, Legal Holidays by Country, Tourism Information Sources; and by an Annotated Bibliography and Chronological, Historic, Folkloric, Calendar, Promotional, Sports, and Subject Indexes

OMNIGRAPHICS

155 W. Congress, Suite 200
Detroit, MI 48226

Omnigraphics, Inc.

Editorial Services provided by Omnigraphics, Inc.,
a division of Relevant Information, Inc.

Pearline Jaikumar, *Managing Editor*

ISBN 978-07808-1362-5
E-ISBN 978-0-7808-1363-2

Library of Congress Cataloging-in-Publication Data

Holidays, festivals & celebrations of the world dictionary : detailing more than 3,300 observances from all 50 states and more than 100 nations. -- 5th edition.

    pages cm.

  "A Compendious Reference Guide to Popular, Ethnic, Religious, National,and Ancient Holidays, Festivals, Celebrations, Commemorations, Holy Days, Feasts, and Fasts, Including Contact Information and Web Sites. Supplemented by Special Sections on Words Relating to Time, Calendar Systems, Phases of the Moon, the World's Major Living Religions, Facts about the U.S. States and Territories, Legal Holidays by State, Presidents of the United States, Facts about Countries around the World, Legal Holidays by Country, Tourism Information Sources; and by an Annotated Bibliography and Chronological, Historic, Ancient, Folkloric, Calendar, Promotional, Sports, and Subject Indexes."

  Includes bibliographical references and indexes.

    ISBN 978-0-7808-1362-5 (hardcover : alk. paper) -- ISBN 978-0-7808-1363-2 (ebook)

  1. Holidays--Dictionaries. 2. Festivals--Dictionaries. I. Omnigraphics,Inc., issuing body. II. Title: Holidays, festivals, and celebrations of the world dictionary.

GT3925.H64 2015

394.2603--dc23   2015000102

Table of Contents

Preface v

Holidays, Festivals, and Celebrations of the World Dictionary 1

Appendices 849

   1. Glossary of Words Relating to Time 851

   2. Calendars throughout History: An Overview of Calendar Systems around the World . . 855

   3. Comparative Table of Calendar Systems 869

   4. Phases of the Moon from 2015 to 2030 Given in Eastern Standard Time 871

   5. Overview of the World's Major Religions 881

   6. Facts about the U.S. States and Territories 885

   7. Legal Holidays by State 917

   8. Tourism Information Sources for the U.S. States and North America 921

   9. Facts about the U.S. Presidents 965

  10. Facts about Countries around the World 979

  11. Legal Holidays by Country 1033

  12. Tourism Information Sources for Countries around the World 1057

  13. Bibliography 1117

Indexes 1143

   1. Chronological Index—Fixed Days and Events 1145

   2. Chronological Index—Movable Days 1189

   3. Special Subject Index 1201

       Arts 1201

       Calendar 1204

       Folkloric 1206

       Food 1209

       Historic 1209

       Promotional 1217

       Religious 1221

       Sporting 1227

   4. General Index 1231

Preface

This revised and expanded fifth edition of *Holidays, Festivals, and Celebrations of the World Dictionary (HFCWD)* contains up-to-date information about more than 3,300 holidays, festivals, celebrations, commemorations, holy days, feasts and fasts, and other observances from all parts of the world, including more than 240 entries that are new to this edition. Entries include events for which people come together for a day or periods of up to a few days or (rarely) weeks for special activities, celebrations, commemorations, or rituals. These events have a story to tell, in that each is significant, unusual, or somehow remarkable. Holidays and festivals for more than 100 countries, as well as events specifically observed in every state of the United States, are included.

The entries cover holidays and festivals that are popular, secular, religious, or a combination thereof. The majority of entries covers events still celebrated or observed, but a few ancient and discontinued events are included because allusions to them still appear in literature or art, or occur in discourse.

Most entries in *HFCWD* have national or wide regional significance, but some local events that are offbeat, colorful, distinctive, or bizarre have also been included, such as the Boryeong Mud Festival, Marche du Nain Rouge, and the Ottery St Mary Flaming Tar Barrels. Entries for well-known days of religious significance, such as Christmas, Rosh Hashanah, and Ramadan, contain information seldom found in other current reference sources.

Audience

HFCWD is intended for elementary, middle, and high schools, academic and public libraries, as well as churches, synagogues, mosques, community affairs groups, and others interested in learning about festive events.

Organization

Main Entries and Alternate Forms

The book is arranged alphabetically by name of holiday. Main entries appear in boldface. All main entries are numbered, and these numbers are used in the indexes. Well-known alternate names of the main entry appear in parentheses immediately after the main entry, e.g., Hanukkah (Chanukah). Common alternate forms appear in boldface within the text of the entry, and cross-references to other entries in the book appear in SMALL CAPITAL letters.

Order of Main Entries

Since people looking for information on a given subject may not know its official title, main entries have been written with the key words first. Thus, words such as *birthday, death of, feast, festa, festival, fête, fiesta, national,* and *international* have been transposed to the end of the main entry, as in Bab, Birth of the; Bastille, Festival de la; and Old-Time Fiddlers' Contest, National.

The rationale for organizing events derived from people's names can be particularly difficult. Some event names use only the person's last name, while other events use the first and last. To simplify the search process for readers, events where a person's name forms the first part of the event name are alphabetized under the person's last name, as in Milk (Harvey) Day and Parker (Charlie) Jazz Festival.

Spelling and Forms Used for Main Entries

HFCWD deals with events that relate to many cultures, the original names of which involve a number of alphabets and non-Roman writing systems. As much as possible, spellings and forms for main entries were standardized for ease of access. The following were used as guides on spelling standardization:

- For Hindu and Islamic calendars and events: *The Encyclopedia of Religion*, Mircea Eliade, ed., Macmillan, 1987.

- For Jewish calendar and events: *The Jewish Holidays: A Guide and Commentary*, Michael Strassfeld, Harper & Row, 1985, as well as *The Encyclopedia of Religion* by Eliade.

- For Asian and African holidays and events no single standard was used. The form used is that appearing most often in the sources consulted. For many Hindu, Islamic, and Asian terms, diacriticals unfamiliar to the non-specialist were omitted.

- General sources consulted were *Encyclopedia Britannica* (15th edition, 1995), *Columbia Encyclopedia* (sixth edition, 2000), *Merriam-Webster's Biographical Dictionary* (1995), and *Merriam-Webster's Geographical Dictionary* (third edition, 1997).

Dates

On the line below the main entry, the date of celebration or observance is given in italics. For those entries whose date is based on a lunar calendar, we have shown the approximate date in the Gregorian calendar followed by the lunar date. The exception is for events based on the strictly lunar Islamic calendar, where only the Islamic month and day are given. See appendix 2, *Calendars throughout History: An Overview of Calendar Systems around the World*, for a detailed explanation of the Islamic calendar.

Religious Holidays

For the most part, entries for religious holidays are spelled and described in terms of the major religion that observes them. If only some followers of a major religion observe a holiday, or if different branches or sects commemorate something different (or nothing at all) on a given holiday, the entry specifies the practice of the particular group. St. John the Baptist's Day, for instance, is recognized by most Christians, and so is described (and indexed) as "Christian," despite the fact that some Christians do not venerate saints. The holy day of Ashura is observed quite differently by Sunni and Shi'ite Muslims, and so both practices are described.

Christian Denominations

For Christianity, references to the West or Western Church generally include the Roman Catholic Church, the branches of the Anglican Communion, and major Protestant denominations. Refer ences to the East or Eastern Church include Orthodox Christians, such as Greek and Russian Orthodox; "separated" churches, such as the Nestorian Church, the Syrian churches, the Coptic Orthodox Church in Egypt, the Armenian Orthodox Church, and the Ethiopian Orthodox Church; and the Uniate churches, or Eastern Catholics, including the Malabar Church in India and the Melchite and Maronite churches.

Contact Information

Names, addresses, phone and fax numbers, and web sites (when available) are included for entries on contemporary public festivals and other events. In some cases, the organization(s) listed are actual sponsors. In others, an embassy or tourist office is given; such agencies are not necessarily responsible for the event, but they are provided as likely sources of information about the event. In a few cases, entries discuss events in several locations, but we have maintained a limit of no more than three contacts per entry. Generally excluded are such religious or contemplative holidays as EASTER, HANUKKAH, KARWACHOTH, and LAYLAT AL-MIRAJ—for which the obvious contact would be a local church, synagogue, temple, or mosque, although in some cases, web sites of churches and religious organizations do provide additional information—as well as holidays that tend to be private or domestic observances, such as MOTHER'S DAY and APRIL FOOLS' DAY. More general contact information is provided in Appendix 8, *Tourism Information Sources for the U.S. States and North America*, and Appendix 12, *Tourism Information Sources for Countries around the World*.

New Entries

More than 240 new entries have been added to this edition. They include religious holidays, historic commemorations, and seasonal events. There are dozens of new entries on holidays and festivals in countries around the world, along with additional coverage of events in the United States. In this new edition coverage of religious holidays, festivals and events related to celebration of the arts, as well as those related to foods and cuisine, has been greatly expanded.

Other Features of this Edition

In addition to adding more than 240 new entries to this new edition, the complete work has been verified and updated, including the 13 appendices and four indexes. A full list of the book's appendices is included below.

Appendices

1. *Glossary of Words Relating to Time*
   This section includes a descriptive listing of words relating to periods of time.

2. *Calendars throughout History: An Overview of Calendar Systems around the World*
   This section includes an overview of the evolution of calendar systems throughout history and throughout the world.

3. *Comparative Table of Calendar Systems*
   This section shows the relationship among various calendar systems, including Gregorian, Jewish, Hindu, Jain, Buddhist, Sikh, and Burmese calendars.

4. *Phases of the Moon from 2015 to 2030 Given in Eastern Standard Time*
   This section explains the importance of the moon to the world's religions and includes charts that show the phases of the moon.

5. *Overview of the World's Major Religions*
   This section provides basic information about the world's major religions, including when and where originated, founder(s), theological orientation, major sacred texts, denominations and sects, estimated number of adherents around the world, and a listing of the main holidays in chronological order by the religion's calendar.

6. *Facts about the U.S. States and Territories*
   This section includes a range of information for each of the 50 states, the District of Columbia, Puerto Rico, and the U.S. territories.

7. *Legal Holidays by State*
   This section lists legal public holidays in each of the states, the District of Columbia, Puerto Rico, and the U.S. territories.

8. *Tourism Information Sources for the U.S. States and North America*
   This section includes tourism information sources for the United States, Canada, and Mexico.

9. *Facts about the U.S. Presidents*

   This section lists all U.S. presidents in the order in which they held office, includes basic biographical information, and lists notable landmarks commemorating them, along with contact information and websites.

10. *Facts about Countries around the World*

    This section provides basic information about the independent nations of the world: official name (in English); capital city; internet country code; flag description; national anthem, motto, and symbols (when available); geographical description of location; total area; brief climate description; proper terms for nationality; population numbers; languages spoken; and information on ethnic groups and religions.

11. *Legal Holidays by Country*

    This section lists legal public holidays around the world in alphabetical order by country.

12. *Tourism Information Sources for Countries around the World*

    This section includes tourism information sources for countries around the world, except the United States, Canada, and Mexico (see Appendix 8). The listings are in alphabetical order by name of the country.

13. *Bibliography*

    This section includes an annotated listing of sources consulted in *HFCWD*, as well as other sources for further reading.

Indexes

Several indexes provide reference to entries (as appropriate) for each of the following categories. In all indexes in this edition, references to entries are given by entry numbers, not page numbers.

1. *Chronological Index—Fixed Days and Events*

   Indexes events that are celebrated at a specific time.

2. *Chronological Index—Movable Days*

   Indexes events whose date of celebration is not fixed, particularly those that are observed according to non-Gregorian calendars and those that depend on the date of Easter.

3. *Special Subject Index*

   Divides events into eight categories:

   Arts—Indexes events that revolve around an art form.

   Calendar—Indexes events that deal specifically with the calendar.

   Folkloric—Indexes events rooted in folklore and tradition.

   Foods—Indexes events that revolve around a food, cuisine, or style of cooking.

   Historic—Indexes commemorations of specific events in history.

   Promotional—Indexes events that promote something, such as a location or activity.

   Religious—Indexes holidays and events related to the beliefs and customs of a faith tradition.

   Sporting—Indexes events that are based on or revolve around sports or games.

   Some events may be categorized in more than one of the above special subjects. For instance, St. Patrick's Day is listed under the Historic Index, because it commemorates a historical person, and the Folkloric Index, for all the folk legends and traditions associated with St. Patrick and his feast day.

4. *General Index*

   Lists names of festivals and holidays by keyword, religious groups, ethnic groups, geographic locations, names of individuals, institutions, and other items of significance appearing within the text of the entries. For example, foods, animals, music, customs, and activities closely associated with an event are indexed—both those that are the subject of an observance and those that play significant roles in observances. Also indexed are celebratory elements common to various cultures.

A

♦ 0001 ♦ **Aban Parab**
*February, March, October; 10th day of Aban, the
eighth Zoroastrian month*

In the Zoroastrian calendar, each of the 30 days of the month
bears the name of the *yazata*, or spiritual being, who is believed to preside over that day. Similarly, each of the 12
months bears the name of the yazata who rules over that
month. When the day and the month both share the same
name, as they do on the 10th of Aban, it is considered a name-
day feast. The yazata of the month of Aban is the female waters. On name-feast days Zoroastrians attend services in a fire
temple, a meeting hall, or a private home.

Because of discrepancies in the calendars used by widely
separated Zoroastrian communities around the world, there
are now three different calendars in use, and the 10th of Aban
can fall either in October, March, or February according to
the Gregorian calendar.

Followers of the Zoroastrian religion, which was founded by
the prophet Zoroaster (or Zarathushtra, who is believed to
have lived around 1200 B.C.E.), today live primarily in Iran
and northwestern India, although smaller communities exist
in Pakistan, Sri Lanka, Canada, the U.S., England, and Australia.

♦ 0002 ♦ **Abbey Road on the River**
Memorial Day Weekend

Even decades after the final Beatles recording, the music of
the Fab Four from Liverpool, England, is still compelling
enough to draw thousands of rock fans together for a single
Beatles event. Abbey Road on the River, which takes place
along the banks of the Ohio River in Louisville, Ky., is the
largest celebration of the band's music in North America. As
many as 25,000 town residents attend—along with Beatles
fans from all over the world—to see dozens of tribute bands
perform on six stages.

The first Abbey Road on the River, in 2002, took place along
the banks of the Cuyahoga River in Cleveland, Ohio. The festivities were moved to their present location in 2006. Once a
three-day affair, the festival has expanded to five days, with

performances by more than 40 bands at the four outdoor
venues of the Riverfront Plaza Belvedere as well as in two
indoor theaters in town.

Festival highlights include shows of complete albums, including a 30-member performance of the *White Album*. In
addition to the live music, the event also offers a film festival, lectures, and vendors selling a variety of merchandise,
collectibles, and artwork.

CONTACTS:
Abbey Road on the River
www.arotr.com

♦ 0003 ♦ **Abbotsford International Air Show**
August

Widely recognized as Canada's national air show, this three-
day event is an opportunity for the aviation industry to display the latest developments in civilian aircraft. Since the
first show was held in 1962, it has included aerobatic performances by the Canadian Armed Forces, the Royal Air Force,
the Snowbirds Jet Team, and the U.S. Air Force's Thunderbirds. Aviation-related equipment is on display, and there
is a large banquet featuring well-known personalities in the
aviation and aerospace fields. The show is held at the airport
in Abbotsford, British Columbia, and is regularly attended
by upwards of 200,000 people.

CONTACTS:
Abbotsford International Airshow Society
1464 Tower St.
Abbotsford, BC V2T 6H5 Canada
604-852-8511 or 855-852-8511; fax: 604-852-6093
www.abbotsfordairshow.com

♦ 0004 ♦ **Abdu'l-Baha, Ascension of**
November 28

The Ascension of Abdul'l-Baha is a holy day in the Baha'i religion that commemorates the death of Abbas Effendi, known
as Abdu'l-Baha, in 1921 in Haifa, Palestine (now Israel). The
eldest son of Mirza Husayn Ali, known as Baha'u'llah, the
prophet-founder of the Baha'i faith, he was named the leader

of the Baha'i community in his father's will, which also appointed him to interpret Baha'i writings. In turn, Abdu'l-Baha appointed his eldest grandson, Shoghi Effendi (1896-1957) as his successor and Guardian of the Cause. Today the affairs of the worldwide Baha'i community are administered by the Universal House of Justice, a body that meets in Haifa and is elected every five years.

CONTACTS:
Bahai International Community
1233 Central St.
Evanston, IL 60201
847-733-3400; fax: 847-733-3578
www.bahai.us

♦ 0005 ♦ Abdullah's (King) Birthday in Jordan
January 30

Since 1999, the year Abdullah II bin al-Hussein succeeded his father, King Hussein, as national monarch, Jordan has celebrated the king's birthday. It is typical on this date for the Royal Hashemite Court of Jordan to publish various well-wishes that arrive from Arab leaders, Western leaders, and other international dignitaries.

Before 2007, the country also observed the day as an official national holiday by closing all its banks and stores. However, that year King Abdullah announced that in order to help "boost productivity and dedication," banks and businesses would remain open on his birthday. He also asked citizens to do the same on the birthday of his late father, another public holiday.

CONTACTS:
Jordan Embassy
3504 International Dr. N.W.
Washington, D.C. 20008
202-966-2664; fax: 202-966-3110
jordanembassyus.org

♦ 0006 ♦ Abha Festival
Six weeks in July-August

Situated in the mountains and blessed with mild weather in an otherwise harsh climate, the city of Adha, Saudi Arabia, is also a popular tourist attraction that boasts amusement parks, a shopping district, and a hotel industry. The Abha Festival, which lasts about six weeks, was established in 1998 to help sustain the city's appeal among tourists. In past years, over 1.5 million visitors have traveled to the city and attended the festival's sports competitions, religious activities, and concerts featuring Arab pop stars. The concert series, which has the distinction of being Saudi Arabia's first public music event, first took place during the inaugural Adha Festival.

The summer festival's main event has consistently been the music program. Its performers cater to younger Saudis, who have been the target audience over the years. Other youth-oriented activities include sailing competitions, horse racing, and soccer.

Addressing general anxieties about the negative impact of popular culture on young festival-goers, organizers ensure

the program maintains moral standards by coordinating with officials of the Commission for the Promotion of Virtue and Prevention of Vice.

CONTACTS:
Saudi Arabia Embassy
601 New Hampshire Ave. N.W.
Washington, D.C. 20037
202-337-4076; fax: 202-944-5983
www.saudiembassy.net

♦ 0007 ♦ Aboakyer Festival
April or May

The Effutu people of Winneba, Ghana, celebrate the **Deer-Hunting Festival** by making an offering to the god Penkye Otu. Two groups known as the Asafo companies, each consisting of about 150 people ranging in age from young boys to grandfathers, compete in a deer hunt that begins at dawn with the pounding of drums and the ringing of bells. When the first deer is caught, the victorious company brings it back alive and presents it proudly to their chief. Then the animal is taken back to the village, where dancing and drumming continue in an effort to placate Penkye Otu so that he will bring them a bountiful year.

CONTACTS:
Ghana Tourism
P.O. Box 4386
Accra Ghana
233-302-666314; fax: 233-302-244611
www.touringghana.com

♦ 0008 ♦ Aboriginal Day, National
June 21

To foster respect and appreciation for the traditions and cultures of Canada's indigenous peoples, the government in 1996 designated the summer solstice as National Aboriginal Day. Long before the national holiday was established, this day of the year had been observed by Canada's Inuit, Métis, and First Nations peoples as a summer celebration commemorating Aboriginal heritage. Coordinating with National Aboriginal organizations, the Canadian government made June 21 an official holiday with the objective of including all citizens in the observance.

Celebrations take place throughout Canada's provinces and territories and are organized by the regional offices of Indian and Northern Affairs Canada and Canadian Heritage. Some festivities are modest celebrations like summer barbecues and picnics, while others exhibit a stronger focus on culture and tradition by holding canoe races, powwows, and awareness events.

Since becoming an official holiday, National Aboriginal Day has been designated the opening day of Celebrate Canada! This 11-day celebration also includes St-Jean Baptiste Day, Canadian Multiculturalism Day, and CANADA DAY.

CONTACTS:
Aboriginal Affairs and Northern Development Canada

Terrasses de la Chaudière
10 Wellington, N. Tower
Gatineau, QC K1A 0H4 Canada
800-567-9604 or 866-553-0554; fax: 866-817-3977
www.ainc-inac.gc.ca

♦ 0009 ♦ Abu Simbel Festival
February 22 and October 22

This festival celebrates the two days of the year on which the light of the rising sun can reach the 180-foot deep innermost chambers of Abu Simbel, the great temple of Ramses II, in Egypt. The temple was designed so that only on these two days in February and October does the sun shine on the four gods in the sanctuary: Ptah, Amen-Re, Ramses, and Re-Hora-khty. This temple, the most colossal in Egypt, was built by Ramses II between 1300 and 1233 B.C.E., and is famous for its four 65-foot statues of the seated Ramses. It is actually two temples—one for Ramses and one for queen Nefertiti—and is extraordinary for its grandeur, beauty, and history. It was unknown to the European world until Swiss explorer Johann Burckhardt found it in 1812. The Italian Giovanni Belzoni excavated the entrance and explored the temple in 1816. In 1964, when the new Aswan Dam was to be built, creating a lake that would have drowned the temple, it was cut into 2,000 pieces and reassembled at a site about 180 feet higher. It is not as perfect as it was at the foot of the cliff—but it was saved.

It is thought that there must have been ritual celebrations in ancient times on the days when the sun penetrated the sanctuary. Today, television covers the event, and people gather to see the sunrise and to meditate. The sun now shines on the sanctuary a day earlier than it did before the temple was moved.

CONTACTS:
Egypt State Information Service
3 Al Estad Al Bahary St.
Nasr City, Cairo Egypt
202-2261-7304
www.sis.gov.eg/En/Default.aspx

♦ 0010 ♦ Academy Awards Ceremony
Late February or March

The glamour and glitz of Hollywood is on full display at the annual movie awards known as the **Oscars** or the Academy Awards. Presented every year since 1929 by the Academy of Motion Picture Arts and Sciences, these awards are presented for outstanding achievements in filmmaking during the preceding year.

Some of the best star-gazing occurs before the actual awards ceremony. That's when some of the film industry's best-known actors and actresses arrive in limousines, wearing everything from tuxedos and designer evening gowns to far less conventional outfits. After the awards—which include Oscars for Best Actor, Best Actress, Best Director, and Best Picture—are handed out, numerous after-show parties are held at various Los Angeles homes and restaurants.

CONTACTS:
Academy of Motion Picture Arts and Sciences
8949 Wilshire Blvd.
Beverly Hills, CA 90211
310-247-3000; fax: 310-859-9619
www.oscars.org

♦ 0011 ♦ Acadian Day
Two weeks in August

The original Acadians were 17th-century French colonists who settled in the area known as Acadia, which covered what is now Nova Scotia as well as Prince Edward Island, and parts of northern Maine and Quebec. Their French-speaking descendants in the Maritime Provinces continue to honor their heritage by holding many local Acadian Day celebrations, usually during the summer months.

Fifty thousand people attend the **Acadian Festival** in Caraquet, New Brunswick, the largest of these celebrations. The festival takes place for 14 days in August each year and includes Acadian dance performances, cabaret, and concerts as well as sporting contests and a blessing of the fleet. The highlight of the festival is "L'Acadie en Fête," a huge celebration involving Acadian musicians, singers, artists, and actors.

CONTACTS:
Festivals Acadiens et Créoles
220 Saint-Pierre Blvd. W.
Ste. 312
Caraquet, NB E1W 1A5 Canada
506-727-2787; fax: 506-727-1995
festivalacadien.ca

♦ 0012 ♦ Acadian Festival
Length varies, usually three-four days at the end of June

The Madawaska Territory, which at one time ran along the Canadian border between Maine and New Brunswick, was settled by a small group of farmers who were chased out of Acadia by the English in the late 18th century. As the settlements grew, they were separated into Canadian and American communities, with Edmundston on the Canadian side and Madawaska and St. David on the American side of the St. John River.

In 1978 the local historical society in Madawaska proclaimed June 28 as Acadian Day in the state of Maine, and since that time it has been the site of an Acadian (or French-Canadian) festival lasting anywhere from one day to a week. Regular events include French music and dancing, an Acadian Supper featuring *pot en pot* and *fougère*, a parade with bands and marching units from both Maine and Canada, and an Acadian mass followed by a procession to the white marble cross that marks the site of the original Acadian settlement. The festival usually coincides with a reunion of the original 13 families who settled here.

CONTACTS:
Madawaska Recreation Department
328 St. Thomas St.

Ste. 101
Madawaska, ME 04756
207-728-3604 or 207-728-3605; fax: 207-728-3611
www.acadianfestival.com

◆ 0013 ◆ Acadiens et Creoles, Festivals
October

A combination of several festivals (food, music, crafts, and more) to celebrate Cajun culture in Lafayette, La., known as the capital of French Louisiana. When they were expelled from Nova Scotia by the British in the 1770s, the French Acadian farmers settled in the area around Lafayette in a region of 22 parishes that came to be known as Acadiana. The word "Cajun" comes from Acadian.

One part of the celebration is the Bayou Food Festival, which offers a range of Cajun cooking from crawfish gumbo to alligator sausage to corn maque-chou. The Louisiana Crafts Festival features handmade Cajun crafts and demonstrations by blacksmiths, decoy carvers, alligator skinners, and storytellers. The Festival de Musique Acadienne features centuries-old music sung in French. Modern crafts are also on exhibit, and lectures and workshops on the Acadian language and history are part of the weekend.

CONTACTS:
Festivals Acadiens et Créoles
P.O. Box 53761
Lafayette, LA 70505
337-534-4274
www.festivalsacadiens.com

◆ 0014 ◆ Accession of H.H. Sheikh Zayed as Ruler of Abu Dhabi
August 6

On August 6, 1966, His Highness Sheikh Zayed bin Sultan Al Nahyan overthrew his brother, Sheikh Shakhbut Bin-Sultan Al Nahyan, in a bloodless palace coup in the Persian Gulf country of the United Arab Emirates (UAE). Sheikh Zayed became the ruler of Abu Dhabi, the country's principal city. In 1971, Sheikh Zayad was appointed president of the country and held that post until his death in 2004. Sheikh Zayed's family had been rulers in the UAE for many years: his grandfather ruled the UAE from 1855 to 1909, and his father ruled from 1922 to 1926.

Sheikh Zayed's reign was marked by reform and the development of a modern, liberalized state. He used his nation's oil wealth to better the lives of his people. Education was his top priority, and many schools and colleges were built under his direction. He promoted sports among young people, both men and women, and built stadiums, training facilities, and a number of youth hostels and centers. Sheikh Zayed also built a modern army with state-of-the-art equipment and training. The troops have participated in UN peacekeeping activities, including the construction of an airport in Kosovo. Unusual in a Muslim nation, the media were allowed a large measure of freedom, although they could not directly criticize Sheikh Zayed or his family. Speaking of his policies, Sheikh Zayed

was quoted as saying, "What is the benefit of wealth if it is not utilized to raise the standard of the people of the country?"

The day of Sheikh Zayed's accession to power is celebrated with a parade featuring floats carrying posters with Sheikh Zayed's portrait and pictures showing the development that the UAE has enjoyed due to his reign. A caravan of camels and other animals follows the floats. Other activities have included an opera concerning the ruler's life.

CONTACTS:
Embassy of the United Arab Emirates
3522 International Ct. N.W
Ste. 400
Washington, D.C. 20008
202-243-2400; fax: 202-243-2432
www.uae-embassy.org

◆ 0015 ◆ Adae-Kese
January

This is the highlight of the ceremonial year among the Ashanti people in Ghana. Adae-Kese commemorates the day on which priest Okomfo Anokye called down from heaven the Ashantis' Golden Stool. Elaborate stools are important fixtures in Ashanti culture. When someone passes away, that person's stool is treasured by his or her survivors and honored periodically. The Golden Stool is that of King Osei Tutu, the founder of the Ashanti kingdom.

During the Adae-Kese festival, people clean their ancestral stools and offer food to the gods and ancestors. The current king and the Golden Stool sit in state, while people from the community and, often, the president of Ghana pay homage to him. All of this takes place in Kumasi, where the king's palace is located. The museum there houses a second, copycat golden stool used to deceive the British, who demanded that the stool be turned over to them after hearing that it was the source of the Ashanti king's powers.

The Adae festival is held every 40 days throughout the year, but the January celebration is the largest and most important.

CONTACTS:
Ministry of Tourism & Diasporan Relations
Ghana Tourist Authority
P.O. Box 4386
Accra Ghana
233-302-666-314; fax: 233-302-244-611
www.touringghana.com

◆ 0016 ◆ Adam's Peak, Pilgrimage to
December-April

A footprint preserved in stone is a sacred site at the top of a mountain in Dalhousie, Sri Lanka. Depending on one's religious tradition, the footprint belongs to Adam (Muslim), the Buddha, St. Thomas (Christian), or Lord Shiva (Hindu). Pilgrims have made the climb for over 1,000 years.

There are two routes to the summit of Adam's Peak, one of which takes about three hours while the other takes seven hours. Though the terrain is rugged, many pilgrims make the ascent by the light of lanterns so they can arrive at the break of dawn and catch a spectacular view of the western coastline. According to local tradition, a woman who reaches the top will be reincarnated as a man.

CONTACTS:
Living Heritage Trust of Sri Lanka
1 Horton Terr.
Colombo 7 Sri Lanka
livingheritage.org

♦ 0017 ♦ Adar Parab
March, April, November; ninth day of Adar, the ninth Zoroastrian month

Adar Parab is one of the "sacred name days" in the Zoroastrian calendar, where the name of the day and the name of the month coincide. Adar, the spiritual being or *yazata* for whom both the day and the month are named, presides over fire and is associated with light and warmth. Parsis—as the Zoroastrians living in India are called—traditionally give their household fires a rest on this day by not cooking and by offering special prayers. It is also customary to recite the portion of the *Avesta* (Zoroastrian sacred writings) known as the *Atash Niyayesh*, "Fire Litany."

Fire is the most important symbol for the followers of Zoroaster (also known as Zarathushtra), a Persian religious leader believed to have lived around 1200 B.C.E. They have fire temples where fires burn constantly, as well as fires that are kindled in prayer halls and private homes for special services performed outside the temple.

The Zoroastrian calendar has 12 months of 30 days each, plus five extra days at the end of the year. Because of discrepancies in the calendars used by widely separated Zoroastrian communities around the world, there are now three different calendars in use, and the 9th of Adar can fall either in March, April, or November.

♦ 0018 ♦ Adelaide Cup
Second Monday in March

The Adelaide Cup is an annual sporting and social event in South Australia that includes horse races, fashion shows, concerts, and gourmet food. Hosted by the South Australian Jockey Club (SAJC), it was declared a public holiday by the South Australian government in 1973. The races begin at noon at the Morphettville Racecourse in Adelaide and continue throughout the day.

The first Adelaide Cup was held in 1864. In 1885 the Australian government banned racecourse betting, forcing organizers to move the event to a different location. The ban was lifted in 1988, and the SAJC re-established the Adelaide Cup that year. Although the event was originally held on the third Monday of May, organizers changed the date to March due to weather concerns. The date change greatly enhanced the financial success of the event, and it has remained in March ever since.

CONTACTS:
Thoroughbred Racing South Australia
Morphettville Racecourse, Morphettville
GPO Box 2646
Adelaide, South Australia 5001 Australia
61-8-8179-9800; fax: 61-8-8179-9891
www.theracessa.com.au

♦ 0019 ♦ Adelaide Festival
February-March

Adelaide, South Australia, metamorphosed from an isolated, culturally deprived city to a major center of art and culture worldwide, thanks to a group of visionary businessmen who originated this annual festival of the arts in 1960. The Adelaide Festival program includes performances, exhibitions, and workshops in dance, music, film, theater, opera, and the visual arts and features artists from all over the world. A writers' week is also featured. Events in the festival take place in the Festival Theatre, parks, churches, the Adelaide Town Hall, and other locations. Over 560,000 people turned out for the 2015 festival.

See also ADELAIDE FRINGE FESTIVAL.

CONTACTS:
Adelaide Festival
Level 9, 33 King William St.
Adelaide, SA 5000 Australia
61-8-8216-4444; fax: 61-8-8216-4455
www.adelaidefestival.org.au

♦ 0020 ♦ Adelaide Fringe Festival
Four weeks in February-March

Originating in the 1970s as an innovative, cutting-edge alternative to the established ADELAIDE FESTIVAL, the Adelaide Fringe Festival today enjoys a synergistic relationship with its sister event, contributing to the vibrant atmosphere of this Australian city during the autumn months. In 2013, the annual Adelaide Fringe Festival was extended from three weeks to four.

The festival features the latest in the underground and experimental arts created by independent artists from Australia, Europe, and the United States. The program includes comedy, dance, film, music, physical theater, dramatic theater, and visual arts. In 2015, the festival featured more than 4000 artists, 1058 shows, and 376 venues. With over 540,000 tickets sold and more than two million people in attendance, the Adelaide Fringe is one of the largest and most popular arts festivals in the world.

CONTACTS:
Adelaide Fringe Office
64 Fullarton Rd.
Norwood, SA 5067 Australia
61-8-8100-2000; fax: 61-8-8100-2020
www.adelaidefringe.com.au

♦ 0021 ♦ Administrative Professionals Week
Last full week of April

Professional Secretaries Week was started in 1952 by Professional Secretaries International—now called the International Association of Administrative Professionals (IAAP)—an organization devoted to the education and professional development of secretaries, executive assistants, information specialists, and office managers. It takes place during the last full week in April, with Administrative Professionals Day observed on Wednesday. Many IAAP chapters sponsor special events throughout the week—such as educational seminars or luncheons with guest speakers for secretaries and their bosses—but Wednesday is the day when managers and executives are supposed to give their office support staff a special token of their appreciation.

How do secretaries want to be recognized on this day? According to the 2001 IAAP survey, most of them want company-wide special events or training and educational sessions. What do they get? Lunch is the most common form of recognition, followed by flowers or other gifts.

CONTACTS:
International Association of Administrative Professionals
10502 N.W. Ambassador Dr.
Ste. 100
Kansas City, MO 64153
816-891-6600; fax: 816-891-9118
www.iaap-hq.org

♦ 0022 ♦ Admission Day
Varies from state to state

Many American states celebrate the anniversary of their admission to the Union by observing a public holiday on or near the actual day. Sometimes the day is referred to by the name of the state—as in Colorado Day, Indiana Day, Nevada Day, or WEST VIRGINIA DAY—and is marked by special celebrations. Other states let the anniversary of their admission pass unnoticed. In Vermont, Admission Day coincides with TOWN MEETING DAY.

For a listing of all states, *see* Appendix.

CONTACTS:
California Department of Parks & Recreation
1416 9th St.
Sacramento, CA 95814
916-653-6995 or 800-777-0369; fax: 916-654-6374
www.parks.ca.gov

♦ 0023 ♦ Advent
From the Sunday closest to November 30 to December 24 in the West; from November 15 to December 24 in the East

The Advent season marks the beginning of the Christian year in Western Christianity. Its length varies from 22 to 28 days, beginning on the Sunday nearest St. Andrew's Day and encompassing the next three Sundays, ending on CHRISTMAS EVE.

In the Roman Catholic Church and those of the Anglican Communion the third Sunday is called Gaudete Sunday, from the first word of the introit, "Rejoice." Rose-colored vestments may replace the purple, and flowers may be on the altar. Originally a period of reflection and penitence in preparation for CHRISTMAS—in much the same way that LENT is in preparation for EASTER—Advent has sometimes been referred to as the **Winter Lent**. But over time the restrictions of Advent have become greatly relaxed. Today it is usually associated with the Advent calendars that parents give their children to help them count the days until Christmas.

In Orthodox (Eastern) Christianity, the church year begins on September 1, and Advent begins on November 15. The Advent fast is called the **Little Lent**, because it's shorter than the Great Lent preceding Easter.

♦ 0024 ♦ Advent (Germany)
Sunday nearest November 30 through December 24

Many German households observe Advent with an Advent wreath. Traditionally fashioned from a fir branch entwined with gold and silver ribbons or bits of red thread, the wreaths also contain holders for four candles. German families display the wreath on a tabletop or suspend it from the ceiling. One candle is lit on each of the Sundays in Advent. An old Roman Catholic tradition called for lighting the candles on Saturday instead. Many German households light a "Star of Seven," a seven-branched candelabrum, on CHRISTMAS EVE, and at midnight carry the lit "star" though the dark to the village church for the Christmas Eve service.

CONTACTS:
Kölner Dommusik
Clarenbachstr. 5 - 15
Cologne 50931 Germany
49-221-94018-10; fax: 49-221-94018-50
www.koelner-dom.de

♦ 0025 ♦ AFC Asian Cup
Every four years

Since 1956, the Asian Football Confederation has held the AFC Asian Cup tournament every four years to determine the best soccer team in Asia. The winner goes on to compete for the FIFA World Cup, the soccer world's highest honor. To avoid conflict over audience with the Olympic Games, which are also held every four years, the Asian Football Confederation held a competition in 2007 and then committed to hold future tournaments every four years from that date forward.

From a seven-team tournament at its first edition, the AFC Cup has grown to a 16-nation tournament watched by an 80,000-strong live audience and over 800 million television viewers. The final tournament comprises two stages: the group stage and the knockout stage. Each team in the group stage plays three games in a group of four, with the winners and runners-up from each group advancing to the single-elimination knockout stage.

Japan has the most cup wins with four, followed by Saudi Arabia and Iran with three wins each. Tournament-host Australia defeated South Korea in the final match of the 2015 Asian Cup, earning the right to compete in the 2017 FIFA World Cup.

CONTACTS:
Asian Football Confederation
AFC House
Jalan 1/155B
Kuala Lumpur 57000 Malaysia
603-8994-3388; fax: 603-8994-2689
www.the-afc.com

♦ 0026 ♦ **Africa Industrialization Day**
November 20

In 1989 the UNITED NATIONS designated November 20 as Africa Industrialization Day. Observances center around mustering international support for the industrialization of Africa.

CONTACTS:
United Nations Industrial Development Organization
1, United Nations Plaza
Rm. DC1-1118
New York, NY 10017
212-963-6890 or 212-963-6885; fax: 212-963-7904
www.unido.org

♦ 0027 ♦ **Africa Malaria Day**
April 25

Africa Malaria Day is sponsored by an international organization called Roll Back Malaria, whose members include representatives from the World Health Organization, UNICEF, the UNITED NATIONS, the World Bank, and various member countries, organizations, and agencies. The goal of this organization is to reduce the worldwide number of malaria cases by one-half by the year 2010.

Malaria kills about 3,000 people a day, which adds up to about 1,000,000 people per year. Most of these people are children, and nine out of ten of them live in sub-Saharan Africa.

Africa Malaria Day is a day dedicated to raising public awareness about malaria prevention and treatment, as well as the economic and social toll the disease takes on poor countries. Activities include special media campaigns, demonstrations of the proper use of treated mosquito netting, lectures about the disease, and other educational events. Roll Back Malaria chose April 25 as the date of their newly created holiday in order to commemorate the April 25, 2000, Summit on Malaria, held in Abuja, Nigeria. The first Africa Malaria Day was held the following year in 2001. The United Nations has declared 2001-2010 as the Decade to Roll Back Malaria.

CONTACTS:
World Health Organization
The RBM Partnership
20, Ave. Appia
Geneva 1211 Switzerland

41-22-791-4318; fax: 41-22-791-1587
www.rollbackmalaria.org

♦ 0028 ♦ **African American Day Parade**
Last Sunday in September

The African American Day parade is the largest black parade in the United States and attracts a crowd of approximately 900,000 annually. Held on the last Sunday of September in the Harlem neighborhood of New York City, the parade progresses up Adam Clayton Powell Boulevard from 111th Street to 142nd Street. The African American Day parade has been held annually since 1969 to promote unity, justice, and economic empowerment. It features many African-American business, social, and political leaders, as well as performers, marchers, and floats representing more than 300 organizations, including a wide range of colleges and bands from throughout the region. Among the participants are step dancers, drum and bugle corps, service organizations, professional associations, philanthropic organizations, cultural heritage groups, and social clubs. The parade celebrates African heritage and black achievement in all areas, and past grand marshals include such luminaries as congressional representative Shirley Chisholm, New York mayor David Dinkins, filmmaker Spike Lee, Reverend Al Sharpton, and actor Denzel Washington.

CONTACTS:
African American Day Parade Inc.
P.O. Box 501
College Stn.
New York, NY 10030
917-294-8107
www.africanamericandayparade.org

♦ 0029 ♦ **African American Women in Cinema**
International Film Festival
Late October or early November

The African American Women in Cinema International Film Festival is a three-day event held in New York City since 1998. The festival celebrates the accomplishments of black and other minority women in the film industry and seeks to expand their professional opportunities. Sponsored by African American Women in Cinema, Inc., a nonprofit organization that works to support minority women filmmakers, the festival takes place in late October or early November and includes film screenings (short and long films), social events, acting workshops, and panel discussions on a variety of subjects in cinema and entertainment. Workshop and discussion forums include such topics as audition techniques, the film editing process, understanding film financing, empowering women through movies, and selecting film music. Events take place at several venues throughout the city. The festival concludes with a brunch and award ceremony on Sunday.

CONTACTS:
African-American Women in Cinema Organization, Inc.
Manhattan

New York, NY
aawic.org

♦ 0030 ♦ African Liberation Day
May 25

While other holidays seek to commemorate the events and achievements of the past, African Liberation Day focuses attention on a goal that has not yet been fully realized: the liberation of all African people. The observance of this day can be traced back to April 15, 1958, when the Conference of Independent African States was held in Accra, Ghana. Attendees declared April 15 African Freedom Day, and between 1958 and 1963 this observance was supported by leaders worldwide, including President John F. Kennedy, MALCOLM X, and Senator Hubert Humphrey in the United States.

As British and European colonies in Africa continued to win their independence during the 1950s and 60s, and as the civil rights movement in the United States began to achieve some success, 31 independent African countries met on May 25, 1963, to form the Organization of African Unity. They changed the name and the date of what now became African Liberation Day. In 1999 the group reorganized into the African Union.

Today, observances worldwide include marches, parades, rallies, and conferences. These events focus on celebrating freedom from colonialism, educating people about the progress of the African liberation movement, and speaking out against oppression. There are also sporting contests and tribal dances, particularly in Chad, Zambia, and other African states where it is a public holiday.

CONTACTS:
African Union
P.O. Box 3243
Roosevelt St. (Old Airport Area)
Addis Ababa W21K19 Ethiopia
251-11-551-7700; fax: 251-11-551-7844
www.au.int

Accra Metropolitan Assembly
P.O. Box 385
Accra Ghana
233-021-663-947; fax: 233-021-667-299
www.ama.gov.gh

♦ 0031 ♦ African Methodist Quarterly Meeting Day
Last Saturday in August

The **Big August Quarterly** of the African Union Methodist Protestant Church takes place annually in Wilmington, Delaware. It honors the establishment of the A.U.M.P. Church in 1813 as the "Mother Church" for African Americans. The first independent black congregation in Wilmington was started by an influential black religious leader named Peter Spencer, who, along with 41 like-minded African Americans, left the town's Asbury Methodist Church in 1805 because its white members refused to let them participate fully in the services. In the years before the Civil War the Big August Quarterly drew slaves from all around, who obtained special passes permitting them to attend the weekend of gospel music, impassioned preaching, and family get-togethers.

Its founders modeled the Big August Quarterly on the quarterly meetings held by Quakers. Many thousands of people from Delaware and its neighboring states came to these stirring religious festivals. Although it no longer draws the crowds it used to, the Big August Quarterly has undergone a resurgence in recent years. It features soul food, musical entertainment, and an opportunity for people to reminisce about the Big August Quarterlies of the past.

♦ 0032 ♦ African World Festival
Third weekend in August

The African World Festival is a cultural festival held annually on the third weekend of August in Detroit, Mich. With more than one million visitors each year, it is one of the largest ethnic festivals in the United States. Sponsored by the Charles H. Wright Museum of African-American History, the festival has been in existence since 1983.

The African World Festival is held at Hart Plaza overlooking the Detroit River and includes entertainment, arts, education, and cultural exhibits. Festival events take place over a three-day weekend, operating from Friday through Sunday. Traditional African dancers and drummers perform, and musicians entertain audiences in the plaza's amphitheater with various styles of African-influenced music, including such genres as reggae, blues, gospel, and jazz. An annual Greek step show features sorority and fraternity dance teams. African and world goods are available from more than 150 vendors in the marketplace, and the Taste of the Diaspora food court offers cuisine ranging from African specialties to all-American favorites. The African Family Village offers arts, crafts, games, spoken word performances, and music for families with children.

CONTACTS:
Charles H. Wright Museum of African American History
315 E. Warren Ave.
Detroit, MI 48201
313-494-5800
thewright.org

♦ 0033 ♦ African/Caribbean International Festival of Life
Independence Day weekend

Introduced in 1993, the African/Caribbean International Festival of Life (IFOL) is a music and culture celebration held in Washington Park in Chicago during the first week of July. The family-oriented festival draws more than 150,000 attendees over a four-day period extending from Thursday through Sunday of Independence Day weekend. IFOL showcases reggae, calypso, world beat, R&B, hip-hop, jazz, blues, and Latin music. In addition, it features dance performances, food, clothing, arts, crafts, and a variety of activities and games designed for family entertainment. IFOL organizers sponsor the event to promote peace, love, and unity among nations, stressing the dual themes of "Bringing nations together" and "Living together as one." Festivalgoers can purchase a one-day pass or a festival pass good for all four days. A portion of the proceeds from the festival is donated to charity to support programs for children in crisis.

CONTACTS:
Martin's International Culture, Inc.
1325 S. Wabash Ave.
Ste.307
Chicago, IL 60605
312-427-0266; fax: 312-427-0268
martinsinterculture.com

♦ 0034 ♦ **African-American Music Appreciation Month**
June

African American Music Appreciation Month is observed in June each year in the United States. Created by music industry executives Kenny Gable and Ed Wright as a way to celebrate and promote black music, the special designation has been proclaimed each year since 1979 by the incumbent U.S. president.

Concerts and activities are typically planned and sponsored on a local level by such organizations as arts councils, chambers of commerce, music associations, museums, charitable foundations, radio stations, and theme parks. At the White House in Washington, D.C., a concert and reception is held each year that features various genres of African-American music, including R&B, jazz, blues, and hip hop. In addition television networks present programming showcasing black performers in concert as well as documentary and feature films about the development and influence of African-American musical forms.

Throughout the country during African American Music Appreciation Month public and private organizations host numerous educational programs and cultural festivals recognizing the achievements of black musicians. In Detroit, Mich., the Charles H. Wright Museum of African American History focuses on a different musical genre each week in a month-long series of concerts, workshops, films, and lectures. Similarly, in the Harlem neighborhood of New York City, an area that was a center of black music and the arts during the Harlem Renaissance of the 1920s, a series of concerts, forums, and ceremonies commemorate the development of jazz, hip hop, and R&B

CONTACTS:
National Museum of African American Music
211 Seventh. Ave. N.
Ste. 310
Nashville, TN 37219
615-301-8724
nmaam.org

♦ 0035 ♦ **Agonalia**
January 9

In Roman mythology, Janus is the god of beginnings and of doorways. The worship of Janus is believed to have been started by Romulus, one of the legendary founders of Rome. Usually depicted with two faces, one looking forward to the future and the other looking back to the past, his image appeared on an early Roman coin with a ship's prow on the reverse side. Roman boys used to toss these coins, calling out "heads or ships" just as youngsters today play "heads or tails." During the festival in honor of Janus known as the Agonalia, the *rex sacrorum* or officiating priest sacrificed a ram. Offerings of barley, incense, wine, and cakes called *Januae* were also common.

Numa Pompilius, the legendary second king of Rome, honored Janus by dedicating the famous *Ianus geminus*, the arcade at the northeast end of the Roman Forum, to him. It was believed that passing through this arcade brought luck to soldiers on their way to war.

CONTACTS:
Italian National Tourist Board
686 Park Ave.
3rd Fl.
New York, NY 10065
212-245-5618; fax: 212-586-9249
www.italiantourism.com

♦ 0036 ♦ **Agriculture Fair at Santarem, National**
10 days beginning first Friday in June

The most important agricultural fair in Portugal is held for 10 days in June each year at Santarém, capital of the rich agricultural province of Ribatejo. Although the focus of the **Ribatejo Fair** is on farming and livestock breeding, there is also acolorful program of bullfighting, folk singing, and dancing, as well as a procession of *campinos*, or bull-herders. Many other European countries exhibit farm animals and machinery at the **Feira Nacional de Agricultura**. Santarém is also the site of an annual gastronomy festival in October, which focuses on traditional cooking from all over the country.

CONTACTS:
Tourism Alentejo and Ribatejo
Republic Sq. 12 - 1
Apartado 335
Beja 7800-427 Portugal
284-313-540; fax: 284-313-550
www.visitribatejo.pt

♦ 0037 ♦ **Agua, La Fiesta de**
First Sunday in October

A festival held in San Pedro de Casta, Lima Department, Peru, the **Water Festival** accompanies the annual cleaning and maintaining of the river canals. The town mayor goes to the cave where Pariapunko, a deity of water, is believed to reside and implores him to flood the community with fresh water. Then La Toma, the gate that holds back the Carhuayumac River, is opened and the water is allowed to course through the newly repaired canals. A procession of horsemen follows the path of the water as it makes its way to the gorge of Carhuayumac.

♦ 0038 ♦ Agwunsi Festival
August-September

Agwunsi, or Agwu, is the god of healing and divination among the Igbo people of Nigeria. He is also the patron of doctors, because he gives herbs and other medicines their power to cure. On Agwunsi feast day, patients who have been healed send animals as a token of gratitude to the doctors who cured them.

♦ 0039 ♦ Air Races and Air Show, National Championship
September, four days ending on second weekend after Labor Day

The National Championship Air Races and Air Show is a four-day nostalgia trip for air buffs, held since 1964 in Reno, Nev. About 95 to 100 aircraft are generally registered for the races, providing some 180,000 spectators with the sight and sound of piston-engine planes flying around closed-pylon race courses. The planes entered include such World War II planes as the powerful P-51 Mustang and the bent-wing Chance-Vought F2G Corsair; the eerie sound the Corsair made was called "whistling death" by the Japanese of World War II. The race is the only one in the world that covers all four classes: Unlimited (vintage and modified warbirds and homebuilt racers), AT-6 (World War II pilot trainers), Formula One (super-midget planes), and Biplane (double-winged barn stormers). Air shows of military demonstrations, parachuting exhibits, and military fly-bys are also some of the events.

CONTACTS:
Reno Air Racing Association
14501 Mt. Anderson St.
Reno, NV 89506
775-972-6663; fax: 775-972-6429
www.airrace.org

♦ 0040 ♦ Airing the Classics
Sixth day of sixth lunar month

In China the **Double Sixth** is the day when Buddhist monasteries examine the books in their library collections to make sure that they haven't been damaged. It commemorates the time when the boat carrying the Buddhist scriptures from India was upset at a river crossing, and all the books had to be spread out to dry. Also known as **Tiankuang Jie**, or **Heaven's Gift Day**, it is traditional in some regions to set linens and books, as well as bath water, out in the sun. Setting aside a special day for "Airing the Classics" is especially important in hot, wet climates, where books are more vulnerable to mold and insects.

♦ 0041 ♦ AirVenture
Late July-early August

Begun in 1953 as a part of the Milwaukee Air Pageant, the AirVenture has grown to become one of the largest conventions of any kind in the world. Sponsored by the Experimental Aircraft Association, the annual event draws together enthusiasts of homemade flying craft, designers of more serious craft, and a host of individuals, companies, and government agencies involved in the aviation and aeronautics industries.

Some 10,000 aircraft of all kinds are on display at the convention. Included in this number are homebuilt airplanes, antique planes, classics, military craft, ultralight flying vehicles, and rotorcraft. In addition, over 500 forums are conducted by aviation leaders, NASA researchers, Federal Aviation Agency personnel, and aircraft designers. Some 800 exhibitors set up booths covering some one million square feet to display their aviation products and services. Workshops explain the details of constructing your own working aircraft. In the afternoon, there is a three-hour air show. In the evening, live entertainment performances feature NASA astronauts, test pilots, and leading aviation personalities. An estimated 750,000 people attend the convention every year.

CONTACTS:
EAA Aviation Center
3000 Poberezny Rd.
Oshkosh, WI 54902
920-426-4800 or 800-564-6322
www.eaa.org/eaa

♦ 0042 ♦ Aizu Byakko Matsuri
September 22-24

Aizu was at one time the sturdiest castle in northeast Japan, but it was destroyed in the battle between the Emperor's forces and the Shogun's forces known as *Boshin-no-eki* in 1868. The *Byakkotai*, or White Tiger Band, a band of young men who vowed to lay down their lives in defense of the castle, saw what they thought was fire rising from the walls. Thinking it had fallen into enemy hands, they kept their vow and killed themselves. To commemorate their courage, there is a procession of 500 warriors, led by the highly selective Byakkotai corps, and a lantern procession through the streets of Aizu Wakamatsu, where the original members of the White Tiger Band are buried.

CONTACTS:
AizuWakamatsu City
3-46 Higashi Sakae-machi
Aizu Wakamatsu, Fukushima Prefecture 965-8601 Japan
81-242-39-1111
www.city.aizuwakamatsu.fukushima.jp

♦ 0043 ♦ Ako Gishi Sai
December 14

Ako Gishi-sai (**Gishi-sai**) is an annual festival held at the Buddhist Sengaku-ji Temple in Tokyo, Japan. Ako Gishi-sai honors the eighteenth-century feudal lord Asano Naganori and his 47 samurai, who represent courage, honor, and loyalty for avenging the death of their lord and then honorably committing suicide. On December 14, the locals gather at the temple to commemorate the event and pay homage at the graves of Asano and his vassals. During the festival, schools and local businesses close, and the town's streets are lined with stalls and colorful lanterns. The highlight of the event is the Gishi Gyoretsu, a procession of 47 artists dressed as samurai, who parade through the streets accompanied by floats depicting the story of Asano. Once the parade reaches the temple grounds, celebrants wait in line to pray and burn incense at the graves.

CONTACTS:
Sengakuji
Takanawa
Minato-ku
Tokyo, 108-0074 Japan
81-3-3441-5560; fax: 81-3-3441-2208
www.sengakuji.or.jp

Japan National Tourism Organization
1 Grand Central Pl.
60 E. 42nd St., Ste. 448
New York, NY 10165
212-757-5640; fax: 212-307-6754
www.jnto.go.jp/eng

♦ 0044 ♦ **Ak-Sar-Ben Livestock Exposition and Rodeo**
September

Billed as the "World's Largest 4-H Livestock Show," the Ak-Sar-Ben ("Nebraska" spelled backwards) Livestock Exposition and Rodeo in Omaha dates back to 1928, when its purpose was to get the state's young people interested in livestock breeding. It started out as a nationwide breed show, but thoroughbred racing became an important part of the event when, during the 1930s, parimutuel racing became legal—as long as it was administered by nonprofit organizations.

The exposition lasts five days and features a World Championship Rodeo, a Catch-a-Calf contest, and entertainment by well-known country and western stars. But the show's main purpose historically has been to showcase 4-H activities.

CONTACTS:
Knights of Ak-Sar-Ben Foundation
6910 Pacific St.
Ste. 102
Omaha, NE 68106
402-554-9600; fax: 402-554-9609
www.aksarben.org

♦ 0045 ♦ **Akshya Tritiya**
April-May; third day of the waxing half of the Hindu month of Vaisakha

The Hindu observance of Akshya Tritiya in India combines fasting and festivities. *Akshya* means "exempt from decay,"

and the devotions performed on this day are believed to last forever. Hindus fast and worship Vishnu, along with his consort Lakshmi, with holy Ganges water, *tulsi* or basil leaves, incense, flowers, lamps, and new clothes. Bathing in the Ganges River is a popular way to demonstrate one's devotion. This is also the day on which the mountain passes of Sri Badrinarain in the Himalayas open again after the long, snowy winter.

Svetambaras Jains also fast on the third day of the waxing half of Vaisakha. They call this day **Aksaya Tritiya**, and it commemorates the fast observed by the first Tirthankara, whose name was Risabha and who was given some sugar cane juice to break his fast. The Svetambaras or "white-clad" Jains are the dominant group in northern India, and they are called this because they believe that monks should be clothed. The other major Jain sect, the Digambaras or "sky-clad" sect, believe that total nudity is required of monks, although Indian law requires that Digambara monks wear a loincloth in public.

♦ 0046 ♦ **Akwambo (Path-Clearing Festival)**
Date varies

How and when the Akwambo Festival is observed by the Fante people, particularly in the Agona and Gomoa regions of Ghana, varies from place to place. It was first observed by the migrant ancestors of these people, whose primary task when they arrived in a new place was clearing paths to the rivers and other watering places. A day was set aside for this purpose, and for clearing the paths leading to farms and other communal places as well. Everyone who used these routes was expected to attend and help in the work or contribute financially.

In some places, path clearing is no longer necessary because there are paved roads. But the festival is still observed, especially at Agona Nkum, where it is part of a week-long celebration. A traditional part of the festivities is the parade of the Asafo groups. Each town has a number of Asafo companies which, during colonial times, functioned as militias. The literal translation of *asafo* is "people of war." Today they are community associations which together include representatives from nearly every family in town, but the military influence is still seen in the flags and weapons carried by members.

On path-clearing day in Agona Nkum the Asafo companies lead a procession beyond the town's borders where they pay homage to Oburata Kofi, the god of the well. Then, amid firing guns, dancing, and drumming, the procession returns to town, where community members meet with the town chief and other leaders to discuss town laws and other communal matters.

CONTACTS:
Ghana Embassy
3512 International Dr. N.W.
Washington, D.C. 20008
202-686-4520; fax: 202-686-4527
www.ghanaembassy.org

♦ 0047 ♦ **Al Bustan International Festival of Music and the Arts**
February and March

The Al Bustan International Festival of Beirut, Lebanon, annually presents a program of music dance, marionettes, and theater, usually centered on a specific theme. Past events have been devoted to the culture of a particular country or city, or to a special subject.

The festival was founded in 1994 to help revive Lebanon's cultural life after 17 years of war. While chamber music dominates the program, the festival also includes works of opera, orchestral music, and choral music. Each year, the festival offers more than 30 performances over the five-week festival period in February and March. During the festival, participating artists offer master classes and workshops at the National Conservatoire in Beirut and other institutions throughout Lebanon. A visual arts exhibition accompanies every festival, and it has commissioned musical works by such contemporary composers as John Taverner.

CONTACTS:
Al Bustan Festival
Mail Box 343
56 Gloucester Rd.
London SW7 4UB United Kingdom
44-207-937-2633
albustanfestival.com

Lebanon Embassy
2560 28th St. N.W.
Washington, D.C. 20008
202-939-6300
www.lebanonembassyus.org

♦ 0048 ♦ **Al Hareed Festival**
April-May

Al Hareed is an important cultural festival celebrated every year in Jazan, Saudi Arabia, a port city on the coast of Red Sea. Sponsored by the government, the event underscores the importance of the Red Sea and its diverse marine life for the Jazan province and Saudi Arabia as a whole. The first event was celebrated in 2004 and since then has become a cultural tradition in the region, with people from all over the kingdom arriving at Jazan to partake in the festivities. The festival's events are actually held on Farazan Island, about 50 km off shore from Jizan. Ferries and small local boats called *flukas* transport cars and people to the island during the festivities. The festival falls around April or May, around the time the Hareed (parrotfish), make their way to the shallow waters of the Al-Hasis Gulf for the breeding season. Although the exact origin of the festival is not known, it is believed that the celebration in its current form grew out of a centuries-old fishing competition on the island.

The highpoint of the festival is the fishing contest. Fishermen throw nets in the narrow gulf to drive the fish toward the shore, where people wait in knee-deep waters to collect them. The contestant with the biggest catch within the allotted time is declared the winner, and is awarded prize money. Interestingly, no fish are sold on this day, and people either present their catch to their friends or extended family. In recent years the festival has evolved to also include other sporting and cultural events.

CONTACTS:
Saudi Commission for Tourism and Antiquities
B.O.Box 66680
Riyadh, 11586 Saudi Arabia
966-11-8808855; fax: 966-0110-8808844
www.scta.gov.sa/en

♦ 0049 ♦ **Alabama Blueberry Festival**
Third Saturday in June

The Alabama Blueberry Festival is a one-day celebration of the blueberry in Brewton, which is in the only area of Alabama still shipping blueberries commercially. The celebration, dedicated to Dr. W. T. Brightwell, whose improved varieties of the Rabbiteye blueberry were introduced here in 1961, features tours of the local blueberry farms. Events include live entertainment, children's rides, arts and crafts, an antique car show, a food contest, and food booths selling all kinds of locally prepared blueberry dishes, among them cobbler, waffles, ice cream and cakes. Attendance is about 28,000.

CONTACTS:
Greater Brewton Area Chamber of Commerce
1010-B Douglas Ave.
Brewton, AL 36426
251-867-3224; fax: 251-809-1793
brewtonchamber.com

♦ 0050 ♦ **Alahamady Be**
First new moon in March

Alahamady Be is NEW YEAR'S DAY in Madagascar, the fourth largest island in the world, located off the southeastern coast of Africa. The Malagasy new year traditionally begins in March. Alahamady Be is celebrated with the appearance of the year's first new moon. Festivities last for two days. People put on their best clothes, feast, give presents, and sing religious songs. The celebration is particularly festive in the capital city of Antananarivo, which means "town of a thousand warriors." The townspeople make their way to the sacred royal hill known as Ambohimanga, meeting at what was once the site of the queen's palace to offer prayers to the departed. When these devotions are completed it's time to eat.

A favorite food is *romazava*, which is made from meat and herbs and eaten with rice. Sausages, vegetables, and wine made from rice or cane sugar often round out the meal. The feasting is an opportunity for families and friends to get together and wish each other luck in the coming year. Because it is not unusual in Madagascar for Christian beliefs to be combined with traditional customs and practices, Christian hymns are often sung on New Year's Day.

CONTACTS:
Madagascar Embassy

2374 Massachusetts Ave. N.W.
Washington, D.C. 20008
202-265-5525; fax: 202 265 3034
www.madagascar-consulate.org

♦ 0051 ♦ **Alamo Day**
March 6

The cry "Remember the Alamo!" has particular significance for the natives of Texas, which was once part of Mexico. In 1836 a garrison of Texans took a stand against the Mexican army at a Franciscan mission in San Antonio named after the grove of cottonwood trees (*alamo* in Spanish) that surrounded it. Led by Lieutenant William Barret Travis, the band of 187 volunteers, including border heroes Davy Crockett and James Bowie, was besieged for 13 days by 3,000-5,000 Mexicans under the leadership of General Antonio López de Santa Anna. Travis refused to surrender and the Alamo was overrun by the opposing army on the morning of March 6. Only women and children among the defenders survived.

The heroic action at the Alamo gave the Texans time to organize the forces necessary to save their independence movement. Six weeks after the Alamo's fall, General Sam Houston defeated and captured Santa Anna at the battle of San Jacinto (*see* SAN JACINTO DAY), forcing him to sign a treaty recognizing Texas' independence. Since 1897, this day has been celebrated as **Texas Heroes' Day**.

The Daughters of the Republic of Texas (DRT) have managed the Alamo since 1905. DRT is an organization founded by daughters of Texas veterans in 1891 to promote the study and celebration of Texas history.

CONTACTS:
Alamo
300 Alamo Plaza
San Antonio, TX 78205
210-225-1391
www.thealamo.org

San Antonio Living History Association
5310 San Pedro Ave.
San Antonio, TX 78212
210-273-1730
salha.org

♦ 0052 ♦ **Alasitas Fair**
January 24

Each year on January 24 a large marketplace in La Paz, Bolivia, is full of merchants who traditionally call out, "*Alasitas*," an Aymara word meaning "buy from me," to potential buyers of their miniature wares. Shoppers can find tiny replicas of just about every kind of object—cars, houses, foods, furniture, clothes, tools, household goods, and, especially, money—and seek those which represent items they would like to have in the coming year. After purchasing the miniature object of one's desire, the next step is to take it to church to have it blessed.

Presiding over all this downsized commerce is Ekeko, an Aymara god of material wealth, fertility, and good luck. Ekeko is represented as a portly little man who wears a backpack full of goods and whose arms are stretched out, as if in an attitude of acquisition. Many people keep ceramic figures of Ekeko in their homes for good luck.

CONTACTS:
Bolivian Embassy
3014 Massachusetts Ave. N.W.
Washington, D.C. 20008
202-483-4410; fax: 202-328-3712
www.bolivia-usa.org

♦ 0053 ♦ **Alaska Day**
October 18

An official holiday in America's 49th and largest state, Alaska Day commemorates the formal transfer of Alaska from Russia to the United States on October 18, 1867. The event, which took place at Sitka, was a sad one for the Russian colonists who had already made Alaska their home, and it must have seemed that Mother Nature was conspiring against them. A strong wind caught the Russian flag during the transfer ceremony, tangling it in the halyards. The seaman who was finally hoisted up to free it dropped the flag by mistake, and another gust swept it into a group of Russian bayonets. The tattered remains were presented to the weeping wife of Prince Dmitri Maksoutsoff, the last Russian governor.

Today the lowering of the Russian flag and the raising of the Stars and Stripes is reenacted every year as part of this five-day festival in Sitka. Other events include a parade and a period costume ball.

After the transfer, Alaska was eventually organized as a territory and maintained this status until it became a state on January 3, 1959 (*see also* Appendix).

CONTACTS:
Alaska Day Festival Committee
P.O. Box 1355
Sitka, AK 99835
907-747-5124 or 907-752-7556
alaskadayfestival.org

♦ 0054 ♦ **Alba White Truffle Fair**
October-November

Alba, Italy is home to numerous varieties of white truffles and is known as the world capital of truffles. Dating back to 1930, the Alba White Truffle Fair celebrates the town's seasonal abundance of this delicacy. The opening event of the fair is a donkey race called the *Palio degli Asini*, which is held on the first Sunday of October. Along with the race, a procession is held where the people dress up in traditional costumes depicting the history of their city. The fair's highlight is the truffle market at the *Cortile della Maddalena*. In addition, dogs compete in a truffle hunt, and spectators can try hunting truffles themselves with the help of well-trained canines. Another notable activity is the truffle-smelling event, in which experts reveal the details of a truffle, from its type to its preferred method of preparation, based solely on its smell. Other events include chef demonstrations, a wine tasting, and cooking classes for children. The fair concludes with the world white truffle auction.

CONTACTS:
Alba White Truffle Fair
Piazza Medford 3
Alba Italy
39-173-361-051
www.fieradeltartufo.org

♦ 0055 ♦ **Albania Independence Day**
November 28

The Albanian people proclaimed their independence from the Turks on this day in 1912. The Turks had first invaded this part of Europe around 1400, but under the leadership of a brave chief named Skanderbeg, the Albanians held them off for more than 20 years. After his death, however, the Turks conquered Albania, and they continued to rule the country for more than 400 years. It wasn't until the end of the Balkan War that Turkish rule was abolished and a proclamation of independence was issued on November 28, 1912.

Independence Day is a public holiday observed throughout Albania and is marked by a festive parade in Tirana, the capital. It is closely followed by Liberation Day on November 29, the day on which the invasions of German and Italian troops during World War II were terminated in 1944.

CONTACTS:
Albania Embassy
1312 18th St. N.W.
4th Fl.
Washington, D.C. 20036
202-223-4942; fax: 202-628-7342
www.embassyofalbania.org

♦ 0056 ♦ **Albania Republic Day**
January 11

Republic Day was a national holiday in Albania, also known as **Anniversary Day**, which commemorated the founding of the Communist government on January 11, 1946, until April 15, 1991, when the first Parliament since the fall of the Soviet Union convened.

CONTACTS:
Albania Embassy
1312 18th St. N.W.
4th Fl.
Washington, D.C. 20036
202-223-4942
www.embassyofalbania.org

♦ 0057 ♦ **Alberta Heritage Day**
First Monday in August

The province of Alberta, Canada, celebrates its cultural heritage on the first Monday of August. The Legislative Assem-

bly of Alberta made this day an official provincial holiday by passing the Heritage Act of 1974, which also decreed that the observance can occur on the preceding Saturday or Sunday.

The holiday's date differs from that of other Canadian heritage celebrations, which are usually held on the third Monday of February. Despite continuous attempts by the Heritage Canada Foundation to make Heritage Day a national holiday, Alberta has maintained its own calendar date.

A notable annual event scheduled just before Alberta Heritage Day is the Crowsnest Pass Doors Open and Heritage Festival. Held since 2006, this tourist-friendly event takes place in the Canadian Rockies and includes heritage hikes, storytelling, and tours of historical sites and local architecture.

CONTACTS:
Alberta Culture and Tourism
Tourism Division
6th Fl., Commerce Pl.
Edmonton, AB T5J 4L6 Canada
780-415-1319
culture.alberta.ca

♦ 0058 ♦ **Albuquerque International Balloon Fiesta**
First full week in October

The Albuquerque International Balloon Fiesta is one of the world's largest gatherings of hot-air balloonists. More than 1,000 balloons, some more than six-stories high, present dizzying colors and designs in the skies of New Mexico for a nine-day fiesta that attracts nearly a million spectators. Besides the daytime ascensions, illuminated balloons light up the night skies. The fiesta also boasts fireworks and food of all sorts.

See also HOT AIR BALLOON CLASSIC.

CONTACTS:
Albuquerque International Balloon Fiesta Inc.
4401 Alameda N.E.
Albuquerque, NM 87113 Canada
505-821-1000 or 888-422-7277; fax: 505-828-2887
www.balloonfiesta.com

♦ 0059 ♦ **Aldeburgh Festival of Music and the Arts**
June

The English fishing village of Aldeburgh, located on the North Sea about 100 miles from London, may seem an unlikely place for an international music festival. But it was here that English composer Benjamin Britten, singer Peter Pears, and writer-producer Eric Crozier—who together led a touring opera company, the English Opera Group—founded the Aldeburgh Festival in 1948. Then as now, the festival embraced the community as both audience member and participant, and sought to bring together established and new artists. Britten and other composers often premiered their works at the festival, many of which were inspired by the people and landscape of Aldeburgh. When the festival grew out of its performance spaces, a new venue, the Snapes Maltings Concert Hall, was built in 1967 on the site of a former malt brewery barn.

Today, in addition to the 17-day festival, activities continue year-round through Aldeburgh Productions and include classical, folk and jazz concerts; opera; contemporary dance; the Britten-Pears School for Advanced Musical Studies; the Snape Proms; and the Easter Festival.

CONTACTS:
Aldeburgh Music
Snape Maltings Concert Hall
Snape, Suffolk IP17 1SP United Kingdom
44-1728-687-100; fax: 44-1728-687-120
www.aldeburgh.co.uk

♦ 0060 ♦ Aldersgate Experience
Sunday nearest May 24

On the evening of May 24, 1738, John Wesley (1703-1791), co-founder of the Methodist Church, visited a house on Aldersgate Street, London, to join a group reading of Martin Luther's preface to the *Epistle to the Romans*. At about quarter to nine, just as they were reading Luther's description of the change that God works in man's heart, Wesley underwent a conversion experience. "I felt my heart strangely warmed," he says in his account of the evening. From that time until his death in 1791, Wesley considered it his mission in life to tell people about his experience and to invite them to share his beliefs. The anniversary of this event is commemorated by the Methodist Church on the Sunday nearest May 24.

♦ 0061 ♦ Alexandra Rose Day
June; Saturday

Sometimes called **Alexandra Day** or simply **Rose Day**, this day commemorates the arrival of Queen Alexandra (1844-1925), wife of the English king, Edward VII, in England on June 26, 1862. In 1902 the much-loved queen founded the Imperial Military Nursing Service, and in 1912 she started Alexandra Rose Day. The Danish-born queen died 13 years later, but the day is still celebrated by selling rose emblems to raise money for hospitals.

See also HOSPITAL WEEK, NATIONAL.

CONTACTS:
Alexandra Rose Charities
5 Mead Ln.
Farnham, Surrey GU9 7DY United Kingdom
44-125-272-6171
www.alexandrarosecharities.org.uk

♦ 0062 ♦ Algeria Independence Day
July 5

On this day in 1962, more than 100 years of French rule in Algeria came to an end as France officially recognized a ref-

erendum for independence that was passed by a vote of the Algerian people on July 1. Algerians had struggled for independence, or at least equality with the French occupants of their land, with organized movements for revolution since the end of World War I. Independence Day is a legal holiday in Algeria.

Another important celebration takes place on ALGERIA NATIONAL DAY, which commemorates the day the successful revolution against the French began.

CONTACTS:
Algerian Embassy
2118 Kalorama Rd. N.W.
Washington, D.C. 20008
202-265-2800; fax: 202-986-5906
www.algerianembassy.org

♦ 0063 ♦ Algeria National Day
November 1

This national holiday, also known as **Revolution Day,** commemorates the day in 1954 Algerians began their revolution against the French, who had ruled since 1830. Huge crowds of people celebrate in the capital city of Algiers on the Mediterranean coast.

CONTACTS:
Algerian Embassy
2118 Kalorama Rd. N.W.
Washington, D.C. 20008
202-265-2800; fax: 202-986-5906
www.algerianembassy.org

♦ 0064 ♦ All Saints' Day
November 1 in the West; first Sunday after Pentecost in the East

In Roman Catholic, Anglican, and many Protestant churches, the first day of November is a celebration of all the Christian saints—particularly those who have no special feast days of their own. Also known as **All-Hallomas** or **All Hallows' Day**, the idea for this holy day goes back to the fourth century, when the Greek Christians kept a festival on the first Sunday after PENTECOST (in late May or early June) in honor of all martyrs and saints. When the Pantheon at Rome was converted into a Christian place of worship in the seventh century, Pope Boniface IV dedicated it to the Virgin and all the martyrs, and the anniversary of this event was celebrated on May 1.

CONTACTS:
Greek Orthodox Archdiocese of Australia, Archdiocesan District of Victoria and Tasmania
221 Dorcas St.
South Melbourne, VIC 3205 Australia
613-9245-9000; fax: 613-9696-3583
www.greekorthodox.org.au

♦ 0065 ♦ All Saints' Day (France)
November 1

Both All Saints' Day, **La Toussaint**, and ALL SOULS' DAY, *Le Jour des Morts,* are widely observed in France. All Saints' Day is, in fact, a legal holiday in France. Church services in memory of all the saints are held on November 1, but by evening the focus turns toward the dead. Cemeteries everywhere are crowded with people who come to clean and decorate the family graves. All Souls' Day, November 2, is dedicated to prayers for the dead who are not yet glorified. Church services are often followed by visits to the churchyard, and families get together to pay homage to the deceased.

In Brittany, pancakes and cider are set out for the dead on the eve of All Souls' Day, and children play practical jokes in the cemeteries—such as placing lit candles inside skulls, or rattling bones in empty pails—to frighten visitors.

♦ 0066 ♦ **All Saints' Day (Louisiana)**
November 1

ALL SAINTS' DAY is celebrated in many areas of the United States where there are large Roman Catholic populations. In New Orleans, for example, it is a legal holiday on which Catholics gather in local cemeteries and decorate the graves with flowers. The descendants of the French Canadian (also known as Acadian or Cajun) settlers around St. Martinsville, Louisiana, observe this day in the traditional French manner by laying wreaths and bouquets on even the most obscure graves and, as darkness falls, by lighting candles throughout the cemeteries in anticipation of ALL SOULS' DAY on November 2.

♦ 0067 ♦ **All Saints' Day and All Souls' Day (Guatemala)**
October 31-November 2

Throughout Latin America, ALL SAINTS' DAY, November 1, and ALL SOULS' DAY, November 2, are treated like a single holiday. In Guatemala, the Indian villagers of Todos Santos (which means "All Saints") stretch these celebrations honoring the dead into a three-day-long affair by adding October 31. Families pay homage to the dead on All Souls' Day by decorating the graves of their loved ones and offering flowers, corn, squash, and orange slices at church. They position them on the floor of the church, pour some coffee into the flower blossoms, and then shake droplets of brandy over the whole display.

These solemn offerings are in stark contrast to the highlight of the festival, wild horse races, in which many of the riders have been drinking since the previous night. In the town of Santiago Sacatepequez people fly huge kites in the graveyard and many attach prayers and notes to their deceased loved ones to the kites' tails.

♦ 0068 ♦ **All Saints' Day and All Souls' Day (Peru)**
November 1-2

In parts of Peru, the normally solemn celebration of ALL SAINTS' DAY and ALL SOULS' DAY gives way to some lively courtship rituals. In Arequipa and Cuzco, for example, many of the young men deliver cakes in the form of a baby, decorated with colored candies to their sweetheart's home. There they hold a mock baptismal ceremony in which they play the role of godfather. This entering into the ritual relationship of *compadrazgo*, or godfathership, often paves the way for marriage later on. On November 2 the young men of Tomaiquiche village visit their girlfriends' homes at dawn to sing to them. The girls reward their suitors by opening a window or door and dousing them with drops of urine. Although this may not seem like a traditional token of love, urine is kept in a closed container in some homes because it is believed to have curative powers.

CONTACTS:
Commission for the Promotion of Peru for Export and Tourism
Calle Uno Oeste 50
Mincetur Bldg.
Fl. 13 and 14
Lima Peru
511-616-7300
www.promperu.gob.pe/english

♦ 0069 ♦ **All Souls' Day**
November 2 in the West; second Saturday prior to Lent and the day before Pentecost in the East

People held festivals for the dead long before Christianity. It was St. Odilo, the abbot of Cluny in France, who in the 10th century proposed that the day after ALL SAINTS' DAY be set aside in honor of the departed—particularly those whose souls were still in purgatory. Today, the souls of all the faithful departed are commemorated. Although All Souls' Day is observed informally by some Protestants, it is primarily a Roman Catholic, Anglican, and Orthodox holy day.

In many Catholic countries, people attend churches, which are appropriately draped in black, and visit family graves on this day to honor their ancestors. In Shropshire and Cheshire, England, children still go out "souling" from house to house, although they are no longer given the traditional "soul cakes" that were supposed to rescue souls from purgatory. The evening of November 1 is often called **All Souls' Eve** and is a time to decorate graveyards and light candles in memory of the dead.

Orthodox Christians commemorate the dead on the second Saturday before Lent begins and on the day before Pentecost.

In Mexico, it is a national holiday called the DÍA DE LOS MUERTOS (or **Day of the Dead**). In the United States, Día de los Muertos is celebrated in areas where there is a large Mexican-American population.

In Portugal, November 2 is known as **Día dos Finados** (All Souls' Day), and the day is observed with special masses and processions to cemeteries. Similar celebrations are held for All Souls' Day in Ecuador, El Salvador, the French West Indies, Macao, and Uruguay.

In Italy **Il Giorno dei Morti** begins at dawn with a solemn Requiem for the dead. Church bells toll and people decorate the graves of their family members with flowers and candles. But Il Giorno dei Morti is not entirely a somber occasion. In Sicily the children who have prayed for the *morti*, souls of the departed, leave their shoes outside doors and windows, where they are filled with gifts. In Rome, it is customary for young people to announce their engagements on All Souls' Day. The man sends the engagement ring to his fiancée in a small white box, which in turn is packed in an oval container filled with *fave dei morti*, "beans of the dead"—little bean-shaped cakes made of ground almonds and sugar combined with eggs, butter, and flour.

♦ 0070 ♦ All Souls' Day (Cochiti Pueblo)
November 2

The Cochiti Pueblo Indians, who occupy the northernmost of the Keresan-speaking pueblos along the Rio Grande west of Santa Fe, refer to this day as **"Their Grandfathers Arrive from the West Feast"** (or **"Their Grandfathers Arrive from the Dead Feast"**). Converted to Catholicism by Spanish missionaries in the late 17th century, the Cochiti Indians regard ALL SOULS' DAY as an opportunity to persuade the visiting spirits of the departed that they have not been forgotten and that their kin are prospering. Each family fasts, setting out bowls of food in the corner of the house and leaving the door open for the returning spirits. The family's material goods—in the form of blankets, shawls, and jewelry—are displayed on the walls, and candles are lit so that the dead can find their way to their former homes. The men congregate in the *kiva*, or ceremonial chamber, where they spend the night singing and cutting up small pieces of food as offerings for the dead.

Similar ceremonies are held at other Indian pueblos in New Mexico. At Taos Pueblo, for example, the church bell rings all night while candles burn and food is brought to the graves in the churchyard. At the Zuni Pueblo around this same time, **Grandmothers' Day** is celebrated by making offerings of food to the dead. The men and boys spend the day going from house to house singing and receiving food.

CONTACTS:
Indian Pueblo Cultural Center
2401 12th St. N.W.
Albuquerque, NM 87104
505-843-7270 or 866-855-7902
www.indianpueblo.org

♦ 0071 ♦ All-American Soap Box Derby
First Saturday in August

The Soap Box Derby is a youth racing program that has been run nationally since 1934. The idea came from an Ohio journalist named Myron Scott, who was assigned to cover a race of gravity-propelled cars built by young boys in his hometown of Dayton and was so impressed by the event that he began to develop a similar program on a nationwide scale. In 1935 the race was moved to Akron because of its hilly terrain, and the following year a permanent track was constructed through the efforts of the Works Progress Administration (WPA).

The World Championship finals held at Derby Downs in Akron consist of three racing divisions: the Stock Division for girls and boys ages 9-16 competing in simplified cars built from kits; the Kit Car Division for youngsters competing in more advanced models, although still using standardized kits and shells; and the Masters Division for girls and boys ages 11-16 who want to test their creativity and design skills. They can build a car from scratch or purchase and assemble a Masters Kit and shell.

Competitors arrive on the Monday before the race and spend the week working on their cars, participating in trial runs, and relaxing before the big race on Saturday. The home-built cars used in the derby today bear little resemblance to derby cars in the 1930s, many of which were actually built out of soap boxes.

CONTACTS:
International Soap Box Derby
P.O. Box 7225
Akron, OH 44306
330-733-8723; fax: 330-733-1370
www.aasbd.org

♦ 0072 ♦ Allen (Richard), Birthday of
February 14

The son of two slaves, Richard Allen (1760-1831) was born in Philadelphia on this day. By the time he was 26 years old, he had saved enough money to buy his way out of slavery, and soon after that he established an African-American congregation that met on Sunday afternoons in St. George's Methodist Church. Because he didn't want his church to exist solely as an arm of a European-American church, Allen bought some land and set up America's first African-American church in an old blacksmith shop. His followers were known as Allenites.

A new church building, completed in 1794, was dedicated by Francis Asbury, America's first Methodist bishop. Allen's work among African Americans expanded at such a rapid rate that in 1816 he had to expand the organization of his church nationwide. Members of the African Methodist Episcopal (AME) Church commemorate the birth of their founder and first bishop on this day.

CONTACTS:
First Episcopal District of the African Methodist Episcopal Church
First District Plaza
3801 Market St.
Philadelphia, PA 19104
215-662-0506 or 215-387-3550; fax: 215-662-0989
www.firstdistrictame.org

African Methodist Episcopal Church
500 8th Ave. S.
Nashville, TN 37203
615-254-0911; fax: 615-254-0912
www.ame-church.com

♦ 0073 ♦ Alma Highland Festival and Games
May, Memorial Day weekend

Like other American cities and towns founded or settled primarily by Scots, Alma, Michigan, celebrates its Scottish heritage by holding a traditional Highland Festival for three days in late May each year. The festival was originated by a local resident who attended the Scottish games in Boston in 1962 and decided that a similar event should be held in Alma, a city founded by Scots and with a Scottish name.

Activities include Scottish athletic events, border collie demonstrations, fiddling contests, an arts and crafts show, piping, drumming, and highland dancing. Participants come from all over the United States and Canada, and some even come from Scotland. The food served at the festival includes meat pies, haggis (a traditional Scottish dish made from the heart, liver, etc. of a sheep or calf, minced with suet and oatmeal, seasoned, and boiled in the stomach of the animal), bridies (hot sausage or meat rolls), and shortbread.

See also GRANDFATHER MOUNTAIN HIGHLAND GAMES AND GATHERING OF SCOTTISH CLANS; HIGHLAND GAMES; and VIRGINIA SCOTTISH GAMES.

CONTACTS:
Alma Highland Festival
110 W. Superior St.
Alma, MI 48801
989-463-8979; fax: 989-463-6588
www.almahighlandfestival.com

♦ 0074 ♦ **Almabtrieb**
September

The **Return from the Mountain Pasture** is an autumn festival that takes place around Salzburg, Austria, and other areas in the German Alps on the day that the cattle are driven down from the mountain pastures to their winter shelter. The cattle are decorated with flowers and the *Sennerinnen,* or herding girls, who lead them wear traditional costumes that vary from place to place. Sometimes the cattle are brought to their final destination on flower-decked boats that ferry them across the mountain lakes. Once the cattle are safely in for the winter, the farmers hold welcome-home feasts which are followed by music, dancing, and singing.

See also ALPAUFZUG and COW FIGHTS.

CONTACTS:
Province of Salzburg
P.O. Box 527
Salzburg 5010 Austria
43-662-8042; fax: 43-662-8042
www.salzburg.gv.at

♦ 0075 ♦ **Aloha Festivals**
September-October

Aloha Festivals is a celebration of Hawaiian culture. Once a week-long event called Aloha Week, it's now a two-month affair with 300 events that starts in Honolulu in early September and runs through the end of October, with a week of festivities on every island of Hawaii. The celebrations include canoe races between the islands of Molokai and Oahu, coronations of royal courts as commemorations of the former Hawaiian monarchy, street parties, cultural events, parades, and pageantry.

CONTACTS:
Aloha Festivals
P.O. Box 15945
Honolulu, HI 96830
808-923-2030; fax: 808-923-2622
www.alohafestivals.com

♦ 0076 ♦ **Alpaufzug**
May or June

Also known as **Alpine Cattle Drive**, an old custom in Switzerland is this springtime "ascent to the mountains," when goats and cows are driven to higher pasture. In the cantons of Appenzell in eastern Switzerland and also in the Alpine canton of Valais, there are picturesque festivals, with herders and their families dressing in traditional costume (the Appenzell men wear red vests and yellow knicker-type pants) and everyone enjoying the cattle show and COW FIGHTS that establish the leader of the herd. In August and September, bringing the herds back down to the valleys, known as *Alpabfahrten*, also prompts festivals, and the cow that has been the greatest milk producer is feted and decked with flowers.

See also ALMABTRIEB.

CONTACTS:
Appenzellerland Tourismus AI
Hauptgasse 4
Appenzell CH-9050 Switzerland
41-71-788-9641; fax: 41-71-788-9649
www.appenzell.ch

♦ 0077 ♦ **Alpenfest**
Third week in July

At an altitude of 1,348 feet, Gaylord is one of the highest incorporated communities in Michigan. Five rivers rise nearby and flow in different directions. Gaylord receives nearly 150 inches of snow each year and the town's main streets are lined with Swiss-style architecture. The annual Alpenfest is basically a celebration of summer.

A highlight of the festival is the "Burning of the Boog." People write their troubles on slips of paper and place them in the Boog—a 300-pound, 10-foot-high monster—which is then burned, giving spectators a chance to watch their troubles literally go up in smoke. The festival also boasts a number of outdoor cafes which host "the World's Largest Coffee Break.".

CONTACTS:
Gaylord Area Chamber of Commerce
319 W. Main St.
P.O. Box 513
Gaylord, MI 49734
989-732-6333 or 800-345-8621; fax: 989-732-7990
www.gaylordchamber.com

♦ 0078 ♦ **Amalaka Ekadashi**
*February-March; 11th day of waxing half of
Hindu month of Phalguna*

Among Hindus, who respect all animate and inanimate
things because they are manifestations of the Universal Spirit, this is a day for worshipping the Alma tree (Amalaka),
where Vishnu is believed to live. An Amalaka tree is ceremo-
nially bathed and watered, a fast is observed, and Brahmans
are given gifts.

Amalaka Ekadashi also marks the beginning of the HOLI or
spring festival in India, where people splash each other with
colored water and red powder (an aphrodisiac), indulge in
eating and drinking, and generally behave in an uninhibited
manner.

♦ 0079 ♦ **Amarnath Yatra**
*July-August; full moon of Hindu month of
Sravana*

Amarnath Yatra is a pilgrimage to the Amarnath cave, high
in the Kashmir Himalayas, near Pahalgam in northern India.
This cave holds a natural ice lingam, the Hindu phallic symbol of Lord Shiva. The trek to the cave, at an altitude of about
12,700 feet, is along narrow, winding mountain trails. The
thousands of pilgrims who make this trip include everyone
from *sadhus* (holy men) walking barefoot over the stones and
snow to wealthy people being carried by coolies. People can
make the yatra, or pilgrimage, for a few months during the
year when the paths are accessible, but the full moon day of
Sravana has special significance to the devout, since tradition
holds that Shiva first made himself manifest in the lingam on
this day.

CONTACTS:
J & K Tourism Development Corporation
Tourist Reception Center
Vir Marg, Jammu Tawi
Jammu, Jammu & Kashmir India
91-191-2579554 or 800-103-1070; fax: 91-191-2549065
jktdc.co.in

♦ 0080 ♦ **Amazon & Galapagos Day**
February 12

Two significant events happened in Ecuadoran history on the
same date: the discovery of the Amazon River headwaters
by Spanish explorer Francisco de Orellana in 1542 and the
incorporation of the Galapagos Islands in 1832. The country
established the Amazon & Galapagos Day holiday during
the presidency of Jaime Roldós Aguilera (1979–1981). Festivities typically focus more attention on the Amazon story and
the biodiversity of that region than on Ecuador's inclusion of
the Galapagos.

According to legend, Orellana and his exploration party of
Spaniards and native peoples successfully arrived from the
city of Quito to the grand river's headwaters only after defeating a group of warrior women known as "the Amazons."

Following their discovery of the river, they sailed its course
to where it emptied into the Atlantic Ocean. The alternative
name for the holiday, **Dia del Oriente** (Orient Day), is a reference to the eastward destination of the explorers.

In observance of the anniversary, Ecuadoran presidents have
visited the Amazon and paid homage to the historic expedition of 1542. Other activities include traditional dances, the
presentation of folklore, and other cultural festivities.

CONTACTS:
Ecuador Embassy
11150 Fairfax Blvd.
Ste. 408
Fairfax, VA 22030
703-383-0077; fax: 703-383-1177
www.galapagos.org

♦ 0081 ♦ **Ambedkar Jayanti**
April 14

Bhimrao Ramji Ambedkar (April 14, 1891- December 6,
1956), also known as B.R. or Babasaheb Ambedkar, was a
jurist, scholar, and the first Law Minister of independent
India who played a central role in drafting the Indian Constitution. Ambedkar was an influential social reformer who
campaigned against discrimination of lower castes in India
and is revered throughout the world as an advocate for the
disadvantaged. His life is honored as Ambedkar Jayanti, a
public holiday observed throughout India on April 14th. On
Ambedkar Jayanti, prominent political leaders pay homage
to Ambedkar's statue at Parliament in New Delhi, while people throughout the country hold rallies, parades, and other
celebrations in his honor. Ambedkar was born in the present
day state of Madhya Pradesh to a family that belonged to the
Dalit caste. Dalits were an oppressed people in India, called
"untouchables" and discriminated against by people of higher castes in all aspects of society. Though he faced oppression
as a child, Ambedkar became highly educated, obtaining advanced degrees from universities in the United States and
Britain. As a leader of the Dalits, Ambedkar helped secure
reforms that gave the people some representation in government. Once law minister, he was a principal architect of the
constitution that granted civil liberties to individuals and
outlawed discrimination against Dalits, and fought to ensure
its passage. In 1990, Dr. B. R. Ambedkar was conferred with
India's highest civilian honor, the Bharat Ratna.

CONTACTS:
Ministry of Tourism
1270 Avenue of the Americas
Ste. 303
New York, NY 10020
212-586-4901; fax: 212-582-3274
tourism.nic.in

♦ 0082 ♦ **American Birkebeiner**
Last weekend in February

The Birkie started in 1973 as a 55-kilometer cross-country ski
race from Hayward, Wis., to Telemark Resort in the neigh-

boring town of Cable, with only 35 skiers competing. Now it is the largest and most prestigious cross-country ski race in North America, an event that attracts top cross-country skiers from all over the world. In addition to the 55-kilometer Birkie, there is also the Kortelopet or "short race" of 23 kilometers, which is open to competitors ages 13 and up. Other races held during the three-day festival include the Barnebirkie (for children) and the 10K Family Fun Ski.

The American Birkebeiner is part of the Worldloppet, an international series of 12 marathon races held in Japan, Switzerland, Sweden, Norway, France, Germany, Austria, Finland, Italy, Canada, Australia, and the United States.

The American race was patterned after the Birkebeiner Rennet in Lillehammer, Norway. During the 13th century, a foreign invader was about to capture Norway's infant prince and heir to the throne. He was saved by two Viking warriors—called "Birkebeiners" for the birch-bark leggings they wore. These men took the child and skied 55 kilometers to safety. The baby eventually became the great Norwegian king, Haakon Haakonsson.

See also VASALOPPET.

CONTACTS:
American Birkebeiner Ski Foundation
10527 Main St.
P.O. Box 911
Hayward, WI 54843
715-634-5025; fax: 715-634-5663
www.birkie.com

♦ 0083 ♦ **American Black Film Festival**
June

Jeff Friday founded the American Black Film Festival (formerly called the Acapulco Black Film Festival) in 1997. This event promotes the works of African-American artists in all spheres of film and television production. The festival has received recognition from such Hollywood luminaries as Denzel Washington, Halle Berry, and Spike Lee. The American Black Film Festival features activities such as gala events, special screenings, awards presentations, and educational opportunities for emerging talent.

CONTACTS:
Film Life Inc.
Chelsea Piers - Pier 62
Ste. 303
New York, NY 10011
646-922-8129
www.thefilmlife.com

♦ 0084 ♦ **American Indian Film Festival**
Early November

The American Indian Film Institute conducts the yearly American Indian Film Festival in San Francisco, California. Originally founded in Seattle, Washington, in 1975 and moved to San Francisco in 1977, the festival is produced by Native Americans and is dedicated to the screening of Native

American films. The American Indian Film Institute's jury judges the movies shown during the festival, with winners announced at the American Indian Motion Picture Awards show every year. The event also includes workshops, discussions, and panel talks.

CONTACTS:
American Indian Film Institute
333 Valencia St.
Ste. 322
San Francisco, CA 94103
415-554-0525; fax: 415-554-0542
aifisf.com/festival/2014

♦ 0085 ♦ **American Indian Heritage Month**
November

In 1914 Red Fox James of the Blackfeet tribe rode a pony 4,000 miles to present his request—endorsed by the governors of 24 states—that a day be set aside in honor of American Indians, or Native Americans, a name many prefer. The first general American Indian Day was observed on the second Saturday in May 1916, but throughout the 20th century, the observance and its date were left to the individual states, and they have varied widely. Since 1995 the month of November has been observed as American Indian Heritage Month.

Few would argue that the plight of American Indians today is not a grim one, with unemployment, illiteracy, and high school drop-out rates among the highest in the country. Although the largest Indian populations can be found in Oklahoma, Arizona, California, New Mexico, and North Carolina, many other states have come up with ways to draw attention to their unique contribution to American culture and to the need for improving their condition. Most celebrations focus on educational and promotional events, displays of Native American art and dance, and agricultural fairs.

CONTACTS:
National Congress of American Indians
Embassy of Tribal Nations
1516 P St. N.W.
Washington, D.C. 20005
202-466-7767; fax: 202-466-7797
www.ncai.org

♦ 0086 ♦ **American Royal Livestock, Horse Show and Rodeo**
October-November

Also known as the **American Royal**, or simply the **Royal**, this is the oldest and one of the largest livestock shows and rodeos in the United States. It dates back to the period just after the Civil War, when Texans returning from the battlefield discovered that their cattle herds had multiplied unchecked. They were forced to conduct massive roundups that reached as far west as Kansas City, Missouri, which soon became a center for the consignment of cattle. Meat packers started building plants there to accommodate the supply, and breeders began to show their stock. The National Hereford Show, held in the Kansas City Stockyards in 1899, is now considered the first American Royal. Over the years the Hereford breeders were joined by breeders of other cattle as well as sheep, swine, and poultry. Draft and carriage horses were first shown at the Royal in 1903.

Although the Royal has suffered some setbacks over the years—including a fire that nearly destroyed the American Royal Building in 1922 and a serious flood in 1951—it has continued to expand. Now more than 270,000 people attend the events at the American Royal Complex, which include the annual World's Largest Barbecue contest. Beginning in June, there are special tours and instruction for school children, 20,000 of whom come to the show to learn more about agribusiness. The main events occur in October and November. The **American Royal Rodeo** is part of the Professional Rodeo Cowboys Association (PRCA) Million Dollar Gold Tour and competitors at the Royal vie for more than $300,000 in prize money during the three-day rodeo event. There are also livestock auctions, horse and livestock shows, country music concerts, barbecue competitions, and a parade through downtown Kansas City that has been called America's largest hometown parade.

CONTACTS:
American Royal Association
1701 American Royal Ct.
Kansas City, MO 64102
816-221-9800; fax: 816-221-8189
www.americanroyal.com

♦ 0087 ♦ **American Solar Challenge**
July

A biannual competition in which participants design, build, and race solar-powered cars in a cross-country event. The cars entered in the race (called "rayce" due to the solar-powered vehicles used) are designed and built by teams of engineering students from about 20 American and Canadian universities. The purpose of the event is "to promote and celebrate educational excellence and engineering creativity."

Originally begun as Sunrayce USA in 1990 and organized by General Motors, the race was renamed the American Solar Challenge in 2001 and the American Solar Challenge in 2005. When the Department of Energy withdrew its support, the 2007 race was cancelled. The event is now sponsored by Toyota and the Crowder College MARET Center. The 2008 race will run some 2,500 miles from Dallas, Texas, to Calgary, Alberta, Canada, while the previous race, in 2005, went from Chicago to Los Angeles. While on the road, each solar-powered car is accompanied by a safety vehicle sporting rooftop hazard flashers; each solar caravan is accompanied by an official observer to keep contestants apprised of possible road problems ahead. The American Solar Challenge is the longest solar-powered car race in the world.

CONTACTS:
Innovators Educational Foundation
P.O. Box 2368
Rolla, MO 65402
americansolarchallenge.org

♦ 0088 ♦ **American West, Festival of the**
July-August

This eight-day festival was started in 1972 by Glen L. Taggart, president of Utah State University in Logan, and takes place from late July to early August. Designed to educate people about America's pioneer and Indian cultures at the close of the 19th century, the festival includes a multimedia historical pageant; a cowboy poetry gathering; an exhibit of Western art, photographs, and engravings; a display of vintage steam tractors; an Old West parade of antique horse-drawn wagons; and demonstrations of pioneer cooking. Various celebrities— including actors Robert Redford, Peter Strauss, and James Drury—have participated in past festivals, and Jimmy Stewart did the taped narration that still accompanies festival events.

Proceeds from the yearly festival have been used to establish a center for the Outlaw-Lawman History Association at Utah State University, a Western Writers' Conference, and two Western magazines. The events are held on the USU campus and in surrounding areas.

CONTACTS:
American West Heritage Center
4025 S. Hwy. 89-91
Wellsville, UT 84339
435-245-6050
www.awhc.org

♦ 0089 ♦ **America's Cup**
Held whenever the Cup is challenged, usually every 3-4 years

The America's Cup races are the world's longest-running international sporting event. The event is named for the trophy, originally called the Hundred Guinea Cup by the Royal Yacht Squadron of Great Britain, that was won by the 100-foot schooner *America* in a race around the Isle of Wight in 1851. The Cup was given by the schooner 's owner, J. C. Stevens, to the New York Yacht Club, which successfully defended it against international challenges for 130 years. In 1984, the challenger *Australia II* defeated the American defender *Courageous* in races off Newport, Rhode Island, marking the end of the longest winning streak in international sports. In 1987, the American challenger *Stars & Stripes*, sailing for the San Diego Yacht Club, regained the Cup in races off Perth, Australia. *Stars & Stripes* successfully defended the cup in 1988 against New Zealand, and in 1992 *America3* retained the Cup for the United States by defeating the Italian boat four races to one.

The race is usually held every three to four years, with challengers coming from England, Canada, France, Sweden, Italy, New Zealand, Australia, Japan, and other countries. The rules require that the defenders and challengers sail in closely matched boats built to the same general specifications, but designs have varied over the years as sailing technology has grown more sophisticated. A new class of boats, the America's Cup class, was introduced in 1991.

The New Zealand team won the Cup in 1995 and again in 2000. The Swiss team took the Cup in 2003 and 2007. The 2007 event was held in Spain, the first time since 1951 that it was held in Europe. After a contentious legal battle over which team would be the challenger for the 2010 regatta, the U.S.'s Golden Gate Yacht Club captured the 33rd America's Cup, defeating Switzerland's Société Nautique de Genève in an unusual best-of-three race series in Valencia, Spain. In 2013, the race featured a new class of boat, a hydro-foiling, wing-sailed catamaran: the AC72. The resulting match between the two final teams was the longest on record both for time and the number of races, with the American team coming from behind to claim victory over New Zealand. In 2017, the race will be held in Bermuda, with Golden Gate Yacht Club defending the America's Cup.

CONTACTS:
America's Cup
Pier 23
Ste. 100
San Francisco, CA 94111
www.americascup.com

♦ 0090 ♦ **Amherstburg Heritage Homecoming**
September

During the period of slavery in America, a secret network of people was established to help slaves escape to freedom. This network became known as the Underground Railroad. The Underground Railroad used several routes, with one route ending in Amherstburg, Ontario.

In 1793, Upper Canada passed the Anti-slave Law, which ended the importation of slaves into Upper Canada. It also granted freedom to all born after that date when they reached the age of 25. This made Upper Canada a safe place for slaves hoping to escape the tyranny of American slave owners. Amherstburg could easily be reached by crossing the Detroit River, which runs between Detroit and Windsor, Ontario, so this became the destination of many escaped slaves.

Amherstburg became a main center in the history and development of the community of black Canadians. Blacks participated in all aspects of business and community life. They were innkeepers, grocers, tobacconists, millers, and shoemakers. The core of the black community was the church. Nazery African Methodist Episcopal Church (now the site of The North American Black Museum) was established in 1848, and the First Baptist Church was established in 1849.

The Amherstburg Heritage Homecoming is an annual multi-family reunion for the families and friends of those whose ancestors found freedom in Amherstburg, and the descendants of those who aided, supported, and welcomed them as citizens and neighbors.

The idea of having a multi-family reunion came up during various family reunions around town. In September 2002, several families got together at the First Baptist Church in Amherstburg to discuss the multi-family reunion idea. During this meeting, the group decided that, if possible, the event should occur on the historic EMANCIPATION DAY date.

Within a few months of this first meeting, an Executive Committee was formed, and many more families became involved. Over the next year, many people worked to make the reunion a reality. This was to be an event where the children could share with pride their heritage and a day where they could remember the sacrifices made by their ancestors to implement an important and positive change.

During the Amherstburg Heritage Homecoming weekend, activities include a re-enactment of the slave crossing, a parade, music, religious services, picnics, arts and crafts, and other fair-type festivities.

♦ 0091 ♦ **Amsterdam Light Festival**
Early December to late January

The city of Amsterdam lights up during winter nights for more than 40 days in December and January for the Amsterdam Light Festival. Founded in 2012-13, the annual event is organized by a public-private partnership involving the municipality, local businesses, and various organizations in the creative sector. Each year a theme is set; for example, in 2014-15, it was "A Bright City." Light artists from all over the world present their works at the festival using the latest in lighting technology.

The Amsterdam Light Festival has two major attractions—the boat route and the walking route. The boat route, called "Water Colors," takes visitors on a cruise along the canals to experience the essence of the festival. The city's various bridges, buildings, and historic structures along the banks of the Amstel River are adorned with works of light art. Museums and cultural institutions across the city are very much a part of the festival, which also features night photography exhibits, walking tours, and lots of eating and drinking.

CONTACTS:
Amsterdam Light festival
Amsterdam The Netherlands
www.amsterdamlightfestival.com/en

Amsterdam Marketing Travel Trade Department
P.O. Box 3331
Amsterdam, 1001 AC The Netherlands
31-20-702-6000; fax: 31-20-625-2869
www.iamsterdam.com/en

♦ 0092 ♦ **Amurdad, Feast of**
July, November, December; seventh day of
Amurdad, the fifth Zoroastrian month

The Feast of Amurdad is one of the "sacred name days" in the Zoroastrian religion, where both the day and the month share the name of the same *yazata* or spiritual being—in this case Amurdad, who presides over plants and is represented by fruits and flowers. Amurdad also stands for immortality.

The Zoroastrian calendar has 12 months of 30 days each, plus five extra days at the end of the year. Because of discrepancies in the calendars used by widely separated Zoroastrian communities around the world, there are now three different calendars in use, and the 7th of Amurdad can fall either in July, November, or December.

Followers of the Zoroastrian religion, which was founded by the prophet Zoroaster (also known as Zarathushtra, who is believed to have lived around 1200 B.C.E.), today live primarily in Iran and northwestern India, although smaller communities exist in Pakistan, Sri Lanka, Canada, the U.S., England, and Australia.

♦ 0093 ♦ An tOireachtas
Early November

The original *Oireachtas,* or "Assembly," dates back to the ancient kingdoms of seventh-century Ireland. In 1897 Conradh na Gaeilge revived the tradition of assembly and discussion that had begun centuries earlier by founding what is now Ireland's oldest annual cultural festival. An tOireachtas is a 10-day celebration of Irish culture and language, and it includes lectures, debates, literary and stage competitions, concerts, art exhibitions, storytelling, and performances of traditional Irish song, music, and dance. A highlight of the festival is the *sean-nós,* or traditional singing in the Irish language. The sean-nós singing competitions culminate in the *Corn Uí Riada,* the final competition for the coveted Ó Riada Trophy.

Sponsored by the Gaelic League, the festival is held in a different venue each year. It is similar to the EISTEDDFOD in Wales and the GAELIC MOD in Scotland.

CONTACTS:
Oireachtas na Gaeilge
6 Sráid Fhearchair
Baile Átha Cliath 2
Éire Ireland
353-1-475-3857; fax: 353-1-475-8767
www.antoireachtas.ie

♦ 0094 ♦ Anant Chaturdashi
August-September; 14th day of waxing half of Hindu month of Bhadrapada

Among Hindus, this is a day for worshipping and meditating on the god Vishnu. A day-long fast is observed, with offerings of fruits, sweets, and flowers to Vishnu. A thread colored in turmeric paste and having 14 knots is tied on the upper right arm while meditating in the belief that it will protect the worshipper from evil and bring prosperity and happiness. ThePandava princes in exile observed this fast on the advice of Sri Krishna and as a result, they defeated the Kauravas and regained their lost kingdom (*see* BHISHMA ASHTAMI).

♦ 0095 ♦ Anastenaria
May 21-23

Anastenaria is a firewalking ceremony in Greece, in the communes of Agia Eleni near Serres and of Langada near Thessalonike. Men and women, some holding red kerchiefs and some carrying icons of St. Constantine and St. Helen—in whose honor the ceremonies are held—dance barefooted on red-hot coals while folk musicians play. The custom is supposed to have originated in an ancient form of worship that was brought by travelers from Kosti in Eastern Thrace and adapted to Christian beliefs.

Firewalking has been practiced in many parts of the world and has been thought at times to ensure a good harvest and at other times to purify the participants.

CONTACTS:
Greek National Tourism Organisation
305 E. 47th St.
2nd Fl.
New York, NY 10017
212-421-5777; fax: 212-826-6940
www.visitgreece.gr

♦ 0096 ♦ Anchorage Festival of Music
June

A major cultural event in Alaska, the Anchorage Festival of Music was established in 1956 by Mary Hale, an arts patron who lived in the city, and Robert Shaw, the world-famous maestro of choral music. Since its inception, this classical music festival has brought local, national, and international orchestral and choral musicians together to perform in chamber recitals and concerts during the month of June. The festival also has an educational component in its Summer Music Conservatory, cosponsored by the Anchorage Festival of Music and the University of Alaska at Anchorage, a program for musicians ages 11-18 with prior instrumental and/or vocal experience. In addition to featuring such works as those of Ludwig van Beethoven (1770-1827), Wolfgang Amadeus MOZART (1756-1791), and Gioacchino Rossini (1792-1868), the festival presents some contemporary classics—hit songs from popular Broadway shows.

CONTACTS:
Anchorage Festival of Music
P.O. Box 100272
Anchorage, AK 99510
907-276-2465
www.anchoragefestivalofmusic.org

♦ 0097 ♦ Anchorage Fur Rendezvous
Begins on the second Friday in February

The Anchorage Fur Rendezvous, also called the **Rondy** and sometimes the **Mardi Gras of the North**, is a 10-day city-wide celebration held in Anchorage, Alaska. The Rondy has its origins in the days when fur trappers, joined by miners, capped off a season of trapping by carousing in Anchorage; this annual rendezvous was formalized as a winter carnival in 1936.

Highlighting the celebration is the World Championship Sled Dog Race, a 75-mile race run in three 25-mile legs on three successive days, starting and ending in Anchorage. Contestants come from throughout the United States. Among the scores of other events and exhibits are parades, the Miners and Trappers Ball, Eskimo blanket tossing, Eskimo dances, a snowshoe baseball game, wristwrestling matches, and performances of an old-time melodrama. Special Alaskan foods sold include sourdough pancakes.

See also IDITAROD TRAIL SLED DOG RACE.

CONTACTS:
Greater Anchorage, Inc
400 D St.
Ste. 110
Anchorage, AK 99501
907-274-1177; fax: 907-277-2199
www.furrondy.net

♦ 0098 ♦ **Andersen (Hans Christian) Festival**
Mid-June through July

Since 1965, the city of Odense, where Danish author Hans Christian Andersen (1805-1875) lived as a child, has honored its native son with festival activities during the summer. Each year, the Hans Christian Andersen Festival presents a choreographed musical production of one of Andersen's fairy tales at the Funen Village outdoor amphitheater. The play is performed once a day, with a cast of about 85 children and young adults. Past performances have included "The Tinder Box," "The Ugly Duckling," "Little Claus and Big Claus," and "Simple Simon." From mid-June through July, the fairy tale castle in the garden behind the Hans Christian Andersen Museum is the site of the Hans Christian Andersen Parade, with 30-minute shows three times a day. Playing the roles of 35 favorite Andersen characters, the troupe performs scenes from the writer's most popular fairy tales.

See also CHILDREN'S BOOK DAY, INTERNATIONAL.

CONTACTS:
H.C. Andersen Festivals
Vintapperstræde 2
2nd Fl.
Odense 5000 Denmark
45-2296-8220
www.hcafestivals.com

♦ 0099 ♦ **Andorra National Day**
September 8

The Principality of Andorra, located in the Pyrénées Mountains between France and Spain, was founded by the Emperor Charlemagne, who recovered the region from the Muslims in 803. (*See also* ST. CHARLEMAGNE'S DAY.) His son later granted part of his empire to the Spanish bishop of Urgell, and by the late 13th century the citizens of Andorra were ruled by two princes, one in Spain and one in France. Until recently, the principality had been governed jointly by the bishop of Urgell and the king, and, later, the president of France.

On September 8, 1278, Andorra's first constitutional document, known as the "Pareatges," was signed. Among other things, it stated that each of the co-rulers would receive a token tribute each year known as the Questia. Originally, the French king received $2 biennially; the bishop $8, plus six hams, six cheeses, and 12 hens in alternate years. On March 14, 1993, the people of Andorra voted to abandon this mode of government and institute a parliamentary system.

The people of Andorra celebrate their National Day by honoring Jungfrau von Meritxell, their patron saint. Pilgrims climb to her hilltop sanctuary near the villages of Encamp and Canillo, where her statue was found by a shepherd under an almond tree (some say a rose bush) blooming out of season. The pilgrims stop to refresh themselves with drinks that have been cooled in the nearby springs, and after the sermon they celebrate by dancing and eating lamb grilled on slabs of slate.

CONTACTS:
Ministry of Tourism, Andorra
Camí de la Grau s/n
Prat del Rull Bldg.
Andorra la Vella AD500 Andorra
376-875-702; fax: 376-860-184
www.visitandorra.com

♦ 0100 ♦ **Angam Day**
October 26

Nauru is an island in the Pacific, about 2,200 miles northeast of Sydney, Australia, and 2,400 miles southwest of Honolulu. Over the past 100 years, the existence of Nauruans has been threatened a number of times—by tribal disputes in the 1870s, which reduced the population to fewer than 1,000, and by an influenza epidemic in 1919. During World War II, two-thirds of the population was deported by the Japanese to the Caroline Islands to build airstrips.

Although the population has increased substantially since then, it is still a cause for concern. Angam Day (angam means "hope") on October 26 commemorates the various occasions when the Nauruan population has reached 1,500, which is considered the minimum number necessary for survival.

CONTACTS:
Permanent Mission of the Republic of Nauru to the UN
801 Second Ave.
Third Fl.
New York, NY 10017
212-937-0074; fax: 212-937-0079
www.un.int/nauru

♦ 0101 ♦ **Angelitos, Los**
October 30

For the Mayan Indians living near Cancún in southeastern Mexico, October 30 was a day devoted to children who had died, the *angelitos,* or "little angels." It was customary for families to put flowers on their doors and to cook up treats for the angelitos who would visit them that night. Los Angelitos marked the beginning of the period during which all the dead were commemorated. Mexicans celebrate the Day of the Dead, or DÍA DE LOS MUERTOS, on ALL SOULS' DAY, November 2.

♦ 0102 ♦ **Angkor Photography Festival**
Late November

The first annual photography event in Southeast Asia, the Angkor Photography Festival takes place in Siem Reap, a town in northwestern Cambodia near the ancient ruins of Angkor. The photographic selections of this exhibition typically focus on the regions of South Asia, Southeast Asia, and the Far East, although the festival welcomes submissions from all over the world.

The festival caters to two genres in the field—humanistic (or concerned) documentary photography and fine art photography. Festivalgoers view works in print exhibitions and outdoor projections set up in different Siem Reap locations.

The festival was co-founded by journalist Gary Knight, photographer Christophe Loviny, and gallerist Jean-Yves Navel in 2005. Their mission—beyond displaying excellent photographs—was to pool the resources of compassionate artists to serve Cambodia's marginalized groups. Each festival, which lasts roughly 10 days, offers youths free workshops led by established photographers. One such workshop offered in 2007 festival used photography to empower women with HIV to document their situation.

CONTACTS:
Angkor Photo Festival & Workshops
B05, Sivatha Blvd
Siem Reap Cambodia
855-12-773-918
angkor-photo.com

♦ 0103 ♦ **Angola Independence Day**
November 11

This national holiday commemorates Angola's formal independence from Portugal on this day in 1975, after battling for autonomy since the beginning of the 20th century.

CONTACTS:
Angola Embassy
2100-2108 16th St. N.W.
Washington, D.C. 20009
202-785-1156; fax: 202-822-9049
www.angola.org

♦ 0104 ♦ **Angola National Heroes Day**
September 17

National Heroes Day in Angola is celebrated on the birthday of the man considered to be the nation's founder, Antonio Agostinho Neto. Born in 1922 in the Bengo province and educated as a doctor, Neto was a powerful force in Angolan history, as well as one of the country's foremost poets. He led the Popular Movement for the Liberation of Angola (PMLA) in the fight for Angola's independence from Portugal. Neto continued to lead that group through years of civil war that raged in Angola after Portugal withdrew and various nationalist groups struggled for power. He also served as Angola's first president, holding office from 1975 until his death in 1979.

National Heroes Day honors Neto, his ideals for his country, and his accomplishments, as well as those who lost their lives in the struggle for Angolan independence. In addition to ceremonies and speeches, special sports events are often held on this day, including competitions in basketball, cycling, football, chess, swimming, volleyball, and other athletics.

CONTACTS:
Angolan Embassy
2100-2108 16th St. N.W.
Washington, D.C. 20009
202-785-1156; fax: 202-822-9049
www.angola.org

♦ 0105 ♦ **Anjou Festival**
July

Every summer the Festival d'Anjou, a celebration of the performing and visual arts held in Angers, France, gives young artists an opportunity to work with and learn from professionals in their fields through the educational workshops offered during the festival. Some of the world's best-known dance and theatrical groups have come to perform at the festival since its founding in 1975. Most of these performances are held either outdoors or inside abbeys, castles, and churches.

CONTACTS:
France Tourism Development Agency
825 3rd Ave.
New York, NY 10022
212-838-7800; fax: 212-838-7855
int.rendezvousenfrance.com

♦ 0106 ♦ **Ann Arbor Art Fair**
A Weekend in July

Established in 1960, the Ann Arbor Art Fair is a group of four independent, contemporary art events. Every year, over 1,000 artists showcase their talents before half a million attendees in Ann Arbor, Michigan. The eclectic festival comprises the original Street Art Fair, the State Street Area Art Fair, the Summer Art Fair, and the South University Art Fair. The festival also hosts children's events as well as music and dance performances by local community groups and professionals.

The first of the four events, the Street Art Fair, takes place on the University of Michigan campus, and begins with a free, kick-off event for the local community. The State Street Area Art Fair presents nearly 300 artists along the streets of Ann Arbor, where visitors peruse contemporary and traditional arts and crafts, including paintings, ceramics, glassworks, jewelry, fiber arts, and wood art. Alongside the art merchants, food vendors offer a diverse selection of cuisines. The Summer Art Fair, run by the Guild of Artists & Artisans, is held in two locations, one on the University of Michigan campus and the other in downtown Ann Arbor. The Guild hosts over 370 exhibitions, as well as demonstrations, training programs, and art therapy sessions. The South University Art Fair is spread across the entire South University area. Combining the nouveau and traditional, the event attracts both local and international artists.

CONTACTS:
Ann Arbor Art Fairs
721 E. Huron St.
Ste. 200
Ann Arbor, MI 48104
734-994-5260; fax: 734-994-0504
www.artfair.org

◆ 0107 ◆ Ann Arbor Film Festival
March

Held annually in Ann Arbor, Michigan, since 1963, the Ann Arbor Film Festival is the longest-running juried venue for independent and experimental cinema in North America. The event features more than 40 programs, consisting of 180 films from at least 20 countries, that are all screened during a six-day period. The festival includes retrospectives, gallery installations, and panel discussions, and is one of the qualifying festivals for the Academy Awards. The Ann Arbor Film Festival pioneered the concept of a travelling film festival, screening movies at 35 universities, museums, and theaters in various American, Canadian, and European cities.

CONTACTS:
Ann Arbor Film Festival
217 N. First St.
Ann Arbor, MI 48104
734-995-5356; fax: 734-995-5396
www.aafilmfest.org

◆ 0108 ◆ Anna Parenna Festival
March 15

Anna Parenna was a Roman goddess who represented the circle or ring of the year—Anna being the feminine form of *annus* (meaning "year") and March, the month her festival was observed, being the first month of the Roman calendar. Anna was usually depicted as the old woman of the year that had just passed, while Mars was the god of the first month of the new year. According to legend, in 494 B.C.E. the ancient Roman *plebs,* or common citizens, fled the city to put political pressure on the patricians (aristocracy), who needed the plebs for the army. They took refuge on the Mons Sacer, a mountain near Rome. They began to run out of food and suffer starvation. Anna, an old woman from Bovillae, brought them cakes every day. When peace was reestablished, the people made her one of their deities and added *Parenna* (meaning "enduring" or "lasting throughout the year") to her name.

On the day of her festival, the plebs of Rome went to the Campus Martius, a large field outside the walls of the city, and lay about on the grass, often pitching tents or constructing simple huts out of stakes and branches with togas stretched across the top. They spent the day drinking, dancing, and singing, returning to the city at night in a state of deep intoxication. As they drank, they often prayed to Anna to let them live as many years as the number of cups of wine they had swallowed.

◆ 0109 ◆ Annakut Festival
October-November; first day of waxing half of Hindu month of Kartika

This Hindu festival is observed on the day following DEWALI in northern India. It celebrates an event in Krishna's life in which he lifted the Govardhan Mountain on his little finger for seven days, to protect the cows and people of Vrindavana (now in the state of Uttar Pradesh) against the deluge of rain sent by Indra, god of the heavens and rains. People come to the nearby town of Vrindavan from all over India to visit and worship at Mount Govardhan on this day. Those who cannot make the trip worship at home and give gifts to Brahmans. Hindus all over the world celebrate this day by preparing hundreds of different food dishes and taking them to temples to offer to the gods.

CONTACTS:
Ministry of Tourism, Government of India
1270 Ave. of the Americas
Ste. 303
New York, NY 10020
212-586-4901; fax: 212-582-3274
tourism.gov.in

◆ 0110 ◆ Annapolis Valley Apple Blossom Festival
Five or six days beginning last week in May

Nova Scotia's Annapolis Valley is widely known for its apple orchards, which begin to flower in late May or early June. The area's first Apple Blossom Festival was held in 1933 in the town of Kentville, but since that time it has grown into a nearly week-long celebration whose events are held throughout the 60 towns and villages of the Annapolis Valley. In addition to a children's parade, sporting events, tours to view the apple blossoms, apple pie baking and eating contests, and a cooking competition, the festival includes the crowning of "Queen Annapolisa," who is chosen from among 18 local princesses.

The festival is also designed to draw attention to the area's historic background as "The Land of Evangeline," the heroine of Henry Wadsworth Longfellow's long narrative poem about the expulsion of a group of Acadians and their subsequent settlement in Louisiana.

CONTACTS:
Apple Blossom Festival Committee
217 Belcher St.
Kentville, NS B4N 1E2 Canada
902-678-8322; fax: 902-678-3710
www.appleblossom.com

◆ 0111 ◆ Annecy International Animation Film Festival
Six days in early June

The Annecy International Animation Film Festival is held annually in June in Annecy, France. As the name suggests, the festival is dedicated to the screening of animated films.

Established animators, film directors, and students attend the event, which takes place in various venues throughout the city and on the outdoor promenade along Lake Annecy. The festival shows around 230 films each year from some of the world's top animation companies. Open-air screenings take place during the evenings. Exhibitions based on the theme of the year, as well as panel discussions on such topics as artistic direction, graphics, and production, round out the festival schedule. At the end of the week, awards are presented in such categories as best feature film, short film, and television film. The International Animation Film Market (Mifa) is a mini-festival within the larger event. Designed for industry professionals, Mifa offers seminars and hands-on workshops focusing on technologies, co-productions, work distribution, promotion, and other activities related to the animation trade.

CONTACTS:
Conservatoire d'art et d'histoire
18 avenue du Trésum
BP 399
Annecy Cedex, 74013 France
334-5010-0900; fax: 334-5010-0970
www.annecy.org/home

♦ 0112 ♦ **Annual Lantern Ceremony**
Eve of Patriots' Day (the third Monday in April)

The Annual Lantern Ceremony takes place every year on the eve of Patriots' Day, a public holiday observed in Massachusetts and Maine on the third Monday in April. Patriots' Day commemorates the American Revolutionary War battles of Lexington and Concord on April 19, 1775. The ceremony is held at the Old North Church in Boston (formal name: Christ Church in the City of Boston), which was built in 1723 and is the oldest standing church building in the city. It permanently entered the American history books on the evening of April 18, 1775. That night, the church sexton, Robert Newman, displayed two lanterns from the church steeple, signaling Paul Revere's fateful message that the British would come to Lexington and Concord "by sea" (i.e., across the Charles River), not by land.

The Annual Lantern Ceremony commemorates the lighting of the two lamps that launched a remarkable episode in U.S. history. The centerpiece of the ceremony each year is a keynote address by a notable leader of the Boston area or beyond. Notable past speakers have included President Gerald Ford, Chief Justice Margaret Marshall, and journalist Nina Totenberg.

CONTACTS:
Old North Church
193 Salem St
Boston, MA 02113
617-858-8231; fax: 617-725-0559
oldnorth.com

♦ 0113 ♦ **Annual Session of the National Baptist Convention, USA**
First Week in September

The Annual Session of the National Baptist Convention, USA, which convenes during the first week of each September in a designated U.S. city, is the major business meeting of the group's boards, auxiliaries, and member churches. It lasts for five days and can attract up to 40,000 delegates. Each annual session typically has a theme, such as "Christian Music for the 21st Century," "The Call to Faithfulness in the Gospel Ministry," or "The Heavenly Vision and the Morals of the Church." During the annual session, delegates deal with business issues. However, they also share Christian fellowship and, through a series of forums, explore such issues as health and wellness, social justice, and empowerment, often with emphasis on their impact on the African-American community. Delegates also hear a keynote speech by the convention's national president and by such guest speakers as Barack Obama.

The National Baptist Convention, USA, founded in 1886, is the country's largest and oldest African-American religious convention, with about 7.5 million members. In September of 2014, the group celebrated their 134th Annual Session in New Orleans, LA.

CONTACTS:
National Baptist Convention, USA, Inc.
1700 Baptist World Center Dr.
Nashville, TN 37207
615-228-6292 or 866-531-3054; fax: 615-262-3917
www.nationalbaptist.com

♦ 0114 ♦ **Annunciation of the Blessed Virgin Mary, Feast of the (Belgium)**
March 25

The Feast of the Annunciation or LADY DAY is known in Belgium as **Notre Dame de la Prospérité**, due to a folk belief that seeds planted on this feast day will certainly sprout. This day is also associated with weather lore: traditional Belgian belief has it that a clear, starry sky before sunrise is a good omen for the next harvest.

According to legend, the Lord asked the animals and birds to pass the Feast of the Annunciation in silent contemplation. When the cuckoo ignored this command and continued its brazen, loud calling, God punished the bird by forbidding it to build its own nest, thus dooming it to wander forever.

CONTACTS:
Annunciation of the Blessed Virgin Mary
289 Spencer St.
Ottawa, ON K1Y 2R1 Canada
613-722-9139
www.annunciationofthebvm.org

♦ 0115 ♦ **Annunciation of the Lord**
March 25

Formerly called the **Annunciation of the Blessed Virgin Mary** by the Roman Catholic Church, this day celebrates the appearance of the Archangel Gabriel to the Virgin Mary announcing that she was to become the mother of Jesus. The date for this feast couldn't have been fixed until the date of CHRISTMAS was established, and obviously the two dates had to be nine months apart. In England, the Feast of the Annunciation is commonly called LADY DAY. Greek Orthodox Christians refer to this day as the Annunciation of the Theotokos.

Annunciation usually falls during LENT, and is kept as a feast day in the midst of the Lenten fast. If it should happen to fall on MAUNDY THURSDAY or GOOD FRIDAY, it is transferred to a date following EASTER. According to medieval superstition, it was a bad omen when Easter and the Annunciation fell on the same day.

In Sweden it was called *Varfrudagen*, "Our Lady's Day." Common pronunciation turned it into *Vaffeldagen*, or "Waffle Day." This is the source of heart-shaped waffle irons: the waffles commemorate the heart of the Virgin Mary.

CONTACTS:
Annunciation of the Theotokos Greek Orthodox Church
1721 Mt. Meigs Rd.
Montgomery, AL 36107
334-263-1366; fax: 334-263-1365
www.agocmal.org

♦ 0116 ♦ **Anthesteria**
February-March

Anthesteria was a spring festival held for three days annually in ancient Athens during the Attic month of Anthesterion (February-March). Its purpose was to celebrate the beginning of spring, the god Dionysus, and the maturing of the wine stored during the previous year. The first day was celebrated by tasting the new wine from the previous vintage. This was known as the Pithoigia, or "opening of the casks." The second day, the Choes, or "pitcher feast," was a merry celebration of the marriage of the chief archon's (magistrate's) wifeto Dionysus. A festival of the dead was held on the third day. This was called the Chutroi, or "feast of pots." This was a time of mourning to honor the dead, and to placate or expel ghosts. The three days of the Anthesteria incorporated the theme of birth-growth-death.

♦ 0117 ♦ **Anthony (Susan B.) Day**
February 15; August 26

Susan Brownell Anthony (1820-1906) devoted her life to the temperance, anti-slavery, and women's suffrage movements. After the Civil War ended in 1865, she focused all of her energies on getting women the right to vote. That goal was achieved in 1920 with the passage of the 19th Amendment to the Constitution of the United States, sometimes called "the Anthony Amendment." She was elected to the Hall of Fame for Great Americans in 1950, and was honored in 1979 when she became the first American woman to have her likeness on a coin: the Susan B. Anthony dollar.

Tributes to Anthony take place on her birthday, February 15, in various parts of the country. Sometimes a memorial ser-

vice is held in the crypt of the Capitol in Washington, D.C., where there is a statue of the pioneers in the women's suffrage movement: Anthony, Elizabeth Cady STANTON, and Lucretia Mott. Ceremonies honoring Anthony are often held at her grave in Rochester, New York, near the home where for more than 40 years she lived and frequently met with other influential reformers. Women's organizations, such as the National Organization for Women (NOW), usually play a major role in sponsoring memorial observances.

Some states observe Susan B. Anthony Day on August 26, the day on which the 19th Amendment was ratified.

CONTACTS:
Susan B. Anthony House
17 Madison St.
Rochester, NY 14608
585-235-6124
www.susanbanthonyhouse.org

♦ 0118 ♦ **Antigua and Barbuda Independence Day**
November 1

Antigua and its dependency, Barbuda, became officially independent from England in 1981. Antigua had been settled by English people as early as 1632. It did not gain self-rule until 1967.

This small state also observes the first Monday and Tuesday in August as a legal holiday known as ANTIGUA CARNIVAL, during which a festival celebrates the islanders' cultural heritage.

CONTACTS:
Antigua and Barbuda Department of Tourism and Trade
25 S.E. 2nd Ave.
Ste. 300
Miami, FL 33131 United States
305-381-6762; fax: 305-381-7908
www.antigua-barbuda.org

♦ 0119 ♦ **Antigua Carnivval**
July-August

Antigua and Barbuda was the first nation in the British Caribbean to abolish slavery, in 1834. This distinction moves Antiguans to celebrate for 11 days in the summer.

The initial Carnival celebrations, which date back to 1957, took place earlier in the year, between May and July. However, the festival was later moved to its current position on the calendar to coincide with the already established celebration of the slaves' emancipation. Today, Antiguans begin celebrating the Carnival in late July and continue until the first Tuesday in August.

Music, competitions, and pageantry dominate the proceedings, most of which take place in the capital city of St. John's. Calypso music can be heard throughout the celebration, and the annual calypso competition produces a Calypso Monarch. Other contests include a steel band competition and two beauty pageants, which crown Caribbean Queen and

Miss Antigua. Every Carnival also features street parades that are famous for their elaborate glittering costumes.

All the proceedings essentially lead up to J'Ouvert, the party on the first Monday in August. At 4:00 A.M. thousands of people fill the streets of St. John's for street dancing, which is accompanied by the sounds of steel drums and brass instruments.

CONTACTS:
National Festivals Office, Antigua and Barbuda
1st Floor Pigotts' Mall
Corner of Market and Redcliffe Streets
St. John's Antigua & Barbuda
268-462-4707 or 268-462-0194
www.antiguacarnival.com

♦ 0120 ♦ **Antigua National Heroes Day**
December 9

Antigua has four citizens who have been designated as National Heroes, and December 9 is a public holiday to honor and celebrate all of them. The date is the birthday of one of the four, Sir Vere Cornwall Bird, the first prime minister of Antigua, who is considered the father of the nation. The others are King Court, who led a slave revolt in 1736; Dame Ellen Georgian Nellie Robinson, a pioneer in education; and Sir Vivian Richards, one of the world's greatest cricket players, who was captain of the West Indies team from 1985 to 1991.

Speeches and ceremonies honor the accomplishments of the National Heroes on this day. Postage stamps were issued memorializing the four National Heroes in 2007. In 2012, in the city of St. John's, the ceremonies commenced with the Service of Recognition at the Salvation Army Citadel, followed by wreath-laying at the St. John's Public Cemetery in Heroes Park, and ended with an exhibition, the "Portrayal of National Heroes."

CONTACTS:
Ministry of Tourism, Civil Aviation and Culture
Nevis St.
St. John's Antigua & Barbuda
268-463-9522
www.antigua.gov.ag

Consulate General of Antigua and Barbuda
3 Dag Hammarskjold Plaza
305 E. 47th St.
6th Fl.
New York, NY 10017
212-541-4119; fax: 646-215-6009
www.abconsulateny.org

♦ 0121 ♦ **Antigua Sailing Week**
April-May

The island nation of Antigua and Barbuda is famous for stiff easterly trade winds, which are ideal for sailing. Thus, it is little wonder that Antigua is the site of a major international sailing event. Organized by the Antigua Hotels and Tourist Association, the Antigua Sailing Week runs from late April into May and draws racing fans and yachting enthusiasts from all over the world.

The first Antigua Sailing Week took place in 1968, when yacht broker Desmond Nicholson and Antiguan hotel owner Howard Hulford recruited a total of 17 boats to participate in a three-day event. Since then the regatta has expanded to include as many as 1,500 sailors and 200 yachts of various sizes that compete in 16 different classes. Nearly every day of Sailing Week, yachts face off in courses of various distances and orientations toward the wind. In 2007, the yachting community celebrated the competition's 40th anniversary.

CONTACTS:
Antigua Sailing Week
Antigua Yacht Club Marina Resort,
English Harbour Antigua & Barbuda
268-734-6366
www.sailingweek.com

♦ 0122 ♦ **Antique and Classic Boat Rendezvous**
Last weekend in July

Every July since 1975, classic wooden yachts of pre-1952 vintage have gathered for the annual Antique and Classic Boat Rendezvous at Mystic Seaport Museum in Mystic, Connecticut. Although some boats built as early as 1890 have participated, most date from the 1920s to the 1940s. Many are one-of-a-kind and have been kept in mint condition by their owners. More than 50 boats from throughout the Northeast participate each year, making it one of the largest gatherings of its kind.

The boats can be viewed at dockside on Friday evening and early on Saturday. Sunday afternoon the vessels begin their colorful parade down the Mystic River to Noank, led by the museum's 84-year-old steamboat, *Sabino*, with a Dixieland jazz band on board. The boats are "dressed" with brightly colored signal flags, and many carry crews in period costumes as they compete for awards in various categories.

♦ 0123 ♦ **Anzac Day**
April 25

A national holiday in Australia and New Zealand, Anzac Day takes its name from the initial letters of "Australia and New Zealand Army Corps." It commemorates the landing of the Anzac troops on the Gallipoli Peninsula in European Turkey on April 25, 1915, during World War I. Like MEMORIAL DAY in the U.S., this day is celebrated with veterans' parades and church services. Observed as a holiday since 1920, Anzac Day now honors those who have died in both world wars as well as in Korea and Vietnam.

CONTACTS:
Anzac Day Commemoration Committee of Queensland
21 Wolverhampton St.
P.O. Box 3246
Stafford, QLD 4053 Australia
61-7-3263-7118; fax: 61-7-3175-0608
www.anzacday.org.au

♦ 0124 ♦ **Aoi Matsuri**
May 15

One of the three major festivals of Kyoto, Japan, the **Holly-hock Festival** is believed to date from the sixth century. The festival's name derives from the hollyhock leaves adorning the headdresses of the participants; legend says hollyhocks help prevent storms and earthquakes. The festival owes its present form to the time in the Heian period (792-1099) when imperial messengers were sent to the Kyoto shrines of Shimogamo and Kamigamo after a plague (or a flood) that came about because the shrines were neglected. Today the festival, which was revived in 1884, consists of a re-creation of the original imperial procession. Some 500 people in ancient costume parade with horses and large lacquered oxcarts carrying the "imperial messengers" from the Kyoto Imperial Palace to the shrines.

See also GION MATSURI and JIDAI MATSURI.

CONTACTS:
National Association of Japan-America Societies
1819 L St. N.W.
Ste. 200
Washington, D.C. 20036
202-429-5545; fax: 202-429-0027
www.us-japan.org

Kyoto Visitor's Guide
Ste. 401, kyotansu ebisugawa bldg, 239-1 Gochome
Yanaginobanba Ebisugawa-agaru
Nakagyo-ku
Kyoto 604-0973 Japan
81-75-253-0321; fax: 81-75-253-0322
www.kyotoguide.com

♦ 0125 ♦ **Apache Maidens' Puberty Rites**
July 4

The Apache Maidens' Puberty Rites are a celebration of the coming-of-age of girls of the Mescalero Apache Tribe, held for four days and four nights around the FOURTH OF JULY in Mescalero, N.M. Besides the puberty rites, there are other events: a rodeo, a powwow with cash prizes for dancers, a parade on July 4, and the nighttime Dance of the Mountain Gods.

The rites are related to the belief that soon after the creation of the world, White Painted Woman appeared in the east as a beautiful young woman, moved to the west, and disappeared when she was old. On the first and last days of the ceremonial, the girls must run around a basket four times, symbolically going through the four stages of life (infancy, childhood, adulthood, and old age). On the last day, their faces are painted with white clay and they enact the role of White Painted Woman, taking on her qualities and preparing for a rewarding adult life. On each of the four nights, the girls dance in the Holy Lodge, which was set up on the first day, while singers sing of the creation and beat time with deer-hoof rattles. The celebrations also involve feasting and elaborate ceremonial dresses.

In the 1800s, the U.S. government forbade the Apaches to congregate, but in 1911 decreed that they could congregate on July 4 to celebrate the nation's birthday. The Apaches then chose that date for their most important cultural ritual as an insult to their conquerors.

CONTACTS:
Mescalero Apache Tribe
P.O. Box 227
Mescalero, NM 88340
575-464-9273
mescaleroapachetribe.com

♦ 0126 ♦ **Apollonian Games**
July 6-13

Apollo was an ancient Greek god, but his fame had spread to Rome where he was adopted as a healing god during a plague in the fifth century B.C.E. A couple of hundred years later, after a setback in the Second Punic War against Hannibal's forces, religious officials decided to appeal to Apollo by holding games in his honor. The Romans first held the **Ludi Apollinares**, or Apollonian Games, in 212 B.C.E. Originally the Games took place on July 13; they turned into an eight-day event due to the event's success.

From the very start, the Apollonian Games showed a Greek influence. There were chariot races and "scenic shows" or theatrical productions—a Greek custom. An ox with gilded horns was sacrificed to Apollo, and everyone feasted. Of the eight days, two were devoted to games and races in the Circus Maximus, a huge outdoor arena, and the other six were devoted to plays in the theaters and market fairs.

See also LUDI; PLEBEIAN GAMES; ROMAN GAMES.

♦ 0127 ♦ **Apparition of the Infant Jesus**
September 18

The ancient Villa de Eten in Peru is inhabited by many descendants of the Mochicas—a pre-Inca culture that flourished in northern Peru from the 3rd century B.C.E. to the 7th century C.E. Town residents still speak the ancient Mochica language, preserved in no other place in Peru. Two of their most important fiestas celebrate the apparitions of the infant Jesus, which took place on June 2 and September 18, 1649. After the second apparition, a tidal wave destroyed the village. The chapel of the apparitions, however, remained standing. Hence the villagers named it *La Capilla de los Milagros* (Chapel of the Miracles).

Townsfolk host a three-day festival commemorating this event, beginning on September 18. Preparations for the fiesta, which include candle making and other festive pursuits, begin several weeks beforehand. A special mass is held on the eve of the fiesta, and it is followed by fireworks and lighted balloons. Festivities continue the following day with a procession to the chapel with the images of Mary Magdalene, St. Peter holding the keys to heaven, and Senor del Mar (Lord of the Sea). Dance groups accompany the procession, each performing to its own tunes and wearing its own distinctive costumes. When the procession returns from the chapel, it stops at altars that have been set up along the way. A huge wheel of fireworks is set off when the procession reaches the church.

CONTACTS:
Commission for the Promotion of Peru for Export & Tourism
Calle Uno Oeste 50
Mincetur Bldg.
Fl. 13 and 14
Lima, San Isidro Peru
51-1-616-7300
www.promperu.gob.pe/english

♦ 0128 ♦ **Apple and Candle Night**
October 31

Another name for HALLOWEEN among children in the Swansea area of Wales. The traditional game of "Apple and Candle" is played by suspending a stick from the ceiling with an apple fastened to one end and a lit candle to the other. The object is to eat the apple without using hands and without getting burned by the swinging candle. To make the game more challenging, players are sometimes blindfolded and the stick is twirled around before the game begins.

See also MISCHIEF NIGHT.

♦ 0129 ♦ **Appleseed (Johnny), Birthday of**
September 26

John Chapman—better known as Johnny Appleseed for his lifelong dedication to planting apple seedlings all over the American Midwest—was born on this day in 1774. While some frontier settlers thought he was a saint, or at the very least a religious fanatic, with his tin pot hat and coffee-sack tunic, the Indians regarded him as a great medicine man since he planted herbs as well as apples.

Since 1962 Johnny Appleseed's birthday has been observed in his hometown of Leominster, Massachusetts, on the first Saturday in June as **Johnny Appleseed Civic Day**. There is usually a ceremony at the monument that marks the site of Chapman's birthplace. In 1966 the day was celebrated with a ceremony marking the issue of a commemorative stamp bearing an image of the pioneer horticulturalist. His birthday is also honored in Ashland, Ohio, where he lived for more than 25 years, and at harvest festivals in apple-growing regions throughout the United States. In fact, the last week in September has been observed as Johnny Appleseed Week in Ohio since 1941.

See also JOHNNY APPLESEED FESTIVAL.

CONTACTS:
Johnny Appleseed Heritage Center, Inc.
c/o 811 Center St.
Ashland, OH 44805
419-289-6137 or 419-651-7680
www.jahci.org

♦ 0130 ♦ **Appleseed (Johnny) Festival**
Third full weekend in September

A legend in his own time, John Chapman—better known as "Johnny Appleseed"—was born in Leominster, Massachusetts, on September 26, 1774. Although facts about his early life are hard to come by, there is a story that he fell in love with a woman named Dorothy Durand and that the families of the two lovers were bitter enemies. When Dorothy's family moved West, Johnny followed. But she died of a broken heart before he found her, the legend says, and many years later he returned to place apple blossoms on her grave.

Chapman knew that there was money to be made in the apple nursery business. By the 1790s he was planting apple trees in western Pennsylvania, and by the turn of the century, he'd moved on to Ohio. He had an uncanny knack for selecting the most advantageous spot near a new settlement, begging or leasing a plot of land to plant his trees, and then selling the saplings to frontier farmers.

Ironically, his trees and apples were never of the best quality, because he refused to improve his stock by grafting superior branches onto his seedlings. One settler in Fort Wayne, Indiana, where Chapman arrived in 1834, complained that his apples were "so sour they would make a pig squeal." It was supposedly in Fort Wayne that he died in 1845, although no one is certain exactly where he is buried.

Chapman has been commemorated in Fort Wayne since 1974 with a two-day fall festival held at Johnny Appleseed Park. The festival includes traditional music and entertainment, demonstrations of pioneer arts and crafts, visits to the alleged gravesite, and discussions with "The Living Lincoln," who talks with visitors about the social issues of the period in history he shared with Johnny Appleseed.

CONTACTS:
Downtown Crystal Lake
25 W. Crystal Lake Ave.
Crystal Lake, IL 60014
815-479-0835; fax: 815-479-0884
www.downtowncl.org

♦ 0131 ♦ **Appomattox Day**
April 9

The Civil War ended on April 9, 1865, in the village of Appomattox Court House, Virginia, when Lieutenant General Ulysses S. Grant of the Union army accepted the surrender of General Robert E. LEE of the Confederacy. The Confederate soldiers were allowed to keep their horses and return to their homes; the officers were allowed to retain their side arms and swords as well. Thus ended the bloody four-year conflict that had cost more than half a million lives.

The most widespread celebration of Appomattox Day took place in 1965 during the Civil War centennial year. Thousands of people attended the ceremonies at the Appomattox Court House National Historical Park. Participants included the Union leader's grandson, Ulysses S. Grant III, as well as Robert E. Lee IV, great-grandson of the Confederate leader. The day was noted across the country—but particularly in the South—with costumed pageants, books and articles reflecting on the war, and concerts of martial music. Although the anniversary is not observed on a yearly basis, reenactments of the historic surrender are held periodically.

CONTACTS:
Appomattox Court House National Historical Park
Hwy. 24
P.O. Box 218
Appomattox, VA 24522
434-352-8987; fax: 434-352-8330
www.nps.gov

♦ 0132 ♦ **April Fools' Day**
April 1

There are many names for this day—including **All Fools' Day**, **April Noddy Day**, **Gowkie Day**, **Huntigowk Day**, and **St. All-Fools' Morn**—just as there are many practical jokes to play on the unsuspecting. One theory about its origin points to Noah as the first "April Fool." It is said that on that day he mistakenly sent the dove out to find dry land after the flood. Another points to the adoption of the Gregorian calendar in 1582, when NEW YEAR'S DAY was officially moved from March 25 to January 1. People who forgot about the change were often mocked by their friends, as they continued to make New Year visits just after the old March date.

The simplest pranks usually involve children who, for example, tell each other that their shoelaces are undone and then cry "April Fool!" when the victims glance at their feet. Sometimes the media get into the act, broadcasting fictitious news items designed to amuse or alarm the public. British television, for example, once showed Italian farmers "harvesting" spaghetti from trees. The French call it **Fooling the April Fish Day** (the fool being the *poisson d'avril*) and try to pin a paper fish on someone's back without getting caught.

In Mexico children play April Fools'-type pranks on December 28, HOLY INNOCENTS' DAY.

♦ 0133 ♦ **Arab International Festival**
Mid-June

The Arab International Festival takes place annually over a three-day weekend in mid-June in Dearborn, Mich. Dearborn's eastern section is noted for its large Arab-American population as well as Arab restaurants, bakeries, and businesses.

The festival was founded in 1996 to showcase and celebrate the heritage and culture of the area's Arab-American residents, as well as the diverse backgrounds of the people of metropolitan Detroit. Ethnic music, performances, food, and merchandise are all featured at the festival, along with amusement rides and such pastimes as coffee-cup reading and henna treatments. As many as 300,000 people have attended the non-alcoholic, family-oriented festival during its opening hours from Friday evening to Sunday night. The festival's sponsors are the local American Arab Chamber of Commerce, the Arab Community Center for Education and Social Services (ACCESS), and the city of Dearborn.

CONTACTS:
American Arab Chamber of Commerce
12740 W. Warren Ave.
Dearborn, MI 48126
313-945-1700; fax: 313-945-6697
www.americanarab.com

♦ 0134 ♦ **Arabic Music Festival**
November

The Arabic Music Festival is an annual event that celebrates classic, traditional Arabic music. The main venue for the event is the Cairo Opera House, which was opened in 1988 after the original building was destroyed by fire in 1971. Located on Gezira Island in the Nile River, the Opera House is part of a cultural district that includes the Museum of Egyptian Modern Arts and the El Hangar Theatre. The Arabic Music Festival was first held there in 1992.

Since then, the festival has been an occasion when the top Arabic instrumentalists, singers, and ensembles from around the world gather to perform. Homage is paid to established performers, and upcoming new talent is frequently introduced here. A cash prize is given to the musical act judged to be the best in the festival. Awards are also given to those who have made significant contributions to the field of Arabic music in the previous year. A conference to discuss topics related to Arabic music is another part of the event.

In 2014, more than 74 musicians from 12 countries participated in the 23rd Arab Music Festival, including Egyptian singers Ali El-Haggar and Amal Maher, Lebanese singer Marouan Khouri and Syrian musician Safwan Bahlawan. The festival honored 14 people who have contributed to the enrichment of Arabic music, including singers Hany Shenouda and Sabah Fakhry and musical instrument maker Nasr Mohamed Tawfik.

CONTACTS:
Egypt State Information Service
3 Al Estad Al Bahary St.
Nasr City
Cairo Egypt
20-2261-7304
www.sis.gov.eg

Cairo Opera House
El Borg Gezira
P.O. Box 11567
Cairo Egypt
20-2737-0603 or 20-2735-0911; fax: 20-2737-0599
www.cairoopera.org

♦ 0135 ♦ **Arapaho Sun Dance**
Mid-summer

The Sun Dance is a major religious event for many Native Americans, including the Cheyenne, Shoshone, and other Plains Indian tribes. The Arapaho people on the Wind River

Reservation, outside Fort Washakie, Wyoming, hold the Sun Dance in mid-summer. To prepare for this sacred ceremony, they create a space for the dance to take place and particular objects are placed within this space, including a buffalo head, symbolizing strength, comfort, and abundance, and fresh sage, which represents the breath of life.

The dancers focus their gaze on the buffalo head as they move toward and away from it. The dance can have many purposes—to cure a loved one who is ill, to bring rain, to avoid death and other calamities, to ensure the tribe's prosperity, or to give thanks. It can last for up to three days.

See also SIOUX SUN DANCE; SOUTHERN UTE TRIBAL SUN DANCE.

CONTACTS:
Wind River Visitors Council
P.O. Box 925
Lander, WY 82520 United States
800-645-6233
www.wind-river.org

♦ 0136 ♦ **Arbaeen**
20th day of Islamic month of Safar

In the year 680 C.E., Imam al-Hussein died during the Battle of Taf in Karbala, Iraq. He was the grandson of the Prophet Mohammad The martyrdom of Hussein was such a pivotal event in Islamic history that it has inspired two Shi'ite Muslim holidays of mourning: ASHURA and Arbaeen. ASHURA, the holy day that commemorates the day Hussein fell to his Sunni enemies, is more widely observed, but Arbaeen still retains significance and elicits fervent expressions from the faithful.

The holy day falls on the 40th day after the anniversary of Hussein's death and marks the date when the martyr's decapitated head, which had been carried off as a trophy to Damascus, was finally reunited with his body.

The most popular way that Iranian Shi'ites observe this holiday is by carrying out *ziarats*—pilgrimages to a holy shrine. The holiest of shrines to Hussein lies in Karbala, the Iraqi city where the fateful seventh-century battle took place. Karbala receives most of its pilgrims from Iraq and Iran. Celebrations have seen Shi'ite-Sunni violence during periods of elevated tension between these two groups.

♦ 0137 ♦ **Arbaeen Pilgrimage**
February 28

In the year 680 C.E., Imam al-Hussein died during the Battle of Taf in Karbala, Iraq. He was the grandson of the Prophet Mohammad and, for Shiite Muslims, one of the three holiest figures in their religion. To commemorate his passing, Shiites from around the world hold the week-long Arbaeen Pilgrimage to his gravesite 40 days after his death. This period of 40 days is the traditional Muslim mourning period following a death. Imam al-Hussein's tomb is in the town of Karbala, about 50 miles south of Baghdad.

Karbala is one of the holiest cities for Shiite Muslims. It has more than 100 mosques and 23 religious schools in its old quarter. For Shiite Muslims, the city is also believed to be a gate to paradise. Many elderly believers come to the city to die, hoping to enter paradise more easily.

During the regime of Iraqi dictator Saddam Hussein, the Arbaeen Pilgrimage was banned. Clashes between pilgrims and the Iraqi military resulted in the arrest of thousands of people and the deaths of hundreds more. Since his overthrow in 2003, the number of people celebrating the Shiite holiday has grown every year. While there have been deaths from attacks made by Sunni suicide bombers, the Arbaeen Pilgrimage has been a largely peaceful affair in which some seven million people participate.

CONTACTS:
Embassy of the Republic of Iraq
3421 Massachusetts Ave. N.W.
Washington, D.C. 20007
202-742-1600; fax: 202-333-1129
www.iraqiembassy.us

♦ 0138 ♦ **Arbor Day**
Last Friday in April

Julius Sterling Morton (1832-1902), one of the earliest American conservationists, settled on the treeless plains of Nebraska in 1855, where he edited the Nebraska City *News* and developed a lifelong interest in new agricultural methods. Believing that the prairie needed more trees to serve as windbreaks, to hold moisture in the soil, and to provide lumber for housing, Morton began planting trees and urged his neighbors to do the same. On April 10, 1872, when he first proposed that a specific day be set aside for the planting of trees, the response was overwhelming: a million trees were planted in Nebraska on that day alone.

All 50 states now observe Arbor Day—usually on the last Friday in April—and the idea has spread to other countries as well. Most observances take place in the public schools, where the value of trees is discussed and trees and shrubs are planted. At the White House, the president, first lady, or a presidential designate plants a special tree on the grounds each year on Arbor Day. But it is in Nebraska City, Nebraska, that Morton is best remembered as the originator of Arbor Day, with celebrations taking place on or near his birthday, April 22. A special ceremony is held at Arbor Lodge, Morton's homestead and one of the earliest known attempts at conservation and beautification in America.

Some states call this day **Bird and Arbor Day**, emphasizing the planting of trees that are attractive to birds.

CONTACTS:
National Arbor Day Foundation
100 Arbor Ave.
Nebraska City, NE 68410
888-448-7337; fax: 402-474-0820
www.arborday.org

♦ 0139 ♦ **Arctic Circle Race**
Mid-April

The first Arctic Circle cross-country ski race was held in Sisimiut, Greenland, in 1996. Organizers bill the event as the "world's toughest ski race" not only because of its length but also because of the uncertain weather conditions and terrain. Athletes must spend two nights camped in a tent in order to complete the race. The event lasts three days and covers 160 kilometers. Dog sleds follow the skiers as a safety precaution. In recent years the event has attracted participants from over 20 countries.

CONTACTS:
Arctic Circle Race Secretariat
P.O. Box 258
Sisimiut 3911 Greenland
299-86-68-30
www.acr.gl

♦ 0140 ♦ **Ardwahist, Feast of**
April, August, September; third day of
Ardwahist, the second Zoroastrian month

The Feast of Ardwahist is considered a "sacred name day" in the Zoroastrian religion because both the day and the month share the name of the same *yazata* or spiritual being—in this case Ardwahist, who stands for truth and righteousness and presides over fire and energy. Ardwahist is represented by the ceremonial fire that plays such a central role in Zoroastrian worship, and that burns continually in most Zoroastrian temples.

The Zoroastrian calendar has 12 months of 30 days each, plus five extra days at the end of the year. Because of discrepancies in the calendars used by widely separated Zoroastrian communities around the world, there are now three different calendars in use, and the 3rd of Ardwahist can fall either in April, August, or September.

Followers of the Zoroastrian religion, which was founded by the prophet Zoroaster (also known as Zarathushtra, who is believed to have lived around 1200 B.C.E.), today live primarily in Iran and northwestern India, although smaller communities exist in Pakistan, Sri Lanka, Canada, the U.S., England, and Australia.

♦ 0141 ♦ **Argentina Flag Day**
June 20 in Rosario; celebrated as a national
holiday on the third Monday in June

The Argentine flag was designed and first raised on February 27, 1812, by Lt.-General Manuel Belgrano, during a battle with the forces of the Spanish crown. Stories about the origin of the design vary, but one popular version states that Belgrano, noting that both Spanish and Independence forces wore the yellow and red of Spain, was inspired to create the new flag of two light blue stripes and one white. The colors are variously said to have been in honor of the Virgin Mary, inspired by the sky, or drawn from a coat of arms of the Span-

ish monarchy. In any case, Belgrano's flag was first raised at the village of Rosario, in two artillery batteries— one on the banks of the Parana River, and another at a site on an island directly opposite Rosario. On June 20, 1816, the Argentine Congress officially approved Belgrano's flag as the symbol of the independent Argentine nation. In later years, a sun was added to the white stripe of the original design. While this is now required on official ceremonial flags, flags without the sun symbol are also used and are known as "ornamental flags."

Belgrano died on June 20, 1820, and this date was declared Flag Day in 1938. It is now celebrated as a national holiday on the third Monday in June, but in Rosario, June 20 is also marked as a civic and school holiday. Across the country, the day may be marked with flag ceremonies and various other celebrations, but in Rosario, the festivities are most extensive. Many of the activities there take place near the National Flag Memorial, a large complex featuring a 70-meter tower commemorating the revolution and containing Belgrano's crypt.

The 50th anniversary of the Flag Memorial was celebrated in 2007. In addition to the usual parades, flag ceremonies, and speeches by government officials, celebrations in Rosario that year featured the inauguration of a new blue-and-white lighting system for the monument. There were also concerts, sporting events, a national artisans fair, and a reenactment of Belgrano's 1812 entry into Rosario.

CONTACTS:
Embassy of Argentina
1600 New Hampshire Ave. N.W.
Washington, D.C. 20009
202-238-6400; fax: 202-332-3171
www.embassyofargentina.us

♦ 0142 ♦ **Argentina Independence Day**
July 9

Independence Day in Argentina is a national holiday commemorating the day in 1816 when delegates from various provinces of the country met at the home of the prominent Bazán family, in Tucumán, to proclaim their independence from Spanish rule. The Bazán home has been preserved and is now a museum known as the Casa Histórica de la Independencia.

The ideal of Argentine independence had been growing for many years before 1816, fostered by the American and French Revolutions. Argentine confidence that a war for independence could be won was bolstered when British forces invaded Buenos Aires in 1806 and 1807, and were driven back by Argentine forces. After much discussion among the various Argentine factions and military campaigns at various places around South America, independence was declared and the United Provinces of South America was formed. Civil war and various forms of government followed, but the date of the original Independence Day celebration has been continuously honored. It is now marked across the country by speeches and patriotic displays, as well as parties, family reunions, and live music.

CONTACTS:
Embassy of Argentina
1600 New Hampshire Ave. N.W.
Washington, D.C. 20009
202-238-6400; fax: 202-332-3171
www.embassyofargentina.us

♦ 0143 ♦ **Argentina National Day of Memory for Truth and Justice**
March 24

Argentina's National Day of Memory for Truth and Justice is a public holiday that commemorates all those who lost their lives or otherwise suffered under the National Reorganization Process, a military dictatorship that seized power in Argentina on March 24, 1976. The junta held power for eight years, and in that time, at least 30,000 citizens were kidnapped, tortured, and executed for their political views. Many of those detained by the secret police were never heard from again, nor were their bodies ever found. Even after democracy was restored, amnesty laws and pardons ruled out trials of those behind the atrocities for several years. The Day of Memory for Truth and Justice is meant not only as a day to remember the dead, but also as a day to continue to seek justice for the human rights violations that were committed during the years of military rule.

In Buenos Aires and around the country, art exhibitions, poetry readings, prayer services, and other cultural events are dedicated to remembering the events of March 24 and its aftermath. In 2013, the day was commemorated in Buenos Aires with posters being placed in a street near the Plaza de Mayo, while residents of San Carlos de Bariloche walked a street decorated with paintings of white head scarves, evocative of the ones worn by mothers looking for their kidnapped children. Argentines living in other countries may also gather on this day for cultural events honoring the victims of the coup and the years of atrocities that followed it.

CONTACTS:
Embassy of Argentina
1600 New Hampshire Ave. N.W.
Washington, D.C. 20009
202-238-6400; fax: 202-332-3171
www.embassyofargentina.us

♦ 0144 ♦ **Argentine National Day**
May 25

Argentina was one of a number of Spanish colonies controlled by the Spanish viceroy in Lima, Peru. When the colonies became too large to be controlled from one site, a separate viceroyalty was formed in 1776, with its headquarters in Buenos Aires.

On May 25, 1810, Buenos Aires declared its independence from the viceroyalty but continued to pledge loyalty to the Spanish crown. May 25 is observed throughout the country as the anniversary of the revolution. Independence from Spain wasn't declared until July 9, 1816—an event that provoked

a long series of civil wars in which rival political leaders fought for national control. Both days are national holidays and are observed with religious services at the cathedral and special performances at the Colón Theatre in Buenos Aires. The city's *Plaza de Mayo* (May Square) was named for the month in which independence was declared.

The Argentine flag is honored with a legal holiday on June 20, **Argentine Flag Day**.

CONTACTS:
Embassy of Argentina
1600 New Hampshire Ave. N.W.
Washington, D.C. 20009
202-238-6400 or 202-238-6401; fax: 202-332-3171
www.embassyofargentina.us

♦ 0145 ♦ **Argungu Fishing Festival**
February-March

The Argungu Fishing Festival is held along a sacred mile of the Sokoto River, a tributary of the Niger River, near Argungu, Kebbi State, in northwestern Nigeria. About 5,000 men from throughout Nigeria take part in the approximately 45 minutes of frenzied fishing. Using nets with calabashes (gourds) as floats, they can catch perch of up to 140 pounds. The largest perch are presented to the emirs, or rulers, who hold the festival.

CONTACTS:
Embassy of the Federal Republic of Nigeria
3519 International Ct. N.W.
Washington, D.C. 20008
202-986-8400; fax: 202-362-6541
www.nigeriaembassyusa.org

♦ 0146 ♦ **Århus Festival**
Nine days beginning first Saturday in September

Since 1965 the Danish city of Århus has been the site of a nine-day festival whose cultural and sporting events run the gamut from opera to fishing competitions. Queen MARGRETHE II traditionally gives the opening speech, followed by a performance by the Danish National Radio Symphony Orchestra. Festival events include jazz, classical, and rock concerts, a cross-country race, public debates, children's programs, poetry readings, and theatrical productions. The New York City Ballet and the Alvin Ailey American Dance Theatre have performed there, as have the Israel Philharmonic Orchestra, the Orchestre de Paris, and such world-renowned soloists as Isaac Stern, Vladimir Ashkenazy, Boris Christoff, and Claudio Arrau.

The program varies from year to year, but the events are always held in a variety of indoor and outdoor sites throughout the city, including the Århus Theater, an art nouveau building from the turn of the 20th century; the new Århus Concert Hall, built in 1981; and the area's many parks, churches, and coffee shops. Århus is also the site of Marselisborg Castle, the Danish royal family's summer residence.

CONTACTS:
Aarhus Festuge
Officersbygningen
Vester Alle 3
Arhus C 8000 Denmark
45-87-30-8300; fax: 45-87-30-8319
www.aarhusfestuge.dk

◆ 0147 ◆ Armed Forces Day (Egypt)
October 6

Armed Forces Day in Egypt is an important national holiday marking the surprise attack on Israel that began the October War of 1973 (also known as the YOM KIPPUR War). Egypt's ally in the war was Syria. The war ended with a cease-fire secured by the United States, and was declared a victory by Egyptian President Anwar Sadat. It strengthened his position and enabled him to seek an honorable peace with Israel. In 1974 and 1975, agreements were signed that paved the way for the return of the SINAI Peninsula to Egypt in April 1982; Israel had occupied the peninsula since the Six-Day War of 1967, in which Egypt had been crushed. In 1977 Sadat made his dramatic trip to Jerusalem to address the Israeli Knesset (Parliament); a year later, Sadat, Israeli Prime Minister Menachem Begin and United States President Jimmy Carter held talks at Camp David, Md., that led to the Israeli-Egyptian peace treaty of 1979.

The holiday is celebrated with grand parades, speeches by government officials, and fireworks. It was while reviewing a military parade on this day in 1981 that Anwar Sadat was assassinated by opponents of peace with Israel.

CONTACTS:
Egypt State Information Service
3 Al Estad Al Bahary St.
Nasr City, Cairo Egypt
202-226-17304
www.sis.gov.eg

◆ 0148 ◆ Armed Forces Day (United States)
Third Saturday in May

Before President Harry S. Truman proclaimed the third Saturday in May as Armed Forces Day in 1949, the three major branches of the United States armed forces—the Army, the Navy, and the Air Force—held elaborate celebrations on three different days during the year. Although the service units continue to celebrate their own days on April 6 (Army), October 27 (Navy), the second Saturday in September (Air Force), and November 10 (Marine Corps), the purpose of Armed Forces Day is to promote the unification of the branches under the Department of Defense (which took place in 1947) and to pay tribute to those serving in all the armed forces.

While commemorations of the individual service units are usually confined to military bases, the celebration of Armed Forces Day entails much broader participation. In addition to the huge parade held on this day each year in New York City, the armed forces often hold "open house" to acquaint the public with their facilities and to demonstrate some of the latest technological advances.

CONTACTS:
U.S. Department of Defense
1400 Defense Pentagon
Washington, D.C. 20301
703-571-3343
www.defense.gov

◆ 0149 ◆ Armenia Constitution Day
July 5

On July 5, 1995, four years after Armenia gained independence from the Soviet Union, the national government adopted a new constitution. Constitution Day, a public holiday, commemorates the creation of a new governmental framework and the beginning of another era for this small country, which for over seven decades had been a Soviet satellite.

The government rewards the public sector with a day off on Constitution Day. Victory Park, located in the capital city of Yerevan, usually stages performances that feature traditional music and dance. Some Armenian communities settled abroad also conduct their own Constitution Day ceremonies.

CONTACTS:
Armenia Embassy
2225 R St. N.W.
Washington, D.C. 20008
202-319-1976; fax: 202-319-2982
usa.mfa.am

◆ 0150 ◆ Armenia Earthquake Memorial Day
December 7

On December 7, 1988, a severe earthquake struck in Armenia, causing catastrophic damage to the entire country's infrastructure and virtually destroying the cities of Spitak, Leninakan (now Gyumri), Kirovakan (now Vanadzor), and Stepanavan. Hundreds of small villages were completely obliterated by the quake and its aftershocks. At its epicenter, the earthquake was estimated to have the destructive force of 10 atomic bombs the size of those dropped on Hiroshima during World War II. More than 25,000 people were killed in the disaster, with another 140,000 injured and more than one million left homeless, in a disaster zone that measured about 30,000 square kilometers.

That day is now remembered each year as a national holiday, marked across the country with prayer, memorial services, and a moment of silence.

CONTACTS:
Armenian Embassy
2225 R St. N.W.
Washington, D.C. 20008 United States
202-319-1976
usa.mfa.am

♦ 0151 ♦ Armenia First Republic Day
May 28

The people of Armenia lived for hundreds of years under foreign domination. Then, in 1917, the Russian Revolution and the collapse of the Russian empire allowed Armenia the opportunity to create a modern republic. The Democratic Republic of Armenia (DRA) was formed in 1918. Also known as the First Republic of Armenia, the DRA was short-lived but important, as it represented the beginning of the modern quest for democracy and independence in Armenia.

The new republic faced serious problems from within and without its borders. In 1920, it was invaded by the Bolshevik Army of Russia and made part of the Transcaucasian Socialist Federative Soviet Republic, and eventually part of the Soviet Union, for more than 70 years. Yet the establishment and brief life of the First Republic is still seen as a proud victory for Armenia. On the holiday, titles and medals are awarded to Armenians of outstanding achievement, and there are speeches by government officials, fireworks displays, concerts, and dancing.

CONTACTS:
Armenian Embassy
2225 R St. N.W.
Washington, D.C. 20010 United States
202-319-1976; fax: 202-319-2980
usa.mfa.am

♦ 0152 ♦ Armenia Independence Day
September 21

On September 21, 1991, the Armenian people voted in favor of independence from the U.S.S.R.; they were granted independence on December 26 of that year, by which time the former Soviet Union had collapsed. Armenia had been part of the Soviet Union since the 1920s.

CONTACTS:
Armenian Embassy
2225 R St. N.W.
Washington, D.C. 20008 United States
202-319-1976
usa.mfa.am/en

♦ 0153 ♦ Armenia Motherhood and Beauty Day
April 7

Motherhood and Beauty Day is a national holiday in Armenia, celebrated each year on April 7. It comes not long after another national holiday, Women's Day, which is celebrated on March 8. Women's Day is meant to honor all women, but Motherhood and Beauty Day is dedicated especially to those who have become mothers.

On this occasion, the unique qualities and beauty of each woman are to be appreciated. Children and adults alike show their affection for their mothers with special visits, cards, and gifts. Sending flowers to one's mother is an especially popular way to mark this holiday. Another tradition associated with Motherhood and Beauty Day is the gift of a twig that has fresh sprouts on it. The symbolism of the budding twig, and the holiday's placement in the springtime, are indicators that the celebration may trace its roots back to ancient fertility cults, such as the cult of Anahit. The month-long period between Women's Day and Motherhood and Beauty Day is unofficially regarded as an ongoing opportunity to celebrate all women.

CONTACTS:
Armenian Embassy
2225 R St. N.W.
Washington, D.C. 20008 United States
202-319-1972
usa.mfa.am/en

♦ 0154 ♦ Armenian Martyrs' Day
April 24

Armenian Martyrs' Day is a day of remembrance for the one million Armenians who died in the Turkish massacre of 191516 On April 24, 1915, Turks arrested Armenian political and intellectual leaders in Istanbul, killing 250 of them. That was the start of deportations, forced marches in the desert, rapes, and imprisonments that killed half the Armenian population in Turkey.

Armenian communities throughout the world observe this day. In the United States, many state governors issue proclamations of remembrance, and special programs, with speeches and prayers, are held in state capitals. There are also special services in Armenian churches.

CONTACTS:
Armenian Embassy
2225 R St. N.W.
Washington, D.C. 20008 United States
202-319-1976; fax: 202-319-2977
usa.mfa.am/en

♦ 0155 ♦ Army-Navy Football Game
December

One of the greatest rivalries in sports, the football game between the U.S. Army and Navy was first played in 1890 at the U.S. Military Academy at West Point, New York. Since then, the Army Black Knights and the Navy Midshipmen have faced off on the field every year. Popularly known as the **Army-Navy Game**, the event attracts a crowd of 50,000 each year, including many enlisted personnel, both at home and abroad. At the game, service men and women killed in action are remembered, and both teams' anthems are sung. To show mutual respect and sportsmanship, the winning and the losing teams stand together in formation and first salute the losing side and then the winning side. The Thompson Cup is awarded to the winning team. The game has a checkered history with many interruptions. In 1893 the game was suspended for five years after an argument between a rear admiral and a brigadier general nearly led to a duel. After the five-year hiatus, the game returned to Philadelphia, the primary home of the game ever since.

CONTACTS:
M&T Bank Stadium
1101 Russell St.
Baltimore, MD 21230
410-261-7283; fax: 410-468-1340
armynavygame.com

United Services Automobile Association
9800 Fredericksburg Rd.
San Antonio, TX 78288
210-531-8722
www.usaa.com

♦ 0156 ♦ **Art Basel**
June

Art Basel is an annual, high-profile art fair that showcases modern and contemporary art from around the world. The event is held each June in Basel, Switzerland, a city with a thriving cultural life that includes many theaters and art museums. About 50,000 artists, museum curators, gallerists, private collectors, and others in the art industry converge in Basel for what is often called the Olympics of the art world. The festival includes paintings, photographs, sculptures, and multimedia works from both established and emerging artists. In addition, Art Basel offers talks, symposiums, and panel discussions on an extensive range of art-related subjects.

The fair was launched in 1970 by three gallerists in Basel with the desire to provide an international platform for the art community. Art Basel also hosts concurrent shows in Hong Kong and Miami Beach each year.

CONTACTS:
MCH Swiss Exhibition (Basel) Ltd.
Messeplatz 10
Basel, 4005 Switzerland
41-58-200-2020; fax: 41-58-206-2194
www.artbasel.com/en

♦ 0157 ♦ **Art Basel (Hong Kong)**
March

Art Basel of Hong Kong is a premier art festival offering an international portal for artists, curators, gallery owners, and private collectors to display works from around the world. Located throughout six exhibition sectors, the show features paintings, sculptures, drawings, photographs, and video art by established masters as well as emerging artists. The event also offers insights into the art world from the perspectives of the artist, curator, and exhibitor. Popularly known as the gateway between East and West, Hong Kong is internationally recognized for its museums, concert halls, and diverse cultural offerings.

The festival traces its roots to 1970, when three gallerists from Basel, Switzerland founded the Art Basel show. Since its beginnings, the festival has grown in terms of its importance in the international art scene and its unparalleled reputation for offering high quality work curated by some of the best in the field. The festival takes place in March as several exhibitions and events run concurrently.

CONTACTS:
Asian Art Fairs Ltd
6/F Luk Kwok Centre
72 Gloucester Rd.
Wan Chai Hong Kong (China)
41-58-200-2020; fax: 41-58-206-2194
www.artbasel.com/en

♦ 0158 ♦ **Art Basel (Miami Beach)**
December

Art Basel is a prestigious gathering of the international art scene that takes place each year in Miami Beach, Florida, a location noted for its spectacular beaches, distinguished art museums, and impressive art deco buildings. The festival showcases works of modern and contemporary artists from leading galleries throughout the world. Founded in 1970 in Basel, Switzerland, the event has become one of the most reputed international art fairs in the world, attracting over 250 galleries and 70,000 visitors each year. Art Basel maintains a longstanding tradition of offering a variety of genres of visual art and for bringing together the best artists, curators, collectors, and art critics worldwide.

The show in Miami Beach is spread across nine divisions, each focusing on a different art form. Besides hosting paintings, sculpture, photography, and video, the festival is also known for its outstanding collection of oversized scale art, with the beach and historical art deco landscapes offering a striking backdrop for these larger-than-life masterpieces.

CONTACTS:
Art Basel U.S. Corp.
c/o MCH Swiss Exhibition (Basel) Ltd.
Messeplatz 10
Basel, 4005 Switzerland
41-58-200-2020; fax: 41-58-206-2194
www.artbasel.com/en

♦ 0159 ♦ **Art Deco Weekend**
A weekend in January

The Miami Design Preservation League was established in 1976 with the purpose of restoring and maintaining the Art Deco buildings of the South Beach area in Miami, Florida. In 1978, Art Deco Weekend began. Each year over 400,000 people gather in January for the festivities. Art Deco Weekend celebrates the heritage and culture of South Beach. Popular events include a costumed dog parade, classic car show, and fashion show, all drawing huge crowds. Emerging fashion designers use the weekend as an opportunity to launch new collections. The classic car cruise is one of the biggest events at the festival, featuring vintage cars, motorcycles, and trucks. Another highlight is the Art Deco district walking tour. Additional walking tours held throughout the weekend are based on specific themes, such as organized crime, the gay and lesbian community, Jewish Miami, neon lights, and cocktails. Art Deco-era clothing, accessories, furniture, and other items are sold during the festival, and talks are given by architects, historians, and preservationists on the importance of the Art Deco movement.

CONTACTS:
Miami Design Preservation League
Ocean Dr. (between 5th and 13th Sts.)
Miami Beach, FL 33139
305-672-2014
www.artdecoweekend.com

♦ 0160 ♦ Art Taipei
October-November

Formerly known as the Taipei Art Fair International, Art Taipei was launched in 1992 in Taiwan. Organized by the Taiwan Art Gallery Association, the annual festival offers a gateway for artists, collectors, and gallerists to view and trade works of art from around the world. The fair features more than 150 galleries and events, including forums, lectures, and panel discussions. Many young artists from Japan, Malaysia, the Philippines, and other parts of Asia participate in the exposition's programs. Exhibits include works of contemporary and modern art in varied genres and mediums, including photography and video. Over the years, Art Taipei has become an important marketplace in the Asian art community, helping to further establish Taiwan's presence in the international art scene.

CONTACTS:
Art Taipei Executive Committee
Taipei World Trade Center, Exhibition Hall 1
No.5, Hsin-Yi Rd., Sec 5
Taipei City, 11011 Taiwan (R.O.C.)
886-2-2725-5200
art-taipei.com

Taiwan Art Gallery Association
2F-1, No. 1
Guangfu S. Rd., Songshan District
Taipei City, 105 Taiwan (R.O.C.)
886-2-2742-3968; fax: 886-2-2742-2088
www.aga.org.tw

♦ 0161 ♦ Artcar Fest
Last weekend in September

Artcar Fest, an annual parade in the San Francisco Bay area since 1997, is dedicated to promoting and celebrating those people who enjoy decorating their cars in artistic ways. The cars are not specially decorated for the event—these cars have been permanently altered in an artistic fashion, are legally registered, and are normally used to go to work, school, and shopping by their owners.

Founded by Philo Northrup and Harrod Blank, two artcar enthusiasts who had been decorating cars since the 1980s, the Artcar Fest parade of cars stretches for more than a mile and takes a full hour to roll by. Many of the owners see themselves as creating mobile sculptural works of art. Some of the designs are whimsical and fun. The Sashimi Tabernacle Choir, for example, is a car decorated with 250 computer-controlled singing fish and lobster sculptures. Together, the fish can perform a repertoire of songs while the car is being driven. The Radio Flyer is a car shaped like a giant red wagon, complete with handle, and named after the famous brand of children's toy wagon.

♦ 0162 ♦ ArtPrize
September-October

A unique international art competition, ArtPrize is held annually in downtown Grand Rapids, Michigan. The event is open to the public, and any artist above the age of 18 can participate. First held in 2009, the competition is the brainchild of Rick DeVos, an American entrepreneur and grandson of Rich DeVos, billionaire philanthropist and cofounder of Amway. Each year ArtPrize gives away large amounts of prize money. Other than two grand prizes worth $200,000 each, there are eight category-based awards worth $20,000 a piece. Some of these categories include two-dimensional, three-dimensional, time-based, and installation art. Half of the event's prizes are judged by public vote, while a jury of art experts decides the other awards. The 19-day festival attracts over 1,500 competitors from nearly 40 countries. Exhibits are scattered over a variety of venues, from sidewalks and coffee shops to a police station. Although considered somewhat unconventional, the festival is hailed as an extremely accessible art show that eschews the exclusivity of many urban art festivals. In recent years, ArtPrize has joined with several local organizations to promote environmentally sustainable practices during the event, such as recycling and composting.

CONTACTS:
ArtPrize HUB
41 Sheldon Blvd. S.E.
Grand Rapids, MI 49503
616-214-7910
www.artprize.org

♦ 0163 ♦ Arts and Crafts Fair, International
October-November, every two years

Burkina Faso, a small sub-Saharan African country with limited natural resources, is continually seeking ways to boost its economy. The International Arts and Crafts Fair, which takes place in the capital city, Ouagadougou, is part of a national development plan that heavily promotes the African handicraft sector. Along with showcasing the works of Burkinabé craftspeople, the 10-day exposition also displays crafts from over 30 other African countries as well as European and Asian nations. Organizers have reported annual attendance totals at over 350,000, making it one of the world's largest handicraft fairs.

The International Arts and Crafts Fair was founded in 1988 by the Salon International de l'Artisanat de Ouagadougou (SIAO), a government organization, and over the years the group has helped expand the Fair's capacity. Exporters from all over the world have traveled to the fair to peruse the many statues, textiles, leatherwork, jewelry, pottery, and ceramics on display. Ever year the SIAO has ensured that an international forum remains a fixture at the exposition. This forum creates opportunities for craftspeople and other industry figures to discuss and seek solutions to ongoing issues in the international handicraft market.

♦ 0164 ♦ **Arts and Pageant of the Masters, Festival of**
July-September

This festival features a display of art works in arty Laguna Beach, Calif., along with breathtaking *tableaux vivants*—living pictures that recreate master art works. Since the 1940s, artists have created the tableaux to reproduce paintings by such varied masters as Leonardo da Vinci, Henri Matisse, and Winslow Homer. They don't stop there; they also transform delicate pieces of jewelry, sculptures, antique artifacts, and even scenes from postage stamps into life-sized works of art. The tableaux, presented for 90 minutes each evening, are created by some 300 models who have used 1,000 yards of fabric and 100 gallons of makeup. Example of a tableau: three gilded men and two gilded styrofoam horses appear in a setting that reproduces a five-inch Scythian gold comb.

CONTACTS:
Festival of Arts / Pageant of the Masters
650 Laguna Canyon Rd.
Laguna Beach, CA 92651
949-494-1145 or 949-464-4282 or 800-487-3378; fax: 949-376-1143
www.foapom.com

♦ 0165 ♦ **Asanha Bucha Day (Asanha Puja Day)**
First full moon of eighth lunar month

Celebrated in Thailand on the first full moon of the eighth lunar month, Asanha Bucha Day marks the first public sermon given by Buddha, which took place at Deer Park in Benares, India. In this initial sermon, Buddha presented the Four Noble Truths to five ascetics. While the ascetics believed in self-mortification, he taught that the cessation of desire was the key to enlightenment. Upon hearing this message, the five men reached enlightenment and became the first Buddhist priests or Sangha. The day also marks the beginning of Vassa, the Buddhist lent period also known as the Rains Retreat.

Ceremonies are held in Buddhist temples throughout the country. Elaborate wax candles are lit and kept burning throughout lent. In the city of Ubon, a Candle Festival is held in which a parade of candles is followed by a contest for best candle design and a beauty contest. In Saraburi, monks from the local temple will walk through the town with their alms bowls. On this day, townspeople will put flowers into their bowls instead of food, and the monks offer these flowers at the temple in honor of the Buddha. Asanha Bucha Day has become a popular day for young Thai men to enter the monkhood.

CONTACTS:
Royal Thai Embassy
1024 Wisconsin Ave. N.W.
Suite 401
Washington, D.C. 20007
202-944-3600; fax: 202-944-3611
www.thaiembassydc.org

♦ 0166 ♦ **Asarah be-Tevet (Fast of the Tenth of Tevet)**
Between December 13 and January 10; Tevet 10

Asarah be-Tevet is a Jewish fast day commemorating the beginning of the siege of Jerusalem by the Babylonians under King Nebuchadnezzar in 586 B.C.E. that was a prelude to the destruction of the First Temple. The fast begins at first morning light on the 10th day of the Jewish month of Tevet.

In Israel it is also a day to remember the victims of the Holocaust. However, Jews outside Israel observe Yom ha-Shoah as HOLOCAUST MEMORIAL DAY.

CONTACTS:
Orthodox Union
11 Broadway
New York, NY 10004
212-563-4000
www.ou.org

♦ 0167 ♦ **Ascension Day**
Between April 30 and June 3; 40 days after Easter

Ascension Day is one of the earliest Christian festivals, dating back to the year 68. According to the New Testament, Jesus met several times with his disciples during the 40 days after his Resurrection to instruct them in how to carry out his teachings. Then on the 40th day he took them to the Mount of Olives, where they watched as he ascended to heaven.

Reflecting both Christian and pagan customs, Ascension Day celebrations include processions symbolizing Christ's entry into heaven and, in some countries, chasing a "devil" through the streets and dunking him in a pond or burning him in effigy—symbolic of the Messiah's triumph over the devil when he opened the kingdom of heaven to all believers.

Other customs attached to this day include "beating the bounds"—switching young boys with willow branches as they are driven along parish boundaries, not only to purify them of evil but to teach them the limits of their parish. This gave rise to the name **Bounds Thursday** in England, where it is also sometimes called **Holy Thursday**, though in the rest of the world that term applies to MAUNDY THURSDAY.

In Germany it is sometimes called Father's Day because Protestant men have *herrenpartien*, "outings," on this day. In Sweden many people go out to the woods at three or four o'clock to hear the birds at sunrise. It is good luck if a cuckoo is heard from the east or west. These jaunts are called *gök-otta*, or "early cuckoo morning."

See also BANNTAG; HOLY THURSDAY.

CONTACTS:
Greek Orthodox Archdiocese of Australia
221 Dorcas St.
South Melbourne, VIC 3205 Australia

613-9245-9000; fax: 613-9696-3583
www.greekorthodox.org.au

♦ 0168 ♦ Ascension Day (Portugal)
Between April 30 and June 3; 40 days after Easter

Also known as *Quinta Feira da Espiga,* or Ear of Wheat Thursday, ASCENSION DAY in Portugal is associated with wishes for peace and prosperity. Traditionally, in rural communities, people gather olive branches, wheat sheaves, poppies, and daisies and fashion them into bouquets. The olive and wheat are symbolic of an abundant harvest; the poppy represents tranquility, and the daisy stands for money. Many Portuguese preserve a sprig of wheat in their homes as a symbol of prosperity. Another Ascension Day custom is to cull healing plants and herbs to be used later in concocting homemade medicines or magic potions.

CONTACTS:
Turismo de Portugal, I.P.
Rua Ivone Silva
Lote 6
Lisbon 1050-124 Portugal
351-211-140-200; fax: 351-211-140-830
www.turismodeportugal.pt/english

♦ 0169 ♦ Ash Wednesday
Between February 4 and March 10

The first day of LENT in the West. For 14 centuries the season of Lent has been a time for self-examination and penitence in preparation for EASTER. The name comes from the Saxon *lengten-tide,* referring to the lengthening of the days and the coming of spring. This 40-day period of abstinence recalls the fasts of Moses, Elijah, and Jesus, all of which—according to scripture—lasted 40 days. It was originally begun in the Western Church on a Sunday. But since Sundays were feast days, in the latter part of the sixth century Pope Gregory I moved the beginning of Lent ahead four days.

Gregory is also credited with having introduced the ceremony that gives this day its name. When public penitents came to the church for forgiveness, the priest would take some ash (made by burning the palms used on PALM SUNDAY of the previous year) and mark their foreheads with the sign of the cross as a reminder that they were but ashes and dust. Eventually the practice was extended to include all who wished to receive ashes.

In the East, ashes are not used, and Lent begins on the Monday before Ash Wednesday.

On Ash Wednesday in Iceland, children try to hook small bags of ashes or stones to the back of people's clothing.

See also SHROVE TUESDAY.

CONTACTS:
CRI/Voice, Institute
4801 N.W. 62nd St.

Oklahoma City, OK 73122
www.crivoice.org

♦ 0170 ♦ Asheville Mountain Dance and Folk Festival
First Thursday, Friday, and Saturday in August

The Asheville Mountain Dance and Folk Festival is the oldest festival of its kind in the country, held since 1928 in Asheville, N.C. Dedicated to traditional southern Appalachian music, it draws more than 400 performers: dulcimer sweepers, tune bow and mouth harp players, mountain fiddlers, and dancers who compete in smooth- and clog-dancing. Bluegrass and old-time bands also are on hand. ("Bluegrass" is not named for the Kentucky grass, but for the Blue Grass Boys, a band formed in 1938 by Bill Monroe, whose style of country popular music is still widely imitated; see also WIDE OPEN BLUEGRASS FESTIVAL).

Other events of the weekend include a quilt show and the Gee Haw Whimmy Diddle World Competition at the Folk Art Center, which usually draws about 50 contestants. The whimmy diddle, an Appalachian whittled folk toy, is a notched wooden gadget with a propeller on one end; when a stick is rubbed across the notches, the propeller spins. The idea of the contest is to control the spin, to make the propeller gee (turn to the right) and haw (turn to the left). The winners of cash prizes are those who get their whimmy diddle to change the direction of rotation the most times. There is also a cash prize for the Most Unusual and World's Largest Whimmy Diddle.

CONTACTS:
Folk Heritage Committee
P.O. Box 1010
Asheville, NC 28802
828-258-6101
www.folkheritage.org

♦ 0171 ♦ Ashokashtami
March-April; eighth day of the waxing half of the Hindu month of Caitra

Lord Lingaraj, a name for the Hindu deity Shiva, receives praise and adoration from Hindus on Ashokashtami, a day in the lunar month of Caitra (March-April in the Gregorian calendar). The festival takes place in Bhubaneswar, a small city in eastern India and the capital of Orissa. Two venerated sites host the festival: the Lingaraja Temple, believed to be the city's oldest temple, and the Rameshwar Temple, located just over a mile away. Thousands of people living in Bhubaneswar and throughout Orissa attend the festival to watch a traditional procession that features a giant wooden chariot carrying a Lingaraj idol and other deities.

The festival is inspired by the world-famous CAR FESTIVAL OF JAGANNATHA, which takes place in Puri, another city in Orissa. For the Ashokashtami procession, the wooden chariot begins at the Lingaraja Temple and, with the assistance of hundreds of attendees, the processional with the heavy cart proceeds to the Rameshwar Temple. Lingaraj and the other deities remain at the temple for four days before they are returned.

CONTACTS:
Odisha Department of Tourism, The Director
Paryatan Bhawan
Museum Campus
Bhubaneswar, Odisha 751 014 India
91-674-243-2177 or 800-208-1414
www.orissatourism.gov.in

♦ 0172 ♦ **Ashura**
First 10 days of Islamic month of Muharram

On the 10th of Muharram in the year 680, Muhammad's grandson Hussein (also spelled Husain) was killed in a skirmish between Sunnis and the small group of Shi'ite supporters with whom he was travelling to Iraq. They had been cut off from water and had suffered for 10 days before the men were killed and the women and children taken to Damascus, Syria, along with the heads of the men. His battlefield grave in Kerbela, about 60 miles southwest of Baghdad, became a pilgrimage site almost immediately, and to this day it remains a devotional center for Shi'ite Muslims around the world. Many aging Shi'ites settle in Kerbela or ask in their will to have their bodies carried to the holy city. So many dead have been sent to Kerbela that the town has been transformed into one vast burial ground.

This Islamic holy day, celebrated in the first month of the Islamic year, was derived by Muhammad from the Jewish fast of YOM KIPPUR; he later changed it to an optional fast day and it is so observed by modern-day Sunni Muslims. But for Shi'ites throughout Asia, the festival is dedicated to Hussein and begins on the first day of Muharram, when people put on their mourning clothes and refrain from shaving or bathing. The story of Hussein's martyrdom is recited in Muslim halls, with as much elaboration as possible. The celebration culminates on the 10th day of Muharram, in a large procession designed as a reenactment of Hussein's funeral, with many men whipping themselves bloody with whips and knives to take on the pain of Hussein. Since the early 19th century, the **Hussein Day** celebration has culminated in the performance of a *ta'ziyah*, or passion play, in which Hussein's life, death, and burial are recreated in a loose sequence of 40 to 50 scenes.

The Fatimid dynasty (969-1171) transferred Hussein's head to Cairo and built the Mosque of the Hasanain ('the two Hasans': Hasan and his brother, Hussein) over the relic. It is an especially holy place and is venerated also by Sunnis.

In India non-Shi'ites frequently take part in the processions, whereas in Iraq they would not be tolerated. Small replicas of Hussein's tomb, called *Ta ziyehs* (from the Arabic *aza*, meaning "mourning"), are carried and buried in the local "Kerbela" grounds: India is so far from Kerbela, Iraq, that Indian Shi'ites consecrate local lands so they, too, may be buried in "Kerbela" grounds.

In Jamaica and Trinidad the festival is called HOSAY and is celebrated by Muslims and Hindus as a symbol of East Indian unity. In Guyana, it is called **Tadja** and is now celebrated by Afro- and Indo-Guyanese, after having been outlawed in the 1930s because of clashes between Muslims and Hindus when it coincided with DURGA PUJA.

In West Africa the holy day is combined with African beliefs, and ensuring prosperity is of uppermost importance: everyone eats as much as possible, inviting poor people to join them, because a full belly ensures prosperity. The Hausa give a fowl or goat's head to each member of the household, which they eat with their backs to each other. In Senegal, Guinea, and Sierra Leone, the dried head and feet of the ram killed at 'ID AL-ADHA are cooked and eaten. Symbolic bathing in rivers and purification by leaping over small fires are followed by torchlight parades and contests.

In Turkey, the 10th of Muharram is called **Yevmi Ashurer**, (day of sweet soup or porridge) and commemorates Noah's departure from the Ark onto Mount Ararat. They must share Allah's gifts with others, so everyone makes *ashurer*, which is a sweet soup or porridge made of boiled wheat, dried currants grain, and nuts, similar to that supposedly made by Noah and stored in the bins of the Ark. Each person is assigned a day to invite his neighbors to come and share it.

CONTACTS:
Embassy of Iraq
3421 Massachusetts Ave. N.W.
Washington, D.C. 20007
202-742-1600; fax: 202-333-1129
www.iraqiembassy.us

♦ 0173 ♦ **Asian Games**
Every four years; November

The Olympic Council of Asia has been organizing the Asian Games since 1951. Every four years, the best athletes from throughout Asia are chosen to compete in the games, which are supervised by the International Olympics Committee.

Not all Asian countries participate in the games. Israel is kept out of the competition due to objections by several Arab nations. Taiwan was kept out for several years due to a conflict with communist mainland China. Australia was disqualified from participation when it was judged to be an Oceanic country. In 1994, the Olympic Council of Asia drew protest for admitting five former Soviet republics into the games.

Among the contests featured at Asian Games are handball, karate, rowing, chess, bowling, and swimming. As in the Olympics, each competition awards a gold, silver, and bronze medal to the three best athletes. A torch is also carried from the site of the last games to the site of the next games, a process that involves some 3,000 persons.

The 2014 Asian Games, officially known as the XVII Asiad, were held in Incheon, South Korea. The Incheon Asiad featured 439 events in 36 sports, with 45 nations and 9,501 athletes (5,823 men and 3,678 women) participating. Fourteen World and 27 Asian records were broken at the event. China won the most medals, followed by South Korea and Japan. The next Asian Games will be celebrated in Jakarta, Indonesia in 2018.

CONTACTS:
Olympic Council of Asia
P.O. Box 6706
Hawalli 32042 Kuwait
965-222-74277; fax: 965-222-74280
www.ocasia.org

♦ 0174 ♦ Aspen Food and Wine Classic
June

The Aspen Food and Wine Classic is an annual, three-day event in June presented by *Food & Wine* magazine. Regarded as a signature event for epicurean food culture, it attracts celebrity chefs and wine connoisseurs from all over the world. The origins of the festival go back to 1983, when Gary Plumley, an Aspen liquor storeowner, joined some restaurateurs in the neighboring village of Snowmass to organize the celebration. Today, the event features the best in culinary talent, presenting an interesting lineup of cooking demonstrations, wine tastings, and panel discussions by renowned chefs and wine experts. The Aspen Food and Wine Classic also serves as a marketing platform, connecting a wide range of products and brands with an audience of 5,000 consumers and industry people.

CONTACTS:
Aspen Chamber Resort Association
425 Rio Grande Pl.
Aspen, CO 81611
970-925-1940 or 800-670-0792; fax: 970-920-1173
www.aspenchamber.org

♦ 0175 ♦ Aspen Music Festival
Late June to late August

One of the finest and most important musical events in the United States, this event was founded in 1949 in Aspen in the Colorado Rocky Mountains. Symphonic orchestra and chamber-music concerts are staged in the white-tented amphitheater designed by Finnish-born architect Eero Saarinen, and smaller presentations in a renovated opera house and a church. Programs range from baroque to modern. Each season new compositions are introduced by "composers in residence"; Virgil Thomson and Aaron Copland have been among them. A school of music operates along with the festival and has an enrollment of more than 900 students.

Aspen was a wealthy silver-mining town in the 1880s, but lost its glitter when silver prices collapsed in the 1890s. Its rebirth began in the late 1930s, largely because of the enterprise of Chicago industrialist Walter Paepcke, who thought Aspen would be suitable for a Platonic community. It is now a popular though pricey skiing resort.

CONTACTS:
Aspen Music Festival and School
225 Music School Rd.

Aspen, CO 81611
970-925-3254; fax: 970-925-3802
www.aspenmusicfestival.com

♦ 0176 ♦ Ass, Feast of the
Around Christmas, December 25

This festival recalling the flight of the Holy Family (Jesus, Mary, and Joseph) into Egypt to escape King Herod reached its peak during the Middle Ages in France. It was customary to have a girl carrying a baby and riding an elaborately decorated ass led through the streets to the church, where a mass was said. But the celebration gradually took on comic overtones, with the priest and congregation imitating the braying of an ass at appropriate times during the service and the ass itself being led into the church and given food and drink. By the 15th century the feast had obviously become nothing more than an occasion for laughter, and it was suppressed thereafter by the Church, although it didn't completely die out until years afterward.

See also FEAST OF FOOLS.

♦ 0177 ♦ Assumption of Our Lady (Santa Marija)
August 15

The Republic of Malta is a small country in the central Mediterranean that consists of seven islands. In 1814, Malta became a crown colony of the British empire. Under British rule, the Maltese Islands helped the Allies during World War Hundreds of Maltese served as soldiers in the British regiments, and Malta allowed the British to use its dockyard and hospitals. Thousands of sick and wounded soldiers were brought to Malta for treatment, thereby earning the country the title of the "Nurse of the Mediterranean."

Malta also played an important role during World War II. The bravery its people showed during the war led to the country being awarded the George Cross, which is now displayed on its flag During World War II, Malta served as a military base for Great Britain's ships, submarines, and military airplanes. For two years, the Axis powers (Italy, Germany, and Japan) attacked Malta, trying to take over the country in an attempt to control the Mediterranean. As supply convoys approached, the Axis military would attack and destroy them. By the summer of 1942, supplies were so low that many Maltese were close to starvation, and the country would soon be forced to surrender.

Operation Pedestal was planned and executed by the British Royal Navy. Fourteen merchant ships carried badly needed supplies to Malta for both the military and civilian population. Those merchant ships were guarded and escorted by 64 warships. The Italian and German air forces were prepared for the convoy and attacked the ships as they approached. The *SS Ohio*, an American oil tanker, soon became a main target. The ship withstood two days of bombings and was severely crippled. However, the Allied warships were able to prop her up and escort her safely to Malta's Valletta Grand

Harbour. Only five of the 14 merchant ships reached Malta. These ships and their crews were met with cheers of joy and appreciation. It gave the people hope that they were saved. Within months after Operation Pedestal, the Axis powers gave up on their attempts to take over Malta.

Today in Malta, the country celebrates the feast of the Assumption of Our Lady, a national holiday that commemorates the success of Operation Pedestal. Many believe that it was through the intervention of Our Lady that Operation Pedestal was able to succeed. On this day, church services across the country start with a prayer of thanksgiving, and the names of the five surviving merchant ships are read.

Feast days, including the feast of Santa Marija, are a big part of life on the Islands. In Malta, this holiday and many of the other holidays are celebrated *festa*-style—with fireworks, decorated streets, and carts throughout the villages selling many different foods, including traditional sweets and delicacies such as Maltese nougat.

CONTACTS:
Malta Tourism Authority
Auberge D'Italie
Merchants St.
Valetta VLT 1170 Malta
356-229-15000; fax: 356-229-15394
www.visitmalta.com

♦ 0178 ♦ **Assumption of the Blessed Virgin Mary, Feast of the**
August 15

Assumption Day, called the **Dormition of the Most Holy Mother of God** in the East, commemorates the belief that when Mary, the mother of Jesus, died, her body was not subjected to the usual process of physical decay but was "assumed" into heaven and reunited there with her soul. Like the IMMACULATE CONCEPTION, the Assumption wasn't always an official dogma of the Roman Catholic Church—not until Pope Pius XII ruled it so in 1950. It was, however, a pious belief held by most Orthodox Christians and some Anglicans. It is regarded as the principal feast day of the Virgin Mother.

This festival may be a Christianization of an earlier Artemis harvest feast, and in some parts of Europe it is still called the **Feast of Our Lady of the Harvest**. The people of Queven, France, actually reenact the Assumption by lowering a wooden angel from the tower of the church and then making her rise again toward "heaven." In Elche, Spain, a two-day enactment of the apocryphal Gospels is performed each year (*see* MYSTERY PLAY OF ELCHE). It is the national holiday of the Acadians in the Maritime Provinces of Canada, and is called *tinta marre* (meaning "a racket"). At 6 P.M. on the 15th, pots and pans are banged, whistles blown, and drums beaten. On the nearest Sunday, boats are decorated and sail past the dock where the priest blesses the fleet. Messina, Sicily, celebrates with a two-week festival including a human tableau of the Assumption and giant figures believed to symbolize the mythical founders of the city, Zancleo and his wife. The girl

who portrays the Madonna is allowed to pardon one criminal.

In São Paulo and other parts of southern Brazil, the feast is called **Nosa Senhora dos Navegantes**, "Our Lady of the Navigators." Pageants are held on decorated canoes, each carrying a captain, a purser, three musicians, and two rowers. They travel to small villages to entertain and feast. Towns may have a church procession with musicians whose costumes and demeanors depict the Three Wise Men.

See also BLESSING OF THE GRAPES; MARYMASS FESTIVAL.

CONTACTS:
Greek Orthodox Archdiocese of Australia (Archdiocesan District of New South Wales & The Australian Capital Territory)
242 Cleveland St.
Redfern, NSW 2016 Australia
61-2-9690-6100; fax: 61-2-9698-5368
www.greekorthodox.org.au

♦ 0179 ♦ **Assumption of the Virgin Mary, Feast of the (Guatemala)**
August 15

Roman Catholics believe that the body of Mary, rather than undergoing death and decay, entered heaven along with her soul, an event that is commemorated in the Feast of the Assumption (*see* ASSUMPTION OF THE BLESSED VIRGIN MARY, FEAST OF THE). In the Guatemalan town of Santa Cruz del Quiché, the Feast of the Assumption is combined with the Fiestas Elenas (August 16-20) and celebrated for nearly a week.

The fiesta's highlight is the famous Snake Dance. Also known as the Dance of the Jesters, this was a Native American dance that the Spanish priests tried to stamp out. They were not successful because the secret societies that executed the dances did so in caves and other secret locations unknown to the Spanish.

The dance involves the use of live snakes, some of them poisonous, which are captured in the mountains and brought back to town in jars. In order to prevent the snakes from poisoning anyone, the venom is removed in advance or else someone sews the snakes' mouths shut. As the energy of the dance reaches its peak the snakes are released and permitted to writhe about on the dance floor. Each of the dancers scoops up a snake and lets it wrap itself around his limbs while continuing to dance. Occasionally the snake goes down a dancer's blouse or jacket, and the audience roars with laughter if the snake manages to escape through a trouser leg.

One of the dancers wears a fur-trimmed suit and carries a stuffed fox. As he lunges at the audience in a threatening way, kids approach him from behind and yank on the fox's tail. According to legend, the stuffed fox represents the earth's fertility, while the serpent symbolizes the rain that bestows life on the earth. It is probably related to the feathered serpent, a predominant Mesoamerican symbol.

CONTACTS:
Instituto Guatemalteco de Turismo
INGUAT- 7 av. 1-17 zona 4
Centro Cívico
Guatemala City Guatemala
502-242-12800
www.visitguatemala.com/en

♦ 0180 ♦ Assumption of the Virgin Mary, Feast of the (Hasselt, Belgium)
Third and fourth Sundays in August every seven years

In Hasselt, the capital of the Belgian province of Limburg, the festival known as *Virge Jesse* (Virgin of the Line of Jesse) takes place on the third and fourth Sundays in August every seven years. Local lore states that in medieval times an image of the Virgin was propped up against a great tree which stood at the crossroads near the present-day site of Hasselt. Those whose journeys took them past the image often stopped there to pray for safe travels and to make an offering to the Virgin. By the 14th century, tales concerning the Virgin's blessings began to attract pilgrims from far and near the image at the crossroads.

Today's ceremonies feature a procession with a dark, ancient image of the Virgin, said by townsfolk to be the same one that once stood against the tree at the crossroads. Bearers carry the image, draped in a black velvet mantle, through town and under a progression of arches that represent important episodes in the city's past.

Assumption Day is an official holiday in Belgium.

CONTACTS:
Belgian Tourist Office
300 E. 42nd St.
14th Fl.
New York, NY 10017
212-758-8130
www.visitbelgium.com

♦ 0181 ♦ Assumption of the Virgin Mary, Feast of the (Italy)
August 15

Colorful processions through the streets and displays of fireworks mark the celebration of the Feast of the Assumption in Italy, as they do in Italian-American communities throughout the United States. In Sicily and rural areas outside of Rome, a **Bowing Procession** is the day's main event. A statue of the Virgin Mary is carried through the town to a ceremonial arch of flowers, where a group of people holding a statue of Christ awaits her arrival. Both statues are inclined toward each other three times, and then the Christ figure precedes that of Mary back to the parish church for a special benediction. The journey to the arch symbolizes Mary's sojourn on earth, the arch itself represents the gate of heaven, and the trip back to the church represents her entrance into heaven.

CONTACTS:
Italian National Tourist Board

686 Park Ave.
3rd Fl.
New York, NY 10065
212-245-5618; fax: 212-586-9249
www.italiantourism.com

♦ 0182 ♦ Aston Magna Festival
Five weekend evenings from early July to early August

The Aston Magna Festival has been held since the 1970s, continuing its tradition of bringing music of the baroque period and beyond to today's audiences using historically accurate instruments and performance practices. The oldest festival of its kind, this annual event in the Berkshires of Massachusetts is an outgrowth of the Aston Magna Foundation for Music and the Humanities, which was founded in 1972 by Lee Elman and harpsichordist Albert Fuller to study all aspects of music composed in the 17th and 18th centuries. Today the mission of the foundation is "to enrich the appreciation of music of the past and the understanding of the cultural, political, and social contexts in which it was composed and experienced."

For five consecutive weekends in July and August, a 21st-century audience can enjoy a musical experience closely resembling that of an earlier era as the works of MOZART, Monteverdi, the Bach family, Schubert, Beethoven, Corelli, Purcell, Haydn, and other composers are performed on period instruments. Concerts are held on Fridays at Bard College, with the same program presented on Saturdays at St. James Church in Great Barrington, Massachusetts. Programs have featured vocal and instrumental works ranging from Elizabethan and Italian madrigals and cantatas to piano sonatas, concertos, and symphonies.

CONTACTS:
Aston Magna Foundation
P.O. Box 28
Great Barrington, MA 01230
413-528-3595 or 800-875-7156
www.astonmagna.org

♦ 0183 ♦ Ataturk Remembrance (Youth and Sports Day)
May 19

On May 19, 1919, Mustafa Kemal Atatürk landed with his forces at the Black Sea town of Samsun, Turkey, to begin his fight against the Allies who had occupied the Ottoman Empire at the end of World War I. Four years later, Atatürk had successfully overcome the last of the Allied forces and Turkey was declared a free republic. He ushered in an era of reform, development, and an increasingly Western approach to government and society. Because Turkish youth have always engaged in sporting events to celebrate the day, it has also become known as **Youth and Sports Day** as well.

In the capital city of Ankara, the celebration of the day begins with a 21-gun salute at 7:00 in the morning, the time when

Atatürk arrived in Samsun. Then the president and other government officials visit the Atatürk Mausoleum before moving on to the 19 Mayis (May 19th) Stadium. Members of the Turkish Air Forces Youth Team have performed parachuting exhibitions in several cities across Turkey.

CONTACTS:
Turkish Coalition of America
1510 H St. N.W.
Ste. 900
Washington, D.C. 20005
202-370-1399; fax: 202-370-1398
www.tc-america.org

♦ 0184 ♦ **Athens Festival**
End of June through September

vThe feeling of ancient Greece comes alive among the ruins every summer in Athens, where the Acropolis and Parthenon help set the stage for the Athens Festival. Harkening back to the city's heritage, music, dance, and theater performancesare presented in the Herod Atticus Odeon, a Roman-style, open-air hillside theater originally built in C.E. 161 that seats thousands. Since 1955 orchestral and chamber music, classical and popular theater, opera, ballet, and modern dance have been performed there by both Greek and international artists, among them the Paris Symphony Orchestra, the Kirov Opera, the Peking Opera, the Alvin Ailey American Dance Theater, the English Bach Festival, the National Theatre of Greece, the Old Vic Company, and the Bolshoi Ballet.

CONTACTS:
Athens Festival
Chatzichristou 23 & Makrigianni
Athens 117 42 Greece
30-210-928-2900; fax: 30-210-928-2941
www.greekfestival.gr/en

♦ 0185 ♦ **Ati-Atihan Festival**
Third week in January

One of the most colorful festivals in the Philippines, held in Kalibo, the capital city of the province of Aklan. Originally falling on the Feast Day of Santo Niño (the infant Jesus), the celebration combines Christian and non-Christian elements.

Its origins are in the 13th century, when 10 families fled Borneo and landed on the Philippine island of Panay. There the resident Ati people gave them land. The Ati (also called Negritos or Pygmies) were small dark people, and after receiving the land, the story goes, the Malayan people blackened their faces to look like the Ati. Years later, the Spanish Christians, having converted much of the country, persuaded the inhabitants to darken their skin, wear warlike clothing, and pretend they were Ati to frighten away the Muslims. They were victorious over the Muslims and attributed their victory to Santo Niño. At that time, religion came into the festival.

Ati-Atihan means "to make like Atis." During the present-day festival, revelers cover their skin with soot and wear Ati costumes that are patchworks of coconut shells, feathers, and fronds. They converge on the main streets and around the town plaza and, to the beat of drums, shout "Hala Bira" ('Go on and fight!'), pound their spears, and repeatedly dance a two-step dance. From a distance, the celebrants look like a solid mass of people lurching and swinging in a frenzied rhythm.

See also DINAGYANG and SINULOG.

CONTACTS:
Kasafi Kalibo Ati-Athihan Foundation, Inc.
2nd Fl. Captain Gil M, Mijares Bldg
Corner XIX Martyrs Rizal St.
Kalibo, Aklan Philippines
63-36-268-6160
www.kaliboatiatihan.ph

♦ 0186 ♦ **Atlanta Film Festival**
April

The Atlanta Film Festival has been held annually since 1976. The event differs from other large film festivals by including genre movies like horror and science fiction. Furthermore, it presents the Pink Peach Award to the best LGBTQ film. Programs at the event include workshops, screenings, panel discussions, and educational events for filmmakers, professionals, and movie lovers alike. The festival also runs the Airport Shorts Program at the Atlanta International Airport, where two hours of short films are shown on 30 screens to 14 million travelers year round.

CONTACTS:
Atlanta Film Festival
25 Park Pl. N.E.
Ste. 800., P.O. Box 5060
Atlanta, GA 30303
678-929-8103
atlantafilmfestival.com

♦ 0187 ♦ **Atlanta Pride Festival**
October 10-11

The Atlanta Pride Festival is a two-day lesbian, gay, bisexual, transgender (LGBT) pride celebration held annually in Atlanta, Georgia and produced by the Atlanta Pride Committee. The event focuses on celebrating identity and promoting the cause of equal rights for the LGBT community. First held in 1971, the 45th Atlanta Pride Festival will take place in 2015. Most Pride Festival events take place at Atlanta's Piedmont Park. Several parades and related events take place before and during the festival. The main Pride Parade is reserved for the second and last day of the festival, which coincides with the October 11th observance of National Coming Out Day.

CONTACTS:
Atlanta Pride Committee Inc
1530 DeKalb Ave. N.E.
Ste. A
Atlanta, GA 30307
404-382-7588; fax: 866-766-9104
atlantapride.org

♦ 0188 ♦ **Atohuna (Friends Made Ceremony)**
Ten days after the first new moon in autumn

Regarded as the most profound of all Cherokee ceremonies, the Atohuna, or Friends Made Ceremony, falls ten days after the Great New Moon Festival and is a celebration of relationships—a time to renew old friendships, reconcile with foes, and forge new bonds. In the broader context, Atohuna represents the cleansing of the body and mind and the divine union between people and the creator. The festival lasts four days and begins with cleansing rites that are carried out in water.

Rekindling the sacred fire is a central part of the ceremony. The fire keeper and his assistants fast for seven days before rekindling the sacred fire, which is believed to have been started by the creator. People are delegated to perform various tasks during Atohuna, such as cleaning, hunting, cooking, and singing of the *Yowah*—sacred chants handed down over generations. The council house (administrative center of the Cherokee) is cleansed by a group of seven men who beat the roof of the house with sycamore wood. As part of the festival, people exchange clothes as a mark of eternal friendship. Atohuna is also the time when people reconcile with elders the fact that many of them might not survive the harsh winter months to come.

CONTACTS:
Cherokee Nation
W.W. Keeler Tribal Complex
17675 S. Muskogee Ave.
Tahlequah, OK 74464
918-453-5000 or 800-256-0671
www.cherokee.org

♦ 0189 ♦ **Audubon Day**
April 26

John James Audubon (1785-1851) was America's foremost ornithological illustrator. After studying drawing in Paris under the French painter Jacques Louis David, Audubon struggled for many years to make a living from his art, shuttling back and forth between Europe and the United States and supplementing his income by giving drawing lessons, turning out portraits, playing the flute or violin at local dances, and at one time running a general store.

In 1820 he began a flatboat excursion down the Mississippi River to seek out new varieties of birds to paint. Eventually he had enough bird portraits to publish in book form. *Birds of America*, produced with the help of engraver Robert Havell, Jr., contains 435 hand-colored plates and was published in "elephant folio" format to accommodate the life-sized portrayals of birds on which Audubon insisted.

After his death in 1851, Audubon's wife Lucy returned to teaching to support herself. One of her students, George Bird Grinnell, became the editor of *Forest and Stream* magazine and in 1886 organized the Audubon Society for the study and protection of birds. Today there are many branches of this organization, known as the National Audubon Society, and it remains dedicated to the conservation of wildlife and natural resources. Its members honor Audubon on his birthday, April 26. In some states, Audubon Day and ARBOR DAY are celebrated together by planting trees in bird sanctuaries.

CONTACTS:
National Audubon Society
225 Varick St.
New York, NY 10014
212-979-3100
www.audubon.org

♦ 0190 ♦ **Auntie Litter's Annual Earth Day Parade and Celebration**
April 22

Auntie Litter's Annual Earth Day Parade and Celebration are held each Earth Day, April 22, in Birmingham, Ala. The character "Auntie Litter," dressed in distinctive stars and green-and-white stripes, is the mascot for an environmental education and awareness program that promotes its green campaign through the Earth Day event.

The message of Auntie Litter is to conserve natural resources, eliminate litter, and to embrace the three Rs: reduce, reuse, and recycle. During Auntie Litter's parade, hundreds of schoolchildren and supporters march for a cleaner Earth. The accompanying celebration features educational exhibits, live entertainment, science demonstrations, and costume competitions. Auntie Litter, Inc., a non-profit organization, was founded in 1990. The Earth Day parade and celebration have been held each year since 1992.

CONTACTS:
Auntie Litter Inc.
1776 Independence Ct.
St 304
Birmingham, AL 35216
205-879-3009; fax: 205-879-3049
auntielitter.org

♦ 0191 ♦ **Austen (Jane) Festival**
Last week of September

Along with being famous for its ancient Roman ruins, the town of Bath, England, is also known as the home of renowned English novelist Jane Austen (1775–1817). The writer's residence in the town, located 100 miles west of London, was short—a mere five years at the turn of the 19th century. However, the author's foray in the city was significant enough to inspire the creation of an annual festival in September.

Since 2001, Austen aficionados have converged on Bath for over a week to celebrate with music, walking tours, films, and the famous Regency Promenade, in which a large group in period costume parade the Georgian terraces of Bath. The festival boasts that it is the largest European promenade featuring the fashion of Britain's Regency era, the period during which Austen wrote. Other well-attended events are workshops, lectures, and readings, which often reference *Northanger Abbey* and *Persuasion*, two Austen novels mainly set in Bath.

Many festival goers delve deeper into Austen's personal history and the influence Bath had on her by visiting the Jane Austen Centre, a permanent exhibit situated in one of the city's Georgian town houses.

CONTACTS:
Jane Austen Centre
40 Gay St.
Bath BA1 2NT United Kingdom
44-122-544-3000
www.janeausten.co.uk

♦ 0192 ♦ Austin City Limits Music Festival
First two weekends in October

When October arrives, the city of Austin, Texas, gears up for the Austin City Limits Music Festival. Musicians from multiple genres, including rock, indie, country, folk, electronic, and hip-hop, play at the festival, which takes place in Zilker Park over the course of two weekends. The festival was conceived in 2002 as an offshoot of the successful PBS television show Austin City Limits.

The Austin City Limits Music Festival features eight stages where approximately 130 artists perform for an estimated 225,000 fans. In addition to the head-turning music, the event offers food from local restaurants, special activities for kids, and handcrafted creations at the Art Market in the center of Zilker Park.

CONTACTS:
Austin City Limits Music Festival
Zilker Park
2100 Barton Springs Rd.
Austin, TX 78704
www.aclfestival.com

Austin Convention & Visitors Bureau
111 Congress Ave.
Ste. 700
Austin, TX 78701
800-926-2282
www.austintexas.org

♦ 0193 ♦ Australia Day
January 26

The anniversary of the first British settlement in Australia on January 26, 1788, was formerly known as **Foundation Day** or **Anniversary Day**. Captain Arthur Phillip and his company of British convicts arrived first at Botany Bay, and when that proved to be an unsuitable location they moved on to Port Jackson, where the city of Sydney was eventually established. They built a penal colony there to help relieve overcrowding in the British prisons.

First officially celebrated in Sydney in 1818, Australia Day has been a public holiday since 1838. It used to be observed on either January 26 or the nearest Monday, but since 1994 it has been observed on January 26 with celebrations all over the country.

CONTACTS:
National Australia Day Council

Old Parliament House
King George Terr.
Parkes, ACT 2600 Australia
61-2-6120-0600
www.australiaday.org.au

♦ 0194 ♦ Australian Open Tennis
January

The Australian Open is the year 's first event in the Grand Slam of tennis, followed by the FRENCH OPEN, the UNITED STATES OPEN, and WIMBLEDON. It is played on synthetic hard courts at Sydney, Australia, and Melbourne, Australia, and known officially as the **Australian Championships.** Tennis took root in Australia in 1880 at the Melbourne Cricket Club. The championship for men began in 1905, and the women's championship in 1922. The matches became an "open" (to both amateurs and professionals) in 1969.

Margaret Smith Court, an Australian known for her powerful serve and volley, is the all-time champion in the women's division of the open; she won the title 11 times between 1960 and 1973. In 1970, she was the second woman to win the Grand Slam; Maureen Connolly had swept the four tournaments in 1953, and Steffi Graf won all four in 1988. Recently, Serena Williams has taken her place alongside the greatest women tennis players of all time with six victories at the Australian Open (2003, 2005, 2007, 2009, 2010, and 2015).

Top multiple winners in the men's division of the Australian Open have been Roy Emerson, who took six titles (1961 and 1962-67); Novak Djokovic with five, including three consecutive titles (2008, 2011-2013, and 2015); Jack Crawford, Ken Rosewall, Pat Wood, Andre Agassi, and Roger Federer who each won four; and Rod Laver, Adrian Quist, and Mats Wilander, who each won three.

CONTACTS:
Tennis Australia
Private Bag 6060
Richmond South, VIC 3000 Australia
61-3-9914-4000; fax: 61-3-9650-2743
www.tennis.com.au

♦ 0195 ♦ Austria National Day
October 26

National Day commemorates the day in 1955 when Soviet occupation forces left Austria, after taking control in 1945. The Austrian State Treaty of May 15, 1955, ensured that Austrians would regain sovereignty over their country on July 27. By October 26, it was once again a free, independent country.

Though a national holiday in Austria, people do not get the day off from school or work, mainly because of the idea that one's country is best served by working. Schools hold special presentations, and the president delivers a speech.

CONTACTS:
Embassy of Austria
3524 International Ct. N.W.

Washington, D.C. 20008
202-895-6700; fax: 202-895-6750
www.austria.org

♦ 0196 ♦ Author's Day, National
November 1

The idea of setting aside a day to celebrate American authors came from Nellie Verne Burt McPherson, president of the Bement (Illinois) Women's Club in 1928. McPherson was a teacher and an avid reader throughout her life. During World War I, when she was recuperating in a hospital, she wrote a fan letter to fiction writer Irving Bacheller, telling him how much she had enjoyed his story, "Eben Holden's Last Day A'Fishin." Bacheller sent her an autographed copy of another story, and McPherson realized that she could never adequately thank him for his gift. Instead, she showed her appreciation by submitting an idea for a National Author's Day to the General Federation of Women's Clubs, which passed a resolution setting aside November 1 as a day to honor American writers. In 1949 the day was recognized by the U.S. Department of Commerce.

Sue Cole, McPherson's granddaughter, was largely responsible for promoting the observation of National Author's Day after her grandmother's death in 1968. She has urged people to write a note to their favorite author on this day to "brighten up the sometimes lonely business of being a writer." Flying the American flag on November 1, according to Mrs. Cole, is another way of showing appreciation for the men and women who have created American literature.

CONTACTS:
Arkansas State Library
900 W. Capitol
Ste. 100
Little Rock, AR 72201
501-682-2053
www.library.arkansas.gov

♦ 0197 ♦ Autumnal Equinox
September 22-23

The sun crosses the plane of the earth's equator twice a year: on or about March 21 (*see* VERNAL EQUINOX) and again six months later, on or about September 22 or 23. On these two occasions, night and day are of equal length all over the world. In the Northern Hemisphere, September 22 or 23 is the first day of autumn.

Autumnal Equinox Day is a national holiday in Japan, observed on either September 23 or 24 to celebrate the arrival of autumn and to honor family ancestors.

See also HIGAN; SHUNBUN-NO-HI.

CONTACTS:
Royal Museums Greenwich
National Maritime Museum
Park Row
Greenwich, London SE10 9NF United Kingdom

44-20-8858-4422; fax: 44-20-8312-6565
www.rmg.co.uk

♦ 0198 ♦ Avani Mulam
August-September; during the Hindu month of Bhadrapada

According to Hindu mythology, the god Indra showed his displeasure with the king of Madurai by sending a drought, during which the river completely dried up. When a sudden, heavy rainfall threatened to flood the river's banks, the king ordered everyone in Madurai to help build a dam to conserve the precious water. The portion of the dam assigned to one old woman was never completed, because she was too busy cooking for the other hungry laborers. One of the workmen who came to her for food was actually the god Sundara, who saved the dam from leaking by throwing a small handful of earth in the gap left by the old woman.

Although Avani Mulam is observed throughout India, the grandest celebration is in Madurai, Tamil Nadu, where an image of Sundara, with a golden basket and a golden spade, is carried in a procession from the river to the temple.

CONTACTS:
Arulmighu Madurai Meenakshi Amman Temple
Madurai, Tamil Nadu India
www.maduraimeenakshi.org

Ministry of Tourism, Government of India
1270 Ave. of the Americas
Ste. 303
New York, NY 10020
212-586-4901; fax: 212-582-3274
tourism.nic.in

♦ 0199 ♦ Aviation Day
August 19

National Aviation Day honors the birthday of the American inventor and early manufacturer of airplanes, Orville WRIGHT (1871-1948), as well as the progress that has been made in manned flight since the Wright Brothers made their historic 120-foot flight at Kitty Hawk, North Carolina, in 1903. President Franklin D. ROOSEVELT proclaimed August 19 as Aviation Day in 1939, and since that time celebrations have been sponsored in a number of states by organizations involved in aviation. Parachute jumping, glider demonstrations, films, airplane rides, and displays of new and antique aircraft are popular events on this day, and open house celebrations are often held at local airports. One of the more impressive observations of Aviation Day occurs when military aircraft fly in formation, often at lower-than-usual altitudes, over airports or other locations where celebrations are being held.

CONTACTS:
First Flight Society
P.O. Box 1903
Kitty Hawk, NC 27949
252-441-1903
firstflight.org

Wright Brothers National Memorial
1401 National Park Dr.
Manteo, NC 27954
252-473-2111; fax: 252-473-2595
www.nps.gov

♦ 0200 ♦ Avignon Festival
July

The month-long **Festival d'Avignon** was founded in 1947 by Jean Vilar, a well-known French actor and director. Invited to direct the first annual drama festival at Avignon, Vilar selected bold and innovative productions to be performed at the Court of Honor at the Popes' Palace (*Palais des Papes*), a large outdoor stage. This new kind of theater attracted an eager audience. In the 1960s Vilar expanded the festival's offerings to include dance, cinema, and musical theater.

The International Centre for Creative Research, a residence for artists, was established in the 1970s at the site of a 14thcentury monastery, with exhibitions and concerts held during the festival. About the same time, fringe theater sprouted in conjunction with the festival. In the 1980s the festival once again reinvented itself by introducing audiovisual media, presenting more international theater productions, and inviting contemporary poets to do readings.

Throughout its evolution, the Avignon Festival has not strayed from the fresh experimentation which was Vilar 's hallmark, thus continuing to attract new audiences after more than 65 years of existence. The festival presents a different program each year, with between 35 and 50 shows from France and all over the world, for a total of 300 performances in about 20 venues, including the Popes' Palace, cloisters, and churches. Most of the shows are created specifically for the Festival, or are being shown for the first time in France. Between 120,000 and 140,000 tickets are sold yearly, and the festival welcomes between 20,000 and 30,000 people to its free events.

CONTACTS:
Festival d'Avignon
Cloître Saint-Louis
20 rue du Portail Boquier
Avignon 84000 France
33-4-90-27-66-50
www.festival-avignon.com

♦ 0201 ♦ Awoojoh
Various

A thanksgiving feast in the West African nation of Sierra Leone, the Awoojoh honors the spirits of the dead, who are believed to have influence over the fortunes of the living. It may be held at any time of year, and the guests include not only friends and relatives but, in a small community, the entire village. The day begins with a family visit to the cemetery, where a libation is poured over the relatives' graves and the dead are invited to join in the thanksgiving celebration. Two kola nuts, one red and one white, are split in half and thrown upon the grave, and the pattern in which they fall is believed to carry a message from the ancestors. It is essential for all family quarrels to be settled before the feast begins.

Many popular African dishes—such as fried bean cakes, fried plantains, rice bread, and "Awoojoh beans"—are served, but the highlight of the meal is an elaborate stew, a portion of which is set out for the dead ancestors or thrown to the vultures, who are believed to embody the souls of the departed. Although the practice of holding a thanksgiving feast originated with the Yoruba, who came to Sierra Leone from Nigeria, Christians and Muslims give them as well.

♦ 0202 ♦ Awuru Odo Festival
Biannually in April

Among the Igbo people of Nigeria, the Odo are the spirits of the dead, who return to the earth to visit their families every two years. They arrive sometime between September and November (*see* ODO FESTIVAL) and depart in April. Before they leave, there is a big theatrical performance known as the Awuru Odo in which masked players, representing the Odo spirits, reenact the story of their visit to the living and the agony of their departure. The performance takes place on a ritual stage in the market square.

Because the Odo festival occurs only once every two years, elaborate preparations are made to welcome the returning spirits. The masks used in the performance are refurbished or new ones are made. Fences are put up around the shrines where the Odo will worship. Many of these preparations are carried out in secrecy by the men, while the women, who are totally excluded from and can have no knowledge of the activities, are responsible for providing enough food for the celebration.

♦ 0203 ♦ Ayathrem (Ayathrima; Bringing Home the Herds)
February, March, October; 26th-30th day of Mihr, the seventh Zoroastrian month

This is the fourth of the six great seasonal feasts known as *gahambars* in the Zoroastrian religion. The gahambars traditionally provided the Zoroastrians, who were at one time a primarily agricultural people, with periodic respites from their labor and an opportunity to give thanks for their earthly blessings. Each of the six gahambars correlated with a phase of agricultural production—midsummer, bringing in the harvest, etc.—and honored one of the six things created by God: sky, water, earth, plants, animals, and humankind. The importance of the gahambars has diminished somewhat, now that so many Zoroastrians live in urban areas, but they are still observed in rural communities where farming rules the patterns of daily life.

The meaning of the word *Ayathrem* is not entirely clear. It is thought to refer to the time of prosperity and nourishment (*thrime* comes from *thrâ*, meaning "to thrive"), which may also be why it is identified with the breeding season for cattle.

The gahambars were typically joyous festivals that included such activities as intricate rituals, specific prayers, and the sharing of food.

The Zoroastrian calendar has 12 months of 30 days each, plus five extra days at the end of the year. Because of discrepancies in the calendars used by widely separated Zoroastrian communities around the world, there are now three different calendars in use, and Ayathrem can fall either in October, March, or February.

♦ 0204 ♦ Ayerye Festival
Between September and December

Fante communities in southern Ghana have organized themselves into local military companies called *asafo* groups for at least the last few hundred years. The Ayerye Festival celebrates and maintains this tradition of local self-defense. When young men come of age, their fathers traditionally give them guns; the Ayerye Festival is a kind of communal initiation occasion, in which the older men share their experience and skills with the new young initiates in order to help prepare them to take their places some day. There are mock battles and competitions designed to help the young men develop their skills.

CONTACTS:
Government of Ghana
Ministry of Communications
P.O. Box M41
Accra Ghana
www.ghana.gov.gh

♦ 0205 ♦ Aymuray (Song of the Harvest)
May 3

The South American Indians known as the Incas had an empire that flourished during the 15th and early 16th centuries and extended along the Pacific coast and Andean highlands from the northern border of what is now Ecuador to central Chile. They celebrated a harvest festival in May, which month they called *Aymuray*, which means "the song of the harvest."

Today, many Quechua Indians, who are descended from the Incas, still live in this region—most of them in Peru, and many continue to celebrate this ancient festival. They choose a tree to be the focus of the action and hang fruit and other objects on its boughs. Then they perform a traditional dance called the *Ayriwa*, "dance of the young corn," around the tree. Singing of the harvest song, the Aymuray, follows, and people shake the tree loose of its gifts and share them amongst each other.

Elsewhere in Peru, Aymuray has been largely combined with the Christian Feast of the EXALTATION OF THE CROSS. There are bonfires and music everywhere, as well as altars with crosses, which people take in processions to church.

♦ 0206 ♦ Ayyam-i-Ha
February 25-March 1

Also known as **Days of Ha**, the Ayyam-i-Ha are intercalary days (extra days inserted in a calendar) in the Baha'i calendar. The calendar is made up of 19 months of 19 days each (361 days), plus the period of four days (five in leap years) of Ayyam-i-Ha added between the 18th and 19th months, which allows for the year to be adjusted to the solar cycle.

The days are set aside for rejoicing, hospitality, gift-giving, special acts of charity, and spiritually preparing for the Baha'i fast, from March 2-20. March 21 is New Year's Day, NAWRUZ, and the first day of the Baha'i calendar.

The new calendar was inaugurated by Mirza Ali Mohammad, known as the BAB, founder of the Babi religion from which the Baha'i faith emerged. Baha'is believe that the new age of unity they foresee should have a new calendar free of the associations of the older calendars.

The Baha'i observe nine days on which work connected with trade, commerce, industry, and agriculture should be suspended. These days are the first, ninth, and 12th days of the Feast of RIDVAN, Nawruz, the anniversaries of the Bab's birth, declaration, and martyrdom, and the birth and ascension of BAHA'U'LAH.

CONTACTS:
U.S. Bahá'í National Center
1233 Central St.
Evanston, IL 60201
847-733-3400
www.bahai.us

♦ 0207 ♦ Azerbaijan Day of the Martyrs
January 20

On January 20, 1990, Soviet troops entered the Azerbaijan capital city of Baku to quell protests by Azerbaijani nationals, who were agitating for freedom from Soviet rule. Shooting down people in the streets, Soviet soldiers were responsible for the deaths of 131 people; 744 others were wounded, and 841 were illegally arrested. The events have come to be known as "Black January." Although the day was very grim, it is considered to be the birth of independent Azerbaijan and a crucial event leading to the collapse of the Soviet Union, due to the public outcry that followed it. The Soviet Union lasted only about one more year after the events in Azerbaijan.

The national holiday on January 20 honors those who died at the hands of the Soviet troops. Flags are flown at half-mast across the country, and a minute of silence is observed at noon. The tragedy is commemorated at Martyrs' Lane, a cemetery and park in Baku where photographs of the victims decorate the tombstones. Here, the president of the nation lays a wreath at the Eternal Fire that honors the dead of Black January.

CONTACTS:
Azerbaijan Republic-State Migration Service
202 Binagadi Hwy.
3123 Block
Binagadi District

Baku, D.C. AZ1114 Azerbaijan
994-12-562-5623; fax: 994-12-562-3702
www.migration.gov.az

♦ 0208 ♦ Azerbaijan Independence Days
May 28; October 18

Azerbaijan observes two independence days. The May 28, 1918, establishment of the Democratic Republic of Azerbaijan provides the occasion for the older independence celebration. Two years later, Azerbaijan came under Soviet rule. By 1991, the growing perestroika (social and economic reform) movement in the former U.S.S.R. created the opportunity for Soviet republics to break free, which, one by one, they proceeded to do. Azerbaijan declared its intention to once again become an independent nation on August 30, 1991. Azerbaijan's new independence day commemorates the declaration of independence made by the Supreme Soviet of Azerbaijan on October 18, 1991. After the U.S.S.R. ceased to exist as a geopolitical entity in December 1991 (which became official on January 1, 1992), Azerbaijan became an official independent state on December 26, 1991.

CONTACTS:
Ministry of Culture and Tourism
1 Azadlyg Ave.
Apt.3
Baku 1000 Azerbaijan
44-912-493-30-02
www.azerbaijan.az

Embassy of the Republic of Azerbaijan
2741 34th St. N.W.
Washington, D.C. 20008
202-337-3500; fax: 202-337-5911
www.azembassy.us

♦ 0209 ♦ Aztec Rain Festival
Varies

For about 100 years the Aztecs ruled much of Mexico until the invasion of the Spanish explorer Hernando Cortes and his troops in 1521. They observed a number of festivals associated with rain and the god of rain and lightning, Tlaloc. One was held in February, when a priest performed various rituals to encourage rainfall at the beginning of the agricultural year.

Another festival was held in March, when flowers had begun to bloom. Because these were the first arrivals of new life from the earth, they were offered to Tlaloc and other rain gods. A third festival to encourage rainfall was held in the autumn. Tlaloc was believed to live in a mountain and at this festival, people fashioned small mountains and images of the gods.

A bit of modern folklore attaches to the Aztec rain god. In 1968 a group of students clambered up a statue of Tlaloc in Mexico City and sat on his head. Some speculated that the god did not take kindly to this and made it pour rain during the OLYMPIC GAMES held in the city that year.

B

♦ 0210 ♦ **Baalbeck Festival**
July and August

The Baalbeck Festival takes place in July and August in the town of Baalbeck, Lebanon. This festival features music, dance, and drama performances by world-famous artists and ensembles. Performances take place Friday and Saturday evenings, in addition to some Thursday and Sunday evenings. They are staged in the town's remarkable Roman ruins, which it bills as the most intact Roman temples in the world. The festival officially began in 1956, though various groups had used the setting in previous years for special performances. Lebanon's long civil war (1975-1996) put a stop to the festival, but the performances resumed again in 1997. The Baalbeck Festival honors Lebanon's historical position as the crossroads of the West and the Middle East by featuring both European art forms, such as opera and ballet, and Middle Eastern music, dance, and poetry. In addition, it commissions new works from writers and composers.

CONTACTS:
Baalbeck International Festival
Karakone El Druze
Osman Ben Affan St
Doursoumian Bldg.
Beirut 1107 Lebanon
961-1-373150; fax: 961-1-373153
www.baalbeck.org.lb

♦ 0211 ♦ **Bab, Birth of the**
October 20

Birth of the Bab is a holy day in the Baha'i religion to celebrate the birthday in 1819 of Mirza Ali Mohammad in Shiraz, Persia (now Iran). In 1844, Mirza Ali declared himself the Bab (meaning "gate") and foretold the coming of one greater than he. The day, on which work is suspended, is a happy social occasion for Baha'is.

See also BAB, DECLARATION OF THE and BAB, MARTYRDOM OF THE.

CONTACTS:
U.S. Bahá'í National Center
1233 Central St.
Evanston, IL 60201
847-733-3400
www.bahai.us

♦ 0212 ♦ **Bab, Declaration of the**
May 22-23

Declaration of the Bab is a joyous Baha'i festival to celebrate the Bab's announcement in 1844 in Shiraz, Persia (now Iran), that he was the "gate" (which is the meaning of Bab) to the coming of the promised one of all religions. This proclamation is considered the beginning of the Baha'i faith, although the religion was founded after the Bab's death.

The Bab, who was born Mirza Ali Mohammad, founded an independent religion known as the Babi faith which grew out of Shi'ite Islam. At the time of this proclamation, the Bab also announced that it was his mission to herald a prophet who would be greater than he (paralleling St. John the Baptist as the forerunner of Jesus; *see* ST. JOHN'S DAY). After his proclamation, the Bab assembled 18 disciples.

This day is holy to Baha'is and a day on which work is suspended. Its observation begins at about two hours after sunset on May 22.

See also BAB, BIRTH OF THE and BAB, MARTYRDOM OF THE.

CONTACTS:
U.S. Bahá'í National Center
1233 Central St.
Evanston, IL 60201
847-733-3400
www.bahai.us

Bahai International Community
866 United Nations Plaza
Ste. 120
New York, NY 10017
212-803-2500; fax: 212-803-2566
www.bic.org

♦ 0213 ♦ **Bab, Martyrdom of the**
July 9

Martyrdom of the Bab is a solemn commemoration of the day in 1850 when the Bab, the first prophet of the Baha'i faith, was executed in Tabriz, Persia (now Iran). Prayers and readings mark the Baha'i holy day, and work is suspended.

After founding the Babi, a new religion growing out of Shi'ite Islam in 1844, the Bab was repeatedly exiled and imprisoned by Muslim rulers and priests who opposed the idea that the Bab would provide another avenue to the truth. They saw the Babis as revolutionaries and heterodox despoilers. A committee of priests demanded the Bab's execution, and he was led to the town square and tied to a post in front of 750 riflemen. The Baha'i's say that shots were fired, but they only severed the ropes binding him. When the smoke cleared, the Bab was found in his cell completing the work he had been doing before the volley of shots—dictating holy words to a scribe. He was taken before a second regiment of riflemen, and this time he was killed. His body was disposed of in a ditch, but was retrieved by his followers and eventually placed in a mausoleum on Mount Carmel in Haifa, Israel, where the Baha'i headquarters is today.

See also BAB, BIRTH OF THE and BAB, DECLARATION OF THE.

CONTACTS:
U.S. Bahá'í National Center
1233 Central St.
Evanston, IL 60201
847-733-3400
www.bahai.us

♦ 0214 ♦ **Babin Den**
January 20

In Bulgaria the old women who helped deliver babies—much like the modern midwife—were called *baba*, or grandmother. It was widely believed that the baby received some of the baba's wisdom, and it was customary for the baby's parents to bring the baba flowers on a particular day each year, called **Grandmother's Day** or **Day of the Midwives**. Eventually the children grew up, but they would continue to visit their baba each year.

Most babies in Bulgaria today are born in hospitals, so the children bring flowers to the doctors and nurses who assisted at their birth. Another traditional activity on this day involves boys dunking girls in the icy waters of rivers and lakes, supposedly to bring them good health in the coming year.

See also GRANDPARENTS' DAY.

♦ 0215 ♦ **Baby Parade**
Second Thursday in August

Started in 1901 by Leo Bamberger, founder of New Jersey's Bamberger's Department Store chain, the Baby Parade that takes place along the boardwalk at the seaside resort of Ocean City on the second Thursday in August each year allows children up to the age of 10 to participate and compete for prizes. There are four different divisions: Division A is for children in decorated strollers, go-carts, wagons, etc., and is further divided into three sections according to the age of the child; Division B features children in comically decorated vehicles, as well as walkers; Division C is for floats; and Division D is for larger commercial and noncommercial floats. The children are reviewed by the judges as they walk or wheel along the boardwalk from Sixth Street to Twelfth Street, and every child who enters receives a sterling silver identification bracelet. Cash prizes are given to the best entry in each division. More than 50,000 spectators are drawn to the **Ocean City Baby Parade** each year.

CONTACTS:
Greater Ocean City Area Chamber of Commerce
Eunice Q. Sorin Visitor & Conference Center
12320 Ocean Gateway
Ocean City, MD 21842
410-213-0552
www.oceancity.org

♦ 0216 ♦ **Bach Festival**
Late July for 10 days during odd-numbered years

Although the Bavarian city of Ansbach, Germany, has no particular connection to Johann Sebastian Bach, it has been the site of a biennial Bach Festival, the **Bachwoche Ansbach**, since 1947. Only music by Bach (or one of his family members) is played, and only on authentic instruments from Bach's time, such as the 1776 fortepiano. Even the concerts are held in buildings that were standing during Bach's lifetime, such as the 15th-century St. Gumbertus Church with its baroque organ.

Well-known vocalists, instrumentalists, and ensembles from all over the world are invited to the 10-day festival to perform Bach's motets, cantatas, organ, and orchestral works. The audience can experience not only the music but the fine acoustics and period architecture of the historic sites where the festival is held. The Palace of Carl Wilhelm Friedrich, for example, allows 500 festival-goers to listen to Bach in its rococo-style ballroom.

CONTACTS:
Bachwoche Ansbach
Brauhausstr. 15
Ansbach D - 91522 Germany
49-981-15037; fax: 49-981-15501
www.bachwoche.de

♦ 0217 ♦ **Bachok Cultural Festival**
May or June

This two-week cultural festival held in Bachok, Kelantan, Malaysia, features traditional Menora and Ma'yong dance-drama troupes, who often perform at Irama Beach. In addition to giant top-spinning and kiteflying competitions, the festival includes *wayang kulit*, or shadow plays, which are not normally seen in public but are performed privately at weddings, anniversaries, and other important celebrations. A puppeteer called *To'Dalang* (Father of the Mysteries) manipulates the puppets from inside an enclosed bamboo stage, and then their shadows are cast upon a screen in front of the audience. Most of the shadow plays are based upon either the *Ramayana* or *Mahabharata* epics from India. The plays are accompanied by a small band of five or six players with drums, a gong, a flageolet (a small, end-blown flute), and sometimes a Malay violin.

◆ 0218 ◆ Bad Durkheim Wurstmarkt (Sausage Fair)
September

Although called Bad Durkheim Wurstmarkt, or **Sausage Fair**, this is actually Germany's biggest wine festival. The name is said to have originated about 150 years ago because of the immense amounts of sausage consumed. Today there are dozens of wheelbarrow stands selling sausage and also chicken and shish-kebab. The religious origins of the feast are traced to 1417, when the villagers sold sausages, wine, and bread from wheelbarrows to pilgrims going to Michelsberg (St. Michael's hill) on MICHAELMAS (ST. MICHAEL'S DAY).

The opening day of the festival features a concert and a procession of bands, vineyard proprietors, and tapsters of the tavern stalls with decorated wine floats. The official opening is conducted by the mayor of Bad Durkheim and the German Wine Queen, and is followed by the tapping of the first cask. The following days are a medley of fireworks, band playing, dancing, and singing through the night. At the three dozen or so tavern stalls, wine is served in glasses called *Schoppen* that hold about a pint. Before the festival is over, some half a million people will have drunk more than 400,000 Schoppen.

From July through late October, there are numerous other wine festivals, mainly in the villages of the Rhine and Moselle valleys. Among them are Bockenheim, Deidesheim, and Schweigen-Rechterbach.

CONTACTS:
German National Tourist Office
122 E. 42nd St.
New York, NY 10168
800-651-7010 or 212-661-7200; fax: 212-661-7174
www.cometogermany.com.

Ehresmann Wine and Beer Hall
Am Hügel 15
Bad Dürkheim 67098 Germany
49-6322-66856; fax: 49-6322-791698
www.duerkheimer-wurstmarkt.de

◆ 0219 ◆ Baekjung
15th day of the seventh lunar month

In Korea the 15th, or full moon day, of the seventh lunar month is observed with Buddhist and folk agricultural traditions. *Baekjung* means "one hundred kinds," referring to the great number of fruits, vegetables, and grains that flourish at this time of year. There are Buddhist ceremonies at which samples of one hundred of these foods are offered to Buddha.

In farming areas, people celebrate this day as a "weeding party" often called *Homi Ssisi* or *Homi ssiggi*—"hoe cleaning," since, by this time in the season, most of the hard work of farming is completed. The farm worker judged to be the hardest worker is feted with a parade around the village. Then his employer provides food and drink for a village-wide party.

◆ 0220 ◆ Baha'i Day of the Covenant
November 26

The Baha'i Day of the Covenant is a Baha'i holy day. It commemorates the covenant BAHA'U'LLAH, founder of the faith, made with humanity and his followers, appointing ABDU'L-BAHA as the head of the Baha'i religion who would interpret Baha'i teachings. Abdu'l-Baha chose the date when followers requested an occasion to remember his importance.

CONTACTS:
Bahai National Center
1233 Central St.
Evanston, IL 60201
847-733-3400 or 800-228-6483
www.bahai.us

◆ 0221 ◆ Bahamas Emancipation Day
First Monday in August

The English settled in the Bahamas during the mid-17th century and brought African slaves with them to work in the cotton fields. Slavery was formally abolished in the British Empire by the Abolition Act of 1833, but it wasn't until 1838 that the slaves in the Bahamas were freed.

Emancipation Day in the Bahamas is observed on the first Monday in August. Businesses are closed, and a regatta is held at Black Point, near Staniel Cay, in the Exuma island group.

See also FOX HILL FESTIVAL.

CONTACTS:
Bahamas Ministry of Tourism
P.O. Box N-3701
Nassau Bahamas
242-302-2000; fax: 242-302-2098
www.bahamas.com

◆ 0222 ◆ Bahamas Independence Day
July 10

The Bahama Islands gained independence from Great Britain at 12:01 A.M. on this day in 1973. The islands had been a British colony for nearly 250 years, but are now a commonwealth, with their own prime minister and parliament.

Businesses are closed on the tenth, a legal holiday, but festivities go on for a week with parades and celebrations. A fireworks display at Clifford Park on July 10 tops off the week.

CONTACTS:
Government of Bahamas
Ministry of Tourism
George St, Bolam House
Bahamas
242-302-2000; fax: 242-302-2098
www.bahamas.gov.bs

◆ 0223 ◆ Bahamas Labor Day
June 7; national holiday is celebrated on first Friday in June

Labor Day is a national holiday in the Bahamas, celebrated on the first Friday in June in order to create a long weekend for workers. The traditional date of Labor Day in the Bahamas, however, is June 7, in commemoration of a significant workers' strike that began on that day in 1942.

Labor Day is meant to honor and celebrate workers and the importance of their contributions to the nation and society. In the capital city, Nassau, thousands of people come to watch a parade through the streets, which begins at midmorning. Bands in colorful uniforms, traditional African *junkanoo* performers, and members of various labor unions and political parties are all part of the procession, which ends up at the Southern Recreation Grounds, where government officials make speeches for the occasion. For many residents and visitors to the Bahamas, the afternoon of Labor Day is a time to relax at home or perhaps visit the beach.

CONTACTS:
Government of Bahamas
Ministry of Tourism
George St, Bolam House
Bahamas
242-302-2000; fax: 242-302-2098
www.bahamas.gov.bs

◆ 0224 ◆ **Baha'u'llah, Ascension of**
May 29

This marks the anniversary of the death in 1892 of Mirza Husayn Ali, known as Baha'u'llah, founder of the Baha'i religion. "Ascension" is not meant literally, but is considered the ascension of the spirit. The day is one of nine Baha'i holy days on which work is suspended. It is observed by gathering together at 3:00 A.M., the time of Baha'u'llah's death in Acre, Palestine (now Israel), for prayers and sometimes readings from Baha'i historical works.

CONTACTS:
Bahai International Community
866 United Nations Plaza
Ste.120
New York, NY 10017
212-803-2500; fax: 212-803-2566
www.bic.org

U.S. Bahá'í National Center
1233 Central St
Evanston, IL 60201
847-733-3400
www.bahai.us

◆ 0225 ◆ **Baha'u'llah, Birth of**
November 12

The anniversary of the birth in 1817 of Baha'u'llah, the founder of the Baha'i religion, is a holy day on which work is suspended. Mirza Husayn Ali, later known as Baha'u'llah ("Glory of God"), was born in Tehran, Persia (now Iran). He was an adherent of Islam, and later a follower of the BAB, who founded the Babi faith, an independent messianic religion. Thirteen years after the Bab's execution in 1850, Husayn Ali declared himself the messenger of God, foretold by the Bab.

See also RIDVAN, FEASTOF.

CONTACTS:
U.S. Bahá'í National Center
1233 Central St
Evanston, IL 60201
847-733-3400
www.bahai.us

◆ 0226 ◆ **Bahia Independence Day**
July 2

The consolidation of Brazilian independence in the state of Bahia is remembered each year with a procession following the path that the Brazilians took when they defeated Portuguese troops there in 1823. Folkloric characters like the *caboclo*, who symbolizes the superiority of native strength over the colonizers, have worked their way into this primarily civic celebration.

◆ 0227 ◆ **Bahrain National Day**
December 16

Bahrain is a small (260 square miles in area) country of islands in the Persian Gulf. After being a British protectorate for more than 100 years, Bahrain became independent in 1971. National Day is a legal holiday observed on December 16 with fireworks, laser shows, and acrobatic and magic performances.

CONTACTS:
Ministry of Industry & Commerce
Diplomatic Area
PO Box 5479
Manama Kingdom of Bahrain
973-17574909; fax: 973-17536277
www.moic.gov.bh

◆ 0228 ◆ **Baile de las Turas (Dance of the Flutes)**
Varies, June-October

Indigenous peoples, including the Ayamas, living in Venezuela's Falcón and Lara states celebrate the Baile de las Turas at various times during the harvest season in thanksgiving for the corn crop. In Maparari, Lara state, Las Turas is held on September 23-24. Roman Catholic-influenced religious processions and services honoring the Virgen Mary blend with traditional religious dance and music over two days. "Tura" refers to the end of the corn harvest as well as to the two different kinds of flutes used in the ceremonies: a smaller, shorter flute which creates a sharp sound and a larger flute with a deeper tone.

◆ 0229 ◆ **Bal du Rat Mort (Dead Rat's Ball)**
First Saturday in March

A huge carnival and ball, Bal du Rat Mort is concentrated in the casino of Ostende, Belgium, but also spread out all over the town. The carnival began at the end of the 19th century, launched by members of the Oostende Art and Philanthropic Circle (Circle Coecilia) who named the affair for a café on Montmartre (a hilly part of northern Paris, home to many artists) where they had whiled away pleasant hours. People are masked at the ball, and there's a competition for the best costume.

CONTACTS:
Toerisme Oostende VZW
Monacoplein 2
Oostende 8400 Belgium
32-59-70-11-99; fax: 32-59-70-34-77
www.visitoostende.be/en

♦ 0230 ♦ Balfour Declaration Day
November 2

Jews, particularly those in Israel, observe Balfour Declaration Day in memory of a turning point in modern Jewish history. On November 2, 1917, Arthur J. Balfour, British Secretary of State for Foreign Affairs, sent a letter to Lord Rothschild indicating that the British government was in favor of establishing a national home for the Jewish people in Palestine. Although this may not seem to be as significant an event as ISRAEL INDEPENDENCE DAY, the Jewish people felt that the British government's commitment to their cause was very important. The day on which it was made has been kept as a semi-holiday ever since.

CONTACTS:
Israel Ministry of Foreign Affairs
9 Yitzhak Rabin Blvd.
Kiryat Ben-Gurion
Jerusalem 9103001 Israel
972-2-530-3111; fax: 972-2-530-3367
www.mfa.gov.il

♦ 0231 ♦ Ball-Catching Festival (Tamaseseri)
January 3

Each year on January 3, two teams of Japanese men wearing only loincloths compete for a ball that weighs about 18 pounds and measures about 12 inches in diameter. It is believed that whoever can raise the ball above his or her head will have good fortune. Because they also believe that merely touching the ball brings good luck, spectators also enter the fray of the competition. Throughout the struggle, the competitors are continuously splashed with cold water, which also soaks the crowd watching the spectacle in cold winter air.

The two ball-catching teams consist of the Land Team, made up of farmers who work the fields, and the Sea team, composed of fisherman. They believe that the size of the harvest or of the catch during the New Year is determined by which team wins the ball and gives it to a waiting Shinto priest— with the winning team bound for the greater yield. A 500-year-old tradition, the ball-catching festival is said to have its roots in the legend of the dragon god (ryujin) offering two balls to the Empress Jingu (170-269). It takes place at Hakozaki Shrine City, Higashi-ku, Fukuoka City, Japan. It is

one of the three main festivals of Kyushu, the southernmost of the four main islands that make up Japan.

CONTACTS:
Japan National Tourism Organization
1 Grand Central Pl.
60 E. 42nd St.
Ste. 448
New York, NY 10165
212-757-5640; fax: 212-307-6754
www.jnto.go.jp/eng

♦ 0232 ♦ Ballet Festival of Miami, International
September

The International Ballet Festival of Miami, held annually over two weeks in September, brings together ballet companies from Europe, Asia, Latin America, and the USA for performances in venues around the city of Miami and Dade County. Produced by the Miami Hispanic Ballet Company, the festival is intended to provide an opportunity for audiences in south Florida to witness the artistry of ballet dancers from around the world, while giving local dancers a chance to showcase their skills alongside these international stars.

In addition to galas and performances in traditional and contemporary styles, the festival includes special performances by young dancers who have won medals in international ballet competitions, a dance-themed film series and art exhibit, and master dance classes and workshops. Each year, the festival also presents two awards. The "A Life for Dance" Award honors an outstanding figure in the dance world, and the "Criticism and Culture of Ballet" Award recognizes a prominent dance critic. The festival will celebrate its 20th anniversary in 2015.

CONTACTS:
Miami Hispanic Cultural Arts Center
111 S.W. 5 Ave.
Miami, FL 33130
305-549-7711
www.internationalballetfestival.org

♦ 0233 ♦ Balserías
On or around February 12

The Guaymía people of Chiriqui Province in Panama meet near February 12 to catch up on tribal affairs. This is also an occasion for the single men to hold an unusual competition amongst each other for available young women. The men line up in rows so that they face each other and hold small logs of balsa, a light wood. The men then try to eliminate each other from the contest by throwing the logs at each other's ankles with such force that they injure each other. The only allowable way for the men to avoid broken bones and other injuries is to constantly leap and dance out of the way of the logs. Those who manage to survive this frenzy intact and without being harmed are allowed to choose from among the young women.

♦ 0234 ♦ Baltic Song Festivals
Summer

Massive festivals of song and dance, emphasizing folk music and national culture, in the Baltic countries of Estonia, Latvia, and Lithuania. These festivals came to symbolize nationhood, especially after the countries came under Soviet domination.

The first all-Estonian song festival, called the *Laulupidu*, was held in Tartu in 1869 with 845 performers singing to 15,000 people. Nationalist leaders, led by J. V. Jannsen, publisher of the first Estonian-language newspaper, had organized the festival to demonstrate that their culture had survived its conquerors.

In 1975 the festival drew 30,000 on stage and 200,000 spectators, and when it ended, the people rose and sang their unofficial anthem, "My Fatherland Is My Love," as tears streamed down their cheeks. The anthem was written during World War II by Lydia Koidula, daughter of Song Festival originator Jannsen, and put to music by Gustav Ernesaks. In 1988, as political activities heightened, there were spontaneous song fests throughout Estonia. Recently, the festival has been held at the Song Festival Amphitheater outside Tallinn.

In Latvia, the first Song Festival was held in 1873 at the Keizardarzs (the Czar 's Garden), a park created in 1721 and named for Czar Peter I. Janis Cimze began collecting the melodies of folk songs in 1869, and these songs, some more than 1,000 years old, were performed by thousands of singers in huge choirs at the first and later festivals.

In Lithuania, each region has its own distinct musical style. Northeastern Aukstaitija, for example, is known for a kind of polyphonic round not found in any other region or in neighboring countries. The rhythms are syncopated, and the rounds sound very dissonant.

The old town of Vilnius is the site each May of "Skamba kankliai," performances by vocalists, instrumentalists, and dancers. Vilnius also hosts the song festival, Dainu Svente, with huge choirs and dancers, every four years. In 2018, the next edition of Dainu Sente will be held in Vilnius in honor of the 100th anniversary of Lithuanian independence.

CONTACTS:
Estonian Song and Dance Celebration Foundation
Pärnu mnt. 10
Tallinn 10148 Estonia
372-627-3120
sa.laulupidu.ee

♦ 0235 ♦ **Baltic-Nordic Harmonica Festival**
July

The Baltic-Nordic Harmonica Festival is an international music festival that celebrates and showcases all types of harmonica playing. It has been held in the historic seaside resort town of Pärnu, Estonia, each year since 2002. Most of the events are held at the Kuursaal, a summer theater that holds several small areas for performances and gatherings. Participants have come from far beyond the Baltic, from countries including Italy, France, Holland, Germany, and the United States. In 2013, more than 2000 people attended the festival.

Participants and visitors attend harmonica workshops, take part in, or listen to, competitions in a number of categories, and may even have a chance to hear something as unusual as a harmonica chorus. The winner of each category receives the title of Baltic-Nordic Champion and can win cash prizes of up to 500 Euros.

CONTACTS:
Director of the festival
Karja 42
Parnu 80018 Estonia
372-5664-3401; fax: 372-443-3313
www.piccolo.ee

♦ 0236 ♦ **Banff Festival of the Arts**
May-August

The Banff Arts Festival grew out of the Banff Centre School of Fine Arts, which was founded in 1933 in this mountain town nestled in the Canadian Rockies. Every summer since 1971, students and faculty of the school, along with internationally renowned artists, have presented a vast array of programs in jazz, vocal jazz, orchestral and chamber music, opera, drama, dance, literature, journalism, visual arts, Aboriginal arts, and film.

CONTACTS:
Banff Centre
107 Tunnel Mountain Dr.
Banff, AB T1L 1H5 Canada
403-762-6100; fax: 403-762-6444
www.banffcentre.ca

♦ 0237 ♦ **Bangabandhu National Mourning Day**
August 15

Bangabandhu National Mourning Day commemorates the anniversary of the death of Bangabandhu Sheikh Mujibur Rahman, the first Prime Minister of Bangladesh. Bangabandhu was assassinated along with most of his family and some supporters on August 15, 1975 in a military coup. He was an important political figure in Bangladesh and played a pivotal role in helping the country achieve independence from East Pakistan. His political party, the Awami League, spearheaded the civil disobedience movement in Bangladesh for which he was arrested and jailed.

Bangabandhu 's daughter Sheikh Hasina, who came to power after his death, instituted the day of remembrance for her father in 1996. The event is observed throughout Bangladesh as a public holiday. The country's flags are hoisted at half-mast, and black flags are raised across state buildings, offices, and educational institutions. Leaders pay homage to the portrait of Bangabandhu at the house where his assassination took place, with the armed forces offering a state salute in honor of the slain leader. The general public visits the Bangabandhu Memorial Museum to pay their respects, while special prayers and almsgiving occur at mosques and other community centers.

CONTACTS:
Bangladesh Tourism Board
Bangladesh House Bldg., Finance Corporation Bhaban (7th Fl.)

22, Purana Paltan
Dhaka 1000 Bangladesh
880-2-9513328
tourismboard.gov.bd

◆ 0238 ◆ Bangladesh Independence Day
March 26

This public holiday celebrates the declaration of the existence of the state of Bangladesh on March 26, 1971. When India gained independence from Britain in 1947, the region that is now Bangladesh was part of Bengal, India. It became East Pakistan and was governed together with West Pakistan as one country. The movement for autonomy in East Pakistan began in 1949. By early 1971, differences between East and West Pakistan had led to war. India entered the war in November in support of East Pakistan, and independence was assured within a month (*see* BANGLADESH VICTORY DAY).

Bangladeshis observe their national holiday of independence in the capital city of Dhaka with memorial ceremonies, a boat race on the Buriganga river, and other festivities.

CONTACTS:
Bangladesh Embassy
3510 International Dr. N.W.
Washington, D.C. 20008
202-244-0183; fax: 202-244-2771
www.bdembassyusa.org

◆ 0239 ◆ Bangladesh Victory Day
December 16

This public holiday in Bangladesh commemorates the end of the war with Pakistan in 1971 and the official creation of the state of Bangladesh, after months of fighting and years of struggle to gain autonomy.

See also BANGLADESH INDEPENDENCE DAY.

CONTACTS:
Bangladesh Liberation War Museum
5 Segun Bagicha
Dhaka 1000 Bangladesh
880-2-955-9091; fax: 880-2-955-9092
www.liberationwarmuseum.org

◆ 0240 ◆ Bank Holiday
Various

In England there are typically six "bank holidays"—week days when the banks are closed for business: NEW YEAR'S DAY, GOOD FRIDAY, EASTER MONDAY, Early May Bank Holidays , Spring Bank Holiday (in late May), August (or Summer) Bank Holiday, CHRISTMAS, and BOXING DAY. These official public holidays were established by law in 1871 and are traditionally spent at local fairgrounds.

In the United States, the Great Depression of 1929 had caused many people to withdraw their savings, and the banks had trouble meeting the demand. In February 1933 the Detroit banks failed and this caused a country-wide panic. President

Franklin D. Roosevelt proclaimed his first full day in office (March 6, 1933) a national "Bank Holiday" to help save the country's banking system. The "holiday" actually lasted 10 days, during which "scrip" (paper currency in denominations of less than a dollar) temporarily replaced real money in many American households.

◆ 0241 ◆ Banntag
Between April 30 and June 3; Ascension Day

In the canton of Basel in Switzerland, this is a day when village citizens walk the village boundaries. *Banntag* means community- or town-boundary day.

Until the Reformation, ASCENSION DAY was a time for the blessing of the fields and checking of boundary markers. The religious aspect of the day declined, and now Ascension Day, which is a public holiday in Basel, is seen as a community festival. Citizens of Basel canton, accompanied by a local official, flag bearers, and musicians, walk along the boundaries to a certain spot where the president of the town council greets them and discusses town topics. In some communities, the walk is followed by a church service and community meal.

CONTACTS:
Basel Tourismus
c/o House of Business
Altmarktstrasse 96
Liestal 4410 Switzerland
41-61-927-6544; fax: 41-61-927-6644
www.baselland-tourismus.ch

◆ 0242 ◆ Baptism of the Lord, Feast of the
January, Sunday following Epiphany

Jesus' baptism by John the Baptist in the River Jordan has always been considered a significant manifestation of Jesus' divinity, and has been celebrated on EPIPHANY by the Orthodox Church since the end of the second century. However, in 1961 the Roman Catholic Church began to celebrate it as a separate feast in its own right. The original date for the feast was January 13, but when the Church calendar was reorganized in 1969, the Feast of the Baptism of the Lord was moved to the Sunday following the Epiphany. The Church omits the observance in years when it coincides with the Epiphany, especially in places like the United States, where celebration of the Epiphany has been shifted from the traditional January 6 observance to the Sunday between January 2 and 8.

See also TIMQAT.

CONTACTS:
Greek Orthodox Archdiocese of Australia
242 Cleveland St.
Redfern, NSW 2016 Australia
61-2-9690-6100; fax: 61-2-9698-5368
www.greekorthodox.org.au
United States Conference of Catholic Bishops
3211 Fourth St. N.E.
Washington, D.C. 20017

202-541-3000
www.usccb.org

♦ 0243 ♦ Barbados Independence Day
November 30

After having been a British colony since the 17th century, Barbados became independent on this day in 1966. A ceremony took place near the capital city of Bridgetown, during which the British flag was lowered and replaced by the Barbados flag, and the national anthem was sung.

Today, festivities extend through the month of November with the National Independence Festival of the Creative Arts.

This is a talent show of all ages in singing, dancing, writing, and acting. On Independence Day, festivities culminate with a parade and the final appearance of performers, and exhibits of art work and photography are on display.

See also BARROW DAY, ERROL.

CONTACTS:
Barbados Tourism Encyclopedia
P.O. Box 16B
Brittons Hill
St. Michael BB11090 Barbados
barbados.org

♦ 0244 ♦ Barbados Jazz Festival
January

Established in 1994 to bring world-renowned jazz performers to the West Indies, the Barbados Jazz Festival has featured such musicians as Luther Vandross, Kenny G, Roberta Flack, and Ray Charles. Indoor performances are held at the Sir Garfield Sobers's Gymnasium and Sunbury Plantation House. There are also open-air concerts at Farley Hill National Park and Heritage Park.

CONTACTS:
Barbados Tourism Encyclopedia
P.O. Box 16B
Brittons Hill
St. Michael BB11090 Barbados
barbados.org

♦ 0245 ♦ Bar-B-Q Festival, International
Second weekend in May

A two-day mouth-watering event in Owensboro, Ky., which calls itself the Bar-B-Q Capital of the World. In the course of the weekend, 10 tons of mutton, 5,000 chickens, and 1,500 gallons of burgoo are cooked and served. Kentucky burgoo is a thick soup made of chicken, mutton, beef, tomatoes, cabbage, potatoes, onions, and corn.

The festival had its beginnings at the turn of the century when the many Roman Catholic churches in the area had summertime picnics in their parishes. Each church had a cooking team to vie with the others in cooking the best barbecue. Eventually, the idea struck someone that there could be a city-wide barbecue if all the church barbecues were combined. Out of that grew the present festival, which now attracts more than 40,000 people.

The barbecue-pit fires are lit on Friday afternoon on the banks of the Ohio River, and the chicken and meat—always mutton, not beef—is barbecued when the coals are red. The Roman Catholic parish chefs still compete, but the cooking contest has expanded to be open to anyone. Events besides cooking and eating include arts and crafts exhibits, bluegrass and country music, street dancing, and contests of pie eating, keg throwing and horseshoe throwing. There are also likely to be political speeches.

CONTACTS:
International Bar-B-Q Festival
P.O. Box 434
Owensboro, KY 42302
270-926-1100 or 800-489-1131
www.bbqfest.com

♦ 0246 ♦ Bard of Armagh Festival of Humorous Verse
Late November

The town of Armagh, Northern Ireland, located southwest of Belfast, is featured in a famous ballad called "The Bard of Armagh." That poem's title inspired the name of the Bard of Armagh Festival of Humorous Verse, an annual three-day event that has taken place since 1993. Poets appear before audiences to recite their works and compete for best poem.

The festival debuted as part of the November Keady Fair before becoming an event in its own right. To determine the official entries, a selection process was established that ensures each poem does not exceed a length of 200 words and features humorous verse suitable for a family audience.

The first two days are devoted to competition heats, which are held at several venues. The third day is devoted to finals, which usually take place at the Armagh City Hotel.

CONTACTS:
John Makem
34 Fergort Rd.
Derrynoose, Armagh Northern Ireland
28-37-531971
www.bardofarmagh.com

♦ 0247 ♦ Barnum Festival
Late May-early July

Bridgeport, Connecticut, was the home of Phineas Taylor Barnum (1810-1891) and the birthplace of Charles Sherwood Stratton (1838-1883), known by his circus name of "General" Tom Thumb, a 28" tall man who was the main attraction of Barnum's 19th-century circus, the Greatest Show on Earth. Barnum was also Bridgeport's mayor in 1875, and his contributions to the city included bringing in new industrial jobs and building a number of parks. Since 1949 he has been honored with a festival beginning in late May and extending through the FOURTH OF JULY. Occasionally it continues through July 5, which is Barnum's birthday, or beyond. The idea behind the festival, which is sponsored by the P.T. Barnum Foundation, Inc., is to get away from Bridgeport's industrial image and to promote the city's circus heritage.

One of the highlights of the festival is the event known as "Champions on Parade," the largest senior drum corps competition in the Northeast. It takes place on the Saturday evening before July 4. On Sunday there is a Barnum Memorial Ceremony at the cemetery where he is buried. Many of the events focus on Barnum's circus background, including entertainment by clowns and a visit to the Barnum Museum, where there is a miniature replica of his circus. The festival is preceded by the selection of an honorary Tom Thumb and Lavinia Warren, Thumb's wife, from among the area's schoolchildren. There is also an honorary Jenny Lind (the Swedish-born soprano who toured the United States under Barnum's sponsorship). Other figures associated with Barnum and his circus are recognized in this way as well.

CONTACTS:
Barnum Festival LLC
c/o 1070 Main St.
Bridgeport, CT 06604
203-367-8495
www.barnumfestival.com

♦ 0248 ♦ Baron Bliss Day
March 9

Baron Bliss Day is a public holiday in Belize honoring Englishman Henry Edward Ernest Victor Bliss (1869-1926). When he died on March 9, Bliss bequeathed his entire estate to Belize City.

On this day each year a morning mass and wreath laying is held at his tomb in the Fort Point area. Then there is a regatta in the harbor, a cycle race, and a kite contest.

♦ 0249 ♦ Barrow (Errol) Day
January 21

A national public holiday that honors Barbados' first prime minister. Errol Barrow was born in 1920, earned a law degree in England, then returned to Barbados. He became finance minister in 1959 and prime minister in 1961. He was reelected in 1966 and, soon after, Barbados became independent of Great Britain (*see* BARBADOS INDEPENDENCE DAY). Barrow was voted out in 1976, but regained office in 1986; he died the next year.

CONTACTS:
Barbados Tourism Encyclopedia
P.O. Box 16B
Brittons Hill
St. Michael BB11090 Barbados
212-986-6516; fax: 212-573-9850
www.barbados.org

♦ 0250 ♦ Bartholomew Fair
August 24

Although ST. BARTHOLOMEW'S DAY isn't really celebrated anymore, for more than 700 years (1133-1855) it was the day on which the Bartholomew Fair was held at Smithfield on the outskirts of London. What began as an opportunity for buying and selling cloth eventually turned into a major event. Almost every type of commodity could be purchased there, and a number of sideshows and other crude sources of entertainment were available as well—earning the Fair its present-day reputation as "the Coney Island of medieval England."

Eventually the entertainment aspects of the Fair outweighed its commercial purposes, and although it was very much a part of English life there was a movement to close it down. In 1822, thousands of people rioted in protest against the threat of closing the Fair. But finally, in 1855, it was permanently abolished.

St. Bartholomew's Day is also known for the massacre of the Huguenots (Protestants) in France, which began at the instigation of Catherine de Medici in Paris on the night of August 23-24, 1572, and spread throughout the country for two more days until between 5,000 and 10,000 had been killed.

♦ 0251 ♦ Bascarsija Nights
July

One of Bosnia and Herzegovina's biggest events, Bascarsija Nights is a month-long celebration of culture. Artistic expressions ranging from street theater to classical symphony make up this festival held in the country's capital, Sarajevo. Over the course of July, about 150,000 people attend between 40 to 50 free events, held in open-air stages throughout Sarajevo and on the city's central stage opposite the Town Hall. Both local and guest artists from other European countries are invited.

Film director Sejfudin Tanovic and other arts enthusiasts began setting up the festival in 1988. Initially, the festival program was extensive but was limited to a single night. Over the years more dates were added until the entire month was booked. The festival gathered more momentum particularly after peace was reached following the Bosnian War (1992–1995).

One well-established tradition of the festival is the opening night performance by the Sarajevo Symphony Orchestra. This prestigious event typically draws a large audience including local and foreign officials. The remaining days are marked by more events offering sophisticated entertainment—theatre, book readings, opera, ballet, art exhibits—as well as popular fare like rock concerts, movie screenings, and folklore presentations.

CONTACTS:
Sarajevo Arts Agency
Cemaluša 1/II
Sarajevo 71000 Bosnia Herzegovina
387-33-207- 921; fax: 387-33-207- 921
www.sarajevoarts.ba

♦ 0252 ♦ Basket Dance
Late September or October

The most important of the three harvest ceremonies performed by the Hopi Indians, the Basket Dance includes various ritual activities that serve to remind people that life is temporary and that they must comply with the Creator's plans. It is observed primarily by women who are members of the Lakon and Owaqöl societies. First they spend several days in a kiva (a sacred ceremonial room) to fast, pray, and chant. Other preparations include creating a sand painting, fashioning prayer plumes from feathers, building an altar, and getting costumes ready.

When the women emerge from the kiva, they chant while presenting baskets to the four directions of the compass, lifting them, then lowering them. Their movements are designed to bring cold, wet weather so that the crops will grow the following spring. Afterward, the women traditionally toss the baskets to the onlookers.

CONTACTS:
Hopi Cultural Center
P.O. Box 67
Second Mesa, AZ 86043
928-734-2401; fax: 928-734-6651
www.hopiculturalcenter.com

♦ 0253 ♦ **Basque Festival, National**
First weekend in July

A sports-music-dance-barbecue celebration of Basque heritage, held annually since 1962 in Elko, Nev. Basque people settled in the West, largely in Nevada and Idaho, in the late 1800s, many becoming shepherds and sheep ranchers.

Participants in the festival wear the traditional red, white, and green of the Basque provinces of Spain. The men also wear the traditional Basque beret.

The festival begins on Friday with social and exhibition dancing. On Saturday there's a parade of more than 50 floats, and major contests of weightlifting, sheep hooking (sheep are hooked with a crook, dragged to a designated spot, and tied by one leg), sheepdog-working, yelling, and dancing the native *jota*. Each year, there is also a three-event contest of log chopping, weightlifting, and a strength-and-endurance event in which contestants race to pluck each of 30 beer cans (they were ears of corn in the old country) from a line and deposit them in a trash can.

Some years, when contestants from Spain are present, there are pentathlons—five-event contests that largely involve lifting, dragging, and walking with enormous weights (for example, a 1,200-pound granite slab is dragged).

On Sunday, the events wind up with a big barbecue of steak, marinated lamb, and spicy sausages called *chorizo*. Music and dancing are important parts of the festival, and *bertsolaris*, troubadours, entertain with song improvisations in the Basque language.

Another Nevada Basque festival is in Reno in July. The Gooding, Idaho, Basque club holds its annual Basque Association Picnic in July.

CONTACTS:
Elko Euzkaldunak Club
1601 Flagview Dr.
PO Box 1321
Elko, NV 89801
775-738-6513
www.elkobasqueclub.com

♦ 0254 ♦ **Basset Hound Games**
Third Sunday in July

The Basset Hound games are held annually at Legion Park in Woodburn, Ore., as a way to bring together Basset Hound owners and their dogs in a day of light-hearted activities. The dogs compete in such custom-tailored Basset Hound events as longest ears, marathon napping, and the best howl. The public is welcome to view the games. The event is run by and raises money for Oregon Basset Hound Rescue, a non-profit group that fosters abandoned Basset Hounds and places them in permanent homes.

The Basset Hound Olympics were launched in 1990 by the Emerald Empire Basset Hound Fanciers as an event where their dogs could compete equally, whether they were show dogs or family pets. From the start, it benefited Basset Hound rescue efforts. It was turned over to the Oregon Basset Hound Rescue in 2007.

CONTACTS:
Oregon Basset Hound Rescue
P.O. Box 20254
Keizer, OR 97307
503-351-0649
www.oregonbassethoundrescue.com

♦ 0255 ♦ **Bastille Day**
July 14

The Bastille was a 14th-century fortress that became a notorious state prison in Paris. An angry mob assaulted the Bastille—which had come to symbolize the French monarchy's oppression of the people—on July 14, 1789, freeing the political prisoners held there and launching the French Revolution.

Although the building itself was razed a year after the attack, the Bastille became a symbol of French independence. July 14 has been celebrated since that time in France as **Fête Nationale**, as well as in French territories in the Pacific, with parades, fireworks, and dancing in the streets. This period in French history is familiar to many through Charles Dickens's portrayal of it in *A Tale of Two Cities*.

In Tahiti and the rest of French Polynesia it is called **Tiurai** or **Heiva**, and is celebrated for most of the month. The festival includes European-type celebrations plus Polynesian competitions that include both men and women, and a play about the enthronement of a Tahitian high chief. The highlight is the nightly folklore spectacle—a competition of music and dance among groups from throughout French Polynesia who have practiced all year for the event.

See also NightWatch.

CONTACTS:
Government Information Service
19 rue de Constantine
Paris 75007 France
33-42-75-80-00
www.france.fr

♦ 0256 ♦ **Bastille Day (Kaplan, Louisiana)**
July 14

The French-speaking town of Kaplan, Louisiana, where most of the inhabitants are descended from French Canadians (Acadians), claims to hold the only community-wide celebration of Bastille Day in the United States. The celebration there on July 14 includes fireworks, amateur athletic competitions, and a "fais do-do" or Acadian street dance.

The custom of observing Bastille Day was started by Eugene Eleazer, a French immigrant who became mayor of Kaplan in 1920. With the exception of a brief interruption during World War II, the town has held its fête every year since 1906. Smaller Bastille Day celebrations are held elsewhere in Louisiana, including New Orleans and Baton Rouge, where French traditions still run strong.

CONTACTS:
Alliance Française de La Nouvelle-Orléans
1519 Jackson Ave.
New Orleans, LA 70130
504-568-0770
af-neworleans.org

♦ 0257 ♦ **Bastille, Festival de la**
Weekend closest to July 14

Because the storming of the Bastille on July 14, 1789, marked an important turning point in the history of France, members of the Club Calumet in Augusta, Maine, chose this day (or the nearest Friday, Saturday, and Sunday) to celebrate the state's French-Canadian (or Acadian) heritage. Events include entertainment by Cajun bands, French folkdancers and Maine cloggers, a huge fireworks display, and a parade through downtown Augusta.

In 1991 the festival honored 85 visitors from Paris—all members of the Sarthois Club who were in this country as part of an exchange with its sister club, Le Club Calumet. But the festival is not limited to the French or descendants of the original Acadian settlers. More than 13,000 visitors come to Augusta each year to participate in the festival. About one-fourth of Maine's current population is of Acadian descent.

See also AcadianFestival.

CONTACTS:
City of Waterville
1 Common St.
Waterville, ME 04901
207-680-4200; fax: 207-680-4207
waterville-me.gov

♦ 0258 ♦ **Bat Flight Breakfast**
Second Thursday in August

Carlsbad Caverns in southern New Mexico was proclaimed a national monument in 1923 not only for its geologic formations but for its teeming bat population. Carlsbad's summer colony of Mexican free-tailed bats, whose numbers vary from one hundred thousand to a million, migrates to the cave each spring. They eat, sleep, digest, communicate, mate, and raise their young while hanging upside-down. The accumulation of guano—a valuable source of fertilizer—can reach depths of up to 40 feet.

Although many visitors to the park witness the bats' spectacular outbound flight at sunset, when they leave the cave in a dense black cloud for their night's feeding in the Pecos River Valley, far fewer are there to witness their return—except those who attend the annual Bat Flight Breakfast. Started in the late 1950s by a group of park employees who wanted to encourage people to witness this natural phenomenon, the breakfast soon became an annual tradition. About 400 people arrive at the cave before sunrise on the second Thursday in August and eat sausages and scrambled eggs in their official yellow "bat breakfast hats" while they wait for the bats to return to their roosts. It is said that the bats generate an eerie sound as they rocket downward with folded wings.

When a television crew was there to film the event in 1989, the bats failed to return as expected. No one is sure how or when they got back into the cave, but 13 hours later, at sunset, they left in droves as usual.

CONTACTS:
Carlsbad Caverns National Park
3225 National Parks Hwy.
Carlsbad, NM 88220
575-785-2232; fax: 505-785-2133
www.nps.gov/cave

♦ 0259 ♦ **Bataan Day**
April 9

A national legal holiday in the Philippines in commemoration of the disastrous World War II Battle of Bataan in 1942, in which the Philippines fell to the Japanese. It is also known as **Araw ng Kagitingan** or **Heroes Day** in the Philippines. Also remembered on this date are the 37,000 U.S. and Filipino soldiers who were captured and the thousands who died during the infamous 70-mile "death march" from Mariveles to a Japanese concentration camp inland at San Fernando. Ceremonies are held at Mt. Samat Shrine, the site of side-by-side fighting by Filipino and American troops.

♦ 0260 ♦ **Bates (Daisy Gatson) Day**
Third Monday in February

Daisy Gatson Bates Day is a state holiday in Arkansas to honor the memory of Daisy Gatson Bates, an American civil rights activist, publisher, and journalist who championed integration efforts in Little Rock, Arkansas. In 1957, Daisy

Bates, then president of the Arkansas chapter of the National Association for the Advancement of Colored People (NAACP), attempted to register nine black students at Little Rock Central High School, which had denied admission to black students in defiance of the 1954 U.S. Supreme Court ruling on desegregation. Several segregationist groups tried to physically block the students from entering the school. The incident attracted national attention, and President Dwight D. Eisenhower intervened by federalizing the Arkansas National Guard and dispatching the army to the school. Daisy Gatson Bates is recognized as a powerful symbol in this fight against school segregation. She organized ministers to escort the nine children to school and remained close with the children by becoming a member of the school's parent-teacher organization.

In 2001, the Arkansas legislature recognized Daisy Gatson Bates Day as an official state holiday. Schools organize classroom activities for students to learn about the civil rights movement, and local events are hosted to honor Bates and her legacy. In 1988, Bates's memoir, *The Long Shadow of Little Rock,* won the National Book Award. She continued to work for civil rights causes, especially in the rural community, until her death in 1999.

CONTACTS:
Arkansas Tourism
1 Capitol Mall
Ste. 4A-900
Little Rock, AR
501-682-1511; fax: 501-324-1525
www.arkansas.com

♦ 0261 ♦ Bath International Music Festival
Late May to early June

Located about 100 miles west of London, the city of Bath was already known for its mineral hot springs and 18th-century architecture when the idea for a music festival germinated and in 1948, a children's festival was held. Lack of funds and public interest nearly extinguished the festival over the next decade, but it gained a new spark with the appointment of violinist Yehudi MENUHIN as artistic director in 1959. During his tenure in the 1960s, the festival became an event of international scope and featured dance, theater, and not-to-be-missed parties in addition to opera and orchestral music. In subsequent years, film presentations, art exhibitions, and children's events were also part of the program.

Today, the 17-day festival presents all types of music—classical, jazz, contemporary, early, world—performed by local and international musicians and features some 150 events, including concerts, lectures, gatherings, workshops, open rehearsals, and educational programs. Festival events take place not only in many of Bath's well-preserved historic buildings, but also in the city streets and on the riverfront.

CONTACTS:
Bath Festivals
Abbey Chambers
Kingston Bldgs.
Third Fl.,

Bath BA1 1NT United Kingdom
44-12-2546-2231
bathfestivals.org.uk

♦ 0262 ♦ Baths of Caracalla
First week in July to second week in August

Originally designed as a social gathering place for men in third-century Rome, the Baths of Caracalla became the unusual setting for open-air opera in 1937. Held every summer, the Bath Operas feature grand Italian operas such as Giuseppe Verdi's *Aida*, which are produced by the Rome Opera Company in lavish style. Ballet performances produced by local and international dance companies are also on the program. The events take place in the evening on one of the world's largest stages—100 feet long and 162 feet wide. While the acoustics are far from ideal, more than 10,000 spectators generally fill the bleachers to enjoy this one-of-a-kind musical extravaganza.

CONTACTS:
Italian National Tourist Board
686 Park Ave.
3rd Fl.
New York, NY 10065
212-245-5618; fax: 212-586-9249
www.italiantourism.com

Superintendence for Archaeological Heritage of Rome
Piazza dei Cinquecento, 67
Ste. 64, Regent St.
Rome 00185 Italy
39-6-480-201; fax: 39-6-678-7689
archeoroma.beniculturali.it/en

♦ 0263 ♦ Battle of Britain Day
September 15

In England, September 15, 1940, is remembered as the day of the biggest daylight bombing raid of Britain by the German Luftwaffe. The German air attacks had begun in June 1940, and beginning September 7 bombs rained on London for 57 consecutive nights. The Royal Air Force (RAF), while greatly outnumbered, had a secret advantage—radar—and the early-warning chain gave RAF pilots a half-hour's notice of German planes taking off from France. The Luftwaffe was finally defeated in April 1941, ending the first extended battle ever fought for control of the air. Winston Churchill, in a speech in August 1940, was referring to the RAF pilots when he said, "Never in the field of human conflict was so much owed by so many to so few."

Today the RAF, as well as civilian aviation organizations, commemorate the anniversary with air displays of various kinds.

CONTACTS:
Royal Air Force Museum
Grahame Park Way
London NW9 5LL United Kingdom
44-20-8205-2266
www.rafmuseum.org.uk

♦ 0264 ♦ **Battle of Flowers (Jersey, Channel Islands)**
Second Thursday in August

First held in 1902 as part of the celebration honoring the coronation of Edward VII and Queen ALEXANDRA, the **Jersey Battle of Flowers** takes place on Jersey in the British Channel Islands every August. It begins with a parade of floats covered in flowers, many of which are quite elaborate and take months to prepare. In past years, floats have included a working windmill and large birds made completely out of flowers. Another popular theme is significant events in the island's history, including the 1871 Battle of Jersey. In addition, each year there is a special float for Miss Battle, the queen of the event.

Spectators no longer engage in a flower-throwing melee after the parade. These days the first event is the town parade two days before the battle, which exposes the year 's exhibits to the public for the first time. Then the "battle" consists of a competition for the finest floats. Finally, a moonlight parade Friday night displays the floats with their illuminations and concludes with a fireworks finale.

CONTACTS:
Jersey Battle of Flowers Ltd
Meadowbank
La Rue des Pres Sorsoleil
St. Lawrence, Jersey JE3 1EE Channel Islands
44-15-3473-0178
www.battleofflowers.com

♦ 0265 ♦ **Battle of Flowers (Vienna, Austria)**
Summer

The Battle of Flowers is the culmination of a huge flower festival in the capital city of Vienna, Austria. Hundreds of floats are elaborately decorated with flowers, often to symbolize a particular aspect of Austrian history or culture. Sometimes they re-create entire scenes from Austrian operettas or ballets. The people of Vienna dress up in their best clothes and hats—similar to what Americans do on EASTER—to watch the parade, which is reviewed by government officials and the leaders of various cultural organizations.

Similar "Battles of Flowers" are held in other Austrian cities, such as Linz, Salzburg, and Innsbruck. A particularly famous one is held on a lake in south Upper Austria known as the Traun See, where barges and boats, rather than floats, are decorated with flowers.

♦ 0266 ♦ **Battle of Germantown, Reenactment of**
First Saturday in October

In October of 1777, George WASHINGTON's battle strategy to recapture Philadelphia from the British called for an assault on the little community of Germantown to the northwest of the city. The British soldiers took refuge in a new stone house, Cliveden, that had just been built by Benjamin Chew. Although the house was pounded by cannon balls, the stone walls withstood the assault and Washington's men were eventually forced to retreat. The thick fog proved to be a decisive factor, hindering the movements of Washington's soldiers at a point where they appeared to be on the verge of winning. Although the Americans were defeated, the Battle of Germantown was considered a moral victory, especially when it was followed two weeks later by the victory of General Horatio Gates at Saratoga.

Since the early 1970s, there has been a reenactment of Washington's defeat by the British in Germantown, now a suburb of Philadelphia, on the first Saturday in October. British and American troops stage a mock battle from house to house. At Cliveden, which now belongs to the National Trust for Historic Preservation, visitors can still see the scars left by American bullets.

CONTACTS:
Cliveden, Inc.
6401 Germantown Ave.
Philadelphia, PA 19144
215-848-1777; fax: 215-438-2892
www.cliveden.org

♦ 0267 ♦ **Battle of New Orleans Day**
January 8

When 5,400 British soldiers attacked near the Chalmette plantation outside New Orleans on January 8, 1815, they were met by a ragtag army of militiamen, sailors, and pirates fighting from behind barricades. The defending U.S. troops were led by General Andrew JACKSON, whose stunning victory—the British suffered some 2,000 casualties, while the Americans lost only eight men—made him a national hero.

This day is no longer as widely celebrated as it was before the Civil War, but it remains a legal holiday in Louisiana, where it is also known as **Jackson Day** or, in honor of Jackson's nickname, as **Old Hickory's Day**. The battlefield is located in Jean Lafitte National Historic Park, which sponsors commemorations and hosts living history encampments during the second weekend in January each year.

CONTACTS:
Louisiana Historical Legacy Inc
P.O. Box 44392
Baton Rouge, LA 70804
225-342-7009; fax: 225-342-3207
www.battleofneworleans2015.com

♦ 0268 ♦ **Battle of Olustee Reenactment**
Weekend in mid-February

The Battle of Olustee Reenactment commemorates the largest battle in Florida during the Civil War. A Confederate victory, the Battle of Olustee (also known as the Battle of Ocean Pond) was fought on February 20, 1864, and a reenactment has taken place on a February weekend each year since 1977.

Knowing that Union soldiers were on the way to secure strategic positions in northeast Florida, Confederate troops fortified a highly defensible position about 10 miles west of Lake City. They occupied a narrow, forested area of dry land with an impassable swamp on one side and a lake on the other. When Union soldiers attacked, the Confederates were able to repel them, though both armies suffered staggering casualties. Each side had about 5,000 men in the battle, but Union losses were heaviest, with 203 killed, 1,152 wounded, and 506 missing. Confederate casualties totaled 93 killed, 847 wounded, and 6 missing.

The Battle of Olustee is also known for the participation of the 54th Massachusetts Regiment, one of the most famous African-American fighting units in the war and the one represented in the film *Glory*. However, other black regiments also took part in the Battle of Olustee, including the 8th United States Colored Troops of Pennsylvania and the 35th United States Colored Troops of North Carolina. Noting the participation of black fighting units in the original battle and its reenactment, Blue/Grey Army, Inc., which sponsors the event, emphasizes that the reenactment and festival are not intended to glorify war or the Confederacy. Rather, through these events the organizers hope to honor the memory of the soldiers who participated on both sides during the Civil War, to encourage the study of local history, and to make known the horror of war. The sponsors state that war "is not something we celebrate, but it is something we should remember."

The reenactment has expanded over the years to include a weekend street festival in Lake City. Associated events include a beauty pageant, history displays and lectures, a music festival, an arts and crafts fair, Blue-Grey 5-K and 1 Mile Fun Runs, and a Blue/Grey Square Dance. Saturdaymorning features the Olustee Civil War Parade, with hundreds of participants in period costumes representing all facets of life during the Civil War. Descendants of the battle also participate. The Battle Reenactment, with about 2,000 reenactors, is the largest annual Civil War reenactment in the Southeast. It takes place at Olustee Battlefield State Park on Sunday afternoon before an audience of as many as 50,000 spectators.

CONTACTS:
Florida Division of Recreation and Parks
3900 Commonwealth Blvd.
Tallahassee, FL 32399
850-245-2157
www.floridastateparks.org

♦ 0269 ♦ **Bawming the Thorn Day**
Saturday nearest Midsummer Day, June 24

This is the day on which people in Appleton, Cheshire, England, celebrate the centuries-old tradition of bawming the thorn, or decorating the hawthorn tree that stands in the center of their town. Children dance around the tree after draping its branches with flowers, flags, and ribbons. According to local legend, the original hawthorn tree was planted there in 1125 by a returning crusader. It was thought to have been a cutting from the hawthorn allegedly planted in Glastonbury, England, by Joseph of Arimathea, who buried Jesus after his crucifixion.

CONTACTS:
Appleton Thorn Village Hall
Stretton Rd.
Appleton Thorn
Warrington WA4 4RT United Kingdom
44-1925 261187
www.appletonthornvillagehall.co.uk

♦ 0270 ♦ **Bay To Breakers**
Third Sunday in May

A footrace, Bay to Breakers is held each year in San Francisco, California. The event was founded in 1912 after the devastating earthquake of 1906, which had destroyed much of San Francisco. The nearly 7.5 mile race takes place on the third Sunday of May, beginning at the Embarcadero, near the San Francisco Bay, and finishing at the Great Highway adjacent to Ocean Beach. Formerly called the Cross City Race, the event is the oldest consecutively run annual footrace in the world.

Typically, the race attracts over 50,000 runners—many in costumes—who are cheered on by more than 100,000 spectators. In addition to the runners, children, the elderly, and families walk the route. A highlight of the race is the centipede run, during which groups of thirteen or more compete while bound together by a bungee cord. While the race is open to people of all ages for an entry fee, professional runners can participate only by invitation. In more recent years, the race has banned alcohol, nudity, and floats from the event.

CONTACTS:
Fort Mason Center
2 Marina Blvd.
San Francisco, CA 94123
415-231-3130
zapposbaytobreakers.com

♦ 0271 ♦ **Bayfest**
Weekend in late September

In Corpus Christi, Texas, Bayfest began in 1976 as a multicultural celebration that provided entertainment for families while also raising money for local charities, which is still its focus today. Festival entertainment includes tejano, mariachi, and other Latin music; rock and roll and country music; a carnival; dancing; and games. Bayfest is held on a beach bordering the Gulf of Mexico and also features ethnic and carnival foods, arts and crafts, fireworks, and the Bayfest Run.

♦ 0272 ♦ **Bayou Classic**
Thanksgiving weekend

The State Farm Bayou Classic is a sporting event held annually in New Orleans, La., that combines the intensity of a great college football rivalry with the pageantry and celebratory atmosphere of a cultural festival. The Bayou Classic centers on the annual football game between two historically black universities: Grambling State University of Grambling,

Louisiana, and Southern University of Baton Rouge. Held each year since 1974, the Classic attracts more than 70,000 football fans to the Louisiana Superdome on Thanksgiving weekend to see the nationally televised game between the Grambling Tigers and the Southern Jaguars.

In addition to such football traditions as tailgate parties and a coaches' luncheon, the Bayou Classic includes numerous fraternity and sorority parties, a battle of the marching bands, a Greek step show, a quiz bowl competition, a gospel music brunch, an employment fair, college fair, fan festival, golf tournament, and community service activity, including building a children's playground in New Orleans one recent year. Altogether more than 200,000 people participate in the Bayou Classic football game and related educational and social events.

CONTACTS:
Bayou Classic
501 Basin St.
Ste. A
New Orleans, LA 70112
504-293-2619; fax: 504-455-7103
www.mybayouclassic.com

♦ 0273 ♦ **Bayreuth Festival**
Late July through end of August

An internationally famous month-long festival in Bayreuth (pronounced buy-ROIT), Bavaria, Germany, celebrating the music of Richard Wagner. It features six to eight Wagner operas and is usually sold out a year in advance. Performances are in the Festspielhaus (Festival Theater) designed by Wagner himself specifically for the presentation of his works. The festival was launched with the first complete performance of the four-opera *Der Ring des Nibelungen* (The Ring of the Nibelung), triumphantly presented in the new Festspielhaus on Aug. 13, 14, 16, and 17, 1876. Except for wartime interruptions, the festival has been staged every year since then. Wagner had moved to Bayreuth in 1874, and lived in the house he called *Wahnfried* (Peace from Delusion) until his death in 1883. During those years, he composed his last work, the sacred festival drama *Parsifal*, and it was produced at Bayreuth in 1882. The festival was directed after Wagner's death by his wife Cosima; their son Seigfried took over as director in 1930, and grandsons Wieland and Wolfgang Wagner revived it after World War II, in 1951.

CONTACTS:
Bayreuther Festspiele
Festspielhügel 1 - 2
Bayreuth 95445 Germany
49-921-78-780
www.bayreuther-festspiele.de/english

♦ 0274 ♦ **Be Kind to Animals Week**
First full week in May

The oldest week of its kind in the United States, Be Kind to Animals Week was first observed in 1915. Established by Dr. William O. Stillman, the leader of the American Humane

Association at the time, this week was dedicated to helping animals and to publicizing the achievements of the nation's humane societies.

Today, Be Kind to Animals Week is observed by thousands of animal shelters across the country. They host special media events, promote education on the humane treatment of animals, and try to remind people of the debt that humankind owes to both wild and domestic animals.

CONTACTS:
American Humane Association
1400 16th St. N.W.
Ste. 360
Washington, D.C. 20036
800-227-4645
www.americanhumane.org

♦ 0275 ♦ **Beaches, Day of the (Día de las Playas)**
December 8

In Uruguay, December 8 is known as the Day of the Beaches because it marks the official opening of the beach season on the coast known as the "Uruguayan Riviera." There are ceremonies in which a priest blesses the waters, sailing regattas, horseback riding competitions, and an international shooting contest at Carrasco. Sometimes this day is referred to as **Family Day** or **Blessing of the Waters Day**.

♦ 0276 ♦ **Bear Society Dance**
Varies

This ritual dance is performed by the Bear Society, an Iroquois Indian group known for its ability to cure the victims of "bear sickness," a type of mental illness of which the victim is aware, but which he or she cannot control. The illness is caused by the bear spirit, and ceremonial foods that would please the spirit are an important part of the ritual. The dance is held in the patient's home or in the longhouse. As part of the ritual, members of the society blow berry juice on the patient.

There are actually two dances: one is a curing rite, and the other can be performed at any time, even without a patient present. The first consists of slow chants, a round dance with a stomp step, and finally the pairing of dancers. Patients cured by the ritual become members of the society.

CONTACTS:
Manataka America Indian Council (MAIC)
P.O. Box 476
Hot Springs, AR 71902
501-627-0555
www.manataka.org

♦ 0277 ♦ **Beargrease (John) Sled Dog Marathon**
First week in February

This annual dog-sledding festival commemorates John Beargrease (1861-1911), the son of a Chippewa chief who was known for delivering mail by sled dog along the North

Shore of Minnesota from 1887 to 1900. Beargrease was often the only connection to the outside world for people living in this remote area in the latter part of the 19th century. For his skill in negotiating the shifting ice on Lake Superior, he was known as the "renowned pilot of Lake Superior."

The festivities begin with a mushers banquet the evening before preparations begin for the big race. The next day veterinarians make sure each dog is marathon-ready, then a cutest puppy contest rounds out the afternoon. On Race Day, opening ceremonies pay respects to John Beargrease before the mushers take off. The Marathon itself is divided into two divisions: Mid-Distance racers follow a 150-mile course, while Marathon mushers cover about 420 miles.

CONTACTS:
Beargrease Sled Dog Marathon
P.O. Box 500
Duluth, MN 55801
218-722-7631
www.beargrease.com

♦ 0278 ♦ Befana Festival
January 5

Sometimes referred to simply as **La Befana**, this is the TWELFTH NIGHT festival in Italy where the *Befana,* a kindly witch, plays much the same role that Santa Claus plays in the United States on CHRISTMAS EVE—giving toys and candy to the children who have been good and a lump of coal or a pebble to those who haven't. According to legend, the Befana was sweeping her house when the Magi, or Three Wise Men, stopped by on their way to Bethlehem. But when they asked her to accompany them, she said she was too busy. She later changed her mind and set out to find the Christ Child, but she got lost. Every year la Befana passes through Italy in her continuing search for the *Gésu Bambino,* leaving gifts for children.

The festival begins on EPIPHANY EVE, when the Befana is supposed to come down the chimney on her broom to leave gifts in children's stockings. In Rome, the Piazza Navona is thronged with children and their parents, who shop for toys and exchange greetings. Bands of young people march around, blowing on cardboard trumpets, and the noise level in the square can be deafening. In the countryside, bonfires are often lit on Epiphany Eve, and people try to predict the weather by watching the direction in which the smoke blows.

See also DÍA DELOSTRES REYES.

♦ 0279 ♦ Beiderbecke (Bix) Memorial Jazz Festival
Third weekend in July

Leon "Bix" Beiderbecke (1903-1931) was an American jazz cornetist, pianist, and composer whose unique style on the horn and tragically short life made him a Jazz Age legend at the age of 28. But it wasn't until 1971, on the 40th anniversary of Bix's death, that the seeds of an annual festival commemorating him were planted. That year, Bill Donahoe's Bix

Beiderbecke Memorial Jazz Band arrived in Bix's hometown of Davenport, Iowa, to pay tribute to him by playing at his gravesite and elsewhere in the city. An enthusiatic response and desire to preserve Bix's memory and music led to the formation of the Bix Beiderbecke Memorial Society, which established the first official festival in 1972. This annual, four-day jazz festival, popularly known as the "Bix Bash," features concerts by some of the world's best jazz bands as well as the Bix Jazz Society Youth Band, tours of Bix's boyhood home, a Bix Jazz Brunch on Sunday, a jazz liturgy at the First Presbyterian Church, and a concert at Bix's grave in Oakdale Memorial Gardens. Many of the concerts are held at LeClaire Park on the banks of the Mississippi River, where musicians perform in a bandshell, as well as indoor venues.

CONTACTS:
Bix Beiderbecke Memorial Society
P.O. Box 3688
Davenport, IA 52808
563-324-7170 or 888-249-5487; fax: 563-326-1732
www.bixsociety.org

♦ 0280 ♦ Beijing Opera Festival
Early December, held triennially

The traditional form of theatre known as Beijing Opera, or Peking Opera, is a national treasure in China. The Beijing Opera Festival is the country's most recognized event featuring this dramatic genre, which distinguishes itself from other opera styles with its elaborate costumes and martial arts displays. Scheduled every three years and always in a different city, the two-week festival is co-organized by the Ministry of Culture, local government, and the Beijing Opera Art Foundation.

About 20 shows are typically featured on each program, and festival organizers bestow awards in various categories to the best productions. The festival also offers workshops in addition to staging performances.

In 1995, the inaugural festival was held in Tianjin, located in northeast China. After the 1998 festival in Beijing, the Ministry of Culture decided to move the next two festivals to southern cities in the hope of fostering greater interest in the region, which has been less engaged historically with Beijing Opera than the northern Chinese.

CONTACTS:
China National Peking Opera Company
No.22, PingAnLi W. St.
XiCheng District
Beijing 100035 China
86-10-58519609
www.cnpoc.cn/en

♦ 0281 ♦ Beiteddine Festival
July and August

The Beiteddine Festival, held in a magnificent 200-year-old palace in this town in the Chouf region of Lebanon, has presented world-class offerings in the arts since 1985. Organizers defied the struggles of Lebanon's civil war by staging this celebration of human culture. Every summer, around 50,000 spectators gather in the Palace's spectacular courtyards to attend different performances. Many performers are Lebanese, but artists from around the world also are invited. The 2014 festival featured artists, programs, and events as varied as: Lebanese diva, Magida El Roumi, Grammy winner Joss Stone, folk singer Katie Melua, Ballet National de Marseille, a theatrical production of "Antigone" by Lebanese director Wajdi Mouawad and a sound and light show inspired by the Metamorphoses of Ovide & Kafka and implemented by ALBA University students.

CONTACTS:
Beiteddine Festival
Starco Center Bloc C
4th Fl.,
Downtown
Beirut Lebanon
961-1-373-430; fax: 961-1-373-440
beiteddine.org

♦ 0282 ♦ **Belarus Independence Day**
July 3

After nearly 70 years under Soviet rule, Belarus declared its sovereignty on July 27, 1990, and issued its declaration of independence on August 25, 1991. Belarus officially became autonomous on December 26, 1991, as did other former Soviet republics. On April 2, 1997, however, a treaty was signed to unite Belarus with the Russian Federation. Thus, Belarus reverted to its earlier Independence Day, July 3, which commemorated the liberation of the capital, Minsk, from German occupation in 1944. April 2 is another public, though working, holiday in Belarus, Unification Day of the Peoples of Belarus and Russia.

CONTACTS:
Belarus Embassy
1619 New Hampshire Ave., N.W.
Washington, D.C. 20009 United States
202-986-1606; fax: 202-986-1805
usa.mfa.gov.by

♦ 0283 ♦ **Belfast Festival**
Late October through early November

A two-week-long arts event held annually since 1962, the Belfast Festival is organized primarily by Queen's University in Belfast. The festival offers a broad selection of artistic genres, including classical music, jazz, comedy, literature, and popular music. The festival program features local and international artists. Luminaries who have appeared throughout the festival's long history include comedian Rowan Atkinson, musicians Jimi Hendrix and Dizzy Gillespie, and actors Laurence Olivier and Billy Connolly.

Founded by Michael Emmerson, a Queen's University student, the festival started as a humble affair but continued to expand over the decades, eventually becoming Northern Ireland's premier arts festival.

By 2006, the program featured 36 venues and audience totals of more than 100,000 people. Around that time, government funding for the festival began to decline. The Save the Belfast Festival Campaign, launched by the *Belfast Telegraph*, successfully recruited a new major funding source and ensured the festival would remain in operation for at least the next few years.

CONTACTS:
Ulster Bank Belfast Festival at Queen's
Lanyon N.
Queen's University
Belfast BT7 1NN United Kingdom
44-28-9097-1034
www.belfastfestival.com

♦ 0284 ♦ **Belgian-American Days**
August

Ghent, Minnesota, named after the famous city in Belgium, is the state's only predominantly Belgian community. The annual Belgian-American Days celebration gives the descendants of Ghent's original Belgian settlers an opportunity to compete in the traditional Belgian sport of *rolle bolle*, which is similar to lawn bowling or Italian bocci. The game is played on bare ground or grass, with stakes set 30 feet apart. The eight-pound disc called a *bolle* is rolled from one stake to the other. The bolle that lands closest to the stake scores. Teams usually consist of three players, and the first team to score eight points wins the game. As many as 300 bollers participate in the championship round held during the event.

Although rolle bolle is the biggest attraction, the festival also features a softball tournament, parades, a firemen's dinner, and a street dance.

♦ 0285 ♦ **Belgium Independence Day**
July 21

This public holiday, also known as the Belgium **National Day**, commemorates Belgium's independence from the Netherlands on July 21, 1831. Belgians had struggled against their rulers for 15 years. A revolt began in 1830, and the next year, the state of Belgium was formed and King Leopold I (1790-1865) was made its first king.

Belgians sing "La Brabançonne," the national anthem, and observe their independence with festivities, especially in the capital city of Brussels.

CONTACTS:
Embassy of Belgium
3330 Garfield St. N.W.
Washington, D.C. 20008
202-333-6900; fax: 202-338-4960
countries.diplomatie.belgium.be/en/united_states

♦ 0286 ♦ **Belize Independence Day**
September 21

On September 21, 1981, Belize gained independence from Britain. Belize was formerly known as British Honduras and had been internally self-governing since 1965.

Independence Day is a national public holiday in Belize. Celebrations begin more than a week before the 21st with dances, pageants, sporting events, and concerts, and culminate with parades and patriotic ceremonies.

CONTACTS:
Belize Tourism Board
Regent St. Ste. 64
P.O. Box 325
Belize City Belize
501-2-227-2420 or 800-624-0686
www.travelbelize.org

Embassy of Belize
2535 Massachusetts Ave. N.W.
Washington, D.C. 20008
202-332-9636; fax: 202-332-6888
www.embassyofbelize.org

♦ 0287 ♦ Belize National Day
September 10

A public holiday in Belize commemorating the Battle of St. George's Caye, fought in 1798 between the Spanish and the English over possession of the area. English loggers had settled in what is now Belize in the early 17th century. British pirates used to hide in the cays there waiting for opportunities to plunder passing Spanish ships. It is also known as **St. George's Caye Day**. Numerous festivities take place on the days leading up to the holiday, including a grand carnival parade.

CONTACTS:
Embassy of Belize
2535 Massachusetts Ave. N.W.
Washington, D.C. 20008
202-332-9636; fax: 202-332-6888
www.embassyofbelize.org

♦ 0288 ♦ Bella Coola Midwinter Rites
November-February

The *kusiut* is a traditional masked dancing society of the Bella Coola, Kimsquit, and other Indian tribes of coastal British Columbia. The society performed dramatic curing dances during the midwinter ceremonial season, which began with the opening rite in November and ended in February. Most involved feats of juggling as well as masked mime. Some were used by initiates to prove that they had received a supernatural "call" to join the society.

Among the more frightening was the series of five *kusiotem* dances: the stomach-cutting dance, the beheading dance, the drowning dance, the burning dance, and the fungus dance. All involved elaborate masks and deception. The beheading dance, for example, was simulated with a false head, and the drowning dance used a dummy and a trap door.

Nowadays membership in the kusiut is open to all men, though the number of spectators is decreasing. As a result, the society's status is deteriorating.

♦ 0289 ♦ Belmont Stakes
June; fifth Saturday after Kentucky Derby

The final race of the Triple Crown of horseracing, the Belmont Stakes is traditionally run on the fifth Saturday after the KENTUCKY DERBY (the third Saturday after the PREAKNESS STAKES). Founded in 1867, it takes place at the Belmont Park Race Track in western Nassau County on Long Island, named for August Belmont, a well-to-do German who played an important role in establishing horseracing in New York.

The horse that sweeps the Triple Crown receives a $1 million bonus in addition to the winner's share of the purses, but in years when no horse wins the Triple Crown, the bonus goes to the horse competing in all three races and scoring the highest on a 5-3-1 point system for finishing first, second, or third. The chances of a single horse winning all three races are relatively slim: in 114 years only 11 horses have managed to do it.

Many breeders pay more attention to the Belmont than they do to the other races when it comes to selecting stud prospects because they believe that in the long run, Belmont winners make better sires.

CONTACTS:
Belmont Stakes Racing Festival
Belmont Park
2150 Hempstead Tpke.
Elmont, NY 11003
516-488-6000 or 844-697-2849
www.belmontstakes.com

♦ 0290 ♦ Beltane
May 1

Beltane (also spelled **Beltine** or **Beltein**) is the Celtic name for the first day of May (*see* MAY DAY), which divided the ancient Celtic year in half. It was believed that each day began with the setting of the sun the night before, so Beltane was celebrated by lighting bonfires to honor the sun god. Cattle were driven through the "Beltane fire"—or between two fires—to protect them from disease before putting them out to pasture for the new season. Sometimes people followed the same ritual to forestall bad luck and to cure barrenness. Contact with the fire was symbolic of contact with the life-giving sun.

Along with LAMMAS (August 1), Hallowmas (ALL SAINTS' DAY, November 1), and CANDLEMAS (February 2), Beltane was one of the British QUARTER DAYS, or term days, when rents were due and debts were settled. The day is still observed in parts of Ireland, the Scottish Highlands, Wales, Brittany, and the Isle of Man, with most of the celebrations revolving around fire and reflecting ancient fertility rites.

See also MIDSUMMERDAY.

CONTACTS:
Order of Bards, Ovates & Druids
P.O. Box 1333
Lewes, East Sussex BN7 1DX United Kingdom
44-1273-470888
www.druidry.org

♦ 0291 ♦ **Benin Independence Day**
August 1

On August 1, 1960, Benin declared its independence from France, ending 70 years as a French colony. Independence Day is a national holiday observed throughout the country, especially in the capital city of Porto Novo.

CONTACTS:
Embassy of the Republic of Benin
2124 Kalorama Rd. N.W.
Washington, D.C. 20008
202-232-6656; fax: 202-265-1996
www.beninembassy.us

♦ 0292 ♦ **Benin National Vodoun Day (Traditional Religions Day)**
January 10

Vodoun is an ancient, African, pantheistic religion. When it was brought to the Americas by African slaves, it was blended with elements of Christianity into what is known as "voodoo." The present African country of Benin, situated on the former kingdom of Dahomey, is known as a center of Vodoun culture, and the city of Ouidah is the home of Vodoun's Supreme Chief, Daagbo Hounon.

Vodoun was scorned and suppressed by European colonists in Dahomey. It continued to be practiced, often in secret, even by those indigenous people who outwardly accepted conversion to Christianity. Benin gained independence in 1960, but Vodoun continued to be banned during the 18 years Mathieu Kerekou was at the head of the government. He found the Vodoun practices and rites unacceptable to the socialist philosophy of his regime.

Kerekou lost power in 1991, and Benin's new democratic government soon showed its respect for Vodoun,which is still practiced by an estimated 65% of the country's population. January 10 was proclaimed National Vodoun Day/Traditional Religions Day, and Vodoun and other traditional religions were given officially recognized status, along with Christianity and Islam. The government, in conjunction with UNESCO, sponsored an event called "Ouidah 92: The First International Festival of Vodoun Arts and Cultures." Works of art were commissioned to honor the ancient kingdom of Dahomey and other aspects of Benin's history and traditions. Because the port of Ouidah was a major point of departure for slave ships, many of the works concerned the slave trade. They are permanently installed throughout the city and are focal points for the celebration of National Vodoun Day/Traditional Religions Day in Ouidah.

The day is celebrated throughout Benin, but most elaborately in Ouidah. There are various processions, Vodoun rituals, dances, and even an international film festival held in conjunction with the holiday. The celebration's central activity, however, is the re-enactment of the journey from the slave auction block in the center of town to the ships in the harbor. Led by the Supreme Chief of Vodoun, followers travel the three-kilometer "Route of the Slaves," pausing to pray and make offerings to the gods and ancestors at the memorials that have been erected along the way. The final stop is a sculpture at the water's edge, called "Gate of No Return." After reaching the end of the route, participants can enjoy music, food vendors, and artists in town and on the beach. Many people of African descent from North and South America visit Benin to make this pilgrimage along the Route of the Slaves.

♦ 0293 ♦ **Bennington Battle Day**
August 16

During the Revolutionary War, Colonel Seth Warner and 350 of his Green Mountain Boys, a group of soldiers from Vermont, played a vital role in defeating the British forces who had come to capture the American supply depot at Bennington, a town in southern Vermont near the New York border. The anniversary of the fighting that took place along the Walloomsac River on August 16, 1777, is a legal holiday in Vermont, and a 306-foot tower has been erected in the town of Old Bennington, two miles west of Bennington proper. A statue of Seth Warner stands nearby. Across the state border in New York's Rensselaer County, the Bennington Battlefield State Park includes the site where the heaviest fighting took place.

The Bennington Battle Monument State Historic Site hosts historic reenacts and displays on the weekend nearest August 16.

CONTACTS:
Bennington Battle Monument
15 Monument Cir.
Old Bennington, VT 05201
802-447-0550
benningtonbattlemonument.com

♦ 0294 ♦ **Bera Festival**
August-September; last Thursday of the Hindu month of Bhadrapada

Wherever there is a large body of water in Bengal, a region encompassing eastern India and Bangladesh, agricultural communities are likely to celebrate the Bera Festival. Holy men known as fakirs supervise the preparation of ornately decorated floats (*bera* means "raft" or "float" in Hindi), which are constructed in honor of Khaja Khizir, the patron saint of the waters. The festival is essentially a Muslim tradition, although it draws from Hindu regional customs. It takes place during the Bangla month of Bhadra, which falls sometime between August and September.

The ancient raft custom existed before the 13th century, but it was only with the arrival of Turkish rulers during that time that the celebration shifted its focus on Khaja Khizir. At that point *nawabs*, or viceroys, of regional cities like Murshidabad and Dhaka became followers of the saint and decreed that the raft festival honor him.

The centerpiece of the festival, the raft, is made out of local banana trunks that are lashed together to make a square platform. On top of the platform are placed 20-foot boats. The float is then decorated with flags, flowers, and other trappings, and finally is pushed into the water to be received by Khaja Khizir.

CONTACTS:
Department of Tourism, Government of West Bengal
New Secretariat Bldg.
1, K. S. Roy Rd.
3rd Fl.
Kolkata, West Bengal 700 001 India
91-33-2225-4723
wbtourism.gov.in

♦ 0295 ♦ Berchtold's Day
January 2

In Switzerland, the day after NEW YEAR'S DAY is known as **Berchtoldstag** and is celebrated primarily by children. Groups of playmates organize parties that feature nut eating and nut games followed by singing and folk dancing. A popular game is the building of "hocks" composed of four nuts placed close together with a fifth balanced on top. The children begin gathering and stockpiling nuts for Berchtold's Day festivities early in the fall.

♦ 0296 ♦ Bergen International Festival
12 days from late May to early June

The Bergen International Festival is the major cultural event in Norway, and features more than 100 events in music, drama, folklore, opera, ballet, and the visual arts. Most of the musical events are held in Bergen's Viking Castle, Haakon's Hall (built in 1250), at the Grieg Concert Hall, at Edvard Grieg's home (known as "Troldhaugen"), and at Lysoen, the island home of composer and violinist Ole Bull. It was, in fact, Edvard Grieg—the composer and founder of the Norwegian nationalist school of music—who originated the idea for a musical festival and who first sponsored such a festival back in 1898. But the Bergen International Festival as it exists today didn't really get started until 1952. Although the primary attraction is music—ranging from classical to jazz, new music from around the world, organ concerts, military band performances, and folklore opera—children's programs, literary events, and art exhibits are featured as well.

CONTACTS:
Bergen International Festival
Vaskerelvsmauet 6
Bergen 5014 Norway
47-55-21-0630; fax: 47-55-21-0640
www.fib.no

♦ 0297 ♦ Bering Sea Ice Golf Classic
Third Saturday in March

This golfing challenge, played on a six-hole course with bright orange golf balls, takes place on the frozen Bering Sea off Nome, Alaska, at a time when the winds can be gale-strength. Par is 41, but winners have claimed scores as low

as23. Entry fees benefit the Lions Club. The tournament, not a wholly serious affair, coincides with the final days of the ID-ITAROD TRAIL SLED DOG RACE that starts about the first of March and ends in Nome about two weeks later.

♦ 0298 ♦ Berlin Biennale
Spring to summer, every other year

The Berlin Biennale is a contemporary arts festival held in Berlin, Germany. It takes place at varying locations throughout the city. Each festival is organized around a theme.

The event was founded in 1995 by Klaus Biesenbach, the director of the KW Institute for Contemporary Art, and a core group of arts patrons. The inspiration for a *biennale* in Germany came from the Venice Biennale. The 1981 demise of Aperto, a forum for young contemporary artists, led to discussions that highlighted the need to increase the profile of contemporary art in Berlin, which fueled the acceleration of the Berlin Biennale project. The aim of the festival is to host an international exhibition of contemporary art and to represent lesser-known young artists. The most important collaborator in the festival is the KW Institute for Contemporary Art, which grants use of its space for exhibitions. Since its founding, the Berlin Biennale has become a magnet for art lovers from around the world.

CONTACTS:
KW Institute for Contemporary Art
Kunst-Werke Berlin e.V.
Auguststraße 69
Berlin, D-10117 Germany
49-30-2434-590; fax: 49-30-2434-5999
www.berlinbiennale.de

♦ 0299 ♦ Berlin Festival of Lights
Ten days in October

Considered one of the best-known light festivals in the world, the Berlin Festival of Lights began in 2005. For ten days in October, light displays illuminate the German city from seven o'clock in the evening until midnight. The light installations convey cultural elements, including popular stories and scenes from history, in addition to their impressive visual artistry. Many national and international artists showcase their creativity at the Berlin Festival of Lights, which attracts nearly two million spectators.Numerous monuments and other buildings in Berlin serve as stages for the festival. Some locations, such as the *Fernsehturm, Berliner Dom, Brandenburger Tor,* and Berlin Cathedral, undergo temporary transformations for the celebration.The Berlin Festival of Lights opens with a ceremony called "Lights On" at the *Potsdamer Platz.* During the ceremony, all the surrounding buildings are illuminated. The festival's artistic use of glass and neon light attracts many enthusiasts. One popular attraction is the LightBeach, which offers dancing and campfires. Other notable activities during the festival include the Mountmitte Night Climbing event, which challenges people with illuminated obstacle courses; 3D-mapping on the buildings in Berlin, with its rhythmic play of lights and shadows; and workshops on night photography.

CONTACTS:
FOL Festival of Lights International Productions GmbH
Savignyplatz 6
Berlin, 10623 Germany
49-30-3186-0113; fax: 49-30-3150-9748
festival-of-lights.de

♦ 0300 ♦ **Berlin International Film Festival**
Ten days in February

The Berlin International Film Festival was founded in 1951, but it has only been held annually in February since 1978. It features films of all genres, lengths, and themes. About 400 films, mostly international and European premieres, are screened every year, and a handful of films compete for the Golden and Silver Bear awards. The festival takes place in several venues in and around Berlin.

A number of categories comprise the Berlin International Film Festival. They include "Competition" for international cinema, "Perspektive Deutsches Kino," which showcases upcoming talent in German films, "Generation" films for the young, and "Berlinale Special" films in honor of cinema personalities. There are also such interesting sections as "Culinary Cinema," featuring food and pleasure, and "Panorama," showcasing independent and art house films. The prestigious festival awards are given in such categories as best film, short film, actor, actress, director, script, documentary, and artistic contribution. Special events also take place concurrently with the festival, the most important of which is the European Film Market, a meeting place for producers, buyers, financiers, distributors, and others in the film industry.

CONTACTS:
Berlin International Film Festival
Potsdamer Straße 5
Berlin, 10785 Germany
49-30-25920-0; fax: 49-30-25920-299
www.berlinale.de/en

♦ 0301 ♦ **Bermuda College Weeks**
March-April

College Weeks began as **Rugby Weeks** in the 1950s, when Ivy League rugby teams came to the island of Bermuda to spend their spring holidays and compete against Bermudian and British teams. But parties and socializing soon took precedence over the rugby competition, and College Weeks became a time for young people from colleges and universities all over the United States to meet in Bermuda and get an early start on the summer season.

The Bermuda government organizes and pays for all of the activities that are scheduled during this period, issuing courtesy cards that entitle college students free admission to everything from a "Get Acquainted" dance at one of the major hotels to beach parties, boat cruises, and steel band concerts. Scores of moped-riding college students take advantage of

the island's hospitality, making Bermuda one of the most popular SPRING BREAK destinations.

♦ 0302 ♦ **Bermuda Day**
May 24

Bermuda Day, formerly COMMONWEALTH DAY, is a public holiday and the highlight of Bermuda Heritage Month. Since 1979, there are a variety of cultural activities during May, including historical exhibits, musical concerts, and thanksgiving services in area churches. Festivities on May 24 include a parade that ends up in the middle of a festival at Bernard Park in Hamilton. It is also a popular day for Bermudians to hit the beaches. Runners participate in a marathon race, and there are also races for cyclists and skaters. May 24 is the beginning of dinghy-racing season—about every other Sunday boaters race in St. George's Harbor.

CONTACTS:
Government of Bermuda
81 Court St.
Hamilton HM 12 Bermuda
441-292-1681; fax: 441-292-2474
www.communityandculture.bm

♦ 0303 ♦ **Bermuda Festival of the Performing Arts**
January-March

The winter season on the island of Bermuda brings on a schedule of performing arts events known as the Bermuda Festival of the Performing Arts, which began in 1976. Yehudi MENUHIN (April 22, 1916-March 12, 1999) was instrumental in organizing the first festival and performed on its 20th anniversary in 1996. Offerings include theater, dance, opera, classical, and modern music performances from around the world. In 2015, world renowned cellist Yo-Yo Ma performed at the Festival's Founders' Recital, which honors the legacy of Mehunin and others who were instrumental in conceiving of the event.

CONTACTS:
Bermuda Festival Ltd
Jardine House
1st Fl., 33/35 Reid St.
Hamilton, HM12 Bermuda
441-295-1291; fax: 441-295-7403
www.bermudafestival.org

♦ 0304 ♦ **Bettara-Ichi**
October 19

The annual **Pickle Market** or **Sticky-Sticky Fair** is held near the Ebisu Shrine in Tokyo, Japan, to supply people with what they will need to observe the EBISU FESTIVAL on the following day, October 20. One of the seven Shinto deities of good luck and the patron deity of tradesmen, Ebisu has a limited following in Tokyo. But the fair that is held the day before is very popular. People buy wooden images of Ebisu, good-luck tokens, and most important of all, the large, white, pickled radish known as *bettara* that is so closely identified with the fair.

The Sticky-Sticky Fair was named after the way the pickled radishes were sold. Stall keepers used to dangle them from a rope so the buyer wouldn't get his hands sticky from the malted rice in which the radishes had been pickled. People would carry them home by swinging them from their ropes, calling out "Bettara! Bettara!" so that others would make way for them. But mischievous young boys would often deliberately swing the sticky pickles around in a crowd to tease the women and girls, who were all dressed up in their holiday clothes.

CONTACTS:
Tokyo Convention & Visitors Bureau
6F, Nisshin Bldg.
346-6 Yamabuki-cho
Tokyo 162-0801 Japan
81-3-5579-2680; fax: 81-3-5579-2685
www.tcvb.or.jp

◆ 0305 ◆ BFI London Film Festival
October

Held in October each year, the 12-day BFI London Film Festival is a prestigious event on London's cultural calendar. The British Film Institute (BFI) launched the festival in 1953 with 20 films, designing it to give the British public an experience parallel to festivals in Cannes, Venice, and Edinburgh. Today, although the festival still caters to public audiences, its world premiere screenings of over 300 films also attract people from film circles and various media around the world.

The gala events that begin and end the festival take place at venues in central London. Question-and-answer sessions follow some of the screenings, offering direct audience engagement with casts and crews as well as behind-the-scenes exposure to filmmaking.

Award categories include the best film for the most creative motion picture; the best British newcomer; the Grierson Award for films with social or cultural significance; and the Sutherland Award for the best directorial debut. The festival also awards the British Film Institute Fellowship in recognition of the work and achievements of outstanding individuals in the art of filmmaking.

CONTACTS:
BFI London Film Festival
21 Stephen St.
London, W1T 1LN United Kingdom
44-20-7957-4777
www.bfi.org.uk/lff

◆ 0306 ◆ Bhai Dooj
Second day of the Hindu month of Kartika

Bhai Dooj is an annual festival celebrated by people who are native to the northern states of India. It is celebrated two days after the major Hindu festival of Diwali, and it falls on the second day of the Bright Fortnight in the Hindu lunar month of Kartika. The festival is a celebration of the bond between brothers and sisters, which it aims to strengthen through a *tika* ceremony performed before Hindu gods. On the day of the festival, rituals are generally carried out in the *pooja* room, or altar, marked out for the gods. Usually a lamp is lit and rituals are performed with a ceremonial plate, the *thali*, which is adorned with sweets, vermillion, and a coconut. The sister prays for the health and long life of her brother and applies a *tika* (a smear of vermillion, saffron, and rice grains) to his forehead. She offers him sweets, along with the coconut that was used in the ceremony. The brother promises to stand by his sister through all hardships.

Like many Hindu festivals, Bhai Dooj is based on legend. Hindu mythology includes a story of Lord Krishna, who slays the demon Narakasura and goes to his sister Subhadra. Subhadra welcomes him with a lamp and sweets, and she smears the protective *tika* on his forehead.

CONTACTS:
Ministry of Tourism, Government of India
1270 Avenue of the Americas
Ste. 303
New York, NY 10020
212-586-4901; fax: 212-582-3274
tourism.nic.in

◆ 0307 ◆ Bhairava Ashtami
November-December; eighth day of the waning half of the Hindu month of Margasirsa

Among Hindus, *Bhairava* means "frightful" or "terrible." He is a manifestation of Shiva, a terrifying character who is worshipped to obtain success, prosperity, the removal of obstacles, and recovery from illness. He is often referred to as *Danda-pani* because he punishes sinners with a *danda* (staff or rod). Another of Bhairava's names is *Swaswa*, which means "he whose horse is a dog." He is often depicted accompanied by a dog or riding on one.

On Bhairava Ashtami Hindus worship Bhairava with sweets and flowers. Dogs everywhere are treated to milk, sweets, and other delicacies. At night, worshippers keep a vigil and spend the time telling stories about Bhairava. They also offer libations to their dead ancestors.

CONTACTS:
Kalapairavar of Sri Kashi Tatcina
Athiyaman Kottai
Salem Bye - Pass Rd.
Dharmapuri, TN 636 705 India
91-91869-51375
kalabairavar.dpi.net.in

◆ 0308 ◆ Bhishma Ashtami
January-February, eighth day of waxing half of Hindu month of Magha or during Hindu month of Kartika (October-November)

In Hindu mythology Bhishma was the son of King Shantanu. When his father decided he wanted to marry a beautiful young maiden named Satyavati, her parents would not permit it because it was Bhishma who was heir to the throne, and if she had sons they could not inherit the kingdom. To allow the marriage to go forward, Bhishma vowed never to marry and have children of his own, nor to accept the crown. Shantanu then married Satyavati, and she bore him two sons.

The two sons died without producing any offspring, but Satyavati had two grandchildren by a son who had been born before she married the king. Bhishma ended up raising these two and taking charge of the training of their children, who were known as the Kauravas and the Pandavas (*see also* ANANT CHATURDASHI). In the battle that was eventually fought between the two groups of offspring, Bhishma sided with the Kauravas and was so badly wounded it was said that there was barely a space of two fingers' width on his body that had not been pierced by an arrow. Since he had been allowed to choose the time of his death, he waited on his death-bed of arrows for 58 days, during which he delivered many religious discourses. He later became the model for modern ascetics who lie on nail-studded beds, and to this day is considered a great example of self-denial, loyalty, and devotion.

During the festival held in his honor, libations are offered to Bhishma with barley, sesame, flowers, and water from the sacred Ganges River.

CONTACTS:
Divine Life Society
P.O. Shivanandanagar,
Tehri-Garhwal, Uttarakhand 249 192 India
91-135-2430040; fax: 91-135-2442046
www.dlshq.org

♦ 0309 ♦ **Bianou**
April

A celebration of the end of the winter season in the market town of Agadés (or Agadéz), Niger. The festivities are held for three days, and start with the sound of distant drumming and chanting of the *muezzin* calling Muslims to prayer. As people assemble, the drummers appear. Behind them come the Tuareg nomads, wearing long blue robes and spinning around in their special dance, the *guedra*. The Tuareg turbans are folded in a way that suggests a cock's comb, since the cock is the symbol of the new season. Agadés is in northern Niger in the Sahara Desert. It was the seat of a Tuareg sultanate in the 15th century, and has been a crossroads for Fulani cattle herders, Tuareg traders, and Hausa merchants. The nomadic peoples also hold an annual gathering in Ingal town in August to take a census, at which time medical care is given by the national government.

See also CAMEL MARKET.

♦ 0310 ♦ **Bible Week, National**
November, begins the Sunday before Thanksgiving

A week devoted to encouraging people to read the Bible, in the belief that it will arouse a positive spiritual force in a world plagued with problems. National Bible Week is promoted by the National Bible Association (originally the Laymen's National Committee), a non-denominational group of businessmen founded in 1940 and devoted to the application of the Golden Rule in daily life. A huge audience listened to the NBC radio program that was broadcast to kick off the first National Bible Week scheduled for December 8-14, 1941; PEARL HARBOR had been bombed just hours before.

CONTACTS:
National Bible Association
488 Madison Ave.
New York, NY 10022
nationalbible.org

♦ 0311 ♦ **Biennale of Sydney**
June to August in even-numbered years

Regarded as Australia's largest and most impressive visual arts show, the Biennale of Sydney is a three-month long event that presents the work of more than 1,600 artists from Australia and around the world. The Biennale was launched in 1973 and is the first of its kind in the Asia-Pacific region. Focusing more on individual artists rather than collective cultural representations, the event includes forums, discussions, and talk shows hosted by distinguished members of the art world. Besides showcasing indigenous and Asian art, the Biennale of Sydney also features many experimental and offbeat works, making it one of the most innovative art events in the region. In addition to art museums and galleries in the city, venues such as the Royal Botanic Gardens and the Sydney Opera House host many new projects. The festival, which is free to the public, receives patronage from both government and corporate sponsors.

CONTACTS:
Biennale of Sydney
Level 4, The Arts Exchange
10 Hickson Rd.
The Rocks, NSW 2000 Australia
61-2-8484-8700; fax: 61-2-9252-8078
www.biennaleofsydney.com.au

♦ 0312 ♦ **Big Iron Farm Show**
Three days in mid-September

The Upper Midwest's largest agricultural exposition, the **Big Iron** is held at the Red River Valley Fairgrounds in West Fargo, North Dakota. Established in 1981 so that farmers would have a place where they could come to view the latest innovations in farming and agricultural equipment, the Big Iron prides itself on being a business event rather than a carnival. In the words of one organizer, "We don't distract people with music, pots and pans, and dog and pony acts." However, for those who would like a little entertainment mixed in, a skid steer rodeo is held each day.

The three-day show regularly attracts more than 70,000 visitors, who come to see not only the farm equipment that is on exhibit but field demonstrations of tillage, crop-spraying, irrigation, and other equipment.

A special program for women takes place on "Ladies' Day." Seminars on such subjects as "Heirloom Art" and "The Changing Role of the Rural Woman" are offered, as well as other activities designed to inform and entertain women who participate in the running of a family farm.

CONTACTS:
Big Iron Farm Show
1805 W. Main Ave.
P.O. Box 797
West Fargo, ND 58078
701-282-2200
bigironfarmshow.com

♦ 0313 ♦ Big Singing
Last Sunday in May

Big Singing in Benton, Kentucky, takes place on the last Sunday in May. The event brings together more than 100 singers trained in the tradition of shape-note singing. Together they enjoy a communal picnic lunch and spend the day singing hymns written in an almost-extinct style of musical notation called shape notes.

A book titled *The Southern Harmony and Musical Companion* increased the popularity of this kind of singing in 19th-century America, and so it is sometimes called Southern Harmony singing. The notation assigns each note a particular shape, thus aiding those who don't read music to figure out the tune. The distinctive harmonies of shape-note singing result from the fact that each part is composed of only four different notes, again making it easier for the singers to learn their part.

The Big Singing in Benton dates back to 1884. Historical records reveal that in the 1920s and 1930s over 10,000 people attended this event annually. As more people became familiar with the melodies and harmonies of American pop music, however, the popularity of shape-note singing faded away. The Benton Big Singing is currently sponsored by the Society for the Preservation of Southern Harmony Singing.

CONTACTS:
WKMS
2018 University Station
Murray, KY 42071
270-809-4359 or 800-599-4737; fax: 270-809-4667
wkms.org

♦ 0314 ♦ Bilby Day, National
Second Sunday of September

Bilbies are nocturnal marsupials in Australia. The animal is not well known compared to the other iconic animals of Australia, the koala and the kangaroo, a fact that conservationists hope to rectify by raising awareness on National Bilby Day. The event takes place in Charleville, a town located west of Brisbane in northeastern Australia, where the bilbies are part of a captive breeding program run by the Queensland Parks and Wildlife Service.

Founded by two local wildlife preservations, National Bilby Day was officially launched in 2005 and arrives at the tail end of Australia's Threatened Species Week. The day's activities are organized by the Save the Bilby Fund, which collects money from year-round fund-raising operations. For past observances, the fund has received a large donation from the manufacturer of a popular chocolate bilby.

A warm-up night, called the "Nocturnal" party, brings people together before the main event the next day. On Bilby Day many of the stalls that are set up cater toward youth. Booths sell bilby stuffed animals and offer face-painting and bilby ears to dress children up like the beloved critters. Choirs perform songs that shed light on the endangered animals, and wildlife experts are on hand to give talks on the current status of bilbies and other endangered species.

CONTACTS:
Save the Bilby Fund
P.O. Box 260
Runaway Bay, QLD 4216 Australia
61-405-384-351; fax: 61-7-5563-8612
www.savethebilbyfund.com

♦ 0315 ♦ Bill of Rights Day
December 15

The first 10 amendments to the U.S. Constitution of 1787—referred to collectively as the Bill of Rights—were ratified on December 15, 1791 (*see* Citizenship Day). This landmark document protected American citizens from specific abuses by their government and guaranteed such basic rights as the freedom of religion, freedom of speech, and freedom of the press. In 1941 President Franklin D. Roosevelt designated December 15 as Bill of Rights Day and called upon Americans to observe it with appropriate patriotic ceremonies.

On December 10, 1948, the United Nations General Assembly unanimously adopted the Universal Declaration of Human Rights, and member countries of the U.N. began to observe December 10 as Human Rights Day. In the United States, the observance extends from December 10 to December 17 and is referred to as Human Rights Week. Since it encompasses December 15, the two events are now observed together and are typically celebrated with essay contests on the importance of freedom and democracy, special radio and television shows, and speeches on the themes of personal freedom and human rights.

In Massachusetts, the week of December 8-15 has been celebrated as Civil Rights Week since 1952. It honors not only the ratification of the Bill of Rights but the adoption of the state's first code of laws, the Body of Liberties, on December 10, 1641.

CONTACTS:
National Constitution Center
Independence Mall
525 Arch St.
Philadelphia, PA 19106
215-409-6600
constitutioncenter.org

♦ 0316 ♦ Billboard Latin Music Awards
April

Since 1989, Billboard magazine has sponsored the week-long Billboard Latin Music Conference in which some 1,000 music executives, musicians, managers, composers, agents, media, and other industry insiders gather for programs, showcases, parties, and networking events.

At the end of the week, the conference presents the Billboard Latin Music Awards in over 50 categories. The awards are chosen based on record sales, radio airplay data, and position on the weekly Billboard music charts. In addition to those awards for musical performance, the conference also bestows the Spirit of Hope Award, for an artist's humanitarian work during the year, and the Lifetime Achievement Award. Since 1999, the awards ceremony has been broadcast on the Telemundo television network.

♦ 0317 ♦ Billiken (Bud) Parade and Picnic
Second Saturday in August

Bud Billiken is the "patron saint" of Chicago's African-American children. Created in 1923 by Robert S. Abbott, the founder of the *Chicago Daily Defender* newspaper, Bud Billiken is a symbol of things as they should be—not necessarily as they are—and his day is primarily a children's event. There is a parade held on the second Saturday in August each year that goes on for several hours, complete with marching bands, baton twirlers, floats holding celebrities and politicians, and units from the Navy, Air Force, and National Guard. The formalities end when the parade reaches Washington Park in the Grand Boulevard area of Chicago, where families have picnics and cookouts.

CONTACTS:
Chicago Defender Charities
700 E. Oakwood Blvd
Fifth Fl.
Chicago, IL 60653
773-536-3710
www.budbillikenparade.org

♦ 0318 ♦ Billy the Kid Pageant
First weekend in August

It was in Lincoln, New Mexico, that the legendary American outlaw Billy the Kid (William Bonney, 1859?-1881) was brought to be hanged in 1881 after a frontier feud known as the Lincoln County War. He made his escape from a building that was once referred to as the Big Store—a combination general store, post office, billiard room, and private hotel that was later used as a courthouse. Today, the building has been restored as a state museum and courthouse.

The reenactment that takes place on the first Saturday and Sunday in August every year features Lincoln residents—many of them descendants of the individuals who originally played a part in the court proceedings and Billy's subsequent escape. First presented in 1940, the pageant involves almost everyone in town and is designed to be as historically accurate as possible. Festival activities surround Billy the Kid's "last escape" throughout the weekend to give the town a late 19th-century feeling, such as weaving and horseshoeing demonstrations, encampments, and an appearance by the Fourth Texas Cavalry.

♦ 0319 ♦ Biological Diversity, International Day for
May 22

In 1994 the United Nations declared December 29 International Day for Biological Diversity. In the year 2000 they changed the date to May 22 in order to draw more attention to the observance. They also wished to honor the May 22, 2000, signing of the Convention on Biological Diversity.

CONTACTS:
Secretariat of the Convention on Biological Diversity
413, Saint Jacques St.
Ste. 800
Montreal, QC H2Y 1N9 Canada
514-288-2220; fax: 514-288-6588
www.cbd.int

♦ 0320 ♦ Birmingham International Center Spotlight
April

Formerly known as the Birmingham Festival of the Arts, this display of performing and visual arts honors a different nation each year, and has been held since 1951 in Birmingham, Ala. A two-week long affair, the festival celebrates the chosen country's theater, literature, history, music, customs, and food with films, lectures, exhibits, and book-and-author luncheons. Traditional dance and folk music ensembles from the honored country perform at the street festival on the third weekend in April amid food and craft booths, storytellers, artists, and musicians.

But the rest of the festival—a renowned educational program—begins in early March when teachers from around the state gather for a workshop to learn about the featured country. Then during the second and third weeks in April they hold events in schools throughout the state highlighting the country's folklore, art, history, and traditions.

CONTACTS:
International Dance Festival Birmingham
c/o DanceXchange
Hippodrome, Thorp St.
Birmingham B5 4TB United Kingdom
44-121-689-3170
www.idfb.co.uk

♦ 0321 ♦ Bishwa Ijtema
Weekend in December-February

Bishwa Ijtema (sometimes spelled Vishwa Ijtema) brings together Muslim believers to Tongi, a northern suburb of the capital of Bangladesh, Dhaka. The three-day event is organized by the Tablighi Jamaat, a missionary organization. English speakers refer to the festival as the World Muslim Congregation (*ijtema* is Arabic for "public gathering"). After the Pilgrimage to Mecca (hajj), it is considered one of the largest Muslim gatherings in the world.

Since 1966, Muslims from Bangladesh and other countries have congregated at Tongi's 190-acre venue along the banks of the Turag River, where they pray, discuss the Quran, and receive instruction from religious scholars. The number of people attending has increased over the decades, expanding to an estimated three million in 2008. Devotees pour into crowded boats and climb rooftops to watch the proceedings. In order to meet the language needs of various believers, translations are provided in English, Arabic, Urdu, and Bangla.

Unlike other Muslim gatherings that may have a political perspective, Bishwa Ijtema forbids political speeches and encourages prayers for harmony and world peace.

CONTACTS:
Bangladesh Parjatan Corporation
83-88, Mohakhali C / A
Dhaka 1212 Bangladesh
880-2-8833229 or 880-2-8834600; fax: 880-2-8833900
parjatan.portal.gov.bd

♦ 0322 ♦ **Bisket Jatra**
April 13 or 14

The festival of the new year in Nepal, **Nava Varsa** or **Navabarsha**, is celebrated with exchanges of greetings and in some areas with ritual bathing. The most important celebration is Bisket Jatra, which means the "festival after the death of the serpent." In Bhaktapur, the new year is celebrated by parading images of gods in chariots. The main attraction of the festival is the erection of a ceremonial pole—a lingam or phallic symbol. This is a peeled tree trunk as much as 80 feet in length that is erected using bamboo and heavy ropes while crowds watch. On New Year's Day, the pole is torn down.

There is a legend behind this ceremonial pole. The daughter of the king of Bhaktapur was insatiable and demanded a new lover every night, but she left her lovers dead by morning. Then a brave prince appeared to try his luck. He managed to stay awake through the night, and saw two thread-like wisps emerging from the princess's nostrils. These wisps turned into poisonous snakes, so the prince drew his sword and killed them. Of course the prince and princess lived happily ever after. This story is recalled with the raising of the pole of Bisket Jatra.

Most holidays in Nepal are set by the lunisolar calendar, but New Year's Day is an exception and always falls in the middle of April.

CONTACTS:
Nepal Tourism Board, Tourist Service Center
P.O. Box 11018
Bhrikuti Mandap
Kathmandu Nepal
977-1-425-6909; fax: 977-1-425-6910
welcomenepal.com

♦ 0323 ♦ **Bite of Seattle**
July

An annual food festival held in Seattle, Washington, since 1982, the Bite of Seattle showcases area restaurants through a series of culinary events, including celebrity-chef cooking demonstrations, wine tastings, and promotional activities by local food companies. Hosted by the Seattle Center, the three-day festival features contests, car shows, movies, and musical performances. Over 100 stalls offer a variety of products from handcrafts to housewares. Local chefs compete in a cook-off, and awards are presented to winning entrants and the top restaurant in Seattle. During the festival, some restaurants contribute to Food Lifeline, a local hunger relief organization.

CONTACTS:
Seattle Center
305 Harrison St.
Seattle, WA 98109
425-295-3262
www.biteofseattle.com

♦ 0324 ♦ **Black and White Ball**
Early June in odd-numbered years

This biennial ball, which began in the 1950s, has been the biggest one-night fundraising event for the arts held in the United States, drawing some 16,000 black-tie partygoers to San Francisco's Civic Center area for music, dancing, food, cocktails, and socializing—all for the benefit of the San Francisco Symphony's education and outreach programs. From 9:00 P.M. until 2:00 A.M., attendees can walk throughout the several-block area to catch an eclectic mix of live music—classical, jazz, rock and roll, blues, swing, funk, reggae, salsa, country— performed by more than 30 groups in 13 indoor and outdoor venues. They can also feast on hors d'oeuvres prepared by nearly 90 of the city's fine dining establishments. In addition to the black and white attire of the revelers, black and white decorations adorn the venues. The high-energy Bash Before the Ball, presented by the San Francisco Symphony's young professional's group, Symphonix, provides a pre-ball warm-up.

♦ 0325 ♦ **Black Christ, Festival of the**
October 21

There are two legends associated with the observance of the **Black Christ Festival** in Portobelo, Panama. One says that during a cholera epidemic on the Isthmus, the people found a crate floating on the water near the beach. When they brought it ashore and opened it, they discovered a statue of a black Christ. They brought it into the church and, within a few days, the cholera had completely disappeared from Portobelo, even though it continued to rage elsewhere.

The other legend concerns a ship carrying the black Christ statue from Spain to Cartagena, Colombia. The ship stopped for supplies in Portobelo, but when it attempted to leave, it was turned back five times by sudden storms. The crew finally threw the crate containing the statue overboard, but local residents rescued it and put it in a place of honor in their church. The image of the black Christ, which is made of dark brown coco-bolo wood, has been credited with everything from miraculous cures to helping the city win the national lottery.

The people of Portobelo honor their patron saint, El Jesús Nazarene, by carrying the statue in procession on a decorated platform through the city streets. Pilgrims come fromall over Panama, as they have for more than 300 years, to celebrate with folk dancing, music, and songs.

See also BLACK NAZARENE FIESTA.

♦ 0326 ♦ Black Christ of Esquipulas, Day of the
January 15

For many people in Central and South America, the pilgrimage to the Black Christ of Esquipulas begins well in advance of the January 15 festival. Quite a number of Indians make the journey to Esquipulas—located in southeastern Guatemala along the borders with El Salvador and Honduras—entirely on foot, and look down upon those pilgrims who travel by horseback or in cars. Many don wide-brimmed straw hats, to which they attach gray Spanish moss and *chiches* (breasts), a yellow fruit that resembles a gourd. Indians making the journey from Quezaltenango blacken their hands with the juice from a special fruit. Folk belief teaches that this act aids Christ in enduring his pain.

Prior to the Spanish Conquest, Indians came to site of modern-day Esquipulas for religious rituals and trade. Once the Spaniards arrived the chief of the local tribes, whose name was Esquipulas, comprehended that it would be useless to resist the Europeans and decided instead to cooperate with them. The Spaniards honored him by founding a town which bore his name. They also built a Roman Catholic church and hired a well-known artist to sculpt a statue of Jesus. Since the local Indians thought that all Europeans were wicked, the priests requested that the artist carve the statue from balsam wood, a wood whose color was close to that of the natives' skin. Over the 400 years that have elapsed since then, the statue has darkened to black due to constant exposure to candle smoke and incense. Many legends involving answered prayers and miraculous cures have enhanced the Black Christ's reputation.

Ceremonial sites resembling altars, built from rocks brought by pilgrims, are scattered through the hills surrounding Esquipulas. The pilgrims stop to pray at these sites in their journeys to and from Esquipulas.

Only Quiché Indians from western Guatemala—believed to be the only Indians in the country who have not intermarried with whites—can perform some of the sacred rituals associated with this pilgrimage, such as dressing the image of the Black Christ. The pilgrimage is a good example of a Christian ritual that is closely tied to the practices of an indigenous population.

♦ 0327 ♦ Black Cowboy Parade
First Saturday in October

A salute to the black cowboys who helped settle the West, held since 1975 in Oakland, Calif. Hundreds of mounted cowboys and marching bands participate in the parade, the only one of its kind in the nation. There are also arts and crafts exhibits and food booths.

CONTACTS:
Oakland Black Cowboy Association (OBCA)
P.O. Box 4889
Oakland, CA 94605
www.blackcowboyassociation.org

♦ 0328 ♦ Black Friday
Various

Black Friday usually refers either to the infamous Wall Street Panic of September 24, 1869, when Jay Gould and James Fisk tried to "corner" the gold market, or to September 19, 1873, when stock failures caused the Panic of 1873. In England, it is often used by workers to describe May 12, 1926, the day on which the General Strike was ended. It is occasionally used to refer to GOODFRIDAY.

Shoppers and retailers in the United States sometimes refer to the day after THANKSGIVING as Black Friday because it marks the beginning of the CHRISTMAS commercial season and is traditionally a frenetic day of shopping.

♦ 0329 ♦ Black Hills Passion Play
June-August

One of Europe's oldest productions, the Passion Play—which recreates events during the last seven days of the life of Christ—was first presented on the American stage in 1932. It was brought to the United States from Germany by Josef Meier, who, until his retirement in 1991, continued to produce and direct the drama three nights a week from early June through the end of August in an outdoor amphitheater in Spearfish, South Dakota.

Known as the Black Hills Passion Play since 1939, when the company settled in Spearfish, the huge outdoor production features Roman soldiers on horseback, a camel caravan, and pigeons escaping from cages as merchants and moneylenders are driven from the Temple.

The amphitheater, which seats 6,000, was built specifically for the Passion Play and claims to have the world's largest stage. A series of permanent sets are used to portray Bethany, the home of Mary and Martha; the palace of Pontius Pilate, the Roman governor; the Temple; the Garden of Gethsemane; the Tomb; and Mount Calvary.

CONTACTS:
South Dakota Historical Society Foundation
900 Governors Dr.
Pierre, SD 57501
605-773-3458; fax: 605-773-6041
www.sdhsf.org

♦ 0330 ♦ Black History Month
February

Black History Month grew out of **Negro History Week**, which was established in February 1926 by African-American historian Carter G. Woodson, who founded the Association for the Study of African-American Life and History. Expanded in 1976 to a month-long observance, this celebration of the contributions and achievements of African Americans was initially designed to encompass the birthday of the abolitionist orator and journalist Frederick Douglass (1817-1895) on February 14 as well as Abraham LINCOLN'S BIRTHDAY. The event is widely observed by schools, churches, libraries, clubs, and organizations wishing to draw attention to the contributions of African Americans.

Douglass was a fugitive slave who assumed this name when, by posing as a sailor, he escaped to New Bedford, Massachusetts. His former master's wife had secretly taught him to read and write, and after his escape Douglass became a skilled orator who lectured widely in favor of abolition. He settled for a while in Rochester, New York, where he founded an anti-slavery newspaper, and eventually ended up in Washington, D.C., where he held a number of government positions. One of his former residences there now houses the Museum of African Art and the Frederick Douglass Institute.

CONTACTS:
Association for the Study of African American Life and History (ASALH)
2225 Georgia Ave. N.W.
Ste. 331
Washington, D.C. 20059
202-238-5910
www.asalh.org

♦ 0331 ♦ **Black Madonna of Jasna Gora, Feast of the**
August 15

The most famous icon in Eastern Europe can be found at the monastery on Jasna Gora, in the city of Czestochowa, Poland. The *Czarna Madonna*, or Black Madonna, is so called because of the dark complexion in the portrait of the Virgin Mary that, according to legend, was painted by St. Luke on a linden wood tabletop built by the apprentice carpenter, Jesus of Nazareth. Each year on August 15, the feast of the ASSUMPTION, hundreds of thousands of pilgrims attend the **Feast of Our Lady of Czestochowa** to seek forgiveness for their sins, recovery from injury or illness, or to offer gratitude for a favor granted. With their rosaries in hand, the pilgrims— some on their knees— climb Jasna Gora, which means the "Hill of Light," to attend mass at the monastery, celebrated above them, on the high monastery walls, by priests in golden chasubles.

More than 80 miracles have been documented at the shrine, which is only one of many dedicated to the Virgin Mary throughout the country. King John II Casimir proclaimed the Virgin Mary to be the Queen of Poland in 1656 after an unlikely victory over the Swedes at Jasna Gora prevented the latter from overrunning the monastery and looting its treasures. Mary is the patron saint of Poland, and Assumption Day is a national holiday.

♦ 0332 ♦ **Black Nazarene Fiesta**
January 1-9

The **Fiesta of Quiapo District** is the largest festival in Manila, Philippines. It is held each year in honor of the Quiapo Dis-

trict's patron saint—the Black Nazarene, a life-sized statue of Jesus carved from blackwood, whose shrine is located in Quiapo's baroque church. The traditional nine-day fiesta featuresnightlyculturalevents,bandconcerts,andfireworks. On the last day of the festival there is a procession of barefoot men pulling a carriage that holds the 200-year-old statue of Christ on the way to Calvary. Those members of the procession who are not pulling the carriage carry candles and circle throughout the district.

See also BLACK CHRIST, FESTIVAL OF THE.

CONTACTS:
Minor Basilica of the Black Nazarene
910 Plaza Miranda
P.O. Box 610
Quiapo, Manila Philippines
63-733-4434; fax: 63-735-8614
www.quiapochurch.com

♦ 0333 ♦ **Black Poetry Day**
October 17

Jupiter Hammon, the first African-American poet to publish his own verse, was born on this day in 1711 and lived most of his life in the Lloyd Neck area of Huntington, Long Island. Hammon was a slave—first to the merchant Henry Lloyd, lord of the Manor of Queen's Village (now Lloyd Neck), and later to Joseph Lloyd, an American patriot who moved to Hartford, Connecticut, during the Revolution. Hammon eventually returned to Lloyd Neck as slave to Joseph's grandson, John Lloyd. Hammon learned how to read and was allowed to use his master's library. On Christmas Day, 1760, he published his first poem, "An Evening Thought," at the age of 49. He went on to publish other poems and a number of prose pieces as well.

Black Poetry Day was first proposed in 1970 by Stanley A. Ransom of Huntington, who was concerned that there were no celebrations to honor the contributions African Americans have made to American life and culture. When Ransom relocated to Plattsburgh, New York, he brought Black Poetry Day with him. Although it is celebrated all over the state, it has yet to be formally proclaimed a state holiday. Oregon has already proclaimed October 17 as Black Poetry Day, and schools elsewhere have taken advantage of the opportunity to encourage African-American students to express their thoughts and feelings through poetry. Other celebrations include inviting guest poets to do readings and meet with students at SUNY-Plattsburgh. In 1985, the African-American poet Gwendolyn Brooks spoke at SUNY-Plattsburgh in honor of Jupiter Hammon's contribution to American culture. Other poets who have visited in the past for Black Poetry Day include Nikki Giovanni, Lucille Clifton, Ntozake Shange, Derek Walcott, Michael Harper, and Yusef Komunyakaa. In 1993 Rita Dove, an African American, was named poet laureate of the United States.

CONTACTS:
SUNY Plattsburgh
101 Broad St.
Plattsburgh, NY 12901
518-564-2000

www.plattsburgh.edu
African American Registry
P.O. Box 19441
Minneapolis, MN 55419
612-822-6831
www.aaregistry.org

◆ 0334 ◆ Black Ships Festival
Third weekend in May in Shimoda, Japan; last full weekend in July in Rhode Island

Kurofune is what the Japanese called the black ships that Commodore Matthew C. Perry anchored off Shimoda, Japan, on July 8, 1853. He forcefully negotiated the Treaty of Kanagawa—the first treaty between the United States and Japan— in 1854. The treaty opened trade between the two countries and ended two centuries of self-imposed isolation for Japan.

In 1934, Shimoda began commemorating the arrival of Commodore Perry and his black ships. It is the site of the first American consulate in Japan, placed there by the Japanese to keep the "barbarians" (Americans) away from the capital, then called Edo. The first consul-general, Townsend Harris, arrived in August 1856. Twenty years later, Shimoda became the sister city to Newport, Rhode Island, where Perry was born.

In 1984, Newport began celebrating a reciprocal Black Ships Festival emphasizing Japanese art, culture, and education. Events include Japanese tea ceremonies, ikebana (flower arranging), origami (paper folding), kendo (martial arts), Sumo wrestling, Japanese kite flying, and traditional Japanese performing arts. In 1986 the Black Ships Festival was expanded to form the Japan-America Society of Rhode Island, which now sponsors the festival and works to develop cooperation and understanding between the citizens of Rhode Island and Japan.

CONTACTS:
Marketing & Events, Inc.
28 Pelham St.
Newport, RI 02840
401-847-7666; fax: 401-846-5600
www.newportevents.com

◆ 0335 ◆ Black St. Benito, Fiesta of the
December 29

This fiesta is celebrated by a number of locales in the state of Zulia, Venezuela, and is especially popular in Bobures. The streets are decorated and people adorn the windows of their homes with white flags two days before the fiesta begins, and the events of December 29 are supervised by the *chimbángueles* or vassals of the saint. After early morning mass, the chimbángueles put St. Benito's statue on a litter and surround it with flowers. They then carry it through the streets while performing an unusual bouncing kind of dance in which they continually move forward and backward to the accompaniment of seven drums, each of which sounds a different tone. They are followed by groups of women who shake green branches in the saint's face. Throughout the long procession, St. Benito's image is sprinkled with perfumes and presented with drinks of homemade whiskey.

When Africans first arrived in Venezuela, they formed brotherhoods to help them preserve their ancient religious practices. Today's chimbángueles are direct descendants of these brotherhoods, and their members are divided according to a rigid hierarchy into chiefs, captains, major-domos, and slaves.

◆ 0336 ◆ Black Storytelling Festival and Conference, National
November

The National Association of Black Storytellers meets annually in November for its National Black Storytelling Festival and Conference. The event, open to both performers and listeners, features workshops and performances by a diverse range of storytellers, including those who dance, play instruments, or recite poetry. All are united by an interest in the African and African-American oral tradition. At the conference, daytime workshops are offered in various aspects of storytelling, while evenings are devoted to concert performances and special story-telling circles. A "master liar's contest" is considered a festival favorite. Also on offer is an African-American market place with cultural instruments, clothing, jewelry for sale, as well as demonstrations, games, and casual storytelling.

The National Association of Black Storytellers was founded by storytellers Mary Carter Smith and Linda Goss in 1982. The first festival of black storytelling was held in 1983 in Baltimore, Md. Its festival and conference now draws thousands of participants and listeners.

CONTACTS:
National Association of Black Storytellers, Inc.
P.O. Box 67722
Baltimore, MD 21215
410-947-1117; fax: 410-947-1117
www.nabsinc.org

◆ 0337 ◆ Blackbeard Pirate Festival
a weekend in late May or early June

The Blackbeard Pirate Festival takes place in Hampton, Va., on a two-day weekend in early June. The festival acknowledges Hampton's history as a key colonial port from which tobacco was exported to England and various manufactured commodities were imported into the new world. The area's wealth attracted the notorious 18th-century Caribbean pirate Blackbeard. The dress, music, and customs of swashbucklers like Blackbeard provide the inspiration for this historical event, which aims to recreate waterfront life in Hampton as it was in 1718. The festival launched in 2000.

The event features tours of replicas of three "tall ships" similar to the ones Blackbeard and his mates may have plundered. A street fair offers live music with historical and maritime themes, as well as refreshments and children's events. Several historical re-enactments can include such incidents as an invasion of Hampton Harbor by pirates seeking revenge for Blackbeard's death and a duel between pirates fighting with pistol and cutlass. Visitors can watch demonstrations of 18th-century crafts, navigation, cooking, and medicine at living history exhibits. The event also features a Grand Pirates Ball for adults, and a Saturday night fireworks display.

CONTACTS:
Virginia Tourism Corporation
901 E. Byrd St.
Richmond, VA 23219
800-847-4882
www.virginia.org

♦ 0338 ♦ Blajini, Feast of the (Sarbatoarea Blajinilor)
April-May; second Monday after Easter

Among rural people in Romania there is a widespread belief in the existence of the *Blajini*, the "Meek" or "Kindly Ones"— a lost race who don't understand the ways of human beings, keep to themselves, and live in a fairy-land "by the Sunday-water." They are beloved by God because of their purity and innocence. On the Monday after EASTER MONDAY, Romanian women and children throw red Easter egg shells on running streams, since they believe that all the world streams eventually flow into a single river, alongside of which live the Blajini. Their hope is that the Blajini will find the shells and know it is time to celebrate the EASTER feast.

♦ 0339 ♦ Blavatsky (Helena Petrovna), Death of
May 8

The anniversary of the death of Helena Petrovna Blavatsky (1831-1891) is commemorated by members of the Theosophical Society, which was founded in New York in 1875 by Blavatsky and Henry Olcott. Theosophy, a pantheistic philosophical-religious system that seeks to learn about reality through mystical experience and by finding esoteric meanings in sacred writings, is regarded as the precursor of American Hinduism. Olcott and Blavatsky moved to India in 1878, and the international headquarters for the Theosophical movement remains in Adyar (near Madras) today.

Blavatsky believed that she possessed extraordinary psychic powers, although in 1884 the Indian press accused her of concocting spiritualist phenomena. When the London Society of Psychical Research declared her a fraud the following year, Blavatsky left India and never returned. She did, however, complete her most important work, *The Secret Doctrine* (1888), an overview of Theosophical teachings, along with numerous other books, before her death in 1891.

CONTACTS:
Theosophical Society in America
1926 N. Main St.
P.O. Box 270
Wheaton, IL 60187
630-668-1571 or 800-669-9425; fax: 630-668-4976
www.theosophical.org

♦ 0340 ♦ Blessed Sacrament, Feast of the
Late July to early August

The **Festival of the Blessed Sacrament** held annually in New Bedford, Massachusetts, coincides with a similar festival on the Portuguese island of Madeira. The American festival, which was first held in 1914, celebrates the safe arrival of the Portuguese immigrants who came to New Bedford in the early 19th century after braving rough seas and stormy weather en route.

The descendants of these immigrants, many of whom served aboard American whaleships, give thanks each year by holding what they would like to think of as the largest Portuguese feast in the world on the first weekend in August. Preparations for the festivities go on throughout the year, and the events include a parade, Portuguese folkloric dancers and singers, Portuguese specialties such as *cabra* (goat) and *bacalhau* (codfish), and a colorful procession to the Immaculate Conception Church. The festival is held at Madeira Field, although the events extend throughout the city. New Bedford, once a thriving New England whaling port, remains home to a large Portuguese-American community.

CONTACTS:
Club Madeirense S.S. Sacramento, Inc.
50 Madeira Ave.
New Bedford, MA 02746
508-992-6911
www.portuguesefeast.com

♦ 0341 ♦ Blessing of the Bikes
Between April and June

In 1996, Father Robert McElwee of the Frontenac Sacred Heart Church in Frontenac, Kans., began a Blessing of the Bikes for local motorcycle enthusiasts. Motorcycles are popular in his part of Kansas, and Father McElwee believed that the blessing ceremony would bring some people into church who might not otherwise attend. He held the event in the spring, just as motorcycle riding season begins. The first blessing involved sprinkling holy water on six motorcycles. But over the years the event began to attract thousands of motorcycle enthusiasts from across the country. The Blessing was so popular in 2005 that Father McElwee needed the assistance of two other priests from nearby parishes. The blessing that year took the three men 45 minutes to complete. For 2006, Father McElwee shared the Blessing of the Bikes with churches in the nearby towns of Joplin, Mo., Fort Scott, Kans., and Pittsburg, Kans. Besides motorcycles, people also bring such wheeled vehicles as children's bicycles and wheelchairs to be blessed.

The celebration includes a number of other events throughout the county, including jumps by the Green Beret Parachute Team, races at the Mo-Kan Dragway, a street concert in Pittsburg, and a concert at Foxtown.

While there is no charge to have a bike blessed, sales of related items such as T-shirts, food, and raffles are used to support scholarships at the nearby Harley-Davidson Technical School and local charities.

CONTACTS:
Cathedral Church of St. John the Divine
112th St. & Amsterdam Ave.
New York, NY 10025
theblessingofthebikes.com

♦ 0342 ♦ Blessing of the Grapes (Haghoghy Ortnootyoon)
Sunday nearest August 15

In ancient times people in Armenia dedicated their grape harvest to Astrik, the goddess of the hearth, in a New Year celebration called *Navasard*. Nowadays the festival is associated with the Feast of the ASSUMPTION, and is celebrated on the Sunday nearest August 15, which is the feast day. No one is supposed to eat grapes until this day, when a tray filled with them is blessed in the church. Each member of the congregation is given a bunch of grapes as he or she leaves, and parties are held after the church ceremony in homes and in the vineyards. It is also traditional for women named Mary to entertain their friends on this, their name day.

CONTACTS:
Diocese of the Armenian Church of America (Eastern)
630 Second Ave.
New York, NY 10016
212-686-0710; fax: 212-779-3558
www.armenianchurch-ed.net

♦ 0343 ♦ Blessing of the Shrimp Fleet
First weekend in May

In the coastal town of Bayou La Batre, the "Seafood Capital of Alabama," the shrimp blessing has been celebrated since 1950. It is usually held on the first Sunday in May. The "main street" of the town, founded in 1786, is actually the bayou, where trawlers are often tied up three or four deep. Shrimp is the mainstay of commercial fishing here, and more than 350 shrimp boats work out of the town, while several hundred other vessels operate in the waters off the port harvesting oysters, crab, and finfish. Seafood products landed in the port have a dockside value of $33 million annually, but the total seafood industry,including processors, is thought to produce $300 million for the local economy. Boat building and repair are also major industries.

The fleet blessing began simply: a priest went up and down the bayou blessing the boats tied to the docks. From the start, a wreath has been lowered into the bayou to honor fishermen lost at sea. Now some 25,000 people come for the highlight and final event of the weekend: the blessing ceremony by the priest of St. Margaret Roman Catholic Church and a parade of between 50 and 100 boats decorated with pennants, bunting, and papier mâché figures. Other events include contests in oyster shucking, shrimp heading, and crab picking; seafood and gumbo dinners; a land parade; a fiddler-crab race for children; and the crowning of the Fleet Queen. The affair is sponsored by St. Margaret Church.

In the port city of Biloxi, Mississippi, **Blessing of the Fleet** is a celebration of the start of the fishing season, where seafood is the major industry. It is also held over the first weekend in May. The blessing began in 1924 when sailing craft made up most of the fleet.

Today up to 80 boats parade past the Blessing Boat, where the pastor of St. Michael's Roman Catholic Church (known as the Church of the Fisherman) stands and bestows the blessings. The boats are decorated with flags and elaborate three-dimensional plywood constructions of such figures as mermaids, shrimp, paddlewheels, and fishnets. There are also schooner races, net-throwing and oyster-shucking contests, the crowning of a king and queen, and street dances known as *fais-do-do*. Supposedly "fais-do-do" was the song sung to children to tell them to go to sleep, and the dance got its name because adults danced when the children slept. The weekend also offers lots of local food—mullet, boiled shrimp, and Biloxi bacon.

CONTACTS:
St. Margaret's Catholic Church
13790 S. Wintzell Ave.
Bayou La Batre, AL 36509
251-689-7544
www.fleetblessing.org

St. Michael Catholic Church
177 First St.
P.O. Box 523
Biloxi, MS 39530
228-435-5578; fax: 228-435-5579
www.stmichaelchurchbiloxi.com

♦ 0344 ♦ Blessing the Sun (Birchat Hahamah)
March-April; every 28 years on the first Wednesday in Jewish month of Nisan

According to Jewish tradition, God made the sun, the moon, and the stars on the fourth day of Creation—a Wednesday, according to ancient reckoning—and once every 28 years the sun returns to the same astronomical position that it held on that day. The Talmud says that the turning point of this 28-year sun cycle occurs at the VERNAL EQUINOX on a Tuesday evening (the first in the month of Nisan) at 6:00 P.M. in Jerusalem. But since the sun is not visible at that time in all parts of the world, the blessing isn't recited until the following morning at sunrise. The blessing is said while standing, and the sun must be visible.

The last blessing of the sun occurred on April 8, 1981, with about 50,000 Jews gathered at the Wailing Wall in Jerusalem, Judaism's holiest shrine. Similar celebrations took place on top of Israel's highest building in Tel Aviv and at the Empire State Building in New York City. The next **Blessing of the Sun** will take place in 2009.

♦ 0345 ♦ Bloomsday
June 16

James Joyce's novel *Ulysses* describes the events of a single day in Dublin: June 16, 1904. First published in Paris in 1922 because it had been banned elsewhere, *Ulysses* caused an uproar when it finally did appear in Ireland, and for a time,

Joyce was reviled by the people of Dublin. But since 1954 Bloomsday—named after the novel's main character, Leopold Bloom—has been a Joycean feast day, observed with a number of events throughout Dublin that commemorate its illustrious author and the lives of his characters. There is a ritual pilgrimage along the "Ulysses Trail" (the path followed by Leopold Bloom), public readings from the novel, costume parties, and parades. Joyce fans can visit the Martello Tower, where the author lived, the James Joyce Centre, and Davy Byrne's Pub, where Leopold Bloom stops on his day-long odyssey. Restaurants specialize in serving the dishes that Bloom ate: kidneys for breakfast, gorgonzola cheese and burgundy for lunch.

CONTACTS:
James Joyce Centre
35 N. Great George's St.
Dublin 1 Ireland
353-1-878-8547
jamesjoyce.ie

◆ 0346 ◆ Blowing the Midwinter Horn
December-January; beginning of Advent through Sunday after Epiphany

The custom of **Midwinterhoorn Blazen** in the province of Overijssel, Netherlands, is believed to have originated more than 2,000 years ago. The local farmers make their winter horns out of pieces of curved birch wood. The horns are about 45 inches long and when soaked in water, they produce a piercing wail that carries for miles over the frozen countryside. Although in pagan times the blowing of the horns was thought to rid the earth of evil spirits, today the horns announce the coming of Christ.

In Oldenzaal, a special melody composed by the area's champion hornblower is played from the four corners of the local church tower, beginning at dawn on ADVENT EVE and continuing until THREE KINGS' DAY (EPIPHANY).

CONTACTS:
Foundation Midwinter Blowing Twenthe
Vijverstraat 1
Ootmarsum, Overijssel 7631 Netherlands
31-541-293-374
midwinterhoornblazentwenthe.nl

◆ 0347 ◆ Blue Dragon Festival (Zhonghe Festival)
Second day of the second lunar month

The Blue Dragon Festival, or the **Zhonghe Festival,** is an annual celebration that heralds the arrival of the rainy season at the end of winter. Dragons, an important symbol in Chinese culture, have long been linked to the elements of nature. The ancient Chinese venerated a dragon symbol on the banks of a lake or river, praying for the spring rain to nurture their fields. The tradition of celebrating the end of winter and the beginning of spring with a dragon festival has continued throughout China, with many provinces across the country maintaining their own distinctive traditions to observe the day. During the festival, people prepare food shaped like the different parts of a dragon: pancakes (the scales), pig's head

(the head), and dumplings (the ears). In China's Shandong province, a mule and horse fair coincides with the Blue Dragon Festival, while in the Shanxi province, people get a haircut—a symbolic act of discarding the old and ringing in the new. As part of the festival in the Chinese countryside, people traditionally rise at dawn to fetch water from the well. They believe that the well is filled with dragon's eggs, and that bringing the eggs home will ensure good fortune for the family in the coming year.

CONTACTS:
China National Tourist Office
370 Lexington Ave.
Ste. 912
New York, NY 10017
212-760-8218; fax: 212-760-8809
www.cnto.org

◆ 0348 ◆ Boat Race Day (Okinawa, Japan)
May; 14th day of fifth lunar month

On Okinawa, the largest of the Ryukyu Islands southwest of Japan, the 14th day of the fifth month is both a religious festival and a sporting event. In Minatogawa, for example, this is the **Festival of the Gods of the Sea**. The villagers first go to the religious sites to make offerings and pray, and then they attend the boat races held in the estuary of the river. In Taira, it is the day on which fishing canoes from Taira race against competitors from the neighboring village of Kawata.

◆ 0349 ◆ Boat Race Day (Thames River)
Late March or early April

This is the annual rowing race between the Oxford and Cambridge University "eights" (as the crews of the eight-oared rowing shells are called) that takes place on the Thames River in England. The race is scheduled to be held on a day when there's an incoming spring tide, which usually occurs in late March or early April. Beginning in Putney and ending four-and-a-half miles downriver at Mortlake, the race attracts large crowds of spectators—many of whom are hoping for the drama of an unexpected capsizing.

CONTACTS:
Great River Race
Taggs Boatyard
44 Summer Rd.
Thames Ditton, Surrey KT7 0QQ United Kingdom
44-20-8398-8141
www.greatriverrace.co.uk

◆ 0350 ◆ Bocuse d'Or
January in odd-numbered years

One of the most prestigious cooking competitions in the world, the Bocuse d'Or is a biennial event that takes place in the historic city of Lyon, France. Named in honor of the event's founder, the famous French chef and gastronome Paul Bocuse, the inaugural Bocuse d'Or took place in 1987. The competition, which features customs and media coverage more commonly found in sporting events, is regarded by many to be the equivalent of a culinary Olympics.In its original format, the Bocuse d'Or brought together 24 chefs from around the world to prepare dishes in a timed competition in front of an audience and a jury of international chefs. Growing interest in the event over the years led to the sponsors to establish over 60 pre-selection events across the continents; top teams from the pre-competition events are chosen to represent 24 countries in the finals. The ultimate competition takes place in a kitchen theater and is witnessed by an audience of spectators and media, along with a 24-member jury. Each team is comprised of a senior and an assistant chef, along with a coach who may communicate with the chefs from an adjacent area. Teams are given 5 hours and 35 minutes to prepare a meat dish and a fish dish, which are judged on their technical skill, creativity, and aesthetics of presentation. The team with the highest overall score receives prize money and a golden statuette of Paul Bocuse.

CONTACTS:
Eurexpo
Boulevard de l'Europe
Chassieu, 69680 France
33-4-7277-6969
www.bocusedor.com

♦ 0351 ♦ **Bodhi Day (Rohatsu)**
December 8

In Japan and other Mahayana Buddhist countries, the enlightenment of the Buddha is celebrated on December 8th as Bodhi Day (Rohatsu).In Japanese, Rohatsu literally translates to *eighth day of the twelfth month*. For a week between the first and eighth of December, monks in Zen monasteries follow the example of the Buddha and participate in a *sesshin*, an intensive retreat in which all of one's time is devoted to meditation, culminating on the final day with Rohatsu. In Theravada Buddhist countries, the anniversaries of Buddha's birth, enlightenment, and death are all observed on Vesak.

Born into a noble family, Siddhartha Guatama (563-483 B.C.E.), set out to find the root cause of the suffering he had witnessed among the commoners. After six years of searching for answers, he sat in mediation under a Bodhi tree and vowed not to rise until he achieved the wisdom he sought. At the end of the eighth day, Siddhartha Guatama attained enlightenment and became the Buddha or 'the awakened one.' In his meditative state, the Buddha is said to have become aware of the principles through which one could be liberated from suffering and achieve nirvana, a state of bliss resulting from the elimination of desire. The Buddha spent the rest of his life disseminating the knowledge he attained.Buddhists all over the world sit in mediation and prayer on Bodhi day. Some may eat rice and milk to symbolize the meal Sujata offered an emaciated Siddhartha Guatama during his meditation to help him regain his strength. It is also customary to light candles in the home, and to string lights on a small fiscus tree, for 30 days to symbolize enlightenment. Families and children will also often make leaf-shaped cookies to represent the Bodhi tree.

♦ 0352 ♦ **Bog Snorkelling Championship, World**
Last Monday in August

Peat bogs are areas of wetlands that are plentiful around the United Kingdom, so in the 1980s folks in the small town of Llanwrtyd Wells, Wales, decided to make annual, if wacky, use of one. They clear a 60-yard path through the black, smelly waters of the Waen Rhydd peat bog outside town. Competitors must traverse the trench twice using any but standard swim strokes. Snorkels and flippers are required wear. A newer event takes place in the same bog in July—the World Mountain Bike Bog Snorkelling Championship; participants in this race can skip the flippers, but still must wear snorkels, as they try to cycle two lengths in the fastest time.

CONTACTS:
Llanwrtyd Tourist Information
Neuadd Arms Hotel
The Square
Llanwrtyd Wells, Wales LD5 4RB United Kingdom
44-1591-610666
www.llanwrtyd.com

♦ 0353 ♦ **Boganda Day**
March 29

In the Central African Republic, Boganda Day marks the anniversary of the death of Barthélémy Boganda, the nation's first prime minister. Boganda was killed in a plane crash on March 29, 1959. He had been a driving force in the creation of the Central African Republic, which became a self-governing republic in 1958. Boganda was also a leader in the movement to unite black African nations. He designed his new country's green, yellow and red flag to represent the ideal of African unity. Boganda was flying between cities in the Central African Republic when his plane went down. At the time of the accident, there was of speculation that sabotage caused the crash.

Boganda Day is a national holiday in the Central African Republic. All banks, official government offices, businesses, and schools are closed.

CONTACTS:
Central African Republic Embassy
2704 Ontario Rd.
Washington, D.C. 20009
202-483-7800; fax: 202-332-9893
www.rcawashington.org

♦ 0354 ♦ **Boggy Bayou Mullet Festival**
Third full weekend in October

A festival of seafood, folk culture, sports, and pageants, the Boggy Bayou Mullet Festival has been held since 1976 in Niceville, Fla. It celebrates the unappreciated mullet, the underdog of seafood, and serves up 10 tons of fried and smoked mullet, plus vast quantities of "mullet dogs," mullet filets on buns. Attendance can reach upwards of 200,000.

Niceville is a small town about 50 miles east of Pensacola in the Florida panhandle. But people kept calling Niceville "Nashville," so, to publicize the town and to promote mullet the Boggy Bayou Festival was begun. Mullet, abundant in the local Gulf waters, is a cheap source of high-quality protein but has had a bad reputation among seafood fanciers because of its feeding habits. Mullet are bottom-feeding vegetarians, and they taste like what they eat. The people of Niceville know that only mullet caught from waters with clean bottoms—like those on Florida's Gulf Coast—are worth eating.

This sleepy bayou town's festival has exploded into a fully rounded affair. It has beauty pageants to name not only the Queen of the Mullet Festival but also Miss Teen Mullet Festival, Junior Miss Mullet Festival, and Little Miss Mullet Festival. Entertainment is on stage all weekend and arts and crafts are on display. Then there is the food. Beyond the mullet, these are samplings from the food booths: Cajun specialties like crawfish pie, gumbo, and gator sausage; American Indian staples of fried bread and *pasole*, which is like pizza; barbecued rabbit, stingray and barracuda on a stick, fried oysters, boiled shrimp, apple dumplings, strawberry pie, and Mexican fried ice cream.

CONTACTS:
Boggy Bayou Mullet Festival Council, Inc.
85 N. Hwy. and College Blvd.
Niceville, FL
mulletfestival.com

♦ 0355 ♦ **Bok Kai Festival**
Usually February or March; second day of second month of Chinese lunar year

The Bok Kai Festival is a two-day event in Marysville, Calif., that began as a Chinese religious event to honor Bok Eye (or Bok I), the god who has the power to control flooding and the waters of irrigation and the rains. The festival, held since the 1880s, is now more of a cultural tribute to the Bok Kai legend.

Chinese immigrants came to northern California in the 1850s to find work in the gold fields or on the railroads being built through the Sierra Nevada mountains. When the railroads were completed, they settled in Marysville, whichbecame the third largest Chinese community in the country, after San Francisco and Sacramento.

Between 1825 and 1862, three floods caused hundreds of fatalities in the Marysville area. In 1865, the Chinese first built a temple on the Yuba River, naming it Bok Kai Mui, meaning temple (Mui) on the north (Bok) side of the stream (Kai). (The temple was destroyed by fire and rebuilt in 1880.) Several gods were placed in the temple, but Bok Eye, meaning Northern or Dark North God, was the central deity. By building the temple in his honor, the Chinese people hoped to protect the city from future flooding.

The celebration of **Bomb Day**—Bok Eye's birthday—began in the 1880s. Today the celebration of Bomb Day with the Bok Kai Festival is a community-wide affair, drawing thousands of visitors from as far as Hong Kong. The day is named for the bombs, huge firecrackers that are fired off during the festival. A parade is another highlight of the festival, and a 150-foot dragon is the highlight of the parade. It winds its way along the parade route on the legs of 100 volunteers, accompanied by floats and marching bands, Clydesdale horses and a Wells

Fargo stagecoach—more than 100 entries in all. The current dragon is the second one to be used in the parade. The first, brought to the United States before 1900, was retired in 1937 and now rests in the temple.

Besides the parade, there are vendors' markets for foods and crafts, demonstrations of martial arts, lion dancing, art displays, and performances by celebrated Chinese artists; these have included a master of Chinese brush painting, a pianist from China, and a composer and poet.

The Bok Kai Temple in Marysville is the only religious shrine to Bok Eye outside of Asia and is a designated historical land-mark.

♦ 0356 ♦ **Bolivia Independence Day**
August 6

Bolivians proclaimed their independence from Spain in 1809, but it took 16 years of struggle to actually gain it in 1825. Spain had ruled the area since the 16th century. The country was named for its revolutionary hero, Simon Bolívar, who, with José SAN MARTÍN, led the Battle of Ayacucho in 1824 that resulted in the end of Spanish rule of Bolivia and Peru.

Independence Day is a public holiday, celebrated over two days including August 6, with parades and dancing in the streets of La Paz and Sucre.

CONTACTS:
Embassy of Bolivia
3014 Massachusetts Ave. N.W.
Washington, D.C. 20008
202-483-4410; fax: 202-328-3712
www.bolivia-usa.org

♦ 0357 ♦ **Bologna Festival**
Last full weekend in July

In 1906 a bologna maker named T. J. Minnie set up his shop in Yale, Michigan. Over the next several decades, a number of other bologna makers settled in Yale, but today only one remains: C. Roy Inc., which produces Yale Bologna. The annual Bologna Festival, established in 1989, is designed to attract true bologna lovers with its booths serving bologna rings, bologna hot dogs, bologna and sauerkraut, and fried bologna sandwiches. A King and Queen Bologna are crowned, and they ride through town on the C. Roy float in the Big Bologna Parade wearing crowns made out of bologna rings.

CONTACTS:
C. Roy Processing, Inc.
444 Roy Dr.
Yale, MI 48097
810-387-3957
croyinc.com

Yale Area Chamber of Commerce
212 S. Main St.
P.O. Box 59
Yale, MI 48097
810-387-9253
www.yalechamber.com

♦ 0358 ♦ Bolshevik Revolution Day
November 7

Bolshevik Revolution Day commemorates the October Revolution of 1917, when the Bolsheviks overthrew the Russian government by seizing power in Petrograd (formerly St. Petersburg, later named Leningrad, and in 1991, after the collapse of the Communist Party, renamed St. Petersburg). The coup took place on November 7 (October 25 on the Julian calendar) and through the years was celebrated as a national holiday marking the start of the Soviet regime. Celebrations were particularly lavish in Moscow, with grand military parades and fly-overs and the Soviet leadership reviewing the parade from atop the Lenin Mausoleum. In Leningrad, the Soviet Baltic fleet sailed up the Neva to drop anchor across from the Winter Palace.

All this ended in 1991. With the Soviet Union disintegrating, the state holiday was still in place, but marches and demonstrations were banned in Moscow. In the newly renamed St. Petersburg, Mayor Anatoly A. Sobchak attended Russian Orthodox services (formerly forbidden) with the Grand Duke Vladimir Kirillovich Romanov, son of a cousin of the last czar.

CONTACTS:
Consulate of the Russian Federation in Houston
1333 W. Loop S.
Ste 1300
Houston, TX 77027
713-337-3300; fax: 713-337-3305
www.rusconhouston.mid.ru

♦ 0359 ♦ Bom Jesus dos Navegantes
January 1

In Salvador, Brazil, the festival known as Bom Jesus dos Navegantes is celebrated on NEW YEAR'S DAY. A procession of small boats decorated with flags and streamers carries a statue of the **Lord Jesus of Seafarers** from the main harbor to the outlying beach of Boa Viagem. Thousands of spectators line Salvador's beaches to catch a glimpse of the spectacle. According to legend, sailors participating in the event will never die by drowning.

A similar procession takes place on the same day in Angra dos Reis, 90 miles south of Rio de Janeiro.

♦ 0360 ♦ Bombing of Darwin, Anniversary of the
February 19

On February 19, 1942, Japanese bomber and fighter planes conducted a devastating air raid on the town of Darwin, the capital city of Australia's Northern Territory. A total of 243 people—service personnel and civilians—died in the attack, which was the first of a long series of bomb raids that the Japanese launched on Darwin and nearby locations during World War II. The bombing on Darwin was the first attack during the war on Australian soil, and it is sometimes called the "Pearl Harbor of Australia," a reference to the Japanese attack on Hawaii in December 1941.

As a tribute to honor the dead and to remember those who defended Darwin, an annual commemoration is held in Bi-centennial Park by the Cenotaph, a marble monument to those slain in World War I. The service begins at 9:30 A.M., and at 9:58, the exact time the attack began in 1942, a World War II air raid siren sounds. During some observances, Australian regiments will re-enact the historic attack. Ground units will shoot their guns, and fighter planes will perform fly-bys over the memorial site.

CONTACTS:
Office of the Official Secretary to the Governor General of Australia
Government House
Dunrossil Dr.
Yarralumla, ACT 2600 Australia
61-2-6283-3533; fax: 61-2-6281-3760
www.gg.gov.au

Freedom of Information, Department of Defence
The Secretary, Campbell Park Offices
Northcott Dr.
Canberra, ACT 2610 Australia
61-2-626-63006; fax: 61-2-6266-2112
www.defence.gov.au

♦ 0361 ♦ Bona Dea Festival
May 1

The ancient Roman festival known as the Bona Dea, or **Maia Maiesta Festival**, was celebrated only by women; no men were allowed to observe or participate in the festivities. Variously described as the sister, daughter, or wife of Faunus, the rustic Roman fertility god, Bona Dea was a deified woman, a chaste matron who was killed by a suspicious husband. Because she revealed her prophesies only to women, Bona Dea's temple was cared for by women, and all of her rites were restricted to women.

The festival of Bona Dea was observed on May 1, the day on which her temple had been dedicated on the Aventine Hill in Rome. The ceremonies were performed by vestal virgins and a group of very respectable matrons, although the rituals associated with the festival apparently included remnants of phallic worship and the telling of indecencies which were not to be repeated to the uninitiated. The observance of the Bona Dea festival undoubtedly contributed to the Roman belief that May was an unlucky month for marriage.

See also MEGALESIA and OPALIA.

♦ 0362 ♦ Bonalu
June-July; Hindu month of Ashada

Bonalu is a month-long religious festival in the southern Indian state of Telengana. Dedicated to goddess Mahakali, an important deity in the Hindu pantheon, the celebration dates back to the early 19th century during a plague epidemic. Legend has it that prayers to Mahakali ended the outbreak, prompting an annual tradition of thanksgiving at various temples across the area. Food is the most significant element of the Bonalu festival. Dressed in finery, women and girls carry brass or earthenware pots filled with rice pudding on their heads to area temples, where devotees welcome them.

The women, who are believed to possess the spirit of the goddess Mahakali, carry the *bonam* (meal) atop their heads, accompanied by a procession of drummers and the temple priest, who carries a copper pot adorned with goddess iconography called the *ghatam*. During such processions, people commonly undergo trance-like states and claim to be oracles. At the culmination of the celebration, all of the *ghatams* from the many temples in the area are carried on richly dressed elephants, converging at the Musi River for a final ritual amid great fanfare.

CONTACTS:
Telangana Tourism Department
"D" Block, 3rd Fl., Secretariat
Hyderabad, Telangana 500 022 India
www.telanganatourism.gov.in

♦ 0363 ♦ **Bonden Festival (Bonden Matsuri)**
February 16-17

At the Bonden (or Bonten) Festival at Yokote in the Akita Prefecture of Japan, each district of the city has a team of 20-30 young men to carry its *bonden* in a race to the Asahio-kayama-jinja shrine. The bonden is a ten-foot bamboo pole, draped with heavy cloth and topped by a circular platform holding a figure of the Animal of the Year, a custom inspired by the traditional east Asian calendar in which each year is named after a particular animal (the rat, ox, tiger, rabbit, dragon, snake, horse, monkey, cock, dog, or boar). As the groups make their way through the city, several from each team carry the bonden, passing it to teammates when they tire. Those carrying the bonden shake and spin it as they go, gradually increasing their pace until, at the end, they are running. The steep incline that leads to the Shinto shrine constitutes the last leg of the race. Here the racers begin to jostle one another, often pushing members of competing teams to the ground in a frenzy to be the first to the top. The team that arrives first wins the privilege of offering its bonden to the *kami*, or god.

There are bonden festivals elsewhere in Japan. At the Kawawatari Bonden Festival, for example, the bonden must be ferried across the river to a shrine on the far bank.

CONTACTS:
Japan National Tourism Organization
1 Grand Central Pl.
60 E. 42nd St.
Ste. 448
New York, NY 10165
212-757-5640; fax: 212-307-6754
www.jnto.go.jp

♦ 0364 ♦ **Bonfim Festival (Festa do Bonfim)**
January; one week to 10 days ending the second Sunday after Epiphany, January 6

There is a church in Salvador, Bahia, Brazil, known as Our Lord of the Happy Ending (*bonfim*). It was built by the captain of a ship that was wrecked off the coast of Bahia in 1875. The captain promised God that if his men survived, he would build a church in gratitude. Today during the Bonfim Festival, hundreds of Brazilian women dress in the traditional white dresses of colonial Bahia and form a procession to the church. The *bahianas* balance jars of water, scented with blossoms, on their heads. The washing of the steps at Bonfim Basilica on the second Thursday after Epiphany is the highlight of the festival.

Though Brazil is nominally a Roman Catholic country, many Brazilians adhere to various Afro-Brazilian cults. Candomblé is one such belief system popular in Bahia, and the Lord of the Happy Ending is Oxalá, a Candomblé deity.

CONTACTS:
Bahia Tourism Authority
Ave. Simon Bolivar
600 - Bahia Convention Center
Salvador, Bahia 41750-230 Brazil
55-71-3117-3000; fax: 55-71-3371-0110
bahia.com.br

♦ 0365 ♦ **Bonfire Night**
Various

There are a number of holidays that are referred to by this name. Guy Fawkes Day (November 5) in England is sometimes called Bonfire Night, and in Scotland the name is applied to the Monday nearest May 24th, the former Empire Day (*see* Commonwealth Day). The original bonfires were actually "bone-fires" in which human or animal bones were burned to appease the gods. But nowadays bonfires are lit primarily for amusement. Other traditional bonfire nights include June 23, the eve of Midsummer Day, when fires were lit to cure disease and ward off evil spirits, and the Winter Solstice, when bonfires heralded the return of the sun.

♦ 0366 ♦ **Bonifacio Day**
November 30

Bonifacio Day commemorates the birthday of Andres Bonifacio y de Castro (1863-1897), a nationalist and revolutionary who many consider to be the father of the Philippine revolution. Since 1921, Bonifacio Day has been a national holiday in the Philippines, and many people visit monuments dedicated to Bonifacio to mark the occasion. In 1892, Andres Bonifacio founded a secret society called the "Katipunan," which led an armed insurgence against the Spanish colonial rulers in the Philippines. Through the Katipunan, Bonifacio inspired the growth of a nationwide movement, and eventually became commander and chief of a revolutionary army. Over time, the Katipunan broke into factions and Bonifacio battled for control with one of his lieutenants, Emilio Aguinaldo, each in charge of competing groups of rebel forces. At the rebels' convention at Terjeros, Aguinaldo secret took an oath as President and Bonifacio refused to recognize the rebel government he formed. Bonifacio was later arrested, tried for treason, and executed on May 10, 1897.

Although it remains controversial that Bonifacio was executed at the hands of rivals in the revolution itself, he is viewed as a treasured national hero in the Philippines who launched the revolution and inspired others to fight for freedom.

CONTACTS:
Department Of Tourism
DOT Bldg., T.M. Kalaw St.
Agrifina Cir.
Manila 1000 Philippines
632-523-8411
www.gov.ph

♦ 0367 ♦ Bonneville Speed Week
Seven Days in August

Bonneville Speed Week is a competition to set speed records on the Bonneville Salt Flats near Wendover, Utah (now called the **World of Speed**). The salt flats were once under Lake Bonneville, which was formed about two million years ago and covered 19,000 square miles in what are now Utah, Nevada, and Idaho. The Great Salt Lake to the east of the flats is all that remains of that prehistoric lake. Bonneville is so flat that it is the only place in the United States where the curvature of the earth can be seen. Its salt surface is as hard as concrete by summer 's end, and the many miles of unobstructed space create an anomaly of nature found nowhere else in the world. These conditions are ideal for land speed racing.

Speed Week has been held since 1949. About 300 cars and motorcycles come here from all over the world to try to break land speed records. The current one-mile automobile speed record was set on October 15, 1997 by Britain's Andy Greene. Greene zipped over the flats in the ThrustSSC at 763.035 mph, the first time the sound barrier was broken on land. The first person to set a speed record on the Bonneville Salt Flats was Teddy Tetzlaff who drove a Blitzen Benz 141 mph in 1914.

CONTACTS:
Utah Salt Flats Racing Association
P.O. Box 27365
Salt Lake City, UT 84127
801-485-2662 or 801-583-3765
www.saltflats.com

♦ 0368 ♦ Boone (Daniel) Festival
First full week in October

Held annually since 1948 in Barbourville, Kentucky, this week-long festival honors the frontiersman Daniel Boone (1734-1820), who in 1775 was the first to carve a trail through the Appalachian Mountains from eastern Tennessee all the way to the Ohio River. For 50 years Boone's "Wilderness Road" was the major route for settlers heading west.

An important part of the festival is the signing of the Cherokee Cane Treaty. Descendants of the original Cherokees who hid in the Smoky Mountains to avoid being forced to move to Oklahoma in 1838-39 sign a treaty each year that provides them with cane, which still grows along the Cumberland River, that they can use to make baskets. Other festival events include an old-fashioned barbecue featuring pioneer and American Indian foods, traditional Indian dances, a long-rifle shoot, and competitions in such activities as hog-calling, wood-chopping, and fiddling.

CONTACTS:
Daniel Boone Festival Inc.
606-627-1750
www.danielboonefestival.com

♦ 0369 ♦ Borglum (Gutzon) Day
August 10

On this day in 1927, sculptor John Gutzon de la Mothe Borglum began carving the faces of four American presidents out of Mount Rushmore in the Black Hills of SouthDakota.

He chose this site because of its smooth-grained granite and the way it dominated the surrounding terrain. It took 14 years to bring the mountain sculpture to its present appearance, but because of delays caused by lack of funds and bad weather, only six and a half years were actually spent in carving. Gutzon Borglum died before the national memorial could be completed, but his son, Lincoln, continued to work on the project until funds ran out in 1941. Since that time no additional carving has been done, nor is any further work planned other than maintenance of the memorial.

The four presidents whose faces emerge from the granite cliffs were chosen as symbols of the birth and growth of the United States during its first 150 years. George WASHINGTON signifies the struggle for independence and the birth of the republic, Thomas JEFFERSON the idea of representative government, Abraham LINCOLN the permanent union of the States and equality for all citizens, and Theodore Roosevelt the 20th-century role of the U.S. in world affairs.

August 10 is observed at Mount Rushmore each year with patriotic music and speeches. The 50th anniversary celebration in 1991 included a formal dedication of the monument and a summer-long extravaganza featuring appearances by former presidents, television personalities, and famous South Dakotans.

CONTACTS:
Mount Rushmore National Memorial
13000 Hwy. 244
Bldg. 31, Ste. 1
Keystone, SD 57751
605-574-2523; fax: 605-574-2307
www.nps.gov
Keystone Chamber of Commerce
110 Swanzey St.
P.O. Box 653
Keystone, SD 57751
605-666-4896 or 800-456-3345
www.keystonechamber.com

♦ 0370 ♦ Borrowed Days
March 29, 30, 31

According to an old Scottish rhyme, the last three days in March were "borrowed" from April, in return for which March promised to destroy three young sheep. But the weather proved to be an obstacle, and the promise was never fulfilled. Other references to the **Borrowing Days** go back even farther. Both an ancient calendar of the Church of Rome and a 1548 book known as the *Complaynt of Scotland* allude to the days at the end of March as being more like winter than spring. Whatever their origin, it seems likely that the wet, windy weather that so often comes at the end of March gave rise to the notion that this month had to "borrow" some additional time.

In the Scottish Highlands, there is an ancient belief that February 12, 13, and 14 were "borrowed" from January, and that it was a good omen for the rest of the year if the weather was as stormy as possible on these days. But if they were fair, no further good weather could be expected through the spring.

♦ 0371 ♦ **Boryeong Mud Festival**
July

The Boryeong Mud Festival takes place in the coastal town of Daecheon, South Korea. First held in 1998, the ten-day event centers on the Boryeong mud flats and attracts millions of people every year. The mineral-rich mud of the region is used in cosmetics due to its therapeutic properties. The event's focal point is Daecheon Beach, where mud from the flats is transported and people enjoy a host of activities, including mud wrestling, a mud pool, a mud prison, mud slides, and mud skiing. Besides mud baths and other cosmetic treatments, participants of the festival experience live music, beauty contests, beach sports, and spectacular pyrotechnical shows.

CONTACTS:
Boryeong Mud Festival Organizing Committee
Daecheon Beach Mud Plaza
Boryeong South Korea
82-10-5438-4865
www.boryeongmudfestival.com

♦ 0372 ♦ **Bosnia and Herzegovina Statehood Day**
November 25

Bosnia and Herzegovina are two adjoining regions in the Balkans that were ruled by Croatian kings in medieval times. They were united into a province under the Turkish Ottoman Empire. From Turkish control, the area passed into Austria-Hungary's realm until Bosnia became part of Yugoslavia in 1918. It was in the capital city of Sarajevo that Austrian Archduke Ferdinand was assassinated, sparking the first World War.

Statehood Day commemorates the November 25, 1943, assembly of the first joint Bosnian and Herzegovinan parliament. In 1946 Bosnia and Herzegovina became part of the newly formed Yugoslav federation.

Bosnia and Herzegovina declared independence from Yugoslavia on March 1, 1992. Bloody conflict between Serbs, Muslims, and Croats escalated into a Serbian ethnic cleansing program to oust the Muslim and Croatian populations, which NATO peacekeeping troops, deployed in 1995-96, stemmed. In March 1994 the Croat and Muslim factions signed an agreement to be united into the Federation of Bosnia and Herzegovina. The Dayton Agreement of December

14, 1995, established a democratic government and constitution.

CONTACTS:
Advisory Council for Bosnia and Herzegovina
1510 H St. N.W.
Ste. 900
Washington, D.C. 20005
202-347-6742
acbih.org
Embassy of Bosnia and Herzegovina
2109 E. St. N.W.
Washington, D.C. 20037
202-337-1500; fax: 202-337-1502
www.bhembassy.org

♦ 0373 ♦ **Bosra Festival**
September 1-10

The city of Bosra, Syria, holds an arts festival during the first 10 days of September. Begun in 1985, the festival features singers, poets, and other performing artists from the Middle East and beyond. Visitors also enjoy displays of visual arts and handicrafts.

♦ 0374 ♦ **Boston Jewish Film Festival**
November

The Boston Jewish Film Festival is an annual, non-competitive film festival that features contemporary cinema based on Jewish themes from around the world. Through its screenings, the festival explores such themes as Jewish identity, its rich culture, and the Jewish experience in relation to world cultures. Films range in subject from the history of the Jews across various countries, to the LGBTQ Jewish experience, to relations between Israelis and Palestinians. The festival is noted for the quality of films that are screened, some of which have gone on to receive honors at the Academy Awards. Although the festival is non-competitive, audience members are given the opportunity to cast ballots for favorite feature film, short film, and documentary. Introductions by visiting artists, question-and-answer sessions, panel discussions, pre-screening music, post-screening concerts, and dance performances are some of the events included at the festival in addition to the screenings.The festival was founded by filmmaker Michal Goldman in 1989, and it has grown from an initial ten screenings to 50 screenings in venues across greater Boston. Over the years, the film festival and its directors have been honored by critics and organizations for their excellence.

CONTACTS:
Boston Jewish Film Festival
1001 Watertown St.
2nd Fl.
West Newton, MA 02465
617-244-9899; fax: 617-244-9894
www.bjff.org

♦ 0375 ♦ **Boston Marathon**
Third Monday in April

The oldest footrace in the United States was first held on PATRIOTS' DAY, April 19, 1897. Organized by members of the Boston Athletic Association (BAA), the race involved only 15 runners. In the 2015 Boston Marathon, 30,000 runners were allowed to participate in the race, with 24,000 spots reserved for time qualifiers. Several thousand additional runners routinely participate on an unofficial basis.

In 1972, it became the first marathon to officially admit women runners, and in 1975 a wheelchair division was created.

The 26.2-mile course begins exactly at noon in Hopkinton, Massachusetts, includes the infamous "Heartbreak Hill" (a section of Commonwealth Avenue in Newton Centre, Massachusetts, that marks the race's 21st mile), and ends near Copley Square in the Back Bay Area.

Well-known American winners of the Boston Marathon include the "old" John Kelley, who won twice and last completed the race in 1992 when he was 84; the "young" John J. Kelley (no relation), who was the first American victor in the post-World War II era; and "Tarzan" Brown, who in 1938 took a break at the nine-mile mark for a quick swim in Lake Cochichuate.

 Among the women, Rosa Mota of Portugal was the first to win three official Boston Marathon titles, though her feat was topped in 2005 by Catherine Ndereba of Kenya, who became the first woman to win four official titles. Rita Jeptoo of Kenya set a women's course record of 2 hours, 18 minutes and 57 seconds during her third marathon win in 2014.

By 1988 the Boston Marathon became the OLYMPIC Marathon trial for nine African countries, leading to what organizers call "the African running revolution." In 1988, a Kenyan runner, Ibrahim Hussein, won the Marathon, becoming the first African to do so. Since then, from 1988 to 2014, all but three winners in the men's division hailed from Africa, including four Ethiopians and the rest of the winners coming from Kenya. Other than the 1990 win by Italian Gelindo Bordin, the 2001 win by Lee Bong-Ju of South Korea, and the 2014 victory by Meb Keflezighi of the United States, the men's field has been dominated by Africans. In 2011, Geoffrey Mutai of Kenya delivering a record-breaking time of 2:03:02 that stands to this day.

CONTACTS:
Boston Athletic Association
185 Dartmouth St.
6th Fl.
Boston, MA 02116
617-236-1652; fax: 617-236-4505
www.baa.org

♦ 0376 ♦ Boston Massacre Day
March 5

Once observed in New Jersey as **Crispus Attucks Day**, March 5 marks the anniversary of the 1770 street fight between a group of colonial American protesters and a squad of British troops quartered inBoston—aneventthatreflected the unpopularity of the British regime in colonial Ameri-

ca and set the stage for the American Revolution. A British sentry was pelted with stones and snowballs by a mob of about 50 people. He called for help, and Captain Thomas Preston sent several soldiers. The soldiers fired and five of the protesters were killed. One of them was Crispus Attucks, a runaway slave who'd spent 20 years as a whaleman. It was Attucks who led the crowd from Dock Square to King Street (now State Street), where the confrontation occurred, and who later became known as the first martyr of the American Revolution.

The name "Boston Massacre" was invented by the colonists and used as propaganda to force the removal of the British troops.

In Massachusetts, the anniversary of the Boston Massacre is observed annually with patriotic songs and speeches recalling Attucks's sacrifice. On the 200th anniversary of the massacre in 1970, and again five years later on the 200th anniversary of the outbreak of the Revolutionary War, the Charlestown Militia Company staged a reenactment of the event.

CONTACTS:
Boston National Historical Park
Charlestown Navy Yard
Boston, MA 02129
617-242-5642 or 617-242-5601
www.nps.gov

The Library of Congress
101 Independence Ave. S.E.
Washington, D.C. 20540
202-707-5000
www.loc.gov

♦ 0377 ♦ Boston Pops
First week in May through middle of July

Henry Lee Higginson, who established the Boston Symphony Orchestra in 1881 to provide culture-hungry Bostonians with classical music, nonetheless believed that in the summer, "concerts of a lighter kind of music" should be presented. On July 11, 1885, his idea became a reality when the audience enjoyed refreshments along with light classics at the first Promenade Concert, held at the Boston Music Hall. It wasn't long before people began to refer fondly to these summer music concerts as "the Pops," a name which became official in 1900. That same year, the Pops moved into the newly built Symphony Hall, which has been its home ever since.

World-class acoustics and the accommodation of cabaret-style seating have made Symphony Hall the perfect indoor venue for the Boston Pops for over one hundred years. Arthur Fiedler led the orchestra into a new era when he was appointed conductor in 1930. Under Fiedler 's direction, the Pops gained a wider audience and national recognition via radio broadcasts (instituted in 1952) and public television presentations (beginning in 1970). In the mid-1970s, two new Pops traditions were established: "Boston's FOURTH OF JULY" on the Charles River ESPLANADE, and Christmas Pops concerts. Composer John Williams, best known for his film scores, was named conductor of the Pops in 1980 after Fiedler 's death. He was succeeded in 1995 by Keith Lockhart, who has led more than 1,500 Boston Pops concerts since arriving from the Cincinnati Pops Orchestra and is now in his nineteenth season as conductor.

Throughout its history the Boston Pops has tailored its programs around American music and musicians, medleys of popular songs, and familiar movements of favorite classical works, and it has featured such artists as Leontyne Price, Itzhak Perlman, Mandy Patinkin, Joel Grey, Doc Severinsen, and Cleo Laine, Susan Tedeschi, Jennifer Hudson, Toby Keith, Neil Diamond, Rascal Flatts, The Dropkick Murphys, Ben Folds, Aimee Mann, Elvis Costello, My Morning Jacket, and The Beach Boys.

Outside of its official concert season at Symphony Hall, where it performs Tuesday through Sunday evenings in spring and summer, the Pops also tours the United States and makes studio recordings, further cementing its reputation as "America's Orchestra.".

CONTACTS:
Boston Symphony Orchestra
301 Massachusetts Ave.
Boston, MA 02115
617-266-1492 or 888-266-1200
www.bso.org

♦ 0378 ♦ **Boston Science Fiction Film Festival**
February

Held at the historic Somerville Theatre in Boston, Massachusetts, the Boston Science Fiction Film Festival is an eleven-day celebration of science fiction movies. The first part of the event is devoted to emerging directors and new features and shorts from around the globe. The festival ends with a marathon event known as the Thon, an endurance screening of classic and new science fiction movies for a continuous 24 hours. The best feature film of the festival is awarded with an exclusive sculpture known as the Gort, modeled after the robot featured in the movie *The Day the Earth Stood Still*. The origins of the festival are rooted in a screening of 14 science fiction films that took place at the Orson Welles Cinema in Cambridge, Massachusetts in 1976. After the Orson Welles Cinema was destroyed by fire in 1986, the venue shifted to the Somerville Theatre.

CONTACTS:
Boston SciFi
106 Jeremy Hill Rd.
Pelham, NH 03076
bostonscifi.com

♦ 0379 ♦ **Botswana Independence Day**
September 30-October 1

Botswana became independent from Great Britain on September 30, 1966. Since 1885, the region had been a British colony called the Bechuanaland Protectorate. The biggest Independence Day festivities are held in the capital city of Gaberones, and includes the singing of the national anthem, "Fatshe La Rona" (Blessed Country).

President's Day is another national holiday, observed on two days in mid-July.

CONTACTS:
Embassy of the Republic of Botswana
1531-1533 New Hampshire Ave. N.W.
Washington, D.C. 20036
202-244-4990; fax: 202-244-4164
www.botswanaembassy.org

♦ 0380 ♦ **Botswana Sir Seretse Khama Day**
July 1

July 1 is the birthday of Sir Seretse Khama, the man who led the nation of Botswana out of colonialism and laid the foundation for a modern democracy in his country. Khama was born in 1921, when Botswana was still known as Bechuanaland, a British protectorate. He was the eldest son of Khama III, the *kgosi* or king of the Bamangwato people. Upon his father's death, Seretse Khama became *kgosi* at the age of four, with his uncle, Tshekedi Khama, acting as his guardian and regent. Khama was educated at boarding schools in South Africa and began college there, but finished his education in England. It was there he met and married Ruth Williams, a white Englishwoman. Shortly thereafter, he returned to his home country with his wife.

The interracial marriage caused an outcry both among tribal leaders and the pro-apartheid leadership of Bechuanaland's powerful neighbor, South Africa. Khama was able to win his own people over, but South African authorities were profoundly threatened by the marriage of a black tribal leader to a white woman. They stirred up a dispute with England regarding the legitimacy of Khama's claims to chieftancy. Due to this pressure from South Africa, Khama and his wife were exiled to England in 1951, and the following year, this exile was declared permanent. By 1956, however, public outcry about the way they had been treated resulted in the couple's return to Bechuanaland.

Khama formed the Bechuanaland Democratic Party and became the last colonial prime minister of Bechuanaland, serving in that post from 1965-66. He was also honored with knighthood in 1966. On September 30, 1966, Bechuanaland became the independent country of Botswana, with Khama as its president. He held this post until his death in 1980. When Botswana became independent, it was widely assumed the country would have to be dependent on one of its wealthier neighbors, for Botswana was so poor that its tax base seemed too small to support the country. Yet through Khama's initiatives, Botswana was able to develop an independent, export-based economy.

Sir Seretse Khama Day is a national holiday, honored across Botswana as a day to remember Khama's contributions to his homeland. In celebrations in Serowe, which is Botswana's capital as well as Khama's birthplace, people proceed from various points to the main town center, where musical and religious groups have gathered. Traditional dances, such as the *tsutsube*, are performed. Speeches and ceremonies are made at the city's statue honoring Khama, and a wreath is laid at his grave in the royal cemetery.

CONTACTS:
Botswana Embassy
1531-1533 New Hampshire Ave. N.W.
Washington, D.C. 20036
202-244-4990; fax: 202-244-4164
www.botswanaembassy.org

♦ 0381 ♦ Bottle Kicking and Hare Pie Scramble, Annual
Between March 23 and April 26; Easter Monday

This 700-year-old event is the highpoint of the local calendar in the small village of Hallaton in Leicestershire, England. Opposing teams from Hallaton and the neighboring town of Medbourne scramble to maneuver two out of three small wooden beer kegs across a goal line in a game that has been described as being "unsurpassed for sheer animal ferocity." The chaos on the field may have something to do with the fact that players drop out of the game from time to time and have "a pint."

The event begins when the local rector blesses the Hare Pie—originally made of hare but now of beef. After handing out slices to some of the villagers, he scatters the remainder on the rectory lawn, where people scramble for it. Then comes the contest for the beer-filled kegs.

Where did these activities originate? According to legend, a village woman was crossing a field when she was attacked by a bull. A running hare diverted the bull's attention and she escaped. She bequeathed a field to the town in gratitude. The connection between the legend and the modern festivities is vague.

♦ 0382 ♦ Boun Phan Vet
October-November; 12th lunar month

In the Laotian capital of Vientiane, rituals honoring events in the country's history as well as the origins of the Laotian people are held on this day in That Luang, the temple where the Buddha's relics have been traditionally housed. Outside the capital Laotians from various communities observe Boun Phan Vet at different times of the year, using the occasion to pay homage to Prince Vessantara, who is believed to be an incarnation of the Buddha. These observances include feasts, dramatic performances, love song contests, rooster fights, and parties at which the villagers entertain neighbors from other villages. This is also a time for young men to be ordained into the *sangha*, or community of Buddhist monks.

♦ 0383 ♦ Boundary Walk (Grenzumgang)
Various

Boundary Walk festivals are held in many German towns. The custom dates back to the Middle Ages, when landownersand church officials, accompanied by armed men, periodically reviewed the boundaries to see that marking stones were in place and that hunting or fishing rights were observed. Eventually town and village boundaries were surveyed in the same way, with a huge feast ending the ceremony.

CONTACTS:
German National Tourist Board
Beethovenstraße 69
Frankfurt 60325 Germany
49-69-974640; fax: 49-69-751903
www.germany.travel

♦ 0384 ♦ Bouphonia (Buphonia)
End of June

The ancient Greek ceremony Bouphonia was held in Athens each year as part of the festival known as **Dipolia** or **Diipolia**. Wheat and barley, or cakes made from them, were placed at the altar of Zeus on the Acropolis. Oxen were driven around the altar, and as soon as one of them nibbled on the grasses or ate the cakes, he was killed with an ax, which was then thrown into the sea. The flesh of the ox was eaten, but his hide was stuffed with straw and sewn together. Then the stuffed animal was set up and yoked to a plow.

According to legend, a man called Sopatrus killed an ox in anger after the animal had eaten some of the cereal he was offering as a sacrifice. He felt so much remorse that he buried the ox and fled to Crete. When a famine ensued, the festival known as Bouphonia was instituted. It was customary for the killing of the ox to be followed by a ceremonial trial for those who had participated in its murder, after which the knife used to slit its throat and the ax used to fell it were thrown into the sea.

♦ 0385 ♦ Bowlegs (Billy) Festival
First full week in June

The oldest and one of the biggest festivals in northwest Florida is held in Fort Walton Beach to commemorate the pirate William Augustus Bowles, also known as Capt. Billy Bowlegs. Bowles arrived in what's now known as the Florida panhandle in 1778 when the Spanish, English, and Americans were maneuvering for control of the Gulf shores. He put together a force of Indians and "White Banditti," created his own throne, and formed the State of Muskogee. To support it, he ran raids on the Gulf of Mexico and on the mainland. He was finally seized and imprisoned in Morro Castle in Cuba, where he starved himself to death in 1803.

This is not a particularly joyous saga, but the light-hearted affair of the Billy Bowlegs Festival goes on for a week. The festival began in 1954 and today attracts about 40,000 spectatorsActivities begin with fireworks on Friday night. The following day, the pirate captain and his red-kerchiefed "krewe" members storm the city from the pirate ship *Blackhawk*. As events move on there are musical concerts, a treasure hunt, arts and crafts, numerous food vendors, and sports events that include a midnight run. More than 100 floats take part in a torchlight parade, and parade participants rain gold doubloons and assorted trinkets on the clamoring crowds.

CONTACTS:
Greater Fort Walton Beach Chamber of Commerce
34 Miracle Strip Pkwy, S.E.
Fort Walton Beach, FL 32548
850-244-8191
www.billybowlegsfestival.com

♦ 0386 ♦ **Boxing Day**
December 26

The term "Boxing Day" comes from the little earthenware boxes that servants, tradespeople, and others who rendered services to the public used to carry around on the day after CHRISTMAS to collect tips and year-end bonuses. Although the custom of distributing gifts (usually money) to public servants and employees has continued, it often takes place before Christmas rather than after, and boxes have nothing to do with it. But the name has remained, and Boxing Day is still observed in England, Canada, Australia, and many other nations. In South Africa, it is known as the **Day of Good Will**. If December 26 falls on a Saturday or Sunday, the following Monday or Tuesday is usually observed as a public or BANK HOLIDAY.

♦ 0387 ♦ **Boy Scouts' Day**
February 8

The Boy Scout movement was started by a British cavalry officer, Robert S. S. Baden-Powell, who was well known not only for his heroic defense of Mafeking in southern Africa during the Boer War, but also for his publication of a military pamphlet, "Aids to Scouting," which emphasized the need for a strong character and outdoor survival skills among British soldiers. King George V ordered Baden-Powell to retire from the military so that he could help British boys learn about camping, hiking, signaling, plant identification, swimming, and other such activities. Baden-Powell's 1908 book, *Scouting for Boys*, was an immediate success, and he devoted the rest of his life to the task of promoting the scouting movement.

The Boy Scouts of America, the nation's largest youth organization, was founded on February 8, 1910. A Chicagopublisher, William D. Boyce, who had experienced the courtesy and helpfulness of a young scout firsthand while staying in London, decided that young American boys needed the same kind of training. Two existing organizations—Dan C. Beard's Sons of Daniel Boone and Ernest Thompson Seton's "Woodcraft Indians"—had already introduced boys to the same idea, and the Sons of Daniel Boone eventually merged with the Boy Scouts of America. Cub Scout "Blue and Gold" dinners, flag ceremonies, parents' nights, shopping center demonstrations, and the presentation of advancement awards are popular ways of celebrating this day, which is part of **Boy Scout Month**, an annual anniversary celebration extending throughout February.

CONTACTS:
Boy Scouts of America-Sam Houston Area Council
2225 N. Loop W.
Houston, TX 77008

713-659-8111 or 877-272-2267; fax: 713-865-9137
www.samhoustonbsa.org

♦ 0388 ♦ **Boys' Dodo Masquerade**
Full moon of Islamic month of Ramadan

A children's entertainment introduced by Muslim Hausa traders during the mid-19th century, the **Dodo Masquerade** performed in Burkina Faso (formerly Upper Volta), has changed considerably over the years, and now reflects the local largely non-Muslim Mossi culture. As the RAMADAN season approaches, boys between the ages of 12 and 16 form groups consisting of a principal singer, a chorus, five or more dancers, a drummer, a few costumed wild animals based on local folklore, and a leader who dresses in military style. The boys decide on their roles and dance steps, which are usually variations on a dozen well-known patterns. Each dancer wears knee bells made from tin can tops and carries two sticks decorated by painting or peeling the bark away in special patterns.

On the night of the full moon during the Islamic month of Ramadan, the boys in their masks and costumes perform their dance for each household or compound while the chorus sings. Younger boys (seven to 12 years of age) started forming their own "Petit Dodo" groups and by the mid-1950s, little boys were dancing Dodo in many Mossi villages.

CONTACTS:
Smithsonian National Museum of African Art
950 Independence Ave. S.W.
Washington, D.C. 20560
202-633-4600; fax: 202-357-4879
africa.si.edu

Embassy of Burkina Faso
2340 Massachusetts Ave. N.W.
Washington, D.C. 20008
202-332-5577; fax: 202-667-1882
burkina-usa.org

♦ 0389 ♦ **Brady (Captain Samuel) Day**
Second week in July

The body of water that is the focal point of the village of Brady Lake, Ohio, has more than aesthetic value to the residents. Captain Samuel Brady, an American frontiersman who fought in the Revolutionary War, was a scout in what was then called the Northwest Territory. He escaped a group of Wyandotte Indians by hiding under the surface of the lake and breathing through a hollow reed. The importance of this event is reflected in the fact that both the community and the lake were named after Captain Brady, and every summer (on a date that has not yet been firmly fixed), the escape is reenacted on the shores of the lake.

When the level of Brady Lake began to drop suddenly in the late 1970s, the residents pulled together to deal with the problems triggered by the water shortage rather than trying to sell their homes in anticipation of falling real estate values.

The Captain Brady Day celebration has become an important unifying event for the people of Brady Lake, who view the lake as a symbol of their solidarity and peaceful way of life.

CONTACTS:
Kent Parks & Recreation
497 Middlebury Rd.
Kent, OH 44240
330-673-8897; fax: 330-673-8898
www.kentparksandrec.com

Cleveland State University Libraries
Main Library
Rhodes Tower 321A
Cleveland, OH 44115
216-687-6998; fax: 216-687-9328
web.ulib.csuohio.edu

♦ 0390 ♦ Braemar Highland Gathering
First Saturday in September

In the 11th century, King Malcolm held a gathering of the Scottish clans in Braemar to test their strength and to choose the hardiest soldiers. Competitors were asked to toss the caber—a pole 16′ to 20′ long and weighing 120 pounds—in such a way that it landed on its other end, much the way loggers used to toss logs across a river. The Braemar Gathering is still an annual event in the village of Braemar in Scotland, and the participants are still required to wear kilts and toss the caber. But the event has been expanded to include traditional Highland dancing, bagpipe music, games, and other athletic competitions as well.

See also HIGHLAND GAMES.

CONTACTS:
Bookings Secretary- Braemar Royal Highland Charity
Society Office
Braemar, Aberdeenshire AB35 5YU United Kingdom
44-13397-41098
www.braemargathering.org

♦ 0391 ♦ Bratislava Music Festival
Late September to early October

With its royal classical musical heritage—Joseph Haydn (1732-1809), Wolfgang Amadeus Mozart (1756-1791), Ludwig van Beethoven (1770-1827), Franz Liszt (1811-1886), and Anton Rubinstein (1829-1894) all performed there—Bratislava was already primed to host an international music festival, founded in 1965 with support from the Ministry of Culture of the Slovak Republic. The two-week festival presents choral, orchestral, and chamber music; opera; musical theater; and ballet. Through a project of the International Music Council and UNESCO, young artists have had the opportunity to perform alongside world-famous musicians at the festival since 1969, launching many professional careers.

CONTACTS:
Slovenská filharm
Reduta
Námestie E. Suchona 1
Bratislava 811 01 Slovakia

421-2-5443-0378
www.filharmonia.sk/en

♦ 0392 ♦ Brauteln
Between February 3 and March 9; Shrove Tuesday

The **Wooing a Bride Ceremony** in Sigmaringen, Germany, is part of a CARNIVAL custom that dates back to 1648. After the Thirty Years' War was over, hunger and disease were widespread in Sigmaringen. This discouraged young men from marrying and starting families. The population dropped so quickly that the mayor offered to reward the first young man brave enough to become engaged with the *Brauteln*, or bride-wooing ceremony, during which the lucky bachelor was carried at the head of a colorful procession around the town square.

Today the custom continues. On SHROVE TUESDAY any man who has married in the last year, who has just moved into town with his wife, or who has arrived at the 25th or 50th anniversary of his marriage is invited to be *brautelt*. Heralds dressed in traditional costumes carry the men around the town pump to the accompaniment of drummers and pipers.

♦ 0393 ♦ Brazil Independence Day
September 7

A declaration of independence was made by Pedro di Alcântara (1798-1834) on this day in 1822. Brazil had been a colony of Portugal since the 16th century. Alcântara, better known as Pedro I, became the first emperor of Brazil in 1823 and ruled until 1831.

Independence Day is a public holiday in Brazil, and there are celebrations in Brasilia, the capital, with parades of military personnel and floats decorated with flowers.

See also INCONFIDÊNCIA WEEK.

CONTACTS:
Brazilian Embassy
3006 Massachusetts Ave. N.W.
Washington, D.C. 20008
202-238-2700
washington.itamaraty.gov.br/en-us

♦ 0394 ♦ Brazil Proclamation of the Republic
November 15

November 15 is a public holiday commemorating the proclamation of the Republic of Brazil during the rule of Pedro II (1825-1891), who reigned from 1831 to 1889.

CONTACTS:
Brazilian Embassy
3006 Massachusetts Ave. N.W.
Washington, D.C. 20008
202-238-2700
washington.itamaraty.gov.br/en-us

♦ 0395 ♦ **Bread and Roses Heritage Festival**
First Monday in September; coincides with
Labor Day in the United States

The Bread and Roses Festival is a one-day, free event held in Lawrence, Mass., each year on LABOR DAY, the first Monday in September. The Festival, which has been held on the town common annually since 1985, commemorates the Bread and Roses Labor Strike that occurred in Lawrence in 1912, when most of the town's 30,000 textile workers walked off the job in protest of low wages and harsh working conditions. Many of the strikers were women and children, including a large proportion of recent immigrants. The strike gained its name from a sign reportedly carried by female protesters, proclaiming, "We want bread and roses, too," indicating that they sought both fair compensation for their work and respect from their employers.

The Festival combines multicultural arts, poetry, dance, and music with themes of labor activism and social protest. Trolley and walking tours visit sites connected with the history of the strike and include exhibits of period artifacts and a demonstration of wool carding and spinning. In addition, information booths, ethnic food, and commemorative merchandise vendors are on site, as well as a petting zoo, pony rides, and a domino tournament.

CONTACTS:
Bread and Roses Heritage Committee, Inc.
P.O. Box 1137
Lawrence, MA 01842
978-309-9740
breadandrosesheritage.org

♦ 0396 ♦ **Bregenz Festival**
July-August

Lake Constance in Bregenz, Austria, provides the setting for the Bregenz Festival, which features opera, symphonic and chamber music, theater, and ballet in a variety of indoor and outdoor venues, including the Festival House on the banks of the lake and a floating stage on the lake itself. The summer festival was established in 1946 to culturally refresh a war-weary public.

CONTACTS:
Bregenzer Festspiele GmbH
Sales Department, Ticket Center
Platz der Wiener Symphoniker 1
Bregenz A-6900 Austria
43-5574-4076; fax: 43-5574-407-400
www.bregenzerfestspiele.com/en

♦ 0397 ♦ **Bridge Crossing Jubilee**
First weekend in March

This annual event in Selma, Alabama, commemorates "Bloody Sunday," which occurred on March 7, 1965, when a group of about 525 African-American demonstrators gathered at Browns Chapel to demand the right to vote. They walked six blocks to Broad Street, then across the Edmund Pettus Bridge, where they were met by more than 50 state troopers and a few dozen possemen on horseback. When the demonstrators refused to turn back, they were brutally beaten. At least 17 were hospitalized, and 40 others received treatment for injuries and the effects of tear gas.

The attack, which was broadcast on national television, caught the attention of millions of Americans and became a symbol of the brutal racism of the South. Two weeks later, the Reverend Martin Luther KING, Jr. and 3,200 civil rights protesters marched the 49 miles from Selma to the state capital, Montgomery—an event that prompted Congress to pass the Voting Rights Act.

Every year on the first weekend in March, the Bridge Crossing Jubilee commemorates both the bloody confrontation at the Pettus Bridge and the march from Selma to Montgomery that followed. Events include a parade, a Miss Jubilee Pageant, a mock trial, and a commemorative march to the bridge. Every five years, celebrants continue all the way to Mont- gomery.

CONTACTS:
Bridge Crossing Jubilee Inc.
209 Broad St.
Selma, AL 36701
334-526-2626
www.selmajubilee.com

♦ 0398 ♦ **Bridge Day**
Third Saturday in October

Bridge Day is both a celebration of the New River Gorge Bridge in Fayetteville, West Virginia, and a day of bliss for daredevils. The bridge, completed in 1977, is the world's longest steel-arch span and is the second highest bridge in the nation (after the Royal Gorge Bridge over the Arkansas River in Colorado). Its arch span is 1,700 feet, with a rise of 360 feet, putting it 876 feet above the New River Gorge National River. On Bridge Day, celebrated since 1980, parachutists jump from the bridge onto the river's banks below. The less bold walk over the bridge. About 200 vendors offer food, crafts, and souvenirs for sale. Attendance is about 150,000.

CONTACTS:
West Virginia Department of Commerce
Capitol Complex
Bldg. 6, Rm. 525
Charleston, WV 25305
304-558-2234 or 800-982-3386; fax: 304-558-1189
www.wvcommerce.org

♦ 0399 ♦ **Bridge Walking (Dari Balgi)**
15th day of the first lunar month

According to Korean folklore, anyone who wants to avoid foot problems for the year should cross a bridge on the night of the 15th, or full moon, day of the first lunar month. Walking over 12 bridges is said to keep away bad luck altogether. Not surprisingly, Koreans of all ages are outdoors on this night looking for bridges to walk across.

The custom of bridge walking goes back centuries. It was particularly popular during the Middle Ages. So many people crowded the bridges that officials decided that men could cross bridges on the full moon night, but women had to wait until the next night. No one knows exactly how or why this custom originated, but the words for "bridge" and "foot" sound alike in Korean.

See also TAEBORUM.

♦ 0400 ♦ Brighton Festival
May

The Brighton Festival, a three-week arts event held each May in Brighton and Hove, England, encompasses art, music, film, literature, dance, and theater. Founded in 1965, the event is the largest annual festival in England. It is critically acclaimed for attracting groundbreaking international artists and hosting world premieres. The festival is designed to promote collaboration between artists and among art forms.

Since 2009, renowned international figures have participated at the Brighton Festival, including visual artist Anish Kapoor, celebrated musician Brian Eno, and democratic leader Aung San Suu Kyi.

The festival begins with a children's parade and pyrotechnics, followed by different events in venues across the city. A popular feature of the festival is the "Artists Open House," where people can visit the homes of various artists. The festival is organized by Brighton Dome, a premiere arts venue in the city.

CONTACTS:
Brighton Dome and Brighton Festival Ltd
12a Pavilion Bldgs., Castle Sq.
Brighton BN1 1EE United Kingdom
44-1273-700-747
brightonfestival.org

♦ 0401 ♦ British Columbia Day
First Monday in August

British Columbia, Canada's westernmost province, joins several other communities in holding a civil holiday on the first Monday in August. For local residents, this day honors the pioneers who established the colony of British Columbia in the 19th century. Although the Legislative Assembly of British Columbia introduced the holiday in 1974, its official status was not ratified until 1996.

There are a number of events that take place in the province's capital, Victoria, but the most popular is the "Symphony Splash," an annual performance of modern and classical music by the Victoria Symphony Orchestra. Held on a barge on the city's Inner Harbor, the concert draws thousands of tourists and locals.

CONTACTS:
British Columbia, Office of Protocol
P.O. Box 9422
Stn. Prov. Govt.

Victoria, BC V8W 9V1 Canada
1250-387-1616; fax: 1250-356-2814
www.protocol.gov.bc.ca

♦ 0402 ♦ British Open
Summer (usually July)

The British Open is the oldest and one of the most prestigious international golf championship tournaments in the world. It is officially the **Open Championship of the British Isles,** but in Great Britain it is known simply as the **Open.** It began in 1860 at the then 12-hole Prestwick course in Scotland and is now rotated among select golf courses in England and Scotland. Scot Willie Park won the first tournament, which is memorable for the tourney's highest single-hole stroke total—21.

Other notable years in the Open:

In 1901, Scot James Braid, who became one of Scotland's greatest golf heroes, won the first of five Open championships.

In 1907, Arnaud Massy of France was the first player from outside Great Britain to win.

In 1910, the Open's 50th anniversary was celebrated at St. Andrews (considered by many to be the premier golf course of the world) in a tempest of a rainstorm that put some of the greens under water.

In 1914, at Prestwick, the great triumvirate of golf, Braid and Englishmen John Henry Taylor and Harry Vardon, entered the match with each having five Open titles behind them. Vardon won with a final total round of 78.

In 1921, Bobby Jones (Robert Tyre Jones Jr.), the legendary golfer and lawyer from Atlanta, Ga., lost his temper at the par-three 11th hole at St. Andrews and shredded his scorecard while the gallery gaped.

In 1926, that same Bobby Jones won the cup; it was the first time in 29 years that an amateur had won.

In 1930, Jones won and went on to sweep the UNITED STATES OPEN and the British Amateur and U.S. Amateur for golfing's Grand Slam, after which he retired. The feat hasn't been equaled. (Later, in 1958, Jones became the first American since Benjamin FRANKLIN to receive the Freedom of the Burgh of St. Andrews.)

In 1973, Gene Sarazen, celebrating his 50th anniversary of play, shot a first-round hole-in-one on the par-three, 126-yard eighth hole (known as the Postage Stamp) at Royal Troon. In the second round, he deuced the hole.

In 1975, American Tom Watson won the first of five championships.

In 1977, Watson and fellow American Jack Nicklaus left the field behind them and dueled to a dramatic final round; Watson won by a stroke with a 72-hole total score of 268.

The Open has a special cachet for golfers since Scotland is considered, if not the birthplace of golf, the place where it developed into its present form played with ball, club, and hole. (At one time, pub doors were the target). The game may actually have originated in Holland, where they called it *kolven*, but golf in Scotland goes back before 1457. That year, Scottish King James II banned "fute-ball and golfe" because they interfered with his subjects' archery practice. The ban didn't take. Golf was confined pretty much to Scotland until 1603 when King James VI of Scotland also assumed the throne of England and brought golf there, even though many English sportsmen sniffily derided it as "Scottish croquet.".

CONTACTS:
Royal and Ancient Golf Club
Beach House
Golf Place
St. Andrews, Fife KY16 9JA United Kingdom
44-13-3446-0000; fax: 44-13-3446-0001
www.randa.org

♦ 0403 ♦ Broadstairs Dickens Festival
June

This nine-day festival commemorating the 19th-century novelist Charles Dickens and his association with the English town of Broadstairs features a play adapted from a different Dickens novel each year. The actors are members of the Broadstairs Dickens Players' Society, and they spend about eight months preparing for their June performance. During the festival, the entire town is transformed: people wander through the streets in Dickensian costumes, play croquet and other games popular during the 19th century, and attend bathing parties and social events with a Victorian theme. There are also concerts of Victorian music, exhibits, and lectures on Dickens.

Charles Dickens lived for many years in Bleak House, overlooking the harbor of Broadstairs. The festival was started by a later inhabitant of Bleak House, Gladys Waterer, in 1936. Although all of Dickens's works have been adapted and performed at the festival at least once, the town's nostalgia for its most famous citizen shows no signs of flagging.

CONTACTS:
Broadstairs Dickens Festival
10 Lanthorne Rd.
Broadstairs
Kent CT10 3NH United Kingdom
44-18-4386-1827
www.broadstairsdickensfestival.co.uk

♦ 0404 ♦ Brotherhood/Sisterhood Week
Third week in February

Every year since 1934, Brotherhood Week has been proclaimed by the president of the United States, sponsored by the National Conference for Community and Justice (formerly, the National Conference of Christians and Jews), and observed by the country as a whole. The original idea was to set aside a week each year when people of all faiths would get together, discuss their differences, and reaffirm the human brotherhood that underlies the variations in their religious beliefs.

Now known as Brotherhood/Sisterhood Week, schools, churches, synagogues, civic groups, and other organizations across America celebrate by bringing together people of different faiths and backgrounds.

The decision to celebrate Brotherhood/Sisterhood Week near WASHINGTON'S BIRTHDAY called attention to George Washington as a symbol of America's commitment to freedom from racial and religious prejudice. When Washington was president he wrote a letter to the Hebrew congregation in Newport, Rhode Island, in which he assured them that in this country there would be "to bigotry no sanction, to persecution no assistance." This quotation has become practically a slogan for the National Conference for Community and Justice which, in addition to organizing this observance, is engaged in a continuing effort to promote interfaith relations.

CONTACTS:
American Conference on Diversity
109 Church St.
New Brunswick, NJ 08901
732-745-9330; fax: 732-745-9419
americanconferenceondiversity.org

National Conference for Community and Justice
820A Prospect Hill Rd.
Windsor, CT 06095
860-683-1039; fax: 860-683-1409
www.nccj.org

♦ 0405 ♦ Bruckner Festival, International
Mid September to early October

Linz, Austria, is the setting for a festival devoted to the works of composer Anton Bruckner (1824-1896), best known for his nine symphonies and three Masses. Although a number of famous composers have lived and worked in Austria— among them Beethoven, Mahler, and Brahms—Bruckner's roots there go back to the fifth century. On the 150th anniversary of his birth in 1974, therefore, it seemed appropriate to institute a festival in his honor.

The Orchestra of Linz and other well-known orchestras perform Bruckner's symphonies, piano and organ compositions, sacred choral and orchestral works, and Masses in the Brucknerhaus, a concert hall built in 1974, as well as in other locations throughout the city. Choral concerts are usually performed in the Augustinian monastery in St. Florian (near Linz) where Bruckner was organist from 1848-55 and where he is buried.

CONTACTS:
Brucknerhaus
Untere Donaulände 7
Linz 4020 Austria
43-732-7612; fax: 43-732-7612
www.brucknerhaus.at

♦ 0406 ♦ Brunei National Day
February 23

Brunei is an independent sultanate on the island of Borneo in the Malay Archipelago. The country is officially named Brunei Darussalam. It had been a British protectorate since 1888. The sultanate gained independence in 1984 and observes its National Day each year on February 23. Many people prepare months in advance to participate in colorful crowd formations, a favorite National Day event, and prayer services take place at mosques around the officially Muslim country.

CONTACTS:
Embassy of Brunei Darussalam
3520 International Ct. N.W.
Washington, D.C. 20008
202-237-1838; fax: 202-885-0560
www.bruneiembassy.org

♦ 0407 ♦ Brussels International Fantastic Film Festival
March-April

The Brussels International Fantastic Film Festival was established in 1983 in Brussels, Belgium. Conducted in various venues in and around Brussels, it focuses exclusively on short and feature films of the horror, thriller, cult, and science fiction genres. More than 60,000 people attend the annual festival, including many international guests.

Apart from the more than 80 films that are shown during the festival, there are various other supplemental events, including the International Body Painting Contest, which was added to the festival in 1987. In the Facial Make-Up Contest, participants transform into zombies and other interesting creatures, and prizes are awarded in the amateur, semi-pro, and special effects categories. The festival also includes a Vampire Ball; a zombie costume parade; the ZomBIFFF'lympics, with zombies taking part in silly Olympic-style games; and a film market by Frontières, which provides film production and financing services to films of the horror genre.

CONTACTS:
Peymey Diffusion A.S.B.L
Rue de la Comtesse de Flandre 8 Gravin van Vlaanderenstraat
Brussels, 1020 Belgium
32-2-201-1713; fax: 32-2-201-1469
www.bifff.net

♦ 0408 ♦ Buccaneer Days
Early April through first weekend in May

During Buccanner Days, the city of Corpus Christi, Tex., by proclamation of the mayor, is under pirate rule, similar to the GASPARILLA PIRATE FESTIVAL in Tampa, Fla. Buccaneer Days, now also known as **Buc Days**, began in 1938 to honor the discovery of Corpus Christi Bay by Spanish explorer Alonzo Alvarez Pineda in 1519. It has become a month-long carnival,calling to mind the days of the early 19th century when the settlement was a hideaway for pirates, who did a brisk trade in contraband. Pirates sail into town, capture the mayor, and demand revelry throughout the city. Events include a professional rodeo, sailboat regattas, parades, sporting events, concerts, a coronation and ball, and fireworks on the bayfront.

♦ 0409 ♦ Budapest Music Weeks
September-October

Music by the Hungarian composers Bela Bartók (1881-1945) and Franz Liszt (1811-1886) is a standby at the music festival held in Budapest from the last week in September through late October each year. But the festival was founded in 1959 to commemorate the 150th anniversary of the death of Franz Josef Haydn (1732-1809), the Austrian composer who spent 30 years at the Esterházy Palace as court composer to Prince Nicolaus Esterházy.

The festival always includes works by Hungarians—Zoltan Kodály (1882-1967), Gyula Illyés, and Zsigmond Móricz as well as Bartók and Liszt—but there are works by composers from other countries as well. Performances of symphonic, chamber, and organ music are held daily, usually in the Budapest Opera House, the Erkel Theatre, the Academy of Music, and in nearby churches and castles. For one week in October, there is a "festival within a festival": the Contemporary Music Series, in which the latest works by Hungarian and foreign composers are premiered.

The Budapest Autumn Festival is held over the last two weeks in October and presents plays, art exhibits, films, and musical and dance performances.

CONTACTS:
Philharmonia Hungary
1094 Budapest
Páva utca 10-12
Budapest Hungary
36-1-302-4961
filharmonia.hu

♦ 0410 ♦ Budapest Spring Festival
April

The Budapest Spring Festival was founded in 1981. It starts during a weekend in early April of every year and continues for over two weeks. The largest cultural event in Hungary, the festival is organized by the city government. Dozens of venues are utilized, including the National Theatre, museums, and the Budapest Music Center, among others. Hungarian as well as international artists participate.

The events of the Budapest Spring Festival include dance, music, literature, theater, opera, and other festivities. Visitors can enjoy world, popular, and jazz music, as well as church music and arias. A large number of concerts are classical, including orchestral programs, solo piano and violin recitals, and string quartet performances. Musicals based on famous literary works and folk dance performances are also celebrated at the festival. Moreover, the works of Shakespeare and his contemporaries are explored in the theater events. The festival also features exhibits related to photography, visual arts, the history of Budapest, and others subjects of cultural interest.

CONTACTS:
Palace of Arts
1, Komor Marcell St.

Budapest 1095 Hungary
361-555-3000 or 361-486-3311
www.btf.hu/videos/trailer

♦ 0411 ♦ **Budget Day**
A Wednesday in March

As a general term, Budget Day refers to the day on which a government official presents the budget for the following year. In England, however, there is a tradition of having the Chancellor of the Exchequer carry the dispatch box containing papers relating to the government's revenues and expenditures for the coming year from the Prime Minister's residence at 10 Downing Street in London to the House of Commons on April 9.

The word "budget" originally referred to a leather wallet or bag, and the Chancellor of the Exchequer carried the government's financial papers in such a bag. The expression "to open one's budget" meant "to speak one's mind." Eventually the word came to stand for the contents of the bag, and the Chancellor of the Exchequer was said to be "opening the budget" when he presented his annual statement to the House of Commons. The modern meaning of the word dates from the mid-18th century.

CONTACTS:
Office for Budget Responsibility
20 Victoria St
London SW1H 0NF United Kingdom
44-207-271-2442
budgetresponsibility.org.uk

♦ 0412 ♦ **Buena Vista Logging Days**
February

In the 1800s, the logging of Minnesota's pine forests near Bemidji was in full swing. During the winter timber harvest, lumberjacks guided teams of Percheron horses, who hauled logs along ice-covered roads. Although the timber industry still works the woods around Bemidji, the golden days of the Minnesota logging boom only lasted 50 years. But the area continues to remember, recreate, and celebrate the skills of the old-time lumberjack by holding a festival at Buena Vista village and logging camp located north of Bemidji. Each year participants dressed in red plaid wool shirts demonstrate log scaling and compete in axe chopping and crosscut-sawing contests. They also guide teams of Percheron, Belgian, and Clydesdale draft horses in log loading and hauling demonstrations.

Visitors are transported to the logging camp aboard horse-powered sleighs and are served lumberjack camp meals all day long. Buena Vista village is also the home of the Lumberjack Hall of Fame, where up to 100 of the old lumberjacks are honored and inducted during the festival. Many of those fabled laborers of the north woods, some of whom are nearly 100 years old, attend the festival each year.

♦ 0413 ♦ **Buenos Aires International Festival of Independent Cinema**
April

One of the most prestigious events in independent filmmaking in Latin America, the annual Buenos Aires International Festival of Independent Cinema (BAFICI) takes place in April at several venues across Buenos Aires, Argentina. For 11 days, the festival showcases some of the most acclaimed independent films from around the world. Founded in 1999, the BAFICI cultivates new film talent with an emphasis on artists from the region. The festival promotes provocative independent films characterized by high risk and commitment.

The festival's standard format includes competitive, non-competitive, and retrospective sections, but in recent years the festival has also experimented with avant-garde and genre films across all sections. Because of the festival's history and identity, BAFICI audiences still look for offbeat films that only such an event can offer. The majority of screenings happen at the Village Recoleta Multiplex and the Junín Cinema. Latin American films are screened with English subtitles, and non-English films with Spanish subtitles. The festival also sets the stage for audiences and media to interact with producers, directors, and casts, and screenings are often followed by question-and-answer sessions.

CONTACTS:
Buenos Aires International Festival of Independent Cinema
Av. Roque Sáenz Peña
Buenos Aires C1035AAQ Argentina
54-11-4393-4670
festivales.buenosaires.gob.ar/es/home

♦ 0414 ♦ **Buenos Aires Rojo Sangre**
October-November

The Buenos Aires Rojo Sangre is devoted to the genres of science fiction, fantasy, and horror. Launched in 2000 to cater to audiences with a craving for the bizarre and the horrific, the festival's competitive format today includes long, medium, and short film categories, as well as independent productions and low budget films that may otherwise miss opportunities to be screened at festivals. In addition to screenings, audiences can enjoy panel discussions and participate in training workshops with some of the masters of the horror genre. While these events are free and open to the public, they are subject to availability. This festival first took place at the University of Buenos Aires and was attended by a modest gathering. The second festival witnessed a surge in participation and was held at the San Martin Cultural Center. Today, the event is attended by thousands of people and boasts over 200 film screenings. It was recently declared a cultural interest event by the Legislature of Buenos Aires.

CONTACTS:
Buenos Aires Rojo Sangre
rojosangre.quintadimension.com

♦ 0415 ♦ **Buergsonndeg**
February-March; first Sunday in Lent

On this day, young people go to hills in the countryside throughout Luxembourg to build bonfires to celebrate the sun and to mark winter's end. Though this custom can be traced to pre-Christian times, in modern times it is associated with LENT.

CONTACTS:
Information and Press Service of the Luxembourg Government
33, Blvd. Roosevelt
L-2450 Luxembourg
352-247-82000
www.luxembourg.public.lu

♦ 0416 ♦ Buffalo Days Powwow
Third weekend in July

UNESCO designated the Head-Smashed-In Buffalo Jump site near Fort Mcleod, Alberta, Canada, as a World Heritage Site in 1981. For more than 5,500 years this natural land formation was used by northern Plains Indians to hunt and slaughter buffalo. Hunters on horseback would herd a large group of buffalo to the edge of the cliff and trigger a stampede so that some would run over the edge to their death. The interpretive center located at the jump provides tours and information and features exhibits on the area's Plains Indian culture.

The Buffalo Days Powwow is held at the site every July. Attendees enjoy dance competitions, foods, crafts, and a teepee village.

CONTACTS:
Alberta Culture & Tourism, Government of Alberta
6th Fl. Commerce Pl.
10155 - 102 St.
Edmonton, AL T5J 4L6 Canada
780-415-1319
culture.alberta.ca

♦ 0417 ♦ Buffalo Soldiers Commemorations
July 28 and other dates

In 1992 the U.S. Congress passed a law designating July 28 as Buffalo Soldiers Day in the United States. This day commemorates the formation on that date in 1866 of the first regular Army regiments comprising African-American soldiers.

African-American soldiers fought for the Union during the Civil War. But it was not until after the war that permanent all-black regiments were established, maintaining the U.S. armed forces policy of segregation. The African-American regiments were deployed in the southwest and in the plains states to serve U.S. interests against Native American tribes, to protect important shipments, and to construct roads and trails. A longstanding debate ranges around the origin of the term "Buffalo Soldier," with some maintaining that the nickname reflected the toughness of the soldiers and others claiming that it was a disparaging racial term used by Native Americans to describe the dark-skinned soldiers they met in battle. The segregated regiments served in the Spanish-American War, World War II, and other conflicts, before being disbanded during the 1940s and 1950s as the U.S. armed forces embraced integration.

Since 1992, Buffalo Soldier Commemorations have been held throughout the country and typically include reenactments,

museum displays, educational forums, prayer services, and dedication or groundbreaking ceremonies for sculptural or other permanent memorials. A monument to the Buffalo Soldiers was dedicated at Fort Leavenworth, Kans., on the first Buffalo Soldiers Day in 1992 by General Colin Powell, who had originated the idea of a memorial to the black soldiers when he was stationed at the fort. Ceremonies and reenactments honoring the Buffalo Soldiers are not limited to July 28, however. Communities throughout the United States present special programs designed to educate audiences about the history of the Buffalo Soldiers throughout the year, particularly during Black History Month in February and on such patriotic holidays as Memorial Day and Veterans Day, with displays of memorabilia and speeches recounting the accomplishments of the troops.

CONTACTS:
Buffalo Soldiers National Museum
3816 Caroline St.
Houston, TX 77004
713-942-8920; fax: 713-942-8912
www.buffalosoldiermuseum.com

Office of the Garrison Commander
290 Grant Ave.
Unit 1
Fort Leavenworth, KS 66027
913-684-4021
garrison.leavenworth.army.mil

♦ 0418 ♦ Buffalo's Big Board Surfing Classic
February

This event features two days of surfing contests at Makaha Beach, Oahu, Hawaii, where the surf is sometimes 20 feet high. The classic is a tribute to "Buffalo" Keaulana, one of the state's premiere watermen. Old-timers ride the waves on the huge wooden surfboards that were used in Hawaii's early days; other events include canoe surfing, team bodyboarding, and tandem surfing. There are also food booths and Hawaiian entertainment.

♦ 0419 ♦ Bulgaria Day of Liberation from Ottoman Domination
March 3

Bulgaria Day of Liberation from Ottoman Domination, celebrated each year on March 3, commemorates the day in 1878 when the Peace Treaty of San Stefano was struck between Russia and Turkey. The signing of this treaty put the nation of Bulgaria back on the map after an absence of about five centuries.

The Ottoman or Turkish Empire had consumed Bulgaria at the end of the 14th century. During the 18th century, a group of Bulgarians began working to revive the national identity of Bulgaria and to encourage Bulgarians to fight for their freedom (*see also* LEADERS OF THE BULGARIAN NATIONAL REVIVAL DAY). In 1876, Georgi Benkowski led a rebellion against the Turks, but it was forcefully put down by the Ottoman forces, and some 30,000 people were killed. In 1877, Czar Alexander II of Russia declared war on the Ottoman Empire, motivated by concern for the Orthodox Christians living in Bulgaria. A joint force of Russian and Bulgarian forces defeated the Ottoman troops at Shipka Pass, which led to the Treaty of San Stefano. Independence did not come instantly; Bulgaria was under Russian administration from 1877 to 1879.

In 1880, March 3 was celebrated in Bulgaria as the anniversary of the enthronement of Alexander II as the Russian Emperor. As Alexander's support had been critical to Bulgarian independence, he was and is seen as a liberator and a hero in Bulgaria. In 1888, March 3 was first observed as Bulgaria's Day of Liberation. It was pronounced a national holiday in 1978 and has been included in the official list of holidays since 1990. The Day of Liberation from Ottoman Domination is considered the most important holiday related to Bulgarian independence. Throughout Bulgaria, citizens pause on this day to pay tribute to those who helped Bulgaria to become a modern, independent country. Festivities marking the day often include parades, concerts, religious services, cultural exhibitions, and fireworks. Those who died fighting for Bulgaria's freedom are honored by the placement of ceremonial wreaths upon their graves.

CONTACTS:
Embassy of the Republic of Bulgaria
1621 22nd StN.W.
Dimitar Peshev Plaza
Washington, D.C. 20008
202-387-0174; fax: 202-234-7973
www.bulgaria-embassy.org

♦ 0420 ♦ **Bulgaria Independence Day**
September 22

On September 22, 1908, Prince Ferdinand (1861-1948) of Bulgaria declared the country's independence from the Turkish Ottoman Empire, which had ruled since the 14th century. In 1944 the former Soviet Union invaded Bulgaria and imposed its communist system for nearly 50 years. Like many other eastern European countries, Bulgaria became an independent republic with a new constitution in 1991. In 1998 the Bulgarian Parliament reinstituted September 22 as Bulgarian Independence Day. It also declared September 6 Unification Day to mark the unification of Bulgaria with Eastern Rumelia, previously under Ottoman control, in 1885.

CONTACTS:
Embassy of the Republic of Bulgaria
1621 22nd St.N.W.
Dimitar Peshev Plaza
Washington, D.C. 20008
202-387-0174; fax: 202-234-7973
www.bulgaria-embassy.org

♦ 0421 ♦ **Bulgarian Education and Culture Day**
May 24

This Bulgarian national holiday—formerly known as **Holy Day of Letters**—promotes Bulgarian culture and honors two brothers, St. Cyril (c. 827-869) and St. Methodius (c. 815-844), missionaries to Moravia. They are believed to have invented

the Slavonic alphabet, also known as the Cyrillic alphabet. What is certain is that through their evangelization efforts, they helped spread the use of the new alphabet, and they are both widely regarded as the country's patrons of education and culture. In 1980, Pope John Paul II declared them patrons of Europe. The brothers started out preaching Christianity in what are now the Czech and Slovak Republics, but their followers fled to Bulgaria when they were persecuted, and Cyrillic became the official alphabet there. It is still used in the former Soviet Union, Serbia, and other Slavic countries as well.

Special religious services, concerts, festivals, and student parades are held throughout Bulgaria on this day, which is also known as **Saints Cyril and Methodius's Day** and **Day of the Founders of the Slavonic Alphabet**. An impressive liturgy, celebrated at the cathedral in Sofia, is one of the high- lights.

CONTACTS:
Bulgarian Cultural and Heritage Center of Seattle (BCHCS)
P.O. Box 6366
Bellevue, WA 98008
seattle-bg.org

♦ 0422 ♦ **Bull Durham Blues Festival**
September

The Carolina blues style of music (also known as Piedmont blues) is different from traditional blues. Rather than expressing stories of bad luck, hard times, and lost love, Carolina blues balance sorrow with celebration. These songs are often light and upbeat, encouraging listeners to dance.

Since 1988, the St. Joseph's Historic Foundation, Inc. (SJHF) has held a blues festival at the Durham Athletic Park in North Carolina, where the Durham Blues baseball team used to play.

The SJHF, an African-American cultural and educational institution, was founded in 1975 to "advance cultural understanding through diverse programs that examine the experiences of Americans of African descent—locally, nationally, and globally." SJHF is deeply rooted in the historic Hayti community of Durham. Funds raised from the Bull Durham Blues Festival support the programs and operations of the Foundation and Hayti Heritage Center, which is the former St. Joseph's African Methodist Episcopal Church, a National Historic landmark. The Hayti District is an area on the southwest edge of Durham, where African Americans settled shortly after the Civil War.

According to the SJHF, the festival serves many purposes. These are as follows: "To increase awareness and appreciation for Durham's rich musical heritage in the Blues, particularly as a showplace for the Piedmont blues style made popular in this part of the Southeast; to increase awareness and appreciation for the Blues as a unique American art form that is reflective of the African American experience; to develop the local audience, particularly within the African American communities in the region, for the Blues which is often more popular overseas than in the United States; to become a national showcase for the finest in contemporary and traditional blues artists in North Carolina and the rest of the United States."

During the three-day festival, many of the best and best-known contemporary blues artists perform for audiences from over 175 North Carolina cities, 25 states, and five countries. As with many music festivals around the country, good food is plentiful in the various restaurants and other venues around Durham.

CONTACTS:
Hayti Heritage Center
804 Fayetteville St.
Durham, NC 27701
919-683-1709; fax: 919-682-5869
hayti.org

♦ 0423 ♦ Bulu Festival
June

To the Dogon people who live in southeastern Mali in West Africa, *bulu* means "rejuvenate." It celebrates the beginning of the planting season. The festival continues for six days during which people ritually renew the life of the community with visits, feasts, and tying up any loose ends amongst each other, as well as their connection with the spiritual realm by offering sacrifices and creating new paintings for sanctuaries. The main communal ritual takes place at the house of the *hogan*, the most powerful priest in the community. Using millet grain saved from the previous year's crop, he enacts a ceremonial planting of grain for the current season in order to encourage a good crop.

♦ 0424 ♦ Bumba-Meu-Boi Folk Drama
June, including June 24, St. John's Day

The Bumba-Meu-Boi is a Brazilian folk drama that is popular in Brazil and especially noteworthy in cities and small towns in the state of Maranhão. The play tells the story of a bull (or, in some versions, an ox) that is slain and then brought back to life. The characters include a sea captain riding a wicker hobby-horse, the bull or ox, the cowboys Chico and Birico, Catirina (the pregnant wife of Chico), the Doctor, and the Chorus. A colorful procession announces the arrival of the players, who sometimes stage playful attacks on the spectators lining the streets. Performances usually take place in a room of the house belonging to the most important family in town, or else in front of a church or in the town's main square.

♦ 0425 ♦ Bumbershoot
September, four days over Labor Day weekend

Bumbershoot is the premier festival of Seattle, Wash., held since 1971 and now a wide-ranging round-up of many arts. It started as Festival '71, but became Bumbershoot in 1973. Bumbershoot is British slang for umbrella, and the festival is supposed to be an umbrella for the arts; the word also calls to mind Seattle's rainy climate.

Bumbershoot draws artists representing diverse genres and forms including music, film, comedy, spoken word, dance, theatre, performance, and visual arts, and also features children's activities, food, and arts and crafts vendors. The festival is held over Labor Day weekend at the Seattle Center, the 74-acre site of the 1962 World's Fair, which includes a variety of indoor and outdoor venues. Attendance to the festival is over 100,000 people. In 2015, Bumbershoot will celebrate its 45th anniversary.

CONTACTS:
Bumbershoot
P.O. Box 9750
Seattle, WA 98109
206-673-5060
bumbershoot.org

♦ 0426 ♦ Bun Bang Fai (Boun Bang Fay; Rocket Festival)
April-May; full moon day of Hindu month of Vaisakha; second weekend in May

Bun Bang Fai is a rain ceremony celebrated in Laos and northeastern Thailand during Buddhist Vesak or Vesakha Puja, observed on the full moon day of the sixth Hindu month (Vaisakha). The Bun Bang Fai (*bun* or *boun* means "festival" in Lao) pre-dates Buddhism and is intended to insure good crops.

In Laos, this is one of the country's wildest celebrations, with music and irreverent dances, processions, and merrymaking. The celebration ends with the firing of bamboo rockets into the sky, supposedly prompting the heavens to commence the rainy season and bring water to the rice fields. Prizes go to the fastest, highest, and brightest rockets.

In Thailand, the celebration is usually on the second weekend in May and is especially festive in Yasothon, with villagers shooting off huge rockets. Before the shooting, there are beauty parades, folk dances, and ribald entertainment.

♦ 0427 ♦ Bunch (Madam Lou) Day
Third Saturday in June

Bunch day is an annual reminder of the rowdy gold-mining days of Central City, Colo., held to honor the town's last madam. The event features bed races, a Madams and Miners Ball, and the selection of a Madam of the Year. In addition, there are tours of old mining rigs and trains that take visitors into the heart of the mountains to see colorful veins of ore.

Central City was settled in the Gold Rush of 1859 and became known as the Richest Square Mile on Earth—some $75 million in gold was mined there. One of the miners was a man named John Gregory, who dug up a fortune. New York newspaper editor Horace Greeley heard about Gregory Gulch and went west to take a look, after which he supposedly wrote, "Go west, young man." The phrase isn't found in his writings, because this advice was first given by John Babsone Soulé in an article for Indiana's *Terre Haute Express*. Greeley reprinted the article in his *New York Tribune* under

Soulé's byline; nevertheless Greeley has been remembered for the inspiring phrase and both Gregory and Soulé have faded into history.

CONTACTS:
Central City
141 Nevada St.
Central City, CO 80427
303-582-5251
www.centralcitycolorado.us

♦ 0428 ♦ Bunka-no-Hi (Culture Day)
November 3

Bunka-no-Hi is a Japanese national holiday on which medals are awarded by the government to those who have made special contributions in the fields of arts and sciences. Winners are not always Japanese; the American Apollo 11 astronauts—Neil Armstrong, Edwin "Buzz" Aldrin, and Michael Collins—are among past honorees. This is also the anniversary of Japan's current constitution in 1946.

The day was formerly celebrated as the birthday of Emperor Meiji, who ruled from 1868 until his death in 1912 and was the great-grandfather of Emperor Akihito (b. 1933). The years of his reign were a time of turning away from feudalism and toward Western rationalism and science, and were known as the age of *bummei-kaika*—"civilization and enlightenment."

Today, this holiday serves to promote the love of freedom, peace, and cultural development.

CONTACTS:
Japanese Cultural & Community Center of Washington
511 – 16th Ave. S.
Seattle, WA 98144
206-568-7114
jcccw.org

♦ 0429 ♦ Bunker Hill Day
June 17

Observed primarily in Boston, Mass., Bunker Hill Day commemorates the Revolutionary War battle of June 1775 between 2,200 British troops under the leadership of General William Howe and half that number of Americans under Colonel William Prescott. In fact, Breed's Hill was fortified, not nearby Bunker Hill, and that is where the British attacked the rebels three times, eventually driving them out of their hastily constructed barricade, but only after losing more than 1,000 men. The American revolutionaries, who had exhausted their small store of ammunition, ended up fighting the British bayonets with the butts of their muskets.

Although the Americans were driven from their fortification and lost some 450 men, the battle boosted their confidence and has always been looked upon as one of the great heroic battles of the American Revolution. A 221-foot granite obelisk in Charlestown, just north of Boston, marks the site of the battle on Breed's Hill, which itself is only 87 feet high. This day is sometimes referred to as **Boston's Fourth of July**.

CONTACTS:
Freedom Trail Foundation
99 Chauncy St.
Ste. 401
Boston, MA 02111
617-357-8300; fax: 617-357-8303
www.thefreedomtrail.org

Boston National Historic Park
Charlestown Navy Yard
Boston, MA 02129
617-242-5642
www.nps.gov/bost

♦ 0430 ♦ Burbank Day
March 7

The birthday of naturalist and plant breeder Luther Burbank (1849-1926) is observed in California in much the same way ARBOR DAY is observed in other states—that is, with activities promoting the value of natural resources and the protection of trees and birds. Burbank moved from his native Massachusetts to Santa Rosa, Calif., in 1875 and spent the rest of his life there experimenting with new varieties of fruits, flowers, and vegetables. Among his other achievements, he is credited with introducing the Shasta daisy. All in all, he developed more than 800 new strains and varieties of fruits, flowers, and forage plants, drawing worldwide attention to the science of plant breeding and helping farmers learn how to use their land more productively.

Burbank was fortunate enough to be honored by the citizens of Santa Rosa during his lifetime. The Rose Carnival was held intermittently between 1894 and his death in 1926. Then, in 1950, the three-day Luther Burbank Rose Festival was instituted. This celebration, which takes place annually in mid-May, includes flower shows, music and sporting events, and a Rose Festival parade. On March 7 a birthday and Arbor Day celebration is held at the Luther Burbank Home and Gardens.

CONTACTS:
Luther Burbank Home & Gardens
204 Santa Rosa Ave.
Santa Rosa, CA 95404
707-524-5445; fax: 707-524-5827
www.lutherburbank.org

The Arbor Day Foundation
100 Arbor Ave.
Nebraska City, NE 68410
888-448-7337
www.arborday.org

♦ 0431 ♦ Burgoyne's (John) Surrender Day
October 17

British General John Burgoyne (1722-1792) is best remembered for his defeat by the colonial American forces in the Saratoga campaign of 1777, during the Revolutionary War. The plan was to have British troops from the north, south, and west unite at Albany, New York, thus isolating New England from the other rebellious colonies. Burgoyne led his troops south from Canada by way of Lake Champlain, capturing Fort Ticonderoga, New York, on July 6, 1777. But they were stopped at the Hudson River by the American forces commanded by General Philip Schuyler and, later, General HoratioGates,withtheassistanceofGeneral Benedict Arnold. Burgoyne was eventually forced to surrender to Gates near Saratoga Springs, New York, on October 17, 1777.

Historians regard the surrender at Saratoga Springs as the turning point in the Revolutionary War. The Americans' victory gave them a psychological advantage and persuaded France to ally itself with the colonists against England, its traditional rival.

The anniversary of Burgoyne's surrender is observed in New York State, particularly in the communities surrounding the Saratoga National Historical Park near Stillwater, New York. A well-known painting of Burgoyne's surrender by John Trumbull hangs in the U.S. Capitol Rotunda in Washington, D.C.

CONTACTS:
Saratoga National Historic Park
648 Rt. 32
Stillwater, NY 12170
518-670-2985; fax: 518-670-2989
www.nps.gov

Saratoga County Chamber of Commerce
28 Clinton St.
Saratoga Springs, NY 12866
518-584-3255; fax: 518-587-0318
battle1777.saratoga.org

♦ 0432 ♦ **Burial of the Sardine**
Between February 4 and March 10; Ash Wednesday, the first day of Lent

The custom of burying a thin slice of meat, nicknamed "the sardine," on ASH WEDNESDAY is common throughout Spain and is thought to have originated in an old fertility custom symbolizing the burial of winter in early spring. The **Entierro de la Sardina** also symbolizes the burial of worldly pleasures and serves as a reminder that people must abstain from eating meat on Fridays throughout the 40 days of LENT. After the burial is over, people attend Ash Wednesday church services.

Another Spanish custom is to make a figure of an ugly old woman out of stucco or cardboard or figures representing the King and Queen of CARNIVAL and to burn or drown these personifications of Carnival on Ash Wednesday or SHROVE TUESDAY.

See also CARNIVALINPANAMA.

♦ 0433 ♦ **Burkina Faso Independence Day**
August 5

Formerly called Upper Volta, Burkina Faso gained independence from France on August 5, 1960, an event commemorated as a national holiday each year. The area had been a French protectorate since the 1890s.

CONTACTS:
Embassy of Burkina Faso
2340 Massachusetts Ave. N.W.
Washington, D.C. 20008
202-332-5577; fax: 202-667-1882
burkina-usa.org

♦ 0434 ♦ **Burkina Faso Republic Day**
December 11

On this day in 1958 Upper Volta (now Burkina Faso) voted to become an independent republic within the French community. It was then internally self-governing until it achieved independence in 1960 (*see* BURKINA FASO INDEPENDENCE DAY). This is considered the most important national holiday in Burkina Faso, with many events held in the capital city of Ouagadougou.

CONTACTS:
Embassy of Burkina Faso
2340 Massachusetts Ave. N.W.
Washington, D.C. 20008
202-332-5577; fax: 202-667-1882
burkina-usa.org

♦ 0435 ♦ **Burning Man Festival**
September, Labor Day weekend

The Burning Man is a counterculture festival held in Nevada's Black Rock Desert near Gerlach over LABOR DAY weekend. Conceived by Larry Harvey in 1986 to honor the SUMMER SOLSTICE, an eight-foot, wooden human figure was burned on Baker Beach in San Francisco in front of a small crowd of about 20. This act of "radical self-expression," as Harvey later called it, would evolve into an annual event drawing thousands of people from all over the world. In 1990 when the police intervened and banned the actual burning of the Man, the event was moved to the desert.

Fueled by the Internet, other media, and word of mouth, Burning Man has become a populist phenomenon, where participants set up a temporary "city," creating their own community, for a few days. "No spectators" is the motto, and people are expected to interact with one another, produce and display artwork and fashion, play music, dance, do spontaneous performances—as long as they actively participate. The 50-foot-high, neon-lit Man towers over Black Rock City until the climax of the festival on Saturday night. While more than 15,000 desert dwellers watch, the figure is ignited and the Man becomes a fiery blaze, with previously loaded fireworks shooting out of him into the night sky. The next day, participants dismantle their city and leave the desert as they found it, with no trace of the Burning Man festivities— until the next year.

CONTACTS:
Burning Man-San Francisco Headquarters
660 Alabama St
San Francisco, CA 94110 United States
415-865-3800
burningman.org

♦ 0436 ♦ **Burning of Judas**
Between March 22 and April 25; Easter

La Quema de Judas takes place throughout Venezuela on the evening of EASTER Sunday. Unlike the many solemn rituals organized by the Roman Catholic Church during HOLY WEEK, Judas burning is a local affair, organized by villages and neighborhoods. The preparations go on all week, beginning with the selection of an appropriate Judas—usually a public figure in the community, but sometimes an individual well known throughout the state or nation—against whom the group has decided to stage a protest. The women construct a life-sized effigy of this person, making sure to include elements of dress or appearance that leave no mistake about its identity. The men build a wooden stand in a central location where the Judas figure will be placed.

On Easter afternoon, the people proceed to the house where the effigy has been stored for safekeeping and demand that Judas Iscariot, the disciple who betrayed Jesus, be turned over for punishment. The Judas effigy is placed on the stand, where everyone gets a chance to hit or kick it. At dusk the leader of the group recites the complaints that the people have against this individual—a document known as "The Testament of Judas," which is often written in verse and quite humorous. Then the event leaders pour gasoline on the Judas and set flame to it. The drinking, dancing, and fireworks continue late into the evening.

Although no one seems to know exactly how the custom originated, accounts of it have been traced back as far as 13th-century Spain.

See also HOLYSATURDAYINMEXICO.

♦ 0437 ♦ Burning of the Ribbons (Queima das Fitas)
May

The Burning of the Ribbons is an eight-day festival that transforms the Portuguese city of Coimbra into a lively festival with music and merriment abounding. The event is centered around a tradition, dating from the 19th century, that is perpetuated by students at the University of Coimbra (theoldest in Portugal). At the end of the second semester (typically in May), the students ceremoniously burn the ribbons (one per day) that represent each of the eight faculties at the institution: Letters, Law, Medicine, Sciences & Technology, Pharmacy, Economics, Psychology & Education Sciences, and Sports Sciences & Physical Education.

Over the course of the eight days, numerous concerts and performances take place. Other highlights include sporting events, a gala ball, and a traditional nighttime serenade at the steps of the Old Cathedral of Coimbra. Thousands of students, townspeople, and tourists gather for the spirited performance. Another high point is the *cortejo*, an elaborate parade featuring floats bearing the respective colors of each faculty. They are accompanied by placards displaying criticisms of particular teachers, of politicians, and of the education system.

CONTACTS:
Turismo de Portugal, I.P.
Rua Ivone Silva

Lote 6
Lisbon 1050-124 Portugal
351-211-140200
www.visitportugal.com

♦ 0438 ♦ Burning of the Socks
March 21, spring equinox

This pungent event takes place in Eastport, Maryland, on the day of the VERNAL EQUINOX. Once a mere suburb of Annapolis, Eastport seceded when the bridge that connected them with the rest of the city was closed for repairs. Local residents reorganized themselves as the "Maritime Republic of Eastport," a little town with an independent spirit, a sense of humor, and a love of local tradition. The town's motto: "We like it this way."

The burning of the socks began in the mid-1970s when a man named Bob Turner, upon leaving his job at the boatyard on the first day of spring, decided to burn his socks in tribute to the coming warmer weather. When he later became the owner of the Annapolis Harbor Boatyard, he invited his employees to stay after work on the first day of spring, burn their socks, and drink a beer in honor of the occasion. Turner's personal custom caught on with others and became a local tradition. The Eastport Yacht Club now organizes the yearly event at which people drink beer, eat oysters, and burn socks, all in the name of driving away winter and welcoming spring.

CONTACTS:
SC Maritime Museum
729 Front St.
Georgetown, SC 29440
843-520-0111
scmaritimemuseum.org

♦ 0439 ♦ Burning the Clavie
January 11

The Burning of the Clavie takes place in Burghead, a fishing village in the region of Moray, Scotland, on January 11, or Old New Year's Eve (*see* OLD CHRISTMAS DAY). Local residents make the clavie themselves by sawing a tar barrel into a larger and smaller half, breaking the larger half into pieces and stuffing it inside the smaller half along with tinder and tar. Once this is done they nail the clavie to a stout post. According to tradition, the clavie must be made without the use of store-bought tools. Therefore a local blacksmith makes the nail, which is hammered to the post with a stone.

At dusk the Clavie King sets the clavie on fire and leads a procession in which the burning barrel is dragged around the harbor and town. The procession stops at the homes of prominent townspeople, and paraders toss a chunk of the clavie through their doors, a custom said to bring good luck to the inhabitants. The parade proceeds to a high headland along the coast, where the flames from the clavie ignite a huge bonfire. At the end of the festivities, the clavie tumbles down the hill. Town inhabitants gather pieces of the clavie to take home with them, using them to light a New Year fire believed to keep witches and evil spirits away for a year.

Because the headland where the bonfire takes place is also the site of a ruined Roman temple, some people believe that the celebration is a survival of an ancient Roman custom. Others trace the festival back to Scandinavia, while another group suspects that it comes from the Druids, members of a pre-Christian religious order that developed among the ancient Celts.

CONTACTS:
Aberdeenshire Council-Buchan Area Office
Arbuthnot House
62 BRd. St.
Peterhead AB42 1DA United Kingdom
aberdeenshire.gov.uk

♦ 0440 ♦ **Burning the Clocks**
December 21-22

Burning the Clocks was instituted in Brighton, England, in 1994 as an end-of-year celebration commemorating the passing of time. Taking place on the Winter Solstice, the event is organized by the local arts charity Same Sky, who created it to bring the community together. Participants make lanterns out of willow branches and paper that are lit and carried in a procession to Brighton Beach, where they are placed on a bonfire to signify the end of one year and the beginning of another.

CONTACTS:
Same Sky
Annexe Studios
Belmont St.
Brighton, BN1 4HN United Kingdom
44-127-357-1106
www.samesky.co.uk

♦ 0441 ♦ **Burning the Devil**
December 7

La Quema del Diablo takes place in Guatemala. Men dressed as devils chase children through the streets from the start of ADVENT until December 7, the eve of the IMMACULATE CONCEPTION. On this day, trash fires are lit in the streets of Guatemala City and other towns, and the devils' reign of terror comes to an end.

CONTACTS:
Guatemalan Embassy
2220 R St. N.W.
Washington, D.C. 20008
202-745-4953; fax: 202-745-1908
www.minex.gob.gt

♦ 0442 ♦ **Burning the Moon House**
February; 15th day of the first lunar month

The festival known as **Dal-jip-tae-u-gee** in the Kyongsang provinces of Korea pays tribute to the moon by watching it rise through a moon house or moon gate—a carefully constructed pile of pine branches which are set on fire. The moon gate is usually built on the top of a hill or at the seashore,

where it is easier to see the moon rise through the flames. Jumping over the flames is believed to ward off evil, and the direction in which the moon gate collapses is an indication of whether the coming year will bring good luck or bad.

In other parts of Korea, a similar moon festival known as **Dal-ma-ji** is celebrated on the eve of the first full moon of the lunar year. People climb hills and build bonfires (without the "gate") to welcome the moon. Various folkloric beliefs concerning the harvest and the weather are associated with the color and brightness of the moon on this night.

See also TAEBORUM.

♦ 0443 ♦ **Burns (Robert) Night**
January 25

Burns Night is the anniversary of the birthday of Scottish poet Robert Burns, who was born in 1759 in a clay cottage that blew down a week later and died in 1796. The day is celebrated not only in Scotland but also in Newfoundland, where there is a sizeable settlement of Scots, and wherever there are devotees of this lusty poet.

The celebrations generally take the form of recitations of Burns's poetry ("Tam O'Shanter" is a standard), the imbibing of quantities of single-malt Scotch whiskey, and the serving of haggis, a Scottish dish made of a sheep's or calf's innards (liver, heart, etc.) cut up with suet and oatmeal, seasoned, and boiled in the stomach of the animal. At the point of the carving of the haggis, it is traditional to recite "To a Haggis," with its line, "Great chieftain o' the pudding race!"

In the course of things, the Selkirk grace is also read: "*Some hae meat, and canna eat/ And some wad eat that want it/ But we hae meat and we can eat/ And sae the Lord be thanket.*" And other favorite lines will be heard—for example, "O, my luve's like a red, red rose," and "O wad some Pow'r the giftie gie us/ To see oursels as others see us!" The evening always ends, of course, with "Auld Lang Syne.".

♦ 0444 ♦ **Burry Man Day**
Second Friday in August

The "Burry Man" has appeared on the streets of South Queensbury, West Lothian, Scotland, annually for over 600 years. He wears a headdress made of flowers that completely hides his face, and his body is costumed with a thick mat of teazle burrs and thistles. With a staff in each hand, he walks from house to house without uttering a word. Nevertheless, people address him politely and often offer him money, in return for which he bestows good fortune on their home.

Some say that the ceremonies of Burry Man Day commemorate King Malcolm III's escape from the British, which he accomplished with the aid of a thick covering of burs and flowers. Another theory contends that the Burry Man is a remnant of an old custom connected with the gathering of fair tolls. This theory draws strength from the fact that he appears on the day before Ferry Fair.

♦ 0445 ♦ **Burundi Independence Day**
July 1

This national holiday commemorates Burundi's independence from Belgium, which had control over the country since the end of World War II, on this day in 1962. Before the war, Germany had counted Burundi among its African territories. Since independence, the country has suffered from devastating ethnic violence between the Hutus, who constitute the majority of the population, and the Tutsis, who are in the minority.

CONTACTS:
Burundi Embassy
2233 Wisconsin Ave. N.W.
Ste. 408
Washington, D.C. 20007
202-342-2574; fax: 202-342-2578
www.burundiembassy-usa.org

♦ 0446 ♦ **Busan International Film Festival**
October

The Busan International Film Festival (BIFF) takes place annually at Haeundae-gu, Busan, in South Korea. First held in 1996, the festival draws more than 200,000 visitors from across the globe. Since 2011, festival events have taken place in a permanent venue, the Busan Cinema Center in Centum City, in addition to other neighboring spaces. Although Korea is the home of the festival, the lineup includes films from all over the Asian continent.The festival is organized into several divisions, including those dedicated to works of Asian filmmakers, debut directors, world cinema, science fiction, and more. The Asian Film Market, launched in 2006, is a festival inside the festival; it provides an opportunity for producers, directors, writers, film organizations, and others to meet, collaborate, and discuss ideas related to production, casting, funding, and project pitching. In addition, 24 young Asian filmmakers are chosen to participate in the 18-day educational program conducted by the Asian Film Academy. The festival also includes conferences on cinema, celebrity meet-and-greet events, and an award ceremony.

CONTACTS:
Bn Cinema Center
3rd Fl.,Biff Hill
120, Suyeonggangbyeon-daero, Haeundae-gu
Busan South Korea
82-1688-3010; fax: 82-51-709-2299
www.biff.kr

♦ 0447 ♦ **Busan Sea Festival**
August

Every August, beginning in 1999, the municipal government of the seaside town of Busan (Pusan) in South Korea has sponsored a nine-day Sea Festival on its main beaches. The festival kicks off with an opening ceremony featuring performances by popular singers and other entertainers and culminates that night in a spectacular fireworks display. Over the course of the festival, a variety of water sports are offered, as well as the Hanbada Festival for the Disabled and championship competitions in windsurfing and beach volleyball.

CONTACTS:
Korea Tourism Organization
10, Segye-ro
Wonju-si, Gangwon-do 220-170 Korea
82-33-738-3000
kto.visitkorea.or.kr

♦ 0448 ♦ **Buskers' Festival**
Late August

"Buskers" are vagabond musicians. They were common in the streets of 14th-century Ferrara, Italy, when it was ruled by the Dukes of Este. They still roam the streets of the world's cities, although they may be difficult to find because they usually have no fixed address and no manager or agent to contact. But Stefano Bottoni, artistic director of Ferrara's Buskers' Festival, manages to track them down and persuade them to come for a seven-day celebration of music that ranges from salsa to Celtic laments, and from MOZART to New Orleans jazz. They are not paid anything, nor are they given a stage to perform on, but since 1988 hundreds of them have wandered the city's narrow streets for a week in August, improvising their own kind of music and jamming with other itinerant musicians. Nearly 700 buskers come from all over the world to perform in Ferrara's squares and alleyways, with its spectacular medieval and Renaissance architecture as their backdrop. The week ends with a jam session in front of the walls of the castle in the center of the town.

CONTACTS:
Ferrara Buskers Festival Association
Mentessi St., 4
Ferrara 44121 Italy
39-532-249-337; fax: 39-532-207-048
www.ferrarabuskers.com

♦ 0449 ♦ **Butter and Egg Days**
First weekend after last Wednesday in April

This is a promotional event in Petaluma, Calif., that recalls the historic days when Petaluma was the "World's Egg Basket," producing millions of eggs that were shipped all over the world. The first Butter and Egg Days was a modest affair in 1983; it now draws about 25,000 for a parade with floats, bands, bagpipers, and children dressed as such things as butter pats and fried eggs. There are also street fairs, an antiques show, an egg toss, a butter-churning contest, and the presentation of the Good Egg award to a Petaluma booster.

The seed of this event was laid in 1918 when the first Egg Day parade was held. With the food shortages of World War I, people were being urged to eat less meat, and Petalumans decided to promote the idea of eating more eggs. Petaluma had the eggs; there were more hatcheries here than anywhere else. In 1878, the incubator developer L. C. Byce had established the Petaluma Incubator Co., which allowed great numbers of baby chicks to be artificially hatched. The town became a thriving poultry center, and boasted the world's only chicken pharmacy. The Egg Days, which ran from 1918 to 1926, brought the town national attention. These were huge celebrations, with nighttime illuminations, balls, chicken rodeos, and parades with gigantic Humpty Dumptys and white leghorn chickens. The chicken-and-egg industry waned in the 1950s, and the dairy industry moved in, which is now honored along with eggs.

CONTACTS:
Petaluma Downtown Association
Historic Depot Stn.
210 Lakeville St.
Petaluma, CA 94952
707-762-9348; fax: 707-283-0528
www.petalumadowntown.com

◆ 0450 ◆ Butter Sculpture Festival
15th day of first lunar month

The celebration of the Buddhist New Year (LOSAR) in Tibet is followed by MONLAM, a two-week prayer festival. On the 15th day, everyone goes to a monastery to view the butter sculptures. The most famous are at Jokhang Monastery in Lhasa, Tibet's capital. Completed over a period of months, the huge sculptures are made out of yak butter pigmented with dyes. They are fastened to 30-foot-high frames for display purposes and illuminated by special butter lamps. Each monastery maintains a workshop where its own artists shape the cold-hardened butter into depictions of legends, or other themes, different each year.

◆ 0451 ◆ Butter Week (Russia)
February-March, the week preceding Ash Wednesday

CARNIVAL is known as Butter Week or **Maslyanitsa** (also rendered Maslenitsa) in Russia because Russians consume so many rich foods throughout this week, the last before the seven-week Lenten fast. *Bliny,* Russian-style pancakes served with sour cream or butter, are eaten all week long and have come to symbolize the feast. People enjoy one rich meal after another as the week proceeds. LENT begins on the Monday following the last Sunday in Butter Week. On this day observant Russian Orthodox Christians remove meat and dairy products from their diets.

Around the turn of the 20th century, the Carnival celebration in St. Petersburg ended with a ceremony in which a folk figure called Prince Carnival rode through town in a cart pulled by 10 horses and bade farewell to the people. He was represented as a tipsy man, sitting before a table covered with food.

When the Prince departed, the people celebrated the end of Carnival with a display of fireworks. In many areas people enjoy winter sports such as skiing, sledding, ice skating, and snowball fights during Butter Week. In some places people mark the end of Carnival by making huge hand-sewn dolls that represent winter and tossing them onto burning bonfires.

◆ 0452 ◆ Buzzard Day
Sunday following March 15

About 75 turkey vultures, also known as turkey buzzards, return to Hinckley, Ohio, each March 15 to spend the summer. While these carrion-eating birds may lack the charm of the SWALLOWS OF SAN JUAN CAPISTRANO, thousands of people celebrate them at the Hinckley Buzzard Day Festival, held since 1958 on the first Sunday after March 15. It features tours, hikes, and talks by naturalists at Metro Park, where the buzzards roost.

The vultures' return was first documented by a park patrolman who logged their arrival date for 23 years. Why the birds return, however, isn't known. One theory recalls the Great Hinckley Varmint Hunt on Dec. 24, 1818, when 475 men and boys lined up along Hinckley's borders and moved inward, slaughtering predators that were killing farm animals. The tons of carrion, of course, provided fine repasts for vulturine tastes.

CONTACTS:
Hinckley Township
1410 Ridge Rd.
Hinckley, OH 44233
330-278-4181; fax: 330-278-2023
www.hinckleytwp.org

◆ 0453 ◆ Byblos International Festival
May-September

The ancient city of Byblos in Lebanon has hosted an international music festival since the late 1960s. Performances of orchestral, chamber music, and jazz concerts are held throughout the summer. There are also plays, operettas, ballet, and modern dance recitals. Most of the events are held in the 12th-century castle built by the Crusaders out of the stones and granite columns of ancient Roman temples and public buildings.

Byblos, also known as Jubayl or Jebeil, is one of the oldest continuously inhabited towns in the world. The precursor of the modern alphabet was developed in Byblos, and the ancient Phoenicians exported their papyrus to the Aegean through the city. The English word "Bible" is derived from *byblos,* the early Greek name for papyrus.

CONTACTS:
Byblos International Festival
Unesco Sq.
Jbeil-Byblos Lebanon
961-9-54-2020; fax: 961-9-54-3030
www.byblosfestival.org

C

♦ 0454 ♦ **Cabrillo Day and Festival**
Week including September 28

Juan Rodríguez Cabrillo was the Portuguese explorer who discovered California on September 28, 1542, when he sailed into the bay that would eventually be called San Diego. He went on to explore the upper California coast, naming both Catalina and San Clemente islands after his ships, but he failed to discover San Francisco Bay before being driven south again by a severe storm.

In the San Diego area, Cabrillo Day celebrations were relatively modest until the early 1960s, when the week-long Cabrillo Festival became a yearly event. Activities include Portuguese-American music and dancing, the placing of a wreath at the base of Cabrillo's statue on Point Loma, and a costumed reenactment of the discovery of San Diego Bay.

CONTACTS:
Cabrillo Festival Inc.
P.O. Box 60718
San Diego, CA 92166
619-225-8909 or 619-218-9890
www.cabrillofestival.org

♦ 0455 ♦ **Cafe Budapest**
October

Cafe Budapest, first held in 1992 and originally billed as the Budapest Autumn Festival, is a festival dedicated to contemporary arts. It starts on the first weekend of October every year and runs for more than two weeks. The festival includes music concerts—classical, pop, contemporary, and jazz—as well as literature, theater, dance, design, and circus arts. Events take place in and around the capital city of Budapest, Hungary, including the Palace of Arts, the Budapest Music Theatre, A38 Ship, and the Liszt Academy, along with the city's pubs and public areas. Cafe Budapest is organized by the city government.

Literature is presented in a unique manner at the Cafe Budapest festival. The authors collaborate with musicians to transport the audience to a world of modern writing as a group called the Literary Traveling Circus. In addition, there are talks and meetings with both Hungarian and international-

ly renowned writers. The thriving contemporary art of photography is on display at the Budapest Photo Street Festival, which showcases photo exhibits of various genres. One can also enjoy Hungarian film screenings, fashion shows, operas, walking tours, and other events.

CONTACTS:
Budapest Festival and Tourism Centre
11 Liszt Ferenc Sq.
Budapest, 1061 Hungary
361-486-3311 or 361-413-0551
cafebudapestfest.hu/photos

♦ 0456 ♦ **Caitra Parb**
March-April; eight days before the full moon of Hindu month of Caitra

A Hindu festival held in Orissa, India, Caitra Parb begins eight days before the purnima (full moon). Throughout the celebration people fast, dance, and hunt. Heads of the families pay homage to their forefathers in the presence of the village priest, or *Jani*, and family members put on festive new costumes. Animal sacrifice plays a prominent part in the celebration, which also signals the beginning of the mango season.

CONTACTS:
Department of Tourism. The Director
Paryatan Bhawan
Museum Campus
Bhubaneswar, Odisha 751 014 India
91-674-2432177 or 800-208-1414
www.orissatourism.gov.in

♦ 0457 ♦ **Caitra Purnima**
March-April; 10 days in Hindu month of Caitra

In southern India, Caitra Purnima is a time for Hindus to worship Chitra Gupta, also known as "the scribe of the gods." Tradition holds that while Brahma was meditating, Chitra Gupta was brought into being. He serves as the scribe to Yama, the ruler and judge of the dead. Some Hindus believe that it is Chitra Gupta who maintains the accounts of their good and bad deeds in the *Agrasamdhani* (main records).

At Kanchipuram, near Madras in Tamil Nadu State, the image of Chitra Gupta is taken out in a procession. Devotees bathe in the holy waters of the River Chitra, which flows from the nearby hills.

CONTACTS:
Tamil Nadu Tourism Development Corporation
Tourism Complex
No.2, Wallajah Rd.
Triplicane
Chennai, Tamil Nadu 600 002 India
91-44-25383333; fax: 91-44-25361385
www.tamilnadutourism.org

♦ 0458 ♦ **Calaveras County Fair and Frog Jumping Jubilee**
Third weekend in May

This event is a four-day county fair, established in 1928, at the Frogtown Fairgrounds near Angels Camp, Calif. It includes the official, original frog-jumping contest based on Mark Twain's story, "The Celebrated Jumping Frog of Calaveras County," as well as a children's parade, livestock competitions, a professional rodeo, a demolition derby, fireworks, and art exhibits. About 3,500 frogs are jumped in daily contests leading up to the Grand Finals on Sunday, in which there are 75 to 100 frog contestants. Jumps are measured from starting point to the landing point of the third hop. The world's record is 21' 53/4 ", set in 1986 by Rosie the Ribiter.

There are cash prizes for winners in various divisions, and anyone breaking Rosie's world record will win $5,000.

Mark Twain wrote the story of the jumping frog in 1865 and claimed it was told to him as the true story of an episode in Angels Camp in 1849. In his story, the original frog, named Dan'l Webster, was owned by one Jim Smiley, who educated it to be a fine jumper. When a stranger came along, Smiley bet him $40 Dan'l Webster could out-jump any frog in Calaveras County. The time arrived for the contest, but the stranger had secretly filled Dan'l Webster with quail shot, and the frog couldn't move. The stranger took the money and left, saying (according to Twain), "Well, I don't see no p'ints about that frog that's any better'n any other frog.".

CONTACTS:
Calaveras County Fair & Jumping Frog Jubilee
2465 Gun Club Rd.
PO Box 489
Angels Camp, CA 95222
209-736-2561
www.frogtown.org

♦ 0459 ♦ **Calendimaggio**
Three days beginning the first Thursday after May 1

According to legend, St. Francis of Assisi used to walk through the streets of Assisi at night, singing. During one of these nocturnal outings, he had a vision of the *Madonna Poverta*, or Lady Poverty, after which he renounced his inheritance and even his clothes and began a new life tending those who suffered from leprosy.

In Assisi, Italy, in early May each year, long processions of *messeri* (gentlemen) and *madonne* (ladies), escorted by knights and esquires, compete with each other in singing and music at the Piazza del Comune. In addition to commemorating the town's patron saint, these singing contests serve as an official welcome to May, which is known as the month of love.

CONTACTS:
Italian National Tourist Board
686 Park Ave. 3rd Fl.
New York, NY
212-245-5618; fax: 212-586-9249
www.italiantourism.com

♦ 0460 ♦ **Calgary Exhibition and Stampede**
July

The 10-day Calgary Exhibition and Stampede, originally called the **Calgary Stampede**, is Canada's largest rodeo event, similar to Cheyenne Frontier Days in the United States. The stampede offers a world-class rodeo competition in saddle bronc and bareback riding, steer wrestling, calf roping, and bull riding, as well as a chuck wagon race that carries a $175,000 prize. Most of the rodeo events are held in the130-acre Stampede Park in downtown Calgary, but there's also a Wild West town called Weadickville (named for Guy Weadick from Cheyenne, Wyoming, who founded the event in 1912), an Indian Village populated by representatives of five Indian tribes from the nearby Plains, a Frontier Casino with blackjack tables and roulette wheels, and agricultural and livestock exhibits.

CONTACTS:
Calgary Stampede
1410 Olympic Way S.E.
Calgary, AB T2G 2W1 Canada
403-261-0101 or 888-883-3828; fax: 403-265-7197
www.calgarystampede.com

♦ 0461 ♦ **Calgary International Children's Festival**
Late May, during the week following Victoria Day

Children, parents, and teachers are entertained and educated every year at the Calgary International Children's Festival. This five-day event takes place in downtown Calgary, located in the Canadian province of Alberta. The festival features storytelling, dance, music, puppetry, and physical comedy, all catering to a young audience. The performances take place in and around the EPCOR CENTRE, located in the Olympic Plaza Cultural District.

The program of the festival, which was launched in 1989, reflects the organizers' emphasis on creativity and cultural sensitivity. Teacher guides are provided to instructors looking to ensure an educational experience for students. A large corps of volunteers helps run the event, and through the financial contributions of donors and sponsors, an outreach program has been established to provide free admission to economically disadvantaged children.

CONTACTS:
Calgary International Children's Festival (CICF)
205 - 8 Avenue SE
Calgary, AB T2G 0K9 Canada
403-294-7414
calgarykidsfest.ca

◆ 0462 ◆ Cali Fair (Sugar Cane Fair, Salsa Fair)
Last week in December

Santiago de Cali, the third-largest city in Colombia, is the capital of one of the country's most prosperous regions, the Valle del Cauca. The rich cultural identity of this city (often called simply "Cali") and the surrounding area have been celebrated each year since 1957 at the Cali Fair. Although it is billed as a "town fair," suggesting a small country festival, the Cali Fair is a major event that draws thousands of local residents and tourists from around the world. Cali is the center of Colombia's sugar industry and is also known as the home of the best salsa dancing in Colombia. The celebration of sugar and salsa is a prominent part of the festival, which is also known as the **Sugar Cane Fair** and the **Salsa Fair.**

The Fair opens with the *cabalgata,* an elaborate cavalcade of riders mounted on fine horses, which moves through the streets of the city. Other parades take place throughout the duration of the Fair. There are numerous artisans selling their crafts, street performers, and other forms of entertainment. There are beauty contests, cultural exhibitions, concerts, and sporting events, including a marathon along the Cali River. A Bullfighting Festival is also part of the celebration. Held at La Plaza de Toros de Cañaveralejo, the Bullfighting Festival showcases the top bulls and matadors from the Americas and Europe.

Many parties and dances take place around the city during the Cali Fair. A salsa marathon is one of many dance events held each year. There are also contests for tango and just about every other kind of Latin American dance. It is said that during Fair time, Cali is the home of the best salsa dancing in the world.

CONTACTS:
Cali-Salsa
Calle 20 ste. Carrera 101A-67
Torre 2, Apto. 1008
Santiago de Cali 760032 Colombia
57-2-3049186
www.cali-salsa.net

◆ 0463 ◆ Calico Pitchin', Cookin', and Spittin' Hullabaloo
March-April; Palm Sunday weekend

This event is a celebration highlighting a tobacco-spitting contest and recalling the 19th-century heyday of Calico, a silver-mining ghost town in southern California about 10 miles north of Barstow. The contest for World Tobacco Spit-

ting Champion began in 1977 and has led to two mentions in the *Guinness Book of World Records* for distance in juice-spitting: Randy Ober of Arkansas spat a record 44' 6" in 1980 and then topped that record the next year with 47' 10". Other contest categories are accuracy in juice-spitting and distance in wad-spitting (wads are required to be at least half an inch in diameter). Contestants have come not only from the United States but also from Great Britain, Germany, and Japan.

The hullabaloo also features a stew cook-off and flapjack racing, plus more standard fare such as a horseshoe-pitching contest, egg-tossing, greased-pole climbing, and bluegrass music.

The date of the event recalls the time of year in 1881 when the miners arrived and named the town Calico because they thought the reds, greens, and yellows of the rock formations looked like a calico skirt. It was the location of one of the largest silver strikes in California, producing about $86 million in silver during the 20 years it flourished. When silver prices sank, so did Calico. In San Bernardino County, Calico is visited by tourists year-round.

◆ 0464 ◆ California Avocado Festival
October

The California Avocado Festival is held every October in Carpinteria, Calif. The three-day, free event features music, arts and crafts, activities (including a golf tournament), and a kids' block party with games, face-painting, and crafts. It also celebrates the avocado. At the Avocado Expo tent, competitors vie to win the awards for best guacamole and biggest avocado. There are cooking demonstrations and a display of the largest vat of guacamole in the world. About 100,000 visitors enjoy each year's avocado celebration.

The festival began in 1986, when a group of community leaders in Carpinteria met to organize an ongoing weekend event to help raise money for local non-profit organizations. Carpinteria is an avocado-growing area located in Santa Barbara County, the third-largest producer of avocados in North America. It seemed natural to put the rough-skinned green fruit at the center of the event. Now the festival benefits more than 40 non-profit groups, whose volunteers work at the festival. And the festival itself is a volunteer-run event, with just one part-time paid staff person. A non-profit group itself, the festival generates its own annual operating revenue.

CONTACTS:
California Avocado Festival
800 Linden Ave.
P.O. Box 146
Carpinteria, CA 93013
805-684-0038; fax: 805-684-0011
avofest.com

◆ 0465 ◆ California Gold Rush Day
Weekend nearest January 24

The anniversary of James W. Marshall's discovery of gold in 1848 while overseeing the construction of a sawmill near

Coloma, Calif., is commemorated with an annual celebration at the Marshall Gold Discovery State Historic Park on the weekend nearest January 24. An employee of John A. Sutter, a wealthy landowner and entrepreneur, Marshall noticed flakes of gold in the streambed as he was inspecting work on the mill. Although Sutter and Marshall tried to keep the discovery secret, over the next year approximately 60,000 to 100,000 gold prospectors flocked to California. The surface deposits of gold eventually dwindled, but both Sutter and Marshall had already been ruined by the gold rush they tried to forestall. Sutter died bankrupt in 1888, and Marshall died five years later, living alone in a crude cabin just a short distance from where he'd first noticed the gleam of metal.

Marshall's cabin is now part of the Marshall Gold Discovery State Historic Park, and Sutter's adobe home is part of a museum and park in Sacramento.

CONTACTS:
Marshall Gold Discovery State Historic Park
310 Back St.
Coloma, CA 95613
530-622-3470
www.parks.ca.gov

Virtual Museum of the City of San Francisco
945 Taraval St.
San Francisco, CA 94116
www.sfmuseum.org

♦ 0466 ♦ Calinda Dance
June 23

The Calinda Dance was a 19th-century Voodoo ritual observed on the eve of ST. JOHN'S DAY in New Orleans. Performed by Sanité Dédé, a Voodoo priestess who confined herself to a very small space and imitated the undulations of a snake, the Calinda was so sensual that in the frenzied group dance that followed it, the dancers tore off their clothing and engaged in an orgy.

Although most Voodoo ceremonies were held in secret, the New Orleans authorities allowed slaves to dance in Congo Square on Sunday afternoons where the authorities could keep an eye on them. This marked the end of the orgy climax and resulted in a combination of the original snake dance with an African war dance. But the Calinda remained so threatening to whites that it was banned as obscene in 1843, shortly before Voodoo enjoyed its greatest popularity under the leadership of Marie Laveau. Laveau presided over the gatherings in Congo Square and turned the St. John's Eve celebration into a public show to which whites and even some newspaper reporters were invited.

♦ 0467 ♦ Cambodia Constitution Day
September 24

After a long and troubled history, Cambodia became a constitutional monarchy in 1993. Constitution Day marks the anniversary of the formal adoption of the Constitution of Cambodia on September 24, 1993. Under the constitution, the king is head of state, but the elected National Assembly has legisla-

tive power. The prime minister is appointed by the king from representatives of the political party with the largest number of seats in the Assembly.

Constitution Day is also the anniversary of the recoronation of King Norodom Sihanouk, twice king of Cambodia (1941–55 and 1993–2004), who was overthrown by General Lon Nol in 1970. Although the King died October 15, 2012 in Beijing, China, his anniversary is still celebrated and September 24 is a national holiday in Cambodia. All banks, state offices, and most businesses are closed.

CONTACTS:
Royal Embassy of Cambodia
4530 16th St. N.W.
Washington, D.C. 20011
202-726-7742; fax: 202-726-8381
www.embassyofcambodia.org

♦ 0468 ♦ Cambodia Independence Day
November 9

Cambodia was a French protectorate for 90 years before it gained independence from France on November 9, 1953. Independence Day, which marks that event, is a national holiday. The principal celebrations are held in the capital city of Phnom Penh, beginning with a morning ceremony at Independence Monument on the crossroads of Norodom and Sihanouk Boulevards, usually with the King of Cambodia in attendance. Later in the day, there is a gala parade held in front of the Royal Palace in Phnom Penh, with colorful floats and marching bands. Shops are adorned with national flags. After dark, the Royal Palace and other important buildings and monuments are lit up. A large fireworks display is held near the riverbanks of the Royal Palace.

CONTACTS:
Royal Embassy of Cambodia
4530 16th St. N.W.
Washington, D.C. 20011
202-726-7742; fax: 202-726-8381
www.embassyofcambodia.org

♦ 0469 ♦ Cambodia National Culture Day
March 3

This event was created in 1999 by the Cambodian government as a way to promote the country's arts and culture. The yearly event is composed of displays, exhibits, live theatrical performances, and conferences held throughout the country. The festival honors the living elder masters in different artistic and cultural fields.

The Ministry of Culture and Fine Arts coordinates many of the events and uses the occasion to take stock of Cambodia's cultural infrastructure, including its historic temples, pagodas, and other landmarks important to the country's heritage and tourism.

CONTACTS:
Ministry of Tourism of Combodia
Lot 3A, St. 169

Veal Vong Commune
Phnom Penh Cambodia
855-2388-4974
www.tourismcambodia.org

♦ 0470 ♦ Cambodia Queen Sihanouk's Birthday
June 18

Her Majesty Norodom Monineath Sihanouk is the mother of King Norodom Sihamoni of Cambodia. The birthday of the Queen Mother is a national holiday in Cambodia, with government offices, schools, and many businesses closed. The holiday is a relatively quiet one, with no lavish festivities normally planned. This is in contrast to the three-day celebration of King Sihamoni's Birthday, which is observed from May 13-15.

CONTACTS:
Ministry of Tourism of Combodia
Lot 3A, St. 169
Veal Vong Commune
Phnom Penh, Prampi Makara Cambodia
855-2388-4974
www.tourismcambodia.org

♦ 0471 ♦ Cambodia Victory Day (Victory over Genocide Day, Nation Day)
January 7

This national holiday is also called **Victory over Genocide Day** and **Nation Day**. It marks the day in 1979 that Vietnamese troops entered Cambodia and began an assault that ended the bloody regime of the Khmer Rouge. It is estimated that as many as two million Cambodians were killed during the nearly four years that Pol Pot of the Khmer Rouge ruled the country. The celebration is viewed with mixed emotions by many Cambodians, since the holiday also marks the beginning of Cambodian dependence on Vietnam.

Victory Day is celebrated with patriotic speeches by government officials, remembrance services for the victims, as well as cultural displays of the era.

CONTACTS:
Royal Embassy of Cambodia
4530 16th St. N.W.
Washington, D.C. 20011
202-726-7742; fax: 202-726-8381
www.embassyofcambodia.org

♦ 0472 ♦ Cambodian New Year (Khmer New Year)
Three days in mid-April (varies according to lunar calendar)

This three-day New Year holiday, also known as **Khmer New Year**, is a major celebration in Cambodia. The first day is called *Moha Sangkran,* which means "New Angel." The tradition on this day is for families to welcome the angel who looks after the world in the coming year. To do so, people clean their houses and themselves and prepare a feast of such traditional foods as peanut curries, noodles, and tree mushrooms. Families bring food to offer Buddhist monks and gather for blessing and prayer. Another activity is the building of a small sand "mountain." Each bit of sand that is added is believed to increase the chance for health and happiness in the coming year.

The second day is known as *Wanabot* or *Vana Bat.* It is a day of gift giving to parents and other elders or persons worthy of respect. Many people also give gifts of charity on this day and perform acts of community service. More sand is added to the mountain.

The final day is called *Loeung Sack.* On this day the monks bless the sand mountains. This is also the day for people to wash their Buddha statues, which is thought to be a kind deed that will bring good luck and long life. The bathing also symbolizes hope for sufficient rainfall for the rice harvest. Many people also spray water on each other in a spirit of fun.

Throughout the new year celebration, children and adults gather to dance and play traditional games. Many streets in Cambodia are crowded with celebrants. The holiday often ends with a fireworks display.

CONTACTS:
Cambodia Tourism Office
262 Monivong Blvd.
Khan Daun Penh
Phnom Penh Cambodia
855-23-213-331 or 855-23-218-585 or 855-23-213-331
www.tourismcambodia.com

Cambodian Coordinating Council
2201 E. Anaheim St.
Ste. 103
Long Beach, CA 90804
www.cam-cc.org

♦ 0473 ♦ Camel and Ostrich Races, International
September, weekend after Labor Day

The International Camel Races are possibly the only camel races in the United States, and are a reminder of a peculiar 19th-century experiment. The races have been held since 1954 in Virginia City, Nev., the one-time mining town that was considered the richest place on earth in the 1860s.

The town is the site of the celebrated Comstock Lode, which yielded nearly $300 million in gold and silver in the two decades after its discovery in 1859. The wealth also gave the territory strategic importance: President Abraham LINCOLN wanted Nevada as a state on the side of the North to support anti-slavery amendments, and he also needed the mineral riches to finance the Civil War. Nevada became a state in 1864, and gold and silver were dug from the mines—with the help, briefly, of camels.

It was thought that camels could work like mules in the mines, and camels in the Federal Camel Corps were shipped to Nevada from Texas (where they were used in the army cavalry). The army had originally brought about 120 camels to the U.S. from Africa and Asia in the mid-1850s to carry cargo from Texas to California. But they didn't last long; their hoofs didn't adapt to the rocky terrain, so they were allowed to roam wild, and apparently died out.

There are some camels kept in town today, though, and others are imported for the races. The three-day race weekend now includes a Camel Hump Ball (a dance and barbecue); a parade with about 70 units, including belly dancers and bagpipe players; and a race of ostriches pulling chariots.

When the camel race was being held in 1961, the movie *The Misfits* was being filmed nearby. Director John Huston came to the races, borrowed a camel, and won.

CONTACTS:
Virginia City Tourism Commission (VCTC) - Visitor Center & Administrative Office
86 S. "C" St.
P.O. Box 920
Virginia City, NV 89440
775-847-7500 or 800-718-7587
www.visitvirginiacitynv.com

♦ 0474 ♦ **Camel Market**
Usually July

An important annual camel-trading fair in Guelmime (also spelled Goulimime or Goulimine), Morocco, a walled town that historically was a caravan center. Located on the northwest edge of the Sahara, the market is attended by the wanderers of the desert—the Shluh (a Berber people from southern Morocco), as well as the blue-veiled Tuareg men known as the Blue Men. The Tuaregs wear a blue *litham*, a double strip of blue cloth worn over the head and covering all but the eyes, sometimes giving their faces a blue tint. They also wear blue robes over their white *djellabahs*. The story is that an English cloth merchant visited the port and trading city of Agadir in the 1500s with calico dyed indigo blue. The Tuaregs liked the blue cloth and have had a predilection for it ever since.

The camel market brings together thousands of these nomads and their camels. They come to sell and trade baby camels as well as animal skins and wool. Hundreds of tents are pitched, and there is constant activity and noise: camel races, shouted bartering, and, at night, performances of the erotic *guedra* dance.

See also BIANOU and CURE SALÉE.

CONTACTS:
Moroccan National Tourist Office
Angle Rue Oued Al Makhazine
Street Zalaga-BP
19-Agdal
Rabat Morocco
212-537-278300; fax: 212-537-674015
www.visitmorocco.com

♦ 0475 ♦ **Cameroon National Day**
May 20

A public holiday commemorating the people's vote to establish a united Republic of Cameroon on May 20, 1972, this day is also known as **Constitution Day**.

CONTACTS:
Cameroon Embassy
3400 International Dr. N.W.
Washington, D.C. 20008
202-265-8790; fax: 202-387-3826
www.cameroonembassyusa.org

♦ 0476 ♦ **Cameroon Youth Day**
February 11

This national holiday in the west African nation of Cameroon celebrates the country's young people. School children and youth groups participate in parades, often accompanied by university students in marching bands. Government officials watch the processions, along with many other onlookers. Businesses sell food and merchandise along the parade routes. Many schools and youth groups also organize art exhibits and sports activities.

The theme of Youth Day is to encourage Cameroon's young people to renounce violence and other unsavory behaviors and to embrace education, sports, and artistic activities. The country's president traditionally makes a nationally broadcast speech on Youth Day, commenting on the achievements of the country's young people and outlining the government's plans to improve education and youth employment opportunities.

♦ 0477 ♦ **Camp Fire Founders' Day**
March 17

The organization originally known as the Camp Fire Girls was founded on March 17, 1910, around the same time that the Boy Scout movement was getting its start in Great Britain (*see* BOY SCOUTS' DAY). Now it is coeducational and is known as Camp Fire USA. The organization stresses self-reliance, and membership is divided into five different age levels, ranging from Sparks (pre-school) to Horizon (grades 9-12). Skilled adults work with these young people in small groups, helping them to become acquainted with nature's secrets and to learn a variety of crafts. Interaction with adults is also emphasized as a way of learning about career choices, hobbies, and other interests.

Camp Fire's founding is observed by the group's members as part of **Camp Fire Boys and Girls Birthday Week**. The Sunday nearest March 17 is **Camp Fire Boys and Girls Birthday Sunday** and is a day when Camp Fire Boys and Girls worship together and participate in their church or temple services.

CONTACTS:
Camp Fire National Headquarters
1100 Walnut Street, Ste. 1900
Kansas City MO, 64106
816-285-2010

♦ 0478 ♦ **Canada Day**
July 1

The British North America Act went into effect on July 1, 1867, uniting Upper Canada (now called Ontario), Lower Canada (now Quebec), New Brunswick, and Nova Scotia into a British dominion. Canadians celebrate this day— which was formerly known as **Dominion Day**—with parades and picnics, somewhat similar to FOURTH OF JULY festivities in the United States.

In Detroit, Michigan, and Windsor, Ontario, which are on opposite sides of the Detroit River and are connected by a vehicular tunnel and the Ambassador Bridge, this is also one of the days on which the International FREEDOM FESTIVAL is held.

CONTACTS:
Canada Place Corporation
100 The Pointe
999 Canada Pl.
Vancouver, BC V6C 3T4 Canada
604-665-9000; fax: 604-775-6251
www.canadaday.canadaplace.ca

Canadian Heritage
15 Eddy St.
Gatineau, QC K1A 0M5 Canada
819-997-0055 or 866-811-0055
www.pch.gc.ca

♦ 0479 ♦ **Canadian International Military Tattoo**
Weekend in late May or early June

An annual event preserving an ancient military tradition, the Canadian International Military Tattoo takes place in Hamilton, a town in the province of Ontario. The evening of entertainment features military bands, drum corps regiments, and pipe bands from Canada and other countries, all performing for residents of Hamilton and the surrounding area. The event often celebrates anniversaries related to Canada's national and/or military heritage and features civilian as well as military musical acts.

The first tattoo took place in 1992 and marked Canada's 125th birthday. In 1999, the Hamilton International Tattoo— as it was then called—faced the threat of being discontinued, but a group of volunteers rallied to preserve it. Around that time the Canadian International Tattoo Association was formed with the sole mission of coordinating the event and ensuring its continuation.

In 2008, the Tattoo celebrated the 400th anniversary of the founding of Quebec City and declared as its theme *Je me souviens*(a popular Quebec slogan that means "I remember").

CONTACTS:
Canadian International Military Tattoo
101 York Blvd
Hamilton, ON L8R 3L4 Canada
905-523-1753
www.canadianmilitarytattoo.ca

♦ 0480 ♦ **Canadian National Exhibition**
August-September

The first Canadian National Exhibition was held in 1879 in Toronto. The fair moved briefly to Ottawa, but it returned to Toronto and was called the **Toronto Industrial Exhibition** until 1921, when the name was changed to reflect its nation-wide appeal. Located on the shores of Lake Ontario, about 10 minutes from downtown Toronto, the fairgrounds occupy 350 acres of lawns, gardens, pavilions, and Victorian-style buildings. Events include an air show, a horse show, celebrity appearances, and much more. The Exhibition claims to be the oldest and largest of its kind in the world.

CONTACTS:
Canadian National Exhibition
Press Bldg. Exhibition Pl.
210 Princes' Blvd.
Toronto, ON M6K 3C3 Canada
416-263-3330; fax: 416-263-3838
theex.com

♦ 0481 ♦ **Canberra Day**
Second Monday in March

Canberra, the capital city of Australia, was founded on March 12, 1913. Unusual in that it is one of the few world capitals planned from the ground up, the city and its giant ornamental pond, Lake Burley Griffin, were built out of a depression in a dusty plain about 200 miles southwest of Sydney.

Originally observed on the third Monday in March, in 2007 the Canberra Day holiday was moved to the second Monday in March in order to bring the observance closer to the day the city was founded. Canberra Day festivities include numerous outdoor events including fireworks and musical performances.

CONTACTS:
Events ACT, Venue and Event Services
Economic Development Directorate
G.P.O. BOX 158
Canberra, ACT 2601 Australia
1300-852-780; fax: 61-2-6205-0776
www.events.act.gov.au

♦ 0482 ♦ **Candelaria (Bolivia)**
February 2

Candelaria or CANDLEMAS is a major holiday in Bolivia, where the Virgen de Candelaria is the country's patroness. The festivities focus on her shrine in the normally placid town of Copacabana on Lake Titicaca, where visitors begin to arrive in the week that precedes the festival. Aymará, Quechua, and Chiriwano Indians can be recognized by their colorful native costumes and musical instruments, and most begin dancing as soon as they arrive and continue till the end of the festival. The image of the Virgin Mary that stands on a revolving platform in the church is not the same one that is carried in the procession on February 2; a duplicate dressed in elaborate robes and precious jewels is used instead, because many years ago it was discovered that every time the statue was moved, big storms or other natural disasters were likely to follow.

◆ 0483 ◆ Candelaria (Peru)
February

A lively celebration of CANDLEMAS is held in Puno, Peru, for about two weeks, including February 2. On that day priests and laypeople form a huge procession that carries the statue of the Virgin Mary through streets carpeted with yellow flowers. Preparations begin more than a week before, however, with church decorating, feasts, and fireworks. By the second week, hundreds of dancers and musicians have arrived to join the main procession, accompanying it with indigenous dances and colorful costumes.

◆ 0484 ◆ Candle Auction
Saturday following April 6

The old custom of "selling by candle" is still observed in scattered locations throughout England, among them the village of Tatworth in Somerset. Every year on the Saturday following April 6, which was LADY DAY according to the old Julian calendar, six acres of valuable watercress-growing land are leased to the highest bidder. The bidders gather behind locked doors in a room illuminated only by a candle stuck to a board. A pin is inserted into the candle an inch below the flame, and the bidding begins as the candle is lit. As the candle burns, the melting wax eventually releases the pin. When the pin falls out, the bidding is closed. The person who got the last bid in before the pin dropped will be able to use the land in the year to come. The idea here is that each bidder will have sufficient time to think before making an offer higher than the one previously presented.

Similar candle auctions are held on different dates at Congresbury, also in Somerset; at Old Bolingbroke, Lincolnshire; at Grimston and Diseworth in Leicestershire; and at Aldermaston in Berkshire, where an acre of church land is let every third year.

◆ 0485 ◆ Candlemas
February 2

After observing the traditional 40-day period of purification following the birth of Jesus, Mary presented him to God at the Temple in Jerusalem. According to a New Testament gospel, an aged and devout Jew named Simeon held the baby in his arms and said that he would be "a light to lighten the Gentiles" (Luke 2:32). It is for this reason that February 2 has come to be called Candlemas (or **Candelaria** in Spanish-speaking countries) and has been celebrated by the blessing of candles since the 11th century. In both the Eastern and Western churches, it is now known as the **Feast of the Presentation of Christ in the Temple**; in the Roman Catholic Church, it was formerly called the **Feast of the Purification of the Blessed Virgin Mary**. In the United States, February 2 is also GROUNDHOG DAY; in Great Britain it is said that the badger comes out to test the weather. The old rhyme is as follows:

If Candlemas Day be dry and fair, The half of winter's to come and mair. If Candlemas Day be wet and foul, The half of winter's gone at Yule.

See also CANDELARIA; MIHR, FESTIVAL OF.

◆ 0486 ◆ Candlewalk
December 31

The American custom of seeing the old year out and the new year in with some type of WATCH NIGHT service can be traced back to England. John Wesley, the founder of the Methodist Church, advocated these kinds of services, believing NEW YEAR'S EVE an appropriate time for religious observance. The first watch night services in the United States were held in St. George's Methodist Church in Philadelphia in the year 1770. Nowadays this type of service may be referred to as a "candlelight" service.

In some areas the African Methodist Episcopal Zion Church holds distinctive Watch Night services. In rural Bladen County, North Carolina, an observance known as the Candlewalk combines pagan fertility rites with the Christian worship of the Virgin Mary. On CHRISTMAS EVE the women and the girls of the church walk deep into the swamp or forest, while the men and boys are threatened with a death curse if they follow. According to local legend, this period of withdrawal is for the purpose of sexual instruction. When the women return, they do so in a single file procession, bearing lighted torches or candles and singing ancient hymns in pidgin English, which some have misidentified as an African language. The women blow out their candles as they come into the church.

The New Year's Eve Watch Night ritual usually takes place close to midnight. It involves prayers, hymns, and sermons. Participants often dress in white and carry lit can- dles.

CONTACTS:
Flushing Area Chamber of Commerce
309 E. Main St.
Flushing, MI 48433
810-659-4141; fax: 810-659-6964
www.flushingchamber.com

◆ 0487 ◆ Candy Dance Arts and Crafts Faire
Last full weekend in September

In 1919, the Candy Dance began in the town of Genoa, in northern Nevada, as a way to raise funds to install street lights. Lillian Virgin Finnegan, daughter of a local judge, proposed a dance where candy would be distributed to dancing couples, followed by a midnight supper at the local hotel. The townswomen made a variety of candies for the occasion, and the event raised enough money to install the needed lights. The following year, however, the town was having trouble paying the electric bill for those lights, and so the Candy Dance returned.

This annual event raising funds to pay for the street lights soon became a popular event, attracting dancers from Reno and Carson City to join the fun. More than two tons of candy is now consumed during the dance weekend. In the 1970s, an arts and crafts fair featuring 300 booths of merchandise was added to the two-day event. Locals dressed as Wyatt Earp and his cohorts roam the town, engaging in gunfights. Activities for children include candle-making, face-painting, and tattoos. The Candy Dance Arts and Crafts Faire, as it is now officially known, provides a substantial part of Genoa's annual operating budget.

CONTACTS:
Genoa Town Office
2289 Main St.
P.O. Box 14
Genoa, NV 89411
775-782-8696; fax: 775-782-2779
www.genoanevada.org

♦ 0488 ♦ Cannes Film Festival
May

The **International Film Festival** held in the resort city of Cannes on the French Riviera is probably the best known of the hundreds of film festivals held all over the world each year. Sponsored by governments, industry, service organizations, experimental film groups, or individual promoters, these festivals provide filmmakers, critics, distributors, and cinema enthusiasts an opportunity to attend showings of new films and to discuss current trends in the industry. The festival at Cannes is held at the Palais des Festivals, and its founding in 1947 marked a resurgence for the film industry, which had been shattered by World War II. The festival has also been responsible for the growing popularity of foreign films in the United States.

Other important film festivals are held in Berlin, London, San Francisco, New York, Chicago, Venice, and Karlovy Vary in the Czech Republic. Some cater to the films of just one country, some to specific subjects, and some are special festivals for student filmmakers.

CONTACTS:
Festival De Cannes, Cinefondation, Marche Du Film
3 rue Amelie
Paris 75007 France
33-1-5359-6100; fax: 33-1-5359-6110
www.festival-cannes.fr/en.html

♦ 0489 ♦ Cannes Shopping Festival
April

Each year in April, the city of Cannes in France hosts an expansive line-up of fashion shows and themed events showcasing the creativity and inspiration of some of the best talent in the fashion world. The Cannes Shopping Festival on the French Riviera is one of the premier events for both international and French fashion designers to display their *haute coutre* collections of clothes and accessories. The show, which is held at the Palais des Festivals et des Congrès, is impres-

sively choreographed and features multiple musical performances. Approximately 300 boutiques display fashion wares ranging from exclusive wedding dresses to casual street wear. The first day is typically devoted to catwalk runways and shows, while the remainder of the festival is filled with gala evenings accompanied by gourmet food and extravagant nightlife. Launched in 2004, the Cannes Shopping Festival is a relative newcomer to the fashion calendar in France. An exclusive event, attendance at the four-day long celebration is by invitation only.

CONTACTS:
Office du Tourisme Palais des Festivals et des Congrès – Cannes
1, boulevard de la Croisette
Cannes, 6400 France
33-4929-98422; fax: 33-49299-8423
www.cannes-destination.fr

♦ 0490 ♦ Cantaderas, Las
Late September or early October

The Fiesta of Las Cantaderas is held in the town of León, Spain. It dates back to a time when four parishes—San Marcelo, Mercado, San Martín, and Santa Ana—were required to contribute four to six young girls, 8-12 years old, as an annual tribute to the Moors. No family could escape this requirement, and any family without a daughter needed to provide a girl and costume her. When the king of León finally freed the population of this burden, the girls sang and danced in the streets to celebrate.

These days the *cantaderas* form a parade, starting at the town hall. They dance and sing their way down the street, directed by a woman called the *sotadera*, who is costumed in a veil and sequined, silk turban. The girls bear fruit baskets or other offerings, which they later give to the bishop. Although civil authorities regard these gifts as a voluntary offering, church authorities still see them as a necessary ceremony going back to feudal times.

CONTACTS:
Tourist Office of Spain
2655 Le Jeune Rd (Gables International Plaza)
Ste. 605
Coral Gables
Miami, FL 33134
305-476-1966; fax: 305-476-1964
www.spain.info

♦ 0491 ♦ Capac Raymi
December

The Capac Raymi was an Inca festival observed around the time of the December solstice (which is the SUMMER SOLSTICE in the Southern Hemisphere and the WINTER SOLSTICE in the Northern Hemisphere). The Inca Empire flourished in the Andean regions of South America, including Peru, Ecuador, and the northern parts of Chile and Argentina during the 15th and 16th centuries, until the Spanish arrived in 1531. The Capac Raymi served as an initiation ceremony for the young men of the ruling class. When the solstice arrived, the boys' ears were pierced in order to insert the large ear spools worn by Inca royalty.

See also INTI RAYMI.

CONTACTS:
Stichting Global Voices
Kingsfordweg 151
Amsterdam 1043GR Netherlands
globalvoicesonline.org

♦ 0492 ♦ Cape Minstrels' Carnival
January

The **Annual Minstrels' Carnival** in Cape Town, South Africa, was inspired by the animated singing and dancing of African-American musicians and singers of the United States. Bands are organized during the year, money is raised to purchase the materials needed for their costumes, and on NEW YEAR'S DAY, Second New Year (January 2), and the week or so that follows, the bands take over the city, displaying their costumes and performing their music in the streets.

This roisterous carnival is offset by string bands, the members of which are decorously dressed and parade with great dignity while playing sacred and other songs during the CHRISTMAS and New Year season.

♦ 0493 ♦ Cape Verde Independence Day
July 5

This public holiday commemorates Cape Verde's independence from Portugal on this day in 1975.

CONTACTS:
Rhode Island Cape Verdean Sub-Committee
P.O. Box 6206
Providence, RI 02940
401-617-9833
ricapeverdeanheritage.webs.com

♦ 0494 ♦ Cape Vincent French Festival
Saturday before July 14

Cape Vincent, New York, is in the Thousand Islands, where Lake Ontario meets the St. Lawrence River, an area with a strong French heritage. At one time, there was so much feeling for NAPOLEON among the local residents that they built a cup-and-saucer style house (a local architectural style in which the ground floor is wider than the second floor) where they hoped he might decide to spend his exile. However, it was one of Napoleon's followers, Le Roy de Chaumont, who first settled here in the 1800s.

Launched in 1968, the festival immediately drew an astounding number of visitors, many of them French Canadians. It takes place, appropriately enough, on the Saturday before BASTILLE DAY and features a wide variety of French foods as well as a pageant and a parade of decorated carts. A French

mass is held at St. Vincent de Paul's Church, and the evening ends with a waterfront display of fireworks.

CONTACTS:
Town of Cape Vincent
1964 NYS Rt. 12E
Cape Vincent, NY 13618
315-654-3660; fax: 315-654-3366
townofcapevincent.org

♦ 0495 ♦ Carabao Festival
May 14-15

A feast in honor of San Isidro Labrador (St. Isidore the Farmer), the patron saint of Filipino farmers, held in Pulilan, Bulacan province, the Philippines. The feast also honors the *carabao*, or water buffalo, the universal beast of burden of the Philippines. Farmers scrub their carabao, then decorate them with flowers to parade with the image of San Isidro. A carabao race is held, and at the finish line, the animals kneel while the parish priest blesses them. The festival is also marked by exploding firecrackers and the performance of the Bamboo Dance, where dancers represent the tinikling bird, a menace to the rice crop. Among the games played is *palo sebo*—climbing a greased pole to get the prize at the top.

See also ST. ISIDORE, FESTIVAL OF; SAN ISIDRO IN PERU, FIESTA OF; SAN ISIDRO THE FARMER, FEAST OF.

CONTACTS:
Provincial Youth, Sports, Employment, Arts & Culture Office
Gat Blas F. Ople Bldg.
Sentro ng Kabataan, Sining at Kultura ng Bulacan
Capitol Compound
Malolos, Bulacan 3017 Philippines
63-44-791-6604; fax: 63-44-791-2480
www.bulacan.gov.ph

♦ 0496 ♦ Caramoor International Music Festival
Mid-June to mid-August

In the 1930s, Walter and Lucie Rosen gave private concerts for their friends in the music room of their Mediterranean-style country estate in Katonah, New York, known as Caramoor. Their devotion to music led to the establishment of the Caramoor Festival in 1946. Small opera productions, chamber music, and children's programs are held in the estate's open-air Spanish courtyard, while the Venetian Theater, which incorporates Greek and Roman marble columns from a 15th-century Italian villa, has a stage large enough to accommodate a symphony orchestra and full-scale opera. Such world-class singers as Beverly Sills, Jessye Norman, and Charles Bressler have performed there, as have well-known instrumentalists Alicia De Larrocha, Misha Dichter, Garrick Ohlsson, and Philippe Entremont. Concerts are held Thursdays through Sundays for nine weeks during the summer. The festival is the summer home of the Orchestra of St. Luke's and St. Luke's Chamber Ensemble.

CONTACTS:
Caramoor Center for Music & the Arts, Inc
149 Girdle Ridge Rd.
P.O. Box 816
Katonah, NY 10536
914-232-5035; fax: 914-232-5521
www.caramoor.org

◆ 0497 ◆ Carberry Day
Friday the 13th

The students and faculty at Brown University in Providence, Rhode Island, celebrate the fictitious academic exploits of Professor Josiah Stinkney Carberry every Friday the 13th. It all began in 1929, when a young faculty member at Brown posted a notice saying that J. S. Carberry would give a lecture on "Archaic Greek Architectural Revetments in Connection with Ionian Philosophy" at eight o'clock, on a certain evening. Ben C. Clough, a retired Latin professor spotted the hoax and decided to join in the fun by inserting the word "not" between "will" and "give." After that, the joke took on a life of its own, and the ubiquitous Professor Carberry began to send postcards and telegrams with news of his latest exotic research trips. Articles under his name began appearing in scholarly journals and, in 1966, Brown gave Carberry a bona fide M.A. degree—awarded, of course, *in absentia*.

On Carberry Day, small brown jugs appear around the campus, and students and teachers fill them with change. The money goes to a book fund that Professor Carberry has set up "in memory of my future late wife, Laura.".

CONTACTS:
Brown University
45 Prospect St.
Providence, RI 02912
401-863-1000
www.brown.edu

◆ 0498 ◆ Caribbean Festival (Feast of Fire)
July

The annual Caribbean Festival in Santiago de Cuba, also known as the **Feast of Fire**, is dedicated to preserving and promoting the cultural traditions of the Caribbean. Casa del Caribe, a cultural center in Santiago de Cuba, organizes the event, along with several other Cuban groups. In addition to numerous performances of music and dancing, there are exhibitions of culinary arts, painting, crafts, drama, religious rituals, and poetry. Each year the festival gives special focus to one of the Caribbean countries. There are academic conferences that explore ways to promote and develop cultural understanding among the Caribbean nations and workshops on storytelling, music, and other traditional arts. Awards are presented to those who have made notable contributions to the culture of the region. Thousands of people from many nations attend the event, enjoying the street festivities and performances at the four main stages and many smaller venues. The "Serpent Parade" is a high point of the Festival, with throngs of dancing people winding their way through the streets of Santiago de Cuba.

◆ 0499 ◆ Caribou Carnival and Canadian Championship Dog Derby
Last weekend in March

The Caribou Carnival is a Canadian festival of winter sports and entertainment that includes competitions in snow and ice sculpting and beard growing. But the highlight of the carnival is the Championship Dog Derby. Offering more prize money than any other dog sled competition in the Northwest Territories, the grueling three-day race takes mushers 150 miles across Great Slave Lake.

In addition to sports, the carnival features a Mushers' Ball, a talent show, fireworks, and an ugly truck and dog contest. It is held in Yellowknife, the capital of the Northwest Territories, a vast region that stretches from the northern boundaries of the Canadian provinces to within 500 miles of the North Pole.

CONTACTS:
City of Yellowknife
4807-52 St.
P.O. Box 580
Yellowknife, NT X1A 2N4 Canada
867-920-5600
www.yellowknife.ca

◆ 0500 ◆ Caricom Day
On or near July 4

CARICOM stands for the "Caribbean Community," an organization established on July 4, 1973, for the purpose of supporting a common market, coordinating foreign policy, and promoting cooperation among the 15 member states of the Caribbean: Antigua and Barbuda, Bahamas, Barbados, Belize, Dominica, Grenada, Guyana, Haiti, Jamaica, Montserrat, St. Kitts-Nevis, St. Lucia, St. Vincent and the Grenadines, Suriname, and Trinidad and Tobago. Caricom Day is celebrated on or around July 4 in Barbados, Guyana, and St. Vincent. In Antigua and Barbuda, it is celebrated on the first Saturday in June.

CONTACTS:
Caribbean Community (CARICOM) Secretariat
P.O. Box 10827
Georgetown Guyana
592-222-0001-75; fax: 592-222-0171
www.caricom.org

◆ 0501 ◆ Carifest
August

The northern climate of Calgary, Alberta, may make the city an unlikely venue for celebrating Caribbean culture. But every summer Carifest helps transform the cold locale into a sunny and vibrant scene with Caribbean music, dancing, and food. After the Toronto Caribana, it is the largest Caribbean festival in Canada.

This five-day affair is organized by the Caribbean Community Council (CCC), which consists of various island association representatives. The CCC established Carifest in 1981 with a mission to offer local Caribbean residents a celebration reminiscent of their homeland. The organization also saw the need to expose all Calgarians to Caribbean culture and to celebrate the city's multicultural character.

The calypso, soca, and reggae music of the Caribbean enlivens the mood at the parade that kicks off the festival week. The procession always includes a special appearance by Miss Carifest, who is selected at a beauty pageant preceding the festival. More music is featured at the main event, the Sunshine Festival, which takes place at Prince's Island Park in downtown Calgary. In addition to its performances, the Sunshine Festival also draws large crowds with crafts and spicy Caribbean food.

CONTACTS:
Caribbean Community Council of Calgary
357 – 1500 14 St. SW
Calgary, AB T3C 1C9 Canada
403-774-1300; fax: 403-774-1300
www.carifestcalgary.com

◆ 0502 ◆ **Carillon Festival, International**
First full week in June

The only event of its kind in the world, the International Carillon Festival in Springfield, Illinois, attracts carillonneurs from France, Belgium, Germany, Brazil, New Zealand, and the Netherlands as well as from the United States. The centerpiece of the festival is the Rees Memorial Carillon, housed in a tower given to the community by Thomas Rees, publisher of the *Illinois State Register* from 1881 to 1933. Rees first became interested in the art and skill of playing bell music while visiting Holland and Belgium. The tower holds 66 bronze bells cast by a 300-year-old Dutch foundry and covering a range of five-and-a-half chromatic octaves. The bells are played manually by means of a keyboard.

The festival, instituted in 1962, features the music of Johann Sebastian BACH (1685-1750), Franz Schubert (1797-1828, *see also* SCHUBERTIADE), Wolfgang Amadeus MOZART (1756-1791), Edvard Grieg (1843-1907), and other compositions arranged for the carillon and played by internationally acclaimed masters of the instrument. The performances take place in Springfield's Washington Park, where listeners can sit the recommended 300 or more feet away.

◆ 0503 ◆ **Carinthian Summer Music Festival**
July-August

Austria, birthplace of Wolfgang Amadeus MOZART, is also home to this summertime classical music festival. For six weeks spanning July and August, the world's most renowned conductors and orchestras perform in various locations in the country's southernmost province, Carinthia.

The performance sites for the festival's symphonic pieces are as impressive as the roster of performing artists, which has included composer Leonard Bernstein and flautist James Galway. Ossiach Abbey, an 11th-century monastery, has re-

mained a main venue site since it hosted the first Carinthian festival, in 1969. Ensembles play at the abbey's church and its baroque hall, Villach's Congress Centre, Glanegg Castle, as well as other scenic settings throughout the mountainous province. The Festival has built its musical reputation on the rare genre known as the "church opera."

Organizers encourage families to take part in the proceedings by offering age-appropriate events for children. For individuals looking for an academic approach, there are instructional courses and opportunities to engage in dialogue with composers and musicians.

CONTACTS:
Office of Carinthian Summer Festival
Gumpendorferstraße 76/2
Vienna 1060 Austria
43-1-596-8198; fax: 43-1-597-1236
www.carinthischersommer.at

◆ 0504 ◆ **Carling Sunday**
Between March 8 and April 11 in the West;
between March 21 and April 24 in the East

Carling Sunday is the fifth Sunday in LENT, and is also known as **Passion Sunday**. Its name possibly derives from "care." It is traditional in Great Britain to eat a dish of parched peas cooked in butter, called a *carling*, said to be in memory of grain Jesus' disciples picked on the Sabbath.

CONTACTS:
Church of England National Office
Church House
Great Smith St.
London SW1P 3AZ United Kingdom
44-20-7898-1000
www.churchofengland.org

◆ 0505 ◆ **Carmentalia**
January 11 and 15

It was unusual in ancient Rome for a single deity to have two separate festival days only a few days apart, and a number of explanations—none of them conclusive—have been offered for why the second festival in honor of the goddess Carmenta was instituted. The only thing that is certain is that the goddess's most prominent characteristic was her gift of prophecy, and that it was primarily women who frequented her temple near the Porta Carmentalis, a gate at the foot of the southern end of the capitol. Carmenta was also a birth-goddess, and although it might seem unusual to celebrate birth in the middle of winter, January happens to be exactly nine months after April, then the most popular time for marriages.

Carmenta had her own priest, or *flamen,* whose duties on her festival days were confined to the preparation of offerings of grain or cereal. There was a taboo against animal skins in Carmenta's cult, perhaps because the slaughter of animals was antithetical to a goddess of birth. The women known as *Carmentes* were similar to midwives—wise old women whose skills and spells assisted women in childbirth, and who had the power to tell their fortunes.

◆ 0506 ◆ Carnaval Miami
February-March

Carnaval is the biggest event in Miami, Fla., honoring Hispanic culture. Held since 1938, it is estimated that one million people attend each year. The highlight and grand finale of the festival is the famous Calle Ocho Open House. This is non-stop, wall-to-wall entertainment along 23 blocks of Southwest Eighth Street (*Calle Ocho*): 40 stages with more than 200 troupes offering live music, dancing, and folkloric performances. There are more than 600 vendors of ethnic food. Other events are the Miss Carnaval Miami beauty contest; a grand *paseo* or parade with floats; limbo dancers, samba groups, and steel bands from the Caribbean; a footrace; a laser display; fireworks; and concerts of international stars.

CONTACTS:
Kiwanis Club of Little Havana
1400 S.W. First St.
Miami, FL 33135
305-644-8888; fax: 305-644-8693
www.carnavalmiami.com

◆ 0507 ◆ Carnea
August-September

The Carnea, also spelled **Karneia**, **Karnea**, or **Carneia**, was one of ancient Sparta's three principal religious festivals—the other two being the Hyacinthia and the Gymnopaidiai— which were observed in many parts of the Peloponnesus as well as in Cyrene, Magna Graecia, and elsewhere. It was the ultimate expression of the cult of Apollo Karneios, the ram god of flocks and herds and of fertility in general. It was held during the month of Carneus (August-September) and dates back to 676 B.C.E. The Carnea was both a vintage festival and a military one, Apollo being expected to help his people both by promoting the harvest and by supporting them in battle. Young men called *staphylodromoi*, or "grape-cluster-runners," chased after a man wearing garlands. It was considered a good omen for the city if they caught him and a bad one if they didn't.

No military operations could be held during this festival, and it is said that the Spartans might not have been defeated by the Persians at Thermopylae if the Carnea hadn't prevented the movement of their main army.

◆ 0508 ◆ Carnival
Various dates, from Epiphany to Ash Wednesday Eve

The period known as Carnival—probably from the Latin *caro* or *carne levara*, meaning "to take away meat" and "a farewell to flesh"—begins anytime after EPIPHANY and usually comes to a climax during the last three days before ASH WEDNESDAY, especially during MARDI GRAS. It is a time of feasting and revelry in anticipation of the prohibitions of LENT.

Carnival is still observed in most of Europe and the Americas. It features masked balls, lavish costume parades, torch processions, dancing, fireworks, noisemaking, and of course feasting on all the foods that will have to be given up for Lent. Ordinarily Carnival includes only the Sunday, Monday, and Tuesday before Ash Wednesday (*see* FASCHING), but sometimes it begins on the preceding Friday or even earlier. In Brazil, Carnival is the major holiday of the year.

See also KARNEVAL IN COLOGNE and SHROVE TUESDAY.

◆ 0509 ◆ Carnival (Argentina)
February-March

The celebration of CARNIVAL in Argentina has decreased in the larger cities, but it remains the most popular celebration of the year in the more sparsely inhabited northern zone. In the province of Jujuy, men and women wearing colorful blankets perform *carnivalito*, a traditional round dance where couples continually vary a few simple figures while their leader waves a handkerchief or ribboned stick and calls out for changes in a high voice. Although this dance at one time was associated with an ancient harvest festival, its significance in this context has been long forgotten. In some places people dance for a few hours a day. These festivities may continue for as long as a month.

The *tincunaco* ceremony is an important part of the Carnival celebration in other areas of Argentina. The ceremony symbolizes the sacred ties that unite a mother and her child's godmother. It takes place under an arch made from a branch taken from a willow tree and decorated with fruit, sweets, cheese, blossoms, and lanterns. The mothers line up on one side of the arch, the godmothers on the other. They move toward one another until they meet under the arch. There they touch foreheads and pass a child made from candy from one to the other. The celebration usually draws to a close with the mock funeral of Pukllay, the spirit of Carnival. One woman, chosen to act as Pukllay's wife, cries about her husband's death. The others tap drums and sing Carnival tunes. Pukllay—usually a rag doll dressed in native costume—is laid to rest in a freshly dug grave showered with blossoms and sweets.

CONTACTS:
National Secretariat of Tourism
Tourist Information Center
Av. Santa Fe 883
Buenos Aires C1059ABC Argentina
54-11-4312-2232 or 54-800-555-0016
www.turismo.gov.ar

◆ 0510 ◆ Carnival (Aruba)
February-March; three days before Ash Wednesday

Preparations for the CARNIVAL celebration on the island of Aruba begin months before the actual event. There is a calypso competition at the end of January, followed by a steel band competition to see who gets to perform in the Carnival parade in Oranjestad. Then there's a tumba contest, "tumba" being the native music of the Netherlands Antilles. The actual celebration begins three days before Ash Wednesday and ends at midnight on Mardi Gras.

The highlight is the Carnival Main Parade, which takes eight hours to wind its way through the streets of Oranjestad. It includes elaborate floats and people in colorful costumes dancing the jump-up, a dance performed to a half-march rhythm. The three-day festival comes to an end with the Old Mask Parade, followed by the traditional burning of "King Momo.".

◆ 0511 ◆ Carnival (Bolivia)
February-March

While Carnival celebrations were formerly held throughout Bolivia, the tendency in recent years has been for people together in the larger cities, such as La Paz, Sucre, Cochambamba, and Oruro, where the dancing and drinking can go on for a week (*see also* Carnival of Oruro). *Pepinos*, masked clowns that wear striped clothing and carry cardboard rods, are found only in La Paz. They wander through the crowds talking in high-pitched voices so that no one will know who they are. Thus disguised they strike at random passersby—who often hit back—with their cardboard batons. Those who wish to dress as pepinos must apply to the police for a special license and wear it throughout the festival so that all can see it. In this way, festivalgoers can identify pepinos that cause injury to people or property.

CONTACTS:
Museum of International Folk Art
706 Camino Lejo
On Museum Hill
Santa Fe, NM 87505
505-476-1200; fax: 505-476-1300
www.internationalfolkart.org

Bolivian Embassy
3014 Massachusetts Ave. N.W.
Washington, D.C. 20008
202-483-4410; fax: 202-328-3712
www.bolivia-usa.org

◆ 0512 ◆ Carnival (Brazil)
Between January 30 and March 5; four days preceding Ash Wednesday

Carnival is the largest popular festival in Brazil, the last chance for partying before Lent. The most extravagant celebration takes place along the eight miles of Copacabana Beach in Rio de Janeiro, where, since the 1930s, the parades, pageants, and costume balls go on for four days, all accompanied by the distinctive rhythm of the samba. The whole city is decorated with colored lights and streamers, and impromptu bands play on every street corner. Banks, stores, and government offices are closed until noon on Ash Wednesday.

The high point of the Carioca (as the natives of Rio are known) Carnival is the parade of the samba schools (*Escola de Samba*), which begins on Carnival Sunday and ends about midday on Monday. The samba schools are neighborhood

groups, many of whom come from the humblest sections of Rio, who develop their own choreography, costumes, and theme songs. The competition among them is as fierce as the rivalry of top sports teams. A single samba school can have as many as two to three thousand participants, so the scale of the parade can only be described as massive. People spend months learning special dances for the parade, and must often raise huge sums of money to pay for their costumes, which range from a few strategically placed strings of beads to elaborate spangled and feathered headdresses. Each samba school dances the length of the Sambadrome, a one-of-a-kind samba stadium designed by Oscar Niemeyer and built in 1984 to allow 85,000 spectators to watch the samba schools dance by. Viewing the parade from the Sambadrome is usually an all-night affair.

In recent years, more and more of Carnival has moved into clubs, the Club Monte Libano being one of the most famous. The Marilyn Monroe look-alike contest held by transvestites on Sugarloaf Mountain is among the most unusual events.

CONTACTS:
Rio-Carnival
Rua Souza Franco 386
201, Vila Isabel
Rio de Janeiro 20551 Brazil
www.rio-carnival.net

◆ 0513 ◆ Carnival (Colombia)
February-March; Friday through Tuesday before Ash Wednesday

From the Friday preceding Ash Wednesday until Shrove Tuesday, the Colombian city of Barranquilla celebrates Carnival. There are costume balls, folklore shows, water festivals, and, on the night before Ash Wednesday, the ceremonial burial of "José Carnaval," the spirit who rules over the festivities. Each *barrio*, or neighborhood, chooses its own beauty queen and holds informal parties, while the city's wealthier inhabitants hold pageants and formal balls, competing to see who can come up with the most ornate costume. *Ron blanco*, the local white rum, is the favored drink, and residents dance in the streets to African and Indian rhythms. The Battle of Flowers on the opening day of the festival involves many elaborate floats decorated with the country's exotic flora.

◆ 0514 ◆ Carnival (Cuba)
Late July to early August

The celebration of Carnival in Havana, Cuba, dates back to the earliest years of the republic, when it featured *comparsas*, or groups of Afro-Cuban dancers, and parades of local officials and other distinguished people in carriages or on horseback. The first floats, many of them imported from New Orleans, appeared in 1908, but from then on, the people of Havana began to design and construct floats of their own and to establish what soon became one of the best-known Carnival celebrations in all of the Americas.

The comparsas remain the highlight of Carnival. About 18 of these dance groups, which come from all parts of the island, entertain Carnival goers with well-orchestrated spectacles of song, dance, and gorgeous costume. Some of the comparsas— composed of ordinary people from all walks of life—have been in existence for nearly 100 years. Each brings its own band and pauses at several points along the parade route to present its choreographic spectacle. This usually includes a conga line, whose characteristic step may represent an attempt to mimic the foot-dragging gait of slaves in chains.

Under the dictatorship of Fidel Castro, Carnival has become somewhat more restrained. Floats and dramatic spectacles are often utilitized for propaganda purposes and to ridicule the country's political enemies. In recent years Carnival has been held over two or more weeks in late July and early August and associated with National Day on July 26 (*see* CUBA LIBERATION DAY).

◆ 0515 ◆ Carnival (Goa, India)
February-March; Saturday through Tuesday before Ash Wednesday

In Goa, a region on the southwest coast of India, CARNIVAL is known as **Intruz** because it leads into the period of LENT. Social conventions are relaxed, and people wearing masks toss *cocotes* and *cartuchos* (small paper packets containing flour and sawdust) at one another, or squirt each other with syringes of perfumed colored water—much like what goes on during the Hindu festival of HOLI. In Panaji, the capital of Goa, there is a huge parade in honor of King Momo, the Lord of the Revels, on SHROVE TUESDAY. There are floats with dancers and bands playing swing music, stilt-walkers dressed up as Walt Disney characters, tableaux, and grotesque figures in African masks. The entire procession can take as long as four hours to pass, ending at the Church of Our Lady of the Immaculate Conception. Afterward, there is dancing in the town squares, public halls, and on the beaches, with older people doing the tango and waltz while the young people dance to popular music. The festivities end at dawn on ASH WEDNESDAY, when most attendees head for church services.

CONTACTS:
Goa Department of Tourism
Paryatan Bhavan
1st Fl.
Panaji, Goa 403 001 India
91-832-2494200; fax: 91-832-2494227
www.goatourism.gov.in

◆ 0516 ◆ Carnival (Haiti)
February-March; three days preceding Ash Wednesday

Although the official CARNIVAL holiday in Haiti takes place during the last three days before ASH WEDNESDAY, the celebration actually begins on the first Sunday after EPIPHANY, when *bandes* or groups of costumed dancers begin to appear in the streets of the cities and suburbs. They often carry a sort of may-

pole, plant it in someone's yard, and then braid a simple pattern with the colored streamers as they dance to the rhythm of drums. The dancers often travel with *marchandes* who sell rum, candy, and rolls from the trays they carry on their heads. After the neighbors have gifted the dancers with a few coins, the whole entourage packs up and moves on to the next location.

The last three days before Ash Wednesday are particularly boisterous and exciting in Port-au-Prince, the capital. Almost everyone appears in costume, blowing noisemakers or playing musical instruments. Floats are pulled through the streets, decorated with bird feathers, palm fronds, flowers, and seashells as well as more mundane materials such as bottle caps, ribbons, and fabric. Because the merrymakers wear masks, they feel free to make fun of political leaders and local institutions. Although the Port-au-Prince celebration is the largest in Haiti, even wilder ones are held in Jacmel, Cap Haitien, Cayes, and Jérémie.

See also CARNIVAL LAMAYOTE; RARA.

◆ 0517 ◆ Carnival (Hungary) (Farsang)
January 6 to Ash Wednesday (February-March)

This is the time of year when most weddings are celebrated in Hungary, and when dances, parties, and festivities are held. In some parts of the country, villagers perform the symbolic burying of King Marrow Bone, who represents life's indulgences. Prince Cibere, whose name recalls the sour bran soup served throughout LENT, begins his 40-day reign on ASH WEDNESDAY.

In southern Hungary, masks known as *busó* that are passed down from one generation to the next are worn during MARDI GRAS. They are made out of carved wood painted with ox blood, with animal skins covering the top and ram's horns emerging from either side. Although at one time only adult married men could wear these masks, young unmarried men now wear them, shaking huge wooden rattles, shooting off cannons, and teasing women with long sticks topped by sheepskin gourds. In Slovenia, these masks have dangling red tongues, and the men wearing them run around in groups carrying clubs covered at one end with the skins of hedgehogs. The Busó parade in Mohács is said to be the biggest carnival event in Hungary.

CONTACTS:
Hungarian National Tourist Organisation
223 E. 52nd St.
New York, NY 10022
212-695-1221
www.gotohungary.com

◆ 0518 ◆ Carnival (Malta)
February-March; before Ash Wednesday

Carnival in Malta includes five days of pre-Lenten festivities, a custom since the 1500s. There are some festivities in the villages, but the main activities are in the capital city of Valletta. Here the traditional events include a parade with floats, brass bands, and participants wearing grotesque masks, as well as open-air folk-dancing competitions. A King Carnival reigns over the festival.

CONTACTS:
Malta Tourism Authority
Auberge D'Italie
Merchants St.
Valletta VLT 1170 Malta
356-2291-5000; fax: 356-2291-5394
www.visitmalta.com

♦ 0519 ♦ Carnival (Martinique and Guadeloupe)
January-March, until Ash Wednesday night

CARNIVAL celebrations on the French Caribbean island of Martinique and its sister island of Guadeloupe begin the Sunday after NEW YEAR'S DAY with weekend parties and dances in the larger cities and towns. But they reach a climax during the last few days before LENT. On the Sunday before Lent, there are parades with marchers in exotic costumes dancing to the beat of the *beguine*, a Congolese ritual dance. Stores and offices are closed on Monday, an official holiday that is spent singing and dancing, with masked balls that go on far into the night. SHROVE TUESDAY is a day for children to dress up in red-devil costumes and carry homemade tridents as they parade through the streets.

The celebration continues right through ASH WEDNESDAY, when thousands of masked, costumed she-devils (many of whom are men in drag) have a parade of their own. Everyone wears black and white, and dark-skinned faces are smeared with ash. Effigies of King Vaval and his alter ego, Bois-Bois, tower over the procession. That night the effigies are burned, and Vaval's coffin is lowered into the ground.

CONTACTS:
Martinique Promotion Bureau/CMT Americas
825 Third Ave.
29th Fl.
New York, NY 10022
212-838-6887
www.martiniquepro.org

♦ 0520 ♦ Carnival (Mexico)
February-March

CARNIVAL celebrations in Mexico vary from one town or region to the next, but almost all involve folk and ritual dances. In Tepeyanco and Papalotla, Tlaxcala State, *paragueros* ("umbrella men") perform exaggerated polkas and mazurkas during Carnival, wearing headdresses shaped like an umbrella. In Santa Ana Chiautempan and Contla, also in Tlaxcala State, *los catrines*—men dressed as women, or "dandies"— carry umbrellas as they mock high-society dances. Other dances performed during Carnival include the *moros, diablos,* and *muertos* taken over from the Spanish, as well as the *arcos* and *pastoras,* which are danced with flowered arches. In Morelos, the Carnival dancers are known as *chinelos.* Although they were formerly disguised as black Africans, nowadays

they wear long embroidered satin gowns, hats topped with ostrich plumes, and masks with horn-shaped black beards.

Carnival in Mexico is known for drama as well as dance. In Zaachila, Oaxaca State, there is a mock battle between priests and devils. In Huejotzingo, Puebla State, an elaborate drama staged over a period of three or four days dramatizes the exploits of the bandit Agustin Lorenzo and the woman with whom he elopes. Carnival is celebrated in Mexico City with fireworks, parades, street dancers, and costume balls.

See also ST. MARTIN'S CARNIVAL.

CONTACTS:
Mexico Tourism Board
Public Relations Liaison
2829 16th St. N.W., 4th Fl.
Washington, D.C. 20009
202-265-9021
www.mexico.us

♦ 0521 ♦ Carnival (Panama)
February-March; four days preceding Ash Wednesday

The celebration of CARNIVAL in Panama begins on the Saturday before ASH WEDNESDAY, when the Carnival Queen and her courtiers enter Panama City. They are greeted by King Momus, the god of gaiety. The Queen leads a parade through the streets, to the accompaniment of *murgas,* or walking bands. Sunday is Pollera Day, when the women bring out the brilliantly colored, hand-embroidered, multilayered *pollera* dresses that are often handed down from one generation to the next. Monday is the day when the *comparasas*—precision dance troupes dressed in elaborate costumes—compete for prizes. On Tuesday, the last day of the celebration, there is a Grand Parade of floats, walking bands, dancers, and all the groups that have performed or paraded on previous days. The festivities continue throughout the night, ending at dawn with the "burial of the fish" ceremony. A mock funeral is held for a dead fish, which is then dumped into the ocean or a swimming pool.

See also BURIAL OF THE SARDINE.

♦ 0522 ♦ Carnival (Peru)
February-March

In Peru, it is customary during CARNIVAL for people to throw water and flour at each other. Sometimes the flour and water are thrown from a balcony on whoever happens to be walking beneath. Groups of young people often stage battles in which the boys throw the girls into fountains or bathtubs and vice versa. At Carnival dances, even well-bred young men and women squirt water at each other from special syringes sold for this purpose. Water-throwing battles are common between sailboats on lakes and in private homes. A particularly colorful celebration is held in Cajamarca.

Although Carnival is celebrated throughout Peru, the events are not as elaborate as those in neighboring Brazil.

◆ 0523 ◆ Carnival (Portugal)
February-March; three days preceding Ash Wednesday

The pre-Lenten festivities in Portugal reach a peak on the last three days before ASH WEDNESDAY. There was a time when the CARNIVAL celebration in Lisbon was characterized by sexual banter and horseplay, with battles involving eggs, oranges, flour, and water. But the present-day public festivities are more restrained. People decorate their cars with masses of flowers, and as the cars parade through town, they pelt their friends and neighbors with blossoms while the bystanders try to retaliate.

There are balls, parties, and dances in the cities, but in rural areas many of the more uninhibited Carnival traditions persist. The *folía* (literally, "madness"), a fertility dance associated with the Portuguese Carnival celebration, is named after the quick and crazy movements of the participants. Mummers and musicians, the burial in effigy of King Carnival, and traditional folk plays are also part of these rural Carnival observances.

CONTACTS:
Turismo de Portugal
Rua Ivone Silva
Lote 6
Lisbon 1050-124 Portugal
351-211-140-200
www.visitportugal.com

◆ 0524 ◆ Carnival (Spain)
February-March; three days preceding Ash Wednesday

CARNIVAL in Spain is an occasion for feasting and partying. Bullfights, masquerade parties, weddings, and dances are held in almost every town and village. The Prado Museum in Madrid resembles a huge street fair, with masqueraders, battles of flowers, showers of confetti, and throngs of vendors. In Catalonia, the northeastern section of Spain, Carnival is observed with the *baile de cintas* or *baile del cordon,* the Spanish ribbon or maypole dance. Another traditional Spanish dance associated with Carnival is *los seises* ("the six"), similar to the English Morris dance. When los seises were on the verge of being suppressed in 1685, they were preserved by papal edict for as long as the costumes lasted. With good care and numerous repairs, they have lasted to this day.

Throwing flowers and confetti at bystanders from blossom-decked cars is another Carnival tradition in Spain. Some towns even stage a battle of flowers. A particularly colorful celebration is held in Valencia, where the orange trees are in bloom at this time of year.

The city of Santa Cruz de Tenerife hosts what many consider the most Brazilesque Carnival celebration in Spain. Parades and musical and dance contests fill the days leading up to ASH WEDNESDAY, when there are fireworks and the traditional BURIAL OF THE SARDINE.

CONTACTS:
Tourist Office of Spain
845 North Michigan Ave.
Ste. 915-E
Chicago, IL 60611
312-642-1992; fax: 312-642-9817
www.spain.info

◆ 0525 ◆ Carnival (Switzerland)
February-March; usually the three days preceding Ash Wednesday

The Swiss actually observe CARNIVAL, or **Fasnacht**, at two different times: in the Roman Catholic cantons, it is observed according to the Gregorian calendar; the Protestant cantons follow the Julian calendar and celebrate it 13 days later.

In Basel, the lights of the city go out at 4:00 A.M., when fife and drum bands perform in the market square. Then members of the Carnival guilds, wearing wild masks and costumes, parade through the streets with lanterns on long poles or perched on their heads, to the accompaniment of pipers and drummers. Frightening masks are also worn during the Carnival celebration at Flums, where they represent such notions as war, death, or disease. At Einsiedeln, "Carnival Runners" dash through the city's thoroughfares from Sunday to ASH WEDNESDAY morning, displaying frightening masks and huge jangling bells strapped to their backs. The masks and bells found in many Swiss Carnival traditions are believed to have survived from ancient times, when people "drove out winter" with loud sounds and frightening masks.

In some parts of Switzerland it is the children who parade through the streets at Carnival, singing and carrying the national flag. The boys dress in costumes that offer clues to their fathers' professions and the girls masquerade as fairies.

CONTACTS:
Swiss National Tourist Office
608 Fifth Ave.
Ste. 202
New York, NY 10020
800-794-7795; fax: 212-262-6116
www.myswitzerland.com

◆ 0526 ◆ Carnival (U.S. Virgin Islands)
Last two weeks in April

Unlike CARNIVAL in New Orleans, Brazil, and elsewhere in the world, where it is a pre-Lenten celebration, the Virgin Islands Carnival is held after EASTER, toward the end of April. It dates back to the days when Danish plantation owners gave their slaves time off to celebrate the end of the sugar cane harvest. Although the first Carnival in 1912 was a great success, it wasn't held again for four decades. Since 1952, it has been an annual event in the capital city of Charlotte Amalie on the island of St. Thomas, and nowadays the Carnival observance in St. Thomas ranks second only to the Trinidad and Tobago Carnival.

Preliminary events begin a week or more beforehand, and the official Carnival period runs from Sunday until midnight the following Saturday. It begins with the opening of Calypso Tent, a week-long calypso song competition for the coveted title of "Calypso King." The celebrations include the crowning of a Carnival Queen, children's parades, a J'Ouvert morning tramp, steel bands, and dancing in the streets. The climax comes on Saturday with the grand carnival parade, featuring limbo dancers, masked figures, and mock stick-fights between Carib Indians and "Zulus." The celebration winds up with one of the most elaborate all-day parades in the Caribbean, featuring the Mocko Jumbi Dancers. These are colorful dancers on 17-foot stilts whose dances and customs derived from ancient cult traditions brought to the islands by African slaves.

CONTACTS:
United States Virgin Islands Department of Tourism
P.O. Box 6400
St. Thomas, VI 00804
340-774-8784; fax: 340-774-4390
www.visitusvi.com

◆ 0527 ◆ Carnival (Venice)
Begins between February 3 and March 9; ending on Shrove Tuesday night

The Carnival celebration in Venice, Italy, is more sophisticated and steeped in tradition than the flashy celebrations that take place in Rio de Janeiro and New Orleans (*see* Carnival in Brazil; Mardi Gras). Costumes for the event are often drawn from the stock characters of Italian popular theater from the 16th through 18th centuries—including Harlequin, a masked clown in diamond-patterned tights; Punchinello, the hunchback; and Pierrot, the sad white-faced clown adapted by the French from the commedia dell'arte. There are also traditional costumed characters such as *La Bautta* (the domino), *Il Dottore* (the professor or doctor of law), and the Renaissance count or countess.

Italian university students, usually in more innovative costumes, pour into Venice as Ash Wednesday draws near. The rhythm of the celebration quickens, evidenced by a number of spectacular costume balls. The costume ball given at Teatro La Fenice—a benefit for charity—is known for attracting film stars, members of European nobility, and other rich and famous people.

◆ 0528 ◆ Carnival Lamayote
February-March; before Ash Wednesday

Carnival, the biggest holiday of the year in Haiti, is distinguished from other Carnival celebrations by the preparation of wooden boxes, decorated with tissue paper and paint, known as *lamayotes*. Haitian boys put a "monster"—usually a mouse, lizard, bug, or other small animal—inside these boxes. During Carnival they dress up in masks and costumes and try to persuade people to pay them a penny for a peek inside their box.

See also Rara.

◆ 0529 ◆ Carnival Memphis
May-June

Carnival celebrations in Memphis, Tennessee, take the form of parties sponsored by the city's "krewes" (private social clubs) throughout the spring. Each Krewe's "king," "queen," and other royal officers are selected each year and preside over some of these functions, the most important of which take place in May and June. Once composed of two separate events—the "Cotton Carnival" attended primarily by whites and the "Cotton Maker's Jubilee" attended primarily by blacks—the event has become slightly more integrated in recent decades. In the one major event open to the public, the Carnival parade, royalty from both black and white clubs ride through the streets together.

Cotton has been an important crop to the people of Memphis since before the Civil War, when the city served as the largest inland port and cotton market in the American South. The Cotton Festival began in 1931—a faint echo of the city's long abandoned Mardi Gras celebrations—as a means of cheering up the populace during the Depression. The Cotton Maker's Jubilee got its start in 1935. Cotton remains an important aspect of the city's economy, as Memphis continues to serve as one of the world's largest cotton markets.

CONTACTS:
Carnival Memphis
4735 Spottswood Ave.
Ste. 103
Memphis, TN 38117
901-458-2500; fax: 901-458-0955
www.carnivalmemphis.org

◆ 0530 ◆ Carnival of Binche
February-March; seven weeks preceding Shrove Tuesday

Carnival of Binche is the most famous pre-Lenten carnival in Belgium and one of the most unusual in Europe. Festivities in Binche, a town of 10,000 population, begin seven weeks before Lent starts and culminate on Mardi Gras with day-long rites of elaborately costumed, orange-throwing clowns called *Gilles*, which means, roughly, "fools" or "jesters." Some 200,000 visitors come for the Mardi Gras weekend.

The Gilles—about 800 men and boys—wear suits stuffed with hay and decorated with appliqued rearing lions, crowns, and stars in the Belgian colors of red, yellow, and black. Heavy bells hang at their waists, and their headdresses—four feet tall and weighing up to seven pounds—are topped by ostrich plumes. In the early morning, the Gilles wear masks with green spectacles and orange eyebrows and moustaches, but these are doffed later in the day when the ostrich headdresses go on. The rites start at daybreak when the Gilles gather in the main square of Binche. To the beating of drums, they march and dance through the streets, stomping their wooden shoes and pelting spectators with oranges. Fireworks at midnight officially end the carnival, but dancing often goes on until dawn of ASH WEDNESDAY.

The most accepted legend explaining the carnival traces its origins to a fete in 1549. Spain had just conquered Peru, and Mary of Hungary, regent of the Netherlands, gave a sumptuous reception at her Binche palace for her nephew, Philip II of Spain. Supposedly, the costumes of the Gilles are patterned on the wardrobe of the Incas, and the thrown oranges represent the Incan gold. A document from 1795 is the earliest to describe the mask of the Gilles.

Some people have suggested that the English word "binge" comes from Binche.

CONTACTS:
Tourist Information Office of Binche
Grand-Place
Binche 7130 Belgium
32-6433-6727; fax: 32-6423-0647
www.carnavaldebinche.be

♦ 0531 ♦ Carnival of Blacks and Whites
January 4-6

The Carnival of Blacks and Whites, held each year in Pasto, Colombia, is one of the oldest Carnival celebrations in South America. In 2002, it was officially declared part of the nation's cultural heritage. This Carnival has four distinct sections, drawn from different aspects of its traditions and history, but the main event commemorated is an annual day of freedom that was granted to slaves during the 1600s. According to tradition, in 1607 there was a slave uprising in Remedios that badly frightened the Spanish masters. The slave population in Popayán played on this fear and demanded at least one day of freedom to offset a similar revolt. They were given January 5 as their own, and on that day they took over the streets, danced to African rhythms, and blackened the city's white walls with coal. This celebration was brought to Pasto by the Ayerbe family in the mid-1800s. By the late 1880s, it had become quite elaborate and had taken on the traditional Carnival use of masks and costumes.

Pre-Carnival festivities begin on December 28, HOLY INNOCENTS' DAY. This day honors the infants slain by King Herod as he sought to destroy the Christ child. In Colombia, it is a day to play pranks on friends and neighbors, usually involving hiding and trying to squirt them other with water. On January 3, pre-Carnival festivities continue with "el Carnavalito," featuring a special children's parade.

The Carnival officially opens on January 4, with a parade that commemorates the arrival in Pasto of the Castañeda family. Some say that the Castañedas are a caricature of the Ayerbe family, while others believe the Castañedas were a large country family that passed through or settled in Pasto in the early 20th century. Whatever the historical truth, in the parade and Carnival the Castañedas are presented as a zany group that includes a pregnant teenaged bride and many

misbehaving children. They are overburdened with luggage, mattresses, and cooking equipment.

The following day, January 5, is the Day of the Blacks, on which the slave revolt is remembered. Revelers celebrate in the streets, and, using special paints and cosmetics designed for the occasion, they paint themselves, their friends, and the town's walls and buildings black. Festivities continue on January 6 with the Day of the Whites. White paints and cosmetics are used as they were the day before, and white powder is also thrown. The Carnival reaches its peak on this day with a final parade consisting of costumed groups, musical and dance ensembles, and elaborate floats that may have been a year in the making.

♦ 0532 ♦ Carnival of Flowers
Late September-early October

The **Toowoomba Carnival of Flowers** held in Queensland, Australia, is responsible for the city of Toowoomba being known as "Australia's Garden City." Since 1950 the eight-day event has included tours of home and city gardens, floral exhibits in all the city shops, a competition for home gardeners, and a special display of exotic and native orchids by the Toowoomba Orchid Society. The highlight of the festival is the Floral Parade, which features thousands of flower-decorated floats and girls in floral costumes. The festival's performing and visual arts section includes theater, music, children's plays, jazz, films, and arts and crafts exhibits.

CONTACTS:
Toowoomba Carnival of Flowers Office
James Cook Centre, Level 1
580-588 Ruthven St
Toowoomba, QLD 4350 Australia
61-131-872
www.tcof.com.au

♦ 0533 ♦ Carnival of Ivrea Orange-Throwing Battle
Week before Lent

The highlight of the annual pre-Lent carnival—held every year for generations in Ivrea, Italy—is the massive orange-throwing battle that involves thousands of combatants in the town's streets and squares. The battle evokes, rather than re-enacts, past events in the town's long history—in this case, key insurrections that the townspeople launched against undesirable leaders. One of the most notorious of these was the medieval Count Raineri di Biandrate, a tyrant who tried to seize maidens' virginity before their weddings. Much of the carnival's activities are inspired by a legendary revolt by the townspeople in 1194 against the Count. They killed him and destroyed his castle, and liberty triumphed.

On the Sunday before LENT, the battle of the oranges is pitted between throwers on foot—who represent the townspeople—and others on decorated horse-drawn wagons, who represent the tyrant's officers. Anyone is welcome to take part. The fight rages all over town, often continuing through MARDI GRAS, or the Tuesday before Lent. The streets become thick with orange peels and the air acrid with their scent. On ASH WEDNESDAY, religious solemnity takes over, and peace is restored for another year.

CONTACTS:
Foundation of the Battle of the Oranges
Antico Palazzo della Credenza
Ivrea 10015 Italy
39-0125-641521
www.storicocarnevaleivrea.it

◆ 0534 ◆ Carnival of Oruro, Bolivia
Between February and March; week preceding Ash Wednesday

The CARNIVAL celebrations in Oruro, Bolivia, continue for an entire week and include music, dancing, eating and drinking, and offerings to *Pachamama*, or Mother Earth. But the highlight is the parade that begins with a series of vehicles carrying items made from gold and silver, jewels, exquisitely embroidered cloth, and antique coins and bills. Next are the Diablos, costumed with horns made from plaster, colored lightbulbs in place of eyes, teeth made from shards of mirrors, and hair fashioned out of tail hairs taken from horses or oxen. They are led by Lucifer and two Satans and accompanied by five cavorting female devils. Then come the Incas, who portray famous people from the time of the Spanish conquest, and the Tobas, who perform war dances. The llama drivers, or *llameros*, are next, followed by the *Callahuallas*, or witch doctors, and a number of other companies, each with its own distinctive costumes and role in the procession. The parade ends with the entry of all the masked groups into the church for a mass in honor of the Virgen del Socavón.

◆ 0535 ◆ Carnival of the Devil
January 2-8 in alternate years

The Carnival of the Devil, held every other year in Riosucio, Caldas, Colombia, is considered so important to Colombia's identity that it has been given official status as part of the nation's cultural heritage. At this unusual festival, a "good" devil is worshipped and celebrated with song and dance. Rather than a representation of absolute evil, he is a playful, happy figure, one who embodies human weaknesses and unsatisfied longings. During the festival, tributes are offered to this devil by artists, poets, writers, and other revelers.

The roots of this festival are very old. It was first officially held in 1847, when the towns of Quiebralomo and Montaña were combined. One of the most striking aspects of the festival is its blending of traditions from different cultures. The people of Quiebralomo had been celebrating the Christian festival of EPIPHANY, or the visit of the Three Wise Men to the infant Jesus, since the 16th century. Even in that celebration, European and African customs had been mixed. Elements from the ancient, native Indian cultures of Colombia were added when the two towns joined their celebrations. These

include worship of the earth, the sun, and the jaguar. The slanted eyes and other features of the big cat (a sacred animal that represents the astral king) have been incorporated into many devil masks. *Guarapo*, a beverage made of fermented maize, is drunk from *calabazos*, or drinking vessels made from gourds.

The festivities begin when the devil takes his throne. Parades, fireworks, bullfights, crafts shows, and other amusements are ongoing, along with contemporary art and music performances by groups known as *cuadrilas*. Spectators and participants alike may dress in colorful devil costumes and masks, which are often painstakingly handcrafted. The costumed revelers represent the main demon's court of lesser devils. At the close of the Carnival, the devil makes a speech promising to return in two years, bringing his little demons back with him.

◆ 0536 ◆ Carnival of the Laetare
Weekend of Laetare Sunday (fourth Sunday of Lent)

Throughout the history of the Catholic Church, various communities designated the fourth Sunday of Lent, known as Laetare Sunday, as a day for carousing—a rare moment of joy in an otherwise somber season. Some believers view the party as a great motivator to persevere through the remainder of their Lent sacrifice. Stavelot, a municipality in the Walloon region of Belgium, developed its own peculiar tradition for this holiday: Carnival of the Laetare, or **Carnival of the Blanc-Moussis (White Brethren)**.

According to legend, the monks of the region joined the carnival celebration in the late 15th century. The local abbotprince did not approve of the monks' participation, and in mocking rebellion, the people subsequently honored the monks by putting on habits themselves. To add fuel to the fire, they even added a laughing mask with a long red nose to the costume.

The many Blanc-Moussis who populate the festival still remain the central focus today. During the parade, which is held on Sunday, the costumed men stand on floats and shower the crowds with confetti and inflated pig bladders. Throughout the weekend, there are also live music performances and fireworks displays.

CONTACTS:
Royal Comité des fêtes de Stavelot
Pré Messire, 1
Stavelot 4970 Belgium
32-8086-3171
www.laetare-stavelot.be

◆ 0537 ◆ Carnival Thursday
Between January 29 and March 4; Thursday before Shrove Tuesday

This is the day on which pre-Lenten celebrations, such as CARNIVAL, traditionally begin, ending several days later on

SHROVE TUESDAY night. These celebrations often take the form of wild revelry, which is perhaps why it also has been referred to as **Mad Thursday**.

◆ 0538 ◆ Carriacou Parang Festival
Weekend before Christmas, December 25

The Carriacou Parang Festival has been held annually since 1977 to sustain the musical tradition of house-to-house serenading by acoustic string bands at Christmas time. Located in the Caribbean Sea, Carriacou is the largest of the sister islands of Grenada, of which it is a dependency. Carriacou is just 13 square miles in size, with a population of mixed Scottish and African ancestry.

The Parang Festival is held in the form of a musical competition. Organized parang groups from villages throughout Carriacou, its neighboring island Petit Martinique, and Grenada compete for cash prizes and a challenge trophy. Groups comprise not more than eight members, all dressed in colorful outfits to reflect the festive season. Some of the instruments used include the bass drum, iron, guitar, quarto, violin, marack (shack-shack), mandolin, saxophone, tambourine, and others. Groups make two appearances, first to perform a "test-piece" Christmas carol selected by the festival committee. In their second appearance, groups perform a song of their choice. Groups are judged on appearance as well as performance.

In 1987, the festival was extended from one day to two, so that international entertainers could perform for the people of Carriacou and Petit Martinique. As a result, the Saturday night of the festival is known as "foreign entertainers' night." The festival was founded and is run by the Mt. Royal Progressive Youth Movement, a non-profit youth organization dedicated to developing its community and serving the less fortunate in society.

CONTACTS:
Carriacou Parang Festival Committee
c/o Mt. Royal Progressive Youth Movement
Mt. Royal, Carriacou Grenada
473-443-7647 or 473-417-8216
www.carriacouparangfestival.com

◆ 0539 ◆ Carthage, International Festival of
Early July to late August

The International Festival of Carthage features classical music, jazz, folk music, theater, films, and ballet. It was founded in 1963 by the Tunisian Ministry of Cultural Affairs to bring foreign productions to Tunisia and to introduce the Tunisian public to the cultures of the West. Both Tunisian and foreign artists and ensembles—many of them from Romania, Spain, France, Germany, the Czech Republic, and the former U.S.S.R.—appear at the festival, which is held in a Roman amphitheater. Well-known American stars who have appeared there include James Brown, Joan Baez, Ray Charles, and Cab Calloway. The two-month Carthage Festival is held concurrently with the Festival of Hammamet, which also includes performances of music, dance, folklore, and theater in an open-air setting.

◆ 0540 ◆ Carthaginians and Romans Fiesta
10 days in late September

Cartegena, located on the Mediterranean Sea in southeastern Spain, is an ancient city steeped in the history of the Carthaginian and Roman Empires. Founded as the central Carthaginian hub in 227 B.C.E., the city was conquered two decades later by the Romans. Today, for 10 days in late September, thousands of local people celebrate the Carthaginians and Romans Fiesta by dressing in period costume and reenacting this pivotal era in history. The festival has been an annual event since 1989.

The festivities open with a ceremonial lighting of a sacred fire, which is followed by the official presentation of the Carthaginian troops and the Roman Legions. During the festival the soldiers stay in Carthaginian and Roman camps, each constructed in a historically accurate style.

Over the next several days, festival attendees witness a series of reenactments, including a Roman circus; the wedding of Carthaginian commander Hannibal and his wife Himilce; the sea battle that preceded the Roman conquest of the city; and the victorious march by the Roman Legions through the streets of Cartegena. On the festival's final day, both sides make one more procession through the city.

CONTACTS:
Tourist Office of Spain
60 E. 42nd St.
Ste. 5300. 53rd Fl.
New York, NY 10165
www.spain.info/en

◆ 0541 ◆ Caruaru Roundup
September

Roundups started out as nothing more than the yearly task of bringing the cattle together in the winter for branding. But in parts of Brazil they have developed into folkloric celebrations involving the participation of hundreds of cowboys who compete in "downing the steers." The roundup in the city of Caruaru in Pernambuco state is one of the largest. In addition to steer-roping contests, viola players and *repentistas* (verse improvisers) entertain the people with their music and rhyming descriptions of the day's activities. Local food specialties are served during the three-day event.

◆ 0542 ◆ Casa Grande Cowboy Days & O'odham Tash
Mid-February

For 44 years, the O'odham Tash Fair and All-Indian Rodeo was held over a weekend in mid-February in Casa Grande,

Ariz. One of the largest Native-American festivals in the United States, it drew dozens of tribes to take part in a celebration of native peoples. In 2010, a dispute between the festival organizers and the city of Casa Grande brought an end to the traditional event.

The following year, the city of Casa Grande revived the O'odham Tash event, merging it with the city's Cowboy Days celebration to create the Casa Grande Cowboy Days & O'odham Tash. Held at the Ed Hooper Rodeo Grounds, the festival highlight is the O'odham Tash All-Indian Rodeo featuring bull riding, wild horse racing, tie-down roping, steer wrestling competitions among the best Native American cowboys and cowgirls from the four O'odham sister tribes. In addition to the rodeo events, the festival includes carnivals, parades, and Native American performances. Proceeds from the events benefit the local community and provide scholarships to local students.

CONTACTS:
Arizona Office of Tourism
1110 W. Washignton St.
Ste. 155
Phoenix, AZ 85007
866-275-5816
www.visitarizona.com

♦ 0543 ♦ **Casals Festival**
February to March

This event is a two-week music festival held in San Juan, Puerto Rico, to celebrate the memory of Pablo Casals (1876-1973), the world-renowned Spanish-born cellist and conductor. An outspoken opponent of Fascism and the regime of Francisco Franco, he was forced to leave Spain and moved to France in 1936. Twenty years later he moved to Puerto Rico, the birthplace of his mother. There he initiated this music festival.

Through the years internationally known artists, among them Rudolf Serkin, Andrés Segovia, Arthur Rubenstein, Isaac Stern, and Yehudi Menuhin (*see also* MENUHIN FESTIVAL), have appeared at the festival. Programs offer a variety of composers, from BACH to Bartók.

CONTACTS:
Casals Festival in Puerto Rico
P.O. Box 41227
San Juan, PR 00940
787-918-1177
www2.pr.gov

♦ 0544 ♦ **Cassinga Day**
May 4

On May 4, 1978, South African forces attacked a SWAPO (South West Africa People's Organization) base located in the old Angolan mining town of Cassinga. Hundreds of Namibians died during the attack. Although Namibia eventually won its political independence in 1990 and is currently ruled by the SWAPO party government, a national holiday is declared every year on the anniversary of the attack to commemorate those who died in their country's struggle for independence.

CONTACTS:
Namibian Embassy
1605 New Hampshire Ave. N.W.
Washington, D.C. 20009
202-986-0540; fax: 202-986-0443
www.namibianembassyusa.org

♦ 0545 ♦ **Castor and Pollux, Festival of**
July 15

In Greco-Roman mythology, Castor and Pollux were twin gods who helped shipwrecked sailors and received sacrifices for favorable winds. Worshipped as the Dioscuri (from the Greek *Dioskouroi*, or "sons of Zeus"), their cult was a popular one in 484 B.C.E., when, according to legend, the twins fought on the side of the Romans in the Battle of Lake Regillus and brought word of their victory to Rome. A temple was built for them in the Forum, and it was here that the annual festival in their honor was celebrated on July 15.

Castor and Pollux were renowned for their athletic ability and are usually depicted as horsemen. They shared the same mother, Leda, but Castor was the son of Tyndareus and was therefore mortal, while Pollux was the son of Zeus and immortal. When they got into an argument with Idas and Lynceus, another set of twins, Castor was slain. Pollux was heartbroken because, as an immortal, he could not join his brother in death. Zeus finally allowed them to stay together, dividing their time between the heavens and the underworld. Eventually they were transformed into the constellation known as Gemini (The Twins), which, before the invention of the compass, was an important aid to navigation.

♦ 0546 ♦ **Castroville Artichoke Food and Wine Festival**
Last weekend in May

The Castroville Artichoke Food and Wine Festival is one of the oldest agricultural festivals in California, held in Castroville, which calls itself the "Artichoke Center of the World." The two-day festival began in 1959 with a barbecue and parade; there is still a parade, and the lead float traditionally carries the Artichoke Queen and a huge green artichoke replica. Other events include a classic car show, a fun run, and displays of "AGROart"—sculptures composed of fruits and vegetables. Food booths offer artichoke cookies and french-fried artichokes. Attendance may reach 14,000.

Castroville, founded in 1863 by Juan Bautista Castro, was an agricultural community from the start. In 1888 sugar beets became an important crop on the land west of Castro's settlement. When beet prices declined in 1921, Andrew J. Molera, the owner of the land, decided to grow artichokes, which were new to the U.S. market. He provided the plants for the first crop and leased the acreage to farmers. By 1925, more than 4,000 acres of artichokes were being cultivated, and by 1929 artichokes were the third largest cash crop of the Salinas Valley.

CONTACTS:
Castroville Festivals
P.O. Box 1041
Castroville, CA 95012
831-633-2465; fax: 831-633-0485
www.artichokefestival.org

♦ 0547 ♦ Caturmas
June through September

The Jains follow an ancient Indian religion popularized by MAHAVIRA. The name of the religion derives from *jinas*, meaning "spiritual victors." There have been 24 jinas so far in this age of the world, according to Jainism. Nonviolence, or *ashima*, is one of Jainism's primary tenets, and devout Jains go to considerable lengths to avoid harming other living beings, including adhering to a vegetarian diet.

Jains observe a retreat known as Caturmas during the rainy season in India, during which travel is curtailed and fasting is frequent. Some speculate that this tradition is based in the Jains' concern for the many small insects that come out during the rainy season, whom they do not wish to kill unnecessarily by traveling about.

CONTACTS:
Federation of Jain Associations in North America
722 S. Main St.
Milpitas, CA 95035
510-730-0204
www.jaina.org

Ahimsa Foundation
21, Skipper House
9, Pusa Rd.
New Delhi, New Delhi 110 005 India
91-11-2875-4012
www.jainsamaj.org

♦ 0548 ♦ Cavalcata Sarda
Second to last Sunday of May

This famous procession—or *cavalcata*—was originally held in Sassari, Sardinia, Italy, more than 900 years ago to celebrate a victory over Saracen invaders. Today the procession consists of costumed groups from over 100 Sardinian villages. Wearing the traditional dress of their region, participants in the Cavalcata Sarda often ride through the streets in ox-drawn carts. After the procession is over, the celebration continues with singing and dancing.

CONTACTS:
Italian National Tourist Board
686 Park Ave.
3rd Fl.
New York, NY 10065
212-245-5618; fax: 212-586-9249
www.italiantourism.com

♦ 0549 ♦ Cavalhadas
50 days after Easter

During the Pentecost season, Brazilian Catholics celebrate Festival of the DIVINE HOLY SPIRIT (Festa do Divino). This festival, believed to have been established by Portugal's Queen Isabel in the 13th century, observes the ascension of Christ into heaven, which is commemorated by Christians worldwide. One distinctly Brazilian tradition during the three-day festival is the Cavalhadas, a ceremony that reenacts the Christian knights' defeat of the Moors on the Iberian Peninsula during the Middle Ages.

Cavalhadas has been an annual observance since 1819. It is held throughout Brazil, although the most popular celebration takes place in the historic city of Pirenópolis in the country's central region. A smaller festival takes place in Amarantina, located farther to the south.

Among the feast's expressly religious activities are masses, processions, and the recitation of novenas. The festival's most-attended event is the staging of the knight tournament itself, which in Pirenópolis occurs in the city's bull ring. All the actors ride on horseback, with the Christian knights, dressed in blue, squaring off against the Moors, in red.

♦ 0550 ♦ Central African Republic Independence Day
August 13; December 1

On December 1, 1958, the region now known as Central African Republic became a republic within the French Community. The republic achieved independence from France on August 13, 1960. Both days are celebrated as national holidays.

CONTACTS:
Kalapairavar of Sri Kashi Tatcina
2704 Ontario Rd.
Washington, D.C. 20009
202-483-7800; fax: 202-332-9893
www.rcawashington.org

♦ 0551 ♦ Central City Opera Festival
Late June to mid-August

Central City Opera Festival is a festival of opera, operetta, and cabaret in the one-time mining town of Central City, Colo. Performances are staged in the Old Opera House, built in 1878 and since restored to its original Victorian elegance. On opening night, "flower girls" present the audience with fresh flowers, which are thrown on stage to the cast at the end of the performance.

Inaugurated in 1932, the **Opera Festival** was not only the first summer opera festival in the country but also the first to espouse singing opera in English, a tradition that continues. *The Ballad of Baby Doe*, an opera that depicts the love story of the real-life silver king, Horace Tabor, who left his wife for the beautiful and much younger Baby Doe, was commissioned by Central City.

Cabaret opera is presented in the historic Teller House next to the Opera House. Built in 1872, this was once the grandest hotel in the west, host to President Ulysses S. Grant and other notables.

One of the presentations is *Face on the Barroom Floor*, which was commissioned on the 100th anniversary of the opera house. The saloon of the Teller House is the site of the "face" made famous in the poem by H. Antoine D'Arcy. The poem tells the story of the drunken vagabond who comes into the bar, asks for whiskey, and explains that he was once a painter who fell in love with beautiful Madeline—and that she was stolen away by his friend. "That's why I took to drink, boys," the vagabond says, and then offers to draw Madeline's portrait on the barroom floor:

Another drink, and with chalk in hand the vagabond began To sketch a face that well might buy the soul of any man. Then, as he placed another lock upon the shapely head,

With a fearful shriek, he leaped and fell across the picture—dead..

CONTACTS:
Central City Opera House Association
400 S. Colorado Blvd.
Ste. 530
Denver, CO 80246
303-292-6700; fax: 303-292-4958
centralcityopera.org

♦ 0552 ♦ **Central Maine Egg Festival**
Fourth Saturday in July

This one-day event in Pittsfield, Maine, was started in 1972 by two journalists who were tired of hearing about their state's potato crop and wanted to focus attention on central Maine's egg and chicken industry. Today its primary attraction is the world's largest skillet—a 300-pound teflon-coated frying pan, five feet in diameter, that is used to cook more than 4,000 eggs for those attending the festival breakfast. The giant skillet, designed and donated by the Alcoa Corporation, is stored in an airplane hangar.

A festival highlight in years past was the World's Largest Egg Contest, in which only chicken eggs could be entered. Since entries came from all over the world, special tests often were conducted to reveal imposters. The winning egg was plated with gold. Other events include an "Egglympics," a chicken barbecue, a street dance, and fireworks.

CONTACTS:
Central Maine Egg Festival
Box 82
Pittsfield, ME 04967
centralmaineeggfestival.org

♦ 0553 ♦ **Cerealia (Cerialia)**
April 19

Ceres was the ancient Roman goddess of grain and of harvests, often identified with the Greek goddess Demeter. Peo-ple held festivals in her honor in various locations, but the Cerealia originated in Rome, where she was worshipped at her temple on the Aventine Hill along with two other deities, Liber (a fertility god) and Libera, his female counterpart. The temple became a center of activity for the plebeians, or common people, who usually suffered when there was a grain shortage.

The festival known as Cerealia was observed at various locations only by Roman matrons, who, for several days preceding the festival, abstained from wine and other carnal pleasures. People who were in mourning were not allowed to appear at the celebration. For this reason, the Cerealia was not observed after the Battle of Cannae, when 50,000 Roman troops were killed by Hannibal.

There is a theory that APRIL FOOLS' DAY is a relic of the ancient Roman Cerealia, also held in April. According to legend, when Ceres's daughter Proserpine was carried off to the underworld by Pluto, Ceres heard the echo of her screams and tried to follow her voice. But it was a fool's errand, for it was impossible to locate the echo's source.

The THESMOPHORIA was a similar festival observed in ancient Greece.

♦ 0554 ♦ **Cervantes Festival, International**
October

Spanish novelist, poet, and playwright Miguel de Cervantes (1547-1616) is best known for his creation of *Don Quixote* (1605), a novel that describes the adventures of an elderly knight and his pragmatic squire, Sancho Panza. Cervantes is honored in a three-week festival held in Guanajuato, Mexico, featuring orchestral music, opera, theater, dance, film, and folklore. At the festival's opening ceremony, statues of Don Quixote and Sancho Panza are lit up by fireworks.

Although most festival events are held in the Teatro Juarez and the Teatro Principal, amateur Mexican actors often give street performances of Cervantes's famous one-act plays in the Plaza de San Roque. Various musical performances are a popular attraction, as are art exhibits, children's theater, and folkloric dance ensembles.

CONTACTS:
Mexico Tourism Board
Viaduct Miguel Aleman
105 Col. Escandon
Mexico City 11800 Mexico
www.visitmexico.com

♦ 0555 ♦ **Chad Independence Day**
August 11

On August 11, 1960, Chad became an independent country after struggling against the French since they first claimed Chad as a French territory in the 1890s.

Celebrations of this national holiday—including parades, dancing, and singing—are often moved to January 11 because of the heavy rains in August.

CONTACTS:
Chad Embassy
2401 Massachusetts Ave. N.W.
Washington, D.C. 20008
202-652-1312
www.chadembassy.us

◆ 0556 ◆ Chad Republic Day
November 28

This national holiday commemorates the establishment of the republic on this day in 1958, which afforded Chad some autonomy, though it was a French territory until it attained full independence (*see* CHAD INDEPENDENCE DAY).

CONTACTS:
Chad Embassy
2401 Massachusetts Ave. N.W.
Washington, D.C. 20008
202-652-1312
www.chadembassy.us

◆ 0557 ◆ Chagu-Chagu Umakko
June 15

People in Morioka, a horse-breeding district of Iwate Prefecture in Japan, hold the Chagu-Chagu Umakko Festival to honor the god of horses. The parade begins at the Komagata-jinja shrine and ends at the Morioka Hachimangu shrine, a distance of just under 10 miles. Using white ropes, people lead richly decorated horses. When they reach the shrine, the riders make an offering of a picture of a horse, and prayers are said for the horses' well-being and the owners' financial success.

Chagu-chagu refers to the sound of the bells that are hung on the horses' heads. *Umakko* comes from *uma*, the word for "horse" in the local dialect. The horses and their riders, mostly young women and children, make a very picturesque sight as they ride along the paths between the rice paddies in summer.

CONTACTS:
Japan National Tourism Organization
1 Grand Central Pl.
60 E. 42nd St.
Ste. 448
New York, NY 10165
212-757-5640; fax: 212-307-6754
www.jnto.go.jp/eng

◆ 0558 ◆ Chakri Day
April 6

A national holiday in Thailand to commemorate the enthronement of Rama I, who founded the Chakri Dynasty in 1782. He was born Chao Phraya Chakri in 1737 and had become Thailand's leading general when a palace coup took place in Thon Buri. Officials invited the general to assume the throne; he did, and one of his first acts was to move the capital across the river to Bangkok. The dynasty he established has headed the country to this day, although the end of absolute monarchy came in 1932. The king was given the title Rama after his death. Ceremonies on April 6 honor his deeds and the founding of Bangkok as the capital.

CONTACTS:
Tourism Authority of Thailand
1600 New Phetchaburi Rd.
Makkasan, Ratchathevi
Bangkok, CA 10400 Thailand
662-250-5500
www.tourismthailand.org

◆ 0559 ◆ Chalanda Marz (First of March)
March 1

In Engadine, located in the Inn River valley of eastern Switzerland, the arrival of spring is celebrated with the ringing of bells. Young people put on herdsmen's costumes with wide leather belts from which they hang as many cow bells as they can collect. Smaller bells hang from their necks or are strapped across their chests. These "herdsmen" are followed by other young boys with bells around their necks who represent the cows. They go from house to house, clanging their bells as loudly as possible to scare off winter and serenading people with traditional spring songs. Sometimes they are given money, but more often they are rewarded with cakes, apples, or eggs. An evening feast is made out of the food, and afterward there are games and dancing. The money goes to the village schoolmaster, who saves it for a class picnic or excursion.

◆ 0560 ◆ Chalk Sunday
Between February 8 and March 14; first Sunday of Lent

In rural Ireland it was at one time customary to brush chalk on single men and women as they entered the church on the first Sunday of LENT. Because Roman Catholics were not permitted to hold weddings during Lent, those who were still unmarried at the beginning of the Lenten season had to remain so until EASTER—if not longer. Back when it was less common for young people to stay single well into their 20s and 30s, marking them with chalk was a way of chiding them for their unmarried status.

◆ 0561 ◆ Chamizal Festival
Early October

The Chamizal Festival, formerly known as the **Border Folk Festival**, has been held at the Chamizal National Memorial in El Paso, Texas, since 1973. It is celebrated in early October and features Latino food, music, and dance as well as traditional crafts and children's activities and entertainment.

The location of the festival is significant, for it was here that Mexican claims to El Chamizal, a wedge of land on the Texas side, were first filed in 1895. The dispute, which involved relocating the Rio Grande's channel, was finally resolved in

1963, an event that is commemorated by the Chamizal National Memorial.

CONTACTS:
National Park Service
Chamizal National Memorial
800 S. San Marcial St.
El Paso, TX 79905
915-532-7273; fax: 915-532-7240
www.nps.gov/cham

♦ 0562 ♦ Chandan Yatra
April-May; beginning on the third day of the waxing half of the Hindu month of Vaisakha and lasting 42 days

Indian Hindus celebrate several festivals during the new year, which in their holiday cycle arrives in Vaisakha, a month falling sometime between April and May. Within Vaisakha there are festivals whose observance takes place during a particular moon phase. One such festival, Chandan Yatra, is held during the waxing half of Vaisakha. During the festival, believers honor various Hindu deities, but most of their devotions are reserved for Lord Jagannatha, an expression of Krishna.

Depending on the festival site, Chandan Yatra lasts between three and six weeks and is celebrated throughout Orissa, a state located on India's eastern coast. Festival locations within Orissa include Puri, Baribapada, Balanga, and one of Hinduism's four holy places, Bhubaneshwar. Traditionally, the most elaborate celebration has always taken place at Puri, which is the final destination of a 42-day-long procession carrying icons of Lord Rama, Lord Krishna, and other deities. The various icons are gathered from temples along the way of the procession. At the final site, a large water tank in Puri called the Narenda, the idols are placed in decorated boats and undergo sacred baths to the accompaniment of music.

Festivals in other towns are typically only three weeks long. They are observed in a similar fashion to the Puri ceremony, with a daily procession from the temple to the water tank.

CONTACTS:
Odisha Tourism
Dept. of Tourism
Paryatan Bhawan
Museum Campus
Bhubaneswar, Odisha 751 014 India
91-674-2432177 or 800-208-1414
www.orissatourism.gov.in

♦ 0563 ♦ Chaomos
At least seven days, including December 21, the winter solstice

Chaomos is the winter festival of the Kalasha (also known as Kalash Kafir) people, who live in valleys in the northwestern corner of Pakistan, about 20 miles north of Chitral. The festival honors Balomain, a demigod who once lived among the Kalasha and did heroic deeds. Every year, his spirit comes to the valleys to count the people, collect their prayers, and take them back to Tsiam, the mythical land where the Kalasha originated, and to Dezao, the omnipotent creator god.

The celebration begins with the purification of women and girls: they take ritual baths, and then have water poured over their heads as they hold loaves of bread cooked by the men. A man waves burning juniper over the head of each woman, murmuring, *"Sooch"* ("Be pure"). On the following day, the men and boys are purified. They, too, take ritual baths and are then forbidden to sit on chairs or beds until evening when the blood of a sacrificed goat is sprinkled on their faces. The celebration continues with singing and chanting, a torchlight procession, dancing, bonfires, and festive eating of special bread and goat tripe.

Kalash means "black," and the people (thought to have descended from Alexander the Great) are called that because of the women's black robes. The Kalasha are among the people who live in Afghanistan in the area called Nuristan ("land of light"). This entire region was once known to the Muslims as Kafiristan ("land of infidels"), but in 1896 the Afghan Kafirs were forcibly converted to Islam. The Kalasha still maintain their old religion, a mixture of ancestor and fire worship. Their pantheon of gods, besides Dezao, includes Sajigor, the "great" god, Mahandeu, the "wise" god, and Surisan, who protects cattle.

Chaomos is one of the four annual festivals of the Kalasha; others are the spring festival in mid-May, the harvest festival in mid-August, and the autumn festival that marks the walnut and grape harvest.

♦ 0564 ♦ Charleston Sternwheel Regatta
Labor Day weekend

The Sternwheel Regatta was a celebration of its river-town history by Charleston, W.Va. The highlights were the sternwheel and power-boat races on the Kanawha River. There were also many other events, including concerts, parades, a car show, a distance run, and the "Anything That Floats Race." The regatta began in 1971 and attracted about a million spectators before it was retired in 2008.

♦ 0565 ♦ Charleston Wine and Food Festival
Five days in the first week in March

The Charleston Wine & Food Festival is a celebration of the food culture and culinary excellence of Charleston, South Carolina. Founded in 2006 by community leaders and volunteers from the area, the five-day event takes place in the first week of March in downtown Charleston, commonly regarded as one of the top food cities of the South. Historic Marion Square is the heart of the festival, where more than 100 culinary activities occur, such as tastings, workshops, seminars, and demonstrations. The Culinary Institute of Charleston organizes the event, which attracts leading chefs, wine sommeliers, and cookbook authors from across the country. The proceeds from the festival benefit local charities and help fund scholarships to local universities.

CONTACTS:
Charleston Wine and Food Festival
P.O. Box 22823
Charleston, SC 29413
843-727-9998
charlestonwineandfood.com

♦ 0566 ♦ **Charlottetown Festival**
June-October

The Charlottetown Festival is devoted entirely to musicals by Canadians. Held from mid-June through mid-October on Prince Edward Island, the festival presents three full-scale musicals every year. One of these is always *Anne of Green Gables*, a story about rural life on the island at the turn of the century, written by island-born novelist Lucy Maud Montgomery. In fact, *Anne of Green Gables* was the first musical presented at the festival when it was founded in 1965.

The festival also offers plays for children, Sunday evening pop concerts, and a series of short plays and musical events. The full-scale musicals and most of the festival's events are held at the Confederation Centre of the Arts in Charlottetown, the capital of Prince Edward Island.

CONTACTS:
Confederation Centre of the Arts
145 Richmond St.
Charlottetown, PEI C1A 1J1 Canada
902-628-1864; fax: 902-566-4648
www.charlottetownfestival.com/en/contact.php

♦ 0567 ♦ **Charro Days Fiesta**
Between January 31 and March 4; four days beginning the Thursday of the weekend before Ash Wednesday

The pre-Lenten festival known as Charro Days has been held each year since 1938 in the border towns of Brownsville, Texas, and Matamoros, Mexico, on opposite sides of the Rio Grande. A major border-crossing point, the two towns have a rich Spanish-Mexican heritage which is reflected in the fiesta. Male residents of the two cities wear the *charro* costume— a cross between the costume worn by the Spanish dons who once ruled Mexico and the Mexican horseman's outfit. Women wear the *china poblana*—a regional costume once worn by a little Chinese girl who was befriended by the Mexicans and has since become a kind of fairy princess to them.

Fiesta events take place in both Brownsville and Matamoros, and include a huge children's parade, costume dances in the street, and other events with Mexican and Latin themes. The festival has been known to attract as many as 400,000 visitors, many of whom wear costumes and participate in the events.

CONTACTS:
Charro Days Fiesta, Inc.
455 E Elizabeth St.
Brownsville, TX 78520
956-542-4245
www.charrodaysfiesta.com

♦ 0568 ♦ **Chavez (Cesar) Day**
March 31

Cesar Chavez Day is an annual commemoration of the famous labor leader. Observed on March 31, Chavez's birthday, the holiday celebrates one of America's greatest champions of social equality. Raised as a migrant farm worker in Arizona, Chavez was deeply moved by the plight of the men, women, and children who labored for meager wages and had little access to basic needs like healthcare and drinking water. Returning from the navy after World War II, Chavez founded the United Farm Workers and began campaigning tirelessly for the cause of farm labor, often in the face of stiff opposition. His movement of reform, called *La Causa*, appealed to many across the country, including religious groups, students, and organized labor. Chavez and his followers engaged in nonviolent tactics like marches, sit-ins, fasts, and pickets, which eventually resulted in winning collective bargaining rights for farm workers.

Becoming a notable figure in California and national politics, Chavez continued to work for the impoverished and marginalized until his death in 1993 at the age of 66. Cesar Chavez Day is observed as a public holiday in California and Colorado and as an optional holiday in Texas. Many Midwestern states also honor the civil rights leader with various celebrations. In the week leading up to March 31, schools focus on the life and work of Chavez, and community leaders make speeches honoring his enduring legacy. The city of Laredo, Texas, observes March as Cesar Chavez Month. A highlight of the celebration is the citizen's march, organized by the League of United Latin American Citizens, when students, labor unions, and community leaders take to the streets to pay their respects to the iconic labor leader.

CONTACTS:
Cesar E. Chavez National Holiday
3325 Wilshire Blvd.
Ste. 1208
Los Angeles, CA 90010
213-387-1974; fax: 213-397-3525
www.cesarchavezholiday.org

♦ 0569 ♦ **Cheese Rolling**
May-June, Monday after Pentecost

In Gloucestershire, England, cheese rolling is believed to have been a popular annual sport for at least 500 years. It is held on WHIT-MONDAY in Birdlip. Cooper's Hill, which is located in Birdlip near Brockworth and is a thousand feet high, is famous for its fine pasture lands. Rolling the cheese down this hill traditionally reminded villagers of their rights to graze their sheep there.

Early in the evening, the event leader, sporting a white smock and top hat, rolls the "cheese" (nowadays, three or four large wooden discs) down the hill. People chase after them, and the first to capture one of the discs receives a small prize. The game is quite tricky, because the descent down Cooper's Hill is very steep, and people often end up tumbling down the side more quickly than the discs.

Cheese rolling is a MAY DAY custom in Stilton, where men and women in teams of four compete to roll the wooden cheese.

♦ 0570 ♦ Cheese Sunday
Between February 8 and 28; Sunday before Lent

The week before Orthodox Christian LENT is known as Cheese or Dairy Week—especially in regions of Greece and Macedonia—because it is the last opportunity for people to eat dairy products. It is usually characterized by dancing, masquerading, and generally uninhibited behavior. At sunset on the final Sunday, people attend an evening church service during which the priest and congregation exchange mutual forgiveness for their sins. The last dish eaten on Cheese Sunday, or **Cheesefare Sunday**, is usually eggs.

Following custom, the last egg left over from the meal may be hung from a string in the middle of the ceiling. People sitting around the table hit it with their foreheads to get it swinging and then try to catch it in their mouths. Another variation of this game is to have someone hold a stick with an egg swinging from a string or thread on the end. People sit in a circle with their mouths open, trying to catch it. The popular saying, "With an egg I close my mouth, with an egg I shall open it again," refers to the hard-boiled Easter eggs that will mark the end of the Lenten fast.

In the Orthodox Church, the second Sunday before the beginning of Great Lent is called Meat Fare Sunday because it is traditionally the last day on which meat may be eaten until EASTER.

♦ 0571 ♦ Cheese Week (Sima Sedmitza)
Between February 8 and 28; week preceding Lent

Bulgarians call the week preceding the start of Orthodox Christian LENT Cheese Week. During this time Bulgarians try to eat up all their cheese, lard, milk, and fish, since these foods will be forbidden in the coming Lenten fast. People visit their parents, godchildren their godparents, and young people call on the elderly during this week, customarily offering a lemon (to men) or an orange (to women).

Young people play a traditional game that involves dangling a piece of Turkish taffy, a bit of cheese, or a hard-boiled egg from the ceiling with a bit of string. One person sets the object in motion while contestants try to catch it with their teeth. In some zones people burn bonfires. The boys jump through the fire while the girls dance around them—possibly a remnant from an ancient custom ensuring fertility.

♦ 0572 ♦ Chelsea Flower Show
Late May

For more than eight decades, England's Royal Horticultural Society (RHS) has held a flower show in London on the grounds of the Royal Hospital in Chelsea. The highlight of this five-day event is the full-sized show gardens that are planted and landscaped in the space of only three weeks by some of Britain's top garden designers. There are also scientific displays of the latest advances in gardening; booths for flower arranging and garden design; and trade stands showing everything from antique garden statuary to the very latest in garden tools and machinery. Experts are also on hand to give people advice on courtyard gardens, window boxes, hanging baskets, and other less elaborate forms of gardening.

The Chelsea Flower Show is followed by other RHS-sponsored shows that span the entire calendar, among them the Hampton Court Palace Flower Show in July, the Westminster Shows held every month in the Royal Horticultural Halls, and the Malvern Spring and Autumn Shows.

CONTACTS:
Royal Horticultural Society
80 Vincent Sq.
London SW1P 2PE United Kingdom
44-84-5260-5000
www.rhs.org.uk

♦ 0573 ♦ Cheltenham International Festival of Music
Early July

Established in 1945 to give first performances of works by British composers, the two-week Cheltenham International Festival of Music has since expanded its scope considerably. Its musical repertoire now includes both British and foreign composers offering operas as well as symphonic, chamber, and choral music. The festival commissions a handful of new works each year and often highlights British works that have been neglected. Composers whose works have premiered there include Malcolm Arnold, Thea Musgrave, Alan Rawsthorne, and Sir Michael Tippett. Special master classes are also offered each year on such subjects as string quartets, piano trios, and brass instruments, while children and adults can participate in other educational programs.

Recitals and chamber music concerts are held in the Pittville Pump Room, Cheltenham Spa's most important Regency structure. Operas are presented in the Everyman Theatre, and symphony concerts take place in the Town Hall. Other locations include local churches, abbeys, and castles. Cheltenham Spa is well known for its mineral springs, its Regency architecture, and its proximity to other attractions in the Cotswold Hills area of England.

CONTACTS:
Cheltenham Festivals
109-111 Bath Rd
Cheltenham, Gloucestershire GL53 7LS United Kingdom
44-844-880-8094
www.cheltenhamfestivals.co.uk

◆ 0574 ◆ Cherokee National Holiday
September, Labor Day weekend

The Cherokee National Holiday has been held since 1953 in Tahlequah, Oklahoma. To commemorate the signing of the 1839 Cherokee Constitution and the establishment of the Cherokee Nation, thousands of Cherokee Indians get together for a four-day celebration in early September. There is an all-Indian rodeo, a native dance competition, a powwow, and a parade with colorful floats and Cherokees in ceremonial dress. Native American arts and crafts—including baskets, flutes, dolls, and jewelry—are on display, and visitors can sample Native American foods. Games and sports offered at the festival include a golf tournament, a horseshoe tournament, a cornstalk shoot, a blowgun shoot, and a traditional Indian marble game.

CONTACTS:
Cherokee Nation
17675 S. Muskogee Ave.
Tahlequah, OK 74464
918-453-5000 or 800-256-0671
www.cherokee.org

◆ 0575 ◆ Cherokee Strip Day
September 16

September 16, 1893, was the date of the last and largest of the "land runs" that opened western Indian territories to white settlement. The Cherokee Strip encompassed more than six million acres of mostly grassy plains where white homesteaders wanted to graze their animals. Anyone who wanted to claim and settle the 160-acre parcels had to line up on the morning of September 16 and race to plant his flag at a chosen spot. The lure of free land attracted an estimated 100,000 prospective settlers, mostly young men who could withstand the harsh climate.

Cherokee Strip Day is a festival day in Oklahoma—particularly in the communities of Ponca City, Enid, and Perry—towns that sprang up as a result of the 1893 run. The celebrations last several days and include parades, picnics, dances, and rodeos.

See also OKLAHOMA DAY.

CONTACTS:
Cherokee Strip Museum
2617 W. Fir Ave.
Perry, OK 73077
580-336-2405
www.cherokee-strip-museum.org

◆ 0576 ◆ Cherry Blossom Festival (Hawaii)
February-March

The Cherry Blossom Festival in Hawaii is an annual Japanese cultural celebration held in Honolulu, usually from mid-February until the first week in April. The beauty of cherry blossoms is almost sacred in Japan, but the cherry blossoms of this festival are purely symbolic; cherry trees don't grow in Hawaii. The festival offers a variety of events: presentations of Kabuki drama, traditional Japanese dances, martial arts, and Japanese films, as well as demonstrations of such arts as weaving and paper-doll making. The celebration was created in 1953 by the Honolulu Japanese community to "bridge the cultural gap by sharing with others the essence of the Japanese heritage."

See also HANAMI.

CONTACTS:
Cherry Blossom Festival
P.O. Box 1105
Aiea, HI 96701
808-949-2255
www.cbfhawaii.com

◆ 0577 ◆ Cherry Blossom Festival (Northern California)
April

More than 2,000 Japanese Americans and performers from Japan participate in this festival in San Francisco's Japantown that takes place over two consecutive weekends in April. Based on HANAMI, a traditional festival in Japan, this celebration of Japanese culture and customs includes exhibitions of Japanese art and dancing, kimono and obi (the sash worn with a kimono) demonstrations, tea ceremonies, and bonsai exhibits. The climax of the festival is a three-hour parade from City Hall to the Japan Center at Post and Fillmore Streets. The parade includes singers and dancers, floats, Akita dogs, Taiko drummers, the Cherry Blossom Queen, and the traditional Taru Mikoshi, a portable shrine piled so high with casks of sake—an alcoholic beverage made from rice—that it takes 100 men to carry it. The festival lasts for seven days, covering two weekends in April. It was first held in 1968 to mark the official opening of San Francisco's Japan Center.

CONTACTS:
Northern California Cherry Blossom Festival
1700 Post St.
San Francisco, CA 94115
415-563-2313
www.sfcherryblossom.org

◆ 0578 ◆ Cherry Blossom Festival, National
Between late March and early April

The National Cherry Blossom Festival in Washington, D.C., is held whenever the cherry trees planted around the Potomac River Tidal Basin bloom—usually between March 20 and April 15. The 3,000 trees were a gift to the city of Washington from the city of Tokyo, Japan, in 1912, and today they are the focal point of a two-week festival celebrating the friendship between the two countries. Most of the original trees died because the water in the Basin flooded their roots. Their replacements were more carefully planted and now thrive. Dates for the festival are set a year in advance to avoid coinciding with EASTER and HOLY WEEK observances.

The festival has been in existence since 1948, although earlier celebrations included re-enacting the original planting and crowning a Cherry Blossom Festival Queen. Today the festivities include formal receptions for the 52 festival princesses (representing the 50 states, the District of Columbia, and the territory of Guam) and a Cherry Blossom parade through downtown Washington.

See also MACON CHERRY BLOSSOM FESTIVAL.

CONTACTS:
National Cherry Blossom Festival
1250 H St. N.W.
Ste. 1000
Washington, D.C. 20005
202-661-7585 or 877-442-5666; fax: 202-661-7599
www.nationalcherryblossomfestival.org

◆ 0579 ◆ Cherry Festival, National
Second week in July

An annual event since 1926, Michigan's National Cherry Festival takes place in Traverse City, "The Cherry Capital of the World," where 70 percent of the world's red cherries are grown. Traditionally held for a full week in July, the time of the cherry harvest, the festival features both traditional and offbeat events involving cherries: cherry pie-eating and cooking contests, a cherry wine competition, displays of cherries and cherry products, free tours of the cherry orchards, a cherry smorgasbord luncheon, and the weighing-in of the world's largest cherry.

The festival began in 1924 with a ceremony to bless the cherry blossoms and ensure a good crop. Now it draws upwards of half a million visitors and includes three major parades, national high school band competitions, canoe races, and a water ski tournament among the more than 100 different events. Former President Gerald R. Ford, a Michigan native, officiated at the festival in 1975.

CONTACTS:
National Cherry Festival
250 E. Front St.
Ste. 301
Traverse City, MI 49684
231-947-4230 or 800-968-3380; fax: 231-947-7435
www.cherryfestival.org

◆ 0580 ◆ Chestertown Tea Party Festival
Late May

When the British passed the Boston Port Act closing the Port of Boston until complete restitution had been made for the tea destroyed during the Boston Tea Party, it unleashed a wave of anger throughout the American colonies. Shortly after the news reached Chestertown, Maryland, the brigantine *Geddes* dropped anchor in Chestertown harbor on May 13, 1774. Word went out that the *Geddes* was carrying a small shipment of tea, and 10 days later a group of local residents boarded the ship and dumped the tea in the Chester River.

Every year during the Chestertown Tea Party Festival the rebellion is reenacted. The local merchants gather at the town park, where they voice their opposition to the British tax on tea. The crowd winds its way down High Street to the river, where the "colonists" board a ship—usually a reproduction of an historic vessel—and throw its cargo of tea (and some of its crew) into the river. Other festival events include a colonial parade with fife and drum corps, exhibits and demonstrations of 18th-century American crafts, walking tours of Chestertown, clog dancing and fiddling, horse-and-carriage rides, and tall ship cruises. Typical Eastern Shore foods are served, such as Maryland fried chicken, barbequed ribs, "chitlins," crab cakes, she-crab soup, and fried clams.

CONTACTS:
Chestertown Tea Party Festival
P.O. Box 526
Chestertown, MD 21620 United States
410-212-6390
www.chestertownteaparty.com

◆ 0581 ◆ Cheung Chau Bun Festival
April-May; date decided by divination; usually about eight days between the end of third lunar month and 10th day of fourth lunar month

This festival is one of the most spectacular events in Hong Kong, celebrated only on Cheung Chau (which means "Long Island" in Chinese), one of the outlying islands of Hong Kong. It is believed that restless ghosts roam the island during the eight-day festival. Some believe they are the spirits of islanders massacred by 19th-century pirates. Others claim they are people who died of a plague in the early 20th century or that they are spirits of people whose remains were disturbed by people building new houses.

Three bamboo-and-paper towers, up to about 60 feet high and covered with sweet pink and white buns, are dedicated to the spirits and intended to placate them. People burn paper replicas of houses, cars, and money. The buns placed highest in the towers traditionally are held to be the luckiest, and people used to climb up the towers in a race to get them. But after a serious accident in 1978, the buns now are passed down the towers.

At the island's Pak Tai Temple, rites are held to honor Pak Tai, known as a Taoist king of the Dark Heaven or the Underworld. He is worshipped as a god of the sea who defeated a demon king and the king's allies, a tortoise and a serpent. The temple holds many small wooden statues of Pak Tai, all with a tortoise under one foot and a serpent under the other.

To pay homage to the animals and fish who serve as residents' food, only vegetarian dishes are served during the festival, and some people also make offerings to the animals' spirits.

In the highlight of the festival, the images of the temple gods are carried in a procession of lion and dragon dancers and children aged about five to eight, who are costumed as legendary Chinese figures. These children seem to float above the procession, but in reality they are held up by poles to which they are attached as adults carry them through the streets.

CONTACTS:
Hong Kong Tourism Board
370 Lexington Ave.
Ste. 1812
New York, NY 10017
212-421-3382; fax: 212-421-8428
www.discoverhongkong.com

◆ 0582 ◆ Cheyenne Frontier Days
Last full week of July

What began in 1897 as an attempt to keep alive the sports and customs of the Old West has grown into a week-long festival that regularly attracts over 300,000 visitors. Cheyenne, Wyoming, was one of the wealthiest cattle-raising cities in the world in the 1880s, and now it celebrates its colorful history by staging one of the world's largest outdoor rodeos. The festival also includes parades of covered wagons, stagecoaches, and other old-time vehicles; ceremonial Indian dances; the crowning of a "Miss Frontier" queen; and pageants recreating events from Cheyenne's past. Cheyenne residents make pancakes for all with batter mixed in a concrete mixer.

CONTACTS:
Cheyenne Frontier Days
4610 Carey Ave.
Cheyenne, WY 82001
307-778-7200 or 800-227-6336; fax: 307-778-7213
www.cfdrodeo.com

◆ 0583 ◆ Chhau Mask-Dance Festival
Mid-April

Chhau is a form of dance rooted in the religious beliefs of Indian folk culture. Different regions of India practice their own unique style of Chhau, incorporating various folk, classical, and traditional elements. The masked dancers are often silent and use stylized movements to illustrate the conflict between good and evil to the accompaniment of drums, pipes, and cymbals. The dramatic situations that give shape to the dances are often drawn from episodes in the *Ramayana* and the *Mahabharata*, two famous epic poems of India.

The Seraikella Chhau dance held every April in the Singhbhum District of Bihar State reflects variations that are unique to the region. The influence of the martial arts can be seen in the dance, but the predominant mood is lyrical. Seraikella is also the home of the Government Chhau Dance School, which sponsors the two-day festival.

In the Mayurbhanj Chhau Dance, also held in the middle of April, the dancers do not wear masks but hold their facial expressions as still as possible, as if to imitate a mask. Unlike other forms of Indian dance, the Chhau dancers use all of the space available to them, and there are many long entrances and sweeping gestures.

CONTACTS:
Ministry of Tourism, Government of India
1270 Ave. of the Americas
Ste. 303
New York, NY 10020 India
212-586-4901; fax: 212-582-3274
tourism.nic.in

Odisha Tourism, The Director
Paryatan Bhawan
Museum Campus
Bhubaneswar 751 014 India
674-2432177
orissatourism.gov.in

◆ 0584 ◆ Chiao Festival (Rite of Cosmic Renewal)
Every 60 years

Also spelled **Jiao**, this ancient festival is traditionally held about every 60 years all over Taiwan. The specific date is determined by a committee of the local priest and town leaders. The Rite of Cosmic Renewal serves to "rededicate" the local temple as well as renew the whole community. The festival can also be held more frequently in order to raise funds for repairing the temple.

People prepare for this important occasion by performing acts of penance and purification, cleansing, repairing and adorning the temple, and inviting the gods and family ancestors to attend the festival, which may last about three days.

Several priests may be enlisted to perform the various rituals of the Chiao Festival, some of which are carried out in private. Public rituals include a presentation of offerings, readings from sacred works, lighting a new fire outside and inside the temple, and dances. People go to enormous effort to prepare a huge banquet for the last day of the festival, to which all the deceased are formally invited by the "floating of the lanterns" the day before. Elaborate floats accompany representatives of each family in the community in a procession to a nearby body of water into which everyone releases a paper lantern on a small raft. The following day the entire community looks like a smorgasbord, with dishes set out in front of homes and more food filling the temple. The festive atmosphere is enhanced by puppet shows, operas, and other attractions.

CONTACTS:
Taipei Economic and Cultural Office in New York
1 E. 42nd St.
4th Fl.
New York, NY 10017
212-317-7300; fax: 212-754-1549
www.taiwanembassy.org

◆ 0585 ◆ Chicago Blues Festival
A weekend in June

The Chicago Blues Festival was first organized in 1984 by the City of Chicago Department of Cultural Affairs and Special Events. The annual festival celebrates blues music and the artists who lived the tradition. It was established a year after the death of renowned blues musician McKinley Morganfield, better known as Muddy Waters, considered "the father of Chicago blues." It takes place over three days at the Petrillo Music Shell in Grant Park, adjacent to the Lake Michigan waterfront. An estimated 500,000 people attend the festival every year. Attendance is free, but tickets are required for food and beverages. The festival showcases music by world-renowned Chicago blues artists Muddy Waters, Howlin' Wolf, and Buddy Guy, among other legends. Performers have included Sunnyland Slim, Jimmy Walker, Willie Dixon, and many others. Panel discussions and lectures also take place, and upcoming musicians are given the chance to perform. In 1988, the organizers started collaborating with the Chicago Public Schools. The resulting program teaches students about the blues genre, including the method of writing a blues song. This project is made possible with the help of the musicians, who remain in residence at the schools, mentoring students for weeks prior to the commencement of the festival. Students are given the opportunity to perform at the festival's opening.

CONTACTS:
Dept. of Cultural Affairs and Special Events
Chicago Cultural Center
78 E. Washington St., 4th Fl.
Chicago, IL 60602
312-744-3315; fax: 312-744-8523
www.cityofchicago.org

♦ 0586 ♦ **Chicago Dancing Festival**
August

The Chicago Dancing Festival is a five-day festival of dance-related events presented at numerous city venues, including outdoor events at Chicago's Millennium Park, the site of the annual festival Grande Finale. The festival features performances by dance companies from Chicago and other cities around the U.S. and the world, representing a variety of dance styles including classical ballet, and contemporary, jazz, and street dance. Unique among festivals of its kind, the Chicago Dancing Festival's events are presented at no cost to the public. Choreographer Lar Lubovitch and dancer, Jay Franke, both Chicago natives, came together in 2006 to establish the Chicago Dancing Company NFP with the goal of producing an annual dance festival. The festival was intended to bring awareness to dance in Chicago and engage the community in the art form by providing access to performances free of charge. The festival debuted in August of 2007, when 8500 people came to Millennium Park to see several leading American dance companies performed for a single night. Since then the festival has continued to grow, now including numerous events taking place over several days, with public participation increasing each year.

CONTACTS:
Chicago Dancing Company NFP
P.O. Box 101043
Chicago, IL 60610
773-609-2335
www.chicagodancingfestival.com

♦ 0587 ♦ **Chicago Gospel Music Festival**
First weekend in June

Since 1985 the city of Chicago, Ill., has celebrated its heritage as the birthplace of gospel music by hosting a three-day festival showcasing local, national, and international performers. The African-American composer Thomas A. Dorsey of Chicago's Pilgrim Baptist Church published the first gospel music in Chicago in 1926. A transplant from Georgia, Dorsey developed a vibrant, upbeat musical style that combined traditional spirituals and hymns with blues and jazz rhythms. In the following decades the genre spread from its roots in the black church to become a significant influence on American music and culture.

Each year the festival hosts about 275,000 fans, who enjoy 50 free performances on three stages in a lakefront setting at Millennium Park. It is the largest free music festival in the world devoted exclusively to gospel music. In addition to the entertainment offerings, the festival hosts a fine art fair, including works in such media as fiber, glass, painting, photography, and wood.

CONTACTS:
City of Chicago
City Hall
121 N. LaSalle St.
Chicago, IL 60602
312-744-5000
www.cityofchicago.org

♦ 0588 ♦ **Chicago International Children's Film Festival**
October

The largest festival in North America celebrating children's films and television, the Chicago International Children's Film Festival is held in Chicago, Illinois each year. Its mission is to promote an international standard of excellence in film and television for children. Talented filmmakers are encouraged to attend, and high-quality films featuring cultural diversity and the affirmation of moral values are showcased at the festival, with the aim of increasing distribution and gaining such works a more widespread audience. Begun in 1983, and growing out of a program started in 1975, the festival reviews thousands of submissions and presents awards in 20 categories, including animation, live-action, shorts, documentaries, and works produced by children. Hundreds of filmmakers, industry professionals, and celebrities routinely attend the event, which includes question-and-answer sessions with children who visit. The festival serves as a qualifying ground for children's films to be nominated for the Academy Awards. The festival was founded by a non-profit organization called Facets and was the first juried, competitive festival of international cinema for children in the United States. Facets distributes films internationally and offers year-round youth programs that focus on films as a catalyst for improving fundamental learning skills. Facets also conducts workshops in which youngsters can learn the techniques involved in making a film.

CONTACTS:
Facets Kids
1517 W. Fullerton Ave.
Chicago, IL 60614

773-281-9075 or 800-331-6197
www.facets.org

♦ 0589 ♦ Chicago International Film Festival
October

An annual film event held in Chicago, Illinois, the Chicago International Film Festival is sponsored by the non-profit organization Cinema/Chicago. The most sought-after award in the festival, the Gold Hugo, denotes an international standard of excellence and signals emerging distinction within the film realm. The festival holds the rare distinction of discovering groundbreaking film directors like Martin Scorsese, John Carpenter, Peter Weir, Rainer Werner Fassbinder, and Victor Erice.

The festival was started in 1964 by Michael Kutza, a graphic artist and filmmaker, whose aim was to provide an alternative to the Hollywood movies that were dominating the theaters in Chicago at the time. The original festival sought the best in international cinema and brought movies that were otherwise unavailable to a Midwestern audience. At many of the festival's screenings, filmgoers are given the unique chance to meet the director, producers, writers, and cast. These seminal members of a film's creative staff generally introduce the films and then facilitate discussions focusing on the work.

CONTACTS:
Cinema/Chicago
30 E. Adams St.
Ste. 800
Chicago, IL 60603
312-683-0121; fax: 312-683-0122
www.chicagofilmfestival.com

♦ 0590 ♦ Chicago International Puppet Theater Festival
Every other January

The Chicago International Puppet Theater Festival was started in 2015 as a biennial event. The mission of the 12-day festival is to establish Chicago as a center for the advancement of the art of puppetry. Conceived and organized by Blair Thomas & Co., a Chicago-based theater troupe founded in 2002, the festival showcases artists from around the globe performing works featuring marionettes, shadow puppets, Bunraku puppets, tiny toy puppets, and various mixed-media puppetry styles. The shows, workshops, and puppeteer symposiums take place in several venues throughout the city, including the Art Institute of Chicago, Chicago Shakespeare Theater, Museum of Contemporary Art, and Field Museum.

CONTACTS:
Chicago International Puppet Theater Festival
P.O. Box 1265
Chicago, IL 60690
www.chicagopuppetfest.org

♦ 0591 ♦ Chicago Jazz Festival
August-September, four days preceding Labor Day

In the 1920s a four-block area along Chicago's State Street, known to the black community as "the Stroll," was the mecca of the jazz world. It was here that jazz took root in the city, establishing Chicago as a center for this uniquely American music. Shortly after the great composer-bandleader Duke Ellington died in 1974, a group of Chicago musicians got together to hold a concert in his honor; after that, the Ellington Concert became an annual event. A similar memorial concert was held for saxophonist John Coltrane in 1978, and the following year these two events merged with the jazz festival already being planned by the Jazz Institute of Chicago. Now it is the most extensive free jazz festival in the world, drawing an estimated audience of 400,000 and featuring such well-known artists as Sarah Vaughan, Ray Charles, Dave Brubeck, Herbie Hancock, George Benson, and Wynton Marsalis.

A number of major jazz events have occurred at the festival, such as the world premiere of Randy Weston's *African Sunrise* by Dizzy Gillespie and the Machito All-Star Orchestra in 1984, or the rendition of "Happy Birthday" sung in honor of Charlie Parker, the great jazz improviser, who was born on August 29, 1920, and died March 12, 1955.

CONTACTS:
Jazz Institute of Chicago
410 S. Michigan Ave. Fine arts bldg.
Ste. 500
Chicago, IL 60605
312-427-1676; fax: 312-427-1684
jazzinchicago.org

♦ 0592 ♦ Chickaban
During Mayan month of Xul

The ancient Mayan feast known as Chickaban, observed at Mani in the Yucatán state of Mexico, was held in honor of the feathered serpent and storm god Kukulcán. Before the feast, the tribal chiefs spent five days fasting, dancing, and worshipping their idols. At the feast itself, offerings were made to Kukulcán, who came down from the sky to join them.

According to the myth, Kukulcán came to the Mayas from the west with 19 attendants, all bareheaded and wearing long robes and sandals. He built Chichén Itzá, the ancient Mayan city, and ruled over the four points of the compass and the four elements of air, earth, fire, and water. Kukulcán is usually depicted with a serpent's body, a jaguar's teeth, and the long plumes of the quetzal bird. He is holding a human head in his jaws and is seated on the cross-shaped symbol of the compass.

♦ 0593 ♦ Chief Joseph Days
Last full weekend in July

Chief Joseph (1840-1904) was the chief of the Nez Perce Indians. When the U.S. government tried to force the Nez Perce Indians to relocate to a reservation in 1877, the chief decided instead to lead about 800 of his followers on a long journey to Canada. After many battles with the white soldiers who were pursuing him and who outnumbered his warriors by ten to one, Chief Joseph and his people were captured within 40 miles of the Canadian border and sent to reservations in Oklahoma, where many of them became ill and died.

Chief Joseph, who spent the rest of his life in exile and who pleaded with President Theodore Roosevelt to let his people return to their ancestral home, is honored with a four-day festival every July in Joseph, Oregon. Established in 1945, the festival features one of the largest rodeos in the Northwest, a traditional Indian dance contest, a Nez Perce encampment and powwow, parades, dances, a golf tournament, and a cowboy church service.

CONTACTS:
Chief Joseph Days Rodeo Office
P.O. Box 13
Joseph, OR 97846
541-432-1015
www.chiefjosephdays.com

♦ 0594 ♦ **Chief Seattle Days**
Third weekend in August

A three-day inter-tribal festival to honor Chief Seattle (1786-1866), for whom Seattle, Washington, is named. He was head of the Suquamish and Duwamish Indian tribes in the Puget Sound area of Washington. His name in the Lushootseed language was *See-ahth*. The festival is held at the Port Madison Indian Reservation in Suquamish, 40 miles south of Seattle. Besides featuring traditional Indian dances and drumming and dancing contests, it has a distinctive northwestern flavor, with salmon and clam bakes and canoe races. Other highlights are a horseshoe tournament, storytelling, and the election of a Chief Seattle Days Queen. The festival closes with the blessing of Chief Seattle's grave.

Chief Seattle and his father were both friendly to white settlers and helped them. He was the first to sign the Port Elliott Treaty in 1855, which set aside reservations for the Suquamish and other Washington tribes.

In a moving speech made in 1854 to a large group of Indians gathered to greet Isaac Stevens, the new United States Indian superintendent, Chief Seattle spoke of the passing away of the Indian tribes, fleeing at the approach of the white man. "Let him be just and deal kindly with my people," he said, "for the dead are not powerless. There is no death, only a change of worlds."

It is uncertain whether Chief Seattle actually uttered these words. The only known translation of Seattle's speech was made from the recollection of Dr. Harvy Smith 33 years later. The waters were made even muddier when, in 1971, Ted Perry, a screenwriter who now teaches at Middlebury College in Vermont, wrote a speech for the Chief that was included in a film on ecology. Mr. Perry knew the script was fiction, but others did not. Perry's apocryphal speech has been attributed to Chief Seattle ever since.

In 1992 a children's book based on an embellished version of Perry's script, *Brother Eagle, Sister Sky* by Susan Jeffers, made the *New York Times* Best Seller list and the great Chief Seattle slipped further into the mists of legend.

CONTACTS:
Suquamish Tribe
18490 Suquamish Way
P.O. Box 498
Suquamish, WA 98392
360-598-3311; fax: 360-598-3135
www.suquamish.org

♦ 0595 ♦ **Children's Day (former Yugoslavia)**
December; three Sundays before Christmas

On the third Sunday before Christmas, known as **Dechiyi Dan** or Children's Day, parents in the former Yugoslavia tie up their children and refuse to release them until they have promised to be good.

And, although many people think that MOTHER'S DAY originated in the United States, Slavs traditionally set aside a Sunday in December to visit their mothers and bring them small gifts. Young children, on the other hand, honor their mothers by tying them up and refusing to release them until they have paid a "ransom" of sweets and goodies. Sometimes the mother hides small gifts under her mattress so that if the children tie her up before she gets out of bed in the morning, she'll have something to offer them. Considering that mothers tied up their children on the previous Sunday, this custom isn't as outrageous as it seems.

The Sunday following Materitse is *Ochichi* or *Ocevi* (Father's Day). Boys and girls tie their fathers to his chair or bed. The ransom in this case is even higher, as the father must promise to buy them coats, shoes, dresses, or other expensive items before they let him go. These promises are usually fulfilled a short time later as CHRISTMAS gifts.

♦ 0596 ♦ **Children's Book Day, International**
April 2

This day, which is observed by countries all over the world, was first suggested by the International Board on Books for Young People (IBBY). They chose Hans Christian Andersen's birthday, April 2, because the Danish author's stories—which include "The Little Match Girl," "The Steadfast Tin Soldier," "The Ugly Duckling," and "Thumbelina"—have been favorites among children of all nationalities. The celebrations include contests in which children illustrate their favorite books, as well as the adoption of foreign pen pals. Every two years the IBBY sponsors the Hans Christian Andersen medals, which are awarded to a children's book author and a children's book illustrator for their contributions to children's literature.

See also ANDERSEN (HANS CHRISTIAN) FESTIVAL.

CONTACTS:
International Board on Books for Young People
Nonnenweg 12
Postfach
Basel 4003 Switzerland
41-61-272-2917; fax: 41-61-272-2757
www.ibby.org

♦ 0597 ♦ **Children's Day**
Various

Many countries have set aside a day on which children are allowed to participate in church services, in government, and in various cultural and recreational activities. In the United States, Children's Day was first celebrated in June 1856 at the Universalist Church in Chelsea, Massachusetts. By 1868 its date had been set on a nationwide basis as the second Sunday in June.

Children's Day is also celebrated in the Democratic Republic of Congo (Dec. 25), Iceland (April 24), Indonesia (June 17), Japan (*see* KODOMO-NO-HI), Nigeria (May 27), and Turkey. The Turkish Children's Day on April 23 gives 400 students the educational opportunity to take seats in the national government in Ankara. The same thing takes place on a smaller scale in cities and towns all over the country.

See also TURKEY NATIONAL SOVEREIGNTY AND CHILDREN'S DAY and URINI NAL.

♦ 0598 ♦ **Chile Battle of Iquique Day (Día de las Glorias Navales)**
May 21

This national holiday in Chile is often called **Dia de las Glorias Navales** in Spanish ("The Day of the Glorious Navy"). From 1879 to 1881, the Chilean navy fought an alliance of Peru and Bolivia in the War of the Pacific (also known as the Chile-Peruvian War). The war grew out of a dispute over export tariffs that Bolivia levied on Chile for nitrate deposits mined in Bolivia's Atacama Province. Peru joined the Bolivian side, and the Chilean navy blockaded the Peruvian port of Iquique. The Chilean victory in the Battle of Iquique on May 21, 1879, was a turning point in a war that Chile eventually won decisively.

The holiday is celebrated throughout Chile with festivals, military parades, and speeches. Sporting events, including boat and bicycle races, are held in honor of the holiday. Many people dress in traditional costumes as a symbol of national pride.

♦ 0599 ♦ **Chile National Unity Day**
First Monday in September

In 1973, Chilean General Augusto Pinochet led a military coup that toppled the government of President Salvador Allende. Allende had been democratically elected, and his administration was replaced by a military dictatorship led by Pinochet. The government created a national holiday, celebrated on September 11, to mark the anniversary of the 1973 military coup. In 1998 the Chilean legislature voted to abolish the September 11 holiday. In its place, the legislature created National Unity Day, which has been celebrated since 1999.

Many Chileans have bitter memories of the years of military rule, when many citizens were arrested and never seen again.

The purpose of National Unity Day is to promote reconciliation and justice in Chile. The holiday is celebrated annually on the first Monday in September.

CONTACTS:
Embassy of Chile
1732 Massachusetts Ave. N.W.
Washington, D.C. 20036
202-785-1746; fax: 202-887-5579
www.chile-usa.org

♦ 0600 ♦ **Chilembwe (John) Day**
January 15

John Chilembwe Day is a national holiday celebrated annually on January 15 (some sources state January 17) in the south-east-African country of Malawi. Reverend John Chilembwe was born in the 1860s in the African nation of Nyasaland, now known as Malawi. A Baptist minister, he spent considerable time abroad in America, where he was exposed to the radical abolitionist thought of John Brown and Booker T. Washington. Returning to Africa, Chilembwe opened a series of schools. Dismayed by the treatment of local peoples at the hands of plantation owners, whom he charged with racism and exploitation, he and a group of 200 followers staged an uprising. They attacked plantations and killed three white staff members along with several African workers. When the revolt failed to gain popular support, Chilembwe tried to flee to neighboring Mozambique. He and a group of his followers were caught and killed on February 3, 1915.

John Chilembwe is now memorialized as a hero for African independence and resistance to colonialism and is celebrated in modern Malawi, which attained its independence in 1964. His image on a Malawi banknote attests to his enduring popularity as a national figure and a symbol of Malawi freedom and patriotism.

CONTACTS:
Malawi Embassy
2408 Massachusetts Ave. N.W.
Washington, D.C. 20008
202-721-0270; fax: 202-721-0288
www.malawiembassy-dc.org

♦ 0601 ♦ **Chilseog (Seventh Evening)**
Seventh day of the seventh lunar month

Chilseog is the Korean version of the SEVEN SISTERS FESTIVAL, based on an old Chinese legend about two stars known as the Herdsman and the Spinning Maiden. The Herdsman star, located in the Aquila constellation, and the Spinning Maiden star, Vega in the Lyra constellation, are in love but can only meet once a year—on the seventh day of the seventh lunar month, when it is believed that crows and magpies fly up into the heavens to form a bridge across the heavenly river, as the Milky Way is called.

On this night it is customary for young Korean women to pray for celestial assistance in sewing and to honor the stars by penning verse about them.

♦ 0602 ♦ Chilympiad (Republic of Texas Chili Cookoff)
Third weekend in September

A chili cookoff in San Marcos, Tex., is called the "largest bowl o' red" competition in the world, which it probably is. Hundreds of chili chefs compete for the state championship, being judged on showmanship as much as recipes. Participation in the Chilympiad is a preliminary to entering the TERLINGUA CHILI COOKOFF in November. Besides the Chilympiad's gastronomic attractions, there are also concerts, arts and crafts, a parade, and carnival.

CONTACTS:
Texas State Historical Association
1155 Union Cir.
Ste. 311580
Denton, TX 76203
940-369-5200; fax: 940-369-5248
www.tshaonline.org

♦ 0603 ♦ China Luoyang Peony Cultural Festival
April

The China Luoyang Peony Cultural Festival celebrates China's national flower, the Luoyang peony, which is a traditional symbol of fame and wealth. The annual celebration first occurred in 1983 in Luoyang, China, an area where the flower is widely grown. Each year, from mid-April to mid-May, the peonies are in full bloom, and local gardens come to life with myriad hues of reds, whites, yellows, and purples. The main venue of the festival is the Luoyang National Peony Garden, which is home to over 400 varieties of the flower, including several rare species. The festival's numerous attendees also visit smaller gardens across Luoyang. The event is often regarded as a doorway to the Chinese city's rich history and culture, including the Longmen Grottoes (a UNESCO heritage site), art museums, and ancient Buddhist temples.

CONTACTS:
Gold Cup Parade Committee
P.O. Box 67
Charlottetown, PE C1A 7K2 Canada
902-626-5098
goldcupparade.ca

♦ 0604 ♦ China National Days
October 1-2

This public holiday commemorates the founding of the People's Republic of China in the capital of Beijing in 1949. Observances take place on October 1-2.

CONTACTS:
China National Tourist Office
370 Lexington Ave.
Ste. 912
New York, NY 10017
212-760-8218; fax: 212-760-8809
www.cnto.org

♦ 0605 ♦ Chinchilla Melon Festival
Third Saturday in February, every two years

A weeklong festival that takes place every two years in the Australian town of Chinchilla, the Chinchilla Melon Festival is a regional agricultural celebration. This area of Queensland grows a quarter of the continent's annual melon crop. Melon-themed events and games are a major part of the festival itinerary. The event was first held in 1994 in an effort to attract tourists and help the rural community that had been struck by drought. After the following year's celebration, the event was changed to a biennial festival in February. Besides featuring a series of popular melon-themed games such as melon bungee and pip-spitting competitions, the festival includes parades, melon carving, rodeos, laser shows, and beach parties.

CONTACTS:
Chinchilla Melon Festival
P.O. Box 556
Chinchilla Qld, 4413 Australia
www.melonfest.com.au

♦ 0606 ♦ Chincoteague Pony Swim and Auction
Wednesday before the last Thursday in July

The Chincoteague Pony Swim and Auction is an annual saltwater roundup of the famous wild ponies of Assateague Island off the Delmarva Peninsula. The volunteer firemen of Chincoteague Island, the largest inhabited island on the Eastern Shore of Virginia, become cowboys for a day. They ride to Assateague, round up as many as 250 or 300 foals, mares, and sires, and then guide them into the water to swim across the channel to Chincoteague. There the ponies are penned in corrals, and the next day some foals are sold at auction and the rest of the herd swims back to Assateague.

Legend says the ponies, which are considered stunted horses rather than true ponies, are the descendants of mustangs that survived a shipwreck of a 16th-century Spanish galleon. Another story holds that the ponies were left behind by pirates who used the island as a hideout and had to leave in a hurry. Still a third (and most probable) version is that English colonists, having brought the ponies to the New World, turned them loose on Assateague and Chincoteague when they began to damage mainland crops.

The annual penning probably started with the colonists, who rounded up foals and yearlings to invigorate their workhorse supply. It took its present form in 1925 when the newly formed Chincoteague Volunteer Fire Company decided to add a fund-raising carnival to the regular pony penning.

Now a week of festivities surrounds the roundup, with midway rides, country music, and oysters and clams to eat. Tens of thousands come to watch the excitement from land and small boats.

A book featuring the event, *Misty of Chincoteague* by Marguerite Henry, was published in 1947 and became a children's classic. A movie based on the book appeared in 1960.

CONTACTS:
Chincoteague Chamber of Commerce
6733 Maddox Blvd.
Chincoteague Island, VA 23336
757-336-6161; fax: 757-336-1242
www.chincoteaguechamber.com

♦ 0607 ♦ Chinhae Cherry Blossom Festival
Early April

The Cherry Blossom Festival is held in Chinhae, South Kyong-sang, Korea, the headquarters of the Korean Navy. The purpose of the festival is to enjoy the thousands of blossoming cherry trees and also to honor Korea's illustrious Admiral Yi Sun-shin. Admiral Yi defeated the Japanese in several sea battles during the latter's invasions of the late 16th century. He is famous for developing "turtle boats," the first iron-clad naval vessels, with 26 cannons on each side; though outnumbered, they proved superior to the Japanese boats. While the cherries bloom, there are daily events—a memorial service, parades, sports contests, music and dance performances, and folk games.

CONTACTS:
Korea Tourism Organization
2 Executive Dr.
Ste. 100
Fort Lee, NJ 07024
201-585-0909; fax: 201-585-9041
english.visitkorea.or.kr

♦ 0608 ♦ Chinkashiki (Fire Control Ceremony)
September 17

Chinkashiki is a ceremony performed by Shinto priests at shrines around Tokyo and elsewhere in Japan. The priests walk in somber procession around a bed of burning coals until they work themselves into a kind of trance. Next, the priests gather up some salt, throw some of it into the fire and smear the remainder on their feet before walking over the burning coals in as dignified a manner as possible. The purpose of the ceremony is to demonstrate to the assembled crowds that Shinto religious beliefs and practices can tame fire and destroy its power to hurt human beings.

Shinto is the indigenous Japanese religious tradition. It has no founder, no official sacred scriptures, and no fixed system of doctrine or ethics, but it relies heavily on traditional rites and festivals.

CONTACTS:
Japan National Tourism Organization
1 Grand Central Pl.
60 E. 42nd St.
Ste. 448
New York, NY 10165
212-757-5640; fax: 212-307-6754
www.jnto.go.jp/eng

♦ 0609 ♦ Chitlin' Strut
November, Friday and Saturday after Thanksgiving

The Chitlin' Strut is a feast of chitlins or chitterlings (hog intestines), held in the small town of Salley, S.C. The affair features a "hawg-calling" contest, country music, arts and crafts, a parade, lots of chitlins (about 8,000 pounds are devoured each year), and chicken for those not enamored of chitlins. (Former President George Bush has said he is a chitlin fan.) Chitlins are prepared by cleaning them well, boiling them until they are tender, and then, after coating them in egg and crumbs, frying them in deep fat until they're crackling crisp.

Salley was named for Col. Dempsey Hammond Salley, who donated the site in the 19th century.

The Chitlin' Strut began in 1966 to raise money for the town's Christmas decorations. The Strut now draws as many as 50,000 people, and Salley, with a population of 700, has used the revenues from it to pay for such necessities as trash cans, signs, and even a fire truck.

CONTACTS:
Salley Chitlin Strut
230 Pine St. N.W.
Salley, SC 29137
803-258-3485
www.chitlinstrut.com

♦ 0610 ♦ Chochin Matsuri (Lantern Festival)
Various

Chochin are cylindrical lanterns made out of paper stretched over a split bamboo frame. These colorful, festive lanterns appear at many Japanese festivals, but they play a special role in Nihonmatsu's Chochin Matsuri on October 4-6 and Akita's Kanto Festival in August. *Kanto* are huge decorations made from 46 chochin hung from a 30-foot pole with nine cross-poles. Each kanto can weigh more than 100 pounds, and there are 160 kanto displayed at the festival in Akita. Not surprisingly, this event is also known as the **Balancing Festival**, since young men perform stunts in which they try to balance the kanto on their chins and foreheads for the entertainment of the crowd.

One of the best-known Chochin festivals is held on August 26-27 in Ishiiki town at Hazu in Aichi Prefecture. The primary attractions are 12 huge chochin, each about 30 feet high and 18 feet across, that are hoisted by means of pulleys up three huge pillars at the Suwa Shrine. According to a local legend, the lanterns commemorate the bonfire that destroyed a dragon who once threatened the shoreline community. As night nears, priests begin to illuminate the lanterns—a process that may take several hours. At the end of the festival the lanterns are lowered after religious dances and songs have been offered.

CONTACTS:
Akita City Hall
1-1-1 Sanno
Akita, Akita Prefecture Japan
81-96-863-2033; fax: 81-96-866-2278
www.city.akita.akita.jp/en/default.htm

◆ 0611 ◆ Choctaw Indian Fair
Begins first Wednesday after Fourth of July

This is a four-day annual gathering of the Mississippi band of Choctaw Indians. Held since 1949 in Philadelphia, Mississippi, it features—besides dances, crafts exhibits, and pageantry—the Choctaw Stickball World Series. Choctaw stickball, the forerunner of lacrosse, is played with long-handled sticks with pouches at the ends for carrying and pitching a leather ball. It is called the "granddaddy of games" and is thought to be the oldest field sport in America. More than 20,000 visitors usually attend the fair.

CONTACTS:
Mississippi Band of Choctaw Indians
101 Industrial Rd.
Choctaw, MS 39350
601-656-5251
www.choctaw.org

◆ 0612 ◆ Choctaw Trail of Tears Walk
May or June

As European settlers migrated west, the Choctaw Indians were forced from their Mississippi and Louisiana settlements. In the 1830s thousands of Choctaw people suffered from starvation, disease, and cold, wet weather for which they were ill-equipped, having had to leave all their possessions behind, and thousands died during the movement to reservations in what is now Oklahoma.

Each year many Choctaw families and friends gather in Skullyville, Oklahoma, where the dead were buried. There is an annual historic reenactment of the walk, known as the "Trail of Tears" walk, and other events. Traditional Choctaw foods are served, and Choctaw baskets, renowned for their intricate patterns, are on display.

CONTACTS:
Choctaw Nation of Oklahoma
P.O. Box 1210
Durant, OK 74702
800-522-6170
www.choctawnation.com

◆ 0613 ◆ Chongmyo Taeje (Royal Shrine Rite)
First Sunday in May

Chongmyo Taeje is a Confucian memorial ceremony held at Chongmyo (or Jongmyo) Shrine in Seoul, Korea, to honor the kings and queens of the Yi, or Joseon, Dynasty (1392-1910). The shrine, in a secluded garden in the center of Seoul, houses the ancestral tablets of the monarchs. Each year elaborate rites are performed to pay homage to them, and a number of royal descendants, robed in the traditional garments of their ancestors, take part. The rites are accompanied by court music and dance. The ceremony is a grand expression of the widespread Confucian practice of honoring ancestors, either at home or at their graves.

CONTACTS:
Cultural Heritage Administration
189, Cheongsa-ro
920, Dunsan-Dong
Seo-gu
Daejeon Korea
82-42-481-3189
jikimi.cha.go.kr/english

◆ 0614 ◆ Christ the King, Feast of
November, Sunday before Advent begins

In 1925, Pope Pius XI established the last Sunday in October as the Feast of Christ the King. He did so in order to remind people of Christ's everlasting authority over the people of the earth, thereby signaling the church's resistance to the rising tide of secular values and ideas in politics as well as in social matters. This Roman Catholic feast day was adopted by the Episcopal Church as well as other churches of the Anglican Communion. In 1970 the Roman Catholic Church moved the feast to the last Sunday before ADVENT begins, as did the Episcopal Church and some other churches in the Anglican Communion.

◆ 0615 ◆ Christkindlesmarkt
Early December through Christmas Eve

Christkindlesmarkt is the biggest and best known of the CHRISTMAS markets of Germany. The market in Nuremberg, Bavaria, Germany, has been held since 1697 in the city's *Hauptmarkt* ("main market"), the site of the famed 60-foot-high *Schöner Brunnen* ("beautiful fountain") and the 600-year-old redstone Church of Our Lady. More than 100 booths are set up to offer only goods directly related to Christmas— dolls, wooden soldiers, tinsel angels, picture books, and painted boxes. Food booths sell Nuremberg's specialties— *Lebkuchen*, or gingerbread, and *Zwetschgenmannlein*, which are little people-shaped confections made of prunes, figs, and raisins, with heads of painted walnuts. A post office branch is set up to cancel letters with a special stamp, and rides are offered in an old horse-drawn mail coach.

The three-week festival is inaugurated with choral singing, the pealing of church bells, and illumination of a crèche. A week or two before Christmas, some 10,000 people parade with lanterns to the Imperial Castle overlooking the city to sing carols. Other major Christmas markets are held in a number of German cities. Munich has the oldest Christmas market; it has been held annually for about 600 years and features daily musical programs. In Rothenburg-on-the-Tauber, the market is a month-long "Winter's Tale" of 150 events that include stagecoach rides, plays, and concerts. In Berlin, a miniature village for children is featured.

CONTACTS:
Nuremberg Convention and Tourist Office
Frauentorgraben 3
P.O. Box 4248
Nuremberg, Bavaria 90443 Germany
49-911-2336-0; fax: 49-911-2336-166
www.christkindlesmarkt.de

♦ 0616 ♦ **Christmas**
December 25

The most popular of the Christian festivals, also known as the **Feast of the Nativity of Our Lord**, Christmas (from "Christ's Mass") celebrates the birth of Jesus of Nazareth. The exact date of Jesus' birth is not known, and for more than three centuries it was a movable feast, often celebrated on EPIPHANY, January 6. The Western Church chose to observe it at the end of December, perhaps as a way of countering the various pre-Christian festivals celebrated around that time of year. Some believe that Pope Julius I fixed the date of Christmas at December 25 in the fourth century. The earliest reference to it is in the Philocalian Calendar of Rome in 336. Although the majority of Eastern Orthodox churches have celebrated the Nativity on December 25 since the middle of the fifth century, those that still adhere to the old Julian calendar—called Old Calendarists—mark the occasion 13 days later, on January 7. The Armenian Churches continue to celebrate OLD CHRISTMAS DAY on January 6.

The Christmas season in the church begins on Christmas Eve and ends on Epiphany, unlike the commercial season that may begin any time after HALLOWEEN.

December 25th is a holy day of obligation for Roman Catholics, who must attend one of the three masses priests are permitted to say in honor of the occasion. These services are celebrated at midnight on CHRISTMAS EVE and at dawn and, usually, mid-morning on Christmas.

As a holiday, Christmas represents a strange intermingling of both Christian and the pagan traditions it replaced. Many of the secular customs now associated with Christmas—such as decorating with mistletoe, holly, and ivy; indulging in excessive eating and drinking; stringing lights in trees; and exchanging gifts—can be traced back to early pagan festivals like the SATURNALIA and ancient WINTER SOLSTICE rites.

Another example is burning the YULE log, which was part of a pre-Christian winter solstice festival celebrating the return of the sun in the middle of winter. Even the Christmas tree, a German custom introduced in Britain by Queen Victoria's husband, Albert, may trace its history back to ancient times .

One of the most universal Christmas traditions is the crèche, a model of the birth scene of Christ, with Jesus in the manger, surrounded by the Holy Family and worshipping angels, shepherds, and animals. Many families have their own crèche, with the three Wise Men set apart and moved closer each day after Christmas until they arrive at the manger on Epiphany. In Austria, the crèche is not put away until CANDLEMAS Day.

In Belgium, the manger also appears in shop windows, constructed of the material sold by the shop: bread at the bakery; silks and laces at dressmakers; a variety of materials from the hardware store; butter and cheese from dairies; and cravats and neckties at the haberdashers.

In Chile the crèche is called a *pesebre*. Some homes leave their doors open so people passing by can come in and say a brief prayer to the *Niño Lindo* (beautiful baby).

In Italy it is a *presépio* and is placed on the lowest shelf of a *ceppo*, which is a pyramid of shelves, lit with candles, used to display secular Christmas decorations and ornaments.

In Poland, where the crèche is called a *yaselko*, it is believed to be the origin of the Christmas folk play called the King Herod play, based on Herod's order to kill all male babies in Bethlehem (*see* HOLY INNOCENTS' DAY). Thirteenth-century Franciscan monks brought the crèche to Poland. Eventually the wax, clay, and wooden figures were transformed into *szopka*, puppets that performed Christmas mystery plays, which told of the mysteries of Christ's life. Later, the monks acted the parts played by the puppets and were called "living szopka." In time, the plays were blended with characters and events from Polish history. The performers are called "Herods" and go from house to house in their villages where they are invited in to sing carols, act, and later to eat and drink with the family.

In Burkina Faso (until 1984 called Upper Volta), in western Africa, the population is mostly in Ouagadougou, the capital, and there the children make nativities (manger scenes) around the entrance to their compound. They are ready on Christmas Day so friends and neighbors can come by and, if they like them, leave a few coins in the dish provided. Some are made of paper and set on a pedestal, others of mud bricks with a thatch roof, while others are in the form of the local round house and have the bricks covered with a coat of concrete and a masonry dome instead of thatch. All of this is ornately decorated with strings of plastic packing peanuts, bits of shiny metal, tinsel, plastic, and flashlight bulbs. Some are modeled after pictures of European churches, but the child who can build a multi-storied nativity is thought very clever. On the wall of the compound behind the nativity is painted a white panel on which are affixed pictures of the Holy Family, crosses, hearts, arrows, stars, and anything else that comes to the mind of the young creator.

In Japan, since the end of World War II, Christmas has become a very popular holiday, even for non-Christians. Christmas dinner is replaced with a commercial Christmas cake, called "decoration cake," (*dekoreshon keki*), covered with ridges and waves of frosting. Grandfather Santa Claus brings the gifts, but stockings are hung on the pipe for the bathtub stove, which is the nearest equivalent to a fireplace in Japanese homes. NEW YEAR'S postcards are much more important than Christmas cards, and the most elaborate use of evergreen trees is also saved for New Year's. Christmas parties are a kind of blending with *bonenkai*, "closing of the year parties," which may only be attended by men and professional women: geishas, waitresses, entertainers. All women can attend Christmas parties, which is one of the reasons why the Japanese consider Christmas to be democratic.

Secular Christmas customs have continued to evolve. The Christmas card didn't become popular until the 19th century in England; Santa Claus's reindeer were an American invention at about the same time. Modern Christmas celebrations tend to focus on the worldly—with such traditions as the office Christmas party, sending out greeting cards, and Christmas specials on television taking the place of church services and other religious observances for many. The movement to "put Christ back into Christmas" has not lessened the enjoyment of this holiday as much for its social and commercial events as for its spiritual significance. The way Christmas is celebrated today is actually no worse—and in many ways much less excessive—than the hedonistic medieval celebration, where the feasting and revelry often extended all the way from Christmas to Candlemas (February 2).

See also GANNA; KOLEDOUVANE; LIGHTING OF THE NATIONAL CHRISTMAS TREE; MISA DE GALLO; and POSADAS.

CONTACTS:
Christian Resource Institute
4801 N.W. 62nd St.
Oklahoma City, OK 73122
www.crivoice.org

◆ 0617 ◆ Christmas (Greece)
December 25

According to Greek folklore, supernatural beings with unusual powers are present upon earth during the 12 days between CHRISTMAS EVE and EPIPHANY. The name for these spirits is *kallikantzari*, and they wander about during the Christmas season causing mischief. They are ugly and unkempt, and their favorite way of getting into the house is through the chimney, much like the traditional Santa Claus. Christmas masqueraders often dress in animal skins to represent these demons of the WINTER SOLSTICE, and their jangling bells are supposed to drive the spirits away. Children born on CHRISTMAS must be baptized immediately to rid them of the evil influence of the kallikantzari.

CONTACTS:
Greek Embassy
2217 Massachusetts Ave. N.W.
Washington, D.C. 20008
202-939-1300; fax: 202-939-1324
www.mfa.gr

◆ 0618 ◆ Christmas (Malta)
December 25

The Republic of Malta is a small country in the central Mediterranean that consists of seven islands. The Maltese Islands have a strong Catholic population that celebrates many religious holidays throughout the year. Because of the strong Catholic influence, several of the holy days are national holidays in Malta.

Religious holidays, such as CHRISTMAS and EASTER, are widely celebrated in Malta. Maltese families tend to be very close-knit, and the holidays are a time to strengthen the sense of community and reinforce family bonds.

On CHRISTMAS EVE, it is traditional to attend Midnight mass and then eat a large Christmas breakfast. In most churches, at 11 P.M. on Christmas Eve there is the "Priedka tat-Tifel," which consists of a young boy (or girl, in some parishes) reciting by heart the events leading up to the Nativity.

On Christmas Day, families prepare large Christmas lunches and give thanks with their relatives for all that they have.

Also, the streets are lined with carts selling a wide assortment of foods, including the more traditional sweets and delicacies. As in many other countries around the world, Maltese families exchange presents at Christmas time.

CONTACTS:
Malta Tourism Authority
Auberge D'Italie
Merchants St.
Valetta, VLT 1170 Malta
356-2-291-5000; fax: 356-2-291-5394
www.visitmalta.com

◆ 0619 ◆ Christmas (Marshall Islands)
December 25

The United Church of Christ in the Marshall Islands of Micronesia has an unusual approach to the traditional lighting of the CHRISTMAS tree. Members of the church's Stewardship Council conceal a decorated tree inside a large wooden cross. While they are singing Christmas carols and hymns, the cross opens slowly and the tree rises from it. The singers set off firecrackers as the tree rises, and then lower their voices and sing more softly as the tree descends back into the cross. When their singing is over, the two sides of the cross come apart and the tree remains standing, symbolic of the birth, death, and resurrection of Christ.

See also KURIJMOJ.

◆ 0620 ◆ Christmas (Norway)
December 25-26

CHRISTMAS, known as **Juledag** in Norway, is generally a quiet day. After attending morning church services, most Norwegians return home to be with their family and friends. December 26, however, is another matter. Referred to as Second Christmas Day, or *Anden Juledag*, it is spent eating, drinking, and going to parties, festivities that continue until January 13. Holiday breakfasts are popular, often accompanied by *aquavit* and other strong drinks. Traditional foods served at these Christmas get-togethers include *lutefisk* (dried cod), *lefse* (a thin potato roll served with butter or cinnamon and sugar), and *fladbröd* (a flat, hard Norwegian bread).

During the German occupation of Norway, when King Haakon was living in England, a Norwegian boat stationed there would be sent to Norway to bring back a Norway spruce each year as a gift for the king at Christmas. The custom of bringing a Norwegian tree to England was continued after the war, and every Christmas a huge Norwegian spruce stands in London's Trafalgar Square.

CONTACTS:
Norwegian Embassy
2720 34th St. N.W.
Washington, D.C. 20008
202-333-6000; fax: 202-469-3990
www.norway.org

♦ 0621 ♦ Christmas (Puerto Rico)
December 25

CHRISTMAS celebrations in Puerto Rico combine island traditions with more contemporary customs, such as Santa Claus and imported Christmas trees. Singers, often dressed as the Three Kings (or Magi), go from door to door singing ancient carols known as *aguinaldos* to the accompaniment of guitars. It is customary to offer gifts to the singer, and over the years the term "aguinaldos" has also come to stand for the gift itself. Sometimes the strolling carolers are asked inside to sample special Christmas dishes, such as roast pig and rice pudding. Christmas pageants and parties, which begin in early December, often extend right up until the Feast of the Three Kings on EPIPHANY (January 6).

In the Dominican Republic, on the island of Hispaniola just west of Puerto Rico, a major Christmas attraction is the animated *nacimiento* (Nativity scene) at the Church of San José. This mechanized toy village features miniature trains and figures of people going about their jobs.

CONTACTS:
Dominican Republic Ministry of Tourism - US Office
136 E. 57 St.
Ste. 805
New York, NY 10022
212-588-1012 or 888-374-6361; fax: 212-588-1015
www.godominicanrepublic.com

♦ 0622 ♦ Christmas (Romania) (Craciun)
December 25

From CHRISTMAS EVE until NEW YEAR'S EVE, boys in Romania go from house to house singing carols, reciting poetry and legends, and carrying the *steaua*, which is a large wooden star covered with gilt paper, decorated with ribbons and bells, and illuminated from within by a burning candle. Dramatic performances of the story of Jesus' birth can be seen in many Romanian towns and villages, with a cast of traditional characters that includes King Herod, the Magi, a clown, and a comical old man. Puppet shows are also popular.

Turte, a special kind of cake consisting of many layers of thin dough with melted sugar or honey and crushed walnuts in between, is the food most often associated with Christmas in Romania. The many-layered dough is representative of the swaddling clothes of the infant Jesus. As the housewife prepares the turte on the day before Christmas Eve, she walks into the yard followed by her husband wielding an ax. They go around to each tree in the yard, and the husband threatens to cut it down because it no longer bears any fruit. The wife intervenes, persuading the husband that the tree will be full of fruit the following summer. The custom may derive from a pagan ceremony.

CONTACTS:
Romanian National Tourist Office
355 Lexington Ave. 8th Fl.
New York, NY 10017
212-545-8484
romaniatourism.com

♦ 0623 ♦ Christmas (Russian Orthodox)
January 7

This celebration of the birth of Jesus is observed by the Russian Orthodox Church under the Julian calendar. The calendar trails behind the Gregorian calendar by 13 days.

Before the 1917 Revolution, Orthodox CHRISTMAS was widely observed in Russia, Ukraine, Belarus, and Georgia. After the Revolution, churches were closed and people practicing religion were persecuted. In 1991, after the Soviet Union had been officially dissolved, Christmas was observed openly and as a state holiday in Russia for the first time in 70 years.

In Moscow, banners were strung up and Nativity scenes were displayed in Red Square. On radio and television, there were nonstop programs telling the Christmas story and showing villagers wearing embroidered folk costumes and carrying tambourines as they made the rounds to offer Christmas bread at every house. On CHRISTMAS EVE, tens of thousands jammed Red Square for performances by choirs and bellringers and gala fireworks over the multi-colored onion domes of St. Basil's Cathedral. Midnight services were celebrated in churches. At the Kremlin, a Christmas charity ball was held to raise money for orphan children.

Before the Revolution, Christmas in Russia was a great feast celebrated with decorated trees, strolling carolers, and gifts. There was a legend of "Father Frost" or "Grandfather Frost," who wore a red robe and black boots and had a long white beard. Tchaikovsky's "Nutcracker Suite" was, of course, associated with the holiday. When Joseph Stalin was in power, some aspects of the old Christmas, such as the tree and the gifts from Grandfather Frost, were added to the New Year's celebrations. Then January 7 became a holiday observed only by those who dared to go to church.

See also OLD CHRISTMAS DAY; RUSSIAN WINTER FESTIVAL.

CONTACTS:
Moscow United Methodist Church
126 Church St.
Moscow, PA 18444
570-842-7251; fax: 570-842-3920
moscowumc.com

♦ 0624 ♦ Christmas (South Africa)
December 25

Because South Africa is in the Southern Hemisphere, CHRISTMAS is a summer holiday. The tinsel and evergreen boughs that decorate homes, churches, parks, and shopping malls offer a stark contrast to the weather, which encourages people to spend the day at the beach or in the shaded mountains. But Christmas traditions persist: English-speaking children hang up their stockings in anticipation of the arrival of Father Christmas, carolers sing by candlelight on CHRISTMAS EVE, and Christmas pageants are performed. One of the most popular activities for children is to produce pantomimes based on such classic tales as "Babes in the Woods." BOXING DAY, December 26, is also observed as a holiday, a time for giving boxes of food and clothing to the poor.

For black South Africans Christmas is a day for feasting and exchanging gifts. It marks the culmination of a Carnival-like week of singing, dancing, and eating.

♦ 0625 ♦ Christmas (Spain) (Pascua de Navidad)
December 25

The **Feast of the Birth** is observed in Spain by attending church services, feasting, and listening to Christmas music. It is a Spanish custom for public servants—such as the mail carrier and the garbage collector—to leave cards with holiday messages for their customers, a reminder of the services they have rendered in the past or hope to render in the coming year. In return, they are given *aguinaldos,* or gifts of money. In Madrid and other large cities, it is not uncommon to see a police officer directing traffic on Christmas Day, surrounded by parcels of all sizes and shapes. Christmas is also a time for processions of the *gigantes,* or giant figures, which dance to the music of fife and drum.

Spanish children receive their gifts at Epiphany, which commemorates the coming of the Magi to Bethlehem, bearing gifts for the Christ child. Children leave their shoes on the window sill or balcony and fill them with straw and carrots or barley for the Magi's horses to eat. In Cadiz, children still observe the traditional rite of "Christmas swinging" on swings that are set up in the courtyards. At one time the custom may have been intended to help the sun in its climb to the highest point in the sky.

♦ 0626 ♦ Christmas (Sweden) (Juledagen)
December 25

Swedes rise early on Christmas to attend *Julotta,* six o'clock church services. The church is lit with hundreds of candles and the congregation sings nativity hymns. In rural areas, lit candles are placed in farmhouse windows and people travel to church by sleigh. Each sleigh carries a torch, and when people arrive at the church they all throw their torches into a bonfire.

Unlike the American Santa Claus, the Swedish Father Christmas, or *jultomte,* is small and thin, more like a leprechaun than a jolly, white-bearded man. The *tomte,* "little man," is a mythical character similar to an elf who can be either troublesome or benevolent, depending on how well he is treated. Because midwinter was considered a dangerous season in pre-Christian times, full of evil spirits, it was important to treat the tomte well by putting out food and drink for him. Over the generations, the jultomte has become a more generous spirit, who distributes gifts rather than receives them. Even when he appears in a red costume with a white beard, however, he is always depicted as being very thin.

See also St. Knut's Day; St. Lucy's Day.

CONTACTS:
Swedish Institute
Box 7434
S-103 91

Stockholm Sweden
46 8-453 78
sweden.se

♦ 0627 ♦ Christmas (Syria)
December 25; January 1

The Syrian Santa Claus is the camel, who brings gifts to children on New Year's Day. According to legend, the youngest of the three camels that carried the Magi to Bethlehem fell down, exhausted by the journey. The Christ child blessed the animal and granted it immortality. Syrian children set out water and wheat for the camel before they go to bed, and when they awake in the morning, they find gifts, or, if they've been naughty, a black mark on their wrists. Another custom associated with the Magi is carried out on Christmas Eve, when vine stems are burned in the middle of the church to warm the Magi after their long journey.

Christmas itself is a family festival in Syria. A special dinner is prepared, and afterward friends and relatives pay social calls on one another. Among Syrian Americans, it is customary to serve guests Oriental coffee and holiday cakes such as *baklawa, burma,* and *mulabas,* as well as nuts, oranges, candies, and Syrian wines.

♦ 0628 ♦ Christmas Bird Count
December 14-January 6

The Christmas Bird Count, also known as CBC, is an international event sponsored annually by the National Audubon Society. Under a system that the society calls "citizen science," volunteers join a count that takes place on one day during the designated CBC period, December 14–January 5. Each group of volunteers, known as a Christmas Bird Count Circle, is assigned a specific geographic area and asked to record the number and species of birds they see. Each circle has a compiler, who organizes the volunteers and records the data that they gather according to a specific methodology. Counts take place in all 50 states, every Canadian province, parts of Central and South America, Bermuda, the West Indies, and Pacific Islands. The data gathered every year helps the Audubon Society and scientists worldwide to understand the status and distribution of bird populations in early winter.

The Christmas Bird Count began at the turn of the last century. At that time, people often competed during the holiday season to see who could shoot the most birds and game. Ornithologist Frank Chapman, an officer in the just-developing Audubon Society, proposed a new holiday tradition—a "Christmas Bird Census" that would encourage people to count birds rather than kill them. At the first count, birders in 25 North American locations spotted about 18,500 individual birds.

The 114th Christmas Bird Count (December 14, 2013 through January 5, 2014) produced an unusually high count of Snowy Owls due to massive storm conditions. A new record was set during that count for total number of observers at 71,659

(60,969 in field plus 10,690 at feeders) who tallied over 66,243,300 birds. Over the decades, generations of volunteers have supplied vital information for the longest-running database in ornithology.

CONTACTS:
National Audubon Society
225 Varick St.
New York, NY 10014
212-979-3000
www.audubon.org

♦ 0629 ♦ Christmas Eve
December 24

Christmas Eve or the **Vigil of Christmas** represents the culmination of the ADVENT season. Like CHRISTMAS itself, Christmas Eve celebrations combine both religious and secular events. Perhaps the most widely anticipated by children is the arrival of Santa Claus—known as *Sinterklass* by the Dutch settlers of New York, who were the first to introduce the idea of St. Nicholas's annual appearance on this day; the original Santa Claus was the tall, saintly looking bishop, Nicholas of Metz. It wasn't until the 19th century that he became the jolly, overweight, pipe-smoking figure in a **red** fur-trimmed suit that children in the United States recognize today. The modern Santa Claus was largely the invention of two men: Clement Moore, who in 1822 wrote his now-famous poem, "A Visit from St. Nicholas," and Thomas Nast, a cartoonist who did numerous illustrations of Santa Claus based on Moore's description. In any case, it is on Christmas Eve that Santa Claus climbs down the chimney and fills the children's stockings that have been hung by the fireplace mantel. Before going to bed children around the world leave milk and food out for the one who brings the presents, be it Santa Claus, the baby Jesus, the Christmas elf of Denmark, the Christmas goat of Finland (called *Joulupukki*), or the Swedish *tomte*, or little man, who resembles Puck or a leprechaun.

The midnight church service celebrating the birth of Jesus Christ is the main Christmas Eve tradition for many Christians of all denominations and even of non-believers, especially if there is a good organist, soloist, or choir. In most European countries, a large but meatless meal is eaten before church, for it is a fast day. Some families, especially those with grown children, exchange gifts on Christmas Eve rather than on Christmas Day. Caroling—going from house to house singing Christmas carols—began in Europe in the Middle Ages. The English brought the custom to America, where it is still very popular.

In Venezuela, after midnight on Christmas Eve, crowds of teenagers roller skate on the Avenida de los Caiboas. After an hour or so, they attend a special early mass called *Misa de Aguinaldos*, "Mass of the Carols," where they're greeted at the door with folk songs. Then they skate home for Christmas breakfast.

In Newfoundland and Nova Scotia, Canada, mummers, or *belsnickers*, go from house to house. Once inside they jog, tell licentious stories, play instruments and sing, and generally act up until the householder identifies the person under the mask. Then the mummer takes off his or her costume and acts like a normal visitor.

In the 19th century, in what is now New Mexico, bundles of branches were set ablaze along the roads and pathways. Called *farolitos* and *luminarias,* these small fires are meant to guide the Travelers to the people's homes on Christmas Eve. Residents are ready to give hospitality to anyone on that night, especially Joseph and Mary with the Christ Child. They wait in faith for the Travelers' three knocks on their door. But modern fire codes overtook the ancient faith, and firefighters began to extinguish the small piles of burning pine branches for fear a spark would start an inferno. Small brown paper bags partially filled with sand and holding a candle eventually replaced the open fires. Inevitably merchants began to sell wires of electric lights to replace the candles, and plastic, multi-colored sleeves to imitate lunch bags, and the modern luminarias began to appear at holidays like HALLOWEEN and the FOURTH OF JULY.

Last-minute shopping is another Christmas Eve tradition, and stores often stay open late to accommodate those who wait until the last minute to purchase their Christmas gifts.

In Buddhist Japan, Christmas Eve is for lovers, a concept introduced by a Japanese pop star and expanded by trendy magazines. It is a Western rite celebrated with a Japanese twist. The day should be spent doing something extra special (expensive), and should end in a fine Tokyo hotel room, most of which have been booked since the previous January; even the cheapest rooms go for exorbitant prices. Being alone on this night is comparable to being dateless on prom night in the United States.

Uncle Chimney is the Japanese version of Santa Claus. Youngsters may be treated to a $29 (or more) barrel of Kentucky Fried Chicken (10 pieces of chicken, five containers of ice cream, and salad) if their parents don't mind lining up for two hours. The reason for the chicken is that many Japanese think Colonel Sanders resembles Santa Claus. Another culinary tradition is strawberry shortcake with a plastic fir tree on top. This was introduced 70 years ago by a Japanese confectioner as a variant of plum pudding. While the origins of this form of Christmas are unclear, many people say it dates from the 1930s, well before the United States occupation in 1945 after World War II.

See also BEFANA FESTIVAL; DÍA DE LOS TRES REYES; GIANT LANTERN FESTIVAL; POSADAS; ST. NICHOLAS'S DAY; "SILENT NIGHT, HOLY NIGHT" CELEBRATION; TOLLING THE DEVIL'S KNELL; WIGILIA.

♦ 0630 ♦ Christmas Eve (Armenia)
January 5 by the Julian calendar; January 18 by the Gregorian calendar

On CHRISTMAS EVE in Armenia it is traditional to eat fried fish, lettuce, and boiled spinach. The spinach is eaten to pay tribute to the Virgin Mary, who, according to legend, ate spinach on the evening before Jesus' birth. After a morning church service on CHRISTMAS Day, the men exchange brief social calls and are served coffee and sweets. On the third day after Christmas, it's the women's turn to make and receive calls.

◆ 0631 ◆ Christmas Eve (Baltics)
December 24

Many people in Estonia attend church on CHRISTMAS EVE. The holiday dinner, which follows the church service, typically includes roasted pig's head or blood sausages, turnips, and potatoes. For dessert there is cranberry soup, and of course plenty of Estonian vodka, which is made from the potatoes for which the country is famous. Many of the Christmas tree ornaments are edible, and real candles—often made by dipping a lamb's wool thread into hot sheep fat—are used to light the tree.

In Latvia, the tree is the only Christmas decoration, and it is laden with gilded walnuts, artificial snow, tinsel, small red apples, and colored candies. After the traditional Christmas Eve dinner, which consists of roast pork, goose and boar's head, and little meat-filled pastries known as *piradzini*, the candles on the tree are lighted and the gifts piled beneath it are distributed and opened.

In Lithuania family members break and consume delicate wafers, or *plotkeles*, on Christmas Eve as a token of peace. The family puts a little hay under the tablecloth as a reminder that Jesus was born in a stable. The *kucios*, or Christmas Eve supper, consists of fish soup followed by cabbage, fried and boiled fish, sauerkraut, and a huge pike served with a hearty, dark gravy. Dessert is *kisielius*, a pudding-like dish that is composed of cream of oats, sugar, and cream.

CONTACTS:
Association Baltic Turkish Culture Academy
A Jakšto St 5,7 LT
Vilnius 01105 Lithuania
370-52151833
www.balturka.lt

◆ 0632 ◆ Christmas Eve (Bethlehem)
December 24

Located only a few miles from Jerusalem in an area that is part of the biblical land of Palestine, Bethlehem is known as the birthplace of Jesus and has long been regarded as a holy place by Christians. A church was eventually built on the site, and the crypt beneath it, known as the Grotto of the Nativity, is reputed to be the site of the original manger. Because there have been so many arguments over the years about which Christian church should control the sanctuary, it is jointly owned by the Armenian, Orthodox, and Roman Catholic churches. A Roman Catholic mass is held there at midnight on CHRISTMAS EVE, and because pilgrims from all over the world attend, most of them end up watching the service on a large closed-circuit television screen in nearby Manger Square. The highlight of the service occurs when a carved wooden figure of the Christ Child is laid in a manger in the Grotto of the Nativity.

Protestants hold an outdoor service in Shepherds' Field where, according to tradition, the shepherds kept watch over the flocks on the first Christmas Eve.

CONTACTS:
Palestine Ministry of Tourism and Antiquities
www.mota.ps/en

◆ 0633 ◆ Christmas Eve (Denmark) (Juleaften)
December 24

The celebration of CHRISTMAS in Denmark actually begins on Little Christmas Eve (December 23) and continues well into the NEW YEAR. It is customary to make enough apple fritters on Little Christmas Eve to last three days. In rural areas, farmers tie a sheaf of grain to a pole in the garden so that the birds can feed from it. Even city dwellers tie bunches of grain to their balconies.

The traditional CHRISTMAS EVE dinner starts with *risengrød* (rice porridge). Like Christmas puddings elsewhere, there is an almond hidden inside the porridge. Whoever finds it receives a prize. The risengrød is followed by roast goose stuffed with prunes and apples and decorated with small Danish flags. After dinner, family members often dance around the Christmas tree, sing carols, and exchange gifts.

The *Julenisse*, or Christmas gnome, is a small bearded man dressed in gray with a pointed red cap who, according to Danish legend, lives in attics or barns and is responsible for bringing a family good or bad luck. On Christmas Eve the Julenisse is given a generous portion of risengrød with an extra helping of butter.

CONTACTS:
VisitDenmark
55 Sloane St
SW1 X9SY London
44-020-7259-5958
www.visitdenmark.co.uk

◆ 0634 ◆ Christmas Eve (Finland) (Jouluaatto)
December 24

Before sitting down to the traditional CHRISTMAS EVE dinner, many Finns go to church and place flowers and lighted candles on the graves of departed family members. Then the family gathers around the table and listens to the head of the household read a Christmas prayer. The meal itself includes *lipeäkala* (the Christmas fish) and ham, various breads, a kind of plum cake known as *torttuja*, and the traditional rice pudding in which an almond has been hidden. According to superstition, the boy or girl who finds it will be married before the next Christmas. The tree is decorated with homemade paper or wooden toys, gingerbread cookies, gilded walnuts, and other treats.

CONTACTS:
Ministry of Foreign Affairs of Finland
P.O. Box 176
Merikasarmi 00023 Finland

358-295-350-000; fax: 358-9-629-840
www.formin.finland.fi

♦ 0635 ♦ Christmas Eve (France) (Veille de Noël)
December 24

CHRISTMAS EVE church services in Paris can be quite elaborate, while those in rural areas of France are usually very simple. No matter where it takes place, the Christmas Mass involves burning candles, Christmas carols, bells, and a crèche or miniature Nativity scene. Most homes also have a crèche. In Provence, the crèche includes not only the Holy Family, but small clay figures called *santons* representing traditional village characters—the butcher, baker, basket maker, flute players, etc.—who come to adore the infant Jesus. In Marseilles, there is a SANTON FAIR in the weeks preceding Christmas that is attended by people from all over Provence who want to purchase the traditional santons, made from molds that have been used for generations.

After the midnight service is over, families return to their homes for the *réveillon*, or traditional Christmas Eve meal, which includes *pâté de foie gras*, oysters, blood sausage, pancakes, and plenty of French wine. It is customary for the newspapers to calculate how many kilograms of blood sausage have been consumed at réveillon. Many families serve goose because, according to a Provençal legend, the goose clucked a greeting to the Wise Men when they drew near the baby Jesus.

In France children leave a pair of shoes out for *Père Noël*, the French gift bringer, to fill with treats.

In some parts of France, people celebrate Christmas Eve with the *Fête des Bergers,* the Shepherds' Mass or Shepherds' Festival. The event revolves around a procession led by shepherds and shepherdesses dressed in traditional, local costumes. A simple farm cart, led by a ram, is decorated with bells, flowers, and candles. The shepherds and shepherdesses put a lamb in the cart and lead it in a procession around the church. Then a shepherd picks up the lamb and gives it to the priest, a gesture that is said to represent the offering of a newborn lamb to the infant Jesus.

CONTACTS:
French Embassy
4101 Reservoir Rd. N.W.
Washington, D.C. 20007
202-944-6000
www.info-france-usa.org

♦ 0636 ♦ Christmas Eve (Italy) (La Vigilia)
December 24

The *presépio*, or Nativity manger, with its miniature figures of the Holy Family, angels, shepherds, and Three Kings plays a major role in the Italian observance of CHRISTMAS and is thought to have originated with ST. FRANCIS OF ASSISI more than 700 years ago. The presépio is set up on the first day of the Novena (the nine days preceding Christmas); on each subsequent morning, the family gathers before the presépio to light candles and offer prayers. Although manger figures are on sale in every market and village fair, in many families the manger is an heirloom that has been handed down for generations. The setting for the manger is usually built at home from cardboard, moss, and bits of twig, and it can be quite elaborate.

Christmas Eve is a family affair. After lighting candles before the presépio, a meatless meal known as the *cenone*, or festa supper, is served. It usually consists of some type of fish (eel is popular among the well-to-do), fowl, artichokes cooked with eggs, fancy breads, and Italian sweets such as *cannoli* (cheese-filled pastry), nougat, and other delicacies.

The YULE log plays a more important role than the Christmas tree. The children may tap it with sticks, requesting certain gifts. Few presents are given on Christmas Eve, since EPIPHANY is the time for gift-giving. The evening concludes with a church service at midnight.

In parts of Calabria and the Abruzzi, itinerant bagpipers, or *zampognari*, come down from the mountains and go from house to house playing pastoral hymns before the homemade mangers. They are given gifts of food or money.

See also BEFANA FESTIVAL.

♦ 0637 ♦ Christmas Eve (Moravian Church)
December 24

Members of the Moravian Church—named after Moravia, a region in the former Czechoslovakia (now part of the Czech Republic)—fled to America to escape persecution in the mid-18th century. They established a number of communities in Pennsylvania, one of which is called Bethlehem and known as "America's Christmas City." As Christmas approaches, the Moravians carry on the Old World tradition of building a Christmas "putz" (from the German word *putzen*, meaning "to decorate") or Nativity scene, which can range from a simple mantle decoration to an elaborate miniature landscape.

On the afternoon of CHRISTMAS EVE, they hold a children's "love feast" consisting of music, meditation, and a simple meal—usually sweet buns and mugs of sweetened coffee—served in the church. Then, after dinner, they assemble again in the church for the Christmas Eve Vigil, a service devoted almost entirely to music. The church lights are dimmed and handmade beeswax candles are distributed to the entire congregation while the children's choir sings a favorite Moravian hymn. A similar observance is held in Winston-Salem, North Carolina, now a historical restoration at which the Moravian way of life is preserved.

CONTACTS:
Moravian Church in North America
1021 Center St.
P.O. Box 1245
Bethlehem, PA 18016
610-867-7566
www.moravian.org

Central Moravian Church
73 W. Church St.
Bethlehem, PA 18018
610-866-5661; fax: 610-866-7256
www.centralmoravianchurch.org

◆ 0638 ◆ Christmas Eve (Switzerland) (HeiligerAbend)
December 24

There are a number of superstitions and folk beliefs surrounding CHRISTMAS EVE in Switzerland. One is the belief that animals gain the power of speech at midnight on Christmas Eve because they were present at Jesus' birth. Farmers give their horses, cows, goats, and other animals extra food on this night, but it's considered bad luck to overhear what the animals say. Old people claim that they can predict the weather for the next 12 months by peeling off 12 layers of onionskin and filling them with salt. Young lovers who want to find out who they will marry are told to drink from nine different fountains while the midnight church bells are ringing on Christmas Eve. If they rush to the church, their future mate will be standing on the steps.

Christkindli, or the Christ Child, who travels in a sleigh pulled by six reindeer, brings Swiss children their gifts. In the area surrounding Hallwil in the canton of Lucerne, a girl dressed in white robes, glittering crown, and a veil portrays the Christ Child. Other children, wearing white garments and carrying baskets of gifts and lanterns, accompany her on her rounds. Some families wait until the Christkindli enters the house to light the candles on the Christmas tree. In many homes the tree is kept hidden until after Christmas Eve supper, when the parlor doors are opened and the tree is displayed in all its glory.

In Zurich cakes known as *Tirggel,* whose main ingredients are flour and honey, are served at Christmas time. The cakes are believed to have originated as a pagan offering. They are made by pushing dough into intricate molds, shaped like characters from folktales, cartoons and other popular subjects. The finished cakes are tough and glossy, so it is not uncommon for them to be kept for months, or even years, and to be used as decorations around the house.

CONTACTS:
Swiss Embassy
2900 Cathedral Ave. N.W.
Washington, D.C. 20008
202-745-7900; fax: 202-387-2564
www.eda.admin.ch/eda/en/home.html

◆ 0639 ◆ Christmas Eve Bonfires
December 22, 23, and 24

The state of Louisiana contains four parishes (the equivalent of counties) called the river parishes, named for their position along the Mississippi River. This cluster of communities, located between Baton Rouge and New Orleans, forms part of the state's Cajun Country, a region that has preserved distinctive ethnic traditions. One such community, St. James Parish, has a popular Cajun tradition that takes place during the three days before CHRISTMAS in the towns of Gramercy, Lutcher, and Paulina.

According to the festival organizers, the tradition of the CHRISTMAS EVE bonfires most likely came from such European countries as France and Germany, the home countries of many early settlers of the St. James area. In those and other European nations, fires commonly marked the Christmas season, as well as St. John the Baptist's Feast Day Eve on June 23. The tradition of fires on these occasions in turn most likely sprang from pagan rituals marking, respectively, the winter and summer solstices.

The Christmas bonfire tradition in Louisiana dates back to the 1880s. There are several theories about how the current practice originated, but the most common explanation is that the bonfires lit the way for the arrival of Papa Noel, the Cajun version of Santa Claus. After World War II, the bonfire structures expanded into more elaborate creations, taking different forms and reaching 25 feet high.

Once restricted to small fires built by family groups, the tradition now calls for dozens of huge blazes lining the levee for miles along the local River Road. Some residents begin building the bonfires the day after Thanksgiving. In the weeks leading up to Christmas, local residents work together to collect materials and to construct the bonfires. A bonfire is lit on each of the two days before Christmas Eve. Then, on Christmas Eve, nearly 100 bonfires are ignited before a large crowd. Fire chiefs give a signal at 7:00 P.M. Christmas Eve (weather permitting) and the fire-tenders simultaneously ignite the fires. The event draws thousands of revelers to the area for the bonfires as well as a series of pageants, music performances, and cook-offs accompanying the main event.

The local community of Lutcher provides a preview of the Christmas Eve bonfires with an annual Festival of the Bonfires that takes place in a public park on a weekend early in December. The three-day event features live music, food, crafts, and carnival rides, as well as the lighting of a single bonfire on each night of the festival. This preview festival celebrated its 18th anniversary in 2007.

CONTACTS:
St. James Parish Welcome Center (Tourism)
1094 U.S. Hwy 61
Gramercy, LA 70052 United States
225-562-2523 or 800-367-7852
www.stjamesla.com

◆ 0640 ◆ Christmas Pastorellas (Mexico)
December 25-January 6

CHRISTMAS Day in Mexico is traditionally a quiet family day, especially following the POSADAS season and the midnight mass known as the *Misa de Gallo,* or "Mass of the Cock," that many attend on CHRISTMAS EVE. But Christmas in Mexico, which extends until DÍA DE LOS TRES REYES (EPIPHANY) on January 6, is also celebrated with *pastorellas,* or pageants, showing how the Wise Men and shepherds overcame obstacles to visit Jesus in the manger in Bethlehem.

These celebrations, which date from colonial days when Spanish missionaries used pageants as a way of teaching Mexicans the story of the Nativity, are performed throughout Mexico in public squares, churches, and theaters. Most of the pageants represent a humorous mix of tradition, politics, and social affairs.

CONTACTS:
Mexico Tourism Board
Viaducto Miguel Alemán
105 Col Escandón
Mexico City, CP 11800 Mexico
800-446-3942
www.visitmexico.com

♦ 0641 ♦ **Christmas Shooting**
Christmas Eve and New Year's Eve

Christmas Shooting is a very noisy custom in Berchtesgaden, Bavaria, Germany. About 200 marksmen gather at midnight above the Berchtesgaden valley and shoot rifles and mortars for an hour. The salvos echoing off the mountains can be heard for many miles. It is believed that the custom of making a loud racket began as a pagan rite to drive away evil spirits.

CONTACTS:
Berchtesgaden Tourismus GmbH
Station Sq. 4
Berchtesgaden 83471 Germany
49-8652-65650-50; fax: 49-8652-65650-99
www.berchtesgadener-land.com

♦ 0642 ♦ **Chrysanthemum Festival**
September-October, including the ninth day of ninth lunar month

The Chrysanthemum Festival was the last of the five sacred festivals of ancient Japan. It lasted over the ninth month and sometimes into the tenth month of the Buddhist lunar calendar, although the ninth day of the ninth month was known as **Chrysanthemum Day**, primarily an occasion for paying visits to one's superiors. Also known as **Choyo**, the festival was a unique tribute to the gardening and artistic skills of the Japanese, who developed a method for growing chrysanthemums within a wire or bamboo frame in the shape of a human figure. The boughs were guided around the frame such that the flowers bloomed only on the outside, clothing the figure in flower blossoms. The heads, hands, and feet of these more-than-life-sized figures would be made of wax or paste, but their costumes were made entirely of chrysanthemums, with blossoms of different sizes and colors used to achieve as realistic an effect as possible.

Formerly, *kiku ningyo* exhibitions were numerous, and could still be seen in the parks of big cities in the early part of the 20th century. But the cost of growing the flowers and erecting the figures became prohibitive, and the exhibits eventually died out. In Japan, Korea, and Okinawa today, Chrysanthemum Day is a fairly unimportant holiday, observed in scattered locations by eating chrysanthemum cakes (a dumpling made from yellow chrysanthemum petals mixed with rice flour) and drinking chrysanthemum wine.

CONTACTS:
Tokyo Convention & Visitors Bureau
Nisshin Bldg. 6Fl.
346-6 Yamabuki-cho, Shinjuku-ku
Tokyo 162-0801 Japan
81-3-5579-2680; fax: 81-3-5579-2685
www.tcvb.or.jp/en

♦ 0643 ♦ **Chuckwagon Races, National Championship**
September, weekend of Labor Day

The National Championship Chuckwagon Races take place at Dan Eoff's "Bar Of" Ranch in Clinton, Ark., each Labor Day weekend from Friday through Sunday. About 150 teams consisting of a wagon and four horses compete in five divisions for the National Champion title. Division winners are awarded silver belt buckles. They also take home a share of $25,000 worth of prizes, including jackets, saddles, and "Chuckwagon Bucks"—prize money that can be spent at the western-themed Trade Show held at the event. The races are for amateurs and open to all. The weekend can attract more than 20,000 spectators, many of whom camp out on the 700-acre ranch.

In addition to chuckwagon racing, events include bronc fanning, so called because riders attempt to calm ornery mounts by fanning them with their cowboy hats. The annual Snowy River Race is a tribute to the film *The Man from Snowy River*, which featured a downhill chase on horseback into a river. The 16 entrants in the race ride their horses up and then furiously down a steep hill, straight into the mouth of a stream, where the race finishes. Live music and dances add to the weekend's festivities.

Eoff and his family launched the races in 1986 as a Labor Day party for friends after attending a chuckwagon race in Cheyenne, Wyoming, in 1985. Eight wagons competed in the first race. More than 30 years later, that party has grown to be the largest chuckwagon race in the United States.

CONTACTS:
Eoff Ranch
2484 Shake Rag Rd.
Clinton, AR 72031
501-745-5250
www.chuckwagonraces.com

♦ 0644 ♦ **Chugiak-Eagle River Bear Paw Festival**
Mid-July

The Bear Paw Festival is a five-day community festival in the towns of Chugiak and Eagle River, near Anchorage, Alaska. Relatively new, it has established itself and achieved popularity with its Ugly Truck and Dog Contest, in which contestants compete for a combined score that rates the lack of beauty of both their vehicles and canine companions. Other events are a parade, a rodeo, arts and crafts displays, a beauty pageant, and carnival rides.

CONTACTS:
Chugiak-Eagle River Chamber of Commerce
P.O. Box 770353
Eagle River, AK 99577
907-694-4702; fax: 907-694-1205
www.cer.org

♦ 0645 ♦ Chulalongkorn Day
October 23

Chulalongkorn Day is a national holiday in Thailand commemorating King Chulalongkorn (Rama V), the king who abolished slavery and introduced numerous reforms when the country was still called Siam. He succeeded to the throne in 1868 when he was 15 years old, was crowned in 1873, and ruled until his death in 1910. He had been a pupil of Anna Leonowens, who taught the young prince about Abraham LINCOLN. The story of her stay in the royal court, and her teaching of the royal children and concubines, was told in Margaret Landon's book, *Anna and the King of Siam*. The book was the basis for the popular Broadway musical, *The King and I*.

CONTACTS:
Tourism Authority of Thailand
1600 New Phetchaburi Rd.
Makkasan, Ratchathevi
Bangkok 10400 Thailand
662-250-5500
www.tourismthailand.org

Government Public Relations Department, Office of the Prime Minister
9 Rama VI Rd.
Soi 30
Bangkok Thailand
66-2-618-2323; fax: 66-2-618-2358
thailand.prd.go.th

♦ 0646 ♦ Chung Yeung
September-October; ninth day of ninth lunar month

A Chinese holiday, Chung Yeung is the second family-remembrance day of the year. It's customary, as on the festival of QING MING, for families to visit the graves of ancestors, tend their gravestones, and make offerings of food, which are eaten after the ceremonies are completed.

It's also traditional on this day for people to go to the hills for picnics and kite-flying. This is done because, according to an ancient legend, a scholar was warned by a soothsayer that disaster would fall on the ninth day of the ninth lunar month. He took his family up into the mountains. When the family returned to their village, they found every living thing dead. They gave thanks that they had been spared. The custom of flying kites stems from traditional lore, which holds that kites can convey bad luck up into the sky.

The day is also known as **Ch'ung Yang**, **Double Nine Day**, and the **Festival of High Places**. It is a public holiday in some places, including Hong Kong and Macau.

CONTACTS:
Hong Kong Tourism Board
370 Lexington Ave.
Ste. 1812
New York, NY 10017
212-421-3382; fax: 212-421-8428
www.discoverhongkong.com

♦ 0647 ♦ Ch'un-hyang Festival
May

This celebration in Namwon, Jeollabuk-do, Korea, honors Ch'un-hyang, a symbol of female virtue. She is the heroine of the ancient Korean story, *Ch'un-hyangjon*, which tells of the love between a commoner and a nobleman. During the festival, her story is reenacted, and other events include a *p'ansori*, or "narrative song" contest, a swinging competition, traditionally enjoyed by young women, and a Miss Ch'un-hyang beauty pageant.

Ch'un-hyang was the daughter of a *kisaeng*, or female entertainer, and she and a nobleman's son, Yi Mongnyong, fell in love and were secretly married. Soon after, he was transferred from Namwon to Seoul. The new governor of Namwon was corrupt and licentious, and he wanted Ch'un-hyang. But even though she was beaten, she didn't give in to his advances. Finally Yi Mongnyong returned to Namwon as provincial inspector. He punished the governor and took Ch'un-hyang as his official bride. To Koreans, this is a favorite tale of love and fidelity and also a symbol of the resistance by common people to privileged classes.

CONTACTS:
Namwon City Hall
60 Sicheong-ro
Namwon, North Jeolla Province 590-701 Korea
82-63-620-6114; fax: 82-63-633-0444
www.namwon.go.kr

Korean Cultural Center
5509 Wilshire Blvd.
Los Angeles, CA 90036
323-634-0280; fax: 323-634-0281
www.korea.net

♦ 0648 ♦ Chuseok (Gawi or Hangawi)
15th day of the eighth lunar month

The MID-AUTUMN FESTIVAL, which is observed in China, Japan, Vietnam, and other Asian countries, is celebrated in Korea as well, where it is called *Chuseok* or **Hangawi**. This fall harvest festival is marked on the 15th day of the eighth lunar month and is a major national holiday in Korea. Like THANKSGIVING in the United States, Chuseok finds many people on the move in Korea as they travel to spend the holiday with their families.

Koreans traditionally begin the day with a religious service at home to remember their ancestors. Then they visit the graves of their departed family members and clear away the weeds and grasses around the tombs; this is not only a symbolic act of honoring their ancestors, but also a practical matter, because of the increased chance for grass fires during the typically dry autumn season. Then people go home and enjoy foods traditional to the season. Various rice-based dishes incorporating fresh fruits and vegetables are popular. Other customary games and activities include wrestling for men, a women's circle song and dance called *Gang-gang-sullae* in the south, and in rural areas, a cow or ox game, in which two men or boys in a cow or ox costume visit each house in the neighborhood and beg for something to eat; if the householder feeds them, they perform a dance. Taking walks in the evening and admiring the moon is also a favorite activity on Chuseok, since the holiday falls on the full moon day of the eighth month.

CONTACTS:
Korea Tourism Organization
2 Executive Dr.
Ste. 750
Fort Lee, NJ 07024
201-585-0909; fax: 201-585-9041
english.visitkorea.or.kr

♦ 0649 ♦ Cinco de Mayo
May 5

Cinco de Mayo or the **Fifth of May** is a national holiday in Mexico commemorating the Battle of Puebla on May 5, 1862, in which Mexican troops under General Ignacio Zaragoza defeated the invading French forces of Napoleon III. Although the battle itself represented only a temporary setback for the French, the Mexicans' victory against overwhelming odds gave them the confidence they needed to persevere until finally triumphing on April 2, 1867.

The anniversary of this event is celebrated not only in Mexico but in many American communities with large Mexican-American populations—especially in the southwestern states of Texas, Arizona, and southern California. The events include parades, patriotic speeches, bullfights, barbecues, and beauty contests. Olvera Street in Los Angeles is particularly known for its Cinco de Mayo celebration.

CONTACTS:
Mexico Tourism Board
800-446-3942
www.visitmexico.com

♦ 0650 ♦ Circumcision, Feast of the
January 1

The Feast of the Circumcision, which commemorates the circumcision of the infant Jesus on the eighth day after his birth, was first observed by the Eastern Orthodox and Roman Catholic churches in the sixth century or earlier and was adopted by the Anglican Church in 1549. It is known by a number of different names: Roman Catholics, who used to call it the **Octave of the Birth of Our Lord** or the **Circumcision of Jesus**, now mark the day as the **Solemnity of Mary, the Mother of God**. Episcopalians call it the **Feast of the Holy Name of Our Lord Jesus Christ**—a reference to the fact that Jesus was officially given his name on this day. Lutherans

refer to it as the **Feast of the Circumcision and the Name of Jesus**. And Eastern Orthodox churches call it the **Feast of the Circumcision of Our Lord**. Old Calendar Orthodox churches observe it 13 days later in accordance with the Julian, or Old Style, calendar.

CONTACTS:
Orthodox Church in America
6850 N. Hempstead Tpke.
Syosset, NY 11791
516-922-0550; fax: 516-922-0954
oca.org

♦ 0651 ♦ Circus Festival of Tomorrow, International (Festival Mondial du Cirque de Demain)
Last weekend in January

The International Circus Festival of Tomorrow is dedicated to celebrating and promoting the talent of young contemporary circus artists below the age of 25. It is conducted every year in Paris at the *Cirque Phénix* in Pelouse de Reuilly, the venue for the festival since 2007. It was founded by Isabelle and Dominique Mauclair in 1977 and was officially recognized in 1979. From 1,000 applications, only about 25 acts are shortlisted for the big show. Those chosen are categorized into two different productions: one called *Cirque de Demain* for ages 16 to 25, and another called *Cirque de l'Avenir* for ages 12 to 16. Some of the acts that comprise the festival include trapeze, tightrope, Korean plank, juggling, acrobatic, and balancing acts. Many experts attend the spectacle, including professional artists, promoters, producers, agents, and successful candidates from previous years. The International Circus Festival of Tomorrow gives budding young artists the opportunity to showcase their talent and often acts as a stepping-stone in their careers. Gold, silver, and bronze medals are presented in all performance categories.

CONTACTS:
International Circus Festival of Tomorrow
Cirque Phenix
Pelouse de Reuilly
Paris, 75012 France
33-1-4055-5056
www.cirquededemain.com

♦ 0652 ♦ Círio de Nazaré
Second Sunday in October

The Brazilian festival known as the Círio de Nazaré is a great "Candle Procession," which attracts pilgrims from all over the country. The Círio de Nazaré has been celebrated since the late 18th century. It traditionally takes place on the second Sunday in October and winds through the city of Belém in the state of Pará on its way to the Nazaré Basilica. There the statue of Our Lady of Nazaré is venerated for 15 days during the festival. The statue is carried on a wooden framework pulled by thousands of people as payment for prayers that have been answered by the saint. The origins of the festival lie in a miracle that is said to have occurred in the early

1700s, when a wooden image of the saint disappeared from someone's home and then reappeared a couple of days later in the same place. To people in Pará, this festival is on a par with CHRISTMAS, with much feasting and exchanging of gifts.

CONTACTS:
Brazilian Tourist Board
SCN Quadra 02 block G Ed
Brasilia, DF 70712-907 Brazil
55-61-2023-8888
www.embratur.gov.br

♦ 0653 ♦ **Citizenship Day**
September 17

Citizenship Day is an outgrowth of two earlier patriotic celebrations. As the anniversary of the signing of the Constitution of the United States in 1787, September 17 was first observed in Philadelphia shortly after the outbreak of the Civil War as **Constitution Day**. Then in 1940 Congress set aside the third Sunday in May as **"I Am an American" Day**, which honored those who had become U.S. citizens during the preceding year. The two holidays were combined in 1952 and called Citizenship Day.

A number of states and cities hold special exercises on September 17 to focus attention on the rights and obligations of citizenship. Schools make a special effort to acquaint their students with the history and importance of the Constitution. Naturalization ceremonies, re-creations of the signing of the Constitution, and parades are other popular ways of celebrating Citizenship Day. Several states observe the entire week in which this day occurs as Constitution Week.

CONTACTS:
National Constitution Center
Independence Mall
525 Arch St.
Philadelphia, PA 19106
215-409-6600
www.constitutioncenter.org

♦ 0654 ♦ **Clean Monday (Kathara Deftera)**
*February-March, Monday of the seventh week
before Orthodox Easter*

Clean Monday, or **Kathara Deftera,** marks the first day of the Eastern Orthodox Lent in Greece. A public holiday in Greece and Cyprus, Clean Monday is a day of purification during Lent, a major liturgical season for many Christian denominations across the world. The day is marked by penitence, abstinence from meat, and renunciation of sin. Greeks often term the Clean Monday celebrations as *koulouma*, which means "abundance and end." Observances of the event vary slightly across the country, with some common practices like the tradition of kite flying being widely observed. While the origin of flying a kite on this day is not exactly clear, many believe it to be symbol for casting off sin and cleansing the soul in preparation for Lent. Special foods mark the day, including shellfish, *lagana* (bread), salad, and *halva* (a tradition-

al sweet). Children make dolls of "Lady Lent" with paper, clay, or dough. To show the importance of fasting, the doll lacks a mouth. In addition, the doll has seven feet to represent the number of Sundays before Easter—children break off a foot on each Sunday of Lent. The Vlachs, a Romanian ethnic minority, perform the Vlach Wedding, a ritual parody of an ancient matchmaking custom with a male impersonating the bride amidst music, dance, and wine drinking.

CONTACTS:
Greek National Tourism Organisation
305 E. 47th St.
New York, NY 10017
212-421-5777; fax: 212-826-6940
www.visitgreece.gr/en

♦ 0655 ♦ **Clearwater County Fair and Lumberjack Days**
Third weekend in September

This international lumberjack event attracts loggers from throughout the world to little Orofino, Idaho (population 3,000). Goldminers came to Orofino to establish the state's first settlements in the 1860s, and more settlers came at the turn of the century to stake out timber claims. Lumbering is now a major part of Orofino's economy. Lumberjack Days began in the early 1940s as a local contest and kept growing.

The events begin on Thursday, a children's parade is held on Friday, and the lumberjack events come on the weekend. The logging competitions include log birling, ax throwing, chopping, chain-saw events, a speed pole climb (130 feet), jack-and-jill sawing, and a skidding, or weight-pulling, contest. The cash prizes total more than $30,000 and attendance is about 6,000.

CONTACTS:
Orofino Chamber of Commerce
P.O. Box 2346
217 1st St.
Orofino, ID 83544
208-476-4335
www.orofino.com

♦ 0656 ♦ **Clipping the Church Day**
First Sunday in July

The old English custom of "clipping the church" entails embracing the church by joining hands around it and performing a simple dance step, advancing and retreating three times. In Guiseley, Yorkshire, the custom traditionally was observed on St. Oswald's Day, August 5, but now takes place in July, during the Festival of Guiseley. There is a special service followed by a procession outside the church where all sing "St. Oswald's Ballad."

In other areas of England, it is observed on whatever day is appropriate to the church calendar. Sometimes a "puppy-dog pie"—a round cake with almond paste on top and a small china dog inside—is baked on the day of the church-clipping ceremony.

Some observers believe that this custom dates back to the ancient pagan festival known as the LUPERCALIA, which included a sacred dance around the altar and the sacrifice of goats and young dogs—hence the puppy-dog pie. At one time it was customary for children to run through the streets after the clipping ceremony crying, "Highgates!".

CONTACTS:
St. Oswald's Parish Church
St Oswald's Institute,
Church St.
Durham DH1 3DQ United Kingdom
44-191-383-0830
www.oswalds.org.uk

♦ 0657 ♦ **Closing the Gates Ceremony**
December 18

The celebration that takes place on this day in Londonderry, Northern Ireland, commemorates the siege of 1688, when James II, at the head of a 20,000-man army, stormed the Protestant city's walls. Londonderry's governor, Colonel Lundy, wanted to surrender and was eventually let down over the walls and permitted to join the king's forces. The governor's scheme to deliver the city to the British was foiled by 13 boy apprentices who managed to shut the Ferryquay Gate just as the British were about to enter the city. The siege lasted for 105 days, during which thousands of Londonderry citizens died of starvation or disease. A ship named the *Mountjoy* finally broke the blockade that had been set up on the River Foyle and brought food to the city's starving inhabitants.

The celebrations held annually on December 18 are set up by the Association of the Apprentice Boys of Derry. The festivities include an historical pageant, the climax of which is the burning of Colonel Lundy's effigy.

♦ 0658 ♦ **Clown Festival, International**
August

Begun in 1995, the International Clown Festival has been held annually at the Bakken amusement park near Copenhagen, Denmark. The festival was founded by the Danish clown Benny Schumann, the grandson of famed European clown Charlie Rivel. The event attracts performing talent from Italy, Belgium, Denmark, Spain, and Russia. While giving the public the chance to see a range of clown performances from around the world, the festival also allows the performers the opportunity to meet and learn from each other as well.

The festival has highlighted both those clowns who perform in the time-honored manner familiar to the general public and those who experiment with different costumes, characters, and approaches. Among the latter are Lars Lottrup, who climbs inside of a large balloon (optional) and disappears; Galina and Yuri Emeliyanovs, the duo known as Pilula, who perform on the high wire with a giant baby carriage; and the Jashgawronsky Brothers, who make music using common garden tools. Two awards are given out (optional) each year: the World Artist and Clown Award and the Golden Nose.

CONTACTS:
International Clown Festival
 Denmark
45-4017-8727
www.clownfestival.dk

♦ 0659 ♦ **CMJ Music Marathon**
October

The CMJ Music Marathon is a five-day annual music event held each October in New York City. Over 120,000 people attend the festival, which focuses on the discovery of new bands and artists in the world of college radio. Named after the *College Music Journal*, the CMJ Music Marathon began in 1981 in a single venue in New York City with just two bands. Today more than 1,400 performers play in over 80 nightclubs and theaters across the city. Along with conferences featuring industry insiders and speakers, the Marathon features College Day, an event for college radio professionals to connect through panels, seminars, performances, and awards.

CONTACTS:
CMJ
115 E. 23Rd St.
3rd Fl.
New York, NY 10113
917-591-4661
www.cmj.com

♦ 0660 ♦ **Coachella Valley Music and Arts Festival**
April

The Coachella Valley Music and Arts Festival is an annual two-weekend event held in Indio, California, each April. This concert features live bands from genres such as rock, indie, hip-hop, and electronica. Art installations and avant-garde sculptures complement the edgy dimension of the festival.

 The event can be traced to 1991 when Pearl Jam organized a concert in Coachella Valley to boycott venues supported by Ticketmaster, establishing the site as a viable festival location. In 1999 Paul Tollet and Goldenvoice founded the festival, and they established it as an annual event in 2001.

One of the largest and most profitable music festivals in the United States, Coachella attracts an audience of 600,000 and grosses $78 million a year.

CONTACTS:
Coachella Valley Music and Arts Festival
81-800 Ave. 51
Indio, CA 92201
888-512-7469
www.coachella.com

♦ 0661 ♦ **Coca-Cola 600**
May, Memorial Day weekend

The Coca-Cola 600 is the longest race of the four big races of the NASCAR (National Association for Stock Car Auto Racing) Sprint Cup circuit (formerly the Winston Cup). The race is held at Lowe's Motor Speedway in Charlotte, N.C. The track, which opened in 1960, installed special lights in 1992 to be the first super speedway ever to have nighttime racing. The track is a mile-and-a-half long, and the 600-mile race covers 400 laps. Lowe's Motor Speedway is also the home track for NASCAR, and many racing teams are based near the speedway.

The Coca-Cola 600 has become a MEMORIAL DAY tradition. In the week preceding the 600, the Charlotte 600 Festival offers a variety of downtown events, including a parade.

During the 55th Coca-Cola 600 in 2014, Jimmie Johnson won the race for the fourth time, second only to Darrell Waltrip who at five wins holds the record for most victories for this event.

See also DAYTONA 500; WINSTON 500; and SOUTHERN500.

CONTACTS:
600 Festival Association
6427 Saddle Creek Ct.
Harrisburg, NC 28075
704-455-5555; fax: 704-455-1900
www.600festival.com

♦ 0662 ♦ Cock Festival
February 2

Popular throughout Castilla and northern Spain, the **Fiesta del Gallo**, or Cock Festival, usually takes place on CANDLEMAS, and it symbolizes the renewal of life or of the harvest. It involves two groups of young people, 12 men and 12 women, who together comprise a kingdom, or *reinado*, with a king and queen who officiate at this and other festivals throughout the year. Young ladies, clothed in white garments and led by the queen, exit the church immediately after the mass and proceed to the town square carrying a live cock. There they meet the mayor of the village whose permission they must ask to kill the cock.

Just how the killing takes place varies from town to town. Sometimes the cock is tied by the legs to a pole, and the queen attacks it with a wooden sword. Sometimes it's buried in the ground with just its head showing. Any young man who wishes to try may be blindfolded, turned around several times, and allowed to attack the cock if he can find it. In some villages of northern Spain, blindfolded men on horseback strike at the cock with wooden swords as it swings from a rope that has been stretched across the street. After the cock is killed, there is a feast.

CONTACTS:
Institute of Tourism of Spain
TURESPAÃ'A C / Capitan Haya 41
Madrid, Madrid CP 28020 Spain
34-91-343-3500
www.spain.info/en_US

♦ 0663 ♦ Collop Monday
Between February 2 and March 8; Monday before Shrove Tuesday

In England, the day before SHROVE TUESDAY was called Collop Monday, a "collop" being a slice of meat or bacon. It was traditionally a day for getting rid of all the meat in the house in preparation for LENT.

♦ 0664 ♦ Colombia Battle of Boyacá Day
August 7

Colombia, known as New Granada in the early part of the 19th century, was then ruled by Spain. Simón Bolívar, the leader of the independence movement in South America, began a military campaign to liberate Colombia in 1817. He achieved a major victory at the Battle of Boyacá on August 7, 1819, when he surprised the Spanish forces crossing a bridge and routed them.

Colombians celebrate this national holiday with parades and festivals throughout the country. Ceremonies take place at the cemeteries where the fallen soldiers of the battle are buried.

CONTACTS:
Embassy of Colombia
2118 Leroy Pl. N.W.
Washington, D.C. 20008
202-387-8338; fax: 202-232-8643
www.colombiaemb.org

♦ 0665 ♦ Colombia Independence Day
July 20

On the day that they celebrate their independence from Spain, Colombians in the capital city of Bogotá often visit an historic place known as *La Casa del Florero* (The House of the Flowerpot). It was here, in the 19th century, that a Colombian storekeeper was asked to lend a large flowerpot to the Spaniards for an important occasion. Rather than let them use it, he broke the flowerpot. A riot ensued—the beginning of the revolt against Spain.

There are Independence Day parades throughout the country on July 20, some with uniformed cavalry performing acrobatic feats on horseback. Schoolchildren march in their uniforms, and dancers perform in the costumes of their region. In the afternoon, people watch athletic games and listen to singing groups perform their favorite folk songs. Because July is a winter month in Colombia, almost everyone wears *ruanas*, which are square shawls of brightly colored wool with a slit in the center for the head, and *alpargates*, or rope-soled canvas sandals.

When Colombia first became a republic in 1819, it included Venezuela, Ecuador, and Panama as well. Venezuela and Ecuador became separate states in 1830, and Panama withdrew in 1903.

CONTACTS:
Colombian Embassy
2118 Leroy Pl. N.W.

Washington, D.C. 20008
202-387-8338; fax: 202-232-8643
www.colombiaemb.org

◆ 0666 ◆ Columbus Day
Second Monday in October

When the Italian explorer Christopher Columbus (1451-1506) persuaded King Ferdinand and Queen Isabella of Spain to provide financial backing for his plan to find a new route to the Orient by sailing west, he was confident that only about 2,400 miles of ocean separated the two continents—a gross underestimation, as it turned out. And when he first landed in the Bahamas on October 12, 1492, he believed that he'd reached the East Indies. Despite these errors in judgment, Columbus is credited with opening the New World to European colonization, and the anniversary of his landing on the Bahamian island of San Salvador is commemorated not only in the United States but in Italy and most of the Spanish-speaking nations of the world.

Also known as **Landing Day**, **Discoverers' Day** (in Hawaii), Discovery Day, **Hispanity Day** in Spain, and in many Latin American countries as **Día de la Raza** or **Day of the Race**, the second Monday in October is celebrated in this country with parades, patriotic ceremonies, and pageants reenacting the historic landing. A mammoth parade up Fifth Avenue in New York City is a Columbus Day tradition.

In 1991, the spirit of political correctness affected Berkeley, California, as Columbus Day was cancelled in favor of Indigenous Peoples Day. Likewise, the Student Senate at the University of Cincinnati declared that myths about Columbus may not be studied or discussed—the University is "a Columbus-myth-free-campus.".

CONTACTS:
Library of Congress
101 Independence Ave. S.E.
Washington, D.C. 20540
202-707-5000; fax: 202-707-2076
www.loc.gov

◆ 0667 ◆ Columbus International Film and Video Festival
November

Promoting the use of films and videos in all forms of education and communication, the Columbus International Film and Video Festival is a six-day celebration held in Columbus, Ohio. Thousands of films, directors, and producers have been honored at this prestigious event. Started in 1952, the gathering is the oldest film festival in the United States. At times, the festival has been included as a qualifying event for the Academy Awards. Promulgating a strong belief that filmmaking and media are important tools not only in education, but also in furthering economic development, organizers staunchly support a rising creative class in Ohio and seek to nurture modes of artistic expression. Film entries are accepted in such categories as documentary, new media, narrative, and experimental film; awards are also bestowed in diverse areas such as the arts, animation, religion and spirituality, and others. Top honorees are presented with a Chris Award, a reference to the festival's namesake, Christopher Columbus. Dr. Edgar Dale, professor of educational media, and his colleagues at Ohio State University founded The Columbus Film Council in 1950, which was the precursor to the current version of the festival. Dale and his colleagues promoted the 16mm film medium and vigorously advocated the use of film as an educational tool. In 1953 their efforts culminated in the Columbus Film Festival, which widely used the 16mm format. Since 1980 the festival has been known as the Columbus International Film and Video Festival.

CONTACTS:
Columbus Film Council
614-444-7460
www.columbusfilmcouncil.org

◆ 0668 ◆ Common Ridings Day
Various dates in June and July

Many Scottish border towns hold a ceremony known as Common Ridings or **Riding the Marches** in June or July. The marches are border districts between England and Scotland and England and Wales. The custom dates back to the Middle Ages, when it was often necessary to reconfirm boundaries destroyed by fire in order to retain royal charters. Originally this was done only as the need arose, but eventually it became a yearly event.

The two main observations of Common Ridings occur in Selkirk and Haywick in June. In Selkirk, the event is combined with a commemoration of the 1513 Battle of Flodden, in which King James IV of Scotland and 10,000 others were killed. The Royal Burgh Standard Bearer leads a cavalcade of 200 riders around the borders of the town common.

CONTACTS:
Hawick Common Riding Committee
11 O'Connell St.
Hawick TD9 9HT United Kingdom
44-1450-378853
www.hawickcommonriding.com

◆ 0669 ◆ Commonwealth Day
Second Monday in March

From 1903 until 1957, this holiday in honor of the British Empire was known as **Empire Day** and was celebrated on May 24, Queen Victoria's birthday. Between 1958 and 1966, it was called **British Commonwealth Day**. Then it was switched to Queen Elizabeth II's official birthday in June, and the name was shortened to Commonwealth Day. It is observed annually on the second Monday in March.

In Canada it is still celebrated on May 24 (or the Monday before) and referred to as **Victoria Day**.

CONTACTS:
Commonwealth Secretariat
Marlborough House
Pall Mall
London SW1Y 5HX United Kingdom
44-20-7747-6500; fax: 44-20-7930-0827
www.thecommonwealth.org

◆ 0670 ◆ Comoros Independence Day
July 6

Comoros proclaimed its declaration of independence from France on this day in 1975, after more than 100 years under French rule. It is commemorated with a national holiday.

CONTACTS:
Honorary Consulate General of Comoros
2923 N. Milwaukee Ave.
Ste. 106
Chicago, IL 60618
312-493-2357; fax: 315-693-2357
comorosconsulatechicago.org

◆ 0671 ◆ Compitalia
Early January

The Compitalia were festivals celebrated in ancient Rome in early January (between the 3rd and the 5th, according to some accounts) in honor of the *lares*, or deities of the household farm and family. *Compita* were places where roads or farm paths crossed each other and were considered sacred. Small tower-like shrines were often built there, and people would hold sacrifices at the shrines at the end of the agricultural year. The shrines were left open in four directions so that the lares had access to them. Sometimes farmers would also hang a broken plough there to indicate that a job was done.

The institution of the Compitalia is attributed to either Tarquin the Proud (also known as Tarquinius Superbus because of his proud and insolent nature) or Servius Tullius. There is some indication that the original sacrifices were human, but that Brutus, the first consul of Rome, eventually substituted dolls and the heads of poppies for human figures. Slaves enjoyed a brief period of freedom during the Compitalia, and the spirit of the ancient festival survived in PLOUGH MONDAY, an occasion for servants to celebrate the completion of their ploughing.

◆ 0672 ◆ Conch Republic Independence Celebration
Week including April 23

In 1982 the United States Border Patrol set up a roadblock on U.S. Highway 1, just north of the Florida Keys. The new checkpoint created massive traffic jams, threatened the region's tourist industry, and angered residents of the Keys, who resented having to prove their American citizenship each time they attempted to drive to the Florida mainland.

On April 23, 1982, after trying in vain to get the courts to stop the blockade, the residents of the Florida Keys, under the leadership of Key West Mayor Dennis Wardlow, seceded from the United States of America. Wardlow announced that the Florida Keys would henceforth become an independent nation known as the Conch Republic. The besieged Republic maintained the secession for one minute, after which time Wardlow surrendered to the United States Navy and called for $1 billion in foreign aid and war relief to restore the damage done to the Keys by the federal government. Though the Republic didn't last, the stunt succeeded in pressuring the U.S. government to lift the roadblocks. Indeed, the motto of the tiny nation later became "we seceded where others failed."

Each year lighthearted residents of the Keys celebrate the short-lived independence of the Conch Republic, which they affirm still exists as a "state of mind." The festival takes place for an entire week surrounding April 23. It features conch-blowing contests, real drag races—in which drag queens race each other down the street—a reenactment of the secession, mock naval battles, bed races, food and crafts booths, a pancake-eating contest, numerous public parties held in bars and clubs, and more.

CONTACTS:
Conch Republic Office of the Secretary General
613 Simonton St.
Key West, FL 33040 Conch Republic
305-296-0213; fax: 305-296-8803
www.conchrepublic.com

◆ 0673 ◆ Concordia Day
November 11

A public holiday on the island of St. Maarten in the West Indies, Concordia Day commemorates the 1648 agreement to divide the island between the Dutch and the French. To this day, St. Maarten is the smallest territory shared by two sovereign states, with only a stone monument and two hand-lettered signs marking the boundary.

Concordia Day celebrates the long-standing peaceful coexistence of the two countries by holding parades and a joint ceremony with French and Dutch officials at the obelisk border monument. November 11 is also the anniversary of the island's discovery in 1493 by Christopher COLUMBUS, who named it after ST. MARTIN, on whose feast day it was discovered.

CONTACTS:
Concordia Language Villages
901 8th St. S.
Moorhead, MN 56562
800-222-4750
www.concordialanguagevillages.org

◆ 0674 ◆ Confederados Reunion
April

The "Confederados" are the descendants of a small band of Southerners who fled the United States at the end of the Civil

War to establish a new life in Brazil. Led by Colonel William Hutchinson Norris, an Alabama state senator who arrived in December 1865 and purchased a large farm about 80 miles northwest of São Paulo, the newcomers found the area's reddish soil reminiscent of Mississippi clay and the climate perfect for growing cotton and watermelons. As the word spread, thousands of Southerners followed—an estimated 2,900 a year landed in Rio de Janeiro between 1867 and 1871, and many more arrived at other Brazilian ports. They settled in a number of places, but the most successful colony was the one started by Norris. Americana, as it is known today, is a center for the textile industry in Brazil.

Many of the Americans missed their homeland and eventually returned there; the number of Confederados living in and around Americana leveled off at about 500 by the turn of the century. They hold four gatherings a year, the largest and most important of which—known as the **Festa Confederada**—takes place in April. In celebration of their heritage, they eat hot dogs and candied apples, drink cold beer, dance in hoop skirts and Civil War uniforms, and display the flag of the Confederate States of America. The April reunion takes place in a small local cemetery between Americana and Santa Barbara, where more than 400 of their ancestors are buried.

CONTACTS:
American City Hall
Av. Brasil, 85
 13465-901 Brazil
55-19-3475-9000
www.americana.sp.gov.br

♦ 0675 ♦ Confederate Memorial Day
Varies from state to state

Observed in memory of the Confederate soldiers who died in the Civil War, Confederate Memorial Day is widely observed in the southern United States. It grew out of a number of smaller, more localized responses to the bloodshed of the War between the States. In Vicksburg, Mississippi, for example, a group of women got together in 1865 to decorate the graves of more than 18,000 men who had been killed during the siege of Vicksburg. A similar event took place the following year in Columbus, Mississippi, where the women laid magnolia blossoms on the graves of the enemy soldiers as well. Today, the last Monday in April is a legal holiday in Mississippi.

The dates on which Confederate Memorial Day is observed vary from state to state and are often linked to some local historical event. In Texas it is called **Confederate Heroes Day**, and is observed on January 19, Robert E. Lee's birthday. Alabama (April 23), Florida (April 23), Georgia (Monday nearest April 26), and South Carolina (May 10) also observe Confederate Memorial Day as a legal holiday. In Tennessee (June 3), the day is a special observance.

♦ 0676 ♦ Confucius's Birthday (Teacher's Day)
September 28

A time to commemorate the birth of the teacher Confucius, perhaps the most influential man in China's history. In Qufu,

Shandong Province, China, the birthplace of Confucius, there is a two-week-long **Confucian Culture Festival**. In Hong Kong, observances are held by the Confucian Society at the Confucius Temple at Causeway Bay near this date.

Confucius, the Latinized version of the name K'ung-fu-tzu, was born in 551 B.C.E. during the Warring States Period and developed a system of ethics and politics that stressed five virtues: charity, justice, propriety, wisdom, and loyalty. His teachings were recorded by his followers in the *Analects* and formed the code of ethics called Confucianism that is still the cornerstone of Chinese thought. It taught filial obedience, respect, and selflessness; the Confucian "golden rule" is "Do not do unto others what you would not want others to do unto you." Confucius died at the age of 73 in 479 B.C.E.

During the Cultural Revolution, Confucianism lost favor, and in the late 1960s Red Guards defaced many of the buildings in Qufu. They have since been restored, and the festival held there from late September into October attracts scholars from China and abroad. The festival opens with a ceremony accompanied by ancient music and dance and includes exhibitions and lectures on the life and teachings of Confucius and on Chinese customs.

Commemorations in Taiwan take the form of dawn services at the Confucian temples. The Confucius Temple in Tainan was built in 1665 by Gen. Chen Yunghua of the Ming Dynasty and is the oldest Confucian temple in Taiwan.

CONTACTS:
Taiwan Government Information Office
4201 Wisconsin Ave. N.W.
Washington, D.C. 20016 United States
202-895-1850; fax: 202-362-6144
www.taiwanembassy.org

♦ 0677 ♦ Congo Independence Day Celebration
August 13-15

The **Three Glorious Days**, or **Trois Glorieuses**, constitute a national holiday in the Republic of Congo, commemorating the independence gained from France on August 15, 1960.

CONTACTS:
Republic of Congo Embassy
1720 16th St. N.W.
Washington, D.C. 20009
202-726-5500; fax: 202-726-1860
www.ambacongo-us.org

♦ 0678 ♦ Congo National Days
March 18; June 5

The Republic of Congo has two historical holidays in addition to its independence day: the assassination of President Marien Ngouabi on March 18, 1977, and the beginning of the civil war on June 5, 1997, which restored President Denis Sassou-Nguesso to power.

CONTACTS:
Republic of Congo Embassy
1720 16th St. N.W.
Washington, D.C. 20009
202-726-5500; fax: 202-726-1860
www.ambacongo-us.org

◆ 0679 ◆ Connecticut Early Music Festival
Two weeks in June

The term "early music" refers to music from the medieval, renaissance, baroque, and classical periods, up to and including Beethoven and Schubert, performed on period instruments.

Since 1983, when harpsichordist Igor Kipnis and flutist John Solum co-founded the Connecticut Early Music Festival, the residents of southeastern Connecticut have been able to hear the music of such composers as Henry Purcell (c.1659-1695), Wolfgang MOZART (1756-1791), Luigi Boccherini (1743-1805), Georg Telemann (1681-1767), Johann Sebastian BACH (1685-1750), François Couperin (1668-1733), Antonio Salieri (17501825 , Christoph Gluck (1714-1787), Arcangelo Corelli (16531713 , Antonio Vivaldi (1678-1741), Claudio Monteverdi (1567-1643), Georg Frideric Handel (1685-1759), Joseph Haydn (1732-1809), Franz Schubert (1797-1828; *see also* SCHUBERTIADE), and Ludwig van Beethoven (1770-1827) performed on such unusual instruments as the cornet, slide trumpet, sackbut, viola da gamba, and the clavichord. The concerts are held in small rooms or churches so that the subtleties of the instruments can be heard—particularly the Noank Baptist Church in Noank and the Harkness Chapel at Connecticut College in New London.

CONTACTS:
Connecticut Early Music Festival
c/o Connecticut College Campus
270 Mohegan Ave.
P.O. Box 5216
New London, CT 06320
860-439-2787; fax: 860-439-2695
www.ctearlymusic.org

◆ 0680 ◆ Constitution Week
Week beginning September 17

Since 2004, the National Constitution Center in Philadelphia, Pa., has hosted Constitution Week, beginning on September 17th, Constitution Day. The event celebrates September 17, 1787, the day the U.S. Constitution was signed. On August 2, 1956, the Congress set aside Constitution Week and asked that the president establish it each year by proclamation. Some presidents, including Ronald Reagan, were faithful in doing so, but the event has lapsed over the years.

Constitution Week begins with a public reading of the Constitution by a rotating group of 100 readers, including politicians, firefighters, nurses, and many others. During Constitution Week, the center provides classrooms across the country with suggested reading lists, class projects, constitution-related games and activities, and other materials to raise the awareness of the nation's children about the U.S. Constitu-

tion. Beginning in 2006, the week also includes the two-day Peter Jennings Institute for Journalists and the Constitution, which brings journalists together to discuss a range of constitutional issues. In addition, a two-day Constitutional Convention composed of adult and youth delegations from all 50 states discuss and debate constitutional issues. The convention releases a "Report Card on the Constitution" in which the health of constitutional practices is evaluated. The convention is videotaped and made available to schools.

The National Constitution Center was established by the U.S. Government in 1988 to promote a greater understanding of the nation's constitution and its relevance in the daily lives of citizens today. The center has over 100 interactive exhibits and displays of film, documents, text, artifacts, and sculpture. It also houses the Annenberg Center for Education and Outreach, which coordinates national educational efforts about the constitution.

◆ 0681 ◆ Constitution Week (Mesa, Arizona)
Week of September 17

Mesa, Ariz., has consistently celebrated the Congressionally established Constitution Week for over 30 years.

Held at the Mesa Amphitheater, the celebration includes a school band concert, the chance for children to meet the Founding Fathers and ask them questions, a Constitution Quiz (the two winning students receive airline tickets to Washington. D.C.), a Boy Scouts parade of flags, the high school color guard ROTC, and live music. Educational activities include information about the lives and activities of America's Founding Fathers, an in-depth examination of the U.S. Constitution and the Bill of Rights, and a class on how to qualify for the Boy Scouts' "Citizenship in the Nation" Merit Badge.

Mesa students at all grade levels learn about the U.S. Constitution during the week. Local politicians visit classrooms to give talks about the legislative process. Mesa students also participate in the National Anthem Project, meant to encourage citizens to sing the country's national anthem.

◆ 0682 ◆ Consualia
August 21 and December 15

The infamous rape of the Sabine women occurred at the first Consualia in ancient Rome. Consus, originally an agricultural deity but also regarded as the god of good counsel and the guardian of secrets, is said to have advised Romulus, the founder of Rome, to abduct the Sabine women as wives for his supporters.

The sanctuary dedicated to Consus in 272 B.C.E. was located on the Aventine Hill in Rome. Sacrifices were held there during his festival, and there were also horse and chariot races in the Circus Maximus, the large arena that lay between the Palatine and Aventine hills. There were actually two festivals in honor of Consus, one on August 21 and the other on December 15.

♦ 0683 ♦ **Coolidge (Calvin) Birthday Celebration**
July 4

The village of Plymouth Notch, Vermont, contains what many consider to be the best preserved and most authentic of all presidential homesites. It was here that Calvin Coolidge (1872-1933), 30th president of the United States, spent his boyhood and was sworn in as president by his father following the death of Warren Harding in 1923. The Coolidge Homestead was donated to the state of Vermont by John Coolidge, the President's son, in 1956. The state eventually acquired his birthplace, the general store and post office owned by his father, the homes of his mother and stepmother, his paternal grandparents' farmhouse, the family church, and the cemetery where the President and six generations of Coolidges are buried.

On the FOURTH OF JULY each year, the anniversary of Coolidge's birth, there is a noontime march from the green near the Plymouth Post Office to the Notch Cemetery, led by a Vermont National Guard colorguard with a bugler and a chaplain. The White House sends a wreath, which is laid at the President's tomb. Townspeople, tourists, and descendants of the Coolidge family listen to a brief graveside prayer service followed by the playing of taps. Next to the President's grave are those of his father, his wife, and his son, Calvin Coolidge, Jr., who died at the age of 16 during his father's White House years.

CONTACTS:
Calvin Coolidge Presidential Foundation, Inc.
P.O. Box 97
Plymouth, VT 05056
802-672-3389; fax: 802-672-3289
coolidgefoundation.org

♦ 0684 ♦ **Cooperatives, International Day of**
First Saturday in July

In 1992 the UNITED NATIONS established International Day of Cooperatives on the first Saturday in July. They chose this date to honor the founding of the International CooperativeAlliance one hundred years earlier. Today the organization represents 760 million people who belong to various cooperatives in 100 countries. In 1994 the United Nations affirmed their commitment to International Day of Cooperatives in recognition of the crucial role that cooperatives play in economic and social development.

CONTACTS:
International Co-operative Alliance
Ave. Milcamps 105
Brussels 1211 Belgium
32-2-743-10-30
ica.coop

♦ 0685 ♦ **Coopers' Dance**
January-February every seven years (2019, 2026, 2033…)

The famous Coopers' Dance, a 500-year-old custom, is performed in Munich, Germany, every seven years throughout the CARNIVAL season. The coopers, who make the barrels in which beer is stored, are highly respected in this city known for its breweries. The most recent Cooper's Dance took place in 2012.

According to tradition, the first Coopers' Dance of the Carnival season is performed on EPIPHANY in front of the MinisterPresident's office building, where thousands of spectators gather in the streets to watch. The dance is performed by 25 colorfully dressed coopers, who swing hoops of fir branches and keep time with the music by beating on barrels with their tools. Individuals, clubs, and other organizations may order a Coopers' Dance to be performed, but so many of these orders come in during Carnival that they cannot all be filled.

CONTACTS:
Munich Tourism Office
Fraunhofer Straße 6
Munich 80469 Germany
49-89-230018; fax: 49-89-230018
www.muenchen.de/int/en

♦ 0686 ♦ **Coptic New Year (Feast of El-Nayrouz)**
September 11

Members of the Coptic Orthodox Church, the native Christian church in Egypt, celebrate the New Year on September 11 because it is the day on which the Dog Star, Sirius, rises in the Egyptian sky, announcing the flooding of the Nile and the new planting season.

To commemorate the martyrs of the church, red vestments and altar clothes are used on this day. A food of special significance on this day is the red date: red recalls the martyrs' blood, the light-colored flesh of the date symbolizes their purity, and the stony pit symbolizes their steadfast faith. The Coptic New Year is also celebrated by Canadians of Egyptian descent and by Egyptian communities elsewhere.

CONTACTS:
Saint Mark Coptic Orthodox Church
11911 Braddock Rd.
Fairfax, VA 22030
703-591-4444
www.stmarkdc.org

♦ 0687 ♦ **Corn Palace Festival**
Last week in August

The world's only Corn Palace was built in Mitchell, South Dakota, in 1892. It was home to the Corn Belt Exposition, designed to encourage farmers to settle in the area by displaying its corn and wheat crops on the building's exterior. A second and larger Corn Palace was built in 1905 to accommodate the growing crowds, and in 1937 a third Corn Palace was completed, this time with the addition of Moorish-looking minarets, turrets, and kiosks. The outside of the Palace is covered entirely with decorations consisting of dock, wild oats, bromegrass, blue grass, rye straw, and wheat tied in bunches. Corn of different colors, sawed in half lengthwise and nailed to the outside walls, is also used to complete the design, which changes every year. The decorating process usually begins in mid-summer and is completed in time for the festival.

Entertainment at the festival has reflected changing public tastes over the years. Stage revues in the 1920s gave way to the "big bands" of the '30s and '40s. Standup comedians and television entertainers in the '50s and '60s have yielded to country and western stars today.

CONTACTS:
Mitchell Corn Palace Festival
604 N. Main St.
Mitchell, SD 57301
605-995-8430 or 800-289-7469
www.cornpalacefestival.com

♦ 0688 ♦ **Cornouaille Festival**
One full week in late July

The Celtic heritage of the Breton people comes alive every year in Quimper, a town in the district of Cornouaille. Located in Brittany, a region in northwestern France, Quimper has hosted this festival of traditional dance, music, storytelling, food, and games for more than 70 years. People dress in Breton costumes, which include elaborate lace bonnets for the women and shallow, brimmed hats for the men. Many of Brittany's inhabitants still speak the ancient Celtic language brought to the region by its first settlers some 2,500 years ago.

CONTACTS:
Cornouaille Festival
BP 71315
Quimper, Cedex 29103 France
33-2-9855-5353; fax: 33-2-9855-3560
www.festival-cornouaille.com

♦ 0689 ♦ **Corn-Planting Ceremony**
February-April

Corn is more than a staple for the Quiché Mayan Indians of Guatemala. In addition to eating it themselves and feeding it to their animals, they use the husks to thatch their huts. The Quiché Mayans also believe that their ancestors were made of ground corn paste.

The corn-planting season begins in February and lasts until April and requires considerable preparation. The fields must be burned and made ready for sowing, and the men who plant the corn perform numerous purification rituals. Churches hold special masses at the beginning of the planting season, and people bring seeds to church for blessings. On the eve of the first day of planting, people light candles, burn incense, and pray for the well-being of their crop. Afterwards, a huge feast and festivities, including fireworks, fortify the farmers before their work begins.

CONTACTS:
Quiche
2a. Avenida 11-01
Zone 4

Santa Cruz del Quiché Quiché
502-59661162
www.visitguatemala.com

♦ 0690 ♦ **Corpus Christi**
Between May 21 and June 24; Thursday after Trinity Sunday

Also known as the **Feast of the Most Holy Body of Christ**, the **Day of Wreaths**, and in France as the **Fête-Dieu**, Corpus Christi is a Roman Catholic festival that has been celebrated in honor of the Eucharist since 1246. In commemoration of the Last Supper on the day before Jesus' crucifixion, worshippers receive Communion and, in some countries, the consecrated bread (or Host) is paraded through the streets, held by the priests in a monstrance. In Spain and Provence, these processions can be quite elaborate, with saints and characters from the Bible following a path decorated with wreaths and strewn with flowers.

In Portugal the feast is known as **Día de Corpo de Deus** and has been one of the major religious observances—both on the mainland and in the Azores—since medieval times. In the city of Ponta Delgada, on San Miguel in the Azores, the people make a flower-petal carpet almost three-quarters of a mile in length. Over this carpet passes a colorful procession of high-ranking clergy and red-robed priests, who are followed by a group of first communicants (those who are to receive communion for the first time)—the young boys wearing dark suits and scarlet capes and the girls wearing white dresses and veils. The climax of the ceremony comes when the bishop raises the silver monstrance and exposes the Blessed Sacrament, the Body of Christ.

CONTACTS:
Turismo de Portugal
Rua Ivone Silva
Lote 6
Lisbon 1050-124 Portugal
351-211-140-200
www.visitportugal.com

♦ 0691 ♦ **Corpus Christi (England)**
Between May 21 and June 24; Thursday after Trinity Sunday

In England, before the Reformation, there was a famous procession in London on CORPUS CHRISTI Day. Beginning at Cheapside, a group of clergymen would move down the street chanting the paternoster, or Lord's Prayer. Over the years they perfected their timing so that just as they reached a certain corner, they sang, "Amen." To this day, there is a street corner in London known as the "Amen Corner," and the street leading to it is known as "Paternoster Row." The procession then turned the corner and proceeded down another street, still known as "Ave Maria Lane."

Although the feast of Corpus Christi is no longer observed in England, there was a time when the city guilds were involved in processions on this day and often performed what were known as Corpus Christi plays. These were pageants based on a scriptural subject or religious mystery, named after the *pagiante*, the large, partitioned cart in which they were presented.

♦ 0692 ♦ Corpus Christi (Germany) (Fronleichnamsfest)
Between May 21 and June 24; Thursday after Trinity Sunday

CORPUS CHRISTI Day in Germany is celebrated with colorful processions where the Sacrament and other holy symbols are carried through villages. Small-town streets are decorated with flowers and greenery, and children dressed in white and wearing wreaths of flowers accompany women in regional costume and local clergy. Sometimes people display pictures of Christ and spread carpets in front of their houses in honor of the day.

The most picturesque of these processions take place in Bavaria, where Corpus Christi is a legal holiday. Some are held on lakes rather than in the streets, with flower-decked boats carrying members of the procession and worshippers across crystal clear waters. The processions at Lake Staffelsee and Lake Chiemsee in Upper Bavaria are among the most dramatic.

CONTACTS:
German National Tourist Board
122 E. 42nd St.
Ste. 2000
New York, NY 10168
212-661-4796; fax: 212-661-7174
www.germany.travel

♦ 0693 ♦ Corpus Christi (Mexico)
Between May 21 and June 24; Thursday after Trinity Sunday

A Roman Catholic holiday commemorating the Eucharist, CORPUS CHRISTI is often observed in Mexico with symbolic battles between the Moors (Muslims) and the Christians, particularly in the states of Puebla and Veracruz. Although costumes vary from one area to the next, the Moors can usually be distinguished by their turbans and crescents, while the Christians often wear either elaborate plumed helmets with visors or derby hats with pink masks. The battle between them may last four or five hours, at the end of which the Moors are defeated and their leader is symbolically buried.

Another spectacle that takes place on Corpus Christi is the *Danza de los Voladores,* or Flying Pole Dance, performed by the Totonac Indians in Papantla in Veracruz State. Four dancers dressed as birds stand on a small platform atop a 70-foot tree that has been stripped of its branches. By carefully winding ropes around the tree and around themselves, they are able to hurl themselves into space and circle the tree 13 times before landing on the ground feet first. The four dancers multiplied by the 13 circles equals 52, the number of years in the ancient Aztec calendar cycle. Other versions of the Flying Pole Dance are performed in Pahuatlan and Cuetzalan, Puebla State.

Religious processions are common in Mexico on Corpus Christi, as is the *reposiar,* a small shrine or altar set up along the procession's path, covered with a lace-trimmed altar cloth and decorated with candles, flowers, and garlands. As the priest makes his rounds of the village, he stops at each of these shrines and gives his benediction. Local tradespeople set up a "mock" market along the path of the procession at which they display miniature objects of their trade. A builder, for example, makes doll houses, while restaurant owners serve small portions of food in miniature dishes and weavers make tiny blankets. The inch-long breads made by the bakers are used by the children as money to buy other miniature wares.

See also MOORS AND CHRISTIANS FIESTA.

CONTACTS:
Mexico Tourism Board
800-446-3942
www.visitmexico.com

♦ 0694 ♦ Corpus Christi (Switzerland) (Fronleichnamsfest)
Between May 21 and June 24; Thursday after Trinity Sunday

Many of the ceremonies observed on CORPUS CHRISTI in Switzerland have come down from the Middle Ages. Although customs may vary from one canton to the next, this festival is almost always observed with elaborate processions of clergy in their best robes, people in picturesque regional costumes, and soldiers in historic uniforms. The priest who leads the procession often walks on a carpet of flowers.

In Fribourg, people decorate their houses with Gobelins (tapestries) as the bishop of Fribourg carries the Holy Sacrament through the streets. In the cantons of Appenzell, the processions include women in native costume, Capuchin monks in their robes, and young girls with white dresses and wreaths of flowers in their hair.

It is customary to throw the church doors open on Corpus Christi and to decorate the altar and aisles with garlands and greens. Outdoor village altars with flowers and candles are often erected in secluded places.

CONTACTS:
Switzerland Tourism
608 Fifth Ave.
New York, NY 10020
800-794-7795; fax: 212-262-6116
www.myswitzerland.com

♦ 0695 ♦ Corpus Christi (Venezuela)
Between May 21 and June 24; Thursday after Trinity Sunday

The Christian feast of Corpus Christi was established in Spanish America by royal decree in the latter part of the 16th century. The celebration was supposed to resemble that held in Spain, with performances and parades of people dressed up as dragons, devils, and giants. Although the dragons and giants have disappeared over the years, the Corpus Christi devils remain an important part of the festival, particularly in San Francisco de Yare in Venezuela.

The devil dancers are welcomed with a blast of fireworks at nine o'clock on the morning of the feast. Spectators gather in the Plaza Bolívar, waiting as the drumbeats become increasingly louder. Then more than 1,000 devils appear, disguised in red garments and horrible-looking masks from which protrude both the horn and the snout of an animal, usually an ox or a pig. Each dancer holds one or more maracas in his right hand and a thin rod from which dangles a small sack in his left. Cowbells and rattles are tied to each dancer's waist, and the noise they make as they leap around and shake the maracas can be deafening.

The appearance of the Sacred Host in the doorway of the church is a sign that the procession around the plaza is about to begin. The devils dance about in a frenzy, while the man at the head of the procession acts as if he is beating them with the whip he carries. When the Sacred Host is taken back to its sanctuary, the devils start crying and attempt to enter the church, but they are shut out. They become increasingly frantic, until finally they fall on their knees and toss their horned masks on the ground as a gesture admitting their defeat.

After the dance is over, the devils go to their leader's house, where everyone dances the *bamba*, a traditional dance of Spanish origin.

CONTACTS:
Venezuelan Consulate General
7 E 51st St.
New York, NY 10022
212-826-1660; fax: 212-644-7471
www.embavenez-us.org/_newyork

♦ 0696 ♦ Cosby Ramp Festival
First Sunday in May

A festival started in 1951 to honor an obnoxious plant—the ramp. Held on Kineuvista Hill near Cosby, Tenn. (which is near Knoxville), the festival is touted as the first and largest of the ramp celebrations.

The ramp, related to the onion, is scientifically designated *Allium triccorcum lilaceae*. The name "ramp" supposedly was a shortening of *rampson*, the name of a similar plant. Devotees of the ramp say it has a mouth-watering, sweet flavor with a hint of garlic; they also concede that it has an astoundingly strong smell—like that of a wild onion multiplied a thousand times. It was once used in medicinal tonics, the theory being that the odor was enough to ward off germs and certainly germy people. It is rich in vitamin C and was the first spring vegetable for mountain people. Ramp harvest festivals of an informal sort are an old Appalachian custom handed down

from the Indians, who taught the European settlers how to cook ramps.

Several days before the festival, a group of ramp pluckers goes into the mountains to pick and clean the ramps. The festival lunch, of course, features fried ramp with eggs cooked with streaked meat, a kind of bacon. The festival music is bluegrass, gospel, and country, and the events include the crowning of the Maid of Ramps. About 5,000 to 6,000 attend.

The Polk County Ramp Festival, a similar but smaller affair, is held in late April in Benton, Tenn. It has bluegrass music all day, and awards are given to the oldest and youngest ramp eaters, the largest family, and the person who has come the farthest distance (winners of this last have even come from outside of the U.S.).

CONTACTS:
State of Tennessee's Department of Tourist Development
312 Rosa L. Parks Ave.
Nashville, TN 37243
615-741-2159
www.tnvacation.com

♦ 0697 ♦ Cosmonauts Day
April 12

On April 12, 1961, Russian cosmonaut Yuri Gagarin became the first man to travel in outer space. His one-hour-and-48-minute flight aboard the Vostok 1 caught the world's imagination and filled the Soviet people with pride. April 12th was declared Cosmonauts Day in Gagarin's honor.

Official ceremonies on this day begin in the Moscow suburb of Korolyov, well-known as the center of Russian rocket production, where officials and former cosmonauts lay flowers at a statue of Gagarin. Participants then walk to Red Square and Gagarin's grave at the Kremlin Wall Necropolis. They then proceed to Gagarin's statue in Cosmonauts Alley, a nearby walkway that leads to the Monument to the Conquerors of Space, and end at Gagarin's grave in the Novodevichy Cemetery.

The general public celebrates the day in a less formal manner. Some place flowers at statues of Gagarin in various cities, while others attend space-themed art and film exhibitions or fashion shows featuring designs based on cosmonaut spacesuits and helmets. Moscow's Institute of Medico-Biological Problems, which produces the food and beverages that cosmonauts use in space, has opened its doors for the general public to taste samples of space food, including vacuum-packed vodka. In 2011, the United Nations General Assembly proclaimed April 12 as International Day of Human Space Flight, coinciding with the 50th anniversary of Gagarin's 1961 flight.

CONTACTS:
Embassy of the Russian Federation
2650 Wisconsin Ave. N.W.
Washington, D.C. 20007
202-298-5700; fax: 202-298-5735
www.russianembassy.org

♦ 0698 ♦ **Costa Rica Annexation of Guanacaste Day (Guanacaste Day, Día de Guanacaste)**
July 25; Monday nearest July 25

Annexation of Guanacaste Day is a Costa Rican national holiday also known as **Guanacaste Day,** or **Día de Guanacaste** in Spanish. It marks the annexation of Guanacaste, the northern part of the Nicoya peninsula, from Nicaragua. The inhabitants of Guanacaste voted to join the state of Costa Rica on July 25, 1824.

The holiday is celebrated with street fiestas, folk dancing, horse parades, and cattle shows. There are organized activities in major parks. Bullfights are a traditional part of the celebration in the Nicoya peninsula, where the holiday festivities typically last for several days.

CONTACTS:
Embassy of Costa Rica
2114 S. St N.W.
Washington, D.C. 20008
202-499-2991; fax: 202-265-4795
www.costarica-embassy.org

♦ 0699 ♦ **Costa Rica Independence Day**
September 15

On this day in 1821, Costa Rica achieved independence, after having been ruled by Spain since the early 1500s. EL SALVADOR, GUATEMALA, HONDURAS, and NICARAGUA also declared independence from Spain on September 15, 1821.

On the evening of September 14, the president traditionally lights a torch representing liberty in the old capital city of Cartago and, on Independence Day, gives a speech to schoolchildren. There are more speeches and dancing in San José, the modern capital.

CONTACTS:
Costa Rican Embassy
2114 S. St N.W.
Washington, D.C. 20008
202-499-2991; fax: 202-265-4795
www.costarica-embassy.org

♦ 0700 ♦ **Costa Rica National Arts Festival**
March or April

One of Central America's most famous celebrations of creative expression, the National Arts Festival in Costa Rica draws international artists from over 30 countries and also serves as a promotional engine for its domestic art scene. The annual weeklong event features theater, dance, music, painting, and the fine arts.

The first festival took place in the national capital of San José in 1989. It was then called the International Theatre Festival and featured the theme "San José for Peace," an allusion to a harmonious political climate that for decades has fostered Costa Rica's rich cultural life. Beginning in 1992, the event became a permanent fixture on the country's calendar and thereafter was known as the National Arts Festival.

Shows and exhibitions take place throughout the month of March. Both the site of the festival and its program alternate each year: in even-numbered years, San José hosts the festival and invites international submissions; in odd-numbered years, a city outside the capital coordinates a plan of events that exclusively features Costa Rican artists.

CONTACTS:
Museum of Contemporary Art and Design
National Centre of Culture (CENAC)
Avenida 3, St. 15/17
San Jose Costa Rica
506-2257-7202; fax: 506-2257-8702
www.madc.cr

♦ 0701 ♦ **Côte d'Ivoire Independence Day**
August 7

Côte d'Ivoire (Ivory Coast) was granted independence from France on August 7, 1960. It had been a French colony since 1893.

Independence Day is a national holiday in Ivory Coast, celebrated with parades, dancing, and fireworks.

CONTACTS:
Cote d'Ivoire Embassy
2424 Massachusetts Ave. N.W.
Washington, D.C. 20008
202-797-0300
www.ambaciusa.org

♦ 0702 ♦ **Cotswold Olimpick Games**
Friday after the last Monday in May

The Cotswold Olimpick Games are an annual sporting event founded in 1612 by attorney Robert Dover under the patronage of King James of England. Dover's Hill, a natural amphitheater in Gloucestershire, was the venue and Dover presided over the games on horseback, majestically attired in the king's favors. Mounted canons fired to indicate the start of the events which included horse racing, sledge hammer throw, shin-kicking, wrestling, and fighting with swords and cudgels. Judges wielding sticks refereed the event and the winners were awarded silver trophies and money. The death of King James in 1625, and later on, the English Civil War, brought the Cotswold Olimpick Games to an end and it wasn't until their revival in the 1960s, when the Games became a regular event.

Today the Cotswold Olimpick Games are held each year on the evening of the Friday after the Spring Bank Holiday. A throwback to the early event, the Games continue to feature a variety of medieval sports, and competitors can register on the evening of the games. An actor on horseback dressed as Robert Dover throws open the event, and thousands of people converge at the venue as participants or spectators. Among the amateur events, the shin-kicking is the most popular, with the participants kicking each other's shins until one falls to the ground. Other events include a five-mile race, tug of war, hammer throw competition, and wheelbarrow relay. After dusk, a bonfire is lit and a torch light procession leads to the town's square where dancing and entertainment follow through the night.

CONTACTS:
Robert Dovers Games Society
 United Kingdom
www.olimpickgames.com

♦ 0703 ♦ Cotton Bowl Game
January 1

This great college football game was inaugurated in 1937 and pits the Southwest Conference champion against another nationally ranked team. The game is preceded by a music festival, an art contest, and a NEW YEAR'S EVE parade of marching bands.

CONTACTS:
Cotton Bowl Classic
AT&T Stadium
One AT&T Way
Arlington, TX 76011
817-892-4800; fax: 817-892-4810
www.goodyearcottonbowl.com

♦ 0704 ♦ Country Christmas Lighted Farm Implement Parade
First Saturday of December

Yakima Valley, Wash., has taken a conventional tradition—the Christmas parade—and added an interesting twist. The Country Christmas Lighted Farm Implement Parade, which takes place in the town of Sunnyside, showcases as many as 70 farm vehicles decorated with hundreds—sometimes thousands—of lights. Some people consider the parade the premier lighted parade of the U.S. northwest.

An annual event since 1989, the parade has drawn as many as 25,000 spectators and has been covered by the national media. Entries in the ceremony include tractors, combines, grape pickers, semi-trucks with flatbeds, and even horse-drawn floats.

The parade route starts in downtown Sunnyside and goes 1.5 miles through the downtown area across Yakima Valley Highway. Other activities that accompany the celebration are a breakfast with Santa and Christmas caroling.

Participants and spectators value the event because it preserves the tradition of a rural Christmas celebration and promotes the agricultural heritage of the Yakima Valley.

CONTACTS:
Sunnyside Chamber of Commerce
451 S. 6th St.
P.O. Box 360
Sunnyside, WA 98944

800-457-8089
www.sunnysidechamber.com

♦ 0705 ♦ Country Dionysia
December

Like the HALOA, the Country DIONYSIA was an ancient Greek celebration that was originally a fertility festival with a strong phallic emphasis. Both were observed during the latter part of the month of Poseideon (December), at the time of year when the days were at their shortest. The Country Dionysia, in fact, was not tied to a single date but was celebrated all over Attica on dates that were determined by local custom. Like CHRISTMAS festivities, it was something that everyone—even slaves—participated in. It was also a time for traditional games, particularly *askoliasmos* ("standing on one leg"), which involved trying to stand on top of a goatskin that had been blown up like a beachball and then covered in grease. There were other contests that also entailed standing on one leg and jumping the longest possible distance, or trying to touch the other players with the leg that was held off the ground.

In its earlier days, the Country Dionysia included a simple procession in which someone carried a jar of wine and a vine, someone dragged a he-goat, someone held a wicker basket of raisins, and someone held a phallus. But over time, it became an elaborate event with gold vessels, expensive costumes, and teams of horses.

CONTACTS:
Athens City Hall
63A Athinas St.
Kotzia Sq.
Athens 10552 Greece
30-210-3722001
www.cityofathens.gr/en

♦ 0706 ♦ Country Music Fan Fair, International
Mid-June

The International Country Music Fan Fair is a country feast of music held over a long weekend in downtown Nashville, Tenn., also known as "Music City, U.S.A." and the home of the Grand Ole Opry. Yearly attractions include stage shows and concerts, autograph-and-picture-taking sessions with big-name stars, some 300 booths and exhibits, fan club banquet dinners, and a celebrity auction. In 2011, the second sellout year in a row, fans were treated to performances by Taylor Swift and to the iconic Dolly Parton making her first Fan Fair appearance in more than three decades.

The Grand Ole Opry was founded by George Dewey Hay, who was called "the Solemn Ole Judge," and began weekly radio broadcasts from Nashville in 1925. The music developed from ballads of rural laborers in the 1920s through the string bands and cowboy music of the 1930s into honky-tonk and rockabilly music after World War II. In 1941, the Opry was staged live at the Ryman Auditorium in Nashville, and in 1974 it moved to Opryland U.S.A. This all led to the Fan Fair, which is billed as "The Closest Thing to Hillbilly Heaven.".

CONTACTS:
CMA Music Festival, Department
1 Music Cir S
Nashville, TN 37203
www.cmaworld.com

♦ 0707 ♦ Cow, Festival of the
January 25

The **Fiesta de la Vaca** takes place in the village of San Pablo de los Montes, in the Spanish province of Toledo, on St. Paul's Day. While the religious procession and mass that are a traditional part of the observance of the feast of San Pablo are going on, a group of young men form a counter-procession in the opposite direction. One of them plays the role of the cow, *La Vaca*, while another is dressed as Mother Sow, *Madre Cochina*. A third is dressed as a shepherd, and there are others ringing cow bells. Every time the group passes the image of the saint, they call out, "Here goes the cow!"

After the mass is over, the mayor and the town councilmen follow the priest to the town hall for the *correr de la Vaca*, or Race of the Cow. La Vaca and the rest of the young men in the group run from the church to the town hall, La Vaca menacing the spectators with his horns. After the Cow arrives at the town hall, the young men are greeted by the mayor, and a celebration with wine follows. Everyone goes home when the church bells ring at noon.

It is believed that the Festival of the Cow is the remnant of a pagan festival and that it survived in opposition to the Christian festivities. Today, however, the two exist quite peacefully side by side.

CONTACTS:
Tourism Office of Spain
60 E. 42nd St.
Ste. 5300 (53rd Fl.)
New York, NY 10165
212-265-8822; fax: 212-265-8864
www.spain.info/en_US

♦ 0708 ♦ Cow Fights
March or April and September or October

Each spring the winner of the cow battles, or **Kuhkämpfe**, held in the canton of Valais, Switzerland, is crowned Queen Cow of the village herds. A championship tournament is held in September or October in Martigny's amphitheater after the cows are herded down the mountains for the winter (*see* ALMABTRIEB). The cow fights began in the 1920s in Martigny, and today crowds fill the streets for the event. Refreshments of choice include wine and sausages, but no beef. The Queen Cow is adorned with a flower garland between her horns and a large bell hanging from a decorated collar. The calf of a Queen Cow can fetch up to 10 times the price of a regular calf.

The term "cow fights" is a bit misleading, however; as a rule, cows don't often exhibit much aggressive behavior, though their owners do. Much of the event consists of cows standing around, grazing, drooling, or even attempting to step out of the fighting arena. Sometimes, though, some cows can be provoked into pushing another cow, letting loose with some barbarous mooing, or—on momentous occasions—butting heads. A group of animal rights activists from Austria descended on the 1993 Fights, but dropped their protest when they witnessed what actually goes on.

See also ALPAUFZUG.

CONTACTS:
Valais/Wallis Promotion
Rue Pré Fleuri 6
PO Box 1469
Sion CH-1951 Switzerland
41-27-327-3590; fax: 41-27-327-3571
www.valais.ch

♦ 0709 ♦ Cow Parade
Varies

The Cow Parade is the world's largest public art exhibition. Since its inception in 1999, the Cow Parade has made appearances in cities all over the world, including Sydney, Auckland, Tokyo, Moscow, Istanbul, Warsaw, Copenhagen, Barcelona, Paris, Buenos Aires, Rio de Janeiro, and Mexico City, as well as over a dozen locations in the U.S.

In each location, the event revolves around fiberglass statues of cows. The undecorated figures are turned over to local artists who then adorn the cows in creative ways. Their designs are frequently based on themes and events with special significance to their locality. After the artists have completed the work on the cows, the statues are displayed in various public locations around the host city. The exhibition continues for several weeks, after which the statues are auctioned off, with proceeds benefiting charities designated by local organizers of the Cow Parade. Besides being a means to raise money for charitable causes, the Cow Parade is meant to bring art to the masses. The cow statues may not represent high art, but they are highly accessible and demonstrate that art can be playful as well as serious.

Although there are some variations, the cows used are usually those created by Pascal Knapp, a Swiss sculptor. The cow was chosen as a subject because of its status as an animal that is known and valued around the world. Knapp designed three cows to be used in the competitions: a standing cow, a grazing cow, and a cow lying at rest.

Since its first staging in 1999, the Cow Parade has grown dramatically. New artists are challenged and inspired by the work of previous entrants and over 10,000 artists worldwide have participated in Cow Parade. More than 5,000 cows have been decorated and have been viewed by more than 250 million people worldwide. Cow Parade events have been staged in 79 cities worldwide since 1999, raising over $30 million for worldwide charitable organizations through the auction of the cows, which takes place at the conclusion of each event.

Miniature replicas of the cows have also become valued collector 's items.

♦ 0710 ♦ **Cowboy Poetry Gathering, National**
Last week in January

The National Cowboy Poetry Gathering is a celebration of the old tradition of cowboy poetry—and of other cowboy art—in the buckaroo town of Elko, Nev.

Poetry by cowboys has a long history; cowboys traditionally recited poetry as they rode on cattle drives, but it was a private, little-known custom. A poem by Allen McCanless published in 1885 has these lines:

My ceiling the sky, my carpet the grass,
My music the lowing of herds as they pass
My books are the brooks, my sermons the stones,
My parson's a wolf on a pulpit of bones…

The gathering, which began in 1985 with about 50 working cowboys, has become a six-day affair that now includes folk music concerts, western dances, exhibits of cowboy gear, and workshops not only on writing but also on such topics as horse-hair braiding and photography. In 1992, the Hispanic *vaquero* (cowboy) was honored with performances and exhibits. Poetry remains the heart of the festival, and the poets—all working ranch people—include men, women, and children as young as six or eight. The poetry includes doggerel and limericks, but is mostly in ballad form with narratives like those of Rudyard Kipling's.

Hal Cannon, director of the Western Folklore Center in Salt Lake City, was the force behind the first gathering, and the Center still sponsors it. The goals of the gathering are to represent the voices of working ranch people through their poetry, music, and folklife; to promote a dialogue between urban and rural people of the American West; and to nurture understanding between pastoral peoples throughout the world. The Center provides a live webcast of events from the Elko Convention Center Auditorium.

At the 31st Gathering in 2015, more than 55 poets, musicians and musical groups from the U.S., Canada, Australia and Mexico performed on seven stages at four different venues. Several representatives of the Baja California Sur ranchero culture attended the Gathering, including vaqueros, storytellers, leatherworkers, traditional cooks, musicians and dancers. The audience has grown from 1,000 people in the first year to roughly 6,000 people in recent years. Tickets go on sale in October and are instant sell-outs. The gathering has spawned other cowboy-poetry festivals throughout the West (*see also* Dakota Cowboy Poetry Gathering).

CONTACTS:
Western Folklife Center
501 Railroad St.
Elko, NV 89801
775-738-7508; fax: 775-738-2900
www.westernfolklife.org

♦ 0711 ♦ **Craftsmen's Fair**
One week in early August

Although craft fairs can be found all over New England during the summer months, the Craftsmen's Fair at Mt. Sunapee Resort in Newbury, N.H., is considered to be the oldest continuously held craft fair, dating back to 1934. The fair features more than 200 craftspeople who sell their work and display their skills through demonstrations in such diverse areas as decoy carving, printmaking, weaving and spinning, basket making, embroidering, pipe making, and blacksmithing. Visitors to the **League of New Hampshire Craftsmen's Fair** can buy clothing, pottery, leaded glass, lampshades, character dolls, marionettes, jewelry, blown glass, leather goods, and just about any other craft they can imagine. There is also a juried craft exhibit, which is open only to members of the League.

CONTACTS:
League of New Hampshire Craftsmen
49 S. Main St.
Ste. 100
Concord, NH 03301
603-224-3375; fax: 603-225-8452
www.nhcrafts.org

♦ 0712 ♦ **Cranberry Day Festival**
Second Tuesday in October

Wampanoag Indians on Martha's Vineyard and Cape Cod, Massachusetts, celebrate Cranberry Day, their most significant annual holiday, on the second Tuesday in October. The tribe cultivates 200 acres of wild cranberries. In earlier times, this festival lasted several days as people harvested the cranberries and used them in festive dishes. These days, children get the day off from school to join the day's activities, which include picking cranberries, a lunch-time bonfire during which stories of previous Cranberry Days and other community legends are told, and a celebration in the evening with dancing, singing, and a huge potluck meal.

CONTACTS:
Wampanoag Tribe of Gay Head (Aquinnah)
20 Black Brook Rd.
Aquinnah, MA 02535
508-645-9265; fax: 508-645-3790
www.wampanoagtribe.net

♦ 0713 ♦ **Cranberry Harvest Festival**
October, Columbus Day weekend

Also known as the **Massachusetts Cranberry Festival**, this annual event has celebrated the harvesting of cranberries inSouth Carver, Massachusetts, since 1949. The idea for the festival came from Ellis D. Atwood, founder of the Edaville Railroad, and Robert Rich of Ocean Spray Cranberries. Rides through the cranberry bogs on the old Edaville steam train are still a popular festival attraction, as are the cranberry-baking and pie-eating contests, the crowning of the Cranberry Queen, and musical and other performances. The highlight of the festival, of course, is the harvesting of the cranberries themselves, which are a traditional part of the American and Canadian Thanksgiving feasts.

CONTACTS:
Cape Cod Cranberry Growers' Association
1 Carver Sq. Blvd.
P.O. Box 97
Carver, MA 02330
508-866-7878; fax: 508-866-4220
www.cranberries.org

♦ 0714 ♦ **Crandall (Prudence) Day**
September, Saturday of Labor Day weekend

The official celebration of Prudence Crandall Day in Canterbury, Connecticut, only dates back to 1987, but Crandall herself has been recognized for some time as a pioneer in the education of young African-American girls. Born in 1803 in Hopkinton, Rhode Island, and educated at the Friends' School in Providence, she established a private academy for girls in Canterbury in 1831. Although her school was widely recognized as one of the state's best, she lost many of her white patrons when she admitted a young African-American girl. Rather than bow to social pressure, she opened another school for "young ladies and little misses of colour"—an act for which she was socially ostracized.

Eventually the Connecticut legislature passed a Black Law (repealed in 1838), which prohibited setting up schools for nonresident African Americans in any Connecticut city or town without the local authorities' approval. Crandall ignored the new law and was arrested, tried, and convicted. Although the verdict was reversed by the court of appeals in July 1834, this only served to strengthen the opposition of the people of Canterbury. Crandall moved to Illinois later that year with her husband, a Baptist clergyman. In a belated attempt to make amends, Connecticut provided Crandall with an annuity. She died in Kansas in 1890. In 1995 the state legislature proclaimed her the official state heroine.

Prudence Crandall Day events include craft demonstrations from the 1830s, period children's games, and at least one activity directly relating to Crandall herself. One year, for example, an actor portraying Crandall gave an interpretation of her character. Most of the festival events are held at the Prudence Crandall Museum, located in the house where Crandall lived and taught.

CONTACTS:
Connecticut Office of Tourism
1 Constitution Plaza
2nd Fl.
Hartford, CT 06103
860-256-2800; fax: 860-270-8077
www.ctvisit.com

Prudence Crandall Museum
1 Constitution Plaza,
2nd Fl.
Hartford, CT 06103
860-256-2800; fax: 860-256-2811
www.ct.gov

♦ 0715 ♦ **Crane Watch**
March-April

There are actually two events in Nebraska that celebrate the world's largest concentration of sandhill cranes: the Crane Watch in Wood River and **Wings Over the Platte** in Grand Island. Both take place during a six-week period in March and April when 70 percent of the world's sandhill cranes— over a half million birds—crowd a 150-mile stretch of the Platte River between Grand Island and Sutherland. Arriving from west Texas, New Mexico, southern California, and central Mexico, the cranes rest and feed in the area before continuing their migration to Canada and Alaska.

The Crane Meadows Nature Center serves as an information center for the many visitors who come to see the cranes, and there are guided tours to the most advantageous viewing areas. Other events associated with the Crane Watch include wildlife displays, outdoor photo seminars, and nature workshops.

CONTACTS:
Kearney Visitors Bureau
1007 Second Ave.
P.O. Box 607
Kearney, NE 68847
308-237-3178 or 800-652-9435; fax: 308-236-9116
visitkearney.org

Grand Island Convention & Visitors Bureau
2424 S. Locust St.
Ste. C
Grand Island, NE 68801
308-382-4400 or 800-658-3178
www.visitgrandisland.com

♦ 0716 ♦ **Crawfish Festival (Breaux Bridge, Louisiana)**
First weekend in May

The Crawfish Festival is a time to celebrate and eat the small crustaceans (also called crayfish and crawdads) in Breaux Bridge, La., a small Cajun village. Since 1959, by act of the state legislature, the village has been officially called the "Crawfish Capital of the World."

Crawfish is related to the lobster, and local folk say the crawfish is really the Acadian lobster that followed them to the bayou lands of southern Louisiana. The Cajuns are descendants of the French Canadians whom the British drove from the colony of Acadia (now Nova Scotia) in the 18th century. They still speak their own patois, a combination of French forms with words borrowed from American Indian, African, Spanish, English, and other languages; they often still live in small, self-contained communities.

The festival is a three-day event, featuring crawfish races (on a special circular table, with betting allowed), a parade, Cajun music night and day, a crawfish cookoff, crawfish races, and a World Championship Crawfish-Eating Contest. In the latter, contestants start out with a dishpan of five pounds of crawfish and eat for two hours. The prize is a trophy and crawfish to take home. As many as 100,000 visitors come to this village of 7,600 for the festival.

CONTACTS:
Breaux Bridge Crawfish Festival Office

P.O. Box 25
Breaux Bridge, LA 70517
337-332-6655; fax: 337-332-5917
www.bbcrawfest.com

♦ 0717 ♦ Crazy Horse Ride and Veterans' Powwow
Early June

The Crazy Horse Ride and Veterans' Powwow are annual events held in early June by members of the Oglala Lakota Sioux tribe of the Pine Ridge Indian Reservation in Pine Ridge, S.D. A four-day day event, it also features a Saturday parade and daily specials and tributes to veterans and soldiers in active duty.

In 1998, Charles Brewer founded the Crazy Horse Ride, to take place just before the Veterans' Powwow, to honor the great Oglala Lakota Sioux warrior chief, Crazy Horse. Brewer also wanted to express gratitude for warrior culture and to pay tribute to all war veterans. The four-day horse ride begins in Fort Robinson, Nebraska, where Crazy Horse was killed in 1877, and it terminates in Pine Ridge at the grounds of the Veterans' Powwow. About 200 people typically take part in the ride, many of them children and young people from the Pine Ridge Indian reservation. The powwow and ride are open to all.

In 2013, the 16th annual ride focused on the theme of renewal after the devastating Great Plains wildfires of the 2012 summer. The procession led into the 25th Annual All Veterans' Oglala Lakota Gathering and Traditional Pow Wow where all armed-service veterans were honored with drumming, dancing, and singing.

CONTACTS:
One Spirit
P.O. Box 3209
Rapid City, SD 57709
570-460-6567
nativeprogress.org

♦ 0718 ♦ Cree Walking-Out Ceremony
Early spring

Among Cree Indians in Canada, it is customary for small children to be carried when they go outdoors until they areinitiated through the Walking-Out Ceremony. The springtime ceremony provides an occasion for the first time a child walks on his or her own (or with a little adult help) outside, signifying movement toward adulthood and greater responsibility. The toddlers' families and friends assemble in a special tent. The children are dressed in traditional costumes and, in some places, are given toy tools and utensils, representing the real tools and utensils they eventually will use. For the walking out, each child walks through the doorway and proceeds about 20 feet to a tree, circles the tree, then returns to the tent, where a huge fuss is made over each child's new accomplishment. After all the toddlers have completed the walk, everyone enjoys a feast.

CONTACTS:
Tourist Office, Ouje Bougoumou
203 Opemiska Meskino

Ouje-Bougoumou, QC G0W 3C0 Canada
888-745-3905; fax: 418-745-3544
www.ouje.ca

♦ 0719 ♦ Creek Green Corn Ceremony
Late summer

This ceremony is a religious harvest festival, not open to the public, held in late summer by the Muskogee-Creek Indians on the ceremonial grounds in Okmulgee, Oklahoma. Each tribal group conducts its own Green Corn Ceremony on one of 12 such Creek ceremonial grounds in the state.

The dances for the ceremony are performed not to the beat of drums, but to the rhythm of turtle and gourd rattles. Women are designated "shell-shakers," and they dance in groups of four with shells (or sometimes today with juice cans filled with pebbles) around their ankles. Children are included in ceremonies from the earliest age: women dancers with babies carry them into the ceremonial circle. One dance, known as the ribbon dance, honors women and is performed only by women and girls.

Other elements of the festival are stickball games and cleansing ceremonies, but the affair is essentially religious. To worship the Great Spirit, Creeks perform rituals relating to wind, fire, water, and earth.

Seminoles and Yuchis in Oklahoma also celebrate the Green Corn. In some ceremonies participants purge themselves with emetics and submit to ceremonial scratching on their legs and arms.

CONTACTS:
Muscogee (Creek) Nation Cultural Center
106 W. 6th St.
Okmulgee, OK 74447
918-549-2434
creekculturalcenter.com

♦ 0720 ♦ Cricket World Cup
Varies

Held every four years, the Cricket World Cup is the premier contest in the sport of cricket, a bat-and-ball sport that originated in England. A series of qualification tournaments are played before the World Cup finals, during which teams from 16 nations square off to determine the world champion. The host country or region for each finals tournament is determined by the sport's governing body, the International Cricket Council (ICC).

Although the sport is centuries old, the tournament itself has only existed since 1975. Around the time of the World Cup's inception, the cricket community was facing pressure to expand its membership, which had previously consisted of a handful of present and former countries of the British Commonwealth. The ICC responded by creating a different kind of membership status for new competitors. By 2007, the ICC had designated six slots in the World Cup Finals for these new teams—the other 10 were reserved for the teams of the old guard, known to cricket fans as Test-playing countries.

The West Indies won the first two tournaments (1975, 1979), India has won twice (1983, 2011), while Pakistan (1992) and Sri Lanka (1996) have each won once. It is Australia that has dominated the competition, however, garnering a World Cup trophy five times (1987, 1999-2007, 2015). The 2015 event was 11th Cricket World Cup, hosted jointly by Australia and New Zealand, with over 93,000 spectators attending the final game. England and Wales will host the next Cricket World Cup in 2019.

CONTACTS:
International Cricket Council (ICC)
St 69, Dubai Sports City
Sh Mohammed Bin Zayed Rd.
Dubai United Arab Emirates
971-4-382-8800; fax: 971-4-382-8600
www.icc-cricket.com

♦ 0721 ♦ **Croatia Anti-Fascist Resistance Day (Anti-Fascism Day)**
June 22

This holiday in Croatia, also called **Anti-Fascism Day**, dates back to the Second World War. After Nazi Germany invaded and conquered Yugoslavia in 1941, Croatia became a German puppet state under a government of Croatian fascists, called the Usta e. One of the resistance groups that sprang up to oppose the fascist government was called the Partisans. It was headed by a half-Croatian Communist leader called Tito (his real name was Josip Broz), who later appointed himself president for life of Yugoslavia.

Anti-Fascist Resistance Day is a national holiday in Croatia. Like most warm weather holidays in the country, it is celebrated with outdoor barbeques and fireworks.

CONTACTS:
Embassy of Croatia
2343 Massachusetts Ave. N.W.
Washington, D.C. 20008
202-588-5899; fax: 202-588-8936
us.mvep.hr/en

♦ 0722 ♦ **Croatia Independence Day**
October 8

This holiday is celebrated in Croatia to mark the day in 1991 that the Croatian Parliament voted to cut constitutional ties with Yugoslavia. The Croatians had declared their independence three months earlier, on June 25 (CROATIA STATEHOOD DAY), but a three-month moratorium was placed on implementation of the decision to give European negotiators a chance to broker an agreement. Those talks failed, and Croatia proceeded with its plan for independence.

Offices, businesses, and schools in Croatia are closed on Independence Day.

CONTACTS:
Embassy of Croatia

2343 Massachusetts Ave.N.W.
Washington, D.C. 20008
202-588-5899; fax: 202-588-8937
us.mvep.hr/en

♦ 0723 ♦ **Croatia Statehood Day**
June 25

Croatians mark this national holiday to commemorate the country's declaration of independence from Yugoslavia on June 25, 1991. This holiday is distinct from the country's Independence Day on October 8, when the implementation of the declaration went into effect.

Offices, businesses, and schools are closed in Croatia on Statehood Day. Wreaths are laid and candles lit at sites of fallen soldiers, including the graves of national heroes. Past celebrations have included a ceremonial line-up of military troops in the central square of the country's capital, Zagreb, and speeches by the country's leaders, including the president.

CONTACTS:
Croatian National Tourist Board,
P.O. Box 2651
New York, NY 10108
croatia.hr/en-GB/Homepage

♦ 0724 ♦ **Croatia Victory and Homeland Thanksgiving Day**
August 5

On this date in 1995 the Croatian Army defeated Serbian forces at the city of Knin in a decisive battle called Operation Storm. The victory enabled Croatia to regain control of the Serbian-declared breakaway Republic of Serbian Krajina.

The main celebration of this national holiday takes place in Knin, where thousands gather to watch a parade and to listen to speeches by the country's leaders. Church bells toll, and wreaths are laid in honor of those who died in the war. The national flag is hoisted on top of the medieval fortress overlooking southern Knin as part of the celebration.

CONTACTS:
Croatian National Tourist Board
P.O. Box 2651
Washington, D.C. 10108
croatia.hr/en-GB/Homepage

♦ 0725 ♦ **Crom Dubh Sunday**
Last Sunday in July

Crom Dubh was an ancient Celtic god believed to live near the town of Cloghane in County Kerry. During the festival of LUGHNASADH, August 1, people would go up to nearby Mount Brandon to pick berries, then join the festivities in Cloghane at the foot of the mountain. The mountain was named for

ST. BRENDAN, who is said to have converted Crom Dubh to Christianity. Thereafter the trek up Mount Brandon became a Christian pilgrimage site.

Today Cloghane hosts a revived Lughnasadh festival over the last weekend in July. In addition to the pilgrimage up Mount Brandon, there are traditional musical and dance performances, poetry readings, sheep-shearing events, boat races, and many other events.

See also REEK SUNDAY.

CONTACTS:
Dingle Tourist Information Office
Strand St.
Dingle Ireland
353-66-915-1188
www.dingle-peninsula.ie

♦ 0726 ♦ **Cromwell's Day**
September 3

As a British general, Puritan statesman, and Lord Protector of England from 1653-58, Oliver Cromwell is remembered today more for his actions as a general and a statesman than for his efforts within the narrow field of Puritanism. Each year the Cromwell Association in England holds a special service near Cromwell's statue outside the Houses of Parliament on September 3. The date is particularly appropriate. It was on this day in 1650 that Cromwell won the battle of Dunbar, inflicting 3,000 casualties and taking 10,000 prisoners at a cost of only 20 British lives. It was on the same day a year later that he won a decisive victory at the battle of Worcester against the Scots. And it was also the day on which he died.

CONTACTS:
Tourist Information Centre, Oliver Cromwell's House
29 St Mary's St.
Ely, Cambridgeshire CB7 4HF United Kingdom
44-1353-662-062; fax: 44-1353-668-518
visitely.eastcambs.gov.uk

♦ 0727 ♦ **Cronia (Kronia)**
Midsummer

In Greek mythology, Cronus (or Kronos) was lord of the universe before the Olympian gods took power. He was the son of Uranus, whom he eventually castrated with a sickle given to him by his mother, Gaea. Once he succeeded his father as ruler of the universe, his reign was so peaceful it was known as the Golden Age. Because he had been warned that one of his children would eventually overthrow him, Cronus swallowed his sons as they were born. But the youngest son, Zeus, managed to escape this fate and was the victor in a 10-year war against his father and the other Titan gods.

The only important festival held in honor of Cronus in classical times was the Cronia, held at Athens, Rhodes, and Thebes in midsummer and resembling the Roman SATURNALIA in terms of the unrestrained behavior that accompanied it. Some say that when Cronus was defeated by Zeus, he fled

to the west and established another Golden Age in Rome, where he was known as Saturn.

Cronus is usually depicted holding a curved object, perhaps the sickle he used to castrate Uranus. After the defeat of Cronus, the universe was divided among his three sons: Zeus ruled the sky, Hades the underworld, and Poseidon the sea.

♦ 0728 ♦ **Crop Over**
Last three weeks in July to first Monday in August

This harvest festival in Barbados was originally celebrated in the 1800s by slaves at the end of the sugar-cane harvest. A procession of carts and animals decorated with flowers would bring the last load of cane to the plantation owner, who would then provide a feast for the laborers. One of the carts carried an effigy known as Mr. Harding, made from sugar-cane refuse and dressed in a black coat, top hat, and mask. The effigy represented the cruel gangdrivers and symbolized the hard times that lay ahead for the laborers until the next crop.

Today, Crop Over is a civic celebration, which was revived in 1974. It takes place during the last three weeks of July and usually ends on the first Monday in August. There are historical displays, craft shows, fairs, cane-cutting contests, open-air concerts, calypso music and dancing, and "stick licking"—a self-defense sport similar to fencing. By the last weekend of the festival, the celebration moves to the island's capital, Bridgetown, which is transformed into a huge open-air bazaar where people can shop and listen to live bands.

Monday is the finale, known as the **Kadooment**—a public holiday—which includes the judging of costumed bands at the National Stadium and a grand calypso procession.

CONTACTS:
Barbados Tourism Authority
800 Second Ave.
New York, NY 10017
212-986-6516 or 800-221-9831; fax: 212-573-9850
www.barbados.org

♦ 0729 ♦ **Crosses, Festival of the (Fiesta de las Cruces)**
Late April

The Mayas of Quintana Roo, Mexico, celebrate the Fiesta of the Patron Crosses in late April. Although its origins are not fully understood, the festival's main feature is an unusual dance or pantomime known as *okoztah-pol*. Festival participants slaughter, cook, and consume a pig. The pig's head is reserved, decorated, and set upon the altar. The following day nine girls, bearing bowls of *pinole* (a powder of toasted corn) and spoons made from agave leaves, circle round a table in the atrium of the church. Two men come into the atrium, one carrying a rattle made from a gourd, the other carrying the decorated head of the pig, which he announces is for sale.

The men barter for the pig's head, while the girls circle nine times in one direction and nine times in the other, keeping track of their circuits by laying cigarettes on the table. The man with the pig's head impersonates the pig, which attempts to escape its captors. The pig impersonater is caught and given to the festival organizer for the price of a hundred cigarettes. Everyone else eats the pinole.

CONTACTS:
Mexico Tourism Board
152 Madison Ave.
Ste. 1800
Newyork, NY 10016
212-308-2110; fax: 212-308-9060
www.cptm.com.mx

♦ 0730 ♦ Crossing of the Delaware
December 25

What is now known as Washington Crossing State Park is the site of the historic event that took place on CHRISTMAS night in 1776, when General George WASHINGTON and the Continental Army crossed the Delaware River just before the Battle of Trenton. **Washington's Crossing of the Delaware** is reenacted on December 25 each year, beginning at Washington Crossing, Pennsylvania (formerly McKonkey's Ferry), and ending on the opposite bank at Washington Crossing, New Jersey.

St. John Terrell, an actor and producer, inaugurated this observance in 1953; he played the part of George Washington himself for a number of years. The costumed actors who cross the river in a specially made Durham boat, similar to those originally used by Washington and his men, try to reproduce the scene exactly as it is depicted in the well-known painting by Emanual Leutze: Vermont's Green Mountain Boys sit in the bow, Gloucester fishermen from Massachusetts man the oars, and General Washington stands with one foot on the gunwale. The actor who portrays Lieutenant James Monroe carries the 13-star flag seen in the painting—an anachronism, since the flag had not been adopted in 1776.

CONTACTS:
Washington Crossing State Park, Department of Environmental Protection
355 Washington Crossing-Pennington Rd.
Titusville, NJ 08560
609-737-0616
www.state.nj.us

♦ 0731 ♦ Cross-Quarter Days
February 1, May 1, August 1, November 1

The cross-quarter days are the four traditional Celtic festivals celebrated by Neopagans. Along with the QUARTER DAYS, they make up the "Wheel of the Year." These holidays "cross" the quarter days (the solstices and the equinoxes) by falling about halfway in between, thus dividing the year into four parts of approximately three months each. They are also known as IMBOLC (February 1), BELTANE (May 1), LAMMAS (August 1), and

SAMHAIN (November 1). These Gregorian calendar dates are less than exact, however; February 6, May 6, August 6, and November 6 actually fall closer to the halfway point between the equinoxes and solstices. (*See also* VERNAL EQUINOX, AUTUMNAL EQUINOX, SUMMER SOLSTICE, WINTER SOLSTICE).

♦ 0732 ♦ Crow Fair
Third weekend in August

The Crow Fair is one of the biggest powwows in the U.S., held since 1918 at Crow Agency, Mont., about 65 miles southeast of Billings. The fair, held Thursday through Sunday, is hosted by the Crow tribe but attracts thousands of other Indians (Peruvian Incas and Alaskan Eskimos were among those attending in 1991), who set up more than 1,000 tepees on the camp grounds.

Dancing at the fair includes not only traditional Plains Indian dances but also the Crow Hop, which is similar to a war dance and is unique to the Crows. It was originally a men's dance, but now women also take part, and all wear clothes of buckskin, feathers, quills, and bells to add a counterpoint to the drum beats.

There are rodeos with cash prizes, horse races, a relay of bareback riding, art exhibits, and demonstrations of such crafts as pipe carving and jewelry designing with turquoise and silver.

CONTACTS:
Crow Fair and Rodeo
P.O. Box 159
Crow Agency, MT 59022 United States
406-638-3808
visitmt.com

♦ 0733 ♦ Cruft's Dog Show
Three days in February

Charles Cruft was an English salesman who went to France to collect orders for "dog cakes" and so impressed the French dog breeders that they invited him to organize the canine section of the Paris Exhibition of 1878. Eight years later Cruft organized his first dog show in London, which won the patronage of Queen Victoria, an ardent dog lover. Now more than 10,000 dogs representing 150 breeds compete for the Best in Show title, and Cruft's Dog Show is considered to be the largest and most widely attended dog show in Britain.

CONTACTS:
Kennel Club Ltd.
1-5 Clarges St.
Piccadilly
London W1J 8AB United Kingdom
44-1296-318-540; fax: 44-20-7518-1058
www.the-kennel-club.org.uk

♦ 0734 ♦ Cuba Liberation Day
January 1; July 26

This national public holiday commemorates the overthrow of the military government of Fulgencio Batista (1901-1973) led by Fidel Castro (b. 1926) that succeeded on January 1, 1959. July 26 is National Day, another public holiday marking the beginning of the revolution Castro led in 1953.

CONTACTS:
Cuban Mission to the U.N.
315 Lexington Ave.
New York, NY 10016
212-689-7216; fax: 212-689-9073
www.cubadiplomatica.cu

♦ 0735 ♦ Cuban Anniversary of the Beginning of the Wars of Independence
October 10

This official holiday in Cuba marks the day in 1868 when Cuba declared its autonomy from Spain. The declaration, called the Grito de Yara, began the Ten Years' War (1868-1878), which was the first of three wars that Cuba fought against Spain for its freedom.

Schools and offices in Cuba are closed on this day.

CONTACTS:
Euromonitor International Ltd
60-61 Britton St
London EC1M 5UX United Kingdom
44-20-7251-8024; fax: 44-20-7608-3149
www.euromonitor.com

♦ 0736 ♦ Cuisinières, Fête des la
Early August

With the possible exception of the celebration at CARNIVAL, this is the most colorful event of the year in the French West Indian island of Guadeloupe. The **Women Cooks' Festival** begins with a morning service at the cathedral and a parade of women in Creole dress. The highlight of the festival is the five-hour feast prepared by the dozen or so members of the Association of Women Chefs. The Creole dishes they prepare include *blaffs* (a fish or shellfish dish in a sauce; the name comes from the sound made by the fish as it is plunged into boiling water), *boudins* (sausage), and *crabes farcis* (stuffed crabs). It has been said that "one fistful of the tiny hot peppers that are vital to Creole cooking is generally considered enough to blow up an average European city.".

CONTACTS:
France Tourism Development Agency
825 Third Ave.
New York, NY 10022
212-838-7800; fax: 212-838-7855
int.rendezvousenfrance.com

♦ 0737 ♦ Cultural Olympiad
Varies

As the name implies, the Cultural Olympiad is the cultural arm of the OLYMPIC GAMES. When it was first held in 1948, the

Olympic Arts Festival took place during the games; but since the Barcelona Games in 1992, it has started immediately after the preceding summer or winter Olympic Games end and continued right up until the next Olympics. At the 2010 Winter Olympics in Vancouver, the Cultural Olympiad presented the Cultural Olympiad Digital Edition. Conforming to the tag-line "Connect.Create.Collaborate." the festival featured national and international artists presenting digital art, music, and cinema. The 2012 London Olympics presented an extensive Cultural Olympiad with the London 2012 Festival. Cultural events occurred across the British Isles, including a World Shakespeare Festival produced by the Royal Shakespeare Company.

CONTACTS:
International Olympic Committee
Château de Vidy
Case postale 356
Lausanne 1001 Switzerland
41-21-621-6111; fax: 41-21-621-6216
www.olympic.org

♦ 0738 ♦ Cup Match
Thursday and Friday before the first Monday in August

The Cup Match is a two-day cricket game held in Bermuda between the teams of Somerset and St. George's. A carnival atmosphere surrounds the cricket grounds, where fans camp and enjoy music, picnics, swimming, and boating. The Bermudian game of chance Crown and Anchor is commonly played in stalls during the Cup Match. Fans not attending the match often camp in parks and beaches on the island, continuing the celebration well into the weekend.

Slavery was abolished in Bermuda on August 1, 1834. This day, commonly known as Emancipation Day, became a time of celebration as communities socialized and played sports, especially cricket. By the late 1800s, cricket matches were usually held on the island during Emancipation Day. In 1902, an official match was organized between the clubs of Somerset and St. George's, and the silver cup used for the event still remains the trophy today. The day was not officially recognized until 1947, when the Bermudan government finally declared two public holidays for the two days of the Cup Match. In 1999 the first holiday was renamed **Emancipation Day** in remembrance of the abolition of slavery. The second holiday, **Somers' Day**, commemorates the arrival of Admiral Sir George Somers to Bermuda.

CONTACTS:
Bermuda Tourism Authority
675 Third Ave.
20th Fl.
New York, NY 10017
212-818-9800; fax: 212-983-5289
www.gotobermuda.com

♦ 0739 ♦ Cure Salée
September-October

The Tuareg, a largely nomadic ethnic group found primarily in Algeria, Niger, Mali, and Libya, converge with their camels and cattle on a place known as Ingal just after the first rains of the season arrive. An oasis in the Sahara region of northern Niger, Ingal has palm groves and date plantations and is a favorite grazing ground. The **Salt Festival** takes its name from the salt contained in the new grass, which is essential to the animals' diet. Each Tuareg group participating in the Cure Salée follows a very specific transhumance or seasonal migration route, some traveling hundreds of miles.

In Tamacheq, the language of the Tuareg, the event is known as **Tanekert** or **Tenekert**. The return of the rains is also celebrated with dancing, singing, and camel races.

CONTACTS:
NOMAD Foundation
307 E. Ojai Ave.
Ste. 103
Ojai, CA 93023
805-646-1706
nomadfoundation.org

♦ 0740 ♦ **Curium Festival (Kourion Festival)**
July

The ancient city of Curium, or Kourion, on the southwest coast of Cyprus, about 12 miles west of Limassol, was buried by volcanic lava in 365. Extensive excavation in recent decades has uncovered a stadium, a basilica and sanctuary of Apollo, and a Roman amphitheater that dates from 50 to 175 C.E. Curium has been the setting for an annual drama festival since 1961. Also known as the **Ancient Greek Drama Festival**, performances are held in the restored amphitheater, which seats 2,400. Both international and Cypriot drama companies participate in the festival, which focuses on the classical Greek dramatists and Shakespeare. There are also moonlight concerts overlooking Episkopi Bay.

CONTACTS:
International Festival of Ancient Greek Drama
38 Regaena St.
Nicosia 1010 Cyprus
357-22-674920; fax: 357-22-680822
www.greekdramafest.com

♦ 0741 ♦ **Custer Buffalo Roundup and Arts Festival**
Weekend nearest last Monday in September or first Monday in October

In South Dakota, buffalo still roam at the Custer State Park in the Black Hills. And every fall, the Old West comes further alive as cowboys, cowgirls, and park staff round up the thundering herd of 1,500 bison and channel the animals into corrals. This annual event helps the park manage and maintain a healthy bison population. Calves are branded and vaccinated, and a number of the animals are sold at auction, which keeps the herd thinned and is an important source of revenue for the park. In addition to the roundup, artists from around the state display their work, and the Custer Chamber of Commerce hosts a chili cook-off.

CONTACTS:
Custer State Park
13329 US Hwy 16A
Custer, SD 57730
605-255-4515 or 605-255-4464
www.custerstatepark.info

♦ 0742 ♦ **Cynonfardd Eisteddfod**
Last Saturday in April

When the Welsh began to emigrate to the United States during the latter part of the 19th century and the early years of the 20th, many were drawn to the coal-mining areas of northeastern Pennsylvania. Among them was a minister, Dr. Thomas C. Edwards, who emigrated in 1870 and established a church society designed to teach English to Welsh children by having them read and memorize music, hymns, songs, poetry, and other literary selections in the tradition of the Welsh EISTEDDFOD. This group became known as the Cynonfardd Literary Society—the Cynon being a stream in South Wales where Edwards had lived as a child. Edwards patterned the society's activities after the Welsh National Eisteddfod, and by 1889 the Cynonfardd Eisteddfod was well established.

Believed to be the oldest continuous Eisteddfod outside of Wales and the only one of its kind in the United States today, the Cynonfardd Eisteddfod was originally held on March 17, ST. PATRICK'S DAY, probably because the coal mines were closed on that day so the Irish miners could celebrate.

Now it is held at the end of April, and the competition is limited to recitations and vocal and instrumental selections. Competitors range in age from under five years old to adults, and the prizes are generally modest—two dollars, for example, for the child under five years who sings the best "Twinkle, Twinkle Little Star," or $50 for the prize-winning senior citizen who sings a Welsh hymn. Literary recitations include selections from the Bible, Henry Wadsworth Longfellow, and other well-known American authors. All performers in both the poetry and music competitions must memorize their selections.

CONTACTS:
Dr. Edwards Memorial Congregational Church
668 Main St.
Edwardsville, PA 18704
570-287-4581
www.dredwardschurch.com

♦ 0743 ♦ **Cyprus Independence Day**
October 1

Cyprus gained independence from Great Britain on August 16, 1960. On that day, British governor Hugh Foot departed amid much ceremony, and Greek Cypriot freedom fighters landed on a plane from Athens with a heroes' welcome. The new Cypriot president, Archbishop Makarios III (1913-1977), gave a speech inspiring Cypriots to improve their new nation.

Independence Day is observed as a public holiday on October 1 each year.

CONTACTS:
Embassy of the Republic of Cyprus
2211 R St. N.W.
Washington, D.C. 20008
202-462-5772; fax: 202-483-6710
www.cyprusembassy.net

♦ 0744 ♦ Czech Festival, National
First full weekend in August

The town of Wilber, Nebraska, site of the annual Czech Festival, has been designated by the U.S. Congress as the "Czech Capital of America." Patterned after the well-known Pennsylvania Dutch Festival in Kutztown (*see* KUTZTOWN FESTIVAL), the purpose of the festival is to recognize contributions of Czech immigrants and to foster Czech culture.

Folk dance groups come from all over the state, and local residents wear Czech costumes and dance the *beseda*, or polka, in the streets. Foods prepared by the town's residents and served at the festival include a number of Czech specialties, such as roast duck, sauerkraut, dumplings, and *kolaches* (sweet buns). There is even a kolache-eating contest.

On the second day of the festival, awards are presented for special achievements in promoting both Nebraska and Czech culture.

CONTACTS:
Nebraska Czechs of Wilber
P.O. Box 652
Wilber, NE 68465 United States
402-821-2667
www.nebraskaczechsofwilber.com

♦ 0745 ♦ Czech Statehood Day (St. Wenceslas Day)
September 28

Czech Statehood Day marks the assassination of Duke Vaclav Wenceslas of Bohemia (western Czech Republic). During his seven-year reign in the 10th century, Wenceslas was known for spreading Christianity among his subjects and helping Prague become the center of trade in central Europe. Wenceslas was murdered by his brother Boleslav on September 28; historians disagree on the precise year, which is thought to be between 929 and 935. Wenceslas was canonized as a saint due to his martyr's death as well as several purported miracles that occurred in the wake of his murder. He is traditionally considered the patron saint of the Czech people. Legends and fictional accounts have sprung up over the centuries about "Good King Wenceslas."

Czech Statehood Day is a public holiday celebrated throughout the Czech Republic. Every year the Czech president awards St. Wenceslas medals to people who contributed to Czech statehood. This ceremony takes place at Prague Castle, where a memorial wreath is placed on the statue of St. Wenc-

eslas. In addition, a pilgrimage takes place at Stara Boleslav, the site of St. Wenceslas' murder.

CONTACTS:
Ministry of Foreign Affairs of the Czech Republic
Loretánské námestí 5
Praha 110 00 Czech Republic
www.czech.cz/en

♦ 0746 ♦ Czechoslovak Independence Day
October 28

The Republic of Czechoslovakia was founded on October 28, 1918, when the National Committee in Prague proclaimed independence from the Austrian Hapsburg emperors and took over the administration of an independent Czechoslovak state. They were supported in this move by President Woodrow Wilson, who sent a note to the Austro-Hungarian foreign minister urging that the various nationalities of the empire be allowed to determine their own political future.

Independence Day was widely celebrated in Czechoslovakia until the Communists seized power there in 1948 and turned it into a Soviet satellite. But it continued to be recognized in the United States with special banquets, addresses, religious services, cultural programs, and the laying of a wreath at the tomb of President Wilson at the Cathedral of St. Peter and St. Paul (also known as the National Cathedral, or Washington Cathedral) in Washington, D.C.

Communities with large Czech or Slovak populations such as New York City, Los Angeles, Wilber, Nebraska, and Newark, New Jersey, may also mark the occasion.

This day should not be confused with Czechoslovak Liberation Day, a national holiday observed on May 9 to commemorate the country's liberation by the Soviet army and U.S. forces at the end of World War II.

CONTACTS:
Embassy of the Czech Republic
3900 Spring of Freedom St. N.W.
Washington, D.C. 20008
202-274-9100; fax: 202-966-8540
www.mzv.cz/washington

D

♦ 0747 ♦ Dae, Feasts of
December-January, April-May, May-June; 1st, 8th, 15th, and 23rd of Dae, the 10th Zoroastrian Month

The Feasts of Dae occur during the month of Dae on the four days that are ruled by Dae, which is the name for the creator aspect of Ahura Mazda, the Wise Lord and primary deity of the Zoroastrian religion. Because there are four days in each month named after and dedicated to the Creator—the 1st, 8th, 15th, and 23rd—there are four name-day feasts in the month of Dae where the same *yazata*, or spiritual being, presides over both the day and the month.

It was on the first of Dae that the king of Persia used to descend from his throne, dressed entirely in white, and suspend the duties of his attendants and make himself available to anyone who wanted to speak to him. He would hold meetings with small landowners and farmers, sharing a meal and reminding them that the continued existence of their culture depended upon each one of them.

The Zoroastrian calendar has 12 months of 30 days each, plus five extra days at the end of the year. Because of discrepancies in the calendars used by widely separated Zoroastrian communities around the world, there are now three different calendars in use, and the Feasts of Dae can fall either in December-January, April-May, or May-June.

Followers of the Zoroastrian religion, which was founded by the prophet Zoroaster (also known as Zarathushtra, believed to have lived around 1200 B.C.E.), today live primarily in Iran and northwestern India, although smaller communities exist in Pakistan, Sri Lanka, Canada, the U.S., England, and Australia.

♦ 0748 ♦ Daedala
Spring

This is the name given to two festivals held in ancient Boeotia, which was a part of Greece, in honor of the reconciliation of Hera and Zeus. According to the myth, Hera and Zeus quarreled and Hera went away to Euboea and refused to return to his bed. To trick her into coming back and on the advice of Cithaeron, Zeus dressed up a carved oak-trunk to resemble a bride and let it be known that he planned to marry Plataea, the daughter of Asopus. Hera was so angry she tore the clothes from the statue, discovered the deception, and was so pleased that the two were reconciled.

The **Little Daedala**, held every six years, involved going to an ancient oak grove and cutting down trees for images. Every 59 or 60 years the **Great Daedala** was held, and all Boeotia joined in the celebration. All the images that had been collected over the years during the Little Daedala were carried to the top of Mt. Cithaeron, where they were burned on an altar along with sacrifices to Zeus and Hera.

♦ 0749 ♦ Dahlonega Gold Rush Days
October

Gold Rush Days are a celebratory reminder in Dahlonega, Ga., of the town's heyday as a gold-rush town. The nation's first major gold rush was here in 1828, and the area around Dahlonega boomed; a federal mint built in 1838 operated for 23 years and coined more than $6 million. Mining continued into the beginning of the 20th century, and today visitors can pan for gold at several locations. The name of the town is pronounced dah-LON-a-gah; it is derived from the Cherokee name *Talonega*, meaning "golden." The festival includes arts and crafts exhibits, country cooking, and beard-growing and hog-calling contests.

CONTACTS:
Dahlonega-Lumpkin County Chamber & Visitors Bureau
13 S. Park St.
Dahlonega, GA 30533
706-864-3711 or 800-231-5543
www.dahlonega.org

♦ 0750 ♦ Daimonji Okuribi (Great Bonfire Event)
August 16

In Japan, the belief that the souls of the dead return to earth during the OBON FESTIVAL gave rise to the custom of lighting great bonfires to guide the souls back to heaven after their yearly visit. This custom is known as Daimonji Okuribi, the Great Bonfire Event. In the city of Kyoto, an enormous flammable structure, built in the shape of the Chinese character *dai*, meaning "big," is set on fire on the hill in back of the Zenrinji Temple. The character is 530 feet tall and 510 feet wide, providing a spectacular display for city residents. The festival begins at 8:00 P.M., when the fires are lit. After this, more fires are lit on other mountains nearby. Hotels charge a fee to those who wish to watch the festival from their roofs, thereby insuring a view of all five okuribi. The banks of the Kamo-gawa River provide another popular viewing area.

According to legend, an apparition of a burning temple once appeared at the foot of the mountain, and this event inspired the yearly bonfires. Similar bonfires are held at Yokote and Hakone on the same night.

CONTACTS:
KYOTO Prefectural Government Tourism Division
Kamigyo Ward
Kyoto City 602-8570 Japan
81-75-432-3221
www.pref.kyoto.jp

◆ 0751 ◆ Daimyo Gyoretsu
Third weekend in August

The Daimyo Gyoretsu is the largest parade of the year in Yuzawa, Japan. It commemorates the annual journey of the *daimyo*, or feudal lord, to Edo (present-day Tokyo) during the Tokugawa period (1600-1868). In order to suppress the possibility of unrest, the Edo shogun, or supreme military ruler, would compel the daimyo from all over Japan to make periodic visits to the capital city. Because the daimyo had to be accompanied by a large entourage, these visits were hugely expensive, leaving them with little money left over for plotting a revolution.

The contemporary Daimyo Gyoretsu consists of a lord's parade and a *mikoshi* parade—mikoshi being the elaborately decorated portable shrines to which the gods were believed to descend during the festivals held in their honor. In addition to the 200 costumed figures who march in these two sections of the parade, there are also floats holding dioramas based on Japanese history and mythology. The tail end of the parade consists of a series of trucks decorated with lanterns that carry dancers, kids, and floats with papier-mâché statues. It is far less formal than what precedes it, and the participants usually wear shorts and brightly colored *happi* coats (traditional Japanese short jackets).

The parade starts at 8:00 in the morning and lasts about five hours, although there is a two-hour break at midday. The route varies slightly from year to year, depending on which of Yuzawa's neighborhoods is in charge of running the parade. Other Japanese cities hold similar Daimyo Gyoretsu festivals, including Hakone on November 3 and Sanjo on May 15-16.

CONTACTS:
Japan National Tourism Organization
1 Grand Central Pl.

60 E. 42nd St.
Ste. 448
New York, NY 10165
212-757-5640; fax: 212-307-6754
www.jnto.go.jp/eng

◆ 0752 ◆ Dakota Cowboy Poetry Gathering
May, Memorial Day weekend

The Dakota Cowboy Poetry Gathering was founded by Bill Lowman, a cowboy poet who had attended a similar event in Nevada in 1985 (*see* COWBOY POETRY GATHERING) and decided that the Badlands of North Dakota should host its own cowboy poetry festival. Two years later the first "Real Cowboy Review" was held in Medora, with 40 poets and musicians participating. The crowds drawn to the event have continued to grow, and the performers often travel long distances to share their poetry, songs, and stories inspired by life on the ranch.

The Medora gathering prides itself on featuring only "the Real Ones"—those cowboys who "have spent a lifetime looking down the top of a cow." It tries to discourage "novelty cowboys, movie cowboys, or rodeo cowboys" who don't really live the life portrayed in their poems. This burgeoning interest in cowboy poetry is largely the result of research done by folklorists who wanted to draw attention to the cowboys' passion for rhyme and tale-spinning and to keep the tradition alive.

CONTACTS:
Medora City Governance
City of Historic Medora
P.O. Box 418-A
Medora, ND 58645
701-623-4828
www.medorand.com

Library of Congress
101 Independence Ave. S.E.
Washington, D.C. 20540 United States
202-707-5000
www.loc.gov

◆ 0753 ◆ Dalai Lama, Birthday of the
July 6

This celebration is held on July 6 for the birthday of the current Dalai Lama, the spiritual and political head of Tibet. The name Dalai means "ocean" and was given to the ruling lama in the 16th century by the Mongol leader Altan Khan. The title suggests depth of wisdom.

The present Dalai Lama, Tenzin Gyatso (b. 1935), who was enthroned in 1940 at the age of five, is the latest in the line that began in the 14th century. Each Dalai Lama is believed to be the reincarnation of the preceding one, and when a Dalai Lama dies, Tibetan lamas search throughout the country for a child who is his reincarnation.

Tibet had been a sovereign country until 1949, when China invaded eastern Tibet and sporadic warfare followed. In 1959, a popular uprising exploded at Lhasa but was suppressed, and the Dalai Lama and most of his ministers and about 80,000 Tibetans escaped across the Himalayas. The Dalai Lama has lived since then in exile in Dharmsala, India. Today there are some 80,000 Tibetans in India, 30,000 in Nepal, and 3,000 in Bhutan.

The birthday is observed today by exiles in India with incense-burning ceremonies to appease the local spirits, family picnics, and traditional dances and singing. The incense burning is a rite pre-dating Buddhism.

See also UNIVERSAL PRAYER DAY.

CONTACTS:
Office of Tibet
1228, 17th St. N.W.
Washington, D.C. 20036
212-213-5010; fax: 703-349-7444
tibetoffice.org

♦ 0754 ♦ Dally in the Alley
Saturday in early September

Dally in the Alley is a one-day visual and performing arts fair that takes place on the Saturday after Labor Day in the North Cass neighborhood of Detroit, Mich. Located in an area with a reputation as a center of creativity and also as a somewhat seedy neighborhood, the Dally began as a community block party and art fair in 1977. The art show expanded into a performing arts festival and moved to its current location in 1982, when it became known as the "Dally in the Alley," the name of an English pub song.

The original festival site was a service alley that dates back to the era when homeowners in the area maintained horses and carriages. Over the years, however, the Dally has expanded beyond the alley proper, taking over neighboring streets with vendor stalls, art displays, and four stages presenting a variety of original music acts throughout the day and night, including rock, techno, hip-hop, folk, country, and jazz artists, among others.

The Dally is sponsored by and benefits the North Cass Community Union, a nonprofit neighborhood organization that supports community preservation issues. Each year more than 30,000 visitors attend the festival, which includes music, a curated art show, poetry and writing workshops, children's activities, food, and refreshments—particularly beer, a beverage closely associated with the founding of the event.

CONTACTS:
North Cass Community Union, Inc.
4632 Second Ave.
Detroit, MI 48201
www.dallyinthealley.com

♦ 0755 ♦ Damba
August

Observed in August by many people in the Northern and Upper Regions of Ghana, Damba may have been originally an Islamic festival, though its real origins are uncertain. There are two parts to the Damba festival: the Somba Damba, which marks MAWLID AL-NABI, the Prophet Muhammad's birthday, and the Naa Damba, which celebrates the naming of Muhammad. The celebration continues for 10 days, with drumming and crowds of dancers in front of the chief's house every night.

The Damba festival includes everyone in the community. Muslims hold evening prayers every night leading up to the Somba Damba, while others join in singing and dancing. But it is the Naa Damba, or chief's celebration, that is the main event. People recite from the Qur'an as they dance near a cow or bull that will be slaughtered for the following feast.

Afterward everyone congregates in front of the chief's house, dressed up in his or her finest garb. As drummers play, the chief and his entourage emerge from the house. Everyone gathers into two semicircles, leaving a large space in the middle for the dancers, the last of whom will be the chief himself.

A highlight of the festival occurs the next day, when horseowners decorate their animals and parade them around town, stopping at the homes of friends. Later in the day a final grand procession marks the official end of the Damba festival.

CONTACTS:
Ghana Permanent: Mission to U.N
19 E. 4th St.
New York, NY 10017
212-832-1300; fax: 212-751-8743
www.ghana.travel

Ghana Tourism Authority
P.O. Box GP 3106
Accra, D.C. 20008 Ghana
233-302-222153
www.ghana.travel

♦ 0756 ♦ Dance Camera West
June

Since 2002, Dance Camera West has been an annual dance media film festival in Los Angeles that brings together dance forms and choreographers from around the world.

The event is open to all styles of dance including ballet, hip-hop, modern dance, postmodern dance, world dance, tap dance, and dance theater. Contemporary, classic, and alternative dance films are all screened at the festival. Screenings are followed by discussion periods with experts in the field.

CONTACTS:
Dance Camera West
2934 1/2 Beverly Glen Cir.
Ste. 292
Los Angeles, CA 90077
310-248-4944
www.dancecamerawest.org

♦ 0757 ♦ Dance Festival Birmingham, International
April-May, every two years

The International Dance Festival Birmingham (IDFB) is a biennial dance celebration that takes place at theaters and public places in Birmingham and the West Midlands area of England. A collaborative effort by the group DanceXchange and the touring company Birmingham Hippodrome, the festival is a major platform for international choreographers and artists of all ages. One of the largest dance events in the world, IDFB was launched in 2008 and is supported by the Birmingham City Council, the Arts Council of England, and various private patrons. The festival boasts an eclectic lineup of international performers. Many works are specifically created for the outdoors, bringing alive the streets and public spaces of Birmingham with dance forms from around the world. Various venues throughout the festival host different activities, including art shows for children, social dance events, and retrospectives on 20th-century master choreographers.

CONTACTS:
c/o DanceXchange
Birmingham Hippodrome
Thorp St.
Birmingham, B5 4TB United Kingdom
44-121-689-3170
www.idfb.co.uk

♦ 0758 ♦ **Dance on Camera**
January-February

Dance on Camera has been held annually in New York City since 1971. Its aim is to promote ballet and contemporary dance personalities through dance film premieres and retrospective programs. The festival is presented and produced by the Dance Films Association, founded by Susan Braun in 1956, in cooperation with the Film Society of Lincoln Center. Dance on Camera also encourages choreographers to pursue filmmaking and educates filmmakers on the history of dance. In addition to film screenings, the festival features panel discussions and a competition for dance films made by high school students. Each year the Susan Braun Award is presented to emerging New York choreographers.

CONTACTS:
Dance Films Association
252 Java St.
Ste. 333
Greenpoint, NY 11222
347-505-8649
www.dancefilms.org

♦ 0759 ♦ **Dance Week Festival**
May-June

Held annually in Zagreb, Croatia, Dance Week Festival is the country's most important dance event. Focusing exclusively on promoting contemporary dance forms, the festival was founded in 1981 by Mirna Zagar and is organized by the Croatian Institute for Movement and Dance. The event provides a venue for the members of the Croatian Choreographic Platform to showcase their talents and is open to artists from all over the world. In addition to large-scale venues in Zagreb's city center, the festival occupies

small non-traditional spaces as well, including courtyards, galleries, and town squares. Dance Week Festival also includes workshops and film screenings.

CONTACTS:
Croatian Institute for Movement and Dance
Biankinijeva 5
Zagreb, 10000 Crotia
385-1-4833-083; fax: 385-1-4641-154
www.danceweekfestival.com

♦ 0760 ♦ **DanceAfrica**
Late May and early June

DanceAfrica is a festival of dance that takes place annually in New York City during the Memorial Day weekend in late May; it then restages on a somewhat smaller scale during the first weekend in June in Washington, D.C. Founded by choreographer Chuck Davis and headquartered at the Brooklyn Academy of Music, the festival began in 1977 as a means of counteracting the negative stereotypes of African dance presented in film and other media. Davis conceived of the festival as a way to provide a "cultural bridge" showing the range and beauty of traditional African dance and its influence on contemporary American dance forms.

Each DanceAfrica festival features an international cast of dancers and musicians and showcases such forms as African folk dance, Afro-Caribbean fusion, and African-American dance theatre. In addition, the weekend includes African music and film presentations, master classes, and an outdoor marketplace featuring African-themed arts, food, clothing, and crafts.

CONTACTS:
Dance Place
3225 8th St. N.E.
Washington, D.C. 20017
202-269-1600; fax: 202-249-7727
www.danceplace.org

Brooklyn Academy of Music (BAM)
Peter Jay Sharp Bldg.
30 Lafayette Ave.
Brooklyn, NY 11217
718-636-4100
www.bam.org

♦ 0761 ♦ **Dancing on the Edge**
July

Dancing on the Edge is an annual event that takes place in Vancouver, British Columbia, to celebrate and promote contemporary Canadian dance. During the festival, Canadian-based dancers perform alongside international artists and companies. Dancing on the Edge has been operating since 1988—supported by local governmental organizations, foundations, art councils, and businesses. The prime venues for the festival are the Finehall Arts Center and the Dance Center.

CONTACTS:
Firehall Arts Centre

280 E. Cordova St. (at Gore Ave.)
Vancouver, BC V6A 1L3 Canada
604-689-0691
www.dancingontheedge.org

♦ 0762 ♦ Dancing Procession
Between May 12 and June 15; Whit Tuesday

The **Sprangprocession** in Luxembourg has been held on Whit Tuesday, which falls 52 days after EASTER, since the eighth century. It honors St. Willibrord (St. Wilfred), the patron saint of Luxembourg, whose feast day is celebrated November 7. The dance that is performed by thousands of participants in the procession through the narrow streets of Echternach has remained basically unchanged. It traditionally involved taking three steps forward and two back to the accompaniment of local bands playing the same melody that was played more than 500 years ago. These days so many people participate, the backward steps are eliminated and instead people step to the left, then to the right. The procession ends up in the basilica, where the remains of St. Willibrord (658-739) are buried.

There are a number of legends that attempt to explain the origin of the Dancing Procession. According to one of them, St. Willibrord came to Luxembourg from northern England to convert the people to Christianity. He saved them from a plague by promising that if they subjected themselves to physical punishment, the plague would end. The people danced to the same tune that is played today, hopping up and down until they were completely exhausted and, as promised, the plague disappeared.

Another story is that a crusader returned from the Holy Land to discover that his dead wife's greedy relatives had taken over his property and branded him a murderer. As he was about to be hanged, he asked permission to play one last tune on his violin. The haunting melody mesmerized the onlookers, who started dancing and were unable to stop. The condemned man walked away from the scaffold, and the procession that is held each year is penance for his unjust condemnation.

A more prosaic explanation is that, in the late eighth century, people afflicted with tremors and various kinds of paralysis reported being healed at St. Willibrord's grave. From that time on, people have performed the dance near his grave for protection from illness. In 1999 University of Kiel neurologist Paul Krack, a native of Echternach, published an article examining the tradition's relationship to outbreaks of hysteric chorea (a disorder that causes involuntary movements) and other movement disorders.

CONTACTS:
Luxembourg City Tourist Office
30 pl. Guillaume II
Luxembourg, LU 1648 Europe
352-22-28-09; fax: 352-46-70-70
www.lcto.lu

♦ 0763 ♦ Dartmouth Winter Carnival
Weekend in February

The students of Dartmouth College in Hanover, New Hampshire, have been celebrating Winter Carnival since 1910, when they decided to hold their own mini-OLYMPICS to shake off the winter blues. Soon other colleges were invited to join in the athletic events, which included ski jumping and snowshoe races. By the 1920s, there were so many parties and balls associated with the weekend that it was called "The Mardi Gras of the North."

The event became even more popular after it was featured in the 1939 movie *Winter Carnival*. Students from other colleges, some as far away as Florida, came to Hanover to join in the fun, and eventually drunkenness and vandalism became a problem.

Carnival events nowadays are limited to Dartmouth students and their guests. Teams from a dozen or so northeastern colleges and universities compete in Nordic and Alpine skiing, ski jumping, hockey, basketball, gymnastics, and other sports. But the highlight for many is the snow sculpture competition on the Dartmouth green. Because snow has been so scarce in some recent winters, the sculptors sometimes have had to rely on snow trucked in from nearby ski areas, scraped off parking lots, and recycled from skating rinks.

CONTACTS:
Dartmouth College
Hanover, NH 03755
603-646-1110
dartmouth.edu

♦ 0764 ♦ Daruma Ichi (Daruma Doll Fair)
Various

Daruma are papier-mâché tumbling dolls that are sold at doll markets held at various times throughout the year. They are symbolic of sturdy character and hard-headedness as well as joy. Custom encourages people to buy dolls that have no eyes painted in. Then the doll owner makes a wish and gives the doll one eye. The other eye is painted in when the wish has been fulfilled.

During the Daruma Ichi held in Takasaki (January 6-7), Tokyo (March 3-4), and other Japanese cities, these dolls are sold in stalls erected on the grounds of shrines or temples. They are similar in shape to the famous Russian "nesting" dolls, and they are often made by farmers as a hobby in their off-hours and sold during the winter months.

CONTACTS:
Japan National Tourism Organization
1 Grand Central Pl.
60 E. 42nd St.
Ste. 448
New York, NY 10165
212-757-5640; fax: 212-307-6754
www.japantravelinfo.com

Tourism and Local Products - DivisionBureau of Tourism, Gunma Prefectural Government
1-1-1 Ote-machi
Maebashi-shi, Gunma 371-8570 Japan

81-27-226-3384; fax: 81-27-223-1197
www.visitgunma.jp/en

♦ 0765 ♦ Dasa Laksana Parvan (Time of the Ten Characteristics)
August-September; fifth to 13th day of the waxing half of Hindu month of Bhadrapada

Dasa Laksana Parvan is a Jain festival observed by the Digambara, or "sky-clad," sect, which is the dominant sect in southern India. Its members are called "sky-clad" because they believe that total nudity is required of monks; even images of the Jinas or spiritual teachers should not be clothed.

This festival usually falls during the latter part of the rainy season, and it may last 10 days instead of eight. Scripture readings focus on different portions of the holy text describing the 10 characteristics to which Jains aspire: forbearance, gentleness, uprightness, purity, truth, restraint, austerity, renunciation, lack of possession, and chastity. The Svetambara, or "white-clad," Jains—the dominant sect in northern India, which believes that monks and images of the Jinas should be clothed—observe a similar festival, known as PARYUSHANA, just before Dasa Laksana Paryan begins.

♦ 0766 ♦ Data Ganj Baksh Death Festival
Islamic month of Safar, days 18-19

This festival is an occasion for massive pilgrimages to the Mausoleum of Data Ganj Baksh in Lahore, Pakistan. Data Ganj Baksh, which means "He Who Gives Generously," was the name given to Syed Ali Abdul Hasan Bin Usman Hujwiri (also rendered Ali Hajweri or al-Hujwiri), a scholar and author who lived most of his life in Lahore and died in 1072. He wrote *Kashful Mahjub* (or *Kashf al-mahjub*), the oldest Persian treatise on Sufism. It is a text on the fundamentals of Sufism and it reviews Islamic mysticism, linking each famous master to a particular doctrine. Ali Hujwiri is one of the most popular saints in Pakistan, and every day hundreds of pilgrims pray at his shrine and ask for blessings and favors. On his *urs* (death festival), thousands throng to the shrine for celebratory activities and prayers.

♦ 0767 ♦ Dattatreya Jayanti
November-December; full moon day of Hindu month of Margasirsa

Dattatreya's birthday is celebrated all over India. One legend has him as the son of Anusuya, an exceptionally devoted and virtuous wife. The wives of Brahma, Vishnu, and Shiva decided to test her virtue by sending their husbands, disguised as beggars, to ask her to give them alms while in the nude. Anusuya avoided the trap by transforming them into babies and suckling them. When her husband, Atri, returned from his morning bath and discovered what had occurred, he turned them into one child with three heads and six hands. The wives begged for their husbands' return, and

when Anusuya restored them to their original forms, they blessed Anusuya, Atri, and their son Dattatreya.

On Dattatreya's birthday, Hindus rise early and bathe in sacred streams, fast, and spend the day in worship and prayer. They also meditate on sacred works that include the *Avadhuta Gita* and *Jivanmukta Gita*. Recently, Dattatreya is identified with the triad of Brahma, Vishnu, and Shiva, for it is believed that portions of these deities were incarnated in him. He is usually depicted with three heads and six hands.

♦ 0768 ♦ Davis Cup
November-December

The Davis Cup is the oldest international men's tennis competition, inaugurated in 1900 and credited with drawing world attention to the game. Tennis was then a young sport; the first U.S. national championship games were played in 1881. The competition was fathered by Dwight F. Davis, who was U.S. doubles champion with Harvard teammate Holcombe Ward in 1899-1901. Davis believed international competition would boost the game's popularity and had a 13-inch-high silver bowl crafted by a Boston silversmith; it was to be called the International Lawn Tennis Challenge Trophy but became known as the Davis Cup.

From the first, the championship was open to all nations. The first games, held at the Longwood Cricket Club in Chestnut Hill, Massachusetts, had only two contestants: a British Isles team and the American team (captained by Davis). The Americans won, 3-0. The Brits did better—but still lost—in 1902. In 1903, they won, and it was not until 1913 that the U.S. regained the cup.

There was growing interest in the cup. Four nations competed in 1919, and that number grew to 14 in 1922 and 24 in 1926. From the start, teams have consisted of two singles players and a doubles team. There are five matches—four singles and one doubles. Each match is awarded one point, and the first team to win three points wins the cup. In women's tennis, the Federation Cup, inaugurated in 1963 and played each year in the spring, is considered the equivalent of the Davis Cup.

The United States has dominated the Davis Cup winning the most victories with 32, but in the 1920s, spurred by William T. ("Big Bill") Tilden II, who was a member of the Davis Cup team for 11 years, they were unstoppable. France won in 1927 and went on to win the next five years up through 1932. Great Britain was a power in the 1930s, and Australia and the United States dominated in the 1940s, 1950s, and 1960s; in the late 1970s and the 1980s the winners had a multi-national flavor. In 1980, Czechoslovakia became the first Communist country to win the Davis Cup. The United States won in 1990, but in 1991, playing in Lyons, France, the French team knocked out the champion U.S. team 3-1 and owned the cup for the first time in 59 years. The French team (led by Guy Forget, Henri Leconte, and coach Yannick Noah) kissed, hugged, leapt over the net, lay down on the court, and danced a conga line. Sweden dominated the 1990s, winning in 1994, 1997, and 1998, but Spain won the Cup in 2000 and four more times in 2004, 2008, 2009, and 2011.

The Davis Cup celebrated its 100th Final in 2012, with the Czech Republic overcoming Spain 3-2 in a down-to-the wire contest at the O2 Arena in Prague. Switzerland won the most recent Davis Cup in 2014.

CONTACTS:
Dwight Davis Tennis Center
5620 Grand Dr.
St. Louis, MO 63112
314-361-0177; fax: 314-361-0191
www.dwightdavistennis.com

International Tennis Federation Bank Ln.
Roehampton
London SW15 5XZ United Kingdom
44-20-8878-6464; fax: 44-20-8878-7799
www.itftennis.com

♦ 0769 ♦ **Davis's (Jefferson) Birthday**
First Monday in June

The only president of the Confederate States of America, Jefferson Davis, was captured and imprisoned after the Civil War but never brought to trial. Since he refused to ask the federal government for a pardon, he went to his grave deprived of the rights of citizenship, including all of his former privileges and properties. It wasn't until October 17, 1978, that his citizenship was restored, posthumously, by President Jimmy Carter when he signed an Amnesty Bill designed to "finally set at rest the divisions that threatened to destroy our nation."

Davis's memory is honored by many white southerners in the United States, and his birthday (June 3) is a legal holiday in Alabama and Florida. In Mississippi the observance is combined with MEMORIAL DAY. In Texas it is observed as CONFEDERATE MEMORIAL DAY, a time when the graves of Confederate soldiers are decorated and memorial ceremonies are held.

At Arlington National Cemetery in Virginia, the Confederate Memorial Services are held each year on the Sunday nearest June 3, and a speaker usually pays tribute to those who died while serving the Confederacy. Another important ceremony is the Massing of the Flags, which is held at the Jefferson Davis Monument in Richmond, Virginia. The flags of the various Southern states are presented in the order in which they seceded from the nation.

CONTACTS:
Civil War Trust Corporate Office
1156 15th St. N.W.
Ste. 900
Washington, D.C. 20005
202-367-1861; fax: 202-367-1865
www.civilwar.org

First White House of the Confederacy
644 Washington Ave.
Montgomery, AL 36104
334-242-1861
www.firstwhitehouse.org

♦ 0770 ♦ **Day of Prayer, National**
First Thursday in May

On the National Day of Prayer, the U.S. president invites Americans of all religious faiths to join together in communal reflection. This celebration seeks to unite people in prayer and bring renewed respect for God. Many Americans participate in prayer and meditation on this day in various churches, synagogues, and temples. In Washington, D.C., government and business leaders, members of the military, and ministers attend a large gathering, which is aired live over television and radio. Prayer services are organized nationwide at community centers and courthouses, some featuring choirs and bands. The National Day of Prayer is not an official holiday; businesses, governmental offices, and public services remain open.

President Harry S. Truman established the National Day of Prayer in 1952, mandating that each subsequent president declare a day of his choice for the observation. In 1988, President Ronald Reagan designated the first Thursday of May as the National Day of Prayer, and every year since the president has issued a proclamation inviting all Americans to observe this day. In 2008, the Freedom From Religion Foundation (FFRF) unsuccessfully filed a lawsuit challenging the designation of a national day of prayer. The case was dismissed after the court cited Abraham Lincoln's references to God in his second inaugural address.

CONTACTS:
National Day of Prayer Task Force
P.O. Box 64225
Colorado Springs, CO 80962
719-519-9560 or 800-444-8828
nationaldayofprayer.org

♦ 0771 ♦ **Days of '76**
Last week in July

This celebration held each year in Deadwood, South Dakota, is an attempt to revive the spirit of the gold rush days. It is timed to coincide as closely as possible with the anniversaries of the deaths of "Calamity Jane" Canary (August 1, 1903) and "Wild Bill" Hickok (August 2, 1876), two of Deadwood's most famous residents.

The festivities begin with a Professional Rodeo Cowboys Association rodeo. Then there is a three-mile-long historical parade that includes floats portraying the various stages of, and characters in, Deadwood's history—from the earliest settlers to the coming of industry and tourism. A kids' carnival and a rodeo are in town during the festival, and street dances featuring country music take place Thursday through Saturday night.

A highlight is the reenactment of the capture and trial of Jack McCall, who shot the much-admired U.S. Marshal James Butler "Wild Bill" Hickok in the back, and who was eventually hanged. The shooting, capture, and trial are reenacted every afternoon from Memorial Day to Labor Day.

Visitors can also tour long-abandoned gold mines and Mount Moriah cemetery where Calamity Jane, the famous frontierswoman, Wild Bill Hickok, and the brilliant young minister Henry Weston "Preacher" Smith are buried.

♦ 0772 ♦ Dayton Air Show
Third weekend in July

Dayton, Ohio, has been a center for aeronautical research and development ever since two of its local residents, Orville and Wilbur WRIGHT, created the first successful flying machine in their bicycle shop and tested their invention just a few miles outside of town.

Dayton began celebrating its heritage as "the birthplace of aviation" by staging informal air shows shortly after the turn of the century, and by the early 1970s, the **Dayton Air Fair** was a regular annual event consisting of flying demonstrations and aircraft displays. By 1988 it was called the **Dayton Air and Trade Show**, reflecting a growing emphasis on the commercial aspects of the aviation and aerospace industry. It was renamed the United States Air and Trade Show in 1990, when it became an international exposition, and through the 1990s the trade show was held biennially. The trade show was discontinued and the event has been renamed again, this time as the Dayton Air Show.

Every year, the third weekend in July is devoted to the air show, which features bi-planes, gliders, helicopters, and jets flown by some of the most famous names in the field of aviation.

Visitors and participants can also visit the United States Air Force Museum, the National Aviation Hall of Fame, the restored Wright Brothers Cycle Shop, and Wright-Patterson Air Force Base, which continues to play a major role in the development of aerospace technology.

CONTACTS:
Dayton Air Show
3800 A Wright Dr.
Ste. A
Vandalia, OH 45377
937-898-5901; fax: 937-898-5121
www.daytonairshow.com

♦ 0773 ♦ Daytona 500
February

The Daytona 500 is the richest of the four biggest NASCAR (National Association for Stock Car Auto Racing) Sprint Cup races (formerly the Winston Cup). It's the final event of Speedweeks at Daytona International Speedway in Daytona Beach, Fla., which lasts more than two weeks. The speedway is a 2.5-mile oval, and racers must complete 200 laps. The all-time champion of the Daytona 500 is Richard Petty, who won seven times (1964, 1966, 1971, 1973, 1974, 1979, and 1981).

The Daytona Speedway, which has a seating capacity of 102,900, has been operating since 1959, but stock-car racing at Daytona dates back to 1936, and car racing has been going on here since the early days of cars. Between 1902 and 1935, 13 automobile speed records were set on the beach by racing greats Barney Oldfield, Sir Henry Segrave, and Sir Malcolm Campbell, who broke existing records five times.

The speedway was the creation of William H. G. (Bill) France, a mechanic and racer who moved to Daytona Beach in 1934 in the heyday of beach racing. He gave up driving to organize and promote races and in 1947 founded NASCAR. He had the idea of building the Daytona track in 1953, but financial and political problems delayed its opening until 1959. When he died in 1992, he was known as the father of stock-car racing.

Today the Speedway presents eight weeks of racing events. Speedweeks starts with a 24-hour endurance race; this race and the 24 Hours of LE MANS (France) are the only two 24-hour races for prototype sports cars in the world.

The stock-car racing world lost one of its legends on February 18, 2001, when seven-time Winston Cup champion Dale Earnhardt, Sr., 49, died from head injuries sustained in a crash during the final lap of the Daytona. His son, Dale, Jr., was in one of two cars ahead of him when he slammed into the wall at about 180 miles per hour in an attempt to overtake Sterling Martin, who was in third place at the time. Michael Waltrip won this particularly dramatic race, which had seen the lead change 49 times and in which an 18-car crash that caused one injury also occurred. Earnhardt characteristically took dangerous risks on the track, earning him such nicknames as "Ironhead" and "Intimidator." During the 2000 season three drivers died in car wrecks from similar injuries: Adam Petty, grandson of racing star Richard Petty, Kenny Irwin, and Tony Roper, so Earnhardt's death raised yet more questions about NASCAR race safety. Finally, in the wake of the 2001 Dale Earnhardt tragedy that shook the racing world to its core, a new era of NASCAR safety was at last ushered in.

In all of Daytona 500 history, there have been only a handful of drivers who have won the race more than once: Richard Petty, the record holder with seven wins; Cale Yarborough with four; Bobby Allison, Dale Jarrett, and Jeff Gordon with three wins each; and Bill Elliot, Sterling Marlin, Michael Waltrip, Matt Kenseth, Jimmie Johnson, and Dale Earnhardt, Jr., have each won twice. The "crown jewels" of the NASCAR circuit are the Daytona 500, the WINSTON 500, the COCA-COLA 600, and the SOUTHERN 500.

CONTACTS:
Daytona International Speedway
1801 W. International Speedway Blvd.
Daytona Beach, FL
386-254-2700
www.daytonainternationalspeedway.com

♦ 0774 ♦ DC Black Pride Festival
Last weekend in May

The D.C. Black Pride Festival is a social, educational, and fundraising festival originating in the African-American lesbian, gay, bisexual, and transgender community of Washington, D.C. The central mission of the festival is to raise awareness of and pride in black lesbians, gays, bisexuals, and transgenders and to support organizations fighting HIV/AIDS and other health issues. The event serves as the model for numerous black pride festivals held throughout the United States.

Held each year since 1991 on the long Memorial Day weekend, the D.C. Black Pride Festival draws about 25,000 to the Washington Convention Center, where displays include a health and wellness fair, as well as specialty merchandise and food vendors. In addition to activities centered in the exhibition hall, entertainment and social events extend throughout the preceding week. Included are a town hall meeting on the state of black gay men's health, workshops on various lifestyle topics, a basketball tournament, and worship services. A fashion show, film festival, comedy showcase, and poetry slam are among the entertainment offerings, and a pageant is held to select Mr. and Ms. D.C. Black Pride. Throughout the festival, various social events offer music, dancing, and refreshments.

CONTACTS:
DC Black Pride
1806 Vernon St. N.W.
Ste. 200
Washington, D.C. 20009
202-347-0555
www.dcblackpride.org

♦ 0775 ♦ DC Caribbean Carnival
Last full weekend in June

Held annually in Washington, D.C., during the last weekend in June, the D.C. Caribbean Carnival is a colorful pageant celebrating the rich cultural life of the Caribbean region. The festival is organized by the nonprofit D.C. Caribbean Carnival, Inc., which conceived the event as a way to foster appreciation of Caribbean culture and to promote cross-cultural understanding.

Since beginning with nine bands in 1993, the carnival has nearly tripled in size, with groups representing every country in the Caribbean. The festival highlight is the opening-day parade that features more than two dozen calypso and steel drum bands accompanied by thousands of costumed masqueraders representing such themes as "Quest for Gold," "Party Time," and "Angels and Jumbies." The parade originates at the intersection of Georgia Avenue and Missouri Avenue N.W. and ends at Banneker Field, where the site has been transformed into "De Savannah," an international marketplace. Entertainment continues throughout the weekend, and craft and food vendors offer regional arts and cuisine. More than 300,000 people attend each year.

CONTACTS:
DC Caribbean Carnival, Inc.
4809A Georgia Ave. N.W.
Ste. 112
Washington, D.C. 20011
202-726-2204; fax: 202-726-8221
www.dccaribbeancarnival.org

♦ 0776 ♦ D-Day
June 6

The day is also known as **Allied Landing Observances Day**. It marks the start of the Allied invasion of occupied France in 1944, which led to the final defeat of Hitler's Germany the following May. The assault, led by U.S. Gen. Dwight D. Eisenhower, was carried out by airborne forces and the greatest armada the world had ever known. About 3,000 ships transported 130,000 British, Canadian, and American troops across the English Channel to land on the beaches of Normandy, which are known historically by their invasion code names: Utah Beach, Omaha Beach, Gold Beach, Juno Beach, Sword Beach.

Airborne troops began parachuting into Normandy at 15 minutes past midnight on June 6, and Landing Craft Transports plowed through the surf to spill troops onto the beaches starting at 6:30 A.M. About 10,000 troops were killed or wounded that day. Each year, simple ceremonies at the Normandy cemeteries commemorate the men who fell.

CONTACTS:
Portsmouth City Museum
Museum Rd.
Portsmouth PO1 2LJ United Kingdom
44-23-9282-6722; fax: 44-23-9287-5276
www.ddaymuseum.co.uk

♦ 0777 ♦ De Diego (Jose) Day
Third Monday in April

Known as the father of the Puerto Rican independence movement, Jose de Diego (1866 -1918) was a statesman, attorney, journalist, and poet who helped found the Unionist Party in 1904 and advocated tirelessly for Puerto Rican independence from both Spain and the United States. Puerto Rican citizens celebrate the day with festivals, music, and dance, while schools, businesses, and government offices typically close.

CONTACTS:
Puerto Rico Tourism
www.seepuertorico.com

♦ 0778 ♦ Dead, Feast for the
Annually or semiannually

An Iroquois Indian ceremony, the Feast for the Dead—the **'Ohgiwe**—is an attempt to placate the spirits of the dead. Sometimes the 'ohgiwe was used as a healing ceremony, for it was believed that an offended spirit could cause sickness or loss of sleep. Often it was held in the longhouse in the spring or fall as a communal ceremony.

The ceremony itself consists of two long dances, a ritual during which pieces of cloth are waved back and forth and distributed to all the singers and dancers, and the ceremonial carrying out of the kettle or drum. There are social dances after the feast is over, and a mock-struggle over special cakes that have been prepared for the dead.

◆ 0779 ◆ Dean (James) Festival
September

James Dean (1931–1955), the legendary film actor and star of *Rebel Without a Cause*, remains the subject of adulation even decades after his early death in an automobile accident. The star's hometown of Fairmount, Ind., contributes to the ongoing tribute by dedicating an annual four-day festival to the icon.

The festival's origins date back to 1975, the same year the Fairmount Historical Museum was founded. Several notables from the town have their own displays, but the main exhibit pays homage to James Dean. During the event, which is officially called **Museum Days/Remembering James Dean**, thousands of fans survey Dean memorabilia and his personal items.

Additional events take place at locations throughout the town. There are free showings of the star's most celebrated films, a James Dean look-alike contest, fashion shows, and a trivia contest. Another tradition, the James Dean Car Show, has existed since 1980.

CONTACTS:
James Dean
10500 Crosspoint Blvd.
Indianapolis, IN 46256
317-570-5000
www.jamesdean.com

◆ 0780 ◆ Decorated Horse, Procession of the
Between May 21 and June 24; Corpus Christi

According to legend, during the Crusades the ship in which the French King Louis IX was traveling and bearing the Eucharist was wrecked on the beach at Brindisi, Puglia province, Italy. The local archbishop salvaged the sacred Host and carried it with him as he rode through the town on a white horse. To commemorate this event, the current archbishop of Brindisi carries the Most Holy Sacrament in a procession that takes place on CORPUS CHRISTI each year. He rides at the head of the procession on a white horse caparisoned in gold, passing through galleries of silk draperies and a constant rain of flowers thrown by spectators. This event is sometimes referred to as the **Procession of the Caparisoned Horse**.

Corpus Christi is celebrated with flowers and colorful processions in other Italian towns and villages as well—those occurring at Genzano and Perugia, Umbria province, being among the more spectacular.

CONTACTS:
Italian Government Tourist Board
686 Park Ave.
3rd Fl.
New York, NY 10065
212-245-5618; fax: 212-586-9249
www.italiantourism.com

◆ 0781 ◆ Deep Sea Fishing Rodeo
Weekend of July 4

This event is the "World's Largest Fishing Rodeo," according to its promoters, and a four-day event staged from Gulfport, Miss. The Mississippi Gulf Coast area is reputed to be one of the world's best natural fish hatcheries, with an abundance of species of fresh-water, salt-water, and deep-sea game fish. The rodeo's fishing waters are the Mississippi Sound of the Gulf of Mexico and the bayous and creeks within a range of 200 miles north of the Mississippi shoreline.

The rodeo began in 1949 and today attracts from 15,000 to 20,000 people and entrants from 48 states. Prizes are awarded for the top weight in 28 categories of fish. Besides fishing, there are also all the peripherals of a festival: arts and crafts exhibits, dances, a midway, fireworks, bands, and the coronation of a Rodeo Queen.

CONTACTS:
Alabama Deep Sea Fishing Rodeo
P.O. Box 16606
Mobile, AL 36616
251-471-0025
www.adsfr.com

◆ 0782 ◆ Defenders' Day
September 12

Defenders' Day, a legal holiday in Maryland, celebrates the anniversary of the battle of North Point. The battle took place near Baltimore on September 12, 1814; two days later, the unsuccessful British attack on Baltimore's Fort McHenry inspired Francis Scott Key to jot down the words of "The Star-Spangled Banner." For this reason the two events are celebrated more or less in conjunction on September 12, a day that is sometimes referred to as **National Anthem Day**.

A 56-foot monument at Calvert and Fayette Streets in Baltimore commemorates the 1814 battle, and the star-shaped Fort McHenry is a national monument and an historic shrine. Defenders' Day is celebrated with a number of patriotic events, including an annual mock bombardment of the fort on the weekend nearest September 12.

CONTACTS:
Fort McHenry National Monument and Historic Shrine
2400 E. Fort Ave.
Baltimore, MD 21230
410-962-4290; fax: 410-962-2500
www.nps.gov

◆ 0783 ◆ Delaware Big House Ceremony
Late October

The Lenape Indians—formerly referred to as Delaware Indians by early European settlers—once lived in what is now New Jersey, southeastern New York, eastern Pennsylvania, Delaware, and parts of western Connecticut, but like many other native peoples, most eventually moved to the western territories. Their faith was known as the Big House Religion, and each autumn the Lenape observed the Big House Ceremony, a 12-day long affair in which members of the tribe would camp around the lodge and celebrate their homecoming. The ceremony included purification rites, a deer hunt, drumming and dancing, and a sacred feast. The Big House was a large log building with doorways positioned facing the east and the west, and was the gathering place for sacred communal observances. The last known Big House Ceremony was held in 1924.

CONTACTS:
Conner Prairie
13400 Allisonville Rd.
Fishers, IN 46038
317-776-6000 or 800-966-1836
www.connerprairie.org

♦ 0784 ♦ Democratic People's Republic of Korea Founding Day
September 9

The founding of North Korea (official name: Democratic People's Republic of Korea) on September 9, 1948, is observed throughout the country as a national holiday. The whole of the Korean peninsula (i.e., present-day North and South Korea) was under the control of Japan from 1910 until the end of World War II. When Japan surrendered in August 1945, the U.S.S.R took control of the northern half of the peninsula, while the southern half came under control of the United States. Despite attempts to unify the two regions, by 1948 it was clear that their sharp political differences made reunification impossible. On August 15, 1949, the Republic of Korea was established in the south. Less than a month later, the Democratic People's Republic of Korea, under the leadership of then-Premier Kim Il-Sung, was founded in the North.

Much of the observance of North Korea's founding day centers on adulating Kim Il-Sung, the founding leader. This is true of many of the political holidays in North Korea, reflecting the "cult of personality" that was a facet of Kim's distinctive political philosophy. The main public celebrations take place in the capital city, Pyongyang, and can include such events as government banquets in the late Kim's honor, political meetings, concerts, and displays of song and dance. Officials and citizens also lay flowers before the monuments to Kim in the capital. Similar displays and flower-laying also take place in towns and cities throughout North Korea.

CONTACTS:
Democratic People's Republic of Korea, Permanent Mission to the United Nations
820 Second Ave.
New York, NY 10017
212-972-3105; fax: 212-972-3154
dprkorea.org.nz

♦ 0785 ♦ Democratic Republic of Congo Independence Day
June 30

The Democratic Republic of Congo (formerly Zaire) gained independence from Belgium on this day in 1960. It had been a Belgian colony since 1907, and powerful movements had struggled for self-rule since the 1950s. The people celebrated the first independence day with fireworks and bonfires in the capital city of Léopoldville (now Kinshasa).

CONTACTS:
Embassy of the Democratic Republic of Congo
1726 M St. N.W
Ste. 601
Washington, D.C. 20036
202-234-7690; fax: 202-234-2609
www.ambardcusa.org

♦ 0786 ♦ Denmark Constitution Day
June 5

This public holiday commemorates the constitution signed on June 5, 1849, that made Denmark a constitutional monarchy, and the one signed on June 5, 1953, that created parliamentary reforms.

A parade takes place in Copenhagen, and other festivities are held in villages throughout Denmark.

CONTACTS:
Royal Danish Embassy
3200 Whitehaven St. N.W.
Washington, D.C. 20008
202-234-4300; fax: 202-328-1470
usa.um.dk

Ministry of Foreign Affairs of Denmark
Asiatisk Plads 2
Copenhagen DK-1448 Denmark
45-33-92-0000; fax: 45-32-54-0533
um.dk

♦ 0787 ♦ Denver Black Arts Festival
Weekend in mid-July

The Denver Black Arts festival, inaugurated in 1987, is an annual cultural exhibition and celebration held each July in Denver City Park West. With more than 100,000 visitors annually, it is one of the largest African-American cultural events in the western United States.

The festival features events from a wide array of art forms. From the performing arts, music shows are featured on four different stages and include African, blues, gospel, hip hop, jazz, reggae, soul, and world beat acts. In addition, dancers perform in a variety of genres, including African, modern, and tap, sharing their talents through dance workshops. A theater emphasizes the strong oral traditions in African and African-American society through presentations of drama, storytelling, and poetry. A musical competition, the "Mile High Challenge," features drum and drill teams from throughout the region. Friday's special events include a program of youth activities designed for those under age 18. On Saturday the "Carnivale du Promenade," also known as the "Boogaloo Celebration Parade," starts at the intersection of Colorado Boulevard and 22nd Avenue and travels through the park to 17th Avenue and Esplanade.

An art fair features visual arts such as carving, drawing, glass works, painting, photography, and textiles as well as a sculpture garden. A number of exhibits allow participants to try techniques and crafts for themselves, including making herd sticks and Kente cloth and adding their work to a mural that is painted throughout the festival. Children may participate in a historical scavenger hunt that invites them to visit various locales within the park to gather information and win prizes.

African goods, including carvings, clothing, and jewelry, are available from vendors in an area known as "Watu Sokoni" ("People's Marketplace"). In addition, a community outreach fair features exhibit booths by clubs, agencies, and other organizations providing health and housing services, as well as employment and education assistance. In a food court area, vendors offer African, Caribbean, and Southern cuisine.

CONTACTS:
Visit Denver, The Convention & Visitors Bureau
1575 California St.
Ste. 300
Denver, CO 80202
303-892-1112 or 800-233-6837
www.denver.org

♦ 0788 ♦ **Departure of the Continental Army**
Saturday nearest June 19

On December 19, 1777, George WASHINGTON and between 11,000 and 12,000 of his Continental Army soldiers marched into Valley Forge, about 18 miles north of Philadelphia, to set up camp for the winter. The men were exhausted, hungry, and poorly equipped. Severe winter weather didn't make their stay at Valley Forge any easier, and they received only irregular supplies of meat and bread. Between 2,000 and 3,000 of the men died from typhus, typhoid, dysentery, and pneumonia before the winter was over.

It was largely through Washington's leadership and the efforts of Baron Friedrich Von STEUBEN that the dispirited army was turned into a well-trained, dependable fighting force by the following summer.

The anniversary of the day the Continental army marched out of Valley Forge in pursuit of the British, who were moving toward New York, is still celebrated with an historic reenactment that takes place on or near June 19 at the Valley Forge National Historical Park each year. In addition, the Army's return to Valley Forge is commemorated on December 19, and there is a muster roll in February.

CONTACTS:
Valley Forge National Historical Park
1400 N. Outer Line Dr.
King of Prussia, PA 19406
610-783-1000; fax: 610-783-1053
www.nps.gov/vafo

♦ 0789 ♦ **Derby Day (Nul)**
Early June

Derby Day is the most prestigious horse race in the world. The idea for the race arose at a dinner party in 1779 and was eventually named for the Earl of Derby, one of the guests who was present that evening. Derby Day is held annually at the Epsom Racecourse in Surrey, England, on the second day of the summer meeting, usually in early June. Many companies in England give their employees the day off so they can join in the picnicking that takes place near the course.

Like its American counterpart, the KENTUCKY DERBY, the festivities surrounding the Derby last far longer than the race itself, which covers a mile and a half and is over in just a few minutes. Only three-year-old colts and fillies can enter, which means that the race can never be won by the same horse twice.

CONTACTS:
Epsom Downs Racecourse
epsom.thejockeyclub.co.uk

♦ 0790 ♦ **Detroit International Jazz Festival**
Labor Day weekend

The Detroit International Jazz Festival (DJF) is a celebration of the jazz music genre held annually in Detroit, Mich., on Labor Day weekend. Billed as the world's largest free jazz festival, the DJF takes place over a period of four days, beginning on Friday evening and concluding on the Monday holiday. It presents more than 100 musical acts on six stages and attracts approximately 750,000 spectators.

Founded in 1980 by philanthropist Robert McCabe and a group of community supporters, the festival was initiated as a means of celebrating the rich musical legacy of the Detroit area, bringing world-class entertainment to the streets of Detroit and revitalizing tourism to the city. The first festivals were located in Hart Plaza, a waterfront park overlooking the Detroit River and Windsor, Ontario, Canada. Associated with the Montreux International Jazz Festival in Switzerland during its first decade, the festival partnered with the Detroit Music Hall from 1991 to 2005.

In 2006 it came under the management of record company executive and philanthropist Gretchen Carhartt Valade. Through Valade's efforts, a nonprofit foundation was established to fund and oversee festival operations, guaranteeing the continuation of DJF and fueling its expansion. The festival area now extends from Hart Plaza three blocks north on Woodward Avenue to Campus Martius Park. Each year the performance lineup includes local and national jazz acts and covers the spectrum of the jazz genre, including funk, fusion, salsa, Afro-rhythms, R&B, and gospel. While such high-profile artists as Herbie Hancock, Dave Brubeck, and Regina Carter headline the show, student ensembles and emerging artists are also featured throughout the weekend, and special programming for young fans is provided at the KidBop area. Refreshments are available at restaurants located within the festival area as well as from food and beverage vendors in Hart Plaza and on the street.

CONTACTS:
Detroit Jazz Festival

19900 Harper Ave.
Harper Woods, MI 48225
313-447-1248; fax: 313-447-1249
www.detroitjazzfest.com

♦ 0791 ♦ Devathani Ekadashi
October-November; 11th day of waxing half of
Hindu month of Kartika

Devathani EKADASHI is a Hindu festival, observed in rural areas, that celebrates the waking of Vishnu. Hindus believe that Vishnu's battle with the great demon Shankhasura was so exhausting that he went to sleep for a period of four months afterward. Each year, Vishnu slumbers from the 11th day of the waxing half of Asadha (June-July) until the 10th day of the waxing half of Kartika (October-November). On the 11th day, he awakens. During his long sleep, Hindu marriages and other ceremonies are not observed.

Hindu women celebrate the festival by fasting, worshipping Vishnu, and singing hymns in praise of various gods and goddesses. Newly ripened crops, such as sugarcane and waternuts, may be eaten on this day for the first time, and it also marks the end of the period during which marriages and other ceremonies cannot be held.

♦ 0792 ♦ Devi Dhura
July-August; the day before and the full moon
day of the Hindu month of Sravana

Held at the same time as RAKSHA BANDHAN, the Hindu festival observed by brothers and sisters in honor of their relationship, a two-day festival is observed in the small Himalayan town of Devi Dhura in Uttar Pradesh, India. Hindus gather at the shrine of Varahi Devi or Bhagwati, an incarnation of Durga. She is the patron goddess of the approximately 200 villages in the area. Animal sacrifices—originally male buffaloes, but often bulls or goats today—are made at the shrine on the day before Raksha Bandhan. Processions from the other villages stream in to Devi Dhura. Generally these are led by dancers, followed by the animals, the priest, and members of the community. As hundreds of goats and bulls are killed, people use the blood to mark their foreheads.

On the second day, the *bagwals* assemble at Kholi Khan, a flat yard next to the shrine. These are groups of men, wearing turbans and carrying sturdy cane shields, who have been selected from six of the villages to participate in an unusual stone-throwing ritual. Each man is given six to eight stones to throw, and the battle that ensues is not a symbolic act but a true fight in which injuries are common and often severe. The stoning can last as little as 20 minutes or as long as two-and-a-half hours, and spectators watch from a safe distance.

Although there are many legends that account for this tradition, none really offers a satisfactory explanation. It is apparently a well-established custom by which Hindus show their faith not only by shedding the blood of animals but also their own. It is believed that the blood lost by the stone-throwing participants amounts to that which would be shed in the sacrifice of one human being.

CONTACTS:
Uttar Pradesh State Tourism Development Corporation Ltd
Rajarshi Purshottam Das Tandon Paryatan Bhavan
C-13, Vipin Khand
Gomti Nagar
Lucknow, Uttar Pradesh India
91-522-2307037; fax: 91-522-2308937
uptourism.gov.in

♦ 0793 ♦ Dew Treading
Between April 30 and June 3; Ascension Day

Both city and country dwellers in the Netherlands continue to observe the old folk custom known as **Dauwtrappen** ("dew treading") on ASCENSION DAY, which is also a public holiday. People take their children to the fields—or, in the case of city dwellers, to the suburbs—to walk through the morning dew and gather spring flowers. According to an old superstition, the Ascension Day dew possesses supernatural growing and healing powers. In the country, it is customary for friends and neighbors to meet each other at an inn for a big breakfast afterward.

♦ 0794 ♦ Dewali (Divali, Deepavali, Festival of Lights)
October-November; 15th day of waning half of
Hindu month of Kartika

The word *dewali* means 'a row or cluster of lights', and the week-long festivities are illuminated by lamps, fireworks, and bonfires. The holiday means different things in different parts of Asia. In northern India it marks the beginning of the Hindu New Year. In Gujarat and Malaysia, families clean and whitewash their homes and draw elaborate designs (called *alpanas*) on their floors with colored powder to welcome Lakshmi, the Hindu goddess of wealth and prosperity. Then they set up rows of little clay lamps, decorating their courtyards, windows, and roofs with light in the belief that Lakshmi won't bless a home that isn't lit up to greet her.

In the Punjab and Mauritius, Dewali celebrates the coronation of Rama (an incarnation of Vishnu) after his conquest of Ravana, the ruler of Sri Lanka, who had stolen his wife. In West Bengal it is a Kali festival. In Maharashtra the lights fend off King Bali, the ruler of the underworld. The Jains commemorate the death of their great hero, MAHAVIRA, on this day, called Deva Dewali, in the city of Pava in Bihar. In Nepal it is TIHAR, a multi-holiday that celebrates the New Year and Lakshmi, sisters honor brothers, and mandalas are prepared for each member of the family.

Dewali is as important to Hindus as CHRISTMAS is to Christians. It is celebrated by the world's 500 million Hindus with gift exchanges, fireworks, and festive (typically vegetarian) meals.

CONTACTS:
Ministry of Tourism, Government of India

1270 Ave. of the Americas
Ste. 303
New York, NY 10020
212-586-4901; fax: 212-582-3274
tourism.nic.in

♦ 0795 ♦ Dhaka International Film Festival
January in even-numbered years

The Dhaka International Film Festival is organized by the Rainbow Film Society in Dhaka, Bangladesh. Its primary goal is to promote Bangladeshi films and connect local artists with the international film industry. The festival was first conducted in 1992, starting as an annual event, but it has run biennially since 1995. It takes place in various venues in Dhaka, and artists from over 50 countries participate.

The festival includes three main types of events: film screenings, conferences, and workshops. Seven categories of films are screened. The Competition section features fictional films from Asia and Australia exclusively. The special jury for this section judges the best film, director, actor, actress, script, and cinematographer. Three films of famous directors from Asia, Africa, Latin America, or Europe are featured in the Retrospective screenings. Cinema of the World includes feature films of all categories. A section is allotted for children's films as well. Independent filmmakers use the festival as a launching pad into the film industry, and a special event is held for screening their works. In addition, female filmmakers are afforded their own category and participate in a conference designed to address women's issues through film. A cinema workshop is held as a parallel event for aspiring filmmakers, with lectures and practical activities led by veterans of the film industry.

CONTACTS:
Rainbow Film Society
B.S. Bhaban, Level 3, Rm. 105
75 Science Laboratory Rd.
Dhaka, 1205 Bangladesh
8802-862-1062
www.dhakafilmfestival.org

♦ 0796 ♦ Dhan Teras
October-November; 13th day of waning half of Hindu month of Kartika

Dhan Teras or **Dhanvantri Trayodashi** is observed two days prior to DEWALI, the Hindu Festival of Lights. It is held in honor of Dhanvantri, the physician of the gods and the father of Indian medicine, whom doctors in particular worship on this day. According to Hindu mythology, the gods and the demons tried to produce the elixir known as *amrita* by churning up the ocean. Dhanvantri rose up out of the water bearing a cup filled with it. He is also credited with inventing the traditional system of Indian medicine known as Ayurveda.

On this day Hindus rise at dawn and bathe, put on new robes, and fast. In the evening, they light an earthen lamp before the door of the house and break their fast. It is considered an auspicious day to purchase new utensils.

♦ 0797 ♦ Dhungri Fair
May

This is a festival celebrated by Hindu women from the hills near Manali, at the north end of the Kullu Valley in the Himachal Pradesh State of India. A small wooden temple known as the Hidimba (or Dhungri) Temple stands among a woods of cedar trees near Manali. The women gather here to honor the goddess Hidimba, who fell in love with Bhima and became his wife in the famous Hindu epic *Mahabharata*, with a traditional dance.

The temple is known for its intricately chiseled door. Hindu legend has it that the craftsman who carved it had his right hand chopped off by order of the king who hired him. The king wanted his temple to stand alone as a great and unique work. However, when the same carver went on to construct a yet more elaborate temple at Chamba, this time using his left hand, the unfortunate worker got his head chopped off.

CONTACTS:
H.P. Tourism Development Corporation Ltd
Ritz Annexe
Shimla, HP 171001 India
91-177- 2652704; fax: 91-177- 2652206
www.hptdc.nic.in

♦ 0798 ♦ Día de la Santa Cruz (Day of the Holy Cross)
May 3

The Day of the Holy Cross, known elsewhere as the EXALTATION OF THE CROSS, is an important one throughout Latin America. Crosses that are normally found in the churches are repaired and repainted, or decorated and carried in procession through the streets.

In Mexico the Day of the Holy Cross is primarily observed by miners, masons, and construction workers. They make elaborately decorated crosses and place them on buildings where they are working. Anyone who is constructing a new building is obligated to throw a party for the workers on this day. Fireworks are set off, and the occasion is treated as a fiesta.

In Peru, Indians hold an all-night vigil on May 2, watching over the wooden crosses they have collected from the churches, roadsides, and mountaintops. The next morning, the crosses are taken to church for the priest's blessing.

In the Andes, the Day of the Cross celebrations have taken the place of the ancient Inca ceremonies known as AYMURAY. In Guatemala, too, the Day of the Cross has replaced an annual pilgrimage to Lake Amatitlán for the purpose of fulfilling certain fertility rites. After the Spanish Conquest, the Spanish priests took advantage of this huge gathering to establish their own Christian celebration. The contemporary festival held in the village of Amatitlán on May 2 and 3 revolves around Indian dancing, music, and water sports as well as prayers and church services.

In Venezuela, the celebration is known as **Velorio de Cruz**. People set up special altars in their homes that include crosses, lighted candles, and images of the saints. Roving musicians and poets from all over the country come to perform in front of these altars. While playing their instruments, they improvise rhymed couplets and other poetic forms.

CONTACTS:
Commission for the Promotion of Peru
Calle Uno Oeste 50
Mincetur Bldg.
Fl. 13 & 14
San Isidro, Lima Peru
51-1-616-7300
www.promperu.gob.pe/english

♦ 0799 ♦ Día de los Charros
September 14

In Mexico the *charros*, whose name means "loud" or "flashy," are skilled horsemen who were originally *rancheros* (ranchers) of mixed Spanish and Indian blood who took pride in their horses and amused themselves by holding riding competitions with each other. They decorated the harnesses with silver and wore elaborately embroidered costumes.

Today's Mexican charros are more sportsmen than cowboys or ranchers. Most belong to one of the many charro associations, each of which has its own ranch and arena for rodeos. It is on September 14, the day before the MEXICO FESTIVAL OF INDEPENDENCE, that many of the charro associations organize parades and rodeos. The *jaripeo*, or rodeo, generally consists of 10 or more events involving special horse-handling skills and exhibitions of various tricks. Bringing a running horse to a full stop by lassoing its front feet is known as a *mangana*, and the *cola* involves riding very close to a running steer and grabbing its tail, which the charro then twists around his own right leg, forcing the steer to fall on its back and do a complete roll. Perhaps the most difficult trick is the *paso de la muerte* (death's pass), where the charro pursues a wild horse, switching from his own horse's saddle to the back of the wild horse at full gallop.

The typical charro's costume features a pair of snug pants together with a long-sleeved top called a *guayabera*, a waist-length jacket, a bow tie, and a sombrero (wide-brimmed hat). These Mexican horsemen generally carry guns, symbolic of the role the charros have played in Mexico's wars.

See also CHARRO DAYS FIESTA.

CONTACTS:
Mexico Tourism Board
800-446-3942
www.visitmexico.com

♦ 0800 ♦ Día de los Muertos
November 2

Día de los Muertos, or **Day of the Dead**, is a national holiday in Mexico and is observed in Hispanic communities throughout the U.S. Many Mexicans believe that the spirits of the dead return to enjoy a visit with their friends and relatives on this day. Long before sunrise, people stream into the cemeteries laden with candles, flowers, and food that is often shaped and decorated to resemble the symbols of death. Children eat tiny chocolate hearses, sugar funeral wreaths, and candy skulls and coffins. But the atmosphere is festive.

In many homes people set up *ofrendas*, or altars, to the departed. These are decked with lighted candles, special foods, and whatever the dead enjoyed when they were alive.

See also ALL SOULS' DAY; ANGELITOS, LOS.

CONTACTS:
Mexico Tourism Board
800-446-3942
www.visitmexico.com

♦ 0801 ♦ Día de los Tres Reyes
January 6

Throughout most of Latin America and Spain, EPIPHANY is called el Día de los Tres Reyes (**Three Kings Day** or **Day of the Wise Men**). It marks the end of the CHRISTMAS season that began on December 16 with POSADAS. In Mexico, on the night of January 5 children stuff their shoes with hay and leave them out for the Wise Men to fill with sweets and gifts—much as children elsewhere leave their Christmas stockings out for Santa Claus to fill on CHRISTMAS EVE. And just as letters to Santa Claus are a popular custom in the United States, Mexican children often write letters to the Magi (the Three Wise Men), listing their good deeds and suggesting what gifts they would like to receive.

In Venezuela, children leave straw by their beds so that the Magi's camels will have something to eat. On the morning of January 6 they awake to find the straw gone and gifts delivered in its place.

See also BEFANA FESTIVAL AND TWELFTH NIGHT.

♦ 0802 ♦ Día de Negritos and Fiesta de los Blanquitos
January 5-6

In Popayán, in Colombia's Cauca Department, the CHRISTMAS season ends with the festivities that take place on January 5 and 6. But rather than honoring the Three Wise Men (*see* DÍA DE LOS TRES REYES), who are said to have reached Bethlehem on January 6, the wild celebration that takes place here comes closer to MARDI GRAS.

During the morning hours of January 5, known as the Día de Negritos or **Day of the Black Ones**, boys equipped with black shoe polish chase the girls and try to smear them with their blackened hands. By evening, older boys have joined in the fun, and no one who dares to leave the house is safe. There are parades in the afternoon with people in costume, decorated cars, and the music of *chirimíasi* (roving groups of musicians who play Colombian music on traditional instruments). At least one member of each group is dressed as a devil carrying a spike or horsewhip, which he uses to tease and frighten spectators. Afterward, the poor crowd into the main square, where beef and other foods donated by the town's wealthier inhabitants are distributed.

The following day, January 6, is known as the Fiesta de los Blanquitos (Festival of the White Ones). Instead of chasing the girls with shoe polish, the boys use talcum powder and wheat flour, which turns into a gluey substance when people dump water from their balconies on the victims. The rowdiness of the two-day celebration is not enjoyed by everyone, however. Older Colombians remember the days when well-dressed gentlemen sauntered beneath the windows of beautiful young women, who favored them by coming to the door and permitting a beauty mark to be dabbed on their faces.

CONTACTS:
Commission for the Promotion of Peru
Calle Uno Oeste 50
Mincetur Bldg
Fl. 13 and 14
Lima 27 Peru
51-1-4224-3131; fax: 51-1-224-7134
www.promperu.gob.pe

◆ 0803 ◆ **Día del Puno**
November 5

Each year a festival takes place in Puno, Peru, during the first week in November to mark the legendary birth of the first Inca ruler, Manco Capac, and his wife Mama Ocllo. It is said that they were the children of the Sun, intended to be the first rulers of the Inca people, and were born on an island in Lake Titicaca. On November 5, the date associated with their birth, a parade of reed boats, called *balsas*, accompanies an elaborately decorated boat that takes a couple playing the roles of Manco Capac and Mama Ocllo to an island in the lake. There the birth is dramatically reenacted.

Festivities include performances of traditional dance and musical groups, sporting events, exhibits, and a crafts fair.

CONTACTS:
Commission for the Promotion of Peru for Export & Tourism
Calle Uno Oeste 50. MINCETUR Bldg.
13 & 14 Fl.
Lima Peru
51-1-616-7300
www.promperu.gob.pe

◆ 0804 ◆ **Diamond Head Crater Celebration**
April or May

In 2006, for the first time in 30 years, music was played inside the Diamond Head Crater on the Hawaiian island of Oahu. The Diamond Head Crater Celebration, created to present Hawaiian culture and music alongside national acts, was organized by Ron Gibson and Mark Mellick of GM Entertainment. The Diamond Head Crater is an extinct volcano outside of the city of Honolulu. It is both a Hawaii state monument and a United States National Natural Landmark.

Crater concerts held during the 1960s and 1970s drew about 40,000 people, but the congestion, parked cars, and trash eventually led to the shows being discontinued. A number of changes were made when the shows were reinstated in 2006. Seating is limited to 7,500 people. Concert-goers are bussed into the site to minimize their impact on the crater environment. Blankets and low-backed beach chairs are permitted in the open-grass seating area.

The six-hour concert has included a number of nationally known musical acts, including the Steve Miller Band, Linda Ronstadt, and Earth, Wind, and Fire. The Honolulu Symphony also performs. The Polynesian Cultural Center presents a program of Pacific island music and dance. A Crater Cabaret presents local musical favorites and dancing. Hawaiian restaurants and breweries provide the food and beverages.

◆ 0805 ◆ **Dicing for the Maid's Money Day**
Last Thursday in January

In the 17th century, dicing (throwing dice) for money was a favorite English pastime in which large sums of money could be won or lost. However, the annual dicing competition that still takes place in Guildford, England, is for the relatively modest sum of 11 pounds, 19 shillings.

In 1674 a local resident named John How established a fund of 400 pounds, which in his will he said he wanted invested and the proceeds distributed each year to a local "maid" or house servant who had served faithfully in the same position for at least two years. The will also stipulated that two servants should throw dice for the gift, and that the one who threw the highest number should receive the entire amount. In 1702, however, another, larger fund was begun by John Parsons. Today, whoever throws the higher number receives the How prize, which is smaller than the Parson prize, which goes to the woman who throws the lower number.

In the presence of the mayor, trustees, and assembled townspeople, the two women chosen to participate in this event each year take turns shaking the dice in a special hide-covered, silver-banded dice box which has been used for this purpose over the past century. According to the official Maid's Money receipt book, the recipients of the prizes in recent years have been older women who have served faithfully in the same family for many years. But the gift was originally designed for young, unmarried women who might need the money for a dowry.

CONTACTS:
Guildford Tourist Information Centre
155 High St.
Guildford, Surrey GU1 3AJ United Kingdom
44-14-8344-4333
www.guildford.gov.uk

◆ 0806 ◆ **Dinagyang**
Last weekend in January

The Dinagyang is a dancing-in-the-streets carnival on the island of Panay in Iloilo City, Philippines, held a week after the ATI-ATIHAN in Kalibo and the SINULOG in Cebu. Like these festivals, Dinagyang venerates the Santo Niño, or Holy Infant. In Iloilo (pronounced EE-lo-EE-lo) the participation of tribal groups adds to the festival's color, but, unlike the exuberant Kalibo crowds, the spectators in Iloilo are quiet.

CONTACTS:
Iloilo Dinagyang Foundation Incorporated
Freedom Grandstand
JM Basa St.
Iloilo City 5000 Philippines
63-33-337-2172; fax: 202-467-9417
dinagyangsailoilo.com

♦ 0807 ♦ **Dinosaur Days**
July

Dinosaur Days is a new celebration of very old bones: the dinosaur fossils that rest in Dinosaur, Colo., near Grand Junction, in the Dinosaur National Monument. About 140 million years ago, when the area of Grand Junction was semi-tropical, dinosaurs roamed here. In 1900, the remains of a brachiosaurus, one of the biggest of the dinosaurs, was found four miles west of downtown. Hence, the Dinosaur Days, which started in 1986 and consist of festivities with a reptilian theme.

A foot race, called the Pterandon Ptrot, starts things off and is followed by a parade of dinosaurs and cave men (anachronisms are allowed) and a street dance (with a rock band, of course) named the Stegosaurus Stomp. There are also lectures and tours at the quarry.

CONTACTS:
Dinosaur National Monument
4545 E. Hwy. 40
Dinosaur, CO 81610
970-374-3000; fax: 970-374-3003
www.nps.gov

♦ 0808 ♦ **Dionysia (Bacchanalia)**
Various dates

The Dionysia was a festival in ancient Greece in honor of Dionysus (also called Bacchus), the son of Zeus and god of wine, fertility, and drama. There were a series of Dionysian festivals: the Oschophoria, the rural or COUNTRY DIONYSIA, the Lenaea, the ANTHESTERIA, the urban Dionysia, and the most famous—the City or Great Dionysia.

The Great Dionysias were held in the spring (March or April) in Athens for five or six days, and their centerpieces were the performances of new tragedies, comedies, and satyric dramas. These took place in the Theater of Dionysus on the side of the Acropolis and were attended by people from throughout the country. The earliest tragedy that survives is *Persai* by Aeschylus, from the year 472 B.C.E. The dramatists, actors, and singers were considered to be performing an act of worship of the god, and Dionysus was thought to be present at the productions.

The City Dionysias were a time of general springtime rejoicing (even prisoners were released to share in the festivities)

and great pomp. The statue of Dionysus was carried in a procession that also included representations of the phallus, symbolizing the god.

Dionysus was both a merry god who inspired great poetry and a cruel god; the Greeks realistically saw wine as something that made people happy and also made them drunk and cruel. Thus, like the god, his festivals seem to have combined contrasting elements of poetry and revelry.

The small rustic Dionysias were festive and bawdy affairs held in December or January at the first tasting of new wine. Besides dramatic presentations, there were processions of slaves carrying the phallus, the singing of obscene lays, youths balancing on a full goat-skin, and the like.

The Leneae, held in Athens in January or February, included a procession of jesting citizens through the city and dramatic presentations. The Oschophoria ("carrying of the grape cluster"), held in the fall when the grapes were ripe, was marked by a footrace for youths.

♦ 0809 ♦ **Dipri Festival**
March-April

The Dipri Festival is a celebration held by the Abidji tribe in Gomon, Côte d'Ivoire (Ivory Coast). The Abidjis are one of about 60 ethnic groups in the country, which became a French colony in 1893 and attained independence in 1960 (*see* CÔTE D'IVOIRE INDEPENDENCE DAY). First, relatives or neighbors meet on the evening before the celebration to reconcile their differences. Then, during the festival, people go into frenzied trances as they are possessed by *sékés*—beneficient spirits— and stumble, dazed, in the street. Some people, supposedly led by the spirits, plunge knives into their bodies and then, with the guidance of the *sékés*, are healed with poultices of raw eggs and herbs. This festival serves several purposes: it resolves conflicts between generations and in the community, it drives away evil spirits, and it purifies the celebrants.

CONTACTS:
Embassy of the Republic of Cote d'Ivoire
2424 Massachusetts Ave. N.W.
Washington, D.C. 20008
202-797-0300
www.ambaciusa.org

♦ 0810 ♦ **Disabled Persons, International Day of**
December 3

The years 1983-92 marked the United Nations Decade of Disabled Persons, a period during which great strides were made in raising awareness and enacting laws to improve the situation of individuals with disabilities. At the conclusion of this 10-year observance, December 3 was proclaimed the International Day of Disabled Persons. The U.N. General Assembly appealed to its members to observe this day with activities and events designed to promote the advantages of integrating disabled persons into every area of social, economic, and political life.

CONTACTS:
United Nations, Department of Public Information
1 United Nations Plaza
Rm. 117
New York, NY 10017
212-963-5610
www.un.org

♦ 0811 ♦ Disarmament Week
October 24-30

The United Nations' Disarmament Week, observed between October 24 and October 30, was established in 1978. It begins on October 24, the anniversary of the founding of the United Nations, now observed as UNITED NATIONS DAY. Observance revolves around raising public awareness of the dangers of the arms race and the need for international disarmament.

CONTACTS:
United Nations Office for Disarmament Affairs
Information and Outreach Branch
UN Plaza, Rm. S-3185
New York, NY 10017
fax: 212-963-4066 or 917-367-1755
www.un.org

♦ 0812 ♦ Discovery Day
November 19; December 5

There are a number of different days referred to by this name, all of which relate to the voyages of Christopher COLUMBUS.

In Trinidad and Tobago, August 1 was Discovery Day, in honor of Columbus's discovery of the two islands on his third voyage to the Western Hemisphere. Since 1985, however, August 1 has been observed as TRINIDAD AND TOBAGO EMANCIPATION DAY. In Haiti, Discovery Day is a legal holiday celebrated on December 5, commemorating its discovery by Columbus in 1492. And in Puerto Rico, which Columbus found on his second voyage in 1493, Discovery Day is celebrated on November 19.

See also MAGELLAN DAY.

♦ 0813 ♦ Distaff Day
January 7

After the 12-day CHRISTMAS celebration ended on TWELFTH NIGHT or EPIPHANY, **St. Distaff's Day** was traditionally the day on which women resumed their chores, symbolized by the distaff, a tool used in spinning flax or wool. It was also called **Rock Day**, from the German word *rocken*—"rock" being another name for the distaff. The "spear side" and the "distaff side" were legal terms used to distinguish the inheritance of male from that of female children, and the distaff eventually became a synonym for the female sex as a whole. Distaff Day was not really a church festival, but it was widely observed at one time in England.

Although the women had to return to work after Twelfth Night was over, the men apparently had plenty of time to amuse themselves by setting the flax on fire, in return for which they would get buckets of water dumped on their heads.

CONTACTS:
Butler County Spinners and Weavers Guild
134 W. Main St.
Worthington, PA 16262
www.butlerguild.org

♦ 0814 ♦ Divine Holy Spirit, Festival of the (Festa do Divino)
May-June; around Pentecost (50 days after Easter)

Portuguese colonists brought their PENTECOST celebration, the **Festa do Divino**, to Brazil in the 17th century. This religious festival is still celebrated today in many Brazilian cities. One of the most traditional celebrations takes place in Diamantina, Minas Gerais State. The week-long festivities include masses and fireworks, culminating in the "parade of the Emperor."

Festa do Divino celebrations can also be found in two of Brazil's most beautiful colonial-era towns: Alcântara, Maranhão State, and Paraty, Rio de Janeiro State. The townspeople dress up in colonial costumes, with many playing the roles of prominent figures from Brazilian history. The climax is a visit from the "Emperor," who arrives with his servants for a procession and mass at the church square. He frees prisoners from the town jail in a symbolic gesture of royal generosity, and strolling musicians known as *Folias do Divino* serenade the townspeople day and night.

The Feast of the Holy Ghost is celebrated by the fishermen living in and around Tietê, São Paulo State, Brazil, and represents a tradition that began several centuries ago in Portugal to commemorate the Descent of the Holy Ghost upon the Apostles. On Pentecost all the fishermen dress in white with sashes and long stocking caps. Each carries an oar in one hand, and during the procession to the river, they form a double line facing each other. As they make an arch by crossing their oars, a dove, symbolic of the Holy Spirit, is carried beneath it on a ribbon-decorated crown.

The townspeople follow the fishermen and the musicians to the river's edge, where all the fishing canoes have been decorated with bunting for the occasion. The white-clad fishermen climb into their canoes, standing while holding their oars upright, and the current carries the floating regatta downstream. The event comes to a close in the parish church, where the men bring their oars to be blessed so they will have a plentiful catch in the coming year.

See also HOLY GHOST, FEAST OF THE.

CONTACTS:
Brazilian Embassy
3006 Massachusetts Ave. N.W.
Washington, D.C. 20008

202-238-2700; fax: 202-238-2827
washington.itamaraty.gov.br/en-us

♦ 0815 ♦ Djibouti Independence Day
June 27

On this day in 1977, Djibouti gained autonomy from France, after more than 100 years under French rule. It is observed as a national holiday.

CONTACTS:
Embassy of Republic of Djibouti
1156 15th St. N.W., Ste. 515
Washington, D.C. 20005
202-331-0270; fax: 202-331-0302

♦ 0816 ♦ Doan Ngu (Summer Solstice Day)
May-June; fifth day of fifth lunar month

Doan Ngu is a celebration of the SUMMER SOLSTICE in Vietnam. Offerings are made to spirits and ghosts and to the god of death to fend off epidemics. In addition, human effigies are burned, providing souls to staff the army of the god of death.

CONTACTS:
Embassy of Vietnam
1233 20th St. N.W.
Ste. 400
Washington, D.C. 20036
202-861-0737; fax: 202-861-0917
www.vietnamembassy-usa.org

♦ 0817 ♦ Doctors' Day
March 30

Since 1933 this day has been set aside to honor America's physicians. It is the anniversary of the day in 1842 on which Dr. Crawford W. Long removed a tumor from the neck of a man while the patient was anesthetized by ether. Dr. Long was the first acclaimed American physician to use ether as an anesthetic agent in a surgical procedure.

Although Doctors' Day highlights the achievement of Dr. Long, the issue of who really discovered general anesthesia is far from clear. In addition to Dr. Long, Gardner Colton, Horace Wells, and Charles Jackson have also claimed credit for the discovery, although some used nitrous oxide gas while others used ether. It was William Thomas Morton who first demonstrated the use of ether as a general anesthetic in front of a gathering of physicians on October 16, 1846, at Massachusetts General Hospital.

The red carnation is the official flower associated with Doctors' Day. The American Medical Association promotes various activities to mark this day, including walk-a-thons and blood drives.

CONTACTS:
American Medical Association

AMA Plaza
330 N. Wabash Ave.
Chicago, IL 60611
800-621-8335
www.ama-assn.org

♦ 0818 ♦ Documentary Edge Festival
May-June

Launched in 2005, the Documentary Edge Festival is an annual celebration of documentary film. The only one of its kind in New Zealand, the event is held in the cities of Auckland and Wellington. The festival showcases award-winning and critically acclaimed documentaries from around the world. In addition to social and educational activities, the event features workshops and interactive question-and-answer sessions with some of the masters of documentary filmmaking. Awards are given for best documentary in various categories, including short, feature, and educational, and a special award is offered for best emerging New Zealand filmmaker. At the conclusion of the event, some of the festival's best films are screened across New Zealand.

CONTACTS:
Documentary New Zealand Trust
P.O. Box 10297 Dominion Rd.
Mt. Eden
Auckland, 1446 New Zealand
649-360-0329; fax: 649-623-0333
documentaryedge.org.nz

♦ 0819 ♦ Dodge City Days
Late July through early August

Dodge City's name alone is enough to conjure up memories of the Old West for the residents of Kansas and the surrounding states who come here to celebrate Dodge City Days every summer. Held annually in late July and early August, the main purpose of the festival is to keep the area's history alive. There are staged shootouts between "Marshal Dillon" and the bad guys, a Professional Rodeo Cowboys Association rodeo, a horse show, and parades featuring costumed characters from the Old West on horseback.

First held in 1960, Dodge City Days now attracts crowds of up to 50,000—most of whom are tourists. In recent years the festival has featured entertainment by top country-and-western music stars, and the events have expanded to include a golf tournament, auto racing, and other decidedly non-traditional activities that have little to do with Dodge City's Old West heritage.

CONTACTS:
Dodge City Area Chamber of Commerce
311 W. Spruce
Dodge City, KS 67801
620-227-3119; fax: 620-227-2957
www.dodgecitychamber.com

◆ 0820 ◆ **Dodge National Circuit Finals Rodeo**
Third week in March

The Dodge National Rodeo event is the finals competition for cowboys competing in the regional circuit system of rodeos, held since 1987 in Pocatello, Idaho. About 200 top cowboys and cowgirls compete each year for their share of a purse worth thousands of dollars and gold championship buckles. Competitions for cowboys are in saddle bronc, bull riding, calf roping, bareback riding, team roping, and steer wrestling; the women compete in barrel racing. For youngsters, there's mutton bustin'—riding sheep. Opening ceremonies spotlight the Pocatello Rodeo Queen and her court. Post-rodeo parties are held each night. Attendance at the finals runs about 40,000.

The circuit system was introduced to allow weekend cowboys who can't compete full-time in rodeos to compete in one of 12 regions in the United States.

See also National Finals Rodeo.

CONTACTS:
Professional Rodeo Cowboys Association
101 Pro Rodeo Dr.
Colorado Springs, CO 80919
719-593-8840 or 800-234-7722; fax: 719-548-4876
www.prorodeo.org

◆ 0821 ◆ **Dodge (Geraldine R.) Poetry Festival**
October in even-numbered years

Since the first Dodge Poetry Festival was held in 1986, the biennial gathering has grown into a four-day event that draws upwards of 5,000 people—including television crews—for what has been described as "a grueling but exhilarating marathon of poetry activity." Readings, panel discussions, and talks by some of America's most famous poets have made the restored village of Waterloo in rural southern New Jersey synonymous with the word "poetry" for the students, writers, and interested spectators who flock to the festival, which is sponsored by the Geraldine R. Dodge Foundation. Mrs. Dodge was a local philanthropist.

Many of the events take place outdoors and include music, food, and strolling performers, giving the whole affair the flavor of a bona fide festival rather than the typical writers' conference. Coverage of the Dodge Festival by the award-winning PBS series "The Power of the Word," hosted by Bill Moyers, is thought to have contributed to the festival's broad public appeal.

The poets who have appeared at the Dodge Festival represent a wide range of the best American and international poets, and the festival has been a place where Poets Laureate share the stage with Slam Champions. Many iconic figures have appeared at the Dodge Festival, including Chinua Achebe, Lucille Clifton, Billy Collins, Bei Dao, Allen Ginsberg, Phillip Levine, Maxine Kumin, Naomi Shihab Nye, Octavio Paz, Adrienne Rich, Charles Simic, Gary Snyder, Derek Walcott, and Korea's most prolific and respected living poet, Ko Un.

CONTACTS:
Geraldine R. Dodge Poetry Program
14 Maple Ave.
Ste. 400
Morristown, NJ 07962
973-540-8442
www.dodgepoetry.org

◆ 0822 ◆ **Dog Days**
July 3-August 11

The Dog Days are known as the hottest days of the year in the Northern Hemisphere and usually occur in July and early August. In ancient times, the sultry weather in Rome during these months often made people sick, and they blamed their illnesses on the fact that this was the time of year when Sirius, the Dog Star, rose at about the same time as the sun. Because Sirius was the brightest star, it was thought to add its heat to the sun, producing hot, unhealthy weather. The ancients used to sacrifice a brown dog at the beginning of the Dog Days to appease the rage of Sirius.

Although there are many different ways of calculating which days in any given year are the dog days, and how long they last, it is impossible to be precise. Nowadays it is generally assumed that they fall between July 3 and August 11—slightly later than they occurred in ancient times.

Because of their association with the Dog Star, various beliefs have sprung up involving the behavior of dogs during this period. In the 16th century it was believed that dogs went mad during the Dog Star season. Another name for this time of year, the **canicular days**, comes from the Latin word *canis* meaning "dog.".

◆ 0823 ◆ **Doggett's Coat and Badge Race**
August 1

Established in 1716 by Thomas Doggett, an actor and one of the owners of the Drury Lane Theatre in London, the **Waterman's Derby** is an annual rowing race held on the Thames River between Old Swan Pier and Cadogan Pier. Six young boatmen who have just completed their apprenticeships must row against the tide for a distance of four and a half miles. The winner receives a new pair of breeches, an orange coat, and—because the original race was to commemorate the crowning of King George I—a badge with the Hanoverian white horse on it. There are cash prizes as well: originally, 10 pounds for the winner, and six, five, four, three, or two pounds for the other rowers, according to the order in which they complete the race. When Doggett died in 1721, he left a legacy that would ensure the continuation of both the race and its prizes.

Nowadays, the prizes are significantly higher, beginning at 250 pounds for first place. The race is administered by the Fishmongers' Company, of which Doggett was a member.

CONTACTS:
Fishmongers' Company
Fishmongers' Hall
London Bridge

London EC4R 9EL United Kingdom
44-20-7626-3531; fax: 44-20-7929-1389
www.fishhall.org.uk

Company of Watermen and Lightermen
16-18 St-Mary-at-Hill
London EC3R 8EF United Kingdom
44-20-7283-2373; fax: 44-20-7283-0477
www.watermenshall.org

♦ 0824 ♦ Dogwood Festival
April

The Dogwood Festival is a night-and-day celebration of the pink and white dogwoods (and azaleas) blooming everywhere in Atlanta, Ga. The founders of the first festival in 1936 thought the event could make Atlanta "internationally known for its beauty during the blooming of the dogwood trees and be the beginning of an annual pilgrimage to the Gate City of the South." The festival comes close to doing that, even though it lapsed during World War II, and didn't really get going again until 1968.

Now this gala event each year attracts about 100,000 people who come not only to see the trees but also for numerous concerts, a hot-air balloon exhibit, an artists market, canine frisbee, and rock climbing. Children's activities include puppet making, games, and a kite-making workshop.

CONTACTS:
Atlanta Dogwood Festival
887 W. Marietta St. N.W.
Studio S-105
Atlanta, GA 30318
404-817-6642; fax: 404-817-9508
www.dogwood.org

♦ 0825 ♦ Dol Purnima
February-March; full moon day of Hindu month of Phalguna

The Dol Purnima festival is celebrated throughout India by followers of Krishna. It occurs on the same day as the birthday of Chaitanya Mahaprabhu (1486-1534), also known as Gauranga, the 16th-century Vishnavite saint and poet of Bengal regarded as an incarnation of Krishna. It is therefore a significant festival for Hindus, who carry an image of Lord Krishna, covered with colored powder and placed in aswinging cradle, through the streets as they sing songs composed especially for the occasion.

CONTACTS:
Mayapur Tourism
Opp Gada Bhavan
Sri Mayapur
Nadia, West Bengal 741313 India
91-3472 245219
www.visitmayapur.com

♦ 0826 ♦ Doleing Day
December 21

It was customary at one time in England on ST. THOMAS'S DAY for the poorer inhabitants of the parish to call on their wealthier neighbors and receive a gift or "dole" of food or money. In return, they would give their benefactors a sprig of holly or mistletoe.

The custom of "going a-gooding," as it was called, gave rise to the name **Gooding Day** in parts of Sussex; in other areas it was referred to as **Mumping (Begging) Day**, since those who had to beg were said to be "on the mump." Children would often spend St. Thomas's Day begging for apples.

♦ 0827 ♦ Dom Fair
November-December

The **Hamburger Dom**, or Dom Fair, is one of the most famous CHRISTMAS fairs in the world. It was named after its original location, which was in the open square in front of the Dom, or cathedral, in Hamburg, Germany. Today the fair is held in the Heiligengeistfeld, or Holy Ghost Field, in the middle of the city. It features booths filled with toys, gingerbread, crafts, and other temptations for holiday shoppers. The Fair begins in November and doesn't close until just before Christmas, giving shoppers from Hamburg and the surrounding area plenty of time to buy their gifts.

CONTACTS:
Hamburg Tourist Board
P.O. Box 10 22 49
Hamburg 20015 Germany
49-40-300-51-300; fax: 49-40-300-51-333
www.hamburg-travel.com

♦ 0828 ♦ Dominica Independence Day
November 3

On this day in 1978, Dominica gained independence from Britain as it became a member of the Commonwealth. It is celebrated as a national holiday for three days, including November 3.

CONTACTS:
Dominica Festivals Committee, Division of Culture
Financial Centre
Kennedy Ave.
1st Fl.
Roseau Dominica
767-448-4833; fax: 767-440-5269
divisionofculture.gov.dm

♦ 0829 ♦ Dominican Republic Independence Day
February 27

In the 1830s Juan Pablo Duarte (1813-1876)—known as "the father of Dominican independence"—organized a secret society known as *La Trinitaria* to fight the Haitians. After a long struggle, independence was finally declared on February 27, 1844. Although disorder, dictatorships, and intermittent peace characterized the Dominican Republic's history until the U.S. Marines occupied it from 1916 to 1924 to keep peace between rival political groups, February 27 is still observed as the country's Independence Day and is celebrated with parades and political meetings.

The site of the proclamation, Independence Park, contains a shrine known as the *Altar de la Patria*, "the nation's altar," honoring the three founders of the Republic—Duarte, Ramón Mella, and Juan Sánchez Ramírez. Duarte's birthday, January 26, is also a public holiday, celebrated as Duarte Day.

Dominican Republicans usually celebrate CARNIVAL along with Independence Day. Thousands gather in the capital, Santo Domingo, for the traditional day-long parade and street party.

CONTACTS:
Dominican Republic Tourism Office
136 E. 57th St.
Ste. 803
New York, NY 10022
212-588-1012 or 888-374-6361; fax: 212-588-1015
www.godominicanrepublic.com

♦ 0830 ♦ Dominican Republic Independence Restoration Day
August 16

During the 19th century, the Dominican Republic won its autonomy from Haiti, only to quickly lose it again over a decade later to Spain. The country reclaimed its freedom after winning a two-year-long war with Spain in 1865. Only 14 men were present for the historic raid that marked the beginning of that war, on August 16, 1863. The freedom fighter Santiago Rodriguez led his small contingent up Capotillo Hill in the capital city, Santo Domingo, where they raised the Dominican flag.

Thus, to pay tribute to its complicated history, Dominicans celebrate independence twice a year: on DOMINICAN REPUBLIC INDEPENDENCE DAY and on Dominican Republic Independence Restoration Day, which commemorates the official beginning of the War of the Restoration in 1863. Celebrations take place throughout the island, but the most prominent celebrations are in Santo Domingo and the other main city, Santiago.

Customary festivities include parades, street fairs, and performances of the national anthem and other compositions. Troops will also present a military review before government officials.

CONTACTS:
Ministry of Tourism, Dominican Republic
136 E. 57th St.
Ste. 805
New York, NY 10022
212-588-1012; fax: 212-588-1015
www.godominicanrepublic.com

♦ 0831 ♦ Dominican Republic Our Lady of Altagracia (Feast of the Virgin of Altagracia, Feast of Our Lady of Altagracia)
January 21

The Virgin Mary is considered by many Catholics to be the patron saint of the Dominican Republic. A cloth painting of Mary that is 13 inches (33 cm) wide by 18 inches (45 cm) high is the focus of a yearly celebration in the island nation. Many religious legends have sprung up over the centuries about the portrait. It was painted by a Spanish artist and brought to the Dominican Republic by two Spanish brothers in the early 1500s. The portrait, which was crowned by a gold and silver tiara by Pope John Paul II in 1978, is located in a basilica in the city of Higuey, in the province of Altagracia.

Every year on January 21, thousands of pilgrims visit the Higuey cathedral to worship. The feast day is a national holiday in the Dominican Republic. It is marked by all-night church services, singing, dancing, and festivals in many Dominican towns.

CONTACTS:
Embassy of the Dominican Republic
1715 22nd St. N.W.
Washington, D.C. 20008
202-332-6280; fax: 202-265-8057
www.domrep.org

♦ 0832 ♦ Dominican Republic Our Lady of Mercedes Day
September 24

A national holiday that illustrates the strong influence of Spanish colonialism and the Catholic Church on Dominican culture, this feast day honors Mary the mother of Jesus, often referred to by Dominicans by her patron saint title—Nuestra Señora de Mercedes (Our Lady of Mercedes). Observance of this celebration dates back to 1615, the year the Mercedians, a Spanish order, established the feast day.

According to legend, before returning to Spain Christopher Columbus placed a cross atop a hill overlooking El Cibao, a region on the northern end of the island. In 1495, during a battle between the Spanish and the native Taino Indians, the Lady of Mercedes appeared, scattering the frightened Indians and thereby securing the Europeans' victory. There were subsequent visitations reported at the site, and eventually settlers marked the spot by erecting a church and pilgrimage site they named Iglesia Las Mercedes.

Every year Iglesia Las Mercedes receives thousands of worshippers, many of whom arrive on the saint's day to pay homage. Another church in Santo Domingo, the Church of Las Mercedes, also attracts many followers on September 24. Typical ceremonies at the church in the capital city include masses throughout the day, the Blessing of the Waters, and a procession from the church through Santo Domingo's Colonial Zone.

CONTACTS:
Embassy of the Dominican Republic
1715 22nd St. N.W.
Washington, D.C. 20008
202-332-6280; fax: 202-265-8057
www.domrep.org

♦ 0833 ♦ Dongji (Winter Solstice)
11th lunar month; around December 21

In Korea the WINTER SOLSTICE falls during the 11th lunar month. Perhaps because the winter solstice month was regarded as the first month of the year under the old calendar system in Korea, many people consider the day of the solstice to be the day on which they become one year older— a kind of communal birthday.

Red bean stew with glutinous rice flour balls is a favorite seasonal dish, particularly on Dongji (also rendered *Tongji*). This food is not only eaten as a means of warding off disease, but is also offered to the family ancestors, spread around the front door or gate of the house, and, throughout the year, prepared and taken to people who are in mourning. The color red is traditionally thought to repel evil spirits and all misfortune.

One legend behind this belief holds that a disobedient son, who happened to dislike red bean porridge, died on Dongji day and became a smallpox spirit. Thus, putting red porridge stew around the house will keep him away.

CONTACTS:
Korea Foundation
1612 K St. N.W.
Ste. 1201
Washington, D.C. 20006
202-419-3400 or 202-419-0497; fax: 202-419-0498
en.kf.or.kr

♦ 0834 ♦ Doo Dah Parade
January

Since 1977, the city of Pasadena, Calif., has been the scene of the Doo Dah Parade, a parody of the nationally known Rose Parade. The Rose Parade is held in conjunction with the Rose Bowl football championship, which is held in the same city.

The Doo Dah Parade encourages outrageous, surreal, and imaginative floats, costumes, and themes from all those who participate. The parade takes place in Old Pasadena. Among the groups who have participated are the Fabulous Sons of Ed Wood, Howdy Krishna, Stupidiotic Evolution, Tequila Mockingbird, Horses on Astroturf, and the Doo Dah House Band. Every year an official queen of the Doo Dah Parade is chosen, and she and her court lead the procession.

Sponsored by the nonprofit Light Bringer Project, the parade raises money for the group's art projects, including the Metro Gallery and the Pasadena Chalk Festival.

♦ 0835 ♦ Dosmoche
February; first lunar month

Early in the new Tibetan Year the Dosmoche festival is held in Leh in the Ladakh region of Jammu and Kashmir State, India. A large *dosmo*, or pole, decorated with streamers and religious symbols is erected. The lamas make a food and drink offering to the Buddha and the gods after the dosmo is in place as a ritual to drive away evil spirits for the new year. Later the

dosmo is torn down and burned, symbolizing that the spirits have been driven away.

CONTACTS:
Moonlight Travels
LBA Shopping Complex
Zangsti
Debi Tou, Leh Ladakh 194101 India
91-1982-202 332
www.ladakhtravels.com

♦ 0836 ♦ Double Tenth Day
October 10

Double Tenth Day is a national holiday in Taiwan to commemorate the Chinese Revolution of October 10, 1911. The revolt marked the end of the Ching, or Qing, Dynasty that had been established in 1644 by the Manchus, and it led to the founding of the Republic of China on January 1, 1912.

It took the Ching rulers several decades to complete their military conquest of China and by 1683, when Taiwan became part of the empire, they governed all of China. The Ching Court's period of glory was in the time of the first three emperors, but after 1795 the court began a slow decline. By the end of the 19th century, Japan and the Western powers had reduced China to what SUN YAT-SEN called a "sub-colony," the court was weak and corrupt, and a group of national capitalists was fomenting uprisings. Sun Yat-sen was one of the leaders of this nationalistic group; he was a Jeffersonian figure who wanted a Western-style government with a parliament and separation of powers.

In October 1911, when a revolt in Wuchang (in the province of Hubei) succeeded, supportive uprisings broke out in other cities. The fall of the Manchus followed. Sun Yat-sen, who was in Denver, Colo., at the time of the October revolt, returned to Shanghai and was elected provisional president of the new republic. He is thought of today as the father of modern China, and his birthday on Nov. 12 is also a national holiday in Taiwan.

For several weeks before Double Tenth Day, the plaza in front of the Presidential Office Building in Taipei, Taiwan, is illuminated. Here there are massive parades and rallies on the holiday, displays of martial arts, folk dancing, and other cultural activities. dazzling display of fireworks is presented over an island in the middle of the Tanshui River.

CONTACTS:
Taipei Economic and Cultural Representative Office in the U.S.
4201 Wisconsin Ave. N.W.
Washington, D.C. 20016
202-895-1800
www.roc-taiwan.org

♦ 0837 ♦ Douglass (Frederick) Day
February 14

Frederick Douglass Day in the United States is celebrated on February 14, the date traditionally believed to have been

205

Douglass's birthday. Born into slavery in 1818 in Maryland, he escaped to freedom in 1838 and eventually made his home in New Bedford, Mass., where he became active in the international abolitionist movement. After the Civil War he served in the U.S. government as a marshal in the District of Columbia and as a minister to the Republic of Haiti and the Dominican Republic.

Each year Douglass's birthday is commemorated with a ceremony at his former home, Cedar Hill, which is now the Frederick Douglass National Historic Site in Washington, D.C. The event, which attracts about 300 people, features speakers on human rights, recitations of excerpts from Douglass's speeches, tours of the home, music performances, and a wreath-laying ceremony. In addition, activities including lectures, readings from his works, and film presentations about his life are also planned in New Bedford, in Rochester, N.Y., where Douglass's grave is located, and in many other locations throughout the country.

CONTACTS:
Frederick Douglass National Historic Site
1411 W. St S.E.
Washington, D.C. 20020
202-426-5961
www.nps.gov/frdo

♦ 0838 ♦ **Down Home Family Reunion**
Third weekend in August

Introduced in 1992, the Down Home Family Reunion is an annual celebration of west African folk life held in Abner Clay Park in Richmond, Va., during the third weekend in August. The reunion draws approximately 25,000 attendees during two days of events and offers music and dance performances, storytelling presentations, traditional foods, a heritage marketplace, and children's activities.

The festival is organized by the Elegba Folklore Society, Inc., a nonprofit group that sponsors the activities in an effort to demonstrate the close connection between west African folk life and the cultural traditions of African Americans. With many hands-on and interactive exhibits, the festival showcases the strong influence of west African culture on life in the American South. Many performers and participants are African. Saturday's activities are free and emphasize family participation in craft demonstrations and a variety of cultural exhibits. Sunday's lineup concludes with a concert at dusk that features music and spoken word performances by national and local acts.

CONTACTS:
Richmond Region Tourism
401 N. 3rd St.
Richmond, VA 23219
800-370-9004
www.visitrichmondva.com

♦ 0839 ♦ **Downtown Hoedown**
Late May or Early June

The Downtown Hoedown is a three-day celebration of country music held annually on Late May or Early June in Detroit, Mich. Since it began as a one-day, outdoor concert in 1983, the Hoedown has become one of the largest events of its kind in the United States and as of 2008 was known as the "World's Largest Free Country Music Concert."

The Hoedown is hosted and sponsored by radio station 99.5 FM WYCD and is considered a premier showcase for new country artists. Among those who have risen to fame after playing at the Hoedown are Garth Brooks, Reba McEntire, Rascal Flatts, and Josh Turner. Musical acts perform on multiple stages Friday through Sunday in a riverfront setting at Hart Plaza, a park along the Detroit River, which borders Detroit and Windsor, Ontario, Canada. Local artists start the show at noon and such Nashville stars as Trace Adkins, Josh Gracin, and Trisha Yearwood headline the show in the evening. In addition to music and dancing, the festival offers food and beverage vendors, mechanical bull rides, and a shopping area. Estimated attendance for the three-day weekend is between 800,000 and one million.

CONTACTS:
Downtown Hoedown
c/o 99.5 WYCD
26455 American Dr.
Southfield, MI 48034
248-327-2900
wycd.cbslocal.com

♦ 0840 ♦ **Dozynki Festival**
August 15

For many Christians around the world, August 15 is the Feast of the ASSUMPTION. But in Poland, it is also a time for celebrating the harvest. During the wheat harvest festival known as **Dozynki Pod Debami**, or **Festival under the Oaks**, the reapers make wreaths out of grain, flowers, nuts, and corn. When they present their wreaths to the master and mistress of the estate on which the wheat is grown, they are invited in for a feast, which is followed by dancing.

For Americans of Polish descent living in Orange County, New York—one of the richest onion-growing areas in the United States—the Dozynki Festival underwent a revival in 1939 under the name of the **Feast of Our Lady of the Flowers**. In the village of Florida, the streets were banked high with piles of onions, and there was a huge parade with floats depicting the arrival of the Polish immigrants in America and various aspects of the onion production industry. There was a costumed pageant in which the onion farmers presented the Lord and Lady of the Manor with a huge wreath of onions and flowers, followed by the Onion Dance, which had been created especially for the festival.

CONTACTS:
Corpus Christi Church
199 Clark St.
Buffalo, NY 14212
716-896-1050
dozynki.corpuschristibuffalo.org

♦ 0841 ♦ Drachenstich (Spearing the Dragon)
Mid-August

This annual event centers around the performance of an open-air play, *Drachenstich*, in Fürth, Germany, in the Bavarian Forest. The climax of the play is a battle between a knight on horseback and a huge (about 50 feet long and 10 feet tall), fire-spewing dragon. The knight, of course, wins—by thrusting his spear into the dragon's throat, thereby piercing a pig'sbladder filled with ox blood. Besides the dragon-sticking, the celebrations include various merrymaking events and a street procession. The play has been performed for about 500 years and is thought to be the oldest folk play in Germany.

CONTACTS:
Drachenstich-Festspiele e.V.
Stadtplatz 4
Furth im Wald, Bavaria 93437 Germany
49-99-735-0970; fax: 49-99-735-0985
www.drachenstich.de

♦ 0842 ♦ Dragon Boat Festival
May-June; fifth day of fifth lunar month

Chu'ü Yüan (343-289 B.C.E.) was a Chinese poet and statesman of the Ch'u kingdom who drowned himself in the Mi Lo River to protest political corruption and injustice. The colorful dragon boat races that take place on lakes and rivers throughout China, Hong Kong, and Taiwan on this day are a reenactment of the search for his body, which was never found. Although the shape of the boats has changed over time, most are narrow shells about 30-feet long with a dragon's head at the prow.

It is said that rice dumplings were cast on the water to lure fish away from the martyr's body. Chinese people in the United States and other countries celebrate the Dragon Boat Festival, which occurs on TUAN WU, or Double Fifth Day, by eating special dumplings made of steamed rice wrapped in bamboo leaves called *tsung tzu* or *zong ze*. This is also a traditional time for performing customs intended to drive away evil spirits and illness.

CONTACTS:
Hong Kong Tourism Board
370 Lexington Ave.
Ste. 1812
New York, NY 10017
212-421-3382 or 800-282-4582; fax: 212-421-8428
www.discoverhongkong.com

♦ 0843 ♦ Druids' Summer Solstice Ceremony
June 20-22

Stonehenge, the ancient stone circle located on Salisbury Plain in Wiltshire, England, is believed to have been built between about 3050 and 1600 B.C.E. The alignment of the monument's stones have led some to theorize that its builders were sun worshippers: at the SUMMER SOLSTICE, when viewed from the center of the monument, the sun rises through the entrance and just between two of the large stones.

In popular lore, Stonehenge has been associated with the ancient Celtic priests known as Druids. However, Stonehenge was built more than 2,000 years before Druids existed. Nonetheless, today modern Druids and other Neopagans gather at Stonehenge for ceremonies, although the date has been pushed forward a couple of days to avoid the crowds of tourists who flock to Stonehenge on the solstice. Wearing white robes and scarlet hoods, the Druids keep a vigil throughout the night, and when the first rays of the rising sun shine on the Altar Stone, they walk in procession around the circle, gathering at the Altar Stone to recite prayers and salute the rising sun.

Neopagans holding ceremonies in the 1980s had several run-ins with the police, so English Heritage—the British government agency that administers the national monument— closed the monument to solstice celebrations. Since 1998, however, English Heritage has gradually been allowing more and more visitors access to the monument. More than 14,000 Druids and other Neopagans peacefully saw in the summer solstice at Stonehenge in 2001.

CONTACTS:
Order of Bards Ovates & Druids
P.O. Box 1333
Lewes, East Sussex BN7 1DX United Kingdom
44-127-347-0888
www.druidry.org

♦ 0844 ♦ Drymiais
March 1-3

In Macedonia, the first three days of March are known as Drymiais and are associated with a number of superstitious beliefs. No trees are pruned or planted during this period because it is believed that they will wither. The same fate awaits trees that are pruned or planted during the last three days of March or on any Wednesday or Friday during the month.

The first day of March is traditionally considered to mark the beginning of spring. One custom is for Macedonian mothers to tie pieces of red and white yarn, twisted together, around their children's wrists on this day (*see also* MARTENITZA). When they see a swallow, the children throw the skein of yarn to the bird as an offering or place it under a stone. If they lift the stone a few days later and find a swarm of ants beneath it, they can expect a healthy and prosperous year.

♦ 0845 ♦ Duarte Day
January 26

The birthday of national hero Juan Pablo Duarte (1813-76) is an official day of remembrance in the Dominican Republic. Dominicans recognize other founding fathers—Ramón Mella and Juan Sanchez Ramírez—but these figures do not figure nearly as prominently in history as Duarte does. Known as the father of national independence, Duarte organized *La Trinitaria* in 1838, a secret resistance group whose efforts against the Haitian occupiers culminated in the Dominican Republic's declaration of independence on February 27, 1844.

Dominicans honor Duarte Day with public fiestas in major towns throughout the country. The stateliest ceremony takes place in Independence Park, located in the capital city, Santa Domingo. The park, which also hosts ceremonies for DOMINICAN REPUBLIC INDEPENDENCE DAY, features *Altar de la Patria* (the nation's altar), a mausoleum to the nation's heroes. On Duarte Day, dignitaries and citizens pay their respects at the gravesites of Duarte, Mella, and Sanchez by adorning the altar with flowers.

CONTACTS:
Dominican Republic Tourism Office
136 E. 57th St.
Ste. 805
New York, NY 10022 United States
212-588-1012 or 888-374-6361; fax: 212-588-1015
www.godominicanrepublic.com

♦ 0846 ♦ **Dublin Irish Festival**
First weekend in August

During the 19th century, a large Irish immigrant population settled in communities throughout the United States. One particular enclave established north of Columbus, Ohio, took the name of the capital of Ireland. In 1987, the first Dublin Irish Festival was held to commemorate the city's rich ethnic heritage.

The first festival was a humble affair, consisting of a small gathering of Irish dancers. The magnitude of the 20th anniversary, with over 93,000 people arriving from all over the world, showed how much the festival had grown in popularity over two decades. That same year, 10,036 festival attendees danced the Irish Jig at one time, setting a Guinness World Record for the largest Irish dance.

One of the festival's main events is the Columbus Feis, in which competitors square off in performances of a Gaelic dance known as the ceilidh (KAY-lee). The Feis, as well as shows taking place on six different stages, comprise the festival's music and dance component. Other activities include listening to storytelling and folklore at three cultural stages, eating traditional Irish food, shopping for imported Irish goods, and watching sheepherding demonstrations.

CONTACTS:
Dublin Irish Festival
6555 Shier Rings Rd.
Dublin, OH 43016
614-410-4545
www.dublinirishfestival.org

♦ 0847 ♦ **Dublin Theatre Festival**
Last Thursday in September to second Saturday in October

The Dublin Theatre Festival is an annual celebration in which artists from Ireland and around the world participate. Founded by Brendan Smith in 1957 to foster cooperation among nations in the aftermath of World War II, the event showcases stories of Dublin and its people—nurturing a sense of community. Shows are held in various locations across the city of Dublin, and the festival includes music, dance, drama, artist talks, and public discussions. Classical dramas as well as works by emerging international theater companies are presented side by side at the event.

CONTACTS:
Dublin Theatre Festival
44 E. Essex St.
Temple Bar
Dublin Ireland
353-1-677-8439; fax: 353-1-633-5918
www.dublintheatrefestival.com

♦ 0848 ♦ **Dubrovnik Summer Festival**
Mid-July to mid-August

Centuries of artistic legacy come to life each year in Croatia at the Dubrovnik Summer Festival, an international festival of music, dance, and theater. Approximately 80 performances, including opera, ballet, drama, art exhibitions, and poetry readings are offered during the course of the festival. They are staged at a variety of open-air and indoor venues, bringing to life the beautiful Renaissance and Baroque architecture of Dubrovnik.

As early as the 1920s, attempts had been made to organize an arts festival in Dubrovnik that would take advantage of the region's rich cultural heritage and its many fine stages. Many performances took place, but planning for a full-fledged festival was not realized at that time. In the aftermath of World War II, there was an upsurge of interest in the arts, as people sought healing and a new identity following the horrors of the war years. As a result, many arts festivals were established at that time, including the Dubrovnik Summer Festival.

The first full festival season in Dubrovnik took place in 1950, and it included orchestra and choral performances, five plays, and an evening of poetry. In 1956, Dubrovnik's annual Games were accepted as a member of the European Festivals Association. In the early years of the festival, the material was almost exclusively Croatian, but as the years passed, the festival expanded to include classics from the wider European tradition, including Shakespeare, Molière, Goethe, and the Greek tragedians. The 65th Dubrovnik Summer Festival was held in 2014 and featured almost 2000 artists from 12 countries, including France, Austria, the USA, Hungary, and Japan. The event boasted ticket sales of over 60,000.

CONTACTS:
Dubrovnik Summer Festival
Od Sigurate 1
Dubrovnik 20000 Croatia
385-20-326-100; fax: 385-20-326-116
www.dubrovnik-festival.hr/en

♦ 0849 ♦ **Dukang Festival**
December 15

The Dukang Festival is a trade fair and festival held in Yichuan in the Henan Province of China. This was the homeland of Dukang, who is supposed to have discovered alcoholic beverages 4,000 years ago (as Dionysus, in Greek mythology, invented wine). A Chinese folk tale tells of Dukang's beverage intoxicating the eight deities, and a poem contains the line, "Who other than Dukang can relieve me of my grief?" Dukang has become a synonym for liquor, and is also the name of a distillery in Yichuan.

The trade fair highlights not only wines and spirits but also cooking oil and food products, electrical appliances, dyes, and other manufactured goods. The festival features performances by opera troupes and dance ensembles.

CONTACTS:
China National Tourist Office
370 Lexington Ave.
Ste. 912
New York, NY 10017
212-760-8218; fax: 212-760-8809
www.cnto.org

♦ 0850 ♦ **Dulcimer and Harp Convention**
Second weekend in June

Founded in 1962 by Jean and Lee Schilling, this annual festival takes place at the Folk Life Center of the Smokies in Cosby, Tenn., which is dedicated to the study and preservation of southern Appalachian folk traditions. There is a modern amphitheater on the Center's 19-acre grounds in the foothills of the Great Smoky Mountains where most of the musical demonstrations and concerts are held. There are also workshops for those who play the musical saw, jew's harp, mountain dulcimer, hammered dulcimer, autoharp, bowed psaltery, and banjo. Both renowned instrumentalists and amateurs from all over the United States attend the two-day festival, which includes jam sessions, craft displays, and special activities for children.

CONTACTS:
State of Tennessee's Department of Tourist Development
312 Rosa L Parks Ave.
Wm Snodgrass/Tennessee Tower
Nashville, TN 37243
615-741-2159
www.tnvacation.com

♦ 0851 ♦ **Dulcimer Days**
June

The hammered dulcimer is a stringed musical instrument in which the strings are beaten with small hammers rather than plucked with the fingers. It is a favorite with American folk musicians, many of whom gather in Coshocton, Ohio, each year for the **Mid-Eastern Regional Dulcimer Championships**. The competition takes place near Roscoe Village, a restored 1830s canal town. In addition to the musical competition there are exhibits, workshops dealing with the hammered and mountain dulcimers—the latter being a narrow folk-zither with three to five metal strings—and jam sessions. The winners of the Dulcimer Days competition are

given a chance to compete in the national competition held each year in Winfield, Kansas.

CONTACTS:
Coshocton Dulcimer Days
600 N. Whitewoman St.
Coshocton, OH 43812
740-545-6265
www.coshoctondulcimerdays.com

♦ 0852 ♦ **Dundee International Guitar Festival**
July

The seaside town of Dundee, Scotland, is hardly a European epicenter; nonetheless, it has become the site of one of Europe's most prominent classical guitar festivals. Virtuosos come from the world's most prestigious conservatories to perform and lead master classes over the course of one weekend. The first festival in 1991 was a local affair, but over the years it has expanded to become an internationally recognized event.

The festival's concerts and educational programs cater particularly to young guitar students. Along with featuring international greats like Paul Galbraith and John Williams, the program also features a Young Artists Platform that puts aspiring guitarists in the spotlight. Many of the instructional subjects are designed in response to students' suggestions; and reduced rates are available for the younger players who cannot afford the full admission.

CONTACTS:
Scotland National Tourism Organization
Ocean Point One
94 Ocean Dr.
Edinburgh EH6 6JH United Kingdom
44-131-524-2121 or 845-859-1006
www.visitscotland.com

♦ 0853 ♦ **Dunmow Flitch Trial**
Every four years in July (2016, 2020, 2024…)

The custom of awarding a flitch of bacon ("flitch" refers to the side of a hog) to any married pair who have neither regretted their union nor quarrelled for a year and a day since their wedding dates back to the 13th century in England. The trial formerly took place on WHIT-MONDAY, but these days it is held every four years in July. Robert Fitzwater instituted the practice during the reign of King Henry III (1216-72), although in the beginning the flitch of bacon was only given to men, since a "happy marriage" at the time was defined as one that was satisfactory to the husband. The wife's views on the success of her marriage were not considered until the beginning of the 18th century.

While kneeling on two sharp stones in the churchyard, the applicant had to take an oath before the prior and villagers of Dunmow that he had never repented of his marriage, waking or sleeping, for a year and a day. If they believed him, he would be carried through the streets in an ancient wooden chair. Given the fact that there were only three prizewinners between 1445 and 1510, it must be assumed that the standard to which the applicants were held was very high.

Today, claimants for the Dunmow Flitch are required to answer questions about their marriage at a mock trial, presided over by a judge. A jury consisting of six spinsters and six bachelors gives the verdict, and the proceedings are usually lighthearted, although there are always some genuine candidates for the flitch as well as those who only take part for amusement.

CONTACTS:
Great Dunmow Town Council Office
Foakes' House
47 Stortford Rd.
Great Dunmow, Essex CM6 1DG United Kingdom
www.uttlesford.gov.uk

♦ 0854 ♦ **Durban International Film Festival**
July

Established in 1979, the Durban International Film Festival is organized annually by the Centre for Creative Arts of the University of Kwazulu-Natal in Durban, South Africa. Over 250 films belonging to various categories are screened every year, but African films receive prime importance. The Centre for Creative Arts collaborates with the Wavescape Surf Film Festival and the Durban Wild Talk Africa Film Festival. Wavescape highlights films related to surfing; Durban Wild Talk focuses on the wildlife of Africa. A handful of films from both festivals are chosen and screened during the Durban International Film Festival.

The festival also features a series of workshops in which filmmakers share their experiences of filming in Africa and participate in professional development activities. The Durban Film Mart is a film finance and co-production market. Through this endeavor, the producers of 20 African films receive an opportunity to promote their projects and talk with financiers about funding them. The Talent Campus Durban program gives shortlisted participants the chance to interact with industry experts through master classes, workshops, and networking events.

CONTACTS:
Centre for Creative Arts
University of KwaZulu-Natal
Howard College Campus
Durban 4041 South Africa
27-31-260-2506; fax: 27-31-260-3074
www.durbanfilmfest.co.za

♦ 0855 ♦ **Durga Puja**
September-October; waxing half of Hindu month of Asvina

There are various Hindu festivals on the Indian subcontinent that celebrate the victory of good over evil.

The festival in Calcutta, India, in the state of West Bengal, honors Durga, who rides a lion and destroys demons. She is one aspect of the Mother Goddess and the personification of energy, and is famous for slaying the buffalo demon, Mahisasura. During the 10 days of Durga Puja, the city becomes one great festival, with deafening music and fireworks. Before the *puja* (a Sanskrit word meaning "worship" or "homage"), artisans have constructed clay figures over straw-and-bamboo frames, some of them 10 feet high. Stages are set up for these figures in neighborhoods throughout the city, and for four days throngs of people admire the clay tableaux, often showing Durga on a lion slaying demons. (Artist Aloke Sen's images have become famous because his demons have the faces of ordinary men and women and represent such evils as lust, anger, vanity, and greed.) On the fourth night, the images, which are genuine works of art and have cost as much as $20,000, are taken down from the stages, placed on bamboo stretchers, and carried—to the music of hundreds of bagpipers and other musicians—to the banks of the Hooghly River and tossed in. As they float toward the mouth of the Ganges, they dissolve back into clay, straw, and bamboo.

Navaratri. In the states of southern India this festival is known as Navaratri (nine nights), and also involves the worship of the goddesses Lakshmi and Sarasvati. Lakshmi is linked with wealth and good luck, and Sarasvati is associated with a river of that name, as well as with fertility, wisdom, and education. The festival is a time for visiting friends and relatives, and houses are decorated with displays of toys and dolls and images of gods. In the state of Gujarat there are nine days of music and dancing devoted to the nine forms of the goddess Ambaji, as well as competitions of *garba* dancing.

Dussehra (or **Dashara**). In other parts of India the festival also celebrates the victory of Lord Rama over Ravana, and is known as Dussehra (or Dashara).

During the 10 days of Dussehra, scenes from the epic poem *Ramayana* are enacted. The epic tells the story of Lord Rama who wins the lovely Sita for his wife, only to have her carried off by evil 10-headed Ravana, demon king of Lanka. Ultimately, Rama slays Ravana, and the forces of good triumph over evil. The dramatizations with music, held throughout northern India, are considered at their best in Delhi. On the 10th day, immense effigies of Ravana, his brother, and his son (all of them stuffed with firecrackers) explode in dramatic bursts of flame and noise (*see also* RAMA LEELA FESTIVAL).

In the northern mountains of Himachal Pradesh, the festival begins with a procession of deities to the town of Kulu from the little hill temples of neighboring villages. Accompanying the deities are villagers blowing large horns, ringing bells, and beating drums. When a deity arrives in Kulu, it is placed before Raghunathji, the presiding god of Kulu Valley, who is in an honored position in a tent. Outside, there is folk dancing and music. On the final day of the festival, a bull is sacrificed as a gift to the gods.

Mysore, in the state of Karnataka, celebrates the victory of goddess Chamundi over demon Mahisasura with regal pomp. The palace of the maharajah is illuminated, there are torchlight and daylight parades, and deities on decorated barges in a floodlit lake. On the final day, there is a grand procession of magnificently caparisoned elephants, the camel corps, the cavalry, and the infantry.

Dasain. In Nepal, the festival is called Dasain, or Bada Dasain. It comes at the end of the long monsoon period when days are clear and the rice is ready for harvesting, and lasts for 10 days.

In Nepal, Buddhists also celebrate this festival and special events are held at Buddhist shrines in Patan and Bhaktapur. The Nepalese also modify the *Ramayana* story to include the goddess Durga's victory over the forces of evil represented by the demon Mahisasura. Since Durga is bloodthirsty, there are thousands of animal sacrifices.

Before the festival begins, Nepalese clean their houses and set up ferris wheels and swings in their villages. On the first day of the festival, a water jug called a *kalash* is filled with holy water, and barley seeds are planted in cow dung on the outside of the jug. During the festival, the seeds are sprinkled with the water, and ceremonies are performed around it.

The first big day of the festival is the seventh day, Fulpati, meaning "day of flowers." A royal kalash holding flowers is carried by Brahmin priests from the ancestral palace in Gurkha to Katmandu. Cannons boom, the king and queen review troops, and then revere the flowers at the Hanuman Dhoka Palace, the old residence of kings.

The eighth night is known as Kalratri, or "black night." At midnight, at Hanuman Dhoka, eight buffaloes and 108 goats are beheaded. During the next day, thousands of buffaloes, goats, and chickens are sacrificed in temples, military posts, and homes as people ask Durga for protection. Blood is sprinkled on the wheels of vehicles, and at the airport, a goat is sacrificed for each Royal Nepal Airlines aircraft.

The 10th day, Vijaya Dashami, commemorates the day that Durga (or Rama) appeared riding a lion to slay the Mahisasura (or Ravana). On this day, people wear the fresh shoots of the barley in their hair and visit older relatives to receive the red *tika* blessing on their foreheads. In towns of the Katmandu Valley, there are masked dances and processions of priests carrying wooden swords, symbolic of the sword used to kill the buffalo demon.

Caitra Dasain, observed in the month of Caitra (March-April), is similar to Bada Dasain, but observed with less pomp. On this earlier occasion, the goddess is worshipped and animal sacrifices are made to her.

CONTACTS:
Ministry of Tourism, Government of India
1270 Ave. of the Americas
Ste. 303
New York, NY 10020
212-586-4901 or 212-586-4902; fax: 212-582-3274
tourism.gov.in

Department of Tourism, Government of West Bengal
New Secretariat Bldg.
1, K. S. Roy Rd.
3rd Fl.
Kolkata, Tamil Nadu 700001 West Bengal

33-2225-4723 or 33-2225-4724
www.wbtourism.gov.in

♦ 0856 ♦ Durham Miners' Gala
Second Saturday of July

With the emergence of coal mining in the 17th century, England began enjoying the fruits of a lucrative industry. But the miners did not always receive fair compensation. Soon after founding the first union in 1869, a group of mine workers in northern England initiated a campaign to lobby their pit bosses, who met regularly to set mining wages at the Royal County Hotel in the city of Durham.

Soon an annual tradition developed in which mine workers arrived at the hotel in grand style, bringing with them brass bands and colorful silk banners that identified their unions. What began as a formal protest became a grand party, and by 1871, the first official Durham Miners' Gala was held.

Today, the gala is less political in nature. It has become more of a heritage celebration of coal mining, an industry that has steadily decreased over the years. The event usually features about 30 community brass bands, which march through the streets of Durham with banners representing member organizations of the National Union of Mineworkers. The procession ends at the Racecourse of Durham University, where attendees gather to hear speeches from trade union leaders and politicians.

CONTACTS:
Durham Miners' Association
P.O. Box 6
The Miners Hall
Durham DH1 4BB United Kingdom
www.durhamminers.org

♦ 0857 ♦ Dutch Liberation Day
May 4-5

Liberation Day, or **National Day**, in the Netherlands celebrates May 5, 1945, the day on which the Nazi forces were driven out of Holland by the Allies. Although the Dutch hadsucceeded in remaining neutral during World War I, the country was invaded by the Nazis in May 1940 and rapidly overrun. Despite the occupation, however, the Dutch managed to make a significant contribution to the Allied cause by building up an effective resistance. The liberation of Holland in 1945, in which the resistance played a leading part, was an important step toward the subsequent defeat of the Nazis.country on May 5 each year, as well as on May 4, Remem-brance Day.

CONTACTS:
National Committee 4 and 5 May
Nieuwe Prinsengracht 89
Amsterdam, VR 1018 Netherlands
31-20-718-3500; fax: 31-20-718-3501
www.4en5mei.nl/english

E

♦ 0858 ♦ **Eagle Dance**
Early spring

Many North American Indians associate the eagle with supernatural powers, particularly the power to control thunder and rain. In the Jemez and Tesuque pueblos in New Mexico, the eagle dance takes place in the early spring. Two dancers, representing male and female, wear feathered caps with yellow beaks and hold wings made out of eagle feathers. They circle each other with hopping and swaying motions.

The Comanches hold an eagle dance where a single dancer imitates the eagle, who according to legend is the young son of a chieftain who was turned into an eagle when he died. Dancers in the Iowa tribe's eagle dance carry an eagle feather fan in their left hands, while the Iroquois eagle dance features feathered rattles and wands.

Among some tribes, eagle feathers are believed to exert special powers. The Sioux wear them in their war bonnets for victory, while the Pawnee, Yuchi, Delaware, and Iroquois Indians use them in ceremonial fans or brushes or as orna- ments.

♦ 0859 ♦ **Earhart (Amelia) Festival**
Weekend closest to July 24

To celebrate the birthday of noted aviator and Atchison native Amelia Earhart, the town of Atchison, Kans., holds the Amelia Earhart Festival on the weekend closest to her July 24th birthday. Earhart was born in Atchison in 1897 and lived there with her grandparents until 1908. The winner of many world records in the history of aviation, Earhart was the first woman to fly across the Atlantic Ocean on her own. In 1937, while attempting to fly around the world, Earhart went missing over the Pacific Ocean and is presumed to have crashed.

The festival began in 1997 to mark the 100th anniversary of the hometown heroine's birth. Among the weekend events are aerobatic performances over the Missouri River, including an exhibition of wing-walking, a birthday party for Earhart, including free cake, an outdoor country music concert, a one-hour trolley tour of Earhart-related sites in town, a children's stage featuring puppet shows and live animals, a toy airplane contest, talks and documentary films about Earhart's life, and a riverside fireworks display set to music.

The Amelia Earhart Pioneering Achievement Award is also presented to a woman who has contributed to the field of aviation.

CONTACTS:
Atchison Chamber of Commerce
200 S. Tenth
P.O. Box 126
Atchison, KS 66002
913-367-2427 or 800-234-1854; fax: 913-367-2485
www.atchisonkansas.net

♦ 0860 ♦ **Earth Day**
April 22

The first Earth Day was observed on April 22, 1970, for the purpose of drawing public attention to the need for cleaning up the earth's air and water and for conserving our natural resources. Since that time the idea has spread, and Earth Day is now observed regularly throughout the United States and in many other countries (though there were some years of slack observance until the late 1980s).

Typical ways of celebrating Earth Day include planting trees, picking up roadside trash, and conducting various programs for recycling and conservation. Schoolchildren may be asked to use only recyclable containers for their snacks and lunches, and environmentally concerned families often try to give up wasteful habits, such as using paper towels or plastic garbage bags.

"Earth" days have been observed by other groups as well. The day of the VERNAL EQUINOX is also observed by some as Earth Day.

CONTACTS:
Earth Day Network
1616 P St. N.W.
Ste. 340
Washington, D.C. 20036
202-518-0044
www.earthday.org

♦ 0861 ♦ **East Timor Independence Day**
May 20

On May 20, 2002, about half of a small island in the Lesser Sundra group became the Democratic Republic of East Timor after being an unwilling and brutalized province of Indonesia for the previous two decades and under Portuguese colonial rule for hundreds of years before that. Among the approximately 200,000 attendees at the independence ceremony in the capital city of Dili were Bishop Carlos Belo and Jose Ramos Horta, who won the NOBEL Peace Prize in 1996 for their efforts toward building the peaceful independence of this Roman Catholic region within Indonesia, the largest Muslim country in the world.

CONTACTS:
Embassy of the United States in Timor-leste
Avenida de Portugal
Praia dos Coqueiros
Dili Timor-leste
670-332-4684; fax: 670-331-3206
timor-leste.gov.tl

♦ 0862 ♦ Easter

Between March 22 and April 25 in the West and between April 4 and May 8 in the East; first Sunday after the first full moon on or following the vernal equinox

Easter is the principal feast of the Christian year, despite the popularity and commercialization that surrounds CHRISTMAS. According to the Gospel of John, Mary Magdalene came to the cave where Jesus had been buried and found the tomb empty. An angel of the Lord told her that Jesus had risen. The anniversary of his resurrection from the dead is joyfully celebrated by Christians every year with special services, music, candlelight, flowers, and the ringing of church bells that had remained silent during LENT.

For Greek Orthodox Christians, the sorrow of GOOD FRIDAY lifts with the service of the Holy Resurrection on Saturday night in a dimly lit church. At midnight, all lights are extinguished, the door to the altar opens and the priest, holding a lighted candle, appears and proclaims that Christ is risen. The congregants light their candles from the priest's, bells ring, people turn to each other and say, *Christos Anesti,* "Christ is risen," and receive the reply, *Alithos Anesti,* "He is risen indeed."

Easter is a movable holiday whose day of observation has for centuries been painstakingly calculated. This is because its day of observance is determined initially by the lunar calendar, like PASSOVER, but then must be put into terms of the solar calendar. The Council of Nicea in 325 C.E. set the formula for calculating the date of Easter still in use today. After many centuries of controversy among Christians, Western Christendom settled on the use of the Gregorian calendar (Eastern Christians use the Julian calendar to determine Easter), decreeing that Easter shall be celebrated on the Sunday after the full moon on or following the VERNAL EQUINOX. If the full moon is on a Sunday, Easter is held the next Sunday. In the East, Easter can occur between April 4 and May 8, but it must come after Passover has ended.

The name for Easter may have come from *Eostre,* the Teutonic goddess of spring and fertility, whose feast was celebrated around this same time. There is also a Germanic goddess named Ostara who was always accompanied by a hare—possibly the ancestor of our modern Easter Bunny. The association of both the rabbit and eggs with Easter is probably the vestige of an ancient springtime fertility rite.

Although Easter has retained a greater religious significance than Christmas, many children in the United States think of it as a time to get new spring clothes, to decorate eggs, and to indulge in the chocolate and jelly beans that the Easter Bunny has left in their Easter baskets.

In Belgium, throughout Walloonia, the priest gives a number of unconsecrated priest's wafers to young children to sell to householders. The proceeds are given to the needy parish families, and the wafers are nailed over the front doors to protect the families from evil.

In Ethiopia, Easter is called **Fasika** and is welcomed in the capital city of Addis Ababa at dawn with a 21-gun salute.

♦ 0863 ♦ Easter (Bulgaria)

Between April 4 and May 8

Although midnight church services are widespread throughout Bulgaria on **Velikden** (The Great Day), or **Vuzkresenie** (Resurrection Day), the EASTER service held in the cathedral in Sofia, the capital, is by far the most impressive. Just before midnight on Easter morning, the traditional hour of Christ's resurrection, a procession of church dignitaries in elaborate vestments follows the archbishop from the cathedral to Alexander Nevsky Square, which is already filled with thousands of worshippers carrying unlighted candles. As the midnight chimes peal, the archbishop blesses the people and the thousands of candles are lit. A service in the cathedral follows.

Easter celebrations in Bulgaria last a full week, known as *Svetla Nedelya,* or the Week of Light, because folklore has it that the sun did not set in Jerusalem for eight days after the resurrection of Christ. One tradition during this week is the national dance known as the *Choro,* which is performed by a circle composed of equal numbers of male and female dancers who begin with a very slow movement that gradually quickens in pace.

CONTACTS:
Embassy of the Republic of Bulgaria
1621 22nd St. N.W.
Dimitar Peshev Plaza
Washington, D.C. 20008
202-387-0174; fax: 202-234-7973
www.bulgaria-embassy.org

Ministry of Economy, Energy and Tourism of Republic of Bulgaria
8 Slavianska St.
Sofia 1052 Bulgaria
359-294-07001; fax: 359-298-72190
old.mee.government.bg

♦ 0864 ♦ Easter (Chile)

Between March 22 and April 25

HOLY WEEK or Semana Santa, the week that precedes EASTER, is a very solemn period in Chile, most of whose inhabitants are Roman Catholic. It is a time to remember the death and resurrection of Christ, and the primary activity for adults is going to church to pray. Children, on the other hand, drag large dolls, who represent Judas, through the streets of their neighborhood in carts or wagons, stopping at houses to request coins. These coins represent the 30 pieces of silver given to Judas for turning Jesus over to the authorities. When the day is over, children set fire to the dolls, under their parents' supervision. On Easter Sunday itself, there are Easter egg hunts and baskets filled with chocolates.

Cuasimodo is the first Sunday following Easter. In the villages and little towns of rural central and southern Chile, religious processions take place, led by priests, who bring Holy Communion to those who are too sick or elderly to make it to church. This is a tradition that extends back more than 100 years, when many Chileans lived too far out in the country to travel to church on Cuasimodo. Because bandits were common and likely to attack the priest, he would usually be accompanied by cowboys known as *huasos*. Although there are no longer any bandits, huasos still like to display their horsemanship on Cuasimodo, when horse-riding contests are frequently held. Today cyclists also escort the priest.

CONTACTS:
Embassy of Chile
1732 Massachusetts Ave., N.W.
Washington, D.C. 20036
202-785-1746
www.chile-usa.org

◆ 0865 ◆ Easter (Cyprus)
Between April 4 and May 8

On EASTER Sunday in Cyprus, fireworks are set off, ships in ports blow their whistles, and bonfires are built to burn Judas. People go home for a late dinner starting with red-dyed hard-boiled eggs and then a special soup and often cheese pie (*tiropita*). It's customary to tap the eggs against each other; whoever cracks the other's egg will have good luck in the coming year. Often there is feasting on lamb roasted on spits over open fires; other traditional foods are *kokoretsi*, a sausage made of lamb innards and herbs, and *lambropsomo*, an Easter bread with a whole red-dyed egg in the center. In the countryside, the feasting is accompanied by fairs and dancing in regional costume. Passersby are offered lamb, red eggs, and wine and are toasted with "Christos Anesti.".

CONTACTS:
Cyprus Tourism Organisation
Leoforos Lemesou 19
Aglantzia, Lefkosia 2112 Cyprus
357-226-91100; fax: 357-223-31644
www.visitcyprus.com

◆ 0866 ◆ Easter (Czech Republic)
Between March 22 and April 25

In the Czech Republic, EASTER (**Velikonoce**) is celebrated as both a religious holy day and a seasonal festival that marks the end of winter.

For breakfast on Easter Sunday (*Nedele velikonocní*), Czechs eat *mazanec*, a traditional raisin-filled sweet bun spiced with nutmeg, topped with almonds, and marked with a cross before baking. Roast lamb or goat is the customary Easter dinner fare. The day itself is filled with preparations for traditional activities that take place the following day on EASTER MONDAY, known as Whipping Monday.

On that day young boys and adolescents visit the homes of girls they admire to sing carols and whip the girls symbolically with pomlázka—pussy willow branches that have been braided into wands and decorated with colored ribbons. In return, the girls give boys such treats as *kraslice* (decorated eggs) or chocolate. The pussy willow branches symbolize youth and fertility. Though the custom is dying out in larger cities, the ritual, which is documented in writings extending back as far as the 14th century, continues in villages.

CONTACTS:
Czech Tourist Authority - CzechTourism
1109 Madison Ave.
New York, NY 10028
212-288-0830; fax: 212-288-0971
www.czechtourism.com

◆ 0867 ◆ Easter (Egypt)
Between April 4 and May 8

EASTER in Egypt is celebrated by the nation's population of Christians, about seven percent of the total population (or 12 million people). The majority of Christians in Egypt belongs to the Coptic Orthodox branch of the church, which is based in Alexandria and Cairo. The Coptic Orthodox Church dates back to the first century and was founded by the apostle Mark, one of the four gospel authors. Significant numbers of Egyptians also belong to various Eastern and Roman Catholic rites, including the Greek Orthodox Church, the Coptic Catholic Church, the Melkite Greek Catholic Church, or to Protestant denominations such as the Coptic Evangelical Church.

In preparation for Easter, the high feast commemorating the resurrection of Jesus, Coptic Orthodox adherents observe a period of LENT comprising 55 days of fasting. During this time all foods derived from animals are prohibited, including meat, fish, eggs, and milk. A diet limited to vegetables and beans is followed during HOLY WEEK, the week leading up to Easter Sunday, and during this period people attend church services every day. On Saturday night, they attend a long Easter Vigil service, which continues through much of the night, ending in the early hours of Easter Sunday morning. Families then return home to break the long period of fasting and celebrate with a feast of roasted turkey or lamb with grape leaves. Children receive small gifts of money or clothing. In Cairo the pope of the Coptic Orthodox Church presides over a national Easter service in the Great Cathedral of St. Mark that is attended by thousands of the congregation as well as numerous government and religious dignitaries. A public holiday celebrating the beginning of spring is held on the day after Easter, and this is a popular day for picnics and visiting family and friends.

CONTACTS:
Tourism Development Authority
Egypt
202-3568-8844; fax: 202-3569-0653
www.tda.gov.eg

♦ 0868 ♦ **Easter (Germany) (Ostern)**
Between March 22 and April 25

The first recorded evidence of a rabbit being associated with EASTER dates from the 16th century in Germany, although the custom may be even older. The Easter hare still brings eggs to German children and hides them in out-of-the-way places, although in the past, the stork, the fox, and the cuckoo have played the same role. In many parts of Germany, little "rabbit gardens" are built for the Easter Bunny, using moss or grass as a nest for the eggs. Egg-gathering and egg-rolling are both popular activities at Easter, as are contests to see who can devour the greatest number of eggs.

Perhaps a remnant of ancient sacrificial rites, bonfires are built on high points of land in northern Germany. Although usually built out of huge piles of tar-soaked barrels and old tree roots and limbs, in the North Rhine-Westphalian village of Luegde, bonfires are made by tying twigs and straw to seven-foot wheels, lighting them, and rolling them down the hill. The flaming wheels, symbolic of the sun, weigh about 800 pounds each. Every time one of them reaches the bottom of the hill, the spectators shout for joy, for it is believed that this will bring a special blessing to the land and a bountiful harvest.

Water is also associated with Easter celebrations in Germany. One old custom entails girls in the Harz Mountains, Thuringia, and other regions rising at dawn to draw "Easter water" from the rivers. If they do so in complete silence and then bathe in the water, they will be blessed with beauty throughout the year. Easter morning dew is used for the same purpose.

"Easter smacks," or *Schmeckostern*, are traditional beatings that the men and women give to each other in various parts of Germany to bring them luck, to protect them from disease, and to keep them young and healthy. The men beat the women on EASTER MONDAY, and the women beat the men on Easter Tuesday. The new life contained by a green branch is supposed to be bestowed on the one who is beaten with it.

♦ 0869 ♦ **Easter (Hollywood, California)**
Between March 22 and April 25

The early Christians believed that on EASTER morning, the sun danced in honor of the resurrection of Christ. This led to the custom of rising before dawn to witness the phenomenon and may be the reason why sunrise services on Easter morning are common throughout the United States.

At the Hollywood Bowl, a huge outdoor amphitheater in the Hollywood Hills, California, the Easter sunrise service is a spectacle on a scale that only Hollywood could produce. First held in 1921, the service is attended by about 30,000 people who spend the night in the stadium. About 50,000 calla lilies decorate the stage, where a huge choir and a symphony orchestra perform the *Hallelujah* chorus from Handel's *Messiah* and traditional Easter hymns. Some 250 teenagers form a "living cross" just after dawn.

CONTACTS:
Hollywood Bowl
2301 N. Highland Ave.
Los Angeles, CA 90068
323-850-2000
www.hollywoodbowl.com

♦ 0870 ♦ **Easter (Italy) (La Pasqua)**
Between March 22 and April 25

In many Italian towns and villages sacred dramas commemorating episodes in the EASTER story or from the Bible are held in the *piazzas* on Easter day. Pastries called *corona di nove* are baked in the form of a crown; in America, these pastries are often made in the shape of rabbits instead. Other traditional foods of the season include *capretto* (lamb) and *agnello* (kid).

In Florence, the Ceremony of the Car, or *Scoppio del Carro*, is held on HOLY SATURDAY. Inaugurated by the ancient Florentine family of de'Pazzi, the custom involves a decorated wooden car filled with explosives, which is drawn into the piazza by white oxen and placed before the cathedral doors. A wire runs from the high altar inside the cathedral to the car in the piazza. As the mass ends, a dove-shaped rocket is ignited at the altar and sent shooting out along the wire. When it reaches the car, it sets fire to the explosives. Tuscan farmers believe that if the rocket does its job well, their harvests will prosper in the coming year. If it fails to ignite the *carro* or if something else goes wrong, their crops in the coming season will be poor.

CONTACTS:
Italian National Tourist Board
686 Park Ave., 3rd Fl.
New York, NY 10065
212-245-5618; fax: 212-586-9249
www.italiantourism.com

♦ 0871 ♦ **Easter (Netherlands) (Paschen, Paasch Zondag)**
Between March 22 and April 25

The lighting of bonfires is a common occurrence on EASTER or Easter Eve in the Netherlands. The fuel is collected weeks in advance, and neighboring towns often compete with each other to see which can build the biggest fire. As the flames get higher, the villagers join hands and dance around the fire. In ancient times, bits of charred wood carried home from the bonfire were believed to protect people's houses from fire and other disasters during the year.

In the village of Denekamp, in the province of Overijssel, two young men who represent the comic characters known as Judas and Iscariot—Judas being "the clever man" and Iscariot being "the stupid man"—prepare the Easter bonfire and help set up the "Easter pole," which is a tall fir tree that has been stripped of its branches, cut down, and carried to the hill where the bonfire will be lit. Judas sets a ladder against the tree, climbs up, and starts auctioning it to the highest bidder. The crowd hoots and jeers at him and at Iscariot, who replaces him. At eight o'clock in the evening the fire is lit, and the townspeople dance and sing a very old hymn whose dialect words and meanings are understood only by local people.

In the eastern Netherlands village of Ootmarsum, the VLÖG-GELEN, or "winging ceremony," is held on Easter Sunday and Monday.

See also EASTER MONDAY IN THE NETHERLANDS.

♦ 0872 ♦ Easter (Norway) (Paske)
Between March 22 and April 25

EASTER in Norway is a popular time to go to mountain resorts and enjoy winter sports. From MAUNDY THURSDAY through EASTER MONDAY, the towns and cities are deserted, but every mountain inn and hotel is packed to overflowing with those who come to ski, skate, toboggan, and enjoy watching others pursue such activities. Ice carnivals, sports competitions, dances, and concerts are also popular, and many mountain resorts hold special out-of-doors Easter services for skiers.

Norwegians who observe the holiday at home dye and decorate Easter eggs after boring small holes in the ends and blowing out the yolk and white, or by carefully cutting the shells in half and then pasting them together again with strips of paper. The decorated eggs are hidden all over the house, and on Easter morning, everyone hunts for the eggs that have been concealed for them by other family members.

♦ 0873 ♦ Easter (Poland) (Wielkanoc)
Between March 22 and April 25

After attending the EASTER church service, Polish families gather to share a cold meal, for the day is considered too sacred to light a fire. The head of the family cuts up a colored egg and gives a piece of it to everyone present. Each person then offers an Easter greeting to the others. The meal itself usually consists of ham, sausages, salads, *babka* (the Polish national cake), and *mazurki*, or sweet cakes filled with nuts, fruit, and honey.

On EASTER MONDAY, people don old clothes and engage in a water-throwing game known as *smigus*. Children often throw decorated eggshells into a stream, in hopes that their Easter wishes will reach those who live beneath the earth.

CONTACTS:
Polish American Journal
P.O. Box 271
North Boston, NY 14110
716-312-8088 or 800-422-1275
www.polamjournal.com

♦ 0874 ♦ Easter (Russia) (Paskha)
Between April 4 and May 8

EASTER is one of the most important holidays of the Russian year. A great deal of attention is devoted to the preparation of *koulich*, a very tall Easter cake made according to a traditional recipe and a major part of the Easter meal that breaks the Lenten fast. Pillows are often placed around the pan while the dough is rising, because any jarring might cause the cake to fall. Husbands often complain that they've been kicked out of the house because their heavy footsteps are disturbing the koulich. The finished cake is usually marked with the initials X and B, which stand for the Russian words meaning "Christ is risen."

On Easter Sunday and Monday the men visit each other, but Easter Tuesday is reserved for the women to call on their friends. In rural areas it is customary for children to swing, dance, and play games and musical instruments on this day. Church bells ring throughout the Easter holiday.

CONTACTS:
Russian Orthodox Church
Department of External Relations
22, Danilovsky val
Danilov monastery DECR MP
Moscow 115191 Russia
749-5633-8428; fax: 749-5633-8428
mospat.ru/en

♦ 0875 ♦ Easter (Spain)
Between March 22 and April 25

After attending EASTER morning mass, many Spanish people throng the cafes and restaurants to break their Lenten fast. In the afternoon, residents of Madrid, Seville, and other cities usually attend bullfights. In villages in southern Valencia, such as Jumilla and Alcañiz, the coming of Easter is marked by a *tamborada*—three days of non-stop drumming. Residents of Hellin are treated to the pounding of 8,000 to 10,000 drums between Holy Wednesday and Easter Sunday.

The shop windows of confectioners and pastry cooks are filled with elaborate displays of cakes around Easter. Sometimes a farmyard is made out of pastry, with hens, cocks, and monkeys. A special pastry known as a *mona* (female monkey) contains a hard-boiled egg, and elaborate and ingenious monas are often given as Easter presents.

In the region of Spain known as Catalonia, HOLY WEEK *pasos* (tableaux) are formed by men standing on each other's shoulders to form a kind of circular pyramid, with a small child standing on the top. Easter pasos often illustrate a biblical scene, such as the Descent from the Cross.

♦ 0876 ♦ Easter (Sweden) (Påskdagen)
Between March 22 and April 25

EASTER in Sweden is a time for winter sports. Thousands of people from Stockholm and other southern cities board special excursion trains and spend the Easter holidays in the northern provinces, where winter sports are at their peak.

On either MAUNDY THURSDAY or Easter Eve, children often dress up as witches and call on their neighbors, much as children in the United States do on HALLOWEEN. Sometimes they slip a secret "Easter letter" under the door or in the mailbox. Bonfires are popular in the western provinces of Sweden, with competitions to see which village can build the biggest fire. The witches and bonfires are reminiscent of pagan ceremonies to ward off evil, and in rural areas people still hang crossed scythes in their stables or paint crosses over their doors to protect themselves against the evil spread by Easter hags flying around on their broomsticks.

CONTACTS:
VisitSweden - Tourism and Travel Information Office
P.O. Box 4649
Grand Central Stn
New York, NY 10163
212-885-9700; fax: 212-885-9710
www.visitsweden.com

♦ 0877 ♦ **Easter (Ukraine)**
Between April 4 and May 8

Decorating eggs is the EASTER custom for which Ukrainians are known all over the world. The *pysanky* eggs are not cooked because the raw egg shell absorbs the color better.

The initial design is drawn on the shell with a *pysar*, or small, metal-tipped writing tool, dipped in beeswax. When the egg is dipped in the first dye (usually yellow, the lightest color), the wax prevents any dye from being absorbed. When the next layer of the design is drawn on the shell, it will remain yellow while the rest of the egg is dyed a darker color (usually orange or red). This layering process continues until the desired artistic effect is achieved. Then the egg is held over a candle flame to melt off the wax and is coated with shellac or varnish. A woman who is particularly adept at decorating Easter eggs is called a *pysarka*.

The eggs are presented as gifts to friends and relatives on Easter morning. One of the decorated eggs that has been hard-boiled is shelled, sliced up, and served at the beginning of the Easter dinner to symbolize the end of the Lenten fast. Sometimes the eggs are used in a game where children try to strike each other's eggs with their own. But due to the eggs' religious significance and the work that goes into decorating them, the shells are never dropped on the ground or discarded. If broken, they are usually thrown into fire or water.

CONTACTS:
Ukrainian Museum
222 E. 6th St.
New York, NY 10003
212-228-0110; fax: 212-228-1947
www.ukrainianmuseum.org

Ukrainian Orthodox Church of the USA
Metropolia Center
135 Davidson Ave.
Somerset, NJ 08873

732-356-0090; fax: 732-356-5556
www.uocofusa.org

♦ 0878 ♦ **Easter (Yaqui Indians)**
Between March 22 and April 25

Although they were originally Mexican, the Yaqui Indians resettled in Arizona, and most of them now live near Tucson or Phoenix. During HOLY WEEK they perform a series of dances and pageants that combine Christian, Native American, and Spanish customs. They act out their own version of the biblical events associated with EASTER, using spectacular masks and costumes and incorporating the complicated symbolism of their native culture as well as such recognizable Christian figures as Jesus, the Virgin Mary, Judas, and Pilate.

When the Yaqui lived in Mexico, a group of ritual clowns known as the Chapayekas played the role of police during the Easter week celebrations. They wore masks made out of goat or wild pig skin with long ears and snouts (*chapayekas* means "long slender noses") and huge horns. They maintained a ritual silence and communicated only by sign language. Today they still play a part in Yaqui Easter observances, performing dances during Easter processions and church services.

CONTACTS:
Pascua Yaqui Tribe
7474 S. Camino de Oeste
Tucson, AZ 85746
520-883-5000; fax: 520-883-5014
www.pascuayaqui-nsn.gov

♦ 0879 ♦ **Easter Egg Roll**
Between March 23 and April 26; Monday following Easter

Starting in the middle of the 19th century, it was customary for young children to roll EASTER eggs on the lawn of the Capitol Building in Washington, D.C. But Congress objected to the damage they inflicted on the grass and in 1878 stationed guards there to halt the practice. President Rutherford B. Hayes, who enjoyed children, said they could use the White House lawn. President Franklin D. ROOSEVELT stopped the custom during World War II, but then it was restored again in 1953 by President Dwight D. Eisenhower.

Today the Egg Roll takes place on the Ellipse behind the White House, and children up to age eight are invited to participate. In addition to rolling their own hard-boiled eggs, the children hunt for about 1,000 wooden eggs—many of them signed by past presidents or celebrities—that have been hidden in the grass. A crowd of up to 10,000 adults and children gathers for the annual event, and sometimes the president greets the crowd from the balcony of the White House.

CONTACTS:
White House
1600 Pennsylvania Ave. N.W.
Washington, D.C. 20500
202-456-7041
www.whitehouse.gov

National Archives and Records Administration (NARA)
Prologue: Quarterly Journal of the NARA
700 Pennsylvania Ave. N.W.
Washington, D.C. 20408
202-357-5000 or 866-325-7208
www.archives.gov

♦ 0880 ♦ Easter Festival (Osterfestspiele)
Begins between March 15 and April 18 and ends between March 22 and April 26; Palm Sunday through Easter Monday

Salzburg's Easter Festival was founded by the famous conductor Herbert von Karajan (1908-1989) in 1967 to honor the works of Richard Wagner (1813-1883), and it remains one of Europe's most elite and elegant music festivals. Those who attend pay top prices, but in return they get to hear some of the world's greatest performers. The Berlin Philharmonic Orchestra is the festival's resident ensemble, and the chorus of the Vienna State Opera or the Choir of the Society of Friends of Music in Vienna perform the choral works. Von Karajan himself conducted all of the concerts, which includethe works of Johann Sebastian BACH (1685-1750), Ludwig van Beethoven (1770-1827), Johannes Brahms (1833-1897), GustavMahler (1860-1911), Wolfgang Amadeus MOZART (1756-1791) and Giuseppe Verdi (1813-1901), until his death in 1989. Now various conductors are invited. A full-scale opera is performed twice during each nine-day festival in the *Grosses Festspielhaus* (large festival hall), which is known for its unique acoustics and seats more than 2,000.

CONTACTS:
Salzburg Easter Festival
Herbert-von-Karajan-Platz 9
Salzburg 5020 Austria
43-662-8045-361; fax: 43-662-8045-790
www.osterfestspiele-salzburg.at

♦ 0881 ♦ Easter Fires
March-April; Easter eve

The tradition of hillside fires on EASTER eve in Fredericksburg, Tex., is thought to have begun many years ago, soon after the town's settlement by German farmers in 1846. A pioneer mother, to calm her children, told them the fires burning on the town's hillside had been lit by the Easter Bunny to boil their Easter eggs. In reality, the fires were those of Indians who were watching the settlement. Since the 1940s the fires have blazed at the Gillespie County Fairgrounds in Fredericksburg in an Easter pageant with a cast of more than 600 that portrays the local legend.

CONTACTS:
Fredericksburg Convention & Visitor Bureau
302 E. Austin St.
Fredericksburg, TX 78624
830-997-6523 or 888-997-3600; fax: 830-997-8588
www.visitfredericksburgtx.com

♦ 0882 ♦ Easter Monday
Between March 23 and April 26; Monday after Easter

Although EASTER Sunday is the culmination of HOLY WEEK and the end of LENT, the following Monday (also known as **Pasch Monday**) is observed as a public holiday in many nations, perhaps to round off the long weekend that begins on GOOD FRIDAY. In London there is a big Easter parade in Hyde Park on this day.

A curious English tradition associated at one time with Easter Monday involved "lifting" or "heaving." Forming what children call a "chair" by crossing hands and grasping another person's wrists, the men would lift the women on Easter Monday—sometimes carrying them for a short distance down the street or to the village green—and on Easter Tuesday the women would lift the men. A similar retaliatory game involved taking off each other's shoes. This is thought to have a connection with the resurrection of Christ. Polish children play *smigus*, a water-throwing game.

CONTACTS:
Hyde Park Office
Rangers Lodge
Hyde Park
London W2 2UH United Kingdom
44-300-061-2000; fax: 44-207-402-3298
www.royalparks.org.uk

♦ 0883 ♦ Easter Monday (Netherlands)
Between March 23 and April 26; Monday after Easter

EASTER MONDAY, or **Paasch Maandag**, is celebrated in the Netherlands with games played with Easter eggs. *Eierrapen*, or hunting for eggs, is a favorite pastime among younger children. *Eiertikken*, or hitting hard-boiled eggs together, is a sport for children of all ages. In rural areas, the eggs are still dyed with coffee grounds, beet juice, onion skins, and other vegetable substances. Then they're packed in baskets and carried to an open field for the eiertikken contest. At a given signal, the children line up and try to break the shell of an opposing team member's egg (the two eggs must be the same color) by knocking them together. The winner keeps the opponent's egg, and the boy or girl who collects the most eggs wins.

Another Easter game, which was popular in the 16th and 17th centuries and was still played in the 20th, is called the *eiergaren*. Played by both children and adults who assemble in the main streets of villages on Easter Monday, the game involves a tub of water with a huge apple floating in it. The tub is placed in the middle of the road and 25 eggs are placed at intervals of about 12 feet along the same road. One person must eat the apple with his hands tied behind his back while a second contestant has to run and gather up all the eggs in a basket before the apple is eaten. Whoever finishes his or her task first is the victor.

CONTACTS:
Netherlands Board of Tourism & Conventions
Prinses Catharina-Amaliastraat 5
Den Haag 2496 XD Netherlands
31-0-70-3705-705
www.nbtc.nl/en

♦ 0884 ♦ **Eastern States Exposition**
September, starts the second Friday after Labor Day

Also known as the **Big E**, the Eastern States Exposition is an agricultural and industrial fair in West Springfield, Mass. It's sponsored by all six New England states and runs to the end of September. The first exposition in 1917 attracted 138,000 visitors; these days, attendance tops one million.

The exposition is known for its Avenue of the States, where each New England state has erected a permanent replica of its original State House. (The New Hampshire State House uses New Hampshire granite for its columns.) In the buildings are displays of state products, for example, Maine potatoes, New Hampshire maple syrup, Vermont cheese, Massachusetts cranberries, Rhode Island clam cakes, and Connecticut apples.

The livestock show is the largest in the East, and the Eastern States Horse Show is one of the oldest and most prestigious equestrian events in the country. Besides hunters, jumpers, harness, and saddle horses, there are draft horses in dress harness.

Today the exposition also features a parade, a circus, and international exhibits.

CONTACTS:
Eastern States Exposition
1305 Memorial Ave. (Rte. 147)
West Springfield, MA 01089
413-737-2443; fax: 413-787-0127
www.thebige.com

♦ 0885 ♦ **Ebisu Festival**
October 20

This Japanese festival is named after Ebisu, one among seven Japanese gods of luck, who is the protector of businessmen and fishermen. According to legend, all the other gods leave their shrines during October, which is known as "the godless month," and gather at the temple of Izumo to discuss issues of great importance. Because he is deaf, Ebisu cannot hear the summons and does not accompany them. The Ebisu Festival, observed on October 20, is a time for members of trade associations and political and literary societies to get together and socialize. Because Ebisu presides over trade and business, the festival is also a time to pray for prosperity. The main celebration takes place in Nara, where the streets leading to the Ebisu shrine are lined with booths selling figures of Ebisu and other objects that stand for wealth and good fortune. In the western part of the country, some shrines celebrate the Ebisu Festival in January.

Ebisu is a folk deity who probably originated in a cult of luck in fishing. To this day, Japanese fishermen bring up stones from the bottom of the sea at the beginning of the fishing season and make them into a shrine to Ebisu. As they cast their nets, they have also been known to call out "Ebisu!" to invoke the god's power. In urban areas, however, the Ebisu Festival is mostly celebrated by merchants, although even here the god is often depicted as carrying a fish.

See also BETTARA-ICHI.

CONTACTS:
Japan National Tourism Organization
1 Grand Central Pl.
60 E. 42nd St.
Ste. 448
New York, NY 10165
212-757-5640; fax: 212-307-6754
www.jnto.go.jp

♦ 0886 ♦ **Echigo-Tsumari Art Triennale**
Every three years in July to September

Launched in 2000 in the Echigo-Tsumari region of Japan, the Echigo-Tsumari Art Triennale is a nouveau art show. Its main objective is known as the Tsumari approach, a kind of community building through art that draws media attention and attracts artists, curators, and others in the art industry. During the festival, hundreds of modern art installations—created by both Japanese and international artists—dot the rural landscape of the area. Art appears in unlikely places, such as abandoned schools, local town centers, and terraced rice fields. Besides viewing works of art in the rural fields and open spaces of the region, visitors enjoy performances from all over the world on stages built in the midst of giant pieces of art and swaying crops.

As part of the revitalization plan for an area that had suffered from earthquakes and depopulation, the Echigo-Tsumari Art Triennale has come to embody *satayoma*, the traditional lifestyle of living in harmony with the land and other people. Urban artists and volunteer groups work with local farmers throughout the festival, inspiring the connection between art, nature, and humanity.

CONTACTS:
Echigo Tsumari Executive Committee
Echigo Tsumari Art Field Information Center Matsudai Nobutai
3743-1 Matsudai
Tokamachi-city, Niigata 942-1526 Japan
81-25-595-6688; fax: 81-25-595-6311
www.echigo-tsumari.jp/eng

♦ 0887 ♦ **Ecuador Independence Day**
August 10

Independence Day, or **National Day**, in Ecuador celebrates its independence movement of 1809. Freedom from Spanish rule was finally achieved on May 24, 1822. That event is commemorated each year on May 24 with another holiday called Battle of Pichincha Day.

Patriotic festivities are held throughout the country, but particularly in the colorful capital city of Quito.

CONTACTS:
Embassy of Ecuador

2535 15th St. N.W.
Washington, D.C. 20009
202-234-7200; fax: 202-333-2893
www.ecuador.org

♦ 0888 ♦ Ecuadoran Civicism & National Unity Day
February 27

Public displays of patriotism are commonplace for Ecuadorans on this national holiday, observed on the anniversary of the Battle of Tarqui in 1822. Leading that military campaign against the Spanish loyalists was Antonio José de Sucre, who is considered the liberator of Ecuador and Peru. In 1948, Ecuadoran president Carlos Julio Arosemena Tola established Civicism and National Unity Day by executive decree.

The flag of Ecuador is prominently featured during the day's celebrations. Along with receiving a public display at government and private buildings, the flag also appears in the traditional ceremonies at schools throughout the country. Students with exemplary academic records will have the honor of being flag bearers in official parades, and all students are expected to deliver an oath and kiss the flag as a symbol of their allegiance.

CONTACTS:
Ecuador Embassy
2535 15th St. N.W.
Washington, D.C. 20009
202-234-7200; fax: 202-333-2893
www.ecuador.org

National Archives of Ecuador
Av. 10 de Agosto N11-539
Santa Prisca Casilla
Quito N11-539 Ecuador
593-2-228-0431
ane.gob.ec

♦ 0889 ♦ Eddy (Mary Baker), Birthday of
July 16

This is the day on which Mary Baker Eddy (1821-1910), founder of the Church of Christ, Scientist, was born. After spending much of her early life as a semi-invalid due to a spinal malady, Eddy suffered a serious fall in 1866 and underwent a healing experience that led her to the discovery of Christian Science. Based on the largely forgotten healing aspects of Christianity, the First Church of Christ, Scientist was established in Boston in 1879, and two years later, Eddy founded the Massachusetts Metaphysical College, where she taught until 1889. She dedicated her entire life to spreading the word about Christianity's power to heal. Her most important written work was *Science and Health with Key to the Scriptures*, published in 1875.

The basic premise of Christian Science is that only mind and spirit are real; matter is an illusion, and therefore subject to decay and dissolution. Sickness and death are only real in that they seem real to humans; through prayer and spiri-

tual development, this error can be overcome. Mary Baker Eddy's birthday is observed by Christian Science churches around the world.

CONTACTS:
Christian Science
210 Massachusetts Ave.
Boston, MA 02115
617-450-2000 or 888-424-2535
christianscience.com

♦ 0890 ♦ Edinburgh International Festival
August

The capital city of Edinburgh (pronounced ED-in-bo-ro), Scotland, is transformed during the last two weeks of August and, in some years, into the first week of September, when it hosts what is probably the most prestigious arts festival in the world. Theater and dance companies, orchestras, chamber groups, and soloists from all over the world perform at the city's major venues, and there are art exhibitions and poetry readings as well. Many important new works have been commissioned specifically for the festival—one of the most famous being T.S. Eliot's *The Cocktail Party*. A highlight of the festival, which has been held since 1947, is the traditional Military Tattoo performed nightly at Edinburgh Castle, which is perched high above the city on a rocky promontory. Marching bands from all over the world perform along with Scottish pipe bands at the tattoo, which ends with a farewell song from a lone piper standing on the floodlit battlements.

There is also a "Fringe Festival" that goes on at the same time—an arena for new talent and amateur entertainers. Although student drama and street theater predominate, the quality of the productions in recent years has sometimes made it difficult to distinguish Fringe events from the "official" ones. The number of Fringe performances has increased dramatically as well—from only a few in 1947 to 49,497 performances of 3,193 shows in 299 venues in 2014, making it the largest arts festival in the world. But the three defining features of the earliest Fringe events still hold true today: none of the performers are officially invited to take part; they must use small and unconventional theater spaces; and they all assume their own financial risks, surviving or sinking according to public demand.

CONTACTS:
Edinburgh International Festival
Cafe Hub
Castlehill
Edinburgh, Scotland EH1 2NE United Kingdom
44-131-473-2099
www.eif.co.uk

♦ 0891 ♦ Edinburgh International Film Festival
June

The Edinburgh International Film Festival (EIFF) is the world's longest-running celebration of cinema. It is held annually for two weeks in the month of June in Edinburgh, Scotland.

The festival was originally established as the International Festival of Documentary Films by John Grierson, the founder of the British documentary movement. Today, the event covers a range of full-length films, documentaries, short films, animated works, and music videos.

The EIFF has turned into an important event for both the local economy and the international film industry. At EIFF, the focus is on talent, discovery, and novelty. In addition to its huge success with audiences, the festival has a big stake in the development of the UK and Scottish film industries.

CONTACTS:
Edinburgh International Film Festival
88 Lothian Rd.
Edinburgh EH3 9BZ United Kingdom
44-131-623-8030; fax: 44-131-229-5501
www.edfilmfest.org.uk

♦ 0892 ♦ Edison (Thomas) Festival of Light
Mid-January through mid-February

Most people associate Thomas Alva Edison (1847-1931) with his famous laboratory in Menlo Park, New Jersey. But when he was 38 years old, a widower and seriously ill, his doctors sent him to Florida for a long vacation. There he discovered giant bamboo growing along the Caloosahatchee River. He established his winter home in Fort Myers and planned to use the bamboo fiber to make filaments for his new incandescent electric lamp bulbs.

The Edison Festival of Light, held annually in Fort Myers for more than three weeks, encompassing his birthday (*see* EDISON'S BIRTHDAY), began as a three-day event in 1938. Highlights of the festival include concerts, the coronation of the King and Queen of Edisonia, a children's parade, fireworks, exhibits of Edison's various inventions, and exhibits of regional inventors. The Grand Parade of Light— a nighttime procession of more than 100 bands, floats, and marching units—is the festival's grand finale. Edison's winter home and his Florida laboratory are open to the public year-round.

CONTACTS:
Edison Festival of Light
1524 Jackson St.
Fort Myers, FL 33901
239-334-2999; fax: 239-334-7418
edisonfestival.org

♦ 0893 ♦ Edison's (Thomas) Birthday
February 11

Although Thomas Alva Edison (1847-1931) is best known as the inventor of the incandescent electric light, his real achievement was to produce the first incandescent lamp of any practical value—one that could be produced inexpensively and distributed widely. In 1882 Edison lost a patent infringement case to Joseph Wilson Swan, who was developing an incandescent light at the same time in England. As a compromise, the two men combined their resources and formed the Edison and Swan Electric Lamp Company.

Edison's genius is credited with a number of other important inventions, among them the carbon transmitter (which brought Alexander Graham Bell's newly invented telephone into gener-al use and led to the development of the microphone), the dic-tating machine, a method for transmitting telegraphic signals from ship to ship (or ship to shore), the Kinetoscope (which made the motion picture a reality), and the phonograph.

See also EDISON FESTIVAL OF LIGHT.

CONTACTS:
Thomas Edison Birthplace Museum
9 N. Edison Dr.
Milan, OH 44846
419-499-2135
tomedison.org

Henry Ford Museum
20900 Oakwood Blvd.
Dearborn, MI 48124
313-982-6001 or 800-835-5237
www.thehenryford.org

♦ 0894 ♦ Edmund Fitzgerald Anniversary
On the Sunday closest to November 10

On November 10, 1975, the 26,000-ton ore carrier *SS Edmund Fitzgerald*, the largest ship on the Great Lakes in its time and known as "The Queen of the Great Lakes," sank during a deadly storm in Lake Superior. In commemoration of that tragedy, a number of events are held.

The primary event is held at the Mariners' Church in downtown Detroit, Mich. As the names of the 29 lost crewmen are read out, a family member or friend of the deceased rings a ship's bell. Beginning in 2006, the church has expanded its service to a 30th ring to remember all those sailors who have been lost on the Great Lakes, some 30,000 lives lost in 6,000 shipwrecks over the years. Marking the 37th anniversary in 2012, a ceremony at the Dossin Great Lakes Museum on Belle Isle commemorated the lives lost on the Edmund Fitzgerald with the lighting of lanterns and an Assembly of the Lost Mariners honor guard. On the Detroit River, a U.S. Coast Guard helicopter escorted a flotilla of U.S. and Canadian vessels as they approached the Museum to receive the commemorative wreath.

CONTACTS:
Dossin Great Lakes Museum
100 Strand Dr.
Belle Isle
Detroit, MI 48207
313-833-5538; fax: 313-833-5342
detroithistorical.org

Mariners' Church of Detroit
170 E. Jefferson Ave.
Detroit, MI 48226
313-259-2206; fax: 313-259-6015
marinerschurchofdetroit.org

♦ 0895 ♦ Egungun Festival
June

The Egungun is a secret society among the Yoruba people of Ede, Oyo State, Nigeria. The major Egungun festival takes place in June, when members of the society come to the market place and perform masked dances. The masks they wear represent ancestral spirits and may cover the whole body or just the face. It is considered dangerous to see any part of the man who is wearing the mask—an offense that was at one time punishable by death.

The masqueraders all dance simultaneously, although each has his own drum accompaniment and entourage of chanting women and girls. The festival climaxes with the appearance of Andu, the most powerful mask. It is believed that the spirits of the deceased possess the masqueraders while they are dancing, and although it promotes a feeling of oneness between the living and the dead, the festival also inspires a certain amount of fear.

CONTACTS:
Kingdom of Oyotunji African Village
56 Braynt Ln.
Sheldon, SC 5129
843-846-8900
www.oyotunji.org

♦ 0896 ♦ **Egypt Revolution Day**
July 23

This national holiday is the anniversary of the military overthrow of the monarchy on July 23, 1952. The new government formally instituted the Republic of Egypt on June 18, 1953. In Cairo on July 23, parades and other festivities take place to commemorate the republic.

CONTACTS:
State Information Service, Egypt Ministry of Information
3 Al Estad Al Bahary St.
Nasr City
Cairo Egypt
20-2-261-7304
www.sis.gov.eg/En

♦ 0897 ♦ **Egyptian Days**
Various

Up until the 17th century in England, these were commonly thought to be unlucky days throughout the year. Popular almanacs would list them as days on which to avoid such important activities as weddings, blood letting (a standard way of treating various illnesses), and traveling. No one knew why certain days were considered unlucky. In fact, which days were Egyptian Days seems to have depended upon which almanac was consulted; apparently, there was never any standard list that was widely circulated.

Although it is not known for sure why they were referred to as the Egyptian Days, it's possible that they were first computed by Egyptian astrologers or were somehow related to the Egyptian plagues. They were also known as the **Dismal Days**, from Latin *dies mali* (meaning "evil days").

CONTACTS:
Egyptian Cultural and Educational Bureau
1303 New Hampshire Ave. N.W.
Washington, D.C. 20036
202-296-3888; fax: 202-296-3891
www.eecous.net

♦ 0898 ♦ **Eight-Hour Day**
Various

Each of Australia's states celebrates the improvements that have been made in working conditions with its own LABOR DAY. The Eight-Hour Day holiday is marked with parades and celebrations to commemorate trade union efforts to limit working hours. In many places, people still chant the unions' slogan: "Eight hours' labor, eight hours' recreation, and eight hours' rest!," which, by happenstance, is the basis of St. Benedict's Rule of Life for religious orders.

In Queensland Labour Day is celebrated on the first Monday in May; in New South Wales, the Australian Capital Territory, and South Australia it's the first Monday in October; in Western Australia it's the first Monday in March; and in Tasmania and Victoria it's the second Monday in March. In New Zealand, Labour Day is observed on the first Monday in October.

CONTACTS:
Victorian Trades Hall Council
Ground Fl.
Old Bldg., Trades Hall, Cnr.
Victoria & Lygon Streets
Carlton South, VIC 3053 Australia
61-3-9659-3511; fax: 61-3-9663-2127
www.vthc.org.au

♦ 0899 ♦ **Eisteddfod**
Early August

The **Royal National Eisteddfod of Wales** dates back to the 12th century. Its purpose is to encourage the preservation of Welsh music and literature, and only those who sing or write in Welsh may enter the competitions. The annual event opens with the blowing of trumpets, followed by all kinds of musical and literary contests—harp playing, solo and choral singing, dramatic presentations, and poetic composition. Prizes and degrees are awarded to the winners.

The National Eisteddfod is held in northern Wales one year and southern Wales the next. Other Eisteddfodau are held in Welsh communities elsewhere from May to November.

See also CYNONFARDD EISTEDDFOD.

CONTACTS:
National Eisteddfod of Wales
40 Parc Ty Glas, Llanisien
Cardiff, Wales CF14 5DU United Kingdom
44-845-300-4090; fax: 44-29-2076-3737
www.eisteddfod.org.uk

♦ 0900 ♦ **Eka Dasa Rudra**
Once every 100 years

Eka Dasa Rudra is a series of processions, ceremonies, and sacrifices held every 100 years at Pura Besakih, the "mother temple" of Bali, Indonesia. The temple, which comprises about 30 separate temples honoring a great variety of Balinese and Hindu gods, was probably built about 1,000 years ago and is on the slopes of the volcanic mountain, Gunung ("Mount") Agung.

On March 17, 1963, the Eka Dasa Rudra was under way when Agung catastrophically erupted and killed more than 1,500 people. Since the sacrifices were interrupted, the Eka Dasa Rudra was started again 16 years later and completed in the period from late February to early May of 1979. Images of gods were carried 19 miles down the mountain to be washed in the sea: entire villages gathered along the route. In all, it is estimated that more than 100,000 people participated in the ritual. The climax came during the Taur rites when 23 priests offered prayers and sacrificed animals—ranging from an eagle to an anteater—to appease forms of Rudra, a Hindu demonic manifestation. Thousands of pilgrims traveled by truck and foot to Besakih.

The complex Balinese religion is largely a blend with Hinduism; the majority of Balinese hold to the Bali Hindu faith, also known as Agama Tirtha.

CONTACTS:
Embassy of The Republic of Indonesia
2020 Massachusetts Ave. N.W.
Washington, D.C. 20036
202-775-5200
www.embassyofindonesia.org

Bali Tourism Board
Jl. Raya Puputan 41
Renon
Denpasar, Bali 80235 Indonesia
62-361-235600; fax: 62-361-239200
www.balitourismboard.org

♦ 0901 ♦ Ekadashi
11th day of each waxing and waning moon

Ekadashi is the Hindi word for "eleventh." Hindus observe 24 11th-day fasts during the course of the Hindu year, although some are more important than others. Each Ekadashi is held in honor of a different Hindu legend and has specific religious duties associated with it. Eating rice, however, is prohibited on all Ekadashi. According to legend, a demon was born of the sweat that fell from Brahma's head on this day, and Brahma instructed it to inhabit the rice grains eaten by people on Ekadashi and to turn into worms in their stomachs.

See also AMALAKA EKADASHI; DEVATHANI EKADASHI; NIRJALA EKADASHI; PUTRADA EKADASHI.

CONTACTS:
Hindu Temple and Cultural Center
3818 212th St. S.E.
Bothell, WA 98021
425-483-7115
www.htccwa.org

♦ 0902 ♦ El Pochó Dance-Drama
January 20

ST. SEBASTIAN'S DAY is celebrated throughout Latin America, but the event that takes place in Tenosique in Tabasco State, Mexico, on this day is unique. The dance-drama known as *El Pochó* involves most of the townspeople and anywhere from 15 to more than 60 dancers. Dancers each play one of three main characters. The *cojóes* are played by men who will engage in a struggle with the *tigres*, also played by men. The *pochoveras* are played by women.

On the morning of January 20 everyone gathers at the pre-arranged location, a house or a plaza. The pochoveras enter in their long skirts and embroidered blouses and perform the initial dance. Then the cojóes enter, wearing masks with exaggerated features, representing the best and worst in humans. Soon the tigres (jaguars) invade the dance space, and the cojóes and tigres play at hunting each other until, finally, they join forces to chase the audience.

CONTACTS:
Mexico Tourism Board
Viaducto Miguel Alemán 105
Col. Escandón
Mexico City 11800 Mexico
www.visitmexico.com

Municipio de Tenosique
Calle 21 Por 26 Sn
Tenosique Centro
Tenosique, Tabasco 86040 Mexico
52-934-342-0036
tenosique.gob.mx

♦ 0903 ♦ El Salvador del Mundo, Festival of
First week in August

The patron saint and namesake of El Salvador—El Salvador del Mundo (the Savior of the World)—is honored with a national festival. Festival proceedings commence the week before the saint's day, on August 6, which is also the same day as the FEAST OF THE TRANSFIGURATION. Some Salvadorans refer to the festival as **Fiestas Agostinos** (August Feasts).

The observance of the festival dates back to 1525, the year that the city of San Salvador, the present-day capital, was founded. The grandest of the celebrations take place in that city, but there are also observances throughout the rest of the country and in Salvadoran communities settled abroad.

The main events of the festival are a religious procession, a large fair, various sporting events, a beauty contest, and a riotous party featuring street floats and dancers. The religious ceremony takes place in front of the national cathedral and entails a spectacle known as *la bajada* (the descent). This ritual features an old wooden image of Christ that is paraded through the streets and then lowered inside a wooden shell. There the sculpture's purple garments are removed, and it emerges from the shell appareled in gleaming white robes, a symbolic representation of Christ's transfiguration.

CONTACTS:
Catholic Community El Salvador del Mundo
Paseo General Escalon
Ste. 5461 Col. Escalon
San Salvador El Salvador
503-2263-0308
www.elsalvadordelmundo.com

♦ 0904 ♦ El Salvador Independence Day
September 15

El Salvador joined with other Central American countries in revolt against Spanish rule in 1821, and revolutionary leader Father José Matías Delgado declared El Salvador to be independent. On this same day, COSTA RICA, GUATEMALA, HONDURAS, and NICARAGUA also declared their independence.

Independence Day is a national holiday in El Salvador.

CONTACTS:
Embassy of El Salvador
1400 16th St. NW
Suite 100, N.W.
Washington, D.C. 20036 United States
202-595-7500
www.elsalvador.org

♦ 0905 ♦ Eldon Turkey Festival
Second Saturday in October

While people in most parts of the United States think about turkeys only as THANKSGIVING day approaches, it is a year-round concern for the turkey farmers of Eldon, Missouri, and the surrounding area, where over two million turkeys are raised annually. There is also a large wild turkey population, which makes turkey hunting a popular local sport.

Since 1986, Eldon has held the Turkey Festival designed to educate the public about domestic turkey production, turkey-farming operations, and the health benefits of turkey-food products. The festival is also an opportunity for numerous conservation and turkey-hunting organizations to provide information on safe hunting practices, wild turkey-calling techniques, and efforts to increase the wild turkey population.

Events at the October festival include turkey races (with the turkeys on leashes), a turkey egg toss, sales of turkey foods, and exhibits on the production of domestic turkeys.

CONTACTS:
Eldon Chamber of Commerce
203 E. First
Eldon, MO 65026
573-392-3752; fax: 573-392-0634
www.eldonchamber.com

♦ 0906 ♦ Election Day
Tuesday following the first Monday in November

Election Day, the day on which Americans vote for their elected officials, is held on the Tuesday after the first Monday in November. Americans vote for their president and vice president every four years on that Tuesday. They vote for their U.S. representatives every two years during even-numbered years, and they vote for their U.S. senators every six years—one-third of the U.S. senators are up for reelection every two years. Americans also vote for their state senators, state representatives, and many local officials on this day.

This date was set by Congress in 1845 to correct abuses caused by having allowed each state to appoint its electors any time before the date in December set for their convening. At that time, the nation was primarily rural, so Election Day was set for late fall, after the harvest would be brought in. At that time, many people would have to travel on foot to their courthouse or county seat to cast their vote, which could take a full day. So Election Day was set on a Tuesday to avoid conflict with Sunday church services.

To encourage people to vote, ten states now consider Election Day a legal holiday, and five additional states require employers to give their employees several hours off to allow them to vote. In other states, some employers give their employees the day off. Even so, millions of Americans do not take advantage of what may be their most valuable privilege.

CONTACTS:
Federal Election Commission
999 E. St. N.W.
Washington, D.C. 20463
202-694-1000 or 800-424-9530
www.fec.gov

♦ 0907 ♦ Election of the Lord Mayor of London
September 29

Since 1546 MICHAELMAS has been the day on which the Lord Mayor of London is elected each year. The election occurs in the Guildhall, in front of which a high wooden fence has been erected. There are a number of doors in the fence, and a beadle of one of the city's Livery Companies, dressed in uniform and a three-cornered hat, waits in back of each door. It is the beadle's job to guard the Guildhall and see that persons without authorization are not allowed into the election ceremony.

Two candidates for the job are chosen from among the city aldermen who have already served a term of office as sheriff. The ceremony begins when the current Lord Mayor, two sheriffs, and 26 aldermen in their scarlet gowns walk from the Mansion House to Guildhall, where they sit on a platform that has been strewn with herbs, a medieval protection against both plague and witchcraft. The candidates proceed to the Aldermen's Court, a body consisting of 13 aldermen whose job it is to interview the candidates and select the one who will serve as mayor.

Once the voting is over, both the new and the old Lord Mayors appear together on the porch of the Guildhall, and then an ornate horse-drawn coach carries them to the Mansion

House, which has been the Lord Mayor of London's official residence since 1753.

See also LORD MAYOR'S SHOW.

CONTACTS:
London Elects - London Election Programme Team
City Hall
The Queen''s Walk
London SE1 2AA United Kingdom
44-20-7983-4444
www.londonelects.org.uk

♦ 0908 ♦ Election of the Mayor of Ock Street
Saturday nearest June 19

The town of Abingdon, England, has long been famous for its Morris dancers, who rank among the best in England. During the 18th century, it was customary for the people of Abingdon to kill and roast a black ox on St. Edmund of Abingdon's Feast Day, or another day nearby. The feast day is June 19, the day before St. Edmund's Fair. The meat would be distributed among the town's needy folk.

In 1700 an argument arose during the ox roast over who would get the horns. It was decided that the only fair way to settle the argument was to have a real fight, so the town was divided into two opposing teams by drawing an imaginary line along Ock Street. Using torches, sticks, stones, and bare fists, the western part of Abingdon, led by a man by the name of Hemmings— one of the town's Morris dancers—took possession of the horns. The crowd hailed him as the "Mayor of Ock Street."

Today, only people who live on Ock Street may vote for the mayor, which they do by placing paper ballots into a soapbox. The winner is usually a member of the Hemmings family, and he toasts his election by drinking from a special applewood chalice, or bowl, with a silver rim, which is believed to be more than 200 years old. He is carried through the streets in a flower-decorated chair by the Abingdon Morris dancers, who follow behind the "hornbearer," a man holding a pole on which is mounted a black-horned ox head. They stop at each of Ock Street's many pubs, where all the dancers have a drink and join in the celebration.

CONTACTS:
Abingdon Traditional Morris Dancers
13 Cheyney Walk
Abingdon OX14 1HN United Kingdom
44-776-666-3213
www.abingdonmorris.org.uk

♦ 0909 ♦ Elephant Festival
Mid-February

The Elephant Festival is held annually in February in the Paklay district of the Sayaboury province in northwestern Laos as a celebration of the Asian elephant. Co-sponsored by the non-profit ElefantAsia conservation organization, the festival also exists to raise awareness of the increasing threat of

extinction that faces the 50,000 elephants throughout Asia. Activities at the event include a majestic parade of more than 70 elephants; offerings of fruit and flowers; an elephant race, show, and museum; a traditional elephant Baci ceremony; as well as the chance to see elephants at their bath. In addition, there are such activities as a tug-of-war contest, a drawing competition, film, music performances, food stalls, and a night market.

CONTACTS:
Lao Elephant Conservation Center
Nam Tien Protected Area
Sayaboury, Sayaboury Province Laos
856-209-659-0665
www.elephantconservationcenter.com

♦ 0910 ♦ Elephant Round-Up
Third weekend in November

The Elephant Round-Up is an internationally famous show of 200 or more trained elephants held annually in the provincial capital of Surin, Thailand. The Suay people of the area have traditionally captured and trained wild elephants to work in the northern Thailand teak forests. The Round-Up gives the trainers the opportunity to demonstrate their elephants' intelligence, strength, and obedience. A tug-of-war is staged where elephants are pitted against Thai soldiers. There are also log-pulling contests, a soccer game with two teams of elephants kicking a giant soccer ball, elephant basketball and other sports. A highlight is the spectacular array of elephants rigged out to reenact a medieval war parade. Besides the elephant demonstrations, there are cultural performances and folk dancing.

CONTACTS:
Tourism Authority of Thailand
1600 New Phetchaburi Rd.
Makkasan
Ratchathevi
Bangkok 10400 Thailand
662-250-5500; fax: 66-02-250-5511
www.tourismthailand.org

♦ 0911 ♦ Eleusinian Mysteries
Lesser Eleusinia in February-March; Greater Eleusinia in September-October

In ancient Athens, the Eleusinia was the most celebrated of all religious ceremonies. Often referred to as the **Mysteries** because anyone who violated the secrecy surrounding the festival rites would be punished by death, the Eleusinia consisted of two celebrations: The Greater Eleusinia was observed for a week or more in September or October; the Lesser Eleusinia was observed in early spring. Those who had been initiated at the lesser mysteries were allowed to participate in the greater mysteries the following year, when the secrets of the festival would be revealed to them.

The Eleusinia was based on the legend of Demeter, a goddess associated with the harvest, and her daughter Persephone, who was carried off by Pluto to live in his underground kingdom. Although the secrecy that accompanied the Eleusinian mysteries has made it difficult to reconstruct exactly what went on there, it is believed that they were intended to encourage a bountiful growing season. The men and women who were initiated during these ceremonies were believed to live happier and more secure lives, and when they died, they were granted a place in the Elysian Fields, the mythical place where the souls of the virtuous went after death.

CONTACTS:
Eleusina Cultural Project
11, Pagkalou & Kimonos St.
Elefsina
Attica 19200 Greece
30-210-556-5613; fax: 30-210-556-5613
aisxylia.gr

Municipality of Elefsina
Xatzidaki and Dimitros St.
Elefsina Greece
30-210-553-7100
www.eleusina.gr

♦ 0912 ♦ **Elfreth's Alley Fete Day**
First weekend in June

Elfreth's Alley is a well-preserved street of privately owned 18th-century homes in Philadelphia. It is the only street in the city that has survived architecturally since the alley first opened in 1702. The 30 houses on the street, dating from 1713 to 1811, have all remained private residences, with the exception of the Mantua Maker's House, which is now a museum open to the public.

The idea of holding an "at home" day dates back to 1934, when a group of residents formed the Elfreth's Alley Association. Now called **Fete Day**, it is a day on which many of the houses are open to visitors, with members of the Association acting as hostesses in Colonial dress. On Fete Day in 1963, the Alley's distinctive character and historical value were officially recognized by its designation as a Registered National Historic Landmark. Over the years the Elfreth's Alley Association has played an active role in renovating the street's cartway and brick sidewalks, as well as saving some of the houses from destruction.

CONTACTS:
Elfreth's Alley Museum
124-126 Elfreth's Alley
Philadelphia, PA 19106 United States
215-627-8680
www.elfrethsalley.org

♦ 0913 ♦ **Elfstedentocht**
December, January, or February

The day of this famous ice skating race in the Netherlands depends on the weather and the thickness of the ice. In the 18th century, young men in the northern part of the country, known as Friesland, would try to skate all the canals that connected the province's 11 towns. Today the **Eleven Cities Race** covers the same 124-mile course, but increasingly mild winters have made its timing less dependable. As many as 16,000 men and women have competed in the race at one time, which takes several hours to complete.

CONTACTS:
Royal Society, the Frisian Eleven Cities
P.O. Box 569
Leeuwarden 8901 BJ Netherlands
31-58-215-5020; fax: 31-58-213-8520
www.elfstedentocht.nl

♦ 0914 ♦ **Elijah Day**
July 20

Considered to be among the greatest of prophets, Elijah is commemorated on this day in both the Roman Catholic and Orthodox churches. An Old Testament Jew who is revered by Jews and Muslims as well, Elijah's story appears in chapters 17 and 18 of the first book of Kings, with the final episode appearing in Second Kings, chapter two. It tells of Elijah's sojourn in the desert, where he was fed every morning and evening by ravens. It also tells about the miracles he performed, replenishing the meal and oil supplies of a widow who fed him despite a severe famine and bringing her son back to life when he died.

The highpoint of Elijah's ministry occurred when he called the priests who worshipped Baal, the pagan fertility god, to the top of Mount Carmel and challenged them to a contest that would prove who was the true God. When the pagan priests failed in their efforts to ask Baal to set fire to their sacrifice, Elijah called on his God, who immediately consumed with fire not only the sacrifice but the altar itself and the dust and water surrounding it. When Elijah died, it is said that he was taken up to heaven in a fiery chariot by a whirlwind.

CONTACTS:
St. Elias Antiochian Orthodox Christian Church
4940 Harroun Rd.
Sylvania, OH 43560
419-882-4037; fax: 419-882-4954

mystelias.com

Ministry of Tourism, Government of Israel
800 Second Ave.
16th Fl.
New York, NY 10017
212-499-5650; fax: 212-499-5655
www.goisrael.com

♦ 0915 ♦ **Elimination of Racial Discrimination, International Day for the**
March 21

International Day for the Elimination of Racial Discrimination is observed annually on March 21, the anniversary of the day in 1960 when, at a peaceful demonstration against the apartheid "pass laws" in Sharpeville, South Africa, police opened fire and killed 69 black South Africans. The observation of this day was initiated by the UNITED NATIONS General Assembly in 1966, when it called on the international community to redouble its efforts to eliminate all forms of racial-discrimination and to remember "the victims of Sharpeville and those countless others in different parts of the world who have fallen victim to racial injustice.".

CONTACTS:
U.N. Human Rights - Office of the High Commissioner
UN Headquarters
Rm S-1310 13th Fl.
Secretariat Bldg.
New York, NY 10017
212-963-5931; fax: 212-963-4097
www.ohchr.org

Emfuleni Local Municipality
Corner Klasie Havenga and Frikkie Meyer Blvd.
Box 3
Vanderbijlpark, Gauteng 1900 South Africa
27-16-950-5000; fax: 27-16-950-5050
www.emfuleni.gov.za

◆ 0916 ◆ Elisabeth (Queen) International Music Competition
May

One of the world's most prestigious music competitions and the largest musical event in Brussels takes place throughout the month of May each year. Open to young competitors from around the world, the competition focuses on violinists one year, composers the next, pianists the third year, and singers the fourth year. It is timed to coincide with the birthday of Queen Elisabeth of Belgium, who supported and encouraged violinist-composer Eugène Ysaÿe when he started the event in 1937.

Although billed as a competition, the public is invited to attend every stage of the contest, from the initial tests at the Royal Conservatory of Music to the winner's performance with full orchestra at the Beaux Arts Palace. Members of the jury, many of whom are past winners of the competition, also perform for the public one evening during the month-long competition, and a distinguished musician is invited to give the opening concert.

CONTACTS:
Secretariat of the Queen Elisabeth Competition
20 Rue aux Laines
Brussels B-1000 Belgium
32-2-213-4050; fax: 32-2-514-3297
www.cmireb.be

◆ 0917 ◆ Elizabeth II (Queen) Birthday
June

Queen Elizabeth II was born on April 21, 1926, but her birthday is officially observed on a Saturday in June by proclamation each year (it may be changed if the weather is really foul). A good explanation for the discrepancy in dates is that April weather is notoriously bad in London.

The celebration includes Trooping the Colour. The "colour" referred to here is the regimental flag. When British soldiers went to battle, it was important that they be able to recognize their flag so they could rally around it. "Trooping the Colour" was a marching display put on for new recruits so they would know what their regiment's flag looked like.

In 1805 the ceremony became an annual event to celebrate the king or queen's official birthday. Today, a different regiment is chosen each year to parade its flag before Queen Elizabeth II, who sits on horseback and inspects the troops in their brightly colored uniforms as they pass before her in London's Horseguards Parade, a large open space in Whitehall. Then she rides in a carriage back to Buckingham Palace. Although the event attracts thousands of tourists, many Londoners turn out for the traditional ceremony as well.

Queen's Birthday is a national holiday in Australia, where it is celebrated on the second Monday in June. It was first observed there in 1788, not long after the country was settled. June 4, the birthday of King George III, was set aside at that time as a holiday for convicts and settlers. After George V died in 1936, the date of his birth, June 3, was set aside to honor the reigning king or queen. Bermuda holds an annual military parade on Hamilton's Front Street in honor of the Queen.

CONTACTS:
Royal Household Public Information Office
Buckingham Palace
London SW1A 1AA United Kingdom
44-20-7930-4832
www.royal.gov.uk

Household Division - Trooping the Colour, Brigade Major
HQ Household Div.
Horse Guards,
Whitehall
London SW1A 2AX United Kingdom
www.householddivision.org.uk

◆ 0918 ◆ Ellensburg Rodeo
September, Labor Day weekend

The Ellensburg Rodeo is the richest rodeo in the state of Washington and also one of the top 25 rodeos of the Professional Rodeo Cowboys Association. Prize money in recent years has been more than $200,000, and an estimated 20,000 people visit Ellensburg on this weekend. Events include a parade and displays of hand crafts, especially weaving and bead work, by the people of the Yakima Indian nation. Yakimas, many in feathered headdress, open each performance of the rodeo with a solemn horseback ride down a steep hill that overlooks the arena.

CONTACTS:
Ellensburg Rodeo Office
609 N. Main St.
Ellensburg, WA 98926
509-962-7831 or 800-637-2444; fax: 509-962-7830
www.ellensburgrodeo.com

♦ 0919 ♦ **Elsie Dairy Festival**
July

The dairy capital of Michigan is appropriately named Elsie in honor of the cow in Borden's ads, and although it has fewer than 1,000 residents, there are 20 working dairy farms in the area. One of them is Green Meadow Farms, which boasts the largest herd of registered Holsteins in the United States.

For three days in July each year since 1986, the town of Elsie serves gallons of ice cream at bargain prices. Green Meadow Farms is open to visitors, and there are competitions in cow milking, ice cream eating, and even milk drinking, with competitors using a baby bottle. The 14-foot-tall fiberglass Holstein in the center of town is a popular place for the festival's 20,000 visitors to have their photographs taken.

CONTACTS:
Elsie Dairy Festival
M-21 Hwy.
N. Hollister Rd.
Elsie, MI 48831
989-277-4826
elsiedairyfest.com

♦ 0920 ♦ **Elul Selichot**
August-September; Jewish month of Elul

Celebrated in the last month of the Hebrew calendar, Elul Selichot is a time for repentance, reconciliation, and self-reflection in preparation for the High Holidays of Rosh Hashanah (the Jewish New Year or Judgment Day) and Yom Kippur (the Day of Atonement). As the end of the year approaches, Jews cast off the bad thoughts, words, and actions of the past year in an effort to become closer to God before judgment on Rosh Hashanah. Jews believe that refusing to engage in introspection and repentance of sin is worse than sin itself. The celebration of Elul Selichot is closely linked to the act of Moses seeking God's forgiveness on behalf of the Israelites. As the New Year approaches, Jews recite a series of penitential prayers and poems before dawn—in addition to customary daily prayers—praising God's mercy. Another important ritual is the daily blowing of the *Shofar*, a hollowed out ram's horn, which encourages repentance and supplication during prayers. Many Jews also visit the graves of relatives and friends during Elul Selichot.

CONTACTS:
Orthodox Union
11 Broadway
New York, NY 10004 USA
212-563-4000
www.ou.org

♦ 0921 ♦ **Elvis International Tribute Week**
Week including August 16

This week-long event pays tribute to rock and roll singer Elvis Presley—"The King of Rock and Roll." The tribute takes place in Memphis, Tenn., largely at Graceland, the 15,000-square-foot mansion that Elvis called home and that is now his gravesite, museum, and a rock and roll shrine.

Born in 1935 in a two-room house in Tupelo, Miss., Elvis moved to Memphis when he was 12, and came to fame in the 1950s with hits like "Hound Dog," "Don't Be Cruel," and "All Shook Up." As a white man singing a black sound, he swept the music world and helped create the Memphis Sound. He was charismatic and sexy and gyrated his hips while performing in a fashion that sent the females in his audiences into a screeching frenzy. This won him the nickname, "Elvis the Pelvis." When he first appeared on television on the "Ed Sullivan Show," the hip shaking was considered too risque, and he was photographed only from the waist up. He appeared in 33 motion pictures and made 45 recordings that sold over a million copies each. He died at Graceland of an overdose of prescription drugs on Aug. 16, 1977.

A candlelight vigil is held on the evening of Aug. 15 at Graceland. Thousands of Elvis's fans, each carrying a candle, pour through the gates and walk to the gravesite. Other events of the week include a Nostalgia Concert by singers and musicians who worked with Presley; a Sock Hop Ball for "flat-top cats and dungaree dolls," in which Elvis songs and other classics of the 1950s and 1960s are played; and an art exhibit and contest, with art depicting Elvis or his home. The Elvis Presley Memorial Karate Tournament draws about 500 competitors from all over the world and reflects Presley's interest in karate—he studied the martial arts for years and was the first movie star to use karate in films.

For those who cannot attend in person, the official Elvis web site provides a live webcast of the vigil.

CONTACTS:
Graceland/Elvis Presley Enterprises Inc.
3734 Elvis Presley Blvd.
P.O. Box 16508
Memphis, TN 38116
901-332-3322 or 901-332-3329 or 800-238-2000
www.graceland.com

♦ 0922 ♦ **Emancipation Day (Canada)**
August 1 or the nearest Saturday

Emancipation Day commemorates August 1, 1834, the date that England's Abolition of Slavery Bill took effect, ending slavery throughout the British Empire. As a result of the law, more than one million slaves were freed in the British colonies, including Canada. While August 1 is not a public holiday in Canada, it is marked by many communities, particularly in Ontario, where many sites of importance to African-Canadian history are located. Public ceremonies typically take place in Toronto, Windsor, Amherstburg, and other cities and towns. But two sites of particular historical interest, the city of Owen Sound and Uncle Tom's Cabin in Dresden, organize Ontario's most prominent Emancipation Day observances. They take place on the Saturday nearest August 1.

Owen Sound was the northern-most terminus for the Underground Railroad, the network of people that helped slaves escape from the American South to the North and to Canada. Many escaped slaves settled in Owen Sound to become integral members of the community. Since 1862, the town has held a picnic to commemorate both Emancipation Day and the U.S. abolition of slavery, which took effect on January 1, 1863. The picnic, attended by local groups and many visitors, has come to incorporate music, crafts, and black-history exhibits as well as food and games.

The Uncle Tom's Cabin site in Dresden comprises the former home of Reverend Josiah Henson and other period buildings, as well as a major exhibit and interpretive centre on black history in North America. Henson, an escaped slave, settled in Ontario in 1830. He established the Dawn Settlement, a community that nurtured former slaves' self-sufficiency and success. Harriet Beecher Stowe used him as the model for the title character in *Uncle Tom's Cabin,* her renowned anti-slavery novel. The Uncle Tom's Cabin site marks Emancipation Day with a day-long program of educational and cultural events, including storytelling, dance, drama, and speeches.

CONTACTS:
Owen Sound Tourism Office
1155 First Ave. W.
Owen Sound, ON N4K 4K8 Canada
519-371-9833 or 888-675-5555
www.owensound.ca

Uncle Tom's Cabin Historic Site
29251 Uncle Tom's Rd.
Dresden, ON N0P 1M0 Canada
519-683-2978; fax: 519-683-1256
www.heritagetrust.on.ca

♦ 0923 ♦ Emancipation Day (Hutchinson, Kansas)
First weekend in August

Emancipation Day typically commemorates the day African-American slaves were freed in the United States. That event is celebrated annually in Hutchinson, Kansas, on the first weekend in August.

During the post-Civil War era, former slaves in the region celebrated Emancipation Day as "Lincoln Day" in Atchinson, Kansas, on September 22. That was the anniversary of the date in 1862 when President Abraham Lincoln issued the Emancipation Proclamation that would take effect the following year. By the late 1890s, the celebration had been moved to Hutchinson in order to take advantage of its more central location. In 1931 the local government proclaimed August 4 Emancipation Day and made it a legal holiday within the African-American community.

Since that time, a program of activities has been conducted each year. While the activities vary somewhat from year to year, the weekend typically kicks off with a social event on Friday night and features a parade on Saturday morning that begins at the intersection of 12th and Main. Following the parade and opening ceremonies, participants gather for a picnic in the park with food and drink vendors. The holiday program also includes sports, such as a basketball, boxing, or golf, as well as a teen night at a local swimming pool. Entertainment includes concerts featuring jazz, blues, or Gospel performers, and the weekend concludes with an ice cream social on Sunday afternoon.

CONTACTS:
Hutchinson Reno Arts & Humanities Council
Festivals Committee
10815 S. Herren Rd.
Hutchinson, KS 67566
620-662-4303
www.hrah.org

Greater Hutchinsion Convention / Visitors Bureau
117 N. Walnut St.
P.O. Box 519
Hutchinson, KS 67501
620-662-3391 or 800-691-4262
www.visithutch.com

Kansas Historical Society
6425 S.W. 6th Ave.
Topeka, KS 66615
785-272-8681
www.kshs.org

♦ 0924 ♦ Emancipation Day (Tallahassee, Florida)
May 20

Emancipation Day in Tallahassee, Florida, is celebrated each year on May 20. That date marks the anniversary of the day in 1865 when Union General Edward M. McCook announced from the steps of his headquarters in central Tallahassee that President Abraham Lincoln had ended slavery in Florida under the terms of the Emancipation Proclamation.

Since 1997 the site of McCook's headquarters, now known as Knott House and open to the public as a state historical museum, has hosted an annual reenactment of the proclamation. A local actor dressed in period costume for the occasion delivers McCook's address from the steps of the white-columned antebellum mansion. A free public celebration follows, with additional speeches, period entertainment, and a picnic across the street in Lewis Park. In addition, trolley tours are conducted to local African-American heritage sites, including a cemetery where African-American Union soldiers were laid to rest.

Long-celebrated by the local African-American community at various sites throughout the area, the observance of Emancipation Day includes a wreath-laying ceremony at Old City Cemetery and a number of educational and cultural functions during the preceding week.

CONTACTS:
Florida Division of Historical Resources
500 S. Bronough St.
R.A. Gray Bldg.
Tallahassee, FL 32399
850-245-6300; fax: 850-245-6454
dos.myflorida.com

♦ 0925 ♦ Emancipation Day (United States)
January 1

President Abraham Lincoln issued his famous Emancipation Proclamation freeing the slaves on January 1, 1863. Although some states have their own emancipation, or freedom, celebrations on the anniversary of the day on which they adopted the 13th Amendment, the most widespread observance takes place on January 1 because it is both a traditional and a legal holiday in all the states. In Texas, and other parts of the South and Southwest, the emancipation of the slaves is celebrated on June 19 or JUNETEENTH, the anniversary of the day in 1865 when General Gordon Granger arrived in Texas to enforce Lincoln's proclamation.

Celebrations are more common in the southern United States, where they frequently center around public readings of the original Emancipation Proclamation.

CONTACTS:
U.S. Government Publishing Office
732 N. Capitol St. N.W.
Washington, D.C. 20401
202-512-1800 or 866-512-1800; fax: 202-512-2104
www.gpo.gov

◆ 0926 ◆ Emancipation Day (Washington, D.C.)
April 16

In Washington, D.C., April 16th is celebrated as EMANCIPATION DAY, commemorating the day in 1862 when President Abraham Lincoln signed into law the District of Columbia Emancipation Act. This law was enacted nine months prior to the Emancipation Proclamation that freed slaves throughout the United States on January 1, 1863. At the time of their emancipation, slaves from the District of Columbia were offered $100 to relocate to colonies outside the United States. In addition, former masters who had remained loyal to the Union during the Civil War were compensated $300 for each freed slave. More than 3,000 slaves were freed under this agreement.

Commemoration of the event was celebrated with parades and festivities annually from 1866 through 1901. The holiday was revived in 2002, and since 2005 the date has been a legal holiday in the District. Events are scheduled throughout the preceding week, including lectures, speeches, reenactments, and a wreath-laying ceremony at the Emancipation Memorial in Lincoln Park near Capitol Hill. The observance culminates in a day of festivities and entertainment that begins with a parade down Pennsylvania Avenue in the morning and ends with evening fireworks on April 16th.

CONTACTS:
DC Emancipation Day Office
1350 Pennsylvania Ave. N.W.
John A. Wilson Bldg.
Rm. 419
Washington, D.C. 20004
202-727-6306
www.emancipationdc.com

◆ 0927 ◆ Emancipation Day Festival
August; varies

On August 1, 1834, the government of Upper Canada formally enacted the Emancipation Proclamation, which freed slaves in Canada. Word of this proclamation spread south to the United States, and thousands of American slaves sought to follow the North Star to find freedom in Canada.

Amherstburg, Ontario, was one of the first communities to hold celebrations in honor of this historic decree. Soon the celebrations spread to other cities, including Windsor. The Emancipation Day celebrations drew tens of thousands of Canadians and Americans. Over the years, Emancipation Day celebrations have included an Emancipation Day parade featuring floats, marching bands, precision drill teams, and dignitaries. The various festivities at Emancipation Day celebrations also included booths selling food and handicrafts.

During the 1930s women of color were often barred from entering mainstream beauty pageants. In 1931 Walter Perry organized the first annual Miss Sepia Pageant in Windsor, which helped bring beautiful and talented young black women into the spotlight. Contestants competed in the evening gown, swimwear, and talent categories. During the Emancipation Day parade, floats featuring the Miss Sepia contestants were always very popular.

CONTACTS:
North American Black Historical Museum
277 King St.
Amherstburg, ON N9V 2C7 Canada
519-736-5433 or 800-713-6336
www.blackhistoricalmuseum.org

◆ 0928 ◆ Ember Days
Four times a year

The Ember Days occur four times a year, at the beginning of each of the natural seasons. Traditionally they are marked by three days of fasting and abstinence—the Wednesday, Friday, and Saturday following, respectively, ASH WEDNESDAY, PENTECOST (Whitsunday), EXALTATION OF THE CROSS, and ST.

LUCY'S DAY. In 1966, the Roman Catholic Church replaced them with days of prayer for various needs and withdrew the obligation to fast. The Anglican Communion still observes them. The four weeks in which these days occur are called Ember Weeks, and the Friday in each of these weeks is known as **Golden Friday**. The word "ember" itself derives from an Old English word referring to the revolution of time.

Some scholars believe that the Ember Days originated with the old pagan purification rites that took place at the seasons of planting, harvest, and vintage. The idea of fasting on these days was instituted by Pope Calixtus I in the third century. By the ninth century it was observed throughout Europe, but it wasn't until 1095 that the dates were fixed. In the Roman Catholic Church and the Church of England, since the sixth century, priests have been ordained on an Ember Saturday.

CONTACTS:
Church of England
Church House
Great Smith St.
London SW1P 3AZ United Kingdom
44-20-7898-1000
www.churchofengland.org

♦ 0929 ♦ **Encaenia Day**
June

In general terms, *encaenia* (pronounced en-SEEN-ya) refers to the festivities celebrating the founding of a city or the dedication of a church. But in Oxford, England, Encaenia Day—sometimes referred to as **Commemoration Day**—is the day at the end of the summer term when the founders and benefactors of Oxford University are commemorated and honorary degrees are awarded to distinguished men and women. The ceremonies take place in the Sheldonian Theatre, designed by Christopher Wren when he was a professor of astronomy at the university, built between 1664-68. Based on a classical amphitheater, the Sheldonian offers an exceptional and often-photographed view from its cupola of Oxford's spires and gargoyles.

CONTACTS:
University of Oxford
Wellington Sq.
Oxford OX1 2JD United Kingdom
44-1865-270-000; fax: 44-1865-270-708
www.ox.ac.uk

♦ 0930 ♦ **Enescu (George) Festival**
August and September (in odd-numbered years)

The George Enescu Festival is held in Bucharest, Romania, over three to four weeks in August and September in odd-numbered years. More than 3,000 musicians, many of them distinguished artists, take part in Romania's celebration of its only famous classical-music composer, George Enescu (1881-1955). In addition to an extensive program of concerts and recitals, prestigious competitions are held at the same time for composers, pianists, and violinists. The rest of the country joins in with related concerts in other parts of Romania.

In 1958, the then-communist regime in Romania launched the festival to honor an artist who had been driven out by their policies: Enescu had died in Paris just three years earlier. Concert venues are centered around Bucharest's Enescu Square and include the Sala Mare a Palatului (Palace Hall) and the Ateneul Roman (Romanian Atheneum), a neoclassical rotunda. Music lovers flock to the festival, whose ticket prices are far lower than many of its counterpart classical-music festivals in Europe.

CONTACTS:
Romanian National Tourist Office
355 Lexington Ave.
8th Fl.
New York, NY 10017
212-545-8484
www.romaniatourism.com

♦ 0931 ♦ **Enkutatash**
September 11

The **Ethiopian New Year** falls on the first day of the Ethiopian month of Maskarem, which is September 11 on the Gregorian calendar. It comes at the end of the rainy season, so the wildflowers that the children gather and the tall grass that rural people use to cover their floors on this day are plentiful. Small groups of children go from house to house, singing songs, leaving small bouquets of flowers, and hoping for a handful of *dabo*, or roasted grain, in return. In some parts of Ethiopia it is customary to slaughter an animal on this day. For traditional reasons this is either a white-headed lamb or a red chicken.

CONTACTS:
Ethiopian Embassy
3506 International Dr. N.W.
Washington, D.C. 20008
202-364-1200; fax: 202-587-0195
www.ethiopianembassy.org

♦ 0932 ♦ **Enlighteners, Day of the (Den na Buditelite)**
November 1

A holiday in Bulgaria, this day commemorates the patriots, writers, and revolutionaries who helped to ignite the spirit of Bulgarian nationalism. Thanksgiving services are held in churches, and elsewhere patriotic speeches, parades, and folk music mark this yearly event. Also known as the **Day of the Awakeners**, it is largely observed by schools and munici-palities.

CONTACTS:
Embassy of the Republic of Bulgaria
1621 22nd St. N.W.
Dimitar Peshev Plaza
Washington, D.C. 20008
202-387-0174; fax: 202-234-7973
www.bulgaria-embassy.org

♦ 0933 ♦ **Eo e Emalani i Alaka i Festival**
Second Saturday in October

The Eo e Emalani i Alaka i Festival is an annual outdoor celebration that takes place, rain or shine, on the second Saturday in October in Koke'e State Park, Kaua'i, Hawaii. It is a joyous commemoration of the journey of Hawaiian Queen Emma Naea Rooke in 1871 from her beach house in Lawa'i to the upper reaches of Kilohana Viewpoint, where she wanted to see for herself the legendary, sweeping views reaching to Wainiha. The Queen, with nearly 100 companions, was led by a legendary guide, Kaluahi, recommended by Eric Knudsen of Waimea.

At the festival, the nature-loving Queen Emma is represented by a woman from the halau (a school where hula-dancing is taught). She and an entourage re-enact Queen Emma's entrance to the mountain meadow, where they are greeted by numerous Hawaiian hula dancers who offer ancient chants and special dances to the royal party. Guests at the free festival are asked to observe royal protocol, such as standing when the Queen enters or leaves the royal tent set up for the occasion. In addition to the historical re-enactment, the day's activities include a photographic exhibit and demonstrations of local crafts, including lauhala (fan and matt) weaving and Ni'ihau shell lei-making. Approximately 2,500 local guests and visitors attend each year's festival, sponsored by the Koke'e Natural History Museum in Kekeha, Kaua'i.

CONTACTS:
Hui o Laka / Kokee Museum
P.O. Box 100
Kekaha, HI 96752
808-335-9975
www.kokee.org

◆ 0934 ◆ Epidaurus Festival
Weekends from July to September

The Epidaurus Festival is marked by theatrical productions of ancient Greek tragedy and comedy at the theater built in the third century B.C.E. in Epidaurus, Greece, about 90 miles southwest of Athens. This open-air theater, the best preserved in Greece, can seat 14,000, and the acoustics are so fine that those seated in the top row can hear a whisper on stage. The performances, also known as the **Festival of Ancient Drama**, are presented by various theaters in the area. Summaries of the Greek-language plays are available to the audience in English.

CONTACTS:
Greek Festival
23 Hadjichristou & Makriyanni St.
Athens 11742 Greece
30-210-928-2900; fax: 30-210-928-2941
www.greekfestival.gr

◆ 0935 ◆ Epiphany (Germany) (Dreikönigsfest)
January 6

Boys dressed up as the Three Kings go from house to house caroling on EPIPHANY in Germany. Because they take with them a long pole from which dangles a star, they are known as Starsingers, or *Sternsinger* (see also EPIPHANY IN SWEDEN and NEW YEAR'S DAY IN GERMANY). In western and southern Germany, salt and chalk are consecrated in church on this day. The salt is given to animals to lick, while the chalk is used to write the initials of the Three Kings—*C.M.B.* for Caspar, Melchior, and Balthasar—over the house and stable doors to protect the household from danger and to keep out the evil spirits.

According to folk belief, a mysterious witch known as *Frau Perchta* (also Berchta or Bertha) wanders about the earth causing trouble between CHRISTMAS and Epiphany. In Upper Bavaria, according to tradition, peasants wearing wooden masks go around cracking whips and symbolically driving out Perchta, who is actually an ancient German fertility goddess and custodian of the dead. It is for this reason that Epiphany is also known as **Perchtennacht**. The Perchta masks, which can be terrifying in their ugliness, are often handed down from one generation to the next.

See also PERCHTENLAUF.

CONTACTS:
Shrine of the Three Holy Kings
Domkloster 3
Köln 50667 Germany
49-221-1794-0200; fax: 49-221-1794-0299
www.koelner-dom.de

◆ 0936 ◆ Epiphany (Labrador)
January 6

The *naluyuks* that visit children on EPIPHANY in Labrador, Canada, are a combination of Santa Claus and the bogeyman. They go from house to house on January 6, their bodies covered in bearskin or an oversized coat with a mask over their faces and a stick in their hands along with a bag of gifts that has been donated ahead of time by parents. Children regard the coming of the naluyuks with great trepidation; Eskimo parents tell tales of a bogeyman figure, the naluyuk, to frighten them into good behavior.

When the naluyuks enter the house, the children perform a Christmas carol or hymn for them, and the naluyuks show their approval by pounding their sticks on the floor. After the singing, the children are asked various questions regarding their behavior over the past year. If the naluyuks are pleased with the answers, they hand each child a gift from their bag.

CONTACTS:
United Church of Canada - Newfoundland and Labrador Conference
320 Elizabeth Ave.
St. John''s, NL A1B 1T9 Canada
709-754-0387 or 709-754-0392; fax: 709-754-8336
www.newlabconf.com

◆ 0937 ◆ Epiphany (Portugal) (Día de Reis)
January 6

EPIPHANY plays and pageants are common in Portugal, particularly in rural areas of the country. Bands of carolers go from house to house singing and begging for gifts. Sometimes family groups visit one another, standing at the door and asking to come in so they can sing to the Christ Child. After they sing their carols, the guests are entertained with wines and sweets.

It is common for parents to give parties for their children on Epiphany Day. The Epiphany cake, or *bolo-rei*, is a favorite tradition at these parties. Baked in the shape of a crown or ring, the cake contains many small trinkets and a single dried bean. Whoever finds the bean is crowned king of the party and must promise to make the cake the following year. At adult parties, the person who finds the bean is expected to pay for the following year's cake.

Epiphany is also a time when the traditional Portuguese dances known as *mouriscadas* and *paulitos* are performed. The latter is an elaborate stick dance in which the dancers, who are usually male but may be dressed as women, manipulate sticks or staves (substitutes for swords) in two opposing lines.

CONTACTS:
All Saints Anglican Church
CP 13
Lagoa, Algarve 8401-901 Portugal
351-282-380-311
allsaintsalgarve.org

AICEP Office in New York
590 Fifth Ave.
4th Fl.
New York, NY 10036
646-723-0299; fax: 212-575-4737
www.embassyportugal-us.org

◆ 0938 ◆ **Epiphany (Russia)**
January 19

On January 19th, members of the Russian Orthodox Church ritually bathe in a river or lake. The day marks the baptism of Jesus Christ in the River Jordan, an event called the Epiphany. Bathing outside on that day, Orthodox Catholics believe, washes away sin. As believers cut holes in the ice with chainsaws and plunge into the frigid water, priests chant prayers to bless the water. Altars and crosses made of ice and snow are sometimes constructed near the bathing site.

Authorities advise against the practice, especially in the freezing temperatures of a Russian winter. Still, in 2006, some 2,000 persons were said to have participated in the ritual in the Moscow area alone.

CONTACTS:
Russian Orthodox Church - Department for External Church Relations
22, Danilovsky val
Danilov Monastery DECR MP
Moscow 115191 Russia
7-495-633-8428; fax: 7-495-633-8428
mospat.ru/en

◆ 0939 ◆ **Epiphany (Spain) (Día de los Reyes Magos)**
January 6

Epiphany is the day when Spanish children receive their gifts, and it is the Three Kings, rather than Santa Claus, who bring them. On Epiphany Eve the children fill their shoes with straw or grain for the Three Kings' horses to eat and place them on balconies or by the front door. The next morning, they find cookies, sweets, and gifts in their place.

In many cities throughout Spain, the Three Kings make a spectacular entry on Epiphany Eve, to the accompaniment of military bands and drummers in medieval dress. The Kings themselves usually ride horses, although in the Canary Islands they arrive by camel. One custom was for groups of people to walk out toward the city boundary to meet the Kings, some carrying ladders and some making a huge racket with horns, bells, and drums. Occasionally, those with ladders would pause in the procession while someone climbed a ladder to look for the Kings.

CONTACTS:
Santa María Cathedral Foundation
Cuchillería, 95
Vitoria-Gasteiz 01001 Spain
34-94-512-2160; fax: 34-94-512-2160
www.catedralvitoria.com/ingles/index.php

Tourist Office of Spain
60 E. 42nd St.
Ste. 5300, 53rd Fl.
New York, NY 10165
212-265-8822; fax: 212-265-8864
www.spain.info

◆ 0940 ◆ **Epiphany (Sweden) (Trettondag Jul)**
January 6

The **Night of the Three Holy Kings** was celebrated in Sweden during the Middle Ages with ecclesiastical folk plays commemorating the Magi's finding of Jesus in the manger. It is still customary for *Stjärngossar*, or Star Boys (*see also* Epiphany in Germany), to present pageants dramatizing the journey of the Three Kings to Bethlehem. They wear white robes and cone-shaped hats with pompons and astronomical symbols on them. They carry paper star lanterns on long poles, illuminated from within by candles.

In rural areas, the Star Boys go from house to house, accompanied by other children dressed in costumes to resemble biblical characters, singing folk songs and hymns. The group almost always includes someone dressed up as Judas, wearing a huge false nose and carrying a purse or money bag jingling with the 30 pieces of silver he received for betraying Jesus.

CONTACTS:
Swedish Church Office
Sysslomansgatan 4
Uppsala 751 70 Sweden
46-18-16-9600
www.svenskakyrkan.se

◆ 0941 ◆ **Epiphany, Christian Orthodox**
January 6 (Gregorian calendar) or January 19 (Julian calendar)

Epiphany is a celebration by the Eastern Orthodox Christian churches of the baptism of Jesus in the River Jordan and the manifestation of his divinity when a dove descended on him. For Orthodox Christians around the world it is called **Blessing of the Waters Day**. In honor of the baptism of Christ, the church's baptismal water is blessed, and small bottles of the holy water are given to parishioners to take home. In many American cities, the priest leads the congregation to a local river which he blesses. Many places throughout the world mark the day with a blessing of the waters and immersion of a cross in seas, lakes, and rivers. At the port of Piraeus, Greece, the local priest throws a cross into the sea, and the diver who retrieves it is thought to be blessed with good luck in the coming year.

In pre-revolutionary Russia, priests and church officials led a procession to the banks of streams or rivers, breaking the ice and lowering a crucifix into the water. Those brave enough to jump into the icy waters to recover the crucifix were thought to be especially blessed. In the north, diving for the cross is frequently done on September 14 (*see* Exaltation of the Cross), when the water is warmer.

The holy day of the Epiphany is celebrated in colorful fashion in Tarpon Springs, Fla., at one time a sea sponge center with the largest sponge market in the world. The community has a strong Greek influence, going back to the beginning of the 20th century when sponge divers from Greece came here to take part in the growing sponge industry. On Epiphany, up to 100 young men from Greek Orthodox churches compete in diving for a gold cross. The cross has been tossed into the bayou by the chief celebrant from the town's St. Nicholas Greek Orthodox Church, and the person who retrieves it will be specially blessed.

Events of this holiday begin the day before with a blessing of the sponge fleet. The next morning, after the church service and a blessing of the waters, there is a parade of school and civic groups led by ecclesiastical dignitaries in their vestments. Many of the paraders wear Greek costume. After the parade, when the cross has been retrieved, the day becomes festive, with bouzouki music, dancing, and feasting, especially on roast lamb. Epiphany has been observed in this manner at Tarpon Springs since 1904, and now attracts about 30,000 people.

In Greece, Epiphany is one of the country's most important church days, especially in the port towns where diving for the cross takes place. After services, on the eve of Epiphany in Cyprus, priests visit houses to cleanse them from demons known as *Kallikantzari*. According to Cypriot tradition, these evil spirits appear on earth at Christmas, and for the next 12 days play evil tricks on people. On the eve of their departure, people appease them by throwing pancakes and sausages onto their roofs, which is where the demons dwell.

See also Epiphany, Feast of the.

CONTACTS:
St. Nicholas Greek Orthodox Cathedral
17 E. Tarpon Ave.
Tarpon Springs, FL 34689
727-937-3540
www.epiphanycity.org

Orthodox Church in America
6850 N. Hempstead Tpke.
Syosset, NY 11791
516-922-0550; fax: 516-922-0954
www.oca.org

♦ 0942 ♦ **Epiphany Eve (Austria)**
January 5

At one time the 12 nights between Christmas and Epiphany were known as "Smoke Nights" in Austria because people went through their houses and barns burning incense. Now the ceremony takes place on only one night, January 5. Also

known as the **Vigil of Epiphany**, there is traditionally a special feast on this night during which an Epiphany cake is served. Three beans are concealed in the cake—two white, one black— and whoever finds a bean in his or her portion gets to dress up as one of the Three Wise Men or Holy Kings. The one with the black bean dresses up as the African king, Balthasar, by rubbing his face with soot or shoe polish. On Epiphany Day the three kings are the guests of honor at the table.

After the Epiphany Eve meal is served, to follow an old custom, the father or head of the household takes a shovelful of coal and burns incense on it. He walks through the house and outbuildings spreading smoke from the incense, followed by the oldest son, who sprinkles holy water in his path. The rest of the family follow, with the youngest child carrying a piece of chalk on a plate that has been blessed in morning mass. After each room and outbuilding has been blessed, the father takes the chalk and writes the initials of the Three Kings—C for Caspar, M for Melchior, and B for Balthasar—over every door leading to the outside. The ritual is believed to protect the household from evil in the coming year.

See also Perchtenlauf.

CONTACTS:
Embassy of Austria
3524 International Ct. N.W.
Washington, D.C. 20008
202-895-6700; fax: 202-895-6750
www.austria.org

♦ 0943 ♦ **Epiphany Eve (France)**
January 5

On the eve of **Le Jour des Rois** ("the Day of the Kings") it is customary in France to give food, clothing, money, and gifts to the parish poor. In Alsace, children go from door to door dressed as the Three Kings, asking for donations of eggs, bacon, and cakes. In Normandy, children make their neighborhood rounds carrying Chinese lanterns and empty baskets, in which they hope to collect food, clothing, and money. In Brittany, someone dressed as a beggar leads a horse, decorated with ribbons and mistletoe, through the streets. There are empty baskets hanging from the saddle in which donations are carried. In Provence and some other parts of southern France, children go out on Epiphany Eve to meet the Three Kings, carrying cakes and figs for the hungry Magi and hay for their camels. Even though they may not meet the Three Kings on the road, they can see their statues standing near the altar of the church, where an Epiphany mass is celebrated at night.

CONTACTS:
Association of Friends of the Coutances Cathedral
1 Rue du Puits Notre Dame
Coutances 50200 France
cathedralecoutances.free.fr

♦ 0944 ♦ **Epiphany, Feast of the**
January 6

One of the oldest Christian feasts (celebrated since the end of the second century, before the establishment of the CHRISTMAS holiday), Epiphany (which means "manifestation" or "showing forth") is sometimes called **Twelfth Day**, THREE KINGS' DAY, DÍA DE LOS TRES REYES (in Latin America), the **Feast of Jordan** (by Ukrainian Orthodox), or OLD CHRISTMAS DAY.

It commemorates the first two occasions on which the divinity of Jesus was manifested: when the Three Kings (or Magi) came to worship the infant Jesus in Bethlehem, and when he was baptized by John the Baptist in the River Jordan and the Holy Spirit descended in the form of a dove and proclaimed him the Son of God. The Roman Catholic and Protestant churches emphasize the visit of the Magi when they celebrate the Epiphany; the Eastern Orthodox churches focus on the baptism of Jesus. The blessing of lakes, rivers, and seas plays a central role in their celebrations.

In France **Le Jour des Rois** (the **Day of the Kings**), sometimes called the **Fête des Rois**, is celebrated with parties for children and adults alike. The highlight of these celebrations is the *galette des rois*, or "cake of the Kings"—a round, flat cake which is cut in the pantry, covered with a white napkin, and carried into the dining room on a small table. An extra piece is always cut, which is traditionally called *le part à Dieu* ("God's share") and is reserved for the first poor person who comes to the door.

The youngest person in the room oversees the distribution of the pieces of cake, one of which contains a bean or tiny china doll. The person who finds this token becomes king or queen for the evening. He or she chooses a consort, and for the remainder of the evening, every move the royal couple makes is imitated and commented upon by the other guests, who take great delight in exclaiming, for example, "The King drinks!" or "The Queen coughs!"

In many parts of France, the celebration begins on the evening of January 5 and involves collecting and distributing food and gifts for the poor (*see* EPIPHANY EVE IN FRANCE).

Now observed by a growing number of Protestants as well as Roman Catholics and Orthodox Christians, Epiphany refers not only to the day itself but to the church season that follows it—a season whose length varies because it ends when LENT begins, and that depends on the date of EASTER.

See also BEFANA FESTIVAL; FOUR AN' TWENTY DAY; EPIPHANY, CHRISTIAN ORTHODOX; TIMQAT; and TWELFTH NIGHT.

CONTACTS:
French Alliance of Oklahoma City
P.O. Box 414
Oklahoma City, OK 73101
405-748-0868
afdokc.org

Union of Diocesan Associations of France
58 Ave. de Breteuil
Paris 75007 France
fax: 33-1-7372-9722
www.eglise.catholique.fr

♦ 0945 ♦ **Equal Opportunity Day**
November 19

At the dedication of the Gettysburg National Cemetery in southern Pennsylvania on November 19, 1863, President Abraham LINCOLN delivered the GETTYSBURG Address. This 270-word speech is considered one of the greatest in American history, though it didn't receive much attention at the time. Equal Opportunity Day is observed at Gettysburg National Cemetery each year, where ceremonies commemorating Lincoln's address are held under the sponsorship of the Sons of Union Veterans and the Lincoln Fellowship of Pennsylvania. Sometimes this day is referred to as **Gettysburg Address Day**.

CONTACTS:
Gettysburg National Cemetery
1195 Baltimore Pike
Gettysburg, PA
717-334-1124
www.nps.gov

♦ 0946 ♦ **Equatorial Guinea Independence Day**
October 12

On this day in 1968, Equatorial Guinea became independent from Spain after being one of its colonies for nearly 300 years. On October 12—the same day on which COLUMBUS DAY is celebrated elsewhere in the world—Equatorial Guinea celebrates its autonomy with a national holiday.

CONTACTS:
Embassy of Equatorial Guinea
2020 16th St. N.W.
Washington, D.C. 20009
202-518-5700; fax: 202-518-5252
egembassydc.com

♦ 0947 ♦ **Equirria**
February 27 and March 14

Tradition holds that Romulus, one of the mythical founders of Rome, began the Equirria. This festival was held on both February 27 and March 14. The Equirria mainly involved racing horses and was dedicated to Mars, the Roman god of war. Scholars don't know why there were two annual Equirrias little more than two weeks apart from each other, but one theory is that these were occasions to publicly begin training horses and men for the military excursions Roman soldiers undertook in the spring. There is also a question of whether the later Equirria was related to the MAMURALIA, also observed on March 14.

CONTACTS:
Italian National Tourist Board
686 Park Ave.
3rd Fl.
New York, NY 10065
212-245-5618; fax: 212-586-9249
www.italiantourism.com

◆ 0948 ◆ Eradication of Poverty, International Day for the
October 17

The UNITED NATIONS named October 17 the International Day for the Eradication of Poverty in 1992. In doing so, the U.N. followed the lead of some non-governmental organizations that had already dedicated the day to promoting awareness of the plight of the extremely poor. The U.N. observance focuses especially on the needs of the destitute in developing countries.

CONTACTS:
United Nations, Department of Public Information
United Nations Headquarters
Rm. DHL-1B-154
New York, NY 10017
212-963-4475
www.un.org

◆ 0949 ◆ Erau Festival
September

This Indonesian festival takes place in Tenggarong, in the province of East Kalimantan on the island of Borneo. Some of the most isolated people in the world live in the surrounding area, where the dense jungle has made contact among neighboring villages difficult and where, until recently, raiding parties were common.

Today the Erau Festival is celebrated for as long as a week around September 24, the anniversary of the city's founding, though many of the ceremonies performed during the festival go back much further. The festival opens with special blessing and purification ceremonies, followed by musical and dance performances, art exhibits, and more traditional Dayak ceremonies.

CONTACTS:
CIOFF Indonesia
Jl. Tomang Utara III / 270
Jakarta 11440 Indonesia
62-21-5657882; fax: 62-21-5657882
www.cioff-indonesia.org

◆ 0950 ◆ Eritrea Independence Day
May 24

Eritrea is a small country on the Red Sea, northeast of Ethiopia, of which it was a part until 1993. Eritreans struggled for 30 years for independence from Ethiopia. Internationally observed elections in 1993 decided the outcome as all but 0.2 percent of Eritreans voted to become independent, which became official on May 24, 1993. A border dispute with Ethiopia caused war from 1998 until 2000, when the UNITED NATIONS resolved the issue.

CONTACTS:
Embassy of Eritrea
1708 New Hampshire Ave. N.W.
Washington, D.C. 20009

202-319-1991; fax: 202-319-1304
www.embassyeritrea.org

◆ 0951 ◆ Eritrean Martyrs' Day
June 20

Following its defeat of Ethiopian government forces in 1991 to establish national independence, Eritrea instituted an official holiday to pay tribute to those who died for the country's liberation. The struggle, which lasted from 1961 to 1991, claimed the lives of an estimated 65,000 freedom fighters and tens of thousands of civilians.

Many Eritreans observe Martyrs' Day by filing into mass mourning processions that conclude at the "Martyrs' Graveyards" located throughout the country. On the eve of Martyrs' Day in 1997, the government expanded the national tribute by opening the National Martyrs' Park, situated in a forest and wildlife preserve outside the capital city, Asmara.

Individuals arrive to pay their respects to the dead by finding names engraved on the National Martyrs' Monument and walking through museums that depict the 30-year struggle for independence.

CONTACTS:
Ministry of Culture and Tourism
P.O. Box 2183
Addis Ababa Ethiopia
251-11-551-2310; fax: 251-11-551-2889
www.tourismethiopia.org/pages/ethiopia.asp

Eritrean Ministry of Tourism
Warsay St.
P.O. Box 1010
Asmara Eritrea
291-115-4100; fax: 291-115-4081
www.eritrea.be

◆ 0952 ◆ Eritrean Start of the Armed Struggle Day
September 1

Between 1961 and 1991 the small country of Eritrea in eastern Africa waged a war of independence against Ethiopia. An important holiday that recognizes Eritrean sacrifices during this prolonged campaign is the Start of the Armed Struggle Day, also known as **Bahti Meskerem**. The day's festivities take place in the country and in Eritrean communities throughout the world.

The anniversary commemorates the first shot fired in 1961 at Mount Adal, in the country's western region. Leading the attack was Idris Hamid Awate, founder of the Eritrean Liberation Army and a celebrated martyr.

In the years since Eritrea's independence was approved by popular referendum in 1993, this anniversary has been less of a war cry against Ethiopia and more an occasion to simply remember the contributions of freedom fighters. Typically, observances include a moment of silence in honor of the martyrs, the singing of the Eritrean national anthem, and public statements by dignitaries.

CONTACTS:
Eritrean Embassy
1708 New Hampshire Ave. N.W.
Washington, D.C. 20009
202-319-1991; fax: 202-319-1304
www.embassyeritrea.org

◆ 0953 ◆ Esala Perahera (Arrival of the Tooth Relic)
July-August; Sinhalese month of Esala

Esala Perahera is a celebration in Kandy, Sri Lanka (formerly Ceylon), that lasts 10 nights and pays homage to the sacred relic believed to be a tooth of the Buddha. Kandy, originally the capital of the independent kingdom of Kandy in the Sri Lankan highlands, is the site of the Dalada Maligava, or Temple of the Tooth, where the relic is kept. The celebration originated in the fourth century when the king of Kandy declared that the tooth be paraded annually so people could honor it.

Processions are held each night for 10 nights, and the tooth is paraded in an elaborate *howdah* (platform) on the back of an ornately decorated elephant. Dozens of richly caparisoned elephants follow, and there are also drummers beating big bass drums and small tom-toms, horn blowers, the famous Kandyan dancers, acrobats, and torch bearers holding aloft baskets of blazing *copra* (coconut meat). Representatives of the major Hindu temples also are part of the processions.

CONTACTS:
Sri Dalada Maligawa
Sri Dalada Veediya
Kandy 20000 Sri Lanka
94-812-234-226; fax: 94-812-205-901
www.sridaladamaligawa.lk

◆ 0954 ◆ Esbat
Full moon of each month; sometimes at the new moon and sometimes at both the full and new moons

"Wicca" is the term used by many believers in modern Neo-pagan witchcraft to describe themselves because it doesn't carry the negative connotations of the words "witch" and "pagan." Many Wiccan covens (assemblies of witches) hold regular meetings, known as Esbats, on the most convenient evening nearest the full and/or new moon. Esbat rituals typically use color, nature symbolism, candles, and symbolic acts to enhance the attributes of a particular moon—the Oak Moon, the Wolf Moon, the Storm Moon, etc. There are 13 moons in one solar year.

The rituals associated with the Esbats, which are usually known by heart, serve as a form of worship, a means of teaching, an aide to meditation, and a form of communication between the worshipper and the gods. Esbat meetings are usually open only to initiates, because they are specifically intended to develop members who are in training for the Wiccan priesthood.

CONTACTS:
Aquarian Tabernacle Church
P.O. Box 409
Index, WA 98256
360-793-1945
www.aquariantabernaclechurch.org

◆ 0955 ◆ Escalade (Scaling the Walls)
Weekend in mid-December

Escalade is a celebration in Geneva, Switzerland, of the victory of the people of Geneva over the attacking French Savoyards. On the nights of Dec. 11 and 12 in 1602, the French soldiers tried to scale the city ramparts, but were ferociously turned back. Among the remembered defenders is Mère Royaume, who poured a pot of scalding soup on the head of a Savoyard soldier.

To mark the victory, people carrying torches and wearing period costumes and armor proceed through the old city on both banks of the Rhone River. Historic figures, like Mère Royaume, are always represented. Shops sell chocolates that look like miniature soup pots. These commemorate Royaume's courageous act. At several points on the route, the procession stops while a herald on horseback reads the proclamation of victory. The procession winds up at St. Peter's Cathedral, where the citizens sing patriotic songs and a huge bonfire concludes the celebration. From there revelers can feast on Mère Royaume's soup and tour the Passage de Monetier. Open to the public only at this time of year, this secret passageway under the Cathedral runs along the old city walls.

On the first Saturday in December a local sports club organizes various races to celebrate, ranging from two to nine kilometers, around the St. Pierre Cathedral. In the evening everyone can participate in the most popular event: the soup pot, or *La Marmite*, race. Runners cover 3.4 kilometers while dressed in costume which can range from witches and skeletons to the more modern and innovative.

CONTACTS:
Switzerland Tourism
608 Fifth Ave.
Ste. 603
New York, NY 10020
212-757-5944 or 800-794-7795; fax: 212-262-6116
www.myswitzerland.com

◆ 0956 ◆ Esplanade Concerts
July 4

Arthur Fiedler (1894-1979), a violinist for the Boston Symphony Orchestra, started this outdoor concert series on July 4, 1929. The first concerts were held under a temporary wooden shell along the banks of the Charles River in Boston, which has since been replaced by the Hatch Memorial Shell, a gift presented to the city in 1940. The concerts are free, and it is not uncommon for hundreds of thousands to gather on the grassy riverbank or listen to the concerts from boats moored in the Charles River lagoon for the FOURTH OF

July holiday. A musically synchronized fireworks display follows the concert.

During the Bicentennial celebration in 1976, the Boston Pops Esplanade Orchestra performed a spectacular rendition of Tchaikovsky's *1812 Overture*. The music was accompanied by the firing of live cannons, the ringing of nearby church bells, and fireworks.

See also Boston Pops.

CONTACTS:
Department of Conservation and Recreation
251 Causeway St.
Ste. 900
Boston, MA 02114
617-626-1250; fax: 617-626-1351
www.mass.gov

♦ 0957 ♦ Essence Festival
Early July

The Essence Music Festival bills itself as the "the nation's largest annual African-American event and gathering of musical talent." The three-day event was launched in 1995. From 1995 through 2005, a combined total of two million fans have taken part in the event. Featured performers have included such renowned African-American musicians as Alicia Keys, Aretha Franklin, Destiny's Child, Earth, Wind & Fire, Gladys Knight, Prince, and Kanye West.

The festival began in New Orleans in 1995 as a one-time event to celebrate the 25th anniversary of *Essence*, the African-American lifestyle magazine, but its success inspired *Essence* to make it an annual event. After the devastation of Hurricane Katrina, the festival temporarily relocated from New Orleans to Houston in 2005. The following year, it returned to New Orleans. According to *Essence* magazine, the festival is a multigenerational event where far-flung African-American families and friends reunite.

CONTACTS:
Essence Magazine
135 W. 50th St.
4th Fl.
New York, NY 10020
800-274-9398
www.essence.com

♦ 0958 ♦ Estonia Independence Day
February 24

On this day in 1918, Estonia issued a declaration of independence from the new Soviet Russia, which was followed by war with the Soviets to maintain Estonian liberty. On February 2, 1920, the war ended with the Tartu Peace Treaty which guaranteed Estonia's independence for all time. The Soviets went on to break this pact, however, and Estonia was under Soviet control for 75 years.

Following a strong independence movement during the late 1980s, Estonia officially declared its independence from the former U.S.S.R. on August 20, 1991, a day which is also commemorated with a public holiday. Latvia and Lithuania had also declared independence from the disintegrating Soviet empire. On September 6, independence was formally recognized by the former Soviet Union.

Estonians celebrate their Independence Day with a parade, church services, speeches, and concerts in the capital city, Tallinn.

CONTACTS:
Ministry of Foreign Affairs, Republic of Estonia
Islandi valjak 1
Tallinn 15049 Estonia
372-6-377-000; fax: 372-6-377-098
vm.ee/en

♦ 0959 ♦ Estonia Restoration of Independence Day
August 20

In the 20th century, Estonia was a sovereign state from 1919 to 1940. At that time, it was forced to become a socialist republic of the Soviet Union. Then, in 1991, the Soviet Union collapsed, and the three Baltic countries of Estonia, Latvia, and Lithuania regained their independence. On August 20 of that year, Estonia formally re-established its independence following a national referendum.

Throughout 2008, the country celebrated its 90th anniversary as a republic. The government encouraged citizens to devote the entire month of August to appreciating the blessings of independence and to remembering the Estonian patriots who suffered through exile and resistance during the Soviet era.

Estonia Restoration of Independence Day is one of three days on which the national flag must be hoisted on state buildings. (The other two days are Estonia Victory Day and Estonia Independence Day.).

CONTACTS:
Estonia Embassy in Washington
2131 Massachusetts Ave. N.W.
Washington, D.C. 20008
202-588-0101; fax: 202-588-0108
www.estemb.org

♦ 0960 ♦ Estonia Victory Day
June 23

In light of the multiple times Estonia has lost its sovereignty, the independence celebration known as Victory Day bears special significance for citizens. This date commemorates the Battle of Vönnu in 1919, in which a joint force of Estonians and Latvians claimed a decisive victory against their Baltic German adversaries. The celebration falls a day before the same date as two time-honored celebrations, Midsummer Day and the St. John's Day (Jaanipäev in Estonian). As a result of the synchronicity of the festivals, various traditions and observances have melded together.

The military triumph in 1919 marked the end of 700 years of German control. The present-day government has framed the holiday as a celebration of Estonian freedom and sovereignty. The president and other dignitaries attend the official Victory Day ceremonies in the capital city, Tallinn. Festivities include a parade, a speech by the president, and a military review.

The holiday transitions from the political to the traditional when the president orders citizens to take torches from the official bonfire held in honor of Victory Day to light the hundreds of bonfires in the country that initiate Midsummer and St. John's Eve celebrations.

CONTACTS:
Estonia Embassy in Washington
2131 Massachusetts Ave. N.W.
Washington, D.C. 20008
202-588-0101; fax: 202-588-0108
www.estemb.org

♦ 0961 ♦ Ethiopia National Day
May 28

A military junta called the Derg brought an end to the Ethiopian Empire and HAILE SELASSIE'S rule September 12, 1974. Haile Selassie (born Tafari Makonnen, 1892-1975) was crowned in 1930, inheriting the throne from a long line of regents. According to tradition, he was the 111th ruler descended from King Solomon and the Queen of Sheba.

The Derg socialist military regime was overthrown by the Ethiopian People's Revolutionary Democratic Front (EPRDF) in 1991, commemorated by the May 28 holiday. A constitution was adopted in 1994 and Ethiopia's first multiparty elections were held in 1995.

CONTACTS:
Ethiopian Embassy
3506 International Dr. N.W.
Washington, D.C. 20008
202-364-1200; fax: 202-587-0195
www.ethiopianembassy.org

♦ 0962 ♦ Ethiopia Patriots' Victory Day
May 5

Emperor Haile Selassie of Ethiopia made a grand entrance into the capital city, Addis Ababa, on May 5, 1941, to mark the end of the Italian occupation. Selassie had deliberately chosen that date because exactly five years earlier, the Italians had entered the city and initiated a period of occupation that halted Ethiopia's long legacy of sovereignty. However, the intervention of British forces and other Allies, as well as the heroics of Ethiopian patriots, helped preserve Ethiopia's independence. Ever since, Ethiopians have annually commemorated Selassie's famous arrival into the capital.

In Addis Ababa, government leaders, diplomats, patriot associations, and city residents turn out to honor veterans who fought in the resistance movement between 1935 and 1941. A dignitary often lays a wreath before one of the city's monu-

ments commemorating Ethiopia's various military victories. Army brass bands also perform to mark the occasion.

CONTACTS:
Ministry of Culture and Tourism
P.O. Box 2183
Addis Ababa Ethiopia
251-11-551-2310; fax: 251-11-551-2889
www.tourismethiopia.org/pages/ethiopia.asp

Ethiopian Embassy
3506 International Dr. N.W.
Washington, D.C. 20008
202-364-1200; fax: 202-587-0195
www.ethiopianembassy.org

Royal Norwegian Embassy in Addis Ababa
P.O. Box 8383
Addis Ababa Ethiopia
251-11-371-0799; fax: 251-11-3711255
www.norway.org.et

♦ 0963 ♦ Ethiopia Victory of Adwa Commemoration Day
March 2

Ethiopia enjoys rare distinction as an African country that successfully shook off European domination for centuries. One pivotal moment of resistance was the Ethiopian army's historic victory over invading Italian troops in the Battle of Adwa. The two-day battle, fought in northern Ethiopia in 1896 and led by Emperor Menelik II, ended on March 2. The great military feat stands as a turning point in the history of modern Africa. The anniversary is thus a significant patriotic holiday for Ethiopians.

Festivities take place throughout the country, with official ceremonies in the capital, Addis Ababa, and Adwa, the historical market town located near the battle site. Past celebrations in the capital have featured addresses by national leaders, with messages focusing on Ethiopia's forefathers and their achievements. People will also leave wreaths at the foot of the Menelik Monument, which commemorates the victory led by the Ethiopian emperor.

The celebration in 2005 was a milestone because it occurred the day before the Italian government returned to Ethiopia the Axum obelisk, a 4th-century relic that the Fascist forces looted during a brief period of conquest and occupation in the 1930s.

CONTACTS:
Embassy of Ethiopia
3506 International Dr. N.W.
Washington, D.C. 20008
202-364-1200; fax: 202-587-0195
www.ethiopianembassy.org

Ministry of Communication and Information Technology-Ethiopia
Mexico Sq. Alta Bldg. 6th Fl.
P.O.Box 1028
Addis Ababa Ethiopia
251-11-550-0191; fax: 251-11- 551-5894
www.mcit.gov.et

◆ 0964 ◆ Ethiopian Sigd Festival
October to November; Heshvan 29

Sigd is a holiday of the Ethiopian Jewish community, celebrated on the 29th day of Heshvan, exactly 50 days after Yom Kippur. The holiday is meant to commemorate the acceptance of the Torah, and the community's commitment to Jewish identity and desire to return to Jerusalem. In 2008, the Knesset designated Sigd as an Israeli national holiday.

During the Sigd celebration in Ethiopia, members of the community begin the day fasting and follow the *kessim* (priests) to the top of a high mountain to pray. The kessim read from the Torah, and the congregants kneel or bow and hold their hands up to the sky, asking for forgiveness of their sins. Trumpets sound at the end of the ceremony, and the participants make a procession down the mountain and on to a festive meal including song and dance. Today in Israel thousands of Ethiopians, known there as Beta Israel, make the pilgrimage to Jerusalem for a ceremony and prayers at the Armon Hanatziv Promenade, from which the old city of Jerusalem can be clearly seen, or at the Western Wall. Following the ceremony the members of the community break their fast with a celebratory meal.

CONTACTS:
Ministry of Tourism, Government of Israel
New York, NY
646-779-6760; fax: 646-779-6765
goisrael.com

◆ 0965 ◆ Eton Wall Game
November 30

Every year on Sᴛ. Aɴᴅʀᴇᴡ's Dᴀʏ, England's prestigious Eton College holds the famous Eton Wall Game, a variety of rugby that has its own highly technical rules and is different from all other forms of the game. The game is played between two teams: the Collegers, who are boys receiving scholarships and living in the old College, and the Oppidans (which means "townspeople"), who live in boarding-houses in town.

The rules are so complex and mysterious that even the spectators are often confused, although the players seem to understand how to play the game. The object of the game is to win goals by maneuvering the ball into the opposing team's "calx," designated by a chalk line on a garden wall at one end of the field and by a mark on a tree at the other. The game is made up of many scrimmages along the brick wall that marks off the college athletic field for which the game is named, and goals are almost never scored.

CONTACTS:
Eton College
Windsor, Berkshire SL4 6DW United Kingdom
44-17-5337-0100
www.etoncollege.com

◆ 0966 ◆ Europalia
October-December

Since its founding in 1969, the European arts festival known around the world as Europalia has presented a comprehensive survey of the diverse cultural and artistic aspects of a specific country. The first several festivals were devoted to European cultures: Italy, the Netherlands, Great Britain, France, Germany, Belgium, Greece, Spain, and Austria. But in 1989 the decision was made to devote the festival to a major culture from outside Europe: Japan. In 1993 the festival's founders moved its focus to the American continent, devoting the three-month festival to a display of cultural events representing Mexico.

While most of the festival events take place in Brussels, other cities in the Netherlands, France, Luxembourg, and Germany also host events, which include art, photography, and craft exhibitions; theater, dance, and orchestral performances; literary and scientific colloquia; and film retrospectives. Europalia '93 Mexico, for example, offered 14 exhibitions, 76 concerts, eight ballet performances, 22 theatrical productions, 17 literary events, 187 films, and nine traditional folk events. Discussions with the well-known writers Octavio Paz and Carlos Fuentes were a highlight of the festival.

CONTACTS:
Europalia International Festival
Ravensteingalerij, 4
Brussels B-1000 Belgium
32-2-504-9120; fax: 32-2-504-9121
europalia.eu

◆ 0967 ◆ European Fine Art Fair
March

The European Fine Art Fair, or **TEFAF Maastricht**, is a ten-day, annual event organized by the European Fine Art Foundation. Held in the city of Maastricht, the Netherlands, the fair is a renowned festival for art, antiques, and design. It was first launched in 1988 with 89 dealers. Today nearly 300 of the world's leading galleries and art dealers from 20 different countries display their wares—ranging from antiquities to 21st-century pieces—at the event. During the fair, collectors, museum representatives, and others in the art industry browse contemporary works, jewelry, antiques, photographs, and paintings by the old masters. **TEFAF Maastricht** is widely respected for its guarantee of authenticity given to objects displayed at the fair. This vetting system for authentication involves hundreds of international experts who examine the pieces with highly sophisticated equipment. Furthermore, **TEFAF Maastricht** maintains its own art loss register, which is the world's largest private database of stolen art. Any objects detected as fraudulent at the fair are removed immediately. A mainstay in the world of fine arts, the festival consistently attracts connoisseurs, collectors, and art lovers from around the world.

CONTACTS:
European Fine Art Foundation
Broekwal 64
Helvoirt 5268 HD Netherlands
31-411-645-090; fax: 31-411-645-091
www.tefaf.com

♦ 0968 ♦ **Evacuation Day**
March 17; September 1; November 25

"Evacuation Day" has been used to describe a number of dates in history on which military forces have withdrawn from a city or country. The best-known evacuation in the United States took place on March 17, 1776, during the early part of the American Revolution. British troops were forced out of Boston when the British commander, General Sir William Howe, conceded defeat to American General George Washington in a move that he hoped would save the British fleet. Bostonians have been celebrating the day ever since. Because of the large Irish-American community in Boston, the popularity of this holiday is often attributed to its being coincident with St. Patrick's Day.

Another well-known evacuation took place a few years later on November 25, 1783, when the British were forced out of New York City.

In England, "Evacuation Day" has also been used to refer to September 1, 1939, and the two days following, when over a million children and adults were evacuated from London and other cities considered to be likely targets for bombing during World War II.

CONTACTS:
Fraunces Tavern Museum
54 Pearl St.
2nd Fl.
New York, NY 10004
212-425-1778; fax: 212-509-3467
frauncestavernmuseum.org

♦ 0969 ♦ **Evamelunga**
September 8

Evamelunga, which means **"The Taking Away of the Burden of Sin"** is a day of thanksgiving for Christians in Cameroon. Families put on their best clothes and flock to the thatched-roof churches, which are decorated with flowers and palm leaves for the occasion. Church choirs and school choruses sing songs expressing gratitude for the arrival of the first missionary who brought them the story of Jesus in the late 19th century. After the church services are over, the feasting and singing continue late into the evening.

CONTACTS:
Presbyterian Church In Cameroon
P.O. Box 19
Buea, South West Province Cameroon
237-332-24-78
www.pccweb.org

♦ 0970 ♦ **Exaltation of the Cross, Feast of the**
September 14; formerly May 3 by Roman Catholics

The holiday known as the Exaltation of the Cross by the Eastern Church, where it is one of the 12 great feasts, is also known as the **Elevation**, **Recovery**, or **Adoration of the Cross**. In the West, it is known as **Holy Cross Day** (by the Anglican Communion), the **Triumph of the Cross** (by Roman Catholics), and also the **Invention of the Cross** (from Latin *invenire*, meaning "to find"). It commemorates three events: the finding of the cross on which Jesus was crucified, the dedication in 335 of the basilica built by Emperor Constantine enclosing the supposed site of Jesus' crucifixion on Golgotha, and the recovery in 629 by Emperor Heraclius of the relic of the cross that had been stolen by the Persians.

According to tradition, St. Helena, mother of Emperor Constantine, found the cross on a visit to Jerusalem, being enabled to identify it by a miracle. Many relics from the cross were distributed among churches throughout the world. (In the late 19th century, Rohault de Fleury catalogued all the known relics in the world; he estimated that they constituted less than one-third of the size of the cross that was believed to have been used.)

In addition, St. Helena discovered the four nails used in the Crucifixion, and the small plaque hung above Jesus that bore the sarcastic inscription "INRI" (*Iesus Nazarenus Rex Iudaeorum*, Latin for "Jesus of Nazareth, King of the Jews"). Two of the nails were placed in Constantine's crown, one was later brought to France by Charlemagne, and the fourth was supposedly cast into the Adriatic Sea when Helena's ship was threatened by a storm on her return journey.

On September 13, 335, bishops met in Jerusalem for the dedication of the basilica of the Holy Sepulchre built by order of Constantine. Many believe this date marks the discovery of the remains of the cross during excavations on the site of the Temple of Venus. On the 14th, a relic enshrined in a silver-gilt receptacle was elevated for veneration.

The relic was taken to Persia in 614 after the Persian army of King Choesroes occupied Jerusalem. When Heraclius of Constantinople defeated the Persians on the banks of the Danube in 629, he brought the sacred relic to Constantinople (now Istanbul). On September 14, 633, it was carried in a solemn procession to the Church of the Holy Wisdom (Hagia Sophia in Greek; Saint Sophia in English) where it was elevated for all to adore, recalling Jesus' words, "And I, if I be lifted up from the earth, will draw all men unto me" (John 12:32).

Former names for this day are **Crouchmas (Cross Mass)**, **Holy Rood Day**, and **Roodmas**, *rood* referring to the wood of which the cross was made.

In the Philippines, there is a nationwide celebration commemorating the discovery of the Holy Cross of Calvary by St. Helena. It is known as **Santacruzan**. Nine-day pageants are held in May with local men and women playing the parts of biblical characters. There are processions with floats of each town's patron saint, and costumed young women and their escorts parade under flower-decked arches. In Lucban, Quezon Province, multicolored rice wafers, called *kiping*, are shaped into the form of fruits and vegetables and displayed as window ornaments.

See also Día de la Santa Cruz; Epiphany, Orthodox; Maskal.

CONTACTS:
Exaltation of The Holy Cross Orthodox Church
10030 N. 32nd St.
Phoenix, AZ 85028
602-867-6025
www.holycrossaz.org

Israel Government Tourist Office
800 Second Ave.
New York, NY 10017
212-499-5650; fax: 212-499-5655
www.goisrael.com

♦ 0971 ♦ **Excited Insects, Feast of**
On or around March 5

Known as Kyongchip or Gyeongchip in Korea and as Ching Che in China, the Feast of Excited Insects marks the transition from winter to spring. It is the day when the insects are said to come back to life after hibernating all winter. In China, it is the day when "the dragon raises his head," summoning the insects back to life, and people perform various rituals designed to prepare for the onslaught and begin the task of restoring fertility to the earth. In Korea, this is one of 24 days in the lunar calendar that marks the beginning of a new season. Farmers prepare their fields and begin planting their barley, cabbage, and other vegetables.

CONTACTS:
China National Tourist Office
370 Lexington Ave.
Ste. 912
New York, NY 10017
212-760-8218; fax: 212-760-8809
www.cnto.org

Korean Tourism Organization
2 Executive Dr.
Ste. 750

Fort Lee, NJ 07024
201-585-0909; fax: 201-585-9041
www.visitkorea.or.kr

♦ 0972 ♦ **Exit Festival**
July

The Exit Festival is a music festival held over four days in July in Novi Sad, Serbia. The first Exit Festival took place at the University of Novi Sad in the summer of 2000, and was part of a student demonstration against the regime of then President Slobodan Milosevic. That year the festival ran for several months as organizers sought to engage young people in support of the cause of ending the repressive regime. In 2001, the festival moved to its present location at the historic Petrovaradin Fortress on the banks of the Danube River. The medieval fortress offers exceptional acoustics for the event, and a unique setting that can accommodate performances on multiple stages at the same time without any loss of sound quality.

Highly regarded among music festivals in the winner of numerous awards, the Exit festival reflects the Serbian spirit of unity, democracy and celebration. The festival line-up each year is comprised of internationally renowned artists performing in variety of genres on the festival's multiple stages. In the surrounding city of Novi Sad, celebrations begin on the eve of the festival and continue though the fours days, with alleyways and bars crowded with locals and visitors from all over Europe.

CONTACTS:
Exit Festival
Petrovaradin Fortress
Novi Sad Serbia
www.exitfest.org

F

♦ 0973 ♦ **Faces Etnofestival**
Weekend in late July or early August

Faces is a multicultural arts festival held annually in Billnäs, Finland, a town in the southern part of the country about 40 miles from Helsinki. Each summer more than 12,000 visitors gather for three days celebrating world cultures with performances in music, dance, theater, and poetry. Ten different stages showcase a range of acts from musical theater and improvisational comedy to reggae, punk, and country. Musicians, actors, clowns, writers, and other participants come from many countries around the world, including Argentina, Sweden, South Africa, Australia, and Russia; Finnish folk and popular music is also highlighted. In addition, workshops, exhibits, and vendors promote fine art, music, crafts, and world cuisine. Yoga, graffiti art, fire dancing, Scandinavian myths, and herbal remedies, are among the many unusual areas of interest included in the program. Activities in the Small Faces area are designed especially for children, including tribal drumming workshops and felting lessons.

The festival, which is sponsored by the humanitarian aid group Etnokult, has been held each year since 1998 as a means of promoting global diversity, equality, and understanding. A symposium held on the festival Saturday challenges those in attendance to reflect on developments in multiculturalism and globalization. The festival's name derives from the idea that coming together in a celebration of diversity helps to give a "face" to otherwise unfamiliar ethnicities and cultures. On the final day of the festival a benefit Peace Concert is held, with proceeds contributing to an international aid project such as hospital construction in a developing nation. The festival operates two campgrounds near the event site for those who wish to stay overnight, with one offering parking for recreational vehicles.

CONTACTS:
Raseborg Tourist Office
Rådhustorget (Town Sq.)
Ekenäs 10600 Finland
358-19-289-2010
www.visitraseborg.com

♦ 0974 ♦ **Fairbanks Winter Carnival**
Second week in March

The Winter Carnival is a week of festivities in Fairbanks, Alaska, highlighted by sled dog races. The carnival opens with the two-day Limited North American Sled Dog Race, and concludes, on the last two days, with the Open North American Sled Dog Race. Other events include dances, a parka parade, a campstove chili contest, a native potlatch, snow- and ice-sculpting contests, snowshoe races and softball, musical and dramatic presentations, and a trade fair.

CONTACTS:
Fairbanks Convention and Visitors Bureau
101 Dunkel St.
Ste. 111
Fairbanks, AK 99701
907-456-5774 or 800-327-5774; fax: 907-459-3757
www.explorefairbanks.com

♦ 0975 ♦ **Fairhope Jubilee**
Summer, usually August

The Jubilee marks a natural phenomenon greeted by the citizens of Fairhope, Alabama, with a rush to the shores of Mobile Bay. Fairhope, on a bluff over the bay, has two miles of beach. At a certain time, when the bay is calm and there is an east wind and a certain feel to the air, bottom-dwelling fish and crustaceans are trapped between a low-oxygen water mass and the shore. They become sluggish because of the shortage of oxygen and can't swim, so townsfolk rush out with buckets, cooking pots, crab nets, long poles, and wash basins to harvest them. The harvest may include flounder, shrimp, blue crab, stingrays, eels, and smaller fish such as shiners, anchovies, and hogchokers.

It's impossible to predict when the phenomenon will occur except that it's always in the summer and usually in August. Sometimes there is more than one occurrence; sometimes it will happen five days in a row. This event depends on a number of very specific circumstances: an overcast day, a gentle wind from the east, a rising tide.

Here's what happens: a deep-water pocket of very salty water stagnates and collects plant matter. This food supply and the warm temperatures cause a population explosion of microorganisms that consume great quantities of oxygen. A gentle east wind comes along and moves the upper-layer water offshore. Then the rising tide pushes the oxygen-poor bottom water toward the shore, and the bottom sea creatures are pushed in front of it. They act as though they're in a stupor because they're trying to get oxygen; they move slowly and don't try to swim. Eels will leave the water and burrow tail-first into the moist sand, leaving their heads in the air with mouths open.

Supposedly the event got its name because the first person seeing the marine migration called out, "Jubilee!".

CONTACTS:
Eastern Shore Chamber of Commerce
327 Fairhope Ave.
Fairhope, AL 36532
251-928-6387
www.eschamber.com

♦ 0976 ♦ Famadihana
Between June and September

The Malagasy people of Madagascar, an island off the southeast coast of Africa, believe that their deceased ancestors have become intermediaries between the living and God. Because they will spend eternity in their new existence, tombs are built to be much sturdier and more elaborately decorated than houses. The Famadihana is a celebration in which people exhume the remains of their ancestors, treat them to a grand feast and party, replace their burial clothes, and then reintern them. The specific date of a family's Famidihana is determined by a spiritual leader, but, for hygenic reasons, it always takes place sometime during the winter months, when the weather is dry.

CONTACTS:
National Tourism Board of Madagascar
Lot IBG 29C Antsahavola
B.P. 1780
Antananarivo 101 Madagascar
261-2022-661-15; fax: 261-2022-661-15
www.madagascar-tourisme.com

♦ 0977 ♦ Family Month, National
Second Sunday in May through the third Sunday in June

National Family Month is observed during the five-week period between MOTHER'S DAY in May and FATHER'S DAY in June. It is timed to coincide with the end of the school year, when families start spending more time together, and also to focus attention on mothers and fathers as the most powerful support system for their children.

National Family Month was started by KidsPeace, a private, not-for-profit organization that has dedicated itself to helping children attain the confidence and develop the courage to face and overcome crises since 1882. KidsPeace has also established National Kids Day, observed on the third Saturday of September. The organization believes that such observances provide opportunities for parents, grandparents, and

caregivers to be more involved in the lives of the children for whom they are responsible. Families are urged to spend time doing things together during this five-week period, whether it is taking a family vacation or simply doing chores around the house.

CONTACTS:
KidsPeace
4085 Independence Dr.
Schnecksville, PA 18078
800-257-3223
www.kidspeace.org

♦ 0978 ♦ Family Week
Begins on the first Sunday in May

In America, Protestant churches, Roman Catholic churches, and Jewish congregations observe **National Family Week**. While each has its own way of celebrating this event, the emphasis is on the strength that a family can find in religion. Members of the congregation are encouraged to examine their own lives from the perspective of how they have contributed to the religious life of their families, and groups often meet to discuss how to deal with social conditions that are having an adverse effect on family life. National Family Week begins on the first Sunday in May and leads up to MOTHER'S DAY and, among Christians, to the **Festival of the Christian Home**.

Many other countries observe a **Family Day**, as well, particularly in Africa. In Angola, Family Day is observed on December 25; in Namibia, December 26. Family Day is also the name by which EASTER MONDAY is known in South Africa.

CONTACTS:
Nelson Memorial United Methodist Church
407 E. Spring St.
Boonville, MO 65233
660-882-6223
www.nelsonmemorialumc.org

Holston Conference of the United Methodist Church
217 S. Rankin Rd.
P.O. Box 850
Alcoa, TN 37701
865-690-4080 or 866-690-4080; fax: 865-690-3162
holston.org

♦ 0979 ♦ Farvardegan Days
March, July, August; 26th-30th days of Spendarmad, the 12th Zoroastrian month, plus five intercalary days

Also known as **Farvadin** or **Farvardin**, this is a Zoroastrian festival celebrated by the followers of Zoroaster in Iran and India. The 10-day **Remembrance of the Departed** commemorates the spirits of the dead (*fravashis*), who have returned to God, or Ahura Mazda, to help in the fight against evil. People perform ceremonies for the departed at home shrines or fire temples.

Farvardegan is celebrated in March by the Fasli sect, July by the Kadmi sect, and August by the Shahenshai sect. Zoroaster (or Zarathushtra) was a Persian prophet and reformer, now believed to have lived around 1200 B.C.E., whose teachings influenced Judaism, Christianity, and Islam. The largest Zoroastrian groups remaining today are in India, where they are known as Parsis, and in Iran.

CONTACTS:
California Zoroastrian Center
8952 Hazard Ave.
Westminster, CA 92683
714-893-4737; fax: 714-894-9577
czc.org

◆ 0980 ◆ **Fasching**
Between February 2 and March 8; the two days before Ash Wednesday

Known in southwest Germany as **Fastnacht**, in Bavaria and Austria as Fasching, and as **Karneval** in the Rhineland, this is a Shrovetide festival that takes place on the two days immediately preceding ASH WEDNESDAY, otherwise known as ROSE MONDAY and SHROVE TUESDAY. It features processions of masked figures, and is the equivalent of MARDI GRAS and the last day of CARNIVAL.

Fastnacht means "eve of the fast," and the wild celebrations that typically take place during this festival are a way of making the most of the last hours before the deprivations of LENT.

In the Black Forest area of southern Germany, these pre-Lenten festivities are called **Fastnet**. The celebrations date back to the Middle Ages and were developed by craftsmen's guilds. Today's carnival clubs (*Narrenzünfte*) still use the same wooden masks and traditional costumes in their parades as their ancestors did. The rites of Fasnet are distinctive: in Elzach, wooden-masked Schuddig Fools, wearing red costumes and large hats decorated with snail shells, run through the town beating people with blown-up hogs' bladders; in Wolfach, fools stroll around in nightgowns and nightcaps; in Überlinger on the Bodensee and Villingen, they crack long whips, toss fruit and nuts to the children, and wear foxes' tails and smiling wooden masks. Carnival ends with *Kehraus*, a "sweeping out."

See also KARNEVAL IN COLOGNE.

CONTACTS:
Evangelical Church in Germany
Herrenhäuser Straße 12
Hanover D-30419 Germany
49-511-2796-0; fax: 49-511-2796-707
www.ekd.de

◆ 0981 ◆ **Fasinada**
July 22

Fasinada is a commemoration of a miraculous event on the tiny island of Gospa od Skrpjela (Our Lady of the Chisels) off Montenegro (formerly in Yugoslavia). The island, according to the story, was once nothing more than a rock. One stormy night, a shipwrecked sailor clung to the rock and vowed that

if he survived he would build a church to the Virgin Mary. He did survive, and sailors dumped stones there until an island was formed; in the 17th century a church was built on the pile of rocks. The festival includes a procession to the island of boats decorated with garlands of flowers and loaded with rocks. The rocks are piled up to reinforce theshores of the island, and then the participants enjoy folk dancing and country sports and games.

CONTACTS:
Embassy of Serbia and Montenegro
2134 Kalorama Rd. N.W.
Washington, D.C.
202-332-0333; fax: 202-332-3933
www.washington.mfa.gov.rs

National Tourism Organisation of Serbia
Cika-Ljubina 8
P.O. BOX 90
Beograd 11000 Serbia
381-011-6557-100; fax: 381-011-2626-767
www.serbia.travel

◆ 0982 ◆ **Fast Day**
Fourth Monday in April

At one time it was customary for the governors of the New England states to proclaim days of public fasting and prayer, usually around the middle of April. But after the Revolutionary War, enthusiasm for the custom began to wane. Because the day's spiritual significance had faded by the 19th century, Massachusetts abolished its Fast Day in 1895 and began to observe PATRIOTS' DAY in its place. Maine followed suit a few years later.

New Hampshire is now the only state that continues to observe Fast Day as a legal holiday, maintaining a tradition that can be traced back to 1679. No longer an occasion for abstinence, it is usually regarded as an opportunity for outdoor recreation and spring chores. Although the date is set by law, the governor of New Hampshire issues a yearly proclamation designating the day on which it will be observed.

CONTACTS:
State of New Hampshire Division of Travel and Tourism Development
172 Pembroke Rd.
P.O. Box 1856
Concord, NH 03302
603-271-2665 or 800-262-6660; fax: 603-271-6870
www.visitnh.gov

◆ 0983 ◆ **Fast for a World Harvest**
November 21

Fast for a World Harvest encourages individuals and organizations to actively participate in the global movement to end hunger and poverty. In fact, the campaign's central mission is to completely eradicate hunger, poverty, and injustice from the world. The Oxford Committee for Famine Relief (OXFAM) started the campaign in 1974 to help feed the world's poor and raise money to assist those affected by natural disasters. Initially, the campaign raised funds independently, without accepting any government grants. As the campaign gained popularity, many volunteers provided the necessary funds and services. There are now Fast for a World Harvest branches across the globe in more than 90 countries.

CONTACTS:
Oxfam America
226 Causeway St.
5th Fl.
Boston, MA 02114
800-776-9326
www.oxfamamerica.org

◆ 0984 ◆ Fastelavn
Between February 2 and March 8; Monday before Ash Wednesday

The Monday before LENT begins is a school holiday for children in Denmark. Early in the morning they enter their parents' bedrooms swinging "Lenten birches"—twigs covered with silk, crepe paper, or ribbon. As they poke or smack their parents they cry out, "Give buns! Give buns!"—referring to the traditional *Fastelavnsboller,* or Shrovetide buns, which their parents give them to put a stop to the beating. This custom probably has its roots in ancient purification rites, where people used to beat one another with switches to drive out evil.

Various games are played with the buns, such as suspending one by string from a chandelier and trying to take a bite of it. Later in the day, the children dress up in costume and go from door to door, where they are given coins, candy, and more buns.

CONTACTS:
Danish Church & Cultural Center
16881 Bastanchury Rd.
Yorba Linda, CA 92886
714-993-6362
www.danishchurchsocal.com

◆ 0985 ◆ Fastens-een
Between February 3 and March 9; the day before Ash Wednesday

The eve or day before ASH WEDNESDAY has been given a number of names in Scotland and northern England, including Fastens-een, **Fastens-eve**, **Fastens-Even**, and **Fastens Tuesday**. All refer to the Lenten season that is about to begin, "Fasten Day" being the Old English form of "Fast Day." **Fastingong** was an early English expression for SHROVE TUESDAY, which was also called **Fastingong Tuesday**. In certain English dialects the word "fastgong" means "fast-going" or "approaching a time of fast."

No matter what the day is called, the day before LENT begins in the West is traditionally a time for carnival-like celebrations.

See also CARNIVAL; COLLOP MONDAY; FASCHING.

◆ 0986 ◆ Father's Day
Third Sunday in June

Sonora Louise Smart Dodd from Spokane, Washington, suggested to her minister in 1910 that a day be set aside for honoring fathers. Her own father was a Civil War veteran who raised his six children on the family farm after his wife died in childbirth. The Ministerial Association and the Spokane YMCA picked up on the idea, and in 1924 Father's Day received the support of President Calvin Coolidge. But it wasn't until 1966 that a presidential proclamation established Father's Day as the third Sunday in June. Although it began as a religious celebration, today it is primarily an occasion for showing appreciation through gift-giving.

See also CHILDREN'S DAY, MOTHER'S DAY.

CONTACTS:
National Center for Fathering
10200 W. 75th St.
Ste. 267
Shawnee Mission, KS 66204
800-593-3237
www.fathers.com

◆ 0987 ◆ Faunalia
December 5 and February 13

In Roman mythology Faunus was a god of the forest who was also associated with fertility. It was believed that eerie noises in the woods came from Faunus. The Faunalia was mostly celebrated by farmers and other rural workers on December 5 with feasting and games. For a time, city-dwellers adopted the festival and observed it on February 13.

Faunus was known as the brother, father, or husband of BONA DEA. Lupercus, the fertility god associated with the LUPERCALIA, was also identified with Faunus, as was Inuus, the fertilizer of cattle. The Fauni, or fauns, were spirits of the forest who resembled the satyrs of Greek legend.

CONTACTS:
Italian National Tourist Board
686 Park Ave.
3rd Fl.
New York, NY 10065 United States
212-245-5618; fax: 212-586-9249
www.italiantourism.com

◆ 0988 ◆ Fawkes (Guy) Day
November 5

On the night of November 4, 1605, 36 barrels of gunpowder were discovered in a cellar beneath the Houses of Parliament in London. The conspirators of the so-called Gunpowder Plot, who planned to blow up King James I and his government to avenge their laws against Roman Catholics, were discovered and arrested, and on January 31 eight of them were beheaded. While Guy Fawkes didn't originate the plan, he was caught red-handed after someone tipped off the king's ministers. And he was among those whose heads were displayed on pikes at London Bridge.

The following year, Parliament established November 5 as a national day of thanksgiving. Children still make effigies of Guy Fawkes and ask passersby for money ("Penny for the Guy") which they spend on fireworks. The effigies are burned in bonfires that night, and fireworks traditionally fill the skies over Britain in remembrance of the failure of the Gunpowder Plot.

CONTACTS:
Britain National Tourism Agency
845 Third Ave.
10th Fl.
New York, NY 10022
212-850-0336
www.visitbritain.org

Library of Congress
101 Independence Ave. S.E.
Washington, D.C. 20540
202-707-5000
www.loc.gov

♦ 0989 ♦ FeatherFest
Late March-Early April

Begun in 2002, the Galveston Island FeatherFest is intended to celebrate the "birds and natural heritage of the Upper Texas Coastal area." Some 300 species of birds are found on Galveston Island in the springtime as they stop at the island during their migration north.

The four-day FeatherFest allows bird enthusiasts the chance to go on field trips to photograph and watch the birds. Prominent environmental writers, naturalists, and artists are the leaders of these field trips. Visitors may also enjoy kayak and boat trips into the wilderness. Seminars, workshops, and lectures on the wildlife in the community are also available. In addition, a FeatherFest Photo Contest is held. Other highlights have included an exhibition of nature photographs at the Galveston County Historical Museum. In the evenings, visitors attend informal gatherings. In 2007, the Houston String Quartet performed an original piece by Houston composer Ken Booker.

CONTACTS:
Galveston FeatherFest & Nature PhotoFest
P.O. Box 1468
Galveston, TX 77553
409-789-8125; fax: 832-459-5533
www.galvestonfeatherfest.com

♦ 0990 ♦ Fellsmere Frog Leg Festival
January

The Fellsmere Frog Leg Festival takes place over four days in January in Fellsmere, Florida. A fundraiser for the city's recreation department that began in 1990, the festival has grown into a signature event for the area with an annual attendance of 80,000 people. Visitors partake of frog leg or alligator

tail dinners, or "frog pops" (frog-on-a-stick) for those who want to sample a smaller portion, in a carnival-like atmosphere featuring live music and dance performances, rides and games, and an arts and crafts fair. Though volunteers at the inaugural festival served only 400 dinners using local frogs, today the festival serves over 5000 pounds of frog legs and 2000 pounds of alligator, which must be shipped in from commercial suppliers to preserve the local crops. The festival also holds two Guinness World Records: one for the most frog legs sold on a single business day, and another for the largest frog leg festival in the world.

CONTACTS:
Fellsmere Frog Leg Festival, Inc.
22 S. Orange St.
P.O. Box 67
Fellsmere, FL 32948
772-571-0250
www.froglegfestival.com

♦ 0991 ♦ Fenkil Day
February 10

Fenkil Day commemorates the historic victory of the Eritrean People's Liberation Front (EPLF) during Operation Fenkil, a military battle that would prove to be a critical turning point in the 30 year-long struggle for independence from Ethiopian colonization. Operation Fenkil was a 72- hour, hard-won battle against superior enemy weaponry that ended on the tenth of February, 1990, when freedom fighters laid siege to the Asmara-Massawa Highway and captured the important port city of Massawa, gaining control of a key part of the Red Sea coastline. Though it would take another fifteen months for the EPLF to finally drive the Ethiopian army from the country, Operation Fenkil is regarded as a symbol of the tenacity and determination of the people of Eritrea, who succeeded in reclaiming their land from the Ethiopian army and setting the stage for complete political and economic emancipation.

Every year, Eritreans from all over the country and the world gather at the Red Sea port of Massawa to celebrate their liberation from colonization and remember those who died in the war. The celebrations often extend over three to four days with the residents of Massawa setting up tents in different locations in the city and holding colorful parades to honor their war veterans. A variety of cultural and sports events are also held as part of the celebrations. The president of Eritrea and other politicians pay homage to those who lost their lives at the war memorial in the Taulud area of Massawa, and the state-run media air official speeches that pay tribute to the Eritrean revolutionaries and urge the youth to uphold the country's sovereignty by emulating the heroic struggles of their freedom fighters.

CONTACTS:
Ministry of Tourism
Tourism Service Center
Harnet Ave.
Asmara Eritrea
291-1-124871
www.eritrea.be

♦ 0992 ♦ **Feralia**
February 21

This ancient Roman festival marked the culmination of a week-long celebration in honor of the *manes*, spirits of the dead. It began on February 13 with the Parentalia, a private celebration in honor of deceased family members, and ended on February 21 with a public celebration known as the Feralia. This was the day on which offerings and gifts were placed on the graves of the deceased and the anniversary of the funeral feast was celebrated. The Feralia was similar to the later Christian holiday, All Souls' Day.

CONTACTS:
Italian National Tourist Board
686 Park Ave.
3rd Fl.
New York, NY 10065 United States
212-245-5618; fax: 212-586-9249
www.italiantourism.com

♦ 0993 ♦ **Fes Festival of World Sacred Music**
May - June

The prevailing spirituality of the holy city of Fez in Morocco was the inspiration for the annual Fes Festival of World Sacred Music, which was launched in 1995. Artists from all over the world perform the sacred music of the world's religions in all its various styles during the week-long festival. The main evening concerts take place at Bab Makina, the reception court of a 14th-century royal palace. The Moorish Palace of Dar Bat'ha is the site of many of the afternoon concerts. Another striking performance site is the Roman ruin of Volubilis, with the ancient Arc of Triumph as a backdrop. The festival, now considered among the world's premier music festivals, draws distinguished artists from the world over, as well as hundreds of enthusiastic visitors each year.

In 2000, festival organizers launched the Festival in the City to run alongside the Sacred Music festival. Free of charge and open to all, it features concerts, Sufi nights, workshops, and art exhibitions, and lends a festive air to the city streets. Another feature of the festival is Fes Encounter, an annual gathering of academics, social activists, and politicians, who debate a pressing current issue, which can range from conflict resolution to social justice.

CONTACTS:
Spirit of Fes Foundation
Sidi Al Khayat
BP 679
Fès 30200 Morocco
212-535-74-0535; fax: 212-535- 63-3989
www.fesfestival.com

Morocco National Tourist Office
104 W. 40th St.
Ste. 1820
New York, NY 10018
212-221-1583; fax: 212-221-1887
www.visitmorocco.com

♦ 0994 ♦ **Festa da Luz (Festival of Light)**
Two weeks beginning the second Sunday in October

The two-week Festival of Light held every year in Belém, Pará State, Brazil, honors Our Lady of Nazareth. Her image is carried through the streets to the cathedral on Saturday night in a *berlinda* or glass enclosure set upon wheels. But it is the Sunday morning procession that is the most important. Church and civic leaders accompany the image as it again rolls through the streets in the berlinda. Behind comes the "Miracle Car"—a heavy platform inscribed with images of the miracles performed by the Virgin—carried on the shoulders of strong men who perform this service as a form of penance. Adults and children of all ages and circumstances follow, many dressed in hair shirts, walking in bare feet, or carrying a heavy load as a form of penance.

The festival takes its name from the lights that decorate the square in front of the church and that outline the building itself. There are booths selling a wide variety of goods and instrumental groups supply continuous music. The pilgrimage that accompanies the Festival of Light dates back to the year 1700 and often draws as many as 100,000 participants.

CONTACTS:
Brazilian Embassy
3006 Massachusetts Ave. N.W.
Washington, D.C. 20008
202-238-2700; fax: 202-238-2827
washington.itamaraty.gov.br/en-us

♦ 0995 ♦ **Festa del Grillo**
Between April 30 and June 3; 40 days after Easter

In most European countries, Ascension Day is a holiday when families go to the country to have picnics or just to spend the day outdoors. On Ascension Day in Florence, Italy, crowds gather in the Cascine—a public park along the banks of the Arno River—to celebrate the Festa del Grillo, or **Cricket Festival**, the chirping cricket being a traditional symbol of spring. Food stalls are set up in the park, and there are balloons and other souvenirs for sale.

Although people used to catch their own crickets, today they can buy them in brightly painted wood, wicker, or wire cages, where they are kept with a large lettuce leaf to sustain them. The children carry their crickets through the park and later hang the cages outside their windows. If the *grillo* sings to them, it means they'll have good luck.

CONTACTS:
Metropolitan City of Florence – Ministry of Tourism
Via Manzoni 16
Florence 50121 Italy
www.firenzeturismo.it

♦ 0996 ♦ **Festival d'Aix en Provence**
July

The Festival d'Aix en Provence was first organized in 1948 by Gabriel Dussurget, a music enthusiast from Paris, and Countess Lily Pastré, who covered the costs of the first festival. It is conducted in the month of July every year in Aix-en-Provence, a city-commune in the south of France. Initially, only music concerts were a part of the festival, but later on operas were included, and at present operas form the crux of the Festival d'Aix en Provence. The prime venue of the festival is the Théâtre de l'Archevêché, but events also take place in the Théâtre de Provence, the Théâtre du Jeu de Paume, and other locales. A prelude to the festival, officially called Aix en Juin, initiated in 2013, takes place in June. A handful of programs covering operas, concerts, recitals, and master classes are held on most evenings throughout the second half of the month. Aix en Juin culminates with a parade and concert at Cours Mirabeau, which coincides with the start of the Festival d'Aix en Provence. Every year the parade honors such opera masters as Handel and Mozart by staging their works.

CONTACTS:
La Boutique du Festival
Palais de l'Ancien Archevêché
Aix-en-Provence, 13100 France
33-43-408-0217; fax: 33-44-263-1374
www.festival-aix.com

♦ 0997 ♦ **Festival des Arts de la Rue (Far de Biarritz)**
A Weekend in May

Founded in 2005, the Festival des Arts de la Rue, or Far de Biarritz, is a celebration of the arts held on the streets of Biarritz, a seaside town in France. The four-day event features an abundance of artistic performances appealing to young and old audiences alike. Over 50 theater companies from France and other countries perform in the squares and parks of Biarritz. During the festival, the public votes for an audience award, and there is also a juried award for the best presentation. While many performances are free, others require tickets to be purchased at designated venues. On numerous stages throughout the town, artists present a diverse assortment of shows, including music, drama, burlesque, mime, acrobatics, and puppetry. The Festival des Arts de la Rue opens with a garden party for the performers and special invitees.

CONTACTS:
Biarritz Evenement
4 avenue de la gare
Biarritz France
33-5-59-22-50-50
www.biarritz-evenement.fr

♦ 0998 ♦ **Festival Du Nouveau Cinema**
October

The Festival du Nouveau Cinéma is a ten-day film festival held in Montreal, Quebec. Its focus is on exhibiting and promoting new trends in cinema and new media. The festival was founded by Claude Chamberlan and Dimitri Eipidès in 1971. Canadian and international artists converge at this annual gathering, which brings together traditional films, multimedia projects, interactive installations, and hybrid forms of movies made possible by digital technologies.

The festival promotes the use of cutting-edge audiovisual practices and has included a range of new-media formats in its presentations, including web series, new forms of television, gamification of films, cinematization of games, and documentary video games. In addition to film screenings, the festival incorporates live proceedings, performances, and interactive sessions. The festival is widely known for its evolving nature and for showcasing new technologies in cinema.

CONTACTS:
Festival Du Nouveau Cinema
3805, St. Laurent Blvd.
Montréal, QC H2W 1X9 Canada
514-282-0004; fax: 514-282-6664
www.nouveaucinema.ca

♦ 0999 ♦ **Festival International des Arts de la Marionette à Saguenay**
July, every two years

Canada's only international puppet festival, the Festival Internationale des Arts de la Marionette à Saguenay, brings together puppet artists from various Canadian provinces and around the world to the Quebec region of Saguenay–Lac-Saint-Jean. Puppetry companies representing nearly every continent put on performances for local residents and puppetry enthusiasts from all over.

The festival was called World Puppet Week when it was first held in 1990. Along with setting up performances, event organizers offered workshops and exhibitions and provided networking opportunities, components that remain part of the six-day festival today.

During the 1990s, the festival attracted the general population with entertaining outdoor shows featuring giant puppets. Many performances take place at an outdoor venue, the Parc de la Riviere-aux-Sables, in the borough of Jonquière, in the city of Saguenay.

CONTACTS:
ManiganSes
3865, rue du Roi – Georges
C.P. 503
Jonquière, QC G7X 7W3 Canada
418-695-4649 or 888-726-8467; fax: 418-695-2873
www.astralopitheque.com/Maniganses

♦ 1000 ♦ **Festival-Institute at Round Top, International**
Early June to mid-July

This teaching institute and music festival was founded by world-renowned pianist James Dick in 1971. Dick wanted to establish a center where talented student musicians could make a smooth transition to a professional career. He started out with a 10-day workshop, but now the institute offers advanced lessons, coaching, and various seminars. The emphasis is still on pianists, but there is also instruction in strings, woodwinds, brass, chamber music, and orchestra. The faculty is composed of internationally known musicians who not only teach at the Institute but perform as soloists at the concerts given there.

Round Top is the smallest incorporated city in Texas, with a population of less than 100. It was named for a building with a rounded roof that was at one time a landmark for arriving stage coaches. Just north of the town square is the scenic 200-acre Festival Hill grounds. Concerts are held in the acoustically excellent 1,200-seat festival concert hall and the Edythe Bates Old Chapel, built in 1883. The campus is open all year to visitors and hosts various events, including an Early Music Festival during MEMORIAL DAY weekend, "August-to-April Concert Series," herb workshops, retreats and conferences, and guided tours.

CONTACTS:
Round Top Festival Institute
248 Jaster Rd.
P.O. Box 89
Round Top, TX 78954
979-249-3129
www.festivalhill.org

♦ 1001 ♦ **Festivities for the Day of National Rebellion**
July 25-27

This three-day national holiday is celebrated throughout Cuba. It commemorates an attack that took place on July 26, 1953, when rebel forces led by Fidel Castro struck the Moncada army barracks in Santiago de Cuba. Although the attack was unsuccessful, it is remembered as the beginning of the rebellion that eventually ousted the dictatorship of Fulgencio Batista in 1959.

The holiday is an occasion for displays of national pride and mass rallies organized by the state. Crowds of 100,000 are common in Havana, where a carnival, live music, singing, dancing, and flag waving mark the occasion. Santiago de Cuba also has a large carnival, and other cities in the country host celebrations as well.

CONTACTS:
National Tourist Information Office
Ministry of Tourism of Cuba
 Cuba
www.cubatravel.tur.cu/en

♦ 1002 ♦ **Festivus**
December 23

The holiday of Festivus first originated on the "Seinfeld" television program in the 1990s. Regular series character Frank Costanza, father of Jerry Seinfeld's friend George Costanza,

invented the holiday when he found that the usual year-end holidays did not fulfill him. Festivus, he explains, is "for the rest of us." To mark Festivus, which he insists his family celebrate, a plain aluminum pole is placed in a bucket of cement. One by one, those present grab the pole and air their grievances about how other people disappointed them in the past year. Frank begins this segment with the phrase: "I gotta lot of problems with some of you people!" After this gripe session comes a contest called the "feats of strength," in which all those present try to subdue the head of the household, and which usually devolves into a wrestling match.

The residents of Erie, Penn., have taken the imaginary holiday of Festivus to heart. Many people in the city and nearby communities throw Festivus parties featuring the aluminum pole and the feats of strength, all in the spirit of good fun.

CONTACTS:
Erie County Tourism
208 E. Bayfront Pkwy.
Ste. 103
Erie, PA 16507
814-454-1000 or 800-524-3743; fax: 814-459-0241
www.visiteriepa.com

♦ 1003 ♦ **Fetes des Lumieres**
Four days around December 8

Fêtes des Lumières is an annual festival celebrated in Lyon, France, for four days around December 8. Most of the city is lit up during the festival. The tradition of celebrating it dates back to December 8, 1852, when the statue of the Virgin Mary was erected next to the Basilica. The statue was supposed to have been unveiled in September of that year, but the plan was disrupted by a flood, and the dedication date was moved to December 8th to take place in conjunction with the Feast of the Immaculate Conception. A storm in 1852 further hindered the festivities, but all was fine by evening, and the people of the city expressed their joy by placing lit candles on their windowsills and balconies. The tradition has grown and has become Lyon's festival of lights; it is now attended by an estimated four million people every year. The events primarily take place in two locations in Lyon—the Basilica of Fourvière and the Place des Terreaux.

The festival is characterized by numerous light installations around the city produced by both local and international artists. One can find interactive, projected, and other types of lighting using the latest technology, along with live music and choreographed recorded sound.

CONTACTS:
Lighting Urban Community International (LUCI Association)
13, rue du Griffon
Lyon, 69001 France
33-42-711-8537
www.fetedeslumieres.lyon.fr

♦ 1004 ♦ **Fiesta Day**
Late February

Held for more than 50 years, Fiesta Day celebrates the multicultural heritage of those who settled Ybor (Ee-bore) City, which is part of Tampa, Florida. Cuban, African-Cuban, Italian, and Jewish immigrants made Ybor City their home in the 1880s, and their influence is still felt in Tampa's Historic District, where this festival takes place. Celebrants can enjoy the diverse food, drink, music, and arts and crafts that reflect the character of Ybor City.

CONTACTS:
Ybor City Development Corporation
City of Tampa
2015 E. 7th Ave.
Tampa, FL 33605
813-274-7936
www.yborcityonline.com

♦ 1005 ♦ Fiesta sa EDSA (People Power Anniversary)
February 25

The Fiesta sa EDSA is a commemoration of the bloodless People Power Revolution in the Philippines on Feb. 22-25, 1986, in which the dictatorial regime of President Ferdinand Marcos was toppled. The revolution began because Marcos and Corazon C. Aquino both claimed victory in a presidential election filled with fraud and violence.

Two key government officers, Minister Juan Ponce Enrile and Armed Forces Vice Chief of Staff Fidel Ramos, rebelled in protest of Marcos's oppression and demanded his resignation. They holed up at military camps at the Epifanio de los Santos Highway (EDSA), which borders Manila on the east. Pro-Marcos forces threatened to annihilate them, but two million unarmed people surged toward the camps. With offerings of flowers, food, and prayers, they provided a human shield and overcame the military's firepower. Fourteen years of Marcos's rule ended, and Corazon C. Aquino became the first woman president of the Philippines (1986-92). Ramos was elected president in 1992 and served until 1998.

The day is marked with ceremonies at the site of the revolution in Quezon City, a part of metropolitan Manila.

CONTACTS:
Embassy of Philippines
1600 Massachusetts Ave. N.W.
Washington, D.C. 20036
202-467-9300; fax: 202-467-9417
www.philippineembassy-usa.org

♦ 1006 ♦ Fiestas Patrias
September 18-19

Fiestas Patrias is the great national two-day holiday in Chile celebrating Independence Day, September 18, and Army Day, September 19. Independence Day commemorates the anniversary of Chile's first movement toward independence from Spain on September 18, 1810, when a group of Chilean leaders took over the government. Spain had colonized much of

South America since the 16th century. By 1814 Chileans were involved in a war with the Spanish, who were opposed to the new local government. The citizens of Chile finally declared their independence on February 12, 1818.

Army Day is observed with a military parade in Santiago, in which the army, navy, air force, and national police display their weapons, equipment, and uniforms. In the days preceding the holiday, *fondas* (fairs) pop up throughout Chile, with carnival rides and food stalls.

Fiestas Patrias is a popular time for Chilean rodeos. *Huasos* or cowboys compete against one another by attempting to pin a calf against the wall of the *medialuna* or arena with their horse—unlike the calf-roping that takes place at American rodeos—and are awarded points based on which part of the horse is touching the calf.

Because September marks the beginning of spring in Chile, Fiestas Patrias is also a popular occasion for kite flying. A favorite sport is kite fighting, in which people cover the kite strings with small sharp pieces of glass in order to try to cut others' kite strings.

CONTACTS:
Embassy of Chile
1732 Massachusetts Ave. N.W.
Washington, D.C. 20036
202-785-1746; fax: 202-887-5579
www.chile-usa.org

♦ 1007 ♦ Fifteenth of Av (Tu be-Av; Hamishah Asar b'Av)
Between July 23 and August 21; Av 15

During the time of the Second Temple in Jerusalem (dedicated between 521 and 517 B.C.E. and destroyed in 70 C.E.), this was a Jewish folk festival in which young women would dress in white and dance in the vineyards, where young bachelors would come to choose their brides.

There are a number of explanations for why the festival was celebrated this way. According to the Talmud, the 15th day of Av was the day when members of different tribes were allowed to intermarry. It was also the day when the cutting of trees to burn on the altar ceased, because the heat of the sun was diminishing and there was some concern that the trees wouldn't dry properly. It's also possible that the holiday was adapted from an ancient SUMMER SOLSTICE festival.

Although in modern times there have been attempts by the new settlements in Israel to turn this day into one of music and folk dancing, the idea doesn't seem to have caught on. The Fifteenth of Av is marked only by a ban on eulogies or fasting.

CONTACTS:
Union of Orthodox Jewish Congregations of America
11 Broadway
New York, NY 10004
212-563-4000; fax: 212-564-9058
www.ou.org

♦ 1008 ♦ Fig Sunday
Between March 14 and April 18; Palm Sunday

The custom of eating figs on PALM SUNDAY gave rise to the name Fig Sunday, or **Fig Pudding Day**, in England, when children would buy figs and either eat them or bring them home to their mothers to make fig pudding. The name may have come from Jesus' cursing of the barren fig tree on the day after his entry into Jerusalem, as told in the 11th chapter of the Gospel of Mark.

CONTACTS:
Saint Barbara Greek Orthodox Church
480 Racebrook Rd.
Orange, CT 06477
203-795-1347
old.saintbarbara.org

♦ 1009 ♦ Fiji Day
October 10

It took 96 years for Great Britain to transfer its claim on Fiji to the island nation's indigenous leadership. However, Fijians still celebrate the date of the signing of the 1874 Deed of Cession, the document that initiated the protracted process that culminated in Fiji's independence in 1970.

The anniversary is celebrated nationwide. The main events take place at the Site of Cession in the town of Levuka, located on the island of Ovalau, and in the present-day capital city, Suva.

In Levuka, festivities focus on the historical aspects of Fiji Day. Fijians will dress up in traditional garb to re-enact of the Deed of Cession. In Suva, leaders, dignitaries, and citizens gather in historic Albert Park for addresses by the president and the prime minister. There is also a parade by military forces, the singing of the national anthem, and a ceremonial firing of cannons. In other communities throughout the islands, Fijians hold oratory contests and stage cultural performances.

CONTACTS:
Tourism Fiji, USA
5777 W. Century Blvd.
Ste. 220
Los Angeles, CA 90045
310-568-1616; fax: 310-670-2318
www.fiji.travel

♦ 1010 ♦ Fiji National Youth Day
Date varies

The island nation of Fiji puts a strong emphasis on national initiatives that serve its young citizens. One of the goals of Fiji's Ministry of Youth and Sports is to increase youth participation in civic life, and in particular, to coordinate programs that help raise the employment rate among the country's youth. National Youth Day highlights this agenda through a series of activities that are coordinated by regional agencies and take place at various locations. The ceremonies are held on a different date each year.

Customarily, the minister who supervises youth initiatives will give a commencement address that officially opens the celebrations, outlines the plan concerning youth, and describes the theme of the year's celebrations. Past celebration themes have included "Tackling Poverty Together" and "Breaking Barriers."

The regional festivities include mural painting, team building activities, youth marches, and competitions in oration and traditional storytelling.

CONTACTS:
Fiji Ministry of Youth and Sports
3 Gordon St. Government Bldg.
P.O. Box 2448
Suva Fiji
679-331-5960; fax: 679-330-5348
www.youth.gov.fj

♦ 1011 ♦ Fiji Ratu Sir Lala Sukuna Day
Last Monday of May

The people of Fiji honor one of the nation's most prominent leaders, Ratu Sir Lala Sukuna, on the Monday nearest his death anniversary (May 30). Sukuna (1888–1958) was a decorated hero in World War I before he became a politician. Over the course of holding various government posts, he helped prepare Fiji for independence from Great Britain. The island nation gained independence in 1970, 12 years after his death.

For many Fijians, memories of the 2000 anniversary are marred by cataclysmic events that took place around the time of the observance. George Speight led a military takeover that briefly removed President Ratu Sir Kamisese Mara and stirred up animosity between native Fijians and Indian residents.

In 2005, the prime minister led an effort to reclaim the holiday's positive connotations by highlighting Sukuna's harmonious economic plan, which protected the land rights of native Fijians but still left room for foreign investment. Adopting a theme of "Unity in Diversity," the celebration included a church service commemorating Ratu Sukuna's life and an exhibition at Fiji Museum devoted to the statesman. Festivities extended for a week and culminated with a final ceremony on the May 30th anniversary.

CONTACTS:
Tourism Fiji - USA
5777 W. Century Blvd.
Ste. 220
Los Angeles, CA 90045
310-568-1616; fax: 310-670-2318
www.fiji.travel

♦ 1012 ♦ Fillmore Jazz Festival
Weekend closest to Independence Day

Sponsored by the Fillmore Merchants Association in San Francisco, Calif., the Fillmore Jazz Festival is the largest free jazz festival in the western United States. The festival comprises two full days and nights of musical entertainment on three stages and occupies Fillmore Street from Jackson to Eddy Streets. An annual event held on the weekend closest to Independence Day, each year it attracts approximately 90,000 visitors from the Bay Area, the state, and throughout North America.

The first Fillmore Jazz Festival was held in 1985 to celebrate the musical heritage of the ethnically diverse Fillmore neighborhood, where such jazz luminaries as Ella Fitzgerald, Duke Ellington, Count Basie, and Billie Holliday performed during the 1940s. In addition to offering performances of standards from the 20th-century golden age of jazz, the lineup features local and national acts offering funk, fusion, salsa, Afro-rhythms, and R&B. The festival showcases the ethnic diversity of the neighborhood through a variety of gourmet food vendors and artists in addition to the entertainment schedule.

CONTACTS:
Steven Restivo Event Services, LLC
P.O. Box 15101
San Rafael, CA 94915
800-310-6563; fax: 415-456-6436
www.fillmorejazzfestival.com

♦ 1013 ♦ Film Festival of India, International
November

The International Film Festival of India (IFFI), held annually in the state of Goa, is the biggest international film festival in the Asian region. By providing a common platform for films from all over the world, the festival promotes friendship and cooperation. The IFFI's founding principles are to discover and support films of all genres, so the screened films represent a variety of aesthetics and content. The festival serves as a venue for film professionals and emerging talent to communicate face-to-face with their counterparts and film lovers across the globe. The IFFI also introduces Indian cinema to a wider audience. Silver and Gold Peacock awards are presented at the festival for actors and directors, along with lifetime achievement, best film, and special jury awards. The IFFI was first held in Mumbai in 1952. The festival toured the cities of Chennai, Delhi, and Kolkata, and it featured 40 full-length films and 100 shorts. It became a competitive event in its third year. In 2004 the location of the festival was shifted to Goa. It is currently organized by the Ministry of Information and Broadcasting, the Directorate of Film Festivals, and the Government of Goa.

CONTACTS:
Festival Director, Ministry of Information and Broadcasting
Sirifort Auditorium Complex
New Delhi, New Delhi 110 049 India
91-11-26499371; fax: 91-11-26499398
www.iffi.nic.in

♦ 1014 ♦ Finland Independence Day
December 6

Sweden and Russia contended for Finland for almost 700 years. The Finnish people lived under Russian control beginning in 1809. The Finnish nationalist movement grew in the 1800s, and when the BOLSHEVIKS took over Russia on November 7, 1917, the Finns saw a time to declare their independence. They did so on December 6 of that same year. This day is a national holiday celebrated with military parades in Helsinki and performances at the National Theater. It is traditionally a solemn occasion that begins with a parade of students carrying torches and one flag for each year of independence.

CONTACTS:
Finnish Tourist Board
c/o Finpro, Porkkalankatu 1
P.O. Box 625
Helsinki 00181 Finland
358-29-469-5650
www.visitfinland.com

Embassy of Finland
3301 Massachusetts Ave. N.W.
Washington, D.C. 20008
202-298-5800; fax: 202-298-6030
www.finland.org

♦ 1015 ♦ Finnish Sliding Festival
First weekend in February

Patterned after the traditional event in Finland that celebrates Fat Tuesday or SHROVE TUESDAY before the beginning of LENT, the Finnish Sliding Festival, or **Laskiainen**, has been held in White, Minnesota, every winter for more than 50 years. It features two large ice slides which are constructed at the edge of Loon Lake. People bring their sleds or toboggans for an exciting ride down the slide onto the frozen expanse of the lake. For those who want more thrills, there is a *vipukelka* which resembles a kind of merry-go-round on ice.

Other activities at the weekend event include log-sawing contests, Finnish music and dance performances, and traditional Finnish foods such as oven pancakes and pea soup.

CONTACTS:
Iron Range Tourism Bureau
111 Station 44 Rd.
Eveleth, MN 55734
218-749-8161 or 800-777-8497; fax: 218-749-8055
www.ironrange.org

Town of White
16 W. 2nd Ave. N.
P.O. Box 146
Aurora, MN 55705
218-229-2813; fax: 218-229-2124
www.townofwhite.com

♦ 1016 ♦ Fire Festivals
February 1, May 1, August 1, November 1

The bonfire has deep symbolic significance in Celtic culture and Neopagan practice. The Greater Sabbats, the four traditional festivals that mark the CROSS-QUARTER DAYS—IMBOLC,

Beltane, Lammas, and Samhain—are often referred to as Fire Festivals. In conjunction with the Quarter Days these four days comprise the Celtic/Neopagan cycle known as the "Wheel of the Year." A bonfire ceremony is customary on the four sabbats among observing Neopagans in the United Kingdom, the United States, and other countries where such traditions are observed.

For three of the Cross-Quarter Days, the symbolic meaning of fire has significance within a sabbat's particular context. For example, for Imbolc (February 1) the emphasis is on the daylight that believers anticipate in the coming spring season. Lighting bonfires during Beltane (May 1) is a way of honoring the sun god. During Samhain (November 1), both the heat and light of fire have great significance since both elements are lacking during the approaching winter.

Historical accounts of bonfires during Lammas are unavailable because the sabbat has only been included in modern-day fire festivals.

CONTACTS:
Pagan Federation
BM Box 7097
London WC1N 3XX United Kingdom
44-208-908-4881; fax: 44-208-908-2093
www.paganfed.org

♦ 1017 ♦ Fire Prevention Week, National
Week including October 9

National Fire Prevention Day is October 9, the anniversary of the Great Chicago Fire of 1871, which killed more than 250 people, left 100,000 homeless, and destroyed more than 17,000 structures. The people of Chicago celebrated their restoration of the city by holding festivities on the anniversary of the fire, but it was the Fire Marshals' Association of North America that decided in 1911 to observe the day in a way that would raise the public's consciousness about fire prevention. President Woodrow Wilson issued the first National Fire Prevention Day proclamation in 1920, and every year since 1925 the week in which October 9 falls has been observed nationwide as National Fire Prevention Week.

Each year the National Fire Protection Association (NFPA) announces a theme for National Fire Prevention Week and sets up programs to educate the public about a particular aspect of fire prevention. Many of these important themes are recurring. In 1994, 2004, 2010, 2014 for example, the theme was the importance of keeping smoke detectors in good working order, and the theme for 1995, 2005, 2006, 2008 and 2013 was avoiding the major causes of home fires. Planning and practicing fire drill escape plans was the theme for 1998, 1999, and 2000, 2003, 2007, and 2012. The NFPA provides a Community Awareness Kit each year to help communities plan fire prevention activities.

CONTACTS:
National Fire Protection Association
1 Batterymarch Park
Quincy, MA 02169
617-770-3000 or 800-344-3555; fax: 617-770-0700
www.nfpa.org

♦ 1018 ♦ Firecracker Festival
January-February

Firecrackers are a traditional element of Tet, the Vietnamese New Year celebration, and one town really takes its firecrackers seriously. Each year 16 families are selected to compete in producing the most spectacular display for the town of Dong Ky in Vietnam's Ha Bac Province. These are no ordinary firecrackers, but huge, elaborately decorated affairs that may require two dozen men to carry and up to $500—more than an average family's annual earnings—to create. Each firecracker is paraded through town and set up on a special tripod for firing. After all the firecrackers have been set off, a panel of judges determines the winning family.

CONTACTS:
Vietnam National Administration of Tourism
Tourism Information Technology Centre
78 Quan Su St.
Hoan Kiem Dist.
Ha Noi Vietnam
84-4-3942-2246; fax: 84-4-3826-3956
www.vietnamtourism.com

♦ 1019 ♦ First Day of Summer (Iceland)
Thursday between April 19-25

In Iceland the First Day of Summer is second in importance only to Christmas and New Year's Day. It is a legal holiday observed on the Thursday that falls between April 19 and April 25, a time of year that marks the end of the long northern winter. The custom of giving gifts on this day was widespread by the middle of the 19th century, although they were usually homemade articles or, in some areas, a share of the fisherman's catch.

Special foods associated with the First Day of Summer include summer-day cakes—flat rye breads up to a foot in diameter—on top of which the day's share of food for each person would be piled. Since the turn of the century it has also been a popular day for young people to give speeches, poetry readings and dramatic performances, or to engage in singing, dancing, and sports.

CONTACTS:
Promote Iceland
Sundagarðar 2
Reykjavik 104 Iceland
354-511-4000; fax: 354-511-4040
www.iceland.is

♦ 1020 ♦ First Foot Day
January 1

The custom of firstfooting, or being the first to cross the threshold of a home in the early hours of New Year's Day, was so popular in England and Scotland during the 19th century that the streets were often more crowded between midnight and one o'clock in the morning than they would normally be at midday. If the "First Foot," traditionally a man, was to bring the family luck, he had to arrive with his arms full of cakes, bread, and cheese for everyone to share. He should be dark-haired, not fair, and must not have flat feet.

Today the custom may still be observed in Britain and in scattered areas of the United States.

CONTACTS:
Scottish Government
Saughton House
Broomhouse Dr.
Edinburgh EH11 3XD Scotland
44-131-244-8504
www.gov.scot

♦ 1021 ♦ **First Fruits of the Alps Sunday**
Fourth Sunday in August

The Alpine dairymen of Vissoie, Valais Canton, Switzerland, show their appreciation to the parish priest by presenting him with cheeses known as *les prémices des Alpes,* or the "first fruits of the Alps," on the fourth Sunday in August every year. Because they live in huts and graze their herds in the mountains all summer, the dairymen rely on the priest's visits so they can attend mass and receive the Holy Sacraments. In return, they give him all the milk their herds yield on the third day after their arrival in the mountains by making it into cheeses.

At the end of August, the justice of the peace of Val D'Anniviers counts, inspects, and weighs the cheeses brought back to Vissoie with the returning herds. After High Mass, the dairymen of the district march in procession to the altar, each carrying his own cheese, and stand before the town's red-and-black-robed magistrates. After giving the first fruits of the Alps to the priest, the dairymen once more form a procession and march to the parsonage, where a feast is held in the courtyard.

♦ 1022 ♦ **First Monday Trade Days**
Thursday through Sunday before first Monday of each month

The First Monday Trade Days are a colossal trading bazaar that each month brings 100,000 to 300,000 people to the small town of Canton, Tex. (population 2,800). This legendary affair in northern Texas has its origins in the 1850s when the circuit court judge came to Canton on the first Monday of the month to conduct court proceedings. Farmers from the area would gather to sell or trade horses, hunting hounds, and other dogs, conduct other business in town, and watch the occasional hanging. The judge no longer holds court in Canton, but the trading event continues.

Now the flea market starts on a Thursday, runs through the weekend, and offers merchandise and food at more than 3,000 exhibition stalls.

Scottsboro, Ala., also has well-known First Monday Trade Days attended by thousands, and this custom is observed in most southern states. Commonly, the markets are held on the streets surrounding the county courthouse. Fiddling and storytelling are often part of the day's activities. The name for the event differs; in some places, it's **Court Day**. In Abingdon, Va., it's **Jockey Day** because of the horse races held along with the trading.

CONTACTS:
First Monday Trade Days
800 Flea Market Rd.
P O Box 665
Canton, TX 75103
903-567-6556; fax: 903-567-2923
www.firstmondaycanton.com

♦ 1023 ♦ **First Night (Boston, Massachusetts)**
December 31

First Night originated in Boston as an annual NEW YEAR'S EVE celebration of the arts. This citywide festival was first held in 1976 to change the drinking and partying that have traditionally marked New Year's Eve celebrations in most American cities into a night of family entertainment. It has proved so successful that 65 other cities in the United States and Canada have followed Boston's lead.

To bring both inner city and suburban communities together, 1,000 artists in Boston offer a wide variety of artistic events and performances at 70 indoor and outdoor sites in Boston's Back Bay, Beacon Hill, South End, downtown, and waterfront areas. In recent years more than one million residents and visitors have been drawn to places in the city where they would not normally walk after dark.

CONTACTS:
First Night Boston
www.firstnightboston.org

♦ 1024 ♦ **Firstborn, Fast of the**
Between March 26 and April 23; Nisan 14

The Fast of the Firstborn is the only fast in the Jewish calendar which is neither an atonement for sin nor a fast of petition. Observed only symbolically by firstborn male Jews on the day before PASSOVER, its main purpose appears to be to remind Jews of the Angel of Death's slaying of the Egyptians' firstborn sons and the miraculous escape of their own sons. The obligation to fast can be avoided by participating in a *siyyum*—the study of a particular passage of the Talmud.

♦ 1025 ♦ **Fisher Poets Gathering**
Three-day weekend in late February

The Fisher Poets Gathering annually brings together poets, musicians, and story-tellers with an interest in fishing, particularly the lives of commercial fishers. Performances and meetings take place in various venues in the historic coastal town of Astoria, Ore., which boasts a still-working waterfront and a rich maritime history.

The centerpieces of the Fisher Poets Gathering are poetry and prose readings, story telling, and open microphone sessions in the evenings. Daytime workshops are available in such areas as creative writing, video-making, painting, and photography. Attendees can also enjoy live music, panels and lectures on fishing-industry issues, and art exhibits. Participants' literary contributions range from poignant personal memoirs to bawdy songs. The gathering was founded in 1998 by local writer Jon Broderick.

CONTACTS:
Astoria-Warrenton Area Chamber of Commerce
111 W. Marine Dr.
Astoria, OR 97103
503-325-6311 or 800-875-6807
www.oldoregon.com

FisherPoets Gathering
Astoria, OR 97103
www.fisherpoets.org

♦ 1026 ♦ Five-Petalled Rose Festival
Third week in June

The Festival of the Five-Petalled Rose takes place in Cesky Krumlov in the Czech Republic. The town prospered during the Renaissance, and today's festival permits residents and visitors to relive some of the town's past glories. Cesky Krumlov's magnificent castle adds to the festival's atmosphere, and some of the events take place there. Festival highlights include swordplay demonstrations, plays and street dramas, processions of people in Renaissance costume, a medieval feast, a historical market, demonstrations of Renaissance crafts, contemporary and Renaissance musical entertainment, and medieval games, military exercises, and dances. The festival takes its name from the five-petalled rose found on the coat of arms of the Rosenbergs, the noble family that lived in the castle during the late medieval and Renaissance periods.

CONTACTS:
Cesky Krumlov Tourism Information Center
Infocentrum
Námestí Svornosti No. 2
Cesky Krumlov 381 01 Czech Republic
420-380-704-621; fax: 420-380-704-619
www.ckrumlov.info

♦ 1027 ♦ Flag Day
June 14

On June 14, 1777, the Continental Congress replaced the British symbols of George Washington's Grand Union flag with a new design featuring 13 white stars in a circle on a field of blue and 13 red and white stripes—one for each state. Although it is not certain, this flag may have been made by the Philadelphia seamstress Betsy Ross who was an official flag-maker for the Pennsylvania Navy. The number of stars increased as the new states entered the Union, but the number of stripes stopped at 15 and was later returned to 13.

President Woodrow Wilson issued a proclamation that established June 14 as Flag Day in 1916, but it didn't become official until 1949. This occurred as a result of a campaign by Bernard J. Cigrand and the American Flag Day Association.

It is observed across the country by displaying the American flag on homes and public buildings. Other popular ways of observing this day include flag-raising ceremonies, the singing of the national anthem, and the study of flag etiquette and the flag's origin and meaning. Each year more than 3,000 schoolchildren form a living American flag at Fort McHenry National Monument in Baltimore, Md., near where Francis Scott Key wrote "The Star-Spangled Banner" (*see also* Defenders' Day).

CONTACTS:
National Park Service
2400 E. Fort Ave.
Baltimore, MD 21230
410-563-3900 or 800-658-8947
www.nps.gov

♦ 1028 ♦ Flagstaff Festival of the Arts
July

This major performing and visual arts festival of Arizona is held in Flagstaff on the campus of Northern Arizona University. The affair began in the early 1960s as a music camp and became a full-fledged festival in 1966. It ran one week that year, and today is a four-week festival with more than 48 events: symphonic and chamber music concerts, ballet, theater, film showings, and art exhibits. From 1966 to 1977, Izler Solomon directed and conducted the festival orchestra, which is composed of musicians from major U.S. orchestras.

CONTACTS:
Flagstaff Visitor Center
1 E. Rt. 66
Flagstaff, AZ 86001
928-213-2951 or 800-379-0065
www.flagstaffarizona.org

♦ 1029 ♦ Flaming Tar Barrels
November 5

Held each year in Ottery St Mary, Devon, England, Flaming Tar Barrels is a tradition dating back hundreds of years. In preparation for the event, the insides of barrels are coated with coal tar and filled with paper and straw. Ranging in size, the barrels are carried in a procession during the day by men, women, and children. At night people light the barrels at various public houses and hotels in the town and carry them on their shoulders. The last barrel is carried to the town square around midnight. Although the exact origins of the festival are unknown, it is most likely a commemoration of England's infamous Gunpowder Plot. On November 5, 1605, a plot by Catholics to assassinate the Protestant King James I was foiled, and the conspirator Guy Fawkes was apprehended and later executed. The tradition of Flaming Tar Barrels concludes with a huge bonfire at St Saviour's Meadow, where an effigy of Guy Fawkes is burned.

CONTACTS:
Ottery St Mary Tourism Information

10b Broad St.
Ottery St Mary, EX11 1BX United Kingdom
44-1404-813964
www.otterystmarytourism.co.uk

◆ 1030 ◆ Flanders Festival
May-November

The Flanders Festival, or **Festival van Vlaanderen**, is one of the longest and most diverse music festivals in Europe. The season extends from spring to late autumn, with events taking place in eight cities spread over the five Flemish provinces of Belgium. In the medieval city of Bruges, for instance, the festival takes place in August and features baroque and early classical music. In Ghent it includes opera as well as symphonic music. Other cities participating in the festival include Antwerp, Brussels-Leuven, Courtrai, Limburg, Mechelen, and Vlaas-Brabant.

Established in 1958, the Flanders Festival grew out of the Brussels World Fair. The world's most famous performers, opera companies, and ensembles perform—often in more than one city—in settings that range from concert halls to abbeys and stadiums.

CONTACTS:
Festival van Vlaanderen Brussel
Rue Zinnerstraat 1
Brussel 1000 Belgium
32-2-548-95-95; fax: 32-2-548-95-90
www.festivalbrxl.be

vzw AMUZ [Flanders Festival-Antwerp]
Kammenstraat 81
Antwerp, NC 2000 Belgium
32-3-202-46-69; fax: 32-3-202-46-64
www.amuz.be

◆ 1031 ◆ Fleadh Cheoil
Late August

The Fleadh Cheoil (Festival of Music) is a national festival that has been promoting Irish traditional music and dance through competition for more than 50 years. It takes place in late August, although the location changes from year to year. The festival also features less formal music sessions and street performances, as well as Irish art, parades, and pag- eants.

CONTACTS:
Comhaltas Ceoltoiri Eireann
32 Belgrave Sq.
Monkstown, Dublin Ireland
353-1-2800-295; fax: 353-1-2803-759
comhaltas.ie

◆ 1032 ◆ Fleet Week (Hampton Roads, Virginia)
October

The Hampton Roads area of southeastern Virginia and northeastern North Carolina features one of the world's largest natural harbors. The cities of Norfolk, Virginia Beach, and Newport News are located here. The U.S. Navy, Marines, Air Force, and Army have facilities in the area, as does NASA.

The Hampton Roads community sponsors an annual Fleet Week to honor the military personnel who are stationed in the area for the work they perform on behalf of the nation. The event is also a celebration of the U.S. Navy's official birthday in October.

Among the Fleet Week activities are a 5K run, a golf tournament, free outdoor music concerts, a chili cook-off, a family day at Norfolk's Town Point Park, and a half marathon run. Military personnel attend the music concerts for free. The Virginia Zoo offers special programming at this time, also free to military personnel and their families.

Local motorcycle enthusiasts sponsor the "Rumble through the Tunnels," a fundraiser in which hundreds of motorcycles ride through several of Hampton Roads tunnels.

Fleet Week ends with a parade of ships and planes along the downtown Norfolk waterfront. Navy tugs spray water into the air, helicopters fly overhead, and frigates, submarines, and landing craft sail by.

CONTACTS:
United States Navy
Chief of Information
1200 Navy Pentagon
Washington, D.C. 20350
www.navy.mil

Naval Station Norfolk Fleet Fest
Public Affairs Office
Norfolk, VI 23505
757-322-2337
www.discovermwr.com

◆ 1033 ◆ Fleet Week (New York City)
May

To give citizens of New York City the chance to meet Navy, Coast Guard, and Marine personnel firsthand, the Navy has sponsored an annual Fleet Week since 1987.

During the week-long event the public is allowed to tour Navy and Coast Guard vessels, including amphibious assault vessels, destroyers, and cruisers. They can also view fighter jets, helicopters, aerial refueler tankers, anti-submarine trackers, bombers, and cargo planes.

Though Fleet Week was canceled in 2013 due to federal budget cuts, the festivities resumed for 2014 with a free concert in Bryant Park to kick-off the week featuring the Navy Band Northeast Pops Ensemble and the U.S. Fleet Forces Band. Fleet Week activities typically include a parade of ships in the harbor, and several competitions, including tug-of-war and eating contests.

◆ 1034 ◆ Fleet Week (San Diego, California)
September

In 1997, community and business organizations in San Diego, Calif., organized the first Fleet Week to honor the sailors and marines who are stationed in that city. Service personnel are thanked for "Serving America Twice," as military personnel and as volunteer workers in the San Diego community. A large number of the sailors and marines use their free time to work as volunteer firefighters, scout leaders, coaches for youth teams, or in other community service positions. By 2001, the annual event was taken over by the newly formed San Diego Fleet Week Foundation. While called a "week," the San Diego Fleet Week lasts for more than a month, with various activities around the city.

San Diego Fleet Week begins with the Port of San Diego Sea and Air Parade featuring Navy aircraft carriers, destroyers, cruisers, submarines, amphibious craft, and frigates, as well as Coast Guard cutters. Military jets and helicopters fly overhead.

Some 100,000 people turn out to watch the parade. Later, naval ships docked at Broadway Pier are open to visitors.

The Marine Corps sponsors a one-day boot camp for civilians interested in experiencing the obstacle course and drill fields used by real recruits. The Marine Corps Air Station Miramar Air Show features vintage airplanes as well as the latest in military aviation. Some 200 booths offer hands-on displays. An evening fireworks display ends the air show.

San Diego State University holds the Fleet Week Football Classic in which their football team plays the U.S. Air Force Academy team.

CONTACTS:
San Diego Fleet Week Foundation
5330 Napa St.
San Diego, CA 92110
619-858-1545; fax: 619-299-9955
www.fleetweeksandiego.org

◆ 1035 ◆ Fleet Week (San Francisco, California)
October

To celebrate the men and women who serve in America's armed forces, San Francisco has held an annual Fleet Week since 1981.

The week-long event features members of the U.S. Navy, Coast Guard, and Marines. After a parade of ships, the public is allowed to visit a number of Navy and Coast Guard vessels docked in San Francisco Bay.

Since 2010, Fleet Week has helped local first responders and military service members prepare for and respond to emergencies that may take place in the Bay Area and around the world. Activities include urban search and rescue training, medical trauma training, and a senior leaders' seminar. Fleet Week returned in 2014 after 2013 activities were cancelled by the federal government shutdown. The event attracted over one million people who watched the Blue Angels air show along the San Francisco Bay waterfront. Other Air Force and Navy aircraft have also participated in Fleet Week, including fighter aircraft and historic planes.

CONTACTS:
San Francisco Fleet Week Association
609 Sutter St.
San Francisco, CA 94102
415-306-0911
www.fleetweek.us

◆ 1036 ◆ Flemington Fair
Late August through Labor Day, first Monday in September

The **New Jersey State Agricultural Fair** is held in Flemington from the end of August and continuing right through LABOR DAY. The event is a traditional agricultural fair that was started by a group of local farmers in 1856, making it one of the oldest state fairs in the country. It features a statewide 4-H lamb show and sale, a tractor pull, a horse and pony pull, and all types of car racing (mini-stocks, modified stocks, midgets, and super sprints). The fair also offers programs and exhibits of flowers, the 4-H organization, nurserymen, and various commercial enterprises.

◆ 1037 ◆ Flemish Community, Feast Day of the
July 11

Each of the autonomous regions of Belgium observes its own feast day. The Feast Day of the Flemish Community is one of several celebrations observed by the citizens of Belgium's autonomous regions, which include three linguistic communities—the Flemish, French, and German. Feast days in other regions of Belgium include FEAST DAY OF THE FRENCH COMMUNITY, FEAST DAY OF THE GERMAN-SPEAKING COMMUNITY, IRIS FEST, and WALLOON REGIONAL DAY.

The Flemish Community, whose political territory encompasses the historic region of Flanders in northern Belgium, celebrates its heritage on the anniversary of The Battle of the Golden Spurs in 1302. The battle, which ended in the Flemish defeat of France, marked the beginning of regional autonomy for this ethnic group.

Many inhabitants believe that if that untrained force of Flemish tradesmen had not overcome their professional French opponents in 1302, the region might still be under French control. The "golden spurs" refer to the 600 spurs that fell from the vanquished French knights on the battlefield, which were retrieved and later preserved as tokens of the Flemish victory.

On the feast day all Flemish governmental offices close for the holiday. Various cities, municipalities, and private groups hold cultural events; local Flemings and those resettled throughout the world pause to give a toast to Flanders; and many individuals gather to hear the minister-president of the Flemish Community deliver a speech marking the anniversary.

♦ 1038 ♦ Flight into Egypt
December 26

Many congregations within the Eastern Orthodox Church commemorate the Holy Family's flight into Egypt on December 26. According to the Gospel of St. Matthew, King Herod wanted to seek out and kill the infant Jesus. But an angel warned Joseph, the husband of Jesus' mother, Mary, of the danger and instructed him to take the family to Egypt for safety and to remain there until Herod's death. Two days later, according to the Gospel, all of the male children under two years of age in Bethlehem were massacred, an event that is commemorated on HOLY INNOCENTS' DAY.

CONTACTS:
Tour Egypt
4119 Adrian St
Lubbock, TX 79415 United States
888-834-1448
www.touregypt.net

♦ 1039 ♦ Float Festival
January-February; night of full moon in Tamil month of Thai (Hindu month of Magha)

The Float Festival is held at the temple city of Madurai in the state of Tamil Nadu, India, to commemorate the birth of Tirumala Nayak, a 17th-century king of Madurai. The center of the festival is the Mariamman Teppakulam pond surrounding a temple on an island. Images of the goddess Meenakshi and her consort are floated on a flower-bedecked raft to the illuminated temple, and a spectacular array of lit floats moves in procession around the pond, accompanied by music and chanted hymns. Thousands of pilgrims from all over India attend this enormously popular festival.

CONTACTS:
Tamil Nadu Tourism Development Corporation
Tourism Complex, No. 2 Wallajah Rd.
Triplicane
Chennai, Tamil Nadu 600 002 India
91-44-2538-3333; fax: 91-44-2536-1385
www.tamilnadutourism.org

♦ 1040 ♦ Floating Lantern Ceremony (Toro Nagashi)
August

This Buddhist ceremony is held in Honolulu, Hawaii, around the anniversaries of the end of World War II and the atomic bombing of HIROSHIMA. The festival is part of the annual Buddhist Bon season of July and August in which the spirits of departed ancestors are welcomed back to earth with prayers, dances, offerings, and by setting afloat more than 1,000 colorful paper lanterns bearing the names of the dead.

See also OBON FESTIVAL.

CONTACTS:
Hawaii Visitors & Convention Bureau
2270 Kalakaua Ave.

Ste. 801
Honolulu, HI 96815
808-923-1811; fax: 808-924-0290
www.hvcb.org

♦ 1041 ♦ Floralia
April 27-May 3

An ancient Roman festival held in honor of Flora, the goddess of flowers and gardens, the Floralia was instituted in 238 B.C.E. It was originally a movable feast whose date depended on the condition of the crops and flowers in any particular year at the end of April and beginning of May.

In 173 B.C.E., after severe storms had proved disastrous for the cornfields and vineyards, the Roman Senate made it an annual festival extending for six days—from April 27, the anniversary of the founding of Flora's temple, through May 3. Traditionally, the first person to lay a wreath or garland on the temple's statue of Flora was destined to have good fortune in the months that followed.

From the beginning, the Floralia was characterized by wild and licentious behavior on the part of the celebrants. The games, dances, and dramatic productions involved in the celebration were usually lewd, and courtesans are said to have performed mimes in the nude. The obscene nature of the festivities was undoubtedly due to their origins in earlier pagan fertility rites designed to promote the earth's fruitfulness. But when the festival was introduced into Rome, it became a good excuse for excessive drinking and carrying on.

The Floralia, which originally featured small statues of Flora that children would decorate with flowers, is believed to have been the precedent for Christian-oriented MAY DAY celebrations, which often included dolls or images of the Virgin Mary.

♦ 1042 ♦ Floralies
April-May, every four to six years

The famous flower festivals of the cities of Ghent and Liège in Belgium combined to hold one joint festival every four to six years at the Hall des Foires de Liège. The first combined festival was held in 2003. Hundreds of horticulturists from around the world show their best products to be judged for cash prizes. The showing attracts about 700,000 visitors.

Ghent was one of the centers of a thriving horticultural industry, and the Floralies there began in 1809 at the Frascati Inn where 50 plants were arranged around a bust of Napoleon. In 1814, it is believed that John Quincy Adams and other U.S. delegates visited the flower show; they were staying in Ghent during negotiations preceding the signing of the Treaty of Ghent, which ended the War of 1812. The Floralies in Liège have been held since 1830.

CONTACTS:
Association of International Floralies
Kortrijksesteenweg 1097A

FLORALIS-Bldg.
4th Fl.
Gent B-9051 Belgium
32-9-241-5091; fax: 32-9-241-5095
www.aifloralies.org

Foire Internationale de Liège
Ave. Maurice-Denis 4
Liege 4000 Belgium
32-4-227-1934; fax: 32-4-227-1895
www.fil.be

♦ 1043 ♦ Florence Musical May (Maggio Musicale Fiorentino)
May-June

The **Florence May Festival** was first held in 1933, and it wasn't long before it had established itself as one of the most important international festivals in Italy. It offers chamber and symphonic music, ballet, and dance, and is recognized as a pioneer in its efforts to revive rare foreign and Italian operas. Most of the larger events are held in the Teatro della Pergola or the more modern Teatro Comunale, home of the festival's resident opera company.

In the past, when operas were staged outdoors, the city fathers had to ban the Vespa motor scooters that young Florentines use to get around, for fear that the noise would ruin the listening experience for festivalgoers.

Many of the world's greatest singers have performed at the festival, among them Maria Callas, Renata Tebaldi, Mario del Monaco, and Boris Christoff. The festival regularly commissions new opera and dance productions, using funds received from the Ministry of Culture.

♦ 1044 ♦ Flores de Mayo (El Salvador)
May

In the late 18th century the Roman Catholic Church set aside the month of May to honor the Blessed Virgin Mary. The religious ceremonies held in honor of the Virgin in El Salvador during this month are called Flores de Mayo (Flowers of May), probably because there are so many wildflowers in bloom at this time of year.

The town of San Vincente celebrates the fiesta in a distinctive way. Each day, between four and five in the afternoon, there is a procession through the streets of town. It starts at the house of the *capitana*, the woman who directs the festival on that day. The women who have worked on the festival and their friends march through town scattering candy, anise seeds, and sweetmeats. Men throw flowers, corn, and grain from the sidelines. At six o'clock the image of the Virgin Mary is carried from the capitana's house to the church in procession, and a second and even more elaborate procession takes place later that night. These processions take place throughout the month-long observance. Each day a different capitana takes charge of the day's activities.

Although "la Flor," as the procession is known, is the highlight of each day's activities, there is also music every morning as men and women playing guitars and marimbas stroll through the streets. Sometimes a jester wearing a mask rides through the town on horseback, handing out announcements of coming events. Another procession takes place at midday, consisting of a parade of cars that have been specially decorated for the fiesta. People wearing masks follow on foot.

CONTACTS:
Church of Jesus Christ of Latter Day Saints
Avenida El Espino
Colonia San Benito
Frente al Redondel Roberto D'Abuisson
Antiguo Cuscatlan El Salvador
503-2520-2631; fax: 503-2520-2654
www.lds.org

♦ 1045 ♦ Flores de Mayo (Philippines)
May 31

Flores de Mayo ("May flowers") festivals take place throughout the Philippines during the month of May. Children create offerings of flowers and bring them to their churches in the afternoon. Parades make their way through towns and villages, with girls wearing traditional costumes followed by their relatives and friends singing Hail Marys.

The festival ends on May 31 with fiestas everywhere. In big cities like Manila, Flores de Mayo is one of the largest festivals of the year, featuring May Queens and fancy dress balls. In the smaller towns and villages, the last day of the month is a day to celebrate the birthday of their patron saint.

CONTACTS:
Philippine Tourism Center
556 Fifth Ave.
New York, NY 10036
212-575-7915; fax: 212-302-6759
itsmorefuninthephilippines.com

♦ 1046 ♦ Floriade
April-October, every 10 years (2022, 2032, 2042…)

Once every 10 years, the Netherlands organizes a World Horticultural Exhibition called the Floriade. The grounds for the 1992 exhibition were the Zoeteneer, outside Amsterdam. They cover 230 acres with lakes, gardens, theme pavilions, restaurants, and environmental displays—including a miniature Netherlands with dykes and canals that visitors can flood and drain at will.

What has been billed as the greatest flower show on earth runs from early April through early October and attracts about three million visitors. Magnificent displays of bulbs and flowers, plants and trees, and fruits and vegetables are divided into seven thematic areas: transport, production, consumer, environment, future, world, and recreation. In addition to the many open-air activities, there are extensive indoor attractions in the numerous halls, greenhouses, and pavilions.

The 2002 Floriade was held in the park in the city of Haarlemmermeer. A unique feature of this event was the milling about of 25 CyberCabs—new, automatically propelled vehicles resembling golf carts—which drove visitors to the top of a hill in the park to enjoy spectacular views of the festival. The first Floriade to be held in the Southeastern quarter of the country took place in the city of Venlo in 2012. The 7th Floriade will be held in Almere in 2022 and will center around the development of a prototype of an entire Green City.

CONTACTS:
Municipality of Almere
Stadhuisplein 1
Almere 1315 HR Netherlands
31-36-539-9911
english.almere.nl

♦ 1047 ♦ Florida Heritage Festival
March-April

The celebration, formerly known as the **De Soto Celebration**, in Florida is in honor of the young Spanish explorer Hernando de Soto (c. 1500-1542), who arrived on the west coast of Florida, probably near Tampa Bay and the present-day town of Bradenton, in 1539. With his band of several hundred conquistadores (conquerors), de Soto set out on a 4,000-mile trek through the wilderness north to the Blue Ridge Mountains, across them, south along the Alabama River to present-day Mobile, across the Mississippi River into what is now Arkansas, and explored further to the south and west. It was the first time a European had explored the North American interior.

The De Soto Celebration held each year from late March through most of April in Bradenton goes back to 1939. In past years, a group of costumed conquistadores would reenact de Soto's landing, coming ashore in longboats and skirmishing with the "Indians" in full view of a grandstand full of spectators then pressing onward until they reached Bradenton, where they would raid the county courthouse. Today they capture the De Soto Square Mall.

Other festival events include a children's parade, a grand parade, a bottle boat regatta, and a seafood fest with live entertainment, arts and crafts, and boat cruises with the conquistadores.

CONTACTS:
Hernando De Soto Historical Society
910 Third Ave. W.
Bradenton, FL 34205
941-747-1998; fax: 941-747-7953
www.desotohq.com

♦ 1048 ♦ Flower Communion
A Sunday in June

The Flower Communion was first held on June 24, 1923 in Prague, Czech Republic. Norbert Capek, who founded the Unitarian Church in Prague, conducted the ceremony, which reflects the Unitarian belief in the oneness of God and human beings. Capek chose flowers for the ritual, a departure from traditional Christian communion services of bread and wine. For the ceremony, attendees bring flowers as representations of themselves to the church. Next the flowers are placed together in a basket and consecrated by the minister. Various hymns and a sermon follow the consecration. The ritual concludes with the congregants taking back a flower from the basket as they leave. In 1940, Capek's wife Maja brought the Flower Communion to America, introducing it to the Unitarian church in Cambridge, Massachusetts.

♦ 1049 ♦ Flower Festivals of St. Rose and St. Margaret Mary Alacoque
August 30 (St. Rose) and October 17 (St. Margaret Mary Alacoque)

On the Caribbean island of St. Lucia, two floral societies known as the Roses and the Marguerites have preserved the royal pageant traditions of their former European colonizers. Each of these groups boasts a royal family as well as a large number of general supporters. They regularly pay tribute to their namesake flowers as well as their patron saints: Rose of Lima (1586–1617) and Margaret Mary Alacoque (1647–1690). The societies no longer enjoy a dominant role in the Caribbean island's social structure but still enjoy a reputation for hosting the *grand fêtes* that mark the respective feast days.

In an intensive process of preparing for the two *fêtes*, the Roses and the Marguerites each hold a series of dress rehearsals known as *séances*. During these events, a main performer, the *shantwel*, leads society members in call-and-response singing accompanied by various folk instruments.

The feast day opens with a church service, which is followed by a street procession presenting the host society's royal entourage. The evening program includes a banquet, the much-awaited performance by the shantwel, and folk dances such as the Quadrille, the *Mappa*, and the *Belair*..

CONTACTS:
St. Lucia Tourist Board
800 Second Ave.
Ste. 910
New York, NY 10017
212-867-2950
stlucianow.com

♦ 1050 ♦ Foire Internationale d'Art Contemporain
October

The Foire Internationale d'Art Contemporain (FIAC) takes place each year in Paris. The event is an exhibition that brings together gallerists, curators, and collectors of contemporary art from across the world. Varied genres of visual art from more than 30 countries are showcased at nearly 200 galleries including the Grand Palais, the Louvre, and other venues. The works chosen for the event undergo a rigorous selection process, which helps to create a balanced and representative collection of international art. The festival also includes educational programs that focus on art history and emerging art scenes. The event features a special section devoted to youth, and the annual Marcel Duchamp Prize is presented to a promising young artist. Other activities on the festival itinerary include musicals, dance, and theater.

CONTACTS:
Foire Internationale d'Art Contemporain
52/54, quai de Dion-Bouton
Puteaux Cedex, 92806 France
33-1-47-56-6420; fax: 33-1-47-56-6429
www.fiac.com/paris/en

♦ 1051 ♦ **Folk Festival, National**
Summer or fall, depending on location

Unlike other music festivals, the National Folk Festival (NFF) does not have a home base. Rather than assuming a permanent residence, this traveling festival works in partnership with a host community for periods of three years. The three-day NFF is a celebration of traditional music, dance, and crafts with an emphasis on the ethnic music styles that have shaped American culture through various eras.

The festival is organized by the National Council for the Traditional Arts (NCTA), which has been producing celebrations of the traditional arts since 1934. The NCTA's aim is to produce a show in the same city for three years, thereby laying the groundwork for a locally produced festival to continue after the National Folk Festival moves on to another city. Since the event is presented free of charge, planning and operations depends largely on the efforts of volunteers.

The traveling framework of the festival has had success in a handful of cities, including Bangor, Maine (host city of NFF in 2002-2004), and Richmond, Va. (2005-2007), which are now sites of regional folk festivals that continue to attract large audiences. Butte, Mont., was chosen to host the festival in the years 2008-2010. During the years 2015-2017, the festival will celebrate its 75th anniversary while taking up residence in Greensboro, North Carolina. Since 1987, the National Folk Festival has been presented to audiences free of charge in 28 cities and drawn crowds of 100,000 to 175,000 annually.

CONTACTS:
National Council for the Traditional Arts (NCTA)
8757 Georgia Ave.
Ste. 450
Silver Spring, MD 20910
301-565-0654; fax: 301-565-0472
ncta-usa.org

♦ 1052 ♦ **Folklore, National Festival of**
Every four years in autumn

Albania celebrates its cultural heritage with the National Festival of Folklore, which takes place in the southern city of Gjirokastra. Since 1968, the festival has drawn local artists and performers; Albanian troupes from neighboring countries like Kosovo, Montenegro, and Macedonia; and performers from more distant countries like Italy, Turkey, and the United States. It is an occasion to present traditional music, folk art,

clothing, and locally made jewelry. The event, which takes place every four years, draws tourists as well as local Albanians.

Gjirokastra, which historians believe was founded as early as the fourth century, has a rich history that is appropriate to the festival's traditional feel. The open square of Gjirokastra Castle, which dates back to the sixth century C.E., is the main performance site. There, dance troupes face off in competitions and singers often perform ballads to the accompaniment of the çifteli, a two-string long-necked mandolin. Crafts people also entice shoppers with their copper jewelry and other wares.

CONTACTS:
Albanian Tourism
Str. "Sermedin Said Toptani"
Tirana Albania
355-42-273-778
www.albania.al

♦ 1053 ♦ **Folkmoot**
Two weeks in mid-to late July

This two-week festival is held in the mountains at the entrance to the Great Smoky Mountains National Park in western North Carolina. It features more than 350 folk musicians and dancers from countries as diverse as Ecuador, Italy, Malaysia, Turkey, Peru, Israel, Slovenia, China, and the Philippines.

Events include a Parade of Nations, a bazaar with local and regional artisans and food vendors, a special children's program, and performances by the folk dancers and musicians. Many of the events take place in the nearby towns of Waynesville and Asheville.

CONTACTS:
Folkmoot USA
112 Virginia Ave.
Waynesville, NC 28786
828-452-2997 or 877-365-5872
www.folkmootusa.org

♦ 1054 ♦ **Fools, Feast of**
On or around January 1

A mock-religious festival popular during the Middle Ages in Europe, particularly France, the Feast of Fools had much in common with the Roman Saturnalia. During the holiday period around Christmas and New Year's Day, various classes of the clergy took turns reversing the normal procedures in the church. On January 1, the Feast of the Circumcision, for example, the priests were in charge; on Holy Innocents' Day, December 28, the choirboys held sway. The group to whom the day belonged would nominate a bishop and archbishop of fools, ordaining them in a mock ceremony and then presenting them to the people. Masked and dressed in women's clothing, they would dance and sing obscene songs, play dice or eat at the altar, burn old shoes in the censers, and engage in other activities that would normally be unthinkable. The revelry died out around the time of the Reformation.

The Feast of Fools was similar, but not identical, to the FEAST OF THE ASS that was observed in France around Christmas time.

CONTACTS:
Festival of Fools
23-25 Gordon St.
Belfast BT1 2LG United Kingdom
44-28-9023-6007; fax: 44-28-9043-4971
foolsfestival.com

♦ 1055 ♦ **Footwashing Day**
Early summer; Sunday

According to the Gospel of John, before the Last Supper Jesus washed the feet of his disciples and instructed them to follow his example of humility and love. Although it was originally performed on MAUNDY THURSDAY, in most American Protestant sects it takes place at other times and occasionally at more frequent intervals.

For some mountain people of Kentucky, this observance takes place only once a year, but the preparations go on for weeks beforehand. On Footwashing Day, the women take turns washing each other's feet, and on the opposite side of the church the men do the same thing. Refreshment stands have been set up so children can eat while their parents are participating in the ritual. After the service, the people who live near the church invite the rest of the participants to eat with them.

CONTACTS:
Grace Communion International
P.O. Box 5005
Glendora, CA 91740
800-423-4444
www.gci.org

♦ 1056 ♦ **Forefathers' Day**
December 21 or 22

Observed primarily in Plymouth, Massachusetts, and by various New England societies throughout the country, Forefathers' Day commemorates the landing of the Pilgrims, who arrived in 1620 on the *Mayflower* and established the second English colony in North America. (The first colony successfully established was in JAMESTOWN, Virginia, in 1607.)

The Old Colony Club of Plymouth was the first group to observe the anniversary in 1769, but since this was only 15 years after the New Style Calendar went into effect, there was some confusion about how many days should be added to the original December 11 date of the landing. All dates before 1700 were supposed to have 10 days added, and all dates after 1700 were supposed to have 11 days added. Somehow a mistake was made, and Old Colony Club members still celebrate Forefathers' Day on December 22. Wearing top hats and led by a drummer, they march down the main street of

Plymouth. After firing a small cannon, they return to their Club for breakfast and toasts to the Pilgrims.

Transplanted New Englanders who have formed New England societies in other parts of the country, however, observe the occasion on December 21, as does the General Society of Mayflower Descendants, which sometimes refers to it as **Compact Day**. The Pilgrim Society, which was founded in 1820 by a group of people interested in the history of Plymouth, holds its annual meeting on December 21 and serves a traditional dinner of succotash, stew, corn, turnips, and beans.

CONTACTS:
Plimoth Plantation
137 Warren Ave.
Plymouth, MA 02360
508-746-1622
www.plimoth.org

♦ 1057 ♦ **Forgiveness, Feast of**
August 1-2

The **Festa del Perdono**, or Feast of Forgiveness, is observed annually in Assisi, Italy, where St. Francis built his humble hermitage, known as the *Porciúncula* ("little portion"), in the 13th century. It was here on a small plot of land containing a ruined chapel that St. Francis experienced his religious conversion and began to preach and gather disciples. He restored the chapel and claimed it as his "portion" or "little inheritance." In 1209 he received papal permission to establish the Franciscan monastic order, the Friars Minor, urging his followers to maintain the chapel as a sacred place.

Porciúncula also refers to the plenary indulgence that used to be given to those who visited this sanctuary on August 2, the date set by Pope Honorius III in 1221. Although in the beginning the indulgence could only be gained in the Porciúncula, the privilege was eventually extended to all churches having a connection with the Franciscan order, and the time for visiting the sanctuary was extended to the period between the afternoon of August 1 and sunset on August 2.

St. Francis instituted the two-day Feast of Forgiveness because it upset him that by going off to fight in the Crusades a sinful man could escape punishment in purgatory. Believing that there should be a more peaceful means to gain salvation, St. Francis received the Pope's permission for Roman Catholics to make an annual pilgrimage to Assisi to renew their relationship with the church.

The August 2 feast was brought to New Mexico by the early Spanish settlers, and it is still observed in the small town of Arroyo Hondo, about 80 miles north of Santa Fe. Although at one time it involved two processions—one beginning at the village church's main entrance and another, a quarter of a mile away, involving only members of the flagellant brotherhood today the celebration in Arroyo Hondo that once drew large crowds has nearly died out.

See also ST. FRANCIS OF ASSISI, FEAST OF.

♦ 1058 ♦ **Fornacalia**
Around February 17

The Fornacalia, or **Feast of Ovens**, was observed no later than February 17, which was also the day of the QUIRINA-LIA festival honoring the ancient Roman god Quirinus. The Fornacalia was designed to benefit the ovens (*fornices*) that parched grain and was held to placate the goddess Fornix, who presided over them. It lasted a week, during which each household made an offering of *far*, flour of the oldest kind of Italian wheat, roasted in the oven and then crushed in an ancient mill and served in the form of cakes. The rituals involved in the Fornacalia were observed primarily by the *curiae*, or tribal divisions of Rome, and it was celebrated in February on different days—one day for the state and one for each of the curiae. According to Ovid, those who were uncertain which curia they belonged to ended up observing this festival on February 17 instead of on the proper day. At this time a general offering of cakes was made by the whole community.

♦ 1059 ♦ **Forty Martyrs' Day**
March 9

The "Forty Martyrs of Sebaste" were Roman soldiers quartered in Armenia in 320. Agricola, the governor of the province, told them that under orders of the Emperor Licinius, they would have to make a sacrifice to the Roman gods. As Christians, they refused to do so. Agricola told them to strip themselves naked and stand on the ice of a nearby pond. All died from exposure during the night. They are greatly revered in the Eastern Christian Church. This day is observed in the Orthodox church in Syria as **Id al-Arba'in Shahid**. In Greece, special foods are prepared: cake with 40 layers of pastry, stew with 40 herbs, 40 pancakes, etc. InRomania, little cakes called *sfintisori* ("little mints") are baked and given to and received from every passerby. *Coliva*, a cake of cooked corn and honey, is also traditional. Farm tools are readied for work, and hearth ashes are spread around the cottage to keep the serpent from entering (each home is said to have a serpent protecting it).

CONTACTS:
Forty Holy Martyrs of Sebaste Antiochian Orthodox Church
340 Eldridge Rd.
Sugar Land, TX 77478
281-240-4845
www.40martyrs.org

♦ 1060 ♦ **Fossey (Dian) Day**
December 27

Over the course of her career, American conservationist Dian Fossey (1932–1985) conducted groundbreaking research on Rwanda's mountain gorillas, a species long victimized by wide-scale poaching. Her advocacy on behalf of the gorillas also helped ensure their preservation. At the age of 53, Fossey was murdered in her cabin at a research center in the Virunga Mountains on December 27, 1985. For Rwandans

and conservationists, the anniversary of her death honors a legacy that draws attention to the plight of a rare animal species and helps promote eco-tourism.

Ceremonies take place in Volcanoes National Park, which is the site of Fossey's murder and contains a permanent memorial to the zoologist. Individuals typically perform traditional dances, while government officials deliver speeches and lay wreaths on her grave site.

CONTACTS:
Dian Fossey Gorilla Fund International, Inc.
800 Cherokee Ave. S.E.
Atlanta, GA 30315
404-624-5881 or 800-851-0203
gorillafund.org

♦ 1061 ♦ **Foster (Stephen) Memorial Day**
January 13

Stephen Collins Foster (1826-1864) was a composer whose popular minstrel songs and sentimental ballads have found a lasting place in American music. When he died at the age of 37, suffering from poverty and alcoholism, he left behind more than 200 compositions—among them "Camptown Races," "Beautiful Dreamer," "My Old Kentucky Home," "Oh! Susanna," "Swanee River," and "Jeanie with the Light Brown Hair."

January 13, the anniversary of Foster's death, was proclaimed as Stephen Foster Memorial Day in 1951. In Florida, this day is part of Stephen Foster Memorial Week, established by the state legislature in 1935.

One of the most widely known observances takes place at the Stephen Foster Center in White Springs, Florida, on the Sunday nearest January 13. The events commemorating Foster's contributions to American music include performances by musical groups from schools and universities throughout the state and daily concerts from the 97-bell carillon tower. During the preceding October, the so-called "Jeanie auditions" (named for Foster's wife, the subject of "Jeanie with the Light Brown Hair") are held to determine the winner of a music scholarship for 18- to 21-year-old Florida women. The winner often appears at the Memorial Week festivities and performs some of Foster's songs.

CONTACTS:
Stephen Foster Folk Culture Center State Park
11016 Lillian Saunders Dr.
US HWY 41 N.
White Springs, FL 32096
386-397-4331
www.floridastateparks.org

♦ 1062 ♦ **Founder's Day**
May 29

Many organizations and institutions celebrate a Founder's Day. In London, the old soldiers at the Royal Hospital in Chelsea hold a Founder's Day parade on May 29, the birthday of Charles II (1630-1685), the hospital's founder and one of England's most popular monarchs. May 29 is also Royal Oak Day (*see* SHICK-SHACK DAY).

CONTACTS:
Royal Hospital Chelsea
Royal Hospital Rd.
London SW3 4SR United Kingdom
44-20-7881-5214
www.chelsea-pensioners.org.uk

♦ 1063 ♦ Four an' Twenty Day
January 18

When England and Scotland switched from the Julian to the Gregorian calendar in 1752, 11 days were dropped to make up for the additional time that had accumulated during the use of the Julian calendar. Four an' Twenty Day (or **Old Twelfth Day**) is a Scottish expression referring to the day on which TWELFTH NIGHT used to be celebrated before the switch.

♦ 1064 ♦ Four Chaplains Day
February 3

Four Chaplains Day honors the four U.S. army chaplains who died rescuing sailors on February 3, 1943 during World War II. The transport vessel was sailing in the North Atlantic when a German submarine torpedoed it. The four chaplains on the ship—Father John Washington, Reverend Clark Poling, Rabbi Alexander Goode, and Reverend George Fox—were all of different faiths. Giving their own life jackets and lifeboats to others, the chaplains helped save many onboard the ship. According to survivors' accounts, the chaplains linked arms and prayed calmly as the ship went down. All four were killed along with 600 others. Prompted by this extreme act of selflessness and sacrifice, Congress proclaimed the first Four Chaplains Day in 1988. Many organizations, including the American Legion, observe the event, and most states and cities issue official proclamations on this day. In honor of Four Chaplains Day, flags are flown at half-staff, and communities hold various services, ceremonies, and programs across the nation. The Episcopal Church observes an official feast day in remembrance of the four men.

CONTACTS:
Chapel of the Four Chaplains
1201 Constitution Ave.
The Navy Yard – Bldg. 649
Philadelphia, PA 19112
215-218-1943; fax: 215-218-1949
www.fourchaplains.org

♦ 1065 ♦ Fourth of July
July 4

In Philadelphia, Pennsylvania, on July 4, 1776, the Continental Congress approved the final draft of the Declaration of Independence. John Hancock, the president of the Congress, was the first to sign the document, using a clear and distinc-tive hand, thus giving rise to the expression "John Hancock" for one's signature.

As the most important national holiday in the U.S., **Independence Day**, often called the Fourth of July, is traditionally celebrated with fireworks displays, family picnics, parades, band concerts, and patriotic speeches. It is observed throughout the United States and U.S. territories.

CONTACTS:
U.S. General Services Administration
Office of Citizen Services and Innovative Technologies
1800 F St., N.W.
Washington, D.C. 20405
844-872-4681
www.usa.gov

♦ 1066 ♦ Fourth of July (Denmark)
July 4

The Fourth of July celebration held in Aalborg, Denmark, each year since 1912 was started by an American of Danish descent, Dr. Max Henius of Chicago. He bought 200 acres of land in Rebild and deeded the land to King Christian X, with the stipulation that his fellow Danish Americans be allowed to celebrate the Fourth of July there every year.

The area is now a national park to which about 35,000 people come to observe America's Independence Day. A replica of the Liberty Bell is rung, the national anthems of both countries are sung by stars from the Royal Danish Opera, military bands perform, and there are bilingual readings of the Declaration of Independence and the Gettysburg Address. As a permanent shrine for Americans of Danish ancestry, there is a replica of the log cabin in which Abraham LINCOLN lived as a young boy.

CONTACTS:
Rebild Tourist Park
Rebildselskabet
Rebildvej 29, Rebild
Skørping DK - 9520 Denmark
45-9839-1440
www.rebildporten.dk

Rebild Office
US Secretariat, Corporate Secretary
1582 Glen Lake Rd.
Hoffman Estates, IL 60169
847-882-2552
www.rebildfesten.dk

♦ 1067 ♦ Fox (George), Death of
January 13

George Fox (1624-1691) was the founder of the Society of Friends, or Quakers, which he organized in 1650 to protest the overly formal religion of his time. An English preacher and missionary, Fox believed that creeds and scriptures were unimportant in religion; all that really counted was the divine light of Christ as it manifested itself in all people. Church was merely a gathering of friends who were guided by the

Inner Light and who were thus able to provide guidance for each other. There was no need for an ordained ministry.

In the early days, the "Friends" set themselves apart from the rest of the world by dressing in black and speaking in biblical style. They were known for their efforts in the abolition of slavery, prison reform, temperance, and education. In the United States, William Penn received a land grant that subsequently became the Quaker colony of Pennsylvania (*see* PENNSYLVANIA DAY). Quakers all over the world observe the anniversary of their founder's death in their meetinghouses.

CONTACTS:
Friends General Conference
1216 Arch St.
Ste. 2B
Philadelphia, PA 19107
215-561-1700; fax: 215-561-0759
www.fgcquaker.org

♦ 1068 ♦ **Fox Hill Festival**
Second week in August

For more than 100 years this day has been celebrated at Fox Hill Village in Nassau, a seaside resort on the island of New Providence in the Bahamas, to commemorate the abolition of slavery. Bahamian foods, singing, and dancing contribute to a carnival atmosphere, although there are services in local churches in the morning that feature gospel and Bahamian religious songs.

See also BAHAMAS EMANCIPATION DAY.

CONTACTS:
Bahamas Ministry of Tourism
P.O. Box N-3701
Nassau 10165 Bahamas
242-302-2000 or 800-224-2627; fax: 242-302-2098
www.bahamas.com

♦ 1069 ♦ **Frameline: The San Francisco International LGBT Film Festival**
June

Frameline: The San Francisco International LGBT Film Festival is a ten-day annual celebration of lesbian, gay, bisexual, and transgender (LGBT) films. The event supports the LGBT community, seeking to improve its visibility through the promotion of film, video, and other forms of media. As the world's largest forum for LGBT films, the festival features around 250 movies, including features, documentaries, shorts, and classics. Among the 400 official guests invited to the event are directors, actors, and distributors from many major studios. The festival also serves as a premier meeting ground for buying theatrical and educational LGBT films in the Northern California region. The festival was first launched in 1977, and it is the oldest and most widely recognized LGBT film event in the world. A popular celebration in the Bay Area, the festival is attended by nearly 60,000 each year. The nonprofit group Frameline also holds year-round exhibitions, including Frameline at the Center, a series of free screenings of socially relevant films.

CONTACTS:
San Francisco International LGBT Film Festival
145 Ninth St.
Ste. 300
San Francisco, CA 94103
415-703-8650; fax: 415-861-1404
frameline.org

♦ 1070 ♦ **Frankenmuth Bavarian Festival**
Second weekend in June

Religious leaders in Bavaria sent a group of 15 Franconians to Michigan's Saginaw Valley in 1845 to set up a mission for the Indians. Although the mission eventually moved elsewhere, the settlement known as Frankenmuth, meaning "courage of the Franconians," retained its Bavarian roots and soon attracted other German immigrants. In fact, for many years after the beginning of the 20th century, German remained the community's principal language.

The Frankenmuth Bavarian Festival, held in June each year to celebrate the town's German heritage, takes advantage of the town's Old World atmosphere and Bavarian architecture, which includes a glockenspiel tower that plays traditional German melodies, while carved wooden figures depict the legend of the PIED PIPER of Hamelin. There is also a replica of the 19th-century Holz Brücke, Frankenmuth's covered wooden bridge that spans the Cass River. The festival features a dance tent resembling a German *biergarten* with German dance bands and beverages, as well as farm tours, arts and crafts displays, a parade featuring the festival's Bavarian Princess, and well-known entertainers of German origin.

CONTACTS:
Frankenmuth Civic Events Council
P.O. Box 333
Frankenmuth, MI 48734
877-879-8919; fax: 989-272-8219
www.bavarianfestival.org

♦ 1071 ♦ **Frankfurt Book Fair (Buchmesse)**
Second week in October

The world's largest annual trade show for the book publishing industry is held annually for five days in Frankfurt, Germany. It attracts exhibitors from about 110 countries and is attended by more than 250,000 people, of whom about 7,000 are publishers, editors, and exhibitors.

Trade fairs have been a tradition in Frankfurt for at least 800 years, and, in even earlier times, its location on the Main River in the heart of the continent made the community a crossroads of trade. Book fairs were held in Frankfurt in the 16th century, when the city had become the center of German publishing. In 1579, the book fairs came under the supervision of the imperial censorship commission, and gradually the center of publishing shifted to Leipzig.

The world wars severely restricted publishing in Europe, but the industry reemerged afterwards. Because Leipzig was in Soviet-controlled East Germany, the publishing trade center moved back to Frankfurt for the first time since about 1650. The book fair had been chiefly an event for German publishers before 1939, but it grew in a few years to be the world's preeminent book fair. In its present international form, the fair is officially dated to 1949.

CONTACTS:
Frankfurt Book Fair
Braubachstraße 16
Frankfurt am Main 60311 Germany
49-69-210-20; fax: 49-69-2102-277
www.buchmesse.de

♦ 1072 ♦ Franklin's (Benjamin) Birthday
January 17

This holiday is a commemoration of the birth of Benjamin Franklin—printer, scientist, inventor, statesman, diplomat, writer, editor, wit, and aphorist. Born in Boston on this day in 1706, Franklin helped edit, and was a signer of, the Declaration of Independence. He also helped to frame the Constitution. The commonsense moralities of his *Poor Richard's Almanac* became catch-phrases in his time and are still quoted today—for example, "Make haste slowly"; "Fish and visitors smell in three days"; "He that goes a-borrowing, goes a-sorrowing."

Franklin invented bifocals, proposed Daylight Saving Time in 1786, and unsuccessfully recommended the wild turkey rather than the bald eagle as the national bird. When he died in 1790 in Philadelphia, he was given the most impressive funeral that city had ever seen: 20,000 people attended.

Since 1991, the Bower Award and Prize in Science—a cash prize of more than $300,000—has been presented on Jan. 17 by the Franklin Institute in Philadelphia to a person who has made a scientific contribution of a practical nature in the manner of Franklin. Also in Philadelphia, the Franklin Institute Science Museum holds a two-day "birthday bash" that often involves people dressing as Franklin. The celebration takes place on the weekend preceding Martin Luther KING, Jr. Day, which is the Monday after Jan. 15.

CONTACTS:
Library of Congress
101 Independence Ave. S.E.
Washington, D.C. 20540 United States
202-707-5000
www.loc.gov

♦ 1073 ♦ Fraternal Order of Real Bearded Santas Reunion and Luncheon
January

The Fraternal Order of Real Bearded Santas (FORBS) is a fraternity of professional Santas based in Orange County, California. The group was founded in 2007 after members of an earlier group, the Amalgamated Order of Real Bearded Santas, resigned in protest from that organization following a series of conflicts that ultimately led to the group's demise. Members of FORBS are required to grow and maintain a real beard for the purpose of portraying Santa Claus. According to the organization's mission statement, its purpose is to "promote the positive image of Santa and to serve the community by providing Santa services" and to "enhance the spirit of Christmas and the joy of being Santa by fostering the spirit of fellowship among our members." The Annual Santa Reunion and Luncheon takes place over a weekend in January and is the most important FORBS social event of the year.

♦ 1074 ♦ Frawardignan, Feast of
April, September, August; 19th day of Frawardin, the first Zoroastrian month

This is a "sacred name day" feast on which the month and day names coincide in the Zoroastrian calendar. But unlike most other name-day feasts, which refer to *yazatas* or spiritual beings, the 19th day of Frawardin honors the spirit of those who are living, dead, and not yet born. On this day a special ceremony is performed in memory of people from the community who have died. This thanksgiving service can be held in a fire temple, a meeting-hall, or a private home.

The Zoroastrian calendar has 12 months of 30 days each, plus five extra days at the end of the year. Because of discrepancies in the calendars used by widely separated Zoroastrian communities around the world, there are now three different calendars in use, and the Feast of Frawardignan can fall either in April, August, or September.

Followers of the Zoroastrian religion, which was founded by the prophet Zoroaster (also known as Zarathushtra, believed to have lived around 1200 B.C.E.), today live primarily in Iran and northwestern India, although smaller communities exist in Pakistan, Sri Lanka, Canada, the U.S., England, and Australia.

♦ 1075 ♦ Freedom Day, National
February 1

National Freedom Day commemorates the abolition of slavery in the United States. On that date in 1865, President Abraham Lincoln signed the 13th Amendment to the U.S. Constitution, making slavery illegal. The purpose of the day is to celebrate the freedom from slavery for all people and to acknowledge the importance of freedom and harmony in American society. Freedom Day is not a federal holiday. Government offices and banks are open for business.

Freedom Day was conceived by U.S. Army Major Richard Robert Wright Sr., a former slave who was a distinguished officer, educator, civil rights activist, and banking entrepreneur. He worked hard to have Freedom Day recognized as a holiday. In 1948, President Harry Truman signed a bill declaring February 1 as National Freedom Day. However, over the years, there have been few formal observances. In fact, a strong drive is underway to adopt June 19, or JUNE-TEENTH, as it is known, as the American holiday to celebrate the end of slavery. This was the date in 1865 when news reached slaves in Texas—two and a half years after the fact—that Lincoln had signed the Emancipation Proclamation. The traditional Texan celebration of the day was revived in recent years and has spread nationwide. Many would like to see it replace February 1 as the national holiday to mark slavery's demise.

CONTACTS:
Library of Congress
101 Independence Ave. S.E.
Washington, D.C. 20540
fax: 202-707-5000
www.loc.gov

♦ 1076 ♦ Freedom Festival, International
Late June to early July

The International Freedom Festival takes place each summer in the neighboring cities of Windsor, Canada, and Detroit, Michigan. The festival began in 1958 as a means of promoting tourism and providing local residents with summertime activities. It celebrates the historically friendly relationship between Canada and the United States. The festival starts in late June and ends in early July to celebrate CANADA DAY on July 1 and the U.S. FOURTH OF JULY. Events have included a rope-pulling contest across the Detroit River, a tug-boat race,a chili-cooking contest, a variety of concerts, carnival rides, a Canada Day parade and party, fireworks displays, and special events for children, the elderly, and the disabled.

CONTACTS:
Parade Company
9500 Mt. Elliott
Studio A
Detroit, MI 48211
313-923-7400; fax: 313-923-2920
www.theparade.org

♦ 1077 ♦ Freedom of Entry Ceremony
April 28

Inaugurated in 2007, this ceremony honors the Royal Malaysian Navy with a series of traditional rituals that date back to medieval times. It takes place in the Malaysian seaport town of Kota Kinabalu on the island of Borneo. Along with the public symbolic gestures that confer the navy's right to protect the city, the ceremony also features several entertaining exhibitions and shows intended to attract tourists.

In the entry ceremony, which borrows from British and Australian military tradition, the navy marches through the city streets with "swords drawn, drums beating, band playing, colors flying, and bayonets fixed." As a public confirmation of the navy's right to march, Kota Kinabalu's Lord Mayor will present a special scroll before the assembled crowd. Another of the ceremony's symbolic elements is the assortment of parade colors, which are meant to help soldiers reassemble in the event of their separation during battle.

Additional events include a boat demonstration, helicopter aerial displays, tours of navy ships, and performances by the navy band and silent drill teams. The inaugural event drew 2,000 people, and government officials announced that they intended to make the ceremony an annual tradition.

CONTACTS:
Sabah Tourism Board
51 Gaya St.
Kota Kinabalu, Sabah 88000 Malaysia
60-3-8821-2121; fax: 60-3-8821-2075
www.sabahtourism.com

♦ 1078 ♦ Freeing the Insects
Late August-early September

There is a festival in Japan on May 28 during which vendors sell insects in tiny bamboo cages. Those who purchase the diminutive pets keep them in or near the house during the summer months so that they can hear their songs in the evening. Then, on a day in late August or early September, they gather in public parks and at temples or shrines to set the insects free. When the creatures realize they have been released, the former captors listen to them burst into their individual sounds.

The custom of freeing the insects, also known as the **Insect-Hearing Festival**, is more common in the countryside. Although no one seems to know its exact origin, it is reminiscent of Italy's FESTA DEL GRILLO, where crickets are purchased in cages and kept as good luck tokens or harbingers of spring.

♦ 1079 ♦ French Community, Feast Day of the (La fête de la Communauté française de Belgique)
September 27

Each of the autonomous regions of Belgium observes its own feast day. Feast Day of the French Community (La fête de la Communauté française de Belgique) is a celebration of linguistic heritage and national independence. Feast days in other regions of Belgium include FEAST DAY OF THE FLEMISH COMMUNITY, FEAST DAY OF THE GERMAN-SPEAKING COMMUNITY, IRIS FEST, and WALLOON REGIONAL DAY.

Three linguistic communities make up Belgium's population—the French, Flemish, and German. There are four million French speakers in Belgium, and most of them live in the federal region of Wallonia, located in the south. Feast Day of the French Community, which largely takes place in the Walloon cities of Namur, Liege, Huy, and Charleroi, is a public assertion of the linguistic and ethnic rights of French speakers. It also marks the historic date in 1830 when the Dutch army withdrew from Brussels to end the union with Holland and its king, William I. This event allowed Belgium to declare its sovereignty.

For the greater part of the 20th century, the holiday took place on the final Sunday of September. The Walloon Assembly, a group leading the burgeoning Walloon Movement, decided in 1975 to switch to the late September date to mark the days in 1830 when Belgians successfully resisted foreign domination. By focusing on this page in history, the leaders hoped to inspire a similar movement of preserving autonomy from Belgium's dominant group, the Flemish speakers of Flanders.

All schools and administrative buildings are closed for the feast day. Past celebrations have extended three days and have offered a program of plays, sports competitions, and free music concerts.

♦ 1080 ♦ French Open Tennis
May-June

Officially known as the **French Championships**, the French Open is one of the four major tournaments that make up the Grand Slam of tennis. (The others are the AUSTRALIAN OPEN, the UNITED STATES OPEN, and WIMBLEDON.) The French National Championship, played at the Stade Roland Garros in Auteil, France, on red-clay courts, was instituted in 1891 but wasn't opened to players from other nations until 1925. It became an open (to both amateurs and professionals) in 1968.

In 1974, Bjorn Borg of Sweden, 18 years old, became the youngest French Open winner. He went on to become a six-time winner—1974, 1975, 1978-81—putting him ahead of the former champion, Henri Cochet, the winner in 1926, 1928, 1930, and 1932. In the women's division, the players who have won the most titles since 1925 have been American Chris Evert Lloyd (seven wins: 1974, 1975, 1979, 1980, 1983, 1985, and 1986) and Australian Margaret Smith Court (five wins: 1962, 1964, 1969, 1970, and 1973). In 1990, 16-year-old Monica Seles of Yugoslavia took the youngest-champion honors from Borg when she beat German Steffi Graf. But Graf went on to win five times (1987, 1988, 1993, 1995, and 1996).

CONTACTS:
French Tennis Federation
Roland Garros Stadium
2 Gordon Bennett Ave.
Paris 75016 France
33-1-4743-4800; fax: 33-1-4743-0494
www.rolandgarros.com

♦ 1081 ♦ French Quarter Festival
Mid-April

The French Quarter Festival celebrates Louisiana's distinctive musical and culinary traditions. Held in New Orleans, the festival features performances by local and other Louisiana musicians as well as those foreign musicians influenced by Louisiana's musical traditions. Scores of bands perform at various sites throughout the French Quarter (also called the Vieux Carré). Sixty local restaurants operate food booths on the festival grounds, offering spectators the best in Louisiana cooking. The festival began in 1983. In recent years close to 300,000 people have attended this three-day event.

CONTACTS:
French Quarter Festivals, Inc.

400 N. Peters St.
Ste. 205
New Orleans, LA 70130
504-522-5730 or 800-673-5725; fax: 504-522-5711
fqfi.org

♦ 1082 ♦ Frieze Art Fair London
October

An international art fair held annually at Regent's Park in London, the Frieze Art Fair includes the work of over 1,000 leading artists. In addition to viewing an eclectic collection of visual art, visitors can also purchase artwork and participate in the Frieze Talks, a program of panel discussions, debates, and guest lectures presented by the fair in collaboration with *Frieze Magazine*. The special event Frieze Masters presents a contemporary take on historical art and features works at nearly 70 galleries. The program includes talks and educational activities that offer a reflection on the ever-changing face of art. Another special program, the Frieze Project, includes commissioned works of artists and a section of performance-based installations.

During the fair, visitors can partake in public tours with an overview of the gallery sections as well as a selection of event highlights and commissioned works. Family tours are available free of cost, while connoisseurs can register for Frieze Bespoke—private tours that provide a customized experience of the fair based on the individual's interest.

CONTACTS:
Frieze Art Fair London
Frieze
1 Montclare St.
London, E2 7EU United Kingdom
'44-203-372-6111
friezelondon.com

Frieze Art Fair New York
247 Centre St.
5th Fl.
New York, NY 10013
212-463-7488
friezenewyork.com

♦ 1083 ♦ Fritter Thursday
Between February 5 and March 11; day after Ash Wednesday

At one time in England, each day of the week during which LENT began had a special name: COLLOP MONDAY, SHROVE TUESDAY, ASH WEDNESDAY, Fritter Thursday, and Kissing Friday. Fritter Thursday took its name from the custom of eating apple fritters—fruit-filled cakes deep-fried in fat—on this day.

♦ 1084 ♦ Frost Saints' Days
May 11, 12, 13

These three consecutive days in May mark the feasts of St. Mammertus, St. Pancras, and St. Servatus. In the wine-growing districts of France, a severe cold spell occasionally strikes at this time of year, inflicting serious damage on the grapevines. Although scientists claim that the unseasonable frost is caused by air currents blowing off a late breakup of polar ice in the north, some in rural France have believed that it is the result of their having offended one of the three saints, who for this reason are called the "frost saints."

In Germany, too, feelings toward these three saints are mixed, especially among those whose livelihood depends on agriculture. They call them "the three severe lords," and farmers believe that their crops are not safe from frost until May 13 has passed. French farmers have been known to show their displeasure over a cold snap at this time of year by flogging the statues and defacing the pictures of Mammertus, Pancras, and Servatus.

♦ 1085 ♦ Fur Trade Days
Second weekend in July

Chadron, Nebraska, was at one time a frontier town with a reputation for lawlessness. Shootouts in the local saloons were a regular occurrence. But in 1893 a local newspaper came up with a way of putting the town's high spiritedness to better use. They organized the 1,000 Mile Horse Race from Chadron to Chicago—a publicity stunt that made Chadron a household name. Nine men, including one former outlaw, competed in the race. John Berry, the winner, reached Chicago in 13 days, 16 hours.

Today Fur Trade Days is an attempt to recreate the excitement of the town's active frontier trading days in the mid-1800s. Activities include a buffalo cookout, horseshoe pitching and buffalo chip-throwing contests, and a primitive rendezvous with a black powder shoot.

CONTACTS:
Chadron Area Chamber of Commerce
706 W. Third St.
P.O. Box 646
Chadron, NE 69337
308-432-4401 or 800-603-2937
www.chadron.com

♦ 1086 ♦ Furrinalia
July 25

Furrina (or Furina) was an ancient Roman deity whose reason for existence has been largely forgotten. She might have been associated with a spring or springs, and some experts regard her as a spirit of the darkness. Others say she was the goddess of robbers. All that is known for certain is that she possessed a grove (on the slopes of the Janiculum, a ridge near the Tiber River), a festival (the Furrinalia, on July 25), and her own *flamen,* or priest, named Furrinalis. Although Furrina belongs to the earliest of Roman religions, the Furrinalia continued to be observed in later Roman times. It was in Furrina's grove that the Roman tribune Gaius Sempronius Gracchus ordered his slave to kill him in 121 B.C.E.

♦ 1087 ♦ Fyr-Bål Fest
Weekend nearest June 21

The Fyr-Bål Fest held every year in Ephraim, Wisconsin, reflects the town's Swedish and Norwegian heritage by incorporating customs traditionally associated with Scandinavian MIDSUMMER celebrations. The two-day festival is presided over by a "Viking chieftain," chosen on the basis of his contributions to the community. On the first evening the chieftain, whose identity has been kept secret, arrives by boat at Ephraim on the shores of Lake Michigan, where he is greeted by children dressed as elves. After a coronation ceremony, he proclaims the official opening of summer and lights a bonfire in which an effigy of the Winter Witch is burned. Other groups along the shores of adjacent Eagle Harbor then light their own bonfires.

In addition to the bonfire, traditional Scandinavian events at the festival include folk dancing and welcome mats in doorways made out of evergreen boughs woven together. There is also a trophy race at the Ephraim Yacht Club.

CONTACTS:
Ephraim Historical Foundation
3060 Anderson Ln.
P.O. Box 165
Ephraim, WI 54211
920-854-9688
www.ephraim.org

G

♦ 1088 ♦ **Gable (Clark) Birthday Celebration**
Saturday nearest February 1

The American film actor William Clark Gable was born in Cadiz, Ohio, on February 1, 1901. For almost a quarter of a century he was Hollywood's leading male star, playing such romantic heroes as Rhett Butler in *Gone With the Wind* (1939).

The Clark Gable Foundation, Inc., was formed in the actor's hometown of Cadiz in 1985 for the purpose of preserving and promoting Gable's memory. Since 1987 it has hosted an annual celebration of Gable's birthday on or near February 1, an event that has been attended by John Clark, Gable's son; Joan Spreckles, his step-daughter; and a number of the original cast members of *Gone With the Wind*. There are booths for Gable memorabilia and showings of his films. The celebration is attended by several hundred collectors and fans.

CONTACTS:
Clark Gable Foundation, Inc.
138 Charleston St
Cadiz, OH 43907
740-942-4989
www.clarkgablefoundation.com

♦ 1089 ♦ **Gabon Independence Day**
August 16-18

Gabon gained official independence from France on August 17, 1960, after more than a century of domination.

August 17 is a public holiday, but celebrations often extend to the days before and after Independence Day, with parades and dancing.

♦ 1090 ♦ **Gaelic Mod**
August

Held in August at the Gaelic College of Celtic Arts and Crafts in St. Ann's, Nova Scotia, the Gaelic Mod is patterned after a similar event observed in Scotland every October. A mod is a competition that involves Gaelic singing, highland dancing, bagpipe playing, and athletic skills—not unlike the Welsh EISTEDDFOD, although the latter is primarily a music and literary event. The Canadian Gaelic Mod includes visits by Scottish clan chiefs and performances by bagpipe bands and highland dance groups. The first mod was held in 1939 when the Gaelic College was founded. Its students and teachers perform all over the world.

CONTACTS:
Gaelic College
51779 Cabot Trail
P.O. Box 80
Englishtown, NS B0C 1H0 Canada
902-295-3411; fax: 902-295-2912
www.gaeliccollege.edu

♦ 1091 ♦ **Gai Jatra**
One week beginning the day after the full moon in August

Gai Jatra is an eight-day carnival-type festival in Nepal, also known as the **Cow Festival**. The largest observances take place in Kathmandu, though people observe Gai Jatra throughout the country. It is sponsored by families who had deaths during the year and is intended to help the dead complete a smooth journey to heaven. Cows are believed to ease the journey and open the gates of heaven with their horns; therefore, during the festival, cows decorated with flowers and teenagers dressed as cows process through the streets. Dancing, singing, and performances satirizing the government and society are also part of the celebrations. These diversions stem from a legend that, after the death of a queen's child, the king sent clowns to console the queen.

CONTACTS:
Nepal Tourism Board
P.O. Box 11018
Bhrikuti Mandap
Nepal
977-1-425-6909; fax: 977-1-425-6910
welcomenepal.com

♦ 1092 ♦ **Gallup Inter-Tribal Indian Ceremonial**
Second week in August, Wednesday through Sunday

This event is a major inter-tribal celebration held at Red Rock State Park near Gallup, New Mexico. The ceremonial originated in 1922, and now more than 50 tribes from the United States, Canada, and Mexico participate. Average attendance is 30,000.

The ceremonial activities include competitive dancing, a barbecue, and all-Indian professional rodeos, in which cowboys compete for silver belt-buckle prizes in such events as calf roping and bronco riding. There are also three evenings of Indian ceremonial dancing, with the Hoop, Deer, Buffalo, and other dances performed by different tribes.

The markets here present some of the country's finest displays of Indian fine arts—Navajo rugs, katchinas, jewelry, pottery, basketry, beadwork, leatherwork, sculptures, and painting. There are also silversmiths, weavers, and potters at work on their crafts.

On Saturday morning, downtown Gallup is the scene of the Ceremonial Parade, with tribal bands playing traditional and contemporary music. It is called the country's only all-Indian non-mechanized parade—all participants are walking, on horseback, or in wagons. On Saturday night, a Ceremonial Queen is crowned.

CONTACTS:
Gallup Inter-Tribal Indian Ceremonial Association
202 W. Coal Ave.
Gallup, NM 87301
505-863-3896
gallupceremonial.com

♦ 1093 ♦ **Galungan**
Every 210 days

Galungan is a major 10-day religious festival commemorating the Balinese New Year that is celebrated throughout the Indonesian island-province of Bali every 210 days. (The Balinese calendar followed for holidays is a 210-day cycle.) This is a Bali Hindu festival (Balinese religion is a mix of traditional Balinese and Hindu practices and beliefs), during which the gods are thought to come to earth. Balinese festivals include rituals in the temples, where small thrones are symbolic seats for the gods to occupy; cockfights, a combination of sport and gambling; offerings of foods, fruit, and flowers to the temple by the women; and card games, music, and dancing.

Numerous temple festivals are held during the year in individual Balinese villages, but Galungan is island-wide.

CONTACTS:
Bali Travel Information
Jalan Raya Puputan 41
Renon
Denpasar, Bali 80235 Indonesia
62-361-235600; fax: 62-361-239200
www.balitourismboard.org

♦ 1094 ♦ **Galway International Arts Festival**
July

Founded in 1978, the Galway International Arts Festival presents a program of performing arts, visual arts, and literature from all over the world. The two-week event takes place each July in the Irish city of Galway, and includes nearly 200 performances in 30 venues across the city. Besides launching Galway as a center for vibrant culture and art, the festival has also nurtured many fledgling arts organizations in Ireland.

Hundreds of thousands of visitors come to Galway to experience a range of festival offerings, from art galleries and street theater to impromptu puppet shows on Galway's cobblestone streets.

CONTACTS:
Galway Arts Festival Ltd
110897, Black Box Theatre
Dyke Rd.
Ireland
353-91-509-700
www.giaf.ie

♦ 1095 ♦ **Galway Oyster Festival**
Last weekend in September

In Galway, Ireland, the opening of the oyster season is celebrated with parties, music, and an oyster-opening competition. A young woman chosen to preside over the activities as the Pearl presents the first oyster to the mayor, who traditionally stands on Clarenbridge Pier in his scarlet robes waiting to open and taste it. Banquets are held in the evening and local pubs serve oysters by the bucketful, washed down by beer.

CONTACTS:
Galway Oyster Festival
Milestone Inventive
58 Lower Salthill
Ireland
353-91-394-637
www.galwayoysterfest.com

♦ 1096 ♦ **Gambia Independence Day**
February 18

Gambia gained independence from Britain on February 18, 1965, and became a constitutional monarchy. On that day, people gathered in Bathurst for music, dancing, and the replacement of the Union Jack with the Gambian flag. A public vote in 1970 made the Republic of the Gambia a British Commonwealth.

Independence Day is a national holiday in Gambia.

CONTACTS:
Embassy of the Gambia
2233 Wisconsin Ave. N.W.
Georgetown Plaza
Ste. 240
Washington, D.C. 20007
202-785-1399 or 202-785-1379; fax: 202-342-0240
www.gambiaembassy.us

♦ 1097 ♦ Gambia Revolution Day
July 22

The tiny country of Gambia, a former British colony in West Africa, celebrates the anniversary of a coup in 1994 that ousted the country's president, Sir Dawda Jawara, and ushered in a military government. Following the bloodless coup, which was staged by a group of soldiers led by Lieutenant Yahya Jammeh, the government made the transition to civilian leadership and the people elected Jammeh president.

The commemoration is essentially a vehicle to show the Gambian people's approval of their president. Since the 1994 coup, there have been a number of public changes to foster support for the celebration: the name of a major park in the capital city, Banjul, was changed from MacCarthy Square to July 22 Square, and the president commissioned the construction of the Arch 22, a tall gateway also in Banjul.

Past celebrations have included the unveiling of new development initiatives as well as cultural festivities. Dissident leaders in Gambia have voiced their disapproval of the anniversary, which they feel does not honor the country's legacy because it commemorates an unconstitutional overthrow of the government.

CONTACTS:
Gambia Tourism Board
P.O. Box 4085
The Gambia
220-446 2491; fax: 220-446 2487
www.visitthegambia.gm

♦ 1098 ♦ Gandhi Jayanti (Mahatma Gandhi'sBirthday)
October 2

A national holiday in India to commemorate the birth of Mohandas Karamchand Gandhi, who came to be known as Mahatma ("great soul") Gandhi. At this time pilgrimages are made from throughout the country to the Raj Ghat on the banks of the Yamuna River in Delhi where Gandhi was cremated. Many communities also hold spinning and weaving sessions in his honor.

Gandhi, often pictured in a simple white cotton robe at a spinning wheel, was the leader of the movement for Indian nationalism, the 20th century's great prophet of nonviolence, and a religious innovator who encouraged a reformed, liberal Hinduism.

He was born in 1869 in Porbandar, India, and educated both in India and England. He went to South Africa as a young lawyer, was shocked by the racial discrimination, and led the African Indians in a nonviolent struggle against repression. Returning to India, he became a dominant political figure, and, in the struggle for independence, was jailed several times. His protests often took the form of fasts.

In the 1930s, he worked for rural people trying to eradicate discrimination against the untouchable caste and promoting hand spinning and weaving as occupations for the poor

and as a way to overcome the British monopoly on cloth. The ashram (a religious retreat center) he established near Ahmedabad became the center of his freedom movement. In the 1940s, he helped heal the scars of religious conflict in Bengal and Bihar; in 1947 his fasting put an end to the rioting in Calcutta. On January 30, 1948, on his way to an evening prayer meeting in Delhi, he was shot and killed by a Hindu fanatic. Albert Einstein was among his great admirers.

CONTACTS:
M.K. Gandhi Institute for Nonviolence
929 S. Plymouth Ave.
Rochester, NY 14608
585-463-3266; fax: 585-276-0203
www.gandhiinstitute.org

♦ 1099 ♦ Ganesh Chathurthi
August-September; waxing half of Hindu month of Bhadrapada

Ganesh Chathurthi is a lively seven- to ten-day long festival to worship the elephant-headed Ganesh, the Hindu god of wisdom and success. He is also the remover of obstacles, so he is also called Vighnesa, or Vighneswara. The festival is especially colorful in the Indian states of Tamil Nadu, Maharashtra, Andhra Pradesh, and Karnataka, and is the best-known event in Bombay.

Everyone pays homage to huge clay images of Ganesh made by highly respected artists, and he is also propitiated with street performances, competitions, processions, and yoga demonstrations. In Bombay, at the end of the week of celebration, as sacred songs are chanted, an image is taken to the sea and immersed to ensure prosperity for both land and water.

It is said that Ganesh, the son of the gods Shiva and Parvati, so annoyed his father one day that Shiva cut off his head. But Shiva then repented, and replaced his head with that of an elephant. Today people ask for Ganesh's help in undertaking new projects.

The story behind the festival in Nepal is that the day, called **Ganesh Chata**, celebrates a bitter dispute between Ganesh and the moon goddess. Therefore, the Nepalese try to stay inside on this night and close out the moonlight.

CONTACTS:
Maharashtra Tourism Development Corporation
C.D.O. Hutments,
Opp. L.I.C. (Yogakshema) Bldg.
Madame Cama Rd.
Mumbai, Maharastra 400 020 India
91-22-2204-4040 or 91-800-229-930; fax: 91-22-2202-4521
www.maharashtratourism.gov.in

♦ 1100 ♦ Ganga Dussehra
May-June; Hindu month of Jyestha

According to Hindu mythology, the Ganges River in India originally flowed only in heaven. In the form of a goddess, Ganga, the river was brought down to earth by King Bhagiratha in order to purify the ashes of his ancestors, 60,000 of whom had been burned under a curse from the great sage Kapila. The river came down reluctantly, breaking her fall on the head of Shiva so that she wouldn't shatter the Earth. By the time she reached the Bay of Bengal, she had touched the ashes of the 60,000 princes and fertilized the entire region.

On Ganga Dussehra, the 10th day of the waxing half of the month of Jyestha, Hindus who are able to reach the Ganges take a dip in the river to purify their sins and remedy their physical ills. The largest crowds assemble at the Uttar Pradesh towns of Hardwar, Mukteshwar, Varanasi, and other locations on the banks of the Ganges that have legendary significance. Those who live far away from the Ganges immerse themselves in whatever river, pond, or sea they can get to on this day.

Part of the Hindu faith includes the hope of bathing in the Ganges at some point during one's life. Upon death, a Hindu's body is generally cremated and the ashes are immersed in its holy water to assure peace for the soul.

See also KUMBH MELA.

CONTACTS:
Directorate of Tourism, Uttar Pradesh
Rajarshi Purshottam Das Tandon Paryatan Bhavan
C-13 , Vipin Khand
Gomti Nagar
Lucknow, Uttar Pradesh India
91-522-230-7037; fax: 91-522-230-8937
www.up-tourism.com

♦ 1101 ♦ **Gangaur**
March-April; first through 18th days of the Hindu month of Caitra

Gangaur is one of the highlights of the festival year in the state of Rajasthan, India. It is observed in celebration of Gauri, another name for Parvati, Shiva's wife. This is largely a girls' and women's festival, but boys and men get to enjoy the elaborate processions that take place in cities around the state, such as Jaipur, Bikaner, Jodhpur, and Udaipur, where there is also a boat procession on Pichola Lake.

The festival begins the day after HOLI and continues for 18 days, during which women fast, dress in their best clothes, adorn themselves with intricate henna designs, and pray—married women, for the well-being of their husbands and marriages, and single women, to find good husbands. The festival culminates with feasting and processions of the goddess' image celebrate the union of Gauri and Shiva, representing happy married life.

CONTACTS:
Ministry of Tourism, Government of India
1270 Avenue of the Americas
Ste. 303
New York, NY 10020
212-586-4901; fax: 212-582-3274
tourism.nic.in

♦ 1102 ♦ **Ganna (Genna)**
January 7

The CHRISTMAS celebration in Ethiopia, which is officially called **Leddat**, takes place on January 7 (see OLD CHRISTMAS), observing the Coptic Orthodox calendar. But it is more popularly known as Ganna, after the game that is traditionally played by boys, young men, and occasionally elders, on this day. According to legend, the shepherds were so happy when they heard about the birth of Jesus that they used their hooked staffs to play ganna—a game similar to field hockey. Pilgrims gather in the spectacular medieval churches in Lalibela for services, music, and food.

♦ 1103 ♦ **Gansabhauet**
November 11

Gansabhauet is an old and peculiar festival involving a dead goose, held only in the country town of Sursee, Lucerne Canton, Switzerland, on St. Martin's Day (see MARTINMAS). A dead goose is hung by its neck in front of the town hall, and young men draw lots to take turns trying to knock it down with a blunt saber. (*Gansabhauet* means "knocking down goose.")

The young men, blindfolded and wearing red robes and big round masks representing the sun, get only one try at the bird. While the men whack at the goose, children's games take place: they scale a stripped tree, race in sacks, and compete in seeing who can make the ugliest face.

Gansabhauet was first mentioned in 1821. Its real origin is uncertain, although it is thought that it may have something to do with the old practice of handing over payment in kind to the landlord.

CONTACTS:
Switzerland Tourism
608 Fifth Ave.
New York, NY 10020
800-794-7795; fax: 212-262-6116
www.myswitzerland.com

♦ 1104 ♦ **Garifuna Settlement Day**
November 19

Garifuna Settlement Day honors the heritage of the Garifuna people, a unique ethnic group in the Caribbean and Central America. Their ancestors were Nigerian captives, who were sent in 1635 from West Africa to the New World to work on plantations and in mines. They were shipwrecked off St. Vincent island, an accident that offered freedom to those who survived. Those who reached the island were taken in by the Carib Indians, who were of South American origin but had lived there for some time. Intermarriage gave rise to the Garifuna, a people that combined the spiritual and artistic traditions of Africa, the Caribbean, and South America.

The Garifuna got along well with the French settlers who arrived later in the 17th century, but when the British came, there was friction. War broke out, and the Garifuna and their French allies eventually surrendered to the superior British forces in 1796. The Garifuna people were then exiled and imprisoned on another island, Baliceaux. More than half of them died there. Those who survived were moved again the following year. Packed onto ships under appalling conditions, they were sent to Roatán Island, near the coast of Honduras. Legends say that the captives hid cassava, one of their staple foods, under their clothing, where it was watered and kept alive by their sweat. Released at Roatán, they quickly settled in Honduras, establishing fishing villages and taking up their former lifestyle.

In 1832, a civil war caused many Garifuna, under the leadership of Alejo Beni, to leave Honduras and settle in Dangriga, Belize. They arrived there on November 19. In 1941, that date was declared Garifina Settlement Day in Dangriga by Thomas Vincent Ramos, one of the community's leaders. In 1943, Garafina Settlement Day was declared a bank and public holiday in the southern districts of Belize, and it is now celebrated throughout the country. The activities often include a reenactment of the landing of the Garifuna in boats. There may be Thanksgiving Masses held in the Catholic churches, followed by long sessions of traditional drumming and dancing. Garifuna crafts and food are sold and displayed. Events to raise awareness and appreciation of Garifuna culture are common, including special days to dress in traditional clothing, a Miss Garifuna Belize beauty pageant, parades, and rallies.

CONTACTS:
National Garifuna Council of Belize
Pablo Lambey Garifuna Cultural Center
59 Commerce St.
 Belize
501-669-0639
ngcbelize.org

Embassy of Belize
2535 Massachusetts Ave. N.W.
Washington, D.C. 20008
202-332-9636; fax: 202-332-6888
www.embassyofbelize.org

♦ 1105 ♦ **Garland Day**
May 12; May 29

On May 12, or **Old May Day**, the children of the Dorset fishing village of Abbotsbury still "bring in the May." They do this by carrying garlands from door to door and receiving small gifts in return. The May garlands are woven by a local woman and her helpers, who are regarded as the town's official garland-makers. Each garland is constructed over a frame and supported by a stout broomstick, which is carried by two young people as they go about the village. Later, the garlands are laid at the base of the local war memorial.

At one time this was an important festival marking the beginning of the fishing season. Garland Day used to center around the blessing of the wreaths, which were then carried down to the water and fastened to the bows of the fishing boats. The fishermen then rowed out to sea after dark and tossed the garlands to the waves with prayers for a safe and plentiful fishing season. This ceremony may be a carry-over from

pagan times, when sacrificial offerings were made to the gods of the sea.

Another Garland Day celebration is held in Castleton, Derbyshire, on May 29 or SHICK-SHACK DAY. The Garland King (or May King) rides on horseback at the head of a procession of musicians and young girls, who perform a dance similar to the HELSTON FLORA DAY furry dance. The "garland" is an immense beehive-shaped structure that fits over his head and shoulders, covered with greenery and flowers and crowned with a special bouquet called the "queen." This is laid at the war memorial in Castleton's marketplace.

CONTACTS:
Peak District National Park Authority
Aldern House
Baslow Rd.
Bakewell, Derbyshire DE45 1AE United Kingdom
44-1629-816200
www.peakdistrict.gov.uk

♦ 1106 ♦ **Garma Festival**
August

Although the Garma Festival is a relatively new event, it celebrates one of the oldest living cultures on earth, the Yolngu of Australia's Northern Territory. The cultural life of this Aboriginal people, whose history stretches back over 40,000 years, is the focus of this festival, which takes place over four days in August. In the spirit of *garma*, a Yolngu word that describes a "two-way learning process," indigenous Australians gather with non-indigenous Australians and international visitors for cultural exchange.

The festival was introduced in 1998 by the Yothu Yindi Foundation, an organization committed to preserving Yolngu culture. Each year people from all over the globe come to Arnhem Land, located in the Northern Territory, for a hands-on experience with the Yolngu.

The centerpiece event of the festival is the daily *bunggul* ceremony, an afternoon gathering that features dances and music performed in traditional dress. Educational activities include classes on how to play the *yidaki* (didgeridoo); fields trips into the bush to collect native plants and foods; and an overview of spear-making. Every year the festival includes an academic forum that investigates issues facing the Yolngu and other indigenous peoples.

CONTACTS:
Yothu Yindi Foundation
Level 2, MET Bldg.
13 – 17 Scaturchio St.
Casuarina, NT 0810 Australia
61-8-8945-5055; fax: 61-8-8945-5011
www.yyf.com.au

♦ 1107 ♦ **Gasparilla Pirate Festival**
Early February

A 164-foot reproduction pirate ship sails up Florida's Tampa Bay and into the Hillsborough River with its cannons booming. About 500 costumed pirates lower themselves over the side and "capture" the city of Tampa and its mayor, raising the pirate flag over city hall. Thus begins the **Gasparilla Pirate Invasion**, one of the nation's largest and best-attended celebrations. The mock invasion is followed by a three-hour victory parade featuring members of a men's club known as Ye Mystic Krewe, which started the pirate festival in 1904.

The festival is named for José Gaspar, an 18th-century Spanish pirate who terrorized the Florida coast from around 1783 until his death in 1821, when he wrapped a length of anchor chain around his waist and leapt into the sea brandishing his sword rather than be captured by a U.S. Navy warship.

CONTACTS:
EventFest, Inc.
1200 W. Cass St.
Ste. 110
Tampa, FL 33606
813-251-3378
www.eventfest.com

♦ 1108 ♦ Gaspee Days
May-June

The British revenue schooner *Gaspee* was sent to the American colonies to reinforce various British revenue laws, including the Townshend Acts of 1767. Because of these laws, colonists had to pay taxes to the British on imported goods they bought from England. As a result, smuggling was common. The colonists at Rhode Island burned the ship on June 10, 1772, in what many regard as the first act of rebellion leading up to the Revolutionary War.

Since 1966 the event has been commemorated in a festival that includes a symbolic reenactment of the burning, a fife and drum muster, and a colonial parade. There are also numerous athletic events and a gala ball. The events, which take place in both Cranston and Warwick, Rhode Island, were proclaimed part of the "Year of the Gaspee" in 1972, the bicentennial of this early stage in the struggle for independence.

See also RHODE ISLAND INDEPENDENCE DAY.

CONTACTS:
Gaspee Days Committee
P.O. Box 1772
Warwick, RI 02888
401-781-1772
www.gaspee.com

♦ 1109 ♦ Gawai Dayak
Late May to early June

Gawai Dayak is a rice harvest festival of the Dayak people of Sarawak, Malaysia, on the northern coast of Borneo. Some aspects of the celebrations have remained essentially the same for centuries. They take place in longhouses, the bamboo-and-palm-leaf structures built on stilts that are shared by 20 or 30 families. At midnight on the eve of Gawai Dayak,

a house elder conducts the chief ritual: while sacrificing a white cock, he recites a poem to ask for guidance, blessings, and a long life. Other events include the selection of the most beautiful man and woman to be king and queen of the harvest, dancing, a feast of rice, eggs, and vegetables, and the serving of traditional *tuak*, rice wine.

CONTACTS:
Sarawak Tourism Board
5th - 7th Fl. Bangunan Yayasan Sarawak
Jalan Masjid
Kuching, Sarawak 93400 Malaysia
60-82-423-600; fax: 60-82-416-700
www.sarawaktourism.com

♦ 1110 ♦ Gay Games
August, every four years (2018, 2022, 2026…)

The Gay Games is a sports and cultural event open to all with the mission of fostering equality, friendship, and pride among LGBT (Lesbian, Gay, Bisexual, Transgender) people, and promoting understanding and respect from the world at large. Launched by Dr. Tom Wadell, an American Olympic Decathlete and social activist, the first Gay Games were held in 1982 in San Francisco. Built around the principles of participation inclusion and personal best, the event does not attempt to find the best gay or lesbian athlete as elite gay and lesbian athletes already participate in the Olympic Games. Rather the Gay Games serve as an open competition to find the best talent among participants of all sexual orientations.

The core programs of the week-long Gay Games presents a multitude of participatory and spectator events. While the sports program includes over 50 sporting events, the cultural program, which also follows the principle of open-participation, includes band and choral performances, cheerleading competitions, and visual arts presentations. Each edition of the Gay Games also includes important memorial events, including exhibition of a new quilt produced for each Games to honor those who have died.

CONTACTS:
Federation of Gay Games
584 Castro St.
Ste. 343
San Francisco, CA 94114
866-459-1261
gaygames.org

♦ 1111 ♦ Gedaliah, Fast of (Tsom Gedalyah, Tzom Gedaliahu)
Between September 8 and October 6; Tishri 3
(first day following Rosh Hashanah)

Nebuchadnezzar, the Babylonian king, destroyed Jerusalem and the First Temple and carried away most of the Jews into slavery in 586 B.C.E. But he left behind a few farmers and families under the supervision of a Jewish governor named Gedaliah ben Ahikam to clean up after the army and to administer affairs in the devastated land. Eventually some Jews who had managed to hide out in the hills came back to the area and joined the thousand or so who had been left behind.

Things progressed well until a few hot-headed traitors, who accused Gedaliah of collaborating with the enemy, murdered him and the small garrison of soldiers Nebuchadnezzar had stationed there. Many of the farmers took their families and fled in terror to Egypt; the rest were either killed or taken to Babylon, bringing about Judah's final collapse. The Fast of Gedaliah commemorates the man who was assassinated at a time when he was needed most.

♦ 1112 ♦ Geerewol Celebrations
Rainy season, late June to mid-September

Geerewol Celebrations are elaborate week-long festivities held by the Wodaabe people of Niger as a kind of male beauty contest. The festivities also serve the important purpose of allowing young men and women to meet prospective mates outside their circle of cousins.

There are two main dances to the celebrations, the *yaake* and the *geerewol*.

The yaake is the dance for demonstrating charm. The men paint their faces with pale yellow or red powder and borders of black kohl around their eyes; they also shave their hairline to heighten the forehead. They dance in a line, leaning forward on tiptoe to accentuate their height, and contorting their faces with rolling eyes, pursed lips, and inflated cheeks. Their charm and personality is judged based on these expressions.

The geerewol is held to select the most beautiful men. In this dance the men line up wearing beads on their bare chests and turbans adorned with ostrich feathers on their heads. For a couple of hours they chant and jump and stomp while selected young unmarried women kneel and scrutinize them. These women are the judges; eventually they walk toward the dancers and indicate their favorites by swinging their arms.

The Geerewol celebration ends at sunrise after an entire night of dancing when the host group presents the departing guests with roasted meat.

CONTACTS:
NOMAD Foundation
307 E. Ojai Ave
Suite-103
Ojai, CA 93023 United States
805-646-1706
nomadfoundation.org

♦ 1113 ♦ General Clinton Canoe Regatta
May, Memorial Day weekend

Originally a re-creation of the historic trip down the Susquehanna River by General James Clinton during the Revolutionary War, this well-known canoe regatta now has three divisions, one for professionals and two for amateurs, based on the type of canoe used. The professional race, which has gained national recognition as the **World Championship**

Flat Water Endurance Race, is the longest one-day race of its kind and covers a 70-mile stretch of the river between Cooperstown and Bainbridge, New York. When it was first held in 1962, it was a one-day affair, but now the regatta and the events associated with it extend for three and a half days over the MEMORIAL DAY weekend. There are cash prizes, and the event attracts canoeists from Canada, Michigan, Minnesota, and Wisconsin.

In addition to the races, a carnival and many other activities for spectators are held at General Clinton Park. It was, in fact, money raised by the races that enabled the Bainbridge Chamber of Commerce to purchase the riverfront land on which the park now stands.

CONTACTS:
Bainbridge Chamber of Commerce
P.O. Box 2
Bainbridge, NY 13733
607-967-8700; fax: 607-967-3157
www.canoeregatta.org

General Clinton Canoe Regatta
P.O. Box 2
Bainbridge, NY 13733
607-967-8700; fax: 607-967-3157
www.canoeregatta.org

♦ 1114 ♦ Georgia Day
February 12

Also known as **Oglethorpe Day**, February 12 commemorates the day in 1733 when James Edward Oglethorpe and 120 other Englishmen landed in Savannah, Georgia, to establish a new colony. The earliest European settlers observed the day by firing salutes and offering toasts in Oglethorpe's honor. For almost 200 years thereafter, the celebrations were confined to major anniversaries of the event, and it wasn't until 1933 that February 12 became a "special day of observance" in the Georgia schools. In 1965 the anniversary of the state's founding was officially proclaimed Georgia Day.

On February 12 there is a procession through the historic town of Savannah and a luncheon. Since 1966 there has been a reenactment of Oglethorpe's landing, with costumed residents playing the roles of Georgia's first European settlers and of the American Indians who greeted them upon their arrival.

CONTACTS:
Savannah Convention and Visitors Bureau
101 E. Bay St.
P.O. Box 1628
Savannah, GA 31401
912-644-6400 or 877-728-2662
www.visitsavannah.com

♦ 1115 ♦ Georgia Harmony Jubilee
Late April

Established in 2004, the week-long Georgia Harmony Jubilee celebrates the 1896 founding of Fitzgerald, Ga., by a group of some 2,000 Northern Civil War veterans and local Southerners. The idea came from Indianapolis newspaper publisher P.H. Fitzgerald, who was impressed when the state of Georgia donated huge quantities of food to help out drought-stricken towns in the North and Midwest. He saw that the wounds of the Civil War had finally healed. Fitzgerald proposed a town where elderly Northern veterans could retire to live with their former enemies. He organized the American Tribune Soldiers' Colony Company, which purchased 60,000 acres of virgin forest in southern Georgia for the project. The city's core is formed by seven streets named after Confederate Civil War generals, seven streets named after Union Civil War generals, and four named after Civil War ships. Sidewalks in the town are painted blue and gray in remembrance of the colors worn by the two armies.

The spirit of harmony—the ability of two former enemies to come together to form a new community 30 years after the end of the American Civil War—is the focus of the annual celebration. Highlights include a staging of *Our Friends, the Enemy,* a play about the town's founding, musical concerts, historical seminars, a tour of historic homes, arts and crafts, and a parade featuring flag bearers from all 50 states.

CONTACTS:
Fitzgerald-Ben Hill Arts Council
P.O. Box 537
Harmony Jubilee Committee
Fitzgerald, GA 31750
229-426-5035
www.harmonyjubilee.com

♦ 1116 ♦ **Georgia Independence Day**
May 26

Georgia Independence Day celebrates the republic's brief period of independence from Tsarist Russia from May 26, 1918, until its forced incorporation into the Soviet Union in 1922. Georgia declared its independence from the former Soviet Union on April 9, 1991, but the national holiday commemorates the country's original independence earlier in the century.

CONTACTS:
Georgia Tourism department
4a, Ingorokva Str.
Tbilisi, 20008 Georgia
995-32-292-2246; fax: 995-32-292-2247
www.visitgeorgia.ge

♦ 1117 ♦ **Georgia Peanut Festival**
October

A harvest festival paying tribute to Georgia's top crop is held in Sylvester, the Peanut Capital of the World. More peanuts are produced in the region around Sylvester than anywhere else in the state, and Georgia accounts for nearly half the U.S.'s peanut production and supplies five percent of the world's total production. Furthermore, Georgia's peanuts are a $2.5 billion industry. In other countries, the end products of peanuts are usually oil and meal; Georgia's harvest is largely used for salted and roasted peanuts and peanut butter.

This festival, which comes at the end of the peanut harvest time, began in 1964. Highlights through the years have included an appearance by George Bush, Sr. in 1979 to kick off his unsuccessful drive for the Republican presidential nomination, and the making of the World's Largest Peanut Butter and Jelly Sandwich in 1987. The sandwich measured 12 1/2 feet by 12 1/2 feet.

Events of the festival include a beauty pageant to choose a Little Miss Peanut, Junior Miss Peanut, and Georgia Peanut Queen; a peanut-syrup-and-pancakes eating contest; a peanut-recipe contest for school children; concerts; clogging exhibitions; a kiddy parade and a grand parade (the state's largest commodity parade) with 150 to 200 entries, including floats, horses, antique cars, and people dressed as peanuts.

CONTACTS:
Sylvester-Worth County Chamber of Commerce
122 N. Main St.
Sylvester, GA 31791
229-776–7718; fax: 229-776-7719
swcountychamber.com

♦ 1118 ♦ **Georgiritt (St. George's Parade)**
March-April, Monday after Easter

St. George is honored each year at Traunstein in Bavaria, Germany, and in other Bavarian villages on EASTER MONDAY to mark April 23, the day on which he is said to have been martyred in 303. The Georgiritt, or St. George's Parade, commemorates the legend of George's victory over the dragon that was threatening the pagan city of Sylene by demanding that humans be sacrificed to feed it. St. George killed the dragon, saved the king's daughter (who was next in line to be sacrificed), and converted Sylene's 15,000 citizens to Christianity.

Because St. George is usually depicted on horseback, the farmers of Traunstein decorate their own horses with garlands and ribbons and ride them across the fields and three times around the parish church. After the local priest blesses the horses and other farm animals, the procession turns toward the village. The festival ends with ritualistic sword dances that have been handed down from medieval times.

See also ST. GEORGE'S DAY.

♦ 1119 ♦ **Geranium Day**
April and May

Since the 1920s this has been a day in England to collect money for the blind. It represents a joint effort by a number of charities dedicated to helping the blind and is organized by the Greater London Fund for the Blind. Although at one time real geraniums were given to those who made donations, these days contributors receive a sticker with a red geranium on it. And there are now two collection days—one in the City of London in April and one in the greater London area in May.

The choice of the geranium—a flower without a strong scent—seems unusual as a symbol for the blind, but it may have been chosen simply because the poppy (*see* MEMORIAL DAY) and the rose (*see* ALEXANDRA ROSE DAY) were already being used for fund-raising purposes. It may also have been chosen for its symbolic meaning: consolation.

CONTACTS:
Greater London Fund for the Blind
12 Whitehorse Mews
37 Westminster Bridge Rd.
London, SE1 7QD United Kingdom
44-20-7620-2066; fax: 44-20-7620-2016
www.glfb.org.uk

♦ 1120 ♦ German Unification Day
October 3

Unity Day celebrates the reunification of East and West Germany that took place on October 3, 1990. In setting the date of the official reunification, West German Chancellor Helmut Kohl wanted to honor the historic events of November 1989, in which the government of East Germany resigned and thousands of citizens scaled the Berlin Wall and began to demolish it. He did not want to overshadow other important November observances, however, such as ALL SOULS' DAY on November 2 and KRISTALLNACHT on November 9-10. He instead chose October 3, because the German Meteorological Association informed him that, on average, the best weather in Germany occurs on that day.

German Unity Day is observed with speeches, marches, and public events, including the government's official Unity Day celebration street festival, which draws about 300,000 people annually. Each year the location changes so that the celebration rotates among all of the German states.

CONTACTS:
German Information Center USA
Embassy of the Federal Republic of Germany
4645 Reservoir Rd., N.W.
Washington, D.C. 20007
202-298-4000
www.germany.info

♦ 1121 ♦ German-American Day
October 6

Descendants of the earliest German settlers have observed October 6 as **German Pioneer Day** or **German Settlement Day** since 1908, commemorating the day on which the first permanent German settlement in America was established at Germantown, Pennsylvania, in 1683. But it wasn't until 1987 that October 6 was formally designated German-American Day by President Ronald Reagan.

According to the Census Bureau's 2010 American Community Survey, the number of self-reported German-Americans increased by 6 million during the last decade to number 49.8 million people—almost as large a group as the nation's 50.5 million Hispanics. German Americans' traditions and institutions have had a wide-ranging impact on the American way of life.

This day is often observed by attending programs and events that promote an understanding of the contributions of German immigrants—for example, lectures on German history, art, music, and literature; exhibits featuring German artifacts; performances of German music and hymns; and church services that acknowledge German-American members of the congregation. Ohio observes German-American Heritage Month throughout October, and smaller celebrations are held in more than 2,000 communities across the country. In recent years, October 6 has also become a time to celebrate GERMAN UNIFICATION DAY (October 3).

CONTACTS:
German American National Congress
4740 N. Western Ave.
Ste. 206
Chicago, IL 60625
773-275-1100 or 888-872-3265; fax: 773-275-4010
www.dank.org

♦ 1122 ♦ German-American Volksfest
July-August

The German-American Volksfest is a cultural fair and carnival held each summer in Berlin, Germany, that celebrates American life and the close relationship of the German and American peoples.

The Volksfest was first celebrated in 1961, closing on August 13th of that year as the Berlin Wall was being erected to separate East and West Berlin. Each summer since that time, visitors to the fairgrounds at the intersection of Clayallee and Argentinische Allee in Berlin-Dahlem have strolled the U.S. Main Street and enjoyed a typical American carnival midway with more than 100 rides and games. Food vendors offer such traditional American fare as hot dogs and hamburgers, and beverage stalls sell beer and wine imported from the United States. Activities include daily bingo games in the casino and a pageant naming Mr. and Miss German-American Volksfest. History and cultural exhibits are also presented, with each year's festival highlighting a unique theme, such as a particular state or region within the United States. Past themes have showcased New Orleans, Louisiana, and the Mississippi riverboat culture of the 19th century, the quaint New England charm of autumn in Massachusetts, and the trend-setting southern California style of Los Angeles. Other exhibits draw attention to modern or historic events that have strengthened German-American relations, such as the Berlin Airlift of 1948.

More than 500,000 people attend the Volksfest each year, enjoying a continuous program of musical entertainment that ranges from country music and rock-n-roll to Motown soul and Memphis blues.

♦ 1123 ♦ German-Speaking Community, Feast Day of the
November 15

Each of the autonomous regions of Belgium observes its own feast day. Of the three linguistic communities that make up

Belgium's population—the Flemish, French, and German—the German-speaking is the least populous. Most individuals of this community reside in a tiny enclave of the Walloon Region that is a separate political entity within the Belgian federal system. This day is an occasion for German speakers to celebrate their ethnic heritage and political autonomy. Feast days in other regions of Belgium include FEAST DAY OF THE FLEMISH COMMUNITY, FEAST DAY OF THE FRENCH COMMUNITY, IRIS FEST, and WALLOON REGIONAL DAY.

Feast Day of the German-Speaking Community was pronounced by parliamentary decree on October 1, 1990, the same day that leaders decided on the German community's emblem and flag. To mark the occasion, regional flags are hung from public buildings in the German-speaking region as well as at locations outside the region with affiliations to the German-speaking community. This holiday falls on the same date as the KING'S BIRTHDAY, a celebration of Leopold I (1790–1865) that has special relevance for the German-speaking community.

♦ 1124 ♦ Gettysburg Civil War Heritage Days
First week in July

The Battle of Gettysburg on July 1-3, 1863, marked a turning point in the American Civil War. It was here that General Robert E. LEE's Confederate army of 75,000 men and the 97,000-man Northern army of General George G. Meade met by chance when a Confederate brigade sent there for supplies observed a forward column of Meade's cavalry. The ensuing battle did not end the war, nor did it attain any major military goals for either the North or the South. But the Confederate army was turned back, and it never recovered from its losses. With 51,000 casualties and 5,000 dead horses, the Battle of Gettysburg ranks as the bloodiest battle in American history.

Every year since 1983 the anniversary of the battle has been commemorated at the Gettysburg National Military Park. Civil War reenactment groups in authentic uniforms, carrying 19th-century weapons of the type used in the battle, demonstrate infantry tactics and drill, cavalry drill, and soldiers' occupations and pastimes. There are also band concerts, a Civil War battle reenactment, lectures by nationally known historians, and a Civil War collectors' show featuring antique arms and uniforms, documents, books, photographs, and personal effects from pre-1865 American military history.

CONTACTS:
G.A.C.
P.O. Box 3482
Gettysburg, PA 17325
800-514-3849
www.gettysburgreenactment.com

♦ 1125 ♦ Gettysburg Day
July 1

The Battle of Gettysburg, which began on July 1, 1863, was a turning point in the Civil War. Under the leadership of General Robert E. LEE, Confederate soldiers were advancing toward Harrisburg, Pennsylvania, when they encountered General George G. Meade's Union forces. On the third day of the battle, Lee ordered his men to attack the center of the Union line in an action that later came to be known as Pickett's Charge. But Meade had anticipated just such a strategy, and the rebels were forced to retreat to Virginia. The toll of missing, wounded, and dead was more than 23,000 for the North and 28,000 for the South.

On the 50th anniversary of the battle, Civil War veterans reenacted Pickett's Charge. There continued to be major observances at the Gettysburg battlefield on all the major anniversaries, although the 75th (in 1938) was the last in which surviving Civil War veterans actually participated. The annual observation takes place throughout the week of July 1 and includes speeches by distinguished guests, a military band concert, and a parade with floats illustrating historic events (*see* GETTYSBURG CIVIL WAR HERITAGE DAYS).

CONTACTS:
Gettysburg National Military Park
1195 Baltimore Pike,
Ste. 100
Gettysburg, PA 17325
717-334-1124; fax: 717-334-1891
www.nps.gov

♦ 1126 ♦ Ghana Farmers' Day
First Friday in December

Much of Ghana's national economy revolves around agriculture, so it is only appropriate that this African country reserves a date to honor its farmers and provide them a day off from their labors. The national administration also uses the occasion to announce its agricultural plans and development policies for the next year.

In 1985 the Provisional National Defense Council, which then constituted Ghana's administration, established the holiday in response to a drought three years before that had imposed serious burdens on farmers and agricultural production. Ghanaian leaders wished to highlight the farmers' struggles and convey their plans to revitalize the agricultural industry. That year's festivities were held in Osino in the Eastern Region, which was most affected by the drought. Similarly, subsequent celebrations have convened in the regions of the country most affected by harvest-time conditions like drought or flooding.

An important component of the day is the awards ceremony, which is held on the regional and the national levels. Judges who have followed farmers' achievements throughout the year bestow prizes for excellence in such categories as husbandry practices, ecological awareness, use of new technology, and contributions to the local community.

CONTACTS:
Ministry of Food and Agriculture
P.O. Box M37
Ghana
233-302-687-223
mofa.gov.gh

♦ 1127 ♦ Ghana Republic Day
July 1

Ghana's Republic Day celebration is one of the most striking in West Africa, due to the fact that the popular attire includes the brightly colored cloth known as the *kenti*. Although at one time each tribe's kenti had a distinctive pattern, weave, and color combination, today most are orange or yellow with a hexagonal pattern. Men wear it draped over one shoulder and around the waist, while women may wear it as a long skirt.

July 1 is the day on which Ghana became an independent republic in 1960. The people also celebrate March 6 as Independence Day—the day in 1957 when British rule ended and Ghana became the first state in the British Commonwealth to be governed by black Africans.

CONTACTS:
Embassy of Ghana
3512 International Dr. N.W.
Washington, D.C. 20008
202-686-4520; fax: 202-686-4527
www.ghanaembassy.org

♦ 1128 ♦ Ghanafest
Last Saturday of July

Ghanafest is a one-day, annual event held on the last Saturday of July and sponsored by the Ghana Club of Chicago and other ethnic associations representing Ghanians in the Chicago area. It attracts about 20,000 participants each year to Chicago's Washington Park. The festival celebrates the history and culture of that west African nation and recognizes the special bond of unity between Ghana and the United States.

Begun in 1987 as the Ga-Dangme HOMOWO Festival of Thanksgiving, Ghanafest acquired its current name in 1990. The festival includes a Ghanian Durbar, or gathering of the royal court. Chiefs, queens, and elders of the traditional council participate in a royal procession, and Ghanian and American officials and guests give speeches.

Entertainers from Ghana perform in a variety of musical styles, and marketplace vendors offer wares ranging from textiles, fine art, and jewelry to foods, including fried fish, Jollof-rice, and okro-soup. The occasion is also used to give community appreciation and achievement awards to notable attendees.

♦ 1129 ♦ Ghanta Karna (Gathyamuga)
July-August; 14th day of waning half of Hindu month of Sravana

This day commemorates the death of Ghanta Karna, or "Bell Ears," a demon with jingling bells in his ears so that he'd never have to hear the name of Vishnu. In Hindu mythology he caused death and destruction wherever he went, until a god in the form of a frog persuaded him to leap into a well, after which the people clubbed him to death and dragged his body to the river to be cremated.

Also known as the **Festival of Boys** because young boys play a primary role in the celebration of Ghanta Karna's death, this day is observed in Nepal by erecting effigies at various crossroads and making passers-by pay a toll. After they've spent the day collecting tolls and preparing for the Ghanta Karna funeral, the boys tie up the effigy with a rope and throw it in the river. Sometimes the effigy is set on fire before being thrown in the water. Young girls hang tiny dolls on the effigy of Ghanta Karna to protect themselves from the monster.

Children also sell iron rings on this day and use the money to buy candy. It is believed that those who have iron nails in the lintels of their homes or are wearing an iron ring will be protected from evil spirits in the coming year.

CONTACTS:
Kathmandu Metropolitan City Office
Bagh Durbar
P.O.Box: 8416
Nepal
977-1-4268506; fax: 977-1-4268509
www.kathmandu.gov.np

♦ 1130 ♦ Ghatasthapana
September-October: Hindu month of Asvina

Ghatasthapana, which means literally "to establish a pot," is the first day of Dashain, an important 15-day religious festival in Nepal. The festival is dedicated to the goddess Durga, an important Hindu deity, and is essentially a celebration of the triumph of good over evil. A significant part of the celebration surrounds a set of intricate rituals conducted on Ghatasthapana. An earthen pot, which is believed to house the goddess Durga, is filled with holy water, smeared in cow dung, and placed on a sand bed in a sacred corner of the house. Next, a collection of leaves from five different trees is placed inside the pot. Strips of red, yellow, and white cloth are then tied around the pot to symbolize power, knowledge, and purity. Mustard or barley seeds are sown in the sand, and the seedlings are given away as offerings at the culmination of the festival. A priest commences the ritual prayers, chanting mantras to appease the goddess. Incense and oil lamps are lit, and offerings of holy grass, fruit, and sweets are made to the goddess. A male member of the household must perform these rituals twice daily, once at daybreak and again at dusk. Although women were traditionally barred from taking part in the rituals, today they are equal participants in this religious rite.

CONTACTS:
Nepal Tourism Board
Tourist Service Center, Bhrikuti Mandap
P.O. Box 11018
Nepal
977-1-4256909; fax: 977-1-4256910
welcomenepal.com

♦ 1131 ♦ Ghode Jatra
March-April; first day of the waxing half of the Hindu Month of Caitra

Ghode Jatra, which translates as "horse parade," is primarily a festival of horses, the highpoint of which is a grand parade performed by the Royal Nepalese Army and Police at Tudikhel, the large open grounds in the heart of the city of Kathmandu. The horse parade is believed to have its origins in the royal cavalcade of the former rulers of Kathmandu on their annual visit to the Bhadrakali temple to worship Lumarhi Devi, the presiding deity there. The festivities have evolved over time into a major tourist attraction, which includes bicycle races, acrobatic shows, and cultural events. While the formal celebrations of the Ghode Jatra attract visitors from Nepal and around the world, several traditions associated with the festival are related to the culture and history of the local population. One custom associated with the Ghode Jatra can be traced to the Newars, the indigenous people of the Kathmandu Valley, who celebrate this festival over several days. Legend has it that the festival marked the victory of the Newars over demons and cannibals who terrorized the people of the valley hundreds of years ago. So whenever the people of Kathmandu returned home with porters and horses after trading in Lhasa, they camped at Tudikhel and ran their horses around in the belief that the clatter of their hooves would drive away the demons and evil spirits. To this day, the Newaris gather around the tree which stands at the center of Tudikhel and offer a traditional meal of rice and meat to appease the gods and ward off the evil forces. A rival celebration to Ghode Jatra takes place at Patan, the area south of the Kathmandu valley, during which an inebriated rider in traditional Newari clothing rides an intoxicated horse, and the loud clamor of the spectators frightens the animal until it bolts as fast as it can while the rider clings to it. A former king of Patan is believed to have established this local event to compete with the grand parade at Tudikhel, as citizens of Patan were not permitted to attend Ghode Jatra in Kathmandu at the time.

CONTACTS:
Nepal Tourism Board
Tourist Service Center, Bhrikuti Mandap
P.O. Box 11018
Nepal
977-1-4256909; fax: 977-1-4256910
welcomenepal.com

♦ 1132 ♦ **Giant Lantern Festival**
December 23-24

This festival is a highlight of CHRISTMAS in the Philippines. In San Fernando, Pampanga, giant lanterns of colored paper and *capiz* shells, some 12 feet in diameter, are lit and carried in a parade. The event attracts crowds of people from Manila and nearby provinces.

CONTACTS:
Secretariat, City Tourism and Investment Promotion Office
2nd Fl. City Hall Bldg.
A. Consunji St.
Brgy. Sto. Rosario
San Fernando, Pampanga Philippines
45-961-5684 or 45-961-8722
giantlantern.ph

♦ 1133 ♦ **Giants, Festival of the (Fête des Géants)**
Begins on the Sunday following July 5

The huge figures that are often carried in procession through the streets of France used to be made of wicker supported by a light wooden frame, but their modern counterparts are usually made of plastic.

For three days and nights during the Fête des Géants in Douai, France, the figure of Gayant is carried through the streets to the accompaniment of drums and church bells. About 25 feet tall and wearing a military uniform, Gayant is followed by his wife, Marie, who is 20 feet high and always dressed in the latest fashion. Then come their three children—Jacquot, Fillion, and the baby, Binbin. The giants leave their home on Rue de Lambres and go to the town hall to salute the mayor, after which they continue on to the Place D'Armes and take part in the carnival festivities.

Another famous procession of the giants takes place in the city of Lille on WHIT-MONDAY, when more than 100 of these fabulous figures are carried through the streets of the town.

CONTACTS:
City of Douai (City of Giants)
Douai Town Hall
83, rue de la Mairie
Douai, 59508 France
33-3-2793-5800; fax: 33-3-2797-7261
www.ville-douai.fr

♦ 1134 ♦ **Giants, Festival of the (Belgium)**
Fourth weekend in August

In many French and Belgian towns, people carry giants—towering figures representing various biblical, historical, or legendary characters—through the streets in their religious and other festival processions.

One of Belgium's more distinctive and colorful pageants, held in Ath (or Aat), highlights the "Marriage of the Giants." The origins of the festival are a little vague, but the giants—Goliath and his bride, strong-man Samson, a warrior named Ambiorix, and several others—are supposed to date from the mid-15th-century Procession of St. Julien. Other figures were added by local guilds over the years, and today the procession is known as **Les Vêpres de Gouyasse**, because it portrays the marriage of Goliath.

The giants, 20-foot-tall figures made of wicker and cloth, are paraded through the streets; men are underneath the figures and see where they're going by peering out through peepholes. Goliath wears a helmet and breastplate, his bride has orange blossoms in her hair, Samson carries a broken column. After they lumber through the streets to the Church of St. Julien, Goliath and his lady are married.

Along with the giants is the legendary horse, Bayard, purported to be able to change size according to the size of his rider. The medieval story has it that four brothers, the sons of Aymon, were carried by the mighty steed Bayard as they fled the wrath of Charlemagne. The horse and its riders were tracked to a high cliff above the Meuse River; the horse gave a tremendous leap and carried the riders to safety across the river. The replica of the horse weighs about three-quarters of a ton and is propelled by a dozen men while four boys ride on its back.

Besides the procession, the day is marked by the shooting of muskets, revelry, eating, drinking, and dancing.

CONTACTS:
Belgian Tourist Office
300 E. 42nd St.
14th Fl.
New York, NY 10017
212-758-8130
www.visitbelgium.com

♦ 1135 ♦ Gibraltar National Day
September 10

The Rock of Gibraltar is a peninsula located on the southern tip of Spain. On September 10, 1967, the people of Gibraltar participated in a national referendum and rejected the option for their small territory to pass under Spanish control. Instead, the Rock of Gibraltar remained a British territory with an arrangement of local sovereignty. Since 1967, Gibraltarians have commemorated the referendum date with celebrations coordinated by the Ministry of Culture.

In recent years, Gibraltar National Day has become an event to foster pride and has extended into Gibraltar National Week. Events leading up to the momentous day are held at different venues and include dance performances, military band concerts, and a governor's parade.

On National Day, people typically dress in the national colors of red and white. A popular tradition is the ceremonial release of 30,000 red and white balloons, each of which represents an individual living on the rock.

CONTACTS:
Gibraltar Tourist Board
Duke of Kent House
Cathedral Sq.
United Kingdom
350-20074950; fax: 350-2007-4943
www.visitgibraltar.gi

♦ 1136 ♦ Gift of the Waters Pageant
First full weekend in August

The tract of land now known as Hot Springs State Park in Thermopolis, Wyoming, originally belonged to the Shoshone and Arapaho Indians. They sold it to the United States in 1886, receiving about $60,000 worth of cattle and food supplies in return. Within the boundaries of the land were several hot mineral springs known for their healing powers. In 1889 the Wyoming State Legislature established the site as a park, stating that one-quarter of the water from the main spring—known as Big Spring, the largest hot mineral spring in the world—was to be set aside for public use. There has been a free bathhouse there since 1902.

The highlight of the event known as the Gift of the Waters Pageant is the reenactment of the signing of the treaty deeding the mineral springs to the people of Wyoming. The role of Washakie, chief of the Shoshones, was originally played by Chief Washakie's son, and later by his great-grandson.

CONTACTS:
Thermopolis Chamber of Commerce
220 Park St.
Thermopolis, WY 82243
thermopolischamber.org

♦ 1137 ♦ Giglio Feast
About two weeks ending July 16

The feast days of Our Lady of Mount Carmel (July 16) and St. Paulinus (June 22) are celebrated together by Italian Americans at the parish of Shrine Church of Our Lady of Mount Carmel in Brooklyn, New York. St. Paulinus (d. 431) was an architect in Nola, Italy, near Naples, who gave himself up to marauders so that a widow's son could be free. In the end, St. Paulinus secured the freedom of all the citizens who had been captured and placed into servitude.

For about two weeks leading up to July 16, there are daily masses and other religious devotions, parties, games, and stands offering Italian sausage, pizza, seafood, and other foods.

The highlights of the festival are the two processions of the giglio (Italian for "lilies"), a huge tower about six stories high and decorated with lilies. On Giglio Sunday, usually the Sunday after July 4, the statue of St. Paulinus is placed atop the giglio and paraded through the parish streets accompanied by a marching band and the singing of the Giglio Song ("O' Giglio 'e Paradiso"). A large boat is also carried to represent the boat that brought St. Paulinus and other freed slaves back home. The procession ends at the church, where there is a special Giglio mass. Afterwards, people retake the streets for the lifting and rotating of the giglio—a tricky feat for the 100 or more men who maneuver the three- or four-ton structure.

On July 16 it all happens again, this time with the giglio carrying the statue of Our Lady of Mount Carmel. One of the notable events of the intervening days is the children's giglio, in which children under 16 do their own parading and lifting with much smaller and lighter structures.

See also LILY FESTIVAL; OUR LADY OF CARMEL, FEAST OF.

CONTACTS:
Our Lady of Mount Carmel Church
275 N. 8th St.
Brooklyn, NY 11211
718-384-0223; fax: 718-384-5838
www.olmcfeast.com

♦ 1138 ♦ Gilroy Garlic Festival
Last full weekend in July

This event is a celebration of garlic in the California town, located in Santa Clara County, that calls itself the Garlic Capital of the World. The claim is made because 90 percent of America's garlic is grown and processed in the area. Humorist Will ROGERS once described Gilroy as "the only town in America where you can marinate a steak by hanging it on the clothesline."

The highlight of the festival is Gourmet Alley with dozens of food booths that use eight tons of garlic in preparing various garlic-flavored dishes, including garlic ice cream. Other events are a Great Garlic Cook-off and Recipe Contest, arts and crafts exhibits, musical entertainment, and a barn dance.

CONTACTS:
Gilroy Garlic Festival Association Inc.
7473 Monterey St.
Gilroy, CA 95020
408-842-1625; fax: 408-842-7337
gilroygarlicfestival.com

♦ 1139 ♦ **Ginem**
December

The Bagobo are a Malay people who live in southeastern Mindanao in the Philippines. In December each year, they observe a ceremony known as the Ginem to thank the spirits for domestic and military successes, to ward off illness, and to drive off the *buso*, a class of demons feared by the Bagobo because they eat the flesh of the dead. At one time the Bagobo went on a skull raid before the Ginem, tying the skulls to ceremonial poles. Today the poles, without skulls, are decorated and carried into the *datu*'s, or chief's, house. A chicken is sacrificed, and offerings of clothes and knives are made in the hope that the spirits will grant a good harvest and health. There is feasting, dancing, and singing until dawn. In areas where the ceremony lasts more than one day, the feasting continues.

♦ 1140 ♦ **Ginseng Festival**
September 5-7

This festival is a celebration of ginseng in Fusong, a county in the Changbai Mountains of China and the largest ginseng grower in the country. The twisted roots of the ginseng, an herb, have for centuries been considered a cure for many ills as well as an aphrodisiac. The people of Fusong have traditionally celebrated the ginseng harvest, and in 1987 the government officially set aside three days for both a festival and a trade fair of ginseng products. The festival features performances of yangko, dragon, and lion dances; story-telling parties with a ginseng theme; art and photo exhibits; and a fireworks display. The trade fair has exhibits not only of ginseng products but also of Chinese medicines and local crafts.

CONTACTS:
China National Tourist Office
370 Lexington Ave.
Ste. 912
New York, NY 10017
212-760-8218; fax: 212-760-8809
www.cnto.org

♦ 1141 ♦ **Gio to Hung Vuong Day**
Tenth day of the third lunar month

The people of Vietnam commemorate the legacy of their ancestors the Kings of the Hung Dynasty on Gio to Hung Vuong Day. With a history dating back 3,000 years, Vietnam was ruled by a succession of 18 kings, known for bringing peace and prosperity to their people. The founding fathers of the dynasty were honored with the Hung Vuong National Altar, built in Phu Tho, in 250 B.C.E. People of Vietnamese heritage congregate at the altar to honor their ancestors. Gio to Hung Vuong Day has been a public holiday since 2007, except during times of social unrest and upheaval.

Vietnamese people worldwide visit their homeland on this day. During the festival, attendees process to the Hung Vuong National Altar on the top of a mountain, where prayers and incense are offered to ancestors. In addition, colorful parades featuring *Banh Chung* rice cakes, folk music, and traditional Vietnamese bronze drums are held throughout the country.

CONTACTS:
Tourism Information Technology Centre
80 Quan Su St.
Hoan Kiem Dist.
Vietnam
84-4-3942-3760; fax: 84-4-3942-4115
vietnamtourism-info.com

♦ 1142 ♦ **Gioco del Ponte**
Last Sunday in June

The *Gioco del Ponte*, or "Battle for the Bridge," in Pisa, Tuscany, Italy, goes back to the 13th century. Following a medieval procession, two teams in full medieval costume take part in a traditional competition which involves a reversal of the usual tug-of-war. About 20 or 30 men from each team line up behind a mechanism on rails and push. The first team to make a "goal" on the opposing side wins; the winner is determined by the best of six matches, or a draw match if both teams win three.

CONTACTS:
Province of Pisa
Piazza Vittorio Emanuele II, 14
Pisa, 56125 Italy
39-50-929777
www.pisaunicaterra.it/en

♦ 1143 ♦ **Gion Matsuri**
July 17

Gion Matsuri is the best-known festival in Japan and the biggest in Kyoto. It began in the year 869 when hundreds of people died in an epidemic that swept through Kyoto. The head priest of the Gion Shrine, now called the Yasaka Shrine, mounted 66 spears on a portable shrine, took it to the emperor's garden, and the pestilence ended. In gratitude to the gods, the priest led a procession in the streets. Except for the period of the Onin War (1467-77), which destroyed the city, the procession has been held ever since.

There are events related to the festival throughout July but the main event is the parade of elaborate, carefully preserved floats on July 17. There are 29 *hoko* ("spears") floats and 22 smaller *yama* ("mountains") floats. The immense hoko weigh as much as 10 tons and can be 30 feet tall; they look like wonderfully ornate towers on wheels. They are decorated with Chinese and Japanese paintings and even with French Gobelin tapestries imported during the 17th and 18th centuries. Just under their lacquered roofs musicians play flutes and drums. From the rooftops of the floats two men toss straw good-luck favors to the crowds. The hoko roll slowly on their big wooden wheels, pulled with ropes by parade participants.

Yama floats weigh only about a ton, and are carried on long poles by teams of men. Life-sized dolls on platforms atop each float represent characters in the story the float depicts.

The towns of Hakata (Fukuoka Prefecture), Narita (Chiba Prefecture), and Takayama (Gifu Prefecture) have imitated the Kyoto celebration and now have their own "Gion" festivals.

See also AOI MATSURI; HAKATA GION YAMAGASA; JIDAI MATSURI.

CONTACTS:
Japan National Tourism Organization
1 Grand Central Pl.
60 E. 42nd St.
Ste. 448
New York, NY 10165
212-757-5640; fax: 212-307-6754
us.jnto.go.jp

♦ 1144 ♦ **Girl Scout Day**
March 12

This observance marks the anniversary of the founding of the American Girl Scouts by Juliette Gordon Low (1860-1927) in Savannah, Ga., in 1912. The day is the focal point of Girl Scout Week, which begins on the Sunday before March 12 and is observed by Girl Scout troops nationwide in various ways—with community service projects, anniversary parties, and plays. The 80th anniversary in 1992 was celebrated with various events, including the kick-off of a national service project on the environment.

CONTACTS:
Girl Scouts of the USA
420 Fifth Ave.
New York, NY 10018
212-852-8000 or 800-478-7248
www.girlscouts.org

♦ 1145 ♦ **Gita Jayanti**
November-December; 11th day of waxing half of Hindu month of Margasirsa

The birthday of the *Bhagavad Gita*—a Sanskrit poem relating a dialogue between Lord Krishna and Arjuna found in the Hindu epic *Mahabharata*—is celebrated by reading and reciting passages from the *Gita* and by holding discussions on its philosophical aspects. This is also a day on which Hindus fast, worship Krishna, and resolve to put more effort into their study of the *Gita*. Why is this day considered the birthday of the *Gita*? Some texts assert that on the 11th day of the waxing half of Margasirsa, Lord Krishna taught Arjuna the sacred lore of the *Gita* on the battlefield of Kurukshetra, and thus made available to the entire human race the poem often referred to as the "Song Celestial.".

♦ 1146 ♦ **Glastonbury Festival of Contemporary Performing Arts**
June

The Glastonbury Festival, dedicated to contemporary music, art, and culture, traces its roots to 1970, and to Worthy Farm in Pilton, England, where it was launched by Michael Eavis. Still hosting the annual June festival, Worthy Farm is located in a scenic valley of streams and limestone bridges. Hundreds of thousands attend Glastonbury, which is recognized as the largest outdoor festival of performing arts in the world.

Run almost entirely by volunteers, Glastonbury is deeply involved with philanthropic causes both global and local, from supporting Green Peace to restoring local barns. The festival strives to attain a zero carbon footprint with its practice of using solar-powered generators and LED lighting technology.

The five-day event boasts over a thousand performances of music, dance, theater, circus, and comedy on its iconic Pyramid stage and smaller stages across the farm. Visitors can shop at over 700 stalls with a variety of food, drink, clothing, and crafts.

CONTACTS:
Glastonbury Festival of Contemporary Performing Arts
Worthy Farm
Worthy Ln.
Pilton, BA4 4BY United Kingdom
44-174-989-0470
www.glastonburyfestivals.co.uk

♦ 1147 ♦ **Glorious Twelfth**
August 12

August 12 is the legal opening of grouse season in Scotland. If the 12th falls on a Sunday, **Grouse Day** is the following day. Because grouse-shooting has always played such a central role in the life of Scottish gentlemen, the occasion is referred to as the Glorious Twelfth and is observed as a social event by Scots around the world.

♦ 1148 ♦ **GLOW Light Festival**
Eight days in November

The city of Eindhoven in the southern Netherlands turns into a city of lights for eight days during the GLOW Light Festival, held annually in November. This free event began in 2006 and is organized by the Forum of Light & Architecture. Lighting artists, both local and international, present designs that incorporate the latest technology, including light projections. The city's buildings, facades, and public spaces are used for the lighting extravaganza. Every year the festival is organized around a theme; for example, "Urban Playground" and "City in Motion" were the themes in 2013 and 2014, respectively. A particular stretch of the city of approximately one kilometer is chosen to exhibit the lighting designs, which are illuminated from 6:30 p.m. until midnight. According to recent statistics, the GLOW Light Festival draws around 650,000 people from across the globe.

CONTACTS:
Stichting GLOW
Begijnenhof 4-6
Postbus 411
Eindhoven, 5600 AK Netherlands
31-40-707-4040
www.gloweindhoven.nl

♦ 1149 ♦ **Glyndebourne Festival Opera**
May-August

Now considered one of the most prestigious opera festivals in the world, the Glyndebourne Festival was founded in 1934 by music lover John Christie and his wife, Audrey Mildmay, who was an opera singer. They built an opera house on the grounds of their Elizabethan estate in Glyndebourne, about 54 miles south of London, and formed an opera company. In the beginning, Christie wanted to stage only Wagnerian operas, but his wife and some of the musicians who helped him put the festival together eventually persuaded him that the emphasis should be on the operas of MOZART. The repertoire expanded even further after Christie's death in 1962, when his son George took over. During the current 11-week season, several full-length operas are presented, at least one of which is by Mozart.

The Glyndebourne Festival has a reputation for spotting and showcasing young talent. It was here that Birgit Nilsson performed in 1951, Joan Sutherland in 1956, and Luciano Pavarotti in 1964. The London Philharmonic Orchestra has been the main ensemble since 1964, and the chorus consists of young British singers who are often selected to sing major roles. The performances start in the late afternoon, and opera-goers are encouraged to bring a picnic dinner so they can eat outdoors and enjoy the grounds during the 85-minute intermission.

CONTACTS:
Glyndebourne Productions Ltd.
Glyndebourne
Lewes, East Sussex BN8 5UU United Kingdom
44-12-7381-2321
www.glyndebourne.com

♦ 1150 ♦ **Goddess of Mercy, Birthday of the**
March-April, 19th day of third lunar month;
October-November, 19th day of 10th lunar
month

The birthday of the Goddess of Mercy is a celebration of Kuan Yin, the *Bodhisattva* ("Buddha-to-be") of infinite compassion and mercy. One of the most beloved of Buddhist deities, he or she is accepted not only by Buddhists but also by Japanese, Chinese, and Koreans. This deity has been depicted as both masculine and feminine and sometimes as transcending sexual identity (with soft body contours but also a moustache).

The *Lotus Sutra*, or scripture, says Avalokitesvara (the deity's Sanskrit name, meaning "the lord who looks in every direction") is able to assume whatever form is needed to relieve suffering. He/she exemplifies the compassion of the enlightened and is known in Tibet as *Spyan-ras gzigs*, "with a pitying look." Kuan Yin, the Chinese name, means "regarder of sounds," or "of the voices of the suffering." The Japanese word for the deity is pronounced "Kannon."

Women especially celebrate Kuan Yin. In Malaysia, hundreds of devotees bearing joss sticks, fresh fruit, flowers, and sweet cakes gather twice a year at temples dedicated to Kuan Yin in Kuala Lumpur and Penang to pray for her benevolence. (She is feminine there and in China, Korea, and Japan.) At the old temple at Jalan Pitt, Penang, puppet shows are staged in celebration of her. In Hong Kong, Kuan Yin is honored on the 19th day of the sixth lunar month at Pak Sha Wan in Hebe Haven.

See also SANJA MATSURI.

CONTACTS:
Tourism Malaysia
120 E. 56th St.
15th Fl.
New York, NY 10022
212-754-1113; fax: 212-754-1116
www.tourismmalaysiausa.com

♦ 1151 ♦ **Going to the Fields (Veldgang)**
Between April 27 and May 21; Monday before
Ascension Thursday

On Rogation Monday (*see* ROGATION DAYS), the inhabitants of the eastern Netherlands village of Mekkelhorst form a procession to the fields to ask God's blessing on all growing things. With the women and girls walking two abreast at the front of the procession, they follow the boundaries of the parish, stopping briefly at an ancient boundary oak and then proceeding to the fields to kneel before a crucifix and pray for a prosperous harvest.

Rogationtide processions like this one are believed to stem from an ancient Roman tradition. The ROBIGALIA is one example of a spring ritual designed to promote the growth of the newly sown crops and to head off diseases that might harm them. Another ancient Roman tradition was to have young maidens visit the fields at the end of May to drive out winter.

♦ 1152 ♦ **Gokarna Aunsi**
Between August and September; during the
waning half of the Hindu month of Bhadrapada

A Hindu festival unique to Nepal, Gokarna Aunsi honors fathers living and dead. Also known as **Kuse Aunsi**, it is celebrated during Bhadrapada, a lunar month in the Hindu calendar. It takes place during the month's dark fortnight, placing it sometime between August or early September.

In Nepalese culture, fathers are highly regarded as the pillars of the family and the community, so the festival has a significant place among religious days. Children with living fathers show their appreciation by giving presents and sweets. After the presentation of gifts, it is customary for sons to touch their fathers' feet with their foreheads, while daughters will touch their hands. This tender gesture is known as "looking upon father's face."

Those whose fathers are deceased also pay tribute. One noteworthy ceremony takes place at the Gokarneswor Mahadeva shrine of Gokarna, a village located just east of Nepal's capital, Kathmandu. The shrine has special significance for Hindus because they believe it was the dwelling site of Shiva, who is attributed with having special affinity with the souls of dead.

CONTACTS:
Nepal Tourism Board
Tourist Service Center
Bhirkuti Mandap
Nepal
977-1-425-6909; fax: 977-1-425-6910
www.welcomenepal.com

♦ 1153 ♦ **Gold Cup Parade**
Third Friday in August

The Gold Cup Parade is the largest street parade in eastern Canada. Held on the third Friday of each August in Charlottetown, Prince Edward Island, the parade features hundreds of floats, as well as marching bands, horses, antique cars, and clowns. The parade winds through the streets of downtown Charlottetown, attracting around 60,000 spectators.

The parade began in 1962 when Frank Acorn and Bill Hancox sought to revive the tradition of Old Home Week as well as the island's harness racing industry. A group of businessmen who were assisting the Charlottetown Driving Park put together the first event. Since then, the parade has become a vibrant feature of the island's summer season. In 1986, the entity was incorporated as the nonprofit Charlottetown Parade Committee, Inc.

CONTACTS:
China National Tourist Office
370 Lexington Ave.
Ste. 912
New York, NY 10017
212-760-8218; fax: 212-760-8809
www.cnto.org

♦ 1154 ♦ **Gold Discovery Days**
Third weekend in July

This five-day festival celebrates the beauty of the Black Hills and the discovery of gold on July 27, 1874, near the present-day city of Custer, South Dakota. The scientific expedition led by General George Custer confirmed the growing speculation about gold in the area and opened the way for a steady influx of eager prospectors. The festival includes a street fair, hot air balloon rally, golf tournament, and musical productions. But the highlight of the event is the Paha Sapa Pageant which recreates this important era in South Dakota's history.

Part one of the pageant depicts the *Paha Sapa*, or sacred land of the Sioux Indians. Part two portrays the lure of gold and the coming of Custer's expedition. In part three the Sioux display their rich cultural heritage by performing ancient ceremonial dances. At the end of the pageant, the entire cast— many of whom have participated since they were children— reappear in special costumes to create a "living flag" of the United States.

CONTACTS:
Custer Chamber of Commerce
615 Washington St.
Custer, SD 57730
605-673-2244 or 800-992-9818
visitcuster.com/chamber

♦ 1155 ♦ **Gold Star Mother's Day**
Last Sunday in September

Since 1936 the last Sunday in September has been designated by the U.S. Congress as Gold Star Mother 's Day in the United States, honoring the mothers of U.S. service men and women who have died at war. The Gold Star mothers' group was founded in the aftermath of World War I by Grace Darling Siebold, whose son George had been killed in an air battle over France in 1918. She found solace in volunteering at a hospital for wounded veterans and in meeting with the mothers of other soldiers who were killed in the war. The group, officially the American Gold Star Mothers, incorporated itself in Washington, D.C., in 1928 with 25 founding members. The organization took its name from the customary symbol used to denote a family member killed in action during the First World War. Families with active service personnel hung banners in their windows with blue stars signaling the number of family members who were in service. If one was killed, the blue star was replaced by a gold star.

As of 2012, the group counted 933 mothers among its membership. Each year Gold Star Mother 's Day is commemorated during several ceremonies in the nation's capital, including flower and wreath laying services at the Vietnam Veterans Memorial Wall and the Tomb of the Unknowns in Arlington National Cemetery. The American Gold Star Mothers' national convention coincides with Gold Star Mother 's Day, and includes a banquet and a reception for veterans at the organization's headquarters in Washington, D.C.

CONTACTS:
American Gold Star Mothers, Inc.
2128 Leroy Pl. N.W.
Washington, D.C. 20008
202-265-0991
www.goldstarmoms.com

◆ 1156 ◆ Golden Chariot and Battle of the Lumecon, Procession of the
June

Held on a Sunday in June in Mons, Belgium, this event commemorates the delivery of the town from the plague in 1349. In the morning, a golden chariot carrying a reliquary of St. Waudru is drawn by white horses through the city, followed by clerics and girls dressed in brocades and lace. In the afternoon, ST. GEORGE, mounted on a steed, fights the dragon (the *lumecon*), a terrible-tailed beast called Doudou. The battle represents the triumph of good over evil. Before the fight starts, spectators sing the "Song of the Doudou" while carillons ring. Much boisterous merrymaking and feasting culminates in the evening with a pageant presented by 2,000 actors, musicians, and singers.

CONTACTS:
Belgian Tourist Office
300 E. 42nd St.
14th Fl.
New York, NY 10017
212-758-8130
www.visitbelgium.com

◆ 1157 ◆ Golden Days
Third week in July

Golden Days is a celebration in Fairbanks, Alaska, of the discovery of gold here on July 22, 1902, and the Gold Rush days that followed. This is the largest summertime event in Alaska. Its 10 days of activities include "Fairbanks in Bloom," billed as the farthest-north flower show, a rubber ducky race, beard and hairy-leg contests, drag races, a golf tournament, concerts, and a grand parade.

There's also a Felix Pedro look-alike contest. Felix Pedrone (remembered as Felix Pedro) was the Italian immigrant who first found gold on a creek near what is now Fairbanks.

CONTACTS:
Greater Fairbanks Chamber of Commerce
100 Cushman St.
Ste. 102
Fairbanks, AK 99701
907-452-1105
fairbankschamber.org

◆ 1158 ◆ Golden Globe Awards Ceremony
January

The Golden Globe Awards is an event that recognizes excellence in movies and television from around the world. The ceremony is held annually in Beverly Hills, California, at the Beverly Hilton Hotel. The awards night is televised in more than 160 countries, and is one of the three most-watched award shows on television after the Academy Awards and Grammy Awards. One of the best-known awards at the event is the Cecil B. DeMille Award for outstanding contribution in the field of entertainment. A continuing tradition at the celebration is the annual selection of a Miss or Mr. Golden

Globe, where the daughter or son of a well-known performer is chosen to assist in the ceremony. The Hollywood Foreign Press Association (HFPA), a non-profit organization composed of international journalists, produces the Golden Globe Awards. The HFPA represents 55 countries and has a combined readership of 250 million. The members of the HFPA interview around 400 actors, directors, and producers each year and watch approximately 300 films.

CONTACTS:
Hollywood Foreign Press Association
646 N. Robertson Blvd.
West Hollywood, CA 90069
www.hfpa.org

◆ 1159 ◆ Golden Horse Film Festival and Awards
November

The Golden Horse Film Festival and Awards, officially known as the **Taipei Golden Horse Film Festival** (TGHFF), is considered the most important film event in Taiwan. Founded in 1962, it is organized by the Motion Picture Development Foundation R.O.C. The Golden Horse Awards competition and the film festival are considered separate events of the festival, and they are given equal importance. The Golden Horse Awards are intended to honor Chinese-language films and are considered the most prestigious of the Chinese film industry. The entries are typically from China, Hong Kong, and Taiwan. They feature a total of 23 categories, including best feature film, animated feature, director, actor, actress, performer, screenplay, and visual effects, among others. The award ceremony is usually held toward the end of the festival. The Taipei Golden Horse Film Festival shows films from all over the world for Taiwanese audiences. A non-competitive event, it screens films of various genres and lengths. It includes such categories as "Made in Taiwan" and "Chinese Indie Vision." In addition to screenings, the festival also offers film reviews, lectures by directors, and other activities.

CONTACTS:
Taipei Golden Horse Film Festival Executive Committee
7F., No.74
Sec.1 Jhonghua Rd.
Taipei City, 10842 Taiwan (R.O.C.)
886-2-2370-0456; fax: 886-2-2370-0366
www.goldenhorse.org.tw

◆ 1160 ◆ Golden Orpheus
June

Named after the Greek god of song and poetry who, according to legend, lived in the Balkan and Rhodope mountains, the Bulgarian popular music competition known as Golden Orpheus is held every summer in Slanchev Bryag (meaning "Sunny Beach"), a resort town on the Black Sea. Musicians from more than 60 countries compete in every category of popular music, including synthesizer, soul, big band, and pop. A prize is given for the best pop song by a Bulgarian composer, and there is an international competition for singers and instrumentalists. World-renowned conductors, directors, and musicologists serve as the jury for the 10-day festival.

♦ 1161 ♦ **Golden Shears World Shearing and Wool-handling Championships**
Late February or March

The Golden Shears World Shearing and Wool-Handling Championships take place every year in late February or early March in Masterton, New Zealand. Participants with all levels of experience compete in shearing, wool handling, and wool pressing as individuals or in teams. There is also a triathlon event. As many as 120 competitors can take part in a single event. This can require more than 700 sheep, as uniform in size as possible. For the competitors, speed, skill, and style are all important in this fiercely competitive activity, which is keenly followed by fans in New Zealand, Australia, and beyond.

The first Shearing World Championships took place in March 1961 at the War Memorial Stadium in Masterton. It was so popular that the local army was called in to control the crowds. Within a few years, seats for the contest were being sold out 12 months in advance. The event's success inspired other communities in New Zealand and other countries to sponsor local shearing contests, and the level of physicality and technique at the championship grew higher. By the late 1980s, competitive shearing and wool handling had become an established, if unorthodox, athletic event.

CONTACTS:
Golden Shears International Shearing Society
The Wool Shed
12 Dixon St.
Masterton, 5810 New Zealand
646-378-8008; fax: 646-378-8009
www.goldenshears.co.nz

♦ 1162 ♦ **Golden Spike Anniversary**
May 10

This reenactment of the completion of America's transcontinental railroad on May 10, 1869, at Promontory Summit, Utah, has been held since 1952. It is supposed to be historically accurate, but differs from accounts of the time, which greatly varied because the crowds kept the members of the press from actually seeing the ceremony. Complicating efforts to reconstruct events, some reporters wrote their stories days before the event occurred.

The building of the transcontinental railroad was a prodigious feat. It was started in 1863, with the Central Pacific working eastward from Sacramento and the Union Pacific laying tracks westward from Omaha. The Central Pacific crews faced the rugged Sierras almost immediately, and also had to have every rail, spike, and locomotive shipped around Cape Horn. Union Pacific had easier terrain, but its crews were harassed by Indians. The Union Pacific crews were Irish, German, and Italian immigrants, Civil War veterans, and ex-slaves. California's labor pool had been drained by the gold rush, so the railroad imported 10,000 Chinese who became the backbone of the labor force.

Today, preliminary events start at 10 A.M., and at 12:30 P.M. two trains—the Central Pacific's "Jupiter" and Union Pacif-

ic's "119" (reproductions of the original locomotives that were present in 1869)—steam from opposite directions on the track and meet at the site of the ceremony where men in period dress speak. Then the Golden Spike and three other spikes are tapped into a special railroad tie; at 12:47 an ordinary iron "last spike" is driven into the last tie to connect the railroads and the message "D-O-N-E" is sent by ham radio to the California State Railway Museum in Sacramento. Originally the message "D-O-N-E" was telegraphed (along lines strung beside the railroad) to San Francisco and Philadelphia. There is then much noise of train whistles, bands playing, and people shouting and hurrahing. A second reenactment is performed at 2 P.M.

There were four ceremonial spikes at the original ceremony. One was the famous Golden Spike; it was engraved on the top, "The Last Spike," and on one side, "May God continue the unity of our Country as the Railroad unites the two great Oceans of the World." That spike was made by San Francisco jewelers from $350 worth of gold supplied by David Hewes, a contractor friend of Central Pacific President Leland Stanford.

The other spikes were a second gold spike, not engraved, a silver spike from Nevada, and an iron spike from Arizona that was clad in silver and topped with gold.

There was also a polished laurel-wood tie for the ceremonial last tie. Four holes had been augered in it, and the ceremonial spikes were tapped into the holes. (Nobody tried to drive a soft gold spike into a hardwood tie.) The engraved Golden Spike and the silver spike are in the possession of Stanford University, and the iron spike from Arizona belongs to the Smithsonian Institution. The second gold spike and the hardwood tie have been lost, probably during the San Francisco earthquake of 1906. The spikes used in the reenactments are replicas.

CONTACTS:
Golden Spike National Historic Site
National Park Service
P.O. Box 897
Brigham City, UT 84302
435-471-2209; fax: 435-471-2341
www.nps.gov

♦ 1163 ♦ **Good Friday**
Between March 20 and April 23; Friday before Easter

There are several theories as to why the day commemorating Jesus' crucifixion is called "Good" Friday. Some scholars think it's a corruption of "God's Friday," while others interpret "good" in the sense of "observed as holy," or to signify that the act of the Crucifixion is central to the Christian view of salvation. It is called **Great Friday** by Orthodox Christians, but it's not surprising that the Friday before EASTER is sometimes referred to as **Black Friday** or **Sorrowful Friday**.

This day has been in the Christian calendar even longer than Easter. And although it was neglected for a long time by Protestant churches, Good Friday has again come into almost universal observance by Christians. From noon to three o'clock many western Christian churches in the U.S. hold the *Tre Ore* (Italian for "three hours," referring to the last three hours Jesus hung on the cross), a service based on the last seven things Jesus said on the cross. Many churches also observe the day by reenacting the procession to the cross as in the ritual of the Stations of the Cross.

In every Orthodox church, the *Epitaphios*, a gold-embroidered pall representing the body of Christ, is laid on a special platform, which is smothered in flowers. During the evening service, the platform is carried out of the church in a procession. The faithful follow, carrying lighted candles and chanting hymns. At squares and crossroads, the procession stops for a prayer by the priest.

Long Friday is another name for Good Friday. In Norway, this day is called **Langfredag**; in Finland, **Pitkäperjantai** (or Long Friday) because it was a day of suffering for Christ.

See also PLEUREUSES, CEREMONY OF.

CONTACTS:
Orthodox Church in America
P.O. Box 675
Syosset, NY 11791
516-922-0550; fax: 516-922-0954
www.oca.org

♦ 1164 ♦ **Good Friday (Belgium) (Goede Vrijdag)**
Between March 20 and April 23; Friday before Easter

Belgian churches are draped in black on GOOD FRIDAY, in memory of Jesus' suffering on the cross, and a general air of sadness prevails in the cities and towns. In rural villages, women often wear mourning on this day. In the afternoon, many attend the three-hour Passion service at the local church.

In Veurne, there is a pilgrims' procession that stops before each of the 18 Stations of the Cross, built there in 1680, to pray and sing hymns. The distance between the different stations is said to correspond to the number of steps (5,751) taken by Christ as he went from Jerusalem to Mount Calvary. The original Stations of the Cross were sites associated with Christ's Passion in Jerusalem and the surrounding area. Pictures or carvings of the Stations of the Cross can often be seen on the walls of Roman Catholic churches.

CONTACTS:
Belgian Tourist Office
300 E. 42nd St.
14th Fl.
New York, NY 10017
212-758-8130
www.visitbelgium.com

♦ 1165 ♦ **Good Friday (Bermuda)**
Between March 20 and April 23; Friday before Easter

The custom of flying kites on GOOD FRIDAY in Bermuda dates back to the 19th century, when a teacher who was having difficulty explaining to his students how Jesus ascended into heaven took them to the highest hill on the island and launched a kite bearing an image of Jesus. When he ran out of string, he cut the line and let the kite fly out of sight. It has been an island tradition since that time for children to fly kites on Good Friday.

Breakfast on EASTER is another Bermudian tradition. It consists of salted cod that has been soaked overnight and then boiled the next day with potatoes. It is served with an olive oil and mayonnaise topping, and sliced bananas on the side.

CONTACTS:
Bermuda Department of Tourism
675 Third Ave.
20th Fl.
New York, NY 10017
212-818-9800 or 800-223-6106; fax: 212-983-5289
www.gotobermuda.com

♦ 1166 ♦ **Good Friday (England)**
Between March 20 and April 23; Friday before Easter

The Friday before EASTER has often been regarded as a day of ill omen by those in rural areas. In England, bread baked on GOOD FRIDAY was marked with a cross to keep the Devil away, and there was a superstition that hanging a "hot cross bun" in the house on this day would protect it from bad luck in the coming year. Sometimes Good Friday buns or cakes remained hanging on a rack or in a wire basket for years afterward, gathering dust and growing black with mold. A piece of Good Friday cake was thought to be especially good for ill cows.

Other Good Friday superstitions include the belief that breaking a piece of crockery on Good Friday would bring good luck because the sharp point would penetrate Judas Iscariot's body. In rural areas, boys often hunted squirrels on this day, because according to legend, Judas was turned into a squirrel.

CONTACTS:
Ministry, Grace Church Nottingham
1 Castle Blvd.
Nottingham, NG7 1FT United Kingdom
44-115-950-2332
gracechurchnottingham.org

♦ 1167 ♦ **Good Friday (Italy)**
Between March 20 and April 23; Friday before Easter

Folk processions with realistic images of the dead Jesus displayed on platforms are common in Italian towns and villages on GOOD FRIDAY. Sometimes the platforms are accompanied by cloaked and hooded worshippers, or by large candles carried aloft on long spiked poles. Funereal music and figures of the grieving Mary and angels holding stained graveclothes accompany the procession. Other objects symbolic of the Passion include the cross, the crown of thorns, and the spear. In the afternoon, there is a church service known as *l'agonia.*

At Santa Croce and other churches in Florence, a custom known as "Thrashing Judas Iscariot" traditionally has been observed on Good Friday. Young boys bring long willow rods tied with colored ribbons to church and at a certain point in the service, they beat the benches loudly with the branches.

CONTACTS:
Italian National Tourist Board
686 Park Ave.
3rd Fl.
New York, NY 10065
212-245-5618; fax: 212-586-9249
www.italiantourism.com

♦ 1168 ♦ Good Friday (Mexico) (Viernes Santo)
Between March 20 and April 23; Friday before Easter

GOOD FRIDAY is a very somber day in Mexico. The churches are often darkened and draped in black. The religious processions that take place on this day represent the funeral that Jesus never had. An effigy of the dead Christ, stained with blood and wearing a crown of thorns, is carried in a glass coffin through the streets. The highlight of these processions is when the statue of Mary, also draped in black, meets the effigy of her crucified son.

The funereal atmosphere is maintained throughout the day. Running, shouting, or using profanity is discouraged, in reverence for the Lord. The mood of those attending church services is very much that of friends and neighbors paying a condolence call on the members of a bereaved family.

See also PASSION PLAY AT TZINTZUNTZAN.

♦ 1169 ♦ Good Friday (Poland) (Wielki Piatek)
Between March 20 and April 23; Friday before Easter

People fast on dry bread and roasted potatoes from GOOD FRIDAY until EASTER Sunday in Poland, but housewives often spend **Great Friday** or **Holy Friday** kneading and rolling out the dough for elaborate Easter cakes. Egg-decorating is also part of the preparations for Easter, and there are three different techniques for decorating eggs: (1) *malowanki* are eggs painted in solid colors with natural substances, such as vegetable skins, roots, or grains; (2) *pisanki* are eggs that are batiked in traditional designs, usually animal or geometrical figures that have been handed down from generation to generation; and (3) *skrobanki* are eggs dyed in solid colors upon which the outlines of birds, flowers, and animals are scratched with a pointed instrument.

In Krakow and other large cities, going from church to church on Good Friday to view the replicas of Jesus' body that are on display traditionally is considered to be an important social event.

See also EASTER IN THE UKRAINE.

♦ 1170 ♦ Good Friday (Spain)
Between March 20 and April 23; Friday before Easter

The religious processions that take place on GOOD FRIDAY in Spain are among the most impressive and elaborate in the world. They are made up of huge *pasos,* or floats, illustrating different scenes in the Passion story and carried by members of various organizations or trade guilds. The pasos are so heavy that it can take 25 or 30 bearers to carry one, and the procession must halt frequently so they can rest.

In Seville, the Good Friday procession dates back to the Middle Ages and includes more than 100 pasos, many of which are elaborate works of art in themselves, with platforms made out of real silver and figures wearing robes embroidered in gold. Among the more outstanding pasos are those portraying the Agony in the Garden, Christ Bearing the Cross, the Crucifixion, and the Descent from the Cross. They are carried by black-robed penitents through the streets of Seville, followed by cross-bearers, uniformed civic leaders, and clergy in magnificent robes.

CONTACTS:
Tourist Office of Spain
60 E. 42nd St.
Ste. 5300 (53rd Fl.)
New York, NY 10165
212-265-8822; fax: 212-265-8864
www.spain.info

♦ 1171 ♦ Goombay!
Last weekend in August

Goombay! is a celebration of African and Caribbean heritage, culture, and arts held during the last weekend of August at Eagle and Market Streets in Asheville, N.C. A free event sponsored by the Young Men's Institute Cultural Center, Inc., the festival has been held each year since 1982. "Goombay" is a Bantu word that refers both to a goatskin drum and to the music played on it; the word is associated with festivals that commemorate the emancipation of slaves in the British territories of the Caribbean in 1834.

Activities are scheduled over three days and include dance and stilt performances, as well as entertainers in a variety of musical styles, such as reggae, R&B, jazz, and Afro-fusion. In addition, festivalgoers may take part in children's games, mask making, demonstrations of traditional crafts, or, for a fee, participate in African percussion lessons with a master drummer. Food is available at the "Isle of Delight Café," which features Caribbean cuisine.

CONTACTS:
YMI Cultural Center
39 S. Market St.
Asheville, NC 28801
828-252-4540
www.ymiculturalcenter.org

♦ 1172 ♦ Gorilla Naming Ceremony (Kwita Izina)
Late June

In Kinyarwandan, a language spoken primarily in Rwanda, *Kwita Izina* means "to give a name." The phrase refers to a long-standing ceremony for naming newborn Rwandan babies. In the 21st century, the tradition has extended to naming newborn mountain gorillas. What was once a humble ceremony among park rangers and wildlife conservationists has become an annual international event.

The Rwanda Office of Tourism and National Parks (ORTPN) launched the first gorilla naming ceremony in 2005 as part of a larger effort to monitor gorillas in Rwanda's jungles and to raise awareness about the various factors that threaten the animals and their habitat.

The ceremony, which since 2007 has been known officially as **Kwita Izina**, is a jubilant affair that includes traditional Rwandan dance and music. Past ceremonies have featured the naming of between 10 and 30 gorillas. Each animal is publicly named by a notable figure from Rwanda or another country—typically a conservationist, successful business person, or international celebrity. A fundraising gala dinner often accompanies the Kwita Izina to raise additional funds for gorilla conservation campaigns.

♦ 1173 ♦ Goschenhoppen Historians' Folk Festival
Second Friday and Saturday of August

The Goschenhoppen region of Pennsylvania, in what is now Montgomery County, was settled in the early 18th century by Mennonite, Schwenkfeldian, Lutheran, Reformed, and Catholic farmers and artisans, most of whom were German immigrants. It remains one of the oldest and most "authentic" Pennsylvania German communities in America. The Goschenhoppen Historians, a group founded in 1963 to study and preserve the culture of the Pennsylvania German, also known as the Pennsylvania Dutch, and related groups, hold an annual Folk Festival at Goschenhoppen Park in East Greenville every summer to educate the public about life in this area during the 18th and 19th centuries and to preserve the traditional skills of the Pennsylvania German people.

Since 1966, when the first Folk Festival was held, the Historians have made every effort to keep the festival as educational and as non-commercial as possible. One of the most interesting aspects is the participation of schoolchildren, who are recruited as apprentices or helpers for the craft demonstrators at the festival. By actively participating in the demonstrations, young people learn traditional skills that might otherwise die out. These include blacksmithing, fishnet making, pewtering, gunsmithing, chair caning, rope making, weaving, and thatch and tile roofing. The Historians also operate a folk life museum and country store.

See also KUTZTOWN FESTIVAL.

CONTACTS:
Goschenhoppen Historians, Inc.
Red Men's Hall, 116 Gravel Pike

P.O. Box 476
Green Lane, PA 18054
215-234-8953
www.goschenhoppen.org

♦ 1174 ♦ Göteborg International Film Festival
January-February

Inaugurated in 1979 and regarded as the leading film event in Scandinavia, the Göteborg Film Festival introduces contemporary Nordic films to the world. It takes place during late January or early February in Gothenburg, a city on Sweden's west coast. From a mere 17-film screening at its launch, Göteborg has grown to nearly 500 films from over 60 countries, making it one of the largest film festivals in the region. The ten-day event attracts hundreds of thousands from Nordic countries and across the world.

The festival program includes features, shorts, and animated films. Offbeat sections include FOCUS films based on a region or theme, the best from Sweden's four Nordic neighbors, and HBTQ-centric films (also known as LGBT). The festival's top prize is the prestigious Dragon Award. Named in honor of the legendary Swedish director, the Ingmar Bergman International Debut Award is given to a film that uses an innovative approach with an existential theme. Göteborg provides a networking forum for promising Scandinavian filmmakers who want to gain exposure through classes, seminars, film screenings, and workshops.

CONTACTS:
Göteborg Film Festival
Olof Palmes plats 1
Göteborg, 41304 Sweden
46-31-339-3000; fax: 46-31-41-0063
www.giff.se/en

♦ 1175 ♦ Gowri Habba
August-September; Hindu month of Bhadrapada

Gowri Habba is a Hindu religious festival celebrated in the southern Indian states of Karnataka, Tamil Nadu, and Andhra Pradesh. Dedicated to the goddess Gowri, the event is primarily observed by women. Typically, married women pray for a happy and peaceful life, while unmarried women pray for a good husband. Various rituals conducted to appease Gowri mark the celebration. Women rise early to bathe and put on new clothes. They place clay idols of the goddess in salvers with grains, while fasting and performing prayer rituals with great fervor. In addition, various offerings of turmeric, vermillion, coconut, beads, bangles, and other sacred articles are made to Gowri. Some of these offerings are also given away to women who visit one another's homes. Women commonly receive a red thread with 16 knots that is tied to the right wrist, a tradition believed to bestow strength, fertility, and benevolence—all aspects of the goddess. Many parents send money and sweets to their married daughters on this day.

CONTACTS:
Department of Tourism, Government of Karnataka
No. 49, 2nd Fl., Khanija Bhavan

Race Course Rd.
Bangalore, Karnataka 560 001 India
91-80-2235-2828; fax: 91-80-2235-2626
www.karnatakatourism.org

♦ 1176 ♦ **Grammy Awards Ceremony**
A Sunday in late January or early February

The Grammy Awards Ceremony, which recognizes the year's most outstanding talent in the music industry, first took place in 1959. The awards are presented annually by The Recording Academy, also known as the National Academy of Recording Arts and Sciences (NARAS) of the United States. The Academy consists of singers, songwriters, engineers, producers, managers, and other professionals of the music industry. The venue for the awards has rotated among New York, Los Angeles, Chicago, and Nashville, but since 2004, the Staples Center in Los Angeles, California, has become the permanent venue. The awards process begins with members of the Academy and record companies submitting eligible recordings for consideration. These entries are reviewed by more than 150 experts from the recording industry and then placed in the appropriate categories for competition, such as Rock, R&B, Jazz, Country, Gospel, New Age, Rap, Classical, and Latin. Selections are also suggested for Album of the Year, Record of the Year, Song of the Year, and Best New Artist. Members narrow down the nominations to five per category, which they then vote on during the final-round ballot process. The winners are announced during the Grammy Awards telecast. Before the ceremony, there is a televised red carpet segment during which star performers pose for the media and fans.

CONTACTS:
Grammy Foundation
3030 Olympic Blvd.
Santa Monica, CA 90404
310-392-3777; fax: 310-392-2188
www.grammy.org

♦ 1177 ♦ **Grand Canyon Music Festival**
September

Since 1983, the Grand Canyon National Park has hosted a three-week series of nine concerts of chamber music that promotes music education in the rural and underserved communities near the park. The event began when musicians Robert Bonfiglio and Clare Hoffman, who were hiking at the park, were asked to play a concert for a retiring park ranger. With community and business support, the event has grown to its present scope.

The concerts take place in the Shrine of the Ages on the South Rim of the Grand Canyon National Park and at the Heard Museum, Scottsdale Community College, and on area Indian reservations. The festival has attracted such award-winning composers as John Corigliano, William Bolcom, and Paul Moravec, and concerts are broadcast on National Public Radio. Since 2001, the festival has also sponsored the Native American Composer Apprentice Project to train young composers to write for string quartets. The 2014 season featured the genre-crossing string quartet ETHEL, The Catalyst Quartet, special guest artist James Bilagody, along with a celebration of the Mississippi River in words and music with composers Eve Beglarian, Guidonian Hand, and Mary Rowell.

CONTACTS:
Grand Canyon Music Festival
P.O. Box 1332
Grand Canyon, AZ 86023
928-638-9215
grandcanyonmusicfest.org

♦ 1178 ♦ **Grand Haven Coast Guard Festival**
July-August

To honor the men and women who serve in the United States Coast Guard, the port city of Grand Haven, Mich., hosts an annual week-long festival. Grand Haven has been nick-named "Coast Guard City USA." It is the site of a Coast Guard Sector Field Office that covers the eastern shore of Lake Michigan.

The Grand Haven Coast Guard Festival includes the National United States Coast Guard Memorial Service at Escanaba Park, which remembers those who have given their lives to protect and serve the United States. The park is named in honor of the USCG cutter *Escanaba,* which was torpedoed while engaged in convey escort duty in the North Atlantic during World War II. A total of 101 crew members lost in the tragedy had been stationed in Grand Haven.

Other events include a Kids Parade, a Parade of Ships, free tours of several Coast Guard vessels, live music, a carnival, a Coast Guard retirees' dinner, and the Grand Parade featuring 120 floats.

CONTACTS:
Grand Haven Coast Guard Festival
113 N. Second St.
Grand Haven, MI 49417
616-846-5940; fax: 616-846-2509
www.coastguardfest.org

♦ 1179 ♦ **Grand Magal of Shaykh Amadou Bamba**
18th day of the Islamic month of Safar

The Grand Magal (or great pilgrimage) of Shaykh Amadou Bamba takes place in Touba, Senegal, on the feast day of Shaykh Amadou Bamba. The Shaykh, who lived from 1850 to 1927, was the country's most revered marabout, or Islamic saint. The pilgrimage is celebrated on the anniversary of the date he was forced by French authorities to depart for a seven-year exile abroad. A charismatic spiritual leader who rejected violence and war, Shaykh Bamba attracted such a large following that the French feared he would challenge their rule. After being allowed to return to Senegal in 1902, he was ordered by the French into a second exile in 1903, this time for four years in Mauritania. In later years, he founded a Sufi order called Mouride (derived from the Arabic word for "student") and began building the Touba mosque, where he was entombed after his death a year later.

Between one and three million pilgrims attend the Grand Magal each year. Among them are members of the Mouride Brotherhood, which is still run by Shaykh Bamba's descendants. Each year, the current head of the Brotherhood addresses the crowd. Pilgrims seek spiritual guidance from Brotherhood leaders, in addition to offering prayers at the Shaykh's tomb. Once their religious duties are complete, devotees partake of the wares of thousands of vendors who sell food, drink, religious tokens, and crafts on the streets of the city.

CONTACTS:
Embassy of Senegal
2215 M St., N.W.
Washington, D.C. 20037
202-234-0540; fax: 202-629-2961
www.ambasenegal-us.org

♦ 1180 ♦ **Grand National**
First Saturday in April

Grand National is the world-famous steeplechase run at the Aintree Racecourse in Liverpool, England. It was started in 1839 by William Lynn, owner of the Waterloo Hotel in Liverpool, as a means of attracting hotel patrons. The first races were at Maghull just outside Liverpool, but the course was moved to Aintree in 1864 and remained unchanged until 1961 when a railing was erected to keep spectators off the course. The next change was in 1990 when the slope at the infamously hazardous Becher's Brook jump was modified because so many horses had been killed there.

The course is four and one-half miles long and has 16 bush fences, of which 14 are jumped twice. The fences average 5'3" high. All have ditches either on the take-off or landing side. The race is limited now to 40 starters, and usually there is a full field. Of the starters, rarely do as many as half finish, and sometimes only as few as three or four. Horses have to qualify by winning three other set races in England, although any horse that wins the MARYLAND HUNT CUP is automatically eligible to run.

Probably the greatest horse to run the Grand National was Red Rum, a big, strong horse that won in 1973, 1974, and 1977. In 1973, Red Rum set a record for the fastest time—9 minutes, 1.90 seconds.

The race became widely known to the general public with the 1944 movie *National Velvet,* based on the 1935 bestseller by Enid Bagnold. It starred Mickey Rooney, playing an ex-jockey, and Elizabeth Taylor as Velvet Brown, the girl who trains "The Pi" for the Grand National steeplechase. When the jockey scheduled to ride proves unsuitable, Velvet cuts her hair and rides to victory herself, but is disqualified when it's discovered she's a girl. Only men could ride originally, but today women are eligible.

CONTACTS:
Aintree Racecourse
Ormskirk Rd.
Liverpool, Merseyside L9 5AS United Kingdom
44-15-1523-2600
aintree.thejockeyclub.co.uk

♦ 1181 ♦ **Grand Prix**
March to November

Formerly part of the international racing series that includes the MONACO GRAND PRIX, the first U.S. Grand Prix was held in 1959 at Sebring, Florida. From 1961 to 1980 it was held at Watkins Glen, N.Y., followed by Detroit (198288 and then Phoenix (1989-91). In 1991, however, the racing committee rejected the Phoenix site, and the Grand Prix was not held in the U.S. again until 2000, when it found a new home at the Indianapolis Motor Speedway. The race takes place in September on a new 2.606-mile course contructed at the Speedway.

Points won in this race count toward the World Championship of Drivers. More than 15 Grand Prix races are held yearly in countries around the world; the season runs from March to November.

Like other Grand Prix races, the race at Indianapolis is for Formula One race cars, which are generally smaller and more maneuverable than the cars used in speedway racing. Engine size, fuel, and other specifications are strictly controlled by the Féderation Internationale de l'Automobile (FIA).

CONTACTS:
Indianapolis Motor Speedway
4790 W. 16th St.
Indianapolis, IN 46222
317-492-8500
www.indianapolismotorspeedway.com

♦ 1182 ♦ **Grande, Fiesta**
December 24-26

Around CHRISTMAS time, thousands of Chilean pilgrims gather to honor the Virgen del Rosario (Virgin of the Rosary), patron saint of miners. The ceremonies take place in the copper-mining town of Andacollo, situated in the Andes mountains. The centerpiece of the festival is a famous three-foot wooden statue of the Virgin that is housed in Andacollo's basilica.

The festival pre-dates the founding of Andacollo in 1891. According to legend, an indigenous man found the statue of the Virgin, which is ascribed with magical powers, in the hills of Peru. The relic later found a permanent shrine in the basilica and thereafter became a sacred pilgrimage site.

The festival's main proceedings take place on December 26, during which a religious dance is performed in indigenous costume. Nearby, cockfighting and horseracing attract participants as alterative secular activities.

Andacollo also hosts a separate celebration, Fiesta Chica, which takes place on the first Sunday of October and coincides with the FESTIVAL OF THE ROSARY. During that ceremony, the venerated statue is transported from the nearby Temple Antiguo to the basilica in a procession that also features indigenous dances.

CONTACTS:
Embassy of Chile
1732 Massachusetts Ave. N.W.

Washington, D.C. 20036
202-785-1746; fax: 202-887-5579
www.chile-usa.org

♦ 1183 ♦ Grandfather Mountain Highland Games and Gathering of Scottish Clans
Second full weekend in July

This largest and best-known Scottish event in America, held since 1956 on Grandfather Mountain near Linville, N.C., opens with a torchlight ceremony at MacRae Meadows at dusk on Thursday. On Friday athletic and other activities begin and in the evening there's a Celtic Jam, followed by a *ceilidh*, or concert of Scottish folk music. On Saturday a 26.2-mile Mountain Marathon climbs a net elevation of 1,000 feet. Competitions are held throughout the day for Highland dancing, piping, drumming, Scottish fiddling, track and field events, and other athletic events. Entertainment includes sheep-herding demonstrations and performances by pipe bands and Scottish performing artists. Another ceilidh, the Tartan Ball, and a Scottish country dance round out the day. Sunday opens with a worship service, followed by more competitions and entertainment, including the colorful Parade of Tartans and the tug of war between the clans.

One of the founders, Donald F. MacDonald, modeled the event after the BRAEMAR HIGHLAND GATHERING, thus the Grandfather Mountain Games are often referred to as **America's Braemar**.

See also ALMA HIGHLAND FESTIVAL AND GAMES; HIGHLAND GAMES; AND VIRGINIA SCOTTISH GAMES.

CONTACTS:
Grandfather Mountain Highland Games
P.O. Box 1095
Linville, NC 28646
828-733-1333; fax: 828-733-0092
www.gmhg.org

♦ 1184 ♦ Grandparents' Day
September, first Sunday after Labor Day

Grandparents' Day is a far more recent invention than MOTHER'S DAY or FATHER'S DAY. It was fostered by Marion McQuade, and a presidential proclamation on September 6, 1979, made it official. It is observed throughout the United States on the first Sunday after LABOR DAY, except in Massachusetts, where it is observed on the first Sunday in October.

There are a number of ways in which grandparents can be honored and their day celebrated. One is to invite real or "adopted" grandparents to school for the day, where they participate in their grandchildren's classes or special assembly programs. Gift giving is not as widespread on this day as it is on Mother's Day or Father's Day.

See also BABIN DEN.

CONTACTS:
National Grandparents Day Council
339 E. J St.

Chula Vista, CA 91910
619-585-8259; fax: 619-585-8259
www.grandparents-day.com

♦ 1185 ♦ Grands Crus, Weekend of the
May

The Weekend of the Grands Crus is an annual wine-tasting event held in Bordeaux, France. Taking place over the course of two days in May, the Weekend of the Grands Crus provides an opportunity for professionals and non-professionals alike to taste many of the finest wines of the region, dine on French cuisine, and visit vineyards and other local landmarks and historic sites of Bordeaux. Each year, owners of the various Bordeaux wineries agree to offer wines for tasting from a pre-selected vintage year, along with another wine of the owner's choice. The Weekend of the Grands Crus is sponsored by the Union des Grands Crus de Bordeaux, an organization established by several local wine producers in 1973 to support this crucial sector of the Bordeaux economy by promoting the vineyards and wines of Bordeaux around the world. Although the Union des Grands Crus de Bordeaux organizes events each year in North America, Europe, and Asia, the Weekend of the Grands Crus is a premier event of the year for the organization and the local community.

CONTACTS:
Union des Grands Crus de Bordeaux
10 cours du XXX Juillet
Bordeaux, 33000 France
33-5-56-51-91-91; fax: 33-5-56-51-64-12
ugcb.net/en

♦ 1186 ♦ Grant's (Bill) Bluegrass Festival
Early August

The oldest and largest bluegrass festival west of the Mississippi is held for five days near Hugo, Okla. The festival began in 1969, organized by Bill Grant as an extension of jam sessions in his home. Attendance the first year was less than 1,000; now more than 20,000 show up. There are band and instrument contests for all ages, non-stop entertainment from 10 A.M. until midnight each day, and jam sessions at all hours.

CONTACTS:
Oklahoma Historical Society
Oklahoma History Center
800 Nazih Zuhdi Dr.
Oklahoma City, OK 73105
405-521-2491
www.okhistory.org

♦ 1187 ♦ Grape Festival
September, Labor Day weekend

The highlight of the Grape Festival held each year in Nauvoo, Illinois, is the historical pageant known as the **Wedding of the Wine and Cheese**. It tells the story of a young French boy who left his unfinished lunch in a limestone cave to keep it cool and then forgot to pick it up. He returned months later and discovered that the bread had grown moldy and spread through the cheese, creating the first blue-veined Roquefort cheese.

In the pageant there is a marriage ceremony celebrating the union of cheese and wine in which a magistrate reads the marriage contract, places it between the wine (carried by the bride) and the cheese (carried by the groom), and circles all three with a wooden hoop symbolizing the wedding ring. The festival also includes parades, a grape stomp, and historical tours.

In the late 1840s, Nauvoo was occupied by French and German Icarians, members of a socialist sect whose creed, "From each according to his ability and to each according to his need," derived from the social-economic philosophy of Karl Marx. The Icarians brought wine-making to the area, and several of their original wine cellars are still used to make the blue cheese that this festival has celebrated for over 50 years. A similar festival is held in Roquefort, France.

CONTACTS:
Nauvoo Tourism Office
1295 Mulholland St.
Nauvoo, IL 62354
217-453-6648
www.visitnauvoo.com

♦ 1188 ♦ **Grasmere Sports**
Late August

This annual event in England's Lake District began in the 1800s to encourage Cumberland and Westmorland wrestling, but it has since expanded to include other traditional Lake District sports. The wrestling competitors stand chest to chest and lock arms behind each other's back. The aim of this subtle form of combat is to throw the opponent to the ground— a goal that many wrestlers struggle all day to achieve while other events are going on elsewhere.

Fell running (a *fell* is a highland plateau), another traditional sport, is an all-out race to the top of the nearest mountain and back. Hound trailing, which reflects the Lake District's importance as a center for fox hunting, is done on foot with packs of hounds who run across the fells after their prey.

Up until 1974, when Cumberland and Westmorland were combined to form Cumbria County, competition between the two rival counties had been fierce.

CONTACTS:
Grasmere Lakeland Sports and Show
The Showfield
Stock Ln.
Grasmere, Cumbria LA22 9SL United Kingdom
44-15-3943-2127
grasmeresports.com

♦ 1189 ♦ **Graveyard Cleaning and Decoration Day**
Between May and early September

In some Southern states—particularly Texas, Kentucky, and Tennessee—a day in summer is set aside for honoring the dead and maintaining the local cemetery. Sometimes called **Grave Day**, Memorial Day, **Decoration Day**, or **Memory Day**, it is a time for families and neighbors to get together, sharing "dinner-on-the-ground" or picnic suppers and listening to sermons. In Pleasant Grove, Kentucky, Grave Day originated as a peace-making ceremony after the Civil War had split Hardin County into two opposing factions.

Graveyard Cleaning Day is often held in July, but it may be observed any time from late May until early September. There usually isn't any connection to official Memorial Day celebrations; the date is a matter of local choice and convenience. In New Orleans, for example, it is customary to whitewash the tombs on All Saints' Day. All of these observations, however, harken back to the ancient Roman festival known as the Parentalia, an uncharacteristically somber occasion on which people decorated the graves of the deceased with flowers and left food in the cemeteries to sustain the spirits of the dead.

♦ 1190 ♦ **Great American Beer Festival**
Three days in late September or early October

The Great American Beer Festival was started in 1982 and has been conducted annually at the Colorado Convention Center in Denver, Colorado, since 2000. The festival consists of a public beer tasting event and a private beer competition. These events garner about 49,000 attendees every year. Organized by the American Homebrewers Association and the Brewers Association of Denver, this world-renowned festival attracts breweries from coast to coast, covering eight U.S. regions: Mid-Atlantic, Midwest, Rocky Mountain, New England, Pacific, Pacific Northwest, Southeast, and Southwest. The Craft Beer & Food Pavilion and the Farm to Table Pavilion feature chefs demonstrating the use of craft brews in a variety of dishes. Attendees also get a chance to evaluate beers by participating in the Beer Judge Certification Program. Breweries offer about 90 beer styles under three broad categories: hybrid, lager, and ale. A team of judges chooses the beer that best represents each category. A Pro-Am competition booth allows professional craft brewers to show off award-winning recipes created by American Homebrewers Association members.

CONTACTS:
Brewers Association
1327 Spruce St.
Boulder, CO 80302
303-447-0816; fax: 303-447-2825
www.greatamericanbeerfestival.com

♦ 1191 ♦ **Great American Brass Band Festival**
Mid-June

This weekend re-creation of the golden age of brass bands in America is held at Centre College in Danville, Ky. About a dozen bands from throughout the U.S. and Canada play Sousa march music, ragtime, and jazz in the New Orleans funeral-march style. A highlight is a band playing overthe-shoulder instruments of the Civil War period; the music blew to the rear of the band so it could be heard by the troops marching behind. The festival begins with a hot-air balloon race, and music then continues through the weekend.

CONTACTS:
Great American Brass Band Festival
320 W. Main St.
Danville, KY 40423
859-319-8426
www.gabbf.org

♦ 1192 ♦ Great American Duck Race
Fourth weekend in August

This uniquely American event started in 1980 in Deming, New Mexico, just to make a little whoopee. Up to 80 live ducks race for cash prizes in an eight-lane chute. There are races that include politicians' heats and a media heat. Other events in the week preceding the duck races are a parade, a lawnmower race, dances, hot-air balloons, an arts and crafts exhibit, an outhouse race, a chili cookoff, a pageant of people dressed like ducks, and a duck contest in which ducks are dressed like people. Race participants come from several states; spectators now number about 20,000, almost double the population of Deming.

Because one duck race a year is not enough, organizers began holding Great American Duck Race II, the Winter Games, over the third weekend in February in 2001. This race is held indoors at the Southwestern New Mexico State Fairgrounds.

CONTACTS:
Great American Duck Race of Deming Inc.
202 S. Diamond
Deming, NM 88030
575-544-0469 or 888-345-1125; fax: 505-544-0774
www.demingduckrace.com

♦ 1193 ♦ Great American Smokeout
Third Thursday in November

It was the *Surgeon General's Report on Smoking and Health* that first gave impetus to grassroots efforts to discourage the smoking of cigarettes. As far back as 1971, the town of Randolph, Massachusetts, had asked its residents to give up tobacco for a day. In 1974 the editor of the *Monticello Times* in Minnesota led the first mass movement by smokers to give up cigarettes, calling it "D-Day" for "Don't Smoke." The idea spread quickly throughout Minnesota and skipped west to California in 1977, where it became known as the Great American Smokeout. The following year it was observed nationwide for the first time, under the sponsorship of the American Cancer Society.

The Smokeout focuses attention not only on cigarette smokers but, more recently, on smokeless tobacco users as well. Activities are generally light-hearted rallies, parades, obstacle courses, contests, skits, parties, etc.—all designed to keep smokers away from their cigarettes for an entire day, in the hope that they will continue the effort on their own.

The Cancer Society encourages nonsmokers to "adopt" smokers on this day and support them as they go through withdrawal from nicotine—a drug that is said to be as addictive as heroin. Schools are particularly active in observing the Smokeout, teaching young people that the easiest way to avoid the health problems associated with smoking is never to start. Businesses, hospitals, and other organizations also sponsor programs and activities designed to increase public awareness of the hazards to which both smokers and those who breathe their smoke are exposed—particularly lung cancer.

In recent years, millions of people have quit for the day, and many of them do not return to the habit.

CONTACTS:
American Cancer Society
250 Williams St. N.W.
Atlanta, GA 30303
800-227-2345
www.cancer.org

♦ 1194 ♦ Great Backyard Bird Count
Mid-February

The Great Backyard Bird Count takes place every year over four days in mid-February throughout the United States and Canada. Volunteers of all ages and experience, known as "citizen scientists," spend at least 15 minutes counting birds from any location—their home, a park, or a schoolyard. Then they report the number of birds and species they have seen via the Internet. This gives scientists a real-time portrait of which birds are where in North America. The event was launched in 1998 by the National Audubon Society and the Cornell University Ornithology Lab.

For the 2015 Great Backyard Bird Count, a record 147,265 bird checklists were submitted by participants from over 100 countries. The 5,090 bird species reported during the four-day count represents nearly half the possible bird species in the world, breaking the previous record for the number of species identified. The website of the Great Backyard Bird Count allows participants to track data, get tips on identifying birds, and enter count-related contests.

CONTACTS:
National Audubon Society
225 Varick St.
New York, NY 10014
212-979-3000 or 800-274-4201
www.audubon.org

♦ 1195 ♦ Great Battle of Hansan Festival (Hansan Daecheop)
August

The Great Battle of Hansan Festival is held annually in Tongyeong-si, Gyeongsangnam-do, South Korea, for four days in August. This colorful and eventful celebration marks the stunning victory of Admiral Yi Sun-sin over the Japanese navy at the Battle of Hansan during the Imjin War (1592-1598).

A re-enactment of the battle in the waters off Tongyeong is the undisputed highlight of the event, but dozens of associated activities are also held in this commemoration of Korea's most revered national hero. They include a commemorative parade; performances of music, dance, and drama; art exhibitions; and lectures. Tongyeong, which some refer to as the "Naples of Asia," is a port city renowned for its beautiful setting and vibrant arts scene. The festival has taken place since the 1960s.

CONTACTS:
Korea Tourism Organization
2 Executive Dr.
Ste. 750
Fort Lee, NJ 07024
201-585-0909; fax: 201-585-9041
www.visitkorea.or.kr

Hansan Daecheop Memorial Foundation
21, Seomun-ro
Tongyeong-si, Gyeongsangnam-do Korea
82-55-644-5222; fax: 82-55-643-4126
english.visitkorea.or.kr

♦ 1196 ♦ **Great Circus Parade**
Mid-July

The Great Circus Parade in Milwaukee, Wisconsin, is a re-creation of a 19th-century circus street pageant. Featuring more than 60 historic circus wagons, 700 horses, wild animals in cages, and hundreds of musicians, clowns, and costumed participants, this annual procession begins with the loading of the half-mile-long circus train at the Circus World Museum in Baraboo. Horses are used to load the flatcars according to traditional circus methods, and the train then embarks on a three-day, 382-mile journey through Wisconsin, arriving in Milwaukee after making several stops at communities in the central and eastern part of the state.

The parade follows a three-mile route through downtown Milwaukee. The wagons are part of the Circus World Museum's collection of historic wagons and show vehicles, many of which have undergone extensive restoration. A display of circus wagons and performances under the Big Top can be seen at Milwaukee's Veterans' Park, which is transformed into the Great Circus Parade Showgrounds for the week of festivities in mid-July.

CONTACTS:
Circus World Museum Foundation
550 Water St. (Hwy. 113)
Baraboo, WI 53913
608-356-8341 or 866-693-1500; fax: 608-356-1800
www.circusworldbaraboo.org

♦ 1197 ♦ **Great Falls Ski Club Mannequin Jump**
Saturday in early April

In the zany sport of mannequin jumping, contestants build a mannequin—which could represent anything from Sponge Bob Square Pants to a Ninja Turtle—and send it flying off a 15-foot ski jump. The audience just marvels and laughs.

Hundreds of spectators come to watch the mannequins fly—and often self-destruct on the way down.

The Great Falls Ski Club Mannequin Jump, which the organizers call "the strangest ski jumping contest on the planet," is held on the first Saturday in April at the Showdown Ski Area in Showdown, Mont. This annual contest has been held since 1995. In addition to the main event, the day's activities feature children's diversions, photography, comedy, and a wide variety of winter sports, including downhill skiing, snowshoeing, snowboarding, and snowmobiling.

CONTACTS:
Great Falls Ski Club
P.O. Box 166
Great Falls, MT 59403
www.greatfallsskiclub.com

♦ 1198 ♦ **Great Locomotive Chase Festival**
First weekend in October

This three-day celebration in Adairsville, Ga., commemorates the storied Civil War locomotive chase that led to the execution of six Union soldiers by the Confederates.

The chase came on April 12, 1862 (the one-year anniversary of the Confederate attack on Fort Sumter), after the Yankee spy, James J. Andrews, stole the Confederate engine named "The General," along with three boxcars and the tender. His plan was to burn the rail bridges between Atlanta and Chattanooga, in order to cut Confederate supply lines.

Andrews swiped the locomotive at Big Shanty (Kennesaw), Georgia, and roared off, stopping to cut telegraph wires and tear up tracks. In due time William A. Fuller, conductor of "The General," who had been having breakfast when his train was stolen, realized something was missing and set off in a handcar with Anthony Murphy. In Adairsville, they boarded the locomotive "Texas," and barreled after "The General" and Andrews, who was trying to reach the bridge at Resaca so he could burn it. The drivers of "The General" kept throwing things on the track to derail the "Texas," but the "Texas" kept in pursuit.

Finally, the Yankee raiders were out of fuel and had nothing left to throw on the track; arriving in Ringgold, Andrews ordered his men to jump and run. They did, but all were apprehended. Andrews and six others were tried and hanged; others were taken as prisoners until being exchanged, and later they received medals from the Union army. The Confederates won the accolades of the Army of the Confederacy.

In 1927, Buster Keaton made the movie *The General* based on the chase, and in 1956, a Disney movie, *The Great Locomotive Chase*, later retitled *Andrews' Raiders*, retold the old story.

Events of the festival include showings of the locomotive-chase movies, a grand parade, beauty pageants, fireworks, and gospel singing. There are also such contests as three-legged races, a marshmallow-spitting contest, a beanbag toss, a balloon toss, and a tug of war. Attendance is estimated at more than 10,000.

Cartersville-Bartow County Convention & Visitors Bureau
P.O. Box 200397
Cartersville, GA 30120
770-387-1357 or 800-733-2280
www.visitcartersvillega.org

♦ 1199 ♦ Great Montana Sheep Drive
August 31

Called "The World's Largest Small Town Parade," the Great Montana Sheep Drive is similar to the annual Running of the Bulls in Pamplona, Spain.

The event, founded in 1989, features hundreds of Montana-bred sheep herded down the six blocks of Main Street in downtown Reed Point, Mont. In a parody of the Spanish bull event, a handful of Reed Point volunteers dressed in black berets and red sashes run ahead of the sheep. There is also a parade, with historic covered wagons and re-enactors dressed in period costumes of the Old West, a log-cutting contest, a shoot-out between two gunfighters, carnival games, and an evening street dance. The lighthearted event has raised money for community projects in the small town (with a population of 185), including a new fire truck and the refurbishing of the town library. Some 12,000 people attend the annual event, making Reed Point one of Montana's largest towns on the weekend of the sheep drive.

CONTACTS:
Reed Point Community Club Inc.
P.O. Box 402
Reed Point, MT 59069
406-780-1476
stillwatercountychamber.com

♦ 1200 ♦ Great Moonbuggy Race
April

The Great Moonbuggy Race is held every April in Huntsville, Ala., by the National Aeronautics and Space Administration (NASA). The race challenges university and high school students in teams of six, to design, assemble, and test-drive a human-powered vehicle suitable for driving on the moon. Teams must carry the unassembled vehicle components to the race starting-point in a container similar in size to those used for the original Lunar Roving Vehicles. The teams must assemble their buggies. Then two team members, a male and a female, drive them over a half-mile-long course that simulates lunar terrain, complete with "craters," "rocks," "lava" ridges, and more. Teams are allowed two runs of the course. Their lowest time is added to the vehicle-assembly time for their final score. Prizes are awarded to the three fastest teams in both the university and high-school categories: cash and a trophy to the first-place winners, and plaques to the others. There are special prizes for most unique and most improved vehicle, a rookie award, and a system safety award. Typically about 50 schools take part in all, from about 15 states, and from as far away as Puerto Rico and Germany.

The Great Moonbuggy Race got its start in 1994 to commemorate the 25th anniversary of the Apollo 11 lunar landing. The

NASA designers of the Lunar Roving Vehicle used by Apollo astronauts were the inspiration for the race. Eight college teams competed the first year, and the race was expanded to include high school teams in 1996.

CONTACTS:
NASA Public Communications Office
NASA Headquarters
Suite 5R30
Washington, D.C. 20546
202-358-0001; fax: 202-358-4338
www.nasa.gov

♦ 1201 ♦ Great New Moon Festival (Cheno i-equa)
October

The Cheno i-equa is one of seven festivals observed by the Cherokee and is regarded as their New Year. Celebrated in October, the ceremony falls on the new moon of autumn and commemorates the creation of earth, which is believed to have taken seven days. Celebrants undertake elaborate cleansing rituals by immersing themselves in a river seven times before participating in the main ceremony, where the most important element is giving thanks to the earth mother.

As with other Cherokee ceremonies, fasting, feasting, and dancing are observed to honor the creator and ancestral spirits. Besides ushering in the New Year, these rituals symbolize the hope that the cycle of nature will be everlasting, whether for good or for bad. During the festival, the priest looks into the *Ulunsuti* (crystal) stones and invokes prayers for the harvest and the welfare of the tribe in the coming year.

CONTACTS:
Cherokee Nation
17675 S. Muskogee Ave.
Tahlequah, OK 74465
www.cherokee.org

♦ 1202 ♦ Great Sami Winter Fair
Begins first Thursday in February

The Lapps, or Samis as many prefer to be called, are a nomadic people of ancient origin who still make their living keeping reindeer herds in the northernmost regions of Norway, Sweden, and Finland, and on the Kola Peninsula of the former Soviet Union. They started holding the Winter Fair, or Market, in Jokkmokk, Sweden, more than 400 years ago, and have continued to hold it in February because this is the time of year when they bring their reindeer to this area. The fourday event draws many visitors who are curious about Sami culture. It includes the marking of the reindeer, reindeer roundup demonstrations, folk music and dance, films, lectures, and the sale of special Sami foods and handicrafts. In 2015 the market celebrated its 410th anniversary.

CONTACTS:
Destination Jokkmokk AB
Stortorget 4
Box 124
Jokkmokk, 962 23 Sweden

46-971-222-50; fax: 46-971-222-59
destinationjokkmokk.se/en

♦ 1203 ♦ Great Schooner Race
First week in July

The Great Schooner Race is held off the shore of Rockland, Maine. Since 1977 the race has featured schooners from the Maine Windjammer Association and a number of other large sailing ships—usually 25 to 30 in all. The race begins at Isleboro Island and ends in Rockland, where the boats parade through Penobscot Bay.

CONTACTS:
Maine Windjammer Association
P.O. Box 1144
Blue Hill, ME 04614
800-807-9463
www.sailmainecoast.com

♦ 1204 ♦ Great Wardmote of the Woodmen of Arden
First week in August

The Great Wardmote, an archery contest organized much the same way it was in medieval times, takes place during the first week in August. It is held in the village of Meriden, which stands in the middle of the once-vast Forest of Arden and claims to be the geographical center of England. Meetings were traditionally held here to discuss the rights and duties of the foresters. In 1785 the various groups of woodmen joined together into one company, the Woodmen of Arden. Today its 80 members attend their annual four-day meeting in August wearing 18th-century dress, including green hats, green coats with gilt buttons, and white trousers.

The woodmen shoot with six-foot bows made of yew and arrows marked with a stamp that denotes their weight in silver. This medieval convention reflects a time when archery was of crucial importance in battle and shooting practice was mandatory in most towns.

CONTACTS:
Visit Britain
845 Third Ave. 10th Fl.
New York, NY 10022
212-850-0336
www.visitbritain.org

♦ 1205 ♦ Great World Theatre
June-September (2020, 2027, 2034, ...)

Performed every several years in Einsiedeln, Switzerland, the play known as **El Gran Teatro del Mundo** (Great World Theatre) is the work of Pedro Calderón de la Barca, a 17th century Spanish dramatist and master of the *auto sacramental*, a type of religious drama in which allegory is used to explain the mysteries of Christianity. In *El Gran Teatre del Mundo*, six representatives of humanity, from beggar to king, face life's

challenges and must account for their actions on Judgment Day. The play is performed in German before the facade of a Benedictine monastery and church with a cast of more than 500 townspeople. After the show, the director invites most of the cast to a Eucharistic banquet—with the exception of the Rich Man, who is sent to hell. The most recent production took place in 2013.

CONTACTS:
Einsiedeln Tourism Information
Hauptstrasse 85
Einsiedeln, 8840 Switzerland
41-55-418-4488
www.einsiedeln-tourismus.ch

♦ 1206 ♦ Grec Festival de Barcelona
July

Every July, the Barcelona City Council hosts the Grec Festival de Barcelona. Founded in 1997, the festival focuses on theater, music, dance, circus, and other stage arts. The title of the festival comes from the name of the main venue, the Teatre Grec, an open-air theater on Montjuïc, a hill near the center of the city. Other venues of the festival in and around Barcelona, Spain, include the Teatre Lliure, Mercat de les Flors, L'Auditori, and other cultural facilities.

The Grec Festival de Barcelona initially featured only theater works, but later on began to include other art forms. It gives prime importance to works by local artists, secondary priority to Catalonian works, and third priority to international productions. The festival starts with an opening performance by a headliner, usually a Catalonian artist or group.

CONTACTS:
Tiquet Rambles
Palau de la Virreina
La Rambla, 99
Barcelona, 08001 Spain
34-93-316-1111
lameva.barcelona.cat/grec/en

♦ 1207 ♦ Greece Independence Day
March 25

This national holiday in Greece celebrates the anniversary of the country's proclamation of independence in 1821 after four centuries of Turkish occupation. The war that followed went on until 1829, when finally the Turkish sultan recognized the independence of Greece. The day is marked with church services and military parades—an especially impressive parade is held in Athens. Greek communities in other parts of the world also observe the day. In New York City, Greece Independence Day is celebrated on the Sunday nearest to March 25 with a parade up Fifth Avenue.

CONTACTS:
Embassy of Greece
2217 Massachusetts Ave. N.W.
Washington, D.C. 20008
202-939-1300; fax: 202-939-1324
www.greekembassy.org

♦ 1208 ♦ **Greek Cypriot National Day**
April 1

This holiday marks the anniversary of the 1955 start of the Greek Cypriot liberation struggle against British colonial forces. The Greek community in Cyprus waged a guerilla campaign against the British in order to gain union with Greece. The Turkish community, which preferred an alliance with Turkey, also took up arms, complicating the struggle.

Greek Cypriot National Day is celebrated in South Cyprus, which is the Greek partitioned part of the island. Almost all public services and most private shops are closed. The holiday is often celebrated with parades in city streets, along with music, dancing and flag waving.

CONTACTS:
Embassy of the Republic of Cyprus
2211 R. St. N.W.
Washington, D.C. 02008
202-462-5772; fax: 202-483-6710
www.cyprusembassy.net

♦ 1209 ♦ **Green Festivals**
Usually in spring and fall

The largest green consumer show in the United States, Green Festivals brings individuals, businesses, and investors together to generate eco-friendly strategies for sustainable living. Originally, the festivals took place in four U.S. cities—San Francisco, Seattle, Chicago, Washington, D.C.—typically in the spring or fall. The events are jointly organized by Global Exchange, a human rights organization, and Co-Op America, an organization committed to social justice and environmental sustainability. Event co-sponsors include a number of non-profits, publications, and other media enterprises.

The first Green Festival was staged in San Francisco, Calif., in 2004, and its success has led to the replication of the event in the other cities. Organizers describe the events as "parties with a purpose." Their offerings are typical of a tradeshow—guest speakers, panel discussions, workshops, career sessions, and commercial exhibitions. Supplementing the festival are various forms of entertainment including films, live music, and organic cuisine.

The capacity of the festivals has grown dramatically since the inaugural year. In 2015, five cities are slated to host Green Festival events, including New York, Washington, D.C., San Francisco, Los Angeles, and Portland. Past festival locations include Austin, Seattle, Chicago and Denver.

Festival directors take pride in visibly demonstrating a commitment to ecological responsibility by reusing, recycling, or composting 96% of the waste generated at the show. Admission discounts are also available to attendees who arrive by bicycle instead of by car—a simple incentive to reduce carbon emissions at the event.

CONTACTS:
Green Festivals Inc.
191 Lyman St.

Ste. 101
Asheville, NC 28801
828-236-0324; fax: 828-254-4287
www.greenfestivals.org

♦ 1210 ♦ **Green George Festival**
April 23

Observed on St. George's Day, April 23, by Romany people (also known as gypsies) in Transylvania, the Green George Festival is a tree-spirit festival in which folkloric beliefs play a major role. A young willow is cut down, decorated with flowers and leaves, and set up in a central place where everyone can see it. Pregnant women may leave a piece of clothing under the tree; if a leaf falls on it by the next morning, they'll have an easy delivery. Sick or elderly people spit on the tree three times, praying for long life and good health.

On April 24, an old custom is for a boy dressed in green leaves and flowers to take three iron nails that have spent three days and three nights in running water, hammer them into the willow, pull them out, and throw them back into the stream. In the evening, Green George appears as a leaf-clad puppet who is also thrown into the stream.

Green George is believed to be a variation on the medieval English Jack in the Green. A relic of European tree worship, Jack in the Green is associated with Pentecost and other celebrations of spring. On May Day in England, he appeared as a boy (typically a chimneysweep) encased in a framework of lath and hoops covered with ivy and holly and wearing a high headdress of leaves.

♦ 1211 ♦ **Green March Day**
November 6

On Green March Day, Moroccans observe the anniversary of the march by the people of Morocco into Spanish-controlled Western Sahara on a call given by King Hassan II. Green March Day is a national holiday and a day Moroccans remember the patriotism and determination of their fellow citizens who laid claim over land in a peaceful and religious manner. Dating back to its independence from Spain in 1956, Morocco sought to bring Western Sahara, formerly known as Spanish Sahara, within its borders. Following an International Court of Justice advisory in 1975 that the people of Western Sahara exercise their right to self-rule, King Hassan II of Morocco announced plans to lead a march into the territory to reclaim it. On November 6, 1975, 350,000 Moroccans who had mobilized in the city of Tarfaya marched unarmed into Western Sahara carrying flags and the Qur'an. On November 9, after the marchers had progressed 10 kilometers into the region, King Hassan ordered them back to Morocco and they returned unharmed. Due to the religious significance of the color green in Islam, the march itself came to be known as the "Green March." In the aftermath of the march, an agreement was reached granting Morocco, Mauritania and Spain joint control of the region. Although Morocco achieved effective control over the Western Sahara in the years that followed, the region has remained in turmoil as the native Sahrawi resisted Moroccan sovereignty.

CONTACTS:
Moroccan National Tourist Office
104 W. 40th St.
Ste. 1820
New York, NY 10018
212-221-1583; fax: 212-221-1887
www.visitmorocco.com

♦ 1212 ♦ **Green River Rendezvous**
Second weekend in July

A reenactment in Pinedale, Wyo., of the days when mountain men, Indians, and traders came together to transact business, trade, drink, holler, and celebrate. The first rendezvous, or gathering, of trappers was held on the Green River, near the present Wyoming-Utah border. After trading posts were established, the rendezvous became less important. The last of these colorful gatherings was held in 1840. A two-hour pageant recreating these rendezvous has been presented by the Sublette County Historical Society since 1936. Celebrations are held over three days, and other events include black-powder shoots and barbecues.

The trappers, traders, and explorers who came to be known as mountain men were a distinctive breed who numbered in their ranks the legendary Jim Bridger, the scout and Indian agent Kit Carson, and William Sublette, who established the area's first trading post. They were satisfying the demand for fur and especially for beaver; the beaver hat was supreme in the world of fashion at the start of the 19th century.

Besides trapping beaver, they also planted the American claim to much of the territory of the American West. For most of the year, they trapped on the tributaries of the Green River, but for several weeks each summer when there was no beaver trapping, they came out of the wilderness and met at a rendezvous site. Trade goods—blankets, coffee, sugar, gunpowder, and cheap whiskey—were brought from Missouri by pack animals and trade wagons, and the trappers brought their beaver skins.

It was a time for more than trading: on one occasion Jim Bridger rode around in a suit of armor that had been brought to him from Scotland. The rendezvous brought together a concentration of explorers and frontiersmen and provided a stepping stone for the settlers who followed. The rendezvous and the era of the mountain men came to an end in the 1840s when the whims of fashion shifted from beaver hats to silk hats, and the race for beaver furs was over.

See also MOUNTAIN MAN RENDEZVOUS.

CONTACTS:
Museum of the Mountain Man, Sublette County Historical Society, Inc.
700 E. Hennick St.
P.O. Box 9090
Pinedale, WY 82941
307-367-4136 or 307-367-4101 or 877-686-6266
museumofthemountainman.com

♦ 1213 ♦ **Greenery Day**
May 4

This day was formerly observed on April 29, the birthday of Emperor Hirohito of Japan (1901-1989), who was the world's longest ruling monarch. His reign included the attempted military conquest of Asia, the attack on the United States at Pearl Harbor, and his country's defeat after the U.S. dropped atomic bombs on Hiroshima and Nagasaki. He also oversaw Japan's post-war resurgence to a position of economic strength and influence. Hirohito renounced his divinity in 1946 and became a symbolic head of state in Japan's new parliamentary democracy.

Today this day is celebrated on May 4 as Greenery Day—**Midori-no-Hi**—with parades featuring elaborate floats, paper lanterns, traditional Japanese costumes, and fireworks. Popular places from which to observe the festivities in Tokyo include Tokyo Tower, the highest structure in the city, and Shiba Park. People also mark the day by planting trees and other activities centered around the appreciation of nature.

Greenery Day is in **Golden Week**, which also includes JAPAN CONSTITUTION MEMORIAL DAY (May 3) and KODOMO-NO- HI (Children's Day, May 5). It is a popular time for people to take vacations and enjoy the spring weather.

CONTACTS:
National Association of Japan-America Societies
1819 L St. N.W.
Ste. 200
Washington, D.C. 20036
202-429-5545; fax: 202-429-0027
www.us-japan.org

Japan Consortium for International Cooperation in Cultural Heritage
13-43 Ueno Koen
Taito-ku
Japan
81-3-3823-4841; fax: 81-3-3823-4027
www.jcic-heritage.jp

♦ 1214 ♦ **Greenland National Day**
June 21

The people of Greenland celebrate National Day on June 21, the longest day of the year. They call the holiday *Ullortuneq* in Greenlandic, which means "the longest day." They celebrate the occasion with communal picnics, shows, and many cultural activities. Since Greenland's current flag was formally instituted on June 21, 1985, they also honor the national flag on this day.

CONTACTS:
Tupilak Travel
Ilivinnguaq 1
P.B. 2291
Nuuk, 3900 Greenland
299-31-32-18; fax: 299-31-32-17
www.nuuk-tourism.gl

♦ 1215 ♦ **Greenville Treaty Camporee**
Usually a weekend in May in odd-numbered years

On June 16, 1795, General Anthony Wayne and representative chiefs of the Allied Tribes of the Northwest Territory met at Fort Greenville to light a ceremonial council fire and work out the terms of a treaty that would open the Northwest Territory to white settlers. The council fire was not allowed to go out until the treaty was finally signed on August 3.

Today, Boy Scouts from Ohio and other parts of the Midwest meet on a weekend nearest in May during odd-numbered years at Greenville City Park to commemorate the treaty. The Miami Valley Council sponsors the weekend, which attracts more than 1,000 Scouts. There are exhibitions of Boy Scout skills, games, competitions, and demonstrations.

CONTACTS:
Miami Valley Council, BSA
7285 Poe Ave.
Dayton, OH 45414
937-278-4825; fax: 937-278-9002
www.miamivalleybsa.org

◆ 1216 ◆ **Greenwood (Chester) Day**
First Saturday in December

Chester Greenwood (1858-1937) made his first pair of "ear protectors" when he was 15 years old. He was granted a patent in 1877 and established an entirely new industry in his hometown of Farmington, Maine, where he continued to refine the design and manufacture of what we now know as earmuffs. By 1918 he was making 216,000 pairs a year, and by 1932 checks and plaids were added to the standard black velvet covering.

Although Greenwood was involved in a number of other business ventures in Farmington and was granted his last patent—for a tempered steel lawn rake—only a few months before he died, it is for his ear protectors that he is primarily remembered. Farmington residents celebrate Chester Greenwood Day on the first Saturday in December (Greenwood was born on December 4) with a parade, flag-raising ceremony, and a foot race. Everyone is encouraged to wear earmuffs for the festivities, including pets.

CONTACTS:
Farmington Downtown Association
P.O. Box 22
Farmington, ME 04938
www.downtownfarmington.com

◆ 1217 ◆ **Grenada Independence Day**
February 7

This is a national holiday commemorating Grenada's independence from Britain on this day in 1974. Britain had held the island since the 18th century, when France ceded it under the Treaty of Paris.

CONTACTS:
Embassy of Grenada
1701 New Hampshire Ave. N.W.
Washington, D.C. 20009
202-265-2561; fax: 202-265-2468
www.grenadaembassyusa.org

◆ 1218 ◆ **Grenada Thanksgiving Day**
October 25

On October 25, 1983, the U.S. and other Caribbean forces invaded Grenada to destabilize the Communist regime that had overthrown the government of Sir Eric Gairy in 1979. Democratic elections were held in December 1984. October 25 is observed as Thanksgiving Day, a public holiday in Grenada.

CONTACTS:
Embassy of Grenada
1701 New Hampshire Ave. N.W.
Washington, D.C. 20009
202-265-2561; fax: 202-265-2468
www.grenadaembassyusa.org

◆ 1219 ◆ **Grey Cup Day**
Late November

The best teams from the Eastern and Western Conferences of the Canadian Football League play against each other in an annual event similar to the SUPER BOWL in the United States. It is called Grey Cup Day after the trophy that is awarded to the winning team—a cup donated by former Canadian Governor-General Earl Grey in 1909.

Parties are held throughout the country so that fans can get together to watch the big game on television. In sports and social clubs, it is not uncommon to set up two televisions so that rival supporters can each watch their own team. Like its American counterpart, the Super Bowl, the Grey Cup is an occasion for widespread drinking and rowdiness.

CONTACTS:
Canadian Football League
50 Wellington St. E.
3rd Fl.
Toronto, ON M5E 1C8 Canada
416-322-9650; fax: 416-322-9651
www.cfl.ca

◆ 1220 ◆ **Groppenfasnacht (Fish Carnival)**
*Between March 1 and April 4; Laetare Sunday
(three weeks before Easter)*

This Lenten celebration in the village of Ermatingen, Thurgau Canton, Switzerland, takes its name from the *Gropp*, a fish a few inches long caught only in the Ermatingen area. The event dates to the time when fishermen celebrated the breaking up of the ice in the spring because they could return to catching fish. A committee of villagers organizes a procession in which children dress as frogs and dwarfs and followa a float that carries a huge Gropp, while men march along carrying antique fishing implements.

CONTACTS:
Groppenkomitee Ermatingen
Hauptstrasse 15
Ermatingen, CH-8272 Switzerland
41-71-664-2473
www.groppenfasnacht.ch

♦ 1221 ♦ **Grotto Day**
August 5; July 25

In England during the late 18th and early 19th centuries, oysters were not considered the rare delicacy they are today and were, in fact, one of the common staples of fishermen's diets. The large number of oysters eaten at that time meant there were lots of shells around. On ST. JAMES'S DAY, which was observed on August 5 before the Gregorian, or New Style, Calendar came into use and on July 25 thereafter, children used the shells to construct small decorative grottoes. Perhaps these were to represent the shrine of St. James in Spain. Sometimes the children begged for pennies as a reward for their efforts. Most of this grotto-building took place in London, and the custom continued right up to the 1950s. St. James the Great was one of the Apostles and brother to ST. JOHN THE EVANGELIST, and the scallop shell was his emblem.

CONTACTS:
St James's Roman Catholic Church
Spanish Pl., 22 George St.
London, W1U 3QY United Kingdom
20-7935-0943
www.sjrcc.org.uk

♦ 1222 ♦ **Groundhog Day**
February 2

There was a medieval superstition that all hibernating animals—not just groundhogs—came out of their caves and dens on CANDLEMAS to check on the weather. If they could see their shadows, it meant that winter would go on for another six weeks and they could go back to sleep. A cloudy day meant that spring was just around the corner. It was the early German settlers known as the Pennsylvania Dutch who attached this superstition to the groundhog. In Germany it was the badger, and in England, France, and Canada it was the bear who was believed to make similar predictions about the weather.

The most famous forecaster in the United States is Punxsutawney Phil, a legendary groundhog in north-central Pennsylvania believed to be nearly a century old. Members of the Punxsutawney Groundhog Club, along with thousands of other people, trek up to Phil's burrow on Gobbler's Knob on February 2 and get the news directly from him. (They also capture the event on film, which is available for viewing from a link on their web site.) Unfortunately, weather researchers have determined that over the years the groundhog has been correct only 28 percent of the time.

Numerous events take place in Punxsutawney over the days surrounding February 2, including group hikes, parties, live entertainment, fireworks, a winter carnival, and the showing of *Groundhog Day*, the 1993 movie starring Bill Murray.

CONTACTS:
Punxsutawney Groundhog Club
200 W. Mahoning St.
Ste. 1
Punxsutawney, PA 15767
814-618-5591; fax: 814-618-5746
www.groundhog.org

♦ 1223 ♦ **Guadalajara International Film Festival**
March

For a week in March, the city of Guadalajara, a cultural hub of Mexico, hosts the prestigious Guadalajara International Film Festival. The festival, which began in 1986, attracts world-famous actors and filmmakers from other top-ranked film festivals. Besides showcasing Mexican and Ibero-American movies on the international stage, the festival serves as a portal for new projects by independent artists across the world. The festival repertoire includes diverse, experimental genres in addition to features, documentaries, and short films. The festival's prestigious Mayahuel Award is determined by an international jury and awarded to the top film across a range of categories.

The festival also provides a forum for the exchange of ideas among notable film personalities and audiences. These educational events are popular with emerging filmmakers, critics, and students from the region.

CONTACTS:
FICG
Nebula 2916
Jardines del Bosque
Guadalajara, 44520 Mexico
52-33-3121-7461
www.ficg.mx

♦ 1224 ♦ **Gualterianas, Festas**
Four days beginning the first Sunday in August

The **Festivals of St. Walter** take place in Guimarães, the 12th-century capital of Portugal. The celebrations, which date back to 1452, include magnificent processions, fireworks, animal fairs, and displays of food and merchandise. Music, ranging from brass bands to modern jazz, can be heard all over the town.

St. Walter (or São Gualter), the town's patron, is represented by an image of a young Franciscan monk who stands in the nave of Senhor dos Passos (Our Lord of the Way of the Cross), the blue-and-white-tiled church that overlooks the town's public garden.

During a Sunday night procession known as the *Procissão Gualteriana*, the image of the saint is carried from the church through the decorated streets of Guimarães while thousands of spectators gather to watch. The procession is followed by a night of fireworks, folk dancing in regional costume, and great activity at the shooting galleries and sideshows that line the streets. The festival culminates on Wednesday with the *Marcha Gualteriana*, a midnight procession of 12 allegorical floats.

CONTACTS:
Municipality of Guimarães
Canon Largo José Maria Gomes
Guimarães, 4804-534 Portugal
351-253-421-200; fax: 351-253-515-134
www.cm-guimaraes.pt

♦ 1225 ♦ Guardian Angels Day
October 2

As early as the ninth century, a day was set aside to honor angels in general and the archangel Michael in particular. This was September 29, the Feast of St. Michael and All Angels or MICHAELMAS. But some people, believing that a particular angel is assigned to watch over each human being,wanted to honor their own personal protectors or guardian angels. A feast in their honor observed in 16th-century Spain was extended to the whole church by Pope Paul V in 1608, and in 1672 Pope Clement X set October 2 as the universal day for the festival.

CONTACTS:
St. Michael the Archangel Roman Catholic Church
490 Arnold Mill Rd.
Woodstock, GA 30188
770-516-0009; fax: 770-516-4664
www.saintmichaelcc.org

♦ 1226 ♦ Guatemala Army Day
June 30

Guatemala's Liberal Revolution, which called for the end of the dictatorship of Vicente Cerna, culminated with a revolt in Guatemala City on June 30, 1871. The coup paved the way for a successful 12-year era under President Justo Rufino Barrios, a leader of the revolution who implemented extensive agrarian reforms as Guatemala's head of state.

Originally known as **Revolution Day**, the anniversary of the 1871 revolt became **Día del Ejército** (Army Day), an official holiday recognizing the service of the armed forces. Typical of most traditional military celebrations, Army Day has been marked over the years by annual parades, usually in Guatemala City, featuring processions of various battalions and divisions.

At the turn of the 21st century, a popular movement grew to force an end to Army Day celebrations. Guatemalan activists began holding a rival event in Guatemala City called the March for Remembrance in honor of the thousands of civilians killed by the repressive military leadership during the country's civil war between 1960 and 1996. The 2007 parade and accompanying protests spawned violence in the streets, and the ongoing campaign of resistance compelled the government to cancel the official parade the following year.

CONTACTS:
Guatemalan Tourism Institute (INGUAT)
7 av 1-17 zone 4, Civic Center
 Guatemala
502-2421-2800
www.visitguatemala.com

Army History of Guatemala - Guatemala Military Museum
24th. Calle 3-81 zone 1
Interior Centro Cultural Miguel Angel Asturias Old Castillo de
San José de Buena Vista

Guatemala
502-2221-4322; fax: 502-2221-4322
museo.mil.gt

♦ 1227 ♦ Guatemala Independence Day
September 15

This is the day on which Guatemala won its independence from Spain in 1821. Four other countries also declared their independence on September 15, 1821: COSTA RICA, EL SALVADOR, HONDURAS, and NICARAGUA.

It is a public holiday during which the buildings in Guatemala City are draped in blue-and-white bunting, and there are parades with schoolchildren marching to the music of military bands. A popular holiday pastime is watching *La Conquista* (The Conquest), a traditional dance where the dancers, in wooden masks and red wigs, reenact the conquest of the Mayan Indians by the Spanish soldier Pedro de Alvarado. The Mayan civilization, which had flourished in Guatemala since 2500 B.C.E., began to decline after 900 C.E. Alvarado, the red-haired Spanish conquistador, began subjugating their descendants in 1523.

CONTACTS:
Embassy of Guatemala
2220 R St. N.W.
Washington, D.C. 20008
202-745-4953; fax: 202-745-1908

Guatemalan Tourism Institute (INGUAT)
7 Av. 1-17 zone 4, Centro Cívico
 Guatemala
502-2421-2800
www.visitguatemala.com

♦ 1228 ♦ Guatemala Revolution Day
October 20

Like another national holiday, GUATEMALA ARMY DAY, this holiday commemorates a historic transfer of Guatemalan power. On October 20, 1944, university students and military leaders aligned to overthrow the dictator Jorge Ubico. Guatemalans fondly remember the replacement government and its executive leader, Juan José Arévalo, who implemented a series of successful labor and agrarian reforms. Arévalo's presidency and that of his successor, Jacobo Arbenz Guzmán, marked a period of political freedom known as 10 Years of Spring.

Music and fireworks mark the day's lively celebrations, the grandest of which are held in the Plaza Mayor in Guatemala City. It is also common on this day for activists to exercise their free speech, a human right that Arévalo championed, and to stage political demonstrations. Some protests draw thousands of people and extend into the next day.

CONTACTS:
Minister of Culture and Sports of Guatemala
6a. St. between 6th and 7th Ave.
The National Palace of Cultural Zone 1

Guatemala
502-2-2230-1750 or 502-2-2230-1755; fax: 502-2-2230-1754
mcd.gob.gt

◆ 1229 ◆ Guavaween
Last Saturday of October

Guavaween is a parade and block party with a Latin flavor in Ybor City, a two-square-mile area in Tampa, Fla. Ybor City grew around the cigar factory established in 1886 by Cuban Vicente Martínez Ybor. From the steps of the factory, José Martí (1853-1895), sometimes called the George Washington of Cuba, exhorted the cigar workers to take up arms against Spain.

The area still has a Latin flavor, and Guavaween is an event to celebrate the culture and have a good time. The "guava" stands for the tropical American fruit, while the "ween" alludes to the festival's resemblance to HALLOWEEN, also observed around this time of year. The parade, with 20 to 50 bands, is led by a woman portraying the mythical "Mama Guava" doing the "Mama Guava Stumble." Many paraders wear costumes lampooning national figures. After the early evening parade, there is partying until the wee hours. Attendance is about 150,000.

CONTACTS:
Ybor City Chamber of Commerce
1800 E. 9th Ave.
Tampa, FL 33605
813-248-3712
ybor.org

◆ 1230 ◆ Gudi Padva
March-April; first day of the waxing half of the Hindu month of Caitra

Gudi Padva marks the beginning of the civil year among Hindus, particularly in the states of Maharashtra, Andhra Pradesh, and Karnataka in central India. The actual New Year (*see* VAISAKH), which begins on the first day of Vaisakha (April-May) is not the same as the beginning of the civil year, which begins on the new moon day of the preceding month, Caitra.

Hindus observe this day by erecting a pole from which hangs a silk banner (a *gudi*) or a piece of women's clothing and a drinking pot. This pole is displayed by sticking it out a window or tying it to the roof or a nearby tree. There are a number of legends associated with the pole, but it generally serves as a good luck symbol.

Other customs associated with this day are visiting friends, bathing, and eating leaves from the *nim* tree, which is believed to bring protection against illness, since this tree has a holy connection with SITALA, the smallpox goddess.

CONTACTS:
Vishva Hindu Parishad
Sankat Mochan Hanuman Mandir Ashram
R.K. Puram Sector 6
New Delhi, Delhi 110022 India
9111- 26178992; fax: 9111-26195527
vhp.org

◆ 1231 ◆ Guelaguetza, La
Two consecutive Mondays after July 16

Also known as **Los Lunes del Cerro**, or **Mondays of the Hill**, this huge dance festival is held in the city of Oaxaca, Oaxaca State, Mexico, on the two Mondays after July 16. Costumed dancers from different *oaxaquena* groups perform in a hilltop arena built exclusively for this event. Seats for the nationally televised festival are expensive, and many of the visiting dance groups must stay in local missions. Although the event is now geared mostly to tourists, it represents a unique opportunity to see regional dances from all the Mexican states.

Guelaguetza comes from the Zapotec language and means "the greatest of courtesies." It refers to the traditional way people exchanged gifts: helping each other build houses, tend to fields, assist with births and deaths. The name became linked with the Mondays of the Hill fiestas in the 20th century. Since the 1930s local craftspeople would give gifts they made to guests assembled for the dances, and in 1951 the event became known as La Guelaguetza. In 1974 the state built a special amphitheater to hold the growing numbers of people attending what is now one of the most popular folk festivals in Mexico.

CONTACTS:
Turismo El Convento De Oaxaca
Calle 5 de Mayo 300 Centro
Oaxaca, 68000 Mexico
951-516-5791; fax: 951-514-0372
oaxacatours.mx/guelaguetza

◆ 1232 ◆ Guinea Independence Day
October 2

Guinea became an independent republic on this day in 1958, after having been a French colony since the late 19th century.

Independence Day is a national holiday celebrated all over the country with parades, dances, and sports competitions, especially in the capital city of Conakry.

◆ 1233 ◆ Guinea Second Republic Day
April 3

Guinea Second Republic Day commemorated an event from history. Guinea was ruled by a dictatorship led by Sekou Touré, who ruled the small West African nation for over 25 years (1958-1984). After Toure's death, a bloodless coup on April 3, 1984 ushered in what many Guineans refer to as the Second Republic, led by former lieutenant Lansana Conté. A military government assumed control of the county until 1993, the year Conté was elected president.

The observation of Second Republic Day was largely orchestrated by the government, and enthusiasm for the celebration waned over the years. In 2010, the country began the transition to democracy.

CONTACTS:
Guinea Embassy

2112 Leroy Pl. N.W.
Washington, D.C. 20008
202-986-4300
guineaembassyusa.com

◆ 1234 ◆ Guinea-Bissau and Cape Verde National Heroes' Day
January 20

Citizens of Guinea-Bissau and Cape Verde have great reverence for Amílcar Cabral (1921–1973), a nationalist leader who was assassinated before he could see his native Guinea-Bissau and nearby Cape Verde achieve independence from Portugal. The two countries, which collaborated in an independence campaign begun in the 1950s, settled on January 20 as their National Heroes' Day because it falls on the anniversary of Cabral's murder. That tragic event further stirred the fire of the liberation movement, and the country became independent in 1974.

A public holiday in Guinea-Bissau and Cape Verde, National Heroes' Day commemorates the legacies of Cabral and other freedom fighters. In years past, the government has issued stamps and bank notes with Cabral's image on National Heroes' Day. Leftist associations in West Africa and throughout the world have observed the day by holding symposiums on the writings and political theories of Cabral.

CONTACTS:
Cape Verdean Museum Exhibit
1003 Waterman Ave.
P.O. Box 14187
East Providence, RI 02914
401-228-7292
www.capeverdeanmuseum.org

◆ 1235 ◆ Guinea-Bissau Independence Day
September 24

After more than 500 years of Portuguese rule, Guinea-Bissau (formerly known as Portuguese Guinea) declared itself an independent republic on September 24, 1973. The U.S. recognized it as such on September 10, 1974, and Portugal followed suit the same day.

September 24 is a national holiday in Guinea-Bissau.

CONTACTS:
American Embassy Dakar
Route des Almadies - BP 49
 Senegal
221-33-879-0000
guinea-bissau.usvpp.gov

◆ 1236 ◆ Guru Arjan, Martyrdom of
May-June; during the Sikh month of Jaith

Guru Arjan (1563-1606) was the fifth of the ten Sikh gurus and the first to be martyred. He became guru in 1581 and is known for many achievements—among them the building of the Golden Temple in the city of Amritsar and compiling the *Adi Granth*, the "First Collection" of Sikh sacred scripture.

Because Guru Arjan was a threat to his power, Jehangir, the emperor of the Mughal Empire, arrested him. Tradition has it that Arjun was tortured to death by being boiled alive while sitting on a burning hot plate. Although he accepted his death peacefully, Arjan left instructions for his successor, Har Gobind, to permit the Sikhs to take up arms to protect the innocent.

People commemorate Guru Arjan's martyrdom by visiting *gurdwaras*, places of worship, for special services. In India, where the weather is exceptionally hot at this time of year, it is traditional for Sikhs to make drinks available to every passerby—a reminder that part of Guru Arjan's torture before his death was being deprived of water.

CONTACTS:
Shiromani Gurdwara Parbandhak Committee
Teja Singh Samundri Hall
Sri Harmandir Sahib Complex
Amritsar, Punjab India
91-183-2553-957-5859; fax: 91-183-255-3919
sgpc.net

◆ 1237 ◆ Guru Gobind Singh, Birthday of
December-January; during the Sikh month of Pausa (Poh)

Born in 1666, Guru Gobind Singh was the last of the ten Sikh gurus. His father, GURU TEGH BAHADUR, was the ninth guru. He is best known for establishing the *Khalsa*, the spiritual brotherhood devoted to defending Sikhism. Guru Gobind Singh is also remembered for his teachings, which include the ideas that living with love, charity, and integrity was more important than observing religious rituals and that men and women are equal.

Guru Gobind Singh was the last guru because, instead of appointing a human successor, he believed that the *Granth Sahib*, the Sikh scriptures, should serve as an eternal Guru to the Sikh community (*see* GURU GRANTH SAHIB, INSTALLATION OF). His birthday is celebrated by Sikhs in India and around the world with festivities similar to those marking the birthday of Guru Nanak (*see* GURU PARAB). They include a three-day-long, continuous reading of the *Guru Granth Sahib*, processions, and the singing of sacred songs. Sporting contests and other games are also popular. Many Sikhs go on pilgrimage to the Golden Temple at Amritsar (*see* GURU ARJAN, MARTYRDOM OF) and to the shrine marking the site of Gobind Singh's birth, Takht Patna Sahib.

CONTACTS:
Guru Gobind Singh Sikh Center
1065 Old Country Rd.
Plainview, NY 11803
516-931-9304
plainview-gurudwara.appspot.com

♦ 1238 ♦ **Guru Granth Sahib, Installation of the**
September-October; during the Sikh month of Asun

GURU GOBIND SINGH, the last of the ten Sikh gurus or spiritual leaders, did not choose a human successor before he died in 1708. Instead, he called his followers together and told them that in the future, the *Adi Granth*, or Sikh scriptures, would serve as Guru. The *Adi Granth* was renamed the Guru Granth Sahib and was installed as the 11th and perpetual Guru to the Sikhs.

The anniversary of the installation of the Guru Granth Sahib is observed with ceremonies in the *gurdwaras*, or houses of worship. These often include readings, the singing of hymns, lectures, and the serving of free meals. A continuous reading of the entire Guru Granth Sahib, which is 1,430 pages long and takes approximately three days to read, may also be conducted. The anniversary of the installation is also a popular day for Sikhs to rededicate themselves to their faith.

CONTACTS:
Baba Makhan Shah Lubana Gurdwara
113-10 101 Ave.
Richmond Hill, NY 11419
718-805-6941
www.worldgurudwaras.com

♦ 1239 ♦ **Guru Har Krishan, Birthday of**
June-July; during the Sikh month of Har

Har Krishan (1656-64) was the eighth of the ten Sikh gurus or prophets on whose teaching the religion is based. He is often referred to as the "Child Guru" because he was only five years old when he succeeded his father, Guru Har Rai, who died in 1661. Har Krishan himself died of smallpox at the age of eight, so he remained a child throughout his brief time as guru.

The anniversary of his birth is celebrated by Sikhs around the world with special services in the *gurdwaras* (houses of worship) and with readings from the GURU GRANTH SAHIB, the Sikh scriptures.

CONTACTS:
Gururdwara Sri Guru Harkrishan Sahib Ji
12 Sherborne St.
Manchester, M3 1FE United Kingdom
44-07882-503-160; fax: 44-161-835-2125
www.gsghks.org.uk

♦ 1240 ♦ **Guru Parab**
October-November; full moon day of Hindu month of Kartika

Guru Nanak (1469-1539), was the founder of the Sikh Dharma faith (Sikhism), which was based on a belief in one god and on the rejection of idolatry and caste distinctions. In Pakistan at Nanak's birthplace, Talwandi (now Nankana Sahib, near Lahore, Pakistan), there is a shrine and a holy tank where thousands of Sikhs congregate on this day for a huge fair and

festival. Here and at Sikh shrines everywhere, the holy scripture, GURU GRANTH SAHIB, is read continuously and recited on Nanak's birthday. Food is distributed, and processions are common.

Nanak was followed by nine other gurus, under whom Sikhism gradually developed. Other Guru Parabs commemorate these later leaders. For example, the Guru Parab in honor of GURU GOBIND SINGH (1666-1708) is observed during the month of Pausa (December-January).

CONTACTS:
Ministry of Tourism, Government of India
1270 Ave. of the Americas
Ste. 303
New York, NY 10020
212-586-4901; fax: 212-582-3274
tourism.gov.in

♦ 1241 ♦ **Guru Purnima**
June-July; full moon day of Hindu month of Asadha

In Hinduism, a guru is a personal teacher or guide who has already attained spiritual insight. The tutorial approach to religious instruction has always been emphasized in India, and in ancient times it was the guru who personally transmitted his knowledge of the Vedas, sacred Hindu books, to his student. The student often lived at the home of his guru and looked up to him with devotion.

Guru Purnima, or **Asadha Purnima,** is the day set aside for the veneration of the guru. In ancient times, when students were educated in ashrams and gurukuls, this was the day they would honor their teachers, pay their fees, and give them presents. It was customary to fast on this day and to seek the guru's blessing.

This day is also known as **Vyasa Purnima** after Rishi Vyasa (ca. fifth century B.C.E.), a famous guru who is said to have compiled the four Vedas, the *Mahabharata*, and the Puranas, a series of 18 epics dealing with creation and the gods in the form of fables, legends, and tales.

CONTACTS:
Nepal Tourism Board
Bhrikuti Mandap
P.O. Box: 11018
Kathmandu, 11018 Nepal
977-1-4256909; fax: 977-1-4256910
welcomenepal.com

♦ 1242 ♦ **Guru Ram Das, Birthday of**
September-October; during the Sikh month of Asun

Ram Das (1534-1581) was the fourth of the ten Sikh gurus and the son-in-law of Amar Das, the third guru. After he was chosen to succeed his father-in-law, his name was changed from Bhai Jetha to Ram Das, which means "God's Servant." His birthday is celebrated during the month of Asun (September-October) in Sikh *gurdwaras*, or houses of worship, with prayers, the singing of hymns, and with readings from the GURU GRANTH SAHIB, the Sikh holy scriptures.

CONTACTS:
Shiromani Gurdwara Parbandhak Committee
Teja Singh Samundri Hall
Sri Harmandir Sahib Complex
Amritsar, Punjab India
91-98148-98451
sgpc.net

◆ 1243 ◆ Guru Tegh Bahadur, Martyrdom of
November-December; during the Sikh month of Magar

Tegh Bahadur (1621-1675) was the ninth of the ten Sikh gurus, or spiritual teachers. His son, GURU GOBIND SINGH, was the last human guru. When Tegh Bahadur was 43 years old, he was installed as guru. The tyrant Aurangzeb was the Muslim emperor of India at the time, and his goal was to make everyone in his domain Muslim. Then, as now, most people living in India were Hindu, though there were also small populations of Sikhs, Jains, and other religious groups. Under Aurangzeb's rule, everyone was forced to convert to Islam under threat of death.

At the behest of a group of Hindu priests, Tegh Bahadur went to Delhi in November 1675 to meet with Aurangzeb, who put him in prison. Legend has it that before Tegh Bahadur was beheaded (since he would not convert to Islam), he wrote a message which read, "I gave my head but not my faith." Guru Tegh Bahadur is remembered for giving his life to preserve the integrity of the Sikh religion.

Sikhs everywhere observe his martyrdom with religious processions and pilgrimages at *gurdwaras*, or houses of worship, with a special devotion to him, and especially at the site of his martyrdom in Delhi where the Gurdwara Sisganj temple was built.

CONTACTS:
Delhi Tourism and Transportation Development Corporation
18-A, D.D.A.SCO Complex
Defence Colony
New Delhi, 110024 Delhi
91-11-24647005; fax: 91-11-24697352
www.delhitourism.gov.in/delhitourism/tourist_place/gtb.jsp

◆ 1244 ◆ Gustavus Adolphus Day (Gustaf Adolfsdagen)
November 6

Gustavus Adolphus (1594-1632) was the king of Sweden (1611-32) who laid the foundations of the modern Swedish state and turned the country into a major European power. By resolving the long-standing constitutional struggle between the crown and the aristocracy, he was able to achieve sweeping reforms in the fields of administrative organization, economic development, and particularly education. Among other things, he created the *Gymnasia* in 1620, which provided for secondary education in Sweden, and gave the University of Uppsala the financial support it needed to flourish.

King Gustav II was killed during the Thirty Years' War while leading a cavalry charge at the Battle of Lützen on November 6, 1632, turning a tactical victory into a national tragedy for the Swedes. The anniversary of his death is observed throughout Sweden with patriotic demonstrations—particularly in Skansen, Stockholm's outdoor museum. Enormous bonfires are built on Reindeer Mountain and processions of students carry lighted torches through the museum grounds.

CONTACTS:
Vasa Museum
Galärvarvsvägen 14
Box 27131
Stockholm, 10252 Sweden
46-8-519-548-00; fax: 46-8-519-548-88
www.vasamuseet.se

◆ 1245 ◆ Guthrie (Woody) Folk Festival
Week of July 14

Fans of folk icon Woody Guthrie (1912–1967) mark his legacy with an annual music festival in his birthplace of Okehmah, Okla. The event is held on the weekend nearest his birthday, July 14.

The festival, introduced in 1998, is a recently created tradition. For the inaugural festival Okemah was treated to performances by folk stars Billy Bragg and Guthrie's son, Arlo Guthrie, as well as to the dedication of a full-body bronze statue of the legend that stands along the town's main street.

Organizing the festival is the Woody Guthrie Coalition, which shares Guthrie's egalitarian vision to bring music to people by maintaining a free admission policy, even for folk music stars like Jackson Browne, Pete Seeger, and the Kingston Trio. Typically, the only concert that charges admission is for raising the festival's funds. This benefit show is usually held at the Crystal Theatre, a venue where Guthrie had performed as a child.

Many music fans stay until the end of the weekend for the final Sunday performance. This concert, called the Hoot for Huntington's, raises money to treat the disease that took Guthrie's life.

CONTACTS:
Woody Guthrie Folk Festival - Woody Guthrie Coalition, Inc.
2805 N. McKinley
Oklahoma City, OK 73106
www.woodyguthrie.com

◆ 1246 ◆ Guyana Independence Day
May 26

This public holiday marks Guyana's independence from Britain on this day in 1966.

Republic Day, or *Mashramani*, is another national holiday, commemorating February 23, 1970, when Guyana became a republic.

CONTACTS:
Guyana Tourism Authority

National Exhibition Center
Sophia
Guyana
592-219-0094 or 592-219-0096; fax: 592-219-0093
www.guyana-tourism.com

◆ 1247 ◆ Gwangiu Kimchi Festival
October or November

The city of Gwangiu in South Korea holds an annual event to celebrate the nation's favorite condiment, kimchi. A fermented, pickled cabbage, kimchi is produced in the autumn in quantities to last through the winter.

The event, which typically runs from Wednesday to Sunday, celebrates everything kimchi. Visitors can learn about the history and different varieties of kimchi on video and through live demonstrations, sample freshly made kimchi, and purchase many types to try at home. The beloved pickle is also the subject of exhibitions about its history, globalization, and manufacture. There are competitions for the best kimchi and the best dish to eat with it. Novices can try their hand at making their own kimchi during a hands-on workshop. In addition to the food-related array of activities, the event treats participants to performances of music and dance ranging from traditional Korean to that of many other nations. Although kimchi has been a feature of Korean cuisine for thousands of years, the festival was launched in the last decade by the city of Gwangiu, which is known for its rich culinary tradition.

CONTACTS:
Gwangiu World Kimchi Cultural Festival Committee
399-3, Maegok-dong
Buk-gu
Gwangju, 149-2 Korea
62-613-3641; fax: 62-613-3629
kimchi.gwangju.go.kr/EN

◆ 1248 ◆ Gyan Panchami
October; fifth day of the waxing half of the Hindu month of Karthik

Gyan Panchami is observed by followers of Jainism, one of the oldest religions in the world, and is regarded as their most important festival. Also known as *Laabh paachami*, the event centers on the worship of *gyan* or knowledge of karma, and underscores the importance of wisdom and morality. On this day, people venerate five types of knowledge: *Mati-Jnan* (knowledge attained through the mind and senses); *Shrut-Jnan* (knowledge acquired from words, signs, and symbols); *Avadhi-Jnan* (knowledge beyond the senses and the mind); *Manah Paryay-Jnan* (knowledge of another's thoughts); and *Keval-Jnan* (knowledge of the past, present, and future).

Traditionally, people clean their homes and perform special *pujas* (prayer rituals) at home and in temples. Religious books and scriptures are worshipped, and students and scholars pray for enlightenment. Some observe a vow of silence for the entire day, while others meditate, fast, and recite holy verses at temples. *Moksha*, or liberation from the cycle of birth and death, is regarded as the main objective of Gyan Panchami.

CONTACTS:
Federation of Jain Associations in North America
Jaina HQ
722 S. Main St.
Milpitas, CA 95035
510-730-0204
www.jaina.org

◆ 1249 ◆ Gyangzê Horse-Racing Festival
Four days in May-June

Masked and costumed dancers and traditional operas dominate the first day of this Tibetan festival. They are performed in the courtyard of the Kumbum, known for its 112 chapels and multi-tiered *stupas* or monuments. But the next three days are devoted to sporting events on horseback, the Tibetans being renowned for their horsemanship. Archers on horseback shoot at targets while riding at full gallop, and some events involve riding yaks instead of horses.

The festival commemorates the highest (in terms of altitude) battle in history, which took place between the Tibetans and the invading British troops in 1903. The British, under the command of Sir Francis Younghusband, slaughtered 600 Tibetans at Guru before moving on to Gyangzê. He then marched into the capital, Lhasa, and forced the acceptance of a trade treaty with the DALAI LAMA, Tibet's ruler.

CONTACTS:
NAVO (Nature Adventure Voyage Off-road)
1-1-503, Fushan International Bldg.
No.28 Shang chi St.
Chengdu, 610041 China
86-28-8611-7722; fax: 86-28-8611-9977
www.china-festival.cn

◆ 1250 ◆ Gynaecocratia
January 8

The Greek title of this observance is a word that means female rule or government. This stab at feminist revolt is of long tradition in northern Greece, where it is common for women to do all the household work and for most men to take life easy in cafes.

Today in the villages of Komotini, Xanthi, Kilkis, and Serres, that standard is reversed for a day when Gynaecocratia is celebrated. The women gather in village cafes to socialize, while the men stay at home cleaning house, tending the babies, and generally looking after household tasks. At dusk, the menjoin their wives in celebrations.

CONTACTS:
Greek National Tourism Organisation
305 E. 47th St.
2nd Fl.
New York, NY 10017
212-421-5777; fax: 212-826-6940
www.visitgreece.gr

H

♦ 1251 ♦ **Hachinohe Enburi**
February 17-20

The people of Hachinohe in Japan celebrate Hachinohe Enburi, an agricultural festival that marks the last days of winter and heralds the arrival of spring. The event, which has been observed for more than eight centuries, is a form of folk ritual performed to usher in a bountiful harvest for the coming year. Following a visit to the Shinra Jinja Shinto shrine, performers parade through the city wearing colorful farming attire and performing dances that showcase traditional farming techniques. Celebrants wear straw-woven shoes with straw gaiters and large headgear called *eboshi* in the shape of horse heads, honoring the importance of animals in traditional agriculture. The festival takes its name from farm tools called *eburi*, which the folk dancers carry while depicting the planting of rice with their unique body movements and songs.

CONTACTS:
Japan National Tourim Organization
1 Grand Central Pl.
60 E. 42nd St., Ste. 448
New York, NY 10165
212-757-5640; fax: 212-307-6754
www.jnto.go.jp/eng

♦ 1252 ♦ **Hadaka Matsuri (Naked Festival)**
January or February, depending on location

Hadaka Matsuri—which means, literally, "naked festival"—is a Shinto tradition observed all over Japan, usually not long after NEW YEAR'S DAY or OSHOGATSU. The young men who participate are naked except for traditional white loincloths known as *fundoshi* or *mawashi*. At the ringing of the temple bell, large numbers of them attempt to climb up a thick rope suspended from the temple ceiling. Because the first to reach the top will have good fortune in the coming year, there is often a good deal of jockeying for position on the rope.

Sometimes the participants in Hadaka Matsuri immerse themselves in a river beforehand to purify themselves. Occasionally several semi-naked young men will carry a *mikoshi*, or portable shrine, in the form of a horse, rice bale, or sake barrel into the river with them.

CONTACTS:
Japan National Tourism Organization
1 Grand Central Pl.
60 E. 42nd St.
Ste. 448
New York, NY 10165
212-757-5640; fax: 212-307-6754
www.jnto.go.jp

♦ 1253 ♦ **Haile Selassie's Birthday**
July 23

Haile Selassie I (1892-1975), emperor of Ethiopia from 1930 to 1974, was born Tafari Makonnen; he became Prince (or *Ras*) Tafari in 1916. Among the Jamaicans known as Rastafarians, Selassie was believed to be the Messiah, and Ethiopia was identified with heaven. Rastafarian theology and political belief was based on the superiority of the black man and the repatriation of black people to Ethiopia.

Ethiopians still celebrate Haile Selassie's birthday. During the years of his reign as emperor, Selassie would stand on the balcony of his palace in Addis Ababa and greet the thousands of well-wishers who gathered there on his birthday.

See also ETHIOPIA NATIONAL DAY and HAILE SELASSIE'S CORONATION DAY.

CONTACTS:
Embassy of Ethiopia
3506 International Dr. N.W.
Washington, D.C. 20008
202-364-1200; fax: 202-587-0195
www.ethiopianembassy.org

♦ 1254 ♦ **Haile Selassie's Coronation Day**
November

The Rastafarians (or Ras Tafarians), members of a political-religious movement among the black population of Jamaica, worship Haile Selassie I, "Might of the Trinity." His original name was Tafari Makonnen (1892-1975), and he was emperor of Ethiopia under the name *Ras* (meaning "Prince") Tafari. Rastafarians consider the Ethiopian emperor the Messiah and son of God, and the champion of their race. Their beliefs, which combine political militancy and religious mysticism, include taboos on funerals, second-hand clothing, physical contact with whites, the eating of pork, and all magic and witchcraft.

The Rastafarians' most important celebration is the anniversary of Haile Selassie's Coronation Day, which occurred on November 2, 1930. The dedication of babies to Ras Tafari, recitations, and singing are typically part of the celebrations on this day.

CONTACTS:
House of His Majesty
Fairfield House
2 Kelston Rd. (via Partis Way)
Bath BA1 3QJ United Kingdom
44-122-546-4165
www.houseofhismajesty.com

♦ 1255 ♦ **Haiti Ancestors' Day**
January 2

Haitians devote the first two days of the calendar year to commemorating the nation's past along with celebrating the new year. The Independence Day festivities that occur on the first day of the year continue into **Jour des Aieux** (Ancestors' Day), an occasion for remembering the founders of Haiti and the individuals who sacrificed their lives during the independence struggle of the early 19th century. The tributes that are held on Ancestors' Day in Haiti and in immigrant communities in major U.S. cities are testimony to the emphasis that Haitian culture places on remembering the country's forefathers.

A large meal often accompanies the day's festivities. Military processions, a common event on Independence Day, may also take place on Ancestors' Day. In years past, particularly during the reign of President Francois Duvalier (1971–1986), the executive leader used this day to deliver radio and television speeches to the nation.

CONTACTS:
Embassy of the Republic of Haiti
2311 Massachusetts Ave. N.W.
Washington, D.C. 20008
202-332-4090; fax: 202-745-7215
www.haiti.org

♦ 1256 ♦ **Haiti Anniversary of the Death of Jean-Jacques Dessalines**
October 17

A former slave, Jean-Jacques Dessalines (ca. 1758–Oct. 17, 1806) played a pivotal role under the command of Toussaint L'Ouverture in the Haitian struggle for independence from France. Following the creation of an independent Haiti, Dessalines ruled Haiti as Emperor Jacques I for two years before he was assassinated in a coup. It is Dessalines' legacy as a freedom fighter and a founding father—rather than his autocratic reign as emperor—that Haitians remember on this official holiday commemorating the anniversary of his death.

Haitians observe the holiday by participating in street parades in the capital city of Port-au-Prince and other cities. In 2012, for the 206th anniversary, Haitian President Michel Martelly and Prime Minister Laurent Lamothe were on hand at an official wreath-laying at the statue of Dessalines. In his speech at the ceremony, President Martelly urged Haitians to "arm themselves with the courage, bravery and patience" of Dessalines and to use the founding father as a role model.

In New York City, which is home to tens of thousands of Haitian immigrants, October 17 is also observed with cultural performances and presentations on Dessalines and Haitian history. The Haitian Lawyers Leadership Network, a U.S.-based political advocacy group, marked the bicentennial of Dessalines' death by holding events throughout the month of October.

CONTACTS:
Embassy of the Republic of Haiti
2311 Massachusetts Ave. N.W.
Washington, D.C. 20008
202-332-4090; fax: 202-745-7215
www.haiti.org

♦ 1257 ♦ **Haiti Battle of Vertières' Day**
November 18

This official public holiday memorializes the last battle for Haitian independence on November 18, 1803, in which Haitian rebels defeated the French colonialists. The victory at Vertières, near the present-day port city of Cap-Haitien, signified the end of a long freedom struggle that stretched out over two major phases. Less than two months after the battle, Haiti became the first black independent republic.

The day was formerly known as **Army Day** or **Armed Forces Day**, and military ceremonies were once the main event. Army parades were staged along the Champs des Mars in the capital city of Port-au-Prince and on the lawn of the National Palace. However, when President Jean-Bertrand Aristide abolished a Haitian army notorious for its brutality in the early 1990s, festival officials phased the armed forces out of the public ceremonies.

The Battle of Vertières Day in 2003 marked the bicentennial anniversary of the victory over the French. In Cap-Haitien, standing before the monument of the Heroes of the Battle of Vertières, then President Aristide gave a stirring speech honoring the victorious soldiers. In 2013, anti-government demonstrators took to the streets of Port-Au-Prince, Haiti, commemorating the Battle of Vertières Day by venting their frustration via protests against the current Martelly government.

CONTACTS:
Toussaint Louverture Historical Society
P.O. Box 4115
Silver Spring, MD 20904
fax: 301-680-9095
toussaintlouverturehs.org

Embassy of the Republic of Haiti
2311 Massachusetts Ave. N.W.

Washington, D.C. 20008
202-332-4090; fax: 202-745-7215
www.haiti.org

♦ 1258 ♦ Haiti Flag and University Day
May 18

An inscription on the Haitian flag's coat of arms reads: "L'Union fait la force" (Unity Makes Strong). National unity is a primary theme of Flag and University Day, which is an independence celebration as well as an occasion to recognize the country's educational system.

For over a century, the celebration was devoted solely to the national emblem. Flag Day became an annual celebration shortly after Catherine Flon sewed the first red and blue flag in 1803, a year before Haiti won its independence from France. Under instructions from Jean-Jacques Dessalines, Haiti's first ruler, Flon used the template of the French flag's tri-color scheme but removed the white stripe. The remaining blue and red stripes symbolized the black and mulatto citizens who made up Haiti's majority population.

The government incorporated University Day as part of the celebration in 1919. Dantes Bellegarde, then minister of public instruction, advocated for the day because he believed that the sanctity of the educational system was being threatened by the U.S. occupation of Haiti that had begun in 1915.

Haitians wave flags throughout the day's parades and fairs, which take place throughout Haiti as well as in New York and Miami, two cities with large Haitian communities. People also attend presentations by experts on the country's flag and Haitian history.

CONTACTS:
Haitian-Americans United Inc.
10 Fairway St.
Ste. 218
P.O. Box 260440
Mattapan, MA 02126
617-298-2976
www.hauinc.org

♦ 1259 ♦ Haiti Independence Day
January 1

The people of Haiti celebrate both NEW YEAR'S DAY and Independence Day on January 1, the day on which they declared their independence from the French in 1804. Thousands of people assemble in the capital city of Port-au-Prince to see the parades and to visit the National Palace on the Champs de Mars. They set off fireworks, dance in the streets, and sing the national anthem, which honors their founder, Jean-Jacques Dessalines, the hero of the anti-French revolt.

According to Haitian custom, whatever happens to someone on January 1 is indicative of what will happen to them during the coming year, motivating even the poorest people to make an effort to put on new clothes, to visit their friends,

and to give and receive gifts in the hope that these efforts will be rewarded in the coming year.

CONTACTS:
Embassy of the Republic of Haiti
2311 Massachusetts Ave. N.W.
Washington, D.C. 20008
202-332-4090; fax: 202-745-7215
www.haiti.org

♦ 1260 ♦ Hakata Dontaku
May 3-4

The largest festival in Japan, Hakata Dontaku is held in Fukuoka City (Fukuoka Prefecture) during Golden Week, the first week in May. This festival attracts more than two million spectators every year because Golden Week is a national holiday encompassing Children's Day (*see* KODOMO-NO-HI), GREENERY DAY, JAPANESE NATIONAL FOUNDATION DAY and JAPAN CONSTITUTION MEMORIAL DAY.

The festival originated in the Muromachi Period (1333-1568) as a procession of the merchants of Hakata, an old section of Fukuoka City, paying their new year visit to the *daimyo*, or feudal lord. The name of the holiday curiously is thought to have derived from the Dutch word *Zondag*, meaning "Sunday," which was broadened to mean "holiday," and corrupted into *Dontaku*.

The festival highlight is a three-hour parade with legendary gods on horseback, floats, and musicians playing *samisens* (a three-stringed instrument similar to a guitar), flutes, and drums.

CONTACTS:
Japan National Tourism Organization
1 Grand Central Pl.
60 E. 42nd St.
Ste. 448
New York, NY 10165
212-757-5640; fax: 212-307-6754
www.japantravelinfo.com

♦ 1261 ♦ Hakata Gion Yamagasa
July 1-15

The GION MATSURI at Kyoto is the model for several other Gion festivals in Japan, and the largest of these is the Gion Yamagasa Festival at Fukuoka. The festival involves townspeople on both sides as well as the creators of the famous Hakata dolls. The elaborate floats for which the festival is famous are called *yamagasa*, and beautiful new dolls are made for them each year.

The festival begins on July 1, when participants purify themselves by collecting sand from the seashore. They put the sand in boxes which are slung beneath the yamagasa. The men wear headbands, *happi* coats, and traditional Japanese loincloths. The highlight of the festival occurs on the morning of July 15, when the Oiyama race is held. This is a five-kilometer race in which teams of 28 men run while carrying yamagasa weighing about a ton. Traditional Noh dramas are performed at the Kushida Shrine in Fukuoka.

CONTACTS:
Fukuoka Convention & Visitors Bureau
1-11-17 Tenjin Chuo-ku
Fukuoka 810-0001 Japan
81-92-733-5050; fax: 81-92-733-5055
www.welcome-fukuoka.or.jp

♦ 1262 ♦ **Hala Festival**
Mid to late February

The Hala Festival has been held in Kuwait every year since 1999 to celebrate the coming of spring and to promote Arab culture and the local economy. The festival begins with an opening carnival and parade, culminating in a lavish fireworks display that draws up to 250,000 people. Over the course of the subsequent two weeks, visitors are able to enjoy such features as performances of music from around the Middle East, exhibitions of calligraphy and cars, sporting events, and religious events. There are also many activities for children. Shopping is a focal point of the festival, with more than 100 local merchants taking part in prize drawings and special offers, including the sale of millions of retail-discount coupons to festival-goers. The city is swathed in lights, mirroring the bright flowers that bloom on the desert to herald the start of spring.

CONTACTS:
Central Agency for Information Technology
Audit Bureau Bldg. Next to Sharq Police Stn.
Ahmed Al Jabir St.
Safat 13009 Kuwait
965-2-242-6077 or 965-2-242-3039; fax: 965-2-240-0222
www.e.gov.kw

♦ 1263 ♦ **Halashashti**
August-September; sixth day of waning half of Hindu month of Bhadrapada

This Hindu festival is often referred to as **Balarama Shashti**, after Krishna's older brother, Balarama, who was born on this day. Balarama's weapon was a plough, so it is also the day on which farmers in India worship the *hala*, or plough. They apply powdered rice and turmeric to the plough's iron blade and decorate it with flowers. A small piece of ground is sanctified and plastered with cow dung, then a small pool of water is dug in the middle and branches of plum, fig, and other fruit trees are planted there. Some women fast all day in the belief that it will ensure happiness, prosperity, and longevity to their sons. When the fast is broken in the evening, there is a great feast and celebration.

CONTACTS:
Bharatiya Kisan Sangh
Gujarat Pradesh Karyalaya
Balram Mandir Parisar
Sector-12 D
Gandhinagar, Gujarat India
91-79-2322-4916; fax: 91-79-5572-8442
www.bksgujarat.org.in

♦ 1264 ♦ **Halcyon Days**
December 14-28

The ancient Greeks called the seven days preceding and the seven days following the WINTER SOLSTICE the "Halcyon Days." According to one legend, the halcyon bird, or kingfisher, nested during this period. Because she built her nest on the water, the gods granted her a respite from storms and high seas so that she could hatch and rear her young.

But Greek mythology has it that Halcyone (or Alcyone), Ceyx's wife and one of Aeolus's daughters, drowned herself when she learned her husband had drowned. The gods took pity on her and transformed them both into kingfishers, and Zeus commanded the seas to be still during these days. Thus it was considered a period when sailors could navigate in safety.

Today, the expression "halcyon days" has come to mean a period of tranquillity, often used as a nostalgic reference to times past.

CONTACTS:
Greek National Tourism Organisation
305 E. 47th St.
2nd Fl.
New York, NY 10017
212-421-5777; fax: 212-826-6940
www.visitgreece.gr

♦ 1265 ♦ **Half Moon Bay Art and Pumpkin Festival**
October, weekend after Columbus Day

This festival, highlighted by a Great Pumpkin Weigh-Off, has been held since 1971 in Half Moon Bay, Calif. The weigh-off winner gets $5 per pound for the heaviest pumpkin; winning pumpkins have weighed in excess of 900 pounds. Other festival features are a Great Pumpkin Parade, arts and crafts, food concessions selling pumpkin bread, pumpkin crepes, pumpkin ice cream, and pumpkin strudel, and entertainment that includes live music, puppet shows, magicians, jugglers, clowns, and professional pumpkin carvers. There are competitions in pumpkin carving and pie eating.

Pumpkins have been grown in the Half Moon Bay area for decades but were used for cattle feed until the 1920s when two farmer brothers decided to try them as human food. That began a surge in pumpkin popularity. The pumpkin festival has also surged; attendance is estimated at 300,000.

CONTACTS:
Half Moon Bay Art & Pumpkin Festival
Main St.
Half Moon Bay, CA 94019
650-726-9652
pumpkinfest.miramarevents.com

♦ 1266 ♦ **Halifax Day**
April 12

Also known as **Halifax Resolves Day**, **Halifax Resolutions Day**, **Halifax Independence Day**, or **Halifax Resolutions of**

Independence Day, this is the day on which, in the spring of 1776, North Carolina's delegates to the Second Continental Congress were given permission to join with representatives from other colonies in declaring their independence from British rule. As the first official sanction of separation from Great Britain, the Halifax Resolutions helped lay the groundwork for the American Revolution.

Halifax Day observances take place in Halifax with reenactments and living history camps.

CONTACTS:
Halifax County Convention and Visitors Bureau
260 Premier Blvd.
Roanoke Rapids, NC 27870
252-535-1687 or 800-522-4282
www.visithalifax.com

♦ 1267 ♦ Halloween
October 31

Halloween has its ultimate origins in the ancient Celtic harvest festival, SAMHAIN, a time when people believed that the spirits of the dead roamed the earth. Irish settlers brought their Halloween customs—which included bobbing for apples and lighting jack-o'-lanterns—to America in the 1840s.

In the United States children go from house to house in costume—often dressed as ghosts, skeletons, or vampires—on Halloween saying, "Trick or treat!" Though for the most part the threat is in jest, the "trick" part of the children's cry carries the implication that if they don't receive a treat, the children will subject that house to some kind of prank, such as marking its windows with a bar of soap or throwing eggs at it. Most receive treats in the form of candy or money. But Halloween parties and parades are popular with adults as well.

Because nuts were a favorite means of foretelling the future on this night, **All Hallows' Eve** in England became known as **Nutcrack Night**. Other British names for the day include **Bob Apple Night**, **Duck** (or **Dookie**) **Apple Night**, **Crab Apple Night**, **Thump-the-door Night**, and, in Wales, APPLE AND CANDLE NIGHT. In the United States it is sometimes referred to as **Trick or Treat Night**.

See also MISCHIEF NIGHT.

CONTACTS:
The Library of Congress
American Folklife Center
101 Independence Ave. S.E.
Washington, D.C. 20540
202-707-5510; fax: 202-707-2076
www.loc.gov

♦ 1268 ♦ Halloween (Ireland)
October 31

In Ireland, HALLOWEEN is observed with traditional foods and customs that are largely based on superstitions or folk beliefs. One of the dishes served is known as *colcannon*, or *callcannon*. It consists of mashed potatoes, parsnips, and chopped onions. A ring, a thimble, a small china doll, and a coin are mixed in, and the one who finds the ring will be married within a year. The one who finds the doll will have children, the one who finds the coin will be wealthy, and the one who finds the thimble will never marry. *Barmbrack*—a cake made with a ring concealed inside—is a variation on the same theme. Whoever gets the ring in his or her slice will be the first to marry. Sometimes there is a nut inside, and the one who finds the nut will marry a widow or widower. If the kernel of the nut is shriveled, the finder will never marry.

Nuts have traditionally played a role in Halloween celebrations in the British Isles. In England, Halloween is known as **Nutcrack Night**. In Ireland, a popular superstition involved putting three nuts on the hearth and naming them after lovers. If one of the nuts cracked or jumped, that lover would be unfaithful; if it began to burn, it meant that he was interested. If a girl named one of the nuts after herself and it burned together with the nut named after her lover, it meant that they would be married.

The jack-o'-lantern, according to the Irish, was the invention of a man named Jack who was too greedy to get into heaven and couldn't get into hell because he had tricked the devil. The devil threw him a lighted coal from hell instead, and Jack stuck it in the turnip he was eating. According to the legend, he used it to light his way as he wandered the earth looking for a final resting place.

CONTACTS:
Brú na Bóinne Visitor Centre
Co. Meath
Donore Ireland
353-41-988-0300; fax: 353-41-982-3071
www.newgrange.com

♦ 1269 ♦ Halloween (Isle of Man)
October 31

In the early part of this century, HALLOWEEN was referred to as **Thump-the-Door Night** on the Isle of Man because boys would gather outside the house of someone they didn't like and bombard the door with turnips or cabbages until the inhabitants gave them some money to make them go away—much like the trick-or-treating that goes on in the United States. As might be expected, the game occasionally got out of control, provoking complaints and sometimes legal action. Eventually it fell out of favor.

Halloween is commonly called **Hollantide** on the Isle of Man because there was a time when it marked the beginning of the church year. This was based on the Celtic custom of beginning the year in November instead of in January.

CONTACTS:
Isle of Man Tourism Division
Dept. of Economic Development
1st Fl., St George's Ct.
Upper Church St.
Douglas IM1 1EX Isle of Man
44-1624-686-766
www.visitisleofman.com

♦ 1270 ♦ Halloween (New Orleans, Louisiana)
October 31

HALLOWEEN is a spooky and macabre celebration in New Orleans, La., when costumed revelers parade up and down Bourbon Street and actors dressed as legendary characters are on the streets to narrate their grisly histories. The sheriff's Haunted House in City Park is a standard feature, and a Ghost Train rolls through the park while costumed police officers jump out of bushes to spook the riders. The Voodoo Museum usually offers a special Halloween ritual in which people may see voodoo rites. Walking tours take visitors to such haunts as Le Pretre House, where a Turkish sultan and his five wives were murdered one night in 1792; it is said that their ghosts still have noisy parties.

On a more solemn note, the St. Louis Cathedral holds vigil services on Halloween, and several masses on ALL SAINTS' DAY. On the afternoon of that day, the archbishop leaves the cathedral for St. Louis Cemetery No. 1 to bless the newly scrubbed and decorated tombs.

CONTACTS:
Molly's at the Market
1107 Decatur St.
New Orleans, LA 70116
504-525-5169; fax: 504-566-0630
www.mollysatthemarket.net

♦ 1271 ♦ Halloween (Scotland)
October 31

Many of the traditional customs associated with HALLOWEEN in Scotland are described in the famous poem of that name by the Scottish poet Robert BURNS, although not all of them are still observed. "Pulling the kail" referred to the custom of sending boys and girls out into the garden (or kailyard) blindfolded. They were instructed to pull up the first plant they encountered and bring it into the house, where its size, shape, and texture would reveal the appearance and disposition of the finder's future husband or wife. It was also believed that by eating an apple in front of a mirror, a young woman could see the reflection of her future mate peering over her shoulder.

Another custom referred to by Burns was known as "The Three Dishes," or *Luggies*. One was filled with clean water, one with dirty water, and one remained empty. They were arranged on the hearth, and as people were led into the room blindfolded, they would dip their fingers into one of the bowls. Choosing the clean water indicated that one would marry a maiden (or bachelor); the dirty water indicated marriage to a widow (or widower). The empty dish meant that the person was destined never to marry.

"Dipping the shift" was another popular superstition regarding marital prospects. If someone dipped a shirt-sleeve in a south-running stream and hung it up by the fire to dry, the apparition of the person's future mate would come in to turn the sleeve.

Superstition surrounded death as well as marriage. It was customary on Halloween for each member of the family to put a stone in the fire and mark a circle around it. When the fire went out, the ashes were raked over the stones. If one of the stones was found out of place the next morning, it means that the person to whom it belonged would die within the year.

CONTACTS:
Scottish Government
St Andrew's House
Regent Rd.
Edinburgh EH1 3DG Scotland
44-1592-874-449
www.scotland.org

♦ 1272 ♦ Haloa
Late December or early January

The Haloa was an ancient Greek festival in honor of Demeter and Dionysus. It took place in Eleusis near the time of the WINTER SOLSTICE. The Haloa is believed to have been an attempt to restore the earth's lost fertility and also, in years when it was obvious that the crops were not growing well, to reverse the course of nature and assist the weak shoots in surviving the winter months.

Only women attended the Haloa. Although there are many theories about what went on there, most involve lewd jokes and games, and uninhibited discussions about sex and illicit love. The celebrants carried sexual organs made out of clay, and pastries made to resemble sex organs were set out on the table. It was believed that such obscene behavior encouraged fertility, and it makes sense in view of the fact that the Haloa was held at a time of year when the fields were frozen and the growth of crops was at a temporary standstill. By manipulating sexual and agricultural symbols, by feasting and carrying on, the women attempted to "warm up" the earth and stimulate its dormant fertility.

CONTACTS:
Greek National Tourism Organisation
305 E. 47th St.
2nd Fl.
New York, NY 10017
212-421-5777; fax: 212-826-6940
www.visitgreece.gr

♦ 1273 ♦ Hambletonian Harness Racing Classic
First Saturday in August

Harness racing's most prestigious race for three-year-old trotters, the Hambletonian is a test of both speed and stamina. Currently held at the Meadowlands Racetrack in East Rutherford, New Jersey, the race dates back to 1926. It is always held on the first Saturday in August and is preceded by a week of other races with purses in the $500,000 range. The purse for the one-mile Hambletonian race is $1.2 million, and the winner usually goes on to take a divisional title.

CONTACTS:
The Hambletonian Society
Cranbury Gates Office Park
109 S. Main St.

Ste.18
Cranbury, NJ 08512
609-371-2211; fax: 609-371-8890
www.hambletonian.org

♦ 1274 ♦ Hana Matsuri (Flower Festival)
April 8

Hana Matsuri is a celebration of the Buddha's birthday, observed in Buddhist temples throughout Japan, where it is known as **Kambutsue**. The highlight of the celebration is a ritual known as *kambutsue* ("ceremony of 'baptizing' the Buddha"), in which a tiny bronze statue of the Buddha, standing in an open lotus flower, is anointed with sweet tea. People use a small bamboo ladle to pour the tea, made of hydrangea leaves, over the head of the statue. The custom is supposed to date from the seventh century, when perfume was used, as well as tea. Festivities often include a procession of children carrying flowers.

See also VESAK.

CONTACTS:
West Los Angeles Buddhist Temple
2003 Corinth Ave.
Los Angeles, CA 90025
310-477-7274; fax: 310-477-6674
westlosangelesbuddhisttemple.org

Japan National Tourism Organization
1 Grand Central Pl.
60 E. 42nd St.
Ste. 448
New York, NY 10165
212-757-5640; fax: 212-307-6754
www.jnto.go.jp

Hatsukaichi City Tourism
1-11-1 Shimohera
Hatsukaichi 738-8501 Japan
81-829-30-9141; fax: 81-829-31-0999
visit-miyajima-japan.com

♦ 1275 ♦ Hanagasa Odori
Varies

One of the largest festivals in the Tohoku region of Japan, Hanagasa Odori is held in Yamagata on August 5-7. Thousands of dancers holding *hanagasa*, which are hats made out of bamboo or rush and decorated with flowers, dance through the city while spectators cheer them on. The rhythmic pulse of the hanagasa songs keeps the dancers moving together as they march down the city streets yelling "Yassho! Makasho!" and twirling their hats to the left, right, up, and down.

The Hanagasa Festival held in Kyoto on October 9 features a procession of people holding large umbrellas decorated with flowers, but the overall effect is similar.

CONTACTS:
Yamagata Tourist Information Center
1-1-1, Kajo Central

Jonanmachi
Yamagata-shi, Yamagata Japan
81-23-647-2333; fax: 81-23-646-6333
yamagatakanko.com.e.db.hp.transer.com

♦ 1276 ♦ Hanami
March-April

The word *hana* means "flower" in Japanese, and *hanami* means "flower viewing." However, appreciation of the cherry blossom in Japan is almost a religion, and therefore hanami has come to refer specifically to cherry blossoms. The pink-and-white blooms last for about two weeks, and during that time people swarm to the parks to picnic, play games, tell stories, and dance. Often companies organize hanami parties for their employees. The season usually starts at the end of March in Kyushu, in early April in the Tokyo area, and in late April in the north of Japan. The most famous viewing place is Yoshinoyama near Nara, where it is said 1,000 trees can be seen at a glance.

See also CHERRY BLOSSOM FESTIVAL.

CONTACTS:
Kyoto City Office (Central Area)
488 Teramachi-Oike
Kamihonnojimae-cho
Nakagyo-ku
Kyoto 604-8571 Japan
81-75-222-3111
www.city.kyoto.jp

♦ 1277 ♦ Handsel Monday
First Monday of the year; first Monday after January 12

A secular holiday, Handsel Monday was important among the rural people of Scotland. "Handsel" was something given as a token of good luck, particularly at the beginning of something; the modern house-warming gift would be a good example. Thus Handsel Monday was an occasion for gift giving at the start of the new year, and it remained a Scottish tradition from the 14th until the 19th century. Eventually it was replaced by BOXING DAY, and the custom of giving farm laborers and public servants some extra money or a small gift on this day continues.

Because Handsel Monday was so widely celebrated among the rural population, many Scottish peasants celebrated **Auld Handsel Monday** on the first Monday after January 12, reflecting their reluctance to shift from the Old Style, or Julian, calendar to the New Style, or Gregorian, calendar.

CONTACTS:
Scotland's national tourist board
Ocean Point One
94 Ocean Dr.
Edinburgh EH6 6JH Scotland
845-859-1006 or 44-0-131-524-2121
www.visitscotland.com

♦ 1278 ♦ Handy (W. C.) Music Festival
July or August

The W.C. Handy Music Festival honors the "Father of the Blues" in the Alabama Quad-Cities of Florence, Muscle Shoals, Sheffield, and Tuscumbia in the northwestern part of the state known as Muscle Shoals.

William Christopher Handy, the son and grandson of ministers, was born in 1873 in Florence, took an early interest in music, and went on to become a prolific composer, performer, orchestra leader, and music publisher despite his father's ministerial influence. In 1911, he wrote an election campaign song for Mayor Edward H. "Boss" Crump of Memphis, Tenn., that became known as the "Memphis Blues" and was one of the works that made him famous. Others included the classic "St. Louis Blues," "Beale Street Blues," and "Careless Love."

Handy, working in the period of transition from ragtime to jazz, fused elements of black folk music with ragtime to create distinctive blues pieces. He also organized a publishing firm, issued anthologies of black spirituals and blues and studies of American black musicians, and wrote an autobiography, *Father of the Blues*, published in 1941. He expressed his philosophy with these words: "Life is like this old trumpet of mine. If you don't put something into it, you don't get nothing out." When Handy died in 1958, a Harlem minister said, "Gabriel now has an understudy."

The festival celebrates not only Handy's musical heritage but also the musical roots of spirituals and jazz. Opening ceremonies are at the W. C. Handy Home & Museum, a log cabin housing Handy's collected papers and memorabilia. His piano and trumpet are on display.

Throughout the festival there is music by nationally known musicians night and day, street dancing, a foot race, folk art exhibits, and music workshops. Events are held in such nontraditional locations as ball fields, parks, and nursing homes, and concerts are performed in the church where Handy's father and grandfather served as pastor, and in restaurants and clubs. The small community of Muscle Shoals, where several events are held, is known in music circles for having given birth to the "Muscle Shoals Sound" through a recording studio that was set up in 1965. Artists as varied as Aretha Franklin, Peggy Lee, Liza Minnelli, Bob Seger, and the Rolling Stones have recorded here.

CONTACTS:
W. C. Handy Music Festival
217 E. Tuscaloosa St.
Florence, AL 35630
256-766-7642
www.wchandymusicfestival.org

♦ 1279 ♦ Han'gul Day
October 9

This day commemorates the invention of the Korean alphabet by scholars under the direction of King Sejong of the Yi Dynasty in 1446.

The Han'gul system consists of 14 consonants and 10 vowels. The symbols for consonants are formed with curved or angled lines; the symbols for vowels are composed of vertical or horizonal straight lines with short lines on either side. Although Sejong made Han'gul the official writing system for the Korean language, it was not used by scholars or upper-class Koreans until after 1945, when Japanese rule came to an end and the influence of Confucianism and Chinese culture waned.

The reign of Sejong (1418-50) was a golden age in Korea, producing—besides the alphabet—the encyclopedic codification of medical knowledge and the development of new fonts of type for printing. (The technique of movable-type printing was developed in Korea in 1234, two hundred years before Johannes Gutenberg's invention in Germany.)

The day is celebrated with Confucian rituals and Choson-period court dances performed at Yongnung, the king's tomb, in Yoju, Kyonggi. Yoju also stages the King Sejong Cultural Festival, which is part of a three-day Grand Cultural Festival, with chanting and processions at Shilluksa Temple, farmers' dances, games such as tug of war, and a lantern parade. In some areas, there are calligraphy contests for both children and adults.

Ceremonies are also held at the King Sejong Memorial Center near Seoul.

CONTACTS:
Korean Tourism Organization
2 Executive Dr.
Ste. 750
Fort Lee, NJ 07024
201-585-0909; fax: 201-585-9041
english.visitkorea.or.kr

♦ 1280 ♦ Hanukkah (Chanukah)
Between November 25 and December 26; from Kislev 25 to Tevet 2

Hanukkah commemorates the successful rebellion of the Jews against the Syrians in the Maccabean War of 162 B.C.E., but the military associations of this festival are played down. What is really being celebrated is the survival of Judaism. After the Jews' victory, they ritually cleansed and rededicated the Temple, then relit the menorah ("perpetual lamp"); hence one of the other names for this celebration, the **Feast of Dedication** (Hanukkah means "dedication" in Hebrew). The story is told that although there was only enough consecrated oil to keep the lamp burning for one day and it would take eight days to get more, the small bottle of oil miraculously lasted for the entire eight days. It is for this reason that Hanukkah is also known as the **Feast of Lights**.

Jewish families today celebrate this holiday by lighting a special Hanukkah menorah, a candelabrum with holders for eight candles, one for each day of celebration, plus a ninth, the shammash, "server," used to light the others. One candle is lit on the first night, two on the second, three on the third, through to the eighth night when all are lit. A special prayer is recited during the lighting, and while the candles burn it is a time for songs and games, including the four-sided toy called the dreidel. Other customs include the giving of gifts, especially to children, and decorating the home—something like the CHRISTMAS celebrations in Christian homes around this same time of year.

CONTACTS:
Jewish Community Center of San Francisco
3200 California St.
San Francisco, CA 94118
415-292-1200; fax: 415-276-1550
www.jccsf.org

Orthodox Union
11 Broadway
New York, NY 10004
212-563-4000; fax: 212-564-9058
www.ou.org

♦ 1281 ♦ Hanuman Jayanti
March-April; Hindu month of Caitra

Hanuman, the Monkey God and a central figure in the great Hindu epic, the *Ramayana*, helped Rama rescue his wife Sita from the demon Ravana; for this Rama decreed the two always be worshipped together. He is revered by Hindus all over India in the form of a monkey with a red face who stands erect like a human. His birth anniversary is observed in the month of Caitra with celibacy, fasting, and reading the *Hanuman-Chalisa*. Hindus visit his temples, of which there are many, to offer prayers on this day and to re-paint his image with vermilion.

CONTACTS:
Jaya Hanuman Temple & Cultural Center
2719, 152nd Ave. N.E.
Redmond, WA 98052
425-818-8277
www.jayahanumantemple.org

Sri Hanuman Temple
390 Cumming St.
Ste. B
Alpharetta, GA 30004
770-475-7701
www.srihanuman.org

♦ 1282 ♦ Harbin Ice and Snow Festival
January 5-February 4

This extravaganza of ice sculptures takes place in the port city of Harbin, the second largest city of northeast China, located in Heilongjiang Province. The sculptures, using themes of ancient legends and stories and modern historic events, depict pavilions, towers, temples, and mythic animals and persons. Located in Zhaolin Park, they shimmer in the sun by day, and at night are illuminated in a rainbow of colors. Theatrical events, art exhibitions, and a photo exhibition mark festival time, and wedding ceremonies are often scheduled at this time in the ice-filled park.

CONTACTS:
Guilin China Travel Service
1-10-4, Sanxing Bldg.

No. 3 Lijiang Rd.
Guilin 541004 China
86-773-267-5596; fax: 86-773-585-9827
www.icefestivalharbin.com

♦ 1283 ♦ Hard Crab Derby, National
September, Labor Day weekend

The first **Hard Crab Derby** was held in 1947. A local newspaper editor dumped a few hard-shell crabs into a circle on Main Street in Crisfield, Maryland. The crab that scurried to an outer circle first was declared the winner, and its owner was awarded a trophy. There doesn't seem to have been any motivation for the race other than the wish to compete with the other derbies that had already been established for horses, automobiles, etc.

Today the National Hard Crab Derby attracts hundred of entries. The Governor's Cup Race, in which entries representing the 50 states compete, takes place on the Saturday of LABOR DAY weekend. There is also a boat-docking contest, a crab-picking contest, and a crab-cooking contest. Parades, beauty contests, concerts, a carnival, and arts and crafts exhibits complete the three-day festival.

CONTACTS:
Crisfield Area Chamber of Commerce
906 W. Main St.
Crisfield, MD 21817
410-968-2500 or 800-782-3913
nationalhardcrabderby.com

♦ 1284 ♦ Hari-Kuyo (Festival of Broken Needles)
February 8 or December 8

Hari-Kuyo is a requiem service for needles held throughout Japan. The ceremony of laying needles to rest harkens back to at least the fourth century C.E. Today the services are attended not only by tailors and dressmakers but also by people who sew at home. Traditionally, a shrine is set up in the Shinto style, with a sacred rope and strips of white paper suspended over a three-tiered altar. On the top tier are offerings of cake and fruit, on the second tier there is a pan of tofu, and the bottom tier is for placing scissors and thimbles. The tofu is the important ingredient; people insert their broken or bent needles in it while offering prayers of thanks to the needles for their years of service. In the Buddhist service, special sutras are recited for the repose of the needles. Afterwards, the needles are wrapped in paper and laid to rest in the sea.

A hari-kuyo is held in Kyoto at the Buddhist Temple Horinji on Dec. 8, and in Tokyo one is held at Asakusa Kannon Temple on Feb. 8.

CONTACTS:
Kyoto City Tourism & Culture Information
239-1 Gochome, Yanaginobanba Ebisugawa-agaru, Nakagyo-ku
#401 Kyotansu Ebisugawa Bldg.
Kyoto 604-0973 Japan
81-75-253-0321; fax: 81-75-253-0322
www.kyotoguide.com

Tokyo Convention & Visitors Bureau
346-6 Yamabuki-cho
Shinjuku-ku
Nisshin Bldg. 6F
Tokyo 162-0801 Japan
81-3-5579-2680; fax: 81-3-5579-2685
www.tcvb.or.jp

♦ 1285 ♦ Harlem International Film Festival
September

The Harlem International Film Festival, which opened for the first time in September 2005 at New York's Columbia University, premieres works of promising international filmmakers. It is known for its diverse and compelling lineup of films from nearly 20 countries as well as its prestigious awards. The five-day event showcases over 60 features, shorts, documentaries, youth projects, and animated films. The annual festival also features the Harlem Spotlight, which presents films produced or directed by Harlem locals, depicting Harlem and its history.

Each year, the festival chooses a country and presents a repertory of its best films. Besides the prestigious Renaissance Award, the festival honors the best feature film with the Brownstone Award. The Mira Nair Award, named in honor of the internationally acclaimed Indian filmmaker and actor, is presented for a rising female filmmaker, and is followed by a host of awards for individual categories, including best screenplay.

CONTACTS:
Harlem International Film Festival
2214 Frederick Douglass Blvd.
Ste. 333
New York, NY 10026
harlemfilmfestival.org

♦ 1286 ♦ Harlem Week
August

Sponsored by the Greater Harlem Chamber of Commerce, Harlem Week is the largest cultural festival in the United States. Participation in Harlem Week and its associated events is estimated to exceed two million people. The festival honors the unique history and importance of the Harlem neighborhood in New York City. This area was the site of an important flourishing in African-American culture known as the Harlem Renaissance during the early 20th century. The Harlem Renaissance marked the emergence of African Americans into the mainstream of the nation's art, music, literature, and culture while simultaneously proclaiming the unique vitality and character of the African-American experience.

When it originated in 1974, Harlem Week was conceived as a single day's celebration of the area's cultural contributions, and sought to revitalize interest in and recognition of the neighborhood's important past. Though the activities have expanded to encompass a wide range of sports, music, and educational events, Harlem Day remains the most important

and event-filled day of the month-long celebration. A street fair, including performance stages, marketplace booths, and food vendors, is located on West 135th Street, and the rich musical heritage of the area is commemorated in numerous performances featuring swing, jazz, Latin, gospel, hip hop, reggae, R&B, and blues music. In addition, the festival includes history tours, fashion shows, an all-star basketball game, a youth tennis tournament, a college fair, a health fair, a children's festival, a senior citizens' party, and an auto show.

CONTACTS:
Greater Harlem Chamber of Commerce
200A W. 136th St.
Harlem, NY 10030
212-862-7200 or 877-427-5364; fax: 212-862-8745
greaterharlemchamber.com

♦ 1287 ♦ Haro Wine Festival (Batalla de Vino)
June 29

The people of Spain's Rioja region douse themselves in red wine during the Haro Wine Festival, which is celebrated on St. Peter's Feast Day in the region's capital city of Haro. The annual event commemorates the area's most important industry, winemaking, and attracts both locals and tourists alike. The festival dates back to the 12th century and is based on a land dispute between the neighboring towns of Haro and Miranda de Ebro over the ownership of the Bilibio cliff. Upon reaching a resolution, Haro town officials marked the boundary on the mountain with purple banners, a practice that turned into a custom repeated every year on the 29th of June. The throwing of the wine started around 1710 and took place after the conclusion of the St. Peter's Day Mass at the chapel on the cliff. The festivities start on the eve of the big day, when the whole town stays up all night and has a party. On the morning of the 29th at seven o'clock, they process to the Bilibio cliff, about five to seven kilometers away from the city. The mayor of Haro hangs the city banner on the highest rock on the mountain. Attendees wear white clothes, which turn purple as the wine hits them, and are armed with squirt guns, spray misters, and buckets to pour the wine on each other. An estimated 50,000 liters of wine gets spilled every year. The wine fight starts after the Mass at the chapel and continues for hours before everyone returns to the city to attend bullfights in the city's arena.

CONTACTS:
Haro Wine Festival
La Rioja
Haro 26200 Spain
www.wine-fight.com

♦ 1288 ♦ Harvest Festival
October

The Harvest Festival of the Iroquois, a confederacy of Native North American tribes, is celebrated in autumn and marks their tradition of thanksgiving for a bountiful harvest. The event, which lasts for four days, is observed in October when all the crops have been harvested and stored and before the men have left for the traditional fall hunt. A group of men called the "keepers of the faith" oversee preparations for the festival. These men announce the dates, organize the feasts, and make thanksgiving speeches in honor of the Great Creator. For the first two days of the event, the Great Feather Dance is performed in full costume. On the third day, the *Ah-do-weh* ceremony is performed, in which participants express gratitude to the natural and spiritual world for all the bounties received. The festival concludes with the bowl game, a game of chance played between clans, or between men and women. The game is symbolic of the struggle of crops against the elements of nature, and the outcome of the game, which follows a complex system of scoring, is believed to foretell the harvest for the following year.

♦ 1289 ♦ Harvest Home Festival
Autumn

Many countries celebrate the end of the summer harvest or the "ingathering" of the crops with a special feast. What became known in England as Harvest Home, or **Harvest Thanksgiving**, was called the **Kirn** in Scotland (from the churn of cream usually presented on the occasion), and probably derived from the ancient LAMMAS celebrations. Eventually it gave rise to the **Harvest Festival** in Canada and THANKSGIVING in the United States.

The autumn harvest feast was usually served in a barn, a tent, or outdoors and was preceded by a church service. Although the earliest harvest feasts were served by a farmer or landowner to his laborers, eventually one big feast for the entire parish became the norm.

See also SZÜRET.

CONTACTS:
The Farmers' Museum
5775 State Hwy. 80 (Lake Rd.)
P.O. Box 30
Cooperstown, NY 13326
607-547-1450 or 888-547-1450; fax: 607-547-1499
www.farmersmuseum.org

County of Wellington, Museum & Archives
74 Woolwich St.
Guelph, ON N1H 3T9 Canada
519-837-2600; fax: 519-837-1909
www.wellington.ca

♦ 1290 ♦ Harvest Moon Days
Full moon nearest September 23

Harvest Moon Days refers to the period of the full moon that falls closest to the AUTUMNAL EQUINOX, around September 23. This is traditionally a time for countries in the Northern Hemisphere to hold their annual harvest festivals.

See also HARVEST HOME FESTIVAL.

CONTACTS:
Harvest Moon Society
10th St.

Clearwater, MB R0K 0M0 Canada
204-873-3858
www.harvestmoonsociety.org

♦ 1291 ♦ Hatch Chile Festival
September, Labor Day weekend

This event pays tribute to the green chili (as it is more commonly spelled outside of New Mexico), New Mexico's state vegetable. The small town of Hatch is the center of the chili-growing industry in the southwestern part of the state. At festival time, the aroma of freshly harvested chilis permeates the town, and a marvelous variety of chilis in all forms can be purchased: fresh green chilis—from the mildest to the hottest, dried red chilis in ornamental braids called *ristras*, red chili powder, chili bread, chili salsa, chili jelly, chili wine, and chili con carne. Besides food, the festival features the crowning of a Green Chile Queen, a skeet shoot, a fiddling contest, a cook-off, and a ristra-making contest.

CONTACTS:
Hatch Chamber of Commerce
P.O. Box 568
Hatch, NM 87937
575-519-4723
www.villageofhatch.org

Hatch Chile Festival Committee
Hatch, NM
505-252-0431
www.hatchchilefest.com

♦ 1292 ♦ Hatfield and McCoy Reunion Festival and Marathon
Three-day weekend in early June

The Hatfield and McCoy Reunion Festival and Marathon are held annually on a three-day weekend in early June in Pikeville, Ky.; Matewan, W.Va.; and Williamson, W.Va. Events take place in all three locations. The festival commemorates a family feud that has entered American lore and has become synonymous with bitter, irresolvable conflict. The feud involved two families who lived on the Tug Fork, a tributary of the Big Sandy River: the Hatfields on the West Virginia side and the McCoys on the Kentucky side. The fight, which ran from 1878 to 1891, apparently began over property rights, was fueled by a love affair between two members of the opposing families, escalated into multiple murders, and eventually necessitated two governors summoning state militia to maintain the peace. In 2003, descendants of both families signed a truce in Pikeville, but they actually had agreed to stop fighting more than a century before.

Centerpieces of the Hatfield and McCoy Reunion Festival are a marathon and half-marathon (motto: "no feudin', just runnin'"), as well as a three-town, all-terrain-vehicle ride. Other highlights include a tug-of-war across the Tug Fork, involving descendants of the feuding clans; a live, dramatic reenactment of scenes from the world's most famous family fight; and an annual feud-site motorcycle ride. In all three towns, live entertainment, tours of Hatfield-McCoy landmarks, activities such as a cornbread contest and pancake break-fast, arts and crafts, and dancing are offered. More than 300 runners typically take part in the running races, and thousands throng the area for the marathon and festival, which launched in 2000.

CONTACTS:
Hatfield McCoy Marathon
201 Central Ave. S.
Williamson, KY 41503
606-625-5092
www.hatfieldmccoymarathon.net

♦ 1293 ♦ Haxey Hood Game
January 6

This centuries-old tradition in Haxey, Lincolnshire, England, can be traced back more than 600 years, when Lady Mow-bray, whose husband owned a large portion of the parish of Haxey, lost her hood to a sudden gust of wind and 13 local men struggled gallantly to retrieve it. She showed her appreciation by staging an annual reenactment of the event, which is believed by some to be the origin of rugby, an English sport that combines soccer with American football.

The game known as **Throwing the Hood**, which takes place on OLD CHRISTMAS DAY (January 6) each year, involves a Lord (who acts as umpire and master of ceremonies), 13 Plough-Boggins (presumably named for the way the original 13 men turned up the soil in their efforts to capture the hood), a Fool, and as many others as care to participate.

After several warm-up rounds with sham hoods, the real contest begins. The participants wrestle over a piece of leather stuffed with straw, coins, and other fillings. The winners carry it back to their village pub, where a victory celebration takes place. Later, the Boggins go from house to house, singing and collecting money for the celebration.

CONTACTS:
Haxey Parish Council, Clerk Office
Haxey Memorial Hall
High St.
Haxey DN9 2HH United Kingdom
44-165-261-8306
haxeyparish.org.uk

Lincolnshire County Council
County Offices, Newland
Lincoln LN1 1YL United Kingdom
44-152-255-2222; fax: 44-152-251-6137
www.lincolnshire.gov.uk

♦ 1294 ♦ Hay-on-Wye Festival of Literature
Late May to early June

This celebration of words and language has been held in Hay-on-Wye, Wales, since 1988. It offers 10 days of comedy, theater, and musical performances in addition to conversations, debates, lectures, interviews, and readings by poets and fiction writers. The festival regularly features some of the most widely known Welsh, Irish, English, European, and American writers in the world, including Margaret Atwood,

Doris Lessing, John Mortimer, William Golding, Anthony Hecht, Joseph Heller, and Jan Morris. Musical performances have included the Welsh National Opera Male Choir and the English Shakespeare Company.

A series of master classes in poetry, short story, and television screenwriting has recently been established for young writers attending the festival whose poems or stories have been published or whose plays have been produced. The master classes include a week of intensive work under the supervision of such renowned writers as Joseph Brodsky, who won the NOBEL PRIZE for Literature in 1980, and the famous Welsh poet and short-story writer Leslie Norris.

CONTACTS:
Hay Festival of Literature & the Arts Ltd
The Drill Hall, 25 Lion St.
Hay-on-Wye HR3 5AD United Kingdom
44-1497-822-620; fax: 44-1497-821-066
www.hayfestival.com

♦ 1295 ♦ Hayti Heritage Film Festival
February

The St. Joseph's Historic Foundation, Inc. (SJHF), was founded in 1975 to advance "cultural understanding through diverse programs that examine the experiences of Americans of African descent-locally, nationally, and globally." It is an African- American cultural and educational institution deeply rooted in the historic Hayti community of Durham, N.C.

African Americans started to settle on the southwest edge of Durham shortly after the Civil War. During the slavery era, the term "Hayti" was used by white people when referring to black settlements. This area originally provided a labor pool for Durham's tobacco warehouses, but it soon began to prosper. When Booker T. Washington visited Hayti in 1911, he described it as "a city of Negro enterprises" whose citizens were "shining examples of what a colored man may become."

The Hayti Heritage Center, which is the former St. Joseph's African Methodist Episcopal Church, sponsors the annual Hyati Heritage Film Festival. The festival celebrates African-American cinema by highlighting established and emerging filmmakers and films while showcasing the contributions and uniqueness of the black artistic tradition in film. The films that are selected embody the richness of black culture and recognize universal themes that exist among all cultures.

CONTACTS:
NYADIFF
535 Cathedral Pkwy.
Ste. 14B
New York, NY 10025
212-864-1760
nyadiff.org

♦ 1296 ♦ Heidi Festival
Mid-June

The town of New Glarus, Wisconsin, has celebrated the annual Heidi Festival since the 1960s. Founded in 1845 by immigrants from the Swiss canton of Glaurus, the town of New Glarus, Wisconsin, continued to attract Swiss immigrants over the years. Today it celebrates its cultural heritage in its yearly Volksfest and Heidi Festival. The Heidi Festival revolves around four performances of *Heidi*, Johanna Spyri's well-known play about a young Swiss shepherdess. The festival also includes opportunities to enjoy Swiss music, food, and dancing.

CONTACTS:
New Glarus Chamber of Commerce
418 Railroad St.
P.O. Box 713
New Glarus, WI 53574
608-527-2095 or 800-527-6838; fax: 608-527-4991
www.swisstown.com

♦ 1297 ♦ **Helsinki Festival**
Late August to early September

The largest cultural event in the Nordic countries is the Helsinki Festival. It grew out of Sibelius Weeks, established in 1951 to honor Finland's most famous composer, Jean Sibelius (*see also* SIBELIUS FESTIVAL). But when the first official Helsinki Festival was held in 1967, it expanded its programming to include music from all periods—rock, jazz, opera, symphonic music, and chamber works—as well as theater, ballet, circus, and art and photo exhibitions.

Among the many musical events is what is known as the Festival Informal, a series where artists and visitors meet informally for "relaxed performances." Events are held in the city's parks and arcades as well as in the modern Finlandia Hall and and the Finnish National Theatre and Opera.

Ensembles that have performed at the 18-day festival include the Helsinki Philharmonic Orchestra, the Royal Philharmonic Orchestra of London, the Moscow Chamber Opera, the Beaux Arts Trio, the Alvin Ailey American Dance Theater, the Groteska Puppet Theatre of Kracow, the Tientsin Acrobat Company of China, and the Ballet Nacional de Cuba.

CONTACTS:
Helsinki Festival
Lasipalatsi, Mannerheimintie 22-24
Helsinki 00100 Finland
358-9-6126-5100
www.helsinginjuhlaviikot.fi

♦ 1298 ♦ **Helston Flora Day**
May 8

According to legend, there was a large stone that at one time blocked off the entrance to hell. One night Satan tried to steal the stone. But on his way through Cornwall, England, he was intercepted by the Archangel Michael, who forced him to drop the stone and flee. The town where he dropped it was called Helston (from Hellstone, or stone of hell), and for many years a large block of granite sat in the yard of a tavern there.

The people of Helston continue to celebrate the Archangel's victory, although no one is quite sure why this celebration has been called "Furry Day." It may derive from the Gaelic word *fer* meaning "a fair," or from the Latin *feriae*, meaning "festival." Some think it's a corruption of "Flora's Day," a reference to the original Roman goddess of flowers (*see* FLORALIA). In any case, today the event is known as Helston Flora Day.

The day's festivities include the "Furry dance," which is performed in the streets by men in top hats and women in fancy dresses, and a trip to the woods in search of flowers and leaves. The original rock has long since been broken up into building stones and used for local construction. Flora Day is held on May 8 except in years when the 8th falls on a Sunday or Monday, in which case it is moved to the previous Saturday.

CONTACTS:
Helston Flora Day Association
117 Meneage St.
Helston TR13 8RL United Kingdom
44-132-657-2063
www.helstonfloraday.org.uk

♦ 1299 ♦ **Hemingway (Ernest) Days Festival**
Week including July 21

This week-long celebration of Ernest Hemingway (1899-1961), the American novelist and short-story writer, is held in Key West, Fla. The festival has been held since 1980 during the week of Hemingway's birthday, July 21. Hemingway made his home in Key West at one time, and his novel, *To Have and Have Not* (1937), is set there. He was awarded the Pulitzer Prize in fiction in 1953 for his short heroic novel about an old Cuban fisherman, *The Old Man and the Sea*, and he received the Nobel Prize for Literature in 1954.

A short-story competition, with a first-place prize of $1,500 and publication of the winning entry in Cutthroat: A Journal of the Arts, drew a total of 938 submissions in 2014. Lorian Hemingway, the writer 's granddaughter and a writer herself, is the coordinator of the story contest.

Other events include a street fair, a Hemingway look-alike contest, a fishing tournament, an arm-wrestling competition, and a party and concert at the Hemingway Home and Museum.

CONTACTS:
Ernest Hemingway Home and Museum
907 Whitehead St.
Key West, FL 33040
305-294-1136; fax: 305-294-2755
www.hemingwayhome.com

♦ 1300 ♦ **Hemis Festival**
Usually in June or July

This three-day Buddhist festival takes place at the Hemis Gompa in the mountainous region of Ladakh in northern

India. This is the largest *gompa* (monastery) in Ladakh and has gold statues, huge stone monuments of Buddha called *stupas* that are studded with precious stones, and an impressive collection of *thangkas*, or big scroll religious paintings.

The festival celebrates the birthday of Guru Padmasambhava, the Indian Buddhist mystic who introduced Tantric Buddhism to Tibet in the eighth century. Tradition says he was a native of Swat (now in Pakistan), an area noted for magicians. Tradition also says he brought on an earthquake in Tibet to get rid of the demons who were delaying the building of a monastery.

The festival attracts people from throughout the mountain areas of Ladakh and Tibet—Muslims and Hindus as well as Buddhists, all dressed in their most colorful clothes. A fair springs up, with stalls selling confections, gems, and crafts.

The highlight of the festival is the Devil Dance of the monks (*see also* MYSTERY PLAY OF TIBET). Demon dancers are costumed as satyrs, many-eyed monsters, fierce tigers, or skeletons, while lamas portraying saints wear miters and opulent silks and carry pastoral crooks. These good lamas, ringing bells and swinging censers, scatter the bad lamas, as they all swirl about to the music of cymbals, drums, and 10-foot-long trumpets. The dance is a morality play, a battle between good and evil spirits, and also expresses the idea that a person's helpless soul can be comforted only by a lama's exorcisms.

CONTACTS:
Tourism Development Authority of Ladakh
Tourist Reception Centre
Leh (Ladakh), Jammu & Kashmir 194101 India
91-1982-252094; fax: 91-1982-252297
leh.nic.in

♦ 1301 ♦ Henley Royal Regatta
Five days in early July

The international rowing competition known as the Henley Regatta was first held in 1839. The long, straight, nearly two-mile stretch of the Thames River about 35 miles west of London made Henley an ideal location for oarsmen to compete— in fact, it was the site of the Olympic rowing competition in both 1908 and 1948, when London hosted the OLYMPIC GAMES. The races became known as "royal" in 1851, when Prince Albert became the first member of the royal family to patronize the event.

The five-day Regatta's many events include races for eight-oared, four-oared, and pair-oared boats as well as sculling races for quadruple, double, and single sculls. The course takes six to seven minutes to row, and there are often two races taking place simultaneously. Although only male oarsmen were allowed to compete for 154 years, an open women's event was introduced in 1993. The so-called "Women's Henley," held annually a few weeks before the Royal Regatta, has grown rapidly in popularity.

In addition to being a world-class rowing competition for oarsmen from a dozen countries and more than 60 colleges

and universities, the Henley Royal Regatta is also a huge lawn party attended by nearly half a million spectators. The hub of social interaction during Regatta week is the Stewards' Enclosure, an exclusive spectators' area located near the end of the course. Parties also take place in tents called "chalets," set up along the banks of the river, as well as in the parking lot, where people serve impressive meals from their cars.

The men traditionally dress in straw hats and rowing blazers and neckties, whose colors indicate what school, college, or club they once rowed for. The women put on their finest summer dresses and hats; short skirts, culottes, or slacks of any kind are forbidden.

CONTACTS:
Henley Royal Regatta
Regatta Headquarters
Henley-on-Thames, Oxfordshire RG9 2LY United Kingdom
44-14-9157-2153; fax: 44-14-9157-5509
www.hrr.co.uk

♦ 1302 ♦ Heritage Holidays
Mid-October

The Heritage Holidays are a five-day celebration of the history of Rome, Ga., which, like its Italian namesake, was built on seven hills. There is also a bronze replica of the Capitoline Wolf outside City Hall. This Roman statue depicting a she-wolf nursing the legendary founders of Rome—Romulus and Remus—was given to the town in 1929 by Benito Mussolini.

Heritage Holidays, however, looks back to different times: it features a re-creation of the famous ride of John Wisdom, who has been called the Paul Revere of the South. During the Civil War, Rome was important to the Confederacy as a rail and manufacturing center. Wisdom, a native of the city who was living in Alabama, was delivering mail when he heard that Yankee soldiers were headed for his hometown. He rode the 67 miles to Rome in 11 hours, wearing out five horses and a mule. The men of Rome set up two old cannons, and the Yanks decided the town seemed too heavily fortified. They surrendered to a smaller Confederate force following them.

Features of the heritage days are a wagon train, parades, riverboat rides, concerts, and a major arts and crafts fair.

CONTACTS:
Greater Rome Convention & Visitors Bureau
402 Civic Center Dr.
Rome, GA 30161
706-295-5576 or 800-444-1834
romegeorgia.org

♦ 1303 ♦ Hermit, Feast of the
September 1

Juan Maria de Castellano is known as a saint among the Hispanic Americans of Hot Springs, New Mexico. He lived in a cave on a mountain peak for three years and slept on the ground. According to legend, he was responsible for a number of miraculous feats, not the least of which was producing water from a rock that had the power to cure blindness and other ills. Once when he had 12 men visit him, the very small amount of food he prepared was sufficient to feed all of them for an entire day.

In the 1930s, the members of the Asociacion de Santa Maria de Guadalupe met twice a year on Hermit's Peak. The second and more important of the two meetings was held on September 1, which came to be known as the Feast of the Hermit. People brought picnics, and some built little huts where they could spend the night. Some came to be cured, while others worked on repairing the fences and clearing the trails. They lit huge bonfires and prayed for the holy man who, like Moses, had caused water to flow from a rock and who, like Jesus, had satisfied the hunger of multitudes.

CONTACTS:
Santa Fe National Forest Headquarters
11 Forest Ln.
Santa Fe, NM 87508
505-438-5300; fax: 505-438-5390
www.fs.fed.us

♦ 1304 ♦ Heurigen Parties
November

St. Martin's Day, November 11, is the traditional time when wine taverns in Austria offer the first new wines of the year. Wine feasts called Heurigen parties abound in these taverns throughout the country and are scheduled according to an official *Heurigenkalender*. Traditional foods served with the new wine include sausage, cheese, and bread. Many taverns also stage operettas and other shows for the season.

CONTACTS:
Vienna Tourist Board
Albertinaplatz / Maysedergasse
Vienna 1010 Austria
43-1-24-555; fax: 43-1-2455-5666
www.wien.info/en

♦ 1305 ♦ Hi Matsuri (Fire Festival)
October 22

Early on the evening of October 22, people light bonfires along the narrow street leading to the Kuramadera Shrine in Kurama, a village in the mountains north of Kyoto, Japan. The bonfires are made with gigantic roots brought in from the nearby forest. Fire is a purifying element, according to Shinto teachings, and the village and its inhabitants are believed to be protected from accidents on this particular night.

Soon after dusk, people light torches: even babies, under the watchful eyes of their parents, are allowed to carry tiny torches made out of twigs. Young men carry large torches, sometimes so large it takes several men to keep them upright. As they walk through the streets, everyone chants rhythmically, "Sai-rei! Sai-ryo!" ("Festival, good festival"). Sometimes a marcher lets a heavy torch fall, and people try

to catch one of the falling sparks because they believe it will bring them good luck.

Around midnight the torches begin to die down and the villagers grow quiet. Everyone gathers around either side of the stairway that takes one to the shrine. The entrance to the stairway has been barred with a rope, which a Shinto priest now cuts. Two groups of strong men carry the two elaborately decorated *mikoshi* or palanquins in which the *kami* or gods are believed to reside when they visit the earth. They take them down the stairway to the outskirts of the village and set them down. Everyone bids farewell to the kami, who must return to their spirit home.

Although no one knows exactly how the Fire Festival originated, some believe it was at one time a test of virility or an initiation rite conducted when a boy reached manhood. Another theory is that it originated in the custom of lighting fires called *mukaebi* to guide gods or spirits from the other world on their visits to earth.

CONTACTS:
Kyoto City – Public Relations Office
488, Teramachi-Oike, Nakagyo-ku
Kyoto 604-8571 Japan
81-75-222-3111
www.city.kyoto.jp/koho/eng

♦ 1306 ♦ Hidrellez Festival
May 6

The Hidrellez Festival is observed in Turkey every May 6. It is marked as the day that two prophets, Hizir and Ilyas, met each other on Earth, and the holiday also is known as **Ruz-I Hizir** (day of Hizir). The word Hidrellez is a fusing of the two names. The festival is a joyous celebration of the coming of spring. The customs associated with it probably derive from various eastern Mediterranean traditions, including Mesopotamian, Anatolian, and pre-Islamic central-Asian Turkish. All of these cultures have numerous, age-old rituals and ceremonies associated with the renewal and rebirth of spring. Many Turks believe that Hizir drank the water of life and is immortal, and that he is able to bestow people with health, happiness, and abundance. He is a symbol of new life, and in some parts of Turkey, people offer sacrifices and votive offerings "for the sake of Hizir" to make their prayers and wishes come true.

People prepare for Hidrellez by thoroughly cleaning their homes, because they believe that Hizir will not visit houses that are not clean. They also purchase fresh new clothes and shoes to wear for the Hidrellez Festival, and prepare special food, such as fresh lamb or lamb's liver. On Hidrellez night, people leave purses and pantries open and put out food bowls, in the belief that Hizir will bring abundance to the homes he visits. If they desire a house or vineyard, they will make a little model of what they want so that Hizir will help them obtain it. Throughout Turkey at Hidrellez time, people perform various ceremonies to improve or to test their luck, believing that fortunes improve with the reawakening of nature in springtime. Such ceremonies typically are carried out in leafy, green places or near sources of water.

CONTACTS:
Ahirkapi Hidrellez Spring Festival Venue
Ahirkapi Park, Çatladikapi
Istanbul Turkey
hidrellez.org

♦ 1307 ♦ Higan
*Week including March 20 or 21 and week
including September 23 or 24*

Higan is a week of Buddhist services observed in Japan at the spring and autumn equinoxes (*see* SHUNBUN-NO-HI and AUTUMNAL EQUINOX) when day and night are of equal length.

Both equinoxes have been national holidays since the Meiji Period (1868-1912). Before World War II, they were known as *koreisai*, "festivals of the Imperial ancestors." After the war, when the national holidays were renamed, they became simply spring equinox and autumn equinox.

Higan is the seven-day period surrounding the equinoxes. It means the "other shore," and refers to the spirits of the dead reaching Nirvana after crossing the river of existence. Thus Higan is a celebration of the spiritual move from the world of suffering to the world of enlightenment and is a time for remembering the dead, visiting, cleaning, and decorating their graves, and reciting *sutras*, Buddhist prayers. *O-hagi*, rice balls covered with sweet bean paste, and sushi are offered. It is traditional not to eat meat during this period. Emperor Heizei instituted the celebration in 806 C.E., when he ordered a week-long reading of a certain sutra for the occasion.

In Okinawa it is a home thanksgiving festival. Barley (*omugi*) or barley cakes with brown sugar are eaten with prayers for good fortune.

CONTACTS:
Zenshuji Soto Mission
123 S. Hewitt St.
Los Angeles, CA 90012
213-624-8658; fax: 213-624-8650
www.zenshuji.org

♦ 1308 ♦ Highland Games
Dates vary

Originally impromptu athletic competitions carried out in the Scottish Highlands as part of a clan gathering, Highland games are now held all over the world, usually under the auspices of a local Caledonian society. Although the Jacobites put an end to the clan assemblies in 1745, the tradition of the games survived, and the first of the modern gatherings was held 90 years later at Braemar (*see* BRAEMAR HIGHLAND GATHERING). Today there are about 40 major gatherings in Scotland alone, as well as in Tauranga, New Zealand, and in several American communities such as Goshen, Connecticut, and

Alexandria, Virginia, where there is a strong Anglo-Scottish presence.

Events at most Highland gatherings include flat and hurdle races, long and high jumps, pole vaulting, throwing the hammer, and tossing the weight (a round stone ball). A unique Highland event is tossing the caber, a tapered fir pole that must be thrown so that it turns end over end and comes to rest with the small end pointing away from the thrower. Competitors who toss the weight or the caber must wear a traditional Scottish kilt. There are also competitions in bagpipe music and Highland dancing.

See also ALMA HIGHLAND FESTIVAL AND GAMES; GRANDFATHER MOUNTAIN HIGHLAND GAMES AND GATHERING OF SCOTTISH CLANS; and VIRGINIA SCOTTISH GAMES.

CONTACTS:
Central Florida Scottish Highland Games
Central Winds Park
1000 E. SR-434
Winter Springs, FL 32708
www.flascot.com

♦ 1309 ♦ Hilaria
March 25

The ancient Romans celebrated the festival of Hilaria for Cybele, the "mother of the gods," and Attis each year on March 25. According to one legend, Cybele fell in love with a human man named Attis. When Attis's attention later strayed to a woman, Cybele made him go insane. He killed himself, after which flowers grew from his blood and his body became a tree. The day of Hilaria, observing this resurrection of sorts, was celebrated with much merry-making and feasting.

CONTACTS:
Italian National Tourist Board
686 Park Ave.
3rd Fl.
New York, NY 10065
212-245-5618; fax: 212-586-9249
www.italiantourism.com

♦ 1310 ♦ Hill Cumorah Pageant
Begins on the third weekend in July

Billed as the largest outdoor pageant in the United States, the Hill Cumorah Pageant is based on the Bible and the *Book of Mormon* and is presented by the Church of Jesus Christ of Latter-Day Saints (popularly called Mormons) in Palmyra, New York, for nine consecutive evenings (excluding Sunday and Monday) beginning on the third weekend in July.

The drama tells the story of the people who lived on the North American continent between 600 B.C.E. and 421 C.E., and how Christ taught these ancient Americans his gospel after his resurrection in Jerusalem. Presented on seven stages, each showing of the pageant can accommodate an audience of 15,000. More than 500 people participate in the pageant on a volunteer basis. Some impressive features of the pageant include water curtains that are used during the "vision" scenes and an erupting volcano.

Hill Cumorah is believed to be the site where, in 1823, the angel Moroni instructed Joseph Smith, the first prophet of the Mormon Church, to look for the secret records, written upon gold plates, that told about the ancient inhabitants of North America—American Indians that the Mormons believe were descended from the Israelites via the tribe of Joseph. Smith was told that the plates were hidden in a hill named Cumorah, located between Palmyra and Manchester, New York. But it was nearly four years before Moroni gave Smith permission to remove the plates and begin their translation. They would eventually be published as the *Book of Mormon* in 1830.

CONTACTS:
Hill Cumorah Visitors' Center
603 SR-21
Palmyra, NY 14522
315-597-5851; fax: 315-597-0165
www.hillcumorah.com

♦ 1311 ♦ **Hina Matsuri (Doll Festival)**
March 3

Hina Matsuri is a festival for girls, celebrated in homes throughout Japan since the Edo Period (1600-1867), when doll making became a highly skilled craft.

A set of 10 to 15 dolls (or *hina*), usually unmatched family heirlooms from various generations, is displayed on a stand covered with red cloth, the stand having at least three and up to seven steps. Dressed in elaborate antique silk costumes, the dolls represent the emperor and empress, ladies-in-waiting, court ministers, musicians, and servants. Replicas of ornate furnishings are part of the display, as are miniature dishes of foods offered to the emperor and empress. People visit each other's homes to admire the dolls.

In parts of Tottori Prefecture, girls make boats of straw, place a pair of paper dolls in them with rice cakes and, after displaying them with the other hina, set them afloat on the Mochigase River. This custom supposedly dates back to ancient times when dolls were used as talismans to exorcize evil; a paper doll cast into a river signified the washing away of human misfortune.

CONTACTS:
Japan National Tourism Organization
340 E. 2nd St.
Little Tokyo Plaza
Ste. 302
Los Angeles, CA 90012
213-623-1952; fax: 213-623-6301
www.japantravelinfo.com

♦ 1312 ♦ **Hippokrateia Festival**
August

This festival is a celebration of Hippocrates, the "Great Physician," on Kos, the Greek island where he was born in about 460 B.C.E. A number of ancient manuscripts bear the name of Hippocrates; the best known of these is the *Aphorisms*, a collection of short discussions on the nature of illness, its diagnosis, prognosis, and treatment. The Hippocratic oath, an ethical code attributed to Hippocrates, is still used in graduation ceremonies at many medical schools. In it, the physician pledges to refrain from causing harm and to live an exemplary personal and professional life.

Throughout antiquity, Kos attracted the sick and infirm who came for healing at the Shrine of Asclepius, the god of medicine. Today the island is a popular resort, featuring fine beaches, the ruins of Roman baths, a Greek theater, and a museum with a huge statue of Hippocrates. The festival includes performances of ancient drama, concerts, a flower show, and a reenactment of the Hippocratic oath.

CONTACTS:
Greek National Tourism Organization
305 E. 47th St.
2nd Fl.
New York, NY 10017
212-421-5777; fax: 212-826-6940
www.visitgreece.gr

♦ 1313 ♦ **Hiroshima Peace Ceremony**
August 6

This ceremony has been held each year since 1947 at the Peace Memorial Park in Hiroshima, Japan, in memory of the victims of the atomic bomb that devastated the city in 1945. (The day was Aug. 5 in the United States, Aug. 6 in Japan.) It was the first time in history that a weapon of such destruction had been used. The American B-29 Superfortress *Enola Gay* carried the bomb, called "Little Boy." The day is sometimes called **Atomic Bomb Day**, but this refers more accurately to the anniversary of the first atomic bomb test on July 16, 1945, at Alamogordo Air Base in New Mexico.

In announcing the bombing, President Harry S. Truman said, "The force from which the sun draws its power has been loosed against those who brought war to the Far East." The immediate death toll was 60,000, at least 75,000 more were injured, and the bomb wiped out more than four square miles—60 percent of the city. One man on the mission described its explosion as a bright, blinding flash followed by a "black cloud of boiling dust" and above it white smoke that "climbed like a mushroom to 20,000 feet." Three days later, on Aug. 9, a second A-bomb, called "Fat Man," was dropped on Nagasaki, razing the center of the city and killing 39,000. On Aug. 15, Japan surrendered, ending World War II.

The peace ceremony is held in the evening, when the city's citizens set thousands of lighted lanterns adrift on the Ota River and prayers are offered for world peace. Other memorial services are also held throughout the world at this time.

CONTACTS:
Hiroshima Peace Memorial Museum

1-2 Nakajimama-cho
Naka-Ku
Hiroshima 730-0811 Japan
81-82-241-4004; fax: 81-82-247-2464
www.pcf.city.hiroshima.jp/index_e2.html

◆ 1314 ◆ Hispanic Heritage Month
September 15-October 15

Since 1989, National Hispanic Heritage Month has been celebrated in the United States from September 15 until October 15. Issued as a presidential proclamation each year, this period of time includes such important Hispanic anniversaries as the independence days of Costa Rica, El Salvador, Guatemala, Honduras, and Nicaragua on September 15, Mexico's Festival of Independence on September 16, and Columbus Day, or Day of the Race, around October 12.

The activities that take place during the month, particularly in cities with large Hispanic populations, focus on how Latinos have made the United States a richer and more interesting place to live. They include performances by Latino musical groups, lectures about Hispanic life, and special awards presentations to Latinos who have made significant achievements in business, education, or the arts. In Washington, D.C., Hispanic members of Congress and other political leaders sponsor an annual dinner at which awards are presented.

CONTACTS:
Hispanic Heritage Foundation
1001 Pennsylvania Ave. N.W.
Washington, D.C. 20004
202-861-9797
www.hispanicheritage.org

◆ 1315 ◆ Historical Regatta
First Sunday in September

Regattas have been a tradition in Italy for more than seven centuries, and this one in Venice is widely known as one of the most beautiful in the world. It marks the return of Caterina Cornaro (1454-1510), the last queen of Cyprus, to Venice. Originally from a noble Venetian family, Caterina's marriage to James II of Lusignan was arranged by leaders in Venice in an effort to claim Cyprus as Venetian territory. It worked, and in 1489 the dethroned Caterina returned to her homeland to a welcome of regattas and celebrations.

For sheer splendor, the Historical Regatta ranks with the Palio of Siena. It begins with a procession of historical boats, all decorated and strewn with flowers, down the Grand Canal, which is itself decked with flags, banners, and tapestries for the occasion. Leading the procession is the "Machina," a vessel of baroque style with oars, elaborate carvings, and golden sculptures, which serves as a grandstand and carries officials and local dignitaries. Then there are various competitions: for young people, for women, and for small gondolas with two oars and crews in 16th-century costume. The races arouse intense enthusiasm among the spectators, and by the

end of the regatta, all of the canals are crowded with boatloads of revelers.

CONTACTS:
Ve.La. SpA
Isola Nova del Tronchetto, 21
Venice 30135 Italy
39-41-2424
www.regatastoricavenezia.it

Veneto Tourism Directorate Office
Palazzo Sceriman
Cannaregio 161
Venice 30121 Italy
39-41-2792-644; fax: 39-41-2792-697
www.veneto.eu

◆ 1316 ◆ Hitachi Furyumono
Early April

This Japanese festival, held in the city of Hitachi in Ibaraki Prefecture, features puppets known as *furyumono*. They perform on huge floats, some nearly 50 feet high, with five tiers. The front part of the float is concealed by large stage doors, which open to the left and right like extended wings to reveal the puppets performing their plays—usually less complicated retellings of dramas from the Edo Period (1603-1867). The puppeteers must lie down while operating the puppets so that the audience won't be able to see them. A single float may carry as many as 25 puppeteers, along with a seven- or eight-piece orchestra.

The rear part of each float is built to resemble a huge rock. Simpler puppet shows illustrating fables and nursery tales are performed here. The puppetry is part of the annual Cherry Blossom Festival in Hitachi.

CONTACTS:
Japan National Tourist Organization
1 Grand Central Pl. 60 E. 42nd St.
Ste. 448
New York, NY 10165
212-757-5640; fax: 212-307-6754
www.jnto.go.jp

◆ 1317 ◆ Hmong New Year
December to January

The Hmong people of Laos mark a 10-day celebration of the New Year to give thanks to spirits and ancestors, as well as to rejoice in a new beginning. They mark the occasion by wearing silk clothing in bright shades of red, green, and white along with ornate silver jewelry. Music is central to the celebration, with tunes played on such traditional instruments as the teun flute and Hmong-style khene pipe. Other traditional activities of the Hmong in Laos include leaf-blowing, ox-fighting, spinning-top competitions, cross-bow demonstrations, and Makkhon, a ceremony that involves young people tossing a ball made of cotton cloth back and forth.

CONTACTS:
Hmong Association of Washington

P.O. BOX 14492
Seattle, WA 98114 United States
253-218-7585
hmongofwa.org

♦ 1318 ♦ Ho Chi Minh's Birthday
May 19

Ho Chi Minh was born on May 19, 1890. Often referred to as the "father of modern Vietnam," Ho Chi Minh spearheaded the Vietnamese people's revolt against French and Japanese occupation. In 1954, after the French and Japanese left, the United States entered the scene, and it was during this struggle that Ho Chi Minh died in 1969. It was another six years before North and South Vietnam united into the Socialist Republic of Vietnam.

On Ho Chi Minh's birthday each year people hold parades in cities, carrying posters depicting him. Many women wear the *ao dai*, traditional Vietnamese dress. Speeches about Ho Chi Minh generally follow the parades.

CONTACTS:
Ho Chi Minh Museum
19 Ngoc Ha - Ba Dinh
Ha Noi Vietnam
84-43-845-5435; fax: 84-43-843-9837
www.baotanghochiminh.vn

♦ 1319 ♦ Hobart Cup Day
On or near January 26

There are a number of famous horse races in Australia each year that are observed as holidays in the states where they take place. Hobart Cup Day is a holiday in Southern Tasmania; it is run in Hobart around AUSTRALIA DAY, January 26. Northern Tasmania observes Launceston Cup Day a month later. In South Australia, Adelaide Cup Day is celebrated in May. And the MELBOURNE CUP, the country's richest handicap race, is held on the first Tuesday in November.

CONTACTS:
Hobart City Council
16 Elizabeth St.
P.O. Box 503
Hobart, TAS 7001 Australia
61-3-6238-2711; fax: 61-3-6238-2186
www.hobartcity.com.au

♦ 1320 ♦ Hobart Royal Regatta
February

The **Royal Hobart Regatta** is a two-day aquatic carnival that includes sailing, rowing, and swimming events as well as fireworks and parades. It is a holiday in Tasmania, Australia, and is held on the Derwent River sometime in early February during Australia's summer season. Hobart is the capital of Tasmania, Australia's southernmost state.

A similar holiday in northern Tasmania is observed on the first Monday in November and is called **Recreation Day**.

CONTACTS:
Royal Hobart Regatta
Main Office Regatta Grandstand Domain 7000
GPO Box 506
Hobart, TAS 7001 Australia
61-3-6234-7249; fax: 61-3-6234-7249
www.royalhobartregatta.com

♦ 1321 ♦ Hobo Convention
One week in mid-August

The small, rural town of Britt, Iowa (population 2,000), seems an unlikely location for a convention of hobos—the unwashed but colorful riders of America's empty boxcars—but for a week each summer its residents play host to this diminishing segment of the population. From across the nation the hobos come to Britt, where they receive free food, sleeping accommodations in empty boxcars, and the adoration of more than 20,000 visitors who want to find out what a hobo's life is really like.

There is a parade, an arts fair, carnival rides, races, and music. But the real action centers on the hobo camp set up by festival organizers on the outskirts of town, where visitors can hear the life stories of these men who have chosen to travel the country unencumbered by family or property.

The hobos are quick to distinguish themselves from tramps and bums. As one explains, "A hobo wants to wander, but he always works for his meals … a tramp wanders, but never does any work; a bum just drinks and wanders." The first Hobo Convention was held in Britt in 1900, and during the 1930s the event attracted hundreds of hobos. But their ranks are thinning, and today the town is lucky if 30 or 40 real hobos show up.

CONTACTS:
Hobo Museum
51 Main St. S.
Britt, IA 50423 United States
641-843-9104
www.hobo.com

♦ 1322 ♦ Hocktide
Between April 5 and May 9; second Monday and Tuesday after Easter

Also known as **Hock Days**, the second Monday and Tuesday after EASTER in England was in medieval times—and in Hungerford, Berkshire, till the present day—associated with collecting dues or rents and money for the church, particularly in rural areas.

There were a number of traditional methods for demanding money, most of them light-hearted rather than threatening. For example, people were often tied up with ropes and had to pay for their release, giving rise to the name **Binding Tuesday**. Or rope might be stretched across the road to stop passersby, who would then have to pay before they were allowed to continue.

In parts of Berkshire, two "Tutti men" in top hats and morning coats—a "tutti" being a small bouquet of flowers—would go from house to house carrying a "tutti pole" decorated with flowers and ribbons. There was also an orange scatterer who threw oranges to the men, old women, and children to keep them busy while the Tutti men went from house to house demanding both money and a kiss from the lady of the house.

In Yorkshire, children were still celebrating **Kissing Day** as recently as the 1950s—widely believed to have derived from hocktide customs.

Hocktide was also one of the QUARTER DAYS.

CONTACTS:
Hungerford Town Council Office
The Library, Church St.
Hungerford, West Berkshire RG17 0JG United Kingdom
44-1488-686195
www.hungerford.org.uk

♦ 1323 ♦ Hogbetsotso Festival
On and around the first Saturday in November

The week-long Hogbetsotso festival commemorates the migration of the Anlo-speaking Ewes, an ethnic group on the eastern coast of Ghana, from the ancient walled city of Notsie in present-day northern Togo to their current home in Ghana. According to legend, the Anlo-Ewes escaped the wicked chief, Ago-Koli, by walking backwards amidst dancing and drumming to war songs. Each year the Anlo-Ewes hold the Hogbetsotso festival, or "Festival of the Exodus," to remember their journey and the brave leaders who guided them.

The Anlo-Ewes begin the observance of Hogbetsotso with a period of peacemaking, during which any outstanding problems are resolved. They perform a ceremony to purify the traditional stool that is an important fixture in Ghanaian culture, and they clean their villages by sweeping and burning garbage. The festival culminates with a grand durbar, or reception, of chiefs and their people, which takes place on the first Saturday of November in Anloga. At the durbar, the chiefs wear bright ceremonial clothing and sit in state, while citizens pay them tribute. The entire festival period is marked by singing, dancing and merry-making. Born of age-old oral legend, the Hogbetsotso festival has been celebrated for generations.

CONTACTS:
Ghana Ministry of Tourism and Diaspora Relations
P.O. Box 4386
Accra Ghana
233-302-666314
www.touringghana.com

♦ 1324 ♦ Hogmanay
December 31

In Scotland and the northern part of England, the last day of the year is known as Hogmanay. There are a number of theories as to where the name comes from—one of them being that it derives from the ancient Scandinavian name for the night preceding the feast of YULE, *Hoggu-nott* or *Hogg-night*. Another is that it comes from the French expression, *Au gui l'an neuf* ("New Year's gift" or "the last day of the year").

Scottish children, often wearing a sheet doubled up in front to form a huge pocket, used to call at the homes of the wealthy on this day and ask for their traditional gift of an oatmeal cake. They would call out, "Hogmanay!" and recite traditional rhymes or sing songs in return for which they'd be given their cakes to take home. It is for this reason that December 31 was also referred to as **Cake Day**.

Today Hogmanay is celebrated much as is NEW YEAR'S EVE around the rest of the Western world, with street and house parties. Such fire ceremonies as torchlight processions and lighting New Year's fires are popular traditions as well.

See also FIRST-FOOT DAY.

CONTACTS:
Festivals Edinburgh
Business Centre 2.6
4 E. Market St.
Edinburgh, Scotland EH8 8BG United Kingdom
44-131-529-7970
www.edinburghfestivalcity.com

♦ 1325 ♦ Hola Mohalla
February-March

Hola Mohalla is a three-day Sikh festival celebrated in Anandpur Sahib, Punjab, India, on the day after HOLI, the colorful water-tossing springtime festival. Mock battles with ancient weapons are staged, and there are also exhibitions of traditional martial arts like archery and fencing. The important Sikh prophet, GURU GOBIND SINGH, started this fair sometime between 1680 and 1700.

CONTACTS:
Ministry of Tourism, Government of India
1270 Avenue of the Americas
Ste. 303
New York, NY 10020
212-586-4901; fax: 212-582-3274
tourism.nic.in

Society for the Confluence of Festivals in India
www.holifestival.org

♦ 1326 ♦ Holetown Festival
Begins in mid-February

The British were not the first European settlers to establish themselves on the Caribbean island of Barbados, but they were the first to remain permanently after they settled in February 1627. The Holetown Festival, which takes place in the historic town of the same name, marks the approximate date of English settlement. A weeklong celebration of history and culture, the festival has been an annual event since 1977.

The opening celebrations are held at the Holetown Monument, which commemorates the settlers' landing. Over the course of the week there are fashion shows, beauty contests, exhibitions, folksongs, an antique car parade, and a carnival at the festival fairgrounds.

Festival organizers ensure that music is integral to the celebration and that a balance exists between the old and the new, the indigenous and the Western. Along with music concerts showcasing authentic Caribbean music and dancing, there are traditional hymns, folksongs, a music festival at the historic St. James Church, and a concert by the Royal Barbados Police Band, in existence since 1889.

CONTACTS:
Barbados Tourism Authority
820 2nd Ave.
Fifth Fl
New York, NY 10017
212-551-4350 or 800-221-9831; fax: 212-573-9850
www.visitbarbados.org

♦ 1327 ♦ Holi
February-March; 14th day of waxing half of
Hindu month of Phalguna

Holi is a colorful and boisterous Hindu spring festival in India, also known as the **Festival of Colors**. This is a time of shedding inhibitions: People smear each other with red and yellow powder and shower each other with colored water shot from bamboo blowpipes or water pistols. Restrictions of caste, sex, age, and personal differences are ignored. *Bhang*, an intoxicating drink made from the same plant that produces marijuana, is imbibed, and revelry reigns.

The name of the festival derives from the name of the wicked Holika. According to legend, an evil king had a good son, Prince Prahlad, who was sent by the gods to deliver the land from the king's cruelty. Holika, the king's sister, decided to kill the prince with fire. Believing she was immune to fire, she held the child in her lap and sat in flames. But Lord Krishna stepped in to save Prahlad, and Holika was left in the fire and burned to death. On the night before the festival, images of Holika are burned on huge bonfires, drums pound, horns blow, and people whoop.

Another tale, related to the practice of water-throwing, is that the small monkey god Hanuman (*see* HANUMAN JAYANTI) one day managed to swallow the sun. People were sad to live in darkness, and other gods suggested they rub color on one another and laugh. They mixed the color in water and squirted each other, and Hanuman thought this was so funny he gave a great laugh, and the sun flew out of his mouth.

There is also the story that the Mongol Emperor Akbar thought everyone would look equal if covered with color, and he therefore ordained the holiday to unite the castes.

The celebrations differ from city to city. In Mathura, Lord Krishna's legendary birthplace, there are especially exu-berant processions with songs and music. In the villages of Nandgaon and Barsnar, once homes of Krishna and his beloved Radha, the celebrations are spread over 16 days. And in Besant, people set up a 25-foot pole called a *chir* to begin the celebrations and burn it at the end of the festival.

In Bangladesh the festival is called **Dol-Jatra**, the **Swing Festival**, because a Krishna doll is kept in a swinging cradle, or *dol*. In Nepal it is called **Rung Khelna**, "playing with color." They build a three-tiered, 25-foot high umbrella and at its base people light joss sticks, and place flowers and red powder. Instead of squirting water, they drop water-filled balloons from upper windows.

In Suriname it is **Holi Phagwa** and also the **Hindu New Year**.

CONTACTS:
Ministry of Tourism, Government of India
1270 Ave. of the Americas
Ste.303
New York, NY 10020
212-586-4901; fax: 212-582-3274
tourism.gov.in

♦ 1328 ♦ Holland Festival
June

Holland (the Netherlands) didn't really have a single composer who could be honored by a festival in a specific city or town—such as the MOZART Festival in Salzburg, Austria (*see* SALZBURG FESTIVAL), or Germany's Wagner Festival in BAYREUTH. Instead, it was decided in 1947 to have a single festival focused on three major cities—Amsterdam, Rotterdam, and the Hague/Scheveningen—that would cover a wide range of artistic and cultural activities and at the same time draw top international artists to the Netherlands.

Nowadays the festival is centered in Amsterdam and lasts 23 days in June with nearly 150 programs. The festival offers not only performances of orchestral and choral works but opera, ballet, contemporary music, dance, theater, and film as well.

The 2015 Holland Festival will launch Michel van der Aa's The Book of Sand, an interactive song cycle inspired by the stories of Jorge Luis Borges, performed by pop singer Kate Miller-Heidke. Another festival focus, Power and the People, addresses the nature of leadership and the position of women. The "Extra Programme" will elaborate on this year's festival themes with 63 events including introductions, post-performance interviews, debates and lectures with artists, writers and thinkers, most of which are free of charge.

CONTACTS:
Holland Festival
Muziekgebouw aan 't IJ Piet Heinkade 1
4th Fl.
Amsterdam 1019 BR Netherlands
31-20-788-2100; fax: 31-20-788-2102
www.hollandfestival.nl

♦ 1329 ♦ Hollerin' Contest, National
Second Saturday in September

Many years ago, the residents of Spivey's Corner, North Carolina, communicated with each other by calling out their greetings, warnings, and cries of distress. They also hollered for their cows, pigs, and dogs to come in. After modern technology supplanted this primitive mode of communication, a local citizen named Ermon Godwin, Jr., decided in 1969 to revive the custom of hollering by holding a day-long competition. In addition to the hollering contests for people of both sexes and all ages, the event includes a pole climb, conch shell-blowing and fox horn-blowing contests, and a watermelon carry. Winners of the competition have demonstrated their skills on nationwide television. Some of the hollerin' can be heard on the contest's web site.

CONTACTS:
Spivey's Corner Fire Department Assistant Chief
P.O. Box 1242
Dunn, NC 28335
910-567-2600
www.hollerincontest.com

♦ 1330 ♦ **Holmenkollen Day**
Week including second Sunday in March

The **Holmenkollen International Ski Meet** is a week-long Norwegian winter festival held at Holmenkollen Hill outside Oslo. It is the main winter sports event of the year and it covers all types of skiing—cross-country racing and jumping as well as downhill and slalom. The world's best skiers meet here to compete for highly coveted prizes.

The high point of the festival comes on Holmenkollen Day, when over a hundred thousand spectators, headed by the king and the royal family, gather at the famous Holmenkollen Hill to watch the ski-jumping event, which has been held here since 1892. Competitors swoop down the 184-foot jump, and the one who soars the farthest wins the coveted King's Cup.

CONTACTS:
Skiforeningen
Kongeveien 5
Oslo 0787 Norway
47-2292-3200; fax: 47-2292-3250
www.skiforeningen.no/english

♦ 1331 ♦ **Holocaust Memorial Day**
Between April 8 and May 6; Nisan 27

Holocaust Memorial Day, or **Yom ha-Shoah,** was established by Israel's Knesset (parliament) as a memorial to the six million Jews slaughtered by the Nazis between 1933 and 1945. It is observed on the 27th day of the month of Nisan, the day on which Allied troops liberated the first Nazi concentration camp at Buchenwald, Germany, in 1945. It is a commemoration that is observed by many non-Jewish people around the world.

CONTACTS:
U.S. Holocaust Memorial Museum
100 Raoul Wallenberg Pl. S.W.
Washington, D.C. 20024

202-488-0400; fax: 202-479-9726
www.ushmm.org

♦ 1332 ♦ **Holocaust Remembrance Day, International**
January 27

International Holocaust Remembrance Day commemorates the liberation of Auschwitz-Birkenau, the largest Nazi concentration camp, in 1945. Death camps like the one at Auschwitz-Birkenau were used to exterminate the six million Jews and others deemed undesirable by the Nazi regime during World War II. International Holocaust Remembrance Day is officially designated by the United Nations, which asks its member states to honor the victims of the Holocaust each year by developing educational programs to prevent any further acts of genocide. On this day, many Holocaust survivors speak about their experiences. Furthermore, there are art exhibitions and musical performances by survivors and their descendants. Universities and schools offer lessons on the importance of remembering the Holocaust.

CONTACTS:
U.S. Holocaust Memorial Museum
100 Raoul Wallenberg Pl. S.W.
Washington, D.C. 20024 USA
202-488-0400; fax: 202-488-0406
www.ushmm.org

♦ 1333 ♦ **Holy Blood, Procession of the**
Between April 30 and June 3; Ascension Day

This procession is a major religious event in Bruges, Belgium, to venerate the Holy Blood of Christ that was brought back from the Second Crusade by Thierry d'Alsace, count of Flanders.

Thierry's bravery in Jerusalem in the battles against the Saracens was legendary. As a reward for his courage, King Baudouin entrusted the count with a vial of a few drops of blood supposed to have come from Christ's wounds and collected from under the cross by Joseph of Arimathea. When Thierry returned to Bruges on April 7, 1150, there was a great celebration: flowers were strewn in the streets, people waved the banners of the city trades, city dignitaries welcomed the heroic count, and the Holy Reliquary was taken in solemn procession to the Chapel of St. Basile.

The present procession commemorates that original one, although it was not a regular celebration until 1820. Today, the activities begin at 11 A.M. with a pontifical mass in the cathedral. The procession gets under way at 3 P.M., lasts about an hour and a half, and closes with a blessing by the bishop.

As the celebration gets under way, every church bell peals in this usually quiet city. Through living tableaux, the procession tells the story of the Bible from the fall of Adam and Eve, on through Abraham and Moses and to the New Testament stories of ST. JOHN the Baptist, the birth of Jesus, the Last Supper, and the Crucifixion on Calvary. Some dozen groups also depict the triumphant return of Thierry d'Alsace to Bruges. When the procession has returned to Burg Square, where it began, the bishop of Bruges lifts the relic of the Holy Blood and blesses the crowd. Visitors come to Bruges from all over the world for the procession.

See also SAN GENNARO, FEAST OF.

CONTACTS:
Basilica of the Holy Blood
Burg 13
Bruges 8000 Belgium
32-50-33-6792
www.holyblood.com

Belgian Tourist Office
300 E. 42nd St.
14th fl.
New York, NY 10017
212-758-8130; fax: 212-355-7675
www.visitbelgium.com

♦ 1334 ♦ **Holy Family, Feast of the**
Sunday after January 6, Epiphany

In the Roman Catholic Church the Holy Family—Jesus, Mary and Joseph—is thought to provide the perfect example of what the family relationship should be like. But it was not until the 17th century that the Holy Family was venerated as a family, and the feast itself was not officially instituted until 1921. Its popularity spread rapidly, and it is now celebrated by Roman Catholics all over the world. Each of the three members of the sacred household at Nazareth are also honored as individuals on their own feast days.

CONTACTS:
Holy Family Catholic Church
919 N.E. 96th St.
Kansas City, MO 64155 United States
816-436-9200
holyfamily.com

♦ 1335 ♦ **Holy Ghost, Feast of the**
March-July

Holy Ghost Season, or **Altura Do Espírito Santo**, has been celebrated in the Azores, Portugal, since the late 15th century. There are actually two types of celebration: the *bodo*, "banquet," and the *função*, "function." Bodos are held in rural *Impérios*—lavishly decorated buildings that are vacant all year except during the festival. The bodo is a large-scale public festival that includes a mass; a children's procession; the ceremonial distribution of meat, bread, and wine; and a number of other activities including an auction, singing competitions, and bullfights.

The função is a small-scale celebration held in private homes. It represents the payment of a personal promise to the Holy Ghost and consists of a series of ritual exchange events, culminating in the coronation of an emperor, the distribution of gifts to the poor, and a communal meal.

Although Holy Ghost season falls primarily between EASTER and TRINITY SUNDAY, urban Impérios have extended the season to July so the same festival props—such as crowns, flags, and other costly items—can be shared among the various regions. Although observation of the feast has nearly disappeared in continental Portugal, it has been carried to Brazil, Canada, Bermuda, and the United States by Portuguese immigrants.

The Holy Ghost celebrations are based on the story of Queen Isabel of Portugal, who loved the poor and pleaded with God to help her starving people. When two ships laden with cattle and grain miraculously appeared in a Portuguese harbor, the Queen served a banquet to the poor and continued this yearly ceremony as an expression of gratitude to God.

See also DIVINE HOLY SPIRIT, FESTIVAL OF THE.

CONTACTS:
Portuguese National Tourist Office
590 Fifth Ave.
4th Fl.
New York, NY 10036
646-723-0299; fax: 212-575-4737
www.embassyportugal-us.org

♦ 1336 ♦ **Holy Innocents' Day**
December 28

Also known as **Innocents' Day** or **Childermas**, this day commemorates the massacre of all the male children two years and under in Bethlehem as ordered by King Herod, who hoped that the infant Jesus would be among them. Not surprisingly, this day has long been regarded as unlucky—particularly for getting married or undertaking any important task. Edward IV of England went so far as to change the day of his coronation when he realized it would fall on December 28.

In ancient times, the "Massacre of the Innocents" was reenacted by whipping the younger members of a family. But over the years the tables turned, and in some countries it has become a day when children play pranks on their elders. In Mexico, Childermas is the equivalent of APRIL FOOL'S DAY.

CONTACTS:
Episcopal Church of the Holy Innocents
135 Marine St.
Beach Haven, NJ 08008
609-492-7571
www.hiecbh.com

♦ 1337 ♦ **Holy Innocents' Day (Belgium)**
(Allerkinderendag)
December 28

HOLY INNOCENTS' DAY is the traditional anniversary of the slaughter of Bethlehem's male children by King Herod, who hoped that the infant Jesus would be among them. According to legend, two of the murdered children were buried in the Convent of Saint Gerard in the province of Namur, Belgium.

Many Belgian children turn the tables on their elders each year on December 28 by locking them up. Early in the morning, they collect all the keys in the house, so that whenever an unsuspecting adult enters a closet or room, they can lock the door behind him or her and demand a ransom—usually spending money, candy, a toy, or fruit. The innocent person who is being held for ransom is called a "sugar uncle" or "sugar aunt."

The tricks played by children on Holy Innocents' Day have been compared to the pranks that children in the United States and elsewhere play on APRIL FOOLS' DAY.

CONTACTS:
Wallonia-Brussels Tourism Office
300 E. 42nd St.
14th Fl.
New York, NY 10017 United States
212-758-8130; fax: 212-355-7675
www.opt.be

♦ 1338 ♦ Holy Prophet and the Martyrdom of Imam Hasan, Death Anniversary of the
28th day of the Islamic month of Safar

On the Islamic calendar, the anniversaries of the deaths of the prophet Muhammad and his grandson, Hasan, are held on the same date. As a successor of the first imam, Ali, Hasan is an important figure among Shi'ite Muslims, particularly the sect known as the Twelvers. His death by poisoning is an especially mournful chapter in Islamic history. This holiday is observed in Shi'ite communities of the Middle East and is an official holiday in Iran, a country with a large Shi'ite majority.

Many followers convene special meetings in houses or mosques called *rawda-khanis* to mourn for these two figures. The ceremony is led by a rawda-khan, a person skilled at reciting the narratives of Islam.

Major ceremonies are also take place in Mashhad, a holy city in Iran. Caravans of mourners known as *azadars* arrive from across Iran and from different countries to pay their respects to the Prophet and Hasan.

CONTACTS:
Imam Mahdi Association of Marjaeya (I.M.A.M.)
22000 Garrison St.
Dearborn, MI 48124
313-562-4626 or 888-747-8264
www.imam-us.org

♦ 1339 ♦ Holy Queen Isabel, Festival of the
Biennially in July

Queen Isabel of Portugal, born in 1271, is best known for the "miracle of the roses." When her husband, who was unsympathetic to his wife's frequent errands of mercy for the poor and afflicted, demanded to know what she was carrying in the folds of her robe, she told him it was roses, even though she was concealing bread for the hungry. When she opened her robe for him to inspect, the loaves of bread had been transformed into roses. She was beatified by Pope Leo X in 1516 and canonized by Urban VIII in 1625.

Historically, Queen Isabel was a strong advocate for peace in the tumultuous times in which she lived. When her husband, Dom Diniz, died in 1325, she retired to the convent of Santa Clara in Coimbra, Portugal, which she had founded. As the patroness of Coimbra, Queen Isabel is honored in early July in even-numbered years with a week of festivities that include religious processions, fireworks, speeches, concerts, and popular amusements.

CONTACTS:
Confraternity of the Holy Queen Isabel
Church of Queen Isabel
High Sta Clara
Coimbra 3040-270 Portugal
351-239-441-674
www.rainhasantaisabel.org

♦ 1340 ♦ Holy Saturday
Between March 21 and April 24 in the West and between April 3 and May 7 in the East; the day before Easter

The Saturday before EASTER Sunday, also called **Easter Even**, is the last day of HOLY WEEK and brings the season of LENT to a close. In the early church, this was the major day for baptisms. Many churches, especially those of the Anglican Communion, still hold large baptismal services on Holy Saturday. It is also known as the **Vigil of Easter** in reference to the fact that Jesus' followers spent this day, after his crucifixion on GOOD FRIDAY, waiting. The Easter, or Paschal, Vigil, the principal celebration of Easter, is traditionally observed the night of Holy Saturday in many churches today. Another name for this day is the **Descent into Hell**, because it commemorates Jesus' descent into and victory over hell.

Slavic Orthodox Christians bring baskets of food to the church for the Blessing of the Pascha (Easter) Baskets on Holy Saturday. The baskets are filled with the foods from which people have abstained during the Lenten fast and which will be part of the Pascha feast. For many inhabitants of Mexican descent in Los Angeles, California, Holy Saturday is the day for a colorful ceremony known as the Blessing of the Animals, which takes place at the Old Plaza Church near Olvera Street.

CONTACTS:
Cathedral of Our Lady of the Angels
555 W. Temple St.
Los Angeles, CA 90012
213-680-5200
www.olacathedral.org

♦ 1341 ♦ Holy Saturday (Mexico) (Sábado de Gloria)
Between March 21 and April 24; day before Easter

In Mexico, HOLY SATURDAY is observed by burning effigies of Judas Iscariot, the disciple who betrayed Jesus to the religious authorities for 30 pieces of silver. Street vendors sell the papier-mâché effigies, which range from one to five feet in height and make Judas look as ugly as possible. The effigies designed for children are stuffed with candies and hung in the patios of private houses. Other effigies are suspended over the streets or hung from lampposts. All have firecrackers attached, which are ignited as soon as the Mass of Glory is over. As the effigies explode, kids jostle one another in an attempt to retrieve the candies and trinkets that are hidden inside.

The church bells, which have been silent since the Wednesday before EASTER, ring on Holy Saturday, and there are folk beliefs associated with the ringing of the bells. For example, it is believed that plants or hair trimmed while the bells are ringing will grow back faster. Children are often smacked on the legs so that they'll grow taller.

See also BURNING OF JUDAS.

CONTACTS:
Mexico Tourism Board
Viaducto Miguel Alemán 105
Col. Escandón
Mexico City 11800 Mexico
800-262-9128
www.visitmexico.com

◆ 1342 ◆ **Holy Thursday**
Between April 30 and June 3; 40 days after Easter

Holy Thursday usually refers to MAUNDY THURSDAY, but in parts of rural England, it traditionally refers to ASCENSION DAY, the day on which Jesus Christ ascended into heaven. The English custom of "well dressing," which may have had its roots in a pagan festival, became associated with Holy Thursday in 1615. There was a severe drought in Derbyshire that year and most of the wells and streams dried up. The only wells that still had water were at Tissington, where people came to get water for their livestock. From that time onward, a special thanksgiving service was held there on Ascension Day, and Tissington became known as "the village of holy wells."

The well-dressing ceremony developed into a full-fledged festival in the 19th century. After delivering his sermon, the priest leads a procession to the wells, which are nearly hidden by screens of fresh flowers fastened to wooden frames. There follows a simple ceremony at each well, asking God to bless and keep the waters pure.

CONTACTS:
Estate Office, Tissington Hall
Tissington
Ashbourne, Derbyshire DE6 1RA United Kingdom
44-13-3535-2200
www.tissingtonhall.co.uk

St Mary's Church
Tissington

Ashbourne, Derbyshire DE6 1RA United Kingdom
44-7758-704452
peakfive.org

◆ 1343 ◆ **Holy Week**
Between March 15 and April 18 in the West and between March 28 and May 1 in the East; the week preceding Easter

Holy Week, the seven days beginning with PALM SUNDAY that precede EASTER, is the most solemn week in the Christian year. It includes MAUNDY THURSDAY, GOOD FRIDAY, and HOLY SATURDAY. The Germans call Holy Week **Still Week** or **Silent Week**, and some Americans call it **Passion Week**, although the season known as Passiontide actually refers to the preceding week.

Passion Sunday or CARLING SUNDAY is the fifth Sunday in LENT (the Sunday *before* Palm Sunday), but since Holy Week was also referred to as Passion Week, this apparently led to the identification of Palm Sunday with Passion Sunday. Since 1970 the Roman Catholic Church has considered the two names to be synonymous, although in 1956 the two Sundays were designated the First Sunday and Second Sunday of the Passion. Another name for the fifth Sunday in Lent is Judica Sunday, from the Introit for the day.

See also PRISONERS, FEAST OF THE; SEMANA SANTA IN GUATEMALA.

CONTACTS:
Orthodox Church in America
6850 N. Hempstead Tpke
P.O. Box 675
Syosset, NY 11791
516-922-0550; fax: 516-922-0954
oca.org

◆ 1344 ◆ **Holy Week (Czech Republic)**
Between March 15 and April 18; the week preceding Easter

In the Czech Republic, each day of HOLY WEEK is associated with traditional customs that combine pagan rituals with those commemorating the death and resurrection of Jesus Christ. The first day of the week, PALM SUNDAY, also known as Flower Sunday, commemorates the arrival of Jesus in Jerusalem. On this day priests bless branches, flowers, and wood that have been brought to church by the congregation. Czech farmers make crosses from the blessed materials and place the crosses in their fields in hopes of a bountiful harvest.

During Holy Week, Czechs undertake spring-cleaning of their homes and may even paint them in an effort to refresh their surroundings after the winter. Chimneys are swept and furniture and bedding aired outside. *Škaredá streda* (Ugly Wednesday is also known as Spy Wednesday in reference to the tradition that it was the day on which Judas Iscariot betrayed Jesus to the Roman authorities. Thursday of Holy Week, known as Holy Thursday or MAUNDY THURSDAY in the English-speaking world, is called *Zelený ctvrtek* (Green

Thursday) in the Czech Republic. On this day Czechs traditionally eat a meal featuring green herbs and vegetables. In the past, children would be sent outside in the morning to bathe in a stream or river, then return home to eat *jidasky*, a pastry shaped into a rope. The braided form of this cake refers to the noose and symbolizes the hanging death of Judas. Spreading jidasky or another bread with honey was believed to offer protection from snakebites throughout the year, and bread with honey was also tossed into wells to assure that they would not run dry during the coming year. Church bells are silenced on Green Thursday and replaced in villages by noisemakers such as wooden rattles. On Good Friday Czech custom calls for wading across a stream barelegged in order to assure good health. In addition, the weather on this day is believed to portend the weather for the rest of the year.

Saturday of Holy Week is known as White Saturday in the Czech Republic and is considered a lucky day to sow seeds. The day concludes with an Easter Vigil religious service and the return of church bells. Preparations for Easter include decorating eggs (*kraslice*) using a variety of methods to create intricate, colorful designs. Typically, the egg white and yolk are removed before the egg is colored. Techniques for applying color include wax-resistance, painting, and scratching the designs onto dyed shells. Boys and young men weave wands from willow branches and decorate them with ribbons. On Easter Monday they use the whips to symbolically spank girls to promote their good health. In return the girls give them a decorated or chocolate egg.

CONTACTS:
Embassy of the Czech Republic
3900 Spring of Freedom St. N.W.
Washington, D.C. 20008
202-274-9100; fax: 202-966-8540
www.mzv.cz

◆ 1345 ◆ Holy Week (Haiti)
Between March 15 and April 18; the week preceding Easter

Holy Week in Haiti is signaled by the appearance of "Monsieur Judas" effigies made out of sawdust and rags. Early in the week these symbolic figures are honored as Jesus' apostles and treasured guests. When Jesus' death is affirmed on Good Friday, however, the effigies disappear—usually hidden by someone in a ravine or cane field just outside town.

On Saturday morning everyone starts hunting for Judas, swinging machetes, knives, and clubs as they shout, "Qui bo' li?" (Where is he?). The search often becomes quite frenzied and every time a Judas is found, the attackers slice him to bits. By midday the remains of these effigies litter the ground. This ritual reenactment of Jesus' betrayal by Judas involves Haitians of all ages and reflects the overall tone of Holy Week celebrations, which are more secular than spiritual.

CONTACTS:
Episcopal Church of Haiti
P.O. Box 1309
Port au Prince 26135 Haiti
509-257-1624
www.egliseepiscopaledhaiti.org

◆ 1346 ◆ Holy Week (Mexico)
Between March 15 and April 18; the week preceding Easter

Although many dramatizations of the events of Holy Week, or **Semana Santa**, take place throughout Mexico, the Passion plays performed in the towns of Taxco, Malinalco, Tzintzuntzan, and Iztapalapa are among the most elaborate. In Malinalco, everyone in town participates in the drama, with the wealthier men taking the parts of Roman soldiers (because they own horses) and less wealthy members of the community representing the Christians, who have no horses but wear brightly colored satin costumes. The young girls are dressed as angels, complete with wings that sparkle in the sunlight.

In Tzintzuntzan, the Passion play starts at 12:00 P.M. on Maundy Thursday and doesn't end until midnight on Good Friday. The play takes place outdoors, in a grove of olive trees near the church, and is known for the professionalism of its actors. The Iztapalapa pageant takes place during Holy Week, and there are several locations throughout the town where scenes are presented. It is best known for its elaborate costumes.

Mexicans are also known for the effigies of Judas that are displayed in the streets on Holy Saturday. Although some of these papier-mâché effigies represent clowns, cowboys, devils, and pirates, the majority portray unpopular politicians or other citizens who have fallen out of public favor.

CONTACTS:
Basilica of Our Lady of Guadalupe
Plaza de las Américas
Núm. 1
Colonia Villa de Guadalupe, Gustavo A. Madero 07050 Mexico
52-55-5118-0500; fax: 52-55-5118-0599
www.virgendeguadalupe.mx

Mexico Tourism Board
800-446-3942
www.visitmexico.com

◆ 1347 ◆ Holy Week (Panama)
Between March 15 and April 18; the week preceding Easter

In Panama, Holy Week is marked by the appearance of devil dancers who wear headdresses that resemble animals' heads and tails made from bells. They visit small villages on Holy Saturday to get rid of evil spirits for the coming year. In larger towns, they participate in public, staged combat with festival participants in angel costumes. Although the devil can be seen as a biblical character, the purifying rites performed by the devil dancers in rural areas probably originate in indigenous traditions.

CONTACTS:
Embassy of Panama
2862 McGill Terr. N.W.
Washington, D.C. 20008
202-483-1407; fax: 202-483-8413
www.embassyofpanama.org

Balboa Union Church
P.O. Box 0843-03040

Balboa
Ancon Panama
507-314-1004
balboaunionchurch.org

♦ 1348 ♦ Holy Week (Philippines)
Between March 15 and April 18; the week preceding Easter

Colorful Passion plays take place throughout LENT in the Philippines (*see* MORIONES FESTIVAL). PALM SUNDAY religious services focus on the joy of Jesus' entry into Jerusalem, and include the blessing of palm branches. Some people visit as many churches as possible on MAUNDY THURSDAY, in a custom known as *visita iglesia* (visit church). Retelling or singing the Passion story is also popular on this day. On GOOD FRIDAY devout Filipinos watch Passion plays, take part in a devotional meditation known as the Stations of the Cross, or participate in public processions of penitents. In some of these, people whip themselves; in others a few people each year will have themselves crucified.

A custom known as *Salubong*, the meeting of the resurrected Jesus and his mother, takes place on EASTER Sunday morning. A religious statue representing Jesus and another representing the Blessed Virgin Mary are taken to the opposite ends of town. People line up behind one or the other image and begin a procession towards a centrally located church. When the two images meet, a children's choir begin to sing, the veil covering Mary's eyes falls away, and a flock of doves is released. Afterwards the images are returned to the church and people attend Easter Sunday mass.

CONTACTS:
Basilica del Santo Niño de Cebu
Osmeña Blvd.
Cebu City Philippines
32-255-6697
basilicasantonino.org.ph

♦ 1349 ♦ Holy Week (Portugal) (Semana Santa)
Between March 15 and April 18; the week preceding Easter

There are exhibits in the churches and street processions illustrating scenes from the Passion of Christ throughout HOLY WEEK in Portugal. In the city of Guimarães, the church of *Senhor dos Passos* shows a different Passion tableau each day of Holy Week. The processions are usually attended by bands of *anjinhos*, or children dressed as angels, with crowns on their heads and fluffy wings attached to their shoulders. The figures of Jesus, which have real hair, eyelashes, and crystal tears, are elaborately dressed in purple velvet robes. The clergy's vestments are also purple, and worshippers watching the procession throw violets at the image of the suffering Jesus.

CONTACTS:
Portugal National Tourist Board
Rua Ivone Silva, Lote 6

Lisbon 1050-124 Portugal
351-211-140-200
www.visitportugal.com

Embassy of Portugal
2012 Massachusetts Ave. N.W.
Washington, D.C. 10036
202-332-3007; fax: 202-223-3926
www.embassyportugal-us.org

♦ 1350 ♦ Homage to Cuauhtemoc (Homenaje a Cuauhtemoc)
August

Cuauhtemoc, the last Aztec emperor, is honored each year with a festival held in front of his statue on the Paseo de la Reforma in Mexico City. After the story of his life and his struggle against the Spaniards has been recited in Spanish and native Indian languages, groups of Conchero dancers perform the dances for which they are renowned. Wearing feathered headdresses trimmed with mirrors and beads and carrying pictures of Christ or various saints, they represent the blending of Indian and Spanish cultures. Most Conchero groups have 50 to 100 dancers, and each dances in his own rhythm and to his own accompaniment. The tempo increases gradually until it reaches a sudden climax, followed by a moment of silence.

Cuauhtemoc is admired for his "bold and intimate acceptance of death," in the words of the Mexican poet Octavio Paz. Paz says that the entry of the Spanish into Mexico precipitated the extinction of the Aztec culture.

CONTACTS:
Mexico Tourism Board
800-446-3942
www.visitmexico.com

♦ 1351 ♦ Homeless Persons' Remembrance Day, National
On or around December 21

Since 1990, the National Coalition for the Homeless and the National Health Care for the Homeless Council have sponsored National Homeless Persons' Remembrance Day to bring attention to the plight of the nation's homeless population and to encourage the public to act on their behalf.

Local groups across the country are encouraged first to determine the number of homeless persons in their community who died in the previous year and then arrange a ceremony to remember them. Candlelight marches, vigils, graveside services, plays and performances, religious services, and public policy advocacy are the suggested ways of remembering. Some groups have read publicly a list of names of the deceased. Because media attention to such issues increases during the holiday season in December, National Homeless Persons' Remembrance Day was in part created to garner a public forum for this issue, and local groups are encouraged to seek out and work with their local media outlets to publicize the event.

CONTACTS:
National Coalition for the Homeless
2201 P St. N.W.
Washington, D.C. 20037
202-462-4822; fax: 202-462-4823
nationalhomeless.org

◆ 1352 ◆ Homowo
Between August and September

Homowo is a harvest festival of thanks to the gods of the Ga (or Gan) people as well as the mark of the new year. *Homowo* means "starved gods," and the festival commemorates the good harvest the Ga were given in ancient times. This harvest came after the famine they endured while traveling to their present home in Ghana.

The festival begins on Thursday and those who have moved away are called *Soobii,* "Thursday people," because that's the day they arrive home for the festival. The following day is the yam festival and the day of twins. All twins who are dressed in white are specially treated all day. Each day there are processions, songs, and dancing until the great day arrives: Homowo, or the **Hunger-Hooting Festival** and open house.

Most homes have enough food in them for a week during the festival. Fish are abundant in Ghana at this time of year, and palm-nut soup, *kpokpoi,* or *ko,* round out the traditional menu. Ko is a kind of grits made with unleavened corn dough and palm oil. The chiefs and elders sprinkle the ko everywhere people have been buried, then go to the prison and personally feed the warders. The following day they visit friends and relatives, reconciling and exchanging New Year's greetings.

CONTACTS:
Ghana Tourist Authority
P.O. Box 3106
Accra Ghana
233-302-682601; fax: 233-302-682510
ghana.travel

◆ 1353 ◆ Homstrom
First Saturday in February

Homstrom is a Swiss festival celebrating the end of winter. In many ways, it is reminiscent of the February 1 mid-winter festival observed by the ancient Celts, known as IMBOLC. One tradition associated with the day is the burning of a straw man who symbolizes Old Man Winter. It is occasionally observed by Swiss-American communities on the first Saturday in February.

CONTACTS:
Swiss National Tourist Office
608 Fifth Ave.
New York, NY 10020
800-794-7795; fax: 212-262-6116
www.myswitzerland.com

◆ 1354 ◆ Honduras Independence Day
September 15

Honduras joined four other Central American countries—Costa Rica, El Salvador, Guatemala, and Nicaragua—in declaring independence from Spain on September 15, 1821. Independence Day is a national holiday and festivities are especially colorful in the capital city of Tegucigalpa.

CONTACTS:
Embassy of Honduras
3007 Tilden St. N.W.
Washington, D.C. 20008
202-966-7702; fax: 202-966-9751
www.hondurasemb.org

◆ 1355 ◆ Honduras Soldiers' Day
October 3

This celebration is held on the birthday of Francisco Morazán (1792–1842), a highly revered Honduran general and statesman. Along with serving as the head of state of his own country, he was also a three-time president of the Central American Federation, a short-lived republic composed of several present-day countries of that region. Morazán's achievements as a military leader in various liberation struggles led the Honduran government to designate his birthday as the official date to honor the country's soldiers.

The day's main celebration is a military parade that takes place in Tegucigalpa, Honduras's capital city. The procession features the service members of every branch of the armed forces, along with dozens of tanks and artillery carriers. The 1997 celebration featured an air display by military helicopters and jet aircraft.

CONTACTS:
Honduran Institute of Tourism
Col. San Carlos
Edif. Europa Apdo.
Tegucigalpa 3261 Honduras
504-2222-2124
www.iht.hn

Honduran Embassy
3007 Tilden St. N.W.
Washington, D.C. 20008
202-966-7702; fax: 202-966-9751
www.hondurasemb.org

◆ 1356 ◆ Hong Kong Arts Festival
Three to four weeks over February and March

This annual celebration of the arts in Hong Kong has been held since 1972. Artists from around the world appear for a diverse program that includes opera, orchestral concerts, chamber music, jazz, dance, film, theater, and exhibits. About 117,000 people attended the 43rd Hong Kong Arts Festival in 2015. The festival featured 1,500 acclaimed artists from around the world in 137 performances, including 16 world premieres and 10 Asian premieres. As the final highlight of the festival, the Bolshoi Ballet performed Balanchine's masterpiece, Jewels.

CONTACTS:
Hong Kong Arts Festival Society Ltd.
12/F 2 Harbour Rd
Rm. 1205
Wanchai Hong Kong
852-2824-3555; fax: 852-2824-3798
www.hk.artsfestival.org

♦ 1357 ♦ Hong Kong International Film Festival
March-April

Regarded as a premier platform in Asia for showcasing new films, the Hong Kong International Film Festival (HKIFF) facilitates cultural exchange, promotes Hong Kong and Chinese movies, and provides a local opportunity to experience cinema from all over the world. Presented by the Hong Kong International Film Festival Society, HKIFF takes place annually during March and April. Screenings of over 300 films from more than 60 countries occur at venues across the city. Launched in 1977, the festival is Hong Kong's largest cultural event today, and is increasingly regarded by independent filmmakers as a forum for the contentious themes that address censorship in China.

Competition sections of the festival include young cinema, the documentary, the short film, the FIPRESCI (International Federation of Film Critics) Prize and the SIGNIS (World Catholic Association for Communication) Award. The non-competition section offers retrospectives of renowned filmmakers and a focus on the history of regional cinema. Film buffs and industry professionals attend seminars, panel discussions, and music performances. Recently, the addition of business and marketing events has added an important new dimension to the festival.

CONTACTS:
Hong Kong International Film Festival Office
21/F, Millennium City 3
370 Kwun Tong Rd.
Kowloon Hong Kong (China)
852-2970-3300; fax: 852-2970-3011
www.hkiff.org.hk/en/index.php

♦ 1358 ♦ Hong Kong Special Administrative Region Establishment Day
July 1

Formerly an occupied territory of the United Kingdom, Hong Kong became a Special Administrative Region (SAR) of China on July 1, 1997. The day is reserved for official celebrations of Hong Kong and its unique "one country, two systems" arrangement with its mainland ally.

Large crowds observe the anniversary by turning out for an official flag-raising ceremony displaying the emblems of Hong Kong and the People's Republic of China. There is also a parade featuring traditional drumming performances and dragon dance troupes.

An alternative tradition has developed since the transfer of power in 1997. Dissenters mark the occasion by holding a massive march in which they protest against the Chinese government with demands that it commit to democratic practices like universal suffrage and the protection of freedom of speech.

CONTACTS:
Hong Kong Tourism Board
370 Lexington Ave.
Ste. 1812
New York, NY 10017
212-421-3382; fax: 212-421-8428
www.discoverhongkong.com

♦ 1359 ♦ Hong Kong WinterFest
Early December to January 1

The Hong Kong WinterFest is a celebration of the holiday season and the coming of New Year. Each year, the Chinese city of Hong Kong hosts this giant event, which many commentators have dubbed as one of the top ten holiday festivals. During WinterFest, Victoria Harbour and the buildings around it become aglow with light installations known as the "symphony of lights." Furthermore, all of Hong Kong adopts a festive look with bright lights and seasonal displays—including a giant lighted Christmas tree in Statue Square. A series of different activities and celebrations takes place during the festival, such as holiday street markets and gourmet food vendors. Visitors also enjoy Christmas concerts, ballets, and other theatrical events at venues throughout Hong Kong. City churches organize carols and other specialty musical programs at parks and malls. The month-long festival concludes with fireworks, signaling the beginning of the New Year.

CONTACTS:
Hong Kong Tourism Board
370 Lexington Ave.
Ste. 1812
New York, NY 10017
212-421-3382; fax: 212-421-8428
www.discoverhongkong.com/eng

♦ 1360 ♦ Hooverfest
August

Hooverfest celebrates the August 10, 1874, birthday of former President Herbert Hoover. The event is hosted by the Herbert Hoover Presidential Library Association of West Branch, Iowa. Hooverfest includes arts and crafts, stage shows, live musical entertainment, a memorial service, and fireworks. The Hoover Presidential Library is situated on a national historic site that includes Hoover's birthplace, his burial site, the library housing the official papers of his administration, and a Quaker meeting house.

A special Hooverball tournament is also held during Hooverfest. Hooverball was invented by White House physician Joel T. Boone as a way to help President Hoover stay fit. The game combines elements from tennis, volleyball, and medicine ball. It is played on a 66-foot by 30-foot court with a volleyball net and either a four-pound or six-pound medicine ball. Teams of two to four players compete against each other. Scoring is the same as in tennis. The game is credited with helping Hoover keep his weight under control. Once popular with the White House staff even after Hoover left office, the game has become less popular in recent years.

CONTACTS:
Hoover Presidential Foundation
302 Parkside Dr.
West Branch, IA 52358
319-643-5327; fax: 319-643-2391
www.hooverassociation.org

♦ 1361 ♦ Hope Watermelon Festival
Second weekend in August

Best known as the birthplace of U.S. President Bill Clinton, Hope, Ark., is also "Home of the World's Largest Watermelons" and hosts the only watermelon festival featuring giant watermelons.

They are indeed large. Hope watermelon growers have been competing to grow the biggest since the 1920s. In 1925, Hugh Laseter created a sensation with a record 136-pounder that was exhibited for a few days and then sent to President Calvin Coolidge. The watermelons kept getting bigger. The 1928 champion was 144 3/4 pounds and was sent to the Rexall Corp. in Boston, Mass., where it "created quite a bit of excitement," according to old accounts.

The first 200-pound melon was grown in 1979 by Ivan Bright and his son Lloyd; seeds from it went for $8 each. That melon broke a 44-year record held by O. D. Middlebrooks, who had grown a 195-pound melon. (It was sent to actor Dick Powell.) In 1985, Lloyd Bright's 10-year-old son Jason produced a 260-pound watermelon that was recorded in the *1992 Guinness Book of World Records*. These melons attain their great size because of the quality of the soil, an early greenhouse start, and careful pruning. Hope farmers also grow average-size watermelons, weighing 30 to 40 pounds.

The Hope Watermelon Festival originated in 1926, lapsed with hard times, was revived in 1977, and has been held annually ever since with attendance at about 50,000. There has been nationwide television and press coverage because of the colossal melons. This is a festival of real down-home Americana: ice cream socials, a big fish fry, softball, a dog show, arm wrestling, arts and crafts booths, musical entertainment, antique car and engine shows, and hot air balloon rides.

The watermelon events include a watermelon toss, a melon-decorating competition, a melon-eating contest, a melon-seed-spitting contest, and a melon-judging and auction. While he was governor of Arkansas, Mr. Clinton visited the festival to compete in the Watermelon 5K Run.

CONTACTS:
Hope-Hempstead County Chamber of Commerce
200 S. Main St.

P.O. Box 250
Hope, AR 71802 United States
870-777-3640; fax: 870-722-6154
www.hopechamberofcommerce.com

♦ 1362 ♦ Hopi Flute Ceremony
Every other year for nine days in mid-August

Like the HOPI SNAKE DANCE, the Flute Ceremony takes place over a nine-day period in the summer on the mesas of northeastern Arizona, where the Hopi Indians live. The two events take place on an alternating basis, with the Snake Dance occurring one year and the Flute Ceremony the next. The purpose of the latter is to encourage rainfall and promote the growth of corn, which is the primary food of the Hopi nation.

The Flute Ceremony takes place in the ancestral rooms of the Flute clan. It begins with a procession into the pueblo led by the clan's chief, who is followed by the Flute boy in his white ceremonial kilt, with a Flute girl on either side wearing feathers in their hair and two white blankets, one of which serves as a skirt.

Many of the rites involved in the Flute Ceremony are actually pantomimes of what the Hopis want their gods to do. For example, the priest may scatter meal on the ground or around the flute altar in imitation of falling rain. Pouring water into the bowl that sits in front of the altar from the six cardinal directions of the world (north, south, east, west, up, down) shows the gods that the priest wants them to send rain from six different directions. Blowing clouds of smoke on the altar shows that he wants rain clouds to appear. And a bullroarer, an instrument that makes a whizzing sound when swung in circles overhead, is used to imitate the sound of thunder.

CONTACTS:
Hopi Cultural Center
P.O. Box 67
Second Mesa, AZ 86043
928-734-2401; fax: 928-734-6651
www.hopiculturalcenter.com

♦ 1363 ♦ Hopi Snake Dance
Every other year in August

The Snake Dance is the grand finale of ceremonies to pray for rain, held by individual Hopi tribes in Arizona every two years. Hopis believe their ancestors originated in an underworld, and that their gods and the spirits of ancestors live there. They call snakes their brothers, and trust that the snakes will carry their prayers to the Rainmakers beneath the earth. Thus the Hopi dancers carry snakes in their mouths to impart prayers to them.

The ceremonies, conducted by the Snake and Antelope fraternities, last 16 days. On the 11th day preparations start for the Snake Dance. For four days, snake priests go out from their village to gather snakes. On the 15th day, a race is run, signifying rain gods bringing water to the village. Then the

Antelopes build a *kisi*, a shallow pit covered with a board, to represent the entrance to the underworld. At sunset on the 15th day, the Snake and Antelope dancers dance around the plaza, stamping on the kisi board and shaking rattles to simulate the sounds of thunder and rain. The Antelope priest dances with green vines around his neck and in his mouth—just as the Snake priests will later do with snakes.

The last day starts with a footrace to honor the snakes. The snakes are washed and deposited in the kisi. The Snake priests dance around the kisi. Each is accompanied by two other priests: one holding a snake whip and one whose function will be to catch the snake when it's dropped. Then each priest takes a snake and carries it first in his hands and then in his mouth. The whipper dances behind him with his left arm around the dancer's neck and calms the snake by stroking it with a feathered wand. After four dances around the plaza, the priests throw the snakes to the catchers. A priest draws a circle on the ground, the catchers throw the snakes in the circle, the Snake priests grab handfuls of them and run with them to turn them loose in the desert.

The HOPI FLUTE CEREMONY takes place in alternate years.

CONTACTS:
Hopi Cultural Center
P.O. Box 67
Second Mesa, AZ 86043
928-734-2401; fax: 928-734-6651
www.hopiculturalcenter.com

Arizona Office of Tourism
1110 W. Washington St.
Ste. 155
Phoenix, AZ 85007
602-364-3700; fax: 602-364-3701
tourism.az.gov

♦ 1364 ♦ Hora at Prislop
Second Sunday in August

The Hora is a dancing festival held at Mount Prislop at the Transylvania-Moldavia border in Romania. The dancers of the hora carry big rings that symbolize the friendship of the people of the regions of Moldavia, Maramures, and Transylvania. The top artistic groups gather at Prislop Pass to present a parade in colorful folk costumes and then a program of songs and dances, ending with the lively peasant horas. Typical food dishes of the area are served and folk art is on display.

CONTACTS:
Romanian National Tourist Office
355 Lexington Ave.
8th Fl.
New York, NY 10017 United States
212-545-8484
www.romaniatourism.com

Transylvania Live
718 B Madison Ave.
Cape May, NJ 08204
866-376-6183
www.visit-transylvania.us

♦ 1365 ♦ Hordad, Feast of
May, September, October; sixth day of Hordad, the third Zoroastrian month

This is considered a "sacred name day" in the Zoroastrian calendar because the same *yazata* or spiritual being, Hordad, rules the day of the week as well as the month. Hordad is a lesser deity who stands for wholeness or perfection; also known as Khordad, this spiritual being shares her name with the third month and the sixth day of the week.

The Zoroastrian calendar has 12 months of 30 days each, plus five extra days at the end of the year. Because of discrepancies in the calendars used by widely separated Zoroastrian communities around the world, there are now three different calendars in use, and the Feast of Hordad can fall either in May, September, or October, according to the Gregorian calendar.

There are about 100,000 followers of Zoroastrianism today, and most of them live in northwestern India or Iran. Smaller communities exist in Pakistan, Sri Lanka, Canada, the U.S., England, and Australia.

CONTACTS:
California Zoroastrian Center
8952 Hazard Ave.
Westminster, CA 92683
714-893-4737; fax: 714-894-9577
czc.org

♦ 1366 ♦ Horn Dance
Monday following first Sunday after September 4

The ancient Horn Dance, believed by many to have originated in Norman times or before, is performed at Abbots Bromley, a small village in Staffordshire, England, as part of the **Wakes Monday** celebration each year. Wakes Monday, the day after the first Sunday following September 4, was at one time part of the Old St. BARTHOLOMEW FAIR. But the Horn Dance is all that remains of the original three-day festival. Although some believe it was once an ancient fertility dance, the Horn Dance probably had something to do with hunting rights and customs in nearby Needwood Forest.

A dozen local men, ranging in age from 12 to more than 50, dress in 16th-century foresters' costumes. Six of them carry reindeer antlers mounted on short wooden sticks. There is also a Hobby Horse, a man playing Robin Hood, a man dressed as a woman who plays the role of Maid Marian, a Fool carrying an inflated bladder on a stick, and a young archer who snaps his bow in time with the music—originally provided by a pipe and tabor but nowadays by a concertina and a triangle.

Beginning at the parish church, the men dance their way around the parish boundaries, stopping to perform at homes and farms along the way. The six deermen, three of whom carry white antlers and three black, take turns "charging" each other while the Hobby Horse prances, the Fool shakes his bladder at the spectators, and Maid Marian takes up a collection. The dancing is over by evening, when everyone adjourns to the local pub or goes home to eat Wakes Cakes, "fair rock candy"—sugar-coated sticks of candy—and brandy snap cookies.

CONTACTS:
Clerk to Abbots Bromley Parish Council
The Hayloft, Marsh Farm Uttoxeter Rd.
Abbots Bromley
Rugeley, Staffordshire WS15 3EJ United Kingdom
44-1283-840891
www.abbotsbromley.com

♦ 1367 ♦ Hortobágy Bridge Fair and International Equestrian Festival
July

This annual event is a showcase of Hungary's fine horses and riders on the Hortobágy, part of the Great Plain of Hungary. The festival also celebrates the famous nine-arched bridge, built in 1833, that crosses the Hortobágy River and is the longest stone bridge in the country.

The Hortobágy National Park is 150 square kilometers in the grassy *puszta* ("prairie") of the Great Plain near the historic city of Debrecen. During the Turkish occupation that began in the 14th century the area was depopulated, and in the 18th century it was used for breeding horses, cattle, and sheep. The equestrian fair is held outside the city and features the famed Lipizzaner horses (from Austrian stock) in dressage exhibitions, the *csikós* (Hungarian cowboy) in colorful embroidered riding costume, carriage parades, pulling contests for draft horses, and other equestrian events. There are also crafts fairs and a peasant market.

CONTACTS:
Hungarian National Tourist Board
223 E. 52nd St.
New York, NY 10022
212-695-1221
www.gotohungary.com

♦ 1368 ♦ Hosay Festival
10th day of Islamic month of Muharram

To Muslims in the Eastern Hemisphere, the **Hussein Festival** is a solemn occasion commemorating the massacre of Hussein and his brother Hassan, grandsons of the prophet Muhammad, on the 10th day of the month of Muharram in 680 (*see* ASHURA). But in Trinidad and Tobago, where the Hosay (or Hussein) Festival was first celebrated in 1884, the traditional procession of mourning has been mixed with various European, African, and Indian rituals to form a unique celebration.

The most popular processions are held in the towns of St. James, Curepe, Tunapuna, Couva, and Cedros. The festival usually begins the evening of Muharram 9 with a solemn procession of flags symbolizing the beginning of the battle of Kerbela, in which Hussein and Hassan were killed. On the second day dancers wearing *tadjahs*—small minaretted tombs made of bamboo, colored tissue, tinfoil, crepe paper, mirrors, and coconut leis—parade through the streets to the accompaniment of African drummers in a ritual that is reminiscent of CARNIVAL (*see* TRINIDAD AND TOBAGO CARNIVAL).

The highlight of the festival occurs on the third night, when the large tadjahs, some of which are six feet tall, are carried through the streets. There are also two moons, representing Hussein and his brother, carried by specially trained dancers. These large crescent-shaped structures are studded with sharp blades and carried on the dancers' shoulders. At midnight, the two moons engage in a ritual embrace to a chorus of cheers from the onlookers.

CONTACTS:
Ministry of Tourism - Trinidad and Tobago
1 Wrightson Rd.
Levels 8 & 9, Tower C
International Waterfront Complex
Port-of-Spain Trinidad and Tobago
868-624-1403; fax: 868-625-1825
www.tourism.gov.tt

Trinidad and Tobago Tourism Development Company
Level 1, Maritime Center
Ste. 29, Tenth Ave.
Barataria Trinidad and Tobago
868-675-7034; fax: 868-638-7962
www.gotrinidadandtobago.com

♦ 1369 ♦ Hoshana Rabbah
Between September 27 and October 24; Tishri 21

On each of the first six days of the Jewish SUKKOT festival, a single stanza of the *Hoshanat* litany is recited (except on the Sabbath) and the congregation circles the reader's platform carrying the four species: a palm branch, citron, three myrtle twigs, and two willow branches, all gathered into a bouquet. But on the seventh day, known as the **Great Hoshana**, the congregation makes seven circuits around the altar, after which the four species are laid down and a bunch of five willow branches is picked up and beaten on the ground three times to symbolize humanity's dependence on rain.

Because Hoshana Rabbah is considered the last possible day on which one can seek forgiveness for the sins of the preceding year, the morning service on this day is very solemn. According to Jewish tradition, on YOM KIPPUR God seals the Book of Life and thus each individual's fate for the coming year. Yom Kippur falls on the 10th day of Tishri.

But since the Middle Ages, Hoshana Rabbah has been regarded as an extension of the deadline for Divine judgment. According to an old Jewish folk belief, notes fell from Heaven on this day informing people of how they had been judged. The traditional Yiddish greeting, *a gute kvitl*, "May you receive a good note," reflects this belief. There is also a popular superstition claiming that a man who doesn't see his shadow on this night is fated to die in the coming year.

CONTACTS:
The Temple Institute
36 Misgav Ladach St.

Jewish Quarter
Old City
Jerusalem 97500 Israel
972-2-6264545; fax: 972-2-6274529
www.templeinstitute.org

Touro Synagogue
4238 Saint Charles Ave.
New Orleans, LA 70115
fax: 504-897-0237
www.tourosynagogue.com

◆ 1370 ◆ Hospital Week, National
Week including May 12

Although Florence Nightingale (1820-1910), the famous nurse and public health activist, spent most of her life in England, it is in the United States that the anniversary of her birth has been celebrated since 1921 as National Hospital Day.

Originally a day set aside in honor of the woman who made nursing a respectable profession and who revolutionized the way hospitals were run, the May 12 observance was expanded to a week-long event in 1953 so that hospitals could use it to plan and implement more extensive public information programs.

Currently sponsored by the American Hospital Association, National Hospital Week provides an opportunity to recognize employee achievements, to educate the community about the services hospitals offer, and to keep the public up to date on technological advances in the health care field.

In 19th-century England, it was customary for each community to designate a **Hospital Saturday** and a **Hospital Sunday**—a time to collect money for local hospitals both on the streets and in the churches. Hospital Saturday later became ALEXANDRA ROSE DAY.

CONTACTS:
American Hospital Association
155 N. Wacker Dr.
Chicago, IL 60606
312-422-3000 or 800-424-4301
www.aha.org

◆ 1371 ◆ Hostos Day
January 11

Eugenio Maria de Hostos (1839-1903) was a Puerto Rican philosopher and patriot who became a leader of the opposition to Spanish colonial rule in the 19th century. He campaigned for the education of women in Brazil, and his books on law and education triggered reforms in other Latin American countries. He even sponsored the first railroad between Chile and Argentina, across the Andes Mountains. The anniversary of his birth is observed as a public holiday in Puerto Rico on the second Monday in January.

CONTACTS:
Puerto Rico Tourism Company

135 W. 50th St.
22nd Fl.
New York, NY 10020
212-586-6262 or 800-223-6530
welcome.topuertorico.org

Puerto Rico Chamber of Commerce
Tetuan St. Ste.100
P.O. Box 9024033
Viejo San Juan, PR 00901
787-721-6060
www.camarapr.org

◆ 1372 ◆ Hot Air Balloon Classic
Early August

The **National Balloon Classic** takes place over about a week in early August from a launch field just outside Indianola, Iowa. When the event was first held in 1970, only 11 balloonists participated, Between 2005 and 2012, the event attracted 100 pilots and 70,000 to 90,000 spectators each year. There are several flights or "tasks" involved in each race, designed to test the pilot's skill in handling his or her balloon. New tasks are added regularly to make the sport more demanding. As a result of the races, Indianola has come to be known as the Balloon Capital of the nation. The city is also the home of the National Balloon Museum.

CONTACTS:
Hot Air Balloon Classic
P.O. Box 346
Indianola, IA 50125
515-961-8415 or 800-359-4692
www.nationalballoonclassic.com

◆ 1373 ◆ Houses and Gardens, Festival of
March-April

One of the nation's oldest and most prestigious house tours is held from mid-March to mid-April in Charleston, S.C. This 300-year-old city has been bombarded by land and sea, devastated by an earthquake, and battered by hurricanes, but it remains a place known for splendid wrought-iron embellished architecture. The port city has 73 pre-Revolutionary buildings, 136 late-18th-century structures, and 600 others built before the 1840s. Among the more interesting areas is Cabbage Row, the model for Catfish Row in DuBose Heyward's novel *Porgy*, on which George Gershwin's opera *Porgy and Bess* was based.

More than 100 homes and gardens, full of blooming azaleas and camellias, are usually included in the festival, which dates from 1947. It features both afternoon and evening candlelight tours, and special candlelight galas with music and wine.

CONTACTS:
Historic Charleston Foundation
40 E. Bay St.
Charleston, SC 29401
843-723-1623; fax: 843-577-2067
www.historiccharleston.org

♦ 1374 ♦ **Houston Livestock Show & Rodeo**
Mid-February to early March

The nation's largest livestock show, with more than 35,000 entries, is held in the famous Astrodome of Houston, Tex. The show is a reminder of the 19th-century days when Houston's shipping trade was based on timber, cotton, and cattle. Things get under way with a downtown parade, and the agenda then includes top celebrity entertainers, pig races, and a chili cook-off.

Since 2003, the rodeo has taken place in the NRG Stadium and Center. Paid attendance for the 2014 event topped over 1.3 million fans.

CONTACTS:
Houston Livestock Show and Rodeo
NRG Center
3 NRG Park
Houston, TX 77054
832-667-1000; fax: 832-667-1134
www.rodeohouston.com

♦ 1375 ♦ **Howl! Festival**
September 5-9

In honor of Beat poet Allen Ginsberg's famous poem "Howl," which was the focus of an obscenity trial in the 1950s, the East Village and Lower East Side of New York City celebrate their own roles in the development of the American counter culture.

Created by local entrepreneur Philip Hartman in 2002 and centered on Tompkins Square Park, the five-day event includes dance, film, theatre, art, poetry, performance, and a host of other artistic activities. In addition, local clubs, restaurants, art galleries, and other venues participate in the celebration. In 2007, the event also included the Carl Solomon Book Expo, named after the Beat writer who was the inspiration for "Howl" and who is credited with getting the first novels of William Burroughs and Jack Kerouac published. In 2013, the festival celebrated its tenth year and featured 350 artists, poets, and performers, including new talent. Earlier festivals included the Charlie Parker Jazz Festival and the Allen Ginsberg Poetry Festival. The event ends with a parade down St. Marks Place.

CONTACTS:
The City of New York
The Arsenal Central Park
830 Fifth Ave.
New York, NY 10065
212-639-9675
www.nycgovparks.org

♦ 1376 ♦ **Human Rights Day, International**
December 10

Observed by the international community every year on December 10, Human Rights Day commemorates the United Nations General Assembly's adoption of the Universal Declaration of Human Rights (UDHR), in Paris, in 1949. The office of the United Nations High Commissioner for Human Rights coordinates activities for the annual celebration. An official observance rather than a public holiday, the event is normally marked by conferences, cultural events, and exhibitions, all concerning the human rights issues that exist in many countries. Every year, Human Rights Day promotes a specific theme that seeks to raise awareness of human rights, underscoring its relevance in daily life. The United Nations Prize in Human Rights and the Nobel Peace Prize are also awarded on this day.

CONTACTS:
Office of the U.N. High Commissioner for Human Rights
www.ohchr.org/EN

♦ 1377 ♦ **Human Towers of Valls**
June 24

On St. John's Day in the city of Valls in the Catalan region of Spain, a touring acrobatic company, or *comparsa*, presents the **Xiquets de Valls**, or "human towers of Valls." The acrobats form human towers or pyramids with four to six men at the base and one or more children at the top. The towers can extend to eight times a man's height, and they are formed to the musical accompaniment of the *gralla*, or native oboe. There is a point during the performance at which the children on top salute, the music ceases, and the entire structure stands immobile for several seconds before collapsing gracefully to the ground.

The companies also create human towers on St. Ursula's Day, October 22, and other fiestas.

CONTACTS:
Tourist Office of Spain
60 E. 42nd St.
Ste. 5300
New York, NY 10165
212-265-8822; fax: 212-265-8864
www.spain.info
Tarragona Tourist Information Center
C/ Major, 39
Tarragona 43003 Spain
34-977-250-795
www.tarragonaturisme.cat

♦ 1378 ♦ **Humana Festival of New American Plays**
March-April

The Humana Festival of New American Plays is an annual gathering of playwrights held in Louisville, Kentucky, since 1976. The Humana Foundation sponsors this event with the assistance of the Louisville-based Actors Theatre. Plays are submitted and selected for production in the months leading up to the festival. The Humana Festival of New American Plays presents both full-length and short ten-minute dramatic works. The event also offers opportunities for spectators to experience behind-the-scenes technical events and the Humana Festival Soiree, which attracts theater veterans from around the United States.

CONTACTS:
Actors Theatre of Louisville
316 W. Main St.
Louisville, KY 40202
502-584-1205
actorstheatre.org

♦ 1379 ♦ Humor and Satire Festival, International
June, during odd-numbered years

Gabrovo, Bulgaria, may seem an unlikely place for the only festival in the world devoted to humor. This town, founded by a blacksmith in the 14th century, has a longstanding reputation for stinginess, and many jokes are told about the length to which its inhabitants will go to avoid spending money. The first humor festival was held there in 1967 in hopes of attracting tourism to the area. Now it is a 10-day event that features a procession of people dressed as their favorite comic figure, a parade of satiric floats, and competitions to see who can get the best laugh. More than a thousand participants from 50 countries—mostly cartoonists, filmmakers, sculptors, artists, and performers specializing in humor and satire—take part in the festival each odd-numbered year, which attracts more than 10,000 spectators.

CONTACTS:
House of Humor and Satire
68, Bryanska St.
P.O. Box 104
Gabrovo 5300 Bulgaria
359-66-807-229 or 359-66-804-945
www.humorhouse.bg

♦ 1380 ♦ Hungary Republic Day
October 23

Republic Day and the 1956 Revolution Anniversary are celebrated on October 23 and originally commemorated the 1956 uprising against Soviet control. On October 23, 1989, in honor of the previous revolution, Hungarians established a new republic, amending the constitution to allow multiparty politics, public assembly, and create separation of power in the government.

CONTACTS:
Ministry of Foreign Affairs and Trade
Bem rakpart 47
Budapest 1027 Hungary
36-1-458-1000; fax: 36-1-212-5918
www.kormany.hu/en

♦ 1381 ♦ Hungary Revolution and Independence Day
March 15

On March 15, Hungarians observe the anniversary of the beginning of the revolution in 1848 against the Habsburg monarchy. The revolutionaries called for the creation of a nation-state with freedom of the press and an independent parliamentary government. In 1989, celebrations were open for the first time since the Soviet invasion, and took place all over the country.

CONTACTS:
Embassy of Hungary
3910 Shoemaker St. N.W.
Washington, D.C. 20008
202-362-6730
washington.kormany.hu

♦ 1382 ♦ Hunters' Moon, Feast of the
Second weekend in October

October was traditionally the time when the *voyageurs*, or traders, came to Fort Ouiatenon (in what is now Lafayette, Indiana) to trade their goods, gossip with the local French settlers, and generally relax and enjoy themselves before setting out on their next journey. Ouiatenon was home not only to the Ouiatenon Indian tribe but also to a number of French families from Canada. The Feast of the Hunter's Moon attempts to reenact as accurately as possible the events that took place there during the mid-18th century.

The two-day festival, which was first held in 1968, begins with the arrival of the voyageurs by canoe on the Wabash River. Events include Indian chants, French folk songs, demonstrations of traditional crafts, and the cooking of typical French and Indian foods over an open fire.

CONTACTS:
Tippecanoe County Historical Association
1001 S. St.
Lafayette, IN 47901
765-476-8411; fax: 765-476-8414
www.tcha.mus.in.us

♦ 1383 ♦ Hurling the Silver Ball
Monday following February 3

St. Ia (or Eia or Ives) is the patron saint of St. Ives, Cornwall. She was one of a group of Celtic missionary saints believed to have reached the southwestern tip of England miraculously by crossing the Irish Sea in a millstone boat. They made a safe landing at the place where St. Ives now stands, and there are parishes and churches throughout Cornwall named after them.

St. Ives celebrates **Feast Monday**, near the Feast of St. Ia on February 3, by playing an ancient game known as hurling. In this case the ball is made of cork encased in silver, which is believed to be very old and is kept in the town clerk's office during the year.

The mayor begins the game by tossing the silver ball against the side of the parish church, which is dedicated to St. Ia. Children then take over, tossing the ball back and forth in what might be described as a kind of "hand football." The game stops promptly at 12 noon, and whoever has the ball in his or her possession at that time receives a cash prize or a medal. The festivities continue in the afternoon with more sporting events, and there is a municipal ball in the evening.

CONTACTS:
Town of St. Ives
St. Ives Town Council
The Guildhall
Street An Pol
St. Ives, Cornwall TR26 2DS United Kingdom
44-17-3679-7840
www.cornwall.gov.uk

♦ 1384 ♦ Hurricane Supplication Day
Fourth Monday in July

Observed in the U.S. Virgin Islands—St. Croix, St. Thomas, and St. John—Hurricane Supplication Day marks the beginning of the hurricane season. Special church services are held to pray for safety from the storms that ravage these and other Caribbean islands. The custom probably dates back to the "rogation" ceremonies which began in fifth-century England—from the word *rogare*, meaning "to beg or supplicate." Rogations usually followed a frightening series of storms, earthquakes, or other natural disasters, although sometimes they took place annually on the ROGATION DAYS that preceded ASCENSION DAY.

At the end of the hurricane season in October there is a **Hurricane Thanksgiving Day**. Church services are held on the third Monday in October so that the islanders can give thanks for being spared the destruction of a major storm.

CONTACTS:
U.S. Virgin Islands Department of Tourism
Office of Film Promotion
P.O. Box 6400
St. Thomas, VI 00804
340-774-8784; fax: 340-774-4390
www.visitusvi.com

♦ 1385 ♦ Hurston (Zora Neale) Festival of the Arts and Humanities
Late January to early February

The Zora Neale Hurston Festival of the Arts and Humanities (also known as the **Zora! Festival**) is an eight-day, multi-disciplinary event held every year in late January to early February in Eatonville, Fla. Zora Neale Hurston was an acclaimed novelist, short-story writer, and playwright. She was also a respected folklorist and anthropologist who devoted herself to preserving the culture of African Americans in the South. She grew up in Eatonville, noted as the oldest incorporated African-American municipality in the United States.

The Zora! Festival was launched in 1990 to showcase her life and work, as well as to celebrate her hometown and the cultural contributions that people of African descent have made to the United States and the world. It features a three-day street festival of the arts, the first day of which is a special education day for school children. The street festival also showcases performances by nationally known acts. During the week prior to the street festival, art exhibits, literary readings, academic presentations, conferences, and lectures, many of them free of charge, are devoted to Hurston and African-American arts in general.

CONTACTS:
The Association to Preserve the Eatonville Community Inc
227 W. Kennedy Blvd.
Eatonville, FL 32751
407-647-3307; fax: 407-539-2192
zorafestival.org

♦ 1386 ♦ Hus (Jan) Day
July 6

Jan Hus Day is celebrated in the Czech Republic to commemorate Jan Hus, an early 15th century Czech priest, theologian, and reformer. Hus was a critic of the Catholic Church's activities during the reign of King Wenceslas IV. Many clergymen had obtained positions of power in the royal administration and had accumulated wealth and property. Hus advocated the idea of a poor Church that limited itself to Biblical teachings and spiritual affairs. Hus was summoned to the ecclesiastical Council of Constance in 1414. When he refused to recant his teachings, Hus wasexcommunicated and burnt at the stake on July 6, 1415. Overthe centuries, Hus has become a symbol of Czech independence and courage.

Jan Hus Day is a national holiday in the Czech Republic. Awreath is placed on his monument in Old Town Square in Prague, and the national flag is flown at all public places.

CONTACTS:
Embassy of the Czech Republic
3900 Spring of Freedom St. N.W.
Washington, D.C. 20008
202-274-9100; fax: 202-966-8540
www.mzv.cz

Prague City Tourism Office
Arbesovo nám. 70/4, Praha 5
Prague 15000 Czech Republic
420-221-714-714
www.praguecitytourism.cz

I

♦ 1387 ♦ I Madonnari Italian Street Painting Festival
May, Memorial Day weekend

This festival celebrating the ancient Italian tradition of street painting was brought to Santa Barbara, Calif., in 1987. Some 200 professional and amateur artists create chalk "paintings"—both reproductions of old masters and original designs—on the Old Mission courtyard. Artist Kurt Wenner has been known for his *trompe l'oeil* paintings in which he transforms sidewalks into fountains or chasms. In 1988, his *Dies Irae*, or "Day of Wrath," was a maelstrom of struggling bodies. He used 200 sticks of chalk for *Dies Irae*.

In Italy in the 17th century, vagabond artists created sidewalk works of chalk art. Because they often painted the Madonna, they were known as *madonnari*. Artists still follow the tradition in the Italian village of Grazie di Curtatone, and Santa Barbara's "I Madonnari" is considered the village's sister festival. Another sister festival is held at San Luis Obispo Mission on the last weekend in April. The art works, masterful as they are, are gone in a week's time.

CONTACTS:
Santa Barbara Festival Office
Children's Creative Project
3970 La Colina Rd.
Ste. 9
Santa Barbara, CA 93110
805-964-4710
www.imadonnarifestival.com

♦ 1388 ♦ Ibu Afo Festival
On or near March 20

The Igbo people of Nigeria celebrate their New Year's Eve around March 20 with a solemn ceremony marking the end of the old year and heralding the arrival of the new. The council of elders who fix the annual calendar determine the exact hour at which the year will end. When it arrives, a wailing noise signals the departing year, and children rush into their houses, lock the doors to avoid being carried away by the old year as it leaves, and bang on the doors to add to the din. As soon as the wailing dies down, the doors are thrown open and everyone greets the new year with spontaneous applause.

CONTACTS:
Nigerian Chamber of Commerce USA
433 N. Camden Dr.
4th Fl.
Beverly Hills, CA 90210
www.ncocusa.com

♦ 1389 ♦ Ice Worm Festival
First full weekend in February

This zany mid-winter festival celebrates the emergence of the ice worm in Cordova, Alaska, where the winters are long and dark and give rise to thoughts of things like ice worms. The highlight of the three-day festival is the procession of a 150-foot-long ice worm (it has a dragon's head) followed by 500 or so paraders. Other events include variety shows, ski events, a survival-suit race, a beauty pageant, music, and dances.

The celebration began in 1961 as a way to shake off the winter blahs, and the legend was born then that an ice worm hibernates during the winter in the Cordova Glacier but starts to hatch or wake up in early February. The worm has gained international fame, and the festival draws great crowds of people.

CONTACTS:
Cordova Chamber of Commerce
404 First St.
Cordova, AK 99574
907-424-7260
cordovachamber.com

♦ 1390 ♦ Iceland Independence Day
June 17

Iceland was proclaimed an independent republic on June 17, 1944. Sometimes referred to as **National Day**, the anniversary of this event is also the birthday of Jón Sigurdsson, the nation's 19th-century leader. A varied program of parades, speeches, sporting competitions, outdoor concerts and shows, and amusements culminates in the evening with dancing in the streets of Reykjavik and other towns.

Another National Day was December 1, the anniversary of the 1918 treaty recognizing Iceland as an independent state under the Danish crown. This is now largely a student celebration.

CONTACTS:
Iceland Tourism Board
Sundagarðar 2
Reykjavík IS-104 Iceland
354-588-1300
www.visiticeland.com

♦ 1391 ♦ **Icelandic Festival**
First weekend in August

The Icelandic Festival, or **Islendingadagurinn**, held in Gimli, Manitoba, each year is one of the oldest ethnic festivals in Canada, dating back to 1890. The Icelandic settlers who emigrated to Canada after their homes in Iceland were destroyed by volcanic eruptions in 1875 wanted to do something to preserve their heritage and customs, and the current festival continues to reflect this interest in Icelandic culture. The events include choral singing and cultural and artistic displays. Participants dress in native Icelandic costumes and eat traditional foods such as smoked lamb and *skyr*, which is similar to yogurt. In recent years a film festival and sporting events have been added to the more traditional offerings.

CONTACTS:
Icelandic Festival of Manitoba
107-94 1st Ave.
Gimli, MB R0C 1B1 Canada
204-642-7417; fax: 204-642-9382
www.icelandicfestival.com

Rural Municipality of Gimli - Municipal Office
62 2nd Ave.
P.O. Box 1246
Gimli, MB R0C 1B0 Canada
204-642-6650 or 866-642-6650; fax: 204-642-6660
www.gimli.ca

♦ 1392 ♦ **Id al-Adha (Feast of Sacrifice; Eid)**
10th through 12th days of Islamic month of Dhu al-Hijjah

This most important feast of the Muslim calendar is the concluding rite of those performing the Hajj or PILGRIMAGE TO MECCA. It is also known as **Id al-Kabir**, the **Great Feast.**

For those not on pilgrimage, Id al-Adha is a three-day festival celebrating Ibrahim's (Abraham's) willingness to obey Allah by killing his son, believed by Muslims to be Ishmael, and not Isaac as written in the Old Testament. Muslims consider Ishmael to be the forefather of the Arabs. According to the Qur'an, Ibrahim had an ax poised over the boy when a voice from Heaven told him to stop. He was allowed to sacrifice a ram instead. Many Muslim families reenact this show of faith by sacrificing a cow, a ram, or a lamb on this day,

using a portion of it for the family feast and donating one- or two-thirds to the poor.

In Turkey this day is called the **Kurban** "sacrificial" **Bayram**. In northern central Africa it is called **Tabaski**. It is an official public holiday in numerous African countries and elsewhere around the world.

See also SALLAH FESTIVAL.

CONTACTS:
Islamic Community Center of Tempe
131 E. 6th St.
Tempe, AZ 85281
480-894-6070; fax: 480-894-6243
www.tempemosque.com

♦ 1393 ♦ **Id al-Fitr (Eid)**
First day of Islamic month of Shawwal

Also known as the **Feast of Fast-Breaking**, or the **Lesser Feast**, Id al-Fitr marks the end of the month-long fast of RAMADAN and the beginning of a three-day feast. It is the second most important Islamic holiday after ID AL-ADHA.

The Id prayer is performed by the whole community at an outdoor prayer ground (*musalla*) or mosque. Then people put on new clothes, children are given presents, and everyone visits relatives and friends. It is the time when everyone asks pardon for all the wrongs of the past year. Village squares have carnival rides, puppet shows, and candy vendors.

It is called **Lebaran** or **Hari Raya** by Indonesians, Thais, and Malaysians. In Turkey, where it is called the **Candy Festival**, or **Seker Bayrami**, this is the day on which children are given candy or money wrapped in handkerchiefs. In Pakistan the special treat associated with this day is *saween*, a spaghetti cooked in milk and sugar, and sprinkled with almonds, pistachios, and dates.

In Malaya, where it is called Hari Raya, they hold open houses. It is the new custom to have one's non-Muslim friends visit to foster more understanding between different religious groups. Muslims in turn will visit Chinese friends during LUNAR NEW YEAR, Hindus during DEWALI, and Christians at CHRISTMAS.

In West Africa, a Mande feast of the virgins has been added to this feast. In western Guinea, young men and women parade all night with floats of animals and boats, singing and dancing; small children sing for presents.

CONTACTS:
American Islamic Association
8860 W. St. Francis Rd.
Frankfort, IL 60423
815-469-1551
www.aiamasjid.org

♦ 1394 ♦ **Id al-Fitr (Nigeria)**
First day of the Islamic month of Shawwal

Among Nigerian Muslims Id al-Fitr—the feast concluding the month-long RAMADAN fast—begins with a procession to the emir's palace. People wear new, festive clothes for the event. The emir is the chief or head of state, and as he sits on his throne, beautifully adorned horses and riders honor him with a *sallah*—a traditional, and dramatic, way of showing respect. One by one, each horseman gallops toward the emir at full tilt and halts only at the last possible moment, then the horseman salutes. The emir's own bodyguards are the last to honor him in this unnerving way. After the sallah is over, the feasting and merrymaking starts. Ox-taming—a special form of bullfighting—is a popular entertainment.

The Islamic religion came to Nigeria around the 11th century with Arabs who crossed the Sahara Desert to trade.

See also SALLAH FESTIVAL.

CONTACTS:
Nigerian Muslim Association of Southern California
9642 S. Western Ave.
Los Angeles, CA 90047
323-940-4646
www.nigerianmuslimassociation.org
Embassy of the Federal Republic of Nigeria
3519 International Ct. N.W.
Washington, D.C. 20008
202-986-8400; fax: 202-362-6541
www.nigeriaembassyusa.org

♦ 1395 ♦ **Idaho International Summerfest**
Midsummer

Every summer Brigham Young University-Idaho, located in Rexburg, invites dancers from different continents to perform folk dance and music. For community leaders and for the university's arts enthusiasts, the Idaho International Summerfest (formerly the Idaho International Dance & Music Festival) is a great opportunity to promote tourism and participate in meaningful cultural exchange.

The university dance directors who founded the festival drew their inspiration from a folk dance tour of Europe they completed in 1983. They envisioned an opportunity to hold a dance event in Rexburg that would attract performers from all over the world. The inaugural festival took place in 1986, and since then the diversity of the team rosters has been notable. Between 1986 and 2006, 172 teams performed from over 55 countries. In recent years, the nearby town of Burley has become a second site of the festival; its version takes place within a week or two of the Rexburg festival.

Opening Ceremonies kick off the festival. Over the course of a week about 10 teams representing different countries perform. Attendees have the opportunity to learn from the visiting dance teams in classes covering various cultures and styles of dance. Beginning in 2014, the Idaho International Summerfest featured a new venue, the Performing Arts Center at Madison High School. The festival has hosted nearly 300 different teams from 60 different countries.

CONTACTS:
Rexburg Chamber of Commerce
127 E. Main St.
Rexburg, ID 83440
208-356-5700 or 888-463-6880; fax: 208-356-5799
rexburgchamber.org

♦ 1396 ♦ **Idaho Regatta**
Last weekend in June

This full-throttle three-day event is held on the Snake River at Burley, Idaho. Burley's population of 9,000 is doubled for the regatta, which is a qualifying race for the American Power Boat Association Western Divisional Championship. A hundred speedboats in 11 inboard limited classes compete for a share of $35,000 in cash prizes—and a mink coat. The regatta has been held since the 1970s, and each year, a coat has been donated as a prize by Lee Moyle, one of the founders of the regatta, and an owner of the Don and Lee Moyle Mink Farm. Boats are entered from throughout the country. They include seven-liter, hydroplanes, super-stock, pro-stock, KRR flat-bottoms, Comp Jets, and stock hydros.

CONTACTS:
Mini-Cassia Chamber of Commere
1177 7th St.
Heyburn, ID 83336
208-679-4793; fax: 208-679-4794
www.minicassiachamber.com

American Power Boat Association
17640 E. Nine Mile Rd.
P.O. Box 377
Eastpointe, MI 48021
586-773-9700; fax: 586-773-6490
www.apba.org

♦ 1397 ♦ **Idaho Spud Day**
Third Saturday in September

Spud Day is a celebration of the potato in Shelley, Idaho. The potato has come to be thought of as *the* crop of Idaho, but the state actually has a number of other important crops: wheat, hay, oats, barley, beans, peas, sugar beets, and fruits. Nonetheless, the spud gets the hurrahs with a festival that began in 1927 and includes a parade, potato-picking and tug-of-war contests, and, of course, potatoes fried, baked, scalloped, mashed, etc. Five thousand free baked potatoes are given to visitors.

CONTACTS:
Shelley City Hall
101 S. Emerson Ave.
Shelley, ID 83274
208-357-3390; fax: 208-357-3998
www.ci.shelley.id.us

Shelley Kiwanis Club
P.O. Box 461
Shelley, ID 83274
208-881-3105
www.idahospudday.com

♦ 1398 ♦ Ides
Various

In the ancient Roman calendar, the ides fell on the 15th day of March, May, July, and October, and on the 13th day of the other months. The Roman emperor Julius Caesar was assassinated on the Ides of March in 44 B.C.E., and Shakespeare's famous reference to this day in his play *Julius Caesar*— "Beware the Ides of March"—is probably the best-known use of the term.

The ancient Romans specified a particular day in the month by relating it to the next calends, ides, or nones. For example, "six days before the Ides of June" meant June 8, since the ides in June fell on the 13th.

Calends, sometimes spelled "kalends," refers to the first day of the month, from which the days of the preceding months were counted backward. The order of the days in each month were publicly proclaimed on the calends. For example, "the sixth of the calends of April" meant March 27, or the sixth day before the first day of April (counting April 1 as the first day.)

The Greeks didn't use the term, which is why the phrase "on (or at) the Greek calends" is a synonym for "never." Occasionally, calends was used to mean Settlement Day, since the first of the month was usually the day on which debts were settled.

The nones fell on the ninth day before the ides. In March, May, July, and October, the nones occurred on the seventh of the month because the ides fell on the 15th. In all the other months, the nones occurred on the fifth or 13th days.

♦ 1399 ♦ Iditarod Trail Sled Dog Race
Early March

The Iditarod is the world's longest and toughest sled dog race, across the state of Alaska from Anchorage on the south central coast to Nome on the Bering Sea just south of the Arctic Circle. It commemorates a 650-mile mid-winter emergency run to take serum from Nenana to Nome during the 1925 diphtheria epidemic. The race, which began in 1973, follows an old frozen-river mail route and is named for a deserted mining town along the way.

About 70 teams compete each year, and the winner is acclaimed the world's best long-distance dog musher. In 1985, Libby Riddles, age 28, was the first woman to win the race, coming in three hours ahead of the second-place finisher. It took her 18 days. Susan Butcher won in 1986, and again in 1987, 1988, and 1990. In 1991, Rick Swenson battled a howling blizzard on the last leg to win and become the first five-time winner (1977, 1979, 1981, 1982). His prize money was $50,000 out of the $250,000 purse. The 1992 winner, Martin Buser, set a record time of 10 days, 19 hours, and 17 minutes. Buser set a new record of 8 days, 22 hours, and 46 minutes when he took his fourth win in 2002. Lance Mackey holds the record for most consecutive wins at four (2007-2010. Dallas

Seavey was the youngest musher to win in 2012, going on to win two more Iditarods in 2014 and 2015. In 2014, Seavey broke all previous record times, crossing the finish in just 8 days, 13 hours, 4 minutes and 19 seconds. Beginning with the 2015 race, the first musher crossing the finish line received a $70,000 check and a new Dodge pickup.

Mushers draw lots for starting position at a banquet held in Anchorage a couple of days before the race. Each musher, with a team of anywhere from 8 to 18 dogs, can expect to face 30-foot snowdrifts and winds of up to 60 miles an hour.

A number of events are clustered around the running of the race. At Wasilla, near Anchorage, Iditarod Days are held on the beginning weekend of the race and feature softball, golf on ice, fireworks, and snow sculptures. Anchorage stages an International Ice Carving Competition that weekend, with ice carvers from around the world creating their cold images in the city's Town Square. At Nome, the BERING SEA ICE GOLF CLASSIC, a six-hole golf tournament, is played on the frozen Bering Sea during the second week of the race.

Various organizations have campaigned against the Iditarod and other sled dog races because of the risks to the dogs and alleged mistreatment. Iditarod organizers provide each dog with a physical examination before the race, yet, according to newspaper reports, it is not unusual for at least one dog each year to die from exhaustion or injuries sustained during the race.

CONTACTS:
Iditarod Trail Committee, Inc.
2100 S. Knik-Goose Bay Rd.
Wasilla, AK 99654 United States
907-376-5155; fax: 907-373-6998
www.iditarod.com

♦ 1400 ♦ Idlewild Jazz Festival
Third Saturday in July

Sponsored by the nonprofit Idlewild Foundation, the Idlewild Jazz Festival is a one-day, outdoor event. It recalls the Jazz Age flourishing of Idlewild, Mich., a resort area in the northwestern part of the state. Known as the "Black Eden" during its heyday in the mid-20th century, Idlewild was a favorite vacation destination for African Americans from such Midwestern cities as Chicago and Detroit. With nearly 25,000 visitors each summer, the area grew to include entertainment venues such as the Flamingo and Paradise jazz clubs, where luminaries including Louis Armstrong, Sarah Vaughan, Sammy Davis Jr., and Count Basie performed during the 1950s.

The festival was conceived in 2002 as a means of paying tribute to that heritage and offering a new generation a connection with the past. The festival takes place in a wooded, lakeside setting on Williams Island and includes a program of music that begins at noon and runs well into the night. In addition, related activities include an art fair, marketplace, and writers' workshop. Food vendors offer refreshments ranging from Jamaican specialties and fish to barbecued wings.

CONTACTS:
Idlewild African American Chamber of Commerce
P.O. Box 435
Idlewild, MI 49642
231-745-4742; fax: 231-301-1074
www.iaacc.com

Lake County Chamber of Commerce
895 Michigan Ave.
P.O. Box 130
Baldwin, MI 49304
231-745-4331
www.lakecountymichigan.com

♦ 1401 ♦ Iduna and Summer Finding
*Vernal Equinox; around March 21 in the
northern hemisphere and around September 23
in the southern hemisphere*

Northern European pagan traditions placed great importance on the official advent of spring known as the vernal equinox. Iduna and Summer Finding, which today are observed by Wiccans and Neo-pagans, are two festivals that celebrate the time of the year in which daylight "overcomes" the night. While they are distinct festivals, both traditions share metaphorical imagery along with the same date.

In Norse mythology, Iduna is the goddess of spring and the keeper of apples of immortality. Her story mirrors that of the Greek goddess Persephone, in which a contriving god abducts her and takes her magical fruit away. She eventually returns, but in the form of a quail, symbolizing the return of the bird from its winter roost. Similarly, Summer Finding focuses on a tradition in which the year's first spotting of a bird or a flower marks the "finding" of the warm season. In some old traditions, whoever discovered the first bird marked the spot with a pole, which is afterwards decorated with flowers.

Among Wiccan and Neo-pagan followers, Summer Finding or Iduna is less commonly observed than Ostara, the equinox festival celebrating the spring goddess of the same name.

CONTACTS:
Pagan Federation
BM Box 7097
London WC1N 3XX United Kingdom
www.paganfed.org

♦ 1402 ♦ Igbi
Sunday nearest February 5

Because February 5 is the day that the sun, it is hoped, will shine for the first time of the year on the village of Khora, and then on Shaitli in the Dagestan region of Russia, the Tsezy (Didoitsy) people celebrate this event marking the middle of winter with a festival known as Igbi.

The name comes from the plural of the Tsezian word *ig*—a ring-shaped bread similar to a bagel—and the baking of these ritual breads plays a central role in the celebration, which involves a number of masked and costumed charac-

ters playing traditional roles. Six *botsi,* or wolves, carrying wooden swords go from house to house collecting the igbi that the women have been baking in preparation for their arrival. The bagels are strung on a long pole known as the *giri,* and those who fail to cooperate are hit with the swords or have their shoes filled with wet snow and ice.

The children get up early on this day, which is now observed on the Sunday nearest February 5 so they don't have to miss school, and go through the village collecting the igbi that have been made especially for them.

Igbi is also a day of reckoning. All through the year the young organizers of the feast have kept notes of the good and bad deeds of the villagers. Now after all the igbi have been collected, there is a ceremony in the center of the village in which the *kvidili*—a traditional figure wearing an animal-skin mask resembling no known animal; lately it looks like a horse with horns and a big mouth like a crocodile—reads out the names of those who have committed a transgression (such as public drunkenness) during the year.

The unlucky ones are dragged to the river and immersed up to their knees through a hole in the ice. Those who are congratulated for their good deeds are handed an ig. At the end of the festival, the kvidili is symbolically slain with a wooden sword.

CONTACTS:
Ministry of Culture of Russian Federation - Federal Agency for Tourism
Myasnitskaya ul. 47
Moscow 101000 Russia
7-495-607-3217
www.russiatourism.ru

Russian American Cultural Heritage Center
www.rach-c.org

♦ 1403 ♦ Imam Ali's Birthday
13th day of the Islamic month of Rajab

Ali ibn Abu Talib was the cousin and son-in-law of the prophet Muhammad. He ruled the Rashidun Empire from 656 to 661. Due to sectarian differences in Islam, he is known variously as the fourth caliph by Sunni Muslims and the first imam by Shi'ite Muslims.

To pay tribute to Ali's special role in the Shi'ite succession, followers have always honored the anniversary of his birth date. The holiday is widely observed in countries with large Shi'ite populations, such as Iraq and Iran. Najaf, the Iraqi city where the imam is laid to rest, is a well-known commemoration site. Throughout the year, the city welcomes Shi'ite pilgrims from Iraq and beyond.

In Iran, Ali's birthday was designated an official holiday during the reign of Nasiru al-Din Shah, in the late 19th century. Today, sermons, speeches, and other events commemorating the imam's birth are overseen by the country's Ministry of Culture and Religious Guidance.

CONTACTS:
Embassy of Iran
2209 Wisconsin Ave. N.W.
Washington, D.C. 20007
202-965-4990; fax: 202-965-1073
www.daftar.org

◆ 1404 ◆ Imam Ali's Martyrdom, Anniversary of
21st day of the Islamic month of Ramadan

Shi'ite Muslims show great reverence toward Ali ibn Abu Talib, the cousin and son-in-law of the prophet Muhammad. As Muhammad's direct descendant, they have conferred distinction on Ali as the first imam. Ali's reign lasted from 656 to 661, the year in which members of a sect known as the Kharijites carried out his assassination, which according to Shi'ite accounts occurred on Ramadan 19. Ali suffered from the stabbing for two days before he died.

Most Shi'ites believe that Ali's tomb lies in Najaf, a present-day city in Iraq. During the year, the Imam Ali Mosque in Najaf attracts pilgrims from throughout Iraq, Iran, and other countries. On his death anniversary, the city's population swells to as many as two million people as pilgrims gather around the imam's holy shrine to pray and mourn.

In addition to observing the death anniversary, some followers observe the date on which Ali was stabbed. It is customary for followers to maintain a round-the-clock vigil to observe the interval between the imam's stabbing and his death.

CONTACTS:
Masjid-e-Ali
47 Cedar Grove Ln
Somerset, NJ 08873
732 564-1331
www.masjid-e-ali.org

◆ 1405 ◆ Imam Sadiq's Martyrdom, Anniversary of
25th day of the Islamic month of Shawwal

Historical accounts differ over the birth year of Ja'far al-Sadiq (699?–765), the sixth Shi'ite imam and founder of an expansion of Islamic *shari'ah* law known as *fiqh*. Records are more certain, however, about the date of his murder, which was believed to be at the hands of the Abbasid ruler al-Mansur. Followers mourn and offer condolences to one another on the death anniversary of this spiritual leader and renowned scholar. It is a public holiday in Iran and is observed in countries with Shi'ite populations.

Many followers observe al-Sadiq's death as they observe other martyr days—with religious processions of mourning and a special meeting called the *rawda-khani*. Convened in houses or mosques, these ceremonies feature *rawda-khans*, individuals who are skilled at reciting Islamic narratives. The retelling of the imam's demise by poisoning often elicits weeping from the audience and other strong expressions of grief.

CONTACTS:
Imam Mahdi Association of Marjaeyah
22000 Garrison St.
Dearborn, MI 48124 United States
313-562-4626 or 888-747-8264
www.imam-us.org

Embassy of Iran
2209 Wisconsin Ave.
Washington, D.C. 20007
202-965-4990; fax: 202-965-1073
www.daftar.org

◆ 1406 ◆ Imbolc (Imbolg)
February 1

One of the "Greater Sabbats" during the Wiccan year, Imbolc celebrates the coming of spring and the recovery of the Earth Goddess after giving birth to the Sun God at Yule. "Wicca" is the name used by many believers in modern Neopagan witchcraft because it doesn't carry the stigma that the terms "witch" or "pagan" carry.

The Greater Sabbats (or Sabbaths) take place four times a year, at the Cross-Quarter Days of February 1, May 1, August 1, and November 1. In ancient days, some of these were huge get-togethers that involved dancing, singing, and feasting which went on all night. Revolving around the changing of the seasons and the breeding of animals, they served as a way to give thanks for the bounties of the earth. Other names for Imbolc include the **Feast of Pan**, **Feast of Torches**, **Feast of Waxing Lights**, and **Oimelc**.

See also Beltane; Lammas; St. Bridget's Day; Samhain.

CONTACTS:
 Pagan Federation
BM Box 7097
London WC1N 3XX United Kingdom
44-560-367-2521
www.paganfed.org

◆ 1407 ◆ Immaculate Conception, Feast of the
December 8

Theological controversy surrounded this festival for centuries, though popular celebration of it dates to at least the eighth century. The argument hinged on the meaning of the word "immaculate," which in this context refers to the belief that Jesus' mother Mary was conceived without original sin, the basic inclination toward wrongdoing that originates from the sin of Adam. Many leading theologians, including St. Thomas Aquinas, questioned the Immaculate Conception.

Although for many years it remained open for debate, in 1854 Pope Pius IX proclaimed it to be an essential dogma of the Roman Catholic Church, and since that time the Feast of the Immaculate Conception has celebrated God's choice of Mary to give birth to His Son. This is also a pious belief held by many Anglicans.

In Guam, this is a legal holiday also known as **Our Lady of Camarin Day**, commemorating a statute of Mary that a fisherman found floating off the coast. It is observed on the fourth Thursday in November.

CONTACTS:
Basilica of the National Shrine of the Immaculate Conception
400 Michigan Ave. N.E.
Washington, D.C. 20017
202-526-8300; fax: 202-526-8313
www.nationalshrine.com

Guam Visitors Bureau
401 Pale San Vitores Rd.
Tumon, GU 96913
671-646-5278; fax: 671-646-8861
www.visitguam.com

♦ 1408 ♦ Immaculate Conception, Feast of the (Argentina)
December 8

Although a number of special fiestas are held in Argentina on December 8, the Feast of the IMMACULATE CONCEPTION of the Virgin Mary, the celebration held in Catamarca stands out. It focuses on the Virgen del Valle, an image of the Virgin Mary that was found in a nearby cave in 1620. Her broad, dark face and narrow eyes marked the Virgen as clearly the product of an indigenous artist.

Every town and hamlet in Catamarca province and in several neighboring provinces has its own replica of the statue, and all bring their images to the provincial capital of San Fernando del Valle de Catamarca for the December 8 procession. Some pilgrims make the journey on foot, which means that they must set out in November to get there on time. Many wear special costumes, and almost everyone also brings brightly hued pennants and flags. They make music with indigenous instruments along the way. When they reach Catamarca, they participate in many of the competitive games associated with the fiesta. The climax of the festival is the procession in which the original image of the Virgen del Valle is escorted through the streets of town while spectators throw white handkerchiefs in the air.

CONTACTS:
National Secretariat of Tourism, Tourist Information Centers
Av. Santa Fe 883
Buenos Aires C1059ABC Argentina
54-11-4312-2232 or 800-555-0016
www.turismo.gov.ar

Secretariat of Tourism
Gral. Roca 50
San Fernando del Valle de Catamarca
Catamarca, Argentina
54-383-4455308
www.turismocatamarca.gob.ar

♦ 1409 ♦ Immaculate Conception, Feast of the (Malta)
December 8

The Republic of Malta is a small country in the central Mediterranean that consists of seven islands. The Maltese Islands have a strong Catholic population that celebrates a wide variety of festivities throughout the religious year.

Maltese families tend to be quite close-knit, and the holidays are a time to strengthen the sense of community and reinforce family bonds. The Maltese people are proud of their religion and parishes, and they go to great lengths to organize and prepare for the celebration day.

Each year many countries, including Malta, celebrate the Feast of the Immaculate Conception on December 8. It is a public holiday set aside to commemorate the birth of the virgin Mary, who is known to the Maltese as "Our Lady without sin." In Malta, this day is one of the feast days celebrated by many Catholics. Feast days are a big part of life on the islands. However, the most important events to all villages are their individual *festas*—celebrations with fireworks, decorated streets, and carts throughout the villages selling many different foods, including traditional sweets and delicacies such as Maltese nougat—honoring their parish patron saint.

CONTACTS:
Malta Tourism Authority
Auberge D'Italie
Merchants St.
Valetta, VLT 1170 Malta
356-2291-5000; fax: 356-2291-5394
www.visitmalta.com

Archdiocese of Malta
P.O. Box 90
Marsa MRS1000 Malta
356-2590-6208 or 356-2124-5350
thechurchinmalta.org

♦ 1410 ♦ Immaculate Conception, Feast of the (Mexico)
December 8

The Feast of the IMMACULATE CONCEPTION of the Virgin Mary is an important day throughout Latin America, but it is especially significant in the Mexican town of San Juan de los Lagos in Jalisco State, where the celebration begins several days in advance. The town's inhabitants temporarily rename the streets where the festival will occur. On Calle de Alegria (Joy Street), for example, there are puppet shows, side shows, games of chance, food stands, and musical performances. On Calle del Azúcar (Sugar Street), all kinds of sweets are sold, including the highly prized *alfajor*, which is a candy made from honey and nuts. And on Calle de las Pieles (Street of Hides), there are exhibitions of animal skins and beautifully made leather goods for sale.

On the morning of December 8, the 11-inch image of the Virgin Mary leaves the local church, carried by priests on a silver litter. Later that afternoon festival organizers put two silver cups on the altar. In one there are scraps of paper bearing the names of devout community members, while the other cup contains blank pieces of paper—with one exception that says "Fiesta de Nuestra Senora de San Juan." Papers are removed two at a time, one from each cup, and the person whose name matches up with the name of the fiesta is in charge of the celebration the following year. Gun shots and ringing bells accompany this news, for it is considered a great honor to be chosen.

CONTACTS:
American Embassy in Mexico City
Paseo de la Reforma 305
Colonia Cuauhtemoc
Mexico City 06500 Mexico
52-55-5080-2000; fax: 52-55-5080-2834
mexico.usembassy.gov

◆ 1411 ◆ Immaculate Heart of Mary, Feast of the
May-June; second Saturday following the second Sunday after Pentecost

It was St. John Eudes who initiated the worship of the Holy Heart of Mary in 1648 by composing a Mass and Office, although the feast failed to be approved by the Congregation of Rites in 1669. Repeated requests over the years for official recognition of the feast were reinforced in 1917 when the Virgin Mary appeared at Fátima, Portugal, and expressed her wish that the devotion be established so that Russia would be saved.

On October 31, 1942, the 25th anniversary of the appearance at Fátima, Pope Pius XII consecrated the entire human race to the Immaculate Heart of Mary, and two years later, a feast under that name was established for August 22, octave of the Feast of the IMMACULATE CONCEPTION. (*See also* OUR LADY OF FÁTIMA DAY.) It was moved to its present date in 1969. Roman Catholics observe this day in honor of Mary and to obtain her intercession for world peace and the practice of virtue.

CONTACTS:
Basilica of the National Shrine of Our Lady of Fatima
1023 Swann Rd.
P.O. Box 167
Lewiston, NY 14174
716-754-7489; fax: 716-754-9130
www.fatimashrine.com

Shrine of Our Lady of the Rosary of Fátima
Apartado 31
Fátima 2496-908 Portugal
351-249-539-600; fax: 351-249-539-605
www.fatima.pt

◆ 1412 ◆ Impruneta, Festa del
Late October

The fair held at Impruneta, outside Florence, Italy, is one of the largest and noisiest of the autumn harvest festivals held all over Tuscany in October.

For weeks before the festival begins, the walls of Florence are covered with posters announcing when the fair will be held. Dating back three centuries, the *festa* originally celebrated the figure of the Virgin Mary which was believed to have been painted by St. Luke. But now it is primarily a celebration of the harvest and a last opportunity before winter to indulge

in the area's special foods and the wines of the Elsa and Pesa valleys.

Chickens, pigeons, and suckling pigs are roasted on spits, and there are tables heaped with home-cured hams and loaves of country-style bread. Other foods associated with the fair include the paper-thin anise cookies known as *brigidini* and almond toffee, which is boiled in iron cauldrons.

CONTACTS:
Italian National Tourist Board
686 Park Ave.
3rd Fl.
New York, NY 10065
212-245-5618; fax: 212-586-9249
www.italiantourism.com

Basilica di Santa Maria all'Impruneta
Piazza Buondelmonti, 28
Impruneta, Florence Province 50023 Italy
39-55-201-1072
www.basilicaimpruneta.org

◆ 1413 ◆ ImPulsTanz: Vienna International Dance Festival
Early July to early August

Originally a festival with an exclusive focus on instruction, ImPulsTanz: Vienna International Dance Festival has become one of the premiere contemporary dance showcases in Europe. The annual program includes more than 200 workshops and 50 productions staged in the city's most important venues.

In 1984, Vienna cultural manager Karl Regenburger and choreographer Ismael Ivo began collaborating to create a dance festival. Their aim was to increase exposure for Austria's contemporary dance scene. For the first four years a handful of instructors offered about 20 workshops in a given festival. By 1988, organizers had added performance pieces to the program. In the years following capacity grew to offer scholarships and career development programs for festival participants. Today instruction is available to dancers of all levels.

In 2012, the festival was awarded the "Bank Austria Kunstpreis," Austria's most prestigious art prize.

CONTACTS:
ImPulsTanz - Vienna International Dance Festival
Museumstraße 5/21
Vienna 1070 Austria
431-523-5558; fax: 431-5-235-5589
www.impulstanz.com

◆ 1414 ◆ Inauguration Day
January 20

From 1789 until 1933, the day on which the newly elected president of the United States began his term of office was March 4—now known as **Old Inauguration Day**. The day was changed to January 20 when the 20th Amendment to the Constitution was passed in 1933. When Inauguration Day falls on a Sunday, the oath of office is administered privately, but the public ceremonies are usually postponed until the following day.

The swearing-in of the president had been held on the East Portico of the Capitol building since Andrew JACKSON's 1829 inauguration. Former president Ronald Reagan changed the site for his inauguration in 1981. Since then, the swearing-in has been held on the West Terrace of the Capitol. This site, which faces out onto the Mall where thousands gather for the event, affords greater visibility for spectators. Reagan reportedly also liked the symbolism of the president facing west, out toward the rest of the country.

At noontime, the chief justice of the United States Supreme Court administers the oath of office to the president, who then delivers an Inaugural Address. This is followed by a colorful Inauguration Parade through the streets of Washington, D.C.

Inauguration festivities are usually somewhat more modest when a president is elected for a second term or when a change in the presidency does not involve a change in the ruling political party.

In the evening inaugural balls are held in a number of different locations, and the president and the first lady try to make a brief appearance at each of them. William Henry Harrison was the first American president to dance at his own inaugural ball, but the exertion proved too much for him. Already suffering from his exposure to the stormy weather during his record-breaking inaugural address (one hour and 45 minutes), he later developed pneumonia and died within a month.

CONTACTS:
 Library of Congress
101 Independence Ave. S.E.
Washington, D.C. 20540
202-707-5000
www.loc.gov

United States Capitol
Capitol Visitor Center
Washington, D.C. 20510
202-226-8000
www.visitthecapitol.gov

♦ 1415 ♦ **Inconfidência Week**
Week including April 21

The *Inconfidência* was a colonial uprising for Brazilian independence from Portugal at the end of the 18th century (*see also* BRAZIL INDEPENDENCE DAY). It is celebrated during the week of April 21 by paying tribute to Joaquim José da Silva Xavier— also known as **Tiradentes** ("tooth-puller") because of his dentistry practice—who became a martyr for independence when the uprising was put down and he was executed.

The Inconfidência Week festivities include performances by orchestras, bands and choirs, and athletic competitions. The city of Ouro Preto is honorarily restored to its former position as state capital of Minas Gerais during the festival.

CONTACTS:
Brazilian Embassy
3006 Massachusetts Ave. N.W.
Washington, D.C. 20008
202-238-2700; fax: 202-238-2827
washington.itamaraty.gov.br

♦ 1416 ♦ **Independence of Cartagena City Day**
Mid-November

On November 11, 1811, Cartagena, Colombia, declared its independence from Spain. The holiday is officially celebrated in Colombia on the Monday closest to November 11. However, festivals and street fairs traditionally take place for days around the actual holiday. There are many parades, including the large and colorful parade through the city of Cartagena, which ends at Plaza Trinidad, where the independence of the city was declared. The culmination of the festivities is the National Beauty Contest, when Miss Colombia is chosen from winners of local beauty pageants around the country.

CONTACTS:
Embassy of Colombia
2118 Leroy Pl. N.W.
Washington, D.C. 20008
202-387-8338; fax: 202-232-8643
www.colombiaemb.org

Cartagena de Indias Corporate Tourism Office
Tourist Pier La Bodeguita
2nd Fl.
Cartagena de Indias Colombia
57-5-6550211; fax: 57-5-6550709
www.cartagenadeindias.travel

♦ 1417 ♦ **India Republic Day**
January 26

This holiday is an important national festival in India celebrating the day in 1950 when India's ties with Britain were severed and the country became a fully independent republic. The holiday is marked with parades and much celebration in all the state capitals, but the celebration in Delhi is especially grand. There is a mammoth parade with military units, floats from each state, dancers and musicians, and fly-overs. The festivities in Delhi actually last for about a week, with special events of all sorts in auditoriums and hotels. Special festivities took place during the year 2000, when India celebrated its 50th anniversary as an independent republic.

England's Queen Victoria had been proclaimed Empress of India in 1877, and it wasn't until 1947 that India won its long fight for freedom. The India Independence Act was passed by the British Parliament in July 1947, and by August 15 the Muslim nation of Pakistan and the Hindu nation of India had become independent dominions. Lord Mountbatten served as governor-general during the transition period. When a new constitution came into effect in 1950 his governor-generalship ended, and India stood fully independent.

Independence Day on Aug. 15 is also a national holiday, but is observed chiefly with speech-making and none of the grandeur of Republic Day.

CONTACTS:
Embassy of India
2107 Massachusetts Ave. N.W.
Washington, D.C. 20008
202-939-7000; fax: 202-265-4351
www.indianembassy.org

Ministry of Communications & Information Technology
(Government of India)
Electronics Niketan, 6
CGO Complex
Lodhi Rd.
New Delhi, Delhi 110003 India
91-11-24301851; fax: 91-11-24363101
deity.gov.in

◆ 1418 ◆ **Indian Arrival Day**
May 30

The people of Trinidad and Tobago observe May 30 as Indian Arrival Day. This holiday honors the nation's citizens of Indian descent and acknowledges their contribution to the social and cultural landscape of Trinidad and Tobago. In particular, it recalls the arrival of the first boats from India in 1845. The boats brought poor people who were made to work as indentured servants, thereby filling the need for cheap labor created by the emancipation of the nation's African slaves in 1838.

The holiday grew out of an observance organized by Indian social activists in 1977, who used the festival to counter anti-Indian prejudice and to encourage ethnic pride in Trinidad's citizens of Indian descent. It was later adopted as a national observance. Today the holiday is celebrated with re-enactments of the arrival of the first ships bringing Indians to Trinidad, parades honoring the history of the nation's Indian citizens and their festivals, and various cultural events.

CONTACTS:
Ministry of Tourism Trinidad & Tobago
1 Wrightson Rd.
Levels 8 & 9, Tower C
International Waterfront Complex
Port-of-Spain Trinidad and Tobago
868-624-1403; fax: 868-625-1825
www.tourism.gov.tt

National Council of Indian Culture
NCIC Nagar
28-38 Narsaloo Ramaya Marg Rd.
Endeavour
Chaguanas, Trinidad Trinidad and Tobago
868-671-6242 or 868-665-6733
www.ncictt.com

National Library and Information System Authority
National Library of Trinidad and Tobago
Hart and Abercromby Streets
Port of Spain Trinidad and Tobago
868-623-6962 or 868-623-7278; fax: 868-625-6096
www.nalis.gov.tt

◆ 1419 ◆ **Indian Market**
Third weekend in August

This showplace for traditional and contemporary Indian art is held on the Plaza of Santa Fe, N.M. The market is the oldest and largest juried competition among Indian artists. It originated as part of the 1922 Fiesta de SANTA FE and continued and grew out of concern that the art forms of the Indian pueblos (villages) were disappearing.

Today more than 800 Indians enter the competition, largely from the 19 New Mexico pueblos and the Apache, Navajo, Hopi, and Ute tribes of the Southwest. Besides the booths of art works, there are numerous food booths, offering such Indian specialties as green chile on fried bread. Indian dances are performed at the courtyard of the Palace of the Governors. A poster-signing ceremony and a benefit art auction precede the market days.

CONTACTS:
Southwest Association for Indian Arts Inc.
P.O. Box 969
Santa Fe, NM 87504
505-983-5220; fax: 505-983-7647
swaia.org

◆ 1420 ◆ **Indianapolis 500**
May, Sunday of Memorial Day weekend

The "Greatest Spectacle in Racing," popularly known as the **Indy 500**, is actually the culmination of a month-long event. It begins the first week in May with the Mayor's Breakfast and parade around the Indianapolis Motor Speedway, the two-and-a-half-mile oval track on which the race takes place. Then there are qualifying races to determine who will participate in the final **Indianapolis 500 Mile Race**, which is held on the Sunday before MEMORIAL DAY.

On the day before the big race, there is a 500 Festival Memorial Parade that draws more than 300,000 spectators to the streets of downtown Indianapolis and features floats, musical groups, and celebrities. The race itself, which has been held in Indianapolis since 1911, regularly attracts about 400,000 spectators to the 559-acre speedway, in addition to 4,000 media people and a nationwide television audience.

The Indy 500 is said to be the largest one-day sporting event in the world.

The official track qualifying record belongs to Arie Luyendyk, whose one-lap speed in 1996 was 237.498 mph. He also holds the record for the fastest time to complete the 500-mile race, set in 1990 when he clocked in at 2:40:58.

The Indy racing car is fueled with a blend of fuels (such as methanol and nitromethane) and usually powered by a turbo-charged engine. Officially, the Indy 500 is a testing-ground for devices that will eventually be used in passenger cars. The annual race has been credited with such automotive improvements as the rearview mirror, balloon tires, and ethyl gasoline.

CONTACTS:
Indy Racing League
4551 W. 16th St.
Indianapolis, IN 46222
317-492-6526
www.indycar.com

Indianapolis Motor Speedway (IMS), LLC.
4790 W. 16th St.
Indianapolis, IN 46222 United States
317-492-8500
www.indianapolismotorspeedway.com

♦ 1421 ♦ **Indonesia Independence Day**
August 17

Indonesia had been a Dutch colony for 300 years when a group of revolutionaries declared independence on August 17, 1945. Indonesians endured four more years of struggle before their independence was formally granted by QUEEN JULIANA of the Netherlands.

This national holiday is celebrated throughout Indonesia with parades, athletic events, and a multitude of cultural and performing arts festivals.

CONTACTS:
Indonesian Embassy
2020 Massachusetts Ave. N.W.
Washington, D.C. 20036
202-775-5200
www.embassyofindonesia.org

♦ 1422 ♦ **Indra Jatra**
September-October; end of Hindu month of
Bhadrapada to early in the Hindu month of
Asvina

Indra Jatra is the most important festival of Nepal, combining homage to a god with an appearance by a living goddess. The festival, lasting for eight days, is a time to honor the recently deceased and to pay homage to the Hindu god Indra and his mother Dagini so they will bless the coming harvests. It furthermore commemorates the day in 1768, during an Indra Jatra (*jatra* means "festival"), that Prithwi Narayan Shah (1730-1775) conquered the Katmandu Valley and unified Nepal.

Legend says that Indra, the god of rain and ruler of heaven, once visited the Katmandu Valley in human form to pick flowers for his mother. The people caught him stealing flowers. Dagini, the mother, came down and promised to spread dew over the crops and to take those who had died in the past year back to heaven with her. The people then released Indra and they have celebrated the occasion ever since.

Before the ceremonies start, a 50-foot tree is cut, sanctified, and dragged to the Hanuman Dhoka Palace in Katmandu. It represents Shiva's *lingam*, the phallic symbol of his creative powers, and shows he's come to the valley. As the pole is erected, bands play and cannons boom. Images of Indra, usu-

ally as a captive, are displayed, and sacrifices of goats and roosters are offered.

Three gold chariots are assembled in Basantpur Square, outside the home of the Kumari, the living goddess and vestal virgin. She is a young girl who was selected to be a goddess when she was about three years old, and she will be replaced by another girl when she begins to menstruate. This indicates she is human.

Two boys playing the roles of the gods GANESH and Bhairab emerge from the Kumari's house to be attendants to the goddess. Then the goddess herself appears in public for the first time, walking on a carpet so her feet don't touch the ground. The crowds go wild. The king bows to the Kumari, and the procession moves off to the palace where it stops in front of the 12-foot mask of the Bhairab. This is the fearsome form of Shiva in Nepal and is displayed only at this time. The Kumari greets the image and rice beer pours from its mouth. Those who catch a drop of the beer are blessed, but even more are those who catch one of the tiny live fish in the beer.

In the following days the procession moves from place to place around Kathmandu. Masked dancers perform every night at the Hanuman Dhoka square dramatizing each of the earthly incarnations of Vishnu. On the final day of the festival the great pole is carried to the river.

CONTACTS:
Nepal Tourism Board - Tourist Service Center
P.O. Box 11018
Bhrikuti Mandap
Kathmandu Nepal
977-1-425-6909; fax: 977-1-425-6910
welcomenepal.com

Kathmandu Metropolitan City Office
Bagh Durbar
P.O. Box 8416
Kathmandu Nepal
977-1-4231481; fax: 977-1-4268509
www.kathmandu.gov.np

♦ 1423 ♦ **Interceltique, Festival**
First Friday in August until second Sunday in
August

Created in 1971, the Festival Interceltique (**Interceltic Festival**) brings together traditional and contemporary expressions of Celtic culture and arts. Approximately 4,500 singers, instrumentalists, visual artists, dancers, professors, and filmmakers—drawn from the traditionally Celtic lands—take part in the event. These lands include Ireland, Scotland, Wales, Cornwall, Galicia (Spain), Asturias (Spain), and Brittany (France). Participants also come from Canada, the United States, and Australia. The festival takes place in Lorient, a town in Brittany, France. It begins on the first Friday in August and lasts until the second Sunday of August. About 350,000 spectators attend the festival annually. Festival organizers hope not only to promote the vitality of Celtic culture, but also to make its artistic contributions known to the rest of the world.

CONTACTS:
Interceltic Festival of Lorient
11 Nayel Space
Lorient 56100 France
33-2-9721-2429
www.festival-interceltique.com

♦ 1424 ♦ Inti Raymi Fiesta
June 24

The **Inti Raymi Festival**, also known as the **Inti Raymi Pageant**, **Sun Festival**, or **Feast of the Sun**, is an ancient WINTER SOLSTICE festival celebrated by the Incas in Peru on June 24. Their ancient empire at one time extended along the Pacific coast of South America from the northern border of modern Ecuador to the Río Maule in central Chile. The Incas believed that their land lay at the center of the earth. They honored Inti Raymi, their sun god, at the foot of La Marca Hills, not far from where the actual equator is now known to be. Their religion embraces both Christian and Indian elements, and they still believe that the sun and moon have god-like powers.

The original Inti Raymi celebration involved animal sacrifices performed by the shaman or priest at the top of the hill of La Marca when the sun reached its zenith at the solstice. Today the main celebration takes place in Cuzco, the 12th-century Incan capital, where there is a special procession and mock sacrifice to the sun, followed by a week-long celebration involving folkloric dances, tours of archeological ruins, and regional arts and crafts displays. Bonfires are still lit in the Andes Mountains to celebrate the rebirth of the sun, and people burn their old clothes as a way of marking the end of the harvest cycle.

CONTACTS:
International Nature & Cultural Adventures (INCA)
1311 63rd St.
Emeryville, CA 94608
510-420-1550; fax: 510-420-0947
www.inca1.com

♦ 1425 ♦ Iowa State Fair
11 days ending third Sunday in August

One of America's foremost state fairs, celebrating agriculture and featuring a life-sized cow sculpted out of 600 pounds of sweet butter, is held for 11 days at the fairgrounds in Des Moines, Iowa. Attracting close to a million people each year, the fair is famous for having inspired the Phil Stong novel, *State Fair*, and three movies based on the novel. Will ROGERS starred in the first movie. The second and third were musicals by Rodgers and Hammerstein and included the now-standard songs "It Might as Well Be Spring" and "It's a Grand Night for Singing."

The fair is also famous for its cow made out of butter. The breed represented varies from year to year. It's kept in a display case cooled to 40 degrees. The most frequently asked question at the fair information booth is, "Where's the butter cow?" (Answer: in the Agriculture Building.)

Sheep are an important feature at the fair, reflecting the fact that Iowa has more sheep farms than any other state. Sheepshearing contests are popular; champions can shear a sheep in 90 seconds. The big boar contest is also popular; the winning animal always weighs in at more than half a ton. There are other competitions as well: checker playing, horseshoe pitching, fiddling, and rolling-pin throwing.

The first Iowa state fair was held in 1854. Memorable moments in the intervening years include the spectacular crash of two trains, one labeled Roosevelt and the other Hoover, which were throttled up at opposite ends of a track. They roared down on each other, crashed, and exploded. The year was 1932, when the presidential candidates were Herbert Hoover and Franklin D. ROOSEVELT.

The fair underwent a period of rapid change between 1880 and 1930, expanding to encompass such activities as horse and auto racing, biplane stunt-flying, high-diving horses, and auto-to-airplane transfers. The American aviator Charles Lindbergh visited the fair in 1927, soon after his triumphant nonstop solo flight across the Atlantic.

CONTACTS:
Iowa State Fair
3000 E. Grand Ave.
P.O. Box 57130
Des Moines, IA 50317 United States
515-262-3111 or 800-545-3247; fax: 515-262-6906
www.iowastatefair.org

♦ 1426 ♦ Iqbal (Muhammad), Birthday of
November 9

In Pakistan, November 9 has been declared a national holiday to celebrate the birthday of Dr. Allama Muhammad Iqbal, a famous Pakistani poet and philosopher.

Iqbal was born in the city of Sialkot in the Punjab province of Pakistan on November 9, 1877. He was an educated man. In college, he studied English literature, philosophy, and Arabic. While in college, he discovered Urdu poetry, and some of his poems were published in 1901. Soon afterward, he gained recognition as a rising star in Urdu literature. He earned a masters degree in philosophy and served as a lecturer in history, philosophy, and political science.

Iqbal spent time in Europe for graduate studies and then taught in England and Germany. During this time, he wrote and lectured on Islamic subjects that helped him gain recognition in literary circles. Iqbal returned to India in 1908 and practiced law until 1934, when his deteriorating health forced him to give up his practice. He died in 1938. His tomb is in Lahore, the capital of the Pakistani province of Punjab.

To honor Iqbal, Pakistan has declared November 9 a national holiday. On this day, a number of functions are held to honor the great poet. Many educational institutions sponsor programs that showcase his life and achievements. In addition to the main function at Iqbal's tomb, the National Museum of Pakistan in Karachi exhibits Iqbal's personal belongings, including his costumes, books, and publications.

CONTACTS:
Tourism Development Corporation of Punjab Ltd.
151-Abubakar Block
New garden Town
Lahore Pakistan
92-42-9923-1647
www.tdcp.gop.pk

◆ 1427 ◆ Iran Islamic Republic Day
Farvardin 12

Most Iranians welcomed Ayatollah Ruhollah Khomeini's campaign to overthrow Mohammad Reza Shah Pahlavi and install a new theocratic government. Millions greeted him in February 1979, when he returned from 15 years of exile. By the end of the following month, the country was prepared to participate on a national referendum to establish an Islamic Republic based on a new constitution. A large majority voted in favor of the measure on March 30 and 31, leading Khomeini to declare on April 1: "This day of Farvardin 12, the first day of God's government, is to be one of our foremost religious and national festivals."

Iranians congregate throughout the country to celebrate Republic Day, also known as **National Day**. Past celebrations have included an address by the Iranian president. The largest public gathering takes place in Revolution Square, located in the capital city of Tehran. Thousands wave the national flag and some performers play music with traditional instruments.

The Iranian calendar differs slightly from the Gregorian calendar, which means the date of commemoration also does not line up with its Gregorian counterpart.

CONTACTS:
Interests Section of the Islamic Republic of Iran
2209 Wisconsin Ave. N.W.
Washington, D.C. 20007
202-965-4990; fax: 202-965-1073
www.daftar.org

◆ 1428 ◆ Iran Petroleum Nationalization Anniversary
Esfand 29

Under the leadership of Prime Minister Mohammed Mossadegh, Iran claimed control of its lucrative oil industry by passing a nationalization law on March 15, 1951. Western countries responded two years later by backing favored leader Mohammad Reza Shah Pahlavi in his successful overthrow of Mossadegh. These events further stirred animosity in Iran against Western countries and fed the nationalist sentiment surrounding the observance of this special anniversary.

Celebrations of this event, also known as the **National Day of Oil**, take place in Iran and in Iranian communities abroad. Past activities have included television shows paying tribute to the 1951 legislation and conferences that focus on oil nationalization as well as Iran's present-day foreign policy.

Because the Iranian calendar differs slightly from the Gregorian calendar, the present-day commemoration falls a few days after March 15.

CONTACTS:
Embassy of Iran
2209 Wisconsin Ave., N.W
Washington, D.C. 20007
202-965-4990; fax: 202-965-1073
www.daftar.org/eng

National Iranian Oil Company
Hafez Crossing, Taleghani Ave.
Tehran Iran
98-616-22-2113
www.nioc.ir

◆ 1429 ◆ Iran Victory Day of the Iranian Revolution
February 11

Few world events during the late 20th century were as pivotal as the Iranian Revolution of 1979, also known as the Islamic Revolution. Ayatollah Ruhollah Khomeini overthrew Shah Mohammad Reza Pahlavi, signaling the end of a 2,500-year era in which autocratic monarchs ruled Iran, formerly Persia. It also marked the rise of Islamic fundamentalism during those years. Iranians celebrate the coup's anniversary and also commemorate the 10 days that led up to Victory Day.

On February 1, 1979, Khomeini returned to Iran to claim power after spending 15 years in exile. To memorialize the historic moment, a helicopter drops flowers on the ayatollah's tomb, in the Behesht-e Zahra cemetery south of the capital city of Tehran. Then, for the next 10 days, people attend film screenings, music performances, and exhibitions inspired by the revolution.

The celebration on February 11, known as the "Dawn of God" (Yaum Allah), usually entails a mass rally and military parade in Tehran.

CONTACTS:
Embassy of Iran
2209 Wisconsin Ave. N.W.
Washington, D.C. 20007
202-965-4990; fax: 202-965-1073
www.daftar.org/eng

Tehran Municipality - Public & International Relations Department
Behesht Ave.
Tehran Iran
98-21-5516-6677; fax: 98-21-5581-2126
en.tehran.ir

◆ 1430 ◆ Iris Fest (Fete de l'Iris)
First weekend of May

Each of the autonomous regions of Belgium observes its own feast day. The Brussels-Capital Region's celebration, called Iris Fest (Fete de l'Iris), is held during the first weekend of May. Feast days in other regions of Belgium include FEAST

DAY OF THE FLEMISH COMMUNITY, FEAST DAY OF THE FRENCH COMMUNITY, FEAST DAY OF THE GERMAN-SPEAKING COMMUNITY, and WALLOON REGIONAL DAY.

Iris Fest is a relatively new festival, as the Brussels-Capital Region only came into existence following the federalization of Belgium in 1989. The festival's main symbol, the iris plant, has been the region's official emblem since 1991.

Many of the weekend's proceedings are held in the city's central square, the Place du Grand Sablon. An established popular act will perform a concert in the square on Saturday, and live jazz concerts are held on Sunday.

On Sunday, the more event-filled of the two days, the Brussels Parliament opens its doors to the public for tours and classical music performances. For La rue en fête, a colorful festival event held throughout Brussels' streets, people gather for parades, theater, and games for kids.

CONTACTS:
Belgian Tourist Office
300 E. 42nd St.
14th Fl.
New York, NY 10017
212-758-8130
www.visitbelgium.com

Belgium Embassy
3330 Garfield St. N.W.
Washington, D.C. 20008
202-333-6900; fax: 202-338-4960
diplomatie.belgium.be/en

◆ 1431 ◆ Ironman Triathlon Championships
Saturday nearest the full moon in October

This extraordinarily grueling international athletic contest has been held since 1978 in Kailua-Kona on Hawaii Island. It consists of a 2.4-mile swim, a 112-mile bicycle race, and, for the final leg, a standard 26.2-mile marathon run. Close to 2,000 stout-hearted men and women participate, preceding the races with a Thursday night party in which they stoke up on carbohydrates. Originally, contestants swam, biked, and ran for the fun and challenge of the event, but cash prizes are now awarded at a banquet the day after the triathlon.

The event is scheduled for the Saturday nearest the full moon in October so that more beach is exposed at low tide, and there is more light from the moon at night. This is the original, but no longer the toughest such contest: double ironmen now challenge triathletes.

CONTACTS:
World Triathlon Corporation
2701 N. Rocky Point Dr.
Ste. 1250
Tampa, FL 33607
813-868-5940; fax: 813-868-5930
www.ironman.com

◆ 1432 ◆ Iroquois Midwinter Festival
January

This festival is the traditional midwinter ceremony of the Iroquois Indians in Canada and the United States, which also serves to usher in the new year. The ceremonies are dedicated to giving thanks to the Master of Life, or Creator, and alsoinclude prayers to Handsome Lake (Ganio'dai'io, 1735-1815), founder of the Iroquois Longhouse religion. The festival lasts eight or nine days. The first few days are concerned with conducting older traditional ceremonies, including the confession and renewal of each person, various other healing and purifying rites, and the False Face dance. The sacrifice of a white dog used to be part of the festival, but this practice has been abandoned. Out of the many ceremonies in the Iroquois tradition, Handsome Lake especially encouraged the Feather Dance, the Thanksgiving Dance, the Personal Chant, and the Bowl Game—known as "the four sacred rituals." The second half of the festival is devoted to fulfilling these.

CONTACTS:
Onondaga Nation Communications
3951 Rt. 11
Onondaga Nation
Nedrow, NY 13120 United States
315-492-1922; fax: 315-469-4717
www.onondaganation.org

Mohawk Council of Kahnawá:ke
P.O. Box 720
Kahnawá:ke, QC J0L 1B0 Canada
450-632-7500; fax: 450-638-5958
www.kahnawake.com

◆ 1433 ◆ Irrigation Festival
First full weekend in May

The Irrigation Festival is the oldest continuous festival in Washington, held since 1896 in Sequim. Originally known as "May Days," the festival celebrated the opening of the first ditch to bring water from the Dungeness River to the arid Sequim prairie. In the early days there were horse races, dancing, a keg of beer hidden in the brush, and tables loaded with food. After a few years, Maypole dances with girls in frilly dresses were a big attraction. The first queen of MAY DAY was chosen in 1908; the first parade was held in 1918; the first queen's float was built in 1948; and a descendant of a pioneer family has been honored as the festival's Grand Pioneer since 1960.

Today, thousands come for a week of activities: a grand parade, a loggers' show, a high school operetta, crafts and flower exhibits, dances, music, and the Ditchwalkers Clam and Spaghetti Dinner.

CONTACTS:
Sequim Irrigation Festival Committee
P.O. Box 2073
Sequim, WA 98382
360-683-6197
www.irrigationfestival.com

◆ 1434 ◆ Islamic Festival
May (odd-numbered years)

Mértola, Portugal, is the site of an Islamic Festival that takes place over four days in May in odd-numbered years. The event celebrates the cultures and peoples of northern Africa and features a wide array of Arab photography, art, cinema, handicrafts, dance, and theater. Seminars cover a variety of subjects, from language to cuisine. Most events are held in the historic town center, which takes on the feel of a "souk," or Arabic market or bazaar. The event is organized by the town council, with the aim of uniting the Portuguese, Spanish, and Islamic cultures that converge in the town's rich history Thousands of visitors flock to the festival, which launched in 2001.

CONTACTS:
Municipality of Mértola - Division of Education, Culture and Social Action
Praça Luís de Camões
Mértola 7750-329 Portugal
351-286-610-100; fax: 351-286-610-101
www.festivalislamicodemertola.com

◆ 1435 ◆ Islamic New Year
First day of the Islamic month of Muharram

The Islamic New Year occurs on the first day of Muharram, the first month in the Islamic calendar. Muharram is one of four especially holy months for Muslims, along with Dhu al-Qadah, Dhu al-Hijjah (when the Pilgrimage to Mecca takes place), and Rajab (when Laylat al-Miraj is celebrated). The name of the month means "sacred."

The first day of Muharram commemorates the flight of the Prophet Muhammad from Mecca, where he had experienced hostility toward his teachings, to Medina in 622, which is considered year one in the Muslim calendar. Muhammad's journey, known as the Hijra, is an important milestone in Islamic history, because it brought the religion to more people. Muhammad was welcomed in Medina and soon had many followers.

Devout Muslims observe New Year's Day by going to mosque to worship and listen to stories about Muhammad and early Muslims. Muslims traditionally make resolutions on this day to live more strongly in accord with the teachings of Islam. Some people may exchange gifts, but this is not a popular custom.

CONTACTS:
Islamic Center of America
19500 Ford Rd.
Dearborn, MI 48128 United States
313-593-0000
icofa.com

◆ 1436 ◆ Isle of Eight Flags Shrimp Festival
First weekend in May

The early part of the 20th century saw the dawn of the shrimp industry in Amelia, Florida, a 13-mile long barrier island on the Atlantic Ocean coast at the northern tip of the state. The island's deep-water harbor proved a hospitable environment and advantageous location from which to harvest what is today the vast majority of Florida's white shrimp crop. To celebrate the shrimp and its importance to the local community and the state, the Isle of Eight Flags Shrimp Festival has been held each year since 1964 on Amelia's Fernandina Beach. The "eight flags" in the festival name refers to the fact that the island was under the dominion of eight different flags in its five century history, beginning with the French in 1562.

Although the food vendors selling shrimp are the highlight of the festival for many of the 150,000 annual attendees, several other popular events take place over the course of the weekend. The festival includes a pirate parade and fireworks, an art, crafts, and antiques show, a Miss Shrimp Festival pageant and other events. On the final day of the festival, a boat parade and the traditional Blessing of the Shrimp Fleet takes place.

CONTACTS:
Isle of Eight Flags Shrimp Festival
102 Centre St.
Fernandina Beach, FL 32034
www.shrimpfestival.com

◆ 1437 ◆ Isle of Wight Festival
June

The Isle of Wight Festival is an annual concert that takes place in Seaclose Park in Newport on the Isle of Wight in the UK, two hours from London by ferry. A major event on Britain's summer calendar, the festival hosts legendary musicians alongside up-and-coming artists. It features both traditional and new music, and welcomes music lovers of all ages.

The festival's history can be traced to the day in 1969 when Bob Dylan drew a crowd of over 150,000 in a field near Godshill on the Isle of Wight. The next year's event was even bigger, with 600,000 watching a lineup that included Jimi Hendrix, The Who, Joni Mitchell, The Moody Blues, Joan Baez, Leonard Cohen, and Miles Davis. Shortly after, Parliament responded to the disarray at the event, known as Britain's Woodstock, by passing the restrictive Isle of Wight Act. After an absence of 32 years, the festival was revived in 2002 for the Queen's Golden Jubilee. Artists who appeared after the revival included David Bowie, the Rolling Stones, Bruce Springsteen, Paul McCartney, Amy Winehouse, and Coldplay. More than 50,000 now attend the event each year.

CONTACTS:
Isle of Wight Festival
Seaclose Park
Newport, Isle of Wight PO30 2QS United Kingdom
isleofwightfestival.com

Isle of Wight Council
Customer Service Centre
County Hall, High St.
Newport, Isle of Wight PO30 1UD United Kingdom
44-198-382-1000
www.iwight.com

♦ 1438 ♦ **Isle of Wight Garlic Festival**
August

The Isle of Wight Garlic Festival is a two-day food and entertainment festival that takes place just outside the village of Newchurch on the Isle of Wight in the United Kingdom. The festival celebrates the best and most pungent garlic grown on the island by the famous Garlic Farm, which boasts a rich history of garlic farming spanning several decades, and is rated as the UK's largest specialty garlic grower. The festival is believed to have originated as a fundraiser for the local community, but it has grown in popularity over the years to also include live music, children's events, and other entertainment.

Regarded as a paean to the versatile bulb, the festival naturally centers around garlic and highlights its use as food and its health benefits. The festival grounds feature cooking demonstrations and marquees filled with garlic products of all types, including garlic fudge and garlic chutneys. In recent years, the festival has become a successful trade fair as well as a fundraiser for charities on the island.

CONTACTS:
Isle of Wight Garlic Festival
P.O. Box 51
Totland Bay
Isle of Wight PO40 0AQ United Kingdom
44-1983-761-475
www.garlic-festival.co.uk

♦ 1439 ♦ **Israel Festival**
May-June

This three-week festival, founded in 1961, is primarily dedicated to Israeli arts and culture, although guest conductors and performers from other countries are featured as well. There are symphony and choral concerts, opera, ballet and modern dance, theater, jazz, folklore, films, and art exhibitions at several locations in Jerusalem.

The Israel Philharmonic Orchestra has performed with guest conductors like Zubin Mehta and Leonard Bernstein, and Israeli dance groups offer both traditional and modern programs. Pablo CASALS and Isaac Stern have played there, Rudolf Nureyev and Merce Cunningham have danced at the festival, and Sir John Gielgud has read Shakespeare there.

CONTACTS:
Israel Festival Office
Jerusalem Israel
israel-festival.org/en

♦ 1440 ♦ **Israel Independence Day**
Between April 16 and May 14; Iyyar 5

Known in Hebrew as **Yom ha-Atzma'ut**, this day commemorates the proclamation of independence by Palestinian Jews and the establishment of a provisional government in Israel on May 14, 1948 (5 Iyyar 5708 on the Jewish calendar).

It is observed with parties, performances, and military parades as well as religious rituals, which include the reading of Psalms. In the United States, Jews celebrate Israel Independence Day by attending concerts, films, parades, Israeli fairs, and other public events. An Israeli Day Parade is held in New York City, but it doesn't always take place on the fifth day of Iyyar.

A popular custom on this day for Israelis is to walk at least a short distance somewhere in the country where they have never walked before.

CONTACTS:
America-Israel Chamber of Commerce
203 N. LaSalle St.
Ste. 2100
Chicago, IL 60601
312-558-1346; fax: 312-346-9603
www.americaisrael.org

Embassy of Israel
3514 International Dr. N.W.
Washington, D.C. 20008
202-364-5500
www.israelemb.org

♦ 1441 ♦ **Istanbul Festivals, International**
Varies

Since the first **International Istanbul Festival** was held in 1973, the Istanbul Foundation for Culture and the Arts has used this event to bridge the cultures of East and West and to promote Turkey's rich cultural heritage.

The original festival has now branched out into four annual festivals and one biennial one: the International Istanbul Film Festival, held in April, the International Istanbul Theatre Festival in May-June, the International Istanbul Music Festival over June and July, and the International Istanbul Jazz Festival in July. The International Istanbul Biennial is held from September to November during odd-numbered years and features contemporary visual art.

CONTACTS:
Istanbul Foundation for Culture and Arts
Nejat Eczacibasi Binasi
Sadi Konuralp Caddesi
No: 5 Sishane
Istanbul 34433 Turkey
212-334-0700; fax: 212-334-0716
www.iksv.org

♦ 1442 ♦ **Isthmian Games**
First month of spring

The Isthmian Games were athletic competitions held in ancient times at Corinth in Greece. They were held during alternate years beginning in 581 B.C.E., with contests in various events, including gymnastics, horse racing, and poetry (the last was open to both men and women). The prize was a crown of celery.

There are differing stories as to the origin of the games; one legend says they were founded by Theseus after he killed the robber chief Sinis. The games were one of the four great national Greek festivals, the others being the OLYMPIC, PYTHIAN, and NEMEAN games. The Isthmian games were especially popular because they offered more amusements than the other three festivals.

CONTACTS:
Greek National Tourism Organisation
305 E. 47th St.
2nd Fl.
New York, NY 10017
212-421-5777; fax: 212-826-6940
www.visitgreece.gr

♦ 1443 ♦ Itabashi Suwa Jinja Ta-Asobi
January or February

The rice crop is crucial to the Japanese, and various rituals are observed to please the *kami*, or god, who is ultimately responsible for a good harvest. These rice-growing rituals can be traced back to ancient times, although the significance of some has been long forgotten. Since spring begins to emerge in January, signalling the nearness of the new planting season, people perform traditional rituals for a good crop. It is not uncommon to see offerings in rice paddies, usually consisting of charms affixed to plants believed to give good luck, such as pine, chestnut, and bamboo during January. The most popular time to observe these rituals is between January 11 and the night of the full moon.

The festival known as Itabashi Suwa Jinja Ta-Asobi, held at the Suwa Shrine in Tokyo, began as a thanksgiving ritual to the god of the rice paddies (*Ta-no-kami*) in return for the granting of a plentiful harvest. There is also a *mikoshi* parade—mikoshi are the portable shrines or palanquins identified with the gods during their visits to earth—singing, and food. One area is set aside for the performance of traditional dances, which include a rice-planting dance, a weeding dance, a chasing-away-the-bird dance, and a fertility dance. At the end of the festival, a big bonfire is lighted and huge drums are played.

CONTACTS:
Itabashi ward office
Itabashi-ku, Tokyo Itabashi chome
No. 66 No. 1
Tokyo 173-8501 Japan
81-3-3964-1111; fax: 81-3-3579-2028
www.city.itabashi.tokyo.jp

Japan National Tourist Organization
1 Grand Central Pl.
60 E. 42nd St.
New York, NY 10165 United States
212-757-5640; fax: 212-307-6754
www.japantravelinfo.com

♦ 1444 ♦ Italian Festival
May, Memorial Day weekend

This event is a weekend festival in McAlester, Okla., in Pittsburgh County, a coal-rich area that drew miners of Italian heritage in the 1880s. The town began as a tent store owned by J. J. McAlester, who discovered and mined the coal here. He was later lieutenant governor of the state. The descendants of the Italian miners celebrate their heritage with folk music, dances, costumes, arts and crafts, and, of course, food, lots of it: 12,000 meatballs, 6,000 sausages, and 200 gallons of spaghetti and sauce.

CONTACTS:
McAlester Italian Festival Foundation, Inc.
P.O. Box 1212
McAlester, OK 74502
918-470-9340
www.themcalesteritalianfestival.org

♦ 1445 ♦ Italian Heritage Parade
Sunday closest to October 12

Since 1869, the city of San Francisco has hosted the annual Italian Heritage Parade, one of the oldest such events in the United States. Originally begun as a way to honor the Italian-American community in San Francisco, the parade has grown to celebrate the October 12 birthday of Christopher Columbus as well.

The parade and many of the related festivities take place in the heavily Italian North Beach area of San Francisco. After services at the Church of Saints Peter and Paul, the parade wends its way from Fisherman's Wharf down Columbus Avenue to Washington Square Park. Floats and marching bands from local community organizations make up the procession. Every year, young girls are chosen from the community to serve as Queen Isabella and her court, named after the Spanish queen who financed Columbus's historic expedition. Dressed in elaborate period costumes, the queen and her court preside over Columbus Day ceremonies throughout the city. The Italian Heritage Parade draws some 400,000 spectators each year.

CONTACTS:
San Francisco Columbus Day Celebration, Inc.
www.sfcolumbusday.org

♦ 1446 ♦ Italy Liberation Day
April 25

Liberation Day is a national holiday commemorating the Allied invasion of Italy in 1943 that led to the overthrow of Mussolini's Fascist rule during World War II.

CONTACTS:
Italian National Tourist Board
686 Park Ave.
3rd Fl.
New York, NY 10065
212-245-5618; fax: 212-586-9249
www.italiantourism.com

♦ 1447 ♦ Itul
December

This highly regarded ritual is a ceremonial dance performed by the Kuba people who live in the Democratic Republic of Congo (formerly Zaire). It takes place on an infrequent basis, not only because the costs and preparation involved are so extensive but also because it can only be held with the king's authorization; the only sponsors (and funders) may be the children of a king.

An Itul performed for a king is held in the dance area of the palace and is considered more refined because the king's wives are professional dancers and singers. If the Itul is open to the public, it takes place in the plaza in front of the palace. Although it is usually held in December, the dates can vary.

The preparations can take up to several months, but the dance itself lasts only a few hours. The villain's role is danced by someone dressed as an animal, and the plot on which the dance is based combines both traditional episodes and those that have been adapted to whatever animal is chosen.

The dance is performed in two parts over two consecutive days. The first part mourns the destruction caused by the enemy-animal, and the second part deals with its capture and killing. There is a chorus of women kneeling in the center who perform the songs and provide a rhythmical accompaniment by beating calabashes or gourd drums on the ground. The dancers move counterclockwise around the chorus, and the king watches the spectacle from a special shelter set off to one side.

The Itul is considered so important that once the word spreads that the ceremony is taking place, Kuba people from all over rush to attend it. It is revived from time to time by kings who fear that their traditional power is being threatened by modern secular life.

CONTACTS:
Embassy of the Democratic Republic of Congo
1726 M St. N.W
Ste. 601
Washington, D.C. 20036
202-234-7690; fax: 202-234-2609
www.ambardcusa.org

♦ 1448 ♦ **Ivy Day**
October 6

October 6 is the anniversary of the death of Charles Stewart Parnell (1846-1891), the famous Irish statesman and leader of the Home Rule Party. He entered the House of Commons when he was only 29 and quickly established a reputation for hostility to England and all things English. He became a hero to the Irish poor, many of whom would try to touch his clothes or kiss his hands and knees when he walked through a crowd.

Parnell fell out of public favor somewhat when he became involved in a divorce case in 1890, and the trauma of rejection by so many of his countrypeople is thought to have contributed to his early death in 1891. But he is a symbol of Irish pride and independence, and his name appears frequently in Irish literature, particularly the poetry of William Butler Yeats and the short story in James Joyce's *Dubliners* called "Ivy Day in the Committee Room."

It is somewhat ironic that the sprig of green ivy traditionally worn on this day—chosen by Parnell himself as an emblem—is a color he apparently intensely disliked.

CONTACTS:
Glasnevin Trust
Glasnevin Cemetery Finglas Rd.
Glasnevin
Dublin 11 Ireland
353-01-882-6500
www.glasnevintrust.ie

♦ 1449 ♦ **Iyomante Matsuri (Bear Festival)**
January-February

Among the Ainu people of the northernmost islands of Japan, especially on Hokkaido, the baiting and killing of a young bear was not considered a brutal act but a ritual send-off to the spirit world. The "divine" cub was ceremoniously fed and cared for, then killed and arranged with fetishes. Some of his own cooked meat and a dish of his own blood, along with cakes and dried fish, were laid before him. He was supposed to bring these gifts to his parents when he arrived in heaven. After a time, Ainu belief has it, he would be reincarnated and return to earth as another cub.

CONTACTS:
Ainu Museum
2-3-4 Wakakusa-cho
Siraoi, Hokkaido 059-0902 Japan
81-1-4482-3914; fax: 81-1-4482-3685
www.ainu-museum.or.jp

♦ 1450 ♦ **Izumo-taisha Jinzaisai**
Late October to early November; 10th lunar month

According to Shinto belief, the gods from all over Japan assemble during the tenth lunar month at the Izumo-taisha Shrine in Taisha-machi, Shimané Prefecture. Local people have dubbed this month *Kamiarizuki*, or "the month when the gods are present." Of course, elsewhere in Japan it is called *Kannazuki*, or "the month when the gods are absent." Numerous rituals honoring the gods take place, including a formal greeting at the beach and a ceremonial procession to the shrine.

CONTACTS:
Japan National Tourist Organization
1 Grand Central Pl. 60 E. 42nd St.
Ste. 448
New York, NY 10165
212-757-5640; fax: 212-307-6754
www.jnto.go.jp

J

♦ 1451 ♦ **Jackalope Days**
Mid to late June

Three days of celebration in Douglas, Wyo., honor the jackalope, an elusive animal that is a cross between a jackrabbit and an antelope (according to the legends of Converse County). The jackalope might be mistaken for a large rabbit except for its antlers, and it might be identified as a small deer, except for its rabbit-like shape.

The jackalope was first seen in 1829 by Roy Ball, a trapper, who was denounced as a liar. Some people still doubt its existence, despite the evidence of numerous stuffed heads on barroom walls. The jackalope is rarely seen because it is a shy animal and comes out of hiding only for breeding with the commonly seen and hornless females, called does, which look like ordinary rabbits. But it breeds only during electrical storms, at the precise moment of the flash when most people are not out wandering around. A 10-foot replica of a jackalope in Centennial Jackalope Square in Douglas attests to the cultural importance of this critter.

Events of Jackalope Days include a downtown carnival, rodeos, a street dance, a parade, the crowning of a rodeo queen, and sports competitions.

CONTACTS:
City of Douglas Administrative Services Office
101 N. Fourth St.
P.O. Box 1030
Douglas, WY 82633 United States
307-358-3462
www.cityofdouglas.org

Douglas Chamber of Commerce
121 Brownfield Rd.
Douglas, WY 82633
307-358-2950; fax: 307-358-2972
www.jackalope.org

♦ 1452 ♦ **Jackson's (Andrew) Birthday**
March 15

Andrew Jackson (1767-1845), the seventh president of the United States (1829-37), became a national hero during the War of 1812 when he successfully fought the British at New Orleans. Jackson's heroic performance came despite the fact

that he was so sick he could barely stand without assistance, and no one knew that a peace treaty had been signed two weeks earlier. His soldiers thought he was as "tough as hickory," resulting in his nickname, "Old Hickory." The anniversary of his birth is a special observance in Tennessee, and the president of the United States usually brings or sends a wreath to be placed on Jackson's grave in the garden at his home, The Hermitage, near Nashville.

Other tributes paid to Jackson during this week include radio speeches and newspaper editorials, school essay contests, and Jackson Day dinners sponsored by the Democratic party, of which he is considered one of the founders. Sometimes these celebrations are held on January 8, BATTLE OF NEW ORLEANS DAY. In Virginia, Jackson's birthday is celebrated in January along with those of Martin Luther KING, Jr. and Robert E. LEE.

CONTACTS:
Andrew Jackson's The Hermitage
4580 Rachel's Ln.
Nashville, TN 37076
615-889-2941; fax: 615-889-9909
www.thehermitage.com

♦ 1453 ♦ **Jacob's Ladder**
May (Main Festival), December (Winter Weekend Festival)

Jacob's Ladder Folk Festival takes place every year over three days in May in Israel at Nof Ginosar on Lake Kinneret. Founded in 1978, the festival is a lively musical and social event that showcases a wide range of folk-music styles, from bluegrass to country rock, from world music to blues, Renaissance, and Irish fiddle music. In 2004, the organizers added an annual indoor festival that takes place over a winter weekend in a hotel in Nof Ginosar. Both events offer, in addition to music, such additional activities as storytelling, dancing, juggling, yoga, tai chi, tractor and trailer tours, swimming, arts and crafts, food booths, and children's shows. Festival-goers in May can camp on-site.

The festival was founded by three members of Kibbutz Machanayim who had settled in Israel from England and the United States in the 1960s. The festival grew out of a monthly folk club that kibbutz members launched in order to perform and listen to the folk and protest songs they had known in their home countries. About 700 fans attended the first festival, held on the grounds of the kibbutz. After numerous moves and significant growth, the festival now draws prominent musicians from Israel and around the world.

CONTACTS:
Jacob s Ladder Festival
Mishol Nimron 2
Katzrin, 12900 Israel
972-4-6850403; fax: 153-4-696-2231
www.jlfestival.com

♦ 1454 ♦ **Jacob's Pillow Dance Festival**
June-August

The second oldest dance festival in the United States (after the Bennington Dance Festival), the Jacob's Pillow Dance Festival takes place for 10 weeks every summer at the historic Ted Shawn Theatre near Lenox, Massachusetts.

Edwin Myers ("Ted") Shawn was an innovative modern dancer and cofounder, with his wife Ruth St. Denis, of Denishawn, the first American modern dance company. In 1933, at his farm named Jacob's Pillow, he founded the Jacob's Pillow Dance Festival as a summer residence and theater for his male dancers. After the group disbanded, Shawn turned Jacob's Pillow into a dance center of international importance—a place where not only ballet but modern and ethnic dance could be presented. Top dancers from all over the world give regular performances throughout the summer to packed houses.

CONTACTS:
Jacob's Pillow Dance
358 George Carter Rd.
Becket, MA 01223
413-243-9919; fax: 413-243-4744
www.jacobspillow.org

♦ 1455 ♦ **Jakarta International Film Festival**
November-December

Indonesia's sole international film festival is held each December in the Indonesian capital of Jakarta. The Jakarta International Film Festival (JIFFEST) attracts tens of thousands of movie fans and industry professionals each year in November and December. Since it began in 1999, JIFFEST has consistently grown to become one of the major international film festivals in Southeast Asia.

Most of the screenings take place at the Pop Up Cinema, the Blitzmegaplex Granda, and the Monas Open Air Cinema. An international jury selects the awards for best Indonesian feature and best Indonesian director. The feature film competition includes awards for top feature script, short fiction script, and documentary script. The festival also hosts a series of training programs and workshops, as well as business events that focus on exploring markets for both local and international films. In 2010, JIFFEST co-organized the Madani

Film Event, an Islamic-themed festival that features panel discussions and screenings.

CONTACTS:
Jakarta International Film Festival
28th AXA Tower Bldg.
Jl. Prof. Dr Satrio kav.18
Jakarta, 12940 Indonesia
62-21-30056090; fax: 62-21-30056091
www.muvila.com/jiffest

♦ 1456 ♦ **Jamaica Festival**
Late July through first Monday in August

Originally called the **Independence Festival of Jamaica** because it ended on the first Monday in August, JAMAICA INDEPENDENCE DAY, the two- to three-week-long event now known as the **Jamaica National Festival of the Arts** emphasizes the cultural roots, conservation, and revival of traditional art forms by ethnic groups—particularly folk music, folk dances, and folk games of African origin—as well as nurturing contemporary arts.

Competitions to determine who will perform at the festival begin early in the year at the local level. After regional and national competitions are held, the best in each category are selected to participate in the final festival programs, which include fine art, photo, and culinary exhibits, music, dance, concerts, plays, and literary readings. The festival has been held in Kingston, Montego Bay, and elsewhere on the island since 1963. A film festival was added in 1977.

CONTACTS:
Jamaica Cultural Development Commission
3 - 5 Phoenix Ave.
Kingston, 10 Jamaica
876-926-5726; fax: 876-960-4521
www.jcdc.gov.jm

♦ 1457 ♦ **Jamaica Independence Day**
First Monday in August

The island of Jamaica became an independent nation with loose ties to the British Commonwealth on August 6, 1962. Before that it had been a founding member of the Federation of the West Indies, a group of Caribbean islands that formed a unit within the Commonwealth of Nations. Allegiance to the British gradually gave way to the emergence of a national identity, and the federation was dissolved.

A public holiday throughout the island, Independence Day is celebrated with a grand parade, traditional music and dancing, arts and crafts exhibits, and agricultural and other events as part of the JAMAICA FESTIVAL.

CONTACTS:
Jamaica Cultural Development Commission
3 - 5 Phoenix Ave.
Kingston, 10 Jamaica
876-926-5726; fax: 876-960-4521
www.jcdc.gov.jm

♦ 1458 ♦ **Jamaica National Heroes Day**
Third Monday of October

In Kingston, Jamaica, National Heroes Park contains a series of statues devoted to key figures in the country's history, including independence leader Alexander Bustamente and pan-African crusader Marcus Garvey. As a way to honor the figures commemorated in this park, the Jamaican government has established National Heroes Day. The holiday officially replaced the celebration for Queen Elizabeth's birthday, although she still receives military honors during ceremonies.

The first group of national heroes was designated in 1965, the year of the centenary celebration of the 1865 Morant Bay Rebellion, a pivotal moment in the quest for independence from Great Britain. The first commemoration took place in 1968. As more heroes were added to the official list over subsequent years, National Heroes Day expanded to become **National Heritage Week**.

A typical ceremony held on the Monday that concludes Heritage Week is the National Heroes Day salute. Local parishes all over the island hold award ceremonies to honor community figures, while at National Heroes Park a main ceremony takes place that features a speech by a national leader, typically the prime minister.

CONTACTS:
Jamaica Tourist Board
5201 Blue Lagoon Dr.
Ste. 670
Miami, FL 33126
305-665-0557 or 800-526-2422; fax: 305-666-7239
www.visitjamaica.com

♦ 1459 ♦ **Jamestown Day**
May 13

Jamestown, Virginia, is the site of the first permanent English settlement in America. A group of 104 settlers sponsored by the London Company (sometimes called the Virginia Company) disembarked about 50 miles from the mouth of the James River on May 13, 1607, and spent a difficult few years fighting famine and disease. Eventually they initiated the tobacco trade that allowed Virginia to become economically self-sufficient. Jamestown also established the first representative government on the continent, brought the first African slaves to the colonies, and built America's first Anglican (Episcopal) church.

On the Sunday nearest May 13, which is officially known as Jamestown Day, a commemorative service is held at the historic site of the original settlement. There are speeches, readings, and choral selections; addresses by British and American officials; and a procession to the Memorial Cross, which marks the town's earliest cemetery, followed by a wreath-laying ceremony.

The 408th anniversary of the founding of the Jamestown Settlement will be celebrated in 2015.

CONTACTS:
Jamestown-Yorktown Foundation
P.O. Box 1607
Williamsburg, VA 23187
757-253-4838 or 888-593-4682; fax: 757-253-5299
www.historyisfun.org

♦ 1460 ♦ **Jamhuri (Kenya Independence Day)**
December 12

The biggest of the national holidays in Kenya, Jamhuri is observed to commemorate the full independence of Kenya from the British in 1963. A year later, the country became a republic with Jomo Kenyatta (c. 1894-1978) the first president. The day is celebrated nationwide but with special events in Nairobi— speeches by the president and other officials, parades, fireworks, and *ngomas* (dances) performed in public plazas.

CONTACTS:
Kenya Tourist Board
c/o Myriad Marketing
6033 W. Century Blvd
Ste. 900
Los Angeles, CA 90045
310-649-7718; fax: 310-649-7713
www.magicalkenya.com

♦ 1461 ♦ **Jammolpur Ceremony**
May

Among the tribe known as the Saora in the hills of eastern India, May is the time for the **Blessing of the Seeds** or Jammolpur ceremony, named for Jammolsum, the god of seed.

Farmers bring some of the seed they will be planting soon to an altar set up for the purpose of blessing the seeds. The altar is placed next to a wall painting a priest has completed that morning. Each element in the painting has a symbolic meaning and power; for example, including birds, deer, and porcupines ensures that these animals will stay away from the young crops. It is common for the Saoras to paint such pictures, which they often do to please a particular god or a deceased ancestor who is giving them trouble. It is also held that the painter is given dreams the night before showing him what to paint.

During the ceremony the priest recites an ancient story and sacrifices a chicken, which is later cooked and eaten. He then pours some wine on the altar and sprinkles some seeds there as well, all the while appealing to the god and ancestors for a good growing season. After the ceremony, the blessed seeds are distributed among the farmers, who take them home and mix them in with the seeds they will sow. At harvest time another ceremony, called Rogonadur, is held.

CONTACTS:
Odisha Department of Tourism
Paryatan Bhawan
Museum Campus
Bhubaneswar, Odisha 751 014 India

91-674-243-2177 or 800-208-1414
www.orissatourism.gov.in

♦ 1462 ♦ Jamshed Navaroz (Jamshed Navroz)
March, July, August; first day of Frawardin, the first Zoroastrian month

The **Zoroastrian New Year** is observed at the VERNAL EQUINOX among the Parsis in India, who are the descendants of the original Zoroastrian immigrants from Iran (formerly Persia). It is traditional for men to dress in white, while women wear colored clothing. Ritual bathing, worship, and the exchange of gifts are part of the celebration. This festival is celebrated in July by the Kadmi sect's calendar and in August by the Shahenshai sect's calendar.

See also NAWRUZ.

CONTACTS:
Ministry of Tourism, Government of India
1270 Ave. of the Americas
Ste. 303
New York, NY 10020
212-586-4901 or 212-586-4902; fax: 212-582-3274
tourism.gov.in

Delhi Zoroastrian Parsis Board of Trustees
c/o Delhi Parsi Dharamshala
Bahadur Shah Zafar Marg
New Delhi, Delhi 110001 India
91-11-2328-8615
delhiparsis.com

♦ 1463 ♦ Janaki Navami
April-May; ninth day of waxing half of Hindu month of Vaisakha

Sita, heroine of the Hindu epic poem *Ramayana*, is supposed to have sprung on this day from a furrow in a field plowed by King Janaka. He named her Sita, which means "furrow of the earth," and raised her as his own child. She was actually the goddess Lakshmi, sent to the earth to bring about the destruction of Ravana and other demons. Many Hindus believe that Sita represents the ideal Indian woman as an embodiment of self-sacrifice, purity, tenderness, fidelity, conjugal affection, and other virtues. Some believe that she appeared in King Janaka's field on the eighth day of the waning half of Phalguna (February-March), and fast on that day instead of the ninth day of Vaisakha.

CONTACTS:
Ministry of Tourism, Government of India
1270 Avenue of the Americas
Ste. 303
New York, NY 10020
212-586-4901; fax: 212-582-3274
tourism.gov.in

Department of Tourism - Government of Bihar
Old Secretariat
Patna, Bihar 800015 India
91-612-2234194; fax: 91-612-2234194
www.bihartourism.gov.in

♦ 1464 ♦ Janmashtami (Krishnastami; Krishna's Birthday)
August-September; new moon day of Hindu month of Bhadrapada

One of the most important Hindu festivals, Janmashtami celebrates the birthday of Lord Krishna, the eighth incarnation of Vishnu and the hero of both rich and poor. Throughout India it is a fast day until the new moon is sighted. Then there are ceremonies and prayers at temples dedicated to Krishna. Rituals include bathing the statue of the infant Krishna and then placing his image in a silver cradle with playthings.

In Mathura, Uttar Pradesh, where Krishna was born, there are performances of Krishna Lila, the folk dramas depicting scenes from Krishna's life. In the state of Tamil Nadu, oiled poles called *ureyadi* are set up, a pot of money is tied to the top, and boys dressed as Krishna try to shinny up the pole and win the prize while spectators squirt water at them.

In Maharashtra, where the festival is known as *Govinda*, pots containing money and curds and butter are suspended high over streets. Boys form human pyramids climbing on each others' shoulders to try to break the pot. These climbing games reflect stories of Krishna, who as a boy loved milk and butter so much they had to be kept out of his reach.

In Nepal, a religious fast is observed on Krishnastami, and Krishna's temple at Lalitpur is visited by pilgrims. People parade in a procession around the town and display pictures of Krishna.

Numerous rich legends tell of Krishna's life. He is supposed to have been adored as a child for his mischievous pranks—tricking people out of their freshly churned butter or stealing the clothes of the cow maidens, called *gopis*, while they bathed in the river. Later, he used his flute to lure the gopis to amorous dalliances. He also defeated the 100-headed serpent Kaliya by dancing it into submission. Paintings, sculpture, and classical dances depict the many episodes of his life. Portraits of him as a child often show him dancing joyously and holding a ball of butter in his hands. Most often he is shown as the divine lover, playing the flute and surrounded by adoring women.

CONTACTS:
Ministry of Tourism, Government of India
1270 Avenue of the Americas
Ste. 303
New York, NY 10020
212-586-4901 or 212-586-4902; fax: 212-582-3274
tourism.gov.in

Uttar Pradesh State Tourism Development Corporation Ltd
Rajarshi Purshottam Das Tandon Paryatan Bhavan
C-13, Vipin Khand
Gomti Nagar
Lucknow, Uttar Pradesh 226010 India
91-522-230-7037; fax: 91-522-230-8937
uptourism.gov.in

New Vrindaban Community
3759 McCrearys Ridge Rd.
Moundsville, WV 26041
304-843-1600
www.newvrindaban.com

♦ 1465 ♦ **Japan Constitution Memorial Day**
May 3

Constitution Memorial Day, or **Kempo Kinen-Bi**, is observed as a national holiday on May 3 and commemorates the adoption of the democratic constitution in 1947. The holiday is part of **Golden Week**, which includes Children's Day, Ko-DOMO-NO-HI, on May 3, and GREENERY DAY, May 4.

CONTACTS:
Fujiyoshida City Hall
International Affairs Desk
6-1-1 Shimoyoshida
Fujiyoshida, Yamanashi 403-8601 Japan
81-0555-24-1236; fax: 81-0555-22-0703
www.city.fujiyoshida.yamanashi.jp

♦ 1466 ♦ **Japan Marine Day**
Third Monday in July

What began in Japan as a celebration of an emperor's historic sea voyage has broadened to become a day of awareness for marine environmental issues. A national holiday, Marine Day (or in Japanese, *Umi no hi*) was established in 1991 by several organizations devoted to ocean conservation. The event's original name was **Marine Commemoration Day**.

This holiday was established in 1941 to mark the return of Meiji the Great (1852–1912), Japan's 122nd emperor, from the northern island of Hokkaido in 1876. The vessel that transported the emperor on the historic voyage, the *Meiji-Maru*, has been preserved as a national treasure and is open for public viewing on Marine Day. Special lectures on other historic ships have been presented at the Tokyo University of Mercantile Marine in conjunction with Marine Day festivities.

With the festival's new focus on marine environmental issues, organizations take advantage of the day to raise awareness by scheduling seaside cleanups and other special events. For Japanese schoolchildren, Marine Day also marks the beginning of their summer vacation.

CONTACTS:
Japan National Tourist Organization
1 Grand Central Pl.
60 E. 42nd St.
Ste. 448
New York, NY 10165
212-757-5640; fax: 212-307-6754
www.jnto.go.jp

♦ 1467 ♦ **Japan National Foundation Day**
February 11

The nationwide holiday known as **Kenkoku Kinen-no-Hi** commemorates the accession to the throne of Jimmu Tenno, Japan's first human emperor, in the year 660 B.C.E. He was believed to be a direct descendant of the gods and is credited with founding the Japanese empire. In fact, this day was originally known as **Empire Day** back in 1872, when the Jap-

anese government first established it as a national holiday. It was abandoned after World War II, then brought back as National Foundation Day in 1966.

It is observed throughout Japan with fireworks and speeches on Japan's position in the world. One of the most elaborate celebrations takes place in Tokyo, where special rites are performed at the Imperial Sanctuary. The emperor and empress, the prime minister, and other high officials attend the ceremony.

CONTACTS:
Japan National Tourist Organization
Little Tokyo Plaza
340 E. 2nd St.
Ste. 302
Los Angeles, CA 90012
213-623-1952; fax: 213-623-6301
www.japantravelinfo.com

♦ 1468 ♦ **Japanese Emperor's Birthday**
December 23

This is a national holiday in Japan honoring the birth of Emperor Akihito (b. 1933). He and his family typically appear on the Imperial Palace balcony to greet visitors, who are invited to enter the grounds on this day.

CONTACTS:
Japan National Tourism Organization
1 Grand Central Pl.
60 E. 42nd St.
New York, NY 10165
212-757-5640; fax: 212-307-6754
www.japantravelinfo.com

♦ 1469 ♦ **Jayuya Festival of Indian Lore**
Mid-November

The **Jayuya Indian Festival** was started in 1969, when new traces of the Taino Indian culture were discovered in and around Jayuya, Puerto Rico. The town of Jayuya was once a center of Taino Indian activity, and many Taino stone carvings can still be seen in nearby caves, even though the tribe itself is extinct. The annual festival is held in mid-November and is timed to coincide with the anniversary of the first sighting of Puerto Rico by COLUMBUS on November 19, 1493.

Festival events include Indian ceremonies and dances as well as concerts featuring *fotutos* (conch shells) as instruments. There is a ceremonial Taino ball game that resembles soccer, and a village (*yukayeque*) of thatched-roof huts that enables visitors to see how the Indians lived. Visitors can attend lectures on the Taino language and customs or take a tour of the caves containing the Indian drawings.

Although Indian arts and crafts are on sale and there are kiosks serving food typical of the island's indigenous population, the Jayuya Indian Festival also has a serious scholarly purpose, which is to educate people about the Taino culture and to encourage more research in this area. Awards are presented each year at the festival to those who have done scholarly work on Puerto Rico's pre-Columbian cultures.

◆ 1470 ◆ **Jazzkaar Festival**
Late April

The Jazzkaar Festival is a 10-day celebration of jazz music held annually in late April in Tallinn, Estonia. Begun in 1990, Jazzkaar culminates the country's observance of international Jazz Appreciation Month and is the largest music festival devoted exclusively to jazz music in the Baltic region of northern Europe. Concerts and associated events are organized and overseen by the Jazzkaar Friends Society.

Performers represent a broad range of jazz variations, including Latin and Middle Eastern traditions, fusion, world beat, and American standards. Among the renowned jazz artists who have visited Jazzkaar are Bobby McFerrin, Chick Corea, Dianne Reeves, Jan Garbarek, John Scofield, Cassandra Wilson, and the Pat Metheny Unity Group. In 2014, Jazzkaar celebrated its 25th birthday and the festival featured the largest number of concerts to date with more than 3,000 performers from 60 countries. The program also showcases numerous musicians from the host country, Estonia.

Concerts take place in a range of venues throughout Tallinn, including clubs, cafes, museums, churches, and theaters. In addition to scheduled performances, additional program events include music competitions, student recitals, lectures, workshops, and special programming on national radio and television. Informal jam sessions often occur at the performance venues after hours and continue late into the night.

CONTACTS:
Society of Friends of the NGO Jazzkaar
Pärnu maantee 30-5
Tallinn, 10141 Estonia
372-666-0030
www.jazzkaar.ee

◆ 1471 ◆ **Jefferson's (Thomas) Birthday**
April 13

Unique among American presidents, Thomas Jefferson (1743-1826) was not only a statesman but a scholar, linguist, writer, philosopher, political theorist, architect, engineer, and farmer. In Europe, he was praised as the foremost American thinker of his time. In the United States, he is remembered primarily as the author in 1776 of the Declaration of Independence. After retiring from government service, Jefferson founded the University of Virginia, which opened in 1825. He died on July 4, 1826, the 50th anniversary of the signing of the Declaration of Independence.

As one of the founders of the Democratic party, along with Andrew JACKSON, he has been honored since 1936 by the Democratic National Committee, which often sponsors official dinners in various locations across the country known as "Jefferson-Jackson Day Dinners." Sometimes these dinners are held on January 8, the anniversary of the BATTLE OF NEW ORLEANS.

At the University of Virginia at Charlottesville, April 13 was observed for many years as **Founder's Day**, but in 1975 the date was shifted to early fall. There is a formal academic procession, after which an address is given by a nationally known figure. This is also the day on which the Thomas Jefferson Award is give to a leading member of the university community.

A birthday commemoration is held each year at Monticello, Jefferson's home in Virginia, as well as at the Jefferson Memorial on the Mall in Washington, D.C.

CONTACTS:
Thomas Jefferson Foundation, Inc.
P.O. Box 316
Charlottesville, VA 22902 United States
434-984-9820 or 800-243-0743
www.monticello.org

◆ 1472 ◆ **Jerash Festival of Culture and Art**
Late July to early August

Jordan's Queen Noor (Lisa Najeb Halaby, b. 1951) played an important role in establishing the visual and performing arts festival that is now held in Jerash every summer. Since 1981 visitors have come to the 2,000-year-old ruins where a Greco-Roman city once stood to hear Jordanian music, to see folkloric dances performed by Jordanian and other Arab groups, and to watch Arab plays and puppet shows. Queen Noor opens the nine-day festival by lighting a symbolic flame in the city forum.

In addition to the music, dance, and theater events, the Jerash Festival also includes an Arab book fair, with titles in both Arabic and English, sponsored by the Jordan Department of Libraries, Documentation, and National Archives.

CONTACTS:
Embassy of the Hashemite Kingdom of Jordan
3504 International Dr. N.W.
Washington, D.C. 20008
202-966-2664; fax: 202-966-3110
www.jordanembassyus.org

◆ 1473 ◆ **Jerusalem Film Festival**
July

The first Jerusalem International Film Festival opened as a three-week event in 1984 with over 100 films, including Israeli premieres and the best in international cinema. Since then, the event has grown in importance, scope, and prestige. Its current format encompasses feature films, documentaries, and television dramas. Films with human rights themes, as well as those dealing with Jewish identity and history, are an important part of the festival.

The festival opens at the Sultan's Pool, an ancient water basin on the west side of Mount Zion. Programs continue at venues ranging from open-air squares in the Old City to the swanky Cinema City, the largest entertainment center in Jerusalem. Besides film screenings, forums, and workshops, the festival hosts a rich array of cultural and educational events, including music and dance performances. Participants in a six-week film workshop produce two short films that provide an original perspective on Jerusalem and Israel, both of which are screened at the festival. The festival's most prestigious award is the Wolgin Prize, established by American philanthropist Jack Wolgin.

CONTACTS:
Jerlem Cinematheque
11 Hebron Rd.
Jerlem, 91083 Israel
972-2-565-4333
www.jff.org.il

◆ 1474 ◆ Jeshn (Afghan Independence Day)
August 19

Jeshn is a celebration of Afghanistan's independence from British control that has been observed throughout the country but with special ceremonies in Kabul. The Treaty of Rawalpindi, signed on August 8, 1919, gave Afghanistan the right to conduct its own foreign affairs. It was the formal conclusion of the brief Third Anglo-Afghan War, which actually ended in May 1919, but August is a slack agricultural period in Afghanistan and therefore a time when more people can celebrate a holiday.

The holiday has been observed with parades, dancing, games, music, and speeches by government figures.

Often the period of Jeshn has been used for major policy announcements. In 1959, one of the more significant events of modern Afghanistan occurred during Jeshn. Prime Minister Mohammad Daoud and other ministers and cabinet and royal family members appeared on the reviewing stand with their wives and daughters exposing their faces. This was a highly dramatic event; until then, women in public always wore the *burka* (an ankle-length tent-like gown and veil that totally covers the head and face, with only a mesh slit to see through). This marked the beginning of abolishing the required burka, and for years afterward most urban upper-class women went about without a veil.

This all changed in 1996 when the fundamentalist Islamic movement, Taliban, took over most of the country and required women to again wear the burka and severely restricted their movements outside the home, forcing most urban westernized Afghan women to give up their careers and education. The Taliban controlled Afghanistan until 2001, when United States and allied forces ousted the Taliban as part of the war against terrorism.

Despite the unsettled conditions in Afghanistan, Independence Day has continued to be observed.

CONTACTS:
Embassy of Afghanistan
2341 Wyoming Ave. N.W.
Washington, D.C. 20008
202-483-6410; fax: 202-483-6488
www.embassyofafghanistan.org

◆ 1475 ◆ Jewish Cultural Festival
June

The ten-day Jewish Culture Festival takes place each year in Cracow, Poland. Centered in the former Jewish district of Kazimierz, the festival offers a wide array of cultural, historical, religious, and culinary events related to Jewish culture, particularly that of the Jews of Poland and Eastern Europe. Lectures, book launches, klezmer-band performances, folk-dancing lessons, and photographic exhibitions are all among the festival's many rich offerings. Festival participants and spectators come from around the world to visit the festival, which has grown significantly since its launch as an annual event in 1994 (prior to that it had occurred on a less regular schedule since 1988).

The aim of the festival organizers, the Jewish Cultural Festival Society, is to pay tribute to and sustain interest in a way of life that once thrived in Poland but has nearly disappeared since World War II. Before the war, the Jewish population of Poland was 3.5 million, but it was decimated by the Holocaust. Today there are only 10,000 self-described Jews living in Poland.

CONTACTS:
Bureau of Jewish Culture Festival
ul. Józefa 36
Cracow, 31-056 Poland
48-12-431-1517; fax: 48-12-431-2427
www.jewishfestival.pl

◆ 1476 ◆ Jhapan Festival (Manasa Festival)
Mid-August; last day of Hindu month of Sravana

Not for the snake-phobic, *Jhampanias*, or snake charmers, gather in the city of Vishnupur, West Bengal State, India, every August for one of the region's most notable annual festivals. Accompanying them, of course, are snakes of all kinds of local varieties, especially dangerous cobras. Jhampanias train their snakes to perform tricks with them, which attendees can observe to their hearts' content. The patron goddess of snakes is Manasa, a daughter of Shiva, and the festival attracts many who follow her cult.

CONTACTS:
Ministry of Tourism, Government of India
1270 Ave. of the Americas
Ste. 303
New York, NY 10020
212-586-4901; fax: 212-582-3274
tourism.gov.in

◆ 1477 ◆ Jhulan Yatra
Between July and August; 17 days preceding the full moon of Sravana

A Hindu festival honoring Lord Jagannatha, Jhulan Yatra is observed in Orissa, a state in India's eastern region, and Bengal, a region shared by India and its eastern neighbor, Bangladesh.

Lord Jagannatha, which is an expression of the deity Krishna, is the reason for music, dancing, and merriment during Jhulan Yatra (also spelled **Jhulan Latra**). This festival takes place over 17 days preceding the full moon of Sravana, a month of the Hindu calendar that falls sometime between July and August. The celebration, which culminates with the full-moon day, takes place ahead of Janmashtami, the festival marking Krishna's birth. Several towns and cities hold official celebrations, but the grandest of them takes place at the Temple of Jagannath in the Orissa town of Puri.

Jhulan Yatra means "swing festival" in Hindi, a reference to the ornately decorated contraption that is specially built to hold the idols of Jagannath and his lover, Radha. Over the course of several nights during the festival, people gather at nighttime to perform songs and dances before the idols. This ritual, known as the *raslila*, dramatizes scenes from Krishna's life. During the festival, people will also visit temples, where they can obtain forgiveness for sins and pray for wealth and prosperity.

CONTACTS:

Sri Jagannath Temple Managing Committee
Grand Rd. Sandhajaga
Sri Nahar
Puri, Odisha 752001 India
91-674-251-1166; fax: 91-674-51-3842
jagannath.nic.in

♦ 1478 ♦ **Jidai Matsuri (Festival of the Ages)**
October 22

Jidai Matsuri is one of the three great festivals of Kyoto, Japan, and also one of the more recent, commemorating the founding of the city as capital in the year 794. A procession of more than 2,000 picturesquely costumed people depict the epochs or ages in Kyoto's history. They parade from the Imperial Palace to the Heian Shrine, which was built in the 18th century as a dedication to the emperors who established Kyoto (then called Heian-kyo) as the capital. The capital was moved in 1868 to Tokyo, and the festival stems from that time. Among the paraders is one representing Gen. Toyotomi Hideyoshi, a patron of the arts under whom Kyoto flourished. He reunified the country after a period of civil war in the Azuchi-Momoyama Period (1573-1600). Wearing full armor, he reenacts an official visit to the emperor.

See also AOI MATSURI and GION MATSURI.

CONTACTS:

Japan National Tourism Organization
1 Grand Central Pl.
60 E. 42nd St.
Ste. 448
New York, NY 10165
212-757-5640; fax: 212-307-6754
www.jnto.go.jp

Heian Jingu Shrine
Nishi Ten-o-cho
Okazaki, Sakyo-ku
Kyoto, 606-8341 Japan

81-75-761-0221; fax: 81-75-761-0225
www.heianjingu.or.jp

♦ 1479 ♦ **Jizo Ennichi**
24th day of each month

Tradition calls for Japanese Buddhists to honor Kshitigarba Jizo on the 24th day of each month with a ritual known as Jizo Ennichi.

Kshitigarba Jizo is a Bodhisattva, or "Buddha-to-be," who is highly regarded by Buddhists in Japan as well as in China, where he is known as Ti-t'sang.

Among Japanese Buddhists, Kshitigarba is known for helping children, women in labor, and the wicked. He is also believed to participate in ushering in the souls of the faithful when they die. He is frequently shown in monk's robes, holding a staff with six rings in his right hand (symbolizing the six dimensions of existence in the realm of desire) and an orb or pearl in his left hand whose symbolic meaning is not known. His statue is most often found outside temples, where he can guide both the dead and the living. Shrines in his honor are set up along roadsides, since he protects travelers as well.

CONTACTS:

Shasta Abbey Buddhist Monastery
3724 Summit Dr.
Mount Shasta, CA 96067 United States
530-926-4208; fax: 530-926-0428
www.shastaabbey.org

♦ 1480 ♦ **Jodlerfests (Yodeling Festivals)**
Summer (end of May through September)

Regional festivals of the art of yodeling are held in the summer months throughout the northern German region of Switzerland. Every two years a national Jodlerfest is held. In 1991, it was in Engelberg and brought together not only yodelers from all over the country but also about 150 players of the Alphorn, a 10- to 15-foot wooden horn with a haunting sound.

The regular annual festivals are held outdoors and feature yodeling clubs, and sometimes soloists, who usually yodel without musical accompaniment. The themes of the songs are related to the mountains, the cows, and the herdsman's life and loves.

Technically, yodeling is a type of singing in which high falsetto and low chest notes alternate. It is supposed to have originated in Switzerland as a way for Alpine cowherds to call from meadow to meadow or to urge on their cows. However, yodeling is also found in other mountain areas in China and North and South America, and among the Aboriginal people of Australia as well as various ethnic groups in Africa.

CONTACTS:

Swiss National Tourist Office
608 Fifth Ave.

New York, NY 10020
800-794-7795; fax: 212-262-6116
www.myswitzerland.com

◆ 1481 ◆ Johnson (Samuel) Commemoration
Saturday following September 18

Samuel Johnson, the English lexicographer, writer, critic, and conversationalist known popularly as Dr. Johnson, was born on this day in 1709. His hometown of Lichfield commemorates its most famous citizen by laying a laurel wreath at the foot of his statue, after which the cathedral choir sings religious songs and intones Dr. Johnson's final prayer while standing on the steps of his birth house. In the evening, there is a candlelight supper based on Dr. Johnson's favorite meal: steak-and-kidney pudding with mushrooms or mutton, with apple tarts and cream for dessert. The guests are served ale and hot punch by people dressed in costumes of the 18th century.

On this same day in Uttoxeter, 18 miles away, the story of Samuel Johnson's quarrel with his father is told to the town's assembled schoolchildren. Michael Johnson, the writer's father, sold books from a stall in the Uttoxeter market, and Samuel's rejection of his father's request for help in manning the stall caused a breach between them that was never healed. After his father's death, Samuel decided that the best way to punish himself for his unforgivable behavior was to stand hatless for hours in pouring rain in the exact location where his father's business had once stood.

The 19th-century American novelist Nathaniel Hawthorne, on a visit to the area, found out the children growing up there did not know the story. Ever since that time, it has been recited to them in the marketplace on this day. Afterwards, one of them lays a wreath on the memorial plaque that marks the place where Dr. Johnson made his penance.

CONTACTS:
Samuel Johnson Birthplace Museum
Breadmarket St.
Lichfield, Staffordshire WS13 6LG United Kingdom
44-1543-264-972; fax: 44-1543-258-441
www.samueljohnsonbirthplace.org.uk

◆ 1482 ◆ Jonquil Festival
First weekend in March

This three-day (Friday through Sunday) festival allows participants to enjoy about 10,000 jonquils in Old Washington Historic State Park in the town of Washington, Ark. The first of these jonquils and daffodils were planted by pioneer families who came here along the Southwest Trail that ran from Missouri to Texas. Washington was the home of the state government after Union troops took Little Rock, Ark., during the Civil War. It is also where James Black, a blacksmith, forged the original Bowie knife for James Bowie in the 1830s.

This festival focuses on the history of Washington; the Pioneer Washington Restoration Foundation, established in 1958, has restored buildings that recreate the period of the early 1800s. Tours are given of these historic buildings. Other events are folk music concerts, food vendors selling funnel cakes (round, greasy, flat cakes made by pouring dough through a funnel onto a grid and sprinkled with powdered sugar) as well as hot dogs and lemonade, an arts and crafts show, blacksmithing, and a special worship service on Sunday morning. The festival attracts about 60,000 visitors.

CONTACTS:
Historic Washington State Park
P.O. Box 129
Washington, AR 71862
870-983-2684; fax: 870-983-2736
www.historicwashingtonstatepark.com

◆ 1483 ◆ Jordan Independence Day
May 25

A treaty signed on this day in 1946 established the constitutional monarchy of the Hashemite Kingdom of Jordan and secured the nation's independence from Great Britain.

Parades through the capital city of Amman mark the celebrations of this national holiday.

CONTACTS:
Jordan Embassy
3504 International Dr. N.W.
Washington, D.C. 20008
202-966-2664; fax: 202-966-3110
www.jordanembassyus.org

◆ 1484 ◆ Jordbruksdagarna
Last full weekend in September

The town of Bishop Hill, Ill., was founded in 1846 by a group of Swedes fleeing religious persecution in the Old World. Their leader, Erik Jansson, sailed across the Atlantic with 1,200 followers, crossed the Great Lakes on steamers, and walked 150 miles to form the colony named with the English translation of Jansson's birthplace in Sweden. Cholera took its toll on the settlers, but their biggest setback was Jansson's murder in 1850. Without his leadership, the colony entered a period of rapid decline and, since it was bypassed by the main railroad line, time stood still there for about a century. As a result, many of the historic buildings remained undisturbed, and in 1984 Bishop Hill was designated a National Historic Landmark.

Many of the descendants of the original colonists still live in Bishop Hill or nearby towns, and they continue to celebrate a number of traditional Swedish holidays. One of these is Jordbruksdagarna, or **Agricultural Days**, a two-day celebration featuring harvest demonstrations, 19th-century crafts and children's games, and ample servings of Colony Stew. The residents of Bishop Hill also celebrate Lucia Nights (*see* ST. LUCY'S DAY), when young women dressed as "Lucias" serve refreshments in the shops and museums.

CONTACTS:
Bishop Hill Heritage Association
103 N. Bishop Hill St.

P.O. Box 92
Bishop Hill, IL 61419
309-927-3899
bishophillheritage.org

♦ 1485 ♦ Jorvik Viking Festival
Mid-February

During the centuries of Viking rule in Europe, York (formerly Jorvik) was a major outpost of the British Isles. The Jorvik Viking Festival, a weeklong festival established in 1985, honors the English city's historical legacy as well as the ethnic heritage of the many Scandinavians who travel to York to participate in the famous re-enactments.

The highlight of the festival is the re-enactment of the Battle of Stamford Bridge, a clash in 1066 between the Normans and the Saxons that marked the end of Viking rule in England. Although the battle actually occurred outside the city, the re-enactment takes place in the Eye of York, a circular grassed area in front of York Castle. Leading up to this main event, the actors perform battle drills and training routines.

Activities of a less violent nature include shopping in a Viking market, the traditional burning of a Viking boat, sword forging demonstrations, and cultural events centered on old Scandinavian tales, dances, and songs.

CONTACTS:
Jorvik Viking Centre
Coppergate
York, YO1 9WT United Kingdom
44-190-461-5505
jorvik-viking-centre.co.uk

♦ 1486 ♦ Joust of the Quintain
Second weekend in September

In the 17th century a tournament known as the Joust of the Quintain was held in Foligno, Perugia, Italy, to commemorate both the equestrian exercises of the early Roman legionnaires and the Joust of the Ring that was popular throughout Europe during the Middle Ages. The tournament was revived in 1946, adhering as closely as possible to the original rules.

The celebration begins on the evening of the second Saturday in September, when the townspeople gather to hear the First Magistrate announce the event. Early Sunday morning there is a parade of people in Renaissance dress, accompanied by musicians and dancers. Ten "knights" representing the city's 10 districts compete on horseback in the actual tournament, which involves galloping past the statue of Mars and trying to remove the ring in its outstretched hand by spearing it with the tip of a lance. The winner receives an ornamental cloak, and a torchlight parade concludes the day's events.

CONTACTS:
Italian National Tourist Board
686 Park Ave.
3rd Fl.
New York, NY 10065

212-245-5618; fax: 212-586-9249
www.italiantourism.com

♦ 1487 ♦ Joust of the Saracens
June and September

The most famous of the Italian jousting festivals, **La Giostra del Saracino** originated during the Crusades (11th-13th centuries), when it was used as a form of propaganda to support the fight to recover the Holy Land from the Muslims. Eight knights representing the four quarters of Arezzo, where the festival takes place, march to the piazza, where an effigy of a Moor or Saracen (i.e., Muslim) has been set up. The effigy is armed with a heavy flail and a shield, which the knights must try to hit in the center with their lances without being touched by the flail. The winner is rewarded with a golden lance on behalf of his district.

CONTACTS:
Associazione Sbandieratori di Arezzo
Piazzetta del Praticino N. ° 7
Arezzo, Tuscany 52100 Italy
39-5752-1857 or 39-347-680-6595; fax: 39-5752-1857
www.sbandieratori.arezzo.it

Institution Giostra del Saracino
Tourist Office, Giostra del Saracino and Folklore
Via Bicchieraia, 26th
Arezzo, 52100 Italy
39-575-37-7462; fax: 39-575-37-7464
www.giostradelsaracinoarezzo.it

♦ 1488 ♦ Jousting the Bear
July 25

Although jousting normally involves two knights charging each other on horseback with lances, the custom has been changed somewhat in Pistoia, Italy, where **La Giostra dell' Orso** is held in July each year. Twelve horsemen representing the town's four districts join in a procession to the Cathedral Square, each accompanied by a group of costumed attendants. They compete against each other in pairs, racing at a gallop toward the effigies of two bears holding targets in their outstretched paws. Points are won by hitting the targets, and the most successful knight is proclaimed Knight of the Golden Spur of Pistoia.

CONTACTS:
Italian Government Tourist Board
686 Park Ave.
3rd Fl.
New York, NY 10065
212-245-5618; fax: 212-586-9249
www.italiantourism.com

♦ 1489 ♦ Jousting Tournament
Third Saturday in June and second Sunday in October

Sponsored by the National Jousting Hall of Fame and held since 1823 in Mount Solon, Va., this tournament for "knights" on horseback is reputed to be America's oldest continuous sporting event. The tourney, recalling the knights of old, is held at the Natural Chimneys Regional Park, where rock formations resemble castle towers.

Jousting contestants gallop full-tilt down an 80-yard course as they try to spear and pluck with their lances three steel rings from crossbars; this exercise is called "running at the ring." The rings are as small as 1/4 " in diameter.

Jousting has been practiced in the United States since the 17th century. Tournaments are also held in Maryland, South Carolina, Virginia, and West Virginia, but the Virginia spectacle is the oldest and the most prestigious. Accompanied by parties, these are high social points of the year. About 150 jousters run at the rings at the Mount Solon tournaments.

♦ 1490 ♦ Jubilee Days Festival
Labor Day weekend

Founded in 1948, Jubilee Days began as a celebration of the harvest and of God's blessings on the community. It has since become a celebration of the unique heritage of Zion, Illinois.

The town was founded in 1901 by the reverend John Alexander Dowie, organizer of the Christian Catholic Church. Wanting to create a city ruled by God, Dowie bought some 6,000 acres of land north of Chicago and founded Zion. All residents were given a 1,100 year lease on the land (Dowie assumed that Christ would return within 100 years and his 1,000 year reign would follow that) and shared in the community's profits. In 1905 Dowie suffered a stroke and was unable to oversee further construction of the new city. He died in 1907 and was succeeded by Wilbur Glenn Voliva. The theme for the 66th Annual Jubilee Days Festival held in 2014 was "Books Can Take You Anywhere." The festival included an arts and crafts festival, a 5k run, a mayor's prayer breakfast, a Zion queen's pageant, entertainment, a parade, and other activities throughout the weekend.

CONTACTS:
City of Zion
2828 Sheridan Rd.
Zion, IL 60099
847-746-4000; fax: 847-746-7167
www.cityofzion.com

♦ 1491 ♦ Juhannus (Midsummer Day)
Saturday between June 20 and June 26

Juhannus is a celebration in Finland of the SUMMER SOLSTICE and of the feast of St. John. Like a medieval holiday, people celebrate at the lake shores where they build bonfires and dance all night. Since this is near the longest day of the year, special late performances are held at open-air theaters in many towns. There are also dances at hotels.

Many customs are remnants of pagan times. In earlier times, the bonfire was supposed to reveal the future. Birch tree branches are brought into the homes to insure future happiness. Even buses and office buildings are adorned with birch

branches. On the Aland Islands, tall poles are decorated with flowers and leaves, and supper tables are decorated with birch and garlands of flowers. The church made the festival ST. JOHN'S DAY, but the celebration has more pagan overtones than Christian ones.

As Finland's Flag Day, Juhannus is also a national holiday.

CONTACTS:
Ministry for Foreign Affairs of Finland
P.O. Box 176
Finland
358-9-1605-5555; fax: 358-9-1605-5799
formin.finland.fi

♦ 1492 ♦ Juliana's (Queen) Birthday
April 30

Juliana Louise Emma Marie Wilhelmina, born on this day in 1909, was queen of the Netherlands from 1948 until 1980, when she voluntarily abdicated in favor of her oldest daughter, Beatrix (b. 1938). Although she aroused controversy from time to time—especially by employing a faith healer in the 1950s and by letting two of her four daughters marry foreigners, she was a popular monarch whose birthday is still celebrated throughout the Netherlands with parades, fun fairs, and decorations honoring the queens of the House of Orange. Queen Juliana died on March 20, 2004, though her birthday remained a national holiday throughout her daughter Beatrix' reign.

On April 30, 2013, Queen Beatrix abdicated the throne and beginning in 2014, the Queen's Day observance was replaced with a celebration of King's Day, honoring her son, King Willem-Alexander.

CONTACTS:
Netherlands Board of Tourism & Conventions
215 Park Ave. S.
Ste. 2005
New York, NY 10003
917-720-1283; fax: 212-370-9507
www.holland.com

♦ 1493 ♦ Juneteenth
June 19

Although President Abraham LINCOLN signed the EMANCIPATION Proclamation on January 1, 1863, it wasn't until two years later that the word reached the slaves in Texas. General Gordon Granger arrived in Galveston on June 19, 1865, with the intention of forcing the slave owners there to release their slaves, and the day has been celebrated since that time in eastern Texas, Louisiana, southwestern Arkansas, Oklahoma, and other parts of the Deep South under the nickname "Juneteenth."

Observed primarily in African-American communities, Juneteenth festivities usually include parades, picnics, and baseball games. Although Juneteenth observances can be found as far west as California, many blacks who originally came from east Texas and surrounding areas choose to return home on the weekend nearest the 19th of June.

CONTACTS:
Juneteenth World Wide Celebration
6003 Bullard Ave.
Ste. 9
P.O. Box 370
New Orleans, LA 70128
504-245-7800; fax: 504 245-9005
www.juneteenth.com

National Juneteenth Museum
2632 N. Charles St.
P.O. Box 7228
Baltimore, MD 21218
410-467-2724
www.juneteenth.com

♦ 1494 ♦ Junkanoo Festival
December 26; January 1

The **Junkanoo Parade and Festival**, held in Nassau's native quarter, combines elements of MARDI GRAS, mummer's parades, and ancient African tribal rituals. It is held on December 26, BOXING DAY, and January 1, NEW YEAR'S DAY. Masqueraded marchers wearing colorful headpieces and costumes that have taken months to prepare dance to the beat of an Afro-Bahamian rhythm called Goombay, which refers to all Bahamian secular music.

The music is played by a variety of unusual native instru-ments, including goat skin drums, lignum vitae sticks, peb-ble-filled "shak-shaks," and steel drums. The name comes from a number of sources. Historically, it referred to the drumbeats and rhythms of Africa, which were brought to the Bahamas by slaves. The term was used during jump-in dances, when the drummer would shout "Gimbey!" at the beginning of each dance. The Ibo tribes in West Africa have a drum they call *Gamby*, from which the name "goombay" probably derived.

The Junkanoo parade, which begins at two o'clock in the morning and continues until sunrise, is followed by the judging of costumes and awarding of prizes. There are Junkanoo parades in Freeport and the Family of Out Islands as well.

In Belize and parts of Guatemala the Junkanoo masqueraders dance from house to house. Their wire-screen masks are painted white or pink, have staring eyes, red lips, black eyebrows, and thin moustaches for men; they are accompanied by two drums and a women's chorus.

In Jamaica, Junkanoo is featured also at political rallies and Independence Day celebrations. There are "root" and "fancy dress" troupes, the latter being more sedate. Their procession contains courtiers; a king and queen preceded by a flower girl; Sailor Boy who uses a whip to keep the audience in line; Babu, an East Indian cowboy with a long cattle prod; and Pitchy Patchy, the latter three being more boisterous than the courtiers. The "root" Junkanoo parade features Amerindians and Warriors, the former dancing with a throbbing rhythm and more body movement; Belly Woman who shakes her belly in time with the music; and Cowhead and other animal characters who butt the crowd. "Root" Junkanoo is usually found in remote villages far from large towns or cities.

There are a number of theories as to where the name "Junkanoo" came from. One is that the festival was started by a West African named Jananin Canno, or from a folkloric figure known in the West Indies, John or Johnny Canoe. Another is that it comes from the French expression *gens inconnus,* or "unknown people," which would seem to refer to the masked dancers.

See also YANCUNÚ, FIESTA DEL.

CONTACTS:
Bahamas Tourist Office
10 Chesterfield St.
London, England W1J 5JL United Kingdom
44-20-73-550800; fax: 44-20-74-919459
www.bahamas.co.uk

♦ 1495 ♦ Juno Caprotina, Festival of
July 7

Juno was the ancient Roman goddess of women and marriage, identified with the Greek goddess Hera. As the highest deity in the Roman pantheon next to Jupiter, her brother and husband, she ruled all aspects of women's lives, including sexuality and childbirth, and served as a kind of guardian angel for women. Along with Jupiter and Minerva, she shared a temple on the Capitoline Hill in Rome; together they were known as the Capitoline Triad. This temple contained Juno's sacred geese, whose cackling, according to Plutarch, saved Rome from the Gauls in 390 B.C.E.

The two most important festivals in honor of Juno were the Juno Caprotina (or **Nonae Caprotinae**) and the MATRONALIA. The former was held under a wild fig tree in the Campus Martius, or Field of Mars, a floodplain of the Tiber River. The kalends or first day of every month were sacred to Juno, and she was also associated with the ancient ceremony of announcing at the new moon the date of the nones (*see* IDES).

The month of June, named after the goddess Juno, is still considered the most popular month for getting married.

♦ 1496 ♦ Just for Laughs Festival
Late July

Every July, Montreal hosts one of the largest comedy festivals in the world. The Just for Laughs Festival, also known as the **Montreal International Comedy Festival**, is a time for comedy fans to catch the best acts and for aspiring comedians to make a foray into the industry.

Two Canadians, Gilbert Rozon and Andy Nulman, founded the festival in 1983 as a small French-language show (called **Juste pour rire**) comprised of only two nights. In 1985, the organizers opened the stage to English-speaking comedians, paving the way for newcomers like *Tonight Show* host Jay Leno and sitcom star Jerry Seinfeld to launch their careers. In the subsequent years, the organizers extended Just for Laughs to 12 days and added a film component to the festival. A TV deal was also inked to attract millions of international viewers.

Today there are more than 1,300 shows and performances, featuring all kinds of comedy as well as juggling and performance art, but the gala shows at Montreal's St. Denis Theatre are always the main event.

CONTACTS:
Just for Laughs
2101 St-Laurent Blvd.
Montreal, QC H2X 2T5 Canada
514-845-3155; fax: 514-845-4140
www.hahaha.com

♦ 1497 ♦ **Jutajaiset Folklore Festival**
Late June, including midsummer's eve

The Jutajaiset Folklore Festival is a 10-day cultural fair held each year in late June in Lapland, the artic region of northern Finland. Jutajaiset celebrates midsummer, a period during which the region—known as the "land of the midnight sun"—experiences 24-hour daylight.

Since beginning in 1972, the festival has been sponsored by the youth folklore society Lapin Nuorison Liitto, first in Sodankylä until 1994 and afterwards in Rovaniemi. It showcases the unique culture of the Sami people of Lapland, with educational programs, local artists, dancers, and musicians. In addition, the festival presents performers from throughout the world, including Estonia, India, Mexico, Russia, and Slovakia. Food and refreshments are available on site.

♦ 1498 ♦ **Juturnalia**
January 11

According to Virgil, Juturna is the sister of Turnus, king of the Rutuli. In return for her virginity, Jupiter gave her immortality. Afterwards she was turned into a fountain of the same name near the Numicus, the river where Aeneas' dead body was found. The waters from this fountain were used in sacrifices, particularly those in honor of the Roman goddess Vesta, and were believed to have curative powers. On January 11, a festival in honor of Juturna was observed by men working on aqueducts and wells. She was also celebrated at the VULCANALIA on August 23 as a protectress against fire.

♦ 1499 ♦ **Juul, Feast of**
December 21 or 22

The Feast of Juul was a pre-Christian festival observed in Scandinavia at the time of the WINTER SOLSTICE. Fires were lit to symbolize the heat, light, and life-giving properties of the returning sun. A YULE (or Juul) log was brought in with great ceremony and burned on the hearth in honor of the Scandinavian god, Thor. A piece of the log was kept as both a token of good luck and as kindling for the following year's log.

In England and in many parts of Germany, France, and other European countries, the Yule log was burned until nothing but ash remained; then the ashes were collected and either strewn on the fields as fertilizer every night until TWELFTH NIGHT or kept as a charm and useful medicine. French peasants believed that if the ashes were kept under the bed, they would protect the house against thunder and lightning, as well as prevent chilblains on the heels during the winter.

The present-day custom of lighting a Yule log at CHRISTMAS is believed to have originated in the bonfires associated with the Feast of Juul.

♦ 1500 ♦ **Juvenalia**
Three days in June

During the Juvenalia festival each year in Krakow, Poland, the students of Jagiellonian University take over the city for three days. After the mayor hands over the keys to the city, they dress up in costumes and masks and parade through the streets making fun of anything they choose. This celebration goes back to a medieval tradition, when new students at the university had to pay a tax to older ones as part of their ritual entry into college life—much like the "hazing" that goes on in fraternities and sororities at American colleges.

CONTACTS:
Tourist Information Network InfoKraków and the Malopolska Tourist Information System
ul. Powisle 11
Kraków, 31-101 Poland
48-12-417-58-10
www.en.infokrakow.pl

♦ 1501 ♦ **JVC Jazz Festival**
Mid-August

Known for many years as the **Newport Jazz Festival**, this event was moved to New York in 1972 and later returned to Newport, Rhode Island, as the JVC Jazz Festival. One of the most important jazz festivals in the world, it features legendary jazz performers as well as up-and-coming new stars and some of the most outstanding big bands, jazz combos, and instrumental and vocal soloists in the country. Dizzy Gillespie, Woody Herman, Ella Fitzgerald, Miles Davis, and Sarah Vaughan have performed there, as have Wynton Marsalis and Spyro Gyra. The first evening's event is usually held at the Newport Casino in the International Tennis Hall of Fame. Subsequent concerts during the three-day festival are held outdoors in Fort Adams State Park, where visitors are encouraged to picnic and relax on the lawn as they listen.

Festival Productions also sponsors JVC Jazz Festivals in other cities worldwide from spring through autumn.

♦ 1502 ♦ **Jyestha Ashtami**
May-June; eighth day of waxing half of Hindu month of Jyestha

This Hindu festival is celebrated at the shrine of Khir Bhawani in Tullamula, Jammu and Kashmir, in honor of their patron goddess, called Ragnya Devi. Pilgrims come from all over to assemble at the shrine, offer prayers and worship at the foot of the goddess, and sing hymns and songs in her praise. *Khir* (rice boiled in milk) is prepared on this day as a food offering. The marble shrine, located about 25 kilometers from Srinagar, India, overlooks a pool formed by spring waters known for their changing colors. Hundreds of Kashmiri Hindus visit the shrine daily.

CONTACTS:
Jammu & Kashmir Tourism Development Corporation
Tourist Reception Centre-Jammu
Vir Marg, Jammu Tawi
Jammu, Jammu & Kashmir India
91-191-2579554; fax: 91-191-2549065
jktdc.in

♦ 1503 ♦ **Jyvaskyla Arts Festival**
July

This cultural festival in Finland was started in 1955 by three well-known figures in the music world: Professor Timo Makinen, composer Seppo Nummi, and Professor Paivo Oksala. It has now expanded beyond musical events to include film, theater, art exhibits, and seminars designed to promote understanding among different national and ethnic traditions. In the past, the festival has included a summer Academy of Chamber Music and performances by world-renowned chamber music groups such as the Bartok Quartet and the London Early Music Group. Festival events are held throughout the city in local churches, museums, theaters, and parks.

CONTACTS:
City of Jyväskylä, Registry Office
P.O. Box 193
Jyväskylä, FI-40101 Finland
358-14-266-0000; fax: 358-14-266-1548
www.jyvaskyla.fi/lang

K

♦ 1504 ♦ **Kaamatan Festival**
May 30-31

Kaamatan is a festival and public holiday in Labuan Territory and the state of Sabah in Malaysia. The festival is celebrated by the Kadazan or Dusun people (also known as the Kadazandusun), the largest indigenous ethnic group in Sabah, which lies on the northern tip of Borneo. Originally headhunters, they were the first native group in Borneo to use the plow. Irrigated (not flooded) rice is their principal crop, and the harvest is a ritual dedicated to the *Bambaazon*, or rice spirit. If the harvest has been good, this is a thanksgiving, and if it has been poor, the ritual is an appeasement of the spirit. The Kadazans believe that spirits reside in natural objects, and rituals are conducted by shamanist priestesses. Besides the solemn aspects of the festival, there is much merrymaking and free flowing of rice wine. This festival is celebrated during most of the month of May throughout the region with carnivals, special exhibits, sports competitions, a beauty pageant and a regatta, all leading up to the rituals on May 30-31 in Penampang.

CONTACTS:
Kadazandusun Cultural Association
Hongkod Koisaan, Km. 8
Penampang Rd.
P.O Box 907
Penampang, Sabah 89509 Malaysia
60-88-713-696; fax: 60-88-713-350
www.kdca.org.my

Sabah Tourism Board
51 Gaya St.
City Centre
Kota Kinabalu, Sabah 88000 Malaysia
60-88-212-121; fax: 60-88-212-075
www.sabahtourism.com

♦ 1505 ♦ **Kakadu Mahbilil Festival**
Early September

The one-day Mahbilil Festival is both a celebration of Australia's indigenous culture and a vehicle for promoting tourism in the Northern Territory. Formerly known as the **Wind Festival**, its festivities take place at Lake Jabiru, located within Kakadu National Park. The national park, a World Heritage Site, adjoins Arnhem Land, which historians conjecture may have been the first territory inhabited by the Aboriginal people.

Aboriginal leaders of Kakadu, who jointly manage the park, invite visitors to join them in celebrating a culture that reaches back 50,000 years. A festival highlight is the Magpie Goose cooking competition, in which contestants show off their best recipes and prepare their meals over a coal fire. Other activities include traditional dancing, market stalls, and live music by local indigenous bands. At the 2014 Mahbilil Festival, activities including a demonstration of indigenous spear-making, painting, and weaving ran throughout the day. The festival also featured art booths, a fun-fair for kids, and a high-energy performance by the Chooky Dancers.

CONTACTS:
Kakadu Tourism
P.O. Box 696
Jabiru, Northern Territory 0886 Australia
800-500-401
www.gagudju-dreaming.com

♦ 1506 ♦ **Kalakshetra Arts Festival**
December-January

The Kalakshetra Foundation, in Tiruvanmiyur in the Tamil Nadu state capital of Chennai, is one of India's most outstanding cultural institutions. It was founded in 1936 and directed for many years by Rukmini Devi Arundale, an Indian woman who married an Englishman and devoted herself to the rejuvenation of Indian dance, music, sculpture, and crafts. Rukmini Devi is also known for choreographing 25 dance-dramas, a traditional Indian art form.

The Kalakshetra Arts Festival, which has been held annually for eight days in December-January since 1951, takes place at the Foundation's College of Fine Arts, a school that specializes in teaching the *Bharatanatyam* and other traditional styles of Indian dance. There are folk dance performances, vocal and instrumental recitals, and of course the famous dance-dramas choreographed by Rukmini Devi and based on themes from *puranas*, or Hindu epics.

CONTACTS:
Kalakshetra Foundation
Central Office
Tiruvanmiyur
Chennai, Tamil Nadu 600 041 India

91-44-24524057; fax: 91-44-24524359
www.kalakshetra.in

◆ 1507 ◆ **Kalevala Day**
February 28

The *Kalevala* is Finland's national epic poem, researched and transcribed by Dr. Elias Lönnrot (1802-1835). Lönnrot and his assistants traveled throughout the country, asking people to tell them whatever they could remember about the folklore surrounding Kalevala, the "Land of Heroes." On February 28, 1835, after years of research, Lönnrot signed the preface to the first edition of the poem. Its more than 20,000 verses brought to life the adventures of such characters as the warrior Lemminkäinen and the blacksmith Ilmarinen, who played a part in the creation of the world when he forged the "lids of heaven." This event marked a turning point in Finnish literature; up to this point, little had been written in the Finnish language. Lönnrot is honored with parades and concerts on this day.

CONTACTS:
Finnish Literature Society
P.O. Box 259
Helsinki, 00171 Finland
358-9-201-131-231
www.finlit.fi

Embassy of Finland, Bucharest
Embassy of Finland
Strada Atena 2 bis
Romania
40-21-230-7504; fax: 40-21-230-7505
www.finland.ro

◆ 1508 ◆ **Kali Puja**
Between September and October; new moon day of Kartika

In the region of Bengal, which encompasses eastern India and Bangladesh, many Hindus regularly honor Kali, an earth goddess of fearsome appearance and a symbol of fertility. Special temples devoted to Kali are located in Dhaka, Bangladesh; Kolkatta and Dakshineswar in India; and other locations throughout the region. During the year believers conduct daily *pujas* (devotional prayers) to Kali, but one particular new-moon day of the year is set aside for a special Kali Puja. This new-moon day, or *amavasya*, takes place during Kartika, the seventh Bengali month falling between October and November. Kali Puja also coincides with Dewali, a well-known celebration observed by Hindus, Sikhs, and Jains in India and other countries.

Kali, like other Hindu deities, assumes many forms. In paintings and sculpture she most commonly bears a dark and violent demeanor and is depicted standing on the chest of her husband, Shiva. (According to Hindu legend, Shiva prostrated himself before Kali in an attempt to pacify her during a killing rampage.) The goddess's fearsomeness is also the source of her strength, which is why during Kali Puja believers make appeals for her protection from harm and ask her to destroy various evils.

Unlike with other festivals, believers will worship Kali at night. Typically, people gather around elaborate *pandals* (shrines) to the goddess around 9 P.M. Priests will then lead a ceremony, which may involve prayers and sacrifices of animals such as goats, sheep, or buffaloes. Worship may continue until as late as 1 A.M. or 2 A.M.

CONTACTS:
Bangladesh Tourism Board
No.22,Bangladesh House Bldg.
Finance Corporation Bhaban
7th Fl.
Purana Paltan, Dhaka 1000 Bangladesh
880-2-9513328
tourismboard.gov.bd

◆ 1509 ◆ **Kallemooi**
Between May 10 and June 13; Saturday before Pentecost

Observed in the North Coast Islands of the Netherlands, the custom known as Kallemooi represents the fishermen's welcome to spring. A tall pole with a transverse arm near the top is erected in the center of the village. A live cock—usually one that has been "borrowed" from a nearby farm—is suspended in a basket from the apex of the crosspiece. An empty bottle is hung from either arm of the structure, which is decorated at the top with the Dutch flag, a green branch, and a placard bearing the word "Kallemooi." For three days and three nights before PENTECOST, or Whitsunday, people feast, make merry, and play Whitsun games. After the fun is over, the rooster is released and returned to its owner.

There has been much speculation about the origin of the word Kallemooi. Some say it can be translated as "calling the May," while others claim it is derived from the word *kalemei*, meaning a "tree without branches" or a bare tree. During the festival, a special drink known as "Kallemooi bitters" is served by all the local inns.

CONTACTS:
Netherlands Board of Tourism & Conventions
215 Park Ave. S
Ste. 2005
New York, NY 10003 United States
917-720-1283; fax: 212-370-9507
www.holland.com

◆ 1510 ◆ **Kamakura Matsuri (Snow Hut Festival)**
February 15-17

Kamakura Matsuri is held in northern Japan in the Akita Prefecture, at the time of year when there is usually deep snow on the ground. The original purpose of the festival was to offer prayers for a good rice crop to Suijin-sama, the water god.

In Yokote and other towns of the region, children build *Kamakura*, snow houses about six feet in diameter resembling Eskimo igloos. They furnish the huts with tatami mats and a wooden altar dedicated to Suijin-sama and have parties in them, while families gather to drink sweet sake and eat rice cakes and fruits. The rice cakes are made in the shape of cranes and turtles, traditional symbols of longevity, and of dogs called *inukko*, thought to guard against devils.

A similar Kamakura Festival is held in Tokamachi in Niigata Prefecture on Jan. 14.

CONTACTS:
Japan National Tourism Organization
1 Grand Central Pl.
60 E. 42nd St.
Ste. 448
New York, NY 10165
212-757-5640; fax: 212-307-6754
www.jnto.go.jp

Akita City
1-1-1 Sanno
Akita, Akita Prefecture Japan
81-18-863-2033; fax: 81-18-866-2278
www.city.akita.akita.jp/en

♦ 1511 ♦ **Kamehameha (King) Celebration**
June 11

A state holiday in Hawaii to celebrate the reign of the island state's first king, this celebration is the only public holiday in the United States that honors royalty.

King Kamehameha I, known as "the Great" (1758?-1819), was the son of a high chief. At his birth it was prophesied that he would defeat all his rivals. He originally was named Paiea, which means "soft-shelled crab." When he grew to manhood he took the name Kamehameha, meaning "the very lonely one" or "the one set apart." By 1810 he had united all the Hawaiian islands and until his death was the undisputed ruler. He promulgated the *mamalahoe kanawai*, or "law of the splintered paddle," which protected the common people from the brutality of powerful chiefs, and he outlawed human sacrifice. He made a fortune for his people with a government monopoly on the sandalwood trade. After his death, he was succeeded by his son, Kamehameha II.

Celebrations extend over much of the month of June. Leis (Hawaiian floral necklaces) are draped on the king's statue across from Iolani Palace, formerly the home of Hawaii's monarchs and now the state capitol in Honolulu, and there is another lei-draping at Kapaau, North Kohala. A floral parade travels from downtown Honolulu to Waikiki; it features a young man who depicts the king wearing a replica of the golden amo-feather cloak and Grecian-style helmet (the originals are kept in Honolulu's Bernice P. Bishop Museum and are displayed on this day). The parade also includes floats and princesses on horseback wearing the *pa'u*, satin riding dresses in the color of their island home. Other events include demonstrations of arts and crafts, a competition of chants and hulas, and a luau, or Hawaiian cookout.

CONTACTS:
Hawaii Information Consortium (HIC)
201 Merchant St.
Ste. 1805
Honolulu, HI 96813
808-695-4620; fax: 808-695-4618
portal.ehawaii.gov

Library of Congress
101 Independence Ave. S.E.
Washington, D.C. 20540
202-707-5000
www.loc.gov

♦ 1512 ♦ **Kapila Shashti**
August-September; every 60 years during the Hindu month of Bhadrapada

According to Hindu astronomers, Kapila Shashti takes place about every 60 years, when several astronomical events coincide during the day.

There is a myth that explains why Kapila Shashti occurs so rarely. It is said that when the sage Narada, who had always been celibate, decided he wanted to have female companionship, he asked the god Krishna, who had 16,008 wives, if he could marry one of them. Krishna asked only that Narada choose a wife who was not in anyone else's company. Since all of them were busy enjoying the company of others, Narada went to bathe in the Ganges River. When he walked out of the river, he discovered that he had been transformed into a woman. He (now "she") married a hermit and had 60 sons, which left her so exhausted that she begged Vishnu to return her to a man. This Krishna granted, but after Narada was a man again, the sons wailed for their mother to feed them. To quiet the turmoil Vishnu granted each son dominion over one year. Each year of the cycle is named after one of Narada's sons. Thus, the cycle is 60 years long. The last day of the cycle is Kapila Shashti, the day when Krishna turned Narada back into a man.

♦ 1513 ♦ **Karatsu Kunchi Festival**
November 2-4

Karatsu Kunchi is an annual autumn festival hosted by the Karatsu-jinja shrine on the island of Kyushu in Japan. Boasting a 400-year history, Karatsu Kunchi is regarded as one of the most important representations of folkloric tradition in the region. The event takes place over three days and centers on massive floats called *hikiyama*, some of which date back to 1816. Weighing as much as three tons each, the floats are made from wood, clay, *washi* (traditional Japanese paper), and cloth fashioned into fantastical animals and mythological creatures. On the first night of the festival, the floats are lit by lanterns and pulled through the streets. The most important part of the festival is the *Otabisho Shinko*, which unfolds on the second day, when the floats are pulled to Nishinohama Beach and dragged through the sand to the accompaniment of drum beats, gongs, and flutes. Karatsu Kunchi concludes on the third day as firefighters dressed in the traditional uniforms of the Edo Period (1603-1868) heave the mammoth floats through the streets, returning them to the Hikiyama Float Exhibition Hall.

CONTACTS:
Karatsu Tourist Association
2935-1 Shinko-machi
Karatsu-City, '847-0816 Japan

81-955-74-3355; fax: 81-955-74-3365
www.karatsu-kankou.jp/english.html

♦ 1514 ♦ Karneval in Cologne
November 11 until Ash Wednesday

Pre-Lenten activities are especially festive in Cologne, Germany. The celebration begins officially on the 11th day of the 11th month at 11:11 P.M., when CARNIVAL societies throughout Germany begin their public activities with singers submitting their latest songs and speakers telling funny tales. The date was originally the end of a fasting period ordered by the church.

During the period from early January until the beginning of LENT, the festival calendar is filled with 300 costume balls, performances of original songs and humorous speeches, and numerous smaller affairs sponsored by such special interest groups as skittle clubs and a rabbit breeders' association. The humorous talks began in 1829, and today audiences clap hands in a slow rhythm to show their approval and whistle to express their disapproval.

These events lead up to the final "crazy days" (*Tolle Tage*) just before ASH WEDNESDAY. During this time, the Lord Mayor of Cologne receives the Triumvirate of Carnival—Prince Carnival, the Cologne Virgin (who, according to tradition, is played by a man), and the Cologne Peasant. The prince represents the prince of joy, the peasant the valor of the men of the town, and the virgin the purity of the city of Cologne, whose city walls the enemy never breached. The prince gets the keys to the city and rules the city until Carnival ends.

On *Weiberfastnacht*, or "Women's Carnival," the Thursday before Ash Wednesday, women take control and cut off the ties of any men within reach. This is revenge—women were excluded from Karneval in the 19th century. On Sunday, there are school and suburban parades.

ROSE MONDAY is the day of Carnival's mammoth parade with decorated floats, giant figures, and bands. Police from surrounding districts are on duty and join the crowds in singing and dancing.

On SHROVE TUESDAY, there are more parades, and crowds cheer the prince and his attendants. That evening, the Carnival season ends with a ball in Gürzenich Hall, the city's 15th-century festival hall. The prince returns the keys of the city, and normalcy is back. On Ash Wednesday, people traditionally eat a fish dinner, and so the restraint of Lent begins.

See also FASCHING.

CONTACTS:
Festival Committee of the Cologne Carnival
Maarweg 134-136
Cologne, D-50825 Germany
49-221-5-7400-0; fax: 49-221-5-7400-37
www.koelnerkarneval.de

♦ 1515 ♦ Karthikai Deepam
Mid-November to Mid-December

Karthikai Deepam is an important annual religious event celebrated by the Tamil people, the largest ethnic group in the southernmost Indian state of Tamil Nadu. Marking the birth of Karthikeya, a Hindu god, the three-day festival is full of ritual. Perhaps its most important rite is the lighting of rows of clay oil lamps—symbols of prosperity—at sundown. The lamps are placed either in the house or on the porch. During Karthikai Deepam, the Tamil prepare traditional sweets, including puffed rice balls and a dessert made of rice flour and sugar. They also light fireworks and visit temples in honor of the event. The festival is also closely linked to a specific ritual known as the "great light," which occurs at the Arunachaleshwarar Temple in the town of Thiruvannamalai in Tamil Nadu. Dedicated to Shiva, who is believed to be the father of Karthikeya, the ritual involves lighting a huge torch atop a hill where thousands of devotees gather each year.

CONTACTS:
Joint Commissioner/Executive Officer
Arulmigu Arunachaleswarar Temple
Thiruvannamalai, Tamil Nadu 606 601 India
91-4175- 252438
www.arunachaleswarartemple.tnhrce.in

♦ 1516 ♦ Kartika Purnima
*October-November; full moon day of Hindu
month of Kartika*

Hindus celebrate Kartika Purnima in honor of the day when God incarnated himself as the Matsya Avatar in fish form. According to Hindu mythology, the purpose of this incarnation was to save Vavaswata, the seventh Manu and progenitor of the human race, from destruction by a deluge. Good deeds done on this day are believed to earn high religious merit. Bathing in the Ganges or in other holy water is considered to be of special religious significance. Hindus spend the day fasting, meditating, and performing charitable acts.

It is also believed the Shankara killed the demon Tripurasura on this day, for which he is also called the Tripurari. Shiva is worshipped on this occasion, and giving a bull (Shiva's mount) as a gift to a Brahman is considered to be an appropriate and significant act. For this reason, it is common to hold cattle fairs on this day.

♦ 1517 ♦ Kartika Snan
October-November; Hindu month of Kartika

The Hindu months of Vaisakha (April-May), Kartika (October-November), and Magha (January-February) are regarded as especially sacred and therefore the most suitable for acts of piety. Throughout the month of Kartika, Hindus bathe in a sacred river, stream, pond, or well early in the morning. On the sacred rivers, such as the Ganges and the Yamuna in India, a month-long bathing festival is held. People set up tents on the riverbank for this purpose, have regular morning baths, eat only a single meal each day, and spend their time in prayer, meditation, and other acts of devotion.

Hindu women in villages and towns get up early in the morning and visit the sacred streams in groups, singing hymns. After their baths, they visit the nearby temples. They also fast and hang lamps in small baskets around their houses or on the tops of the bamboo along the river. These lamps are kept burning throughout the month. The women also worship the Tulsi plant, which is considered sacred and is cultivated in homes and temples. When Tulsi leaves are put into any water, it becomes as holy as water from the Ganges. Tulsi leaves offered to Vishnu during the month of Kartika are said to please him more than the gift of a thousand cows.

◆ 1518 ◆ Kartini Day
April 21

Kartini Day is an Indonesian holiday commemorating the birth in 1879 of Raden Ajeng Kartini, one of the country's national heroes and a pioneer in the emancipation of Indonesian women. Throughout Indonesia women wear their national dress to symbolize their unity, and the nation enjoys parades, lectures, and various school activities.

Lady Kartini, the daughter of a Javanese nobleman who worked for the Dutch colonial administration, was exposed to Western ideas when she attended a Dutch school. When she had to withdraw from school because she was of noble birth, she corresponded with Dutch friends telling of her concern both for the plight of Indonesians under colonial rule and for the restricted lives of Indonesian women. She married in 1903 and began a fight for the right of women to be educated and against the unwritten but all-pervading Javanese law, *Adat*.

She died in 1904 at the age of 25, after the birth of her first child. Her letters were published in 1911 under the title, *Door duisternis tot licht* ("Through Darkness into Light"), and created support for the Kartini Foundation, which opened the first girls' school in Java in 1916.

CONTACTS:
Asia-Pacific Human Rights Information Center
8F, CE Nishihonmachi Bldg.
1-7-7 Nishihonmachi, Nishi-ku
Osaka, 550-0005 Japan
816-6543-7002; fax: 816-6543-7004
www.hurights.or.jp

Indonesian Embassy
2020 Massachusetts Ave. N.W.
Washington, D.C. 20036
202-775-5200
www.embassyofindonesia.org

◆ 1519 ◆ Karwachoth
October-November; fourth day of waning half of Hindu month of Kartika

Observed by married women in Hindu families, the Karwachoth festival is a day-long fast in honor of the Hindu god Shiva and goddess Parvati, whom they hope will bring prosperity and long life to their husbands. It is also a time for mothers to bless their married daughters and present them with gifts. Virgins and widows are not allowed to participate in the celebrations, which begin at dawn when the women bathe and put on new clothes. The day is devoted to worshipping Shiva and Parvati, and the fast is broken at night when the moon rises.

See also Savitri-Vrata.

◆ 1520 ◆ Kasone Festival of Watering the Banyan Tree
Mid-April to May; full moon day of Burmese month of Kasone

The most important of the 12 Burmese festivals of the months, **Kasone Full Moon Day**—sometimes known as **Buddha Day**—celebrates the birth and the enlightenment of the Buddha at the foot of the banyan tree. Buddhists in Myanmar (Burma) gather at monasteries and precept halls to practice meditation, to make charitable donations, and to observe the precepts of Buddhism. Another ritual associated with this day is the pouring of water, both individually and collectively, to celebrate the preservation of the banyan tree. Because Kasone is a hot, dry month, fish are often transferred from streams, ponds, and tanks to places where there is more water.

◆ 1521 ◆ Kasuga Matsuri
March 13

The Kasuga Shrine in Nara is one of the most beautiful and ancient in Japan. Every year on March 13 a festival is held there with elaborate ceremonies and performances that recall the shrine's heyday. The *hiki-uma* horse ceremony, where a sacred horse is led in procession through the streets, and the elegant *Yamato-mai* dance performed by Shinto women are reminiscent of the culture and customs of the Nara and Heian Eras. Construction of the Kasuga Shrine was started during the Nara period (710-784) and was completed in the first years of the Heian period (794-1185).

CONTACTS:
Japan National Tourism Organization
1 Grand Central Pl.
60 E. 42nd St.
Ste. 448
New York, NY 10165
212-757-5640; fax: 212-307-6754
www.jnto.go.jp

◆ 1522 ◆ Kataklysmos, Feast of (Festival of the Flood)
Between May 10 and June 13; coincides with Christian Pentecost

This religious and popular festival is celebrated only on Cyprus, with its roots in both the Bible and Greek mythology. The Greek word *kataklysmos*, meaning "flood," refers to the

Bible's story in the book of Genesis, and a Greek creation story.

In Genesis 6:5-9:1, God decided all humankind was corrupt and that he would bring a flood to destroy all life—except for Noah, his wife, their sons and their sons' wives, and male and female specimens of every beast and fowl. Noah built an ark for this menagerie, and they all lived on it while it rained for 40 days and 40 nights, eventually landing, it is thought, on Mt. Ararat. (*See also* ASHURA.) When the flood ended, God told Noah and his family to be fruitful and replenish the earth.

In the Greek story, Zeus decided to destroy the earth because of human wickedness. Floods covered the earth, leaving only a spot of dry land on top of Mt. Parnassus. After it had rained nine days and nine nights, a great wooden chest drifted to the spot. Within it were Deucalion, the son of Prometheus, and his wife Pyrrha. Prometheus, knowing the flood was coming, had told his son to build the chest and embark in it.

Coming down from the mountain into a dead world, Deucalion and Pyrrha heard a voice telling them to "cast behind you the bones of your mother." They realized the earth was the mother, and stones her bones. They began to throw the stones, and the stones took human shape. They were called Stone People, and rescued the earth from desolation.

Biblical scholars have suggested that the flood described in Genesis is based on the one from ancient Mesopotamian literature, especially in the Gilgamesh Epic, whose hero is called Ut-Napishtim. In this story, the gods bring on the flood because mankind is so noisy they cannot sleep. After the flood, Ut-Napishtim is made a god.

The Kataklysmos festivities, held in seaside towns, usually last from Saturday through Monday. They include games, folk dancing, boat races, swimming competitions, feasting, and the singing of *tchattista*, improvised verses sung in competition. Everyone joins in throwing water at each other, which symbolizes the purification of body and soul. Larnaca is especially known for its celebration of Kataklysmos, and other festivals are held in Limassol, Paphos, Polis, Agia Napa, and Paralimni.

CONTACTS:
Cyprus Tourism Organization
Leoforos Lemesou 19
Aglantzia Lefkosia, 2112 Cyprus
357-22-691-100; fax: 357-22-331-644
www.visitcyprus.com

♦ 1523 ♦ **Kataragama Festival**
June-July; 10 days and nights prior to full moon day of Hindu month of Asadha

Kataragama is considered one of the 16 holiest pilgrimage sites in Sri Lanka and is venerated not only by Hindus but by Buddhists and even Muslims. There is a shrine there dedicated to SKANDA, the Hindu god of war, and his consort Valli. Their union is commemorated by taking the god's *yantra*, or

icon, from his temple to the temple dedicated to Valli at the opposite end of the town square. It is carried on the back of an elephant to the accompaniment of conch shells and the clamor of thousands of pilgrims, both Hindu and Buddhist, who gather in Kataragama to watch and to undergo penances.

The climax of the festival is the fire-walking ceremony, where devotees walk across a bed of red-hot embers without burning their feet. Other pilgrims walk on shoes with interior spikes, pull carts with lines attached to hooks in their flesh, or dance until they are completely exhausted.

The festival, which is also known as the **Perahära**, concludes at the exact hour of the full moon with a water-cutting ceremony. The priest, along with Skanda's yantra, is lowered into the river. He draws a mandala in the riverbed with a sword and then bathes the god's image. After this symbolic exercise, the pilgrims plunge themselves into the sacred stream in the belief that it will wash away their sins.

♦ 1524 ♦ **Kati Bihu**
Middle of October

Bihu is a series of cultural festivals in the northeastern Indian state of Assam. The different festivals are celebrated three times during the year, each coinciding with a distinctive phase in the farming calendar. While two of the Bihu celebrations are associated with New Year and the harvest season, Kati Bihu, or the **Kongali Bihu,** which means "the festival of the poor," marks the fallow season when the granaries are empty and rice paddies have only just been sown. The festival centers on the worship of deities and the basil plant—a sacred symbol for Hindus. Rituals and offerings also inform much of the event's activities. Earthen lamps are lit in front of granaries and rice fields to usher in a good harvest. To demonstrate compassion, celebrants feed a rice preparation to cattle, caring for their livestock even in times of want. Additionally, people chant prayers, cast spells to ward off evil spirits, and light sky lamps hung from bamboo poles stuck in the rice paddies. These lamps are believed to guide souls to heaven, while also providing the practical benefit of attracting insects away from crops.

CONTACTS:
Directorate of Tourism, Govt. of Assam
Station Rd.
Panbazar
Guwahati, Assam 781 001 India
91-361- 2547102 or 91-361-2542748; fax: 91-361-2547102
assamtourism.gov.in

♦ 1525 ♦ **Kattestoet (Festival of the Cats)**
Second Sunday in May; parade every three years (2015, 2018, 2021…)

A peculiar celebration to commemorate an event involving cats, Kattestoet is held in Ieper (Ypres), West Flanders, Belgium. There are different stories about how the festival began. One story says that in 962, Baudoin III, count of Flanders, threw several live cats from his castle tower to show that he wasn't awed by cats. The animals had historically been worshipped as creatures related to witches, and Baudoin, a recent Christian convert, was demonstrating that he didn't believe in such pagan ideas.

Another story is that cats in great numbers were needed in the Middle Ages to battle mice and rats. The Cloth Hall, where yearly sales of cloth and garments were held, attracted mice, and cats were set free to devour the mice. But once the sales were over, the rodent problem disappeared and there was a cat problem. The solution seemed to be to hurl the live cats from the belfry.

In the celebration today, about 2,000 people, dressed as cats, witches, and giants, march in a parade to the tune of bagpipes. Floats depict the history of the town and of feline figures— Puss in Boots, the Egyptian cat-headed goddess Bast, and others. The climax of the celebration comes when a jester throws toy witches and stuffed cloth cats from the town belfry.

CONTACTS:
Ypres Tourist Office
Cloth Hall
Ypres, B-8900 Belgium
32-57-239-220; fax: 32-57-239-275
www.toerismeieper.be/en

◆ 1526 ◆ Kaustinen Folk Music Festival
Third week in July

Scandinavia's largest international festival of folk music and dance, Finland's Kaustinen Folk Music Festival was founded in 1968 to preserve Finnish folk music, dance, and art. Only Finnish amateur groups participated in the beginning, but in recent years the festival has included performances by groups from Japan, Greenland, Canada, the United States, and other foreign countries. There are scheduled performances in local banquet halls as well as impromptu sidewalk jam sessions and open air competitions among musicians and dancers. Special events include the Kaustinen Cavalcade, a display of local musicians' talents, and a grand folk music parade.

CONTACTS:
Kaustinen Folk Music Festival
Kansantaiteenkeskus
Jyväskyläntie 3
Kaustinen, 69600 Finland
358-40-172-9566 or 358-40-358-2413
kaustinen.net

◆ 1527 ◆ Kawagoé Matsuri
Every two years on October 14-15

Only during the Kawagoé Matsuri can festivalgoers view the enormous, elaborate floats of old Edo (the old name for Tokyo). This is because there are now so many telephone and power lines crisscrossing the streets of Japanese cities that it has become almost impossible for these large floats to participate in parades. Instead, the *mikoshi*, or portable shrines, are often used.

The *hon-matsuri*, or full festival, is held every other year. More than 20 richly decorated parade floats, thought to be reproductions of floats from Tokyo's Kanda-jinja Shrine, are carried through the streets of Kawagoé. In the evening, the floats come together and bump into one another in the center of town—a ceremony known as *Hikkawasé*. *Hyashi* bands— which play traditional Japanese music on the flute, drum, *shamisen* (three-stringed lute), and other instruments—also spar with one another musically, trying their best to interrupt the others' rhythm.

CONTACTS:
Kawagoe City Tourist Information Office
24-9 Wakitamachi
Kawagoe, Saitama 350-1122 Japan
81-49-222-5556; fax: 81-49-226-4102
www.city.kawagoe.saitama.jp

◆ 1528 ◆ Kazakhstan National Days
Various

The central Asian nation of Kazakhstan celebrates a number of important holidays. These include New Year's Day (January 1-2), International Women's Day (March 8), Nauryz Meiramy, or Nawruz (March 22), Unity of the Kazakh People Day (May 1), Victory Day (May 9), Constitution of the Republic of Kazakhstan Day (August 30, 1995), Republic Day (October 25, 1991), and Independence Day (December 16, 1991).

CONTACTS:
Embassy of Kazakhstan
1401 16th St. N.W.
Washington, D.C. 20036
202-232-5488
www.kazakhembus.com

◆ 1529 ◆ Keaw Yed Wakes Festival
Sunday of or following August 24

Keaw Yed means "cow's head" in Lancastrian dialect, and *Wakes* refers to the annual feast held in Westhoughton, Lancashire, on the Sunday of or following St. Bartholomew's Day, August 24 (*see* Bartholomew Fair).

Dating back more than 400 years, the Wakes started out as a religious festival featuring a grand rushbearing procession in which a cart filled with new rushes, to replace those used in the church pews, moved through the town, ending up at the church where special services were held. After the sermon, the children were given "rush money" to spend at the fair.

But over time, the rushbearing ceremony faded and the festival became primarily an opportunity for merrymaking. (*See also* Rushbearing Festival.) The foods traditionally served at the festival included pork pasties and frumenty (also called furmenty or furmety), a porridge made from boiled wheat seasoned with sugar, cinnamon, and raisins.

There have been several attempts to explain the association of the cow's head with the Wakes. One story says that some of the town's wealthier citizens donated a cow to be publicly roasted and distributed to the poor. But rivalry between two factions in town led to a brawl, and the cow's head went to the victors, who were then referred to as "Keaw Yeds" by their rivals.

◆ 1530 ◆ Keene Pumpkin Festival
October

Every year since 1991, the town of Keene, N.H., has held the Pumpkin Festival, in which tens of thousands of carved and lit pumpkins are displayed on scaffolding. In 2013, a total of 30,581 pumpkins were displayed, establishing a new world record for the most jack-o-lanterns lit at the same time and place.

Scaffolding standing some 50 feet high is set up on Gilbo Avenue, Railroad Square, and Main Street in downtown Keene. The scaffolding is arranged as walls and as four massive towers. Pumpkins are carved and displayed in rows on the scaffolding. Local businesses often have a number of pumpkins carved to spell out an advertising slogan. Community groups will carve out mottos. Individuals carve faces or names. In the evening, candles are lit within each pumpkin to form great flickering orange walls that light up the crowds.

Related activities include the largest children's costume parade in New England, a pumpkin pie eating contest, and a pumpkin seed spitting contest. In 2014, large parties of visting youth and local college students became unruly, leading to a series of riots that required significant police response and marred the reputation of the event nationally. Responding to safety concerns, the Keene City Council voted to deny a permit for the 25th Annual Pumpkin Festival, which was to take place in October 2015. The mayor and festival organizers vowed to develop safety plans that will enable the festival to be held in the future.

CONTACTS:
Let it Shine, Inc.
P.O. Box O
Keene, NH 03431
pumpkinfestival2014.org

◆ 1531 ◆ Keiro-no-Hi (Respect-for-the-Aged Day)
Third Monday in September

Keiro-no-Hi is a national holiday in Japan set aside as a day to honor the elderly. At community centers entertainments are held and the guests are given small keepsakes and gifts of food—for example, rice cakes dyed red and white, the traditional Japanese colors of happiness.

◆ 1532 ◆ Keller (Helen) Festival
Last weekend in June

A three-day festival in Tuscumbia, Ala., to honor Helen Keller and her remarkable life. Born in Tuscumbia in 1880, she was left blind, deaf, and mute by illness at the age of 19 months. After Helen's parents appealed to Alexander Graham Bell for help in educating the child, 20-year-old Anne

Mansfield Sullivan, partially blind and a graduate of the Perkins School for the Blind in Boston, arrived and taught the child by pressing objects and a manual alphabet into Helen's palm. Helen learned to read and write and later graduated cum laude from Radcliffe College. She became widely known for her writings, and toured the world to promote opportunities for other blind and deaf persons. Samuel L. Clemens (Mark Twain) was so moved by her spirit that he likened Miss Keller to St. Joan of Arc.

Festival events include art exhibits, stage shows, musical entertainment, sports tournaments, a parade, and historic tours. At Miss Keller's birthplace, Ivy Green, visitors can see the pump at which Helen learned her first word, "water." The house contains a library of Braille books, a Braille typewriter, and other mementos.

The Miracle Worker, the play by William Gibson about Helen Keller and Anne Sullivan, has been presented since 1962 on Friday and Saturday nights in late June and July on the grounds of Ivy Green. The play opened in New York in 1959, won the Pulitzer Prize in 1960, and was made into a movie in 1962.

◆ 1533 ◆ Kelly (Emmett) Clown Festival
First weekend in May

Houston, Missouri, is the hometown of Emmett Kelly, who was the world's most famous clown. Kelly was born on December 9, 1898, in Sedan, Kansas, but his Irish father moved the family to a farm near Houston when he was six years old. Kelly developed an interest in cartooning, and by the time he left Houston to seek work in Kansas City at the age of 19, he had gained a reputation as an entertainer with his "chalk talk" act, which involved telling a story while sketching on paper with colored chalk.

Best known for his role as "Weary Willie," a sad-faced tramp dressed in tattered clothes who was originally one of his cartoon characters, Kelly worked for a number of circuses and in 1952 made his motion picture debut in *The Greatest Show on Earth*. He died in Sarasota, Florida, on March 28, 1979—opening day for the Ringling Bros. and Barnum & Bailey Circus in New York.

Houston's Emmett Kelly Clown Festival began in 1988 and is timed to coincide with the opening of the circus season in May. Among the 700 or 800 clowns who participate in the two-day festival are Emmett Kelly's son (Emmett Kelly, Jr.) and grandson (Joseph Kelly), both of whom continue the "Weary Willie" tradition. In addition to the clown parade and performances of clown stunts and skits, there are a number of "chalk talk" storytelling events.

◆ 1534 ◆ Kenka Matsuri (Roughhouse Festival)
October 14-15

The Kenka Matsuri (Roughhouse Festival) or **Nada Festival** takes place in October in Shirahama, a suburb of the city of Himeji, Japan. Thousands flock to the shrine where the festival is held, first paying their respects to the *kami,* or gods, and then settling in for the entertainment: a procession of *mikoshi*— portable shrines or palanquins that are elaborately carved and decorated, and that can weigh as much as a thousand pounds. The roughhousing starts as teams of mikoshi-bearers jostle each other for position in the procession to the Matsubara Hachiman Shrine. Once they reach the shrine, the palanquin-bearers spin their heavy burden, tilt it to one side, raise it up high in the air, and let it crash to the ground—difficult maneuvers designed to thrill the crowd and win the kami's approval.

The festival ends when the kami are ready to depart for their spirit home. The mikoshi engage in a final battle in an open field, where thousands of cheering spectators take sides and and egg them on. Festival officials eventually call a halt to the mayhem, and the battered mikoshi are returned to the shrine, where they will be repaired and stored until the next year's festival.

See also YAYA MATSURI.

CONTACTS:
Japan National Tourism Organization
1 Grand Central Pl.
60 E. 42nd St.
Ste. 448
New York, NY 10165
212-757-5640; fax: 212-307-6754
www.jnto.go.jp

♦ 1535 ♦ **Kent State Memorial Day**
May 4

When students at Kent State University in Ohio decided to hold a rally to protest the incursion of U.S. military forces into Cambodia during the Vietnam War, no one thought it would end in a national tragedy or that it would mark a turning point in public opinion about the war. But when the Ohio National Guard started firing indiscriminately at the crowd, four Kent State students were killed and nine were wounded—one of whom was paralyzed from the waist down. The next year, three students were convicted on rioting charges, but the eight guardsmen involved in the tragic incident were never tried. A lawsuit brought by the parents of the slain and wounded students ended in an out-of-court settlement.

A candlelight vigil takes place at the Kent State campus every year on May 4, the anniversary of the 1970 shootings. It begins at midnight on May 3, when a candlelight procession winds its way around the campus and stops in a parking lot near the university's Prentice Hall. There, for the next 12 hours, rotating teams of sentinels stand in the places where Allison Krause, Sandy Scheuer, Bill Schroeder, and Jeff Miller were killed. The vigil is coordinated by the May 4 Task Force, a group led by a Kent State graduate and dedicated to promoting campus awareness and preventing a repetition of the violence.

Although the university refused to discuss the tragedy for 10 years after it occurred, nowadays it is commemorated open-ly—to the point where the May 4 Memorial is featured prominently in the college catalog and a course is offered on "May 4th and Its Aftermath." There are four permanent scholarships named for the dead.

CONTACTS:
Kent State University
800 E. Summit St.
Kent, OH 44240
330-672-3000
www.kent.edu

♦ 1536 ♦ **Kentucky Derby**
First Saturday in May

The Kentucky Derby is the greatest and most glamorous horse race in America, run since 1875 in Louisville, Ky. Also known as the **Run for the Roses** because of the garland of roses draped on the winning horse, it is a one-and-one-quarter-mile race for three-year-old thoroughbreds and is the first race in the Triple Crown; the others are the PREAKNESS and the BELMONT STAKES. The site of the race is hallowed Churchill Downs, the track known for its twin spires, built in 1895.

The race is usually run in slightly over two minutes, but in 1964, Northern Dancer was the first to win the Derby in two minutes flat. In 1973, the great Secretariat, fondly known as Big Red, won in 1:59 2/5. That was the only time the Derby was raced in less than two minutes until Monarchos clocked in at 1:59.97 in 2001. Ridden by Ron Turcotte, Secretariat then went on to take the Triple Crown, exploding from the pack to win the Belmont by an unprecedented 31 lengths.

The Derby took its name from the English horse race that was started in 1780 by the 12th Earl of Derby, and Kentuckians hoped to duplicate the social panache of the Epsom Derby (*see* DERBY DAY). They did, in a different way. The Derby became Louisville's major social occasion of the year; women to this day wear their most stylish hats to the racetrack, and there are numerous lavish Derby breakfasts and parties.

Traditional food includes Kentucky ham and beaten biscuits. And, of course, the Derby wouldn't be the Derby without mint juleps, the bourbon-and-mint drink served in cold silver julep cups or in special iced commemorative glasses at the track. Parties are not confined to Louisville; throughout the country and the world, Derby parties are held to watch the race on television. Stephen FOSTER's "My Old Kentucky Home," the official state song, is played as the horses parade to the post, and spectators in Louisville and far away stand and sing and (sometimes) dab their eyes.

Attendance at Churchill Downs is usually 120,000 to 130,000 people—most of them watching what they can from the infield and a select few, often including royalty, from Millionaires Row high in the clubhouse.

Derby Day is the finale of the 10-day Kentucky Derby Festival—a series of events that include a sternwheel steamboat race on the Ohio River, a Pegasus parade, fireworks, concerts, and a coronation ball.

CONTACTS:
Kentucky Derby Festival
1001 S. Third St
Louisville, KY 40203 United States
502-584-3378 or 800-928-3378; fax: 502-589-4674
www.kdf.org

◆ 1537 ◆ Kenya Madaraka Day
June 1

The Republic of Kenya, on the eastern coast of Africa, is surrounded by Somalia, Ethiopia, Sudan, Uganda, and Tanzania. In the mid-1800s, British settlers arrived in East Africa. They eventually established the East African Protectorate in 1895, which promoted European settlement in some of the most fertile parts of Kenya, forcing the native Kenyans from their land. In some areas, especially in the arid northern half of the country, there were few British settlers.

Even before Kenya was officially made a British colony in 1920, European settlers were allowed to participate in government. However, Africans were prohibited from direct political participation until 1944, at which time a few appointed (but not elected) African representatives were allowed to sit in the legislature.

Between 1952 and 1959, Kenyans began to rebel against British colonial rule and its land policies. This rebellion took place almost exclusively in the highlands of central Kenya, which were home to the Kikuyu people. Detention camps and restricted villages were established to contain the Kikuyu insurgents. Tens of thousands of Kikuyu died in these areas and in the fighting, compared to approximately 650 British deaths.

Following the rebellions, Africans were given many more opportunities to participate in politics. The first elections to elect Africans to the Legislative Council took place in 1957. On June 1, 1963, Kenya became a self-governing country when Jomo Kenyatta, an ethnic Kikuyu and head of the Kenya African National Union (KANU), became the first prime minister. On December 12, 1963, Kenya became an independent nation.

June 1 is a public holiday in Kenya. The day is set aside to commemorate the day that Kenya became a self-ruling nation. On this day, the main event takes place at Nyayo Stadium in Nairobi. The President addresses the nation, and the uniformed military, singers, and traditional dancers from around the country provide entertainment for the crowds.

The day is full of festive activities, including family picnics and games in the public parks. Many people take this opportunity to go back to their hometowns for the occasion, and often a big meal of goat or chicken is prepared for the special day. Retail business in Nairobi is slower on this day, while public transportation to up-country areas is heavier than normal.

◆ 1538 ◆ Kenya Mashujaa Day (Heroes Day)
October 20

Jomo Kenyatta, the founding father of Kenya, was a hero in the struggle for freedom and the nation's first president, leading the country from independence in 1963 until his death in 1978. Until 2010, October 20 was observed as Kenyatta Day, recognizing the day in 1952 when Kenyatta was arrested, tried, and imprisoned for his involvement in the anti-colonial movement. In a 2010 national referendum, Kenyans adopted a new constitution which included numerous democratic reforms. Following the promulgation of the constitution, Kenyatta Day was renamed as Mashujaa Day, also known as **Heroes' Day**, to pay tribute to all those who took part in Kenya's liberation struggle, as well as those who have made positive contributions to the nation's well-being. Mashujaa Day is celebrated in much the same way that Kenyatta Day was observed. The president inspects an honor guard and addresses the nation from Nairobi's Nyayo Stadium, where a military parade and ceremony also take place.

◆ 1539 ◆ Kenya Moi Day
October 10

The Republic of Kenya is on the eastern coast of Africa. It is surrounded by Somalia, Ethiopia, Sudan, Uganda, and Tanzania. British settlers arrived in East Africa in the mid-1800s and eventually promoted European settlement in some of the most fertile parts of Kenya, forcing native Kenyans from their land.

Kenya was officially made a British colony in 1920. European settlers were allowed to participate in government, while Africans were not allowed to participate directly in the political arena.

After many years, Africans were given opportunities to participate in politics. The first elections to elect Africans to the Legislative Council took place in 1957. On June 1, 1963, Kenya became a self-ruling country, and then it became an independent country on December 12 of that same year. Kenya's first president was Jomo Kenyatta, an ethnic Kikuyu and head of the Kenya African National Union (KANU).

In 1978, Daniel arap Moi became the second president of Kenya. Though his presidency was marred by controversy with accusations of election fraud, corruption, and human rights violations, Moi was very popular among the people of Kenya for his philosophy of peace, love, and unity then known as Nyayo.

In 1989, parliament passed a law declaring October 10 as a public holiday in honor of President Moi and his achievements, which continued to be observed long past his retirement in 2002. Following the promulgation of the new Kenyan Constitution in 2010, Moi Day was removed from the list of official public holidays. The new law notwithstanding, the government has continued to urge citizens to dedicate the day to philanthropic and nation-building causes in keeping with Moi's legacy.

◆ 1540 ◆ Kenya Skydive Boogie
November

Every November, the skies over Diani in Kenya bloom with colorful parachutes during the three-week-long Sky-dive Boogie, a major event that typically attracts dozens of divers from at least 15 countries. They include members of skydiving clubs and specialist skydive formation teams, as well as novices who may choose a tandem jump for their first sky-diving experience. Participants appreciate the excellent weather, wind, and logistical conditions at Diani: because it is located at sea level, divers can experience a full one-minute accelerated free fall from 14,000 feet, compared with the average free-fall duration of 30 seconds. Divers land directly on the beach outside their hotel, and after a short rest, can climb back aboard a plane at Ukunda airstrip, 10 minutes away.

With such convenient logistics, some participants have been able to fit up to 19 dives in a single day. The Boogie was launched in 1989 by Harro Trempeneau of Kenya Skydivers, the group that still organizes it.

CONTACTS:
Kenya Tourism Board
Kenya-Re Towers, Ragati Rd.
P.O. BOX 30630
Nairobi, 00100 Kenya
254-20-2711-262; fax: 254-20-271-9925
ktb.go.ke

♦ 1541 ♦ Keretkun Festival
Late autumn

The Chukchi people of northeastern Siberia hold a two- or three-day celebration in late autumn known as the Keretkun Festival, in honor of the "owner" of all the sea animals on which they depend for their livelihood. The purpose of the festival is to symbolically return all the animals that had been killed during the hunting season to the sea, thus replenishing the resource that had been plundered. Objects used in the celebration include a special net made out of reindeer tendons, painted oars, statues of birds, and a small wooden image of Keretkun, which is burned at the end of the festival.

A similar festival is held by the Koryak people, another group that depends upon sea animals for survival. The **Seal Festival** is held at the end of the hunting season in November, and the participants plead with the animals they've killed to return to the sea and let themselves be caught again next year. The dead animals are represented by stylized likenesses made out of seaweed.

CONTACTS:
Committee For Sports And Tourism Of Chukotka Ao
18a Lenin St
Anadyr city, Chukotka AO 689000 Russia
742-722-66745; fax: 742-722-64398
www.visitchukotka.com

♦ 1542 ♦ Keukenhof Flower Show
Late March-late May

The world's largest flower show takes place in Lisse, South Holland, Netherlands, at the Keukenhof, a former 15th-cen-

tury estate and hunting lodge that has been turned into a park dotted with lakes. As many as five or six million bulbs blossom here between late March and the end of May, either in hothouses or in the flowerbeds that border the ponds and fountains. There is a museum in Lisse devoted to the history and cultivation of bulbs, and young girls (*meisjes*) in 15th-century dress sell guidebooks to help acquaint visitors withthe 800 varieties of tulips, hyacinths, and daffodils that fill the 70-acre park with color. Thousands of people flock to the gardens each spring, although some prefer to view the bulbs from the windows of the Leyden-Haarlem train.

CONTACTS:
Bezoekadres
Stationsweg 166A
Lisse, 2161 Netherlands
31-252-465-555; fax: 31-252-465-565
www.keukenhof.nl

♦ 1543 ♦ Kewpiesta
Third weekend in April

The Kewpie doll, which was very popular in the 1920s and 1930s, was the creation of Rose O'Neill, a writer, artist, and sculptor from the Ozark region of Missouri. Modeled on her baby brother, the kewpie doll had a pointed tuft of hair at the top of the head.

The annual four-day event known as Kewpiesta is held in Branson, about 10 miles south of O'Neill's homestead. Planned and sponsored by members of the National Rose O'Neill Club, the festival includes tours of O'Neill's birthplace, a Kewpie doll look-alike contest, and special displays in store windows. It is held in April, which is the month during which O'Neill died in 1944 as well as the start of the tourist season in the Ozarks.

CONTACTS:
Internationl Rose O'Neil Club Foundation
P.O. Box 668
Branson, MO 65616
www.irocf.org

♦ 1544 ♦ Khamis al-Amwat
Between March 26 and April 29; Thursday after Easter

Also known as **Dead Remembrance Thursday**, the observation of this day by Muslims was instituted by Saladin the Magnificent (1137-1193) to offset the widespread celebration in Jordan of EASTER by the Christians and of PASSOVER by the Jews. It is a day to pay respects at burial grounds and offer dyed eggs to children. Before World War II, it became a three-day holiday, which included **Ziyarit al-Nabi Musi**, a visit to the shrine of Moses, or simply **al-Ziyara**, "the Visit."

In Jerusalem on Saturday of HOLY WEEK (*see* HOLY SATURDAY), Muslims hold the feast of Nebi Mousa for the same reason. Peasants from the countryside arrive in great numbers and go to the mosque near the Dome of the Rock. Old green war banners are unfurled and there is a parade to the shrine of Moses near the Dead Sea which can last for several hours.

♦ 1545 ♦ Khomeini (Ayatollah), Death Anniversary of
Khordad 14

An estimated 6 to 11 million people gathered for the funeral of Ayatollah Ruhollah Khomeini, who had led as Supreme Leader of Iran from 1979 until his death on June 3, 1989. Observances of his death anniversary today do not draw as many participants as did his funeral. But the **Heart-Rending Departure of the Great Leader of the Islamic Republic of Iran**, as the celebration is officially known, is still widely commemorated throughout the country. The event draws thousands of foreigners to the Khomeini mausoleum, a massive structure near Tehran that has become an established pilgrimage site for Shi'ite Muslims.

As with many Shi'ite holidays of mourning, the anniversary of Khomeini's death is marked by dramatic expressions of grief. Many people display black flags and carry posters of the ayatollah. Along with visiting the leader's mausoleum, people will also spend the day in Khomein, the village of his birth, and in Qom, the holy city where he received his Islamic training.

In 2008, Iran held a special five-day celebration that included speeches by Ayatollah Ali Khamenei and the country's president, Mahmoud Ahmadinejad.

The Iranian calendar differs slightly from the Gregorian calendar, which means the date of commemoration also does not line up exactly with its Gregorian counterpart.

♦ 1546 ♦ Khordad 15 Revolt, Anniversary of the
Khordad 15

Mohammad Reza Shah Pahlavi was the monarch of Iran from 1941 to 1979. During his reign, on June 5, 1963, the government arrested Ayatollah Ruhollah Khomeini, an event that proved to be pivotal in building support for the resistance against the Shah and his Western-supported regime.

The authorities had apprehended Khomeini two days after he delivered an incendiary speech to Islamic students at a *madrassa*. In several towns throughout Iran, large numbers of citizens turned out to demonstrate against the government upon hearing news of Khomeini's arrest. The country was in a state of upheaval for six days, and thus was born the Movement of Khordad 15, named after the Iranian calendar date on which the ayatollah was arrested.

Demonstrations continued on the anniversary of the arrest for 15 years leading up to Khomeini's rise to power. In 1975, one fateful rally held in Khomeini's hometown of Qom was crushed by the Iranian army, resulting in the deaths of many protesters.

In February 1979, millions greeted Khomeini when he returned from 15 years of exile. By the end of the following month, Iranians passed a national referendum to establish an Islamic Republic based on a new constitution. The Shah was removed from power, and Khomeini installed a theocratic government.

Protests became less common after 1979, since Khomeini successfully had fulfilled the mission of the Khordad 15 movement. In the years following the ayatollah's death in 1989, which occurred on Khordad 14, the elaborate memorials for the revered leader began overshadowing the observances of the anniversary the following day.

♦ 1547 ♦ Khordad Sal
March, July, August; sixth day of Frawardin, the first Zoroastrian month

The Parsis of India, descendants of the original Zoroastrian immigrants from Iran (formerly Persia), celebrate the birthday of their founder on this day. Zoroaster (or Zarathushtra, c. 1200 B.C.E.) was a Persian prophet and religious reformer whose ideas combined both monotheism and dualism in the worship of Ahura Mazda, the Wise Lord, and his evil opponent, Ahriman. The largest group of Zoroastrians today can be found in India, where they are known as Parsis (or Parsees), although there are still isolated groups of Zoroastrians in Iran.

Zoroaster's birth is observed in March by the Fasli sect, in July by the Kadmi sect, and in August by the Shahenshai sect.

See also FARVARDEGAN DAYS.

♦ 1548 ♦ Kiamichi Owa-Chito (Festival of the Forest)
Third weekend in June

A celebration of southeastern Oklahoma's forestry industry and of the culture of the Choctaw Indians of the area, Kiamichi Owa-Chito is held in Beavers Bend Resort Park near Broken Bow. Shortleaf and loblolly pines are abundant in the region, which is the heart of Oklahoma's timberland. The mistletoe, Oklahoma's state flower, also flourishes here. The Forest Heritage Center in the park has exhibits that include petrified logs, tools of the forestry industry, and dioramas.

Sporting events of the festival include canoe races, archery, and log birling (log rolling). Other activities range from contests in turkey and owl calling and a spelling bee to art and photography exhibits and musical entertainment—gospel singing, fiddling, and bluegrass.

CONTACTS:
Oklahoma Forestry Services
Department of Agriculture
Food and Forestry
2800 N. Lincoln Blvd.
Oklahoma City, OK 73105
405-522-6158; fax: 405-522-4583
www.forestry.ok.gov

♦ 1549 ♦ **Kiddies' Carnival**
Between January and March; the week before Carnival

The country of Trinidad and Tobago, located in the West Indies, offers a CARNIVAL celebration for children that mirrors the famous parades for adults. The week before Carnival begins children march in a big parade of their own. The children themselves choose a theme (such as "Arabian Nights") and, with the help of adult family members, create costumes that illustrate their theme. Dressed in beautiful costumes the children sing and dance their way down the streets, moving to Calypso music or doing the "jump-up," a popular Trinidadian dance.

CONTACTS:
National Library and Information System Authority of Trinidad and Tobago
National Library Bldg.
Hart and Abercromby St.
Trinidad and Tobago
868-623-6962; fax: 868-625-6096
www.nalis.gov.tt

West Indian American Day Carnival Association
323-325 Rogers Ave.
Brooklyn, NY 11225
718-467-1797
wiadcacarnival.org

♦ 1550 ♦ **Kiel Week**
Last full week in June

Kiel Week is an international sailing regatta in Kiel, Germany, at which the world's leading yachters compete. Craft of all sorts—sail, motor, and muscle-powered—race on the waters of the Kiel Fjord. Kiel, once the chief naval port of Germany, is a center of inshore and deep-sea fishing, and was host for the sailing races of the 1972 OLYMPIC GAMES.

Kiel Week began in 1882 with 20 yachts. Today there are well over 1,000 yachts competing in three classes of races—international, Olympic, and offshore regattas—as well as more than 1,000 events ranging from talks by international political leaders to such cultural events as art exhibits, theater, and music.

♦ 1551 ♦ **Kilkenny Arts Festival**
Mid-August

Kilkenny Arts Festival, one of Ireland's oldest and largest international arts festivals, is held annually over 10 days in August in the medieval town of Kilkenny in southeast Ireland. A group of classical music enthusiasts founded the festival in 1974. It now presents an extensive program of music, including classical, jazz, world and traditional styles, as well as theatre, dance, visual art, literature, film, and young people's events. In addition, the festival features lively street performances. The non-profit Kilkenny Arts Festival is dedicated to presenting leading Irish artists, as well as international artists who would not otherwise be seen in Ireland. Drawn by

the festival's reputation for innovation and high standards, about 80,000 visitors partake of the festival each year.

CONTACTS:
Kilkenny Arts Festival
11 Patrick's Ct.
Patrick St.
Ireland
353-56-776-3663; fax: 353-56-775-1704
www.kilkennyarts.ie

♦ 1552 ♦ **Killing the Pigs, Festival of**
September

In rural areas of Estonia, the Festival of Killing the Pigs traditionally has been celebrated sometime in September. Each village has a few men who are skilled in time-honored methods of slaughtering animals and preparing the meat. On the day of the festival, the women prepare a meal of pork, vodka, and "blood bread"—flour mixed with the animal's blood that is boiled, and then often fried, before it is eaten. After the meal is over, neighbors get together and spend the evening singing and dancing.

♦ 1553 ♦ **Kim Il-Sung, Birthday of**
April 15

The birthday of the late North Korean leader Kim Il-Sung on April 15, 1912, is marked as a public holiday throughout North Korea (official name: Democratic People's Republic of Korea). The holiday is known as the **Day of the Sun**. All over the country, people lay floral wreaths and baskets before the hundreds of statues that commemorate Kim. The main observances take place in the capital city Pyongyang, where officials of numerous organizations and citizens lay flowers at one of the nation's grandest monuments to Kim, located on Mansu Hill.

The late leader's birthday celebration often coincides with the Araring Festival, named after a famous Korean folk song. During the renowned mass games of the festival, up to 100,000 participants take part in various large-scale synchronized dance and gymnastics displays in Pyongyang's 150,000-seat May Day stadium. Tens of thousands of well-trained school children create an effect close to animation in the stadium's stands by flashing colored flashcards in intricately timed routines.

Kim Il-Sung ruled North Korea from 1945 until his death in 1994. Known in his country as the "Great Leader," he is proclaimed in the national constitution as the "eternal president." The current leader of North Korea is his son, Kim Jong-Il. Both men are publicly adulated under the "cult of personality" that was part of Kim Il-Sung's distinctive political philosophy. Today, North Korea is a Communist country with a repressive government.

♦ 1554 ♦ **Kim Jong-Il, Birthday of**
February 16-17

The birth date of North Korean leader Kim Jong-Il (February 16, 1941) is marked with a two-day public holiday observed throughout the country. Large-scale public celebrations— including mass gymnastics displays, musical performances, fireworks, and military demonstrations—are centered in the capital city of Pyongyang. Smaller-scale displays take place in towns and villages throughout North Korea (official name: Democratic People's Republic of Korea). Special horticultural exhibitions feature the Kimjongilia, a flower cultivated to bloom around Kim's birthday. In a country with food and energy shortages, the government also often marks Kim's birthday by allotting North Koreans extra food or electricity.

The Kims have ruled the country since 1945, when Kim Jong-Il's father, Kim Il-Sung, took control of the northern half of the Korean Peninsula. His son was designated his successor in 1980. When the father, Kim Il Sung, died 1994, the son, Kim Jong-Il, became the country's leader. His official title is chairman of the national defense commission, but he is proclaimed in his country as the "sun of the 21st century." Both he and his father are publicly adulated under the "cult of personality" that was part of Kim Il-Sung's distinctive political philosophy. Today, North Korea is a Communist country with a repressive government.

♦ 1555 ♦ **Kinderzeche (Children's Party)**
Third full week in July

Kinderzeche is a festival in Dinkelsbühl, Bavaria, Germany, to honor the children who saved the town during the Thirty Years' War of 1618-48. In 1632, according to legend, the Swedish commander, a Colonel Sperreuth, threatened destruction of the town (which endured eight sieges during the war). The town council was debating its response, when a gatekeeper's daughter named Lore proposed gathering a group of children together to appeal to Sperreuth. The council agreed to let her try. As the Swedish troops rode into town, the children sang, and Lore with her small band of children appeared before the commander, knelt, and asked his mercy. The commander's heart softened; he spared the town, and told the citizens, "Children are the rescuers of Dinkelsbühl. Always remember the debt of thanks you owe them."

The celebration today is a reenactment of the event, with participants (most of them Dinkelsbühl residents) in the costume of 17th-century town councilors and soldiers. Highlights of the festival include the parade of the Dinkelsbühl Boys' Band and a performance of a medieval sword dance, in which dancers stand on top of a pedestal of crossed blades. About 300,000 visitors attend the festival.

Dinkelsbühl is about 20 miles from Rothenburg-on-the-Tauber, Germany, which also commemorates an event of the Thirty Years' War with the MEISTERTRUNK PAGEANT.

CONTACTS:
Tourist service Dinkelsbühl - TSD
Altrathausplatz 14
Dinkelsbuhl, D-91550 Germany
49-9851-902-470; fax: 49-9851-902-419
www.dinkelsbuehl.de

♦ 1556 ♦ **King (Martin Luther, Jr.), Birthday**
Federal holiday: third Monday in January;
birthday: January 15

In 1955 Rosa Parks, a black seamstress in Montgomery, Alabama, refused to obey a bus driver's order to give up her seat to a white male passenger. She was fined $14 for her defiance of the Jim Crow (segregationist) law that required blacks to sit in the rear of buses, and if the bus were crowded, to give up their seat to a white passenger. The incident led to a citywide bus boycott and raised its leader, the young black Baptist minister Dr. Martin Luther King, Jr., to national prominence.

King went on to establish the Southern Christian Leadership Conference, to win the Nobel Peace Prize, and to play an active role in the civil rights movement of the 1960s. He was in Memphis, Tennessee, on April 4, 1968, organizing a strike of the city's predominantly black sanitation workers, when he was shot to death at the age of 39 by James Earl Ray.

Martin Luther King Day is a federal holiday, the only one that honors a person who was not a president; federal government offices are closed on that day. It has become a focal point for recognition of African-American history and the American civil rights movement led by Dr. King. It is also a legal holiday in all 50 states, since New Hampshire signed its King holiday legislation into law in 1999. In Alabama it became **Martin Luther King and Robert E. Lee's Birthday**, observed on the third Monday in January. The same day in Virginia is called **Lee-Jackson-King Day**, combining Dr. King's birthday with those of Robert E. Lee and Andrew "Stonewall" Jackson (*see also* LEE DAY, ROBERT E. and JACKSON'S BIRTHDAY, ANDREW). In schools, the day is often observed with special lessons and assembly programs dealing with Dr. King's life and work.

See also BRIDGE CROSSING JUBILEE.

CONTACTS:
King Center
449 Auburn Ave. N.E.
Atlanta, GA 30312
404-526-8900
www.thekingcenter.org

♦ 1557 ♦ **King (Martin Luther, Jr.) Drum Major**
       for Justice Parade, Battle of the Bands &
       Drum Line Extravaganza, National
Monday in mid-January

The National Martin Luther King Jr. Drum Major for Justice Parade, Battle of the Bands & Drum Line Extravaganza is a celebration held annually in St. Petersburg, Fla., on the BIRTH- DAY OF MARTIN LUTHER KING JR. federal holiday. The event is organized by the Martin Luther King Jr. Holiday & Legacy Association Inc. and led by Sevell Carescale Brown III, whose original idea gave rise to the celebration. Through a grand pageant showcasing the talents of black college students, Brown sought to honor Dr. King's legacy as a "drum major for justice" while encouraging young people to aspire to higher education. The first parade was held on January 20, 1986, the year that Dr. King's birthday was first commemorated as a federal holiday.

To participate in the parade and competition, marching bands travel from historically black colleges and universities throughout the South, including Alabama, Arkansas, Georgia, Mississippi, North Carolina, South Carolina, and Texas. Among the participants are Bethune Cookman University, Florida A & M University, Morehouse College, and the 300-member Historically Black Colleges & Universities All-Star Band, with members drawn from several schools. The parade, which begins at the intersection of Third Avenue South and Dr. Martin Luther King Jr. Street, travels 1.3 miles to South Vinoy Park and is attended by approximately 100,000 spectators. Following the parade, a high-energy band competition gets underway at Tropicana Field Dome Stadium. Scholarships are available to participating band members, and an awards banquet is held on the Friday preceding the parade.

CONTACTS:
MLK National Parade
P.O. Box 12732
St. Petersburg, FL 33733
727-388-9494
www.mlknationalparade.org

♦ 1558 ♦ King's Day (Koningsdag)
April 27

King's Day, or Koningsdag, commemorates the birthday of the king of the Netherlands. Since 1890, the day had been celebrated as Queen's Day, or Koninginnedag, commemorating the birthday of the queen. Following Queen Beatrix's abdication in 2013, however, the Dutch welcomed their first king in over a century when Willem-Alexander ascended to the throne. Observed as a national holiday in the Netherlands, the day is synonymous with the color orange, an allusion to the House of Orange, the royal dynasty of the Netherlands. The color orange is ubiquitous, from banners and clothing, to food and drinks. Revelers with their hair dyed orange fill the streets and squares, often sporting accessories such as a crown or a lion, which are the royal insignia. Across the country, and particularly in Amsterdam, Arnhem, Utrecht and The Hague, the celebrations begin the previous evening with concerts and parties, and celebrants singing "Het Wilhelmus," a 16th century ode to William of Orange and his fight for the Dutch people. The royal family often makes public appearances on this day, and local orange committees stage performances centered on historic events.

CONTACTS:
Amsterdam Marketing Travel Trade Department
P.O. Box 3331
Amsterdam, 1001 AC The Netherlands
31-20-702-6000; fax: 31-20-625-2869
www.iamsterdam.com/en

♦ 1559 ♦ Kingdom Days
Last weekend in June

This annual festival in Fulton, Missouri, was based on a Civil War confrontation between a Union general and the local militia. On July 28, 1861, there was a battle near Calwood that left 19 dead and 76 wounded. In an effort to spare Callaway County any further bloodshed, Colonel Jefferson Jones sent a letter to General John B. Henderson, commander of the Union military forces in northeastern Missouri. Jones requested that the county be left alone to conduct its own business and to control its own destiny. Henderson, perhaps fearing stiff resistance, agreed to the truce and signed the treaty that designated Callaway County a "kingdom," separate from both the U.S. and the Confederacy. No shots were fired, no one was injured, and the disagreements between the two military units were settled peacefully.

This event was only one of the historic reenactments that took place during the Kingdom Days festival. Others were more humorous, such as the "shotgun" Civil War-era wedding in 1991. Other events have included a parade, bed races, a "baby derby" in which babies up to 18 months old crawl 10 feet to the finish line, a hot air balloon rally, and a pig-kissing contest.

CONTACTS:
Fulton Area Chamber of Commerce
409 Court St.
Fulton, MO 65251
573-642-3055; fax: 573-642-5182
www.fultonmochamber.com

♦ 1560 ♦ King's Birthday (Belgium)
November 15

King Leopold I (1790-1865) of Belgium was named after ST. LEOPOLD, whose feast is celebrated on this day. He was the first leader of Belgium after it achieved independence from the Netherlands in 1831, and reigned until his death. Also known as **Dynasty Day**, or **Fête de la Dynastie**, the day is a major observance particularly among Belgium's German-speaking community.

CONTACTS:
Embassy of Belgium
3330 Garfield St. N.W.
Washington, D.C. 20008
202-333-6900

diplomatie.belgium.be/en

Belgian Monarchy, Royal Palace
Rue Brederode, 16
Brussels, 1000 Belgium
32-2-551-2020
www.monarchie.be

♦ 1561 ♦ King's Birthday (Denmark)
March 11

Though no longer observed, the birthday of Frederick IX of Denmark (1899-1972) was a national holiday in that country, marked by patriotic speeches and parades. Soldiers in uniform would march down the main street of Copenhagen, the capital, accompanied by military bands. This was also an occasion for singing Denmark's two national anthems, "Kong Kristian Stod Ved Hojen Mast" ("King Kristian Stood Beside the Lofty Mast") and "Der Er Et Yndigt Land" ("This Is a Lovely Land"). The words of the former were written by Johannes Ewald and translated into English by the well-known American poet, Henry Wadsworth Longfellow.

Frederick IX became king of Denmark in 1947 and ruled until his death in 1972. He is remembered for the encouragement he gave to the Danish resistance movement against the German occupation during World War II. In fact, from 1943-45 he was imprisoned by the Germans along with his father, Christian X.

Frederick's daughter, Margrethe, is the current queen of Denmark (*see* Queen Margrethe's Birthday).

CONTACTS:
Embassy of Denmark
3200 Whitehaven St. N.W.
Washington, D.C. 20008
202-234-4300; fax: 202-328-1470
usa.um.dk

♦ 1562 ♦ **King's Birthday (Lesotho)**
July 17

Veneration for royalty is still customary for the Basotho, the majority group living in the Kingdom of Lesotho. As recently as 1993, the monarch of Lesotho, a tiny country enclosed within South Africa, had full executive power. Accordingly, the birthday of monarch King Letsie III is a momentous occasion.

Born in 1963, King Letsie is the son of King Moshoeshoe II, who became Lesotho's first monarch after the country gained full independence from Great Britain in 1966. Letsie briefly claimed rule between 1990 and 1995, the years when Moshoeshoe II was in exile. With his father's death in 1996, Letsie permanently inherited the throne, although by this stage a newly introduced constitution had demoted Lesotho's status to "living symbol of national unity," which essentially meant he no longer possessed executive or legislative powers.

Many citizens honor the king on his birthday by attending his parade, at which he appears in regal attire and is usually accompanied by his wife, Queen Masenate Mohato Seeiso. In 2003, the royal family announced that in the years to come the official festivities will change location each year to ensure that more residents of the country's ten districts can enjoy greater participation in the celebration.

CONTACTS:
Royal Palace Secretariat
P.O. Box 527
Government Office Complex Phase 1 Qhobosheaneng
 Lesotho
266-22-316-332; fax: 266-223-10102
www.gov.ls/king

♦ 1563 ♦ **King's Birthday (Thailand)**
December 5

This national holiday celebrates the birthday of Thailand's King Bhumibol Adulyadej (b. 1927), the country's longest-reigning monarch who ascended to the throne in 1946. Bangkok blooms with decorations, which are especially lavish in the area of the floodlit Grand Palace. Full dress ceremonies, including a Trooping of the Colors by Thailand's elite Royal Guards, are performed at the palace.

CONTACTS:
Thai Embassy
1024 Wisconsin Ave. N.W.
Ste. 401
Washington, D.C. 20007
202-944-3600; fax: 202-944-3611
www.thaiembassydc.org

♦ 1564 ♦ **Kingsburg Swedish Festival**
Third weekend in May

This festival pays tribute to the Swedish heritage of Kingsburg, Calif. The event began in 1924 as a luncheon to commemorate the midsummer celebration of the harvest in Sweden. Today it's a full-fledged festival running from Thursday through Sunday of the third weekend in May and attracts about 25,000 visitors. Traditional Swedish costumes are worn, and Swedish food is eaten—Swedish pancakes, Swedish pea soup, a smorgasbord. Events include a Parade of Trolls, raising of the May Pole, folk dancing, arts and crafts displays, a horse trot, and live entertainment.

CONTACTS:
Kingsburg District Chamber of Commerce
1475 Draper St.
Kingsburg, CA 93631
559-897-1111
www.kingsburg-chamber-of-commerce.org

♦ 1565 ♦ **Kiplingcotes Derby**
Third Thursday in March

The Kiplingcotes Derby, which is run along the Wolds Way in Yorkshire, England, on the third Thursday in March, dates back more than 450 years, making it the longest-running "flat race" (as opposed to the steeplechase, which involves jumping over obstacles) in England. The route along which the horses run measures four miles in length and cuts through five different parishes, supposedly following an ancient Roman road. It begins near South Dalton and finishes near Kiplingcotes Farm in the parish of Middleton-on-the-Wolds.

The minimum weight that every rider must achieve is 10 stone (140 lbs.), and they are weighed beforehand to weed out cheaters who may have filled their pockets with heavy pieces of metal. The entrance fee paid by each competitor will be awarded to the second-place finisher while the winner takes home the interest on the shares of stock provided in 1618 by the district's landowners to finance the race in future years. It is never a large sum, however, and the prestige of winning is worth more than the actual prize money.

One year, when no riders had signed up for the race, officials took a cart-horse around the track rather than interrupt the centuries-old custom. In addition, in 2001 the race was cancelled due to the outbreak of foot and mouth disease throughout England; however, one rider ceremoniously rode the course.

CONTACTS:
Yorkshire Tourist Board
Dry Sand Foundry
Foundry Sq.
Holbeck
Leeds, LS11 5DL United Kingdom
44-113-322-3500
www.yorkshire.com

Market Weighton Town Council
2 Linegate
Market Weighton
East Yorkshire, YO43 3AR United Kingdom
44-1430-871-430
www.marketweightontowncouncil.gov.uk

♦ 1566 ♦ Kiribati Gospel Day (National Church Day)
July 10

The Republic of Kiribati is a group of 33 coral islands in the central Pacific Ocean, about 2,500 miles southwest of Hawaii. The islands of Kiribati are divided into three groups: the Gilbert Islands, the Phoenix Islands, and the Line Islands. Of the 33 islands, 21 are inhabited. Approximately 90% of the population lives on the Gilbert Islands; only one of the Phoenix Islands (Kanton Island) and three of the Line Islands are permanently inhabited.

European settlers began arriving in Kiribati in the 1800s. In 1892, the Gilbert Islands agreed to become a British protectorate. They became part of a British colony (along with the Ellice Islands and Banaba) in 1916. Over the next 20 years, the Line and Phoenix Islands were incorporated. The republic gained independence from the United Kingdom on July 12, 1979.

Included among the European settlers were missionaries from various denominations. Today, the predominant religions in Kiribati are Roman Catholic (52%) and Protestant (40%). Other religions include Seventh-Day Adventist, Muslim, Baha'i, Latter-day Saints, and Church of God.

On Gospel day, the Roman Catholic and Protestant churches host a celebration that is usually held at the Bairiki National Stadium in the capital, South Tarawa. A combined service is conducted by one of the heads of the two churches. Following the service, the people celebrate in the *maneaba* (center of the village) with local dances, choir, and religious songs performed by different groups from the two churches.

♦ 1567 ♦ Kiribati Independence Day
July 12

This island group in the middle of the Pacific Ocean was known as the Gilbert Islands until its independence from Britain on July 12, 1979. Independence Day is observed as a national holiday.

CONTACTS:
Consulate of Kiribati
95 Nakolo Pl.
Honolulu, HI 96819
808-834-7603; fax: 808-834-7604
www.consularcorpshawaii.org

♦ 1568 ♦ Kiribati National Health Day
Mid-April

The Republic of Kiribati (pronounced Kiribas) is a group of 33 coral islands in the central Pacific Ocean, about 2,500 miles southwest of Hawaii. The islands of Kiribati are divided into three groups: the Gilbert Islands, the Phoenix Islands, and the Line Islands. All of the islands, except for Banaba in the Gilbert Islands, are atolls (ring-shaped islands with central lagoons). The capital of Kiribati is Tarawa, an atoll in the Gilbert Islands.

Most of the Kiribati atolls are just over 19 feet above sea level and surrounded by barrier reefs. This makes an ideal setting for fishing, snorkeling, scuba diving, swimming, and other water sports.

There are few natural resources found throughout Kiribati. The country's agricultural products include copra (dried coconut meat from which coconut oil is extracted), taro, breadfruit, sweet potatoes, and other vegetables. The main industries are fishing, handicrafts, and tourism. World War II battle sites, game fishing, and ecotourism are some of the more popular attractions.

Every year, the people of Kiribati celebrate National Health Day. It is a public holiday set aside to encourage people to live a healthy lifestyle. This includes not only being active, but also taking time to relax. The Health Department coordi-nates several sports competitions throughout the day, includ-ing soccer, volleyball, softball, boxing, basketball, and cycling. In addition, most people take time to relax and enjoy their hobbies.

CONTACTS:
Ministry of Health & Medical Services
P.O. Box 268
Bikenibeu, Tarawa Kiribati
686-281-00; fax: 686-285-12
www.health.gov.ki

♦ 1569 ♦ Kiribati World Teachers' Day
October 6

The Republic of Kiribati is a group of 33 coral islands in the central Pacific Ocean, about 2,500 miles southwest of Hawaii.

European settlers began arriving in Kiribati in the 1800s. In 1892, the Gilbert Islands agreed to become a British protectorate. They became part of a British colony (along with the Ellice Islands and Banaba) in 1916. Over the next 20 years, the Line and Phoenix Islands were incorporated. The republic gained independence from the United Kingdom on July 12, 1979. Today, the official language in Kiribati is English.

The main languages are English, Gilbertese, and Austronesian.

The constitution of Kiribati requires children between the ages of 6 and 15 years old to attend school. Primary school includes grades 1 through 6, and Junior Secondary School (JSS) includes grades 7 through 9. Once students complete JSS, they may choose to continue on to secondary schools or to pursue vocational or technical careers. Students must successfully complete secondary school in order to attend a higher education institution.

Kiribati joined the United Nations Educational, Scientific, and Cultural Organization (UNESCO) on October 24, 1989. By September 2006, Kiribati had 14 schools participating in UNESCO's Associated Schools Project Network (ASPnet), a network of schools dedicated to promoting quality education.

To show their respect and appreciation for teachers in Kiribati, October 6 has been declared World Teachers' Day. It is a national holiday set aside to acknowledge that teachers contribute greatly to the development of the country's most important resource—people. On World Teacher's Day, the activities include local dancing, singing, and sporting events. Also, the Kiribati Teachers College in Tarawa is open to the public, allowing people to visit the school and learn more about it.

CONTACTS:
Kiribati National Tourism Office
P.O. Box 487
Betio
 Kiribati
686-25-573
www.kiribatitourism.gov.ki

◆ 1570 ◆ **Kiribati Youth Day**
August 7

The Republic of Kiribati is a group of 33 coral islands in the central Pacific Ocean, about 2,500 miles southwest of Hawaii. The islands of Kiribati are divided into three groups: the Gilbert Islands, the Phoenix Islands, and the Line Islands. All of the islands, except for Banaba in the Gilbert Islands, are atolls (ring-shaped islands with central lagoons). Most of the Kiribati atolls are just over 19 feet above sea level and surrounded by barrier reefs. This makes an ideal setting for fishing, snorkeling, scuba diving, swimming, and other water sports.

The constitution of Kiribati requires children between the ages of 6 and 15 years old to attend school. Primary school includes grades 1 through 6, and Junior Secondary School (JSS) includes grades 7 through 9. Once students complete JSS, they may choose to continue on to secondary schools or to pursue vocational or technical careers. Students must successfully complete secondary school in order to attend a higher education institution.

August 7 in Kiribati has been declared Youth Day. The purpose of this national holiday is to promote healthy lifestyles among the youth in Kiribati. Like HEALTH DAY in Kiribati, some of the main events of the day center on sports competitions soccer, volleyball, boxing, tennis, basketball, and other traditional games such as local wrestling and more. For those youths not participating in the sporting events, there are also local dancing and singing competitions. Youth from the different districts and islands in Kiribati compete in these various events. Afterwards, a youth beauty pageant is held.

CONTACTS:
Ministry of Communication, Transport and Tourism Development
P.O. Box 487
Betio, Tarawa Kiribati
686-26003; fax: 686-26193
www.president.gov.ki

◆ 1571 ◆ **Kite Meeting, International**
April

The International Kite Meeting is a nine-day, international kite competition. This annual event takes place on the beaches of Berck-sur-Mer in the popular Opal Coast region of northern France. Held since 1987, the festival attracts over half a million spectators. The competition boasts many unusual and intricate styles of kites, such as jellyfish, lobsters, octopuses, panda bears, boats, and cartoon characters. Kites are judged based on construction material, size, and other factors. Many diverse styles and methods of kite flying are found at the event, including synchronized kite flying and *Rokkaku*, the Japanese art of kite fighting. In addition to kiting, the event features a wide variety of other entertainment, from comedy and poetry to wind gardens—exhibits featuring flowers, sand, windmills, and scarecrows.

CONTACTS:
France Tourism Development Agency
825 Third Ave.
New York, NY 10022
212-838-7800; fax: 212-838-7855
int.rendezvousenfrance.com

◆ 1572 ◆ **Kiwanis Kids' Day**
Fourth Saturday in September

The National Kids' Day Foundation and Kiwanis International first came up with the idea of setting aside a day to focus on children and their welfare in 1949. Kiwanis International eventually assumed responsibility for the program and re-named it Kiwanis Kids' Day.

On the fourth Saturday in September, local Kiwanis clubs sponsor activities designed to show the community's appreciation of and pride in its children. The actual program for the day varies from one club to the next, but some of the more popular activities include parades, picnics and field days, theater parties, free admission programs, poster contests, fishing derbies, talent shows, and youth recognition banquets. The idea is to show youngsters that they are an important part of the community and that the community wants them to be good citizens.

CONTACTS:
Kiwanis International Foundation
3636 Woodview Trace
Indianapolis, IN 46268
317-217-6254 or 800-549-2647; fax: 317-471-8323
www.kiwanis.org/foundation

♦ 1573 ♦ Klo Dance
Autumn

A harvest celebration among the Baoulé people of Côte d'Ivoire (Ivory Coast) in western Africa, the *klo* dance takes place during the fall harvest season and is similar to HALLOWEEN in the United States. Groups of young boys dressed from head to toe in strips of palm leaves go from house to house, dancing to the accompaniment of sticks beaten together. They ask for "treats"—yams, manioc, or peanuts— and sing a song of thanks if they are given any. But if they are refused, their "trick" is to sing teasing songs and to scold the woman of the house for being stingy. Afterward, the boys take their treats into the bush to eat them.

♦ 1574 ♦ Klondike Days Exposition
Late July

For 10 days in late July every year since 1962, the city of Edmonton, Alberta, Canada, has commemorated the Gold Rush of 1898 and its impact on what was originally a small agricultural town. People dress up in Klondike costumes— long dresses, stockings, and lace-up boots for the women, frontier wear for the men. A two-hour parade through the city's downtown area kicks off the festivities, followed by a band competition at Clark Stadium. There is a gold-panning competition at the Chilkoot Gold Mine and chuckwagon racing. Gambling at a Klondike-style casino is a popular diversion. Klondike garden parties and pancake breakfasts are held throughout the city, which was once the starting point for the overland trip to the Yukon.

♦ 1575 ♦ Klondike Gold Discovery Day
Third Monday in August

On August 17, 1896, George Washington Carmack discovered gold at Bonanza Creek in northwestern Canada's Yukon Territory. His discovery triggered a huge gold rush and an enormous influx of American miners and traders. More than 30,000 poured into the Klondike region over the next couple of years, sparking the formation of Dawson and the construction of the Yukon narrow-gage railway. But the Klondike boom was short-lived, and by 1900 most of the miners had given up and were replaced by companies using mechanical mining techniques. To this day, mining remains the area's most important industry.

Also known as **Discovery Day**, this important event in Canada's history is observed as a public holiday in the Yukon. The city of Dawson celebrates with various special events, including a parade, musical entertainment, bathtub races, and, of course, panning for gold.

CONTACTS:
Department of Tourism & Culture
Government of Yukon
P.O. Box 2703
Whitehorse, YT Y1A 2C6 Canada
867-667-5340 or 800-661-0494
www.travelyukon.com

♦ 1576 ♦ Klondike International Outhouse Race
September, Sunday of Labor Day weekend

First held in 1977, the Klondike International Outhouse Race takes place annually in the gold rush city of Dawson in Canada's Yukon Territory. A serious athletic event for some— and an opportunity for less serious competitors to indulge in what can only be described as "bathroom humor"—the race involves four-person teams, each pulling an outhouse on wheels. Many of the teams compete in outrageous costumes and cover their outhouses with appropriate graffiti or equip them with such modern-day comforts as telephones and carpeted seats.

There are two basic types of competitors: the serious runners, who train rigorously for the event and are sent off in the first heat of the three-kilometer race; and those who never make it any further than the first bar on the course, or who reach the finish line from the wrong direction. There are awards for the best dressed as well as the fastest, and the grand trophy is a wooden outhouse with an engraved plaque.

CONTACTS:
Klondike Visitors Association
P.O. Box 389
Dawson City, YT Y0B 1G0 Canada
867-993-5575 or 877-465-3006
www.dawsoncity.ca

♦ 1577 ♦ Knabenschiessen
Second weekend in September

The Knabenschiessen is a marksmanship contest in Zurich, Switzerland, for boys and girls aged 12 to 17. The custom dates to the 17th century when all boys were required to practice their shooting during summer holidays. The final rifle match was a kind of examination. Today, the rifles used are like those that are issued in the army. Prizes are awarded, and the winner is named King, or Queen, of the Marksmen. A huge amusement park is set up for the Knabenschiessen, and there is a parade and market.

CONTACTS:
Zürich Tourism Convention Bureau
Stampfenbachstrasse 52
Zurich, 8006 Switzerland
41-44-215-4030; fax: 41-44-215-4099
www.zuerich.com

Protect Society of Zurich city
Uetlibergstr. 341
Zurich, 8045 Switzerland
41-44-462-99-55; fax: 44-462-9965
www.knabenschiessen.ch

♦ 1578 ♦ **Kneeling Sunday**
Between May 24 and June 27; 50 days after Easter

In Orthodox Christianity, Pentecost (or Whitsunday) is known as Kneeling Sunday. After the liturgy, the congregation kneels while the priest makes three invocations, one of which is a prayer for the repose of the dead. In some rural parts of Greece, the worshippers place flowers from their gardens on the ground in front of them as they kneel, and they burn candles to light the way for the souls of the departed. Sometimes they cover their eyes with rose petals, believing that if their eyes are open when the souls of their loved ones pass by, they will be recognized, and the grief that accompanies this recognition will make it impossible for the soul to leave the earth.

CONTACTS:
United States Conference of Catholic Bishops
3211 Fourth St. N.E.
Washington, D.C. 20017
202-541-3000
www.usccb.org

♦ 1579 ♦ **Kodomo-no-Hi (Children's Day)**
May 5

Kodomo-no-Hi is a national holiday in Japan that was known as Boys' Day from the ninth century, but became a day for both boys and girls in 1948. Today the day is observed largely with family picnics, but some still practice the old custom of flying wind socks in the shape of carp, a common Japanese food fish. Households with sons erect tall bamboo poles outside the home and attach streamers in the shape of carp for each son. The carp supposedly represents the strength, courage, and determination shown in its upstream journeys. The festivities are part of **Golden Week**, which also includes Greenery Day (May 4) and Japan Constitution Memorial Day (May 3).

CONTACTS:
National Association of Japan-America Societies, Inc
1819 L St. N.W.
Ste. 200
Washington, D.C. 20036
202-429-5545; fax: 202-429-0027
www.us-japan.org

♦ 1580 ♦ **Kojagara**
September-October; full moon day of Hindu month of Asvina

The word "Kojagara" is a combination of two terms, *Kah* and *jagara*, which means "who is awake?" This is what the goddess Lakshmi says when she descends to the earth on the night of the full moon in the month of Asvina. She blesses all those who are awake with wealth and prosperity, so the festivities go on all night. Kojagara is a harvest festival and is celebrated throughout India.

There is a folk tale about a king who fell into dire financial straits. When his queen observed the fast and night vigil in honor of Lakshmi, the goddess of wealth, their fortunes were reversed and prosperity returned to them.

♦ 1581 ♦ **Kokila Vrata**
Every 20 years, on the full moon day of the intercalary month when it falls in the Hindu month of Asadha

A *kokil* is a cuckoo, and this day, which honors Sati, the wife of Shiva, is known as Kokila Vrata because Sati is believed to have once been changed into a cuckoo as a punishment.

According to Hindu mythology, Sati's father, Daksha, agreed to her marriage to Shiva only reluctantly. Daksha hosted a religious feast one day and excluded the couple. Sati appeared at the feast anyway, and soon involved her father in a quarrel over his refusal to accept Shiva as his son-in-law. In anger and vengeance Sati leaped into the sacrificial fire where she burned to death. Since this was considered a sin, she returned to life as a cuckoo in order to make reparation.

Hindus observe Kokila Vrata by eating only one meal per day during the month. They fast entirely on the last day of the month. People also may worship a live cuckoo or an image of one.

♦ 1582 ♦ **Koledouvane**
December 24-25

Koledouvane is the ritual singing of Christmas carols that takes place in Bulgaria each year on December 24 and 25. The *koledari*, or "carol singers," go from house to house and wish people good health and prosperity. Although their dress and ornaments differ from region to region, the *koledarka*, a long oak stick covered with elaborate carving, is a traditional accessory.

A similar ritual, called *Sourvakari*, is carried out on New Year's Day. Those who go from house to house wishing people a Happy New Year carry a decorated dogwood twig, which they use to tap people on the back as they deliver their good wishes. The near coincidence of the two customs can probably be explained by the switch from the Julian to the Gregorian calendar. They have survived as separate celebrations, even though they are closely related in meaning.

♦ 1583 ♦ **Kolkata International Film Festival**
November

The Kolkata International Film Festival is an annual event held in the city of Kolkata, in the State of West Bengal, India. It features a wide selection of world cinema and is attended by millions of fans from the city. The open, progressive, and accommodating atmosphere of the festival is aided by the government's liberal support of the arts. The film festival is organized by the Nandan West Bengal Film Center, which was founded in 1985 with the help of acclaimed Bengali film director and Academy Award winner Satyajit Ray. The festival began in 1995, and within a couple of years of its inception, it received recognition from the International Federation of Film Producers Association (FIAPF) in Paris, the international authority governing film festivals.

CONTACTS:
Kolkata International Film Festival
1/1 A J C Bose Rd.
Kolkata, West Bengal 700 020 India
91-33-2223-1210; fax: 91-33-22235744
www.kff.in

♦ 1584 ♦ Kopenfahrt (Barrel Parade)
Between February 3 and March 9; Shrove Tuesday

The **Kope Festival** on Shrove Tuesday has been observed by the salt miners of Lüneburg, Lower Saxony, Germany, since the 15th century. Originally the *Kope,* a wooden barrel filled with stones, was dragged through the narrow streets of the town by *Salzjunker,* or young journeymen salters, on horseback. They were followed by a long procession of local officials, salt mine laborers, and townspeople.

Today the **Kope Procession** has become a folk, rather than a historical, event. As the riders attempt to guide the Kope through the streets, trumpeters blast their instruments as loudly as possible in an attempt to unnerve the horses. Once the Kope is brought to the mouth of the salt mine, it is set on a huge pile of wood and burned. Following the bonfire is a ceremony initiating the Salzjunker into the Guild of Master Salters.

Some believe that the Kopenfahrt bonfire was originally a pagan ceremony symbolizing the sun god's triumph over the forces of darkness. In any case, the festival was revived in 1950 and is now a regular part of the old mining town's annual Carnival celebration.

♦ 1585 ♦ Korea Liberation Day
August 15

This Korean holiday commemorates the surrender of Japan to the Allies in 1945, liberating Korea from Japan's 35-year occupation. The day also commemorates the formal proclamation of the Republic of Korea in South Korea in 1948, but it is a national holiday in both Koreas.

See also Samil-Jol.

CONTACTS:
Korea Tourism Organization
5509 Wilshire Blvd.
Ste. 201
Los Angeles, CA 90036
323-634-0280; fax: 323-634-0281
kto.visitkorea.or.kr/eng.kto

Embassy of the Republic of Korea
2320 Massachusetts Ave. N.W.
Washington, D.C. 20008
202-939-5663; fax: 202-342-1597
usa.mofa.go.kr/english/am/usa/main

♦ 1586 ♦ Korea National Foundation Day
October 3

This national holiday in the Republic of Korea (South Korea), also known as **Tangun Day** and **Gaecheon-jeol**, commemorates the legendary founding of the Korean nation in 2333 B.C.E. by Tangun.

Prince Hwan-ung left heaven to rule earth from Mt. T'aebaek. In his kingdom were a bear and a tiger who wished to become humans. Hwan-ung told them that if they remained in a cave for 100 days eating nothing but mugwort and garlic, they would become like people. The tiger got bored, but the bear lasted it out and became a beautiful woman. She and Hwan-ung bore a son called Tangun Wanggom, meaning Sandalwood King. When he grew up, he built his own city at the present site of P'yongyang (now the capital of North Korea) and called his new kingdom Choson, meaning "morning freshness" or "morning calm." The book *Samguk Yusa,* written in 1289, records this story. The myth is important in that it links the Korean people with a heavenly origin.

The holiday is celebrated with ceremonies at the ancient rock altar of Tangun, on the summit of Mt. Mani on Kanghwa Island, about 25 miles west of Seoul.

CONTACTS:
Korea Tourism Organization
10 Segye-ro
Wonju-si
Gangwon-do, 220-170 Korea
82-33-738-3000
kto.visitkorea.or.kr

♦ 1587 ♦ Korean War Veterans Armistice Day, National
July 27

July 1998 marked the 45th anniversary of the signing of the treaty that ended the Korean War, which lasted from 1950 through 1953. To mark the anniversary, President Bill Clinton proclaimed July 27 a national day of recognition to commemorate the more than 37,000 U.S. service personnel who lost their lives during the war. In doing so, the president called "upon all Americans to observe this day with appropriate ceremonies and activities that honor and give thanks to our distinguished Korean War veterans."

Since that time, National Korean War Veterans Armistice Day has been celebrated each July in community memorial services throughout the country and with speeches and a wreath-laying ceremony at the Korean War Veterans Memorial on the Mall in Washington, D.C. The ceremonies in the nation's capital have attracted as many as 5,000 participants and have included such dignitaries as Ambassador Lee Tae Sik of the Republic of Korea and U.S. Vice President Dick Cheney. As directed by the president's proclamation, U.S. flags are flown at half-staff on July 27th in remembrance of the U.S. personnel who lost their lives during the 37 months of combat in Korea.

CONTACTS:
Korean War Veterans Memorial - National Park Service

900 Ohio Dr. S.W.
Washington, D.C. 20024
202-426-6841
www.nps.gov/kowa

♦ 1588 ♦ Kosovo Independence Day
February 17

Kosovo, a border state between Serbia and Albania in southeastern Europe, has witnessed a long history of strife between its predominantly Albanian population and Serbian minority. When Serbia launched a brutal campaign of ethnic cleansing on Kosovo's Albanian population, killing thousands, a mass exodus ensued. NATO intervened and ended the bloodshed. Consequently, Kosovo became a United Nations protectorate with a provisional government. On February 17, 2008, the United Nations declared Kosovo an independent sovereign state. Thousands of ethnic Albanians poured into the nation's capital city of Pristina, singing, dancing, and waving flags. Each year on February 17, the city holds parades with military, police, and fire units. This day is also marked with official speeches, fireworks, and concerts. However, in recent years a deep economic crisis has dampened Independence Day celebrations, with the Kosovo government calling for new austerity measures to help weather the stormy economic climate.

CONTACTS:
Ministry of Foreign Affairs
Ministry of Foreign Affairs Bldg.
Str."Luan Haradinaj
Prishtinë, 10000 Kosovo
381-38-200-11-087
www.mfa-ks.net/?page=2,1

♦ 1589 ♦ Kristallnacht (Crystal Night)
November 9-10

A 17-year-old Jew named Herschel Grynszpan assassinated the third secretary at the German embassy in Paris on November 7, 1938, to avenge the expulsion of his parents and 15,000 other Polish Jews to German concentration camps. His act gave the German Nazis the excuse they had been looking for to conduct a *pogrom,* or "organized massacre." Crystal Night, or **Night of the Broken Glass**, gets its name from the shattered glass that littered the streets two nights later, when the windows of Jewish-owned shops and homes were systematically smashed throughout Leipzig and other German and Austrian cities in a frenzy of destruction that resulted in the arrest and deportation of about 30,000 Jews.

Crystal Night marked the beginning of the Nazis' plan to rob the Jews of their possessions and to force them out of their homes and neighborhoods. Although the so-called "Final Solution" (to kill all European Jews) had not been publicly suggested at this point, the Nazis' actions on this night left little doubt as to what the fate of German Jews would be if war broke out. Today Jews everywhere observe the anniversary of this infamous event by holding special memorial services.

In Germany, Kristallnacht coincides with the anniversary of another famous, if very recent, event: the breaching of the Berlin Wall in 1989. The coincidence of the two observances is seen by many as symbolic of the conflicts of German history.

CONTACTS:
Simon Wiesenthal Center
9760 W. Pico Blvd.
Los Angeles, CA 90035
motlc.wiesenthal.com

United States Holocaust Memorial Museum
100 Raoul Wallenberg Pl. S.W.
Washington, D.C. 20024
202-488-0400
www.ushmm.org

♦ 1590 ♦ Ksamavani
September; first day of the waning half of Asvina

Jainism, a religion that originated in ancient India, advocates peaceful coexistence. Forgiveness is thus regarded as a sacred act and is foundational to spiritual health. In the spirit similar to that of Paryushana, a better known Jain festival, Ksamavani invites believers to ask for and receive forgiveness. It takes place in India and in Jain communities abroad during the lunar month of Asvina, which falls between September and October.

On Ksamavani, every member of the Jain community approaches family members, neighbors, colleagues, and co-workers and asks them for forgiveness for harms done. The other person can be anyone, irrespective of his or her social standing, and the offenses could be committed knowingly or unknowingly. The ritual is intended to help repair severed ties and relations. It is also a required act for anyone looking to attain the ultimate goal of nirvana, the term for the liberation of the soul.

♦ 1591 ♦ Ksan Celebrations
Friday evenings in July and August

Dances and accompanying songs are performed by the 'Ksan, or Gitxsan, Indians in a longhouse in the Indian Village in Hazelton, British Columbia, Canada. They are generally a celebration of the important things of life, such as breathing and being at one with the cosmos.

The dances are said to go back to pre-history; they were revived in 1958, and the 'Ksan dancers have since performed in New York City, San Francisco, Seattle, Kansas City, Missouri, and even Australia.

Box-shaped skin drums provide the beat for the dances. Songs, besides being about cosmic events, are sometimes songs of marriage, songs of divorce, or what are known as "happy heart songs" about almost anything. Performers must be *Git 'Ksan*, meaning "People of the 'Ksan" (named after the nearby Skeena River).

Because the homeland of the Git 'Ksan is far inland, it was overlooked by the Spaniards and Russians who explored the coast in the 1700s, and fur traders didn't stay here because the climate is too humid for good fur. As a result, the 'Ksan culture has been maintained without outside influences.

CONTACTS:
Ksan Historical Village and Museum
Box 440
Hazelton, BC V0J 1Y0 Canada
250-842-5544; fax: 250-842-6533
www.ksan.org

♦ 1592 ♦ Kuhio (Prince) Day
Monday on or near March 26

Prince Jonah Kuhio Kalanianaole (1871-1921) was a young man when the Hawaiian monarchy was overthrown in 1893. As a member of the royal family, he fought for the restoration of the monarchy and spent a year as a political prisoner. He lived abroad for a number of years after his release, but eventually returned to his native land and was elected as the first delegate to represent the Territory of Hawaii in the U.S. Congress in 1903. He was reelected and served 10 consecutive terms until his death in 1921.

Because he worked so hard to preserve the old Hawaiian customs and traditions and to take care of the dwindling number of Hawaiian natives, Prince Kuhio has been revered by his people. His birthday is commemorated on the island of Kauai, where he was born, with a week-long Prince Kuhio Festival during the latter part of March. The festival pays tribute to him by featuring such traditional Hawaiian events as outrigger canoe races, hula dancing, and performances of Hawaiian music.

CONTACTS:
Association of Hawaiian Civic Clubs
P.O. Box 1135
Honolulu, HI 96807
aohcc.org

♦ 1593 ♦ Kumbh Mela (Pitcher Fair)
Every 12 years on a date calculated by astrologers (2013, 2025, 2037...)

The Kumbh Mela involves mass immersion rituals by Hindus near the city of Allahabad (the ancient holy city of Prayag) in the north-central state of Uttar Pradesh, India. Millions of pilgrims gather to bathe at the confluence of the Ganges and Yamuna rivers, which is also where the mythical river of enlightenment, the Saraswati, flows. The bathers wash away the sins of their past lives and pray to escape the cycle of reincarnation. *Sadhus*, or holy men, carry images of deities to the river for immersion, and the most ascetic sadhus, naked except for loincloths, their faces and bodies smeared with ashes, go in procession to the waters, escorting images borne on palanquins. The Ganges is not only a sacred river but is the source of all sacred waters. The junction of the three rivers at Allahabad is called the *sangam* and is considered by some the holiest place in India.

The *mela* (fair) is thought to be the largest periodic gathering of human beings in the world; a vast tent city appears, temporary water and power lines are installed, and 10 pontoon bridges are laid across the Ganges. Movies of Hindu gods and heroes are shown from the backs of trucks, and plays recounting Hindu mythology are performed. Merchants lay out all manner of goods.

The story behind the mela is that Hindu gods and *asuras*, or demons, fought for a *kumbh*, or pitcher, carrying *amrit*, the nectar of immortality. The god who seized the kumbh stopped at Prayag, Hardwar, Nasik, and Ujjain on his way to paradise. The journey took 12 days (which are longer than earthly days), and therefore the mela follows a 12-year cycle.

A purification bathing ceremony called the *Magh Mela* is also held each spring in Allahabad. It is India's biggest yearly religious bathing festival. Although the Magh Mela attracts a million people, more or less, the Kumbh Mela dwarfs it!

See also GANGA DUSSEHRA.

CONTACTS:
Uttar Pradesh Tourism Department, Directorate of Tourism
Rajarshi Purshottam Das Tandon Paryatan Bhavan
C-13, Vipin Khand,
Gomti Nagar
Lucknow, Uttar Pradesh India
91-522-2307037; fax: 91-522-2308937
www.up-tourism.com

♦ 1594 ♦ Kunta Kinte Heritage Festival
Last weekend in September

The Kunta Kinte Heritage Festival is a two-day event held at the Anne Arundel County Fairgrounds in Crownsville, Md., that celebrates the heritage and culture of African Americans. The festival, which draws about 8,000 visitors annually, is named in honor of Kunta Kinte, a Gambian youth who was forced into slavery in the United States during the late 18th century. His descendant, Alex Haley, listened to family stories he heard from his grandmother and became inspired. He researched his family history and published it in 1976 in the worldwide bestseller *Roots*.

First held in 1987, the Kunta Kinte Heritage Festival was conceived as an opportunity both to celebrate the contributions of African Americans to American culture and to educate younger generations about their history. The festival is held on the last weekend of September each year to reflect Kinte's arrival on the slave ship *Lord Ligonier* at the Annapolis port on September 29, 1767. Music and entertainment range from African dancers to Caribbean steel drum bands, jazz bands, gospel choirs, and hip hop acts. Family activities are emphasized, including games, storytelling, instrument-making, and mask-decorating. A Family Education Tent also offers exhibits and information on a variety of education, career, and health topics as well as information on social groups and political action organizations.

♦ 1595 ♦ Ku-omboka
Usually February or March

Ku-omboka, which means "getting out of the water," is a floodtime festival observed by the Lozi people of Zambia.

When the Zambezi River begins its annual flooding of the Barotzé flood plains, thousands of boats and canoes, led by the chief on his royal barge, make their way to higher ground. When the Lozi reach their new seasonal home at Limulunga, they celebrate with singing and dancing. In July, when the floods have receded, they return to the lowlands.

◆ 1596 ◆ Kupalo Festival
June 24; Midsummer's day and night

A Ukrainian and Russian festival also called **Ivan Kupalo**, dating back to pagan days, Kupalo traditionally is celebrated by young unmarried men and women and boys and girls. The festival takes its name from the god of summer and fertility: Kupalo sleeps in the winter and each spring awakens and shakes the tree he's been under, making the seeds fall as a sign of the year's harvest. During the day and night of the celebration, boys and girls decorate a sapling tree with flowers, seeds, and fruit, call it Kupalo, and dance and sing special songs to please this image of the god.

In other events of the day, young women gather flowers to make a wreath that is tossed into a river; the spot where the wreath reaches the shore indicates the family the girl will marry into. Another custom for girls is to make an effigy of Marena, the goddess of cold, death, and winter. After singing special songs, they burn or drown the effigy to cut the goddess's power over the coming winter; winters in Ukraine are very harsh.

Young men sometimes go into the forest to look for a special fern that only blooms (according to the legend) on the night of MIDSUMMER. They take with them a special cloth, white powder, and a knife. If they find the fern and are strong enough to ward off the enticements of wood nymphs, they draw a circle with the white powder and sit and wait for the fern to bloom. When it does, they cut the blossom with the knife and put the flower in the special cloth. They must never, ever, tell anyone they have found the fern, or they will lose the luck and power it gives. The people's rationale behind this story is that it explains why some people have more talent and luck than others.

The celebrations to a greater or lesser degree are popular in both Ukraine and among Ukrainians in the United States.

◆ 1597 ◆ Kurijmoj
September-October through mid-January

Kurijmoj is a four-month CHRISTMAS celebration lasting from late September or early October through mid-January in the tropical Marshall Islands. For these Marshallese people, this is the Christmas season. December 25 itself is called *ronoul lalim raan*, "The Twenty-Fifth Day." Preparations begin in March or April, after EASTER. Kurijmoj is celebrated by people who had been living on the atoll of Enewetak in the Marshall

Islands and were forced to move from their homes to the atoll of Wujlan in 1947 so that the U.S. could test atomic bombs on their islands. They were able to return 33 years later.

People begin forming singing and dancing groups called *jepta* and practice together in early October. The jepta groups compete with each other in church at ADVENT with songs, dances, jokes, food, and a "money tree" constructed like a piñata, and again on the Sunday nearest NEW YEAR'S DAY. Each group chooses a theme which often has a biblical foundation, such as the birth of Jesus, the Gospel word, or God's plan. The "money tree" is really more like a parade float, decorated on the outside according to the group's theme and filled on the inside with gifts for the minister of the church. Nowadays the dances resemble a mixture of hula-style dances and Japanese bon dances.

Games are also played during this holiday. In *karate*, the women in a jepta play at being Japanese warriers and loot a men's jepta. In *kalbuuj*, the men of one jepta capture and "arrest" the women of another jepta and confine them to a "jail" the men have created from women's cooking and sleeping houses in the town until the women agree they are well-treated and have no reason to leave. Before the relocation, kalbuuj was a regular game, but since the people have returned to Enewetak, it has been attempted only a few times because the women were traditionally captured after returning from gathering fronds from which to make various handicrafts for the festival. After their return, the plants were not large enough to produce good fronds, so the women's pretext for leaving the town was gone.

The feast on Christmas Day is the largest of the year, with roasted pig, coconuts, rice, bread, fried doughnuts, and *bwiro*, a special treat made from breadfruit. After a short church service at 6 A.M., people divide up the food baskets they have worked hard to prepare and exchange them with each other. By 10 A.M. the jeptas are assembling at the church to perform and compete with each other, dressed up in new clothes, often wearing leis of flowers in their hair and around their necks and other accessories, which are promptly seized by spectators as well as by members of competing jeptas (though people are left wearing at least minimal clothing), who in turn adorn the jepta members with sprays of perfume. Each jepta performs up to 20 songs, so this is a day-long event.

◆ 1598 ◆ Kuta Karnival
September or October

One of the most important annual festivals in Indonesia, the nine-day Kuta Karnival has been held in Bali since 2002. Similar to the CARNIVAL and MARDI GRAS events found in other countries, the Kuta Karnival is a time when all the usual rules of behavior are set aside.

For several nights during the Kuta Karnival, the streets of Bali are crowded with people eating and drinking. Among the festivities is a parade with floats, antique cars, a Chinese dragon, and hundreds of traditional Balinese dancers dressed in colorful costumes. Because Bali has long been a popular destination for surfers from around the world, there are also a number of surfing competitions during the carnival for competitors of all age groups. There are swimming, beach volleyball, and skateboarding contests, a wide range of live music performances, cabaret shows, and children's events, including clowns, craft making, balloons, and games. Sporting events include matches sponsored by the World Boxing Association and the World Women's Tennis organizations.

♦ 1599 ♦ **Kutztown Festival**
Week including 4th of July

The **Pennsylvania Dutch Folk Festival** in Kutztown, Pennsylvania, is an annual celebration of Pennsylvania Dutch foods, crafts, and customs. Although many people identify the "Pennsylvania Dutch" with the Amish people, the Mennonites, or with the Holland Dutch, the name actually came from the Yankee pronunciation of *deutsch,* meaning "German." But the Pennsylvania Dutch are not simply transplanted Germans, either. Their folk culture is peculiarly American, and they encompass a number of national and religious groups.

The Kutztown Festival acquaints visitors with all aspects of Pennsylvania Dutch culture. There are special foods—such as apple butter, *rivvel* soup (rivvels are like dumplings), and the fruit pies which the Pennsylvania Dutch claim to have originated. Traditional artisans featured at the fair include tinsmiths, weavers, pretzel-makers, candlemakers, cigar-makers, potters, and quilters.

There are reenactments of a Pennsylvania Dutch funeral feast and demonstrations of *nipsi*—a complicated game that involves batting a piece of wood and then "bidding" the number of hops that the opposing team will require to get from where the wood landed back to home base. There is even a seminar on Pennsylvania Dutch cooking. One of the fair's most interesting figures is the *Fraktur* painter, who illuminates birth and baptismal records and book plates with bright colors and flowing scrollwork.

CONTACTS:
Kutztown Folk Festival
P.O. Box 306
Kutztown, PA 19530
888-674-6136
www.kutztownfestival.com

♦ 1600 ♦ **Kuwait Liberation Day**
February 26

After Iraqi President Saddam Hussein's troops invaded Kuwait on August 2, 1990, several countries in the United Nations formed a military coalition—including troops and equipment from the U.S., France, and Britain, and financial assistance from West Germany and Japan—to force them out. Five days later, the first U.S. forces arrived in Saudi Arabia. Operation Desert Storm began on January 17, 1991, and for five weeks, U.S. and British air forces relentlessly bombed

Baghdad. This was followed by four days of a ground war which resulted in Hussein's troops leaving Kuwait.

February 26 is a national holiday in Kuwait celebrating the end of Iraq's military presence in Kuwait.

CONTACTS:
Kuwait Embassy
2940 Tilden St. N.W.
Washington, D.C. 20008
202-966-0702
www.kuwaitembassy.us

Kuwait Cultural Office
3500 International Dr. N.W,
Washington, D.C. 20008
202-364-2100; fax: 202-363-8394
www.kuwaitculture.com

♦ 1601 ♦ **Kuwait National Day**
February 25

This national holiday commemorates Kuwait's independence from Britain in 1961. Though internally governed by the Sabah family, Britain had handled its foreign affairs since 1899.

CONTACTS:
Kuwait Cultural Office
2940 Tilden St. N.W.
Washington, D.C. 20008
202-966-0702
www.kuwaitembassy.us

♦ 1602 ♦ **Kuwana Ishitori Matsuri**
July 10-12

The Kuwana Ishitori Matsuri, or **Collect Stones Festival**, commemorates the days when many stones had to be transported by cart to build a shrine. There is a procession of floats, adorned with beautiful cloth, tapestries, and lanterns, through the town of Kuwana, Japan, on July 10, to represent the means by which the rocks were once transported. At midnight the floats all meet at the local shrine, and then each float goes back to the locale it came from. On July 11, there is a presentation of stones at the shrine, followed by a series of processions that lasts till nightime the following day. Then people assemble near the floats, watch the lighting of the float lanterns, and listen to the crashing drum music that fills the air.

♦ 1603 ♦ **Kwafie Festival**
November-January

The Kwafie Festival is celebrated in Dormaa Ahenkro, Berekum, and Nsuatre in the Brong Ahafo Region of Ghana to commemorate the bringing of fire to the area, said to have been accomplished by ancestors who emigrated to this region long ago. The celebration lasts about three days and can occur in either November, December, or January. In Dormaa

Ahenkro the festival begins with an evening torchlight procession from the palace to the house where the sacred stools are kept. The ancestors are worshipped with libations, then the procession returns to the palace. The next morning everyone gathers at the palace where the chief presides over the "laying of logs," or *Nkukuato*, in which lower-level officials bring in logs on their shoulders to give the chief. The highest ranking official chooses three logs to begin the fire, which is then used for cooking a ritual meal.

Later in the day an even grander procession carries the ancestral stools to a nearby body of water for ritual purification. Other sacred ceremonies are also performed. Then the final day of the festival is marked by joyous dancing, music, and feasts on the palace grounds.

CONTACTS:
Ghana Tourism Authority
P.O. Box GP 3106
Ghana
233-302-682601; fax: 233-302-682510
www.ghana.travel

♦ 1604 ♦ **Kwakiutl Midwinter Ceremony**
November through February

The Kwakiutl are one of the Indian tribes who inhabit the northwestern coast of the United States, stretching from northern California to southeastern Alaska. They believe that long ago, before their people even existed, powerful supernatural animals—including bears, wolves, seals, ravens, bees, owls, and killer whales—held dominion over the world. These beings endowed early humans, who were the ancestors of today's Kwakiutl, with a measure of that power.

During their winter ceremonial season, the Kwakiutl acknowledge and reaffirm their connection with the supernatural world by performing sacred dance dramas, or *tseka*. The performers dress in strips of cedar bark and wear masks elaborately designed to invoke the spirits of their supernatural forebears. The dances themselves illustrate characters and incidents from Kwakiutl mythology.

♦ 1605 ♦ **Kwanzaa**
December 26-January 1

An African-American celebration of family and black culture, Kwanzaa is thought to be observed by five million Americans and perhaps 10 million others in Africa, Canada, the Caribbean, and parts of Europe. The holiday was created in 1966 by Maulana Karenga, chairman of the Black Studies Department at California State University in Long Beach.

In Swahili, Kwanzaa means "first fruits of the harvest," and first-fruit practices common throughout Africa were adapted by Karenga for the celebration.

Each day of the seven-day festival is dedicated to one of seven principles: *umoja* (unity), *kujichagulia* (self-determination),

ujima (collective work and responsibility), *ujamaa* (cooperative economics), *nia* (purpose), *kuumba* (creativity), and *imani* (faith).

Families gather in the evenings to discuss the principle of the day, and then light a black, red, or green candle and place it in a seven-branched candleholder called a *kinara* to symbolize giving light and life to the principle. On the evening of Dec. 31, families join with other members of the community for a feast called the *karamu*. Decorations are in the red, black, and green that symbolize Africa, and both adults and children wear African garments.

Increasingly, colleges and museums are holding Kwanzaa events during some of the days. For example, in Chicago, an African Market is held on Dec. 28 by the Ujamma Family, a black self-help group. In New York City, the American Museum of Natural History celebrates Kwanzaa with an African Marketplace, poetry, folktales, and music.

CONTACTS:
African American Cultural Center
3018 W. 48th St.
Los Angeles, CA 90043
323-299-6124; fax: 323-299-0261
www.officialkwanzaawebsite.org

♦ 1606 ♦ **Kyokusui-no-En**
April 29; first Sunday in March

In ancient Japan high-ranking people entertained themselves with a custom called Kyokusui. They filled a lacquer wine cup with *sake* (rice wine) and placed it in a stream. Participants sitting on a bank downstream tried to write a five-line poem before the sake reached them. They would then snatch the cup out of the stream and drink the sake.

The poems were written on a strip of thick paper known as a *tanzaku*. Most of the poems were *waka*, which is a traditional form in Japanese poetry. It has five lines with a total of 31 syllables: five syllables in the first line, seven in the second, five in the third, and seven in the fourth and fifth lines (5-7-5-7-7).

Kyokusui-no-En is a reenactment of this ancient pastime held April 29 in Kyoto. A similar ceremony is performed in Fukuoka on the first Sunday in March.

CONTACTS:
Fukuoka Prefecture Tourist Association
7-7 Higashikoen
Hakata-ku
Fukuoka-shi, Fukuoka 812-8577 Japan
81-92-645-0019; fax: 81-92-645-0020
www.crossroadfukuoka.jp/en

♦ 1607 ♦ **Kyrgyz Independence Day**
August 31

Kyrgyzstan declared independence from the Soviet Union on August 31, 1991, along with other central Asian republics as the Soviet empire crumbled. Located along the famed Silk Road, the trade route connecting the eastern and western parts of Eurasia, the country is mostly mountainous, part of the Tien-Shan, or Celestial Mountains. Independence Day is a national public holiday in the Kyrgyz Republic.

CONTACTS:
Kyrgyz Embassy
2360 Massachusetts Ave. N.W.
Washington, D.C. 20008
202-449-9822; fax: 202-386-7550
www.kgembassy.org

L

♦ 1608 ♦ **La Paz Day**
July 16

Bolivia was officially established as an independent country on August 6, 1825, an event now commemorated each year on BOLIVIA INDEPENDENCE DAY. The capital city of La Paz, however, celebrates its own Independence Day on July 16. The holiday commemorates the date in 1809 when Pedro Domingo Murillo led a revolt of *mestizos,* or those of mixed European and South American heritage, against the Spanish authorities. Murillo's uprising was the second against the Spanish in the space of a few months. Murillo declared Upper Peru, as Bolivia as then known, to be an independent state, but 16 years of struggle were necessary to make his declaration a reality. July 16 is now a municipal holiday in La Paz, and the day is celebrated with parades, concerts, fireworks, and dances.

CONTACTS:
Embassy of the Plurinational State of Bolivia
3014 Massachusetts Ave. N.W.
Washington, D.C. 20008
202-483-4410; fax: 202-328-3712
www.bolivia-usa.org

♦ 1609 ♦ **Laba Festival**
Eighth day of the 12th lunar month

The Laba Festival falls just ahead of the Chinese New Year and is profoundly linked to ancient Chinese culture and Buddhism. Although exact explanations surrounding the origin of the event vary, many believe that the celebration goes back over 3,000 years, occurring under different names during the Xia, Shang, and Zhou dynasties. The festival may derive from an ancient sacrificial ritual performed to appease ancestors, ward off ill health, and secure a good harvest. During the 10th-century Song dynasty, the event commemorated the day Buddha attained enlightenment. *Laba,* or rice porridge, is central to the festival, although its recipe and ingredients vary from region to region. The porridge is usually prepared with rice, beans, nuts, and dried fruit, and may be eaten sweetened or salted. At some Buddhist temples, monks prepare the porridge as an offering to the Buddha and then distribute it among the people. Another common practice is to pickle garlic cloves on this day. The garlic is then cured

for three weeks and eaten with dumplings for the Chinese New Year.

CONTACTS:
Bejing Foreign Affairs Office
No.2, Zhengyi Rd.
Dongcheng District, Beijing 100744 China
fax: 8610-6519-2775
www.ebeijing.gov.cn

♦ 1610 ♦ **Labor Day**
First Monday in September

Although workers' holidays had been observed since the days of the medieval trade guilds, laborers in the United States didn't have a holiday of their own until 1882. This was the year when Peter J. McGuire, a New York City carpenter and labor union leader, and Matthew Maguire, a machinist from Paterson, N.J., suggested to the Central Labor Union of New York that a celebration be held in honor of the American worker. Some 10,000 New Yorkers paraded in Union Square, New York, on September 5 of that year—a date specifically chosen by McGuire to fill the long gap between the FOURTH OF JULY and THANKSGIVING.

The first Labor Day observance was confined to New York City, but the idea of setting aside a day to honor workers spread quickly, and by 1895 Labor Day events were taking place across the nation. Oregon, in 1887, was the first state to make it a legal holiday, and in 1894 President Grover Cleveland signed a bill making it a national holiday. The holiday's association with trade unions has declined, but it remains important as the day that marks the end of the summer season for schoolchildren and as an opportunity for friends and families to get together for picnics and sporting events.

Labour Day is celebrated in England and Europe on May 1. In Australia, where it is called EIGHT HOUR DAY, it is celebrated at different times in different states, and commemorates the struggle for a shorter working day. In Antigua and Barbuda, Labor Day is observed on May 6; in the Bahamas, it's June 7; in Bermuda, Sept. 2; in Jamaica, May 23; and in Trinidad and Tobago, June 19. Labor Day is observed on the first Monday in September throughout the United States, in Canada, and in Puerto Rico. In Japan, November 23 is **Labor Thanksgiv-**

ing Day, or **Kinro Kansha-no-Hi**, a legal holiday set aside to honor working people and productivity.

CONTACTS:
U.S. Department of Labor
200 Constitution Ave. N.W
Washington, D.C. 20210
202-693-4676 or 866-487-2365; fax: 202-693-4674
www.dol.gov

◆ 1611 ◆ LaborFest
July 5 through July 31

LaborFest is a cultural and arts festival centered in San Francisco, Calif., that advances workers' rights and commemorates the achievements of the labor movement of the early 20th century. The festival comprises a three-week program of free and paid-admission events, including book and poetry readings, issue-centered discussion forums, an international film festival, music and theater performances, and historical tours and presentations. Held annually since 1994, LaborFest promotes solidarity among workers and includes performers, films, and presenters from around the world.

The festival begins each year on July 5th, the anniversary of "Bloody Thursday," when two union workers were killed by police while supporting a strike by longshoremen and maritime workers on the San Francisco docks in 1934. The deaths on that day catalyzed workers throughout the city to walk off their jobs in what became known as the General Strike of 1934. At LaborFest, boat, bus, walking, and bike tours visit historic sites related to the strike and the history of organized labor in San Francisco. On July 31, the last night of the festival, a closing party is held, featuring a music concert celebrating working-class life.

◆ 1612 ◆ Lac Long Quan Festival
Six days in late March-early April

This six-day festival, held in the Vietnamese village of Binh Minh, honors the legendary king Lac Long Quan. According to tradition his wife, Au Co, "hatched" (in the sense of laying an egg) 100 people, who ended up populating what is now the Ha Tay Province.

During the festival people celebrate their ancestors with offerings of fruit and flowers paraded by young women accompanied by folk musicians, then elders bestow blessings on the offerings. Although Lac Long Quan and Au Co are the focus of the proceedings, Buddha is also included and considered a special guest.

CONTACTS:
Vietnam National Administration of Tourism
80 Quan Su Str.
Hoan Kiem
Vietnam
84-4-3942-3760; fax: 84-4-3942-4115
www.vietnamtourism.com

◆ 1613 ◆ Ladouvane
December 31; June 24

Ladouvane, or the **Singing to Rings**, is a Bulgarian fertility ritual. Traditionally, young girls drop their rings, together with oats and barley (symbols of fertility), into a cauldron of spring water. The rings are tied with a red thread to a bunch of ivy, crane's bill, basil, or some other perennial plant, and the cauldron is left out overnight. Ritual dances are performed around the cauldron and the girls' fortunes are told.

In western Bulgaria, the Central Balkan Range, and along the Danube River, Ladouvane is observed on NEW YEAR'S EVE. In the rest of the country, it is observed on MIDSUMMER DAY.

◆ 1614 ◆ Lady Day
March 25

Lady Day is the name in England for the Feast of the ANNUNCIATION. This day was originally called **Our Lady Day**, a name that applied to three other days relating to the Virgin Mary: the IMMACULATE CONCEPTION (December 8), the NATIVITY OF THE BLESSED VIRGIN MARY (September 8), and the ASSUMPTION OF THE BLESSED VIRGIN MARY (August 15). It commemorates the archangel Gabriel's announcement to Mary that she would give birth to Jesus, and is often referred to simply as The Annunciation. Lady Day is one of the QUARTER DAYS in England and Ireland when rents are paid and tenants change houses. In France it is called **Nôtre Dame de Mars** ("Our Lady of March").

◆ 1615 ◆ Lady Day among Samis
March 25

In the Sami region of Finland, villages such as Inari and Enontekio celebrate a festival on LADY DAY that usually occurs within the EASTER season. Sami people travel from remote homesteads to participate in a special church service, which is typically succeeded by such outdoor activities as lasso-throwing and skijoring, a sport in which skiers are pulled by reindeer over a frozen lake. Because the festival draws everyone together, March 25 is also a popular time for weddings.

◆ 1616 ◆ Lag ba-Omer
18th day of the Jewish month of Iyyar, or the 33rd day of the 50 days that separate Passover and Shavuot

The name of this Jewish holiday means "thirty-three omer," an *omer* being a sheaf of barley or wheat. In the biblical book of Leviticus, the people were commanded by Jehovah to make an offering of a sheaf of barley on each of the 50 days between PASSOVER and SHAVUOT. After the evening service, the number of the day was solemnly announced, and in time this ceremony came to be known as "the counting of the omer."

Why the 33rd day of this period was singled out may have something to do with an ancient pagan festival of the forest that was celebrated at this same time. Another story claims that the plague that had been decimating the students of Rabbi Akiba in the second century suddenly and miraculously stopped on this day. In any case, the mid-harvest festival of Lag ba-Omer represents a break in the otherwise solemn season between Passover and Shavuot.

♦ 1617 ♦ Lajkonik
Between May 21 and June 24; first Thursday after Corpus Christi

The most popular folk festival in Krakow, Poland, Lajkonik (or the **Horse Festival**) has lost touch with its medieval roots, but is believed to commemorate the horseman who carried the news of the Tartar defeat during the 13th-century Tartar invasions. A group of 18 costumed people gathers in the courtyard of the Norbertine Monastery in a suburb of Krakow. They include a standard-bearer in the traditional dress of a Polish nobleman, a small band of musicians, and a bearded horseman in oriental costume riding a richly draped but rather small wooden hobby-horse. This is the Lajkonik, originally called the Horse or the "Zwierzyniec Horse," named for the town where the monastery is located, and now the unofficial symbol of Krakow.

After performing a ceremonial dance for the vicar and the nuns, the procession leaves the monastery and moves in the direction of the city. The horseman collects money from the crowds lining the streets, tapping each donor with his rod to bring them good luck; they then join the procession. Eventually the parade ends up in the market square for the climax of the ritual. The city officials greet the horseman in front of the town hall. He dances for the assembled dignitaries and receives from them a sack of money and a glass of wine, which he consumes after toasting the well-being of the city.

The festival was first sponsored by the guild that furnished wood to Krakow and the salt mines. In the past the actors came from the Boatman congregation who, since the Middle Ages, have floated timber down the Vistula River to Krakow. Now they tend to be Krakow factory workers.

♦ 1618 ♦ Lakshmi Puja
September-October; Hindu month of Asvina

The annual festival in honor of the Hindu goddess Lakshmi is held in the autumn, when Hindus of all castes ask for her blessings. Lights shine from every house, and no one sleeps during the celebrations.

Lakshmi is traditionally associated with wealth, prosperity, and good luck. In later Hindu literature, she appears as the dutiful wife of the god Vishnu and is typically portrayed massaging his feet while he rests on the cosmic serpent, Shesa. She remains a popular Hindu goddess to this day in India, where she is a special patron of shopkeepers.

See also TIHAR.

♦ 1619 ♦ Lammas
August 1

Possibly one of the four great pagan festivals of Britain—the LUGNASADH—Lammas was known as the **Gule of August** in the Middle Ages. It celebrated the harvest, and was the forerunner of the THANKSGIVING celebrated in the United States and Canada. In medieval England, loaves made from the first ripe grain were blessed in the church on this day—the word *lammas* being a short form of "loaf mass." Lammas Day is similar in original intent to the Jewish Feast of Weeks, also called SHAVUOT or PENTECOST, which came at the end of the PASSOVER grain harvest. A 15th-century suggestion was that the name derived from "lamb" and "mass," and was the time when a feudal tribute of lambs was paid.

In the Scottish Highlands, people used to sprinkle their cows and the floors of their houses with menstrual blood, which they believed was especially potent against evil on this day. It was also one of the QUARTER DAYS in Scotland, when tenants brought in the first new grain to their landlords.

Along with CANDLEMAS, WALPURGIS NIGHT, and HALLOWEEN, Lammas is an important day in Neopagan calendars.

A phrase used from the 16th to the 19th century, "at Latter Lammas Day," meant "never.".

♦ 1620 ♦ Lammas Fair
July

Although it is no longer the important trade fair it was at one time, the Lammas Fair is still held for three days every July in Exeter, England. The opening ceremonies, which date back to medieval times, include a procession from the guildhall by two sergeants carrying a blue-and-white pole decorated with flowers and ribbons, from which a large stuffed white glove is suspended. At noon, the sergeants march to the four ancient gates of the city and proclaim the fair open before returning to the guildhall, where the mayor announces the event.

The custom of displaying a glove to open the fair dates back to ancient Saxon times, when permission to hold a market or fair had to be obtained first from a local judge and then ratified by the king, who sent one of his gloves as a token of his approval. It was reinstituted in 1939, after having been discontinued for a number of years.

CONTACTS:
Exeter City Council
Civic Center Paris St.
Exeter, Devon EX1 1JN United Kingdom
44-13-9227-7888; fax: 44-13-9226-5265
www.exeter.gov.uk

♦ 1621 ♦ Lamp Nights (Kandil Geceleri, Candle Feasts)
Five nights on the Muslim calendar: the 12th of Rabi al-Awwal; first of Rajab; 27th of Rajab; 15th of Shaban; and 27th of Ramadan

Turkish Muslims keep mosques lit all night five times a year in order to commemorate five religious festivals associated with events in the life of the prophet Muhammad: Mawli- dal-Nabi, the Birthday of the Prophet Muhammad (12th of Rabi al-Awwal); the Conception of the Prophet Muhammad (1st of Rajab); Laylat-al-Miraj, the Prophet Muhammad's Night Journey and Ascent (27th of Rajab); Laylat al- Ba- ra'ah, the Night of Forgiveness (15th of Shaban); and Laylat al-Qadr, the Night of Power (27th of Ramadan). As a whole, these commemorative evenings are known as **Kandil Geceleri**. Kandil means "candle," and the name translates as **Candle Feasts** or Lamp Nights.

On these special nights, Turkish Muslims believe that a special holiness prevails. They attend prayer services at the mosque and engage in such devotional activities as reciting poems or singing songs about the Prophet Muhammad. Ring-shaped sesame-seed biscuits known as *Kandil Simidi* are associated with Lamp Nights, as are *Lokma,* fritters drenched in sweet syrup. In past generations, young people paid visits to their elders on Lamp Nights as a sign of respect, though in recent times a phone call is considered by many to be sufficient.

The custom of Lamp Nights dates to the 16th century, when Sultan Selim II ordered that lamps or candles be placed in mosque minarets to announce the five special holy days. On Lamp Nights in modern times, mosques are brightly illuminated with electric lights, including garlands of bulbs looped between minarets. Some strict Muslims dislike the displays, believing that they imitate the Orthodox Christian practice of displaying lights at Christmastime to mark the birth of Christ.

♦ 1622 ♦ Land Diving
April and May

On Pentecost Island in Vanuatu, a nation consisting of 80 islands in the southwest Pacific that has been independent since 1980, land diving, or **Nagol**, is a centuries-old fertility ritual that is the precursor of what is known in the United States as "bungee jumping." Tree branches, trunks, and vines from the forest are used to create a tower—about 85 feet tall—while the yams are being harvested in April and May.

Facing a test of resolve and courage, island men and boys ascend the tower with liana vines they have personally selected for strength and accurate length. One end of each vine is tied to the ankle and the other to the tower. Before jumping, the diver gives voice to his innermost thoughts, so that the entire crowd may hear what could be his last words, should he not survive the fall. After the diver leaps off the tower, the vines stretch nearly to the ground and the diver ducks his head out of the way and lets his shoulders touch the land— just barely—to symbolically fertilize the earth for the next year's yam crop. During the ritual, the entire village assembles under the tower to dance, sing, and encourage the divers.

Although land diving originated as an agricultural ritual, today it is also a tourist attraction and source of income for villagers in the southern part of the island, who charge a high entry fee for visitors wishing to take photographs or shoot videos.

♦ 1623 ♦ Landing of d'Iberville
Last weekend in April

This event is a commemoration of the landing in 1699 of Pierre LeMoyne d'Iberville at a spot on Biloxi Bay that is now Ocean Springs, Miss. The arrival of d'Iberville and 200 colonists established the Louisiana Colony for King Louis XIV of France; the territory stretched from the Appalachians to the Rocky Mountains and from Canada to the Gulf of Mexico. D'Iberville built Fort Maurepas here, the first significant structure erected by Europeans on the Gulf Coast.

A replica of the fort is the backdrop for the reenactment of the landing. This pageant boasts a costumed cast representing both the notables of d'Iberville's fleet as well as the welcoming Biloxi Indians. The part of d'Iberville is always played by a celebrity, usually from the political world. However, in 1984, Col. Stuart A. Roosa, an Apollo 14 astronaut, played the explorer. In the reenactment, d'Iberville with his officers debarks and wades ashore, plants a cross in the sand, and claims the land for Louis XIV. The Indians, at first wary, invite the French to their village to smoke a peace pipe. The reenactment was first staged in 1939.

The celebration begins on Friday night with a covered dish supper at the civic center. On Saturday night, there is a formal-dress historic ball and pageant, with the presentation of d'Iberville, his officers, and the Cassette Girls. These were young orphan women who had been taught by Catholic nuns in Paris; they made the long trip to the Gulf Coast to become the brides of the men settled in the territory. They were called Cassette Girls because of the cases each carried that contained their trousseaus. The reenactment takes place on Sunday and is followed by a grand parade. There are also exhibits and street and food fairs.

CONTACTS:
Ocean Springs Chamber of Commerce - Main Street - Tourism Bureau
1000 Washington Ave.
Ocean Springs, MS 39564
228-875-4424; fax: 228-875-0332
www.oceanspringschamber.com

♦ 1624 ♦ Landsgemeinde
Last Sunday of April

Landsgemeinde is an open-air meeting to conduct cantonal business, held once a year in Appenzell, in the canton of Appenzell Inner-Rhoden in Switzerland. At the meeting, citizens vote on representatives for cantonal offices and on budget and tax proposals. Voting is by raised hands.

The assembly is a tradition that dates back to the very early days of the Swiss state. Women may wear richly embroidered national costumes, and men swords. Other districts in central and eastern Switzerland also have these assemblies, each with distinct customs. In Stans, for example, the blowing of a horn signals the time to walk to the meeting place outside the town; the horn is a reminder of the ancient call to battle.

Landsgemeinde has echos in the town meetings of the United States (*see* TOWN MEETING DAY).

♦ 1625 ♦ Landshut Wedding
Late June to late July, every four years (2017, 2021, 2025 . . .)

This pageant in Landshut, Bavaria, Germany, recreates a lavish 15th-century wedding—that of Duke George the Rich of Bavaria and Princess Hedwig from Poland, which took place in 1475. There were 10,000 guests, and records state that they ate 333 oxen, 275 fat pigs, 40 calves, and 12,000 geese.

Today the festivities are spread over three weeks, with the wedding reenactments on weekends—a play and dances on Saturdays; the historical wedding procession, followed by a concert, on Sundays. During the week, historical dances are performed, and some 2,000 residents dressed as medieval burghers roam the streets. There are also jesters parading, armored knights on horseback, and wandering minstrels.

CONTACTS:
Die Forderer e.V. Landshut
Spiegelgasse 208
Landshut, 84028 Germany
49-871-229-18; fax: 49-871-2746-53
www.landshuter-hochzeit.de

♦ 1626 ♦ Lanimer Festival
Week in early June

The people of Lanark, Scotland, dedicate an entire week to inspecting and celebrating the boundary stones that enclose the territory gifted to them by King David I of Scotland in the 12th century. This week-long event, known as the Lanimer Festival, features public decorations, a parade of civic officials, marching bands, and a series of tableaux. Because people carrying birch branches march in the procession, it is also known as **The Birks**.

A standard-bearer, selected each year by the town council, starts off the second, midday procession. The procession passes by each of the boundary stones, stopping occasionally for sports and horse races. The days' activities close with the town clerk's pronouncement that the boundaries remain in good condition, and a 900-year-old bell rings in celebration.

CONTACTS:
Lanimer Festival-Secretary
The Howe
12 Leslie Rd.
Glasgow, G41 4PY United Kingdom
44-141-423-6408
www.lanarklanimers.co.uk

♦ 1627 ♦ Lantern Festival (Yuan Hsiao Chieh)
January-February; 15th day of first lunar month, fourth day of first lunar month in Tibet

The Lantern Festival is a festival of lights that ends the LUNAR NEW YEAR, or Chinese New Year, celebrations and marks the first full moon of the new lunar year.

In China, it's traditional for merchants to hang paper lanterns outside their shops for several days before the full-moon day.

On the night of the festival, the streets are bright with both lanterns and streamers, and people go out in throngs to see the displays. The most popular lanterns are cut-outs of running horses that revolve with the heat of the candles that light them. Other customs include eating round, stuffed dumplings and solving "lantern riddles"—riddles that are written on pieces of paper and stuck to the lanterns. In many areas, children parade with lanterns of all shapes and sizes. It's also thought to be a good night for young women to find husbands. In Penang, Malaysia, single women in their best dresses stroll along the city's promenade, and some parade in decorated cars followed by musicians.

Tibetan Buddhists celebrate the day as MONLAM, or Prayer Festival, and in Lhasa, the butter sculptures of the monks are famous (*see* BUTTER SCULPTURE FESTIVAL). In China's Gansu Province, the Lhabuleng Monastery is the site of sculptured butter flowers made by the lamas and hung in front of the main scripture hall. On the day before the full moon, a dance is performed by about 30 masked lamas to the music of drums, horns, and cymbals. The protagonists are the God of Death and his concubines; they dance with others who are dressed as skeletons, horned stags, and yaks.

In 1990, the Taipei Lantern Festival was first held in Taiwan's capital city. It's held at the Chiang Kai-shek Memorial Hall and features high-tech lanterns with mechanical animation, dry-ice "smoke," and laser beams. In recent years, theme lanterns were modeled after the Chinese zodiacal animals for those years. Sculptor Yuyu Yang has produced elaborate structures for the festival, including a dragon that was 40 feet high with a skin of a stainless-steel grid and 1,200 interior light bulbs that shone through to make it look like a gigantic hand-made paper lantern. Laser beams shot from the dragon's eyes, and red-colored smoke spewed from the mouth. Another year, he created three 33-foot-high goats made of acrylic tubes with colored lights shining from the inside.

The festival also offers musical and folk art performances, a procession of religious and folk floats, and troupes of performers entertaining with martial arts demonstrations, stilt-walking, and acrobatics.

In Hong Kong, anyone who has had a son during the year brings a lantern to the Ancestral Hall, where the men gather for a meal.

The Lantern Festival is supposed to have originated with the emperors of China's Han dynasty (206 B.C.E.-221 C.E.), who paid tribute to the universe on that night. Because the ceremony was held in the evening, lanterns were used to illuminate the palace. The Han rulers imposed a year-round curfew on their subjects, but on this night the curfew was lifted, and the people, carrying their own simple lanterns, went forth to view the fancy lanterns of the palace.

Another legend holds that the festival originated because a maid of honor (named Yuan Xiao, also the name of the sweet dumpling of this day) in the emperor's household longed to see her parents during the days of the Spring Festival. The resourceful Dongfang Shuo decided to help her. He spread the rumor that the god of fire was going to burn down the city of Chang-an. The city was thrown into a panic. Dongfang Shuo, summoned by the emperor, advised him to have everyone leave the palace and also to order that lanterns be hung in every street and every building. In this way, the god of fire would think the city was already burning. The emperor followed the advice, and Yuan Xiao took the opportunity to see her family. There have been lanterns ever since.

CONTACTS:
Taipei Economic and Cultural Representative Office in the US
4201 Wisconsin Ave. N.W.
Washington, D.C. 20016
202-895-1800
www.roc-taiwan.org

Asia New Zealand Foundation
Level 16
Fujitsu Tower, 141 The Terr.
Wellington, 6011 New Zealand
64-4-471-2320; fax: 64-4-471-2330
asianz.org.nz

♦ 1628 ♦ **Lantern Festival (Korea)**
Eighth day of the fourth lunar month

In Korea, Buddha's birthday is observed on the evening of the eighth day of the fourth lunar month and is known as *Deungseog* or "lantern evening." A couple of days beforehand, some households hang a lantern-holder, a pole decorated with a pheasant's tail feather (or branch of pine) and colorful strips of silk. Then, on the evening of the eighth, they hang one lantern for each person in the family and light them. Tradition holds that the more brilliant the household can make its lantern display, the luckier it will be.

Although many types of lanterns are used, some of the most popular resemble a tortoise, duck, ship, drum, lotus flower, heron, carp, watermelon, or sun and moon.

Monks began the custom of hanging lanterns for Buddha's birthday during the middle of the Silla dynasty (seventh-eighth century). As Confucianism took stronger hold during the Yi dynasty (1392-1910), it fell into decline. Later in the 20th century many Koreans revived the tradition, though nowadays it is not as widespread. Still, temples all over South Korea hold celebrations in honor of the Buddha on this day with elaborate lantern displays, particularly in Seoul, where there are festivals at major temples with special religious services, other spiritual activities, games, crafts, and a huge lantern parade.

See also VESAK.

CONTACTS:
Korea Tourism Organization
10 Segye-ro
Wonju-si
Gangwon-do, 220-170 Korea
82-33-738-3000
kto.visitkorea.or.kr

♦ 1629 ♦ **Lantern Night at Bryn Mawr College**
Mid-November

Traditions help build a feeling of community at Bryn Mawr, a women's college near Philadelphia, Pennsylvania, where the induction ceremony of Lantern Night has welcomed freshwomen since the late 1880s. The ceremony takes place in the courtyard of the Cloisters, a quadrangle with a pond at the center. The first-year students process into the courtyard, and the sophomores place candlelit lanterns behind each one. Upperclass women sing a hymn in ancient Greek to the goddess of wisdom, Athena, and freshwomen respond in kind. The ceremony in the Cloisters is followed by a stepsing, in which the students of all classes gather together for fellowship and the singing of lighthearted songs outside of Taylor Hall, on the administration building's steps.

CONTACTS:
Bryn Mawr College
101 N. Merion Ave.
Bryn Mawr, PA 19010
610-526-5000
www.brynmawr.edu

♦ 1630 ♦ **Lanterns Festival**
End of Islamic month of Ramadan

A trader known as Daddy Maggay introduced the custom of parading with lanterns in Freetown, Sierra Leone, during the 1930s. The original lanterns were simple hand-held paper boxes, lit from within and mounted on sticks. They were carried through the streets of Freetown in celebration of the 26th day of RAMADAN, also known as the **Day of Light** or **Lai-Lai-Tu-Gadri**, when the Qur'an was sent to earth by Allah (*see* LAYLAT AL-QADR).

As the years passed, the celebration—and the lanterns—grew larger. Heavy boots, originally worn as protection from the crowds, came to be used to produce drum-like rhythmical beats on the paved streets since some Muslims discourage using drums. Maggay's group was called *bobo*, the name for their distinctive beat. Neighborhood rivalries, based on competition in lantern building, often erupted in violence.

By the 1950s the Young Men's Muslim Association had taken over the festival in hopes of reducing the violence through better organization. The lanterns—which by that time were elaborate float-like structures illuminated from within and drawn by eight-man teams or motor vehicles—were divided into three categories for judging: Group A for ships; Group B for animals and people; and Group C for miscellaneous secular subjects. Prizes were awarded to the top three winners in each group, based on creativity and building technique.

◆ 1631 ◆ Larentalia
December 23

In ancient Rome, the *lares* were the beneficient spirits of household and family. Along with the *penates* (the gods of the storeroom) and the *manes* (spirits of the dead), they were worshipped privately within the home. Eventually they came to be identified with the spirits of the deceased. Each household had its own *lar*, to whom a prayer was addressed every morning and for whom special offerings were made at family festivals.

During the Larentalia, observed on December 23, offerings were made to the dead, especially at the shrine of Acca Larentia, the nurse of Romulus and Remus, the legendary founders of Rome. A sacrifice was offered on the spot where Acca Larentia was said to have disappeared.

See also COMPITALIA; FERALIA; PARENTALIA.

◆ 1632 ◆ Lasseters Camel Cup
Early July

What began in 1971 as a friendly camel race between two Alice Springs Lions Club members has grown into a major Australian event that generates more than $250,000 annually for charity. Camels thrive in Alice Springs, which has one of the driest and harshest climates in Australia, and therefore it is not surprising that camel races play the same role there that horse races do in other, less arid parts of the country (*see* HOBART CUP DAY; MELBOURNE CUP DAY).

Today the Camel Cup takes place at Blatherskite Park in Alice Springs and is only one of several camel-oriented events, which are accompanied by the eating and beer-drinking that are a hallmark of so many Australian festivals. Other events include polo on camels, helicopter rides, rickshaw races, the Miss Camel Cup competition, and fireworks.

CONTACTS:
Alice Springs Town Council
93 Todd St.
Alice Springs, NT 0871 Australia
61-8-8950-0500; fax: 61-8-8953-0558
www.alicesprings.nt.gov.au

◆ 1633 ◆ Last Great Day
October; Tishri 22

A one-day festival observed by the United Church of God, the Last Great Day immediately follows the Feast of Tabernacles in the seventh month of Tishri, the Hebrew calendar. The Feast of Tabernacles and the Last Great Day are Holy Days that represent for believers the final steps of God's plan for the fate of the world and his people. As prescribed by the United Church of God, which is a Christian sect, believers observe all seven of the Holy Days. For the Last Great Day, they are invited to meditate on the eternal life that awaits God's loyal followers.

The Last Great Day is described in the Book of Revelation as a scene proceeding a 1,000-year-long reign of Christ. Standing before a "great white throne and him who was seated on it," the dead are told whether they have been ordained a life in heaven or if they will suffer eternal damnation in the Lake of Fire. The day has a corollary in the Old Testament's Book of Leviticus, which contains a description of a final day of a series of feasts during which people continuously present God their offerings.

CONTACTS:
United Church of God
P.O. Box 541027
Cincinnati, OH 45254
513-576-9796; fax: 513-576-9795
www.ucg.org

◆ 1634 ◆ Latin Festival (Feriae Latinae)
April

The Latin Festival was held in Rome for more than a thousand years, making it one of the longest-lived Roman festivals. The original **Feriae Latinae** was held by a group of ancient Latin tribes, who lived a simple pastoral life and worshiped Jupiter on the Alban Mount, about 13 miles outside Rome. All wars came to a halt for the observance. There was a sacrifice of a young white cow who had never been yoked as well as a ritual pouring of milk rather than wine, since the grape had not yet been introduced into Italy. After the sacrifice to Jupiter, the meat of the cow was used for a communal meal. A curious sight accompanied the ritual—little dolls or puppets made to look like people, called *oscilla*, bobbed from tree branches. Some have suggested these may have been symbolic of human sacrifice in earlier times, but others assert they were probably a kind of good-luck emblem.

By the period of the later Republic, the Romans had taken over the ceremony and they commemorated the early Latin peoples, most of whose settlements had by then disappeared. The Latin Festival was normally held in April, before military activities for the year got underway. A temple to Jupiter was built on the site in the sixth century B.C.E. and Romans would gather at the temple Jupiter to participate in the traditional libation and animal sacrifice. Afterward, feasting and games went on for two days.

◆ 1635 ◆ Latina, Fiesta
October

The Fiesta Latina takes place on one Saturday every October in Asheville, N.C. A celebration of Latino culture and community, it features Latino music, dance, food, and arts and crafts. It also provides opportunities for local businesses, organizations, and public-health agencies to reach the local Latino community with informational displays and services.

The festival began in 1999, when an Asheville museum sponsored a textile exhibition by Latin-American artists. Officials at the Asheville Latin Americans for Advancement Society decided to use the exhibit as a launch pad for a broader event to reflect many aspects of Latino culture. The event is now affiliated with the Young Men's Institute Cultural Center, a long-standing African-American socio-cultural institution in Asheville.

CONTACTS:
YMI Cultural Center
39 S. Market St.
Asheville, NC 28801
828-257-4540
www.ymiculturalcenter.org

◆ 1636 ◆ Latter-Day Saints, Founding of the Church of
April 6

April 6, 1830, is the day on which Joseph Smith formally established the Church of Jesus Christ of the Latter-Day Saints (also known as Mormons) in Fayette, New York. Three years later the anniversary of the Church's founding was celebrated for the first time, with a meeting of about 80 people on the Big Blue River in Jackson County, Missouri. After that, there were no "birthday" celebrations until 1837, when a general conference was held to conduct church business and to observe the anniversary. Eventually the idea of holding an annual conference became an established custom, and it was always scheduled to encompass the April 6 founding date.

CONTACTS:
The Church of Jesus Christ of Latter-Day Saints-Church Music and Cultural Arts Office
50 N.E. Temple St
20th Fl.
Salt Lake City, UT 84150
801-240-3959
www.lds.org

◆ 1637 ◆ Latvia Independence Day
November 18

Independence Day marks Latvia's declaration of independence from German and Russian occupation on November 18, 1918. The country remained independent until World War II, when it was absorbed by the Soviet Union. Like the other Baltic republics, Latvia proclaimed its independence from Soviet Russia in 1991, on August 21.

CONTACTS:
Embassy of Latvia
2306 Massachusetts Ave. N.W.
Washington, D.C. 20008
202-328-2840; fax: 202-328-2860
www.mfa.gov.lv/en

◆ 1638 ◆ Law Day
May 1

It was the American Bar Association that persuaded President Dwight D. Eisenhower in 1958 to set aside a special day to commemorate the role of law in the United States and to remind people of the contrast between democratic government under the law and the tyranny of Communism. But it wasn't until 1961 that a joint resolution of Congress designated May 1 as Law Day, and President John F. Kennedy asked Americans to display the flag and observe the occasion with appropriate programs—typically mock trials, courthouse tours, special radio and television programs, library exhibits, and essay contests. Most Law Day exercises today are sponsored by the American Bar Association in cooperation with state and local bar associations.

The first of May was previously known as LOYALTY DAY, another attempt to play up the virtues of democracy and to cast Communism in a negative light. It is no coincidence that in the former U.S.S.R., MAY DAY was the great holiday for massive military reviews and other demonstrations of armed power.

CONTACTS:
American Bar Association
321 N. Clark St.
Chicago, IL 60654
312-988-5000 or 800-285-2221
www.americanbar.org

◆ 1639 ◆ Laylat al-Bara'ah (Shab-Barat)
Eve of the 15th day of the Islamic month of Shaban

This holy day is known as Laylat al-Bara'ah ("Night of Forgiveness") in Arabic and SHAB-BARAT in Persian. Followers observe the date by holding a vigil throughout the night. They congregate at the local mosque to pray, read the Qur'an, and set off fireworks. Like other Islamic traditions, the festival reflects the common elements as well as the differences between the religion's Shi'ite and Sunni sects.

Sunnis regard the holiday exclusively as a night in which one's fate for the upcoming year is determined. According to Sunni lore, every individual's destiny is recorded on a corresponding leaf on the Tree of Life. When Allah shakes this tree on the 15th of Shaban, he fixes the next year's course of events.

Simultaneous to observing these destiny traditions of Laylat al-Bara'ah, Shi'ites also celebrate the BIRTHDAY OF THE TWELFTH IMAM, a figure of paramount importance in the Shi'ite faith who is expected to redeem the world upon his second coming.

◆ 1640 ◆ Laylat al-Miraj
27th day of the Islamic month of Rajab

Laylat al-Miraj commemorates the ascent of the Prophet Muhammad into heaven. One night during the 10th year of his prophecy, the angel Gabriel woke Muhammad and traveled with him to Jerusalem on the winged horse, Burak. There he prayed at the site of the Temple of Solomon with the Prophets Abraham, Moses, Jesus, and others. Then, carried by Gabriel, he rose to heaven from the rock of the Temple Mount, where the Dome of the Rock sanctuary now stands. Allah instructed him regarding the five daily prayers that all Muslims must observe. Muslims today celebrate the evening of the 27th day of Rajab with special prayers. This day is also known as the **Night Journey**, or the **Ascent**.

♦ 1641 ♦ Laylat al-Qadr
One of the last 10 days of Islamic month of Ramadan

Laylat al-Qadr commemorates the night in 610 during which Allah revealed the entire Qur'an (Muslim holy book) to Muhammad. It was then that the angel Gabriel first spoke to him, and was thus the beginning of his mission. These revelations continued throughout the remainder of his life. Children begin studying the Qur'an when they are very young, and they celebrate when they've read all 114 chapters for the first time. Many adults try to memorize the entire Qur'an. The common belief that this day occurred on the 26th or 27th of Ramadan has no Islamic base. It seems to have originated in Manicheism where the death of Mani is celebrated on the 27th of the fasting month. This day is also known as the **Night of Power** or **Night of Destiny**.

See also LANTERNS FESTIVAL.

♦ 1642 ♦ Laytown Strand Races
September

A carnival atmosphere pervades the Laytown Strand Races, a unique horse race run on a beach track by the Irish Sea in Laytown, County Meath, Ireland. Horses, owners, trainers, and bookmakers mingle with horse-lovers, racing fans, party-goers, sun worshippers, and food and beverage vendors on the beach as the tide recedes and the races begin.

CONTACTS:
Laytown Races
9 Palace St.
Drogheda, County Louth Ireland
353-41-9842111
www.laytownstrandraces.ie

♦ 1643 ♦ Lazarus Saturday
Between March 27 and April 30; Saturday before Palm Sunday

In Russia and in all Eastern Orthodox churches, the Saturday before PALM SUNDAY (or Willow Sunday) is set aside to honor Lazarus, whom Jesus raised from the dead. Pussywillows are blessed at the evening service in the Russian Orthodox Church, and the branches are distributed to the worshippers, who take them home and display them above their icons. It was an ancient folk custom for people to beat their children with willow branches—not so much to punish them as to ensure that they would grow up tall and resilient like the willow tree.

On this day in Greece, Romania, and the former Yugoslavia, one custom is for groups of children to carry willow branches from house to house and sing songs and act out the story

of Jesus raising Lazarus from the dead. In return, they receive gifts of fruit and candy. They believe the resurrection of Lazarus is symbolic of the renewal of spring, which is why the *Lazarouvane* (the celebration of ST. LAZARUS'S DAY in Bulgaria) focuses on fertility and marriage.

CONTACTS:
Orthodox Church in America
P.O. Box 675
Syosset, NY 11791
516-922-0550; fax: 516-922-0954
oca.org

♦ 1644 ♦ Le Mans Motor Race
June

The motor racing circuit in the city of Le Mans, capital of the Sarthe department of France, has been the scene of important races since 1914, although it wasn't until 1923 that the first 24-hour sports car race for which the course is now famous was held. Over the years the **Le Mans 24-Hour Grand Prix d'Endurance** has had a significant impact on the development of sports cars for racing, resulting in some prototype sports cars that are not far behind Formula I racing cars in terms of power and speed. The original course was rough and dusty, with a lap distance of just under 11 miles. Eventually the road surface was improved, the corners were eased, and the lap distance was reduced to just over eight miles. Part of the course is still a French highway, now flanked by permanent concrete stands for spectators and the pits, where refueling and repairs are done. A serious accident at Le Mans in 1955, in which a French driver and 85 spectators died, led to a number of course improvements.

The all-night racing at Le Mans is a favorite spectacle for motor racing fans. One of the major attractions is the opportunity to watch what goes on in the pits. Although most Grand Prix races can now be run without refueling or tire changing, the highly efficient work of the teams' mechanics still plays an important part in long-duration races like the one at Le Mans.

♦ 1645 ♦ Leaders of the Bulgarian National Revival Day (National Enlighteners Day)
November 1

Bulgaria's native culture is rich and ancient, but at one time, it seemed in danger of being lost forever. Bulgaria was under the rule of the Ottoman Empire for almost five centuries, and the Empire's Turkish authorities suppressed any expression of unity or national pride by the Bulgarian people. Bulgaria had poor schools and no other institutions in place to protect and preserve its heritage. Under such conditions, the country's traditional culture could not thrive.

That situation underwent a dramatic reversal during the period known as the Bulgarian National Revival. This cultural renaissance began in the 18th century and is divided into three stages: the early period, including the 18th century and the early part of the 19th century; the middle period, lasting from roughly the 1820s until the Crimean War, which ended in 1856; and the late period, dating from the Crimean War until Bulgaria's liberation from the Ottoman Empire in 1878, as a result of the Russo-Turkish War.

During the Revival, a number of well-educated Bulgarians made a conscious effort to awaken feelings of pride and unity among their countrymen, in part because they felt that such feelings were necessary if Bulgaria were ever to regain its freedom from Ottoman rule. They did this by working to develop Bulgarian literature that would call to mind past glories and hopes for a better future. They worked to establish modern schools, and within a few decades, 1,500 primary schools were in operation throughout the country. This, in turn, allowed more young Bulgarians to further their educations at the great universities of Europe and Russia. Within a short while, the country had a well-educated elite, which took control of the arts and newspapers in Bulgaria.

National pride and unity were greatly reinforced by these efforts, which are credited with paving the way to successful opposition to Ottoman rule. On November 1, Bulgaria celebrates a national holiday to honor and remember those visionaries who did so much to establish a sense of national pride and to lay the foundation for Bulgarian liberation. The holiday was declared official in 1922, but was suspended in 1945 after Bulgaria came under Communist rule, as part of the former Soviet Union. After the dissolution of the Soviet Union, celebration was resumed in 1990 and made official again in 1995.

Across Bulgaria, Leaders of the Bulgarian National Revival Day (sometimes called **National Enlighteners Day**) is an occasion to pay tribute to all those committed to culture and education. It is traditionally a day to give awards to outstanding teachers, actors, and artists of all sorts. Since the 1930s, it has been a tradition in cities and towns throughout the country to hold parades honoring students and teachers. In the capital city of Sofia, the parade progresses beneath huge portraits of those leaders who nourished Bulgaria's cultural rebirth.

CONTACTS:
Bulgarian Embassy
1621 22nd St. N.W.
Dimitar Peshev Plaza
Washington, D.C. 20008
202-387-0174 or 202-299-0273; fax: 202-234-7973
www.bulgaria-embassy.org

♦ 1646 ♦ **Leap Year Day**
February 29

The earth actually takes longer than 365 days to complete its trip around the sun—five hours, 48 minutes, and 45 seconds longer, to be precise. To accommodate this discrepancy, an extra day is added to the Gregorian calendar at the end of February every four years (but not in "century" years unless evenly divisible by 400, e.g., 1600 and 2000, but not 1700). The year in which this occurs is called Leap Year, probably because the English courts did not always recognize February 29, and the date was often "leaped over" in the records.

There's an old tradition that women could propose marriage to men during Leap Year. The men had to pay a forfeit if they refused. It is for this reason that February 29 is sometimes referred to as **Ladies' Day** or **Bachelors' Day**. Leap Year Day is also **St. Oswald's Day,** named after the 10th-century archbishop of York, who died on February 29, 992.

See also Sadie Hawkins Day.

CONTACTS:
U.S. Naval Observatory
Naval Meteorology and Oceanography Command
1100 Balch Blvd.
Stennis Space Ctr.
www.usno.navy.mil

♦ 1647 ♦ **Lebanon National Day**
November 22

Also known as **Independence Day**, this national holiday commemorates Lebanon's independence from France on this day in 1943.

CONTACTS:
Embassy of Lebanon
2560 28th St. N.W.
Washington, D.C. 20008
202-939-6300; fax: 202-939-6324
www.lebanonembassyus.org

♦ 1648 ♦ **Lebanon Resistance and Liberation Day**
May 25

A recently established tradition in Lebanon, this day celebrates the end of Israel's 22-year-long military occupation, which occurred in 2000. That year Israel completed its withdrawal from the country's southern region. Immediately after, the cabinet under Lebanese prime minister Salim al-Hoss declared the public holiday on May 25.

Conferences, rallies, and speeches commemorating the anniversary are commonplace, particularly in southern Lebanon, the region most directly affected by Israel's intervention. In 2000, tens of thousands rejoiced over the retreat of the Israeli defense forces by swarming around public locales in the former war zone. Many displaced individuals were able to return after spending years away from their home communities. The anniversary's political significance has endured for the Lebanese, particularly in view of the renewed combat between Israel and Hezbollah paramilitary forces in 2006.

Resistance and Liberation Day can also be an occasion to turn public attention to the country's ongoing reconstruction efforts. Such was the case for the 2007 anniversary, when Lebanese leaders marked the day by announcing the reopening of the Zahrani bridge, an important road link destroyed in a July 2006 Israeli air strike.

CONTACTS:
Embassy of Lebanon
2560 28th St. N.W.

Washington, D.C. 20008
202-939-6300; fax: 202-939-6324
www.lebanonembassyus.org

◆ 1649 ◆ Lee (Ann) Birthday
February 29

Ann Lee (1736-1784) was a leader in the religious movement known as the Shakers. She left England in 1774 to establish Shaker communities throughout New England and New York state, as well as in Kentucky, Ohio, and Indiana. "Mother Ann," as she was known to her followers, believed that sexual desire was the original sin and people must be celibate in order to be closer to God. Shaker communities were known for their inventions (which include the flat broom and the clothespin), their architecture, and their furniture design as well as their commitment to celibacy, communal ownership of property, prayer, and separation from the world. They were pioneers in scientific stock breeding, crop rotation, and food preservation. The only active Shaker community that remains today is at Sabbathday Lake in Poland Spring, Maine.

Since there are less than a dozen Shakers alive, Ann Lee's birthday is no longer celebrated on a large scale, but there are numerous events commemorating the history of the Shaker movement that take place at several sites and museums devoted to Shakerism.

CONTACTS:
United Society of Shakers
707 Shaker Rd.
New Gloucester, ME 04260 United States
207-926-4597
www.maineshakers.com

◆ 1650 ◆ Lee (Robert E.) Day
Third Monday in January

The Confederate General Robert Edward Lee was born on January 19, 1807. He was in charge of the military and naval forces of Virginia during the Civil War, building a reputation as a brilliant military strategist and a man who inspired great loyalty among his troops. By the time he was appointed general-in-chief of all the Confederate armies, the South's defeat was imminent. Lee's subsequent surrender to General Ulysses S. Grant at the Appomattox Court House in 1865 marked the end of the war (*see* Appomattox Day).

In 1889 Georgia became the first state to make Lee's birthday a legal holiday. Other states observing Lee's birthday each year include Alabama, Arkansas, Kentucky, and Mississippi. Texas observes Lee's birthday as **Confederate Heroes Day**.

CONTACTS:
Arlington House, The Robert E. Lee Memorial
George Washington Memorial Pkwy
c/o Turkey Run Park
McLean, VA 22101
703-235-1530; fax: 703-235-1546
www.nps.gov

◆ 1651 ◆ Leeds International Film Festival
November

The Leeds International Film Festival (LIFF) is one of the most important public film events in the United Kingdom. Boasting a diverse panorama of works that reach beyond the realm of mainstream cinema, the LIFF was founded in 1987 and maintains a reputation for innovative programming. The festival includes features, documentaries, animated shorts, retrospectives, cult and fantasy movies, as well as locally produced short films. The festival is also open to movies in the music video and the short dance film genres. Each of the categories features cash prizes for the winning films. In addition, LIFF offers the World Animation Award and the Louis Le Prince International Short Film Award, which qualify entrants at the Academy Awards. The Leeds festival routinely attracts top names among filmmakers, actors, and other special guests. The festival is held in Leeds, a city in West Yorkshire, England, and is presented by the Leeds City Council. Films are screened at various venues throughout the city, from grand cinema halls to clubs.

CONTACTS:
Leeds International Film Festival
Town Hall
The Headrow
Leeds, LS1 3AD United Kingdom
44-113-2478-398
www.leedsfilm.com

◆ 1652 ◆ Lei Day
May 1

This is a celebration of Hawaii's state symbol of friendship. In 1928 Mrs. John T. Warren came up with the slogan, "Lei Day is May Day," and the holiday has been held there ever since. The events of the day include state-wide lei competitions. Leis are garlands made of flower blossoms, seeds, leaves, ferns, and pods. There is the crowning of a Lei Queen in Honolulu, and assorted exhibits and hula performances. The queen's coronation is accompanied by chanting and the blowing of conch shells.

On the day after the celebration, leis from the state-wide competitions are ceremoniously placed on the graves of Hawaii's royalty at the Royal Mausoleum in Nuuanu Valley.

◆ 1653 ◆ Leiden Day
October 3

In 1573 the Dutch city of Leiden (or Leyden) was besieged by the Spaniards. Thousands were dying from disease and hunger, but when a group of desperate citizens pleaded with the Burgomaster to surrender, he replied that he had sworn to keep the city safe and that it was better to die of starvation than shame. His stubbornness heartened the people, and finally the river dikes were cut so that the Dutch army could sail in over the flooded fields and save the city. A statue of the heroic Burgomaster, Adrian van der Werff, was later erected in Leiden's Church of Saint Pancras.

According to legend, the first person to emerge from the besieged city on October 3 was a young orphan boy. In the deserted Spanish camp, he discovered a huge pot of stew that was still hot. He summoned the townspeople, who enjoyed their first hot meal in several months. Known as *Hutspot met Klapstuk*, the mixture of meat and vegetables is still served on this day, along with bread and herring.

♦ 1654 ♦ Leif Erikson Day
October 9

The Viking explorer known as Leif the Lucky or Leif Erikson (because he was the son of Eric the Red) sailed westward from Greenland somewhere around the year 1000 and discovered a place he named Vinland after the wild grapes that grew there. No one really knows where Vinland was, but some historians believe that Erikson landed in North America 488 years before Columbus sailed into the New World. The only evidence that this may have happened are a few Viking relics found in Rhode Island, Minnesota, and Ontario. In 1960, the site of a Norse settlement was discovered at L'Anse aux Meadows, at the northern tip of Newfoundland. The site dates from about the year 1000, but it has not been definitively linked to Leif Erikson's explorations.

Because the date and place of Erikson's "discovery" of North America were uncertain, members of the Leif Erikson Association arbitrarily chose October 9 to commemorate this event—perhaps because the first organized group of Norwegian emigrants landed in America on October 9, 1825. But it wasn't until 1964 that President Lyndon B. Johnson proclaimed this as Leif Erikson Day.

States with large Norwegian-American populations—such as Washington, Minnesota, Wisconsin, and New York—often hold observances on this day, as do members of the Sons of Norway, the Leif Erikson Society, and other Norwegian-American organizations. October 9 is a commemorative day in Iceland and Norway as well.

CONTACTS:
Leif Erikson Lodge
2245 N.W. 57th St.
Seattle, WA 98107
206-783-1274; fax: 206-783-1726
leiferiksonlodge.com

♦ 1655 ♦ Lemon Festival
Late January through mid-February

Since the 1930s the town of Menton, France, has celebrated its annual Lemon Festival for three weeks beginning in late January or February. Festival organizers expect about 300,000 people to visit the town during the festival in order to enjoy the parades—featuring larger-than-life-sized figurines made entirely of citrus fruit, a specialty of the region—and other activities. Performances of local folk music and dance also take place during the festival. In addition, visitors may stroll by scenes from famous stories reconstructed out of citrus fruits and displayed in one of the city's parks. The Lemon Festival

coincides with another important local event, the Orchid Festival. Those who attend this exhibit of orchid specimens may also sample regional foods and view the work of local artists.

CONTACTS:
Office De Tourisme De Menton
8, Ave. Boyer BP
Menton cedex, 239 06506 France
33-4-9241-7676
www.tourisme-menton.fr

♦ 1656 ♦ Lemuralia
May 9, 11, 13

In ancient Rome the *lemures* were the ghosts of the family's dead, who were considered to be troublesome and therefore had to be exorcized on a regular basis. The lemures were generally equated with larvae or evil spirits, although some people believed that the lemures included the *lares*, or "good spirits," as well (*see* Larentalia).

The Lemuralia or **Lemuria** was a yearly festival held on the ninth, 11th and 13th of May to get rid of the lemures. Supposedly introduced by Romulus, the legendary founder of Rome, after he killed his twin brother Remus, this festival was originally called the **Remuria**. Participants walked barefoot, cleansed their hands three times, and threw black beans behind them nine times to appease the spirits of the dead. On the third day of the festival, a merchants' festival was held to ensure a prosperous year for business. The period during which the Lemuralia was held—the entire month of May—was considered to be an unlucky time for marriages.

♦ 1657 ♦ Lent
Begins between February 4 and March 10 in West and between February 15 and March 21 in East; 40-day period, beginning on Ash Wednesday in the West and on the Monday seven weeks before Easter in the East; ends on Easter eve, Holy Saturday

Self-denial during a period of intense religious devotion has been a long-standing tradition in both the Eastern and Western churches. In the early days, Christians prepared for Easter with a strict fast only from Good Friday until Easter morning. It wasn't until the ninth century that the Lenten season, called the **Great Lent** in the East to differentiate it from the Advent fast called Little Lent, was fixed at 40 days (with Sundays omitted)—perhaps reflecting the biblical importance attached to the number 40: Moses had gone without food for 40 days on Mt. Sinai, the children of Israel had wandered for 40 years with little sustenance, Elijah had fasted 40 days, and so did Jesus, between his baptism and the beginning of his ministry.

In the Western church further extensions led to a no-longer-existing "pre-Lent" season, with its Sundays called Septuagesima (roughly 70 days before Easter), Sexagesima (60), and Quinquagesima (50)—all preceding the first Sunday of Lent, Quadragesima (40).

The first day of Orthodox Lent is called Clean Monday.

For centuries the Lenten season has been observed with certain periods of strict fasting, and with abstinence from meat, and in the East, also from dairy products, wine, and olive oil, as well as giving up something—a favorite food or other worldly pleasure—for the 40 days of Lent. Celebrations such as Carnival and Mardi Gras offered Christians their last opportunities to indulge before the rigorous Lenten restrictions.

See also Ash Wednesday; Cheese Sunday; Mothering Sunday; Shrove Monday; Shrove Tuesday.

♦ 1658 ♦ Leonhardiritt (St. Leonard's Ride)
November 6 or nearest weekend

Also called **Leonhardifahrt**, this is a celebration of St. Leonhard, the patron saint of horses and cattle, observed in various towns of Bavaria, Germany. Traditionally, processions of elaborately harnessed horses draw decorated wagons to the local church. Some people also bring their cattle to be blessed. A contest of whip-cracking often follows the procession. Among the towns where Leonard's Ride is held are Bad Tölz, Rottenbuch, Bad Füssing, Waldkirchen, and Murnau. November 6 is the name-day of the saint and the traditional day of the procession, but some towns now hold their rides on a weekend near that date.

♦ 1659 ♦ Lesotho Independence Day
October 4

Formerly Basutoland, the Kingdom of Lesotho was formally granted its independence from Great Britain on this day in 1966. It had been a British colony since the 1860s.

Before the flag-changing ceremonies at midnight to symbolize Lesotho's new autonomy, a colorful procession took place as King Moshoeshoe II (b. 1938) paraded in full regalia leading 100 chiefs into the capital city of Maseru.

CONTACTS:
High Commission Of The Kingdom Of Lesotho
1820-130 Albert St.
Ottawa, ON K1P 5G4 Canada
613-234-0770; fax: 613-234-5665
www.lesothocanada.gov.ls

♦ 1660 ♦ Lewis and Clark Festival
June

This five-day festival commemorates the Lewis and Clark expedition, an early exploration of the vast wilderness of what is now the northwestern United States. The expedition was sponsored by the U.S. government and led by President Thomas Jefferson's secretary Meriwether Lewis (1774-1809) and U.S. Army officer William Clark (1770-1838).

Lewis and Clark covered a total of about 8,000 miles. Starting near St. Louis in May 1804, they journeyed up the Missouri River, across the Rocky Mountains, and along the Columbia and other rivers to the Pacific coast. They returned to St. Louis in September 1806 with maps of their route and the surrounding regions; specimens and descriptions of plant, animal, and mineral resources; and information about the native peoples of the West. The success of the expedition enabled the United States to claim the Oregon region, which included what are now the states of Oregon, Washington, and Idaho.

The Lewis and Clark Festival in Great Falls, Montana, celebrates the expedition's stay there in 1805. Giant Springs Her-itage State Park is the site of living history reenactments and encampments, where visitors can experience what daily life was like in the early 19th century, watch interpretive demon-strations, and eat typical expedition fare. The festival also features lectures at the Lewis and Clark Interpretive Center, exhibits, seminars, tours of historic sites, float trips, nature hikes, and a treasure hunt.

CONTACTS:
Lewis & Clark Foundation
1101 15th St. N.
PO Box 398
Great Falls, MT 59401
406-791-7732
www.lewisandclarkfoundation.org

♦ 1661 ♦ Li Ch'un
February 4 or 5

Li Ch'un is Chinese for "spring is here." This is one of 24 days in the Chinese calendar marking a change of season. The celebration of spring in some places has involved a procession of local dignitaries, dancers, singers, and musicians. Some of these carried a platform holding an ox and his driver made of paper. Each year the Chinese almanac, the *T'ung Shu*, gives specific instructions about the most auspicious colors to use in creating the ox and driver.

People also traditionally mount a post with feathers outside their homes. The sight of feathers floating in the breeze means that spring has officially arrived.

♦ 1662 ♦ Liberalia
March 17

Liber and Libera were ancient Roman fertility deities, worshipped along with Ceres. The triad of Ceres, Liber, and Libera was identified with the Greek deities Demeter, Dionysus, and Persephone. At the festival held in honor of Liber and Libera on March 17, young Roman boys who had come of age wore the *toga virilis* for the first time. In the ancient Italian town of Lavinium, a whole month was consecrated to Liber. The various rituals carried out during this time were designed to ensure the growth of newly planted seeds.

See also Cerealia.

♦ 1663 ♦ Liberia Armed Forces Day
February 11

On this day, Liberians honor the soldiers of the country's armed forces. Festivities often include regiment parades and a public address from the Liberian president or the commander-in-chief. Since the day's first observance in 1957, the holiday has evoked mixed memories for Liberians, as the army has been linked with the chaos that plagued the country at the end of the 20th century.

Unlike many of its African neighbors, Liberia steered clear of military coups during the relatively peaceful years under President W. V. S. Tubman (1944–71). However, the army did help carry out the repressive policies of the dictators who succeeded Tubman. Between 1989 and 2003, during two consecutive civil wars, Liberians suffered numerous atrocities by soldiers, as well as by rebel fighters.

For a short period following the war, this holiday received no fanfare because the country's implosion left Liberians with no army to honor. In 2007, however, the defense ministry introduced a newly restructured contingent, which paraded through the main streets of the capital city, Monrovia, before hundreds of attendees.

CONTACTS:
Embassy Of Liberia
5201 16th St. N.W.
Washington, D.C. 20011
202-723-0437; fax: 202-723-0436
www.liberianembassyus.org

♦ 1664 ♦ **Liberia Flag Day**
August 24

The Liberian flag bears a striking resemblance to the American flag, a visual reminder of the historically close ties between this West African country and the United States. Eleven horizontal stripes—six red and five white—represent the signers of the Liberian Declaration of Independence, while the single white star that sits in the flag's upper left corner signifies Liberia's former position as the sole free black state in Africa.

Flag Day, a patriotic day paying homage to Liberia's national emblem, is an official public holiday. Citizens and public buildings display their flags, and parades often feature schoolchildren and military units. The holiday was first observed in an 1847 convention, when the founding fathers approved the flag's design along with establishing the new republic.

CONTACTS:
Embassy Of Liberia
5201 16th St. N.W.
Washington, D.C. 20011
202-723-0437; fax: 202-723-0436
www.liberianembassyus.org

♦ 1665 ♦ **Liberia Independence Day**
July 26

This especially important Liberian holiday is celebrated with a parade, a party for the diplomatic corps in Monrovia, and a grand ball in the evening. Similar events are held throughout the country. The day commemorates the signing of the Declaration of Independence in 1847 by the various settlements of the country, establishing the first independent black republic in Africa.

The nation that is now Liberia was settled in the early 1800s by freed American slaves under the auspices of the American Colonization Society. The capital city, Monrovia, is named after U.S. President James Monroe. The first settlers arrived on Providence Island in 1822. Other settlers followed, and they united in 1838. After independence, elections were held, and Joseph Jenkins Roberts was elected the first president in January 1848.

CONTACTS:
Liberian Embassy
5201 16th St. N.W.
Washington, D.C. 20011
202-723-0437; fax: 202-723-0436
www.liberianembassyus.org

♦ 1666 ♦ **Liberia National Redemption Day**
April 12

On April 12, 1980, 13 soldiers stormed Liberia's executive mansion, killing President William R. Tolbert and 26 other government leaders. Shortly after the massacre, 13 cabinet members were publicly executed. The soldiers were led by Samuel Kanyon Doe, a member of the ethnic Krahn tribe who immediately declared himself president of Liberia and set up a military regime called the People's Redemption Council. He also declared that in the coming years April 12 would be National Redemption Day.

Doe associated his regime with *redemption* because he believed that as a member of Liberia's long-repressed indigenous majority, he would lead a restructuring of the country's power base. His rule, however, was not the welcome change that many anticipated. Instead, his regime was marred by corruption and severe political abuses from April 1980 until his death on September 9, 1990.

For Doe's political opponents, National Redemption Day was a time to memorialize the many individuals who were killed during that tragic month in 1980. Today, many Liberians observe the anniversary by remembering the slain.

CONTACTS:
Embassy Of Liberia
5201 16th St. N.W.
Washington, D.C. 20011
202-723-0437; fax: 202-723-0436
www.liberianembassyus.org

♦ 1667 ♦ **Liberia National Unification Day**
May 14

This annual observance draws attention to one of the most pressing issues facing Liberians throughout their history: the animosity between the Americo-Liberian elite and the indigenous majority. Under the leadership of President William V. S. Tubman, who led from 1944 to 1971, the divide between these two groups was diminished. In his inaugural address, Tubman introduced his National Unification Policy, which featured among other things an extension of the vote to women and to the country's indigenous people. The official anniversary, sometimes referred to as **Unification and Integration Day**, emerged as a means to draw support for the policy.

The day reminds Liberians to remember what they hold in common and not to dwell on how they diverge. While the friction between Americo-Liberians and indigenous has abated throughout history, a general focus on national unity is still an urgent current issue for this oft-divided country, devastated by two consecutive civil wars between 1989 and 2003.

CONTACTS:
Embassy Of Liberia
5201 16th St. N.W.
Washington, D.C. 20011
202-723-0437; fax: 202-723-0436
www.liberianembassyus.org

♦ 1668 ♦ Liberian Fast and Prayer Day
2nd Friday in April

Liberians reserve Fast and Prayer Day for collective reflection and self-discipline. The observance of the day is not mandatory since the constitution provides for freedom of religion. Nonetheless, many believe this national observance is in keeping with the spiritual convictions of Liberia's founding fathers. As President W. V. S. Tubman stated in an address commemorating a national fast, the country was established on a "deep and well-founded belief and trust in God through prayer."

The day historically has been observed by Christians, as Liberian Muslims more commonly dedicate the Islamic month of Ramadan to fasting and prayer. While officially the observance spans only 24 hours, the time of fasting and prayer can extend to an entire week. In addition, certain circumstances may prompt a spiritual leader to call for a special week of prayer separate from the one that is held annually. In February 1966, under President Tubman's direction, the country prayed in accordance with the dying wishes of Reverend J. D. K. Baker of the Protestant Episcopal Church. His hope, according to Tubman, was for citizens to pray "for the peace, security and safety of the Liberian State and for the peace and brotherhood of mankind throughout the world.".

♦ 1669 ♦ Liberian President W. V. S. Tubman's Birthday
November 29

The influence of William V. S. Tubman (1895-1971), Liberia's president for 27 continuous years, was so great that his birthday was established an official holiday while he still held office. The national legislature declared the holiday in response to a citizens' appeal made in 1952. Decades after his death, Liberians still celebrate the national hero's birthday, also known as **Goodwill Day**.

Tubman was a popular leader for a number of reasons. Born in Harper, he was the first president not to claim allegiance to the elite power center of Monrovia, a fact that endeared him to the country's indigenous majority. His Unification Policy extended the vote to women and to indigenous people. Perhaps his greatest political achievement, however, was his Open Door policy, which attracted much-needed foreign investment to Liberia.

The most elaborate festivities for Tubman's birthday have always taken place in his native city, Harper, where activities may extend for three days. One Tubman Birthday tradition that has endured for decades is the Queen Rally. This beauty pageant also doubles as a fund-raiser, in which contestants representing civic groups compete for money prizes, which are awarded for public works projects.

♦ 1670 ♦ Libya Day of Arafa
Ninth day of Dhu al-Hijjah, the 12th month of the Islamic lunar calendar

The Islamic nation of Libya recognizes the Day of Arafa as a public holiday. **Waqf al Arafa** (translated as Day of Arafa, Day of Arafat, or **Day of Repentance**) is an Islamic religious observation marked by prayer, fasting, and penitence. One of the five pillars of Islam is the requirement that every able-bodied Muslim make a pilgrimage to Mecca, a city in Saudi Arabia, at least once during his or her lifetime if financially possible. This journey is known as Hajj, the annual PILGRIMAGE TO MECCA that occurs during Dhu-al-Hijjah, the 12th and last month of the Islamic calendar.

The ninth day of Dhu-al-Hijjah is known as the Day of Arafa. On this holy day those conducting Hajj gather on the Plain of Arafat and nearby Mount Arafat—a granite hill east of Mecca also referred to as the Mountain of Mercy—where the prophet Muhammad delivered his final sermon. The pilgrims' experience on the Plain of Arafat is often cited as the height of the annual journey to Mecca and this time spent in prayer and reflection is that which validates a Muslim's participation in Hajj. Many Libyan Muslims and those in other countries fast, perform acts of devotion, and pray for forgiveness of their sins on this day. The observation of Day of Arafa begins at dawn and ceases at sunset. The following day marks the major Muslim festival ID-AL-ADHA.

♦ 1671 ♦ Libya Declaration of Jamahiriya Day (Declaration of the People's Authority Day)
March 2

On March 2, Libyans celebrate Declaration of Jamahiriya Day, also known as **Declaration of the People's Authority Day**. In observance of this public holiday, schools and businesses are closed throughout the country. Citizens attend speeches and rallies in honor of the founding of the Jamahiri-ya, which has no official translation. The term, which is derived from the Arab word for republic, roughly means "state of the masses," "people's authority," or "people's power."

The term Jamahiriya was created by Libyan leader Colonel Muammar Qaddafi, who defined it as a "state run by the people without a government" and characterized it as a political advancement for all humankind. This political philosophy is sometimes termed the Third Universal Theory and is an amalgamation of socialism and Islam. On September 1, 1969, Qaddafi staged a coup d'état, overthrowing the Libyan monarchy and establishing a socialist, Islamic republic. Upon taking power he changed the name of the country to the Socialist People's Libyan Arab Jamahiriya. In theory, under Jamahiriya, Libya would be ruled by the people themselves through local councils. In practice, however, Libya is governed by an authoritarian state.

CONTACTS:
The Libyan Ministry of Tourism
Bab Albahr
Near Tripoli Seaport
Libya
218-21-336-4621; fax: 218-21-336-4605
www.temehu.com

♦ 1672 ♦ **Libya Revolution Day**
September 1

This national holiday commemorates the revolution, led by Col. Muammar Qaddafi (b. 1938), that ousted King Idris I (Muhammad Idris el-Senussi, 1890-1983), who had ruled since 1952, and established a republic known as the People's Arab Jamahiriyah on this day in 1969.

CONTACTS:
Embassy Of Libya
2600 Virginia Ave. N.W.
Ste. 300
Washington, D.C. 20037
202-944-9601; fax: 202-944-9606
dev.bogatest.com

♦ 1673 ♦ **Lighting of the National Christmas Tree**
December

On a selected night in December, the president of the United States lights the national Christmas tree at the northern end of the Ellipse in Washington, D.C., to the accompaniment of orchestral and choral music. The lighting ceremony marks the beginning of the two-week **Pageant of Peace**, a huge holiday celebration in the nation's capital that includes seasonal music, caroling, 50 state Christmas trees, and a burning YULE log.

CONTACTS:
President's Park
White House Liaison
1100 Ohio Dr. S.W.
Washington, D.C. 20242 United States

202-208-1631 or 800-877-8339; fax: 202-208-1643
www.nps.gov/whho/index.htm

♦ 1674 ♦ **Lights, Festival of**
Mid-November to January

The biggest event of the year in Niagara Falls, New York, is its Festival of Lights, which is held for about eight weeks during the CHRISTMAS holiday season. The falls themselves are illuminated, as are displays throughout the town featuring more than 200 life-sized storybook characters in dozens of animated scenes. There is an arts and crafts show, a toy train collectors' show, a boat show, a doll show, and magic shows. There are also numerous sports tournaments. Musical events include performances by internationally known singers, gospel choirs, bell choirs, steel drum bands, jazz groups, and blues bands. During the festival more than half a million lights adorn the city, which was the site of the world's first commercial hydroelectric plant in 1895.

♦ 1675 ♦ **Lights, Festival of (Ganden Ngamcho)**
November-December; 25th day of 10th Tibetan lunar month

This Tibetan Buddhist festival commemorates the birth and death of Tsongkhapa (1357-1419), a saintly scholar, teacher, and reformer of the monasteries, who enforced strict monastic rules. In 1408 he instituted the Great Prayer, a New Year rededication of Tibet to Buddhism; it was celebrated without interruption until 1959 when the Chinese invaded Tibet. He formulated a doctrine that became the basis of the Gelug (meaning "virtuous") sect of Buddhism. It became the predominant sect of Tibet, and Tsongkhapa's successors became the DALAI LAMAS, the rulers of Tibet.

During the festival, thousands of butter lamps (dishes of liquid clarified butter called *ghee,* with wicks floating in them) are lit on the roofs and window sills of homes and on temple altars. At this time people seek spiritual merit by visiting the temples.

CONTACTS:
Kopan Monastery
Kapan Village
Ward 5
Nepal
977-1-4821 268
kopanmonastery.com

♦ 1676 ♦ **Lilac Festival**
Ten days in May

The annual Lilac Festival in Rochester, New York, celebrates the abundance of lilacs in the city's Highland Park. Horticulturalist John Dunbar began the garden with 20 varieties of the flowering shrub in 1892. The festival began six years later as a one-day event for people to enjoy the recently adorned park. Frederick Law Olmstead, who also designed Central Park in New York City, finished the development of Highland Park.

Today this is a ten-day festival during which visitors admire more than 1,200 lilac bushes of more than 500 varieties. In addition to viewing the flowers, visitors to the Lilac Festival can also sample a wide array of international foods and enjoy concerts, art shows, and other free festival events.

CONTACTS:
The Springut Group Inc
26 S. Goodman St.
Ste. A
Rochester, NY 14607
585-473-4482 or 800-677-7282; fax: 585-473-7645
www.rochesterevents.com

◆ 1677 ◆ Lily Festival (Festa dei Giglio)
Begins June 22

The week-long Lily Festival in Nola, Napoli, Italy, honors San Paolino (St. Paulinus), the town's patron saint. Legend has it that the festival began in the fourth century as a "welcome home" celebration when Paolino, who had placed himself in slavery to release a local widow's son, returned from Africa. Eight tradesmen representing the town greeted him by strewing flowers at his feet.

Eventually the eight tradesmen were represented by sticks covered in lilies, and over the years the lily sticks (*gigli* in Italian) grew longer and more ornate. Today they are from 75 feet to nearly 100 feet high. Since they weigh about 50 tons, it takes 40 men to carry each one. After a traditional blessing is given, the crowd throws flowers into the air and begins a costumed procession that meanders through the narrow streets of the town, led by a boat carrying a statue of San Paolino and featuring the eight huge gigli, each of which is surrounded by its own symphony orchestra.

See also GIGLIO FEAST.

CONTACTS:
Italian Government Tourist Board
686 Park Ave.
New York, NY 10065
212-245-5618; fax: 212-586-9249
www.italiantourism.com

◆ 1678 ◆ Lim Festival
January-February; 13th day of first lunar month

The Lim Festival is an alternating-song contest, held in the commune of Lung Giang, about 18 miles from Hanoi, in the Bac Ninh Province of Vietnam. This is a courtship event, in which girls and boys of different villages carry on a singing courtship dialogue. The singers take part in what is a vocal contest with set rules; one melody, for example, can only be used for two verses of the song, and therefore there is considerable improvising. The storylines of the songs tell of daily events. Young men and women practice them while they are at work in the rice fields or fishing. There is also a weaving competition for young women.

Other Lim Festivals takes place in other villages in the province with processions and games such as human chess and wrestling.

◆ 1679 ◆ Limassol Wine Festival
Early September

This event is an annual celebration of the wine of Cyprus, lasting nearly two weeks and held in the Municipal Gardens of Limassol, the center of the wine-making industry. Wineries there compete to create the most original and decorative booths, and every evening pour out from barrels free samples of their wine. People sitting at picnic tables may watch exhibits of traditional wine pressing. There are also musical, theatrical, and dance performances.

◆ 1680 ◆ Lincoln's (Abraham) Birthday
February 12

Abraham Lincoln, the 16th president of the United States, also called the Great Emancipator, the Rail Splitter, and Honest Abe, was born on Feb. 12, 1809. President throughout the Civil War, he is known for his struggle to preserve the union, his issuance of the EMANCIPATION PROCLAMATION, and his assassination less than two weeks after the Confederate surrender at Appomattox Court House in 1865 (*see* APPOMATTOX DAY).

A wreath-laying ceremony and reading of the Gettysburg Address at the Lincoln Memorial in Washington D.C., are traditional on Feb. 12. Because the Republican party reveres Lincoln as its first president, Republicans commonly hold Lincoln Day fundraising dinners, as the Democrats hold JACKSON Day dinners.

Lincoln's actual birthday, Feb. 12, is a legal holiday in 11 states: California, Connecticut, Illinois, Indiana, Iowa, Kentucky, Michigan, Missouri, New Jersey, New York, and West Virginia. In most other states, Lincoln's and George Washington's birthdays are combined for a legal holiday on the third Monday in February called either PRESIDENTS' DAY or Washington-Lincoln Day.

CONTACTS:
Lincoln Memorial, National Park Service
2 Lincoln Memorial Cir., N.W.
Washington, D.C. 20037
202-426-6841
www.nps.gov

Library Of Congress
101 Independence Ave., S.E.
Washington, D.C. 20540
202-707-5000
www.loc.gov

◆ 1681 ◆ Lindenfest
Second weekend in July

A 600-year-old linden tree in Geisenheim, Germany, is the center of this annual festival celebrating the new wine. As the oldest town in the Rhineland region, Geisenheim is renowned for its vineyards, and during the **Linden Tree Festival** people come from all over the world to taste the wine, visit the vineyards, and make pilgrimages to Marienthal, a Franciscan shrine in a nearby wooded valley. The ancient linden tree is decorated with lights for the three-day festival, and folk dancing and feasting take place beneath its branches.

◆ 1682 ◆ **Lismore Lantern Parade**
June 21

Observed during the winter solstice (June 21 in the southern hemisphere), the Lismore Lantern Parade in New South Wales, Australia, is a relatively new festival honoring an ancient seasonal observance. In 1994 leaders in Lismore established the parade in hopes of revitalizing the town's declining business district. Festival founders selected the longest night of the year to honor the cycles of the seasons, and they selected the lantern as the central motif because they recognized it as a common symbol of hope among a number of cultures.

Every year around Easter, Lismore community groups begin preparing for the parade, offering workshops to construct the parade's original artwork. Volunteers travel from all over southeastern Australia to help make lanterns, costumes, and puppets. The parade is accompanied by other festivities, including a Carnival Dance, music shows, and street theater.

Attendance has grown dramatically since 1994, from a few hundred people to over 25,000, some of whom come from overseas.

CONTACTS:
Lismore Lantern Parade
81 Orion St.
Lismore, NSW 2480 Australia
61-2-6622-6333; fax: 61-2-6622-1962
www.lanternparade.com

◆ 1683 ◆ **Literacy Day, International**
September 8

Established by the UNITED NATIONS to encourage universal literacy, this day has been observed since 1966 by all countries and organizations that are part of the United Nations system. It was a direct outgrowth of the World Conference of Ministers of Education in Tehran, Iran, which first called for the eradication of illiteracy throughout the world. Observances are sponsored primarily by UNESCO (United Nations Educational, Scientific, and Cultural Organization) and include the awarding of special literacy prizes.

Prizes are also awarded by the International Reading Association and the Japanese publisher Shoichi Noma to literacy programs that have made a significant difference. For example, in 1984 the Noma Prize was given to the Bazhong District in the People's Republic of China, where the literacy rate had been raised from 10 percent to 90 percent over a 35-year period.

CONTACTS:
UNESCO
7, place de Fontenoy
Paris, 75352 France

33-1-4568-1000
www.unesco.org

◆ 1684 ◆ **Lithuania Independence Day**
February 16

This is a national holiday in Lithuania marking the declaration of independence from Austrian, Prussian, and Russian occupation on February 16, 1918.

Today the anniversary is celebrated with festivals and fireworks, particularly in the capital city of Vilnius.

CONTACTS:
Lithuanian Embassy
2622 16th St. N.W.
Washington, D.C. 20009
202-234-5860; fax: 202-328-0466
usa.mfa.lt/usa/en

◆ 1685 ◆ **Lithuania Restoration of Statehood Day**
March 11

Lithuania had been independent for only 12 years when the Soviets occupied the country in 1940. The people voted for self-rule in February 1990, and the new democratically elected parliament declared independence from the U.S.S.R. on March 11, 1990. Beginning the next month, the Soviet Union began an economic blockade against Lithuania and eventually resorted to violence against people holding vigil around the capital buildings on January 13, 1991. Outrage from around the world stopped the attack. Within a year the influence of perestroika (Mikhail Gorbachev's social reform policies) and independence movements in the other Soviet states brought about the disintegration of the Soviet Union.

Restoration of Statehood Day is an official holiday in Lithua- nia.

CONTACTS:
Lithuanian Embassy
2622 16th St. N.W.
Washington, D.C. 20009 United States
202-234-5860; fax: 202-328-0466
usa.mfa.lt/usa/en

◆ 1686 ◆ **Lithuania State Day (Coronation of King Mindaugas)**
July 6

Lithuania State Day is a national holiday observed on July 6. On this day, Lithuanians honor the coronation of Mindaugas, who became the first and only king of a unified Lithuania in 1253, bringing the Baltic people together under his leadership. In 2003 Lithuanians celebrated the 750th anniversary of his crowning with a series of cultural activities, including operas, folk music concerts, folk dance performances, parades, and festivals.

Mindaugas founded the first independent Lithuanian state in 1240. Fearing that Lithuania would be unable to withstand attacks from neighboring groups, Mindaugas sought help from the Teutonic Knights, a religious military order that had established power in the southeastern Baltic region. In gratitude for their support, Mindaugas became a Roman Catholic in 1251. He is generally credited with bringing Christianity to the country for the first time, although the people of the Baltic region eventually rebelled against their compulsory Christian conversion, and many returned to pagan beliefs following his assassination in 1263.

CONTACTS:
Office Of The Seimas
Gedimino pr. 53
 Lithuania
370-5-239-6060
www3.lrs.lt

Lithuanian Embassy
2622 16th St. N.W.
Washington, D.C. 20009
202-234-5860; fax: 202-328-0466
usa.mfa.lt/usa/en

♦ 1687 ♦ **Little Big Horn Days**
Weekend nearest June 25

This festival is a commemoration in Hardin, Mont., of the Old West and particularly of the most famous Indian-U.S. cavalry battle in history, Custer's Last Stand. An hour-long reenactment of that battle, known as the Battle of Little Big Horn, is staged each night of the three-day festival near the actual site of the original battle, which occurred June 25, 1876.

The battle reenactment is performed by more than 200 Indian and cavalry riders. Among them are descendants of the Indian scouts who rode with Colonel George Armstrong Custer, who led more than 200 men to battle and to death. The pageant is based on the notes and outline prepared by Joe Medicine Crow, a tribal historian, and was originally sponsored by the Crow Agency, administrator of the Crow Reservation. The first presentation of the drama was in 1964. It continued for a number of years before lapsing and then being restored to life in 1990.

Other events of the weekend are a historical symposium, a street dance, a Scandinavian dinner, and a parade.

CONTACTS:
The Hardin Area Chamber of Commerce and Agriculture
10 E. Railway St.
Hardin, MT 59034
406-665-1672; fax: 406-665-3577
www.thehardinchamber.org

♦ 1688 ♦ **Little League World Series**
Late August

Little League baseball began in 1939 with only three teams. It was incorporated under a bill signed into law by President Lyndon B. Johnson in 1964. Ten years later the law was amended to allow girls to join Little League teams. It is now played by over 2.5 million boys and girls between the ages of nine and twelve in 48 countries. The field is a smaller version of the regulation baseball diamond, with bases 60 feet apart and a pitching distance of 46 feet.

Every year in August the Little League World Series is held at Howard J. Lamade Field in Williamsport, Pennsylvania, location of the International Headquarters of Little League Baseball and home of the Little League Museum. First-round games are held on Monday, Tuesday, and Wednesday, with every team guaranteed a minimum of three games. Those who advance to the championship game end up playing as many as five games. The U.S. and International Championships are on Thursday, and Friday remains an open date, in case of rain. The series finale is played on Saturday.

World Series games are also held in August for Junior League Baseball (ages 13-14), Senior League (ages 14-16), and Big League (ages 16-18).

CONTACTS:
Little League International Baseball and Softball
539 US Rt. 15 Hwy
P.O. Box 3485
Williamsport, PA 17701
570-326-1921; fax: 570-326-1074
www.littleleague.org

♦ 1689 ♦ **Living Chess Game (La Partita a Scácchi Viventi)**
Second weekend in September in even-numbered years

Every two years the main piazza in Marostica, Italy, is transformed into a giant chessboard. More than 500 townspeople wearing elaborate medieval costumes portray chessmen and act out a living game: knights in shining armor ride real horses, castles roll by on wheels, and black and white queens and kings march from square to square to meet their destinies. Thousands of spectators watch from bleachers, cheering loudly when a castle is lost and moaning when there is an impending checkmate. The local players begin rehearsing in March for the two-and-a-half hour performances. Some start out as pawns and over the years work their way up to become knights, kings, and queens.

The basis for the game is an incident that took place in 1454, when Lionora, the daughter of the lord of the castle, was being courted by two rivals. They challenged each other to a deadly duel but were persuaded to engage in a game of chess instead. Even today, the moves in the game are spoken in an ancient dialect, including the final *scácco matto!* (checkmate).

CONTACTS:
Associazione Pro Marostica
Piazza Castello, 1
Marostica, 36063 Italy
39-0424-72127; fax: 39-0424-72800
www.marosticascacchi.it

♦ 1690 ♦ Llama Ch'uyay
July 31

The Llama Ch'uyay in Sonqo, Bolivia, near La Paz, is the ritual in which llamas are made to drink a "medicine." The llamas are gathered together in a corral and, one at a time, they are forced to drink bottles of *hampi*, a concoction made from *chicha* and *trago* (two kinds of liquor), sugar, barley mash, soup broth, and special herbs. A large male may consume more than five bottles, while baby llamas usually drink only half a bottle. Three bottles is considered a normal dose. After the animals drink their medicine, they are decorated with colored tassels made out of yarn. After the feeding, people may also toss more chicha onto the animals. A similar ritual is performed for horses on July 25, the feast of Santiago (*see* St. James's Day).

♦ 1691 ♦ Lochristi Begonia Festival
Last weekend in August

A colorful celebration of the national flower of Belgium, held in Lochristi (six miles from Ghent), where 30 to 33 million flowering tubers are produced each year on more than 400 acres. For the festival, residents create enormous three-dimensional floral tableaux for a parade of flower-decked floats. These depict a different theme each year—for example, the world's favorite fairy tales. Besides the tableaux, arrangements of millions of yellow, red, orange, and white blossoms on beds of sand turn the town's main street into a carpet of flowered pictures. Other events are band concerts and tours to the begonia fields.

The tuberous begonia was originally a tropical plant. It takes its name from Michel Bégon, a French amateur botanist who was an administrator in the West Indies at the time of Louis XIV. The plant reached England in 1777, and Belgium began cultivating the begonia in the middle of the 19th century.

Because the commercial value of the begonias comes from their tubers, or underground stems, the farmers of Lochristi discarded the blossoms before the festival was begun in 1946 and put them to good use.

♦ 1692 ♦ Lohri
Around January 14; during Hindu month of Magha

Lohri is a traditional seasonal festival in India celebrating winter's end and the returning prominence of the sun to the Northern Hemisphere. Among Hindus and Sikhs Lohri is a particularly special occasion for families who have had a baby during the previous year; families may celebrate with a feast and family members and friends often give gifts to the new child. This is also a traditional day for young unmarried Sikh women to pray for a good marriage, which custom is said to derive from the association of a 16th-century matchmaker named Dulla Bhutti with Lohri. Another old tradition is for children to go door to door singing for candy from the neighbors, not unlike Halloween in the United States.

Throughout India Lohri today is widely celebrated at night with bonfires and dancing. People eat seasonal nuts and candies and also throw them into the fire.

See also Magh Sankranti.

CONTACTS:
Ministry of Tourism, Government of India
1270 Ave. of the Americas
Ste. 303
New York, NY 10020
212-586-4901; fax: 212-582-3274
tourism.nic.in

Uttarakhand Tourism Development Board
Pt.Deendayal Upadhaya Paryatan Bhawan
Near ONGC Helipad
Garhi Cantt
Dehradun, Uttarakhand 248 001 India
91-135-2559987; fax: 91-135 -2559988
uttarakhandtourism.gov.in

♦ 1693 ♦ Loi Krathong
October-November; full moon night of 12th lunar month

Loi Krathong is an ancient festival held under a full moon throughout Thailand, considered to be the loveliest of the country's festivals. After sunset, people make their way to the water to launch small lotus-shaped banana-leaf or paper boats, each holding a lighted candle, a flower, joss sticks, and a small coin. Loi means "to float" and Krathong is a "leaf cup" or "bowl."

There are several legends linked to the origins of this festival. One holds that the festival began about 700 years ago when King Ramakhamhaeng of Sukhothai, the first Thai capital, was making a pilgrimage on the river from temple to temple. One of his wives wanted to please both the king and the Lord Buddha, so she created a paper lantern resembling a lotus flower (which symbolizes the flowering of the human spirit), put a candle in it, and set it afloat. The king was so delighted he decreed that his subjects should follow this custom on one night of the year. Fittingly, the ruins of Sukhothai are the backdrop on the night of Loi Krathong for celebrations that include displays of lighted candles, fireworks, folk dancing, and a spectacular sound-and-light presentation.

A second legend traces the festival to the more ancient practice of propitiating the Mother of Water, Me Khongkha. The aim is to thank Me Khongkha and wash away the sins of the past year. The coins in the lotus cups are meant as tokens to ask forgiveness for thoughtless ways.

In yet another story, the festival celebrates the lotus blossoms that sprang up when the Buddha took his first baby steps.

A similar celebration is held in Washington, D.C., at the reflecting pool near the Lincoln Memorial. Dinner and participation are by paid ticket, but anyone passing can watch the adult, child, and teen dances and the exhibition of martial arts; and after dark, the floating candles.

CONTACTS:
Tourism Authority of Thailand
611 N. Larchmont Blvd.
1st Fl.
Los Angeles, CA 90004
323-461-9814; fax: 323-461-9834
www.tourismthailand.org

♦ 1694 ♦ Lollapalooza
August

Lollapalooza is an annual music festival that takes place during the summer in Grant Park in Chicago, Illinois. Bands from various musical genres, mostly from alternative rock, heavy metal, and hip-hop, perform at the venue to a diverse audience. Lollapalooza is often credited with helping spread alternative music to the mainstream and exposing hip-hop to a wider audience. In addition to its concert lineup, Lollapalooza provides a forum for political, environmental, and charitable organizations to raise awareness among the more than 100,000 attendees.

Lollapalooza was conceived in 1991 by singer Perry Farrelll as a farewell tour for his band Jane's Addiction. Its goal was to bring fans and artists of different types of music together on one stage, thereby highlighting lesser-known bands and exposing fans to new kinds of music. Many up-and-coming bands received exposure at Lollapalooza, including Nine Inch Nails and Pearl Jam. Another aim of the event was to bring music from the West Coast and East Coast to Middle America. As described by Perry Farrelll, the term "lollapalooza" was derived from the expression meaning something or someone unique, excellent, or exceptional. In 2004 the event was cancelled. The next year, the festival saw its rebirth when Farrell, along with Capital Sports & Entertainment, purchased the rights to the festival. The 2005 event introduced fresh ideas in keeping with the original spirit of the festival, and it turned into a three-day weekend with a lineup of over 100 bands. The event has been held annually ever since, and Grant Park has been locked in as the venue through 2021.

CONTACTS:
Lollapalooza
Grant Park
337 E. Randolph St.
Chicago, IL 60601
888-512-7469
www.lollapalooza.com

♦ 1695 ♦ London Bridge Days
Last week in October

Given its location, this is one of the stranger and more unexpected festivals in all of the United States. Held in Lake Havasu City in the Arizona desert, the festival is a week-long celebration of all things English and of the London Bridge that spans a channel of the Colorado River. This London Bridge was built in 1831 to span the River Thames in London, England. Opening festivities at the time included a banquet held on the bridge and a balloon ascending from it. Like its predecessor mentioned in the nursery rhyme, which was completed in 1209, this bridge was falling down until Robert P. McCulloch, Sr., of the McCulloch Oil Corp., bought 10,000 tons of the granite facing blocks, transported them from foggy Londontown to sunny Arizona, rebuilt the bridge stone by stone, and dedicated it on Oct. 10, 1971. The Bridge Days are a commemoration of that re-opening.

A replica of an English village next to the bridge is the center of festival activities. There are English costume contests, a parade, a ball, musical entertainment, arts and crafts exhibits, a "quit-rent" ceremony (*see* PAYMENT OF QUIT RENT), and a Renaissance Festival. Lake Havasu City is a planned community and resort on the banks of Lake Havasu, which is fed by the Colorado River and impounded by the Parker Dam.

CONTACTS:
Lake Havasu Convention & Visitors Bureau
314 London Bridge Rd.
Lake Havasu City, AZ 86403
928-453-3444 or 800-242-8278
www.golakehavasu.com

♦ 1696 ♦ London, Festival of the City of
June-July

First held in 1963, the Festival of the City of London was designed to show off the historic "square mile" in the heart of the city. The churches, cathedrals, halls, and other landmarks in this area have served as the setting for the festival's concerts, operas, and theater productions ever since. An open-air production of Gilbert and Sullivan's *Yeoman of the Guard*, staged in the Tower of London to commemorate its 900th anniversary during the festival's first year, has since become a regular event.

Concerts are given by both British and international artists, orchestras, and chamber music groups. There are band concerts, dance recitals, prose and poetry readings, art and photographic exhibits, and a series of ethnic cultural events. Street theater and traveling miracle plays round out the festival's offerings.

CONTACTS:
City of London Festival
Fitz Eylwin House
25 Holborn Viaduct
London, EC1A 2BP United Kingdom
44-845-120-7502
www.colf.org

♦ 1697 ♦ Long (Huey P.) Day
August 30

Huey Long was the colorful and often controversial governor of Louisiana from 1928 until 1932. Although he was impeached only a year after he'd been elected, he refused to yield the governorship to his lieutenant governor, a political enemy, and held on to the office until someone he liked better was elected. By then he'd been elected to the U.S. Senate, where he took what many considered to be an extreme stand on the redistribution of wealth, and openly rebelled against the administration of Franklin D. Roosevelt, a fellow Democrat.

In 1934-35 Long reorganized the Louisiana state government and set up what amounted to a dictatorship for himself. He exercised direct control over the judiciary, the police, firefighters, schoolteachers, election officials, and tax assessors while still serving as a U.S. Senator. As he was leaving the state capitol building on September 8, 1935, he was shot and killed by Dr. Carl Weiss, the son-in-law of one of his many political enemies.

Despite his controversial political activities, Long was revered by the rural people of the state, who supported his Share-Our-Wealth Society promising a minimum income for every American family. His birthday, August 30, is a special observance in Louisiana which the governor can declare a legal holiday. It has been observed since 1937.

♦ 1698 ♦ Looking Glass Powwow
August

This powwow, held by the Nez Perce Indians each August in Kamiah, Idaho, celebrates the memory of Chief Looking Glass, who was killed in the Nez Perce War of 1877. Nez Perce (meaning "pierced nose" and pronounced NEZ-purse) is the name given by the French to a number of tribes that practiced the custom of nose-piercing. The term is used now to designate the main tribe of the Shahaptian Indians who, however, never pierced their noses.

Other major annual powwows of the Nez Perce are the Mata'Lyma Powwow and Root Feast in Kamiah the third weekend in May with traditional dancing, and the Chief Joseph and Warriors Memorial Powwow the third weekend in June in Lapwai.

CONTACTS:
Nez Perce Tribal Executive Committee
P.O. Box 305
Lapwai, ID 83540
208-843-7342; fax: 208-843-7354
www.nezperce.org

♦ 1699 ♦ Lord Mayor's Show
Second Saturday in November

The second Friday in November is **Lord Mayor's Day** in London, the day on which the city's Lord Mayor is admitted to office. The following day is the Lord Mayor's Show, a series of civic ceremonies that culminate in a parade to the Law Courts held since 1215. At one time the Lord Mayor rode on horseback or traveled by state barge along the Thames, but today he rides from Guildhall to the Law Courts in a scarlet and gold coach drawn by six matched horses. This is the only time the mayoral coach is used; the rest of the time it is kept in the Museum of London.

Accompanying the coach is an honor guard of musketeers and pikemen in period dress, as well as many bands and nu-

merous floats decorated to reflect the interests or profession of the new Lord Mayor. This colorful pageant dates back to the 13th century, when King John gave the citizens of London a charter stating that the Mayor was to be elected on September 29 and that he was to present himself either to the King or to the Royal Justices to be officially installed.

See also Election of the Lord Mayor of London.

CONTACTS:
Museum Of London
150 London Wall
London, EC2Y 5HN United Kingdom
44-20-7001-9844
www.museumoflondon.org.uk

City of London Corporation
Guildhall
P.O. Box 270
London, EC2P 2EJ United Kingdom
44-20-7606-3030
www.cityoflondon.gov.uk

♦ 1700 ♦ Lord's Evening Meal (Memorial)
March-April; Nisan 14

The Lord's Evening Meal, also known as the **Memorial**, is a religious commemoration of the Last Supper and death of Jesus Christ observed by Jehovah's Witnesses. Jehovah's Witnesses consider this event to be the only religious celebration specifically supported by the Bible. The Lord's Evening Meal is conducted after sunset, and it includes discussion of the meaning and importance of the wine and bread used in the event. Within the community of believers, only a minority of adherents is allowed to partake in the ritual of the bread and wine. Jehovah's Witnesses believe that when they celebrate the **Memorial,** they become one with Jesus Christ and receive forgiveness from sins.

CONTACTS:
Jehovah's Witnesses
25 Columbia Heights
Brooklyn, NY 11201
718-560-5000
www.jw.org/en

♦ 1701 ♦ Los Isleños Fiesta
Late March

The Los Isleños Fiesta is held annually on a weekend in late March in Saint Bernard, La., near New Orleans, to celebrate the culture and heritage of "los isleños." This is the name given to more than 2,000 immigrants from the Canary Islands in Spain to Louisiana, and their descendants. The original settlers were sent to Louisiana from 1778 to 1783 to populate and defend the area, and many of them lived in St. Bernard.

The festival features visitors from the Canary Islands, who perform folk music and dances. Craftsmen and women are on hand to demonstrate traditional isleños crafts. Other activities include a children's area, heritage events, a mini museum, and ethnic food and drink. In a reflection of more recent settlers to St. Bernard, the festival also includes an Irish-Italian-Isleños parade. The Los Isleños Heritage and Cultural Society celebrated its 38th annual Isleño Fiesta in 2014 in St. Bernard Village.

CONTACTS:
Los Isleños Heritage & Cultural Society Museum
1345-1357 Bayou Rd.
St. Bernard, LA 70085
504-277-4681
www.losislenos.org

♦ 1702 ♦ Losar
December-January; first day of first Tibetan lunar month

Losar is the new year in Tibet, according to the Tibetan calendar, which is in use throughout the Himalayan region; the date is determined by Tibetan astrologers in Dharmsala, India.

Before the new year, bad memories from the old year must be chased away, so houses are whitewashed and thoroughly cleaned. A little of the dirt collected is thrown away at a crossroads where spirits might dwell. A special dish called *guthuk* is prepared; in it are dumplings holding omens: a pebble promises life as durable as a diamond; cayenne pepper suggests a temperamental personality; a piece of charcoal would mean the recipient has a black heart. On the last day of the old year, monks conduct ceremonies to drive out evil spirits and negative forces. In one such ritual, the monks, in grotesque masks and wigs and exotic robes, perform a dance in which they portray the struggle between good and evil (*see* MYSTERY PLAY OF TIBET).

On the first day of the year, people arise early to place water and offerings on their household shrines. In the three days of the celebration, much special food and drink is prepared. This is a time of hospitality and merrymaking, with feasts, dances, and archery competitions.

Tibet was invaded by the Chinese in 1949, and the DALAI LAMA, the spiritual and political head of Tibet, has been in exile since 1959. Much of the Tibetan culture has been suppressed, but festivals are still observed in a modest way in Tibet and by Tibetans in exile.

Tibetan exiles in India celebrate Losar by flocking to the temple in Dharmsala where the Dalai Lama lives. On the second day of the new year, he blesses people by touching their heads and giving them a piece of red-and-white string. People tie the blessed string around their necks as a protection from illness.

In Bodhnath, on the eastern side of Kathmandu, Nepal, crowds of Tibetan refugees visit the *stupa* there to watch lamas perform rites. Copper horns are blown, there are masked dances, and a portrait of the Dalai Lama is dis- played.

CONTACTS:
Tibet Homestay
9, Old Rajpur
Dehra Dun, Uttrakhand 248 009 India
www.tibethomestay.com

♦ 1703 ♦ Lotus, Birthday of the
24th day of sixth lunar month

The lotus flower is one of the great symbols of Buddhism. In fact, Buddha is often depicted standing on a lotus flower. This flower, which begins its life in mud under water, pushes up to the surface and rests on top. For this reason the lotus represents life as well as transcendence.

The Birthday of the Lotus is observed at the time of year when lotuses bloom, and people flock to Beijing to see them in its moats and ponds—much as they do in Japan and in Washington, D.C., during cherry blossom time (*see* CHERRY BLOSSOM FESTIVAL). Special lanes for rowboats are cut through the thick layer of lotus blossoms that cover the lakes of the Winter Palace in Beijing.

♦ 1704 ♦ Louisiana Shrimp and Petroleum Festival
September, Labor Day weekend

This festival combines a celebration of an old industry and a newer one in Morgan City, La., which once called itself the Jumbo Shrimp Capital of the World. In 1947, oil was discovered offshore, and it was decided to combine the tribute to shrimp with a tribute to oil.

The celebration was originally known as the **Shrimp Festival and Blessing of the Fleet**. It began in 1937 as a revival of the Italian custom of blessing fishing fleets before they set out to sea, but from the first it also included boat races, a dance, a boat parade, and free boiled shrimp. After the world's first commercial offshore well was drilled in the Gulf of Mexico below Morgan City, the shrimp industry was outstripped in economic importance by the petroleum industry, and petroleum seeped into the festival. The highlight, though, is still the Blessing of the Fleet and a water parade, with hundreds of boats taking part. Other events of this festival, one of the state's premier affairs, are fireworks, an outdoor Roman Catholic mass, arts and crafts displays, Cajun culinary treats, musical performances, and the coronation of the festival King and Queen.

CONTACTS:
Louisiana Shrimp & Petroleum Festival
712 Second St.
P.O. Box 103
Morgan City, LA 70380
985-385-0703; fax: 985-385-4628
www.shrimpandpetroleum.org

♦ 1705 ♦ Louisiana Sugar Cane Festival
Last weekend in September

The Sugar Cane Festival pays tribute to this important crop in New Iberia, La., which lies on the Bayou Teche. The Teche country is known as the "Sugar Bowl of Louisiana." The festival, which began in 1937 and now is participated in by 13 of the 17 sugar-producing parishes of the area, begins on Friday with a Farmers' Day. Highlights of the day are agriculture, homemaking and livestock shows, and a boat parade down Bayou Teche. On Saturday, there's a children's parade and the crowning of Queen Sugar at a ball, and on Sunday, the new Queen Sugar and King Sucrose reign over a parade. Other features are a blessing of the crops and a *fais-do-do*, a dance party.

CONTACTS:
Louisiana Sugar Cane Fair & Festival Association
P.O. Box 9768
New Iberia, LA 70562
337-369-9323
www.hisugar.org

◆ 1706 ◆ Low Sunday
Between March 29 and May 2; Sunday after Easter

The Sunday following the "high" feast of EASTER, it is also known as **Quasimodo Sunday**, **Close Sunday**, or **Low Easterday**. "Low" probably refers to the lack of high ritual used on Easter, and not to the low attendance usual on this day. The name Quasimodo Sunday comes from the Introit of the mass which is said on this day. In Latin it begins with the phrase *Quasi modo geniti infantes*—"As newborn babes...." The famous character Quasimodo in Victor Hugo's novel, *The Hunchback of Notre Dame*, is said to have been found abandoned on this day, which marks the close of Easter week.

◆ 1707 ◆ Loyalty Day
May 1

The U.S. Veterans of Foreign Wars designated the first day of May as Loyalty Day in 1947. The intention was to direct attention away from the Communist Party in the United States, which was using U.S. MAY DAY rallies to promote its doctrines and sign up new members. The idea caught on, and soon Loyalty Day was being celebrated throughout the country with parades, school programs, patriotic exercises, and speeches on the importance of showing loyalty to the United States. In Delaware, for example, Loyalty Day was marked by a special ceremony at Cooch's Bridge, where the Stars and Stripes were first displayed in battle. And in New York City, the Loyalty Day parade routinely attracted tens of thousands of participants.

Dissent over American intervention in Vietnam eventually eroded the popularity of Loyalty Day, and in 1968 only a few thousand marchers turned out for the traditional parades in Manhattan and Brooklyn, while 87,000 people participated in the Vietnam peace march in Central Park. Loyalty Day was later replaced by LAW DAY.

CONTACTS:
Loyalty Days Foundation
P.O. Box 75
Long Beach, WA 98631
360-642-4441
loyaltydayslongbeach.com

◆ 1708 ◆ Lu Pan, Birthday of
June-July; 13th day of sixth lunar month

This holiday commemorates the birth of the Taoist patron saint of carpenters and builders. Said to have been born in 507 B.C.E., Lu Pan, a versatile inventor, is sometimes called the Chinese Leonardo da Vinci. In Hong Kong, people in the construction industry observe the day with celebratory banquets to give thanks for their good fortune in the past year and to pray for better fortune in the year to come. They also pay their respects at noon at the Lu Pan Temple in Kennedy Town.

Lu Pan, an architect, engineer, and inventor, is credited with inventing the drill, plane, shovel, saw, lock, and ladder. His wife is said to have invented the umbrella. Because his inventions are indispensable to building, it is common practice at the start of major construction projects for employees to have feasts, burn incense, and offer prayers to Lu Pan so that he may protect them and the construction work from disaster.

◆ 1709 ◆ Lucerne International Festival of Music
Mid-August to mid-September

The first **Lucerne Festival** was held in 1938, when Arturo Toscanini (1867-1957) was persuaded by the city of Lucerne, Switzerland, to conduct a concert at the Tribschen estate, formerly the home of composer Richard Wagner and recently turned into the Wagner Museum.

Because cultural life in Switzerland was not interrupted by World War II, the festival was able to attract many famous conductors and performers who were war refugees. In addition to Toscanini, other well-known participants in the early days of the festival include Bruno Walter (1876-1962), Vladimir Horowitz (1903-1989), Fritz Busch (1890-1951), Artur Schnabel (1882-1951), Pablo CASALS (1876-1973), Herbert von Karajan (1908-1989), and Rudolf Serkin (1903-1991).

Ernest Ansermet (1883-1969), Fritz Busch, and Bruno Walter formed the Swiss Festival Orchestra in 1943, and it has been the festival's mainstay ever since. Comprised of the best musicians in Switzerland who come together specifically for the Lucerne Festival and cannot be heard elsewhere, the orchestra is joined by other national groups—among them the Lucerne Festival Choir, the Lucerne Festival Strings, and the Lucerne Vocal Soloists—as well as internationally known orchestras from other countries. The program offers a balance of symphonic and chamber music as well as master classes, young artists' matinees, and a concert for seniors and persons with disabilities. The theme for the 2014 Summer Festival was "Psyche," and the 2015 theme is "Humor.".

CONTACTS:
Lucerne Festival
Hirschmattstrasse 13
Luzern, CH-6002 Switzerland
41-41-226-4400; fax: 41-41-226-4460
www.lucernefestival.ch

◆ 1710 ◆ Ludi
Various

Ludi was the word used for public games in ancient Rome. These were holidays devoted to rest and pleasure. The **Ludi Megalenses** were held every year from April 4-10 from 191 B.C.E. onwards in honor of Cybele, the Roman Mother Goddess, whose image had been brought to Rome in 204 B.C.E. (*see* MEGALESIA). The **Megalensian Games** were followed by the **Ludi Ceriales** in honor of Ceres, the ancient goddess of cereals, from April 12-19 (*see* CEREALIA). Then came the **Ludi Florales** in honor of Flora, the goddess of flowers, from April 27-May 3 (*see* FLORALIA). The Ludi Florales were followed by a period of hard work in the fields, and the next games didn't occur for seven weeks. The **Ludi Apollinares**, or APOLLONIAN GAMES, held in honor of Apollo, went on from July 613 The **Ludi Romani**, or ROMAN GAMES, instituted in 366 B.C.E., lasted from September 4-19. And the **Ludi Plebei**, or PLEBEIAN GAMES, which were first held somewhere between 220 and 216 B.C.E., took place November 4-17.

All in all, there were 59 days devoted to these traditional games in the Roman calendar before the time of Sulla, who became dictator of the Roman Republic in 82 B.C.E. They were considered to be the *dies nefasti*—days on which all civil and judicial business must be suspended for fear of offending the gods.

♦ 1711 ♦ **Lughnasadh**
August 1 or a nearby Sunday

The Lughnasadh was a pre-Christian festival in Ireland associated with the ancient Celtic god Lugh. Occurring at the beginning of the harvest season, the Lughnasadh was a time for gathering berries and other early fruits of the season. Many of the hilltop sites where people came to pick berries were later taken over by the Roman Catholic Church and turned into pilgrimage sites. This is the case in County Mayo, where on the last Sunday in July thousands of pilgrims still climb to the summit of "the Reek," or Croagh Patrick, Ireland's holiest mountain. That day is known as REEK SUNDAY, and a series of masses are held in a small oratory on the top of Croagh Patrick. This is where St. Patrick is said to have spent the 40 days of LENT, and it was from this mountaintop that he is said to have driven all the venomous serpents into the ocean, thus explaining why there are no snakes in Ireland. Lughnasadh was also a popular time to hold fairs. Today it is observed by many Neopagan groups.

See also CROM DUBH SUNDAY; ST. PATRICK'S DAY; TAILTE FAIR.

♦ 1712 ♦ **Luilak**
Between May 9 and June 12; Saturday before Pentecost

Luilak, or **Lazybones Day**, is a youth festival celebrated in Zaandam, Haarlem, Amsterdam, and other towns in the western Netherlands. The celebration begins at four o'clock in the morning on the Saturday before PENTECOST, when groups of young people awaken their neighbors by whistling, banging on pots and pans, and ringing doorbells. Any boys or girls who refuse to get up and join the noisemaking are referred to as *Luilak*, or "Lazybones," a name that is said to have originated in 1672 when a watchman named Piet Lak

fell asleep while French invaders entered the country. Thereafter he was referred to as *Luie-Lak*, "Lazy Lak." In many parts of the country *Luilakbollen*, or "Lazybones Cakes," traditionally baked in the shape of fat double rolls and served with syrup, are a specialty of the season.

Children celebrate Luilak by making little wagons, often shaped like boots and decorated with branches and thistles, known as *luilakken*. Pulling the wagons over the cobblestone streets can generate enough friction to set the wheels smoking. The children then either watch while their luilakken go up in flames or else dump them in the canals.

In Haarlem, Luilak marks the opening of the celebrated Whitsun flower market in the Grote Markt at midnight (*see* MERCHANTS' FLOWER MARKET).

♦ 1713 ♦ **Lumberjack World Championships**
Last weekend in July

At the turn of the century Hayward, Wisconsin, was one of the most active logging towns in the northern United States. Nowadays Hayward is known primarily as the site of the largest lumberjack competition in the country. Lumberjacks and logrollers from New Zealand, Australia, Canada, England, and the United States come to Hayward to compete in one- and two-man buck sawing, power sawing, a variety of chopping events, and the speed climbing contest, where loggers climb up and down a 90-foot fir pole in less than 30 seconds. There is also a lumberjack relay race, with teams consisting of one speed climber, one "river pig" (logroller), two-man crosscut saw partners, and one standing-cut chopper.

The three-day event takes place at the end of July in the Lumberjack Bowl, a large bay of Lake Hayward that was once used as a giant holding pond for the North Wisconsin Lumber Company and is now used for the World Logrolling Championships. The sport of "birling" or logrolling originated in New England and then moved west. Lumberjacks in overalls, woolen shirts, and high boots learned to maneuver a floating carpet of logs, using their pike poles to break up log jams. A working skill soon became a pastime and then a sporting event. Today's competitors dress in shorts and t-shirts or bathing suits and wear special birling shoes. Competitors stand on a floating log and try to roll each other off balance and into the water.

CONTACTS:
Lumberjack World Championships
P.O. Box 666
Hayward, WI 54843
715-634-2484
www.lumberjackworldchampionships.com

♦ 1714 ♦ **Lunar New Year**
Between January 21 and February 19; first day of first lunar month

The Lunar New Year has certain variations from country to country, but they all include offerings to the household god(s), housecleaning and new clothes, a large banquet, ancestor worship, and firecrackers.

It is the most important and the longest of all Chinese festivals, celebrated by Chinese communities throughout the world. The festival, believed to date back to prehistory, marks the beginning of the new lunar cycle. It is also called the **Spring Festival**, since it falls between the WINTER SOLSTICE and VERNAL EQUINOX. It is the day when everyone becomes one year older—age is calculated by the year not the date of birth.

Activities begin in the 12th month, as people prepare food, clean their houses, settle debts, and buy new clothes. They also paste red papers with auspicious writings on the doors and windows of their homes.

On the 24th day of the 12th month, each Kitchen God leaves earth to report to the Jade Emperor in heaven on the activities of each family during the past year. To send their Kitchen God on his way, households burn paper money and joss sticks and give him offerings of wine. To make sure that his words to the Jade Emperor are sweet, they also offer *tang kwa*, a dumpling that finds its way into the mouths of eager children.

The eve of the new year is the high point of the festival when family members return home to honor their ancestors and enjoy a great feast. The food that is served has symbolic meaning. Abalone, for example, promises abundance; bean sprouts, prosperity; oysters, good business.

This is also a night of colossal noise; firecrackers explode and rockets whistle to frighten away devils. An old legend says that the lunar festival dates from the times when a wild beast (a *nihn*; also the Cantonese word for "year") appeared at the end of winter to devour many villagers. After the people discovered that the beast feared bright lights, the color red, and noise, they protected themselves on the last day of the year by lighting up their houses, painting objects red, banging drums and gongs, and exploding bamboo "crackers." The explosions go on till dawn, and continue sporadically for the next two weeks.

In Hong Kong, it is traditional after the feast to visit the flower markets. Flowers also have symbolic meaning, and gardeners try to ensure that peach and plum trees, which signify good luck, bloom on New Year's Day.

On the first day of the new year, household doors are thrown open to let good luck enter. Families go out to visit friends and worship at temples. Words are carefully watched to avoid saying anything that might signify death, sickness, or poverty. Scissors and knives aren't used for fear of "cutting" the good fortune, and brooms aren't used either, lest they sweep away good luck. Dragon and lion dances are performed, with 50 or more people supporting long paper dragons. There are acrobatic demonstrations and much beating of gongs and clashing of cymbals.

An ancient custom is giving little red packets of money (called *hung-pao* or *lai see*) to children and employees or service-people. The red signifies good fortune, and red is everywhere at this time.

On the third day of the holiday, families stay home, because it's supposed to be a time of bad luck. On the fourth day, local deities return to earth after a stay in heaven and are welcomed back with firecrackers and the burning of spirit money. According to legend, the seventh day is the anniversary of the creation of mankind, and the ninth day is the birthday of the Jade Emperor, the supreme Taoist deity. He is honored, not surprisingly, with firecrackers.

In most Asian countries, people return to work after the fourth or fifth day of celebration. In Taiwan, New Year's Eve, New Year's Day, and the two days following are public holidays, and all government offices, most businesses, restaurants, and stores are closed. The closings may continue for eight days.

By the 13th and 14th days, shops hang out lanterns for the Yuen Siu or LANTERN FESTIVAL, the day of the first full moon of the new year and the conclusion of the celebration.

In Chinese, the lunar new year is known as **Ch'un Chieh**, or "Spring Festival." It was formerly called **Yuan Tan,** "the first morning," but the name was changed when the Gregorian calendar was officially adopted by the Republic of China in 1912. To differentiate the Chinese new year from the Western new year, January 1 was designated *Yuan Tan*. Today in China and in other eastern nations, January 1 is a public holiday, but the Spring Festival is the much grander celebration.

Celebrations vary from country to country and region to region. In some towns in the countryside of Yunnan province in China, for example, an opera is performed by farmers. The Chinese communities in San Francisco and New York City are especially known for their exuberant and ear-splitting celebrations. In China, celebrations were banned from the onset of the Cultural Revolution in 1966 until 1980 when dragons and lions once again appeared on the streets.

In Vietnam, where the holiday is called TET, the ancestors are believed to return to heaven on the fourth day, and everyone has to return to work. On the seventh day, the *Cay Nev* is removed from the front of the home. This is a high bamboo pole that was set up on the last day of the old year. On its top are red paper with inscriptions, wind chimes, a square of woven bamboo to stop evil spirits from entering, and a small basket with betel and areca nuts for the good spirits.

In Taiwan it is called **Sang-Sin**. Small horses and palanquins are cut from yellow paper and burned to serve as conveyances for the Kitchen God.

The New Year's feast is first laid before the ancestor shrine. About seven o'clock, after the ancestors have eaten, the food is gathered up, reheated, and eaten by the family. The greater the amount of food placed before the shrine, the greater will be the reward for the new year.

After the banquet, oranges are stacked in fives before the ancestor tablets and household gods. A dragon-bedecked red cloth is hung before the altar. The dragon is the spirit of rain and abundance, and the oranges are an invitation to the gods to share the family's feasting.

In Korea **Je-sok**, or **Je-ya**, is the name for New Year's Eve. Torches are lit in every part of the home, and everyone sits up all night to "defend the New Year" from evil spirits. In modern Seoul the church bells are rung 33 times at midnight. While the foods may vary, everyone, rich and poor alike, has *duggook* soup, made from rice and containing pheasant, chicken, meat, pinenuts, and chestnuts.

Many games are played. Among the most unusual is girls seesawing. In early times Korean men stopped some of the sterner sports and forbade women to have any outdoor exercises. Korean girls then took to using a seesaw behind their garden walls. But they do it standing up—so as to get a possible glimpse of their boyfriends, as they fly up and down.

In Okinawa's villages there is the custom of new water for **Shogatsu**, the new year. About five o'clock in the morning youngsters bring a teapot of fresh water to the homes of their relatives. There a cupful is placed on the Buddhist god shelf, or the fire god's shelf in the kitchen, and the first pot of tea is made from it.

See also Losar, Narcissus Festival, and Sol.

CONTACTS:
International Buddhist Society
9160 Steveston Hwy
Richmond, BC V7A 1M5 Canada
604-274-2822; fax: 604-271-1121
www.buddhisttemple.ca

♦ 1715 ♦ Lupercalia
February 15

This was an ancient Roman festival during which worshippers gathered at a grotto on the Palatine Hill in Rome called the Lupercal, where Rome's legendary founders, Romulus and Remus, had been suckled by a wolf. The sacrifice of goats and dogs to the Roman deities Lupercus and Faunus was part of the ceremony. Luperci (priests of Lupercus) dressed in goatskins and, smeared with the sacrificial blood, would run about striking women with thongs of goat skin. This was thought to assure them of fertility and an easy de-

livery. The name for these thongs—*februa*—meant "means of purification" and eventually gave the month of February its name. There is some reason to believe that the Lupercalia was a forerunner of modern Valentine's Day customs. Part of the ceremony involved putting girls' names in a box and letting boys draw them out, thus pairing them off until the next Lupercalia.

♦ 1716 ♦ Luxembourg National Day
June 23

This public holiday is also known as **Grand Duke Day,** since it is the birthday of Jean (b. 1921), the Grand Duke of Luxembourg. It is also the day on which the country celebrates its independence. Although formerly ruled by the Netherlands and Belgium, the grand duchy raised its own flag for the first time in 1890. It remained politically neutral until after its liberation from the Germans at the end of World War II, when it joined the North Atlantic Treaty Organization.

On the eve of the national holiday, Dudelange hosts a torchlight procession, and the castle at Wiltz hosts a fête in the courtyard. In Esch-sur-Alzette, there are athletic competitions and other festivities. Fireworks, parades, special religious services, public concerts, and dancing comprise the elaborate celebration in the capital city of Luxembourg.

On National Day people assemble in the capital, not only to celebrate their independence but also to observe the official birthday of the Grand Duke, who succeeded his mother, the Grand Duchess Charlotte, in 1964. Although Luxembourg covers less than a thousand square miles, the people there identify strongly with their country and speak their own language, known as Luxembourgeois.

CONTACTS:
Luxembourg National Tourist Board
68-70, boulevard de la Pétrusse
Luxembourg, L-2320 Luxembourg
352-4282-8210; fax: 352-4282-8230
www.visitluxembourg.com/en

Embassy Of Luxembourg
2200 Massachusetts Ave. N.W.
Washington, D.C. 20008
202-265-4171
washington.mae.lu/en

M

♦ 1717 ♦ **Maafa Commemoration**
Third week in September

The Maafa Commemoration is an annual week-long remembrance of the Transatlantic Slave Trade and the experience of Middle Passage. The word Maafa, a Kiswahili word meaning catastrophe, is increasingly being applied to those historical events.

The commemoration, held at the St. Paul Community Baptist Church in Brooklyn, N.Y., centers around a dramatic presentation put on by the church's drama ministry. "The Maafa Suite … A Healing Journey" depicts the history of African Americans, from Africa to the Jim Crow South. As many as 100 performers in music, dance, and theatre contribute to "The Maafa Suite." The work's creators describe it as a transformative psychodrama that aims to educate and heal the collective memory of African Americans. It is open to the public by paid ticket. Other events during the week include lectures, worship services, Maafa museum tours, a Garden of Gethsemane sweat lodge, and special activities for senior citizens and young people, many of them free of charge. The commemoration first took place in 1995. The play has toured to other African-American churches in the United States, and many churches have created their own Maafa commemorations.

CONTACTS:
St. Paul Community Baptist Church
859 Hendrix St.
Brooklyn, NY 11207
718-257-1300; fax: 718-257-2988
www.spcbc.com

♦ 1718 ♦ **Mabon**
Autumnal (Fall) Equinox, September 22 or 23 in the northern hemisphere

Archaeological findings of prehistoric cultures in the British Isles reveal that important festivals observed the year's equinoxes and solstices. In ancient history, Celtic peoples observed these days as the four QUARTER DAYS: Ostara (VERNAL EQUINOX), Litha (SUMMER SOLSTICE), Yule (WINTER SOLSTICE), and Mabon (AUTUMNAL EQUINOX). Today, Wiccans and Neo-pagans, who draw many traditions from Celtic culture,

retain the Mabon tradition. Some communities refer to the day simply as "autumn harvest" or "autumn *sabbat.*"

According to Welsh legend, Mabon was a magical youth renowned for his hunting skills. His mother held him captive in a cave, but the warrior Culhwch, with the aid of several animals of the forest, came to the boy's rescue. For many present-day believers, Culhwch's search for Mabon symbolizes everyone's search for the inner child.

Typical Wiccan and Neo-pagan celebrations of Mabon, which take place throughout the world, are circle ceremonies that recognize various harvest themes. A ceremonial site—often an altar—will be decorated with items like corn, apples, wine, or black and white candles (the light and dark colors represent the equinox). Participants may tell stories, light candles, chant, dance, or recite invocations.

♦ 1719 ♦ **MacArthur (Douglas) Day**
January 26

Douglas MacArthur (1880-1964), five-star general and supreme commander of the Allied forces in the Southwest Pacific during World War II, was born on this day in Little Rock, Arkansas. Although MacArthur retired from the U.S. Army in 1937, he was recalled to active duty in July 1941. Promoted to general in December 1944, he was appointed commander of all U.S. army forces in the Pacific four months later. After the U.S. dropped an atomic bomb on Hiroshima on August 6, 1945, it was MacArthur who supervised the surrender ceremony in Tokyo. As commander of the Allied occupation of Japan from 1945-51, MacArthur directed the demobilization of Japanese military forces and the drafting of a new constitution.

Many people felt that MacArthur was imperious and egotistical, while to others he appeared warm, courageous, and even humble. Everyone seemed to agree that he possessed superior intelligence and a rare ability to command. His birthday is observed in his home state of Arkansas, where he is widely remembered as one of the state's most famous sons.

♦ 1720 ♦ **Macedonian Ilinden (St. Elijah's Uprising Day)**
August 2

August 2 is an official holiday in Macedonia commemorating the nation's first modern statehood. In 1903, Macedonian Christian nationalists led a rebellion against the Turkish Ottoman Empire. The rebels staged an uprising on August 2 of that year, a date that also marked the Christian feast day of Ilinden, or the prophet Elijah's ascension into heaven. During the uprising, approximately 30,000 Macedonian fighters waged war against 300,000 Turkish troops, declaring Macedonian independence upon liberating the town of Krusˇevo and establishing the Krus? evo Republic. The republic didn't last, however; the nationalists were crushed by the Turks in November 1903 after months of intense violence.

Still, the Ilinden uprising has become a cultural cornerstone in the mythology of modern Macedonia and is acknowledged as an important precursor to the establishment of the present-day Republic of Macedonia. In 2003, Macedonians celebrated the 100th anniversary of the Ilinden uprising with commemorative coins, memorial services, a wide range of art and history exhibitions, and literary works that pay tribute to this memorable date in the Macedonian struggle for freedom and justice.

♦ 1721 ♦ Macedonian Independence Day
September 8

Macedonians celebrate their country's sovereignty on September 8. A former Yugoslav republic, Macedonia became independent in fall 1991 upon the breakup of the Socialist Federal Republic of Yugoslavia. Prior to that point, the longstanding independence movement in Macedonia was gaining renewed momentum after a buildup of nationalistic sentiment encouraged by local artists and intellectuals. On January 25, 1991, the Assembly of the Republic of Macedonia passed a resolution demanding federal reconfiguration and naming itself the sole power in the country. On August 23 of that year the assembly drafted a new constitution, which guaranteed sovereignty, democracy, human rights, and the rule of law. Macedonia declared its independence after a referendum held on September 8, 1991, in which 95% of participants voted for an independent Macedonia. After considerable debate, the constitution was accepted on November 17, 1991.

♦ 1722 ♦ Macedonian National Uprising Day
(Day of Macedonian Uprising in 1941; Macedonian Revolution Day)
October 11

October 11 marks the anniversary of the beginning of the Macedonian people's uprising against fascism during World War II. This holiday is observed through formal ceremonies at which the prime minister and other dignitaries deliver addresses acknowledging the significance of this revolt to the spirit of Macedonian independence. In conjunction with this holiday, the Macedonian Parliament recognizes accomplishments in the areas of science, culture, art, and journalism through the "October 11" life achievement awards.

During the Second World War, the Axis powers controlled the Kingdom of Yugoslavia, of which Macedonia was part. On October 11, 1941, the people of Macedonia began to organize and mount an armed insurrection against their Bulgarian and Italian occupiers with an attack on the local Axis-power headquarters in the city of Prilep, located in the Vardar region of Macedonia. Partisans staged a simultaneous uprising against the fascists in the city of Kumanovo. The October 11 rebellion launched the war for liberation from fascist occupation, which coincided with the rise of the communist movement in Macedonia.

♦ 1723 ♦ Macker (Gus) Basketball
January-October; varies according to host city

This 3-on-3 basketball tournament—and party—takes place on the streets of more than 70 cities across the United States. The **Gus Macker 3-on-3 Basketball Tournament** grew out of a low-wager backyard competition when, in 1974, Scott McNeal assembled 17 friends at his parents' house in the western Michigan city of Lowell, near Grand Rapids, to play a basketball tournament with six teams of three people each.

Apparently realizing that this kind of event could have larger popular appeal, McNeal adopted the moniker "Gus Macker" and began holding Macker tournaments once a year in Belding, Michigan. National media attention from the likes of *Sports Illustrated* and ABC's "Wide World of Sports" sparked inquiries from communities around the country, and in 1987 McNeal began taking the Macker on tour.

In 1992 the Macker was honored by the Basketball Hall of Fame as the Official 3-on-3 Tournament. Indoor Mackers were introduced in 1994 so that the games could proceed during winter months in northern cities. Several Canadian cities have begun to participate as well.

The Macker is notable for its stringent guidelines for having a positive, family-oriented event and its insistence on donating proceeds to local charities. Since 1987, the Macker tour has expanded, holding a total of 972 tournaments annually in more than 75 cities, with over 2.2 million players–male and female from seven years old to over 50–and more than 23 million spectators. As of 2014, the Macker has raised approximately $15,000,000 for charity.

CONTACTS:
Macker Basketball, LLC.
107 E. Main St.
Ste. 3
Belding, MI 48809
616-794-1445; fax: 616-794-1472
www.macker.com

♦ 1724 ♦ Macon Cherry Blossom Festival
Mid-March

This festival celebrates the blooming (traditional date of full bloom is March 23) of the Yoshino cherry trees in Macon, Ga., which calls itself the Cherry Blossom Capital of the World. Cherry trees in Macon date back to 1952, when William A.

Fickling discovered a mystery tree on his lawn. It was identified as a Yoshino flowering cherry, a native of Japan. Fickling learned to propagate the trees, and began giving them to the community; today Macon has 170,000 Yoshino cherry trees given by the Fickling family—30 times more than the number in Washington, D.C. The festival honors Fickling, known as "Johnny Cherry seed," and has as its themes love and international friendship.

The 10-day celebration, started in 1982, includes the 10-mile Cherry Blossom Trail, and now offers about 250 activities. Among the events are parades, aircraft displays and fly-ins, a fashion show, fireworks, concerts, a bed race, a lantern-lighting ceremony, and the fire department's Pink Pancake Breakfast. Macon has many antebellum mansions spared by Gen. William T. Sherman on his Civil War march to the sea, so there are several house and garden tours.

The city continues donating trees: about 15,000 are given to area residents for planting each spring.

See also Cherry Blossom Festival.

CONTACTS:
Macon Cherry Blossom Festival
794 Cherry St.
Macon, GA 31201 United States
478-330-7050; fax: 478-330-7067
www.cherryblossom.com

♦ 1725 ♦ Madagascar Independence Day
June 26

This national holiday commemorates Madagascar's independence from France on this day in 1960. **Republic Day** is another public holiday in Madagascar, held on December 30, the day the new constitution went into effect. The country became a republic in 1975.

CONTACTS:
Embassy Of Madagascar
2374 Massachusetts Ave. N.W.
Washington, D.C. 20008
202-265-5525; fax: 202-265-3034
www.madagascar-embassy.org

♦ 1726 ♦ Madagascar Martyrs' Day
(Commemoration Day, Insurrection Day)
March 29

Madagascar Martyrs' Day, also known as **Commemoration Day** or **Insurrection Day**, officially memorializes those who died in the Revolt of 1947 against the French. Madagascar had been a French colony since 1896 and then was named an overseas territory within the French Union in the 1946 constitution. Although the French constitution accorded the people of Madagascar full citizenship, its assimilationist policies contradicted the goal of independence for Madagascar. Consequently, Malagasy nationalists formed a movement for autonomy from France.

On March 29, 1947, the people staged a nationalist uprising against colonial forces that eventually spread to one-third of the island. After months of fighting and the arrival of additional troops from France, the colonial army was able to regain control of the island. Casualties from the conflict were reported as high as 80,000 and as low as 8,000, depending on the source. French military courts tried the leaders of the revolt and executed 20. According to some reports, other court hearings resulted in 5,000 to 6,000 convictions with a range of penalties from imprisonment to capital punishment. On March 29 the Malagasy government and people remember those patriots who sacrificed their lives in this rebellion for their country's freedom.

CONTACTS:
Embassy Of Madagascar
2374 Massachusetts Ave. N.W.
Washington, D.C. 20008 United States
202-265-5525; fax: 202-265-3034
www.madagascar-embassy.org

♦ 1727 ♦ Madara Kijinsai (Demon-God Event)
April 17

According to an old Japanese legend, when the 14th-century Rakuhoji Temple in Yamatomura burned down, the demon god Madara summoned a number of demons and rebuilt the temple in seven days. Then the demons danced around a bonfire to celebrate their accomplishment and to express their hopes for the temple's future success.

Today, men dress up like demons and, on horseback, climb the 145 stairs to the Rakuhoji Temple. There are also demon dances to commemorate those who saved the temple from oblivion. Since the event takes place in April when the cherry trees are in bloom, many spectators come to Yamatomura not just to see the Demon-God Event but also to view the blossoming trees.

♦ 1728 ♦ Madeleine, Fête de la
July 22

The **Magdalene Festival** is observed in St. Baume, a forested region of Provence, France, on the anniversary of the death of Mary Magdalene. An unfounded ninth-century legend has it that she set out from Palestine in a small boat and miraculously arrived on the shores of Provence. Wandering eastward from Les Saintes-Maries-de-la-Mer, she came to *la fôret de la Baume*, "the forest of the cave," a grotto where she spent 33 years living on wild roots and berries doing penance for her sins.

Thousands of pilgrims have visited *la Sainte Baume*, the holy cave, since the 13th century. Although July 22 is the most popular pilgrimage date, the shrine is visited throughout the year. At one time a journey to the grotto was considered especially important for engaged couples, who went there to ensure a fruitful marriage. More recently, young girls have scrambled up the wooded hillside to ask for the Magdalene's help in finding a husband.

CONTACTS:
France Tourism Development Agency
825 Third Ave.
New York, NY 10022
212-838-7800; fax: 212-838-7855
int.rendezvousenfrance.com/en

♦ 1729 ♦ MadFest Juggling Festival
Usually second or third weekend of January

Since 1962, the Madison Area Jugglers have welcomed fellow jugglers every year to their headquarters at the University of Wisconsin in Madison. The MadFest Juggling Festival's reputation has been bolstered by the success of the Madison Area Jugglers' world champion passing team, The Mad 5.

The festival is an occasion for jugglers at all levels to share the tricks of the trade and watch world-class performers. The festivities are also open to unicycling, yo-yoing, and other forms of object manipulation. Beginning in 2006, the Wisconsin State Yo-Yo Contest was added to the festival's proceedings.

The festival usually takes place from Thursday to Saturday. Throughout the festival there is open juggling, during which the jugglers show up at the university's field house to practice or just mingle with other jugglers. Saturday night is reserved for the MadFest Juggling Extravaganza at the Wisconsin Union Theater, where special guest jugglers perform along with other musical and comedy acts.

CONTACTS:
MadFest Juggling Festival
2222 E. Washington Ave.
Madison, WI 53704
madjugglers.com

♦ 1730 ♦ Madison County Covered Bridge Festival
Second weekend in October

The Madison County Covered Bridge Festival takes place annually on the second weekend in October in and around Winterset, Iowa. The town is located in Madison County, noted for its historic wooden covered bridges. These structures became world-famous with the success of the best-selling 1992 novel, *The Bridges of Madison County,* by Robert James Waller, and the subsequent film of the same name. The festival, which pre-dates the book and movie, was launched in 1970.

The Covered Bridge Festival celebrates not just Madison County's vintage bridges, but all things old-fashioned. In addition to bridge tours, the weekend's festivities include demonstrations of such traditional activities as sheep shearing, wool spinning, and soap making. The non-stop entertainment includes barbershop quartets, square dancers, and cloggers, plus quilts and antiques are on display. Children are invited to take part in a spelling bee championship, and a parade of antique cars is a highlight of the weekend.

CONTACTS:
Madison County Chamber Of Commerce
73 Jefferson St.
Winterset, IA 50273
515-462-1185; fax: 515-462-1393
www.madisoncounty.com

♦ 1731 ♦ Magellan (Ferdinand) Day
March 6

The island of Guam, largest and southernmost of the Mariana Islands in the Pacific Ocean, about 3,000 miles west of Hawaii, was found on this date in 1521 by the Portuguese navigator Ferdinand Magellan. He named the island Ladrones, meaning "thieves," because of the way, according to Magellan, the inhabitants behaved. The island was formally claimed by Spain in 1565, and was later ceded to the United States as a prize at the end of the Spanish-American War. Today, Guam is the site of major U.S. military installations.

Guamanians celebrate their island's founding with an official holiday on the first Monday in March with fiestas and sailboating. This day is also known as **Discovery Day**.

CONTACTS:
Guam Visitors Bureau
401 Pale San Vitores Rd.
Tumon, GU 96913
671-646-5278
www.visitguam.com

♦ 1732 ♦ Magh Bihu
Middle of January

Bihu is regarded as one of the most important and ancient festivals in the northeastern state of Assam in India. A series of different events that are celebrated three times during the year, the Bihu celebration coincides with distinct phases in the farming calendar. Magh Bihu, one of the three festivals, falls on the 11th month of the Hindu calendar and is observed by the Assamese with feasts and parties. Also known as **Bhogali Bihu,** which means "festival of food," Magh Bihu marks the end of the harvest season and celebrates the food culture of the region. Households begin the festivities a few weeks early by preparing traditional sweet and savory dishes. On the eve of the event, celebrants erect a canopy out of bamboo and thatch for a feast, which is accompanied by drumming and singing. The following morning, people rise early to bathe and gather in fields, where they light a bonfire, throwing rice cakes and nuts as offerings to the fire god. Other celebrations involve buffalo fights and traditional Assamese games. Similarly, the urban populace of the region light small bonfires and organize cookouts with friends and relatives.

CONTACTS:
Directorate of Tourism, Govt. of Assam
Station Rd.
Guwahati, Assam 781 001 India
91-361- 2547102, 91-361-2542748; fax: 91-361-2547102
assamtourism.gov.in

♦ 1733 ♦ **Magh Sankranti**
Usually around January 14; Hindu month of Magha

In celebration of the sun's movement back toward the Northern Hemisphere, people in Nepal visit holy bathing spots during this festival in the Hindu month of Magha. Some actually bathe in the shallow water, but the weather is usually quite chilly and most are content to splash water on their hands and faces and sprinkle it on their heads. People also spend the day sitting in the sun, massaging each other with mustard oil, which is also used by mothers to bless their children. Foods traditionally served on this day include *khichari*, a mixture of rice and lentils; sesame seeds; sweet potatoes; spinach; and home-made wine and beer. Traditional gifts for the priests are a bundle of wood and a clay fire pot.

This holiday is also celebrated all over India, where it is called **Makar Sankranti** or, in some parts of India, Lohri.

CONTACTS:
Sikkim Tourist Information Centre
New Sikkim House
14, Panchsheel Marg
Chanakyapuri
New Delhi, Delhi 110 021 India
91-11-26115346
sikkimtourism.gov.in

♦ 1734 ♦ **Magha Puja (Maka Buja, Full Moon Day)**
March-April; full moon night of third lunar month

This important Buddhist holy day is celebrated in India, Laos (as **Makha Bouxa**), and Thailand, where it is a national holiday. The day commemorates the occasion when 1,250 followers ordained by the Buddha arrived by coincidence at Veluvan Monastery in Rajagriha, Bihar, India, to hear him lay down monastic regulations and predict his own death and entry with Nirvana in three months' time. On this day there are sermons in the temples throughout the day, and monks spend the day chanting. The people perform acts of merit-making, such as offering food to monks and freeing captive birds and fish. After sunset, monks lead followers in walking three times around the chapels of monasteries. Each person carries flowers, glowing incense, and a lighted candle in homage to the Buddha. In Laos, the ceremonies are especially colorful at Vientiane and at the Khmer ruins of Wat Ph near Champasak.

♦ 1735 ♦ **Magha Purnima**
January-February; full moon day of Hindu month of magha

Like Kartika Purnima, this is a Hindu bathing festival. Magha is considered to be one of the four most sacred months, and Hindus believe that bathing in the Ganges on this day is a great purifying act. When they cannot get to the Ganges, they bathe in the sea or in any holy stream, river, or tank (a pool or pond used to store water). Great bathing festivals are held at various places along the banks of the Yamuna, Sarayu, Narmad, and other holy rivers, and people walk for miles to have a bath. There is a large tank that is considered holy at Kumbhkonam, near Madras, which is also a popular destination since Hindus believe that on this particular day, the Ganges flows into the tank.

Magha Purnima is a day for fasting and charities. Early in the morning, libations are offered to dead ancestors, while donations of food, clothes, and money are given to the poor. Then Brahmans are fed and given *dan-dakshina* (offerings) according to one's means and capacity.

♦ 1736 ♦ **Maghi**
January-February; during Sikh month of Magh

Guru Gobind Singh and his Khalsa, a defense militia of "soldier-saints" he formed, were attacked by the Mughal army at Anandpur. It is said that 40 of his close followers let fear get the best of them and ran away, but they later repented and joined the Guru at Muktsar. There they gave their lives in the Battle of Muktsar in December 1705—an act of self-sacrifice that enabled them to achieve liberation from the cycle of rebirth.

Maghi is a day for honoring these men, who are now known as the Forty Immortals. Sikhs in India and elsewhere observe the holiday by visiting their local *gurdwara* (house of worship) and listening to the recitation of sacred hymns. The observance is particularly solemn at Muktsar in Punjab State, India, where the slaughter occurred.

CONTACTS:
Punjab Heritage And Tourism Promotion Board
Archives Bhawan
lot No 3, Sector 38 A,
Chandigarh, Punjab 160 036 India
91-172-2625950; fax: 91-172-2625953
www.punjabtourism.gov.in

♦ 1737 ♦ **Magna Carta Day**
June 15

The Magna Carta was the "great charter" of English liberties, which the tyrannical King John I was forced by the English nobility to sign on June 15, 1215. Although this day does not appear in the official calendar of any church, it is a day of great religious significance throughout the English-speaking world. One of the 48 personal rights and liberties guaranteed by the Magna Carta was freedom of worship; in fact, the opening words of the document were, "The Church of England shall be free."

The Magna Carta is regarded as one of the most important documents in the history of political and human freedom. Although it may seem remote to Americans, who sometimes take freedom for granted, for the English this date marks the first time that the basic belief in the value of the individual was recognized by the ruling government.

CONTACTS:
U. S. National Archives and Records Administration

700 Pennsylvania Ave., N.W.
Washington, D.C. 20408
866-272-6272
www.archives.gov

♦ 1738 ♦ **Magnolia Blossom Festival**
Third weekend in May

The Magnolia Blossom Festival is an annual event that takes place during the third weekend in May in Magnolia, Arkansas, located in the southwest corner of the state. Held for the first time in 1989, the Magnolia Blossom Festival has grown to become one of the largest festivals in Arkansas, with attendance each year many times larger than the population of the small community.

Festival events take place around Magnolia's downtown square and include an art show, a treasure hunt, a fishing competition, and a 5K race. The highlight of the festival, however, is the **World Championship Steak Cook-off**, the event that has given this small town's festival a nationwide reputation. On Saturday morning of the festival weekend, over 80 "steak teams" from around the country begin the day taking part in the Parade of the World Championship Steak Cook-Off Chefs down Main Street. The teams then line the town square with their cookers and begin preparing thousands of sixteen ounce rib-eye steaks to be served to that afternoon to the competition's judges and the public. The Steak Cook-off winner is awarded prize money and the Governor's Cup trophy.

CONTACTS:
Magnolia/Columbia County Chamber of Commerce
P.O. Box 866
211 W. Main St.
Magnolia, AR 71754
870-234-4352
www.blossomfestival.org

♦ 1739 ♦ **Mahamastakabhishekha (Grand HeadAnointing Ceremony)**
March-April; every 10-15 years during the Jain month of caitra

The huge image of Bahubali (also known as Gomateshwara), who was the son of the first Jaina *tirthankara* (spiritual guide), was sculpted out of rock at Shravanabelagola in the District of Hassan, Karnataka State, India, and dedicated on March 13, 981. The image of Bahubali, which at 57 feet stands higher than the Colossus of Rhodes, honors a Jaina ascetic who gave up his kingdom and renounced the world after a conflict with his brother, who was the crown prince, made him realize how selfish and acquisitive people really were.

The Grand Head-Anointing Ceremony, as the event is known, only takes place when a certain conjunction, a coincidence of astrological events, occurs—every 10-15 years. Huge numbers of Jaina devotees attend the ceremony. Special scaffolding is set up behind the statue to hold Jaina monks and priests, who pour 1,008 pots of holy liquid—consisting of water, coconuts, plantains, *ghee* (clarified butter), sugar,

almonds, dates, poppy seeds, milk, curds, sandalwood gold foil, silver foil, and precious gems and coins— over its head. Attendees shout in devotion as the statue is ritually bathed.

CONTACTS:
Department of Tourism, Government of Karnataka
Khanija Bhavan
Race Course Rd.
Ste. 49, 2nd Fl.
Bangalore, Karnataka 560 001 India
91-80-2235 2828; fax: 91-80-2235 2626
www.karnatakatourism.org

♦ 1740 ♦ **Mahavira Jayanti**
March-April; 13th day of waxing half of Hindu month of Caitra

A major Jain festival in India, Mahavira Jayanti is dedicated to Vardhamana (6th century B.C.E.), who came to be known as Mahavira, meaning "great hero" of the Jains. The festival celebrates his birthday, and is marked with prayers, fasting, and recitations. The holiday is observed with special fanfare by eastern Indians at Pawapuri in the state of Bihar, where Mahavira was born near the modern town of Patna. Another large celebration is held at the Parasnatha temple in Calcutta.

Mahavira, a contemporary of the Buddha, is regarded by the Jains as the 24th and last in a series of *Tirthankaras*, or enlightened teachers or "ford-makers," and present-day Jainism is traced to his life and teachings. For 121/2 years, he was an ascetic, wandering about, begging for food, and wearing little. Then he found enlightenment, became a *Jina*, meaning "conqueror," and a Tirthankara. He taught for 30 years before he died. Jainism today continues to be an ascetic religion, practiced by about 3.5 million people. They reject any action that could harm a living being, and some, therefore, wear masks over their mouths to prevent the chance of breathing in and thus killing an insect. Jains, with a strong literary tradition, have played an important role in conserving the writings of non-Jain Hindu authors.

See also Dewali.

♦ 1741 ♦ **Maidens' Fair on Mount Gaina**
Third Sunday in July

The Maidens' Fair is a major folk festival held at Mount Gaina in Transylvania, Romania. It was originally a marriage fair,where young men came to choose their future wives, but is now an opportunity for people to display their talents in handicrafts, costume making, singing, and dancing. Thousands of people gather for the events of the fair, which include dance competitions and concerts by folk bands and singers. Other aspects of the festival are feasts and bonfires, and the chanting of satirical verses during certain folk dances.

CONTACTS:
Romanian National Tourist Office
355 Lexington Ave.
8th Fl.
New York, NY 10017

212-545-8484
romaniatourism.com

♦ 1742 ♦ Maidyarem (Maidhyairya; Mid-Year or Winter Feast)

December-January, May, June; 16th-20th days of Dae, the 10th Zoroastrian month

Maidyarem is the fifth of the six great seasonal feasts, known as *gahambars*, of the Zoroastrian religion. It was traditionally celebrated at a point in the agricultural year when, due to extreme cold, all work came to a halt. The name comes from the word *airya*, which means "rest."

The six gahambars were typically joyous festivals that included such activities as special rituals and prayers, and the sharing of food. Although they lasted five days, the fifth day was the only one spent in actual celebration; the other four were for preparation and anticipation of the day's feasting, when families or neighborhoods would get together. These seasonal feasts were designed to give those who worked from dawn to dusk on farms a respite from their labors. Today, with so many Zoroastrians living in urban areas, the importance of the gahambars has diminished.

The Zoroastrian calendar has 12 months of 30 days each, plus five extra days at the end of the year. Because of discrepancies in the calendars used by widely separated Zoroastrian communities around the world, there are now three different calendars in use, and Maidyarem can fall either in December-January, May, or June according to the Gregorian calendar.

There are only about 100,000 followers of Zoroastrianism today, and most of them live in northwestern India or Iran. Smaller communities exist in Pakistan, Sri Lanka, Canada, the U.S., England, and Australia.

♦ 1743 ♦ Maidyoshahem (Maidhyoishema; MidSummer Feast)

June-July, October-November, November-December; 11th-15th days of Tir, the fourth Zoroastrian month

This festival is the second of the six great seasonal festivals, known as *gahambars*, of the Zoroastrian religion. Each of the six gahambars correlates with a phase of agricultural production and honors one of the six things created by God: sky, water, earth, plants, animals, and humankind. Maidyoshahem was linked to the creation of the waters.

Traditionally, the gahambars were joyous festivals that lasted five days and provided farm workers with a much-needed respite from their labors. The first four days were spent in preparation for the feasting that took place on the fifth day. Today, however, so many Zoroastrians live in urban areas that the importance of the gahambars has diminished somewhat.

The Zoroastrian calendar has 12 months of 30 days each, plus five extra days at the end of the year. Because of discrepan-

cies in the calendars used by widely separated Zoroastrian communities around the world, there are now three different calendars in use, and Maidyoshahem can fall either in June-July, October-November, or November-December, according to the Gregorian calendar.

See also TIRAGAN.

♦ 1744 ♦ Maidyozarem (Maidhyoizaremaya; MidSpring Feast)

April-May, September, October; 11th-15th days of Ardwahist, the second Zoroastrian month

Maidyozarem is the first of the six great seasonal feasts, known as *gahambars*, of the Zoroastrian religion. It is observed from the 41st to the 45th day after NAWRUZ or New Year's Day. Each of the six gahambars correlates with a phase of agricultural production and honors one of the six things created by God: sky, water, earth, plants, animals, and humankind. Maidyozarem—which means "mid-spring"—is linked to the creation of the sky, and the spiritual being associated with this festival is Shahrewar, who presides over metals and minerals and is represented by the consecrated implements used to tend the sacred fire in Zoroastrian temples.

Traditionally, the gahambars were joyous festivals that lasted five days and provided farm workers with a much-needed respite from their labors. The first four days were spent in preparation for the feasting that took place on the fifth day. Today, however, so many Zoroastrians live in urban areas that the importance of the gahambars has diminished somewhat.

The Zoroastrian calendar has 12 months of 30 days each, plus five extra days at the end of the year. Because of discrepancies in the calendars used by widely separated Zoroastrian communities around the world, there are now three different calendars in use, and Maidyozarem can fall either in April-May, early September, or early October, according to the Gregorian calendar.

♦ 1745 ♦ Maifest

Third weekend in May

The original Maifest in Hermann, Missouri, was a children's festival founded in 1874. The festival was revived in 1952 as a German ethnic festival for people of all ages. Held the third weekend in May, the festival offers German folklore, songs, music, and food in celebration of the arrival of spring. Black beer, cheese, sausage, crackers, and bratwurst are served, and there are band concerts and musical shows.

CONTACTS:
Brenham Maifest
P.O. Box 1588
Brenham, TX 77834
www.maifest.org

♦ 1746 ♦ Maimona (Maimuna)

Between March 28 and April 25; day after Passover

Jews in North Africa commemorate the philosopher and rabbi, Moses Maimonides (1135 or 1138-1204), on the evening of the last day of PASSOVER and the day that follows. Since the news of Maimonides's death in 1204 reached many Jews during Passover, they were not able to mourn his passing, as custom would normally dictate, by eating bread and an egg. So they postponed it until the following day.

In Libya on this day, each family member receives the *maimona* (from an Arabic word meaning "good fortune")—a small loaf of bread with an egg baked inside, which they eat with slices of lamb.

In Morocco, people dress up or wear costumes. Special displays of food are arranged on tables, including pitchers of milk and bowls of flour with eggs, broad green beans, stalks of wheat, and dates. Surrounding the bowls are honey, fruit, nuts, cookies, lettuce, wine, and a type of pancake known as *muflita*. After going to the synagogue, people stop to bless their friends and sample the refreshments at each home. A lettuce leaf, representing prosperous crops, is dipped in honey, symbolizing sweetness, and given to each guest. Wherever possible, people dip their feet in streams, rivers, or the sea.

◆ 1747 ◆ Maine Lobster Festival
Five days including first weekend in August

Claiming to be the "Original Lobster Festival," the event known as the Maine Lobster Festival has been held in the fishing port of Rockland since 1948. The festival's emphasis is on marine foods and exhibits, with special events such as lobster crate- and trap-hauling races, a Maine cooking contest, the crowning of a Maine Sea Goddess, and a lobster-eating competition. There is also musical entertainment and a big parade, featuring the Sea Goddess, Sea Princesses, and King Neptune and his court.

Although many towns in Maine hold annual lobster festivals, some have gone bankrupt by offering visitors all the lobster they can eat for a ridiculously low price. Although the prices have gone up, the lure of an inexpensive lobster meal remains one of the primary reasons people attend these festivals. At the Rockland festival, the price of the lobster meal is based on the current market price. But the lobster is fresh, and it is steamed in the world's largest lobster cooker.

CONTACTS:
Maine Lobster Festival
P.O. Box 552
Rockland, ME 04841
207-596-0376 or 800-576-7512
www.mainelobsterfestival.com

◆ 1748 ◆ *Maine* Memorial Day
February 15

Memorial Day *February 15* The American battleship *Maine*, which had been sent to Cuba to rescue any Americans who might be endangered by the Cubans' unrest under Spanish rule, was blown up while sitting at anchor in Havana harbor on February 15, 1898. Many in the United States assumed that the Spanish were responsible for the ship's destruction, since American sympathies were clearly with the Cubans. But despite the fact that 260 men died, the question of responsibility for the explosion was never really settled. The Spanish-American War was declared in April, and "Remember the *Maine!*" is the slogan that has been associated with it ever since.

February 15 was observed for many years by the U.S. Navy and by Spanish-American War veterans' associations in Havana and the United States. Some naval units still participate in local observances. This day is sometimes called **Battleship Day** or **Spanish-American War Memorial Day**.

Special observances marked the 100th anniversary of the battleship's destruction in 1998 at Key West, Florida, the ship's last port-of-call before heading to Havana.

CONTACTS:
Searsmont Town Office
37 Main St. S.
P.O. Box 56
Searsmont, ME "04973 United States
207-342-5411; fax: 207-342-3495
searsmont.com

Naval History and Heritage Command
805 Kidder Breese St. S.E.
Washington Navy Yard, D.C. 20374
202-433-7880
www.history.navy.mil

◆ 1749 ◆ Making Happiness Festival
Ninth and 10th days of first lunar month

Some villages in Taiwan observe the **Tso-Fu Festival**, or "making happiness" festival, soon after the LUNAR NEW YEAR. This observance honors the gods as well as women who have borne sons during the past year. On the ninth, village leaders round up images of gods from homes and shrines and head a procession to the temple, which includes musicians as well as people carrying banners and banging gongs. Once there, the new mothers make special offerings of "new-male cakes" called *hsin-ting ping*, while everyone else gives other sacrifices. The next day a special feast is held for the village leaders, the elderly, and the mothers, who now hand out new-male cakes to everyone except other new mothers. The festival concludes with the collection of the images of the gods from the temple and their return to their regular homes.

CONTACTS:
Taipei Economic and Cultural Office in New York
1 E. 42nd St.
9th Fl.
New York, NY 10017
212-867-1632; fax: 212-867-1635
go2taiwan.net

Ministry of Foreign Affairs, Republic of China (Taiwan)
3731 Wilshire Blvd.
Ste. 700
Los Angeles, CA 90010
213-389-1215; fax: 213-383-3245
www.roc-taiwan.org

◆ 1750 ◆ **Malawi Freedom Day**
June 14

Malawi Freedom Day is a public holiday celebrating the end of the corrupt totalitarian regime that ruled the country for nearly three decades. In 1966, two years after becoming an autonomous nation free from the British government, the African country of Malawi established a new constitution and became a single-party state. Dr. Hastings Kamuzu Banda, leader of the conservative Malawi Congress Party (MCP), became the nation's first president. In 1971, Banda was declared president for life, a position he retained until the 1990s with the help of the paramilitary wing of the MCP.

In 1993, however, growing domestic unrest and pressure from church leaders and the international community forced Banda to allow a public referendum. The Malawian people were asked to decide between continued one-party rule and a multiparty democracy. On June 14, 63% of voters opted to end one-party rule and Banda's regime in favor of democratic leadership. National elections were conducted on May 17, 1994, and the United Democratic Front candidate Bakili Muluzu won the presidency.

CONTACTS:
Embassy of the Republic of Malawi
2408 Massachusetts Ave.N.W.
Washington, D.C. 20008
202-721-0270; fax: 202-721- 0288
www.malawiembassy-dc.org

◆ 1751 ◆ **Malawi Martyrs' Day**
March 3

March 3 is celebrated each year as a national holiday in Malawi honoring the political heroes who gave their lives in the struggle against British colonialism. Malawians often attend church services on March 3 and offer prayers for departed freedom fighters. In addition, Radio Malawi plays tribute music to remember those martyred during the 1959 crisis in Central Africa.

For most of the 19th century, the African nation of Malawi (formerly called Nyasaland) was a British colony. Beginning in the early- to mid-20th century, however, the country's indigenous people began attempts to achieve independence from British rule. During the 1950s, Britain united Malawi with the Federation of Northern and Southern Rhodesia (now known as Zambia and Zimbabwe), a venture that led to widespread resentment of colonial domination. In response, in an effort to attain independence, Malawians formed their own political parties and plotted violent retaliations and acts of sabotage. On March 3, 1959, British forces declared a state of emergency and orchestrated Operation Sunrise, arresting prominent Malawian nationalists and other dissidents. Fury over the arrests of these resistance leaders precipitated the deaths of more than 20 demonstrators. In total, 51 were killed, over 1,300 were detained, and many more were wounded during the state of emergency, which lasted until 1960.

CONTACTS:
Malawi Ministry of Tourism & Culture
Tourism House
Off Convention Dr.
Private Bag 326
Malawi
265-1-775-499; fax: 265-1-770-650
www.visitmalawi.mw

Embassy of the Republic of Malawi
2408 Massachusetts Ave. N.W.
Washington, D.C. 20008
202-721-0270; fax: 202-721-0288
www.malawiembassy-dc.org

◆ 1752 ◆ **Malawi Republic Day**
July 6

Also known as **National Day,** this holiday commemorates Malawi's independence from Britain on this day in 1966. The area had been known as Nyasaland. At midnight on July 5-6, 1966, 40,000 people cheered the changing of the flag at Central Stadium, ushering in Malawi's autonomy.

Today ceremonies and prayer services are held at stadiums in Blantyre, Mzuzu, or the capital city of Lilongwe.

CONTACTS:
Ministry of Foreign Affairs and International Cooperation
P.O. Box 30315
Lilongwe, 3 Malawi
265-1-789-088; fax: 265-1-788-482
www.foreignaffairs.gov.mw

◆ 1753 ◆ **Malaysia Birthday of SPB Yang di-Pertuan Agong**
June 2

Malaysia practices a system of government based on a constitutional monarchy and parliamentary democracy. The head of state is the king, also known as Seri Paduka Baginda (SPB) Yang di-Pertuan Agong. Although the term king is used, this is not a hereditary position. The SPB Yang di-Pertuan Agong is also the highest commander of the Malaysian armed forces. The federal head of government is the prime minister.

The SPB Yang di-Pertuan Agong is one of three bodies that make up the Malaysian Parliament. The other two are the Senate (Dewan Negara) and the House of Representatives (Dewan Rakyat). The Yang di-Pertuan Agong is elected to a five-year term. According to the Malaysian Constitution, only the Conference of Rulers has the power to elect and appoint the Yang di-Pertuan Agong. The Conference of Rulers is a council comprised of state rulers who deliberate on questions of national policy and other important matters.

Every year, June 2 is set aside as a national holiday in Malaysia to celebrate the birthday of the current and past SPB Yang di-Pertuan Agongs.

CONTACTS:
Malaysia Tourism Promotion Board
120 E. 56th St.

15th Fl.
New York, NY 10022
212-754-1113; fax: 212-754-1116
www.tourism.gov.my

Embassy of Malaysia
3516 International Ct. N.W.
Washington, D.C. 20008
202-572-9700; fax: 202-572-9882
www.kln.gov.my

♦ 1754 ♦ Malcolm X's Birthday
May 19

Malcolm X, whose original name was Malcolm Little (1925-1965), was an outspoken leader in the black nationalist movement of the 1960s. He converted to the Muslim faith while serving time in prison for burglary, and upon his release began touring the country on behalf of the Nation of Islam, led by Elijah Muhammad. In 1964 he was suspended from the sect and started his own religious organization. But hostility between Malcolm's followers and the rival Black Muslims escalated. He was assassinated at a rally in Harlem shortly after his PILGRIMAGE TO MECCA.

Because during most of his career Malcolm X advocated violence (for self-protection) and had a reputation for fanaticism and racism, his leadership was rejected by most other civil rights leaders of his day. But, as reflected in his *The Autobiography of Malcolm X, as Told to Alex Haley,* his pilgrimage to Mecca changed his outlook. After performing the pilgrimage rites, Malcolm composed and sent a letter back home. It read, in part: "For the past week, I have been utterly speechless and spellbound by the graciousness I see displayed all around me by people *of all colors....* There were tens of thousands of pilgrims ... from blue-eyed blonds to black-skinned Africans. But we were all participating in the same ritual, displaying a spirit of unity and brotherhood that my experiences in America had led me to believe never could exist between the white and the non-white."

His birthday, May 19, is still observed in most major American cities with a large African-American population.

CONTACTS:
Malcolm X Memorial Foundation
3448 Evans St.
Omaha, NE 68111
402-881-8104
malcolmxfoundation.org

Malcolm X Grassroots Movement
P.O. Box 471711
Brooklyn, NY 11247
718-254-8800
mxgm.org

♦ 1755 ♦ Maldives Embraced Islam Day
Varies

The Republic of Maldives is an island nation comprised of approximately 1,190 islands in the Indian Ocean. In 1153, Maldives converted from Buddhism to Islam. The main events and festivals in Maldives follow the Muslim calendar.

Children receive religious education both at home and in school, and all children learn the Arabic alphabet. According to legend, the country converted to Islam as follows: Long ago, Rannamaari, an evil sea-demon, came out from the sea once a month and threatened to destroy everything unless a virgin was sacrificed. Every month the people of the island chose a young girl by lot and left her alone in a small temple as a sacrifice.

One day, a young man named Yousuf Shamsuddin-al Tabrezi arrived on the island. He stayed in the house of a poor couple in Malé. When the daughter of the house was selected for the next sacrifice, Yousuf decided to disguise himself as a girl and take her place in the temple. He went to the temple that night and continuously recited the Holy Quran. The demon came that night, but as it got closer to the temple, it heard the words of the Quran and turned away.

When the islanders went to check on Yousuf in the morning, they were amazed to find him alive and still reciting the Quran. He told them that it was the powers of the Holy Quran that had saved him. He called upon the king to embrace Islam so that the island could be free from the wrath of the demon. The King took his advice and converted to Islam and ordered all of his subjects to do the same.

CONTACTS:
Ministry of Tourism, Republic of Maldives
5th Fl. Velaanaage
Block 20096-Ameeru Ahmed Magu
Maldives
960-302-2200; fax: 960-332-2512
tourism.gov.mv

Ministry of Home Affairs
10th Fl.
Velaanaage
Maldives
960-332-1752; fax: 960-332-4739
en.homeaffairs.gov.mv

♦ 1756 ♦ Maldives Independence Day
July 26

This group of islands in the Indian Ocean had been under British control since 1887 until its full independence on this day in 1965. Independence Day is a national holiday in Maldives.

Maldives became a republic on November 11, 1968, an event commemorated with another national holiday, **Republic Day**. Festivities are held for two days, including November 11.

CONTACTS:
Maldives Marketing & PR Corporation
Velaanaage, Ameer Ahmed Magu
4th Fl.
Maldives
960-332-3228; fax: 960-332-3229
www.visitmaldives.com

♦ 1757 ♦ Maldives National Day
First day of Rabi-al-Awwal, the third month in the Islamic calendar

The Republic of Maldives is an island nation comprised of approximately 1,190 islands in the Indian Ocean. The people of the islands had easy access to precious cowry shells (historically used as currency and in jewelry) and ambergris (a substance produced in the digestive system of sperm whales and used in perfumes). These valuable resources attracted the attention of Portuguese explorers. In 1558, the Portuguese attacked the Maldives islands, killed the country's sultan, and established their own rule. For the next 15 years, the Portuguese ruled the country, despite the islanders' wishes for its former leadership. Among other rules, the Portuguese tried to force Christianity on the Maldivians, who were an Islamic people.

In 1573, a Maldivian named Muhammad Thakurufaanu and his brothers killed the Portuguese leader Andreas Andre and recaptured the island of Malé. Thakurufaanu served as sultan for 12 years, during which time he formed an army, introduced coins, and improved trade and religious observances. His dynasty lasted for the next 132 years.

Today, Maldives celebrates National Day to commemorate the historic event in which Thakurufaanu overthrew the Portuguese rulers. Celebrations on this holiday, which falls on the first day of Rabi-al-Awwal (the third month in the Islamic calendar), consist of parades and root marches in the streets of Malé and other islands.

CONTACTS:
Maldives Ministry of Tourism
5th Fl. Velaanaage
Block 20096 Ameeru Ahmed Magu
Maldives
960-302-2200; fax: 960-332-2512
tourism.gov.mv

Ministry of Home Affairs
Velaanaage
10th Fl.
Maldives
960-332-1752; fax: 960-332-4739
en.homeaffairs.gov.mv/?page_id=231

♦ 1758 ♦ Mali Independence Day
September 22

Mali gained its independence from France on September 22, 1960. As a colony since the 1890s, it was known as French Sudan. In ancient and medieval times Mali had a prominent role in a series of illustrious empires that spanned western Africa.

Also known as **Republic Day**, this is an important national holiday in Mali.

CONTACTS:
American Embassy in Bamako
ACI 2000, Rue 243
Porte 297
Mali
223-2070-2300; fax: 223-2070-2479
mali.usembassy.gov

Malian Cultural Center
151 W. 136 St.

Rm. 208
Harlem, NY 10036
347-577-6330
umaca.org

♦ 1759 ♦ Mallard Ceremony
January 14 every 100 years (2001, 2101, 2201, 2301…)

The **Mallard Feast** or **Mallard Day** ceremony held once every 100 years at All Souls College in Oxford commemorates the college's founding in 1438. Henry Chichele, archbishop of Canterbury at the time, wanted to establish a college at Oxford in memory of those who had perished in the wars between England and France. While he was considering where such a college might be located, he had a dream that when the foundations were being dug, a fattened mallard was found stuck in the drain or sewer. He decided to heed the omen and, when the digging began at the location specified in his dream, a huge mallard was indeed found—a sure sign that his college would flourish.

Although no one is sure exactly when the first commemoration of this event was held, the ceremony itself has remained unchanged. The Fellows of the college nominate the Lord of the Mallard. He in turn appoints six officers, who march before him carrying white staves and wearing medals with the image of the mallard engraved on them. When the Lord is seated in his chair, the officers carry him around the quadrangle three times and sing a traditional song. After that, they climb up to the college roof in a torchlight procession and sing the song again, loudly enough for most of the town to hear. Eventually they retire to their common rooms to drink wine and continue their merrymaking.

CONTACTS:
All Souls College University of Oxford
All Souls College
Oxford, OX1 4AL United Kingdom
44-1865-279379
www.all-souls.ox.ac.uk

♦ 1760 ♦ Malta Freedom Day
March 31

The Republic of Malta is a small country in the central Mediterranean that consists of seven islands. In 1814, Malta became a crown colony of the British empire. Under British rule, the Maltese Islands helped the Allies during World War I. Hundreds of Maltese served as soldiers in the British regiments, and Malta allowed the British to use its dockyard and hospitals. Thousands of sick and wounded soldiers were brought to Malta for treatment, thereby earning the country the title of the "Nurse of the Mediterranean."

Malta also played an important role during World War II. The bravery its people showed during the war led to the country being awarded the George Cross, which is now displayed on its flag. On September 21, 1964, Malta was granted independence from Britain. On December 13 of that same year, Malta became a republic within the Commonwealth, with the President as head of state.

Although Malta gained independence in 1964, the British armed forces did not completely leave until March 31, 1979. It was at that time that the Maltese Prime Minister, Dom Mintoff, demanded that the British either pay a higher rent for their bases or withdraw. This freed Malta of foreign military occupation for the first time in history.

In Malta, Freedom Day is a public holiday that commemorates the day the last of the British military left the Maltese Islands. On this holiday, a ceremony is held at the War Memorial in Floriana. The main events of the day take place around the Freedom Day Monument in Vittoriosa. In the afternoon, a competitive regatta is held in Grand Harbour, where food and drink booths are set up along the harbor. The participants compete in traditional Maltese boats called *id-dg-hajsa Maltija*.

CONTACTS:
Malta Tourism Authority
Auberge D'Italie
Merchants St.
Valetta, VLT 1170 Malta
356-2291-5000; fax: 356-2291-5394
www.visitmalta.com

♦ 1761 ♦ **Malta Independence Day**
September 21

Malta Independence Day is a nationwide celebration of Malta's independence, achieved on this day in 1964. Malta was under the control of various political entities from its earliest days. In the early 19th century, the Maltese acknowledged Great Britain's sovereignty, but through the years various constitutions were in force, and in the 20th century, self-government was repeatedly granted and suspended. Malta's heroic stand against the Axis in World War II won a declaration that self-government would be restored at the end of the war, and indeed self-government under another constitution was granted in 1947. It was revoked in 1959, restored in 1962, and independence was finally granted in 1964. Ten years later, on Dec. 13, 1974, Malta became a republic—December 13 is a national holiday and horse races at Marsa commemorate that event.

Independence Day is celebrated with parades and festivities throughout the country.

See also VICTORY DAY.

CONTACTS:
Malta Tourism Authority
1st Fl. Auberge D'Italie
229, Merchants St.
Valetta, VLT 1170 Malta
356-2291-5114; fax: 356-2291-5394
www.mta.com.mt

♦ 1762 ♦ **Malta Republic Day**
December 13

The Republic of Malta is a small country in the central Mediterranean that consists of seven islands. In 1814, as part of the Treaty of Paris, Malta became a crown colony of the British empire. The colony was used as a shipping waystation and fleet headquarters. Because of its close proximity to the Suez Canal, it was considered to be a very important outpost to the British territories in India.

On September 21, 1964, Malta was granted its independence from Britain. According to its 1964 constitution, Queen Elizabeth II would initially serve as the supreme leader of Malta, with a Governor-General serving as executive authority on her behalf. On December 13, 1974, Malta became a republic within the Commonwealth, with the President as head of state.

To commemorate the day the country became a republic, December 13 has been declared Republic Day in Malta. On this day, a big feast is held and Malta's National Anthem is played and/or sung at the end of all masses. In addition, the President of Malta presents national awards, namely the Order of Merit and *Gieh ir-Repubblika.* These awards inspire a sense of patriotism, as they are awarded as a token of appreciation for those who honor their country through their achievements and service to their community.

Although Malta gained independence in 1964, the British armed forces did not completely leave until March 31, 1979. This was the first time in Malta's history that the country was free of foreign military. To commemorate this day, the people of Malta celebrate FREEDOM DAY.

CONTACTS:
Malta Tourism Authority
Auberge D'Italie
Merchants St.
Valletta, VLT 1170 Malta
356-2291-5000; fax: 356-2291-5394
www.mta.com.mt

Consulate of Malta
P.O. Box 1104
Duvall, WA 98019
425-788-3120; fax: 425-696-9374
consulatewashington.tripod.com

♦ 1763 ♦ **Malta Sette Guigno (Commemoration of Uprising of June 7, 1919)**
June 7

The Republic of Malta is a small country in the central Mediterranean that consists of seven islands. In 1798 Napoleon Bonaparte invaded Malta and took power. The people of Malta did not want to be under French rule, so the country asked the British to help compel the French to leave. In 1799, the British Navy forced the French to withdraw. The Treaty of Paris, signed on May 30, 1814, made Malta a crown colony of the British empire.

Under British rule, the Maltese Islands helped the Allies during World War I. Hundreds of Maltese served as soldiers in the British regiments, and the country allowed the British to use its dockyard and hospitals. Thousands of sick and wounded soldiers were brought to Malta, thereby earning the country the title of the "Nurse of the Mediterranean."

Although the war brought jobs to the country, the wages were relatively low. Many Maltese found it hard to make ends meet. The high cost of living created serious problems for many Maltese. These factors and others prompted riots in Valletta on June 7, 1919. During the riots, four Maltese were killed by British troops. The victims included Guzeppi Bajada, Manwel Attard, Wenzu Dyer, and Karmenu Abela. This tragic event became known as the Sette Guigno Riots.

The 1919 riots impelled the country to establish the first responsible government in Malta in 1921. It was the first time Maltese citizens could elect Maltese members of Parliament.

Today, Malta recognizes the anniversary of the riots as a national holiday. Every year on June 7, Malta holds a commemorative ceremony at Palace Square in Valletta, in front of the House of Representatives. Bouquets of flowers are placed on the monument of the Sette Guigno victims at Addolorata (Our Lady of Sorrows) cemetery. The commemorative celebration also includes marches by the Police Corps and the playing of the national anthem L-Innu Malti, and a moment of silence in memory of the four fallen men.

CONTACTS:
Heritage Malta
Ex Royal Naval Hospital
Triq Marina
Kalkara, KKR1524 Malta
356-2295-4000; fax: 356-2122-2900
heritagemalta.org

♦ 1764 ♦ Mamuralia
March 14

According to one Roman myth, Mamurius was a smith who was run out of the city because the shields he had made for the Roman soldiers failed to protect them when they were substituted for the sacred shield that had fallen from heaven. Another explanation for the ceremonies held on this day is that Mamurius, whose name was a variation of Mars, represented the old year, which had to be driven away on the day preceding the first full moon of the new Roman year. In any case, the rite that took place on March 14 involved leading a man wearing only animal skins through the streets of Rome. He was pursued and beaten with long white rods until he was driven out of the city.

The Mamuralia was unusual in that no other Roman festival occurred on an even-numbered day. One explanation is that the festival was originally held on the IDES of March, but was moved back a day so that people could attend both the horseraces known as the EQUIRRIA and the ANNA PARENNA FESTIVAL held on March 15.

CONTACTS:
Italian National Tourist Board
686 Park Ave.
3rd Fl.
New York, NY 10065 United States

212-245-5618; fax: 212-586-9249
www.italiantourism.com

♦ 1765 ♦ Mandi Safar
During Islamic month of Safar

Mandi Safar is a Muslim bathing festival unique to Malaysia. This holiday, which is observed during the month of Safar, was originally believed to commemorate the last time Muhammad was able to bathe before his death. Muslims wearing bright colors visited beaches for a religious cleansing of the body and soul with water. There is no mention of the rite in the Qur'an (the Muslim holy book), and orthodox Muslims consider it nothing more than a picnic. It continues as a merry holiday. The best-known gathering places are the beaches of Tanjong Kling, near Malacca, and of Penang.

CONTACTS:
Malaysia Tourism Promotion Board
120 E. 56th St.
15th Fl.
New York, NY 10022
212-754-1113; fax: 212-754-1116
www.tourism.gov.my

Department of Islamic Development Malaysia
Federal Government Administration Centre
Level 4-9 Block D7
Putrajaya, Wilayah Persekutuan 62519 Malaysia
603-8886-4000; fax: 603-8889-2039
www.islam.gov.my

♦ 1766 ♦ Manger Yam
November 25

Like the NEW YAM FESTIVALS held in some African countries, Manger Yam is a harvest celebration of the yam crop observed in Haiti, a country mainly comprised of descendants of slaves from west Africa. Because Haitians, too, depend upon the yam crop, they hold the Manger Yam, named after the French *manger*, which means "to eat."

It is considered taboo to eat any of the new yams before the festival for fear of falling ill or bringing ruin to the yam crop. This is also an occasion on which families reunite to celebrate together. In Voodoo, or more properly, Vodoun, belief, it is very important for people to maintain relationships with the dead, as well as with each other and the gods, so the deceased are included in the Manger Yam as well as in other ceremonies and festivals.

In the Voodoo service, the priest or priestess leads prayers to the dead and to the gods and offers the first yams to them. After the ceremony, people feast on yam dishes and enjoy music and dancing.

CONTACTS:
Haiti Cultural Exchange
c/o FiveMyles Gallery
558 St. Johns Pl.
Brooklyn, NY 11238 United States
347-565-4429
haiticulturalx.org

♦ 1767 ♦ **Mani Rimdu**
Usually November

This Tibetan Buddhist festival is held at the Tengboche *gompa* (monastery) in Solu Khumbu district high in the Himalayas of Nepal. Merely getting there requires at least a six-day hike in the mountains. But the scenery—which includes Mt. Everest and several lower but equally impressive peaks—is magnificent for those who make it.

Mani Rimdu is a thousand-year-old Buddhist epic that is re-enacted in the courtyard of the monastery. It takes place under a full moon, and begins when masked dancers enter the courtyard in silence. The same re-enactment takes place at the Thami monastery in May or June, although festival organizers in both locations recently have started requesting that foreigners who want to witness the event pay a fee.

CONTACTS:
Nepal Tourism Board, Tourist Service Center
P.O. Box 11018
Bhrikuti Mandap
Nepal
977-1-425-6909; fax: 977-1-425-6910
welcomenepal.com

Chiwong Monastery
Boudha-6
P.O. 8043
Nepal
977-14-479305
chiwongmonastery.com

♦ 1768 ♦ **Manitoba Sunflower Festival**
Last weekend in July

The Mennonites were members of an evangelical Protestant sect that originated in Europe in the 16th century and was named for Menno Simon, a Dutch priest. They began emigrating to North America in the late 17th century and lived primarily as farmers, retaining their German language. A number of Russian Mennonites settled in Manitoba, Canada, where their heritage is still celebrated in the towns along the so-called Mennonite Trail.

Because the Mennonites were the first to extract the oil from sunflower plants, the city of Altona in southern Manitoba has chosen to honor its Mennonite heritage with an annual **Sunflower Festival** during the last weekend in July. Since 1965 the festival has attempted to revive the Mennonite culture by offering performances of "low German" humor and by serving a number of Mennonite foods such as *schmaunfat, veriniki, pluma moose, borscht,* and *rollkuchen.* A special sunflower ice cream is made especially for the festival. Less "authentic" activities include the Great Ping Pong Ball Drop, motorcross races, pancake breakfasts, and a huge farmers' market.

CONTACTS:
Town of Altona
111 Centre Ave.
P.O. Box 1630
Altona, MB R0G 0B0 Canada
204-324-6468; fax: 204-324-1550
altona.ca

Manitoba Music
1-376 Donald St.
Winnipeg, MB R3B 2J2 Canada
204-942-8650; fax: 204-942-6083
www.manitobamusic.com

♦ 1769 ♦ **Manly Man Festival and Spam Cook-Off, National**
Father's Day weekend (June)

In 1991 in Roslyn, Wash., a group of male camping buddies got together to create the National Manly Man Festival and Spam Cook-Off. This spoof event displays the alleged manliness of those who attend. Now organized by the Order of the Manly Men, which claims 1,000 members nationwide, the event includes such manly activities as eating bugs, bucking bellies together in greeting, and preparing and eating a variety of Spam-related foods. Spam chowder and Spam quiche are two of the favorites. Those who enter the Spam cook-off can win trophies donated by the Hormel Corp., maker of the canned meat product.

In addition to the Spam-related activities, there is also a parade of manly vehicles down Roslyn's main street (women can participate providing their vehicle is "manly" enough), a tool-belt competition, a softball game, and the selection of the Spam queen, who qualifies based on submitting a 100-word essay. Those men who attend the National Manly Man Festival receive an official membership card, a beer mug, and a certificate proving their manliness. Honorary Order of the Manly Men memberships have been granted to actors Kurt Russell and Bruce Willis, Governor Arnold Schwarzenegger, and former football coach Mike Ditka.

CONTACTS:
City of Roslyn
201 S. 1st St.
P.O. Box 451
Roslyn, WA 98941
509-649-3105; fax: 509-649-3174
www.ci.roslyn.wa.us

♦ 1770 ♦ **Mar del Plata International Film Festival**
November

The Mar del Plata International Film Festival is an event held in November in Mar del Plata, a beach resort in Argentina. Inaugurated in 1954, the festival was intended to be an artistic and cultural event rather than a competitive one, and so it remained simply an exhibition of selected international movies for several years. During the 1970s and 1980s, the festival suffered several interruptions as a result of political upheavals in the country. The festival was reestablished in 1996, and has since 2008 has been a regular on the international film festival circuit. Today, the Mar del Plata International Film Festival provides an international springboard for Latin American films, and also presents the best of international films to the domestic audience. As the only film festival in Latin America to be recognized by the FIAPF (International Federation of Film Producers Association), the festival has evolved over the years to offer a thorough perspective on world cinema. Every year the festival includes over 300 titles in a variety of genres, along with special presentations and retrospectives. The Astor awards are given to the winners in the international competition section; the best Latin American, Argentine, and short films are also recognized with awards.

CONTACTS:
Mar del Plata International Film Festival
Av. Belgrano 1586
9th Fl.
Buenos Aires, 1093 Argentina
54-11-4383-6904
www.mardelplatafilmfest.com

◆ 1771 ◆ Maralal Camel Derby
August

The Maralal Camel Derby takes place annually over three days in August in Maralal, Kenya, located about 180 miles north of Nairobi in the country's Northern Region. First held in 1990, it welcomes entrants from all over the world, who compete against Kenyan champions in professional and amateur races. The professional camel races are regarded by many as a serious international sport. The race course runs through desert areas with conditions presenting varying levels of difficulty. Camels are available for hire (handlers optional) to anyone who wants to saddle up and take part.

In addition to the camel races, other competitive events include donkey rides for children and bicycle races of 18 miles and 26 miles. Also featured are colorful displays of local dancing. The spectacular festival, organized by Yares Safaris, draws visitors from around the globe, but it has a serious side. The camel races are intended to create awareness of the rapid desertification of Kenya and the benefits that camels can bring to desert inhabitants.

CONTACTS:
Kenya Tourism Board, c/o Myriad Marketing
6033 W. Century Blvd.
Ste. 900
Los Angeles, CA 90045
310-649-7718; fax: 310-649-7713
www.magicalkenya.com

◆ 1772 ◆ Marbles Tournament, National
Late June

The annual National Marbles Tournament began in 1922, when Macy's Department Store in Philadelphia sponsored a promotional tournament. The Scripps-Howard Newspapers sponsored the event until 1955, when the city of Wildwood, New Jersey, and a group of volunteers interested in preserving the game decided to sponsor the event jointly. Traditionally held for five days near the end of June in this New Jersey seaside resort town, the tournament features a competition among champions selected in elimination contests throughout the country. The national boy and girl champions each receive a trophy and a plaque as well as a $2,000 scholarship.

Although there are many games that can be played with marbles—such as Potsies, Poison, Passout, Chassies, Puggy,

Black Snake, and Old Boiler (reportedly a favorite with Abraham Lincoln)—the game played in the national tournament is called Ringer. It is played by placing 13 marbles in the form of a cross in a 10-foot circle. The marbles inside the circle are called "migs" or "miggles." Players alternate shots using a "shooter" or "taw," and the winner is the first one to shoot seven miggles out of the ring.

CONTACTS:
Greater Wildwoods Tourism Improvement and Development Authority
4501 Boardwalk
Wildwood, NJ '08260 United States
609-729-9000 or 800-992-9732; fax: 609-846-2631
www.wildwoodsnj.com

◆ 1773 ◆ Marche du Nain Rouge
Sunday following the Vernal Equinox

A costumed parade held in Detroit, Michigan, the Marche du Nain Rouge is a community event observed every year to drive away the Nain Rouge, a red dwarf, which according to legend is a harbinger of doom to the city. Held on the Sunday following the vernal equinox, the event revolves around a 300-year-old legend involving the founder of Detroit, Antoine de la Mothe Cadillac. It is said that Cadillac had a vision of the Nain Rouge and though warned to avoid him, fought him off valiantly. Many believe Cadillac was cursed to doom by the Nain Rouge, as years later he died penniless in France. For the centuries that followed, Detroiters honored the courage of Cadillac, but believed the Nain Rouge continued to taunt the city during difficult times.

During the march, costumed characters wind their way along the streets of the city, including some dressed as the Nain Rouge himself, who is intended to be banished by the groups that follow. One group, La Bande du Nains, is a group of citizens who claim heritage from the various continents of the world. Armed with sticks, canes, pots, and pans, they chase the red devil to a final destination: a bonfire that consumes an effigy of the Nain Rouge to rid the city of this mythical imp and his malevolent curse. Though the parade to drive away the Nain Rouge is the central focus of the event, it is followed by parties, music, and celebrations meant to signify the hope for good fortune to follow.

◆ 1774 ◆ Mardi Gras
February-March; two weeks before Ash Wednesday

The most flamboyant of Mardi Gras (from the French for "fat Tuesday") celebrations in North America culminates in a riot of parades and throngs of laughing, drinking, dancing people in the streets of New Orleans, La.

The Mardi Gras celebrations symbolize New Orleans, "The City that Care Forgot," to most people. The festivities actually start on Jan. 6 (Epiphany) with a series of private balls. The tempo picks up in the last two weeks of the Carnival season, when the streets ring with 30 separate parades organized by committees called *krewes*. The parades consist of marching jazz bands and lavishly decorated two-story floats carrying the costumed and masked krewe royalty who toss "throws" to pleading spectators; these are beads or bonbons or the coveted Mardi Gras doubloons. Each of the parades has 15 to 20 floats, all decorated to express a certain theme.

Two of the biggest and most elaborate parades, the Krewe of Endymion and the Bacchus parade, take place on the weekend before Mardi Gras. On the day of Mardi Gras, designated the "Day of Un-Rule," the traditional parades spotlight Rex, King of Carnival and Monarch of Merriment, in the morning, and Comus, God of Revelry, by torchlight at night. On that same evening the private balls of Rex and Comus are held. At midnight, the madness of Carnival ends, and LENT begins, and a million or so spectators and participants face sobriety.

New Orleans had its first organized Mardi Gras parade in 1857. It consisted of two floats and was presented by the first Carnival society, the Mistick Krewe of Comus, its name alluding to John Milton's masque, *Comus*. The parade was apparently well received; it was one of the first local institutions revived after the Civil War.

Mardi Gras in New Orleans is the best known, but not the oldest Mardi Gras. A two-week pre-Lenten celebration in Mobile, Ala., stands alone as the oldest celebration of Mardi Gras in the country. It was first observed in 1703 by the French who had founded the port city the year before. When the Spanish occupied Mobile in 1780, they moved it to the eve of the TWELFTH NIGHT of CHRISTMAS and paraded in grotesque costumes and masks. The celebrations were suspended during the Civil War, but were revived in 1866 by Joe Cain, a town clerk who togged himself out as an Indian chief and rode through the streets in a charcoal wagon. The old Mardi Gras societies reappeared, and new ones evolved.

Today a different mystic society parades each evening in the two weeks before Lent, and balls are held that are open to everyone. Mardi Gras itself, the day before ASH WEDNESDAY, is a legal holiday in the state of Louisiana.

Galveston, Texas, has a 12-day period of whoop-de-do leading up to the actual day of **Fat Tuesday** in this barrier-island city of Texas. About 200,000 spectators are attracted to the Mardi Gras festival, which was first held here in 1867. Though it died out at the turn of the century, it was revived in 1985. Growing bigger every year, this celebration features masked balls, royal coronations, Cajun dances, jazz performances, and, of course, numerous parades with dramatic floats.

See also CARNIVAL and SHROVE TUESDAY.

CONTACTS:
Galveston Island Visitors Center
2328 Bdwy.
Galveston, TX 77550
409-797-5144 or 888-425-4753
www.galveston.com

New Orleans Convention and Visitors Bureau
2020 Saint Charles Ave.
New Orleans, LA 70130 United States
504-566-5011 or 800-672-6124; fax: 504-566-5046
neworleanscvb.com

Mobile Bay Convention & Visitors Bureau
1 South Water St.
Mobile Bay, AL 36602
251-208-2000 or 800-566-2453; fax: 251-208-2060
www.mobile.org

♦ 1775 ♦ **Mardi Gras (France)**
Between February 3 and March 9; Tuesday before Ash Wednesday

MARDI GRAS (Fat Tuesday) is the last day of CARNIVAL, the three-day period of uninhibited celebration that precedes LENT. The festivities in France are particularly colorful in southern cities like Cannes, Menton, and Grasse, all in Alpes-Maritimes department, where people go out in the streets in costume and indulge in all sorts of noisy pranks, such as tooting tin horns and pelting passersby with confetti and flowers. Each town, in fact, has its own *bataille de fleurs* (battle of flowers) right before Lent, with people in flower-decked cars and floats driving for hours along the streets and boulevards, throwing flowers at each other.

One of the great celebrations of Europe is the carnival at Nice, where grotesque, caricatured figures parade down the Avenue de la Gare—among them giant cabbages and carrots, gnomes, devils on horseback, nymphs, and fairies. King Carnival, dressed in striped hose and a slashed doublet, leads the parade from his throne on a float draped with purple velvet. On the night of Mardi Gras, the King Carnival effigy is burned at the stake.

In Paris and some other French cities, butchers observe Carnival with the fête of the *Boeuf Gras*, or Fat Ox. An ox decked with garlands of greenery, flowers, and ribbons is led through the streets in procession, followed by a triumphal cart bearing a young boy known as the "King of the Butchers." The crowd pays tribute to him by blowing horns and throwing confetti, flowers, and sweets.

See also NICE CARNAVAL.

CONTACTS:
Rendez-vous en France
825 Third Ave.
New York, NY 10022
212-838-7800; fax: 212-838-7855
int.rendezvousenfrance.com

♦ 1776 ♦ **Mardi Gras Film Festival**
February to March

The Mardi Gras Film Festival, which takes place each year during the Gay and Lesbian Mardi Gras in Sydney, Australia, features screenings of lesbian, gay, bisexual, and transgender (LGBT) films from around the world. Although LGBT films have been a part of the Sydney Mardi Gras since 1986, the current film festival was established in 1993 when *Queer Screen,* an organization of Sydney filmmakers and students, took control of the festival to develop it as a community-produced event. Over two decades, the festival has grown to become one of Australia's largest film festivals, and one of the most highly-respected and important LGBT film festivals in the world.

Presenting up to 50 films over the course of two weeks, the festival program includes traditional feature films, short films, and documentaries. Each year, several films make their world premiere at the festival. At the conclusion of the festival, audience awards are announced recognizing the Best Feature and the Best Documentary.

CONTACTS:
Queer Screen
Ste. 5, Level 1
66 Oxford St.
Darlinghurst, NSW 2010 Australia
612-9332-4938; fax: 612-9332-4319
queerscreen.org.au

♦ 1777 ♦ Margaret Mead Film Festival
October

The Margaret Mead Film Festival is an event sponsored by the American Museum of Natural History in New York and is held annually every fall. The focus of the festival is to bring challenging subjects and films involving a wide range of issues and perspectives to the fore. Documentaries, animation, hybrid, and experimental films that promote an understanding of diversity and highlight different cultural heritages are included at the festival. A premier showcase for experimental documentaries and films exploring indigenous peoples, the festival is known for being one of the first to exhibit diverse, extraordinary subject matter. For example, *Paris Is Burning*, a film about the urban transgender ballroom community in New York City, was screened at the festival in 1990.

The festival is named after Margaret Mead, a renowned anthropologist who worked at the Museum of Natural History. It was founded in 1977 during the year of her 75th birthday. Her studies are recognized for popularizing cultural anthropology and advancing its academic standing and appeal. She was one of the first anthropologists to integrate visual media in her work, which focused on studying specific aspects of visual communication. The festival exemplifies Mead's concept that films could be used as tools for varied cultures to understand and learn from each other.

The Margaret Mead Filmmaker Award, presented annually, recognizes filmmakers who embody the essence, vitality, and innovation that Mead exhibited in her anthropology research and fieldwork.

CONTACTS:
American Museum of Natural History
Central Park W. at 79th St.
New York, NY 10024
212-769-5305; fax: 212-769-5329
www.amnh.org/explore/margaret-mead-film-festival

♦ 1778 ♦ Margrethe's (Queen) Birthday
April 16

The birthday of Queen Margrethe II (b. 1940) is observed in the capital city of Copenhagen, where people congregate in the courtyard of Amalienborg, the royal palace. Carrying small Danish flags, children cheer and sing for the Queen, refusing to go home until she comes out to greet them. She often appears on the balcony at lunchtime and makes a speech, which is followed by a changing of the Royal Guard in its scarlet dress uniforms.

CONTACTS:
Amalienborg Museum
Christian VIII"'s Palace
Copenhagen, 1257 Denmark
45-3312-2186
www.kongernessamling.dk

Office of the Lord Chamberlain
Det Gule Palæ
Amaliegade 18
Copenhagen, 1256 Denmark
45-3340-1010; fax: 45-3340-2777
kongehuset.dk

♦ 1779 ♦ Marian Days
First weekend of August

In 1975 the Congregation of the Mother Co-Redemptrix, a Vietnamese religious order, established a new campus in Carthage, Mo. The order's priests and brothers were among tens of thousands of Vietnamese citizens who came to the United States to escape the turmoil of the Vietnam War (1959–1975). Many Vietnamese Catholics believed their safe passage to America was the result of the Virgin Mary's intervention. Marian Days, which the small town of Carthage has hosted since 1977, is a time for Vietnamese Catholics to honor the Mother of Jesus and recognize the protection she offered to refugees.

Despite its small size, Carthage somehow manages to handle the influx of more than 70,000 visitors for the summer celebration. Attendees come from all over the country; some stay in nearby hotels, and others camp on the grounds of the Catholic order's 28-acre campus or in residents' backyards. A festival area is arranged before the weekend for church groups to erect food tents and various displays.

The weekend's events, which include daily Masses, penance ceremonies, benedictions, and religious lectures, lead up to the Saturday celebration, which consists of a parade for the Virgin Mary as well as a fireworks and balloon ceremony. The weekend closes with a final mass that is recited in Vietnamese and translated into English.

CONTACTS:
Congregation of the Mother Co-Redemptrix
1900 Grand Ave.
Carthage, MO 64836
417-358-7787; fax: 417-358-9508
dongcong.net

Carthage Convention & Visitors Bureau
402 S. Garrison Ave.
Carthage, MO 64836
417-359-8181
visit-carthage.com

◆ 1780 ◆ **Marino Wine Festival**
First weekend in October

The Italian town of Marino is located in the area southeast of Rome known as the Castelli Romani, after the numerous castles, palaces, and Renaissance villas that dot the landscape. Marino is known as a wine town, and there are about a hundred *cantine*—small, nondescript taverns where tourists and residents can buy the local wine, which is often siphoned from a large vat and poured into an empty mineral water bottle, for a very low price. It's not surprising, then, that during the town's wine festival in early October the new grape harvest is celebrated by letting the previous year's wine gush freely from the Moors Fountain. Crowds of Romans eager to escape the city descend upon Marino with jugs, bottles, and thermoses to fill. The wine is free for the taking and is the perfect accompaniment to a *porchetta* sandwich, the filling made by slowly roasting pig over a woodfire with fresh garlic, rosemary, and olive oil.

CONTACTS:
Italian National Tourist Board
686 Park Ave.
3rd Fl.
New York, NY 10065
212-245-5618; fax: 212-586-9249
www.italiantourism.com

Gourmet's International Srl/GmbH
Via Bernhard-Johannes-Str.
Merano, BZ 39012 Italy
39-47-321-0011; fax: 39-47-323-3720
www.meranowinefestival.com/en

◆ 1781 ◆ **Marion County Ham Days**
Last full weekend in September

This event is a weekend celebration of the famous Kentucky smoked ham, held in Lebanon (Marion County), Ky., since 1970. The affair started with a simple country ham breakfast served to about 300 people on the street; now about 50,000 folks show up. Breakfast (ham cured in Marion County, eggs, biscuits with local honey, fried apples) is still served on Saturday and Sunday, but there is more: a "Pigasus Parade" with more than 100 floats, a Pokey Pig 5-kilometer run, a crafts and antiques show, a hog-calling contest, a hay-bale toss, and a hot air balloon race.

CONTACTS:
Marion County Chamber of Commerce
239 N. Spalding Ave.
Lebanon, KY 40033
270-692-9594
www.marioncountykychamber.com

◆ 1782 ◆ **Mariposa Folk Festival**
First weekend in July

This three-day folk music festival is the oldest in Canada, where it has served as a model for many smaller festivals. Since 1961 the festival has presented a broad spectrum of folk music—from Kentucky blues to Indian chanting—by performers from all over Canada, the United States, Britain, Africa, and Australia. The events are held on the grounds of Tudhope Park in Orillia, Ontario, about 60 miles north of Toronto.

The Mariposa Festival helped pioneer the workshop concept, emphasizing the importance of establishing a dialogue between the artist and the audience. In addition to the workshops hosted by festival musicians, there is a "folk-play" area where a family can work with a particular performer, who shares his or her special talents with both children and their parents.

CONTACTS:
Mariposa Folk Foundation
10 Peter St. S.
Orillia, ON L3V 5A9 Canada
705-326-3655; fax: 705-326-5963
www.mariposafolk.com

◆ 1783 ◆ **Maritime Day, National**
May 22

The day chosen to commemorate the contribution of American commercial shipping is, appropriately, the day on which the *Savannah* left its home port in Georgia in 1819 to attempt the first steam-propelled crossing of the Atlantic. So unusual was it to see a steam-powered vessel in those days that when the *Savannah* passed the naval station at Cape Clear, Ireland, the authorities thought she was on fire and quickly dispatched a royal cutter to assist her. In reality, the *Savannah* was equipped with sails and only relied on her engines for about 90 hours of the journey.

It was President Franklin D. ROOSEVELT who first proclaimed May 22 as National Maritime Day in 1933. Since that time observations of this day have grown in popularity, particularly in American port cities. Ships are opened to the public, maritime art and essay contests are held, and parades and band concerts are common. Environmentalists sometimes take advantage of the attention focused on the country's maritime heritage on this day to draw attention to pollution and deterioration of maritime environments, particularly in large commercial ports like New York City.

CONTACTS:
U.S. Department of Transportation - Maritime Administration
1200 New Jersey Ave. SE
W. Bldg.
Washington, D.C. 20590
202-366-4000 or 800-996-2723
www.marad.dot.gov

U.S. Maritime Service
1200 New Jersey Ave. S.E.
Washington, D.C. 20590
www.usmm.org

◆ 1784 ◆ **Marlboro Music Festival**
Mid-July to mid-August

It was the noted violinist Adolf Busch who came up with the idea of establishing a summer community for musicians that would free them from the pressures and restrictions of concert life. Every summer since 1951, a group of artists from all over the world has gathered in Marlboro, Vermont, to exchange musical ideas. The Marlboro Music School, which holds an eight-week session each summer, is primarily a place where students or those who are just starting out on their professional careers can study contemporary and classical chamber music.

During the five-week festival, the general public has an opportunity to hear the results of their collaborations. But the primary emphasis at Marlboro is on rehearsing the works that the participants themselves have selected, rather than on performing them for the public.

Although many noted musicians have been associated with Marlboro, perhaps the best known is Pablo CASALS, the world-famous cellist who conducted the Marlboro Festival Orchestra and taught master classes there from 1960 to 1973.

CONTACTS:
Marlboro Music Festival
2472 S. Rd.
Brattleboro, VT 05301
802-254-2394; fax: 802-254-4307
www.marlboromusic.org

◆ 1785 ◆ Marley's (Bob) Birthday
Week of February 6

A week-long Bob Marley Birthday celebration takes place every year over the course of the week of his birth date (February 6, 1945). Events center in and around the Bob Marley museum in Kingston, Jamaica. The museum is located at 56 Hope Road, where Marley lived during the 1970s and recorded many of the reggae-music albums for which he is famous. The celebration typically encompasses such events as symposia on Marley's life and work, films, lectures, learning activities for children, and of course a series of concerts celebrating Marley's music. In the past, Marley's four sons have performed to benefit Ghetto Youths, a charity that two of Marley's sons founded to help young artists get started in the music business.

The birthday celebration is sponsored by Tuff Gong Records International, the landmark Caribbean record company founded by Marley in 1965, which also runs the Bob Marley Foundation. Since Marley's death in 1981, the birthday celebration has grown in momentum, and it now draws hundreds of fans to his hometown.

CONTACTS:
Tuff Gong International
220 Marcus Garvey Dr.
Kingston, Jamaica 11 West Indies
876-923-9380; fax: 876-923-4657
tuffgong.com

The Rita Marley Foundation
56 Hope Rd.
Jamaica
876-978-2991
www.ritamarleyfoundation.org

◆ 1786 ◆ Maroon Festival
January 6

When Jamaica was a Spanish territory in the 16th century, African slaves were brought in to work the plantations. The Spanish, disappointed by the lack of gold on the island, eventually left and the former slaves fled to the mountains. During the 17th and 18th centuries, the island's British inhabitants were often harassed or attacked by the descendants of these well-armed and organized fugitive slaves, who were called Maroons (having been marooned or deserted by their owners). By 1738 the Maroons had been given permission to settle in the northern part of the island.

The annual Maroon Festival is held at Accompong on January 6, and commemorates the 1759 signing of the peace treaty with the English and establishment of the town of Accompong. It is celebrated with traditional dancing and singing, maroon feasts and ceremonies, the blowing of the *abeng*, and the playing of maroon drums.

CONTACTS:
Visit Jamaica
5201 Blue Lagoon Dr.
Ste. 670
Miami, FL 33126
305-665-0557 or 800-526-2422; fax: 305-666-7239
www.visitjamaica.com

◆ 1787 ◆ Marrakech Popular Arts Festival
Mid-July

The annual five-day national festival of popular arts is held in Marrakech, Morocco, every July. It showcases folk singers, dancers, theater troupes, fortune-tellers, fire-swallowers, and snake charmers from all over Morocco, as well as a variety or artists and entertainers from Europe, Asia, and South America, including China, Peru, and Ukraine. Performances take place at outdoor venues all over the city, with the major events centered in the ruins of the 16-century Badi Palace or the Djemma el Fna (main town square). Launched in the mid-1960s, the festival is one of the longest-running of its kind.

CONTACTS:
Foundation des Festivals de Marrakech
Theatre Royal
Avenue Mohammed VI
Morocco
212-52-443-2021
www.marrakechfestival.com

◆ 1788 ◆ Marriage Fair
September

This mass engagement and marriage *moussem*, or "festival," is held in the remote village of Imilchil in the Atlas Mountains of Morocco. As many as 30,000 people of the Ait Hadiddou tribe, a Berber clan, gather for the three days of the moussem. Also known as the **Fiancée Festival**, this is a combined trade fair and pageant of public courtship, instant engagement, and the immediate exchange of marriage vows. The festival solves the problem of meeting a mate in a society where isolation is the norm: the men spend half a year moving with their flocks to upland pastures, while the women stay in the villages, planting crops and weaving rugs.

Families and their herds of sheep and donkeys stream onto the Imilchil plateau at dawn of the first day. They sell or barter their wool, meat, grain, and vegetables, while tradesmen set up tents of pottery, rugs, and tools. Musicians beat tambourines, games are played, and acrobats perform. The center of their Islam-influenced devotions is the tomb of the holy man Sidi Mohammed el Merheni. It's not certain when he lived but it's known that the marriages he blessed were happy.

The courtship proceeds with women wearing a peaked headdress and striped wool capes over white dresses. Their eyes are outlined with kohl and their cheeks are rouged. The prospective grooms, wearing white robes and turbans, weave in pairs through the clusters of brides-to-be. A man speaks to a woman, the woman nods assent, and if the family approves, the couple will enter the wedding tent to seek approval from a representative of the Ministry of Justice in Rabat. Brides who have not been previously married will leave the moussem with their fathers, and be welcomed by their grooms' families with a feast later in the year. Women who are divorcées or widows will go directly to live with their husbands. (Ait Hadiddou women are free to divorce and remarry.)

When a woman consents to marriage, she tells her suitor, "You have captured my liver." The Ait Hadiddou consider the liver to be the soul of love because it aids digestion and well-being.

CONTACTS:
Moroccan National Tourist Office (New York)
104 W. 40th St.
Ste. 1820
New York, NY 10018 United States
212-221-1583; fax: 212-221-1887
www.visitmorocco.com/index.php/eng

♦ 1789 ♦ **Marshall Islands Constitution Day**
May 1

In 1943, during World War II, the Allied forces—the United States, Britain, France, Union of Soviet Socialist Republics (USSR), Australia, Belgium, Brazil, Canada, China, Denmark, Greece, Netherlands, New Zealand, Norway, Poland, South Africa, and Yugoslavia—invaded the Marshall Islands. By 1944, the Allied forces occupied the Marshall Islands. At the end of World War II, the United States was given effective power in the Marshall Islands. Throughout their occupation, the United States conducted nuclear weapons testing on the islands (*see also* REMEMBRANCE DAY).

On May 1, 1979, the Marshall Islands constitution was signed, establishing it as a self-governing country. In 1982, the Marshall Islands officially changed its name to the Republic of the Marshall Islands.

Constitution Day is a public holiday in the Marshall Islands. On this day of celebration, people gather together for a parade to commemorate their independence. Also as part of the celebration, field-day contests are held between all private and public schools, entities within the community itself, and more. Some of these contests include basketball, women's softball, men's baseball, volleyball, soccer, tug-of-war, and various track-and-field events.

CONTACTS:
Marshall Islands Visitors Authority (MIVA)
P.O. Box 5
Majuro, 96960 Marshall Islands
692-625-6482; fax: 692-625-6771
www.visitmarshallislands.com

Embassy of the Republic of the Marshall Islands
2433 Massachusetts Ave., N.W.
Washington, D.C. 20008
202-234-5414; fax: 202-232-3236
www.rmiembassyus.org

♦ 1790 ♦ **Marshall Islands Fishermen's Day**
First Friday in July

In the Marshall Islands, Fishermen's Day is a public holiday that is sponsored by the Marshalls Billfish Club. During the Fishermen's Day contest, competing fishermen go out into the ocean and attempt to catch the most, the biggest, or the heaviest fish in any of several categories. Because the boats often leave between 5:30 and 6:00 A.M., competitors usually register the evening before the actual contest day. The fishing often lasts as late as 5:00 P.M., at which time the fish are weighed and measured.

The Marshall Islands is well known to have some of the best sport-fishing conditions in the world. In 1981, four friends, Tom Micheals, Wally Milne, Ramsey Reimers, and Ronnie Reimers, founded the Marshalls Billfish Club so that they could be invited to compete in the Hawaiian Invitational Billfish Tournament (HIBT) championship in Kona, Hawaii. During their first time competing in this tournament, the Marshalls Billfish Club won with a 711-pound marlin caught by Ramsey Reimers. That fish remains in the top ten for that competition.

The win at the 1981 HIBT inspired the four friends to set up an annual tournament in the Marshall Islands every July. They recruited many volunteers to help plan and run the very first tournament in July 1982. The Marshall Islands government endorsed the club, local businesses made contributions, and several off-island supporters also contributed to the event. Since then, the event has become a national holiday and a source of enjoyment to hundreds of people each year.

The Marshalls Billfish Club now has a Board of Directors, consisting of seven elected directors and four appointed positions (President, Vice President, Director, and Secretary). There are now over 200 members in the club.

CONTACTS:
Marshall Islands Billfishclub
P.O. Box 1139

Majuro, MH 969690 Marshall Islands
692-625-7491
www.billfishclub.com

♦ 1791 ♦ Marshall Islands Gospel Day
First Friday in December

Gospel Day in the Marshall Islands is similar to THANKSGIVING day in the United States. The only difference between the two countries' celebrations is that the Marshallese people attend church on this day to commemorate the first missionaries who brought the light of God to the Marshall Islands.

Today, most Marshallese are Protestants. In general, the Marshallese people are very religious. In the Republic of the Marshall Islands, Sundays are set aside for rest and relaxation and attending church services.

The largest church in the Marshall Islands is the United Church of Christ; however, many other Protestant denominations have churches in the Marshall Islands, including Assembly of God, Baptist, and Seventh Day Adventists. In addition, the Catholic Church has established a strong presence in the islands. And more recently, the Church of Latter-day Saints has also become established.

CONTACTS:
Embassy of the Republic of the Marshall Islands
2433 Massachusetts Ave., N.W.
Washington, D.C. 20008
202-234-5414; fax: 202-232-3236
www.rmiembassyus.org

♦ 1792 ♦ Marshall Islands Lutok Kobban Alele
Last week of September

The inhabitants of Micronesia's Marshall Islands have long kept a tradition centered on the *alele,* a soft-sided basket handmade from the native pandanus plant. This treasured item contains a family's most valuable possessions, and according to Marshallese custom, passes through generations in the trust of the family's eldest female.

The phrase "Lutok Kobban Alele" means pour out the valuable contents of the basket. The event of the same name is a weeklong festival that honors the basket as a national symbol and celebrates Marshallese culture in general. The inaugural festival was held in 1986, the year that the Marshall Islands ended a long era under U.S. administration. In years past, the festival has been sponsored by the Marshall Islands Alele Museum.

Festivities conclude with an official ceremony on MANIT DAY, a public holiday observed on the last Friday of September. Activities take place in the capital city of Marjuro and include performances by Marshallese singers and dancers, feasts promoting local foods, traditional storytelling, and demonstrations of basket weaving and cooking.

CONTACTS:
Marshallese Educational Initiative, Inc.
P.O. Box 875

Fayetteville, AR 72702 United States
479-365-6755
www.meius.org

Alele Museum, Library and National Archives
P.O. Box 629
Majuro, MH 96960 Marshall Islands
692-625-3372; fax: 692-625-3226
alelemuseum.tripod.com/Index.html

♦ 1793 ♦ Marshall Islands Manit Day (Marshall Islands Custom Day)
Last Friday in September

Cultural values and customs in the Marshall Islands are known as *manit*. Manit Day is part of the annual cultural festival LUTOK KOBBAN ALELE, which is the last week of September. The purpose of Lutok Kobban Alele is to promote and preserve the Marshallese culture.

The Manit Day celebration takes place near the Alele Museum, Library, and National Archive, which displays exclusive and original artifacts of the Marshall Islands. On Manit Day, people from the general public can set up a booth outside the museum to sell their handicrafts, food, drinks, etc. Many Marshallese handicrafts are known for their high quality and use of natural products. Woven baskets, fans, hats, wall hangings, purses, mats, coasters, and Marshallese stick charts are made from such raw materials as coconut, pandana leaves, and likajir shells. Popular Marshallese products also include such coconut oil products as hand soaps and laundry detergents. These products are good for the skin, but they do not harm the environment.

As part of the celebration, children from all of the public schools have the opportunity to perform dances, sing songs, perform skits, or tell folklore stories. In addition, some local traditional contest games, including coconut husking and basket weaving, are often conducted.

CONTACTS:
Alele Museum, Library and National Archives
P.O. Box 629
Majuro, MH 96960 Marshall Islands
692-625-3372; fax: 692-625-3226
alelemuseum.tripod.com

Missionary Ventures International
5144 S. Orange Ave.
P.O. Box 593550
Orlando, FL 32809
407-859-7322; fax: 407-856-7934
www.mvi.org

♦ 1794 ♦ Marshall Islands President's Day
November 17

The Republic of the Marshall Islands has designated November 17 as President's Day, a day to remember the nation's first president, Amata Kabua. Kabua started his career as a school teacher and rose to become paramount chief of the Island of Majuro and head of state of the Marshall Islands. He served five terms as president of the Marshall Islands, beginning in

1979 when the country became independent and continuing until his death in 1996.

There are no organized activities or events on this day.

CONTACTS:
Office of the President, Republic of the Marshall Islands
P.O. Box 2
Majuro, MH 96960 Marshall Islands
692-625-2233; fax: 692-625-4021
www.rmi-op.net

♦ 1795 ♦ Martenitza
March 1

Every year on March 1, people in Bulgaria present each other with *martenitzas*—two joined tassels of red-and-white woolen thread resembling a simple CHRISTMAS decoration symbolizing health and happiness. The custom originated with the ancient Thracians, and the first martenitzas had silver or gold coins attached to them. Today it is most widespread in Bulgaria, although the Martenitza is also celebrated in southern Romania, Albania, Greece, and Cyprus.

The rites are varied. In some regions, women dress completely in red on this day. In northeastern Bulgaria, the lady of the house traditionally tosses a red cloth over a fruit tree, or spreads a red woolen cloth on the fields for fertility. In stock-breeding areas, a red-and-white thread is tied to the cattle. Bulgaria is the only country where this particular fertility custom seems to have survived. In Greece the "March" is tied to the wrist or big toe of children to protect them from the March sun. They remove it when they see the first swallow or stork, signs of springtime. On Cyprus it is hoped that one's skin will be as red (healthy) as the string. In Canada, Bulgarian-Macedonians throw the string out for the first robins to use in their nests.

See also DRYMIAIS.

CONTACTS:
Stara Zagora Tourist Information Centre
27, Ruski Blvd.
Stara Zagora, 6000 Bulgaria
359-42-627-098; fax: 359-42-627-098
www.tour.starazagora.bg/en

Embassy of the Republic of Bulgaria
1621 22nd St. N.W.
Dimitar Peshev Plaza
Washington, D.C. 20008
202-387-0174 or 202-299-0273; fax: 202-234-7973
www.bulgaria-embassy.org

♦ 1796 ♦ Martinmas
November 11

This is the feast day of St. Martin of Tours (c. 316-397), one of the most popular saints of the Middle Ages. It is said that when he heard that he had been elected bishop of Tours, he hid himself in a barn. A squawking goose gave away his hiding place, and the day is still celebrated with roast goose dinners. Another popular legend involves St. Martin's cloak, which he divided with his sword, giving half to a shivering beggar.

In Germany and northern Europe, Roman Catholics commemorate St. Martin while Protestants commemorate Martin Luther's baptismal day (*see* MARTINSFEST).

For rural people, Martinmas comes at a happy time of year: the crops are in, the animals have been slaughtered, the new wine is ready, and the hard work of summer and autumn is over. It's no surprise, then, that St. Martin is the patron saint of tavern keepers, wine-growers, and drunkards. There is a good deal of weather lore associated with this day. Spells of mild autumn weather that Americans refer to as "Indian summer" are called "St. Martin's summer" or "a Martinmas summer" in Europe and England. It was once a QUARTER DAY. Nowadays, in England, this day is more remembered as Armistice Day (*see* VETERANS DAY).

In Belgium, where it is called **Sint Maartens Dag**, St. Martin's Day is a favorite holiday among children. Like ST. NICHOLAS, St. Martin visits them on the feast day eve bringing them gifts. On November 11 apples and nuts are tossed into children's rooms while they stand with their faces turned to the wall. *Gauffres*, little waffle cakes, are particularly popular on St. Martin's Day.

This day is also an important festival in the Netherlands. There it is known as **Beggar's Day**, and boys and girls serenade their neighbors and beg for goodies. In many towns the children light a bonfire and dance and shout around it. Then they march in processions with lanterns made from scooped-out turnips, carrots, or beets.

In other European countries, St. Martin's Day is regarded as a time to give thanks for the harvest and is often observed with feasting. Goose is the traditional meal. In Sweden, November 11 is known as **Martin's Goose Day** (**Marten Gas**). In France, *mal de Saint Martin* (St. Martin's sickness) is the name given to the upset stomach that often follows overindulgence. There is also an impressive ceremony at St. Martin's shrine in Tours on this day.

See also HUERIGEN PARTIES; QUADRILLES OF SAN MARTIN; ST. MARTIN'S DAY IN PORTUGAL.

CONTACTS:
Belgian Tourist Office
300 E. 42nd St.
14th Fl.
New York, NY 10017
212-758-8130
www.visitbelgium.com

St. Martin of Tours
220 Central Ave.
Bethpage, NY 11714
516-931-0818
www.smtbethpage.org

♦ 1797 ♦ Martinmas (Ireland)
November 11

There are a number of superstitions and folk beliefs associated with MARTINMAS in Ireland. One is that you must have roast goose for dinner or risk eating no more goose in the coming year. (According to legend, when St. Martin heard that he had been elected Bishop of Tours, he hid himself in a barn but was given away by a squawking goose.) In any case, it is traditional to kill a sheep, lamb, kid, pig, calf, or cow on St. Martin's Eve and eat the meat on **St. Martin's Day**, after sprinkling the animal's blood in the four corners of the house as well as on the walls, threshold, and floor. A dot of blood is even smeared on the forehead of each family member in the belief that it will protect them from evil for one year. The shedding of blood may also be a survival of the time when animals were killed right before winter because it was difficult to find fodder.

On the Aran Islands off the western coast of Ireland, there is a legend that when St. Martin stopped at the house of a poor woman and asked for something to eat, she sacrificed her child because she had no meat to offer him. But when he left the house, the woman found her child still asleep in his cradle. Aran Islanders sacrifice an animal on Martinmas in memory of this miracle, and feed roast cock or goose to any beggar who comes to the door on November 11.

Fishermen in Ireland will not go fishing on Martinmas, believing that if they do, they will meet a horseman riding over the sea, followed by a terrible storm. It is also considered bad luck to turn a wheel of any kind—car, mill, or spinning—on this day.

CONTACTS:
Church of Ireland House
Church Ave.
Rathmines, Dublin 6 Ireland
353-1-497-8422; fax: 353-1-497-8821
www.ireland.anglican.org

National Tourism Development Authority
88-95, Amiens St.
Ireland
353-1-884-7101
www.failteireland.ie

♦ 1798 ♦ Martinsfest
November 10-11

Martin's Festival in Germany honors both St. Martin of Tours (*see* MARTINMAS and ST. MARTIN'S DAY IN PORTUGAL) and Martin Luther (1483-1546), the German theologian and leader of the Protestant REFORMATION.

In Düsseldorf, a man dressed as St. Martin rides through the streets followed by hundreds of children. Many carry lanterns made from hollowed-out pumpkins. It is thought that the rites associated with St. Martin's Day may have originated as an early thanksgiving festival in honor of Freya, the ancient German goddess of plenty.

While German Roman Catholics honor St. Martin on this day, Protestants honor Martin Luther, who was born on November 10, 1483, and baptized on the 11th. In Erfurt, where Martin Luther attended the university, there is a procession of children carrying lanterns. This ends in the plaza in front of the cathedral and the Severi Church. With their lanterns the children form the "Luther rose," or the escutcheon of Martin Luther.

CONTACTS:
German Lutheran Church - Deutsche Evangelische
Kirchengemeinde Washington DC
10012 Kendale Rd.
Potomac, MD 20854
301-365-2678
www.glcwashington.org/english

German National Tourist Office
122 E. 42nd St.
Ste. 2000
New York, NY 10168
212-661-4796; fax: 212-661-7174
www.germany.travel/en

German Information Center USA, Embassy of the Federal
Republic of Germany
4645 Reservoir Rd. N.W.
Washington, D.C. 20007
202-298-4000
www.germany.info

♦ 1799 ♦ Martyrdom of Joseph and Hyrum Smith
June 27

Members of the Church of Jesus Christ of Latter-Day Saints, also known as Mormons, commemorate the day on which their founder, Joseph Smith, and his brother, Hyrum, were murdered in the city jail in Carthage, Illinois, in 1844. Joseph Smith had announced his candidacy for the U.S. presidency earlier that year, and he had been attacked by a group of Mormon dissenters for his political ambition and his alleged polygamy: There is evidence that he may have married as many as 50 wives, although he acknowledged only his first.

As the mayor of Nauvoo, Ill., Smith saw to it that the press used to print the opposition newspaper was destroyed. Threats of mob violence followed, and Smith and his brother were eventually jailed on charges of treason. Although the brothers had been promised protection by the governor, a mob of men with blackened faces stormed the jail on June 27 and killed them, thus elevating them to the status of martyrs.

CONTACTS:
Illinois Nauvoo Mission, The Church of Jesus Christ of Latter-day
Saints
975 Young St.
P.O. Box 215
Nauvoo, IL 62354
217-453-2237 or 217-453-1122
www.historicnauvoo.net

Church of Jesus Christ of Latter-Day Saints
50 E. N. Temple St.
Fl. 7
Salt Lake City, UT 84150
801-240-1000
www.lds.org

♦ 1800 ♦ Martyrs' Day (Lebanon)
May 6

Martyrs' Day has been observed as a public holiday since 1970 to honor the fallen heroes of Arab nationalism. The date, May 6, was selected to commemorate the 21 Arab intellectuals who were hanged on that date in 1916 in Beirut, Lebanon, and Damascus, Syria, by an official of the occupying Ottoman Empire.

On Martyrs' Day, ceremonies of public commemoration are led by government officials in Beirut at Martyrs' Square, named in honor of the murdered nationalists. Officials and citizens also lay wreaths at martyrs' monuments in Beirut and throughout the country.

CONTACTS:
Ministry of Tourism
550 Central Bank St. Hamra
P.O.Box 11
Beirut, 5344 Lebanon
961-1-340-940; fax: 961-1-340-945
www.destinationlebanon.gov.lb

◆ 1801 ◆ Martyrs of North America, Feast of the
October 19

The **Feast of the North American Martyrs** commemorates the death of eight priests who were killed by the Iroquois,mortal enemies of the Huron Indians, with whom the priests had been working for 34 years. There was a great deal of missionary activity being carried out in what is now Canada and upstate New York during the 1600s, and many of the devoted missionaries who worked among the Indians in the area extending from Nova Scotia to the Great Lakes met with torture and often cruel death. The eight who are remembered on this day are St. Rene Goupil (1608-1642), St. Isaac Jogues (1607-1646), St. John Lalonde (d. 1646), and their companions, French Jesuits who died in 1649. They were canonized together in 1930, and a shrine built for them at Auriesville, New York, holds a novena (a traditional Roman Catholic ritual of prayer lasting nine days) each year over nine days including October 19.

CONTACTS:
Shrine of Our Lady of Martyrs
136 Shrine Rd.
Fultonville, NY 12072
518-853-3033; fax: 518-853-3051
www.martyrshrine.org

◆ 1802 ◆ Marya
July-August; third day of waning half of Hindu month of Sravana

When Gautama sat down under the Bo tree to await Enlightenment, Mara, the Buddhist Lord of the Senses and satanic tempter, tried a number of strategies to divert him from his goal. Disguised as a messenger, Mara brought the news that one of Gautama's rivals had usurped his family's throne. Then he scared away the other gods who had gathered to honor the future Buddha by causing a storm of rain, rocks, and ashes to fall. Finally, he sent his three daughters, representing thirst, desire, and delight, to seduce Gautama—all to no avail.

In the city of Patan, Nepal, a procession on this day commemorates the Buddha's triumph over Mara's temptations.

A procession of 3,000 to 4,000 people, carrying gifts—usually butter lamps—for Lord Buddha, moves through the city from shrine to shrine. Some wear masks and others play traditional Nepalese musical instruments. The devil dancers and mask-wearers in the parade often pretend to scare the children who line the streets by suddenly jumping out at them.

CONTACTS:
Ministry of Culture, Tourism and Civil Aviation
Singha Durbar
Nepal
977-1-421-1992; fax: 977-1-421-1758
www.tourism.gov.np

Buddhist Council of the Midwest
1812 Washington St.
Evanston, IL 60202
847-869-5806; fax: 847-869-5806
www.buddhistcouncilmidwest.org

◆ 1803 ◆ Maryland Day
March 25

Maryland Day, or **Founder's Day**, commemorates the landing of the first colonists there in 1634, and the first Roman Catholic Mass they celebrated. Named after Henrietta Maria, the consort of King Charles I (1600-1649) of England, Maryland was the first proprietary colony on the American mainland. George Calvert, Lord Baltimore (1580?-1632), was appointed by the king as proprietor, and as a Catholic he hoped to establish a refuge for other Catholics who had been persecuted in Anglican England. He was succeeded as head of the colony by his son, Cecilius Calvert (1605-1675), the second Lord Baltimore, who brought 200 more colonists over from England.

CONTACTS:
Maryland Office of Tourism Development
401 E. Pratt St.
14th Fl.
Baltimore, MD 21202
410-767-6288 or 866-639-3526; fax: 410-333-6643
visitmaryland.org

Annapolis & Anne Arundel County Conference & Visitors Bureau
26 West St.
Annapolis, MD 21401
410-280-0445 or 888-302-2852; fax: 410-263-9591
www.visitannapolis.org

Four Rivers Heritage Area
The Arundel Center
44 Calvert St.
Annapolis, MD 21401
410-222-1805
fourriversheritage.org

◆ 1804 ◆ Maryland Hunt Cup
Last Saturday in April

A steeplechase that has been run in Maryland since 1894, the Hunt Cup is considered the premier such horse race in America and one of the toughest steeplechases in the world. It's a timber race: the jumps are over stout post-and-rail fences rather than hedges as in the English GRAND NATIONAL. Since 1922, it has always been held in Glyndon, the locale of the Green Spring Valley Hounds, a hunt club. The course is four miles long and has 22 fences, none of which is jumped twice. The highest fence is the 16th at 4′10″, while the most spectacular, causing the most spills, is the 4′6″ third fence, near the beginning of the race before the horses are well warmed up.

The first race was held to settle a dispute between two hunt clubs, Green Spring Valley Hounds and the Elkridge Hunt, over which had the better fox-hunting horses. Originally only for club members, the race was opened to all comers in 1903, and a rivalry between Pennsylvania and Maryland horses began and still endures.

At the first race, a silver cup and $100 were awarded to the winner. Today there is still a cup, but the purse has grown to $65,000. Memorable horses have been Mountain Dew, a three-time winner in the 1960s; Jay Trump, also a three-time winner in the 1960s and the winner of the English Grand National in 1965; and Ben Nevis, twice a winner, who took seven seconds off the course record in 1978. Ben Nevis, who also won the English Grand National, was a small horse but a spectacular athlete.

The Hunt Cup was originally only for men, but women were allowed to enter in the late 1970s, and in 1980 Joy Slater was the first woman to take the prize.

Tailgate parties are held before the race, and a hunt ball after it is attended by riders, trainers, jockeys, owners, and members of the two local hunt clubs. It's considered the social event of the season.

CONTACTS:
Maryland Office of Tourism Development
401 E. Pratt St.
14th Fl.
Baltimore, MD 21202
410-767-6288 or 866-639-3526; fax: 410-333-6643
visitmaryland.org

Maryland Steeplechase Association (MSA)
P.O. Box 651
Lisbon, MD 21765
410-489-7826; fax: 410-489-7828
www.marylandsteeplechaseassociation.com

♦ 1805 ♦ Maryland Seafood Festival
September

The Maryland Seafood Festival has been held since the 1960s. This three-day festival held in early September features the preparation and sale of seafood dishes, especially Maryland regional favorites. Many children's and family activities are available, such as beach bingo, face painting, and a beach volleyball contest. Local restaurants participate in a Crab Soup Cookoff. The festival takes place at Sandy Point State Park in Annapolis, Maryland. It coincides with the annual "Save the Bay Day," sponsored by the Chesapeake Bay Foundation.

CONTACTS:
Maryland Seafood Festival
Sandy Point State Park
1100 E. College Pkwy
Annapolis, MD 21409
410-353-9237
www.mdseafoodfestival.com

♦ 1806 ♦ Marymass Festival
Second and third weeks in August

The Marymass Festival is famous for its horse races, believed to be the oldest in Europe. It is named after Mary, the mother of Jesus and is held near August 15, the Feast of the ASSUMPTION. But it also honors Mary (1542-1587), queen of Scots, who is said to have visited Irvine and enjoyed the festivities in 1563. In addition to the horse races, there is a parade, the crowning of a Marymass queen, fireworks, and other events.

CONTACTS:
Marymass Festival
C/O The HAC, Harbour St.
Irvine, Ayrshire KA12 8PZ United Kingdom
44-79-1474-9221
www.marymass.com

♦ 1807 ♦ Marzas
February 28-March 1

On the last night of February and the first of March in Spain, young *marceros*, or March serenaders, wander through the streets singing songs to their girlfriends and asking for donations of food and sweets to celebrate the arrival of spring. The term *marzas* refers both to the traditional songs they sing and to the gifts they receive. Although the songs themselves vary, they always mention the month of March and the coming of spring, leading many to believe that the tradition has its roots in pagan rituals celebrating the passing of winter.

CONTACTS:
Ministry of Culture
Plaza del Rey, 1
Madrid, 28004 Spain
91 701 74 81
www.mecd.gob.es

Embassy of Spain – Cultural Office
2375 Pennsylvania Ave. N.W.
Washington, D.C. 20037
202-728-2334; fax: 202-496-0328
www.spainculture.us

♦ 1808 ♦ Marzenna Day
Saturday or Sunday nearest March 21

A festival day along the Vistula River in Poland, Marzenna Day is a spring ritual particularly enjoyed by young people. A *Marzenna* is a straw doll about three or four feet tall and dressed in rags, a striped shirt, a hat, and lots of ribbons. On this day near the first day of spring (*see* VERNAL EQUINOX), the townspeople, dressed in costume, accompany the Marzenna to the river and throw her in. Not only is this act a final farewell to winter, but it also recalls an old legend about a young man whose faith in one god was so great that he was able to save a girl who was about to be sacrificed to appease the gods of storms and floods. After the doll is thrown into the water, the people welcome spring with singing and dancing.

CONTACTS:
Polish National Tourist Office
5 Marine View Plaza
Ste. 303 b
Hoboken, NJ 07030
201-420-9910
www.poland.travel/en-us

♦ 1809 ♦ **Masi Magham**
February-March; full moon day of the Hindu month of Magha

The Masi Magham festival is observed every 12 years during the full moon of the Hindu month of Magha, although a smaller festival takes place annually. Hindus flock to Kumbakonam in southern India to bathe in the Maha-Magha tank, where the waters of nine holy rivers are said to be mixed: the Ganges, the Yumma, the Godavari, the Saraswati, the Narmada, the Cauvery, the Kumari, the Payoshni, and the Sarayu. Bathing in the sacred tank (or pool) purifies them of their sins.

The Masi Magham festival is also a time for gift-giving, particularly in support of charitable institutions. One way of measuring the size of one's gift to the poor is to give one's weight in gold, a custom known as *Tulabhara*. Sometimes the gold collected in this way is used to renovate the 16 temples that have been built over the years near the site of the sacred tank.

In Malaysia, the Masi Magham is a two-day festival celebrated by the Chettiyar (a Tamil merchant caste) community in Malacca. The image of Subramanya, a Hindu god, is taken in procession to the temple known as Sannasi Malai Kovil, formerly the home of a famous ascetic who had the power to heal. Oratorical contests are held and dramas are staged at the temple, and at the end of the day, the statue is taken back through the streets of Malacca to Poyyatha Vinayagar Kovil, where it remains for another year.

CONTACTS:
Tamil Nadu Tourism Development Corporation
Tourism Complex
No. 2 Wallajah Rd.
Triplicane
Chennai, Tamil Nadu 600 002 India
91-44-2538-3333; fax: 91-44-2536-1385
www.tamilnadutourism.org

DrikPanchang Registered Office
Flushing Meadows, Outer Ring Rd.
403 B-Block
Doddanakundi
Bangalore, Karnataka 560 037 India
91-80-4211-6503
www.drikpanchang.com

♦ 1810 ♦ **Maskal**
September 27

Maskal ia a Christian festival in Ethiopia to commemorate the finding of the True Cross, the cross on which Christ was crucified. (*Maskal* means "cross.") The celebration comes at the end of the rainy season in the Ethiopian spring, when fields are blooming with yellow flowers known as the maskal flowers. In communities throughout the nation, a tall pole called a *demara* is set up and topped with a cross. Families place smaller demaras against the big one, and in the evening they are made into a huge bonfire. Religious ceremonies are performed around the bonfire, with songs and dancing. The ashes of the burned-out fire are considered holy, so the people place the powder of the ashes on their foreheads.

See also EXALTATION OF THE CROSS.

CONTACTS:
International Ethiopian Evangelical Church
7930 Eastern Ave.N.W.
Washington, D.C. 20012
202-726-8529
www.eecdc.org

Ethiopian Community Association of Chicago
1730 W. Greenleaf Ave.
Chicago, IL 60626
773-508-0303; fax: 773-508-0309
www.ecachicago.org

♦ 1811 ♦ **Masters Golf Tournament**
First full week in April

Known to golf fans everywhere as **The Masters**, this annual tournament has been held at the exclusive Augusta National Golf Club in Georgia since it was first started there in 1934 by Bobby Jones, who designed the course. It has long been associated with names like Ben Hogan, Sam Snead, Arnold Palmer, and Jack Nicklaus. Former U.S. President Dwight Eisenhower often played the course and stayed in a cottage to the left of the 10th tee that is still called "Ike's Cottage."

The qualifying rounds are held on Thursday and Friday of the four-day tournament, and the top 44 finishers participate in the final round. The top 24 finishers are automatically invited back the next year and do not have to qualify again. In addition to the cash prize, the winner of the tournament, which has been referred to as "golf's rite of spring," receives a trophy and a green blazer. Each year on the Tuesday night before the tournament, there is a Champions Dinner attended by past winners and hosted by the defending champion— all of them wearing their distinctive green jackets.

It wasn't until September 1990 that the Augusta National Golf Club admitted its first black member, Ron Townsend, president of the Gannett Television Group. Had the Club refused to admit a black man, it is likely that the Masters would no longer have been held there, since the PGA (Professional Golfers' Association) now has rules forbidding discriminatory membership practices.

Seven years later, Tiger Woods, an African-American player, broke a 32-year tournament record and became golf's newest sensation.

CONTACTS:
Augusta National, Inc.
2604 Washington Rd.
Augusta, GA 30904
706-667-6000
www.masters.com

Augusta Convention & Visitors Bureau
1450 Greene St. Ste. 110
P.O. Box 1331
Augusta, GA 30901
706-823-6600 or 800-726-0243; fax: 706-823-6609
www.visitaugusta.com

♦ 1812 ♦ **Mata Tirtha Snan (Mother's Day)**
Mid-April to early May; last day of the waning half of the month of Baisakh

One of the most popular and widely celebrated festivals in Nepal, Mata Tirtha Snan, also known as **Mata Tirtha Aunsi**, is an important cultural cog in the country's family-oriented society. It falls on the local month of Baisakh, the first month of the Nepali Year, and is celebrated by honoring one's mother in various ways, typically with gifts and sweets. Children who live away from their parents usually journey back home to spend the day with their mothers.

Folklore has it that a cowherd whose mother had died was so distraught that he travelled to a pond in the forest to pay homage and make offerings. To his amazement, his mother's face appeared in the water and accepted his gifts. Today, this spot is known as Mata Tirtha, a holy bathing site not far from the capital city of Kathmandu and the destination of a ritualistic pilgrimage by people whose mothers have passed away. The spot has two pools, a larger one for bathing and a smaller one where a person may "see their mother's face". It is widely believed that a pilgrimage to Mata Tirtha will ensure that one's mother's soul remains in peace, a belief that has cemented this festival in Nepal's rich cultural heritage.

CONTACTS:
Kathmandu Metropolitan City Office
Bagh Durbar
P.O.Box 8416
Kathmandu, 8416 Nepal
977-4268506; fax: 977-1-4268509
www.kathmandu.gov.np

♦ 1813 ♦ **Matralia**
June 11

The Matralia was an ancient Roman festival in honor of Mater Matuta, who is often confused with the Greek dawn goddess, Leucothea. Modern authorities describe Mater Matuta, who has no mythology but whose cult was widespread in ancient times, as a goddess of the dawn's light and of childbirth—the dawn being a lucky time to give birth. She was also a deity of matrons, and only matrons and freeborn women were allowed to participate in the festival held at her shrine in the round temple known as the Forum Boarium.

Not much is known about what went on during the Matralia, but it appears that only the wife of a first marriage was

allowed to decorate the image of the goddess. No female slaves were allowed in the temple—except for one, who was driven out after being slapped on the face. The women offered prayers primarily on behalf of their nieces and nephews; their own children were considered to be of secondary importance. They made offerings of flowers and often arrived at the temple carrying their relatives' children in their arms.

CONTACTS:
Italian National Tourist Board
686 Park Ave.
3rd Fl.
New York, NY 10065
212-245-5618; fax: 212-586-9249
www.italiantourism.com

World Monuments Fund
350 Fifth Ave.
Ste. 2412
New York, NY 10118
646-424-9594; fax: 646-424-9593
www.wmf.org

♦ 1814 ♦ **Matriculation, Feast of the**
February

The Feast of the Matriculation is a noisy and lighthearted celebration for university students in Italy. It is observed in various university cities, but the festivities are especially lively in Padua, where everyone in town as well as students from other parts of the country participate. The students march through the streets of Padua in noisy groups wearing the many-colored hats of their respective colleges. They all congregate at the famous Caffé Pedrocchi, where the celebration continues. Although no one is exactly sure what gave rise to this feast, it is apparently a very old tradition.

CONTACTS:
National Italian American Foundation
1860 19th St. N.W.
Amb. Peter F. Secchia Bldg.
Washington, D.C. 20009
202-387-0600; fax: 202-387-0800
www.niaf.org

American Association of Teachers of Italian
John D. Calandra Italian American Institute Queens College/CUNY
25 W. 43rd St.
17th Fl.
New York, NY 10036
212-642-2094
www.utm.utoronto.ca

♦ 1815 ♦ **Matrimonial Tea Party**
Between May 11 and June 14; Whit-Monday, Monday after Pentecost

Known locally as **Goûter Matrimonial** or **Déjeuner Matrimonial**, the Matrimonial Tea party that takes place on WHIT-MONDAY every year in écaussinnes-Lalaing in Belgium is an opportunity for young, unmarried women to entertain eligible bachelors. The first Matrimonial was organized by a young man named Marcel Tricot early in the 20th century.

At 9 o'clock in the morning, the visiting unmarried men, who must appear in full bridegrooms' dress and wear a symbolic cup on their lapels, are greeted at the town hall and invited to write their names in an official guest book. Then there are receptions, speeches by local officials, sightseeing tours, band concerts, and plenty of opportunity for the bachelors to walk through the streets, which are decorated with streamers, pennants, and humorous poems appropriate to the occasion.

At three in the afternoon the annual tea is announced. One of the young women welcomes the bachelors in the name of all of the "old maids" in écaussinnes-Lalaing. The "tea" consists of coffee, beer, and locally made sweets, and it is followed by folk dancing and merrymaking that continues for most of the night. No statistics are available concerning the success of the event in terms of matchmaking.

CONTACTS:
Belgian Tourist Office
300 E. 42nd St., 14th Fl.
New York, NY 10017
212-758-8130
www.visitbelgium.com

♦ 1816 ♦ Matronalia
March 1

Also known as the **Matronales Feriae**, the Matronalia was an ancient Roman festival in honor of Juno, the goddess of women. It was observed on March 1, the day on which her temple was dedicated. The cult of Juno was established by the king of the Sabines, Titus Tatius, and the Matronalia celebrated not only the sacredness of marriage as an institution but the peace that followed the first marriages that took place between Roman men and Sabine women.

It was customary for married women to form a procession to Juno's temple, where offerings were made to the goddess. At home, women received gifts from their husbands on this day and held feasts for their female slaves. They also prayed for marital peace and harmony.

CONTACTS:
Italian National Tourist Board
686 Park Ave.
3rd Fl.
New York, NY 10065 United States
212-245-5618; fax: 212-586-9249
www.italiantourism.com

♦ 1817 ♦ Matsu, Birthday of
23rd day of third lunar month

This holiday celebrates the birthday of the Chinese deity Matsu (or Ma-cho or Mazu), the Goddess of the Sea who is venerated by fishermen for protecting them from storms and disasters at sea. People pay homage to her on her birthday at the Meizhou Mazu Temple on Meishou Island, Fujian Province, China, on Taiwan, and in other Chinese communities.

One Chinese legend says that the goddess was born in about 960 and, because she never cried in the first month of her life, was named Lin Moniang, *moniang* meaning "quiet girl." She began to read when she was eight, studied Buddhist and Taoist scriptures, became a believer in Buddhism at 10, studied magic arts when she was 12, and at 28 achieved nirvana and became a goddess. She is worshipped because she is believed to have performed many miracles during her life. Courts in successive dynasties issued decrees to honor her with such titles as "Holy Princess" and "Holy Mother."

In Taiwan, the story is that Matsu, a girl from Hokkien Province in China, took up the fishing trade to support her mother after her fisherman father died. One day she died at sea, and because of her filial devotion, she came to be worshipped as a deity. During World War II, when American planes started to bomb Taiwan, many women prayed to Matsu, and it is said that some women saw a girl dressed in red holding out a red cloth to catch the falling bombs.

She is known as A-Ma, or the Mother Goddess, on Macao. The legend there says A-Ma was a beautiful young woman whose presence on a Canton-bound ship saved it from disaster. All the other ships in the fleet, whose rich owners had refused to give her passage, were destroyed in a storm.

Whatever the story, people whose lives depend on the sea visit the goddess' temples on her birthday.

On Taiwan, the most famous celebration site is the Chaotien Temple in Peikang. Built in 1694, it is Taiwan's oldest, biggest, and richest Matsu temple. A carnival-like atmosphere prevails during the **Matsu Festival**, with watermelon stalls, cotton candy stalls, and sling-shot ranges set up along roadsides. There are parades of the goddess and other gods through village streets, where altars bearing sacrifices of food and incense have been set up. Hundreds of thousands of people pour out of buses and arrive on foot at Peikang. Many of them make pilgrimages from the town of Tachia about 60 miles north, spending a week visiting about 16 Matsu temples along the route. Peikang becomes so crowded it's hard to move, and the firecrackers are deafening. It has been estimated that 75 percent of all firecrackers manufactured on Taiwan are exploded in Peikang during the Matsu Festival; afterwards the remnants of the firecrackers lie two inches deep on the streets.

See also Tin Hau Festival.

CONTACTS:
Taipei Economic and Cultural Office in New York
1 E. 42nd St.
4th Fl.
New York, NY 10017 United States
212-486-0088; fax: 212-421-7866
www.roc-taiwan.org

♦ 1818 ♦ Maundy Thursday
Between March 19 and April 22 in West and between April 1 and May 5 in East; Thursday before Easter

Also known as **Green Thursday** in Germany from the practice of giving a green branch to penitents as a sign that their penance was completed; **Shere** or **Sheer Thursday**, meaning "free from guilt"; **Paschal Thursday**, **Passion Thursday**, or **Holy Thursday**, it is the day preceding GOOD FRIDAY.

It commemorates Jesus' institution of the Eucharist during the Last Supper, celebrated by Christians since the middle of the fourth century. The practice of ceremonial footwashing in imitation of Jesus, who washed his disciples' feet before the Last Supper as a sign and example of humility and love, has been largely discontinued in Protestant churches. However, the Roman Catholic Church and the Anglican Communion still celebrate the rites of Maundy Thursday, which may include handing out special coins known as "Maundy money" to the aged and the poor, instead of footwashing. Also on this day, the sacramental Holy Oils, or chrism, are blessed.

The name "Maundy" probably comes from the Latin *mandatum*, or "commandment," referring to Jesus' words after he washed the feet of his disciples: "A new commandment I give unto you, that you love one another as I have loved you" (John 13:34).

CONTACTS:
Orthodox Church in America
6850 N. Hempstead Tpke
P.O. Box 675
Syosset, NY 11791 United States
516-922-0550; fax: 516-922-0954
www.oca.org

♦ 1819 ♦ **Mauni Amavasya**
January-February; 15th day of waning half of Hindu month of Magha

Complete silence is observed on the day known to Hindus as Mauni Amavasya. Because bathing during Magha, one of the most sacred Hindu months, is considered to be a purifying act, many Hindus camp out along the banks of the Ganges River throughout the month and bathe daily in the sacred river. But the bathing and fasting end with the observance of Mauni Amavasya, a day for worshipping Lord Vishnu and circumambulating the peepal (a type of ficus) tree, which is mentioned in the *Bhagavad Gita* and is regarded as holy.

For many Hindus, the celebration takes place at Prayag, a well-known pilgrimage center where the Ganges, Yamuna, and Saraswati rivers flow together. Some live here for a full month, practicing rituals and ceremonial sacrifices known as *Kalpa-Vas*. Religious discourses and services are held daily, and the worshippers who come here eat only one meal a day or confine their diet to fruit and milk.

CONTACTS:
Hindu Community and Cultural Center
1232 Arrowhead Ave.
Livermore, CA 94551 United States
925-449-6255; fax: 925-455-0404

♦ 1820 ♦ **Mauritania Independence Day**
November 28

This national holiday commemorates Mauritania's independence from France on November 28, 1960, after more than 50 years under French rule.

CONTACTS:
U.S. Embassy in Nouakchott, Mauritania
288, rue 42-100, (rue Abdallaye)
BP 222
Nouakchott, 20520 Mauritania
222-4525-2660; fax: 222-4525-1592
mauritania.usembassy.gov

♦ 1821 ♦ **Mauritius Independence Day**
March 12

This national holiday commemorates the day in 1968 when Mauritius gained independence from Britain, after being under its rule since the early 19th century.

CONTACTS:
Mauritius Tourism Promotion Authority
Victoria House
St Louis St.
4-5th Fl.
Mauritius
230-210-1545; fax: 230-212-5142
www.tourism-mauritius.mu

♦ 1822 ♦ **Maverick Sunday Concerts**
Sundays from July to early September

Hervey White, a novelist, poet and architect, purchased a piece of farmland he named "Maverick" just outside of Woodstock, New York, around the turn of the century. Within a few years, White had built a "music chapel" there and organized a Sunday afternoon concert series designed to give professional orchestral musicians an opportunity to play chamber music during the off-season. The series was under way by 1916, making the Maverick Sunday Concerts the oldest continuous chamber music series in the United States.

The concerts, which take place on Sunday afternoons from July to early September, are held in an unusual rustic concert hall made of locally cut and milled oak, pine, and chestnut. There are 56 paned windows in the front gable, a huge porch along one side, and seating for an audience of 400. The programming runs the gamut from traditional music for quintets, quartets, trios, and duos to the very latest contemporary compositions. Many of the works performed there in the past were composed by Alexander Semmier, who directed the Maverick concerts from 1954 to 1969. There have also been world premieres by noted Hudson Valley composers and performances by the Tokyo String Quartet, the Dorian Woodwind Quintet, the Beaux Arts Quartet, the Manhattan String Quartet, and the Cremona Arts Trio.

CONTACTS:
Maverick Concerts
120 Maverick Rd.
P.O. Box 9
Woodstock, NY 12498

845-679-8217
www.maverickconcerts.org

♦ 1823 ♦ **Mawlid al-Nabi (Maulid al-Nabi;
Prophet's Birthday)**
12th day of the Islamic month of Rabial-Awwal

Mawlid al-Nabi celebrates the birth of Muhammad, the founder of Islam. Born in Mecca around 570, he was a shepherd and a trader who began to receive revelations from God when he was 40 years old. Over the next 23 years he not only established a religion but brought an unprecedented political unity to Arab tribes. Muhammad's birth began to be observed as a public holiday about the 12th century, except by conservative sects such as the Wahhabis who do not celebrate any human. They believe that to do so would detract from the worship of God. It is celebrated with the recitation of litanies in mosques, and with firecrackers and gift-givingthroughout the Middle East and countries with prominent Muslim populations. In Burkina Faso and parts of Ghana the holiday is called DAMBA and in Indonesia, SEKATEN. The Prophet's birthday is a legal holiday in more than 30 countries around the world.

CONTACTS:
Islamic Supreme Council of America
17195 Silver Pkwy.
Ste. 401
Fenton, MI 48430
810-593-1222; fax: 810-815-0518
www.islamicsupremecouncil.org

♦ 1824 ♦ **May Day**
May 1

Many of the customs associated with the first day of May may come from the old Roman FLORALIA, or festival of flowers. These include the gathering of branches and flowers on MAY DAY EVE or early May Day morning, the choosing and crowning of a May Queen, and dancing around a bush, tree, or decorated pole, the maypole. The sports and festivities that are held on this day symbolize the rebirth of nature as well as human fertility. In fact, the ritual drinking and dancing around the maypole in colonial America so horrified the Pilgrim Fathers that they outlawed the practice and punished the offenders. This is probably why May Day has remained a relatively quiet affair in this country.

In Communist countries, May Day has been transformed into a holiday for workers, marked by parades that are an occasion for displaying military strength. The May Day Parade in Red Square, Moscow, has long been a spectacular example, though less so in recent years with the dissolution of the Soviet Union and the resulting relaxation of Cold War tensions. Perhaps in reaction to such displays, Americans instituted LOYALTY DAY and LAW DAY on this same date. In Great Britain, May 1 is LABOR DAY. More than 50 other countries also celebrate Labor Day in honor of workers on May 1.

See also VAPPU.

CONTACTS:
Industrial Workers of the World
P.O. Box 180195
Chicago, IL 60618 United States
773-728-0996
www.iww.org

♦ 1825 ♦ **May Day (Czech Republic) (Prvého
Máje)**
May 1

The traditional maypole associated with MAY DAY in western Europe, the United States, and elsewhere plays a central role in the celebration of May 1 in the former Czechoslovakia (now the countries of the Czech Republic and Slovak Republic). On May Day Eve, boys traditionally plant maypoles underneath their girlfriends' windows, so that the girls will wake up and see them first thing in the morning. In some villages, it is customary to raise a maypole beneath the window of the most popular girl in town. The maypole is said to represent the girl's life; the taller it is, the longer she will live. Sometimes it is a small tree, decorated with ribbons and colored eggshells.

Bands give concerts in village squares on May Day, and musicians go from house to house, singing. As a traditional spring festival, May Day has been a time for Czechs and Slovaks to sing, dance, and take pleasure in the beauty of the season.

See also MAY DAY EVE IN THE CZECH REPUBLIC.

CONTACTS:
Czech Tourist Authority – CzechTourism
1109 Madison Ave.
New York, NY 10028 United States
212-288-0830; fax: 212-288-0971
www.czechtourism.com

♦ 1826 ♦ **May Day (France)**
May 1

In France the celebration of MAY DAY is inextricably linked to flowers. It is considered good luck to wear lilies-of-the-valley on this day, and it is believed that any wishes made while wearing the flowers are bound to come true. Sometimes sprays of pressed lilies are sent to distant friends and loved ones. In southern France the flower vendors sell lilies-of-the-valley on every street corner.

The **First of May** has political overtones in France as well, and it is a public holiday officially observed as LABOR DAY. Political demonstrations, speeches, and parades are common on this day—similar to May Day celebrations in England, Russia, and other countries.

CONTACTS:
France Tourism Development Agency
825 Third Ave.
New York, NY 10022
212-838-7800; fax: 212-838-7855
int.rendezvousenfrance.com

◆ 1827 ◆ May Day (Scandinavia)
May 1

In Scandinavia, the celebration of MAY DAY actually begins on April 30, WALPURGIS NIGHT. But the big event of the day is a mock battle between summer and winter, usually represented by two husky young men. Summer always wins, and winter is buried in effigy.

In the Swedish university town of Uppsala, students wearing white caps gather together to hear songs and speeches. Huge bonfires, also associated with Walpurgis Night, are popular in many areas of Sweden. Political speeches, parades of labor organizations, and public demonstrations take place on May 1 as well.

There is a superstition in Norway, dating back to pre-Christian times, about hearing the cuckoo's first call in spring: If the call comes from the south, the year will be good; if it is heard from the north, one will become ill or die in the coming year; if it comes from the west, one will be successful; and if it comes from the east, one will be lucky in love. For this reason, traditional Norwegian calendars show a bird perched in a tree on the mark for May 1.

CONTACTS:
VisitSweden
P.O. Box 4649
Grand Central Stn.
New York, NY 10163
212-885-9700; fax: 212-885-9710
www.visitsweden.com

◆ 1828 ◆ May Day (Spain)
May 1

Many Spanish MAY DAY customs are believed to have pagan origins (*see* FLORALIA). At the end of April, young people (in some villages, only bachelors) choose a tall pine tree to use as a maypole and set it up in the plaza. They decorate it with ribbons, beads, and eggshells, and as they dance around it they sing May songs. The ceremonies around the tree continue for several days, and on the last day of the month the tree is sold to raise money for refreshments or a dinner.

La Maya refers to both the girls who take part in the May Day celebrations and to the May Queen. It is traditional for a group of boys and girls to choose a queen, sit her on a couch or chair, and dance around her on May Day. They sing love songs, or *coplas*, in which they ask for food and money from everyone who passes by, and then use the contributions for a feast or banquet.

In some areas, the May Queen has been replaced by a *Cruz de Mayo*, or May cross. An altar is set up with candles, a white cloth, and a cross decorated with flowers and ribbons. There is dancing around the altar and requests for food and money. Sometimes young girls carry the wooden May crosses through the streets, asking for contributions. It is possible that this custom resulted from the confusion of May Day with the Feast of the Holy Cross, formerly observed by the Roman Catholic Church on May 3 (*see* EXALTATION OF THE

CROSS), and still observed by Catholics in Latin America (*see* DÍA DE LA SANTA CRUZ).

CONTACTS:
Tourist Office of Spain
60 E. 42nd St.
Ste. 5300, 53rd Fl.
New York, NY 10165
212-265-8822; fax: 212-265-8864
www.spain.info

◆ 1829 ◆ May Day Eve (Czech Republic)
April 30

According to an old Czech superstition, witches try to enter people's homes on the eve of MAY DAY and do them harm. At one time it was customary to sprinkle sand or grass on the doorstep, in the belief that the witches had to count the grains or blades before entering the house. Now the "Burning of the Witches" ceremony is observed in some parts of the country by building bonfires on the mountain tops. Brooms that have been dipped in pitch are plunged into the fire and then held aloft like torches.

In Postupice, a town in the Bohemian region, a Maypole and Burning of the Witches Festival is held April 30-May 1 every year. The young men put up a maypole, decorated with ribbons and colored wreaths, in the village square on the afternoon of April 30. The next day, both men and women dress up in peasant costumes, weaving the ribbons in and out as they dance around the maypole and celebrate the coming of spring. The burning of the witches takes place afterward, when the villagers throw their broomsticks into the bonfire and burn the witches in effigy. People gather around the bonfire to drink brandy or beer and roast sausages as they watch the witches burn.

CONTACTS:
Czech-Moravian Confederation of Trade Unions
nám. W. Churchilla 2
Praha, Praha 3 11359 Czech Republic
420-23-446-2138
www.cmkos.cz

◆ 1830 ◆ May Day Eve (Ireland)
April 30

According to Irish legend, the fairy people fight among themselves on the eve of MAY DAY. Every seven years, the combat is especially intense, for they compete with one another for the crops, taking the best ears of wheat, barley, and oats as their prize. By mixing the barley with dew gathered from a mountain top at midnight, they make a strong liquor. One drink is believed to set them dancing for 24 hours without pausing to rest.

The custom of celebrating May Day Eve with bonfires or with a May bush decorated with candles can be traced back to the pagan feast of BELTANE, which marked the summer's beginning. In Ireland, a horse's skull was often burned in the bonfire. On November Eve (October 31) in County Cork, a procession led by a man called "The White Mare," who was dressed in a white robe and carried a symbolic horse's head, went from house to house soliciting contributions of money and food. Because fairies and the spirits of the dead were believed to roam around on this night, food was left out to ward off their mischief.

CONTACTS:
Independent Workers Union
55 N. Main St
Ireland
353-21-427-7151
www.union.ie

♦ 1831 ♦ **May Day Eve (Italy)**
April 30

In Modena, Italy, if tradition is followed, the boys of the town sing May songs under the village windows on the eve of MAY DAY. A talented musician is often asked to sing to the sweethearts of the others, and the boys compete with one another to see who can compose the most persuasive lyrics. On the Sunday following, it is customary for the boys to appear with empty baskets at the houses they have serenaded. The families fill the baskets with things to eat.

May Day itself, or *Calendimaggio*, bears little resemblance to the original pagan spring festival once celebrated in ancient Rome. Modern-day Italians attend horse races, fireworks exhibitions, and various types of competitions and lotteries which are held throughout the country on May 1.

CONTACTS:
Italian Confederation of Workers Union
Via Po n. 21
Rome, 00198 Italy
39-68-4731
www.cisl.it

♦ 1832 ♦ **May Day Eve (Switzerland) (Maitag Vorabend)**
April 30

Certain villages in the Seeland and Burgdorf regions of the canton of Bern in Switzerland still observe the ancient custom of planting the *Maitannli*, or May pine tree. Boys from the village steal into the forest after dark on May Day Eve, April 30, and cut down small pine trees, which they deck with flowers and ribbons and plant under their sweethearts' bedroom windows, at the front gate, or occasionally on the roof. The young man who plants the symbolic tree is usually welcomed and entertained by the girl and her family. Girls who have a reputation for being arrogant or unpopular sometimes find a grotesque straw puppet in place of the traditional Maitannli.

CONTACTS:
Switzerland Tourism Board
608 Fifth Ave.
New York, NY 10020
212-757-5944 or 800-794-7795; fax: 212-262-6116
www.myswitzerland.com

♦ 1833 ♦ **May Festival, International**
May

Germany's second oldest music festival (after the BAYREUTH FESTIVAL) is the **Wiesbaden May Festival**, founded in 1896. Kaiser Wilhelm II came to Wiesbaden, which is about 26 miles west of Frankfurt, to officiate at the grand opening.

The month-long festival offers eight or nine full-length operas performed in the original language, symphonic concerts, ballet, drama, experimental theater, and mime. Most of the festival events are held in the rococo-style Hessian State Theater, the Kleines Haus (a small auditorium for plays), and the Kurhaus (for symphonic concerts). Among the world-renowned groups that have been invited to perform at the festival are the Netherlands Dance Theatre, Japan's Red Buddha Theatre, the Salzburg Marionettes, the Hamburg State Opera, the Berlin State Opera, the Zurich Opera, the Welsh Philharmonic Orchestra Cardiff, and the Greek National Ballet.

CONTACTS:
German National Tourist Office
122 E. 42nd St.
Ste. 2000
New York, NY 10168
212-661-4796; fax: 212-661-7174
www.germany.travel

Wiesbaden Tourist Information Center
Marktplatz 1
Wiesbaden, 65183 Germany
49-611-1729-930; fax: 49-611-1729-798
www.wiesbaden.de

♦ 1834 ♦ **Mayberry Days**
Last full weekend in September

This annual event celebrates "The Andy Griffith Show," a weekly television comedy show about the adventures of a small-town sheriff in a fictional town called Mayberry that was produced from 1960 to 1968 and remains on the air in syndication. The festival was first held in 1990 in actor Andy Griffith's home town of Mount Airy, North Carolina, to celebrate the show's 30th anniversary. Since that time it has grown into a three-day event that attracts fans of the show from all over the United States and Canada.

Highlights of the festival include concerts by the Doug Dillard Band (Doug Dillard appeared on the show as one of the Darling boys, a mountain family that visited Mayberry), a "Sheriff's Choice" golf tournament, and Colonel Tim's Talent Time, which is modeled after the talent show that takes place in one of the program's episodes. There is also a parade, a Mayberry trivia contest, a pie-eating contest, a barbecue cook-off, and a silent auction. Actors associated with the show are often special guests at the festival, and watching reruns of old shows is a favorite activity.

CONTACTS:
Surry Arts Council
218 Rockford St.
P.O. Box 141

Mount Airy, NC 27030
336-786-7998; fax: 336-786-9822
www.surryarts.org

♦ 1835 ♦ **Mayfest, International**
May

International Mayfest is a five-day celebration of the arts—performing, visual, and literary—held in Tulsa, Okla. One of the largest festivals in the state, the event features a juried art fair and theatrical presentations. In the past, these varied works have been staged: *Three Penny Opera, Our Town,* and *Revenge of the Space Pandas.* There is also a variety of musical entertainment and ethnic foods from all corners of the globe.

CONTACTS:
Tulsa International Mayfest, Inc.
400 S. Main St
Tulsa, OK 74103
918-582-6435
www.tulsamayfest.org

♦ 1836 ♦ **Mayoring Day**
May

In England, this is the day on which the new mayor of a town or borough parades through the streets. If it takes place on a Sunday, it is often called **Mayor's Sunday** and is celebrated with a church service. In Rye, Sussex, the old tradition of the "hot-penny scramble" is carried out on this day. The new mayor throws hot pennies to the children, who then scramble to pick them up. This custom probably dates back to the time when Rye minted its own coins, and they were distributed while still hot from the molds.

CONTACTS:
Rye Tourist Information Centre
4/5 Lion St.
Rye, East Sussex TN31 7LB United Kingdom
44-1797-229049
www.visit1066country.com

♦ 1837 ♦ **Maytime Festival, International**
Last weekend in May

A festival center since the 12th century, the city of Dundalk in County Louth, Ireland, is the home of the International Maytime Festival and also of the International Amateur Theatre Association. It is the festival's aim to improve amateur theater standards and to bring together outstanding amateur theater groups from all over the world. Over 200 events are presented each year in the Dundalk Town Hall auditorium. There are also a number of "fringe" events, such as a children's afternoon theater and a lunchtime theater, that are presented in other locations.

Amateur theater groups wishing to participate in the International Maytime Festival are judged on the basis of their work by the International Amateur Theatre Association's center in their own country. Theater groups from throughout the British Isles, the United States, and eastern Europe have appeared at the festival in recent years.

CONTACTS:
International Amateur Theatre Association
19, Dorset Ave.
London, UB2 4HF United Kingdom
www.aitaiata.org
Dundalk Community Tourist Office
Market Sq.
Dundalk, Louth Ireland
353-42-9352111
www.discoverireland.ie

♦ 1838 ♦ **McClure Bean Soup Festival**
Second Tuesday through Saturday in September

When a group of Civil War veterans met on the second floor of the Joseph Peters Blacksmith Shop in Bannerville, Pennsylvania in 1883 to organize a Grand Army of the Republic Post, they probably had no idea that their actions might some day lead to a bean soup festival. But when they served a special bean soup at their first meeting, it was such a hit that they eventually invited the public to a "real Civil War bean soup dinner" in 1891. Today, thousands of gallons of bean soup are prepared in 35-gallon kettles, 16 of which can be heated simultaneously over a special battery of wood-fire furnaces set up for the occasion. The cooks, all of whom wear Civil War uniforms, take turns stirring the soup with wooden ladles for 180-minute shifts.

As the Civil War veterans died out, their sons took over the festival, which is now held at the Henry K. Ritter Camp #65 Sons of the Union War Veterans. It takes place for two full days and five nights, usually a Tuesday through Saturday in September, and includes political speeches, exhibits, parades, nightly entertainment, and amusement rides. The recipe for the soup is based on the original Civil War recipe, and it is served to over 70,000 people.

CONTACTS:
McClure Bean Soup Festival and Fair
Ohio St.
McClure, PA 17841
717-543-5467
mcclurebeansoupfair.com

♦ 1839 ♦ **Mecklenburg Independence Day**
May 20

The citizens of Mecklenburg County, North Carolina, would like to think that their ancestors were the first to call for independence from the British when they adopted the Mecklenburg Declaration of Independence on May 20, 1775. But historians now believe that the resolutions calling for independence that had been sent to the Second Continental Congress in Philadelphia were never actually presented there.

Even though the Mecklenburg patriots may not have been the first to declare their independence from British rule, their actions represent an important step on the road to the American Revolution.

CONTACTS:
Charlotte Visitor Info Center
501 S. College St.
Charlotte, NC 28202
704-331-2700 or 800-231-4636
www.charlottesgotalot.com

Mecklenburg County Government Office
Valerie Woodard Center
3205 Freedom Dr.
Charlotte, NC 28208
704-336-7600
charmeck.org

♦ 1840 ♦ Medora Musical
June-September, Labor Day

Theodore ("Teddy") Roosevelt, the 26th president of the United States, spent two years ranching in the Dakota Territory as a young man. When the Spanish-American War was declared in 1898, Roosevelt resigned his position as assistant secretary of the Navy under President William McKinley and organized the First Volunteer Cavalry, nicknamed the "Rough Riders," and took them to Cuba. His colorful exploits, particularly in the Battle of Santiago, made him a national hero.

Every night from mid-June through LABOR DAY in Medora, North Dakota, there is a musical extravaganza known as the Medora Musical—a patriotic song-and-dance salute to Teddy Roosevelt and his Rough Riders. The musical is performed in a natural amphitheater featuring an outdoor escalator to get people to their seats. The colorful buttes and ravines of the Badlands form a dramatic backdrop for the Broadway-class variety show.

CONTACTS:
Theodore Roosevelt Medora Foundation
P.O. Box 198
Medora, ND 58645
701-623-4444 or 800-633-6721
www.medora.com

City of Historic Medora
P.O. Box 418-A
Medora, ND 58645
701-623-4828
www.medorand.com

♦ 1841 ♦ Meenakshi Kalyanam (Chitrai Festival)
Between March and May; during Hindu months of Caitra or Vaisakha

The marriage of the goddess Meenakshi, an incarnation of Parvati, and Lord Sundereswarar (also known as Lord Shiva), is celebrated in Madurai, Tamil Nadu, India. The rituals are observed at the Meenakshi Temple, one of the biggest temple complexes in India, most of it built between the 12th and 18th centuries. There is a huge procession, with chariots carrying the temple images, dressed in special robes and jewels, through the streets. The people, in celebrating the marriage of the deities, also commemorate their own marriages. This festival is also celebrated in Malaysia, where it is known as PANGUNI UTTIRAM.

CONTACTS:
Sri Meenakshi Temple Society
17130 McLean Rd.
Pearland, TX 77584
281-489-0358; fax: 281-489-3540
www.emeenakshi.org

♦ 1842 ♦ Megalesia
April 4

The cult of the Phrygian goddess Cybele (also known as Kybele, the Great Mother or Magna Mater; *see also* BONA DEA and OPALIA) was established in Rome on this day in 204 B.C.E., when her image was installed in the temple of Victory on the Palatine Hill. Eventually her own temple was built on the same hill, but April 4 continued to be set aside as a commemoration of the foreign goddess' arrival in Rome.

Her festival was given a Greek name, the Megalesia, and in the beginning, no Roman citizens were allowed to take part in it. But over time it spread to the streets of Rome, where Cybele's image was carried in a chariot drawn by lions with her castrated priests leaping and gashing themselves in a frenzy of devotion. The procession went from the Palatine to the Circus, where games known as LUDI and plays known as *ludi megalenses* were held. The task of keeping the festival under Phrygian control—and within the bounds of propriety—eventually proved to be difficult, and the Megalesia became little more than a holiday celebrated in honor of the Magna Mater.

CONTACTS:
Italian National Tourist Board
686 Park Ave.
3rd Fl.
New York, NY 10065
212-245-5618; fax: 212-586-9249
www.italiantourism.com

♦ 1843 ♦ Meiji Setsu
November 3

This day was formerly observed as the birthday of the Emperor Meiji (1852-1912), who ruled Japan from 1868 until his death. Meiji Tenno abolished feudalism, raised the people's standard of living, and secured Japan's reputation as a great world power. It was during his reign that Japan made rapid progress toward becoming a modern nation by using Western institutions, technology, and learning as its model. It was during this period that a constitution was adopted, a parliament was convened, civil and criminal laws were codified, and an educational system was established. Railways were built, and electric lights and telephones were put into use.

Today, November 3 is still a national holiday, but it is known as BUNKA-NO-HI, or Culture Day.

CONTACTS:
Meiji Jingu Intercultual Research Institute
1-1 Yoyogi-Kamizono-cho
Shibuya-ku
Tokyo, 151-8857 Japan
81-3-3379-9338; fax: 81-3-3379-9374
www.meijijingu.or.jp/english

♦ 1844 ♦ Meistertrunk Pageant (Master Draught Pageant)
Between May 8 and June 11; Pentecost

This celebration in the medieval town of Rothenburg-on-the-Tauber, Germany, commemorates a gargantuan drinking feat in 1631. The pageant is staged for four days ending on WHIT-MONDAY, and the play itself, *Meistertrunk*, is also performed on various occasions during the summer. The best known of the Bavarian history plays, *Meistertrunk* dramatizes a chronicled event of the Thirty Years' War: the town was threatened with destruction by Imperial troops led by the famed general, Johann Tserclaes Tilly. The general saw the state wine beaker and decided to play a game with the town's life at stake. If a council member could drink off the entire beaker of wine—about a gallon—in one draught, Tilly promised to spare the town. Burgomaster George Nusch accepted the challenge and emptied the beaker in one mighty gulp and the town was saved.

The play is performed out of doors with the entire town a stage. Tilly's troops are camped outside the city walls, and in the market square costumed children plead with the general. The same beaker that Nusch drained in 1631 is used in the reenactment.

A parade precedes the play, and the "Shepherds' Dance" is performed after it in the market square. The dance, dating to 1516, is in honor of St. Wolfgang, the patron saint of shepherds, and recalls the time a member of the shepherds' guild raced from his pastures to warn the city of the approach of an enemy.

CONTACTS:
Meistertrunk Managing Committee
Jagerstrasse 4
Rothenburg ob der Tauber, 91541 Germany
49-9861-5292
www.meistertrunk.de

♦ 1845 ♦ Meitlisonntag
Second Sunday in January

In the Seetal district of Aargau, Switzerland, the girls of Meisterschwanden and Fahrwangen hold a procession on the second Sunday in January known as Meitlisonntag, "Girls' Sunday." They dress in historical uniforms and stage a military parade before an all-female General Staff. The custom dates from the Villmergen War of 1712, a conflict in which the women of Meisterschwanden and Fahrwangen played a vital role in achieving victory. The military procession is followed by a popular festival.

CONTACTS:
Meisterschwanden Local government
Hauptstrasse 10
Meisterschwanden, 5616 Switzerland
41-56-676-6666; fax: 41-56-676-6660
www.meisterschwanden.ch

♦ 1846 ♦ Melbourne Cup Day
First Tuesday in November

The only public holiday in the world dedicated to a horse race, Melbourne Cup Day has been observed in Melbourne, Victoria, Australia, since the first Cup race was held there in 1867. The event actually features seven races, including the grueling handicap race of just under two miles, which is run by some 20 thoroughbreds for a purse worth $4 million. The story of Phar Lap, the legendary New Zealand thoroughbred who won the Cup in 1930 after nearly being shot by unscrupulous gamblers, was made into a movie—*Far Lap* (1984), directed by Simon Wincer—that made the Cup an event familiar to people all over the world.

Cup Day is not only a legal holiday in the state of Victoria, but is observed throughout the world in offices where Australians work. For those who attend, it is a particularly glamorous event. The champagne flows, huge sums of money are wagered, and the women wear lavish hats while the men turn out in grey top hats and dark morning suits. There are similar races held in other Australian states (*see* HOBART CUP DAY), but the Melbourne Cup is still the number one classic of the Australian horseracing circuit.

A six-week festival, known as the **Spring Racing Carnival**, leads up to the big day and lasts well into November.

CONTACTS:
Victoria Racing Club Limited
400 Epson Rd.
Flemington, VIC 3031 Australia
61-3-0072-7575
www.melbournecup.com

Tourism Australia
2029 Century Park E. Ste. 3150
Mailbox 358
Los Angeles, CA 90067
310-695-3200; fax: 310-695-3201
www.tourism.australia.com

♦ 1847 ♦ Melbourne Festival
October

A multi-arts festival held over 17 days in various venues across Melbourne, Australia, the annual Melbourne Festival features some of the finest national and international artists and companies. The Melbourne Festival connects diverse communities of artists with the vibrant art scene of the city. A unique ensemble of artistic performances make up the festival program, including dance, music, theater, circus, visual arts, and multimedia. Beyond the performances, educational classes such as workshops, master art courses, and artist conversations are also presented. In addition, the festival hosts a plethora of food-related activities and family-friendly events. The Melbourne Festival first opened in 1986 and was organized by the famous Italian American composer Gian Carlo Menotti. Besides ticketed activities, the festival offers a host of free exhibitions and other events.

CONTACTS:
Melbourne Festival
Level 2, Yarra Bldg.
Federation Sq.
Melbourne, VIC 3000 Australia
61-3-9662-4242; fax: 61-3-9662-4141
www.melbournefestival.com.au

◆ 1848 ◆ Melbourne International Comedy Festival
Late March to mid-April

The Melbourne International Comedy Festival is Australia's largest annual cultural event, featuring as many as 230 different shows and drawing as many as 400,000 attendees. The festival was founded in 1987 by two comedians, Barry Humphries and Peter Cook.

For three and a half weeks, Melbourne becomes a comedy metropolis, with many activities taking place at the city's Town Hall. The main event in festivals past has been the Opening Night Gala, which features an all-star lineup.

Along with enjoying standup comedy, festival attendees also check out theatre events, street performance, and short films.

Comedians who stand out from the rest of the pack receive official awards at the end of the festival.

Every year festival planners maintain a strong focus on fostering new comedic talents. In the months preceding the big event, competitions are held throughout Australia to determine who will perform at the main stage in Melbourne. Comedians of nearly all ages are welcomed: there is a Class Clown contest for youths between ages 9 and 17 in addition to the Raw Comedy open-mic competition for adult artists.

CONTACTS:
Melbourne International Comedy Festival
240 Exhibition St.
Melbourne, Victoria 3000 Australia
fax: 613-9245-3700
www.comedyfestival.com.au

◆ 1849 ◆ Melbourne International Film Festival
July-August

Launched in 1952, the Melbourne International Film Festival (MIFF) is Australia's biggest annual film event. One of the oldest film festivals in the world, MIFF presents critically acclaimed works from Australia and around the world. In addition to its screening program for current cinema, the event features retrospectives, workshops, discussions, and a host of other cultural activities. MIFF premieres many local films and promotes the work of Australia's rising filmmakers. The festival usually extends over a three-week period and includes a four-day skills development program for

young directors. There are two categories of awards offered each year: the MIFF Shorts Awards and the People's Choice Awards for most popular narrative feature and documentary.

CONTACTS:
Melbourne International Film Festival
Level 3, Block Ct.
290 Collins St.
Melbourne, VIC 3000 Australia
61-3-8660-4888
miff.com.au

◆ 1850 ◆ Memorial Day
Last Monday in May

Memorial Day is a legal holiday, formerly known as **Decoration Day**, proclaimed annually by the president to honor U.S. citizens who have died in war. Since 1950, by congressional request, the day is also set aside to pray for permanent peace.

Both religious services and patriotic parades mark the day's celebrations. In the national official observance, a wreath is placed on the Tomb of the Unknown Soldier in Arlington National Cemetery in Virginia. One of the more moving observances is at the Gettysburg National Cemetery in Pennsylvania, where schoolchildren scatter flowers over the graves of unknown soldiers of the Civil War.

The association of poppies with fallen soldiers was popularized by the poet John McCrae, who wrote the lines "In Flanders fields the poppies blow/Between the crosses, row on row." Flanders was the site of heavy fighting during World War I, and for many who wrote about it later, the poppy came to symbolize both the beauty of the landscape and the blood that was shed there. Poppies are sold by veterans' organizations around the holiday.

The practice of decorating graves of war dead began before the close of the Civil War. However, an officially set day was established in 1868 when Gen. John A. Logan, commander-in-chief of the Grand Army of the Republic, issued an order naming May 30 as a day for "strewing with flowers or otherwise decorating the graves of comrades who died in defense of their country during the late rebellion." The day became known as Decoration Day, but as it was extended to include the dead of all wars, it took the name Memorial Day.

CONTACTS:
Gettysburg National Military Park
1195 Baltimore Pike
Ste. 100
Gettysburg, PA 17325
717-334-1124; fax: 717-334-1891
www.nps.gov

Arlington National Cemetery
Arlington, VA 22211
877-907-8585; fax: 703-614-0619
www.arlingtoncemetery.mil

Sons of Union Veterans of the Civil War
1 Lincoln Cir. at Reservoir Park
Ste. 240

Harrisburg, PA 17103
717-232-7000; fax: 717-412-7492
www.suvcw.org

♦ 1851 ♦ Memorial Day Luminaria at Fredericksburg National Cemetery
Saturday in late May

Memorial Day Luminaria at Fredericksburg National Cemetery was created to honor those "who have given their lives for their country." Each year on the Saturday closest to Memorial Day, hundreds of volunteers from the Commonwealth Girl Scout Council and the Boy Scouts of America set, light, and maintain candles on the graves of more than 15,300 U.S. soldiers who are buried in Fredericksburg National Cemetery. Graves receiving luminaria include thousands of those who died during the Civil War in addition to several hundred burials from other periods in American history.

The vigil, which was first held in 1996, runs from 8:00 PM to 11:00 PM, and includes walking tours of the Marye's Heights gravesite and "Taps" performed each half hour. The cemetery remains open until all the luminarias have gone out. Between 3,000 and 6,000 visitors take part in this event each year.

CONTACTS:
Fredericksburg and Spotsylvania National Military Park
120 Chatham Ln.
Fredericksburg, VA 22405
fax: 540-371-1907
www.nps.gov/frsp

♦ 1852 ♦ Memphis in May International Festival
May

This month-long festival in Memphis, Tenn., focuses on a different nation's culture each year, with exhibitions, lectures, films, performing arts presentations, sporting events, and student exchange programs.

Beginning on the first weekend in May, the festival opens with the Beale Street Music Festival—Beale Street being "the birthplace of the blues." The second festival weekend features a salute to the year's honored country with special exhibits and events showcasing the music, food, art, and dance of the country. The third weekend is an international barbecue competition, dubbed the "Superbowl of Swine," and the fourth weekend is the Great Southern Food Festival, including music and storytelling.

Festival events take place at Memphis's riverfront park, museums, botanical gardens, galleries, hospitals, theaters, shopping malls, and universities. The festival ends with the Sunset Symphony playing a concert of music from the featured country and then for the finale, Tchaikovsky's *1812 Overture*, complete with live cannons and an impressive display of fireworks.

CONTACTS:
Memphis in May International Festival
56 S. Front St

Memphis, TN 38103
901-525-4611; fax: 901-525-4686
www.memphisinmay.org

♦ 1853 ♦ Menuhin Festival
Mid-July through early September

The fashionable resort town of Gstaad, Switzerland, is the setting for an annual summer music festival founded in 1956 by the world-renowned violinist Yehudi Menuhin (b. 1916). Menuhin's name and status have attracted internationally known soloists, orchestras, and chamber music groups to the festival—among them the Zurich Chamber Orchestra, the Chamber Music Ensemble of the Academy of St. Martin-in-the-Fields, and the Zurich Collegium Musicum. Students from the Menuhin School in London and the International Menuhin Music Academy in Gstaad are also invited to perform at least one concert each season. Menuhin's sister, Hepzibah, and son, Jeremy, have performed as soloists at the festival.

Although the emphasis is usually on chamber music and solo recitals, large orchestral pieces are occasionally performed as well. Chamber music concerts are given in the cone-roofed chapel at Saanen.

CONTACTS:
Gstaad Menuhin Festival & Academy AG
Postfach 65
Gstaad, 3780 Switzerland
41-33-748-8338; fax: 41-33-748-8339
www.gstaadmenuhinfestival.ch

♦ 1854 ♦ Mercè, Festa de la
September

Nearly 400 events celebrate the patron saint of Barcelona, La Madonna de la Mercè, each year for a few days including September 24. In years past, the Madonna's feast was observed with religious processions, but these days the processions are augmented by the city's liveliest party of the year with fireworks, street art, live music and dancing, acrobats forming human towers, and sporting events.

CONTACTS:
Barcelona City Council
Placa Sant Jaume, 1
Barcelona, 08002 Spain
fax: 34-93-402-7000
merce.bcn.cat

♦ 1855 ♦ Merchants' Flower Market
Between May 10 and June 13; the seventh Sunday after Easter

Whitsunday, or PENTECOST, in the Dutch city of Haarlem is the day on which the famous flower market opens in the *Grote Markt* (Great Market). Flower merchants arrive in the afternoon or early evening to set up displays of their flowers on tables and carts. When all the flowers have been arranged, the lights are turned off. As midnight approaches, the market square fills with people. As the bells begin to ring in the steeple of St. Bavo's Church, floodlights go on and thousands of tulips, daffodils, irises, and geraniums appear as if by magic. The festival continues all night until eight o'clock in the morning, with dancing to the sound of barrel organs. People buy herring, pastries, and ice cream from food vendors as well as flowers to place in their windows or on their dining-room tables in celebration of Whitsuntide.

See also LUILAK.

CONTACTS:
Netherlands Board of Tourism & Conventions
215 Park Ave. S.
Ste. 2005
New York, NY 10003
917-720-1283; fax: 212-370-9507
www.holland.com

Haarlem Tourist Information Office
Grote Markt 2
Haarlem, 2011 Netherlands
fax: 31-23-531-7325
www.haarlemmarketing.co.uk

♦ 1856 ♦ **Merdeka Day**
August 31

Merdeka Day is a national holiday in Malaysia to commemorate its *merdeka*, or independence, from the British in 1957. Parts of Malaysia were under the rule of various foreign powers for centuries, but by the 1920s all the states eventually comprising Malaysia were ruled by Britain. The Federation of Malaya was founded in 1957 and Malaysia was formed in 1963.

The streets of towns and cities are decorated on this day, and there are numerous parades, exhibitions, and stage shows.

CONTACTS:
Malaysia Tourism Promotion Board
120 E. 56th St.
15th Fl.
New York, NY 10022
212-754-1113; fax: 212-754-1116
www.tourism.gov.my

♦ 1857 ♦ **Merengue Festival (Festival de Merengue)**
Last week in July-first week in August

The merengue is a lively Caribbean dance that originated in Haiti and the Dominican Republic. Its main characteristic is a limping side-step, and it corresponds to the rumba of Cuba or the samba of Brazil.

The world's most famous merengue festival takes place in Santo Domingo, the Dominican Republic's capital city, where outdoor stages are set up along the city's waterfront, and top bands play merengue music while couples swirl and shake to the fast-paced, pulsating rhythms.

In addition to watching the performances and competitions among merengue dancers, festivalgoers can enjoy the music of DJs and bands on the street, imbibe rum and beer, and eat the signature pork sandwiches, *chimichurris*.

CONTACTS:
Dominican Republic Tourism Office
136 E. 57th St.
Ste. 805
New York, NY 10022
212-588-1012 or 888-374-6361; fax: 212-588-1015
www.godominicanrepublic.com

♦ 1858 ♦ **Merrie Monarch Festival**
March-April; week after Easter

The Merrie Monarch Festival is a week of festivities in Hilo honoring Hawaii's King David Kalakaua (1836-1891), who reigned from 1874 to 1891, and gave the United States exclusive rights to maintain a naval station at PEARL HARBOR. The week's events, starting on EASTER, close with the world's largest hula competition on the last three nights. The top hula schools (*hula halau*) compete in ancient and modern hula.

CONTACTS:
Hawaii Tourism Authority
1801 Kalakaua Ave.
Honolulu, HI 96815
808-973-2255; fax: 808-973-2253
www.hawaiitourismauthority.org

♦ 1859 ♦ **Meskwaki Powwow**
Mid-August

The Meskwaki Powwow is held annually on the second weekend of August at the home of the Meskwaki Tribal Nation in Tama, Iowa. It is Iowa's only all-Indian powwow, held at the only Native American settlement in the state. Traditional dancing is at the heart of the event. Featured performers in colorful tribal regalia execute such ceremonial dances as the Victory Dance, which honors soldiers and veterans, and the Buffalo Dance, which reaches back to the tribe's days as active hunters. Among the other dozen or so showcased dances are the Friendship Dance, War Dance, and Pipe Dance. The event also offers arts and crafts and special exhibits. All are welcome to attend.

The annual Meskwaki Powwow has been held since 1913. It grew from the tribe's Green Corn Dance, which accompanied the harvesting of crops each year. From 1902 to 1912, the Meskwaki nation held "field days," a week-long festival of dancing, horse-racing, and games that did not accompany a harvest. In 1912, the Meskwaki chief asked a group of men to plan the following year's field days. In 1913, the event, now called a powwow, was held at the same location it occupies today. More social than spiritual, the present-day powwow still is a reaffirmation of hope, kinship, and friendship, according to tribe members.

CONTACTS:
Meskwaki Annual Powwow Association
1504 305th St

Tama, IA 52339 United States
meskwakipowwow.com

♦ 1860 ♦ Messiah Festival
March-April; eight days during Easter week

The first Messiah Festival in Lindsborg, Kansas, was held in 1882 by a group of Swedish immigrants under the leadership of Dr. and Mrs. Carl Swensson. Using the voices of local townspeople, the Swenssons established what is now known as the Bethany Oratorio Society, a group of 400 singers that includes faculty and students from Bethany College and a 50-member symphony orchestra. Other groups that perform at the annual festival include the Bethany College Choir and the Bethany Community Symphony Orchestra.

The program consists primarily of choral works, oratorios, and solo recitals, often by guest soloists such as Barbara Hocher, D'Anna Fortunato, Ronald Corrado, and Susan von Reichenback. All concerts are held at the college's Presser Auditorium. Lindsborg's Messiah Festival is often referred to as the "Oberammergau of the Plains." (*See also* Oberammergau Passion Play.).

CONTACTS:
Bethany College
335 E. Swensson St.
Lindsborg, KS 67456
785-227-3380
www.bethanylb.edu

Lindsborg Convention & Visitors Bureau
104 E. Lincoln St.
P.O. Box 70
Lindsborg, KS 67456
888-227-2227; fax: 785-227-8687
www.lindsborgcity.org

♦ 1861 ♦ Mevlana, Festival of
Mid-December

This nine-day festival is held in Konya, Turkey, the home of the religious sect known as the Mevlevi. Sometimes referred to as the "Order of the Whirling Dervishes" for the prominent role that ritual dance plays in their weekly observance of *sama* (congregational music), the sect was founded in the 13th century by Mevlana Celaleddin Rumi, one of Turkey's greatest poets and mystics. Their practices were banned in the early part of the 20th century, but in 1954 Konya was given permission to revive the ritual dances. For nine days each year in December, the dervishes dance to the accompaniment of chanting and the music of flute, zither, and drums. Their turning and whirling motions are supposed to represent communion with the Divine.

The Mevlana Festival also offers lectures on the Mevlevis and special exhibits of art that date back to the 11th century.

CONTACTS:
DC Tourism Office
2525 Massachusetts Ave. N.W.
Washington, D.C. 20008

800-367-8875; fax: 202-612-6800
www.tourismturkey.org
Embassy of Turkey
2525 Massachusetts Ave. N.W
Washington, D.C. 20008
202-612-6700; fax: 202-612-6744
www.washington.emb.mfa.gov.tr

♦ 1862 ♦ Mexico Festival of Independence
September 15-16

The **Fiesta Patrias** celebrates the anniversary of Mexico's independence. Although the festival itself goes on for the greater part of a week, it comes to a dramatic climax at 11 o'clock on the night of September 15 in Mexico City as crowds of merrymakers wait for the president to appear on the balcony of the National Palace and proclaim the famous *Grito de Dolores* ("cry of Dolores")—the "call to freedom" that the priest Miguel Hidalgo y Costilla (1753-1811) of the town of Dolores used to rouse the peasant population to fight for their independence in 1810. The people respond by cheering *Viva México!* and shooting off pistols and fireworks.

The Festival of Independence is celebrated in smaller communities throughout Mexico in much the same way, with the local mayor reciting the *Grito de Dolores* at precisely 11 o'clock.

The following day is Independence Day, which is celebrated with fireworks, the ringing of cathedral bells, and a huge military parade. One of the big events on Independence Day is the drawing for the National Lottery. Tickets are inexpensive, and the winner becomes an instant millionaire. Almost everyone watches the drawing on television or listens to the radio to see who wins.

CONTACTS:
United States-Mexico Chamber of Commerce California Regional Chapter
1800 Century Park E.
Ste. 300
Los Angeles, CA 90067
310-922-0206; fax: 310-598-4188
www.usmcocca.org

♦ 1863 ♦ Meyboom
August 9

One of the oldest folk traditions in Belgium, Meyboom is an amalgamation of Belgian folklore, patron-saint celebration, and traditional neighborhood rivalry. In 2008, the people of Belgium observed the 700th anniversary of the festival. As in centuries past, the event was marked with a procession of giant puppets and the planting of a *meyboom* (Dutch for "may tree").

The legend is told by a local fraternity known as the Brotherhood of Saint-Laurent's Companions. In 1213 a wedding party was attacked by marauders from the village of Leuven, located about 20 miles east of the capital city, Brussels. A group of archers came to the victims' rescue, and in reward, the duke gave them permission to plant a maypole on the eve of their patron saint's feastday, St. Laurent. The first celebration took place in 1208.

Today, in keeping with tradition established by the Brotherhood, a young tree is planted on the corner of Rue des Sables and Rue du Marais in Brussels. Before the official planting, a throng of merrymakers gathers for the tree's presentation at Place des Sablons. Then a procession of trumpeters and costumed giants accompanies the tree to its final destination. Time is of the essence, since according to custom, if the *meyboom* is not planted by 5:00 P.M. the city will be cursed and the good fortune destined for the locals will be transferred instead to the people of Leuven.

CONTACTS:
Confrérie des Compagnons de Saint-Laurent (Meyboom)
Rue Roger van der Weyden, 18/20
Brussels, 1000 Belgium
www.meyboom.be

♦ 1864 ♦ **Miami/Bahamas Goombay Festival**
Early June

The Miami/Bahamas Goombay Festival is held over two days in early June each year in Coconut Grove, Fla. It was founded to commemorate the cultural and historical influence of South Florida's first black residents: the workers and craftsmen who arrived in Miami in the early 1800s to build the first hotel in Coconut Grove.

Launching in 1976, the free festival celebrates the music, art, culture, and heritage of the Bahamas and of multi-ethnic Miami with a parade, performances, ethnic food, and a variety of basketball and music activities. The event is named for the traditional music of the Bahamas, which blends African and colonial European influences. Goombay, which means "rhythm" in the Bantu language, is also the name for the goatskin drum that provides the beat for this type of Bahamian music. The festival, which was established as a non-profit organization by William R. Rolle and nine other activists, now draws about 300,000 participants to its colorful attractions.

CONTACTS:
Miami/Bahamas Goombay Festival in Coconut Grove, Inc.
4716 Brooker St.
Miami, FL 33133 United States
305-446-0643; fax: 305-446-6265
www.goombayfestivalcoconutgrove.com

♦ 1865 ♦ **Mi-Carême**
Between March 8 and April 11; fourth Sunday in Lent

This break from the strictness of LENT has traditionally been observed in France, Belgium, and various islands of the French West Indies—including Guadeloupe, St. Barthélemy, and Martinique. In Paris, it is customarily celebrated with the **Fête des Blanchisseuses**, or laundresses, who choose a queen from each of the various metropolitan districts. The

district queens and the queen of queens chosen by them ride through the streets on a float, followed by their costumed courtiers and ladies-in-waiting. Then there is a colorful ball for the washerwomen that night.

In Belgium, **Mid-Lent** or **Half-Vasten** is the day when someone dresses up as the Count of Mid-Lent and distributes gifts to children.

CONTACTS:
Rendez-vous en France
825 Third Ave.
New York, NY 10022
212-838-7800; fax: 212-838-7855
int.rendezvousenfrance.com

Association Cœurs Sœurs
14 rue des Thermopyles
Paris, 75014 France
33-6-2667-7639
carnaval-des-femmes.org

♦ 1866 ♦ **Michaelmas**
September 29 in the West; November 8 in the East

The **Feast of the Archangel Michael**, or the **Day of St. Michael and All Angels**, is a traditional feast day in the Roman Catholic, Anglican Communion, and Orthodox churches. The cult of ST. MICHAEL, traditionally regarded as the leader of the heavenly host of angels, probably originated in the East, then spread to the West by the fifth century. The Roman Catholic feast honors the archangels Michael, Gabriel, and Raphael, while in the East and the Anglican communion, Michael and all the angels are honored.

Churches dedicated to Michael can be found in Asia and throughout coastal Europe, usually in places where Michael is reputed to have saved the community from the threat of a monster or giant. The ninth-century abbey Mont St. Michel, off the coast of Normandy, France, once held the shield worn by Michael in his fight against the dragon.

There is an old saying that if you eat goose on Michaelmas you won't have to worry about money for a year. When tenants paid their rent on this day (*see* QUARTER DAYS), it was customary to include "one goose fit for the lord's dinner." Feasting on goose dinners is still part of the Michaelmas tradition, particularly in Ireland.

CONTACTS:
Church of St. Michael
424 W. 34th St.
New York, NY 10001
212-563-2575
www.stmichaelnyc.com

Bishop"s Castle Michaelmas Fair
The Porch House
High St.
Bishop"s Castle, Shropshire SY9 5BE United Kingdom
44-158-863-8154
www.michaelmasfair.co.uk

476

♦ 1867 ♦ **Michaelmas (Norway)**
September 29

In Norway, **Mikkelsmesse** is the time of year when cows and goats are herded down from the mountain farms, or *saeters*, to the valley homesteads. Almost all farms of any importance have saeters, which are similar to summer camps and are normally operated by women. Cattle and other animals are put out to pasture in the lush mountain meadows, and, traditionally, the girls—usually the eldest daughters of the family—milk and tend the animals and make butter, goat's cheese, and other dairy products for sale or for use on the farms throughout the winter. When the girls return to their family homes in late September with their tubs of butter and well-fed animals wearing garlands of flowers, it is an occasion for dancing, singing, and feasting.

CONTACTS:
Norway Tourism Information Center
655 Third Ave.
18th Fl.
New York, NY 10017
212-885-9700; fax: 212-885-9710
www.visitnorway.com

♦ 1868 ♦ **Michigan Brown Trout Festival**
Third through fourth weekend in July

You don't have to be a professional charter captain or even a local fisherman to participate in the Michigan Brown Trout Festival, which has been held in Alpena on the shores of Lake Huron since 1975. The main event is the two-day Super Tournament, which pits boat against boat. Cash prizes are awarded to those who catch the largest fish (by weight) in each of five divisions—brown trout, salmon, lake trout, steelhead, and walleye—each day and over the course of the week-long festival.

Tens of thousands of people come to Alpena to enjoy not only the fishing competitions but the sailboat races, entertainment, and other festival events. The lucky person who catches Big Brownie, a specially tagged brown trout, during the festival wins a $50,000 savings bond. But the luck that is familiar to fishermen everywhere has plagued those attending the festival as well: no one has ever collected.

Michigan is also home to the National Trout Festival, which dates back to 1933. About 40,000 fishermen and visitors come to the small town of Kalkaska, which has 275 miles of trout streams and 85 lakes stocked with brown, brook, rainbow, and lake trout. This festival is timed to coincide with the opening of trout season, which is the last Saturday in April throughout Michigan.

CONTACTS:
Michigan Brown Trout Festival
400 E. Chisholm St.
Alpena, MI 49707
989-590-2480
www.alpenami-browntrout.com

♦ 1869 ♦ **Michigan Renaissance Festival**
August-September for seven consecutive weekends

Visitors who walk through the turreted gates of the annual Renaissance Festival in Holly, Michigan, are made to feel as if they're stepping back into the 16th century. The festival has a permanent, 200-acre site which is set up to resemble a European village. Festival activities, which are designed to entertain and educate, include theater, games, and equestrian events as well as displays and demonstrations of Renaissance crafts and cooking. The entire event, which takes place over seven consecutive weekends beginning in mid-August, is based on the theme of a harvest celebration in which visitors are encouraged to participate. They can try their hand at archery or dueling, sample roasted turkey drumsticks, observe the arts of glassblowing, pewter casting, and blacksmithing, and witness a Tournament of Chivalry in which costumed knights on horseback joust on the gaming field.

The popularity of Renaissance festivals began with their introduction in California during the 1960s. Such events are now held in Detroit, Minneapolis, Kansas City, Kansas, and Largo and Sarasota, Florida, and in many other cities across the country. Attendance at the Holly festival has grown to more than 150,000 since it was first held in 1980.

CONTACTS:
Michigan Renaissance Festival
12600 Dixie Hwy
Holly, MI 48442
248-634-5552 or 800-601-4848; fax: 248-634-7590
www.michrenfest.com

♦ 1870 ♦ **Mid-Autumn Festival**
Full moon nearest September 15; 15th day of eighth lunar Month

This festival to honor the moon goddess is a national holiday in China and a day celebrated throughout the Far East and in Asian communities all over the world. It is also known as the **Moon Cake Festival**. In Korea, it is called **Hangawi** or CHUSEOK; in Vietnam **Trung Thursday**; in Hong Kong **Chung Ch'iu**; and in Taiwan **Tiong-chhiu Choeh**.

Family reunions are traditional on this day, giving it some resemblance to the American THANKSGIVING. People travel long distances to be together for exchanging presents, feasting, and eating moon cakes. The ingredients of the cakes and the celebration vary according to the region.

In Taiwan, people have picnics and climb mountains to have a better view of the moon. Besides eating moon cakes, people eat pomeloes, a sweet local fruit. The Chinese word for pomelo sounds like the Chinese word for "blessing," so this is considered an especially good time to indulge in pomeloes. It's also a time for lovers to tryst.

In Malaysia, Vietnam, and other areas, it is a children's festival. They parade through the streets on the night of the festival with candle-lit paper lanterns, some of them white and round like the moon, others like all sorts of animals. Dancers parade with dragons made of paper and cloth, and firecrackers are lit after the parades. In Hong Kong children also carry paper lanterns, and many people spend the evening on the beaches watching the moon and the many bonfires that are lit on this night.

In Suzhou, China, a celebration is held in the Museum of Chinese Drama and Opera, with spectators seated at small porcelain tables where they eat moon cakes, drink jasmine tea, and watch a program of Chinese classical music, ballad-singing, acrobatics, and comic scenes from operas.

In Japan, the custom of *tsukimi*, or "moon-viewing," is observed at the same time as the Chinese festival—at the time of the full moon nearest September 15. People set up a table facing the horizon where the moon will rise, and place offerings on the table to the spirit of the moon. These would include a vase holding the seven grasses of autumn, cooked vegetables, and *tsukimi dango*, moon-viewing dumplings made of rice flour. Moon-viewing festivals are held at Hyakkaen Garden, Mukojima, Tokyo, and on Osawa at Daikakuji Temple in Kyoto, where the moon is watched from boats with dragons on their bows.

There are 20 to 30 varieties of moon cakes, which in their roundness are symbolic of family unity. Some are made of lotus seed paste, some of red bean paste, some with mixed nuts, and some have a duck egg in the center. In some regions, the moon cakes are crusty, while in others they are flaky.

There are also varying versions of the origins of the festival, which is thought to go back to the ninth century. One version has it that the Chinese, looking at the dark side of the full moon, saw a hare or rabbit, which was able to make a potion for immortality. The festival was the rabbit's birthday, and people sold rabbits on the streets. Moon cakes were made to feed the rabbits. Another version says that the day marks the overthrow of the Mongol overlords in ancient China; the moon cakes supposedly hid secret messages planning the overthrow.

The more accepted version is that the day is a harvest festival at a time when the moon is brightest. At this time of year, as the weather gets colder, people want a day to rest and enjoy life.

CONTACTS:
China National Tourist Office in the US
370 Lexington Ave.
Ste. 912
New York, NY 10017
212-760-8218; fax: 212-760-8809
www.cnto.org

Taipei Economic and Cultural Representative Office in the US
1 E. 42nd St.
4th Fl.
New York, NY 10017
212-486-0088; fax: 212-421-7866
www.taiwanembassy.org

♦ 1871 ♦ **Mid-Autumn Festival (Singapore)**
Full moon nearest September 15

The MID-AUTUMN FESTIVAL, sometimes known as the **Moon Cake Festival**, is observed by Chinese communities around the world. In Singapore, the mooncakes served during the festival recall a 14th-century uprising against the Mongols, when word of the revolt was spread by concealing the message in cakes that were then smuggled out to compatriots. Today the cakes are often sold along with lanterns and are filled with either a sweet bean paste or with melon and lotus seeds, and may be flavored with orange peels, egg yolks, or other spices. On the night of the Mid-Autumn Festival, children all over Singapore have parades so they can show off their lighted lanterns. There are also lantern-making contests, Chinese costume-making competitions, lion and dragon dances, and concerts.

CONTACTS:
Singapore Tourism Board
1156 Avenue of the Americas
Ste. 702
New York, NY 10036
212-302-4861; fax: 212-302-4801
www.stb.gov.sg

Chinatown Festivals Organising Committee
Kreta Ayer Community Club
28A Kreta Ayer Rd.
Singapore, 088995 Singapore
65-6222-3597
chinatownfestivals.sg

♦ 1872 ♦ **Middfest International**
Three days in late September-early October

Middletown, Ohio, is home to the annual festival of international culture known as Middfest. Designed to promote world understanding, friendship, and peace, the festival highlights the culture of a different country each year. Performers, artists, and dignitaries from the featured country come to Middletown and stay with local families. During the week preceding the three-day festival, they perform in nearby communities, give talks, and demonstrate their art and skills.

Countries that have been invited to participate since the festival's inception in 1981 include Luxembourg, Mexico, Egypt, Brazil, Japan, Switzerland, Canada, Italy, India, and Ireland. Included in the celebration are museum-quality exhibits, ethnic dances, and menus from all over the world. Lectures, workshops, films, and special interest activities are also scheduled throughout Middfest weekend.

CONTACTS:
Butler County Visitors Bureau
8756 Union Centre Blvd.
West Chester, OH 45069
513-860-4194 or 888-462-2282; fax: 513-860-4195
www.gettothebc.com

City of Middletown
1 Donham Plaza
Middletown, OH 45042
513-425-7766
www.cityofmiddletown.org

♦ 1873 ♦ **Midimu Ceremony**
June-October

The Midimu ceremony is a masked dance ritual celebrating the end of the three-year initiation period for Makonde boys and girls. Although the Makonde originally lived in Malawi, Zambia, and Zimbabwe, they have migrated to Tanzania and Mozambique as well. During the dry season, which occurs between June and October, a group of the men inform their families that they must take a long trip. There is a public farewell ceremony, and then they disappear for 10 to 15 days. During this time they go from one village to the next and perform the masked dances of the Midimu ceremony, visiting the house of each new initiate and, after portraying various mythical stories in dance, receive honey, meat, jewelry, and occasionally money in return.

The Midimu ceremony always begins at night during the time when the moon moves from the quarter to the half phase. It usually follows a happy event—such as a successful hunt, a good haul of fish, or a bountiful harvest.

CONTACTS:
Tanzania Tourist Board
The Bradford Group
347 Fifth Ave.
Ste. 1205
New York, NY 10016
212-447-0027; fax: 212-725-8253
www.tanzaniatouristboard.com

♦ 1874 ♦ **Mid-Lent (Italy)**
  Between March 8 and April 7; fourth Sunday in Lent

In Italy **Mezza Quaresima**, or Mid-Lent, is a day of respite from the otherwise severe restrictions of LENT. Parties, dances, and street celebrations take place throughout the country, and many feature effigies of *Quaresima* that resemble a lean, witch-like old hag—in stark contrast to the fat man who represents CARNIVAL.

In Abruzzi, according to custom, the effigy of Quaresima is pierced with seven feathers and suspended on a rope stretched across the street. On each Saturday in Lent the villagers pluck out one feather to signify the end of one of the seven weeks of the Lenten season.

CONTACTS:
Italian National Tourist Board
686 Park Ave.
3rd Fl.
New York, NY 10065
212-245-5618; fax: 212-586-9249
www.italiantourism.com

Agriturismo Castiglione
Fraz. Basilica 77
Sansepolcro
Arezzo, 52037 Italy
39-575-750066; fax: 39-575-744477
www.agriturismocastiglione.it/en

♦ 1875 ♦ **Midnight Sun Festival**
  June 21

The Midnight Sun Festival is a celebration of the SUMMER SOLSTICE in Nome, Alaska, where the sun shines for better than 22 hours a day in the peak of summer. In Nome, the longest day of the year is feted on two days with a street dance, blanket toss, barbecue, Monte Carlo night (gambling), Eskimo dances, a parade, and a mock bank hold-up and jail. A river raft race has been held at midnight on June 21 since the 1960s. Various homemade rafts paddle down a one- to two-mile course on the Nome River, and the winning team claims a fur-lined honey bucket, which is passed on from year to year. A softball tournament, with about 20 men's and women's teams competing for trophies, precedes the day of the solstice. Games start at about 10 P.M.

Various places in Alaska celebrate the midnight sun in various ways: Skagway throws a dance, and at Tok in 1990, the Frigid Poets Society began the practice of climbing a mountain to watch the sun not set.

In Fairbanks, a midnight baseball game is played without artificial lights. The home team, Fairbanks Goldpanners (the name recalls the gold-rush days of early Fairbanks), is reputed to be one of the best semi-pro teams in the nation. The solstice is also marked with department store sales. On the day before the baseball game, there is a Midnight Sun Run, a 10-kilometer race attracting local and national runners, with refreshments and entertainment at the finish.

This excessive activity at midnight may be at least partly explained by the function of the pineal gland. In humans, this pinecone-shaped gland is thought to produce the hormone melatonin that circulates through the body and triggers two reactions—drowsiness and reduced sex drive. Light inhibits melatonin production and thus makes it easier to do with less sleep when the sun shines. Hence, baseball games at midnight. (It is also a fact that 72 percent of Alaska babies are conceived between May and September.).

CONTACTS:
Fairbanks Convention and Visitors Bureau
101 Dunkel St.
Ste. 111
Fairbanks, AK 99701
907-456-5774 or 800-327-5774; fax: 907-459-3757
www.explorefairbanks.com

♦ 1876 ♦ **Midnight Sun Intertribal Powwow**
  July

Since 2001, the Midnight Sun Intertribal Powwow has been held in Fairbanks, Ala. Drawing together members of many tribes from across North America, the powwow is designed to bring together the diverse Native American traditions found in Alaska. Besides the native Athabascan and Eskimo tribes in Alaska, members of other tribes from across the United States and Canada have also moved to the state. Making these tribal members aware of each others' traditions and finding common ground among them all is the primary goal of the powwow. Bringing these traditions to the attention of the general public in a favorable light is another goal.

The Midnight Sun Intertribal Powwow begins with a blessing of the grounds. Entertainment includes dance groups from several tribal traditions and drum groups playing native music. Some dancing events are open to visitors. Booths sell foods, native crafts, and costumes. The last event of the pow-wow is the release of an eagle into the air.

CONTACTS:
Fairbanks Arts Association
Alaska Centennial Center for the Arts Pioneer Park
2300 Airport Rd.
Fairbanks, AK 99707
907-456-6484; fax: 907-456-4112
fairbanksarts.org

Fairbanks Convention & Visitors Bureau
101 Dunkel St.
Ste. 111
Fairbanks, AK 99701
907-456-5774 or 800-327-5774; fax: 907-459-3757
www.explorefairbanks.com

♦ 1877 ♦ **Midsummer Day**
June 24, or nearest Friday

This ancient pagan festival of the SUMMER SOLSTICE, originally kept on June 21, is celebrated in Europe and Scandinavian countries in much the same way as BELTANE was celebrated in Ireland. Bonfires are still lit in some places on **Midsummer Eve** as a way of driving out evil and renewing reproductive powers. At one time it was believed that all natural waters had medicinal powers on this day, and people bathed in streams and rivers to cure their illnesses. Midsummer Day is also sacred to lovers. Shakespeare's romantic comedy, *A Midsummer Night's Dream,* reflects the traditional spirit associated with this festival.

The Swedish begin their **Midsommar** celebration on the Friday before Midsummer Eve and continue through Sunday. Every town and village sets up a maypole, or *Majstang,* which is decorated with flowers, leaves, and flags. In Rattvik, Sweden, on Lake Siljan, the festivities are held on a pier. The province of Dalarna, where some of Sweden's oldest wooden cottages have been preserved, is a popular place to spend the Midsommar festival weekend.

The Swedes call Midsommar "the day that never ends," because the sun doesn't begin to set until 10:00 P.M. and it rises again at 2:00 A.M. In areas of Norway and Sweden that lie above the Arctic Circle, the sun shines brightly 24 hours a day for six weeks.

When June 24 was designated ST. JOHN'S DAY by the Christian Church, the fires that had been associated with the pagan festival were reinterpreted to symbolize St. John, whom the Lord had once called "a burning and shining light." But the pre-Christian elements surrounding Midsummer Day never really disappeared, and the Feast of St. John has long been associated with solstitial rites. This day is also one of the official QUARTER DAYS in England.

In Estonia, St. John's Eve is a national holiday known as **Voidupuha**, or **Victory Day**, commemorating the 1919 Battle of Vonnu in which Estonia regained control from Baltic-German rule; because celebrations extend into the night, the next day, June 24, is also a public holiday.

See also CALINDA DANCE; INTI RAYMI FESTIVAL; JUHANNUS; KUPALO FESTIVAL; ST. HANS FESTIVAL.

CONTACTS:
Pagan Federation
BM Box 7097
London, WC1N 3XX United Kingdom
fax: 44-560-367-2521
www.paganfed.org

♦ 1878 ♦ **Mihr, Festival of**
February

The Church of Armenia, proud of its ancient lineage and determined to retain its national character, has made it a point to keep a number of pagan ceremonies alive by investing them with Christian significance. This seems to be the case with the Festival of Mihr, the ancient god of fire. This pagan spring festival was originally observed by lighting fires in Mihr's honor in the marketplace, and by lighting a lantern that burned throughout the year in the temple. When Christianity was introduced in Armenia early in the third century, fires were lit on this day in the church courtyards, and people danced around them or jumped through the flames.

The modern-day Armenian celebration of the Presentation of Christ in the Temple or CANDLEMAS retains many elements of the pagan Festival of Mihr.

CONTACTS:
Armenian Travel Bureau
24B Bagramyan Ave.
Armenia
374-10-563-321; fax: 374-10-561-327
www.atb.am

Armenian Aryan Order Office
Agatangueghos 7
Rm. 241
Armenia
374-1052-3875 or 818-238-0011
www.hayary.org

♦ 1879 ♦ **Mihragan**
February, March, October; 16th day of Mihr, the seventh Zoroastrian month

Mihragan probably was adapted from the ancient Persian Feast of MITHRA. The 16th of Mihr is considered a "sacred name day" because both the day and the month share the name of the Zoroastrian spiritual being or *yazata* known as Mihr (or Meher, or sometimes Mithra), who presides over justice and who is traditionally identified with the sun. In the Zoroastrian religion, name-day feasts are cerebrated with special religious services which may be performed in a fire temple, a meeting hall, or a private home by either priests or laypeople.

Mihragan is the festival of the AUTUMNAL EQUINOX, and as such, it should occur exactly six months after the festival of the VERNAL EQUINOX, JAMSHED NAVAROZ, which falls on the first day of the first Zoroastrian month. Because the month is Mihr, it was thought to be more appropriate to celebrate the festival on the day—in this case, the 16th—that bears the same name as the month.

Mihragan is also associated with a legendary ancient event—the day on which the heroic Faridun ascended the throne of Persia after killing the mythical evil ruler Zohak.

The Zoroastrian calendar has 12 months of 30 days each, plus five extra days at the end of the year. Because of discrepancies in the calendars used by widely separated Zoroastrian communities around the world, there are now three different calendars in use, and Mihragan can fall either in February, March, or October according to the Gregorian calendar.

There are only about 100,000 followers of Zoroastrianism today, and most of them live in northwestern India or Iran. Smaller communities exist in Pakistan, Sri Lanka, Canada, the U.S., England, and Australia.

CONTACTS:
Iranian Zoroastrian Association
106 Pomona Dr
Suffern, NY 10901 United States
iza-anjoman.org

◆ 1880 ◆ Milan Trade Fair
April

The Milan Trade Fair was originally started in 1920 to allow Italy and other European countries to display their products. It grew into a 10-day event in April hosting 35,000 manufacturers from 110 countries, 25 of whom had their own pavilions. Although the trade fair is a boost for Milan's economy, the city was chosen primarily because of its geographical proximity to the rest of Europe. Today the center hosts more than 70 shows year round. There are also buildings devoted to the products of the various regions of Italy, with displays of leathercrafts, jewelry, textiles, graphic arts, fashions, and ceramics.

CONTACTS:
Fiera Milano SpA
Piazzale Carlo Magno 1
Milano, Lombardy 20149 Italy
39-02-4997-1 or 800-82-0029; fax: 39-02-4997-7379
www.fieramilano.it

◆ 1881 ◆ Milk (Harvey) Day
May 22

Harvey Milk (May 22, 1930 – November 27, 1978) was a politician and gay rights activist who won a seat on the San Francisco Board of Supervisors in 1977, becoming the first openly gay person elected to public office in California. Milk ran for office three times before he finally was elected as a city supervisor. While in office, he became a close ally of Mayor George

Moscone, and led the Board to pass a strict gay rights ordinance for the city. On November 27, 1978, Harvey Milk and George Moscone were assassinated by Dan White, a Board colleague who had resigned but wanted to be reinstated. White had often clashed with Milk on policy matters and opposed the increasing tolerance of homosexuality.

Harvey Milk Day was established in 2009 as a day of special significance by the California legislature and signed into law by then Governor Arnold Schwarzenegger. Schools across the state observe the day by teaching about Milk's life and educating students about discrimination against gays and lesbians. In 2009, Harvey Milk was posthumously awarded the Presidential Medal of Freedom.

CONTACTS:
Harvey Milk Foundation
P.O. Box 5666
Fort Lauderdale, FL 33310
916-443-3855
milkfoundation.org

◆ 1882 ◆ Mill Valley Film Festival
October

The Mill Valley Film Festival is an 11-day non-competitive event held by the California Film Institute in Mill Valley, California, for the purpose of promoting and celebrating film as art and education. Founded in 1977 by Mark Fishkin, it ranks among the top 10 film festivals in the U.S. The internationally renowned festival showcases the best of American independent and foreign cinema, exhibiting works by more than 200 filmmakers from around the world, and is attended by approximately 60,000 people. The festival has a reputation for launching the careers of new filmmakers and presenting new films. Some of the past movies screened at the festival have gone on to win Academy Awards. Categories for films include U.S. Cinema, World Cinema, Valley of the Docs, Children's Film Festival, 5@5 (a daily shorts program), and Active Cinema (an initiative for activist movies). The films are usually screened at the Christopher B. Smith Rafael Film Center in San Rafael, the Sequoia Theater in Mill Valley, the Cinema in Corte Madera, and the Lark Theatre in Larkspur.

CONTACTS:
California Film Institute
1001 Lootens Pl.
Ste. 220
San Rafael, CA 94901
415-383-5256; fax: 415-383-8606
www.mvff.com

◆ 1883 ◆ Mille Miglia
May

The three-day endurance rally in Italy for vintage racing cars known as the Mille Miglia, or **Thousand Miles**, began in 1927 as an all-out race, and it took about 20 hours to cover the course. By 1938, the roads had improved to the point where it took only about 12 hours, and the all-time record of 10 hours, seven minutes, 48 seconds was set in 1955. This meant that the driver had to average nearly 100 miles per hour on roads that drivers normally would hesitate to traverse at 40. A tragic accident in 1957, in which one of the racers, his navigator, and 11 spectators were killed, led to a ban against racing on public roads and brought the Mille Miglia to an abrupt halt.

The event was reorganized in 1977 with different rules. Although it still features vintage racing cars from the 1920s through the 1950s and the same roads, drivers are given three days—rather than 10 hours—to cover the thousand miles. Driving in ordinary traffic, the competitors have to average a set number of miles per hour on 34 timed sections of the course, 19 of which are driven over particularly challenging and scenic stretches of road.

The route begins in Brescia, goes east to Verona, and then southeast to Ferrera, where the drivers spend the night. Early the next morning they leave for Ravenna, follow the coast to Rimini, and then head into the mountains, where they must cover some of the most serpentine and beautiful roads in the world. The drivers spend the second night in Rome and on the third day make a 12-hour dash back to Brescia via Viterbo, Siena, Florence, and Bologna.

CONTACTS:
1000 Miglia S.r.l.
Via Enzo Ferrari 4/6
Brescia, 25134 Italy
39-051-093-8313
www.1000miglia.eu

♦ 1884 ♦ Min, Festival of
Autumn

Min was an ancient Egyptian god, often identified with Amun and Horus. As the god of fertility and rain, he was frequently represented holding a thunderbolt. Ancient Egyptians also associated Min with a bull, in which form he was also believed to be present at the annual harvest festival held in his honor. There were processions at the temple in Luxor, where the god also may have been offered lettuce, considered an aphrodisiac.

CONTACTS:
Tour Egypt
4119 Adrian St.
Lubbock, TX 79415 United States
888-834-1448
www.touregypt.net

♦ 1885 ♦ Minehead Hobby Horse Parade
April 30-May 1

In England and Wales, hobby horses have been a part of celebrations welcoming spring as far back as anyone can remember. In the waterfront town of Minehead, Somerset, the "sailors' horse" has a boat-shaped frame 7-10 feet long, which is carried on the shoulders of a man whose body is concealed by a canvas curtain that hangs to the ground. His head is covered by a painted tin mask and a tall dunce cap.

Through a slit in the canvas, he can reach out his hand for contributions from spectators. Hundreds of rainbow-colored ribbons stream from the top of the horse, fluttering in the wind as he cavorts about town to the accompaniment of a drum and an accordion. Most of the money that is collected by the hobby horse and his companions is spent in the local pub afterwards, although some of it is supposed to go to charitable causes.

On MAY DAY Eve the horse sets out promptly at midnight, ending up at Whitecross (a crossroads to the west of town, the former site of a maypole) on May Day morning. Later in the afternoon the group goes to the nearby village of Dunster and pays its respects to the lord of the local castle. The hobby horse performs again in the square at Dunster that evening.

A similar ceremony is held in Padstow, Cornwall, where "Old 'Obby 'Oss" is a ferocious-looking monster with snapping jaws and sharp teeth. During the dance that represents the culmination of the Padstow ceremony, the horse goes through a ritualistic death and rebirth—an indication, perhaps, of the ceremony's roots in ancient fertility rites driving out winter and welcoming spring.

CONTACTS:
Padstow Tourist Information Centre
The Red Brick Bldg.
N. Quay
Padstow, PL28 8AF United Kingdom
44-18-4153-3449; fax: 44-18-4153-2356
www.padstowlive.com

Minehead Town Council
The Town Hall
The Parade
Minehead, Somerset TA24 5NB United Kingdom
44-16-4370-7213; fax: 44-16-4370-5152
www.mineheadtowncouncil.co.uk

♦ 1886 ♦ Minneapolis Aquatennial Festival
Ten days, including the third full week in July

The Aquatennial Festival takes place in Minneapolis, one of America's coldest cities, during the one time of the year it's most likely to be warm and rain-free, according to meteorologists. It is not only a celebration of summer but of the region's many rivers and lakes. Of the nearly 50 events in the festival, one of the most popular is the Milk Carton Boat Race, a competition for vessels made entirely from milk cartons. In 1993, the largest-ever boat was entered—a 100-foot, 25,000-milk carton vessel resembling an aircraft carrier with a "cargo" of nearly 150 people, honoring veterans of Operation Desert Storm.

First held in 1940, the Aquatennial Festival also features such events as the evening Torchlight Parade and the Grande Day Parade, a sand castle competition, a sailing regatta, a triathlon, and a fireworks display. More than 800,000 people attend the 10-day annual festival.

CONTACTS:
Minneapolis Downtown Council
81 S. 9th St.

Ste. 260
Minneapolis, MN 55402
612-376-7669; fax: 612-338-0634
www.aquatennial.com

♦ 1887 ♦ Miramichi Folk Song Festival
August

Miramichi, a timber port along the St. Lawrence River in Canada, also refers to a type of ballad or narrative song associated with Canadian lumber camps. Miramichi became the newest city in the province of New Brunswick when in 1995 the towns of Newcastle and Chatham, as well as several area villages, combined to incorporate one city. The Miramichi Folk Song Festival, held over three to five days in August, is devoted entirely to songs and ballads in the miramichi "come all ye" style that tell stories of adventure, tragedy, and romance. While most of the songs are performed without accompaniment, they are often followed by tunes played on the fiddle, mouth organ, accordion, or guitar. There are also step-dancing and tap-dancing contests.

Founded in 1958, the festival features local folk singers and musicians as well as groups from all over Canada and the United States.

CONTACTS:
Miramichi Folk Song Festival
100 Newcastle Blvd.
Beaverbrook Kin Centre
Miramichi, NB E9B 1W1 Canada
506-622-1780
www.miramichifolksongfestival.com

♦ 1888 ♦ Miriam's Yahrzeit
March-April; Nisan 10

Miriam's Yahrzeit is a commemoration to honor Miriam, the sister of Moses and one of the most important women in early Hebrew history. *Yahrzeit* is the practice of remembering the anniversary of a loved one's death, observed according to the date and the Hebrew calendar, and typically includes lighting a candle at sunset and reciting *Kaddish*, the mourner's prayer.

When the Egyptian Pharoah decreed that all Hebrew boys would be drowned in the Nile River, Miriam, the prophetess, predicted that her brother Moses would be saved. Having hidden the baby Moses for three months, Miriam's mother instructed her to take the child to the Nile in a waterproof basket, hoping the river would carry him to safety. On that day the Pharaoh's sister was bathing in the Nile, noticed the basket, and took pity on the on the newborn. Miriam approached the Pharaoh's sister and persuaded her unknowingly take Moses' own mother as his nurse. This act ensured that Moses would be raised by his mother until he was adopted into the Egyptian family. Many years later, Miriam would help her brothers Moses and Aaron guide the Jewish people through the desert toward the Promised Land, revealing a source of water that came to be known as Miriam's Well.

♦ 1889 ♦ Misa de Gallo
December 16-24

Misa de Gallo is the start of the CHRISTMAS season in the Philippines, blending Christian tradition with the harvest thanksgiving of the ancient Filipinos.

As the first cockcrows are heard at dawn on Dec. 16, bells of the Roman Catholic churches ring, brass bands parade through towns, children fire small bamboo cannons, and skyrockets burst—all to awaken people for the Misa de Gallo, called **Cock's Mass** in English and **Simbang Gabi** in Tagalog. Each morning of the festival families walk to churches for mass at dawn. Then, on Dec. 24, there is a midnight mass. After the services, people congregate in food stalls that have been set up around church patios or go home for traditional breakfasts of rice cakes and ginger tea or cocoa.

Legend says the Cock's Mass started in the 1700s when a Spanish priest thought that blending native custom with Catholic ritual would help spread the faith. Filipinos had long celebrated good harvests with festivals of thanksgiving, and the priest called the farmers together at harvest time to thank God for good fortune and to pray for a good harvest in the coming year.

CONTACTS:
Philippine Tourism Center
556 Fifth Ave.
New York, NY 10036
212-575-7915; fax: 212-302-6759
www.experiencephilippines.org

Philippine Catholic Lay Mission
78 Simoun St. cor. Banaue
Brgy. Sto. Domingo
Quezon City, 1114 Philippines
63-2-712-20-53
www.philcatholiclaymission.com

♦ 1890 ♦ Mischief Night
November 4

The idea of letting children have a "lawless night" originated in England, and was often celebrated on MAY DAY EVE (April 30) or on HALLOWEEN. But in the mid-17th century, when GUY FAWKES DAY (November 5) became a national holiday, Guy Fawkes Eve became the most popular night for mischief in England, Australia, and New Zealand, where it is sometimes called **Mischievous Night** or **Danger Night**.

CONTACTS:
Tourism Australia (US)
2029 Century Park E. Ste. 3150
Mailbox #358
Los Angeles, CA 90067 United States
fax: 310-695-3200
www.tourism.australia.com

Christchurch & Canterbury Tourism
Botanic Gardens, Rolleston Ave.
PO Box 2600
New Zealand
fax: 64-3-379-9629
www.christchurchnz.com

♦ 1891 ♦ **Misisi Beer Feast**
October; Twamo

The ritual harvest feast known as the **Misisi** takes place in Uganda after the millet harvest each year. The Sebei people make a beer out of the *misisi* ("grain that is left on the ground") after the millet stalks have been gathered and placed in granaries. Misisi also refers to the cobs of maize that are too small to be worth storing. In addition to beer, the feast includes maize meal, steamed plantains, and a bullock, ram, or chickens.

A special group of close relatives is invited to the feast, and the host's father (or some other elder) pours the beer from a libation gourd or *mwendet* and offers it to a friend, saying, "Please accept this beer; I am still alive and let us enjoy it together." Libations are poured with the right hand, inside the house or *kraal,* naming the host's father, brothers, mother, mother's brothers, grandparents, father-in-law, brothers-in-law, and all deceased members of the clan who still have living descendants. Libations are poured for the evil spirits with the left hand, outside the kraal, naming deceased relatives who are jealous because they never had children, or those who cursed them in life.

The Misisi Beer Feast is usually held during the month called Twamo, which is around the same time as the month of October. Mukutanik, an adaptation of Misisi, is held at CHRISTMAS. In areas of Uganda where the millet ripens sooner, it is held earlier.

CONTACTS:
Uganda Tourism Board
42 Windsor Crescent, Kololo
P.O. Box 7211
Uganda
256-414-342-196; fax: 256-414-342-188
www.visituganda.com

♦ 1892 ♦ **Miss America Pageant**
September

What began in 1921 as an attempt by the Business Men's League of Atlantic City, New Jersey, to keep tourists in town after LABOR DAY has developed into an American institution. The week-long event that begins when the winners of the 50 state pageants arrive on Monday includes evening gown, swimsuit, and talent competitions; a parade along Atlantic City's famous boardwalk; and, on Saturday evening, final judging of the 10 semifinalists and five finalists, culminating in the crowning of the new Miss America shortly before midnight. Bert Parks, who hosted the pageant on television for 25 years, was renowned for his patented rendition of "There She Goes," the song that is traditionally sung as the new Miss America walks down the runway in Convention Hall for the first time. In addition to a year of travel and lucrative personal appearances, the winner receives a $50,000 scholarship.

The Miss America Pageant has had its ups and downs over the years—notably the 1968 protests by members of the women's liberation movement, who lit a symbolic fire in a trashcan and threw in a brassiere, some fashion magazines,

and makeup— giving rise to the labeling of feminists as "bra-burners." Vanessa Williams, the first African American to win the pageant, was also the first to be dethroned when it was revealed in July of 1984 that she had once posed nude for *Penthouse* magazine. But many former Miss Americas have gone on to achieve successful careers as models, actresses, or television personalities, or in public service— among them Phyllis George (Miss America 1971), Mary Ann Mobley (1959), and Bess Myerson (1945).

CONTACTS:
Miss America Organization
222 New Rd.
Ste. 700
Linwood, NJ 08221
609-653-8700; fax: 609-653-8740
www.missamerica.org

♦ 1893 ♦ **Mithra, Feast of**
January, February, September; first day of Mihr, the seventh Zoroastrian month

This is a lesser feast celebrated on the first day of the seventh month by Zoroastrians, who are followers of the Persian prophet, Zoroaster (also known as Zarathushtra, believed to have lived around 1200 B.C.E.). Because there are only about 100,000 Zororastrians in the world and their communities are often widely separated, they actually use three different calendars: the Fasli, the Shahanshahi, and the Kadmi calendars, which means that their festivals have three different dates according to the Gregorian calendar. The Feast of Mithra coincides with the AUTUMNAL EQUINOX in the Fasli calendar.

Mithra is an alternate name for the spiritual being Mihr, who is charged with overseeing contracts and fair dealing. Mithra is also responsible for avenging people who have broken contracts or who have not dealt fairly with one another. Some scholars believe that he is the basis for the Roman god by the same name.

Of the modern-day followers of Zoroastrianism, most live in northwestern India (where they are known as Parsis) or Iran. Smaller communities exist in Pakistan, Sri Lanka, Canada, the U.S., England, and Australia.

See also MIHRAGAN.

CONTACTS:
Iranian Zoroastrian Association
106 Pomona Dr
Suffern, NY 10901 United States
iza-anjoman.org

♦ 1894 ♦ **Miwok Acorn Festival**
Usually weekend after fourth Friday of September

This is an annual two-day event of the Miwok (which means "people") Indians, held at the Indian Grinding Rock State Historic Park near Sacramento, Calif. The park was a gathering place for Indians for thousands of years until Europeans settled there in 1848 at the time of the Gold Rush. This is an ancient harvest festival, largely religious, with ceremonial rites and traditional dances. It celebrates the acorn, just as Indians in the east have harvest festivals for the turkey, and in the south and southwest for corn. Acorns were a staple of the California Indians' diet, and were ground to make soup and meal for bread.

CONTACTS:
Tuolumne Me-Wuk Tribal Council
19595 Mi-Wu St.
P.O. Box 699
Tuolumne, CA 95379
209-928-5300; fax: 209-928-1677
www.mewuk.com

♦ 1895 ♦ Mnarja (Imnarja; Feast of St. Peter and St. Paul)
June 29

Mnarja is the principal folk festival of Malta and a public holiday there, thought to have been originally a harvest festival. It is held in Buskett Gardens, a park with extensive vineyards and orange and lemon orchards not far from Mdina, Malta's medieval capital. The name of the festival is a corruption of the Italian *luminaria*, meaning "illumination," since in long-ago times, the bastions around Mdina were illuminated by bonfires for the event. At one time, Mnarja was such a popular and important feast that a husband traditionally promised his bride on their wedding day that he would take her to Buskett on Mnarja Day every year.

Festivities begin on the eve of Mnarja with an agricultural show that continues through the next morning and folk-singing (*ghana*) and folk-music competitions. The traditional food of the evening is fried rabbit. On the following day, bareback horse and donkey races bring the feast to an end. The winners receive *paljj*, "embroidered banners," which they donate to their town church.

See also St. Paul's Shipwreck, Feast of; Sts. Peter and Paul Day.

CONTACTS:
Malta Tourism Authority
Auberge D'Italie
Merchants St.
Valletta, 1170 Malta
356-2291-5000; fax: 356-2291-5394
www.visitmalta.com/en

♦ 1896 ♦ Mobile International Festival
November

Founded in 1982, the Mobile International Festival is meant to share the many cultures of the Mobile, Ala., community with the public.

The festival begins with an opening ceremony and a parade of flags. The Mobile Civic Center houses native dancers, costumes, crafts, musical concerts, acrobats, martial arts, puppet theatre,

art gallery, and cuisine from such countries as Japan, Korea, Ireland, Kenya, China, Greece, Panama, Indonesia, Mexico, Nepal, and India. Visitors are given a "passport" when they enter the festival and collect a stamp as they visit each country's cultural exhibit. In 2012, the Mobile International Festival added a focus on STEM (Science, Technology, Engineering, and Math) to its education program, encouraging festival members to emphasize STEM from a global perspective in their exhibits. The theme of the 31st Annual Mobile International Festival held in 2014 was "Let the Games Begin." Festival attendees were able to play games native to over 70 countries. As part of the festival's dedication to STEM, exhibitors highlighted how those games utilize math and strategic thinking.

CONTACTS:
Mobile International Festival
2900 Dauphin St.
Mobile, AL 36606
251-208-1555
www.mobileinternationalfestival.org

♦ 1897 ♦ Mobile-Phone Throwing World Championship
Last week in August

The Mobile-Phone Throwing World Championship takes place during the last week of August in Savonlinna, Finland. The light-hearted event offers several categories for men, women, and teams: original, which is based only on the distance of throw and requires a traditional "over the shoulder" toss; freestyle, with no age limits, based on the distance of the throw, style, aesthetics, and creative choreography; and juniors, which requires an "over the shoulder" throw, but is limited to children 12 years old and under. Contest organizers provide contestants with mobile phones to throw in the World Championship. They include a variety of brands and models, and all are fitted with batteries. First-place winners get a new mobile phone.

The competition was created in part to highlight Finland's vital role in developing mobile-phone technology. Direct-dial car phones were introduced in Finland in 1971, and as early as 1981, Finland and its Nordic neighbors Sweden, Norway, and Denmark had access to a public mobile telephone network. Since the inaugural Mobile-Phone Throwing World Championship in 2000, several countries have introduced their own national championships, including Belgium, the Czech Republic, Germany, Norway, Spain, Switzerland, and the United Kingdom. The United States held its first national championship in Massachusetts in 2008.

Dries Feremans holds the men's world throwing record of 110.42 meters, set in Belgium in 2014. For the women, Tereza Kopicová holds the record of 60.24 meters, set in the Czech Republic in 2012.

CONTACTS:
Savonlinna Festivals
Puistokatu
Savonlinna, 57100 Finland
358-44-511-2323
www.mobilephonethrowing.fi

♦ 1898 ♦ **Mochi N o Matsuri**
Eighth day of 12th lunar month

The **Rice Cake Festival** is a minor public holiday native to Okinawa. The rice cakes, called *mochi* or *muchi*, are red or white and cylindrical, about four inches long and one inch in diameter. They are wrapped in the leaf of the *sannin* plant or in sugar cane leaves. On the morning of the eighth day of the 12th lunar month, the cakes are placed on a special shelf while prayers are said. Then they are served to guests or hung by string around the room.

CONTACTS:
Japan National Tourism Organization
1 Grand Central Pl.
60 E. 42nd St.
Ste. 448
New York, NY 10165
212-757-5640; fax: 212-307-6754
www.jnto.go.jp

♦ 1899 ♦ **Mohawk Trail Concerts**
Weekends in July

The Mohawk Trail is a stretch of 67 miles along Route 2 from Greenfield in northern Massachusetts to the New York boundary. It was originally an Indian path, then a route for covered wagons and stagecoaches. Nowadays it is favored by tourists, particularly during the New England fall foliage season.

The Mohawk Trail Concerts began in 1970 as a series of chamber music performances by musicians who spent the summer in and around Charlemont, a rural area 120 miles northwest of Boston. One of the founding musicians, violinist-composer Arnold Black (1923-2000), eventually became the artistic director for what evolved into a weekend concert series that now extends through the month of July, with other special concerts throughout the year. Performances are given in the Federated Church of Charlemont, where the audiences hear both well-known musicians and young artists in a varied program of classical, contemporary, jazz, and folk music.

Beginning with the 46th season in 2015, Mohawk Trail Concerts will be under the directorship of cellist Mark Fraser, founding member of the Adaskin String Trio, who will take the reins from Ruth Black, director from 2000-2014.

CONTACTS:
Mohawk Trail Concerts
75 Bridge St.
P.O. Box 75
Shelburne Falls, MA 01370
413-625-9511
www.mohawktrailconcerts.org

♦ 1900 ♦ **Mohegan Homecoming**
Third weekend in August

The Mohegan Homecoming, which takes place in Uncasville, Connecticut, on the third weekend in August each year, is a modern festival that has evolved from the pre-Columbian

thanksgiving ceremony held by the Indians to thank their creator for the corn harvest. Up until 1941 the Mohegans held a Green Corn Festival, also known as the Wigwam Festival, but later the event was billed as a "homecoming"—a time for Mohegan Indians living in all parts of the world to come home and renew their roots. It is an opportunity to conduct tribal business, such as the installation of new chieftains and medicine women, and to update one another on tribal matters. Foods served at the festival include succotash, clam chowder, and other New England specialties; other events include traditional dancing, storytelling, and arts and crafts displays.

CONTACTS:
Mohegan Tribe
13 Crow Hill Rd.
Uncasville, CT 06382 United States
860-862-6100
www.mohegan.nsn.us

♦ 1901 ♦ **Moldova Independence Day**
August 27

The Republic of Moldova is situated between Romania and Ukraine, and it has often by occupied by surrounding nations. In 1359, the Moldovan feudal state was formed. In 1812, the Russian-Turkish Peace Treaty was signed. In accordance with the treaty, the Russian empire annexed the eastern part of Moldova, making it a Russian province. In 1918, the country united with Romania. This unity lasted till 1940, when the Soviet Union annexed the country. Moldova functioned as a territorial entity within the Soviet Union until the late 20th century.

On August 27, 1991, the Republic of Moldova became an independent and sovereign state. To commemorate this momentous occasion, the country celebrates Independence Day every year on August 27. As part of the celebrations, the Moldovan President addresses the people of the country with a festive speech. Public concerts, fairs, and outdoor activities are held in Chisinau, the capital of Moldova, and in other cities around the country. On August 27, 2001, the first military parade was held in Chisinau to celebrate the first 10 years of the country's independence.

CONTACTS:
Republic of Moldova
1 Piata Marii Adunari Nationale
Chisinau, MD-2033 Moldova
373-22-820-900; fax: 373-22-820-930
www.moldova.md

♦ 1902 ♦ **Moldova Memorial Easter (Moldova Grave-Visiting Day)**
Monday after Easter Monday

The most prevalent religion in Moldova is Christianity; in fact, almost half of the population belongs to the Eastern Orthodox Church. The two most important religious holidays in Moldova are Christmas and Easter. The day of

Orthodox Easter changes from year to year, falling on the first Sunday after the first new moon following the day of the spring equinox. A six-week fast precedes the holiday, and the traditional foods served on Easter are similar to those served on Christmas.

In Moldova, the Easter celebration lasts two days—Easter Sunday and Easter Monday, which is the official public holiday. One week after Easter Monday is Memorial Easter. On this day, people visit and take care of the graves of their deceased relatives.

CONTACTS:
Orthodox Church of Moldova
Metropolitan Foreign Relations Department
12 Ciuflea St.
Chisinau, MD-2001 Moldova
373-27-8266
en.mitropolia.md

Tourism Agency of the Republic of Moldova
53, Hincesti St.
Chisinau, 2028 Moldova
373-2222-6634
turism.gov.md

◆ 1903 ◆ **Moldovan Language Day**
August 31

Limba Noastra, or **Our Language Day**, is a public holiday in Moldova, which is the official name of the former Moldavian Soviet Socialist Republic, a historic region of northeastern Romania. On August 31, 1989, Moldova became the first Soviet republic to pass a law declaring its language, Moldovan, to be the official language of the republic. The language law also formally proclaimed that Moldovan and Romanian were the same. The Soviets had insisted that Moldovan was a different language from Romanian in order to promote the idea that Moldova and Romania were separate nations.

Second in importance only to MOLDOVA INDEPENDENCE DAY on August 27, Language Day is celebrated with ceremonies at the burial sites of individuals linked to the struggle for cultural rights of Romanians, especially Romanian poets and writers.

CONTACTS:
Voiaj International
Bd. Negruzzi, 4/2
Chisinau, MD-2001 Moldova
373-22-54-6464; fax: 373-22-88-2882
voiaj.md

◆ 1904 ◆ **Mollyockett Day**
Third Saturday in July

Mollyockett was a Pequawket Indian who lived among the early settlers of western Maine. Born between 1730 and 1740, she lived in the area now known as Bethel after 1770 and made frequent trips throughout the Androscoggin Valley and into northern New Hampshire, Vermont, and Quebec. She was known as an "Indian doctress" who treated the white settlers of New England as well. One of her most famous patients was the infant Hannibal Hamlin, whom she found near death and cured with warm cow's milk. He grew up to become Abraham LINCOLN's vice president. Mollyockett was also known as a storyteller, famous for her tales of buried Indian treasure.

The local festival that is currently known as Mollyockett Day in Bethel, Maine, started out in the 1950s as a fundraising event for families in need of assistance. In 1970 the name was changed in honor of the Indian woman whose generosity and self-reliance have become legendary. The festival includes a parade, foot races, rubber ducky race, and Maine lobsters.

CONTACTS:
Bethel Area Chamber of Commerce
8 Station Pl.
P.O. Box 1247
Bethel, ME 04217
207-824-2282 or 800-442-5826; fax: 207-824-7123
www.mollyockettdays.com

◆ 1905 ◆ **Monaco Grand Prix**
May

One of the last true road circuits, the Monaco GRAND PRIX winds through the streets of Monte Carlo, along the harbor, and through a tunnel. It is a Formula One motor race, which refers to very specific rules governing the car's weight, maximum number of cylinders, fuel, and engine cylinder capacity. First run in 1929, the Monaco Grand Prix has a lap distance of 1.95 miles with an unusually high number of corners, which demand constant gear-changes and maximum concentration from the drivers. In 1955 an Italian car skidded and ended up in the harbor, underscoring the dangerous and unusual nature of this race.

Formula One cars are single-seaters, although prior to the 1920s the mechanic rode in the car as well. The engine is located in the rear, and the driver, protected by special clothing, a crash helmet, and goggles, steers with a very small wheel from a reclining position, to reduce air drag to a minimum.

Grand Prix races are held all over the world and are approximately 200 miles in length. But most are now run on specially constructed courses designed to simulate road conditions.

CONTACTS:
Automobile Club of Monaco
23 Boulevard Albert 1er
Monaco, 98000 Monaco
fax: 377-9315-2600
acm.mc

Monaco Government Tourist and Convention Bureau
565 Fifth Ave.
23rd Fl.
New York, NY 10017
212-286-3330 or 800-753-9696; fax: 212-286-9890
www.visitmonaco.com

♦ 1906 ♦ **Monkey God, Birthday of the**
September

This holiday is a celebration by Chinese Taoists of Tai Seng Yeh, the popular Monkey God, who sneaked into heaven and acquired miraculous powers; he is thought to cure the sick and absolve the hopeless. He is the godfather of many Chinese children.

In Singapore, Taoist mediums go into a trance to let the god's spirit enter their bodies; then, possessed, they howl and slash themselves with knives, and scrawl symbols on scraps of paper that are grabbed by devotees. There are also puppet shows and Chinese street opera performances at Chinese temples.

CONTACTS:
Tiong Bahru Qi Tian Gong temple
44 Eng Hoon St.
Singapore, 169786 Singapore
65-6220-2469; fax: 65 62220352
www.qitiangong.com

Singapore Tourism Board
1156 Ave. of the Americas
Ste. 702
New York, NY 10036
212-302-4861; fax: 212-302-4801
www.stb.gov.sg

♦ 1907 ♦ **Monkey Party**
November-December

Yongyuth Kijwattananuson first offered this banquet to the long-tailed macaque monkeys who live in the city of Lop Buri, Thailand, in 1988 to thank them for making his hotel so attractive to visitors. It has since become an institution, especially for the hundreds of monkeys who normally spend their time begging and stealing food from townspeople and tourists. Dozens of chefs prepare numerous dishes featuring fruit and vegetables on tables covered with red tablecloths and then wait for the monkeys to overcome their fear of the spectators, loudspeakers, and media people who assemble to cover the event. Once they realize it's safe, the monkeys eventually approach the tables to feast on the offerings, playing and throwing food in the process. According to local legend, some of the monkeys can be seen disembarking from trains the morning of the event, though it is more likely that the majority, at least, are local inhabitants.

CONTACTS:
Tourism Authority of Thailand
611 N. Larchmont Blvd.
1st Fl.
Los Angeles, CA 90004
323-461-9814; fax: 323-461-9834
www.tourismthailand.org

♦ 1908 ♦ **Monlam (Prayer Festival)**
Usually February; 4th-25th days of first Tibetan lunar month

The greatest festival in Tibet follows the Tibetan New Year (LOSAR) celebrations, and commemorates the miraculous powers of Buddha. The two-week festival was started in the 14th century by Tsongkhapa, the great reformist monk, to ensure that the new year would be successful and prosperous. It is a time to attend examinations of and make offerings to monks, to light butter lamps, and above all to socialize, get the latest news, and watch sports events such as wrestling, archery, and horse racing. On the 15th day celebrants throng to Lhasa's famous Jokhang temple, where monks have created enormous butter sculptures. (*See* BUTTER SCULPTURE FESTIVAL.) A procession around the Barkor, the old city of Lhasa, carries a statue of Maitreya, the future Buddha.

When the Chinese denounced religious observances in 1959, the festival died. It was revived again in 1986, and has been observed since, although not with the grandeur of earlier days.

CONTACTS:
Office of Tibet
1228, 17th St. N.W.
Washington, D.C. 20036
212-213-5010; fax: 703-349-7444
tibet.net

♦ 1909 ♦ **Monterey Jazz Festival**
Third or fourth weekend in September

This festival is a three-day celebration of jazz held since 1958 outside Monterey, Calif., at the Monterey Fairgrounds, where seven stages accommodate dozens of acts and 40,000 fans. Jimmy Lyons, a West Coast disc jockey, is credited with starting the first festival, and since then it has attracted top jazz artists. Among the many who have appeared are Dizzy Gillespie, Woody Herman, Thelonius Monk, Gerry Mulligan, Odetta, and Pee Wee Russell. The festival has boasted a number of world premieres: Duke Ellington's *Suite Thursday*, Lalo Schifrin's *Gillespiana*, and Charles Mingus's *Meditations on Monterey* are a few of them.

The atmosphere is jazzy and cosmopolitan. Booths outside the arena sell food for every taste, from sweet-potato pies to tacos to beef teriyaki.

CONTACTS:
Monterey Jazz Festival Administrative Office
9699 Blue Larkspur Ln.
Ste. 204
Monterey, CA 93940
831-373-3366 or 888-248-6499; fax: 831-373-0244
www.montereyjazzfestival.org

♦ 1910 ♦ **Montreal Jazz Festival**
Last weekend in June through first week in July

What has been called the most important cultural event in Canada and the largest jazz festival in the world, the **Festival International de Jazz de Montréal** has attracted some of the greatest names in jazz—including Miles Davis, Pat Metheny, Ray Charles, and Dizzy Gillespie. More than a million people come to the festival, about one-fourth of them from outside Montreal. Although the first festival in 1980 featured only about 20 performances, the 1995 event had 2,000 artists performing in 400 concerts.

Montreal's streets are closed for the 11 days of the festival to make room for the outdoor performances, which take place rain or shine, and represent a mix of traditional, modern, and innovative jazz. Marking the 35th anniversary of the Montreal Jazz Festival, the 2014 event was considered to be the biggest and best jazz event in the world, with more than 2 million music-lovers viewing 3,000 musicians in 650 concerts.

CONTACTS:
Festival International de Jazz de Montreal
400 Maisonneuve Blvd. W.
Ninth Fl.
Montreal, QC H3A 1L4 Canada
514-523-3378 or 855-299-3378; fax: 514 525-8033
www.montrealjazzfest.com

♦ 1911 ♦ **Montreal World Film Festival**
August

The Montreal World Film Festival is held each August. It was created to celebrate cultural diversity and promote understanding through international cinema. With its selection of 400 films from over 80 countries, the festival celebrates established filmmakers, supports innovation, discovers new talent, and provides a meeting place for both film professionals and the general public. It is one of the oldest film festivals in Canada and the only competitive one in North America that has accreditation from the International Federation of Film Producers Association.

CONTACTS:
Montreal World Film Festival
1432 de Bleury St.
Montréal, QC H3A 2J1 Canada
514-848-3883; fax: 514-848-3886
www.ffm-montreal.org/en/home.html

♦ 1912 ♦ **Montreux International Jazz Festival**
July

The most widely known jazz festival in Europe is held in Montreux, Switzerland, for about two weeks in July. There are big band, blues, country and western, jazz rock, folk jazz, and avant garde jazz concerts, most of which are held inside the Convention Centre's Stravinski Auditorium and Miles Davis Hall. Other concerts and jam sessions are held on the terrace and in the gardens of the Casino and on boats cruising Lake Leman. Most of the bands, combos, and soloists who have appeared at Montreux are American: Oscar Peterson, Dizzy Gillespie, Ella Fitzgerald, Count Basie, Miles Davis, Ray Charles, and Buddy Rich, to name just a few. Attention is also paid to up-and-coming talent, sometimes from countries as far away as Japan and Brazil. The Montreux Festival has been an annual event since 1967 and inspired the Detroit International Jazz Festival, a sister jazz festival held every year over Labor Day weekend in Detroit, Michigan.

CONTACTS:
Montreux Jazz Festival Foundation 2
2m2c / Avenue Claude Nobs 5
Montreux, 1820 Switzerland
fax: 41-21-966-4444
www.montreuxjazz.com

♦ 1913 ♦ **Moon Day**
July 20

The first man to walk on the moon was American astronaut Neil Armstrong. On July 20, 1969, he and his fellow astronaut, Edwin E. "Buzz" Aldrin, left the command module *Columbia* and landed the lunar module *Eagle* on the moon's Sea of Tranquillity. Armstrong's first words as he stepped out on the lunar surface were heard by an estimated 600 million television viewers around the world: "That's one small step for a man, one giant leap for mankind."

Air Force Lieutenant Colonel Michael Collins, pilot of the *Columbia,* continued to circle the moon for the 211/2 hours during which Armstrong and Aldrin conducted their experiments. The information they collected about the moon's soil, terrain, and atmospheric conditions made an enormous contribution to knowledge of the universe and future space exploration. The Apollo 11 mission was completed eight years after President John F. Kennedy told Congress he believed that the United States could put a man on the moon before the decade ended.

CONTACTS:
NASA Public Communications Office
NASA Headquarters
Ste. 5R30
Washington, D.C. 20546
202-358-0001; fax: 202-358-4338
www.nasa.gov

♦ 1914 ♦ **Moore (Billy) Days**
Third weekend in October

Billy Moore Days celebrate the pioneer who established a stage stop, general store, and saloon in what became Avondale, Ariz. Avondale and the other Tri-City towns of Goodyear and Litchfield Park commemorate Billy Moore with a carnival, arts and crafts fair, golf tournament, burro races, car show, a street dance, and a 100-unit parade in which assorted politicians and the Arizona Maid of Cotton take part. The celebration has been held since 1954.

Billy Moore's story is surrounded by legend. He is supposed to have belonged to the gang of guerrillas led by William Clarke Quantrill, but historians think he was a young blacksmith with the gang, not one of the pillagers. Whatever he was, he was exiled by the governor of Missouri for his part in the Quantrill gang, and he headed out for Arizona Territory in 1867. Before setting up business, he either had a run-in with an outlaw or was attacked by Apaches; in any event, he was seriously injured, and a Yaqui Indian woman who later became his wife nursed him back to health.

In the late 1880s Moore bought 280 acres of land at the stage stop known as Coldwater for 25 cents an acre under the Desert Lands Act of 1877. He became a justice of the peace and was postmaster at the Coldwater station until 1905, when the post office was moved to a different location because liquor and the mail were being distributed from the same station in violation of the law. Billy Moore died in 1934 at the age of 92.

CONTACTS:
Arizona Office of Tourism
1110 W. Washington St.
Ste. 155
Phoenix, AZ 85007
602-364-3700; fax: 602-364-3701
tourism.az.gov

City of Avondale
11465 W. Civic Center Dr.
Avondale, AZ 85323
623-333-1000
www.ci.avondale.az.us

♦ 1915 ♦ **Moors and Christians Fiesta**
April 22-24

Moors and Christians fiestas are celebrated throughout the year all over Spain to commemorate various battles between the two groups. But it is the **Fiesta of Alcoy** in the province of Alicante that is one of the most colorful. Coinciding with the feast day of St. George on April 23, the fiesta commemorates the victory of the Christians over the Moorish leader al-Azraq in 1276.

The three-day event begins on the morning of April 22 with the ceremonial entry of the Christians, symbolizing the forces that assembled to defend the town of Alcoy in the 13th century. The Moors arrive in the afternoon, dressed in exotic Oriental costumes. On April 23 the relic of St. George is carried in procession from his temple to the parish Church of Santa Maria, where a mass is sung. On the third day the battle is reenacted and an apparition of St. George appears on the battlements of the castle.

In the 15th, 16th, and 17th centuries, fiestas of Moors and Christians were danced. It is believed that this type of celebration eventually crossed the sea to England and became the familiar Morris dance.

CONTACTS:
Tourist Office of Spain
60 E. 42nd St.
Ste. 5300 (53rd Fl.)
New York, NY 10165
212-265-8822; fax: 212-265-8864
www.spain.info

♦ 1916 ♦ **Moose Dropping Festival**
Second weekend in July

When the snow melts on Denali (Mount McKinley) during the Alaskan summer, the citizens of nearby Talkeetna start gathering moose droppings in preparation for their annual July festival. Varnished moose droppings are turned into jewelry and other decorative and useful objects. Some droppings are also put aside for such festival events as the Moose Nugget

Toss, where participants throw them at a target resembling a moose. The Mountain Mother Contest is another festival highlight. These supermoms show what they're capable of by mastering a number of feats within a short time period, such as carrying a baby doll and grocery bags across a river, changing diapers, splitting wood, and baking a pie.

CONTACTS:
Moose Dropping Festival
c/o Talkeetna Historical Society
P.O. Box 76
Talkeetna, AK 99676
907-733-2487
www.talkeetnahistoricalsociety.org

♦ 1917 ♦ **Moravian Music Festival**
Mid-June for one week in odd-numbered years

When the Moravian Church established its first American communities in the 18th century, the settlers continued to nurture their musical heritage in worship as well as in daily life—virtually interchangeable for the Moravians, for whom music was an essential component of life. As such, singing, playing instruments, and composing music were second nature to most Moravians.

Thor Johnson, the son of a Moravian minister, helped 20th-century America rediscover Moravian music when he conducted the first Early American Moravian Music Festival in Bethlehem, Pennsylvania, in 1950. Later that decade, the Moravian Music Foundation was established in North Carolina to preserve and publish the music in the archives of the Moravian Church in America.

What is now known as the Moravian Music Festival is held every two years, in cities within the northern and southern provinces of the Moravian Church in America. The archives managed by the Moravian Music Foundation provide the choral, orchestral, and chamber music performed at the festival. In addition to concerts and recitals, the festival presents seminars and workshops.

CONTACTS:
Moravian Music Foundation
Archie K. Davis Center
457 S. Church St.
Winston-Salem, NC 27101
336-725-0651; fax: 336-725-4514
moravianmusic.org

♦ 1918 ♦ **Moreska Sword Dance**
July 29; July-August

The Moreska Sword Dance is a ritual dance of medieval knights that has been performed every July 29 for centuries. The dance takes place in Korcula, the main town of the island of Korcula off the coast of the former Yugoslavia (now within Croatia), in honor of the town's patron saint, Theodore. The dance-cum-pageant, with many clashes of steel, symbolizes the battle against the Turks when Korcula was under the control of the kings of Bosnia in the late 14th century.

A spirited and athletic dance, it also has been performed in other parts of Europe. There is historical evidence, for example, that the Moreska, whose name is derived from the Spanish word for "Moorish," was danced in 1156 in Lerida, Spain, to portray the expulsion of the Moors from Aragon. Originally performed only on July 29, it is now presented within the six-week **Festival of Sword Dances** running through July and August, though the grandest performance is still on the 29th. Korcula has hosted the festival since 1997 to celebrate and preserve the 400-year-old tradition of sword dancing.

From the 15th century, Korcula was under the control, successively, of Venice, Austria, France, Britain, again Austria, and Italy, until being ceded to Yugoslavia after World War I. It was under Italian occupation in World War II and liberated by Yugoslavian partisans in 1944-45. Marco Polo is supposed to have been born on Korcula.

See also Moors and Christians Fiesta.

CONTACTS:
Korcula Tourist Board
Obala dr. Franje Tudmana 4
Korcula, 20260 Croatia
385-20-715-701; fax: 385-20-715-866
www.visitkorcula.eu

♦ 1919 ♦ **Morija Arts and Cultural Festival**
Two events; one in April and one in October

The legacy of European colonialism and other historic forces have inhibited the indigenous culture of the Kingdom of Lesotho, an enclave within South Africa. The primary objective of the Morija Arts and Cultural Festival, promoted as the country's premier annual cultural event, is to revive the cultural life of the Sotho people. Additionally, the festival boosts tourism and the sale of traditional African crafts.

Established in 1999, the festival takes place in a large village of Morija in the Maseru district. It is coordinated by Morija Museum & Archives, with financial support from the Royal Family, the Lesotho government, and various churches, private donors, and nongovernmental organizations.

Originally held in October, the three-day festival was moved to April in 2008. Its agenda has remained consistent with past celebrations and has included cultural exhibits, night concerts, and workshops for various artists and performers. A second festival component, the Morija Festival Cultural Competitions, takes place in early October. The competitions serve to increase the participation of Sotho youth, a special priority for Morija Museum & Archives, and include primary and high school groups, as well as community cultural groups. Though the Cultural Competitions began with a focus on traditional dance, they now include traditional instruments and games, poetry, art, and drama. In 2013 the Morija museum sought to bring dramatized dance programs into local high schools.

CONTACTS:
Morija Museum & Archives
P.O. Box 12

Morija, 190 Lesotho
266-2236-0308; fax: 266-2236-0308
www.morija.co.ls

♦ 1920 ♦ **Moriones Festival**
Begins between March 15 and April 18; Holy Week

One of the more popular and colorful of the many Passion plays—folk dramas that retell the story of Jesus' arrest, trial, and crucifixion—is performed before Easter in the Philippines. Held on the island-province of Marinduque with participants wearing masks and costumes of Roman soldiers, Moriones tells the story of the legendary Roman soldier, Longinus, who is said to have been blind in one eye. As he pierced the side of the crucified Jesus, a drop of the blood cured his blindness. The first thing he saw with both eyes was Christ's passage to heaven. According to the legend Longinus announced this good news. The Roman warriors, however, wanted to stop this report and captured him.

Many local men take part in the Marinduque play, performing the roles of Roman soldiers. They wear large wooden masks covered with black beards and painted with enormous black eyes, open mouths, and pink flesh. The masks disguise their identities, as their participation serves as an act of humble religious devotion rather than an attempt to garner public recognition. Longinus escapes from the Roman soldiers three times in the Marinduque Passion play, but cannot evade capture on the fourth attempt. The Roman soldiers lead Longinus to a scaffold, but he continues to declare his faith in Christ. The Moriones cut his head off and carry it through town, while bringing his body along on a stretcher.

CONTACTS:
Philippines Department of Tourism
556 Fifth Ave.
New York, NY 10036
212-575-7915; fax: 212-302-6759
www.experiencephilippines.org

♦ 1921 ♦ **Mormon Pioneer Day**
July 24

After their founder, Joseph Smith, was murdered in 1844, the Mormons—members of the Church of Jesus Christ of Latter-Day Saints—moved westward from their settlement in Nauvoo, Illinois, under the leadership of Brigham Young. When Young surveyed the Salt Lake Valley on July 24, 1847, he proclaimed, "This is the right place." Thousands of Mormon pioneers followed him over the next two decades, many of them pushing their belongings in handcarts.

The original 40-acre plot with log houses where the Mormons settled is the modern Salt Lake City, and the day on which Young chose the site is celebrated not only in Utah but in surrounding states with significant Mormon populations, such as Idaho, Arizona, Nevada, Wyoming, and California. Other states observe their own **Pioneer Day** at different times of the year.

CONTACTS:
Utah Office of Tourism
Council Hall / Capitol Hill
300 N. State St.
Salt Lake City, UT 84114
801-538-1900 or 800-200-1160
www.visitutah.com

Salt Lake Visitor Information Center
90 S. W. Temple
Salt Lake City, UT 84101
801-534-4900 or 800-541-4955
www.visitsaltlake.com

◆ 1922 ◆ Morocco Independence Day
November 18

Independence Day, also known as **Fete de l'Independence**, is a national holiday commemorating Morocco's independence from France on November 18, 1927; a secret treaty in 1904 had divided Morocco between France and Spain.

Throne Day, March 3, was also a public holiday, commemorating the anniversary of King Hassan II's accession in 1961. When King Hassan II died in 1999, his son, Mohammed VI (b. 1963), became king, and now it is his birthday on August 21 that is celebrated, along with July 30, his coronation day.

Other public holidays in Morocco include: August 20, the anniversary of the king's and people's revolution, and November 6, the anniversary of the Green March in 1975. In order to claim the Western Sahara for Morocco, more than 300,000 Moroccans marched into the territory, which the Spanish still controlled; Spanish troops left the area by early 1976.

CONTACTS:
Moroccan National Tourist Office (MNTO)
104 W. 40th St.
Ste. 1820
New York, NY 10018
212-221-1583; fax: 212-221-1887
www.visitmorocco.com

◆ 1923 ◆ Moro-Moro Play
April or May

The term *moro-moro* refers to a type of folk drama performed in villages throughout the Philippines, usually during fiestas. Although each village's moro-moro is a little different in terms of treatment, all are full of romance and melodrama, and the highpoint is always a battle between Muslims and Christians. Local people write the script, which is in verse, and some performances include quite elaborate scenery and costumes. Music and dance are also part of the production.

One of the most notable moro-moros is held in San Dionisio in Rizal Province, where the drama is performed in the church and the village square every spring, usually in April or May.

See also MOORS AND CHRISTIANS FIESTA.

CONTACTS:
Philippine Tourism Center
556 Fifth Ave.
New York, NY 10036
212-575-7915; fax: 212-302-6759
www.experiencephilippines.org

National Commission for Culture and the Arts, Philippines
633 General Luna St.
Intramuros
Philippines
63-2527-2192
www.ncca.gov.ph

◆ 1924 ◆ Morris Rattlesnake Roundup
Second weekend in June

In 1956, when the first **Rattlesnake Roundup** was held in Morris, Pennsylvania, more than 400 of the poisonous snakes were caught and sold to leather craftsmen and zoos. But their numbers have dwindled since that time, and the trend has been toward the protection of endangered species—even poisonous ones. Now only about 25 to 35 snakes are found each year, and by law they must be returned to the wild. The roundup is sponsored by the local fire department and about 80 hunters participate, catching the snakes with tongs and forked sticks. Most of the snakes are 30"-45" long.

CONTACTS:
Wellsboro Area Chamber of Commerce
114 Main St.
Wellsboro, PA 16901
570-724-1926
www.wellsboropa.com

◆ 1925 ◆ Moscow International Film Festival
June-July

With its debut in 1935, the Moscow International Film Festival (MIFF) is one of the oldest film festivals in the world, although it had to wait until the 1960s to become an annual event. During that time, a new generation of filmmakers began to experiment with bold themes that mirrored the socio-political changes in the country. The festival aims to create a worldwide audience for Russian film, and to promote cultural exchange between Russia and other nations.

Taking place in Moscow, the MIFF's ten-day program includes features, shorts, and documentaries, as well as non-competition and retrospective sections. Films by master directors fill the competition section, with screenings at the Rossiya Theater, the Multiplex Cinema October, and the Khudozhestvenny. The highest honor at the festival is the Golden George Award. Legendary film personalities from across the globe attend red carpet events. MIFF also hosts promotional events for international distributors and producers, who attend festival screenings as well as forums and roundtables.

CONTACTS:
Moscow International Film Festival
11 bld. 1
Maly Kozikhinsky Ln.

Moscow, 123001 Russia
7-495-725-2622; fax: 7-495-725-2622
www.moscowfilmfestival.ru/miff36/eng

◆ 1926 ◆ Moshoeshoe's Day
March 11

Moshoeshoe (also called **Mshweshwe** or **Moshesh**, and pronounced mow-SHOO-shoo; c. 1790-1870) was a leader in South Africa who organized a group of tribes to fight the Zulu warlord, Shaka. He called his followers the Basotho (or Basuto) people, and although they succeeded in fending off the Zulu, they were eventually drawn into a war with the Europeans who started settling their territory. Moshoeshoe and the Basotho retreated into the mountains, and from this position they were able to keep the European invaders at bay. In 1868 the Basotho nation became a British protectorate known as Basutoland, and in 1966 it became the independent kingdom of Lesotho within the British Commonwealth (*see* LESOTHO INDEPENDENCE DAY).

The Basotho people continue to honor their founder on this day with a solomn wreath-laying ceremony in the capital city of Maseru, along with sporting events and traditional music and dancing.

CONTACTS:
Ministry of Tourism, Environment and Culture
P.O. Box 52
Maseru, 100 Lesotho
266-22313034; fax: 266-22310194
www.gov.ls

◆ 1927 ◆ Most Precious Blood, Feast of the
Formerly July 1

In the Roman Catholic Church, July was the month of the Most Precious Blood—referring to the blood of Jesus, which ever since the time of the Last Supper has been regarded by Christians as possessing redemptive power. But it wasn't until 1849 that a specific day was chosen for general observance of this festival. At that time Pope Pius IX was forced into exile while Rome was under attack by the French. One of his companions, who happened to be a general officer of the Fathers of the Most Precious Blood, tried to convince the Pope to promise that if he regained his papal lands he would establish this festival as a universal observance. The Pope, of course, said he didn't want to bargain with God, but that he would extend the festival to the whole church anyway. Since he reached this decision on the day before the first Sunday in July, it was originally the first Sunday that was dedicated to the Most Precious Blood. But Pius X moved the feast to the first day of July. In 1969 it was suppressed altogether and is no longer on the church calendar.
SOURCES:DAYSCUSTFAITH-1957, P. 166RELHOLCAL-2004, P. 99.

CONTACTS:
American TFP
P.O. Box 341
Hanover, PA 17331
717-225-7147 or 888-317-5571; fax: 717-225-7382
www.tfp.org

◆ 1928 ◆ Mothering Sunday
March-April; fourth Sunday in Lent

It was the custom in 17th-century England for Christians to pay their respects on the fourth Sunday in LENT to the "Mother Church" where they had been baptized. Also known as **Misers**, or **Mid-Lent**, **Sunday**, this day usually included a visit to one's parents—to "go a-mothering," as it was called back then. It was common practice to bring a cake or trinket for the mother of the family. In England the favorite gift was the simnel cake, a saffron-flavored fruitcake topped with almond paste.

In the Roman Catholic Church and the Anglican Communion, the fourth Sunday in Lent is known as **Laetare Sunday**. The Introit of the Mass begins with the word "Rejoice" (*laetare* in Latin), marking a slight respite in the solemn Lenten season, hence the terms Mid-Lent Sunday and **Refreshment Sunday**. Priests may wear rose-colored vestments to mass, instead of the usual purple for Lent, so the day is also called **Rose Sunday**. Also on this day the pope blesses the Golden Rose, an ornament resembling a spray of roses, symbolizing spiritual joy.

CONTACTS:
Ely Diocesan Office
Bishop Woodford House
Barton Rd.
Ely, CB7 4DX United Kingdom
44-135-365-2700 or 44-135-366-3579
www.ely.anglican.org

◆ 1929 ◆ Mother-in-Law Day
Fourth Sunday in October

Modeled on the celebration of MOTHER'S DAY and FATHER'S DAY, **Mother-in-Law's Day** was first celebrated on March 5, 1934, in Amarillo, Texas, where it was initiated by the editor of the local newspaper. The observance was later moved to the fourth Sunday in October.

Mothers-in-law have never enjoyed the widespread respect and devotion that mothers have received over the years, and the rising divorce rate has given the whole concept of in-laws a less permanent place in the national imagination. This may be part of the reason why Mother-in-Law Day has failed to catch on like Mother's Day, Father's Day, and even GRANDPARENTS' DAY. But many people feel that mothers-in-law deserve a special day of their own, if for no other reason than for their good humor in enduring the many jokes that have been told about them.

◆ 1930 ◆ Mother's Day
Second Sunday in May

The setting aside of a day each year to honor mothers was the suggestion of Anna M. Jarvis of Philadelphia, Pennsylvania, whose own mother had died on May 9, 1906. She held a memorial service and asked those attending to wear white carnations—a gesture that soon became a tradition. By 1914

President Woodrow Wilson had proclaimed a national day in honor of mothers, and some people still wear carnations on the second Sunday in May—pink or red for mothers who are living and white for those who have died.

Sometimes Mother's Day is confused with Mothering Sunday, an English holiday that falls on the fourth Sunday in Lent. But Mother's Day is now observed in England as well, and the traditions associated with Mothering Sunday have been largely forgotten. A number of Protestant churches have designated this day as the **Festival of the Christian Home**.

See also Children's Day.

CONTACTS:
American Mothers, Inc.
1701 K. St. N.W.
Ste. 650
Washington, D.C. 20006
877-242-4264
www.americanmothers.org

Visit Philadelphia
30 S. 17th St.
Ste. 2010
Philadelphia, PA 19103
215-599-0776 or 800-537-7676
www.visitphilly.com

♦ 1931 ♦ **Mothman Festival**
September

In 1966 the first sightings of a creature that came to be known as Mothman were first reported in the small town of Point Pleasant, W.Va., Mothman was said to have two glowing red eyes, large wings, and a height of six or seven feet. Witnesses reported him flying along the dark roads around town, especially near the old weapons plant where the government stored explosives during World War II. The story soon caught national attention. As the stories of Mothman died down, reports of UFO sightings, of animal mutilations, and of mysterious "men in black" began circulating. The collapse of the nearby Silver Bridge in December 1967, in which 46 cars fell into the Ohio River, was also thought to be connected with the odd events. Since then, Point Pleasant has become, like Roswell, N.Mex., one of the leading sites for those who investigate strange phenomena.

Since 2001 the Mothman Museum of Point Pleasant has sponsored the Mothman Festival. Those interested in the Mothman phenomena and in such paranormal topics as ghosts and UFOs gather in the town. Merchandise booths are set up along the town's main streets, and posters, books, T-shirts, and a host of other products are available. Music concerts are also held along the river.

CONTACTS:
Mothman Museum
400 Main St.
Point Pleasant, WV 25550
304-812-5211
mothmanmuseum.com

♦ 1932 ♦ **Motorcycle Week (Bike Week)**
First week in March

Bike Week is the largest motorcycle meet in the world, held for 10 days in Daytona Beach, Fla. The event began in 1937, as an outgrowth of automobile races. These had been started years earlier on Daytona's Ormond Beach by Henry Ford, who had a mansion and was testing cars there. It was suspended for a few years during World War II, but the 50th anniversary was celebrated in 1991, with half a million people attending.

The highlight of the week is the Daytona 200 race, which attracts competitors from all over the world and is considered one of the most prestigious motorcycle road races in the world. Other race events include a three-hour U.S. Endurance Championship race and vintage motorcycle races on Classics Day. The events take place in the Daytona Beach Municipal Stadium, with a quarter-mile banked oval track, and on the Daytona International Speedway.

Motorcyclists come from around the world, and most bring their motorcycles with them. A popular feature of the week is a mammoth parade of over 5,000 motorcycles. Parade watchers include large contingents of elderly people, some of whom hold signs saying "Grandmothers Love Biking" and other slogans. Concerts and trade shows are held throughout the week.

CONTACTS:

♦ 1933 ♦ **Mount Cameroon Race**
Last Sunday in January

The annual "mad race" requires athletes to run up and down Mt. Cameroon (13,353 ft.) in the central African country of Cameroon. The race is the most difficult in Africa; the course is so steep that runners have to carry poles, and temperatures can vary from a humid 80 degrees F. at the start of the race to freezing at the summit. On the night before the race, local people make sacrifices to appease the mountain spirits. Thousands of spectators watch the race, in which about 250 runners usually participate; the winner's time can be under four hours.

CONTACTS:
Cameroon Visit
Sonac St. Mankon
P.O BOX 801
Cameroon
7-9655-085-041
www.cameroonvisit.com

♦ 1934 ♦ **Mount Ceahlau Feast**
Second Sunday in August

A folk event that has ancient roots, the Mount Ceahlau Feast is held at Durau, Romania, at the foot of Mount Ceahlau. Themountain was considered sacred to the Dacians, the ancestors of the present Romanians, and was the scene of their annual celebrations. In those days, people climbed to the summit to greet the sun with religious ceremonies and feasts. Today there are demonstrations of such sports as wrestling and foot racing, and exhibits and sales of folk art.

CONTACTS:
Romanian National Tourist Office
355 Lexington Ave.
8th Fl.
New York, NY 10017
212-545-8484
www.romaniatourism.com

♦ 1935 ♦ Mount Fuji Climbing Season, End of
On or near August 26

Climbing Mount Fuji is such a popular sport in Japan that the climbing season has a formal opening and closing. It begins on July 1, when the six most popular routes for the journey up the mountain are opened for the summer, and ends with a fire festival in the city of Fujiyoshida on or near the evening of August 26. Huge torches more than 10 feet high and several feet in circumference are set up along the streets, and families pile up firewood in front of their houses. At about 5 P.M., two portable shrines are brought down from the mountain and carried through the main street of Fujiyoshida. About an hour later, all the torches and family bonfires are lit simultaneously. The flames continue long past midnight, and thousands of spectators flock to the town to witness the spectacle.

CONTACTS:
Fujiyoshida City Hall - International Affairs Desk
6-1-1 Shimoyoshida
Fujiyoshida, Yamanashi 403-8601 Japan
81-555-24-1236; fax: 81-555-22-0703
www.city.fujiyoshida.yamanashi.jp/div/english/html

♦ 1936 ♦ Mount Hagen Show
Late August

This gathering, known as a sing-sing, in Papua New Guinea provides an opportunity for outsiders to experience the ceremonial drumming, dancing, and other displays of tribal culture of hundreds of Western Highland clans. Performers wear their traditional tribal garb, often with body paint and an elaborate headdress made of feathers. The annual Mount Hagen show, staged more for tourists than for the locals, includes a competition that encourages decorative costumes and wild dancing to the accompaniment of nonstop drumming. Ritualistic sing-sings performed by individual tribes are also held throughout the highlands, but these are more private ceremonies.

CONTACTS:
Papua New Guinea Tourism Promotion Authority in USA
1334 Parkview Ave.
Ste. 300
Manhattan Beach, CA 90266
310-545-4200; fax: 310-545-4221
www.papuanewguinea.travel

Niugini Eco Tourism Services Ltd
Sect 47 Lot 61 Warakum

P.O. Box 1377
Mt Hagen, 281 Papua New Guinea
675-542-3552 or 675-7155-6046; fax: 675-542-3555
www.png-tourism.com

♦ 1937 ♦ Mount Isa Rodeo and Mardi Gras
August

For three days in August, Mount Isa, a city in the outback of Queensland, hosts Australia's largest rodeo in grand style. Begun in 1959 by three of the city's Rotary Clubs, the rodeo has contributed more than $3.8 million to local charities and community groups during its history. Among the offerings are the Rodeo Mardi Gras, with a Friday night parade of floats through the central business district; an annual "Best Dressed Premises" contest during the week leading up to the rodeo, in which businesses decorate their premises in a rodeo theme and encourage their staffs to wear rodeo-style costumes; and a fairground on blocked-off city streets in central Mount Isa, with carnival rides, entertainment, and food from Friday afternoon until early Saturday morning.

As for the main event, the rodeo attracts competitors from all over the world, with individual events including bull riding, saddle and bareback bronco riding, steer wrestling, team roping, and rope and tie.

CONTACTS:
Mount Isa Mines Rotary Rodeo Office
19 Marian St.
P.O. Box 353
Mount Isa, QLD 4825 Australia
617-4743-2706; fax: 617-4743-8435
www.isarodeo.com.au

♦ 1938 ♦ Mountain Man Rendezvous
September, Labor Day weekend

The Mountain Man Rendezvous is a celebration of 19th-century history at Fort Bridger, Wyo. This town was founded in 1842 as a trading post by mountain men Jim Bridger and Louis Vasquez. It was established as a stronghold by Mormons in 1853, and taken over by the U.S. Army in 1959. In the great westward migration, streams of wagon trains passed through Fort Bridger for points west.

The Mountain Man Rendezvous began in 1973 and today attracts about 45,000 visitors over four days. The days of 1820-40 are reenacted with people in calico and buckskins, furs and feathers. A teepee village is set up where campers wear clothing of the period, and there is a traders' row where replicas of pre-1840 items are for sale. Other activities include competitions in tomahawk throwing and archery, costume and cooking contests, black-powder shoots, and Indian tribal dances.

See also GREEN RIVER RENDEZVOUS.

CONTACTS:
Fort Bridger Rendezvous Association
234 S. 300 W.

Lehi, UT 84043
fortbridgerrendezvous.net

♦ 1939 ♦ Mountain State Forest Festival
Last weekend in September through first week in October

This festival is an eight-day celebration of the timber industry—one of West Virginia's biggest industries—in the small town of Elkins. The 60th annual festival was held in 1996, but the event actually has its origins in the 1930 three-day "fall homecoming" held to call attention to the area's scenic attractions. The festival was suspended during World War II. Today attendance tops 100,000.

A highlight of the festival is the crowning of Queen Silvia, who wears an elaborate embroidered velvet gown. Usually the governor crowns the queen, but in 1936, President Franklin D. ROOSEVELT did the honors. After his address, a pageant was presented that was based on the ancient Egyptian myth of creation.

Events today salute the timber industry but also include non-timber events. Hence, there are forestry and wood-products exhibits and lumberjack contests along with a horseshoe tournament, live musical entertainment, a motorcycle race, arts and crafts exhibits, and a mammoth buckwheat cake and sausage feed. Buckwheat cakes are a local favorite. There are additionally several parades, including a fireman's parade with antique and modern fire equipment.

CONTACTS:
Mountain State Forest Festival
101 Lough St.
P.O. Box 388
Elkins, WV 26241
304-636-1824; fax: 304-636-4020
www.forestfestival.com

♦ 1940 ♦ Movement Electronic Music Festival
Memorial Day Weekend

Movement Electronic Music Festival (formerly the Detroit Electronic Music Festival)is a four-day celebration of electronic dance music held annually on Memorial Day weekend in Detroit, Mich. Developing out of the techno (or "house") music scene that originated in the city's dance clubs during the late 1980s and '90s, the festival presents an entertainment lineup that features DJs and music acts from the local area as well as from around the globe.

Since its inception in 2000, it has become one of the largest electronic music festivals in the United States. Events take place Friday through Monday on multiple stages at Hart Plaza, a park along the Detroit River, which borders Detroit and Windsor, Ontario, Canada. More than one million attendees participated in the first three festivals, which were free to the public, but that number declined after paid admission was required beginning in 2003. The festival attracted approximately 107,300 people in 2012.

In addition to live music, the festival hosts a market area with food and beverage vendors as well as merchandise stalls and social action organizations. Movement Electronic Music Festival is produced by Paxahau Promotions Group and financially supported by the City of Detroit and a number of commercial sponsors.

CONTACTS:
Movement Electronic Music Festival
Hart Plaza
1 Hart Plaza
Detroit, MI 48226
movement.us

♦ 1941 ♦ Moving Day
May 1; May 25

The idea of packing up one's belongings and changing residences on a particular day has been a tradition in many countries. In 19th-century America, May 1st was the normal day for the inhabitants of Boston and New York to change their place of residence, since leases normally expired on this day.

In Scotland, it was called **Flitting Day** and took place on May 25. The decision of whether to "sit or flit" was up to the tenant, but "flitting" seemed to be more common. On Flitting Day they had to vacate their houses by noon, which often meant a great upheaval for the family during the preceding day or two. But apparently the novelty value of flitting outweighed the boredom of sitting. In some parts of Scotland, this occurs on May 1, and is also called **Term Day**.

In Norway, Moving Day or **Flyttedag** takes place sometime during the autumn months. But rather than being a day for changing residences, it is a day when servants searching for employment flock to the larger towns and cities dressed in the costumes of their native villages. Sometimes they ride in small carts or wagons, piled high with painted trunks or bundles of clothing and other possessions. While city residents take advantage of this opportunity to interview their help for the coming year, the servants seeking employment often try to sell their produce, farm animals, and handicrafts on the street.

CONTACTS:
Québec City Tourism Head Office
399, rue Saint-Joseph Est
Québec, QC G1K 8E2 Canada
877-783-1608; fax: 418-641-6290
www.quebecregion.com

♦ 1942 ♦ Moxie Festival
Second weekend in July

Moxie, originally a nerve tonic, was invented in 1876 by Dr. Augustine Thompson of Union, Maine. In 1884 it became a carbonated beverage whose main ingredient was gentian root. The Moxie Festival in Lisbon, Maine, began as an autograph session for Frank Potter, the author of *The Moxie Mystique,* in 1982. Within a few years the event had grown to include a pancake breakfast, parade, car show, craft fair, chicken barbecue, and firemen's muster.

Although Moxie is no longer widely available, those who remember it describe it as a kind of precursor to Coca Cola. The drink can still be found in Maine, where it is quite popular. About 10,000 people attend the festival each year.

CONTACTS:
Town of Lisbon
300 Lisbon St.
Lisbon, ME 04250
fax: 207-992-8997
moxiefestival.com

♦ 1943 ♦ **Mozambique Independence Day**
June 25

This national holiday commemorates Mozambique's independence from Portugal, attained on this day in 1975 after 10 years of warfare and nearly half a century of Portuguese rule.

♦ 1944 ♦ **Mozambique Lusaka Agreement Day**
September 7

In December 1992, Zambia's Ministry of Tourism convened wildlife law enforcement officers from eight eastern and southern African countries in Lusaka, Zambia. The purpose of this meeting was to discuss ways to stop the illegal trade of wild plants and animals from these countries. During this meeting, the group developed the Lusaka Agreement on Co-operative Enforcement Operations Directed at Illegal Trade in Wild Fauna and Flora.

Following this initial meeting, several working group meetings were held among members of the Convention on International Trade in Endangered Species of Wild Fauna and Flora (CITES), Interpol, and U.S. Fish & Wildlife Service, as well as London University lawyers for the Foundation for International Environment Law Development (FIELD). The Lusaka Agreement was formally adopted on September 8, 1994, and the agreement took effect on December 10, 1996.

There are currently six parties to the agreement: The Republics of Congo (Brazzaville), Kenya, Tanzania, Uganda, Zambia, and the Kingdom of Lesotho. The Republics of South Africa, Ethiopia, and the Kingdom of Swaziland are signatories.

As part of the agreement, the Lusaka Agreement Task Force was launched on June 1, 1999. This permanent inter-governmental task force was set up to coordinate activities in and among the states affected by the Lusaka Agreement. The task force is responsible for conducting investigations into violations of national laws involving the illegal trade of wild fauna and flora. The headquarters for the Lusaka Agreement Task Force is located in Nairobi, Kenya.

To show support for this important agreement, September 7 has been declared Lusaka Agreement Day in Mozambique. It is a public holiday throughout the country.

CONTACTS:
Lusaka Agreement Task Force
Chui Crt KWS HQs
Langata Rd.
P.O. Box 3533
Nairobi, 00506 Kenya
254-722-204-008
lusakaagreement.org

♦ 1945 ♦ **Mozambique Peace Day**
October 4

The United States Institute of Peace (USIP) is an independent, nonpartisan, national institution that was established in 1985. It is funded by the United States Congress to help prevent and resolve violent international conflicts, promote post-conflict stability and development, and increase conflict management capacity, tools, and intellectual capital worldwide.

To accomplish these goals, the Institute shares its knowledge, skills, and resources with others and directly engages in peace-building efforts around the world. The Institute is comprised of experts from the government, military, non-governmental organizations (NGOs), academia, and the private sector. In addition, the Institute partners with non-profit organizations, academic institutions, government agencies, international organizations, and the military. The USIP played an instrumental role in brokering the peace in Mozambique.

On October 4, 1992, after approximately 15 years of armed conflict throughout the Republic of Mozambique, Joaquim Alberto Chissano, President of the Republic of Mozambique, signed the Mozambique General Peace Agreement in Rome, Italy. The signing of this agreement essentially put an end to the country's civil war.

To commemorate this day, the Republic of Mozambique has declared October 4 as Peace Day.

CONTACTS:
UNICEF Ave do Zimbabwe
1440 Maputo
Mozambique
fax: 258-21-481100
www.unicef.org/infobycountry/mozambique_contact.html

United States Institute of Peace
2301 Constitution Ave. N.W.
Washington, D.C. 20037
202-457-1700
www.usip.org

♦ 1946 ♦ **Mozart (Wolfgang Amadeus), Birthday of**
January 27

Wolfgang Amadeus Mozart was born in Salzburg, Austria, on this day in 1756 and died only 35 years later, on December 5, 1791. An extraordinarily precocious child, he began performing at the age of three and was composing by the age of five. Mozart represents the high point of the late 18th-century

Viennese Classical style, and his achievements in composing operas, chamber music, symphonies, and piano concerti have earned him a reputation as one of the greatest musical geniuses of all time.

Mozart's birthday is observed by musical societies all over the world, who often give concerts of his music on this day. The city of his birth also honors him every summer with the SALZBURG FESTIVAL—which has become so closely identified with him that it is often referred to as "The Mozart Festival"—and at the end of January with MOZART WEEK.

CONTACTS:
Austrian Tourist Office, Inc.
61 Broadway
Ste. 1701
New York, NY 10006
212-944-6880
www.austria.info

♦ 1947 ♦ Mozart Festival (Mozartfest)
June-July

The only time Wolfgang Amadeus Mozart (1756-1791) spent in Würzburg was when he stopped there for some coffee while traveling between Salzburg and Frankfurt, but the German city has hosted a Mozart Festival in early summer each year since 1922, with the exception of a nine-year interruption during and after World War II. Daily concerts of Mozart's symphonies, concertos, sonatas, motets, sacred vocal works, and operas are performed from early June to early July, with little repetition due to the vast number of such works.

Würzburg's churches, palaces, and fortresses often serve as locations for the concerts, the most impressive being Prince Bishop's Residence, considered one of Europe's most stunning baroque palaces. Mozart's *Eine kleine Nachtmusik* is performed on Saturday evenings in the torchlit garden of the Residence, while indoor concerts are given in the elaborate baroque *Kaisersaal* (Imperial Hall), which has a ceiling fresco painted by Giovanni Tiepolo (1696-1770), the great Italian artist.

Musical groups that have performed at past festivals include the Würzburg Philharmonic Orchestra, the Bambert Symphony Orchestra, the Prague Chamber Orchestra, and the Amadeus Quartet.

CONTACTS:
Mozart Festival in Würzburg
Rückermainstr. 2
Wurzburg, 97070 Germany
49-931-372-336; fax: 49-931-373-939
www.mozartfest.de

♦ 1948 ♦ Mozart Week (Mozartwoche)
Last week in January

Wolfgang Amadeus Mozart was born on January 27, 1756. Every January since 1956, his birthday has been celebrated by the people of Salzburg, Austria, where he was born, with a music festival devoted entirely to his works. Along with his chamber music and symphonies, Mozart's operas are often given in concert form. The festival also prides itself on presenting many of his lesser known works, which are seldom performed elsewhere.

The principle ensembles for the festival are the Vienna Philharmonic Orchestra and the Mozarteum Orchestra, under the leadership of both native and guest conductors. The concerts are given in a number of sites associated with Mozart's life, including the Mozarteum Building, St. Peter 's Church, the Salzburg Cathedral, and even Mozart's home.

In 2016, Mozart's 260th birthday anniversary will be recognized at the event, along with the 175th anniversary of Salzburg's Mozarteum Orchestra, founded in 1841 with the help of Mozart's widow and sons.

CONTACTS:
Salzburg City Tourist Office
Alpenstraße, P+R-Parkplatz
Salzburg, 5020 Austria
43-662-8898-7360
www.salzburg.info

Stiftung Mozarteum Salzburg
Schwarzstr. 26
Salzburg, 5020 Austria
43-662-889-400
www.mozarteum.at

♦ 1949 ♦ Mule Days
May, Memorial Day weekend

A raucous salute in Bishop, Calif., to that workhorse of the ages, the mule. Bishop is an outfitting point for pack trips and lies between California's two highest mountain ranges. The entire region depends on mules to transport people and gear into the High Sierra.

Mule Days was started in 1969 by mule-packers who wanted to have a good time and initiate their summer packing season. Now about 50,000 people show up in Bishop (population 3,500) for the Thursday-through-Monday celebration.

A highlight is the Saturday morning 250-unit parade, billed as the world's largest non-motorized parade. It includes pack strings from local pack stations and national parks, a sheep-drawn wagon, llamas (used for sheepherding), and a rider on a Brahma steer. The pack loads demonstrate how mules haul such various necessities as machinery, wood, and outhouses into remote areas. Other events include mule-shoeing contests and such muleback cowboy events as steer roping and barrel racing. The weekend's wildest events are "packers' scrambles," where about 50 packers scramble to catch mules, pack and saddle them, and race away with horses and cattle. About 40 horses, two dozen cattle, and 80 mules raise the dust in the arena during the scrambles.

Draft horses and miniature horses also put in appearances, and there are mule shows and sales, western art, barbecues, and country dances. Motels are booked solid a year in advance. Ronald Reagan attended Mule Days in 1974 when he was California's governor.

Mules are the sterile progeny of male asses or donkeys and mares (female horses). The rarer offspring of male horses and female donkeys are called hinneys. Mules have been beasts of burden for at least 3,000 years.

CONTACTS:
Mule Days Celebration
1141 N. Main St.
Bishop, CA 93514 United States
fax: 760-872-4263
www.muledays.org

♦ 1950 ♦ Mulid of Shaykh Yusuf Abu el-Haggag (Moulid of Abu el-Haggag)
Two weeks prior to the beginning of the Muslim observance of Ramadan

The Mulid of Shaykh Yusuf Abu el-Haggag celebrates the patron shaykh of Luxor, Egypt, with a two-day street festival that draws Muslims and visitors alike. It takes place two weeks prior to the start of Ramadan in the ninth month of the Islamic lunar calendar. The festival highlight is the procession of large boats, an Islamic symbol for the journey toward spiritual enlightenment, through the city's labyrinthine streets. Entertainment includes tahtib, or a stick fight accompanied by beating drums, horse races, dance, and music.

The shaykh, though born in Damascus, is highly honored in Luxor, where he established a spiritual retreat, or *zawiyah*.

CONTACTS:
Tour Egypt
4119 Adrian St.
Lubbock, TX 79415
888-834-1448
www.touregypt.net

♦ 1951 ♦ Multicultural Festival, National
February

Every February in Civic, the central district of Canberra, Australia, the National Multicultural Festival pulses with music, color, food, and dancing. This event celebrates the rich traditions of communities from Europe and Asia who settled in Australia in the late 18th century. Originally a modest one-day event in conjunction with 1981's Australia Day celebrations, the festival has grown into a three-day mega-celebration drawing hundreds of thousands of local and international visitors, and making millions of dollars for the Australian Capital Territory economy.

Administered by the office of multicultural affairs, the festival has booths from around the world, offering traditional foods and wares. One of the high points of the festival is the vibrant Fringe Event, which showcases visual and performance art.

♦ 1952 ♦ Munich Opera Festival
July

Although Munich, Germany, may be best known for its OKTOBERFEST, it is also the home of one of the world's great opera festivals. The focus is on three composers who were associated with the city in some way: Richard Strauss (1864-1949), who was born there; Richard Wagner (1813-1883), some of whose operas premiered there; and Wolfgang Amadeus MOZART (1756-1791), some of whose operas were first performed in the rococo Residenz Theater, a former royal palace. But other operas have been staged there as well, particularly those by Gaetano Donizetti (1797-1848), Gioacchino Rossini (1792-1868), Ruggero Leoncavallo (1858-1919), Pietro Mascagni (1863-1945), and other Italian composers. About 16 operas are normally presented during the month-long festival, along with one or two ballets and a few recitals.

Most of the operas are staged in the Nationaltheater, home of the Bavarian State Opera. Some of the events take place in the Cuvilliés-Theater, a horseshoe-shaped rococo theater that was destroyed in World War II and then rebuilt according to its original plan. There is an hour-long intermission to allow patrons time to eat dinner.

CONTACTS:
Munich Opera Festival
Bayerische Staatsoper
Max-Joseph-Platz 2
Munich, D-80539 Germany
49-89-218-501; fax: 49-89-218-511-33
www.staatsoper.de/en

♦ 1953 ♦ Muñoz-Rivera Day
July 17

Luis Muñoz-Rivera was born on this day in 1859 in Barranquitas, Puerto Rico. A statesman, journalist, and patriot who devoted his life to the cause of Puerto Rican independence, Muñoz-Rivera was instrumental in obtaining Puerto Rico's charter of home rule from Spain in 1897 and served as secretary of state and later president of the first autonomist cabinet. However, when the United States put an end to his country's short-lived experiment with home rule, Muñoz-Rivera resigned. He eventually went to live in the U.S., where he continued to advocate Puerto Rican independence by publishing a magazine to acquaint North Americans with the plight of his homeland. He died in 1910 just before the passage of the Jones Bill, which gave Puerto Rico a large measure of self-government.

Muñoz-Rivera's birthday is a public holiday in Puerto Rico. His hometown of Barranquitas holds a three-day crafts fair every July that is timed to coincide with the birthday anniversary celebration. The fair tries to keep traditional skills and crafts alive by passing them on to the young.

CONTACTS:
Puerto Rico Tourism Company
135 W. 50th St
22nd Fl
New York, NY 10020
800-223-6530; fax: 212-586-6262
welcome.topuertorico.org

The Library of Congress
101 Independence Ave. S.E.

Washington, D.C. 20540
202-707-5000
www.loc.gov

♦ 1954 ♦ Muscat Festival
January to February

Muscat Festival has been sponsored annually since 1998 by the municipal government of Muscat, Oman. It takes place over several weeks in late January and early February. The festival is a showcase of Oman's traditional Arabian arts and culture, with a wide array of performances, exhibitions, sports, and children's activities, as well as such modern spectacles as a Formula 2 powerboat championship race. Over the course of the festival, which takes place at indoor and outdoor venues all over the city, as many as three million people take part.

CONTACTS:
Muscat Festival
Amerat Park
Oman
968-800-77-222
www.muscat-festival.com

♦ 1955 ♦ Mushroom Festival
First weekend in May

Richmond, Missouri, isn't the only town that claims to be the "Mushroom Capital of the World." Kennett Square, Pennsylvania, and Stover, Missouri, share this distinction as well. But Richmond is known for its highly prized morel mushrooms, which resemble a deeply pitted or folded cone-like sponge at the top of a hollow stem. The highlight of the annual Mushroom Festival, which has been held in Richmond since 1980, is the Big Morel Contest. Other events include a parade, crafts, a carnival, mushroom eating, and much more. Mushroom hunters flock to the town's wooded areas in search of the morel, known as the "Golden Fleece of mushrooms" because it is hard to find and has never been successfully cultivated.

Widespread morel hunting during the festival has necessitated an informal code of ethics among hunters. The rules include asking permission to hunt on privately owned lands, avoiding damage to the delicate fungi by inadvertently "stomping" small morels concealed by leaves, and dividing the day's booty with one's fellow "morellers." Above all, the hunters must refrain from revealing where they found their prize-winning specimens.

CONTACTS:
Richmond Area Chamber of Commerce
104 W. N. Main St.
Richmond, MO 64085
816-776-6916; fax: 816-776-6917
www.richmondchamber.org

♦ 1956 ♦ Music and Dance Festival, International
June-July

One of the most important music and dance festivals in Europe, the festival in Granada, Spain, celebrated its 64th year in 2015. It features an array of international orchestras and performers in settings of incomparable grandeur, such as the Alhambra (a 14th-century palace built for the Moorish kings), the adjoining Renaissance palace of Charles V, and the theater of the Generalife Gardens.

CONTACTS:
Festival Internacional de Música y Danza de Granada
Corral del Carbon, 2ª planta
c/ Mariana Pineda s/n
Granada, E-18009 Spain
34-958-221-844
www.granadafestival.org

♦ 1957 ♦ Mut l-ard
May 17

This is believed to be the first day of summer in Morocco, and the word *mut l-ard* means "death of the earth." Various rituals performed on this day by different tribes are designed to ward off evil and danger. For example, it is believed that rising at dawn and taking a bath will strengthen the body, and there is a taboo against sleeping, which is believed to result in a loss of courage. A special dish made from barley, fresh milk or buttermilk, and the root of a plant called *bûzeffur* is prepared and eaten on this day in the belief that it will make the people strong and ward off evil. In some areas it is believed that a husband's affections will waver on this day, and that the wife should therefore make herself as attractive as possible by using cosmetics.

CONTACTS:
Moroccan National Tourist Office (New York)
104 W. 40th St.
Ste. 1820
New York, NY 10018
212-221-1583; fax: 212-221-1887
www.visitmorocco.com

♦ 1958 ♦ Myanmar Armed Forces Day
March 27

The Union of Myanmar, known as Burma until 1989, is in southeast Asia. It is bordered by China, Laos, Thailand, Bangladesh, and India.

Throughout most of the 1800s, Burma was ruled by the British. In 1819, the British invaded Burma and took over parts of the country. By 1886, they had control over the entire country and made it a province of India, which was also under British control.

In 1930 a Burman named Saya San led a major armed rebellion against the British. San was executed by the British, but he inspired other Burmese to demand independence.

Aung San, an outspoken student leader, continued the fight for Burma's independence. He was eventually arrested, but he escaped to China, where he collaborated with the Japanese. The Japanese promised San that if he helped to overthrow the British, they would make Burma an independent nation. San helped the Japanese oust the British, and the Japanese ruled Burma from 1942 until 1945. By then it had become clear to San that the Japanese had no intention of handing Burma back to its people. On March 27, 1945, he helped the World War II Allied forces remove the Japanese from power.

Today, Myanmar celebrates Armed Forces Day on March 27 to commemorate the day that Aung San rebelled against the Japanese. The day is celebrated with a military parade and fireworks. Since 1989, the Tatmadaw, the Myanmar military, has made it a tradition to pardon several prisoners on Armed Forces Day.

CONTACTS:
Myanmar Tourism Marketing Office
Rm. 4-B, Nilar Condo
No. 204, Bo Myat Htun Rd.
Myanmar
95-9502-9602
www.tourismmyanmar.org

◆ 1959 ◆ Myanmar Independence Day
January 4

The southeast Asian country of Burma, renamed Myanmar in 1989 by its military government, was under the control of the British for more than a century. During World War II, the Japanese captured Burma and created a puppet state, which came to an end when the Japanese were driven out at the end of the war in 1945. The Burmese people were unwilling to return to British rule, and when they were given their independence on January 4, 1948, they refused to join the British Commonwealth.

The capital, Yangon (formerly Rangoon), is decorated for the Independence Day festivities. Most of the people dress in their national costume, which consists of an *aingyi* (blouse or shirt) and a *longyi* (skirt). Women draw the longyi to one side, fold it back to the opposite side, and tuck it in at the waist, while men tie theirs in front. The Burmese are unusual in that they have kept their national dress longer than most other southeast Asian countries. Although men often wear regular Western shirts, on Independence Day they're more likely to put on their collarless Burmese shirts. A dish known as *panthay khowse* (noodles and chicken) is traditionally served on this day, as is *nga sak kin* (curried fish balls). The preferred beverage is tea.

CONTACTS:
Embassy of the Republic of the Union of Myanmar
2300 S. St. N.W
Washington, D.C. 20008
202-332-3344; fax: 202-332-4351
www.mewashingtondc.com

◆ 1960 ◆ Myanmar Martyrs' Day
July 19

The Union of Myanmar, known as Burma until 1989, is bordered by China, Laos, Thailand, Bangladesh, and India.

Throughout most of the 1800s, Burma was ruled by the British. Under British rule, the Burmese people were considered second-class citizens. Over time, this led to discontent among the Asian population, and they began to organize independence movements. Toward the turn of the century, in an effort to appease the Burmese citizens, the British gave them a bit more autonomy. However, this was not enough to satisfy the Burmese. In 1930, a Burmese man named Saya San led an armed rebellion against the British. San was executed by the British, but he served as an inspiration to other Burmese.

Aung San, a student at Rangoon University, was an outspoken proponent of Burmese independence. He collaborated with the Japanese to overthrow the British empire. The Japanese promised San that if he helped to overthrow the British, they would make Burma an independent nation. With San's help, the Japanese succeeded in removing the British from power in 1942. The Japanese then ruled Burma, but it soon became clear to San that the Japanese had no intention of handing Burma back to its people. He sided with the Allies during World War II, and on March 27, 1945, he helped them remove the Japanese from power.

The British granted Burma its independence in 1947. On July 13, 1947, Aung San gave his last public speech. In this speech, he urged his fellow Burmese to mend their ways and be more disciplined. On July 19, 1947, Aung San and six of his cabinet members, including his older brother, were assassinated during an Executive Council meeting. His political adversary, U Saw, was found guilty of participating in the assassinations and was later executed for his part in the killings.

July 19 has been declared Martyr's Day, a national holiday on which the people of Myanmar remember their slain leader Aung San. On this day, the country holds a moment of silence, and a ceremony is held as family members of Aung San and the other assassinated cabinet members lay wreaths on their tombs.

Unfortunately, the promise of an independent nation was short-lived. Burma was initially a democratic republic until 1962, when General Ne Win led a military coup d'etat. Since that time, the country has been ruled by a military government. In 1990, multi-party elections were held and the main opposition won a landslide victory, but the repressive military junta refused to hand over power. The United States has refused to recognize the name Myanmar, which has been used since 1989 by the military government, and continues to use the nation's previous name, Burma.

Today, Aung San's daughter, Aung San Suu Kyi, has followed her father's lead. She is very involved in the political struggle for human rights and has called for a democratic government. She has been placed under house arrest several times. While under house arrest, she was awarded several awards for democracy and human rights, including the Nobel Peace Prize in 1991.

CONTACTS:
Myanmar Tourism Marketing Office
Room 4-B, Nilar Condo

No. 204, Bo Myat Htun
Myanmar
95-9502-9602 or 95-9502-9603
www.tourismmyanmar.org

♦ 1961 ♦ **Myanmar Peasants' Day**
March 2

The Union of Myanmar, known as Burma until 1989, is in southeast Asia. It is bordered by China, Laos, Thailand, Bangladesh, and India. The population consists of 135 ethnic groups.

In the 1800s, Burma was conquered by Great Britain, which made it a province of India (also under British control). In the 1900s, Burma first became a self-governing colony then became independent in 1948. The country was initially a democratic republic until 1962, when General Ne Win led a military coup d'etat. Since that time, the country has been ruled by a military government. In 1990, multi-party elections were held and the main opposition won a landslide victory, but the repressive military junta refused to hand over power. The United States has refused to recognize the name Myanmar, which has been used since 1989 by the military government, and continues to use the nation's previous name, Burma.

The predominant industry in Myanmar is agriculture. At one point, Myanmar was the biggest exporter of rice in Asia, but now their line of agricultural products is more diverse—beans, peas, black matpe, maize, sesame and by products, Niger seeds, various spices (coriander, dry ginger, turmeric, red chili, onions, and more), timber, and rattan.

The country could not support these agricultural activities without the peasant workers. To show their appreciation for the peasants' contribution to Myanmar society, the country has declared March 2 Peasants' Day. It is a national holiday.

It was also on this day in 1962 that Burmese General Ne Win led the military coup. The country holds parades on this day to honor him.

CONTACTS:
Myanmar Tourism Marketing
Rm. 4-B, Nilar Condo
No. 204, Bo Myat Htun Rd.
Myanmar
95-9502-9602
www.tourismmyanmar.org

♦ 1962 ♦ **Myanmar Union Day**
February 12

The Union of Myanmar, also known as Burma, has declared February 12 a national holiday. Union Day commemorates the day in 1947 that Bogyoke Aung San, a Burmese nationalist leader, helped to unify all of Burma.

When Britain annexed Burma in 1886, the country was not unified: central Burma was inhabited by Burmese people, while the outlying areas were inhabited by ethnic minori-

ties. The British continued to govern Burma into the 20th century. In the 1930s, Aung San led student protests, causing the British government to imprison him. He fled to Japan in 1940, returning in 1941 with the invading Japanese as head of the Burma Independence Army (BIA). He later served as minister of defense in the puppet government headed by Ba Maw. Aung San became disillusioned with the Japanese and handed the BIA over to the Allies in 1945.

Aung San helped establish the Anti-Fascist People's Freedom League (AFPFL), the Burmese political organization that led the struggle for Burma's independence from Great Britain. He emerged after the World War II as de facto prime minister of British Burma and negotiated the agreement that won Burma its independence. On February 12, 1947, Aung San and leaders from national groups across the country signed the "Panglong Agreement." That action unified Burma and demanded that the British government restore independence to all of Burma. But Aung San did not live to see it: he was assassinated on July 19, 1947, before the country officially became independent on January 4, 1948.

Five days before Union Day, an annual relay of the Union flag begins. A ceremony to mark the start of the relay is held at City Hall. The flag is carried through 45 townships before arriving at People's Square on Pyay Road for a Union Day ceremony.

CONTACTS:
Myanmar Tourism Marketing
Rm. 4-B, Nilar Condo No. 204
Bo Myat Htun Rd. (Middle Block)
Myanmar
95-9502-9602 or 95-9502-9603
www.tourismmyanmar.org

♦ 1963 ♦ **Mystery Play (Elche)**
August 14-15

El Misterio d'Elx, or the Mystery Play of Elche, is a medieval drama about the death and assumption of the Virgin Mary that takes place in August on the Feast of the ASSUMPTION in Elche, a town in Valencia, Spain. The first part of the play is performed on August 14, the day before the feast, and it deals with the death of the Virgin and the ascension of her soul to heaven on a throne, or *araceli*, carried by five angels. In the second part, performed on August 15, the Virgin is buried and the Gate of Heaven opens. The araceli descends a second time and takes the Virgin away. She is crowned at the heavenly portal while organ music plays, bells ring, and firecrackers explode.

The mystery play is performed from a raised platform in the sanctuary of the Church of La Merced. It is considered by many to be one of Spain's greatest religious dramatic survivals, and it is believed to date back to the early 13th century.

CONTACTS:
Tourist Info Valencia
Calle Paz, 48
Valencia, 46003 Spain
34-963-986-422; fax: 34-963-986-421
en.comunitatvalenciana.com

♦ 1964 ♦ Mystery Play (Tibet)
January-February; last day of Tibetan year

Originally performed by a devil-dancing cult to drive out the old year along with its demons and human enemies, this annual dramatic presentation was known to Tibetans as the **Dance of the Red-Tiger Devil** and to Europeans as the **Pageant of the Lamas** or the Mystery Play of Tibet. Under Buddhist influence, it was seen as symbolizing the triumph of the Indian missionary monks, led by Padmasambhava (*see also* HEMIS FESTIVAL and PARO TSHECHU), over pagan devils, and more recently, it has been changed to represent the assassination of Lang-darma, the king who tried to rid Tibet of Lamaism. Despite its many transformations over the years,

however, the play continues to retain the devil-dancing features of its earliest form.

It is performed on the last day of the year in the courtyards of Buddhist temples or monasteries and continues for two days. A group of priests in black miters is confronted by one group of demons after another, which they manage to exorcize. On the second day, a dough effigy representing the enemies of Tibet and Lamaism is dismembered and disemboweled. Pieces of the effigy are thrown to the audience, who eat them or keep them to use as talismans. The play is followed by a burnt offering and a procession.

See also LOSAR.

N

◆ 1965 ◆ NAACP Image Awards
Early March

The NAACP Image Awards is an annual event held in March at a gala ceremony in Los Angeles that is broadcast during prime time on the Fox Television Network. The awards are presented by the National Association for the Advancement of Colored People, the long-established American civil rights organization. The awards recognize exceptional performances and achievements in the arts by people of color. They also honor outstanding champions of social justice. The 36 award categories include music, television, motion pictures, and literature, in addition to such honorary awards as the Chairman's Award, the President's Award, and the Image Awards Hall of Fame. Past winners form a roll call of exceptional achievers, from Stevie Wonder to Barak Obama.

The awards were established by the Beverly Hills/Hollywood branch of the NAACP in 1967, at the peak of civil-rights activism in the United States. Troubled by the generally negative portrayal of the black experience in popular media, the chapter founded the awards to honor the best actors, writers, producers, and directors of color, and to recognize those in the entertainment industry who supported them. The NAACP has long been involved in the struggle for greater and more positive representation of African Americans in popular media, beginning with a protest of the 1915 film *Birth of a Nation*, by D.W. Griffiths.

◆ 1966 ◆ Naadam
July 11-13

This Mongolian festival, sometimes spelled **Nadaam**, spotlights three major sports events. Its history goes back to the 13th century when Marco Polo described a gathering of 10,000 white horses. Mongolian chieftains, after meeting for parleys, competed in horse racing, archery, and wrestling, the "three manly games" for a Mongolian. Later, the fairs included women and were held in July or August when the pastures were lush and the horses well-fed.

Today Naadam is held from July 11 (Revolution Day, a legal holiday in Mongolia) to July 13 in provinces throughout the country. The chief Naadam is in the stadium in Ulaanbaatar, the capital. In Inner Mongolia (the Inner Mongolia Autonomous Region of China), Naadam is celebrated on July 20-26 on the Gogantala Pasture and at Lake Salim in the prefecture of Xinjiang. Other Naadams are held as people desire.

The fairs bring together the nomadic people who pitch a city of *yurts* or *gers*, felt tents. Wrestling is usually the first event; at Ulaanbaatar, several hundred participants make a grand entrance in special tight-fitting costumes that leave the chest bare, proving the wrestler is male, though today wrestlers often wear only tight shorts and boots. A legend has it that long ago many men were once defeated by a woman, thus the costume had to expose the chest. Titles awarded to top wrestlers are Falcon, Elephant, Lion, and Titan, and their prizes are silk scarves and horses.

The second sport is archery, a sport of great antiquity—sixth-century Mongols hunted hares with bows and arrows while riding at full speed. Modern contests are both on foot and horseback.

The last of the traditional sporting events is horse racing. In the national Naadam, the featured race is for children from around the ages of 6-10 who cover cross-country courses ranging from 5 to 30 kilometers. When night falls, a bowed stringed instrument called a *matouqin* is played, and people sit by their yurts talking, dancing, and drinking aromatic butter tea and *kumys*, a drink made of fermented mare's milk.

CONTACTS:
Discover Mongolia Travel Co., Ltd.
1101, Metro Business Center
Baga toiruu, 6th khoroo
Sukhbaatar district
 Mongolia
976-7012-0011; fax: 976-7012-0022
www.discovermongolia.mn

◆ 1967 ◆ Naag Panchami
July-August; waxing half of Hindu month of Sravana

A Hindu festival celebrated throughout India and Nepal, dedicated to the sacred serpent, Ananta, on whose coils Vishnu rested while he was creating the universe. According to

Hindu belief, snakes can bring wealth and rain, and unhappy ones can cause a home to collapse. Therefore milk and flowers are offered to snakes, especially cobras; snake deities; or painted snake images at shrines. Because snakes are also worn by Shiva, hundreds of snakes are released at the Shiva temples in Ujjain, Madhya Pradesh, where Shiva lived after destroying a demon, and in Varanasi, Uttar Pradesh, considered the religious capital of the Hindu faith. In Jodhpur, Rajasthan, huge cloth *naags*, or cobras, are displayed.

CONTACTS:
Greater Cleveland Shiva Vishnu Temple
7733 Ridge Rd.
Parma, OH 44129
440-888-9433
www.shivavishnutemple.org

♦ 1968 ♦ **Nabanna**
November to December; during the Hindu
month of Agrahayana (Margasirsa)

The harvest festival of Nabanna (sometimes spelled **Navanna**) is a very popular ceremony among the Hindu rice growers of Bangladesh and West Bengal, India. It typically honors the Goddess Lakshmi, who symbolizes wealth and fertility, and takes place during Agrahayana, a Bangla month that falls between November and December.

According to folk custom, a community cannot enjoy the new rice crop until Lakshmi is first offered *nabanna* ("new food" or "new rice" in Bangla). Farmers will cut and husk a special variety of rice and typically offer it prepared as rice porridge. In some cases, ancestral spirits and local deities are also the intended recipients of the offering. Other customs during the festival include greeting the moon with lamps, giving children gifts and sweetened milk, and offering rice and other types of food to crows. According to folklore, the flight patterns of the birds that pick up the food can foretell a community's fortunes.

The celebration in the capital, Dhaka, differs from those in agricultural regions, as residents employ the holiday to make a political statement and reassert Bangladesh's cultural independence from Pakistan.

♦ 1969 ♦ **Nabekamuri Matsuri (Pan-on-Head Festival)**
May 8

The Nabekamuri or Pan-on-Head Festival held in Sakata at the Chikuma Shrine is one of the most unusual of all Japanese festivals. Its roots can be traced back to a time when a previously married woman arrived in Sakata balancing a pan on her head, perhaps to signify her domestic history. Today, about a dozen children march in a parade through town, wearing enormous papier-mâché pans on their heads that are tied under their chins. Other parade participants include lion dancers, people wearing Noh play costumes, flutists, and young girls carrying sacred mirrors.

♦ 1970 ♦ **Nagoya City Festival**
October

An annual secular festival in Nagoya, Aichi Prefecture, Japan, started by the city's merchants in 1955 to give thanks for their prosperity. It features a parade of about 700 participants depicting historical figures in period costume, among them Oda Nobunaga, Toyotomi Hideyoshi, and Tokugawa Ieyasu, the three feudal warlords who unified the country at the end of the 16th century.

CONTACTS:
Nagoya Convention and Visitors Bureau
Nagoya Chamber of Commerce and Industry, Bldg. 11F
10-19, Sakae 2-Chome
Naka-ku
Nagoya, 460-0008 Japan
81-5-2202-1145
www.nagoya-info.jp

City of Nagoya
1-1, Sannomaru 3-chome
Naka-ku, Nagoya 460-8508 Japan
81-52-972-3064; fax: 81-52-962-7134
www.city.nagoya.jp

♦ 1971 ♦ **Namahage Festival**
February 13-15 or weekend including second
Sunday in February

A *namahage* is a man dressed as a demon, wearing a grotesque mask and cape made of straw, and carrying a wooden pail and a wooden kitchen knife. Namahages traditionally appear on New Year's Eve at residents' homes to warn children and new wives not to be lazy (*see* OMISOKA). In 1964 the city of Oga adapted what was originally, and still is, a community event that occurs in people's homes into a public festival that welcomes tourists. The Shinzan Shrine is the site for the festivities, also known as the **Namahage Sedo Matsuri** or the **Demon Mask Festival**. In the dark, tens of people disguised as namahage parade down from the mountains and head to the shrine for music and dancing. As early as the 12th century, priests at the shrine would make a fire and pray as they baked rice cakes for the namahage. Today a bonfire and rice cakes still await the arrival of the namahage.

CONTACTS:
AKITA Prefecture
1-1 Sanno Yonchome
Akita, 010-0951 Japan
81-18-860-1111
www.pref.akita.lg.jp

Oga Board of Education, Lifelong Learning Division Cultural Asset Team
Funagawa-aza-izumidai 66-1
Oga City, Akita Prefecture 010-0595 Japan
81-185-24-9103; fax: 81-185-24-9156
www.namahage-oga.akita.jp/english

♦ 1972 ♦ **Namibia Heroes Day**
August 26

The Republic of Namibia, formerly South West Africa, is the 31st largest country in the world. There are 13 named regions in Namibia.

For over 100 years, Namibia was under oppressive occupation—first by the Germans, starting in 1884, and then by the Afrikaners of South Africa, starting in 1920. During both the German and South African occupations, the Namibian people lost rights to their land, minerals, and resources. Many were forced to work as indentured laborers or work on white-owned farms.

In 1946, the United Nations declared Namibia a trust territory, giving the country rights of self-determination, but South Africa was not willing to give up control. As the apartheid system of segregation spread across South Africa, Namibia was also affected. In 1966, the United Nations officially dissolved South Africa's authority over Namibia, but South Africa ignored this action and continued to rule Namibia.

August 26, 1966, marked the start of nearly 30 years of violence in Namibia. On this day, the South West Africa People's Organization (SWAPO) attacked a group of forces from the South African Colonial Apartheid regime at Ongulumbashe. For the next 24 years, the People's Liberation Army of Namibia (PLAN) and the South African Colonial Apartheid regime were at war. On March 21, 1990, Namibia officially gained independence from South Africa.

To honor those who lost their lives fighting for national freedom, Namibia has designated August 26 as Heroes' Day. On this day, thousands of Namibians gather at Ongulumbashe to celebrate. During this full day of celebration, representatives from all 13 regions give performances and cultural presentations, including traditional praise songs and dances. In addition, there is a re-enactment of the battle of Ongulumbashe, which concludes with the raising of the Namibian flag in the same manner as the real fighters did after each triumph during the war.

In Namibia's capital city of Windhoek, the Heroes' Acre national monument was erected to honor the freedom fighters.

CONTACTS:
Namibia Tourism Board
1st Fl. Channel Life Towers
39 Post St. Mall
Private Bag 13244
Namibia
264-61-2906000; fax: 264-61-254848
www.namibiatourism.com.na

Ministry of Defence Namibia
Private Bag 13307
Namibia
264-61-2049111
www.mod.gov.na

♦ 1973 ♦ **Nanakusa Matsuri (Seven Herbs or Grasses Festival)**
January 7

A Japanese ceremony dating back to the ninth century, also called **Wakana-setsu** or "**Festival of Young Herbs**," or **Jin-**

jitsu "**Man Day**" because it occurs on the zodiacal day for "man." After an offering to the clan deity in the morning, participants partake of *nanakusa gayu*, a rice gruel seasoned with seven different herbs that is said to have been served for its medicinal value to the young prince of the Emperor Saga (ruled 810-824). The herbs are shepherd's-purse, chickweed, parsley, cottonweed, radish, as well as herbs known as *hotoke-no-za* and *aona* in Japanese.

♦ 1974 ♦ **Napa Valley Mustard Festival**
February and March

Since 1994, the Napa Valley Mustard Festival has been held in the Napa Valley of northern California. It is held in winter, when the wild mustard plant is in bloom. During this time, the wild mustard plant transforms the dormant vineyards of the region into rolling yellow and green expanses.

The Napa Valley region, known for its vineyards, began the festival to bring tourists to the area during the off season. It has since grown to be a regional celebration of the area's arts, food, and culture. The six-week long festival features art and photography contests, special gourmet dining events, a jazz concert, a marketplace at COPIA: The American Center for Wine, Food and the Arts featuring foods and mustards from around the world, the World-Wide Mustard Competition Awards Ceremony, and Napa Valley Chefs' Mustard Recipe Competition. The World-Wide Mustard Competition has 19 categories ranging from sweet-hot to classic Dijon. More than 500 restaurants, wineries, and food companies participate in the festival.

CONTACTS:
Napa Valley Mustard Festival
P.O. Box 3603
Yountville, CA 94599
707-938-1133; fax: 707-938-0123
www.mustardfestival.org

♦ 1975 ♦ **Napoleon's Day**
May 5

Napoleon Bonaparte, emperor of France from 1804-15, is one of the most celebrated individuals in European history and still has many admirers in France. Often referred to as "Le Corse" (from Corsica, where he was born) or "Le Petit Caporal" (the little corporal) for his short stature, Napoleon is best known for the zeal with which he pursued the military expansion of France and for his reforms, which left a lasting mark on the judicial, financial, administrative, and educational institutions of not only France, but much of western Europe.

After finally abdicating in favor of his son on June 22, 1815, Napoleon was exiled to the island of St. Helena in the southern Atlantic with a small group of followers. He died there on May 5, 1821, at the age of only 51. But his legend grew, and in 1840 his remains were taken from St. Helena back to Paris, where a magnificent funeral was held. He was finally entombed under the gold-plated dome of the Church of

Saint-Louis, one of the buildings in the compound of the Hô-tel des Invalides, where his descendants and admirers still congregate on May 5 each year to attend a commemorative mass.

See also CAPE VINCENT FRENCH FESTIVAL.

CONTACTS:
Napoleon Foundation
7 rue Geoffroy Saint-Hilaire
Paris, 75005 France
33-1-5643-4600
www.napoleon.org

◆ 1976 ◆ Narak Chaturdashi
October-November; 14th day of waning half of Hindu month of Kartika

The day after DHAN TERAS is celebrated by Hindus as Narak Chaturdashi. It is dedicated to Yama, the god of Naraka, or Hell. Bathing at dawn on this day is considered essential; in fact, those who bathe after the sun has risen risk losing their religious merit. After bathing, Hindus offer libations to Yama three times in the hope that he will spare them the tortures of hell. A fast is observed and in the evening, lamps are lit in Yama's honor.

CONTACTS:
Office Of The District Magistrate - Hapur
Diet Campus
Hapur, UP 245101 India
91-122-2304833
hapur.nic.in

◆ 1977 ◆ Narcissus Festival
January or February

A celebration in Honolulu, Hawaii, to usher in the Chinese or LUNAR NEW YEAR. There are a queen pageant and a coronation ball, Chinese cooking demonstrations, food booths, and arts and crafts exhibits. A parade features lion dances and fireworks. The first Narcissus Festival was held in 1950, narcissus blossoms being chosen as a symbol of hope that Chinese culture would have a renaissance in Hawaii.

CONTACTS:
Chinese Chamber of Commerce of Hawaii
8 S. King St.
Ste. 201
Honolulu, HI 96813
808-533-3181
www.chinesechamber.com

◆ 1978 ◆ Nariyal Purnima (Coconut Day)
July-August; full moon day of the Hindu month of Sravana

Nariyal (or Narali) Purnima, Coconut Day, is celebrated by Hindus in western India in the union territory of Daman and Diu, on India's west coast, and in the nearby state of Maharashtra at the end of the monsoon season. This is the time of

year when the fishing and water-trade season begins again, and, in thanks, people gather at the shores and throw coconuts into the Arabian Sea as offerings to Varuna, the sea god. Why coconuts? For one thing, because the nut of the coconut appears to have three eyes, it is associated with the god Shiva, who is represented as having three eyes. For another, coconut kernals are a standard offering to the gods. Finally, many consider breaking a coconut to bring good luck to any new venture, such as the beginning of the trade sea-son.

CONTACTS:
Administration of Daman and Diu
Tourism Department
Paryatan Bhavan
Moti Daman, Daman 396210 India
fax: 91-260-2255104
www.daman.nic.in

◆ 1979 ◆ Narsimha Jayanti
April-May; 14th day of waxing half of Hindu month of Vaisakha

According to Hindu mythology, this is the day on which Vishnu appeared as the Narsimha, or Man-Lion, to free the world from the demon king, Hiranyakasipu. The king, who had forbidden the worship of anyone but himself, was very annoyed to discover that his own son, Prahlada, was an ardent devotee of Vishnu. He tortured Prahlada in an attempt to convert him, but the child remained unmoved in his devotion. Then the king tried to kill Prahlada by having him trampled by elephants and thrown off precipices, but again without success. Eventually Hiranyakasipu became so enraged that he rushed to kill Prahlada with his own sword, asking the child, "Where is your savior?" It was at this moment that Vishnu stepped from behind a nearby pillar in the form of Narsimha—half-lion, half-man—and tore the king to pieces.

On this day, Hindus fast, meditate, and pray for the spiritual fortitude of Prahlada. Sometimes they demonstrate the depth of their devotion by giving cows, grain, gold, robes, and other goods to the poor and the Brahmans as acts of charity.

◆ 1980 ◆ NASA Day of Remembrance
Last Thursday of January

To commemorate and honor those who have died in America's space program, NASA established the Day of Remembrance in 2004. The day particularly focuses on those astronauts who died in three NASA space tragedies: the three astronauts who died in the *Apollo 1* fire on January 27, 1967 (Roger Chafee, Gus Grissom, and Ed White); the seven astronauts who died in the Shuttle *Challenger* disaster of January 28, 1986 (Gregory B. Jarvis, Christa McAuliffe Ronald E. McNair, Ellison S. Onizuka, Judith A. Resnik, Francis R. Scobee, and Michael J. Smith); and the seven astronauts who died in the Shuttle *Columbia* tragedy of February 1, 2003 (Micahel P. Anderson, David Brown, Kalpana Chawla, Laurel Salton Clark, Rick D. Husband, William C. McCool, and Ilan Ramon). The day also remembers those NASA employees who died in training accidents, car crashes, and maintenance accidents, including the helicopter crew who perished while engaged in the Columbia debris recovery effort.

NASA headquarters in Washington, D.C., observes the day with remarks by a number of high-ranking officials and astronauts and a roll call of all those who have died. The event is broadcast by closed-circuit television to NASA facilities throughout the world. At Cape Canaveral in Florida, a minute of silence is observed at noon. Flags at all NASA facilities are flown at half-staff.

CONTACTS:
National Aeronautics and Space Administration
Ste. 5R30
NASA Headquarters
Washington, D.C. 20546 United States
202-358-0001; fax: 202-358-4338
www.nasa.gov

♦ 1981 ♦ Nashville Film Festival
April

The Nashville Film Festival in Nashville, Tennessee, celebrates the art of filmmaking by presenting the work of independent and international filmmakers. The festival was founded in 1969 by Mary Jane Coleman and was originally known as the Sinking Creek Film Celebration. Because Nashville is the capital of country music in America, the festival includes various workshops emphasizing film music and promoting collaboration among singers, songwriters, and film professionals. Categories of films screened at the festival include world cinema, independent film, and documentaries. Filmmakers take more than $37,000 in prize money in addition to television broadcasting rights, and winners in the short feature and animation categories qualify immediately for the Academy Awards. Other award categories include best LGBT film, best film by a black filmmaker, and best Hispanic film. Achievement awards are also given for on-screen and off-screen talent.

CONTACTS:
Nashville Film Festival
161 Rains Ave.
Nashville, TN 37203
615-742-2500
nashvillefilmfestival.org

♦ 1982 ♦ Natal Day in Nova Scotia
First Monday in August

Several of Canada's provinces observe a holiday on the first Monday in August. In Halifax, the capital of Nova Scotia, and throughout the province, this day is known as Natal Day in celebration of the municipality's birthday. Its official name is **Alexander Keith's Natal Day**, in recognition of the prominent local brewer and politician who lived in the 19th century. The holiday's main organizer is the Halifax Regional Municipality.

In 1895, local leaders made plans for an official celebration to mark the arrival of the railway, slated for August of that year. In response to the news that the tracks had not yet been completed, the leaders decided to keep the date but alter the celebration to remember the municipality's birthday instead.

Family activities take place during the few days leading up to Natal Day. In Halifax there is a concert and a fireworks show at Angus L. Macdonald Bridge in the harbor. Dartmouth, a neighbor city, has in past years hosted its own fireworks show at Lake Banook Cove. It also hosts the Dartmouth Natal Day Road Race, a running competition held since 1907.

CONTACTS:
Alexander Keith's Natal Day Festival
Halifax-Dartmouth Natal Day Steering Committee
P.O. Box 1749
Halifax, NS B3J 3A5 Canada
902-490-6773
www.natalday.org

♦ 1983 ♦ Natchez Spring and Fall Pilgrimages
March-April and October

These events, held since 1932 in Natchez, Miss., attract about 75,000 people to tour the county's antebellum houses. Women in hoop skirts welcome visitors to the mansions and their gardens of azaleas, camellias, olive trees, and boxwood hedges.

Natchez, situated on 200-foot bluffs overlooking the Mississippi River, was named for the Natchez Indians. It was founded by the French in 1716, and was the first European settlement on the river. It had a golden era in the 60 years after Mississippi became a territory in 1798. The town was an important river port, and wealthy citizens had vast plantations and built magnificent homes. Thirty-one of these, some owned by descendants of the original families, are open for the spring tours. They include such spectacular homes as Longwood, the largest octagonal house remaining in the United States, and Auburn, an imposing mansion with a free-standing stairway to the second floor.

Besides the tours, there are candlelight dinners in Magnolia Hall, a mansion that houses a costume museum, and presentations four times a week of the "Confederate Pageant," a lavish musical with local performers in costume presenting vignettes of the Old South. "Southern Road to Freedom," presented by the Holy Family Choir, is a musical tribute to the struggles and victories of African Americans in Natchez from colonial days to the present, and is performed three times a week.

During the celebration in October, there is another mansion tour. During the three-week Natchez Fall Pilgrimage there are 18 homes open to tours.

CONTACTS:
Natchez Pilgrimage Tours
640 S. Canal St.
P.O. Box 347
Natchez, MS 39121
601-446-6631 or 800-647-6742
www.natchezpilgrimage.com

♦ 1984 ♦ **Natchitoches Christmas Festival**
Late November through New Year's Eve

Named after a Native American tribe, Natchitoches (pronounced *Nack-a-tish*) is the oldest permanent settlement in the Louisiana Purchase Territory. It is also home to one of the oldest community-based holiday celebrations in the country. Since 1927, both townspeople and visitors have made the festival a fixture in their holiday routine.

The Natchitoches Christmas Festival keeps families entertained for over six weeks. The Festival of Lights, held the weekend before Thanksgiving, opens the season with a brilliant display of Christmas lights in the Downtown Historic District. Natchitoches coordinates with Shreveport-Bossier City, Louisiana, and six Texas cities to join together a Trail of Lights that stretches between all the municipalities.

The Christmas Festival, which draws more than 100,000 people, is the premier event of the festival season. The Christmas Festival is observed with a parade, an assortment of river bank booths, arts and crafts, and a traditional fireworks show over Cane River Lake. The fireworks tradition dates as far back as the late 1930s.

The festivities continue up until the New Year's Eve celebration, with guided tours of holiday homes, nightly excursions by streetcar or carriages, and additional fireworks shows that are held each Saturday evening.

CONTACTS:
Natchitoches Convention and Visitor's Bureau
781 Front St.
Natchitoches, LA 71457 United States
800-259-1714; fax: 318-352-8072
www.christmasfestival.com

♦ 1985 ♦ **Nations, Festival of (Minnesota)**
First weekend in May

Minnesota's largest ethnic celebration, the Festival of Nations takes place in St. Paul, a city of great ethnic diversity. Nearly 100 different ethnic groups (up from 65 in the 1980s) participate in this event, which has been presented by the International Institute of Minnesota since 1932 and features costumes, folk craft demonstrations, and cultural exhibits. Folk dance and music performances run continuously and showcase performers from Greece, Egypt, Ireland, Polynesia, Norway, Ecuador, Armenia, and many other countries.

Food is one of the festival's main attractions. Past offerings have included sausage with kraut (Czech), falafel sandwiches (Palestinian), beef pita pockets (Oromo people of Ethiopia and Kenya), spinach pie (Egyptian), choux a la creme (French strawberry cream puff), and syrnyk (Ukrainian cheesecake). Visitors who are thirsty can find mango milk shakes (Indian), green tea (Japanese), and egg coffee (Finnish). Sidewalk cafes serve authentic food from more than four dozen countries.

CONTACTS:
International Institute of Minnesota
1694 Como Ave.

St. Paul, MN 55108
651-647-0191
www.iimn.org

♦ 1986 ♦ **Nations, Festival of (Montana)**
Eight days beginning first Saturday in August

A celebration of the multi-ethnic heritage of Red Lodge, Mont. In its early days, Red Lodge was a coal-mining town where miners who came from a number of European nations established their own communities. This festival began in 1950 to honor the different ethnic traditions. Today there is dancing, singing, and eating. Special foods are served by representatives of England, Scotland, Ireland, Wales, Germany, Finland, the Scandinavian countries, Italy, and the several nationalities that made up the former Yugoslavia. Eight days of events wind up with an All Nations Parade followed by a street dance.

CONTACTS:
Red Lodge Area Chamber of Commerce
701 N. Broadway
P.O. Box 988
Red Lodge, MT 59068
406-446-1718 or 888-281-0625
redlodgechamber.org

♦ 1987 ♦ **Native American Ceremonies in June at Devils Tower**
June

Devils Tower is an 867-foot-tall rock formation located in northeast Wyoming. For centuries, it has been the sacred site of Native American religious and cultural ceremonies. These include vision quests, sweat-lodge rites, prayer offerings, pipe ceremonies and the group ritual known as the Sun Dance. The Lakota Sioux, Cheyenne, Eastern Shoshone, Crow and Kiowa are among more than 20 Native American tribes that honor Devils Tower as a holy place and a vital cultural resource. In more recent times, Devils Tower also has become a popular site for tourists and for rock climbers.

June is an especially active and significant month for Native American ceremonies at Devils Tower because of the occurrence of the summer solstice. On June 21, various tribes hold private and sacred services at the tower's base. As a result, in 1995 the U.S. National Park Service, which maintains the tower as a national monument, asked climbers to refrain voluntarily from visiting during June in order not to disrupt religious ceremonies. In 1996, the Park Service also banned guided tours during June. Though these moves were controversial, with at least one law suit filed in response, many climbers respect the voluntary ban. Park officials have noted a decrease of up to 85 percent of normal climbing activity in June.

CONTACTS:
Devils Tower National Monument
P.O. Box 10
Devils Tower, WY 82714
307-467-5283
www.nps.gov

♦ 1988 ♦ **Native American Music Awards (Nammys)**
October or November

Begun in 1998, the Native American Music Awards (nicknamed the **Nammys**) honor the best musicians and composers in the Native American and aboriginal music fields. Sponsored by the Native American Music Association, the Nammys promote Native American music by bringing it to the attention of a national audience.

The Nammys honor some 30 categories of music, ranging from Artist of the Year and Best Female Artist to Flutist of the Year and Best Pow Wow Recording. Some of the categories are specific to traditional Native American music. Other categories are more general, covering Native American artists who perform rock, jazz, or New Age music. Some 200 recordings are typically evaluated for the awards. The awards show, which takes place at a casino, has been broadcast on satellite television.

The Native American Music Association also maintains the world's largest archive of Native American music, containing 7,000 recordings. It promotes the hiring and training of Native Americans in the music and performance industries and presents musical concerts throughout the United States.

CONTACTS:
Native American Music Association
511 Avenue of the Americas
Ste. 371
New York, NY 10011
212-228-8300; fax: 646-688-6883
www.nativeamericanmusicawards.com

♦ 1989 ♦ **Native Islander Gullah Celebration**
February

The Native Islander Gullah Celebration takes place annually over four weekends in February on Hilton Head Island, S.C. The event showcases the rich history and heritage of the island's Gullahs, the name for people of African origin inhabiting the islands and coastal areas of the southeastern United States. The word also refers to the language of these people, a rich mix of English and various African languages. The event was founded in 1996 to promote economic opportunities for minority business owners in Hilton Head and to boost tourism to the area, as well as to highlight Gullah arts, crafts, food, and history.

Entertainment at the celebration includes storytelling, traditional gospel music, African dance, and popular R&B and jazz. An expo provides demonstrations in such traditional arts and crafts as sweet-grass basket-making, indigo dying techniques, African "long-strip" quilting, and weaving fish nets. Other events include film and theatrical presentations and literary celebrations, with an emphasis on the vivid folklore, superstitions, and oral traditions of the Gullahs. A cultural symposium sponsors panel discussions of the Gullah language and culture.

CONTACTS:
Hilton Head Island Gullah Celebration
P.O. Box 23452
Hilton Head Island, SC 29925
fax: 843-255-7304
www.gullahcelebration.com

♦ 1990 ♦ **Nativity of the Blessed Virgin Mary, Feast of the**
September 8

Only three births are celebrated in the whole Christian calendar: the Virgin Mary's, St. John's on June 24, (St. John's Day), and Jesus Christ's on December 25 (Christmas). Although it is not known where the September 8 date of Mary's birth originated, it seems to have been established by the end of the seventh century. In the Coptic and Abyssinian churches, the first day of every month is celebrated as the birthday of the Virgin Mary.

There are a number of legends describing the Virgin Mary's birth. Most early works of art show Mary and her mother, Anne, surrounded by elaborate furnishings and ancient Hebrew decorations, with a choir of angels hovering overhead. There are more festivals in honor of Mary than of any other saint—among them the Feasts of the Immaculate Conception the Annunciation, the Purification or Candlemas, and the Visitation.

In Malta there is a regatta in the capital, Valletta, in celebration of the defeat of the Turks by the Knights of St. John of Jerusalem on this day in 1565, and the end of the Axis siege in 1943 (*see* Victory Day).

In northern Europe, the **Feast of the Nativity of Our Lady** functioned as a traditional harvest festival—a time to give thanks to Mary for the bounty of the fields and to ask her to protect the crops until they were harvested. Native Americans in the United States often observe September 8 with traditional Indian harvest dances in Mary's honor, following mass in the local Roman Catholic mission church.

CONTACTS:
Marian Library/International Marian Research Institute
University of Dayton
300 College Park
Dayton, OH 45469
fax: 937-229-1000
www.udayton.edu

Women for Faith & Family
P.O. Box 300411
St. Louis, MO 63130
314-863-8385; fax: 314-863-5858
www.wf-f.org

♦ 1991 ♦ **Nativity of the Blessed Virgin Mary, Feast of the (Germany)**
September 8

Farmers of the Black Forest region of Germany customarily bring their horses to St. Märgen on this day to be blessed by the local priest. The horses wear traditional harnesses with well-polished brass, which are decorated with flowers. Streamers of ribbon are woven into their manes and tails. Both the farmers and their wives may wear the traditional costumes of the Black Forest valley.

Long known as the center of a famous horse-breeding area, St. Märgen is especially noted for the sturdy horses that work the neighboring farms. September 8, the Feast of the NATIVITY OF THE BLESSED VIRGIN MARY, is known in the Black Forest region as **Pferdeweihe**, or the **Blessing of Horses**.

♦ 1992 ♦ **Nativity of the Blessed Virgin Mary, Feast of the (Peru)**
September 8

The Feast of the NATIVITY OF THE BLESSED VIRGIN MARY is widely celebrated in Peru, with festivities often beginning on September 1 and lasting for more than a week. It is one of only three birthdays observed by the Roman Catholic Church, the others being CHRISTMAS and John the Baptist's birthday (*see* ST. JOHN'S DAY).

Several towns in the Mantaro Valley of the Huancayo area hold large fiestas in honor of the Virgen of Cocharcas in the days surrounding September 8. In the village of Sapallango, for example, the festival includes a dance reenactment of the death of an Incan ruler, fireworks, and bullfights. Other Peruvian areas that celebrate the Virgin's nativity include Cuzco, Chumbivilcas, Cajamarca, and Loreto.

♦ 1993 ♦ **Nativity of the Theotokos**
September 8

The Greek word *theotokos* means "god-bearer," or "mother of God." The feast known as the **Nativity of Our Most Holy Lady, the Theotokos** (or simply as the Nativity of the Theotokos) is observed in Orthodox Christian churches on September 8. Western Christian churches celebrate the feast on the same day, but call it the NATIVITY OF THE BLESSED VIRGIN MARY.

The feast of Mary's nativity is believed to have originated in the East, probably in Syria or Palestine, some centuries ago. It was already a major celebration in Jerusalem by the end of the fifth century, and by the seventh century it had become established in the Roman liturgy. By the 11th century, the observation of this feast had spread throughout the Christian world.

Mary was declared to be *Theotokos* as a result of the Council of Ephesus, held in 431. A major item on the Council's agenda was the theological controversy over Mary: Was she the mother of the incarnate Son of God, or had she given birth to a human being who was later united to the Son of God? The Council condemned the latter viewpoint as heretical.

CONTACTS:
Nativity of the Theotokos Monastery
121 St. Elias Ln.
Saxonburg, PA 16056

724-352-3999
www.nativityofthetheotokosmonastery.org
Greek Orthodox Archdiocese of Australia
242 Cleveland St.
Redfern, NSW 2016 Australia
61-2-9690-6100; fax: 61-2-9698-5368
www.greekorthodox.org.au

♦ 1994 ♦ **Nauru Independence Day**
January 31

This island in the Pacific Ocean gained independence from Great Britain on January 31, 1968. It had been governed by Australia. Independence Day is a national holiday in Nauru.

CONTACTS:
Embassy of the Republic of China (Taiwan), Yaren, Republic of Nauru
1 Civic Center
Nauru
674-557-3333
www.taiwanembassy.org/NR

Permanent Mission of the Republic of Nauru to the United Nations
801 Second Ave.
Third Fl.
New York, NY 10017
212-937-0074; fax: 212-937-0079
www.un.int/nauru

♦ 1995 ♦ **Navajo Mountain Chant**
Nine days at the end of winter

Among the Navajo Indians of Arizona, the nine-day Mountain Chant marks a transition in the seasons. It takes place in late winter, at the end of the thunderstorms but before the spring winds arrive. The chant is also considered a healing ceremony, performed not only for individuals who are sick but to restore order and balance in human relationships.

The Mountain Chant is based on a legend that chronicles the adventures of Dsilyi Neyani, the eldest son of a wandering Navajo family. He is captured by the Utes while hunting one day, but he manages to escape. During his long journey to rejoin his family, he encounters many hazards and learns a great deal about magic and ceremonial acts—rituals that play an important role in the Mountain Chant. He is gone so long that when he finally returns, his family is now the size of a tribe and relaying his adventures to them takes several days. The rituals he brings back are so compelling that messengers are immediately dispatched to find more witnesses to what he has learned.

The Chant consists of four ceremonies, all based on the same legend. Perhaps the most moving ceremony takes place on the final day, when the medicine man emerges from the lodge or hogan at sunset and begins to chant, while a circle of evergreens eight to ten feet tall—each concealing a man holding the tree—moves to create a circular enclosure with a bonfire in the center. The bonfire is lit, and later in the evening dancers whose bodies are covered in white clay (to protect their skin from the heat) rush into the circle and perform.

♦ 1996 ♦ Navajo Nation Fair at Window Rock
Early September

The Navajo Nation Fair at Window Rock is a five-day gala billed as the "World's Largest American Indian Fair," held in Window Rock, Ariz., the capital of the Navajo Nation. More than 100,000 visitors attend the fair, which dates back to 1947. It features a parade through the Window Rock area and a rodeo with more than 900 cowboys and cowgirls from eight different Indian rodeo associations. Other events include horse races, an inter-tribal powwow, a Miss Navajo Nation competition, an Indian fry-bread contest, a baby contest, country and western dances, Indian song and dance competitions, and agricultural and livestock exhibits. Arts and crafts exhibits are also part of Navajo fairs: the Navajos are famous for turquoise and silver jewelry, sand paintings, and woven rugs. The art of weaving was taught to Navajo women, their lore says, by Spider Woman, one of the Holy People from the underworld.

The Navajo Reservation covers 17.5 million acres and is the largest in the United States.

See also Shiprock Navajo Nation Fair.

CONTACTS:
Navajo Nation Fair Office
P.O. Box 2370
Window Rock, AZ 86515
928-871-6647; fax: 928-871-6637
www.navajonationfair.com

♦ 1997 ♦ Navajo Night Chant
Nine days in late fall or early winter

The nine-night ceremony known as the Night Chant or the Nightway (Yei Bei Chei) is believed to date from around 1000 B.C.E., when it was first performed by the Indians who lived in Canyon de Chelly (now eastern Arizona). It is considered to be the most sacred of all Navajo ceremonies and one of the most difficult to learn, because it involves memorizing many songs, prayers, and the complicated designs used in sand paintings. Like the Navajo Mountain Chant, the Night Chant is basically a healing ritual, designed both to cure people who are sick and to restore the order and balance of human relationships within the Navajo universe.

The Night Chant begins when the medicine man—a combination doctor-priest who has learned the intricate and detailed practices that are essential to the chant—emerges from the lodge leading the dancers, who represent the gods. The medicine man intones a long healing prayer for those who are sick and performs several other ritual acts. Then the dancers begin. The chant itself is performed without variation and has a hypnotic effect on the listeners.

♦ 1998 ♦ Nawruz (Naw roz; No Ruz; New Year)
Beginning about March 21 for 13 days

The first day of spring (*nawruz* means "new day") celebrated by all religious groups in Iran and Afghanistan. In India, it is celebrated by the Parsis as Jamshed Navaroz. The holiday is pre-Islamic, a legacy of Zoroastrian Persia. It is also called **Ras al-Am**. In Afghanistan it is celebrated as **Nauruz**; in Kashmir as **Nav Roz**; and in Turkmenistan, it's **Novrus Bairam**. Nawruz is also celebrated in Kazakhstan, Kyrgyzstan, Uzbekistan, and Azerbaijan.

The origins of Nawruz are obscure, but it is generally thought to have been a pastoral festival marking the change from winter to summer. Legends have grown up around the holiday. In Afghanistan, where it is also **Farmer's Day**, an ugly old woman named Ajuzak is thought to roam around when Nawruz begins. If it rains on Nawruz, she is washing her hair and the spring plantings will thrive. The Achaemenid kings (559 B.C.E.-330 B.C.E.) are known to have celebrated Nawruz, probably with gift-giving. Farmers decorate their cows and come into the city for an annual agricultural fair with prizes. Betting on kite flying is a sport for later in the day.

A special event, *jandah bala kardan* ("raising of the standard"), is held on Nawruz at the tomb of Hazrat Ali in Mazar-i-Sharif in northern Afghanistan. The *jandah*, or standard, is raised in the courtyard of the shrine, and stays there for 40 days. Thousands visit the shrine to touch the staff to gain merit, and the sick and crippled touch it hoping for cures. The standard comes down at a time when a distinct kind of red tulip blooms and then soon fades; at this time, people visit friends and wish each other long lives and many children.

Buzkashi, the national game of Afghanistan, is usually played on Nawruz, especially in Mazar-i-Sharif. *Buzkashi* means "goat-grabbing," and the object of the game is for a team of horse riders to grab the carcass of a goat placed in a pit, carry it around a goal post, and put it back in the pit. The game is supposed to have developed on the plains of Mongolia and Central Asia, sometimes using a prisoner-of-war instead of a goat; now a dead calf is usually used. It's a ferocious game occasionally producing fatalities; there are several hundred horsemen (*chapandaz*) on each team, and they gallop at breakneck speed, lashing at horses and each other with special buzkashi whips.

Special Afghan dishes on Nawruz are *samanak*, a dessert made of wheat and sugar, and *haft-mewah* ("seven fruits")—a compote of walnuts, almonds, pistachio nuts, red and green raisins, dried apricots, and a fruit called *sanjet*.

In Iran, Nawruz is an event lasting 13 days, during which people wear new clothes, give gifts, and visit friends and relatives. Banquet tables traditionally hold seven foods starting with the letter S. Plates with sprouting wheat symbolize fertility, as do eggs, which are colored. Other symbols on the table are a mirror, candlesticks, and a bowl of water with a green leaf in it. The 13th day after No Ruz is Sizdah-Bedar or "13th day out" and everyone picnics in the country or on rugs in city parks. The idea is to get out of their houses, taking any bad luck with them.

For the Baha'i, the day also marks the end of the 19-day fast, from March 2-20, when Baha'i abstain from food and drink from sunrise to sunset as a reminder that one's true nature is spiritual rather than material.

See also Ayyam-i-Ha.

CONTACTS:
Permanent Mission of the Republic of The Gambia to the United Nations
800 Second Ave.
Ste. 400F
New York, NY 10017
212-856-9820; fax: 212-949-6640
www.un.int/gambia

♦ 1999 ♦ **Nawruz (Kazakhstan)**
Around March 21

The people of Kazakhstan celebrate Nawruz around the time of the Vernal Equinox. This holiday, rendered Nauryz in Kazakhstan, celebrates the start of the new year and is the most festive of all the nation's holidays. Indeed Kazakhs sometimes call it *Ulys Kuni,* meaning "the first day of the new year," or *Ulystyn uly kuni,* "the great day of the people."

Special activities take place to commemorate the occasion, including horse races, games, and all kinds of merrymaking. People dress in their best clothing, prepare large and tasty meals, exchange well-wishes and congratulations, and visit friends and family. Since the activities that take place on Nauryz are thought to foretell one's fortune for the year, people try to include an abundance of food and other good things in their celebrations.

The main meal takes place around noon, and is introduced and concluded by the mullah's recitation of, a prayer honoring the ancestors. At the end of the feast, the oldest male blesses all those present so that they may prosper in the year to come. The number seven is considered a lucky number for this festival. It represents the seven days of the week. In the course of the celebrations, elderly men will be presented with seven cups of a special festival beverage called *nauryz-kozhe.* The beverage is itself made from seven grades of seven different kinds of grain.

♦ 2000 ♦ **Ncwala**
December or January; actual date determined by astrologers

The most sacred of the national ceremonies of the independent kingdom of Swaziland, the Ncwala is the "first fruits festival." Held at the Royal Kraal (residence) at Ludzidzini outside the capital of Mbabane, it is a six-day ritualized festival of song, dance, folklore, and martial display, focusing on the king as the source of fertility and the symbol of power and unity.

In what is known as the "little iNcwala," representatives from the Bemanti people, having journeyed to the shores of the Indian Ocean in the neighboring country of Mozambique to gather foam from the water, return to the Kraal and the celebrating begins. Then, unmarried young men go out to the countryside to collect branches of the lusekwane shrub (a kind of acacia) which will be used in the bonfire at the end of the festival.

During the main ceremony, warriors dance and chant to persuade the king (who has secluded himself) to return to his people. He finally appears wearing a black-plumed headdress, dances the king's dance and eats part of a pumpkin, paving the way for all to enjoy the harvest. On the last day people feed a bonfire with bedding and other items from the old year, a cleansing for a fresh start to the new agricultural year.

CONTACTS:
Swaziland Ministry of Tourism & Environmental Affairs
Income Tax Bldg.
2nd Fl. Mhlambanyatsi Rd.
P.O. Box 2652
Mbabane, H100 Swaziland
268-2404-6162
www.gov.sz

♦ 2001 ♦ **N'cwala**
February 24

In 1835 the Ngoni tribe, an offshoot of the Zulus, left South Africa and moved into what is now the country of Zambia. The festival known as N'cwala celebrates the tribe's satisfaction with its environs since that time and also marks the beginning of the harvest. This is a festival of thanksgiving and people congregate in the village of Mutenguleni, including the paramount chief, where the celebration takes place on February 24. Groups of dancers display their skills for the paramount chief, who traditionally chooses one group as having outdone the others, which is no small feat, given that Ngoni dancers are renowned throughout the region. The chief is also responsible for being the first to sample the season's new foods and blessing it for the people.

CONTACTS:
Zambia Tourist Board
First Fl. Petroda House
Great E. Rd.
P.O. Box 30017
Zambia
260-211-229087; fax: 260-211-225174
www.zambiatourism.com

♦ 2002 ♦ **NEBRASKAland DAYS**
12 days in mid-June

This celebration of Nebraska's Western heritage is held in North Platte, the home of Colonel William "Buffalo Bill" Cody. This famous buffalo hunter, U.S. Army scout, and Indian fighter eventually became a touring showman, organizing his first Wild West exhibition in 1883. His stars included Annie Oakley and Chief Sitting Bull. Since 1965 the NEBRASKAland DAYS celebration has honored North Platte's most famous citizen by bestowing the Buffalo Bill Award on a well-known Western film star. Past winners have included Andy Devine, Gene Autry, Henry Fonda, Slim Pickens, and Wilford Brimley.

Other highlights of the festival include the Buffalo Bill Rodeo; the Frontier Review, which tells the story of the West in song and dance; entertainment by top country and western performers; a parade; and a Chuckwagon Pork Breakfast.

CONTACTS:
NEBRASKAland Days
509 E. 4th St.
Ste. G
North Platte, NE 69103
308-532-7939 or 888-313-5606
www.nebraskalanddays.com

◆ 2003 ◆ Nebuta Matsuri
August 2-7

Nebuta Matsuri, the main festival of Aomori Prefecture in Japan, features processions of huge, elaborately painted papier-mâché figures called *nebuta*. The festival supposedly originated when Sakanoue-no-Tamuramaro (758-811) was sent here to put down a rebellion. He won by raising dummy soldiers along the skyline, making the enemy think his army was bigger than it was.

Today in the capital city of Aomori, the nebuta figures, up to 49 feet wide and 26 feet high, depict ferociously scowling samurai warriors. Illuminated from within by candles, they glow as they are carried through the streets at nightfall. Spectators wear hats made of flowers and dance in the streets.

A similar but smaller festival is held in Hirosaki Aug. 1-7. Here, the nebuta are fan-shaped and depict warriors on one side and beautiful women on the other.

CONTACTS:
Japan National Tourism Organization
1 Grand Central Pl.
60 E. 42nd St.
Ste. 448
New York, NY 10165
212-757-5640; fax: 212-307-6754
www.japantravelinfo.com

Japan Consortium for International Cooperation in Cultural Heritage
13-43 Ueno Koen, Taito-ku
Tokyo, 110-8713 Japan
81-3-3823-4841; fax: 81-3-3823-4027
www.jcic-heritage.jp

Aomori Tourism and Convention Association, Aomori Nebuta Executive Committee
Aomori Port Passenger Ship Terminal Bldg. 2F
1-4-1 Yanagawa
Aomori, 038-0012 Japan
81-17-723-7211; fax: 81-17-723-7215
www.atca.info

◆ 2004 ◆ Neighbor Day
Sunday before Memorial Day weekend

In 1993, following a local hate crime incident between teenagers that left one dead and another in jail, the town of Westerly, R.I., instituted Neighbor Day to promote the idea that all citizens should "Love Thy Neighbor as Thyself."

Citizens of Westerly celebrate Neighbor Day by getting to know better other people in their community. Town officials and local business leaders sponsor and host social gatherings to foster interactions between residents. Private individuals host open houses for their neighbors and friends. Friendly contacts via mail, email, or telephone are also encouraged.

The concept of a Neighbor Day has been promoted by Westerly and adopted in several other cities: Providence, R.I., celebrates a National Neighborhood Day, while Seattle, Wash., celebrates a Neighbor Appreciation Day.

CONTACTS:
Town of Westerly
45 Broad St
Westerly, RI 02891
www.neighbordayworldwide.com

◆ 2005 ◆ Nemean Games
Probably August

Ancient Greek games, one of four ancient Greek festivals involving games, held every second year in the sanctuary of Zeus in the valley of Nemea in the northeastern part of the Greek Peloponnesus. Little is known of these games before 573 B.C.E. Legend says they may have been originated by Hercules after he slew the lion of Nemea—one of his 12 labors. He killed the lion by driving it into a cave and strangling it. The games consisted of gymnastic, equestrian, and musical contests. Winners were crowned with a garland of wild celery.

See also ISTHMIAN GAMES; PYTHIAN GAMES; and OLYMPIC GAMES.

CONTACTS:
Society for the Revival of the Nemean Games
P.O. Box 2016
Nemea, GR- 205 00 Greece
30-27460-24125; fax: 30-27460-24125
nemeangames.org

◆ 2006 ◆ Nemoralia
August 13

The Nemoralia was an ancient Roman festival in honor of the goddess Diana held at Nemi, in the territory of Aricia about 16 miles southeast of Rome. As the goddess of the hunt, Diana presided over the forests of Aricia. There was a grove, or *nemus*, there that adjoined a famous shrine dedicated to the goddess, and her priest was known as *rex nemorensis*, or "king of the grove." By custom, the rex nemorensis was a runaway slave who attained his royal office by murdering his predecessor.

Diana was worshipped throughout Rome and Latium (now western Italy) on August 13, the day on which her temple on the Aventine Hill had been dedicated by Servius Tullius. But her most famous cult was in Aricia, where the Nemoralia was observed to protect the vines and the fruit trees as well as to celebrate Diana's power. Some experts believe that the Christian Feast of the Dormition, or ASSUMPTION on August 15, eventually incorporated the harvest-blessing element of the ancient Nemoralia. It is still common in some parts of the Orthodox Christian Church for worshippers to make offerings of new wheat and cakes to the Theotokos on that day.

◆ 2007 ◆ **Nenana Ice Classic**
Late February

Alaska's oldest tradition, a legal game that allows people to bet on when the massive ice cover on the Tanana River will break up. The Classic is kicked off in late February in Nenana (which has a population of about 570) with a winter carnival known as Tripod Days. At this time, a 1,500-pound spruce tripod is set into the ice of the Tanana River with a rope leading to a watchtower and clock. Two to three months later when the ice starts to move, a siren will sound, and when the tripod has moved 100 feet downstream, a meat cleaver stops the hands of the clock. This becomes the official time of the breakup. This setup of tripod, tower, clock, and cleaver has been the same since 1936 and has never failed.

Throughout Alaska, people place $2.50 bets in red gas cans with their predictions on the month, day, and hour of the ice's breakup. In early April, Nenana residents collect and sort the tickets. The earliest breakup ever recorded was April 20, 1940, at 3:27 A.M., and the latest May 20, 1964, at 11:41 A.M.

Wagering on the Nenana River ice began informally in 1906 when Jimmy Duke, owner of a roadhouse on the banks of the Tanana, started wagering with his chum Adolph "Two Cord" Nelson on the breakup day. In 1913, railroad engineers surveying the site for a bridge got in on the betting, and a pool started. In 1917, they started keeping records, and that year has been marked as the first official year of the Nenana Ice Classic. Now it's part of Alaskan lore, and the red betting cans are sometimes called the first spring flower. In 1990, 152,000 tickets were sold, and after deductions for taxes and expenses, the purse was $138,000. In 2000 the jackpot was worth a record-breaking $335,000. In 2014, despite printing 300,000, the Ice Classic sold out of tickets, setting a record for both ticket sales and for the size of the jackpot–a grand total of $363,627.

CONTACTS:
Nenana Ice Classic
P.O. Box 272
Nenana, AK 99760
fax: 907-832-5446
www.nenanaakiceclassic.com

◆ 2008 ◆ **Nepal Democracy Day**
February 18

Also known as **Rashtriya Prajatantra Divas**, this holiday commemorates the introduction of a democratic system of government in Nepal, which had been ruled by the Rana family since the mid-19th century.

Two other national holidays in Nepal are Unity Day, January 11—celebrating the unification of the various principalities into one country more than 200 years ago—and Constitution Day, November 8—observing the adoption of a new Nepalese constitution in 1990.

◆ 2009 ◆ **Nepal Republic Day**
May 29

In 2008, following years of protests and subsequent peace negotiations, Nepal's newly elected Constituent Assembly voted to end the country's 240-year long monarchy, forcing the abdication of the last Nepali monarch, Gyanendra Shah. The Constituent Assembly then formally declared Nepal to be a federal democratic republic and elected the country's first president. Nepal celebrated its first Republic Day on May 29, 2009 with celebrations in the capital city of Kathmandu and across the nation. Thousands marched in the streets singing, dancing, and lighting fireworks. A special event presided by national leaders and foreign dignitaries was organized at the Tundikhel Army Pavilion, and the foundation stone for a Republic Monument was laid in the heart of the capital. Republic Day is observed as a national holiday and celebrated with military parades and vibrant cultural events.

◆ 2010 ◆ **Neri-Kuyo**
August 16, every three years (2011, 2014…)

A Buddhist ceremony held every three years at Joshinji Temple in Tokyo, Japan, to celebrate the coming to earth of the Bodhisattvas. They are Buddhas-to-be who have undertaken a quest for enlightenment and have vowed to save all beings before they attain Buddhahood.

One of the best-known vows taken by a Bodhisattva is this:

Living beings are countless— I vow to save them all.
Passions are inextinguishable— I vow to extinguish them all.
Dharma truths are measureless— I vow to master them all.
The Buddha-way is unexcelled— I vow to attain it.

For the Neri-Kuyo in Tokyo, a curved wooden bridge is erected between two of the temple buildings, and local people dressed as Amitabha Buddha and 24 other Bodhisattvas file slowly across the bridge and back again. Wearing golden masks and haloes and fanned by attendants, they repeat this ceremony three times a day.

◆ 2011 ◆ **Netherlands Military Tattoo**
September

The Netherlands Military Tattoo takes place every year over five days in September in Ahoy Rotterdam, the Netherlands. It is one of the biggest and best-known displays of military drumming, bag piping, band music, and precision marching in Europe. Drawing on long-standing military tradition, the Netherlands Military Tattoo has been performed for the public since 1978. The ticketed event takes place in an indoor arena.

The word tattoo derives from the Dutch phrase *Doe den tap toe*(literal translation: 'Turn off the taps'), because drummers used to be sent out into Dutch garrison towns at curfew to remind tavern keepers to turn off the beer taps so soldiers would return to barracks.

CONTACTS:

Netherlands Military Tattoo
National Tattoo - Support Bureau
P.O. Box 10151
Vught, GC 5260 Netherlands
www.nationaletaptoe.nl

♦ 2012 ♦ **Nevis Tea Meeting**
Full moon night in summer

The pageant known as the **Tea Meeting** held on the island of Nevis in the West Indies probably developed from church fund-raising events in the 19th century. The characters include a King, his Queen, and their court. The King and Queen sit on a stage while costumed members of the audience get up and perform for them—singing, dancing, reciting poetry, or giving a speech. Tea (or some other hot drink) is served and ceremonial fruit, cakes, and kisses from the King and Queen are auctioned off. Then the King and Queen and their court give ironic speeches, followed by more audience acts. If there is enough participation from the audience, the pageant can go on all night. It is common for scoffers in the back of the room to make loud and obscene comments throughout the performance.

CONTACTS:

Nevis Tourism Authority
P.O. Box 184
Main St.
Charlestown, Nevis West Indies
407-287-5204
www.nevisisland.com

♦ 2013 ♦ **New Brunswick Day**
First Monday in August

Like several other Canadian provinces, New Brunswick has made the first Monday of August a provincial holiday. The official day, which legislation enacted in 1976, seeks to boost tourism to New Brunswick as well as shine a spotlight on local heritage. The site of the official celebration rotates each year.

The New Brunswick Department of Tourism, Recreation and Heritage organizes the heritage activities leading up to Monday, which typically entail flag-raising ceremonies, speeches by dignitaries, and live entertainment. In 1990, the department initiated a new tradition, the awarding of the New Brunswick Day Merit Award. This honor is bestowed on local citizens for their efforts in one of six categories: art and culture, business, community leadership, environment, sport and recreation, and volunteer services.

CONTACTS:
Tourism, Heritage and Culture

P.O. Box 12345
Campbellton, NB E3N 3T6 Canada
800-561-0123
www.tourismnewbrunswick.ca

♦ 2014 ♦ **New Church Day**
June 19

New Church Day refers to the Church of the New Jerusalem, founded in London in the late 18th century by the disciples of Emanuel Swedenborg, the Swedish scientist, philosopher, and theologian. In 1817, the General Convention of the New Jerusalem in the U.S.A. was founded in Philadelphia.

Swedenborg's followers believe that in 1757 there was a great judgment in the spiritual world, and that as a result the evil spirits were separated from the good and a new heaven was established. At that time Jesus called his apostles together and told them to preach the new doctrines in the new heaven, just as he had told them to do 16 centuries earlier on earth. All of this took place on June 19 and 20. June 19 is also the date on which Swedenborg's disciples met in 1770 to organize the Church of the New Jerusalem. Every year on this day members of the New Church, called Swedenborgians, meet to conduct important church business and to commemorate the church's founding.

CONTACTS:
New Church (General Church of the New Jerusalem)
P.O. Box 743
Bryn Athyn, PA 19009
267-502-4900
www.newchurch.org

♦ 2015 ♦ **New Deal Festival**
Mid-July, one Saturday

The New Deal Festival celebrates the heritage of Arthurdale, W.Va., as the first of about 100 "New Deal" communities established during the Great Depression by President Franklin D. Roosevelt. In 1934 and 1935, the federal government resettled 165 disadvantaged families from nearby coal-mining communities to the 1,000-acre site that was named Arthurdale after its original owner, Richard Arthur. Families were settled in new homes with amenities then unusual for rural dwellers, such as electricity and indoor plumbing. They were encouraged to be self-sufficient by growing food and raising animals, and soon the town had established its own church, post office, and high school.

Such planned towns were a cherished project of First Lady Eleanor Roosevelt, and she visited Arthurdale many times to distribute high school diplomas or Christmas gifts to residents. In 1985, residents established a heritage non-profit organization to purchase land and restore historic buildings to preserve the unique history of the community. They began to mark the town's founding and to celebrate its legacy with the New Deal Festival.

The festival features educational events, such as museum tours, lectures, and book signings. A mountain crafts and antique sale is held, and there are demonstrations of such skills as weaving and blacksmithing. Participants can enjoy live music and story-telling, an antique tractor and car display, and an appearance by "Eleanor Roosevelt," played by an actress.

CONTACTS:
Arthurdale Heritage, Inc.
P.O. Box 850
Arthurdale, WV 26520
304-864-3959; fax: 304-864-4602
www.arthurdaleheritage.org

♦ 2016 ♦ **New England Folk Festival**
Third weekend in April

The first New England Folk Festival was held in 1944, and for 25 years it was held in different locations throughout New England. Now its permanent home is in Natick, Massachusetts, and all of the festival's events are held in and around Natick High School. The emphasis is on folk dancing: Morris dancing teams from all over the country perform at the festival, and there are square and contra dances, folk dance workshops, and many other events for folk dance enthusiasts. There are also instrumental jam sessions, national food booths, and displays of ethnic crafts, such as Ukrainian EASTER eggs and colored scrimshaw.

The festival is unusual in that those who attend are encouraged to participate by bringing along their musical instruments and joining in any impromptu or scheduled jam sessions or workshops. Attendees are also encouraged to dance with any group they choose.

CONTACTS:
New England Folk Festival Association
P.O. Box 2789
Acton, MA 01720
617-299-1590
www.neffa.org

♦ 2017 ♦ **New Fire Ceremony**
Every 52 years

Among the ancient Aztec people of what is now Mexico, the year was divided into 18 months of 20 days each, plus a five-day "unlucky" period. There was also a ritualistic period of 260 days, which was composed of 13 months with 20 named days in each month. When one cycle was superimposed on the other, it resulted in a "century" of 52 years. Although festivals were observed each month, the most impressive and important occurred at the end of the 52-year cycle, when people feared that the world would be destroyed. It was known as the New Fire Ceremony because the old altar fire was extinguished and a new one was lit, symbolizing the new lease on life that the dawn of a new cycle represented.

Just before dusk on the day of the ceremony, all fires in the Valley of Mexico were put out. Huge crowds of people followed their priests from Mexico City to a temple several miles away on the Hill of the Star. Because the hill permitted

them to view the heavens in all directions, it was here that the priests waited for a celestial sign telling them that the world would end or that a new century would begin. If the constellation known as the Pleiades passed the zenith, life would continue as it had. But if it failed to do so, the sun and stars would be changed into wild beasts who would fall to the earth and devour all the people, after which an earthquake would complete the destruction.

As soon as the heavenly signal received a favorable interpretation, burning torches were carried by runners throughout the valley to relight the fires in each house.

CONTACTS:
Mexicolore
28 Warriner Gardens
London, SW11 4EB United Kingdom
44-20-7622-9577; fax: 44-20-7498-0173
www.mexicolore.co.uk

♦ 2018 ♦ **New Jersey Offshore Grand Prix**
August

Formerly known as the **Benihana Grand Prix Power Boat Regatta** and before that as the **Hennessy Grand Prix**, this race is not only one of the largest offshore power boat races in the country but a festival as well, with a beauty pageant, band concerts, and fireworks taking place at the popular beach resort of Point Pleasant. The race runs along the Atlantic coast of New Jersey attracting more than 250,000 spectators to the state's beaches.

When the regatta was first held in 1964, it covered a 265-mile course around Long Island. But it was eventually moved to the Jersey shore, where there were more open beaches and clear waterways. In addition to the large number of onshore spectators, about 3,000 power boats watch the race from the water.

CONTACTS:

♦ 2019 ♦ **New Orleans Jazz and Heritage Festival**
Late April to early May

A 10-day feast for the ears, the eyes, and the stomach held in New Orleans, Louisiana. The festival's forerunner was the New Orleans International Jazz Fest organized in 1968 to celebrate the city's 250th anniversary. Among the jazz greats on hand were Louis Armstrong and Duke Ellington. After it disbanded, George Wein, the founder of the famed Newport Jazz Festival (*see* JVC JAZZ FESTIVAL), urged the initiation of a festival to celebrate the regional culture of New Orleans, and in 1970 it was underway. A high spot in the festival was the evening when Eubie Blake, then 95 years old, was honored as a ragtime and jazz pioneer; he played several of his own tunes, including "I'm Just Wild About Harry" and "Memories of You."

Today it brings together thousands of musicians, artisans, and cooks who do their thing for more than half a million visitors. The concerts feature not only traditional and contemporary jazz, but also other music forms developed in New Orleans: ragtime, country, Cajun, zydeco, gospel, folk, and Latin. Food tents serve a multitude of indigenous foods, such as jambalaya, andouille, crawfish bisque, gumbo, frog legs, and so on. Hundreds of artisans also display their crafts.

CONTACTS:
New Orleans Jazz & Heritage Festival & Foundation, Inc.
336 Camp St.
Ste. 250
New Orleans, LA 70130
504-410-4100
www.nojazzfest.com

♦ 2020 ♦ New Orleans Wine and Food Experience
May

A four-day celebration of local restaurants and international wineries, the New Orleans Wine and Food Experience takes place every May, with all money raised going to non-profit organizations. Special themed dinners are featured, as well as seminars and tastings.

CONTACTS:
New Orleans Wine and Food Experience
P.O. Box 4248
New Orleans, LA 70178
504-934-1474; fax: 504-596-3663
www.nowfe.com

♦ 2021 ♦ New Vision Arts Festival
Every other year in October-November

A biennial event that debuted in 2002, the New Vision Arts Festival takes place in Hong Kong and offers a platform for artists from across the world. Hosted by the government of Hong Kong, the event focuses on commissioned works in dance, music, and theater. The festival also features workshops, classes, talks, and meet-the-artist sessions. One of the highlights of the event is a mentorship program, which offers an opportunity for young writers to learn the nuances of various performing arts and theatrical work. While the festival includes work from international and multicultural artists, its main focus is on Asian works.

CONTACTS:
Leisure and Cultural Services Department
Level 5, Administration Bldg.
Hong Kong Cultural Centre, Tsimshatsui, 10 Salisbury Rd.
 Hong Kong (China)
'852-2370-1044; fax: 852-2371-4171
www.newvisionfestival.gov.hk/2014/en

♦ 2022 ♦ New Yam Festival
End of June

Celebrated by almost every ethnic group in Nigeria, the New Yam Festival is observed annually at the end of June. It is considered taboo to eat the new yam before this festival. The high priest sacrifices a goat and pours its blood over a symbol representing the god of the harvest. Then the carcass is cooked and a soup is made from it, while the yams are boiled and pounded to make *foofoo*. After the priest has prayed for a better harvest in the coming year, he declares the feast open by eating the pounded yam and the soup. Then everyone joins in, and there is dancing, drinking, and merrymaking. After the festival is over, new yam may be eaten by anyone in the community.

Among the Igbo people, the yam crop is considered sacred, and anyone who steals yam is banished. This is because the original yam is believed to have grown out of the flesh of two children who had been sacrificed so that the other Igbo children wouldn't starve. At the New Yam Festival, each household places four or eight new yams on the ground and cuts small pieces off the head and the tail. The yams are then cooked with palm oil and chicken, and the meal is considered to be a symbolic reenactment of the original sacrifice.

Among the Yoruba people, where the New Yam Festival is known as **Eje**, the celebration is more elaborate. It takes place over two days and consists of purification rites, presentation rites, divining rites, and thanksgiving rites. In one divination rite, a recently harvested yam is divided into two parts. They are thrown on the ground, and if one lands face up and the other face down, this is considered a positive sign for the life of the community and the success of crops in the coming year. If both fall face down or face up, problems lie ahead.

♦ 2023 ♦ New Year for Trees
Around December 23

Today, several groups in Great Britain and Ireland practice what they believe to be ancient Druidism. They hold Druidic festivals at the beginning of spring, summer, autumn and winter. They observe December 23 as the New Year for Trees, because it falls right after the WINTER SOLSTICE, which marks the rebirth of the sun and the start of a new year according to the tree calendar.

See also TU BISHVAT.

♦ 2024 ♦ New Year's Day
January 1

Celebrating the first day of the year on the first day of January is a relatively modern practice. Although the Romans began marking the beginning of their civil year on January 1, the traditional springtime opening of the growing season and time for major military campaigns still held on as the popular New Year celebration.

William the Conqueror decreed that the New Year commence on January 1, but practice in England was still variable. Even after the Gregorian calendar was adopted by all Roman Catholic countries in 1582, Great Britain and the English colonies in America continued to begin the year on March 25 in accordance with the old Julian calendar. It wasn't until 1752 that Britain and its possessions adopted the New Style (Gregorian) calendar and accepted January 1 as the beginning of the year.

New Year's Day is a public holiday in the U.S. and in many other countries, and is traditionally a day for receiving visitors and recovering from NEW YEAR'S EVE festivities. A favorite pastime in the United States is watching football games on television—especially the ROSE BOWL game in Pasadena, California, the COTTON BOWL in Dallas, Texas, the SUGAR BOWL in New Orleans, Louisiana, and the ORANGE BOWL in Miami, Florida. A number of parades are also televised on New Year's Day, one of the most famous being the Mummers' Parade in Philadelphia, Pennsylvania. New Year's is a time for making resolutions for the coming year—promises that are loudly proclaimed and then often forgotten.

See also HOGMANAY; LUNAR NEW YEAR; OSHOGATSU; ST. BASIL, FEAST OF; SOL.

CONTACTS:
Philadelphia Mummers Museum
1000 S. Second St.
Philadelphia, PA 19147
215-336-3050
www.phillymummers.com

◆ 2025 ◆ New Year's Day (Denmark) (Nytaarsdag)
January 1

In towns and cities throughout Denmark, the New Year marks the beginning of one of the most important social seasons in the calendar. Men and women attend church services and later call on relatives and friends to wish them a Happy New Year. These social calls only last about a half hour, but they go on for almost two weeks. Wine and small cookies are usually served during these visits.

Young people usher in the New Year by banging loudly on their friends' doors and throwing pieces of broken pottery that they have collected during the year against the sides of their houses.

◆ 2026 ◆ New Year's Day (France)
January 1

Known as **Le Jour de l'An** or **Le Jour des étrennes** for the gifts that are exchanged on this day, NEW YEAR'S DAY in France is a time for family reunions, visits, and greeting cards or letters. Tradespeople traditionally send their errand boys or girls to deliver gifts to their patrons. The baker, for example, might send a *brioche*, while the butcher might send a chicken and the dairyman some eggs. Those who deliver the gifts are usually given wine or money. Servants and clerks often receive an extra month's pay as a New Year's gift, while family and friends give each other chocolates, flowers, preserved fruit, and *marrons glacés*, or candied chestnuts.

In the afternoon, men pay social calls on their women friends and young people visit their elders. In the evening, a formal dinner is usually held at the home of the family's eldest member. Since relatives come from far and wide to attend these reunions, they are usually very large and festive affairs.

◆ 2027 ◆ New Year's Day (Germany)
January 1

According to German folk tradition, **Neujahr** is a time of new beginnings, and the first day of the year must be lived as you hope to live during the next 12 months. Housewives put forth an extra effort to make sure their homes are in order, and everyone wears new clothes. People avoid unpleasant tasks and try not to spend money, although they often jingle the coins in their pockets for good luck. People exchange greeting cards, but the giving of gifts is confined to those who have served the family throughout the year—for example, the mail carrier, janitor, and cleaning person.

◆ 2028 ◆ New Year's Day (Lithuania)
January 1

Lithuanians have nicknamed NEW YEAR'S EVE "Little Christmas Eve," because the holidays are celebrated in comparable ways. After eating dinner people sit up to welcome the start of the new year. Like CHRISTMAS EVE, New Year's Eve furnishes Lithuanians with an important opportunity for fortune telling. Many New Year's Eve superstitions taught young men and women a wide variety of charms that would reveal something of their future mates.

People watch the weather on NEW YEAR'S DAY carefully, as it is believed to predict the weather for the coming year. Human activities are also viewed as indicators of future events. People try to smile and be kind to one another, as this means that they can expect the same throughout the year. People hope to hear good news when they rise on New Year's Day. The first piece of news they hear, whether good or bad, reveals the kind of news they will receive in the year to come.

◆ 2029 ◆ New Year's Day (Malta)
January 1

The Republic of Malta is a small country in the central Mediterranean that consists of seven islands. The Maltese Islands have a strong Catholic population that celebrates a wide variety of events throughout the religious year. Religious holidays are widely celebrated in Malta. Most Maltese families are very close-knit, and the holidays are a time to strengthen the sense of community and reinforce family bonds.

In Malta, the arrival of the New Year is celebrated on both a secular level and a religious level. Starting on NEW YEAR'S EVE, most Maltese celebrate by going out for dinner and/or attending a party to ring in the New Year. For NEW YEAR'S DAY, most Maltese celebrate on a secular level by going out for lunch or organizing family lunches. On a religious level, many Maltese celebrate the Feast of Mary Mother of God. Across the country, religious new year celebrations are held in churches and chapels. Practicing Catholics in Malta are expected to observe the Feast of Mary Mother of God by attending mass on this day.

CONTACTS:
Malta Tourism Authority
Auberge D'Italie

Merchants St.
Valletta, VLT 1170 Malta
356-2291-5000; fax: 356-2291-5394
www.visitmalta.com

♦ 2030 ♦ New Year's Day (Netherlands) (Nieuwjaarsdag)
January 1

The first day of the New Year in the Netherlands is spent eating holiday cakes, breads, and waffles, visiting friends, and drinking *slemp*, a traditional New Year's hot beverage made with milk, tea, sugar, and spices. Traditional baked specialties include *knijpertjes*, or "clothespins," which have been popular since the Middle Ages, and a long decorative loaf known as *duivekater*. These and other holiday cakes and pastries are served with slemp, which was originally sold to skaters from stalls on the ice-covered canals.

In Zeeland, Overijssel, and other areas, boys go from house to house ringing bells and wishing people a Happy New Year. Sometimes they bang on a homemade drum called a *rommelpot*, or "rumble pot," and beg for pennies. It is possible that the rommelpot was originally intended to frighten away evil spirits at the start of the New Year.

CONTACTS:
Netherlands Board of Tourism & Conventions
215 Park Ave. S.
Ste 2005
New York, NY 10003 United States
917-720-1283; fax: 212-370-9507
www.holland.com

♦ 2031 ♦ New Year's Day (Portugal) (Ano Novo)
January 1

In Portugal, the New Year begins with special church services. Afterward, friends and relatives visit each other's houses, greeting each other with "Boas Festas" (Happy Holidays) and exchanging good wishes. In addition, people often make promises about how they will live their lives in the coming year.

In northern Portugal, children go through the neighborhood singing old songs called *janeiras* ("January songs"), which are thought to bring luck in the coming year. Sometimes a band of local musicians will go through the streets, stopping to play a special selection when they pass the house of someone they know.

There are many traditions and folk beliefs concerning NEW YEAR'S DAY. People tend to mind their manners, believing that how they conduct themselves on this day foreshadows their behavior for the coming year. If they should pay off a debt on New Year's Day, they are likely to end up paying for the next 12 months. It is the custom in Portugal on NEW YEAR'S EVE to choose 12 grapes from a bunch, and to eat them one after another just as the clock strikes 12, offering New Year's wishes to everyone in the room. This act is supposed to guarantee happiness in the coming year.

CONTACTS:
Turismo de Portugal, I.P
Rua Ivone Silva
Lisbon, 1050-124 Portugal
351-211-140-200
www.visitportugal.com/en

♦ 2032 ♦ New Year's Day (Romania) (Anul Nou)
January 1

Children welcome the New Year in Romania with an ancient fertility rite called *samanatul*, or "sowing." They stuff their pockets with corn and go from house to house, throwing corn at people and greeting them with wishes for a long life. In some parts of Romania, the *sorcova*—a stick to which flowers are tied—is used instead of corn. The flowers are from twigs plucked on St. ANDREW'S EVE and forced into blossom by CHRISTMAS. Rather than throwing corn at people, the children brush their faces lightly with the sorcova. This custom may be a survival from ancient Roman times, when people saluted one another with laurel branches.

Romanians also celebrate NEW YEAR'S DAY by exchanging gifts. Servants, the poor, and the young often receive gifts of money.

♦ 2033 ♦ New Year's Day (Russia)
January 1

Under the Communist system NEW YEAR'S DAY largely replaced CHRISTMAS as the major winter festival in the former Soviet Union (*see* RUSSIAN WINTER FESTIVAL). Since the dissolution of the Soviet Union, however, this, or NEW YEAR'S EVE, is still the day on which Grandfather Frost visits and brings gifts for children. Within the walls of Moscow's Kremlin, there was a huge party at the Palace of Congresses attended by as many as 50,000 children. Entertainment at the party included the arrival of *D'yed Moroz*, or Grandfather Frost, wearing a white beard, red robe, and a hat trimmed in white fur and riding a Sputnik-drawn sleigh or some other outlandish vehicle. There were also troops of folk dancers, magicians, clowns, and tumblers who performed for the children. Older Muscovites celebrated New Year's by attending dances at schools, clubs, theaters and union halls. Outside of Moscow, the same festivities took place on a more modest scale.

Caviar, smoked fish, roast meats, and other treats were served in honor of the holiday. Among the many cakes and sweets served were *babka*, a yeast coffee cake made in a round pan, and *kulich*, a fancy fruitbread of Ukrainian origin made in three tiers to symbolize the Trinity.

♦ 2034 ♦ New Year's Day (Switzerland) (Neujahrstag)
January 1

The Swiss celebrate NEW YEAR'S DAY with amateur dramatic performances, visits with friends, and feasting on roast goose with chestnut stuffing, New Year's bread, and *birewegge*, or pear pie, which looks like a shiny loaf of bread and has a rich filling of pears and raisins. Goose necks filled with ground giblets, seasoning, and other ingredients are a favorite delicacy when sliced thin and served as a between-meal snack. Although the holiday is generally a quiet one, children often hide on New Year's morning, startling their parents when they jump out to give them New Year's greetings.

According to Swiss folklore, the first day of January is full of omens and predictions. A red sky, for example, signifies storms, fire, and war in the coming year. Meeting a woman the first thing on New Year's Day is thought to bring bad luck, while encountering a man or a child is looked upon as a good sign.

◆ 2035 ◆ New Year's Eve
December 31

The last day of the year is usually greeted with mixed emotions—joy and anticipation on the one hand, melancholy and regret on the other. Some celebrate by attending midnight church services, while others congregate in public places like Times Square in New York City, or Trafalgar Square in London, Glasgow's George Square or Edinburgh's Iron Kirk to count down the closing seconds of the old year. In the United States, people congregate at parties, some lasting all night, and many people spend New Year's Eve in front of the television watching other people celebrate. In recent years, celebrations in time zones all over the world have also been televised, so viewers can celebrate several times in one night, if they wish.

In Scotland, December 31 is known as **Old Year's Night**, or HOGMANAY. Although there are a number of theories about the derivation of the name, the tradition it refers to involves handing out pieces of oat-cake to poor children, who go from door to door calling out "Hogmanay!" In the United States, the Scottish song "Auld Lang Syne," with lyrics by poet Robert BURNS, is sung at almost every New Year's Eve celebration, while in London, the Scots at St. Paul's Churchyard toast and sing.

In Denmark the New Year is "shot in" with a thunderous explosion of fireworks, rockets, and Chinese pistols. In some villages, young people play pranks such as those done on HALLOWEEN in the United States.

Iceland has bonfires to clean up trash and elf dances, because elves are believed to be about on this night and might want to stop and rest on their way.

Neapolitans believe it brings luck to throw pots and dishes out the windows at midnight.

On the last two days of the year in Japan, a fire watch is implemented to prepare for the New Year, their most important holiday. Young men gather into groups then go to separate parts of the towns. They carry a clapper which they sound every few yards, crying out, "take care with fire."

Armenian families spend the night at home feasting. During the celebration, the neighbors, one at a time, lower a basket of presents down the chimney, then it is the recipients' turn to go to their neighbors.

Romanian boys used to go around to their neighbors with a *plugusorul*, a little plough, which may be a remnant of the Roman OPALIA, the festival to the goddess of abundance, Ops. Later they changed to a homemade drum that sounds like a bull, which is what pulls the plough through the meadow. They ring cow bells and crack whips and recite hundreds of verses of their country story at the top of their lungs.

See also FIRST NIGHT; LADOUVANE; OMISOKA.

CONTACTS:
Times Square Alliance
1560 Broadway
Suite 800
New York, NY 10036 United States
212-768-1560; fax: 212-768-0233
www.timessquarenyc.org

◆ 2036 ◆ New Year's Eve (Australia)
December 31

The major cities of Australia host spectacular events on New Year's Eve, with tens of thousands of people turning out to watch fireworks and take part in various events. Most cities offer free public transport and run extra buses and trains to manage the large crowds. Although New Year's Eve is not a public holiday in Australia, most government offices and schools are either closed or operate with a limited staff.

CONTACTS:
Tourism Australia
2029 Century Park E., Ste. 3150
Mailbox No.358
Los Angeles, CA 90067
310-695-3200; fax: 310-695-3201
www.australia.com

◆ 2037 ◆ New Year's Eve (Brazil)
December 31

One of the most exotic NEW YEAR'S EVE celebrations in the world takes place along the beaches of Brazil—particularly Copacabana Beach in Rio de Janeiro, where thousands of followers of Candomblé, a religion practiced in Brazil, meet to pay homage to the ocean goddess, YEMANJÁ (or Iemanjá). Dressed in white and carrying fresh flowers, candles, and *cachaça* (sugarcane alcohol), they flock to the beach around 10 o'clock and lay out tablecloths surrounded by candles and covered with gifts for the goddess. Animal sacrifices are not uncommon.

The ceremony reaches its peak at midnight, when fireworks go off and people rush into the water—shrieking, sobbing, or singing—carrying their flowers and gifts for Yemanjá. If the waves carry their gifts out to sea, it means that the goddess was satisfied and they can go home happy. It is considered an ill omen if the ocean throws back their gifts.

◆ 2038 ◆ **New Year's Eve (Ecuador)**
December 31

Many Ecuadorians celebrate the Old Year, *Año Viejo*, on December 31 by stuffing an old shirt and pair of pants with straw and sewing them together to make an effigy of a man. With a hat on his head, a pipe in his mouth, and a cane in his hand, the scarecrow figure sits in a chair in front of the house, sometimes under an arch made of cypress branches. Someone draws up a mock "last will and testament" listing various family members' faults that must be done away with. At midnight, or earlier if there are small children in the house, someone reads the will aloud and everyone makes jokes about its contents. Then the straw figure is lit with a match, and the faults of the Old Year go up in flames. Sometimes the old man's "widow" goes from house to house, dressed in black and begging for contributions to charity.

After the straw men have burned and the widows have come in from the streets, everyone sits down to enjoy the spiced foods typically served on this night. The most popular is a crisp fried pastry in the shape of a doughnut, which is dipped into a brown sugar syrup.

◆ 2039 ◆ **New Year's Eve (Germany) (Silvesterabend)**
December 31

In different areas of Germany, it is considered lucky to eat certain foods on the last night of the old year. Carp is served frequently, not only in homes but in fashionable city restaurants. Another favorite is *Silvesterabend* punch, a hot drink made from red wine flavored with cinnamon and sugar. *Feuerzangenbowle*, or "fire tongs punch," has special cones of sugar, soaked in liquor, suspended over the punch bowl. When they are set aflame, the alcoholic sugar drips into the hot wine below. In Baden, a special dried pea soup is considered to bring good luck when served on NEW YEAR'S EVE. Along the lower Rhine, "little New Year" yeast cookies are baked in the form of spiral wreaths, pretzels, or circles. Everyone leaves a bit of each food served on his or her plate until after midnight in the belief that it will ensure a well-stocked pantry in the coming year.

According to ancient Germanic folk belief, the only way to drive out demons, devils, and other evil spirits on the last night of the year is by making noise. Grown men can be seen riding hobby horses up and down the streets of German villages on New Year's Eve at midnight, and *Buttenmandl* ("Little Butten Men"), who are peasants dressed in straw clothing and deerskin animal masks, ring bells and drag clanking chains through the streets in an effort to drive out evil spirits.

In the Bavarian Alps, shooting parties are still popular. Sometimes members of shooting societies will climb a mountain and shoot off 500 or more old mortars in unison. (*See* CHRISTMAS SHOOTING.)

In the Bavarian town of Oberammergau, a "star singer" carrying a large illuminated star on a long pole leads a New Year's Eve procession that lasts for several hours (*see also* EPIPHANY IN GERMANY). He sings a song that summarizes the events of the past year and extends good wishes for the year to come, accompanied by members of the Passion Play orchestra (*see also* OBERAMMERGAU PASSION PLAY).

New Year's pranks are common in Germany, such as chocolates with mustard inside, sugar lumps with spiders inside, and firework dogs that produce a string of black, sausage-like material when burned. Among young people, "lead-pouring" parties are popular. They drop a little melted lead into a bowl of cold water and read each other's fortunes by interpreting the shapes the metal assumes.

◆ 2040 ◆ **New Year's Eve (Spain)**
December 31

In Spain, it is customary for families to gather on NEW YEAR'S EVE in small groups to celebrate the coming of the New Year. Shortly before midnight, bags or bunches of grapes are distributed. When midnight arrives, everyone eats one grape for each stroke of the clock. Eating all 12 grapes before the clock is finished striking ensures good luck in the New Year. The grapes are usually washed down with muscatel wine. So firmly entrenched is the grape-eating custom that in theaters and cinemas, the show is often interrupted at midnight on New Year's Eve so that the audience can eat the grapes and drink the wine they've brought with them.

NEW YEAR'S DAY is spent visiting family and friends, feasting, and exchanging cards and gifts. Eating and drinking well on this day is believed to guarantee an abundance of food and drink in the coming year.

◆ 2041 ◆ **New Year's Parade of Firemen (Dezomeshiki)**
January 6

Each year on January 6, the Tokyo Fire Department hosts a parade of vehicles and a display of ladder stunts to remind citizens of the dangers of fire and to pray for a safe year. The event dates from the Edo Period (17th through 19th centuries), when great fires struck several times. The New Year's Parade of Firemen originated then, with firemen praying in front of the shrine of Ueno Toshogu for a safe, fire-free year ahead. In those days, the main fire-fighting technique was to tear down the buildings near the source of the fire to prevent it from spreading. Ladders were indispensable tools, because the firefighters had to climb the roofs of the buildings, and they needed great agility and strength to scale the ladders.

The highlight of the present-day Parade of Firemen hearkens back to this tradition, as men dressed as firemen from the Edo period perform circus-like acrobatic stunts on bamboo ladders. In addition to the ladder displays, the event features large-scale fire-fighting and emergency drills, and a parade of more than 100 fire engines and helicopters. Similar events are held on January 6 throughout Japan, but the Tokyo event is considered the most spectacular.

CONTACTS:
Japan National Tourist Organization
1 Grand Central Pl.
60 E. 42nd St.
Ste. 448
New York, NY 10165
212-757-5640; fax: 212-307-6754
www.jnto.go.jp

♦ 2042 ♦ New York City Marathon
First Sunday in November

The New York City Marathon began in 1970 as a race four times around Central Park. But in 1976, Fred Lebow and the New York Road Runners Club, the world's largest running club and the race's sponsor, decided to get corporate support, invite top runners from all over the world, and to run the course through all five New York boroughs.

Unlike the BOSTON MARATHON, which is run primarily through the countryside and small towns, the New York course is urban, beginning at the tollbooth plaza at the end of the Verrazano-Narrows Bridge on Staten Island and progressing across the bridge through Brooklyn, Queens, Manhattan, and the Bronx before finishing in Manhattan's Central Park.

About 30,000 runners compete in the race, and over a million New Yorkers turn out to watch. In addition to cash prizes ranging from $65,000 for the first-place finishers to $7,500 for fifth place, thousands more in bonuses are handed out each year.

The marathon has had a positive effect on New York City's public image, which has suffered because of its high crime rate and frequent clashes between ethnic groups. The runners who compete regularly in New York say that the crowds are enthusiastic and friendly, and city dwellers look upon it as a time to forget racial and ethnic differences and cheer the runners on.

Like most things in New York City, its marathon is amazing. Rosie Ruiz, well known for being disqualified for cheating in the Boston Marathon, was thrown out in New York for taking the subway to the finish line.

Then there's race organizer Fred Lebow: although an avid runner he had never run New York until he was struck by brain cancer. Then in 1992, the cancer in remission, this 60-year-old Romanian-born escapee from the Holocaust finally ran the 26.2 mile course. His companion on his heroic run was his good friend and nine-time New York winner, Grete Waitz of Norway. Lebow's time: 5 hours 32 minutes 34 seconds.

In 1992 Australian-born Lisa Ondieki set a new women's course record of 2:24:40 and won a $30,000 bonus in addition to the standard $20,000 purse and Mercedes-Benz automobile. Willie Mtolo, a 28-year-old Zulu from South Africa, won his first major international marathon in 1992. This was a special victory for him since he had been unable to compete outside his homeland until that year: South African athletes

had suffered a 21-year political embargo. Mtolo's time: 2 hours 9 minutes 29 seconds.

In the 2000 race, runners came from more than 150 countries, and over 100 contenders competed in the Marathon's first official wheelchair and handcycle division. Several scheduled runners were lost in the 2001 terrorist attack on the World Trade Center, and some relatives and friends signed up to run in their places. The Road Runners Club dedicated the 2001 Marathon to the victims of the attacks.

Course records for the New York City Marathon have been set by two Kenyan runners: Margaret Okayo in the 2003 women's race, with a time of 2 hours, 22 minutes, 31 seconds, and Geoffrey Mutai in the 2011 men's race with a time of 2 hours, 5 minutes, 6 seconds.

For the marathon's 40th anniversary in 2009, Meb Keflezighi became the first American winner since 1982. After the 2012 New York City Marathon was cancelled due to the devastating effects of Superstorm Sandy, a record 50,740 runners participated in the 2013 race with 50,304 of them finishing, breaking the previous record of 47,340 finishers set in 2011.

CONTACTS:
New York Road Runners
9 E 89th St.
New York, NY 10128 United States
212-860-4455
www.nyrrc.org

♦ 2043 ♦ New York Film Festival
September - October

The Film Society of Lincoln Center organizes the prestigious New York Film Festival. Founded in 1962 by Amos Vogel and Richard Roud, the event celebrates national and international cinema from both established and emerging directors. Its central goals are to encourage the work of new filmmakers and create awareness of film as an art form by providing access to a diverse array of movies. The festival presents features and shorts, along with experimental film and video productions. A selection committee chooses approximately 30 feature films to comprise the event's main itinerary. Many of the best movies screened at top international film festivals such as those in Cannes and Venice are also featured at the New York Film Festival. In addition to this event, the Film Society of Lincoln Center provides year-round programming, presenting numerous premieres, retrospectives, and symposia.

CONTACTS:
Film Society of Lincoln Center
70 Lincoln Center Plaza
New York, NY 10023
212-875-5610 or 888-313-6085
www.filmlinc.com

♦ 2044 ♦ New York Gay Pride March
June

In the early morning of June 28, 1969, police conducted a raid at the Stonewall Inn, a popular gay bar in New York City's Greenwich Village. Tensions between police and the gay community erupted following the raid, leading to days of violent protests and demonstrations. The Stonewall Riots, as they are known today, quickly grew in significance beyond the local reaction to police harassment, inspiring worldwide solidarity and serving as a catalyst for the modern gay civil rights movement. In June 1970, New York City would host the nation's first gay pride march to commemorate the anniversary of the Stonewall Riots. Within a decade, pride marches were being held in most major cities in the United States and around the world.

Today, the New York Gay Pride March is the signature event of **Pride Week**, a week-long celebration of lesbian, gay, bisexual, and transgender culture. Dozens of parade floats accompany several hundred groups representing businesses, community organizations, and politicians on a march down Fifth Avenue. Pride Week also includes a rally commemorating the one that took place in Washington Square Park one month after the Stonewall Riots, along with parties, family events, and a day-long street fair called PrideFest.

CONTACTS:
Heritage of Pride, Inc
154 Christopher St.
Ste. 1D
New York, NY 10014
212-807-7433; fax: 212-807-7436
www.nycpride.org

♦ 2045 ♦ New York International Children's Film Festival
February-March

The New York International Children's Film Festival supports the creation and dissemination of thought-provoking films for children and teens aged three to 18 years. The festival's aim is to help children learn to appreciate the arts and stimulate discussions among peers, families, and members of the film community. The lineup includes selected movies from such genres as animation, live action, documentary, and experimental film. Around 100 films are screened at the festival, narrowed down from 2500 international submissions. Other festival events include gala premieres, retrospectives, question-and-answer sessions with filmmakers, workshops, receptions, and award ceremonies.

Over 25,000 people visit the festival every year and, since the year 2000, all shows have been sold out in advance. The festival was founded in 1997 by Eric Beckman and is currently produced and organized by the film distributor GKIDS. Originally held for a week, it has grown into a four-week event that is the largest film festival in the United States for young people and a qualifier for the Academy Awards.

CONTACTS:
New York International Children's Film Festival
225 Broadway
Ste. 2610
New York, NY 10007
212-349-0330
www.gkids.com

♦ 2046 ♦ New York International Fringe Festival
Two weeks in August

The New York International Fringe Festival, or **FringeNYC**, celebrates experimental theater. It was founded in 1997 and takes place on more than 20 stages in downtown Manhattan, predominantly on the Lower East Side, in the East Village, and in Greenwich Village. It is produced by The Present Theatre Company, Inc. Artists participate in the annual festival through a rigorous selection process. Around 200 companies from all over the world are chosen to perform some 1,200 shows, spanning such genres as puppetry, opera, comedy, drama, and musical theater. In addition to the theater productions, there are other types of events held during the festival. For example, FringeU is a series of lectures and discussions with playwrights that focuses on the creative process. FringeJR showcases theater performances intended specifically for children five to 12 years old. Similarly, FringeHIGH is an event that stages shows for teens. One can also enjoy the festival outdoors with FringeAL FRESCO productions. FringeART is about getting involved in various art projects, such as making puppets out of scrap materials. More than 75,000 people attend the festival every year.

CONTACTS:
Present Company
518 E. 6th St.
Ste. BW
New York, NY 10009
917-745-3397
www.fringenyc.org

♦ 2047 ♦ New Zealand Festival
Late February to early March during even-numbered years

For three weeks every two years, artists, writers, and performers from all over the world come to Wellington, New Zealand, to showcase their talents in music, dance, theater, opera, literature, and the visual arts. The New Zealand Festival offers everything from Afro-Cuban dance music to the Viennese opera of Richard Strauss, from classical ballet to cutting-edge theater, and much more. The *New Zealand Post* Writers and Readers Week also takes place within the festival. In addition, the festival highlights the work of contemporary Maori and other indigenous artists.

CONTACTS:
New Zealand Festival
St James Theatre
77-87 Courtenay Pl.
Wellington, 6011 New Zealand
64-4-473-0149; fax: 64-4-471-1164
www.festival.co.nz

♦ 2048 ♦ **New Zealand National Agricultural Fieldays**
Second week of June

The largest agricultural show in New Zealand takes place for three days during the second week in June in Hamilton, and attracts visitors from more than 40 countries. There are exhibits covering every type of rural activity, demonstrations of how to use the latest farm equipment, and contests in such areas as hay-baling, wire-fencing, tractor-driving, and helicopter log-lifting.

Other agricultural shows in New Zealand include the Agricultural and Pastoral Show at Auckland in late November and the Canterbury Agricultural and Pastoral Show in mid-November. In a country that in 1990 had more than 60 million sheep and only 3.3 million people, these regional agricultural shows attract the kind of audience that is usually associated with major athletic competitions.

See also ROYAL SHOWS.

CONTACTS:
NZ National Agricultural Fieldays team
Private Bag 3015
Hamilton, 3240 New Zealand
64-7-843-4499; fax: 64-7-843-8572
www.fieldays.co.nz

♦ 2049 ♦ **Newfoundland Discovery Day**
Monday nearest June 24

Newfoundland distinguishes itself from several other Canadian provinces by celebrating its provincial holiday on a different calendar date. Most Canadian provinces and territories observe the holiday on the first Monday of August, but Newfoundlanders have selected June 24 because that historic date marks Italian explorer John Cabot's discovery of the region in 1497.

In 1997 Newfoundland celebrated the 500th anniversary of Cabot's landfall. A modern-day replica of the explorer's ship, the *Matthew,* was built, and sailors reenacted the historic journey from Bristol, England, to Newfoundland. Thousands of people gathered in the town of Bonavista at the site where historians conjecture Cabot landed. There they welcomed the ship at the end of its seven-week voyage. Among the dignitaries who attended were England's Queen Elizabeth and Prince Philip along with Newfoundland premier Brian Tobin.

♦ 2050 ♦ **Newport Folk Festival**
August

The Newport Folk Festival is an annual folk music festival that takes place at the Fort Adams State Park in Newport, Rhode Island. The event features music from the traditions of folk, blues, country, bluegrass, and folk rock. Since the 1990s, alternative country, indie folk, and folk punk bands have been featured as well. The Newport Folk Festival was founded in 1959 by George Wein, who also created the Newport Jazz Festival. Such major stars as Joan Baez and Bob Dylan were among those musicians introduced at this festival. The festival promotes a broad range of musical genres and performers. In the 1960s, country and blues singers such as Johnny Cash and Howlin' Wolf performed at the festival, and Mississippi Delta blues singers who faded from popularity during the 1940s were later rediscovered at Newport. The festival was discontinued in 1971, but was revived in 1985 and has been running uninterrupted since. National Public Radio's online music site has been involved in recording performances at the festival and streaming them on the Internet, and much of the history of the festival has been captured via live recordings. Since 1998, the Newport Folk Festival Tour has traveled around the United States as part of the festival.

CONTACTS:
Fort Adams State Park
90 Fort Adams Dr.
Newport, RI 02840
800-745-3000
www.newportfolk.org

♦ 2051 ♦ **Newport Harbor Christmas Boat Parade**
December 17-23

Newport Harbor Christmas Boat Parade is a week-long nightly parade of boats at Newport Beach, Calif. The area has one of the largest concentrations of pleasure craft in the world—more than 9,000 boats are docked at the harbor. More than 150 boats of all kinds, wildly decorated with lights that depict Santa Claus, snowmen, snowflakes, and other symbols of winter, join the parade. Some boats carry huge inflated figures (an enormous Grinch in an engineer's cap appeared in 1990) and many play music. The vessels range from rowboats to tugs to elegant yachts.

The floating parades actually started in 1908 as a FOURTH OF JULY spectacular. (The Fourth parades are no more.) John Scarpa, a real-estate broker was trying to sell some property, and to promote it he lit up a gondola and eight canoes with Japanese lanterns and paraded around the harbor. This developed into the **Illuminated Water Parade**, and was a highlight of the Fourth for years. In 1946, the city got a barge, put a tree and carolers on it, and towed it around the harbor, and that began the current December parades. They are considered the "granddaddy" of water parades, the biggest in the nation. About a million spectators watch them during the festival's seven days.

CONTACTS:
Newport Beach Chamber of Commerce
20351 Irvine Ave.
Ste. C-5
Newport Beach, CA 92660
949-729-4400; fax: 949-729-4417
www.newportbeach.com

♦ 2052 ♦ **Newport Music Festival**
Two weeks in mid-July

In 1969 the Metropolitan Opera in New York City decided to establish its summer home in Newport, Rhode Island. The fog and humidity, however, played havoc with the artists' delicate instruments, and it quickly became apparent that Newport wasn't the place for outdoor opera. But the grand rooms of its famed waterfront mansions provided an ideal setting for chamber music. Using members of the Metropolitan Opera Orchestra, the festival in its infancy paved the way for the "Romantic revival," which soon spread worldwide.

The Newport Music Festival still offers music of the Romantic era (1825-1900) but in recent years it has expanded its offerings and now presents a wide spectrum of composers and performers. Dozens of world premieres of forgotten or lost minor masterpieces by well-known composers, such as the four-handed *Andante Cantabile* by Claude Debussy (1862-1918), have taken place here, as have the North American debuts of many now-famous international and American artists, such as the young Dimitris Sgouros. More than 60 concerts are presented during the two-week festival, which has developed a reputation for programs so rare and varied that they draw music-lovers from thousands of miles away.

CONTACTS:
Newport Music Festival (Rhode Island Arts Foundation at Newport, Inc.)
850 Aquidneck Ave.
Middletown, RI 02842
401-846-1133
www.newportmusic.org

♦ 2053 ♦ **Newport to Bermuda Race**
June in even-numbered years

One of the oldest sailing races in the international calendar, the race from Newport, Rhode Island, to Bermuda was initiated by Thomas Fleming Day, editor and founder of *Rudder* magazine. At the time, most existing ocean races were for yachts of more than 100 feet, and Day wanted to see a race for smaller yachts (less than 40 feet overall). The first such race, in 1904, was run from Brooklyn, New York, to Marblehead, Massachusetts, a distance of 330 nautical miles. The following year it went from Brooklyn to Hampton Roads, Virginia (250 miles). In 1906, the finish was in Bermuda.

The Bermuda races died out in 1910, but they were revived in 1923 under the sponsorship of the Cruising Club of America (CCA). Since 1924 the race has been sailed biennially in June. The starting point was moved from New London, Connecticut, to Montauk, Long Island. But now the race is run from Narragansett Bay off Newport to St. David's Head, Bermuda—a distance of 635 nautical miles. Sponsored jointly by the CCA and the Royal Bermuda Yacht Club, the Newport to Bermuda Race is now part of the Onion Patch trophy series, which consists of this and three local, unnamed races.

CONTACTS:
Bermuda Tourism
675 Third Ave.
20th Fl.
New York, NY 10017
212-818-9800 or 800-223-6106; fax: 212-983-5289
www.gotobermuda.com

♦ 2054 ♦ **Ngan Duan Sib (Tenth Lunar Month Festival)**
September-October; 10th lunar month

In the city of Nakhon Si Thammarat in Thailand, a festival is held during the tenth lunar month to feed the ghosts of ancestors for their annual visit among the living. Buddhist tradition holds that they reside in hell and because of sins they committed when they were alive, these spirits have very small mouths, which makes them constantly hungry. So during the Tenth Lunar Month Festival people try to placate the unworldly visitors with gifts and food designed to fit into tiny mouths.

A major event is a parade of food to the temple. Floats carry gifts and foods resembling such objects as clothing, coins, games, and boats—everything the spirits will need, including transportation back to their home. A popular sweet is called *la*, a toffee-like cookie or candy made from rice flour, brown palm sugar, and egg yolks thin enough to fit in the ghosts' small mouths. Tables are set up on the temple's front grounds to hold the food when the parade arrives. After allowing the ghosts a few minutes with the food, children are permitted to sample the treats.

It is traditional for children, and men, to dress up as ghosts and skeletons during the festival and prowl around, menacing people and begging for money—much like the trick-or-treating that goes on in the United States at HALLOWEEN.

♦ 2055 ♦ **Nganja, Feast of**
April

A harvest custom in Angola, the Feast of Nganja is primarily celebrated by children. On a day in April, when the harvest is ripe, they go out to their family fields and gather some fresh corn. In small groups they go to the woods, where they build campfires and roast their corn on the cob. But the real excitement of the feast lies in the game that is played while the corn is being cooked. Without warning, a child from one group may jump up and steal the corn from another. The robbing and plundering is good-natured, although there are always a few children who end up with no corn at all.

A similar children's feast held in Angola during the harvest months of February, March, and April is known as the Feast of Okambondondo. This all-night celebration is held indoors, with the girls doing all the cooking and the meal itself being served in the kitchen just before dawn.

CONTACTS:
SOS Children's Villages
Terrington House
13-15 Hills Rd.
Cambridge, CB2 1NL United Kingdom
www.our-africa.org

♦ 2056 ♦ **Ngmayem Festival**
March; in some areas October

The Ngmayem Festival is a harvest celebration that takes place in March in Manya Krobo in southeastern Ghana. The festival has been held annually since 1944 to foster tribal unity, but it commemorates the end of a famine that occurred hundred of years ago.

The festival derives its name from the historic importance of *ngma*, or millet, to the survival of the tribe, though that grain now is cultivated mainly for ritual purposes. Traditional foods associated with Ngmayem include mashed yam, palm soup, roasted corn, and meal. Festivities and rites are planned throughout the harvest month, and these may include dances, marriages, naming ceremonies, and other rituals designed to strengthen relationships and allegiances within the tribe. Events during the main festival week include blessings, cleansing ceremonies, thanksgiving services, visitation of royal tombs, and commemoration of ancestors. Festivalgoers dress in colorful attire and adorn themselves with beads.

Krobo leaders also conduct a *durbar,* or court reception, in which tribe members meet with chiefs to discuss the government and administration of the group and to hear updates on development projects and political issues affecting the people, such as water rights and border disputes. Beginning in the 2000s, a Ngmayem Festival was also celebrated annually in October in Dodowa to celebrate the harvest, foster tribal unity, and educate younger generations about their history.

CONTACTS:
Ghana Tourism Authority
P.O. Box GP 3106
 Ghana
233-302-222153
www.ghana.travel

National Commission on Culture
1 Gamal Abdul Nasser Ave. Private Mail Bag
Ministries P.O.
 Ghana
233-21-661030
www.ghanaculture.gov.gh

♦ 2057 ♦ **Ngoc Son Temple Festival**
Autumn

The Ngoc Son Temple sits on a little island in Hoan Kiem Lake in Hanoi, the capital of Vietnam. The lake is named after a 500-year-old legend. It was said that a divine tortoise lived in the lake. When China ruled Vietnam, the tortoise gave a warrior named Le Loi a sword with sacred powers. This Le Loi wielded to liberate Vietnam, eventually becoming Emperor Le Thai To. Later he went out on the lake to give the sword back to the tortoise, who took it, then disappeared into the lake's depths—thus, the lake's name means "Lake of the Restored Sword."

The Ngoc Son, meaning "Jade Mound," Temple honors three Vietnamese saints—a doctor, La To, a writer, Van Xuong, and a martial artist, Quan Vu—and one patriotic hero, Tran Hung Dao. The annual festival commemorates these ancestors with

a procession from Hanoi which crosses a bridge to the temple. Some play traditional instruments along the way. At the temple a special worship service is held, then everyone enjoys a feast.

CONTACTS:
Vietnam National Administration of Tourism
80 Quan Su
Hoan Kiem Dist
Vietnam
84-4-942-1061
www.vietnamtourism.com

♦ 2058 ♦ **Ngondo Festival**
November-December

For the majority of the Sawa, an ethnic group composed of various coastal peoples of Cameroon, guidance comes from the Jengu water spirits. The annual Ngondo Festival is a special occasion for Sawa chiefs to petition these spirits for prophecies and warnings and to communicate those messages to a gathered assembly. The event, which lasts a few weeks, takes place on the banks of the Wouri River in the country's most populous city, Douala. Various cultural activities accompany the discernment process of the festival.

It is possible for the Sawa to receive the same message twice. Such was the case with the 2007 festival, when chiefs announced for the second year in a row that Sawa sons and daughters should focus more intently on joint and constructive action.

Sawa chiefs deliver their messages at the water feast that officially closes the Ngondo Festival. Activities preceding the water feast include traditional wrestling competitions, art exhibitions, choral singing, round table conferences, a trade fair, a canoe race, and a Miss Ngondo pageant.

♦ 2059 ♦ **Nguillatun**
Usually March

The Mapuche Indians live in southern Chile and west central Argentina, particularly in the province of Neuquén. The name *Mapuche* means "people of the earth." The autumn harvest usually comes in March and for the Mapuche, this is a time to say special prayers to give thanks and ask for fertility and protection from floods, droughts, and other disasters. A special *nguillatun* (gee-ya-TOON), or prayer ceremony, is held at harvest time and is led by a *machi*, a religious leader who is usually a woman. People apply blue and white paint to their faces—colors which are considered spiritually positive. For two to four days the Mapuche pray, sing, dance and feast.

♦ 2060 ♦ **Nicaragua Battle of San Jacinto Day**
September 14

In Nicaragua, the month of September is full of celebratory activities across the country to commemorate the 1856 battle at Hacienda San Jacinto and Nicaraguan independence.

Starting on September 1, people hang the Nicaraguan flag around their homes, and the Central American Patrimonial Festivities begin. An inaugural ceremony at the Plaza de los Honores del Palacio Presidencial kicks off the week-long festival during which school marching bands from across the country combine music and choreography to compete against bands from other schools. The final contest is held at the National Stadium in Managua, where the groups compete in front of judges for the title of best musical group in the country.

Also during the month of September, a burning torch is carried through Central America, from Guatemala to Costa Rica. It is passed from hand to hand by the best students and other outstanding individuals from each municipality. Each person carries the torch for no more than 100 meters. The total run is 387 kilometers and involves more than 8,000 students. When the torch reaches the National Cultural Palace, the president kicks off folkloric events that occur throughout the day. On September 13, the national flag is hung at all schools and the national anthem is broadcast in across the country.

September 14 is a national holiday dedicated to the anniversary of the independence of Central America and the battle at San Jacinto. Starting at 7:30 in the morning, the president awards the Presidential Medallion to the best students and teachers from around the country at the Plaza de la Fé Juan Pablo Segundo. Marching bands from 100 schools in the capital (approximately 15,000 students) and bands from the National Army and the Police participate in a parade that day.

The celebrations conclude on September 15 with the reading of the Act of Independence of Central America in all state schools throughout Nicaragua.

CONTACTS:
Consulate Of Nicaragua In Washington D.C.
1627 New Hampshire Ave. N.W.
Washington, D.C. 20009
202-939-6531; fax: 202-939-6574
consuladodenicaragua.com

♦ 2061 ♦ Nicaragua Independence Day
September 15

Nicaragua shares its Independence Day with four other Central American countries—Costa Rica, El Salvador, Guatemala, and Honduras—all of which declared their independence from Spain on September 15, 1821. There is a parade in the capital city of Managua, and the president and other public officials give speeches. Nicaraguans also celebrate Independence Day by attending cockfights and bullfights. But unlike bullfights in other countries, the Nicaraguan matador does not kill the bull. Instead, he tries to mount it and ride it rodeo-style.

♦ 2062 ♦ Nice Carnaval
January-February; three weekends before Shrove Tuesday

Dating back to the late 13th century and deriving, some believe, from ancient rites of spring, the Carnival celebration in Nice, France, is one of the Mediterranean resort town's most picturesque spectacles. It actually begins about three weeks before Shrove Tuesday with the arrival of King Carnival. The next two Saturdays and Sundays are filled with processions, confetti battles, and masked balls. The processions of floats, each accompanied by marchers or riders on horseback wearing elaborate costumes, draw large crowds. There are also parades of "big heads," large heads representing various personages made of pasteboard, and huge panels of light illustrating the year's theme decorate the Place Messena, the carnival grounds in the heart of Nice. During the last five days before Shrove Tuesday, a grand *charivari*, or street party, ensues with roving musicians, singers, and actors mingling with onlookers. On Shrove Tuesday, King Carnival is burnt in a bonfire on the shore and fireworks close out the long pre-Lenten celebration.

Flowers play an important role in the Nice Carnaval, for it is in the south of France that the flowers for French perfume are grown. During the festivities, there are several afternoons devoted to *Bataille de Fleurs*, Parades of Flowers, consisting of some 20 floats, all meticulously decorated with 4,000-5,000 fresh flowers.

CONTACTS:
Office du Tourisme Et des Congrès
5 Promenade des Anglais
BP 4079
Nice, 06302 France
33-892-707-407; fax: 33-4-9214-4649
en.nicetourisme.com

♦ 2063 ♦ Nicodemus Emancipation and Homecoming Celebration
Last weekend in July

The Nicodemus Emancipation and Homecoming Celebration is held annually the last weekend in July to celebrate the abolishment of slavery in the United States. It also celebrates Nicodemus, an all-black town in northwest Kansas that was settled by former slaves fleeing the south in 1877 after the post-Civil War Reconstruction period had ended. The town was named after a legendary slave who reportedly bought his own freedom. The town is the only still-living all-black community west of the Mississippi founded by former slaves. Originally settled by 350 freed slaves, it now has a permanent population of about 40 people. The town, which comprises five historic buildings, was declared a National Historic Site in 1998. Only one building is open to visitors.

The Emancipation and Homecoming Celebration has taken place every year since 1878. The event includes such attractions as a parade, a fashion show, military displays, and descendants' program, which draws relatives of the original town settlers from across the country.

CONTACTS:
Nicodemus National Historic Site
510 B1 Washington Ave.

Nicodemus, KS 67625
785-839-4233; fax: 785-839-4325
www.nps.gov

♦ 2064 ♦ Niger Republic Day
December 18

On August 3, 1960, Niger gained full independence from France, after having been a colony since 1922. Niger had voted to become a republic on December 18, 1958. August 3 is a national holiday celebrating Independence Day, while December 18 is Republic Day.

CONTACTS:
Embassy of the Republic of Niger
2204 R St. N.W.
Washington, D.C. 20008
202-483-4224; fax: 202-483-3169
www.embassyofniger.org

♦ 2065 ♦ Nigeria National Day
October 1

Also known as **Independence Day**, this national holiday commemorates the autonomy of Nigeria that officially began October 1, 1960, after being under British control since 1900. Nigeria became a federal republic with a new constitution on October 1, 1963. In 1966 some military officers staged a coup and ruled until other army officers overthrew them in 1975. Civilian rule was restored on the anniversary of freedom, October 1, 1979. The city of Lagos was the capital until 1986, when the government center moved to Abuja.

CONTACTS:
Embassy of the Federal Republic of Nigeria
2204 R. St. N.W.
Washington, D.C. 20008
202-483-4224; fax: 202-483-3169
www.embassyofniger.org

♦ 2066 ♦ Night of the Radishes
December 23

Night of the Radishes is a festival that dates from the 19th century that combines art, agriculture, and religion. It is held in the *zócalo*, or main square, in Oaxaca, Mexico, 300 miles south of Mexico City. The radish made its first appearance here during the Spanish colonial period, and in commemoration Oaxaqueños carve them into elaborate shapes and display them on **La Noche de Ratanos**. The radishes, the same red-skinned, white-fleshed roots commonly eaten in salads, grow to yam-size here and are each uniquely shaped by growing through the rocky soil.

Indian families harvest these vegetables, combine and sculpt them into elaborate forms depicting biblical scenes, especially the nativity of Jesus. Historical and Aztec themes are also represented. After the awarding of cash prizes and ribbons, a fireworks display caps the night.

During the festival and throughout the CHRISTMAS season, an-

other custom is observed: people buy small pottery bowls filled with sweet fried dough called *buñuelos*. After they eat the dough, they fling the bowl violently to the ground. The walks become thick with pottery shards.

♦ 2067 ♦ Night Watch
July 13

La Retraite aux Flambeaux, or the Night Watch, is a half-holiday in France that is celebrated on the eve of BASTILLE DAY. The lights in Paris are darkened in remembrance of the day in 1789 when the Bastille fell. Colorful processions of soldiers, patriotic bands, and people bearing torches and Chinese lanterns march through the streets, followed by crowds of spectators. The procession usually ends at the home of a prominent citizen, who offers the torch- and lantern-bearers something to drink.

♦ 2068 ♦ Niiname-sai
November 23-24

Niiname-sai, which translates as the "the festival of new crops," has been a ritual celebration at Shinto shrines since the early 19th century. Rice—Japan's staple crop—holds a significant place in the country's history and economy. The festival traces its roots to the ancient ritual of *shinsen*, or offerings of the first harvest of rice made to the deity. The grand thanksgiving ceremony begins at the imperial palace, when the emperor of Japan makes an offering of the season's first harvest to the *Amaterasu-omikami* (Sun Goddess) and other deities. Following this, Shinto shrines all over the country perform the ceremony, which takes on the form of a national event.

Two raised platforms, one for the deity and another for the emperor, are built inside the imperial palace, and the emperor makes offerings of rice porridge, sake, and steamed rice from the newly harvested crop. The food is served to the deity in Kashiwa (containers made from woven beech leaves). Two offerings are made, one at dusk on November 23 and a second at dawn the next day. Shinto believes that the emperors of Japan are direct descendants of the *Amaterasu-omikami*, and that the sharing of food with the *Kami* (ancestral spirits) symbolizes a spiritual communion with ancestors.

CONTACTS:
Tsubaki Grand Shrine of America & Tsubaki Kannagara Jinja
17720 Crooked Mile Rd.
Granite Falls, WA 98252
360-691-6389
www.tsubakishrine.org

Atsuta Shrine Office
1-1-1 Jingu
Atsuta-ku
Nagoya, 456-8585 Japan
81-52-671-4151
www.atsutajingu.or.jp/en

♦ 2069 ♦ Niman Festival
July

The Niman, or **Going Home Ceremony**, takes place in the Hopi Indian pueblos of northeastern Arizona. After entering the pueblos in February, the *katchinas*, ancestral spirits impersonated by men wearing elaborate masks, leave again in July. During the six months when they are present in the pueblo (*see* Powamû Ceremony), the katchinas appear in a series of dances, of which the Niman is the last. For the Going Home Ceremony, up to 75 dancers representing katchinas spend an entire day singing and dancing. They give bows, arrows, and other gifts to the boys and katchina dolls to the girls before returning to their mountain homes.

♦ 2070 ♦ Nine Imperial Gods, Festival of the
First nine days of ninth lunar month

As celebrated today in Singapore, the Festival of the Nine Imperial Gods derives from an ancient Chinese cleansing ritual. The festival begins with a procession to a body of water. There a Taoist priest prays for the spirits of the Gods to enter an urn of burning incense. The procession then carries the urn to a temple, where worshippers can bring offerings. Outside the Tou Mu Kong temple, near Kangkar, Singapore, people are informed of the Gods' presence by the raising of nine oil lamps dangling from a bamboo pole. Worshippers enter the temple by crossing a specially constructed bridge. By crossing the bridge, devotees trust that they are cleansed of all evil from the previous year.

Chinese operas known as *wayang* shows—some of which take two or more days to complete—are often performed during the nine days of the festival.

On the ninth day, a final procession takes the urn back to the water's edge, where it is placed in a small boat to carry the Gods back to the heavens.

CONTACTS:
Singapore Tourism Board
1156 Ave. of the Americas
Ste. 702
New York, NY 10036
212-302-4861; fax: 212-302-4801
www.stb.gov.sg

♦ 2071 ♦ Nineteen Day Fast
March 2 – 20

The Nineteen-Day Fast is an obligatory fast observed by members of the Baha'i faith during a nineteen day period in the month of Ala, just prior to the Baha'i new year. During Ala, Baha'i's between the ages of 15 and 70 fast from sunrise to sunset, abstaining completely from food and drink. Those who are travelling or engaged in heavy labor, as well as the elderly, the sick, and pregnant and nursing mothers, are exempt from the fast.

The founder of the Baha'i faith, Baha'u'llah, laid down the guidelines for the Nineteen-Day Fast in the *Kitáb-i-Aqdas* (Most Holy Book), the faith's central text. The fast is a spiritual exercise, symbolic of restraint from selfishness and phys-

ical desires, and its purpose draw the individual closer to god. The Nineteen-Day Fast is one of the greatest obligations among Baha'i's, and is similar to the fasting periods seen in many other religions, including Ramadan in Muslim culture.

CONTACTS:
National Spiritual Assembly of the Bahá'ís of the United States
U.S. Bahá'í National Center
1233 Central St.
Evanston, IL 60201
847-733-3400 or 800-228-6483
www.bahai.us

♦ 2072 ♦ Nino Fidencio Festival
October

In 1938, a local healer named El Nino Fidencio was allegedly murdered in the northeast Mexican town of Espinazo. Rumors spread that doctors, jealous of his healing abilities, had killed him.

Born Jose Fidencio Sintora Constantino in 1890, Fidencio displayed an early talent for herbal remedies. Soon, people from nearby towns would journey to Espinazo to see the *curandero,* or mystical healer, and be cured. In 1928, radical Mexican president Plutarco Elias Calles came to Espinazo to arrest the healer Fidencio for practicing medicine without a license. But Fidencio is said to have cured the president and his ailing daughter, which brought him and his healing miracles to national attention. Upon his death in 1938, rumors spread that Fidencio had been murdered. Detractors claim that Fidencio was an alcoholic who drank himself to an early death.

For a week each October, thousands of pilgrims flock to Espinazo to place flowers at the tomb of El Nino Fidencio and hold spontaneous rituals involving sacred songs, herbs, and various oils and potions. Those afflicted with disease bathe themselves in a small pond near the tomb that is said to contain healing waters. These rituals draw on Catholic ceremony as well as ancient Aztec beliefs and peasant folklore. Again drawing on Catholic teachings, pilgrims call Fidencio "El Guadalupano," or the son of the Virgin of Guadalupe, a Mexican saint. Despite warnings from the Catholic Church to stay away from this heretical pilgrimage, thousands of otherwise devoutly Catholic Mexicans come to remember the legendary village healer.

♦ 2073 ♦ Nippy Lug Day
Between February 6 and March 12; Friday following Shrove Tuesday

A "lug" at one time referred to the ear-flap of a man's cap, but in Scotland and northern England it became a synonym for the ear itself. In 19th-century Scotland, schoolchildren called their teachers "nip-lugs" because they often pulled their pupils' ears as a disciplinary measure. In Westmorland, England, it was traditional at one time for children to pinch each other's ears on the Friday following Shrove Tuesday, giving rise to the name Nippy Lug Day.

♦ 2074 ♦ **Nirjala Ekadashi**
*May-June; 11th day of waxing half of Hindu
month of Jyestha*

Of the 24 EKADASHI or 11th-day fasts observed during the course of the Hindu year, Nirjala Ekadashi is one of the more important. No food or even water is taken on this day, which is an act of extreme devotion since the month of Jyestha is very hot. Both men and women observe a strict fast and offer *puja* (worship) to Vishnu to ensure happiness and forgiveness of their sins. *Panchamrata* is prepared by mixing together milk, ghee (clarified butter), curds, honey, and sugar. It is then offered to the image of Vishnu, which has been draped in rich clothing and jewels, with a fan placed beside it. Hindus meditate on Vishnu as the Lord of the Universe and worship the deity with flowers, lamps, water, and incense.

Some Hindus believe that faithful observance of the fast and other rituals on Nirjala Ekadashi ensures happiness, salvation, longevity, and prosperity. Those who can afford to do so give clothes, grains, umbrellas, fans, and pitchers filled with water to the Brahmans.

♦ 2075 ♦ **Nisei Week**
Early August

Nisei Week is an annual Japanese-American festival in the Little Tokyo area of Los Angeles, Calif. Little Tokyo is the social, cultural, and economic center for the Japanese and Nisei community of southern California. The Nisei are people of Japanese descent born and raised in the United States. Held since 1934, this week-long festival features a parade, a carnival, Japanese folk dancing, celebrity appearances, and a prince and princess pageant. There are special exhibits of bonsai, flower arranging, doll making, tea ceremonies, and other Japanese arts. Sports competitions and demonstrations include jiu-jitsu and karate. Attendance is about 50,000.

CONTACTS:
Japanese American National Museum
100 N. Central Ave.
Los Angeles, CA 90012
213-625-0414 or 800-461-5266; fax: 213-625-1770
www.janm.org

♦ 2076 ♦ **Niue Peniamina Gospel Day**
Fourth Friday in October

Niue is a tropical island northeast of New Zealand that is approximately 269 square meters in size, with a population of approximately 1,500 people. It is one of the world's smallest self-governing states. Although the country was annexed to New Zealand in 1901, it gained sovereignty in 1974. The country still uses the New Zealand currency today.

Niue is believed to have been settled between 400 and 1100 CE by people from Samoa, Tonga, and the Cook Islands. Captain James Cook discovered the island in 1774 but met much resistance from the Niuans.

Niue Peniamina Gospel Day derives from the nation's conversion to Christianity. In 1830, John Williams, of the London Missionary Society, traveled to Niue, determined to convert the islanders to Christianity. He kidnapped two local boys named Niumaga and Uea to try to educate and convert them. Several months later, the boys returned to Niue, but the Niuans no longer accepted them. The islanders eventually killed Uea and his father.

Niumaga continued to face rejection by his fellow Niuans, so he and his friend, Peniamina Nukai, left for Samoa. Peniamina worked as a servant for Dr. George Turner, a famous missionary. While working for Dr. Turner, Peniamina learned to read and write, and he converted to Christianity.

On October 26, 1846, Peniamina returned to Niue, bringing with him his Christian beliefs and ideals. He preached to his fellow islanders and began to convert many to Christianity.

Today, Niue remains a deeply Christian country. Sunday is truly a day of rest; as a result most businesses are closed, and very few activities are conducted on Sunday. For example, fishing, diving and boating are not allowed on Sundays.

Every year, on the fourth Friday of October, Niuans observe Peniamina Gospel Day as a national holiday to celebrate the day that Peniamina brought Christianity to the island.

CONTACTS:
Niue Tourism Office
Visitor Information Centre
Niue Island
683-4224; fax: 683-4225
www.niueisland.com

♦ 2077 ♦ **Nizhni Novgorod**
Varies

The great medieval fair held at Nizhni Novgorod, Russia, began in the 16th century at the monastery of St. Macarius, a popular place of pilgrimage. It grew so large that the little town of Makaraev could barely accommodate it, and when it burned to the ground in 1816, it was relocated to a new town that had been built expressly to house it. The new city was located on the sandy plains where the Oka and Volga rivers flower together, making it an ideal spot for international trade. It was called Nizhni Novgorod or "Lower New City."

Nizhni Novgorod was largely a barter fair and entirely a market of direct trade, where no merchant placed orders for goods he could not inspect. Everything sold was displayed there, including cloth, furs, hides, cotton, iron, and half-wild horses. Although the height of the fair was in August, caravans and sailboats began to arrive in June. The bishop of the Russian Orthodox Church officially opened the fair with a solemn service on July 15th, but the real fair couldn't begin until the tea boats arrived, having sailed up the Volga River at the end of their 7,000-mile journey from China. Once the price of tea was determined, the prices of all the other goods was set and the trading began in earnest. This usually occurred during the first few days of August.

More than 200,000 traders took up residence in Nizhni Novgorod for the duration of the fair, and they spent most of their time smoking and drinking tea and making verbal agreements that they sealed with a handshake. By 1900, the fair was doing business worth more than $100 million a year. But during several periods—the Revolution in 1917, civil wars, and periods of famine—desperate Russians from nearby cities went down to the deserted fair and dismantled the stone and brick buildings to get at their wooden window and door frames, which they burned to stay warm.

The Soviet government under Lenin reopened the fair in 1923, but seven years later the Stalin regime abolished all 18,000 Russian fairs because they were not a part of the Kremlin-controlled trade program. The fairgrounds reopened in 1991 after the collapse of the Soviet Union. It has been modernized and now hosts major exhibition events year-round.

CONTACTS:
Russian Embassy
2650 Wisconsin Ave. N.W.
Washington, D.C. 20007
202-298-5700; fax: 202-298-5735
www.russianembassy.org

♦ 2078 ♦ Nobel Prize Ceremony
December 10

Nobel Prizes are awarded each year to people, regardless of nationality, deemed by committees to have made the most significant practical efforts toward the well-being of the human race. In his will, the Swedish inventor Alfred Nobel (1833-1896) directed that the income from his $9 million estate be used to fund five annual prizes for the most important discoveries or inventions in the fields of physics, chemistry, and physiology or medicine; for the most distinguished literary work of an idealistic nature; and for the most effective work in the interest of international peace. The first Nobel Prizes were awarded in 1901, but a sixth prize—in economics—was added in 1969.

Prize winners receive the awards, each worth a little over $1 million, at a special ceremony in Stockholm, Sweden, on December 10, the anniversary of Alfred Nobel's death in 1896. The peace prize is awarded in Oslo, Norway.

CONTACTS:
Nobel Foundation
Sturegatan 14
P.O. Box 5232
Stockholm, SE-102 45 Sweden
46-8-663-0920; fax: 46-8-660-3847
www.nobelprize.org

♦ 2079 ♦ Noel Night
First Saturday in December

Noel Night is a community holiday celebration that takes place on the first Saturday of December in the University Cultural Center area of Detroit, Mich. The area encompasses such institutions as Wayne State University, museums devoted to art, science, history, and African-American history, and numerous churches, restaurants, and shops. The event area extends from Ferry Street to Willis Street on the north and south and from St. Antoine to Cass Avenue on the east and west, including the main thoroughfare Woodward Avenue, which is closed to automobile traffic during the festival.

Held annually since 1973, Noel Night offers dozens of unique holiday displays and activities, including horse-drawn carriage rides, a living nativity scene, musical and comedy performances, holiday lighting, and an ice sculpture competition. A community sing-a-long led by the Salvation Army Band concludes the festivities, which take place between 5:00 P.M. and 9:30 P.M. Restaurants and street vendors offer holiday foods and refreshments, including soups, roasted almonds, and hot chocolate, and museums offer free admission during the festival.

CONTACTS:
Midtown Detroit, Inc.
3939 Woodward Ave.
Ste. 100
Detroit, MI 48201
313-420-6000; fax: 313-420-6200
midtowndetroitinc.org

♦ 2080 ♦ Nomaoi Matsuri (Horse Festival)
July 23-25

Eight villages take part in the Horse Festival held in Haramachi, Japan, in July. Hibarino moor provides the open space where men on horseback wearing ancient armor and helmets reenact a military muster that was originally organized by a former lord of the fief. Other festival events that take place on the moor include the breaking of wild horses, horse races, and games, while in town there is a procession of men and their horses and a parade of shrine floats.

CONTACTS:
Japan National Tourist Organization
1 Grand Central Pl.
60 E. 42nd St.
Ste. 448
New York, NY 10165
212-757-5640; fax: 212-307-6754
www.jnto.go.jp

♦ 2081 ♦ Nombre de Jesús
February 1-15

The two-week fair known as Nombre de Jesús takes place in the village of San Pedro Nonualco in El Salvador. The celebration centers on two images of the Christ Child—one with blond hair and blue eyes, and the other with black hair and black eyes—which are sent from the nearby town of Cojutepeque. The light-complexioned Christ Child is the best-loved image, and people cover it with money and gifts as it passes. The major-domo of the fiesta is usually the fortunate one who gets to keep this image in his house during the two weeks.

People do traditional dances in a circle around the veiled figure of the blond infant—an activity that Catholic priests have tried, unsuccessfully, to discourage. Although many different local foods are served, a favorite is the dove-shaped candy called *chancaca*, made of ground corn and sugar, that young men traditionally present to their sweethearts.

◆ 2082 ◆ Nordic Fest
Last full weekend in July

The Nordic Fest held annually in Decorah, Iowa, prides itself on preserving the area's Norwegian heritage without resorting to commercialism. From Friday night through Sunday of the last full weekend in July, the festival offers arts and crafts displays, dances, lectures, concerts, sporting events, and museum visits. Both the Norwegian-American Museum and the Porter House Museum are open to visitors, and there is a walking tour of the Home of the Trolls—a troll being the Norwegian version of the pixie or elf. The festival begins with a parade and Norse Fire Celebration, and the events that follow are all designed to highlight a particular aspect of Decorah's Norwegian heritage. Scandinavian dancers perform, Norse plays are put on for the children, and special Norwegian and English church services are held.

The festival has been held annually in Decorah since 1967. The Luther College Women's Club had sponsored a Scandinavian Festival Day since 1936, and eventually it was expanded to the present three-day event.

CONTACTS:
Nordic Fest
507 W. Water St.
Decorah, IA 52101
563-382-3990 or 800-382-3378; fax: 563-382-5515
www.nordicfest.com

◆ 2083 ◆ Normandy Impressionist Festival
April to September, every three years

Founded in 2010, the Normandy Impressionist Festival celebrates the lives and works of the 19th-century French Impressionists. Held each year in the Normandy region of France, the celebration features over 300 events, focusing on artists such as Claude Monet, Eugene Boudin, Camille Pissarro, and Auguste Renoir, among others. The festival brings together masterpieces from around the world, with international art experts presenting contemporary interpretations on Impressionism. The event is open to the public and seeks to engage professional and amateur artists through a range of educational activities held at schools and cultural centers. Beyond Impressionist art, the festival also presents musical, theatrical, and literary events, which are often held at local *guinguettes*, the traditional French outdoor restaurants first made famous by the Impressionists.

CONTACTS:
Impressionist Normandy Association
14bis avenue Pasteur
Cedex 1
Rouen, BP 589-76006 France
www.normandie-impressionniste.eu

◆ 2084 ◆ Norsk Høstfest
Second week in October

All five Scandinavian countries—Denmark, Finland, Iceland, Norway, and Sweden—are represented at the annual Scandinavian heritage festival known as Norsk Høstfest that has been held in Minot, North Dakota, since 1978. The festival includes performances by top entertainers, one of whom is selected by the previous year's ticketholders as the "People's Choice" and many of whom are either Scandinavian or Americans of Scandinavian descent. There are also Swedish accordion players, Scandinavian folk dancers, and Lakota flute players, who perform at the Høstfest complex on North Dakota's state fairgrounds in Minot. The complex includes five stages, 40 food booths, and dozens of demonstration areas for craftsmen and artisans—among them the highly skilled *rosemalers*, or "folk painters." The Viking Age Club sets up an authentic encampment to show how the North Plains Scandinavian settlers lived.

Food is a big part of the five-day festival, which features traditional Scandinavian delicacies. More than 60,000 visitors come to Minot to sample Swedish sweet bread, *søt suppe* (fruit soup), *potet klub* (potato dumpling), Icelandic cake, *røm mergrøt* ("red porridge," a rhubarb pudding), Danish kringle (pretzel-shaped cookie), *lefse* (a thin, potato cake spread with butter and cinnamon and folded over), and *lutefisk* (cod soaked in lye and then boiled). A similar Scandinavian festival, the Hjemkomst Festival, is held in June in Fargo.

CONTACTS:
Norsk Hostfest Association
P.O. Box 1347
Minot, ND 58702
701-852-2368; fax: 701-838-7873
hostfest.com

◆ 2085 ◆ North American Indian Days
Second week in July

One of the largest gatherings of United States and Canadian Indian tribes, held in Browning, Montana, the hub of the Blackfeet Indian Reservation in the northwest mountains of the state. The powwow grounds fill up with teepees for four festive days of traditional Indian dancing, games, and sporting events. There are also exhibits of arts and crafts—beadwork, quill and feather work, moccasins and other leather goods.

CONTACTS:
Montana Governor's Office of Indian Affairs
State Capitol Bldg.
2nd Fl. Rm. 202
P.O. Box 200801

Helena, MT 59620
406-444-3702; fax: 406-444-1350
tribalnations.mt.gov

Browning Area Chamber of Commerce
124 2nd Ave. N.W.
P.O. Box 469
Browning, MT 59417
406-338-2344; fax: 406-338-2605
www.browningchamber.com

♦ 2086 ♦ North American International Auto Show
Two weeks in January

The North American International Auto Show (NAIAS) is an automobile exhibition held each year in Detroit, Mich., which is known as the Motor City. In addition to presenting cars that will be available to consumers in the upcoming model year, each year dozens of concept vehicles that have never been seen in North America or in the world are unveiled during the show.

The NAIAS is one of the oldest and largest automobile exhibitions in the world. It began in 1907 when the Detroit Auto Dealers Association formed and decided to showcase their offerings to the public. It has been held nearly every year since then, with the exception of several years during and after World War II.

The Detroit Auto Show began as a gathering in a riverside park and moved to various locations throughout the City of Detroit, finally locating in its current setting at Cobo Center in downtown Detroit in 1965. It has been called NAIAS since 1989, a name change that reflects the participation of automobile manufacturers from around the world. The show runs annually during the final two weeks in January, with the first week reserved for media and industry insiders and the second week open to the public. Since 1976 a black-tie charity ball has taken place on the eve of the public opening of the show. The 2015 Auto Show was attended by 808,775 people, surpassing the 2014 total of 803,451. Fifty-five new vehicles were introduced, and 5,025 journalists from 60 countries and 40 U.S. states attended. Charity preview guests, numbering 13,350, helped raise $5.3 million for children's charities.

CONTACTS:
North American International Auto Show
1900 W. Big Beaver
Ste. 100
Troy, MI 48084
248-643-0250; fax: 248-637-0784
www.naias.com

♦ 2087 ♦ North American Wife-Carrying Championship
October

The North American Wife-Carrying Championship began in 2000. The WIFE-CARRYING WORLD CHAMPIONSHIP, held in Sonkajärvi, Finland, inspired contest organizers in Maine to develop a North American competition. The American competition takes place at the Sunday River Ski Resort in Bethel, Maine. As in the world championship, a man may carry a woman other than his wife. Penalties apply for dropping one's "wife." The couple who completes the course in the shortest length of time wins. The course measures 278 yards and includes two 39" hurdles, sand, grass, sharp turns, and a waist-deep pond. Winners fly to Finland to represent North America in the world championship.

CONTACTS:
Sunday River Ski Resort
15 S. Ridge Rd.
P.O. Box 4500
Newry, ME 04261
207-824-3000 or 800-543-2754; fax: 207-824-5110
www.sundayriver.com

♦ 2088 ♦ North Korea Victory Day
July 27

Victory Day marks the end of the Korean War, the three-year conflict between North Korea (official name: Democratic People's Republic of Korea), which was backed by the U.S.S.R. and China, and South Korea (official name: Republic of Korea), which was supported by the United Nations and United States. On July 27, 1953, the opponents signed an armistice that formally ended the war. The document ended overt hostilities, but it was not a permanent peace treaty between the nations. North and South Korea remain separate entities and occupy essentially the same territory they did when the war began. The border zone known as the demilitarized zone (DMZ) is heavily guarded on both sides, including almost 40,000 U.S. troops on the south side. Today, North Korea (official name: Democratic People's Republic of Korea) is a Communist country with a repressive government.

Victory Day is a public holiday observed throughout North Korea. Officials and citizens mark the occasion by laying wreaths and flowers at military cemeteries and monuments nationwide. In the capital city, Pyongyang, public celebrations can include displays by military personnel, dance performances, and youth oratorical events. In addition, officials take part in public wreath- and flower-laying ceremonies at national monuments in the city.

CONTACTS:
Permanent Mission of the Republic of Korea to the United Nations
335 E. 45th St.
New York, NY 10017
212-439-4000; fax: 212-986-1083
un.mofat.go.kr

♦ 2089 ♦ North Pole Winter Carnival
Early March

The North Pole Winter Carnival is a weekend celebration of winter in North Pole, Alaska, a suburb of Fairbanks. North Pole was named by Con Miller, a man who bought a Fairbanks trading post in 1949. When he cleaned it out, he found a SantaClaus suit and started wearing it on trips to the interior to buy furs and sell supplies. A few years later he built a new trading post southeast of Fairbanks, called it Santa Claus House, and named the town around it North Pole. The town now has a government and a post office. It also has the Winter Carnival which features the North Pole Championship Sled Dog Race, a dog weight-pulling contest, carnival rides and games, food booths, crafts bazaars, and live entertainment.

CONTACTS:
City of North Pole
125 Snowman Ln.
North Pole, AK 99705 United States
907-488-8583; fax: 907-488-3002
www.northpolealaska.com

♦ 2090 ♦ Northern Games
July

A showcase for traditional Inuit and Indian sports and culture, the Northern Games are held in the Northwest Territories of Canada in July each year. They feature traditional dances, drumming competitions, arts and crafts displays, and the "Good Woman" Contest, which gives Northern women a chance to demonstrate their skill in such areas as animal skinning and bannock baking. The games are held in Inuvik and draw competitors from Alaska, Yukon Territory, and Labrador as well.

CONTACTS:
Town of Inuvik
P.O. Box 1160
Ste. 2 Firth St.
Inuvik, NT X0E 0T0 Canada
867-777-8600; fax: 867-777-8601
inuvik.ca

♦ 2091 ♦ Northwest Folklife Festival
May, Memorial Day weekend

The Northwest Folklife Festival is an international four-day event started in 1972 in Seattle, Wash., that draws performers and artisans from Washington, Oregon, Idaho, Alaska, and the Canadian province of British Columbia. The emphasis is on amateur performers and ethnicity with some 100 countries represented. Events include music and dance on 17 stages; demonstrations by artisans of such skills as leather tanning, boatbuilding, blacksmithing, and broom making; and an International Food Village that offers food from more than 30 nations.

The festival spans the MEMORIAL DAY weekend, starting on Friday and winding up on Monday.

CONTACTS:
Northwest Folklife
158 Thomas St.
Ste. 32
Seattle, WA 98109
206-684-7300; fax: 206-684-7190
www.nwfolklife.org

♦ 2092 ♦ Norway Constitution Day (Syttende Mai)
May 17

May 17, 1814, marks both Norway's declaration of independence from Sweden and the day on which its constitution was signed. At that time, however, the king of Sweden still ruled Norway, and true independence didn't come until 1905, when the union with Sweden was dissolved and Norway chose its own king. Nevertheless, this day remains the great spring festival in Norway, and today it is celebrated primarily by young people.

The children's procession in Oslo, the capital city, is the largest of many school parades throughout the country. Marching behind their school bands and banners, the children pass under the balcony of the Royal Palace in salute to the king. Students who are about to graduate from secondary school and enter college cheer and spin their tasseled caps in the air on bamboo canes. In the afternoon, many neighborhoods have celebrations of their own so that children who are too young to participate in the school parades may march near their homes. Everyone joins in the procession, waving Norwegian flags, leading dogs, and pushing baby carriages. Eventually they congregate in the town square to listen to patriotic speeches and play games.

May 17 has been celebrated since the 1820s and is sometimes referred to as **Norway's National Day** or **Norway's Liberation Day**.

See also SYTTENDE MAI FEST.

CONTACTS:
Norwegian Ministry of Foreign Affairs
7. juni-plassen/ Victoria Terrasse
PO Box 8114 Dep.
Oslo, N-0032 Norway
47-2395-0000; fax: 47-2395-0099
www.regjeringen.no/en

♦ 2093 ♦ Nuestra Señora de Itatí
July 16

The town of Itatí is situated on the banks of Argentina's Paraná River. Two days before the well-known festival of Neustra Señora de Itatí, which is held on July 16, thousands of pilgrims begin to arrive from San Luis de Palmar in a seemingly endless procession of people on horseback, in carts, and on foot, carrying flags and an image of St. Louis. Festival goers arrive from all over Argentina as well, not only to honor Nuestra Señora but to enjoy the nightly festivities of drinking and games of chance.

Worship services take place on the 16th in the huge basilica that guards the copper statue of the Virgin, which is more than 24 feet high. Pilgrims even ascend up into the statue until their heads reach the Virgin's crown.

CONTACTS:
National Secretariat of Tourism, Tourist Information Centers

Av. Santa Fe 883
Buenos Aires, C1059ABC Argentina
54-11-4312-2232 or 800-555-0016; fax: 54-11-4302-7816
www.turismo.gov.ar/eng/menu.htm

♦ 2094 ♦ Nuestra Senora de Peñafrancia, Feast of
Third week of September

A grand fiesta devoted to Our Lady of Peñafrancia, held in Naga City on the Bicol peninsula in the Philippines. Some 200 years ago a Spanish official attributed the recovery of his ill daughter to the lady and built a shrine to her in Naga City, starting the devotion to her that has lasted into the present.

This is the biggest festival of the Bicol region; it starts with a nine-day novena at the Naga Cathedral. A procession then carries the image of the Virgin to a pagoda on a festooned barge, which is surrounded by a flotilla of smaller boats. The people on the smaller boats chant prayers and hymns as they proceed along the river. Meanwhile, on the shore, pilgrims from other Bicol provinces kneel and pray as the barge passes by. When the water-borne pagoda has finished its journey, there are shouts of "Viva la virgen!" and the image is taken back to its shrine.

CONTACTS:
Philippine Tourism Center
556 Fifth Ave.
New York, NY 10036
212-575-7915; fax: 212-302-6759
www.tourism.gov.ph

♦ 2095 ♦ Nuits de Fourvière
Late June to early September

The city of Lyon, France, was called "Lugdunum" in Roman times, and the city's old Roman theater, the Théâtre Romain de Fourvière, is still used for public performances. This large outdoor arena seats 3,000 people and is the principal venue in a summer festival known as the Nuits de Fourvière, or Nights of Fourvière. This festival includes music, ballet, and theater events. Musical performances range from opera and symphonic music, to world and pop music. The Nuits de Fourvière begins in June and ends in September, though most of the performances take place in July.

CONTACTS:
Les Nuits de Fourviere
1 Cléberg St.
Lyon, 69005 France
33-4-7257-1540; fax: 33-4-7257-1549
www.nuitsdefourviere.com

♦ 2096 ♦ Nunavut Day
July 9

In relation to Canada's other provincial holidays, Nunavut Day is a new observance because the territory of Nunavut is itself new. Canada's northernmost territory was established on July 9, 1993, through a land claim signed by the national government and the Inuit of the Nunavut Settlement Area. Territory leaders first designated Nunavut Day on April 1, but in 1999 they settled on the present date to commemorate the historic land agreement, which conferred self-governing powers to the territory.

Most of the day's activities take place in Nunavut's hub and capital city, Iqaluit. Festivities include barbeques, parades, traditional Inuit games, and feasts featuring local cuisine of caribou, walrus, and arctic char. In recent years, the day's program has also included organized tournaments of cribbage, checkers, and Scrabble.

CONTACTS:
Government of Nunavut
P.O. Box 1000
Stn 200
Iqaluit, NU X0A 0H0 Canada
867-975-6000 or 877-212-6438; fax: 867-975-6099
www.gov.nu.ca

♦ 2097 ♦ Nusardil
Seventh Sunday after Pentecost (June)

Assyrian Christians celebrate Nusardil to commemorate the church's baptism ceremony. But the origins of the ceremony are said to date to pre-Christian times. Assyrian pagans worshipped gods of fire, air, and water. Sprinkling water on the path of a pagan religious procession was a common practice meant to show respect. When St. Thomas converted the Assyrians to Christianity in the first century C.E., he resorted to a mass baptism because of the many people involved. His splashing of water on a crowd of people, combined with the earlier pagan tradition, led to the current practice.

Traditionally, Nusardil participants splash or spill water on each other in a ritualistic way. Even those not associated with the celebration may get splashed for fun. Today, children also use squirt guns or similar devices to spray water on each other and on their elders. While the ceremony has its serious side, it is also a lighthearted occasion. Assyrian churches in America will often have a picnic on Nusardil. Food and a variety of outdoor games are combined with the water splashing ceremony.

CONTACTS:
Holy Apostolic Catholic Assyrian Church of the East -
Archdiocese of Australia, New Zealand and Lebanon
P.O. Box 621
Fairfield, NSW 2165 Australia
612-9610-8680
assyrianchurch.org.au

♦ 2098 ♦ Nuuk Snow Festival
Third weekend in March

In 1994 the town of Nuuk, Greenland, held its first snow-sculpture festival. It has since become an annual event, scheduled for the third weekend in March. It attracts contestants from all over Greenland, as well as from Canada, the United States, Sweden, Norway, Finland, and Denmark.

Festival organizers give each team of sculptors a compressed block of snow. The teams then set to work, transforming the square block into an amazing variety of shapes. Their efforts are displayed in a sculpture park that is illuminated at night, creating beautiful lights and shadows on the sculptures. Prizes for the best sculptures are awarded on the fourth day of the festival.

CONTACTS:
Visit Greenland
Hans Egedesvej 29
P.O. Box 1615
Nuuk, 3900 Greenland
299-34-28-20
www.greenland.com/en

♦ 2099 ♦ NXNE (North by Northeast)
June

NXNE, or **North by Northeast,** is a five-day multimedia festival held in Toronto, Canada, that includes film, music, art, comedy, and interactive digital media. Since 1994, the event has brought together musicians, artists, comedians, and filmmakers from all over the world. NXNE is held in venues throughout downtown Toronto, including the public space of Yonge-Dundas Square, which features the main stage for headlining musicians. Volunteers largely run the festival—in 2012 over 1,000 volunteers helped to run NXNE.

CONTACTS:
NXNE
189 Church St.
Toronto, ON M5B 1Y7 Canada
416-863-6963; fax: 416-863-0828
nxne.com

♦ 2100 ♦ Nyambinyambi
Spring

The annual planting festival called the **Rain-Calling or Nyambinyambi,** is observed by the Kwangali people of Namibia, who believe that the land must be cleansed before the rain can fall and the fields can be planted. The chief sends his grandson out to cut down a tree, which is erected at the entrance gate to the village. The people lay their planting tools, seeds, pumpkins, and hunting weapons at the base of the tree and pray to the god known as Karunga, or Kalunga, to bring them a plentiful harvest and a good hunting season. In the Songhay's region of Niger, this is called **Genji Bi Hori**, "Black Spirit Festival." They also pray that rain will fall soon after the ceremony, which is believed to rid the country of bad luck.

The Songhay rain-bringing ceremony is held at the end of the hot dry season. Known as **Yenaandi** ("the act of cooling off") or the **Rain Dance**, it is usually held on a Thursday, the *Tooru* ("gods") sacred day, and is addressed to the four principal Tooru deities: Dongo, the god of thunder; Cirey, the god of lightning; Moussa Nyori, the god of clouds and wind; and Hausakoy, the god of blacksmithing.

♦ 2101 ♦ Nyepi
March

The people of Bali in Indonesia celebrate the Vernal Equinox and the New Year by driving the devils out of the villages and then observing a day of stillness, known as Nyepi or Njepi. It is believed that when spring arrives and the rainy season ends, the Lord of Hell, Yama, sweeps the devils out of Hades. The devils then fall on Bali, making it necessary to purify the entire island.

First the evil spirits are lured out of their hiding places with an elaborate offering of food, drink, money, and household utensils. Samples of every seed and fruit and of every animal used as food are all laid out in an eight-point star representing the Rose of the Winds. Then the evil spirits are driven out of the village by the strong incantations and curses of the priests, and by the people who run through the streets with their faces and bodies painted, lighting firecrackers, carrying torches, beating the trees and the ground, and banging drums, tin cans, and anything else they can find to make noise to drive the demons away. Animal sacrifices play an important role in the ceremony, because blood is believed to cleanse the impure earth.The following day, Nyepi, marks the start of the New Yearand the arrival of spring. It is observed with the suspension of all activity: no cooking or fires, no sexual intercourse, and no work of any kind are permitted.

O

♦ 2102 ♦ Oakley (Annie) Festival
July

The legendary markswoman known as Annie Oakley was born Phoebe Ann Moses near Willow Dell, Ohio, on August 13, 1860. Her father died when she was very young, and Annie learned to shoot game for her family with her father's rifle. At the age of 15 she was invited to participate in a shooting match in Cincinnati with Frank Butler, a champion marksman. She won the match and married Butler a year later. Together they toured the country with their shooting act, "Butler and Oakley," and in 1884 they joined Buffalo Bill's Wild West Show. They performed with the show throughout Europe and the United States for 17 years, including a command performance for Queen Victoria during her Jubilee year (1887). Annie and Frank returned to Ohio in the 1920s to be near their family and friends. She died in Greenville on November 3, 1926, and he died 18 days later.

The Annie Oakley Festival in Greenville commemorates "Little Miss Sure Shot" (as she was dubbed by the great Sioux Indian chief, Sitting Bull) with shooting and sports competitions and demonstrations of hide tanning, knife throwing, bead working, and other activities associated with the Old West. There is a tour of Annie Oakley's gravesite and a Miss Annie Oakley Shooting Contest for young girls. A highlight of the festival is the Annie Oakley Days Parade.

CONTACTS:
Darke County Visitors Bureau & Welcome Center
421 S. Broadway
Greenville, OH 45331 United States
937-548-5158 or 800-504-2995; fax: 937-548-2385
www.visitdarkecounty.org

♦ 2103 ♦ Oath Monday
July

A centuries-old custom in Ulm, Germany, that combines politics and pageantry. Each year in July, the bürgermeister, or mayor, gives a policy speech in the market square, listens to the public discussions, and then, after the ringing of a bell, takes an oath swearing to stand "for rich and poor" in all matters "of the public weal."

Events then shift to the Danube River and a waterborne parade called the *Nabada*. Rafts and boats are decorated with tableaux of papier-mâché figures that satirize local and regional politics. With them are floating bands and private boats. Later, back on land, a medieval pageant is presented.

The oath-taking began in 1397 when the city was on the verge of bankruptcy. The nobles, who had been running the city, agreed to sit down with representatives of the guilds—groups of merchants and craftsmen. At the close of the negotiations, the guilds had a majority on the city council, the citizens had the right to a hearing before major city decisions were made, and the Solemn Oath was established, ending the privileges of the aristocracy.

CONTACTS:
Tourist-Information Ulm/Neu-Ulm
Münsterplatz 50
Ulm, 89073 Germany
49-731-161-28-30; fax: 49-731-161-16-41
www.tourismus.ulm.de

♦ 2104 ♦ Oberammergau Passion Play
May through October, once every decade in years ending in zero

The most famous of Passion plays, held since the 17th century in the small woodcarving village of Oberammergau, Germany, in the Bavarian Alps.

The play, depicting the story of Christ's suffering, crucifixion, and resurrection, is presented in six hours by a cast of about 2,000. All performers are villagers, and the 600 with speaking parts are required to have been born in Oberammergau. The role of Mary is traditionally played by an unmarried woman. Close to half a million people attend the productions, which are staged in an open-air theater seating 5,000.

Legend says that the play was first performed in 1634 in fulfillment of a vow. The plague was sweeping Europe, and the Oberammergau elders swore to God that they would reenact the Passion of Christ if he would spare the remaining villagers; already a fifth of the population had been lost. The plague passed by, and the play has been performed since then (shifting to decennial years in 1700), except in 1870 during the Franco-Prussian War and during World War II. In modern times, the play has aroused protests that the 1860 text had anti-Semitic overtones. Director Christian Stückl and assistant director Otto Huber revised the text and music for the 2000 Passion Play in response to those concerns.

CONTACTS:
Tourist-Information Oberammergau
Eugen-Papst-Str. 9a
Oberammergau, Bavaria 82487 Germany
49-882-292-2740; fax: 49-882-292-2745
www.ammergauer-alpen.de

♦ 2105 ♦ **Obon Festival**
July 13-15; August 13-15

Also called the **Bon Festival** or **Festival of the Dead**, this is the time when the dead revisit the earth, according to Japanese Buddhist belief. Throughout Japan, in either July or August, depending on the area, religious rites and family reunions are held in memory of the dead.

On the first evening of the festival, small bonfires are lit outside homes to welcome the spirits of ancestors. A meal, usually vegetables, rice cakes, and fruit, is set out for the spirits, and for two days they are spoken to as though they were present. On the final day (July 15 or Aug. 15), farewell dumplings are prepared, and another bonfire is lit outside the house to guide the spirits back. The climax is the *Bon Odori*, "dance of rejoicing," folk dances held in every town by the light of paper lanterns, to comfort the souls of the dead. Some Bon-Odori dances are especially famous—one being the **Awa Odori** of Tokushima, which is accompanied by puppet shows and groups of musicians parading night and day.

At midnight some families gather the leftover rice cakes and food and take them to the waterfront. They are placed in a two- or three-foot-long boat made of rice straw with a rice straw sail; a lit paper lantern is on the bow and burning joss sticks at the stern. The breeze carries the boats, sustaining the spirits on their outward trip.

Obon celebrations are also held in Japanese communities throughout the world. About 500 people usually take part in the Bon-Odori in Chicago in July, and there are noted celebrations in several California cities.

♦ 2106 ♦ **Obzinky**
Late August or early September

There are two harvest celebrations in the Czech and Slovak Republics. One of them, known as **Posviceni**, is the church consecration of the harvest. The other, Obzinky, is a secular festival where the field workers celebrate the end of the harvest by making a wreath out of corn, ears of wheat or rye, and wildflowers. Sometimes the wreath is placed on the head of a pretty young girl, and sometimes it is placed in a wagon along with decorated rakes and scythes and pulled in procession to the home of the landowner. The laborers present the wreath and congratulate their employer on a good harvest,

after which they are invited to participate in dancing and feasting at the farm owner's expense. Foods served at the feast traditionally include roast pig, roast goose, and *Kolace*—square cakes filled with plum jam or a stuffing made from sweetened cheese or poppy seed. Beer and *slivovice*, a prune liquor, accompany the food.

The woman who binds the last sheaf is known as the *Baba* ("old woman") in some areas. In others, the Baba is a doll made from the last sheaf of grain and decorated with ribbons and flowers. Like the wreath, the Baba is carried in procession to the landlord's home, where it occupies a place of honor until the next harvest.

A similar harvest festival, known as the **Nubaigai,** is held in Lithuania. Here, too, a Baba is borne in procession to the farm; sometimes the worker who bound the last sheaf is wrapped up in it. But the harvest wreath is carried on a plate covered with a white linen cloth, and as the procession advances, the reapers sing an old song about how they rescued the crop from a huge bison that tried to devour it.

♦ 2107 ♦ **Octave of Our Lady, Consoler of the Afflicted**
April-May; third through fifth Sundays after Easter

The **Octave of Notre Dame la Consolatrice des Affligés** or **Our Lady of Luxembourg** is observed in Luxembourg beginning on the third Sunday after EASTER and lasting from eight to 15 days. Since 1666, when Luxembourg-Ville was dedicated to the patronage of Mary the Consolatrice and the keys of the city were entrusted to her statue in the cathedral, she has been regarded as the capital city's protector, and her festival is the country's most outstanding religious celebration. Colorful banners are hung across the streets, and the route of the procession is lined with fir trees. Brass bands, Boy Scouts, Girl Guides, school and church groups, and small children dressed as priests, bishops, and cardinals start the procession, scattering rose petals. The image of the Virgin follows, dressed in dark blue velvet embroidered with gold and jewels. The symbolic key of Luxembourg-Ville hangs from one of her wrists.

According to legend, the statue was discovered in a hollow oak in 1624 by some Jesuit students. They took it to the Jesuit college church (now the cathedral) and placed it on the altar. That night the figure vanished mysteriously and was later found in the oak. The same thing occurred a second time, at which point the church fathers realized that the Virgin wished to remain outside the fortress walls. They built a tiny chapel for the image in 1625, which became a pilgrimage center. The chapel was destroyed in the French Revolution, but the image was miraculously saved and eventually installed in the cathedral's main altar. When NAPOLEON I made his triumphal entry into the fortress after the Revolution, a little girl officially presented him with the keys on a crimson cushion. "Take them back," he told her. "They are in good hands.".

CONTACTS:
Luxembourg National Tourist Board
68-70, boulevard de la Pétrusse
Luxembourg
352-42-82-82-10; fax: 352-42-82-82-30
www.visitluxembourg.com/en

♦ 2108 ♦ October Feasts
October

The October Feasts have been held every year in the city of Guadalajara in the state of Jalisco, Mexico, since 1965. Throughout the month residents and visitors enjoy a variety of cultural events that celebrate local and international culture, including opera, jazz and other musical performances, art exhibits, folk dances, ballet, theater, and food. Attendees can also find amusement park rides, bungee jumping, and a haunted house billed as "one of the largest in Latin America.".

♦ 2109 ♦ October Horse Sacrifice
October 15

In ancient Rome, a chariot race was held in the Field of Mars on October 15. After the race was over, the right-hand horse of the winning chariot was killed as a sacrifice to Mars. The head was cut off first, and there was a fight between the inhabitants of two different quarters of the city to see who could seize the head and place it in a designated spot. As soon as the tail was cut off, it was rushed to the king's hearth so that the blood would fall on the hearth. The rest of the blood was preserved until April 21, when it was mixed with other blood in a special ceremony and given to shepherds to burn, since they believed that the smoke would purify their flocks (*see* PARILIA).

The symbolic elements of the October Horse Sacrifice—the race, the choice of the right-hand horse, the blood, the hearth, and the necklace of loaves that was hung around the horse's head—all have strong associations with fertility. Although the horse sacrifice may have started out as a fertility rite, it later became a martial one.

♦ 2110 ♦ October War of Liberation Anniversary
October 6

In Syria, the anniversary of the Arab-Israeli War of 1973 is celebrated on October 6, the day the hostilities started with a surprise attack by Syrian and Egyptian forces that caught the Israelis off guard during the Jewish fast of YOM KIPPUR. Although the Arab armies were turned back, they inflicted heavy casualties on Israel and reclaimed some of the land they had lost in the Six-Day War. Also known as **Tishrin**—after the month of October in which the war started—the celebration tends to play up the Arab soldiers' role in the war with special television broadcasts glorifying the conflict, art exhibits, plays, films, concerts, rallies, and wreath-laying ceremonies. No mention is made of the fact that 6,000 Syrians died in the conflict, or that Israeli troops reached the outskirts of Damascus.

In Egypt, October 6 is Armed Forces Day, commemorating the Egyptians' role in the October War. Anwar Sadat, the hero of that war, was assassinated on October 6, 1981, while viewing the Armed Forces Day parade.

See also ARMED FORCES DAY (EGYPT).

♦ 2111 ♦ Odalan (Temple's Birthday)
Various

Hindus in Bali, an island in Indonesia, celebrate the birthday of their local temple every 210 days. Odalans commemorate the anniversary of a temple's consecration. Because the Balinese Pawukon calendar is 210 days long, this happens roughly every seven months according to the Gregorian calendar. Most often, odalans last about three days, though the festivities can go on for a week or more.

Before an odalan, people are busy preparing food and other offerings and decorating the temple. An odalan consists of worship services, presentations of such offerings as food, money, and flowers in the temple, and special anointings. After religious services, there are huge feasts, music and dancing, and puppet plays.

♦ 2112 ♦ Odo Festival
December-August, biannually

The Odo festival marks the return of the dead (*odo*) to visit the living in the northern Igbo villages of Nigeria. Lasting in some places from December until August, the festival has three distinct stages: the arrival of the odo, their stay with the living, and their departure. The first stage is observed with ritual celebrations and festivities welcoming the returning spirits of the dead. Then there is a stretch of six or more months during which the spirits of the dead interact with their living relatives and visit their ancestral homes. Their final departure is a very emotional affair (*see* AWURU ODO FESTIVAL), since they will not return for two more years.

Odo plays, featuring certain stock characters identified by their costumes and the manner in which they interact with the audience, are usually performed at the return and staying stages of the odo journey. Most of the roles are played by men, while the women function as chorus members and sometimes as spectators. The performers wear costumes traditionally made from plant fiber, leaves, beads, and feathers, although more durable cloth costumes are becoming more common in contemporary Odo plays. A musical accompaniment, featuring xylophones, drums, and rattles, is known as *obilenu* music, meaning "that which lies above.".

♦ 2113 ♦ Odunde Festival
Early June

The Odunde Festival takes place annually on the streets of south Philadelphia over the second weekend in June. Odunde means "Happy New Year" in the language of the Yoruba people of Nigeria. A celebration of the African new year, the Odunde Festival centers on a vibrant procession to the Schuylkill River, where participants make offerings of flowers and fruit to the River Goddess Oshun. Oshun is one of 401 orishas, similar to Christian saints, revered in the Yoruba religion, Ifa. Drumming, singing, incantations, and prayers accompany the procession and offerings. All are welcome to take part in the parade and ceremonies.

The festival also features a wealth of entertainment, from rap to fashion shows to tap dancing to African dance. African-centered food, crafts, clothing, and jewelry are on offer. The festival also has incorporated such events as a reception for ambassadors and an African business symposium. Founded in 1975 with a $100 grant, the popular, free festival welcomes as many as 500,000 participants over its three days.

CONTACTS:
Odunde, Inc.
2308 Graysferry Ave.
P.O. Box 21748
Philadelphia, PA 19146
215-732-8510
odundefestival.org

♦ 2114 ♦ Odwira
September

Odwira is a celebration of national identity by the Akan or Asante people of Ghana, once known as the Gold Coast. The festival originated centuries ago as a time for people to assemble after the yam harvest, and was inaccurately called the Yam Festival by non-Africans.

The kingdom of Ashanti, which is now the region of Ashanti, became rich and powerful in the late 1600s under its first ruler, Asantehene ("King") Osei Tutu. He is believed to have initiated the festival with the additional purpose of reinforcing the loyalty of the subjugated chiefs. The nation he built up withstood the British until 1901. He built a palace at Kumasi, and to further strengthen the nation, he and a priest, Okomfo Anokye, introduced the legendary Golden Stool. Supposed to have been brought down from heaven, it was thought to enshrine the nation's soul and became a symbol of the bond between all Ashanti people. Tutu also set down laws for life and religion. Much of this culture still survives.

During Odwira, the national identity is reinforced with purification ceremonies: a priest in each town prepares a purification bundle of certain tree branches and shoots, and in the evening carries it out of town and buries it. The Golden Stool is carried in a procession and placed on a throne without touching the ground. Huge umbrellas to protect participants from the sun add to the color of the procession. Drums and horns provide music.

CONTACTS:
Ministry of Tourism & Diasporan Relations, Ghana Tourist Board
P.O. Box 4386
Ghana
233-302-666314; fax: 233-302-244611
www.touringghana.com

♦ 2115 ♦ Ohio River Sternwheel Festival
September, weekend after Labor Day

A sternwheeler is a boat propelled by a paddle wheel at the stern or rear of the vessel. At one time they were a common sight along the Ohio River, although many have fallen into decay or have been turned into floating restaurants.

The riverfront town of Marietta, Ohio, is home to two of the sternwheelers that remain in working order and is the site of an annual Sternwheel Festival celebrating the heyday of the riverboat during the 19th century. Anywhere from 25 to 30 sternwheelers arrive in Marietta during the first week in September for the festival, which begins on the Friday after LABOR DAY.

Outdoor concerts, calliope music, entertainment by singers and dancers, and the crowning of Queen Genevieve of the River take place on Saturday, and on Sunday there are sternwheel races. Two of the largest and best-known sternwheelers, the *Delta Queen* and the *River Queen*, participate in the festival every year.

CONTACTS:
Ohio River Sternwheel Festival
P.O. Box 2109
Marietta, OH 45750 United States
800-288-2577
www.ohioriversternwheelfestival.org

♦ 2116 ♦ Oklahoma Day
April 22

After forcing the Indians to move west of the Mississippi River during the early decades of the 19th century, Congress set aside a vast area including all of what is now Oklahoma and called it the Indian Territory, telling them the land would be theirs forever. But eventually the U.S. government reneged on its policy in response to pressure from railroad companies and land-hungry homesteaders. Part of the Indian Territory was opened to white settlement by allowing "land runs," in which homesteaders raced across the border to stake their claim to 160-acre plots offered free of charge. Those who managed to sneak across the line before the official opening were called "sooners," which is how Oklahoma came to be nicknamed "the Sooner State." The land run of April 22, 1889, paved the way for the organization of the Oklahoma Territory in 1890, and for Oklahoma's statehood in 1907.

Also known as **Oklahoma 89ers Day**, the celebrations on April 22 focus on the town of Guthrie, the site of the original land office about 80 miles from the starting border. In 1915, the "89ers," as the original participants came to be called, reenacted the land rush, and each year Guthrie observes its anniversary with an 89ers festival. Elsewhere in Oklahoma, the day is celebrated with parades, rodeos, and events based on the land rush theme.

See also CHEROKEE STRIP DAY.

CONTACTS:
Oklahoma Historical Society
Oklahoma History Center
800 Nazih Zuhdi Dr.
Oklahoma City, OK 73105
405-521-2491
www.okhistory.org

Guthrie Chamber Of Commerce
212 W. Oklahoma Ave.
Guthrie, OK 73044
405-282-1947 or 800-299-1889
www.guthrieok.com

♦ 2117 ♦ Oklahoma Historical Day
October 10

The early history of Oklahoma is replete with stories about a French family named Chouteau. Major Jean Pierre Chouteau and his half-brother, René Auguste, monopolized the fur trade with the Indians, and in 1796 Chouteau established the first permanent non-Indian settlement within the boundaries of what is now Oklahoma when he built a cabin to serve as a headquarters and trading post in Salina. Chouteau's birthday, October 10, became a legal holiday known as Oklahoma-Historical Day in 1939, and a major annual celebration, also called **Chouteau Day**, is held in Salina each year, though it is no longer a state holiday.

CONTACTS:
Oklahoma History Center
800 Nazih Zuhid Dr.
Oklahoma City, OK 73105
405-521-2491; fax: 405-522-5402
www.okhistory.org

♦ 2118 ♦ Okmulgee Pecan Festival
Third weekend in June

The Okmulgee Pecan Festival is a nutty festival in Okmulgee, Okla., that made the *Guinness Book of World Records* in 1988 for the world's largest pecan pie. The pie had a diameter of 40 feet, and it weighed about 16 1/2 tons. Even with the help of the culinary arts department of the Oklahoma State University Technical Branch in Okmulgee, this was an enormous task. So in 1990 the big event was a pecan cookie with a diameter of 32 feet and a weight of 7,500 pounds. That was a bit of a chore, too. In 1991, it was decided to keep it simple and celebrate with the "World's Largest Pecan Cookie and Ice Cream Party." More than 15,000 cookies and 5,000 single servings of vanilla ice cream were served.

Okmulgee, a name that means "bubbling waters" in the Creek language, is the capital of the Creek Nation. It is also an area that raises a lot of pecans; some 600 acres near Okmulgee are devoted to growing pecans. The festival began in 1984 and has been voted one of the top 10 festivals in the state. Besides

large pecan concoctions, it offers a carnival, a pecan bake-off, a pie-throwing booth, arm-wrestling contests, the crowning of a Pecan Prince and Princess, and a turtle race.

CONTACTS:
City of Okmulgee The Chamber of Commerce
112 N. Morton
Okmulgee, OK 74447
918-756-6172; fax: 918-756-6441
www.okmulgeeonline.com

♦ 2119 ♦ Okpesi Festival
September

The Igbo people of Nigeria believe that failure to perform this annual rite will bring bad luck not only to the individual but to the entire community. It must be carried out by every male child whose father has died, for it is a ceremony in honor of the Igbo ancestors, or *ndioki*. Also known as **Itensi**, the ritual begins with a blood sacrifice of cocks, after which the blood is spread on wooden altars built specifically for the purpose. The sacrifice is followed by a feast during which communion is achieved both among the living and between the living and the dead.

See also ODO FESTIVAL.

♦ 2120 ♦ Oktoberfest
Late September through early October

The first Oktoberfest was held on October 12, 1810, in honor of the marriage of Crown Prince Ludwig of Bavaria to Princess Therese von Saxony-Hildburghausen. Since that time it has become, above all else, a celebration of German beer. The Lord Mayor of Munich, Germany, opens the first barrel, and the 16-day festival begins. Both citizens and tourists flock to this event, which is marked by folk costume parades in which brewery horses draw floats and decorated beer wagons through the streets. Oktoberfest celebrations modeled on the German festival are also held in cities throughout the United States.

CONTACTS:
Munich Tourist Office
Sendlinger St. 1
Munich, 80331 Germany
49-89-233-96-500; fax: 49-89-233-30-233
www.munich-tourist.de

♦ 2121 ♦ Okunchi Matsuri
October 7-9

Regarded as among the most unusual festivals in Japan, the Okunchi Festival in Nagasaki dates back to the 17th century, when many Chinese lived in the city and when both Dutch and Chinese traders regularly anchored their ships there. For many years, the ruling shogun of Japan barred foreigners from other Japanese ports, and the few Dutch and Chinese ships that were allowed to stop in Nagasaki were the country's only point of contact with the non-Japanese world. The

Okunchi Festival pays tribute to these traders by presenting both a Dutch dance and a Chinese dragon dance, along with processions, street fairs, and other entertainment.

The Dutch and Chinese dances are performed in an open area at the beginning of the many stairs that go to the Suwa Shrine. Civic authorities and priests view the ceremony from the stairs, while the rest of the audience sits on risers flanking the performance area. Two young women execute the Dutch dance, one of whom wears a false mustache and plays the part of a man. The two dancers bend at the waist, exchange coy smiles, and flirt with each other, to the amusement of the crowd. The Chinese dance features four dragons made out of cloth stretched over flexible frames. Each dragon conceals about a dozen dancers, who help it "dance" with snakelike motions by maneuvering the black rods attached to its body. The dragon dance reenacts the legendary battle between darkness, symbolized by the dragon, and light, symbolized by the sun—a golden globe atop a long pole. Needless to say, the sun always wins.

In addition to the dances, the Okunchi Festival also features the traditional procession of the *mikoshi*—the ornate palanquin on which the local deity is believed to descend for a ride as it is carried through the streets. The festival ends when the empty mikoshi returns to the shrine after the god has departed.

A similar Okunchi Festival is held at the end of October in Karatsu in Saga Prefecture.

CONTACTS:
Japan National Tourist Organization
1 Grand Central Pl. 60 E. 42nd St.
Ste. 448
New York, NY 10165
212-757-5640; fax: 212-307-6754
www.jnto.go.jp

♦ 2122 ♦ Old Christmas Day
January 6 or 7

In addition to being the Feast of the EPIPHANY, January 6 is known as Old Christmas Day. When England and Scotland switched over from the Julian to the Gregorian calendar in 1752, 11 days were dropped to make up for the calendar discrepancy that had accumulated with the use of the Julian calendar. In all subsequent years, CHRISTMAS arrived 11 days early. Many people, especially in rural areas, had trouble accepting the loss of these 11 days, and continued to recognize the holidays of the Julian calendar as Old Christmas, Old CANDLEMAS, Old MIDSUMMER DAY, etc. Russians and Ukrainians celebrate this holiday on January 7.

See also CHRISTMAS (RUSSIAN ORTHODOX).

♦ 2123 ♦ Old Fiddler's Convention
Second week in August

A five-day concert in the small town of Galax, Va., the Old Fiddler's Convention spotlights old-time music in an out-

door setting. The convention was organized in 1935 as a fundraising event by members of Moose Lodge No. 733 and was dedicated to "keeping alive the memories and sentiments of days gone by." About 25,000 people now attend.

Hundreds of contestants take part, competing for cash prizes and trophies in categories that include guitar, mandolin, dulcimer, dobro, clawhammer and bluegrass banjo, clog or flatfoot dancing, and folk singing.

CONTACTS:
Old Fiddler's Convention
P.O. Box 655
Galax, VA 24333
276-236-8541
www.oldfiddlersconvention.com

♦ 2124 ♦ Old Pecos Bull and Corn Dance
August 2

On the **Feast of Porcingula** (named after the shrine of their patron saint, Santa Maria de los Angeles, in Portiuncula, Italy), Indians at the Jemez Pueblo in New Mexico hold a celebration that combines both traditional Indian and Roman Catholic elements. On August 1, the day before the feast, six Indian priests wearing white shirts and trousers with red headbands and sashes come out of the ceremonial kiva and circle the plaza, chanting. Then the dancers are summoned to the kiva to prepare for the next day's corn dance.

On August 2, a mass is sung in honor of Santa Maria de los Angeles, after which the priest of Jemez accompanies her image to the shrine that has been set up for her in the plaza. The Pecos "bull," named after the people who were forced to abandon the Pecos Pueblo in favor of Jemez in 1838, is really a dancer carrying a framework that resembles a bull. Throughout the two days of the festival, the bull is prodded with sticks and tormented in mock bullfights. The men and boys who play the role of matador are less than flattering in their imitations of white men, which usually draw laughs from the spectators. There is a feast for the bull and the bullfighters, and after that the corn dance is performed before Santa Maria's shrine.

CONTACTS:
Department of Tourism, Jemez Pueblo
7413 Hwy. 4
Jemez Pueblo, NM 87024
575-834-7235
www.jemezpueblo.com

♦ 2125 ♦ Old Saybrook Torchlight Parade and Muster
Second Saturday night in December

In 1970 the Colonial Saybrook Fifes and Drums, under the leadership of Bill Reid, revived the tradition of a CHRISTMAS torchlight parade. In early December each year, in colonial America, the village militia would muster with their fifes and drums and march to the town green carrying torches and lanterns. When they heard the fifes and drums pass, the townspeople would follow behind the militia, also carrying torches and lanterns, to the green where a community meeting and carol sing would take place. It is thought that the event originally commemorated ADVENT.

Old Saybrook, Connecticut (population 10,000), is located at the mouth of the Connecticut River on Long Island Sound and was settled in 1635. It is the only community in the United States that is known to have revived this tradition.

The modern-day procession follows the traditional ritual with no less than 58 fife and drum corps from as far away as Virginia, New Jersey, and New York made up of 35 people per unit on average, plus support groups. The corps are sometimes led by Santa Claus himself and the marchers often augment their colonial-style costumes with seasonal decorations. For example, Christmas lights sparkle on tricornered hats, and silver tinsel hangs from flintlock rifles. The fifes and drums play not only colonial martial music but also the joyous and peaceful songs of Christmas. Citizens of the town and thousands of visitors join the march carrying torches and lanterns to the town green for a community carol sing led by the high school band.

CONTACTS:
Old Saybrook Chamber of Commerce
1 Main St.
Old Saybrook, CT 06475
860-388-3266; fax: 860-388-9433
www.oldsaybrookchamber.com

♦ 2126 ♦ Old Silvester
December 31, January 13

The custom known as **Silvesterklausen** in the small town of Urnäsch in Appenzell Outer Rhoden Canton, Switzerland, is performed both on December 31, *New* Silvester Day (ST. SYL-VESTER'S DAY), and on January 13, or *Old* Silvester Day. (The two dates reflect the change from the Julian, or Old Style, calendar to the Gregorian, or New Style, calendar in 1582.)

The men of the village, wearing masks, costumes, and heavy harnesses with bells, traditionally walk in groups from house to house—or, in the surrounding countryside, from one farm to the next—singing wordless yodels. The friends and neighbors who receive them offer them a drink before they move on to the next house. The yodelers are usually so well disguised that their neighbors don't recognize them.

♦ 2127 ♦ Old Spanish Days
Early August

This five-day fiesta held in Santa Barbara, California, in early August draws heavily on the area's Spanish-American and Mexican-American heritage. The celebration begins with the Fiesta Pequeña, or "Little Festival," on the steps of the Santa Barbara Mission, the 10th of the 21 Spanish missions built in California by Fray Junípero Serra and his successors. The opening ceremonies include Spanish and Mexican songs and dances, the traditional fiesta blessing, and the introduction of ST. BARBARA, who is portrayed by a local citizen. The next

few days are filled with flamenco guitarists, Mexican folklore dancers, and other performances at the Lobero Theatre, the site of the first Old Spanish Days festival in 1924.

The highlight of the week is the historical parade, featuring floats that depict various episodes in Santa Barbara's history, marching bands and precision drill teams, costumed flower girls, and horses in ornate silver trappings. Other popular events include the children's parade and the rodeo and stock horse show.

CONTACTS:
Old Spanish Days in Santa Barbara, Inc.
129 Castillo St.
P.O. Box 21557
Santa Barbara, CA 93101
805-962-8101 or 805-965-3021
www.oldspanishdays-fiesta.org

♦ 2128 ♦ Oldenburg International Film Festival
September

The five-day Oldenburg International Film Festival is regarded as one of the most offbeat events in Europe with eclectic, innovative films from across the world. Launched in 1994, the festival takes place in September each year at Oldenburg in northwestern Germany. Dubbed by the media as the European Sundance, an allusion to the famous American independent film festival, Oldenburg showcases filmmaking that goes far beyond typical blockbuster and box office fare. The Oldenburg is probably the only festival in the world that screens part of its program in a local prison, where convicts and glitterati together share the cinematic experience.

The audience votes for the independent feature and short film that will receive the German Independence Award. The best actor is honored with the Seymour Cassel Award. In 1994, Oldenburgische Landesbank (OLB), a German bank and longtime sponsor, added glamour to the festival with the OLB Walk of Fame, where film luminaries walk a starlit path inside the bank.

CONTACTS:
Internationales Filmfest Oldenburg
Bahnhofstr, 15
Oldenburg, D-26122 Germany
49-441-925-08-55; fax: 49-441-939-255-24
www.filmfest-oldenburg.de/en

♦ 2129 ♦ Older Persons, International Day of
October 1

The UNITED NATIONS General Assembly decided to set aside October 1 as International Day for the Elderly in 1990 (later designated as the International Day of Older Persons), at which time it asked its member nations to contribute to the Trust Fund for Ageing, which supports projects in developing countries that benefit the elderly.

By designating a day when governments are supposed to focus on what they can do to provide for the elderly, the U.N. hopes not only to forestall problems related to the aging of the population but to focus attention on the promise that a maturing population holds for social, economic, cultural, and spiritual undertakings. The United Nations also set aside the year 1999 as the International Year of Older Persons.

CONTACTS:
United Nations, Department of Public Information
Rm. S-1070L
New York, NY 10017
212-963-6842; fax: 212-963-6914
www.un.org

♦ 2130 ♦ Old-Time Country Music Contest and Festival, National
September, week before Labor Day

Created by Bob Everhart as part of America's bicentennial celebration in 1976, the National Old-Time Country Music Contest and Festival in Avoca, Iowa, is now the largest gathering of public domain music-makers and listeners in the United States.

Sponsored by the National Traditional Country Music Association, the festival's purpose is to preserve the music that, in Everhart's words, has been "prostituted, violated, diluted, and in many instances altered so dramatically that it is no longer recognizable as a traditional American art form." There are more than 30 competitions in such varied musical genres as ragtime, polka, Cajun, mountain, folk, cowboy, Western, swing, yodeling, and gospel. The festival also includes songwriting contests and the National Bluegrass Band Championships. Non-musical events include storytelling and cowboy poetry contests and arts and crafts displays.

CONTACTS:
National Traditional Country Music Association
P.O. Box 492
650 Main St.
Anita, IA 50020
712-762-4363
www.ntcma.net

♦ 2131 ♦ Oldtime Fiddlers' Contest and Festival, National
Third full week in June

The National Oldtime Fiddlers' Contest and Festival is a major musical event in the United States, held for a full week in Weiser, Idaho, where fiddling was first heard in 1863. A way station was established that year at Weiser, and people traveling through in covered wagons stopped for rest and recreational fiddling. In 1914, the first fiddling contest was held, but interest petered out until 1953 when Blaine Stubblefield, a fiddle fan and member of the local chamber of commerce, initiated a fiddling competition. In 1963, in conjunction with Idaho's Centennial, the competition officially became the National Oldtime Fiddlers' Contest.

Awards are given for the national champion in several categories; this is big-time fiddling, with contestants having won their spot through competitions in other states. Besides

music, there is a fiddlers parade, street dancing, and sing-alongs; another attraction is the National Fiddlers' Hall of Fame here. Attendance is about 10,000.

CONTACTS:
National Oldtime Fiddlers Inc.
2235 Paddock Ave.
P.O. Box 447
Weiser, ID 83672
208-414-0255; fax: 208-414-0256
www.fiddlecontest.org

♦ 2132 ♦ Ole Time Fiddlers and Bluegrass Festival
May, Memorial Day Weekend

A festival for genuinely old-time fiddlers, the Ole Time Fiddlers and Bluegrass Festival is held at Fiddler's Grove Campground in Union Grove, N.C. The festival was organized in 1970 by Harper A. Van Hoy as a serious musical venture, and admission is limited to 5,000 people to attract those who want to hear what Van Hoy has called the "purest mountain music this side of the Mississippi."

A special contest category is for fiddlers who must meet these criteria: they are over 55 years old, have had no formal musical training, and have learned from fiddlers older than themselves. There are competitions for all the major instruments of traditional American music, including autoharp, banjo, fiddle, harmonica, and mandolin. Workshops are conducted for most of the instruments played in competition, as well as in shape-note singing, storytelling, clog dancing, and children's folk music. Additionally, there are arts and crafts and food.

CONTACTS:
Fiddler's Grove Festival
1819 W. Memorial Hwy.
Union Grove, NC 28689
704-682-1350
www.fiddlersgrove.com

♦ 2133 ♦ Olney White Squirrel Count
October

The community of Olney, Ill., boasts a population of rare white squirrels. It is believed that the animals first appeared in the area just after the American Civil War. For many years, the city in southern Illinois has been concerned with preserving the squirrels. Ordinances prohibit cats and dogs, the squirrels' natural enemies, from running loose. Feeding stations have been set up in residential neighborhoods where the squirrel population is high. Laws give the squirrels the right-of-way on city streets, while residents are fined if they try to leave town with one of the animals.

Every year an official count is done to determine how the white squirrel population is surviving. No actual count as such is conducted. Rather, professors from nearby Central College, with the help of volunteers, try to gauge whether the number of animals is increasing or decreasing and whether any migration is taking place. The numbers have varied over the years. Most observers tend to believe that the white squirrel population has increased not only in the town of Olney, but in the surrounding countryside as well. The annual count was brought to national attention in 2002 during the 100-Year White Squirrel Celebration. In addition to the annual count, the event included a parade, a 5K race, the dedication of a statue to the white squirrel, and an official blessing of the animal.

CONTACTS:
City of Olney
300 S. Whittle Ave.
Olney, IL 62450
618-395-7302; fax: 618-395-7304
www.ci.olney.il.us

◆ 2134 ◆ Olympic Games
Winter Games every four years (2018, 2022, 2026…); Summer Games every four years 2016, 2020, 2024…)

The world's oldest sports spectacular, the first known Olympiad was held in 776 B.C.E. in Olympia, Greece. It is believed the festivals began before 1400 B.C.E. The modern games, which until recently were held roughly every four years in different countries, were revived in 1896 by Baron Pierre de Coubertin of France. Those 1896 summer games took place in Athens, with 13 nations sending about 300 male athletes to compete in 42 events and 10 different sports. Now nearly 200 nations send thousands of male and female athletes to the Olympics, and hundreds of millions watch the events on television. Some winter sports were included in early years of the modern Olympics, but the Winter Games as a separate event didn't begin until 1924.

In ancient Greece, four national religious festivals—the Olympic Games, the PYTHIAN GAMES, the NEMEAN GAMES, and the ISTHMIAN GAMES—were major events; the Olympic Games, honoring Zeus, were especially famous. Records tell of Olympic Games every four years from 776 B.C.E. to 217 C.E. when, with Greece under Roman domination, the games had lost their religious purpose and the athletes vied only for money. They were abolished by the Roman emperor, Theodosius I. It is generally believed, however, that the festival consisted not only of sporting contests, but of the presentation of offerings to Zeus and other gods. At first, these were simple foot races; later the long jump, discus and javelin-throwing, wrestling, boxing, *pancratium* (a ferocious combination of boxing and wrestling), and chariot racing were added. Poets and dramatists also presented works. The games opened with trumpet fanfares and closed with a banquet.

Modern Olympics comprise Summer Games, held in a large city, and Winter Games, held at a resort. Since 1994, the games are still on a four-year cycle, but two years apart: Winter Games in 2014, 2018, 2022, etc., and Summer Games in 2012, 2016, 2020, etc. There are 41 approved sports for the Summer Games. The Winter Games consist of 15 approved sports.

Today, the opening ceremonies highlight a parade of the athletes led by those from Greece, in honor of the original Games, followed by the athletes from the other nations, in alphabetical order according to the spelling in the country's language; the host country enters last.

After the Games are declared open, the dramatic lighting of the Olympic flame occurs. A cross-country relay runner carries a torch first lit in Olympia, and ignites the flame that burns for the 15-16 days of the games. Thousands of runners, representing each country between Greece and the host country, take part in the four-week torch relay. This is followed by a spectacular production of fireworks, strobe lights, fly-overs, music, dance, and assorted entertainment.

The Winter Games of 1992, held in Albertville, France, were historic in their reflection of dramatic political changes. The Soviet Union had broken up in August 1991, and athletes from five former Soviet republics competed as representatives of the Commonwealth of Independent States or United Team, and the Olympic flag, not that of the U.S.S.R., was raised for the winners.

The first and second-place medals are both made of silver but the first place has a wash of gold; the third-place medal is bronze.

The Olympics are supposed to be nonpolitical but have been marked (and marred) by politics. In 1936, Adolf Hitler, who called blacks an inferior race, opened the Olympics in Berlin, Germany, as a propaganda show. It was thus a great triumph for humanity when Jesse Owens, a black man from Ohio State University, won four gold (first place) medals. He won the 100- and 200-meter dashes and the running broad jump, and was on the winning 400-meter relay team. Hitler ducked out of the stadium so he wouldn't have to congratulate Owens.

In 1972, the Games in Munich, Germany, were struck with horror when 11 Israeli athletes were killed by Arab terrorists.

The 1980 Games were opened in Moscow by Communist Party chairman Leonid I. Brezhnev, but athletes from the United States, Canada, West Germany, Japan and 50 other countries didn't participate. Their countries boycotted the event in protest of the Soviet invasion of Afghanistan. Terrorism again struck the Games in Atlanta in 1996.

Prominent Olympics participants have included:

Jim Thorpe, an American Indian and one of the greatest all-round athletes of all time, won gold medals for the decathlon and pentathlon in 1912. The following year, he was stripped of the medals when an investigation showed he had played semiprofessional baseball. He died in 1953, and the medals were restored to his family in 1982.

Paavo Nurmi, known as the "Flying Finn," won nine gold medals in long-distance running in three Olympics—in 1920, 1924, and 1928. On an extremely hot day at the Paris Summer Games in 1924, Nurmi set Olympic records in the 1,500-meter and 5,000-meter runs. Two days later, he won the 10,000-meter cross-country race. In 1928, he set a record for the one-hour run, covering 11 miles and 1,648 yards. His

1924 wins were considered the greatest individual performance in the history of track and field.

The Norwegian skater Sonja Henie won three gold medals—in 1928, 1932, and 1936. In 1924, at the age of 11, she was the youngest Olympian contestant ever (she finished last that year). She thrilled crowds by incorporating balletic moves into what had been standard skating exercises.

Emil Zatopek, a Czech long-distance runner, won three gold medals in 1952 and set Olympic records for the 5,000- and 10,000-meter races and for the marathon.

Larisa Latynina, a gymnast from the Ukraine, won 18 Olympic medals over the course of three consecutive Olympics (1956, 1960, 1964) and held the record for most medals for 48 years until surpassed by American swimmer Michael Phelps in 2012. With her nine gold metals, Latynina stands among the greatest Olympians. Her record for individual event medals still stands at 14.

Jean-Claude Killy, known as "Le Superman" in his native France, won three gold medals in Alpine ski events at Grenoble, France, in 1968.

Mark Spitz, a swimmer from California, became the first athlete to win seven gold medals in a single Olympics (1972). He set world records in four individual men's events, and won the remaining medals in team events. These teams also set world records. Spitz, 22 at the time, was so popular for a while that his photo was a pinup poster.

Michael Phelps turned in an even more spectacular performance. At the 2004 Olympics he won six gold medals, but that was just the warm up. In 2008, he set a new record by winning eight gold medals—in the 100- and 200-meter butterfly; the 200-meter freestyle; the 200- and 400-meter individual medley; the 4x100-meter medley relay; and the 4x100- and 4x200-meter freestyle relay. He set new world records in seven of those events, all but the 100-meter butterfly. At this third Olympics in 2012, Michael Phelps won four more gold medals, one each for the 100-meter butterfly, the 200-meter medley, the 4x200-meter freestyle, and the 4x100-meter medley. His total of 22 Olympic medals, including 18 gold medals, earned him the distinction of being the most decorated Olympian of all time.

Also in 2012, Usain Bolt helped his Jamaican relay teammates breaking the world record for the 4x100-meter for the second time–the first was in 2008. The legendary sprinter set an Olympic record for the 100-meter, with a time of 9.63 seconds, and increased his medal total to six gold medals won in two Olympic appearances.

See also CULTURAL OLYMPIAD.

CONTACTS:
International Olympic Committee
Chateau de Vidy
Case postale 356
Lausanne, 1001 Switzerland
41-21-621-6111; fax: 41-21-621-6216
www.olympic.org

Olympic Museum
1, quai d'Ouchy
Lausanne, 1006 Switzerland
41-21-621-6511
www.olympic.org/museum

♦ 2135 ♦ **Omak Stampede and Suicide Race**
Second weekend in August

The Omak Stampede and Suicide Race includes three days of professional rodeo in Omak, Wash. What makes this different from other rodeos is the World Famous Suicide Race which was featured on the 1980s television program, "Ripley's Believe It or Not." This is a terrifying hoof-thundering gallop by 15-20 mounted horses down an almost vertical hill, across the Okanogan River, and then into the rodeo arena. Four of these races are held, one after each rodeo performance.

The rodeos top off a week of activities which include Indian ceremonies, dances, and stick games, a type of gambling, at an Indian teepee village. (Much of the town of Omak is on the Colville Indian Reservation; the name Omak comes from the Indian word *omache*, meaning "good medicine.") Other events are a Not Quite White Water Raft Race, a western art show, a grand parade, a kiddies' parade, and dances. Attendance is 20,000 to 30,000.

Animal rights activists have protested the race because of the extreme danger to the horses. Since 1983, at least 15 horses have died in the race or been euthanized after injuries sustained in the race.

CONTACTS:
Progressive Animal Welfare Society
15305 44th Ave. W.
Lynnwood, WA 98087
425-787-2500; fax: 425-742-5711
www.paws.org

♦ 2136 ♦ **Oman National Day**
November 18-19

This holiday in Oman observes the birthday of Sultan Qaboos Bin Said (b. 1940) on November 18, but festive events continue through the 19th as well. His accession to the throne took place on July 23, 1970. National Day events include parades, pageantry, an equestrian show, a marine festival, fireworks, and, every five years, an elaborate military show.

CONTACTS:
Embassy Of Oman Cultural Division
8381 Old Courthouse Rd.
Ste. 130
Vienna, VA 22182
571-722-0000; fax: 571-722-0001
www.omani.info

♦ 2137 ♦ **Ombashira Matsuri**
Early April to mid-May, every six years

This ceremony, which takes place in Suwa, Japan, and represents a symbolic rebuilding of the Suwa-taisha Shrine, has four parts. The first is called *Yamadashi*, "taking the tree from the forest," a spirited event in which many people participate in cutting down a large fir tree, known as *ombashira*. The second part is *Satobiki*, "parading it through the streets." Men dressed as *daimyo*, or feudal lords, march in this parade, singing special woodcutters' folk songs known as *min'yo*. In the third part of the ceremony, known as *Kawawatashi*, the tree is carried across the river. In the festival's grand finale, called *Hikitaté*, the log is planted upright at a corner of the four shrines by tying ropes to the top and pulling it until it is vertical.

This event takes place once in six years, in the Year of the Monkey and the Year of the Tiger. Because felling the tree and transporting it to the shrine is a long process, the festival begins in early April and ends in the middle of May.

CONTACTS:
Japan National Tourist Organization
1 Grand Central Pl. 60 E. 42nd St.
Ste 448
New York, NY 10165
212-757-5640; fax: 212-307-6754
www.jnto.go.jp

♦ 2138 ♦ **Omisoka**
December 31

New Year's Eve in Japan is observed by settling financial accounts (*kake*), eating a special noodle dish known as *okake*, which is hot soup over noodles, and taking a hot bath followed by a well-earned rest. Widely celebrated on December 31, Omisoka marks the end of the preparations for New Year's celebrations, which go on for the next three days. It is a popular time for visitors to drop in to exchange New Year's greetings over cups of hot sake and decorated *mochi* cakes.

The city of Ashikaga, 50 miles north of Tokyo, is the site of the 1,200-year-old Saishoji temple, headquarters for the Akutai Matsuri, the "naughty festival," or "festival of abusive language." On New Year's Eve there, participants walk (or take a bus) up a dark mountain road led by a man blowing a *horagai*, a shell that is supposed to fend off bad tidings. Some carry lanterns and wear cardboard hats bearing the picture of Bishamonten, one of the seven gods of fortune in Japanese Buddhism. The Saishoji temple was built in honor of this god.

The festival originated more than 200 years ago so repressed workers could let off steam; therefore, this is not simply a midnight stroll. Those hiking toward the temple atop the 1,000-foot-high hill scream curses into the night. They curse politicians, teachers, bad grades, low pay, and any other complaints of modern daily life in Japan. They release pent-up frustrations with words they ordinarily would not say directly to anyone. *Bakayaro* is one of the words most frequently heard. It means, roughly, "you idiot."

After the 40-minute walk the crowd storms into the temple, the bell is rung, prayers are offered, and the cursing continues. But when the new year arrives at midnight, the curses

end and more typical celebration begins. Then the celebrants turn to another unique ceremony: when the priest calls the name of each worshipper, the individual kneels with a wide red lacquer bowl at his or her lips. Sake is then poured onto the person's forehead, runs across his or her face, into the bowl and is consumed. All this occurs while the priest reads the worshipper's personal wishes for the new year to the pounding of a taiko drum. This ceremony is supposed to ensure that happiness will flow in the new year.

On Omisoka, people wearing kimonos fill the streets as they go to visit shrines. But millions watch the "Red and White Song Contest" on TV. This marathon song festival, first organized in 1950, has become an indispensable ritual of the New Year. The show, lasting up to four hours, usually has 50 performers, 25 on each team. The Red team is comprised of women, the White team men. When the performances are over, the audience and a panel of judges decide which team won. Typical past performances include an orchestra playing Mozart and a group singing Okinawan folk music; a bit less typical was a female singer in a gown of feathers that made her look like a bird; as she finished her song she flapped her arms and flew away, suspended by a wire.

The TV show ends shortly before midnight in time for an older tradition: the tolling of the great bells in Buddhist temples at midnight. Priests strike the bells 108 times, a reminder of the 108 human frailties or sins in Buddhist belief. By the end of the 108 strokes of the bell, the impure desires of the old year have been driven away.

An ancient folk ritual of a very different sort is observed on the Oga Peninsula, Akita Prefecture, on New Year's Eve. Young men play the part of hairy devils called NAMAHAGE, dressing in grotesque red and blue masks and straw cloaks. They stomp through the streets shouting, "Any wicked people about?" and then pound on people's doorways, the idea being to frighten children and newly married women so that they won't be lazy. After being admitted to a home, they sit down for rice cakes, first scaring the wits out of children with stories of what will happen to them if they are naughty.

See also OSHOGATSU.

CONTACTS:
Japan National Tourism Organization
1 Grand Central Pl.
60 E. 42nd St.
Ste. 448
New York, NY 10165
212-757-5640; fax: 212-307-6754
www.jnto.go.jp

Ashikaga City Office
3-2145 Honjo
Ashikaga, Tochigi Prefecture 326-8601 Japan
81-284-20-2222
www.city.ashikaga.tochigi.jp

♦ 2139 ♦ **Omizutori Matsuri (Water-Drawing Festival)**
March 1-14

Omizutori Matsuri is marked by religious rites, officially called **Shuni-e**, that have been observed for 12 centuries at the Buddhist Todaiji Temple in the city of Nara, Nara Prefecture, Japan. During this period of meditative rituals, the drone of recited sutras and the sound of blowing conchs echo from the temple. The high point comes on March 12, when young monks on the gallery of the temple brandish burning pine-branch torches, shaking off burning pieces. Spectators below try to catch the sparks, believing they have magic power against evil.

At 2 A.M. on March 13, the ceremony of drawing water is observed to the accompaniment of ancient music. Buckets are carried to a well, and the first water of the year is drawn and offered to the Buddha. Then the monks perform a final dramatic fire dance to the beating of drums.

For many Japanese, the Omizutori signals the start of spring.

CONTACTS:
Japan National Tourist Organization
1 Grand Central Pl.
60 E. 42nd St. Ste. 448
New York, NY 10165
212-757-5640; fax: 212-307-6754
www.jnto.go.jp

♦ 2140 ♦ Ommegang
First Thursday in July and the previous Tuesday

A medieval pageant presented on the Grand-Place of Brussels, Belgium, and one of the country's most popular attractions. The pageant in its present form dates only from 1930, the year of the centenary of Belgium, but it is a reenactment of the Ommegang of 1549. And that Ommegang had gone back at least to 1359, when it was first recorded.

The word *ommegang* is from the Flemish words *omme* ("around") and *gang* ("march"), and was a word used for processions around monuments. The present Brussels Ommegang is linked to the story of Béatrice Soetkens.

The year was 1348. Béatrice, a poor but honest woman, was told by the Virgin Mary to go to Antwerp to get a miracle-making statue. Béatrice ordered her husband to start rowing his boat to take her to Antwerp, and there she was able to get the statue, despite the interference of the sexton. On the way back to Brussels, her husband, exhausted, had to stop rowing, but the drifting boat safely arrived in Brussels at a spot where archers practiced. A church was built there, and every year the statue was carried around under the protection of the "Grand Serment," the Archery Guild.

That was the start of the Ommegang. At first wholly religious, in time profane elements were mingled. The royal princes were admirers of the Ommegang, and details of the 1549 Ommegang are known through the works of Juan Christobal Calvete de Estrelle, the chronicler of Philippe II, son of Charles V. The 1549 Ommegang was dedicated to Charles.

The Ommegang disappeared after 1810, but has been the same since its 1930 revival. It is preceded by strolling musi-

cians, followed by a parade of people representing the magistrate and various city officials; the court of Marie of Hungary, with pages, ladies-in-waiting, and a hunting group of dogs and falcons; and the Court of Charles V, with mounted knights bearing banners. Many of those representing the court figures are descendants of the original noble families.

Then the actual procession takes place, led by the Knight of Peace and the Theban trumpets. Participants include trade groups with floats, archers and crossbowmen, and stilt walkers and groups of dancers and Gilles (clowns) dancing around symbolic animals: the legendary horse Bayard and the four sons of Aymon [*see* GIANTS, FESTIVAL OF THE (BELGIUM)] surrounded by eagles, a pelican, unicorn, dragon, lion, and serpent.

CONTACTS:
Ommegang - Brussels Events
Rue des Tanneurs, 180
Brussels, 1000 Belgium
32-2-512-19-61; fax: 32-2-502-68-35
www.ommegang.be

♦ 2141 ♦ Onam
August-September; four days during Hindu month of Bhadrapada

A harvest festival and a celebration of ancient King Mahabali in the state of Kerala in India. This is Kerala's biggest festival, lasting 10 days and featuring dancing, feasting, and displays of elaborately designed carpets of flowers. It's famous for the races of the so-called snake boats held at Champakulam, Aranmulai, and Kottayam. The boats are designed in all shapes—with beaks or kite tails—and have crews of up to 100 men who row to the rhythm of drums and cymbals.

The festival honors King Mahabali, who was sent into exile in the nether world when gods grew jealous of him. He's allowed to return to his people once a year, and the boat races, cleaned homes, carpets of flowers, clapping dances by girls, and other events are the welcome for him.

CONTACTS:
Department of Tourism, Government of Kerala
Park View
Opposite to Museums Compound
Thiruvananthapuram, Kerala 695 033 India
91-471-2321132 or 800-425-4747; fax: 91-471-2322279
www.keralatourism.org

Ministry of Tourism, Government of India
1270 Ave. of the Americas
Ste. 303
New York, NY 10020
212-586-4901; fax: 212-582-3274
tourism.nic.in

♦ 2142 ♦ Onwasato Festival
August

Observed by the Igbo people of Nigeria, the Onwasato Festival marks the beginning of the harvest season and is celebrated by feasting on the new crops, particularly yams. The highlight of the festival is the thanksgiving ritual in which the senior member of each family kills a fowl in the *Obu* (the father's sitting-house), sprinkles the blood on the *Okpensi* (the family symbol), and gives thanks to the family's ancestors. The feathers are then removed and scattered on the threshold of the compound—a sign that the people have forsaken all evil for the coming season. Of all the many fowl that are killed, one is roasted and set aside, while the others are used for the first day's feasting. On the second day of the festival, all the members of the extended family meet in the senior member's Obu and share the fowl that has been set aside in a ritual known as the "handing round of fowl," or *Inya Okuku*.

♦ 2143 ♦ **Opal Festival**
March-April, Easter weekend

The South Australian town of Coober Pedy is known for its opal mines, producing about 70 percent of the world's opals. In the early 20th century, newcomers to the area—explorers, miners, construction workers, soldiers returning from World War I—built underground dugouts in which to live because of the harsh environment of the outback, with its excessive heat and minimal water supply. Thus, the town came to be called "kupa piti" or "white man in a hole" by the aboriginal people.

Celebrated over EASTER weekend, Coober Pedy's annual Opal Festival includes such competitive events as the mine rescue demonstration, stein holding competition, beer belly contest, tug-of-war, tossing the sausage, triathlons for men and women, games and races for children, football, and the multicultural dance and singing competition. While the fun begins on Thursday night with the festival cabaret, Saturday is the main day, kicking off with a morning street parade featuring a marching band, mining equipment, and floats and culminating in a fireworks display and a dance at night. Throughout the festival, the opal walk leads festivalgoers from shop to shop to view rare and beautiful specimens, and dugout tours are available. There are also displays of local handicrafts, along with food and drink tents, stage acts, aboriginal dancing, and music.

CONTACTS:
District Council of Coober Pedy
Lot 773 Hutchison St
P.O. Box 425
Coober Pedy, SA 5723 Australia
61-8-8672-4600; fax: 61-8-8672-5699
www.cooberpedy.sa.gov.au

♦ 2144 ♦ **Opalia**
December 19

The ancient Roman fertility goddess Ops was known by several different names—among them Rhea, Cybele, BONA DEA, Magna Mater (*see* MEGALESIA), Thya, and Tellus. She married Saturn and was the mother of Jupiter, and was usually portrayed as a matron, with a loaf of bread in her left hand and her right hand opened as if offering assistance. There were actually two festivals in her honor. The Opalia was observed

on December 19, when it is believed that a sacrifice to Ops was made in the temple of Saturn. On August 25, the Opiconsivia, the sacrifice took place in the Regia or king's house.

Not much is known about what actually took place during the Opalia. There is even some disagreement as to whether Ops was the wife of Saturn or the wife of Consus. The fact that the Opalia was held four days after the CONSUALIA on December 15, and that the Opiconsivia was held four days after the festival in honor of Consus on August 21 has been used to support the theory that Ops was actually the wife of Consus. In any case, it appears that women played an important role in the festival. Because Ops was a fertility goddess, she was often invoked by touching the earth.

♦ 2145 ♦ **Open Marathon, International**
Mid-October

The International Open Marathon is a modern-day marathon in Greece run by male and female athletes of all ages. The race retraces the course of the Greek soldier, Pheidippides, who ran from the battlefield at Marathon to Athens to bring news of the Athenian victory over the Persians, a distance of about 25 miles. The starting line today is in the village of Marathon and the finish line is at the Olympic Stadium in the heart of Athens.

A mound in Marathon marks the grave of 192 Athenian soldiers killed in the 490 B.C.E. victory.

CONTACTS:
Greek National Tourism Organization
305 E. 47th St.
2nd Fl.
New York, NY 10017
212-421-5777; fax: 212-826-6940
www.visitgreece.gr

♦ 2146 ♦ **Opening of the Underground Caves Day (Te Kauki Nanganga')**
November 20

The end of World War II is marked annually by the people of Butaritari Island (northern islands of the independent republic of Kiribati, located in the Central Pacific Ocean). Each year, they open the caves that were built to shelter them during WWII. Accompanied by a celebration, the event takes place on the anniversary of the day the caves initially were opened after the war ended in 1945.

Traditionally, the people of Butaritari would gather in the maneaba (meeting house), and older citizens would share their stories and experiences of the struggle between U.S Marines and Japanese soldiers for control of the island. The event's main activities take place in Ukiangang village on Butaritari Island, featuring singing, dancing, feasting, and indoor and outdoor games.

CONTACTS:
Kiribati National Tourism Office
P.O. Box 487

Betio, Tarawa Kiribati
686- 25573
www.gotokiribati.com.au

◆ 2147 ◆ Orange Bowl Game
January 1

One of the older post-season college football games, first played in 1935, in which the two top teams meet at the 75,521-seat LandShark Stadium in Miami, Florida, to play for the national championship every four years. Top teams also contend during the years in which the national championship is determined in one of the other three bowl cities—Pasadena, California's ROSE BOWL, New Orleans, Louisiana's SUGAR BOWL, and Phoenix, Arizona's Fiesta Bowl—which alternately host the biggest college football game of the year.

The game is preceded by a NEW YEAR'S EVE Orange Bowl Parade along Biscayne Boulevard. A parade more on the satirical side is the King Mango Strut held each year near Jan. 1 in Coconut Grove, Florida.

CONTACTS:
Orange Bowl Committee
14360 N.W. 77th Ct.
Miami Lakes, FL 33016
305-341-4701; fax: 305-341-4771
game.orangebowl.org

◆ 2148 ◆ Orange Day (Orangemen's Day)
July 12

Sometimes referred to simply as **The Twelfth** or **The Glorious Twelfth**, this is the anniversary of the Battle of Boyne, which took place in Ireland on July 1, 1690, when the old Julian calendar was still in use. Ireland was under English rule at the time, and the trouble began when James II, who was Roman Catholic, was deposed in 1668 and his throne was given to William of Orange, a Protestant. Each side raised an army of about 30,000 men, and the two clashed on the banks of the Boyne River. The Protestants won a decisive victory, but that was hardly the end of the conflict. The Catholics formed underground societies designed to restore the line of James, and the Protestants countered by forming the Orange Order, committed to maintaining the link with Protestant England. As Irishmen left Ireland and England for the New World, lodges of Orangemen were formed in Canada and the United States, where Orange Day is still observed by Protestant Irish.

◆ 2149 ◆ Oregon Bach Festival
June-July

The Oregon Bach Festival began in 1970. The German organist and conductor Helmuth Rilling and his co-founder, Royce Saltzman, former President of the American Choral Directors Association, organized the event to celebrate the musical works of Johann Sebastian Bach. The festival started as a series of classes and concerts at the University of Oregon at Eugene. Later on, full-scale choral and orchestral performances were included in the sessions.

Several special events take place during the festival, including a master class in conducting, which has been part of the festival for more than 40 years; a summer program for high school vocalists presented by the Stangeland Family Youth Choral Academy (SFYCA); and a choral workshop for professionals held in conjunction with the SFYCA. The Organ Institute offers classes, seminars, workshops, and other thought-provoking sessions on the works of Bach to auditioned organists. The Oregon Bach Festival Composers Symposium provides composers with workshops, reading sessions, and performances of their works.

CONTACTS:
Oregon Bach Festival
1257 University of Oregon
Eugene, OR 97403
541-346-5666 or 800-457-1486; fax: 541-346-5669
oregonbachfestival.com

◆ 2150 ◆ Oregon Brewers Festival
Last full weekend in July

During the last full weekend of July, Portland hosts the Oregon Brewers Festival at Tom McCall Waterfront Park on the banks of the Willamette River. The festival is dedicated to celebrating the tradition of craft beer produced in microbreweries across the country. Approximately 85,000 people flock to this annual beer-tasting event, which is among the nation's longest running. Over 85 breweries participate by offering samples of more than 30 different styles of handcrafted beer.

The festival kicks off with the Oregon Brewers Brunch and a parade down the streets of Southeast Portland, over the Hawthorne Bridge, to the site of the festival. In addition to a wide range of beer, the event features home-brewing demonstrations, live music, and a variety of food vendors.

CONTACTS:
Portland Brewers Festival Association of Oregon
7424 S.W. Beaverton Hillsdale Hwy.
Portland, OR 97225
www.oregonbrewfest.com

◆ 2151 ◆ Oregon Dune Mushers' Mail Run
March; dates vary according to the tide schedules

The Oregon Dune Mushers' Mail Run takes place every year, with teams of 4 to 12 dogs in different class groups completing a 75-mile course between North Bend and Florence, Ore. Traveling through the Oregon Dunes National Recreation Area, about 15-20 teams take two to three days to complete the run. It is non-competitive, designed only to test the endurance of the dogs and their "mushers," who ride in wheeled carts.

The event commemorates early American history, when the strength of humans and animals, and their mutual co-operation, were essential to the settling of the United States. The course, which runs along the Pacific coast on roads, trails, and over huge sand dunes, also harkens back to the days before 1914, when a railway tunnel finally was completed in the Gardiner area of Oregon. Prior to that date, beaches commonly were used as highways. Even today, the beach area between the low-tide mark and the mean high-tide mark is under the jurisdiction of Oregon's highway system.

The Oregon Dune Mushers' Mail Run was conceived in 1977 by dog musher Jim Tofflemire after he ran the famous 1,200-mile-long IDITAROD TRAIL SLED DOG RACE from Anchorage to Nome, Alaska. He had struggled to raise the funds for the race, and he wanted to help others raise money while also experiencing the unique mushing conditions on the Oregon coast. In keeping with his original vision, the Oregon run includes a distinctive fund-raising element. Each musher carries three commemorative stamped envelopes and is required to have the stamps cancelled in the three communities that the race course passes through: North Bend, Lakeside, and Florence. The envelopes then are sold as a fundraiser to benefit the Oregon Dune Mushers. The organization often uses the proceeds to send mushers to the Iditarod Race.

CONTACTS:
Oregon Dune Mushers
P.O. Box 841
North Bend, OR 97459
541-677-8393
www.oregondunemushers.com

♦ 2152 ♦ Oregon Shakespeare Festival
February through early November

The Oregon Shakespeare Festival was founded in 1935 in Ashland, Oregon. Initially limited to performing plays written by William Shakespeare on an outdoor stage called the Allen Elizabethan Theatre, the company began staging the works of other playwrights in 1970, when its second venue—the Angus Bowmer Theatre—was built. A third theatre, the Black Swan, opened in 1977 and was replaced by the Thomas Theatre in 2002. The additional spaces have allowed the festival to stage modern and contemporary works, in addition to maintaining its original commitment to producing the works of Shakespeare. As one of the major theater festivals in North America, the Oregon Shakespeare Festival serves as an educational source for teachers and holds numerous supplemental events, including roundtables, seminars, discussions, dinners, and fundraisers.

CONTACTS:
Oregon Shakespeare Festival
15 S. Pioneer St.
Ashland, OR 97520
541-482-2111; fax: 541-482-0446
www.osfashland.org

♦ 2153 ♦ Original Gullah Festival
May, the weekend before Memorial Day

The Original Gullah Festival is held annually in Beaufort, S.C., on the weekend before Memorial Day. Founded in 1986, its aim is to promote awareness of local customs and culture through the arts. The three-day event features such entertainment as jazz, blues, reggae, and gospel musicians; storytelling and dance performances; arts and crafts displays; museum exhibits; and a variety of food vendors.

The term Gullah, or Geechee, is used to refer to the African-American people and culture descended from slaves brought from Africa to the coastal region of South Carolina and the Georgia Low Country. Because of its relative geographic isolation in island communities, Gullah culture retained distinctly African and Caribbean features, including traditional foods, crafts, folk beliefs, and language.

The Original Gullah Festival was founded by Rosalie Pazant, her three daughters, and a family friend, inspired by a discussion of the "good old days" of celebrating Memorial Day in the African-American community. Pazant is still president of the board of directors that organizes and oversees the event, along with an executive committee. From 35 people at the first festival, the attendance has expanded to as many as 70,000 over the festival's three days.

CONTACTS:
Original Gullah Festival of SC, Inc.
P.O. Box 73
Beaufort, SC 29901
843-321-9288
theoriginalgullahfestival.org

♦ 2154 ♦ Osaka International Festival
April

Founded in 1958 as a meeting place for Eastern and Western cultures, the Osaka International Festival presents classical music performed by orchestras, chamber ensembles, and solo artists from Japan and other countries. The program also includes dance, drama, and opera, with performances given in the 2,709-seat Osaka Festival Hall, one of the largest and most modern in the Far East. The Comedie Française, Vienna Burgtheater, and Théâtre de France Renaud-Barrault have performed there, as have the New York City Ballet, the Alwin Nikolais Dance Theatre, and the Ballet Aztlan de Mexico.

Every Osaka Festival features classical Japanese Noh dance-dramas and Kabuki theatrical performances. The Bunraku Puppet Theatre also presents traditional Japanese dramas using dolls that are two-thirds human size. The two-week festival is scheduled to take place in April, which is cherry-blossom time in Osaka.

CONTACTS:
Japan National Tourism Organization
1 Grand Center Pl.
60 E 42nd St.
Ste. 448
New York, NY 10165
212-757-5640; fax: 212-307-6754
www.japantravelinfo.com

♦ 2155 ♦ Oshogatsu (New Year's Day)
January 1

This is the "festival of festivals" in Japan, also known as **Ganjitsu**, actually celebrated for several days. Government offices, banks, museums and most businesses are closed from NEW YEAR'S DAY, a national holiday, through January 3.

From the middle of December, streets are decorated with pine and plum branches, bamboo stalks, and ropes festooned with paper. Traditional home decorations are small pine trees with bamboo stems attached, which are placed on either side of the front entrance to represent longevity and constancy. For weeks before New Year's, people clean house and purchase new clothes for the children; this is also a time for exchanging gifts, sending greeting cards, and paying off personal debts.

On New Year's Day, it's traditional to pray at the household altar and to eat special foods, for example, steamed rice that has been pounded into small, round, gooey cakes called *mochi*. Herring roe is eaten for fertility, black beans for health, dried chestnuts for success, and porgy and prawns are omens of happiness.

Business resumes on Jan. 4, and the holiday period is over on Jan. 7 when decorations come down as part of the festival of NANAKUSA MATSURI.

See also HADAKA MATSURI; OMISOKA; UTAKAI HAJIME.

CONTACTS:
Japan National Tourist Organization
1 Grand Central Pl.
60 E. 42nd St.
Ste 448
New York, NY 10165
212-757-5640; fax: 212-307-6754
www.jnto.go.jp

♦ 2156 ♦ Osorezan Taisai
July 20-24

Mt. Osoré, located on the Shimokita Peninsula in the north of Honshu, Japan, is a spiritual center for many Japanese. It is known as a place where departed souls congregate. During the Osorezan Taisai Festival, or **Osorezanrei Grand Festival**, people flock to the mountain at Mutsu City, Aomori Prefecture, where psychics endeavor to summon the spirits of the dead by chanting. The priests who cross the weathered slopes of the mountain in procession add to the festival's grim and ghostly atmosphere.

♦ 2157 ♦ Ostara
Around March 22

Ostara, which coincides with the VERNAL EQUINOX, is one of the four pagan QUARTER DAYS, along with Litha (SUMMER SOLSTICE), Mabon (AUTUMNAL EQUINOX), and YULE. It is observed by those who follow Wicca (modern witchcraft) and Neopaganism by lighting fires to commemorate the return of light in the spring and to honor the god and goddess.

Also known as Eostre or Alban Eilir, Ostara is also regarded as a time of fertility and conception. In some Wiccan tradi-

tions, it is marked as the time when the goddess conceives the god's child, which will be born at the WINTER SOLSTICE.

♦ 2158 ♦ Otsa Festival
Between August and November

The Ekperi people of eastern Nigeria celebrate the annual three-day Otsa Festival to purify their land and promote community solidarity. Masquerade plays are held in which primarily male members of the community wear masks and colorful costumes. Women play the role of "mother" to each play, accepting donations to pay for masks and costumes required for the performance.

While the masquerades vary from village to village and borrow elements from other villages as well as from neighboring tribes, certain key factors seem to be common throughout the region. On Otsa eve, a giant figure named Umese, wearing a mask and clad in locally woven cloth, goes from house to house. This giant dances and sings and collects donations to pay for the coming masquerades. The first of the Otsa day masquerades is performed by young boys who wear ragged cloth masks and costumes that have been created by the village's elderly men. These costumes are said to contain "medication" that will protect the boys from harm and, in a larger sense, protect the village as well. Later masquerades feature performers dancing and wearing masks made from cloth or carved wood. Some performers dance on behalf of certain segments of the community, such as the hunters, and their headdress will reflect these concerns. A dancer performing on behalf of the village's children, for example, may wear toy dolls. Several new performances are added each year while others are dropped or revised. Some 30 masquerades are usually performed during the Otsa Festival.

♦ 2159 ♦ Our Lady Aparecida, Festival of
October

Brazil's patron saint, the Virgin Mary *Aparecida* ("she who has appeared"), is honored with a 10-day festival in the city near São Paulo that bears her name. Legend has it that after a poor day's catch, fishermen cast their nets into the Paraiba do Sul River and pulled up a small statue of the Virgin Mary, carved out of black wood. When they cast their nets again, they came up full of fish. This was the first miracle attributed to the saint, and the city of Aparecida with its beautiful church built to house the statue is now the destination of many pilgrimages.

Nossa Senhora de Aparecida is celebrated during the month of October, but the 12th is a legal public holiday in Brazil to honor the saint.

♦ 2160 ♦ Our Lady of Carmel, Feast of
July 16

Our Lady of Carmel (the *Madonna del Carmine*) is the patroness of the city of Naples, Italy. Her festival is celebrated with dancing, singing, and magnificent fireworks displays. Brightly decorated wax replicas of human body parts used to be sold at booths near the church, and people suffering from various physical ailments appealed to the Madonna to restore their health by offering her these replicas of the diseased portions of their bodies.

Her feast is also observed by Italian Americans in the United States. For example, it is part of the elaborate GIGLIO FEAST celebrated in Brooklyn, New York.

See also TIRANA, LA.

CONTACTS:
Our Lady Of Mount Carmel Church
275 N. Eighth St.
Brooklyn, NY 11211
718-384-0223; fax: 718-384-5838
www.olmcfeast.com

♦ 2161 ♦ Our Lady of Fátima Day
May 13

This Portuguese holiday commemorates the appearance of the Virgin Mary to three children, aged 7 to 10, from the village of Fátima in 1917. The first appearance to the dos Santos children—Lucia, and her cousins, Jacinta and Francisco— took place on May 13, 1917, when they saw what they thought was lightning and a lady appeared to them from the top of a nearby tree. No one really took their story seriously, however, until the same thing began to occur on the 13th of every month. Each time the children went to see the Virgin, they were accompanied by an increasingly large crowd of adults. She appeared to them for the last time on October 13, in the presence of about 70,000 onlookers, when she revealed she was Our Lady of the Rosary. She told them to recite the rosary daily, and asked that a church be built for her.

Eventually the cult of Our Lady of Fátima spread, a basilica was built, and pilgrimages to the isolated shrine became common. Two great pilgrimages take place each year on May 13 and October 13, with smaller groups making their way to Fátima around the 13th day of each month in between. July 13 is considered Our Lady of Fátima Day because it was two months after the Virgin's first appearance that a large number of adults witnessed the same miracle: the sun seemed to dance, tremble, and finally fall. It took 20 years for the event to be investigated, authenticated, and the cult granted acceptance by the Pope.

CONTACTS:
Our Lady of the Rosary Library
11721 Hidden Creek Rd.
Prospect, KY 40059
502-425-9738
www.olrl.org

Tourism Central Portugal
John Mendonca
8 St.
Aveiro, 3800-200 Portugal
351-234-420-760; fax: 351-234-428-326
www.turismodocentro.pt

♦ 2162 ♦ Our Lady of Guadalupe, Feast of (United States)
December 12

The Feast of OUR LADY OF GUADALUPE is celebrated by Roman Catholics in the southwestern United States, where the Spanish influence is still strong. At the pueblo just north of Taos, New Mexico, there is an impressive torchlight procession on December 12. At the Jemez Pueblo, *matachines* (clowns or buffoons) perform a variety of Indian ceremonial dances. At churches and plazas throughout New Mexico, Texas, and Arizona, such traditional Indian dances as the arc and arrow, gourd, braid, feather, palm, owl, and snake dances are performed on this day.

Several masses are held on this day at Our Lady of Guadalupe Church in San Diego, California, where the *mañanitas*, or "good morning song," is sung to the Virgin Mary, and *mariachis*, strolling musicians, perform in the Virgin's honor.

CONTACTS:
Indian Pueblo Cultural Center
2401 12th St. N.W.
Albuquerque, NM 87104
505-843-7270 or 866-855-7902
www.indianpueblo.org

American Indian Chamber of Commerce of NM
2401 12th St. N.W.
Ste. 5-S
Albuquerque, NM 87104
505-766-9545; fax: 505-766-9499
www.aiccnm.com

♦ 2163 ♦ Our Lady of Guadalupe, Fiesta of
December 12

Nuestra Señora de Guadalupe is the patron saint of Mexico, and on December 12 thousands of pilgrims flock to her shrine at the famous Church of Guadalupe outside Mexico City. On the evening of December 11 crowds have already gathered for mariachi-led singing and special ceremonies at midnight, which are carried on national television.

This great religious festival commemorates the appearance of the Virgin Mary on Tepeyac hill just north of present-day Mexico City. According to legend, she identified herself to an Indian convert named Juan Diego in the early morning of December 9, 1531, and told him to tell the bishop to build her a shrine there. When the bishop refused to believe the story, the Virgin filled Diego's homespun blanket with Castillian roses, which did not normally grow in Mexico, as proof of his vision. When Juan opened the blanket to show the bishop the roses, they had vanished. In their place was an image of Mary on the blanket. It soon adorned the newly built shrine and has hung there for four centuries without any apparent deterioration or fading of colors.

The story of Juan Diego and the Virgin is reenacted in a puppet show each year, and relics of Our Lady of Guadalupe are sold in the streets. It is said that only the French shrine at Lourdes and the one at Fátima attract as many pilgrims (*see* Our Lady of Fátima Day and Our Lady of Lourdes, Feast of).

She is the patron saint of Peruvian students, and of all of Central and South America. In El Salvador, it is called *Día del Indio* ("Day of the Indian").

In 1990, Pope John Paul II beatified Juan Diego, a necessary step on the way to sainthood.

CONTACTS:
Mexico Tourism Board
152 Madison Ave.
Ste. 1800
New York, NY 10016 United States
212-308-2110
www.visitmexico.com

♦ 2164 ♦ Our Lady of Lourdes, Feast of
February 11

The Feast of Our Lady of Lourdes commemorates the first of 18 appearances of the Virgin Mary to a 14-year-old French peasant girl, Bernadette Soubirous. The young girl's visions occurred between February 11 and July 16, 1858, near the town of Lourdes. The Virgin led her to a nearby grotto, and the miraculous spring that appeared there has been associated ever since with the power to heal.

Pilgrimages to the grotto were authorized in 1862, and the Feast of Our Lady of Lourdes was extended to the entire Roman Catholic Church in 1907. Some five million people a year make the pilgrimage to Lourdes, making it one of the world's major pilgrimage sites. Many of them are sick, and the cures they report are reviewed by a special medical bureau. As of 1976, the Church had accepted only 63 of these cures as miraculous.

CONTACTS:
Sanctuary Our-Lady of Lourdes
1 Ave., Monseigneur Theas
Lourdes, 65108 France
33-5-6242-7878; fax: 33-5-6242-7877
en.lourdes-france.org

♦ 2165 ♦ Our Lady of Nazaré Festival
September 8-18

Nazaré has been called "the most picturesque town in Portugal," and thousands of tourists flock here every summer to paint, film, and photograph the quaint fishing village. The Church of Our Lady of Nazareth was built near the place where the Virgin Mary is said to have saved the life of Fuas Roupinho, who was pursuing a white deer when a sudden sea mist arose and caused him to lose his bearings. The Virgin halted his horse in its tracks—a hoof-print is still visible—and, as the mist cleared, Roupinho discovered that he was on the brink of a cliff, 300 feet above the ocean. Today the town is built on two levels, the lower one extending along the beach. A pilgrimage chapel overlooks the town from the upper level.

The name *Nazaré* comes from a statue of the Virgin brought back here from Nazareth, the childhood home of Jesus, by a monk in the fourth century. The annual 10-day festival that takes place in the town's main square begins on September 8, the anniversary of the miracle, and includes bullfights, musical concerts, and folk dancing.

Some of the best and most dangerous fishing in all of Portugal goes on here. Fishermen have to negotiate a treacherous barrier reef with a difficult swell that often capsizes entire boats with their crews. Therefore, the Nazaré fishermen, who carry the Virgin's statue on their shoulders in three festive processions, are the focus of the event.

CONTACTS:
Tourism Central Portugal
John Mendonca, 8 St.
Aveiro, 3800-200 Portugal
351-234-420-760; fax: 351-234-428-326
www.turismodocentro.pt

♦ 2166 ♦ Our Lady of Solitude, Fiesta of
December 18

The **Virgen de la Soledad**, or Our Lady of Solitude, is the patroness of the state of Oaxaca, Mexico. According to legend, she first appeared in the city in 1543 when a man leading 12 burros arrived in town one night and discovered the next morning that there was a 13th among them. The mysterious animal passed away almost instantaneously, and when the man opened the huge chest it was carrying he discovered an almost life-sized image of the Virgin. A church was built on the site, which was discovered to lie over an immense deposit of silver, and the sealed entrance to the mine can still be seen to the right of the main aisle. Legend has it that the priest used to descend into the mine when it was dark and carry out silver through a tunnel that led to the church.

Preparations for the fiesta begin several days before December 18, when carnival rides and food and gambling booths are set up in the vicinity of the church. For several evenings there are *calendas*, processions of men and women carrying colored paper lanterns illuminated by candles and poles topped with figures of birds, boats, and other objects made out of flowers, leaves, or colored paper. There are also floats with various themes and huge papier-mâché caricatures of well-known individuals.

Thousands of pilgrims come from all over the state of Oaxaca to see the Virgin, who is dressed in velvet and satin gowns and who wears an emerald-and-diamond-studded crown for the fiesta. Despite her elegant attire, however, she is the patron saint of Mexican sailors, and a folktale holds that she often disappears from her niche at night and comes back at daybreak wet with drops of sea water.

♦ 2167 ♦ Our Lady of Sorrows Festival
Friday, Saturday, and Sunday closest to August 20

The pilgrimage to the church of Our Lady of Sorrows, or **Nossa Senhora da Agonia**, in Viana do Castelo, Portugal, is one of the country's most colorful religious festivals. Sometimes called the **Pardon of Our Lady of Sorrows**, it includes a procession in which the image of the Virgin Mary is carried over flower-strewn streets. Participants also enjoy fireworks on the River Lima, a parade of carnival giants and dwarfs, bullfights, and regional singing and folk dancing.

CONTACTS:
Turismo de Portugal, I.P.
Rua Ivone Silva
Lote 6
Lisbon, 1050-124 Portugal
351-211-140-200
www.visitportugal.com/en

♦ 2168 ♦ Our Lady of the Angels, Feast of
August 2

Our Lady of the Angels or **Nuestra Señora de los Angeles** is the patron saint of Costa Rica. Although her feast day, August 2, is observed throughout the country, the celebration focuses on Cartago, where the black stone said to bear her image is housed in the basilica that was erected on the spot where she is said to have appeared more than 300 years ago to a poor Indian girl who was gathering firewood.

On August 2 each year the small black stone image of the Virgin rides through the streets in a religious procession from the basilica to the church of St. Nicholas, where it remains until the first Saturday of September. The entire route of the procession is decorated with carpets of flowers and colored sand, and there are floats depicting various religious scenes and events. At one time many worshippers used to follow the procession dressed as Indians with strange designs painted on their faces. Although they claimed that they were fulfilling a special vow to the Virgin, church authorities prohibited the practice in 1958 because it was regarded as pagan superstition. Instead, penitents must follow the route of the procession in bare feet while balancing heavy stones on their heads or shoulders.

CONTACTS:
Our Lady of Sorrows
1728 Oxmoor Rd.
Homewood, AL 35209
205-871-8121; fax: 205-871-8180
www.ourladyofsorrows.com

♦ 2169 ♦ Our Lady of the Good Death Festival
Begins on the Friday nearest August 15

The state of Bahia in northeastern Brazil is largely populated by Afro-Brazilians, descendants of the estimated 3.5 million slaves brought to the country during the transatlantic slave trade. Among this segment is a well-known Afro-Catholic group called *Irmandade da Boa Morte* (Sisterhood of Good

Death), founded in 1823 by freed female slaves living in the town of Cachoeira. A major celebration observed by the sisterhood is the Our Lady of the Good Death Festival, a unique version of the FEAST OF THE ASSUMPTION OF THE BLESSED VIRGIN MARY. Intermixed with the feast's Catholic traditions are the sisterhood's expressions of Candomblé, a separate religion with origins in the Yoruban culture of West Africa.

Over three days, the several dozen women who constitute the sisterhood hold mass and processions dramatizing Mary's death. It is a time of mourning as well as celebration for Mary's ascension into heaven, upon which she becomes *Nossa Senhora da Gloria* (Our Lady of Glory).

One way the sisters depart from Catholic festival observance is by worshiping Orishás, which are Yoruban spirits that represent major forces of nature. There are also performances of the samba de roda (ring samba). These non-Catholic expressions of the festival and other Candomblé practices have attracted criticism from Brazilian church leaders.

CONTACTS:
Bahia Tourism Authority
Salvador, Bahia Brazil
55-71-3103-3103
bahia.com.br

♦ 2170 ♦ Our Lady of the Rock, Festival of
Every Sunday in October

The church of **Nossa Señora da Penha**, Our Lady of the Rock, rises up from a 300-foot-high granite boulder on the outskirts of Rio de Janeiro, Brazil. A number of legends accounts for the church's unusual location, one of which is that a man sleeping at the foot of the boulder was rescued from being eaten by a crocodile by the Virgin's miraculous intervention.

Pilgrims travel to the church every Sunday during the month of October. Some climb the 365 stone steps that have been carved out of the granite entirely on their knees because they have made a pledge to the Virgin, while others carry huge candles and wax images of body parts that she has cured. The large square at the base of the rock is filled with stalls selling food and drink with which the pilgrims can refresh themselves. Ferris wheels, carousels, games, and fireworks enliven the festivities. In the city of Rio De Janeiro, the festival is considered second in importance only to CARNIVAL.

Local people say that a man once caught his foot on the top step and tumbled back down the steps. Assuming that the strange downward progression represented the fulfillment of a promise made to the Virgin, the other pilgrims politely moved to the side as he passed by.

♦ 2171 ♦ Ouray Ice Festival
January

The Ouray Ice Festival is an ice-climbing competition and exposition held annually in January in Ouray, Colo. In addition to the main contest, which tests ice-climbers' skill and speed, competitions are held for such feats as axe-throwing and tight-rope walking across a gorge. Also on offer are manufacturers' displays of specialty equipment, film and slide-show presentations, and a climbing wall for children. Anyone can register to compete.

The first Ouray Ice Festival was held in January 1996, promoted by Jeff Lowe, an ice-climbing pioneer.

CONTACTS:
Ouray Ice Park, Inc.
P.O. Box 1058
Ouray, CO 81427 United States
970-325-4288
ourayicepark.com

♦ 2172 ♦ **Outback Festival**
September in odd-numbered years

In 1895 A. B. "Banjo" Patterson wrote "Waltzing Matilda," the song that is most closely identified with the Australian outback. The song was based on an incident that occurred at Dogworth Station near Winton, Queensland, and it was in Winton that the ballad was first sung in public. Today Winton is host to the biennial Outback Festival, which celebrates Australia's pioneer traditions. There are parades, picnics, historic tours, safaris, rodeos, sheep-shearing and whip-cracking demonstrations, pigeon races, and sports competitions at the festival, which is held in September, at the end of the Australian winter.

The Bronze Swagman Award is presented at the festival for the best "bush verse"—similar to COWBOY POETRY in the United States. Entries are accepted from all over the world, but the poems must be written in English and must portray an "Australian Bush" theme.

CONTACTS:
Outback Festival Inc.
P.O. Box 24
Winton, QLD 4735 Australia
61-7-4657-1558
www.outbackfestival.com.au

♦ 2173 ♦ **Ovoo Worship Festival**
June

Although the date varies by location, the Ovoo Worship Festival takes place in rural areas throughout Mongolia during the month of June. Ovoos are shrines at which individuals can make offerings for safe journeys or economic well-being. They are constructed out of rocks, tree branches, leaves, and other materials to form a kind of pyramid shape. Inside may be some kind of representation of God. Small towns and villages pay homage at the ovoos in June and hold festivals featuring Buddhist prayers, special food, and horse races. The people also usher in the growing season as they honor the ovoos, praying for a fruitful harvest.

♦ 2174 ♦ **Owara Kaze-no-Bon Festival**
September 1-3

Owara Kaze-no-Bon is a festival steeped in folklore and celebrated by the people of the small town of Yatsuo-machi in Japan. The three-day celebration begins on September 1, which is associated with natural disasters and calamity according to the traditional Japanese calendar, and centers on prayers for a bountiful harvest and protection from bad weather. Although there are many accounts of the origin of the festival, the most plausible is that the *Bon* rituals—historically observed by the Japanese to honor the spirits of their ancestors—have continued on as a harvest festival with folk music and dance.

Most of the celebrations take place after dark, when the town takes on a festive look with thousands of paper lanterns decorating homes and streets. Men dress in traditional *happi* coats, and women wear summer kimonos with black sashes. Donning braided straw hats called *amigasa*, young men and women dance throughout the night to folk music. Accompanied by traditional Japanese musical instruments, dancers perform in groups on the sloping streets of the town. These unique dance steps are passed down from the elders to the younger generation as a form of folk art.

CONTACTS:
Japan National Tourim Organization
1 Grand Central Pl., 60 E. 42nd St.
Ste. 448
New York, NY 10165
212-757-5640; fax: 212-307-6754
www.jnto.go.jp/eng

♦ 2175 ♦ **Ox Cart Festival**
Second weekend of February

In Thailand, oxen are conventionally used for plowing rice paddies. But for one weekend in February, they become race animals in a famous competition set in the central region's Phetchaburi Province. A tradition that dates back to the reign of King Rama V (1868–1910), the Ox Cart Festival celebrates an agricultural custom and is an opportunity for Thai officials to promote tourism in Phetchaburi Province and the rest of the country.

According to tradition, rice farmers of Amphoe Ban Laem, a village in Phetchaburi, would mark the end of the harvest season by harnessing oxen to unused carts and racing them for a distance of nearly 1,000 feet. It was, and still is, an occasion for gambling between ox owners and spectators. Wagers typically center around bottles of *lao khao*, a strong form of rice whisky. Once only a local phenomenon, the competition grew in popularity until King Rama V decided to hold races at Bangkok's Royal Palace, where thousands of people attended. Soon after, it became part of the capital's celebrations to mark the Thai New Year.

The Ox Cart Festival has been an official annual event in Phetchaburi Province since 1998. There are multiple races staged throughout the province, but the best known takes place in Amphoe Ban Laem.

CONTACTS:
Tourism Authority of Thailand
1600 New Phetchaburi Rd.

Makkasan
Ratchathevi
Bangkok, 10400 Thailand
662-250-5500
www.tourismthailand.org

♦ 2176 ♦ **Oxi Day**
October 28

Oxi Day, also known as Ochi or Ohi Day, commemorates the day during World War II that the Prime Minister of Greece refused to allow Benito Mussolini's army to enter and occupy the country, despite Mussolini's threat that his superior forces would destroy Greece if it offered any resistance. A public holiday in Greece, Oxi Day is celebrated across the country with military parades, including naval parades in coastal towns, and special services held in Orthodox churches. It is also a public holiday in Cyprus.

At 3 o'clock in the morning on October 28, 1940, Benito Mussolini sent the Italian Ambassador to Greek Prime Minister Ioannis Metaxas with an ultimatum: allow the Italian troops amassed on the border with Albania to enter Greece unopposed, or face certain destruction at the their hands. Despite his army's small size and inferior weaponry, Metaxas simply responded with "Oxi" (pronounced o-hee), meaning "No" in Greek. Though Mussolini's troops did launch an attack, they met fierce and unexpected resistance by the Greek army.

Eventually, Hitler's army was forced to come to Mussolini's aid, and the Germans finally occupied Greece. Nevertheless, the time spent and German casualties incurred would prove crucial factors in the outcome of the war overall. On Oxi Day Greeks around the world also remember the bravery of their countrymen, about whom Winston Churchill said, "Hence we will not say that Greeks fight like heroes, but we will say that heroes fight like Greeks." The 75th anniversary of Oxi Day will be celebrated in 2015. .

♦ 2177 ♦ **Ozark Folk Festival**
Second weekend in October

The Ozark Folk Festival in Eureka Springs, Ark., was first held in 1948 to preserve the music and folklore of the Ozarks. For two or three days, musicians, mostly nonprofessional, gather to play mountain music on fiddles, banjos, jackass jawbones, harmonicas, dulcimers, and other non-electrified instruments. Only traditional Ozark music is allowed, and that means it must be at least 70 years old. Some of the music dates back to Elizabethan times. Also on the menu are performances by jig, clog, and square-dance groups, crafts displays, and a Festival Queen contest.

Eureka Springs, about 50 miles north of Fayetteville, is the oldest health spa in the Ozarks, and the winding streets and houses are much the same as they were in the 1880s.

P

♦ 2178 ♦ **Pacific Northwest Festival**
August

Most opera companies shy away from Richard Wagner's *Der Ring des Nibelungen* because of the technical difficulties involved in staging the work and because it is assumed that only audiences in Wagner's native Germany will have the stamina to sit through the entire four-opera cycle. But in 1975, the Seattle Opera proved not only that the *Ring* could be staged, but that it could draw huge audiences. Under the direction of Glenn Ross, the Seattle Opera started its annual Wagner festival, performing the uncut *Ring* cycle in German the first week and in English the second week with an augmented orchestra. All operas are performed in the Seattle Opera House, which had been remodeled for the 1962 World's Fair.

Some of the world's finest Wagnerian performers have participated in the Pacific Northwest Festival over the years, among them Herbert Becker, Ingrid Bjoner, Philip Booth, Ute Vinzing, Paul Crook, and Malcolm Rivers. When General Director Speight Jenkins decided in 1985 to stage an entirely new production of *Die Walkure*, one of the operas in the *Ring* cycle, he was booed for his innovative approach by those who preferred the more traditional production.

See also BAYREUTH FESTIVAL and RAVELLO MUSIC FESTIVAL.

♦ 2179 ♦ **Pack Monday Fair**
Monday following October 10

The Pack Monday Fair, which used to be called St. Michael's Fair because it is held on the Monday following Old MICHAELMAS Day, is held in Sherborne, England. It begins shortly after midnight on Sunday, when a band of young people lock arms and march through the streets of Sherborne blowing bugles, horns, and whistles, and banging metal pots, tea-trays, and garbage can lids together. Locals call this noise-making brigade "Teddy Roe's Band," a tradition that has persisted for several centuries even though town authorities have tried to stamp it out.

The people of Sherborne say that a man named Teddy Roe once served as the chief mason involved in the reconstruction of the Sherborne Abbey Church. A fire that took place in the late 15th century destroyed much of the church. The workers who rebuilt the church completed the fan-vaulting in 1490. Legend has it that when the workers finished they "packed" the instruments of their trade and paraded in triumph through the main avenues of town, led by Teddy Roe. Another explanation asserts that Teddy Roe had no connection with the abbey, but that he came to Sherborne later and revived the ancient tradition of the Pack Monday Fair, which had lapsed. Yet another theory is that banging on pots and pans originated in the pagan custom of making loud noises to frighten away evil spirits.

CONTACTS:
Sherborne Tourist Information Centre
The Manor House
Newland
Sherborne, Dorset DT9 3NL United Kingdom
44-19-3581-2807; fax: 44-19-3581-2611
www.sherbornetown.com

♦ 2180 ♦ **Paczki Day**
Thursday before Lent in Poland; Tuesday before Lent in the United States

Paczki Day is a day in early to mid February in Poland and the United States on which a rich, jelly- or crème-filled doughnut is traditionally eaten in anticipation of the 40 days of fasting required during the religious season of LENT. In Poland, the observance of Paczki Day is known as *Thusty Czwartek*, or Fat Thursday; in the United States, Polish-Americans celebrate Paczki Day on Fat Tuesday, the day before ASH WEDNESDAY, which signals the beginning of Lent. Since at least the Middle Ages, consuming butter or lard was prohibited during the observance of Lent in Poland. In the final days before the fast began, households traditionally used up their stores of these products by preparing rich foods such as cakes and pastries. Paczki are made of dense, rich dough that is deep-fried and may be filled with fruit-flavored jam or crème; they are often glazed or coated with powdered sugar.

In the United States, areas with large Polish-American populations—such as Chicago, Cleveland, and Detroit—have widely adopted the custom of eating paczki in the days prior to the start of Lent, with many Polish neighborhoods taking on a festival atmosphere as patrons flock to ethnic bakeries for authentic paczki. In the largely Polish-American community of Hamtramck, Michigan, free, continuous entertainment is provided throughout the day, an annual paczki-eating contest is held, and radio stations broadcast live from the scene. Throughout the community, bars open as early as 7:00 AM on Paczki Day and offer traditional Polish cuisine, including pierogi, golumpki, and kielbasa; in addition, many serve specialty items including "paczki shots" or liquor-filled paczki.

CONTACTS:
City of Hamtramck
3401 Evaline
Hamtramck, MI 48212
313-876-7700
www.hamtramck.us

Embassy of The Republic of Poland
2640 16th St. N.W.
Washington, D.C. 20009
202-499-1700; fax: 202-328-6271
www.washington.mfa.gov.pl/en

♦ 2181 ♦ **Pafos Aphrodite Festival Cyprus**
Late August-early September

The Pafos Aphrodite Festival Cyprus is held each year at the medieval Castle Square in Pafos, Cyprus. Cyprus is an island nation whose cultural heritage dates back more than 9,000 years, taking in Greek temples, Roman art, and artifacts from numerous other periods. The festival was established by various organizations in the Pafos district in the hope of establishing and promoting the locality as a center of high-profile cultural events. In 1998, the government granted annual funding for the Pafos Aphrodite Festival Cyprus.

The first show, performed in 1999, was Verdi's *Aida*. Ensuing years have seen the performance of *La Traviata, Rigoletto, Tosca, Zorba the Greek,* and *Turnadot.* Each year, the performance is subtitled in English and Greek.

CONTACTS:
Pafos Aphrodite Festival Cyprus
P.O. Box 60032
Pafos, 8100 Cyprus
357-26822218; fax: 357-26220221
www.pafc.com.cy

♦ 2182 ♦ **Pageant of the Golden Tree**
Every five years, two days in late August

The Pageant of the Golden Tree, which is celebrated in the historic town of Bruges, Belgium, has been an official celebration of national history and local tradition since 1958. The tradition behind the festival dates back to medieval times. In 1468, a pageant was held commemorating the wedding of Princess Margareth of York and Charles the Bold, Duke of Burgundy and Count of Flanders. The central emblem of the tournament was a Golden Tree, which stood in the center of the market square where jousting knights competed for a prize horse.

The festival is held on two consecutive nights. The main event, which is performed for thousands of Belgians and tourists, is the dramatization of the historic pageant, including the grand entrance of the wedding party and the medieval tournament. In addition to these performances, as many as 2,000 actors representing about 100 groups parade through the streets of Bruges on floats, accompanied by giant puppets.

The celebration that took place in 2002 marked a modernization of the event. Bruges leaders, taking advantage of the city's European Union-designated status as a Cultural Capital, shed light on the region's modern history, in particular the period during which local magistrates and guilds gained more power under the ruling sovereigns.

CONTACTS:
Belgian Tourist Office
300 E. 42nd St.
14th Fl.
New York, NY 10017
212-758-8130
www.visitbelgium.com

Royal Committee Initiative Brugge vzw
Ter Walle 5
Sint-Michiels, 8200 Belgium
comitevoorinitiatief.be

♦ 2183 ♦ **Paine (Thomas) Day**
January 29

Thomas Paine (1737-1809) was a propagandist and humanitarian whose influential pamphlet, *Common Sense,* is credited with persuading the American colonies to declare their independence from Great Britain. Six months after the publication of *Common Sense* in January 1776, the Declaration of Independence was signed. While Paine was serving in George WASHINGTON'S army during the Revolutionary War, he wrote his inspirational tract, *The Crisis,* whose opening line was the famous, "These are the times that try men's souls."

On the Sunday nearest January 29, Paine's birthday, he is honored by members of the Thomas Paine National Historical Association in New Rochelle, New York. They lay a wreath at his monument in the Thomas Paine Memorial Museum, which houses some of his letters and personal effects. The museum is located on Paine's former farmland, and the cottage in which he lived is only a short walk away. This day is also known as **Common Sense Day**, to encourage the use of good sense in protecting the rights of all people.

CONTACTS:
Thomas Paine National Historical Association
983 N. Ave.
New Rochelle, NY 10804
www.thomaspaine.org

♦ 2184 ♦ **Paitishahem (Patishahya; Feast of Bringing in the Harvest)**
January, February, September; 26th-30th days of Shahrewar, the sixth Zoroastrian month

Paitishahem is the third of the six great seasonal feasts, known as *gahambars*, of the Zoroastrian religion. Each of the six gahambars correlated with a phase of agricultural production—in this case, bringing in the harvest—and honored one of the six things created by God: sky, water, earth, plants, animals, and humankind.

Traditionally, the gahambars were joyous festivals that lasted five days and provided farm workers with a much-needed respite from their labors. The first four days were spent in preparation for the feasting that took place on the fifth day. Today, however, so many Zoroastrians live in urban areas that the importance of the gahambars has diminished somewhat.

The Zoroastrian calendar has 12 months of 30 days each, plus five extra days at the end of the year. Because of discrepancies in the calendars used by widely separated Zoroastrian communities around the world, there are now three different calendars in use, and Paitishahem can fall either in January, February, or September according to the Gregorian calendar.

There are only about 100,000 followers of Zoroaster (also known as Zarathushtra, believed to have lived around 1200 B.C.E.) today, and most of them live in northwestern India or Iran. Smaller communities exist in Pakistan, Sri Lanka, Canada, the U.S., England, and Australia.

♦ 2185 ♦ Pakistan Day
March 23

This national holiday is also known as **Republic Day,** and is the anniversary of a 1940 resolution calling for a Muslim country for Muslim Indians. On the same day in 1956, Pakistan became an Islamic republic within the British Commonwealth.

Pakistan Day is celebrated with parades and fairs.

CONTACTS:
Embassy of Pakistan
3517 International Ct. N.W
Washington, D.C. 20008 United States
202-243-6500; fax: 202-686-1534
www.embassyofpakistanusa.org

♦ 2186 ♦ Pakistan Independence Day
August 14

On this day in 1947, Pakistan gained independence from Britain. Pakistan had been part of the immense British colony of India since the 18th century.

Independence Day is a national holiday observed in much the same way as PAKISTAN DAY.

CONTACTS:
Embassy of Pakistan
3517 International Ct. N.W
Washington, D.C. 20008 United States
202-243-6500; fax: 202-686-1534
www.embassyofpakistanusa.org

♦ 2187 ♦ Pakistan Kashmir Solidarity Day
February 5

On February 5, 1990, Pakistanis protested against Indian rule in an armed uprising. Nawaz Sharif, who was the main opposition leader and the chief minister of Punjab at that time, put advertisements in newspapers calling for a nationwide strike on February 5 to enable the people "to pray for God's help for the success of jihad in Kashmir." More than 80,000 Kashmiris lost their lives during the demonstrations.

Pakistan People's Party Government leader Benazir Bhutto responded by declaring the day a public holiday, naming it Kashmir Solidarity Day. It is a national holiday, so government offices, banks, schools, and colleges are closed for the day. Along many of the major roads in the capital city, banners are displayed to show Pakistan's solidarity with the Kashmirs.

On Kashmir Solidarity Day across the country and in Pakistan-occupied Kashmir, a five-minute period of silence is observed to remember those who were killed during the uprising, and politicians around the country lead prayers of tribute. In addition, every province plans their own events, including rallies or processions, seminars, and speeches.

In a message on Kashmir Solidarity Day in 2015, President Mamnoon Hussain called upon the international community to come to the aid of the Kashmiris. "The right to self-determination is a revered principle of international law. But even after more than 67 years, this fundamental right is being denied to the people of Jammu and Kashmir." He added, "Today, while paying homage to the memory of thousands of Kashmiri martyrs who have laid down their lives for a legitimate cause, we express solidarity with the Kashmiri brethren and salute their sacrifices and determination in holding high the banner of freedom to defend their dignity and honour." Prime Minister Nawaz Sharif assured the Kashmiri people that the people of Pakistan will always stand with them. "I am sure that in not too distant a future the Kashmiris will achieve their cherished goal."

CONTACTS:
Embassy of Pakistan
3517 International Ct. N.W
Washington, D.C. 20008
202-243-6500; fax: 202-686-1534
www.embassyofpakistanusa.org

♦ 2188 ♦ Palau Independence Day
October 1

The Republic of Palau is a small island nation in the southern Pacific Ocean, near the Philippines, Indonesia, and Papua New Guinea. For the last 4,000 years, Palau has been settled by people from various countries. Originally, migrants from Indonesia settled in Palau. In the 18th century, the British had a more prominent presence. In the 19th century, the Spanish influence dominated the country. After the Spanish-American War, Spain sold Palau to Germany in 1899.

In 1914, the Treaty of Versailles gave Japan control over Palau. Under Japanese rule, the Palauan culture shifted the economy from a level of subsistence to a market economy, and individual property ownership became more common.

In 1947, after World War II, Palau became one of six island districts that became part of the Trust Territory of the Pacific Islands that were to be administered by the United States. As part of its mandate, the United States was to improve Palau's infrastructure and educational system so that it could eventually become a self-sufficient nation.

Palau approved a new constitution in 1981, and then signed a Compact of Free Association with the United States in 1982. The Compact went into effect on October 1, 1994, making Palau an independent nation.

Palau has dedicated this day as a national holiday. Palau Independence Day is the most celebrated holiday of the year. On this day, the nation celebrates events that include cultural feasts and symposiums.

CONTACTS:
Palau Visitors Authority
P.O. Box 256
Palau
680-488-2793; fax: 680-488-1453
www.visit-palau.com

Embassy of the Republic of Palau
1701 Pennsylvania Ave. N.W.
Ste. 300
Washington, D.C. 20006
202-452-6814; fax: 202-452-6281
www.palauembassy.com

♦ 2189 ♦ **Palio, Festival of the**
July 2, August 16

The **Palio of the Contrade** is a horse race that has been held twice a year in Siena, Tuscany, Italy, since the 13th century. The race features Siena's 17 *contrade*, or "ward organizations." In the Middle Ages these were rival military companies, but they are now social clubs. In each race, 10 of Siena's 17 contrade compete, hiring a professional jockey and selecting his attendants. The 10 contrade that will participate are determined by a drawing. Each contrade also has its own animal symbol, flag, color, museum, church, and motto. In medieval costume and with banners flying, the riders form a procession that carries the *Palio,* painted silk standards, through the city streets.

The race itself is run in the city's main square, the Piazza del Campo. There is intense rivalry, distrust, cheating, fixing, and bribery and frequent fights. The jockeys ride bareback, each holding a whip, which he can use on his opponents' horses as well as on his own. Riders for the finalist contrade race three times around the Piazza, and the winning contrade receives the Palio to hang on its church until the next festival. Revelry and merrymaking continue until dawn, and the winning jockey is honored with a victory dinner.

The second big race, held on August 16, is known as **Madonna del Voto Day**, in honor of the Virgin Mary.

CONTACTS:
Italian National Tourist Board
686 Park Ave.
3rd Fl.
New York, NY 10065
212-245-5618; fax: 212-586-9249
www.italiantourism.com

♦ 2190 ♦ **Palio of the Goose and River Festival**
June 28-29

In the Middle Ages the Leap of the Goose was a test of swimming skill for the local boatmen in Pavia, Lombardy, Italy. Now it is a combined rowing and swimming relay race held at the end of June each year. Competitors leap from a raft at the end of the race and try to reach a goose suspended in air. Geese apparently played an important part in the city's history, acting as sentries when Pavia was besieged by the Gauls. In the procession through the streets of Pavia that precedes the competition, live geese are carried in cages.

There is also a Tournament of the Towers in which teams of six men from each of the city's nine wards try to knock down each other's wooden towers in a mock battle. A final battle involves the Beccaria Tower, which can only be approached by gangplanks. The winners set the tower on fire.

CONTACTS:
Italian Government Tourist Board
686 Park Ave.
3rd Fl.
New York, NY 10065 United States
212-245-5618; fax: 212-586-9249
www.italiantourism.com

♦ 2191 ♦ **Palm Sunday**
Between March 15 and April 18 in the West and between March 28 and May 1 in the East; the Sunday before Easter

During the Jewish PASSOVER celebration, Jesus rode into Jerusalem and was given a hero's welcome by the people, who had heard of his miracles and regarded him as the leader who would deliver them from the domination of the Roman Empire. They carried palm branches, a traditional symbol of victory, and spread them in the streets before him, shouting "Hosanna, glory to God" (John 12:12,13). Palms are still used in church services on this day, which is the beginning of HOLY WEEK, and Jesus' triumphal entry into Jerusalem is often reenacted with a procession—the most impressive being the one in Rome, where the pope, carried in ST. PETER'S CHAIR, blesses the palms.

At the beginning or end of the service, the palms are distributed to the congregation. In some countries, where palms are not available, branches of other trees—particularly pussy willow, olive, box, yew, and spruce—are used. They are later hung up in houses for good luck, buried to preserve crops, or used to decorate graves. Other names for this day include **Passion Sunday**, FIG SUNDAY, **Willow Sunday**, **Branch Sunday**, **Blossom Sunday,** and, in France, **Rameaux.**

CONTACTS:
United States Conference of Catholic Bishops of Catholic Bishops
3211 Fourth St. N.E.
Washington, D.C. 20017
202-541-3000
www.usccb.org

♦ 2192 ♦ Palm Sunday (Austria)
Between March 15 and April 18; the Sunday before Easter

PALM SUNDAY commemorates Jesus' entry into Jerusalem, where he was greeted by people waving palm branches. In Austria and the Bavarian region of Germany, farmers make *Palmbuschen* by attaching holly leaves, willow boughs, and cedar twigs to the tops of long poles. After the Palmbuschen have been blessed in the local church, the farmers set them up in their fields or barns to ward off illness, to protect their crops from hail and drought, and to preserve their families from other disasters. The Palmbuschen are kept there throughout the year.

See also PALM SUNDAY (GERMANY).

♦ 2193 ♦ Palm Sunday (Finland)
Between March 15 and April 18; the Sunday before Easter

Instead of the traditional palm branches used in PALM SUNDAY observances elsewhere, birch branches are used in rural areas of Finland. Children may gather the branches or willow switches in the woods and decorate them with paper flowers and cloth streamers. According to custom, on the Saturday or Sunday before EASTER, known as **Willowswitch Saturday** and **Willowswitch Sunday**, they go from house to house and spank the woman of the house lightly while reciting a Finnish refrain wishing her good health. The woman then uses a switch on her livestock in the same way. The switches are eventually collected and saved, to be used again the first time the cattle are driven to pasture in the new year. The children return on Easter to receive a treat.

Pussywillow or birch branches are also used to foretell the arrival of spring. Once they are cut, the days are counted until the buds on the branches open; this is how many weeks it will take for the trees in the forest to bud.

CONTACTS:
Ministry for Foreign Affairs Finland
P.O. Box 176
Helsinki, FI-00023 Finland
358-9-1605-5555; fax: 358-9-629-840
formin.finland.fi

♦ 2194 ♦ Palm Sunday (Germany) (Palmsonntag)
Between March 15 and April 18; the Sunday before Easter

Although PALM SUNDAY customs vary from one part of Germany to the next, all celebrate the resurgence of life as symbolized by the arrival of spring. In the Black Forest, people decorate tall poles with pussywillows, heart or cross motifs, and long multicolored ribbon streamers. They set the decorated poles up in front of their houses and later carry them in procession to the local church, where they are blessed by the priest.

In Bavaria, branches from 12 different kinds of wood are cut, then bent and fastened to long poles in a semicircular shape and decorated with glass beads to resemble glittering trees. The trees are carried in procession to the church, blessed by the priest, and then set up in the farmers' fields to protect the crops and ensure a bountiful harvest.

One of the more unusual Palm Sunday customs in Germany is the *Palm Esel*, or wooden Palm Donkey, symbolic of the ass upon which Jesus entered Jerusalem. This survival of an ancient folk custom is carried to the village church. People believe that if they touch the Palm Donkey, they will share in the blessing that emanated from the humble ass that once carried Jesus.

See also PALM SUNDAY (AUSTRIA).

CONTACTS:
UK-German Connection
34 Belgrave Sq.
London, SW1X 8QB United Kingdom
44-20-7824-1570
www.ukgermanconnection.org

♦ 2195 ♦ Palm Sunday (Italy) (Domenica delle Palme)
Between March 15 and April 18; the Sunday before Easter

On PALM SUNDAY, the piazzas in front of most small Italian churches are filled with people dressed in spring clothes and vendors selling olive and palm branches. The olive branches are often gilded or painted silver, and the palms are braided into crosses and decorated with roses, lilies, or other flowers. After the palms have been blessed in the church, they are often exchanged as a peace offering or sign of reconciliation between those who have quarreled. In Rapallo, a center for the silk industry, silkworms' eggs are taken to church on Palm Sunday to be blessed.

The most impressive Palm Sunday observance, however, takes place in Rome. The pope, carried in ST. PETER'S CHAIR on the shoulders of eight men, comes out of St. Peter's Basilica to bless the palms. After the service, the golden palms are distributed among the clergy and the olive branches are distributed to the congregation. Then the thousands of worshippers who have gathered in St. Peter's Square march through the basilica and around the portico, emerging from one door and re-entering through another to symbolize the entry of Jesus into Jerusalem. The procession eventually makes its way to the high altar, where mass is said. Some of the palm branches are saved and later burned to make the next year's ASH WEDNESDAY ashes. The rest are given to the people to take home, where they are treasured as protection against evil, particularly lightning and storms.

CONTACTS:
Italian Government Tourist Board
686 Park Ave.
3rd Fl.
New York, NY 10065
212-245-5618; fax: 212-586-9249
www.italiantourism.com

♦ 2196 ♦ Palm Sunday (Netherlands) (Palm Zondag)
Between March 15 and April 18; the Sunday before Easter

The *Palmpaas*, or "Easter palm," in the Netherlands is a stick between 18" and 54" long to which a hoop has been attached. The hoop is covered with boxwood and decorated with colored paper flags, eggshells, sugar rings, oranges, raisins, figs, chocolate eggs, and small cakes. There are figures of swans or cocks on top that are made out of baked dough. Sometimes there are contests for the most elaborate Palmpaas. Children in rural areas of the Netherlands go from one farm to the next with their Palmpaas, singing nonsense verses in which they ask for Easter eggs, sometimes for use in the popular Easter sport of *eiertikken*, or egg tapping.

With its egg and bird decorations, it seems likely that the Palmpaas was originally a fertility symbol that represented the arrival of spring in the village and the resurgence of life after winter. In some Roman Catholic areas, the Palmpaas are blessed by the local priest and then saved as protection against lightning and sore throats during the coming year.

CONTACTS:
Netherlands Board of Tourism & Conventions
215 Park Ave. S.
Ste. 2005
New York, NY 10003
917-720-1283; fax: 212-370-9507
www.visitholland.nl

♦ 2197 ♦ Palm Sunday (United States)
Between March 15 and April 18; the Sunday before Easter

Programs of sacred music are performed in many American towns and cities on PALM SUNDAY. They are often sponsored by and held in churches, but may be part of the musical community's regular concert series. These programs usually begin on or before Palm Sunday and may continue throughout HOLY WEEK. Some of the more popular pieces performed at these concerts include Bach's *St. John Passion* or *St. Matthew Passion*, Handel's *Messiah*, Gounod's *La Rédemption*, Haydn's *Seven Last Words*, Beethoven's *Christ on the Mount of Olives*, and Sir John Stainer's *Crucifixion*. Bethany College's MESSIAH FESTIVAL in Lindsborg, Kansas, has been held during Holy Week for over 100 years.

In addition to musical performances, plays or pageants dealing with Holy Week themes are often performed on Palm Sunday as well. The same group that performs the BLACK HILLS PASSION PLAY in South Dakota all summer for many years portrayed the last seven days in the life of Christ during Holy Week at an amphitheater near Lake Wales, Florida.

In St. Augustine, Florida, the Blessing of the Fishing and Shrimp Fleet takes place on Palm Sunday. Shrimp trawlers and other fishing boats, as well as many privately owned vessels, circle past the City Yacht Pier to receive the local priest's blessing.

Many people place the palm branches that have been blessed in the churches on Palm Sunday behind religious pictures and statues in homes, stores, and restaurants.

CONTACTS:
St. Augustine, Ponte Vedra & The Beaches Visitors & Convention Bureau
29 Old Mission Ave.
St. Augustine, FL 32084
800-653-2489
www.floridashistoriccoast.com

United States Conference of Catholic Bishops of Catholic Bishops
3211 Fourth St. N.E.
Washington, D.C. 20017
202-541-3000
www.usccb.org

♦ 2198 ♦ Pan American Day
April 14

April 14, 1890, is the day on which the First International Conference of American States adopted a resolution forming what is now known as the Organization of American States (OAS). The original member countries include Argentina, Bolivia, Brazil, Chile, Colombia, Costa Rica, Cuba, the Dominican Republic, Ecuador, El Salvador, Guatemala, Haiti, Honduras, Mexico, Nicaragua, Panama, Paraguay, Peru, the United States, Uruguay, and Venezuela. Since 1967, 14 more countries have joined: Barbados, Trinidad and Tobago, Jamaica, Grenada, Suriname, Dominica, St. Lucia, Antigua and Barbuda, St. Vincent and the Grenadines, the Bahamas, St. Kitts and Nevis, Canada, Belize, and Guyana.

The purpose of the OAS, which has remained basically unchanged since that time, is to strengthen peace and security in the Western Hemisphere by promoting understanding among the various countries of North, Central, and South America. The International Union of American Republics (now called the Pan American Union)—the central permanent agency and general secretariat of the OAS—designated April 14 as Pan American Day in 1930, and it was first observed the following year.

Although each member country holds its own celebration, it is at the Pan American Union building in Washington, D.C., that one of the largest observances takes place. Students from all over the Western Hemisphere travel to Washington where, against a backdrop of flags in the courtyard of the House of the Americas, they perform a program of folk songs and dances. Ceremonies are also held in Miami and in other cities with large populations from Latin American countries.

CONTACTS:
Organization of American States
17th St. & Constitution Ave. N.W.
Washington, D.C. 20006
202-370-5000; fax: 202-458-3967
www.oas.org

♦ 2199 ♦ Panafrican Film and Television Festival of Ouagadougou
February-March in odd-numbered years

The Panafrican Film and Television Festival of Ouagadougou, also known as *Festival Panafricain du Cinéma et de la Télévision de Ouagadougou* (FESPACO), is a biennial event established in 1969. It is conducted in Ouagadougou, the capital of Burkina Faso, West Africa. In addition to a revolving theme pertaining to the art of filmmaking, the festival focuses on the promotion of films having any connection to Africa, whether in terms of their narrative, the persons involved, their setting, or any other aspect. Over 150 films are selected in feature, short film, documentary, and other categories. The Stallion of Yennenga award is given to the African film that best demonstrates "Africa's realities." Other awards include the Oumarou Ganda Prize for the best first film, the Paul Robeson Prize for the best film by a director of the African diaspora, and honors for best screenplay, original score, actor, actress, and sound editing, among other categories. The festival also includes the African International Film and TV Market (MICA), which provides filmmakers with the chance to market their work and find appropriate financiers.

CONTACTS:
FESPACO (Panafrican Film & Television Festival of Ouagadougou)
Ouagadougou 01
 Burkina Faso
226-2530-8370
www.fespaco.bf/en

♦ 2200 ♦ Pan-African Film Festival
February

The Pan-African Film Festival was introduced in Los Angeles, California, in 1992 with the aim of promoting cultural understanding among people of African descent through film. More than 150 movies from around the world are screened at the Baldwin Hills Crenshaw Plaza. Students are able to view films about topics such as youth issues, literacy, and self-esteem free of charge. Awards are presented for best narrative feature, narrative short, documentary, and director-first feature. Community forums are also a major part of the festival.

CONTACTS:
Pan African Film Festival Office
6820 La Tijera Blvd
Ste. 200

Los Angeles, CA 90045
310-337-4737; fax: 310-337-4736
www.paff.org

♦ 2201 ♦ Panama Independence Days
November 3; November 28

Panama celebrates two Independence Days: November 28, the anniversary of freedom from Spain, and November 3, the anniversary of independence from Colombia. Both are national holidays. After gaining independence from Spain on November 28, 1821, Panama joined the Republic of Greater Colombia. For 50 years, Panama struggled for complete autonomy. In 1903, Colombia and Panama disagreed on whether to let the U.S. build a canal at Panama. With U.S. backing, Panama broke away on November 3, 1903, and the canal was built.

November 3 is celebrated with parades and fireworks in Panama City.

CONTACTS:
Panama Embassy
2862 McGill Terr. N.W
Washington, D.C. 20008
202-483-1407; fax: 202-483-8413
www.embassyofpanama.org

♦ 2202 ♦ Panathenaea
July or August

Panathenaea is the most important of the ancient Greek festivals, celebrated in Athens in honor of Athena, the patron goddess of that city. The lesser festival was held every year, and the Great Panathenaea every fourth year much more elaborately. The date was the 28th of the Attic month of Hecatombaeon (July or August).

In the yearly celebrations, there were musical and athletic contests, animal sacrifices, and a procession. The procession of the Great Panathenaea was an especially grand affair and is pictured on a frieze of the Parthenon. The *peplus*, a garment with an embroidered depiction of the battle of the gods and the giants, was rigged like a sail on a ship with wheels and carried through the city to the Acropolis. The procession included priests leading a train of animals that would be sacrificed, maidens carrying sacrificial implements, warriors, old men with olive branches, and horses. The festival ended with the sacrifice of oxen and a banquet.

CONTACTS:
FHW
Poulopoulou 38
Athens, 118 51 Greece
212-254-5000; fax: 212-254-3838
www.ime.gr

♦ 2203 ♦ Pancake Day
Between February 3 and March 9; Shrove Tuesday

For the people of Olney, England, and Liberal, Kansas, Pancake Day is more than another name for Shrove Tuesday. The old custom of making pancakes on the Tuesday preceding Ash Wednesday has survived in the form of a Pancake Race. Ladies of both towns run a 450-yard course, flipping pancakes as they go. Participants must wear a skirt, an apron, and a headscarf, and must toss their pancakes in the air three times as they run. The winner of the Kansas race is announced by a transatlantic phone call to Olney immediately after it is over.

The Olney race dates back to 1445. According to the legend, a housewife who was making pancakes heard the bell summoning her to church and was in such a hurry that she ran along the road with the frying pan still in her hand. The Liberal, Kansas, race has been run since 1950. It only lasts about a minute, but it draws a good deal of media attention and is followed by pancake-eating contests, a parade, and children's races.

CONTACTS:
Pancake Day of Liberal
318 N. Lincoln Ave.
Liberal, KS 67905
620-624-6423
www.pancakeday.net

Olney Centre
High St
Olney
Buckinghamshire, MK46 4EF United Kingdom
44-1234-711679; fax: 44-1234-241107
www.olneytowncouncil.gov.uk

♦ 2204 ♦ **Panchadaan**
*August-September, third day of waning half
of Hindu month of Bhadrapada; July-August,
eighth day of waxing half of Hindu month of
Sravana*

The **Alms Giving Festival** in Nepal is based on the Dangatha chapter of the *Kapidawdan*, an ancient Buddhist text, stating that those who donate food and clothing to beggars on this day will be blessed with seven great gifts: health, happiness, longevity, wisdom, wealth, fame, and children. All Buddhists, rich or poor, go from door to door in large groups begging for alms. They are usually well received in Nepalese homes—even non-Buddhist people give food or money to the Buddhist beggars on this day.

In Patan and elsewhere in Nepal, Panchadaan is observed on the eighth day of the waxing half of Sravana. In Kathmandu and Bhadgaon, it is observed on the third day of the waning half of Bhadrapada.

♦ 2205 ♦ **Panguni Uttiram (Panguni Uthiram)**
*March-April; 10 days including full moon day of
Hindu month of Caitra*

The full moon day of Caitra is the day on which the Hindu god Shiva married the goddess Meenakshi at Madura, Indonesia.

The 10-day Hindu festival that follows also celebrates the marriage of Subramanya to Theivanai, adopted daughter of Indra.

Panguni Uttiram is a popular festival in Malaysia, where the worship of Subramanya is widespread. There are fairs on the temple grounds and processions in which Hindu gods and goddesses are carried through the streets in chariots. In Kuala Lumpur, Subramanya and his consort are taken from the Sentul temple in an elaborately decorated chariot through the city streets. Free meals are served throughout the day to visitors. At Bukit Mertajam, a fire-walking ceremony is held on this day.

In India, this festival is known as Meenakshi Kalyanam.

CONTACTS:
Malaysian Tourism Promotion Board
818 W. Seventh St.
Ste. 970
Los Angeles, CA 90017
213-689-9702; fax: 213-689-1530
www.tourism.gov.my

♦ 2206 ♦ **Papa Festival**
January

According to tradition, Okomfo Anokye, the founder of the Ashanti nation in Ghana used the following method for choosing a location for the capital city: he planted two trees and decided to establish the seat of government at whichever site's tree grew. The tree planted at Kumasi flourished, thus Kumasi is the capital of the Ashanti Region. The other tree, planted at Kumawu, died. Still, each year in January the people of Kumawu remember their past.

The festival is named for the local god and begins with a procession of ancestral stools, or thrones, to a nearby river, where they are cleansed. Then a bonfire is lit and burns all night. The next morning, the chief makes an offering to all the chiefs who have passed on. Finally, a procession takes the chief, carried in a palanquin, to the site where the legendary tree was planted for the ritual slaughtering of a cow or bull. Later, there is a scramble of young men to cut a piece of the meat. Those who attempt to do so are often beaten back with whips and branches, but those who succeed in escaping with their portion are regarded with admiration, especially by the young women in the crowd of spectators.

CONTACTS:
Ghana Tourism Authority
P.O. Box GP 3106
Ghana
233-302-682601; fax: 233-302-682510
www.ghana.travel

Embassy of Ghana
3512 International Dr. N.W.
Washington, D.C. 20008
202-686-4520; fax: 202-686-4527
www.ghanaembassy.org

♦ 2207 ♦ Papua New Guinea Independence Day
September 16

This national holiday celebrates Papua New Guinea's independence on this day in 1975. In the late 19th century Germany laid claim to the northeastern section of the island, while Britain ruled the southeastern section. Britain left its section to Australia in 1902, which occupied the German area in 1914, and eventually administered the whole area until independence, though it is still part of the British Commonwealth.

In 2000, Papua New Guinea celebrated its silver jubilee (25th) anniversary of independence with a flag-raising ceremony, a parade, and musical and dance performances in the capital city, Port Moresby. In 2015, the 40th anniversary of independence will be observed.

CONTACTS:
Embassy of Papua New Guinea
1779 Massachusetts Ave. N.W.
Ste. 805
Washington, D.C. 20036
202-745-3680; fax: 202-745-3679
www.pngembassy.org

♦ 2208 ♦ Parada del Sol
Late February

In 1951 the town of Scottsdale, Ariz., began an annual Sunshine Festival. The event featured a parade through the downtown that led to the city park for a family barbeque. In 1954, the newly-formed Scottsdale Jaycees took over the event and renamed it the Parada del Sol.

Wanting to use the Parada del Sol to highlight Scottsdale's Old West heritage, the Jaycees adopted the slogan "The West's Most Western Town" to promote the event. They added Western-style staged gunfights and holdups to the festival. In 1956 a Professional Rodeo Cowboys Association-sanctioned rodeo was added. Over the years, the rodeo has been held at different sites around Scottsdale, including the Scottsdale Stadium and the Rawhide Western Town. It is now located at the Equidome Arena at WestWorld in north Scottsdale.

Since 1959 the Parada del Sol has begun with the Hashknife Pony Express run from the town of Holbrook to Scottsdale, the only pony express service still officially authorized by the U.S. Postal Service. This delivery is followed by the two-mile parade itself, held on a Saturday, which features 150 floats and some 1,000 horses. The parade ends in Old Town, where spectators can go for a block party with food, drinks, games, live music, and pony rides for the children. The three-day rodeo begins on the following Friday.

CONTACTS:
Parada del Sol
P.O. Box 292
Scottsdale, AZ 85252
480-990-3179
www.paradadelsol.rodeo

♦ 2209 ♦ Paraguay Independence Day
May 14 and 15

Paraguayans set aside two days to celebrate their independence from Spain, which they won on May 14, 1811, after a bloodless revolution led by Dr. José Gaspar Rodríguez Francia (1766-1840). Dr. Francia was also instrumental in the design of Paraguay's flag, which is the only national flag in the world that is different on both sides.

The most elaborate Independence Day parade is in the capital, Asunción. People may wear traditional clothes as they stroll down the streets: for the men, fancy shirts, broad-brimmed straw hats, ponchos, a *faja* (sash) around the waist, and full trousers known as *bombachas*; for the women, blouses with lace inserts and brightly colored embroidery, full skirts with many layers of petticoats underneath, and a *rebozo* or shawl similar to the Spanish mantilla. *Sopa Paraguay*, a traditional Independence Day dish, is served on this day because it is only on special occasions that the poor can afford to buy the eggs and cheese that go into the soup.

CONTACTS:
Embassy of Paraguay
2400 Massachusetts Ave. N.W.
Washington, D.C. 20008
202-483-6960; fax: 202-234-4508
www.mre.gov.py/embaparusa/en/index-eng.html

♦ 2210 ♦ Pardon of Nossa Senhora dos Remédios
Early September

Both religious and secular activities play a part in the Pardon of Nossa Senhora dos Remédios, a pilgrimage to the Sanctuary of Our Lady of the Remedies in Lamego, Portugal, a small town known for its port wine and smoked ham. Great numbers of pilgrims climb the monumental staircase up to the baroque church, but the highlight of the festival is the triumphal procession on the last day, in which thousands of country people in local costume participate. There is also a battle of flowers, a folklore festival, fireworks, sports contests, and handicraft exhibitions.

CONTACTS:
Portuguese National Tourist Office
590 Fifth Ave.
4th Fl.
New York, NY 10036
www.visitportugal.com/en

♦ 2211 ♦ Pardon of Ste. Anne d'Auray
Last weekend in July

In the 17th century in Brittany, the story goes, Sт. Anne, mother of the Virgin Mary, appeared to a peasant named Yves (or Yvon) and told him that she wanted to see her ruined chapel rebuilt. Yves reported this to his bishop, who at first refused to believe him, but eventually changed his mind. Soon afterward, a broken image of St. Anne was found in a field nearby, and people started making contributions so that the effigy could be enshrined. A church was built in Auray and soon it became a place of pilgrimage for believers all over France.

The **Pardon of St. Anne** remains one of Brittany's most picturesque festivals. On their knees, 20,000 devout Roman Catholics mount the *Scala Santa,* the sacred stairway leading to the chapel containing St. Anne's statue. Many Bretons attending the festival wear the ornate headdresses and embroidered costumes for which their province is famous. They come to pay homage to St. Anne and pray she will grant their requests.

CONTACTS:
Association of Shrine Towns of France
267, rue Jean-Marie Vianney
France
33-4-7408-1076; fax: 33-4-7408-1542
www.villes-sanctuaires.com

♦ 2212 ♦ Parentalia
February 13

This was an ancient Roman festival held in honor of the *manes,* or souls of the dead—in particular, deceased relatives. It began a season for remembering the dead, which ended with the FERALIA on February 21. This week was a quiet, serious occasion, without the rowdiness that characterized other Roman festivals. Everything, including the temples, closed down, and people decorated graves with flowers and left food—sometimes elaborate banquets—in the cemeteries in the belief that it would be eaten by the spirits of the deceased.

February 22 was devoted to forgiveness and the restoration of friendships broken during the preceding year.

♦ 2213 ♦ Parilia (Palilia)
April 21

This ancient Roman festival was held in honor of Pales, the protector of shepherds and their flocks—although some say it was named after *pario,* meaning "to bear or increase." Pales was sometimes regarded as male, and therefore similar to Pan or Faunus, and sometimes as female, and therefore related to Vesta, or Anna Parenna (*see* ANNA PARENNA FESTIVAL). In any case, the Parilia was a pastoral rite that was observed not only in rural areas but also in Rome, where it coincided with the city's founding in 753 B.C.E. In fact, it is believed that Romulus, one of the legendary founders of Rome, played a significant role in the cleansing and renewal rituals associated with the Parilia.

Although no sacrifices were offered, lustrations (purifying ceremonies) were carried out with fire and smoke. The blood that had been preserved from the OCTOBER HORSE SACRIFICE six months earlier was burned, as were bean shells and the ashes of the cattle sacrificed at the CEREALIA. The stables were purified with smoke and swept out with brooms. There were also offerings to Pales of cheese, boiled wine, and millet cakes. In rural areas, heaps of straw were set ablaze, and

shepherds and their flocks had to pass over or through them three times. The festival ended with a huge open-air feast.

♦ 2214 ♦ Paris Air and Space Show
June in odd-numbered years

The biennial **Salons Internationaux de l'Aéronautique et de l'Espace** is held at Le Bourget Airport just outside of Paris—the airfield where Charles Lindbergh landed after his historic nonstop flight from New York in 1927. It attracts more than half a million visitors who come to see exhibits of aircraft, launching and ground equipment, missile propulsion units, navigational aids, anti-aircraft detection devices, and other aeronautic equipment.

On the last day of the 11-day event there is a special flying demonstration that has occasionally been marred by spectacular crashes. In 1989, for example, a Soviet MiG-29 flying only 580 feet above the ground in a maneuver designed to display its slow-speed handling suddenly plummeted earthward, burying its needle-shaped nose eight feet into the rain-softened turf before bursting into flames. The pilot was fortunate enough to have ejected in time and sustained only minor injuries.

The 39th biennial Paris Air Show was held in 1991, just a few months after the Persian Gulf War, and a worldwide recession had threatened to scuttle the event. But the role played by high technology aircraft in the Allied victory over Saddam Hussein attracted a record number of exhibitors—approximately 1,700 from 38 countries—and spectators. The 1999 show hosted 1,895 exhibitors from 41 countries and more than 250,000 visitors.

CONTACTS:
Salons International De L'Aeronautique Et De L'Espace
Le Bourget, Paris 93350 France
www.siae.fr

♦ 2215 ♦ Paris Autumn Festival (Festival d'Automne)
Mid-September through late December

The Autumn Festival marks the return of Parisians from their August holidays and the start of the city's cultural season. When it was founded in 1972, the festival incorporated two existing events—Semaines Musicales Internationales and the Festival of International Dance—with theater and art exhibitions. It now encompasses film, photography, and other contemporary arts on an international scale.

Most of the theater presentations are experimental in some way, and they have included productions by Richard Foreman's Ontological Hysteric Theatre from the United States, Peter Stein's Schaubuhne am Halleschen Ufer from West Berlin, Denmark's Odin Teatret, Poland's Teatr Cricot 2, and Taganka Theatre from the former U.S.S.R.

Composers whose works have been performed there include Pierre Boulez, György Ligeti, John Cage, and Iannis Zenakis.

Martha Graham's, Merce Cunningham's, and Maurice Béjart's dance companies have performed at the festival, as have the New York Philharmonic, the London Sinfonietta, and the Orchestre de Paris. Events are held in numerous locations throughout Paris, among them the Pompidou Center, the Théâtre de Chaillot, and the Théâtre des Champs Elysées.

CONTACTS:
Fall Festival in Paris
156, rue de Rivoli
Paris, 75001 France
33-1-5345-1700; fax: 33-1-5345-1701
www.festival-automne.com

♦ 2216 ♦ **Parker (Charlie) Jazz Festival**
Last weekend in August

The Charlie Parker Jazz Festival is a free event sponsored by the City Parks Foundation in New York City. Held annually since 1993, the event comprises two concerts held over a weekend in late August to commemorate Parker's birthday, August 29, 1920. Known to jazz followers as "Yardbird" or more simply "Bird," Parker was one of the most innovative and influential jazz saxophonists of the 20th century. His works are particularly noted for their complexity and virtuoso improvisation, which continue to attract critical admiration more than 50 years after his death in 1955.

The festival concerts take place at Marcus Garvey Park in Harlem and Tompkins Square Park in the East Village, neighborhoods in which Parker lived and worked. In 2014, the 22nd edition of the Charlie Parker Jazz Festival featured both jazz veterans and up-and-coming stars alike. Highlights included The Wallace Roney Orchestra, young Jazz singer Brianna Thomas, and "The Marriage of Latin Music & Jazz," a panel discussion led by Joe Conzo Sr., Latin music historian and publicist and confidante of the late Tito Puente.

CONTACTS:
City Parks Foundation
830 Fifth Ave.
New York, NY 10065
212-360-1399; fax: 212-360-8283
www.cityparksfoundation.org

♦ 2217 ♦ **Parks (Rosa) Day**
First Monday following February 4

Rosa Parks Day is an observance in California that commemorates the birthday of Rosa Parks, an Alabama-born African American woman widely known for her role in the civil rights movement. In 1955, Parks was travelling home from work on a Montgomery, Alabama bus when she was asked to vacate her seat for a white man, a standard practice in America at the time. Parks refused to give up her seat and risked arrest for violating the law. Along with Dr. Martin Luther King Jr., the influential civil rights leader, she joined the boycott of the Montgomery public transportation system, which lasted more than a year. In 1956, the U.S. Supreme Court decreed the law of segregation unconstitutional. Parks also played an active role in the civil rights movement as secretary of the Montgomery chapter of the National Association for the Advancement of Colored People (NAACP), and later, as advisor of the NAACP Youth Council.

Parks was recipient of many awards and honors in her lifetime, including the Presidential Medal of Freedom, the nation's highest civilian honor. Widely regarded as the mother of the civil rights movement, she continues to inspire generations due to her courageous act of civil disobedience and her dedication to the concepts of human rights and freedom. The first commemoration of Rosa Parks Day occurred in 2000. Church leaders, politicians, schools, and social organizations celebrate the day with a series of events and activities to remember and honor Parks and her struggle against racial discrimination. The Rosa Parks bus, a symbol of the fight for social justice, is on display in the Henry Ford Museum in Dearborn, Michigan, in her memory.

♦ 2218 ♦ **Paro Tsechu**
Early spring on a date set by the lamas, or 10th-15th days of second lunar month

One of the most popular festivals of Bhutan, a principality northeast of India in the Himalayas, is held in the town of Paro. (*Tsechus* means "tenth day" and relates to the birth of the Buddha. It is used as "festival" is used in English.)

The Paro festival is held over five days to commemorate the life and deeds of Padmasambhava [*see also* MYSTERY PLAY OF (TIBET)]. Known in Bhutan as Guru Rinpoche, he was a mystic who lived in the eighth century and brought Buddhism to Bhutan from Tibet.

The purpose of this festival is to exorcize evil influences and to ensure good fortune in the coming year. The highlight of Paro events comes before dawn on the last day when a huge appliqued scroll known as the *Thongdrel* is unfurled from the top of the wall of the *Dzong* (the monastery and district center). It is displayed to onlookers in the courtyard until just before the first rays of the sun touch it. The Thongdrel is said to have the power to confer blessings and provide respite from the cycle of existence. It is a type of *thangka* (a religious scroll of any size) and is so big that it covers the three-story wall of the Dzong, and it depicts the life of the Guru Rinpoche, his various peaceful manifestations, and his consorts.

Dressed in their best clothes, people bring dried yak meat and *churra*, a puffed rice dish, to the Dzong and watch masked dancers. A series of dances, called *cham*, are performed for the festival. One of these, the Black Hat Dance, tells of the victory over a Tibetan king who tried to wipe out Buddhism; those who watch the dance are supposed to receive great spiritual blessings. The Dance of the Four Stags commemorates the vanquishing of the god of the wind by Guru Rinpoche. The god rode on a stag, and the guru commandeered the stag as his own mount. Another dance, the Deer Dance, tells the story of Guru Rinpoche teaching Buddhism while traveling through the country on the back of a deer. The dances are performed by monks who play the roles of deities, heroes, and animals dressed in brilliantly colored silks and brocades. They wear carved wooden or papier mâché masks symbolizing the figure they portray.

The dances are accompanied by the music of drums, bells, gongs, conch-shell trumpets, and horns. Some horns are so long that they touch the ground.

Other activities include folk dancing and singing and lewd performances by clowns called *atsaras*. Many of the dances and performances are typical of Tibetan Buddhist traditions also observed in Tibet and the Ladakh area of India.

CONTACTS:
Bhutan Travel Bureau
P.O. Box 126
Bhutan
975-2-323251; fax: 975-2-323695
www.tourism.gov.bt/activities/festivals

♦ 2219 ♦ **Parshurama Jayanti**
April-May; third day of waxing half of Hindu month of Vaisakha

According to Hindu mythology, it was Parashurama (Rama with an Ax) who destroyed the evil Kshatriya kings and princes 21 times, including the thousand-armed warrior, Arjuna. His birthday, Parashurama Jayanti, is therefore observed with fasting, austerities, and prayer. It is also a day to worship Lord Vishnu, of whom Parashurama is believed to be the sixth incarnation. To Hindus, Parashurama represents filial obedience, austerity, power, and brahmanic ideals.

Parashurama's story is told in the *Mahabharata* and in the Puranas, or Hindu epics. He also appears in the *Ramayana*, where he challenges Ramachandra, the seventh avatar or incarnation of Vishnu, to a test of strength. When it becomes apparent that he is losing, Parashurama pays homage to Ramachandra and retires to the Himalayas. The Malabar region on the southwest coast of India is believed to have been founded by Parashurama.

♦ 2220 ♦ **Parshva, Birthday of**
December-January; 10th day of the waning half of the Jain month of Pausa

Parshva was the 23rd Jina or Tirthankara (spiritual guide) of Jainism. He lived during the ninth century B.C.E., for about 100 years, according to legend. He became a wandering ascetic when he was 30 years old and later founded what is considered the original white-clad (Svetambara) monks in the Jaina tradition. His birth is celebrated by Jains on the 10th day of the waning half of Pausa (December-January), particularly in Bihar and West Bengal, where he gained a large following.

The parents of MAHAVIRA (6th century B.C.E.), the 24th Tirthankara and "Great Hero" of the Jain religion, were adherents of Parshva's spiritual teachings. Although

Mahavira is much better known, Jains believe that he did not found a new religion so much as provide guidance for a tradition that had already been established.

♦ 2221 ♦ **Partridge Day**
September 1

This is traditionally the day on which the partridge-hunting season opens in England. Just as Grouse Day in Scotland (*see* GLORIOUS TWELFTH) was often referred to as St. Grouse's Day, Partridge Day was sometimes called **St. Partridge's Day**.

♦ 2222 ♦ **Paryushana**
August-September; Hindu month of Bhadrapada

Like most other Jaina festivals, the Paryushana festival is observed by focusing on the 10 cardinal virtues: forgiveness, charity, simplicity, contentment, truthfulness, self-restraint, fasting, detachment, humility, and continence. Believers ask those whom they may have offended to forgive them, and friendships that have lapsed during the year are restored.

The Paryushana festival is observed all over India in the month of Bhadrapada (August-September), but on different dates. The Svetambara Jainas observe it for eight days, and then the ten-day celebration of the Digambara Jainas begins.

♦ 2223 ♦ **Pascua Florida Day**
On or near April 2

Although no one knows for certain the date on which Ponce de León (1460-1521) landed at Florida in 1513, it is widely believed that he first stepped ashore somewhere between St. Augustine and the mouth of the St. Johns River on April 2. He named the land Pascua Florida because it was Eastertime. *Pascua* is a Spanish word meaning "Easter," and *Florida* means "flowering" or "full of flowers." (In Scotland and northern England, another name for EASTER was Pasch Day; among Orthodox Christians it is called Pascha.)

The Florida state legislature designated April 2 **Florida State Day** in 1953, but when it falls on a Saturday or Sunday, the holiday is observed on the preceding Friday or the following Monday. The week ending on April 2 is known as Pascua Florida Week, a time when both school children and adults are encouraged to attend special programs devoted to the area's discovery and history.

♦ 2224 ♦ **Passion Play at Tzintzuntzan**
Between March 19 and April 22; Thursday and Friday before Easter

The *Penitentes*, or penitents, are a lay brotherhood of religious flagellants. In Mexico on GOOD FRIDAY, they often participate in Passion plays dramatizing the events of the closing days in the life of Jesus. One of the most complete and colorful Passion plays is the one staged in Tzintzuntzan in the state of Michoacán. Performed in an olive grove near the church, the play begins at noon on the Thursday preceding EASTER with a representation of the Last Supper and continues until midnight on Good Friday. The penitents wear black loincloths and face-coverings, lashing their own bare backs and wearing chains that bite into the flesh of their ankles. They carry heavy crosses in imitation of Jesus. In Passion plays elsewhere in Mexico, the penitents hold bundles of cacti on their shoulders while candles burn into the palms of their hands.

CONTACTS:
Mexico Tourism Board
Viaducto Miguel Alemán 105 Col
Escandón, Chiapas 11800 Mexico
800-262-9128 or 800-446-3942
www.visitmexico.com

♦ 2225 ♦ Passover
Begins between March 27 and April 24; Nisan 15-21 (or 22)

Also known as **Pesah**, **Pesach**, or the **Feast of Unleavened Bread**, Passover is an eight-day celebration (seven days in Israel and by Reform Jews) of the deliverance of the Jews from slavery in Egypt. It is one of the three PILGRIM FESTIVALS (*see also* SHAVUOT and SUKKOT). According to the book of Exodus, when Pharaoh refused to let Moses lead the Jews out of Egypt, God sent a number of plagues—including locusts, fire, and hailstones—but Pharaoh still was unmoved. A 10th and final plague, during which the Angel of Death was sent to kill the Egyptians' first-born sons, finally persuaded Pharaoh to relent. All the Jews had been instructed to sacrifice a lamb and sprinkle the blood on their doorposts so that the Angel would "pass over" and spare their sons.

Jewish families today eat a ceremonial dinner called the *Seder* at which they retell the story of the Exodus from Egypt and eat various symbolic foods—including meat of the paschal lamb, bitter herbs (recalling the harsh life of slavery) and wine (symbolizing the fruitfulness of the earth). The *matzoh*, a flat, unleavened bread, is meant to symbolize the haste with which the Jews left: they didn't have time to let their bread rise before baking it. In strictly religious Jewish homes today, all foods made with leavening are prohibited during this season.

See also FIRSTBORN, FAST OF THE.

CONTACTS:
Union of Orthodox Jewish Congregations of America
11 Broadway
New York, NY 10004
212-563-4000
www.ou.org

♦ 2226 ♦ Patriot Day
September 11

Patriot Day in the United States commemorates the anniversary of the terrorist attacks that took place on September 11, 2001, in New York City, N.Y.; Washington, D.C.; and in the skies above Shanksville, Penn. On that day,

hijackers associated with the al Qaeda terrorist organization commandeered four commercial airliners and planned to intentionally crash them into several sites. They flew two of the planes into the Twin Towers of the World Trade Center in lower Manhattan and one into the Pentagon in the nation's capital. The fourth plane, which was believed to be headed either to the White House or to the U.S. Capitol, crashed in a field in rural Pennsylvania after passengers on the plane figured out the hijackers' intentions and resisted them.

As designated by an act of Congress in December 2001, each year the president proclaims a day of national observance in memory of the more than 2,700 people who lost their lives in the attacks. Throughout the nation, flags are flown at half-staff and a moment of silence is observed at 8:46 A.M. Eastern time, the exact moment the first plane flew into the North Tower of the World Trade Center.

Observances take place at each of the three sites of attack. In New York, the site of the greatest loss of life, a memorial service takes place during the morning of September 11 each year; moments of silence are observed at the exact times that the planes crashed into the towers and that the towers collapsed. Surviving family members recite the names of the deceased. On the evening of September 11, a light display known as the Tribute in Light fills the sky with beams of light in the space formerly taken up by the World Trade Center towers. In Washington, D.C., victims of the attacks are remembered at a public wreath-laying ceremony in Arlington National Cemetery as well as a private ceremony at the Pentagon for family and friends of those who died. In Shanksville, Pennsylvania, a memorial service is also held near the crash site of United Airlines Flight 93, the only hijacked aircraft that did not reach its intended target. The ceremony in Pennsylvania includes tolling of the bells and reading a list of victims.

In addition to the services planned at the sites of the attacks, memorial tributes are held throughout the United States, particularly at state and municipal government buildings, public safety offices, and fire stations. These events typically include patriotic remarks, observance of moments of silence, and wreath-laying ceremonies.

CONTACTS:
Arlington National Cemetery
Arlington, VA 22211
703-614-0619 or 877-907-8585
www.arlingtoncemetery.mil

New York City
Office of the Mayor
City Hall
New York, NY 10007
212-639-9675
www.nyc.gov

♦ 2227 ♦ Patriots' Day
Third Monday in April

The battles of Lexington and Concord, Massachusetts, marked the beginning of the American Revolution on April 19, 1775. This is a legal holiday in Massachusetts and Maine.

Although no one really knows who fired the first shot on the Lexington green—"the shot heard 'round the world," in the words of Ralph Waldo Emerson—the British proceeded from Lexington to Concord, where there was a second bloody confrontation at North Bridge.

Residents of Maine and Massachusetts have observed Patriots' Day since the 18th century with costume parades, flag-raising ceremonies, and reenactments of the battles and the famous rides of Paul Revere and William Dawes, who were sent to warn their comrades in Concord of the British troops' approach. The BOSTON MARATHON, one of the most famous of the world's marathon races, is run each year on Patriots' Day. Sometimes this day is referred to as **Lexington Day** or **Battles of Lexington and Concord Day**.

CONTACTS:
Concord Chamber of Commerce
15 Walden St.
Ste. 7
Concord, MA 01742
978-369-3120; fax: 978-369-1515
www.concordchamberofcommerce.org

Lexington Chamber of Commerce
1875 Massachusetts Ave.
Lexington, MA 02420
781-862-2480
lexingtonchamberofcommerce.vpweb.com

♦ 2228 ♦ **Paul Bunyan Show**
First full weekend in October

Paul Bunyan is the mythical hero of lumberjacks in the United States, and many tall tales have been passed down about his adventures with Babe the Blue Ox and Johnny Inkslinger. Among other things, these tales describe how he created Puget Sound and the Grand Canyon, and how his hotcake griddle was so large that it had to be greased by men using sides of bacon for skates. The first Bunyan stories were published in 1910, and within 15 years he had become a national legend.

Since 1952 the **Paul Bunyan Festival,** sponsored jointly by the Ohio Forestry Association and Hocking College in Nelsonville (which grants a degree in forestry) has focused on wood products and forestry conservation. It is the lumber industry's opportunity to familiarize visitors with the journey wood takes from the forest to finished products and an opportunity for both professional and student lumberjacks to test their skills in chopping and sawing. Teams of draft horses compete in a log-skidding contest—an operation that is performed today by heavy machines—and turn-of-the-century steam logging equipment is on display. Billed as the largest live forestry exposition in the East, the show gives visitors an opportunity to see both traditional and modern logging techniques in action.

CONTACTS:
Ohio Forestry Association Inc.
1100-H Brandywine Blvd.
Zanesville, OH 43701
614-497-9580; fax: 614-497-9581
www.ohioforest.org

♦ 2229 ♦ **Pausha Dashami**
December-January; tenth day of the Hindu month of Pausha

In Jainism, one of the world's oldest religions, Pausha Dashami celebrates the birth of Parshvanath, one of the 24 *thritankaras,* or saints. The event extends over three days with fasting, meditation, and ritual prayers forming much of the observances. During Pausha Dashami, a grand religious fair takes place at Sankheshwar, an important Jain pilgrimage center located in western India. Devotees gather in large numbers to observe *Upavas Attham,* the practice of austerity and renunciation in Jainism. They abstain from food during the three days, and some restrict themselves to just drinking boiled water. This observance is believed to bestow prosperity and spiritual happiness on the person. In Jain temples across India and abroad, *bhajans* (mass singing of devotional songs), *abhisheks* (libations), and *arathi* (offering of lamps lit with camphor) make up part of the festival's rituals.

♦ 2230 ♦ **Payment of Quit Rent**
September 29

One of London's oldest and most unusual events, the annual Payment of Quit Rent, takes place at the Royal Courts of Justice on MICHAELMAS, September 29. The ceremony symbolizes the city of London's payment to the Crown for two parcels of land: the first, known as The Forge, is thought to have been the old tournament ground for the Knights of the Templars, who rented it in 1235 for an annual payment of horseshoes and nails. The second, a piece of land in Shropshire known as The Moors, came into the city's possession during the reign of Henry VIII and was rented from the Crown for an annual payment of a bill-hook and a hatchet.

During the first part of the ceremony, the City Solicitor counts out six huge horseshoes from Flemish war horses and 61 nails. He gives them to the Queen's Remembrancer, who keeps them in his office until the following year. During the second part, the City Solicitor demonstrates how sharp the blades of the bill-hook and hatchet are by cutting up a bundle of twigs. These, too, are presented to the Queen's Remembrancer, who is dressed in his wig and ceremonial robes.

CONTACTS:
British National Tourism Agency
845 Third Ave.
10th Fl.
New York, NY 10022
212-850-0336
www.visitbritain.org

♦ 2231 ♦ **Payson Rodeo**
Third weekend in August

The Payson Rodeo is a rodeo, parade, and general Wild West three-day weekend in the cowboy-and-cattle country of Payson, Ariz. The first Payson rodeo was held in 1885, and it's been held ever since with no interruptions, not even for war, making it the world's oldest continuous Professional

Rodeo Cowboys Association rodeo. Events of the weekend include the parade with floats, dancers, and cowboys, country music, a chili cookout, and arts and crafts. Total attendance is usually about 30,000.

CONTACTS:
Rim Country Regional Chamber of Commerce
100 W. Main St.
Payson, AZ 85547 United States
928-474-4515 or 800-672-9766 ; fax: 928-474-8812
www.rimcountrychamber.com

♦ 2232 ♦ Peace, International Day of
September

The day of the opening session of the UNITED NATIONS General Assembly, and a day proclaimed by the U.N. to promote the ideals of peace. The first official observance of the day was in September 1982.

At the United Nations the day is marked with a special message by the secretary-general, who then rings the Japanese Peace Bell and invites people throughout the world to reflect on the meaning of peace.

Special events are organized in various countries, and in the United States the mayors of a number of cities issue proclamations for the day.

CONTACTS:
United Nations
Department of Public Information
Rm. S-1070L
New York, NY 10017
212-963-6842; fax: 212-963-6914
www.un.org

♦ 2233 ♦ Peanut Festival, National
Mid-October

The National Peanut Festival is a nine-day festival in Dothan, Ala., honoring the peanut, a multimillion-dollar crop in Alabama. A highlight is the Goober Parade, for which the streets are paved with peanuts by a giant cement mixer that moves along the line of march throwing out a ton of peanuts, while parade watchers scramble for them. It is said the parade attracts as many as 200,000 spectators. Other events include the selection of Peanut Farmer of the Year, a cooking contest of peanut dishes, crafts exhibits, fireworks, a beauty pageant, and live entertainment.

The festival began in 1938, was discontinued during World War II, and resumed in 1947. Revenues from the festival help the economy not only of Dothan but of neighboring areas of Florida and Georgia. Plains, Ga., the home of peanut farmer and former President Jimmy Carter, is just over the state border.

The peanut and its potential became nationally if not internationally known because of the work of George Washington Carver, who in 1896 became head of agricultural research at Tuskegee Institute in Tuskegee, Ala. His research program ultimately developed 300 derivative products from peanuts, including cheese, flour, inks, dyes, soap, and cosmetics. The research was crucial to the South's economy; the peanut crop freed farmers of their dependence on cotton, which depleted the soil and could be wiped out by boll weevils. When Carver arrived in Tuskegee, the peanut was not recognized as a crop; within the next 50 years, it became the South's second largest cash crop after cotton. Carver was the guest of honor at the first Peanut Festival in 1938.

CONTACTS:
National Peanut Festival Association Inc.
5622 Hwy. 231 S.
Dothan, AL 36301
334-793-4323; fax: 334-793-3247
www.nationalpeanutfestival.com

♦ 2234 ♦ Pearl Harbor Day
December 7

Pearl Harbor Day marks the anniversary of the Japanese raid on Pearl Harbor in 1941, bringing the United States into World War II and widening the European war to the Pacific.

The bombing, which began at 7:55 A.M. Hawaiian time on a Sunday morning, lasted little more than an hour but devastated the American military base on the island of Oahu in the Hawaiian Islands. Nearly all the ships of the U.S. Pacific Fleet were anchored there side by side, and most were damaged or destroyed; half the bombers at the army's Hickam Field were destroyed. The battleship USS *Arizona* sank, and 1,177 sailors and Marines went down with the ship, which became their tomb. In all, the attack claimed more than 3,000 casualties— 2,403 killed and 1,178 wounded.

On the following day, President Franklin D. ROOSEVELT addressed a solemn Congress to ask for a declaration of war. His opening unforgettable words: "Yesterday, December 7, 1941—a date which will live in infamy—the United States of America was suddenly and deliberately attacked by naval and air forces of the Empire of Japan." War was declared immediately with only one opposing vote, that by Rep. Jeannette Rankin of Montana.

In the months that followed, the slogan "Remember Pearl Harbor" swept America, and radio stations repeatedly played the song of the same name with these lyrics:

Let's remember Pearl Harbor, as we go to meet the foe,

Let's remember Pearl Harbor, as we did the Alamo.
We will always remember, how they died for liberty,

Let's remember Pearl Harbor, and go on to victory.

Many states proclaim a Pearl Harbor Remembrance Day, and each year, services are held on December 7 at the *Arizona* Memorial in Pearl Harbor. The marble memorial, built over the sunken USS *Arizona* and dedicated in 1962, was designed by architect Albert Preis, a resident of Honolulu who was an Austrian citizen in 1941 and was interned as an enemy alien.

In 1991, on the 50th anniversary of the attack, commemorations were held over several days in Hawaii.

The observances began on Dec. 4, designated as Hawaii Remembrance Day. Ceremonies recalled the death of civilians in downtown Pearl Harbor. One of them was Nancy Masako Arakaki, a nine-year-old Japanese-American girl killed when anti-aircraft shells fell on her Japanese-language school.

On Dec. 5, Survivors Day, families of those present in Pearl Harbor in 1941 attended ceremonies at the *Arizona* Memorial. Franklin Van Valkenburgh, the commanding officer of the USS *Arizona*, was among those remembered; he posthumously won the Medal of Honor for his heroism aboard ship.

Dec. 6 was a Day of Reflection, intended to focus on the gains since the war rather than on the losses of the day.

On Pearl Harbor Day itself, former President George Bush, who received the Distinguished Flying Cross for heroism as a Navy pilot in the Pacific during World War II, spoke at ceremonies beginning at 7:55 a.m. at the *Arizona* Memorial. Other dignitaries were all Americans; no foreign representatives were invited, out of political prudence. Other events included a parade, a flyover by jet fighters, an outdoor concert by the Honolulu Symphony presenting the premiere of *Pearl Harbor Overture: Time of Remembrance* by John Duffy, and a wreath-laying service at the National Memorial Cemetery of the Pacific in the Punchbowl overlooking Honolulu. And finally, at sunset on Pearl Harbor Day, survivors and their families gathered at the Arizona Visitors Center for a final service to honor those who died aboard the battleship in 1941.

CONTACTS:
Library of Congress
101 Independence Ave. S.E.
Washington, D.C. 20540
202-707-5510; fax: 202-707-2076
www.loc.gov

USS Arizona Memorial
1 Arizona Memorial Pl.
Honolulu, HI 96818
808-423-7300; fax: 808-422-7623
www.nps.gov

Naval Historical Center
805 Kidder Breese S.E.
Washington Navy Yard
Bldg. 76
Washington, D.C. 20374
202-433-4882
www.history.navy.mil

♦ 2235 ♦ Pendleton Round-Up and Happy Canyon
Mid-September

One of the best-known rodeos in the West, held since 1910 in the small ranch town of Pendleton, Ore. The home of internationally known saddle makers, Pendleton is also the heart of Oregon's wheat-producing region. The week-long round-up started as a celebration of the end of the wheat harvest. Happy Canyon was inaugurated four years later when two local men decided the entertainment at a local fair was of poor quality and too expensive. The Happy Canyon

shows at first depicted historical episodes and evolved into the present-day Happy Canyon Pageant, a presentation by Northwest Indian tribes that features a teepee encampment and ceremonial dancing. Nowadays, each day of the rodeo begins with a cowboy breakfast (ham, eggs, flapjacks) at Stillman Park and ends with the pageant.

In between, the rodeo features the standard competitions approved by the Professional Rodeo Cowboys Association—bronco riding, bareback riding, Brahma bull riding, steer wrestling, and calf and steer roping. Additionally, there are wild horse and stagecoach races and wild-cow milking.

CONTACTS:
Pendleton Round-Up and Happy Canyon Association
1205 S.W. Court Ave.
Pendleton, OR 97801
541-276-2553 or 800-457-6336; fax: 541-276-9776
www.pendletonroundup.com

♦ 2236 ♦ Penitents, Procession of the (Belgium)
Last Sunday in July

The Procession of the Penitents is a religious procession in Veurne (or Furnes), West Flanders, Belgium. Penitents in coarse robes and hoods walk barefoot through town, many carrying heavy wooden crosses. The procession, to the sound of drumbeats, is interspersed with scenes depicting biblical events. In some, costumed people dramatize Old and New Testament characters. In others there are carved wooden figures on platforms. At the end of the procession, bishops parade carrying the Sacred Host; and as the Sacrament passes, spectators quietly kneel. After the procession is over there is a *kermess*, or fair, in the marketplace. The celebration traditionally draws large crowds.

Two legends account for the origins of the procession. One says that it dates back to 1099 when crusader Count Robert II of Flanders returned from Jerusalem with a fragment of the True Cross. The other traces it to 1644 when townsfolk carried crosses in a reenactment of the last walk of Jesus before his crucifixion. The procession was to seek intercession against the plague and an outbreak of war between the Spanish and French.

CONTACTS:
Tourist Office for Flanders - Brussels
620 Eighth Ave.
44th Fl.
New York, NY 10018
212-584-2336
www.visitflanders.com

Tourist Office for Flanders - Brussels
Place Saint-Denis 16
Veurne, 8630 Belgium
32-58-33-55-00; fax: 32-58-33-55-19
www.veurne.be

♦ 2237 ♦ Penitents, Procession of the (Spain)
Between May 3-June 6; the week preceding Pentecost

During the week before PENTECOST on the Spanish side of the Pyrénées near the French border, a procession of penitents, covered from head to toe in black except for their eyes, makes its way from the village of Burgos to the Abbey of Roncesvalles. With heavy wooden crosses tied to their backs, they struggle up the steep two-mile path that leads to the abbey, chanting a doleful *Miserere*. After attending mass there, the penitents make their confessions without removing the black hoods that hide their faces.

Since the penitents come from five surrounding villages, each parish performs its own penitential march over a five-day period. According to legend, the procession originated as an act of penance among 23 families seeking atonement for the sins they had committed during the year.

CONTACTS:
Navarre Tourist Office
Avenida Roncesvalles, 4
Pamplona, 31002 Spain
34-848-42-04-20
www.turismo.navarra.es

Orreaga-Roncesvalles Tourist Office
Antiguo Molino
Colegiata de Roncesvalles, s/n
Roncesvalles, 31650 Spain
34-948-760-301; fax: 34-948-760-301
www.spain.info

♦ 2238 ♦ **Pennsylvania Day**
On or near October 24

The state of Pennsylvania was named for William Penn, who was born in London on October 24, 1644. As a young man he joined the Quakers, who were at that time considered a radical religious group, and eventually he used his inheritance from his father to establish a Quaker colony in the New World. He put a great deal of thought and planning into how his colony would be governed, and insisted that the colonists treat the Indians with respect. The colony thrived, its population growing from about 1,000 in 1682 to more than 12,000 seven years later.

Pennsylvanians have always held large celebrations on major anniversaries of Penn's birth, and in 1932 the governor proclaimed October 24 as **William Penn Commemoration Day**, or simply **Penn Day**. This day was also commemorated with a special pageant held in Jordans, Buckinghamshire, England, where Penn and his family are buried. Since that time celebrations have tended to be local rather than statewide. In recent decades, the week of October 24 has been celebrated as **Pennsylvania Week**.

Any observation using his name would undoubtedly have made William Penn turn over in his grave, as he was outspoken in his opposition to the practice of naming streets, cities, states, or anything else after people.

CONTACTS:
Pennsylvania Historical and Museum Commission
State Museum Bldg
300 N. St

Harrisburg, PA 17120
717-787-3362
www.portal.state.pa.us

♦ 2239 ♦ **Pennsylvania Dutch Folk Festival**
First week in July

The Pennsylvania Dutch Folk Festival has been held since the 1950s. The festival, which began in Kutztown, Pennsylvania, has been forced to search for a new location in recent years, landing in Schuykill and then in Adamstown. The festival offers demonstrations of traditional Pennsylvania Dutch crafts, such as quilting, folk music and dancing, Pennsylvania Dutch foods, an old-fashioned country auction, a recreation of daily life in a traditional Pennsylvania Dutch community, children's activities, and more.

CONTACTS:
Kutztown Folk Festival
P.O. Box 306
Kutztown, PA 19530
888-674-6136
www.kutztownfestival.com

♦ 2240 ♦ **Pentecost**
Between May 10 and June 13 in West and between May 24 and June 27 in East; seventh Sunday after Easter

As recorded in the New Testament in Acts 2, it was on the 50th day after EASTER that the Apostles were praying together and the Holy Spirit descended on them in the form of tongues of fire. They received the "gift of tongues"—the ability to speak in other languages—and immediately began to preach about Jesus Christ to the Jews from all over the world who had flocked to Jerusalem for the Feast of SHAVUOT. (Pentecost, from the Greek word meaning "fiftieth," is also one of the names for the second of the three Jewish PILGRIM FESTIVALS.) Christian Pentecost thus became not only a commemoration of the Holy Spirit's visit, but also the birth of the Christian Church. It was on roughly this same day, centuries earlier, that Moses received the Ten Commandments on Mt. Sinai and the Jewish religious community got its start.

The English call it **White Sunday**, or **Whitsunday**, after the white garments worn on Pentecost by the newly baptized. Although it is not certain when Pentecost began to be observed by Christians, it may have been as early as the first century. The period beginning with the Saturday before Whitsunday and ending the following Saturday is known as **Whitsuntide**, or in modern times simply as **Whitsun**.

Whitsunday has been linked to pagan spring rites, such as the English custom of Morris dancing and the drinking of "Whitsun ale." In Scotland, Whitsunday was one of the QUARTER DAYS. In Estonia and Finland, eggs are dyed as at Easter because their hens don't lay until this time. In Germany it is called **Pfingsten**, and pink and red peonies, called *Pfingstrosen*, or "Whitsun roses," are the symbols along with birch trees. Some churches lower a carved dove into the congregation and call this "swinging the Holy Ghost." Cattle are decorated and an overdressed person is said to be "dressed like a Whitsun ox." A holdover pagan game is called "hunting the green man," or *Laubmannchen*—a young man dressed in leaves and moss hides, and children hunt for him.

See also KNEELING SUNDAY; PINKSTER DAY.

CONTACTS:
Christian Resource Institute
4801 N.W. 62nd St.
Oklahoma, OK 73122
801-497-0946
www.cresourcei.org

Orthodox Church in America
6850 N. Hempstead Tpke
P.O. Box 675
Syosset, NY 11791
516-922-0550; fax: 516-922-0954
www.oca.org

♦ 2241 ♦ People's Army of North Korea, Founding of the
April 25

The founding of the People's Army of North Korea (official name: Democratic People's Republic of Korea) in 1932 is marked every year with a national public holiday. The main celebration takes place in the capital city of Pyongyang and includes oratorical meetings, where various officials praise the army's exploits. Public displays can also include parades, gun-salutes, fireworks, choruses, dance displays, and drum-beating.

According to the country's official government news agency (Central Korean News Agency of the Democratic People's Republic of Korea), the year 2007 marked the 75th anniversary of the army's founding. While many sources list February 8, 1948, as the army's official start-date, other sources note that earlier versions of the army launched in the 1930s. The North Korean government apparently observes 1932 as the date of the army's founding. Despite the nation's small size, the People's Army of North Korea ranks as the fourth largest military in the world, noted the U.S. Department of Defense in 2013, with an estimated four to five percent of the nation's 24 million people on active duty and another 25 percent assigned to reserve units.

CONTACTS:
Permanent Mission of the Republic of Korea to the United Nations
335 E. 45th St.
New York, NY 10017
212-439-4000; fax: 212-986-1083
un.mofa.go.kr/english/am/un/mission/location/index.jsp

♦ 2242 ♦ Peppercorn Ceremony
Day near April 23

This ceremony has been a tradition on the island of Bermuda since 1816, when a lease to the State House in St. George

(the seat of Bermuda's government from 1620-1815) was granted to the mayor, aldermen, and common council of St. George in trust by the members of the Masonic Lodge for the annual rent of one peppercorn. The date for the annual rent payment was originally December 27, the feast of ST. JOHN THE EVANGELIST, but it was changed to the most suitable day nearest April 23, ST. GEORGE'S DAY, in honor of the patron saint for whom the town is named.

On the day of the Peppercorn Ceremony, the governor of Bermuda arrives at the State House with great pomp in a horse-drawn carriage, is welcomed by the mayor of St. George, and receives a key to the State House for the purpose of holding a meeting of Her Majesty's Executive Council, which upholds the conditions of the lease. The rent of one peppercorn is delivered on a velvet pillow and members of the Executive Council proceed to the State House for their meeting.

The old State House building, with mortar made of turtle oil and lime, was constructed in 1619 and is believed to be the first stone building in Bermuda. Until the capital was moved to Hamilton in 1815, Parliament met there. Bermuda's Parliament is the third oldest in the world (after Iceland and England).

CONTACTS:
Bermuda Tourism
675 3rd Ave.
20th Fl.
New York, NY 10017
212-818-9800 or 800-223-6106; fax: 212-983-5289
www.gotobermuda.com

♦ 2243 ♦ Perchtenlauf
January 6

The Perchtenlauf in Austria is usually held on EPIPHANY, but in some areas it is celebrated at a later date. The *Perchten* are old masks, usually of witches and fearsome animals, that have been handed down from generation to generation. People wearing the masks run through the village beating drums, ringing bells, singing, shouting, and making as much noise as possible to scare winter away—an ancient custom that can be traced back to pre-Christian times. Another tradition associated with the Perchtenlauf is the cracking of whips—again, an attempt to drive out winter.

Dancing also plays a part in the celebration. The *Perchtentanz* takes place when the procession of masked figures stops in the main square of the village and everyone begins to dance wildly, making even more noise than before. The Perchten dances of Imst and Thaur in Tirol are particularly well known for their brightly colored old masks. Another notable Perchten pageant takes place in the Gastein Valley village of Bad Gastein in the state of Salzburg.

See also EPIPHANY (GERMANY).

CONTACTS:
Austrian National Tourist Office
61 Broadway,
Ste. 1701
New York, NY 10006

212-944-6880; fax: 212-730-4568
www.austria.info

Perchtenhauptmann
Auhausgasse 199/2
Flachau, 5542 Austria
43-664-2381-815
www.perchtenlauf.at

♦ 2244 ♦ Perseids
Visibility peaks around August 10-12

Meteors, also called shooting stars or falling stars, are seen as streaks of light in the sky that result when a small chunk of stony or metallic matter enters the Earth's atmosphere and vaporizes. A meteor shower occurs when a number of meteors enters the Earth's atmosphere at approximately the same time and place. The shower's name is usually derived from the constellation (or a star within it) from which the shower appears to originate.

Since the year 36 C.E. there have been records of an annual meteor shower known as the Perseids (because it appears to originate in the constellation Perseus) that is most observable during the nights of August 10-12. Observers everywhere except the South Pole can see as many as 60 meteors an hour streak across the sky on what is often referred to as the **Night of the Shooting Stars**.

♦ 2245 ♦ Perth International Arts Festival
January-February

Originally designed as a program of cultural entertainment for students attending evening and summer classes at the University of Western Australia, the Perth International Arts Festival has grown into one of Australia's major arts festivals. It offers drama, dance, music, opera, films, art exhibits, children's programs, and even sporting events at locations throughout the city.

Although the focus is on Australian performing artists, international groups appear there on a regular basis, including England's Chichester Festival Theatre Company, the National Theater of the Deaf from the United States, Spain's Madrid Flamenco Company, and the Stratford National Theatre of Canada.

Plays performed at the festival range from the classics to contemporary works by Australian and English dramatists. The month-long festival also features open-air folk music concerts and dancing, street theater, parades, improvisations, and other dramatic performances.

CONTACTS:
Perth International Arts Festival
3 Crawley Ave.
Crawley, WA 6009 Australia
61-8-6488-5555
2015.perthfestival.com.au

♦ 2246 ♦ Peru Battle of Angamos
October 8

The War of the Pacific (1879-1883), also known as the Saltpeter War, began when Chile and Bolivia fought for control of a portion of the Atacama Desert, which was full of valuable minerals.

On October 8, 1879, the Chilean Navy captured Peru's ironclad steam-propelled warship, the *Huáscar*, and killed the captain, Admiral Miguel Grau. After this battle, the Peruvians lost their momentum against the Chilean forces. Chile gained control over the seas and was thus able to invade Peru and Bolivia.

October 8 is a national holiday in Peru. This day is set aside to remember the lost Battle of Angamos. On this day, military and civil parades are held, and celebrations are held to honor the heroic deeds of Admiral Miguel Grau and his role in the Battle of Angamos.

CONTACTS:
Embassy of the United States in Peru
Avenida La Encalada cdra. 17 s/n
Surco
Lima, 33 Peru
51-1-618-2000; fax: 51-1-618-2397
lima.usembassy.gov

♦ 2247 ♦ Peru Independence Day
July 28-29

Peru had been a colony of Spain for nearly 300 years when Simon Bolívar (1783-1830), along with José SAN MARTÍN (1778-1850), led the Battle of Ayacucho in 1824 that resulted in the end of Spanish rule of Bolivia and Peru. San Martín had declared independence on July 28, 1821, but Peru's sovereignty was not secured until Bolívar's forces defeated the Spanish at Ayacucho. Bolívar then became the ruler of Peru (*see also* BOLIVIA INDEPENDENCE DAY).

Celebrated all over Peru, Independence Day is a public holiday. In the south, festivities also take place on July 25, ST. JAMES'S DAY.

CONTACTS:
Commission for the Promotion of Peru for Export and Tourism
Calle Uno Oeste No. 50
Mincetur Bldg. Fl. 13 and 14,
San Isidro, Lima Peru
51-1-616 7300
www.promperu.gob.pe

♦ 2248 ♦ Peyote Dance (Híkuli Dance)
January

To the Tarahumara (who call themselves Rarámuri) and Huichol Indians of northern Mexico, peyote, or *híkuli*, is the mescal button, derived from the tops of a cactus plant and used as a stimulant or hallucinogen during religious ceremonies. In October and November, they head for eastern Chihuahua to gather peyote. The peyote will be used in January in the dance that follows the deer hunt, because peyote is identified with deer. The dancers paint symbolic designs, such as corn, squash, and fruit, on their faces. They ingest peyote to induce a supernatural state and to encourage the growth of crops. The dance is characterized by sudden jumping and twisting movements; the beat is set by rubbing deer bones together or shaking deer-hoof rattles.

♦ 2249 ♦ Pffiferdaj
First Sunday in September

An Alsatian festival of medieval origin, Pffiferdaj—also known as the **Day of the Strolling Fiddlers**, or **Fiddlers' Festival**—is celebrated in the city of Ribeauvillé, France, an area widely known for its wines. In the Middle Ages the Ribeaupierre family started a musicians' union here, and every September the musicians of Alsace gathered to pay homage to the lord of Ribeaupierre by forming a procession to the church of Notre Dame du Dusenbach.

Today the custom continues. Wine flows freely from the fountain in front of the town hall, and a procession of fiddlers and other musicians, often playing old instruments, makes its way through the town. Their costumes and floats recall life in the Middle Ages.

CONTACTS:
Ribeauville & Riquewihr Tourist Office
BP 90067
Ribeauville Cedex, 68153 France
3-89-73-23-23; fax: 3-89-73-23-29
www.ribeauville-riquewihr.com

♦ 2250 ♦ Phagwa
Full moon day in March

The Hindu festival of Phagwa celebrates the VERNAL EQUINOX and the start of the Hindu New Year (*see* VAISAKH). In Trinidad and Tobago, a Carnival spirit has gradually pervaded the festivities, which now combine both secular and religious elements and are no longer confined to Hindus. The celebration includes bonfires (to symbolize the destruction of Holika, the evil sister of King Hiranya Kashipu; *see also* HOLI) and Chowtal-singing competitions, which mix religious and secular music and are heavily influenced by calypso. The spraying of *Abeer* powder, a red vegetable dye made into a bright fuchsia liquid, gives everyone's hair and skin a tie-dyed effect.

Band competitions, similar to those held at Carnival (*see* TRINIDAD AND TOBAGO CARNIVAL), are held at several locations throughout the island. There are also reenactments of the legend of Holika, complete with oriental costumes, crowns, jewelry, and flowers.

CONTACTS:
National Library and Information System Authority of Trinidad and Tobago
National Library Bldg.
Hart and Abercromby St.
Trinidad and Tobago
868-623-6962; fax: 868-625-6096
www.nalis.gov.tt

♦ 2251 ♦ Phchum Ben
September or October

The 15-day period also known as **Prachum-Ben** in Cambodia is dedicated to rituals for the dead. It occurs during the rainy season when skies are usually overcast, and the darkness seems an appropriate time for Yama, God of the Underworld, to let the souls of the dead visit their families. The traditional offering to the dead consists of *ben*—special cakes made of glutinous rice mixed with coconut milk and other ingredients—arranged on a platter around a centerpiece and placed on a pedestal. Sometimes the rice is formed into a cone called *bay bettbor*, with flags, flowers, and joss sticks used to decorate the top. During this time a monk says prayers at the tombs of the dead.

♦ 2252 ♦ Philadeplphia Flower Show
February-March

First held in 1829, the Philadelphia Flower Show was originally hosted by the Pennsylvania Horticultural Society, which was America's first horticultural association. Since 1996 the festival has taken place at the Pennsylvania Convention Center. Each year more than 200,000 people attend the indoor event, which has a specific annual theme. The show includes installations created by many professional landscapers as well as artistic flower arrangements by individuals, families, and school groups. The exhibition also includes talks on various horticultural topics such as flower arranging and organic gardening.

CONTACTS:
Pennsylvania Horticultural Society
100 N. 20th St.
5th Fl.
Philadelphia, PA 19103
215-988-8800; fax: 215-988-8810
phsonline.org

Pennsylvania Convention Center
12th & Arch Sts.
Philadelphia, PA 19107
215-988-8800
theflowershow.com

♦ 2253 ♦ Philippines Independence Day
June 12

As a result of the Spanish-American War, the United States became involved in the Filipino struggle for independence at the end of the 19th century. The Americans called back Emilio Aguinaldo (1869-1964), the exiled rebel leader, and helped him bring centuries of Spanish rule to an end. Aguinaldo declared the islands independent on June 12, 1898. But the U.S. acquired the Philippines after signing the Treaty of Paris in 1899, and it wasn't until July 4, 1946, that the islands were granted full independence.

For many years, Filipinos set aside July 4 to celebrate their own independence and to acknowledge their longstanding ties to the United States. But in 1962, President Diosdada

Macapagal changed the date to June 12, the anniversary of Aguinaldo's initial declaration of independence from Spain. The U.S. ambassador often speaks at Independence Day ceremonies in Manila, which include a military parade and the pealing of church bells. After the official ceremonies are over, Filipinos devote the remainder of the day to recreation. There are games and athletic competitions, fireworks displays, and Independence Day balls. In Hawaii, which has a large Filipino population, there are often Filipino fiestas celebrating Philippine heritage.

CONTACTS:
Philippine Information Agency
Media Center Bldg.
Visayas Ave Brgy, Vasra
 Philippines
63-2-772-7600
news.pia.gov.ph

♦ 2254 ♦ Phra Buddha Bat Fair
February-March

This annual festival takes place at the Phra Buddha Bat or Phra Phutthabat temple (the Shrine of the Holy Footprint), a hill temple in Saraburi, Thailand, where the Holy Footprint of the Buddha is enshrined. This is one of the most sacred places in Thailand, and pilgrims throng here during the festival to pay homage. The festival features performances of folk music and a handicraft bazaar.

CONTACTS:
Tourism Authority of Thailand
1600 New Phetchaburi Rd.
Makkasan
Ratchathewi, Bangkok 10400 Thailand
662-250-5500
www.tourismthailand.org

♦ 2255 ♦ Pickett (Bill) Invitational Rodeo
Various weekends from February through November

The Bill Pickett Invitational Rodeo, in operation since 1984, is a series of rodeo competitions in the United States that features the nation's only touring black rodeo. The event is named in honor of Bill Pickett (1870-1932), the first African American selected to the Rodeo Hall of Fame in Oklahoma City, Okla.

The tour begins in February in Memphis, Tenn., and draws more than 100,000 annually. During the regular season, cowboys and cowgirls compete in weekend events in cities throughout the country. Events include bareback riding, barrel racing, bull riding, calf roping, steer undecorating, and bulldogging. Bulldogging, also known as steer wrestling, is an event created by the rodeo's namesake, who performed in the famous 101 Ranch Wild West Show with "Buffalo Bill" Cody, Will Rogers, and Tom Mix. A timed event, it features a cowboy on horseback racing a 600- to 700-pound bull, grabbing onto its horns, jumping out of his saddle, and wrestling the bull to the ground—all within a few seconds.

The top 10 finishers in each event at the end of the season in September are invited to compete in the championship rodeo held in November in Las Vegas, Nev. The championship festivities include a number of social and sporting events, with a formal reception for the participants and a golf tournament.

CONTACTS:
Bill Pickett Invitational Rodeo
P.O. Box 39163
Denver, CO 80239
303-373-1246; fax: 303-373-2747
www.billpickettrodeo.com

♦ 2256 ♦ Pickle Festival
Third weekend in August

The small town of Linwood, Michigan, is a center for pickle growing and processing. Since 1977 it has hosted a three-day festival in honor of its native product. Because so many local residents grow their own cucumbers and develop their own pickling recipes, there is a pickle-canning contest. Another popular event is the pickle-eating contest. Competitors are timed to see how long it takes them to unwrap and eat a pickle. The first one who is able to whistle afterward wins.

CONTACTS:
Great Lakes Bay Regional Convention & Visitors Bureau
515 N. Washington Ave.
2nd Fl.
Saginaw, MI 48607
989-752-7164 or 800-444-9979
www.gogreat.com

♦ 2257 ♦ Pied Piper Open Air Theater
Sundays, mid-May through mid-September

A dramatization of the legend of the Pied Piper of Hamelin, presented on an open-air stage in Hamelin (or Hameln), Germany.

According to the legend, in 1284 Hamelin was infested with rats. A stranger appeared, wearing an outlandishly colored (pied) coat, and he promised to free the town of its plague of vermin if they would pay him a set sum of money. The town agreed, and the piper began playing his pipes, and all the rats and mice came out of the houses and gathered around the piper. He led them to the Weser River, walked into it, and they followed him and were drowned. But the citizens refused to pay the piper. He left, angry. On June 26, he returned, dressed as a hunter and wearing a red hat. He played his pipes, and this time children followed him. He led 130 children out of the town and to the Koppenberg hill where they disappeared—forever. Only two children remained behind. One was blind, and couldn't see where the children went, and one was mute.

Research tends to discredit the legend. One theory is that the ratcatcher was Nicholas of Cologne, who led thousands of German children on the disastrous Children's Crusade in

1212. Another holds that the story stemmed from the arrival of a labor agent who lured many young men to Bohemia with the promise of good wages.

Fortunately, the people of Hamelin don't let research get in the way of a good story. Today, the children of Hamelin are the principal performers in the play, and their number is limited to 130 in keeping with the legend.

Robert Browning, the English poet who wrote the poem "The Pied Piper of Hamelin" to amuse a sick child, described the vermin this way: *Rats!*

They fought the dogs and killed the cats,
And bit the babies in the cradles,
And ate the cheeses out of the vats,
And licked the soup from the cooks' own ladles…

When the piper arrived and began to play, Browning wrote,

…out of the houses the rats came tumbling.

Great rats, small rats, lean rats, brawny rats,
Brown rats, black rats, gray rats, tawny rats …
Brothers, sisters, husbands, wives—
Followed the Piper for their lives.

And then when the piper led the children off to Koppenberg, a portal opened wide, the piper and the children entered, and—

When all were in to the very last,
The door in the mountainside shut fast..

CONTACTS:
Hameln Marketing and Tourismus GmbH
Deisterallee 1
Hameln, D-31785 Germany
49-5151-957-82-3; fax: 49-5151-957-84-0
www.hameln.com

♦ 2258 ♦ **Piedigrotta, Festival of**
September 7-9

Held in Naples, Italy, for three days in September, the Festival of Piedigrotta is known primarily for its noise and gaiety. According to one legend, it commemorates the destruction in 44 C.E. of a site that had formerly been the scene of pagan orgies, and the building of a chapel in its place. A second explanation is that the chapel was built in 1356 after the Blessed Virgin Mary had appeared to a priest, a nun, and a man named Peter and ordered its construction. In any case, the festival is a particularly joyful one, with processions, fireworks, and some very unusual puppet shows. Visitors to Naples during festival time discover that it is almost impossible to get any sleep.

♦ 2259 ♦ **Pig Festivals**
Various

For the Bundi people of Papua New Guinea, the Pig Festival is an event of enormous importance that encompasses dozens of social ceremonies and political events. Among other things, it is a time when tribe members must settle their debts, and it provides opportunities to trade goods. Marriage ceremonies, initiation ceremonies, bride-price payments, menstruation and courtship ceremonies also take place during the period of the Pig Festival. The *kanam*, a Bundi dance performance that represents the animals and birds that live in the forest, is frequently performed at pig festivals.

♦ 2260 ♦ **Pig's Face Feast**
Sunday following September 14

A number of explanations have been offered for the custom of eating pig's face, or pork-chop, sandwiches on the Sunday following Holy Cross Day (September 14; *see* EXALTATION OF THE CROSS) in the Cotswold village of Avening, England. One involves the love of Matilda of Flanders (d. 1083), who later became the wife of William the Conqueror, for Brittric, Lord of Gloucester. When Brittric refused to reciprocate, Matilda married William and then, as Queen, ordered Brittric's imprisonment and, eventually, his death. She later repented and built a church at the place where Brittric had once ruled as lord of the manor. The church was completed on September 14, Holy Cross Day, and the Queen is said to have held a boar's head dedication feast. The wild boars were so delicious that the people of Avening continued to celebrate their church dedication by eating the same meat. Another legend says that the feast commemorates the slaying of a troublesome wild boar, which took place on or around this date.

Today there is an evening anniversary service in Holy Cross Church at Avening, after which the villagers participate in an 11th-century banquet headed by Queen Matilda and other historic characters in period costume. Pork sandwiches are also served in the local pubs.

CONTACTS:
Holy Cross Church, Avening Parish Council
77 Pheasant Way
Cirencester, Gloucestershire GL7 1BJ United Kingdom
44-12-8538-0041
www.avening-pc.gov.uk

♦ 2261 ♦ **Pii Mai**
April 13-15

Thailand's Pii Mai, or the **Lao New Year,** falls between April 13 and 15 on the Gregorian calendar. One of the most significant holidays in Thailand, Pii Mai marks the end of the dry season and the start of the rainy season. The celebration is symbolic of rebirth and purification. The three-day festival commences with *Sangkhan Luang,* the last day of the old year, when people clean their homes and gather at rivers or temple grounds to build sand mounds in order to earn blessings. On the second day, *Sangkhan Nao,* people socialize and enjoy themselves. A favorite tradition involves throwing water on friends and passersby. Day three, called *Sangkhan Kheun,* is the first day of the New Year and the most significant day of the festival. People visit their elders, bringing flowers and scented water to seek blessing and forgiveness. During this time, families also observe the *Su khwan* or *Baci,* a ritual that marks births, marriages, and other rites of passage. Tying white threads of cotton or silk on the right wrist serves as a symbol of peace, prosperity, and good health. *Baci* celebrants believe this tradition restores balance and harmony to the individual and community.

CONTACTS:
International Lao New Year Festival committee
c/o Center for Lao Studies
65 Ninth St.
San Francisco, CA 94103
415-680-4027; fax: 415-565-0204
www.laonewyear.org

♦ 2262 ♦ **Pike Festival, National**
May

The National Pike Festival (also known as the National Road Festival) is literally the "world's longest festival"—90 miles of events along Route 40 in southwestern Pennsylvania and parts of West Virginia and Ohio. The original section of the road (or "pike," as in turnpike road) from Baltimore to Cumberland, Maryland, was Thomas JEFFERSON'S idea in 1806. The section between Cumberland and Wheeling, West Virginia, was the first road to receive federal funding in 1811.

Since 1974 the festival has commemorated America's first transportation link from the East to the western frontier. It was originally designed as a Bicentennial event in Pennsylvania, but the idea caught on quickly, and towns along Route 40 in nearby states were eager to add their own events.

The festival begins on a weekend in mid-May as locales from western Maryland through southwestern Pennsylvania and eastern Ohio celebrate "the road that made the nation." Wagon trains originating from all parts travel along the route known as the National Road. When they set up camp for the night, there are bonfires and other entertainment to which the public is invited. Inns, taverns, toll-houses, and other historic buildings along the route host tours and special ceremonies.

CONTACTS:
James Shaull Wagon Train Foundation, Inc.
9811 National Pike
Big Pool, MD 21711
301-791-3246
www.nationalpikefestival.org
National Road Heritage Corridor
65 W. Main St.
Ste. 103
Uniontown, PA 15401
724-437-9877; fax: 724-437-6550
www.nationalroadpa.org

♦ 2263 ♦ **Pilgrim Festivals**
Various

The ancient Israelites were expected to celebrate three pilgrim festivals: PASSOVER, SHAVUOT, and SUKKOT. They are referred to in Hebrew as the *shalosh regalim,* "three (foot) pilgrimages," because the Bible commanded that they be observed "in the place the Lord your God will choose." Adult males over the age of 13 traditionally made a pilgrimage to Jerusalem on these three occasions. But after the Temple there was destroyed, the law requiring pilgrimages lapsed. The obligation to rejoice on the three pilgrim festivals—by eating meat, drinking wine, and wearing new clothes—continued.

Today, Jews come from all over the world to spend these festivals in Jerusalem. But now they tend to be sorrowful voyages, made for the purpose of mourning the destruction of the Temple. It is for this reason that Jews traditionally gather at the Wailing Wall—the only remaining retaining wall of the Temple Mount, site of the First and Second Temples, built during the first century B.C.E. in the reign of Herod.

CONTACTS:
Ministry of Tourism, Government of Israel
New York, NY
646-779-6760; fax: 646-779-6765
www.goisrael.com

Israel Government Tourism Office
36 Misgav Ladach St.
Jewish Quarter, Old City
Jerusalem, 97500 Israel
972-2-6264545; fax: 972-2-6274529
www.templeinstitute.org

♦ 2264 ♦ **Pilgrim Progress Pageant**
Every Friday during August

It was on Plymouth Rock in what is now Plymouth, Massachusetts, that the Pilgrims landed in December 1620 to found their first permanent settlement north of Virginia. More than half of the 102 people who sailed on the *Mayflower* to the New World died of exposure, illness, and hunger by the end of the first winter.

An annual series of parades is organized by the General Society of Mayflower Descendants. Each Friday in August at 6:00 P.M., a group of men, women, and children dressed as Pilgrims form a procession up Leyden Street to the site of the former Fort-Meetinghouse on Burial Hill, now the Church of the Pilgrimage on Main Street. When they reach the site of the old fort, they reenact the church service that was held by the survivors at the end of that first winter in 1621. The pageant has been held every August since 1921 and also takes place on THANKSGIVING Day.

CONTACTS:
Destination Plymouth
134 Court St
Plymouth, MA 02360 United States
508-747-0100; fax: 508-747-3118
www.visit-plymouth.com

♦ 2265 ♦ **Pilgrim Thanksgiving Day (Plymouth, Massachusetts)**
Last Thursday in November

Ten thousand visitors flock to Plymouth, Massachusetts, on THANKSGIVING Day to watch the annual procession from Plymouth Rock to the First Parish Church, where the congregation sings the same psalms sung by the original Pilgrims more than three and a half centuries ago. Each marcher represents one of the men, women, and children who survived the 1620 trip from England aboard the *Mayflower* to form the settlement known as Plimoth Plantation.

The modern-day Plimoth Plantation is a living-history village that recreates Pilgrim life in 1627. Costumed actors and historians carry out many of the same activities performed by the original Pilgrims, such as sheep-shearing, building houses, planting crops, weeding gardens, and cooking. Each November Plimoth offers a variety of programs as well as period dining that features original Thanksgiving Day foods.

CONTACTS:
Plimoth Plantation
137 Warren Ave.
Plymouth, MA 02360
508-746-1622
www.plimoth.org

♦ 2266 ♦ **Pilgrimage of Our Lady of Valme**
Each Sunday in October

The Romería (pilgrimage) of Our Lady of Valme involves a cross-country pilgrimage. The image of Our Lady of Valme is kept in the parish church of Dos Hermanas, but on this day she is carried in an elaborate procession to the shrine of Valme, on a hill overlooking Seville, Spain. Legend has it that King Ferdinand III stopped here on his way to free Seville from the Moors. He prayed to the Virgin Mary, *"valme"* (bless me), and promised a sanctuary for her if he was successful.

Accompanied by children in carriages, decorated floats, local men on horseback carrying silver maces, and Andalusian cavaliers and their ladies in regional dress, the cart bearing the statue of the Virgin Mary dressed in a blue velvet cloak is drawn by oxen with gilded horns and garlands of flowers around their necks. The pilgrims walk behind, and there is laughter, hand-clapping, and singing with tambourine accompaniment. Every so often fireworks are set off so the pilgrims in Valme can judge the progress of the procession.

It takes about three hours to reach the sanctuary, then the cavaliers open the gates, everyone rushes inside, the statue is carried in at shoulder height, and the mass begins. Afterwards, there is dancing, singing, and drinking until sunset, when the image is escorted back to Dos Hermanas.

CONTACTS:
City of Dos Hermanas
Constitution Sq. No.1
Dos Hermanas, CP 41701 Spain
34-954-919-500
www.doshermanas.es

♦ 2267 ♦ **Pilgrimage of Saut d'Eau**
July 16

Although it falls at the same time as a church holiday honoring OUR LADY OF CARMEL, the pilgrimage to the church in Ville-Bonheur, Haiti, combines both Christian and Voodoo beliefs. There is a sacred grove just outside Ville-Bonheur where, according to legend, the Virgin Mary once appeared on top of a palm tree. When people started neglecting the local church and worshipping the palm tree instead, the priest ordered it chopped down. Since no one wanted to kill the tree, the priest did it himself. Then he found people coming to pay honor to the roots, so he had those ripped out. Shortly thereafter the priest suffered a stroke and died. The people interpreted his death as a sign of the correctness of the vision.

The pilgrimage to this holy place, known as Saut d'Eau (waterfall), involves following a steep, winding trail and walking along a pebbly stream-bed for several hundred yards. Pilgrims eventually reach a place where two waterfalls tumble from a precipice more than 100 feet high—a kind of natural cathedral where rainbows are common in the mist that rises from the falls. This is the home of Damballah-wedo and other African deities who play a part in the Haitian religious practice known as Voodoo, or Vodoun.

Some worshipers tie colored cords, which they have purchased as offerings to the African *loa* (deities), to the sacred trees at the foot of the falls, while others bathe in the water. The pilgrims gather up a small bit of dirt from the base of the trees and carry it home in their handkerchiefs. These same pilgrims can be seen later in the day paying their respects to the Virgin in the local church—further evidence of the way in which this pilgrimage has brought together Christian and Voodoo beliefs.

CONTACTS:
Embassy of the Republic of Haiti
2311 Massachusetts Ave. N.W.
Washington, D.C. 20008 United States
202-332-4090; fax: 202-745-7215
www.haiti.org

♦ 2268 ♦ **Pilgrimage of the Dew**
May-June; Friday before Pentecost to Tuesday following

This colorful procession, known as the **Romería del Rocío**, or Pilgrimage of the Dew, begins during the week preceding Whitsunday, or PENTECOST, in towns and villages of Andalusia, Spain. The pilgrims' destination is the church of El Rocío in Almonte, Huelva, where a small statue of the Virgin known as *La Blanca Paloma* ("the White Dove") resides. They travel in two-wheeled, white-hooded farm carts, drawn by oxen wearing bells, flowers, and ribbon streamers. Some of the carts are set up as moving shrines to the Virgin, and the pilgrims themselves are dressed in regional costumes.

On Pentecost, the pilgrims file past the church of El Rocío and pay homage to La Blanca Paloma. There are fireworks at midnight, followed by dancing and singing until dawn. On Monday, the image of the Virgin is carried in solemn procession through the streets of Almonte. Being chosen to bear the statue on one's shoulders is considered a special privilege, eagerly sought by those who wish to receive special indulgence during the coming year. The procession is accompanied by the chanting of priests and the shouts of the pilgrims, who call out "Viva la Blanca Paloma!" as they wend their way through the town.

CONTACTS:
Provincial Tourism Board of Huelva
Calle Fernando el Católico, 14
2ª planta
Huelva, 21003 Spain
34-959-257-467
www.turismohuelva.org

Andalusia Tourist Community
c/o La Empresa Pública Turismo Andaluz, S.A.
Calle Compañia 40
Málaga, 29008 Spain
34-951-29-9300; fax: 34-951-29-9315
www.andalucia.org

♦ 2269 ♦ Pilgrimage to Chalma
January 1-5

Chalma is a small Mexican town located in a deep canyon. Five hundred years ago, the Aztecs made pilgrimages to a nearby cave, where they brought offerings of flowers and incense to a stone idol known as Otzocteotl, God of the Caves. After the Spanish conquest of Mexico, two Augustinian missionaries attempted to convert the people to Christianity but failed. Finally they brought a large cross made of wood to the cave, hoping to erect it in place of the idol. But when they entered, they found the stone image smashed to pieces and, in the place where it stood, a life-sized crucifix. As the local people learned of this remarkable occurrence, they were quickly converted to Christianity.

The cave became such a popular place of pilgrimage that in 1683, the image of Christ, known as the Señor de Chalma, was moved to the altar of a church that had just been built to house it. This is where pilgrims from all over Mexico come during the first five days of January to ask the Señor's blessing for the coming year and to express their gratitude for the favors he has granted them in the year that has just ended. Pilgrimages also take place in February, August, September, and often during HOLY WEEK and at CHRISTMAS.

♦ 2270 ♦ Pilgrimage to Mecca (Hajj)
Eighth-13th days of Islamic month of Dhu al-Hijjah

At least once in a lifetime, every Muslim man or woman (if she is accompanied by a male protector) with the means and the opportunity to do so is expected to make a pilgrimage to Mecca, the city in Saudi Arabia where Muhammad was born. It is one of the "five pillars" (fundamental duties) of Islam, and must be performed during the special pilgrimage season. The Qur'an (Muslim holy book) says the founder of this pilgrimage was Abraham.

The pilgrims wear two sheets of seamless white cloth and perform elaborate rites at the Grand Mosque of Mecca and in the immediate vicinity, which require about six days to complete. The focal point is the Kaaba, a 15-foot high stone structure that stands in the center court of the Grand Mosque of Mecca. In one corner of the court is the Black Stone, believed to have been brought by the angel Gabriel to Moses when he was rebuilding the Kaaba. It is a symbol of eternity because of its durability and is not worshipped, but is rather a sanctuary consecrated to God, and toward which all Muslim prayers are oriented.

Among the stages of the pilgrimage are walking around the Kaaba seven times, sacrificing a ram, ox, or camel, gathering at the Mount of Mercy and "standing before God" from noon to sunset, and throwing pebbles at three pillars at Mina, which represent Satan's tempting Abraham not to sacrifice his son. (*See* ID AL-ADHA.)

It is not uncommon for two million or more Muslims to participate in the pilgrimage, which has forced Saudi Arabia and other countries to explore new methods for freezing, preserving, and distributing the meat that is produced by so many sacrifices. The huge crowds have also challenged Saudi authorities as hundreds of people have been killed during stampedes in recent years.

At the end of the pilgrimage, it is customary to visit the tomb of Muhammad at Medina before returning home. Returning pilgrims, wearing the green scarf of the Hajj, are met by family and friends who have rented taxis and decorated them with palm branches and the families' best rugs. The pilgrim's house has been decorated with palm-leaf arches, and sometimes outlined with lights. In Kurdish and Egyptian villages, the doorways will also have designs suggesting the journey. Then a feast and party finish the welcome home.

CONTACTS:
Ministry of Hajj Portal
P.O. Box 2475
Al-Shasha District, Makkah Mukarramah Kingdom of Saudi Arabia
966-12-5506621
haj.gov.sa

Saudi Arabian Embassy
601 New Hampshire Ave. N.W.
Washington, D.C. 20037
202-337-4076; fax: 202-944-5983
www.saudiembassy.net

♦ 2271 ♦ Pilgrimage to Moulay Idriss
Late August or September

The most important *moussem*, or "festival," in Morocco is held in the holy city of Moulay Idriss. Moulay Idriss I was the eighth-century imam (Muslim prayer leader) who united the Berbers and founded the city of Fez and the first dynasty of Morocco; he is supposed to have had 500 wives, 1,000 children, and 12,000 horses. His burial place is the white Mausoleum of Moulay Idriss. The town named for him grew up around the tomb after his death.

This moussem lasts several weeks and alternates between prayers and celebrations. A feature is the *fantasia*, a great charge of horses and costumed riders who fire their rifles into the air and perform equestrian stunts as they gallop. There are also bazaars and singing and dancing.

CONTACTS:
Moroccan National Tourist Office
104 W. 40th St.
Suite 1820
New York, NY 10018
212-221-1583; fax: 212-221-1887
www.visitmorocco.com

♦ 2272 ♦ **Pilgrimage to Qoyllur Riti**
May-June

Although CORPUS CHRISTI processions are common, the pilgrimage to Qoyllur Riti in Peru is unique. The journey involves a dangerous climb up a glacier near Cuzco to honor an apparition of Jesus that was witnessed there in 1780, although it is believed that a related custom took place there before the arrival of Christianity. It is sometimes called the Star Snow Festival (*Qoyllur* means "star") because it takes place at a time when the constellation known as the Pleiades first becomes visible in the night sky.

The pilgrimage is one of the biggest celebrations of the year, and the festivities go on for nearly two-and-a-half weeks. On Wednesday morning, ringing church bells rouse townspeople by 4 A.M. They rise and begin to sweep streets, construct fruit stands, and make ready temporary altars in anticipation of the procession. In the outlying parishes, images of the saints are prepared for their entrance into Cuzco. While men bear the images in turns, women tote beverages and food in their wraps. All of these smaller processions arrive around 11 o'clock at Cuzco at the church of Santa Clara, where they do honor to the Virgin of Bethlehem, who is the guardian of Cuzco.

The big procession forms the next day, with everyone wearing the native dress of his or her region. Those who make it to the top of the glacier, which is 16,000 feet above sea level, erect a cross, recite prayers, and light candles. The mountain is said to be a home for the spirits of those who have committed mortal sins. But the climb is also believed to strengthen the pilgrims, many of whom are young men, making them more able to avoid falling under the influence of harmful powers. On the journey down the mountain, the pilgrims often carry blocks of ice, which some regard as possessing the power to heal the sick. Many others water their fields with the melted ice in the belief that it is holy water.

CONTACTS:
Embassy of Peru
1700 Massachusetts Ave. N.W
Washington, D.C. 20036
202-833-9860; fax: 202-659-8124
www.embassyofperu.org

Cuscoperu.com e-commerce SCRL
U.V. Mariscal Gamarra 5-H Pje. Retamas

Cusco, 08003 Peru
51-84-263-646; fax: 51-84-263-646
www.cuscoperu.com

♦ 2273 ♦ **Pilgrimage to Shrine of Father Laval**
September 9

An annual pilgrimage by thousands of people of all faiths to the shrine of Roman Catholic priest Père Jacques Désiré Laval in Port Louis, Mauritius. Father Laval came to Mauritius in 1841 and devoted himself to the spiritual improvement of the emancipated slaves until his death in 1864. The pilgrimage is held on the day of his death. It originated on the day the priest was buried, when more than 30,000 weeping people followed his bier as he was taken for burial opposite the Ste. Croix Church. A monument to him has since been erected there. Many masses are celebrated at the shrine on the memorial day, starting early in the morning. A vigil ends the day. Miracles of healing are attributed to Father Laval, who was beatified in 1979 in Rome by Pope John Paul II.

CONTACTS:
Mauritius Tourism Promotion Authority
Air Mauritius Centre
5, President John Kennedy St.
11th Fl.
Mauritius
230-210-1545; fax: 230-212-5142
www.mauritius.net

♦ 2274 ♦ **Pilgrimage to Souvenance**
Early April

Every Easter for over 200 years, hundreds of devotees of voodoo journey to the Haitian village of Souvenance to visit a holy temple. The village, some 90 miles north of the capital city of Port-au-Prince, was founded by freed slaves from the West African country of Dahomey, now called Benin, and is considered to be a direct link to the ancients. The village temple is one of the most important sites of the voodoo religion.

During the five-day ceremony, devotees dress in white and wearing white scarves wrapped around their heads. The ceremony includes drumming, dancing, chanting, and sacrificing such animals as bulls, rams, and goats. The sacrificed animals, with slit throats, are passed among the believers so that the blood soaks the white garments they wear. Some believers hold the dead animals above themselves so that the blood drips down onto their heads. The sacrifices are devoted to the warrior god Ogoun. Worshippers dance throughout the night, imbibing rum and cane liquor and ingesting various herbs. The loas, or gods, are believed to take possession of some of the worshippers during the service. Voodoo is one of three state-recognized religions in Haiti, and some two thirds of the population is said to participate in its rites.

CONTACTS:
Embassy of the Republic of Haiti
2311 Massachusetts Ave. N.W.

Washington, D.C. 20008 United States
202-332-4090; fax: 202-745-7215
www.haiti.org

♦ 2275 ♦ Pilgrimage to the Tomb of Sunan Bayat
21st day of the Javanese month of Mulud

Islamic Pilgrims flock to the tomb of the Sufi saint, Sunan Bayat, in Tembayat, Java, Indonesia, each year on the anniversary of his birth. This type of birthday pilgrimage is known as a "mulid," or anniversary, festival. Sunan Bayat was a 16th-century non-Muslim king who gave up his wealth and privilege in order to pray, preach, and meditate. Many Indonesians consider Sunan Bayat to be one of the nine Sufi saints who converted the people of the island of Java to Islam. Others count him as an honorary tenth member of the exalted group.

Pilgrims visit his mountain-top tomb year-round, but the mulid pilgrimage is considered to be especially auspicious for pilgrims. The last leg of the pilgrims' journey begins in a modern parking lot at the foot of the staircase leading up the mountain. Here visitors can use modern facilities for the ritual washing that is required before formal prayers can be offered. Visitors also must buy a ticket to gain entry to the burial compound. They then ascend to the tomb up a winding staircase, where small stalls along the way offer food, drink, and religious tokens.

Once at the tomb, pilgrims rely on an attendant, seated in the antechamber, who prays on their behalf, alternating prayers with a recitation of the first chapter of the Islamic Holy Book, the Koran, in Arabic. As they enter the pitch darkness of the tomb itself, pilgrims often lay flowers at the graves of Sunan Bayat and his two wives, who are buried on either side of him. According to local custom, new buds will appear suddenly on the flower stalks as a sign that the saint is willing to answer a pilgrim's prayers. Because many Javanese Muslims believe that a saint's *barakah*—or grace—is strongest in the evening, they visit late and remain at the burial complex until at least midnight. Others pay extra money to sleep on the site in order to best absorb Sunan Bayat's *barakah*.

CONTACTS:
Department of Tourism Marketing, Lao Ministry of Information, Culture and Tourism
Lane Xang Ave.
P.O. Box 3556
 Lao PDR
856-2121-2251
www.tourismlaos.org

Embassy of the Republic of Indonesia
2020 Massachusetts Ave. N.W.
Washington, D.C. 20036
202-775-5200
www.embassyofindonesia.org

♦ 2276 ♦ Pine Battle of Vinuesa
August 14-16

The Pine Battle or *Pinochada* of Vinuesa in the province of Soria, Spain, takes place in an area where the nobility once built a number of hunting lodges and where King Juan I located his main residence in the 14th century. The town of Vinuesa stands at the opening of a valley and is cradled on both sides by hills studded with pine trees. Tradition dictates that Juan II had the pines planted as a gift memorializing the pleasant times he had there hunting with his father.

On August 14, two tall pine trees are erected at the entrance to the village and in the main square. There is a ceremony in the church that evening at which the mayor's wife makes an offering to Our Lady of the Pine, an image of the Virgin that is attached to a pine trunk in a recess above the altar.

On the morning of August 15, two fraternities representing the town's two patrons, Our Lady and SAN ROQUE, join in a procession to the church. There they perform a *revolteo*, a flag-twirling ceremony which takes place at many festivals in Spain. Later that afternoon there is a procession to a nearby field, where ceremonial dances are performed and there is another revolteo. The second day of the festival ends with a twilight procession featuring an image of the Virgin that is a replica of the 11th-century original.

On the final day of the festival, there is a ceremonial mock battle in which the women of Vinuesa attack the men with pine branches. The explanation for this is that centuries ago, when an image of the Virgin was found between two pine trees near the boundary between Vinuesa and Covaleda, a quarrel broke out over who would get to keep the image. After several hours of fighting, the men of Vinuesa asked for reinforcements, and their wives arrived to help them. The women tore branches from the pine trees and used them to strike their opponents in the eyes, thus winning the battle for Vinuesa.

♦ 2277 ♦ Pingxi Sky Lantern Festival
Mid-January to mid-February at Chinese New Year

The Pingxi Sky Lantern Festival takes place annually near Taipei, Taiwan, to celebrate the Chinese New Year. Thousands of paper lanterns are lit and sent floating to the sky, a traditional method of sending wishes to deities to grant. Because of the risk of fire, Pingxi is the only area of Taiwan where sky lanterns can be released legally on account of its mountain location and significant annual rainfall.

CONTACTS:
Tourism Bureau, Republic of China (Taiwan)
9F., No.290, Sec. 4, Zhongxiao E. Rd.
Da-an District
Taipei City, 10694 Taiwan (R.O.C.)
886-2-2349-1500
www.eventaiwan.tw

♦ 2278 ♦ Pinkster Day
Between May 10 and June 13; 50 days after Easter

When PENTECOST (Whitsunday) became part of the Christian calendar in northern Europe, the name underwent numerous transformations. In Germany it became *Pfingsten,* and the Dutch called it *Pinkster.* When the Dutch settled in New York, they called the feast of Pentecost "Pinkster Day."

By the beginning of the 19th century, Albany had become a center for this celebration, which took place on Capitol, or "Pinkster," Hill and consisted of a week-long carnival dominated by the city's African-American population. It is said that their African-inspired dancing and music horrified the staid Dutch settlers, and by 1811 Pinkster Day had been legally prohibited by the New York state legislature.

◆ 2279 ◆ Pirates Week
Last week in October

Pirates Week is a Cayman Islands festival celebrating the history of Grand Cayman, at one time a favorite haunt for pirates and buccaneers. The entire island is transformed into a pirate encampment for the week-long festival. There is a mock invasion of George Town, parades, pageants, and the trial of the pirates. Everyone dresses up in costumes, and the singing, dancing, and food fairs that are held throughout the island all revolve around a pirate theme.

The Cayman Islands—from the Spanish *caimán,* meaning "alligator"—were apparently unoccupied when first sighted by COLUMBUS in 1503. Although frequented by Spanish, English, and French ships, they were not claimed by anyone until they were ceded to the British in 1670 and settlers started arriving. Before long, the islands' remote location made them an ideal stopover for pirates.

CONTACTS:
Pirates Week Administration
10 Shedden Rd.
P.O. Box 51
Grand Cayman, KY1-1101 Cayman Islands
1-345-949-5078; fax: 1-345-949-5449
www.piratesweekfestival.com

◆ 2280 ◆ Pitra Visarjana Amavasya
September-October; waning half of Hindu month of Asvina

During this two-week festival in India, no male family member is allowed to shave, nor is it permissible to cut hair, pare nails, or wear new clothes. It is a time for honoring ancestors by making special offerings of food and water, especially *khir,* or rice boiled in milk. Brahmans (priests, members of the highest Hindu caste) are often invited to partake of these special foods in the belief that they will ensure that the offerings reach the souls of departed family members. It is usually the eldest son or senior member of the family who performs the rituals associated with this festival.

◆ 2281 ◆ Plague Sunday
Last Sunday in August

When the plague reached the village of Eyam, Derbyshire, England, in 1665, about three-fifths of the town's population was wiped out. But under the leadership of Vicar William Mompesson, the villagers displayed both courage and selflessness, voluntarily isolating themselves from other villages in the parish and requesting that their food and medical supplies be dropped off at a point outside the village. The disease eventually became so virulent that the vicar had to hold open-air services for his dwindling congregation in a place up in the hills known as Cucklet Dell.

Every year on the last Sunday in August, a procession of clergy, standard bearers, choir members, and musicians forms at Eyam's parish church and slowly proceeds up the road leading toward the Dell. Hundreds of villagers, tourists, hikers, cyclists, and parents with baby carriages fall in behind them, finding seats on the grassy slopes of the Dell's natural amphitheater. A simple sermon pays tribute to the plague victims and the 74 villagers who survived.

CONTACTS:
Eyam Parish Church
Parish Office, Church St.
Eyam, Derbyshire S32 5QU United Kingdom
44-14-3363-0930
www.eyam-church.org

◆ 2282 ◆ Planting the Penny Hedge
Between April 29 and June 2; eve of Ascension Day

The Penny Hedge—"penny" meaning penance—is a fence of interlaced stakes and boughs that is built along the water's edge at Boyes Staith, near Whitby, England. It is set up early in the morning on the eve of ASCENSION DAY and should be sturdy enough to survive three tides.

According to the local legend, in 1159 three noblemen were out hunting a wild boar. When the animal took refuge in a hermitage occupied by a monk from Whitby Abbey, the holy man closed his door and refused to release it. The hunters were so angry that they beat the monk with their staves to the point of death. When the abbot of Whitby arrived on the scene, he decided that the hunters should receive a heavy punishment, but the dying monk convinced him otherwise. Instead, the abbot ordered them to build a hedge every year on the shore of Whitby Harbor while the bailiff blew a horn, announced a summary of their offences, and shouted, "Out on ye!" The first hedge was set up in 1160.

Today the story of the crime is no longer recited during the performance of the task, nor is the hedge still built by the descendants of the murderers. It is usually the harbor master himself who continues the tradition by building the hedge, while church and civil dignitaries, along with townspeople and visitors, look on.

CONTACTS:
Whitby Museum
Pannett Park
Whitby, North Yorkshire YO21 1RE United Kingdom

44-1947-602908
www.whitbymuseum.org.uk

♦ 2283 ♦ Plebeian Games (Ludi Plebeii)
November 4-17

The Roman leader Flaminus is thought to have instituted the Plebeian Games in 220 B.C.E. They originally may have been held in the Circus Flaminius, which he built. Later, they may have moved to the Circus Maximus, a huge open arena between the Palatine and Aventine hills. The Games were dedicated to Jupiter, one of whose feast days was November 13. The Games themselves took place from November 15-17 and included horse and chariot races and contests that involved running, boxing and wrestling. The first nine days of the festival (November 4-12) were devoted to theatrical performances.

See also APOLLONIAN GAMES; LUDI; ROMAN GAMES.

♦ 2284 ♦ Pleureuses, Ceremony of
Between March 20 and April 23; Friday before Easter

This GOOD FRIDAY ceremony takes place at the Church of Romont in Switzerland. Held since the 15th century, the ceremony begins with a reading from the Bible of the Passion of Christ (the last seven days of his life). The congregation then begins its procession through the village streets. The weepers or mourners (the *Pleureuses*) are veiled in black attire resembling nuns' habits, and walk slowly behind a young girl portraying the Virgin Mary. She walks behind a penitent wearing a black hood and carrying a large cross. The mourners carry the symbols of the Passion on scarlet cushions: a crown of thorns, a whip, nails, a hammer, tongs, and St. Veronica's shroud (Veronica was a woman in the crowd who, as Christ passed her carrying the cross, wiped his face and his image was, according to legend, imprinted on the cloth). During the procession, the town resounds with chants and prayers.

CONTACTS:
Romont Tourism Office
Rue du Chateau 112
Romont, 1680 Switzerland
41-26-651-9055; fax: 41-26-651-9059
www.romont.ch

♦ 2285 ♦ Plough Monday
January, first Monday after Epiphany

This ancient rustic English holiday, also called **Fool Plough** or **Fond Plough**, or **Fond Pleeaf**, survived into the late 1800s. It is thought to have started in the days of the medieval Roman Catholic Church, when farmers, or ploughmen, kept candles called plough-lights burning in churches before the images of saints.

Once a year, on the Monday after EPIPHANY (before ploughing begins), or sometimes at the end of LENT (to celebrate the end of ploughing), they gathered in villages to ask for money to pay for the plough-lights. The Reformation of the 16th century ended this homage to saints, but not the day's celebration as a time to return to labor after the CHRISTMAS festivities.

By the 19th century, the day was observed with music, dancing, processions, and collecting money through trick-or-treat type means. "The Bessy"—a man dressed up to look ridiculous in women's clothing—and "The Fool," wearing animal skins or a fur cap and tail, solicited money from door to door so they could buy food and drink for their merrymaking. The ploughmen dragged a beribboned plough from house to house, shouting "God speed the plough," and if a home owner failed to make a contribution, they ploughed up his front yard. The money collected was spent not on plough-lights but on ale in the public houses.

The custom of blessing the plough on the prior day, Plough Sunday, was still observed in some areas in the 20th century.

♦ 2286 ♦ Poetry Festival of Medellín, International
June-July

One of the largest poetry events in the world, the International Poetry Festival of Medellín is more than a typical gathering of poets and critics. Since its inception in 1991, the festival has been a politically charged platform for artists and intellectuals to demand more peaceful government policies for Medellín and the rest of Colombia, which has been long ravaged by political violence. Because of the festival's dissident stance, the Colombian government has refused to offer financial support, although outside funding has come from several European countries.

The International Poetry Festival in Medellín was founded as a means to promote creativity and artistic consciousness amidst the brutality of the country's long-running drug wars. The festival's organizers, The Prometeo Art and Poetry Corporation, formed that group after launching a poetry publication called Prometeo. Their aim was to use poetry to restore and renew their country's social fabric and to mobilize people to improve society.

The festival was an immediate success and grew quickly, now taking place over eight days. Poets from South America and around the world give free recitals in public parks, university theatres, prisons, schools, and libraries. The events attracting the largest audiences are the opening reading and the closing ceremony, which typically draw several thousand people. Residents of the city and visitors from far and wide flock to the festival to join in the intense enthusiasm and creative energy that are hallmarks of the event.

In 2014, the festival featured 70 poets from 39 different countries. For the 25th anniversary of the Medellín International Poetry Festival in 2015, 90 poets from over 40 countries will attend. Over 150 poetry, musical, academic, and artistic events are planned. In honor of the festival's anniversary, the winner of the first ever René Char World Poetry Award will be announced. Also part of the festival, the World Poetry Summit for Peace in Colombia will include panels, conferences and dialogues between world poets who have taken part in peace and conflict resolution processes.

CONTACTS:
Corporation of Art and Poetry Prometeo
Carrera 50 A
No. 60-22 Barrio Prado Center
 Colombia
57-4-2549495
www.festivaldepoesiademedellin.org

Embassy of Colombia
2118 Leroy Pl. N.W.
Washington, D.C. 20008
202-387-8338; fax: 202-232-8643
www.colombiaemb.org

♦ 2287 ♦ Poetry Month, National
April

Established by the Academy of American Poets in 1996, National Poetry Month centers attention on the contributions and accomplishments of American poets. Activities during the month-long event, which is celebrated primarily by educational institutions, libraries, bookstores, and nonprofit organizations throughout the United States and Canada, include poetry readings, poetry festivals, displays and exhibits, workshops, and other events designed to help Americans of all ages learn more about poetry and its place in our contemporary culture.

CONTACTS:
Academy of American Poets
75 Maiden Ln.
Ste. 901
New York, NY 10038
212-274-0343; fax: 212-274-9427
www.poets.org

♦ 2288 ♦ Polar Bear Swim Day
January 1

Since 1920, a group of hardy swimmers has celebrated NEW YEAR'S DAY by plunging into the frigid waters of Vancouver's English Bay. As crazy as it sounds, the custom has spread to the United States, where chapters of the American Polar Bear Club have established themselves in a number of states known for their cold winter weather. In Sheboygan, Wisconsin, more than 300 daring swimmers—many of them in costume—brave the ice floes of Lake Michigan to take their New Year's Day swim. About 3,000 to 4,000 spectators stay bundled up on the beach and watch. The Sheboygan event has gradually expanded into a day-long festival, with a brat-fry, a costume contest, and live entertainment.

CONTACTS:
Sheboygan County Chamber of Commerce
621 S. 8th St.
Sheboygan, WI 53081
920-457-9491; fax: 920-457-6269
www.sheboygan.org

Greater Vancouver Convention and Visitors Bureau
200 Burrard St.
Ste. 210
Vancouver, BC V6C 3L6 Canada
604-682-2222; fax: 604-682-1717
www.tourismvancouver.com

♦ 2289 ♦ Polish Constitution Day
May 3

May 3, known in Poland as **Swieto Trzeciego Maja**, is a patriotic legal holiday honoring the nation's first constitution, adopted in 1791. It introduced fundamental changes in the way Poland was governed, based on the ideas of the French Revolution, and represented an attempt to preserve the country's independence. Although the May 3rd Constitution (as it was called) represented a great advance for the Polish people, it also aroused the anxieties of neighboring countries and eventually led to the Second Partition two years later.

CONTACTS:
Polish American Cultural Center
6501 Lansing Ave.
Cleveland, OH 44105
216-883-2828
new.polishcenterofcleveland.org

Embassy of the Republic of Poland
2640 16th St. N.W.
Washington, D.C. 20009
202-499-1700; fax: 202-328-6271
www.washington.mfa.gov.pl

♦ 2290 ♦ Polish Independence Day
November 11

This national holiday commemorates the re-creation of the state of Poland at the end of World War I. On November 11, 1918, Poland was granted independence after having been partitioned under the rule of Prussia, Austria, and Russia for more than 100 years. After the Soviet system took over the country, the holiday was abolished. But in 1989, after the Communist government fell, Independence Day was once again a national holiday.

See also POLISH SOLIDARITY DAY.

CONTACTS:
Embassy of The Republic of Poland
2460 16th St. N.W.
Washington, D.C. 20009
202-499-1700; fax: 202-328-6271
washington.mfa.gov.pl/en

♦ 2291 ♦ Polish Liberation Day
July 22; January 17

July 22 is the anniversary of the day on which the KRN (National Home Council) established the Polish Committee of National Liberation (PKWN) in 1944, the first people's government in the country's thousand-year history. The PKWN manifesto issued on this date proclaimed that its first priorities were complete liberation from the Nazis and the freeing of ancient Polish lands on the Baltic Sea and Odra River, as well as the democratization of the country.

In the city of Warsaw, January 17 is observed as Liberation Day. It was on this day in 1945 that the city was freed from Nazi oppression by Soviet troops. Special ceremonies are held at the Monument to the Unknown Soldier in Warsaw's Victory Square.

CONTACTS:
Embassy of The Republic of Poland
2460 16th St. N.W.
Washington, D.C. 20009
202-499-1700; fax: 202-328-6271
washington.mfa.gov.pl

♦ 2292 ♦ **Polish Solidarity Day**
August 31

This marks the day in 1980 when the Polish labor union Solidarnosc (Solidarity) was formed at the Lenin Shipyards in Gdansk. Under the leadership of Lech Walesa, an electrician at the shipyard, 17,000 workers had staged a strike earlier in the year to protest rising food prices. An agreement was finally reached between the Gdansk strikers and the Polish Communist government, allowing free unions to be formed, independent of the Communist Party.

Solidarity was formally founded on September 22 and consisted of about 50 labor unions. But when the union stepped up its demands, staging a series of controlled strikes throughout 1981 to pressure the government for free elections and economic reforms, Premier Wojciech Jaruzelski was subjected to even greater pressure from the Soviet Union to put a stop to the group's activities. On December 13, 1981, martial law was declared, the fledgling union's legal status was terminated, and Walesa was put under arrest. He was released in November 1982, and martial law was lifted six months later.

After almost a decade of struggle, Solidarity was finally granted legal status on April 17, 1989, clearing the way for the downfall of the Polish Communist Party. The Polish labor union's successful struggle marked the beginning of similar changes in other Communist-bloc countries in Europe, many of whom overthrew their Communist leaders and took the first steps toward establishing more democratic forms of government. Solidarity's founding is celebrated not only in Poland but by Polish Americans in the United States, with demonstrations and programs in support of Polish workers.

CONTACTS:
NSZZ Solidarnosc
Shafts Piastowskie 24
Gdansk, 80-855 Poland
48-58-308-44-80; fax: 48-58-308-42-19
www.solidarnosc.org.pl

♦ 2293 ♦ **Polka Festival, National**
May, Memorial Day weekend

The National Polka Festival takes place in Ennis, Texas, on Memorial Day Weekend. Founded in 1966, this festival attracts 50,000 people to Ennis for a Saturday and Sunday filled with Czech music, food, folk dance, folk costumes, and crafts. A Saturday morning parade composed of floats, marching bands, clowns, groups of kids, seniors, and representatives from civic organizations kicks off the event. The town's four halls, all with spacious dance floors, host bands at various times throughout the day. On Sunday morning visitors may attend a Polka mass.

CONTACTS:
Ennis Convention & Visitors Bureau
002 E. Ennis Ave.
Ennis, TX 75119
972-878-4748 or 888-366-4748
www.visitennis.org

National Polka Festival
Ennis, TX
www.nationalpolkafestival.com

♦ 2294 ♦ **Polytechneio Day**
November 17

Polytechneio Day commemorates the civil uprising on November 17, 1973 against the Greek military regime that had suppressed civil rights and committed various atrocities against dissenters for years. The uprising grew from events occurring at the National Technical University of Athens, also known as the Polytechneio, months earlier in February 1973. Law students at the University of Athens organized demonstrations and barricades inside the law school as a form of protest against the junta, which had banned student elections in universities across Greece and had implemented forcible drafting of students. Popular indignation rose against the junta following the arrest and torture of student demonstrators. On November 14, student meetings at the Polytechneio concluded with sloganeering against the oppressive regime and the U.S. government's support for the Greek junta. The next day, the students shut the doors to the Polytechneio and staged a sit-in. Thousands filled the streets near the University expressing solidarity with the students. The following day, a radio station broadcast the students' message about their struggle to the city of Athens. By evening, crowds had swelled and violent clashes between police and demonstrators resulted in multiple injuries. Despite imposition of a curfew, people continued to protest. On November 17, the government sent a tank to break down the gates of the Polytechneio. The students resisted, culminating in the loss of 88 lives and hundreds of injuries. Although the November revolt did not topple the dictatorship immediately, the event remains one of the most significant in contemporary Greek history as a symbol of the struggle for freedom, democracy, and social justice. In 1996, the Greek parliament declared November 17 as a national holiday, and many educational establishments hold commemorative services to honor the memory of those who lost their lives in the uprising.

CONTACTS:
Greek National Tourism Organisation
305 E. 47th St.

New York, NY 10017
212-421-5777; fax: 212-826-6940
www.visitgreece.gr/en

◆ 2295 ◆ Pongal
Mid-January

A colorful four-day harvest and thanksgiving celebration in southern India, Pongal honors the sun, the earth, and the cow. It is called Pongal in the state of Tamil Nadu; **Karnataka** in Andhra Pradesh; and **Makara Sankranti** in Gujarat.

The first day is called Bhogi Pongal and is for cleaning everything in the house. On the second day, freshly harvested rice and *jaggery* ('palm sugar') are put to boil in new pots. When the mixture bubbles, people cry out, "Pongal!" ('It boils.') The rice is offered to Surya, the sun, before people taste it themselves, thus the second day is called Surya Pongal. On the third day, called Mattu Pongal (Festival of the Cow), village cows and oxen are bathed, decorated with garlands of bells, beads, and leaves, and worshipped.

On the fourth day, known as Kanyapongal, the festival of Jallikattu takes place in villages near Madurai in Tamil Nadu as well as in Andhra Pradesh. Bundles containing money are tied to the sharpened horns of bulls. The animals are paraded around the village and then stampeded. Young men who are brave enough try to snatch the money from the bulls' horns.

In Ahmedabad in the state of Gujarat, the celebration is a time of competitive kite-flying, and is termed the **International Kite Festival**. The skies are filled with kites, and kite makers come from other cities to make their multicolored kites in all shapes. As darkness falls, the battle of the kites ends, and new kites soar aloft, each with its own paper lamp, so that the sky is filled with flickering lights.

CONTACTS:
Tamil Nadu Tourism
Tourism Complex
No. 2 Wallajah Rd.
Triplicane
Chennai, Tamil Nadu 600 002 India
91-44-2538-3333; fax: 91-44-2536-1385
www.tamilnadutourism.org

Indiatourism Delhi
Indiatourism , 88 Janpath
New Delhi, Delhi 110 001 India
91-11-23320342; fax: 91-11-23320109
www.tourism.nic.in

◆ 2296 ◆ Pooram
April-May; Hindu month of Vaisakha

One of the most spectacular festivals of southern India, this is a celebration in Trichur (or Thrissur), Kerala, dedicated to Lord Shiva. People fast on the first day of the festival and the rest of the days are devoted to fairs, processions, and fireworks displays. The highlight of the pageantry comes when an image of the deity Vadakkunathan is taken from the temple and carried in a procession of temple elephants ornately decorated with gold-plated mail. The Brahmans riding them hold colorful ceremonial umbrellas and whisks of yak hair and peacock feathers. The elephants lumber through the pagoda-shaped gateway of the Vadakkunathan temple and into the village while drummers beat and pipers trill. Fireworks light the skies until dawn.

CONTACTS:
Department of Tourism, Government of Kerala
Park View
Thiruvananthapuram, Kerala 695 033 India
91-471-2321132 or 800-425-4747; fax: 91-471-2322279
www.keralatourism.org

◆ 2297 ◆ Pori International Jazz Festival
Mid-July

Pori, Finland, is 150 miles northwest of Helsinki—far enough north to guarantee 19 hours of daylight during the summer jazz festival that has been held there since 1966. It offers up to 10 major concerts and numerous smaller concerts as well as jam sessions, films, a children's program, and many informal musical events in the city's cafes, restaurants, jazz clubs, and art galleries. All styles of jazz—from traditional to contemporary, dixieland, blues, and swing—are represented. Performers at past festivals have included Herbie Hancock, Chuck Mangione, Ornette Coleman, Dizzy Gillespie, Sonny Rollins, and B.B. King as well as Scandinavian jazz artists. The major concerts are held in an outdoor amphitheater on Kirjurinluoto Island, a natural park in the heart of the city. There are also lectures, films, and exhibitions on jazz and its influence.

CONTACTS:
Pori Jazz Office
Pori Jazz 66
Pohjoisranta 11 D
Pori, 28100 Finland
358-10-391-6000; fax: 358-2-646-9630
www.porijazz.fi

◆ 2298 ◆ Portland Rose Festival
June

The Portland Rose Festival is a month-long salute to the rose in Portland, Ore., and certainly one of the sweetest-smelling festivals anywhere.

The "City of Roses" has been putting on a rose festival since 1907 and claims now to produce the biggest celebration of the rose in the world. To justify such a claim, the festival offers more than 60 events. These include an air show, musical concerts, fireworks, the Portland Arts Festival, tours and cruises on visiting U.S. and Canadian Navy ships, and boat and Indy-class car races.

The salute starts with the coronation of the Rose Queen, and continues with parade after parade, including a starlight parade, called the second largest lighted parade in the United States, the largest children's parade, and the climax—a grand floral parade, with dozens of rose-bedecked floats. On the final days of the festival, the Portland Rose

Society stages the Rose Show, the oldest and largest rose show in the country, with about 20,000 individual blossoms exhibited.

Portland is thought to have started its life as a rose city in the early 19th century, when traders brought with them seeds of the wild rose of England. It flourished as the Oregon Sweet Briar. Settlers brought more roses, and then in 1888, Mrs. Henry L. Pittock held a rose show in her front yard, and that evolved into today's festival.

The parade is one of two major floral parades in the country, the other being the better known TOURNAMENT OF ROSES in Pasadena, Calif., every NEW YEAR'S DAY.

CONTACTS:
Portland Rose Festival Foundation
Rose Bldg.
1020 S.W. Naito Pkwy.
Portland, OR 97204
503-227-2681; fax: 503-227-6603
www.rosefestival.org

♦ 2299 ♦ Portland Liberation Day
April 25

Liberation Day, or **Liberty Day**, is a public holiday commemorating the military coup on this day in 1974 that removed Marcello Caetano (1906-1980) from power, reflecting the opposition of many Portuguese to their government's military policies and wars in Africa.

CONTACTS:
Portugal National Tourist Board
Rua Ivone Silva St.
Lote 6
Lisbon, 1050-124 Portugal
351-211-140-200
www.visitportugal.com

♦ 2300 ♦ Portugal National Day
June 10

Also known as **Camões Memorial Day** and **Portugal Day**, this national holiday observes the death anniversary of Luis Vas de Camões (1524-1580), Portugal's national poet. His epic work, *The Lusiads* (1572), was based on the voyage to India of Portuguese explorer Vasco de Gama.

This national holiday is observed with patriotic speeches, games, and costumed citizens in the capital city of Lisbon.

CONTACTS:
Embassy of Portugal
2012 Massachusetts Ave. N.W.
Washington, D.C. 20036
202-350-5400; fax: 202-462-3726
www.embassyportugal-us.org

♦ 2301 ♦ Portugal Republic Day
October 5

This national holiday commemorates the establishment of the Portuguese Republic on this day in 1910, which ended over two centuries of the monarchical rule of the Portuguese royal family, the House of Braganca.

CONTACTS:
Embassy of Portugal
2012 Massachusetts Ave. N.W.
Washington, D.C. 20036
202-332-3007; fax: 202-223-3926
www.embassyportugal-us.org

♦ 2302 ♦ Portugal Restoration of Independence Day
December 1

This public holiday commemorates the restoration of Portugal's independence from Spain on December 1, 1640. Philip II (1527-1598) of Spain assumed control of Portugal in 1580 upon the death of Henry, prince of Portugal, and the "Spanish captivity" lasted for 60 years. Revolution began in Lisbon, and in 1640, the Portuguese dethroned Philip IV (1605-1665; grandson of Philip II) and reclaimed independence for Portugal.

CONTACTS:
Embassy of Portugal
2012 Massachusetts Ave. N.W.
Washington, D.C. 20036
202-332-3007; fax: 202-223-3926
www.embassyportugal-us.org

Tourism of Portugal
Rua Ivone Silva St.
Lote 6
Lisbon, 1050-124 Portugal
351-211-140-200; fax: 351-211-140-830
www.visitportugal.com

♦ 2303 ♦ Posadas
December 16-24

This nine-day CHRISTMAS celebration in Mexico commemorates the journey Mary and Joseph (the parents of Jesus) took from Nazareth to Bethlehem. Reenacting the couple's search for shelter (*posada* in Spanish) in which the infant Jesus might be born, a group of "pilgrims" will knock on someone's door and ask the owner to let them in. Although they may initially be refused, the master of the house finally invites them to enter, and the Posadas party begins. The children are blindfolded and given a chance to break the *piñata* (a clay or papier-mâché animal that hangs from the ceiling and is filled with candy and toys) by swinging at it with a stick. The posadas are repeated for nine evenings, the last occurring on CHRISTMAS EVE.

The MISA DE GALLO, or Mass of the Cock (so-called because it's held so early in the day), ends after midnight, and then there are fireworks and, in some towns, a special parade with floats and *tableaux vivants* representing biblical scenes.

In small Mexican villages, there is often a procession led by two children bearing images of Joseph and Mary riding a burro. The adult members of the group carry lighted tapers and sing the Litany of the Virgin as they approach each house. There is also a famous Posadas celebration on Olvera Street in Los Angeles.

CONTACTS:
Embassy of Portugal
2012 Massachusetts Ave. N.W.
Washington, D.C. 20036
202-350-5400; fax: 202-462-3726
www.embassyportugal-us.org

◆ 2304 ◆ Poson
May-June; full moon day of Hindu month of Jyestha

This festival, also called **Dhamma Vijaya** and **Full Moon Day**, celebrates the bringing of Buddhism to Sri Lanka (formerly Ceylon). It is second in importance only to Vesak. The story of this day is that King Devanampiya Tissa was chasing a deer in the forest of Mihintale when someone called out his name. He looked up and saw a figure in a saffron-colored robe standing on a rock with six companions. The robed figure was the holy patron of Sri Lanka, Arahat Mahinda, the son of Emperor Asoka of India, who was a convert to Buddhism from Hinduism. He had sent his son and companions as missionaries to Ceylon in about 251 B.C.E. Mahinda converted King Devanampiya Tissa and the royal family, and they in turn converted the common people. Mahinda, who propagated the faith through works of practical benevolence, died in about 204 B.C.E.

While the holiday is celebrated throughout Sri Lanka, the major ceremonies are at the ancient cities of Anuradhapura and Mihintale. There, historical events involving Mahinda are reenacted, streets and buildings are decorated and illuminated, and temples are crowded. In Mihintale people climb to the rock where Arahat Mahinda delivered his first sermon to the king. An important part of the festival is paying homage to the branch of the Bodhi Tree brought to Sri Lanka by Mahinda's sister, Sanghamita. This is the tree that Gautama sat under until he received enlightenment and became the Buddha.

CONTACTS:
Sri Lanka Tourism Promotion Bureau
No. 80, Galle Rd.
Colombo, 00300 Sri Lanka
94-112-426-900; fax: 94-112-440-001
www.srilanka.travel

◆ 2305 ◆ Potato Blossom Festival
July

Founded in 1937 to celebrate Maine's primary food crop, the potato, this festival is held the third weekend in July in Fort Fairfield, Maine, when the potato blossoms are in bloom. Fort Fairfield is the nation's largest potato producer. From 1937 to 1960, the festival was held in a series of towns in northern Maine before Fort Fairfield was officially chosen as the permanent site.

Potato-related events include the Jr. Miss Potato Blossom Pageant, a potato recipe contest, a potato picking contest, and mashed potato wrestling. Other events include musical concerts, bicycle races, a household pet show, an antique farm equipment show, a human chess game, a tractor pull, a two-hour parade, and fireworks. In 1950, the Potato Blossom Festival sponsored the first marathon race to be held in the state of Maine.

CONTACTS:
Fort Fairfield Chamber of Commerce
18 Community Center Dr.
Fort Fairfield, ME 04742
207-472-3800; fax: 207-472-3810
fortcc.org

◆ 2306 ◆ Potato Days
October

In Norway during the fall potato harvest, it was customary to give children a week off school to help in the fields. Norwegian farmers would put in a request for a certain number of children and feed them during their week of employment. Although this arrangement is no longer as common as it was up until the 1950s, children still help harvest the potatoes on their families' farms, and the traditional fall vacation is still known as the potato vacation, or *potetserie*.

A similar arrangement can be found in the United States, especially in states where there are many small farms producing a single crop. In northern Maine, children also harvest potatoes, and in Vermont some schools give their students time off to help pick apples.

◆ 2307 ◆ POW/MIA Recognition Day, National
Third Friday in September

A national observance honoring prisoners of war and service members missing in action, National POW/MIA Recognition Day is held on the third Friday of September each year. The day's observation first began in 1979, when Congress mandated that the U.S. and POW/MIA flags be flown together to remember the day. The event begins with a presidential address that pays tribute to POWs and MIA individuals and urges Americans to remember the contributions of these men and women. In addition, the Pentagon hosts a commemoration ceremony for former POWs and their families. The ceremony is presided over by the Department of Defense and a keynote speaker addresses the gathering. Concurrent observances of the event are held across the country at schools, universities, state capitols, and veteran's organizations. Many states hold veteran's rallies, joint prayers, and other ceremonies and remembrances to commemorate the event.

CONTACTS:
National League of POW/MIA Families
5673 Columbia Pike
Ste. 100
Falls Church, VA 22041
703-465-7432
www.pow-miafamilies.org

♦ 2308 ♦ Powamû Ceremony
February

The Hopi Indians believe that for six months of the year ancestral spirits called the *katchinas* leave their mountain homes and visit the tribe, bringing health to the people and rain for their crops. The Hopi who live at the Walpi Pueblo in northeastern Arizona celebrate the entry of the Sky Father (also known as the Sun God) into the pueblo in February by dramatizing the event in a ceremony known as Powamû. The Sky Father, represented by a man wearing a circular mask surrounded by feathers and horsehair with a curved beak in the middle, is led into the pueblo from the east at sunrise. There he visits the house and *kiva* (underground chamber used for religious and other ceremonies) of the chief, performing certain ceremonial rites and exchanging symbolic gifts.

A similar sequence of events is performed in July during the NIMAN FESTIVAL. At this time, the Sky Father is ushered out of the pueblo. In the intervening months, it is assumed that he remains in the village or nearby, making public appearances in masked dances from time to time.

CONTACTS:
Hopi Cultural Center
P.O. Box 67
Second Mesa, AZ 86043
928-734-2401; fax: 928-734-6651
www.hopiculturalcenter.com

Arizona Office of Tourism
1110 W. Washington St.
Suite 155
Phoenix, AZ 85007
602-364-3700; fax: 602-364-3701
tourism.az.gov

♦ 2309 ♦ Prague Kolache Festival
First Saturday in May

The Prague Kolache Festival is held every year on the first Saturday in May in Prague, Okla. The event celebrates the rich Czech heritage of the city's founding families, who settled in the area around the turn of the last century. The event is named after a Czech pastry that consists of a sweet roll with a fruit center. The first Kolache Festival took place in 1951, as a dress rehearsal for a celebration of the town's 50th birthday in 1952. The popular event carried on annually through 1955, when a 10-year lapse occurred. It has now been held consistently since 1965.

The festival draws as many as 30,000 people to a town of just 2,500 residents. Organizers estimate that 50,000 kolaches are consumed each year. A contest for the best homemade kolache, bread, and wine is a highlight of the festival. It also features an arts-and-crafts show, amusement-park-style carnival, and parade showcasing antique tractors and colorful Czech folk clothing. A variety of free entertainment, ethnic food and drink, and Czech dancing and costume competitions round out the day. Topping it off is the crowning of the Kolache Festival "royalty." By custom, the newly crowned queen opens the evening's popular polka street dance, which carries on until 10:00 that night.

CONTACTS:
Prague Kolache Festival
1107 N. Broadway Ave.
Prague, OK 74864
405-567-4866
www.praguekolachefestival.com

♦ 2310 ♦ Prague Spring International Music Festival
Three weeks in May

When the Prague Spring International Music Festival was organized in 1946, the Czech Philharmonic Orchestra was celebrating its 50th year and was given a prominent place on the program that first year. But orchestras, musical ensembles, and performing artists from around the world participate in this three-week festival, which presents symphonic, chamber and vocal music; jazz; opera; musical theater; and world premieres of Czech and other contemporary composers. The festival always opens with the symphonic poems of Czech composer Bedrich Smetana (1824-1884), *Ma Vlast* (My Country), and concludes with Ludwig van Beethoven's (1770-1827) Ninth Symphony. In addition, the Prague Spring Competition, founded one year after the festival itself, showcases the instrumental talents of young musicians.

CONTACTS:
Prague Spring
Hellichova 18
Prague, 118 00 Czech Republic
420-2-5731-2547; fax: 420-2-5731-3725
www.festival.cz

♦ 2311 ♦ Prayer for Christian Unity, Week of
January 18-25

The Week of Prayer for Christian Unity, as organized by the World Council of Churches, dates back to 1964. Calls for Christian unity and efforts to bring Christians of various denominations together in worship can be traced back at least 200 years earlier, however. In 1908, the Rev. Paul Watson proposed a week-long observance dedicated to Christian unity to be scheduled between the feasts of ST. PETER'S CHAIR (January 18) and ST. PAUL (January 25), the two great leaders of the first Christians. The World Council of Churches maintains these dates. Each year an inter-denominational committee selects a scriptural theme and prepares the outlines of a worship service for each day of the Week of Prayer. Individual congregations are free to use the material as is, or vary it to suit local practices and traditions.

CONTACTS:
World Council of Churches
P.O. Box 2100
Geneva, CH-1211 Switzerland
www.oikoumene.org/en

♦ 2312 ♦ Preakness Stakes
Third Saturday in May

The 10-day **Preakness Festival** or **Maryland Preakness Celebration** culminates in the running of the Preakness Stakes, the "middle jewel of the Triple Crown" of horseracing—the other two being the KENTUCKY DERBY and the BELMONT STAKES. Held at Baltimore's Pimlico Race Course, the Preakness was first run on May 27, 1873. The festival leading up to the race features recreational, sporting, and cultural events— including hot air balloons, a 5K run, and a parade.

CONTACTS:

Maryland Jockey Club
Pimlico Race Course
5201 Park Heights Ave.
Baltimore, MD 21215
410-542-9400 or 877-206-8042
www.marylandracing.com

♦ 2313 ♦ Premio Lo Nuestro Latin Music Awards
February

Since 1989, the Univision television network has been awarding the Premios Lo Nuestro Latin Music Awards. Some 35 categories of music and performance are honored. It is the oldest such awards program in the United States.

The televised awards ceremony features live performances by nominated musical acts along with music videos. Journalists and media celebrities from throughout Latin America come to the event. Among those artists who have won the awards are Ricky Martin, Gloria Estefan, Jennifer Lopez, Aventura, and Ivy Queen. While originating from the United States, the Premio Lo Nuestro Latin Music Awards program is broadcast throughout Latin America.

CONTACTS:
Univision Communications, Inc.
9405 N.W. 41st St.
Miami, FL 33178
305-471-3900
corporate.univision.com

♦ 2314 ♦ Presentation of the Blessed Virgin Mary, Feast of the
November 21

The Feast of the Presentation of the Blessed Virgin Mary was first celebrated by the Greeks in about the eighth century andwas not adopted by the Roman Catholic Church until the later Middle Ages; no one is quite sure when this festival was first introduced. As related in the apocryphal Book of James, it commemorates the presentation of the three-year-old Mary in the Temple to consecrate her to the service of God. Many have confused this festival with the Feast of the Presentation of Christ in the Temple, otherwise known as CANDLEMAS.

CONTACTS:
Mary Page, Marian Library/International Marian Research Institute
University of Dayton
300 College Park
Dayton, OH 45469
937-229-1000
www.udayton.edu

♦ 2315 ♦ Preservation of the Ozone Layer, International Day for the
September 16

In 1994, the UNITED NATIONS established September 16 as International Day for the Preservation of the Ozone Layer. The date honors the September 16, 1987, signing of the Montreal Protocol on Substances that Deplete the Ozone Layer. Nations may observe the day with activities that support the aims of the Protocol.

CONTACTS:
United Nations, Department of Public Information
Rm. S-1070L J, K, L
New York, NY 10017 United States
212-963-4664; fax: 212-963-0077
www.un.org

♦ 2316 ♦ Presidents' Day`
Third Monday in February

The passage of Public Law 90-363 in 1968, also known as the "Monday Holiday Law," changed the observance of WASHINGTON'S BIRTHDAY from February 22 to the third Monday in February. Because it occurs so soon after LINCOLN'S BIRTHDAY, many states—such as Hawaii, Minnesota, Nebraska, Wisconsin, and Wyoming—combine the two holidays and call it Presidents' Day or **Washington-Lincoln Day**. Some regard it as a day to honor all former presidents of the United States.

See also Appendix.

♦ 2317 ♦ Pretzel Sunday
Between March 8 and April 7; fourth Sunday in Lent

On **Bretzelsonndeg** in Luxembourg, it is the custom for boys to present their sweethearts with decorated pretzel-cakes. If a girl wants to encourage the boy, she reciprocates with a decorated egg on EASTER Sunday. If the pretzel-cake is large, the egg must be large also; a small cake warrants a small egg.

The custom is reversed during LEAP YEAR, when girls give cakes to boys on Pretzel Sunday, and boys return the favor with eggs at Easter. Married couples often participate in the exchange of cakes and eggs as well.

♦ 2318 ♦ Primrose Day
April 19

Benjamin Disraeli, Earl of Beaconsfield, novelist, and twice prime minister of England, died on this day in 1881. When he was buried in the family vault at Hughenden Manor, near High Wycombe, Queen Victoria came to lay a wreath of primroses, thought to be his favorite flower, on his grave. Two years later the Primrose League was formed to support the principles of Conservatism which Disraeli had championed. The organization's influence ebbed after World War I, but Primrose Day is remembered in honor of Disraeli and his contribution to the Conservative cause.

CONTACTS:
Greater London Authority
The Queen's Walk
City Hall
London, SE1 2AA United Kingdom
44-20-7983-4000; fax: 44-20-7983-4057
www.london.gov.uk

♦ 2319 ♦ **Prince's Birthday in Liechtenstein**
August 15

The Prince's Birthday is a national holiday in Liechtenstein. This 60-square-mile country (population around 32,000) gets almost 25 percent of its revenue from selling postage stamps. The country is a constitutional monarchy headed by Prince Franz Joseph II, who turned over actual power to his son, Hans-Adam (b. 1945), in 1984. It was founded at the end of the 17th century when Johann Adam von Liechtenstein, a wealthy Austrian prince, bought land in the Rhine valley from two bankrupt counts. In 1719, he obtained an imperial deed creating the country. That date is considered the official birth of the nation. Members of the Liechtenstein family have ruled the country ever since.

Franz Joseph II was born on Aug. 16, 1905, but his birthday is celebrated on Aug. 15, the day of the Feast of the ASSUMPTION. Celebrations take place in the capital city of Vaduz. People come from the countryside for the festivities which include an open house at the prince's home and castle, Schloss Vaduz, dancing in the streets, special food in the cafes, and fireworks in the evening.

CONTACTS:
Princely House of Liechtenstein
Furstenhaus von Liechtenstein
Schloss Vaduz, Vaduz 9490 Liechtenstein
423-238-1200; fax: 423-238-1201
www.fuerstenhaus.li/en

♦ 2320 ♦ **Prinsjesdag**
Third Tuesday in September

The state opening of Parliament in the Netherlands takes place on the third Tuesday in September at the 13th-century Ridderzaal, or Knights' Hall, in The Hague. Queen Beatrix rides to Parliament in a golden coach drawn by eight horses. She is received by the two houses of Parliament—the Upper House and the Lower House, corresponding to the Senate and the House of Representatives in the United States—to whom she addresses her speech outlining the government's intended majority program for the coming year.

A similar ceremony is observed in Great Britain (*see* STATE OPENING OF PARLIAMENT).

CONTACTS:
Government Information Service
Courtyard 19
P.O. Box 20001
Hague, EA 2500 Netherlands
www.koninklijkhuis.nl

♦ 2321 ♦ **Prisoners, Feast of the**
Between March 15 and April 18; Tuesday before Easter

Popayán, Colombia, is famous for the beauty of its HOLY WEEK celebrations, which include the traditional blessing of the palms on PALM SUNDAY and a procession between rows of waving palm branches. But one of the more unusual ceremonies held during this week is called the Feast of the Prisoners.

A procession of litters covered with plates and bowls of food and cases of soft drinks arrives at the local prison on Tuesday afternoon, accompanied by government officials, the archbishop in ceremonial garb, and schoolgirls with more things to eat. The prisoners are gathered in the courtyard to listen to various addresses. One of them who is approaching the end of his sentence is selected to sit, guarded and manacled, at a special table. He symbolizes Barrabas, the man in the biblical EASTER story whom the crowd clamored to free instead of Jesus. As people walk by the chosen prisoner they deposit gifts of food or money for him to retrieve when he is set free at the end of the day. That night there is a candlelight procession in which large decorated litters depict scenes from the Passion of Christ or bear images of the saints.

Although no one knows how far back Popayán's Holy Week traditions extend, historical records indicate that Easter ceremonies were being held there in 1558.

CONTACTS:
Embassy of Colombia
2118 Leroy Pl. N.W.
Washington, D.C. 20008
202-387-8338; fax: 202-232-8643
www.colombiaemb.org

♦ 2322 ♦ **Puccini Festival**
Every June-August

The Puccini Festival is held annually each summer in Torre del Lago in Tuscany, Italy, to honor and celebrate Giacomo Puccini (1858-1924), the Italian composer of such beloved operas as *La Boheme* and *Madame Butterfly*. Over the course of each summer from June through August, the festival presents distinguished and often innovative productions of Puccini's works. More than 40,000 music lovers attend ticketed festival concerts and operas each summer. The productions take place in an open-air theatre close to the Villa Mausoleum, where Puccini lived and worked. In addition to musical performances, such collateral events as talks and art exhibitions having to do with Puccini's life and work are held throughout the area all summer.

The festival was founded in 1930 by Giovacchino Forzano, a playwright and librettist, and Pietro Mascagri, a friend from Puccini's school days. Shortly before he died, Puccini had written in a letter to Forzano of his desire to "listen to one of my operas in the open air." Six years after the maestro's death, his friend honored his wish by mounting a production of *La Boheme* on the lakeshore in front of Puccini's house, on a provisional stage built on piles in the lake. The festival has thrived ever since. In 1966, the performances moved to a large amphitheatre on reclaimed land near the lake harbor. Four to five opera productions each season attract about 40,000 spectators to the Teatro dei Quattromila, the new, state-of-the-art, open-air theatre that is the centerpiece of a cultural park celebrating Puccini and his achievements.

CONTACTS:
Italian National Tourist Board of North America
686 Park Ave.
3rd Fl.
New York, NY 10065
212-245-5618; fax: 212-586-9249
www.italiantourism.com

Puccini Festival Foundation
Via the bogs
Torre de Lago Puccini, LU 55049 Italy
39-0584-350567; fax: 39-0584-341657
www.puccinifestival.it

♦ 2323 ♦ Puck Fair
August 10-12

A traditional gathering that dates back hundreds of years, Puck Fair is a three-day event held in Killorglin in County Kerry, Ireland. A large male goat is decorated with ribbons and paraded through the streets on the first day, which is known as Gathering Day. The goat, known as King Puck, presides over the fair from his "throne," an enclosure on a three-story platform in the town square. The main event of the second day, known as Puck's Fair Day, is a livestock show. On the third day, known as Scattering Day or Children's Day, King Puck is led out of town to the accompaniment of traditional Irish music. People come from all over Europe and the United States to attend the fair.

CONTACTS:
Puck Fair Ltd.
c/o K.C.Y.M.S
Mill Rd.
Killorglin, County Kerry Ireland
353-66-976-2366; fax: 353-66-976-2366
www.puckfair.ie

♦ 2324 ♦ Puerto Rico Constitution Day
July 25

Puerto Rico Constitution Day is the anniversary of the day on which Puerto Rico changed from a territory to a commonwealth and adopted its new constitution in 1952. Sometimes referred to as **Commonwealth Day**, July 25 is a legal holiday throughout the island. It is celebrated with parades, speeches, fireworks, and parties.

The most interesting thing about the relationship between Puerto Rico and the United States is its voluntary nature. Under the commonwealth arrangement, islanders elect a governor and a legislature as well as a resident commissioner who is sent—with a voice but not a vote—to the U.S. Congress in Washington, D.C. The relationship remains permanent for as along as both parties agree to it, but it can be changed at any time by mutual consent. The reason Puerto Rico became a commonwealth rather than an independent republic or a state is that the election of 1948 failed to produce a majority vote in favor of either of these alternatives.

CONTACTS:
Puerto Rico Tourism Company
135 W., 50th St., 22nd Fl.
New York, NY 10020
212-586-6262 or 800-223-6530
welcome.topuertorico.org

Puerto Rico Hotel & Tourism Association
Doral Bank Plaza, Calle Resolución #33
Ste. 701-B
San Juan, PR 00920
787-758-8001; fax: 787-758-8091
www.prhta.org

♦ 2325 ♦ Pulaski Day
October 11; first Sunday in October

Count Casimir Pulaski was already a seasoned fighter for the cause of independence when he first arrived in America in 1777 to help General George WASHINGTON and the Continental Army overthrow the British. While still a teenager he had fought to preserve the independence of his native Poland, and when he was forced to flee his country he ended up in Paris. There he met Benjamin FRANKLIN and Silas Deane, who were impressed by his military background and arranged for him to join the American revolutionaries.

Although he was put in charge of the mounted units and given the title Commander of the Horse, Pulaski had trouble maintaining his soldiers' respect. He spoke no English and was unwilling to take orders from anyone, including Washington. Eventually he resigned from the army and raised an independent cavalry corps, continuing his fight for the colonies' independence. It was on October 11, 1779, that the Polish count died while trying to free Savannah, Georgia, from British control.

The president of the United States proclaims October 11 as Pulaski Day each year, and it is observed with parades and patriotic exercises in communities in Georgia, Indiana, Nebraska, and Wisconsin. The biggest Pulaski Day parade takes place in New York City on the first Sunday in October, when more than 100,000 Polish Americans march up Fifth Avenue.

CONTACTS:
General Pulaski Memorial Parade Committee Inc
79-17 Albion Ave.
Queens
New York, NY 10007
718-383-0505
www.pulaskiparade.org

♦ 2326 ♦ Punjabi American Festival
May

Since 1994, the Punjabi American Heritage Society has sponsored the annual Punjabi American Festival in Yuba City, Calif. The event is meant to celebrate the Punjabi culture of Northern India and to introduce young Punjabi-Americans to their heritage. Many Punjabi immigrants have settled in the Yuba City area of California. The festival is the largest of its kind in North America.

The Punjabi American Festival is a day-long event held at the Yuba-Sutter Fairgrounds in Yuba City. It begins with the playing of the National Anthem, followed by children reciting a Punjabi prayer. Featured are Bhangra dance groups, which contain both male and female dancers in colorful costumes performing songs and intricate dances. Traditionally, Bhangra dances are performed to celebrate harvest time. There are also other ethnic folk dancers and musical performers, Punjabi comedy skits, arts and crafts, movies, children's games, and over 50 booths selling traditional foods, clothing, and jewelry. Over 300 children participate in the stage performances. A number of prominent Punjabis from across the country are also honored by the Punjabi American heritage Society during the festival. The money raised is used towards cultural projects in the Yuba City community.

CONTACTS:
Punjabi American Heritage Society
P.O. Box 621
Yuba City, CA 95992
530-844-0247
www.punjabiheritage.org

♦ 2327 ♦ Punkin Chunkin World Championship
October-November

A celebration held the first weekend after Halloween in Sussex County, Del., since 1986, the Punkin Chunkin World Championship involves shooting pumpkins as far as possible using homemade catapults, trebuchets, slingshots, or pneumatic air cannons. No prizes are offered except for bragging rights.

There are various levels of competition based on the type of machine used and the age of participants. Pumpkins are weighed beforehand, the competing teams are given three minutes to prepare and load their machines, and then each team in turn is given the chance to launch their projectile. Each team gets the best of three shots. Judges on ATVs ride out in the field to mark and measure the distance each pumpkin traveled. Pumpkins that break apart in midair are considered

"pie" and are disqualified. The 2013 event included 72 teams and drew more than 20,000 people. The event grossed more than $100,000 in ticket sales and associated revenues, most of which is distributed in scholarships to a variety of community organizations. The popular Punkin Chunkin festivals are said to have spread to some 50 other locations across America.

♦ 2328 ♦ Punky (Punkie) Night
Last Thursday in October

In the English village of Hinton St. George, Somerset, it is traditional for both children and adults to walk through town carrying "punkies," or lanterns made from carved-out mangel-wurzels, or mangolds (a variety of beet), with candles in them. Some say that the custom originated when parish women made crude vegetable lanterns to guide their husbands home after a long evening at the local pub. October 28 was traditionally the date for the Chiselborough Fair, and it was not uncommon for the men to drink too much and get lost in the fields on their way home.

Although this custom is observed in other English towns, the celebration at Hinton St. George is by far the best established. There is a procession of children carrying punkies through the streets, begging for money, and singing the "punky song." A prize is given out for the best carved punky. There is no evidence that the name "punky" came from "pumpkin," but the custom is very similar to what takes place on HALLOWEEN in the United States, where carved, candlelit pumpkins are displayed in windows and on doorsteps.

♦ 2329 ♦ Puppeteers, Festival of
Early July

The art of making and performing with puppets has enjoyed a resurgence in the decades since World War II—particularly in the Czech Republic, where puppet ensembles proliferated after 1945. Every summer since 1951, a nationwide festival of puppeteers has been held in Chrudim. Puppeteers from other countries are often invited to participate in the festival.

In addition to the performances of puppet theaters, there are discussions and seminars on the art of puppetry.

Other international puppet festivals have been held in Barcelona, Spain; Braunschweig, Germany; Bielski-Biala, Poland; Bialystok, Poland; Bochum, Germany; and Washington, D.C.

CONTACTS:
City of Chrudim
The Old Town Hall.
The Ressel Sq. 1
Chrudim, 537 01 Czech Republic
420-469-622-959; fax: 420-469-645-821
www.chrudim.eu/en.html

♦ 2330 ♦ Purim
Between February 25 and March 25; Adar 14

Six hundred years before the Christian era, most Jews were slaves in Persia. The Persian prime minister Haman, who generally hated Jews and particularly hated a proud Jew named Mordechai, persuaded King Ahasuerus (Xerxes I) to let him destroy the empire's entire Jewish population. Haman cast lots (*pur* is Akkadian for "lot") to find out which day would be the most auspicious for his evil plan, and the lots told him that things would go especially well on the 14th of Adar. This is why Purim is also called **The Feast of Lots**.

The king did not realize that his own wife, Esther, was Jewish, and that Mordechai was her cousin, until she pleaded with him to spare her people. Haman was hanged, and his position as prime minister was given to Mordechai.

Ahasuerus granted the Jews an extra day to vanquish Haman's supporters, so the rabbis decreed that in Jerusalem and other walled cities, Purim should be celebrated on 15 Adar and called *Purim Shushan*, Hebrew for "Susa," the Persian capital. In leap year, the 14th (or 15th in Jerusalem) Adar is known as *Purim Katan*, "the lesser Purim."

The Old Testament Book of Esther is read aloud in synagogues on the eve and morning of Purim, and listeners drown out every mention of Haman's name by jeering and stamping their feet. Purim is also a time for sharing food with friends and for charity to the poor.

See also PURIMS, SPECIAL.

◆ 2331 ◆ **Purims, Special**
Various

Just as Jews throughout the world celebrate their escape from the evil plot of the Persian prime minister Haman (*see* PURIM), many individual Jewish communities commemorate their deliverance from specific calamities by observing their own Purims. The **Padua Purim**, for example, observed on 11 Sivan, celebrates Jews' deliverance from a major fire in Padua, Italy, in 1795. The **Baghdad Purim**, observed on 11 Av, celebrates the conquest of Baghdad by the Arabs and the defeat of the Persians. The **Snow Purim**, observed on 24 Tevet, celebrates the major snowstorm in Tunis that caused extensive damage and injury elsewhere but left the Jewish quarter of the city untouched. And the **Hitler Purim**, observed in Casablanca, Morocco, on 2 Kislev, commemorates the city's escape from German domination during World War II.

CONTACTS:
Orthodox Union
11 Broadway
New York, NY 10004
212-563-4000
www.ou.org

◆ 2332 ◆ **Purple Heart Day**
August 7

Purple Heart Day is observed in the United States and commemorates the establishment in 1782 of the Badge of

Military Merit, an award created by George Washington to honor soldiers for their distinguished action in battle. The Purple Heart was not used after the Revolutionary War, but was restored in 1932 as an honor for those who have been wounded or killed in battle.

On August 7 throughout the country, local chapters of the Military Order of the Purple Heart sponsor services to remember and honor medal recipients from their communities. Taking place in a variety of locations, including parks, cemeteries, and state capitols, these ceremonies often feature prayers, military music, reminiscences by award recipients, and speeches by government and military officials. In some communities a picnic or potluck follows. Services are also scheduled at the National Purple Heart Hall of Honor in New Windsor, N.Y. The Hall of Honor opened in 2006 and is dedicated to collecting and preserving the stories of those who have earned a Purple Heart medal. It is located on the site of Washington's last encampment and the site where the first modern recipients of the Purple Heart were awarded their medals in 1932.

CONTACTS:
National Purple Heart Hall of Honor
374 Temple Hill Rd.
New Windsor, NY 12553
845-561-1765 or 877-284-6667; fax: 845-569-0382
www.thepurpleheart.com

◆ 2333 ◆ **Pushkar Mela**
October-November; full moon day of Hindu month of Kartika

Pushkar Mela is a camel fair and one of the best known of the Hindu religious fairs of India. It is held at Pushkar, the place where it is said a lotus flower slipped out of Lord Brahma's hands. Water sprang up where the petals fell and created the holy waters of Pushkar Lake. A temple to Brahma on the shore of the lake is one of the few temples in India dedicated to Brahma. Pushkar is in the state of Rajasthan, a vast desert area dotted with oases and populated with wild black camels.

The commercial side of the fair features the sale of about 10,000 camels. Sheep, goats, horses, and donkeys are also sold there. Countless stalls offer such camel accouterments as saddles and blankets embellished with mirrors, bangles, brass utensils, and brass-studded belts. Camel races are a highlight. In the "camel rush" people jump onto camels, and the camel that holds the most people wins a prize.

On the night of the full moon (*Kartika Purnima*), devotees bathe in the waters of the lake and then make offerings of coconut and rice at the Brahma temple.

CONTACTS:
PushkarFestivals
C-811, Ground Fl.
Sushant Lok-1
Gurgaon, New Delhi 122002 India
91-124-4636800 or 866-374-7068; fax: 91-124-4636880
www.pushkarfestivals.com

♦ 2334 ♦ **Putrada Ekadashi**
July-August; 11th day of waxing half of Hindu month of Sravana

The Hindu EKADASHI, or 11th-day fast known as Putrada Ekadashi, is observed primarily by parents who want to produce a son. A fast is observed, Vishnu is worshipped and meditated upon, and the Brahmans are fed and presented with robes and money. Fasting and piety on this day are believed to ensure the conception of a boy, especially for those who sleep in the same room where Vishnu has been worshipped.

Would-be parents are also expected to observe the Ekadashithat falls in the waning half of the month of Sravana.

It is known as KamadaEkadashi.Ekadashi,ortheWish-Fulfillingthey were held every four years on the plain near Delphi.Competitions in instrumental music, singing, drama, and recitations in verse and prose were primary, but there were also athletic and equestrian contests modeled on those at Olympia. The prize was a crown of bay leaves.

♦ 2335 ♦ **Pythian Games**
Every four years in August

The Pythian Games were ancient Greek games considered next in importance to the OLYMPIC GAMES. From 586 B.C.E.,.

Q

♦ 2336 ♦ **Qatar Independence Day**
September 3

This national holiday celebrates Qatar's full independence from Britain on this day in 1971.

CONTACTS:
Embassy of State of Qatar
2555 M St. N.W.
Washington, D.C. 20037
202-274-1600; fax: 202-237-0061
www.qatarembassy.net

♦ 2337 ♦ **Qiantang River Tidal Bore Watching Festival, International**
18th day of the eighth lunar month

The rare phenomenon known as the tidal bore, in which a tidal wave roars up a river, has always attracted thousands of spectators. Scientists have designated the massive wave that travels up the Qiantang River in China's eastern region the world's largest tidal bore. More than 300,000 people gather for this natural wonder during the autumn full moon, on a day when the gravitational pull on the water is greatest.

Yanguan Town in Haining, Hangzhou, is the best place to watch the tidal event and thus has become the host site of the festival. It coincides with the MID-AUTUMN FESTIVAL (or Moon Cake Festival), a holiday celebrated throughout the Far East. Festivalgoers in Haining practice the old custom of eating moon cakes, a staple pastry of the Mid-Autumn Festival.

The Qiantang waves have been recorded as high as 30 feet. Some attendees decide to watch from a close distance, which has resulted in drownings during years when the tide is especially strong. One popular safe vantage point is the multi-storied Liuhe Pagoda, an ancient famous structure located near the river.

♦ 2338 ♦ **Qing Ming Festival (Ching Ming Festival)**
Fourth or fifth day of third lunar month

The Qing Ming Festival is a day for Chinese throughout the world to honor their dead. *Qing Ming* means "clear and bright," and refers to the weather at this time of year. It is a Confucian festival that dates back to the Han Dynasty (206 B.C.E. to 221 C.E.), and it is now a Chinese national holiday. It is computed as 105 days after the WINTER SOLSTICE, Tong-ji.

The day is observed in the countryside with visits to ancestral graves to sweep, wash, repair, and paint them. Offerings of food, wine, incense, and flowers are made, firecrackers are set off, and paper money is burned at the graveside, so that the ancestors will have funds to spend in the afterworld. (The Chinese traditional belief is that the afterlife is quite similar to this life, and that the dead live a little below ground in the Yellow Springs region.)

In ancient China, people spent Qing Ming playing Chinese football and flying kites. Today, they picnic and gather for family meals. In the cities, though, it has been changed to a day of patriotism with placement of memorial wreaths only to Chinese revolution heroes in a few state-run public cemeteries.

The day is also called **Cold Food Day** (in Korea, **Han Sik-il**; in Taiwan, **Han Shih**) because, according to an ancient legend, it was taboo to cook the day before.

In Taiwan, yellow paper strips about 3 x 2 inches, are stuck in the ground of the grave, as is shingling. This symbolically maintains the home of one's ancestors. Then the prayers and food offerings are done.

See also THANH-MINH AND ULLAMBANA.

♦ 2339 ♦ **Quadragesima Sunday**
Between February 8 and March 14; first Sunday in Lent in West

The name for the first Sunday in LENT is derived from the Latin word meaning "fortieth." The first Sunday of the Lenten season is 40 days before EASTER. The other "numbered" Sundays, all before Lent, are Quinquagesima ("fiftieth"), Sexagesima ("sixtieth"), and Septuagesima ("seventieth"). These are reckoned by an approximate number of days before Easter; only Quadrigesima is close to the actual count. These names, as well as "Pre-Lent," are no longer used, the calendar now referring to the number of Sundays after EPIPHANY, e.g. first Sunday after Epiphany, second Sunday after Epiphany, and so on until ASH WEDNESDAY, then, first Sunday in Lent.

♦ 2340 ♦ Quadrilles of San Martin
November 11

Every year on San Martin's Day (*see* MARTINMAS), the Quadrilles of St. Martin—often described as an "equestrian ballet"—have been held in the old Colombian town named after the saint. Forty-eight expert riders, all male and mounted on Creole horses, divide into four groups and take their places at the four corners of the town's large square.

Each group of riders is dressed to represent a different ethnic group that has played a part in Colombia's past: The Moors (Arabs) wear turbans and white, Oriental-looking robes and carry scimitars; the Spaniards wear black riding jackets, white breeches, tall boots, and cowboy hats and carry sabers; the Blacks wear exotic African headgear and animal skins and carry long machetes; and the Indians wear feather headdresses, breastplates, and elaborate necklaces and are armed with bows and arrows.

The performances reenact various events in Colombia's history, including the battles between the Spanish and the Moors and the wars of independence waged against Spain. Although the acts themselves are carefully staged, they often involve improvisation requiring fast riding and split-second timing.

After the Quadrilles are over, residents and visitors gather in the square's open-air cafes to drink *aguardiente,* the local anise-flavored liquor, to eat *ternara a la llanera,* or barbecued baby beef, and to watch the fireworks displays that are set off over the city. Participation in the Quadrilles is an honor that is handed down from one generation to the next among the city's oldest families.

See also MOORS AND CHRISTIANS FIESTA.

CONTACTS:
Embassy of Colombia
2118 Leroy Pl. N.W.
Washington, D.C. 20008
202-387-8338; fax: 202-232-8643
www.colombiaemb.org

♦ 2341 ♦ Quarter Days
Various

The four traditional quarter days in England, Northern Ireland, and Wales are LADY DAY (March 15), MIDSUMMER DAY (June 24), MICHAELMAS (September 29), and CHRISTMAS Day (December 25). They mark off the four quarters of the year and the times at which rents and other payments are due. It was also customary to move into or out of a house on a quarter day.

In Scotland the quarter days are CANDLEMAS (February 2), PENTECOST (or Whitsunday, the seventh Sunday after Easter), LAMMAS (August 1), and MARTINMAS (November 11).

See also CROSS-QUARTER DAYS.

♦ 2342 ♦ Quartier d'été
Mid-July to mid-August

From mid-July to mid-August the city of Paris, France, hosts an outdoor arts festival, featuring more than 200 performances and 450 guest artists. Events take place in concert halls, gardens, parks, squares, and alongside the city's monuments. The menu of events includes music, dance, theater, film, and circus performances, as well as storytelling and visual arts exhibits. The festival began in 1990.

CONTACTS:
Paris Convention and Visitors Bureau
25, rue des Pyramides
Paris, 75001 France
en.parisinfo.com

♦ 2343 ♦ Quebec City Festival of Sacred Music
October-November

The Quebec City Festival of Sacred Music includes all musical forms, as long as they are spiritually inspired. This open-minded policy has resulted in festival programs featuring such diverse style as gospel, Negro spirituals, Gregorian chants, Celtic music, and throat singing.

The event's founder, local Quebec City priest Mario Dufour, believed that sacred music was so beautiful and spiritually edifying that a festival should be organized around it. He also envisioned that the music genre could connect with enthusiasts over many religious and linguistic boundaries. His own St. Roch Church was the suggested venue for the inaugural festival held in 1997, which at that time was the first of its kind in North America. The church has hosted the 11-day event ever since.

Over the years, world-renowned international performers have been selected for the program, and the event has become an established part of the Quebec City's cultural cal- endar.

♦ 2344 ♦ Quebec Winter Carnival
Late January to mid-February

Winter carnivals are common throughout Canada, but the celebration of winter that has been held since the mid-1950s in Quebec City ranks among the great carnivals of the world. It begins with the Queen's Ball at the Château Frontenac, a hotel resembling a huge medieval castle in the center of the city, and a parade of illuminated floats.

The International Ice Sculpture Contest, featuring artists from several northern countries, is held at Place Carnaval. More than 40,000 tons of snow are trucked in to construct a large snow castle, which is illuminated at night and which serves as a mock jail for those who fail to remain smiling throughout the celebration. Bonhomme Carnaval, the festival's seven-foot-high snowman mascot dressed in a red cap and traditional sash, roams the streets teasing children and looking for people to lock up in the Ice Palace. The festival drink is caribou, a blend of white alcohol and red wine.

An unusual festival event is the hazardous race of steel-bottomed boats on the semi-frozen St. Lawrence River. Each boat has a team of five, and its members must maneuver around ice floes and occasionally drag their boats over large patches of ice.

An interesting feature of this festival is the way it is financed. A principal source of income for the Carnaval Association is the candle, or "bougie," sale. People who buy the bougies increase the chances that their representative "duchess" (and there are a number of duchesses chosen from all over Quebec) will be selected as Carnaval Queen. They also get a chance to participate in a giant lottery. More than 10,000 people participate in the sale and distribution of candles on "Bougie Night.".

CONTACTS:
Carnaval de Quebec
205, boulevard des Cèdres
Quebec, QC G1L 1N8 Canada
418-626-3716; fax: 418-626-7252
carnaval.qc.ca/en

◆ 2345 ◆ Quecholli
280th day of the Aztec year; end of 14th month

Mixcoatl was the Aztec god of the chase, also known as the Cloud Serpent. He had deer or rabbit characteristics, was identified with the morning star, and, as one of the four creators of the world, made fire from sticks just before the creation of man. The festival in his honor, known as Quecholli, was observed with a ceremonial hunt. According to the civil cycle of the Aztec calendar—which consisted of 18 months of 20 days each, plus five unlucky days—Quecholli was celebrated at the end of the 14th month. This was also the day on which weapons were made.

CONTACTS:
Embassy of the United States in Mexico City
Paseo de la Reforma 305
Colonia Cuauhtemoc, Mexico City 06500 Mexico
11-52-55-5080-2000; fax: 11-52-55-5080-2005
mexico.usembassy.gov

◆ 2346 ◆ Queen's Birthday (Thailand)
August 12

Queen's Birthday is a nationwide celebration in Thailand of the birthday of Her Majesty Queen Sirikit (b. 1932). Throughout the country, buildings are decorated to honor the queen, but the most splendid are in Bangkok, where buildings and streets are brilliant with colored lights.

CONTACTS:
Wat Buddharangsi of Miami
15200 S.W. 240th St.
Miami, FL 33032
305-245-2702; fax: 305-245-2702
thaitemplemiami.com

Foreign Office, Government of Thailand
Public Relations Department
9 Rama VI Rd., Soi 30
Bangkok, 10400 Thailand

66-2-618-2323; fax: 66-2-618-2358
thailand.prd.go.th

◆ 2347 ◆ Queen's Day (England)
November 17

This is the day on which Queen Elizabeth I ascended to the throne in 1558 upon the death of her sister, Queen Mary I. Often referred to as the Virgin Queen because she never married, Elizabeth reigned for 44 years—a period that came to be known as the Elizabethan Age because it marked England's rise as a major European power in commerce, politics, and the arts.

The anniversary of her coronation was celebrated for more than 300 years after her reign ended, primarily as a holiday for those working in government offices. After the Gunpowder Plot was exposed in 1605, two years following Elizabeth's death, the day was marked by anti-papal demonstrations, which included burning the pope in effigy. **Queen Elizabeth's Day** eventually merged with the celebration of GUY FAWKES DAY.

CONTACTS:
Official Website of The British Monarchy
Buckingham Palace
London, SW1A 1AA United Kingdom
44-20-7930-4832
www.royal.gov.uk

◆ 2348 ◆ Queenship of Mary
August 22

Mary, the mother of Jesus, was identified with the title of "Queen" at least as early as the 13th century. Artists often depicted her as wearing a crown or being crowned as she was received into heaven. When Pope Pius XII solemnly defined the dogma of the ASSUMPTION of Mary in 1950, he stated that she was raised body and soul to heaven, "to shine resplendent as Queen at the right hand of her Son."

On October 11, 1954, during the Marian year that marked the centenary of the proclamation of the dogma of the IMMACULATE CONCEPTION of Mary, Pope Pius XII established the feast of the Queenship of Mary on May 31. After the Second Vatican Council, the feast (classified as an obligatory memorial) was changed to August 22 so that it would follow the Feast of the Assumption on August 15.

◆ 2349 ◆ Queer Lisboa: International Queer Film Festival
September

Queer Lisboa: International Queer Film Festival was launched for the first time in 1997 when the Lesbian and Gay Association of Portugal asked Brazilian-born artist Celso Junior to screen a retrospective of gay films from his personal collection. Today, the festival is the only event of its kind in Portugal and takes place at the impressive Sao Jorge Cinema in the heart of Lisbon. The festival's competition section in feature films, documentary, and short films carry a cash award and is judged by an international jury. The non-competition section includes retrospectives, along with special screenings that focus on the works of a particular filmmaker, a specific theme, or a country.

CONTACTS:
Queer Lisboa: International Queer Film Festival
Casa do Cinema
Rua da Rosa
Lisbon, 1200-385 Portugal
351-91-376-5343
queerlisboa.pt/en

♦ 2350 ♦ **Quintaine, La**
Second Sunday in November

St. Leonard, the patron saint of prisoners, is honored each year in the French town of St.-Léonard-de-Noblat by a ceremony in which 30 men carry the *quintaine,* a three-foot-high box painted to resemble a prison, to the church to be blessed. Afterward they mount it on a post and strike it with mallets as they gallop by on horseback. Fragments of the smashed quintaine are said to bring good luck and to make hens lay eggs.

CONTACTS:
Saint-Leonard-de-Noblat Tourism Office
Place du Champs de Mars
Sainte Leonard-de-Noblat, 87400 France
33-5-5556-2506; fax: 5-55-56-36-97
www.tourisme-noblat.fr

♦ 2351 ♦ **Quirinalia**
February 17

Quirinus was an ancient Roman deity who closely resembled Mars, the god of war. His name is associated with that of the Quirinal, one of the seven hills on which Rome was built and the site of an ancient Sabine settlement that was the seat of his cult. Eventually Quirinus was identified with Romulus, one of the legendary founders of Rome, and his festival on February 17, the Quirinalia, coincided with the date on which Romulus was believed to have been deified. This festival was also associated with the advent of spring warfare, when the shields and weapons of the army, which had been purified and retired for the winter, were brought out. The temple dedicated to Quirinus on the hill known as the Quirinal was one of the oldest in Rome.

R

♦ 2352 ♦ **Räben-Chilbi**
Second Saturday in November

Every year on the second Saturday in November, the town of Richterswil, a picturesque town on Lake Zurich in Switzerland, celebrates a holiday named Räben-Chilbi. This holiday centers on a very common vegetable—the turnip.

Räben-Chilbi is the largest turnip festival in Europe. On this day, school classes and clubs prepare for the "Räbeliechtli" procession, for which displays made from carved turnips lit with candles make their way around town. Approximately 26 tons of turnips and 50,000 candles are used each year. This statistic earned the festival a place in the *Guinness Book of Records* in 1998.

The whole town is also decorated for the occasion. The carved turnips are on display in the windows of the homes and buildings along the route. In addition, a wide variety of music and entertainment are part of the celebrations.

CONTACTS:
Switzerland Tourism
608 Fifth Ave.
New York, NY 10020
800-794-7795; fax: 212-262-6116
www.myswitzerland.com

♦ 2353 ♦ **Race of the Ceri**
May 15

The Race of the Ceri (Candles) held in Gubbio, Umbria, Italy, every May 15 is thought by some to have originated in pre-Christian times because its date coincides with the IDES of May in the pagan calendar, but the better-founded explanation is that it commemorates the city's patron, St. Ubaldo Baldassini (d. 1160). The candles for which the event is named were originally made of wax but are now heavy, tower-like wooden structures reinforced with iron bands. These are taken in procession to the Piazza dei Consoli, where the teams of bearers who carry them pause to rest. Then, upon a signal, the bearers run with the candles up to the top of Mount Ingino, where they are offered to St. Ubaldo, whose feast is observed the following day.

CONTACTS:
Italian National Tourist Board
630 Fifth Ave.

3rd Fl.
New York, NY 10065
212-245-5618; fax: 212-586-9249
www.italiantourism.com

♦ 2354 ♦ **Race Relations Sunday**
Sunday nearest February 12

This day is observed on the Sunday nearest Abraham LINCOLN'S BIRTHDAY because of the role he played in freeing the slaves during the Civil War. Up until 1965 it was sponsored by the National Council of Churches, but since that time, sponsorship has been taken over by individual denominations within the National Council. A number of Roman Catholic groups observe Race Relations Sunday as well, and some Jewish organizations observe it on the preceding Sabbath. Although it was originally conceived in 1924 as an opportunity to focus on improving relations among all races, the longstanding racial conflict between whites and African Americans in the United States has made this the focal point in recent decades.

There are a number of other observances dealing with race relations at this same time in February. The NAACP (National Association for the Advancement of Colored People) was established on Lincoln's Birthday in 1909, and members of this organization combine the observance of Race Relations Sunday with their organization's founding and with the birthday of the black abolitionist and early human rights activist Frederick Douglass on February 7, 1817.

♦ 2355 ♦ **Race Unity Day**
Second Sunday in June

Race Unity Day is observed worldwide by Baha'is and others with meetings and discussions. The day was begun in 1957 by the Baha'i National Spiritual Assembly in the United States, with the purpose of focusing attention on racial prejudice.

The Baha'is see racism as a major barrier to peace, and teach that there must be universal recognition of the oneness of all humans to achieve peace.

CONTACTS:
U.S. Bahá'í National Center
1233 Central St.
Evanston, IL 60201
847-733-3400 or 800-228-6483
www.bahai.us

♦ 2356 ♦ **Radha Ashtami**
August-September; eighth day of waning half of Hindu month of Bhadrapada

This Hindu holiday celebrates the birth of Radha, who was the mistress of the god Krishna during the period of his life when he lived among the cowherds of Vrindavana. Although she was the wife of another *gopa* (cowherd), she was the best-loved of Krishna's consorts and his constant companion. Some Hindus believe that Radha is a symbol of the human soul drawn to the ineffable god Krishna, or the pure, divine love to which the fickle, human love returns.

Images of Radha are bathed on this day and then dressed and ornamented before being offered food and worship. Hindus bathe in the early morning and fast all day to show their devotion to Radha.

♦ 2357 ♦ **Radunitsa**
Ninth day after Eastern Orthodox Easter, which is the first Sunday after the first full moon on or following the vernal equinox

The Slavic peoples of Eastern Europe observe Radunitsa as an Orthodox Christian holiday. This day of remembrance for the dead arrives nine days after Easter. In Belarus, a country that sits on Russia's western border, Radunitsa is a state holiday.

The holiday's origins are not Christian but pagan, thus dating back to ancient times. Many pagan believers of the region once devoted the day to ritual wailing and left gifts of eggs on the graves of the deceased. During the middle ages, churches tried to suppress this tradition's observance, but in subsequent centuries the church adopted the pagan customs into the Easter rites. The dyed eggs left for the dead, for instance, have evolved to symbolize Christ's surfacing from the tomb.

The spirit of Radunitsa is joyful in the midst of mourning. (In Slavic languages, *Radunitsa* and its variations mean "Joy Day.") Believers anticipate that the dead will triumph over death as Christ did following his crucifixion. Eating paschal (Easter) foods is a popular way to celebrate. Congregations will gather to eat eggs as well as pancakes, grains like *kutya* or *kulichi,* and a type of gingerbread called *prianiki.*.

CONTACTS:
Embassy of Belarus
1619 New Hampshire Ave. N.W.
Washington, D.C. 20009
202-986-1606; fax: 202-986-1805
usa.mfa.gov.by

National Tourism Agency
Kirova St. 8/2
19 Pobediteley Ave.
Belarus
375-17-226-9900; fax: 375-17-226-0272
eng.belarustourism.by

Orthodox Church in America
P.O. Box 675
Syosset, NY 11791
516-922-0550; fax: 516-922-0954
oca.org

♦ 2358 ♦ **RAGBRAI**
Last full week in July

A bicycle ride (not race) across the state of Iowa, RAGBRAI is billed as the oldest, longest, and largest bicycle-touring event in the nation and possibly the world. The sponsor from the start has been the *Des Moines Register,* and RAGBRAI stands for **Register's Annual Great Bicycle Ride Across Iowa**. The field is limited to 8,500, and participants are chosen through a drawing.

The ride began in 1973 when Don Kaul, a *Register* columnist who worked out of Washington, D.C., was challenged by another columnist, John Karras, to bicycle across the state to learn about Iowa. The challenge was accepted, and both decided to ride. Karras wrote an article telling about the plan and inviting readers to go along: at the start of the race, there were 300 riders, and 115 rode the distance. One of these was 83-year-old Clarence Pickard, who rode a woman's bike from border to border.

The ride was intended as a one-time event, but interest was such that it continued the next year, and the next, when it got the RAGBRAI name. The route is different each year but always runs from west to east. Distances average 471 miles; the longest was the 540 miles of RAGBRAI XIII in 1985. According to tradition, riders dip their rear tires in the Missouri River at the start of the tour and seven days later dip their front tires in the Mississippi River when they finish. Multi-day touring rides have been organized in other states since RAGBRAI started.

CONTACTS:
RAGBRAI
715 Locust St.
P.O. Box 622
Des Moines, IA 50303 United States
800-474-3342
www.ragbrai.org

♦ 2359 ♦ **Raid on Redding Ridge**
First weekend in June

Held at Putnam Memorial State Park, reenactors portray the British invasion of Connecticut in 1777. Other activities include encampments of both British and American soldiers, artillery demonstrations, infantry drills, and crafts of the Revolutionary period. Spectators are kept a safe distance away, but they are encouraged to observe and ask questions.

♦ 2360 ♦ Rainforest World Music Festival
July/August

Musicians and music enthusiasts from all over the world gather on the large island of Borneo, Malaysia, to celebrate indigenous culture and artistic diversity at the Rainforest World Music Festival. This three-day event features a diverse group of performers hailing from various islands of the Malaysian archipelago, neighboring countries of Southeast Asia, and around the world.

The festival is organized by the Malaysia Tourist Board and takes place at the Sarawak Cultural Village, an ethnic-themed park situated in Borneo's jungle. Since 1997, the program has featured a balance of cultural education and entertaining performances. Both the festival and the village attract tourists who are engaged in indigenous customs and expressions and may already be familiar with such exotic instruments as the boat lute, jaw harp, and nose flute.

Over the years events have been organized in conjunction with the music festival, including the Folk Art Forum, which addresses issues of cultural exchange and economic sustainability for folk artists, and the Rainforest World Craft Bazaar, inaugurated in 2008 as an opportunity for indigenous peoples to sell their wares and demonstrate their various skills as craftspeople.

♦ 2361 ♦ Raksha Bandhan
July-August; full moon day of Hindu month of Sravana

This day, sometimes also referred to as **Brother and Sister Day**, is celebrated in some parts of India by brothers and sisters to reaffirm their bonds of affection, as well as to perform a ritual of protection. A sister ties a bracelet, made of colorful threads and amulets, called a *rakhi* on her brother's wrists. The brother in turn may give his sister gifts—a piece of jewelry or money—while promising to protect her.

In Nepal it is a festival for both Hindus and Buddhists, for which they may even attend each others' temples. The Brahmins put the golden threads around everyone's wrist; it is worn until Dewali.

♦ 2362 ♦ Rally Day
Late September or early October

In liturgical Protestant churches, Rally Day marks the beginning of the church calendar year. It typically occurs at the end of September or the beginning of October. Although not all Protestant churches observe this day, the customs associated with it include giving Bibles to children, promoting children from one Sunday school grade to the next, welcoming new members into the church, and making a formal presentation of church goals for the coming year.

♦ 2363 ♦ Ram Roasting Fair
May-June; Tuesday after Pentecost

The town of Kingsteignton in Devonshire, England, observes an annual custom every year on Whit-Tuesday (*see* WHIT-MONDAY) that is said to date back to pre-Christian times, when the village suffered from lack of water. The people prayed to their gods for help, and almost immediately a new spring rose in a meadow nearby. The spring, known as Fair Water, never ran dry, even during the hottest of summers. A live ram was slaughtered as a thanksgiving offering.

After Christianity arrived in Devonshire, a live lamb was carried through the streets on Whit-Monday in a cart covered with lilacs and laburnum, and everyone who met it was asked to contribute something toward the cost of the next day's ceremony. On Tuesday, the ram was killed and roasted whole, and slices of the meat were sold cheaply to the poor.

Today, the people of Kingsteignton still observe the annual ram roasting—usually a deer roasting, because rams are more costly and harder to come by. Local butchers in long white coats turn the spit over a huge log fire, while the crowds amuse themselves with sports and MAY DAY festivities. In the evening, the deer is cut up and distributed to the holders of lucky numbers, since there is not enough meat for everyone.

♦ 2364 ♦ Rama Leela Festival
September-October; near the 10th day of waxing half of Hindu month of Asvina

The Hindu festival of Dussehra (*see* DURGA PUJA), observed on the 10th day of the waxing half of Asvina, celebrates the victory of the legendary hero Rama over the demon Ravana. The Rama Leela (or Ramalila) is a cycle of pageant plays based on the Hindu epic, *Ramayana,* which details the life and heroic deeds of Rama. Around the time of Dussehra, therefore, the Rama Leela is performed in towns and cities through northern India—most notably at Agra, Allahabad, Rama Nagar, and Varanasi. The performances last between seven and 31 days, during which the *Ramayana* is constantly recited to the accompaniment of music.

Perhaps the most important of these performances takes place for 31 days in Rama Nagar, where the scenes are enacted at various set locales in the form of processions depicting various scenes from the *Ramayana.*

CONTACTS:
Uttar Pradesh State Tourism Development Corporation Ltd.
Rajarshi Purshottam Das Tandon Paryatan Bhavan
C-13, Vipin Khand,
Gomti Nagar
Lucknow, Uttar Pradesh India
91-522-2308993; fax: 91-522-2308937
uptourism.gov.in

♦ 2365 ♦ Ramadan
Ninth month of the Islamic year

The month of Ramadan traditionally begins with the actual sighting of the new moon, marking the start of the ninth month in the Islamic lunar calendar. Authorities in Saudi Arabia are relied upon for this official sighting. With the exception of children, the sick, and the very old, devout Muslims abstain from food, drink, smoking, sex, and gambling from sunrise to sunset during this period.

This holiest season in the Islamic year commemorates the time when the Qur'an, the Islamic holy book, is said to have been revealed to Muhammad. This occurred on LAYLAT AL-QADR, one of the last 10 nights of the month. Fasting during the month of Ramadan is one of the Five Pillars (fundamental religious duties) of Islam. It is a time for self-examination and increased religious devotion—similar to the Jewish period from ROSH HASHANAH to YOM KIPPUR and the Christian LENT.

Many West Africans have a two-day carnival, similar to SHROVE TUESDAY, before Ramadan starts.

Because it is based on the Islamic lunar calendar, which does not use intercalated days to stay aligned with the solar calendar's seasons, Ramadan moves through the year, occurring in each of the seasons over time.

The **Fast of Ramadan** ends when the new moon is again sighted and the new lunar month begins. It is followed by the ID AL-FITR, Festival of Breaking Fast, which lasts for three days and is marked by feasting and the exchange of gifts.

♦ 2366 ♦ Ramanavami (Ram Navami)
March-April; ninth day of waxing half of Hindu month of Caitra

The Hindu festival of Ramanavami celebrates the birth of Rama, who was the first son of King Dasaratha of Ayodhya. According to Hindu belief, the god Vishnu was incarnated in 10 different human forms, of which Rama was the seventh. He and his wife, Sita, are venerated by Hindus as the ideal man and wife. Because Rama is the hero of the great religious epic poem, the *Ramayana,* Hindus observe his birthday by reciting stories from it. They also flock to temples, such as that in Ayodhya in Uttar Pradesh, where the image of Rama is enshrined, and chant prayers, repeating his name as they strive to free themselves from the cycle of birth and death.

CONTACTS:
Uttar Pradesh State Tourism Development Corporation Ltd.
Rajarshi Purshottam Das Tandon Paryatan Bhavan
C-13, Vipin Khand,
Gomti Nagar
Lucknow, Uttar Pradesh 226010 India
91-522-230-7037; fax: 91-522-230-8937
www.up-tourism.com

♦ 2367 ♦ Ramayana Ballet
Full moon nights from May to October

The most spectacular dance-drama on the island of Java, Indonesia, is held on an open-air stage at the Prambanan Temple near Yogyakarta. The ballet is a contemporary abbreviated version of the Hindu epic, the *Ramayana,* unfolding over the four nights to tell the story of Prince Rama banished from his country to wander for years in the wilderness. More than 100 dancers and players in *gamelans* (percussive orchestras) present spectacles of monkey armies, giants on stilts, and clashing battles. The rich carvings—lions and *Ramayana* scenes—of the Prambanan temple complex in the background are spotlighted by the moon.

CONTACTS:
Ministry of Tourism, Republic of Indonesia
Sapta Pesona Bldg.
Jl. Medan Merdeka Barat No. 17
Jakarta, 10110 Indonesia
21-383-8167; fax: 21-384-9715
www.indonesia.travel

♦ 2368 ♦ Rand Show
March-April; during the Easter season

Also known as the **Rand Easter Show**, the Rand Show was founded in 1895. This South African industrial, commercial, and agricultural show is similar to what a huge state fair is like in the United States. The Rand Show was sponsored by the Witwatersrand Agricultural Society, but has been owned by Kagiso Media since 1999. It is considered to be the most important event of its kind in South Africa. It features agricultural, industrial, and livestock exhibitions, equestrian shows, live entertainment, and an amusement park. The most popular feature is the consumer goods display. Hundreds of thousands of people attend the Rand Show each year, which is held at the Expo Centre in Johannesburg.

CONTACTS:
Rand Show
Cnr Nasrec & Rand Show
 South Africa
27-11-494-2894; fax: 27-11-494-5004
www.randshow.co.za

♦ 2369 ♦ Rara (Ra-Ra)
February-April; weekends in Lent

In Haiti the celebration of CARNIVAL is known as Rara for the groups of people who come down from the hills to dance in processions on the weekends throughout LENT and particularly during EASTER week. It begins by calling on Legba, who appears as Carrefour, the guardian of thresholds and crossroads.

Each Rara band consists of a musical group, a band chief, a queen with attendants, a women's choir, and vendors selling food. The group's leader often dresses like a jester and twirls a long baton known as a *jonc*. On SHROVE TUESDAY night, the Rara bands perform a Bruler Carnival in which they carry out the ritual burning of various carnival objects then make a cross on their forehead with the ashes. Rara has deep ties with Voodoo and its resemblance to other Carnival celebrations is largely superficial.

See also CARNIVAL LAMAYOTE.

CONTACTS:
Embassy of the Republic of Haiti
2311 Massachusetts Ave. N.W.
Washington, D.C. 20008 United States
202-332-4090; fax: 202-745-7215
www.haiti.org

♦ 2370 ♦ Rasa Leela Festival
August-September; Hindu month ofBhadrapada

JANMASHTAMI is the birthday of Krishna, the eighth incarnation of the Hindu god Vishnu, which is observed on the new moon day of the month of Bhadrapada. In the city of Mathura in Uttar Pradesh, an important center of Indian art and the birthplace of Krishna, a month-long festival is held during Bhadrapada. The Rasa Leela play cycle, a traditional operatic ballet based on the Krishna legend, is performed throughout the month. In other Indian cities, such as Manipur, the festival has been shortened. The Rasa Leela (or Ras-Lila) Festival takes its name from the *ras*, or dance, of Krishna, the divine flute-player, and his consort, Radha.

CONTACTS:
Directorate of Tourism, Uttar Pradesh
Rajarshi Purshottam Das Tandon Paryatan Bhavan
C-13, Vipin Khand,
Gomti Nagar
Lucknow, Uttar Pradesh 226 010 India
91-522-2308993; fax: 91-522-2308937
www.up-tourism.com

♦ 2371 ♦ Rath Yatra
June-July; second day of waxing half of Hindu month of Asadha

Rath Yatra is an outpouring of tens of thousands of pilgrims to honor Jagannath, Lord of the Universe, in Puri in the state of Orissa, India. Jagannath, worshipped primarily in Orissa, is a form of Krishna (though the term applies also to Vishnu), and the Jagannath Temple in Puri is one of the largest Hindu temples in the country.

During the festival, wooden images of Jagannath, his brother, Balbhadra, and his sister, Subhadra, are taken in procession in three huge chariots or carts that look like temples and are called *raths*. They go from the Jagannath Temple to be bathed at Gundicha Mandir, a temple about a mile away; the gods are installed there for a week before being brought back to the Jagannath Temple. This is such a popular festival because all castes are considered equal, and everyone has to eat the food prepared by low caste men at the shrine.

The main chariot has a striped yellow-and-orange canopy 45 feet high with 16 wheels, each seven feet in diameter. It is occupied by scores of riders and pulled by thousands of devotees. Because the moving chariot becomes an inexorable force that could crush anything in its path, the name of the god entered the English language as "**Juggernaut**."

The festival is also known as the **Jagannath Festival**, or **Car Festival**. Others are held in Varanasi, Uttar Pradesh State, in Mahesh, a suburb of Calcutta, West Bengal State, and other areas, but the most impressive Rath Yatra is at Puri.

CONTACTS:
Director, Department of Tourism, Government of Odisha
Paryatan Bhawan
Museum Campus
Bhubaneswar, Odisha 751 014 India
91-674-2432177 or 800-208-1414
www.orissatourism.gov.in

♦ 2372 ♦ Ratification Day
January 14

Most people associate the end of the Revolutionary War with the surrender of Lord Cornwallis at YORKTOWN, Virginia, in 1781. But it was almost two years later that the Treaty of Paris was signed. It then had to be ratified by the Continental Congress and returned to England within six months. As members of the Congress arrived in Annapolis, Maryland, to ratify the treaty, it became apparent that they needed delegates from two more states to constitute a quorum. With prodding from Thomas JEFFERSON, the delegates from Connecticut finally arrived, and South Carolina Congressman Richard Beresford was dragged from his sickbed in a Philadelphia hotel room. Once everyone was assembled, the treaty was quickly ratified on January 14, 1784, and the American Revolution was officially ended. But it was still too late to get it back to England by the March deadline, since an ocean crossing took at least two months. Fortunately, Britain was willing to forgive the delay.

The Old Senate Chamber in Maryland's historic State House at Annapolis has been preserved exactly as it was when the ratification took place. On January 14, the same type of flag that was displayed in 1784—with 12 stars in a circle and the

13th in the center—flies over the State House and many other buildings in Annapolis. The ceremony that takes place inside varies from year to year, but it often revolves around a particular aspect of the original event. One year, for example, the original Treaty of Paris was put on display in the rotunda.

CONTACTS:
Library of Congress
101 Independence Ave. S.E.
Washington, D.C. 20540
202-707-5000; fax: 202-707-2076
www.loc.gov

Maryland State House
c/o Maryland State Archives
100 State Cir.
Annapolis, MD 21401
410-974-3901 or 800-811-8336; fax: 410-974-3275
msa.maryland.gov

♦ 2373 ♦ **Rato (Red) Machhendranath**
April-May; Hindu month of Vaisakha

The chariot procession known as Rato (Red) Machhendranath is the biggest event in Patan, Nepal. The festival honors Machhendranath, the god of rain and plenty, who is worshipped by both Hindus and Buddhists in different incarnations, and has shrines at both Patan and in the village of Bungamati, a few miles south of Patan. The festival, held when the monsoon season is approaching, is a plea for plentiful rain.

The image of the god, a carved piece of red-painted wood, is taken from the shrine in the Pulchowk area at the start of the festivities and paraded around the city in several stages on a wheeled chariot. The chariot is a huge wooden wagon that is towed by hundreds of devotees. Finally, after a month of being hauled about, the chariot is dismantled, and the image is conveyed to Bungamati to spend six months at the temple there.

A similar but shorter festival, the Sweta (or White) Machhendranath, is held in Kathmandu in March or April. The image of the god is taken from the temple at Kel Tole, placed on a chariot and pulled from one historic location to another. When it arrives in the south of the city, the chariot is taken apart, and the image is returned to its starting place.

CONTACTS:
Nepal Tourism Board, Tourist Service Center
Bhrikuti Mandap
P.O. Box 11018
Nepal
977-1-4256909; fax: 977-1-4256910
welcomenepal.com

♦ 2374 ♦ **Rat's Wedding Day**
19th day of first lunar month

The Rat's Wedding Day is observed in some Chinese households on the 19th day of the first lunar month. It is customary to go to bed early so that the rats have plenty of time to en-

joy themselves. Food is left out for them in the hope that it will dissuade the more ravenous rodents from disturbing the householder's kitchen. If a very large rat takes up residence in a house, it is regarded as the "Money Rat" and is treated well on this day, for its arrival indicates that the householder will prosper.

♦ 2375 ♦ **Ravello Music Festival**
Mid-July

When German composer Richard Wagner (1813-1883) visited the famous Villa Rufolo in 1880 in Ravello, Italy, he was so impressed by its beauty that he used it as the setting for *Parsifal,* his final opera. Fifty years after his death, the residents of Ravello held a commemorative concert at the Villa, and 20 years later, in 1953, another commemorative concert of Wagnerian music was given. Since then the concerts have been held annually. They last about a week and focus entirely on music composed by Wagner, by composers who influenced (or were influenced by) him, and by composers with whom he had some connection. Most take place in the gardens of the 13th-century Villa Rufolo, the church of Santa Maria Gradillo, and the park, with its view of the Bay of Naples.

See also Bayreuth Festival and Pacific Northwest Festival.

CONTACTS:
Ravello Concert Society
RCS - Piazza Duomo
Ravello, SA 84010 Italy
39-089-8424082; fax: 39-089-858249
www.ravelloarts.org

Ravello Foundation
Piazza Duomo
Ravello, 84010 Italy
39-89-858422; fax: 39-89-8586278
www.ravellofestival.com

♦ 2376 ♦ **Ravinia Festival**
June-September

Chicago's 12-week festival of classical music, theater, and dance takes place in Highland Park, one of the city's northern suburbs. Although today the festival can boast performances by some of the world's most distinguished conductors, soloists, symphony orchestras, and dance companies, its history since 1904 has been punctuated by periodic financial crises and, in the 1940s, a fire that destroyed the Ravinia Park pavilion. But since that time the festival has rebounded, expanding to include pop, jazz, and folk music as well as several weeks of theater performances. Nearly half a million people attend the festival each year.

CONTACTS:
Ravinia Festival
P.O. Box 896
418 Sheridan Rd.
Highland Park, IL 60035 United States
847-266-5000
www.ravinia.org

♦ 2377 ♦ Reconciliation, Day of
December 16

The South African legal holiday known as the Day of Reconciliation was established on December 16, 1838, in commemoration of the victory of the Voortrekkers over Dingane (also spelled Dingaan) and the Zulus. It was formerly called Day of the Covenant. The "covenant" it refers to is the vow that Andries Pretorius (1798-1853) and the Voortrekkers made with God as they prepared for the Battle of Blood River: that if they were victorious, the day would be observed as a Sabbath and a church would be built in gratitude.

The original name for this holiday was **Dingaan's Day**. Then it was called **Day of the Vow** during apartheid. After South Africa renounced apartheid and held its first democratic election in 1994, the day remained a legal holiday but acquired a new name to reflect its new focus—promoting national unity and healing.

CONTACTS:
Government of South Africa
Tshedimosetso House, 1035 Frances Baard St.
Hatfield
 South Africa
27-12-473-0000
www.gov.za

♦ 2378 ♦ Reconciliation Week, National
May 27-June 3

Australia sets aside the week between May 27 and June 3 to honor the culture and history of its Aborigines and Torres Strait Islanders and to promote reconciliation and forgiveness for the treatment that these indigenous peoples have suffered at the hands of white Australians. Since it was first held in 1996, National Reconciliation Week has featured various activities designed to promote understanding between indigenous and non-indigenous Australians, such as the People's Walk for Reconciliation across the Sydney Harbor Bridge in 2000.

The starting and ending dates of the commemoration are important anniversaries: On May 27, 1967, 90 percent of Australians voted to eliminate parts of their country's constitution that were discriminatory against indigenous Australians, and on June 3, 1992, the High Court of Australia ruled on the Eddie Mabo case, acknowledging the rights of indigenous Australians by rejecting the idea that Australia had been uninhabited until the first British settlers arrived.

Since 1998, this week-long celebration has encompassed National Sorry Day on May 28. An inquiry into the forcible removal of Aboriginal and Torres Strait Island children from their families led to a recommendation that a formal day of apology be declared, offering the community an opportunity to get involved in activities acknowledging the impact of the policy of forcible removal on these people. Australians are encouraged to sign local "Sorry Books" or to register their apologies electronically.

CONTACTS:
Reconciliation Australia

Old Parliament House
King George Terr.
Parkes, ACT 2600 Australia
61-2-6273-9200; fax: 61-2-6273-9201
www.reconciliation.org.au

♦ 2379 ♦ Red Earth Native American Cultural Festival
Second weekend in June

One of the largest such events in the country, the Red Earth Native American Cultural Festival is held in Oklahoma City and draws participants from more than 150 American Indian tribes. The three-day festival features arts and crafts, dancing, and parades.

The name Oklahoma means "red people," being derived from two Choctaw words, *okla*, meaning "people," and *humma*, meaning "red." There are 35 tribes with tribal councils now living in Oklahoma. Their population is more than 175,000, the second largest of any state in the nation.

CONTACTS:
Red Earth Inc.
6 Santa Fe Plaza
Oklahoma City, Ok 73102 United States
405-427-5228; fax: 405-427-8079
www.redearth.org

♦ 2380 ♦ Red Flannel Festival
First Saturday of October

During a cold winter in 1936, flannel shirt merchants in Cedar Springs, Mich., stumbled upon an opportunity to boost the sales of their warm garments. In response to an editorial written by Cedar Springs' local press, a national news story showed appreciation for red flannel longjohns. The welcome press helped elicit numerous orders from all over the country, and the town's subsequent windfall gave birth to a celebration of local industry known as the Red Flannel Festival, first held in 1939.

With the closure of the Red Flannel Factory in 1994, the fates of the local business and the festival were in jeopardy. But local business women kept red flannel production going, and dedicated volunteers managed to preserve the festival tradition.

The event, also called **Red Festival Day**, has its share of distinctive traditions. Scheer's Lumberjack Show celebrates Michigan's lumber legacy, featuring demonstrations by real lumberjacks who chop wood, speed-climb trees, and throw axes. The Keystope Kops, the icon of the festival, circulate the crowd to "arrest" offenders who do not wear the obligatory red.

Other festivities include a Prince and Princess Contest, a grand parade, a 5K run and walk, and a window decorating contest, in which contestants conjure up their best red flannel displays. Two other established traditions, the Horseshow Throwing Contest and the Red Flannel Queen Scholarship Pageant, date back to the inaugural festival.

CONTACTS:
Red Flannel Festival
21 E. Maple St.
P.O. Box 43
Cedar Springs, MI 49319
616-696-2662
redflannelfestival.org

♦ 2381 ♦ Red Waistcoat Festival
First or second weekend in July

The **Festa do Colete Encarnado**, or Red Waistcoat Festival, celebrates the *campionos*—the cowboys who watch over the bulls in the pasturelands of the Ribatejo in Portugal, and who traditionally wear red vests, green stocking caps, blue or black trousers, and red sashes. Supposedly the best bulls for bullfighting are those that have been allowed to roam freely in the vast, rich pastures for which this part of the country is famous, and bullfights play a big part in the festival. But unlike bullfighting elsewhere, no one gets hurt and it's against Portuguese law to kill the bull.

A highlight of the festival is the traditional running of the bulls through the streets of Vila Franca de Xira, which is about 20 miles from Lisbon. In addition to bullfighting, there are folk dances, fireworks, and various competitions for the campionos, including the Ribatejan fandango, a competitive dance for men only.

CONTACTS:
Portugal Tourism
866, Second Ave.
8th Fl.
New York, NY 10017
646-723-0200; fax: 212-764-6137
www.visitportugal.com

♦ 2382 ♦ Redentore, Festa del
Third Sunday in July

Festa del Redentore, or **Feast of the Redeemer**, is celebrated in Venice, Italy—one of only two remaining provincial religious festivals surviving in Venice. (The other is at the church of the Salute on the Grand Canal, which commemorates deliverance from the plague, but is more religious in nature.)

It also marks the end of the plague in the late 16th century, when the people of Venice dedicated a church on Guidecca Island to Jesus the Redeemer and vowed to visit it every year. They continue to keep their promise by building a bridge of boats across the Guidecca and Grand canals, across which worshippers can walk back and forth during the celebration.

At dawn, the boats all go out to the Lido to watch the sun rise over the Adriatic Sea. During the festival the cafes, shops, canals, and the church are decorated with lights. When the bridge of boats closes at around nine o'clock, a fireworks display begins.

Services inside the Church of the Redentore, which include masses commemorating the redeeming power of Jesus, are quite solemn in comparison to what is going on outside—a festival that has been described as the "Venetian Bacchanal.".

CONTACTS:
Italian Government Tourist Board
686 Park Ave.
3rd Fl.
New York, NY 10065 United States
212-245-5618; fax: 212-586-9249
www.italiantourism.com

♦ 2383 ♦ Reed Dance
Late August or early September

The Reed Dance is the culmination of a week-long coming-of-age ceremony for young girls in Swaziland. They gather in the royal city of Lobamba and spend several days along the riverbank gathering reeds for the Queen Mother. They use the reeds to rebuild the screens that surround the Queen Mother's *kraal*, or enclosure. The Reed Dance is performed for the Queen Mother near the end of the ceremony, when the girls, dressed in bead skirts and beautiful jewelry, perform complicated steps done in perfect time, tossing reeds high into the air. Since the Reed Dance, also known as **Umhlanga**, is not a sacred ceremony, visitors are welcome to watch.

CONTACTS:
Swaziland Ministry of Tourism
Income Tax Bldg. 4th Fl.
P.O. Box 57
 Swaziland
268-2404-2644; fax: 268-2404-4851
www.gov.sz

♦ 2384 ♦ Reek Sunday
Last Sunday in July

In County Mayo, thousands of pilgrims climb Croagh Patrick on the last Sunday in July to pray on the spot where Ireland's patron saint, St. Patrick, is believed to have started his ministry. Those wishing to maximize the arduousness of the journey ascend the 2,510-foot mountain, known locally as the Reek, in bare feet and at night. The traditional time to begin the ascent is midnight and the climb takes about three hours. There are stopping points along the way where pilgrims pray before continuing. Many visit the small chapel at the top where masses are celebrated.

Croagh Patrick has been a pilgrimage site since at least the 12th century and possibly as far back as the seventh century.

See also Crom Dubh Sunday.

CONTACTS:
Westport Tourist Office
Bridge St.
Westport, Mayo Ireland
353-98-25711
www.westporttourism.com

Croagh Patrick Visitor Centre
Teach na Miasa
Murrisk, Co. Mayo Ireland

353-98-64114; fax: 353-98-64115
www.croagh-patrick.com

♦ 2385 ♦ Reformation Day
October 31

When Martin Luther (1483-1546), a German monk and religious reformer, nailed his 95 "theses" (or propositions) to the church door in Wittenberg on October 31, 1517, his only intention was to voice his opinions about certain practices and customs in the Roman Catholic Church, in the hope that someone would engage him in a public debate.

Instead, so many people agreed with his ideas that they spread throughout western Europe and touched off a religious revolt known as the Reformation. As a result, many Christians broke their centuries-old connection with the Roman Catholic Church and established independent churches of their own, prime among them being the Lutheran Church.

October 31 is observed by most Protestant denominations as Reformation Day, and the preceding Sunday is known as **Reformation Sunday**. In Germany, the day is sometimes referred to as **Luther's Theses Day**.

See also MARTINSFEST.

CONTACTS:
St. Paul's Lutheran Church
12022 Jerusalem Rd.
Kingsville, MD 21087
410-592-8100
www.stpaulskingsville.org

♦ 2386 ♦ Regatta of the Great Maritime Republics
Late May

The great maritime republics of Italy for which this event is named are Pisa, Genoa, Amalfi, and Venice. Although they no longer enjoy the wealth and power of medieval days, since 1956 the four cities have commemorated their former greatness with a friendly battle to rule the seas. The location rotates among the cities each year. Before the regatta begins, there is an elaborate parade with people dressed in period costume. Then the longboats—which were blessed by then Bishop Angelo Roncalli before he became Pope John XXIII— decorated to represent each of the republics take off on a 2,000-meter race.

CONTACTS:
Province of Pisa
Piazza Vittorio Emanuele II, 14
Pisa, 56125 Italy
50-929777
www.pisaunicaterra.it

♦ 2387 ♦ Reggae Sumfest
July

The largest reggae event in the world, Reggae Sumfest, takes place each July in Montego Bay, Jamaica. The annual festival features the world's best-known reggae performers as well as salespeople hawking such island specialties as curried goat, bammy and fish, sugarcane, and jelly coconut. This is one of the world's premier musical events, attracting up to 50,000 people.

Reggae originated as the music of the Jamaican poor, reflecting social discontent and the Rastafarian movement. Jamaican-born reggae star Bob Marley, who died of brain cancer at the age of 36, transformed the island-bred music into an international craze. He is venerated in Jamaica much as ELVIS Presley is in the United States, and his former house and studio in Kingston, called Tuff Gong, is still a center for some of the more serious reggae music being produced today.

CONTACTS:
Jamaica Tourist Board
5201 Blue Lagoon Dr.
Ste. 670
Miami, FL
305-665-0557 or 800-233-4582; fax: 305-666-7239
www.jtbonline.org

♦ 2388 ♦ Reindeer Driving Competition
Late March

The Sami people who live in the northern parts of the Scandinavian countries round up their herds of reindeer between December and March every year to count, sort, slaughter, and mark their animals in much the same way that cattle and sheep are rounded up in the United States and elsewhere. Round-ups usually last from one to three days and often include athletic competitions. In late March in Inari, Finland, men and women compete on cross-country skis as they try to herd 100 reindeer over a 3 1/4-mile course. The fastest time wins the competition.

CONTACTS:
Northern Lapland Tourism
Kiehinen
Kelotie 1 / Siula
Saariselka, 99830 Finland
40-168-7838
www.saariselka.fi

♦ 2389 ♦ Rei-tai-sai
October 11-13

Rei-tai-sai is an annual thanksgiving festival celebrated at the Tsubaki Grand Shrine, one of the oldest Shinto shrines in Japan. Located in Suzuka, the shrine is dedicated to Sarutuhiko Okami, the leader of the earthly *kami*, or spirits. This autumn festival is important for the local community, as it marks the first celebration after what was traditionally a month-long period of abstinence in September. The event shares common elements with other Rei sai ceremonies followed at Shinto shrines in Japan. During the festival, the shrine is cleansed, and ritual prayer and food offerings are made to the deity.

CONTACTS:
Tsubaki Grand Shrine of America & Tsubaki Kannagara Jinja
17720 Crooked Mile Rd.

Granite Falls, WA 98252
360-691-6389
www.tsubakishrine.org

Tsurugaoka Hachimangu
2-1-31 Yukinoshita
Kamakura, Kanagawa 248-8588 Japan
81-467-22-0315; fax: 81-467-22-4667
www.tsurugaoka-hachimangu.jp

◆ 2390 ◆ Remembrance Day
March 1

The Republic of the Marshall Islands consists of 29 atolls in the North Pacific Ocean. An atoll is a group of coral islands that form a ring around a shallow lagoon.

After World War II, the United States occupied the Marshall Islands for several decades. In 1946, the United States began a nuclear testing program in the Marshall Islands to test post-World War II nuclear weapons.

In 1954, the United States detonated Bravo, the most powerful hydrogen bomb ever tested by the United States, on Bikini atoll. The fallout radiation from the test forced the evacuation of Marshallese and U.S. military personnel on four of the atolls. Many of the people exposed to the radiation began to experience nausea, vomiting, and itching skin and eyes. Those who were most heavily exposed suffered skin burns and later hair loss. The U.S. Atomic Energy Commission issued a statement to the press calling Bravo a "routine atomic test" and stating that some Americans and Marshallese were "unexpectedly exposed to some radioactivity. There were no burns. All were reported well."

Throughout the remainder of the 1950s, the U.S. government declared the islands safe for rehabitation and returned the islanders to their homes. The U.S. government gave the islanders money and set up trust funds to compensate for the damages, and nuclear testing continued. By 1963, the first thyroid tumors began to appear among those who had been exposed to the Bravo test, and U.S. doctors noticed a higher than normal incidence of growth retardation among young islanders. In 1969, the Atomic Energy Commission stated, "There's virtually no radiation left and we can find no discernible effect on either plant or animal life."

By the mid-1970s, it became clear that the damage was much more extensive than originally reported. Throughout the 1980s and 1990s, the U.S. government set up trust funds for the Marshallese residents and paid the victims millions of dollars in total.

On **Remembrance Day** (formerly Memorial and Nuclear Victims Day), Marshallese people from the four atolls that were affected by the bomb and fallout gather to pray and commemorate their atolls and those who were killed during the bomb testing.

CONTACTS:

Atomic Heritage Foundation
910 17th St. N.W.

Ste. 408
Washington, D.C. 20006
202-293-0045
www.atomicheritage.org

Trust Liaison for the People of Bikini
P.O. Box 1096
Majuro, MH 96960 Marshall Islands
692-625-3177; fax: 692-625-3330
www.bikiniatoll.com

◆ 2391 ◆ Repentance and Prayer Day
Last Wednesday before November 23

Repentance and Prayer Day is a day of religious observance for Protestants in the German state of Saxony. Some may attend church services on this day, while others choose to spend time at home in quiet reflection and prayer, seeking forgiveness for wrong-doing. The day falls on the last Wednesday before November 23rd, and 11 days before Advent. Since 1893, Repentance and Prayer Day has been celebrated on its present date, save for a brief period during World War II when the observance was moved to the following Sunday. At various points the day was recognized as a public, non-working holiday only in certain regions, whereas at other times, including from 1990 to 1994, the day was accepted as a public holiday throughout Germany. Seeking to raise funds for federal nursing care insurance in 1994, the German government proposed that workers give up the Repentance and Prayer Day holiday and instead work on that day without pay. All of the German states agreed to the proposal except Saxony, which elected to charge its workers higher taxes but retain the Repentance and Prayer Day holiday.

◆ 2392 ◆ Repudiation Dtay
November 23

The Stamp Act of 1765 forced the American colonies to pay a tax on various official documents and publications, such as legal papers, liquor permits, lawyers' licenses, and school diplomas. The tax on newspapers and pamphlets was particularly burdensome, as it was based on the number of printed sheets and advertisements in each publication. The tax had to be paid in British pounds sterling, which made it even more expensive. In defiance of the new law, the court of Frederick County, Maryland, declared that it would carry on its business without the tax stamps required by the Act. In March 1766, the Act was rescinded by Parliament.

The date on which the Stamp Act was repudiated, November 23, has been observed for many years as a half-holiday in Frederick County to commemorate this courageous act. It has been customary for the Daughters of the American Revolution (DAR) to meet in the courthouse on this day and to listen while the clerk of the circuit court reads the original 1765 decision.

◆ 2393 ◆ Restoration of Independence of the Republic of Latvia
May 4

The Restoration of Independence of the Republic of Latvia from the USSR is marked as a national public holiday in Latvia every May 4. On that date in 1990, Latvia's Supreme Court re-declared the country a free democratic parliamentary republic. Following a transitional period, full independence was attained on August 21, 1991.

Prior to World War I, present-day Latvia was divided into several provinces ruled by the Russian Empire. After the upheaval of the First World War, Latvian pro-independence forces joined together to create a provisional parliament, the Latvian People's Council. On November 18, 1918, the group proclaimed Latvia an independent and democratic republic. The country celebrates every November 18 as LATVIA INDEPENDENCE DAY, a national holiday. Since 1920, Latvia has been acknowledged continuously by other countries as an independent state, despite occupations by Nazi Germany from 1941 to 1945, and by the Soviet Union from 1940 to 1941 and 1945 to 1991. After Latvia's Supreme Court re-declared the country a free republic on May 4, 1990, its *de facto* independence was restored on August 21, 1991.

CONTACTS:
Embassy of Latvia
2306 Massachusetts Ave., N.W.
Washington, D.C. 20008
202-328-2840; fax: 202-328-2860
www.latvia-usa.org

♦ 2394 ♦ Restoration of the Aaronic Priesthood Commemoration
May 15

The Restoration of the Aaronic Priesthood Commemoration is a Mormon liturgical observation. According to Mormon belief, on May 15, 1829, John the Baptist appeared before Joseph Smith and Oliver Cowdery near Harmony, Pennsylvania, and bestowed a special authority on the two men. Called the Aaronic Priesthood, this power allowed the men the ability to baptize and serve as ordained ministers. Mormons observe the day with a modest outdoor celebration, usually at a nearby park or other local site. Members of the Aaronic Priesthood participate in a sacramental service as part of this event. The bishop conducts the service, while the priests administer the sacrament with help from the deacons. Members of the Church of Jesus Christ of Latter-Day Saints also sing various musical pieces and hold talks about the healing power of faith during the celebration.

CONTACTS:
Church of Jesus Christ of Latter-day Saints
50 East North Temple St.
7th Fl.
Salt Lake City, UT 84150
801-240-1000
www.lds.org

♦ 2395 ♦ Return Day
November, the Thursday after Election Day

In the early 19th century, the rural residents of Sussex County, Delaware, had to travel all the way to Georgetown, the county seat, to cast their ballots on ELECTION DAY. The roads were rough, the weather was often bad, and many of the men were uneasy about leaving their families behind.

In 1828, the General Assembly adopted new election laws establishing polling places in the "hundreds," as the political subdivisions of the county were called (probably referring to the early English "group of 100 hides," the number of land units necessary to support one peasant family). While this spared voters from having to travel, they had no way of finding out the results of the election because there were no county newspapers. The tabulations were rushed to Georgetown by couriers, and the results were read two days later from the courthouse steps. Many of the farmers in the surrounding areas would take a day off and travel to Georgetown with their families to hear the announcement and to join in the festivities, which included cockfights, band concerts, and open-air markets. The winning candidates were often carried around the town green in an impromptu victory celebration.

Of course, there is no longer any need to wait two days to hear election results (with the notable exception of the 2000 election). But the residents of Georgetown continue the tradition, which includes a formal announcement of the results on the Thursday after the Presidential Election Day. There are parades, picnics, military displays, and, of course, politicking. Both the winners and the losers circulate among their supporters. Street vendors sell roast oxen, which has been cooked on a spit, and there is a parade down Market Street reminiscent of the days when farmers would arrive in town in their wagons and ox-drawn carts.

CONTACTS:
Georgetown Historical Society
108 E. Main St.
PO Box 376
Georgetown, MA 01833 United States
978-352-7364
www.georgetownhistoricalsociety.com

♦ 2396 ♦ Reversing Current, Festival of the (Water Festival; Bonn Om Tuk)
Late October or November

The Festival of the Reversing Current is a festival and national holiday to celebrate a natural phenomenon in Cambodia. Tonle Sap, a lake, is connected to the Mekong River by the Tonle Sap River, which normally flows south from the lake. But during the rainy season, from mid-May to mid-October, the flood-swollen Mekong backs up and flows backward through the Tonle Sap River into the lake. The depth of the lake jumps from seven feet to 35 feet, and the total surface quadruples. The normal southward flow returns when the dry season starts. Because of the phenomenon, the Tonle Sap lake is an extremely rich source of freshwater fish.

The festival, held at the time when the Tonle Sap returns to its normal direction, is a time of fireworks, merrymaking and races of pirogues, or long canoes, at Phnom Penh.

CONTACTS:
Royal Embassy of Cambodia
4530 16th St. N.W.
Washington, D.C. 20011
202-726-7742; fax: 202-726-8381
www.embassyofcambodia.org

Tourist Information Center - Cambodia
#262 Monivong Blvd.
Khan Daun Penh
 Cambodia
855-23-218-585; fax: 855-23-213-331
www.tourismcambodia.com

♦ 2397 ♦ Reykjavik Arts Festival (Listahátí í Reykjavík)
Late May to early June in even-numbered years

Originally called the **North Atlantic Festival**, this nearly three-week-long festival highlights the performing and visual arts. Vladimir Ashkenazy, the famous pianist and an Icelandic citizen, founded the festival with Ivar Eskeland, former director of the Nordic House in Reykjavik. While Eskeland was primarily interested in establishing a Nordic arts festival, Ashkenazy wanted it to be international in scope. The two men combined their goals, and the first festival was held in 1970.

Since that time the festival has seen performances by violinist Yehudi MENUHIN, flutist James Galway, conductor André Previn, bassist Boris Christoff, and the London Sinfonietta. Artists and companies from Austria, Denmark, Germany, France, Greenland, Norway, Sweden, and the United States have also performed there. The festival is well attended not only by local people but by tourists as well.

CONTACTS:
Reykjavik Arts Festival
Laekjargata 3
Reykjavik, 101 Iceland
354-561-2444
www.artfest.is

♦ 2398 ♦ Rhode Island Independence Day
May 4

Rhode Island was the first and only state to declare its independence from England entirely on its own. Relations between the colony and its British rulers had deteriorated rapidly after the 1772 incident in which Rhode Island colonists boarded and burned the British revenue cutter, the *Gaspee*, which had been patrolling the coastal waters in search of local smugglers (*see* GASPEE DAYS). On May 4, 1776, both houses of the General Assembly renounced the colony's allegiance to Great Britain—a full two months before the rest of the colonies followed suit on July 4 (*see* FOURTH OF JULY).

Rhode Islanders celebrate this event during May, which is Rhode Island Heritage Month, with flag-raising ceremonies, cannon salutes, and parades of local patriotic, veterans', and scouting organizations.

♦ 2399 ♦ Rice-Planting Festival at Osaka
June 14

There are many rituals associated with the growing of rice in Japanese farming communities. June marks the beginning of the rainy season, and transplanting usually takes place during June and July. In many rural celebrations, young women in costume perform rituals including planting seedlings while singing rice-planting songs to the accompaniment of pipes and drums. Sometimes women light fires of rice straw and pray to the rice god. Shinto priests are often asked to offer prayers for a good harvest season.

On June 14 in Osaka, thousands congregate to observe a group of young kimono-clad women plant rice and sing in the sacred fields near the Sumiyoshi Shrine. Working rhythmically to the music, the young women appear to be participating in a dance rather than the hard work of planting.

CONTACTS:
Osaka Government Tourism Bureau
4-4-21 Minamisenba, Chuo-ku
Resona Semba Bldg
Fifth fl.
Osaka, 542-0081 Japan
81-6-6282-5900; fax: 81-6-6282-5915
www.osaka-info.jp

♦ 2400 ♦ Richmond Fossil Festival
First weekend of May, held biennially

The Australian town of Richmond, located in northwest Queensland, celebrates its archaeological treasures every two years at its Kronosaurus Korner and Richmond Marine Fossil Museum. The festival is also a celebration of the town's outback identity, with a number of traditional community events including a loader pull, a rodeo, and a rock-throwing competition. It has been observed since 2002.

Scheduled events on the opening day, Friday, include a fossil-finding expedition, a school concert, and the rodeo. Saturday focuses on Kronosaurus Korner, the site of a parade, novelty events, and the famous physical contest known as the World Champion Moonrock Throwing Competition, which challenges men to heave a rock weighing over 59 pounds.

On Sunday, festivalgoers attend the Show and Shine Car Show. On Monday, the festival closes with more archaeological activities including "fossicking" (sifting for fossils) and a fossil preparation workshop.

CONTACTS:
Richmond Shire Council
50 Goldring St.
Richmond, QLD 4822 Australia
61-7-4741-3277; fax: 61-7-4741-3308
www.richmond.qld.gov.au

♦ 2401 ♦ Ridvan, Feast of
April 21-May 2

The Feast of Ridvan is a Baha'i celebration to commemorate a 12-day period in 1863. That's when the Baha'i founder, Baha'u'llah (which means "Glory of God"), made the declaration that he was God's messenger for this age—the one foreseen by the Bab to be a prophet of the same rank as Abraham, Moses, Jesus, Muhammad, Buddha, Krishna, and Zoroaster. The first, ninth, and 12th days of the period are holy days when work is suspended. The celebration starts at sunset, April 20, the eve of Ridvan.

When he made his declaration, Baha'u'llah was staying outside Baghdad, Iraq, at a garden he called *Ridvan*, meaning "Paradise." On the first day, he declared his manifestation to his family and close associates. On the ninth day other followers joined him, and the declaration of his station became public knowledge. On the 12th day, he left the garden.

Nineteen years earlier, the Bab had prophesied that one greater than he would come (*see* BAB, DECLARATION OF THE); Baha'u'llah's proclamation stated that he was the "promised one." He set forth the form of the Baha'i religion, teaching the unity of all religions and the unity and brotherhood of all mankind. He wrote more than 100 works of sacred literature.

CONTACTS:
Baha'i National Center
1233 Central St.
Evanston, IL 60201
847-733-3400 or 800-228-6483
www.bahai.us

♦ 2402 ♦ Riley (James Whitcomb) Festival
Begins first Thursday in October

James Whitcomb Riley (1849-1916), a poet best known for his nostalgic dialect verse, is honored in his hometown of Greenfield, Indiana, with a three-day festival held around his birthday on October 7 each year. Most of the events are held near the Riley Birthplace Museum, the house where the poet spent his childhood, although there are poetry contests, programs in the local schools, and parades through the streets of downtown Greenfield as well.

The festival was started in 1911 by Minnie Belle Mitchell, an author who wanted schools and literary clubs to observe the poet's birthday. The governor of Indiana proclaimed October 7 as **Riley Day** soon afterward, and Riley attended the celebration in 1912, finding himself smothered in bouquets of flowers as his car paraded down the street.

Today Riley is best remembered for such poems as "When the Frost is on the Punkin," "The Raggedy Man," and "Little Orphan Annie," which later inspired both the Raggedy Ann and Andy dolls as well as the Orphan Annie comic strip, which was successfully brought to Broadway as the musical *Annie*.

CONTACTS:
Riley Festival
312 E. Main St.
Ste. C
Greenfield, IN 46140 United States

317-462-2141; fax: 317-467-1449
www.rileyfestival.com

♦ 2403 ♦ Rio de Janeiro International Film Festival
October

Over the last 10 years, the annual Rio de Janeiro International Film Festival in Brazil has established itself as the largest film festival in Latin America. Every year 25,000 visitors view more than 400 movies showcased in 30 theaters in the city. The festival features an international division that includes 300 films from roughly 60 countries, presented in 12 non-competitive thematic programs. The "World Panorama" division highlights the best of international directors, the "Expectation" class consists of emerging directors in the international scene, and "Midnight Movies" comprises experimental films. The festival also serves as a showcase for contemporary Brazilian cinema, and the "Premiere Brazil" category features dramas, documentaries, and short films of Brazilian origin that vie for the prestigious "Trofeu Redentor" award. This category focuses on making the culture of Brazil more visible to an international audience. A "Focus" category at the festival selects one country each year to promote its national cinema, with the added intention of improving international commercial ties. The festival is also noted for its RioMarket, a business center offering discussions on key issues within the film industry, and its networking events for industry professionals. The festival is a merger of the Rio Cine Film Festival and the Mostra Banco Nacional de Cinema—an event that occurred in 1999.

CONTACTS:
Rio Festival
Street Teresa Guimarães, 70
Botafogo
Rio de Janeiro, 22280-050 Brazil
55-21-3515-4450
www.festivaldorio.com.br/en

♦ 2404 ♦ Risabha's Nirvana and Mauni Amavasya
January-February; 14th and 15th day of the waning half of the Hindu month of Magha

Jains, a religious minority who are most heavily concentrated in India, honor 24 spiritual guides named Tirthankaras. Foremost among these divine beings is the original Tirthankara, Risabha. According to Jain tradition, Risabha lived 600,000 years ago. He is credited with establishing the first Indian emperor and instituting fundamental social conventions for humans. Jains in India and other countries celebrate Risabha's Nirvana and Mauni Amavasya over two days in Magha, a Jain lunar month that falls between January and February.

Jains revere Tirthankaras for attaining nirvana, a state of total liberation from an endless cycle of birth and death. On the Nirvana day of Risabha, known in southern India as **Jinaratri**, believers remember their spiritual guide's liberation at Mount Kailash, a mythic site of the Himalayas range in Tibet known to Jains as Ashtapada. They typically observe the day with processions.

Mauni Amavasya takes place on the next day, and for Svetambara Jains, the religion's dominant sect, it is a time for silent reflection.

CONTACTS:
JAINA - Federation of Jain Associations in North America
722 S. Main St.
Milpitas, CA 95053
510-730-0204
www.jaina.org

Ministry of External Affairs
Government of India
35 A S. Block
New Delhi, New Delhi 110011 India
11-23011650
www.mea.gov.in

♦ 2405 ♦ Rishi Panchami
August-September; fifth day of waxing half of Hindu month of Bhadrapada

Hindus devote the day of Rishi Panchami to the Sapta Rishis, also known as the seven seers or mental sons of Brahma: Bhrigu, Pulastya, Kratu, Pulaha, Marichi, Atri, and Vasistha. An earthenware or copper pitcher filled with water is placed on an altar sanctified with cow dung. The seven seers are then worshipped with betel leaf, flowers, camphor, and lamps. Only fruits are eaten on this day.

Rishi Panchami is primarily a women's festival, but men may observe it for the well-being and happiness of their wives. Devi Arundhati, the wife of Rishi Vasistha and a model of conjugal excellence, is also worshipped on this day.

♦ 2406 ♦ River Kwai Bridge Week
Last week in November

River Kwai Bridge Week in Kanchanaburi, Thailand, commemorates World War II's infamous Death Railway and the River Kwai (Khwae Noi) Bridge. Between 1942 and 1945, more than 16,000 Allied prisoners of war and 49,000 impressed Asian laborers were forced by the Japanese to build a railway through the jungle from Bangkok, Thailand, into Burma (now Myanmar), and it is said that one person died for every railway tie on the track. At the Kanchanaburi War Cemetery, commemorative services are held every April 25 for the 6,982 American, Australian, British, and Dutch prisoners of war buried there.

The bridge became known as a symbol of the horrors and futilities of war through the novel, *The Bridge Over the River Kwai,* by Pierre Boulle and the 1957 movie based on it, *The Bridge on the River Kwai.* During the week-long events, the reconstructed bridge (it was bombed during the war) is the setting for sound-and-light presentations, and there are also historical exhibitions and rides on World War II-era trains.

CONTACTS:
Tourism Authority of Thailand
1600 New Phetchaburi Rd.
Makkasan
Ratchathevi, Bangkok 10400 Thailand
66-2-250-5500; fax: 66-2-250-5511
www.tourismthailand.org

♦ 2407 ♦ River to Reef Festival
First Sunday in October

"Celebrating Our Way of Life" is the theme of the River to Reef Festival held in the town of Mackay, located on the eastern coast of Australia in Queensland. The celebration's name refers to the two natural landmarks of Mackay: the Pioneer River and one of the country's most popular tropical destinations, the Great Barrier Reef.

The celebration, which has taken place since 2005, offers food, dance, music, and other activities typically found at a family festival. Most events are held at the main stage, located alongside the Pioneer River. Children are treated to a concert that kicks off with a procession by a colorful "river serpent." Rock bands square off in a competition that includes a performance of an original song having a "River to Reef" theme. Other activities include a fashion show, a culinary competition, a show featuring fire-twirling performances, a riverside carnival, and a boat show.

CONTACTS:
Mackay Regional Council
P.O. Box 41
Mackay, QLD 4740 Australia
61-7-4961-9444 or 1300-622-529; fax: 61-7-4944-2400
www.mackay.qld.gov.au

♦ 2408 ♦ Rizal Day
December 30

A national holiday in the Philippines, Rizal Day commemorates the execution of the national hero, Dr. José Rizal, on this day in 1896. Flags fly at half-staff throughout the country, and special rites are led by the president at the 500-foot obelisk that is the Rizal Monument in Manila.

Rizal, born in 1861 in the Philippines, was a doctor who studied medicine in Spain, France, and Germany. He was also a botanist, educator, man of letters, and inspiration for the Philippine nationalist movement. Writing from Europe and denouncing the corrupt ruling of the Philippines by Spanish friars, he became known as a leader of the Philippine reform movement.

He wrote the novel, *Noli me tangere* (1886; *The Lost Eden,* 1961), for which the Spanish administration deported him shortly after he had returned to the Philippines in 1887. He again returned to the Philippines in 1892 and founded a nonviolent reform movement, as a result of which he was exiled to the Philippine island of Mindanao, where he established a school and hospital.

Rizal had no direct role in the nationalist insurrection; nevertheless, he was arrested, tried for sedition, and executed by a firing squad. On the eve of his execution, he wrote the poem "Mi Ultimo Adiós," meaning "My Last Farewell." The poem, in the original Spanish and translated into other languages, is transcribed on a marble slab near the Rizal Monument.

CONTACTS:
Philippines Department of Tourism
556 Fifth Ave.
New York, NY 10036
212-575-7915; fax: 212-302-6759
www.tourism.gov.ph

♦ 2409 ♦ Road Building
April

In areas of Nigeria where the Igbo live, especially Mbaise, there is a festival in April known as **Emume Ibo Uzo**, or Road Building. It is a time for everyone in the community to get together and maintain the major thoroughfares by clearing and leveling them. This festival was particularly important in the days before government-sponsored road building became common.

♦ 2410 ♦ Roberts's (Joseph Jenkins) Birthday
March 15

Joseph Jenkins Roberts (1809–1876), Liberia's first and seventh president, led the movement for an independent Liberia, established in 1848. Along with being a celebration of the forefather's birth, this day (also known as **J. J. Roberts Day**) is an occasion to pay homage to Liberia's historical role as Africa's oldest republic.

Born a free man in Norfolk, Virginia, Roberts moved to Liberia, which was originally a colony, in 1829, part of a group of former slaves and slave descendants organized by the American Colonization Society. As lieutenant-governor and then governor of the colony, Roberts led Liberia through its transition into a sovereign republic.

In many respects, Roberts's birthday stands apart from other holidays that recognize Liberian notables because he was a member of the established Americo-Liberian elite, a group historically criticized for wielding control over the country's indigenous population for more than a century.

CONTACTS:
Library of Virginia
800 E. Broad St.
Richmond, VA 23219
804-692-3500
www.lva.virginia.gov

Ministry of Foreign Affairs, Government of the Republic of Liberia
Capitol Hill
Liberia
www.mofa.gov.lr

♦ 2411 ♦ Robigalia
April 25

The ancient Romans knew how much damage certain fungi could do to their crops, but they attributed these diseases to the wrath of the gods. Robigus was the Roman god who personified such blights, and the annual festival known as the Robigalia was designed to placate him. It was believed that prayers and sacrifices made on this day, April 25, would head off the mildew, rust, wilt, and other blights that so often devastated their crops.

♦ 2412 ♦ Robin Hood Festival in Nottinghamshire, England
Week in late July to early August

The Robin Hood Festival takes place for one week in late July to early August every year in Sherwood Forest, an ancient woodland in Nottinghamshire, England. The event celebrates the life and times of one of the most popular outlaws in the world: Robin Hood. Activities and entertainment include children's theater, strolling players, jesters, jousting, and music. There are demonstrations in such aged arts as falconry and long-bow-shooting, and a medieval market offers a variety of goods. As many as 75,000 visitors take part in the week's activities. The festival is free, with nominal charges for some performances and activities. It has taken place every year since 1975.

Robin Hood is a legendary figure who is portrayed as a romantic medieval bowman who lived as an outlaw in Sherwood Forest, outsmarting and stealing from the wealthy to help the poor and oppressed. Whether or not Robin Hood was based on a real person is a question debated by historians to this day. While several possible candidates have been identified, there is no conclusive evidence pointing to a single man. Some historians believe that the Robin Hood myth may have originated in the pre-Christian belief in a nature spirit or god of the forest.

CONTACTS:
Sherwood Forest Country Park
Sherwood Forest Visitor Centre
Edwinstowe, Nottinghamshire NG21 9HN United Kingdom
44-115-300-500-8080
www.nottinghamshire.gov.uk/robinhoodfestival

♦ 2413 ♦ Robin Hood Festival in Sherwood, Oregon
Mid-July; Friday and Saturday

The Robin Hood Festival has taken place in Sherwood, Ore., every year since just after World War II. At that point in the town's history, the economy was slow, and local core businesses were threatened by a new commercial area at Highway 99 called Six Corners. Inspired by the need to help, and also by the re-release of the classic 1938 film *The Adventures of Robin Hood,* Sherwood's civic leaders decided to capitalize on the legend connected to their town's name. Initially, a group of World War II veterans in Robin Hood costumes made appearances at movie theaters where the film was showing. They were so popular that they were invited back, and soon they were invited to appear at various festivals in the Portland area. It eventually led to the creation of the popular Sherwood event.

The Robin Hood Festival features a parade, a knighting ceremony, live music, comedy, and dancing. Each year a Maid Marian is crowned. Food and plenty of community spirit round out the event.

CONTACTS:
Sherwood Robin Hood Festival
P.O. Box 496
Sherwood, OR 97140
503-625-4233
www.robinhoodfestival.org

♦ 2414 ♦ Robinson (Jackie) Day
April 15

Jackie Robinson Day is celebrated throughout Major League Baseball (MLB) in honor of Jackie Robinson, the first African American to play professional baseball in the MLB. In the first half of the 20th century, baseball was segregated. Robinson and other African Americans played in the Negro Leagues, but discrimination prevented them from playing in the MLB. On April 15, 1947, Robinson played his first professional game for the Brooklyn Dodgers. In addition to breaking the color barrier, he went on to be named Rookie of the Year and later the National League's Most Valuable Player. A six-time All-Star, he was elected in 1962 to the Baseball Hall of Fame in Cooperstown, New York.

To commemorate Robinson's achievements, activities are planned each year at all MLB stadiums on April 15th, or the date closest to that on which a baseball game is scheduled. Home teams coordinate activities for the tribute, which may include pregame award presentations, special guests throwing the first pitch, prizes for fans in attendance, and appearances by other legendary baseball stars. Jackie Robinson Day has been celebrated each year since 2004, with Robinson's widow, Rachel, and other family members taking part in the annual ceremonies.

To honor Robinson in 2007, many players donned special jerseys emblazoned with the number 42, Robinson's number that had been permanently retired from baseball in 1997. In the years since 2007, the tradition has been repeated, with players, managers, coaches and umpires wearing number 42 in honor of Jackie Robinson. In 2014, the 67th anniversary of Jackie Robinson's debut was celebrated at Historic Dodgertown in Vero Beach, Florida, with a minor league exhibition game.

CONTACTS:
Jackie Robinson Foundation
1 Hudson Sq.
75 Varick St.
2nd Fl.
New York, NY 10013
212-290-8600; fax: 212-290-8081
www.jackierobinson.org

♦ 2415 ♦ Robots at Play
August

Robots at Play is an international festival of robotics, intended to promote the understanding, use, and enjoyment of robots in everyday life. The festival, held in Denmark, includes exhibits of robots at work; areas where visitors can play games with robot opponents, dance with robots, and otherwise interact with them; art featuring robots; robot films; and a professional conference on robotics. There is a robot-building competition for children, an area featuring robots built from scrap material, and a designer's competition with a prize of 75,000 DK, sponsored by the Fionia Bank.

The designers' competition encourages entrants to combine robotic function, good design, and artistry. In 2006, the first year of the competition, the top prize was taken by Huggable, a robotic teddy bear designed by Dan Stiehl and Cynthia Breazeal, a team from the Massachusetts Institute of Technology. Huggable was designed to mimic the attributes of a companion animal such as a cat or dog in order to provide the therapeutic benefits that real animals have been shown to provide to the elderly and infirm. In 2007, the prize was won by the team of Hideki Kozima, from Japan, and Marek Michalowski, from the United States, for their robot Keepon. A small unit with a soft, rubbery skin, Keepon featured cameras in its eyes and a microphone in its nose. It was designed to interact with young children and aid in the study of their nonverbal play.

CONTACTS:
Innovation Network RoboCluster
Princess Grace
Palace 1
Odense, 5230 Denmark
45-6550-3652
www.robocluster.dk

♦ 2416 ♦ Rock Ness
Weekend in early June

The shores of the world-famous Loch Ness outside Inverness, Scotland, is the site of this summer music festival featuring acts from the diverse genres of electronic, dance, and rock. Despite its remote location in the Scottish Highlands, the event drew as many as 35,000 music fans.

The first Rock Ness took place on June 24, 2006, with a bill favoring electronic acts. A successful attendance draw inspired organizers to extend the event to a full weekend the following year. Exposure for the event increased again in 2008 when performances were televised for the first time on Channel 4, a major British network. That year organizers also featured a more diverse program, with the dance acts performing on Saturday and the rock bands playing on Sunday.

Following a successful event in 2013, the festival was cancelled in 2014 and 2015 due to scheduling conflicts and financial difficulties. Amid growing fears over the future of the festival and the impact of its loss on the Inverness economy, the concert organizers have vowed to make serious efforts to restore the event in the future.

CONTACTS:
Rock Ness Limited
Almack House,
28 King St.
London, SW1Y 6QW United Kingdom
www.rockness.co.uk

Scotland Information Centre
Ocean Point One
94 Ocean Dr.
Edinburgh, EH6 6JH Scotland
44-131-472-2222; fax: 44-131-472-2250
www.visitscotland.org

♦ 2417 ♦ Rodgers (Jimmie) Festival
May

This country music festival in Meridian, Miss., salutes the life and music of Jimmie Rodgers on the anniversary of his death on May 26, 1933. Rodgers was born in Meridian in 1897 and left school at 14 to work on the Mississippi and Ohio Railroad; later, during his singing career, he was known as the "Singing Brakeman." He learned to play the guitar and banjo, and learned the blues from black railroad workers. Mr. Rodgers's music blended blues with the sounds of country, work, hobo, and cowboy songs. In 1925, because tuberculosis prevented him from working any longer for the railroad, he became a performer, and quickly a best-selling recording artist.

Today he is considered the Father of Country Music. Among his recordings that had a lasting influence on popular singers were "Blue Yodel No. 1," "Brakeman's Blues," and "My Time Ain't Long." The Jimmie Rodgers Memorial and Museum in Meridian has exhibits of his guitar, concert clothing, and railroad equipment he used.

The week-long festival highlights top musical stars and features a talent contest and a beauty contest.

CONTACTS:
Jimmie Rodgers Museum
1725 Jimmie Rodgers Dr.
Meridian, MS 39307
601-485-1808
www.jimmierodgers.com

♦ 2418 ♦ Rogation Days
Between April 30 and June 3; Monday, Tuesday, and Wednesday preceding Ascension Day

Since medieval times, the three days before Ascension Day (called Holy Thursday in Great Britain) have been known as Rogation Days (from *rogare*, "to pray"). Both the Roman Catholic and Protestant churches set them aside as days of abstinence and prayer, especially for the harvest.

In many churches in the United States **Rogation Sunday**, the fifth Sunday after Easter, has been known as **Rural Life Sunday** or **Soil Stewardship Sunday** since 1929—a day when the religious aspects of agricultural life are emphasized. It is also known as **Cantate Sunday** because the Latin Mass

for this day begins with the first words of Psalm 98, *Cantate Domino*, "Sing to the Lord."

The Rogation Days also had a secular meaning at one time in England, where they were called **Gang Days** or **Gange Days**—from the Saxon word *gangen*, meaning "to go." There was a custom of walking the parish boundaries during the three days before Holy Thursday (Ascension Day), the procession consisting of the priests and prelates of the church and a select number of men from the parish. Later, these Rogation Days were set aside for special local celebrations. In 19th-century Dorsetshire, for example, a local festival called the Bezant was held each year on Rogation Monday.

♦ 2419 ♦ Rogers (Roy) Festival
First weekend in June

With his wife Dale Evans, Roy Rogers was one of America's best-known singing cowboys. The couple starred in a popular television series, "The Roy Rogers Show," which ran from 1951 to 1957, and featured his horse, Trigger, and dog, Bullet.

Since 1984, Rogers has been honored in his hometown of Portsmouth, Ohio, with an annual festival sponsored by the Roy Rogers-Dale Evans Collectors Association. The four-day event includes displays of Roy Rogers memorabilia, tours of Roy Rogers's boyhood home, and special performances by old-time Western stars such as the late Lash LaRue, "King of the Bullwhip." There are showings of Roy Rogers's films and television programs, and Western memorabilia collectors set up booths to sell and exchange their wares.

Proceeds from the annual event go into a Roy Rogers Scholarship Fund that pays for a needy student to attend Shawnee State University in Portsmouth. Rogers's son, Roy (Dusty) Rogers, Jr., a cowboy singer in his own right, often attends the festival.

CONTACTS:
Roy Rogers
c/o Roy Rogers - Dale Evans Collectors Association
P.O. Box 1166
Portsmouth, OH 45662
740-259-1195
www.royrogersfestival.org

♦ 2420 ♦ Rogers (Will) Day
November 4

The birthday of America's "cowboy philosopher" is observed in Oklahoma, where he was born on November 4, 1879, when it was still the Indian Territory (*see* Oklahoma Day). After his first appearance as a vaudeville entertainer in 1905 at Madison Square Garden, he developed a widespread reputation as a humorist. He went on to become a writer, a radio performer, and a motion-picture star, best loved for his gum-chewing, homespun image.

Will Rogers died in a plane crash on August 15, 1935, while flying with the well-known aviator, Wiley Post. A monument to the two men was erected at the site of the crash near Point Barrow, Alaska. Rogers's birthday was first observed in 1947, with a celebration at the Will Rogers Memorial near the town of Claremore where he was born. Beneath the statue of Rogers at the memorial is printed the statement for which he is best remembered: "I never met a man I didn't like.".

CONTACTS:
Will Rogers Memorial Museums
1720 W. Will Rogers Blvd.
Claremore, OK 74017
918-341-0719 or 800-324-9455
www.willrogers.com

♦ 2421 ♦ Rogonadur
December-January

The Saora people, who live in the hills of eastern India and worship their own gods rather than those of the Hindus, celebrate a harvest festival in December or January known as Rogonadur, which refers to a type of bean known as the red gram. The festival, which lasts several days, is preceded by a religious ceremony a week or so before, in which the priest makes an offering of new gram to the gods and appeals to them to visit for the festival.

Bunches of fresh gram decorate village homes and shrines for the celebration, which includes dancing and music at each shrine. In the mornings people make private offerings of gram to the gods in their homes before heading outside to start the communal festivities. After a few days, the priest holds a concluding ceremony, makes a final offering, then dismisses the gods.

See also JAMMOLPUR CEREMONY.

♦ 2422 ♦ Roman Games (Ludi Romani)
September 4-19

Like the PLEBEIAN GAMES, the Roman Games were held in honor of Jupiter. They date back to the dedication of the temple to Jupiter on the Capitoline hill on September 13, 509 B.C.E., making them the most ancient of the ancient Roman games. Originally a one-day event, by the time of Caesar the Games lasted a full 15 days.

A grand procession to the Circus Maximus, a huge arena just outside Rome, signalled the beginning of the festival. Along with the athletes, the procession included charioteers, dancers, musicians playing flutes and lyres, men dressed in goatskins to look like satyrs, images of the gods, and the animals who were to be sacrificed came last.

Events included boxing, running, and wrestling contests, occasional mock battles, and two- and four-horse chariot races. Sometimes the drivers were accompanied by partners on foot, who, after a chariot crossed the finish line, had to race each other back to the other end of the arena to decide the entire contest.

See also APOLLONIAN GAMES; LUDI.

♦ 2423 ♦ Romania National Day
December 1

The national holiday of Romania has been celebrated since 1990, after the fall of Romanian Communist Party head Nicolae Ceausescu, with military parades, speeches and a holiday from work. This day marks the unification in 1918 of Romania and Transylvania and the formation of the Romanian state within its present-day boundaries. Romania's full independence had been recognized in 1878, but Transylvania had remained outside the new state. On December 1, a Romanian assembly passed the resolution of unity celebrated on National Day.

CONTACTS:
Romanian Embassy
1607 23rd St. N.W.
Washington, D.C. 20008
202-332-4846; fax: 202-232-4748
washington.mae.ro

♦ 2424 ♦ Rondo Days Celebration
Third week of July

The Rondo Days Celebration launched in 1983 as a showcase for the rich African-American culture and heritage of the Rondo community in St. Paul, Minn. Rondo, the city's vibrant, predominantly black neighborhood, was destroyed and its people displaced in the 1960s by the construction of the I-94 freeway. Recreating the energy and spirit of Rondo and bringing together former residents and other Minnesotans and visitors was the inspiration for the celebration's founders, Marvin "Roger" Anderson and Floyd Smaller. The celebration is now run by a non-profit organization.

The event takes place during the third week of July in St. Paul. A celebration of multi-cultural food, art, music, and activities, it now draws up to 35,000 visitors a year. Other highlights include a community parade, a free dinner honoring the community's senior citizens, and a five-kilometer fun walk and run. There also is an annual, hotly contested drill-team competition drawing squads from across the country.

CONTACTS:
Rondo Avenue, Inc.
1360 University Ave. W.
Ste 140
St. Paul, MN 55104
651-315-7676; fax: 651-538-6511
rondoavenueinc.org

♦ 2425 ♦ Roosevelt (Franklin D.) Day
January 30

Franklin Delano Roosevelt (1882-1945) was the 32nd president of the United States and the only one elected to four terms of office. He fell ill from polio in 1921, but regained partial use of his legs. His administration extended from the darkest days of the Great Depression to the Japanese attack on PEARL HARBOR. He never lived to see the final Allied victory at the end of World War II, however; he was stricken with a massive cerebral hemorrhage and died at the Little White House in Warm Springs, Georgia, on April 12, 1945.

Roosevelt's birthday is observed by family members, friends, and representatives of various organizations at his home at Hyde Park, New York. The ceremony begins at 11:00 A.M., when a color guard from the U.S. Military Academy at West Point marches into the rose garden where the President is buried and takes its place before his grave. Wreaths are laid, and a family member places cut flowers on the grave. The superintendent of the military academy presents the "President's Wreath," a prayer is offered, and the event concludes with three volleys from a ceremonial firing squad.

CONTACTS:
Roosevelt-Vanderbilt NHS
4097 Albany Post Rd.
Hyde Park, NY 12538
845-229-9115
www.nps.gov/hofr

♦ 2426 ♦ Roots Festival
May or June during even-numbered years

The first Roots Festival took place in the west African country of the Gambia in 1996. The event derives its name from African-American writer Alex Haley's book *Roots*, in which he traces his ancestry back to the Gambian village of Juffureh. Sponsored by Gambia's Department of State for Tourism and Culture, the Roots Festival aims to memorialize the enslavement and transportation of millions of Africans. It also serves to build bridges between the African diaspora and the people of the Gambia, in order to celebrate and strengthen African cultural identity and to encourage trade and business ties. The festival includes music and dance performances, plays, tours of African cultural sites, opportunities to participate in Gambian rite of passage rituals, a beauty contest, a fashion show, and a seminar on business opportunities in Gambia. This biennial festival takes place in even-numbered years in the capital city of Banjul.

CONTACTS:
Gambia Tourism Authority
P.O. Box 4085
Kotu, Gambia West Africa
220-446-2491; fax: 220-446-2487
www.visitthegambia.gm

♦ 2427 ♦ Ropotine (Repotini)
Between April 7 and May 18; third Tuesday after Easter

This Romanian festival is celebrated exclusively by women, who take advantage of this day to turn the tables on their husbands. It is the one day of the year when women are the masters: they feast all day, and they can punish men for any slights they may have suffered. Traditionally, women get together and make household utensils out of straw and clay, particularly a shallow baking dish for bread, known as the *tzesturi*, used to bake rolls and cakes which they hand out to children and the poor "to keep away wars.".

♦ 2428 ♦ Rosary, Festival of the
First Sunday in October

The rosary is a string of beads used by Roman Catholics to count a ritual series of prayers consisting of 15 paternosters ("Our Fathers," also known as the Lord's Prayer), and 150 *Ave Marias*, or "Hail Marys." The rosary is divided into 15 decades—each decade containing one paternoster marked by a large bead and 10 Ave Marias marked by 10 smaller beads. As the prayers are recited, the beads are passed through the fingers, making it easier to keep track of the sequence.

The festival, observed on the first Sunday in October, was established by Pope Pius V under the name of Santa Maria de Victoria (St. Mary of Victory). But the name was changed by Gregory XIII to Festival of the Rosary. Among the events for which the faithful in the former Yugoslavia give thanks on this day is the victory of Prince Eugene over the Turks at Belgrade in 1716.

CONTACTS:
Holy Rosary Parish of The Roman Catholic Archdiocese of Baltimore MD
408 S. Chester St.
Baltimore, MD 21231
410-732-3960; fax: 410-675-4917
www.holyrosarypl.org/en

♦ 2429 ♦ Rose Bowl Game
January 1

The Rose Bowl Game is the oldest and best known of the post-season college football bowl games, held in Pasadena, Calif., the home of the TOURNAMENT OF ROSES. The first Rose Bowl game was played in 1902 between Michigan and Stanford; the Michigan Wolverines, coached by Fielding H. "Hurry Up" Yost, demolished the Indians, 49-0. Yost was known for his "point-a-minute" teams, and the Michigan 11 had racked up 550 points in 11 winning games, unscored on and untied, before the bowl encounter. Willie Heston, one of the great all-time backs, led the team to victory.

Football gave way to chariot races after that first game, but football came back to stay in 1916. Among the notable highlights in the years since then was the wrong-way run in 1929. The University of California was playing Georgia Tech. Roy Riegels, the center and captain of California's Golden Bears, picked up a Tech fumble, started toward the Tech goal line, and then, facing a troop of Tech defenders, cut across the field and started toward his own goal line, 60 yards away. Players on both sides gaped. Finally Benny Lom, a Bears halfback, ran after Riegels and grabbed him at the three-yard line. Tech players bounced him back to the one. California tried a punt, but it was blocked and the ball rolled out of the end zone. The officials declared a safety, and Georgia Tech won the contest by one point.

From 1947 to 1998 the Rose Bowl brought together the champions of the Midwest Big Ten and Pac Ten (Pacific Ten) Conferences; since 1999, the top two ranked teams in any conference have played here. Numerous other bowl games have come along since 1902: the ORANGE BOWL in Miami, the SUGAR BOWL in New Orleans, and the COTTON BOWL in Dallas started games in the mid-1930s, and by the 1980s there were 16 bowl games in late December or on NEW YEAR'S DAY.

CONTACTS:
Pasadena Tournament of Roses
391 S. Orange Grove Blvd.
Pasadena, CA 91184
626-449-4100
www.tournamentofroses.com

♦ 2430 ♦ **Rose Festival**
May-June

According to legend, a Persian trader brought rose bush cuttings to the Balkans hundreds of years ago to provide attar for his lady's perfume. Bulgaria still supplies 90 percent of the world's rose attar, and roses are raised for food and medicinal purposes as well.

The 10-day festival that celebrates Bulgaria's role in the cultivation and export of roses is held in Kazanlak, a small town in what is known as the Valley of the Roses. It begins with a procession of farmers and young people dressed in native costume and carrying baskets for the ritual picking of the rose petals. Even the queen of the pageant is selected not for her beauty but for her rose-picking ability. After she is crowned, she leads a long chain dance into Kazanlak, where her arrival is the signal to begin the Parade of Roses. Rose-decorated floats, costumed paraders, and folk dancers follow a route that winds through all the nearby towns. Afterward, there are picnics featuring Bulgarian foods. Folk dance and song programs complete the festival activities.

The Rose Festival is always held in late May and early June, the blooming season for roses. It takes 3,300 pounds of rose petals to make two pounds of rose attar.

CONTACTS:
Embassy of the Republic of Bulgaria
1621 22nd St. N.W.
Dimitar Peshev Plaza
Washington, D.C. 20008
202-387-0174; fax: 202-234-7973
www.bulgaria-embassy.org

♦ 2431 ♦ **Rose Monday**
Between February 2 and March 8; Monday
before Lent

Germany is famous for its CARNIVAL celebrations, which reach a climax on Rose Monday, the day before SHROVE TUESDAY. More than 400 Carnival balls are held in Munich alone, and Rose Monday celebrations are held in Cologne, Düsseldorf, Mainz, Münster, and Berlin as well. In addition to balls and parades, which take place in small towns as well as the cities, the day is observed by singing songs, often with haunting tunes, that have been composed especially for Carnival.

Because it is the last time for hi-jinks before LENT, **Rosenmontag** is characterized by a free-for-all atmosphere in which the

normal rules of behavior are relaxed. It is not uncommon, for example, for people to go up to strangers on the street and kiss them.

The German name for the day, *Rosen Montag*, or "Roses Monday," is a mispronunciation of the original name *Rasen Montag*, meaning "rushing Monday" or "live-it-up Monday.".

CONTACTS:
German Information Center
4645 Reservoir Rd. N.W.
Washington, D.C. 20007
202-298-4000
www.germany.info

♦ 2432 ♦ **Rose of Tralee Beauty Contest**
Last full weekend in August

The village of Tralee in County Kerry is famous for a festival that is unique in Ireland: the annual beauty contest for the "Rose of Tralee." Held during a long weekend in late August, the festivities begin with the playing of a harp by a woman belonging to a Kerry family in which harp-playing has been a traditional occupation for generations. There are also horse races and competitions in singing, dancing, and storytelling, but it is the beauty contest that draws the most attention. Contestants come from Ireland, Britain, the United States, and even Australia, although the winner must be of Kerry descent.

"The Rose of Tralee," a popular Irish ballad, was written by William Pembroke Mulchinock, who lived just outside the village of Tralee and fell in love with a girl who was a servant in one of the nearby houses. To put a stop to the relationship, his family sent him to India, where he served as a soldier for three years. He returned to Tralee just in time to see the funeral procession of the girl he loved, who had died of a broken heart. In the public park just outside of Tralee there is a memorial to the ill-fated lovers.

CONTACTS:
Rose of Tralee
Ashe Memorial Hall, Denny St.
Tralee, County Kerry Ireland
353-66-712-1322
www.roseoftralee.ie

♦ 2433 ♦ **Rosh Hashanah**
Between September 6 and October 4; Tishri 1
and 2

Rosh Hashanah marks the beginning of the **Jewish New Year** and the first two of the 10 High Holy Days (*see* TESHUVAH) that conclude with YOM KIPPUR, the Day of Atonement. Unlike the secular NEW YEAR'S DAY observance, this is a solemn season during which each person is subject to review and judgment for the coming year. It is a time of prayer and penitence, and is sometimes called the **Day of Remembrance** or the **Day of Blowing the Shofar**. The story of Abraham is read in the synagogue, and the blowing of the *shofar* ("ram's horn") serves as a reminder that although Abraham, in obedience to God, was willing to sacrifice his son, Isaac, God allowed him to sacrifice a ram instead. The plaintive sound of the shofar is also a call to penitence.

Orthodox Ashkenazim (Jews whose ancestors came from northern Europe) observe the ceremony of Tashlikh, a symbolic throwing of one's sins into a body of water, on the first day of Rosh Hashanah; Kurds jump into the water; kabbalists shake their garments to "free" themselves from sin. All debts from the past year are supposed to be settled before Rosh Hashanah, and many Jews ask forgiveness from friends and family for any slights or transgressions of the concluding year.

Jews celebrate the New Year by eating a special rounded loaf of challah bread, symbolic of the continuity of life, as well as apples dipped in honey, symbols of sweetness and health.

CONTACTS:
Orthodox Union
11 Broadway
New York, NY 10004 United States
212-563-4000; fax: 212-564-9058
www.ou.org

Union for Reform Judaism
633 Third Ave.
New York, NY 10017 United States
212-650-4000
www.urj.org

♦ 2434 ♦ **Roswell UFO Festival**
Early July

Around July 4, 1947, a UFO (unidentified flying object) allegedly crashed near Roswell, a farming and ranching community in southeastern New Mexico. According to some reports, the bodies of four aliens were found at a site around 30 miles from Roswell. Mack Brazel worked on a ranch southeast of Corona, New Mexico, where he found strange debris on July 5. The next day he went to Roswell to show it to the Chaves County sheriff, who in turn passed the information along to officials at Roswell Army Air Field (RAAF). An investigation was begun and a press release about the crash was released by the RAAF. The headline in the July 8 *Roswell Daily Record* read, "RAAF Captures Flying Saucer on Ranch in Roswell Region." But the Army-Air Force changed its story the next day, claiming that the debris was from a weather balloon.

The "Roswell Incident" has remained a subject of controversy for years. In September 1994 the Air Force produced a report which asserted that the recovered object was in fact a spy balloon flown as part of the then-top-secret Project Mogul. On the 50th anniversary of the event in 1997 the Air Force issued a report designed to put continuing rumors about a cover-up to rest. That report claimed the retrieved bodies were actually crash-test dummies (even though such experiments did not begin until 1953).

The town of Roswell celebrates its reputation as the UFO capital of the United States with a week-long festival in early July, which has been officially designated as "Alien Month."

Activities include a UFO parade, an alien puppet show, concerts, and special exhibits. The UFO Museum and Research Center invites UFO experts from around the world to speak at the festival, which combines traditional FOURTH OF JULY barbecues and fireworks with serious discussion of UFO reports.

CONTACTS:
Roswell Chamber of Commerce
131 W. 2nd St.
Roswell, NM 88201
575-623-5695 or 877-849-7679
www.roswellnm.org

♦ 2435 ♦ **Rousa, Feast of**
Between April 29 and June 2; the 25th day after Easter

In parts of Greece, the **Feast of Mid-Pentecost**, which occurs on the 25th day after EASTER, is called the Feast of Rousa (or Rosa). On this day, a special ceremony is performed to ward off scarlatina, or scarlet fever. The children bake rolls out of flour, butter, honey, sesame oil, and other ingredients which they have collected from their neighbors. Along with other foods, these are eaten at a children's banquet, which is followed by singing and dancing. Central to the ceremony, however, is the baking of special ring-shaped cakes, which can only be made by a girl whose name is unique in the neighborhood and which must be baked in a specially built oven.

After the banquet is over, these ring-shaped cakes are divided among the children and hung up to dry. If any of the children who participated in the feast come down with scarlet fever or any similar disease, a piece of the cake is pounded and sprinkled over their skin, which has already been smeared with molten sugar, honey, or sesame oil. This is believed to be an infallible cure.

While the name of this feast is widely believed to come from the crimson rash that accompanies scarlet fever, it may also be a remnant of the old Roman festival known as Rosalia, or Feast of the Roses.

CONTACTS:
Greek National Tourism Organisation
305, E. 47th St.
2nd Fl.
New York, NY 10017 United States
212-421-5777; fax: 212-826-6940
www.visitgreece.gr/ | www.gtp.gr

City of Athens Convention and Visitors Bureau
7 Xenofontos Str
Athens, 105 57 Greece
30-21-03253123; fax: 30-21-03216653
www.athensconventionbureau.gr

♦ 2436 ♦ **Rousalii**
May-June; Pentecost or Trinity Sunday, Sunday after Pentecost

In Romania, PENTECOST or the week after, including TRINITY SUNDAY, is the time when the Rousalii, the three daughters of an emperor who were ill-treated during their lives on earth and later became goddesses, set out to cause misery and mischief wherever they could. Traditional Romanian belief holds that during the period from Trinity Sunday to St. Peter's Day (June 29), the Rousalii roam over the earth, causing high winds and storms. People may be caught up in whirlwinds, or children may be snatched from the arms of their mothers if they venture outdoors or travel any distance from home.

On the eve of Rousalii, it is traditional to place a twig of wormwood under your pillow. Because medicinal herbs supposedly lose their potency for several weeks after Rousalii, it is considered unwise to gather any herbs from the fields until at least nine weeks have passed.

♦ 2437 ♦ Route 66 Festival
Summer

Known as the "Mother Road" and "America's Main Street," Route 66 once carried travelers across the southern part of the United States for over 2,400 miles, passing through some of Arizona and New Mexico's most scenic areas. But when Interstate 40 was built in the 1960s, Route 66 was bypassed, causing great economic hardship to the communities—some of them Native American—that depended on the highway for their livelihood. Entire towns were boarded up, and miles of the road bed were replaced with cornfields.

The movement to "Save Historic Route 66" by promoting heritage tourism along the historic highway began in the late 1960s and has been going on ever since. Route 66 festivals have been held in several towns and cities located along the old highway, particularly Landergin, Texas, Albuquerque, New Mexico, and Clinton, Oklahoma, where the Route 66 Museum is located. They feature such events as lectures by authors who have written books about the highway, the showing of films involving Route 66, photographic and art exhibits, and music by such well-known performers as the late Bobby Troup, best remembered for his hit song, "Get Your Kicks on Route 66."

In 2014, the Route 66 International Festival in Kingman, Arizona, celebrated the "Mother Road" with an exhibit of Route 66 authors, artists and collectors, and a film festival featuring movies that were filmed on Route 66, in Kingman, or showcase Andy Devine.

CONTACTS:
Oklahoma Route 66 Museum
2229 W. Gary Blvd.
Clinton, OK 73601
580-323-7866
www.route66.org

New Mexico Route 66 Association
1430 Central Ave. N.W.
Albuquerque, NM 87121
505-385-1410
www.rt66nm.org

♦ 2438 ♦ Royal Ascot
Mid-June

The racecourse on Ascot Heath in Berkshire, England, is the site of a world-famous horse race also called the **Royal Meeting**, that was initiated in 1711 by Queen Anne. The Royal Ascot race meeting goes on for four days in June each year and culminates in the event known as the **Ascot Gold Cup**, a race that is nearly two miles long for horses more than three years old. Although the Gold Cup race was established in 1807, the original cup was stolen 100 years later.

A major social and fashion event as well as a sporting one, the Royal Ascot race is usually attended by the British sovereign and receives widespread media coverage. It has even given its name to a type of broad neck-scarf traditionally worn by well-dressed English gentlemen at the races.

CONTACTS:
Ascot Racecourse
Ascot
Berkshire, SL5 7JX United Kingdom
44-84-4346-3616; fax: 44-13-4463-1273
www.ascot.co.uk

♦ 2439 ♦ Royal Brunei Armed Forces Day
May 31

The formation of the Royal Brunei Armed Forces took place on May 31, 1961. Brunei had been a British protectorate since 1888, dependent on the British armed forces for its defense. In 1961, some 60 Brunei recruits began training as part of a transition period toward complete independence for the country, which occurred in 1984. The Royal Brunei Armed Forces maintain close ties with the British military forces, as well as those of Malaysia and Singapore. They also regularly cooperate in exercises with the armed forces of New Zealand, Australia, and the United States.

The formation of the Royal Brunei Armed Forces is commemorated each year. Around the country, there may be parades and military displays put on by various units of the armed forces. In the capital city of Bandar Seri Begawan, the occasion is usually commemorated at the Taman Haji Sir Omar Ali Saifuddien in the city center. Events include a military parade and such military demonstrations as parachuting exhibitions or mock battles. In 2007, the Royal Brunei Armed Forces marked the anniversary by giving special presents to those children who were celebrating their first birthday on that day. The children were given special souvenirs of the occasion, and bank accounts were opened in their names.

♦ 2440 ♦ Royal Easter Show
March-April; one week during the Easter holiday

The largest and best-attended of the Australian agricultural fairs, the Royal Easter Show was first held in 1822 as a way of promoting the country's agricultural industry and helping people sell their products. Now it attracts more than a million visitors each year and has expanded to include sports competitions, fashion and flower shows, and celebrity performances, in addition to the usual agricultural and industrial exhibits.

The show was held at the Moore Park Showground in Sydney every year from 1882 to 1997, although it was canceled during the 1919 influenza epidemic and during World War II, when the showground was occupied by the Australian army. Sponsored by the Royal Agricultural Society of New South Wales, the Royal Easter Show has been held since 1998 at the Sydney Showground at Homebush Bay and attracts more than 600 exhibitors each year and is similar to some of the larger American state fairs, such as the Iowa State Fair and the Eastern States Exposition.

See also Royal Shows.

CONTACTS:
Sydney Royal Easter Show
1 Showground Rd.
Sydney Olympic Park
Sydney, NSW 2127 Australia
61-2-9704-1111; fax: 61-2-9704-1122
www.eastershow.com.au

♦ 2441 ♦ **Royal Ploughing Ceremony**
Early May

The Royal Ploughing Ceremony is an ancient Brahman ritual held on a large field near the Grand Palace in Bangkok, Thailand. It celebrates the official start of the annual rice-planting season and is believed to ensure an abundant rice crop. The king presides over the rituals, in which the participants wear scarlet and gold costumes and oxen wear bells.

The Brahmans are a small Hindu group in Thailand, numbering only a few thousand families, but they have considerable influence. Royal and official ceremonies are almost always performed by them. The national calendar is prepared by Brahmans and the royal astrologers. Brahman rites blend with those of Buddhism, the dominant Thai religion.

CONTACTS:
Tourism Authority of Thailand
611 N. Larchmont Blvd.
1st Fl.
Los Angeles, CA 90004
323-461-9814; fax: 323-461-9834
www.tourismthailand.org

♦ 2442 ♦ **Royal Shows**
April, July, August, September, October

More than 500 agricultural shows are held in Australia each year, but the annual Royal Shows, held in each of the state capitals, are famous for their outstanding livestock, agricultural, and industrial exhibits as well as their competitive events. More than four and one-half million people visit the **Royals** each year.

The **Royal Queensland Show**, noted for its unusual display of tropical plants and flowers from all over the state of Queensland, is held in August. The **Hobart Royal Show** is held in mid-October. The **Royal Melbourne Show**, the **Royal Adelaide Show**, and the **Perth Royal Show** are held in

September. The Royal Easter Show, held at Sydney's 71-acre show grounds in early to mid-April, is the most popular of the country's Royal Shows. All of the Royals feature attractions such as sheepdog trials, wood chopping, and tree-felling contests, and the uniquely Australian camp drafts— an unusual rodeo event in which cattle are driven over a course that tests both horse and rider.

Other agricultural shows include **Alice Springs Show**, **Tennant Creek Show**, **Katherine Show**, and **Darwin Show**—all observed in the Northern Territory during the month of July.

CONTACTS:
Tourism Australia (US)
2029 Century Park E. Ste. 3150
Mailbox #358
Los Angeles, CA 90067
310-695-3200; fax: 310-695-3201
www.tourism.australia.com

♦ 2443 ♦ **Ruhr Festival**
May-June

Germany's Ruhr Valley is known as a coal-mining and industrial center, and the annual cultural festival celebrated in Recklinghausen continues to reflect the needs and issues of the area. The festival grew out of an informal arrangement in 1946 between the artists of the Hamburg State Opera and the people of the mining town of Recklinghausen. In return for desperately needed coal to keep their theater's heating system from freezing, performers from Hamburg would go to Recklinghausen to perform their plays and operas. A new theater was built there in 1965 with the motto, "Coal I Gave for Art—Art I Gave for Coal."

The vast majority of the people who attend the festival's theater productions, concerts, and exhibitions are industrial workers, and the local trade unions lend their financial support. Events at the Ruhr Festival often address an economic or industrial theme, and there are scientific and political seminars covering new technological developments and their implications for working people.

CONTACTS:
Ruhr Tourismus GmbH
Centroallee 261
Oberhausen, 46047 Germany
49-1806-181620
www.ruhr-tourismus.de/en

♦ 2444 ♦ **Rukmini Ashtami**
December-January; eighth day of waning half of Hindu month of Pausa

Vaishnavite Hindus believe that Rukmini, Lord Krishna's primary wife and queen, was born on this day. According to the *Harivansha Purana*, she fell in love with Krishna but was already betrothed to Shishupala, king of Chedi. As she was going to the temple on her wedding day, Krishna carried her off in his chariot. They were pursued by Shishupala and Rukmin, her brother, but Krishna defeated them and eventually married her.

The fast known as Rukmini Ashtami is observed by women, both married and unmarried. Rukmini, Krishna, and Pradyumna, their son, are worshipped. A Brahman priest is also fed and given *dan-dakshina*, or charitable gifts, on this day. Many middle-class Hindus believe that observance of this fast ensures conjugal happiness and prosperity, and that it will help them find good husbands for unmarried girls.

◆ 2445 ◆ Rumi Festival
September to early October

Each September, the Rifa Ma'rufi Order of America, the American branch of an established Sufi Muslim order, sponsors a festival to honor the 13th-century poet and Sufi Islamic mystic Jelaluddin al-Rumi. Held in Chapel Hill and Carrboro, North Carolina, the event attracts hundreds of people to readings of the poets work, Rumi-related lectures, and performances of the music and dance for which the order are renowned. For devotees, music and dance are channels to spiritual ecstasy. Its members are best known in the West as "whirling dervishes" because of their dance rituals that involve spinning in place for extended periods of time.

The Rumi Festival, which spans several days, is held in September (often running into early October) to honor Rumi's birth month and to mark the re-birth of his popularity in the United States and abroad. It was inspired by the famous URS OF JELALUDDIN AL-RUMI, or Whirling Dervish Festival, held every December in Konya, Turkey. The American festival launched in 1997. It is hosted by the Rifai Ma'rufi Order of America, with participation and support from the University of North Carolina Seminar for Comparative Islamic Studies.

CONTACTS:
Carolina Center for the Study of the Middle East and Muslim Civilizations
3023 FedEx Global Education Center
301 Pittsboro St.
CB 7582
Chapel Hill, NC 27599
919-962-2034; fax: 919-843-2102
mideast.unc.edu

Chisholme Institute
Chisholme House
Hawick, Scottish Borders
Roberton, Scotland TD9 7PH United Kingdom
44-145-088-0215
rumifestival.org

Iranian Cultural Society of North Carolina
P.O. Box 32217
Raleigh, NC 27622
icsnc.org

◆ 2446 ◆ Runeberg (Johan Ludvig), Birthday of
February 5

Johan Ludvig Runeberg (1804-1877) is widely regarded as Finland's greatest poet. His work embodied the patriotic spirit of his countrymen and, because it was written in Swedish, exerted a great influence on Swedish literature as well.

One of his poems, "Vårtland" ("Our Country"), became the Finnish national anthem.

Schools throughout Finland are closed on Runeberg's birthday. Busts and pictures of him are displayed in shop windows, particularly in Helsinki, with rows of white candles placed in the foreground. A special ceremony is observed at Runeberg's monument in the Esplanade, where his statue is decorated with garlands of pine and spruce, suspended between four huge torches. Students lay wreaths of flowers at the foot of the monument and sing the national anthem. At night the torches are lit, and lighted candles burn in the windows of houses and apartments.

CONTACTS:
Ministry of Foreign Affairs of Finland
Laivastokatu 22 A
MKA2
Helsinki, 00160 Finland
358-295-350-000; fax: 358-9-1605-5002
formin.finland.fi

◆ 2447 ◆ Running of the Bulls in Mexico
Sunday following August 15

The running of the bulls that takes place on the Sunday following the Feast of the ASSUMPTION in Huamantla, Tlaxcala, Mexico, is considered to be far more dangerous than the famous running of the bulls in Pamplona, Spain, during the SAN FERMIN FESTIVAL. This is because the bulls are released from cages in nine different locations, making it almost impossible for those who are trying to outrun the bulls to anticipate the direction from which they are coming or the path that they are likely to follow through the maze of streets that lead to the arena. In Pamplona, the bulls are all released in one location, and they follow a well-known route to the bullring.

This particular running of the bulls dates back to the time when the Spanish conquistadores first brought cattle to Mexico, and the custom of running the bulls through the streets of Huamantla was observed every year until it began to fade around 1700. A group of local people revived the tradition in the 1920s as part of the **Assumption Fiesta**.

CONTACTS:
Government of Tlaxcala
Plaza de la Constitucion No.3
Tlaxcala, Tlaxcala 90000 Mexico
52-246-465-0900
www.tlaxcala.gob.mx

◆ 2448 ◆ Rushbearing Festival
Saturday nearest August 5

The custom of rushbearing in England dates back more than 1,000 years, perhaps to an ancient Roman harvest festival. Young girls would cover the floor of the parish church with rushes and fasten elaborate flower garlands to the walls. After the invention of floor coverings eliminated the need for rushes, the original ceremony gradually evolved into a flower festival, similar to MAY DAY celebrations, with sports, folk dancing, and floral processions.

Modern-day rushbearing ceremonies still take place in Great Musgrave, Ambleside, Grasmere, and Warcop in Westmorland, although Grasmere claims to be the only community where the rushbearing tradition has remained unbroken since ancient times. The poet William Wordsworth was largely responsible for keeping the custom alive there during the early 19th century. He and his sister, Dorothy, lived at Dove Cottage in Grasmere from 1799 until 1808.

Most rushbearing festivals begin with a procession of children carrying flower garlands and wood-framed bearings with rushes woven into traditional designs and ecclesiastical emblems. When they reach the parish church, they scatter rushes over the floor and arrange the garlands and bearings around the altar and against the church walls. There is a religious service, after which the entire village participates in sports, Maypole dancing, and other festivities. Most rushbearing events take place in July and August, often on the Saturday nearest ST. ANNE'S DAY (July 26) or St. Oswald's Day (August 5).

CONTACTS:
Grasmere Tourist Information Centre
Red Bank Rd.
Grasmere, Cumbria LA22 9SW United Kingdom
44-1539-4352-45
www.visitcumbria.com

◆ 2449 ◆ Russell (C. M.) Auction
Third weekend in March

The C. M. Russell Auction features an art auction, a celebration of western artist Charles M. Russell, and a western-style good time in Great Falls, Mont., where Charley Russell had his home and studio. The affair began in 1969 to raise money for the C. M. Russell (as he signed his paintings) Museum, which was then just getting started. Events include seminars, dance demonstrations by the Blackfeet Indians, an exhibit of paintings and sculpture of western artists and an auction of their works, and a Quick Draw, in which artists have 30 minutes to draw any subject they want. Their quick draws are then auctioned. There is also a chuckwagon brunch and a Charley Russell Birthday Party (he was born March 19, 1864, and died in 1926).

Charley Russell, a cowboy artist who was also the author of a collection of stories and sketches, *Trails Plowed Under*, depicted the early days of cowpunchers and Indians in Montana and Wyoming. In an introduction to *Trails Plowed Under*, Will ROGERS wrote that there will never be "the Real Cowboy, Painter and Man, combined that old Charley was." Charley Russell wrote about himself: "I am an illustrator. There are lots better ones, but some worse." His paintings now are coveted by collectors and worth millions.

CONTACTS:
C. M. Russell Museum
400 13th St. N.
Great Falls, MT 59401

406-727-8787; fax: 406-727-2402
www.cmrussell.org

◆ 2450 ◆ Russian Winter Festival
December 25-January 5

The Russian Winter Festival is a festival of arts and a time of holiday partying largely in Moscow, Russia, and somewhat less grandly in other cities of the former Soviet Union. In Moscow, there are circuses, performances of Russian fables for children, and other special theatrical presentations as well as traditional outdoor parties with troika (sled) rides, folk games, and dancing around fir trees. On NEW YEAR'S EVE, children wait for gifts from "Grandfather Frost"—who wears a red robe and black boots and has a white beard—and his helper, Snow Girl.

In the past, Grandfather Frost was associated with CHRISTMAS, but religious holidays were stamped out after the 1917 Revolution. After the dissolution of the Soviet Union in 1991, people began to openly revive old traditions, and Grandfather Frost may again become a Christmas figure, though Santa Claus has also become popular in Russia.

CONTACTS:
Russian National Tourist Office
224 W. 30th St.
Ste. 701
New York, NY 10001
646-473-2233 or 877-221-7120; fax: 646-473-2205
www.russia-travel.com

◆ 2451 ◆ Rwanda Independence Day
July 1

This national holiday celebrates Rwanda's independence from Belgium on July 1, 1962, after nearly 50 years of Belgian rule.

CONTACTS:
Rwanda Embassy
1875 Connecticut Ave.
N.W.Ste. 540
Washington, D.C. 20009
202-232-2882; fax: 202-232-4544
www.rwandaembassy.org

◆ 2452 ◆ Rwanda Liberation Day
July 4

The Republic of Rwanda is a landlocked country in central Africa. It is bordered by Uganda, Tanzania, Burundi, and the Democratic Republic of Congo.

Rwanda's original inhabitants were the Tutsi and Hutu people. The country was ruled by Tutsi kings until the Europeans began arriving in 1894. Rwanda became a German colony in 1899, but the Belgian military from Zaire took control of the country in 1915. After World War I, Rwanda became a mandate territory of the League of Nations under the administration of Belgium.

The Belgian rulers established discriminatory practices throughout the country, leading the Batutsi king and his chiefs to form the Union Nationale Rwandaise (UNAR), a political party that demanded independence. In response, the Belgian authorities created another party called Parmehutu. In 1959, under the Belgian supervision, the Parmehutu began the massacre of hundreds of thousands of Batutsi. On July 1, 1962, the United Nations terminated the Belgian trusteeship and granted full independence to Rwanda.

On July 5, 1973, Major General Juvenal Habyarimana led the military and took power. He dissolved the National Assembly and the Parmehutu Party and abolished all political activity. In December 1978, Rwandans overwhelmingly endorsed a new constitution and elected Habyarimana as president. He was re-elected in 1983 and again in 1988. In response to public pressure for political reform, President Habyarimana announced in 1990 his plans to transform Rwanda's one-party state into a multi-party democracy. Later that year, Rwandan exiles, primarily ethnic Tutsis, formed the Rwandan Patriotic Front (RPF) and invaded Rwanda. A cease-fire took effect on July 31, 1992.

On April 6, 1994, an airplane carrying President Habyarimana and the President of Burundi was shot down, and both presidents were killed. The Rwandan Army and militia groups immediately began rounding up and killing all Tutsis and moderate Hutus throughout the country. As many as 800,000 Tutsis and moderate Hutus had been killed by July. On July 4, 1994, the RPF took over Kigali, and the war ended on July 16. This is now known as the Rwandan genocide.

Today, Rwandans across the country celebrate the anniversary of their liberation on July 4. The main celebrations take place at Amahoro Stadium in Kigali. Delegations from Ethiopia, the Democratic Republic of Congo, Burundi, Uganda, South Africa, Tanzania, and Zimbabwe attend the colorful ceremony that includes a military parade, music, dancing, and recitals. The president addresses the nation, calling on the people to reflect on the past tragedies of Rwanda and the

successes that have been made since 1994 to rebuild and develop the country. The celebrations in Kigali also include an official state reception and a football game between Rwanda and Uganda. Similar ceremonies are held around the country to mark Liberation Day.

◆ 2453 ◆ Rwanda National Heroes' Day
February 1

The Republic of Rwanda is a landlocked country in central Africa, bordered by Uganda, Tanzania, Burundi, and the Democratic Republic of Congo. Rwandans celebrate Heroes' Day on February 1. National celebrations take place starting early in the morning with the laying of wreaths at the Heroes' Cemetery at Remera, Kigali, by the president, officials of the government, and the families of the country's heroes.

National Heroes' Day commemorates events that occurred after April 6, 1994, when Rwandan President Juvenal Habyarimana and the president of Burundi were killed when their airplane was shot down. After that, the Rwandan military began to systematically kill all Tutsis and moderate Hutus. Local officials and government-sponsored radio stations called on ordinary citizens to kill their Tutsi neighbors. Hundreds of thousands of Tutsi and moderate Hutus were killed. This is now known as the Rwandan genocide. Victims of this genocide are remembered on Heroes' Day.

During the Rwandan genocide, rebels surrounded the Nyange Secondary School and asked the students to identify the Tutsi students. When a group of students refused to do this, the rebels killed them. This heroic act is also remembered on National Heroes' Day. Wreaths are laid at Nyange in memory of students who stood against the rebel forces. The national Heroes' Day celebration at Nyange features songs, dances, and poems praising the virtues and good example of the national heroes. The people are reminded of the great value in service to the country that the national heroes have shown those who are still alive.

S

◆ 2454 ◆ Saba Saba Day
July 7

July 7 marks the day when the ruling party of Tanzania, known as TANU (Tanganyika African National Union), was formed in 1954. The TANU Creed is based on the principles of socialism as set forth in the TANU Constitution. Also known as **Saba Saba Peasants' Day** or **Industrial Day**, it is officially celebrated in a different region of the country each year with traditional dances, sports, processions, rallies, and fairs.

Tanzania, perhaps best known as the home of Mount Kilimanjaro, was formed in 1964 when Tanganyika merged with Zanzibar.

CONTACTS:
Embassy of the United Republic of Tanzania
1232 22nd St. N.W.
Washington, D.C. 20037
202-884-1080; fax: 202-797-7408
tanzaniaembassy-us.org

◆ 2455 ◆ Sabantui
Spring

Sabantui, or the **Festival of the Plow**, was originally an agricultural celebration of the planting season. The date is now set each year by the president of the Republic of Tatarstan. The festival is held in Kazan on the Volga River. The events include climbing a greased pole to reach a cock in a cage on top and "smashing the crocks," a variation of Pin-the-Tail-on-the-Donkey in which a blindfolded player who has been spun around several times tries to break open crockery pieces that contain prizes. There are also wrestling matches, foot and horse races, and lots of music and food.

Sabantui is also celebrated by Tatars living in Belarus. People of Tatar ancestry in Turkey observe Tepresh in June, a similar festival marking the end of the planting season.

CONTACTS:
Tatarstan Department of Foreign Affairs
Kremlin
Kazan, Tatarstan 420014 Russian Federation
495-769-0310; fax: 843-292-0283
www.justrussia.ru

◆ 2456 ◆ Sabbat
Eight times a year, on the solstices, equinoxes, and Cross-Quarter Days

The eight Sabbats are the major holidays celebrated by members of the various Neopagan religions that have flourished in the United States since the mid-1960s. Although normally observed on the VERNAL EQUINOX, SUMMER SOLSTICE, AUTUM- NAL EQUINOX, WINTER SOLSTICE, and CROSS-QUARTER DAYS (February 1, May 1, August 1, and November 1), the Sabbats may sometimes be displaced from their traditional dates in order to fall closer to that of a specific Neopagan festival.

Since 1970, the outdoor celebration of Sabbats in the United States has increased in popularity on both the local and national levels. Although local gatherings may attract a few hundred people, there is now an annual cycle of festivals—approximately one for each Sabbat in each major region of the United States—that is regularly attended by thousands of Neopagan adherents. The Sabbat ritual typically combines drama, poetry, music, costume, and dance.

◆ 2457 ◆ Sabbath of Rabbi Isaac Mayer Wise
Last Sabbath in March

Isaac Mayer Wise (1819-1900), a prominent American rabbi, is generally considered the pioneer of Reform Judaism in America. In 1875 he founded the Hebrew Union College in Cincinnati for the training of rabbis and was its president until his death. Wise also helped organize the Union of American Hebrew Congregations in 1873 and the Central Conference of American Rabbis in 1889.

Reform Judaism began in Germany during the European Age of Enlightenment in the 18th century, when some Jews were struggling to reconcile their traditional beliefs with modern thought and learning. Reform Jews abandoned many ancient ceremonial traditions and stressed ethical teachings over ritualistic observance. Rabbi Wise was the leader who brought these reforms to the United States. Adherents to Reform Judaism honor both the birth and death of Rabbi Wise on the last Sabbath in the month of March.

CONTACTS:
Union for Reform Judaism
633 Third Ave.
New York, NY 10017
212-650-4000 or 855-875-1800
www.urj.org

◆ 2458 ◆ Sacaea
Five days, including the vernal equinox, March 21 or 22

Sacaea was an ancient five-day Babylonian New Year festival associated with Anaitis, the Syrian war goddess identified with the Greek goddess Athena. It was characterized by drunkenness and licentious behavior as well as a reversal of the usual customs and relationships. Slaves ruled their masters throughout the festival, and a mock king was selected from among the criminals. After being feasted and honored for five days, the mock king was executed, thereby serving as a surrogate for the real king, who was supposed to die each new year when a new king was born.

The festival was instituted by Cyrus, king of the Persians, when he marched against the Sacae, or people of Scythia. In order to detain the enemy, he set out tables laden with delicacies to which they were unaccustomed. While they lingered over the food, he was able to destroy them.

◆ 2459 ◆ Sacred Heart of Jesus, Feast of the
Between May 22 and June 25; Friday after Corpus Christi

The Feast of the Sacred Heart of Jesus is a solemnity (meaning a festival of the greatest importance) in the Roman Catholic Church celebrated on the Friday after CORPUS CHRISTI. It is devoted to the symbol of Jesus' love for all humanity and is a significant holiday in Colombia.

◆ 2460 ◆ Sadie Hawkins Day
Usually first Saturday in November

Sadie Hawkins Day was created as a day when spinsters can legitimately chase bachelors; if caught, the men are obliged to marry their pursuers. Artist Al Capp invented the unpretty but hopeful Sadie Hawkins and her day in his comic strip, *L'il Abner*, some time in the 1930s. In the following decades, Sadie Hawkins Days, usually featuring dances to which males were invited by females, were popular on school campuses. Celebrations are rarer now.

Capp's long-running *L'il Abner*, named for its good-looking but not-too-bright hero, injected the hillbilly characters of Dogpatch into American culture.

◆ 2461 ◆ Safari Rally
July

The Safari Rally, a grueling weekend auto race, takes place on a 2,550-mile circuit over unpaved roads. Starting outside Nairobi, Kenya, the route is considered the toughest in the world; the roads climb in and out of the Great Rift Valley, and there are severe changes in climate. Furthermore, it's the rainy season when the race is held, and the roads can turn into virtual swamps. There are usually about 100 entrants, and fewer than 10 to 20 finish.

The rally began as part of the celebrations marking the coronation of QUEEN ELIZABETH II in 1953 and was called the **Coronation Rally**. It generated such interest that it was continued and renamed the **East African Safari,** with Kenya, Uganda, and Tanzania on the route. Since 1974, it has been confined to Kenya. Nairobi gets rally fever at this time of year. The city is hung with flags, and cars sprayed to look like rally cars zoom around the streets. Thousands of spectators watch the race at various points along the route.

CONTACTS:
Embassy of the Republic of Kenya
2249 R St. N.W.
Washington, D.C. 20008
202-387-6101; fax: 202-462-3829
www.kenyaembassy.com

◆ 2462 ◆ Saffron Rose Festival
Last Sunday in October

Saffron, the world's most expensive spice, is harvested from the stigmas of the autumn-flowering *Crocus sativus*. Much of the world's saffron comes from Spain's La Mancha region, and it is used to flavor French bouillabaisse, Spanish paella, cakes, breads, cookies, and the cuisines of East India, the Middle East, and North Africa. It takes 35,000 flowers to produce one pound.

The Saffron Rose Festival held in the town of Consuegra each year celebrates this exotic crop, which must be harvested by hand so that the valuable stigmas are not crumpled. Hosted by a national television personality, the celebrations include parades and contests, traditional folk dancing, and the crowning of a pageant queen. Costumed characters from CERVANTES's 17th-century novel, *Don Quixote*, stroll among the crowds who flock to Consuegra for the fiesta.

CONTACTS:
Tourist Office of Spain
60 E. 42nd St.
Ste. 5300 (53rd Fl.)
New York, NY 10165
212-265-8822; fax: 212-265-8864
www.spain.info/en_US

◆ 2463 ◆ Sahara National Festival
November or December

The Tunisian city of Douz is considered the gateway to the Sahara Desert. It is also the site of the annual Sahara National Festival, when nomads and Bedouins from all over the country gather to compete in camel races and to perform traditional music. There is also a poetry contest, a traditional wedding ceremony, and greyhound racing. The time of the week-long festival—which celebrates the date harvest—varies according to the weather, but usually takes place in November or December. A date marketplace is set up during the festival, usually on a Thursday, and fresh dates as well as *lagmi* (the juice of the date palm, fermented in the sun) are sold. Other items for sale at the market, which draws as many tourists as tribesmen, include camels, incense, ebony, rugs, desert flowers, caftans, and Berber tapestries.

CONTACTS:
Embassy of Tunisia
1515 Massachusetts Ave. N.W.
Washington, D.C. 20005 United States
202-862-1850; fax: 202-862-1858
www.tunconsusa.org/#!contact/c24vq

♦ 2464 ♦ Saigon Liberation Day
April 30

In the mid-20th century, Vietnam was divided into two separate nations. Civil war broke out between North Vietnam, which was allied with the communist regime in China, and South Vietnam, which was allied with the French and the United States. On April 30, 1975, the Vietnam War officially came to an end as communist North Vietnamese tanks rolled onto the grounds of the Presidential Palace in the South Vietnamese capital city of Saigon. The war was a victory for the communist forces and a defeat for the American military. U.S. armed forces were forced out of the country, while the democratic government of South Vietnam was removed from power.

To mark the anniversary of their military victory, the Vietnamese hold celebrations throughout the month of April. The capture of each major city or region by North Vietnamese forces during that month is celebrated locally on the day it happened. The celebrations culminate on April 30th, when the entire nation celebrates the final victory in Saigon (now named Ho Chi Minh City).

In Ho Chi Minh City, there are military parades featuring marching bands and Vietnam War veterans. Costumed dancers reenact the shooting down of American warplanes. Fireworks are shot off to mark the hour when the South Vietnamese government officially surrendered. The president and other high-ranking officials normally give speeches from the nation's capital in Hanoi. In 2005, the government released some 7,500 political prisoners as part of an amnesty to mark the occasion.

♦ 2465 ♦ Saigusa Matsuri
June 17

For hundreds of years the citizens of Nara, Japan, have searched the surrounding mountains for lilies, gathering them each summer in preparation for the **Lily Festival** at the Isagawa Shrine. The lilies are placed in a Shinto shrine where seven ladies wearing white robes perform a blessing ceremony over them, and a Shinto priest carries a large bundle of the flowers to the altar as an offering. Then the seven women perform a special dance in which they wave lily stalks in a motion designed to ward off the problems brought on by the wet weather typical this time of year. Afterwards, the lilies are mounted on a float and taken out in a procession through the streets of Nara, where it is believed that they will purify the air.

♦ 2466 ♦ Saintes Festival of Ancient Music
Mid-July

Saintes, an ancient Roman city about 16 miles inland from the Atlantic coast of southwest France, is the setting for a week-long festival of medieval and Renaissance music in July. Concerts are held in some of the town's most famous sites, including Abbaye aux Dames, built in the 11th century, and St. Eutrope Church, with its ancient Roman crypts.

Although the artists who perform there are not always as well known as those who perform at the Festival of International Contemporary Arts, which takes place at the same time only 40 miles away in La Rochelle, performers at Saintes have included the Ensemble Vocal and Instrumental of Nantes, the Ensemble Polyphonique de Paris, and Le Collectif de Musique Ancienne de Paris. For music lovers whose tastes span the centuries, the combination of the two festivals is ideal.

CONTACTS:
Abbaye aux Dames, the Musical City
11 Place de l'Abbaye
Saintes, 17104 France
33-5-46-97-4848
www.abbayeauxdames.org

France Tourism Development Agency
825 Third Ave.
New York, NY 10022
212-838-7800; fax: 212-838-7855
int.rendezvousenfrance.com

♦ 2467 ♦ Saints, Doctors, Missionaries, and Martyrs Day
November 8

Since the Reformation the Church of England has not added saints to its calendar. Although there have certainly been many candidates for sainthood over the past 450 years, and many martyrs who have given their lives as foreign missionaries, the Church of England has not canonized them, although a few are commemorated on special days. Instead, since 1928 it has set aside November 8, exactly one week after ALL SAINTS' DAY, to commemorate "the unnamed saints of the nation."

See also ST. CHARLES DAY.

♦ 2468 ♦ Sakata Chauth
January-February; fourth day of the waning half of the Hindu month of Magha

Hindu men and women fast on this day in honor of GANESH, the Hindu god of wisdom with the head of an elephant, because it is believed to be the day of his birth. After being bathed first thing in the morning, the statue of Ganesh is worshipped with sweets and balls made of *jaggery* (a coarse, dark sugar made from palm trees) and sesame seeds. When the moon rises the fast is broken, and the moon god is worshipped and offered water. The day-long fast observed on Sakata Chauth is believed to ensure wisdom, a trouble-free life, and prosperity.

♦ 2469 ♦ **Sallah (Salah) Festival**
10th day of Islamic month of Dhual-Hijjah

ID AL-ADHA is an occasion of much pomp and ceremony in Nigeria, where it is also known as the **Durbar Festival**. This is the culmination of the Muslim PILGRIMAGE TO MECCA and a day of communal prayer. People throng together in their best regalia. Processions of nobles on horseback are led by the emir to the prayer grounds. After a prayer service, the emir, dressed in white and carrying the historic sword of Katsina, is seated in state on a platform. Groups of men take turns galloping up, reining in so their horses rear up at the last moment, and salute the emir. He raises the sword in response. Later, there is entertainment by musicians, acrobats, jesters, and dancers. Niger and some other African countries also celebrate the day with elaborate festivities.

See also ID AL-FITR (NIGERIA).

CONTACTS:
Embassy of the Federal Republic of Nigeria
3519 International Ct. N.W.
Washington, D.C. 20008
202-986-8400; fax: 202-362-6541
www.nigeriaembassyusa.org

♦ 2470 ♦ **Salvation Army Founder's Day**
April 10

April 10 is the day on which William Booth (1829-1912), founder of the international religious and charitable movement known as the Salvation Army, was born in Nottingham, England. His work as a pawnbroker in London acquainted Booth with all forms of human misery and economic suffering, and his conversion to Methodism led to a career as a Methodist lay preacher and eventually as an independent evangelist.

With the help of his wife, Catherine Mumford, he established the East London Revival Society, which soon became known as the Christian Mission and later the Salvation Army, characterized by its military ranks, uniforms, flags, bands, and regulation books. Booth's work encompassed social reform as well as religious conversion, and he set up children's and maternity homes, food and shelter stations, and agencies for helping discharged criminals. The Salvation Army expanded to the United States in 1880, and today it has outposts in more than 80 countries.

Although Booth's birthday is observed to varying degrees at Salvation Army outposts around the world, a major celebration was held on the organization's centennial in 1965. In the United States, there were open houses at Salvation Army institutions, special commemorative religious services, and other anniversary events. In London, a centennial congress was held in the Royal Albert Hall. The Salvation Army regards 1865 as the year of its founding because on July 2 that year, William Booth first preached at an open-air meeting in London's East End, a slum district notorious for its poverty and crime rate.

CONTACTS:
Salvation Army
International Headquarters
101 Queen Victoria St.
London, EC4V 4EH United Kingdom
44-207-332-0101
www.salvationarmy.org

♦ 2471 ♦ **Salzburg Festival**
July-August

Although the city of Salzburg, Austria, did little to honor its most famous native son during his lifetime, it has been making up for the oversight ever since. The Salzburg Festival is so closely identified with Wolfgang Amadeus MOZART (1756-1791) that it is often referred to simply as the **Mozart Festival**. Although it features musical events by a wide variety of composers and performances by internationally celebrated musicians, conductors, singers and instrumentalists, the festival has always paid special homage to Mozart—especially so in 1991 during the Mozart bicentennial celebration.

The festival takes place at the end of July and through most of August at different venues throughout the city. Most of the operatic and large orchestral pieces are performed in the Festspielhaus, while other performances take place in the Landestheater. Chamber music concerts are usually given in the hall of the Mozarteum, and the Residenz is the scene for serenade concerts held by candlelight. Visits to Mozart's birthplace at Getreidegasse 9 are especially popular during the festival.

CONTACTS:
Salzburg Festival
Hofstallgasse 1
Salzburg, Salzburg 5020 Austria
43-6628-0450
www.salzburgerfestspiele.at

♦ 2472 ♦ **Samhain (Samain)**
November 1

This ancient Celtic harvest festival was celebrated at the beginning of winter. According to Celtic folklore, this was the day when the souls of the dead and other supernatural entities gathered and would have access to the human realm— thus giving rise to the fears about ghosts and goblins that we now associate with HALLOWEEN, or Samhain Eve.

♦ 2473 ♦ **Sàmi Easter Festival**
March to April, depending on the date of Easter

The Sàmi Easter Festival takes place annually during Easter week in Kautokeino, Norway. The Sàmi people are the indigenous people of the northernmost Nordic regions, including northern Norway. Festival activities include tours by reindeer-drawn sleigh, ice fishing, and snowmobiling. There are art exhibitions and several concerts, with some featuring traditional yoik, as well as modern music of the Samis. The festival is also host to the annual reindeer-racing world-cup race. A highlight of the event is an outdoor drive-in cinema for snowmobiles, known as the Ice Cinema. A film festival runs every year in conjunction with the Sàmi festival, with a variety of films on offer for viewing indoors or out. The main festival launched in 1972, with the film festival debuting in 1997.

CONTACTS:
Royal Norwegian Embassy in Washington
2720 34th St. N.W.
Washington, D.C. 20008 United States
202-333-6000; fax: 202-469-3990
www.norway.org

♦ 2474 ♦ Sàmi National Holiday
February 6

The Sàmi people (formerly known as Lapplanders) are indigenous to the arctic area of the Nordic countries, including Norway, Sweden, Finland, and Russia. Many Sàmi make a living in reindeer husbandry and fishing. Nature is very important to the Sàmi.

The Sàmi have not always had an easy life in Norway. At the end of the 1800s, the Norwegian government implemented policies of Norwegianization, which required everyone to conform to the Norwegian way of life. Schools were not allowed to teach Sàmi language or culture. However, attitudes changed by the mid-1950s, and Norwegian authorities recognized the importance of maintaining the Sàmi culture. Since then, policies have been modified to reflect these changing attitudes, and Norway now embraces the Sàmi language, traditions, and culture.

February 6 is recognized as Sàmi National Holiday in Norway, Sweden, Finland, and Russia. This day is full of activities that celebrate the Sàmi culture. Sàmi National Holiday was first celebrated in 1993 and has become a popular event and a time for the indigenous Sàmi people to celebrate their cultural identity.

CONTACTS:
Royal Norwegian Embassy in Washington
2720 34th St. N.W.
Washington, D.C. 20008
202-333-6000; fax: 202-469-3990
www.norway.org/embassy

♦ 2475 ♦ Samil-jol (Independence Movement Day)
March 1

The Korean national holiday Samil-jol celebrates the anniversary of the independence demonstrations in 1919 protesting the Japanese occupation. (*Samil* means 'three-one,' signifying third month, first day.) Japan had taken over Korea in 1910, depriving Koreans of many of their freedoms. The March 1 movement was a turning point; an estimated two million people took to the streets in peaceful demonstrations, and a declaration of independence was read at a rally in Seoul. The demonstrations were met with thousands of arrests, and close to 23,000 Koreans were killed or wounded. Independence leaders formed a provisional government abroad, and there were major anti-Japanese rallies in the 1920s, but independence didn't come until 1945 with Japan's surrender and the end of World War II. The day is marked with the reading of the 1919 Declaration of Independence at Pagoda Park in Seoul.

See also KOREA LIBERATION DAY.

CONTACTS:
Embassy of the Republic of Korea
2450 Massachusetts Ave. N.W.
Washington, D.C. 20008 United States
202-939-5600; fax: 202-797-0595
usa.mofa.go.kr/english/am/usa/main

♦ 2476 ♦ Samoa Independence Day
June 1

Samoa (called Western Samoa until 1997) gained independence from New Zealand on January 1, 1962. Because the rainy season in Samoa comes in January, however, celebrations are held in June on the first day of the month.

CONTACTS:
Permanent Mission of Samoa to the UN
800 Second Ave.
Ste. 400 J
New York, NY 10017
212-599-6196
www.un.int/samoa

♦ 2477 ♦ Samvatsari
August-September; Hindu month of Bhadrapada

Samvatsari is celebrated by the followers of Jainism, one of the oldest religions in the world. The festival, which falls on the final day of the eight-day religious event called Paryushana, is considered one of the holiest days in the Jain calendar. Essentially a monastic practice, the celebration is filled with rituals, prayers, and contemplation. Many of the rituals are based on the tenet of harmlessness—unwillingness to harm any living creature by thought, word, or action—which is one of the main pillars of Jainism. During Samvatsari, devotees dress as religious ascetics and seek atonement for their transgressions, both voluntary and involuntary, by uttering the words "Micchami Dukkadam," which mean, "may all the evil that has been done be fruitless." The event is also a time for reflection, introspection, and a cleansing of the soul to rid the self of all impurities. Jains from all over the world visit temples to listen to spiritual leaders and perform prayer rituals.

CONTACTS:
Federation of Jain Associations in North America
Jaina HQ
722 S. Main St.

Milpitas, CA 95035
510-730-0204
www.jaina.org

♦ 2478 ♦ **San Antonio, Fiesta**
Ten days including April 21

The Fiesta San Antonio is a 10-day extravaganza of events held since 1901 in San Antonio, Tex., including SAN JACINTO DAY, April 21. The fiesta celebrates the 1836 Battle of San Jacinto that won Texas' independence from Mexico, and is much more than a simple independence celebration. The distinctive highlight of the fiesta is the Battle of Flowers Parade alongside the ALAMO. Merrymakers originally pelted each other with flowers, but now people crush *cascarones*, decorated eggshells filled with confetti, on each others' heads. Another focal event is "A Night in Old San Antonio," which actually goes on for four nights, bringing thousands into La Villita—"the little town," the earliest residential area of the city, now restored—for block dancing and more than 200 booths selling all kinds of ethnic foods. Some 150 other events include concerts, flower and fashion shows, sporting events, art fairs, a *charreada* (Mexican rodeo), dances and pageants with people in lavish costume, torchlit floats in the Fiesta Flambeau Parade, and decorated barges in the San Antonio River Parade.

CONTACTS:
Fiesta San Antonio Commission
2611 Broadway
San Antonio, TX 78215
210-227-5191 or 877-723-4378; fax: 210-227-1139
www.fiesta-sa.org

♦ 2479 ♦ **San Blas, Fiesta of**
February 3

San Blas is the patron saint of Paraguay, and his feast day, February 3, is observed throughout the country. Asunción and other large cities host religious processions, and the smaller villages often have bullfights on this day. Flowers, ribbons, and paper money (attached to the tail) adorn the bull. Because this event is a humorous commentary on bullfighting rather than a real bullfight, the goal is not to kill the bull. Instead, bullfighters try to grab hold of the bull and remove the money from its tail without getting hurt.

See also ST. BLAISE'S DAY.

CONTACTS:
Embassy of the Republic of Paraguay
2400 Massachusetts Ave., N.W.
Washington, D.C. 20008
202-483-6960; fax: 202-234-4508
www.mre.gov.py

♦ 2480 ♦ **San Diego Comic-Con International**
A weekend in July

The San Diego Comic-Con International is an annual event that draws around one million visitors, including many film stars, writers, cartoonists, authors, and producers. It was founded in 1970 by comic book fans. Since 1991, the San Diego Convention Center in San Diego, California, has hosted the event.

Close to 700 programs take place in the event's exhibit hall, which spans over 600,000 square feet. During the show, the hall comes alive with comic book, movie, and science fiction characters. One popular program at the convention is the Comic-Con International Independent Film Festival, during which viewers and industry experts screen films in the genres of action, animation, documentary, horror, comedy, and fantasy. Educational and academic programs like the Comic Arts Conference are also part of the event. Moreover, the Will Eisner Comic Industry Awards, considered the Oscars of the comic book industry, are announced at the convention.

CONTACTS:
Comic-Con International
P.O. Box 128458
San Diego, CA 92112
www.comic-con.org

San Diego Convention Center
111 W. Harbor Dr.
San Diego, CA 92101
619-525-5000
visitsandiego.com

♦ 2481 ♦ **San Estevan, Feast of**
September 2

The Feast of San Estevan is a harvest dance and annual feast day in the Indian pueblo of Acoma in New Mexico. Acoma is a cluster of adobes atop a barren mesa 367 feet above a valley. It was established in the 12th century and is the oldest continuously inhabited community in America. Only about 50 people now live there year-round, but Acoma people from nearby villages return for feast days and celebrations.

The mesa is dominated by the mission church of San Estevan del Rey, which was completed in 1640 under the direction of Friar Juan Ramirez. All the building materials, including massive logs for the roof, had to be carried from the valley below. Supposedly Friar Juan had gained both the confidence of the Acoma people and access to the mesa by saving an infant from a fall off the mesa's edge. His delivery of the child back to the mother was considered a miracle.

A mass and procession begin the feast day. The statue of the patron saint, ST. STEPHEN (San Estevan in Spanish) is taken from the church to the plaza where the dances are performed from 9:00 A.M. to 5:00 P.M. There are 15 or so different dances—Bear, Butterfly, and Rainbow are some of them.

Acoma also has two rooster pulls, one in June and one in July. These are religious sacrificial ceremonies, during which prayers are offered for rain, for persons who need help, and for the country. Animal rights activists have protested the sacrificial aspect of these rites.

CONTACTS:
Indian Pueblo Cultural Center

2401 12th St. N.W.
Albuquerque, NM 87104 United States
505-843-7270 or 866-855-7902
www.indianpueblo.org

♦ 2482 ♦ San Fermin Festival
July 6-14

The festivities surrounding this well-known festival in Pamplona, Spain, honoring the city's bishop, begin with a rocket fired from the balcony of the town hall. Bands of *txistularis* (a Basque word pronounced chees-too-LAH-rees)—with dancers, drummers, and *txistu* players (a musical instrument like a flute)—and bagpipers march through the town and its suburbs playing songs announcing the "running of the bulls," an event that has taken place here for 400 years. Each morning, young men, dressed in typical Basque costumes, risk their lives running through the streets of Pamplona ahead of the bulls being run to the bullring where the bullfights will be held. Perhaps the best-known portrayal of this scene occurs in Ernest Hemingway's novel, *The Sun Also Rises*..

CONTACTS:
Pamplona Tourist Office
Avenida Roncesvalles 4
Pamplona, Navarre 31001 Spain
484-842-0420
www.turismo.navarra.es/eng/fijos/contacto

♦ 2483 ♦ San Francisco Ethnic Dance Festival
June

The annual San Francisco Ethnic Dance Festival was founded in 1978 to promote the diverse dance companies of the San Francisco Bay area in California. This unique event provides artists with the opportunity to express their cultural and ethnic heritage through the medium of dance. Dance companies and soloists audition in over a hundred different dance genres, including classical, sacred, social, and folk, among others. Many international groups, from Senegalese *Kaolack* dancers to Mexican *folkorico* dancers, perform at the festival. This combination of international artists, all from different socioeconomic backgrounds, occupations, and lifestyles, helps the festival create a mosaic of contemporary cultures. Some performers are second- or third-generation dancers who preserve and reinvent the work of the festival's pioneers. The event is mainly held at the Palace of Fine Arts in San Francisco with four performances each weekend of June.

CONTACTS:
World Arts West, Fort Mason Center
2 Marina Blvd., Bldg. D
Ste. 230
San Francisco, CA 94123
415-474-3914; fax: 415-474-3922
worldartswest.org

♦ 2484 ♦ San Francisco, Fiesta of
September 26-October 4

In Quibdó, Colombia, the Fiesta of San Francisco is one of the biggest celebrations of the year. The town is divided into eight sections, and each is responsible for putting up its own decorations and altars in preparation for the procession on October 4, which is the highlight of the festival. But several days of sports—which include boxing, horse-racing, cycling, and pig-catching contests—precede this. The streets are filled with people dressed up as devils, savages, and various animals, and there are dancing and fireworks every night. Mock bullfights are held with *vacalocas* (crazy cows), which are wooden cows or bulls with flaming horns.

On the final day, there is an afternoon procession in which everyone—the local police, schoolchildren, religious organizations, and members of the general public—accompany the statue of ST. FRANCIS as it is carried through the streets of Quibdó.

CONTACTS:
Embassy of Colombia
2118 Leroy Pl. N.W.
Washington, D.C. 20008 United States
202-387-8338; fax: 202-232-8643
www.colombiaemb.org

♦ 2485 ♦ San Francisco International Film Festival
April

The San Francisco International Film Festival is the longest-running film festival in the Americas. Sponsored by the San Francisco Film Society, it was first launched in 1957 by film exhibitor Irving "Bud" Levin, who started the event as a philanthropic endeavor to expose local citizens to the art form of cinema and secure a place for San Francisco in the international art scene. The festival successfully introduced foreign films to the American public. The two-week festival features more than 150 films, including features, documentaries, animated shorts, experimental work, and digital media presentations. It attracts an audience of approximately 70,000 people each year. Other activities at the festival include seminars, industry panel events, award functions, tributes, and retrospectives.

CONTACTS:
San Francisco Film Society
39 Mesa St., Ste. 110
The Presidio
San Francisco, CA 94129
415-561-5000; fax: 415-440-1760
www.sffs.org

♦ 2486 ♦ San Francisco Pride
Last weekend in June

San Francisco Pride, also known as the San Francisco **Lesbian, Gay, Bisexual, and Transgender (LGBT) Pride Celebration,** is a festival and parade to celebrate the community of LGBT people and promote equality for all. First observed in Golden Gate Park in 1970, the festival has been held every year since except one. In 2014, the estimated attendance at the parade and festival was 1.7 million people, making it the largest event to date. According to the mission statement of the San Francisco Lesbian Gay Bisexual Transgender Pride Celebration Committee, the purpose of the event is to "educate the world, commemorate our heritage, celebrate our culture, and liberate our people." The event also has a charitable purpose, with over $2.4 million in proceeds donated since 1997 to support local LGBT organizations and other health and welfare groups. San Francisco Pride will celebrate its 45th anniversary in 2015, with the theme of "Equality without Exception."

CONTACTS:
San Francisco Pride
1841 Market St.
Fourth Fl.
San Francisco, CA 94103
415-864-0831; fax: 415-864-5889
www.sfpride.org

♦ 2487 ♦ San Francisco Street Food Festival
A Weekend in August

The San Francisco Street Food Festival celebrates the variety of different cuisines found on Folsom Street in the city's Mission District. First held in 2009, the annual event is organized by La Cocina, a female-led culinary incubator that helps women get started in food businesses. On Friday night, a large family-style meal is served to all attendees. On the following day, the main food activities take place from 11:00 a.m. to 7:00 p.m. More than 80 vendors sell various items related to international food culture and cooking. On Sunday, entrepreneurial conferences are presented on such food-industry-related topics as securing finance, overcoming barriers to entry, and choosing real estate.

♦ 2488 ♦ San Francisco's Day (Lima, Peru)
August 4 and October 4

On Santo Domingo's Day, August 4, and again on St. Francis's (San Francisco's) Day on October 4, there is a fiesta in Lima where the two saints and their churches exchange greetings. A procession sets out from each church, complete with its own music, major-domo, and image of the saint carried on a litter. The two groups meet in the plaza under a decorated triumphal arch, at which point the litters are lowered in commemoration of the historical meeting between the two men, who died only five years apart in the 13th century. Church bells ring and fireworks are set off, with elaborate banquets to follow at the monasteries of the saint whose day is being celebrated.

See also ST. FRANCIS OF ASSISI, FEAST OF.

CONTACTS:
Commission for the Promotion of Peru
Calle Uno Oeste 50
Mincetur Bldg,
13 & 14th Fl.
Peru
511-616-7300
www.promperu.gob.pe

♦ 2489 ♦ San Gennaro, Feast of
September 19

San Gennaro, or St. Januarius, fourth-century bishop of Benevento, is the patron saint of Naples, Italy. According to legend, he survived being thrown into a fiery furnace and then a den of wild beasts, but was eventually beheaded during the reign of Diocletian. His body was brought to Naples, along with a vial containing some of his blood. The congealed blood, preserved since that time in the Cathedral of San Gennaro, is claimed to liquefy on the anniversary of his death each year— an event that has drawn crowds to Naples since 1389.

Scientists have recently come up with a possible explanation for the phenomenon: certain substances, including some types of mayonnaise, are normally thick gels that can be liquefied instantly by shaking or stirring. Left standing, such liquids soon revert to gels. The answer may never be known because, to date, the Roman Catholic Church has forbidden opening the vial and analyzing its chemical nature.

The Society of San Gennaro in New York City's "Little Italy" section began holding a San Gennaro festival on Mulberry Street in 1925. Since 1996, however, the festival has been organized by the Figli (Children) of San Gennaro, an organization within the Archdiocese of New York City. The 11-day event attracts nearly two million spectators. It includes processions carrying a statue of St. Januarius from the shrine at Most Precious Blood Church as well as a street fair. One of the goals of the event is to find a mate for the festival queen, who more often than not has married within two years after her festival reign. Proceeds from the festival go to low-income schools and parishes on the city's Lower East Side. In 2001, the festival was cancelled due to the nearby terrorist attacks of September 11. Instead, the church held a memorial service followed by a candlelight procession of the statue of the saint.

See also HOLY BLOOD, PROCESSION OF THE.

CONTACTS:
Italian National Tourist Board
686 Park Ave.
Third Fl.
New York, NY 10065
212-245-5618; fax: 212-586-9249
www.italiantourism.com

♦ 2490 ♦ San Geronimo Feast Day
September 29-30

San Geronimo Feast Day is the feast day for St. Jerome, the patron saint of Taos Pueblo, probably the best known of the 19 Indian pueblos (villages) in New Mexico. For 1,000 years, the Tiwa-speaking Taos Indians have lived at or near the present pueblo. In the 1540s Spanish soldiers arrived, thinking they had discovered one of the lost cities of gold. The gold-brown adobe, multi-story structures are the largest existing pueblo structures of their kind in the U.S., unchanged from the way they looked to the Spaniards, and are still the home of about 1,500 residents.

The feast day commences on the evening of Sept. 29 with a sundown dance, followed by vespers in the San Geronimo Mission. On the following day, there are foot races in the morning, and in the afternoon, frightening looking "clowns" with black-and-white body paint and wearing black-and-white costumes climb a pole; the act has secret religious significance to the Taos. An Indian trade fair offers Indian crafts and foods for sale.

The Taos Pueblo is also known for its CHRISTMAS celebrations, lasting from Christmas Eve through Dec. 29. On CHRISTMAS EVE, there is a pine torch procession from the church through the plaza, and on Christmas Day, the Deer Dance is often performed.

CONTACTS:
Taos Pueblo Tourism
120 Veterans Hwy.
Taos, NM 87571
575-758-1028
www.taospueblo.com

♦ 2491 ♦ San Ildefonso Firelight Dances
January 22-23

These late January festivities mark a highlight in the ceremonial year at San Ildefonso Pueblo near Santa Fe, New Mexico. January 23 is the pueblo's feast day, celebrated with a special church service and dances, such as the Buffalo, Comanche, and Deer dances. The dances are a way of paying respect and giving thanks for the animals on which people depend for food and other materials. On the evening before, there are bonfires and a firelight procession.

CONTACTS:
Pueblo de San Ildefonso
02 Tunyo Po
Santa Fe, NM 87506
505-455-2273
www.sanipueblo.org

Indian Pueblo Cultural Center
2401 12th St. N.W.
Albuquerque, NM 87104
505-843-7270 or 866-855-7902
www.indianpueblo.org

♦ 2492 ♦ San Isidro in Peru, Fiesta of
First two weeks in May

ST. ISIDORE is the patron saint of agriculture, and in the agricultural community of Moche, Peru, the celebration of his festival (May 15) lasts throughout the first two weeks in May. Every night during this period the image of San Isidro, garbed in simple clothes and a hat woven from straw, spends the night at a different farm. The image is placed on an outdoor altar decorated with whatever fruits and vegetables that particular farm produces, and there is considerable competition among the farmers to exceed each other in setting up these altars. After the saint leaves, the altar is taken down and the fruit is distributed among neighbors and guests. A band escorts the saint to the home of his next host.

The saint is returned to the church in Moche on the afternoon of May 14. The straw hat is removed and a silver one put in its place, along with a velvet cape embroidered with gold, in preparation for the procession on May 15. On the nights of May 14 and 15, devil dancers wearing horned masks roam the countryside, taking from small farms whatever they can lay their hands on. Because they are known as the "devils of San Isidro," their deeds go unpunished.

CONTACTS:
Embassy of Peru
1700 Massachusetts Ave. N.W.
Washington, D.C. 20036
202-833-9860; fax: 202-659-8124
www.embassyofperu.org

Commission for the Promotion of Peru for Export and Tourism
Calle Uno Oeste 50
San Isidro, Lima Peru
511-616-7300; fax: 511-224-7134
www.promperu.gob.pe

♦ 2493 ♦ San Isidro of Seville, Feast of
April 4

St. Isidro or Isidore (c. 560-636) was born in Cartagena, Spain, and eventually became bishop of Seville, a post formerly held by his older brother, St. Leander. St. Isidro is known for creating schools throughout the country and, especially, his writing of the *Etymologies*, an encyclopedic treatment of all kinds of subjects ranging from mathematics to theology. His feast day is celebrated not only in Spain, but in many Latin American countries as well.

In Río Frío, Colombia, April occurs in autumn and is typically very dry. On San Isidro's feast day, April 4, townspeople process the saint's image around the streets and hope that he will help bring some much-needed rain. The procession traditionally takes two steps forward, then one step backward, and so on, with the idea that if it drags out long enough, some rain may fall before the festivities end. If no rain falls, the people who had been singing praises to St. Isidro during the procession may well begin to insult and swear at him.

♦ 2494 ♦ San Isidro the Farmer, Feast of
May 15

The **Feast of St. Isidore the Ploughman** is celebrated in Madrid, Spain, with eight days of bullfighting at the Plaza de Toros, colorful parades, and many artistic, cultural, and sporting events. Street vendors sell pictures of the saint, small glass or pottery bells believed to ward off harm from thunder and lightning, and whistle-stemmed glass roses, which provide a noisy accompaniment to the feasting and dancing that go on.

San Isidro (c. 1070-1130) is the patron saint of Madrid and also of farmers. He worked on a farm outside Madrid. According to legend, one day, as his master was spying on him to see how hard he was working, an angel and a yoke of white oxen appeared at Isidro's side. He was canonized in

1622, and local farmers still attend a special mass on his feast day, May 15. The Festival of San Isidro is celebrated in other Spanish towns as well, particularly León and Alicante.

San Isidro is also the patron saint of Saipan, capital of the Northern Mariana Islands in the western Pacific Ocean near Guam. While dance groups practice, men form hunting and fishing parties to provide food, and youth organizations clean and prepare the festival site. The fiesta begins at the end of a novena (nine days of prayers and special religious services). It features games of skill and traditional dances with prizes for the winners, and a great variety of foods.

Philippine towns and villages also commemorate St. Isidro. In Quezon Province, ornaments made from rice meal dyed in bright colors, called *kiping*, are attached to the fronts of houses. Townspeople and the priest parade through town and when that's over, the kiping are eaten.

See also CARABAO FESTIVAL and ST. ISIDORE, FESTIVAL OF.

CONTACTS:
Madrid Municipal Office of Tourist Information
Plaza Mayor, 3
Spain
34-91-366-5477
www.madridcitytourist.com

♦ 2495 ♦ **San Jacinto Day**
April 21

Fresh from his March 1836 victory at the Battle of the ALAMO, General Antonio López de Santa Anna (1795?-1876) of Mexico proceeded eastward until he encountered the Texan army general, Samuel Houston (1793-1863), at a place called San Jacinto, about 22 miles east of the present-day city of Houston. Raising the now familiar cry of "Remember the Alamo!" Houston's 900 soldiers defeated the Mexican force of nearly 1,600 in a battle that lasted only 18 minutes. Santa Anna was taken prisoner and forced to sign a treaty pledging his help in securing independence for Texas, which was annexed by the United States in 1845.

A legal holiday in Texas, San Jacinto Day is celebrated throughout the state but particularly in San Antonio, where the highpoint of the 10-day SAN ANTONIO FIESTA is the huge Battle of Flowers parade winding through miles of the city's downtown streets.

CONTACTS:
Texas State Historical Association
1400 W. Highland St.
Denton, TX 76201
940-369-5200; fax: 940-369-5248
www.tshaonline.org

♦ 2496 ♦ **San José Day Festival**
March 19 and September 19

The San José Day Festival at Laguna Pueblo, about 45 miles west of Albuquerque, New Mexico, used to take place only on ST. JOSEPH'S DAY, March 19. But today it is also celebrated on September 19, when freshly harvested crops can be sold and festivities enjoyed in the summer weather.

The fiesta's events reflect both traditional Laguna events and the Roman Catholic influence common to the pueblos. There are Catholic masses and processions honoring St. Joseph as well as traditional Laguna dancing. Attendees, including other native peoples, can also enjoy a carnival with rides, numerous food stands, and sporting events. One of the largest draws is the annual All-Indian Baseball Tournament in September; Laguna boasts five semi-pro baseball teams.

CONTACTS:
Indian Pueblo Cultural Center
2401 12th St. N.W.
Albuquerque, NM 87104 United States
505-843-7270 or 866-855-7902
www.indianpueblo.org

♦ 2497 ♦ **San Juan and San Pedro Festivals**
June 24; June 29

The celebrations of ST. JOHN'S DAY (June 24) and ST. PETER'S DAY (June 29) in Tobatí, Paraguay, have much in common. Both have a religious element, with special masses, and a traditional folk element, with a game called *Toro Candil*. In this game, someone plays the toro, or bull, by wearing a hide-covered frame with a bull's skull attached to the front and chasing everyone around. His horns are wrapped with rags drenched with kerosene and set on fire, so that when darkness falls and he chases spectators through the streets, the flaming horns make the game more exciting.

Other costumed characters who play a part in the game include a *ñandú guazú* (a rhea, which is similar to an ostrich) and men playing Guaycurú Indians dressed in rags with faces painted black. The ñandú—actually a child inside a small leaf-covered cage—follows the bull around, and pesters him. The Guaycurú chase women around and threaten to abduct them. Other participants in the festival carry blazing torches and menace women—a remnant, perhaps, of the ancient festivals observed on June 24 with bonfires and the practice of walking barefoot over live coals (*see also* MIDSUMMER DAY).

CONTACTS:
Embassy of Paraguay
2400 Massachusetts Ave. N.W.
Washington, D.C. 20008 United States
202-483-6960; fax: 202-234-4508
www.mre.gov.py/embaparusa/en/index-eng.html

♦ 2498 ♦ **San Juan de Dios, Fiesta of**
March 7-8

San Juan de Dios (St. John of God) was born in Portugal in 1495. He was a soldier for Spain for some years, but after his troop was disbanded in 1536, he took up a life as a shepherd. John underwent a period of emotional and spiritual difficulty when he was around 40. With the assistance of a priest, he found some stability and decided to devote his life to God, eventually establishing a house in Granada for the sick and the poor. John fell ill after rescuing a man who was in danger of drowning in a flood, and he died in 1550 when he was 55. A religious order, the Brothers Hospitallers, was founded in his honor, and thereafter he was known as John of God and the patron saint of hospitals.

In Puno, Peru, San Juan de Dios is celebrated with a two-day fiesta. On March 7, llamas bring in dry wood for bonfires in a parade with flute and drum music, and in the evening bonfires blaze. The next day, St. John of God's feast day, a procession takes the saint's image through the streets of Puno, and dancers and musicians create a festive atmosphere around the church.

CONTACTS:
Commission for the Promotion of Peru
Calle Uno Oeste 50, Edificio Mincetur
Pisos 13 y 14
Lima, Lima 27 Peru
511-616-7300; fax: 511-224-7134
www.promperu.gob.pe

♦ 2499 ♦ San Juan Pueblo Feast Day
June 24

San Juan Pueblo Feast Day is a day to honor St. John the Baptist, the patron saint of the San Juan Pueblo, near Espanola, New Mexico. The pueblo, where the first New Mexican capital was founded by the Spaniards in 1598, is headquarters today for the Eight Northern Indian Pueblos Council.

The San Juan feast day observations, like those of other New Mexican pueblos, combines Roman Catholic ritual with traditional Indian ceremonies.

The celebration begins on the evening of June 23 with vespers and mass in the Church of St. John the Baptist. After the services, St. John's statue is carried to a shrine prepared for it in the pueblo's plaza. This procession is followed by a one-mile run in which anyone can participate; a "sing" by the pueblo war chiefs, or officers; a procession of singers and runners; and two Buffalo dances, each presented by two men and one woman wearing buffalo costumes.

The actual feast day begins with a mass, and is followed by an assortment of dances, which usually include Buffalo, Comanche, and Green Corn (harvest) dances. Men beat drums and chant as the dancers, arrayed in long lines and wearing body paint and elaborate costumes with feathers and beads, move slowly and rhythmically to the beat. Vendors sell jewelry, crafts, and assorted souvenirs, and a carnival with a ferris wheel and carousel is also part of the celebration.

See also ST. JOHN'S DAY.

CONTACTS:
Ohkay Owingeh Pueblo
491 Old Santa Fe Trail
Santa Fe, NM 87501 United States
505-827-7400; fax: 505-827-7402
nmtourism.org

♦ 2500 ♦ San Lorenzo, Día de
August 10

St. Laurence of Rome was a deacon under Pope Sixtus II in the third century. According to legend, St. Laurence was cooked alive on a gridiron, a few days after the pope was martyred. In the midst of his torture, it is said he suggested that his tormentors turn him over to ensure that he would be well-roasted. His feast day is August 10.

As the patron saint of Zinacantan, Chiapas State, Mexico, San Lorenzo is honored with a five-day festival that takes place August 7-11 each year. The highlight is a procession, interrupted periodically by a dance performed by the *Capitanes*. Each dancer holds one foot out in front while hopping on the other foot for a time, then they shift so that the opposite foot is held out. Thousands attend the festival, which includes a huge open market and a fireworks display.

♦ 2501 ♦ San Marino Anniversary of the Arengo
March 25

The Republic of San Marino, a landlocked nation surrounded by Italy, is the smallest republic in the world. It is also the oldest existing state in Europe.

The Arengo was the first form of government in the Republic of San Marino. Under this form of government, all of the patriarchs assembled to decide on important matters dealing with public life in San Marino. This was workable while the population of San Marino was small. But as the population continued to grow, they needed a new means of governing the country.

In 1243, the first two Consuls, the Captains Regent, were elected to office for a period of six months. Every six months, new Captains Regent were appointed. From that point, the Arengo did not meet as an assembly of Patriarchs until March 25, 1906. By then, it was much different from its original form and purpose. The Arengo was still part of community life and met twice a year, in April and October. When new regents were elected, every patriarch could send petitions and requests of public interest to the Grand and General Council.

The Arengo still exists today. Twice a year, the citizens of San Marino can send requests of public interest to the Grand and General Council through their regents. Within one month the regents must decide whether the requests will be discussed in the Council.

March 25 in San Marino is a national holiday that commemorates the Arengo of 1906, which marked the birth of a Parliament elected directly by the people. On this day, all of the military corps appear in full-dress uniform in front of Palazzo Begni. A laurel wreath is placed on the monument to the Fallen, and the ceremony continues with a mass in the Basilica to thank the founder saint. All of the corps participate in a parade through the streets of the old town center.

CONTACTS:
Republic of San Marino Tourist Office

Contrada Omagnano 20
San Marino
378-549-882914; fax: 378-549-882575
www.visitsanmarino.com

◆ 2502 ◆ San Marino Investiture of New Captains Regent
April 1 and October 1

The Republic of San Marino, a landlocked nation surrounded by Italy, is the smallest republic in the world. It is also the oldest existing state in Europe.

The first form of government in San Marino was the Arengo. Under this form of government, all of the patriarchs assembled to decide on important matters dealing with public life in San Marino. This was workable while the population of San Marino was small. But as the population continued to grow, they needed a new means of governing the country.

In 1243, the first two Consuls, the Captains Regent, were elected to office for a period of six months. Every six months, new Captains Regent were appointed. This form of rule has continued to date.

Every April 1 and October 1, the Heads of State are installed in office in a traditional ceremony that follows the centuries-old protocol.

According to the rules, the ceremony begins at 9.45 A.M. with a flag-raising ceremony in Piazza della Libertà, by the Guard of Honour of the Great and General Council, the Militia, and the Military Band. Between 10:00 A.M. and 1:00 P.M., the Captains Regent, the Authorities, and the Diplomatic and Consular Corps, dressed in traditional costumes, are escorted by the Military Corps in a parade that winds along the narrow streets of the old town center. After a ceremony at Palazzo Valloni and in the Basilica del Santo, they meet again in the Government Building, where the exchange of powers takes place between the Captains Regent who have just terminated their mission and the new Captains Regent who are about to guide the republic for the next six months. These ceremonies are open to the public. In fact, the public and visitors to the country are encouraged to witness these time-honored ceremonies.

An important part of this ceremony is when the Official Speaker makes a speech relating to major problems or issues of international importance.

◆ 2503 ◆ San Marino Liberation Day (Feast Day of Saint Agatha)
February 5

The Republic of San Marino, a landlocked nation surrounded by Italy, is the smallest republic in the world. It is also the oldest existing state in Europe.

Republic of San Marino was twice occupied by military forces, but only for a few months each time: in 1503 by Cesare

Borgia, known as Valentino, and in 1739 by Cardinal Giulio Alberoni. Freedom from Borgia came after the tyrant died, while in the case of Cardinal Alberoni, civil disobedience was used to protest against this abuse of power.

In 1739, Cardinal Alberoni invaded San Marino and occupied the country. For the next several months, the people of San Marino protested the occupation and appealed to the Vatican. Clandestine messages were sent to obtain justice from the Pope. The Pope recognized the rights of San Marino and on February 5, 1740, he restored the country's independence.

Today, San Marino celebrates Liberation Day on February 5 to mark the anniversary of the liberation of San Marino. As part of the celebration, there is a public procession from the city of Borgo Maggiore to the capital city of San Marino proper. In addition, various civic celebrations take place throughout the day.

February 5 in San Marino is also dedicated to Saint Agatha, the "co-patron" of the city. Special services are held on this day. In San Marino, Saint Agatha is second only to Saint Marinus, the legendary stone-mason and philosopher who is said to have founded the original city of San Marino.

◆ 2504 ◆ San Martín Day
Monday after August 17

This national holiday in Argentina honors José Francisco de San Martín, who died on this day in 1850.

Spain had ruled what is now Argentina, as well as nearly all the rest of South and Central America, since the 16th century. Born in 1778 in a town called Yapeyú, San Martín, formerly a soldier in the Spanish army in Europe, came home in 1812 to fight in the revolution against Spain. He led forces across the Andes—an unprecedented accomplishment—to defeat the Spanish in Chile and Peru. The victories he led assured independence from Spain for much of the region.

After passing the torch to Simon Bolívar, another famous South American revolutionary leader (*see also* BOLIVIA INDEPENDENCE DAY), San Martín resigned in 1822. He left Argentina in 1824, and lived out his life in exile in France.

CONTACTS:
Embassy of Argentina
1600 New Hampshire Ave. N.W.
Washington, D.C. 20009 United States
202-238-6400; fax: 202-332-3171
embassyofargentina.us/embassyofargentina.us/en/theembassy/main.htm

◆ 2505 ◆ San Miguel, Fiesta de
September 29

On ST. MICHAEL'S DAY in Taypi, La Paz Department, Bolivia, there is a fiesta that demonstrates the importance of both maintaining and crossing the boundaries that exist between communities. Two dance groups—one from Taypi and the other from Ranikera, about three hours walking distanceaway—meet in the town square for religious ceremonies and dance performances. Both groups perform at the same time, but do so as individual units, without mingling with the other group. They also maintain their boundaries while eating and resting, each group at one far end of the square. Five communal meals are served, with dancing in between, while spectators from other nearby towns observe the proceedings without entering the festival space.

CONTACTS:
Embassy of Bolivia
3014 Massachusetts Ave. N.W.
Washington, D.C. 20008 United States
202-483-4410; fax: 202-328-3712
www.bolivia-usa.org

♦ 2506 ♦ **San Pedro International Costa Maya Festival**
July or August

Ambergris Caye is the largest island of Belize and a major historical site of the Mayan empire, a vast pre-Colombian civilization that extended from Honduras to Mexico. It is also the site of the San Pedro International Costa Maya Festival, an annual event that celebrates the region's Mayan heritage and entices tourists from around the world. Performing at the festival are dancers, musicians, and other entertainers who represent the five countries of the Mundo Maya (Maya World): Mexico, Belize, Guatemala, Honduras, and El Salvador.

The festival began after several leaders of a Belizean chamber of commerce were inspired by a Honduran cultural celebration in 1991. They decided to launch their own party the following year. They set up the festivities in San Pedro Town, the main hub on Amergris Caye. The event's original name was the International Sea & Air Festival, a reference to the aircraft and sea vessels that attendees used to travel to the festivities.

Today, the weeklong festival is considered the biggest in Belize. The opening night is devoted to the Reina de la Costa Maya (Queen of the Mayan Coast), a beauty pageant that has been held since 1996. Each successive night is devoted to highlighting a different Mundo Maya country. Performers from all countries gather for Sunday's grand finale show.

Musicians perform a wide range of music including reggae, salsa, merengue, and traditional Maya. Dancing often accompanies the music performances and enhances the display of traditional culture.

CONTACTS:
Belize Tourism Board
64 Regent St.
P.O. Box 325
Belize
501-227-2420 or 800-624-0686
www.travelbelize.org

Embassy of Belize
2535 Massachusetts Ave. N.W.
Washington, D.C. 20008
202-332-9636; fax: 202-332-6888
www.embassyofbelize.org

♦ 2507 ♦ **San Roque, Fiesta of**
Week beginning the first Sunday in September

San Roque is the patron saint of Tarija, Bolivia, whose natives, known as *chapacos*, are a mixture of Spaniards and Tomata Indians.

The townspeople wear their best and most colorful clothes—and decorate their dogs—for the fiesta in San Roque's honor that begins on the first Sunday in September. There are processions of the saint's image, which has also been brightly adorned, throughout the week which go through the streets, stopping at the hospital and area churches. Participants in the processions include dancers, singers, musicians, and people who've made personal vows.

The celebration of San Roque is said to go back to colonial times, when a plague devastated the city. After the Spanish colonists prayed to San Roque, the disease reportedly subsided, thus the people began an annual fiesta in thanksgiving.

CONTACTS:
Embassy of Bolivia
3014 Massachusetts Ave. N.W.
Washington, D.C. 20008 United States
202-483-4410; fax: 202-328-3712
www.bolivia-usa.org

♦ 2508 ♦ **Sandburg Days Festival**
Three days in April

This festival honors Carl Sandburg (1878-1967), a Pulitzer Prize-winning American poet and biographer of Abraham LINCOLN. It is sponsored by the Carl Sandburg Historic Site Association, located at the home where Sandburg was born in Galesburg, Illinois. Literary, history, sporting, theatrical, musical, and children's events are held at the Sandburg house, Knox College, and other venues in Galesburg during the three-day festival, as well as a golf tournament and a folk concert.

As a poet, Sandburg is best known for writing about American cities, particularly Chicago, and for incorporating American folklore in his poems. He also published a highly acclaimed autobiography, *Always the Young Strangers* (1953), which described his boyhood in Galesburg.

CONTACTS:
Carl Sandburg Historic Site Association
2163 E. Main St.
Galesburg, IL 61401
309-343-2485
www.visitgalesburg.com

♦ 2509 ♦ **Sandcastle Competition**
Usually July

The Sandcastle Competition is a cash-prize arts competition in the most ephemeral of media, sand and water, held since 1981 in Imperial Beach, Calif. Close to 250,000 spectators come for the parade, the food booths, the fireworks, the band concert—and the sand-castle building. This is no child's play; about 400 amateur and professional contestants compete for cash prizes totaling more than $20,000. Professionals make money building huge sand castles in malls and hotels.

There are specific rules regarding the construction of the castles: no adhesives can be used, but water spray rigs are allowed to keep the art works from drying out and blowing away; teams can number up to 10, but no substitutions are permitted.

In the past, the sand sculptures have represented assorted animals from the nearby San Diego Zoo, including hippos, lions, elephants, and creatures of the sea. One "castle" was a sand sofa with a sand man seated on it, a sand dog by his side, a sand television set, and a sand beer can. The sculpting is always scheduled for a Sunday, and by Sunday night the elaborate works of art, some 14 feet long, are lost to high tide.

The date of the festival is set through checking oceanographic tide tables to make sure the sculpting happens on a day when the tide is lower than normal. Events preceding the Sunday competition are a casual-dress Sandcastle Ball on Friday night, a community breakfast, parade, children's sand-sculpting contest, art exhibits, and fireworks. On Sunday, there's nothing but sculpting and live music.

♦ 2510 ♦ Sanghamita Day
May-June; full moon day of Hindu month of Jyestha

Observed by Buddhists in Sri Lanka (formerly Ceylon), this day celebrates the arrival of Sanghamita, daughter of Emperor Asoka of India, in 288 B.C.E. According to legend, Buddhism was first brought to Sri Lanka by a group of missionaries led by Mahinda, Asoka's son. Mahinda later sent for his sister, Sanghamita, who arrived with a branch from the Bodhi tree at Gaya, sacred to Buddhists as the tree under which the Buddha was sitting when he attained Enlightenment. The sapling was planted in the royal city of Anuradhapura, where Sanghamita founded an order of nuns. Buddhists still make pilgrimages to the city on this day to see what is believed to be the oldest documented tree in the world.

See also POSON.

CONTACTS:
Sri Lanka Tourism
No. 80, Galle Rd.
Colombo, 3 Sri Lanka
411-242-6900; fax: 411-244-0001
www.srilanka.travel

♦ 2511 ♦ Sango Festival
Early November

Sango has an extremely prominent cult among the Oyo people of Nigeria. Because Sango, a former Oyo ruler, is identified with thunder and lightning, the festival held in his honor takes place toward the end of the rainy season in early November and features various ceremonies connected with rain magic.

On the first day of the seven-day festival, women form a procession to the river, where they sink a hollow calabash gourd filled with special medicines to mark the beginning of the dry season. The *Timi*, or king, meets the worshippers at a place near the river, accompanied by drummers, trumpeters, and a huge crowd of onlookers. The women of the palace put on a special musical performance praising all the tribe's rulers throughout its history.

The remainder of the week is devoted to similar performances of music and dance before the Timi, although their real purpose is to please and entertain the god Sango. The main performer each day dances in a self-induced trance-like state, during which it is believed that he speaks with the voice of Sango and is impervious to pain. The festival concludes on the seventh day with a procession of fire in which a worshipper carries a large pot containing a sacred flame that brings blessings to all parts of the village.

CONTACTS:
Embassy of the Federal Republic of Nigeria
3519 International Ct. N.W.
Washington, D.C. 20008 United States
202-986-8400; fax: 202-362-6541
www.nigeriaembassyusa.org

♦ 2512 ♦ Sani Gourmet
May

Sani Gourmet is an international food festival hosted by the Sani Resort Hotel in the Chalkidiki region of Greece. The event features cuisine from Mediterranean and Asian cultures, including Near-East countries such as Iran, Azerbaijan, and Georgia. Restaurants host tastings and other programs, such as cooking demonstrations, workshops, discussions, and wine tastings.

CONTACTS:
Sani Gourmet
55, N. Plastira St.
Thessaloniki, 54250 Greece
2310-317-327; fax: 2310-317-881
www.sanigourmet.gr/En

♦ 2513 ♦ Sanja Matsuri (Three Shrines Festival)
Weekend near May 18

One of the most spectacular festivals in Tokyo, Japan, Sanja Matsuri honors Kannon, the GODDESS OF MERCY (known as Kuan Yin in Chinese), and three fishermen brothers who founded the Asakusa Kannon Temple in the 14th century. *Sanja* means "three shrines," and, according to legend, after the brothers discovered a statue of Kannon in the Sumida River, their spirits were enshrined in three places. The festival has been held each year since the late 1800s on a weekend near May 18. Activities are focused on the Asakusa Temple and Tokyo's "Shitamachi," or downtown area.

More than 100 portable shrines called *mikoshi*, which weigh up to two tons and are surmounted by gold phoenixes, are paraded through the streets to the gates of the temple. Carrying them are men in *happi* coats—the traditional short laborers' jackets—worn to advertise their districts. There are also priests on horseback, musicians playing "sanja-bayashi" festival music, and dancers in traditional costume. On Sunday, various dances are performed.

CONTACTS:
Asakusa Shrine
2-3-1 Asakusa, Taito
Tokyo, 111-0032 Japan
81-3-3844-1575; fax: 81-3-3841-2020
www.asakusajinja.jp

Tokyo Convention & Visitors Bureau
Nisshin Bldg. 6F
346-6 Yamabuki-cho
Shinjuku-ku
Tokyo, 162-0801 Japan
81-3-5579-2680; fax: 81-3-5579-2685
www.tcvb.or.jp

◆ 2514 ◆ Sanno Matsuri
Every two years in June

Held in Tokyo at the Hié Shrine, the Sanno Matsuri is held every two years, alternating with the Kanda Matsuri at the Kanda Shrine. During the Edo era (1603-1867) when Japan was ruled by the shogun, this festival was attended by the shogun himself. More than 40 festival floats were paraded through the streets, although today only three *mikoshi* (portable shrines) are seen.

People in special holiday outfits jam into the shrine complex. On June 15, the shrine's mikoshi and gilded lions' heads are brought out for the main parade, along with the *dashi* (festival floats or carts) sent by each of the surrounding districts. They are accompanied by about 400 participants dressed in costumes of the Heian Era (9th-12th centuries). The *miko*, shrine maidens, perform *kagura*—sacred dance and music in honor of the gods.

A good-luck ceremony associated with the Sanno Matsuri is known as the *Chi-no-Wa Shinji*. It involves passing—twice to the left and once to the right—through a big circle woven together with *chigaya* (a kind of grass) attached to a frame made of bamboo.

CONTACTS:
Tokyo Convention & Visitors Bureau
Nisshin Bldg. 6 Fl.
346-6 Yamabuki-cho
Shinjuku-ku, Tokyo 162-0801 Japan
81-3-5579-2680; fax: 81-3-5579-2685
www.tcvb.or.jp/en

◆ 2515 ◆ Sant' Efisio, Festival of
May 1-4

Although nearly every town and village in Sardinia, Italy, has its own festival, one of the most important is the **Sagra di Sant' Efisio** at Cagliari, which commemorates the martyrdom of a third-century Roman general who was converted

to Christianity and was credited with saving the town from the plague. In early May a procession accompanies a statue of St. Efisio, Sardinia's patron saint, through the streets of Cagliari to the church of Pula, the town where he suffered martyrdom. Three days later the statue returns to Cagliari. Several thousand pilgrims on foot, in carts, or on horseback, wearing costumes that date from the 17th century and earlier, take part in the procession, which culminates in a parade down Cagliari's main avenue that is said to rival the parade on ST. PATRICK'S DAY in New York City.

CONTACTS:
Italian National Tourist Board
686 Park Ave.
3rd Fl.
New York, NY 10065
212-245-5618; fax: 212-586-9249
www.italiantourism.com

◆ 2516 ◆ Santa Fe Chamber Music Festival
July-August

This festival in Santa Fe, New Mexico, started in 1973 and has since produced a range of musical programs from the baroque to the modern. The festival began impressively: the acclaimed cellist Pablo CASALS (1876-1973) was the first honorary president, and artist Georgia O'Keeffe (1887-1986) produced the first of her now-famous posters and program covers. Fourteen artists presented six Sunday concerts that first year; now dozens of musicians of international acclaim take part. Youth concerts, open rehearsals, in-state tours to Indian reservations and small communities, out-of-state tours, and National Public Radio broadcasts have expanded the audiences.

Santa Fe, with its ancient tri-ethnic culture, has a great roster of historic buildings, and from time to time they serve as concert halls. For instance, chamber music concerts have been presented in the Romanesque Cathedral of St. Francis, built in 1869; the Palace of the Governors, in continuous use since 1610; and the 18th-century Santuario de Nuestra Señora de Guadalupe, where altar bells rather than dimming lights signal the end of intermissions.

CONTACTS:
Santa Fe Chamber Music Festival
P.O. Box 2227
Santa Fe, NM 87504 United States
505-983-2075 or 888-221-9836
www.santafechambermusic.com

◆ 2517 ◆ Santa Fe, Fiesta de
September, weekend after Labor Day

The Fiesta de Santa Fe is a religious and secular festival said (without much argument) to be the oldest such event in the country. It dates to 1712 and recalls the early history of Santa Fe, New Mexico.

The Spanish *conquistadores* were ousted from Santa Fe in 1680 in a revolt by the Pueblo Indians. Led by Don Diego de Vargas, the Spanish peacefully regained control in 1693. Vargas had promised to honor *La Conquistadora*, the small statue of the Virgin Mary that is now enshrined in St. Francis Cathedral, if she granted them success. The first procession was held in 1712 to fulfill that promise.

The festivities start the Thursday night after LABOR DAY with the burning of Zozobra, or Old Man Gloom, a 50-foot-high fabric and wood effigy whose yearly immolation began in 1926. Thousands watch and shout "Burn him!" when the effigy groans and asks for mercy. Fireworks announce the end of Gloom. The next morning there is a mass. Then comes the grand procession: Vargas and the fiesta queen, *la reina*, lead the way on horseback to the town plaza, escorted by the *Caballeros de Vargas,* Vargas's guards or manservants, who are also on horseback.

Afterwards, spectators make their way to the plaza for the start of three days of dancing, street fairs, a grand ball, and a parade with floats satirizing local politicians. The fiesta ends Sunday night with a mass of thanksgiving and a candlelight procession to the Cross of Martyrs overlooking Santa Fe.

CONTACTS:
Santa Fe Fiesta Council Inc.
P.O. Box 4516
Santa Fe, NM 87502 United States
505-913-1517
www.santafefiesta.org

♦ 2518 ♦ **Santa Fe Opera Festival**
End of June through August

The internationally acclaimed Santa Fe Opera Festival began in 1957 and survived the burning of the opera house in 1967. It is now staged in an open-air opera "house" atop a mesa outside Santa Fe, New Mexico, that was renovated from 1996 to 1998.

The Gala Opening Celebration includes an Opera Ball to benefit apprentice programs for young artists, and, on opening night, a festive reception, tailgate parties (with tablecloths and caviar and people in formal dress) and, after the performance, waltzing for the entire audience.

CONTACTS:
Santa Fe Opera
P.O. Box 2408
Santa Fe, NM 87504
505-986-5955 or 800-280-4654
www.santafeopera.org

♦ 2519 ♦ **Santa Inés, Fiesta of**
Week preceding the Sunday nearest January 21

The Mayas of Yucatán, Mexico, celebrate this fiesta in the town of Dzitas, which is located near the well-known Chichén Itzá ruins. The preparation of foods for the fiesta, especially the grinding of the maize for the cakes known as *arepas*, takes place on the Wednesday preceding the Sunday nearest January 21, which is the most important day. Some of

these cakes are consumed right away by the *cargadores*, as the men in charge of the fiesta are known, and some are offered to visitors, whom villagers expect will donate funds toward the cost of the festival.

The highlight of the Santa Inés Fiesta is an organized Mayan dance known as a *jarana*. A thatched enclosure is built especially for the dance, which is performed by Maya young people. Dancing couples face one another, the men with their hands in back of them and the women lifting their skirts just a bit. The dance floor may hold more than 200 pairs of dancers at a time, and the jarana is considered a good opportunity to meet young people of the opposite sex.

On the final Sunday another ritual, called the pig's head dance, is held to transfer authority to those who will organize the following year's fiesta. Some of the dancers carry roasted pigs' heads decorated with colored paper flags. At the end of the dance, each new cargador receives one of the pig heads from his predecessor, a symbol of the authority and responsibility that has been conferred on him.

CONTACTS:
Mexico Tourism Board
225 N. Michigan Ave.
Ste 1850
Chicago, IL
786-621-2909
www.mexico.us

♦ 2520 ♦ **Santa Isobel, Fiesta of**
July 4

Santa Isobel is the great fiesta of the Yaqui Indians of southern Arizona and Mexico, observed on July 4. It features the coyote dance—a ceremonial dance performed for soldiers, chiefs, and pueblo officials who have died, as well as at certain specific fiestas. Three men, each wearing the head and hide of a coyote and holding a bow which they strike with a piece of cane, perform a slow step in a crouching position, stamping the ground with the flat of their feet to the accompaniment of a water drum. All night long the dancers advance toward and retreat from the drum, their motions mimicking those of a coyote. Just before dawn, a plate of meat is placed in front of each of the dancers. Each man picks the meat up in his teeth, just as a coyote would, and delivers it to the drum.

CONTACTS:
Pascua Yaqui Tribe
7474 S. Camino de Oeste
Tucson, AZ 85746
520-883-5000; fax: 520-883-5014
www.pascuayaqui-nsn.gov

♦ 2521 ♦ **Santa Rita, Fiesta of**
MAy 22

It is said that when St. Rita was a child, she wanted to become a nun, but she ended up marrying to please her parents. Her husband turned out to be abusive, unfaithful, and, about 20 years into their marriage, was involved in some activity that got him murdered. Rita then fulfilled her childhood dream and joined a nunnery at Cascia, Italy. Her ministry as a nun focused on caring for the ill and troubled until she died of tuberculosis in 1447.

Villagers in Apastepeque, San Vicente Department, El Salvador, celebrate Santa Rita's feast day, May 22, with a dance-drama called the Dance of the *Tunco de Monte*, or Wild Pig. This is an Indian dance going back to pre-Christian times and is popular among Indians all over El Salvador. One person dresses in pig skins and pretends to be a pig, while other dancers portray various other stock characters. They enact the chasing and, finally, killing of the pig. At the concluding "feast" the hunter who has caught the pig alternates between praying to Santa Rita for the welfare of the village and cracking jokes.

CONTACTS:
Monastero Santa Rita
Santa Rita Ave., 13
Cascia, PG 06043 Italy
39-762-210-743; fax: 39-767-860-743
www.santaritadacascia.org

♦ 2522 ♦ **Santa Rosalia Fishermen's Festival**
September, weekend after Labor Day

St. Rosalia is the patron saint of Palermo, and Sicilian Americans living in Monterey, California, observe a two-day festival in her honor in the hope that she will protect their fishermen at sea and provide an abundant catch.

The Santa Rosalia Fishermen's Festival dates prior to World War II, when a statue of the saint was taken in procession from San Carlos Church to fishermen's wharf. A blessing of the fleet followed, and the statue of Santa Rosalia was returned to the church for a concluding religious ceremony. By the early 1950s, however, the festival had expanded to include fireworks, parades, water events, contests, and colorful fishing nets decorating the streets of downtown Monterey.

Today the festival also celebrates Italian heritage with a traditional bocci ball competition, Italian music and food, and an arts and crafts fair.

CONTACTS:
Monterey County Convention & Visitors Bureau
P.O. Box 1770
Monterey, CA 93942
888-221-1010
www.seemonterey.com

♦ 2523 ♦ **Santamaría (Juan) Day**
Mid-April

Juan Santamaría is remembered as a national hero in Costa Rica. The country had been threatened in 1856 by William Walker, an American imperialist who planned to use his mercenary army to conquer Central America and use its citizens for slave labor. Walker had already taken control of Nicaragua and organized a similar invasion of Costa Rica.

Santamaría, a 19-year-old drummer boy from the town of Alajeula, was part of the makeshift militia that fought Walker's forces. On April 11, 1856, Santamaría volunteered for a dangerous assignment. There are conflicting stories about his actions, which either set fire to Walker's fort or his ammunitions store. In any event, Santamaría was killed in the process, and Walker's forces were eventually repelled.

Juan Santamaría Day is actually a week-long festival of parades, concerts, dancing, and marching bands throughout the country, with the biggest celebrations in Alajeula. The official holiday, when schools, government offices, and businesses are closed, is usually on April 11, the anniversary of Santa María's death. But the official date has been changed in recent years. If April 11 occurs during Easter week or on a weekend, the national holiday is celebrated on the closest Monday.

CONTACTS:
Consulate General of Costa Rica
2112 S. St. N.W.
Washington, D.C. 20008
202-499-2991; fax: 202-265-4795
www.costarica-embassy.org

♦ 2524 ♦ **Santander International Festival of Music and Dance**
July-August

Santander, a resort town in northern Spain on the Atlantic coast, is not only a popular summer vacation destination but also the home of an international music and dance festival that has been held there since 1951. The month-long festival offers symphonic, choral, and chamber music; recitals; classical and Spanish dance; and jazz. Although the programs are chosen more for their broad appeal than for their adventurousness, some of the great international ensembles of the world have performed at Santander. Events are held at the Festival Palace of Cantabria, which opened in 1991 opposite the Bay of Santander, as well as at various churches, monuments, and historic sites around the city.

CONTACTS:
Palace of Festivals Cantabria
Gamazo, s/n.
Santander, 39004 Spain
34-942-361-606; fax: 34-942-364-780
www.palaciofestivales.com

♦ 2525 ♦ **Santo Toribio Fiesta**
April 27

According to legend, St. Toribio arrived in La Villa de Macate, Peru, at a time when the stream that had supplied the town with water had gone dry. The inhabitants were about to prepare to move elsewhere when St. Toribio knocked his staff against the rocks that surrounded the spring three times, releasing a torrent of water.

On April 27, there is a fiesta held in La Villa de Macate where this miracle is reenacted. After a procession in which the saint's image is carried to the place where the miracle occurred, the priest strikes the same rock three times with a staff, and the water, which has been temporarily diverted, again floods the streambed.

CONTACTS:
Commission for the Promotion of Peru for Export and Tourism
Calle Uno Oeste 50
Mincetur Bldg.
13 & 14 Fl.
Peru
51-1-616-7300
www.promperu.gob.pe

♦ 2526 ♦ Santon Fair
December

Santons are the small, colored clay figures that appear in crèches throughout France at CHRISTMAS. Thousands of people come from all over to purchase their santons at the Santon Fair, which takes place during the month of December in Marseilles. In addition to the usual biblical figures, a number of local figures, garbed in traditional Provençal clothing, can be purchased at the fair. They are made by local families who have passed down the molds and models from generation to generation since the 17th century.

♦ 2527 ♦ Sao Paulo Gay Pride Parade
May June

The São Paulo Gay Pride Parade, held each June in Brazil's most populous city, is an event to celebrate gay identity and promote gay rights. Though the inaugural parade in 1997 drew only 2,000 participants, the parade has grown significantly every year since and is now the second largest annual event held in the city after the Formula One Grand Prix. In 2006, the Guinness Book of World Records named the São Paulo Gay Pride Parade the largest pride parade in the world. Still widely viewed as the world's largest, the parade has attracted the participation of 3,000,000 people in recent years. Beginning at the Museum of Art of São Paulo, parade marchers and rolling floats wind through the heart of downtown São Paulo to Roosevelt Square, often taking eight hours to traverse the 2.6 mile route. The parade is the highlight and culmination of a week-long gay pride celebration that includes concerts, dance performances, street fairs, and educational events. The 20th anniversary São Paulo Gay Pride Parade will take place in 2016.

CONTACTS:
Sao Paulo Gay Pride Parade
245 S.E. 1st St.
Ste. 311
Miami, FL 33131
305-722-5447 or 866-930-6020; fax: 305-722-7398
www.gaypridebrazil.org

♦ 2528 ♦ São Tomé and Principe National Independence Day
July 12

On this day in 1975, São Tomé and Principe gained official independence from Portugal and became a democratic republic. July 12 is a national holiday in São Tomé and Principe.

CONTACTS:
Navetur, Sao Tome and Principe Tourism Agency
Rua Viriato da Cruz
P.O. Box 227
São Tomé and Principe
239-222-2122 or 239-222-1748
www.navetur-equatour.st

Permanent Mission of Sao Tome and Principe to the UN
400 Third Ave.
Ste. 1807
New York, NY 10017
212-651-8116; fax: 212-651-8117
www.un.int

♦ 2529 ♦ Sapporo Snow Festival (Yuki Matsuri)
February 5-11 (or February 6-12 if February 11 falls on a Saturday or Sunday)

An exuberant celebration of snow and ice held since 1950 in Sapporo, the capital city of the Japanese island of Hokkaido. In 1974, the first international Snow Statue Contest was held. The week's activities feature a colorful parade and competitive events in winter sports. What particularly draws more than two million tourists, though, is the display of colossal ice sculptures along the main street and snow statues in Odori Park.

Because of the shortage of snow in the festival area, thousands of tons of snow are trucked in from the suburbs. The sculptures are spectacular—intricately carved and often several stories high. About three weeks before the festival the work begins: a wooden frame is built and packed with snow; after the snow has hardened the frame is removed and the carving begins. A different theme is chosen each year for the sculptures.

CONTACTS:
Sapporo Snow Festival - Tourism Department
60 E. 42Nd St.
Ste. 448
New York, NY 10165
212-757-5640; fax: 212-307-6754
www.jnto.go.jp

♦ 2530 ♦ Sarasota Circus Festival and Parade
January

Colossal! Spectacular! The Sarasota Circus Festival and Parade is a non-stop circus early in the year in the capital of the circus world, Sarasota, Fla. The festival has included a parade in downtown Sarasota. Events include shows of magic, juggling, clowning, dog stunts, knife throwing, and various other acts all day long. In addition, there are outdoor "thrill shows"—performers on high sway poles, on high wires, and on motorcycles on high wires. And there are displays of miniature circuses, arts and crafts, and a circus art and photography show.

Sarasota was put on the circus map in 1927 when John Ringling, one of the founding Ringling brothers, decided to make Sarasota the winter headquarters for the Ringling Bros. and Barnum & Bailey Circus. They moved in 1960 to nearby Venice, but Sarasota was by then established as a circus mecca, and many circus people now make their year-round homes there. Furthermore, the city is home to the Circus Hall of Fame and the Ringling Museum of the Circus. John Ringling's palatial home, Ca d'Zan, completed in 1925, can be seen there, along with the John and Mabel Ringling Museum of Art, which has a fine collection of the art work of Peter Paul Rubens.

CONTACTS:
Circus Arts Conservatory
2075 Bahia Vista St.
Sarasota, FL 34239
941-355-9335; fax: 941-355-7978
circusarts.org

♦ 2531 ♦ **Saratoga Festival**
June-August

The Saratoga Performing Arts Center in Saratoga Springs, New York, is the summer home of the New York City Ballet, the Philadelphia Orchestra, and the Spa Summer Theater. The festival held there every summer includes not only performances by these groups, but also a four-week summer school program for talented high school students interested in dance, orchestra and jazz studies, and theater. Ballet and orchestral performances take place in a partially enclosed amphitheater, and visitors often arrive a few hours early to picnic on the grass and enjoy the spacious grounds of the Saratoga Spa State Park, where the center is located.

The Saratoga Festival has seen a number of world premieres, among them the 1976 premiere of Gian Carlo Menotti's first symphony (*see* SPOLETO FESTIVAL USA) and the 1974 world premiere of the ballet, *Coppelia.* The summer theater performs both classical and contemporary plays in the center's 500-seat theater.

CONTACTS:
Saratoga Performing Arts Center
108 Avenue of the Pines
Saratoga Springs, NY 12866
518-584-9330; fax: 518-584-0809
www.spac.org

♦ 2532 ♦ **Sasquatch! Music Festival**
Memorial Day Weekend

Since 2002, fans of independent rock music have converged on central Washington for the Sasquatch! Music Festival, a three-day outdoor music festival in May. This event, which offers a serene view of the Columbia River gorge, is a welcome change from the dirt and the grime of many outdoor concert settings. The Gorge Ampitheatre has achieved acclaimed status as one of North America's premiere outdoor venues.

The Sasquatch! lineup usually features about two dozen bands, performing on the three stages of the Gorge Ampitheatre. Bands

not on the main bill perform on the Yeti Stage and the Wookie Stage. At the Sasquatch Mainstage, fans have the option of milling in the front or catching the music further back on the grassy hillside. The festival's organic approach and eco-friendly policy is bolstered by its purchase of carbon offsets.

CONTACTS:
SASQUATCH! Music Festival
754 Silica Rd. N.W.
Quincy, WA 98848
www.sasquatchfestival.com

♦ 2533 ♦ **Sata-Häme Accordion Festival**
Early July

Every summer, the Finnish town of Ikaalinen draws accordion players from all over Europe and as far away as South America to the Sata-Häme Accordion Festival. During festival week, they perform in the Finnish Folk Musician Championships and the finals of the Gold and Silver Accordion competitions. For some 30 years, festival goers have also enjoyed the free outdoor concerts held on Lake Kyrösjärvi, in the parks of Wanha Kauppala, and around the town. Accordion lessons and workshops are also offered.

CONTACTS:
Sata-Hame Accordion Festival
Karhoistentie 3 L 2a
Ikaalinen, 39500 Finland
358-43-217-0800
en.satahamesoi.fi

♦ 2534 ♦ **Satchmo SummerFest**
Early August

The Satchmo SummerFest is a celebration of the music and legacy of jazz musician Louis "Satchmo" Armstrong, who was born in New Orleans, La., on August 4, 1901. The four-day weekend festival takes place in early August in the city's French quarter. It started in 2001 as a commemoration of the centenary of the beloved performer's birth, and was such a success that it was adopted as an annual event by French Quarter Festivals, Inc.

At the center of the festival is jazz music performed on three stages devoted, respectively, to traditional jazz, contemporary jazz, and brass bands. Participants also honor Armstrong with an annual exhibit of art on a Satchmo theme, with awards for outstanding entries. There are speakers' seminars on the history of music, jazz exhibits, a children's stage, and a jazz-themed Catholic mass. Also featured is a "Satchmo Strut" through New Orleans' live music district, and plenty of New-Orleans-style food, including a red-beans-and-rice luncheon.

CONTACTS:
French Quarter Festivals Inc.
400 N. Peters St.
Ste. 205
New Orleans, LA 70130
504-522-5730 or 800-673-5725; fax: 504-522-5711
fqfi.org

♦ 2535 ♦ **Saturnalia**
December 17-23

This ancient Roman WINTER SOLSTICE festival began on December 17 and lasted for seven days. It was held in honor of Saturn, the father of the gods, and was characterized by the suspension of discipline and reversal of the usual order. Grudges and quarrels were forgotten; businesses, courts, and schools closed down; wars were interrupted or postponed; slaves were served by their masters; and masquerading or change of dress between the sexes often occurred. It was traditional to offer gifts of imitation fruit (a symbol of fertility), dolls (symbolic of the custom of human sacrifice), and candles (reminiscent of the bonfires traditionally associated with pagan solstice celebrations).

Households would select a mock king to preside over the festivities, which were characterized by various kinds of excesses—giving rise to the modern use of the term *saturnalian,* meaning "a period of unrestrained license and revelry.".

♦ 2536 ♦ **Saturnalia Roman Festival**
Second Sunday in January

The winter solstice celebration of Saturnalia, once a festive observance throughout the Roman Empire, was eventually subsumed by the celebration of Christmas. In the small Welsh village of Llanwrtyd Wells, located in an area that still features Roman structures and artifacts, residents devote a weekend to this long-forgotten holiday honoring the god Saturn.

Llanwrtyd Wells, which prides itself as the "wacky festival capital of the world," takes a tongue-in-cheek approach to the observance, which is organized to draw tourists as well as relive Roman culture. The festival's gladiator chariot race, for example, accompanies a winter beer festival and features mountain bikes towing barrels instead of proper horse-drawn chariots.

This event and others attract attendees dressed in the requisite togas and laurel hats. Festival goers remain in costume for the Saturnalia Ramble, a marked walk through the Welsh countryside along old Roman roads. To enhance the celebration, local pubs and restaurants offer Roman-themed food.

♦ 2537 ♦ **Saudi Arabia National Heritage and Folk Culture Festival (Janadriyah Festival)**
Two weeks in February/March

Janadriyah, a town located outside Riyadh, Saudi Arabia, is the site of an annual camel race every year that dates back to the early 1970s. The event attracted the country's traditionalists because it exemplified the older customs of Saudi Arabia, a country whose steps at modernization have been a source of national concern in recent decades.

Seeking to promote the traditional nature of this event and other customs, Saudi Arabian Crown Prince Abdullah ibn Abd al-Aziz and the National Guard established the National Heritage and Folk Culture Festival in 1985. The camel race remains the central event of this annual two-week festival, popularly called the **Janadriyah Festival**, but other activities promoting time-honored expressions and practices round out the program. Classical forms of poetry, dance, theater, and music are all featured, as well as exhibitions of traditional crafts.

About 3,000 camels and their jockeys compete in the big race before a large crowd, which typically includes Saudi Arabia's reigning monarch. Nearby the site of the race stands a permanent "heritage" village, where artisans like carpenters, blacksmiths, metalsmiths, and cobblers demonstrate their crafts. The village usually features a *beit sha'ar,* a Bedouin tent that offers spectators a vivid picture of nomad life.

Each night ends with nightly readings of poetry, lectures on Arabic literature, and music and dance performances by troupes from throughout the Arabian Peninsula.

CONTACTS:
Royal Embassy of Saudi Arabia
601 New Hampshire Ave., N.W.
Washington, D.C. 20037
202-342-3800
www.saudiembassy.net

♦ 2538 ♦ **Savitri-Vrata (Savitri Vow)**
May-June; 13th day of waning half of Hindu month of Jyestha

Savitri-Vrata is observed by Hindu women in honor of the legendary princess Savitri. She loved her husband, Satyavan, so much that she refused to leave him when he died, eventually persuading Yama, King of Death, to give him back. Women whose husbands are alive spend the day fasting and praying, anointing their husbands' foreheads with sandalwood paste, and showering them with gifts of food and flowers. Women whose husbands have died beg to be delivered from the miseries of widowhood in a future existence. The *vrata,* or vow, is a ritual practice observed by Hindu women for a period of 14 years to obtain their wish.

See also KARWACHOTH.

♦ 2539 ♦ **Savonlinna Opera Festival**
Early July to early August

The Savonlinna Opera Festival is a month-long music festival in Savonlinna, Finland. Considered one of Europe's most important musical events, it began in 1967 with a performance of Beethoven's *Fidelio.* In 1992, for its 25th anniversary, *Fidelio* was presented again, as well as George and Ira Gershwin's *Porgy and Bess,* produced by Opera Ebony of New York and conducted by Estonian maestro Eri Klas.

The main site of the festival is the Olavinlinna Castle, the best-preserved medieval fortress in Finland. It was built in 1475 and named by Swedes and Finns on the lookout for raiding Russian armies.

CONTACTS:
Savonlinna Opera Festival Office
3301 Massachusetts Ave. N.W.
Washington, D.C. 20008
202-298 5800; fax: 202-298-6030
www.finland.org

◆ 2540 ◆ Schäferlauf
August 24 or the following weekend

St. Bartholomew's Day is celebrated in Markgröningen and other towns in the Swabia district of Germany with a barefoot race among shepherds and shepherdesses of the Black Forest. The first known race in Markgröningen was in 1445. Today in Markgröningen, an international music festival is held the weekend before the race. Children of active shepherds still race barefoot, and the winning shepherd and shepherdess are given a sheep or a large mutton roast. After the race there are other pastoral activities, such as a shepherds' dance and a water-carriers' race in which contestants must balance a pail of water on their heads and pour it into a tub at the finish line.

CONTACTS:
City of Markgroningen
Marktplatz 1
Groningen, 71706 Germany
49-7145-13-245; fax: 49-7145-13-131
www.markgroeningen.de

◆ 2541 ◆ Schemenlauf
Between January 26 and March 3; week preceding Ash Wednesday

The Schemenlauf, or **Running of the Spectres**, takes place during the Carnival season at Imst, Austria, in the Tirolean Alps. The roots of this traditional Austrian celebration can be traced back to the Middle Ages, when people believed that the densely wooded mountain slopes were populated by good and evil spirits with the power to prevent or promote the growth of seeds in the ground. To ward off the evil spirits, they resorted to mummery and wore frightening masks (*see* Perchtenlauf) as they danced through the village making as much noise as they could. Originally the festival may have been a way of welcoming spring.

Only men are allowed to participate in the Schemenlauf at Imst. About 400 *Schemen* ("spectres") join the procession, often stopping to invite spectators to join them in the traditional circular dance. Visitors come from all over the world to see this colorful festival, which is followed by a night of revelry reminiscent of Mardi Gras celebrations elsewhere.

CONTACTS:
Embassy of Austria
3524 International Ct. N.W.
Washington, D.C. 20008
202-895-6700; fax: 202-895-6750
www.austria.org

Imst Tourismus
Johannesplatz 4
Imst, 6460 Austria

43-54-126-9100; fax: 43-54-126-9108
www.imst.at

◆ 2542 ◆ Schubertiade
Mid-June

When Austrian composer Franz Schubert (1797-1828) participated in concerts put on for a small group of friends and fans, these intimate gatherings became known as "Schubertiads." Since 1976, the festival in honor of Schubert's music known as Schubertiade has attempted to recreate this tradition. Under the artistic direction of Hermann Prey, who retired as artistic director in 1984, a 10-year cycle of Schubert's symphonies, songs, and piano concertos has been planned in the exact order in which they were composed, with chamber music, choral music, and operas performed in between. Since 1984, however, the program has also included works by composers other than Schubert.

Initially the concerts were given at the Palace of Hohenems in Hohenems, Austria, with the Alps rising in the background. During the 1990s the festival moved to Feldkirch, and now the Schubertiade is held in the village of Schwarzenberg at the Angelika-Kauffmann-Saal, a beautiful timber-framed hall, at the Kleine Dorfsaal next door, and at the Hotel Post in the neighboring village of Bezau.

A number of ensembles known for their interpretations of Schubert's work have participated in the festival, including the Brandeis Quartet, the Franz Schubert Quartet, the Amadeus Quartet, and the Vienna Philharmonic Orchestra.

CONTACTS:
Schubertiade GmbH
Schweizer Str. 1
Hohenems, 6845 Austria
43-5576-72091; fax: 43-5576-75450
www.schubertiade.at

◆ 2543 ◆ Schützenfest (Marksmen's Festival)
July

This event in Germany is a tradition going back 400 years. There are a number of marksmen's festivals held during the summer months. The biggest of these, in Hannover, is held for 10 days at the beginning of July and attracts about 200,000 spectators. It features merry-go-rounds, other carnival rides, and food booths, many serving sausage. The fair is highlighted by Europe's longest festival procession. There are marksmen's brass-and-pipe bands, paraders in folk costumes, floats, and horse-drawn carriages. Other notable marksmen's festivals are in Düsseldorf in July and in Biberach in Baden-Württemberg in June or July. The Biberach festival has been celebrated every year since 1649 and features a procession of more than 1,000 costumed children.

CONTACTS:
Hannover Marketing und Tourismus
Ernst-August-Platz 8
Hannover, 30159 Germany
49-511-12345-111; fax: 49-511-12345-112
www.hannover.de

◆ 2544 ◆ Schutzengelfest (Festival of the Guardian Angel)
Second Sunday in July

Schutzengelfest is a religious and social occasion in northern Switzerland observed since the 17th century. Its setting is the *Wildkirchli*, or "chapel in the wild," a cave in the Alpstein mountain range in the Appenzell Innerrhoden Canton. A Capuchin monk decided in 1621 that the cave, which is now renowned for prehistoric finds, was an ideal place for a mountain worship service. In 1679, Paulus Ulmann, a priest in nearby Appenzell, set up a foundation to ensure that services would continue.

The festival starts at 10 A.M. when a priest or monk from Appenzell conducts the worship service. Then, a yodelers' choir gives a festive concert, and participants start walking to the villages of Ebenalp or Aescher for feasting and dancing.

CONTACTS:
Switzerland Tourism
608 Fifth Ave.
New York, NY 10020
800-794-7795; fax: 212-262-6116
www.myswitzerland.com

◆ 2545 ◆ Schwenkfelder Thanksgiving (Gedaechtnisz Tag)
September 24

The Schwenkfelders who now live in Pennsylvania Dutch country are the descendants of a small Protestant sect that sprang up in Germany around the time of the Reformation. They were followers of Caspar Schwenkfeld (1489-1561), a Silesian Reformation theologian who founded the movement called "Reformation by the Middle Way." He and his followers separated themselves from orthodox Protestant circles and formed the small societies and brotherhoods that still survive in the United States as the Schwenkfelder Church, or "Confessors of the Glory of Christ."

In 1733, a handful of Schwenkfeld's followers arrived in Philadelphia, and a second group emigrated from Germany on September 22, 1734. The next day they swore their allegiance to the British king, then they spent the following day, September 24, expressing their gratitude to God for having delivered them from persecution. In the Pennsylvania Dutch counties where Schwenkfelders still live, this day is observed as a special THANKSGIVING Day.

CONTACTS:
Central Schwenkfelder Church
2111 Valley Forge Rd.
Lansdale, PA 19446
610-584-4480; fax: 610-584-5761
www.centralschwenkfelder.com

◆ 2546 ◆ Sea, Festival of the (Seamen's Day, Sjomannadagur)
First weekend in June

The Festival of the Sea is based on the Icelandic tradition of Seamen's Day, an occasion to honor all who make their living from the sea. It takes place annually, primarily in the city of Reykjavík, but also in fishing towns and villages nationwide.

Traditionally, fishermen compete during the festival in swimming and rowing races and other tests of strength, including the popular tug-of-war. However, the festival has been modernized in recent years, and now includes numerous cultural activities, parades, arts-and-crafts activities for kids, food fairs (featuring sea food in particular), and sailing competitions. In addition, newer residents of Iceland are given the opportunity to share the cultures of their homelands. Tourists come from far and wide to participate in the fun and to view boats and ships as they rest in the harbors.

◆ 2547 ◆ Sea Islands Black Heritage Festival
Mid-August

The Sea Islands Black Heritage Festival is a cultural festival held annually at Epworth by the Sea in St. Simons Island, Ga. The festival celebrates the local Gullah heritage and provides a means of preserving and promoting African culture in the diaspora.

The term Gullah, or Geechee, is used to refer to the African-American people and culture descended from slaves brought from Africa to the coastal region of South Carolina and the Georgia Low Country. Because of its relative geographic isolation in island communities, Gullah culture retained distinctly African and Caribbean features, including traditional foods, crafts, folk beliefs, and language.

Sponsored by A Project for Cultural Affairs (APCA), the Sea Islands Black Heritage Festival takes place on a weekend in mid-August and showcases Gullah/Geechee culture through storytelling, music, art, and such crafts as basket weaving, quilting, and preserve making. An opening night party is held on Friday night, and on Sunday visitors may tour sites connected with local black history. A special Children's Corner offers family activities throughout the weekend, including games, storytelling, crafts, and drumming.

◆ 2548 ◆ Sea Music Festival
Second weekend in June

The only event of its kind in the Western Hemisphere, the annual Sea Music Festival takes place during the second weekend in June at Mystic Seaport Museum in Mystic, Connecticut. Since 1980 the ships and exhibits representing a 19th-century maritime village along the Mystic River have been the backdrop for more than 40 musicians and chantey (pronounced SHANT-ee) singers from around the world. The festival, attracting about 10,000 visitors, is a tribute to the music that has been an integral part of shipboard life since the 16th century.

The festival offers performances of chanteys, or sailors' work songs, as well as "forebitters"—songs sung for entertainment. Most of the lyrics and melodies are of British or Irish origin, although many incorporate American fiddle tunes, African-American minstrel ditties, older ballads, and the popular music of the time. Chanteys helped the sailor maintain the rhythm of a tedious job. In fact, it was considered bad luck to sing a chantey when no work was being done.

The event features daytime and evening concerts Thursday through Sunday, symposia, workshops, and a dance. There is also a special preview concert for museum members that highlights a well-known performer each year.

CONTACTS:
Mystic Seaport
75 Greenmanville Ave.
PO Box 6000
Mystic, CT 06355
860-572-0711
www.mysticseaport.org

♦ 2549 ♦ Sea Offering Ceremonies
Varies

Offering ceremonies are an important practice in some Javanese religious groups. These ceremonies are often conducted by fishermen in coastal towns at various times of the year as their way of giving thanks to the sea god for their livelihood and of asking for his protection during the coming year.

In some places the Sea Offering Ceremony coincides with a major Muslim holiday. At Klidang Beach in Central Java, for example, it is held as part of ID AL-FITR. In Malang, East Java, it coincides with MAWLID AL-NABI, the Prophet Muhammad's birthday observance.

The offering ceremony held every August in Tegal, Central Java, is in many ways characteristic. There is a feast and a puppet show the night before the ceremony. In the morning, the fishermen bring their offerings down to the beach. A convoy of decorated boats sets out to sea, and the offerings— which often include food, flowers, or a bull's head— are thrown into the water.

♦ 2550 ♦ Seafair
July-August

Seafair is an annual summer festival for residents of and visitors to the Greater Puget Sound region of northwest Washington state. The three-week festival features more than 40 educational, cultural, and sporting events, most of which are water-related. It begins with the Pirates' Landing at Alki Beach in West Seattle and includes concerts, a torchlight parade, hydroplane races on Lake Washington, and Bon Odori (Japanese folk dancing) performances (*see also* OBON FESTIVAL). Local businesspeople are honored by being named Commodores, and scholarships are awarded to the festival Queen and Sea Princesses. Seafair claims to be one of the largest festivals in the United States, attracting more than 54 million visitors annually.

CONTACTS:
Seafair

2200 Sixth Ave.
Ste. 400
Seattle, WA 98121
206-728-0123
www.seafair.com

♦ 2551 ♦ Seagull-Calling Contest
First Saturday in May

The annual Seagull-Calling Contest is held at Marina Park in Port Orchard, Wash., on the first Saturday in May. Contestants of all ages can vie for the title of "Best Seagull Caller in the Country." There are solo, duet, trio, and group categories. Prizes are also awarded for such categories as the most seagulls lured, best costume, most authentic call, and cutest call. Baiting is permitted, so many of contestants bring such delicacies as greasy French fries to lure the gulls. Bribing the judges is not only allowed, it is encouraged. The event is free of charge, and usually draws between 40-50 contestants and many onlookers.

Conceived as a one-off publicity stunt for the centennial of Port Orchard in 1986, the contest has become a beloved event, much covered by national television programs.

♦ 2552 ♦ Sealing the Frost
Early April

The Cuchumatan Indians of Santa Eulalia in northern Guatemala hold a rather risky ceremony every year early in the planting season. The town of Santa Eulalia is perched high in the mountains and the Indians traditionally believe that the cold frost resides in a crack over the edge of a cliff outside town. In order to protect the new crops from a late frost, the religious leaders in town lead a procession to the cliff. They tie a rope around the waist of one of the leaders and lower him over the edge where he fills in the crack with cement to keep the frost in.

♦ 2553 ♦ Seattle International Dance Festival
June

The Seattle International Dance Festival, which takes place annually over two weeks in June, is an event dedicated specifically to celebrating and promoting contemporary dance forms from around the world. In addition to the dance performances, the festival features an educational institute that gives local dancers an opportunity to attend master classes and workshops with international artists and prepare a program to be presented at the festival. The purpose of the Seattle International Dance Festival is to engage the public in appreciation of contemporary and experimental dance by providing access to diverse performances in a festival environment the community can enjoy. Seattle's Khambatta Dance Company presented the first festival in 2006, and the company continues to act as festival producers. Since 2009, the festival has established a strong presence in the city's South Lake Union neighborhood, and a that community's continued development is a particular focus of festival organizers. South Lake Union hosts Art on the Fly, an outdoor street fair and dance party that kicks of the festival, a closing night cabaret-style performance in which the venue is not revealed until 24 hours in advance, along with numerous other related events.

CONTACTS:
Seattle International Dance Festival Beyond the Threshold
5609 34th Ave. S.W.
Seattle, WA 98126
206-552-0694; fax: 206-552-0694
www.seattleidf.org

♦ 2554 ♦ Seattle International Film Festival
May-June

The Seattle International Film Festival (SIFF) is renowned for discovering new talent and screening eclectic films. This 25-day festival is Seattle's best-known film event. It features around 450 American and international films, including several world premieres, with an annual audience of 150,000. The mission of SIFF is to promote film as a powerful medium that can bring about extraordinary transformation. The festival features movies from major and independent American studios as well as films from Latin America, Europe, Africa, and Asia. SIFF seeks to encourage cross-cultural understanding and education through film. An interesting component of SIFF is the "Secret Festival," which is a screening of four films. A select audience attends the event without knowing what will be shown, and viewers must sign an oath not to reveal what they see.

SIFF was co-founded by Dan Ireland and Darryl MacDonald in 1976. The duo also founded the Egyptian Theater at the former Masonic Temple on Seattle's Capitol Hill, which remains a prime venue for SIFF. Additionally, other locations are used as festival venues during the event, including the SIFF Cinema at Seattle Center.

CONTACTS:
Seattle International Film Festival
305 Harrison St.
Seattle, WA 98109
206-464-5830; fax: 206-264-7919
www.siff.net

♦ 2555 ♦ Sebring 12-Hour Race
March

The **International Grand Prix Sports Car 12-Hour Endurance Race** held every year in March ranks with the INDIANAPOLIS 500 and LE MANS as one of the three great auto races in the world. Held in Sebring, Florida, since 1950, the event draws nearly 100,000 spectators and has featured such world-renowned drivers as Mario Andretti, Juan Fangio of Argentina, and Stirling Moss of England.

CONTACTS:
Sebring International Raceway
113 Midway Dr.
Sebring, FL 33870

863-655-1442
www.sebringraceway.com

♦ 2556 ♦ Sechseläuten
Third Monday of April and preceding Sunday

This colorful springtime festival in Zurich, Switzerland, ushers in spring by exploding the *Böögg* ("snowman"), the symbol of winter. *Sechseläuten* means the "six-o'clock ringing," and the present custom stems from the 14th-century practice of ringing the cathedral bells at six in the evening (instead of wintertime seven) to proclaim the earlier end of the spring and summer work day. The first ringing of the six o'clock bell was a good excuse for a celebration.

Festivities begin with a children's parade on Sunday, with the children in historical costumes and accompanied by the Böögg, which is stuffed with cotton wadding and firecrackers. On Monday, members of the guilds (formerly, associations of craftsmen, but now social groups) parade through the flag-festooned city in medieval costumes, accompanied by bands. Everyone converges at Sechseläutenplatz on the shore of Lake Zurich at six that evening, the bells ring, groups on horseback gallop around the Böögg to the music of a hunting march, and then the Böögg explodes and burns. Torchlight parades go on into the night, and feasts are held at guild halls.

♦ 2557 ♦ Seged
November; 29th day of eighth lunar month

Seged is a religious festival of unclear origin observed only by Ethiopian Jews known as the Falashas or the Beta Israel. It begins with a procession up a hill to the place where the ritual will be held. The participants wear clean, preferably white, clothes with colored fringe, symbolic of the state of purity in which they have kept themselves by avoiding sexual intercourse and bodily contact with non-Falashas for seven days. The priests, who lead the procession, sing prayers and carry the *Orit* (the Jewish scriptures in Geez—an ancient local language—written on parchment) and other holy books wrapped in colored cloth. Everyone who climbs the hill carries a stone, which is placed on an already existing circular wall marking the holy area where the Orit will be placed.

The ceremony itself includes a commemoration of the dead, where those who wish to honor their deceased relatives place a seed of grain on the stone wall for each relative and say a special prayer. There are also readings from the Orit and donations of money to the priests. After the service is over, the procession moves back down the hill to the prayerhouse, where food for the communal meal—usually *indjära* (bread), *kay wot* (meat stew), and *t'alla* (beer)—is distributed. The remainder of the day is spent in non-religious festivities, especially singing and dancing to the music of *masänqos* (one-stringed bowed lutes).

♦ 2558 ♦ Seijin-no-Hi (Adults Day; Coming-ofAge Day)
Second Monday in January

This national holiday in Japan honors those who reached their 20th birthday (voting age) in the previous year. Gatherings, usually with speakers, are held in community centers where the honorees show off their new adult finery. A traditional archery contest is held on this day at Sanjusangendo Temple in Kyoto, with people from throughout Japan participating. Until 2000, Seijin-no-Hi was observed on January 15, but now it is celebrated on the second Monday in January.

CONTACTS:
Japan National Tourism Organization
1 Grand Center Pl.
60 E 42nd St.
Ste. 448
New York, NY 10165
212-757-5640; fax: 212-307-6754
www.jnto.go.jp

♦ 2559 ♦ **Sekaten**
12th day of the Muslim month of Rabial-Awwal

The Prophet Muhammad's birthday, MAWLID AL-NABI, is a public holiday in Indonesia and is celebrated with the festival of Sekaten on the island of Java. Religious ceremonies, including recitations from the Qur'an, the Muslim holy book, coexist with traditional Javanese dances and music.

In the city of Yogyakarta, a procession of *gamelan* musical instruments begins at the palace, or *keraton*, and parades to the Great Mosque. A gamelon is a group of mostly percussion instruments, such as gongs, drums, and xylophones, that comprise an Indonesian orchestra. Gamelans are stored in the palace, but come out for this festive occasion to provide music for worshippers and spectators. Javanese dances and shadow puppet plays are also performed on Sekaten.

CONTACTS:
Lintang Buana Tourism Services
Jl. Siwalan Kerto Timur 1
No.42
Indonesia
231-843-4556; fax: 231-843-7599
www.javatourism.com

♦ 2560 ♦ **Semana Criolla (Gaucho Festival)**
Between March 15 and April 18; during Holy Week

Gauchos—Latin American cowboys—are highly revered in Uruguay, where for more than 150 years they fought the Indians and ruled the plains. Semana Criolla, a three-week festival that pays tribute to gauchos, coincides with the observance of HOLY WEEK. In the Prado, a park in Montevideo, men in typical gaucho dress—high boots, baggy pants, ponchos, and cowboy hats—compete against each other in horsemanship, lassoing, and bronco-busting, much like a rodeo in the western United States.

The bronco-busting is the highlight of the gaucho festival, and contestants come from all over the country to undergo a screening process designed to select the best applicants for the competitions. There is as much emphasis on elegant costumes and beautiful saddles as there is on the skills involved, and occasionally female gauchos make a name for themselves by appearing in this event.

CONTACTS:
Embassy of Uruguay
1913 I (Eye) St. N.W.
Washington, D.C. 20006
202-331-1313; fax: 202-331-8142
www.mrree.gub.uy

Ministry of Tourism of Uruguay
Rambla 25 de agosto S/N
Uruguay
598-1885
www.turismo.gub.uy

♦ 2561 ♦ **Semana Santa (Guatemala)**
Between March 15 and April 18; Palm Sunday to Easter

Semana Santa, or HOLY WEEK, is without doubt the biggest occasion of the year in Antigua, the old colonial capital of Guatemala, and one of the largest EASTER celebrations in the New World. Thousands of tourists and believers come to the city to witness this massive display of religious theater. The entire Passion play, beginning with Jesus' entry into Jerusalem on PALM SUNDAY and ending with his Resurrection on Easter, is reenacted in the streets of Antigua—complete with armor-clad Roman soldiers on horseback, who charge through the town early on GOOD FRIDAY looking for Jesus. Men in purple robes and accompanied by Roman soldiers take turns carrying *andas* ("floats") through the streets.

CONTACTS:
Guatemala Tourism Commission
7 av. 1-17 zona 4
Centro Cívico
Guatemala
502-242-12800; fax: 305-442-1013
www.visitguatemala.com

♦ 2562 ♦ **Semik**
May-June; seventh Thursday after Easter

In pre-revolutionary Russia, Semik—from *semy,* meaning "the seventh"—took place on the seventh Thursday after EASTER and was observed primarily by young girls. They would go to the woods and pick birch branches, decorating them with ribbons and wreaths. Then they would throw the wreaths into the nearest brook or river. If the wreath stayed on the surface, it meant that they would be married in a year, but if it sank, it meant that they would remain single—or, if married, would soon be widowed. In some areas the wreaths were hung on trees, and as long as they remained there, the girls would have good fortune. Another custom associated with the Semik was the performance of traditional songs and dances by young girls and boys in the forest, often around a decorated birch tree.

In pagan times, the Semik was the feast of a wood god, celebrated at the time of year when the new leaves first appeared on the trees. Since it was the young girls who spent most of their time in the forest picking berries and mushrooms while the women worked in the fields, it is likely that the wreaths hung on the trees were at one time an offering to the wood god.

See also WIANKI FESTIVAL OF WREATHS.

♦ 2563 ♦ Sending the Winter Dress
October-November; first day of 10th lunar month

This is the day on which the Chinese send winter clothes to their dead ancestors. They are not real items of clothing but paper replicas. People display the paper clothes in their homes before wrapping them up and addressing them. That done, families proceed to the graves of their departed ones and burn the packages.

This is one of three annual occasions in remembrance of ancestors who have passed on; the other two are CHUNG YEUNG and QING MING.

♦ 2564 ♦ Senegal Independence Day
April 4

For many years, Senegal was controlled by various European powers, and France gradually began gaining control over the area in the 17th century. On April 4, 1960, Senegal won its independence from France. Today, April 4 is a national holiday celebrated all over the country, but festivities are particularly grand in the capital city of Dakar.

CONTACTS:
Embassy of Senegal
2215 M St. N.W.
Washington, D.C. 20037
202-234-0540; fax: 202-629-2961
www.ambasenegal-us.org

♦ 2565 ♦ Senj International Summer Carnival
August

Carnival events are most traditionally held in early spring, in conjunction with LENT, but the masquarade and party spirit of the Carnival are transplanted to early August each year on the eastern shore of the Adriatic Sea. There, in the city of Senj, Croatia, the Senj International Summer Carnival has been held since 1967. Revelers from around the world come to attend the four-day event. Likewise, while many of the parade participants are drawn from local talent, many come from other nations, including Sweden, Austria, and Italy. The festivities reach their height on Saturday, when the main Carnival procession, made up of about 3,000 costumed revelers, makes its way through the streets of Senj, watched by crowds numbering as many as 25,000 people.

CONTACTS:
Tourist Board Senja
Old St. 2
Senj, 53270 Croatia
385-53-881-068; fax: 385-53-881-219
www.tz-senj.hr

Croatian Embassy
2343 Massachusetts Ave. N.W.
Washington, D.C. 20008
202-588-5899; fax: 202-588-8937
us.mvep.hr

♦ 2566 ♦ Señor de los Milagros
October 18-28

A religious brotherhood affiliated with the church of Las Nazarenas in Lima, Peru, has maintained an annual devotional procession that began in the 17th century. This devotion centers on a painting of Christ, known as Señor de los Milagros, or Lord of the Miracles. The artist of the painting was an Angolan man brought to Peru as a slave in the 1600s. He lived on a plantation in the Pachacamilla area of Lima and there painted the image of the crucified, brown-skinned Jesus on a wall. This wall painting survived several attempts to erase it and at least one earthquake, in 1746. For these reasons, area Roman Catholics believed it to be an unusual image of Christ that required protection and special attention.

Many men are required to carry the two-ton litter upon which rests the portion of the wall with the painting of Señor de los Milagros. Held between October 18-28, the procession attracts thousands of people, making it one of the most well attended processions in South America. This time of year is sometimes referred to as Purple Spring, because October is springtime in Peru and because nearly everyone dresses in purple for the occasion.

Along the route—which starts at the church of Las Nazarenas and winds its way through the streets of Lima until it reaches the church of La Merced—food stands offer numerous delicacies, especially the traditional favorite sweet, *Turron de Doña Pepa*. The throngs of people who visit Lima in October for the Señor de los Milagros can also attend a series of bullfights at the Plaza de Acho.

CONTACTS:
Mission Dolores Parish
3321 Sixteenth St.
San Francisco, CA 94114
415-621-8203; fax: 415-621-2294
missiondolores.org

Embassy of Peru
1700 Massachusetts Ave. N.W.
Washington, D.C. 20036
202-833-9860; fax: 202-659-8124
www.embassyofperu.org

♦ 2567 ♦ Señor de los Temblores Procession
Monday before Easter

There is a legend in Peru that early in the 17th century, some men from the port city of Callao discovered an unusual box while out fishing. The shape of the floating box led them to believe that a crucifix might be concealed within, and they brought news of their discovery to Lima church authorities. The church authorities wanted the box brought to them, but it was so heavy that no one was able to lift it. When they resolved to have the box taken to Ayacucho, the box also became mysteriously heavy. But when someone suggested it be sent to Cuzco, the box suddenly lightened—which all present interpreted as a sign that the image in the box desired to go there.

Shortly after it was installed in a chapel of the unfinished cathedral in Cuzco, the city was hit by the terrible earthquake of 1650. The earth shook for three days, and it didn't stop until the crucifix was taken from the undamaged church and carried into the streets. Thereafter, it was called el Señor de los Temblores (Lord of the Earthquakes), and the people believed that it protected Cuzco from earthquakes for almost 300 years.

To commemorate this event, the Quechua Indians of Cuzco take the Lord of the Earthquakes out in procession every year on the Monday before EASTER. Before it leaves the church, however, it is carefully dusted and dressed in white, lace-trimmed panties, which are then covered first with a white loincloth and then with a black velvet one. The statue wears no clothes on its arms or chest, although it wears a curly wig topped by a gold crown. It is carried in the procession by 30 men bearing a heavy litter made of solid silver, and Quechua Indians carrying lighted candles lay down a "carpet" of red flower petals for the Señor to pass over. With church officials bringing up the rear, the procession stops at various churches throughout the city, where the litter enters the church. Few brave a look directly into the Señor's face, as tradition holds that a single glance from the statue indicates that one will die in the year to come.

Although Cuzco suffered a serious earthquake in 1941, the Indians maintain faith in the image's power to protect them.

CONTACTS:
Peru Export and Tourism Promotion Agency
Calle Uno Oeste 50, Edificio Mincetur
Pisos 13 y 14
San Isidro
Peru
51-1-616-7300
www.promperu.gob.pe/english

♦ 2568 ♦ Serbia Statehood Day of the Republic
February 15

The Republic of Serbia is a landlocked nation in central and southeastern Europe. For over 300 years, starting in 1459, Serbia was under the control of Turkish Ottoman rule. Because the Serbian people were being oppressed by the Ottoman sultans, many migrated to other parts of the Balkan Peninsula.

On February 15, 1804, Serbian patriot Djordje Petrovic Karadjordje led an uprising against the Ottoman to gain independence. This uprising lasted over nine years, but in the end the Ottoman remained in control. A second uprising, led by Milos Obrenovic, occurred in 1815 and lasted two years. The second uprising was successful, and Serbia formally gained independence from the Ottoman Empire in 1829.

In 2001, the Serbian Parliament declared February 15 a state holiday to commemorate the day in 1804 that the first Serbian uprising against the Turks began. A ceremony is held in Orasac to celebrate the first Serbian uprising and constitution (signed in 1835), which led to the creation of the modern Serbian state. The main celebrations include festive concerts, film and theater premiers, exhibitions, and many other events.

♦ 2569 ♦ Serreta, Festa da
September 8-15

The Festa da Serreta that has been held annually since 1932 in Gustine, California, is based on a similar festival held on the island of Terceira in the Azores, from which many of Gustine's residents emigrated. It is held in honor of *Nossa Senhora dos Milagres*, "Our Lady of Miracles," for whom a 16th-century priest built a small chapel in the Azorean village of Serreta.

The week-long festival attracts thousands of visitors. Highlights include the *Bodo do Leite* ("Banquet of Milk") fresh-drawn from the cows as is the practice in the Azores. There are also *cantorías ao desafio* (extemporaneous song contests), which draw contestants from all over California and even some Azoreans.

The image of *Nossa Senhora* is carried in a procession from the church to a portable chapel, or *capela*, that is brought out specifically for use on this occasion. A group of women sit in the chapel and watch over the donations of money that are left there. Another festival event is the traditional bullfight, which takes place in a rectangular arena. The bull is held by a long rope, his horns are padded, and the men do not so much fight him as play with him.

♦ 2570 ♦ Seton (Mother) Day
December 1

The Company of the Daughters of Charity, a community of Catholic women ministering to the "poorest of the poor," was founded in France in 1633 by St. Vincent de Paul and Louise de Marillac. In 1809 an American woman, Elizabeth Ann Bayley Seton (1774-1821), modeled her Emmitsburg, Maryland-based community after the French Daughters, which she called the American Sisters of Charity. The French and American congregations united in 1850 and formed an international community of women serving the poor worldwide.

On September 14, 1975, Mother Seton, as she is known to her followers, became the first American-born saint to be canonized by the Roman Catholic Church. The Sisters of Charity of St. Vincent de Paul continue to observe December 1 as the anniversary of the founding of their order. Many also observe January 4, the day she died, as her feast day (*see* ST. ELIZABETH ANN SETON, FEAST OF).

CONTACTS:
Sisters of Charity Center
6301 Riverdale Ave.
Bronx, NY 10471
718-549-9200
www.scny.org

Daughters of Charity of St. Vincent de Paul
Seton Provincialate
26000 Altamont Rd.
Los Altos Hills, CA 94022
650-941-4490; fax: 650-949-8883
www.daughtersofcharity.com

♦ 2571 ♦ **Setsubun (Bean-Throwing Festival)**
February 3 or 4

Setsubun is a ceremony observed in all major temples throughout Japan to mark the last day of winter according to the lunar calendar. People throng temple grounds where the priests or stars such as actors and sumo wrestlers throw dried beans to the crowd who shout, "Fortune in, goblins out!" Some people also decorate their doorways with sardine heads, because the evil spirits don't like their smell. Beans caught at the temple are brought home to drive out evil there.

CONTACTS:
Japan National Tourist Organization
1 Grand Central Pl.
60 E. 42nd St.
Ste. 448
New York, NY 10165
212-757-5640; fax: 212-307-6754
www.jnto.go.jp

♦ 2572 ♦ **Seven Sisters Festival**
July-August; seventh day of seventh lunar month

The Seven Sisters Festival is a celebration for would-be lovers, observed in China, Korea, Taiwan, and Hong Kong. It is based on an ancient Chinese legend and is also known as the **Maiden's Festival**, **Double Seventh**, **Chhit Sek**, and CHILSEOG. In the legend, an orphaned cowherd is forced from his home by his elder brother and sister-in-law, who give him only a broken-down cart, an ox, and a tiny piece of land. The ox, called Elder Brother the Ox, takes pity on the cowherd, and tells him that on a certain day seven girls will visit earth from heaven to bathe in a nearby river. If the young man steals the clothes of any one of the girls, she will marry him.

The cowherd steals the clothes of the Seventh Maiden. They fall in love, marry, and live happily for three years, when she is ordered back to heaven by the gods. When the cowherd dies, he becomes immortal, but the Queen Mother of the Western Heaven keeps the two apart by drawing a line across the sky—the Silver River, or Milky Way. They can cross this only once a year, on the seventh day of the seventh month, on a bridge formed by thousands of magpies.

On the sixth day of the seventh month, unmarried men pay homage to the cowherd, and on the seventh day, young unmarried women make offerings of combs, mirrors, paper flowers, and powder puffs to the Seventh Maiden. The festival is celebrated chiefly at home, but in Hong Kong young women also visit Lover's Rock on Bowen Road on Hong Kong Island to burn *joss* ('incense') sticks, lay offerings at the rock, and consult soothsayers.

See also TANABATA.

CONTACTS:
Hong Kong Tourism Board
5670 Wilshire Blvd.
Ste 1230
Los Angeles, CA 90036 United States
323-938-4582; fax: 323-938-4583
www.discoverhongkong.com

♦ 2573 ♦ **Seville Fair**
April

Over the past century, the Seville Fair, also known as the **April Fair**, has developed into one of Spain's major spectacles. Originally a market for livestock, the fair with its multi-colored tents, wreaths, and paper lanterns now transforms the city of Seville. The singing, dancing, and drinking go on for a week, and a sense of joyousness pervades the city. The week's activities include a parade of riders and a number of bullfights held in the Plaza de la Maestranza (equestrian parade ground)—now considered the "cathedral" of bullfighting.

CONTACTS:
Seville Tourism Consortium
Plaza de San Francisco
19 Bldg Laredo
Seville, 41004 Spain
349-554-71232
www.visitasevilla.es

♦ 2574 ♦ **Seward's Day**
Last Monday in March

When William Henry Seward, secretary of state for President Andrew Johnson, signed the treaty authorizing the purchase of Alaska from Czarist Russia for $7 million on March 30, 1867, most Americans thought he was crazy. They called it "Seward's folly," "Seward's icebox," and "Johnson's polar bear garden." But public opinion quickly changed when gold was discovered in the region.

Since that time, Alaska's natural resources have paid back the initial investment many times over. Its natural gas, coal, and oil reserves, in addition to its seafood and lumber industries, have proved to be far more valuable than its gold. Unfortunately, Seward did not live to see his foresight commemorated as a legal holiday in the state of Alaska. The purchase of Alaska is now widely regarded as the crowning achievement of both William Seward and President Johnson. (*See* ALASKA DAY.).

CONTACTS:
Library of Congress
101 Independence Ave. S.E.
Washington, D.C. 20540
202-707-5000; fax: 202-707-2076
www.loc.gov

♦ 2575 ♦ Seychelles Independence Day
June 29

Also known as **Republic Day**, Seychelles Independence Day is a national holiday that commemorates Seychelles' transition to an independent republic on this day in 1976. It had been a British colony since 1903. Before that, it was a dependency of Mauritius, which was ruled by France.

When Seychelles became independent, the people had a three-month-long party.

CONTACTS:
Seychelles Tourism Board
800 Second Ave.
Ste. 400C, Forth fl.
New York, NY 10017
212-972-1785; fax: 212-972-1786
www.seychelles.travel

♦ 2576 ♦ Seychelles Liberation Day
June 5

Less than a year after gaining independence (see above), a coup overthrew the government. Two major political parties had developed in Seychelles, the Seychelles Democratic Party (SDP) and the Seychelles People's United Party (SPUP). James Mancham, the leader of the SDP party, which won the majority vote, became president, and France Albert Rene became prime minister. Rene's supporters led the overthrow and ousted Mancham on June 5, 1977, an event commemorated as a public holiday on Liberation Day.

CONTACTS:
Republic of Seychelles to the UN
800 Second Ave.
Ste 400C, 4th fl
New York, NY 10017 United States
212-972-1785; fax: 212-972-1786
www.seychelles.travel

♦ 2577 ♦ Seychelles National Day
June 18

The Republic of Seychelles comprises 115 islands in the western Indian Ocean. Seychelles was first settled by the French in 1770 and remained in French hands until Napoleon was defeated at Waterloo. In 1814, Seychelles was ceded to Britain under the Treaty of Paris.

Under the British rule, the population of Seychelles doubled, and important estates that produced coconut, food crops, cotton, and sugar cane were established.

Seychelles gained independence from Britain in 1976 and became a republic within the commonwealth. The republic was under single party rule until December 4, 1991, when President France Albert René announced a return to the multiparty system of government. On June 18, 1993, a new constitution was approved, and the first multiparty presidential and legislative elections were held in July.

June 18th is known as National Day in Seychelles. This national holiday commemorates the implementation of a multiparty democracy. On this day, thousands of people attend celebratory events that include parades, a flower show, music, and a presidential speech.

CONTACTS:
Department of Information Communications Technology
P.O. Box 737
3rd Fl. Caravelle House
Seychelles
248-428-6609; fax: 248-432-2720
www.ict.gov.sc

♦ 2578 ♦ Shab-Barat
14th day of Islamic month of Sha'ban

Shab-Barat (or **Shab-i-Barat, Shaaban**) is a time when Muslims—particularly those in India and Pakistan—ask Allah to forgive the people they know who have died. They often spend the night in mosques praying and reading the Qur'an, and they visit graveyards to pray for the souls of their friends and ancestors. They also celebrate Allah's mercy by setting off fireworks, illuminating the outsides of their mosques, and giving food to the poor.

Also known as **Laylat al-Bara'ah**, or the **Night of Forgiveness**, Shab-Barat is a time of intense prayer in preparing for RAMADAN, for it is believed that this is the night on which God fixes the destinies of humans for the coming year and sins are absolved.

♦ 2579 ♦ Shad Festival
Last full weekend in April

Since 1981, the city of Lambertville, N.J., has celebrated the Shad Festival, honoring the annual return of the shad fish to the Delaware River to spawn. Because of water pollution in the area many years ago, the shad—also called river herring—were almost wiped out. But a major cleanup of area pollution brought the commercial fish back to the region. The festival also promotes the preservation of the environment and of the Delaware River ecosystem.

The two-day street festival features an arts show, cooking demonstrations, and live music concerts. Local nonprofit and community volunteer organizations use the event as a fundraiser by selling food and other items. A poster auction raises money for college scholarships for local students. There are also demonstrations of how the local fishing community catches shad with nets. The Shad Festival has won the Governor's Conference on Tourism Best Event Award three times.

CONTACTS:
Greater Lambertville – New Hope Chamber of Commerce
59 N. Union St.
Lambertville, NJ 08530
609-397-0055
www.glnhcc.org

♦ 2580 ♦ Shah Abdul Latif Death Festival
14th-16th days of Islamic month of Safar

This festival commermorates the death of poet-musician
Shah Abdul Latif (1689-1752) at Bhit Shah, Sindh, Pakistan.
He was one of the most beloved of Pakistan's mystic Sufi
poet-musicians who founded a music tradition based on
popular themes and using folk melodies. He was the author
of the *Risalo*, the best-known collection of romantic poetry
in the Sindhi language; its heroes and heroines have become
symbols of the oppression of Sindh by foreign occupiers.

At Latif's *urs*, or "death festival," a huge fair takes place outside the poet's shrine. There are wrestling matches (a popular
entertainment in Sindh), a circus, theater, and numerous food
and souvenir booths. Inside the shrine the atmosphere is
quiet, and there is devotional singing by well-known Sindh
groups. The main event of the urs is a concert at which the
annual Latif Award is presented to the best performers.

CONTACTS:
Culture Tourism and Antiquities Department - Government of
Sindh
7th Fl.
New Sindh Secretariat Bldg. No.1
Karachi, Sindh Pakistan
92-21-99222885; fax: 92-21-99222886
web.culture.gos.pk

♦ 2581 ♦ Shaheed Day
February 21

Shaheed or **Shahid Day** is a national day of mourning in
Bangladesh. Before becoming an autonomous country in
1971 (*see* BANGLADESH INDEPENDENCE DAY), this land had
been East Pakistan ever since all of India gained independence from Britain in 1947. As East Pakistan, the country was
poorer and less powerful than West Pakistan (now Pakistan),
where the central government was. East Pakistan paid its
taxes to West Pakistan, which gave East Pakistan little economic support in return. In addition, West Pakistan wanted
to make its language, Urdu, the only official language of both
Pakistans. Most of the people in East Pakistan spoke Bengali
(some of the Indian region of Bengal became East Pakistan
in 1947), and they were strongly opposed to the restriction
of the use of their language in government and commerce.

In 1952 university students held protests which erupted in
violence. Lives were lost, and as a memorial, people form a
procession from the Azimpur graveyard on February 21 each
year.

CONTACTS:
Embassy of Bangladesh

3510 International Dr. N.W.
Washington, D.C. 20008
202-244-0183; fax: 202-244-2771
www.bdembassyusa.org

♦ 2582 ♦ Shahi Durbar
Last week in February

The annual fair known as Shahi Durbar takes place in the
town of Sibi in the Baluchistan Province of Pakistan. The
event goes back to the 15th century when it centered around
a gathering of tribal elders (*durbar* means "royal gathering"),
and it is still an occasion for local politicians to speechify and
debate each other. But it also features an agricultural fair, a
handicraft market, and numerous sporting events, including horse racing, tent pegging, wrestling, and cockfighting.
Relatively few foreigners come to the fair, but it represents a
unique opportunity to observe the traditional customs and
costumes of the tribal people of Baluchistan.

CONTACTS:
Consulate General of Pakistan
12 E. 65 St.
New York, NY 10065
212-879-5800; fax: 212-517-6987
www.pakistanconsulateny.org

Pakistan Tourism Development Corporation (PTDC)
22-Saeed Plaza
Blue Area
Jinnah Ave.
Pakistan
92-51-921-9699; fax: 92-51-921-9729
www.tourism.gov.pk

♦ 2583 ♦ Shahrewar, Feast of
January, August, December; fourth day of
Shahrewar, the sixth Zoroastrian month

The Feast of Shahrewar is one of the "sacred name days"
in the Zoroastrian religion, where the day and the month
share the name of the same *yazata* or spiritual being—in
this case, Shahrewar, who represents Desirable (or Benevolent) Dominion and who presides over metals and minerals.
Because there are actually three different Zoroastrian calendars in use by widely separated Zoroastrian communities,
the Feast of Shahrewar occurs in either January, August, or
December.

Among the followers of Persian prophet Zoroaster (also
known as Zarathushtra, believed to have lived around 1200
B.C.E.), a name-day feast is observed with religious ceremonies in fire temples, meeting halls, or private homes.

There are only about 100,000 followers of Zoroastrianism
today, and most of them live in northwestern India or Iran.
Smaller communities exist in Pakistan, Sri Lanka, Canada,
the U.S., England, and Australia.

♦ 2584 ♦ Shaker Festivals
Various

Shakers are members of the United Society of Believers in Christ's Second Appearing, a celibate sect founded in 1747 in England. The Society, an offshoot of the Quakers, adopted ritual practices such as shaking, shouting, dancing, whirling, and singing in tongues, hence the nickname "Shakers." Communal settlements were established in the United States by Shaker leader Ann LEE, an Englishwoman known to her followers as Mother Ann and thought to be the first of the Believers to experience the constant indwelling of the spirit of Christ. She came to America in 1774 and founded the first Shaker church in what is now Watervliet, New York. The Shaker movement later spread throughout New England, Kentucky, Ohio, and Indiana. It reached its peak in the 1840s with a total membership of about 6,000. By 1905 the movement counted only 1,000 adherents. Today less than a dozen Shakers remain, living together in a small community at Sabbathday Lake, Maine.

The simple lines of Shaker furniture and other crafts strongly influenced American furniture design. What's more, craftspeople from these inventive communities designed the first screw propeller, rotary harrow, clothespin, and other items.

A number of Shaker festivals take place at Shaker museums and historic villages across the country. In South Union, Kentucky, the Shaker Museum hosts "Civil War Days" in mid-August, a two-day recreation of life in South Union's Shaker community during the Civil War. In late September the Museum sponsors "Harvest Day," an event that allows visitors to experience a day in a Shaker community around harvest time in the 1870s.

The Shaker Village of Pleasant Hill, Kentucky, holds a "Day of Releasement" in late July, in which visitors experience life in a Shaker community on a day off from work. They also celebrate a "Shaker Fourth" on the FOURTH OF JULY, recreating a typical Shaker Independence Day. Various Shaker villages and museums honor Mother Ann Day on August 5, in which they celebrate the life of Shaker leader Ann Lee.

CONTACTS:
Shaker Woods
217 SR-7
Columbiana, OH 44408
330-482-0214; fax: 330-482-0215
www.shakerwoods.com

♦ 2585 ♦ **Shakespeare's (William) Birthday**
April 23

No one really knows the exact date of William Shakespeare's birth, although he was baptized on April 26, 1564, and died on April 23, 1616. April 23 is also ST. GEORGE'S DAY, and this may be why it was decided to observe the birth of England's greatest poet and dramatist on the feast day of England's patron saint. Special pageants are held at Stratford-up-on-Avon in Warwickshire, where Shakespeare was born and where thousands of tourists go each year to see his plays performed.

♦ 2586 ♦ **Shalako Ceremonial**
Late November or early December

One of the most impressive of the Pueblo Indian dances, the Shalako Ceremonial is held at the Zuni Pueblo in southwestern New Mexico. In this ceremony of all-night dancing and chants, houses are blessed, the dead are commemorated, and prayers are offered for good health and good weather in the coming year. The dance features towering masked figures with beaks who represent messengers from the rainmakers. They make clacking noises as they approach designated houses, and once inside the houses, they remove their masks, chant, and share food. Other figures taking part in the ceremonial are rain gods, warriors carrying whips, and the fire god, who is depicted by a young boy. The dancing goes on all through the cold night. The following morning, there are foot races.

CONTACTS:
Indian Pueblo Cultural Center
2401 12th St. N.W.
Albuquerque, NM 87104
505-843-7270 or 866-855-7902
www.indianpueblo.org

♦ 2587 ♦ **Sham el-Nessim**
Between April 5 and May 9; Monday after
Coptic Easter

A national holiday and folk festival in Egypt, the Sham el-Nessim has been observed for thousands of years as a day to smell the breezes and celebrate spring. *Nessim* means "zephyr," the spring breeze, and *sham* means "to breathe in." While the date is set by the Coptic calendar, the holiday is now a non-religious national holiday observed by everyone as a family affair.

Traditionally, people pack picnics to have outings along the Nile River or in parks. Certain food is specified for the occasion: the main dish is *fessikh*, a kind of salted fish, and it's also traditional to have *mouloukhiya* (stuffed vine leaves) and eggs with decorated, colored shells. The foods are believed to prevent disease, and the eggs symbolize life. Vast numbers of fish are eaten in Cairo on Sham al-Nessim.

Other traditions call for placing freshly cut flowers at doors and windows, and putting a clove of garlic at the head of each bed to prevent boredom and fatigue for those who lie there.

At the time of the pharaohs, spring was celebrated with gifts of lotus flowers to wives or loved ones, and families enjoyed river outings on flower-decorated barges and *feluccas* (small sailing vessels).

CONTACTS:
Egypt State Information Service (SIS)
3 Al Estad Al Bahary St.
Nasr City, Cairo Egypt
20-2261-7304
www.sis.gov.eg

♦ 2588 ♦ **Shambhala Music Festival**
First Week in August

The largest electronic music event in Canada, the Shambhala Music Festival is an annual five-day celebration held on a 500-acre cattle ranch in the West Kootenay Mountains near Nelson, British Columbia. Incorporating the beauty of its natural surroundings, the festival features DJs and other artists from around the world. Run by the Bundschuh family since 1998, the festival eschews corporate sponsorship and uses only the help of more than 2,000 volunteers, who manage six stages at various locations on the site.

CONTACTS:
Shambhala Music Festival Ltd.
7790 British Columbia 3
Salmo, BC V0G 1Z0 Canada
250-352-7623
www.shambhalamusicfestival.com

♦ 2589 ♦ **Shanghai International Film Festival**
June

Founded in 1933, the Shanghai International Film Festival (SIFF) is regarded as a major international event in East Asia, and reflects China's growing economic and cultural status in the early 21st century. Taking place in Shanghai each June, the festival hosts four main programs. Most notable is the competition section and its prestigious Golden Goblet Award and Asian New Talent Award, both juried by highly respected international filmmakers. The SIFF Market serves as a major trade platform for Chinese films. The SIFFORUM, a comprehensive educative platform, disseminates information through a series of lectures, workshops, and master classes. The International Film Panorama offers a plethora of official selections, retrospectives, and gala screenings from world cinema. Hollywood and Asian celebrities dazzle the red carpet at the opening gala of the festival.

With wide media coverage, over 800 films are screened in 35 cinemas across the city, attracting hundreds of thousands of moviegoers and film professionals. However, unlike festivals held in Hong Kong or Taiwan, SIFF faces the challenges of meeting the strict laws of the Chinese state, while also striving to appeal to a global audience.

♦ 2590 ♦ **Shankaracharya Jayanti**
April-May; fifth or 10th day of waxing half of Hindu month of Vaisakha

Although he is believed to have lived between 788 and 820, Hindu tradition says that Adi Shankaracharya, one of India's greatest saint-philosophers, flourished in 200 B.C.E. He revived Brahmanism and raised Vedanta philosophy to new heights, producing a number of original philosophical works and commentaries on the Upanishads, Vedanta Sutras, and the *Bhagavad Gita*. Shankaracharya also composed many popular hymns, worked numerous miracles, and urged Hindus to devote themselves to God in all of his many forms and incarnations.

Shankaracharya's birthday, known as Shankaracharya Jayanti, is celebrated on the fifth day of Vaisakha in southern India and on the 10th day in northern India. It is usually spent fasting, meditating, and studying Shankaracharya's works.

CONTACTS:
Administrator Sringeri Sharada Peetham
Sringeri Mutt
Chickmagalur, Karnataka 577139 India
91-8265-250123; fax: 91-8265-250792
www.sringeri.net

♦ 2591 ♦ **Sharad Purnima**
September-October; full moon day of Hindu month of Asvina

Hindus devote this day to the moon god, Hari. In the belief that *amrit* (elixir) is showered on the earth by moonbeams, they prepare *khir* (milk thickened with rice and mixed with sugar) on this day and offer it to Hari amid the ringing of bells and chanting of hymns. The mixture is left out in the moonshine all night so that it may absorb the amrit falling from the moon. The resulting khir is believe to possess special qualities. In the evening, the moon god is worshipped and offered food. The next morning, the specially prepared khir is given to the devotees.

♦ 2592 ♦ **Shavuot (Shabuoth)**
Between May 16 and June 13; Sivan 6-7

Shavuot ("weeks") is the second of the three PILGRIM FESTIVALS (*see also* PASSOVER and SUKKOT). It follows Passover by 50 days and is also known in English as *Pentecost* from the Greek word meaning "fiftieth" (like the Christian PENTECOST, which comes 50 days after EASTER). It is also called the **Feast of Weeks** or **Feast of the Harvest**, because it originally marked the end of the seven weeks of the Passover barley harvest and the beginning of the wheat harvest. At one time, all adult male Jews were expected to bring their first *omer*, or "sheaf," of barley to the Temple in Jerusalem as a thanksgiving offering. Today dairy dishes are associated with Shavuot, particularly cheese blintzes.

After the period of Jewish slavery in Egypt, Shavuot took on a new meaning: it celebrated Moses' return from the top of Mt. Sinai with the two stone tablets containing the Ten Commandments, the most fundamental laws of the Jewish faith, and is therefore also known as the **Festival of the Giving of the Law**. Orthodox and Conservative Jews in the Diaspora celebrate two days of Shavuot as full holidays, while Reform Jews and those living in Israel observe only the first day.

See also LAG BA-OMER.

CONTACTS:
Orthodox Union
11 Broadway
New York, NY 10004
212-563-4000; fax: 212-564-9058
www.ou.org

♦ 2593 ♦ **Sheboygan Bratwurst Days**
First weekend in August

Sheboygan Bratwurst Days is a celebration in Sheboygan, Wis., that is scented with the smoke from 3,000 to 4,000 bratwursts being grilled. Sheboygan, billing itself the "Bratwurst Capital of the World," or alternatively, the "Wurst City of the World," is the home of several large sausage factories that ship bratwurst around the country and of numerous smaller markets that make tons of brat. (*Brat*, incidentally, rhymes with *cot*, not *cat*.) The celebration's main event is a parade led by a 13-foot-tall balloon Bavarian figure in lederhosen who is known as the *Bratmeister*, or "sausage master." In 1991, a highlight of the parade was a float carrying giant twin brats—two 130-pound brats on a hard roll made from 40 pounds of dough.

The point of the festival is to eat brats, and the smell of them cooking on outdoor grills permeates the city. There are a brat-and-pancake breakfast and a brat-eating contest. Other events include band concerts, a magic show, wrestling matches, competitions for children, and a stumpf-fiddle contest. The stumpf fiddle is an instrument combining bells, springs, BB-filled pie plates, wood blocks, and taxi horns on a wooden pole with a rubber ball at the bottom.

Germans settled in Sheboygan in the 1830s and 1840s and immediately began making sausage. In 1953, to celebrate the city's 100th birthday, a Bratwurst Day was held in August. The mayor's proclamation noted that the city "has achieved national fame and recognition for the exclusive manufacture of a special kind of roasting sausage . . ."

The celebration was canceled in 1966 because it had become too rowdy. In 1978, Bratwurst Days came back for the city's 125th anniversary. Today the festival attracts about 50,000 people.

CONTACTS:
Sheboygan Jaycees
P.O. Box 561
Sheboygan, WI 53082
920-803-8980
www.sheboyganjaycees.com

♦ 2594 ♦ **Sheelah's Day**
March 18

Even the Irish aren't exactly sure who Sheelah was. Some say she was St. Patrick's wife; some say his mother. But one thing that they all seem to agree on is how this day should be celebrated: by drinking whiskey. The shamrock worn on ST. PATRICK'S DAY is supposed to be worn on the following day as well, until it is "drowned" in the last glass of the evening. If someone should drop his shamrock into his glass and drink it before the "drowning ceremony" takes place, he has no choice but to get a fresh shamrock and another glass.

CONTACTS:
Department of Foreign Affairs and Trade
Iveagh House
80 St Stephen's Green
Dublin, 2 Ireland
353-140-82000
www.dfa.ie

♦ 2595 ♦ **Shellfish Gathering (Shiohi-gari)**
April 4

April 4 is approximately the date on which the tide is usually at its lowest in Japan. Families dress in brightly colored clothing and gather in coastal areas where the shellfish are known to be plentiful. They go out in boats decorated with red and white bunting and wait until the tide goes out and strands them on the bottom. Then they dig for clams, which they often cook and eat on the spot for lunch. Fishermen living nearbyare more than willing to supplement their efforts, selling clams from their own stock to those whose digging has been unsuccessful. Most people buy a bag of shellfish to take home as well. The maritime police are usually kept busy rescuing those who go out too far and are caught by the incoming tide.

♦ 2596 ♦ **Shembe Festival**
First day in July to the last Sunday

The Shembe Festival, named for Isaiah Shembe (c. 1870-1935), the sect's founder, is one of three annual festivals observed by the Nazareth Baptist Church (Church of the Ama Nazaretha). It takes place at the Ematabetulu village near Inanda, South Africa. The other two are the October festival, observed at Judia near Ginginglovu, and the January festival observed on Inhlangakazi Mountain. All aspects of worship, ritual, dress, and festivals were established by Shembe in 1911. The church's beliefs are a mixture of pagan, Old Testament, and Christian ideas.

The **July Festival** is the most popular of the three, and church members come from all over South Africa to attend it. Some live in temporary encampments for the festival, which begins on the first day of July and ends on the last Sunday. Throughout this period there are alternate days of dancing and rest. The sacred dancing that takes place on the final Sunday usually draws large numbers of spectators. Other activities during the festival include sermons by a variety of preachers, testimonies by church members, and prayer for the sick.

The men and women dance separately, and their costumes vary considerably. The two male groups of dancers, for example, are the Njobo and the Iscotch. The Njobo, who are mostly older men, wear traditional Zulu dress, as do the female groups. But the younger male dancers of the Iscotch group wear a long white smock with a tasseled hem over a black pleated kilt, a white pith helmet, black army boots with black-and-white football socks, and a light green tie bearing icons of the prophet Shembe and other church leaders.

The dances, which can last an entire day, involve rows of 50 or more dancers, each of which takes its turn at the front and then gradually works its way to the back, allowing those who tire to leave the group without being noticed.

CONTACTS:
South African Tourism Board
Bojanala House
90 Protea Rd.
Chislehurston, Johannesburg 2196 South Africa
271-189-53000 or 278-312-36789; fax: 271-189-53001
www.southafrica.net

♦ 2597 ♦ Shemini Atzeret
Between September 27 and October 25; Tishri 22

Shemini Atzeret, or "eighth day of solemn assembly," is actually the eighth day of the festival of SUKKOT, but it is celebrated as a separate holiday dedicated to the love of God. The second day of Shemini Atzeret is known as SIMHAT TORAH and is also celebrated separately by Orthodox and Conservative Jews. Most Reform Jews celebrate Shemini Atzeret concurrently with Simhat Torah.

In ancient times, prayers for rain were recited on this day—a practice that is still part of Orthodox services. It is also one of four Jewish holidays on which the *Yizkor*, or memorial rite for the dead, is observed. The other three are YOM KIPPUR, the second day of SHAVUOT, and the last day of PASSOVER.

CONTACTS:
Orthodox Union
11 Broadway
New York, NY 10004
212-563-4000; fax: 212-564-9058
www.ou.org

♦ 2598 ♦ Shenandoah Apple Blossom Festival
Early May

This four-day celebration of the apple orchards of Virginia's Shenandoah Valley is held in Winchester, the state's apple center. The festival was inaugurated in 1924 to publicize the area's historic, scenic, and industrial assets. Its motto was: "The bounties of nature are the gift of God." Winchester was settled in 1732, and George Washington, an early landlord in the area, required each tenant to plant four acres of apples.

The festival comes when the orchards are in bloom. Over 250,000 people visit to enjoy the pink and white blossoms and the special events, including the coronation of Queen Shenandoah, a title once held by Luci Baines Johnson, former President Lyndon B. Johnson's youngest daughter. The 2001 Queen was Tyne Vance, granddaughter of former President Gerald R. Ford. Other attractions are parades, concerts and band competitions, a circus, fireworks, a 10K run, children's activities, a car show, and celebrity appearances. The 2012 Queen was Jazmyn Dorsett, daughter of National Football League running back Tony Dorsett.

CONTACTS:
Shenandoah Apple Blossom Festival, Inc.
135 N. Cameron St.
Winchester, VA 22601
540-662-3863; fax: 540-662-7274
thebloom.com

♦ 2599 ♦ Shepherd's Fair
Two weeks beginning the third or fourth Sunday in August

Also known as the **Schueberfouer** or **Schuebermesse**, the Shepherd's Fair held in Luxembourg City at the end of August every year dates back to 1340, when it was founded by John the Blind, count of Luxembourg and king of Bohemia. Originally a market for the wool and sheep merchants of medieval Europe, the Shepherd's Fair has shifted its focus over the years. Today it is geared toward entertainment rather than commerce, with carousels, food stands, and candy booths everywhere. Practically the only remnant of the original fair is the *Marche des Moutons*, (March of the Sheep), a parade of sheep decorated with ribbons and led by shepherds in folkloric costumes, accompanied by a band playing an ancient tune known as the *Hammelsmarsch*, or "Sheeps' March.".

CONTACTS:
Luxembourg National Tourist Board
68-70, boulevard de la Pétrusse
Luxembourg, L-2320 Luxembourg
352-42-82-82-10; fax: 352-42-82-82-30
www.visitluxembourg.com

♦ 2600 ♦ Shichi-Go-San (Seven-Five-Three Festival)
November 15

Shichi-Go-San is an ancient Japanese celebration that marks the special ages of seven, five, and three. It has long been traditional for families to take girls aged seven, boys of five, and all three-year-olds, dressed in their finest, to the neighborhood Shinto shrine where their birth is recorded. There they are purified, and the priest prays to the tutelary deity for their healthy growth. At the end the priest gives each child two little packages: one containing cakes in the form of Shinto emblems (mirror, sword, and jewel), and the other holding sacred rice to be mixed with the evening meal. Afterwards, there are often parties for the children, and customarily they are given a special pink hard candy, called "thousand-year candy," to symbolize hopes for a long life. Because Nov. 15 is not a legal holiday, families now observe the ceremony on the Sunday nearest that date.

Legend says that the custom started because parents believed their children's mischievousness was caused by little worms that somehow entered their bodies. The visits to the shrines were to pray that the mischief-making worms would depart. A more likely story is that the festival began in the days when children often died young, and parents gave thanks for those who survived.

CONTACTS:
Center for Intercultural Communication
1-1-1-609 Iwado-Kita
Komae-shi, Tokyo 201-0004 Japan
81-3-3430-1780; fax: 81-3-3430-1740
www.cichonyaku.com

◆ 2601 ◆ **Shick-Shack Day (Shik-Shak Day, Shicsack Day, Shig-Shag Day)**
May 29

The *Oxford English Dictionary* suggests that this day takes its name from a corruption of *shitsack*, a derogatory term for the Nonconformists, Protestants who did not follow the doctrines and practices of the established Church of England. It was later applied to those who did not wear the traditional sprig of oak on May 29, or **Royal Oak Day**—the birthday of Charles II and the day in 1660 on which he made his triumphal entry into London as king after a 12-year interregnum.

The association of Charles II (1630-1685) and the oak tree dates back to 1651 when, after being defeated by Oliver CROMWELL in battle, legend has it he took refuge from his pursuers in an oak tree behind a house known as Boscobel. *Shick-shack* has since become synonymous with the oak-apple or sprig of oak itself, and May 29 is celebrated—particularly in rural areas of England—in memory of the restoration of King Charles and his preservation in the Royal Oak. Also called **Oak Apple Day**, **Oak Ball Day**, **Bobby Ack Day**, **Yack Bob Day**, **Restoration Day**, or **Nettle Day**.

◆ 2602 ◆ **Shigmo Festival**
February-March; Hindu month of Phalguna

The Shigmo Festival, or **Shigmotsav**, is the traditional Hindu spring festival that is celebrated in the state of Goa in India. This two-week event begins with participants paying homage to the gods of the Hindu pantheon. Shigmotsav is celebrated in cities throughout Goa and is known for being one of the most colorful and visually exciting events in India. The festival is particularly famous for the elaborate floats that fill the streets of the Goan city of Panaji. During the 14 days of the event, Hindus typically abstain from eating meat and drinking alcohol.

CONTACTS:
Goa Tourism Development Corporation Ltd.
Paryatan Bhavan
2nd Fl.
Panaji, Goa 403 001 India
91-832 -2437132 or 91-832 -2437728; fax: 91-832-2437433
goa-tourism.com

◆ 2603 ◆ **Shilla (Silla) Cultural Festival**
October in even-numbered years

The Shilla Cultural Festival is an exuberant three-day festival, one of Korea's biggest and most impressive, to celebrate the country's ancient Shilla Kingdom. The celebrations are held in Kyongju, the capital of the Shilla Kingdom, and throughout the Kyongju Valley, where there is a great treasure of historic buildings: the Sokkuram Grotto, one of Asia's finest Buddhist shrines with a granite dome; Ch'omsongdae, a seventh-century bottle-shaped stone structure that is the world's earliest known extant observatory; royal tombs; palaces; and pleasure pavilions. The Shilla Kingdom in the southeastern portion of what is now Korea flourished from 57 B.C.E. to 935

C.E., and defeated two rival kingdoms, unifying all three in 676. The Unified Shilla Period is considered a golden age of Buddhist arts and especially of granite Buddhist sculpture.

The festival features concerts, wrestling matches, Buddhist pagoda dancing, games and contests, and lavish processions with elaborate floats.

CONTACTS:
Korea National Tourism Organization
2 Executive Dr.
Ste. 750
Fort Lee, NJ 07024
201-585-0909; fax: 201-585-9041
english.visitkorea.or.kr

◆ 2604 ◆ **Shinbyu**
September 2

Shinbyu is a Burmese Buddhist initiation ceremony for boys. According to traditional beliefs held by many Buddhists, every person should enter a monastery for a time in order to deepen their understanding of the Buddhist religion. This is what the Shinbyu ceremony is about. Parents dress their sons in robes and fancy headdresses that resemble the costume that the Buddha wore before he renounced his life as a prince. The boys ride white horses through the streets in parade and enjoy a sumptuous banquet provided by their parents. Afterwards the boys go to the temple, where their heads are shaved and they enter into the monastic life for a period of time that typically lasts from three days to three months.

◆ 2605 ◆ **Shinju Matsuri Festival**
Late August-early September

The Shinju Matsuri Festival, also known as the **Festival of the Pearl**, is a 10-day celebration of the multicultural heritage of Broome, a tourist town in Western Australia. In the late 1800s, a wealth of pearls was discovered in the region, drawing fortune seekers from Japan, Malaysia, China, and Europe. In celebrating Shinju Matsuri, held annually since 1970, Broome relives those glorious boon days and celebrates the town's distinct ethnic heritage.

During the festival, Broome's Chinatown district is the site of a float parade as well as the waking of Sammy, a Chinese festival dragon. There are also tributes to the town's pearling history, a Mardi Gras festival, a Carnival of Nations, Dragon Boat Races, traditional and contemporary art exhibits, and a Gala Ball. A fireworks ceremony closes the week's festivities.

CONTACTS:
Shinju Matsuri Events Managers
7 Blackman St.
Broome, WA 6725 Australia
61-89-192-6461
www.shinjumatsuri.com.au

◆ 2606 ◆ **Shinnecock Powwow**
September, Labor Day weekend

The Shinnecock Indians, like many other Native Americans, host a major powwow over the long LABOR DAY weekend. People travel from all over the United States, and beyond, to attend. The Shinnecock Powwow has been held for more than 50 years. Events include arts, crafts, music, storytelling, and, of course, dancing competitions.

The Shinneock Indians are part of the Algonquian nation of Indians. "Shinnecock" means "those who live where the land flattens." A good portion of their 500-acre reservation is tidal marshland. The Shinnecock have been known as whalers and fishermen, and many of the foods served at the powwow reflect their historical links to the sea.

CONTACTS:
Shinnecock Indian Nation Tribal Office
P.O. Box 5006
Southampton, NY 11969
631-283-6143; fax: 631-822-1270
www.shinnecocknation.org

♦ 2607 ♦ **Shinran-Shonin Day**
May-June

Shinran-Shonin (1173-1262) was a Japanese Buddhist monk and a disciple of Honen, the founder of the Pure Land sect of Buddhism in Japan. Although Shinran did not wish to oppose his teacher by founding a new denomination, he did strive to clarify how the principles of Pure Land Buddhism were constituted, and the school of Buddhism he founded is therefore known as the "True Pure Land School," or Jodo Shin-shu.

Shinran thought that people achieved salvation through faith rather than through religious practices. Therefore, he disagreed with the celibacy and hardships imposed by monastic Buddhism. Although Shinran was not the first Buddhist monk to marry, his marriage signified the point in history where Japan began to turn in the direction of lay Buddhism. Shinran-Shonin Day is observed in May or June by Japanese Pure Land Buddhists.

♦ 2608 ♦ **Shiprock Navajo Nation Fair**
Usually first weekend of October

Also known as the **Northern Navajo Fair**, this fair began in 1924 and is considered the oldest and most traditional of Navajo fairs. It is a harvest fair held in Shiprock, New Mexico, the largest populated community of the Navajo Nation.

The fair coincides with the conclusion of an ancient healing ceremony, the NAVAJO NIGHT CHANT. This is a nine-day chant known as the *Yei Bei Chei*, and is a complex ritual usually conducted after the first frost. Parts of the ceremony may be witnessed by the public. Among the more colorful public rituals are *Two Yei's Come* and the grand finale in which sacred masked dancers begin a dance late Saturday night and continue into the pre-dawn.

After watching the healing ceremony, spectators go on to other events of the fair such as an all-Indian rodeo, an inter-

tribal powwow, a livestock show, a carnival, the Miss Northern Navajo Pageant, Indian arts and crafts exhibits, and a Saturday morning parade.

See also NAVAJO NATION FAIR AT WINDOW ROCK.

CONTACTS:
Northern Navajo Nation Fair Office
Fair Director
P.O. Box 2120
Shiprock, NM 87499
505-918-7624
northernnavajonationfair.org

Navajo Tourism Department
P.O. Box 663
Window Rock, AZ 86515
928-810-8501; fax: 928-810-8500
www.discovernavajo.com

♦ 2609 ♦ **Shishi Odori (Deer Dance)**
Various

The Shishi Odori or **Deer Dance** of Japan's Ehime Prefecture dates back to the early 17th century. Young boys wearing deer masks with antlers beat small drums known as *kodaiko* and act out a search for the female deer who tries to conceal herself. At the Uwatsuhiko Shrine at Uwajima, the *Yatsushishi-odori*, or Eight Deers Dance, performed in late October, is particularly graceful and is one of the highlights of the autumn festivals held in the Ehime Prefecture.

A Shishi Odori is also held at Hananomaki in Iwate Prefecture. Eight men wearing deer masks perform a sunlight, moonlight, and starlight dance; a measured, ceremonial dance; and a dance that tells the story of a deer's life. This kind of dancing is usually performed during the month of March, but only at the request of visitors.

CONTACTS:
Japan National Tourism Organization
1 Grand Central Pl.
60 E. 42nd St.
Ste. 448
New York, NY 10165
212-757-5640; fax: 212-307-6754
www.japantravelinfo.com

♦ 2610 ♦ **Shivaratri**
February-March; 14th day of waning half of Hindu month of Phalguna

A Hindu holiday observed throughout India and Nepal. Legend says that on this night Lord Shiva, the great god of destruction (who is also the restorer), danced the Tandav, his celestial dance of Creation, Preservation, and Destruction. Hindu devotees of Shiva eat only once on the day before this "Night of Shiva," and then fast and tell stories about him. In India, pilgrims throng the Shiva shrines in Chidambaram (Tamil Nadu), Kalahasti (Andhra Pradesh), and Varanasi (Uttar Pradesh), where special celebrations are held. Mandi in Himachal Pradesh becomes one big party. Devotees carry deities on temple chariots, and there are folk dances and folk music.

Hundreds of thousands make the pilgrimage to Pashupatinath Temple in Kathmandu, Nepal, for worship, feasting, and ritual bathing in the holy Bagmati River.

In Port Louis, Mauritius, wooden arches covered with flowers are carried to Grand Bassin, to get water from the holy lake to wash the symbols of Shiva.

CONTACTS:
Sri Siva Vishnu Temple
6905 Cipriano Rd.
Lanham, MD 20706
301-552-3335; fax: 301-552-1204
www.ssvt.org

Ministry of Tourism, Government of India
1270 Ave. of the Americas
Ste. 303
New York, NY 10020
212-586-4901 or 212-586-4902; fax: 212-582-3274
tourism.gov.in

♦ 2611 ♦ Shravani Mela
July-August; in the Hindu month of Sravana

Shravani Mela is an annual pilgrimage celebrated at the Baba Baidyanath Temple, located in the northeastern state of Jharkhand in India. Every year devotees make the journey from the sacred river Ganges at Sultanganj in Bihar to the Baba Baidyanath Temple. Participants come from as far away as Nepal, Bhutan, and other countries across the world. Many saffron-clad *sadhus,* or ascetics, in India make this journey on foot carrying water from the Ganges to make an offering to Shiva, the presiding deity of the temple. The holy water is carried in urns fastened to a bamboo pole called a *kanwar,* which the pilgrim balances on his shoulders. The entire pilgrimage route reverberates with chants of *Bol Bam,* an invocation believed to generate psychological strength and enthusiasm among the devotees to help them on their arduous journey.

Individuals who undertake the pilgrimage are required to observe a vow of celibacy and uphold all moral virtues during the holy month. They have to keep their body and mind pure, walk bare-footed, and do charitable deeds while they carry the holy water. This pilgrimage originated in Hindu mythology. According to legend, Shiva (a primary god of the Hindu trinity) swallowed the venom of a deadly snake that was threatening to destroy the universe. The other gods in the Hindu pantheon offered Shiva the sacred waters of the Ganges to reduce the effects of the poison. The Shravani Mela is believed to be a ritual enactment of this religious story.

CONTACTS:
Department of Tourism, Govt. of Jharkhand
Jharkhand Tourist Information Centre
Deoghar, Deoghar India
91-6432-222422
www.jharkhandtourism.in

♦ 2612 ♦ Shrimp Festival, National
Second weekend in October

A waterside festival held for four days in Gulf Shores, Ala., drawing crowds estimated at 200,000. This festival began in this shrimping and resort area in 1971 as a one-day event to liven things up after LABOR DAY. The big event was a shrimp-cooking contest, and shrimp dishes have been in the forefront since. About 30 percent of the food vendors' fare includes shrimp, with lots of jambalaya and kabobs. Also on the menu are such dishes as shark and Greek foods including seafood gyros (pronounced YEER-ohs). Events of the festival include a children's art village, an air show, live musical entertainment, and arts and crafts displays.

CONTACTS:
Coastal Alabama Business Chamber, Special Events Director
3150 Gulf Shores Pkwy.
Gulf Shores, AL 36542
251-968-6091
myshrimpfest.com

Coastal Alabama Business Chamber
3150 Gulf Shores Pkwy.
P.O. Drawer 3869
Gulf Shores, AL 36542
251-968-6904; fax: 251-968-5332
www.mygulfcoastchamber.com

♦ 2613 ♦ Shrove Monday
Between February 2 and March 8; Monday before Ash Wednesday

Many countries celebrate Shrove Monday as well as SHROVE TUESDAY, both days marking a time of preparation for LENT. It is often a day for eating pastry, as the butter and eggs in the house must all be used up before Lent. In Greece it is known as **Clean Monday** and is observed by holding picnics at which Lenten foods are served. In Iceland, the Monday before Lent is known as **Bun Day**. The significance of the name is twofold: It is a day for striking people on the buttocks with a stick before they get out of bed as well as a day for eating sweet buns with whipped cream. The latter custom is believed to have been introduced by Danish and Norwegian bakers who emigrated to Iceland during the late 19th century.

♦ 2614 ♦ Shrove Tuesday
Between February 3 and March 9; day before Ash Wednesday

There are a number of names in the West for the last day before the long fast of LENT. The French call it MARDI GRAS (meaning "Fat Tuesday"), because it was traditionally a time to use up all the milk, butter, and eggs left in the kitchen. These ingredients often went into pancakes, which is why the English call it PANCAKE DAY and still celebrate it with games and races that involve tossing pancakes in the air.

Other names include **Shuttlecock** (or **Football**) **Day**, after sports associated with this day; **Doughnut Day**; **Bannock** (or **Bannocky**) **Day** (a bannock being the Scottish equivalent of a pancake), and **Fastingong** (meaning "approaching a time of fast"). The name "Shrove Tuesday" is derived from the Christian custom of confessing sins and being "shriven" (i.e., absolved) just before Lent.

In northern Sweden, people eat a meat stew. In the south, they eat Shrove Tuesday buns called *semlor*, made with cardamom, filled with almond paste, and topped with whipped cream.

No matter what its name, the day before ASH WEDNESDAY has long been a time for excessive eating and merrymaking. The Mardi Gras parade in New Orleans is typical of the masquerades and dancing in the streets that take place in many countries on this day as people prepare for the long Lenten fast.

See also CARNIVAL; CHEESE SUNDAY; CHEESE WEEK; FASCHING; FASTENS-EEN.

CONTACTS:
British National Tourism Agency
845 Third Ave.
10th Fl.
New York, NY 10022
212-850-0336
www.visitbritain.org

♦ 2615 ♦ Shrove Tuesday (Bohemia)
Between February 3 and March 9; day before Ash Wednesday

In the Bohemian region of the Czech Republic, a mummer known as the "Oats Goat" traditionally is led from house to house on SHROVE TUESDAY. He dances with the women of the house, and in return they feed him and give him money. Like the Fastnachtsbär (or Shrovetide Bear) in parts of Germany, the Oats Goat is dressed in straw and wears horns on his head. He is associated with fertility; at one time it was widely believed that dancing with the Fastnachtsbär ensured the growth of crops.

♦ 2616 ♦ Shrove Tuesday (Estonia)
Between February 3 and March 9; day before Ash Wednesday

Schools are closed in Estonia on the last day before LENT, known as **Vastla Päev**, and children often spend the entire day sledding. At night, their mothers serve a traditional SHROVE TUESDAY soup, which is made from pigs' feet boiled with dried peas or lima beans. After dinner, the children play with the *vuriluu kont*, or the bones left over from the pigs' feet soup. A hole is drilled in each bone and a doubled rope is inserted through the hole. When the contrivance is manipulated in a certain way it causes a terrific rattle, which delights the children and is a traditional way to end the day's celebration.

♦ 2617 ♦ Shrove Tuesday (Finland)
Between February 3 and March 9; day before Ash Wednesday

Children in Finland often spend SHROVE TUESDAY, a school holiday, sledding and enjoying other outdoor sports. According to an old folk saying, the better the coasting and the longer the hills one rides on **Laskiaispäivä**, the more bountiful the coming harvest will be. A typical Finnish meal on this day would include pea soup and *blini*, or rich pancakes, served with caviar and *smetana*, a kind of sour milk. A typical dessert consists of wheat buns filled with almond paste, placed in deep dishes, and eaten with hot milk.

There are many folk beliefs surrounding Shrove Tuesday. At one time, women would not spin on this day, believing that if they did, no flax would grow the following summer. Men refrained from planing wood, the common wisdom being that if farm animals walked on the chips made by the planes, their feet would become swollen and sore.

♦ 2618 ♦ Shrove Tuesday (Netherlands)
Between February 3 and March 9; day before Ash Wednesday

The day preceding the Lenten fast is known as **Vastenavond** (Fast Eve) in the Netherlands, where it is a time for feasting and merrymaking. In the provinces of Limburg and Brabant, it is customary to eat pancakes and *oliebollen*, or rich fried cakes with currants, raisins, and apples added. Brabant specializes in *worstebrood*, a special kind of bread that appears ordinary on the outside but is filled with spiced sausage meat.

In the southern part of the country, the CARNIVAL season lasts for three days, beginning on the Sunday before ASH WEDNESDAY. In other areas, the celebration is confined to one day. The farmers of Schouwen-en-Duiveland, on the island of Zeeland, still observe the old Vastenavond custom of gathering at the village green with their horses in the afternoon. The animals are carefully groomed and decorated with paper roses. The men ride their horses down to the beach, making sure the animals get their feet wet. The leader of the procession toots on a horn. It is possible that this custom originated in an ancient spring purification rite, when blowing horns was believed to drive away evil spirits and getting wet was a symbolic act of cleansing.

♦ 2619 ♦ Shrove Tuesday (Pennsylvania Dutch)
Between February 3 and March 9; day before Ash Wednesday

Among the Pennsylvania Dutch, work is taboo on SHROVE TUESDAY, just as it is on other religious holidays. There is an old superstition that if a woman sews on Shrove Tuesday, she will prevent her hens from laying their eggs. Some believe that sewing on this day means that the house will be visited by snakes during the spring and summer.

A special kind of cake or doughnut known as a *fasnacht* is eaten on this day. Rectangular with a slit down the middle, it is often soaked with molasses and then dunked in saffron tea. Sometimes the fasnachts were crumbled and fed to the chickens in the belief that it would prevent the hawks from snatching the chicks in the spring. Another old custom associated with Shrove Tuesday is "barring out," or locking the teacher out of the local school. In many areas, CHRISTMAS is barring-out day.

♦ 2620 ♦ Shrovetide (Norway) (Fastelavn)
Between February 3 and March 9; Sunday before Ash Wednesday

Formerly observed on the Monday before ASH WEDNESDAY, Fastelavn, or **Shrove Sunday**, is a holiday that Norwegian children anticipate eagerly. They rise at dawn and, armed with *fastelavnsris* (decorated birch or evergreen branches), they go from room to room and strike with their branches anyone who is still in bed. The children receive a hot cross bun for every victim they spank.

The fastelavnsris can be quite elaborate, often decorated with tinsel and paper streamers or brightly colored paper roses. Sometimes a doll with stiff, full skirts is tied to the topmost branch. The curious custom of switching with branches may be traced to an ancient pagan rite heralding the fruitfulness of spring.

♦ 2621 ♦ Shunbun-no-Hi (Vernal Equinox Day)
March 21

In Japan, where the VERNAL EQUINOX is a national holiday, the entire week during which the equinox occurs is called HIGAN, which means "other shore." According to Buddhist belief, a river divides this world and the next; it is only by crossing the river, which entails resisting temptation's powerful currents, that one attains enlightenment.

The observance of Vernal Equinox Day began during the reign of seventh-century Prince Shotoku. It became a national holiday during the Meiji period. Visiting the family cemetery is a popular activity on this day, and people tend to regard it as a happy event. Although no meat is served during the week, *o-hagi*, soft rice balls covered with sweetened bean paste, are popular, as is rice and vegetables with a vinegar-based sauce. Shunbun-no-Hi is a day set aside to honor nature and to show respect for growing things.

CONTACTS:
Japan National Tourism Organization
1 Grand Central Pl.
60 E. 42nd St.
Ste. 448
New York, NY 10165
212-757-5640; fax: 212-307-6754
www.jnto.go.jp

Japanese Center for Intercultural Communications
1-1-1-609 Iwado-Kita
Komae-shi, Tokyo 201-0004 Japan
81-334-301-780; fax: 81-334-301-740
www.cichonyaku.com

♦ 2622 ♦ Shwedagon Pagoda Festival
February-March; full moon day of the Burmese month of Tabaung

The people of Myanmar (formerly Burma) celebrate their local pagodas or temples on the full moon day in the month of Tabaung (February-March in the Gregorian calendar). Visitors to the pagoda take the opportunity to make offerings and to pray. Many people construct a pagoda out of sand, a custom thought to bring good luck.

The largest celebration is held at the Shwedagon Pagoda in Yangon (formerly Rangoon), the capital city of Myanmar. This ancient temple, which is more than 2,500 years old, is 300 feet tall and has a dome covered in gold and precious jewels. People selling flowers, incense, and little gold Buddhas line the steps leading to the pagoda, hoping to sell their wares to people who want to leave an offering at the shrine. Souvenirs, in the form of papier-mâché dolls, hand-woven baskets, cloth and pottery, are for sale in the bamboo stalls clustered at the foot of the pagoda.

The dome of the Shwedagon Pagoda, with its two tons of gold and more than 5,000 diamonds, glitters so brightly that it can often be seen by airplanes flying overhead.

CONTACTS:
Embassy of the Republic of the Union of Myanmar
2300 S. St. N.W.
Washington, D.C. 20008
202-332-3344; fax: 202-332-4351
www.mewashingtondc.com

♦ 2623 ♦ Siaosi Tupou I (King) Day
December 4

Located in the Pacific Ocean some 1,250 miles north of New Zealand, the island nation of Tonga consists of about 150 islands, 36 of which are inhabited, with a population of about 120,000. King George Tupou I, also known by his Tongan name of King Siaosi Tupou I, was the first king of the Pacific island nation. He took on the title on December 4, 1845, and the date is a Tongan national holiday.

Born into the extensive royalty of Tonga, Tupou wanted to be named king at an early age. But he was not recognized by the chiefs because he came from the small island of Ha'apai. Tupou resorted to military engagement to secure the cooperation of some chiefs. A series of political maneuvers over some 15 years, including earning the backing of local missionaries by promising to spread Christianity in the region, eventually made the ambitious Tupou to be legally named king of all the Tongan islands.

Tupuo's rule was marked by a number of landmark events. He abolished serfdom and introduced the nation's first written laws. He opened the country's first parliament and introduced its first constitution. He also forbade the purchase of Tongan land by foreigners, hoping in this way to stop what he saw as the exploitation of his people. Tupou ruled as king in a constitutional monarchy with legally-defined powers until his death in 1893.

Tonga honors King Tupou I for establishing much about their country, both good and bad, that still distinguishes it today.

CONTACTS:
Tonga Consulate General
1350 Bayshore Hwy
Ste 610
Burlingame, CA 94010
650-685-1001; fax: 650-685-1003
www.tongaconsul.com

♦ 2624 ♦ Sibelius Festival
First two weeks in October

Jean Sibelius (1865-1957) was a Finnish composer known for his seven symphonies and many symphonic poems for orchestra. Most of the symphonic poems are based on the *Kalevala*, Finland's national epic poem. But his most famous work is *Finlandia*, which was first performed in Helsinki in 1900. Because it expressed so much national pride and patriotism, the work became the anthem of the Finnish independence movement, and for many years the Russians refused to allow its performance.

From 1951 to 1965 Helsinki hosted Sibelius Weeks as an annual musical tribute to the composer; after 1965 the festival expanded to become the HELSINKI FESTIVAL. Today an annual Sibelius Festival is held in the town of Järvenpää during the first two weeks in October.

CONTACTS:
City of Jarvenpaa
Seutulantie 12 (First fl.)
P.O. Box 41
Jarvenpaa, 04401 Finland
358-9-2719-2880
www.jarvenpaa.fi

♦ 2625 ♦ Sierra Leone Independence Day
April 27

This national holiday celebrates the day Sierra Leone became independent from Britain in 1961.

Independence Day festivities are especially elaborate in the capital city of Freetown.

CONTACTS:
Embassy of Sierra Leone
1701 19th St. N.W.
Washington, D.C. 20009
202-939-9261; fax: 202-483-1793
embassyofsierraleone.net

♦ 2626 ♦ Signal: Prague Light Festival
October

Signal: Prague Light Festival is an artistic light show that has become one of the most popular cultural events in the Czech Republic. During the event, the city of Prague, with its historic buildings, streets, parks, and squares, is transformed into a virtual gallery of visual art. More than 30 artists showcase their talents through various interactive lighting and audiovisual installations, including laser beams, strobe lights, and light sculptures. One of the innovative technologies common to the festival is video mapping, which uses lasers to project images onto a structure. Signal: Prague Light Festival features works by international and Czech artists, many of whom premiere their installations at the event. Some of the city's famous landmarks for outdoor lighting and video mapping exhibits include the Old Town Square, Hybernia Palace, the Fruit Market, the Church of St. Ludmila, Charles Bridge, and the Museum Kampa. The annual festival was first held in 2013, drawing 250,000 visitors.

CONTACTS:
SIGNAL Festival
Kubelíkova 27
Praha, 13000 Czech Republic
www.signalfestival.com

♦ 2627 ♦ Sihanouk (King) Commemoration Day
October 15

The nation of Cambodia observes October 15 as a public holiday to commemorate King Norodom Sihanouk, the most respected ruler who led the country to independence from France in 1953. Known as the "King-father of Cambodia," Sihanouk is greatly revered for his contributions to national reconciliation and unity during the long period of political and social instability in the country. In 2004, Sihanouk voluntarily abdicated the throne in favor of his son, the current King Norodom Sihamoni. Upon his death on October 15, 2012, Cambodia announced a week of mourning, and a government decree required all ministries, and public and private institutions to observe the day and honor the former ruler in accordance with Cambodian traditions. The decree also mandated Cambodian embassies and consulates- general to foreign countries to honor the late King with appropriate observances. Most of the celebrations take place in the capital city of Phnom Penh, where pagodas and other places of worship hold commemorative ceremonies, and the Ministry of Information airs programs on the late King's biography and achievements.

♦ 2628 ♦ Silent Days
Begins between March 19 and April 22;
Thursday, Friday, and Saturday before Easter

The last three days of HOLY WEEK—MAUNDY THURSDAY, GOOD FRIDAY, and HOLY SATURDAY—were at one time referred to as the **Swidages**, from an Old English word meaning "to besilent." From this came Silent Days or **Still Days**—three days during which the church bells in England remained silent. The bells were rung again at the EASTER Vigil service.

♦ 2629 ♦ "Silent Night, Holy Night"
December 24

The world's best known Christmas carol, "Silent Night, Holy Night," was written and composed by Franz Gruber and Father Josef Mohr. The carol was first performed on CHRIST-

MAS EVE, 1818, at St. Nickola Church in Oberndorf, Austria. This event is commemorated in Oberndorf, Hallein, Wagrain, Salzburg, and other towns in the state of Salzburg by holding a candlelight procession on December 24. Everyone sings the carol as they march to the church and again when they are inside. It is usually sung in various languages to honor the many nations where the birth of the Christ child is celebrated.

CONTACTS:
Silent Night Society (e.V.)
Stille-Nacht-Platz 7
Oberndorf bei Salzburg, A-5110 Austria
43-6649-3099-19
www.stillenacht.at/en

♦ 2630 ♦ Simadan Festival
February-April

Simadan is a folk festival celebrating the sorghum harvest on the island of Bonaire in the Netherlands Antilles. Sorghum is a cereal grass, and it was at one time a staple for the island's natives. Farm owners, known as *kunuku*, enlist the aid of their friends, family, and neighbors to harvest the crop. To give thanks for the assistance and the abundant harvest, they hold a Simadan consisting of traditional food, song, and dance.

Foods served at the festival include goat soup, *funchi* (similar to finely textured grits), *giambo* (okra soup), *repa* (sorghum-based pancakes), and *boontji kunuku* (beans). The music features back-and-forth singing from one group to another accompanied by such instruments as the guitar, marimba, *bari* (drum), *karko* (conchshell), and triangle. Hand-clapping also drives the rhythm. The *wapa*, a Simadan dance, involves rows of dancers moving and interacting with each other to a steady beat.

In the past, Bonaireans stored their food in the *Mangasina di Rey*, or Storehouse of the King, located in the village of Rincon. At the height of the harvest season, the kunuku would make a thanksgiving offering of sorghum seed, which would be blessed by the priest and stored in the Mangasina di Rey. This took place during EASTER and was known as Simadan di Pastor. This particular festival continues to be celebrated in Rincon and Nikiboko.

CONTACTS:
Bonaire Government Tourist Office, Adams Unlimited
80 Broad St. 32nd Fl.
Ste. 3202
New York, NY 10004 United States
212-956-5912 or 800-266-2473; fax: 212-956-5913
www.tourismbonaire.com

♦ 2631 ♦ Simbra Oilor (Sheep Counting)
May

Simbra (or Sambra) Oilor is a rural folk festival held in parts of Romania, including Transylvania and Banat. In May people herd sheep to the mountains for summer grazing. But before they leave, on the morning of Simbra Oilor all the sheep are milked in order to estimate how much cheese each

will produce. This cheese will then be paid throughout the summer to those who own the sheep. Afterwards, there is a community potluck feast.

In some places a similar festival is held in the fall when the sheep are brought back down from the mountains.

CONTACTS:
Romanian National Tourist Office
355 Lexington Ave.
8th Fl.
New York, NY 10017
212-545-8484
www.romaniatourism.com

♦ 2632 ♦ Simhat Torah
Between September 28 and October 26; Tishri 22 or 23

or 23 This Jewish holiday, which follows SUKKOT, celebrates the annual completion of the public reading of the Torah, or the first five books of the Bible, and the beginning of a new reading cycle. The hand-lettered scrolls of the Torah are removed from the Ark (a box-like container) and paraded around the synagogue—and sometimes through the streets—amidst singing and dancing. Simhat Torah means "rejoicing in the law," which is as good a description as any of what takes place on this day. To be chosen as the Bridegroom of the Law—to read the final verses of the last book, Deuteronomy—or the Bridegroom of the Beginning—to read the opening verses of the first book, Genesis—is considered a great honor.

In Israel and among Reform Jews, this festival is observed on the 22nd day of Tishri, concurrently with SHEMINI ATZERET; all other Jews celebrate it separately on the 23rd day. Israelis also hold a second *hakkafot* ("procession around the synagogue") on the night after Simhat Torah, frequently accompanied by bands and choirs.

Simhat Torah customs have varied from country to country. In Afghanistan all the scrolls are taken out of their Arks and heaped in a pyramid almost to the synagogue's roof. In Cochin, China, a carpet was laid on the courtyard flagstones, coconut oil lamps were heaped in a pyramid in front of the synagogue entrance, and the scrolls of the Law carried around the outside of the synagogue. One synagogue in Calcutta, India, has 50 scrolls, and the women go from scroll to scroll, kissing them. At the end of the holiday a Simhat Torah ball is held and a beauty queen chosen. Young Yemeni children are taken to the synagogue for the first time on this holiday.

In southern France, two mourners stand on either side of the reader, crying bitterly as the death of Moses is related. The Bridegrooms of the Law in Holland are escorted home in a torchlight parade accompanied by music. A crown from one of the Torah scrolls was placed on the head of every reader in medieval Spain, and in some places in eastern Europe, the reader wore a large paper hat decorated with bells and feathers.

CONTACTS:
Union for Reform Judaism
633 Third Ave.
New York, NY 10017
212-563-4000
urj.org

Orthodox Union
11 Broadway
New York, NY 10004
212-650-4000
www.ou.org

◆ 2633 ◆ Sinai Liberation Day
April 25

This legal holiday in Egypt commemorates the final withdrawal of Israeli troops on this date in 1982 under the 1978 Camp David agreement between Egypt and Israel to return the Sinai Peninsula to Egypt.

CONTACTS:
State Information Service
3 Al Estad Al Bahary St.
Nasr City, Cairo Egypt
20-2261-7304
www.sis.gov.eg/En

◆ 2634 ◆ Singapore Food Festival
July

The Singapore Food Festival is a national event held every July that showcases the culinary traditions of Singapore. Launched for the first time in 1994, the festival not only celebrates Singapore's local cuisine, but also acknowledges the influence of the country's multicultural heritage on its culinary landscape. Eateries throughout the country brim with activity during this month-long festival and offer a wide array of flavors that attract food-lovers from inside and outside the country. Besides savoring signature dishes of Chinese, Malay, Indian, and Peranakan cuisine, visitors also experience new versions of traditional flavors. The festival, which is organized by the Singapore Tourism Board, also hosts heritage food trails, culinary workshops, contests, and a variety of other food events. Since its inception, the festival has witnessed a steady increase in attendance, both from tourists as well as professionals from the food and beverage industry. The large scale of the event has helped market Singapore as a food capital of Southeast Asia.

CONTACTS:
Singapore Tourism Board
1 Orchard Spring Ln.
Tourism Ct.
Singapore
65-6736-2000; fax: 800-736-2000
www.yoursingapore.com

◆ 2635 ◆ Singapore National Day
August 9

Singapore National Day is a public holiday in Singapore to commemorate its independence. Singapore was the administrative seat for the Straits Settlements, a British crown colony, from 1867 until it was occupied by Japan in World War II. It was restored to Britain in 1945, became a part of Malaysia in 1963, and became independent in 1965. The holiday is celebrated with a spectacular parade, cultural dances, and fireworks.

CONTACTS:
Singapore Embassy
3501 International Dr. N.W.
Washington, D.C. 20008 United States
202-537-3100; fax: 202-537-0876
www.mfa.gov.sg

◆ 2636 ◆ Sinhala Avurudu
April 13 or 14

Sinhala Avurudu, or New Year, is celebrated in Sri Lanka (formerly Ceylon) as a non-religious festival by both Sinhalese and Tamils. The exact hour of the new year is determined by astrologers, and often the new year does not begin when the old year ends. The few hours between the new and old year are known as the *nona gathe* ("neutral period"), and all activities, including eating and drinking, must stop for that time.

In the villages the new year traditionally begins with lighting a fire in the kitchen and wearing new clothes. The color of these clothes is determined by an almanac. The ceremonies reach a climax with an anointing ceremony. Oil is mixed with an herbal paste and a family elder rubs this oil on the heads of all the family members as they sit with a white cloth under their feet. The holiday is also a day of public festivities, including sports, games, dancing, and special dinners.

CONTACTS:
Sri Lanka Tourist Board
Sri Lanka Tourism Head Office
No. 80, Galle Rd.
Sri Lanka
11-94-11-244-0001; fax: 94-11-244-0001
www.srilanka.travel

◆ 2637 ◆ Sinjska Alka
First weekend in August

Sinjska Alka is a day of jousting on horseback in the small town of Sinj, near Split in Croatia. The festival commemorates a victory of a peasant army over the Turks in 1715, even though the 60,000 Turks outnumbered the Sinj warriors by three to one. The annual tournament was supposedly instituted soon after the 1715 victory.

On this day, young men who have trained throughout the year ride horses headlong down the steep 140-yard run and try to spear an iron ring, or *alka*, suspended from a rope about nine feet off the ground. The ring has a diameter of six inches and within it is another two-inch ring. The jouster who most successfully spears the rings in three tries is the winner and receives a sash and silver medal. The band plays a triumphal march and shots are fired for all top scorers.

Before the contest, there is a ceremonial procession through the streets. The contestants march through Sinj accompanied by their mace bearers and shield bearers wearing 18th-century costumes decorated with gold and silver.

CONTACTS:
Viteska Sinj Alka Society
Šetalište Alojzija Stepinca 2
Sinj, 21230 Croatia
385-21-821-542; fax: 385-21-821-113
www.alka.hr

Sinj Tourist Board
12 Put Petrovca
Sinj, 21230 Croatia
385-21-826-352; fax: 385-21-660-360
www.visitsinj.com

♦ 2638 ♦ Sinulog Festival
Third weekend in January

The Sinulog Festival takes place on the island of Cebu in the Philippines, held at the same time as the frenzied ATI-ATIHAN FESTIVAL in Kalibo and the more sedate DINAGYANG in Iloilo City. The word *sinulog* is derived from the rootword *sulog*, meaning "river current"; the dancing of the festival is thought to flow like a river.

The festival celebrates both early Cebuano culture and the history of the Christianization of Cebu, combining the pageantry of early years with today's Christian ritual. An image of Cebu's patron saint, the Santo Niño ("the Holy Child," Jesus), is carried in a procession along the streets, while drums beat in the ritual for a bountiful harvest and revelers dance in the streets.

CONTACTS:
Sinulog Foundation, Inc.
Cebu City Sports Center
Osmeña Blvd.
Cebu City, 6000 Philippines
63-32-253-3700; fax: 63-32-254-5010
www.sinulog.ph

Philippine Department of Tourism
556 Fifth Ave.
New York, NY 10036
212-575-7915; fax: 212-302-6759
www.philippinetourismny.org

Cebu City Tourism Commission
Osmeña Blvd.
City Library Bldg.
Cebu City, 6000 Philippines
63-32-412-4355; fax: 63-32-412-4355
www.cebucitytourism.org

♦ 2639 ♦ Sioux Sun Dance
Late June

Although many North American Indian tribes hold ritual dances in honor of the sun and its life-giving powers, the Sioux were known to hold one of the most spectacular. Usu-

ally performed during the SUMMER SOLSTICE, preparations for the dance included the cutting and raising of a tree that would be considered a visible connection between the heavens and earth, and the setting up of teepees in a circle to represent the cosmos.

Participants abstained from food and drink during the dance itself, which lasted from one to four days, and decorated their bodies in the symbolic colors of red (sunset), blue (sky), yellow (lightning), white (light), and black (night). They wore deerskin loincloths, wristlets and anklets made out of rabbit fur, and carried an eagle-wing bone whistle in their mouths. The dance often involved self-laceration or hanging themselves from the tree-pole with their feet barely touching the ground. Sometimes the dancers fell unconscious or tore themselves loose, which was considered evidence that they'd had a visionary experience. After the dance, they were allowed to have a steam bath, food, and water.

See also ARAPAHO SUN DANCE; SOUTHERN UTE TRIBAL SUN DANCE.

CONTACTS:
Akta Lakota Museum & Cultural Center
St. Joseph"s Indian School
1301 N. Main St.
Chamberlain, SD 57325
800-798-3452
aktalakota.stjo.org

♦ 2640 ♦ Sister's Meals Festival
15th-16th day of the third lunar month

Sisters' Meal Festival is celebrated by the Miao people, an ethnic group in the Guizhou province of southwestern China. A version of Valentine's Day, the Sisters' Meal Festival encourages young women to wear their best traditional costumes to meet their suitors. Bullfights, dragon boat races, and village fairs are among the activities featured during the event. Women gather at the riverside to cook sticky rice, which they dye using natural color extracts of wild flowers and leaves picked in the mountains. The grains of rice are dyed blue, white, pink, and yellow to represent the seasons, and are offered to potential suitors in a parcel that also conceals a written message much like fortune cookies. The wooden drum dance and *Lusheng* music from a traditional reed instrument are other important elements of this festival. As the girls dance to the drum beats, suitors arrive from neighboring villages in the hope of finding their future wife. As dusk falls, made partners seal their romance by antiphonal singing.

CONTACTS:
China National Tourist Office
370 Lexington Ave.
Ste. 912
New York, NY 10017
212-760-8218; fax: 212-760-8809
www.cnto.org

♦ 2641 ♦ Sitala Ashtami
March-April; eighth day of the waxing half of the Hindu month of Caitra

Sitala Ashtami is a Hindu festival honoring Sitala, goddess of smallpox. She is named for the chill typically experienced during high fever. She is believed to have the power to protect people from smallpox and to give people smallpox, and her blessings are invoked for protection against the disease.

On this day, Hindu women visit the nearest Sitala shrine in the morning, offering the goddess rice, homemade sweets, cooked food, and holy water mixed with milk. In some places colorful fairs are held near Sitala's shrines, and there is merry-making, dancing, feasting, and the buying and selling of wares.

♦ 2642 ♦ Sithinakha
May-June; sixth day of waxing half of Hindu month of Jyestha

This is the birthday of the Hindu god Kumara, also known as SKANDA, the god of war and son of Shiva. Kumara has six heads because he was nursed by the karttikas—six women who, as stars, comprise the Pleiades. For this reason he is also called *Karttikeya,* "son of Karttikas." The six heads also represent the six senses (including extrasensory perception). He has a large following under the name *Subrahmanya,* meaning "dear to the Brahmanas."

Most Hindus observe this day with a ritual purification bath followed by processions to the temples to honor Kumara. It is also considered a good opportunity to clean out wells and tanks, because the snake gods are off worshipping on this day and it's safe to enter their habitats.

In Nepal, eight different kinds of cakes, made from eight different grains, are offered to Kumara on his birthday, and for this reason Sithinakha is sometimes referred to as the **Cake Festival.** Lotus-shaped windmills are often set on rooftops at this time, to symbolize the end of bad times and the onset of holier days.

♦ 2643 ♦ Sitka Summer Music Festival
First three weeks in June

The Sitka Summer Music Festival is a series of concerts featuring internationally known musicians, held during the first three weeks in June in Sitka, Alaska. Chamber music concerts are held on Tuesdays, Fridays, and Saturdays, and there are programs ranging from classical to pop. The concerts are given in the Centennial Building auditorium, which has a wall of glass behind the stage. Since the nights are light in June, the audience can look at mountains, eagles, water, and mist while listening to the music. Violin virtuoso Paul Rosenthal founded the festival in 1972, producing the first musical event with four other musicians, and going on to emphasize a repertoire of 18th- and 19th-century classics.

CONTACTS:
Sitka Summer Music Festival
104 Jeff Davis St.
Anchorage, AK 99835
907-747-6774
www.sitkamusicfestival.org

♦ 2644 ♦ Sizdah Bedar
April 1st or 2nd, the 13th day after Nawruz

Sizdah Bedar is an annual celebration that falls on the 13th day of the first month of the Iranian calendar. Traditionally, Iranians have spent the day outdoors with friends and family in an attempt to dispel the evil effects associated with the number 13. The celebration of Sizdah Bedar in Iran goes back to the sixth century; its origins are deeply rooted in Persian mythology and Zoroastrianism. Ancient Iranians believed that on this day the angel of rain would vanquish the demon of drought. As a result, they celebrated outdoors and sought divine blessing by sacrificing sheep in hope of a good harvest, strong family, and renewed kinship within the tribe.

People continue to celebrate the day, leaving towns and cities and heading to the woods or mountains to sing, dance, and enjoy nature. Young women knot together blades of grass and make a wish for a good husband and a fulfilling life. Older men play traditional games like backgammon, while youth ride horses and play pranks. At the end of the celebrations, before returning home, they perform the ritual of discarding the *Sabzeh*—sprouts of seven grains prepared as part of the New Year tradition. They believe that the *Sabzeh* has absorbed all of the sicknesses and calamities waiting to befall the family in the coming year. Throwing away the grains is a symbol of rebirth, positive thought, and new hope.

♦ 2645 ♦ Sjomannadagur (Seaman's Day)
First Sunday in June

Sjomannadagur is a day honoring the role that fishing and fishermen have played in Icelandic history, celebrated in the coastal towns and cities of Iceland. Sailors take the day off, and the Seaman's Union sponsors many events. These include competitions in rowing and swimming, tugs-of-war, and sea rescue competitions. On the more solemn side, medals are awarded for rescue operations of the past year. Most celebrations begin with a church service and a trip to the local cemetery to honor sailors lost at sea. Afterward there are children's parades, dances, outdoor cookouts, and bonfires in the evening. The proceeds from the day's events throughout the country go to the national fund that supports old seamen's homes.

CONTACTS:
Promote Iceland
Sundagarðar 2
Reykjavík, 104 Iceland
354-511-4000; fax: 354-511-4040
www.iceland.is

♦ 2646 ♦ Skanda Sashti
October-November; six days beginning the sixth day of the waxing half of the Tamil month of Aippasi (Hindu month of Asadha)

Skanda is a son of Shiva. He is also known as Subrahmanya, especially in southern India. According to Hindu mythology, Shiva cast his seed into fire, where it was afterwards received by the river goddess Ganga (the Ganges River), who "gave birth" to Skanda. She hid him among the rushes on the bank of the river, where he was found by the six *karttikas* (the Pleiades) and raised by them, for which reason he has six heads and is often referred to as Skanda-Karttikeya. He was born for the purpose of destroying Taraka, a demon whom the gods particularly wanted to get rid of. The festival known as Skanda Sashti celebrates Taraka's defeat.

The focus of the celebration is the six holy places in southern India associated with Skanda, especially in the state of Tamil Nadu. Thousands of Hindus gather at each of these temples to sing hymns, chant psalms, and dramatize scenes from the god's life. Hindus believe that observing this festival ensures success, prosperity, happiness, and peace.

See also SITHINAKHA.

CONTACTS:
Murugan Temple of North America
6300 Princess Garden Pkwy.
Lanham, MD 20706
301-552-4889; fax: 301-552-5043
www.murugantemple.org

Tiruchendur Sri Subrahmanya Swami Temple
Tiruchchendur, Tamil Nadu 628 215 India
91-4639-242-221
www.tiruchendurmurugantemple.tnhrce.in

♦ 2647 ♦ Skipjack Races and Land Festival
September, Labor Day weekend

A skipjack is a kind of sail-powered fishing boat popular in the 19th century. Around the turn of the 20th century over 1,000 skipjacks worked the waters off Deal Island, Maryland. By 1960, only 40 remained. It was then that local enthusiasts revived the skipjack races, which dated back to 1871 but had only been organized in 1921. The revived races have continued since 1960, scheduled for LABOR DAY weekend. People from all over the state come to Deal Island harbor on that weekend, to cheer on the skippers of these traditional craft and to honor the contribution that the fishing industry has made to the region's history.

CONTACTS:
Dorchester Skipjack Committee, Inc.
P.O. Box 1224
Cambridge, MD 21613
410-228-7141
www.skipjack-nathan.org

Somerset County Tourism
P.O. Box 243
Princess Anne, MD 21853
410-651-2968 or 800-521-9189
visitsomerset.com

♦ 2648 ♦ Slovak Republic Independence Day
January 1

On January 1, 1993, the Slovak Republic peacefully split off from the Czech Republic and became an independent country. Other national holidays include Constitution Day, commemorating the ratification of the Slovak Republic's constitution on September 1, 1992; National Uprising Day, August 29, observing Slovakia's battle against Nazi Germany in 1944; and July 5, Sts. Cyril and Methodius Day.

CONTACTS:
Embassy of the Slovak Republic
3523 International Ct. N.W.
Washington, D.C. 20008
202-237-1054; fax: 202-237-6438
www.mzv.sk/washington

♦ 2649 ♦ Slovenia National Day
June 25

Slovenia declared its independence from Yugoslavia on June 25, 1991, after elections in 1990 showed that 88% of the people wished to secede from Yugoslavia. Previously, Slovenia, which is a little smaller than New Jersey, was part of the Austria-Hungarian kingdom. It joined with Serbia, Croatia, and Montenegro at the end of World War I, and this federation was called Yugoslavia after 1929.

CONTACTS:
Embassy of the Republic of Slovenia
2410 California St. N.W.
Washington, D.C. 20008
202-386-6601; fax: 202-386-6633
www.washington.embassy.si

♦ 2650 ♦ Smithsonian Folklife Festival
Last weekend in June to first weekend in July

Since 1967 the Festival of American Folklife has been held on the National Mall in Washington, D.C., to celebrate the richness and diversity of American and world cultures. Since that time the Festival has presented more than 15,000 musicians, craftspeople, storytellers, cooks, workers, performers, and other cultural specialists from every region of the United States and from more than 45 other nations. Recent festival programs have included musicians from the former Soviet Union, demonstrations of African-American coil basketry and Italian-American stone-carving, the performance of a Japanese rice-planting ritual, and exhibits illustrating the occupational cultures of working people—taxicab drivers, firefighters, waiters, and railway workers.

The Festival is designed to expose visitors to people and cultures who would not ordinarily be heard in a national setting. It emphasizes folk, tribal, ethnic, and regional traditions in communities throughout the U.S. and abroad. Each year the festival features a particular state (or region) and country. One year, for example, the featured region was "Family Farming in the Heartland." More than 100 farmers from 12 Midwestern states came to the nation's capital to talk to visitors about changes in farming methods and farm life, and to demonstrate both modern and traditional farming skills. The featured country was Indonesia, and there were demonstrations of Buginese boat-building and traditional mask carving, in addition to an all-night Indonesian shadow-puppet show.

CONTACTS:
Smithsonian Center for Folklife and Cultural Heritage
600 Maryland Ave. S.W.
Ste. 2001, MRC 520
Washington, D.C. 20024
202-633-6440; fax: 202-633-6474
www.folklife.si.edu

♦ 2651 ♦ Smithsonian Kite Festival
Late March

The Kite Festival held on the Mall in Washington, D.C., every spring is co-sponsored by the Smithsonian Resident Associate Program and the National Air and Space Museum. First held in 1966, the festival was started by Dr. Paul Garber, a kite fancier and historian emeritus of the National Air and Space Museum. Until his death in 1992, Dr. Garber served as master of ceremonies for the festivities.

A major focus of the annual festival is the competition for hand-made kites, which must be capable of flying at a minimum altitude of 100 feet for at least one minute. Kites are judged on the basis of appearance (design, craftsmanship, beauty) as well as on performance (takeoff, climb, angle, recovery). Trophies are awarded in many categories—for example, airplane, bird figure, box-kite, spacecraft, and delta—and age groups. Participants come from all regions of the United States as well as several foreign countries. Immediately following the kite display program, a kite-building workshop is held for members of the Smithsonian Resident Associate Program.

CONTACTS:
Smithsonian Associates
1100 Jefferson Dr. S.W.
P.O. Box 23293
Washington, D.C. 20026
202-633-3030; fax: 202-786-2034
smithsonianassociates.org

♦ 2652 ♦ Smithville Fiddlers Jamboree and Crafts Festival
Weekend near July 4

Acclaimed enough to have been the subject of an hour-long documentary on national television, the Fiddlers Jamboree and Crafts Festival held every year on a weekend near the FOURTH OF JULY in Smithville, Tennessee, celebrates the style of country music popularly known as bluegrass. Musical competitions are held in 24 different categories, including fiddle, banjo, mandolin, guitar, dulcimer, harmonica, folk singing, gospel singing, buck dancing, and clog dancing.

There are also musical performances, both formal and impromptu, as well as more than 200 booths where working artists and craftspeople display their work. Most of the events are held on a stage set up in front of the DeKalb County Courthouse. The highlight of the festival is a head-to-head contest between the best of the fiddlers. The winner receives a cash prize and the Berry C. Williams Memorial Trophy, named after the festival's founder.

CONTACTS:
Smithville Fiddlers' Jamboree
P.O. Box 83
Smithville, TN 37166
615-597-8500
smithvillejamboree.com

♦ 2653 ♦ Snan Yatra
May-June; full moon day of Hindu month of Jyestha

This Hindu bathing festival is held in Puri, Orissa, India. Images of the gods Jagannath, Balbhadra, Subhadra, and Sudarshan are brought in a grand procession to the bathing platform for their ceremonial baths. As mantras from the Vedas, or Hindu sacred writings, are recited, consecrated water is poured over the deities. Then they are dressed in ceremonial robes before going into seclusion for 15 days. For Hindus, this is an occasion for rejoicing and merrymaking.

♦ 2654 ♦ So Joo Festival: The Eve of St. John's Feast Day
June 23

June 23, the eve of the Feast of St. John the Baptist, is celebrated each year in Porto, Portugal, with a curious ritual. Festival-goers tap each other on the head with plastic hammers or leeks. Some say the gesture indicates romantic interest, others claim it brings good luck to the recipient. The custom can be traced to the 19th century, when long-stemmed garlic flowers were used in mid-summer games, and in turn, to pagan times. Indeed, the fireworks, music, all-night dancing, and colorful processions that feature on St. John's Eve are more closely allied to pagan summer solstice rituals than religious observances. A large amount of wine is drunk, and grilled sardines are consumed. The festival is also known as "So Joo," which is an anglicized form of the Portuguese words for Saint John.

♦ 2655 ♦ Sofia Music Weeks
May-June

Sofia, Bulgaria, is one of Europe's oldest cities and thus an appropriate site for an international classical music festival. For the three weeks of this festival, the capital city's most stately concert halls—including Bulgaria Hall and the National Palace of Culture—open their doors to opera companies, ballet companies, symphonies, orchestras, and other artists. The festival also includes an educational component for classical music students.

The festival first took place in 1971 and expanded throughout that decade. By 1982 it had earned a membership in the European Festivals Association. Although all international performers are welcomed and appreciated, festival organizers ensure representation for national artists. Past years have featured the Sofia Philharmonic, Sofia Opera, Bulgarian Radio Symphony Orchestra and Mixed Choir, and Sofia Soloists Chamber Ensemble. Music selections will often celebrate great native composers.

Beyond the performances, the festival program offers symposiums on music theory, photograph exhibitions, screenings of filmed operas, and master classes for young musicians and singers.

CONTACTS:
Sofia Music Weeks International Festival Foundation
National Palace of Culture
1 Bulgaria Sq.
Sofia, 1414 Bulgaria
359-2-986-1527; fax: 359-2-954-9086
www.worldnn.com/pp/smw

♦ 2656 ♦ Sokjon-Taeje Memorial Rites
Second and eighth lunar months

The Sokjon-Taeje (or Seokjeon-Daeje) Memorial Rites began centuries ago in China to commemorate the contributions of ethical philosopher CONFUCIUS. The Rites are no longer held in China, but they continue to be observed twice a year, in the spring and in the autumn, at the important Songgyung-wan University in Seoul, South Korea. Confucianism has had a deep and lasting impact on Korean culture. Among other things, Confucius taught respect for one's elders and those in authority, which is a legacy Koreans hold to today.

Students participate in the somber ceremony, which includes offerings of food and wine to Confucius, traditional dances and costumes, and poem recitations.

♦ 2657 ♦ Sol
January-February; first day of first lunar month;
January 1-2

One of the biggest holidays of the year in Korea, Sol, or LUNAR NEW YEAR, is celebrated largely by rural people and is a two-day national holiday. January 1 and 2, also national holidays, are celebrated more by residents of cities. On Sol, tradition calls for families to gather in their best clothes and for children to bow to parents and grandparents to reaffirm family ties. A soup made of rice dumplings called *duggook* is always served, and it is customary to play *yut*, a game played with wooden blocks and a game board. Young girls see-saw standing up. During early Confucianism, women were not allowed any outdoor exercises. See-sawing this way bounced them above their enclosing walls, and they could see their boyfriends. This made see-sawing a love sport and not exercise. It is still very popular.

CONTACTS:
Korea Tourism Organization (KTO)
2 Executive Dr.
Ste. 750
Fort Lee, NJ 07024
201-585-0909 or 888-868-7567; fax: 201-585-9041
english.visitkorea.or.kr

♦ 2658 ♦ Solidarity with the Palestinian People, International Day of
November 29

In 1977, the General Assembly of the UNITED NATIONS declared November 29 International Day of Solidarity with the Palestinian People. On December 1, 2000, the Assembly reaffirmed the U.N.'s responsibility to work towards the peaceful creation of a Palestinian homeland and lauded those countries that observed the International Day of Solidarity with the Palestinian People.

CONTACTS:
United Nations, Department of Public Information
1 UN Plaza. Rm. DC1-1106
New York, NY 10017
212-963-6842; fax: 212-963-6914
www.un.org/en

♦ 2659 ♦ Solomon Islands Independence Day
July 7

The Solomon Islands in the southwest Pacific gained independence from Britain on this day in 1978. They had been under British control since 1900. Independence Day is a national holiday throughout the islands.

CONTACTS:
Permanent Mission of Solomon Islands
800 Second Ave.
Ste. 400 L
New York, NY 10017
212-599-6192; fax: 212-661-8925
www.un.int

♦ 2660 ♦ Somalia Independence Day
July 1

Somalia became an independant, unified country on July 1, 1960. In colonial times, Somalia was divided up between Britain and Italy. The northern part of the region was British Somaliland, and other areas belonged to Italy. June 26 is the anniversary of independence of British Somaliland from Britain in 1960, while July 1, 1960, is the day the former Italian Somaliland became independent from Italy. On July 1, 1960, both areas were united as the Republic of Somalia.

Following a government overthrow in 1991, the country disintegrated into civil war until a transitional national government was established in October 2000. The transition process ended in 2012 when a new provisional constitution was passed and Somalia was reformed as a federation with a permanent central government. That same year, 275 members of parliament were appointed, who subsequently elected a new president.

CONTACTS:
Ka Joog Organization
1420 Washington Ave. S.
Minneapolis, MN 55454
612-255-3524; fax: 612-255-3523
www.kajoog.org

♦ 2661 ♦ Song of Hiawatha Pageant
Last two weekends in July and first weekend in August

Pipestone, Minnesota, was named for the soft red stone used by the Native American Dakota tribe to make their ceremonial pipes. The Dakotas believe that their tribe originated here, and that the stone was colored by the blood of their ancestors.

On weekends in late July and early August each year, the story of Hiawatha (Haionhwat'ha, fl. c.1570)—the chief of the Onondaga tribe immortalized in Henry Wadsworth Longfellow's poem, "Song of Hiawatha"—is told in symbolic pantomime with traditional Indian music and dances. The audience watches the performance from the opposite side of a quiet reflecting pool that lies at the bottom of the pipestone quarry where the pageant is held.

The Great Spirit appears at the top of the cliff, where he shows his children the pink stone and makes a calumet or peace pipe. With the last whiff on his pipe, the Great Spirit disappears in a cloud of smoke. The Three Maidens, who once guarded the place where the Great Spirit lived, can be seen in the form of three huge boulders. The pageant ends with the death of Hiawatha and his departure on a "long and distant journey.".

CONTACTS:
Pipestone Chamber of Commerce
117 Eighth Ave. S.E.
P.O. Box 8
Pipestone, MN 56164
507-825-3316 or 800-336-6125
www.pipestoneminnesota.com

♦ 2662 ♦ **Songkran**
Around April 12-15 (when the Sun enters Aries)

Songkran is the traditional NEW YEAR in Thailand and a public holiday. The celebration actually lasts for three days in mid-April, and takes the form of religious ceremonies as well as public festivities. Merit-making ceremonies are held at Buddhist temples, water is sprinkled on Buddhist images, and captive birds and fish are freed. Water-splashing on the streets is also a part of the festivities, especially among young people. The young do not splash older people, but instead sprinkle water on their hands or feet to honor them.

The celebration is held with special élan in Chiang Mai with beauty contests, parades, dancing, and, of course, water splashing.

See also WATER-SPLASHING FESTIVAL.

CONTACTS:
Tourism Authority of Thailand
61 Broadway
Ste. 2810
New York, NY 10006
212-432-0433; fax: 212-269-2588
www.tourismthailand.org

♦ 2663 ♦ **Sonoma Country Harvest Fair**
First weekend in October

The Sonoma County Harvest Fair is an event conducted annually in Santa Rosa, California. It is a celebration of local food and drink, with a major emphasis on the different varieties of wine, beer, and cider produced in the area. More than 150 wineries take part in the fair in addition to restaurants and food vendors.

CONTACTS:
Sonoma County Harvest Fair
1350 Bennett Valley Rd.
Santa Rosa, CA 95404
707-545-4200
www.harvestfair.org

♦ 2664 ♦ **Soul Saturdays (Saturday of Souls)**
Dates vary with most in February through May

Soul Saturdays are a series of Saturdays set aside in the liturgical calendar of Eastern and Greek Orthodox Catholic Churches for the remembrance of those who have died. These days occur on designated Saturdays before and during the seasons of LENT and EASTER: the first two are observed on the two Saturdays before Lent begins, the third Saturday of Souls coincides with the first Saturday of Lent, and the fourth Soul Saturday takes place on the Saturday before PENTECOST, the close of the Easter season.

Saturday holds special significance in the religious calendar as the day on which the crucified Jesus lay dead in the tomb before his resurrection. On each Soul Saturday a special service is held where prayers are offered in memory of those who have died and a list of the names of the dead is recited. Participants attending the services prepare *kollyva*, a dish made of sweetened, boiled wheat kernels, raisins, almonds, and pomegranate seeds that is traditionally associated with funerals and memorial services in Greece and Eastern Europe. In addition to attending religious services, participants often visit the graves of departed family members on Soul Saturdays, to clean and decorate the burial sites.

CONTACTS:
Orthodox Church in America
6850 N. Hempstead Tpke
Syosset, NY 11791
516-922-0550; fax: 516-922-0954
oca.org

♦ 2665 ♦ **Sound Symposium**
July in even-numbered years

The Sound Symposium is an international music and arts festival held every two years in St. John's, Newfoundland, Canada. The symposium features an eclectic mix of artists whose work involves the innovative or masterful manipulation of sound, and hopes to inspire rising artists to explore new avenues in music, performance art, and the visual arts.

Performances take place in a variety of locales, from concert halls to the streets, and from old army bunkers to the beach. They include dance, theater, performance art, gallery exhibitions, and all kinds of music. Participants may sample new expressions in jazz, electronic music, percussion, rock and roll, classical, folk music, experimental music, world music, improvisational music, and experiments with newly invented instruments. The musicians who participate in the "Harbor Symphony," for example, board boats and play compositions written for the various whistles and horns on board. Symposium participants may also join workshops led by the guest artists.

CONTACTS:
Sound Symposium
c/o Sound Arts Initiatives, Inc
P.O. Box 23232
St. John's, NL A1B 4J9 Canada
709-753-4630; fax: 709-753-4630
www.soundsymposium.com

♦ 2666 ♦ South Africa Freedom Day
April 27

In 1652, the Dutch East India Trading Company set up a station in Cape Town, South Africa, to service passing ships. After that, European pioneers began to colonize South Africa. In 1657, colonial authorities started giving land to the European settlers. As more Europeans arrived and built their farms, the need for land and labor grew. The settlers began spreading into other areas, and they brought people from East Africa and Madagascar to serve as slaves.

By the mid-1700s, even though there were more slaves than European colonists in South Africa, the white colonists continued to maintain power and authority. Throughout South Africa the minority white population practiced apartheid, an official policy of segregation that involved discrimination against non-white citizens in political, legal, and economic matters. Black South Africans faced stifling discrimination in all areas of their lives. Intense pressure from other countries forced the South African government to put an end to the practice of apartheid. In February 1990, South African President Frederik Willem de Klerk ended apartheid in the county.

On April 27, 1994, the Republic of South Africa held its first democratic elections. The African National Congress (ANC), an important black organization formed to fight for the freedom and rights of all black citizens, won the election. The new ANC-led government began the reconstruction and development of the country and its institutions, bringing with it socio-economic change that improved the lives of all South Africans, especially the poor.

Every year, the Republic of South Africa celebrates Freedom Day, a public holiday that commemorates the anniversary of the historic day in 1994. Special cultural events and exhibitions are held in various venues around Cape Town, the legislative capital of South Africa, and other locations around the country.

CONTACTS:
South African Embassy
3051 Massachusetts Ave. N.W.
Washington, D.C. 20008
202-232-4400; fax: 202-265-1607
www.saembassy.org

Ministry of Tourism, Government of South Africa
120 Plein St.
3rd Fl., Rm. 328
South Africa
27-21-465-7240; fax: 27-21-465-3216
www.gov.za

♦ 2667 ♦ South Africa Heritage Day
September 24

On September 24, 1995, the Republic of South Africa celebrated its first Heritage Day. The day was declared a national holiday by the first democratically elected government of South Africa, which was elected on April 27, 1994. According to the Department of Arts, Culture, Science and Technology, the word heritage is defined as "that which we inherit: the sum total of wild life and scenic parks, sites of scientific or historical importance, national monuments, historic buildings, works of art, literature and music, oral traditions and museum collections together with their documentation." To help South Africans celebrate their heritage, this day has been set aside to recognize all aspects of South African culture, including creative expression, historical inheritance, language, food, and the land in which they live.

During his speech on Heritage Day in 1996, President Nelson Mandela said, "When our first democratically elected government decided to make Heritage Day one of our national days, we did so because we knew that our rich and varied cultural heritage has a profound power to help build our new nation.

We did so knowing that the struggles against the injustice and inequities of the past are part of our national identity; they are part of our culture. We knew that, if indeed our nation has to rise like the proverbial phoenix from the ashes of division and conflict, we had to acknowledge those whose selfless efforts and talents were dedicated to this goal of non-racial democracy."

The government of the Republic of South Africa determines a theme for each year's celebrations. That first Heritage Day celebration in 1995 focused on composer Enoch Sontonga, the creator of a hymn that was adopted as the national anthem, His gravesite was declared a national monument, and his music was highlighted.

CONTACTS:
Ministry of Tourism, Government of South Africa
17 Trevena St. Tourism House, Sunnyside
Private Bag X424
Pretoria, 0001 South Africa
27-12-444-6769; fax: 27-12-444-7027
www.gov.za

♦ 2668 ♦ South Africa National Arts Festival
(Grahamstown Festival)
Late June through early July

Grahamstown, South Africa, is the site for what is purportedly the world's largest arts festival after Britain's Edinburgh Arts Festival. Since the inaugural festival in 1974, this small city in the Eastern Cape has increasingly drawn more people for the 11-day National Arts Festival (also known as the **Grahamstown Festival**), and has expanded its number of shows from 60 to more than 500. Organized by the Grahamstown Foundation, the festival takes both South African and international entrants.

The festival program manages an even balance of sophisticated and popular entertainment. Performances cross the spectrum from opera, cabaret, and jazz to stand-up comedy and folk music. The Fringe Festival, which in some years has featured up to 200 performances, attracts fans of more unconventional art.

The festival's largest theater venue is the 1820 Settlers National Monument. Smaller productions, which include those on the festival's fringe program, take place in any of the town's available public halls or large rooms.

Grahamstown has also gained a reputation for the enormous street market that materializes during the festival and bolsters the region's economy. Traders come from all over the Eastern Cape and set up stands in public parks and market squares to sell homemade and manufactured products.

CONTACTS:
National Arts Festival
1820 Settlers Monument
P.O. Box 304
Grahamstown, 6139 South Africa
270-46-603-1103; fax: 270-46-622-3082
www.nationalartsfestival.co.za

♦ 2669 ♦ **South Africa Republic Day**
May 31

A referendum held in South Africa on October 6, 1960, narrowly approved the formation of the Republic of South Africa, although "colored" voters were excluded as part of the country's long-standing policy of racial segregation known as apartheid. The closeness of the vote—52.14 percent in favor, 47.42 percent opposed—reflected the mixed feelings of both the Afrikaners and the British settlers, although the former generally supported the idea.

The Union of South Africa became the Republic of South Africa on May 31, 1961, thus severing its long-standing ties to the old British Empire.

Also on this date in 1902 the Boer War ended. The Treaty of Vereeniging was signed by representatives of the South African Republic and the Orange Free State who had been waging war with Great Britain since October 12, 1899. Eight years later, the Union of South Africa was inaugurated, uniting the Cape of Good Hope, Natal, the Transvaal, and the Orange Free State.

CONTACTS:
South African Tourism
500 5th Ave.
20th Fl., Ste. 2040

New York, NY 10110
212-730-2929 or 800-593-1318; fax: 212-764-1980
www.southafrica.net

South African History Online
349 Albert Rd.
Woodstock
Cape Town, 7925 South Africa
27-21-447-4365; fax: 27-21-447-2875
www.sahistory.org.za

♦ 2670 ♦ **South Africa Women's Day**
August 9

On August 9, 1956, a protest march was held at the Union Buildings in Pretoria, South Africa, the country's main government offices. Approximately 20,000 women participated in a peaceful march to protest against policies that restricted the rights of African women. These policies were intended to "tighten up control of movement of African women to town, registration of their service contracts, and a compulsory medical examination for all African women town-dwellers." They were protesting in part against pass laws, which governed the movement of all blacks, with special restrictions for women. The law required all black women to carry passes, which were special identification documents to show that they were allowed to enter areas that were for white people only.

The Federation of South African Women (established in 1954 to set up a broad-based women's organization) staged the protest march to challenge the idea that "a woman's place is in the kitchen." When the women arrived at the Union Buildings, they carried petitions signed by more than 100,000 people to give to J.G. Strijdom, the prime minister. Then they sang a freedom song composed specifically for the march: *Wathint' abafazi, Strijdom! Wathint' imbokodo uzo kufa! (Now you have touched the women, Strijdom! You have struck a rock! You will be crushed!)*

This song has come to represent the women's movement in South Africa.

Every year, on August 9, people gather at the Victoria & Alfred Waterfront Amphitheatre in Cape Town to celebrate National Women's Day. South African men, women, and children celebrate the achievements of women—not only from South Africa but also from all over the world. This day is celebrated to remind people of the contributions and achievements women have made to society and for women's rights, and to acknowledge the difficulties and prejudices many women still face.

Leading up to National Women's Day is the annual Women in Focus program, workshops that are intended to enlighten, inform, and entertain women with a series of innovative and celebratory programs.

CONTACTS:
V&A Waterfront Head Office
Victoria Wharf
Victoria & Alfred Waterfront
2nd Fl.,

South Africa
27-21-408-7500; fax: 27-21-408-7505
www.waterfront.co.za

♦ 2671 ♦ South Africa Youth Day
June 16

Throughout the history of South Africa, black citizens have suffered from segregation and oppression by the white leaders. In 1953, the South African government passed the Bantu Education Act, which included provisions for the establishment of a Black Education Department in the Department of Native Affairs to develop a curriculum that addressed the "nature and requirements of the black people." The aim of this curriculum was to provide black South Africans with an education that would give them only the skills necessary to serve their own people or to work in labor-intensive jobs under whites. Blacks were not to receive an education that would lead them to seek positions they would not be allowed to hold in society. The Bantu Education Act also declared that Afrikaans, a Dutch dialect, was to be used on an equal basis with English in secondary schools.

By 1975, black students began to fight against their lower-class status. They started to protest not only the fact that Afrikaans was a mandatory part of their education, but also the segregated schools and universities, poor facilities, overcrowded classrooms, and poorly trained teachers.

On June 16, 1976, more than 20,000 students from Soweto began a protest march. Police were called to the scene, and violent riots broke out. These riots lasted eight months, during which time approximately 700 people, many of them youths, were killed.

June 16 has been set aside as Youth Day (previously known as Soweto Day), a public holiday across the Republic of South Africa, to commemorate the day the protests began and to honor the youth who lost their lives during the riots.

Ceremonies, parades, and historic exhibitions are part of the celebrations across South Africa.

CONTACTS:
Ministry of Tourism - South Africa
120 Plein St.
Fl. 3 Rm. 328
South Africa
27-21-465-7240; fax: 27-21-465-3216
www.gov.za

♦ 2672 ♦ South Carolina Peach Festival
Mid-July

The South Carolina Peach Festival is a 10-day festival in Gaffney, S.C., to salute the state's peach industry. Events of the festival include a parade, beauty pageants, country music concerts, and peach desserts. Gaffney's year-round tribute to the peach is the eye-catching "peachoid," a one-million-gallon water tank in the shape and color of a peach with a great metal leaf hanging over it.

CONTACTS:
Cherokee County Chamber of Commerce
225 S. Limestone St.
Gaffney, SC 29340
864-489-5721
www.cherokeechamber.org

♦ 2673 ♦ South Korea Constitution Day
July 17

Constitution Day, July 17, is observed as a national holiday in South Korea on the anniversary of the date that the country's constitution was declared in 1948. It was declared a public holiday in October 1948. Apart from the display of flags in public places, citizens and officials do little to formally celebrate the occasion, although events such as marathons are often held on the day. Following a restructuring of the South Korean public sector work force to adhere to a 40-hour work week, Constitution Day will no longer be a free day for workers as of 2008; however, it still will be observed as a day of commemoration.

The entire Korean peninsula (i.e., present-day North and South Korea) was under the control of Japan from 1910 until the end of World War II. When Japan surrendered in August 1945, the U.S.S.R. took control of the northern half of the peninsula, while the southern half came under control of the United States. Despite attempts to unify the two regions, by 1948 it was clear that their sharp political differences made reunification impossible. South Korea held its first democratic elections and selected members for the National Assembly before the national constitution was proclaimed on July 17. On August 15, 1948, the Republic of Korea was established in the south with Syngman Rhee as the first President. Less than a month later, the Democratic People's Republic of Korea, under the leadership of then-Premier Kim Il-Sung, was founded in the North.

CONTACTS:
Embassy of the Republic of Korea
2450 Massachusetts Ave. N.W.
Washington, D.C. 20008
202-939-5600; fax: 202-797-0595
usa.mofa.go.kr

♦ 2674 ♦ South Korea Memorial Day
June 6

South Korea (official name: Republic of Korea) has designated June 6 as a national holiday to honor soldiers and civilians who sacrificed their lives for their country during the Korean War, 1950-1953. The main ceremony of remembrance is held at the National Cemetery in the capital city, Seoul.

Throughout the country, officials and citizens pray and lay flowers at the graves of the war dead. Citizens display the flag of South Korea, which is called Tae-guk-gi, on the front doors of their homes to commemorate the civilians and soldiers who died in war. Memorial Day was declared a public holiday on April 19, 1956.

CONTACTS:
Embassy of the Republic of Korea
2450 Massachusetts Ave. N.W.
Washington, D.C. 20008
202-939-5600; fax: 202-797-0595
usa.mofa.go.kr/english/am/usa/main

♦ 2675 ♦ South Sudan Independence Day
July 9

After a bloody, five-decade struggle, South Sudan gained its independence from Sudan in July of 2011. Celebrations erupted at midnight, and tens of thousands thronged the streets of the capital Juba, hoisting flags, singing, and dancing. Since achieving independence, the country has been plagued by disputes over its oil reserves, inter-ethnic wars, and rivalries within its ruling party. This turmoil has plunged the new nation back into chaos and marred its political stability and economic development, bringing it to the brink of a full-blown humanitarian crisis. Despite these problems, the country continues to celebrate its independence day in the capital city and to a lesser extent elsewhere in the nation. The day is marked by speeches, parades, and dances, with choirs singing the country's national anthem. In addition, the Christian population of South Sudan holds community-wide prayer services across the country.

♦ 2676 ♦ Southern 500
November

The Southern 500 is the oldest southern stock-car race, held in Darlington, S.C., since 1950. The race, which draws about 80,000 spectators, is one of the four so-called crown jewels in the NASCAR (National Association for Stock Car Auto Racing) Sprint Cup circuit and is considered the forerunner of those races. The others are the DAYTONA 500 (in Florida), the WINSTON 500 (Talladega, Ala.), and the COCA-COLA 600 (Charlotte, N.C.).

The first of the southern super speedways, the Darlington track was promoted and built by Harold Brasington, a sometime racing driver, and a group of Darlington citizens. The track was built on land owned by Sherman J. Ramsey, a farmer, and he insisted that his minnow pond not be disturbed. So the track had to skirt around it. Sports writers dubbed the oddly configured raceway the "Lady in Black," supposedly because it was fickle with drivers, like a mysterious woman. The winner of the first race in 1950 was Johnny Mantz.

CONTACTS:
Darlington Raceway
1301 Harry Byrd Hwy.
P.O. Box 500
Darlington, SC 29532
843-395-8900 or 866-459-7223; fax: 843-393-3911
www.darlingtonraceway.com

NASCAR Foundation
1 Daytona Blvd.
6th Fl.
Daytona Beach, FL 32114

877-515-4483
www.nascar.com

♦ 2677 ♦ Southern Ute Tribal Sun Dance
Mid-July

The Southern Ute Tribal Sun Dance is a ritual ceremony of ancient origin held by the Southern Ute Indians in Ignacio, Colo., often on the Sunday and Monday after the FOURTH OF JULY. The dancers who perform the ceremony are chosen from those who dream dreams and see visions, and they fast for four days before the dancing. While the public is allowed to attend, dress must be circumspect, and women are not allowed who are "on their moon," that is, having their menstrual period.

The Sun Dance was at one time performed by most Plains tribes, and usually involved self-torture. The Utes, however, did not practice this.

See also ARAPAHO SUN DANCE; SIOUX SUN DANCE.

CONTACTS:
Southern Ute Indian Tribe
P.O. Box 737
356 Ouray Dr.
Ignacio, CO 81137
970-563-0100
www.southernute-nsn.gov

♦ 2678 ♦ Southwestern Exposition Livestock Show & Rodeo
Last two weeks of January

This event is the oldest continuously running livestock show in the United States, held since 1896 in Fort Worth, Tex. The exposition calls to mind Fort Worth's past when it was considered the capital of the southwestern cattle empire, and stockyards ringed the city. The world's first indoor rodeo was featured here in 1918.

Events of the exposition include a parade, horse shows, a midway, big-name entertainers, and $600,000 in show premiums and rodeo purses. The more than 17,000 head of livestock include beef and dairy cattle, sheep, swine, goats, horses, donkeys, mules, pigeons, poultry, sheepdogs, and llamas. The latter have been found to be more effective against coyotes than guns, dogs, electric fences, or chemical repellants. About 500 of them guard sheep in the Rocky Mountain region.

CONTACTS:
Southwestern Exposition Livestock Show and Rodeo
P.O. Box 150,
Fort Worth, TX 76101
817-877-2400; fax: 817-866-7823
www.fwssr.com

♦ 2679 ♦ Soyaluna (Hopi Soyal Ceremony)
December 22

The Hopi Indians traditionally believed that at the time of the WINTER SOLSTICE, the sun had traveled as far from the earth as he ever did. Only the most powerful humans could persuade the sun to turn around and come back to the pueblo. The purpose of Soyaluna, which is still held among the Hopi who live on the mesas of Arizona, is to prevent the disappearance of the sun at the time of year when the days are at their shortest.

The main ceremony takes place in the *kiva*, a large, circular underground room that can only be entered by climbing down a ladder through a hole in the ceiling. Hopi priests prepare the kiva by scattering cornmeal around the floor. On the west wall of the kiva, a stack of corn serves as an altar, surrounded by stalks and husks. Each family has given some corn to make the altar. At the solstice, everyone assembles in the kiva for rituals designed to bring the sun back for another agricultural year.

CONTACTS:
Hopi Cultural Center
P.O. Box 67
Second Mesa, AZ 86043
928-734-2401; fax: 928-734-6651
www.hopiculturalcenter.com

♦ 2680 ♦ **Spamarama**
April or May

Spamarama is an annual salute to Spam, the canned lunch meat, that has been held in Austin, Texas, since 1978. Spamarama—"the official pandemonious potted pork party"— includes the Spam Cook-Off in which chefs vie to offer the best presentation of Spam, the Spam Jam (live musical entertainment), and the Spam-Alympics (events include a Spam relay race, a Spamburger-eating contest, and a Spam toss). The festival, which is also a charity event, has no association with Hormel Foods Corp., the company that produces the canned meat.

Hormel's main office is located in Austin, Minnesota, where the Spam Museum opened in September 2001.

CONTACTS:
Spamarama
Waterloo Park-403 E. 15th
Austin, TX 78701
512-834-1827
www.spamarama.org

♦ 2681 ♦ **Special Olympics**
February and June-July

The Special Olympics is an international program of year-round sports training and athletic competition for more than one million children and adults with mental retardation. It was founded by Eunice Kennedy Shriver, who organized the first International Special Olympics Summer Games at Soldier Field in Chicago in 1968. Five years earlier, Shriver had started a day camp for people with mental retardation, and she quickly saw that they were far more capable in sports and physical activities that many experts thought.

Today, athletes from 160 countries participate in local, national, and international competitions in 26 summer and winter sports, such as basketball, cycling, gymnastics, soccer, floor hockey, alpine skiing, figure skating, and aquatics. There are Special Olympics chapters in all 50 states of the U.S., and about 25,000 communities have Special Olympics programs. The Special Olympics World Summer Games are held every four years in early summer (June-July) and the Special Olympics World Winter Games are held every four years in February. The president of the United States often attends the opening ceremonies, during which the Special Olympic Cauldron is lit.

CONTACTS:
Special Olympics
1133 19th St. N.W.
Washington, D.C. 20036
202-628-3630 or 800-700-8585; fax: 202-824-0200
www.specialolympics.org

♦ 2682 ♦ **Spendarmad, Feast of**
February, June, July; fifth day of Spendarmad, the 12th Zoroastrian month

The Feast of Spendarmad is one of the "sacred name days" in the Zoroastrian religion, where the day and the month share the name of the same *yazata*, or spiritual being—in this case, Spendarmad, who represents Holy Devotion and who presides over the earth. In the past, the Feast of Spendarmad was also a special feast for women, whose husbands would give them presents on this day. Such gift giving is still a part of the festival in some areas, but the practice is no longer widespread.

Among the followers of Zoroaster (also known as Zarathushtra, believed to have lived around 1200 B.C.E.), the Persian prophet, a name-day feast is an occasion for religious ceremonies which can be performed in a fire temple, meeting hall, or private home. Because there are actually three different Zoroastrian calendars in use by widely separated Zoroastrian communities, the Feast of Spendarmad occurs either in February, June, or July in the Gregorian calendar.

There are only about 100,000 followers of Zoroastrianism today, and most of them live in northwestern India or Iran. Smaller communities exist in Pakistan, Sri Lanka, Canada, the U.S., England, and Australia.

♦ 2683 ♦ **Spiedie Fest and Balloon Rally**
Early August

The Spiedie Fest and Balloon Rally takes place annually in Otsiningo Park in Binghampton, N.Y., over three days in early August. The Spiedie Fest began in 1983 when a few families got together to decide who had the best recipe for *spiedie*—a regional delicacy of Italian descent. It consists of small pieces of marinated meat that are skewered and grilled, then served on Italian bread or a roll with fresh marinade on top. In 1985, the families decided to move the cooking contest to a local park and to feature five hot-air balloons, as well as a children's area. The aim was a community event that was fun, safe, and inexpensive. Recently, more than 100,000 have attended each festival, which now incorporates one of the leading hot-air balloon rallies in the United States. Besides bolstering local pride, the event benefits the community, with all profits going to charities in local Broome County.

The centerpieces of the festival are five balloon launches (weather permitting) at dawn and dusk, and the spiedie cooking contest. Other highlights are an antique car display, a craft show featuring more than 200 vendors, a sand volley-ball tournament, and a five-kilometer run/walk. There also are live music acts, a variety of food, and celebrity appear-ances.

CONTACTS:
Spiedie Fest Balloon Rally Expo, Inc.
P.O. Box 275
Westview Stn
Binghampton, NY 13905 United States
607-765-6604; fax: 607-205-1502
www.spiediefest.com

♦ 2684 ♦ **Spirit Burying**
January-February; second to 15th days of the first lunar month

Spirit burying, or *Mae-gwi*, is a new year custom common in rural areas of Korea. Farmers form bands and process around the village, visiting each home. In some areas the farmers wear masks and costumes and perform a traditional drama; in others they march around banging gongs and playing other musical instruments. Each household rewards the band with food, drink, or money. Any money collected is then put into a general community fund. Traditional belief has it that such activity will subdue evil spirits and provide for the village's protection in the coming year.

See also SOL; TAEBORUM.

♦ 2685 ♦ **Spiritual Baptist (Shouters) Liberation Day**
March 30

The people of Trinidad and Tobago observe March 30 as Spir-itual Baptist (Shouters) Liberation Day. This national holiday, instituted in 1996, honors an African-American religious sect once outlawed in Trinidad and Tobago. The Spiritual Baptists originally came to the islands as former American slaves, who had fought for the British in the Revolutionary War. Their style of worship combined African and Ameri-can Baptist beliefs and practices. Services include bell ring-ing, shouting, and high-volume singing and chanting. The colonial government of Trinidad and Tobago accused the Spiritual Baptists of disturbing the peace. In 1917, the gov-ernment forbade the group (nicknamed the "Shouters") from practicing their religion. This law was overturned in 1951. The recently established national holiday honors the Spiri-tual Baptists' long struggle against religious persecution. It is observed with speeches and religious services.

CONTACTS:
Ministry of Tourism Trinidad and Tobago
1 Wrightson Rd.
Levels 8 & 9, Tower C
International Waterfront Complex
Trinidad and Tobago
868-624-1403; fax: 868-625-1825
www.tourism.gov.tt

♦ 2686 ♦ **Spock Days/Galaxyfest**
Second weekend of June

Vulcan, a town located in the Canadian province of Alberta, has an inadvertent yet auspicious connection with the highly successful Star Trek franchise: it has the same name as the species to which the character Dr. Spock belongs. Since 1991 the annual celebration now known as Spock Days/Galaxy-fest has boosted tourism and brought into town fans eager for another celebration of the cult phenomenon that has been spawned by the Star Trek movies and TV shows.

There are two structures in Vulcan that build upon the town's Star Trek connection: the replica of the famous starship U.S.S. *Enterprise*, which stands at the town's main entrance, and the Vulcan Tourism and Trek Station, which opened to the public in 1998 and is the base of operations for Spock Days/ Gal-axyfest.

Initial there were two festivals: the VulCon, the original cel-ebration, and the Spockdays Rodeo that was added later. In 2002 the events were combined to take place over one long weekend. Typically, events include a costume contest, a Klingon-inspired stunt-game competition, a Galaxy Awards Banquet, and appearances by cast members from Star Trek shows.

CONTACTS:
Vulcan Tourism
115 Centre St. E.
P.O. Box 1161
Vulcan, AB T0L 2B0 Canada
403-485-2994
www.vulcantourism.com

♦ 2687 ♦ **Spoken Word Festival, Calgary International**
March-April

The Calgary Spoken Word Society was created in 2003 by poet Sheri-D Wilson to promote spoken word poetry locally, provincially, nationally, and internationally, through perfor-mance and education. The Society sponsored the first annual Calgary International Spoken Word Festival in 2004. A rous-ing success, it consisted of four events featuring artists from across Canada. Each year since the event has expanded, with more artists and more events. Today, the festival includes more than a dozen events featuring a wide range of voices and viewpoints.

In addition, the Spoken Word Society has created other events throughout the year to promote spoken word poetry.

In 2005, it launched the monthly Calgary Poetry Slam, which gives up-and-coming poets the opportunity to perform. Also in 2005, the Society created the Word Travels program, which places poets in Calgary area high schools. This program presents an innovative approach to literacy, using the accessibility of Spoken Word to introduce students to the world of literature, speak to students in their own language, and give them the voice to speak in their own.

The 10th annual Calgary Spoken Word Festival was held in 2013 and featured 100 artists in 28 events and seven languages. Events included two poetry slams, a collectible poetry program, two panel discussions, and seven workshops. In 2013, The Word Travels presented five school events and 18 poet-in-school happenings.

♦ 2688 ♦ Spoleto Festival USA
May-June

Pulitzer Prize-winning composer Gian Carlo Menotti founded the **Festival of Two Worlds** in Spoleto, Italy, in 1958, and brought it to Charleston, South Carolina, under the name **Spoleto USA** in 1977. The annual 17-day international arts festival focuses on new works and productions, and routinely offers more than 100 events in opera, chamber music, symphonic concerts, theater, dance, and art. In recent years, the festival has also offered jazz and other newer musical performances.

CONTACTS:
Spoleto Festival USA
14 George St.
Charleston, SC 29401
843-722-2764; fax: 843-723-6383
spoletousa.org

♦ 2689 ♦ Spring Break
February-April

Spring Break is an annual celebration of spring—and of school vacations—by an estimated two million college students who whoop it up, sunbathe, party, drink, dance, and listen to loud music.

From the early 1950s until 1985, Fort Lauderdale, Fla., was a prime destination. In 1960 the movie, *Where the Boys Are* (based on the Glendon Swarthout novel of the same name), featuring Connie Francis, George Hamilton, and Yvette Mimieux, was all about spring break. It gave Fort Lauderdale great national exposure. But the hordes of students got to be too much; by 1985, 350,000 people took over the city for six weeks and tied up not just traffic but the legal system. Fort Lauderdale started clamping down, and now only about 20,000 students visit.

Popular destinations today include Panama City Beach, Fla., Daytona Beach, Fla., South Padre Island, Tex., Palm Springs, Calif., the Bahamas, Jamaica, and Mexico. To lure the spring breakers, various towns and resorts spend millions of dollars and offer an abundance of free activities, including beach sports, concerts, movie premieres, and contests.

CONTACTS:
Panama City Beach Convention & Visitors Bureau
17001 Panama City Beach Pkwy
Panama City Beach, FL 32413
850-233-6503 or 800-722-3224
www.visitpanamacitybeach.com

Cancun Convention & Visitors Bureau
Cancun Center
1st. Flr., Blvd. Kukulcan
Hotel Zone
Cancun, Q.Roo 77500 Mexico
52-998-881-2745; fax: 52-998-881-2774
cancun.travel

City of South Padre Island Convention & Visitors Bureau
7355 Padre Blvd.
South Padre Island, TX 78597
956-761-3000 or 800-767-2373; fax: 956-761-3024
www.sopadre.com

♦ 2690 ♦ Spring of Culture
March

The first Arab state to discover oil, the Persian Gulf country of Bahrain has enjoyed dramatic economic development since the first half of the 20th century. In recent decades, government organizations have worked toward making its national arts program as robust as its oil industry. The Spring of Culture Festival, held every March in the capital city of Manama, helps fulfill this cultural mission and promotes tourism to the country. The festival is organized by the Sector of Culture and Heritage with the support of the Economic Development Board.

Thanks to its reputation as a meeting place between the East and the West, Spring of Culture is able to attract performers from all over the world. The festival was first held in 2006. In its first few years, the proceedings sometimes continued into April to overlap with the internationally known Bahrain Formula One Grand Prix, also held in Manama.

National, regional, and international artists converge on Manama to perform poetry readings, music, theater, and dance. Experts also present lectures and hold workshops. A survey of past performers illustrates the diversity of the performers: over the years the event has featured a Lebanese musician, a Senegalese singer, an Algerian-French thinker, and a Japanese drumming troupe.

CONTACTS:
Economic Development Board of Bahrain
Seef Tower
7th, 8th, 12th, 13th & 16th Fl.
P.O. Box 11299
 Bahrain
973-1758-9999; fax: 973-1758-9900
www.bahrainedb.com/en

♦ 2691 ♦ Springtime Festival
Begins between March 11 and April 15; four successive Thursdays before Orthodox Easter

Celebrated by people of all religious faiths, the Springtime Festival is a regional celebration throughout the Bekáa (or

Beqaa) Valley in eastern Lebanon. It takes place during LENT, on four successive Thursdays preceding the Eastern Orthodox EASTER.

The first Thursday, known as Thursday-of-the-Animals, is a day of rest for domestic working animals, whose heads are decorated with a spot of henna, which is symbolic of blood and life. On the following Thursday, known as Thursday-of-the-Plants, young children and unmarried girls wash themselves in water scented with crushed flowers. Next is Thursday-of-the-Dead, a day for visiting the graves of family and friends. Last is Thursday-of-the-Jumping, or Day of the Jumping, when people living in the mountains come down by the thousands to the plains to join in the festival activities. They visit the tomb of Noah, which is outside Zahle, and then the shrine of the Wadi Zaour, a locally popular Muslim saint, in Anjar, a town that was an Armenian refugee village in the 1940s. There they receive blessings for good health. Eventually everyone returns to the villages, where there is dancing in the streets and even on the mosque grounds.

◆ 2692 ◆ **Spy Wednesday**
Between March 19 and April 22; Wednesday before Easter

The Wednesday before EASTER Sunday is the day on which the disciple Judas Iscariot made the deal to betray Jesus. In order to arrest Jesus without exciting the populace, Judas led the Jewish priests to the Garden of Gethsemane, near Jerusalem, where Jesus had gone at night to pray with the other 11 disciples after the Last Supper (*see* MAUNDY THURSDAY). Judas identified Jesus by kissing him and addressing him as "Master." For this he was paid 30 pieces of silver, the price of a slave in the Old Testament.

The name "Spy Wednesday" is said to be of Irish origin, although the Bible never refers to Judas as a spy. His surname, Iscariot, is believed by some to be a corruption of the Latin *sicarius*, meaning "murderer" or "assassin.".

CONTACTS:
Desiring God
2112 Broadway St. N.E.
Suite 150
Minneapolis, MN 55413
888-346-4700; fax: 612-338-4372
www.desiringgod.org

◆ 2693 ◆ **Sri Lanka National Day**
February 4

The former British colony of Ceylon changed its name in 1972 to Sri Lanka, which means "Blessed Isle." Sri Lankans commemorate the granting of their independence from Great Britain on February 4, 1948, with public gatherings throughout the island and special services in the temples, churches, and mosques. There are also parades, folk dances, processions, and national games.

CONTACTS:
Embassy of Sri Lanka

2148 Wyoming Ave. N.W.
Washington, D.C. 20008
202-483-4025; fax: 202-232-7181
slembassyusa.org

◆ 2694 ◆ **St. Agatha Festival**
February 3-5

Sant' Agata is especially revered in Catania, Sicily, where her relics are preserved in a silver casket. The beautiful young Sicilian virgin was put to death in the third century because she refused to yield to the advances of a Roman prefect. Among the tortures she is said to have endured was having her breasts cut off, and to this day she is the patron saint of nursing mothers and women suffering from diseases of the breast.

On February 3, 4 and 5 each year, a silver bust of St. Agatha wearing a jewel-encrusted crown is carried in procession from the cathedral to Catania's various churches. Included in the procession are the *ceri*, huge wooden replicas of candlesticks which are carved with episodes from the saint's martyrdom. The streets are lined with streamers and flowers, and illuminated by strings of colored lights after dark. The festival ends with a fireworks display in the piazza.

CONTACTS:
Regional Minister of Tourism, Sport and Entertainment
Via Emanuele Notarbartolo, 9
Palermo, Sicily 90141 Italy
39-91-7078030; fax: 39-91-7078212
pti.regione.sicilia.it

◆ 2695 ◆ **St. Agnes's Eve**
January 20

The eve of St. Agnes's Day (January 21) has long been associated with various superstitions about how young girls might discover the identity of their future husbands. According to one such belief, a girl who went to bed without any supper on this night would dream of the man she was to marry. John Keats used this legend as the basis for his well-known poem, "The Eve of St. Agnes," in which a young maid dreams of her lover and wakes to find him standing at her bedside.

St. Agnes herself was martyred sometime during the fourth century, when she may have been only 12 or 13 years old, because she had consecrated herself to Christ and refused to marry. She was later named the patron saint of young virgins. In art St. Agnes is often represented with a lamb or sometimes with a dove with a ring in its beak.

◆ 2696 ◆ **St. Alban's Day**
June 22

St. Alban is the first and best known of all the English saints and martyrs. He was a soldier living as a pagan in the town of Verulamium, probably during the third century, when a Christian priest named Amphibalus, pursued by Roman persecutors, begged for refuge in his house. Alban took him in and was soon converted by him and baptized. When he could conceal Amphibalus no longer, Alban changed clothes with him and gave himself up as the priest. The deception was soon discovered, however, and Alban was brought before the governor, condemned, and beheaded.

There are a number of legends concerning St. Alban's execution. One is that when the crowd that gathered to watch the beheading was too large to get across the small bridge leading to the execution place, St. Alban said a prayer and caused the waters to divide. Another is that when he asked for a drink of water, a spring gushed forth from the ground in front of him. Supposedly, the soldier who was appointed to kill St. Alban refused to do so, and was beheaded along with the saint.

A shrine was later erected in Verulamium, and the town was renamed St. Albans. The cathedral hosts a festival each year on a weekend near St. Alban's Day, when pilgrims gather for special services, a procession, and other events.

CONTACTS:
Cathedral & Abbey Church of St Alban
St. Albans
Hertfordshire, AL1 1BY United Kingdom
44-17-2786-0780; fax: 44-17-2785-0944
www.stalbanscathedral.org

♦ **2697** ♦ **St. Andrew's Day**
November 30

St. Andrew, the brother of ST. PETER, was the first apostle called by Jesus, but he is primarily known today as the patron saint of Scotland, though he was also chosen to be patron saint of Russia. According to the apocryphal and unreliable Acts of St. Andrew, he went to Greece, and having converted the proconsul's wife there, he was condemned to be crucified. Fastened to an X-shaped cross by cords rather than nails, he eventually died of thirst and starvation.

St. Andrew's association with Scotland didn't come about until four centuries after his death, when some of his relics were brought there. Although there are a number of churches throughout England and Scotland that bear St. Andrew's name, many associate it with the famous St. Andrew's golf course near Dundee. Some Scots continue the custom of wearing a "St. Andrew's cross" on November 30, which consists of blue and white ribbons shaped like the letter X. The tradition for this form of a cross began no earlier than the 13th century.

This is also a major feast in Lapland and a time for weddings and meeting new people.

CONTACTS:
Visit St Andrews
70 Market St.
St. Andrews, Fife KY16 9NU Scotland
44-1334-472021
www.visitstandrews.com

St. Andrews Church of Scotland
Chaussée de Vleurgat 181
Brussels, 1050 Belgium
www.churchofscotland.be

♦ **2698** ♦ **St. Andrew's Eve (Noc Swietego Andreja)**
November 29

The eve of ST. ANDREW'S DAY is a special night for young Polish girls who want to find husbands. They play *Andrzejki*, or "Andrew's games," a kind of fortune telling. Young girls break off dry branches from cherry trees, place them in wet sand, and tend them carefully for the next few weeks. If the branch blooms by CHRISTMAS, it is believed that they will marry within the year. Pouring liquid wax into cold water is another popular method of foretelling their romantic futures. The shapes into which the wax hardens often provide clues with which they can read their fate. The boys try to foretell their own futures on St. Catherine's Eve (*see also* ST. CATHERINE'S DAY, November 25).

The patron saint of both Russia and Scotland, St. Andrew's name means "manly" or "courageous," making him an appropriate target for the appeals of young girls seeking lovers. Andrzejki are popular among Polish Americans as well, where they include peeling apples to see what letter the apple peel seems to form when thrown over the peeler's left shoulder.

Austrian peasant women also forced fruit tree branches, but they brought them to Christmas mass and believed they gave them the ability to see all the witches in the congregation.

♦ **2699** ♦ **St. Anne's Day**
July 26

In 1650, a group of Breton sailors built a tiny frame church at the place where the town of Beaupré, Quebec, Canada, now stands. They wanted to honor of St. Anne, the traditional name for the mother of the Virgin Mary and wife of Joachim or ST. JOSEPH (the apostle James names her in his Letter). The sailors had been caught in a vicious storm at sea and vowed that if St. Anne would save them, they would build her a sanctuary at the spot where their feet first touched land. In 1658, the people of the village built a new and larger church, and it was then that the first of St. Anne de Beaupré's miraculous cures took place, when a local man suffering from rheumatism came to the church and walked away in perfect health. Since that time thousands of cures have been reported at the Basilica of Sainte Anne de Beaupré, which has been called the "Lourdes of the New World" after the famous shrine in France.

St. Anne is the patron saint of Canada. The pilgrimage to her shrine in Beaupré is one of the major pilgrimages on the North American continent. Romanies from Canada and the United States also arrive to celebrate Santana ("St. Anna"). They camp on the church property, prepare a *slava* feast of special foods for and prayers to St. Anne, and visit their families (*see* PARDON OF STE. ANNE D'AURAY).

CONTACTS:
Basilica of Sainte-Anne-de-Beaupré
10018, Avenue Royale
Saint Anne de Beaupre, Quebec G0A 3C0 Canada

418-827-3781; fax: 418-827-8771
www.sanctuairesainteanne.org

♦ 2700 ♦ St. Anthony of Padua, Feast of
June 13

St. Anthony of Padua (1195-1231) is the patron saint of people who lose things and of children. He has also become, like ST. FRANCIS OF ASSISI, a patron saint of animals. In the days before automobiles, people in Rome sent their horses and mules to St. Anthony's Church to be blessed on this day. The Feast of St. Anthony is also celebrated by many Puerto Rican communities, as well as by American Indians in the southwestern United States. In New Mexico, for instance, traditional Indian dances are held on **San Antonio's Day** in the pueblos at Taos, San Juan, Santa Clara, San Ildefonso, Sandia, Cochiti, and elsewhere.

One of the most outstanding celebrations is held in New York City's Greenwich Village. St. Anthony's Shrine Church on West Houston and Sullivan Streets, in the heart of one of the original Little Italy sections of New York, boasts the oldest Italian Roman Catholic congregation in the city and is the site of a 10-day festival that combines religious observance and the carnival atmosphere of a street fair. Masses are held all day on June 13, and a procession bearing the statue of St. Anthony through the streets begins at seven o'clock that evening. Thousands of people are drawn to the festival, which extends from the weekend before the actual feast day through the weekend following it.

In the village of El Pinar, Granada, Spain, a novena ends with the Rosary on St. Anthony's Eve. Then a fiesta begins with a parade of huge papier-mâché heads of historical and imaginary characters (called *gigantes* "giants" and *cabezudos* "big-heads"), on 10-foot-tall wire frames and dressed in long robes. This parade is accompanied by a band playing *pasodobles* (a quick, light march often played at bullfights). Boys toss firecrackers, small children hide in terror, fireworks are set off, street dancing begins, and carnival booths are set up. On the 13th, the parade begins at 9 A.M. After a noon High Mass, the statue of St. Anthony is paraded through the village for three hours. The band plays and pairs of men in two lines dance the *jota* (a complex dance using the rhythm of boot-heels and castanets). When the dancers tire, they are replaced by eager onlookers. At their return to the church, they block the door to keep St. Anthony from going in so the dancing can go on. Parishioners lay money at the feet of the statue for the support of the church for the coming year.

St. Anthony of Padua was born in Lisbon, Portugal, in 1195, and is the patron saint of Portugal. The festivities held here in his honor begin on the evening of June 12 with an impressive display of *marchas*, walking groups of singers and musicians, who parade along the Avenida da Liberdade. The celebration continues the next day with more processions and traditional folk dancing.

Throughout the month of June, children in Lisbon prepare altars in the saint's honor, covering boxes and tables with white paper and decorating them with candles and pictures of St. Anthony. They beg "a little penny for San António"

from passersby, but the money—once used to restore the church of San António da Sé after its destruction by an earthquake in 1755—is now put toward a children's feast.

Because he is considered the matchmaker saint, St. Anthony's Eve is a time when young people write letters asking António for help in finding a mate. Another custom of the day is for a young man to present the girl he hopes to marry with a pot of basil concealing a verse or love letter.

CONTACTS:
Shrine Church of Saint Anthony of Padua
154 Sullivan St.
New York, NY 10012
212-777-2755; fax: 212-673-6684
www.stanthonynyc.org

♦ 2701 ♦ St. Anthony the Abbot, Feast of
January 17

St. Anthony the Abbot was one of the earliest saints, and, if St. Athanasius's biography of him is correct, Anthony lived more than 100 years (251-356). Living as a hermit, Anthony nonetheless attracted disciples and ventured out occasionally to become involved in the doctrinal controversies of his day. Eventually he came to be regarded as a healer of animals as well as of people. The order of Hospitallers of St. Anthony, founded during the 12th century, endeavored to keep animals in good health by hanging bells around their necks. His feast day is celebrated in Mexico and other parts of Latin America by bringing household pets and livestock into the churchyard, where the local priest blesses them with holy water. All the animals are carefully groomed and often decorated with ribbons and fresh flowers.

In some Latin American cities, the **Blessing of the Animals** takes place on a different day—often on HOLY SATURDAY, the day before EASTER. Hispanic people and others in the United States often celebrate the Blessing of the Animals on this day as well. In Los Angeles, the procession of animals to Our Lady of the Angels Church follows a cobblestone path that was laid by Mexican settlers more than 200 years ago.

♦ 2702 ♦ St. Augustine of Hippo, Feast of
August 28

St. Augustine's career as a Christian got off to a slow start. The son of a pagan father and a Christian mother, he spent most of his youth in dissipation and promiscuity. He was 32 years old when he converted to Christianity in 386 after undergoing conflicts within himself on how he was living and what he believed; hearing St. Ambrose preach was said to have influenced him as well. A few years later he became bishop of Hippo in North Africa. For the next 40 years he was a teacher, writer, preacher, and theologian who exerted a profound influence on the development of Christian doctrine. He is best known for his spiritual autobiography, the *Confessions*, which detail the excesses of his youth, his career as a teacher of rhetoric, his years as a believer in Manicheism and Platonism, and his belated conversion to Christianity. It is primarily for his writings that he is known as the patron saint of theologians and scholars and one of the "Four Latin Fathers" of the Christian Church.

St. Augustine also typifies the Christian who has been converted slowly, as exemplified by his well-known prayer, "O God, make me pure—but not yet." When a company of Spanish soldiers landed on the coast of Florida on St. Augustine's Day in 1565, they named the U.S.'s oldest European community after him.

♦ 2703 ♦ St. Barbara's Day
December 4

Scholars doubt that St. Barbara existed as more than a legend that emerged during the second century. The story is that her father locked her away in a tower to prevent her from ever marrying. When she became a Christian he tried to kill her, then turned her in to the pagan authorities. Then he was killed by a bolt of lightning.

In parts of France, Germany, and Syria, St. Barbara's Day is considered the beginning of the CHRISTMAS season. In southern France, especially in Provence, it is customary to set out dishes holding grains of wheat soaked in water on sunny window sills. There is a folk belief that if the "St. Barbara's grain" grows quickly, it means a good year for crops. But if it withers and dies, the crops will be ruined. On CHRISTMAS EVE, the grain is placed near the crèche as a symbol of the coming harvest. There is a similar custom in Germany and the Czech and Slovak republics, where cherry branches are placed in water and tended carefully in the hope that they will bloom on Christmas Eve. In Syria, St. Barbara's Day is for feasting and bringing food to the poor.

In Poland, St. Barbara's Day is associated with weather prophecies. If it rains, it will be cold and icy on Christmas Day; if it's cold and icy, Christmas will be rainy.

♦ 2704 ♦ St. Barnabas's Day
June 11

Before England adopted the Gregorian calendar in 1752, June 11 was the day of the SUMMER SOLSTICE. In addition to being the longest day of the year, it was also St. Barnabas's Day (or **Barnaby Day**), and this association gave rise to the old English jingle, "Barnaby bright, Barnaby bright, the longest day and the shortest night." It was customary on this day for the priests and clerks in the Church of England to wear garlands of roses and to decorate the church with them. Other names for this day were **Long Barnaby** and **Barnaby Bright**.

♦ 2705 ♦ St. Bartholomew's Day
August 24

St. Bartholomew is the patron saint of beekeepers and honey-makers, and for this reason it was traditional in England for the honey crop to be gathered on August 24. Since the main ingredient in mead—an ancient alcoholic drink that is

still made in some parts of England today—is honey, the Blessing of the Mead is also observed on St. Bartholomew's Day.

In ancient Rome, mead was offered to the gods of love and fertility. Although few people today still believe that drinking mead will help a marriage produce children, the drink is still believed to have curative powers.

In St. Mount's Bay, Cornwall, a special ceremony is held by the Almoner of the Worshipful Company of Mead Makers. It begins with a church service, and then the participants move to the Mead Hall, where the Almoner, who is also the vicar of the parish, blesses the mead that has been fermenting for two years and pours it into a special cup. The mead can then be moved to a storage vat. In the past, mead was traditionally drunk from a bowl, known as a mazer, made from birds-eye maple with a silver rim.

See also BARTHOLOMEW FAIR; SCHÄFERLAUF; STOURBRIDGE FAIR.

CONTACTS:
Visit Britain
2029 Century Park E.
Ste. 1350
Los Angeles, CA 90067
310-481-2989
www.visitbritain.org

♦ 2706 ♦ St. Basil, Feast of
January 1

NEW YEAR'S DAY and the feast day for Agios Vasilis (St. Basil) are one and the same in Greece and Cyprus, and for all Orthodox Christians. Celebrations begin on NEW YEAR'S EVE when Agios Vasilis is believed to visit each house, blessing the people and their belongings and animals, and bringing presents to the children. Nowadays, the parish priest goes around and blesses the homes of his flock.

On New Year's Day, a cake called the *Vassilopita*, or "St. Basil's bread," is ceremoniously sliced, according to varying traditions going back to Byzantine times. Usually the first slice is cut for Jesus Christ, the next is for the house, and the following for absent family members. A coin has been baked in the cake, and the person finding the coin will be the luckiest member of the family that year.

St. Basil was a monk and church father who left many influential writings, including a defense of the study of pagan writings by Christians. He was born about the year 329 and was declared a saint soon after his death on Jan. 1 of the year 379 in Caesarea (in present-day Israel).

♦ 2707 ♦ St. Blaise's Day
February 3

The association of St. Blaise (or **Blase**, or **Blasius**) with the blessing of throats can be traced to a number of sources.

According to one story, as he was being led to his own execution in 316, he miraculously cured a child who was suffering from a throat infection. Another story has it that he saved the life of a boy who was choking on a fishbone. In any case, St. Blaise, since the sixth century in the East, has been the patron saint of people who suffer from throat afflictions, and celebrations on this day in the Roman Catholic Church often include the blessing of throats by the priest. In Paraguay, the religious services are followed by a holiday festival (*see* SAN BLAS, FIESTA OF).

Among the many tortures said to have been suffered by this saint was having his body torn by iron combs similar to those used at one time by wool-combers in England. St. Blaise thus became the patron saint of wool-combers as well, and his feast day has traditionally been celebrated in English towns where the woolen industry is important.

In Spain they bake small loaves, called *tortas de San Blas* ("San Blas's loaves") or *panecillos del santo* ("little breads of the saint"). They are blessed during mass, and each child eats a bit to prevent him or her from choking during the year.

♦ 2708 ♦ St. Brendan's Day
May 16

St. Brendan, who lived in the sixth century, is one of the most popular Irish saints. In addition to founding a number of monasteries, including the one at Clonfert in Galway, Ireland, he was alleged to be the author of *Navigatio Brendani*, the story of his journey with a crew of four monks to a land across the ocean (the tale, however, is thought to have been written in the 10th century). No one, including St. Brendan himself, knew exactly where he had been when he returned, but a number of legends concerning the journey developed over the centuries—one of which claims that he actually reached the American continent.

In 1977, an Irishman named Tim Severin built a boat out of leather like the one described in *Navigatio* and set out to follow St. Brendan's instructions. After 50 days at sea, he ended up in Newfoundland, giving credence to the theory that St. Brendan reached America 1,000 years before COLUMBUS.

♦ 2709 ♦ St. Bridget's Day
February 1

St. Bridget (or **Brigid**, or **Bride**) is the female patron saint of Ireland. She has also been identified with an ancient pagan goddess. Her feast day, February 1, was traditionally the first day of spring and of the new year in rural Ireland because it marked the start of the agricultural season. Legends about Bridget associate her with abundance and fertility; her cows, for example, allegedly gave milk up to three times a day. She is credited with an almost endless number of miracles and was buried in the same church at Downpatrick where the bodies of ST. PATRICK and ST. COLUMBA lie. She lived during the sixth century and probably established the first Irish convent, around which the city of Kildare eventually grew.

Many old customs and folk beliefs are associated with St. Bridget's feast day. For example, people would not perform any work on this day that involved turning or twisting, or that required the use of a wheel. It was also customary on the eve of the saint's day for the oldest daughter of the family to bring a bundle of rushes to the door. Playing the role of St. Bridget, she would distribute the rushes among the family members, who would make crosses from them and, after the crosses were sprinkled with holy water, hang them throughout the house. Because St. Bridget is said to have woven the first cloth in Ireland, a cloth known as the *Brat Bhride*, or "Bridget's cloak," was left outside on the steps, and during the night it was believed to acquire special healing powers.

The custom of having women propose marriage to men during LEAP YEAR can also be traced to St. Bridget. As legend has it, she complained to St. Patrick about the fact that men always took the initiative and persuaded him to grant women the right to do so during one year out of every four. Then Bridget proposed to Patrick, who turned her down but softened his refusal by giving her a kiss and a silk gown.

♦ 2710 ♦ St. Catherine's Day
November 25 (suppressed in 1969 in the Roman Catholic Church)

St. Catherine is now thought to have been a folkloric figure rather than a historical person; for that reason, her feast day is no longer observed in the Roman Catholic Church calendar. According to apocryphal writings, St. Catherine of Alexandria was sentenced to death by Emperor Maxentius for her extraordinary success in converting people to Christianity in the fourth century. He placed her in a torture machine that consisted of wheels armed with sharp spikes so that she would be torn to pieces as the wheels revolved. She was saved from this grim fate by divine intervention, but then the Emperor had her beheaded. The "Catherine Wheel" in England today is a type of firework that revolves in pinwheel fashion. In the United States, the "cartwheels" performed regularly by aspiring gymnasts repeat the motion of St. Catherine on the wheel of torture.

In 18th-century England, young women in the textile districts engaged in merry-making or "catherning" on this day, which is sometimes referred to as **Cathern Day**. As the patron saint of old maids, St. Catherine is still celebrated in France by unmarried women under 25, especially those employed in the millinery and dressmaking industries. They wear "Catherine bonnets" on November 25— homemade creations of paper and ribbon. The French expression *coiffer Sainte Catherine* (to don St. Catherine's bonnet), is used to warn girls that they are likely to become spinsters.

♦ 2711 ♦ St. Catherine's Day (Estonia)
November 25

Estonian folklorists believe that the customs associated with Kadripäev, or ST. CATHERINE'S DAY in Estonia, may date back to pre-Christian times. The holiday is strongly associated with women and their traditional activities, such as herding. People dress up in light-colored clothing, symbolizing winter's snow, and visit their neighbors, singing songs and offering blessings for the family's sheep and other herd animals. In return householders offer them cloth, wool, or food. An old superstition connected with the day forbade such activities as shearing and weaving, and sometimes knitting and sewing, as a means of protecting the sheep. Estonians associate Kadripäev with the arrival of winter.

CONTACTS:
Estonian Institute
Suur-Karja 14
Tallinn, 10140 Estonia
372-6-314-355
www.einst.ee

♦ 2712 ♦ St. Cecilia's Day
November 22

Not much can be said with confidence about St. Cecilia's life. According to her apocryphal acts, which date from the fifth century, she was a Roman from a noble family who was put to death in the second or third century for her Christian beliefs. How she became the patron saint of music and musicians is not exactly known, but according to legend she played the harp so beautifully that an angel left heaven to come down and listen to her. In any case, the Academy of Music in Rome accepted her as its patron when it was established in 1584.

In 1683, a musical society was formed in London especially for the celebration of St. Cecilia's Day. It held a festival each year at which a special ode was sung. The poet John Dryden composed his "Ode for St. Cecilia's Day" in 1687 for this purpose. By the end of the 17th century it was customary to hold concerts on November 22 in St. Cecilia's honor—a practice which has faded over the years, but there are still many choirs and musical societies that bear her name.

♦ 2713 ♦ St. Charlemagne's Day
January 28

Charlemagne wasn't actually a saint at all; he was an emperor and the first ruler of the Holy Roman Empire, crowned in 800 by Pope Leo III. But because of his great interest in education, French college students refer to him as a saint and a hero. Although he was never able to read and write himself, Charlemagne, whose name means "Charles the Great," founded the University of Paris. In fact, his reign was marked by a huge cultural revival, including significant advances in scholarship, literature, and philosophy.

St. Charlemagne's Day is still celebrated by college students in France, who hold champagne breakfasts at which professors and top students recite poems and give speeches.

♦ 2714 ♦ St. Charles's Day
January 30

Charles I, crowned king of England in 1625, was illegally executed on Jan. 30, 1649, primarily for defending the Anglican Church. His body was secretly buried in Windsor Castle. He was widely acclaimed as a martyr. A royal decree ordered a special service on this day to be in the Book of Common Prayer from 1662 to 1859. It also ordered it to be a day of national fasting. The anniversary of this event is commemorated by the Society of Charles the Martyr with an annual service at the site of his execution in Whitehall, London. St. Charles is the only post-Reformation figure to be honored in this way by the Church of England.

See also SAINTS, DOCTORS, MISSIONARIES AND MARTYRS DAY.

CONTACTS:
Society of King Charles the Martyr
22 Tyning Rd.
Winsley
Bradford-on Avon, BA15 2JJ United Kingdom
skcm.org

♦ 2715 ♦ St. Christopher's Day
May 9 in the East and July 25 in the West

The lack of reliable information about St. Christopher's life led the Roman Catholic Church to lessen the significance of his feast in its universal calendar in 1969. But he is still widely venerated—especially by travelers, of whom he is the patron saint. According to the most popular legend, Christopher became a ferryman, carrying people across a river on his strong shoulders while using his staff for balance. One day he carried a small child across, but the weight was so overwhelming that he almost didn't make it to the other side. When he did, the child revealed himself as Christ, explaining his great weight by saying, "With me thou hast borne the sins of the world." The name Christopher means "Christ-bearer."

St. Christopher's Day is observed by members of the Christopher movement in the United States, whose mission is to encourage individual responsibility and positive action. Founded by a member of the Roman Catholic Maryknoll order, the movement has its headquarters in New York City and embraces people of other denominations as well.

In Nesquehoning, Pennsylvania, St. Christopher's Day is the occasion for the **Blessing of the Cars**. The custom began in 1933, when the pastor of Our Lady of Mount Carmel Church started blessing automobiles on the feast day of the patron saint of travelers because he himself had been involved in three serious car accidents. Sometimes it takes an entire week to bless all the cars that arrive in Nesquehoning from throughout Pennsylvania and other nearby states. In recent years other Catholic churches in the area have taken up the custom and perform their own blessing ceremonies. (*See also* ST. FRANCES OF ROME, FEAST OF.).

CONTACTS:
Christophers
5 Hanover Sq.
22nd Fl.
New York, NY 10004

212-759-4050 or 888-298-4050; fax: 212-838-5073
www.christophers.org

♦ 2716 ♦ St. Clare of Assisi, Feast of
August 11

There were a number of women who joined the Second Order of St. Francis, but the first and most famous was St. Clare (c. 1194-1253). The daughter of a wealthy and noble family, she heard St. Francis preach about his rule of poverty and penance and, at the age of 18, left home to dedicate herself to the Franciscan way of life. She was joined 16 days later by her sister, Agnes. Other women, referred to as the Poor Ladies, were eventually drawn to the hard life that Clare had chosen, and the religious order that she and Francis founded is known today as the Poor Clares (*see also* ST. FRANCIS OF ASSISI, FEAST DAY OF).

Clare outlived Francis, who died in 1226, by 27 years. Although she was ill and confined to her bed for most of this time, she was a tireless proponent of the so-called "Primitive Rule," which calls for perpetual fasting except on Sundays and CHRISTMAS. In addition to their vows of poverty, chastity, and obedience, the Poor Clares also take a vow of enclosure, which means that they never leave the convent.

Clare died in 1253 and was canonized on August 12, 1255. Her feast day, which was observed for centuries by Roman Catholics and some Episcopalians, was eventually moved to August 11, the date of her death according to the revised Roman Catholic calendar and some other calendars.

♦ 2717 ♦ St. Columba's Day
June 9

Along with ST. BRIDGET and ST. PATRICK, St. Columba (c. 521-597), also known as **Colm Cille**, **Columeille**, or **Columcille**, is a patron saint of Ireland. Although he led an exemplary life, traveling all over Ireland to set up churches, schools, and monasteries, he is chiefly remembered for his self-imposed exile to the island of Iona off the Scottish coast.

According to legend, Columba felt that he was responsible for the battle of Cuildremne, where 3,000 men were killed, and resolved to atone for his actions by winning 3,000 souls for Christ. He landed at Iona on the eve of PENTECOST, and proceeded to found a monastery and school from which he and his disciples preached the gospel throughout Scotland. Although he had been forbidden to see his native country again, he returned several years later, allegedly blindfolded, to save the poets of Ireland, who were about to be expelled because they had grown so arrogant and overbearing.

St. Columba is also associated with the story of how the robin got its red breast. When Columba asked the robin who landed on his window sill to sing him a song, the robin sang the story of the crucifixion and how he had pulled the thorns out of Christ's forehead and, in doing so, had been covered with his blood.

♦ 2718 ♦ St. Crispin's Day
October 25

According to legend, Crispin and his brother Crispinian traveled from Rome to the French town of Soissons, where they preached and earned a living as shoemakers, offering shoes to the poor at a very low price and using leather provided by angels. The people of Soissons built a church in their honor in the sixth century, and since that time they have been known as the patron saints of shoemakers and other workers in leather. People who wore shoes that were too tight were said to be "in St. Crispin's prison."

This is also the day on which the French and English armies fought the battle of Agincourt in the middle period of the Hundred Years War (1415). The association between the feast day and the battle is so strong that writers sometimes use "St. Crispin's Day" as an expression meaning "a time of battle" or "a time to fight." This day is also called the **Feast of Crispian**, **St. Crispian's Day**, **Crispin's Day**, **Crispin Crispian**, and the **Day of Crispin Crispianus**.

♦ 2719 ♦ St. David's Day
March 1

The patron saint of Wales, St. David was a sixth-century priest who founded an austere religious order and many monasteries and churches, and eventually became primate of South Wales. His day is observed not only by the people of Wales but by Welsh groups all over the world. There are large communities of Welsh throughout the United States— particularly in Pennsylvania, Ohio, Wisconsin, and Florida—who celebrate St. David's Day with performances of choral singing, for which the Welsh are noted (*see also* EISTEDDFOD). The St. David's Society of New York holds an annual banquet on March 1, and the Welsh Society of Philadelphia, which was established in 1802, celebrates with eating, drinking, and songs.

The leek, Wales' national symbol, is often worn on St. David's Day. According to legend, when St. David was leading his people to victory against the Saxons, he commanded them to wear leeks in their hats to avoid being confused with the enemy. In the United States, the daffodil has replaced the leek.

CONTACTS:
Welsh Society of Philadelphia
P.O. Box 7287
Saint Davids, PA 19087
www.philadelphiawelsh.org

♦ 2720 ♦ St. Demetrius's Day
October 26 in the East and October 8 in the West

St. Demetrius is the patron saint of Salonika (Thessalonike) in northeastern Greece, near where he was martyred, perhaps during the fourth century. His feast day marks the beginning of winter for farmers, and a spell of warm weather after October 26 is often called "the little summer" or "the summer of St. Demetrius." It is a day for opening and tasting the season's new wines. St. Demetrius is also the patron saint of soldiers.

October 26 is also the anniversary of the liberation of Salonika from the Turks in 1912.

♦ 2721 ♦ St. Denis's Day
October 9

Also known as St. Dionysius, St. Denis is the patron saint of France. According to legend, Pope Clement sent him to what is now France to establish the Church there, during the reign of Emperor Decius (249-251), but the pagans who greeted him did not treat him well. When he came to Paris as their first bishop, they threw him to the wild beasts, but the beasts licked his feet. Then they put him in a fiery furnace, but he emerged unharmed. The most widely repeated legend is that they beheaded him on Martyr's Hill—the place now known as Montmartre in Paris—but he miraculously picked up his head and carried it for two miles before expiring at the site where the Church of St. Denis was later built.

Denis has also been identified with St. Dionysius the Areopagite, legendarily portrayed as a convert of ST. PAUL.

♦ 2722 ♦ St. Dismas's Day
March 25; second Sunday in October

According to the Bible, two thieves were crucified with Jesus. The one on his right, traditionally called Dismas, repented and was promised, "Today thou shalt be with me in Paradise" (Luke 23:43). He is therefore the patron saint of persons condemned to death. In the United States, the National Catholic Prison Chaplains' Association, by special permission from Rome, observes the second Sunday in October as **Good Thief Sunday** and holds masses in American prisons in honor of St. Dismas. March 25 is also the Feast of the ANNUNCIATION.

♦ 2723 ♦ St. Dunstan's Day
May 19

St. Dunstan (c. 909-988) was the archbishop of Canterbury. According to legend, St. Dunstan was such a good man that Satan felt his activities had to be watched all the time. One day, when Dunstan was working at the monastery forge, he looked up and saw the devil peering at him through the window. He quickly pulled the red-hot tongs from the coals and grabbed the devil's nose with them, refusing to let go until he promised not to tempt him any more. Howling in pain, Satan ran and dipped his nose in nearby Tunbridge Wells to cool it off, which is why the water there is sulphurous. St. Dunstan is buried in Canterbury Cathedral. He is the patron saint of blacksmiths, jewelers, and locksmiths.

CONTACTS:
Guild Church of St Dunstan-in-the-West
186A Fleet St.
London, EC4A 2HR United Kingdom

44-20-7405-1929
www.stdunstaninthewest.org

♦ 2724 ♦ St. Dymphna's Day
May 15

According to legend, St. Dymphna (or Dimpna) was the daughter of a seventh-century Irish king. She fled with her priest to Geel, Belgium, to escape her pagan father's demand for an incestuous marriage. There she was found by the king, who killed her and the priest.

St. Dymphna came to be known as the patron saint of the insane, and for centuries mental patients were brought to the site of her relics in Geel, where the townsfolk looked after them. An infirmary was eventually built next to the Church of St. Dymphna, and by 1852 Geel was placed under state medical supervision.

Today there is a large, well-equipped sanatorium for the mentally ill in Geel, known throughout the world for its "boarding out" system, which allows harmless mental patients to be cared for as paying guests in the homes of local citizens. On May 15 special church services are held and a religious procession moves through the streets carrying a stone from St. Dymphna's alleged tomb—a relic that at one time was applied to patients as part of their therapy.

CONTACTS:
National Shrine of St. Dymphna
206 Cherry Rd. N.E.
P.O. Box 4
Massillon, OH 44648
330-833-8478
www.natlshrinestdymphna.org

Belgian Tourist Office
300 E. 42nd St.
14th Fl.
New York, NY 10017
212-758-8130
www.visitbelgium.com

♦ 2725 ♦ St. Elizabeth Ann Seton, Feast of
January 4

The first native-born American to be declared a saint, Elizabeth Ann Seton (1774-1821) was canonized in 1975. She was the founder of the first religious community for women in the United States, the American Sisters of Charity, and she was responsible for laying the foundations of the American Catholic school system. She also established orphan asylums, the forerunners of the modern foundling homes and child-care centers run today by the Sisters of Charity.

Special services commemorating Elizabeth Ann Seton's death on January 4, 1821, are held on major anniversaries at the Chapel of St. Joseph's Provincial House of the Daughters of Charity in Emmitsburg, Maryland, the headquarters for her order of nuns, and at Trinity Episcopal Church in New York City, of which she was a member before her conversion to

Roman Catholicism in 1805. More than 100,000 people attended her canonization ceremony at St. Peter's Basilica in Rome. On that same day, over 35,000 pilgrims flocked to Emmitsburg, where six masses were said in honor of the new saint.

See also SETON (MOTHER) DAY.

CONTACTS:
National Shrine of Saint Elizabeth Ann Seton
333 S. Seton Ave.
Emmitsburg, MD 21727
301-447-6606; fax: 301-447-6061
www.setonheritage.org

◆ 2726 ◆ St. Elmo's Day
June 2

The day that is known as St. Elmo's Day is actually **St. Erasmus's Day**, in honor of a third-century Italian bishop who is thought to have suffered martyrdom around the year 304. Erasmus was a patron saint of sailors and was especially popular in the 13th century. He is often referred to as Elmo, a variation of Erasmus.

Sometimes at sea on stormy nights, sailors will see a pale, brushlike spray of electricity at the top of the mast. In the Middle Ages, they believed that these fires were the souls of the departed, rising to glory through the intercession of St. Elmo. Such an electrical display is still referred to as "St. Elmo's Fire."

◆ 2727 ◆ St. Evermaire, Game of
May 1

The **Spel van Sint Evermarus**, or the Game of St. Evermaire, is a dramatic reenactment of the slaying of eight pilgrims in Rousson (Rutten), Belgium, on their way to the Holy Land in 699. After spending the night at a farmhouse, the story goes, the saint and his seven companions were murdered by a robber.

This event is portrayed by the townspeople of Rousson, Belgium, each year on the first day of May in the meadow near the Chapel of St. Evermaire. Following a procession around the casket believed to contain the saint's bones, costumed villagers representing St. Evermaire and his companions are attacked by 50 "brigands" riding heavy farm horses and led by Hacco, the legendary assailant. By the end of the drama, the saint and the seven pilgrims lie dead.

Although the event was not commemorated for 200 years after its occurrence, the inhabitants of Rousson have faithfully presented their play for the past 10 centuries.

CONTACTS:
Belgian Tourist Office
300 E. 42nd St.
14th Fl.
New York, NY 10017
212-758-8130
www.visitbelgium.com

◆ 2728 ◆ St. Frances Cabrini, Feast of
December 22; November 13

The first American citizen to be proclaimed a saint of the Roman Catholic Church, Francesca Xavier Cabrini (1850-1917) was born in Italy. After serving as a nurse and a teacher in her native country, and seeing the miserable conditions under which so many orphans lived, she became a nun and was appointed superior of the orphanage at Codogno. Known thereafter as Mother Cabrini, she founded the Missionary Sisters of the Sacred Heart in 1880 and established a number of other schools and orphanages. Nine years later she and six of her nuns landed in New York, where they had been sent to help the Italian immigrants. She went on to establish orphanages, schools, and hospitals in many American cities, as well as in Europe and South America. She was canonized on July 7, 1946, and her feast day is December 22.

St. Frances Cabrini's feast day is commemorated in many places, but particularly at Mother Cabrini High School in New York City, in whose chapel she is buried. November 13, the day on which she was beatified, is also observed at every establishment of the Missionary Sisters of the Sacred Heart.

CONTACTS:
Missionary Sisters of the Sacred Heart of Jesus
MSC Mission Offices, Stella Maris Province
610 King of Prussia Rd.
Radnor, PA 19087
610-902-1039; fax: 610-971-0396
www.mothercabrini.org

◆ 2729 ◆ St. Frances of Rome, Feast of
March 9

St. Frances of Rome (1384-1440), also known as Francesca Romana or Frances the Roman, was a model for housewives and widows. In her 40 years of marriage to Lorenzo Ponziano, it is said there was never the slightest dispute or misunderstanding between them. Despite the death of her children, her husband's banishment, and the confiscation of their estates, she continued to nurse the sick, care for the poor, and settle disputes wherever she went.

Eventually she founded a society of women who pledged to offer themselves to God and to serve the poor. Known at first as the Oblates of Mary, they were afterwards called the Oblates of Tor de Specchi, after the building in which they were housed. When she died, St. Frances's body was removed to Santa Maria Nuova in Rome, which is now known as the church of Santa Francesca Romana. She is the patron saint of widows.

St. Frances's feast day is observed on March 9, the date on which she died. Because she is also the patron saint of motorists—although no clear reason for this is given—it is customary for Italian drivers to flock to the Colosseum in Rome for the blessing of their cars. Crowds also visit Tor de Specchi and Casa degli Esercizi Pii (formerly her home, the Palazzo Ponziano), whose rooms are opened to the public on this day.

See also ST. CHRISTOPHER'S DAY.

CONTACTS:
Italian Government Tourist Board
686 Park Ave.
3rd Fl.
New York, NY 10065
212-245-5618; fax: 212-586-9249
www.italiantourism.com

◆ 2730 ◆ St. Francis of Assisi, Feast of
October 3-4

The most important festival of the Franciscan calendar in Assisi, Italy, the feast of St. Francis (1181-1226) commemorates the saint's transition from this life to the afterlife. For two days the entire town is illuminated by oil lamps burning consecrated oil brought from a different Italian town each year. A parchment in St. Francis's handwriting, believed to be the saint's deathbed blessing to his follower, Brother Leo, is taken to the top of the Santa Maria degli Angeli basilica— built in the 16th century around St. Francis's humble hermitage known as the *Porciúncula*—and the people are blessed by the pope's representative (*see* FORGIVENESS, FEAST OF).

In the United States, it is not uncommon for people to bring their pets to church to be blessed on St. Francis's feast day, because of his love for animals as expressed in his *Canticle of Creatures*.

See also ST. ANTHONY THE ABBOT and SAN FRANCISCO.

CONTACTS:
Italian National Tourist Board
630 Fifth Ave.
3rd Fl.
New York, NY 10065
212-245-5618; fax: 212-586-9249
www.italiantourism.com

◆ 2731 ◆ St. Gabriel, Feast of
Around December 28

St. Gabriel is one of the most popular Ethiopian Orthodox saints and believed to intercede on behalf of those who pray to him more than other saints. Thousands of Orthodox Christians, Muslims, Greeks, Armenians, and tribal people make a pilgrimage on his feast day to Kullubi, Ethiopia. Many carry boulders on their backs in a show of piety, and women often carry babies named after the saint to the local church's baptismal font, as St. Gabriel has a reputation for granting the requests of women who wish to become pregnant.

Most of the pilgrims set up campsites and usually listen to High Mass over loudspeakers, since the church at Kullubi is very small.

CONTACTS:
St. Gabriel the Archangel Catholic Church
6303 Nottingham Ave.
St. Louis, MO 63109
314-353-6303
www.stgabrielstl.org

◆ 2732 ◆ St. Gens, Festival of (La Fête de St. Gens)
Sunday following May 15; first weekend in September

St. Gens, patron saint of the fever-afflicted, was born in Monteux, France, which he is said to have saved from a great drought in the 12th century. He is honored twice annually in his native Provence: first, at Monteux on the Sunday following May 15, and again, at Beaucet, on the first Saturday and Sunday in September. The ceremonies held on both occasions are similar, consisting of a procession with the saint's image, prayers for the sick, and supplications for rain.

According to legend, St. Gens retired to a desert place near Mont Ventoux, where he worked the land with a team of oxen. One day a wolf attacked and ate one of the oxen. St. Gens made the wolf pay by hitching him with the remaining ox and forcing him to plow the land.

CONTACTS:
Church of St. Genevieve
7087 Goiffon Rd.
Centerville, MN 55038
651-429-7937; fax: 651-653-0071
stgens.org

◆ 2733 ◆ St. George's Day
April 23; November 23

Nothing much is known for certain about St. George, but the patron saint of England is popularly known in medieval legend for slaying a vicious dragon that was besieging a town in Cappadocia. After being fed two sheep a day, they became scarce and people had to be given instead—beginning with the king's daughter. She was on her way to the dragon's den to be sacrificed when she met St. George, who insisted on fighting the dragon and, according to another legend, eventually stunned it with his spear. Making a leash out of the princess's sash, he let her lead the monster back to the city like a pet dog. When the people saw what had happened, they were converted to Christianity. To this day, St. George is often depicted with a dragon.

St. George's Day, sometimes referred to as **Georgemas**, has been observed as a religious feast as well as a holiday since the 13th century. In the United States, there are St. George's societies in Philadelphia, New York City, Charleston, S.C., and Baltimore, Maryland, dedicated to charitable causes that hold annual dinners on this day.

St. George's Day is celebrated on November 23 as a national holiday in the Republic of Georgia. A festival is held at the cathedral of Mtskheta, the old capital and religious center of Georgia.

See also GEORGIRITT; GOLDEN CHARIOT AND BATTLE OF THE LUMECON, PROCESSION OF THE; ST. GEORGE'S DAY IN BULGARIA; ST. GEORGE'S DAY IN SYRIA.

CONTACTS:
Embassy of Georgia
1824 R St. N.W.

Washington, D.C. 20009
202-387-2390; fax: 202-387-0864
usa.mfa.gov.ge

◆ 2734 ◆ St. George's Day (Bulgaria)
May 6

ST. GEORGE'S DAY, or **Gergiovden,** is one of the most important celebrations in Bulgaria. It marks the start of the stock-breeding season. The sheep are turned out to graze on the eve of this day because the dew is believed to have curative powers. Special foods are served the following day, traditional songs are sung, and both livestock and their pens are decorated with blossoming willow twigs.

Traditional rural Bulgarian belief holds that someone who is born on this day is blessed with wisdom and beauty. In some areas a lamb is slaughtered, and the door sill is smeared with its blood to protect the house from witches, illness, and other forms of bad luck.

◆ 2735 ◆ St. George's Day (Syria) (Id Mar Jurjus)
April 23

In Syria, where he is known as Mar Jurjus, St. George is honored not only by Christians but by Muslims, who know him as al-Khidr and at one time identified him with the prophet ELIJAH. There are shrines dedicated to St. George throughout the country, and several monasteries mark sites where the saint is said to have revealed himself. One of the most important is the monastery at Humeira, near Tripoli, Syria, where both Christians and Muslims from all over Syria attend a folk festival each year on ST. GEORGE'S DAY, April 23.

CONTACTS:
Saint George Orthodox Church
6 Atwood Ave.
Norwood, MA 02062
781-762-4396; fax: 781-255-1871
www.stgeorgenorwood.org

◆ 2736 ◆ St. Giles Fair
Monday and Tuesday after the Sunday following September 1

The St. Giles Fair, held in Oxford, England, dates back even further than Oxford University. It is the only one remaining of the five great fairs once held in Oxford, and it still occupies its original site on St. Giles Street.

When it started more than 800 years ago, St. Giles was an important trade fair. Today it features sports and popular amusements, including "dodge-em" cars, swing-boats, and gaily painted "roundabouts" (rotaries). Booths sell holiday foods and other merchandise, and visitors flock to the fair from throughout Oxfordshire and the surrounding counties.

St. Giles serves as the patron of the physically disabled, and according to legend the fair was situated outside the walls of the city because townsfolk did not want lame people and beggars to enter the city. The St. Giles Fair is held on the Monday and Tuesday after the Sunday following his feast day, which is September 1.

CONTACTS:
St. Giles' Church
10 Woodstock Rd.
Oxford, OX2 6HT United Kingdom
44-1865-311198
www.st-giles-church.org

◆ 2737 ◆ St. Gregory's Day
March 12

St. Gregory was a sixth-century monk who became a pope. He is said to have invented the Gregorian chant. Popular legend attributes many acts of kindness to St. Gregory. One is that he freed frogs from the ice of early spring. Another is that he loved beggars and fed them at his own table with food served on golden plates.

St. Gregory is also the patron saint of schoolchildren and scholars. In Belgium, schoolchildren rise early on March 12 and parade through the streets dressed as "little soldiers of St. Gregory." They carry a big basket for gifts and are accompanied by a noisy drummer. One of them is dressed as Pope Gregory in gaudy vestments and a gold paper crown. The young girls in the procession wear big shoulder bows that resemble the wings of a butterfly. They march from house to house, pausing at each door to sing a song and to ask for treats.

The procession always includes a group of angels, because the legend says that when Gregory was walking through the slave market at Rome, he saw a group of handsome young English youths. Upon learning their nationality, he exclaimed, "Were they but Christians, they would truly be *angeli* [angels], not *Angli* [Anglo-Saxons]!".

CONTACTS:
St. Gregory the Great Orthodox Church
1443 Euclid St. N.W.
Washington, D.C. 20009
202-299-0479
www.stgregoryoc.org

◆ 2738 ◆ St. Gudula's Day
January 8

St. Gudula (or Gudule) is the patron saint of Brussels, Belgium. According to legend, Satan was so envious of her piety and influence among the people that he often tried to extinguish her lantern as she returned from midnight mass. But as she prayed for help, an angel would re-light the candle.

She died in 712, and her relics were moved to Brussels in 978. Since 1047 they have remained in the church of St. Michael, thereafter named the Cathedral of St. Gudula. Her feast day is observed with great solemnity in Brussels, particularly at the cathedral that bears her name.

◆ 2739 ◆ St. Hans Festival
June 24

Like other MIDSUMMER DAY celebrations, the St. Hans (St. John) Festival in Norway combines both pagan and Christian customs. This festival was originally held in honor of the sun god, for the ancients believed that the sun's change of course at the SUMMER SOLSTICE was an important event. The gates of the upper and lower worlds stood wide open at this time, and supernatural beings such as trolls and goblins roamed the earth.

After Christianity was introduced, the Norwegian midsummer festival was linked to the birth of John the Baptist (*see* ST. JOHN'S DAY), and it became known as **Sankt Hans Dag**, or **St. John's Day**. But some of the ancient customs and superstitions surrounding Midsummer Day have persisted. Only a century ago it was still common for Norwegians to hide their pokers and to carve a cross on their broomsticks as a way of warding off witches who might otherwise use these household items for transportation. The present-day custom of decorating with birch boughs also has its roots in ancient times, when the foliage was considered a symbol of the life force that awakens in Nature in the spring and early summer.

The festival of St. Hans is still celebrated in Norway much as it has been for hundreds of years. On *Jonsok*, or St. John's Eve, Norwegians who live near the fjords head out in their boats, which are decorated with green boughs and flowers, to get the best possible view of the St. John's bonfires on the mountains.

CONTACTS:
Royal Norwegian Embassy
2720 34th St. N.W.
Washington, D.C. 20008
202-333-6000; fax: 202-333-3990
www.norway.org

◆ 2740 ◆ St. Herman Pilgrimage
August 9 and two adjoining days

The St. Herman Pilgrimage takes place for three days on and near August 9 on Kodiak Island and nearby Spruce Island in Alaska. The pilgrimage marks the anniversary of the canonization of St. Herman by the Russian Orthodox Church in 1970. It is attended by the church's clergy and faithful Christians from Alaska, the lower 48 states, and often from other countries. The event includes services at the Holy Resurrection Cathedral in Kodiak, as well as a boat trip to Spruce Island, where St. Herman lived as a hermit in the first half of the 19th century, lovingly serving the native people and God. At Spruce Island, divine services take place at the chapel of Ss. Sergius & Herman, which was founded by St. Herman himself. Pilgrims may drink from a spring thought to be invested by St. Herman with miracle-working properties. They also pray at the remains of St. Herman, where the saint's hat and his cross and chain are displayed. In Kodiak, other pilgrimage activities include tea with the bishop and a grand banquet. Also on offer are educational talks and displays.

Saint Herman was born in Russia in 1756. As a hermetic monk, he was asked in 1793 to join a mission to North America. The group traveled to Kodiak Island to spread the news of Christianity to the native Aleut people. Eventually Herman moved to Spruce Island, where he prayed, fasted, built a chapel, and devoted himself to serving the people. His deep spirituality and healing powers led to his glorification as a saint in 1970. The first canonized American saint, Herman was also known as the Wonder Worker of Alaska.

CONTACTS:
Orthodox Church in America, Diocese of Alaska
P.O. Box 210569
Anchorage, AK 99521
907-677-0224; fax: 907-677-0646
www.doaoca.org

Orthodox Church in America
6850 N. Hempstead Tpke
P.O. Box 675
Syosset, NY 11791
516-922-0550; fax: 516-922-0954
oca.org

◆ 2741 ◆ St. Hilary's Day
January 13 or 14

St. Hilary of Poitiers (c. 315–c. 367) was a French theologian who, as bishop of Poitiers, defended the divinity of Christ against Arianism, which affirmed that Christ was not truly divine because He was a "created" being. The so-called "Hilary term," beginning in January at Oxford and Dublin universities, is named after him. At one time the phrase also referred to a term or session of the High Court of Justice in England. According to tradition St. Hilary's Day—observed on January 13 by Anglicans but on January 14 by Roman Catholics—is the coldest day of the year.

◆ 2742 ◆ St. Hubert de Liège, Feast of
November 3

St. Hubert (d. 727) is the patron saint of hunters, dogs, and victims of rabies. His feast day is especially honored at the church named for him in the little town of St. Hubert, Luxembourg Province, Belgium, on the first weekend in November. People who live in the Forest of Ardennes bring their dogs to the church to be blessed, and St. Hubert's Mass marks the official opening of the hunting season. In some places special loaves of bread are brought to the mass to be blessed, after which everyone eats a piece and feeds the rest to their dogs, horses, and other domestic animals to ward off rabies.

According to legend, St. Hubert was once more interested in hunting than he was in observing church festivals. But on GOOD FRIDAY one year, while he was hunting, he saw a young white stag with a crucifix between his antlers. The vision was so powerful that he changed his ways, became a monk, and was eventually made bishop of Liège. The site of this event is marked by a chapel about five miles from St. Hubert.

Thousands of pilgrims visit St. Hubert's shrine at the Church of St. Hubert each year. Among the artifacts there are his hunting horn and mantle, supposedly given to him by the Virgin Mary—a thread of which, when placed on a small cut on the forehead, is supposed to cure people who suffer from rabies. His relics are enshrined at the cathedral in Liège.

CONTACTS:
St. Hubert Tourist Information Office
Rue Saint-Gilles 12
Saint-Hubert, B-6870 Belgium
32-61-61-30-10; fax: 32-61-61-54-44
www.saint-hubert-tourisme.be

♦ 2743 ♦ St. Ignatius Loyola, Feast of
July 31

St. Ignatius Loyola (1491-1556) founded the Society of Jesus, the Roman Catholic religious order whose members are known as Jesuits. Now the largest single religious order in the world, the Jesuits are known for their work in education, which St. Ignatius believed was one of the best ways to help people. In the United States, which currently has more Jesuits than any other country, they train hundreds of thousands of high school, college, and university students every year. St. Ignatius is the patron saint of retreats and those who attend retreats.

The Feast of St. Ignatius is celebrated by Jesuits everywhere, but particularly in the Basque region of Spain where he was born. The largest Basque community in North America, located in Boise, Idaho, holds its annual **St. Ignatius Loyola Picnic** on the last weekend in July—an event often referred to as the **Basque Festival**. Every five years Boise's Basque Organization holds Jaialdi ("Big Festival"), the International Basque Cultural Festival, which features Basque music, dancing, food, sports, and more. (*See also* BASQUE FESTIVAL, NATIONAL.) The first Basques settled in the United States in 1865.

CONTACTS:
Church of St. Ignatius Loyola
980 Park Ave.
New York, NY 10028
212-288-3588
www.stignatiusloyola.org

Basque Museum & Cultural Center
611 Grove St.
Boise, ID 83702
208-343-2671
www.basquemuseum.com

♦ 2744 ♦ St. Isidore, Festival of
Mid-May

Although indigenous fertility rites were outlawed when Mexico was conquered by the Spaniards and converted to Catholicism, a few pre-Hispanic festivities have survived— often overlaid with Christian meaning. One of these is the Festival of St. Isidore in Metepec, where farmers honor their patron saint around the time of his feast day, May 15. The men dress up as women and accompany their plows and oxen, which have been decorated with flowers, in a procession to the fields.

In Acapantzingo, Morelos State, there is a sowing festival in mid-May that includes a folk play and ritual dances, while in Matamoros, Tamaulipas State, there is a procession in honor of St. Isidore followed by dances that depict the events of the Spanish conquest.

See also SAN ISIDRO IN PERU, FIESTA OF; SAN ISIDRO THE FARMER, FEAST OF.

CONTACTS:
St. Isidore Catholic Church
625 Spring Ave. N.E.
Grand Rapids, MI 49503
616-459-4731
www.saintisidorechurch.org

♦ 2745 ♦ St. James's Day
July 25 in the Western Church; April 30 in the Eastern Church

The Apostle James the Great (d. 44) was martyred by Herod. Also known as Santiago, he is the patron saint of Spain. His feast day is celebrated in the Western Church on July 25, the anniversary of the day on which, according to Spanish tradition, his body was miraculously discovered in Compostela, Spain, after being buried there for 800 years. A church was built on the site, which later became the town of Santiago de Compostela, once a place of pilgrimage second only to Jerusalem and Rome. St. James's Day is still celebrated in Compostela with a weeklong festival that features a mock burning of the 12th-century cathedral and an elaborate fireworks display.

The Indian pueblos of New Mexico, which were the target of early Spanish missionary efforts, also observe St. James's Day. At the **Fiestas de Santiago y Santa Ana**, held annually in the Taos Pueblo on July 25 and 26 (or the nearest weekend), the corn dance is performed in honor of both St. James and ST. ANNE, the mother of the Virgin Mary, whose feast day follows Santiago Day. Ritual dances also take place in the Santa Ana, Laguna, and Cochiti pueblos. At Acoma Pueblo, Santiago's Day is celebrated by holding a rooster pull.

In Loíza, Puerto Rico, the **Fiesta of St. James the Apostle** or **Fiesta de Santiago Apóstol** is the biggest celebration of the year. It focuses on three images of the saint—the *Santiago de los Muchachos* (St. James of the Children), the *Santiago de los Hombres* (St. James of the Men), and the *Santiago de las Mujeres* (St. James of the Women)—which are carried from the homes of the *mantenedoras* (keepers) who have kept guard over them all year to a place near the sea known as *Las Carreras*, "the racetracks."

Santiago de los Hombres begins the procession, stopping in front of the house where another saint is kept. This second image joins the first and the procession continues until all three end up at Las Carreras, where the traditional ceremony of racing with the flags of the saints takes place. Farm workers and fishermen dress in traditional costumes and perform music and dances of African origin. St. James's Day is also a popular choice for baptisms and marriages.

His feast day in the Eastern Church is April 30.

CONTACTS:
Puerto Rico Tourism Company
135 W. 50th St.
22nd Fl.
New York, NY 10020
212-586-6262 or 800-223-6530
welcome.topuertorico.org

Library of Congress
101 Independence Ave., S.E.
Washington, D.C. 20540
202-707-5000; fax: 202-707-2076
www.loc.gov

♦ 2746 ♦ St. Joan of Arc, Feast Day of
May 30; May 9

The second patron saint of France (the first is ST. DENIS) and one of the best known of all the saints, Joan of Arc—whom the French refer to as Jeanne d'Arc, the "Maid of Orleans," for the role she played in saving the city of Orleans from the British in the 15th century—was a young, pious peasant girl from the village of Domremy. In 1428 she heard voices she identified as ST. MICHAEL, ST. CATHERINE, and St. Margaret telling her to help the dauphin, Charles VII, recover his kingdom from the British. Her mission was accomplished within 15 months, but Joan was captured by the king's enemies, tried for witchcraft and heresy, and burned at the stake in Rouen on May 30, 1431.

St. Joan's Day is celebrated on May 30 everywhere except in the city of New Orleans, Louisiana, where she is honored on May 9, the day after the anniversary of her dramatic rescue of the French city for which New Orleans was named. In France, the **Fête de Jeanne d'Arc** is observed with special ceremonies in Rouen and Orleans, where the streets are decorated with banners, garlands, and portraits of the teenage girl who was canonized in 1920, five centuries after she led the French forces to victory and brought about the coronation of Charles VII at Reims.

CONTACTS:
St. Joan of Arc Feast Day
63 Columbus Ave.
Farmingville, NY 11738
631-846-1089
www.joanofarc.us

Rouen Tourism Office
25 Place de cathÉdrale
Rouen, 76000 France
33-2-3208-3254; fax: 33-2-3208-3249
www.rouentourisme.com

♦ 2747 ♦ St. John Lateran, Feast of the Dedication of
November 9

This Roman Catholic observance commemorates Pope Sylvester's consecration of the Basilica of the Most Holy Savior commonly known as St. John Lateran, in Rome on November 9, 324. Churches as they are known today—that is, buildings set apart as places of worship—did not exist for the first two centuries of the Christian era; believers gathered in each other's homes. Thus, the pope's public dedication of this church at the beginning of the fourth century was a first in Christianity and merited a special celebration.

St. John Lateran began as the mansion of a wealthy Roman family named Laterani until it was given to the Christians, serving as the residence of popes for a thousand years. The home was built around a great hall, and this hall became the church. It was called a "basilica," a word that originally described an oblong hall, rounded at one or both ends, where public assemblies were held. A baptistry was added and dedicated to St. John the Baptist, and since the 12th century, the church has been known as St. John Lateran.

♦ 2748 ♦ St. John the Baptist, Martyrdom of
August 29

St. John the Baptist was beheaded by King Herod because he had denounced Herod's marriage to Herodias, the wife of his half-brother Philip (Luke 3:19, 20), an illegal union according to Jewish law. Herodias' daughter by a former marriage, by legend called Salome, pleased Herod so much with her dancing that he swore to give her whatever she wanted. At her mother's urging she asked for the head of John the Baptist on a platter (Matthew 14:3-12). Herod, grief-stricken over having let himself be maneuvered into killing a good and innocent man, later had the head concealed within the palace walls to spare it any further indignities. It remained there until after the discovery of the holy cross by St. Helena, an event which drew many pilgrims to Jerusalem. Two of them found the head after St. John appeared to them in a vision.

The Martyrdom of St. John the Baptist—also known as the **Feast of the Beheading** in the Eastern Orthodox Church—has been celebrated by Christians since the fourth century. The observance started at Sebaste (Samaria), where the Baptist was believed to have been buried.

See also EXALTATION OF THE CROSS; ST. JOHN'S DAY.

♦ 2749 ♦ St. John the Evangelist's Day
December 27

John the Evangelist, also called **St. John the Divine**, was thought to be not only the youngest of the Apostles but the longest-lived, dying peacefully of natural causes at an advanced age. Although he escaped actual martyrdom, St. John endured considerable persecution and suffering for his beliefs. He is said to have drunk poison to prove his faith (so he is the patron saint of protection against poison), been cast into a cauldron of boiling oil, and at one point banished to the lonely Greek island of Patmos, where he worked among the criminals in the mines. He remained healthy, vigorous, and miraculously unharmed throughout these trials and returned to Ephesus where it is believed he wrote the Gospel according to John. He is also believed to be the author of the New Testament Book of Revelation, though many scholars disagree.

See also ST. STEPHEN'S DAY.

CONTACTS:
Church of St.John the Evangelist
11 Fourth Ave. S.W.
Rochester, MN 55902
507-288-7372; fax: 507-288-7373
www.sj.org

♦ 2750 ♦ **St. John's Eve (Germany) (Johannisnacht)**
June 23

The SUMMER SOLSTICE, or *Sommersonnenwende*, in Germany is observed by lighting the *Johannisfeuer*, or St. John's fire. Young boys often try to leap through the flames, and young lovers join hands and try to jump over the fire together in the belief that if they succeed, they will never be parted. Cattle driven through the bonfire's ashes are believed to be safe from danger and disease in the coming year.

According to German folklore, the water spirits demanded a human victim on MIDSUMMER DAY. But contrary to the danger this implies, people often went out and bathed on St. John's Eve in streams or rivers to cure disease and strengthen their legs. In the Thuringia region, wreaths were hung on the doors because it was believed that St. John the Baptist walked through the streets on this night, and that he would bow to any door with a wreath on it.

♦ 2751 ♦ **St. John's Day**
June 24

It is unusual for a saint's day to commemorate his birth rather than his death, but John the Baptist (d. c. 29) and the Virgin Mary are the exceptions here. (*See* NATIVITY OF THE BLESSED VIRGIN MARY, FEAST OF THE). Roman Catholics, Eastern Orthodox Christians, Anglicans, and Lutherans honor St. John on the anniversary of his birth; the Roman Catholic and Orthodox churches commemorate his death as well, on August 29 (*see* ST. JOHN THE BAPTIST, MARTYRDOM OF).

John was the cousin of Jesus, born in their old age to Zechariah and Elizabeth, a kinswoman of the Virgin Mary. John was the one chosen to prepare the way for the Messiah. It is a pious belief of many that he was sanctified—that is, freed from original sin—in his mother's womb when she was visited by Mary. (*See* VISITATION, FEAST OF THE.) He lived as a hermit in the wilderness on a diet of honey and locusts until it was time to begin his public ministry. He preached repentance of sins and baptized many, including Jesus (*see* EPIPHANY). He denounced King Herod and his second wife, Herodias, and it was she who vowed revenge for John's condemnation of her marriage, and who had her daughter, Salome, demand the Baptist's head on a platter.

Many St. John's Day customs date from pre-Christian times, when June 24 was celebrated as MIDSUMMER DAY. Celebrations in some areas still bear the hallmarks of the old pagan SUMMER SOLSTICE rites, such as bonfires, dancing, and decorating with flowers. For the French in Canada, the **Feast of the Nativity of St. John the Baptist** is one of the biggest celebrations of the year, especially in Quebec. The **San Juan Fiesta** in New York City takes place on the Sunday nearest June 24 and is the year's most important festival for Hispanic Americans.

St. John's Day (**Día de San Juan**) is a major holiday throughout Mexico. As the patron saint of waters, St. John is honored by decorating fountains and wells and by bathing in local streams and rivers. The bathing begins at midnight—often to the accompaniment of village bands—and it is customary for spectators to throw flowers among the bathers. In Mexico City and other urban centers, the celebration takes place in fashionable bath-houses rather than rivers, where there are diving and swimming contests as well. Street vendors sell small mules made out of cornhusks, decorated with flowers and filled with sugar cane and candy.

A family of yellow-flowered plants, commonly called St. John's-wort, is used by voodoo conjurors and folk medicine practitioners to ward off evil spirits and ensure good luck. In the southern United States, all species of the plant are called John the Conqueror root, or "John de Conker," and all parts of it are used: the root, leaves, petals, and stems. The plant's imagery is often mentioned in African-American folklore and blues music.

The leaves, and often the petals, contain oil and pigment-filled glands that appear as reddish spots when held to the light. According to legend, these spots are John the Baptist's blood, and the plant is most potent if rituals are performed on his birthday.

See also SAN JUAN AND SAN PEDRO FESTIVALS; SAN JUAN PUEBLO FEAST DAY; ST. HANS FESTIVAL.

♦ 2752 ♦ **St. John's Day (Guatemala)**
June 24

Día de San Juan or ST. JOHN'S DAY has been observed by some Guatemalan Indians, especially those in Camotan, Chiquimula Department, and San Juan Sacatepéquez, Guatemala Department, with a traditional dance known as *Los Gigantes* (The Giants). It is based on a story from the Popol Vuh, the sacred book of the Quiché Mayan Indians, but it also incorporates two events from the Bible: the beheading of St. John the Baptist and David's struggle against Goliath. The dancers wear red, blue, yellow and white costumes; these colors symbolize the four directions of the compass. Some dancers also wear veils, which refers to an ancient belief that at one time the sun and moon had faces that were veiled. Using their swords, dancers outline the path the sun takes when it rises and sets in both the opening and closing sequences of the dance.

♦ 2753 ♦ **St. John's Day (Portugal)**
June 24

Both ST. JOHN'S DAY and St. John's Eve (*see also* MIDSUMMER DAY) are widely celebrated in Portugal with parades, pageants, bullfights, fireworks, and other popular amusements. Many of the traditional rites connected with fire, water, and love are still observed here as well. Young people dance around bonfires and couples often leap over these fires, holding hands. Mothers sometimes hold their children over the burning embers, and cattle and flocks are driven through the ashes—all to take advantage of the curative powers of St. John's fires. Similar traditions focus on water, which on St. John's Eve is supposed to possess great healing power.

One of the most interesting St. John's Day celebrations takes place in Braga and is known as the *Dança de Rei David*, or Dance of King David. The role of King David is always performed by a member of a certain family living near Braga, and the dance itself probably dates back to medieval times. The King is dressed in a tall crown and voluminous cape. Ten shepherds or courtiers who accompany him wear velvet coats in brilliant colors and turban-style hats. Shepherds play ancient tunes on their fiddles, flutes, and triangles. As they parade through town this group stops frequently to perform the ritualistic Dance of King David.

CONTACTS:
Portuguese National Tourist Office
590 Fifth Ave.
4th Fl.
New York, NY 10036
351-646-723-0200
www.visitportugal.com

♦ 2754 ♦ **St. John's Day (Puerto Rico)**
June 24

Wading or bathing in the water on ST. JOHN'S DAY is a tradition that many see as symbolic of John the Baptist baptizing Jesus. In Puerto Rico, **San Juan Day** is observed by gathering at the beaches to eat, dance, drink, build bonfires, and bathe in the Caribbean. At midnight, revelers take a swim in the ocean, a tradition based on the biblical scene in which John, the cousin of Jesus, baptizes him. Over the years, the religious significance of the event has been overshadowed, and today bathing in the water is believed to bring good luck in the coming year.

The annual St. John the Baptist Day parade in Camden, New Jersey, has been going on since the 1950s, not long after the first Puerto Ricans began migrating there to take jobs in the Campbell Soup factory. Billed as the only organized parade in the city, the event is eagerly anticipated by the area's thousands of Hispanic Americans, many of whom line the parade route from Cooper and Second Streets to Wiggins Park along the waterfront. There is a competition for the best float and a steady procession of salsa dancers, folk dancers, and beauty queens. The parade marks the culmination of a week of festivities including a banquet, art exhibits, and a flag-raising ceremony—that honor the area's Hispanics.

In Hartford, Connecticut, a San Juan Bautista Festival has been held on the Saturday nearest June 24 since 1979. Sponsored by the San Juan Center, Inc., it includes Puerto Rican food and entertainment, particularly bands that play Puerto Rican music and use traditional instruments of the homeland. Although the Hartford festival is designed to give the area's Puerto Rican population an opportunity to celebrate their heritage, it draws many other people as well.

CONTACTS:
Puerto Rico Tourism Company Office
135 W. 50th St.
22nd Fl.
New York, NY 10020
212-586-6262 or 800-223-6530
welcome.topuertorico.org

♦ 2755 ♦ **St. John's Eve (Denmark)**
June 23

Known in Denmark as **Sankt Hans Aften**, St. John's Eve occurs near the longest day of the year and therefore is an occasion for national rejoicing. Huge bonfires, often topped with tar barrels or other flammable materials, light up the night sky for miles around. Sometimes an effigy of a witch, perhaps a pagan symbol of winter or death, is thrown on the fire. Along the coast, fires are built on the beach or shore. People go out in their boats to watch them burn and to sing romantic songs. Sometimes there are speeches, singing games, dances, and fireworks as well.

Midsummer Eve is also a popular time for Danes to leave their year-round homes and go to vacation cottages on the coast.

CONTACTS:
Embassy of Denmark
3200 Whitehaven St. N.W.
Washington, D.C. 20008
202-234-4300; fax: 202-328-1470
usa.um.dk

♦ 2756 ♦ **St. John's Eve (France) (La Vielle de la Saint Jean)**
June 23

The custom of lighting bonfires on the eve of ST. JOHN'S DAY has been said to originate with the ancient Druids, who built fires at the SUMMER SOLSTICE in honor of the sun god. Bonfires are still an important part of the festivities on St. John's Eve in France, where participants contribute something to burn. Traditionally, the village priest often lights the fire and leads the townspeople in the singing of hymns and the chanting of prayers.

In upper Brittany, St. John's fires are built around tall poles, which are set on the hilltops. A boy named Jean or a girl named Jeanne provides a bouquet or wreath for the pole and kindles the fire. Then the young people sing and dance around it while it burns. Sometimes the fire is replaced by a burning torch thrown skyward or by a wagon wheel covered with straw, set ablaze, and rolled downhill.

At sea, Breton fishermen traditionally put old clothing in a barrel, hoist it up the mainmast, and set it afire so that other ships in the fishing fleet can share the celebration.

There are many folk beliefs associated with St. John's Eve. One is that strewing the ashes from the St. John's fires over the fields will bring a good harvest. Another is that leaping over the dying embers guarantees that the crops will grow as high as the jumper can jump. In the sheep-raising Jura district, shepherds drive their flower-decked animals in a procession and later nail the flower wreaths to their stable doors as a protection against the forces of evil.

CONTACTS:
France Tourism Development Agency
825 3rd Ave.
New York, NY 10022
212-838-7800; fax: 212-838-7855
int.rendezvousenfrance.com/en

♦ 2757 ♦ St. John's Eve (Greece)
June 23

A custom still practiced in some rural Greek villages on ST. JOHN'S DAY is a procession of young boys and girls escorting the *Kalinitsa*, the girl considered the most beautiful in the neighborhood. On St. John's Eve, the young people gather at the Kalinitsa's house and dress her up as a bride, with a veil and a garland of flowers around her neck. The procession itself is led by a young boy holding a rod. He is followed by the Kalinitsa, who is in turn followed by four "ladies in waiting" and a little girl holding a parasol over the Kalinitsa's head. Other girls and boys accompany them, and they go around the village singing a song about drawing water for the sweet basil. If they should encounter a procession from another neighborhood at a crossroad, the parasols are lowered over the Kalinitsas' faces so they won't set eyes on each other. On the following day, June 24, the children gather at the Kalinitsa's house for a party.

Another old Greek custom, known as the *Erma*, is for two people who have chosen each other for friends to plant some seeds in a basket and raise them in darkness a few weeks before St. John's Day. On St. John's Eve they exchange plants and pledge their friendship by shaking hands three times over a fire.

CONTACTS:
Greek National Tourism Organisation
305, E. 47th St.
2nd Fl.
New York, NY 10017 United States
212-421-5777; fax: 212-826-6940
www.visitgreece.gr/ | www.gtp.gr

♦ 2758 ♦ St. John's Eve (Ireland)
June 23

The Irish still celebrate St. John's Eve with bonfires, dancing, omens, and prayers. People build fires on the hillsides and feed the flames with fragrant boughs. As the fires burn low, both old and young people customarily join hands and jump over the embers in the belief that it will bring an abundant harvest. Young Irish girls used to drop melted lead into water on St. John's Eve. They would then look for clues about their future in whatever shape the lead assumed.

According to Irish folklore, the soul leaves the body on this night and wanders about until it reaches the place where death will eventually strike. This belief was so widespread at one time that people routinely sat up all night on St. John's Eve to keep their souls from making the trip.

♦ 2759 ♦ St. John's Eve (Spain)
June 23

La Víspera de San Juan in Spain is dedicated to water and fire. Fireworks displays are common and *bogueras*, or bonfires, are lit in the city of Alicante, as well as villages, hilltops, and fields. In the Pyrénées, folk beliefs surround the bonfires and their charred remains, which are considered protection from thunderstorms. Cinders from the fires can also be mixed with the newly sown crops or put in the garden to ensure rapid growth. In other places people believe that cabbages planted on St. John's Eve will come up within 24 hours, and that beans will be ready by ST. PETER'S DAY, six days later. Folkloric beliefs also focus on water. Walking through the dew or bathing in the sea on this day is believed to promote beauty and health.

Young girls traditionally believe that San Juan will help them see into their future. By placing a bowl of water outside the window and breaking an egg into it at midnight on St. John's Eve, they try to read their destiny in the shape the egg assumes. Similarly, pouring melted lead into a bowl of water at noon gives clues as to what kind of man they will marry.

In the province of Asturias, a dance known as the *corri-corri* is performed on ST. JOHN'S DAY by six women with one man pursuing them. The sexual motif of the dance links it to the fertility rites associated with MIDSUMMER DAY in ancient times. In the Basque region, men perform the *bordón-danza*, or sword dance, in two facing lines, wearing white shirts and breeches, red sashes and berets, and carrying long sticks in place of the traditional swords. The fact that this dance is performed most commonly on St. John's Day suggests a connection with ancient SUMMER SOLSTICE rites.

Pastry shops in Spain sell special cakes shaped like the letter J on St. John's Eve, which may be decorated with pink sugar roses and elaborate scrolls.

CONTACTS:
Valencia Tourist Office
Avda. Cortes Valencianas, 59
Valencia, 46015 Spain
34-902-101-505; fax: 34-963-606-430
www.visitvalencia.com

♦ 2760 ♦ St. John's Eve and Day (Latvia) (Jans vakars)
June 23-24

The three-day MIDSUMMER festival known as **Ligo Svetki** is Latvia's greatest feast of the year. It begins on St. John's Eve, when boys and girls meet in the village squares. The boys chase the girls and, in accordance with an ancient custom, beat them with cattail switches. Then the young people gather flowers, herbs, and grasses to make wreaths that will be used in ceremonies the following day.

They also practice *Ligo* songs, which are based on the traditional Latvian *daina*, a short, unrhymed song in which epic and lyric elements are mixed. Sometimes the songs take the form of singing contests in praise or blame of the various men in town who are named Janis (or John): One group of singers praises a certain Janis for the prosperity of his farm and livestock, while another points out that his garden is full of weeds, his barnyard is littered with rubbish, and his servants are lazy. These songs serve as a reminder to everyone that their homes must be ready for the guests who will arrive on the following night—the boys and girls who arrive armed with their wreaths and place them on the heads of Janis and his wife.

As in many other countries, lighting bonfires is a tradition in Latvia on St. John's Night. Young people jump over the fires in the belief that it will ensure a good harvest. Others wave Ligo torches and perform typical Latvian folk dances, such as the *Trisparu deja*, the *Jandalins*, the *Ackups*, and the *Sudmalinas*. In some Latvian towns, arches made from birch branches and wildflowers are placed in front of the houses, and the ceremonies associated with the Ligo feast are performed beneath these fragrant canopies.

♦ 2761 ♦ St. Joseph the Worker, Feast of
May 1

A public holiday in Malta, celebrated with festivities throughout the country. In Valletta, a highlight of the mass conducted by the archbishop in St. John's Cathedral is the blessing of the tools and products of laborers and craftsmen.

St. Joseph, the husband of the Virgin Mary, was a carpenter who taught Jesus his craft. He is the patron saint of workers, laborers, carpenters, cabinetmakers, and joiners. In 1955, Pope Pius XII established the Feast of St. Joseph the Worker on May 1 as a counter-celebration to the Communists' MAY DAY celebrations honoring workers.

CONTACTS:
Malta Tourism Authority
Auberge D'Italie
Merchants St.
Valletta, VLT 1170 Malta
356-2291-5000; fax: 356-2291-5394
www.mta.com.mt

♦ 2762 ♦ St. Joseph's Day
March 12-19

The feast of the foster-father of Jesus, known as **Dia de San Giuseppe**, is widely observed in Italy as a day of feasting and sharing with the poor, of whom he is the patron saint. Villages prepare a "table of St. Joseph" by contributing money, candles, flowers, or food. Then they invite three guests of honor—representing Jesus, Mary, and Joseph—to join in their feast, as well as others representing the 12 Apostles. They also invite the orphans, widows, beggars, and poor people of the

village to eat with them. The food is blessed by the village priest and by the child chosen to represent Jesus; then it is passed from one person to the next. The **Feast of St. Joseph** is celebrated by Italians in the United States and in other countries as well.

In Valencia, Spain, it is a week-long festival called **Fallas de San Jose (Bonfires of St. Joseph)**. It has its roots in medieval times when, on St. Joseph's Eve, the carpenters' guild made a huge bonfire out of the wood shavings that had accumulated over the winter to honor the carpenter patron saint, St. Joseph. This act marked the end of winter and was the last night on which candles and amps would have to be lighted. In fact, the carpenters often burned the *parot*, or wooden candelabrum, in front of their shops.

Nowadays the parots have become *fallas*, or huge floats of intricate scenes made of wood and papier-mâché, satirizing everything from the high cost of living to political personalities. On St. Joseph's Eve, March 18, the fallas parade through the streets. At midnight on March 19, the celebration ends with the spectacular ceremony known as the *crema*, when all the fallas are set on fire. One *Ninot*, or "doll," from each falla is chosen, and before the fire the best one is selected and preserved in a special museum. Another highlight is the *crida*, which consists of a series of public announcements made from the Torres de Serrano by the Queen of the Fallas and the city mayor. The festival is said to reflect the happy and satirical nature of the Valencians.

See also SAN JOSÉ DAY FESTIVAL and SWALLOWS OF SAN JUAN CAPISTRANO.

CONTACTS:
Italian National Tourist Board
686 Park Ave.
3rd Fl.
New York, NY 10065
212-245-5618; fax: 212-586-9249
www.italiantourism.com

Valencia Tourism
Avda. Cortes Valencianas, 59
Valencia, 46015 Spain
34-902-101-505
www.visitvalencia.com

♦ 2763 ♦ St. Jude's Day
October 28

Because St. Jude is believed to have been martyred with St. Simon in Persia, where they had gone to preach Christianity, their feast is celebrated jointly on October 28, thought to be the date on which their relics were moved to old St. Peter's basilica. Aside from the fact that they were both apostles, little is known about Simon and Jude. The New Testament refers to "Judas, not Iscariot" to distinguish Jude the Apostle from the Judas who betrayed Jesus.

Since St. Jude is the patron saint of hopeless causes, the saint day is observed particularly by students, who often ask for his help on exams. St. Jude and St. Joseph traditionally are the most important saints to Roman Catholics in Buffalo,

New York, where people buy St. Jude medals to help them win over impossible odds or achieve the unachievable.

◆ 2764 ◆ St. Kitts and Nevis Independence Day
September 19

Saint Kitts and Nevis is officially called the Federation of Saint Kitts and Nevis. An island nation in the West Indies in the Leeward Islands, it consists of the islands of Saint Kitts, Nevis, and Sombrero. Most of the people on these islands are descendants of Africans who were originally brought to the islands as slaves.

In 1493, Christopher Columbus landed on Saint Kitts and named the island Saint Christopher, after his patron saint. During this same voyage, Columbus also landed on Nevis. It wasn't until 1623 that English colonists began to settle on Saint Christopher's Island. At that time, the English shortened its name to Saint Kitts Island. In 1628, English colonists began to settle on Nevis. For the next 100 years, the British and French formed a rivalry for control over the islands. In 1782, the British took permanent control over the islands.

The islands, along with nearby Anguilla, were united in 1882. They joined the West Indies Federation in 1958 and remained in that association until its dissolution in 1962. Saint Kitts, Nevis, and Anguilla became a self-governing state of the United Kingdom in 1967. Anguilla seceded in 1980, and Saint Kitts and Nevis gained independence on September 19, 1983.

Every year, the people of Saint Kitts and Nevis celebrate Independence Day on September 19. Various celebrations take place across the islands on this day, including a cultural program of dance, live music, local food, and traditional displays.

CONTACTS:
St. Kitts Tourism Authority
350 Fifth Ave.
59th Fl.
New York, NY 10118
914-949-2164 or 800-582-6208
www.stkittstourism.kn

Permanent Mission of St. Kitts & Nevis to the United Nations
414 E. 75th St.
5th Fl.
New York, NY 10021
212-535-1234; fax: 212-535-6854
www.stkittsnevis.org

◆ 2765 ◆ St. Kitts and Nevis National Heroes Day
September 16

Saint Kitts and Nevis is officially called the Federation of Saint Kitts and Nevis. An island nation in the West Indies in the Leeward Islands, it consists of the islands of Saint Kitts, Nevis, and Sombrero. Most of the people on these islands are descendants of Africans who were originally brought to the islands as slaves.

In 1493, Christopher Columbus landed on Saint Kitts and named the island Saint Christopher, after his patron saint. During this same voyage, Columbus also landed on Nevis. It wasn't until 1623 that English colonists began to settle on Saint Christopher's Island. At that time, the English shortened its name to Saint Kitts Island. In 1628, English colonists began to settle on Nevis. For the next 100 years, the British and French formed a rivalry for control over the islands. In 1782, the British took permanent control over the islands.

The islands, along with nearby Anguilla, were united in 1882. They joined the West Indies Federation in 1958 and remained in that association until its dissolution in 1962. Saint Kitts, Nevis, and Anguilla became a self-governing state of the United Kingdom in 1967. Anguilla seceded in 1980, and Saint Kitts and Nevis gained independence on September 19, 1983.

In 1998, the Saint Kitts and Nevis federal Parliament passed the National Honours Act. Through this act, various awards and acknowledgements were established, including a National Heroes Day. On this day, the country honors those who have distinguished themselves for the good of the islands. The first National Heroes Day was celebrated on September 16, 1998. The first National Hero was the late Robert L. Bradshaw, the first Premier of the Associated State of Saint Kitts, Nevis, and Anguilla.

CONTACTS:
St. Kitts Tourism Authority
Pelican Mall
P.O. Box 132
Basseterre, St. Kitts 10021 Saint Kitts and Nevis
869-465-4040; fax: 869-465-8794
www.stkittstourism.kn

◆ 2766 ◆ St. Knut's Day
January 13

Tjugondag Knut, or St. Knut's Day, marks the end of the Yuletide season in Sweden. King Canute (or Knut) ruled Denmark, England, and Norway in the 11th century; his feast day is January 13. Rather than letting the holidays fade quietly, Swedish families throughout the country hold parties to celebrate the final lighting (and subsequent dismantling) of the CHRISTMAS tree. After letting the children eat the cookies and candies used to decorate the tree, and after packing the ornaments away in their boxes, it is customary to hurl the tree through an open window.

In Norway, January 13 is known as **Tyvendedagen**, or **Twentieth Day**, since it is the 20th day after Christmas. It is observed in much the same way, with parties and the dismantling of the Christmas tree. But instead of throwing the tree out the window, it is customarily chopped up and burned in the fireplace.

◆ 2767 ◆ St. Lazarus's Day
Between March 27 and April 30; Saturday before Palm Sunday

In Bulgaria, St. Lazarus's Day (**Lazarouvane** or **Lazarovden**) is the great Slavic festival of youth and fertility and doesn't have much to do with Lazarus himself. The day takes its name from a series of ritual games and songs studied in advance by young girls during LENT. Although there are many versions of the ritual, they all have a common focus, which is the "coming out" of girls who are ready to be married. Particular attention is paid to dress, which usually involves colorful traditional costumes and heavy jewelry. In former times, the people of Bulgaria believed that the more elaborate the rituals devoted to marriage, the better the chances for happiness, long life, and a house full of children.

See also LAZARUS SATURDAY.

♦ 2768 ♦ **St. Leopold's Day**
November 15

St. Leopold (1073-1136), the patron saint of Austria, was buried in the abbey he had established in Klosterneuburg, Lower Austria. His feast day is observed there with the ceremony known as **Fasselrutschen**, or the **Slide of the Great Cask**, in the abbey's wine cellar. Participants climb the narrow staircase that leads to the top of the cask, which was sculpted by a famous Viennese woodcarver and holds 12,000 gallons of wine, and then slide down its smooth surface to a padded platform at its base. The faster the trip down, according to tradition, the better luck the person will have in the coming year.

St. Leopold's Day is also known as **Gaense Tag**, or **Goose Day**, because the traditional evening meal served on this day is roast goose. Mid-November marks the beginning of the new wine season, and all over Austria there are wine-drinking picnics and parties around this day, known as HEURIGEN PARTIES.

CONTACTS:
Tourismusverein Klosterneuburg
Bahnhof Kierling / Bahnsteig 1
Niedermarkt 4
Klosterneuburg, A-3400 Austria
43-22-433-2038
tvs.reps.at/info

Austrian Consulate General
31 E. 69th St.
New York, NY 10021
212-737-6400; fax: 212-585 1992
www.bmeia.gv.at/en

♦ 2769 ♦ **St. Lucia Independence Day**
February 22

The West Indies island of St. Lucia celebrates its national independence holiday on February 22. On that day in 1979 the country gained full independence from Britain. St. Lucia had been a British colony since 1814.

CONTACTS:
Consulate General of Saint Lucia in New York
800 2nd Ave.
5th Fl.

New York, NY 10017
212-697-9360; fax: 212-697-4993
saintluciaconsulateny.org

St Lucia Tourism Board
800 Second Ave.
Ste. 910
New York, NY 10017
212-867-2950 or 800-456-3984
stlucianow.com

♦ 2770 ♦ **St. Lucy's Day**
December 13

According to tradition, St. Lucy, or Santa Lucia, was born in Syracuse, Sicily, in the third or fourth century. She was endowed with a fatal beauty that eventually attracted the unwanted attentions of a pagan nobleman, to whom she was betrothed against her will. She is the patron saint of the blind because in an attempt to end the affair, she supposedly cut out her eyes, which her suitor claimed "haunted him day and night." But God restored her eyes as a reward for her sacrifice. She was then probably killed by a sword thrust through her throat. Because of this she is the patron saint for protection from throat infections.

St. Lucy allegedly blinded herself on the shortest, darkest day of the year (*see* WINTER SOLSTICE), and she later became a symbol of the preciousness of light. Her day is widely celebrated in Sweden as **Luciadagen**, which marks the official beginning of the CHRISTMAS season. Lucy means "light," and to the sun-starved inhabitants of Scandinavia, she often appears in a shining white robe crowned by a radiant halo.

It is traditional to observe Luciadagen by dressing the oldest daughter in the family in a white robe tied with a crimson sash. Candles are set into her crown, which is covered with lingonberry leaves. The younger girls are also dressed in white and given haloes of glittering tinsel. The boys— called *Starngossar*, or Star Boys—wear white robes and tall cone-shaped hats, made of silver paper, and carry star-topped scepters.

The "Lucia Bride" with her crown of burning candles, followed by the Star Boys, younger girls, and dancing children, called *tomten*, or "gnomes," wakens each member of the household on the morning of December 13 with a tray of coffee and special saffron buns or ginger cookies.

Although this is a family celebration, the Lucia tradition nowadays is observed in schools, offices, and hotels as well. Specially chosen Lucias and their attendants visit hospitals to cheer up the sick and elderly. The largest public celebration in Sweden takes place in Stockholm, where hundreds of girls compete for the title of "Stockholm Lucia."

From Sweden the Lucy celebrations spread to Finland, Norway, and Denmark. Swedish immigrants brought St. Lucy's Day to the United States, and the Swedish customs survive in Swedish-American communities throughout the country.

In Rockford, Illinois, for example, the St. Lucy's Day program is staged by the Swedish Historical Society at the Erlander Home Museum. The young woman chosen as Lucia on this day has to meet certain criteria, such as participation in Swedish classes, contributions to Swedish culture, or membership in one of Rockford's many Swedish societies.

At Bethany College in Lindsborg, Kansas, freshmen in the women's dormitories traditionally are awakened at three o'clock in the morning by a white-clad Lucia bearing coffee and baked goods. St. Lucy's Day is also observed by Swedish Americans in Minneapolis-St. Paul, Seattle, Chicago, and San Diego.

CONTACTS:
St. Lucy's Church
949 Scranton St.
Scranton, PA 18504
570-347-9421; fax: 570-341-8252
www.stlucy-church.org

♦ 2771 ♦ St. Marinus Day
September 3

This is the official foundation day of the Republic of San Marino, a landlocked area of less than 30 square miles on the Adriatic side of central Italy. The oldest independent country in Europe, San Marino takes its name from St. Marinus, who lived in the fourth century. According to legend, he was a deacon and stonemason working on an aqueduct one day when a woman wrongly identified him as the husband who had deserted her. She pursued him into the mountains, where he barricaded himself in a cave until she eventually gave up. He spent the rest of his life on Monte Titano as a hermit. The present-day city of San Marino was built on the site where his original hermitage was believed to be.

CONTACTS:
San Marino Tourism Office
Contrada Omagnano, 20
San Marino
378-549-882914; fax: 378-549-882575
www.visitsanmarino.com

♦ 2772 ♦ St. Mark, Fair of (Feria de San Marcos)
Mid-April to early May

The Fair of St. Mark, which is held annually for nearly a month in Aguascalientes, dates back to the early 17th century and remains one of Mexico's most famous fiestas. It is primarily a showcase for the country's more than 200 forms of ritual and folk dance, each of which has its own meaning, mythology, history, and pageantry. There are also commercial and art exhibits, cockfights, bullfights, sports competitions, parades, and a battle of flowers. The wandering musicians known as *mariachis* give concerts, and regional folk dance groups from all over Mexico perform in the San Marcos Gar- den.

CONTACTS:
Mexico Tourism Board

152 Madison Ave.
Ste. 1800
New York, NY 10016
212-308-2110; fax: 212-308-9060
www.visitmexico.com

♦ 2773 ♦ St. Mark's Day
April 25

Although he is often assumed to be one of the Apostles, Mark was much too young at the time to be more than a follower of Jesus. He is known primarily as the author of one of the four Gospels, which biblical scholars believe is based on what he learned from his close friend and traveling companion, ST. PETER. St. Mark the Evangelist is also associated with Venice, Italy, where the church bearing his name was built over the place where his relics were taken in 815.

In England, it was believed that if you kept a vigil on the church porch from 11 o'clock on St. Mark's Eve until one o'clock in the morning, you would see the ghosts of all those who would die in the coming year as they walked up the path and entered the church. Young girls believed that if they left a flower on the church porch during the day and returned for it at midnight, they would see a wedding procession, including an apparition of their future husband, as they walked home. Because it involved an all-night vigil, St. Mark's Day eventually came to be associated with various forms of licentious behavior, which is why the parochial clergy in the Middle Ages decided that the day should be one of abstinence.

♦ 2774 ♦ St. Mark's Day (Hungary)
April 25

In Hungary, St. Mark's Day is also known as **Buza-Szentelo** or the **Blessing of the Wheat**, during which people follow their priest or minister in a procession to the wheat fields where the crop is blessed. They return to the village carrying spears of the blessed wheat, which some believe has healing powers. The fields are again blessed when harvesting begins on June 29, STS. PETER AND PAUL DAY.

♦ 2775 ♦ St. Maron's Day
February 9

St. Maron (also spelled *St. Maroun*), the patron saint of Lebanon, was a monk who died in 410 C.E. After his death his disciples, the forefathers of the Maronite Christian sect, migrated from the Monastery of St. Maron in Syria to Mount Lebanon, where a large segment of Maronite Christians are settled today.

The **Feast of St. Maron**, as it is known in Lebanon, does not have the cultural significance for its citizens that it had in past eras, a change in great part due to the country's changing demographics along religious lines. Today Maronites only make up one-quarter of the Lebanese population (between one-half and one million). Many Lebanese Christians immigrated to North and South America, Europe, and Australia to escape the conditions of a long civil waged between 1975 and 1991.

In Lebanon and abroad, the most common ceremony of the feast day is the Maronite liturgy, which is a distinctive blend of Catholic doctrine, Arabic music, and singing in Syriac-Aramaic, a classical language that was spoken by Jesus.

CONTACTS:
Eparchy of Saint Maron of Brooklyn
109 Remsen St.
Brooklyn, NY 11201 United States
718-237-9913; fax: 718-243-0444
www.stmaron.org

◆ 2776 ◆ St. Martha, Coffin Fiesta of
July 29

St. Martha was the sister of Mary and Lazarus who pleaded with Jesus to bring her dead brother back to life. Jesus did so, and because Martha played such an important role in this story, folk beliefs often assign her the power of granting miraculous cures.

In San Xosé de Ribarteme, in the province of Pontevedra in the region of Galicia, Spain, near the northern border of Portugal, the *ofrecidos*—people who have made a vow to St. Martha—lie in open coffins during a procession that takes place after High Mass on St. Martha's feast day. Most of the ofrecidos are women, but there are always a few men as well. They hire the coffins from the church, usually because they themselves or a member of their family has recently been cured by St. Martha's intervention. Most wear coarse net tunics called *mortajas* (shrouds) to indicate that they represent the "living dead.".

CONTACTS:
Saint Martha Church
8523 Georgiana Ave.
Morton Grove, IL 60053
847-965-0262; fax: 847-965-2535
www.saintmarthachurch.org

◆ 2777 ◆ St. Martha's Day
Last weekend in June

Martha was the sister of Mary and of Lazarus, whom Jesus raised from the dead (*see also* LAZARUS SATURDAY and ST. LAZARUS'S DAY). She is best known for her role in the Lord's visit to the house she shared with her two siblings in Bethany. While Mary sat and listened to their guest, Martha was busy serving and cleaning up. When she complained, Jesus told her that what Mary was doing was just as important as housework. For this reason, Martha is known as the patroness of housewives, cooks, and laundresses.

Martha's second, and legendary, claim to fame is that she killed a dragon who was ravaging the Provençal countryside, hiding on the wooded banks of the Rhone and periodically feeding on flocks and men. She overcame the beast by sprinkling holy water on him, then she bound him with her belt and led him into town, where the townspeople stoned him to death. A church was built on the site of this alleged event in what is now known as Tarascon in Provence, France.

Every year on the last weekend in June a procession takes place there that commemorates St. Martha's power. In the first procession, eight men representing those devoured by the dragon walk next to its spiked body and manipulate the tail and jaws, which snap at the crowd of spectators. In the second procession, the dragon trots along behind a young girl representing St. Martha. Traditionally, she is dressed in white and leads the dragon leashed on her crimson ribbon belt.

See also STES. MARIES, FÊTE DES.

CONTACTS:
Parish Ste Marthe Quatre Chemins
3, rue Condorcet
Pantin, Paris 93500 France
33-1-48-45-02-77; fax: 33-1-48-46-38-26
stemarthe.free.fr

◆ 2778 ◆ St. Martin's Carnival
February-March; Tuesday of Carnival week

The highlight of CARNIVAL celebrations in the village of Huixquilucan, Mexico, is a mock battle between two local churches. In the church of St. Martin, an image of the saint on horseback is given a new suit and sombrero each year. Across town, in the church of San Juan, a humble statue of the Virgin Mary appears in a pink dress and white veil and crown. According to local legend, St. Martin mounts his horse nightly and goes to visit the Virgin at San Juan church. Members of the San Juan church resent the implications of this legend and insist that their Virgin would not accept any male visitor at night, whether saint or ordinary mortal.

The argument comes to a head on Tuesday of Carnival week, when the two churches battle each other late in the afternoon. Both sides use firecrackers, rotten eggs, eggshells filled with paint, and even sticks and stones as weapons, and the battle continues for a couple of hours. Finally, the authorities call a halt to the event, and both sides claim victory.

CONTACTS:
St Martin promotional office
825 Third Ave.
29th Fl.
New York, NY 10022
fax: 212-838-7855
www.stmartinisland.org

St. Martin of Tours Catholic Church
11967 Sunset Blvd.
Los Angeles, CA 90049
310-476-7403; fax: 310-476-0290
www.saintmartinoftours.com

◆ 2779 ◆ St. Martin's Day (Portugal)
November 11

In many European countries, the celebration of St. Martin's Day is associated with slaughtering animals, and Portugal is no exception. On the **Feast of São Martinho** people roast chestnuts, drink red Portuguese wine, and butcher a pig. There is a St. Martin's Day Fair at Golegã, in Ribatejo, that features a famous horse show at which some of the country's finest thoroughbreds are displayed. Another well-known St. Martin's Day Fair is held at Penafiel, in Trás-os-Montes. The parades and celebrations that are held in towns and villages throughout Portugal on this day are usually more secular than Christian in flavor.

See also MARTINMAS.

CONTACTS:
Portugal National Tourmst Board
866 Second Ave.
8th Fl.
New York, NY 10017
646-723-0200; fax: 212-764-6137
www.visitportugal.com

Feira Nacional do Cavalo (Golegã Horse Fair)
Largo do Marquês de Pombal, 25
Golegã, 2150-130 Portugal
351-24-997-6302; fax: 351-24-997-7114
feiradagolega.com

Hudson Portuguese Club
13 Port St.
Hudson, MA 01749
978-568-1541
www.hudsonportugueseclub.org

♦ 2780 ♦ **St. Martin's Eve (Estonia) (Mardi Päev)**
November 10

Traditionally, children in Estonia go from door to door at dusk on St. Martin's Eve in much the same way that American children trick-or-treat on HALLOWEEN. Their refrain is, "Please let us in because Mardi's fingers and toes are cold," and if they are not welcomed into the house and given treats, they retaliate by singing rude and uncomplimentary songs. Usually they're ushered into the kitchen, where such delicacies as apples, nuts, cookies, and raisin bread are handed out. Turnips—one of the few winter vegetables in Estonia—are another prized gift, as is *viljandi kama*, a kind of meal comprised of 15 different grains and dried vegetables mixed with sour milk, sugar, and cream that is regarded as a special treat. Well-to-do families give children bags of viljandi kama on Martin's Day to show how prosperous they are.

♦ 2781 ♦ **St. Mary's County Oyster Festival**
Third weekend in October

Oyster festivals are common in areas where the oyster industry has survived. But the festival that has been held at the start of the oyster season in Leonardtown, Maryland, since 1967 has a special significance for those skilled in the fine art of oyster shucking. The highlight of the October festival is the National Oyster Shucking Championship to see who can open the most oysters as quickly and neatly as possible. The winner of this contest goes on to compete in the GALWAY OYSTER FESTIVAL in Ireland the following year.

The season's new oysters are served in every imaginable way: raw on the half-shell with sauce, steamed, fried, and stewed in a broth. The two-day festival also offers cooking demonstations and live musical entertainment.

CONTACTS:
St. Mary's County Oyster Festival
42455 Fairgrounds Rd.
Leonardtown, MD 20650
301-863-5015
usoysterfest.com

♦ 2782 ♦ **St. Matthias's Day**
February 24

The story of how St. Matthias was elected to replace Judas Iscariot as one of the 12 apostles after Judas committed suicide can be found in the Bible's Book of Acts (1:15-26). It was Peter who declared that the number of apostles should be restored to 12, and the choice of who would succeed Judas was made by casting lots. Two men were nominated— Matthias and Joseph—and the lot fell upon Matthias.

There is no historical record of Matthias's deeds or death. His fame rests almost entirely upon the fact that he took the betrayer Judas' place, although legend claims that he was stoned and beheaded in Ethiopia in 64 C.E.

♦ 2783 ♦ **St. Médardus's Day**
June 8

St. Médardus, or Médard, who lived from about 470 to 560, was the bishop of Vermandois, Noyon, and Tournai in France. Because he was the patron saint of farmers and good weather, he has come to play a role in weather lore similar to that of the English ST. SWITHIN. In Belgium he is known as the rain saint, and there is an old folk rhyme that says, "If it rains on St. Médard's Day, it will rain for 40 days.".

♦ 2784 ♦ **St. Mennas's Day**
November 11

There are actually two different saints by the name of Mennas. One was born in Egypt and enlisted in the Roman army. He hid in a mountain cave in Phrygia to avoid persecution, but then boldly entered the arena at Cotyaeum and proclaimed that he was a Christian—an act of courage for which he was beheaded in 295. The second St. Mennas was a Greek from Asia Minor who became a hermit in the Abruzzi region of Italy and died in the sixth century.

In Greece, St. Mennas's Day is observed by shepherds. Because he has the power to reveal where lost or stolen objects lie, his name is invoked by shepherds who have lost their sheep, or who wish to protect their flocks from wolves. Shepherds' wives refrain from using scissors on St. Mennas's Day. Instead, they wind a thread around the points of the scissors— a symbolic action designed to keep the jaws of wolves closed and the mouths of the village gossips shut. St. Mennas's Day is also regarded as the beginning of the winter season.

♦ 2785 ♦ St. Michael's Day
September 29 in the West and November 8 in the East; first Sunday in October

Coming at the end of the harvest season, St. Michael's Day has traditionally been a day for giving thanks and for celebrating the end of the season of hard work in the fields.

In Finland **Mikkelin Paiva** is observed on the first Sunday in October. In the countryside, servants are hired and next year's labor contracts signed. The harvesters celebrate the end of their labors on Saturday night by holding candlelight dances. The observation of Mikkelin Paiva replaced an earlier festival known as **Kekri**, which was celebrated by each landowner as soon as his crops were safely in the barns. The "Kekri" (spirits of the dead) were rewarded with a feast for their help with the farm work. The Kekri festival was probably a remnant of some form of ancestor worship.

In Ethiopia, where St. Michael's Day is observed on November 8, people attend services at any churches consecrated to *Mika'el*. The celebrations include chanting and dancing by the clergy, and a procession carrying the holy ark, or *tabot*, out of the church and then, later in the day, returning it. The services are followed by singing and dancing, an occasion for young men to possibly find a bride.

See also MICHAELMAS; SAN MIGUEL, FIESTA DE; TIMQAT; TURA MICHELE FAIR.

CONTACTS:
Saint Michael Center for the Blessed Virgin Mary
P.O. Box 8461
Honolulu, HI 96830
808-943-7088 or 800-505-MARY; fax: 808-943-6120
www.saintmichaelusa.org

♦ 2786 ♦ St. Modesto's Day
December 18

St. Modesto is the patron saint of farmers in Greece. His feast day is celebrated with various rituals in honor of farm animals. Sometimes a special mass is said for the cattle. In Lemnos, *kollyva* (cooked wheat berries) and holy water are mixed with their fodder, while in Lesbos, the holy water is sprinkled on the fields to ward off locusts and disease. For horses and oxen, December 18 is a day of rest.

The Eastern Orthodox Church reserves this day to commemorate St. Modestus, who was patriarch of Jerusalem from 631 to 634. He had been abbot of St. Theodosius's Monastery in the desert of Judah, and was administrator of Jerusalem during the captivity of St. Zacharias in Persia. Modestus is known for a sermon he preached on the bodily ASSUMPTION of the Virgin Mary into heaven.

♦ 2787 ♦ St. Nichiren's Pardon, Festival of
September 11-13

At the Botamochi Temple in Kamakura, Japan, this festival honors St. Nichiren (1222-1282), considered to be Japan's most fervent Buddhist priest. Born the son of a poor fisherman, Nichiren established Kamakura as the homebase for his extensive and energetic missionary efforts. But the energy and self-confidence with which he devoted himself to political and social events soon aroused the distrust of the government and other Buddhist sects. He was banished to the peninsula of Izu in 1261, but later pardoned. This only increased his attacks on the other sects and he was finally exiled to the island of Sado in the Sea of Japan in 1271. After four years there, he returned and spent the rest of his life on Mount Minobu, now the site of the main Nichiren temple. Nichiren spent the remainder of his life teaching the monks of his sect and continuing his missionary work.

Today there are several million Nichiren Buddhists. The Festival of St. Nichiren's Pardon is observed by members of the Nichiren sect with massive demonstrations and the loud chanting of prayers attributed to Nichiren, accompanied by the beating of drums. At Kamakura, people make offerings of *botamochi*, rice balls covered with sweet bean paste, in his honor.

CONTACTS:
Soka Gakkai International
Josei Toda International Center
15-3 Samon-cho
Shinjuku-ku, Tokyo 160-0017 Japan
81-3-5360-9811; fax: 81-3-5360-9881
www.sgi.org

♦ 2788 ♦ St. Nicholas's Day
December 6

Very little is known about St. Nicholas's life, except that in the fourth century he was the bishop of Myra in what is now Turkey. One of the legends surrounding him is that he saved three sisters from being forced into prostitution by their poverty-stricken father by throwing three bags of gold into their room, thus providing each of them with a dowry. This may be the source of St. Nicholas's association with gift giving.

On December 6 in the Netherlands, St. Nicholas, or *Sinterklass*, still rides into town on a white horse, dressed in his red bishop's robes and preceded by "Black Peter," a Satanic figure in Moorish costume who beats the bad children with a switch while rewarding the good children with candy and gifts. He is the patron saint of sailors, and churches dedicated to him are often built so they can be seen off the coast as landmarks.

The American Santa Claus, a corruption of "St. Nicholas," is a cross between the original St. Nicholas and the British "Father Christmas." The political cartoonist Thomas Nast created a Santa Claus dressed in furs and looking more like King Cole—an image that grew fatter and merrier over the years, until he became the uniquely American figure that adorns thousands of cards, decorations, and homes throughout the CHRISTMAS season. Although Americans open their gifts on Christmas or CHRISTMAS EVE, in the Netherlands, Switzerland, Germany, and some other European countries, gifts are still exchanged on December 5, St. Nicholas's Eve, or December 6, St. Nicholas's Day.

CONTACTS:
St. Nicholas Cathedral
3500 Massachusetts Ave. N.W.
Wahington, D.C. 20007
202-333-5060
www.stnicholasdc.org

Netherlands Board of Tourism & Conventions
215 Park Ave. S.
Ste. 2005
New York, NY 10003
917-720-1283; fax: 212-370-9507
www.holland.com

♦ 2789 ♦ **St. Nicholas's Day (Greece)**
December 6

As the patron saint of ships and seamen, St. Nicholas is very important to the Greeks, so many of whom have traditionally made their living at sea. Many Greek ships, from the smallest fishing boat to the largest commercial vessel, carry an icon of the saint on board. Seamen honor St. Nicholas on his feast day, which falls at a time of year when storms grow more frequent, by burning a light before this icon and saying prayers for the safety of their boat or ship.

CONTACTS:
St Nicholas Center
109 W. 12th St.
Holland, MI 49423
www.stnicholascenter.org

♦ 2790 ♦ **St. Nicholas's Day (Italy)**
May 7-8

The **Festa di San Nicola** is celebrated in Italy on May 7 and 8, the anniversary of the transfer of the saint's relics by a group of 11th-century sailors from Bari, who risked their lives to rescue St. Nicholas's body from Muslims who threatened to desecrate his tomb at Myra in Asia Minor. This is the same St. Nicholas who is associated with CHRISTMAS and the giving of gifts to children. Therefore he is the patron saint of children.

Thousands of pilgrims come to the Basilica of San Nicola in Bari, Puglia, to worship at the saint's tomb and to ask for his help. Nicholas is also the patron saint of sailors. There is a procession on this day in which a group of Barese sailors take the saint's image down to the water, where it is placed on a flower-decked boat and taken out to sea. Hundreds of small craft carrying pilgrims and fishermen accompany the vessel, and at night the statue is returned to its place of honor on the altar of San Nicola's crypt.

CONTACTS:
St Nicholas Center
109 W. 12th St.

Holland, MI 49423
www.stnicholascenter.org

Basilica San Nicola
Largo Abate Elia, 13
Bari, 70122 Italy
39-80-573-7111; fax: 39-80-573-7261
www.basilicasannicola.it

♦ 2791 ♦ **St. Olav's Day**
July 29

The feast day of St. Olav (995-1030), also known as **Olsok,** was at one time observed throughout Norway, although today the primary celebration takes place in Trondheim. It commemorates the death of Olav Haraldsson—the second King Olav—at the Battle of Stiklestad in the year 1030. By 1070, work had begun on Nidaros Cathedral, which was erected over King Olav's grave and drew crowds of pilgrims during the annual Olsok days throughout the Middle Ages. Although it is said that King Olav did not display many saintly qualities during his reign (1015-28), he was responsible for introducing Christianity, and legend has embellished his reputation over the years, so that today he is also considered the champion of national independence.

St. Olav is the patron saint of Norway, and his name is identified with the highest Norwegian civilian decoration. The anniversary of his death is still marked by religious services, fireworks, and public merry-making. Every year the battle in which he died is reenacted by a large and colorful cast, occasionally drawing a well-known actor such as Liv Ullman, during the **St. Olav Festival** in Trondheim.

In the Faroe Islands, this is known as **Olavsoka,** or "St. Olav's Wake," a national holiday. Parliament opens on the 29th, but the festivities—that include dancing, rock concerts, sports events, speeches, drinking, a parade of members of *Logting* (parliament) to the church for a sermon then back for the opening session—begin the night before and continue into the early hours of the 30th.

♦ 2792 ♦ **St. Patrick's Day**
March 17

The patron saint of Ireland, St. Patrick, was born about 390 in Roman Britain—scholars disagree as to exactly where—and died around 461. His grandfather was a Christian priest, and his father a deacon and an official of the Roman Empire in Britain. He is said to have been kidnapped at the age of 16 by Irish raiders and sold into slavery in Ireland; he escaped after six years, and received his religious training in continental monasteries. After being consecrated a bishop, he returned to Ireland about 432 as a missionary. The association of St. Patrick with the shamrock stems from his supposed use of its three-part leaf to explain the concept of the Holy Trinity to his largely uneducated listeners (*see* TRINITY SUNDAY).

St. Patrick's Purgatory has been a famed site of pilgrimage since the early 13th century. It is on Station Island in Lough Derg in County Donegal where St. Patrick had a vision promising that all who came to the sanctuary in penitence and faith would receive an indulgence for their sins. Additionally, if their faith remained strong, they would be allowed a glimpse of the tortures of the damned and the joys of the redeemed.

The **Feast of St. Patrick** is celebrated by Roman Catholics, the Anglican Communion, and Lutherans on March 17. The day is also popularly celebrated, particularly in the U.S., by "the wearing of the green," with many people of Irish and other extractions wearing some item of green clothing. Parties featuring corned beef and cabbage, and even the drinking of beer dyed green with food coloring are also part of this celebration of Irish heritage.

The St. Patrick's Day Parade in New York City, which dates back to 1762, is the largest in the United States and a major event for Irish Americans. More than 125,000 marchers participate, stopping at St. Patrick's Cathedral on Fifth Avenue for the blessing of the archbishop of New York. In Boston the St. Patrick's Day Parade goes back even farther, to 1737. In fact, during the siege of Boston which forced the British evacuation on March 17, 1776, General George WASHINGTON used "Boston" as the day's secret password and "St. Patrick" as the appropriate response (*see* EVACUATION DAY).

See also REEK SUNDAY and ST. PATRICK'S DAY PARADE IN SAVANNAH.

CONTACTS:
St. Patrick's Festival
St. Stephen's Green House,
Earlsfort Terr.
Dublin, 2 Ireland
353-1-676-3205; fax: 353-1-676-3208
www.stpatricksfestival.ie

♦ 2793 ♦ St. Patrick's Day (Ireland)
March 17

The observation of ST. PATRICK'S DAY is universal but traditionally less frenzied in Ireland than it is in the United States. Instead of the massive parades, rowdy parties, and commercialism of U.S. celebrations, many Irish spend the day attending Mass, wearing sprigs of real shamrock, and hailing each other with the traditional St. Patrick's Day greeting: "Beannacht na feile Padraig oraibh"—"May the blessings of St. Patrick be with you." Since 1996, however, Dublin has hosted a colorful St. Patrick's Festival. It lasts four days and features musical performances, street theater, fireworks, and a grand parade.

Because it falls during LENT, St. Patrick's Day is anticipated as a reprieve from the deprivations of the period preceding EASTER. It is a time when children can gorge themselves on sweets and adults can indulge in a pint at the local pub. A traditional St. Patrick's Day dinner usually includes colcannon—a dish made of mashed potatoes, butter, onions, and kale.

CONTACTS:
St. Patrick's Festival
St. Stephen's Green House

Earlsfort Terr.
Dublin, 2 Ireland
353-1-676-3205; fax: 353-1-676-3208
www.stpatricksfestival.ie

♦ 2794 ♦ St. Patrick's Day Encampment
Weekend nearest March 17

The winter of 1779-80 was a time of discouragement and despair for the Continental Army. General George WASHINGTON set up camp in Morristown, New Jersey, that year so he could rest and reassemble his men. The soldiers' winter routine was bleak and monotonous. There was so much work to be done that they did not even celebrate CHRISTMAS. General Washington did, however, grant his men a holiday on March 17, ST. PATRICK'S DAY. A good portion of the American army was Irish, and political changes taking place in Ireland at the time found a sympathetic following among the American revolutionaries.

The St. Patrick's Day Encampment of 1780 is reenacted each year at the Jockey Hollow Encampment Area in Morristown. Between 30 and 40 men and their camp followers set up camp for the weekend and perform more or less the same chores and activities that Washington's men performed, although the trend toward milder winters has robbed the event of some of its authenticity. The original March 17 encampment was not the first St. Patrick's Day celebration in America; the first celebration took place in Boston in 1737.

♦ 2795 ♦ St. Patrick's Day Parade (Savannah, Georgia)
March 17

One of the oldest and biggest parades in the country, held since 1824 in Savannah, Ga., a city with a long Irish history. The oldest Irish society in the United States, the Hibernian Society, was formed in Savannah in 1812 by 13 Irish Protestants. The next year they held a private procession that was a forerunner to the present St. Paddy's parade. The first public procession is recorded in 1824, and public parades have been held ever since. There have been only six lapses of this parade: for wars, sympathy for the Irish Revolution, and for an unrecorded reason. The first floats appeared in 1875; according to reports of the time, one carried two women representing Ireland and America, and another had 32 women for the 32 counties of Ireland.

Today the parade, which follows a route through the city's historic district, comprises between 200 and 300 separate units, including family groups, commercial floats, Georgia and out-of-state high school bands, and military bands and marching units. The day begins with mass at the Cathedral of St. John the Baptist. Members of the Fenian Society of Savannah, formed in 1973, start things off with a members' breakfast of green grits before they form a marching unit. The other main activity is eating. The fare is predominantly green—grits, beer, doughnuts, etc. Crowds are estimated at anywhere from 300,000 to 500,000.

See also ST. PATRICK'S DAY.

CONTACTS:
St. Patrick's Day Parade Committee
5 W. Liberty St.
P.O. Box 9224
Savannah, GA 31412 United States
912-233-4804; fax: 912-233-8244
www.savannahsaintpatricksday.com

♦ 2796 ♦ St. Paul, Feast of the Conversion of
January 25

Saul of Tarsus, a highly educated, devout Jew, was converted to Christianity on the road to Damascus not long after the death of Jesus Christ. Later he was known as Paul and through his life, his teachings, and his writings became the most influential leader in the history of the church. According to tradition, he was beheaded during Nero's persecution of Christians about the year 67.

At St. Paul's Chapel in New York City, the oldest church building in Manhattan, the path through the graveyard that is routinely used as a shortcut between Broadway and Fulton Street is closed for 48 hours, beginning on the eve of the Feast of the Conversion of St. Paul.

At one time the weather on this day was linked to predictions about the coming year. Fair weather on St. Paul's Day was said to presage a prosperous year; snow or rain an unproductive one. Clouds meant that many cattle would die, and a windy day was said to be the forerunner of war.

In memory of Sts. Paul and Peter, the World Council of Churches sponsors the Week of PRAYER FOR CHRISTIAN UNITY, which begins on January 18, the feast of ST. PETER'S CHAIR, and ends on January 25.

See also STS. PETER AND PAUL DAY.

♦ 2797 ♦ St. Paul Winter Carnival
Last week of January to first week of February

This 10-day winter festival was established in 1886 in response to a newspaper story from the East that described St. Paul, Minnesota, as "another Siberia, unfit for human habitation." A group of local businessmen set out to publicize the area's winter attractions, and the first winter carnival featured an Ice Palace in St. Paul's Central Park constructed by a Montreal contractor.

Since that time, an entire legend has developed about the founding of St. Paul. This legend is reenacted each year. The main players are Boreas, King of the Winds, the Queen of the Snows, and the fire god, Vulcanus, who storms the Ice Palace but is persuaded by the Queen to submit to Boreas and let the people enjoy their carnival celebration.

Highlights include ice golf, skating, skiing, and sled dog races, softball on ice, ice carving and snow sculpture contests, and a parade featuring antique sleighs and cutters.

CONTACTS:
St. Paul Festival & Heritage Foundation
429 Landmark Center
75 W. 5th St.
Saint Paul, MN 55102
651-223-4700; fax: 651-223-4707
www.wintercarnival.com

♦ 2798 ♦ St. Paul's Shipwreck, Feast of
February 10

This feast is a commemoration in Malta of the shipwreck of St. Paul on the island in 60 C.E., an event told about in the New Testament. Paul, the story says, was being taken as a prisoner aboard ship to Rome where he was to stand trial. When storms drove the ship aground, Paul escaped and was welcomed by the "barbarous people" (meaning they were not Greco-Romans). According to legend, he got their attention when a snake bit him on the hand but did him no harm, and he then healed people of diseases. Paul stayed for three months in Malta, converting the people to Christianity (Acts 27:1-28:11). Paul is the patron saint of Malta and snakebite victims.

The day is a public holiday, and is observed with family gatherings and religious ceremonies and processions.

See also MNARJA.

CONTACTS:
Malta Tourism Board
Auberge D'Italie
Merchants St.
Valletta, VLT 1170 Malta
356-2291-5000; fax: 356-2291-5394
www.visitmalta.com

♦ 2799 ♦ St. Peter's Chair, Festival of
January 18

In ancient times it was the custom in many dioceses for Roman Catholics to observe the anniversary of the date on which the diocese first received a bishop. Perhaps the only remaining observance of this type takes place at the Vatican in Rome, where St. Peter is honored as bishop of Rome and the first pope. The current pope, wearing his triple crown and vestments of gold cloth, is carried in his chair of state on this day in a spectacular procession up the nave of St. Peter's Basilica. He is deposited behind the altar on a richly decorated throne that enshrines the plain wooden chair on which St. Peter is believed to have sat. The ceremony dates back to at least 720 and is regarded as one of the most magnificent ecclesiastical observances to be held at St. Peter's.

CONTACTS:
St. Peter's Basilica
Piazza San Pietro
Città del Vaticano
Vatican City, 00120 Italy
39-06-6988-3731
w2.vatican.va

Italian National Tourist Board
686 Park Ave.

3rd Fl.
New York, NY 10065
212-245-5618; fax: 212-586-9249
www.italiantourism.com

♦ 2800 ♦ St. Peter's Day (Belgium)
June 29

Sint Pieter (as he is called in Belgium), who walked across the water to reach Jesus, is honored each year on June 29 by Belgian fishermen, mariners, and others who are exposed to the dangers of the sea. The **Blessing of the Sea** ceremony is performed at Blankenberge and other seaport towns in West Flanders near the saint's day. After a special church service is held, a procession of clergy, church dignitaries, and seamen carry votive offerings, flowers, and garlands down to the shore. Then the priests board the boats and go out to bless the waves.

Although the custom has died out in all but a few rural areas, the building of bonfires is traditional on St. Peter's Day in Belgium. Years ago, children trundled wheelbarrows from one farm to the next in search of wood for St. Peter's fires. As the flames grew higher and higher, the children danced in a ring around the bonfire. People still light candles on this night and say the rosary in commemoration of St. Peter.

See also STS. PETER AND PAUL DAY.

CONTACTS:
Tourism Leuven
Townhall
Naamsestraat 3
Leuven, 3000 Belgium
32-1620-3020; fax: 32-1620-3003
www.leuven.be

♦ 2801 ♦ St. Peter's Fiesta
Weekend nearest June 29

Honoring the patron saint of fishermen, **St. Peter's Day** is celebrated in fishing villages and ports all over the world. Perhaps the largest American celebration takes place in Gloucester, Massachusetts, where St. Peter's Fiesta has been celebrated by the Italian-American fishing community for several decades. The life-sized statue of St. Peter donated by an Italian-American fishing captain in 1926 provided a focal point for the celebration, and the Sunday morning procession carrying this statue from the St. Peter's Club to an outdoor altar erected on the waterfront is still the highlight of the two-day festival. The mass that follows is usually celebrated by a visiting bishop or cardinal, who also officiates at the Blessing of the Fleet that afternoon.

Other festival events include seine boat (formerly used to haul in the catch) races and a "greasy-pole" contest in which competitors try to retrieve a red flag from the end of a well-greased pole suspended over the water.

The 2000 film *The Perfect Storm* dramatized the dangers Gloucester fishermen face.

CONTACTS:
St. Peter's Fiesta Committee
P.O. Box 3105
Gloucester, MA 01930
978-375-2542
www.stpetersfiesta.org

♦ 2802 ♦ St. Placidus Festival
July 11

Sankt Placidusfest is a religious procession held on July 11 at Disentis, Switzerland, in honor of St. Placidus, who was murdered near the Benedictine abbey that he and St. Sigisbert helped establish there in 614. A wealthy landowner, Placidus donated the land for the abbey, joined the religious order as a monk, and was later beheaded for defending the abbey's ecclesiastical rights.

Every year the relics of St. Placidus and St. Sigisbert are carried in a solemn procession from the abbey to the parish church and back through the village to the abbey. Traditionally, during the ceremonies, parishioners in colorful folk costumes chant the old, and very long, "Song of St. Placidus.".

♦ 2803 ♦ St. Polycarp's Day
February 23 (formerly January 26)

St. Polycarp (c. 69-c. 155) was a disciple of ST. JOHN THE EVANGELIST and one of the earliest fathers of the Christian Church. He became bishop of Smyrna in 96 and, when the persecution of Christians was ordered by Roman Emperor Marcus Aurelius, he was condemned to be burned at the stake. But according to legend, the fire formed an arch over his head and his body was left unharmed. When a spear was plunged into his heart, so much blood poured out that it quenched the flames. He finally succumbed, although the date of his martyrdom has been questioned, with some asserting it took place sometime between 166 and 169. That would have made him an astonishing 120 years old. Scholars believe there are good reasons for the original date of 155, however, which would have made him 86 when he was martyred.

Polycarp's friends and fellow Christians got together afterward to discuss how they might best carry on his memory. In fact, it was the martyrdom of St. Polycarp that gave rise to one of Christianity's richest traditions: the annual commemoration of the anniversary of a saint's death, a practice that didn't become universal until the third century. The earliest of these observances consisted of a memorial banquet, but by the fourth century they included a vigil service followed by celebration of the Eucharist.

CONTACTS:
St. Polycarp catholic church
8100 Chapman Ave.
Stanton, CA 90680
714-893-2766; fax: 714-898-6675
www.stpolycarp.org

◆ 2804 ◆ St. Rocco's Celebration (Rokovo)
August

St. Rocco's Celebration, or **Rokovo** as it is also known, has its roots in the feast day of St. Rocco. This saint, sometimes referred to as Rok, is the patron saint of the Catholic parish in the town of Virovitica, Croatia. Rocco was born into a noble family in France in c. 1295. Orphaned at an early age, he was taken in by a wealthy uncle, but eventually took a vow of poverty and began the life of a religious pilgrim. Bubonic plague was prevalent at the time, and Rocco is said to have miraculously healed many sufferers by praying for them.

His feast day, August 16, is the center of the St. Rocco's Celebration, although the celebration goes on for two or three weeks in total. The festival was first held in 1992, and in that year, August 16 was also designated the Day of the Town of Virovitica. The events, which are jointly organized by the Town of Virovitica and its Tourist Board, include music and dance performances, sports competitions, and art and historical exhibitions.

CONTACTS:
St. Rocco Church
3205 Fulton Rd.
Cleveland, OH 44109
216-961-8331; fax: 216-961-1845
www.stroccocleveland.org

◆ 2805 ◆ St. Roch's Day
August 16

Also known as Roque or Rock, St. Roch (c. 1295-c. 1327) was a Frenchman who went on a pilgrimage to Rome. The plague struck while he was there, and, legend has it, he spent his time healing the afflicted by miraculous means. Eventually he contracted the disease himself and retreated to a forest to die alone. But his faithful dog brought him food every day, and he recovered enough to return to his home in Montpelier. He had changed so much, however, that no one recognized him. He was arrested as a spy and died in prison.

Known as the patron saint of the sick and the plague-stricken, St. Roch is honored annually throughout Italy. In Florence there is a flower festival that includes a 14th-century historical costume parade, races, and competitions. In Realmonte, Sicily, the saint's poverty is recalled with a procession of people dressed in rags who carry a shabby picture of the saint.

In Spain, SAN ROQUE festivals are held every August around A Coruña Province. They feature traditional dances of farmers and seamen and processions in honor of St. Roch.

CONTACTS:
St. Roch Church
10 Saint Roch Ave.
Greenwich, CT 06830
203-869-4176; fax: 203-618-0341
www.strochchurch.com

◆ 2806 ◆ St. Rose of Lima's Day
August 30

St. Rose was the first canonized saint of the Americas, born in Lima, Peru, in 1586. She is the patron saint of Central and South America and the Philippines. When her parents tried to persuade her to marry, she began a self-imposed exile in the summerhouse in the yard, where she lived as a Dominican nun and inflicted severe penances on herself. She died in 1617 and was canonized in 1671.

On her feast day a candlelight procession takes place from her shrine in the church of Santo Domingo to the cathedral. Adults wear purple robes, while children wear white ones. People sing religious hymns as they accompany the rose-covered image to the cathedral. St. Rose's Day is a public holiday throughout Peru.

CONTACTS:
Saint Rose of Lima
11701 Clopper Rd.
Gaithersburg, MD 20878
301-948-7545; fax: 301-869-2170
www.strose-parish.org

◆ 2807 ◆ St. Sarkis's Day
January 21

In Armenia St. Sarkis is associated with predictions about love and romance. It is customary for young lovers to put out crumbs for birds and watch to see which way the birds fly off, for it is believed that their future spouse will come from the same direction. It is also traditional to leave some *pokhint*—a dish made of flour, butter, and honey—outside the door on St. Sarkis's Day. According to legend, when St. Sarkiswas battling the Georgians, the roasted wheat in his pocket miraculously turned into pokhint.

CONTACTS:
St. Sarkis Armenian Church
1805 Random Rd.,
Carrollton, TX 75006 United States
972-245-6995; fax: 972-245-5228
www.stsarkis.org

◆ 2808 ◆ St. Sava's Day
January 14 in the West and December 5 in the East

St. Sava (1174-c. 1235) was a Serbian noble of the Nemanya dynasty who renounced his right to the throne and chose instead to become a monk. While his brother was crowned king, Sava became archbishop of Serbia and the cultural and spiritual leader of his people. He was the founder of the Serbian Orthodox Church and played a central role in education and the beginnings of medieval Serbian literature.

As the patron saint of the former Yugoslavia, St. Sava, or Sveti Sava, is commemorated on the anniversary of his death with special church services, speeches, and choral singing. Schoolchildren sing, dance, and recite poems in his honor.

CONTACTS:
Saint Basil Church

27450 N. Bradley
Lake Forest, IL 60045 United States
847-247-0077; fax: 847-247-0088
stbasilchurch.org

♦ 2809 ♦ St. Sebastian's Day
January 20

St. Sebastian is known as the patron saint of archers for reasons that are all too obvious: legend has it that when his two brothers were imprisoned for being Christians, he went to visit them and to encourage them to stand by their faith, converting many of the other prisoners and their visitors in the process. His actions drew attention to his own beliefs, however, and he was condemned to die by being tied to a stake and shot with arrows until his body resembled a pincushion. When a Christian woman came to claim his body for burial, she discovered that he was still alive and nursed him back to health. Undaunted, he confronted his persecutors again. This time they succeeded in killing him, and his body was thrown into the great sewer of Rome in 288. All that is known with reasonable surety is that Sebastian lived, was an early martyr, and was buried on the Appian Way in Rome.

In Zinacantán, Chiapas State, Mexico, there is a nine-day celebration in honor of St. Sebastian, extending from January 17 to January 25, that marks the transfer of authority from the Big Alcalde (or chief magistrate) to his successor. At the end of the festival, the outgoing Big Alcalde is escorted with his articles of office to the house of the incoming Big Alcalde. There is an elaborate ritual during which he hands over an image of San Sebastián and other symbols of his authority. The festival also features a jousting pantomime, dancing to the rhythm of a special drum, two feasts, and a mock healing ceremony. The connection between the **Día de San Sebastián** festivities and the martyrdom of St. Sebastian, however, remains obscure.

People in the city of Rio de Janeiro, Brazil, also celebrate the feast day of their patron saint with church services, colorful religious processions, and other festivities.

See also EL POCHÓ DANCE-DRAMA.

CONTACTS:
Saint Sebastian Catholic Church
801 Broad Ave.
Belle Vernon, PA 15012 United States
724-929-9300; fax: 724-930-7611
www.saintsebastianchurch.org

♦ 2810 ♦ St. Spyridon (Spiridion) Day
December 12 in the East and December 14 in the West

St. Spyridon is the patron saint of Corfu, Zakynthos, and Kephalonia; these are among the Ionian Islands located off the western coast of Greece. Although he was born a shepherd in Cyprus, he became bishop of Tremithus and was renowned for his rustic simplicity. He supposedly attended the Nicene Council (325) and defended the Apostolic faith against the Arians. After his death in c. 348, his relics were brought from Cyprus to Constantinople and then to Corfu in 1456. Every year a sacred relic of the saint, dressed in costly vestments, is carried through the streets on his feast day. Colorful folk festivities complete the day-long celebration. This day is celebrated on December 14 in the Roman Catholic Church.

CONTACTS:
St. Spyridon Greek Orthodox Church
3655 Park Blvd.
San Diego, CA 92103
619-297-4165; fax: 619-297-4181
stspyridon.org

♦ 2811 ♦ St. Stephen's Day
December 26

On this day in c. 35, St. Stephen became the first Christian martyr. The New Testament book of Acts records that Stephen was chosen by the Apostles as one of the first seven deacons of the church in Jerusalem. He was later denounced as a blasphemer by the Sanhedrin, the Jewish council in ancient Palestine, and stoned to death. St. Stephen is the patron saint of bricklayers.

December 26, 27, and 28, otherwise known respectively as St. Stephen's Day, ST. JOHN THE EVANGELIST'S DAY, and HOLY INNOCENTS' DAY, are considered examples of the three different degrees of martyrdom. St. Stephen's death is an example of the highest class of martyrdom—that is to say, both in will and in deed. St. John the Evangelist, who showed that he was ready to die for Christ but was prevented from actually doing so, exemplifies martyrdom in will, but not in deed. And the children who lost their lives in the slaughter of the Innocents provide an example of the martyrdom in deed but not in will.

In many countries, St. Stephen's Day is celebrated as an extra Christmas holiday. In England, it is known as BOXING DAY. In Austria, priests bless the horses because St. Stephen is their patron. In Poland tossing rice at each other symbolizes blessings and recalls Stephen's stoning. And in Ireland, boys with blackened faces carrying a paper wren, go about begging and "hunting the wren." The hunting of the wren is most likely a carryover from an old belief that the robin, symbolizing the NEW YEAR, killed the wren, symbolizing the Old, at the turning of the year.

See also SAN ESTEVAN, FEAST OF.

CONTACTS:
St.Stephens Knanaya Church
182 Main St.
Maynard, MA 01752
978-897-9285
www.ststephensknanayachurch.org

Dingle Tourist Office
Strand St.
County Kerry
Ireland
www.dingle-peninsula.ie

♦ 2812 ♦ **St. Stephen's Day (Hungary)**
August 20

Hungary celebrates three national days, according to a 1991 state mandate. The founding of Hungary is commemorated on August 20, which is also the feast day of the founder of the country, St. Stephen of Hungary (c. 975-1038). He assumed the kingship in 1000 and worked to unite the various clans into a single Christian state. In 1950 the day was changed to Constitution Day by the communist regime, but since 1990, it has again celebrated St. Stephen.

CONTACTS:
Szent István Bazilika, Budapest
Hercegprímás St. 7th
Budapest, H-1051 Hungary
36-1-317-28-59; fax: 36-328-07-73
en.bazilika.biz

♦ 2813 ♦ **St. Swithin's Day**
July 15

When Swithin, the bishop of Winchester, England, died in 862, he was buried according to his wish, outside the cathedral in the churchyard, in a place where the rain from the eaves poured down. Whether this request was prompted by humility on his part or a wish to feel "the sweet rain of heaven" on his grave, it was reversed after his canonization, when clerical authorities tried to move his remains to a site within the church. According to legend, the heavens opened and there was a heavy rainfall—a show of the saint's displeasure that made it impossible to remove his body. This led to the popular belief that if it rains on St. Swithin's Day it will rain for 40 days; but if it is fair, it will be dry for 40 days. Swithin is the patron saint of rain, both for and against it.

CONTACTS:
Saint Swithun's Church
C/- The Vicarage
191 Hither Green Ln.
Hither Green, London SE13 6QE United Kingdom
44-20-8852-5088
www.saintswithuns.org.uk

♦ 2814 ♦ **St. Sylvester's Day**
December 31

St. Sylvester (d. 335) was pope in the year 325, when Emperor Constantine declared that the pagan religion of Rome was abolished and that Christianity would henceforth be the official religion of the Empire. Although it is unclear exactly what role, if any, St. Sylvester played in this important event, he is always given at least some of the credit for stamping out paganism.

Because St. Sylvester's Day is also NEW YEAR'S EVE, it is celebrated in Switzerland by lighting bonfires in the mountains and ringing church bells to signal the passing of the old year and the beginning of the new. It is a day for rising early, and the last to get out of bed or to reach school are greeted with shouts of "Sylvester!" In some Swiss villages, grain is threshed on specially constructed platforms to ensure a plentiful harvest in the coming year (*see also* OLD SILVESTER).

St. Sylvester's Eve is celebrated in Austria, Hungary, and Germany. It is not uncommon in restaurants and cafes for the owner to set a pig loose at midnight. Everyone tries to touch the pig because it is considered a symbol of good luck. In private homes, a marzipan pig may be hung from the ceiling and touched at midnight.

CONTACTS:
St.Sylvester Catholic Church
2157 N. Humboldt Blvd.
Chicago, IL 60647
773-235-3646; fax: 773-489-0974
www.stsylvesterchurch.com

♦ 2815 ♦ **St. Sylvester's Day (Madeira)**
December 31

In many European countries, December 31, in addition to NEW YEAR'S EVE, is also the observance of ST. SYLVESTER'S DAY, the feast day of Pope Sylvester (314-335). In Madeira, a group of eight Portuguese islands off the northwest coast of Africa, one of the world's most impressive fireworks displays takes place on the evening of this day, which is known as the Great Festival of St. Sylvester. The noise of the fireworks resounds over the Bay of Funchal, the islands' capital, where oceanliners make a special stop so that passengers can watch the celebrations.

CONTACTS:
St. Sylvester Roman Catholic Church
68 Ohio Ave.
Medford, NY 11763
631-475-4506
stsylvesterli.org

♦ 2816 ♦ **St. Tammany's Day**
May 1

During the Revolutionary War, the American troops were amused by the fact that the "Redcoats" (i.e., the British) had a patron saint: ST. GEORGE, who had a reputation for protecting English soldiers. So they decided to adopt a patron saint of their own, and chose for the purpose a disreputable 17th-century Delaware Indian chief named Tammanend. They dubbed him "St. Tammany" or "St. Tamina," chose May 1 for his festival, and celebrated the day with pompous and ridiculous ceremonies.

After the revolution Tammany Societies were eventually formed in many cities and towns, representing middle-class opposition to the power of the aristocratic Federalist Party. In the early 19th century the Society of Tammany became identified with the Democratic party. But the society's tendency to dole out gifts to the poor and to bribe political leaders— among them the notorious "Boss" Tweed of New York City— made the name "Tammany Hall" (the building in which the organization had its headquarters in New York City) synonymous with urban political corruption.

◆ 2817 ◆ St. Teresa's Day
October 15

St. Teresa of Ávila (1515-1582) was a Spanish Carmelite nun and reformer who recognized that the discipline in convents had relaxed to the point where they were little more than social clubs. In 1562, amidst intense opposition, she withdrew from the big convent she had entered in 1535 and established a small house with only 13 members known as the Reformed, or Discalced, Carmelites. Teresa's nuns devoted themselves to a rigorous way of life that had been largely forgotten in most monastic orders. They never left the convent, they maintained almost perpetual silence, they lived in austere poverty, and, as a symbol of their humility, they wore sandals instead of shoes—thus the designation "discalced," which means "barefoot." Before she died, Teresa had established 17 such communities. She was canonized by Pope Gregory XV in 1622.

Every year in Ávila, Spain, there is a huge celebration in honor of St. Teresa on October 15. The day is filled with religious services, parades, dances, games, and feasts, and the streets are decorated with banners and flowers. St. Teresa of Ávila is often colloquially referred to as "Big St. Teresa" to distinguish her from St. Teresa of Lisieux, a 19th-century Carmelite nun and author.

CONTACTS:
St Teresa Church
141 Henry St
New York, NY 10002 United States
212-233-0233
www.stteresany.org

◆ 2818 ◆ St. Thomas's Day
December 21 by Malabar Christians and Anglicans; July 3 by Roman Catholics; October 6 in the East

St. Thomas the Apostle was dubbed "Doubting Thomas" because, after the Resurrection, the other Apostles told him that they had seen Jesus, and he wouldn't believe them until he had touched Jesus' wounds himself. When the Apostles left Jerusalem to preach to the people of other nations, as Jesus had instructed them to do, tradition says Thomas traveled eastward toward India. In Kerala, the smallest state in India, the Malabar Christians (or Christians of St. Thomas) claim St. Thomas as the founder of their church. For them his feast day is a major celebration. Thomas is the patron saint of India and Pakistan.

In December Mayan Indians in Chichicastenago, Guatemala, honor the sun god they worshiped long before they became Christians with a dangerous ritual known as the *palo voladore*, or "flying pole dance." Three men climb to the top of a 50-foot pole. As one of them beats a drum and plays a flute, the other two wind a long rope attached to the pole around one foot and jump. If they land on their feet, it is believed that the sun god will be pleased and that the days will start getting longer—a safe bet in view of the fact that St. Thomas's Day coincides with the WINTER SOLSTICE.

CONTACTS:
Saint Thomas Church
1 W. 53rd St.
New York, NY 10019
212-757-7013
www.saintthomaschurch.org

◆ 2819 ◆ St. Thorlak's Day
December 23

Thorlak Thorhalli (1133-1193) was born in Iceland and, after being educated abroad, returned there to become bishop of Skalholt in 1177 or 1178. He was canonized by the Icelandic parliament five years after his death, even though the Roman Catholic Church has never officially confirmed the cult. His day traditionally marks the climax of CHRISTMAS preparations for Icelanders. It is associated with housecleaning and clothes washing, as well as the preparation of special foods. The *hangiket*, or smoked mutton, for Christmas was usually cooked on this day, and in the western fjords, the ammonia-like smell of skate hash cooked on St. Thorlak's Day is still considered a harbinger of the holiday season.

◆ 2820 ◆ St. Tryphon's Day (Montenegro and Bulgaria) (Trifon Zarezan)
February 1 or February 14 (varies)

The patron saint of gardeners, St. Tryphon is believed to have been born in Phrygia and was put to death by the Roman emperor Diocletian in about 250. Today, he is a popular figure among vine growers in Bulgaria and Montenegro. It is thus appropriate in those countries that St. Tryphon's Day, or **Trifon Zarezan**, coincides with the beginning of the pruning season in February. Roman Catholics living in other countries observe the saint's day on November 10.

Accompanying the saint's day in Bulgaria and Montenegro is a secular tradition that has developed in the vineyard districts. Seeking a blessing from the saint, growers will sprinkle wine on their vineyards before commencing an evening celebration of feasting and drinking.

Celebrations of a more somber nature take place in the Catholic and Orthodox churches of the two countries. One of the most widely attended ceremonies takes place in the Montenegrin city of Kotor at the Cathedral of St. Tryphon, built in the 12th century in honor of the saint.

See also VINEGROWER'S DAY.

CONTACTS:
Orthodox Church in America
6850 N. Hempstead Tpke
P.O. Box 675
Syosset, NY 11791
516-922-0550; fax: 516-922-0954
oca.org

◆ 2821 ◆ St. Urho's Day
March 16

719

St. Urho, whose name in Finnish means "hero," is credited with banishing a plague of grasshoppers that was threatening Finland's grape arbors. His legend in the United States was popularized in the 1950s, largely through the efforts of Professor Sulo Havumaki of Bemidji State University in Minnesota. After being celebrated as a "joke holiday" for several years in the Menahga-Sebeka area, the idea spread to other states with large Finnish populations.

The actual celebrations, which are largely confined to Finnish communities, include wearing St. Urho's official colors—Nile green and royal purple—drinking grape juice, and chanting St. Urho's famous words, "Grasshopper, grasshopper, go away," in Finnish. In some areas there is a ceremonial "changing of the guard"—in this case, two makeshift guards carrying pitchforks or chainsaws (to cut down the giant grasshoppers) who meet and exchange clothing, including humorous or unusual undergarments.

The similarities between this day and ST. PATRICK'S DAY, observed on March 17, can hardly be overlooked. St. Patrick, who is believed to have driven the snakes out of Ireland, is widely regarded as a rival to St. Urho and his grasshoppers. There is some evidence that native Finns who have visited friends and relatives in the U.S. are taking the St. Urho's celebration back to Finland with them.

♦ 2822 ♦ St. Vaclav's Day
September 28

Also known as **St. Wenceslas** (c. 907-929), St. Vaclav was a Bohemian prince who became the patron saint of the former Czechoslovakia. He was raised a Christian and eventually took over the government, encouraging the work of German missionaries who were trying to Christianize Bohemia. His zeal antagonized his non-Christian opponents, his brother among them, and he was eventually murdered by his brother or his brother's supporters. A few years later, his remains were transferred to the Church of St. Vitus in Prague, which became a popular pilgrimage site in the medieval period.

St. Vaclav's Day is a holiday throughout the Czech Republic. The virtues of "Good King Wenceslas" have been memorialized by the popular 19th-century Christmas carol of that name, though it rests on no historical basis.

♦ 2823 ♦ St. Vincent and the Grenadines Independence and Thanksgiving Day
October 27

A group of islands in the West Indies, St. Vincent and the Grenadines gained independence from Britain on October 27, 1979, and citizens celebrate their freedom with this national holiday.

CONTACTS:
St. Vincent/The Grenadines Tourist Office
801 2nd Ave.
21 Fl.
New York, NY 10017 United States

212-687-4981; fax: 212-949-5946
www.visitsvg.com

♦ 2824 ♦ St. Vincent and the Grenadines National Heroes Day
March 14

St. Vincent and the Grenadines is a nation comprised of a group of more than 30 islands, with St. Vincent being the largest of the islands. St. Vincent and the Grenadines are part of the Windward Islands in the Caribbean Sea.

Every March, the country celebrates Heroes and Heritage month. Throughout the month, the country learns about and remembers the past by holding cultural events and Indigenous People's Day celebrations. Many Vincentians make an annual pilgrimage to the Grenadine island of Balliceaux to pay homage to the fallen indigenous people, many of whom were later exiled to the region that became Belize and other parts of Central America.

March 14 is National Heroes Day. On this day, the country honors their national hero, Chief Joseph Chatoyer. He led the nation in preventing the Europeans from colonizing the islands. On March 14, 1795, Chatoyer was killed by British troops at Dorsetshire Hill. A monument honoring Chatoyer stands on this spot. As part of the Heroes Day celebration, a wreath-laying ceremony is held at the obelisk at Dorsetshire Hill.

CONTACTS:
St. Vincent & The Grenadines Tourist Office
801 Second Ave.
21st Fl.
New York, NY 10017
212-687-4981 or 800-729-1726; fax: 212-949-5946
www.visitsvg.com

♦ 2825 ♦ St. Vincent's Day
January 22

São Vicente is the patron saint of Lisbon, Portugal. St. Vincent of Saragossa was a deacon who was arrested along with Bishop Valerius. While Valerius was banished, Vincent was tortured and martyred in Spain under Diocletian's authority around the year 304. According to legend, his body was thrown to be devoured by vultures, but it was defended by a raven. Then his body was cast into the sea, but it came to shore and was buried.

St. Vincent's feast day is January 22. In Lisbon, people celebrate St. Vincent's Day with processions and prayers. But in the surrounding rural areas, there are a number of folk traditions associated with this day. Farmers believe that by carrying a resin torch to the top of a high hill on January 22, they can predict what the coming harvest will be like. If the wind extinguishes the flame, the crops will be abundant; if the torch continues to burn, a poor growing season lies ahead.

CONTACTS:
St. Vincent's Cathedral

1300 Forest Ridge Dr.
Bedford, TX 76022
817-354-7911; fax: 817-354-5073
www.stvincentscathedral.org

St. Vincent Church
164 W. Market St.
Akron, OH 44303
330-535-3135; fax: 330-535-4160
www.stvincentchurch.com

Portugal National Tourist Board
866 Second Ave.
8th Fl.
New York, NY 10017
646-723-0200; fax: 212-764-6137
www.visitportugal.com

♦ 2826 ♦ St. Vitus's Day
June 15

According to legend, St. Vitus was raised as a Christian by his nurse and his foster father. All three suffered persecution and were eventually put to death for their beliefs around 303, when Vitus was still a young boy. A chapel was later built in his honor at Ulm, Germany, and it was believed that anyone who danced before his shrine there on June 15, St. Vitus's Day, would be assured of good health in the coming year.

Whether the motions of the enthusiastic dancers resembled the symptoms of those suffering from any of the diseases known as chorea, or whether people who suffered from disorders of the nervous system were often miraculously cured at the shrine is not known for certain, but chorea is commonly referred to as "St. Vitus's dance" for the violent motions that accompany the disease. St. Vitus is the patron saint not only of those suffering from epilepsy and other disorders of the nervous system, but of actors and dancers as well.

♦ 2827 ♦ St. Vladimir's Day
July 15

St. Vladimir's Day is the official feast day of Vladimir the Great, the first Christian ruler of Kiev, Ukraine. Born in 958, Vladimir was a staunch follower of Slavic paganism. His early life was filled with warfare and cruelty, including acts of human sacrifice. After the killing of a Christian man and his son, Vladimir started to question his pagan faith and consider the advantages of Christianity, especially in political terms. Consequently, he sent envoys to Constantinople to investigate a possible Byzantine alliance. Eventually, Vladimir converted to Christianity, undergoing a total transformation. He stopped waging wars, and he ordered the destruction of pagan temples and the building of Christian churches and monasteries in their place. Vladimir died on July 15, 1015. On his feast day, the faithful hold vigils and special church services to celebrate the saint.

♦ 2828 ♦ Stånga Games
Four days including second weekend of July

The Stånga Games, often referred to as the "Gotlandic Olympics," have been held on Gotland Island in the Baltic Sea since 1924. They are the Swedish equivalent of Scotland's Braemar Highland Gathering, with competitive games and sports played the way they were in Viking times (late 700s to 1100 C.E.). Ancient square-and-border-ball is a popular team event in which the ball is hit with the hand or kicked with the foot, and teams must try to gain as much of their opponents' ground as possible. The Gotlandic pole-throwing contest is much like "tossing the caber" in Scotland. Another game, the Stone, is similar to horseshoes. It uses two stones, one made of stone and one of metal, which the players throw with the object of landing them as near as possible to the post. In the Gotlandic pentathlon, the participants compete in five events: a run, a game similar to the Stone, a high jump, pole throwing, and Cumberland wrestling. Other games include kick astride, hook the bottom, rule the roast, tug-of-pole, and breaking the ox.

CONTACTS:
Stanga Games
Neptungatan 4
Visby, 621 41 Sweden
46-498-207-067; fax: 46-498-215-474
www.stangaspelen.com

♦ 2829 ♦ Stanton (Elizabeth Cady) Day
November 12

Elizabeth Cady Stanton (1815-1902) was a pioneer in the struggle for women's rights. After graduating from the Troy Female Academy (now known as the Emma Willard School), one of the first schools devoted to providing better education for women, she married journalist and abolitionist Henry Brewster Stanton—although she carefully omitted the word "obey" from their wedding ceremony.

With a group of other women, she helped organize the first women's rights convention, held at Seneca Falls, New York, in 1848. This is where Stanton drew up her famous bill of rights for women, which included the first formal demand for women's suffrage in the United States. But it was her partnership with Susan B. Anthony, beginning in 1851, that galvanized the women's rights movement. Together they organized the National Woman Suffrage Association, planned suffrage campaigns, spoke out in favor of liberal divorce laws, and fought for political, legal, and industrial equality for women. Stanton died, however, 18 years before the 19th Amendment to the Constitution, granting women the right to vote, became law in 1920.

Governor Herbert Lehman of New York declared November 12 Elizabeth Cady Stanton Day in 1941. Stanton's birthday has long been observed by women's rights groups throughout the United States, particularly the National Organization for Women (NOW).

CONTACTS:
Elizabeth Cady Stanton House
National Park Service
32 Washington St.
Seneca Falls, NY 13148

315-568-2991; fax: 315-568-2141
www.nps.gov

Library of Congress
101 Independence Ave. S.E.
Washington, D.C. 20540
202-707-5000; fax: 202-707-2076
www.loc.gov

◆ 2830 ◆ Star Festival
January-February; 18th day of Chinese lunar year

In traditional Chinese belief, gods have great influence on people's lives and reside on the stars and planets. When LUNAR NEW YEAR is over, therefore, a day is set aside for men and boys to worship the Star Gods. Women are traditionally forbidden to participate in the ceremony, which consists of setting up a small table or altar in the courtyard of the house with a very simple food offering—usually sweetened rice balls. Two pictures are placed on the altar, one of the Star Gods and another of the cyclical signs associated with them. Inside a sealed envelope is a chart of lucky and unlucky stars. The father of the household prays to whichever star was associated with his birthday, then lights special lamps, made of red and yellow paper and filled with perfumed oil, that have been arranged around the altar. They burn out quickly, then each son of the house goes to the altar to relight three of the lamps in order to honor his star. If their flames burn brightly, it means he will have good luck in the coming year.

CONTACTS:
Star festival
Ueno-sho 25
Hiyoshicho
Prefecture Nantan, Kyoto Prefecture Japan
www.thestarfestival.com

◆ 2831 ◆ State Fair of Texas
Late September through the beginning of October

Not surprisingly, the State Fair of Texas is one of the nation's biggest state fairs, claiming more than three million visitors to the 200-acre Fair Park in Dallas. The fair began in 1887, and in 1952 Big Tex, its symbol of bigness, arrived. Big Tex is a 52-foot-tall cowboy with a 30-foot chest and 7'8" biceps, wearing a five-foot-high, 75-gallon cowboy hat. The cowboy stands in the middle of the fairgrounds booming out welcomes and announcements. The skeleton of the cowboy was built in 1949 to be the world's tallest Santa Claus for a CHRISTMAS celebration in Kerens, Tex. It was sold to the State Fair, and Dallas artist Jack Bridges used baling wire and papier-mâché to create the cowboy that debuted in 1952. The following year, a motor was installed to move the cowboy's jaw in sync with a voice mechanism, and Big Tex has been booming ever since. Among fair events are a college football game, concerts, and parades.

CONTACTS:
State Fair of Texas
3921 Martin Luther King Blvd.
P.O. Box 150009

Dallas, TX 75210
214-565-9931; fax: 214-421-8710
www.bigtex.com

◆ 2832 ◆ State Opening of Parliament
Early November

This colorful British ritual is observed at the beginning of November when the members of Parliament return after the long summer recess. Crowds assemble in the streets of Westminster, an inner borough of Greater London, in hopes of catching a glimpse of the Queen as she arrives in her horse-drawn coach, dressed in royal robes of state and escorted by the Household Cavalry. The Queen is not allowed to enter the House of Commons because she is not a commoner, so after being met by the Lord Chancellor she is led straight to the House of Lords. Seated on a magnificent throne and surrounded by various church and state officials in their robes, she reads aloud the speech that has been written for her by members of the government outlining their plans for the coming session.

An interesting tradition that accompanies the opening of Parliament is the searching of the cellars of both Houses. This goes back to 1605, when GUY FAWKES and his accomplices tried to blow the Houses up.

CONTACTS:
United Kingdom Parliament, Parliamentary Education Unit
London, SW1A 2TT United Kingdom
44-20-7219-3074; fax: 44-20-7219-2570
www.parliament.uk

◆ 2833 ◆ Ste. Genevieve, Jour de Fête à (Days of Celebration)
Second full weekend in August

Ste. Genevieve became the first permanent settlement in the state of Missouri when the French arrived in 1725. At one time it rivaled St. Louis in size and importance, and the town still prides itself on its authentic 18th- and 19th-century architecture.

The annual Jour de Fête that has been held in mid-August each year since 1965 not only celebrates the area's French heritage but is a German and Spanish festival as well. Historic homes dating back to 1770 are opened to the public, people dress in colonial costumes, and arts and crafts are on display.

CONTACTS:
Jour de Fete Arts & Crafts Festival
P.O. Box 132
Ste. Genevieve, MO 63670
saintegenevievejourdefete.com

◆ 2834 ◆ Steinbeck (John) Festival
May

Salinas, California, birthplace of famous American author John Steinbeck (1902-1968), has hosted a yearly literary festival in his honor since 1980. Steinbeck, who was awarded the NOBEL PRIZE for literature in 1962, wrote extensively about the people, places, and social conditions of his homeland in California's central coastal region. The festival gives Steinbeck fans an opportunity to visit many of the places that formed Steinbeck's worldview and inspired his works. The four-day event features lectures on aspects of Steinbeck's work and life, tours, performances of plays and screenings of movies based on Steinbeck's stories, and a book fair. The festival also sponsors a short story contest, the winner of which receives a cash prize of $1,000.

CONTACTS:
National Steinbeck Center
1 Main St.
Salinas, CA 93901
831-796-3833; fax: 831-796-3828
www.steinbeck.org

♦ 2835 ♦ **Stes. Maries, Fête des**
May 24-25

According to a French legend, St. Sarah, patron saint of gypsies, was the Egyptian handmaid of Sts. Mary Jacoby and Mary Salome, and all three were shipwrecked off the Provençal coast of France. The three holy women supposedly died in the small Provençal village of Les Saintes Maries-de-la-Mer, where their remains are said to be preserved in the 15th-century church of Les Saintes-Maries. The relics of St. Sarah are deeply venerated by the Romanies, or gypsies, of southern France, who try to worship at her shrine at least once during their lives.

The highlight of the service held at the church during the **Festival of the Holy Maries** occurs when the flower-decked reliquary of the Maries is lowered slowly through a trap door in the ceiling. On the second day of the festival, there is a procession down to the sea for the blessing of the painted wooden vessel known as the "Bark of the Saints." The bark holds a silver urn which is believed to contain some of the bones of the saints. Thousands of devout pilgrims make the journey to Les Saintes Maries-de-la-Mer each year.

CONTACTS:
Saintes-Maries-de-la-Mer Office of Tourism
5 av. Van Gogh
Saintes-Maries-de-la-Mer, 13460 France
33-4-9097-8255; fax: 33-4-9097-7115
www.saintesmaries.com/en

♦ 2836 ♦ **Steuben (Baron Friedrich) Day**
September 17

Baron Friedrich Wilhelm Ludolf Gerhard Augustus von Steuben (1730-1794) was an experienced Prussian soldier who came to America in 1777 and volunteered to serve in the Continental army without rank or pay. He was sent to join General George WASHINGTON at Valley Forge, where he trained Washington's men in the intricacies of military drill, earning himself the sobriquet "Drill Master of the American Revolu-

tion." Steuben led one of Washington's divisions at the Battle of YORKTOWN, and his experience in siege warfare helped the American troops achieve the victory that soon brought the Revolutionary War to an end. In gratitude for his contributions, he was granted American citizenship and given a large piece of land in the Mohawk Valley and a yearly pension.

Steuben's birthday, September 17, was first celebrated by members of the Steuben Society of America, an organization founded in 1919 by U.S. citizens of German descent. The Society now has branches in many states, which observe the anniversary with patriotic exercises. At Valley Forge State Park in Pennsylvania, there is a Steuben birthday celebration featuring German music and speeches at the monument to him erected in 1915. There are also Steuben Day parades in New York City, Philadelphia, and Chicago on or near the Prussian hero's birthday.

CONTACTS:
Steuben Day Observance Association of Philadelphia and Vicinity, Inc.
8601 Roosevelt Blvd.
Philadelphia, PA 19152
215-332-3400; fax: 215-332-6050
www.steubenparade.com

Steuben Society of America
6705 Fresh Pond Rd.
Ridgewood, NY 11378
718-381-0900
www.steubensociety.org

♦ 2837 ♦ **Stewardship Sunday**
Second Sunday in November

This is the day on which many churches in the United States and Canada begin their campaign for financial support in the coming year. The term "stewardship" refers to Christian and Jewish teaching that all creation belongs to God and that each man and woman is an agent or steward to whom God's property is entrusted for a while. On this Sunday each year, churches appeal to their members' sense of responsibility as stewards of the money God has entrusted to them.

CONTACTS:
Reformed Church in America
4500 60th St. S.E.
Grand Rapids, MI 49512
616-698-7071 or 800-968-3943; fax: 616-698-6606
www.rca.org

♦ 2838 ♦ **Stickdance**
Spring

Observed by the Athabascan Indians of Alaska, Stickdance is a week of ceremonies to grieve for the dead. The ancient ceremony, usually held long after the deaths of those memorialized, is now observed only in two villages on the Yukon River—Kaltag and Nulato.

Each evening of the ceremony, people go to the community hall with traditional foods—moose, salmon, beaver, rabbit, ptarmigan (a kind of grouse)—for a meal called a *potlatch*.

After the meal, the women stand in a circle, swaying and chanting traditional songs for the dead. The hall becomes more crowded each night. On Friday night, as the women dance in a circle, the men carry in a tall spruce tree stripped of branches and wrapped in ribbons. The tree is erected in the center of the room and wolf and fox furs are draped on it. The people then dance around it and chant continuously through the night. In the morning, the men tear the furs and ribbons from the stick and carry it away to the Yukon River, where they break it into pieces and throw the pieces on the river's ice.

On Saturday night, people representing the dead are ritually dressed in special clothes. Somberly, they leave the hall and go to the river where they shake the spirits from their clothing. On their return to the hall, the mood becomes festive; gifts are exchanged and a night of celebration begins. The following morning the people who have represented the dead walk through the village shaking hands with people, sharing food and drink, and saying farewell.

Stickdance is held at irregular intervals, since it takes months or longer to prepare for it. People must choose those who will represent the dead being honored and make their clothes, and they must also save up to buy gifts.

The Athabascans, who may have descended from bands who crossed from Asia, have lived in Alaska longer than the Eskimos have and speak a language that is in the same family as that spoken by Navajos and Apaches.

♦ 2839 ♦ **Stiftungsfest**
Last weekend in August

Appropriately enough, Minnesota's oldest continuous festival is held in the town of Norwood-Young America. Loosely translated as "founders' day," Stiftungsfest was created in 1861 by the Young America Pioneer Maennerchor (men's choir) as a way of bringing the music of old Germany to the new world. Well-known bands and singing groups from Germany as well as local groups perform during the three-day event, which includes a traditional German beer garden, a Heritage Tent showcasing German arts and crafts, and a Grand Parade.

CONTACTS:
Stiftungsfest Committee
P.O. Box 133
Norwood Young America, MN 55368
952-467-1812
www.stiftungsfest.org

♦ 2840 ♦ **Stir-Up Sunday**
November-December; Sunday before Advent

The collect for the Sunday preceding ADVENT in the Church of England begins, "Stir up, we beseech Thee, O Lord, the wills of thy faithful people." But the other "stirring up" that takes place on this day is more literal: the stirring of the bat-

ter for the traditional CHRISTMAS pudding, which must be prepared weeks in advance. It is customary for each member of the family to take turns stirring the pudding with a wooden spoon (symbolic of Jesus' crib), which is thought to bring good luck. The stirring is done clockwise, with eyes closed, and the stirrer makes a wish.

♦ 2841 ♦ **Stockton Asparagus Festival**
Last weekend in April

This two-day celebration takes place in Stockton, Calif., the heart of the region that claims to be the "Asparagus Capital of the Nation." In fact, California accounts for about 90 percent of the fresh-market asparagus production in the country, and most of that asparagus comes from Stockton's San Joaquin Delta region.

The festival began in 1986 to promote the asparagus and it now draws 80,000 spectators to the region's various events. These include about 50 food booths in Asparagus Alley, a wine-tasting booth, a fun run (some runners wear asparagus spears in their headbands), a car show of some 200 antique and classic cars, arts and crafts, live entertainment, and children's activities.

There's also a recipe contest; among the past winning entries are enchiladas and lasagna made, of course, with asparagus. Other popular asparagus dishes served include asparaberry shortcake (it is said the asparagus gives a nutmeg flavor to the strawberries), asparagus-and-beef sandwiches, and asparagus bisque.

The festival is also a time to promulgate information about the asparagus. Fair-goers learn that asparagus is a source of vitamins A and C; the first trainload of asparagus was sent east from California in 1900; the Greeks and Romans used asparagus as a medicine for bee stings, dropsy, and toothache, and also as an aphrodisiac.

CONTACTS:
San Joaquin Asparagus Festival
1658 S. Airport Way
Stockton, CA 95206
209-466-5041; fax: 209-466-5141
sanjoaquinasparagusfestival.net

Stockton Asparagus Festival
125 Bridge Pl.
Stockton, CA 95202
209-938-1555 or 877-778-6258
www.visitstockton.org

♦ 2842 ♦ **Stonewall Rebellion, Anniversary of the**
June 27

The Stonewall Inn was a gay bar in New York City's Greenwich Village that was raided by the police on June 27, 1969. Police frequently monitored the bar and undertook occasional raids in the past, but on that Friday night, the encounter turned explosive. As the outraged crowd threw stones and bottles, the police retaliated by aiming a fire hose against it. Eventually, more police arrived and subdued what had turned into a riot.

Today, the Stonewall Rebellion is regarded as a turning point in the history of the gay rights movement. It is commemorated in New York, Philadelphia, and other U.S. cities with parades, memorial services for those who have died of AIDS, and other activities designed to draw attention to the ways in which homosexuals have been discriminated against.

CONTACTS:
Stonewall Veterans Association
70-A Greenwich Ave.
Ste. 120
Manhattan, NY 10011
212-627-1969; fax: 718-294-1969
www.stonewallvets.org

♦ 2843 ♦ Store Bededag
Between April 18 and May 21; fourth Friday after Easter

A public holiday in Denmark, Store Bededag is a nationwide day of prayer which has been observed since the 18th century, when King Christian VII's prime minister, Count Johann Friedrich Struensee, decided that one great day of prayer should replace the numerous penitential days observed by the Evangelical Lutheran Church, the state church.

The eve of **Common Prayer Day** is announced by the ringing of church bells. In former times, it was customary for Copenhagen burghers to greet the spring by putting on new clothes and strolling around the city ramparts. Then they went home and ate *varme hveder*, a small square wheat bread, served hot. Today, people still dress in their spring finery and eat the traditional bread, but now they walk along the famous Langelinie, the boulevard that faces Copenhagen's waterfront.

CONTACTS:
Store Bededag
Vimmelskaftet 47
Copenhagen, DK-1161 Denmark
45-3348-0500
www.kristendom.dk

♦ 2844 ♦ Storytelling Festival, National
First weekend in October

A three-day festival in Jonesborough, Tenn., the National Storytelling Festival was started in 1973 to revive the ancient folk art of storytelling. The popularity of storytelling seemed to be dying, replaced by radio, television, and movies. The first festival was the idea of Jimmy Neil Smith, a Jonesborough schoolteacher who became executive director of the festival's sponsor, the National Association for the Preservation and Perpetuation of Storytelling (now known as the Storytelling Foundation International), which was formed in 1975 and is headquartered in Jonesborough. That first event drew about 60 people. At first, people sat on bales of hay, then the festival moved to kitchens and parlors and porches, and finally into the large tents that are used now. The festival has inspired scores of similar events around the country as well as college courses in storytelling.

About 6,000 people now attend to listen to storytellers relate ghost stories, sacred stories, ballads, tall tales, myths, legends, and fairy tales. Restaurants set up food booths, and a resource tent provides tapes and other material. The 20th-anniversary celebration in 1992 brought together more than 80 storytellers who had all appeared at previous festivals. A highlight was a special ghost-story concert by tellers of supernatural tales.

See also TELLABRATION and YUKON INTERNATIONAL STORYTELLING FESTIVAL.

CONTACTS:
International Storytelling Center
116 W. Main St.
Jonesborough, TN 37659
423-753-2171 or 800-952-8392; fax: 423-913-1320
www.storytellingfestival.net

♦ 2845 ♦ Stourbridge Fair
Began August 24 for three weeks

In the 17th century the Stourbridge Fair, held at Stourbridge (or Sturbridge) near Cambridge, was England's chief place of exchange. It was established around 1200 as a benefit for the local lepers' hospital, and it was put on by the town and Cambridge University beginning on ST. BARTHOLOMEW'S DAY, August 24, and continuing for about three weeks. It was held at Duddery Square, where all the cloth and clothing shops were located. Merchants and wholesalers could buy everything from Italian silks to furs from the Baltics and linen from Flanders. Those who attended the fair would bring home souvenirs known as "fairings"—originally relics or images of saints, but later trinkets of all sorts or gingerbread in the shape of hobby-horses covered with gilt. The fair was held for the last time in 1855.

Although there were other amusements for fairgoers, including rope dancing and puppet shows, those who wanted to see the greatest entertainers of England and Europe would go to London for the BARTHOLOMEW FAIR, which was held at this same time of year.

CONTACTS:
CambridgePPF
Wandlebury Ring
Gog Magog Hills
Babraham, Cambridgeshire CB22 3AE United Kingdom
44-12-2324-3830
www.cambridgeppf.org

♦ 2846 ♦ Stratford Festival
April-November

What started in Stratford, Ontario, in 1953 as a six-week Shakespearean drama festival under the artistic leadership of Alec Guinness and Irene Worth has since expanded into a 26-week event drawing an audience of half a million people. All of Shakespeare's plays have been performed here over the years, as well as works by Sophocles (c. 496-406 B.C.E.), Henrik Ibsen (1828-1906), Jean-Baptiste Molière (1622-1673),Anton Chekhov (1860-1904), Richard Sheridan (1751-1816), Samuel Beckett (1906-1989), and a number of Canadian playwrights. The festival's repertory company, known as the Stratford Company, goes on tour during the months when the festival is not in session.

CONTACTS:
Stratford Festival
55 Queen St.
P.O. Box 520
Stratford, ON N5A 6V2 Canada
519-273-1600 or 800-567-1600
www.stratfordfestival.ca

♦ 2847 ♦ **Strawberry Festival**
June

The Strawberry Festival is one of several annual festivals held by Iroquois Indians. At Tonawanda, N.Y., the people congregate in their longhouse to hear a lengthy recitation of the words of Handsome Lake (Ganio "Día Io," 1735-1815). In 1799 this Seneca prophet delivered a message calling for cooperative farming, abstention from hard drink, abandonment of witchcraft and magic, the prohibition of abortion, and other instructions. This is the basis of today's Longhouse religion.

Following the recitations and speeches are ceremonial dances accompanied by chants and the pounding of turtle-shell rattles. Lunch follows, with a strawberry drink and winding up with strawberry shortcake. The Iroquois say, "You will eat strawberries when you die," because strawberries line the road to heaven.

Other traditional Iroquois celebrations include the IROQUOIS MIDWINTER FESTIVAL, a Maple Dance held when maple syrup and sugar are made, a Planting Festival, and the Green Corn Dance, at which the principal dish is succotash, made not just with corn and lima beans but also with squash and venison or beef.

CONTACTS:
Owego Strawberry Festival
Owego, NY
www.owegostrawberryfestival.com

♦ 2848 ♦ **Struga Poetry Evenings**
Mid-June

The annual international poetry festival known as Struga Poetry Evenings was launched in 1962 with a series of readings by Macedonian poets in honor of Konstantin and Dimitar Miladinov, brothers born in the early 19th century. Both were known as great writers, teachers, and intellectuals, and many consider Konstantin Miladinov to be the founder of

modern Macedonian poetry. The Struga festival opens each year with his poem "Longing for the South."

The festival takes place over five days in late August, drawing about 20 Macedonian and 30 international poets, who take part in readings and symposia. The festival also typically features an art exhibit, workshops in poetry-related subjects, and leisure activities. A festival centerpiece is the international poetry reading, Meridians, held after the opening ceremony. The presentation of special awards are always highlights of the festival. The Miladinov Brothers Award acknowledges the best poetry book by a Macedonian author in the period between two festivals, and the Struga Bridges Award, presented jointly by the festival and UNESCO, recognizes the best debut poetry book by an author of any country. A festival jury also selects one poet as the Gold Wreath Award winner, who presides as laureate over the festival.

CONTACTS:
Struga Poetry Evenings
P.O. Box 109
Struga, 6330 Macedonia
389-46-786-270; fax: 389-46-786-280
www.strugapoetryevenings.com/?lang=en

♦ 2849 ♦ **Sts. Cosmas and Damian Day**
September 27

Legend has Cosmas (also Cosme or Cosmo) and Damian as twin brothers from Syria who were brought up in the Christian faith and who devoted their lives to medicine. As doctors they refused payment for their services, instead asking those who benefited from their healing to believe in Christ. What can be reasonably asserted is that they probably lived and were martyred in Syria during or before the fifth century.

In Brazil, the feast of Cosmas and Damian is celebrated on September 27 and it is traditional to give candy to children, since the saints are patrons of children. Yoruban mythology, which lives on through African Brazilians, tells of another set of holy twins, who are often associated with Cosmas and Damian.

♦ 2850 ♦ **Sts. Peter and Paul Day**
June 29

It is said that St. Peter and St. Paul were both martyred on June 29, and for this reason their names have been linked in various observances around the world. In Malta, the feast of St. Peter and St. Paul is a harvest festival known as MNARJA. In Peru, the **Día de San Pedro y San Pablo** is celebrated in fishing villages because St. Peter is the patron saint of fishermen. Processions of decorated boats carrying an image of the saint are common, and sometimes a special floating altar is set up, with decorations made out of shells and seaweed.

In Valparaíso, Chile, this sort of procession has been going on since 1682.

In Trinidad fishermen first go out to catch fish to give to the poor and as they return, the Anglican priest blesses them and the sea. Then the partying begins. After the priest leaves, bongo and bele dances are done to honor St. Peter.

CONTACTS:
St. Anthony Messenger Press and Franciscan Communications
28 W. Liberty St.
Cincinnati, OH 45202
513-241-5615
www.americancatholic.org

♦ 2851 ♦ **Students' Fight for Freedom and Democracy, Day of (Struggle for Freedom and Democracy Day, World Students' Day)**
November 17

In 1939, Nazi troops invaded Czechoslovakia and took over the country, installing a dictatorship. Student-led demonstrations against the occupation in late October and early November 1939 led to the death of several students, most notably, Jan Opletal of Charles University in Prague. On November 17, the day Opletal was to be buried, more protests were held. Nazi troops subsequently executed nine student leaders, closed all universities, and sent many students to a concentration camp.

November 17 became a date of national recognition for Czechs after World War II. The date took on greater significance on November 17, 1989, when Czech students gathered 50 years after the original protest, this time to demonstrate against the communist regime. This marked the beginning of the so-called Velvet Revolution to reestablish a democratic government.

The Day of Students' Fight for Freedom and Democracy is a national holiday in the Czech Republic. People gather and light candles near a "V for Victory" memorial plaque on National Avenue in Prague. Ribbons in the national colors of red, blue, and white are often worn. Music associated with the 1989 protest is played, and the national flag is flown in all public places.

CONTACTS:
Embassy of the Czech Republic
3900 Spring of Freedom St. N.W.
Washington, D.C. 20008
202-274-9100; fax: 202-966-8540
www.mzv.cz

♦ 2852 ♦ **Sturgis Motorcycle Rally**
First Monday of August through following Sunday

A mammoth yearly rally of 250,000 or so motorcyclists in small Sturgis, S.D. (population 7,000), formerly called the **Black Hills Motorcycle Classic**. There are races, merrymaking, band music, and usually some misbehavior, including arrests for drunken driving. There tend to be numerous accidents with injuries, and sometimes, fatalities. Motorcycle

drag racing runs eight days, and other official events include bike shows, a swap meet, monster truck races, Tough Man and Tough Woman Contests (the titles determined by fights in which biting and kicking but not much else are forbidden), and a fireworks show. The rally also includes unofficial events, especially weddings; bikers find it romantic to get married during the rally, and 100 or more couples get married there every year.

The rally began in 1938 when Clarence (Pappy) Hoel, a local motorcycle dealer, invited some fellow bikers to a get-together. His wife, Pearl, made hot dogs, potato salad, and iced tea for the crew. The rally has been held ever since, except for two years during World War II, and has become part of biker lore.

CONTACTS:
City of Sturgis Rally and Events Department
1040 2nd St.
Ste. 201
Sturgis, SD 57785
605-720-0800
www.sturgismotorcyclerally.com

♦ 2853 ♦ **Stuttgart Festival of Animated Film**
May

First launched in 1982, the Stuttgart Festival of Animated Film (ITFS) is both a German cultural event and a commercial enterprise for filmmakers, directors, and distributors. The annual festival screens the latest works in animation, which range from simple cartoons to 3D computer-generated movies. Stuttgart hosts screenings at various venues, such as the open-air cinema in the city's historic *Schlossplatz* or the many indoor theaters in the city center. In addition to its films, the festival includes many special programs, such as school and studio presentations, master classes, and retrospectives at the Mercedes-Benz Museum and the Wilhelma Zoo. As one of the most important international film festivals in Germany, ITFS features awards ceremonies, after-parties, live music, and comedy acts. Its international competition is spread over multiple categories, including awards for trick animation, cartoons, and features. Furthermore, the festival honors animated works that significantly impact the film industry and fashion world.

♦ 2854 ♦ **Styrian Autumn (Steirischer Herbst)**
October-November

Dedicated to the avant-garde in music, drama, literature, and the fine arts, this month-long festival in Austria celebrates spontaneity and experimentation. Founded in 1968, its goal is to remove the barrier between the producers and consumers of culture by presenting world premieres of plays, operas, and musical works by contemporary artists, workshops and symposia on 20th-century composers, exhibitions of contemporary art, and a variety of fringe events that include circus acts and multimedia shows. Ticket prices are purposely kept low, and many festival events are offered free of charge. There are also interdisciplinary symposia. The festival takes its name from the province of Styria, whose capital city, Graz, is where the work of Austria's modernists is performed and displayed.

CONTACTS:
Steirischer Herbst Festivalbu ro
Sackstrasse 17
Graz, 8010 Austria
43-316-823-007; fax: 43-316-823-007-77
www.steirischerherbst.at

◆ **2855** ◆ **Sudan Independence Day**
January 1

Sudan became an independent republic on NEW YEAR'S DAY in 1956, after having been a joint British-Egyptian territory since 1899.

Independence Day is celebrated as a national holiday with elaborate festivities in the capital city of Khartoum.

CONTACTS:
Embassy of The Republic of Sudan
2210 Massachusetts Ave.
Washington, D.C. 20008
202-338-8565; fax: 202-667-2406
www.sudanembassy.org

◆ **2856** ◆ **Sugar Ball Show (Sugar-Coated Haws Festival)**
16th through 18th days of first lunar month

This temple festival is held at the Haiyunan Buddhist convent of Sifang District in Qingdao, Shandong Province, China. Set for the day of the first spring tide, this festival has been held since the convent was built in the 17th century near the end of the Ming Dynasty. Originally fishermen observed this time to pray for safety and a good harvest. Now sugar balls, also called *haws*—yams, oranges, and dates dipped in hot syrup and then cooled until crisp—colorfully displayed on long skewers, are specialties of the fair. About 200,000 people attend the show.

◆ **2857** ◆ **Sugar Bowl Classic**
January 1

New Orleans, Louisiana, has been host to football and lots of hoopla since the Sugar Bowl originated there in 1935. That first game took place in the depths of the Great Depression, and since then the Sugar Bowl has survived many difficulties, including a World War and a devastating hurricane.

The first Sugar Bowl took place in 1935 between Tulane University's Green Wave, unbeaten in the South, and Temple University's Owls, the only unbeaten team in the North. The Green Wave and the Owls waged an exciting contest in which Tulane overcame a 14-point deficit to win, 20-14. Since then, the annual event has included a team from the Southeastern Conference. Alabama has the most wins with eight

(many with legendary coach Bear Bryant), and Louisiana State is next with six wins. In 2009, the Sugar Bowl celebrated its 75th anniversary.

The Sugar Bowl has been played in New Orleans every year except 2006 when, for the only time in the history of the game, it was played away from the city. This was soon after the devastating Hurricane Katrina, which killed hundreds of people and destroyed thousands of homes and businesses. The New Orleans Superdome was left standing, but badly damaged. So in 2006, the Sugar Bowl staff moved to Georgia and put on the game in the Georgia Dome. The game moved back to New Orleans the following year. In January 2015, the Sugar Bowl hosted a college football playoff semifinal game between Ohio State and Alabama. In 2016 and 2017, the Sugar Bowl will feature the SEC and Big 12 conference champions.

CONTACTS:
Allstate Sugar Bowl
1500 Sugar Bowl Dr.
New Orleans, LA 70112 United States
504-828-2440; fax: 504-828-2441
www.allstatesugarbowl.org

◆ **2858** ◆ **Sukkot (Sukkoth, Succoth)**
Begins between September 20 and October 18; Tishri 15-21

After their escape from slavery in Egypt, the Jews wandered in the desert for 40 years under the leadership of Moses. For much of the time they lived in huts, or *sukkot*, made of wooden frames covered with branches or hay. The festival of Sukkot, also known as the **Feast of Tabernacles** or the **Feast of Booths**, commemorates this period in Jewish history. It is also one of the PILGRIM FESTIVALS (*see also* PASSOVER and SHAVUOT).

The traditional way of observing Sukkot was to build a small booth or tabernacle and live in it during the seven-day festival. Nowadays Orthodox congregations build a *sukkah* in the synagogue, while Reform Jews make miniature models of the ancient huts and use them as centerpieces on the family table. Although linked to the Exodus from Egypt, Sukkot also celebrates the fall harvest and is sometimes referred to as the **Feast of the Ingathering**.

A major part of the festival is the four species: a palm branch, citron, three myrtle twigs, and two willow branches. These are tied together and waved at different points in the service, to "rejoice before the Lord."

Like other Jewish holidays, Sukkot begins at sundown on the preceding evening. The seventh day of Sukkot is known as HOSHANA RABBAH and is the last possible day on which one can seek and obtain forgiveness for the sins of the previous year— an extension of the YOM KIPPUR or the Day of Atonement. The eighth day of Sukkot is known as SHEMINI ATZERET, and the day after that is called SIMHAT TORAH, which is now celebrated as a separate holiday by Orthodox and Conservative Jews.

CONTACTS:
Orthodox Union
11 Broadway
New York, NY 10004
212-563-4000
www.ou.org

Union for Reform Judaism
633 Third Ave.
New York, NY 10017
212-650-4000
urj.org

♦ 2859 ♦ Sumamao, Fiesta de
December 26

The Argentine ritual drama known as *sumamao*, which means "beautiful river," is named after the location in which it is traditionally performed—near the Rio Dulce. It used to take place in a deserted chapel near the river, but nowadays it is sponsored by a ranch owner, who sets up a small altar on his property.

On San Esteban's (St. Stephen's) Day, December 26, an avenue of *arcos*, or arches—made from trees that have been stripped of their branches except for a tuft on top and tied together by cords hung with *ichas* (cakes in the form of puppets)—leads up to the altar. The drama begins at dawn with trumpets and fireworks, followed by a slow procession of men on horseback through the arches. The rest of the drama unfolds throughout the day, culminating in the demolition of the arcos and the eating of the ichas. A fiesta concludes the celebration.

The sumamao is primarily an agricultural ritual aimed at winning the favor of the gods by offering sacrifices and exorcizing evil spirits. Social dances—including the *zamba*, the *gato*, and the *chacarera*—have replaced the orgiastic behavior that followed the ritual in ancient times.

♦ 2860 ♦ Suminuri Matsuri
January 15

Suminuri Matsuri is a New Year tradition observed for more than half a millennium in a district of Matsunoyama, Niigata Prefecture, Japan. People adorn their homes and streets with decorations made of paper, tree branches, and bamboo for Oshogatsu, New Year's Day. After the holiday they take down the decorations and burn them, keeping the ashes for the Suminuri Festival. People take their ashes outside and mix them with some snow, then rub the concoction on each other's faces for luck in the new year.

♦ 2861 ♦ Summer Festival
July 4

There is something for everybody on the Fourth of July in Owensboro, Ky. A highlight has been the "Anything That Goes and Floats Race," in which contestants must have a vehicle that gets them to the Ohio River and then floats them for a decent distance on the river. Vehicles that have made it into the water include bicycles attached to a canoe, a skateboard tied to a plastic raft, and large pontoons powered by bicycles on land and paddlewheels in the water.

Other events include musical entertainment, sporting events, and, of course, fireworks.

CONTACTS:
Kentucky Department of Travel and Tourism
Capital Plaza Tower
500 Mero St.
22nd Fl.
Frankfort, KY 40601
502-564-4930 or 800-225-8747
www.kentuckytourism.com

♦ 2862 ♦ Summer Solstice
June 21-22 (Northern Hemisphere); December 21-22 (Southern Hemisphere)

There are times during the year, respectively in each hemisphere, when the sun is at its furthest point from the equator. It reaches its northernmost point around June 21, which is the longest day of the year for those living north of the equator, and its southernmost point around December 22, which is the longest day for those living in the Southern Hemisphere. The summer solstice marks the first day of the summer season— the word solstice is from the Latin word, solstitium, meaning "sun-stopping," since the point at which the sun appears to rise and set stops and reverses direction after this day. Although it was very common to celebrate the summer solstice in ancient times, modern American observations are comparatively rare. But there are a number of solstice observances held by New Age and Neopagan groups throughout the United States. *See also* Capac Raymi; Doan ngu; Druids' Summer Solstice Ceremony; Midnight Sun Festival; Midsummer Day; Ysyakh.

CONTACTS:
Myrtle Beach Area Chamber of Commerce
1200 N. Oak St.
P.O. Box 2115
Myrtle Beach, SC 29578
843-626-7444 or 800-356-3016; fax: 843-448-3010
www.visitmyrtlebeach.com

♦ 2863 ♦ Sun Fun Festival
First week in June

Sun Fun Festival is a beach festival at Myrtle Beach, S.C., to celebrate the state's Grand Strand, a 60-mile stretch of white-sand ocean beach. Myrtle Beach is the central city on the strand and so the fitting place for this five-day celebration that includes an air show, beauty pageants, beach games, music and dance performances, and a sandcastle-building contest. The record for the world's longest sandcastle was set here in 1990—the castle measured 10½ miles long. As many as 200,000 people attend.

◆ 2864 ◆ Sun Pageant Day
January-March

It is not uncommon for towns in the northern part of Norway to observe **Solday**, or **Sun Day**, when the sun reappears at the end of January or in early February. In Narvik, Nordland County, for example, Sun Pageant Day is celebrated in early February.

The sun's reappearance is particularly welcome for the people of Rjukan, Telemark County, which is nestled so deeply in a narrow valley that the sun doesn't shine there from early October to mid-March.

Although the date of the Sun Pageant in Rjukan varies from year to year, it always entails weeks of preparation. The town square is decorated with tall ice columns topped by flaming torches. At one end there is a throne on a raised wooden platform for the "Prince of the Sun," who leads a procession of costumed figures into the square and officially begins the celebration. The eating, singing, folk dancing, and fireworks continue for most of the day and night.

CONTACTS:
Telemark Tourist Information Office
Uniongata 18
Kunnskapsverkstedet
Skien, 3732
47-35-90-0020; fax: 47-3590-0021
www.visittelemark.com

◆ 2865 ◆ Sun Yat-sen, Birthday of
November 12

Sun Yat-sen (1866-1925) was the leader of the Chinese Nationalist Party (Kuomintang). He served as the first provisional president of the Republic of China (1911-12) and later as its de facto ruler (1923-25). Because he possessed an exceptionally broad knowledge of the West and developed a grand plan for China's industrialization, he is known as "the father of modern China."

Sun Yat-sen's birthday is a holiday in Taiwan. The anniversary of his death, March 12, is observed as Arbor Day in Taiwan.

See also DOUBLE TENTH DAY.

CONTACTS:
Dr. Sun Yat-sen Foundation
45 N. King St.
Honolulu, HI 96817
www.sunyatsenhawaii.org

◆ 2866 ◆ Sundance Film Festival
Ten days in mid-January

Originally held in Salt Lake City and known as the United States Film Festival, since 1984 the Sundance Film Festival has been organized by the Sundance Institute, founded by actor and director Robert Redford. It is an internationally recognized showcase for independent films, many of which would not ordinarily be seen by distributors and studios. Although most are American, Canadian and other foreign films are also screened during the 10-day festival, held in Park City, Utah, every January. The highlight of the festival is the American Independent Dramatic and Documentary Competition, where new American independent films are given their premieres. Judges for the competition have included well-known directors, screenwriters, and film critics.

Many emerging independent filmmakers now look to the Sundance Film Festival as their first opportunity to present their films before an audience. Filmgoers and the entertainment industry look to the Festival for the discovery of new talent and as a champion of films that challenge audiences and expand the boundaries of the art of filmmaking.

CONTACTS:
Sundance Institute
1825 Three Kings Dr.
P.O. Box 684429
Park City, UT 84060
435-658-3456; fax: 435-658-3457
www.sundance.org

◆ 2867 ◆ Sunday of Orthodoxy
First Sunday of Lent in the Christian Orthodox calendar

The first Sunday of Lent in the Christian Orthodox church commemorates the victory in the eighth century of the Orthodox over the iconoclasts, who denounced the use of icons and destroyed them. On this day, worshippers hear readings from the Syndicon, a text that declares the suitability of using icons in prayer and worship both public and private.

See also SUNDAY OF ST. GREGORY PALAMAS, SUNDAY OF THE HOLY CROSS, and SUNDAY OF ST. JOHN CLIMACOS.

CONTACTS:
Orthodox Church in America
6850 N. Hempstead Tpke
P.O. Box 675
Syosset, NY 11791
516-922-0550; fax: 516-922-0954
oca.org

◆ 2868 ◆ Sunday of St. Gregory Palamas
Second Sunday of Lent in the Christian Orthodox calendar

The Christian Orthodox church dedicates the second Sunday in Lent to St. Gregory Palamas, who was born in Constatinople around 1296 C.E. Along with several members of his family, he entered a monastery on Mt. Athos after the death of his father. Gregory believed that, although God ultimately is unknowable, humanity can experience God's power through the Christian sacraments and mystical experience, both of which are possible only through the Incarnation of Christ. Gregory believed that a dedicated focus on the son of God can open believers' hearts and minds to God's work in their own lives.

See also SUNDAY OF ORTHODOXY; SUNDAY OF THE HOLY CROSS; and SUNDAY OF ST. JOHN CLIMACOS.

CONTACTS:
Orthodox Church in America
6850 N. Hempstead Tpke
P.O. Box 675
Syosset, NY 11791
516-922-0550; fax: 516-922-0954
oca.org

♦ 2869 ♦ Sunday of St. John Climacos
Fourth Sunday in Lent in the Orthodox Christian calendar

Orthodox Christians dedicate the fourth Sunday of Lent to St. John Climacos, born in Syria in 525 C.E. Although surnamed Scholasticas, St. John often is called "Climacos," meaning "of the ladder." This refers to his most important holy writing, The Ladder of Divine Ascent, which details in 30 parts, or steps, all the Christian virtues. Employing many parables and historical touches drawn from monastic life, it is considered by many to be a cornerstone of literature of spiritual struggle and growth.

St. John was well educated, but chose to abandon scholarship for spirituality. John went to Mt. Sinai, which was known for its holy monks, to find a teacher. Under the guidance of a monk named Martyrius, he practiced Christian virtues. After his mentor's death, John retreated into isolation for 20 years, where he studied the lives of the saints and became one of the most learned men of the Church. At age 70, John was persuaded to become leader of a group of monks. His guidance was so effective and renowned that the pope, St. Gregory the Great, gave him a large sum of money for the hospital of Sinai, where many pilgrims stayed. After only four years in the leadership position, John returned to his hermit's life of spiritual contemplation.

See also SUNDAY OF ORTHODOXY; SUNDAY OF ST. GREGORY PALA- MAS; and SUNDAY OF THE HOLY CROSS.

♦ 2870 ♦ Sunday of St. Mary of Egypt
Fifth Sunday of Great Lent under the Orthodox moveable cycle, and also on April 1 under the fixed Orthodox cycle

The Sunday of St. Mary of Egypt is celebrated by Orthodox Christians on the fifth Sunday of Great Lent and also on April 1. St. Mary was a sinful, lustful woman who repented and became devout. She is seen as the least worthy person, but through God's mercy she became a treasure chosen by God. Among stories told about St. Mary, there is a tale of the time she attempted to enter a church in Jerusalem, but was driven back by an unseen force, although her companions entered without delay. This prompted Mary to open her heart and to pray to the mother of Jesus, the Virgin Mary. After she begged forgiveness, she again attempted to enter the holy place, and found that the same sort of force that previously had prevented her entry now propelled her forward. Mary of Egypt is also said to have retired to the desert to live as a hermit, having received a divine message to do so. Not long before she died, she encountered St. Zosimas of Palestine, a venerable monk who gave her a mantle to wear and who related her story to the faithful. St. Mary of Egypt is revered as a patron saint of penitent women.

On the fifth Sunday of Great Lent, St. Mary of Egypt is the subject of sermons during the Divine Liturgy. On this day, Orthodox priests typically bless dried fruit after the services.

CONTACTS:
Orthodox Church in America
6850 N. Hempstead Tpke
P.O. Box 675
Syosset, NY 11791
516-922-0550; fax: 516-922-0954
oca.org
Saint Mary of Egypt Orthodox Church
1765 Woodstock Rd.
Rosewell, GA 30075
770-640-1780
www.stmaryofegypt.org

♦ 2871 ♦ Sunday of the Holy Cross
Third Sunday of Lent under the Christian Orthodox calendar

On the third Sunday of Lent in the Orthodox Christian faith, believers are exhorted to contemplate the cross upon which Christ was crucified. It is day of extensive fasting and deep prayer. Meditation on the Holy Cross calls upon believers to consider their own mortality, but more importantly, to consider Christ in his passion and subsequent resurrection.

See also SUNDAY OF ORTHODOXY; SUNDAY OF ST. GREGORY PALA- MAS; and SUNDAY OF ST. JOHN CLIMACOS.

CONTACTS:
Orthodox Church in America
P.O. Box 675
Syosset, NY 11791
516-922-0550; fax: 516-922-0954
oca.org

♦ 2872 ♦ Sunday School Day
First Sunday in May

In the Polynesian kingdom of Tonga, a group of islands whose inhabitants are primarily Methodist, the first Sunday in May is known as **Faka Me**, or Sunday School Day. The children rise early and bathe in the sea, after which they put on the new clothes that their mothers have made: *valas*, or kilts, for the boys and new dresses for the girls. Then they all go to church, where the youngest children sing a hymn or recite a verse of scripture in front of the congregation and the older children present biblical dramas.

At the feast that always follows a church service, the children sit on mats spread on the ground. A variety of Polynesian specialties—including roast pig, lobster, chicken, and fish steamed in coconut milk, and potato-like vegetables called *ufi*—are served to the children by the adults on long trays made of woven coconut fronds known as *volas*. The parents stand behind their children and fan them to keep them cool as they eat.

Sunday School Day is observed in various ways by Protestant children in other countries as well.

See also WHITE SUNDAY.

♦ 2873 ♦ Sundiata, Festival
Third weekend in February

Held each year since 1981, the Festival Sundiata is a celebration of African-American heritage, culture, arts, and history held at Seattle Center in Seattle, Wash., during the third weekend of February. Admission to the festival is free, and events are spread over four days, from Thursday through the Monday holiday celebrating WASHINGTON'S BIRTHDAY. Festival Sundiata draws approximately 50,000 participants from the Pacific Northwest.

The fair is named in honor of Sundiata Keita, a historic king of the Mali Empire in West Africa, whose 13th-century reign is remembered as a time of great cultural and economic achievement. Organized by the Sundiata African American Cultural Association, the festival emphasizes entertainment, art, and education. Activities include music, percussion, and dance performances, lectures, storytelling, cooking demonstrations, and interactive craft exhibits, such as mask making. Festival Sundiata also features an art exhibition showcasing black artists in various media, including painting, sculpture, textiles, photography, and multimedia, which remains open to the public during the week following the festival.

CONTACTS:
Sundiata African American Cultural Association
P.O. Box 24723
Seattle, WA 98124
866-505-6006; fax: 206-420-6184
www.festivalsundiata.org

♦ 2874 ♦ Super Bowl Sunday
Usually last Sunday in January

The day of the championship game of the National Football League, which marks the culmination of the American professional football season. The game is played at a preselected site, always either a warm-weather city or one with a covered stadium. The contestants are the winners from each of the league's two divisions, the American Football Conference and the National Football Conference.

The first game was played on Jan. 15, 1967, in the Los Angeles Coliseum; the Green Bay Packers beat the Kansas City Chiefs by a score of 35-10. Since then, the games have been identified by Roman numerals (e.g., Super Bowl II in 1968), and, in keeping with this pretension, are surrounded by hoopla reminiscent of Roman imperial excess. Fans vie for Super Bowl tickets, and corporations woo clients with lavish Super Bowl trips.

Nationwide, the day is celebrated with at-home parties to watch the game on television, and many, many people watch: about 40 million viewers in the U.S. out of about 800 million around the world tune in to the Super Bowl. At sports bars, fans gather to watch wall-sized television screens, drink beer, and cheer.

CONTACTS:
National Football League
345 Park Ave.
New York, NY 10154 United States
212-450-2000; fax: 212-681-7573
www.nfl.com

♦ 2875 ♦ Superman Celebration
June

Since 1978 the town of Metropolis, Ill., celebrates the popular D.C. Comics hero Superman with an annual event. According to his comic book adventures, Superman lives in the city of "Metropolis," which is usually taken to be New York. But Metropolis, Illinois, argues otherwise and celebrates the character as a hometown boy. A 15-foot bronze statue of the character stands in the town's Superman Square.

The four-day Superman Celebration features appearances by artists and writers who create the Superman comic books and actors from various television series, including the 1950s Superman series and the more recent "Smallville" series, which chronicles the adventures of Superman as a boy. An outdoor film festival includes documentaries about the superhero and screenings of his movies and television programs. In addition, a comics art gallery, a Jeopardy-style quiz game featuring Superman trivia questions, a Superdog contest, a superhero parade, and live music round out the festivities. The town's Super Museum, housing the world's largest collection of Superman-related items, hosts a memorabilia auction and dinner.

CONTACTS:
Super Museum
517 Market St.
Metropolis, IL 62960
618-524-5518
www.supermuseum.com

Metropolis Tourism Commission
516 Market St.
Metropolis, IL 62960
877-424-5025; fax: 618-524-4780
www.supermancelebration.net

♦ 2876 ♦ Suriname Independence Day
November 25

Suriname had been under Dutch control for more than 200 years when it gained independence on this day in 1975, which is observed as a national holiday.

CONTACTS:
Embassy of the Republic of Suriname
4301 Connecticut Ave. N.W.
Ste. 460
Washington, D.C. 20008
202-244-7488; fax: 202-244-5878
www.surinameembassy.org

♦ 2877 ♦ Surya Sashti
October-November; sixth day of the waxing half of the Hindu month of Kartika

The observance of Surya Sashti includes a three-day fast for married Hindu women with children. They must abstain even from drinking water, and yet they must make offerings of food and water as they worship Surya, the sun god, and keep an all-night vigil.

On the following day, women bathe before sunrise, worship the rising sun, and break their fast. Brahmans, who are members of the highest Hindu class, are fed and given gifts on this day. Hindu women believe that by keeping the fast and observing the festival's other rules, they will be guaranteed good health, longevity, and the happiness of their children and husbands.

CONTACTS:
Shri Surya Narayan Mandir Inc.
92-17 172 St.
Jamaica, Queens
New York, NY 11433 United States
347-809-4373
www.shrisuryanarayanmandir.org

♦ 2878 ♦ Susuharai (Soot Sweeping)
December 13

In Japan, many people choose to give their houses a thorough cleaning at year's end. Worn or broken furniture and utensils and items that have been lost are replaced. New *tatami* mats, which are the thick straw mats on which people sit and sleep, are brought in, and damage to the paper sliding doors in traditional Japanese houses is repaired. In some areas, it is customary to tie pounded rice cakes (*mochi-bana*, "rice-cake flowers") to the branches of willow trees as an offering to the gods. Friends and co-workers may also throw "year-end forgetting parties" known as *bonen-kai*.

♦ 2879 ♦ Svenskarnas Dag
Fourth Sunday in June

One of the largest festivals in the United States celebrating the traditions of a specific ethnic group, Svenskarnas Dag honors the Swedish heritage of the people of Minneapolis, Minnesota, and the longest day of the year. When the festival first started in 1934 it was observed in August, but in 1941 the day was changed to the fourth Sunday in June so that it would coincide with midsummer observances in Sweden (*see* MIDSUMMER DAY).

Held in Minnehaha Park in Minneapolis, the festival includes a band concert, Swedish folk dancing, choral group performances, and the crowning of a Midsummer Queen. A national celebrity of Swedish descent is often asked to officiate at this one-day event, which attracts more than 100,000 visitors each year.

CONTACTS:
Svenskarnas Dag Committee
5008 38th Ave. S.
Minneapolis, MN 55417
612-825-8808; fax: 612-825-8808
www.svenskarnasdag.com

♦ 2880 ♦ Svetitskhovloba
July 13 and October 14

Built in the 11th century, the Svetitskhoveli Cathedral is located in the historical town of Mtskheta in Georgia. It is one of the principal worship sites of the Georgian Orthodox faith and the place where many local monarchs have been crowned and laid to rest. It has also inspired a major Georgian Orthodox holiday, Svetitskhovloba, which is celebrated two days of the year.

Svetitskhovloba pays homage to this cathedral, whose name means "Life Giving Pillar," as well as to the relic that it is believed to hold: the cloak of Christ, or as believers call it, the "Tunic of God." During the holiday, Christians gather for collective prayer in the cathedral and to remember the Twelve Apostles. Then, for the day's main ceremony, pilgrims from Georgia and other nearby countries congregate for a mass baptism at the junction of the Aragvi and Kura rivers. Children as well as adults are baptized.

The first observance of the year, on July 13, arrives the day after the Georgian celebration of STS. PETER AND PAUL DAY. The second observance, on October 14, is also known as **Mtskhetoba** (Day of Mtskheta).

CONTACTS:
Patriarchate of Georgia
1 Erekle II's Sq.
Georgia
995-2299-0378; fax: 995-2298-7114
www.patriarchate.ge

♦ 2881 ♦ Swallow, Procession of the
March 1

The Procession of the Swallow takes place in Greece on March 1 as a celebration of the arrival of spring. Children go from house to house in pairs, carrying a rod from which a basket full of ivy leaves is hung. At the end of the rod is an effigy of a bird made of wood with tiny bells around its neck. This is the "swallow," the traditional harbinger of spring.

As they proceed through the village, the children sing "swallow songs" that go back more than 2,000 years. The woman of the house takes a few ivy leaves from the basket and places them in her hen's nest in the hope that they will encourage the hen to produce more eggs. The children receive a few eggs in return, and they move on to the next house. The ivy, which is green all year round, is symbolic of growth and fertility, and it is believed to have the power to bring good health to hens and other animals.

♦ 2882 ♦ Swallows of San Juan Capistrano
March 19 and October 23

San Juan Capistrano was the name of a mission built on the Pacific Coast by Father Junipero Serra in 1777. Even after the buildings collapsed in an earthquake 35 years later, thousands of swallows continued to nest in the ruins of the church. Local people noticed that the swallows tended to fly south on October 23, the death anniversary of St. John of Capistrano, and returned on March 19, ST. JOSEPH'S DAY.

Beginning in 1940, the sentimental love song "When the Swallows Come Back to Capistrano" (words and music by Leon René) was recorded by a variety of artists. This brought attention to the event and media attention further made it known. A Swallow Festival is held each year at the mission in San Juan Capistrano near Los Angeles, California, around the time of the birds' return. Also known as the **Fiesta de las Golondrinas**, it features what is billed as the largest non-motorized parade in the country. In addition to the Swallow Festival, the Mission hosts various cultural and historic events throughout the year.

CONTACTS:
Mission San Juan Capistrano
26801 Ortega Hwy.
San Juan Capistrano, CA 92675
949-234-1300
www.missionsjc.com

San Juan Capistrano Civic Center
32400 Paseo Adelanto
San Juan Capistrano, CA 92675
949-493-1171; fax: 949-493-1053
www.sanjuancapistrano.net

♦ 2883 ♦ Swan Upping
Third week in July

The tradition of marking newborn swans goes back six centuries, to a time when most of the swans on England's public waters were owned by the queen. Later the members of two livery companies (trade guilds), the Company of Dyers and the Company of Vintners, were given the right to keep swans on the Thames River between London and Henley.

Every year since 1363, the Queen's swan master and the swan wardens of the two livery companies row up the Thames, starting at Blackfriars in the center of London and continuing upstream to Abingdon, and "up" all the swan families into the boats, where they are marked with identification numbers. There are very specific rules governing how ownership

is decided, and the six boats, each flying a large silk flag as they row up the river, form a procession that has changed little over the centuries.

CONTACTS:
British Monarchy Official Web Site
Public Information Office
Buckingham Palace
London, SW1A 1AA United Kingdom
44-20-7930-4832
www.royal.gov.uk

♦ 2884 ♦ Swarupa Dwadashi
December-January; twelfth day of the waning half of the Hindu month of Pausa

Swarupa Dwadashi is a fast observed by Hindu women in the month of December or January. On this day, Hindu women seek the blessings of Vishnu, one of three supreme deities in the Hindu pantheon, and participate in a fast that is meant to bestow beauty, happiness, and healthy children on the seeker. According to Hindu mythology, the goddess Parvathi empathized with women who lacked physical beauty, so Shiva told her that women could attain both beauty and happiness by fasting on the twelfth day of the waning phase of the moon.

On Swarupa Dwadashi, women offer special prayers and participate in rituals extolling Vishnu. *Homams*—offerings of dried cow dung burned in a consecrated fire—are performed at homes and temples, and it is customary to offer 108 oblations to the sacred fire on this day. At the culmination of the festival, Brahmans, who are regarded as the highest order of people in traditional Indian society, are fed and offered gifts. After the rituals are completed, women break their fasts.

CONTACTS:
Ministry of Tourism, Government of India
3550 Wilshire Blvd.
Ste. 204
Los Angeles, CA 90010
213-380-8855; fax: 213-380-6111
tourism.nic.in

♦ 2885 ♦ Swaziland Independence Day
September 6

Independence Day is a national holiday in Swaziland. On this day in 1968, Swaziland became self-governing after having been ruled by Britain since 1903. This national holiday was also known as **Somhlolo Day** or **Sobhuza Day**, named after Sobhuza II (1899-1982), king of Swaziland from 1921 until his death. In 1973, he disregarded the constitution passed upon independence and assumed supreme power.

CONTACTS:
Embassy of the United States, Mbabane Swaziland
7th Fl. Central Bank Bldg.
Mahlokohla St.
P.O. Box 199
Swaziland
268-404-6441; fax: 268-404-5959
swaziland.usembassy.gov

◆ 2886 ◆ Swedish Flag Day
June 6

Constitution and Flag Day commemorates the adoption of the Swedish constitution on June 6, 1809, and the ascension of Gustavus I to the throne on June 6, 1523. It is observed throughout Sweden with patriotic meetings, parades, and the raising of flags. In Stockholm the main celebration takes place at the Stadium, where the Swedish national anthem is sung by a chorus of several thousand voices, and King Carl XVI Gustav awards flags to various schools, sports clubs, and other organizations. In the evening the celebration continues at Skansen, the oldest open-air museum in Europe.

CONTACTS:
Government Offices of Sweden
Rosenbad 4
Stockholm, SE-103 33 Sweden
46-8-405-1000
www.government.se

Stiftelsen Skansen
Box 27807
Stockholm, 11593 Sweden
46-8-442-8000
www.skansen.se

◆ 2887 ◆ Swedish Homage Festival
Second weekend in October in odd-numbered years

Svensk Hyllningsfest, or the Swedish Homage Festival, is a biennial event held for three days during the second week in October in Lindsborg, Kansas. It honors the Swedish pioneers who first settled the area and celebrates the heritage of Lindsborg's Swedish-American population. More than 50,000 people attend the festival, which started in 1941 and is now held only in odd-numbered years.

Events include a parade; Swedish folk dancing, singing, and band music; Swedish arts and crafts displays; and a huge *smörgasbord,* or hot and cold buffet.

CONTACTS:
Svensk Hyllningsfest
P.O. Box 323
Lindsborg, KS 67456
www.svenskhyllningsfest.org

◆ 2888 ◆ Sweetest Day
Third Saturday in October

More than 40 years ago, a man from Cleveland came up with the idea of showing the city's orphans and shut-ins that they hadn't been forgotten by distributing small gifts to them on a Saturday in October. Over the years, other Clevelanders took up the idea of spreading cheer not only to the underprivileged but to everyone. The celebration of what came to be called Sweetest Day soon spread to Detroit and other American cities.

This holiday is unusual in that it is not based on any one group's religious beliefs or on a family relationship. Because it falls midway between FATHER'S DAY and CHRISTMAS, however, it has come to be regarded as a merchandising opportunity. Although it is still supposed to be an occasion to remember others with a kind act, a word of encouragement, or a long-overdue letter, local merchants in cities where Sweetest Day is observed usually get together and promote the day as a time to purchase gifts.

◆ 2889 ◆ Sweetwater Rattlesnake Round-Up
Second weekend in March

Billed "The World's Largest Rattlesnake Round-Up," this is one of several rattlesnake round-ups in Texas. It was started in 1958 by ranchers in Sweetwater to thin out the snakes plaguing them and their livestock, and now the average annual catch is 12,000 pounds of Western Diamondback Rattlesnake. Some 30,000 spectators watch the goings-on.

The round-up is sponsored by the Sweetwater Jaycees, who stress the focus on safety (hunters are governed by state hunting laws) and the benefits of the round-up. The round-up supports various Jaycee charitable causes.

The weekend events include snake-handling demonstrations and the awarding of prizes for the most pounds and the biggest snake. There are also a Miss Snake Charmer Queen Contest, a parade, rattlesnake dances with country bands, and a rattlesnake meat-eating contest. A cook shack fries and serves more than 4,000 pounds of rattlesnake meat each year.

Other Texas rattlesnake round-ups are held from February through April in Cleburne, Brownwood, Big Spring, San Angelo, Jacksboro, Gainesville, and Freer. A number of other southern states also have rattlesnake round-ups.

In recent years, state departments of natural resources and conservation organizations have warned of the health risks of eating rattlesnakes caught at round-ups. In addition, the Humane Society has condemned the cruelty to snakes during these events and argues that rattlesnakes actually present relatively little danger to livestock—and that holding round-ups increases the chances that humans will be bitten.

CONTACTS:
Sweetwater Texas Chamber of Commerc
810 E. Broadway St.
Sweetwater, TX 79556
325-235-5488; fax: 325-235-1026
sweetwatertexas.org

◆ 2890 ◆ Swiss National Day
August 1

A nationwide celebration of the Swiss Confederation, observed with torchlight processions, fireworks, shooting contests, and folkloric events. The day commemorates the occasion in 1291 when representatives of the three original cantons of Schwyz, Uri, and Unterwalden met on the Rutli meadow and swore an oath of alliance and mutual defense to lay the foundations of the Confederation.

In 1991, yearlong 700th-anniversary festivities set different themes for the different language areas. A celebration of the Federal Pact of 1291 was the theme for the German-speaking region; a Four Cultures Festival, demonstrating cultural diversity, for the French-speaking region; and a Festival of Solidarity, illustrating Switzerland's role in the international community, in the Romansh- and Italian-speaking areas.

CONTACTS:
Embassy of Switzerland
2900 Cathedral Ave. N.W.
Washington, D.C. 20008
202-745-7900; fax: 202-387-2564
www.eda.admin.ch

♦ 2891 ♦ SXSW (South by Southwest)
March

SXSW, also known as **South by Southwest**, is a ten-day event comprised of three concurrent festivals that take place in Austin, Texas. The inaugural South by Southwest Music and Media Conference was held in 1987. Organizers hoped to create an event to draw artists and music industry professionals from around the country to Austin, giving local musicians the opportunity to perform for a wider audience. The performances would take place in the context of a conference atmosphere, providing a forum for discussion about music industry issues and trends and a network to help participating artists build their careers. Austin's eclectic musical history and vibrant music nightclub scene helped the event capture national attention immediately, with 700 participants taking part in the first year. By the second year, the festival was receiving applications from artists and conference participants from around the world. Combining musical performances with lectures, panel discussions, and a trade show and expo, the music conference now attracts 28,000 attendees each year, including over 2000 local, national, and international musical acts performing on 100 stages throughout downtown Austin. SXSW is known as one of the largest music conferences of its kind in the world.

In 1994, the festival added two additional conferences to the slate of events: the film festival SXSW FILM, and SXSW Interactive (formerly SXSW Multimedia) focusing on emerging technologies. Both events follow the same model as the music festival, combining conference events with artistic performance; together the Film and Interactive events attract over 50,000 participants every year.

CONTACTS:
SXSW, LLC
P.O. Box 685289
Austin, TX 78768
512-467-7979
sxsw.com

♦ 2892 ♦ SXSW (South by Southwest) Film
March

SXSW (South by Southwest) Film is an annual, international festival held for nine days in Austin, Texas. It provides a forum for new talent in filmmaking and creates a supportive community for artists to share their ideas. The event brings together many in the movie industry, including filmmakers, screenwriters, actors, film crews, and distributors. The festival features a range of programming, from documentaries to comedies. The event also includes an intensive, five-day conference on filmmaking and movie marketing. In addition, the conference features workshops, keynote addresses, mentorship activities, and group sessions led by industry experts. The festival concludes with an awards night, which includes prizes for poster and title design, audience choice prizes, and various other special commendations. Many of Austin's venues screen movies during SXSW, such as the Paramount Theater, Vimeo Theatre, Topfer Theater, and Stateside Theater. Shuttle services connect many of the venues and most are within walking distance of each other. There are also satellite screenings at other theaters in Austin during the festival.

CONTACTS:
SXSW, LLC
P.O. Box 685289
Austin, TX 78768
512-467-7979
sxsw.com

♦ 2893 ♦ Sydney Festival
January

The Sydney Festival reflects the culture of the city of Sydney, Australia. The festival was established in 1977 by the Sydney Committee, the NSW State Government, and the City of Sydney. It takes place from the second week to the final week of January every year. The Festival is the largest of Sydney's annual cultural celebrations, drawing more than 500,000 people for free events and over 200,000 people for ticketed events. It takes place in more than 30 venues in and around the city, including the Sydney Opera House and Town Hall.

Many forms of entertainment comprise the Sydney festival, including music, theater, dance, opera, circus, and cabaret. One can also find a range of family-oriented events and installations. Popular international artists from across the globe contribute to the high caliber of talent on display. The festival also provides opportunities for Australian artists to premiere their works, and it encompasses contemporary as well as traditional performances. Special events of the festival include the Parramatta Opening Party at Centenary Square, a disco at the Information and Cultural Exchange, a circus, a dance at the Riverside Theaters, and more.

CONTACTS:
Sydney Festival Office
Level 5, 10 Hickson Rd.
The Rocks, NSW 2000 Australia
61-2-8248-6500; fax: 61-2-8248-6599
www.sydneyfestival.org.au

♦ 2894 ♦ **Sydney Film Festival**
June

Beginning in 1954, the Sydney Film Festival brings the best in new, international cinema to Australia. Held over a span of 12 days, this annual event is one of the world's longest-running celebrations of the medium. Its lineup includes features, shorts, documentaries, animation, and retrospectives. Audiences are treated to over 250 screenings at various venues across Sydney's central business district. For its first 50 years the festival was not competitive. However, in 2007 the New South Wales government funded an official international competition, and the festival now presents many awards across various categories. The festival also features the annual Travelling Film Festival (TFF), which provides an opportunity to screen national and international features, shorts, and documentaries in over 20 locations across Australia.

CONTACTS:
Sydney Film Festival
Level 2, 10 Hickson Rd.
The Rocks, NSW 2000 Australia
612-8220-6600; fax: 612-9252-7596
www.sff.org.au

♦ 2895 ♦ **Sydney Gay and Lesbian Mardi Gras**
Late February to early March

The Sydney Gay and Lesbian Mardi Gras is an annual parade and two-week festival to celebrate Lesbian, Gay, Bisexual, Transgender (LGBT) pride. Produced by the Sydney Gay and Lesbian Mardi Gras organization, the event originally grew out of the gay rights marches of the late 1970s.

The Mardi Gras Parade is the highlight event of the festival, attracting thousands of marchers in colourful costumes to walk along the 1.1-mile route. Numerous floats are exhibited in the parade, along with fireworks displays. Another important festival event is Fair Day, a picnic-like celebration for people of all ages that takes place in Victoria Park.

CONTACTS:
Sydney Gay and Lesbian Mardi Gras
94 Oxford St.
Ste. 6
Darlinghurst, NSW 2010 Australia
61-2-9383-0900; fax: 61-2-9383-0966
www.mardigras.org.au

♦ 2896 ♦ **Syria Martyrs' Day**
May 6

In 1916, a meeting of Arab intellectuals in Paris called for the liberation of all Arab countries from Turkish rule. In response, Turkish Sultan Abdul Hamid appointed Jamal Pasha the governor of Damascus. Jamal Pasha ordered mass arrests of dissidents. When a group of Syrian nationalists refused to renounce their views, they were hanged in al-Murjeh square in Damascus on May 6, 1916. The executions sparked Arab resistance throughout the Ottoman Empire. An Arab army led by Sharif Hussein of Mecca soon defeated the Turks. The Ottoman Empire collapsed at the end of World War I.

To commemorate the heroic event, the Syrian president lays a wreath at the martyrs' monument at Qasyoun Mountain. The president hosts a banquet in the evening for the children of the Syrian martyrs. The day is celebrated with fireworks, parades, military air shows, and speeches.

CONTACTS:
Embassy of United State of America
Mansur Str. No. 2
Rawda
Abu Rumaneh, Damascus Syria
963-3391-444; fax: 963-3391-3999
www.syriatourism.org

♦ 2897 ♦ **Syria National Day**
April 17

This national holiday commemorates the withdrawal of French troops on this day in 1946, when Syria proclaimed its independence after more than 20 years of French occupation. It is also known as **Independence Day** and **Evacuation Day**.

CONTACTS:
Syrian Consulate in Sydney, Australia
Level 1, 366B Darling St.
Balmain, NSW 2041 Australia
61-2-9818-3087; fax: 61-2-9818-1360
www.syrianembassy.org.au/english

♦ 2898 ♦ **Syttende Mai Fest**
Weekend nearest May 17

Norway Constitution Day is celebrated each year by descendants of Norwegian immigrants who first settled in Spring Grove, Minnesota. The town, incorporated in 1889, was the first Norse settlement in Minnesota, and the Norwegian language can still be heard in the town's streets and cafes. The Syttende Mai Fest offers ethnic foods, folk music and costumes, a show of traditional Norwegian arts and crafts, and a grand parade led by the "King of Trolls." Young children dressed as creatures known as *Nisse* roam the streets during the festival, wearing green caps and playing tricks on people. Unlike the trolls, who thrive on darkness and are known for making things go wrong, the Nisse bring luck and help out with household tasks. During the festival, the store windows often feature displays with trolls or Nisse peeking out.

Other Minnesota towns celebrating Syttende Mai with special festivities include Hendricks, Milan, Wahkon, and Willmar. Syttende Mai is celebrated by Norwegian communities in other states as well. The celebration in Stoughton, Wisconsin, takes place on the weekend nearest May 17 and features folk dancing, a Norwegian smorgasbord, and demonstrations of *rosemaling* (painted or carved floral designs) and *hardanger* (a form of pulled thread embroidery).

CONTACTS:
Stoughton Chamber of Commerce

532 E. Main St.
Stoughton, WI 53589
608-873-7912 or 888-873-7912; fax: 608-873-7743
www.stoughtonwi.com

♦ 2899 ♦ Szüret

Late October

Since wine is the national drink of the Hungarian people, the Szüret, or **Grape Gathering**, is a time for great celebration. In fact, many peasant marriages take place after this yearly festival. As they have done since ancient times, the grape gatherers make an enormous "bouquet" out of grapes and two men carry it on a pole in procession to the vineyard own-er's home, accompanied by musicians, clowns, and young girls dressed in white wearing flower wreaths on their heads. When they reach their destination, they hang the cluster of grapes from the ceiling and accept the vineyard owner's invitation to join in the feasting and dancing.

A traditional game known as "robber" is often played during the festival, either as the grapes are being gathered or during the dancing that takes place later. While several men guard the bouquet of grapes, the others try to steal the fruit off the vines. Anyone who gets caught is dragged before a mock judge and forced to pay a penalty—usually by performing a song, a solo dance, or a pantomime while his companions make fun of him.

T

♦ 2900 ♦ **Ta Chiu**
December 27

Ta Chiu is an annual Taoist festival celebrated in Hong Kong. Originating around the late-19th century, the three-day event centers on bringing peace, health, and renewed life to the community. A particularly important aspect of Ta Chiu is the elaborate ceremony performed by Taoist priests for the "Three Pure Ones"—the Gods, Ghosts, and Pure Spirits. The ritual is said to cure ailments and offer protection and spiritual renewal. Before the festival begins, home altars and temples are sanctified and people take baths, wear clean clothes, and abstain from meat and sex. During Ta Chiu, the faithful offer prayers to various idols and shrines. In celebration of the spirit of renewal, live birds and fish are released from captivity, and priests go door-to-door collecting unwanted items, which are placed in a large paper boat and set afire. In addition, people's names are written on pieces of paper and attached to a paper horse, which is burned in the belief that the names will reach heaven. At midnight, after the various ceremonies have concluded, a communal feast is enjoyed. In more recent times, the festival has become somewhat less religious, with towns organizing celebrations featuring Chinese operas and carnivals.

♦ 2901 ♦ **Ta Mo's Day**
Fifth day of 10th lunar month

Ta Mo (or Bodhidharma) was a sixth-century Indian monk who founded the Ch'an school of Buddhism in China, known in Japan as Zen Buddhism. Information about his historical existence is quite sketchy. But he is said to have believed that the Law of Buddha could only be understood through contemplation, without the aid of books or rituals. According to legend, he spent nine years meditating in front of a cave wall, during which time his legs fell off. The Japanese, to whom he is known as DARUMA, have a legless doll, constructed in such a way that no matter how it is placed on the ground, it always returns to a sitting position.

There is another legend that Ta Mo cut off his eyelids in a fit of anger after falling asleep during meditation. When they fell to the ground, his eyelids took root and grew up as the first tea plant. This legend is the basis for the practice among Zen monks of drinking tea to stay awake during meditation. Members of the Ch'an (or Zen) sect of Buddhism observe the fifth day of the 10th month as Ta Mo's Day. People in Japan customarily give Daruma dolls to those who have worked hard to achieve a goal.

CONTACTS:
USA Shaolin Temple
446 Broadway
2nd Fl.
New York, NY 10013
212-358-7876; fax: 212-358-7879
www.usashaolintemple.org

CloudWater Zendo
14436 Puritas Ave.
Cleveland, OH 44135
216-889-1393
www.cloudwater.org

♦ 2902 ♦ **Ta'anit Esther (Fast of Esther)**
Between February 13 and March 13; Adar 13

The **Fast of Esther** commemorates the three days that Queen Esther fasted before petitioning her husband, King Ahasuerus (Xerxes I) of Persia, to spare the Jews of her country from destruction by Haman, the Persian prime minister, in the sixth century B.C.E. (*See* PURIM.)

Ordinarily observed on the 13th day of the Jewish month of Adar, Ta'anit Esther is observed on the preceding Thursday (Adar 11) when Adar 13 falls on the Sabbath.

This date was originally a minor festival commemorating Judah Maccabee's defeat of the Syrian general Nicanor, known as the "Day of Nicanor." In time it gave way to the present Fast of Esther.

CONTACTS:
Orthodox Union
11 Broadway
New York, NY 10004
212-563-4000
www.ou.org

♦ 2903 ♦ **Tabuleiros Festival (Festa dos Tabuleiros)**
Four days in mid-July every third year

The town of Tomar in Portugal has been celebrating the Tabuleiros ("headdresses") Festival for 600 years as a way of expressing gratitude for the harvest and charity for the poor. The highlight of the festival is the procession through town of hundreds of girls in traditional headdresses selected from Tomar and the surrounding communities.

The foundation of the headdress, which weighs about 33 pounds and must be at least as tall as the girl who carries it, is a round basket covered with a linen cloth. An elaborate framework of bamboo sticks and wires holds up 30 small loaves of bread arranged in five rows. Flowers made of colored paper disguise the wires and the entire structure is topped with a white dove or Maltese cross. The priest blesses the bread, and the girls keep their tabuleiros for the entire year to ward off sickness. This is also a time for making donations to the poor and the afflicted.

CONTACTS:
Turismo de Portugal, I.P.
Rua Ivone Silva, Lote 6
Lisbon, 1050-124 Portugal
351-211-140-200; fax: 351-211-140-830
www.visitportugal.com

♦ 2904 ♦ **Taeborum (Daeboreum)**
February; 15th day of the first lunar month

Taeborum marks the first full moon of the LUNAR NEW YEAR in Korea (*see* SOL) and is at least as important as that holiday. Many customs and games are traditional on this day, which is also sometimes called the Great Fifteenth. The Fifteenth, or Full Moon Day, marks the end of the New Year season in Korea and is regarded as the final opportunity to ensure good luck for the coming year. It is considered lucky on this day for people to routinely repeat their actions nine times—particularly children, who compete with each other to see how many "lucky nines" they can achieve before the day is over.

It is common to celebrate the Great Fifteenth with kite flying and kite fighting, which is done by covering the strings with glass dust and then crossing them so that they rub together as they fly. The string held by the more skillfully manipulated kite eventually cuts through the string of the less successful kite, sending it crashing to the ground.

Another popular sport on this day is the tug-of-war. In some areas, an entire town or county is divided into two opposing teams. It is widely believed that the winners will bring in a plentiful crop and will be protected from disease in the coming year.

See also BRIDGE WALKING; BURNING THE MOON HOUSE; SPIRIT BURYING; TORCH FIGHT.

CONTACTS:
Korea Foundation
67 Suha-dong, Jung-gu
19th Fl., Mirae Asset CENTER1
Bldg. W. Tower
Seoul, 100-759 Korea
82-2-2151-6546; fax: 82-2-2151-6592
www.koreana.or.kr

♦ 2905 ♦ **Tagore (Rabindranath), Birthday of**
May 7

This date commemorates the birth of Rabindranath Tagore (1861-1941), the great poet, philosopher, social reformer, dramatist, and musician of Calcutta, India. Born into a family of painters, writers, and musicians, Tagore possessed talents for all those creative professions. In 1913, he was the first non-European to win the NOBEL PRIZE for literature. The Tagore family has been important in India's cultural history from the 19th century and is especially revered in Calcutta. Rabindranath Tagore's birthday is celebrated with a festival of his poetry, plays, music, and dance dramas. There are discussions at schools and universities of his ideas on education and philosophy, and screenings of films based on Tagore's short stories and novels made by filmmaker and Calcutta native, Satyajit Ray.

CONTACTS:
Ministry of Culture India
322- C Wing Shastri Bhawan,
New Delhi, New Delhi 110115 India
91-11-23381431
rabindranathtagore-150.gov.in

♦ 2906 ♦ **Taiiku-no-Hi**
October 10

Taiiku-no-Hi, or **Health-Sports Day**, is a national legal holiday in Japan set aside to promote good physical and emotional health through athletic activity. Since 1966 it has been observed on the anniversary of the first day of the OLYMPIC GAMES held in Tokyo in 1964.

♦ 2907 ♦ **Tailte Fair (Teltown Fair)**
Mid-July to mid-August

Tailte was the foster mother of Lugh, an ancient Celtic god and patron of fairs. The Tailte (or Teltown) Fair, held in ancient Ireland for more than 2,000 years, was an early harvest festival in which the first fruits of the harvest were sacrificed to the spirit of Tailte, who was further honored by funeral games. Each chieftain brought his best athletes—runners, jumpers, spear throwers, and horsemen—as well as his harpists and poets and storytellers, who competed like the athletes for prizes of gold rings and jeweled ornaments. The Tailteann Games, as they were known, were last held in 1169, and the Irish have since revived them. The fair itself lasted until 1806.

See also LUGHNASADH.

♦ 2908 ♦ **Taiwan Armed Forces Day**
September 3

Founded in 1955, Armed Forces Day in Taiwan honors that country's military and celebrates their victory over the Japanese in World War II. Called in Taiwan the War of Resistance, that struggle actually began before World War II when Japan invaded the Chinese mainland.

The day is marked by military parades featuring special units chosen for their precision and outstanding performance. A troop-cheering by the onlookers is also part of the celebration, as are educational activities covering the history of the war period and the role played by the Taiwanese military in defeating the enemy. A speech is delivered by the national defense minister in which he honors those soldiers who fought in the War of Resistance and their surviving families. The day is also marked by the members of the armed forces having a rare day off from work.

CONTACTS:
Taipei Economic and Cultural Representative Office
4201 Wisconsin Ave. N.W.
Washington, D.C. 20016
202-895-1800
www.taiwanembassy.org

♦ 2909 ♦ Taiwan Peace Memorial Day
February 28

Following the end of World War II, the island of Taiwan won independence from Japan, and the Chinese Nationalist government officially took over the island. On February 28, 1947, misunderstandings between the new government and the native residents led to an uprising that was brutally suppressed. A period known as the White Terror ensued, in which thousands of Taiwanese were killed or imprisoned. For years, the period was never discussed in public, and official textbooks did not mention it. But in 1995, President Lee Teng-hui made a formal apology for the incident. Since then, other steps have been taken to heal the wounds. The February 28 Incident Memorial Foundation was founded to compensate victims and their families and to restore the good names of those who were wrongly accused.

February 28 has been named Peace Memorial Day and is marked by memorial services for the victims, concerts, art exhibitions, and group runs. Taiwan's president attends a ceremony in which he rings a ceremonial bell, bows to the victims' families, and hands them a certificate acknowledging that they are guilty of no crime. The day is also referred to as "228 Memorial Day" in reference to the original date of the 28th day of the second month: 2/28.

CONTACTS:
Taipei Economic and Cultural Representative Office
4201 Wisconsin Ave. N.W.
Washington, D.C. 20016
202-895-1800
www.taiwanembassy.org

♦ 2910 ♦ Tajikistan Day of National Unity
June 27

On June 27, 1997, a treaty was signed between Islamic rebels and the Russian-backed Tajikistan government, bringing to an end a bloody five-year-long civil war. The day is remembered as the Day of National Unity.

To mark the one-year anniversary of the treaty, 100 members of the rebel group United Tajik Opposition were officially sworn in as members of the Tajik Army. On the Day of National Unity in 2007, the Tajik parliament passed a law granting amnesty to all rebels who had fought against the government, provided they had not committed murder, rape, human or drug trafficking, or terrorism. Some 2,000 prison inmates were released under the new law. The 2007 commemoration also marked the opening of 11 new buildings in the city of Dushanbe.

In a speech on the 16th anniversary of Tajikistan National Unity Day in 2013, President Emomali Rahmon congratulated the crowd gathered in the capital city of Dushanbe and invited all the people of Tajikistan to respect the values of unity, peace, tranquility, and stability, and to celebrate the prosperity of their country.

CONTACTS:
Embassy of the Republic of Tajikistan
1005 New Hampshire Ave. NW
Washington, D.C. 20037
202-223-6090; fax: 202-223-6091
www.tjus.org

♦ 2911 ♦ Tajikistan Independence Day
September 9

On September 9, 1991, Tajikistan officially declared its independence from the distintegrating Soviet Union. Independence Day is celebrated with parades, solomn services, theatrical events and pageantry. July 22 is another national holiday, celebrating the Tajik language.

CONTACTS:
Embassy of the Republic of Tajikistan
1005 New Hampshire Ave. N.W.
Washington, D.C. 20037 United States
202-223-6090; fax: 202-223-6091
www.tjus.org

♦ 2912 ♦ Takayama Matsuri
April 14-15 and October 9-10

Held twice a year in Japan, in the spring and the autumn, the Takayama Festival is famous for its elaborately decorated *yatai*, festival floats. These were first used at Kyoto's Gion Matsuri, and later appeared in other parts of the country. Twelve of these floats appear at the April festival, held at Takayama's Hié Shrine, and 11 participate in the October festival at the Sakuragaoka-hachimangu Shrine. They are so highly decorated—with beautiful fabrics, lacquered wood, and patterned metals—that they are often referred to as "Yomeimon in motion," a reference to the famous gate at the Toshogu Shrine in Nikko. Some yatai feature performances of *kabuki*, puppet plays, often performed by cleverly designed mechanical marionettes.

A highlight of the festival is the parade of metal gongs known as *tokeigaku*, which produce a unique kind of folk music. There is also a *Shishi-mai*, or Lion Dance, originally used by Japanese farmers to ward off wild boars and other animals that threatened their crops.

CONTACTS:
Japan National Tourism Organization
1 Grand Central Pl.
60 E. 42nd St
Ste. 448
New York, NY 10165
212-757-5640; fax: 212-307-6754
www.jnto.go.jp

♦ 2913 ♦ **Take Our Daughters to Work Day**
Fourth Thursday in April

Sponsored by the Ms. Foundation for Women since 1993, this is a day dedicated to girls between the ages of nine and 15, who are encouraged to go to work with their parents, grandparents, or other adults in their lives. The purpose is to support girls' development and to help them stay focused on their future during adolescence. Spending a day at work with an adult, it is hoped, will increase girls' interest in planning their own education and careers, and will inspire educators, employers, and parents to redress the inequalities in job opportunities for women.

CONTACTS:
Take Our Sons & Daughters to Work Foundation
209 E. Fearing St.
Ste 1
Elizabeth City, NC 27909
800-676-7780
www.daughtersandsonstowork.org

♦ 2914 ♦ **Také-no-Nobori**
Sunday near July 15

The origins of this rain festival go back to 1504, a year in which there was no rain all summer in what is now the Nagano Prefecture of Japan. Villagers appealed to their god and were rewarded with three days of rain in a row. Thankful, they made an offering to the god of two especially fine pieces of cloth, sufficient to make two kimonos.

Today people in Uedo City continue this tradition each year on a Sunday near July 15. People trek up to the shrine on Mount Ogamidake and offer pieces of homemade cloth to the god.

CONTACTS:
Japan National Tourism Organization
1 Grand Central Pl.
60 E. 42nd St.
Ste. 448
New York, NY 10165
212-757-5640; fax: 212-307-6754
www.jnto.go.jp/eng

City of Uedo, Citizens' Affairs Division
Ote 1-11-16, Nagano-ken
Ueda-shi, Nagano-ken 386-8601 Japan
81-2-6822-4100; fax: 81-2-6822-6023
www.city.ueda.nagano.jp

♦ 2915 ♦ **Tako-Age (Kite Flying)**
April, May, June

Kite-flying battles are a favorite sport in Japan, and numerous kite festivals take place in the spring. In the battles, the object is to cut down other kites by means of skillful maneuvering; broken glass embedded in the kite lines also helps.

The kite festivals of Nagasaki are held in April and May, with teams of as many as 20 people controlling colossal kites up to 25′ x 30′ in size.

In Hamamatsu in Shizuoka Prefecture, a kite festival is held on the beach May 3-5. It is thought to have originated in the mid-16th century when the lord of one of the fiefdoms celebrated the birth of a son by flying a giant kite. It is the biggest event now in the western region of the prefecture, with more than 1,000 kites sparring in the sky. Other festival events include parades of 50 floats in the evenings.

In Shirone in Niigata Prefecture, two teams on opposite banks of the Nakanokuchi River wage kite battles in mid-June. This festival supposedly dates back some 300 years when the people of one village accidentally crashed a huge kite onto a neighboring village.

CONTACTS:
Japan Kite Association
1-12-10 Nihonbashi
Chuoh-ku, Tokyo 103-0027 Japan
81-3-3275-2704; fax: 81-3-3273-0575
www.tako.gr.jp

♦ 2916 ♦ **Tallgrass Film Festival**
October

The Tallgrass Film Festival is a five-day film festival that takes place in Wichita, Kansas. It is the largest independent film festival in the state of Kansas and a hallmark of the cultural landscape of Wichita. The festival spotlights independent films that would otherwise not be screened in the region. The event is renowned in the independent filmmaking community, and filmmakers across the United States and around the world participate in it. In addition to screening more than 180 films from around the world, the festival features galas, filmmaker workshops, panels, and legendary parties. The festival is produced by the Tallgrass Film Association, which was founded by Kansas native Timothy Gruver. The first edition of the festival was held in 2003 by Gruver, who envisioned a festival along the lines of the Telluride Film Festival. He wanted to create a festival for the love of film and for the audience. Prior to the third edition of the festival in 2006, Gruver passed away, but his vision was continued by the Tallgrass Festival board members and remains strong.

CONTACTS:
Tallgrass Film Festival
212 N. Market
Wichita, KS 67206
316-303-9292
www.tallgrassfilmfest.com

♦ 2917 ♦ **Tam Kung Festival**
May; eighth day of fourth lunar month

A celebration of the birthday of the god Tam Kung is held at the Tam Kung Temple in Shau Kei Wan on Hong Kong Island. Like Tin Hau, Tam Kung is a popular deity among fisherfolk. He is a Taoist child-god, whose powers were apparent when he was only 12 years old. His greatest gift was controlling the weather, but he could also heal the sick and predict the future. Residents of the Shau Kei Wan area believe he saved many lives during an outbreak of cholera in 1967. His birthday is marked with a grand procession, Cantonese opera, and lion and dragon dances.

◆ 2918 ◆ Tammuz, Fast of the 17th of (Shivah Asar be-Tammuz)
Between June 17 and July 24; Tammuz 17

The **Fast of Tammuz** commemorates the breaching of the walls of Jerusalem in 586 B.C.E., when the Babylonians conquered Judah, destroyed the Temple, and carried most of the Jewish population off into slavery. But this destruction had a happy ending: after 70 years the people returned and rebuilt the Temple. Then the Roman army breached the walls of Jerusalem in the year 70 C.E., dooming both the city and its Temple for the second time. This time the destruction and the scattering of the people—known as the Diaspora—had a far more tragic finality. Jews remain scattered over the face of the earth to this day. Other sad events associated with this day are the shattering of the first Tablets of the Law by Moses, and the collapse of the sacrificial system caused by the Roman invasion in 70 C.E.

The Fast of Tammuz begins Three Weeks of mourning lasting until Tisha be-Av.

See also Asarah be-Tevet.

CONTACTS:
Orthodox Union
11 Broadway
New York, NY 10004
212-563-4000; fax: 212-564-9058
www.ou.org

◆ 2919 ◆ Tanabata (Star Festival)
July 7, August 6-8

This Japanese festival is based on a Chinese legend of parted lovers who are identified with two of the brightest stars in the night sky. In the legend, Vega, representing a weaver-princess, is permitted by the king to marry the simple cowherd, Altair. But after they marry, the princess neglects her weaving and the herdsman forgets his cows, so the king separates them, making them live on opposite sides of the River of Heaven, as the Milky Way is known in Japan. On the seventh day of the seventh month, the lovers are able to meet when a flock of magpies makes a bridge across the river. If it's rainy, the lovers have to wait another year.

The festival is observed throughout Japan, with people hanging colorful strips of paper on bamboo branches outside their homes. It is an especially colorful occasion in Sendai (Miyagi Prefecture), where it occurs a month later, on August 6-8. The whole city is decked out with paper streamers and works of origami, the Japanese art of paper folding.

See also Chilseog; Seven Sisters Festival.

CONTACTS:
Japan National Tourism Organization
1 Grand Central Pl.
60 E. 42nd St.
Ste. 448
New York, NY 10165
212-757-5640; fax: 212-307-6754
www.jnto.go.jp/eng

Sendai Tanabata Festival Support Association
2-16-12 Honcho
Aoba-ku
Sendai-shi, Miyagi 980-0014 Japan
81-22-265-8185
www.sendaitanabata.com

◆ 2920 ◆ Tangata Manu (Birdman Ceremony)
Spring

Sometime around the 14th century, different groups on Easter Island, also known as Rapanui, were at war with each other, perhaps over a lack of food caused by a mini ice age. Some scholars theorize that the islanders began the Tangata Manu, or *Manutara*, as a way of resolving their conflicts.

Each tribal chief would select a young man to compete with representatives from other tribes in an egg hunt. Each man swam to a nearby island in search of the first egg laid by a seabird known as a tern. This process could take as long as a month. The chief of the first one to swim back with the egg was called the "birdman" for the year.

Carvings of the Birdman—represented as a bird-headed man whose hand grasps an egg—can be found all over Easter Island.

◆ 2921 ◆ Tanglewood Music Festival
July-August

Tanglewood is a 210-acre estate donated in 1937 by Mrs. Gorham Brooks. Located in the Berkshire Mountains of western Massachusetts, it is the summer home of the Boston Symphony Orchestra. What was originally known as the Berkshire Festival started in 1936 and in 1940 became part of the Berkshire Music Center, now the Tanglewood Music Center, where advanced American and foreign musicians come to study and perform for nine weeks each summer.

The festival includes concerts by the Boston Symphony and the Berkshire Music Center Orchestra as well as chamber music, jazz, choral and vocal concerts, and music theater productions. In early August there is a Festival of Contemporary Music that focuses on new works, some of which have been specially commissioned for the festival.

The grounds at Tanglewood open about two hours prior to the concerts so people can picnic on the lawns. More than

350,000 people come to Tanglewood over the course of the festival each summer.

CONTACTS:
Boston Symphony Orchestra
297 W. St.
Lenox, MA 01240
413-637-1600
www.bso.org

♦ 2922 ♦ Tango Festival
Late February-early March

Historians say tango evolved as a dance form in Buenos Aires, Argentina, toward the end of the 19th century. It is thus fitting that the city would host a festival devoted to the dance. Since 1999, the Tango Festival has invited aficionados to immerse themselves in the step routines of this romantic art form.

Dance performances are the centerpiece of the festival, which is popular among natives as well as tourists. Typically, on the last Friday of February a performance at *La Selección Nacional de Tango* will launch the festival; then, for the next nine days events are held at multiple locations, including concert halls, clubs, and *barrios*.

The festival does not restrict itself to dance performances, however. Past festivals have featured original musical pieces performed by musical troupes from neighboring countries as well as from Europe. There are also photo exhibits, classes, and a trade fair offering tango records, books, and clothing and accessories.

CONTACTS:
Buenos Aires Convention & Visitors Bureau
Pabellón Ocre, 1° Piso, Oficina 5
Juncal, 04431 Argentina
5411-4777-5930
www.buenosairesbureau.com

♦ 2923 ♦ Tango-no-Sekku (Boys' Day Festival)
May 5

The Boys' Day Festival in Japan dates back to the Tokugawa period (1603-1867). For centuries, Japanese farmers had frightened off harmful insects by hanging brightly colored banners and scary figurines in their fields. These later came to resemble warriors and rather than being placed in the fields, they were kept in the house to encourage young boys to imitate samurai warriors' courage—a practice approved by that era's rulers. In the latter part of the 18th century, people decided that the indoor display wasn't enough, and they started flying tubular wind-socks in the form of carp from poles outside their houses. To commemorate the old days, however, families set up tiers of shelves bearing figures of warriors and their equipment—armor, helmets, swords, etc. These miniature figures were treasured and kept for the festival from one year to the next.

The celebration, since 1945, of KODOMO-NO-HI, or Children's Day, was intended to replace Tango-no-Sekku. But in fact, many of the activities associated with May 5—which include sumo wrestling, *kendo* (fencing with bamboo staves), and climbing competitions—tend to focus on boys.

♦ 2924 ♦ Tano Festival (Dano-nal; Swing Day)
May-June; fifth day of fifth lunar month

An ancient spring agricultural festival in Korea, the Tano Festival started as a planting ritual and a time to pray for a good harvest. It falls in the farming season between the planting of rice seedlings and their transplanting to the paddy fields. With the lunar SOL or New Year's Day and MID-AUTUMN FESTIVAL, it is one of the country's three great festivals on the lunar calendar. Festivities in the countryside include swinging contests for girls: swings are suspended from tall poles or bridges, and the girls, sometimes in pairs, try to ring a bell with their feet as they swing. Boys and men sometimes compete in this, but usually they take part in *ssirum*, native Korean wrestling, a sport that can be dated to 400 C.E. Today ssirum matches are nationally televised.

In the usually sleepy east coast town of Kangnung, the festival goes on for nearly a week. Activities include a mask dance-drama of ancient tradition and shaman *kut*, ritualistic ceremonies combining theatrics with music and dance.

The ceremonies are performed by a shaman, or *mudang*, a priestess who is able to appease spirits to prevent natural disasters. The mudang is also a talented performer with supernatural powers when in a trance. A long-lived indigenous shamanistic faith of uncertain origin involves the worship of spirits and demons who reside in natural objects—rocks, mountains, trees, and so on. Shamanists also believe the dead have souls, and that the mudangs can mediate between the living and the departed.

Korea is nominally more than 70 percent Buddhist and more than 15 percent Christian, but it actively remains about 90 percent shamanist.

♦ 2925 ♦ Tanzania Independence Day
December 9

Tanzania Independence Day is a celebration of independence from the British in 1961 of Tanganyika, which merged with Zanzibar in 1964 to become Tanzania. The day is a national holiday celebrated with parades, youth leagues marching before the president at the stadium in Dar es Salaam, school games, cultural dances, and aerobatics by the air force.

CONTACTS:
Embassy of the United Republic of Tanzania
1232 22nd St. N.W.
Washington, D.C. 20037
202-939-6125; fax: 202-797-7408
tanzaniaembassy-us.org

♦ 2926 ♦ Tanzania Union Day
April 26

On April 26, 1964, the East African countries of Tanganyika and Zanzibar merged to form the United Republic of Tanzania. Union Day celebrates this merger.

In the city of Dar es Salaam, speeches and a parade mark Union Day. Dignitaries from nearby countries join Tanzanian government officials in these festivities.

In 2004, to mark Union Day, then President Benjamin Mkapa pardoned nearly 4,500 prisoners who had been sentenced for minor crimes or who had less than three years to serve of a longer sentence.

CONTACTS:
Embassy of the United Republic of Tanzania
1232 22nd St. N.W.
Washington, D.C. 20037 United States
202-939-6125; fax: 202-797-7408
tanzaniaembassy-us.org

♦ 2927 ♦ **Tarantula Fest and Barbecue**
First Saturday of October

The tarantula mating season begins in mid-August and lasts through early November, and northern California's Henry W. Coe State Park sees plenty of the spiders crossing its roads during this time of year. Park rangers view the mass exodus as a great opportunity to hold a festival and a barbecue complete with typical fare as well as tarantula cookies and suckers.

The bolder attendees of the festival go for the tarantula-handling. Some even muster the courage to pose for pictures as the spiders crawl on their faces (this particular breed of tarantula is docile and its venom is virtually harmless). Plenty of other proceedings accompany the main event. The Tarantulas, the park's jug music "house band," usually perform. There are also displays of non-native tarantulas, merchandise for sale, and a raffle. The park's visitor center also opens up for people to learn more about tarantulas and the park, which covers 87,000 acres, making it the largest state park in northern California.

CONTACTS:
Henry W. Coe State Park
Pine Ridge Association
9100 E. Dunne Ave.
Morgan Hill, CA 95037
408-779-2728
coepark.net

♦ 2928 ♦ **Tarnetar Mela**
August-September; three days in the Hindu month of Bhadrapada

This famous fair is held in Tarnetar, a small town in India's Gujarat State. People from area tribes wear their most exquisite clothes for the three-day event, particularly young unmarried people, since the fair is mainly an occasion for them to find spouses. Young men carry magnificently decorated *chhatris* (umbrellas)—a sight for which the fair is renowned—to signal their availability to young women. The Trinetreshwar, or temple of Shiva, provides the grounds for the fair, which abound in food stalls, craft and cattle exhibits, sporting events, and lots of dancing.

Adding to the prospective matrimonial atmosphere is the traditional belief that connects Tarnetar with the marriage between Draupadi and Arjuna, the warrior-hero of the Hindu epics, the *Mahabarata* and the *Bhagavad Gita*.

CONTACTS:
Gujarat Tourism Corporation
Udyog Bhavan, Block No. 16
4th Fl Sector-11
Gandhinagar, Gujarat 382011 India
91-79-23222523 or 800 200 5080; fax: 91-79-23238908
www.gujarattourism.com

♦ 2929 ♦ **Tartu Hanseatic Days**
Late June-July

Tartu, Estonia, is an ancient city first mentioned in written works in the year 1030. Situated on the Baltic Sea, it was one of the influential cities belonging to the Hanseatic League, a powerful group of allied cities during the Middle Ages that controlled trade on the Baltic, and to some extent the North Sea as well. At the time, Tartu was an important meeting place for tradesmen from Germany, Sweden, Russia, and other lands. In 1986, the Hanseatic Days celebration was established to preserve this aspect of Tartu's heritage. It has since become one of the most important cultural events in all of Estonia.

During Hanseatic Days, those attending the festivities have ample opportunity to learn about life in medieval times. Festival staff members dress in period costume and carry out a variety of authentic activities. Agricultural practices and skilled trades are demonstrated. There are processions, cultural programs, knights tournaments, concerts, and exhibitions of folk art and handcrafts. Entertainment is also provided by wandering jesters, dance and musical companies, circus performers, and street theater groups. Performances by symphonies and choirs are also common at this time. Special events are organized for children, and there is a rowing race held on the Emajogi River, which runs through Tartu.

In addition to celebrating the past, Hanseatic Days is a time for representatives of the Hanseatic cities to come together and look to the present and future. In seminars and conferences, attendees meet to discuss ways to create strong partnerships and use the Hanseatic alliance in the years to come.

CONTACTS:
Tartu Convention Bureau
Raekoja plats 20
Tartu, 51004 Estonia
372-744-1464
www.visittartu.com

♦ 2930 ♦ **Taste of Chicago**
10 days extending from the last week of June through the first week of July

Taste of Chicago is the largest food festival in the United States and one of the most popular tourist attractions in Illinois. Begun as a one-day celebration of Chicago's diverse cuisine in 1980, the Taste of Chicago quickly grew into a 10-day food and entertainment spectacle that attracts more than 3.5 million visitors each year. The first Taste festival was held in a three-block area of Michigan Avenue on July 4, 1980. However, with attendance more than triple the anticipated 75,000 visitors, the festival relocated the following year to nearby Grant Park on the Lake Michigan waterfront. In addition to extending the length of the festival from one day to 10, organizers also expanded the number of vendor restaurants to 70 and offered a full range of local and national music acts to entertain festivalgoers. Over the years additional entertainment and education programs were added, including cooking classes, family-themed crafts, fitness demonstrations, and world culture exhibits.

While the Taste of Chicago extends from late June into early July, the most popular day to attend is July 3, when a schedule of celebrity music performers culminates in a spectacular municipal fireworks display over Lake Michigan.

CONTACTS:
City of Chicago
121 N. LaSalle St.
City Hall
Chicago, IL 60602
312-744-5000
www.cityofchicago.org

♦ 2931 ♦ Tater Days
First weekend and Monday in April

Considered the oldest trade day in the U.S., Tater Days is now a celebration of the sweet potato in Benton, Ky. The event started in 1843 when sweet potatoes were a staple crop of the area. Today the "tater" is honored with a parade, fleamarket, gospel music, arts and crafts exhibits, and a Miss Tater Day contest. Most of the food served is some kind of sweet potato concoction.

CONTACTS:
Kentucky Department of Travel and Tourism
500 Mero St.
Capital Plaza Tower
22nd Fl.
Frankfort, KY 40601
502-564-4930 or 800-225-8747
www.kentuckytourism.com

♦ 2932 ♦ Ta'u Fo'ou
January 1

New Year's Day in Tonga, a Polynesian island kingdom in the South Pacific, is reminiscent of CHRISTMAS EVE celebrations in the United States and western Europe, when carolers go from house to house singing Christmas songs. But because the new year arrives in the middle of the Southern Hemisphere's summer, when schoolchildren are on holiday and the weather is warm, the caroling custom has a cultural

twist. Boys and girls go from house to house singing hymns, rounds, and other songs that they have created specifically for the occasion. Instead of offering them hot chocolate or coffee, their friends and neighbors show their appreciation by offering fruit or cool drinks. Sometimes the children will be given a piece of *tapa*, Polynesian bark cloth.

♦ 2933 ♦ Taungbyon Spirit Festival
Eight days before the full moon in August

Part circus, part multinational marketplace, the Spirit Festival in Taungbyon, Myanmar, commemorates the Brother Lords, two brothers who lived in the 11th century. Condemned to die for their laziness, the brothers were recognized as spirit-gods after their deaths. The festival includes folk dramas, ceremonial dances, and opportunities to gamble and socialize. Images reflecting the pre-Buddhist animist traditions of the Burmese people are daubed with ceremonial oils and taken through the streets in procession. Shamans (intermediaries between the natural and the spirit worlds) hold many assemblies during the fair.

CONTACTS:
Embassy of the Republic of the Union of Myanmar
2300 S. St. N.W.
Washington, D.C. 20008
202-332-3344; fax: 202-332-4351
www.mewashingtondc.com

♦ 2934 ♦ Tazaungdaing
October-November; full moon day of Burmese month of Tazaungmone

The Tazaungdaing festival was observed in Burma (now officially called Myanmar) even before the spread of Buddhism. It was held in honor of the God of Lights, and it marked the awakening of the Hindu god Vishnu from his long sleep. Burmese Buddhists later attached their own religious significance to the festival, saying that this was the night that Siddhartha's mother, sensing that her son was about to discard the royal robes of his birth and put on the robes of the monkhood, spent the entire night weaving the traditional yellow robes for him. To commemorate her achievement, a weaving contest is held at the Shwe Dagon Pagoda in Rangoon (now called Yangon). Another festival activity is the offering of *Kathin* robes to the Buddhist monks to replace the soiled robes they have worn throughout the rainy season. This offering ceremony begins on the first waning day of THADINGYUT and continues until the full moon night of Tazaungmone.

The Tazaungdaing festival is celebrated by sending up fire balloons and lighting multicolored lanterns, especially at the Sulamani Pagoda in Tavatimsa. Sometimes called the **Tawadeintha Festival**, this day commemorates the return of Gautama Buddha from his visit to heavenly Tawadeintha to visit his mother's reincarnated spirit. Holy men with lit candles illuminated his path back to earth.

CONTACTS:
Embassy of the Union of Myanmar
2300 S. St. N.W.

Washington, D.C. 20008 United States
202-332-3344; fax: 202-332-4351
www.mewashingtondc.com

◆ 2935 ◆ Taziyeh
Ninth day of Islamic month of Muharram

For Shi'ite Muslims, the martyrdom of the Prophet Muhammad's grandson, Hussein, is one of the more critical events in Islamic history. In 680 C.E., Hussein and a small group of Shi'ite supporters clashed with Sunnis in Karbala, a city in present-day Iraq, and were killed. The Shi'ite holiday of Ashura commemorates Hussein's death and the days leading up to it. The 10 days make up the initial days of Muharram, the first month of the Islamic year.

Iranian Shi'ites mark the eve of Ashura by celebrating Taziyeh, which is named after the passion play of the same name. Performances of *taziyeh* are common in Iraq, Pakistan, and India, as well as in Iran, but only in Iran has the tradition developed into a formal holiday. The word *taziyeh* means "consolation" and signifies the blessing that performers are believed to receive by imitating the sacred events that befell the prophet's family. Sometimes the shows coincide with religious processions.

After experiencing its heyday in the 19th century, *taziyeh* performances dropped off since they were written off as a folk custom for the lower classes. During the Iranian Revolution in 1979, clerics re-authorized the tradition and *taziyeh* experienced a resurgence, with more elaborate productions and greater attendance numbers.

CONTACTS:
Asia Society And Museum
725 Park Ave.
at 70th St.
New York, NY 10021
212-288-6400; fax: 212-517-8315
asiasociety.org

◆ 2936 ◆ Teachers' Day in the Czech Republic
March 28

March 28 is the birthday of Jan Amos Komensky (1592-1670; his name is also rendered John Comenius), a noted educational reformer and theologian in the former Czechoslovakia. Komensky was the first person to write an illustrated textbook for children. Published in 1658, it was pocket-sized and used for teaching Latin words. Komensky was also a proponent of compulsory education who pointed out the state's obligation to provide kindergarten training and schooling. It has been traditional for children to honor him on Teachers' Day, or **Komensky Day**, by bringing flowers and gifts to their teachers. The day is also observed with lectures, music, and educational activities.

◆ 2937 ◆ Teej (Tij; Green Teej)
July-August; third day of waxing half of Hindu month of Sravana

Teej is a way to welcome the monsoon, the season when the wind from the Indian Ocean brings heavy rainfall. The festival is celebrated especially in the dry, desert-like state of Rajasthan in northwestern India. Because the monsoon augurs good crops and fertility, this is also a celebration for women and is dedicated to the Hindu goddess, Parvati, consort of Lord Shiva and patron goddess of women. On this day, she is supposed to have been reunited with Shiva.

On Teej women traditionally paint delicate designs on their hands and feet with henna. Specially decorated swings are hung from trees in every village, and women swing on them and sing songs in praise of Parvati. Married women go to their parents' home and receive gifts of clothes and jewelry. There are also local fairs and processions carrying the image of the goddess.

In Jaipur, the capital of Rajasthan, women dressed in their finest go out to the main temple with flowers and brass vessels filled with water to worship the goddess and sing her praise. A palanquin carrying an image of Parvati is carried through the streets in a procession of decorated elephants, camels, horses, chariots, dancers, and musicians.

On this day in Kathmandu, Nepal, Hindu women visit Pashupatinath Temple to worship Shiva and Parvati. Ritual bathing in the sacred Bagmati River is supposed to wash away the sins of the past year.

CONTACTS:
Department of Tourism , Art & Culture, Government of Rajasthan
Paryatan Bhawan
Khasa Kothi Hotel Campus
M.I. Rd.
Jaipur, Rajasthan 302001 India
91-141-5110598
www.rajasthantourism.gov.in

◆ 2938 ◆ Tejano Conjunto Festival
Mid-May

Conjunto music originated in the late 19th century in southern Texas, where the mingling of Germanic and Mexican cultures produced a unique folk music. The German settlers introduced the accordian, to which the Mexicanos added the Spanish bajo sexto guitar for a new kind of music. "Tejano" refers to conjunto music as it is played in Texas, which differs from the "Norteño" conjunto played in northern Mexico.

The Tejano Conjunto Festival held for five days in mid-May every year in San Antonio, Texas, is the largest festival of its kind in the world. Since 1982 it has featured some of the best Tejano conjunto artists performing traditional, popular, and progressive conjunto music. The festival also includes an induction ceremony for the Conjunto Music Hall of Fame, a poster contest, art exhibits, a silent auction, and awards presentations held at San Antonio's Guadalupe Theater and Rosedale Park.

CONTACTS:
Guadalupe Cultural Arts Center
723 S. Brazos St.

San Antonio, TX 78207
210-271-3151
www.guadalupeculturalarts.org

♦ 2939 ♦ Tekakwitha (Kateri) Feast Day
July 14

The first Native American to be beatified, Kateri Tekakwitha (1656–1680) is a venerated figure among both Catholics and Native Americans as well as the patroness of ecology and the environment. Catholic churches—in particular those named after her or based in places connected to her legacy—hold mass on her feast day, during which congregants may offer prayers to God through her intercession.

Known as the "Lily of the Mohawk," Tekakwitha was born in upstate New York to a Christian Algonquin mother and a non-Christian Mohawk father. She was baptized in 1656. Acutely aware that her newfound faith did not make her popular with her village, she moved to a Christian community near Montreal, Canada. Up until her death at the age of 24, she devoted herself to prayer, fasting, and service. Witnesses at her deathbed reported that her facial scars, left by a bout with smallpox, suddenly disappeared after she died. Her legacy has inspired a campaign for her sainthood. In 1980 Pope John Paul II declared her "Blessed"—the last designation made by the Church before someone officially becomes a saint.

Among the North American churches and shrines sites that have noteworthy feast day celebrations are the National Kateri Shrine in Fonda, New York, where she had her first encounter with Christianity; and the Kateri Center at the Saint Francis-Xavier Mission at Kahnawake, Quebec, where she lived following her conversion.

CONTACTS:
National Saint Kateri Shrine
3628 State Hwy 5
P.O. Box 627
Fonda, NY 12068
518-853-3646
www.katerishrine.com

♦ 2940 ♦ Tell (Wilhelm) Festival
September, Labor Day weekend

New Glarus, Wisconsin, was settled by a group of Swiss immigrants in 1845 and is still referred to as "Little Switzerland." It is the location of several annual events designed to draw attention to the area's Swiss heritage. These include the HEIDI FESTIVAL in June and the VOLKSFEST in August. But one of the most popular is the Wilhelm Tell Pageant that has been performed each year on LABOR DAY weekend since 1938.

The highlight of the William Tell story, of course, is the famous "apple scene" where the imprisoned patriot is given a chance at freedom if he can shoot an apple off his son's head. The play includes performances by the famous New Glarus yodelers and the costumed usherettes, who perform Swiss folk dances. The play is given in Swiss-German on Sunday afternoon and in English on Saturday and Monday. The pageant weekend includes dancing on the green, Swiss singing, and other traditional Swiss forms of entertainment.

See also WILLIAM TELL PLAY.

CONTACTS:
New Glarus Chamber of Commerce
418 Railroad St.
P.O. Box 713
New Glarus, WI 53574
608-527-2095 or 800-527-6838
swisstown.com

♦ 2941 ♦ Tell (William) Play
Thursdays and Saturdays from late June to early September

The Swiss legendary hero William Tell symbolized the struggle for individual and political freedom. When he defied the Austrian authorities, he was forced to shoot an apple off his son's head in order to gain his freedom. He was later arrested for threatening the governor's life, saved the same governor's life en route to prison, escaped, and ultimately killed the governor in an ambush. These events supposedly inspired the Swiss people to rebel against Austrian rule.

Although there is no hard evidence to support William Tell's existence, the story of his test as a marksman has passed into folklore. German dramatist J. C. Friedrich von Schiller (1759-1805) wrote a play about Tell in 1804. Set in the environs of Altdorf, the legendary site of the apple-shooting incident, Schiller's play has been performed at an open-air theater in Interlaken, Switzerland, since 1912.

See also WILHELM TELL FESTIVAL.

CONTACTS:
Tell Open-Air Theatre Interlaken
Tellweg 5
Matten, 3800 Switzerland
41-33-822-3722
www.tellspiele.ch

♦ 2942 ♦ Tellabration
Third weekend in November

A nationwide night of storytelling, Tellabration was started in 1988 by storyteller J. G. ("Paw-Paw") Pinkerton. The event began with storytelling going on in six communities in Connecticut. The next year, Texas and Missouri also had Tellabrations, and by 1991, storytelling on this night was happening in 72 communities in 27 states, as well as in locations in Bermuda and Canada. Eventually, the length of Tellabrations extended to a weekend. In 1999 people held Tellabrations in 42 states and 14 countries. Proceeds of the event go toward developing the archives of Storytelling Foundation International (formerly the National Association for the Preservation and Perpetuation of Storytelling) in Jonesborough, Tenn.

Pinkerton originated the event as a way to encourage storytelling for adults, feeling that storytelling keeps culture alive. He grew up in a small Texas town listening to family stories—especially those told by his grandfather who had herded cattle in the early days of Texas. Pinkerton became a mining executive and, after retiring in 1988, devoted his time to promoting storytelling from his Connecticut home.

See also STORYTELLING FESTIVAL, NATIONAL and YUKON INTERNATIONAL STORYTELLING FESTIVAL.

CONTACTS:
National Storytelling Network
P.O. Box 795
Jonesborough, TN 37659 United States
423-913-8201 or 800-525-4514; fax: 423-753-9331
www.storynet.org

♦ 2943 ♦ **Telluride Film Festival**
September, Labor Day weekend

A three-day celebration of the silver screen in Telluride, Colo., the Telluride Film Festival features free outdoor showings in Elks Park with the audience bundled in blankets and sleeping bags. The festival attracts celebrity film makers, actors, and film scholars from all over the globe for national and international premieres and viewings of experimental filmmaking, retrospectives, and tributes.

CONTACTS:
Telluride Film Festival
800 Jones St
Berkeley, CA 94710 United States
510-665-9494; fax: 510-665-9589
www.telluridefilmfestival.org

♦ 2944 ♦ **Telluride Hang Gliding Festival**
Second week in June

The largest hang gliding event in the country is held in Telluride, Colo., the small mountain resort that began life as a mining town and is known today as the "festival capital of the Rockies." Top hang gliders from throughout the world come here to soar and spin above Town Park. On the last day of the six-day event, in the competition for the World Acrobatic Championship, fliers skid, loop, somersault, and pirouette from the heights of the ski mountain, trailing colored smoke from their wingtips.

CONTACTS:
Telluride Tourism Board / Chamber of Commerce
630 W. Colorado Ave.
P.O. Box 1009
Telluride, CO 81435
888-355-8743
www.visittelluride.com

♦ 2945 ♦ **Telluride Horrow Show**
October

The Telluride Horror Show is a three-day genre film festival showcasing the year's most macabre films produced across the world. The annual event first opened in 2010 and takes place in the mountain resort town of Telluride, Colorado. People come to see 20 feature films and 30 short films, screened in Telluride's historic Sheridan Opera House and Nugget Theatre, both just a block apart on Telluride's main street. Visitors can choose from an eclectic selection of horror, suspense, thriller, dark fantasy, sci-fi, and dark comedy movies.

The festival traditionally opens with a pig roast, a kind of horror scene itself, with the pig—head and all—splayed on a giant platter. Renowned writers and directors of the horror genre take the stage to participate in special question-and-answer sessions after the screenings. The event closes with a horror theme party for the organizers, sponsors, and guests.

CONTACTS:
Telluride Horrow Show
P.O. Box 182
Telluride, CO 81435
970-708-3906
www.telluridehorrorshow.com

♦ 2946 ♦ **Telluride Jazz Festival**
First weekend in August

This festival consists of three days of jazz in Telluride, Colo. Top artists produce jazz of all schools—traditional, Chicago, blues, big band, and Latin. The music happens both indoors—at the historic Sherman Opera House and at various pubs—and outdoors at the Town Park Pavilion. The festival began in 1977.

Telluride also boasts a three-day Bluegrass and Country Music Festival in late June, and a Chamber Music Festival held during two weekends in August. A special feature of that festival is the gourmet dessert concert, when fancy treats are served with the music, and the concert closes with a classical jam session.

CONTACTS:
Telluride Bluegrass Festival
P.O. Box 769
500 W. Main St.
Lyons, CO 80540
303-823-0848 or 800-624-2422; fax: 303-823-0849
www.bluegrass.com

♦ 2947 ♦ **Ten Days on the Island**
Late March-early April, biennially

Every two years, arts enthusiasts travel to Tasmania, an island off the southern coast of Australia, for Ten Days on the Island. First launched in 2001, this biennial festival celebrates island culture and showcases local and international art in all major forms: dance, theatre, music, opera, film, and literature. The festival's organizer, Tasmania's Department of Tourism, Arts and the Environment, markets the festival with the double aim of drawing tourists and boosting employment for local artists and arts practitioners.

There are on average 200 ticketed and free performances and exhibitions, held at roughly 40 locations in the island's capital, Hobart, and throughout the state of Tasmania. Estimates of past events have counted 160,000 attendants. The festival has drawn more international artists over the years, and in 2007, it began offering regional tours of theater productions.

CONTACTS:
Ten Days on the Island
71 Murray St.
G.P.O. Box 1403
Hobart, Tasmania 7000 Australia
61-3-6210-5700; fax: 61-3-6210-5799
www.tendays.org.au

Tasmanian Government Tourism Agency
420 Washington St.
Elmhurst, IL 60126
630-758-0108
www.tourismtasmania.com.au

♦ 2948 ♦ **Tenjin Matsuri**
July 24-25

The Tenjin Festival in Japan honors the scholar and statesman Sugawara Michizane (845-903), who was deified as Tenjin after his death and regarded as the god of literature. The festival began about 950 C.E. as a purification rite. Today, the Tenjin Festival opens at the Temmangu Shrine with the beating of the *Moyooshi Daiko*, a drum about five feet in diameter. It lies flat in a cart and is struck by several men, known as *Ganji*, wearing tall peaked red hats. Other participants in the procession do everything in their power to prevent the drummers from drumming. They remove the platform on which the drum sits and tilt it in every direction, but the drummers keep striking it furiously. The drum-cart is followed by a masked figure on horseback who represents Sarutahiko, the deity who led all the other gods to Japan. There are Lion Dancers to drive away evil spirits, costumed children, and various carts and palanquins carrying local dignitaries and the mayor of Osaka.

Most important is the *mikoshi*—the heavy, ornately decorated portable shrine in which the soul of Tenjin is believed to reside. In the evening, the parade moves to the river, with numerous barges and boats carrying glowing lanterns, while bonfires illuminate the banks. Fireworks mark the end of the festival, and the barges are towed back up the river so that the sacred objects can be returned to the shrine by morning.

CONTACTS:
Japan National Tourism Organization
1 Grand Central Pl.
60 E. 42nd St.
Ste. 448
New York, NY 10165
212-757-5640; fax: 212-307-6754
www.jnto.go.jp/eng

Japan National Tourism Organization
2-1-8 Tenjimbashi
Kita-ku
Osaka City, 530-0041 Japan
81-6-6282-5900
www.osaka-info.jp

♦ 2949 ♦ **Tennessee Walking Horse National Celebration**
August-September, 11 days ending the Saturday before Labor Day

This festival features 11 days and nights of pageantry and competition for more than 2,000 Tennessee Walking Horses in Shelbyville, Tenn., the "Walking Horse Capital of the World." The horses compete for more than $650,000 in prizes and the title of World Grand Champion. The celebration is the nation's largest horse show in terms of spectators (close to 250,000 fans come to this town of 13,000) and the second largest in numbers of entered horses.

The blood lines of the Tennessee Walking Horse are traced back to the Thoroughbred, the Standardbred, the Morgan, and the American Saddle Horse. It was bred pure in the early days of Tennessee for the threefold purpose of riding, driving, and general farm work. Today, it's a pleasure mount and a show horse with distinctive high-stepping gaits.

The three natural gaits of the Tennessee Walker are the flat-foot walk, the running walk, and the canter. The flat-foot walk, the slowest, is a diagonally opposed movement of the feet. The running walk starts like the flat-foot walk and, as speed increases, the hind foot overstrides the front track. It is the only gait of a horse where the forefoot strikes the ground a mere instant before the hindfoot. The canter is a rhythmic motion known as the "rocking-chair" movement.

The Shelbyville celebration began in 1939, at the initiative of horse owner Henry Davis of Wartrace, Tenn., who thought his county should celebrate its most important asset. The celebration has been held ever since without interruption.

Besides the horse shows, the celebration features an equestrian trade fair, horse sales, an arts-and-crafts festival, and America's largest barn decoration competition. The barns and stalls are elegantly decorated with brass lanterns, chandeliers, fine art, rugs, and expensive furnishings.

CONTACTS:
Tennessee Walking Horse National Celebration
P.O. Box 1010
Shelbyville, TN 37162
931-684-5915; fax: 931-684-5949
www.twhnc.com

♦ 2950 ♦ **Terlingua Chili Cookoff**
First full weekend in November

The Terlingua Chili Cookoff is a contest of chili chefs held in Terlingua, Tex., an abandoned mining town near the Big Bend desert area in the southwestern part of the state. More than 200 cooks from as many as 30 states and occasionally from foreign countries show up to prepare the official state dish, and thousands of spectators drive or fly in. Humorists Wick Fowler and H. Allen Smith staged the first cookoff in 1967, deciding to locate it in the hot desert because it was a contest for a hot dish. It has become such an institution that the number of entrants has to be kept down by earning points at preliminary cookoffs, especially the CHILYMPIAD.

CONTACTS:
Original Terlingua International Championship Chili Cookoff
1400 Mockingbird Dr.
Grapevine, TX 76051
972-935-2402; fax: 972-351-0024
www.abowlofred.com

Chili Appreciation Society International
P.O. Box 39
Terlingua, TX 79852
432-371-2595 or 888-227-4468
www.casichili.net

♦ 2951 ♦ Terminalia
February 23

In ancient Rome, February 23 marked the end of the year and was therefore an appropriate time to honor Terminus, the god of boundaries and landmarks. The terminus, or boundary stone marking the outer limits of Rome, stood between the fifth and sixth milestones on the road to Laurentum. During the observance of the Terminalia, property owners would gather there—or at the boundary stones that marked their private lands—to place garlands around the stone and offer sacrifices. Afterward there would be singing and socializing among family members and servants.

Ceremonies that involve marking boundaries are common in England and Scotland as well (*see* ASCENSION DAY and COMMON RIDINGS DAY).

♦ 2952 ♦ Teshuvah
September-October; during the month of Tishri between Rosh Hashanah and Yom Kippur

The ten days between ROSH HASHANAH and YOM KIPPUR are known to Jews as Aseret Yemey Tushuvah, or **Ten Days of Penitence**. They are a time for reflection, introspection, and repentance, during which people apologize to one another for any wrongs they may have committed during the previous year. The Hebrew word *teshuvah* means "turning." According to tradition, an unfavorable verdict about one's behavior may be changed by repentance and charity. Each day the famous prayer of confession, which begins "Our Father, our King," is recited at the service in the temple.

In Palestine, pilgrimages are made during this period to the tomb of Rachel and other sacred burial places, as well as to the graves of relatives. In other countries, it is customary to visit the local cemetery. No weddings or banquets may be held during these days, and scholarly Jews spend their time reading and studying the sacred books.

The atmosphere during this time is not one of sadness but of thoughtfulness and kindness. Jews often greet one another by saying, *Gemar Hatimah Tovah*, which means, "May the final verdict be favorable.".

CONTACTS:
Union of Orthodox Jewish Congregations of America
11 Broadway
New York, NY 10004 United States
212-563-4000; fax: 212-564-9058
www.ou.org

♦ 2953 ♦ Tet
January-February; first to seventh days of first lunar month

The Vietnamese New Year, Tet, is an abbreviation for **Tet Nguyen Dan**, meaning "first day." This is the most important festival of the year, signifying both the beginning of the year and of spring. It's also seen as a precursor of everything that will happen in the coming year, and for that reason, efforts are made to start the year properly with family reunions, paying homage to ancestors, and wiping out debts.

At the start of the festival, the Spirit of the Hearth goes to the abode of the Emperor of Jade to report on family members. The spirit should be in a good frame of mind, so a tree is built of bamboo and red paper to ward off evil spirits. At midnight the New Year and the return of the Spirit of the Hearth are welcomed with firecrackers, gongs, and drums. The festival then continues for a week, with special events on each day. A favorite food of the festival is *banh chung*, which is made of sticky rice, yellow beans, pig fat, and spices wrapped in leaves and boiled for half a day.

Tet became known worldwide in 1968 for the Tet Offensive of the Vietnam War. The LUNAR NEW YEAR truce was shattered on Jan. 31 with attacks by North Vietnam and the National Liberation Front against more than 100 South Vietnamese cities. The United States embassy in Saigon was attacked and parts of it held by the Viet Cong for six hours; the headquarters of U.S. Gen. William Westmoreland at Tan Son Nhut Airport outside Saigon was also attacked. The city of Hue was captured. The attacks were repulsed, and the U.S. and South Vietnam claimed victory. But television viewers had seen the ferocity of the attack and the flight of Saigon residents, and the offensive led to increased movements in the United States to end the war.

CONTACTS:
Vietnam National Administration of Tourism
80 Quan Su St
Hoan Kiem Dist
Vietnam
84-4-3942-2246; fax: 84-4-3826-3956
www.vietnamtourism.com

♦ 2954 ♦ Texas Citrus Fiesta
Third full weekend in January

An annual festival held in Mission, Tex., the Texas Citrus Fiesta salutes the Texas citrus industry and, especially, the Texas Ruby Red Grapefruit. Mission, in the Rio Grande Valley, was founded by the Catholic Missionary Society of the Oblate Fathers, who built a mission here in 1824. They also are credited as the first community to plant citrus fruit in the region, which is now famous for the Ruby Red Grapefruit.

Among the events of the fiesta are a style show featuring garments made of Rio Grande Valley agricultural products: dried orange peel, seeds, and onion skins are used in creating costumes that range from ballgowns to bikinis. Other events include parades, the coronation of a Citrus Queen, arts and crafts, and food and games.

CONTACTS:
Texas Citrus Fiesta
220 E. 9th St.
Mission, TX 78572
956-585-9724; fax: 956-585-9728
www.texascitrusfiesta.org

♦ 2955 ♦ Texas Folklife Festival
Early June

Often described as "the largest block party in Texas," the Texas Folklife Festival was founded in 1972 by O. T. Baker, exhibits manager at the Institute of Texan Cultures, as a celebration of the state's ethnic cultures and pioneer heritage. There are demonstrations of the crafts, work skills, costumes, foods, and customs of about 40 different ethnic groups living in Texas today. Visitors can learn how to make a cowhide chair, for example, or the proper way to pickle olives. There have been lessons in Swiss yodeling, splitting shingles, and blacksmithing, as well as musical performances by German oompah bands, Czech accordionists, and Dutch singers. The fourday festival is sponsored by the Institute of Texan Cultures and is held at HemisFair Park in downtown San Antonio.

CONTACTS:
UTSA's Institute of Texan Cultures
801 E. Cesar E.
Chavez Blvd
San Antonio, TX 78205
210-458-2300
www.texancultures.com

♦ 2956 ♦ Texas Independence Day
March 2

A legal holiday in Texas, March 2 commemorates both the convention at Washington-on-the-Brazos held on this day in 1836, when delegates prepared for the separation of Texas from Mexico, and the birthday of Sam Houston (1793-1863), who led the Texans to victory over the Mexicans in the battle of SAN JACINTO. The convention formed an interim government, drew up a constitution, and made Sam Houston commander-in-chief of the Texan military forces. But their work was interrupted by the invading Mexican army. It wasn't until the following month that the Republic of Texas forced the issue of independence at the battle of San Jacinto. Texas is the only state to celebrate independence from a country other than England.

March 2 is also known as **Sam Houston Day** and **Texas Flag Day**, although these are "special observance days" rather than legal holidays. This period in Texas history, beginning with the Washington-on-the-Brazos convention and ending with Sam Houston's decisive victory at San Jacinto, is celebrated each year during "Texas Week.".

CONTACTS:
Washington-on-the-Brazos State Park
P.O. Box 305
Washington, TX 77880
936-878-2214
tpwd.texas.gov

♦ 2957 ♦ Texas Rose Festival
Third week in October

An annual tribute to roses in Tyler, Tex., center of the region that produces more than a third of the field-grown roses in the United States. Tyler's Municipal Rose Garden, one of the largest rose gardens in the country, covers 14 acres and has some 30,000 rose bushes, representing more than 400 varieties. They blossom among pines, fountains, gazebos, and archways, peaking in May but continuing through October. The five-day festival features the coronation of a Rose Queen, a rose show, a parade of floats decorated with roses, and tours of the rose gardens. There are also arts and crafts shows, a square-dance festival, and a symphony concert.

CONTACTS:
Texas Rose Festival Association
420 Rose Park Dr.
Tyler, TX 75702
903-597-3130; fax: 903-597-3031
www.texasrosefestival.com

♦ 2958 ♦ Thadingyut
September-October; full moon of Thadingyut

For Buddhists, the period that begins with the full moon day of the 11th lunar month and continues until the full moon day of the 12th lunar month marks the end of the Buddhist Lent and the beginning of the *Kathin*, or pilgrimage season. Also known as **Robe Offering Month**, this is a time when Buddhists make pilgrimages to various temples, bringing food and gifts—particularly new robes—to the monks. In Myanmar (formerly Burma), Thadingyut is the day on which the Buddha completed his preaching of the *Abhidhamma*, or "philosophy," and it is sometimes referred to as **Abhidhamma Day**. In Laos, it is called **Boun Ok Vatsa**, or the **Festival of the Waters**, as it is a popular time for pirogue (canoe) races. In Thailand, it is called **Tod Kathin**—the *kathin* being a wooden frame on which scraps of cloth were stretched before being sewn together to make into robes.

See also TAZAUNGDAING; WASO.

CONTACTS:
Ministry of Hotels and Tourism - Myanmar
Building No. 33
Myanmar
95-67-406129
www.myanmartourism.org

♦ 2959 ♦ Thailand Constitution Day
December 10

In 1932 Thailand's absolute monarchy was replaced with a constitutional monarchy. King Rama VII oversaw the transfer of power. Under the newly instituted constitution of that time, the monarchy remained in place and the king was designated the head of state, head of the armed forces, upholder of all religions, and sacred and inviolable in his person.

In practice, however, while the monarchy is still held in esteem by the people, real power in Thailand has often been held by the military. Reflecting the country's volatile politics, Thailand has had a series of 18 constitutions or charters since 1932, the latest one being adopted in 2007. All of them have allowed for a constitutional monarchy with greater or lesser power. Celebrations on Constitution Day involve the people thanking the monarchy for granting them a chance to take part in running the country.

CONTACTS:
Royal Thai Embassy
1024 Wisconsin Ave. N.W.
Washington, D.C. 20007
202-944-3600; fax: 202-944-3611
www.thaiembdc.org

♦ 2960 ♦ **Thailand Coronation Day**
May 5

On May 5, 1950, King Bhumibol Adulyadej was crowned Rama IX of Thailand, the ninth king of the Chakri dynasty. Ever since, the day has been celebrated as Coronation Day in Thailand.

The celebration begins on May 3 with Buddhist monks holding a service at the Amarindra Vinichai Hall in the Grand Palace. A high monk delivers a sermon and scriptures are read in honor of the Chakri family ancestors. On May 4th, the Chief of Brahmin priests reads out the official proclamation of Coronation Day. In the evening, Buddhist priests perform a chanting ceremony. On May 5, the Buddhist monks are given a feast and the king wears his full regalia. At noon, the Royal Thai Army and Navy each give a 21-gun salute. Later in the day, the king awards medals and decorations to those citizens who have done outstanding services for the state.

CONTACTS:
Royal Thai Embassy
1024 Wisconsin Ave. N.W.
Ste. 401
Washington, D.C. 20007
202-944-3600; fax: 202-944-3611
www.thaiembdc.org

♦ 2961 ♦ **Thaipusam (Thai Poosam)**
January-February; three to 12 days in Hindu month of Magha

Thaipusam is a dramatic Hindu festival celebrated in India, Malaysia, Sri Lanka, Singapore, South Africa, Mauritius, and elsewhere. The day marks the birthday and victory of the Hindu god Subramaniam, also known as Lord Murugar, over the demons, and is a time of penance and consecration

to the god, usually involving self-mortification in a test of mind over pain.

In Malaysia, the festival is a public holiday in the states of Perak, Penang, and Selangor. In Georgetown, Penang, a statue of Subramaniam—covered with gold, silver, diamonds, and emeralds—is taken from the Sri Mariamman temple along with his consorts, Valli and Theivanai, and placed in a silver chariot. Then begins a grand procession to his tomb in the Batu Caves, near the capital city of Kuala Lumpur, where the statue is carried up 272 steep steps, and placed beside the permanent statue kept there. The next day about 200,000 people begin to pay homage, while movies, carousels, and other entertainments are provided for their amusement.

The most intense form of penance and devotion is the carrying of *kavadee*—a wooden arch on a wooden platform—which the Tamil people of Mauritius practice in a unique way—much more elaborately and solemnly than in other countries. Devotees, both male and female, abstain from meat and sex during the sacred 10 days before the festival. Each day they go to the temple (*kovil*) to make offerings, and in Port Louis, at Arulmigu Sockalingam Meenaatchee Amman Kovil, Murugar and his two consorts are decorated differently each day to depict episodes in the deity's life.

On the eve of the celebration, devotees prepare their kavadees and decorate them with flowers, paper, and peacock feathers. They may be built in other shapes, such as a peacock or temple, but the arch is most common. The next morning, priests pour cow milk into two brass pots and tie them to the sides of each kavadee. Fruits, or *jagger* (a coarse, brown sugar made from the East Indian palm tree), may also be placed on the platform. Then religious ceremonies are performed at the shrines to put the bearers in a trance. When ready, penitents have their upper bodies pierced symmetrically with *vels*, the sacred lance given to Lord Subramaniam by his mother, Parvati; some also have skewers driven through their cheeks, foreheads, or tongues.

The procession then begins, with the devotees carrying the kavadees on their shoulders. Some penitents draw a small chariot by means of chains fixed to hooks dug into their sides; some walk to the temple on sandals studded with nails. Groups of young men and women follow, singing rhythmic songs. Each region may have 40 to 100 kavadees, but in places like Port Louis there may be 600 to 800. At the temple, the kavadee is dismounted, the needles and skewers removed by the priest, and the milk in the pots—which has stayed pure—is poured over the deity from head to foot. The penitents then go out and join the crowds.

Some believe carrying the kavadee washes away sins through self-inflicted suffering; others say the kavadee symbolizes the triumph of good over evil.

In Durban, South Africa, these rites last 12 days and are also performed during Chitray Massum in April-May.

CONTACTS:
Malaysian Tourism Promotion Board
818 W. Seventh St.

Ste. 970
Los Angeles, CA 90017
213-689-9702; fax: 213-689-1530
www.tourismmalaysiausa.com

♦ 2962 ♦ Thanh-Minh
Fifth day of third lunar month

Thanh-Minh (which means "pure and bright") in Vietnam is a day to commemorate the dead. Families brings flowers, food, incense, and other offerings to the graves of deceased relatives. Sometimes they visit the graves a few days in advance to prepare for Thanh-Minh by raking or sweeping the surrounding area and painting the tombs.

See also QING MING FESTIVAL.

♦ 2963 ♦ Thanksgiving
Fourth Thursday in November (U.S.); second Monday in October (Canada)

The Pilgrim settlers of New England were not the first to set aside a day for expressing their gratitude to God for the harvest. The Greeks and the Romans paid tribute to their agricultural goddesses, the Anglo-Saxons celebrated LAMMAS and HARVEST HOME FESTIVAL, and the Jews have their eight-day SUKKOT, or Feast of Tabernacles. The first American Thanksgiving was entirely religious, and took place on December 4, 1619, when a group of 38 English settlers arrived at Berkeley Plantation on the James River. Their charter decreed that their day of arrival be celebrated yearly as a day of thanksgiving to God.

But most Americans think of the first "official" Thanksgiving as being the one that took place at Plymouth Colony in October 1621, a year after the Pilgrims first landed on the New England coast. They were joined in their three-day feast by Massasoit, the chief of the Wampanoag Indians, and about 90 of his fellow tribesmen.

The Episcopal Church and many states declared Thanksgiving holidays, but it wasn't until 1863 that President Abraham LINCOLN proclaimed the last Thursday in November as a national day to give thanks. Each year thereafter, for 75 years, the president proclaimed the same day to be celebrated. In 1939, however, President Franklin D. ROOSEVELT moved it one week earlier to allow more time for Christmas shopping. Finally, Congress ruled that the fourth Thursday of November would be the legal federal holiday of Thanksgiving after 1941. Canadians celebrate their Thanksgiving on the second Monday in October.

Today Thanksgiving is a time for family reunions and traditions, most of which center around the preparation of an elaborate meal featuring turkey and a dozen or so accompanying dishes. Although some people go to special church services on Thanksgiving day, far more line the streets of Philadelphia, Detroit, and New York City, where huge parades are held. In many places Santa Claus arrives in town on this day, and the widespread sales that begin in department stores the next day mark the start of the CHRISTMAS shopping season.

See also PILGRIM THANKSGIVING DAY; SCHWENKFELDER THANKS-GIVING.

CONTACTS:
Library of Congress
101 Independence Ave. S.E.
Washington, D.C. 20540
202-707-5000
www.loc.gov

♦ 2964 ♦ Thargelia
May-June

This ancient Greek festival was celebrated in Athens on the sixth and seventh days of the ancient Greek month of Thargelion (which fell sometime between late May and early June) to honor Apollo. In addition to offerings of first fruits, or the first bread from the new wheat, it was customary to select two condemned criminals (either two men or a man and a woman) to act as scapegoats for community guilt. First they were led through the city and then driven out and banished. If circumstances warranted a greater sacrifice, they were killed—either thrown into the sea or burned on a pyre. On the second day of the festival there was an offering of thanksgiving, a procession, and the official registration ceremony for individuals who had been adopted.

CONTACTS:
Greek National Tourism Organisation
305 E. 47th St.
2nd Fl.
New York, NY 10017 United States
212-421-5777; fax: 212-826-6940
www.visitgreece.gr/ | www.gtp.gr

♦ 2965 ♦ That Luang Festival
Full moon in November

This annual weeklong festival takes place in Vientiane, the capital city of Laos, at the time of the full moon. The festival is centered in and around That Luang Stupa, the country's most sacred Buddhist temple, which is the National Symbol of Laos. During the festival, hundreds of monks from all over the country gather to chant, pray, and accept alms and gifts of flowers and food from local people. Buddhists consider giving to the monks beneficial, and they give willingly, without accepting thanks. The monks, for their part, share their takings with the poor of the city.

On the evening of the full moon, the monks take part in a sacred procession. This is capped off by a grand fireworks display and revelry through the night in which entire families take part. Dancing, music, drinking, and eating go on far into the night. During the day, an international trade fair takes place in the city that showcases tourism in Laos and other countries in the region. Vendors selling goods and trinkets on the streets add to a carnival-like atmosphere.

CONTACTS:
Embassy of Lao People's Democratic Republic
2222 S .St. N.W.
Washington, D.C. 20008

202-332-6416; fax: 202-332-4923
www.laoembassy.com

◆ 2966 ◆ Thay Pagoda Festival
March-April

This Vietnamese festival, which varies in length, is held in honor of Buddhist monk Dao Hanh, who lived during the Ly Dynasty (1009-1225 C.E.). Dao Hanh was said to have invented what is known as *mua roi can*, "water puppetry," an activity that plays an important part in the festival. The puppet shows take place on the pond in front of the pagoda. The puppeteers stand mostly underwater behind a curtain in order to control the puppets' actions on a stage on the water's surface.

In addition to water puppet performances, the festival features firecracker competitions, folk singing, rowing contests, and mountain-climbing events. It is held in the village of Thay (or Thuy Khe village) in the Quoc Oai District of Ha Tay Province.

CONTACTS:
Vietnam National Administration of Tourism
80 Quan Su St.
Hoan Kiem Dist.
Vietnam
84-4-3942-3760; fax: 84-4-3942-4115
www.vietnamtourism.com

◆ 2967 ◆ Thesmophoria
*Late October or early November; three days
during ancient Greek month of Pyanopsion*

Thesmophoria was an ancient Greek festival held in honor of Demeter Thesmophoros, the goddess of the harvest and fertility and the protectress of marriage; it is unclear whether this festival was named after the goddess or vice versa. It was celebrated by women, perhaps only married women, and lasted three days, between the 11th and the 13th (some say between the 14th and the 16th) of the month of Pyanopsion (which fell between October and November), at the time of the autumn sowing of the new crops.

According to Greek mythology, Demeter's daughter, Kore, was gathering flowers near Eleusis one day when she was abducted by Pluto, god of the underworld, and taken away to his subterranean kingdom. By lowering pigs into chasms in the earth, the women commemorated the abduction of Kore. Some of the women had to enter the underground chambers themselves and bring up the putrefied remains of the pigs that had been cast there the year before. The rotten flesh was placed on altars and mixed with seed corn, which was then sown in the fields as a kind of magical fertilizer to ensure a good crop. The women fasted on the second day, and on the third they celebrated the magic of fertility in the animal as well as the plant kingdoms.

In Athens and other Greek cities, the women who celebrated the Thesmophoria dressed in white robes and observed a period of strict chastity for several days before and during the ceremony. They would strew their beds with herbs that were supposed to ward off venereal diseases and sit on the ground to promote the fertility of the corn that had just been sown. Although the festival itself was taken very seriously, it was not uncommon for the women to joke among themselves, as if in doing so they could cheer the goddess Demeter, who suffered greatly over the loss of her daughter.

The Romans had a similar festival in honor of Ceres, called the CEREALIA.

◆ 2968 ◆ Thimithi Fire-Walking Ceremony
*October-November; during the Tamil month of
Aipasi*

The Thimithi Fire-Walking Ceremony takes place in Singapore's Sri Mariamman Temple during the Tamil month of Aipasi (which corresponds to the Hindu month of Kartika; Tamil people hail from southern India). This Tamil Hindu observance is part of a two-month festival in which various scenes from the great Hindu epic, the *Mahabharata*, are reenacted by devotees and the epic itself is read aloud in installments.

During the Thimithi Fire-Walking Ceremony followers of the goddess Draupadi—who plays a major role in the *Mahabharata*—walk across a bed of red-hot coals. This observance begins at 2:00 A.M. in the Sri Srinivasa Perumal Temple. The fire walking takes place more than 12 hours later, at 5:00 P.M. The Padukalam (Battle Field) ceremony, based on a battle scene from the *Mahabharata*, takes place before the fire-walking event. The *Mahabharata* tells that after an 18-day-long war Draupadi volunteered to walk on hot coals in order to demonstrate her purity.

Today's worshippers do so to show their faith in the goddess. They begin by making offerings at Draupadi's shrine. Then they receive bracelets of yellow string, in which a piece of turmeric and a sprig of margosa leaves are entwined. In addition they are prepared for their ordeal with three whip lashes across the wrist. Then they form a procession leading to the Sri Mariamman Temple, where the bed of hot coals awaits them. After crossing the coals, devotees splash through a pit of milk, set up as a means of soothing the skin on their feet. Local historians trace the Thimithi Fire-Walking Ceremony at this temple to the 1840s.

CONTACTS:
Hindu Endowments Board
397 Serangoon Rd
Singapore, 218123 Singapore
65-6296-3469; fax: 65-6292-9766
www.heb.gov.sg

◆ 2969 ◆ Thimphu Tsechu
September-October

Thimphu Tsechu is a three-day festival of religious ceremonies and costumed dances held in Thimphu, the capital city of Bhutan. *Tsechu* means "tenth day" and is used in much the same way as "festival" is used in English. Many of the dances performed at the tsechu are designed to teach lessons about how one's behavior on earth affects the afterlife, while others are believed to influence the actions of the spirits or to purify sacred ground.

Perhaps the most famous and exotic of the *cham* dances performed at the festival is the Dance of the Drummers from Dametsi, thought to have been introduced by a saint who lived in the 16th century. The dance represents the vision of the heavenly castle of Guru Rinpoche, which the saint saw in a dream. It is performed by 12 men who wear animal masks and yellow skirts. They bang on beautifully adorned drums to celebrate the victory of Mahayana Buddhism. They jump about and execute complex patterns, which symbolize the playful antics of the gods and spirits of the afterlife.

CONTACTS:
Tourism Council of Bhutan
P.O. Box 126
Bhutan
975-2-323251; fax: 975-2-323695
www.tourism.gov.bt

♦ 2970 ♦ **Thingyan**
Mid-April; during Burmese month of Tagu

The three-day feast of the New Year in Burma (now officially called Myanmar) is also known as the **Water Festival** because of the custom of throwing or squirting water on others. The festival has been traditional for centuries; King Narathihapate (1254-1287) built enclosed corridors running from his palace to the banks of the Irrawaddy River; inside them he and his courtiers reveled in water throwing.

During the celebration, pots of clear cold water are offered to monks at monasteries to wash or sprinkle images of Buddha. Everyone else gets drenched; young men and women roam the streets dousing everybody with buckets of water or turning hoses on them. On the final day, the traditional Burmese New Year, birds and fish are set free, and young people wash the hair of their elders. The water-splashing custom originated with the idea that through this ritual the bad luck and sins of the old year were washed away. Now splashing people is more a frolicsome thing to do and also a way of cooling off. This is the hottest time of year in Burma, and temperatures can sizzle above 100 degrees.

See also LUNAR NEW YEAR and SONGKRAN.

CONTACTS:
Embassy of the Republic of the Union of Myanmar
2300 S. St. N.W.
Washington, D.C. 20008
202-332-3344; fax: 202-332-4351
www.mewashingtondc.com

♦ 2971 ♦ **Third Prince, Birthday of the**
April-May; eighth and ninth days of fourth lunar month

This Chinese Taoist festival honors the Third Prince, a miracle-working child-god who rides on the wheels of wind and fire. In Singapore, Chinese mediums in trances dance, slash themselves with spiked maces and swords, and write charms on yellow paper with blood from their tongues. There is also a street procession of stilt-walkers, dragon dancers, and Chinese musicians.

CONTACTS:
Singapore Tourism Board
1156 Avenue of the Americas
Ste. 702
New York, NY 10036
212-302-4861; fax: 212-302-4801
www.mfa.gov.sg

♦ 2972 ♦ **Thjodhatid**
First weekend in August

Thjodhatid is a three-day "people's feast" celebrated in the Vestmannaeyjar area (or Westmann Islands) of Iceland. The festival commemorates the granting of Iceland's constitution on July 1, 1874, which permitted the nation, long under the control of Denmark, to handle its own domestic affairs. Because of foul weather, the island people of Vestmannaeyjar weren't able to attend the mainland celebration, so they held their own festival at home a month later. They've been holding this month-late celebration ever since.

Most of the festivities take place in Herjólfsdalur on Heimaey Island. Enormous bonfires are built, and there are sporting events, dancing, singing, and eating and drinking. People come from the mainland for this event, so the island is filled with campers.

CONTACTS:
Permanent Mission of Iceland to the UN
800 Third Ave.
36th Fl.
New York, NY 10022
212-593-2700; fax: 212-593-6269
www.iceland.is

♦ 2973 ♦ **Thorrablót (Thorri Banquet)**
February

Thorrablóts, which are held in February in towns throughout Iceland, are midwinter feasts featuring traditional Icelandic foods and beverages that may be repugnant to visitors with nonadventurous taste buds. The fare includes *hákarl* (a gamey shark); ram's testicles; *lundi* (broiled puffin birds); *blódmör* (sheep's blood pudding); and seal and whale meat. Dessert may be more palatable for non-natives: *skyr*, made from curd and dried wild crowberries. The locals wash everything down with a schnapps nicknamed "black death." Live music and dancing accompanies the feasting.

CONTACTS:
Icelandic Tourism Board
Sundagarðar 2
Reykjavík, D.C. 104 Iceland

354-511-4000; fax: 354-511-4040
www.iceland.is

◆ 2974 ◆ Three Archbishops, Day of the
January 30

In Greece during the 11th century there was a popular controversy over which of the three fourth-century archbishops—Basil the Great, Gregory the Theologian, or John Chrysostom—was the greatest saint of the Greek Orthodox Church. In 1081 Bishop John of Galatia resolved the problem by reporting that the three saints had appeared to him in a vision to say that they were all equal in the eyes of God. Their equality is celebrated on this day, which is also known as the **Holiday of the Three Hierarchs**. In Greek schools special exercises are held in honor of the three, who supported the classical Greek tradition at a time when many early Christians were opposed to all non-Christian literature.

◆ 2975 ◆ Three Choirs Festival
Third full week in August

One of Europe's oldest continuing music festivals, the Three Choirs Festival alternates among the three English cathedral cities of Gloucester, Worcester, and Hereford. The festival traditionally opens at the host cathedral with a performance by a choir and orchestra. Concerts during the rest of the weeklong event take place either in the cathedral or in local theaters and historic homes.

Records show that the festival was founded before 1719, and that it was held, as it is now, in succession at the three cathedrals. In the early days of the festival, it was customary for two or more wealthy patrons—called stewards—to underwrite the cost of the event. Today, subscribers to the festivals are still referred to as stewards, and money collected at the doors of the cathedral following a performance still benefits the Charity for the Relief of Widows and Orphans of Clergy, which has been affiliated with the festival since 1724.

CONTACTS:
Three Choirs Festival Association
7c College Green
Gloucester, GL1 2LX United Kingdom
44-84-5652-1823
www.3choirs.org

◆ 2976 ◆ Three Kings Day in Indian Pueblos
January 6

Three Kings Day in Indian Pueblos is the day for the installation of new officers and governors at most of the 19 Indian pueblos in New Mexico. The inaugural day begins with a church ceremony during which four walking canes, the symbols of authority, are passed on to the new governor. The governor is honored with a dance, which starts in mid-morning and is usually some form of an animal dance—often the EAGLE, Elk, Buffalo, and Deer dances. Spirited and animated, they are considered a form of prayer. Each dance is very

different from the others, and the same dance differs from pueblo to pueblo, although certain aspects are similar. In the Deer Dance, for example, dancers "walk" holding two sticks that represent their forelegs. They wear elaborate costumes and antler headdresses.

New Mexico's 19 pueblos are: Acoma, Cochiti, Isleta, Jemez, Laguna, Nambe, Picuris, Pojoaque, Sandia, San Felipe, San Ildefonso, San Juan, Santa Ana, Santa Clara, Santo Domingo, Taos, Tesuque, Zia, and Zuni. Each of them celebrates its saint's feast day as well as other occasions with dances and ceremonies that are an expression of thanksgiving, prayer, renewal, and harmony with nature. Many dances tell stories, legends, or history. Besides the feast days and Three Kings Day (EPIPHANY), most pueblos observe these other major holidays: NEW YEAR'S DAY, EASTER, and CHRISTMAS, which is often celebrated for two to five days.

CONTACTS:
Indian Pueblo Cultural Center
2401 12th St. N.W.
Albuquerque, NM 87104
505-843-7270 or 866-855-7902
www.indianpueblo.org

◆ 2977 ◆ Three Weeks
Begins between June 17 and July 24 and ends between July 17 and August 14; from Tammuz 17 until Av 9 until Av 9

The 17th of Tammuz, also known as **Shivah Asar be-Tammuz**, marks the day on which the walls of Jerusalem were breached by the Babylonians under Nebuchadnezzar (*see also* ASARAH BE-TEVET). The three-week period between this day and the ninth of Av (*see* TISHA BE-AV) is known in Hebrew as the period **Bén ha-Metsarim**, in reference to Lamentations 1:3, which describes the city of Jerusalem as having been overtaken by her persecutors "between the straits."

Because this period is associated with the destruction of the Temple, it is a time of mourning for the Jewish people. As the days draw closer to the ninth of Av, the signs of mourning increase in severity. Although there are differences between Ashkenazi and Sephardic customs, the restrictions include not shaving or cutting one's hair, not wearing new clothes, nor eating fruit for the first time in season. Beginning with the first day of Av, the Ashkenazi custom is not to eat any meat nor drink any wine until after Tisha be-Av, while Sephardim refrain from meat and wine beginning with the Sunday preceding the ninth of Av. On Tisha be-Av itself, it is not permitted to eat or drink, to wear leather shoes, to anoint with oil, to wash (except where required), or to engage in sexual relations. On each of the three Sabbaths during the Three Weeks, a special prophetic passage of the Old Testament, known as a *haftarah*, is read.

CONTACTS:
Orthodox Union
11 Broadway
New York, NY 10004
212-563-4000
ou.org

♦ 2978 ♦ Tiananmen Square Anniversary
June 4

Each year thousands of people in Hong Kong, China, gather on June 4 to commemorate the anniversary of the Tiananmen Square massacre with a candlelight vigil. On that same date in 1989, Chinese government tanks rolled into Beijing's Tiananmen Square killing hundreds of demonstrators calling for democratic reforms in China and injuring 10,000 more. The Chinese government has suppressed similar commemorative efforts in other Chinese cities, but since Hong Kong was a British colony until 1997, the tradition of the candlelight vigil took hold there. Since 1997 the Chinese government has discouraged the Hong Kong commemorations and pressured foreign news correspondents not to cover the yearly event.

In 2014, between 100,000 and 180,000 people gathered for a ceremony at Victoria Park in Hong Kong to commemorate the 25th anniversary of the Tiananmen Square crackdown, the largest crowd since 1989. Even as heightened security on mainland China has attempted to expunge all memory of the Tiananmen bloodshed from Chinese consciousness, Hong Kong remained the only city on Chinese soil where any public commemoration of the anniversary could even take place. Across the harbor from the well-attended vigil in Victoria Park, 3,060 people gathered at a much smaller event, calling for established pro-democracy parties to be more assertive in challenging the Beijing government.

CONTACTS:
Beijing Foriegn Affairs Office
No.2, Zhengyi Rd.
Dongcheng District
Beijing, 100744 China
fax: 8610-6519 2775
www.ebeijing.gov.cn

♦ 2979 ♦ Tichborne Dole
March 25

The custom of handing out a dole, or allotment of flour, to the village poor in Alresford, Hampshire, England, dates back to the 12th or 13th century. Lady Mabella Tichborne, who was on her deathbed at the time, begged her husband to grant her enough land to provide an annual bounty of bread to the poor, who were suffering from a recent failure of the wheat crop. Her husband, in a less charitable frame of mind, snatched a blazing log from the fire and said that his wife could have as much land as she was able to crawl across before the flames died out. Although she had been bedridden for years, Lady Mabella had her servants carry her to the fields bordering the Tichborne estate and miraculously managed to crawl across 23 acres. With her dying breath, she proclaimed that if her heirs should ever fail to honor the bequest, the family name would die out.

On March 25, or LADY DAY, each year, villagers in need of assistance gather at the porch of Tichborne House to claim their portion of the gift: a gallon of flour for adults, half as much for children. The fields across which Lady Mabella dragged herself are still known as "The Crawls.".

CONTACTS:
Hampshire County Council
Tourism Section, Dept. of Economy
Transport & Environment
Elizabeth II Ct. W.
Winchester, SO23 8UJ United Kingdom
44-196-284-6005; fax: 44-196-287-8131
www.hants.gov.uk

♦ 2980 ♦ Tihar
October-November; waning half of Hindu month of Kartika

Tihar is a five-day Hindu festival in Nepal that honors different animals on successive days. The third day of the festival, LAKSHMI PUJA, dedicated to the goddess of wealth, is known throughout India as DEWALI.

On the first day of the festival, offerings of rice are made to crows, thought to be sent by Yama, the god of death, as his "messengers of death." The second day honors dogs, since in the afterworld dogs will guide departed souls across the river of the dead. Dogs are fed special food and adorned with flowers. Cows are honored on the morning of the third day; they, too, receive garlands and often their horns are painted gold and silver.

The third day is the most important day of the festival, when Lakshmi will come to visit every home that is suitably lit for her. Consequently, as evening falls, tiny candles and butter lamps flicker in homes throughout the country.

The fourth day is a day for honoring oxen and bullocks, and it also marks the start of the new year for the Newari people of the Kathmandu Valley. On the fifth day, known as Bhai Tika, brothers and sisters meet and place *tikas* (dots of red sandalwood paste, considered emblems of good luck) on each other's foreheads. The brothers give their sisters gifts, and the sisters give sweets and delicacies to their brothers and pray to Yama for their brothers' long life. This custom celebrates the legendary occasion when a girl pleaded so eloquently with Yama to spare her young brother from an early death that he relented and the boy lived.

CONTACTS:
Nepal Tourism Board
Bhrikuti Mandap
P.O. Box 11018
Nepal
977-1-4256909; fax: 977-1-4256910
welcomenepal.com

♦ 2981 ♦ Time Observance Day
June 10

Emperor Tenchi (or Tenji) of Japan (626-671) is credited with making the first water clock, a device that measured time by the amount of water leaking out of a vessel. Because keeping track of time was not standard practice in the seventh century, the Japanese honor their 38th emperor on June 10, the day on which he first ordered the hour to be announced by sounding temple bells and drums.

The **Rokoku Festival**, or **Water Clock Festival**, is held on this day at the Omi Jingu Shrine in the city of Otsu, Shiga Prefecture, where the emperor's water clock is housed.

While placing so much emphasis on keeping track of the time may sound odd to Americans, it is important to remember that the Japanese were traditionally lax in such matters, often failing to announce the time when a meeting or function would begin because it depended on the readiness of the person in charge.

♦ 2982 ♦ Timor Santa Cruz Massacre Day (National Youth Day)
November 12

The Santa Cruz Massacre Day (**National Youth Day**) remains among the most significant anniversaries for veterans of the Timorese independence movement, which was active during the Indonesian occupation between 1975 and 1999. In 1991, 271 protesters—many of them students—disappeared or were killed at the Santa Cruz cemetery in the Timor-Leste capital, Dili. That massacre sparked international outrage and kept the spotlight on the Indonesian occupation until it ended in 1999.

Before Indonesia withdrew forces, the anniversary of the Santa Cruz Massacre inspired several political protests, in towns and cities of Timor-Leste and among sympathetic communities throughout the world. In 1994, on the third anniversary, a group of Timorese activists scaled the fence of the U.S. embassy in Jakarta, Indonesia, to request political asylum.

The tone of the day was and remains mournful. During the occupation years, Timorese often lit candles, and it was often an occasion for public figures to rally the people. On the fifth anniversary of the massacre, NOBEL Peace Prize–winner José Ramos-Horta called on Timorese to begin a new phase of their campaign for self-determination.

CONTACTS:
Embassy of the Democratic Republic of Timor Leste
4201 Connecticut Ave.
NW Ste 504
Washington, D.C. 20008 United States
202-966-3202; fax: 202-966-3205
www.timorlesteembassy.org

♦ 2983 ♦ Timor-Leste Anniversary of the Indonesian Invasion
December 7

During Indonesia's 24-year occupation of its smaller neighbor, East Timor, the Timorese began commemorating historical dates, including the anniversary of the invasion of Indonesian forces on December 7, 1975. The arrival of the Indonesians initiated a period of occupation in which about 200,000 Timorese were killed. Today, in the Democratic Republic of Timor-Leste (internationally recognized since 2002), this anniversary remains an occasion to mourn those who were killed and to seek redress for crimes committed during the occupation.

Beginning in 1976, the year Indonesia annexed the nation then known as East Timor, the Timorese established a tradition of gathering in the capital, Dili, to commemorate the anniversary of the invasion and stage a public protest over Indonesia's actions. Candlelight vigils and commemorative church services also became common throughout the country and around the world. An historic demonstration took place on the 20th anniversary in 1995, when 112 East Timorese and supporters temporarily occupied Russian and Dutch embassies in Jakarta, the capital of Indonesia.

In the years since Timor-Leste achieved independence, human rights and other political groups have marked milestone anniversaries of the invasion by continuing to demand justice for the occupation's victims.

CONTACTS:
Embassy of the Democratic Republic of Timor Leste
4201 Connecticut Ave. N.W.
Ste. 504
Washington, D.C. 20008
202-966-3202; fax: 202-966-3205
www.timorlesteembassy.org

♦ 2984 ♦ Timor-Leste Proclamation of Independence Day
November 28

After the East Timorese declared independence from Portugal on November 28, 1975, it took over two decades to fulfill the promise of freedom. Their plans were foiled by neighboring Indonesia, which carried out its own occupation of its neighbor between 1975 and 1999. A second date, EAST TIMOR INDEPENDENCE DAY, was established when the Democratic Republic of Timor-Leste, as it is officially known, finally became a free state on May 2, 2002.

Observances for the November 28 anniversary honor the veterans of the independence movement. State leaders and other dignitaries usually participate in a parade, and the president of the country often bestows medals of honor to distinguish individuals who fought for the country's freedom.

CONTACTS:
Embassy of the Democratic Republic of Timor Leste
4201 Connecticut Ave. N.W.
Ste. 504
Washington, D.C. 20008
202-966-3202; fax: 202-966-3205
www.timorlesteembassy.org

♦ 2985 ♦ Timqat (Timkat)
January 19-20

Because the Ethiopian CHRISTMAS, called GANNA, falls on January 7, EPIPHANY (Timqat) is celebrated on January 19. Timqat celebrates the baptism of Jesus in the Jordan River. It begins at sunset on Epiphany Eve, when people dress in white and go to their local church. From the church they form a procession with the *tabot,* or holy ark, in which the ancient Israelites put the Tablets of the Law, or Torah, the first five books of the Old Testament. Ethiopians do not believe it was lost, but that it is now preserved in the Cathedral of Axum in Ethiopia (each Ethiopian Orthodox church has a blessed replica of the tabot as well). They accompany it to a lake, stream, or pond. It is placed in a tent, where it is guarded all night while the clergy and villagers sing, dance, and eat until the baptismal service the following morning. At dawn the clergy bless the water and sprinkle it on the heads of those who wish to renew their Christian vows. Then the procession, again bearing the tabot, returns to the church. The festivities continue until the following day, January 20 or the Feast of St. Michael.

Ethiopian religious processions are characterized by the priests' richly colored ceremonial robes, fringed, embroidered umbrellas, and elaborately decorated crosses. The national sport of *guks* is often played at Timqat. Warriors with shields of hippopotamus hide, wearing lion-mane capes and headdresses ride on caparisoned horses and try to strike each other with thrown bamboo lances.

CONTACTS:
Embassy of Ethiopia
3506 International Dr. N.W.
Washington, D.C. 20008
202-364-1200; fax: 202-587-0195
www.ethiopianembassy.org

♦ 2986 ♦ **Tin Hau Festival**
23rd day of third lunar month

This birthday festival in Hong Kong celebrates Tin Hau, queen of Heaven and goddess of the sea. Also known as Tien-hou or Matsu, she is one of the most popular deities in Hong Kong; there are about 24 Tin Hau temples throughout the territory, and fishermen often have shrines to her on their boats. Her story dates back many centuries. It is said that she was born with mystical powers in a fishing village in Fukien Province, and that as a young girl she saved her two brothers from drowning during a storm. Today she is revered for her ability to calm the waves and to guarantee bountiful catches, and for her protection from shipwrecks and sickness.

The festivities include parades, performances of Chinese opera, and the sailing of hundreds of junks and sampans, decked out with colorful streamers, through Hong Kong's waterways to the temples. The temple in Joss House Bay is especially known for its festival, which attracts thousands of fisherfolk. The original temple was built southwest of the present temple in 1012 by two brothers who said their lives were saved by the statue of Tin Hau that they clutched when they were shipwrecked. A typhoon destroyed that temple, and descendants of the brothers built another one on the present site in 1266.

See also MATSU, BIRTHDAY OF.

CONTACTS:
Hong Kong Tourist Office
9-11/F Citicorp Centre

18 Whitfield Rd.
China
852-2807-6543; fax: 852-2806-0303
www.discoverhongkong.com

♦ 2987 ♦ **Tiragan**
July, November, December; 13th day of Tir, the fourth Zoroastrian month

Tiragan is a Zoroastrian celebration in honor of Tishtrya, a deity identified with rain as well as Sirius, the Dog Star. It is held during the *gahambar* or seasonal feast of MAIDYOSHA-HEM, also known as the Mid-Summer Feast. The followers of Persian prophet Zoroaster (also known as Zarathushtra, believed to have lived around 1200 B.C.E.), believe that dogs belong to the good part of creation and that they serve as helpers to mankind. Dogs are also thought to possess the ability to see spiritual beings. Much like the celebration of HOLI in India and of SONGKRAN in Thailand, the festival's activities include splashing people with water.

The 13th day of Tir is also associated with a legendary event during the reign of King Minochiher, when a dispute about the boundary between Iran and Turan (a region in what is now southeastern Iran) was decided by the throwing of an arrow (tir) by an archer named Erekhsha.

There are only about 100,000 followers of Zoroastrianism today, and most of them live in northwestern India or Iran. Smaller communities exist in Pakistan, Sri Lanka, Canada, the U.S., England, and Australia.

♦ 2988 ♦ **Tirana, La**
About a week, including July 16

Each July tens of thousands of pilgrims set up camp in the small village of La Tirana, in the Tarapacá region of northern Chile. July 16 is the feast day of the Virgen del Carmen and the highlight of the festival (*see also* OUR LADY OF CARMEL). On that day there is a colorful, musical procession of images of the Virgen and Jesus around the village accompanied by more than 100 dance groups in elaborate costumes. Dancers who attend the festival practice traditional Andean dances all year round for the event, and many view their dancing as an act of devotion to the Virgen. During the rest of the time people wander the markets that have sprung up, worship at the chapel that houses the image of the Virgen, and participate in masses and other religious activities organized by the Diocese of Iquique.

CONTACTS:
Embassy of Chile
1732 Massachusetts Ave. N.W.
Washington, D.C. 20036
202-785-1746; fax: 202-887-5579
chileabroad.gov.cl/estados-unidos/en

♦ 2989 ♦ **Tirupati Festival**
August-September; about nine days during Hindu month of Bhadrapada

Tirupati, Andhra Pradesh, India, is considered an essential pilgrimage center for every devout Hindu. The shrine there, one of the richest temples in the world, is situated on the seven Tirumala hills. Since Tirupati is the seat of Lord Venkteshwara, a manifestation of Lord Vishnu, Venkteshwara is also known as the "Lord of the Seven Hills." The grand festival, called *Bhramotsavam*, is held at Tirupati during the month of Bhadrapada for about nine days, during which Hindus gather to seek Lord Venkteshwara's blessings for material and spiritual gains.

Hindus who make a pilgrimage to Tirupati during the festival in the month of Bhadrapada often shave their hair off as a votive offering. Parents bring very young children there to perform their first tonsure (the act of clipping the hair) at the feet of the image of Lord Venkteshwara.

CONTACTS:
Ministry of Tourism - Government of India
1270 Avenue of the Americas
Ste. 303
New York, NY 10020
212-586-4901; fax: 212-582-3274
tourism.nic.in

Tirumala Tirupati Devasthanams
TTD Administrative Bldg.
K.T. Rd.
Tirupati, Andhra Pradesh 517 501 Indian
91-877-2233333 or 800-425-4141; fax: 91-877-2264217
www.tirumala.org

Tourism Information Center - Government of Andhra Pradesh
1st Fl.
D Block
Hyderabad, Andhra Pradesh 500022 India
91-40-23456717 or 800-42-545454
www.aptourism.gov.in

♦ 2990 ♦ Tisha be-Av
Between July 17 and August 14; Av 9

The Jewish **Fast of Av** is a period of fasting, lamentation, and prayer in memory of the destruction of both the First and Second Temples in Jerusalem. When the Babylonians under Nebuchadnezzar destroyed the First Temple in 586 B.C.E., the Jews rebuilt it, but continued the fast day. Then the Second Temple was destroyed by the Romans under Titus, who burned it down in 70 C.E., and a long period of exile began for the Jews.

The Fast of Av begins at sunset the previous day and lasts for more than 24 hours. The nine days from the beginning of the month of Av through Tisha be-Av mark a period of intense mourning for the various disasters and tragedies that have befallen the Jewish people throughout history.

See also ASARAH BE-TEVET and THREE WEEKS.

♦ 2991 ♦ Tivoli Gardens Season
Mid-April to late September

Tivoli Gardens is a renowned entertainment center that has been a summer attraction in the middle of Copenhagen, Denmark, since 1843. There are orchestral, jazz, and rock concerts; ballet; and Italian pantomimes featuring Pantaloon, Columbine, and Harlequin performed with the original musical scores. Another favorite entertainment is the Tivoli Guards, a band comprised of youngsters dressed in uniforms similar to those worn by the Royal Guard. At night the gardens dazzle with laser light shows and fireworks.

CONTACTS:
Tivoli Gardens
Tivoli A/S, Vesterbrogade 3
Copenhagen, 1630 Denmark
45-33-15-10-01
www.tivoligardens.com

♦ 2992 ♦ *To Kill a Mockingbird* Annual Production
April-May

A two-act dramatization of Harper Lee's novel *To Kill a Mockingbird* is presented over several weekends each spring at the courthouse in Lee's hometown, Monroeville, Ala. Presented by amateur players from the community, the production draws hundreds of fans of the Pulitzer-Prize-winning novel, published in 1960.

The first act generally is performed outdoors, with the action moving into the historic 1903 courtroom for Act Two. Members of the audience are chosen to portray the jury in one of the play's climactic scenes. The courthouse setting is highly prized, because it inspired the set created for the trial scenes in the popular 1962 film version of *To Kill a Mockingbird*. The movie starred Gregory Peck as Atticus Finch, the principled attorney fighting racism in 1930s Alabama.

Lee, who never wrote another book, still lives in Monroeville, but is said never to have attended the production based on her masterpiece. Monroeville began hosting performances in 1990, and it has transformed the town into a destination for tourists. Paid tickets to the performances sell out quickly in advance.

CONTACTS:
Monroe County Heritage Museums
86 N. Alabama Ave.
Monroeville, AL 36460 United States
251-743-2879; fax: 251-743-2189
www.monroecountymuseum.org

♦ 2993 ♦ Togo Independence Day
April 27

Togo became independent on this day in 1960, after being under French control from the end of World War I. Independence Day is a national holiday in Togo.

CONTACTS:
Embassy of Togo
2208 Massachusetts Ave. N.W.
Washington, D.C. 20008
202-234-4212; fax: 202-232-3190
www.togoleseembassy.com

◆ 2994 ◆ Togo National Liberation Day
January 13

On January 13, 1967, Togo president Nicolas Grunitzky, of mixed Kabye, Ewe, and Polish heritage, was overthrown by Gnassingbé Eyadema, who remained president of Togo until 2005. He was succeeded by his son Faure Gnassingbé. Bowing to both internal and international pressure, Faure Gnassingbé agreed to step down and hold a general election. He won that election, was reelected in 2010, and will run for a third term in 2015. National Liberation Day celebrates the accession to power of his father, Gnassingbé Eyadema.

To celebrate National Liberation Day, the Togo military joins with civilian bands to mount several colorful parades down the Boulevard du Mono in the city of Lomé. Dissident groups have long opposed the celebrations, noting that January 13, 1963, saw the assassination of the nation's first president, Sylvanus Olympio. Because of the conflicting events that have happened on the same day in Togo history, President Gnassingbé in 2005 took a step toward appeasing his critics by publicly calling Sylvanus Olympio the true father of Togo's independence. In 2008, he called for an end to the public celebrations on National Liberation Day. The army would celebrate the day quietly on their own military bases, while the civilian population was urged to pray for national reconciliation.

CONTACTS:
Embassy of Togo
2208 Massachusetts Ave., N.W.
Washington, D.C. 20008
202-234-4212; fax: 202-232-3190
www.togoleseembassy.com

◆ 2995 ◆ Tohono O'odham Nation Rodeo
Three days in February

The Tohono O'odham Nation Rodeo has been a tradition for more than 60 years. Thousands of visitors come to Sells, Arizona, for the event each year for three days of rodeo and festivities in February. Dancers from tribes nationwide recreate ceremonial dances designed to bring rain, cure illness, or prepare for war, while Native American cowboys and cowgirls compete for $40,000 in prize money in such events as bareback riding, saddle bronc riding, bull riding, calf roping, steer wrestling, and barrel racing. Craft shows highlight the work of local Tohono O'odham and Pima artists and craftspeople, along with Maricopa pottery and baskets and Hopi kachina dolls.

The Tohono O'odham Nation, which in 1986 changed its name from Papago (meaning "Bean People") to Tohono O'odham (which means "Desert People"), have lived in the desert regions of what is now Arizona and Mexico for centuries. They are renowned for their ability to grow food in the desert, and the festival features lots of traditional Indian foods, including fry bread and barbecue.

CONTACTS:
Tohono O'odham Nation

P.O. Box 837
Sells, AZ 85634
520-383-1800; fax: 520-383-3263
www.tonation-nsn.gov

◆ 2996 ◆ Toh-shiya
Sunday closest to January 15

Toh-shiya is an archery contest held at the Sanjusangen-do Temple in Kyoto, Japan. The event is also known as **New Year Archery,** since the first arrows of the New Year are shot at this contest. Expert archers, along with the young, participate in this free event, which is a sort of coming-of-age ritual. Girls dressed in kimonos enter adulthood by drawing their bows at the event. Legend has it that master archers were able to hit their targets from the northern and southern ends of the temple, which is the longest wooden structure in the world. An archer named Wasa Daihachiro is said to have hit 8,132 arrows in a 24-hour period in 1688.

CONTACTS:
Japan National Tourism Organization
1 Grand Central Pl.
60 E. 42nd St., Ste. 448
New York, NY 10165
212-757-5640; fax: 212-307-6754
www.jnto.go.jp/eng

◆ 2997 ◆ Toji (Winter Solstice)
December 22

The earliest mention of WINTER SOLSTICE celebrations in Japan dates back at least to 725 C.E. and comes from records left by Emperor Shomu. It is an especially happy time for farmers, because it marks the time of year when the days begin to grow longer and the sun nearer. Many of the customs associated with Toji are still observed in rural areas; they include enjoying citrus baths, eating foods made from pumpkins (which is believed to bring good luck), and offering gifts to one's ancestors. Servants and workers are often given a day off, and many shrines sponsor bonfires.

CONTACTS:
Shingon Head Temple Toji [Kyoogokokuji]
1 Kujocho
Minami Ward
Kyoto, Kyoto Prefecture 601-8473 Japan
81-75-691-3325; fax: 81-75-662-0250
www.toji.or.jp

◆ 2998 ◆ Tok Race of Champions Dog Sled Race
Late March

The last race of the Alaska dog-mushing season, held since 1954 in Tok, which claims to be the Dog Capital of Alaska. Mushers from Alaska, Canada, and the lower 48 states participate in six-dog, eight-dog and open-class events for cash prizes.

Tok, a trade center for nearby Athabascan Indian villages, is also a center for dog breeding, training, and mushing. It's not quite certain where the name of the town came from; some say it derives from a native word meaning "peace crossing," and others believe the village was originally called Tokyo and shortened to Tok during World War II.

CONTACTS:
Tok Dog Mushers Association
P.O. Box 45
Tok, AK 99780
www.tokdogmushers.org

◆ 2999 ◆ Tolling the Devil's Knell
December 24

To celebrate the birth of Christ and the death of the Devil, All Saints Minster Church in Dewsbury, Yorkshire, rings its bell the same number of times as the number of the year (for example, 2,000 times in 2000) on Christmas Eve. The tolling starts at 11:00 P.M., stops during the church service from midnight to 12:45, and is then resumed until the years have been tolled away. The custom has been going on for almost 700 years, although there was an interruption in the early 19th century and again during World War II, when all bell-ringing was banned except to signal enemy invasion.

Although no one seems to remember exactly how the custom started, there is a legend that says Sir Thomas Soothill donated the tenor bell to the parish church as a penance for murdering a young boy servant and then trying to conceal his body. The bell has been called "Black Tom of Soothill" since the 13th century, and **Tolling Black Tom** is supposed to keep the parish safe from the Devil for another 12 months.

CONTACTS:
Dewsbury Minster, Serving the people of Dewsbury
Rishworth Rd.
Dewsbury, West Yorkshire WF12 8DD United Kingdom
44-19-2445-7057
www.dewsburyminster.org.uk

◆ 3000 ◆ Tom Sawyer Days, National
Week of July 4

Sponsored by the Hannibal, Missouri, Jaycees, the National Tom Sawyer Days celebration began in 1956 with a Tom Sawyer Fence Painting Contest and a Tom and Becky competition. Three years later, all of the events relating to the fictional character originally created by Mark Twain in his 1876 novel were combined with the traditional Fourth of July celebration in Hannibal, and Independence Day was officially proclaimed "Tom Sawyer Day." In 1961 it became a national event, and today the festival spans five days and includes a number of unique competitions.

Contestants for the fence-painting competition, who must be 10 to 13 years old, come primarily from the 10 states bordering the Mississippi River. They are judged on the authenticity of their costumes (which must be based on details from Mark Twain's book), the speed with which they can whitewash a four-by-five-foot section of fence, and the quality of their work.

The Frog Jump Competition is another of the festival's highlights, drawing up to 300 children and their pet frogs, each of whom is allowed three jumps. Competitors for the Tom and Becky competition must be eighth graders living in Hannibal, and the winners serve as goodwill ambassadors for the year.

See also Calaveras County Fair and Frog Jumping Jubilee.

CONTACTS:
Hannibal Jaycees
P.O. Box 484
Hannibal, MO 63401
573-221-3231
www.hannibaljaycees.org

◆ 3001 ◆ Tomatina (Tomato Battle)
Last week in August

Regardless of which legend one believes, what began in 1945 as a few tossed tomatoes as a show of disdain for the repressive Franco regime—or during a feud among friends—or by a fan unhappy with a musician's performance—has developed into full-fledged tomato warfare in Buñol, Valencia, Spain, during the last week in August. La Tomatina also happens to coincide with the town's patron saint festival, and while the tomato battle itself takes place on a Wednesday, the festivities last for a week.

Residents prepare for the impending food fight by protecting their storefronts and homes with plastic, donning special clothing, and imbibing alcohol. Thousands of pounds of tomatoes are trucked into town and dropped off at the Plaza del Pueblo, Buñol's main square, and the light-hearted battle commences. Although anyone is fair game when it comes to choosing a target, La Tomatina offers a good opportunity for males and females to meet and flirt with each other. This community-sanctioned tomato bath leaves both the festival-goers and the streets covered with pulp, seeds, and juice, but after the cleanup, celebrants continue to enjoy the festival's fireworks, parades, food, and music.

CONTACTS:
Tomatina Festival Spain
Plaza de Tetuán, 5
Valencia, 46003 Spain
34-96353-2562
www.latomatina.org

◆ 3002 ◆ Tonga Emancipation Day
June 4

June 4 is a national holiday in the Kingdom of Tonga, celebrating its full independence from Britain. Located in the Pacific Ocean some 1,250 miles north of New Zealand, the island nation of Tonga consists of about 150 islands, 36 of which are inhabited. With a population of about 120,000, Tonga is ruled by a royal family that goes back to 1831.

On June 4, 1863, King George Tupuo I abolished the system of serfdom in the island nation of Tonga. The historic occasion is remembered on Emancipation Day, which is celebrated just after the conclusion of the annual three-day Ha'apai Festival. The Ha'apai Festival begins on Tonga's outer islands and ends on Lifuka Island on June 4th. Both the festival and Emancipation Day are marked with feasts and dancing.

CONTACTS:
Consulate General of Tonga in San Francisco
1350 Bayshore Hwy.
Ste. 610
Burlingame, CA 94010
650-685-1001; fax: 650-685-1003
www.tongaconsul.com/home

Tonga Ministry of Information & Communications
1st Fl.O.G. Sanft & Sons Bldg.
Western Corner of Taufa'ahau Rd. & Wellington Rd.
Tonga
676-28-170; fax: 676-24-861
mic.gov.to

♦ 3003 ♦ **Tonga Heilala Festival**
Week of July 4

Located in the Pacific Ocean some 1,250 miles north of New Zealand, the island nation of Tonga consists of about 150 islands, 36 of which are inhabited. With a population of about 120,000, Tonga is ruled by a royal family that goes back to 1831.

The Heilala Festival celebrates the flowering of the heilala, Tonga's national flower. The Festival begins with the birthday celebration for Tonga's King Tupou VI, which takes place on July 4th, and then continues for the following week.

The weeklong Heilala Festival features a host of events, including a Miss Heilala Pageant, parades of floats, processions, and music festivals. The streets of Tongatapu are covered with colorful flowered arches, while decorative lights illuminate the Royal Tomb at Mala'ekula and the Royal Palace. Among the live entertainment is the dance group Lakalaka from Vavau, which features some 1,000 dancers. In addition to food, drinks, and live music, there are also traditional crafts on display. A night-time torch-lighting ceremony, named Tupakapakanava, involves a group of participants carrying flaming torches of dry reeds along the northern coastline of Tongatapu. The evenings often end with gatherings around beach bonfires.

CONTACTS:
Tonga Ministry of Information & Communications
Western Corner of Taufa"ahau Rd. & Wellington Rd.
1st Fl, O. G. Sanft & Sons Bldg.
Tonga
676-28-170; fax: 676-24-861
www.mic.gov.to

Tonga Consulate General
1350 Bayshore Hwy.
Ste. 610
Burlingame, CA 94010
650-685-1001; fax: 650-685-1003
www.tongaconsul.com

♦ 3004 ♦ **Tonga National Day**
November 4

On November 4, 1875, King George Tupou I gave his consent to the constitution of the new nation of Tonga. Celebrated for many years as **Tonga Constitution Day**, the government of Tonga in 2006 renamed the holiday Tonga National Day and pronounced it an occasion to celebrate the country's heritage as a whole.

Located in the Pacific Ocean some 1,250 miles north of New Zealand, the island nation of Tonga consists of about 150 islands, 36 of which are inhabited. With a population of about 120,000, Tonga is ruled by a royal family that goes back to 1831. King George Tupou I conquered the islands that now make up Tonga and granted his people a constitution guaranteeing their rights in 1875. His great-grandson, King George Tupou II, signed a treaty of friendship with England in 1900 that made Tonga a protected state. Tonga achieved complete independence in 1970 and became a member of the United Nations in 1999.

CONTACTS:
Tonga Consulate General
1350 Bayshore Hwy
Suite 610
Burlingame, CA 94010
650-685-1001; fax: 650-685-1003
www.tongaconsul.com

♦ 3005 ♦ **Tono Matsuri**
September 14-15

This autumn festival in Japan, observed in the hope that it will bring a good harvest, provides an excellent display of traditional Japanese arts. There is a Sʜɪsʜɪ Oᴅᴏʀɪ dance, performed to the accompaniment of taiko drums; *Taué-odori*, a rice-planting dance; *kagura* (sacred music and dance) performances; and *Yabusamé* (horseback archery) demonstrations. There is also a children's parade, called *Chigo-gyoretsu*. A distinctive genre of festival music, known as *Nambubayashi*, is performed on the grounds of the Tonogo-hachimangu Shrine in Tono.

CONTACTS:
Japan National Tourism Organization
1 Grand Central Pl.
60 E. 42nd St.
Ste. 448
New York, NY 10165
212-757-5640; fax: 212-307-6754
www.jnto.go.jp

Iwate Prefecture Tourism Association
Moriokaekinishitori Chome
No. 9 No. 1 (Marios 3F)
Morioka, Iwate Prefecture 020-0045 Japan
81-19-651-0626; fax: 81-19-651-0637
www.japan-iwate.info

♦ 3006 ♦ **Torch Festival**
24th through 26th days of sixth lunar month

The Torch Festival is a traditional holiday of many of the Yi people in Yunnan and Sichuan Provinces in China. Revelers dress in fine clothes, and the girls are especially colorful in embroidered gowns and headdresses of all colors. Celebrations begin with the sound of firecrackers, followed by folk dancing, athletic contests in such sports as pole-climbing and wrestling, and a bullfight. At night, huge bonfires are lit, dancers whirl around them, and a parade of people carrying torches brightens the night.

CONTACTS:
Yunnan Provincial Tourism Information Center
Yunnan Tourism Bldg.
No. 678 Dianchi Rd.
Kunming, Yunnan Province 650200 China
86-0871-96927
en.ynta.gov.cn

♦ 3007 ♦ Torch Fight
February; 15th day of the first lunar month

Torch fights are still popular in some rural areas in Korea to celebrate the first full moon of the LUNAR NEW YEAR (SOL). Neighboring farming villages form their own teams and fight each other with torches made of burning bundles of straw. Young men and boys do the fighting, and the number of torches they use depends on the number of people in their families. A hill is usually the designated battleground, and the torch-bearers gather there and wait for the full moon to rise, at which point a gong signals the beginning of the battle.

The fighting consists of members of each team rushing their opponents, brandishing their lit torches. While no one usually gets hurt in this game, participants generally go home with singed hair and clothing.

See also TAEBORUM.

CONTACTS:
Korea National Tourism Organization
737 N. Michigan Ave.
Ste. 910
Chicago, IL 60611
312-981-1717 or 800-868-7567; fax: 312-981-1721
english.visitkorea.or.kr

♦ 3008 ♦ Tori-no-ichi (Rooster Festival)
November

The **Rooster Festival** in Japan takes its name from the mythological rooster who helped bring the sun god out from hiding in a cave, and the bird became a symbol of material well-being. Many members of the Shinto sect who observe this festival are wealthy merchants and speculators, and the bamboo rakes that can be seen everywhere at this time are called *kumade*. People carry these rakes, usually decorated with good-luck emblems and the smiling face of the laughing goddess Okame, because they represent the power to pull toward them anything they desire. Some of the rakes are small enough to be worn in a woman's hair, while others are so large and heavily decorated that it takes several men to

carry them through the streets. Sometimes, signs advertising restaurants or shops are hung from them and used throughout the year.

CONTACTS:
Japan National Tourism Organization
1 Grand Central Pl.
60 E. 42nd St.
Ste. 448
New York, NY 10165
212-757-5640; fax: 212-307-6754
www.jnto.go.jp/eng

♦ 3009 ♦ Toronto Caribana (Toronto Caribbean Carnival)
Summer; varies

Since 1967, Toronto, Canada, has hosted a multi-week summer festival called Caribana, also known as the **Toronto Caribbean Carnival**. The festival was originally created as a community heritage project for Canada's Centennial year. It is the largest Caribbean festival in North America, bringing in more than one million people each year.

Caribana is a Trinidad-style carnival that includes music, dance, food, and costumes from Jamaica, Guyana, the Bahamas, Brazil, and other cultures represented in Toronto. The main event of the festival is the mile-long Caribana Parade, which is one of the largest in North America. The parade participants dress in brilliant costumes, and dozens of trucks fill the parade route all day, carrying artists giving live performances in soca, calypso, steel pan, reggae, and salsa.

In addition to the parade, main events include a two-day Olympic Island Caribbean Arts Festival, a calypso competition, a Caribana king and queen pageant, parties, Caribbean food, outdoor concerts, music, and dance. These events are intended to celebrate the community's heritage and culture.

This festival is similar to Calgary's annual CARIFEST celebration.

CONTACTS:
Caribana (Tourist Info)
215 Spadina Ave.
Ste. 400
Toronto, ON M5T 2C7 Canada
647-693-4441
www.caribana.com

♦ 3010 ♦ Toronto International Film Festival
First week of September

Second in size only to the Cannes Film Festival in France, the Toronto International Film Festival is considered one of the world's most prestigious artistic events. As such, it features some of the year's most anticipated films, attracts leading stars in the movie business, and serves as a major networking and educational opportunity for industry professionals.

Established by the Toronto International Film Festival Group, the festival was first held in 1976. From its inception, the event intended to attract worldwide attention yet simultaneously promote the domestic film industry. Today, people attend several showcases of Canadian-made films.

Festival organizers pride themselves on creating a public festival, which means film submissions from all over are accepted and screenings are open to the public as well as to the media and the film industry. The Toronto International Film Festival Group reports that it handles more than 300,000 public and industry admissions. From this group of films, Toronto theaters host screenings of over 300 films, representing about 50 different countries.

In spite of its lasting reputation for highlighting independent and international cinema, the festival has attracted attention and controversy since the 1990s for the submissions from Hollywood and the grand film marketing campaigns that promote them.

CONTACTS:
Toronto International Film Festival Group
350 King St. West
Toronto, ON M5V 3X5 Canada
416-599-8433
www.torontointernationalfilmfestival.ca

♦ 3011 ♦ Toronto Veg Food Fest
First weekend in September

The Toronto Veg Food Fest is an annual festival that takes place over the first weekend in September at Toronto's Harbourfront Centre. The festival includes over one hundred different food vendors, including local restaurants and bakeries, and a free, three-day program of presentations, workshops, documentary screenings, cooking demonstrations, live music, and children's events. Organized and presented by the Toronto Vegetarian Association for over thirty years, the Toronto Veg Food Fest is one of the oldest of vegetarian food festivals in the world. The purpose of the festival is to provide an opportunity for the public to access vegetarian foods, to raise awareness about the diversity of vegetarian cuisine, and to promote the health and environmental benefits of meatless meals. Every year, more than 40,000 people attend the festival.

CONTACTS:
Toronto Vegetarian Association
17 Baldwin St.
2nd Fl.
Toronto, ON M5T 1L1 Canada
416-544-9800
vegfoodfest.com

♦ 3012 ♦ Torta dei Fieschi
August 14

When Count Fieschi of Lavagna in Genoa, Italy, was married in 1240, he invited his guests—and everyone else in town—to share a cake that was more than 30 feet high. The citizens of Lavagna haven't forgotten his generosity, and each year they celebrate the event on August 14. Dressed in costumes, they

parade to the town square, where they pin to their clothes a piece of paper (blue for men, white for women) on which a word is written. When they find someone wearing the same word, the couple is given a piece of "Fieschi's cake.".

CONTACTS:
Italian Government Tourist Board
686 Park Ave.
3rd Fl.
New York, NY 10065
212-245-5618; fax: 212-586-9249
www.italiantourism.com

♦ 3013 ♦ Toshogu Haru-No-Taisai (Great Spring Festival of the Toshogu Shrine)
May 17-18

This festival—also known as the **Sennin Gyoretsu**, or **Procession of 1,000 People**—provides the most spectacular display of ancient samurai costumes and weaponry in Japan. The Toshogu Shrine, in Nikko, Tochigi Prefecture, was built in 1617 to house the mausoleum of Tokugawa Ieyasu (1543-1616), the first of the Tokugawa shoguns. The festival originated in honor of the reburial of Ieyasu in the new mausoleum.

On the first day of the festival, dignitaries and members of the Tokugawa family make offerings to the deities of the shrine. Also on this day, warriors on horseback shoot at targets with bows and arrows. On the morning of May 18 more than 1,000 people take part in the procession from Toshogu to Futarasan Shrine, including hundreds of samurai warriors with armor, helmets, and weaponry. Also marching are priests with flags; men with stuffed hawks representing huntsmen; men in fox masks to honor the fox spirits that protect the shrine; and musicians with drums and bells.

CONTACTS:
Tochigi Prefecture
1-1-20 Hanawada
Utsunomiya, Tochigi Prefecture 320-8501 Japan
81-28-623-3165; fax: 81-28-623-2199
www.pref.tochigi.lg.jp

♦ 3014 ♦ Tour de France
July

The Tour de France is the world's greatest bicycle race and also the annual sports event with the most viewers—an estimated one billion who watch television coverage beamed around the world and 14.6 million who stand by the roadside.

The tour, started in 1903, takes place mostly in France and Belgium, but also visits Spain, Italy, Germany, and Switzerland. It is divided into 21 timed stages, or legs, over three weeks, and has become a French national obsession. The newspaper sports columnist Red Smith once wrote that "an army from Mars could invade France, the government could fall, and even the recipe for sauce Béarnaise be lost, but if it happened during the Tour de France nobody would notice."

The route and distance of the tour is different each year, averaging 3,500 kilometers (about 2,100 miles, or the distance from Chicago to Los Angeles). It always includes strenuous mountain passes and a finale in Paris. The number of riders is limited to 180, and the rider with the lowest cumulative time for all stages is the winner. There have been four five-time winners: Jacques Anquetil (1957, 1961-64), Eddy Merckx (1969-72, 1974), Bernard Hinault (1978, 1979, 1981, 1982, 1985), and Miguel Indurain from Spain (1991-95). Merckx, a Belgian who seemed almost immune to pain, is considered the all-time greatest cycler. He competed in 1,800 races and won 525 of them. In 1986, Greg LeMond was the first American to win the tour. He was nearly killed in a 1987 hunting accident, and endured accidents and operations during the next two years, but came back to win the tour in 1989 and again in 1990.

American and former Olympian Lance Armstrong narrowly survived cancer diagnosed in 1996 and went on to win the Tour from 1999 to 2005—the first person to win seven times. In 2012, however, in response to a report of the United States Anti-Doping Agency indicating that Armstrong engaged in widespread use of banned substances and practices, the Union Cycliste Internationale formally stripped him of his seven Tour de France victories.

The first tour in 1903 was organized as a publicity stunt by Henri Desgranges, bicyclist and publisher of the cycling magazine *L'Auto*. On July 1, 1903, 60 bikers started from the Alarm Clock Café on the outskirts of Paris, and three weeks later Maurice Garin was the winner, and the tour was born. In 1984, the Tour Feminin, a special women's race, was added to the tour, and is now a stage race of about 1,000 kilometers, run concurrently with the final two weeks of the men's tour. The first winner was an American, Marianne Martin.

CONTACTS:
Amaury Sport Organisation
France
33-1-4133-1561
www.aso.fr

♦ 3015 ♦ **Tournament of Roses (Rose Parade)**
January 1

The Rose Parade is one of the world's most elaborate and most photographed parades, held every New Year's Day in Pasadena, Calif. The parade is made up of about 50 floats elaborately decorated—and completely covered—with roses, orchids, chrysanthemums, and other blossoms that portray the year's theme. Additionally there are more than 20 bands, 200 horses and costumed riders, a grand marshal, a Rose Queen, and the Queen's princesses. The parade is five and one-half miles long, attracts about one million spectators along the route and picks up about 350 million television viewers around the world.

The first festival, called the Battle of Flowers, was held on Jan. 1, 1890, under the auspices of the Valley Hunt Club. The man responsible was Charles Frederick Holder, a naturalist and teacher of zoology. He had seen battles of the flowers on the

French Riviera (*see* MARDI GRAS IN FRANCE), and figured California could do something similar; his suggestion resulted in a parade of decorated carriages and buggies followed by amateur athletic events. The parade evolved gradually. Floral floats were introduced, and in 1902 the morning parade was capped by a football game, which was replaced in following years by chariot races. In 1916, football came back, and the ROSE BOWL GAME is now traditionally associated with the parade.

In 1992, the theme of the tournament was "Voyages of Discovery," and it kicked off the Columbus Quincentennial. Co-grand marshals were Cristobal Colon, a descendant of Christopher COLUMBUS, and Colorado Rep. Ben Nighthorse Campbell, a Cheyenne chief.

CONTACTS:
Tournament of Roses
391 S. Orange Grove Blvd.
Pasadena, CA 91184
626-449-4100
www.tournamentofroses.com

♦ 3016 ♦ **Town Meeting Day**
First Tuesday of March

An official state holiday in Vermont, this is the day on which nearly every town elects its officers, approves budgets, and deals with other civic issues in a daylong public meeting of the voters. It more or less coincides with the anniversary of Vermont's admission to the Union on March 4, 1791 (*see* Appendix). Vermonters pride themselves on their active participation in these meetings, which often include heated debates on issues of local importance.

CONTACTS:
Vermont League of Cities & Towns
89 Main St.
Ste. 4
Montpelier, VT 05602
802-229-9111; fax: 802-229-2211
www.vlct.org

♦ 3017 ♦ **Trafalgar Day**
October 21

This is the anniversary of the famous naval battle fought by the British off Cape Trafalgar, Spain, in 1805. The British navy, under the command of Viscount Horatio Nelson (1758-1805), defeated the combined French and Spanish fleets, thus eliminating the threat of NAPOLEON's invasion of England. The victory that cost Lord Nelson his life was commemorated by the column erected in his honor in London's Trafalgar Square. Ceremonies on Trafalgar Day, or **Nelson Day**, include a naval parade from London's Mall to Trafalgar Square, where a brief service is held and wreaths are placed at the foot of Nelson's Column.

CONTACTS:
National Maritime Museum
Park Row
Greenwich
London, SE10 9NF United Kingdom

www.rmg.co.uk
Greater London Authority
City Hall, The Queen's Walk
More London
London, SE1 2AA United Kingdom
44-20-7983-4000
www.london.gov.uk

♦ 3018 ♦ Transfer Day
Last Monday in March

On March 31, 1917, the U.S. government formally purchased the Virgin Islands from Denmark for the sum of $25 million—about $295 an acre. Located about 34 miles east of Puerto Rico, the U.S. Virgin Islands consist of about 50 small islets and cays in addition to the three large islands of St. Thomas, St. John, and St. Croix. The United States purchased them primarily for their strategic importance, and they are still considered a vital key to the defense of the Panama Canal Zone and the Caribbean.

Transfer Day is usually observed with a parade and other public festivities. There was a major celebration in 1967, 50 years after the transfer took place, with events that underscored Danish-American friendship and a reenactment of the original transfer ceremony of 1917. The climax of the year-long semi-centennial celebration came when the governors of all 50 states as well as Guam, Puerto Rico, and American Samoa landed in St. Thomas for the 59th National Governors' Conference. Danish-American Week was observed at the same time.

CONTACTS:
Library of Congress
101 Independence Ave. S.E.
Washington, D.C. 20540
202-707-5000
www.loc.gov

♦ 3019 ♦ Transfiguration, Feast of the
August 6

As described in the first three Gospels, when Jesus' ministry was coming to an end, he took his three closest disciples—Peter, James, and John—to a mountaintop to pray. While he was praying, his face shone like the sun and his garments became glistening white. Moses (symbolizing the Law) and ELIJAH (symbolizing the prophets) appeared and began talking with him, testifying to his Messiahship. Then a bright cloud came over them, and a voice from within the cloud said, "This is my beloved Son, with whom I am well pleased; listen to him." The disciples were awestruck and fell to the ground. When they raised their heads, they saw only Jesus (Matthew 17).

Observance of this feast began in the Eastern church as early as the fourth century, but it was not introduced in the Western church until 1457. It is observed by Roman Catholics, Orthodox Christians, Lutherans, and Anglicans; most Protestants stopped observing it at the time of the REFORMATION.

The mountaintop on which the Transfiguration took place is traditionally believed to be Mount Tabor, a few miles east of Nazareth in Galilee. However, many scholars believe it was Mount Hermon, or even the Mount of Olives.

♦ 3020 ♦ Transpac Race
Begins early July in odd-numbered years

It was in 1906, the year of the great San Francisco earthquake, that the first yacht race across the Pacific was held. Because of the earthquake, only three yachts participated, ranging in length from 48 feet to 115 feet overall. The course was from Los Angeles to Honolulu.

The Transpac Race was originally held in even-numbered years, with a long break between 1912 and 1923, and another interruption, after the Japanese attack on Pearl Harbor, between 1941 and 1947. It is currently held in odd-numbered years and is sponsored by the Transpacific Yacht Club.

The finish can be close: in the 1965 race, with 55 yachts participating, there were fewer than 100 yards between the first two finishers as they struggled up the Molokai Channel. One had lost her main boom and the other's boom was badly damaged.

CONTACTS:
Transpacific Yacht Club
1508 Santiago Dr.
Newport Beach, CA 92660
949-646-0089
www.transpacyc.com

♦ 3021 ♦ Trial of Louis Riel
July-August

Louis Riel (1844-1885) was the leader of the métis, Canadians of mixed French and Indian ancestry. He became their champion in the struggle for Canadian unification during the late 19th century and was twice elected to the House of Commons but never seated. He became a U.S. citizen in 1883, but returned to Canada two years later to lead the North-West Rebellion. Defeated, he was eventually tried for treason, convicted, and hanged at Regina, Saskatchewan, on November 16, 1885.

The transcripts of Riel's five-day trial are the basis for a full-length courtroom drama that is performed in July and August in Regina. Riel's life and death are seen today as symbolic of the problems between French and English Canadians.

CONTACTS:
Tourism Regina
1925 Rose St.
Regina, SK S4P 3P1 Canada
306-789-5099 or 800-661-5099; fax: 306-352-1630
www.tourismregina.com

Library and Archives Canada
395 Wellington St.
Ottawa, ON K1A ON4 Canada
613-996-5115 or 866-299-1699; fax: 613-995-6274
www.bac-lac.gc.ca/eng

◆ 3022 ◆ **Tribeca Film Festival**
April

The Tribeca Film Festival was founded in 2002 in response to the terrorist attacks on the World Trade Center on September 11, 2001. In the wake of the attacks, one section of New York City—the Lower Manhattan neighborhood of Tribeca, located near the World Trade Center site—had suffered significant financial losses. The festival's founders—actor Robert De Niro, film producer Jane Rosenthal, and philanthropist Craig Hatkoff—believed a festival devoted to music, culture, and independent film would restore Lower Manhattan as a major center for filmmaking and would generate opportunities for artists in the independent film world.

Spanning a week in April, the Tribeca Festival showcases movies at various theaters in Tribeca and throughout Manhattan. Juries decide on the best films in competitions in the categories of documentary, feature, and short film. In addition to the film screenings, there are also panel talks, music performances, and workshops for aspiring filmmakers.

In its initial years the festival fulfilled its goals to promote Tribeca and bolster the film industry. The event has recorded up to 1 million attendees and has featured more than 200 films. In 2006, the film festival entered into a partnership with Tropfest, the world's largest short film festival held in Australia. The following year, Tropfest@Tribeca was established as a freestanding festival that is held in September.

CONTACTS:
Tribeca Film Institute
32 Avenue of the Americas
27th Fl.
New York, NY 10013
212-274-8080 Fax 212-274-8081
tribecafilminstitute.org

◆ 3023 ◆ **Tribute of the Three Cows**
July 13

This unusual event takes place on the Pierre St. Martin, located in the Pyrénées Mountains between Spain and France, on July 13 every year. Representatives of the French Pyrenean valley of Barétous and those of the Spanish Pyrenean valley of Roncal meet at the summit at 10 o'clock in the morning and pile their hands on top of each other's in a show of friendship. Then the French hand over three cows, which must be healthy two-year-olds. The Spaniards prepare a banquet afterward, which is cooked over fires made from wood that is hauled up the mountain by mules.

This tribute was imposed by treaty in 1375, when the two valleys were at war with each other, and the Roncal cowmen emerged as the victors. Such local treaties were often made without the consent of the national governments, and a number of them are still adhered to. But the annual Tribute of the Three Cows is by far the most unusual and picturesque.

CONTACTS:
Tourist Office of Spain

60 E. 42nd St.
Ste. 5300 (53rd Fl.)
New York, NY 10165
212-265-8822; fax: 212-265-8864
www.spain.info

Permanent Mission of Spain to the United States
245 E. 47th St.
36th Fl.
New York, NY 10017
212-661-1050; fax: 212-949-7247
www.spainun.org

◆ 3024 ◆ **Tricky Women Festival of Animated Films**
March

The Tricky Women Festival of Animated Films celebrates the achievements of women in the field of animation. Taking place each year in Vienna, Austria, the event's primary aim is to provide an international competition for women in the genre. The five-day festival promotes the importance of the genre by showcasing innovative and challenging films that debunk the myth that animation merely encompasses cartoons for children. The event's competition section is restricted to short films, while the noncompetition section includes documentaries and feature films. Awards and cash prizes go to the female directors of the works, and each participant may enter more than one film in the competition as long as the work is not a repeat entry from a previous year. In addition to the awards ceremony, the festival includes an artist-in-residence program.

◆ 3025 ◆ **Trigo, Fiesta Nacional del (National Wheat Festival)**
February

For more than 40 years the city of Leones in Córdoba Province, Argentina, has held an annual tribute to farmers and the wheat harvest. A blessing of the new wheat takes place at a special morning mass. Young women vie to be selected as the Wheat Queen. There is a parade of floats and farm vehicles, and prizes for the finest wheat.

CONTACTS:
Embassy of Argentina
1600 New Hampshire Ave. N.W.
Washington, 20009
202-238-6400; fax: 202-332-3171
www.embassyofargentina.us

National Secretariat of Tourism, Tourist Information Centers
Santa Fe 883
Argentina
54-11-4312-2232 or 800-555-0016
www.turismo.gov.ar/indexfse.html

◆ 3026 ◆ **Trinidad and Tobago Carnival**
Between February 2 and March 8; Monday and Tuesday before Ash Wednesday

One of the most spectacular and frenzied Carnival celebrations before Lent, the Trinidad and Tobago Carnival is a nonstop 48-hour festival in which almost everyone on the island participates. It started out in the late 19th century as a high-spirited but relatively sedate celebration involving a torchlight procession in blackface called *canboulay*—from *cannes brulées*, or "burned cane"—patterned after the procession of slaves on their way to fight fires in the cane fields. There was also music in the streets and masked dancing, although slaves were not permitted to wear masks. With the emancipation of the slaves, Carnival became a free-for-all with raucous music and displays of near-nudity. The government tried to crack down on the celebrations, but in 1881 there were canboulay riots in which 38 policemen were injured. After that, a law was passed that forbade parading before six o'clock in the morning on Carnival Monday. That moment is still known as *jouvé* (possibly from *jour ouvert*, or "day-break").

Today the main events are the two carnival day parades, which involve 25 to 30 costumed bands, each with about 2,500 marchers and its own king and queen. There is a calypso competition in which steel bands and calypso composers vie for the title of "Calypso Monarch." Few get any sleep during the two-day celebration, and the event ends with the *las lap*, which is a wild, uninhibited dance in the streets.

CONTACTS:
National Library and Information System Authority
National Library Bldg.
Hart and Abercromby St. S
Trinidad and Tobago
868-623-6962; fax: 868-625-6096
www.nalis.gov.tt

♦ 3027 ♦ Trinidad and Tobago Emancipation Day
August 1

Since 1985, August 1 has been celebrated in Trinidad and Tobago as Emancipation Day, rather than Columbus Discovery Day, as in former years. Slavery was abolished in 1833 throughout the British Empire, and eventually slaves in the colony of Trinidad and Tobago were freed. The day begins with an all-night vigil and includes religious services, cultural events, processions past historic landmarks, addresses by dignitaries, and an evening of shows with a torchlight procession to the National Stadium.

CONTACTS:
Ministry of Tourism
International Waterfront Complex
Levels 8 & 9, Tower C,
1 Wrightson Rd.
Trinidad and Tobago
868-624-1403; fax: 868-625-1825
www.tourism.gov.tt

National Library and Information System Authority of Trinidad and Tobago
National Library Bldg.
Hart and Abercromby St.
Trinidad and Tobago
868-623-6962; fax: 868-625-6096
www.nalis.gov.tt

♦ 3028 ♦ Trinidad and Tobago Film Festival
September

Founded in 2006, the Trinidad and Tobago Film Festival is held annually in the island republic and features works by artists of the Caribbean and the international community. In 2015, in an effort to support and improve the Caribbean film industry, the event instituted a Caribbean Film Mart and Regional Film Database, which will be used to market Caribbean movies in the global marketplace.

CONTACTS:
Trinidad and Tobago Film Festival
199 Belmont Circular Rd.
Trinidad and Tobago
868-621-0709; fax: 868-621-3473
www.ttfilmfestival.com

♦ 3029 ♦ Trinidad and Tobago Independence Day
August 31

After being subjected to British rule since 1802, Trinidad and Tobago became an independent commonwealth state on this day in 1962.

This national holiday is celebrated amid a Carnival atmosphere, with an elaborate military parade accompanied by calypsos at the Queen's Park Savannah. Religious services are varied to accommodate the Yoruba Orisha, Hindu, Muslim, Baptist, and other faiths represented in the citizenry. Later in the day, awards are presented at the National Awards Ceremony to those who have notably served their country.

CONTACTS:
National Library and Information System Authority
National Library of Trinidad and Tobago
Hart and Abercromby St.s
Trinidad and Tobago
868-623-6962; fax: 868-625-6096
www.nalis.gov.tt

♦ 3030 ♦ Trinidad and Tobago Republic Day
September 24

The country of Trinidad and Tobago consists of two islands in the Caribbean just northeast of Venezuela. The islands became British colonies during the 19th century and in 1889 were joined into one colony. On August 31, 1962, Trinidad and Tobago gained independence from England. On August 1, 1976, the nation became a republic. To mark the occasion, September 1—the date when the nation's first parliament met—has become Republic Day. The holiday was removed from the calendar from 1999 to 2002 to make room for Spiritual Baptist (Shouters) Liberation Day. But it returned in 2002 and remains today.

Republic Day is normally celebrated with a parade and other festivities, including dances and feasts. The Royal Oak Derby, Trinidad and Tobago's most important horse race, is normally run on this day as well. The nation's president always gives a speech stressing that being a republic means that all citizens are to assume responsibility for their own actions as the price of freedom.

CONTACTS:
Embassy of the Republic of Trinidad and Tobago
1708 Massachusetts Ave. N.W.
Washington, D.C. 20036
202-467-6490; fax: 202-785-3130
www.ttembassy.org

◆ 3031 ◆ Trinity Sunday
Between May 17 and June 20; first Sunday after Pentecost in the West and Monday after Pentecost in the East

Trinity Sunday differs from other days in the Christian calendar in that it is not associated with a particular saint or historic event. Instead, it is a day that celebrates the central dogma of Christian theology: that the One God exists as three persons with one substance—as the Father, the Son, and the Holy Spirit. The idea of a festival in honor of the Trinity was first introduced by Stephen, bishop of Liège, Belgium, in the 10th century. But it took several more centuries for a feast in honor of so abstract a concept to find its way into the church calendar. It became popular in England perhaps because of the consecration of Thomas à Becket on that day in 1162, but it wasn't until 1334 that it became a universal observance decreed by Pope John XXII. The day after Trinity is sometimes referred to as Trinity Monday.

Tradition has it that St. Patrick of Ireland used a shamrock as a symbol of the "three-in-one," triune God.

◆ 3032 ◆ Triple Crown Pack Burro Races
July-August

Every year, three races of pack burros and human runners take place in the Colorado Rocky Mountains. The first leg of the triple crown starts in Fairplay and is held the last weekend in July. The second leg, the first weekend in August, starts in Leadville. The final race is two weeks later in Buena Vista.

The first organized pack burro races were held in 1949 along a route over Mosquito Pass between Leadville and Fairplay; in 1979, the Buena Vista race became the final leg of the triple crown. The races cover from 15 to 30 miles over 13,500-foot mountain passes, sometimes in snow, and generally take the 20 to 25 entrants three to four hours. Women run a different, shorter course than men. Contestants can't ride their burros, but must run alongside them. (They can and frequently do push the animals.) Winners of individual races get cash prizes.

The word *burro* is Spanish and means "donkey." The history of these animals in the West goes back to the Gold Rush days of the 1800s when pack burros carried great loads of machinery and supplies to mining camps. Pack burro racing is thought to have started in those times.

The race days are surrounded by a variety of activities and are now major events in the small Colorado towns. In Buena Vista, for example, there are duck races, storytellers, and gold panning. Fairplay has llama races, and Leadville holds contests in mine drilling events. There's also a triple crown outhouse race; each town in the burro triple crown stages an outhouse race, with definite rules (e.g., one member of the outhouse team must sit in the outhouse during the race wearing colored underwear and/or a bathrobe).

CONTACTS:
Leadville Boom Days
P.O. Box 596
Leadville, CO 80461
719-293-4896
www.leadvilleboomdays.com

◆ 3033 ◆ Trois Glorieuses
Third weekend in November

The **Three Glorious Days** to which the name of this French wine festival refers occur in November in Côte d'Or Department, Burgundy, in eastern France. The festival is observed in three different wine-producing centers. On the first day, at the Château of Clos Vougeot, the Confrerie des Chevaliers du Tastevin put on their red robes and square toques (a type of soft hat popular in the 16th century) to receive their new members—the *tastevin* is a small silver cup used to taste wines. This event is followed by a pig dinner during which hundreds of bottles of wine are uncorked. The second day of the festival takes place at Beaune, where a wine auction is held at the Hospice de Beaune, whose cellars are open to the public. On the third and final day in Meursault, everyone who has taken part in the work of the wine harvest is invited to a huge banquet. There is folk dancing and merrymaking as the festival draws to a close.

The Confrérie des Chevaliers du Tastevin was formed in 1934 to put the French wine industry back on its feet after a number of disastrous vintage failures. They hold a series of wine-tasters' banquets throughout Burgundy, but the most elaborate ones are part of this three-day festival.

CONTACTS:
Confrérie des Chevaliers du Tastevin
2 rue de Chaux
Nuits Saint Georges, F-21700 France
33-3-8061-0712; fax: 33-3-8062-3709
www.tastevin-bourgogne.com/en

◆ 3034 ◆ Trumpets, Feast of
September; Tishri 1

The first day of Tishri, the seventh month of the Hebrew calendar, has religious significance for Jewish people and two sects of Christianity: Seventh-Day Adventists and the United Church of God. The day has different meanings for these groups. Jewish people celebrate the beginning of Tishri, which falls sometime between September and October, as Rosh Hashanah. The Christian group knows the holiday as the Feast of Trumpets. The day's significance is revealed in the biblical book of Revelation, in which a prophecy states that a seventh or "last" trumpet will announce the second coming of Jesus Christ, who will deliver the followers of God in heaven.

The Feast of Trumpets is the fourth of the seven Holy Days whose observance is central to the faith of the United Church of God. These days prefigure God's plan for creation, which he has revealed in the context of a spiritual harvest. The Days, also known as Feasts, are explained in detail in the Book of Leviticus, which recounts God's instructions to Moses about how to celebrate the feasts.

CONTACTS:
United Church of God
P.O. Box 541027
Cincinnati, OH 45254
513-576-9796; fax: 513-576-9795
www.ucg.org

♦ 3035 ♦ Tsagaan Sar (Mongolian New Year)
Between end of January and beginning of March

The New Year in Mongolia is determined by a lunar calendar and marks the beginning of spring. People generally celebrate for three days with lots of visiting, feasting, music, and sporting events. *Tsagaan Sar* means "white month," a reference to the milk and other dairy foods which become more plentiful in the spring.

People begin getting ready for the holiday about a month ahead of time, making repairs to and cleaning living quarters and sheds, preparing food in advance, and buying or fashioning gifts. The night before New Year's Day is *Bituun*, the occasion for parties to say goodbye to the old year.

After the New Year has begun, people often wear new clothes and spend at least a couple of days paying brief visits to family members, friends and neighbors, giving a small, inexpensive gift to each, then returning home to be themselves the recipients of visitors and gifts. Many *gers*, the tents in which Mongolian nomads live, resound with music played on traditional string instruments and overflow with special festive foods and drinks during the holiday.

CONTACTS:
Embassy of Mongolia
2833 M St. N.W.
Washington, D.C. 20007
202-333-7117; fax: 202-298-9227
mongolianembassy.us

Mongolian National Chamber of Commerce & Industry
MNCCI Bldg. Mahatma Gandhi St.
15st khoroo, Khan-Uul district
Ulaanbaatar, 17011 Mongolia
976-11-327176; fax: 976-11-324620
en.mongolchamber.mn

♦ 3036 ♦ Tsunahiki Matsuri
June

The tug-of-war is a traditional way to pray for a plentiful harvest throughout Japan and it is a popular event around the country. Several annual tugs-of-war take place in Okinawa Prefecture, and the one in Yonabaru, which is said to be about 400 years old, is one of the more famous. Thousands of people take part, dividing themselves into the East and West teams. Each team parades half of the rope, which can be three to five feet thick, to the beach, where they are connected by wooden poles, and then tugged on furiously by both sides until a winner is proclaimed.

See also Underwater Tug-of-War Festival.

CONTACTS:
Okinawa Convention and Visitors Bureau
1831-1 Oroku
Naha, Okinawa 901-0152 Japan
81-98-859-6123; fax: 81-98-859-6221
www.ocvb.or.jp

♦ 3037 ♦ Tsurugaoka Hachiman Shrine Matsuri
September 14-16

After the opening ceremonies are held on September 14, the annual celebration at the Tsurugaoka Hachiman shrine in Kamakura, Japan, begins on the 15th with a parade of three *mikoshi*, portable shrines to which the spirits of the gods are believed to descend during the festival. But the highlight occurs the following day, when the Yabusame takes place. It features three men on horseback in hunting clothes called *karishozoku*, which date from the Kamakura Era (1192-1333) and feature wide-brimmed, high-crowned hats with chin straps and elaborate kimono-style robes. The horsemen, all of whom are top-rated archers, ride down a straight track about 850 feet long near the shrine's entrance. Three targets are set up along the route, and the archers shoot their arrows at them while travelling at a high rate of speed.

In feudal times, Yabusame was an arrow-shooting game in which samurai warriors, under the guise of being contestants, showed off their battle skills. Today it is primarily a form of entertainment.

CONTACTS:
Japan National Tourism Organization
1 Grand Central Pl.
60 E. 42nd St.
Ste. 448
New York, NY 10165
212-757-5640; fax: 212-307-6754
www.jnto.go.jp/eng

♦ 3038 ♦ Tu Bishvat (Bi-Shevat; B'shevat; Hamishah Asar Bishevat)
Between January 16 and February 13; Shevat 15

Tu Bishvat, also known as **New Year for Trees**, is a minor Jewish festival similar to Arbor Day. It is first referred to in the late Second Temple period (515 B.C.E.-20 C.E.), when it was the cut-off date for levying the tithe on the produce of fruit trees. When Jewish colonists returned to Palestine during the 1930s, they reclaimed the barren land by planting trees wherever they could. It became customary to plant a tree for every newborn child: a cedar for a boy and a cypress or pine for a girl.

Today the children of Israel celebrate Tu Bishvat with tree planting and outdoor games. In other countries, Jews observe the festival by eating fruit that grows in the Jewish homeland—such as oranges, figs, dates, raisins, pomegranates, and especially almonds, the first tree to bloom in Israel's spring.

CONTACTS:
Union for Reform Judaism
633 Third Ave.
New York, NY 10017
212-650-4000
urj.org

♦ 3039 ♦ **Tuan Wu (Double Fifth)**
May-June; fifth day of fifth lunar month

The Double Fifth holiday is celebrated throughout China but is most popular south of the Yangtze River. It is also a festive holiday in Taiwan, Hong Kong, and among Chinese Americans. One reason why dragon boat races are often held on this day is that dragon boats are believed to offer protection against disease, particularly for the paddlers. Another reason is that Ch'ü Yüan (c. 343-c. 289 B.C.E.), a renowned minister of the Ch'u kingdom and a famous poet, threw himself into the Mi Lo River on the fifth day of the fifth month. When the people heard about his suicide, they all jumped into their boats and paddled out to save him, but it was too late. So they wrapped rice in bamboo leaves or stuffed it into sections of bamboo tube and floated it on the river to provide sustenance for his spirit. It is traditional to prepare and eat sticky rice dumplings known as *zong ze* or *tzung tzu* on this day in honor of the drowned poet Ch'ü Yüan.

Charms made from chunks of incense are used to ward off the so-called "five poisonous things"—which vary in different parts of China depending upon the climate and the local animal life. In Taiwan, for example, the five poisonous things are wall-lizards, toads, centipedes, spiders, and snakes. The charms are made in the shape of these harmful creatures, and sometimes small cakes resembling the creatures are eaten on this day.

Another custom associated with the Double Fifth is the placing of mugwort plants in the doorposts of each house. These branches are supposed to frighten evil spirits away and preserve those living in the house from summer diseases. Those who take a bath at noon on the fifth day of the fifth month are believed to be immune from illness for one year.

See also Dragon Boat Festival.

♦ 3040 ♦ **Tubman (Harriet) Annual Pilgrimage**
Memorial Day weekend

The Harriet Tubman Annual Pilgrimage is held every Memorial Day weekend at her gravesite and former home in Auburn, N.Y. In addition to a ceremony at Tubman's grave, there are commemorative activities, including a banquet.

Many of the activities take place on the 30-acre site of her residence. The site also contains other historic buildings, such as the home for aged people that Tubman established and where she herself received care before her death at age 93.

Harriet Tubman was an African-American abolitionist and humanitarian born in 1820. A former slave, she is most famous for leading hundreds of slaves to freedom via the "Underground Railroad," a network of abolitionists and safe houses. This heroic accomplishment led to her being defined as the "Moses of her People." After the abolition of slavery, Tubman worked tirelessly to help the poor, the elderly, and freed slaves, and to further the rights of women.

CONTACTS:
Harriet Tubman Home
180 S. St.
Auburn, NY 13201
315-252-2081
www.nyhistory.com

♦ 3041 ♦ **Tucson International Mariachi Conference**
Last week in April

Mariachi is traditional Mexican folk music with vocal, instrumental, and dance components. A small group of musicians typically sing and play some combination of the following instruments—guitar, *vihuela* (a small guitar-like instrument), *guitarrón* (a larger bass-like instrument), violin, and trumpet. Mariachi music also lends itself to the rhythmic *zapateado* dance, where the performers' boot heels act as percussion instruments.

Since the early 1980s, Mexican music enthusiasts have gathered in Arizona every April for the five-day Tucson International Mariachi Conference. Attendees take part in cultural workshops geared toward young people, enjoy performances by top mariachi bands, and join in the fun at the Fiesta de Garibaldi, an outdoor street festival offering food, arts and crafts, dance, and music.

CONTACTS:
Tucson International Mariachi Conference
c/o La Frontera Center
504 W. 29th St.
Tucson, AZ 85713
520-838-3908; fax: 520-792-0654
www.tucsonmariachi.org

♦ 3042 ♦ **Tucson Meet Yourself Festival**
Second weekend in October

The annual folk and ethnic festival known as Tucson Meet Yourself has been held in Tucson, Arizona, since 1974. Designed to promote southern Arizona's wide mix of cultures—which includes Mexican-, Czechoslovakian-, Italian-, German-, and Indian-American groups—the festival features formal presentations of traditional music and dance, demonstrations by folk artists and craftspeople, and workshops in which various experts on ethnic customs and traditions hold informal discussions, give lessons, and organize games.

Food, however, is the festival's primary attraction. Dozens of food booths, each operated by a non-profit organization identified with a specific cultural heritage and elaborately decorated to represent elements of "the old country," are set up throughout the park in which the event is held. Although American-Indian and Mexican-American specialties predominate, the booths have featured Irish, Finnish, Hungarian, Ukrainian, Greek, Armenian, Vietnamese, Japanese, Sri Lankan, and many other ethnic dishes, giving the festival the well-earned nickname of "Tucson Eat Yourself.".

CONTACTS:
Tucson Meet Yourself
P.O. Box 42044
Tucson, AZ 85733
520-621-4046
www.tucsonmeetyourself.org

◆ 3043 ◆ Tulip Time
Second weekend in May

When a group of high school students in Pella, Iowa, staged an operetta called *Tulip Time in Pella* in 1935, the only tulips growing in the town were in wooden pots. But the musical performance gave the local chamber of commerce an idea for promoting the town's Dutch heritage. They hired tulip specialists from the Netherlands to teach them how to plant and care for tulips. Then they planted thousands of bulbs and got the local historical society started preserving the town's Dutch buildings and heirlooms.

Today Pella (named "city of refuge" by the first Dutch immigrants, who were fleeing religious intolerance in their homeland) has been renovated to resemble a typical village in the Netherlands. During the festival, townspeople dress in Dutch provincial costumes and engage in such activities as street scrubbing, authentic Dutch dancing and folk music, and tours of the formal tulip gardens. One of these gardens features a Dutch windmill and a pond shaped like a wooden shoe.

Unlike most local festivals, Tulip Time is not a commercial event. There are no souvenir stands or food booths, although the local shops, museums, and restaurants offer a wide variety of Dutch specialties. Many of the events take place at the Tulip Torne, a tower with twin pylons more than 65 feet high that was built as a memorial to the early Dutch settlers.

CONTACTS:
Pella Historical Society & Museums
507 Franklin St.
Pella, IA 50219
641-628-4311
www.pellahistorical.org

◆ 3044 ◆ Tulip Time Festival (Holland Michigan)
May

The Tulip Time Festival is an annual one-week celebration of Dutch heritage held in Holland, Michigan. Tulips are the main attraction: 4.5 million flowers bloom in the city's streets, parks, and public attractions. Other than tulips, the celebration boasts parades, marketplaces, food vendors, beer tents, and children's activities. A popular attraction is the *klompen* dance, a Dutch folk dance performed in wooden shoes. In addition, there are carnival rides, arts and crafts fairs, concerts, theatrical shows, cycling, and a marathon for adults and children.

The Tulip Time Festival is the largest celebration of Dutch heritage in America and the third largest small-town festival in the nation. In 1927, Lida Rogers, a biology teacher at the local high school, suggested that the town adopt the tulip as its official flower because of the town's close Dutch ties. The next year, the mayor purchased a large quantity of tulip bulbs from the Netherlands. Initially held as a four-day event, the Tulip Time Festival was expanded to a ten-day-long celebration in 1991. In 2001, the festival was shortened to eight days to better coincide with the peak blooming period of the flowers.

CONTACTS:
Tulip Time Festival, Inc.
74 West 8th St.
Holland, MI 49423
616-396-4221; fax: 616-396-4545
www.tuliptime.com

◆ 3045 ◆ Tulsa Indian Arts Festival
First weekend in February

The Tulsa Indian Arts Festival features exhibitions of the work of Native American fine artists, dancing, music, auctions, storytelling, and such foods as corn soup, meat pies, and fry bread. Artists also provide educational demonstrations for the many schoolchildren who often attend. People from more than 60 tribes live in Oklahoma, whose name comes from the Choctaw meaning "red people.".

CONTACTS:
Greater Tulsa Indian Art Festival
9521 B Riverside Pkwy.
Box 358
Tulsa, OK 74137
918-298-2300 or 866-442-1846
tulsaindianartfestival.com

◆ 3046 ◆ Tulsidas Jayanti (Birthday of Tulsidas)
July-August; seventh day of the waxing half of the Hindu month of Sravana

The Indian poet Tulsidas (1532-1623) is best known for his retelling of the epic *Ramayana* in Hindi, the language of the common people. Another work, *Ramcaritmanas* ("The Holy Lake of the Deeds of Rama"), has been so influential that it is often referred to as "the Bible of North India." In fact, he and his works are so greatly revered that tradition regards him as a reincarnation of Valmiki, the legendary author of the *Ramayana*.

Tulsidas wrote that he was the son of a brahman, a member of the highest Hindu caste, but his parents didn't want to keep him because of the astrological interpretation of the planets and stars dominant at the time of his birth. Therefore they turned Tulsidas over to a Hindu holy man who raised him. Tulsidas went on to marry a woman with whom he was very much in love. Apparently, at some point she told him, "If you loved Rama half as much as you love this perishable body, your sorrows would be over," which is credited with awakening his devotion to Rama and changing the course of his life.

Many Hindus believe that Tulsidas died on the same day that he was born. They spend this day fasting and performing works of charity. Reading and reciting the *Ramayana* is another popular activity, as are discussions, lectures, seminars, and symposia on his life and works.

♦ 3047 ♦ Tunarama Festival
Late January

Running since 1961, the Tunarama Festival promotes the tuna fishing industry along Boston Bay in Port Lincoln, South Australia. It is organized as a free event, and is sponsored by businesses, tourism bodies, and the local council. In addition to fireworks, shows, and parades, the Tunarama Festival features the World Championship Tuna Toss, in which contestants compete for cash prizes by throwing large tunas.

CONTACTS:
Port Lincoln Tunarama Incorporated
P.O. Box 40
8 King St.
Port Lincoln
Australia 5606
Phone: 61-8-8682-1300
www.tunarama.net

♦ 3048 ♦ Tunisia Independence Day
March 20

Independence Day is a public holiday commemorating a treaty signed on this day in 1956 that formally recognized Tunisia's independence from France. It had been a French colony since the 1880s.

CONTACTS:
Embassy of The Republic of Tunisia
1515 Massachusetts Ave. N.W.
Washington, D.C. 20005
202-862-1850; fax: 202-862-1858
www.tunconsusa.org

♦ 3049 ♦ Tunisia Republic Day
July 25

This public holiday in Tunisia is held on the anniversary of the vote to abolish monarchical rule and found the republic on July 25, 1957.

CONTACTS:
Embassy of Tunisia

1515 Massachusetts Ave. N.W.
Washington, D.C. 20005 United States
202-862-1850; fax: 202-862-1858
www.tunconsusa.org

♦ 3050 ♦ Tunisia Revolution and Youth Day
January 14

The Tunisian Revolution, popularly known as the Jasmine Revolution, began in December 2010 with street protests over unemployment, corruption, inflation, widespread poverty, and a lack of political freedoms. Many protesters were injured or killed by the ruling regime's security forces during the unrest. Month-long demonstrations eventually led to the ouster of President Zine El Abidine Ben Ali in January 2011, the formation of a national unity government, and the election of a Constituent Assembly. The state successfully transformed from a dictatorship to a modern democracy in 2014, when the Constituent Assembly ratified a constitution and parliamentary and presidential elections for a permanent government took place.

Since 2012, Revolution and Youth Day has been observed to commemorate the events and the youth of the country who comprised the majority of the protestors. Tunisians gather in the Tunis, the capital city, to celebrate the political changes and remember those who died for the cause. The Tunis clock tower is draped with red and white cloth, and political parties march through the city waving flags and shouting slogans. An official ceremony takes place at the presidential palace.

♦ 3051 ♦ Tupou VI (King), Birthday of
July 4

The birthday of the sovereign of the island nation of Tonga has been observed as a public holiday since the early 19th century. King Tupou VI, the younger brother and successor of the late King George Tupou V, served as Tonga's High Commissioner to Australia until his brother's death on March 18, 2012. Although, the monarch's birthday falls on July 4th, the actual celebrations extend throughout the first week of July, and coinciding with observance of the coronation of the King and his Queen Nanasipau'u.

While traditional dancing, singing, parades, and church services mark the celebrations, the highlight of the events is the annual **Heilala Festival** held in Nuku'alofa, the capital of Tonga. The festival runs for nine days leading up to the birthday celebration, which culminates with a military parade, a thanksgiving service at the Royal Palace, and a luncheon.

♦ 3052 ♦ Tura Michele Fair (Augsburg Day)
September 29

On St. Michael's Day in Augsburg, Bavaria, there is an annual autumn fair that attracts visitors from all over Germany. One of the fair's chief attractions is the hourly appearance of figures representing the Archangel Michael and the Devil that are built into the foundation of Perlach Turm, or Tower, called *Tura* in local dialect. The slender structure, 225 feet high, standing next to Peter's Kirche (church) was originally a watch tower, but it was heightened in 1615 and converted into a belfry. Whenever the tower bell strikes on St. Michael's Day, the armor-clad figure of the Archangel appears and stabs with his pointed spear at the Devil writhing at his feet.

Although the figures were destroyed during World War II, they were later replaced. For over four centuries spectators have gathered around the Tura to watch the symbolic drama reenacted on St. Michael's Day.

CONTACTS:
Regio Augsburg Tourismus GmbH
Schiessgrabenstrasse 14
Augsburg, D-86150 Germany
49-821-502-070; fax: 49-821-502-0745
www.augsburg-tourismus.de

♦ 3053 ♦ Turkey National Sovereignty and Children's Day
April 23

This festival was started in 1920 by Mustafa Kemal Atatürk, the founder of the Turkish Republic, who recognized how important children were to his country's future and dedicated this day to them. On this national public holiday, Atatürk is honored with special services in Ankara, Turkey's capital city, at the monument built for him. Afterwards a children's program takes place in which children from around the world wear festive traditional costumes and dance and sing. In Istanbul, a similar celebration is held in the national soccer stadium.

Environmental scouts, similar to Boy Scouts in the United States, often observe this day by planting trees.

CONTACTS:
Turkish Coalition of America
1510 H St. N.W.
Ste. 900
Washington, D.C. 20005
202-370-1399; fax: 202-370-1398
www.tc-america.org

Embassy of the Republic of Turkey
2525 Massachusetts Ave. N.W.
Washington, D.C. 20008
202-612-6700; fax: 202-612-6744
www.washington.emb.mfa.gov.tr

♦ 3054 ♦ Turkey Republic Day
October 29

The Turkish Republic was founded by Mustafa Kemal Atatürk in 1923 after the fall of the Ottoman Empire. Kemal was named the first president on October 29, a full republican constitution was adopted the following April, and all members of the Ottoman dynasty were expelled from the country. Although Islam remained the state religion for several years,

this clause was eventually removed from the constitution and in April 1928, Turkey became a purely secular state.

The public celebration, which lasts for two days, includes parades, music, torchlight processions, and other festivities in honor of the founding of the republic. The largest parades are held in Ankara and Istanbul.

CONTACTS:
Embassy of the Republic of Turkey
2525 Massachusetts Ave. N.W.
Washington, D.C. 20008
202-612-6700; fax: 202-612-6744
www.washington.emb.mfa.gov.tr

♦ 3055 ♦ Turkey Victory Day
August 30

Turkey Victory Day honors the founder of modern Turkey, Mustafa Kemal Atatürk, and the military victory over the Greeks in 1922. In 1923, Turkey was established as an independent republic. The holiday is a celebration of the nation's military, the republic Atatürk founded, and the spirit of the Turkish people to resist tyranny and rule by outsiders.

Victory Day is celebrated throughout Turkey and on the island of Cyprus. The primary celebration is held at Atatürk's Mausoleum in the city of Ankara. Leading military officials visit the tomb to lay a ceremonial wreath. Veterans come from all over Turkey to attend the event. Wreaths are also placed on various statues of Atatürk found throughout the city. A ceremony including military and governmental officials is then held at the Atatürk Culture Center. Military leaders later retire to the General Staff headquarters to greet dignitaries from the country's major political parties, parliamentary and judicial officials, and the prime minister. A ceremony is also held at the War Academy in Istanbul, while marches are held in major cities across the country.

CONTACTS:
Embassy of the Republic of Turkey
2525 Massachusetts Ave. N.W.
Washington, D.C. 20008
202-612-6700; fax: 202-612-6744
www.washington.emb.mfa.gov.tr

♦ 3056 ♦ Turkish Wrestling Championships
July

Yagli gures, or "grease wrestling," is Turkey's most popular sport. An annual wrestling tournament has been held in July at Kirkpinar, near the Turkish-Greek border, for more than six centuries. The competitors cover their bodies and their leather knee breeches with oil, making it extremely difficult to get a grip on one's opponent. Although the Turks have proved their superiority at wrestling at many OLYMPIC GAMES, this national form of the sport requires exceptional skill and strength training.

CONTACTS:
Embassy of the Republic of Turkey

2525 Massachusetts Ave. N.W.
Washington, D.C. 20008
202-612-6700; fax: 202-612-6744
www.washington.emb.mfa.gov.tr

◆ 3057 ◆ Turkmenistan Independence Day
October 27-28

This national holiday commemorates Turkmenistan's independence from the U.S.S.R. on October 27, 1991. Turkmenistan and other republics were gradually able to establish their own autonomous states due to the relaxation of Soviet rule influenced by the policy of perestroika. When the Soviet Union ceased to exist in December 1991, their independence was assured.

CONTACTS:
Embassy of Turkmenistan
2207 Massachusetts Ave., N.W.
Washington, D.C. 20008
202-588-1500; fax: 202-280-1003
turkmenistanembassy.org

◆ 3058 ◆ Turkmenistan National Days
Various

The newly independent (1991) nation of Turkmenistan celebrates a large number of national holidays honoring Turkmen arts, popular culture, religion, civics, and history. Memory Day (January 12) commemorates the Turkmen tribesmen massacred by Russian Imperial troops at the Battle of Goek-Tepe in 1881. On May 9, Victory Day, the nation memorializes the end of World War II (1945). Remembrance Day (October 6) recalls those who died in the earthquake that devasted the country in 1948. Neutrality Day (December 1) promotes the government's official policy of neutrality in international affairs, while Good Neighborliness Day (December 7) publicizes Turkmenistan's intent to be a good neighbor to other countries. Turkmen Bakhsi Day (July 14) pays tribute to Bakhsi, the ancient literary genre of oral epics still popular in Turkmenistan. Horse Day (April 27) celebrates Turkmenistan's outstanding horses and the cultural tradition of horse breeding. The nation's fine oriental carpets and the women who weave them are praised on Carpet Day (May 25).

Other national holidays include NEW YEAR'S DAY (January 1), RAMADAN (moveable), National Flag Day (February 19), International WOMEN'S DAY (March 8), Novruz-Bairam, or NAWRUZ (March 21), A Drop of Water Is a Grain of Gold Day (April 6), Revival and Unity Day (May 18), Holiday of the poetry of Magtymguli (May 19), Kurban-Bairam (ID AL-ADHA; moveable), Day of Election of the First President (June 21), Turkmen Melon Holiday (July 10), Student Youth Day (November 17), and Harvest Holiday/Bread Day (November 30).

CONTACTS:
Embassy of Turkmenistan
2207 Massachusetts Ave. N.W.
Washington, D.C. 20008
202-588-1500; fax: 202-280-1003
turkmenistanembassy.org

◆ 3059 ◆ Turon
December; the week after Christmas

A Polish peasant festival observed in the week following CHRISTMAS, Turon may be a remnant of an ancient festival in honor of the winter god Radegast. *Turon* is a Polish word for "bull" or "ox." People wear several different animal disguises as they go from house to house singing carols and receiving food and drink from their neighbors in return. Other traditional costumes worn in the celebration represent a wolf, a bear, and a goat. The original turon symbolized frost, consuming vegetation with its huge mouth.

CONTACTS:
Association Of The Sons Of Poland
333 Hackensack St.
Carlstadt, NJ 07072
201-935-2807; fax: 201-935-2752
sonsofpoland.org

◆ 3060 ◆ Turtle Days
Mid-June

The origins of this unusual festival, held in Churubusco, Indiana, can be traced back to 1948, when a farmer named Gale Harris spotted a huge turtle one day while patching his roof. Since the lakes around town were known as prime turtle-breeding grounds, the turtle's appearance was not surprising. But its apparent size was—four or five feet wide and six feet long, according to Harris and others who glimpsed it. Harris tried every way he could think of to capture the monster, but the turtle always managed to escape. Finally he went to the lengths of pumping water out of the lake, but just as there remained only about an acre of water in the lake, Harris got appendicitis. By the time he recovered from surgery, it had rained, ruining the dams and refilling the lake.

The town decided to capitalize on all the publicity it had received—newspapers around the country had been reporting on the search for the turtle, now dubbed Oscar, "the Beast of 'Busco"—and organize a community festival. The first Turtle Days festival was held in 1950. Now held annually in mid-June, the event features a parade with a turtle float, booths selling turtle soup, and turtle races.

CONTACTS:
Turtle Days Association, Inc.
P.O. Box 187
Churubusco, IN 46723
260-416-6311
www.turtledays.com

◆ 3061 ◆ Turtle Independence Day
July 4

Since 1989, the Mauna Lani Resort in Hawaii has taken in baby Hawaiian green sea turtles from the Sea Life Park Hawaii by Dolphin Discovery in Oahu, Hawaii. Staffers raise the turtles in salt water ponds located on the resort hotel's grounds until they reach maturity and can be released into the wild. Baby turtles are only a few inches across, while mature turtles must be between 18 and 24 inches across. Every Fourth of July, a Turtle Independence Day is held in which turtles old enough and large enough to live in the ocean are brought down to the hotel's beach and let go. The hotel estimates that they have raised and released 125 turtles since the program began.

Because it is observed on the island of Hawaii, Turtle Independence Day serves as a way to promote a species native to the state. It is also an opportunity for families to learn more about the creatures. In addition to the release of the mature turtles, which is open to the public, the hotel also has entertainment, games, canoe rides, and educational displays for the children during the event.

CONTACTS:
Mauna Lani Resort
68-1400 Mauna Lani Dr.
Kohala Coast, HI 96743
808-885-6622; fax: 808-881-7000
www.maunalani.com

♦ 3062 ♦ **Tuvalu Independence Day**
October 1

Independence Day is the only national celebration in Tuvalu. The nation of Tuvalu consists of nine islands in the South Pacific with a total surface area of 10 square miles. Settled by Polynesian people some 3,000 years ago, Tuvalu came to the attention of the larger world in the 19th century when the British colonized the islands. Called the Elice Islands by the British, they played a crucial role during World War II as a key airbase in the fight against Japan. Achieving independence in 1978, the islands renamed themselves Tuvalu, which means "eight islands," a reference to the eight out of nine islands which have been inhabited for centuries.

Independence Day is marked in the capital city of Funafuti with an official government flag raising ceremony followed by a parade of policemen and schoolchildren. Similar events are held in smaller communities throughout the country. In addition to several days of feasting and dance, the Independence Day Sports Festival is held, in which citizens enjoy a number of sporting competitions.

CONTACTS:
Consulate of Tuvalu in New York
800 Second Ave.
Ste. 400 B
New York, NY 10017
212-490-0534; fax: 212-937-0692
tuvalu.visahq.com

Ministry of Foreign Affairs, Trade, Tourism, Environment &
Labour, Government of Tuvalu
Private Mail Bag
Vaiaku, Funafuti Tuvalu
688-20840
www.timelesstuvalu.com

♦ 3063 ♦ **Twelfth Imam, Birthday of the**
15th day of the Islamic month of Shaban

Among Shi'ite Muslims, Muhammad al-Mahdi holds distinction as a direct descendant of the prophet Muhammad and the 12th and last imam. More important, followers believe he achieved immortality during his earthly life in the late ninth century, and that after a long departure, he will return as the savior of the world.

Iran, a country with the largest Shi'ite population, holds birthday celebrations in various towns and cities. Typical festivities include picnics, firework displays, and outdoor concerts. Qom, considered the holiest of Iranian cities next to Mashhad, is a popular celebration site. Many worshippers visit the Jamkaran Mosque, located on the city's outskirts. According to local belief, Imam Mahdi delivered a prophecy in 974 locating his eventual return at this mosque site. A tradition has emerged in which visitors to the mosque leave their wishes and personal requests for the imam.

CONTACTS:

♦ 3064 ♦ **Twelfth Night**
January 5-6

The evening before EPIPHANY is called **Epiphany Eve**, or Twelfth Night, and it traditionally marks the end of the CHRISTMAS season, also called **Twelfthtide** in England. Since **Twelfth Day** is January 6, there is some confusion over exactly when Twelfth Night occurs, and it is often observed on the night of Epiphany rather than the night before.

Twelfth Night is an occasion for merrymaking, as reflected in Shakespeare's comedy, *Twelfth Night*. Celebrations reflect ancient WINTER SOLSTICE rites encouraging the rebirth of the New Year and also the Magis' visit to the Christ child.

Pageants held on this night typically include fantastic masked figures, costumed musicians, and traditional dances, such as the Abbots Bromley Antler Dance, or HORN DANCE, in England. Customarily, the Twelfth Night cake is sliced and served and the man who gets the hidden bean and the woman the pea are the king ("King of the Bean" or "Lord of Misrule") and queen for the festivities.

♦ 3065 ♦ **Twenty-Four:Seven Theatre Festival**
July

The 24:7 Theatre Festival is a weeklong event held in Manchester, England. Taking place at nontraditional locations, the event showcases emerging talent in all areas of theater production—from writers to technicians. Founded in 2004 by David Slack and Amanda Hennessey, the 24:7 Theatre Festival is best known for helping participants fine-tune their works for production. The event is supported by many high-profile actors in theater, film, and television, and is among the Arts Council England National Portfolio Organizations.

CONTACTS:
24:7 Headquarters
Astley & Byrom House
21-23 Quay St.
Manchester, M3 3JD United Kingdom
44-845-408-4101
www.247theatrefestival.co.uk

♦ 3066 ♦ Twins Days Festival
First full weekend in August

The Twins Days Festival, which takes place every year in Twinsburg, Ohio, began in 1976 as part of the town's bicentennial celebration. Since then it has become an international event, drawing twins from as far away as Japan and Nigeria. It is listed in the *Guinness Book of World Records* as the World's Largest Annual Gathering of Twins. The festival now draws nearly 3,000 sets of twins.

Events include the "Double Take Parade," Twins Talent Show, panel discussions, a golf tournament, and contests for the twins (and triplets) who look most alike and least alike, the youngest twins, those who have traveled the farthest, etc.

About a third of the sets of twins who come to the festival are not identical, and participants are assured they do not have to come dressed alike, although many choose to do so. Individuals who have lost a twin are encouraged to come as well. A similar event, known as Twin-O-Rama, is held in mid-July in Cassville, Wisconsin.

CONTACTS:
Twins Days Festival Committee
9825 Ravenna Rd
Twinsburg, OH 44087
330-425-3652; fax: 330-425-7280
www.twinsdays.org

♦ 3067 ♦ Tynwald Ceremony
July 5

The Isle of Man, located off the coast of England in the Irish Sea, was once the property of the Vikings. It was here that they established their custom of holding an open-air court for the settling of disputes and the passing of laws. They held their "Thing," or tribal parliament, in an open space, usually near a hill or mound, because they feared the magic associated with roofed buildings and wanted everyone to have easy access to the meeting.

Today, the Tynwald Ceremony—whose name comes from the Norse *Thing vollr*, meaning a fenced open parliament—is held at St. John's on Tynwald Hill. According to local lore, this hill contains soil from each of the Isle of Man's 17 ancient parishes. The ceremony takes place on July 5, which is Old MIDSUMMER DAY, when the Lieutenant-Governor of the Isle of Man exits a special service at St. John's Chapel and is accompanied to the hill by church and state officials. The chief justice reads a brief summary of every bill that has been passed during the year—first in English, and then in Manx, the old language of the island. This formality, once concluded, symbolizes the fact that the inhabitants of the Isle of Man have acknowledged the acts of the British Parliament and have incorporated them into the laws of their land.

CONTACTS:
Office of the Clerk of Tynwald, The Parliament of the Isle of Man
Tynwald
Legislative Bldg.
Finch Rd.
Douglas, Isle of Man IM1 3PW United Kingdom
44-16-24-685500; fax: 44-16-24-685504
www.tynwald.org.im

♦ 3068 ♦ Tyre Festival
Late July-early August

Tyre, located in southern Lebanon, is an ancient Phoenician city and a UNESCO World Heritage Site that dates back to the third millennium B.C.E. In recent decades, the historic city has also been traumatized by conflict between extremist elements and the Israeli Defense Forces. Organizers eager to bring joy to a city populace long plagued by bombs and the climate of war established the Tyre Festival in 1996, a summer celebration of Lebanese culture and music. The festival is held at Tyre's Al-Bass archaeological site, which features large Roman ruins of a necropolis (ancient cemetery) and a stadium. Local and international artists perform at the festival. Past programs have included concerts by solo vocalists, choirs, and Arabic orchestras; dance performances; marionette shows; and music concerts featuring a traditional stringed instrument called the oud.

CONTACTS:
Lebanon Ministry of Tourism
550 Central Bank St. Hamra
P.O. Box 11
Beirut, 5344 Lebanon
961-1-340-940; fax: 961-1- 340-945
mot.gov.lb

U

♦ 3069 ♦ **Uesugi Matsuri**
April 29-May 3

This Japanese festival, held in Yonezawa, commemorates the illustrious warrior Uesugi Kenshin (1530-1578), known for his strong principles and for staying away from women all his life. He fought battles in the hopes of becoming emperor of Japan, but he became ill and died while leading an assault on Kyoto. Uesugi Kenshin is also remembered for his role in a series of five battles, fought on a triangular island in the middle of the Matsukawa river, known as the Battles of Kawanakajima. It was here that he faced his arch-enemy Takeda Shingen, the ruler of a neighboring state. Both men passed away due to natural causes before either accomplished a conclusive victory.

The Uesugi Matsuri commemorates the warrior and his soldiers with mock battles and various costumed events, as well as a *Musha Gyoretsu*, a parade of warriors of the Sengoku (Warring States) Era.

CONTACTS:
Japan National Tourism Organization
Yamagata Tourism Information Center
1-1-1, Kajo Central
Jonan-machi, Yamagata 990-8580 Japan
81-2-3647-2333
www.jnto.go.jp

♦ 3070 ♦ **Uganda Independence Day**
October 9

This national holiday commemorates Uganda's independence from Britain on this day in 1962, after 70 years of British rule. Uganda became a republic in 1963 on its one-year independence anniversary.

CONTACTS:
Embassy of the Republic of Uganda
5911 16th St. N.W.
Washington, D.C. 20011
202-726-7100; fax: 202-726-1727
washington.mofa.go.ug

♦ 3071 ♦ **Uganda Liberation Day**
January 26

Uganda has had a troubled history in the recent past, with European colonization followed by political and military unrest, several coups, and a succession of rulers, including the ruthless dictator Idi Amin. Uganda Liberation Day marks the events of January 26, 1986, when the military junta was overthrown by the National Resistance Army following a five-year civil war. Yoweri Kaguta Museveni assumed the presidency at that time. His reign has been marked by relative stability and economic growth, although marred by his intervention in the civil war in the Democratic Republic of the Congo.

On the evening before celebration of Uganda Liberation Day, fireworks are exploded over the capital city of Kampala. The next day, a parade involving all branches of the Uganda military is held either at the Kololo Independence grounds or at the Kololo airfield, just outside Kampala. The country's president presides over the occasion. Ugandan schoolchildren are normally bussed in for the day. Other festivities include a bull roast on the grounds of Makerere University. Throughout the country, the general public marks the day with sporting events and hearty feasts.

CONTACTS:
Embassy of the Republic of Uganda
5911 16th St. N.W.
Washington, D.C. 20011
202-726-7100; fax: 202-726-1727
washington.mofa.go.ug

♦ 3072 ♦ **Uganda Martyrs Day**
June 3

On June 3, 1886, the country of Uganda's first Christian converts were executed in the town of Namugongo. Then known as Buganda, the country had just begun attracting the attention of Catholic and Anglican missionaries. Sons of many of the region's leading families had converted to Christianity. The king of Buganda, Mwanga II, saw this conversion as a sign of treachery against his authority. He arrested 45 of the young Christian men and had them brought to him at Namugongo. When the converts refused to renounce their faith, they were burned alive on a funeral pyre.

To commemorate the event, Christian pilgrims from all over Uganda journey to Namugongo and the town's Anglican church. In 2003, an estimated 800,000 pilgrims participated in the event. Uganda's vice-president and other high-ranking officials also attended.

During the reign of Uganda's dictator Idi Amin, a Muslim, another massacre of the 19th century was also commemorated. Amin was angered that a massacre of some 70 Muslims in 1857 had never been honored or officially remembered, so he had a small mosque erected across the road from the Anglican church in Namugongo. Amin was ousted from power in 1979 before he could complete a planned larger mosque. Soldiers of his successor, Obote II, reportedly slaughtered pigs on the site, desecrating the land and rendering it unsuitable for Muslim religious activities.

CONTACTS:
Embassy of the Republic of Uganda
5911 16th St. N.W.
Washington, D.C. 20011
202-726-7100; fax: 202-726-1727
www.ugandaembassy.com

♦ 3073 ♦ Uganda National Heroes Day
June 9

Uganda National Heroes Day honors all those who sacrificed themselves to better the lives of the Ugandan people. Unfortunately, the holiday is one of the most divisive days in the Ugandan year. What constitutes a hero, and who specifically should be honored, are matters of debate in the country. Many of the heroes officially recognized by the government are fallen soldiers who died during Uganda's civil war in the 1980s. But the scars of that war, and the memories of crimes committed by both sides against the Ugandan people, are still in evidence today. There is no widespread agreement as to which of that war's fallen should be honored.

Some citizens have argued for remembering less controversial heroes, such as the Ugandan doctor who detected a deadly Ebola outbreak before it spread.

CONTACTS:
Embassy of the Republic of Uganda
5911 16th St. N.W.
Washington, D.C. 20011
202-726-7100; fax: 202-726-1727
washington.mofa.go.ug

♦ 3074 ♦ Uhola Festival
Varies

Observed by the Dakarkari people in Nigeria, the Uhola Festival is preceded by a housecleaning period during which the villages, the shrines, and the surrounding hills are cleaned up and put in order. This time is dominated by the drinking of local beer, called *m'kya*. The *Yadato*—boys and girls from wealthy families—go into seclusion for a four-week period prior to the Uhola, where they are properly fed and fattened, and encouraged to rest up for the celebration.

On the first day of the festival, the Yadato must dance in front of the chiefs' palace and present the chiefs with Uhola gifts. The celebration then moves to the village square, where they continue to dance and sing songs satirizing prostitutes, unmarried pregnant girls, irresponsible men—even political figures. The highlight of the second day of the festival is the wrestling contest, which also takes place in the village square. Sometimes the Dakarkari wrestle against other tribes, and the victor in each match receives a prize from the chief. The wrestling, prize giving, and speeches continue for about four more days, until the priest declares that the festival is over.

Only girls who are engaged to be married are allowed to participate in the Uhola. Their future husbands must have completed their *golmo*—a period of farm labor in lieu of paying for their brides. After the Uhola, the girls move into their prospective husbands' homes, while new boys go into golmo.

CONTACTS:
Embassy of the Federal Republic of Nigeria
3519 International Ct., N.W.
Washington, D.C. 20008
202-986-8400; fax: 202-362-6541
www.nigeriaembassyusa.org

♦ 3075 ♦ Ukraine Constitution Day
June 28

On June 28, 1996, the country of Ukraine adopted a new constitution. Having gained independence in 1991 following the collapse of the Soviet Union, Ukraine began working on drafting a new constitution. Five years of work were required before the final document was written and approved by the country's parliament. The constitution created a democratic form of government that guarantees human rights and freedoms for its citizens under the rule of law.

Since it is a fairly new holiday, traditions have not yet been established to celebrate the day. In Kiev, popular Ukrainian musicians and singers give concerts in Maidan Nezalezhnosty Square.

CONTACTS:
Embassy of Ukraine
3350 M St. N.W.
Washington, D.C. 20007
202-349-2963; fax: 202-333-0817
usa.mfa.gov.ua

♦ 3076 ♦ Ukraine Independence Day
August 24

On this day in 1991, just after a failed coup in Moscow, Ukraine declared its independence from the U.S.S.R. On December 1, 1991, 90 percent of the people voted for independence.

CONTACTS:
Embassy of Ukraine
3350 M St. N.W.
Washington, D.C. 20007
202-349-2963; fax: 202-333-0817
usa.mfa.gov.ua/en

♦ 3077 ♦ Ukraine Unification Day (National Reunification Day)
January 22

On January 22, 1919, the Ukrainian People's Republic and the West Ukrainian People's Republic merged into a single nation. In a ceremony held in the city of Kiev, the two separate nations agreed to become the nation of Ukraine.

The Ukrainian People's Republic had been formed in January 1918 from Ukrainian land that had formerly been part of Russia. The West Ukrainian People's Republic was created in 1918 from land that had formerly been part of the Austro-Hungarian Empire. This was the first time that the Ukrainian people had established a single nation out of all the territory they occupied.

The day became an official holiday in 1999. In 2008, Ukrainian president Victor Yushchenko proposed that the holiday be renamed **National Reunification Day**. The day was remembered in 1987 when hundreds of thousands of people joined hands in a 550-kilometer long human chain stretching from the capital city of Kiev to the city of Lviv in western Ukraine.

CONTACTS:
Embassy of Ukraine
3350 M St. N.W.
Washington, D.C. 20007
202-349-2963; fax: 202-333-0817
usa.mfa.gov.ua

♦ 3078 ♦ Ukrainian Harvest Festivals
Varies; usually mid-October

Ukrainian harvest festivals have some elements in common with state and county fairs in the United States: stalls where farmers display their best produce of the season for prizes, games, and entertainment. In the great farming regions of Ukraine, known as "the breadbasket of Europe," harvest festivals have been celebrated for millennia. It is traditional to bake loaves of bread at harvest time with decorative images suggestive of the new crops, such as stalks of wheat.

Modern festivals often feature a parade to the fairgrounds, such sporting competitions as tugs-of-war, sack jumping, soccer, volleyball, and basketball, and musical, dance, and comedic performances.

Ukraine is also known for the *hopak*, a dance in which men hold their arms out, crouch down close to the floor and shoot their legs out in quick movements. This dance is said to have originated as a Ukrainian military exercise.

CONTACTS:
Alberta Tourism Division
6th Fl. Commerce Pl.
10155 - 102 St.
Edmonton, AB T5J 4L6 Canada
780-415-1319
culture.alberta.ca/about/contact-us

♦ 3079 ♦ Ullambana (Hungry Ghosts Festival; All Souls' Feast)
July-August; full moon or 15th day of seventh lunar month

A Buddhist and Taoist festival probably dating back to the sixth century and CONFUCIUS, Ullambana is observed in China as well as throughout the rest of eastern Asia. A legend attaches to this feast's origins: a Buddhist monk named Moggallana sought to save his mother from hell, where she went after her death because of her greed. The Buddha proposed that Moggallana and his fellow monks offer money, apparel, and food on behalf of all the souls he would encounter there. Moggallana did as the Buddha suggested and so rescued his mother. Because it illustrated the Chinese virtue of honoring one's parents, Ullambana became the best-loved Buddhist festival in China, and from there it spread to Japan, Korea, and other east Asian countries.

It is believed that during this month the souls of the dead are released from purgatory to roam the earth. In Taiwan the day is called "opening of the gates of Hell." This makes it a dangerous time to travel, get married, or move to a new house.

Unhappy and hungry spirits—those who died without descendants to look after them or who had no proper funeral (because they were killed in a plane crash, for example)—may cause trouble and therefore must be placated with offerings. So people burn paper replicas of material possessions like automobiles, furniture, clothing, and paper money ("ghost money") believing that this frees these things for the spirits' use. Joss sticks are burned, and offerings of food are placed on tables outside people's homes. Prayers are said at all Chinese temples and at Chinese shops and homes, and *wayang* (Chinese street opera) and puppet shows are performed on open-air stages.

Families in Vietnam remember the souls of the dead by visiting their graves. It is known as **Yue Lan**, **Vu Lan Day**, **Day of the Dead**, and **Trung Nguyen**. The festival, the second most important of the year after TET, is observed throughout the country in Buddhist temples and homes and offices. To remember the dead, families perform the *dan chay*, an offering of incense at graves. An altar at home is prepared with two levels—one for Buddha with offerings of incense, fruit, and rice, and one for departed relatives with rice soup, fruit, and meat. It is considered best if offerings include the *tan sinh*, three kinds of creatures—fish, meat, and shrimp—and the *ngu qua*, five kinds of fruit. Money and clothes made of votive papers are also burned at this time.

CONTACTS:
Consulate of Vietnam
866 United Nations Plaza
Ste. 435
New York, NY 10017
212-644-0594; fax: 212-644-5732
vietnam.embassy-online.net

Ministry of Foreign Affairs, Republic of China (Taiwan)
4201 Wisconsin Ave. N.W.
Washington, D.C. 20016
202-895-1800
www.taiwanembassy.org

◆ 3080 ◆ **Ullr Fest**
Late January to early February

A winter festival in Breckenridge, Colo., this celebration recognizes Ullr, the Norse god of winter and a stepson of Thor. Highlights are a parade, skiing and other sporting events, and a snow sculpture championship.

CONTACTS:
Breckenridge Tourism Office
111 Ski Hill Rd.
Breckenridge, CO 80424
888-251-2417; fax: 970-453-7238
www.gobreck.com

◆ 3081 ◆ **Umoja Karamu**
Fourth Sunday in November

The African-American holiday of Umoja Karamu, which means "unity feast" in Kiswahili, celebrates family members' commitment to one another. Established in 1971 by Brother Edward Sims, Jr., the feast was observed on the fourth Sunday in November, a date set by the Temple of the Black Messiah in Washington, D.C. African-American churches and families in several states continue to celebrate the festival, although it is not as widely observed as Kwanzaa.

Five periods of African-American life, each symbolized by a particular color, provide the framework for the Umoja Karamu ceremony: 1) the family in Africa, before slavery in America (black); 2) the enslaved family in America (white); 3) the family freed from slavery (red); 4) the family struggling for true liberation (green); 5) the family anticipating the future (orange or gold). Narratives, music, and foods relating to each period are part of the ceremony.

CONTACTS:
African American Registry
P.O. Box 19441
Minneapolis, MN 55419
612-822-6831
www.aaregistry.org

◆ 3082 ◆ **Underwater Tug-of-War Festival**
January 15

It's not the Polar Bear Swim, but the annual tug-of-war in Mihama, Fukui Prefecture, does involve people jumping into cold waters in the middle of winter. This is a ritual connected with the local Shinto shrine. Legend has it that a huge snake once menaced the waters of Hiruga Lake, which opens out into the Sea of Japan. The people drove the snake away by taking a huge rope, bigger than the snake, into the water. Today, young men struggle in a tug-of-war while standing in the lake. The rope symbolizes the snake, and the tug-of-war continues until the rope is pulled apart or cut in two. The event also serves as a ritual appealing for a good fishing season.

◆ 3083 ◆ **United Arab Emirates National Day**
December 2

This national holiday commemorates the December 2, 1971, expiration of a British treaty that inhibited self-rule for the sheikhdoms on the Persian Gulf in the eastern Arabian peninsula, and the union of seven of the sheikhdoms in the former Trucial States to become the United Arab Emirates. The Emirates' major cities celebrate National Day December 2-3.

CONTACTS:
Embassy of United Arab Emirates
3522 International Ct. N.W.
Ste. 400
Washington, D.C. 20008
202-243-2400; fax: 202-243-2432
www.uae-embassy.org

◆ 3084 ◆ **United Nations Day**
October 24

The international peacekeeping organization known as the United Nations was formally established on October 24, 1945, in the wake of World War II. Representatives from the United States, Great Britain, the Soviet Union, and China first met in August and September of 1944 at the Dumbarton Oaks estate in Washington, D.C., to discuss the problems involved in creating such an agency, and the results of their talks became the basis for the United Nations Charter that was ratified the following year. Although it has not always been successful in maintaining world peace, the U.N. has served as an important international forum for the handling of conflicts in the Middle East, Korea, Somalia, the former Yugoslavia, and other troubled areas.

Each member nation observes October 24, and in some places the entire week is known as **United Nations Week**. In the United States, events taking place on this day include parades, international fairs, and dinners featuring foods from different countries. It is also common to hold debates and discussions designed to acquaint the public with the U.N.'s functions. Schools frequently observe United Nations Day by holding folk festivals that teach students the music, songs, and dances of different countries, or by organizing special programs focusing on their geography, products, government, and culture.

CONTACTS:
U.N. Headquarters
First Ave. at 46th St.
New York, NY 10017
www.un.org/en

◆ 3085 ◆ **United Solo Theatre Festival**
October-November

The United Solo Theatre Festival is the largest theater event in the world featuring one-person performances. Founded by Omar Sangare in 2010, the festival takes place annually on Theatre Row in New York City. Open submissions for solo acts are solicited in categories such as dance, drama, poetry, stand-up, improvisation, performance art, magic, puppetry, and multimedia. The performers include new talent as well as renowned solo artists. Participating theater companies are allowed to generate income from ticket sales for up to eight shows and are exposed to media attention and reviews. The best shows of the festival are honored at the United Solo Showcase in Europe.

CONTACTS:
Theatre Row
410 W. 42nd St.
New York, NY 10036
unitedsolo.org

◆ 3086 ◆ United States Open Championship in Golf
Four days ending the third Sunday in June

The **U.S. Open**, conducted by the United States Golf Association, is the oldest golf tournament in North America, and was first held in 1895. More than 6,000 professional and amateur golfers vie for only 156 available places. Unlike the MASTERS, which is an invitational tournament, the U.S. Open is for anyone good enough to survive the qualifying rounds.

Rather than being played on the same course each year, its location changes. It is traditionally played on the nation's best courses, such as Merion in Philadelphia, Oakland Hills in Birmingham, Mich., Baltusrol in Union County, N.J., Winged Foot in Mamaroneck, N.Y., and Pebble Beach on the Monterey Peninsula of California. Since the 1930s, it has been the U.S.G.A.'s practice every 10 to 15 years to take the Open back to certain courses that have demonstrated they can produce a rigorous test for the world's top golfers. The tournament itself takes four days. There is a qualifying round followed by three days of 18 holes each, for a total of 72 holes.

The U.S. Open is one of the most difficult golf championships to win. Its list of champions includes Bobby Jones, Walter Hagen, Gene Sarazen, Ben Hogan, Arnold Palmer, Jack Nicklaus, Lee Trevino, Tom Watson, and Tiger Woods. The 1913 tournament, which was won by an unknown 20-year-old store clerk named Francis Ouimet, is considered to have marked the transformation of golf in America from an elite game to a public pastime.

CONTACTS:
United States Golf Association
P.O. Box 708
Far Hills, NJ 07931
908-234-2300; fax: 908-234-1883
www.usga.org

◆ 3087 ◆ United States Open Tennis
September

The **U.S. Open** is the final tournament in the four events that make up the Grand Slam of tennis. (The others are the AUSTRALIAN OPEN, the FRENCH OPEN and WIMBLEDON.) Also known as the **U.S. Championships**, the games are played on hard courts at Flushing Meadows Park in Queens, N.Y. They had been played from 1915 to 1978 in Forest Hills, also in Queens. Separate amateur and professional open championships were held in 1968 and 1969, and the tournament became exclusively an open in 1970.

The U.S. National Lawn Tennis Association was established in 1881, and the first official U.S. National Championship was played under its auspices that year in Newport, R.I. The first women's championship was played in 1887. The golden age at Forest Hills is considered to have been the 1920s when William T. "Big Bill" Tilden II dominated the game. He was U.S. Open champion seven times: 1920-25 and 1929. Other seven-time winners were Richard Sears (1881-87) and William Larned (1901, 1902, 1907-11). Jimmy Connors took the title five times (1974, 1976, 1978, 1982, 1983). In the women's championships, Molla Bjurstedt Mallory is the all-time champ; she won eight times (1915-18, 1920-22, 1926). Helen Wills Moody won seven times (1923-25, 1927-29, 1931). "Little Poker Face," as she was called, also won eight Wimbledons and four French Opens.

Ranking near the top of the excitement scale were the wins in the U.S. Championships that sewed up the Grand Slam championship. In 1938, Don Budge was the first to win all four Grand Slam titles. The feat wasn't equaled until 1962 when Rod Laver won all four. Then he did it again in 1969. In 1953, Californian Maureen Connolly became the first woman to sweep the Grand Slam titles. Known as "Little Mo," she had won her first U.S. Championship at the age of 16 in 1951. A horse-riding accident in 1954 cut her career short, and she died in 1969. Women who have won all Grand Slam titles since then are Margaret Smith Court in 1970 and Steffi Graf in 1988.

CONTACTS:
United States Tennis Association
70 W. Red Oak Ln.
White Plains, NY 10604
914-696-7000
www.usopen.org

◆ 3088 ◆ United Tribes International Powwow
Early September over four days

The United Tribes International Powwow takes place every year over a four-day weekend in early September at United Tribes Technical College in Bismarck, N.Dak. The event typically draws 20,000 to see more than 1,500 drummers and dancers representing about 70 Native-American tribes. Contests are held for all age groups in singing, dancing, and drumming. Other festival events include a parade, a softball tournament, arts and crafts, and a national Miss Indians pageant for contestants between the ages of 17 and 26. The event also hosts such visiting cultural performers as a Maori dance troupe from New Zealand.

The powwow is affiliated with United Tribes Technical College, which was founded in 1969 to serve the academic and cultural requirements of American-Indian students and their families. The powwow launched the same year. A non-alcohol event, the powwow is open to all. Free camping is available at the site. The winner of many awards, the powwow is considered a premier cultural event of North Dakota.

CONTACTS:
United Tribes Technical College
3315 University Dr.
Bismarck, ND 58504
701-255-3285
www.uttc.edu

♦ 3089 ♦ Universal Prayer Day (Dzam Ling Chi Sang)
Usually June or July; 14th to 16th days of fifth Tibetan lunar month

Universal Prayer Day is a Tibetan Buddhist festival and a time for spiritual cleansing. During this time, people hang prayer flags on tree tops, burn juniper twigs, and build bonfires to worship the Buddha and local gods. Fire in the Tibetan culture is symbolic of cleansing. Family picnics are also common during the festival.

This is also the time of the once-a-year display of the famous giant *thangkas*, scroll paintings, at Tashilhunpo Monastery in Shigatse, Tibet. Tashilhunpo (which means "heap of glory"), the seat of the Panchen Lamas, once had more than 4,000 monks. But the monastery was disbanded by the Chinese in 1960, and only a few hundred monks remain.

At this time, three huge thangkas with images of the Buddha are displayed for three days on a nine-story wall on the monastery grounds. Thangkas, which are made in all sizes, were first known in Tibet in the 10th century, and were used in monastery schools as teaching devices. They were always consecrated before they were hung.

Panchen Lamas came into being in the 17th century when the fifth Dalai Lama gave the title *panchen*, meaning "great scholar," to his beloved tutor. The tutor was then found to be the reincarnation of Amitabha, the Buddha of infinite light, and subsequent Panchen Lamas are new incarnations. As with Dalai Lamas, when a Panchen Lama dies, a search is conducted for an infant boy who is the new incarnation.

See also DALAI LAMA, BIRTHDAY OF THE.

CONTACTS:
Office of Tibet
1228, 17th St. N.W.
Washington, D.C. 20036
212-213-5010; fax: 703-349-7444
tibetoffice.org

♦ 3090 ♦ University of Pennsylvania Relay Carnival
Seven days, beginning on the Sunday before the last weekend in April

The **Penn Relays** is the oldest and largest track and field event in the United States. The first relay meet held on the campus of the University of Pennsylvania in Philadelphia was on April 21, 1895, but even back then the tents and the festival atmosphere contributed to its reputation as a carnival rather than just a series of races. Since that time, the Penn Relays have served as a springboard for athletes who later went on to win OLYMPIC medals—such as Carl Lewis, Joan Benoit, Edwin Moses, and Frank Shorter. It is also a breeding ground for rising track and field stars, with more than 700 high school teams and 180 college teams participating.

The event begins on the Sunday before the last weekend in April (unless that day is EASTER, in which case the Relays begin a week earlier) with a 20-kilometer road race. There is a heptathlon and a decathlon on Tuesday and Wednesday, and the rest of the week is filled with walk, sprint, distance, and field events for athletes of all ages and abilities—including Special Olympians (*see also* SPECIAL OLYMPICS). More than 70,000 spectators are drawn to the event, which receives wide press coverage.

CONTACTS:
Penn Relays Office
219 S. 33rd St.
Philadelphia, PA 19104
215-898-6145
www.thepennrelays.com

Penn Athletics
Weightman Hall
235 S. 33rd St.
Philadelphia, PA 19104
215-898-6151; fax: 215-573-2161
www.pennathletics.com

♦ 3091 ♦ Up-Helly-Aa
Last Tuesday in January

This ancient fire festival is observed by people of Lerwick in the Shetland Islands. In pre-Christian times their Norse ancestors welcomed the return of the sun god with YULE, a 24-day period of feasting, storytelling, and bonfires. The last night of the festival was called Up-Helly-Aa, or "End of the Holy Days."

Today a group known as the Guizers builds a 31-foot model of a Viking longship, complete with a dragon's head and many oars, in honor of those Viking invaders who decided to remain in Scotland. On the night of Up-Helly-Aa, the Guizers dress in Norse costumes and helmets and carry the boat to a large open field. There they throw lit torches into the ship and burn it.

Up-helly-Aa originally referred to EPIPHANY, or January 6—the day when the Yuletide holidays came to an end. The shifting of the date to the end of January probably reflects the change from the Julian to the Gregorian calendar in 1752. This day is also referred to as **Uphaliday, Uphelya, Up-Helly-Day, Uphalie Day,** or **Uphalimass.**

CONTACTS:
Up Helly Aa Committee
Galley Shed
St Sunniva St.
Lerwick, Shetland ZE1 0HL United Kingdom
www.uphellyaa.org

Promote Shetland
Shetland Museum & Archives

Hay's Dock
Lerwick, Shetland ZE1 0WP United Kingdom
44-159-598-9898
visit.shetland.org

♦ 3092 ♦ Urini Nal (Children's Day)
May 5

Urini Nal has been a national holiday in South Korea since 1975. Schools are closed and parks are packed with children. Events of the day may include wrestling and martial arts exhibitions, dancing, and the presentation of puppet shows and plays. Cake shops give away rice cake favors. The holiday is intended to forge the bonds of family life.

♦ 3093 ♦ Urs Ajmer Sharif
First through sixth days of the Islamic month of Rajab

This is the *urs*, death anniversary, of the Sufi saint Khwaja Muin al-Din Muhammad Chishti (or Moinuddin Muhammad Chishti, 1142-1236), who founded a major Sufi order in India. His tomb, known as the Dargah, is located in Ajmer, Rajasthan, India, considered by many South Asian Muslims to be the most important PILGRIMAGE site next to Mecca.

The saint is often referred to as Gharib Nawaz, meaning "protector of the poor," because he spent much of his life in service to the less fortunate. He also had a great love of devotional music, believing it had the potential to enhance one's spirituality. Such songs, called *qawwali*, are sung during his death festival. Chishti is said to have retreated into solitude six days before he died, thus his urs is celebrated not only on the anniversary of his death, but also on the preceding five days.

In addition to special religious services, offerings, prayers, and other ceremonies, a huge fair takes over the town of Ajmer during the urs. Vendors sell food and religious items, and some of the finest poets of the Urdu language gather to provide readings.

CONTACTS:
Government of Rajasthan, Department of Tourism Art & Culture
Paryatan Bhawan, M.I. Rd.
Khasa Kothi Hotel Campus
Jaipur, Rajasthan 302001 India
91-141-511-0598
www.rajasthantourism.gov.in

Khawaja Gharib Nawaz Shrine
123, Faiz Manzil, Imam Bada
Khadim Mohalla, Dargah Sharif
Ajmer, Rajasthan 305001 India
91-887-530-0786
www.khawajagharibnawaz.com

♦ 3094 ♦ Urs of Baba Farid Shakar Ganj
Fifth, sixth, and seventh days of the Islamic month of Muharram

Urs of Baba Farid Shakar Ganj is marked every year to commemorate the death anniversary of the great Punjabi poet and Sufi Muslim saint, Baba Farid Shakar Ganj, born in 1188 C.E. He is known as the first Punjabi saint and the father of Punjabi culture. On his death anniversary, pilgrims from around the world visit his shrine-like tomb, or *mazar*, in Pakpattan, Pakistan. On this occasion, Bahashti Darwaza (Paradise Door), made of silver and overlaid with gold flowers, is opened to allow thousands of devotees to pass through over the course of the three-day occasion. The anniversary also is marked with folk music and ecstatic dancing by the faithful. This commemoration has taken place every year for more than 750 years.

CONTACTS:
Pakistan Tourism Development Corporation
Flashman's Hotel
The Mall, Rawalpindi Cantt
Pakistan
92-51-927-2811; fax: 92-51-927-1588
www.tourism.gov.pk

♦ 3095 ♦ Urs of Jelaluddin al-Rumi (Whirling Dervish Festival)
Week leading up to December 17

Each year up to a million people flood Konya, Turkey, on the anniversary of the death of the poet and Sufi Islamic mystic Jelaluddin al-Rumi. The prolific and influential poet was born in 1207 in what is now Afghanistan. After spending most of his life in present-day Turkey, he died there in 1273. Rumi's teachings are the basis for the Sufi Muslim order known as Mevlevi in Turkish and Malawi in Arabic. The order uses music and dance to experience spiritual ecstasy, and its members are most commonly known as "whirling dervishes" because of their dance rituals that involve spinning in place for extended periods of time.

During the week leading up to December 17, lights bejewel the town of Konya, shop keepers offer special merchandise, and thousands of visitors arrive to partake of exhibits and lectures related to Rumi and the Mevlevi order. Festival-goers also visit Rumi's tomb, situated in an extensive Mevlevi complex, which comprises one of Turkey's most-visited museums. The climax of the festival week takes place on December 17, when Mevlevis perform their whirling dance wearing costumes that feature white trousers, a full white overskirt, and tall cylindrical hats. Each of these items represents an aspect of the dancer's ego, which is symbolically overcome during the dance by the performer's spirit ascending to love and truth. Before the dance, Rumi's poems are recited and prayers offered. The dance occurs in seven parts, each of which has a particular meaning. The whirling, which is said to mirror the circular movements of creation, from an atom's particles to the planets' orbits, occurs in the fifth section. Muslims and non-Muslims alike attend the striking, world-renowned display. It inspired the RUMI FESTIVAL, held annually in North Carolina to honor the beloved poet and his teachings.

CONTACTS:
Turkish Culture & Tourism Office
2525 Massachusetts Ave. N.W.

787

Washington, D.C. 20008
202-612-6800
www.tourismturkey.org

♦ 3096 ♦ Uruguay Constitution Oath Taking Day
July 18

The country of Uruguay adopted its first constitution on July 18, 1830, shortly after becoming an independent country in 1928. Although it adopted other constitutions in 1917, 1934, 1952, and 1967, the 1830 version laid the groundwork upon which all later versions have relied. The 1830 constitution, modeled after the American and French constitutions, created executive, legislative, and judicial branches of government. The legislative branch consists of a senate and a house of representatives. Later constitutions checked the powers of the president and provided for a separation of church and state. Constitutional amendments adopted in 1976 strengthened the political powers of the country's military.

To commemorate the adoption of Uruguay's first constitution, speeches are given by government officials and a parade featuring a military band, mounted cavalry, and soldiers is held in the capital city of Montevideo.

CONTACTS:
Consulate General of Uruguay
420 Madison Ave.
Sixth Fl.
New York, NY 10017
212-753-8582; fax: 212-753-1603
www.consuladouruguaynewyork.com

♦ 3097 ♦ Uruguay Independence Day
August 25

This national holiday commemorates the declaration of independence from Portuguese rule on this day in 1825. By 1828, Uruguay was officially autonomous.

Patriotic ceremonies are held in the capital city of Montevideo, with speeches and the singing of the national anthem.

CONTACTS:
Embassy of Uruguay
1913 I (Eye) St. N.W.
Washington, D.C. 20006
202-331-1313; fax: 202-331-8142
www.mrree.gub.uy

♦ 3098 ♦ Usokae
January

Usokae, or the **Bullfinch Exchange,** is held in Dazaifu City, Japan at a shrine dedicated to the ancient poet and scholar Sugawara no Michizane. According to legend, Sugawara's good fortune is represented by the bullfinch. At the annual New Year celebration, participants bring small wooden bullfinch figures they received the year before to exchange for new ones in the hope of changing bad luck to good luck. The

Shinshoku, or priests, of the shrine surreptitiously hand out the shrine's twelve golden bullfinches to random worshippers in the crowd. Those who get the bullfinches are said to receive good fortune for the year. On the same evening, a fire festival takes place and the shrine is enveloped in smoke and flames.

CONTACTS:
Japan National Tourism Organization
1 Grand Central Pl.
60 E. 42nd St., Ste. 448
New York, NY 10165
212-757-5640; fax: 212-307-6754
www.jnto.go.jp/eng

♦ 3099 ♦ Utah Arts Festival
Late June

The Utah Arts Festival was founded in 1977 in Salt Lake City and is now a five-day event held on stages and in the streets, plazas, and galleries. Hundreds of booths are set up for regional foods and for exhibits of sculpture, painting, pottery, folk arts, and photography. In a Children's Art Yard, stories are told of Utah's mining days and natural history. Live performances of contemporary, jazz, bluegrass, folk, and salsa music as well as dance, theater, symphony, and opera performances are presented on three stages.

CONTACTS:
Utah Arts Festival
230 S. 500 W.
Ste. 120
Salt Lake City, UT 84101
801-322-2428
uaf.org

♦ 3100 ♦ Utakai Hajime (Imperial Poem-Reading Ceremony)
Mid-January

Utakai Hajime, the Imperial Poem-Reading Ceremony, is a centuries-old New Year 's tradition in Japan. The first historical reference to this custom dates back to 1267. The ceremony took place off and on over the years, but has been a regular annual event since 1879. It takes place in the Matsunoma Stateroom at the Imperial Palace in Tokyo and is attended by the emperor, empress, other members of the imperial family, judges, and guests. Many people, including people outside Japan, write poems for this annual competition and the chance to read one's winning poem in this company.

The initial poetry readings are those composed by members of the public, followed by those by the royal family, ending with the poem written by the emperor, which is read five times. The poems are traditionally written in *tanka* style. These are traditional short poems of only five lines and 31 syllables: the first line has five syllables, the second has seven, the third has five, and the last two lines each have seven. In poems they composed for the 2015 ceremony, Emperor Akihito presented an image of the fall harvest, while Empress Michiko expressed her love of reading.

CONTACTS:
Japan Echo Inc.
Nippon Press Center
2-2-1 Uchisaiwaicho
Bldg. 2F
Chiyoda-ku, Tokyo 100-0011 Japan
81-3-5510-5401; fax: 81-3-3519-3519
www.japanecho.co.jp

♦ 3101 ♦ **Ute Bear Dance**
May, Memorial Day weekend

An ancient ceremony of the Southern Ute Indians, the Ute Bear Dance is now held on the Sunday and Monday of MEMORIAL DAY weekend in Ignacio, Colo. Originally the ritual was held in late February or early March, at the time when bears awaken from their hibernation. It stemmed from the belief that the Utes were descended from bears, and the dance served both to help the bears coming out of hibernation and to gain power from them, since bears were believed to cure sickness and to communicate with people in the Spirit World.

Today the dance is largely a social occasion, and is what is called a women's dance, since the women ask the men to dance. This practice is rooted in the habits of bears: supposedly the female bear wakes first and then chases the male bear. In earlier days, two bears—a man and woman wearing bearskins, with red paint around their mouths to suggest the bloody ferocity of the bears—romped around a corral, the female chasing the male, and both responding ferociously toward anyone who might laugh. In the present-day dance, lines of women and men advance toward each other, gradually dancing in pairs. The dancing goes on until sunset, when there is a feast.

CONTACTS:
Southern Ute Tribal Council
356 Ouray Dr.
P.O. Box 737
Ignacio, CO 81137
970-563-0100
www.southern-ute.nsn.us

♦ 3102 ♦ **Uzbekistan Constitution Day**
December 8

On December 8, 1992, the new constitution of Uzbekistan was signed, creating a democratic system of government for the newly-independent country.

Uzbekistan was created in 1924 by the communist government of the Soviet Union. The traditional boundaries of Central Asia were redefined under the communists to make nationalistic or ethnic opposition to the central government more difficult. Uzbekistan remained a part of the Soviet Union until the collapse of the communist regime, becoming an independent nation in 1991.

On Constitution Day, the country's president usually broadcasts a message of greeting to the Uzbekistan people in which he reiterates the democratic ideals of the constitution and outlines what steps the government has taken to ensure those ideals are carried out.

On Constitution Day in 2007, the Uzbekistan senate passed a law liberalizing criminal punishments. Under this new law, women, young people under the age of 18, men over 60, and foreign citizens who have been arrested for a first crime will no longer be imprisoned. Prison sentences for nonviolent crimes were also reduced.

CONTACTS:
Embassy of Uzbekistan to the United States
1746 Massachusetts Ave. N.W.
Washington, D.C. 20036
202-887-5300; fax: 202-293-6804
www.uzbekistan.org

♦ 3103 ♦ **Uzbekistan Independence Day**
September 1

The Republic of Uzbekistan was one of the central Asian republics of the former Soviet Union until 1991, when it and other republics declared their independence from theU.S.S.R. Independence Day, September 1, is celebrated throughout the country with parties, music, and exhibits.

CONTACTS:
Embassy of Uzbekistan
1746 Massachusetts Ave. N.W
Washington, D.C. 20036 United States
202-887-5300; fax: 202-293-6804
www.uzbekistan.org

V

♦ 3104 ♦ **Vaisakh**
April-May; first day of Hindu month of Vaisakha

Vaisakh is the Hindu New Year and a harvest festival, celebrated primarily in northern India and Bangladesh with temple worship, ritual bathing in rivers, and a New Year's fair. For Sikhs, it is their most important holy day.

In Malaysia and India, especially in the Indian state of Punjab, where the gospel of the Sikhs began, Vaisakh (also spelled **Baisakh**) is particularly significant. On this day in 1689 GURU GOBIND SINGH chose the five leaders (called the *Panch Pyare*, or "Beloved Five") who formed the Khalsa, the militant fraternity of the Sikhs. There the holiday is celebrated in the temples, with a 48-hour reading of the GURU GRANTH SAHIB (the Sikh holy book), prayers, hymns, and sermons. Castelessness, an important Sikh principle, is emphasized by everyone eating and sitting together. Afterwards, there is feasting and dancing of the *bhangra*, a popular and athletic folk dance for men, depicting the entire farming year.

In the Indian state of Kerala, the festival is known as **Vishu**. Activities include fireworks and what is called *Vishu Kani*, a display of grain, fruits, flowers, gold, new cloth, and money, which is supposed to ensure a prosperous year.

The festival is called **Bohag Bihu** in Assam, and there it is celebrated for a week with music, folk dances, and community feasting. Traditions include decorating cattle, smearing them with turmeric, and giving them brown sugar and eggplant to eat. Also during this time, there is a day on which young people look for marriage partners. The girls wear beautiful scarves, and the boys look for the most lovely orchids; they present these to each other and then dance.

CONTACTS:
Punjab Heritage And Tourism Promotion Board
Archives Bhawan
Plot No 3, Sector 38 A
Chandigarh, Punjab 160036 India
91-172-2625950; fax: 91-172-2625953
www.punjabtourism.gov.in

♦ 3105 ♦ **Vaitarani**
November-December; 11th day of the waning half of the Hindu month of Margashirsha

Vaitarani is the river that, according to Hindu belief, runs between the earth and the underworld, which the dead must cross to reach the realm of Yama, who is the ruler and judge of the dead. It plays much the same role in Hindu mythology that the River Styx plays in Greek mythology. Because this river is said to be filled with all kinds of filth, blood, and moral offenses, Hindus believe that it can only be crossed with the aid of a cow. It is for this reason that cows are given in charity to Brahmans where there is a death in the community.

On the day known as Vaitarani, devout Hindus observe a fast and other prescribed rituals. In the evening they worship a black cow, who is bathed in fragrant water and has sandal paste applied to her horns. Brahmans are given gifts of food, clothes, and a cow made out of gold or silver.

♦ 3106 ♦ **Valdemar (King) Day**
June 15

According to legend, Danish King Valdemar II set out to conquer the pagan Estonians and convert them to Christianity. During the night of June 15, 1219, the Estonians made a surprise attack on the Danish camp. As he raised his arms toward heaven to pray for help, the Danish archbishop discovered that as long as he could hold his arms up, the Danes were able to push back the enemy. But when they dropped from weariness, the Estonians gained ground. Eventually a red banner with a white cross floated down from the sky and, as the archbishop caught it, he heard a voice from the clouds say that the Danes would win if they raised this banner before their enemies. A messenger took the banner to King Valdemar, and the Danes won the battle.

Schools, sports organizations, and Boy Scout troops in Denmark often hold pageants on June 15, also known as **Flag Day**, in which they reenact the story of the *Dannebrog* (the Danish flag) and King Valdemar. The red and white flag can be seen flying everywhere on this day in honor of its miraculous first appearance.

CONTACTS:
Embassy of Denmark
3200 Whitehaven St. N.W.
Washington, D.C. 20008 United States
202-234-4300; fax: 202-328-1470
usa.um.dk

◆ 3107 ◆ Valentine's Day
February 14

St. Valentine is believed to have been a Roman priest who was martyred on this day around 270. How he became the patron saint of lovers remains a mystery, but one theory is that the Church used the day of St. Valentine's martyrdom in an attempt to Christianize the old Roman LUPERCALIA, a pagan festival held around the middle of February. Part of the ancient ceremony entailed putting girls' names in a box and letting the boys draw them out. Couples would thus be paired off until the following year. The Church substituted saints' names for girls' names, in the hope that the participant would model his life after the saint whose name he drew. But by the 16th century, it was once again girls' names that ended up in the box. Eventually the custom of sending anonymous cards or messages to those one admired became the accepted way of celebrating **St. Valentine's Day**.

Valentine's Day has been the occasion for such events as underwater weddings and "kiss-ins" and "hug-ins"—in 1999, about 3,000 couples in Belarus attempted to set a new world record for the largest kiss-in (previously held by 1,600 couples in Spain); in 2002 more than 1,000 students and teachers at a South African high school went for the world's biggest hug-in.

CONTACTS:
France Tourism Development Agency
825 Third Ave.
New York, NY 10022
212-838-7800; fax: 212-838-7855
int.rendezvousenfrance.com

◆ 3108 ◆ Valley of the Moon Vintage Festival
Last full weekend in September

Valley of the Moon Vintage Festival is California's oldest wine festival, held since the late 1890s in Sonoma, the cradle of the state's wine industry. Located in Sonoma Valley, which Jack London made famous as the "Valley of the Moon," the city was founded in 1835 by Gen. Mariano Guadalupe Vallejo. In 1846, the Northwest became part of the United States, and, on June 14 of that year, American settlers invaded Sonoma, captured Vallejo and his Mexican garrison, and raised an improvised Bear Flag to proclaim California a republic. On July 9, the flag was replaced by the Stars and Stripes.

In the 1850s, Hungarian nobleman Count Agoston Haraszthy planted thousands of cuttings from European grape vines to establish the Buena Vista Winery, now the state's oldest premium winery, becoming the father of California's wine industry. In 1863, a double wedding united the two prominent wine-making families—the Vallejos and the Haraszthys.

The three-day festival focuses on this history, presenting re-enactments of the 1846 Bear Flag Revolt and of the double wedding. There are also wine tastings, parades, live music, a blessing of the grapes, a firemen's water fight, and grape stomps.

CONTACTS:
Valley of the Moon Vintage Festival
P.O. Box 652
Sonoma, CA 95476
707-996-2109
valleyofthemoonvintagefestival.com

◆ 3109 ◆ Valmiki Jayanti
September-October; full moon day of the Hindu month of Asvina

This festival celebrates the birthday of the poet Valmiki, whom Hindus believe to be the author of the epic poem *Ramayana*. A contemporary of Rama, the hero of the *Ramayana*, Valmiki himself is represented as taking part in some of the scenes he relates. No one knows for certain when the poem was written; estimates range from 500 to 300 B.C.E., with portions added between 300 B.C.E. and 200 C.E.

On Valmiki's birthday, people make processions and carry his portrait through the main streets of towns and villages. Members of the disadvantaged Indian classes pay particular homage to Valmiki, from whom they claim they are descended.

CONTACTS:
Bhagban Valmik Temple
V.P.O. Shankar ,Patti Takhar ,
Teh. Nakodar
Distt. Jalandhar, Punjab 144042 India
91-97792-70161
www.bhagwanvalmikitemple.com

◆ 3110 ◆ Vaman Dwadashi
August-September; 12th day of Bhadrapada

According to Hindu belief, the god Vishnu turned himself into a dwarf, Vamana, to trick Bali, who conquered and ruled the kingdom of Indra, into giving up some of his domain. This story appears in the Hindu epic, the *Ramayana*. Devout Hindus worship both Vishnu and Bali with a fast beginning on the 11th day of Bhadrapada and keeping an all-night vigil. Offerings and mantras are made to an image of Vamana. Onthe 12th, Hindus rise at dawn, bathe, continue to worship the image of Vamana, then, finally, break their fast with a festive meal. It is primarily women who observe this day, and they often invite a young Brahman boy to the celebration—a boy to represent the short height of Vamana, and a Brahman because it is believed that good fortune will come to those who give alms to Brahmans. Thus the boy is given such gifts as shoes and an umbrella.

◆ 3111 ◆ Vancouver Writer's Fest
October

Widely considered the best literary festival in Canada, the Vancouver Writers' Fest attracts more than 16,000 every year and gives participants a chance to mingle with well-established national and international authors. The celebration aims at increasing book readership among children and gives a platform to local and international undiscovered writers. Created in 1988, the festival takes place at various locations on Granville Island in British Columbia. The event features activities such as readings, panel discussions, a writing contest for young people, and a literary cabaret.

CONTACTS:
Vancouver Writer's Fest
202-1398 Cartwright St.
Vancouver, BC V6H 3R8 Canada
604-681-6330
www.writersfest.bc.ca

♦ 3112 ♦ Vandalia Gathering
May, Memorial Day weekend

A folk festival held on the state capitol grounds in Charleston, W.Va., the Vandalia Gathering serves to exhibit the best of the state's traditional arts, music, dance, crafts, and food. Events include music by fiddlers, banjo players, and lap-dulcimer players, clogging, craft demonstrations, liars' contests, storytelling, and an exhibition of quilts made by West Virginia's top quilters. Held since 1976, the festival attracts about 35,000 people.

See also WEST VIRGINIA DAY.

CONTACTS:
WV Division of Culture and History, The Cultural Center
Capitol Complex, 1900 Kanawha Blvd., E.
Charleston, WV 25305 United States
304-558-0220; fax: 304-558-2779
www.wvculture.org

♦ 3113 ♦ Vanuatu Custom Chiefs Day
March 5

Among the 83 islands that compose the island nation of Vanuatu are many that have rejected European influence and instead prefer to live according to their traditional customs. While customs vary widely throughout the islands, village life, subsistence farming, a belief in magic, and rule by chiefs are common.

In 1977 a National Council of Chiefs was set up by the government to advise and propose ways to ensure the preservation of traditional ways of life through Vanuatu. These tribal chiefs are honored on March 5 of each year, which is a public holiday. Celebratory activities on this day include sporting events, carnivals, agricultural fairs, and arts festivals.

CONTACTS:
Vanuatu Tourism Office, Vanautu
Level 1, Pilioko House
P.O. BOX 209
Vanuatu
678-22515
vanuatu.travel

♦ 3114 ♦ Vanuatu Father Walter Lini Day
February 21

A former Anglican priest, Father Walter Lini became the first prime minister of the newly independent country of Vanuatu in 1980. His term in office was marked by tensions with several larger countries, including France and the United States. Lini strongly opposed French atom bomb testing in the Pacific and supported the independence movement in the French colony of New Caledonia. He also called for a reduced American naval presence in the region and resisted efforts of foreigners to develop or invest in Vanuatu. After establishing relations with Libya, Cuba, and Vietnam, Lini also pushed for what he called "Melanesian socialism"—a system based on the traditional Polynesian idea that a people's land is owned in common. Lini left office in 1991 and passed away in 1999.

Despite those who remember him for his authoritarian ways, Lini is honored on February 21 as the father of Vanuatu's independence. To mark the 25th anniversary of the country's independence, the 2005 celebration of Father Walter Lini Day included a special remembrance service at the Tagabe Anglican Church. Prime minister Ham Lini, Walter Lini's brother, presided over a ceremony in which a floral wreath was placed on the late priest's grave. In 2015, Prime Minister Joe Natuman made a speech in honor Father Walter Lini at his gravesite at Nazareth, and also made a presentation to the Lini family on the occasion.

CONTACTS:
Vanuatu Tourism Office, Vanautu
Level 1, Pilioko House
P.O. BOX 209
Vanuatu
678-22515
vanuatu.travel

♦ 3115 ♦ Vanuatu Independence Day
July 31

The most important national holiday in Vanuatu, Independence Day is celebrated throughout the country. It marks the end of colonial rule by the French and British. This archipelago of 83 islands is located about 1,000 miles northeast of Australia.

The first Europeans to visit Vanuatu were Spanish explorers in 1605, but it was the French who established the first permanent settlements in the 1850s. By the early 1900s, the islands were ruled under a joint French-British agreement. In the 1960s, secessionist ideas began to spread throughout the island chain, and in May 1980 an insurrection in Tanna brought the matter to the forefront. Self-rule came to Vanuatu in July of that same year. Father Walter Lini, a former Anglican priest, became the country's first prime minister.

The largest Independence Day celebrations take place in the capital city of Port Vila. A number of sporting events are held, as well as canoe and yacht races in the harbor. A military parade takes place in Independence Park. Dancing takes place and aerobics groups from throughout Vanuatu perform, and a string band competition is held.

CONTACTS:
Vanuatu Tourism Office, Vanautu
Level 1, Pilioko House
P.O. BOX 209
Vanuatu
678-22515
vanuatu.travel

♦ 3116 ♦ Vanuatu Unity Day
November 29

The nation of Vanuatu is an archipelago of 83 islands, 113 languages, and a host of different tribal groups. To celebrate the unification of differing groups into one nation, Unity Day was established on November 29. On that day in 1977, unrest in the islands, then under French-British administration, caused a great loss of life. Such internal division is something that present-day Vanuatu citizens do not want to see repeated.

To celebrate this day, representatives from all of Vanuatu's peoples come to the capital city of Port Vila. High chiefs from all the islands attend the festivities, which include performances by native dancers in their traditional dress and a parade. Music concerts and sporting events are also part of the celebration. Ordinary citizens usually observe the day with picnics or by camping.

CONTACTS:
Vanuatu Tourism Office, Vanautu
Level 1, Pilioko House
P.O. Box 209
Vanuatu
678-22515
vanuatu.travel

♦ 3117 ♦ Vappu
May 1

Vappu is a national holiday and celebration of the coming of spring in Finland. This traditional festival rejoicing the end of the long northern winter is also Labor Day, and factories that are said to "never close" do close on May 1 and Christmas Day.

For students (and even gray-bearded former students), the "anything goes" celebration begins at midnight on the eve of May Day, called Vapunaatto, when they wear white student caps and indulge in anything not indecent or criminal. It's traditional in Helsinki for students to wade across the moat that surrounds the statue of Havis Amanda, a mermaid, and place their caps on her head. There are balloons, streamers, horns, and masks everywhere, and few get much sleep. On May Day itself, the students lead processions through the streets of Helsinki, and then enjoy carnivals and concerts. Workers in most provincial towns generally gather in more solemn fashion to celebrate with speeches and parades.

CONTACTS:
Ministry for Foreign Affairs of Finland
P.O. Box 176
Finland

358-9-1605-5555; fax: 358-9-1605-5799
formin.finland.fi

♦ 3118 ♦ Vaqueros, Fiesta de los
Last full week in February

Fiesta de los Vaqueros is a weeklong event in Tucson, Ariz., featuring the "world's longest non-motorized parade" and the largest outdoor midwinter rodeo in the United States. The fiesta starts with the parade—a two-mile-long procession of more than 200 entries, including such old horse-drawn vehicles as buckboards, surreys (with or without the fringe on top), western stagecoaches, and Conestoga wagons. The first parade was in 1925; now about 200,000 people line the parade route.

The eight days of rodeo include the standard events as well as daily Mutton Bustin' contests. In these, four- to six-year-olds test their riding skills on sheep. There are also demonstrations by Appaloosa trick stallions and by the Quadrille de Mujeres, a women's precision-riding team.

CONTACTS:
Tucson Rodeo Parade Committee and Museum
4823 S. 6th Ave.
Tucson, AZ 85714
520-294-1280
www.tucsonrodeoparade.com

♦ 3119 ♦ Vasaloppet
Late February to first Sunday in March

The biggest cross-country ski race in the world takes place in Sweden on the first Sunday in March each year. The course begins on the border between Norway and Sweden, in a huge frozen field outside the village of Sälen, and ends 54 miles away in the Swedish town of Mora. The race was named for a young Swedish nobleman, Gustav Vasa, who persuaded the people of Mora to help him drive out the Danes in 1520. He later ruled the country for almost 40 years as King Gustavus I.

More than 8,000 men compete in the annual race, which for even the strongest skier takes over five hours to complete. Because they consider this to be a test of their manhood, many Swedish men celebrate their 50th birthdays by entering the race. More than 325,000 have officially completed the Vasaloppet since the race became a national ski festival in 1922. Numerous other ski events take place over the last week in February leading up to the main Vasaloppet race.

CONTACTS:
Vasaloppet Mora
P.O. Box 22
Mora, MN 55051
800-368-6672; fax: 320-679-4840
www.vasaloppet.us

♦ 3120 ♦ Vasant Panchami (Basant Panchami)
January-February; fifth day of waxing half of Hindu month of Magha

Vasant Panchami is a festival of spring, celebrated throughout India among Hindus and Sikhs at the end of January or in early February. People wear bright yellow clothes, the color of the mustard flower that heralds the onset of spring, and mark the day with music, dancing, and kite-flying.

In Shantiniketan, West Bengal, the festival is celebrated with special lavishness in honor of Sarasvati, the Hindu goddess of learning and the arts. Her images are taken in procession to rivers to be bathed, and books and pens are placed at her shrine.

Many five-year-old Sikh children begin attending school for the first time on this day because Sikhs believe it a sacred time for children to begin their education.

In recent years, many young people observe Vasant Panchami (also spelled **Basant Panchami**) by exchanging tokens of affection, similar to VALENTINE'S DAY in the United States.

CONTACTS:
Department of Tourism, Government of West Bengal
New Secretariat Bldg.
1, K. S. Roy Rd.
3rd Fl.
Kolkata, West Bengal 700001 India
91-33-2225-4723
www.wbtourism.gov.in

♦ 3121 ♦ **Vasanth Navaratri**
March- April; in the waxing phase of the moon in the Hindu month of Chaitra

Vasanth Navaratri, or **Chaitra Navaratri,** celebrates the nine forms of the Hindu goddess Shakti and is one of the nine-night *Navaratris* held annually; the Vasanth Navaratri is held in spring. The festival has its roots in Hindu mythology, but exact origins vary across India's geographical regions. In Hinduism, Shakti is the mother goddess, representing all creative power. According to the traditional Hindu calendar, the month Chaitra is the first month of the year, and Vasanth Navaratri celebrates the Hindu New Year. Each day of the event is represented by a different color, worn by participants on corresponding days. Hindus frequently fast in the daylight hours during the festival and feast after sundown. One of the most important rituals of Vasanth Navaratri—performed before midday on the first day of the festival—is the filling of the *kalasha* pot with offerings to Durga, one of Shakti's nine forms. The event culminates on the ninth day with a birthday celebration for Lord Rama, one of the forms taken by the god Vishnu.

CONTACTS:
Ministry of Tourism, Government of India
3550 Wilshire Blvd.
Ste. 204
Los Angeles, CA 90010
213-380-8855; fax: 213-380-6111
tourism.nic.in

♦ 3122 ♦ **Vatsa (Ho Khao Slak)**
June-July to October-November; full moon of Asadha to the full moon of Karttika

Vatsa, also known as **Ho Khao Slak**, is the Laotian observance of WASO or the Buddhist Rains Retreat. It begins later in the year than the traditional season observed in many other Buddhist communities, and the customs associated with it are also slightly different in Laos. But it is still a three- or four-month period when Buddhist monks must stay in one place in retreat rather than remain on the move.

People draw the name of a monk in the local monastery and bring him a gift of food, flowers, or one of the eight essential items that Buddhist monks are permitted to own (a robe, an alms bowl, a belt, a razor, a needle, a filter with which to strain water, a staff, and a toothpick). Parents often give toys and candy to their children as well. At the end of the festival, boat races are held on the rivers at Vientiane, Luang Phabang, and Savannakhet.

♦ 3123 ♦ **Vegetarian Festival**
September-October; first nine days of ninth lunar month

The Vegetarian Festival is an annual nine-day affair observed on the island of Phuket off southwestern Thailand by residents of Chinese ancestry. During the nine days, observers eat only vegetarian foods. The festival begins with a parade in which devotees wear white, and continues with ceremonies at temples, performances of special feats by ascetics, and acts of self-mortification—walking on hot coals, piercing the skin, and so on. The festival celebrates the beginning of the month called "Taoist Lent," when devout Chinese abstain from meat. It is thought, however, that the self-mortification acts are derived from the Hindu festival of THAIPUSAM.

CONTACTS:
Tourism Authority of Thailand
611 N. Larchmont Blvd.
1st Fl.
Los Angeles, CA 90004 United States
323-461-9814; fax: 323-461-9834
www.tourismthailand.org

♦ 3124 ♦ **Vendimia, Fiesta de la**
Second week in September

Spain is famous for its sherry, and some of the best sherry comes from the southwestern part of the country, in a district known as Jerez de la Frontera. This is said to be one of the few remaining places where the juice of the grapes is extracted by trampling them in huge wooden vats, or *lagares*. Although most people think this is done with bare feet, the participants actually wear specially designed hobnail boots.

In mid-September Jerez de la Frontera holds its **Grape Harvest Festival**, or Fiesta de la Vendimia, which includes flamenco dancing, *cante jondo* singing (a distinctive and deeply moving variety of Spanish gypsy song), and bullfighting. There is also an official "blessing of the grapes" and the season's first wine before the statue of San Ginés de la Jara, the patron saint of the region's winegrowers. The blessing is part of a colorful pageant held at the Collegiate Church of Santa

Maria. All of the events that take place during the festival pay tribute in one way or another to wine sherry, the area's most famous product.

CONTACTS:
Tourist Office of Spain
60 E. 42nd St.
Ste. 5300 (53rd Fl.)
New York, NY 10165
212-265-8822; fax: 212-265-8864
www.spain.info/en_US

◆ 3125 ◆ Venezuela Battle of Carabobo Day
June 24

The Battle of Carabobo was fought in Venezuela on June 24, 1821, between the Spanish, led by Field Marshal Miguel de La Torre, and the Venezuelan freedom fighters, led by Simón Bolívar. It was fought some 30 kilometers from the town of Valencia in Venezuela. The battle was one-sided; Bolívar 's men suffered only one casualty for every 15 inflicted on the Spanish. Irish, Welsh, and English volunteers fought on Bolívar 's side, comprising the British Legion. Their victory led to the independence of Venezuela. The day is sometimes celebrated in Venezuela as Army Day.

At the site of the battle is the Alley of Glory, along which a number of low pillars hold busts of the soldiers who fought in the battle. The alley leads to the Triumphal Arch, which features two female figures representing peace and victory. Below the arch is the tomb of the unknown soldier, guarded by two soldiers wearing uniforms from the time of Bolívar.

The Battle of Carabobo Day is marked by a nationally-televised, day-long military parade in Carabobo. In 2014, more than 6000 members of 40 military units took part in the celebration of the 193rd anniversary of the Battle of Carabobo. President Nicolás Maduro delivered a speech at the event and also awarded several military honors.

CONTACTS:
Embassy of the Bolivarian Republic of Venezuela in the United
1099 30th St. N.W.
Washington, D.C. 20007
202-342-2214; fax: 202-342-6820
eeuu.embajada.gob.ve

◆ 3126 ◆ Venezuela Independence Day
July 5; April 19

Revolutionary struggle against Spanish rule began in Venezuela in 1810. On July 5, 1811, a group of citizens in Caracas became the first in South America to proclaim a formal declaration of independence from Spain. Forces led by Simón Bolívar assured independence in 1821.

April 19 is another national holiday, known as both Declaration of Independence Day and Day of the Indian.

CONTACTS:
Venezuelan Consular Office
1099 30th St. N.W.

Washington, D.C. 20007
202-342-2214; fax: 202-342-6820
eeuu.embajada.gob.ve

◆ 3127 ◆ Venice Biennale (La Biennale)
In odd-numbered years

The Venice Biennale, or **La Biennale**, was launched in 1893 by a resolution of the Venice City Council to commemorate the silver anniversary of King Umberto and Margherita of Savoy. Venice Biennale is one of the most prestigious cultural events in the world for promoting contemporary art. The festival showcases a variety of artistic genres, including visual art, music, dance, architecture, film, and theater. Currently, 88 countries participate in the event, with exhibitions held in the Central Pavilion and 29 other venues representing the various nations participating in the event. The Biennale Musica is a venue for the world premiere of new compositions, orchestras, ensembles, and soloists. The Venice International Film Festival, taking place in Lido, Italy, is the oldest film festival in the world and has remained a vital part of the Venice Biennale. The Biennale Theatre, created in the 1990s, originally set out to perform Venetian classics and has now evolved to include contemporary theatrical works. In addition, the festival hosts theater workshops, which serve as a meeting ground for playwrights, directors, actors, and stage designers from around the world.

CONTACTS:
La Biennale di Venezia
Ca' Giustinian
San Marco 1364/A
Venice, 30124 Italy
39-041-5218711; fax: 39-041-2728329
www.labiennale.org/en

◆ 3128 ◆ Venice Film Festival
August-September

The Venice Film Festival is the world's oldest international film festival. It is part of the Venice Biennale, a group of diverse performing and visual art events hosted by the Venice City Council. The annual event takes place in August or early September in Lido, a picturesque beach resort in Venice.

The festival began in 1932 under the Italian fascist regime. First called the Exhibition of Cinematographic Arts, and originally non-competitive, the festival screened American director Rouben Mamoulian's *Dr. Jekyll and Mr. Hyde* as its debut. The event returned with a competitive section and the Mussolini Cup award for best foreign film and best Italian film. After World War II, the Mussolini Cup was replaced by the Golden Lion for the best film, which remains the highest honor. Besides its world premieres, which are screened at the historic Palazzo del Cinema, the festival is known for its galas, glamour, red carpets, and celebrities.

CONTACTS:
Venice Film Festival
Ca' Giustinian
San Marco 1364/A

Venice, 30124 Italy
39-041-5218711; fax: 39-041-5218854
www.labiennale.org/en

♦ 3129 ♦ Verdur Rock
Last weekend of June

Verdur Rock, a music festival held in the French-speaking region of Belgium known as Wallonia, offers amateur rock bands a rare shot at playing before a large audience. As many as 10,000 gather for the free one-day event at the Verdur Theater, an open-air venue standing on top of the historic citadel of Namur. The festival was founded in 1985 and is coordinated by the Youth Service de la Ville de Namur.

Over the years organizers have negotiated a balance between established international and Belgian performers and the "Young Talents," local French-speaking bands who earn stage slots by beating out other competitors. Concert performers include past Verdur Rock winners and the victor of the Cégep Rock contest, a sister festival held in Montreal, Canada, also catering to amateur acts.

CONTACTS:
Verdur Rock Festival
Youth Service
Esplanade de l'Hôtel de Ville
Namur, 5000 Belgium
32-81-24-6090; fax: 32-81-24-7149
www.verdur-rock.be

♦ 3130 ♦ Vermont Maple Festival
Last weekend in April

Vermont is the official maple capital of the world, and the maple festival held there each spring is really a statewide celebration. Maple sugaring—the process of tapping maple trees, gathering the sap, and boiling it in the sugarhouse to produce syrup—was a main source of income for the early settlers in Vermont as well as their main source of sweets. The sugaring industry flourished until World War II, when the number of producers dropped sharply. In the 1940s, 1950s, and 1960s, the growing emphasis on dairy farming resulted in the suspension of many sugaring operations. Although there has been a resurgence of interest in recent years, mild winters have taken their toll on the maple sugar crop because cold nights are needed to make the sap flow.

Since 1968 the three-day festival in St. Albans has promoted Vermont maple products through educational exhibits, sugaring equipment displays, essay contests, syrup competitions, maple cooking contests, and a parade. In addition to maple syrup, the festival gives visitors an opportunity to sample maple cream, maple candy, and maple sugar on snow.

CONTACTS:
Vermont Maple Festival
P.O. Box 255
St. Albans, VT 05478 United States
802-524-5800
www.vtmaplefestival.org

♦ 3131 ♦ Vernal Equinox
March 21 or 22

The vernal equinox, Latin for "of spring" and "equal night," is one of the two occasions during the year when the sun crosses the equator, and the days and nights everywhere are nearly of equal length. It marks the beginning of spring in the Northern Hemisphere and the beginning of autumn in the Southern Hemisphere.

See also AUTUMNAL EQUINOX; HIGAN; NYEPI; SHUNBUN-NO-HI.

CONTACTS:
NASA Public Communications Office
NASA Headquarters
Ste. 5R30
Washington, D.C. 20546
202-358-0001; fax: 202-358-4338
www.nasa.gov

Lab for Particles and Fields
Code 672
Goddard Space Flight Center
Greenbelt, MD 20771
301-474-4527
www.istp.gsfc.nasa.gov

♦ 3132 ♦ Vernal Equinox (Chichén Itzá)
March 21

Chichén Itzá, located on Mexico's Yucatán Peninsula, is one of the country's biggest and best preserved Mayan ruins. Every year on the VERNAL EQUINOX, the angle of the sunlight hitting the enormous El Castillo pyramid creates a shadow that gives the illusion of a snake slithering down its side. The Mayans believed that this was Kukulcán, the feathered snake god known to the Aztecs as Quetzalcoatl.

Researchers were not aware of the annual awakening of the serpent god until 30 to 40 years ago, but since that time tourists have converged on the site on March 21—although the serpent can be seen up to four days before or after the equinox. Visitors enjoy folk dancers, musicians, and poets while they wait for the moment of the serpent's appearance, when the hours of sunlight equal the hours of darkness. Although the serpent can also be seen at the AUTUMNAL EQUINOX in September, this is during the rainy season and cloudy weather often spoils the effect.

CONTACTS:
Merida Tourism Office
Calle 56-A no. 242 between 56-B and 60
Colonia Alcalá Martín
Mérida, Yucatán 97050 Mexico
52-999-925-5186
www.merida.gob.mx/turismo/contenido/informacion_in/
informacion.htm

♦ 3133 ♦ Verrazano (Giovanni da) Day
April 17

Observed in New York state, Verrazano Day commemorates the discovery of New York Harbor by the Italian navigator

Giovanni da Verrazano on April 17, 1524. With the backing of King Francis I of France, Verrazano sailed his ship *La Dauphine* to the New World, reaching the Carolina coast in March 1524 and then sailing northward, exploring the eastern coast of North America. In addition to discovering the present-day site of New York City's harbor, he also discovered Block Island and Narragansett Bay in what is now Rhode Island, plus 32 islands off the coast of Maine, including Monhegan. Verrazano was the first European explorer to name newly discovered sites in North America after persons and places in the Old World.

In naming the Verrazano-Narrows Bridge, New York gave Verrazano official recognition. Spanning New York Harbor from Brooklyn to Staten Island, the 4,260-foot suspension bridge, built between 1959 and 1964, succeeded the Golden Gate Bridge in San Francisco as the world's longest suspension bridge until the Humber Bridge was completed in 1981 in Kingston upon Hull, England. Upon its completion in 1998, Japan's Akashi-Kaikyo Bridge took over the title with a span of over 6,500 feet.

♦ 3134 ♦ **Vesak (Wesak; Buddha's Birthday)**
April-May; full moon of Hindu month of Vaisakha; April 8

This is the holiest of Buddhist holy days, celebrating the Buddha's birth, enlightenment, and death, or attaining of Nirvana. While these anniversaries are observed in all Buddhist countries, they are not always celebrated on the same day. In Theravada Buddhist countries, all three anniversaries are marked on the full moon of Vaisakha. In Japan and other Mahayana Buddhist countries, the three anniversaries are usually observed on separate days—the birth on April 8, the enlightenment on December 8, and the death on February 15.

Vesak is a public holiday in many countries, including Thailand, Indonesia, Korea, and Singapore.

This celebration differs from country to country, but generally activities are centered on the Buddhist temples, where people gather to listen to sermons by monks. In the evening, there are candlelit processions around the temples. Homes are also decorated with paper lanterns and oil lamps. Because it's considered important to practice the virtues of kindness to all living things, it's traditional in some countries to free caged birds on this day. In some areas, booths are set up along streets to dispense food. In Burma (Myanmar), people water the Bodhi tree with blessed water and chant prayers around it (*see* KASONE FESTIVAL OF WATERING THE BANYAN TREE).

The Buddha was born as a prince, Siddhartha Gautama, at Lumbini in present-day Nepal, an isolated spot near the border with India, and Lumbini is one of the most sacred pilgrimage destinations for Buddhists, especially on Vesak. A stone pillar erected in 250 B.C.E. by the Indian emperor Asoka designates the birthplace, and a brick temple contains carvings depicting the birth. Another center of celebrations in Nepal is the Swayambhunath temple, built about 2,000 years ago. On this day it is constantly circled by a procession of pilgrims. The lamas in colorful silk robes dance around the

stupa (temple) while musicians play. On this day each year, the stupa's collection of rare *thangkas* (embroidered religious scrolls) and mandalas (geometrical and astrological representations of the world) is shown on the southern wall of the stupa courtyard.

Sarnath, Uttar Pradesh, India, is the place where the Buddha preached his first sermon, and a big fair and a procession of relics of the Buddha highlight the day there. Bodh Gaya (or Buddh Gaya) in the state of Bihar is also the site of special celebrations. It was here that Siddhartha Gautama sat under the Bodhi tree, attained enlightenment, and became known as the Buddha, meaning the "Enlightened One."

Gautama was born about 563 B.C.E. into a regal family and was brought up in great luxury. At the age of 29, distressed by the misery of mankind, he renounced his princely life and his wife and infant son to become a wandering ascetic and to search for a path that would give relief from suffering. For six years he practiced severe austerities, eating little. But he realized that self-mortification wasn't leading him to what he sought. One morning, sitting in deep meditation, under a ficus tree now called the Bodhi tree, he achieved enlightenment, or awakening. This was at Bodh Gaya in about 528 B.C.E., when Gautama was 35 years old. In the years that followed, he laid down rules of ethics (*see* MAGHA PUJA) and condemned the caste system. He taught that the aim of religion is to free oneself of worldly fetters in order to attain enlightenment, or Nirvana, a condition of freedom from sorrow and selfish desire. The Buddha trained large numbers of disciples to continue his work. He died in about 483 B.C.E.

From its start in northern India, Buddhism spread throughout Asia. The religion grew especially after Asoka, the first great emperor of India, adopted it as his religion in the third century B.C.E. and traveled about preaching and building hospitals and monasteries. He also sent his son, Mahinda, to preach the tenets of Buddhism in Sri Lanka (*see* POSON). The Buddhism practiced in Southeast Asia is the oldest form of the religion, known as Theravada Buddhism, or "The Way of the Elders." As Buddhism went north, into Nepal, Bhutan, Tibet, China, Korea, and then Japan, it took a different form called Mahayana Buddhism, or "The Great Vehicle."

Vesak, or **Wesak**, is also known as **Waisak** (Indonesia), **Wisakha Bucha** (Thailand), **Buddha Jayanti** (Nepal and India), **Phat Dan Day** (Vietnam), **Buddha Purnima** (India), **Kambutsu-e** or HANA MATSURI (Japan), **Full Moon of Kason** (Myanmar), **Vixakha Bouxa** (Laos) and sometimes the **Feast of the Lanterns**.

See also BUN BANG FAI and SONGKRAN.

CONTACTS:
South Putuo Temple
515 South Rd.
Siming, 361005 China
www.nanputuo.com

♦ 3135 ♦ **Veterans Day**
November 11; second Sunday in November in Great Britain

On November 11, 1918, the armistice between the Allied and Central Powers that halted the fighting in World War I was signed in Marshal Ferdinand Foch's railroad car in the forest of Compiègne, France. In the United States, the name **Armistice Day** was changed to Veterans Day in 1954 to honor those who have served their country in other wars as well.

In Great Britain, Canada, and France, it is dedicated primarily to those who died in either of the world wars. The British, Australians, and Canadians call it **Remembrance Day**. In England it is also known as **Poppy Day** for the red paper flowers sold by the British Legion to benefit veterans. In the U.S. veterans groups sell poppies on MEMORIAL DAY.

An attempt in 1971 to make Veterans Day conform to the "Monday Holiday Law" by scheduling it on the fourth Monday in October triggered widespread resistance, and seven years later it was moved back to the traditional November 11 date. In many places the 11th day of the 11th month is celebrated by observing a two-minute silence at 11:00 in the morning, the hour at which the hostilities ceased.

CONTACTS:
U.S. Department of Veterans Affairs
1722 I St. N.W.
Washington, D.C. 20421
800-827-1000 or 800-273-8255
www.va.gov

Canada Veterans Affairs
61 Hyperion Ct.
Ste. 04
Kingston, ON K7K 7K7 Canada
866-522-2122
www.veterans.gc.ca/eng

Australian War Memorial
G.P.O. Box 345
Canberra, ACT 2601 Australia
61-2-6243-4211; fax: 61-2-6243-4325
www.awm.gov.au

♦ 3136 ♦ **Veterans Day (Emporia, Kansas)**
November 11 and the preceding week

Veterans Day was founded in Emporia, Kansas, on November 11, 1953, and that city commemorates the holiday with a special program of events each year. For decades, November 11 was observed in the United States as Armistice Day, the anniversary of the end of World War I. But in 1953 the City of Emporia created a special program to honor all veterans, not just those from the 1914 to 1918 era. The idea attracted notice and gained support among lawmakers in other states and in the U.S. Congress, which passed a bill changing the name of the federal holiday the following year.

In recognition of its unique role in defining Veterans Day, Emporia celebrates the holiday with 10 days of special events, including museum exhibits, running and walking races, essay and poster contests, discussion panels, war films, luncheons, entertainment, and memorial luminaria. Sponsored by the Emporia Chamber of Commerce and Convention & Visitors Bureau, most events are free and open to the public. In addition to a blood drive, the Veterans Administration

Health Center collects personal care items and clothing to be delivered to inpatient and outpatient programs for veterans in need. On the Saturday preceding the Veterans Day federal holiday, a parade sponsored by the Veterans of Foreign Wars (VFW) is held on Commercial Street in downtown Emporia, and a memorial service follows. Veterans Day concludes with a free dinner for all veterans at a local restaurant.

CONTACTS:
Emporia Chamber of Commerce and Convention & Visitors Bureau
719 Commercial St.
Emporia, KS 66801
800-279-3730; fax: 620-342-3223
www.emporiakschamber.org

♦ 3137 ♦ **Veterans Homecoming (Branson, Missouri)**
November 5 through 11

Veterans Homecoming in Branson, Missouri, is the largest Veterans Day commemoration in the United States, with more than 50,000 veterans and their families attending annually. Events extend over the week before November 11, and include special entertainment performances, lectures, social receptions, reenactments, and military memorials. The Branson Veterans Task Force, which organizes the celebration, maintains a headquarters at Branson's Celebration Hall, where veterans and active duty personnel can receive a free lunch daily throughout the week. Special tributes to veterans take place throughout the town, including the world's largest flying American flag, a salute to the troops on the showboat *Branson Belle,* and candlelight memorials remembering those who lost their lives in war. Each day "Reveille" and "Retreat" signal the beginning and the end of the day's activities, and throughout the week visitors enjoy free performances by military bands and drill teams. On Veterans Day a parade sponsored by the American Legion proceeds through downtown Branson. Throughout the week special discounts are given to veterans at various dining and retail establishments as well as museums, shows, and hotels.

CONTACTS:
Branson Veterans Task Force
The Falls Shopping Center
3625 Falls Pkwy
Ste. W
Branson, MO 65616
417-337-8387
www.bransonveterans.com

♦ 3138 ♦ **Veterans Pow Wow**
Early November

The annual Veterans Pow Wow in Topeka, Kans., honors service veterans and active-duty U.S. service personnel on a date close to Veterans Day in early November. Hosted since 2001 by the Awi Akta District of the Northern Cherokee Nation of the Old Louisiana Territory, the event was held at Washburn University before moving to the Gage Park Zoo Shelter House in 2007.

The Pow Wow uses traditional Native American dancing and drumming. It includes a color guard from the local community and a special tribute to a veteran from among tribe members. Dancers and musicians in formal regalia participate in a drum circle and gourd dancing; all drums are welcome. The event, which includes Native American craft and food vendors, is attended by about 400 people.

CONTACTS:
Awi Akta District of the Northern Cherokee Nation of the Old
Louisiana Territory
4327 S.W. 17th Terr.
Topeka, KS 66604
www.awiakta.org

♦ 3139 ♦ **Victory Day (Our Lady of Victories Day)**
September 8

This national holiday in Malta celebrates the lifting of two sieges:

In 1565, the Hospitallers, or the Knights of the Order of St. John of Jerusalem, with 6,000-9,000 men, held Malta against a four-month siege by some 29,000 Ottoman Turks. The onslaught left half the knights dead, but the Turks didn't fare well either—the knights used the heads of Turkish captives as cannonballs, and the defeat of the Turks humbled the Ottoman Empire. (Malta was under the control of the knights, a religious and military order of the Roman Catholic Church dedicated to tending the sick and poor and warring against Muslims, from 1530 until June 1798, when NAPOLEON took possession of the island.)

During World War II, the island fought off Axis powers (Germany and Italy) despite three years of severe air bombardment. In April 1942, air-raid alerts averaged about 10 a day; the ruins included the Royal Opera House in Valletta, destroyed by a German bomb. British Prime Minister Winston Churchill called Malta "our only unsinkable aircraft carrier."

On April 15, 1942, England's King George VI awarded the island of Malta the George Cross, Britain's highest decoration for civilian gallantry, to "honour her brave people … to bear witness to a heroism and devotion which will long be famous in history." This was the first time a medal was conferred on any part of the commonwealth. At this time, Britain also declared that self-government would be restored at the end of hostilities.

The holiday is celebrated with parades, fireworks, and a colorful regatta and boat races in the Grand Harbour at Valletta. A highlight of the boat races is that of the *dgnajsas*, oared taxi boats with painted designs. They are thought to date back to Phoenician times (800 B.C.E.).

See also MALTA INDEPENDENCE DAY.

CONTACTS:
Malta Tourism Authority
Auberge D'Italie
Merchants St.
Valletta, VLT 1170 Malta

356-2291-5000; fax: 356-2291-5394
www.visitmalta.com

♦ 3140 ♦ **Victory Day (Russia)**
May 9

Victory Day is a national public holiday in the Russian Federation. It celebrates the defeat of Nazism and the end of World War II on European soil. On this day people remember the 27 million Russian civilians and soldiers who perished during the war. Each year on May 9 people crowd Moscow's Red Square for solemn rites of remembrance—one minute of silence and cannon or gun salutes—as well as traditional musical and dance performances. Veterans may attend wearing their uniforms and medals. Many leave flowers at memorials and graves. TV stations often air films about World War II.

CONTACTS:
Embassy of the Russian Federation
2650 Wisconsin Ave. N.W.
Washington, D.C. 20007
202-298-5700; fax: 202-298-5735
www.russianembassy.org

♦ 3141 ♦ **Vidalia Onion Festival**
Last weekend in April to early May

There are no tears during this tribute to Georgia's state vegetable, the sweet Vidalia onion, which is said to be burp-free, good for digestion, *and* tearless. The festival is held in Vidalia (nearby Glenville has a rival onion festival, usually a week earlier) at the height of the harvest season, which extends from mid-April to early June.

This onion is an interesting vegetable, officially the F-1 hybrid yellow granex, a round white onion with a yellow skin. Local folks hail it as the "world's sweetest onion," and, in fact, it has a sugar content of 12.5 percent, making it as sweet as a Valencia orange. If the seed is planted anywhere but Georgia, however, it becomes a normal sharp-tasting onion, probably due to the soil. Therefore, the name Vidalia may be given only to onions grown throughout 13 Georgia counties and parts of seven other counties (by act of the state legislature and federal directive).

According to a local story, Vidalia onions have been known since 1931, when a farmer discovered the onions didn't make him cry and so got a premium price for them even during the Depression. But they didn't become widely known until Delbert Bland of Bland Farms, a big onion producer, started a marketing campaign and mail-order onion business in 1984. In 1990, the sweet-onion business in Georgia amounted to about $35 million.

The celebration of the onion includes standard festival fare—music, a street dance, a fishing rodeo and expo, and a fun run. It also has a competition for Miss Vidalia Onion (a beautiful high school or college woman). Other beauty pageant winners are Miss Vidalia Onion Seed (ages 3-5), Miss Vidalia Onion Sprout (ages 6-9), Miss Spring Onion (ages 10-12), and Miss Junior Vidalia Onion (ages 13-16). Finally, there are onion-eating contests, and a Vidalia Onion Cook-Off, which produces cakes, breads, and muffins made with onions.

CONTACTS:
Vidalia Area Convention and Visitors Bureau
100 Vidalia Sweet Onion Dr.
Ste. A
Vidalia, GA 30474
912-538-8687; fax: 912-538-1466
www.vidaliaarea.com

◆ 3142 ◆ **Vienna Festival**
May-June

This six-week festival, founded in 1951, regularly attracts more than a million people to the city of Vienna, Austria. There are hundreds of performances of music, opera, ballet, and drama by some of the best-known Austrian and foreign companies in the world—including the Royal Shakespeare Company, the Merce Cunningham Dance Company, the Martha Graham Dance Company, the Noh Theater of Japan, and the Malegot Ballet of St. Petersburg.

Like the EDINBURGH INTERNATIONAL FESTIVAL, the Vienna Festival also includes many "fringe" events offered by independent theater, dance, and musical groups.

CONTACTS:
Vienna Festival
Lehargasse 11/1/6
Vienna, 1060 Austria
43-1589-2222; fax: 43-1589-2249
www.festwochen.at

◆ 3143 ◆ **Vienna Jazz Festival (Jazz Fest Wien)**
June-July

As its name suggests, this annual Viennese event is all about jazz. Regarded as one of the most prominent music festivals of its kind, the Vienna Jazz Festival attracts over 60,000 visitors and participants from all over the world. The concerts are held in various indoor and open-air venues throughout the city, including the Vienna State Opera, the cultural complex *MuseumsQuartier*, and the Town Hall Square. Featuring world-class jazz musicians as well as performers from other genres such as pop, rock, blues, soul, and folk, the Vienna Jazz Festival has been a summer tradition since 1991.

CONTACTS:
Verein Jazz Fest Wien
Lammgasse 12/8
Vienna, A-1080 Austria
431-712-4224; fax: 431-712-3434
www.viennajazz.org/en

◆ 3144 ◆ **Vietnam Ancestors Death Anniversary**
10th day of the third lunar month (April)

Traditionally, Vietnamese families will remember the death of an ancestor on the anniversary of his or her death. Family members gather for the festive occasion to enjoy a banquet. It is customary to include at least one member of each generation of the family, even if this involves traveling a great distance. Foods include personal favorites of the deceased as well as chicken, a prized meat in Vietnam. In central Vietnam, it is customary to make stuffed rice flour balls. Special anniversary desserts are also prepared, desserts which are made only during this event. Because of the time and effort involved, wealthier families often hire caterers to prepare the food.

The deceased ancestor is thought to return for a visit on this day. He or she is ritually greeted at the beginning of the occasion. In addition to the banquet, offerings are made on the family altar and incense sticks are burned in honor the ancestor as well as the *cong*, or "God of the Home." The *Thanh hoang*, or "God of the Village," is also honored.

Until recently, the Ancestors Death Anniversary was observed only on the actual day of the death. But the Vietnamese government standardized the celebration to an annual observance to be held on the 10th day of the third lunar month, which occurs in April.

CONTACTS:
Ministry of Culture, Sports and Tourism - Vietnam National Administration of Tourism
1233 20th St. N.W.
Ste. 400
Washington, D.C. 20036
202-861-0737; fax: 202-861-0917
www.vietnamembassy-usa.org
Ministry of Culture, Sports and Tourism - Vietnam National Administration of Tourism
02 Nui Truc St.
Ba Dinh District
Vietnam
84-4-3943-7072; fax: 84-4-3826-3956
vietnamtourism.gov.vn

◆ 3145 ◆ **Vietnam National Day**
September 2

The Socialist Republic of Vietnam observes its declaration of independence from France as a national holiday. On this day in 1945 HO CHI MINH (1890-1969) proclaimed the establishment of the Democratic Republic of Vietnam. To celebrate Vietnam's national holiday, people gather in major cities, including Hanoi, for speeches, parades, fireworks, and other festivities.

CONTACTS:
Embassy of Vietnam
1233 20th St. N.W.
Ste. 400
Washington, D.C. 20036
202-861-0737; fax: 202-861-0917
www.vietnamembassy-usa.org

◆ 3146 ◆ **Vietnam Veterans Memorial Anniversary**
November 11

The Vietnam Veterans Memorial Anniversary commemorates the dedication of the Vietnam Veterans Memorial in Washington, D.C., on November 13, 1982. Known commonly as "The Wall," the black granite Memorial is set within Constitution Gardens on Constitution Avenue between 21st and 23rd Streets. It lists the names of 58,256 U.S. service personnel who were killed while serving in Vietnam between 1957 and 1975.

Development and construction of the Memorial was overseen by the Vietnam Veterans Memorial Fund, Inc., a private organization that raised money for the project through donations and held an open competition for design proposals. The winning design was submitted by Maya Lin, a native of Ohio who was a student at Yale University at the time her design was chosen. In 1984 the Vietnam Veterans Memorial was brought under the oversight of the National Park Service.

Each year on Veterans Day, the anniversary of the Memorial's dedication is celebrated with a special ceremony, including speakers and a military color guard. As many as 10,000 veterans, family, and friends have gathered to participate in the Veterans Day observance. In 2007, the 25th anniversary of the Memorial, a special program included speeches by General Colin Powell and representatives of veterans' and family service organizations, including the American Gold Star Mothers, Gold Star Wives, and others. Musicians performed patriotic hymns and "Taps," and representatives of the armed services and family groups placed memorial wreaths.

CONTACTS:
Vietnam Veterans Memorial Wall
National Park Service
900 Ohio Dr. S.W.
Washington, D.C. 20024
202-426-6841
www.nps.gov/vive

♦ 3147 ♦ Vignerons, Fête des (Winegrowers' Festival)
August, approximately every 20-25 years

Held only five times during each of the 19th and 20th centuries in Vevey, Switzerland, the Fête des Vignerons is a pageant of music, dance, and song depicting the passage of the seasons in winegrowing country and honoring the most talented workers in the vineyards. It lasts more than two weeks and has a cast of thousands, drawn from the local population. The pageant takes place in an open-air theater, specially constructed each time the festival is held, with Lake Geneva and the mountains beyond as a backdrop. The festival was last held in 1999.

CONTACTS:
Confrerie des Vignerons
Rue du Chateau 2
Vevey, 1800 Switzerland
41-21-923-8705; fax: 41-21-923-8706
www.fetedesvignerons.ch

♦ 3148 ♦ Viking Festival
Mid-June

The annual Viking festival has been held since 2000 in the town of Hafnarfjordur, Iceland. During the festival, held near the summer solstice in mid-June, Viking-culture enthusiasts from around the world display reconstructions of Viking garb, handicraft, and traditions, ranging from weddings to sword and archery fights. The festival typically draws about150 "Vikings" from Iceland and many foreign countries. They include hand-picked woodcarvers, stone carvers, other craftsmen, storytellers, and show fighters. In addition to Viking displays, the festival offers its thousands of spectators and visitors a market; live music, dance, and drama; guided walks; and art exhibitions.

CONTACTS:
Scandinavian Tourist Boards
655 Third Ave.
Ste. 1810
New York, NY 10017
213-885-9700
www.goscandinavia.com

Hafnarfjörður Information Centre
Strandgata 6
Hafnarfjordur, 220 Iceland
354-585-5500; fax: 354-585-5509
www.hafnarfjordur.is

♦ 3149 ♦ Viña del Mar International Song Festival
Third week in February

The seaport of Viña del Mar in Valparaiso, Chile, is one of South America's most popular attractions and also the site of one of the continent's biggest music events, the Viña del Mar International Song Festival (Festival Internacional de la Canción de Viña del Mar). The weeklong festival attracts thousands of people, including many tourists, and is broadcast in 21 countries.

An annual event established in 1960, the festival takes place at an outdoor amphitheatre called the Quinta Vergara. From its inception, the festival has held a song competition that traditionally features performers from about 10 Spanish-speaking countries. There is also a program featuring folk musicians and an international show that includes English-speaking as well as Latin performers.

CONTACTS:
Chile National Tourism Service
Av Providencia
Ste. 1550
Chile
56-22-731-8310
www.sernatur.cl

♦ 3150 ♦ Vinalia
April 23, August 19

There were two ancient Roman festivals that were sacred to Venus and known as the Vinalia. The first, observed on April 23, was called the Vinalia Priora; the second, on August 19, was the Vinalia Rustica. Both festivals, it seems, were originally sacred to Jupiter. But after the worship of Venus was introduced into Rome in the second century B.C.E., its popularity spread so quickly that the older association with Jupiter gradually faded.

April 23 was probably the day on which the wineskins were first opened, the new wine having been brought into Rome just a few days earlier. Libations from the newly opened skins were made to Jupiter (later Venus, who was a deity of gardens and therefore of vineyards as well). After the libation, the wine was tasted. Winegrowers were warned not to bring the new wine into the city until the Vinalia had been proclaimed on the *nones*, or the ninth day before the IDES of the month.

There is some confusion about what went on at the August festival. Some believe that this—not April 23—was the day on which the new wine was brought into Rome. Others say that the Vinalia Rustica was a rite designed to protect the vintage that would follow from disease, storms, and other harmful influences.

♦ 3151 ♦ Vincy Carnival
Late June to early July

Carnival festivities take place on the Caribbean island of St. Vincent from late June to early July. Touring musical groups, led by one or two "maskers" who act as leaders, are a primary feature of the celebrations. The leaders are usually dressed as traditional characters—among them the Devil, Wild Indian, Bold Robber, and the hump-backed Bruise-ee-Back. Each group may perform a song written for the occasion by its leader, and usually acts out some kind of violent argument that will amuse or scare the onlookers and persuade them to donate some money. The songs are mocking or even slanderous in nature, and usually concern an individual or event associated with a particular locale. The band members typically dress in costumes based on that of their leader, but sometimes they merely blacken their faces, dab crude slogans and faces onto their white t-shirts and pants, and wear *washikongs* (tennis shoes) and strangely constructed hats.

CONTACTS:
St. Vincent and the Grenadines Tourist Information Office
801 Second Ave.
21st Fl.
New York, NY 10017
212-687-4490; fax: 212-949-5946
www.gov.vc

♦ 3152 ♦ Vinegar Festival, International
Mid-June Saturday

The International Vinegar Festival, a celebration of the sour liquid condiment, takes place every year on one Saturday in mid-June in Roslyn, S.Dak. The family-friendly day features a parade, live entertainment, cooking demonstrations, a handicrafts market, and food vendors. Participants can enjoy such activities as a vinegar-tasting party and making crafts from vinegar bottles. A centerpiece of the festival is billed

as the "mother of all vinegar contests," with vinegars from around the globe presented for judging to a panel of chefs.

The festival was launched in 2000 as a means to help the tiny town of Roslyn stay economically vibrant. A committee called CARE (Committee for the Advancement of Roslyn and Eden) sought a niche to draw visitors, and they found it thanks to a local writer named Lawrence Diggs, also known as "Vinegar Man." A food scientist, he is a collector of vinegars and the author of *Vinegar: Appreciating, Making, and Enjoying Vinegar*. He helped to found a vinegar museum in Roslyn, housed in a building donated by the city, which has been featured by such prestigious food journals as *Bon Appetit* and *Gourmet*.

CONTACTS:
International Vinegar Museum
502 Main St.
P.O. Box 201
Roslyn, SD 57261
605-486-0075
internationalvinegarmuseum.com

Vinegar Man
P.O. Box 41
Roslyn, SD 57261
www.vinegarman.com

♦ 3153 ♦ Vinegrower's Day
February 14

This pre-harvest vineyard festival in Bulgaria involves pruning the vines and sprinkling them with wine. Ritual songs and dances are performed in hopes of a plentiful grape harvest. In some areas, a "Vine King" is crowned with a wreath of twigs from the vineyards. Everyone treats him with great respect, for it is believed that fertility depends on the King's happiness.

Participation in the **Trifon Zarezan** festivities is something that both locals and foreign tourists look forward to. Visits to well-known Bulgarian vineyards are organized, the vines are pruned, and guests are given an opportunity to sample the local wine and foods.

See also ST. TRYPHON'S DAY.

CONTACTS:
Ministry of Foreign Affairs of the Republic of Bulgaria
2, Aleksandar Zhendov Str
Sofia, 1113 Bulgaria
359-2-948-2999
www.mfa.bg

♦ 3154 ♦ Vintage Computer Festivals
First weekend of November

By offering a huge display of old computer hardware, software, and ephemera, Vintage Computer Festivals provide to the public a hands-on perspective on the computer revolution, as well as the simple pleasure of playing with old computers. The success of the main festival, which is held in

California's Silicon Valley, has spawned regional festivals in New England and Europe. The first European version of the festival took place in 2000, and the first East Coast version was held the following year.

Computer collector Sellam Ismail founded the festival with a mission to network with collectors and advance research on the history of the computer. At the first festival, in 1997, collectors exchanged stories, traded equipment, listened to talks by established industry figures, and attended workshops on vintage computer collecting. This basic format of the event has not changed, even as the festival has expanded.

In addition to the main exhibit and the speaker presentations, there is a side event known as the Vintage Computer Film Festival, which screens films on vintage computing as well as technological development.

CONTACTS:
Vintage Computer Festival
2442 Research Dr.
Livermore, CA 94550 United States
925-294-5900
www.vintage.org

♦ 3155 ♦ Vintners' Procession
Thursday after July 4

The Worshipful Company of Vintners (Winemakers) of the city of London holds its annual procession on the Thursday following July 4, the Feast of the Translation of St. Martin. Starting at 5:30 P.M., they walk from the Vintners' Hall in Upper Thames Street to the church of St. James, Garlickhythe. Two wine porters, dressed in top hats and white smocks and carrying birch brooms, lead the procession, sweeping the road of any "foulness" so that Company officials don't slip or soil their fur and velvet robes—the type of event that occurred more often in 1205, when a court order decreed that the roads be swept first and that the Master, Wardens, and Brethren be provided with herbal nosegays to sniff so they wouldn't be offended by any "noxious flavours or other ill vapours."

The Company of Vintners was once one of the wealthiest and most influential of London's ancient guilds or livery companies. Today it has the right to export and import all spirits from and to the Port of London, or anywhere within a three-mile limit.

CONTACTS:
Worshipful Company of Vintners
Vintners' Hall, Upper Thames St.
London, EC4V 3BG United Kingdom
44-20-7236-1863; fax: 44-20-3432-6670
www.vintnershall.co.uk

♦ 3156 ♦ Virgen de Los Angeles Day
August 2

Costa Rica honors its patron saint, La Virgen de los Angeles (also known as La Negrita), on this national holiday. La Negrita is a statue of the Virgin Mary with Baby Jesus in her arms. The statue is carved in dark wood, which is how La Negrita ("little dark one") earned its name. The statue is housed in the Basilica Virgen de Los Angeles in Cartago, next to a small stream. Many Costa Ricans believe both the statue and the stream have curative powers. A legend about the statue dates back to August 2, 1635, when a local woman found the statue in the woods and took it more than once to her home, but the statue kept returning to the spot where she first saw it.

People from all over the country come to Cartago on August 2 to celebrate the mass at the Basilica, pray to Little Negrita, and collect water from the stream. Many pilgrims come on foot, after journeys of several days. Celebrations of the holiday include street fairs, live music, and feasts throughout Costa Rica.

CONTACTS:
Embassy of Costa Rica
2112 S. St.
Washington, D.C. 20008
202-499-2991; fax: 202-265-4795
www.costarica-embassy.org

♦ 3157 ♦ Virgin of the Pillar, Feast of the
October 12

According to an ancient legend, the Virgin Mary appeared to Santiago, or St. James the Apostle, when he was in Saragossa (Zaragoza), Aragón, Spain. She spoke to him from the top of a pillar, which he interpreted as a sign that he should build a chapel where the column stood. *Nuestra Señora del Pilar* has since become a major pilgrimage center.

The Feast of the Virgin of the Pillar is observed with special masses and processions in honor of *La Virgen*. The *Gigantes*— giant cardboard and canvas figures concealing the men who dance behind them—are brought out especially for the occasion. Often representing Spanish kings and queens or famous literary and historical figures, they can be 20- to 30-feet tall. The *cabezudos*, or "big heads," on the other hand, are grotesque puppets with huge heads which are meant to poke fun at certain professions or personalities. Also characteristic of the festival are *jota* contests in which Aragon's regional folk dance is performed to the accompaniment of guitars, mandolins, and lutes.

See also ST. JAMES'S DAY.

CONTACTS:
Zaragoza Tourist Board
Plaza de Ntra. Sra. Del Pilar, s/n.
 Spain
34-976-721-100
www.zaragoza.es

♦ 3158 ♦ Virginia Scottish Games
Fourth weekend in July

Alexandria, Virginia, was founded by Scotsmen in 1749 and named for Scottish merchant John Alexander. The city celebrates its Scottish heritage with a two-day Celtic country fair featuring bagpipe bands, world-class athletes, Celtic dancers, a national fiddling championship, and an international harp competition.

One of the most colorful attractions is the Highland dancing, which involves hundreds of competitors ranging in age from preschoolers to adults. The highlight of the athletic contests is the caber toss, which is part of a seven-event competition known as the Highland Heptathlon. These contests trace their origins to the ancient HIGHLAND GAMES of northern Scotland, where military chiefs demonstrated their strength at annual clan gatherings.

See also ALMA HIGHLAND FESTIVAL AND GAMES; GRANDFATHER MOUNTAIN HIGHLAND GAMES AND GATHERING OF SCOTTISH CLANS.

CONTACTS:
Virginia Scottish Games Association
P.O. Box 1338
Alexandria, VA 22313
www.vascottishgames.org

♦ 3159 ♦ Visitation, Feast of the
May 31

On this day Christian churches in the West commemorate the Virgin Mary's visit to her cousin Elizabeth. After learning that she was to be the mother of Jesus, Mary went into the mountains of Judea to see her cousin, the barren wife of Zechariah, who had conceived a son who would come to be known as John the Baptist. According to the Gospel of Luke, Elizabeth's baby "leaped in her womb" (1:41) at the sound of Mary's voice. It was at this moment, according to the belief of some Roman Catholics, that John the Baptist was cleansed from original sin and filled with heavenly grace. Mary stayed with Elizabeth for three months and returned home just before John was born.

See also ST. JOHN'S DAY.

CONTACTS:
Marian Library/International Marian Research Institute
University of Dayton
300 College Park
Dayton, OH 45469
937-229-1000
www.udayton.edu

♦ 3160 ♦ Visvakarma Puja
August-September; end of Hindu month of Bhadrapada

Dedicated to Visvakarma, the patron god of all Hindu artisans, the **Festival of Tools** is a workers' holiday in India dedicated to each individual's most important tool or instrument. A pitcher representing the god is set in a place of honor in every home and shop, and before it the people lay their most important tool. Students might place one of their schoolbooks there, musicians would place the instrument they play, artists would put their favorite brushes before the

pitcher, tailors their scissors, gardeners their rakes, fishermen their nets, etc. A candle is lit in front of the pitcher, and sometimes incense is burned or scented water is sprinkled over the tool. Workers give thanks for their tools and implore Visvakarma's help in plying their trade.

After this ceremony is over, people gather in parks or public places and spend the rest of the day with games and feasting.

CONTACTS:
Department of Tourism, Government of West Bengal
1, K. S. Roy Rd.
New Secretariat Bldg.
3rd Fl.
Kolkata, West Bengal 700001 India
91-33-22254723; fax: 91-33-22254565
wbtourism.gov.in

♦ 3161 ♦ Vivid Sydney
May-June

Vivid Sydney is an 18-day annual extravaganza of music, lights, and art in Sydney, Australia. Hundreds of international artists participate in the event, which is enjoyed by more than one million visitors from Australia and around the world. The festival includes special programs like Vivid Music— an expansive line-up of local and international music shows at the Sydney Opera House. Each year the event transforms the sails of the Opera House into giant, colorful canvases filled with video-mapped images and projections. During the festival, visitors can walk the harbor and peruse a series of light sculptures and installations. Other highpoints of the event include workshops, panel discussions, product launches, and award presentations. The platform called Vivid Ideas attracts some of the best creative minds from Australia and other countries. Vivid Sydney incorporates a wide variety of food options, from gourmet dining to popular street foods. The Vivid Night Markets offer a selection of clothes, jewelry, home furnishings, and other bric-a-brac. Public transport is available to help navigate the festival, with extra buses and trains provided during the event.

CONTACTS:
Destination NSW
Level 2, 88 Cumberland St.
Sydney, NSW 2000 Australia
61-2-9931-1111; fax: 61-2-9931-1490
www.vividsydney.com

♦ 3162 ♦ V-J Day (Victory over Japan Day)
August 14

V-J Day commemorates the anniversary of Japan's surrender to the Allies in 1945, ending World War II. The atomic bombs dropped on HIROSHIMA on Aug. 6 and Nagasaki on Aug. 9, and the Soviet Union's invasion of Manchuria in the previous week made the surrender inevitable. The announcement of the surrender by President Harry S. Truman set off street celebrations from coast to coast in the United States. In New York City, Times Square was jammed with people embracing and dancing. In Naples, Italy, the Andrews Sisters had just finished singing "Don't Sit Under the Apple Tree" to U.S. troops when Maxine Andrews was given a slip of paper and read the news; joyous bedlam ensued.

The official end of the war didn't come until Sept. 2, when Gen. Douglas MacArthur accepted the Japanese surrender from Gen. Yoshijiro Umezu aboard the USS *Missouri* in Tokyo Bay. He said, "Today the guns are silent. A great tragedy has ended…. The holy mission has been completed." President Truman declared Sept. 2 as official V-J Day.

V-J Day is a legal holiday only in the state of Rhode Island, where it is called Victory Day. In Connecticut, the tiny village of Moosup (a section of the town of Plainfield) claims to have the only V-J Day parade in the country. Sponsored by the local American Legion post, it began small in 1961 and now features more than 200 units—marching bands, floats, civic groups, color guards, and Gold Star Mothers (women who lost a son or daughter in war)—and attracts some 10,000 spectators.

CONTACTS:
Naval Historical and Heritage Command
805 Kidder Breese St. S.E.
Washington Navy Yard
Washington, D.C. 20374
202-433-7880
www.history.navy.mil

American Legion National Headquarters
700 N. Pennsylvania St.
P.O. Box 1055
Indianapolis, IN 46206
317-630-1200; fax: 317-630-1223
www.legion.org

National Archives and Records Administration
700 Pennsylvania Ave. N.W.
Washington, D.C. 20408
202-357-5000 or 866-325-7208
www.archives.gov

♦ 3163 ♦ **Vlöggelen**
Between March 22 and April 25; Easter Sunday and Monday

As practiced in the eastern Netherlands village of Ootmarsum, the Vlöggelen, or **Winging Ceremony**, is believed to be the remnant of an ancient spring fertility rite. It is a ritualistic dance through the narrow cobbled streets led by eight unmarried men, linked to form a human chain that advances slowly, "like birds on the wing." The dancers enter the front doors of shops, inns, farmhouses, and barns, emerging through the back doors to the melody of an old Easter hymn with so many verses that the dancers must read the words pinned to the back of the person in front of them. Later, the men fetch firewood for a huge bonfire that night. In recent years, the tradition has drawn criticism from the Dutch Council of Christians and Jews, because the lyrics of the song blame the Jews for Jesus' death.

See also Easter Monday in the Netherlands.

♦ 3164 ♦ **Vohuman, Feast of**
January, May, June; second day of Vohuman, the 11th Zoroastrian month

The Feast of Vohuman is one of the "sacred name days" in the Zoroastrian religion, where the day and the month share the name of the same *yazata*, or spiritual being—in this case, Vohuman, who represents Good Mind (or Good Thought) and who presides over animals. Because there are actually three different Zoroastrian calendars in use by widely separated Zoroastrian communities, the Feast of Vohuman occurs either in January, May, or June.

Among the followers of Persian prophet Zoroaster (also known as Zarathushtra, believed to have lived around 1200 B.C.E.), a name-day feast is an occasion for religious services which can be performed in a fire temple, meeting hall, or private home.

There are about 100,000 followers of Zoroastrianism today, and most of them live in northwestern India or Iran. Smaller communities exist in Pakistan, Sri Lanka, Canada, the U.S., England, and Australia.

♦ 3165 ♦ **Volksfest**
First Sunday in August

Founded in 1845 by immigrants from the Swiss canton of Glaurus, the town of New Glarus, Wisconsin, continued to attract Swiss immigrants over the years. Today it celebrates this cultural heritage in its yearly Volksfest and Heidi Festival. The Volksfest Festival honors Swiss National Day, which takes place on August 1. The citizens of New Glarus have switched the day of their observance to the first Sunday in August, however. Festivities take place in Tell Shooting Park, one-half mile north of town. They include performances of Swiss music by various choral groups, yodeling, *thalerschwingen* and accordion music, Swiss folk dancing, and flag throwing. Frequently a representative from the Swiss Embassy or Swiss government will attend as an honored speaker.

CONTACTS:
New Glarus Chamber of Commerce
418 Railroad St.
P.O. Box 713
New Glarus, WI 53574
608-527-2095 or 800-527-6838; fax: 608-527-4991
swisstown.com

♦ 3166 ♦ **Volunteer Day for Economic and Social Development, International**
December 5

In 1985 the United Nations established December 5 as International Volunteer Day for Economic and Social Development. The Assembly hoped that in so doing, it would draw favorable attention to the contribution made by these volunteers, and thus inspire more people to serve the world community as volunteers.

CONTACTS:
United Nations, Department of Public Information
Rm. S-1070L, United Nations
New York, NY 10017
212-963-6842; fax: 212-963-6914
www.un.org

♦ 3167 ♦ **Voodoo Music Experience**
Late October

The Voodoo Music Experience is an annual music festival that takes place in New Orleans, La., over a three-day weekend in late October. The event debuted in 1999 with the aim of showcasing the verve and diversity of New Orleans' renowned music scene, as well as bringing famed acts to the city. More than 120 musicians performed at the event in 2007.

Performers are grouped into three categories: "Le Ritual" for established musicians; "Le Flambeau" for artists who reflect New Orleans' musical history and traditions; and "Le Carnival" for musicians and performance artists from New Orleans' underground art and bohemian scene.

The Voodoo Music Experience is famous for it's quirky programming, and has featured varied, high-profile national and international acts along with local Louisiana musicians. The festival has hosted over 2000 artists since its inception. In 2014, the festival attracted more than 100,000 people, making it one of the largest crowds in the event's 16-year history.

♦ 3168 ♦ **Vulcanalia (Volcanalia)**
August 23

Vulcan was the ancient Roman god of volcanic or destructive fire—not to be confused with the Greek god Hephaestus, who was the god of the blacksmith's forge and therefore a kindly fire god. In offering sacrifices to Vulcan, it was customary to burn the whole victim—usually a calf or a boar—rather than reserving a part of the animal, as was common when worshipping other gods.

The Vulcanalia, or festival in honor of Vulcan, was held on August 23, right at the time of year when forest fires might be expected and when the stored grain was in danger of burning. For this reason Vulcan's cult was very prominent at Ostia, where Rome's grain was stored. At the Vulcanalia, which was observed in Egypt, in Athens, and in Rome, the priest or flamen Volcanis performed a sacrifice, and the heads of families burned small fish they had caught in the Tiber River.

It was the Emperor Augustus who divided the city of Rome into small districts to facilitate fire fighting, and who was honored as Volcanus Quietus Augustus.

W

♦ 3169 ♦ Waila Festival
Late May

Since 1989, the Arizona Historical Society has sponsored the annual Waila Festival in Tucson, Ariz. Waila (pronounced Why-la) is a native music of the Tohono O'odham Indian tribe of southern Arizona. Waila uses such instruments as the accordion, alto saxophone, guitars, and drums. Similar to the Polish polka or Scottish folk dances, waila is a lively, danceable music. The event celebrates the 100-year-old musical form, promotes local groups playing the music, and brings the traditions and culture of the Tohono O'odham tribe to the attention of a wider public.

The Waila Festival is held on the grounds of the University of Arizona. Four waila bands perform and the spectators spread out blankets and lawn chairs to enjoy the music. Dancing is encouraged. Traditional foods like tepary beans, squash, corn soup, and cholla buds are for sale.

CONTACTS:
Arizona Historical Society, Tucson Main Museum
949 E. Second St.
Tucson, AZ 85719
520-628-5774
www.arizonahistoricalsociety.org

♦ 3170 ♦ Waitangi Day
February 6

A national public holiday in New Zealand, February 6 commemorates the signing of the 1840 Treaty of Waitangi, in which the Maori natives agreed to coexist peacefully with the European settlers. Although it was first declared a national day of commemoration in 1960, Waitangi Day was not observed as a public holiday outside the North Island until it became **New Zealand Day** in 1973. It was observed as such until 1976, when it again became known as Waitangi Day.

The town of Waitangi is located on the Bay of Islands at the northern end of the North Island, and the day on which the treaty was signed is observed there by the Royal New Zealand Navy and the Maoris each year.

Because of continued discrimination against them, some Maoris protested the occasion during the 1980s. In 1988 the New Zealand government cancelled the national commemoration ceremonies and has attempted to reorganize the observance in later years. But the protests continued through the 1990s and early 2000s.

CONTACTS:
Ministry for Culture and Heritage
P.O. Box 5364
New Zealand
64-4-499-4229; fax: 61-4-499-4490
www.nzhistory.net.nz

♦ 3171 ♦ Wakakusayama Yaki (Mount Wakakusa Fire Festival)
January 15

This event, held near the Japanese city of Nara, is, along with DAIMONJI OKURIBI, one of the ancient capital's most thrilling spectacles. It takes place on Mt. Wakakusa, a series of three smooth, round hills just over 1,000 feet high located east of the city. Fireworks are ignited, and at six o'clock in the evening, priests from the temples of Todai-ji and Kofuku-ji set fire to the dry grass on the slopes. The whole mountain turns into a flaming beacon that lights up the night sky and can be seen for miles.

Also known as the **Mt. Wakakusa Dead Grass-Burning Event**, the festival commemorates the historic burning of the hill 10 centuries ago during a friendly disagreement about the boundaries of the two major temples and a shrine in Nara. Kofuku-ji's five-story pagoda, built in the 8th century, is the second highest in all of Japan. The silhouette of this temple, seen against the fires on Mt. Wakakusa, is one of Japan's best-known images.

CONTACTS:
Nara Prefectural Government
30 Nobori-oji-cho
Nara, 630-8501 Japan
81-0742-27-8477; fax: 81-0742-23-0620
www.pref.nara.jp

♦ 3172 ♦ Walking Days
May-June, Whit-Monday week

Throughout Lancashire and Yorkshire, England, Walking Days are an important feature of community life. Each town or village has its own parade of children from schools and churches of all denominations. Traffic is held up, the shops are closed, and thousands of spectators come from all the surrounding towns to watch the procession, which can take more than three hours to pass. The children are often dressed in white, and the girls wear veils or wreaths and carry bouquets of flowers. In Manchester, the procession takes place on WHIT-MONDAY, while other communities usually celebrate their Walking Days on the following Friday or Sunday.

This northern English custom may have originated with the traditional "Club Walks," which were ceremonial walks to church made by various social and other groups. In Warrington, Lancashire, Walking Day is June 28—the traditional date of the Newtown and Latchford Heath Races. It was the rector of Warrington who initiated the custom in 1835 to publicize a negative aspect of the horse races: the fact that parents who lost money on the horses often brought poverty upon their children.

CONTACTS:
VisitBritain
845 Third Ave.
10th Fl.
New York, NY 10022
212-850-0336
www.visitbritain.org

Warrington Museum & Art Gallery
Museum St.
Cultural Quarter
Warrington, WA1 1JB United Kingdom
44-1925-442399; fax: 44-1925-443257
www.warringtonmuseum.co.uk

♦ 3173 ♦ **Wall Street Rat Race**
May

This unusual 2.5-mile race features Wall Street runners who don business suits instead of fitness gear, pump cellular phones and briefcases instead of hand weights, and follow a route that takes them through the heart of New York City's financial district. Both individual runners and teams participate, and prizes are awarded not only to the top three male and female finishers but also to the runner wearing the "zaniest costume." Since 1987 the Carey Wall Street Rat Race, coordinated by the New York Runners Club and sponsored by Carey Limousine, has raised money for Very Special Arts (VSA), an international nonprofit organization that serves children and adults with disabilities. VSA offers programs in visual arts, drama, dance, music, and creative writing through schools, cultural institutions, health and rehabilitation organizations, and associations for people with disabilities.

CONTACTS:
New York Road Runners Club
9 E. 89th St.
New York, NY 10128 United States
212-860-4455
www.nyrr.org

♦ 3174 ♦ **Walloon Regional Day**
Third Sunday in September

Each of the autonomous regions of Belgium observes its own feast day. September is a month of celebration for Belgium's Walloon Region. In addition to the local traditional festivities, Walloon Regional Day takes place on the third Sunday of the month, and the FEAST DAY OF THE FRENCH COMMUNITY is held in Wallonia during September. Feast days in other regions of Belgium include FEAST DAY OF THE FLEMISH COMMUNITY, FEAST DAY OF THE GERMAN-SPEAKING COMMUNITY, and IRIS FEST.

Established as a federal state in 1993, Wallonia is Belgium's largest region, making up 55 percent of the country's territory. Yet Walloon Regional Day is a new celebration that is not as popular or as commonly observed as the more established regional days. The main festivities take place in the regional capital, Nemur.

CONTACTS:
Belgium Embassy
3330 Garfield St. N.W.
Washington, D.C. 20008
202-333-6900; fax: 202-338-4960
countries.diplomatie.belgium.be/en/united_states

♦ 3175 ♦ **Walpurgis Night (Walpurgisnacht)**
April 30

People who lived in the Harz Mountains of Germany believed for many centuries that witches rode across the sky on the eve of St. Walpurga's Day to hold a coven on Brocken Mountain. To frighten them off, they rang church bells, banged pots and pans, and lit torches topped with hemlock, rosemary, and juniper. The legend of Walpurgis Night is still celebrated in Germany, Austria, and Scandinavia with bonfires and other festivities designed to welcome spring by warding off demons, disaster, and darkness, particularly the towns of Schierke-am-Brocken, Blankenburg, Elend, and Bad Suderode in the German state of Saxony-Anhalt.

St. Walpurga (or Walburga) was an eighth-century English nun who later became a German abbess. She is the patron saint against dog bites and rabies. On the eve of May 1 her remains were moved from Heidenheim to Eichstätt, Germany, where her shrine became a popular place of pilgrimage. Legend has it that the rocks at Eichstätt give off a miraculous oil possessing curative powers. She is the saint who is also associated with protection against magic.

CONTACTS:
German National Tourist Office
122 E. 42nd St.
Ste. 2000
New York, NY 10168
212-661-4796; fax: 212-661-7174
www.germany.travel

♦ 3176 ♦ **Wampanoag Powwow**
Weekend nearest July 4

It was Massasoit, chief of the Wampanoag Indians, who made a peace treaty with the Pilgrims who settled at Plymouth, Massachusetts, in 1620. Most of the tribe was later wiped out in what was known as King Philip's War, but the survivors fled to Martha's Vineyard and Nantucket, or joined the Cape Cod Indians who had remained neutral in the struggle.

For centuries Wampanoag Indians have held annual pow-wows during the summertime, which have been opportunities for tribal members to reunite in one place for feasts and traditional ceremonies and other activities. Today, more than 1,000 Wampanoag Indians live in Mashpee, Massachusetts, and hold their annual powwow over the FOURTH OF JULY weekend. One traditional game played is known as "fireball." It is similar to soccer but is played with a flaming ball. Fireball is a "medicine game"; men who participate believe that the bruises, burns, and other wounds they suffer during the game will relieve a loved one's illness.

CONTACTS:
Mashpee Wampanoag Tribal Council Tribal Offices
483 Great Neck Rd. S.
P.O. Box 1048
Mashpee, MA 02649
508-477-0208; fax: 508-477-1218
www.mashpeewampanoagtribe.com

♦ 3177 ♦ Wangala (Hundred Drums Festival)
November, after harvest

A festival that lasts several days and celebrates the harvest, Wangala is held in the Garo Hills of the state of Meghalaya in northeastern India. It involves a ceremony led by the village-priest, climaxing in a dance to the sound of 100 drums and the music of gongs, flutes, and trumpets.

CONTACTS:
Directorate of Tourism, Government of Meghalaya
3rd Secretariat Nokrek Bldg.
Lower Lachumiere
Shillong, Meghalaya 793001 India
91-364-2500736; fax: 91-364-2226054
www.megtourism.gov.in

♦ 3178 ♦ Waratambar
August

Waratambar is observed by members of the Christian population of Papua New Guinea, who comprise more than half of the country's four million people. It is a day for giving thanks to the Lord for what Christianity has done for people throughout the world. Farmers and their families take time off work to participate in the celebration, which focuses on singing and dancing. The songs express an appreciation of and closeness to nature and all creatures; the dances dramatize tribal wars. Costumes worn by the dancers are traditionally handmade—of ferns, moss, leaves, flowers, and other natural materials.

Waratambar is observed on different days in August in different provinces. In New Ireland, the date is August 24.

CONTACTS:
Embassy of Papua New Guinea
1779 Massachusetts Ave. N.W.
Ste. 805
Washington, D.C. 20036 United States
202-745-3680; fax: 202-745-3679
www.pngembassy.org

♦ 3179 ♦ Warei Taisai
July 22-24

This Japanese festival is held in Uwajima in late July. Hundreds of ships dock in the harbor, all decorated with flags. In town, there is the parade of the *Ushioni*, a creature that looks like a combination of a whale and a dragon that is carried through the streets by 15 to 20 young people.

Another festival highlight is the *Hashiri-komi* ceremony, a procession of young people carrying portable shrines called *mikoshi* into the sea while rockets explode all around them. The Warei Tasai festival dates back to the 18th century and is the highlight of the summer festival season in Ehime Prefecture.

CONTACTS:
Japan National Tourist Organization
1 Grand Central Pl.
60 E 42nd St.
Ste. 448
New York, NY 10165
212-757-5640; fax: 212-307-6754
www.japantravelinfo.com

♦ 3180 ♦ Warri Festival, National
October-November

Warri, the national board game of Antigua and Barbuda, stirs up enough devotion to warrant an annual competition. Antiguans inherited this board game from their West African slave ancestors, who played it on Caribbean sugar plantations in the 19th century. Despite attempts by slave owners to phase the game out, the tradition survived into the present age and eventually penetrated the arena of international competition.

The game consists of a thick wooden board with 12 pockets containing pieces or counters called *nickars*. These pieces typically are identical shells that can be found on Antigua's beaches.

The game can be played with two or more players. Using arithmetic skill, a Warri player beats his or her opposition by capturing 25 counters.

Competition at the National Warri Festival is organized into several classes, including the Masters, Seniors, Juniors, and the Novice Division. There are also open competitions for women and schools. Antiguans, who take pride in their national game, are perennial favorites to win the competition.

CONTACTS:
Antigua and Barbuda Department of Tourism and Trade
25 S.E. 2nd Ave.
Ste. 300

Miami, FL 33131
305-381-6762; fax: 305-381-7908
www.antigua-barbuda.org

Antigua Hotels & Tourist Association
Island House
Newgate St.
P.O. Box 454
Antigua & Barbuda
268-462-0374; fax: 268-462-3702
www.antiguahotels.org

♦ 3181 ♦ **Warsaw Autumn Festival**
September

Officially called the **International Festival of Contemporary Music**, the Warsaw Autumn Festival's offerings in its early years were more conservative than the name would seem to indicate. Today more experimental music and world premieres are performed along with classical standbys of the 20th century.

Established in 1956 by a group of Polish composers who wanted to bring other East European as well as West European countries together, the festival has presented the work of Luciano Berio, Michael Tippett, Krzysztof Pendericki, Witold Lutoslawski, and other 20th-century composers.

The concerts, which continue for about 10 days in September, are held in the National Philharmonic building, the Royal Castle, and other venues around the city. Orchestras that have performed in these locations include the Scottish National Orchestra of Glasgow, the Tokyo Metropolitan Symphony Orchestra, the Polish Chamber Orchestra, and the National Philharmonic Orchestra and Choir of Warsaw.

CONTACTS:
Warsaw Autumn Festival
Rynek Starego Miasta 27
Warsaw, 00-272 Poland
48-22-831-0607; fax: 48-22-831-0607
www.warszawska-jesien.art.pl

♦ 3182 ♦ **Warsaw International Film Festival**
October

Each October, the Warsaw Film Festival celebrates the art of Polish filmmaking. This international event began in 1985 when Warsaw Film Week was created under the directorship of the famous Polish cultural activist and film distributor Roman Gutek. The festival has become increasingly important in Eastern Europe, garnering inclusion in the prestigious FIAPF (International Federation of Film Producers Association) alongside acclaimed film festivals in Cannes and Venice.

Competitive categories include international features, debut and second movies, avant-garde, documentary, and short films. The non-competitive sections include special screenings of new films by famous international directors, films from other leading international festivals, and Polish classics by acclaimed directors. Screenings take place at the Kinoteka, the Palladium, and the Kino Luna, some of the best cinemas in the city, and are often followed by interactive sessions among cast, crew, and audience.

CONTACTS:
Warsaw Film Foundation
P.O. Box 816
Warszawa 1, 00950 Poland
fax: 48-22-621-4647
www.wff.pl/en/

♦ 3183 ♦ **Washington State Apple Blossom Festival**
May

The oldest blossom festival in the United States, this event has been held annually in Wenatchee, Washington, since 1920 (with the exception of the World War II years). It began with a suggestion from Mrs. E. Wagner, a Wenatchee resident who wanted to see something similar to the celebration held in her native New Zealand when the apple orchards were in bloom. Originally called **Blossom Days**, the event grew in size and popularity until it reached its current status as an 11-day festival drawing up to 100,000 spectators.

In 1947 the name of the festival was officially changed from the **Wenatchee Apple Blossom Festival** to its present name, although it continues to be held in Wenatchee, the "Apple Capital of the World." In addition to seeing the Wenatchee Valley orchards in full bloom, the events include parades, a foodfest, a marching band competition, and sporting events. In 1967 the Aomori Apple Blossom Festival in Japan became Wenatchee's "sister festival," and the two towns have exchanged visitors a number of times.

CONTACTS:
Washington State Apple Blossom Festival
2 S. Chelan Ave.
P.O. Box 2836
Wenatchee, WA 98807
509-662-3616; fax: 509-665-0347
www.appleblossom.org

♦ 3184 ♦ **Washington's (George) Birthday**
February 22; observed third Monday in February

George Washington's birthday was not always celebrated in the United States as widely as it is today. The date itself was in question for a while, since the Gregorian calendar was adopted in England during Washington's lifetime and this shifted his birthday from February 11 to February 22 (*see* OLD CHRISTMAS DAY). Then there was a period when Washington's association with the Federalist party made the Antifederalists (or Jeffersonian Republicans) uncomfortable, and they put a damper on any official celebrations. It wasn't until Washington's death in 1799 that such feelings disappeared and he was regarded as a national hero.

As commander-in-chief of the Continental Army during the American Revolution and as the first president of the United States, George Washington looms large in American literature and legend. By the centennial of his birth in 1832, celebrations were firmly established, and his name had been given not only to the nation's capital, but to a state and more than 20 cities and towns. The federal government combined Washington's birthday with that of another famous American president, Abraham LINCOLN as PRESIDENTS' DAY, observed on the third Monday in February.

At his death in 1799 Washington was a lieutenant general, then the highest military rank in the United States. That same year Congress had established the nation's highest military title, General of the Armies of the United States, intending it for him, but he didn't live to receive it. Subsequently, he was outranked by many U.S. Army officers, so in 1976 Congress finally granted it to him. He is now the senior general officer on Army rolls; General John J. Pershing is the only other officer to have been so honored—he received it in September 1919 for his work during World War I.

See also WASHINGTON'S BIRTHDAY CELEBRATION IN ALEXANDRIA, VIRGINIA and WASHINGTON'S BIRTHDAY CELEBRATION IN LOS DOS LAREDOS.

CONTACTS:
Library of Congress
101 Independence Ave. S.E.
Washington, D.C. 20540
202-707-5000
www.loc.gov

♦ 3185 ♦ Washington's (George) Birthday Celebration (Alexandria, Virginia)
Third Monday in February and preceding weekend

Every year, Alexandria, Va., hosts an array of activities devoted to George Washington, including the nation's largest parade honoring the Father of Our Country. Alexandria calls itself Washington's hometown; he kept a townhouse there, was one of the city's original surveyors, organized the Friendship Fire Company, and was a vestryman of Christ Church Parish and Charter Master of Masonic Lodge No. 22. A reminder of the president's association with the Masons is the George Washington Masonic National Memorial, a 333-foot-tall replica of the ancient lighthouse in Alexandria, Egypt.

Celebrations of Washington's birthday have been held in Alexandria since the president's lifetime. The first parade to honor him was in 1798, when he came from his Mt. Vernon home to review the troops in front of Gadsby's Tavern.

The present-day festivities get off to an elegant start over the weekend with a banquet followed by the George Washington Birthnight Ball in Gadsby's Tavern, a duplication of the birthday-eve parties held in Washington's lifetime. People wear 18th-century dress, and the banquet toasts to Washington are usually delivered by people who are prominent in current events and who reflect Washington's military background. In 1991, former chairman of the U.S. Joint Chiefs of Staff Gen. Colin Powell (later Secretary of State under President George W. Bush) proposed the toast. His name and face became widely known during the Persian Gulf War of 1991.

On Monday is the big parade. It lasts two hours and usually draws about 75,000 spectators. George and Martha Washington are depicted, along with other colonial personages. The paraders include a number of Scottish bagpipe groups (the city was founded by Scots), Masonic units, equestrian groups, color guards, fife and drum corps, and horse-drawn carriages.

See also WASHINGTON'S BIRTHDAY.

CONTACTS:
Library of Congress
101 Independence Ave. S.E.
Washington, D.C. 20540
202-707-5000; fax: 202-707-8366
www.loc.gov

♦ 3186 ♦ Washington's (George) Birthday Celebration (Los Dos Laredos)
First half of February

This is a two-week celebration in honor of George Washington, held since 1898 by Laredo, Tex., and its sister city on the other side of the Mexican border, Nuevo Laredo. The two Laredos (*los dos Laredos* in Spanish) are linked by history and by three bridges across the Rio Grande. Founded by the Spanish in 1755, Laredo has been under seven different national flags. Both cities also celebrate Mexico's Independence Day during Expomex in September (*see also* MEXICO FESTIVAL OF INDEPENDENCE).

Washington's birthday events include dances, fireworks, mariachi music, a fun run, a jalapeno-eating contest, and parades with lavishly decorated floats.

CONTACTS:
Washington's Birthday Celebration Association
1819 E. Hillside Rd.
Laredo, TX 78041
956-722-0589; fax: 956-722-5528
wbcalaredo.org

♦ 3187 ♦ Waso (Buddhist Rains Retreat)
June-July to September-October; full moon of Buddhist month of Waso to full moon of Buddhist month of Thadingyut

Waso is a three-month period when monks remain in monasteries to study and meditate. At other times of the year, monks wander the countryside, but this is the time of monsoons in Southeast Asia, and the Buddha chose this period for retreat and prayer so they wouldn't walk across fields and damage young rice plants. However, even in China, Japan, and Korea—countries that don't have monsoons—the Waso is observed. It is also known as the **Buddhist Lent**. In Cambodia and India it is called **Vassa** or **Vossa**. In Burma (now Myanmar) and Thailand it is called **Phansa**, **Waso**, **Wasa**, or **Wazo Full Moon Day**; and in Laos, VATSA.

The months are considered a time of restraint and abstinence. Weddings are not celebrated, and people try to avoid moving to new homes. Many young men enter the priesthood just for the retreat period, and therefore many ordinations take place. The new young monks have their heads shaved and washed with saffron, and they are given yellow robes. Many lay people attend the monasteries for instruction.

The day just prior to the retreat commemorates the Buddha's first sermon to his five disciples, 49 days after his enlightenment.

In Thailand, the start of the retreat, called Khao Phansa, is observed in the northeastern city of Ubon Ratchathani with the Candle Festival, in which beeswax candles carved in the shapes of birds and other figures, several yards high, are paraded and then presented to the temples. In many places, a beeswax candle is lit at the beginning of Waso and kept burning throughout the period. In Saraburi, people offer flowers and incense to monks who walk to the hilltop Shrine of the Holy Footprint where they present the offerings as tribute (*see also* Phra Buddha Bat Fair). It is traditional everywhere for people to bring food and other necessities to the monasteries.

The end of this period, called **Ok-Barnsa**, or **Full Moon Day of Thadingyut**, is a time of thanksgiving to the monks, and also, according to legend, the time when the Buddha returned to earth after visiting his mother in heaven and preaching to her for three months. During the month of celebration (known as **Kathin**), lay people present monks with new robes and other items for the coming year.

Boat races are held on the rivers in Laos at Vientiane, Luang Phabang and Savannakhet, and in Thailand at numerous places. A special ceremony takes place in Bangkok when elaborate golden royal barges, rowed by oarsmen in scarlet, proceed to Wat Arun (the Temple of Dawn), where the king presents robes to the monks.

At Sakon Nakhon in northeastern Thailand, people build temples and shrines from beeswax and parade them through the streets to present them at temples. After the presentations, there are regattas and general festivities.

In Myanmar, a Festival of Lights called the **Tassaung Daing** or Tazaungdaing Festival is held at this time, when the moon is full. Homes are lit with paper lanterns, and all-night performances are staged by dancers, comedians, and musicians. A major event of the festival is an all-night weaving contest at the Shwe Dagon pagoda in Rangoon (officially called Yangon); young unmarried women spend the night weaving robes, and at dawn they are offered to images of the Buddha at the pagoda. Similar weaving competitions are held throughout the country.

See also Thadingyut.

CONTACTS:
Tourism Authority of Thailand
611 N. Larchmont Blvd.
1st Fl.
Los Angeles, CA 90004
323-461-9814; fax: 323-461-9834
www.tourismthailand.org

♦ 3188 ♦ **Watch Night (Bolden, Georgia)**
December 31

Watch Night services are held every New Year's Eve at 10:00 P.M. at Mt. Calvary Baptist Church in the village of Eulonia, near Bolden, Ga. The heart of the event is a "ring-shout" performance by the McIntosh County Shouters. Call-and-response singing, counter-clockwise dance movements, and interlocking rhythms created with hand-clapping and stick beating on the wooden floor are key elements of the ring-shout, which has indisputable roots in African tradition. The ring-shout was written about by outsiders as early as 1845, but many believed it had died out until this church's group of performers came to light in 1980. The McIntosh County Shouters have since been featured in concerts, on television, and on a CD. The Watch Night service is open to all.

Watch Night is a solemn yet joyful Christian vigil on the last night of the year in which hymns, testimonies, and prayers are shared. Because the Emancipation Proclamation freeing slaves in the United States went into effect at midnight on January 1, 1863, African Americans have invested the occasion with added significance. Some even refer to Watch Night as Freedom's Eve.

♦ 3189 ♦ **Watch Night Service**
December 31

The custom of holding a "Watch Night" service on New Year's Eve was started in America by St. George's Methodist Church in Philadelphia in 1770. The custom has since been adopted by a number of denominations throughout the country. Methodists, Presbyterians, and others gather in their churches on the night of December 31. A five-minute period of silence is observed right before midnight, when a hymn of praise is sung.

Sometimes New Year's Eve is referred to as **Watch Night**, a time for people to gather and celebrate as they see the old year out and the new year in.

CONTACTS:
Historic St. Georges United Methodist Church
235 N. 4th St.
Philadelphia, PA 19106
215-925-7788
www.historicstgeorges.org

♦ 3190 ♦ **Water-Drawing Festival**
Begins between September 20 and October 18; night following the first day of Sukkot and each night of the festival thereafter

The name of this ancient Jewish festival comes from Isaiah 12:3, which says, "Therefore with joy shall ye draw water out of the wells of salvation." The water-drawing ceremony, also known as **Simhat bet ha-Sho'evah**, was a matter of dispute between Pharisees, who regarded it as an oral tradition handed down from Sinai, and the Sadducees, who saw no basis for it and often showed outright contempt for the entire ritual. The more the Sadducees opposed it, the more emphasis the Pharisees placed on the water libation, which was considered a particularly joyful occasion and was performed in the temple on the night following the first day of Sukkot and then on each remaining night of the festival. Huge bonfires were lit throughout Jerusalem and the people stayed up dancing and singing for most of the night, often dozing off on each other's shoulders.

There have been attempts to revive the water-drawing festival in a more modern form, primarily among Israel's contemporary *kibbutzim,* or agricultural communities.

CONTACTS:
Union of Orthodox Jewish Congregations of America
11 Broadway
New York, NY 10004 United States
212-563-4000; fax: 212-564-9058
www.ou.org

♦ 3191 ♦ Watermelon Thump
Last full weekend in June

This is a celebration of the watermelon harvest in Luling, Tex. The chief watermelon-related events are watermelon judging, a watermelon auction, watermelon-eating competitions, and watermelon seed-spitting contests leading to a Championship Seed Spit-Off. Among other activities are a parade, a carnival, and the coronation of the Watermelon Thump Queen.

CONTACTS:
Watermelon Thump
421 E. Davis St.
P.O. Box 710
Luling, TX 78648
830-875-3214; fax: 830-875-2082
www.watermelonthump.com

♦ 3192 ♦ Watermelon-Eating and Seed-Spitting Contest
Second Sunday in September

The only event of its kind sanctioned by the United States Department of Agriculture, the Watermelon-Eating and Seed-Spitting Contest held since 1965 in Pardeeville, Wisconsin, is attended by up to 9,000 people—eaters, spitters, and spectators. It takes eight people an entire day to cut up the 4,500-5,000 watermelons used in the contest. This festival also includes a watermelon volleyball competition, watermelon carving and growing contests, a parade, and a T-shirt design contest. But it is the eating and spitting contests that most people come to see.

Tongue-in-cheek rules for the spitting contest are strictly enforced: professional tobacco spitters are not eligible; denture wearers must abide by the judge's decision if their teeth go further than the seed; and no one is allowed to propel their seeds through a pipe, tube, or other hollow object. There is a team spitting competition, a couples' spitting competition, and separate competitions for men and women.

CONTACTS:
Pardeeville Watermelon Festival
P.O. Box 163
Pardeeville, WI 53954 United States

608-535-9139
pardeevillewatermelonfestival.com

♦ 3193 ♦ Water-Splashing Festival (Dai New Year)
Mid-April

The Dai people of southwestern Yunnan Province of China celebrate the birthday of Buddha (*see* VESAK) and the new year in the middle of April with the Water-Splashing Festival. In tropical Xishuangbanna, a land of elephants and golden-haired monkeys, the celebration begins with dragon-boat races and fireworks displays. On the second day, people visit Buddhist temples. The third day, which is New Year's Day, is the high point. Dressed in colorful local costumes, people carry buckets and pans of water to the temple to bathe the Buddha, and they then splash water at each other. The water symbolizes happiness and good health. It washes away the demons of the past year and welcomes in a new year of good harvests, better livestock, and increased prosperity.

CONTACTS:
Yunnan Provincial Tourism Information Center
Yunnan Tourism Bldg.
No. 678 Dianchi Rd.
Kunming, Yunnan Province 650200 China
86-0871-12301
en.ynta.gov.cn

♦ 3194 ♦ Watts Festival
August

The Watts Festival is held every August over a three-day weekend in Los Angeles. The event began in 1966 as a celebration of African-American cultural awareness, community pride, and political consciousness in the wake of the riots that took place over six days in the Watts area of the city in 1965. It also was founded as a commemoration of the 34 people who died in the disturbance. The Watts Festival is now billed as one of the longest-running African-American cultural celebrations in the United States.

The festival features 16 distinct programs: an art exhibit, business exhibits, a carnival, a children's village, community forums, concerts, food and drink concessions, a fashion show, a film festival, the Goodwill Ambassador Scholarship, a performing arts stage, a senior citizens' pavilion, social service agencies, a "Spirit of Watts" tour, a sports village, and a custom car, bike, and van show. The concerts are a highlight of the festival, and such world-class performers as Stevie Wonder, James Brown, and Nancy Wilson have volunteered their talents to the Watts Summer Festival.

CONTACTS:
Watts Summer Festival, Inc.
8391 Beverly Blvd,
Ste.433
Los Angeles, CA 90048
323-954-8988
www.blacknla.com

♦ 3195 ♦ Wayne Chicken Show
Second Saturday in July

This lighthearted one-day event takes place in Wayne, Nebraska, a town that is known primarily as a pork capital. But, as one of the festival's organizers admits, "We didn't want to make fun of pigs," and since there were some egg-processing plants and chicken farms in the area who were willing to contribute to the cause, the Wayne Chicken Show was "hatched" in 1981. Billed as an "eggszotic egg-stravaganza," up to 15,000 people witness competitions in rooster crowing, chicken flying, egg dropping and catching, and a national cluck-off whose winner has appeared on the Tonight Show. There are prizes for the oddest egg, the most beautiful beak, and the best chicken legs on a human. The eggs and chefs for the free "omelette feed" are donated by egg producers in the area.

CONTACTS:
Wayne Chicken Show
108 W. 3rd St.
Wayne, NE 68787
402-375-2240
www.chickenshow.com

♦ 3196 ♦ WCSH Sidewalk Art Festival
Saturday in late August

The WCSH 6 Sidewalk Art Festival is held every year on a Saturday in late August in Portland, Maine. More than 300 artists typically display their work at the outdoor event, which draws thousands of visitors to the festival area. The exhibit is juried, with cash prizes for first, second, and third place. For the fourth prize, the WCSH 6 Purchase Prize, cash is awarded, plus the winning art work becomes part of the permanent art collection of the festival sponsor, local television station WCSH 6. August 2007 marked the 42nd anniversary of the festival. Its organizers bill it as the largest and oldest one-day art show in northern New England.

CONTACTS:
City of Portland
389 Congress St.
Portland, ME 04101
207-874-8721
www.portlandmaine.gov

♦ 3197 ♦ Wear Red Day, National
First Friday in February

Wear Red Day is a national campaign jointly promoted by the Department of Health and Human Services (HHS) and the American Heart Association (AHA) that focuses on creating awareness of heart disease, particularly among women. Introduced in 2002, the event serves as an alert for women to protect themselves against cardiovascular disease. Red was chosen as the color to wear during the campaign due to its conspicuousness, likeness to the heart, and ability to convey the serious nature of the issue.

Since its launching, the program has joined with other women's health groups as well as community and corporate partners to create a national movement aimed at motivating women to learn more about their heart. The campaign also addresses health disparities in African American and Hispanic women through special events and public education. On Wear Red Day, people are urged to wear red clothing and host a Wear Red Day tribute with family, colleagues, or the local community. As part of the campaign, organizers host road shows, fundraisers, and the Red Dress Collection Fashion Show, which occurs every February during New York Fashion Week.

CONTACTS:
American Heart Association
7272 Greenville Ave.
Dallas, TX 75231
800-242-8721
www.goredforwomen.org

♦ 3198 ♦ Wedding Festivities (Galicnik, Macedonia)
July 12

It was common practice at one time in the former Yugoslavia for men to leave their villages or even to emigrate in search of higher paying work. On a specific day they would all return to their villages and mass wedding celebrations would be held. Galicnik is one of the last strongholds of this ancient custom, and on St. Peter's Day each year a multiple wedding feast is held. It begins on St. Peter's Eve with a torchlight procession of brides to three fountains where water is drawn for a purification ceremony. The most interesting feature of the wedding ceremony itself is that brides, bridegrooms, and guests knock their heads together. The first night of the marriage is spent in a complicated hide-and-seek game and the newlyweds do not sleep together. There is a great feast on the second day and that night the marriages are consummated.

Because the village of Galicnik is cut off from the rest of the world by snow for much of the winter, it is transformed during the summer, when many former residents and tourists come for the July 12 wedding festivities. Similar village wedding ceremonies are held in the Slovenian towns of Ljubljana (end of July) and Bled (mid-August).

CONTACTS:
Macedonia Ministry of Culture
Bul. Ilenden bb
Skopje, 1000 Macedonia
389-2-3116-180; fax: 389-2-3213-767
macedonia.usembassy.gov

♦ 3199 ♦ Week of Solidarity with the Peoples of Non-Self-Governing Territories
Begins May 25

In 1999 the General Assembly of the United Nations asked the special committee on decolonization to honor the week beginning May 25 as the Week of Solidarity with the Peoples of Non-Self-Governing Territories. In 1972 the United Nations established this same week as the Week of Solidarity with the Colonial Peoples of Southern Africa and Guinea (Bissau) and Cape Verde Fighting For Freedom, Independence and Equal Rights. They chose May 25 as the starting date since it had already been established as AFRICAN LIBERATION DAY.

CONTACTS:
United Nations, Department of Public Information
1775 K St.
Ste. 400
Washington, D.C. 20006
202-331-8670; fax: 202-331-9191
www.un.org

♦ 3200 ♦ Weifang International Kite Festival
April

The Weifang International Kite Festival has been held annually in the Shandong province of China since 1984. More than 10,000 kites from more than 40 countries compete in the event for the title of Kite King. The festival begins with an opening ceremony in which representatives from participating countries march into a massive soccer stadium, joining singers, acrobats, and traditional Chinese drummers. The next day teams meet on the grounds to fly their handmade kites made from bamboo.

CONTACTS:
Weifang International Kite Festival Office
Weifang, 261041 China
86-536-809-6863; fax: 86-536-809-6863
cnikf.com/en

China National Tourist Office
370 Lexington Ave.
Ste. 912
New York, NY 10017
212-760-8218; fax: 212-760-8809
www.cnto.org

♦ 3201 ♦ West Virginia Day
June 20

West Virginia Day is a state holiday in West Virginia to celebrate its joining the Union in 1863 as the 35th state. The creation of the state was a result of the Civil War. The settlers of western Virginia defied the state's vote to secede from the Union, and President LINCOLN justified the "secession" of West Virginia from Virginia as a war act. He proclaimed its statehood in April of 1863 and on June 20 West Virginia formally entered the Union as an anti-slave state. The western Virginians' movement for independence from Virginia had actually started long before the Civil War; as early as 1776, western Virginians had the idea of establishing a separate colony called Vandalia, named for Queen Charlotte, wife of British King George III, who believed herself to be a descendant of the Vandals of early Europe.

The day is marked with ceremonies at the state capitol in Charleston and at the West Virginia Independence Hall in Wheeling. It was there that the conventions were held to declare West Virginia's independence from Virginia.

CONTACTS:
West Virginia Archives and History
1900 Kanawha Blvd.
E. Bldg. 9
Charleston, WV 25305
304-558-0230; fax: 304-558-4193
www.wvculture.org

♦ 3202 ♦ West Virginia Italian Heritage Festival
September, Labor Day weekend

This three-day street festival in Clarksburg, W.Va., celebrates Italian culture. The festival began in 1979 and attracts from 175,000 to 200,000 visitors for tastes of food, music, dance, crafts, and sports. A queen, known as Regina Maria, reigns over the festivities. Distinctively Italian events are a bocci tournament, a homemade wine contest, a pasta cookoff (prizes for the best red sauce and best white sauce) for both professional and amateur cooks, and Italian religious observances. There are also strolling musicians, organ grinders, and puppeteers.

About 40 percent of Clarksburg's population is of Italian descent. Italians came here around the turn of the century for plentiful coal-mining jobs and it is said the mountains are reminiscent of those in northern Italy.

CONTACTS:
West Virginia Italian Heritage Festival
340 W. Main St.
P.O. Box 1632
Clarksburg, WV 26302
304-622-7314; fax: 304-622-5727
www.wvihf.com

♦ 3203 ♦ West Virginia Strawberry Festival
Usually late May or early June

A long-standing, good-tasting tradition in Buckhannon, W.Va., the center of a strawberry-growing region. The festival began in 1936, was suspended during World War II, and celebrated its 50th anniversary in 1991 with a block-long strawberry shortcake. Visitors, who numbered about 100,000, got free samples.

The festival focuses on what can be done culinarily to the strawberry: there are pancake breakfasts with strawberry jam, strawberry syrup, and fresh strawberries. There's a strawberry recipe contest, with recipes for such delights as strawberry cakes, pies, and cookies, kiwi-and-strawberry pizza, chicken glazed with strawberries, and strawberry stirring sticks (take drinking straws and fill with strawberries). The festival includes the coronation of a king and queen, a Strawberry Party Gras (a street festival of music and dancing), strawberry auctions, the sweetest strawberry tasting contest, an antique car show, and contests and parades.

CONTACTS:
West Virginia Strawberry Festival Association Inc
P.O. Box 117
Buckhannon, WV 26201
304-472-9036; fax: 304-472-9037
www.wvstrawberryfestival.com

♦ 3204 ♦ **Western Stock Show, National**
Mid-January

The National Western Stock Show is the world's largest live-stock exhibition and the show of shows in Denver, Colo. This is a 16-day trade show for the ranching industry, drawing visitors from throughout the U.S. as well as Mexico and Canada. On view at the stock show are more than 20,000 Hereford, Angus, Simmental, Shorthorn, and Longhorn cattle. Plus Arabian, Morgan, draft, miniature and quarter horses, and ewes, llamas, and yaks. Transactions in the millions of dollars are daily events; the livestock auctions as a matter of course can bring six figures for a single bull.

There are also daily rodeos, with more than 1,000 professional cowboys and cowgirls taking part in calf roping, bull and bronco riding, steer wrestling, and barrel racing. Sheep-shearing contests, displays for children, exhibits and sales of livestock supplies, and exhibitions of Western paintings are other features.

More than half a million people attend, among them ranchers wearing belt buckles with diamonds and boots with the value of diamonds.

CONTACTS:
National Western Stock Show
4655 Humboldt St.
Denver, CO 80216
303-296-6977 or 866-464-2626; fax: 303-292-1708
www.nationalwestern.com

♦ 3205 ♦ **Wexford Festival Opera**
Late October

The Wexford Festival Opera is best known for its staging of obscure or seldom-heard operas from the 17th to the 20th centuries. Held in a small seaport community in the southeastern corner of Ireland since 1951, the festival has based its success on its choice of rare operas and relatively unknown singers, many of whom have later become quite famous.

Three operas are staged during the two-week festival in Wexford's Georgian-style Theatre Royal, built in 1832. Some of the unusual operas presented there include Bedrich Smetana's *The Two Widows,* Joseph Haydn's *Il Monde della Luna,* and Francesco Cavalli's *Eritrea,* which had not been performed since 1652.

The festival also features choral and symphonic concerts and a fireworks display.

CONTACTS:
National Opera House
High St.

Ireland
353-53-912-2400; fax: 353-53-912-4289
www.wexfordopera.com

♦ 3206 ♦ **Whale Festivals (Alaska)**
Various

Gray whales are native to the northern Pacific Ocean. They spend their summers in the Bering Sea but migrate every year to the waters off the coast of Mexico, where female whales give birth to their young. Since the whales prefer to hug the coast as they make their long journey, they are often visible to those living in seaside towns. Several towns along the migration route have begun to celebrate the whales' yearly appearances by hosting whale festivals. Other whale species also make this yearly migration, and are sometimes seen in coastal waters as well.

In Alaska, the towns of Sitka and Kodiak both hold whale festivals. Kodiak's Whalefest takes place in April, as the whales pass by on their way to their summer feeding grounds. Besides watching the whales—which can be done on land—festivalgoers can attend lectures, films, storytelling and children's events, radio talk shows, crafts workshops, art exhibits, and more.

The Sitka festival takes place in November. Sitka festivalgoers most commonly spot humpback whales, but also catch glimpses of gray whales, orca (killer) whales, dall, and harbor porpoises. Festival organizers coordinate a program of whale-watching tours, special presentations by marine biologists, and performances by Native and Russian dance troupes.

CONTACTS:
Sitka WhaleFest
834 Lincoln St.
Sitka, AK 99835
907-747-8878
sitkawhalefest.org

Alaska Department of Fish and Game
1255 W. 8th St.
P.O. Box 115526
Juneau, AK 99811
907-465-4110; fax: 907-465-6094
www.adfg.alaska.gov

♦ 3207 ♦ **Whale Festivals (California)**
March

Several whale festivals take place in the state of California. Gray whales are native to the northern Pacific Ocean. They spend their summers in the Bering Sea but migrate every year to the waters off the coast of Mexico, where female whales give birth to their young. Since the whales prefer to hug the coast as they make their long journey, they are often visible to those living in seaside towns. Several towns along the migration route have begun to celebrate the whales' yearly appearances by hosting whale festivals.

Santa Barbara's festival occurs in March, when gray whales pass by on their way north to Alaska and the Bering Sea. In addition to whale-watching opportunities, the festival also

818

includes a street fair, complete with live music, dance, and other forms of entertainment, lectures, a rubber duck race, storytelling, displays of art and crafts, and information about whales.

Dana Point, California, also holds its Festival of Whales on two consecutive weekends in March. This event features a street fair, musical entertainment, an art show, educational events and presentations, and a parade.

The neighboring northern California towns of Mendocino and Fort Bragg hold their whale festivals on consecutive weekends in March. Their celebrations include whale-watching cruises, wine tasting, seafood chowder tasting, nature walks, and visits to the Cabrillo Point lighthouse.

CONTACTS:
Dana Point Festival of Whales
34675 Golden Lantern
Dana Point, CA 92629
949-496-1045 or 888-440-4309
www.dpfestivalofwhales.com

Santa Barbara Whale Festival
500 E. Montecito St
Santa Barbara, CA 93103 United States
805-966-9222 or 800-676-1266; fax: 805-966-1728
www.santabarbaraca.com

◆ 3208 ◆ Wheat Harvest (Transylvania)
Late summer

In Transylvania, a region of Romania that was at one time part of Hungary, the gathering of the wheat harvest in late summer reflects traditional customs that have been largely supplanted by modern agricultural methods elsewhere. Here the owner of a farm must still rely on friends and neighbors to gather the crops. When the last sheaf is harvested, a wreath made of wheat and wild flowers is taken to the farmer's house by young girls in traditional dress. The other farm laborers lie in wait for the procession and carry out a mock ambush by drenching everyone in water. When the landowner first appears in the harvest field, the harvesters tie him up and demand a ransom for his release.

When the procession arrives at the landowner's house, poems in his honor are recited. The wreath is hung in a special place where it will remain until the next harvest. There is a feast for everyone, followed by dancing to the music of a gypsy band. A special delicacy associated with the harvest feast is gingerbread cookies. In fact, elaborately shaped and decorated gingerbread cookies are considered a part of the region's folk art tradition.

◆ 3209 ◆ Wheat Harvest Festival (Provins, France)
Last weekend of August

The small village of Provins in north-central France celebrates its wheat harvest at the end of the summer. On the last Saturday and Sunday of August, villagers decorate their homes and shops with wheat and wildflowers. There are also exhibits of antique farming tools and parades featuring har-

vest floats pulled by tractors. The villagers reenact ancient rituals involving wheat and perform demonstrations of how the grain is separated, ground, and baked to make bread.

◆ 3210 ◆ Whe'wahchee (He'dewachi; Dance of Thanksgiving)
August

Whe'wahchee is the annual dance and celebration of the Omaha Indian tribe of Nebraska, held on the Omaha Reservation in northeastern Nebraska. The ceremonies take place near a pole, usually made out of a cottonwood or willow tree, which represents numerous sacred beliefs.

The 188th dance was held in 1991, making this the oldest powwow in the United States. LEWIS AND CLARK encountered the Omahas in 1803 and mentioned the **Omaha Dance of Thanksgiving** in their journal.

CONTACTS:
Omaha Tribe of Nebraska
P.O. Box 368
Macy, NE 68039
402-837-5391; fax: 402-837-5308
omaha-nsn.gov

Nebraska Folklife Network
5620 Hunts Dr.
Lincoln, NE 68512
402-420-5442; fax: 402-420-5442
nebraskafolklife.org

◆ 3211 ◆ Whistlers Convention, International
Third week in April

This convocation of whistlers in Louisburg, N.C., is highlighted by whistlers' contests for children, teenagers, and adults. Held since 1974, it grew out of a folk festival.

The convention features a school for whistlers and a concert in which the performer is usually someone who can both sing and whistle. On the Sunday after the contest, whistlers whistle at church services and on Monday give demonstrations in schools.

The grand champion in 1992 was Sean Lomax of Murrieta, Calif., who whistled the First Movement of Beethoven's Fifth Symphony and a selection from Bizet's *Carmen*. This is serious whistling.

This convention isn't a big event, but it is the only one in the United States, and in 1992 it attracted people from 10 states and three Canadian provinces. In addition, Masaaki Moku, a whistler from Osaka, Japan, was there; he whistled the Japanese national anthem for the contest audience.

CONTACTS:
Town of Louisburg N.C.
110 W. Nash St.
Louisburg, NC 27549
919-496-4145; fax: 919-496-3895
www.townoflouisburg.com

Public Radio International
401 2nd Ave. N.

Ste. 500
Minneapolis, MN 55401
612-338-5000
www.pri.org

♦ 3212 ♦ White Nights
June

This celebration marks the time of year in St. Petersburg (formerly Leningrad), Russia, when the nights are so short that the sky appears white, or light grey, and twilight lasts only 30 or 40 minutes. The city, with its many buildings painted in pastel shades of lavender, green, pink, and yellow, has a particularly beautiful charm during the white nights. The city is full of various cultural events to celebrate this summer twilight. The Mariinsky Theatre presents a special program of ballets, operas, and symphonic concerts. In addition, there is a chamber music festival and an international jazz festival.

CONTACTS:
St. Petersburg City Administration
Smolny
St. Petersburg, 191060 Russia
7-812-576-71-23; fax: 7-812-576-73-45
gov.spb.ru

♦ 3213 ♦ White Nights
The days before, during, and after the full moon, generally the 13th, 14th, and 15th of each month

According to suggestions in Islamic folklore, the days before, during, and after a full moon are likely to be especially blessed or lucky. On these dates, the skies are bathed in the silvery light of the full or nearly full moon, making the nights "white." In the Islamic calendar, months begin on the first day of the new moon and last for 29 or 30 days; therefore, the White Nights generally occur on the 13th, 14th, and 15th of each month.

Many Muslims worldwide consider the White Nights a good time to observe optional fast days. Shia Muslim officials recommend extra prayers on White Nights that fall during the months of Rajab, Shaban, and Ramadan. Some believe that special blessings will come to those who observe this teaching.

CONTACTS:
Islamic Society of North America (ISNA)
6555 S. County Rd. 750 E.
P.O. Box 38
Plainfield, IN 46168
317-839-8157
www.isna.net

♦ 3214 ♦ White Sunday
Second Sunday in October

This is a special day celebrated in the Christian churches of both American Samoa and the country of Samoa to honor children. Each child dresses in white and wears a crown of white frangipani blossoms. The children line up and walk to church, carrying banners and singing hymns, while their parents wait for them inside. Instead of the usual sermon, the children present short dramatizations of Bible stories such as the good Samaritan, Noah's ark, and the prodigal son. After the performance is over, the children return to their homes, where their parents serve them a feast that includes roast pig, bananas, taro, coconuts, and cakes. They are allowed to eat all they want, and in a reversal of the usual custom, **Lotu-A-Tamaiti** is the one day of the year when the adults don't sit down to eat first.

See also SUNDAY SCHOOL DAY.

CONTACTS:
Samoa Tourism Authorit
P.O. Box 2272
Samoa
685-63500; fax: 685-20886
www.samoa.travel

♦ 3215 ♦ Whit-Monday (Whitmonday)
Between May 11 and June 14; Monday after Pentecost

The day after Whitsunday (PENTECOST) is known as Whit-Monday, and in Great Britain it is also the **Late May Bank Holiday** (*see* BANK HOLIDAY). The week that includes these two holidays, beginning on Whitsunday and ending the following Saturday, is called Whitsuntide.

Until fairly recently, Whit-Monday was one of the major holidays of the year in Pennsylvania Dutch country. In the period from 1835 to just after the Civil War, Whit-Monday was referred to as the "**Dutch Fourth of July**" in Lancaster, Pennsylvania, where rural people came to eat, drink, and be entertained. In Lenhartsville, another Pennsylvania Dutch town, Whit-Monday was known as **Battalion Day**, and it was characterized by music, dancing, and military musters. So much carousing went on that one Pennsylvania newspaper suggested that the name "Whitsuntide" be changed to "Whiskeytide."

See also WALKING DAYS.

♦ 3216 ♦ Whole Enchilada Fiesta
Late September

The Whole Enchilada Fiesta is marked by lots of red chili, lots of corn meal, lots of cheese, and lots of people. This festival in Las Cruces, New Mexico, draws about 100,000 people who scramble to get a taste of the world's biggest enchilada. It's 10 feet long and is made of 750 pounds of stone ground corn for the dough, 75 gallons of red chili sauce, and 175 pounds of cheese. The enchilada is prepared as the climactic Sunday afternoon event: while thousands watch and cheer, giant tortillas are lifted from 175 gallons of bubbling vegetable oil and smothered with the chili sauce and cheese and served. Before this grand moment, there will have been a parade, street dances, arts and crafts exhibits, and a fun run. Las Cruces is the largest business center in southern New Mexico, but its economic foundation is agriculture, and chilis are a big crop.

See also HATCH CHILE FESTIVAL.

CONTACTS:
Whole Enchilada Fiesta
P.O. Box 8248
1515 E Hadley Ave
Las Cruces, NM 88006 United States
575-523-3111
www.enchiladafiesta.com

♦ 3217 ♦ Whuppity Scoorie
March 1

On March 1 every year, Lanark's parish church bell rings exactly at 6 P.M., after a four-month silence. As the bell begins to ring, children in this Scottish town parade three times round the church, dangling pieces of string with paper balls attached at the other end. Then they start striking one another with the paper balls in a play fight. Pennies are then tossed to the ground, which heightens the children's enjoyment as they rush to collect them.

One explanation for the origin of this festival is that it can be traced back to pagan times, when people believed that making a great deal of noise would scare away evil spirits and protect the crops from damage. Another is that an English soldier, who once sought refuge in the church from Scottish defender William Wallace (c. 1270-1305) and his men, had to circle it three times before the doors were opened, crying "Sanctuary!" while Wallace's men pursued him, crying "Up at ye!"—the phrase from which festival's name is believed to have derived.

CONTACTS:
Visit Scotland
Ocean Point One
94 Ocean Dr.
Edinburgh, Scotland EH6 6JH United Kingdom
44-131-524-2121
www.visitscotland.com

♦ 3218 ♦ Wianki Festival of Wreaths
June 23

On St. John's Eve in Poland, young girls traditionally perform a ritual that can be traced back to pagan times. They weave garlands out of wild flowers, put a lit candle in the center, and set them afloat in the nearest stream. If the wreath drifts to shore, it means that the girl will never marry, but if it floats downstream, she will find a husband. If the wreath should sink, it means that the girl will die before the year is out. Since the boy who finds a wreath, according to the superstition, is destined to marry the girl who made it, boys hide in boats along the riverbanks and try to catch their girl-friends' wreaths as they float by.

A variation on this custom, known as the Wianki Festival of Wreaths (*wianki* means "wreath" in Polish), is observed by Polish Americans in Washington, D.C., on this same day every year. The wreaths are made out of fresh greens, the candles are lit at twilight, and they're set afloat in the reflecting pool in front of the Lincoln Memorial. Because there is no current, the wreaths don't drift much at all. But young men gather around the pool anyway, in the hope that the wind will blow their girlfriends' wreaths toward them.

See also MIDSUMMER DAY and SEMIK.

CONTACTS:
Polish-American Arts Association
P.O. Box 9442
Washington, D.C. 20016
www.paaa.us

♦ 3219 ♦ Wicklow Gardens Festival
May 1 to July 31

In County Wicklow, Ireland, more than 20 private gardens are open to the public in May and June for the Wicklow Gardens Festival. The Wicklow climate is especially conducive to gardening, and the county itself is known as the "Garden of Ireland." The gardens participating in the festival range from the grounds surrounding large, historic houses to cottage gardens. Some of the gardens date back to the 17th century, while others have been planted more recently. Some are open year round. Others are closed to the public except during the festival. Many of the gardens that charge entrance fees during the festival donate the money to local charities.

CONTACTS:
Wicklow County Council
County Buildings
Whitegates
Ireland
353-404-20100; fax: 353-404-67792
www.wicklow.ie

♦ 3220 ♦ Wide Open Bluegrass Festival
Two days in late September or early October

This festival for bluegrass music fans follows a week-long trade show of the International Bluegrass Music Association (IBMA), held the third week in September in Owensboro, Ky. Owensboro was the choice for the event's location because Bill Monroe (1912-1996)—the founder of the seminal bluegrass group, The Blue Grass Boys, and father of bluegrass music—was born in Ohio County, 30 miles from the city. More than 40 bluegrass groups perform, and proceeds from admission sales go to a trust fund for IBMA members.

CONTACTS:
International Bluegrass Music Association
608 W. Iris Dr.
Nashville, TN 37204
615-256-3222 or 888-438-4262; fax: 615-256-0450
www.ibma.org

♦ 3221 ♦ Wiener Festwochen
May-June

Wiener Festwochen is an arts and cultural festival held for six weeks in the months of May and June in Vienna, Austria. The festival began in 1951 to promote postwar Vienna as a cultural destination and demonstrate Austria's will to survive the ravages of World War II. The City Hall Square becomes an outdoor venue that features classical music, operas, and plays enjoyed by countless tourists. The festival also includes exhibitions, films, video installations, and talks by artists. Events are held at multiple venues, including the Burgtheater, the Museum Quarter, the State Opera, the Kunsthalle Wien, and the Wiener Konzerthaus. The festival presents art from cities throughout Europe, while at the same time promoting and showcasing the creative life in Vienna. The mission of the festival is to provide local and international audiences with access to unique, innovative events and to mount extraordinary productions on a grand scale.

CONTACTS:
Wiener Festwochen Gesellschaft m.b.H.
Lehárgasse 11/1/6
Vienna, 1060 Austria
431-589-220; fax: 431-589-2249
www.festwochen.at

♦ 3222 ♦ Wife-Carrying World Championships
Early July

The annual Wife-Carrying World Championships have been held in Sonkajärvi, Finland, since the 1990s. The residents of Sonkajärvi trace the idea of wife carrying back to a 19th-century bandit named Rosvo-Ronkainen. In order to join his band, prospective robbers had to prove themselves by running a kind of obstacle course. In those days thieves sometimes did carry off women from rival villages, so local residents combined the two ideas, inventing wife-carrying contests.

Just as in times past, the wife you carry off does not have to be your own. Today's male contestants may carry any woman over the age of 17 who weighs at least 49 kilos (107.8 lbs.). (Lighter contestants can enter if they carry weights that bring them up to 49 kilos.) The course measures 253.5 meters in length and includes one water obstacle and two dry land obstacles. Any contestant that drops his "wife" is fined 15 seconds. The couple that completes the course in the shortest length of time wins. In addition to a medal, the winning couple receives the wife's weight in beer. The contest includes a special division for men who actually carry their own wives.

Only about 30 couples compete in these world championships. These contestants include the winners of the NORTH AMERICAN WIFE-CARRYING CHAMPIONSHIP in Bethel, Maine.

The Wife-Carrying World Championship is sponsored by the Association of Sonkajärvi Entrepreneurs and the local government, and is part of the three-day long Sonkajärvi County Fair, which also includes a beer barrel-rolling contest.

CONTACTS:
Sonkajärven Eukonkanto Oy
Rutakontie 21
Sonkajärvi, 74300 Finland

358-40-675-0027 or 358-40-776-6263
www.eukonkanto.fi
Sonkajärvi Municipal Authority
Rutakontie 28
Sonkajärvi, 74300 Finland
358-40-6750-001; fax: 358-17-2727-017
www.sonkajarvi.fi

♦ 3223 ♦ Wigilia
December 24

Christians in Poland, like Christians around the world, regard the entire period from CHRISTMAS EVE (December 24) to EPIPHANY (January 6) as part of the CHRISTMAS season. Although their customs and the timing of their specific Christmas celebrations may differ from village to village, it all occurs during these two weeks. *Wigilia* means "to watch" or "keep vigil" in Polish. It takes place on Christmas Eve and commemorates the vigil that the shepherds kept on the night of Christ's birth. But it's very possible that the celebration goes back to pre-Christian times. Showing forgiveness and sharing food were part of the Poles' ancient WINTER SOLSTICE observance, a tradition that can still be seen in what is known as the *Gody*—the days of harmony and goodwill that start with the Wigilia and last until Epiphany, or Three Kings Day.

Because some people still cling to the ancient belief that wandering spirits roam the land during the darkest days of the year, it is not uncommon for Poles to make an extra effort to be hospitable at Christmas time, leaving out a pan of warm water and a bowl of nuts and fruits for any unexpected visitors.

♦ 3224 ♦ Wild Horse Festival (Soma-Nomaioi)
July 22-25

The Wild Horse Festival, or **Soma-Nomaioi**, takes place annually in Soma City and Minami-Soma City in Fukushima Prefecture in eastern Japan. The festival occurs over four days, July 22-25. It is a historical re-enactment of military exercises that are more than 1,000 years old.

In the event's highlight, on July 24, about 600 mounted samurai warriors in replicas of traditional Japanese armor gallop across the vast Hibarigahara plain and vie for 40 shrine flags propelled into the air by fireworks. On the same day, 12 armored Samurai warriors compete in a 1,000-meter race. Other colorful spectacles include opening ceremonies at three shrines on July 23; a procession on July 24 summoned by conch shell horn and war drums; and the Nomagake ritual on July 25. During the latter event, white-clad wranglers capture horses with their bare hands and offer them at the Odaka Shrine. These military exercises are thought to have originated in the 10th century, and they have been re-enacted for hundreds of years. Thousands of visitors come to witness the colorful spectacle and amazing equestrian skills.

CONTACTS:
Japan National Tourist Organization
1 Grand Central Pl.

60 E. 42nd St.
Ste. 448
New York, NY 10165
212-757-5640; fax: 212-307-6754
www.jnto.go.jp

♦ 3225 ♦ Wilder (Laura Ingalls) Pageant
July, over three consecutive three-day weekends

The Laura Ingalls Wilder Pageant is held every July over three consecutive three-day weekends in De Smet, S.Dak., where the beloved author came of age in the late 19th century. The pageant features a play based on one of Wilder's autobiographical novels, such as *Little House on the Prairie or The Long Winter*. The plays are produced and performed outdoors by about 100 local volunteers on a 30-acre site purchased in 1974 especially for this purpose by the Laura Ingalls Wilder Pageant Society. The site is nestled between the site of the actual Ingalls homestead, the big slough, and Silver Lake—all locations made famous by Wilder's books. Pageant-goers can enjoy a pioneer-themed gift shop and café, as well as music and free wagon rides while they wait for each evening's show to start.

The inspiration for the Laura Ingalls Wilder Pageant was a 1951 radio dramatization of *The Long Winter*, which is set in De Smet. Local people gained permission to turn the radio play into a drama, which they performed for free in 1955 at the town's high-school auditorium. In 1968, a group of De Smet actors revived the play for a summer arts festival. Its success prompted volunteers to launch the Laura Ingalls Wilder Pageant as an outdoor family play to celebrate the life and works of De Smet's hometown author. The Laura Ingalls Wilder Pageant Society, a non-profit organization, was founded in 1973 and the pageant site was purchased a year later. People from all over the world now gather there to celebrate the family values and pioneering spirit captured forever by Wilder's books.

CONTACTS:
Laura Ingalls Wilder Pageant
P.O. Box 154
De Smet, SD 57231 United States
800-776-3594 or 800-880-3383
www.desmetpageant.org

♦ 3226 ♦ Wilderness Woman Competition
First weekend in December

In the midst of Winterfest, celebrated the entire month of December in Talkeetna, Alaska, a tongue-in-cheek competition for unmarried women takes place that pokes fun at the lack of eligible females in this northernmost state. Sponsored by the Talkeetna Bachelor Society, the Wilderness Woman Competition puts single ladies in the driver's seat—of a snowmobile— to snake through an obstacle course. After completing a number of other tasks, including the preparation of food,contestants must bring their homemade snack and a beer to a football-watching bachelor—quite a fantasy in this town at the foot of Mount McKinley where men far

outnumber the women. The Bachelor Auction and Ball follow the competition.

CONTACTS:
Talkeetna Chamber of Commerce
P.O. Box 334
Talkeetna, AK 99676
www.talkeetnachamber.org

♦ 3227 ♦ Wildlife Film Festival, International
Week in mid-April

Since 1978, the world's top wildlife filmmakers and producers have gathered in Missoula, Montana, for eight days every spring to share their ideas, techniques, and products with others in their field and with interested members of the public. Today, about 200 new films are presented for viewing, with a special showing of films for children. There is a wildlife parade as well as workshops and panel discussions at different venues in downtown Missoula, and about 10,000 people attend the annual event. In 2013 the festival organizers launched a year-round film screening series. The 38th annual festival took place in 2015.

CONTACTS:
International Wildlife Film Festival
718 S. Higgins Ave.
Missoula, MT 59801 United States
406-728-9380; fax: 406-728-2881
www.wildlifefilms.org

♦ 3228 ♦ Williams (Roger) Day
February 5

Roger Williams was the founder of the American Baptist Church. Born in Wales, he arrived in the Massachusetts colony on this day in 1631 and soon found himself in profound disagreement with the local Puritans. The latter admitted no distinction between crime and sin, while Williams contended that the civil authorities only had a right to punish those who had committed a civil offense. The argument led to a court trial in 1635, and soon afterward Williams was banished from the colony. He fled south to what is now called Providence and founded the Rhode Island colony. Under his leadership, the people of Rhode Island were the first to establish a Baptist congregation on American soil (in 1638) and the first to build a community based on this principle of religious liberty.

Baptists in the United States still celebrate the day of his arrival in America. The First Baptist Meeting House in Providence holds its annual Forefathers Service in May, honoring Williams as its founder and often using the 18th-century order of worship.

CONTACTS:
Roger Williams National Memorial, National Park Service
282 N. Main St.
Providence, RI 02903
401-521-7266
www.nps.gov

First Baptist Church in America
75 N. Main St.
Providence, RI 02903
401-454-3418
www.fbcia.org

♦ 3229 ♦ Williams (Tennessee) New Orleans Literary Festival
Late March

Admirers of the work of American playwright Tennessee Williams (1911-1983) gather together to celebrate his work—and that of other southern writers—at the Tennessee Williams New Orleans Literary Festival. The five-day event, scheduled in late March, features performances of plays, master classes, literary tours of the city, concerts, a book fair, poetry and prose readings, and a wide variety of lectures and discussions led by scholars, writers, and performers. The festival closes with a tea party, a play, and a "Stella-Shouting Contest," in which festivalgoers compete to imitate Stanley Kowalski's bellowing cry of "Stella!" as performed by actor Marlon Brando in the movie version of Tennessee Williams's play, *A Streetcar Named Desire*.

CONTACTS:
Tennessee Williams/New Orleans Literary Festival
938 Lafayette St.
Ste. 514
New Orleans, LA 70113 United States
504-581-1144 or 800-990-3378
www.tennesseewilliams.net

♦ 3230 ♦ Wimbledon
Late June to early July; six weeks before first Monday in August

The oldest and most prestigious tennis tournament in the world, the **Lawn Tennis Championships** at Wimbledon are held for 13 days each summer, beginning six weeks before the first Monday in August, on the manicured courts of the All England Lawn Tennis and Croquet Club. The first competition in 1877 was supposedly an attempt to raise money to purchase a new roller for the croquet lawns, and it featured only the men's singles event. Today the world's best tennis players compete for both singles and doubles titles that are the most coveted in tennis. The event is watched on television by tennis fans all over the world, many of whom get up at dawn or conduct all-night vigils around their television sets so as not to miss a single match. Members of the English royal family often watch the finals from the Royal Box.

The Centre Court at Wimbledon, where the championships are held, is off-limits to members and everyone except the grounds staff. On the Saturday before the competition begins, four women members of the club play two or three sets to "bruise" the grass and make sure the courts are in good shape.

CONTACTS:
All England Lawn Tennis and Croquet Club
Church Rd.

Wimbledon
London, SW19 5AE United Kingdom
44-20-8944-1066; fax: 44-20-8947-8752
www.wimbledon.org

♦ 3231 ♦ Wind Festival
First day of second lunar month

In the rural districts of Korea's Kyongsang-namdo and Kyongsang-pukto Provinces, a grandmother known as *Yungdeung Mama* comes down from heaven every year on the first day of the second lunar month and returns on the 20th day. If she brings her daughter with her, there is no trouble; but if she brings her daughter-in-law, who is an epileptic, it means that a stormy wind known as *Yungdeung Baram* will wreck ships and ruin the crops. To prevent such devastation, farmers, fishermen, and sailors offer special prayers and sacrifices to Yungdeung Mama and her daughter-in-law. Tempting foods and boiled rice are set out in the kitchen or garden, and little pieces of white paper containing the birthdates of family members are burned for good luck: the higher the ashes fly, the better the luck. Sometimes altars are made out of bamboo branches with pieces of cloth or paper tied to them. Sacrifices are laid under the altars, which remain standing until the 20th day of the month.

CONTACTS:
Korea Tourism Organization (KTO)
2 Executive Dr.
Ste. 750
Fort Lee, NJ 07024
201-585-0909 or 888-868-7567; fax: 201-585-9041
english.visitkorea.or.kr

♦ 3232 ♦ Windjammer Days
Tuesday and Wednesday in late June

The annual Windjammer Days Festival in Boothbay Harbor, Maine, celebrates the U.S. Coast Guard's 200 years of service to coastal Maine. The festival is also a salute to the large sailing merchant ships that once carried trade along the New England coast. The locals claim that this festival, which has been going on since 1963, was the original gathering of "tall ships," although they are for the most part sailing schooners rather than the full-rigged clipper ships and barks that have gathered in New York, Boston, and other port cities for more recent celebrations.

There is an antique boat parade as well as tours of Navy and Coast Guard ships. Band concerts, seafood, and fireworks add to the merrymaking.

In the 19th century the Boothbay region played an active role in the shipping trade, carrying lumber to South America and the West Indies. There was a time when more than a hundred of these coastal vessels might have been seen in Boothbay Harbor, waiting out a spell of bad weather.

CONTACTS:
Boothbay Harbor Region Chamber of Commerc
P.O. Box 356

Boothbay Harbor, ME 04538 United States
207-633-2353
www.boothbayharbor.com

♦ 3233 ♦ **Wings 'n Water Festival**
Third weekend in September

This two-day event celebrates the coastal environment of southern New Jersey. It is sponsored by the Wetlands Institute, an organization dedicated to conserving coastal salt marshes and educating the public about marshland ecology. Since 1983 the Institute has held the Wings 'n Water Festival in September every year to raise funds for its various educational and research projects as well as to raise public awareness of the salt marsh by offering activities that relate to its unique environment.

Salt marsh safaris and boat cruises, a decoy and decorative bird-carving show, exhibits of naturalist and maritime art, and a wildlife craft market are among the events. There is also a Black Lab retriever demonstration, musical entertainment featuring traditional American instruments, and various booths serving oysters, clams on the half shell, chowders, "shrimpwiches," Maryland hard-shelled crabs, and Maine lobster. Festival events are held along a 15-**mile** stretch of the South Jersey coast that includes Avalon, Stone Harbor, and Cape May Court House.

CONTACTS:
Wetlands Institute
1075 Stone Harbor Blvd.
Stone Harbor, NJ 08247
609-368-1211; fax: 609-368-3871
www.wetlandsinstitute.org

♦ 3234 ♦ **Winnipeg Folk Festival**
Second weekend in July

The largest event of its kind in North America, the Winnipeg Folk Festival is essentially a music festival featuring bluegrass, gospel, jazz, Cajun, swing, Celtic, and other performers from Canada and around the world. Held at Birds Hill Park, about 19 miles northeast of Winnipeg, the festival has seen performances by such world-renowned artists as Odetta, Bonnie Raitt, Bruce Cockburn, Pete Seeger, Eric Bogle, Ladysmith Black Mambazo, and Billy Bragg. There are concerts, jam sessions, a juried handicrafts village, children's performances, and folk dancing. The festival was started in 1974 by Mitch Podolak, a veteran in the folk music field, and although it only lasts for three days, it also operates on a year-round basis as a folklore and music center.

CONTACTS:
Winnipeg Folk Festival
203-211 Bannatyne Ave.
Winnipeg, MB R3B 3P2 Canada
204-231-0096 or 866-301-3823; fax: 204-231-0076
www.winnipegfolkfestival.ca

♦ 3235 ♦ **Winston 500**
April

This 500-mile stock-car race is Alabama's biggest sporting event. It's held at the Talladega SuperSpeedway, known as the "World's Fastest Speedway." The Winston 500 is one of the Big Four NASCAR (National Association for Stock Car Auto Racing) events in the Sprint Cup Series (formerly the Winston Cup). The other big events are the Daytona 500, the Coca- Cola 600, and the Southern 500. The Winston is considered the fastest of the four. The winner in Talladega in 1991 was 51-year-old Harry Gant, who had never won two races in a row in his 11 years on the circuit and was the surprise of the season. He won four straight in 1991, beginning with the Southern 500 at Darlington International Raceway in South Carolina. "Age don't have nothing to do with it," Gant said about the streak. His day's work at Talladega driving an average speed of 165.62 miles an hour entitled him to $81,950.

Talladega, which opened in 1969, has 83,200 permanent grandstand seats and each year attracts more than 350,000 spectators.

CONTACTS:
NASCAR Foundation
1 Daytona Blvd.
Sixth Fl.
Daytona Beach, FL 32114
877-515-4483
www.nascarfoundation.org

Talladega SuperSpeedway
3366 Speedway Blvd.
Talladega, AL 35160
877-462-3342; fax: 256-761-4717
www.talladegasuperspeedway.com

♦ 3236 ♦ **Winter Festival of Lights**
Early November through late January

A premier light show in Wheeling, W. Va., the Winter Festival of Lights started in 1985 and is now considered a rival of the light show at Niagara Falls (*see* Lights, Festival of). More than a million people visit each year to see two million lights on the downtown Victorian buildings, dozens of giant displays, 200 lighted trees, and about 10 miles of drive-by light displays with architectural and landscape lighting designed by world-famous lighting designers. Some 300 acres of the city's Oglebay Park (a former private estate that was left to the city) are covered with animated light displays that depict symbols of Hanukkah and Christmas and general winter scenes. There are also nighttime parades and storefront animations.

CONTACTS:
Wheeling Area Chamber of Commerce
1310 Market St.
2nd Fl.
Wheeling, WV 26003
304-233-2575; fax: 304-233-1320
www.wheelingchamber.com

Library of Congress
101 Independence Ave. S.E.
Washington
DC, 20540

202-707-5000
www.loc.gov

♦ 3237 ♦ Winter Solstice
June 21-22 (Southern Hemisphere); December 21-22 (Northern Hemisphere)

This is the shortest day of the year, respectively in each hemisphere, when the sun has reached its furthest point from the equator. It also marks the first day of winter.

The winter solstice has played an important role in art, literature, mythology, and religion. There were many pre-Christian seasonal traditions marking the winter solstice, and huge bonfires were an integral part of these ancient solar rites. Although winter was regarded as the season of dormancy, darkness, and cold, the gradual lengthening of the days after the winter solstice brought on a more festive mood. To many peoples this return of the light was cause for celebration that the cycle of nature was continuing.

See also Dongji; Haloa; Inti Raymi Fiesta; Juul, Feast of; Soyaluna; Toji; Yule.

CONTACTS:
Public Communications Office
NASA Headquarters
Ste. 5R30
Washington, D.C. 20546
202-358-0001; fax: 202-358-4338
www.nasa.gov

♦ 3238 ♦ Winter Solstice (China)
December 23

The Chinese honor the god T'ien at the Winter Solstice. According to tradition, this is the day on which the ancient emperors of China would present themselves before T'ien at the Forbidden City in the capital of Beijing to offer sacrifices. Today, people commemorate the longest night of the year by visiting temples and serving feasts in their homes to honor deceased family members.

The imperial winter solstice ceremonies were closed to all foreigners and almost all Chinese. When the monarchy ended in 1912, the imperial rites were discontinued. Nevertheless, the people of Hong Kong still observe the winter solstice by taking a day off to feast with their families and present offerings to their ancestors.

CONTACTS:
Beijing Foreign Affairs Office
No.2, Zhengyi Rd.
Dongcheng District
Beijing, PRC 100744 China
fax: 8610-6519-2775
www.ebeijing.gov.cn

♦ 3239 ♦ Winterlude
10 days in February

A midwinter civic festival held in Ottawa, Canada, Winterlude is primarily a celebration of winter sports. The Rideau Canal, which has been referred to as "the world's longest skating rink," is nearly eight kilometers (five miles) long and provides an excellent outdoor skating facility. There is also snowshoeing, skiing, curling (a game in which thick heavy stone and iron disks are slid across the ice toward a target), speedskating, dogsled racing, barrel jumping, and tobogganing. For those who prefer not to participate in the many sporting events, there is an elaborate snow sculpture exhibit known as Ice Dream. Nearly half a million people attend the 10-day festival each year.

CONTACTS:
National Capital Commission
202-40 Elgin St.
Ottawa, ON K1P 1C7 United Kingdom
613-239-5353
www.ncc-ccn.gc.ca

♦ 3240 ♦ Wisconsin Cheese Curd Festival
Late June

The Wisconsin Cheese Curd Festival takes place in the state's cheese curd capital of Ellsworth, Wisconsin, and is presented by the Ellsworth Area Chamber of Commerce. An annual occurrence, the event features a parade as well as craft and food vendors, musical entertainment, 5K and 10K races, a basketball tournament, and a cheese curd eating contest.

CONTACTS:
Ellsworth Area Chamber of Commerce
P.O. Box 927
Ellsworth, WI 54011
715-273-6442
www.ellsworthchamber.com

♦ 3241 ♦ Wizard of Oz Festival
Third weekend in September

The story of Oz, originally created by author L. Frank Baum in his 1900 children's book *The Wonderful Wizard of Oz*, has become an enduring tale for the ages. In 1939, the classic film *The Wizard of Oz* was released, based on Baum's book. Since 1982, the story has come to life again every September in the town of Chesterton, Ind., as townspeople dress up and portray Dorothy, the Scarecrow, the Tin Man, the Cowardly Lion, Glinda the Good Witch, and other characters. A huge sculpture of the Tin Man overlooks the proceedings from the top of a downtown building. The festival also serves as a reunion site for actors who played the Munchkins in the film—many come every year to meet fans and participate in the annual hour-long Oz Fantasy Parade, Munchkin autograph parties, a Munchkin celebrity dinner and dance, and a Munchkin breakfast.

As if all this were not enough, the festival also has a town crier competition, Auntie Em's pie contest, a juried arts and crafts display, Oz memorabilia collectors' gatherings, and a teddy bear parade and tea party.

CONTACTS:
Duneland Chamber of Commerce
220 Broadway
Chesterton, IN 46304
219-926-5513; fax: 219-926-7593
www.chestertonchamber.org

♦ 3242 ♦ **Wolf Trap Summer Festival Season**
May-September

Located just 30 minutes from downtown Washington, D.C., in Vienna, Virginia, Wolf Trap Farm Park for the Performing Arts hosts musical performances on a year-round basis. But Wolf Trap is best known for the Summer Festival Season. Recent seasons have featured productions by the New York City Opera, the National Symphony Orchestra, the Kirov Ballet from Leningrad (now St. Petersburg, Russia), the Bolshoi Ballet, and the Joffrey Ballet as well as performances by Ray Charles, Johnny Cash, John Denver, Willie Nelson, Emmylou Harris, and jazz trumpeter Wynton Marsalis.

Concerts are held in the 6,900-seat Filene Center, about half of which is exposed to the open sky. Many concertgoers bring a picnic supper and dine on the grass. Smaller concerts are held during the festival as well as off-season in the pre-Revolutionary, 350-seat German Barn.

CONTACTS:
Wolf Trap Foundation for the Performing Arts
1645 Trap Rd.
Vienna, VA 22182
703-255-1900
www.wolftrap.org

♦ 3243 ♦ **Wolfe (Thomas) Festival**
October 3

The Thomas Wolfe Festival is a celebration of the writer's birth in 1900 in Asheville, N.C. The celebrations usually extend several days beyond the actual birthday and include dramatizations of Wolfe's works, the performance of musical compositions based on his writings, workshops conducted by Wolfe scholars, and a walking tour of "Wolfe's Asheville." This includes a visit to Riverside Cemetery, where Wolfe and members of his family, as well as some of the people he fictionalized in his novels, are buried.

The center of the celebration is the Thomas Wolfe Memorial State Historic Site, the boarding house run by his mother, where Thomas Wolfe grew up. It still has the sign dating back to his mother's time hanging over the porch, "Old Kentucky Home." In his famous first novel, *Look Homeward, Angel*, published in 1929, Wolfe fictionalized Asheville as Altamont and called the boarding house "Dixieland."

Other works by Wolfe include *Of Time and the River*, published in 1935, and *The Web and the Rock* and *You Can't Go Home Again*, both published after his death in 1938.

CONTACTS:
Thomas Wolfe Memorial
52 N. Market St.

Asheville, NC 28801
828-253-8304
wolfememorial.com

♦ 3244 ♦ **Women's Day, International**
March 8

Not only is this day commemorating women one of the most widely observed holidays of recent origin, but it is unusual in that it began in the United States and was adopted by many other countries, including the former U.S.S.R. and the People's Republic of China. This holiday has its roots in the March 8, 1857, revolt of American women in New York City, protesting conditions in the textile and garment industries, although it wasn't proclaimed a holiday until 1910.

In Great Britain and the United States, International Women's Day is marked by special exhibitions, films, etc., in praise of women. In the former U.S.S.R., women received honors for distinguished service in industry, aviation, agriculture, military service, and other fields of endeavor.

CONTACTS:
United Nations, Global Teaching and Learning Project
14, avenue de la Paix
Geneva, CH 1211 Switzerland
41-22-917-4896; fax: 41-22-917-0123
www.unog.ch

♦ 3245 ♦ **Wood (Grant) Art Festival**
Second Sunday in June

American artist Grant Wood (1892-1942) is best known for his painting, *American Gothic*, of a dour-looking farmer holding a pitchfork as he stands with his daughter in front of their 19th-century Gothic revival farmhouse. The annual Grant Wood Art Festival in Stone City-Anamosa, Iowa, celebrates the area's heritage as "Grant Wood Country" with juried art exhibits, children's and adults' "Art Happenings," dramatic and musical presentations, and guided bus tours of Stone City.

Born in Anamosa, Wood traveled to Europe several times, where he was exposed to Flemish and German primitive art. But he eventually returned to Iowa to paint the scenes he knew best in the clean-cut, realistic style for which he became famous. He established an art colony in the Stone City valley in 1932-33, and replicas of the colorful ice wagons used as housing by the students and instructors serve as a backdrop for the exhibits of contemporary artists during the festival.

The original *American Gothic*—one of the most widely parodied paintings in the world—is on display at the Chicago Art Institute.

CONTACTS:
Grant Wood Art Gallery
124 E. Main St.
Anamosa, IA 52205
319-462-4267
www.grantwoodartgallery.org

◆ 3246 ◆ Wood (Henry) Promenade Concerts
Mid-July to mid-September

Popularly known as **The Proms**, the nine-week concert series that has been held in London since 1895 presents solo recitals, operas, symphonies, chamber music, and popular music to enormous audiences. Tens of thousands of listeners tune in to the concerts on their radios or televisions, and 7,000-8,000 crowd into the Royal Albert Hall. The series is named after Henry Wood, a pianist and singing teacher who served as conductor at the Proms for 46 years and who is credited with establishing its first permanent orchestra, introducing young and aspiring musicians to the public, and attracting the primarily youthful crowd that attends the Proms every year. The idea for the series came from France, where "promenade concerts"—in other words, concerts where strolling around and socializing took precedence over listening to the music—were popular.

A highlight of the Proms is "Last Night," which occurs on a Saturday in mid-September. *Fantasia of Sea Songs*, composed by Henry Wood, is a traditional part of the Last Night program, as is a setting of Blake's "Jerusalem" and Elgar's "Pomp and Circumstance." Many festival patrons wear party hats, throw streamers, and chant rhymes similar to those heard at football games as the festival draws to a close.

CONTACTS:
BBC Proms Box Office
Royal Albert Hall, Kensington Gore
London, England SW7 2AP United Kingdom
www.bbc.co.uk

◆ 3247 ◆ Wooden Boat Festival
Late June to early July

Since 1977, the Lake Union Wooden Boat Festival has been held each year from late June to early July in Seattle, Wash. The festival runs during the week preceding Independence Day and celebrates the maritime heritage of the Northwest region. Attracting about 10,000 participants each year, the Wooden Boat Festival is sponsored by the Center for Wooden Boats, a "hands-on maritime museum" located at the south end of Lake Union on Valley Street. The Center is dedicated to preserving the traditions and skills of small craft sailing. It maintains a fleet of historic craft, which are available to rent from its livery year-round, though not during the festival. The Wooden Boat Festival includes boatbuilding demonstrations, storytelling, boat rides and races, sailing lessons, safety education, knot tying, and model boat workshops. Food and music add to the festival atmosphere.

CONTACTS:
Center for Wooden Boats
1010 Valley St.
Seattle, WA 98109
206-382-2628; fax: 206-382-2699
cwb.org

◆ 3248 ◆ Woodward Dream Cruise
Third Saturday in August

Since 1995, the one-day Woodward Dream Cruise has featured a parade of cars driving down a 16-mile stretch of Woodward Avenue in the suburbs just north of Detroit, Mich. Owners of antique cars, muscle cars, custom cars, street rods, and special interest cars participate.

The first Dream Cruise was held in 1995 as a one-time event to raise funds for a children's soccer field. It attracted a crowd of 250,000, more than 10 times the number anticipated. The event proved so popular that it has grown into an annual event and has occurred each year since then, on the third Saturday in August. More than 40,000 classic cars travel the route from 9:00 A.M. to 9:00 P.M. Spectators line up along the sidewalks with folding chairs and blankets to watch the parade of interesting cars.

Car clubs, radio stations, and the automobile industry have taken an active role. Street rods and concept cars from North America and around the world participate in the Dream Cruise, which has developed into a multi-community street festival, with entertainment stages, food and merchandise vendors, parades, and automotive displays. It is arguably the largest one-day auto event in the world.

Woodward Avenue has a long automotive history. The second person to ever drive a car on Woodward Avenue was Henry Ford in 1896. In the 1950s and 1960s, Woodward Avenue was the Detroit area's most popular spot to go "cruising," driving slowly up and down the street to show off your car and to see the cars of others. The Dream Cruise reflects a past era, when youth in the area often "cruised" Woodward Avenue at night, driving muscle cars, visiting drive-in restaurants, looking for friends, or engaging in street races. Because the Dream Cruse particularly celebrates the heyday of the automobile from that time period and Detroit's prominence in the automobile industry, some of those who drive cars in the Woodward Dream Cruise wear 1950s style clothing and play "oldies" rock music from their car radios.

The Woodward Dream Cruise, Inc., is a nonprofit organization that coordinates the efforts of the nine communities involved in the event. Sales of Dream Cruise merchandise raise money for nearly 100 local charities.

The Woodward Dream Cruise has inspired similar cruises in nearby Macomb County, northeast of Detroit. Various "Gratiot Cruises" take place on Gratiot Avenue, another main thoroughfare once known for cruising.

CONTACTS:
Ferndale Downtown Development Authority
149 W. Nine Mile Rd.
Ferndale, MI 48220
248-546-1632
www.downtownferndale.com

◆ 3249 ◆ Workers' Party of North Korea, Founding of the
October 10

The founding of the ruling Workers' Party of North Korea (official name: Democratic People's Republic of Korea) on

October 10, 1945, is marked as a national holiday throughout the country. Some historians cite the party's founding date as June 30, 1949, when the North Korean and South Korean communist parties merged. However, the North Korean government recognizes the earlier date, on which a meeting took place to found the "North Korea Bureau of the Communist Party of Korea."

The main public celebrations of the Founding of the Workers' Party take place in the capital city of Pyongyang. Commemorative dance and song performances, evening galas, and oratorical meetings all can be elements of the holiday observance. Similar speeches and performances also are featured in towns and cities throughout the country.

CONTACTS:
Permanent Mission of the Republic of Korea to the United Nations
335 E. 45th St
New York, NY 10017
212-439-4000; fax: 212-986-1083
un.mofat.go.kr

♦ 3250 ♦ World AIDS Day
December 1

In order to promote more social tolerance and a greater awareness of HIV (human immunodeficiency virus) and AIDS (acquired immune deficiency syndrome), the World Health Organization (WHO) declared December 1 as World Aids Day in 1988. Every year various global agencies, including the American Association for World Health, take the lead in coordinating this day and in educating people about HIV/AIDS, which has claimed nearly 22 million lives in the 20 years since the first AIDS cases were diagnosed.

In the United States, local communities, organizations, and schools have observed World AIDS Day by displaying sections of the NAMES Project AIDS Memorial Quilt, each square of which represents an individual who has died of AIDS; exhibiting their own artwork focusing on the AIDS crisis; disseminating education and prevention materials; collecting personal care and food items for centers that serve AIDS patients; and holding candlelight memorial services, among many other events.

CONTACTS:
World Health Organization
20 Ave. Appia
Geneva, 1211 Switzerland
41-22-791-2111; fax: 41-22-791-3111
www.who.int

♦ 3251 ♦ World Champion Bathtub Race
Fourth Sunday of July

In 1967, the British Columbian city of Nanaimo decided to mark its centennial anniversary with a race in its Nanaimo Harbor. Thus was born the International World Championship Bathtub Race, the main event of the four-day Nanaimo Marine Festival.

The 36-mile race features homemade entries that have the shape and design of a tub and run on a boat motor that does not exceed eight horsepower. The original 1967 race featuring the first 200 "tubbers" posed some dangers, convincing organizers of the need for formal rules and safety precautions. Today's racers must follow all guidelines and their craft must meet certain specifications that have been established by the Loyal Nanaimo Bathtub Society.

Nanaimo's businesses participate by having their own "Bath-tub Spirit" competition, which involves decorating their workplaces in the Marine Festival theme. Other festival events include a Sail Past on Wheels Fun Parade, a "Kiddies Karnival," and a fireworks show.

CONTACTS:
Loyal Nanaimo Bathtub Society
373 Franklyn St.
Nanaimo, BC V9R 2X5 Canada
250-753-7223; fax: 250-753-7244
bathtubbing.com

♦ 3252 ♦ World Championship Crab Races
February

This sporting event in Crescent City, Calif., features races of the nine- to 11-inch Dungeness crabs that are caught off this northern California coastal city. The crabs are urged down a four-foot raceway, prizes are awarded, and the winning crab gets a trip back to the harbor for a ceremonious liberation. This is also an eating event: throughout the day about 3,000 pounds of fresh cracked crab are served.

The event began in 1976, but its origins are older. Traditionally, local fishermen returned to port after a day of crabbing and celebrated the catch by racing their liveliest crabs in a chalked circle.

CONTACTS:
Crescent City & Del Norte County Chamber of Commerce
1001 Front St.
Crescent City, CA 95531
800-343-8300
www.delnorte.org

♦ 3253 ♦ World Championship Hoop Dance Contest
Early February

The World Championship Hoop Dance Contest annually draws dancers from around North America to compete in the traditional art of Native-American intertribal hoop dance. Individual performers may use as few as four to as many as 50 hoops, manipulating them to create such designs as globes or butterflies. Each dancer incorporates aspects of his or her distinctive culture into the dance, with emphasis on grace, speed, and athleticism.

The event takes place on the first weekend in February at the Heard Museum in Phoenix, Ariz. Over the course of the two-day event, dancers compete in five age divisions, ranging from under five to 40-plus. They vary in experience from near-beginner to top champions. The contest has been held every year since 1991. Its sponsor, the Heard Museum, specializes in Native American arts and artifacts.

CONTACTS:
Heard Museum
2301 N. Central Ave.
Phoenix, AZ 85004
602-252-8840; fax: 602-252-9757
heard.org

♦ 3254 ♦ **World Creole Music Festival**
Last weekend of October

Creole music, language, and culture are sources of national pride for the island nation of Dominica, as they are for peoples throughout the Caribbean, Latin America, and other regions where Creoles have settled. The World Creole Music Festival is a three-day event showcasing this distinctive music and culture. It is held in Dominica's capital city, Roseau, and other cities on the island during the country's independence celebrations. The festival has become a major tourist event, drawing thousands of visitors from the French Caribbean, North America, and other regions of the world.

The festival has been a great financial boon for Dominica's tourism industry. According to the coordinating organization, the Dominica Festivals Commission, the inaugural festival in 1997 drew 10,000 "paid patrons." By 1999 this total more than doubled. The Commission has also established what it describes as "fringe activities"—Creole in the Park and Zouk on the River—as part of a strategy to stimulate development of local Dominican business communities.

The festival's performers, who are Dominican or travel to the island from other Creole-speaking locations, perhaps have benefited the most from the exposure. The festival has brought attention to a diverse set of musical genres that are directly or indirectly associated with Creole music, including cadence-lypso, zouk, soukous, bouyon, and zydeco.

CONTACTS:
Dominica Festivals Committee
Ground Fl., Financial Center
Dominica
767-448-4833; fax: 767-440-5269
www.wcmfdominica.com

♦ 3255 ♦ **World Cup**
June-July, every four years (2018, 2022, 2026…)

The World Cup is the world series of soccer. Since 1930 (except during World War II), the international championship games have been played every four years, sandwiched between the OLYMPIC GAMES. The series was started under the auspices of the Fédération Internationale de Football Association (FIFA) and is now the best attended and most-watched sporting event in the world. According to FIFA estimates, about 700 million viewers worldwide watched the final match of the 2010 World Cup.

Soccer is also called football or association football; the word soccer comes from assoc., an abbreviation for "association." It originated in England in the public schools (which are actually more like American private schools), and spread to universities and then into local clubs, attracting more and more working-class players. British sailors took the game to Brazil in the 1870s, and businessmen carried it to Prague and Vienna in the 1880s and 1890s. Belgium and France began an annual series of games in 1903. In 1904, international competition was such that FIFA was formed, and by 1998, it claimed more than 200 member associations in 77 nations. In 1946, the trophy was named the Jules Rimet Cup for the president of FIFA from 1921 to 1954.

From its inception the World Cup has been played on a rotating basis between Europe and the Americas, but in 2002, Korea and Japan co-hosted the World Cup in Asia for the first time.

The first Women's World Cup tournament was held in 1991, sixty-one years after the men's first FIFA World Cup. It was the first cup ever taken by the United States. There have been six women's championships since 1991, won by four different national teams. The United States (1991, 1999) and Germany (2003, 2007) have both won twice, with Norway (1995) and Japan (2011) each winning once. The upcoming Women's World Cup will take place in Canada in 2015, and in France in 2019.

The first World Cup was played in Montevideo, Uruguay, and Uruguay won. Brazil has won the World Cup five times; Italy and Germany have each won four times. Argentina and Uruguay have each captured two Cups, while Spain, France and England have won one each. Brazil's wins came in 1958, 1962, 1970, 1994, and 2002; the first three happened under the leadership of Edson Arantes do Nascimento, better known as Pelé and sometimes as the *Pérola Negra*, or "Black Pearl." A Brazilian national hero and at the time one of the best-known athletes in the world, the 5'8" Pelé combined kicking strength and accuracy with the knack of anticipating other players' moves. He announced his retirement in 1974 but in 1975 signed a three-year $7 million contract with the New York Cosmos; after leading them to the North American Soccer League championship in 1977, he retired for good.

The next two World Cups will be hosted by Russia in 2018 and Qatar in 2022.

CONTACTS:
International Federation of Association Football
Strasse 20
P.O. Box 8044
Zurich, 8044 Switzerland
41-43-222-7777; fax: 41-43-222-7878
www.fifa.com

♦ 3256 ♦ **World Day for Water**
March 22

In 1992 the UNITED NATIONS declared March 22 World Day for Water. Programs associated with the day draw attention to the ways in which proper water resource management contributes to a nation's economic and social vitality.

CONTACTS:
United Nations Environment Programme
Regional Office for North America
900 17th St. N.W.
Ste. 506
Washington, D.C. 20006
202-974-0465
www.unep.org

United Nations, Department of Public Information
Information Centre
1775 K St., Ste. 400
Washington, D.C. 20006
202-331-8670; fax: 202-331-9191
www.un.org

♦ 3257 ♦ World Day of Prayer
First Friday in March

The idea of designating a day for Christians to pray together was suggested in 1887 by the Presbyterian Church in the United States. Today, the observance has spread to other denominations, all of which hold the same service—translated, of course, into the appropriate language—on the first Friday in March. In each community, one church is selected for the service, and throughout the day women of all denominations come and go, each staying as long as she wishes, to take her place in this worldwide chain of prayer.

It is the Church Women United movement that organizes the observance and selects a theme upon which women around the world focus as they join together in prayer. The praying starts as soon as the sun crosses the International Date Line and travels westward around the globe.

CONTACTS:
Church Women United, The Interchurch Center
475 Riverside Dr.
Ste. 243
New York, NY 10115
212-870-2347 or 800-298-5551; fax: 212-870-2338
www.churchwomen.org

♦ 3258 ♦ World Day to Combat Desertification and Drought
June 17

In 1994 the UNITED NATIONS established World Day to Combat Desertification and Drought on June 17. The date coincides with the June 17, 1994, signing of the Convention to Combat Desertification. Observances draw attention to the need for cooperation between nations in order to stop desertification and respond to drought.

CONTACTS:
United Nations Office at Geneva
Palais des Nations
14, avenue de la Paix
Geneva, CH 1211 Switzerland
41-22-917-4896
www.un.org

♦ 3259 ♦ World Development Information Day
October 24

In 1972 the United Nations established World Development Information Day on October 24. The purpose of this observance is to raise awareness about world economic development and the programs devised by the U.N. to promote development. The date was chosen to coincide with UNITED NATIONS DAY and the adoption of the International Development Strategy for the Second United Nations Development Decade.

CONTACTS:
United Nations Office, Development and Human Right Section
Room S-1040
New York, NY 10017
212-963-3771; fax: 212-963-1186
www.un.org

♦ 3260 ♦ World Environment Day
June 5

The UNITED NATIONS General Assembly designated June 5 World Environment Day in 1972. The date was chosen because it marked the opening day of the United Nations Conference on the Human Environment in Stockholm, Sweden, which led to the establishment of the United Nations Environment Programme, based in Nairobi, Kenya. The conference was convened again 20 years later, in the hope that nations would recapture the enthusiasm of the 1972 conference and take up the challenge of preserving and enhancing the environment.

The General Assembly urges countries and organizations to mark this day with activities that educate people about threats to the environment and encourage them to strike a balance between development and concern for the earth's future.

CONTACTS:
United Nations Foundation
1750 Pennsylvania Ave. N.W.
Ste 300
Washington, D.C. 20006
202-887-9040; fax: 202-887-9021
www.unfoundation.org

♦ 3261 ♦ World Eskimo-Indian Olympics
Mid-July

The World Eskimo-Indian Olympics is a gathering in Fairbanks, Alaska, of Native people from throughout the state and Canada to participate in three days of games of strength and endurance. Events include the popular blanket toss, which originated in whaling communities as a method of tossing a hunter high enough to sight far-off whales. The tossees are sometimes bounced as high as 28 feet in the air. Also on the program are a sewing competition, a seal-skinning contest, Native dancing, and such events as the knuckle-hop contest, in which contestants get on all fours and hop on their knuckles. The winner is the one who goes the farthest.

CONTACTS:
World Eskimo-Indian Olympics
400 Cushman, ste. a
P.O. Box 72433
Fairbanks, AK 99707
907-452-6646; fax: 907-456-2422
www.weio.org

♦ 3262 ♦ World Food Day
October 16

Proclaimed in 1979 by the conference of the Food and Agriculture Organization (FAO) of the UNITED NATIONS, World Food Day is designed to heighten public awareness of the world food problem and to promote cooperation in the struggle against hunger, malnutrition, and poverty. October 16 is the anniversary of the founding of the FAO in Rome, Italy, in 1945.

CONTACTS:
United Nations Food and Agriculture Organization
Liaison Office for North America
2121 K St.
Ste. 800B
Washington, D.C. 20037
202-653-2400; fax: 202-653-5760
www.worldfooddayusa.org

United Nations Food and Agriculture Organization
14, avenue de la Paix
Geneva, CH 1211 Switzerland
41-22-917-4896; fax: 41-22-917-0123
www.unog.ch

♦ 3263 ♦ World Invocation Day (Festival of Goodwill)
Spring, during the full moon in Sagittarius

World Invocation Day, also known as the **Festival of Goodwill**, is a holiday observed by the Arcane School and the churches and organizations descended from it. The Arcane School was established by Alice A. Bailey in 1923 as a training school for adult men and women in meditation techniques and the development of spiritual potential.

The focus of this observance is a prayer written by Bailey, known as the Great Invocation, which is recited by people at meetings around the world. This festival is the forerunner of recent examples of "worldwide prayer meetings," such as the Harmonic Convergence in 1988.

CONTACTS:
Arcane School c/o Lucis Trust
120 Wall St.
24th Fl.
New York, NY 10005
212-292-0707; fax: 212-292-0808
www.lucistrust.org

♦ 3264 ♦ World Malaria Day
April 25

World Malaria Day, observed annually on April 25th, was first instituted by the World Health Organization during its 2007 World Health Assembly. Malaria is a major cause of death in Sub Saharan Africa and Latin America, as well as parts of the Middle East and Europe. This global public health campaign focuses on the need for sustained investment in the control and eradication of the disease. Malaria Day aims to strengthen cooperation between countries in affected areas, encourage new donors on behalf of global partnerships, and enable research institutions to present their findings on control and treatment. World Malaria Day was originally celebrated as Africa Malaria Day on April 25, 2000 at the Abuja summit; it was attended by representatives from 44 malaria-endemic countries in Africa. Each year the event sets new targets and re-energizes partners to make the world malaria-free. The Roll Back Malaria Partnership, launched at the second World Malaria Day, is an organization of over 500 partners designed to mobilize resources and coordinate efforts to achieve the goals set by the Global Malaria Action Plan.

CONTACTS:
World Health Organization
1 Dag Hammarskjold Plaza
885 Second Ave., 26th Fl.
New York, NY 10017
646-626-6060; fax: 646-626-6080
www.who.int

♦ 3265 ♦ World Peace Festival
Saturday in early August

The World Peace Festival is celebrated annually on a Saturday in early August at the World Peace Sanctuary in Amenia, N.Y. Described by its organizers as a day of prayers of peace and gratitude, the festival is devoted to a culture of peace. It celebrates all that unites the world's diverse cultures. The day includes a flag ceremony honoring all the nations of the world and the distinctive heritage of each. In an Interfaith Pavilion, representatives of such faiths as Jain, Muslim, Baha'I, and Native Americans share their traditions. Visitors also can wander a Peace Labyrinth. In addition, the event features live music, children's activities, international food and drink vendors, and not-for-profit booths selling crafts and goods from around the world. The event has been celebrated every year since 1990.

The festival sponsor, the World Peace Prayer Society, is associated with the Department of Public Information at the United Nations. It is non-religious, non-political, and non-profit. It aims to support harmony, peace, and goodwill among all citizens of the world. Anyone is welcome to join the World Peace Prayer Society, via its web site, and admission is free. All that is asked of members is that they take into their hearts and lives the prayer "May peace prevail on earth.".

CONTACTS:
World Peace Prayer Society
26 Benton Rd.
Wassaic, NY 12592
845-877-6093; fax: 845-877-6862
www.worldpeace.org

♦ 3266 ♦ World Population Day
July 11

World Population Day was established by the Governing Council of the UNITED NATIONS Development Programme to focus public attention on the issue of population growth. Schools, businesses, and organizations around the world are urged to observe July 11 with speeches, programs, and activities that address population issues and encourage people to think of solutions to the health, social, and economic problems associated with population growth. World Population Day is an outgrowth of the Day of Five Billion, which was observed on July 11, 1987, to mark the approximate date when the world's population reached five billion.

With the world population at 7 billion people in 2011 (up from 2.5 billion in 1950), the United Nations predicts that figure will rise to between 8.3 and 10.9 billion by 2050. For 2014 World Population Day, the UNITED NATIONS called for support of the largest-ever generation of youth (1.8 billion) with the theme "Investing in Young People.".

CONTACTS:
United Nations Population Fund (UNFPA)
605 Third Ave.
New York, NY 10158
www.unfpa.org

♦ 3267 ♦ World Religion Day
Third Sunday in January

World Religion Day was initiated in 1950 by the National Spiritual Assembly of the Baha'i faith in the United States. The purpose was to call attention to the harmony of the world's religions and emphasize that the aims of religion are to create unity among people, to ease suffering, and to bring about peace. The day is observed with gatherings in homes, public meetings and panel discussions, and proclamations by government officials.

CONTACTS:
U.S. Bahá'í National Center
1233 Central St.
Evanston, IL 60201
847-733-3400
www.bahai.us

♦ 3268 ♦ World Rock Paper Scissors Championship
October

Since 2002, the World Rock Paper Scissors (RPS) Society has hosted an annual championship in Toronto, Ontario, Canada, to find the world's best player of the childhood game. The familiar game is usually used to settle everyday disputes between children. It involves displaying one's hand in three positions: as a "rock" (fist), "paper" (flat, palm down), or "scissors" (first two fingers). To determine the winner of each round, the rules are as follows: rock breaks scissors, scissors cut paper, and paper covers rock. The game is sometimes known as **Rochambeau**.

Some 500 game enthusiasts from around the world participate in the championship to win a total of $10,000 in prizes. There are no eligibility requirements to attend or play. A fee of $40 is charged. Two players go against each other with a referee standing by to determine the winner of each match. The original 500 players are whittled down to the last two players, and the outcome of their match determines the champion. The contest takes place at a Toronto bar.

Besides the prize money, champions have appeared as guests on such TV programs as "Late Night with Conan O'Brien" and the "Ellen Degeneres Show." The World Rock Paper Scissors Society claims a history going back to 1842 London and boasts some 2,300 members worldwide. It also sponsors a series of RPS tournaments in other cities around the world.

CONTACTS:
World RPS Society
The Trilogy Bldg.
69 Helena Ave.
Toronto, ON M6G 2H3 Canada
518-595-4470
www.worldrps.com

♦ 3269 ♦ World Santa Claus Congress
Late July

The World Santa Claus Congress is held every July at the Bakken amusement park in Klampenborg, Denmark. The three-day event typically brings together more than 100 Santa Clauses from a more than a dozen countries, including Japan and Venezuela. The Santas, who may attend by invitation only, must submit proof of professional Santa status—for example, a videotape of themselves serving as Santa Claus at a shopping mall. During the congress, the Santas can take professional development courses in such subjects as how to walk like, laugh like, and exude the generous spirit of Santa-Claus. They dance around a Christmas tree and enjoy a traditional Danish Christmas feast of roast pork, cabbage, and rice pudding. By tradition, the Santas also travel by antique fire engines and buses to a nearby beach for an annual dip in the sea. The congress has taken place at Bakken every year since July 1963, when an entertainer at the park invited a group of Danish Santas to a children's party.

CONTACTS:
Bakken
A/S Bakken
Dyrehavevej 62
Klampenborg, DK-2930 Denmark
45-3963-3544
www.bakken.dk

♦ 3270 ♦ World Series
October

Also known as the **Fall Classic**, this best-of-seven-games play-off is between the championship baseball teams of the American and National Leagues. Games are played in the home parks of the participating teams, but the Series is truly a national event. For many it marks the spiritual end of summer and is a uniquely American occasion—like the Fourth of July.

The first World Series was played in 1903 between the Boston Red Sox and the Pittsburgh Pirates. There was a lapse in 1904, but the Series resumed in 1905 and has been played annually ever since. The seven-game format was adopted in 1922.

Highlights of the Series mirror the symbolism of life that some see in the game itself; they include moments of athletic perfection and of human error, of drama and of scandal.

The scandal came when eight team members of the Chicago White Sox (ever afterwards to be known as the Black Sox) were accused of conspiring with gamblers to lose the 1919 World Series. Star left fielder "Shoeless" Joe Jackson admitted his part in the scandal, and on leaving court one day, heard the plea of a tearful young fan, "Say it ain't so, Joe."

Brooklyn Dodgers catcher Mickey Owen brought groans from fans with an error that has resounded in Series history. He let a ball get away from him—in 1941, in the ninth inning, on the third strike, with the Dodgers ahead of the New York Yankees by one run. The Yankee team revived and went on to win. Fifteen years later, in 1956, Yankee pitcher Don Larsen gave fans a rare thrill when he pitched a perfect game (no hits, no walks, no runners allowed on base) against the Dodgers, beating them 2-0. It remains the only perfect game pitched in a Series. Both these World Series were called Subway Series, because New York City fans could commute by subway from the Dodgers' Ebbets Field in Brooklyn to Yankee Stadium in the Bronx.

Another dramatic moment came in the 1989 Series. On Oct. 17, at 5:04 P.M., while 60,000 fans were waiting for the introduction of the players at San Francisco's Candlestick Park, an earthquake struck and the ballpark swayed. Players and fans were safely evacuated (although 67 people in other parts of the city died in the quake), and 10 days later the Series resumed in the same park. The Oakland Athletics mowed down the San Francisco Giants in four straight games.

CONTACTS:
MLB Advanced Media, L.P.
75 Ninth Ave.
5th Fl.
New York, NY 10011
512-434-1542 or 866-800-1275
mlb.mlb.com

♦ 3271 ♦ **World Space Week**
October 4-10

In 1999 the United Nations designated October 4 through October 10 as World Space Week. The week celebrates the contributions that space science and technology have made to improving life on earth. October 4 was chosen to commemorate the former U.S.S.R.'s October 4, 1957, launch of Sputnik, the first manmade satellite in space. October 10 honors the 1967 signing of the U.N. Treaty on Principles Governing the Activities of States in the Exploration and Use of Outer Space.

CONTACTS:
United Nations, Department of Public Information
Palais des Nations
14, avenue de la Paix
Geneva, CH 1211 Switzerland
41-22-917-1234; fax: 41-22-917-0123
www.un.org

♦ 3272 ♦ **World Wristwrestling Championships**
Second Saturday of October

These competitions are the original world championship matches in wristwrestling, which is similar to but slightly different from armwrestling. The one-day competitions, held in Petaluma, Calif., since 1962, originated in Mike Gilardi's Saloon in 1957. A bank building has now replaced Gilardi's. The excitement generated by the first backroom bar contests led Bill Soberanes, a columnist for the *Petaluma Argus-Courier*, to transform the bar sport into an international championship.

Fifty men entered the first world championship in 1962. The final pairings that year pitted David-and-Goliath contestants Earl Hagerman, at 5'8", and Duane Benedix, 6'4". In four seconds, Hagerman won. There was only one division at that time; now there are several weight divisions for men and women. Contestants number from 250 to 300 with wrestlers coming from as far away as Australia, Germany, and Russia. The event has been viewed by a TV audience of 200 million. Sometimes there are cash prizes; other times there are none. In the past a purse of more than $5,000 has been split among the winning contestants. But medals and trophies are always awarded.

CONTACTS:
Petaluma Visitors Program
210 Lakeville St. Hwy 116
Petaluma, CA 94952 United States
877-273-8258
www.visitpetaluma.com

♦ 3273 ♦ **WorldFest-Houston International Film Festival**
April

The WorldFest-Houston International Film Festival is one of the oldest celebrations of independent film. It was first launched in 1961 under the name Cinema Arts: An International Film Society. The ten-day festival features a diverse lineup of independent American and international films in 12 major categories, as well as works in such genres as television, music videos, and unproduced screenplays. The festival presents its prestigious Remi Statuette to the winners of each major category. The event also has a tradition of honoring a different country each year and showcasing the country's best films. In addition to screenings, the WorldFest-Houston International Film Festival offers a series of workshops and classes on finance, distribution, and promotion of independent cinema.

CONTACTS:
WorldFest-Houston

9898 Bissonnet St.
Ste. 650
Houston, TX 77036
713-965-9955 or 866-965-9955; fax: 713-965-9960
worldfest.org

◆ 3274 ◆ World's Biggest Fish Fry
Last full week in April

A spring festival in Paris, Tenn., the World's Biggest Fish Fry makes use of the catfish in nearby Kentucky Lake. The fish fry began in 1954, and by the next year more than 1,600 pounds of catfish were served. Now, some 13,000 pounds of catfish are cooked, and about 100,000 people show up in this town of 10,000 to eat, fish, and look around.

Events include a car show, arts and crafts exhibits, a two-hour parade and a smaller Small Fry Parade, and the coronation of a Queen of the Tennessee Valley and a Junior King and Queen. In the Fishing Rodeo, prizes are awarded for the biggest bass and biggest crappie, which must be caught in Kentucky Lake using legal sport equipment. Besides fried fish to eat, there are hush puppies, small deep-fat fried corn meal balls; some say these were originally made and tossed to puppies to keep them from begging while meals were being prepared.

CONTACTS:
Paris-Henry County Chamber of Commerce
2508 E. Wood St.
Paris, TN 38242
731-642-3431 or 800-345-1103; fax: 731-642-3454
www.paristnchamber.com

◆ 3275 ◆ World's Championship Duck-Calling Contest and Wings Over the Prairie Festival
November, Thanksgiving week

This contest is an annual sporting event in Stuttgart, Ark., the "Rice and Duck Capital of the World." The first duck-calling contest was held in 1936 and attracted 17 contestants. The winner that year was Thomas E. Walsh of Mississippi who was awarded a hunting coat valued at $6.60. Today, there are hundreds of participants in the various calling events (including the women's, intermediate, and junior world's championships). The main World's Championship contest is limited to between 50 and 80 callers who have qualified in sanctioned state and regional calling events. These elite duck callers vie for a prize package worth $15,000. This celebration of the waterfowl hunting season is held when the rice fields around Stuttgart have been harvested and the ducks have ample opportunity for feeding. The duck hunting here is billed as the finest in the world.

Ducks are called by blowing a "duck call," a device about the size of a cigar. Originally the callers had to demonstrate four calls—the open-water call, the woods call, the mating call, and the scare call. Now contestants are judged on the hail, or long-distance, call; the mating, or lonesome-duck, call; the feed, or chatter, call; and the comeback call. Judges sit behind a screen so they can't see the contestants. And since 1955, a "Champion of Champions" contest for former World Champions has been staged every five years.

The related events that have sprung up around the contest have been formalized as the Wings Over the Prairie Festival. Included are fun shoots, an arts and crafts fair, a sportsmen's dinner and dance, a 10K race, children's duck-call clinics, and a duck-gumbo cookoff. In 1957 the Grand Prairie Beauty Pageant debuted in which a Queen Mallard is crowned.

CONTACTS:
Stuttgart Chamber of Commerce
507 S. Main
P.O. Box 1500
Stuttgart, AR 72160 United States
870-673-1602; fax: 870-673-1604
www.stuttgartarkansas.com

◆ 3276 ◆ World's Largest Salmon Barbecue
Late June or early July

Some 5,000 pounds of salmon are barbecued for close to 5,000 visitors in the city of Fort Bragg on the northern coast of California. Besides salmon freshly caught in local waters and freshly barbecued, the menu offers corn on the cob, salad, hot bread, and ice cream. The feasting is followed by fireworks and dancing. The event is sponsored by the Salmon Restoration Association of California, and proceeds from it help restore the once abundant salmon runs on the rivers of the area.

CONTACTS:
Salmon Restoration Association
P.O. Box 1448
Fort Bragg, CA 95437
www.salmonrestoration.com

◆ 3277 ◆ Wrangler National Finals Rodeo
Begins first Friday in December

Rodeo's premier event, sometimes called the SUPER BOWL of rodeos, is a 10-day affair that has been held since 1985 in Las Vegas, Nev. The Wrangler National Finals Rodeo, which offered a record $2.45 million in prize money in 1991, is reserved for the top 15 contestants in each of seven events: bareback riding, steer wrestling, team roping, saddle bronc riding, calf roping, women's barrel racing, and bull riding. The winners are considered the world champions in their event. There is also a world all-around champion.

The national finals debuted in 1959 in Dallas, moved to Los Angeles in 1962 and to Oklahoma City in 1965, where it stayed until its move to Las Vegas 20 years later. Attendance is about 85,000.

The rodeo is preceded by the Miss Rodeo America Pageant. Events during the 10 days of rodeo include a Professional Rodeo Cowboys Association convention and trade show, horsemanship competitions, a hoedown, the National Finals Rodeo Christmas Gift Show, cowboy poetry gatherings, style shows, a golf invitational, fashion shows, and dances. The World Champions Awards Banquet is the grand finale.

See also DODGE NATIONAL CIRCUIT FINALS RODEO.

CONTACTS:
Professional Rodeo Cowboys Association
101 Pro Rodeo Dr.
Colorado Springs, CO 80919
719-593-8840; fax: 719-548-4876
www.prorodeo.org

♦ 3278 ♦ **Wright Brothers Day**
December 17

It was on the morning of December 17, 1903, that Wilbur and Orville Wright became the first men to fly and control a powered heavier-than-air machine. Orville Wright took his turn at piloting on this particular day and his historic 12-second flight (120 feet) near Kitty Hawk, North Carolina, was witnessed by only a handful of observers. It wasn't until the brothers went on to set additional flight records that they received widespread acclaim for their achievements. Their original plane (patented in 1906) can be seen today at the National Air and Space Museum in Washington, D.C.

Although Wright Brothers Day has been observed in one way or another and under various names throughout the United States almost since the flight took place, the more notable observations include the annual Wright Brothers Dinner held in Washington, D.C., by the National Aeronautic Association. Celebrations are also held in North Carolina at Kitty Hawk and in Dayton, Ohio, where the brothers were born and where they opened their first bicycle shop in 1892.

Events on December 17 traditionally include a "flyover" by military aircraft and a special ceremony held at the Wright Brothers National Memorial, a 425-acre area that features a 60-foot granite pylon on top of Kill Devil Hill, where the Wright Brothers' camp was located. The flyover takes place at precisely 10:35 A.M., the time of the original flight in 1903.

A week of special events in 2003 marked the 100th anniversary of the Wright brothers' flight. There were aviation exhibits and programs, air shows and fly-bys, and visiting astronauts. An attempted re-enactment of the original flight, however, was thwarted by bad weather.

CONTACTS:
Wright Brothers National Memorial
1401 National Park Dr.
Manteo, NC 27954
252-473-2111; fax: 252-473-2595
www.nps.gov/wrbr

♦ 3279 ♦ **Wurstfest (Sausage Festival)**
Begins on the Friday before the first Monday in November

A festival billed as "The Best of the Wurst," Wurstfest is held in the town of New Braunfels, Tex., to celebrate the sausage-making season and recall the town's German heritage. New Braunfels was settled in 1845 by German immigrants led by Prince Carl of Solms-Braunfels, a cousin of Queen Victoria. The prince chose lands along the Comal and Guadalupe rivers, envisioning a castle on the riverbanks. But the rigors of the wilderness proved too much, and he abandoned his castle plans and went home, while those who had followed him were left behind. They were decimated by starvation and disease, but the survivors eventually prospered, finding abundant water and rich soil.

The ten-day "salute to sausage" features polka music, German singing and dancing, arts and crafts, sporting events, a *biergarten*, and German food—especially sausage.

CONTACTS:
Wurstfest Assocation of New Braunfels
P.O. Box 310309
New Braunfels, TX 78131
830-625-9167 or 800-221-4369; fax: 830-620-1318
wurstfest.com

♦ 3280 ♦ **Wuwuchim**
November

Wuwuchim is the new year for the Hopi Indians, observed in northeastern Arizona. This is thought to be the time when *Katchina* spirits emerge from *Shipap*, the underworld, to stay a short time on earth. It is the most important of Hopi rituals because it establishes the rhythms for the year to come. For several days, prayers, songs, and dances for a prosperous and safe new year are led by the priests in the *kivas*, or ceremonial chambers. The men of the tribe dance, wearing embroidered kilts, and priests from the Bear Clan chant about the time of creation. It may also serve as an initiation rite for boys.

CONTACTS:
Hopi Cultural Center
P.O. Box 67
Second Mesa, AZ 86043
928-734-2401; fax: 928-734-6651
www.hopiculturalcenter.com

X

♦ 3281 ♦ Xilonen, Festival of
Eight days beginning on June 22

This ancient Aztec festival was held in honor of Xilonen, the goddess of maize (corn); she is also known as Chicomecoatl. Like many other Aztec ceremonies, this one involved human sacrifice. Each night unmarried girls formed a procession to a temple carrying young green corn as an offering to the goddess. They wore their hair long and loose, which represented their unmarried status and also may have been suggestive of the long tassles of ripe corn. A slave girl was chosen to represent the goddess and dressed to resemble her. On the last night she was sacrificed in a ceremony for Xilonen.

CONTACTS:
Embassy of Mexico
1911 Pennsylvania Ave. NW
Washington, D.C. 20006 United States
202-728-1600
embamex.sre.gob.mx/eua

♦ 3282 ♦ Xipe Totec, Festival of
March

Among the Aztec Indians of Mexico, Xipe Totec was a god of war. The observance of his festival, also known as **Tlacax- ipehualiztli**, took place in March according to the Gregorian calendar. Xipe Totec was often referred to as "Our Lord the Flayed One" (or, "the Flayer"), and statues and other images of him show the god wearing a human skin.

The Festival of Xipe Totec was an occasion for Aztec warriors to mimic the god. They killed their prisoners of war, often cutting their hearts out, and removed their skins from their bodies. They would then wear these skins for the entire 20-day month and hold mock battles, after which they would discard the now-rotting skins into caves or bury them.

Many scholars have noticed an agricultural metaphor in this practice—likening the wearing of human skin to the process by which a seed grows inside a rotting hull before emerging as a fresh shoot—but more recent scholarship has tended to discredit any connection between Xipe Totec, the donning of skins, and Aztec agricultural rituals.

Y

♦ 3283 ♦ Yale-Harvard Regatta
Usually during first weekend in June

This famous college crew race has been held since 1865 between arch-rivals Yale and Harvard on the Thames River (pronounced THAYMZ) in New London, Connecticut. The event, which claims to be the oldest crew competition in the country, is timed to coincide with the turning of the tide, either upriver or downriver. It begins with a two-mile freshman race, followed by a two-mile combination race featuring the best rowers from all classes. Then there is a three-mile junior varsity race. But the highlight is the four-mile varsity race.

Prior to World War II, crowds of up to 60,000 used to line the banks of the Thames to watch the race, but nowadays only a third as many come to watch—many of them by boat.

CONTACTS:
Harvard Crew, Harvard University
65 N. Harvard St.
Boston, MA 02163
617-496-2476
gocrimson.com

♦ 3284 ♦ Yam Festival at Aburi
September or October

This is an annual harvest festival celebrating the new yam crop and Ntoa, god of the harvest, observed in the town of Aburi in Ghana's Eastern Region. The festival is preceded by a 40-day period of somberness to encourage farmers to continue overseeing the gathering of the harvest. Even funerals are considered inappropriate, although if someone does die during this time, it is customary to sacrifice a sheep to appease the god and then to hold as brief a funeral as possible. It is also forbidden for any new yam to be brought to town before the festival, since no one should enjoy the new crop until it has been presented and offered to Ntoa.

The festival begins in the morning with a purification procession: one man goes to the spring to fill a pot of water; as he carries it through the streets, another man carries a sapling and periodically dips the sapling into the water and sprinkles water along the path while saying a ritual prayer. Later in the day a priest in a white robe emerges from the fetish house, where he has been confined throughout the 40 days, and leads a procession through the town, stopping at certain points to slice three chips off a new yam tuber he carries. It is believed that if two or more of these peelings fall with the skin side down, the year will be full of good fortune. If, however, the peelings fall with the skin side up, it bodes ill for the coming year. An attendant usually makes sure this doesn't happen, though. Then prayers and an offering of palm wine, drinking water, eggs, new yam, and a sheep are made to Ntoa, and a ceremonial feast follows.

See also NEW YAM FESTIVAL.

CONTACTS:
Embassy of Ghana
3512 International Dr. N.W.
Washington, D.C. 20008
202-686-4520; fax: 202-686-4527
www.ghanaembassy.org

♦ 3285 ♦ Yancunú, Fiesta del
December 25-January 6

The *Baile del Yancunú* takes place in the northern coastal towns of Honduras around CHRISTMAS and EPIPHANY. Its roots lie in African folk traditions rather than in Christianity, however. It is said that performing the dance insures abundance in the coming year. This area of the country is inhabited mainly by Caribs, people who trace their ancestors back to African slaves imported from St. Vincent during the colonial era.

The dancers, all men, wear brightly colored long-sleeved shirts, skirts that resemble kilts, knee-high stockings, and masks made from metallic cloth and paint. Strings of seashells hang from various parts of their bodies, which make a rustling sound as they dance. There are six to 12 dancers in each group and four drummers who strike their instruments with their palms. Members of these groups speak in different dialects, which becomes apparent when they begin to dance, a performance they accompany by singing and yelling. Sometimes the dancers form a circle, with pairs in the center dancing the principal role.

See also JUNKANOO FESTIVAL.

CONTACTS:
Embassy of Honduras
3007 Tilden St. N.W.
Washington, D.C. 20008 United States
202-966-7702; fax: 202-966-9751
www.hondurasemb.org

♦ 3286 ♦ **Yarmouth Clam Festival**
Third weekend of July

Held in a small town in southern Maine, the Yarmouth Clam Festival has been a New England tradition since 1965. For a few days, the town expands to as much as 15 times its size, receiving nearly 120,000 visitors.

The event is a great introduction to the many methods of clam preparation. Festival goers have their choice of steamed clams, whole fried clams, clam strips, clam cakes, clam chowder, and fried clams in batter, among other traditional festival fare. Along with celebrating Yarmouth's seafood, the festival is also a fundraiser, with proceeds from the seafood booths helping to support over 35 local nonprofit organizations.

Other clam-related activities include clam-shucking contests and It's Clamtastic!, a competition added to the festival in 2006. Taking place on the Thursday before the festival officially opens, the competition invites people to sample and judge seafood platters from local restaurants.

Beyond sampling clams and other seafood, attendees can choose from a number of other activities including rides, games, live music, an antique show, a parade on Friday night, and a fireworks show on Saturday.

CONTACTS:
Yarmouth Chamber of Commerce
162 Main St.
Yarmouth, ME 04096
207-846-3984
clamfestival.com

♦ 3287 ♦ **Yaya Matsuri (Shouting Festival)**
February 1-8

Like the Kenka Matsuri (Quarrel Festival) held in Himeji, the Yaya Matsuri held in Owase, Japan, during the first week in February features *mikoshi*, portable shrines, carried through the streets by groups of young men who meet and deliberately crash into each other. The festival takes its name from their shouts—"Yaya! Yaya!"—as they run into one another. Although the origin of this unusual custom is not known, houses located along the route of the procession usually have to put up protective fences to ensure that their property is not damaged.

Several special events, including dances, are held during the weeklong festival. On the last night, there is a ceremony at the Owase Shrine to determine who will participate in the festival the next year.

CONTACTS:
Japan National Tourist Organization

1 Grand Central Pl. 60 E. 42nd St.
Ste. 448
New York, NY 10165
212-757-5640; fax: 212-307-6754
www.jnto.go.jp

♦ 3288 ♦ **Yellow Daisy Festival**
Second weekend in September

The Yellow Daisy Festival is a tribute to a rare flower, the yellow daisy, or *Viguiera porteri*, that blooms on Stone Mountain near Atlanta, Ga. The flowers, two and one-half feet tall, grow in granite crevices, sprouting in April and not blooming until September, when they give the mountain a golden blanket. They wilt if they are picked and seem to thrive only in the crevices. They were first discovered in 1846 by Pennsylvania missionary Thomas Porter, who sent a specimen to noted botanist Asa Gray for identification. Gray decided it was the *Viguiera* genus, comprising about 60 other species that grow largely in Central America and Mexico. The only other place in the United States the yellow daisy has been identified is California, but there the plant is larger and woodier.

The festival, held since 1969 at Georgia's Stone Mountain Park, offers tours to view the daisy and much more: one of the South's largest arts and crafts shows, live music, and children's activities.

CONTACTS:
Stone Mountain Park
1000 Robert E. Lee Blvd
Stone Mountain, GA 30083
800-401-2407
www.stonemountainpark.com

♦ 3289 ♦ **Yemanjá Festival**
February 2

Yemanjá is a major festival of the Candomblé religion in the Rio Vermelho district of Salvador, Bahia state, Brazil. *Maes-de-santo* and *filhas-de-santo* (men and women mediums, or followers of the saints) sing and dance from daybreak on, summoning *Yemanjá*, or *Iemanjá* (the goddess of the ocean), to the festival. Offerings are placed in boats and carried down to the sea, where they are set afloat. Thousands of people flock to the coast for the festivities.

See also New Year's Eve in Brazil.

♦ 3290 ♦ **Yemen Independence and National Days**
May 22; November 30

Independence Day in Yemen is November 30, a national holiday to commemorate Yemen's independence from the British. It was won on that day in 1967, when evacuation of British soldiers was complete and the leading political group, the National Liberation Front, declared the formation of the independent state of the People's Republic of South Yemen. The British had occupied key portions of the country since the 1830s.

National Day observes the official proclamation of the unification of the Yemen Arab Republic (North Yemen) and the People's Democratic Republic of Yemen (South Yemen) on May 22, 1990. An agreement to a common constitution, government, and economy between both had been signed the day before.

CONTACTS:
Embassy of the Republic of Yemen
2319 Wyoming Ave. N.W.
Washington, D.C. 20008
202-965-4760; fax: 202-337-2017
www.yemenembassy.org

♦ 3291 ♦ Yemen Revolution Days
September 26; October 14

Yemen observes two Revolution Days: one commemorates the revolutionary movement that overthrew the monarchy of Imam Muhammad al-Badr on September 26, 1962, and helped pave the way for the creation of the Yemen Arab Republic. Before that could occur, however, British occupation of the area remained another force impeding independence. Revolts against the British then ensued in 1962-63, and by 1967, the British granted Yemen its sovereignty (*see* YEMEN INDEPENDENCE AND NATIONAL DAYS). These revolts are commemorated on October 14.

CONTACTS:
Embassy of the Republic of Yemen
2319 Wyoming Ave., N.W.
Washington, D.C. 20008
202-965-4760; fax: 202-337-2017
www.yemenembassy.org

♦ 3292 ♦ Yom ha-Zikkaron
Between April 15 and May 13; Iyyar 4

In Israel, the **Day of Remembrance** honors those who died fighting for the establishment of the Israeli state. It is observed on the day preceding Yom ha-Atzma'ut, or ISRAEL INDEPENDENCE DAY. During Shahavit (the morning service), a candle is lit in memory of fallen soldiers, the ark is opened, and Psalm 9, "Over the death of the son," is recited. This is followed by a prayer for the war dead and other prayers for lost relatives. The service concludes with a reading of Psalm 114.

At the end of the day, sirens are sounded and a few minutes of silence are observed throughout Israel. At sundown, Yom ha-Atzma'ut begins and the mood shifts to one of celebration.

CONTACTS:
Union of Orthodox Jewish Congregations of America
11 Broadway
New York, NY 10004 United States
212-563-4000; fax: 212-564-9058
www.ou.org

♦ 3293 ♦ Yom Kippur
Between September 15 and October 13; Tishri 10

Also known as the **Day of Atonement** or **Yom ha-Din**, the **Day of Judgment**, Yom Kippur is the holiest and most solemn day in the Jewish calendar, and the last of the 10 High Holy Days, or Days of Penitence (*see* TESHUVAH), that begin with ROSH HASHANAH, the Jewish New Year. It is on this day that Jews acknowledge transgressions, repent through confession, then make atonement to God to obtain his forgiveness, with the hope of being inscribed in the Book of Life. It is not uncommon for Jews to spend the entire 24 hours at the synagogue, where five services are held.

Yom Kippur is a strict day of fasting; not even water may be taken from sundown to sundown. It is also a day of reconciliation for those who have done each other harm during the past year and a day of charity toward the less fortunate. It is the only fast day that is not postponed if it falls on the Sabbath.

CONTACTS:
Union for Reform Judaism
633 Third Ave.
New York, NY 10017
212-650-4000 or 800-875-1800
urj.org

Orthodox Union
11 Broadway
New York, NY 10004
212-563-4000
www.ou.org

♦ 3294 ♦ Yom Yerushalayim
Between May 9 and June 6; Iyyar 28

Jerusalem Day commemorates the capture and reunification of Jerusalem during the Six-Day War (on 28 Iyyar 5727 on the Jewish calendar—June 7, 1967), after which Israel gained possession of the Old City of Jerusalem, which had been under Jordanian rule, and other Arab lands. It is the most recent addition to the Jewish calendar and is observed primarily in Israel.

Although there are no specific rituals connected with this relatively new holiday, it is common to recite the Hallel (Psalms 115-118), Psalm 107, and the Aleinu, or concluding prayer. Because this day falls during the LAG BA-OMER period—which begins on the second night of PASSOVER and continues through SHAVUOT—the mourning customs traditionally observed during this time are suspended for the day.

CONTACTS:
Union of Orthodox Jewish Congregations of America
11 Broadway
New York, NY 10004
212-563-4000
www.ou.org

♦ 3295 ♦ York Festival and Mystery Plays
July during even-numbered years

From 1350 until 1570, a series of "mystery plays"—dramas recounting the story of mankind from the Creation to the

Last Judgment—were produced in the city of York, England, on CORPUS CHRISTI by the medieval craft guilds. The event was revived in 1951. Since 1998 the plays have been staged on wagons, as they were in medieval times, which move to different sites within the city as they are performed. The York Early Music Festival, which takes place annually, incorporates the mystery plays into its program during even-numbered years.

CONTACTS:
National Centre for Early Music, York Early Music
Foundation
St. Margaret's Church
Walmgate, York Y01 9TL United Kingdom
44-90-0463-2220; fax: 44-90-0461-2631
www.ncem.co.uk

♦ 3296 ♦ Yorktown Day
October 19

On October 19, 1781, Lord Cornwallis surrendered his British and German troops to General George WASHINGTON'S Allied American and French troops at Yorktown, Virginia. Although the peace treaty recognizing American independence was not ratified until January 14, 1784, the fighting was only sporadic in the intervening two years, and the Battle of Yorktown is widely considered to mark the end of the Revolutionary War.

There has been some sort of patriotic observance of this day since its first anniversary in 1782. But since 1949, Yorktown Day activities have been planned and sponsored by the Yorktown Day Association, composed of representatives from 13 different patriotic and government organizations.

Events held at the Colonial National Historical Park in Yorktown include a commemorative ceremony at the French Cemetery and the placing of a wreath at both the French Monument and the Monument to Alliance and Victory. There are other patriotic exercises, 18th-century tactical demonstrations, a parade of military and civilian units, and musical presentations by fife and drum units from all over the eastern United States. The events are often attended by visiting French dignitaries.

CONTACTS:
Colonial National Historic Park
National Park Service
P.O. Box 210
Yorktown, VA 23690
757-898-3400 or 757-898-2410; fax: 757-898-6346
www.nps.gov

Yorktown Preservation Society
P.O. Box 405
Yorktown, VA 23690
www.ypsva.org

♦ 3297 ♦ Young's Birthday
June 1

Often referred to as "the American Moses," Brigham Young led thousands of his religious followers across 1,000 miles of wilderness from their Illinois settlement to find refuge in what is now Salt Lake City, Utah. He became the second president of the Church of Jesus Christ of the Latter-day Saints, whose members are also known as Mormons. The anniversary of Young's birth on June 1, 1801, is observed by Mormon churches worldwide, as is July 24, the date on which he arrived in the Salt Lake Valley in 1847 (*see* MORMON PIONEER DAY).

CONTACTS:
Church of Jesus Christ of Latter-day Saints
50 N.E. Temple St.
Rm. 1888
Salt Lake City, UT 84150
801-240-3959; fax: 801-240-1187
www.lds.org/?lang=eng

♦ 3298 ♦ Ysyakh
June 21-22

This is a celebration of the midnight sun, observed in the Yakut region in the northeastern part of Russia on the SUMMER SOLSTICE. In 1992 the Yakut Autonomous Soviet Republic became the Republic of Sakha (the Yakut people's name for themselves) within the Russian Federation.

The festivities include foot races, horse races, and often sled dog and reindeer races. Folk dancing and feasting—primarily on boiled beef and *kumiss*, or fermented mare's milk—complete the celebration, which often goes on all night.

CONTACTS:
Tourist Agency of the Republic of Sakha
Yaroslavsky Str. 30/1,
Office 66
Yakutsk, Republic of Sakha 677018 Russian Federation
7-411-235-1144; fax: 7-411-235-11-44
www.yakutiatravel.com

♦ 3299 ♦ Yudu Nal
15th day of the sixth lunar month

Yudu, which means "washing one's hair in flowing water," is a tradition that goes back to the Silla period (7th-9th centuries) in Korean history. It has been the custom on this day to go on picnics near a moving body of water, a stream, river, or waterfall, and to bathe and wash one's hair. Folklore has it that doing so will ward off fever and other heat-related ills. In any case, swimming in a cool stream is a refreshing way to beat hot summer weather. In modern times people also call this activity *mulmaji*, "greeting the water.".

♦ 3300 ♦ Yukigassen Festivals
February and March

Yukigassen contests are organized snowball fights. They take place in several countries, including Japan and Finland. The Mt. ShowaShinzan International Yukigassen takes place in Sobetsu, Hokkaido Prefecture, Japan, each February. The event began in 1988, and consists of matches between two teams of seven players, each armed with 90 snowballs. Teams compete in rounds of plays until one emerges as the overall winner and is awarded a cup.

In 1995 the town of Kemijärvi, Lappi Province, Finland, inspired by its sister city of Sobetsu, began to host its own Yukigassen competition. Its festival, held in March, also attracts competitors from around the world.

CONTACTS:
International Alliance of Sport Yukigassen
Sobetsu Information Center
384-1, Aza-Takinomachi, Usu-gun
Sobetsu, Hokkaido Japan
81-1-4266-2244; fax: 81-1-4266-2800
www.yukigassen-intl.com

♦ 3301 ♦ **Yukon International Storytelling Festival**
First weekend in June

Storytellers have come from all over the world to regale audiences at the Yukon International Storytelling Festival in Whitehorse, Yukon, though a great many come from the polar regions. Located north of the Arctic Circle, the Yukon Territory in northwestern Canada has hosted the festival since 1988. Storytellers and other entertainers perform in three tents over the three-day event. There are also drum dances and other musical and dance performers.

See also STORYTELLING FESTIVAL, NATIONAL and TELLABRATION.

CONTACTS:
Department of Tourism and Culture
100, Hanson St.
P.O. Box 2703
Whitehorse, Yukon Canada
867-667-3053 or 800-661-0408; fax: 867-393-7005
www.tc.gov.yk.ca

Department of Tourism and Culture
2269 Chestnut St.
Ste. 627
San Francisco, CA 94123
415-388-3022; fax: 415-388-3018
en-corporate.canada.travel

♦ 3302 ♦ **Yule**
December 22; December 25

Also known as **Alban Arthan**, Yule is one of the "Lesser Sabbats" of the Wiccan year, thought to be a time when ancient believers celebrated the rebirth of the sun god and the lengthening of the days. This took place annually around the time of the WINTER SOLSTICE and lasted for 12 days.

The SABBATS are the eight holy days generally observed in modern witchcraft (Wicca) and Neopaganism. They revolve around the changing of the seasons and agricultural events, and have been celebrated outdoors with feasting, dancing, and performances of poetry, drama, and music. There are four "Greater Sabbats," falling on February 2 (*see* IMBOLC), April 30, July 31, and October 31 (*see* SAMHAIN). The Lesser Sabbats fall on the solstices and equinoxes.

Yule, or **Yule Day**, is also an old Scottish expression for CHRISTMAS day, "Yule," deriving from the old Norse word *jól*, referring to a pre-Christian winter solstice festival. CHRISTMAS EVE is sometimes referred to as "Yule-Even."

See also JUUL, FEAST OF.

♦ 3303 ♦ **Yuma Lettuce Days**
March

Held annually, Yuma Lettuce Days celebrates the agricultural abundance of Yuma, Arizona. Originally held at a historic state park, the event was moved in 2015 to the University of Arizona's Yuma Agricultural Center, a working research farm, which allows visitors to learn about growing methods as well as sample fresh produce. A harvest dinner, which happens one or two days prior to the festival, marks the start of Yuma Lettuce Days. The event features local food and supports the Yuma County Ag Producers Scholarship Fund. A variety of activities take place during the festival, including cooking demonstrations by celebrity chefs, a vegetable carving session, and local restaurant tastings. Yuma Lettuce Days also features cooking contests, a farm equipment display, and various food and beverage vendors.

CONTACTS:
Yuma Lettuce Days
6485 W. 8th St.
U of A Yuma Agricultural Center
Yuma, AR 85364
928-376-0100
www.yumalettucedays.com

Z

♦ 3304 ♦ **Zambia Farmers Day**
August 7

Farmers Day celebrates the country of Zambia's agricultural sector, praises their efforts in providing crops to feed the country, and gives them a day to relax from their labors. Governmental officials normally give speeches outlining the advances in the harvest of crops, particularly maize. But average citizens enjoy a variety of sporting events that are held on the Farmers Day weekend. In 2005 Mobil Oil Zambia began sponsoring the Zambia Closed Tennis Championship on Farmers Day. Other events include soccer cham- pionships.

CONTACTS:
Embassy of the Republic of Zambia
2419 Massachusetts Ave. N.W.
Washington, D.C. 20008
202-265-9717; fax: 202-332-0826
www.zambiaembassy.org

♦ 3305 ♦ **Zambia Heroes Day**
First Monday in July

In 1964, Zambia won its freedom from England and became an independent nation. Those who fought in that freedom struggle are honored and remembered each year on Heroes Day. The somber day is a public holiday and all Zambians take the day off work.

In 1974 then-president Dr. Kenneth Kaunda presented a gift to the nation to honor its heroes: a statue of a man with no shirt or shoes and defiantly raising a chained hand into the air. Erected in the capital city of Lusaka, the one-and-a-half-ton bronze statue has become the rallying point for any holiday, march, or remembrance in which freedom plays a role. Both government and opposition groups often hold rallies at the statue.

In 2004 Zambian vice-president Nevers Mumba proposed that Heroes Day be refocused to include the members of the Zambian soccer team who died in a plane crash in 1993. Eighteen members of the winning team died when the Zambian Air Force jet they were riding in crashed off the coast of Gabon.

CONTACTS:
Embassy of the Republic of Zambia
2419 Massachusetts Ave. N.W.
Washington, D.C. 20008 United States
202-265-9717; fax: 202-332-0826
www.zambiaembassy.org

♦ 3306 ♦ **Zambia Independence Day**
October 24

On this day in 1964, the British colony of Northern Rhodesia became the independent Republic of Zambia, after decades of nationalist struggle.

For two days, including October 24, celebrations and parades are held all over Zambia, but the most elaborate are in the capital city of Lusaka. Labor and youth organizations march along with the armed forces with dancing and music. Various tribal dances from all over the country are performed in Independence Stadium, and there are gymnastics performances by children. October 24 is also the occasion for the final game of the annual Independence Soccer Trophy.

CONTACTS:
Embassy of the Republic of Zambia
2419 Massachusetts Ave. N.W.
Washington, D.C. 20008 United States
202-265-9717; fax: 202-332-0826
www.zambiaembassy.org

♦ 3307 ♦ **Zambia Unity Day**
First Tuesday in July

Because Zambia is composed of several different tribal groups, the founders of the country promoted the idea of national unity as a means to keep the young nation from falling apart. Zambia Unity Day was created to help foster solidarity between the diverse groups that make up the country.

The slogan "One Zambia, One Nation" is used to signify the goal of the holiday. Remembrance speeches on Unity Day stress that people of varying backgrounds and political beliefs had come together to work for Zambian independence. That spirit must be maintained for Zambia to grow in the future.

CONTACTS:
Embassy of the Republic of Zambia
2419 Massachusetts Ave. N.W.
Washington, D.C. 20008
202-265-9717; fax: 202-332-0826
www.zambiaembassy.org

♦ 3308 ♦ Zanzibar International Film Festival
July

The Zanzibar International Film Festival (ZIFF) is a festival primarily for films from Africa and the Dhow countries (Gulf countries, India, Pakistan, Iran, and Indian Ocean islands). It is arguably the largest cultural event in East Africa. The festival, which centers on a specific theme each year, takes place in various venues near the seafront in historic Stone Town, the cultural heart of Zanzibar, Tanzania.

The revelry begins with an opening parade consisting of drummers, musicians, and acrobats. In addition to film screenings, festivities include musical performances, literary events, filmmaking workshops, historical tours of the city, and visual arts exhibitions. The Main Panorama event screens over 100 films, while the Women's Panorama event focuses on cinema as a vehicle for female empowerment. The celebration also includes a special event for Swahili films exclusively. The festival reaches the rural and underprivileged areas in and around Zanzibar through the Village Panorama event, and the ZIFF Awards ceremony honors the best talents in regional and international cinema. The African Films Development Awards night recognizes individuals and organizations for their contributions to the African film industry.

CONTACTS:
Ngome Kongwe
P.O. Box 3032
Tanzania
255-773-411-499; fax: 255-777-419-955
www.ziff.or.tz

♦ 3309 ♦ Zanzibar Revolution Day
January 12

In December 1963, the African island of Zanzibar won independence from England. A month later, on January 12, 1964, a revolution led by John Okello of the Afro-Shirazi Party overthrew the sultan who ruled Zanzibar. Okello's revolution was bloody. Black citizens of Zanzibar believed that Arab and Indian businessmen, who ran most of the island's commerce, had been unfairly installed by the English colonists. Within the first few days, some 17,000 Arabs and Indians were killed. Many more fled the country, leaving their belongings and businesses to be confiscated by the new government without compensation. Abeid Karume was named president and the country's name changed to the People's Republic of Zanzibar.

Karume began a program of befriending the communist nations of China, East Germany, and the Soviet Union. He accepted their financial aid and technical advisors. The new government seized and nationalized Arab- and Indian-owned businesses and ousted most Europeans from the country. By 1972, Karume's autocratic rule led to widespread dissatisfaction. In April of that year, gunmen assassinated Karume in the Afro-Shirazi Party headquarters. Since his death, Zanzibar (now a semiautonomous part of Tanzania since merging with neighboring Tanganyika) has moved to a more free-market approach to trade, working hard to develop a tourist industry.

Zanzibar Revolution Day marks the occasion of the revolt that installed Karume as president. His son, Amani Karume, is now the island's president. Celebrations are held at the Amaan Stadium and a wreath is officially placed at the gravesite of Abeid Karume.

CONTACTS:
Embassy of the United Republic of Tanzania
1232 22nd St. N.W.
Washington, D.C. 20037
202-884-1080; fax: 202-797-7408
tanzaniaembassy-us.org

♦ 3310 ♦ Zarthastno Diso
April, May, June; 11th day of Dae, the 10th Zoroastrian month

This is the day on which the followers of Zoroaster (or Zarathushtra), the Persian prophet and religious reformer, commemorate their founder's death, at one time believed to have occurred in 551 B.C.E. He is now believed to have lived around 1200 B.C.E. Zoroaster was a figure associated with occult knowledge and the practice of magic on the one hand, and on the other, with the monotheistic concept of God familiar in modern-day Christianity and Judaism. The largest group of his followers are the Parsis of India, although they can also be found in isolated areas of Iran, and elsewhere around the world.

Zoroaster's death is observed in April by the Fasli sect of Zoroastrians, in May by the Kadmi sect, and in June by the Shahenshai sect.

♦ 3311 ♦ Zimbabwe Defense Forces Day
August 15

To honor the nation's armed forces, Zimbabwe holds a special celebration annually on August 15. Despite the economic problems that plague the African country, including inflation over 400 percent and unemployment of 70 percent, the nation spends enormous amounts of its wealth on military equipment and training for its defense forces. President Robert Mugabe has explained that opposition to Zimbabwe's controversial land reform program, which involves confiscating farm land owned by whites to give to black military veterans, has pushed him to ensure that the country can defend itself from aggressive foreign powers.

In 2013, thousands of people countrywide commemorated the 33rd Zimbabwe Defense Forces Day. In the capital of

Harare, President Robert Mugabe inspected the honor guard and delivered his key note address to a crowd gathered at the National Sport Stadium. There was a fly-over by four Air Force jets during a rendition of the Zimbabwe national anthem, with parachute displays by the Zimbabwe Defense Forces.

CONTACTS:
Embassy of Zimbabwe
1608 New Hampshire Ave. N.W.
Washington, D.C. 20009 United States
202-332-7100; fax: 202-483-9326
www.zimbabwe-embassy.us

♦ 3312 ♦ Zimbabwe Heroes' Day
August 9

To honor those members of the armed forces who gave their lives to defend Zimbabwe, the nation holds an annual day of remembrance for them on August 9.

Celebrations are held at the National Heroes Acre, where fallen heroes are buried, in the capital city of Harare. Families of the dead lay wreaths on the graves. The country's president visits each grave and speaks with the families. Nearby, special stands are installed to seat spectators. Young people march from the center of the city to the site, singing revolutionary songs as they march. A variety of musical groups perform, including church choirs and war veterans' choirs, and schoolchildren recite poems about revolutionary struggle. Dance groups perform traditional *itshomani* and *injukwa* dances.

Similar ceremonies are held throughout the country. In the city of Masvingo, celebrations are held at the Masvingo Provincial Heroes Acre. Drum majorettes, boy soldiers, and war veterans march from the suburb of Pangolin to the memorial site. The president's speech is read to the crowd, and music and dance programs are presented.

CONTACTS:
Embassy of the Republic of Zimbabwe in Stockholm
P.O. Box 3253
Stockholm, 103 65 Sweden
46-8-7655-380
www.zimembassy.se

♦ 3313 ♦ Zimbabwe Independence Day
April 18

Independence Day is the major holiday in Zimbabwe, which means "stone dwelling" in Bantu. Like much of Africa, the area that is now Zimbabwe was long controlled by Europeans. Cecil Rhodes formed the British South Africa Company in 1889 to colonize the region, and European settlers began arriving in the 1890s. Rhodes's company governed the country until 1922 when the 34,000 European settlers chose to become a self-governing British colony, Southern Rhodesia. In 1923, Southern Rhodesia was annexed by the British Crown.

A fight for independence took place in the 1970s. An independent constitution was written for Zimbabwe in London in 1979. Independence followed on April 18, 1980. The white minority finally consented to multiracial elections in 1980, which Robert Mugabe won in a landslide.

Independence Day is celebrated in every city and district of the nation with political rallies, parades, traditional dances, singing, and fireworks.

CONTACTS:
Embassy of Republic of Zimbabwe in Canberra
7 Timbarra Crescent, O'Malley
Australia
61-2-6286-2281; fax: 61-2-6290-1680
zimembassycanberra.org.au

♦ 3314 ♦ Zimbabwe National Unity Day
December 22

Begun in 1997, National Unity Day celebrates the coming together of Zimbabwe's two political parties, the Zanu-PF and PF Zapu (one representing the Shona-speaking and the other the Ndebele-speaking peoples). These two groups had fought together against the colonial government of Rhodesia in the 1970s. Upon independence, however, and the creation of Zimbabwe, the two parties often clashed over the political direction the country should take. Violence erupted between them in the 1980s. Since the merger, the government of Zimbabwe has explained that the move has resulted in a government of unity in which all factions of the population are represented without conflict.

Among the celebrations to mark National Unity Day are a number of sporting events, including a soccer championship in which the winning team receives the Unity Cup. In the city of Masvingo, the general public and leading political figures gather at the Great Zimbabwe National Monuments for a concert featuring a number of popular singers and musicians.

CONTACTS:
Embassy of Zimbabwe
1608 New Hampshire Ave.
Washington, D.C. 20009 United States
202-332-7100; fax: 202-483-9326
www.zimbabwe-embassy.us

♦ 3315 ♦ Zurich Festival
June-July

Originally called the Zurich May Festival, this international music, dance, and theater festival in Switzerland was founded in 1909 by Alfred Reucker, director at the time of the Zurich Opera House, because the opera season usually ended in April, and singers and actors needed more work. It was patterned after the BAYREUTH FESTIVAL, with the primary emphasis on opera, but since that time it has expanded to include orchestral and chamber music, vocal and instrumental recitals, ballet, and art exhibits.

Past performers at the festival have included the Royal Shakespeare Company, Tokyo's Red Buddha Theatre, the Netherlands Dance Theatre, Belgium's Ballet of the 20th

Century, and the Abafumi Company of Uganda. Exhibits in city museums are set up to coincide with the festival, and there are master classes for young musicians.

CONTACTS:
Zurich Festival
Ramistrasse 4
Zurich, 8001 Switzerland
41-44-269-990; fax: 41-44-269-90-99
www.zuercher-festspiele.ch

♦ 3316 ♦ **Zwiebelmarkt (Onion Market)**
Fourth Monday in November

Zwiebelmarkt is a great celebration of onions and the principal festival of Bern, the capital of Switzerland, known for its bear pit and mechanical clock that displays a parade of wonderful mechanical figures every hour. The onion market is said to date back to the great fire of 1405, after which farmers of the lake region of Canton Fribourg were given the right to sell their products in Bern because they helped rebuild the city. This story is probably a made-up one, since the first documented mention of onions came in the middle of the 19th century.

Farmers at hundreds of stalls offer for sale more than 100 tons of strings of onions, as well as other winter vegetables and nuts. There is a carnival spirit, with confetti battles, people dressed in disguises, and jesters doing satires of the year's events.

CONTACTS:
Bern Tourism
Amthausgasse 4
P.O. Box 177
Berne, 3000 Switzerland
41-31-328-1260; fax: 41-31-328-1269
www.bern.com/en

♦ 3317 ♦ **Zydeco Music Festival (Southwest Louisiana)**
Early September

The American music known as Zydeco was originally called "La La," which is Creole French for "house dance." The Creoles are the descendants of the original French and Spanish settlers of the Gulf States, particularly Louisiana. It was traditional at one time for the Creole community to help each other with harvest-related work. Once the tasks were completed the fun would begin when they celebrated with a La La, using such instruments as the scrubboard (*frottoir*), spoons, fiddle, triangles, and an accordion to create a musical accompaniment.

Later, during hard times, a family might hold a La La on a Saturday night at their home. They would move all the furniture out of a room, charge a small fee to get in, and sell gumbo and beverages. The music played at these informal gatherings was later called "Zydeco"—from *les haricots*, the French word for snapbeans—by Clifton Chenier, a well-known Zydeco musician.

In 1981 a group of Louisiana citizens, concerned that Creole and Zydeco music was disappearing, organized the Southwest Louisiana Zydeco Music Festival. The first Zydeco Festival was held the following year in a farmer's field on the outskirts of Opelousas. Today the festival is sponsored by the Southern Development Foundation and features Creole food along with performances by well-known Zydeco bands.

CONTACTS:
City of Opelousas, Tourism Information Center
828 E. Landry
Opelousas, LA 70570
337-948-6263 or 800-424-5442; fax: 337-948-6263
www.opelousas.info

Appendices

1. Glossary of Words Relating to Time 851

This section includes a descriptive listing of words relating to periods of time. All terms are defined in two separate lists: first by number referred to, then alphabetically.

2. Calendars throughout History: An Overview of Calendar Systems around the World 855

This section includes an overview of the evolution of calendar systems throughout history and throughout the world.

3. Comparative Table of Calendar Systems 869

This section shows the relationship among various calendar systems, including Gregorian, Jewish, Hindu, Jain, Buddhist, Sikh, and Burmese calendars.

4. Phases of the Moon from 2015 to 2030 Given in Eastern Standard Time 871

This section explains the importance of the moon to the world's religions and includes charts that show the phases of the moon.

5. Overview of the World's Major Religions 881

This section provides basic information about the world's major religions, including when and where originated, founder(s), theological orientation, major sacred texts, denominations and sects, estimated number of adherents around the world, and a listing of the main holidays in chronological order by the religion's calendar.

6. Facts about the U.S. States and Territories 885

This section lists for each of the 50 states: the date of admission; information about observances, if applicable; state nicknames, mottoes, animals, flowers, and other symbols; reference sources noting the admission day; and selected state offices to contact for further information, including web sites. For territories, listed are year of association with the U.S.; nicknames, mottoes, flowers, and other symbols; and web sites and offices to contact.

7. Legal Holidays by State 917

This section lists legal public holidays in each of the states, the District of Columbia, the Commonwealth of Puerto Rico, and the U.S. territories.

8. Tourism Information Sources for the U.S. States and North America 921

This section includes tourism information sources for the United States, Canada, and Mexico.

9. Facts about the U.S. Presidents **965**

This section lists all U.S. presidents in the order in which they held office, their birth dates and places, spouses, death dates and places, burial sites, political parties, nicknames, and career highlights. It also lists notable landmarks commemorating them, along with contact information and web sites.

10. Facts about Countries around the World **979**

This section provides basic information about the independent nations of the world: official name (in English); capital city; internet country code; flag description; national anthem, motto, and symbols (when available); geographical description of location; total area; brief climate description; proper terms for nationality; population numbers; languages spoken; and information on ethnic groups and religions.

11. Legal Holidays by Country **1033**

This section lists legal public holidays around the world in alphabetical order by country.

12. Tourism Information Sources for Countries around the World **1057**

This section includes tourism information sources for countries around the world, except the United States, Canada, and Mexico (see Appendix 8). The listings are in alphabetical order by name of the country.

13. Bibliography **1117**

This section includes an annotated listing of sources cited or consulted in HFCWD, as well as other sources for further reading.

APPENDIX 1

Glossary of Words Relating to Time

A descriptive listing of words relating to periods of time is included below. Many of the words are adjectives in form, but also are commonly used as nouns, e.g., the bicentennial of the U.S. Constitution. All terms are defined in two separate lists: first by number referred to, then alphabetically.

Listed by Number

diurnal, per diem, quotidian
daily; of a day

nocturnal
nightly; of a night

nichthemeron
a period of 24 hours

semidiurnal
twice a day

hebdomadal
weekly; a period of seven days

semiweekly
twice a week

biweekly
every two weeks
twice a week

fortnightly
once every two weeks

triweekly
every three weeks
three times a week

novendial
a period of nine days

monthly, tricenary
relating to a period of one month
thirty days

bimonthly
every two months
twice a month

semimonthly
twice a month

bimester
relating to a period of two months

trimester
relating to a period of three months

trimonthly
every three months
three times a month

biquarterly
twice every three months

biannual
twice a year (not necessarily at equally spaced intervals)

triannual
three times a year

semiannual, semiyearly, semestral
every half year or six-month period

annual, solennial, quotennial, per annum
yearly; once a year

biennial, biennium, biyearly, diennial
relating to a period of two years

triennial, triennium
relating to a period of three years

quadrennial, quadrennium, quadriennial
relating to a period of four years

quinquennial, quintennial, quinquennium
relating to a period of five years

sexennial, sextennial
relating to a period of six years

septenary, septennial, septennium
relating to a period of seven years

octennial
relating to a period of eight years

851

novennial
relating to a period of nine years

decennary, decennial, decennium
relating to a period of 10 years

undecennial
relating to a period of 11 years

duodecennial
relating to a period of 12 years

quindecennial
relating to a period of 15 years

septendecennial
relating to a period of 17 years

vicennial, vigintennial
relating to a period of 20 years

tricennial, trigintennial
relating to a period of 30 years

quinquagenary, semicentennial, semicentenary
relating to a period of 50 years

centenary, centennial, centennium, centurial
relating to a period of 100 years

quasquicentennial
relating to a period of 125 years

sesquicentenary, sesquicentennial
relating to a period of 150 years

bicentenary, bicentennial, bicentennium
relating to a period of 200 years

tercentenary, tricentennial, tercentennial
relating to a period of 300 years

quadricentennial, quatercentennial
relating to a period of 400 years

quincentenary, quincentennial
relating to a period of 500 years

sexcentenary
relating to a period of 600 years

septicentennial
relating to a period of 700 years

antemillennial, premillennial
relating to the period before the millennium

millennial, millennium
relating to a period of 1000 years; 10 centuries

postmillennial
relating to the period after the millennium

sesquimillennium
relating to a period of 1500 years; 15 centuries

bimillenary, bimillennial, bimillennium
relating to a period of 2000 years; 20 centuries

perennial
occurring year after year

plurennial
lasting for many years

aeonial
everlasting

Listed Alphabetically

aeonial
everlasting

annual
yearly; once a year

antemillennial
relating to the period before the millennium

biannual
twice a year (not necessarily at equally spaced intervals)

bicentenary, bicentennial, bicentennium
relating to a period of 200 years

biennial, biennium
relating to a period of two years

bimester
relating to a period of two months

bimillenary, bimillennial, bimillennium
relating to a period of 2000 years; 20 centuries

bimonthly
every two months
twice a month

biquarterly
twice every three months

biweekly
every two weeks
twice a week

biyearly
relating to a period of two years

centenary, centennial, centennium, centurial
relating to a period of 100 years

decennary, decennial, decennium
relating to a period of 10 years

diennial
relating to a period of two years

diurnal
daily; of a day

duodecennial
relating to a period of 12 years

fortnightly
once every two weeks

hebdomadal
weekly; a period of seven days

millennial, millennium
relating to a period of 1000 years; 10 centuries

monthly
relating to a period of one month
thirty days

nichthemeron
a period of 24 hours

nocturnal
nightly; of a night

novendial
a period of nine days

novennial
relating to a period of nine years

octennial
relating to a period of eight years

per annum
yearly; once a year

per diem
daily; of a day

perennial
occurring year after year

plurennial
lasting for many years

postmillennial
relating to the period after the millennium

premillennial
relating to the period before the millennium

quadrennial, quadrennium, quadriennial
relating to a period of four years

quadricentennial
relating to a period of 400 years

quasquicentennial
relating to a period of 125 years

quatercentennial
relating to a period of 400 years

quincentenary, quincentennial
relating to a period of 500 years

quindecennial
relating to a period of 15 years

quinquagenary
relating to a period of 50 years

quinquennial, quinquennium, quintennial
relating to a period of five years

quotennial
yearly; once a year

quotidian
daily; of a day

semestral, semiannual
every half year or six-month period

semicentenary, semicentennial
relating to a period of 50 years

semidiurnal
twice a day

semimonthly
twice a month

semiweekly
twice a week

semiyearly
every half year or six-month period

septenary
relating to a period of seven years

septendecennial
relating to a period of 17 years

septennial, septennium
relating to a period of seven years

septicentennial
relating to a period of 700 years

sesquicentenary, sesquicentennial
relating to a period of 150 years

sesquimillennium
relating to a period of 1500 years; 15 centuries

sexcentenary
relating to a period of 600 years

sexennial, sextennial
relating to a period of six years

solennial
yearly; once a year

tercentenary, tercentennial
relating to a period of 300 years

triannual
three times a year

tricenary
relating to a period of one month
thirty days

tricennial
relating to a period of 30 years

tricentennial
relating to a period of 300 years

triennial, triennium
relating to a period of three years

trigintennial
relating to a period of 30 years

trimester
relating to a period of three months

trimonthly
every three months
three times a month

triweekly
every three weeks
three times a week

undecennial
relating to a period of 11 years

vicennial, vigintennial
relating to a period of 20 years

APPENDIX 2

Calendars throughout History: An Overview of Calendar Systems around the World

This section provides information on calendars in various parts of the world and within major religious traditions. Following a general historical overview, these calendars will be discussed in the order in which they were developed or established:

Calendars throughout History: An Overview
    Ancient Egyptians and Babylonians Systematize Their Calendars
    Babylonians and Egyptians Disagree
    The Solar System Affects the Length of the Year
    The Gap between the Lunar and Solar Cycles

Chinese Calendar

Calendars of India
    India's Original Calendar
    The Saka Era Calendar
    Hindu Calendar
    Jain Calendar
    Cyclical Eras
    Buddhist Calendar
    Sikh Calendar

Mayan and Aztec Calendars

Babylonian Calendar
    Zoroastrian Calendars

Roman Julian Calendar

Jewish Calendar

Islamic Calendar

Gregorian Calendar

Christian Liturgical Calendar
    Old and New Calendars
    Western Liturgical Calendars
    Orthodox Liturgical Calendars

Baha'i Calendar

Calendars throughout History: An Overview

The calendar is so ordinary, and yet so important, that one can hardly imagine a time when it did not exist. It is a fundamental commodity of life. Its significance is so great that in some cultures the institution and maintenance of dating systems have sacred status, and they fall under the jurisdiction of religious authorities.

Around the globe, through centuries of human history, a wide range of different calendars have been used to order time in a systematic manner—a need that all human civilizations share. Today, the Western Gregorian calendar serves as an international standard for business and diplomatic purposes. On the world's stage, this is a recent development, and people of various religions, nations, and societies still employ many other calendars to mark the passing of time. The characteristics of these calendars are as diverse as the societies that developed them. All calendars, however, serve the common purpose of enabling people to work together to accomplish specific goals.

In the broadest sense, a calendar consists of the set of rules that a society uses to determine which days are ordinary and which days are holy, or holidays.

Thousands of years ago, before the beginning of the written historical record, people lived in small tribal societies based on hunting and gathering. Activities were likely coordinated by word of mouth, and time-keeping methods were fairly uncomplicated. People probably used days as indications of time, and perhaps they even recognized periods similar to months through observing changes in the moon's appearance. They would have observed seasonal and annual patterns, but without a formal system of reckoning them. Almost certainly, their needs did not demand anything as complex as a decade or century.

Over the course of time, people began living in agricultural communities with larger populations and diversified work forces. This shift required that people become more interdependent. For example, if farmers and city dwellers were going to conduct business efficiently, they must come to the marketplace at the same time. As a result, the need for a tool to arrange societal events became apparent.

Ancient Egyptians and Babylonians Systematize Their Calendars

The first two cultures that influenced the development of the Western Gregorian calendar were the Babylonians and Egyptians. Both shared similar characteristics—an agricultural base, a large population spread over a significant expanse of land, and a need to gather together at regular intervals to observe religious festivals. The responsibility for forming a central time-reckoning system so that people would know when to arrive at these festivals was placed in the hands of the respective religious communities.

To develop their calendars, both groups followed similar approaches. They divided time into three major divisions— what we now recognize as days, months, and years—and then went about calculating the exact duration of each category. The questions faced by the ancient Babylonians and Egyptians were the same questions all subsequent calendar makers have had to address:

- How long is a day?
- How long is a month?
- How long is a year?

These values may seem obvious to a modern observer, but it took centuries of ongoing observations, measurements, and calculations to set them.

The Day

The basic building block of all calendars is the day. The length of the day is set by the amount of time in which the earth completes one rotation on its axis. During the fifth century B.C.E. (Before Common Era, which is equivalent to the term B.C.), the Babylonians divided this duration of time into 24 segments that we now know as hours. However, because accurate measurement of seconds and even minutes was not possible until the 16th century C.E.
(Common Era, equivalent to A.D.), the length of those hours has not always been fixed.

The day was given scientific regularity only with the development of accurate clocks, the demand for which was a byproduct of the interest in maritime navigation that came with the Renaissance.

The Month

Although dividing the day into hours and seconds was important, a method of ordering a succession of days into larger units of time was also necessary for long-term planning. The development of what we now call a month, which is based on the orbit of the moon around the earth, grew out of such an attempt to organize days.

A lunar month, the period of a complete cycle of the phases of the moon, lasts approximately 29.5 days, is easy for all to recognize, and short enough to be counted without using large numbers. .Its simplicity and minimal ease of observation (if one discounts cloudy skies) led to its great significance, and it was widely used as the basis for calendars in many cultures. The length of each month varied according to the culture. For example, the Babylonians alternated between 29- and 30-day months, while the Egyptians fixed them at 30 days.

The Seasons and the Year

Perhaps the most difficult issue faced by calendar makers was establishing the length of the year. The problem inherent in the use of a lunar calendar is that the cycles of the sun, not the moon, determine the seasons, the predictability of which is essential to the success of agriculture. Although measuring a complete cycle of seasons may not seem complicated, it created significant problems for many calendar systems.

Each season in a cycle was marked by weather changes. Some seasons were warm, others cold; some had high levels of precipitation, others low. This cycling of the seasons originally defined the year—a period of time important to agrarian cultures that depended heavily on the ability to predict optimal planting and harvesting times.

Each season contained several new moons or months. The cycling of the moon and the cycling of weather patterns were not synchronized. This led to different systems for measuring a year's length.

Babylonians and Egyptians Disagree

In the fifth century B.C.E., the Babylonians and Egyptians both arrived at a specific number of days in the year, but their conclusions were different. The Babylonians claimed that the year was 360 days long while the Egyptians more accurately estimated the year at 365 days. The discrepancy between the two lengths of the year is puzzling.

One possibility for the difference is that the Babylonians simply miscalculated. This is unlikely, however, in light of their sophisticated astronomical and mathematical systems. Another explanation is that they rounded their figure from 365 to 360 to facilitate the interaction of the year with their base-12 numerical system.

The problem with the Babylonians' five-day omission was that the months would not stay in line with the seasons of the year. Each year the beginning of each month would occur at least five days earlier in relation to the position of the sun. Eventually, the months would be completely dissociated with the seasons in which they originally occurred. To correct this problem, the Babylonians periodically added months to the calendar, a process termed intercalation, which can also be used to add "leap" days or weeks.

The Babylonians were not the only people to face the problem of keeping the months coordinated with the seasons. Even though the Egyptians calculated the length of the year more accurately, they too realized that their determination was not exactly perfect.

The Solar System Affects the Length of the Year

Precise division of a year into months or days is impossible because the seasons, the phases of the moon, and the ever-cycling periods of daylight and nighttime are determined by the earth's relationship to the sun and the moon. The movements of these heavenly bodies do not neatly coincide with the mathematical systems of any human civilization.

The quest to discover the secrets of how the universe fits together has motivated astronomers throughout history. In the second century C.E., Ptolemy, a Greek astronomer, formulated the theory that the earth was the center of the universe and that the sun, stars, moon, and other planets revolved around it. In the 15th century C.E., the Polish astronomer Copernicus advocated the notion that the earth rotated on an axis and, along with the other heavenly bodies in the solar system, revolved around the sun. Shortly after the Copernican assertion, Galileo presented supporting evidence based on observations he had made using his invention, the telescope.

The Gap between the Lunar and Solar Cycles

We now understand that an 11.25-day difference exists between the 354-day lunar cycle on which the months are based and the 365.25-day solar cycle that determines the seasons. Calendar systems have applied three main strategies in their search for a solution to this discrepancy.

The first, called a lunar calendar, ignores the seasons and allows the lunar (moon) cycle to be the basis of the year, as the Islamic calendar does. A second is called a lunisolar calendar. It involves an elaborate system of calculations to add days or months to the lunar year until it coincides with the solar year. The Jewish calendar is one example. The third system, which originated with the Egyptians, is the pure solar calendar. It allows the sun to determine not only the seasons but the length of the months as well.

Chinese Calendar

The Chinese calendar, widely used in Asian countries, is based on the oldest system of time measurement still in use, with its origin believed to be 2953 B.C.E. Part of the reason that the Chinese calendar has survived intact for so long is that, until the middle of the 20th century, the document was considered sacred. Any changes to the calendar were tightly controlled by imperial authorities, and the penalty for illegally tampering with the time-keeping system was death. Until the rise of Communism in China during the 20th century, the official calendar was presented to the emperor, governors, and other dignitaries in an annual ceremony. Since 1912, the Gregorian calendar has been in use for civic purposes.

The Chinese New Year takes place on the new moon nearest to the point that is defined in the West as the 15th degree of the zodiacal sign of Aquarius. Each of 12 months in the Chinese year is 29 or 30 days long and is divided into two parts, each of which is two weeks long. The Chinese calendar, like all lunisolar systems, requires periodic adjustment to keep the lunar and solar cycles integrated, therefore an intercalary month is added when necessary.

The names of each of the 24 two-week periods sometimes correspond to festivals that occur during the period. Beginning with the New Year, which takes place in late January or early February, these periods are known by the following names: Spring Begins (New Year), the Rain Water, the Excited Insects, the Vernal Equinox, the Clear and Bright, the Grain Rains, the Summer Begins, the Grain Fills, the Grain in Ear, the Summer Solstice, the Slight Heat, the Great Heat, the Autumn Begins, the Limit of Heat, the White Dew, the Autumnal Equinox, the Cold Dew, the Hoar Frost Descends, the Winter Begins, the Little Snow, the Heavy Snow, the Winter Solstice, the Little Cold, and the Great Cold.

Calendars of India

Throughout its history, India has used a plethora of calendars and dating systems, which have included two basic types: a civil calendar that changed with each new regime and a religious calendar maintained by the Hindus. Although each geographical region had its own Hindu calendar, most of the calendars shared some elements that they gleaned from a common heritage.

India's Original Calendar

India's first time-reckoning system emerged before 1000 B.C.E. It was based on astronomical observations and consisted of a solar year of 360 days comprising 12 lunar months. The discrepancy between the length of the solar and lunar years was corrected by intercalating a month every 60 months.

In 1200 C.E., the Muslims brought the use of their calendar to India for administrative purposes, and in 1757 the British introduced the Gregorian calendar. Even so, each separate state maintained a calendar that its citizens used in their daily interactions. Throughout India's colonial days, the entrenchment of these local calendars created havoc for the central government because any given date would yield up to six different interpretations throughout the country. The difficulties continued as an indigenous government took control in 1947.

The Saka Era Calendar

When India became a unified and independent nation, the differences among regional calendars included more than 30 methods for determining the beginning of the era, the year, and the month. These variations in the Hindu calendar were the culmination of nearly 3,000 years of history.

In 1952, the Calendar Reform Committee was established and charged with task of devising a unified system that would adhere to modern astronomical calculations and accommodate the calculation of dates for religious festivals. As a result of the committee's work, the National Calendar of India was adopted in 1957.

The National Calendar of India is a 12-month lunisolar calendar with traditional Hindu month names. Some months are 30 days in length; others are 31 days. The year is 365 days long, with an extra day added to the end of the first month every four years (coinciding with leap years in the Gregorian calendar).

The National Calendar of India counts years from the inception of the Saka Era (S.E.)—the spring equinox in 79 C.E. In the year in which it was adopted, the first day of the first month (Caitra) was Caitra 1, 1879 S.E., which corresponded to March 22, 1957 C.E. Using the Gregorian calendar for comparison, the year 1926 in the Saka Era began on March 22, 2004 C.E.

Dates for religious festivals, which depend on lunar and solar movements, are calculated annually by the India Meteorological Department, although regional variations still exist. For administrative purposes, the Indian government currently follows the Gregorian calendar.

Hindu Calendar

Although each geographical region of India has had its own calendar, all are based on an ancient calendar, the earliest time measurement system in India, found in texts thought to date from as early as 1000 B.C. Of the multitudinous regional Hindu calendars, used only for religious holidays, the majority divide an approximate solar year of 360 days into 12 months. Each day is 1/30th of a month, with the intercalation of a leap month every 60 months. Time measurements based on observations of the constellations are used along with the calendar. Each month is divided into two fortnights: *krsna* (waning or dark half) and *sukla* (waxing or bright half). In southern India, the month begins with the new moon. In other parts of the country, the full moon is considered to be the beginning of the month. Many references to the Hindu calendar (depending on the source) are given as follows: month, fortnight (either S=waxing or K=waning), and number of the day in that fortnight, e.g., Rama Navami: Caitra S. 9.

The names of the Hindu months (with variant spellings) are given below, with the Burmese name for the month in brackets:

Caitra or Chaitra [Tagu]: March-April

Vaisakha [Kasone]: April-May

Jyeshta or Jyaistha [Nayhone]: May-June

Ashadha or Asadha [Waso]: June-July

Sravana [Wagaung]: July-August

Bhadrapada [Tawthalin]: August-September

Asvina [Thadingyut]: September-October

Kartika or Karttika [Tazaungmone]: October-November

Margasirsa or Margashirsha [Nadaw]: November-December

Pausa or Pausha [Pyatho]: December-January

Magha [Tabodwei]: January-February

Phalguna [Tabaung]: February-March

Jain Calendar

The Indian calendars generally have lunar months, but the duration of an average year is a sidereal year. The dates of most all the Jain festivals are calculated using such a lunisolar calendar. In northern India, the beginning of the month occurs at the full moon. This means that the first fortnight is waning. People in southern India typically mark the beginning of the month at the new moon and the first fortnight is waxing. Jains begin the new year in the autumn with the Diwali festival commemorating the liberation (achievement of Nirvana) of their founder, Nataputta Mahavira. The Hindu new year generally occurs in the spring; however, in Gujarat, the Hindu new year also starts with Diwali.)

Mahavira's achievement of Nirvana (at his death) in 527 B.C.E. also serves as the epoch for the Jain calendar. Diwali 2004 C.E., for example, begins the year 2531 V.N.S. (Vira Nirvana Samvat).

Cyclical Eras

The Jain concept of how time cycles through progressive and regressive eras also differs from the Hindus'. Jains believe that a complete cycle of time consists of twelve separate units. Of these, six represent deteriorating conditions and six represent improving conditions. The third and fourth units of both half-cycles represent times when neither extreme predominates. Only during these units can the Tirthankaras be born.

Currently, the earth is experiencing the fifth unit in the declining part of the time cycle. Risabha, the first Tirthankara of the current age, is said to have been born during the third unit; Mahavira was born at the close of the fourth. Each of the last two units in the declining half-cycle has a duration of 21,000 years.

The months of the Jain calendar are given below. The names of the Jain months are nearly the same as those of the Hindu months, but the Jain new year begins in Kartika, rather than in Caitra.

Kartika: October-November

Margasira: November-December

Pausa: December-January

Magha: January-February

Phalguna: February-March

Caitra: March-April

Vaisakha: April-May

Jyestha: May-June

Asadha: June-July

Sravana: July-August

Bhadrapada: August-September
Asvina: September-October

Buddhist Calendar

The Buddhist calendar, which originated in India, has even more pronounced variations among different geographic locations than the Hindu calendar, with which it shares many common elements. Buddhism spread outside India following the death of the Buddha (Siddhartha Gautama) in 483 B.C.E. Among the Buddhist sects, even the method for determining the date of the new year is not uniform. Theravada Buddhists (those primarily in Sri Lanka, Laos, Burma/Myanmar, Thailand, and Cambodia), using a Hindu calendar as their basis, calculate the months by the moon and the new year by the sun's position in relation to the twelve segments of the heavens, each named for a sign of the zodiac. The solar new year begins when the sun enters Aries, usually between April 13th and 18th. The lunar months alternate between twenty-nine and thirty days in length. The first lunar month is usually sometime in December, except for the Burmese Buddhist calendar, which begins in April (see Hindu Calendar above for Burmese names). Periodically, the seventh month has an intercalary day, and an intercalary month is added every few years. Cambodia, Laos, and Thailand refer to the months by number. Tibetan Buddhists, whose calendar has been heavily influenced by the Chinese calendar, begin their new year at the full moon nearest to the midpoint of Aquarius. Mahayana Buddhists (those primarily in Tibet, Mongolia, China, Korea, and Japan) base their holidays on Buddhist, Chinese, or Gregorian calendars.

Sikh Calendar

The Sikh calendar dates from the religion's inception in the 15th century C.E. It is a lunar calendar that is based on the moon's movement from one zodiac sign into the next rather than on the phase of the moon. The dates of some festivals, however, derive from the phase of the moon. The beginning of a new month is called the Sangrand. It is announced in the Sikh house of worship (gurdwara) but it is not a festival day.

Sikh festivals are marked on a special calendar called the Sikh Gurpurab Calendar. A gurpurab is a date commemorating births, deaths (and martyrdoms), or other important events associated with the lives of the 10 Sikh human *Guru*s or with the Sikh scriptures, the *Guru Granth Sahib*. The Gurpurab Calendar also notes the anniversary dates of historic incidents important to the Sikh faith.

The Sikh Gurpurab Calendar begins with the month of Chait (March/April), showing its inspiration from the Hindu calendar. The Sikh New Year celebration, however, falls on the first day of the second month, Basakh.

The Sikh have used several calendars since their religious tradition began in the 15th century. Over time, the lunar calendar, called the Bikrami calendar, was used predominantly. The Bikrami calendar consisted of 12 months averaging 29.5 days. This yields a year that is approximately 11 days shorter than the solar year. To keep the lunar calendar in line with the solar seasons, the Sikh calendar intercalated an extra lunar month whenever two new moons occur within the same solar month. The 13th lunar month then took the name of the solar month in which it fell. The names of the regular 12 lunar months are listed in the *Guru Granth Sahib*.

The solar component of the Bikrami calendar, however, did not correspond exactly to the natural solar year—every 70 years a discrepancy equal to one day accrued. To resolve this problem, two calendars were developed to accurately match the natural solar year: the Nanakshai Calendar, which is based on Guru Nanak's birth, and the Khalsa Calendar, which is based on the founding of the Khalsa. In 1999 C.E., the Sikhs adopted the Nanakshai Calendar. Although the choice generated some controversy, it is now used to observe all Sikh religious holidays, and has grown increasingly popular, especially among Sikh communities outside India.

The Nanakshai calendar is devised in a manner that maintains consistency with the western Gregorian calendar so that holidays always fall on the same day of the year. It begins with the month of Chait (Chait 1 falls on March 14) and contains five months of 31 days and seven months of 30 days. The last month usually contains 30 days, but in leap years, an extra day is added.

The Nanakshai calendar counts years from Guru Nanak's birth in 1469 C.E. The year Nanakshai 547 begins in the year 2015 C.E.

The months of the Nanakshai calendar, along with variant spellings, are given below.

Chait or Chet: March-April
Basakh or Vaisakhi: April-May
Jaith or Jeth: May-June
Har or Harh: June-July
Sawan: July-August
Bhadro or Bhadon: August-September

Asun or Asu: September-October

Katik: October-November

Magar or Maghar: November-December

Poh: December-January

Magh: January-February

Phagan or Phagun: February-March

Mayan and Aztec Calendars

The Mayan and Aztec civilizations both used what is commonly referred to as the Mesoamerican calendar. This ancient calendar may have derived from the Olmec civilization, which thrived between 1300 and 400 B.C.E. in what is now southeastern Mexico, along the Gulf. The Mesoamerican calendrical system, which probably originated between 1000–900 B.C.E., employed not just one calendar, but a system of two interconnecting calendars: a 260-day calendar and a 365-day calendar. These two calendars ran alongside each other. Every 52 years, a named day from the 260-day calendar would be the same as a named day from the 365-day calendar (there are 18,980 days in 52 years, and 18,980 is the least common multiple of both 365 and 260). This 52-year cycle was observed by both the Mayans and the Aztecs.

Mayan civilization, in what is now southeastern Mexico, Belize, and portions of Guatemala and Honduras, flourished between about 300–900 C.E., a period known as the Classical Mayan era. The Mayans used the 260-day calendar—known as the *tzolkin*—for sacred purposes, and the 365-day solar-based calendar—called the *haab*—for agricultural purposes. The Mayan calendar system employed glyphs, small pictorial inscriptions, to represent such time periods as a day, a month, and a year, as well as to represent specific months of the year and specific days in the months. Each day was named for a god who was thought to be manifest as that day. The days' numbers were written using a combination of dots and bars. The 260-day Mayan calendar was divided into 13 months of 20 named days. The 365-day calendar was divided into 18 months of 20 named days plus a brief month of five days, called *Uayeb*, or "ominous days." The 52-year Mayan cycle is known as the Calendar Round. The 260-day system is thought to be the only one of its kind in the world. Scholars are not certain what the significance of 260 is, though some have noted that the average duration of human pregnancy is approximately 260 days long. In addition, the Mayans had a highly developed knowledge of astronomy, and 260 was a number significant in calculating the appearance of Venus—the planet identified with the Mayan god Kukulcan, known as Quetzalcoatl to the Toltec people, who flourished in Mesoamerica (and dominated the Mayans) from the 10th century to the middle of the 12th century.

Mayans also developed the Long Count, an extensive system of time-reckoning which attempted to encompass the time of the world from its creation to its end. The Mayans are thought to have developed the Long Count between 400 B.C.E. and 100 A.D. From this system, they dated the current creation to have occurred in 3114 B.C.E. (or 3113 B.C.E., by some contemporary calculations), and current dates are calculated by counting the number of days from this creation date.

The Aztecs—they called themselves Mexica—dominated Mesoamerica after the Toltec empire collapsed, from the early 1300s up until the Spanish began colonization in the early 1600s. Like the Mayans, the Aztecs used the 260-day calendar divided into 13 months of 20 days; they called it *tonalpohualli*, or "count of day." Their 365-day calendar also consisted of 18 months of 20 days plus a period of five days, which the Aztecs believed to be unlucky. The Aztecs also named their days after deities, but, unlike the Mayan system, Aztec numerical notation consisted only of dots. Aztecs probably did not use a Long Count. At the end of their 52-year cycle—which they called *xiuhmolpilli*, or "year bundle"—the Aztecs celebrated the new beginning with a great renewal ceremony (see NEW FIRE CEREMONY).

Today, the 365-day civil calendar predominates throughout the region, though some contemporary Mayans also continue to use the 260-day calendar to observe sacred festivals.

Babylonian Calendar

Babylonian, Sumerian, and Assyrian astronomers living in the Mesopotamian Valley hundreds of years B.C.E.

developed calendars that would influence the later Roman Julian and Gregorian calendars. These calendars were based on the phases of the moon and were closely related to the religious life of the cultures that developed them. The influence of the Mesopotamian civilizations on the global art of calendar making was far-reaching because many of the techniques they developed were adopted by future societies.

Of the various cultures that thrived in the Mesopotamian valley, the Babylonians seem to have most significantly influenced calendar making. Many details of the evolution of the Babylonian calendar have been lost over the centuries, but it is known that the calendar was lunar in nature, had a system of intercalation, had months divided into seven-day units, and had days with twenty-four hours.

Because these early calendar makers were pioneers in the field, they were among the first to be confronted with the discrepancy between the lunar and solar cycles—a problem that had the potential to render any calendar system ineffective. To reconcile the two natural courses, the Babylonians worked out a schedule whereby an extra month was periodically intercalated. The process of intercalation, termed *iti dirig*, seems to have been rather arbitrary at first, but by 380 B.C.E. a formal system was adopted adding an extra month in the third, sixth, eighth, eleventh, seventeenth, and nineteenth years. Many other cultures, including the Greeks, developed similar intercalation schemes which may have drawn their inspiration from the Babylonian model.

Although the origin of the week has been a subject of much research and debate among scholars since the time of Plutarch (46-119 C.E.), most agree that the Babylonians are the primary source for the week in the Western civil calendar. Many researchers also conclude that the Babylonians devised the week as a part of their religious practices. They have observed that years, months, and days all reflect natural cycles, but the week does not. This observation has led to some questions: Why does the week have seven days? Why are the days named after celestial bodies? Why are the days not arranged according to the order of the planets in the solar system? Many proposed solutions to these quandaries have surfaced over the course of time.

Details of the Babylonian calendar are few, but some are known. It appears that the major festival was the New Year celebration which took place in the spring of the year during the Babylonian month of Nisanu. On the first day of the festival, a ritual marriage was performed between the king and the high priestess, who symbolized the sovereignty of the land. On this day, the Babylonian creation myth (called *Enuma elish* from its opening words, "When on high") was read aloud. On the fifth day, Rites of Atonement were observed. During the Rites the king, as a representative of the people, endured a ritual of abasement to atone for the sins of the people against the gods. On the seventh day, the Festival of the Sun, or spring equinox, took place.

Zoroastrian Calendars

Zoroastrianism originated in Iran. The religion's founder, the prophet Zoroaster, was thought to have lived around 1200 B.C.E.. Zoroastrianism flourished and waned in concert with the success of the Persian Empire. By the time of the Sasanian dynasty (226-651 B.C.E.), Zoroastrianism was made the empire's official religion. After the Muslim conquest of Persia in the middle of the seventh century, however, many Zoroastrians migrated to India, particularly the western state of Gujarat, where they became known as the "Parsi" (meaning "Persian") community.

The Zoroastrian calendar derived from the ancient Babylonian calendar, except that the former's days and months were dedicated to spiritual beings. In the mid-18th century, some Parsis adopted the Iranian calendar and called it the *qadimi* calendar, giving rise to the Zoroastrian sect known as Kadmi. Others remained with the traditional religion and calendar, though it was a month behind the Kadmi calendar, and were referred to as Shenshais, often rendered Shahanshahis. In 1906, the Fasli sect was founded. It advocated the use of a calendar closer to the Gregorian one, in which the new year would always begin at the vernal equinox and which would add an extra day every four years.

All three Zoroastrian calendars have the same twelve 30-day months with five intercalary days called *Gatha* coming at the end of the twelfth month. The differences are in how each reconciles the lunar year with the natural solar year. As a result, a single date on each Zoroastrian calendar corresponds to three different Gregorian dates. For example, in 2014, the first day of the first month (Frawardin 1) fell on March 21 according to the Fasli calendar, on July 19 according to the Kadmi calendar, and on August 18 according to the Shahanshai calendar.

The Zoroastrian month names and approximate English meanings are:

Frawardin or Fravardin (Humanity) March-April*

Ardwahist or Ardibehest (Truth and Righteousness) April-May

Hordad or Khordad (Perfection) May-June

Tir (Sirius, the Dog Star) June-July

Amurdad or Amardad (Immortality) July-August

Shahrewar or Sherever (Benevolent Dominion) August-September

Mihr or Meher (Fair Dealing) September-October

Aban or Avan (Water or Purity) October-November

Adar or Adur (Fire) November-December

Dae or Deh (Creator) December-January

Vohuman or Bahman (Good Mind) January-February

Spendarmad or Aspandarmad (Holy Devotion) February-March

***Gregorian month ranges corresponding to the Fasli calendar**

Roman Julian Calendar

Julius Caesar ordered the change of the reformed Roman lunar calendar to a solar-based one in 46 B.C.E. The intercalation of ninety days corrected a growing discrepancy between the seasons and the months in which they had traditionally fallen. Prior to this intercalation, the Roman civic year had come to be about three months "ahead" of the seasons, so spring began in June. The year 46 B.C.E. was assigned 445 days to make the adjustment; it was called *ultimus annus confusionis,* "the last year of the muddled reckoning." The new calendar, based on the Egyptian solar calendar, provided for a year of 365 days with an additional day in February every fourth year. The addition of this leap year and day gives the Julian year an average length of 365.25 days—very close to the actual solar cycle. The Julian calendar (O.S., or Old Style) remained in civic use in the West for more than 1,600 years, is still the basis of the "Old Calendarist" Orthodox Christian liturgical calendar, and is used by all Orthodox Christian churches to determine the date of Easter.

Jewish Calendar

The Jewish calendar is based on a lunar model. This means that the phases of the moon determine when a month begins and ends. In early Hebrew society, the High Priest appointed watchmen to look for the new moon. When it appeared, the watchmen would report back to the High Priest who would proclaim the beginning of a new month. The system of observing the new moon became impractical after the destruction of the Temple in 70 C.E. and the subsequent Diaspora of the Jews (the scattering of the community into distant geographic areas). The central system for proclaiming a new month could not adequately meet the needs of a dispersed population.

In 358 C.E., Hillel II introduced a permanent calendar based on mathematical and astronomical calculations, eliminating the need for eyewitness sightings of the new moon with which the new month begins. Even though individual enclaves of Jews were often completely isolated from one another, they were able to maintain a sense of unity and identity partly because of their common religious calendar and observances.

From the time of Hillel II until the present, the Hebrew calendar has evolved into one of the most intricate systems of time reckoning in existence. The calendar includes such elements as varying year lengths, varying month lengths, and leap years—all of which are designed to meet the requirements of Judaic law regarding the celebration of feasts, festivals, and holidays.

Only slight modifications were made to Hillel's calendar, and it has remained unchanged since the tenth century. A day is reckoned from sundown to sundown, a week contains seven days, a month is either twenty-nine or thirty days long, and a year has twelve lunar months plus about eleven days, or 353, 354, or 355 days. To reconcile the calendar with the annual solar cycle, a thirteenth month of thirty days is intercalated in the third, sixth, eighth, eleventh, fourteenth, seventeenth, and nineteenth years of a nineteen-year cycle; a leap year may contain from 383 to 385 days. The civil calendar begins with the month of Tishri, the first day of which is Rosh Hashanah, the New Year. The cycle of the religious calendar begins on Nisan 15, Passover (Pesach). According to Hebrew scholars, the era used to number the years of the Jewish calendar (designated anno mundi or A.M.) had its epoch in the year of Creation which they believe was 3761 B.C.E.

The names of the months of the Jewish calendar were borrowed from the Babylonians. The pre-exilic books of the Bible usually refer to the months according to their numerical order, beginning with Tishri, but there are four months mentioned with different names: Nisan/Abib, Iyyar/Ziv, Tishri/Ethanim, and Heshvan/Bul:

Nisan: mid-March to mid-April

Iyyar: mid-April to mid-May

Sivan: mid-May to mid-June

Tammuz: mid-June to mid-July

Av: mid-July to mid-August

Elul: mid-August to mid-September

Tishri: mid-September to mid-October

Heshvan: mid-October to mid-November

Kislev: mid-November to mid-December

Tevet: mid-December to mid-January

Shevat: mid-January to mid-February

Adar: mid-February to mid-March

*The intercalary month of Adar II is inserted before Adar as needed.

Islamic Calendar

The Islamic calendar, called *hijri* or Hegirian, is still strictly lunar-based. Moreover, the *actual* beginning of a month depends on the sighting of the new moon. Traditionally, if the sky is overcast and the new moon is not visible, the previous month runs another thirty days before the new month begins. However, the *practical* beginning of a month is according to astronomical calculations of lunar cycles. The Islamic era begins July 16, 622 C.E., the date of the hegira or flight into exile of the Prophet Muhammad from Mecca to Medina.

There are twelve Islamic lunar months, some of twenty-nine, others of thirty days; these yield 354 days in the Islamic year. The fixed holidays set in the Islamic calendar thus move "backward" about ten days each year in relation to the Gregorian calendar. In roughly thirty-six years, Ramadan, the Islamic holy month of fasting, moves back through the entire solar year. The Islamic day runs from sundown to sundown.

Other calendars were developed in Islamic countries for the sake of agriculture, which depends on a solar calendar. The Coptic calendar, a variation of the Julian, was used until recently, but is now limited primarily to Egypt and the Sudan, countries with large Coptic populations. The Turkish fiscal calendar, also Julian-based, was used in the Ottoman Empire. Nowadays, the Gregorian calendar is followed nearly everywhere for civic purposes, and the Islamic calendar determines only the days of religious observance. Saudi Arabia is one exception, and, at least officially, employs the Islamic calendar as the calendar of reference.

The names of the Islamic months are an ancient reflection of the seasons of the solar year:

Muharram: the sacred month

Safar: the month which is void

Rabi al-Awwal: the first spring

Rabi ath-Thani: the second spring

Jumada-l-Ula: the first month of dryness

Jumada-th-Thaniyyah: the second month of dryness

Rajab: the revered month

Shaban: the month of division

Ramadan: the month of great heat

Shawwal: the month of hunting

Dhu al-Qadah: the month of rest

Dhu al-Hijjah: the month of pilgrimage

Gregorian Calendar

By the late 16th century, the difference between the Julian calendar and the seasons had grown to ten days because the Julian year, averaging 365.25 days, was slightly longer than the actual length of a solar year, which, by modern calculation, is known to be 365.242199 days long. This error of 11 minutes 14 seconds per year amounted to three days every 400 years. Fixed holy days began to occur in the "wrong" season, both for the church and for farmers, who used certain holy days to determine planting and harvesting. Pope Gregory XIII ordered the reform that deleted ten days from the year 1582; in that year, October 15 was the day after October 5. This change, coupled with the elimination of leap days in "century" years unless evenly divisible by 400 (e.g., 1600, 2000), corrected the calendar so that today only occasional "leap seconds" are needed to keep months and seasons synchronized. The Gregorian calendar also set January 1 as the beginning of the new year. At first adopted only in Roman Catholic countries, the Gregorian calendar (N.S., or New Style) gradually came to be accepted throughout the West, and today has become the calendar used by most of the world, at least for business and government.

Christian Liturgical Calendars

Clearly visible within the Christian liturgical calendar are elements of both the Hebrew and Greek time-keeping systems. Most immediately recognizable, however, are the influences of the Jewish calendar. The movable feasts within Christianity, such as Easter and Pentecost, have connections to Hebrew celebrations.

Today, many branches of Christianity follow similar calendars to mark the holy days of the year. The calendar focuses attention on special incidents in Jesus's life and also provides for the remembrance of many saints and historical events. It includes two types of dates: movable feasts, which are typically established based on their relationship to the Feast of the Resurrection (Easter), and fixed holidays.

Western Liturgical Calendar

The western Christian liturgical year begins in late November with a season called Advent. Four weeks long, Advent provides a time during which Christians prepare for Jesus's birth. Advent is followed by Christmas and the Christmas season during which Jesus's birth is celebrated. Epiphany, in early January commemorates Jesus's appearance to the Gentiles (non-Jews). Lent is a season of introspection and penance in preparation for Easter. It concludes with Holy Week, when events in the last week of Jesus's life are highlighted. The Easter season begins on Resurrection Sunday and lasts until Ascension Day, commemorating Jesus's ascension into heaven. The season of Pentecost begins with the celebration of the coming of the Holy Spirit. The longest season of the year, Trinity, completes the cycle.

The revised Roman Catholic calendar of 1969 changed some of the days on which certain saints were honored. Once universally honored days became only locally honored. According to Catholic law, followers are obligated to participate in Mass weekly on either a Saturday evening or Sunday morning and on six other days identified as holy days of obligation: Christmas, Solemnity of Mary, Ascension, Assumption of the Blessed Virgin, All Saints Day, and Immaculate Conception.

Orthodox Liturgical Calendars

In the Orthodox Church, holidays and feast days are determined by two different calendars, the Julian Calendar and the Gregorian calendar. There are five main elements to the Orthodox liturgical calendar: the daily cycle, the weekly cycle, the Paschal cycle, the cycle of fixed feasts, and the cycle of eight tones.

In contrast to practice in many other Christian Churches of starting the liturgical year with the first Sunday in Advent, the Orthodox liturgical year begins on September 1. In the Ecumenical Patriarchate this is observed as the Day of the Environment, with the role in the salvation of the world of the Theotokos, the mother of God, being emphasized. The Nativity of the Virgin Mary on September 8 and her Dormition on August 15 come at opposite ends of the liturgical year. Other than those included among the twelve great feasts, the other Marian feast day is December 9, the Conception of the Virgin by St. Anne.

March 25, the Annunciation, is another major feast of the Theotokos, but it is also a feast of the Conception of Christ and begins a series of feasts of the Lord. The Nativity of the Lord, as well as the Visit of the Magi, is observed in the Orthodox Church on December 25. The Circumcision of Jesus falls on January 1, the feast of Saint Basil the Great. For the Orthodox Christian, Epiphany, or Theophany as it is sometimes known, is January 6 and commemorates Christ's baptism. The feast of the Transfiguration is held on August 6.

The Paschal cycle begins four weeks before Lent, on the Sunday of the Pharisee and the Publican. Lent itself begins on Pure Monday and ends on Lazarus Saturday, the day before Palm Sunday. The Passion, the Mystical Supper, the Agony, Betrayal, Trial, Sufferings, Death, Burial and Glorious Resurrection, the Assumption into Heaven of the Lord, and the Sending of His Holy Spirit upon the Apostles are all celebrated in the feasts of the Paschal cycle. The cycle ends with Pentecost Sunday, the feast of the Holy Trinity, and the Sunday of All Saints.

In addition to the special feast days of the Lord or of Mary, every day on the Orthodox Calendar commemorates some saint. These may be saints venerated by all of Christendom, Latin Church saints from early centuries, saints particular to a specific locale, or the Righteous, or Dikaios, of the Old Law. Somewhat anachronistically, the Maccabees are commemorated as though they were Christian martyrs. The Maccabees were the family of Mattathias who, in 167 B.C.E., led the Jewish revolt against Antiochus IV Epiphanes. Even some Latin Church saints from after the Great Schism are recognized, and some Latin feasts, such as Corpus Christi, are observed.

In the medieval period of the Church, all music was organized on the basis of a system of eight tones. These tones continue to have not only musical significance but a calendrical significance as well. Beginning the first Sunday after Easter, St. Thomas Sunday, each successive week uses the texts and music of the next of the eight tones for its offices. Each day of the week has its distinctive hymns and verses for each of these eight tones. The book which contains the texts for each day's services for all eight tones is called the Parakletike.

Baha'i Calendar

The Baha'i calendar was established by the Bab in his writings and later confirmed by Baha'u'llah with some modifications and additions. Baha'u'llah set the year 1 of the Baha'i era at the Bab's declaration in 1844 C.E. The Baha'i calendar, called the Badí (meaning "wondrous"), is based on the solar year and begins on the vernal equinox in the Northern Hemisphere, normally March 20 or 21. It consists of 19 months, each with 19 days. Four intercalary days—called AYYAM-I-HA, the Days of Ha—occur after the 18th month in regular years, while five are inserted in leap years. Nineteen multiplied by 19 equals 361, plus four intercalary days equals 365. But the number 19 was chosen for more than its mathematical convenience. The Baha'i religion's first prophet, Mirza Ali Mohammad (also known as the BAB), devised a calendar for the new religion. He had 18 followers, thus these 19 original Babis are remembered in the calendar's structure.

On the first day of each of the nineteen months of the Baha'i year, in each locality the Baha'i community gathers for the Nineteen-Day Feast. The Feast has three parts: a devotional service consisting of prayers and readings from the sacred writings; a meeting of the Baha'i community for consultation on local affairs; and a social occasion with hospitality and fellowship.

Each Baha'í month is named for an attribute of God:

Bahá (Splendor) March 21

Jalál (Glory) April 9

Jamál (Beauty) April 28

Azamat (Grandeur) May 17

Núr (Light) June 5

Rahmat (Mercy) June 24

Kalimát (Words) July 13

Kamál (Perfection) August 1

Asmá (Names) August 20

'Izzat (Might) September 8

Mashiyyat (Will) September 27

'Ilm (Knowledge) October 16

Qudrat (Power) November 4

Qawl (Speech) November 23

Masá'il (Questions) December 12

Sharaf (Honor) December 31

Sultán (Sovereignty) January 19

Mulk (Dominion) February 7

Ayyam-i-Ha (Days of Ha; intercalary days): February 26-March 1 (February 26-March 2 in leap years)

'Alá' (Loftiness) March 2 (month of fasting)

APPENDIX 3

Comparative Table of Calendar Systems

The Gregorian calendar is based on the solar cycle of 365 days per year, while the Jewish, Hindu, and Burmese calendars are based on the lunar cycle of 29.5 days per month. The first day of the lunar months depicted here is typically the day of the new moon. The lunar months can overlap with the Gregorian months near which they fall. This is reflected in the chart below. While the Burmese calendar is essentially identical to the Hindu, the names of the months differ and are thus represented below. An asterisk (*) denotes the months in which the various New Years fall.

Gregorian Calendar	Jewish Calendar	Hindu, Jain, Buddhist and Sikh Calendar	Burmese Calendar
January*	Shevat	Magha	Tabodwei
February	Adar	Phalguna	Tabaung
March	Nisan	Caitra*	Tagu*
April	Iyyar	Vaisakha*	Kasone
May	Sivan	Jyeshta	Nayhone
June	Tammuz	Ashadha	Waso
July	Av	Sravana	Wagaung
August	Elul	Bhadrapada	Tawthalin
September	Tishri*	Asvina	Thadingyut
October	Heshvan	Kartika	Tazaungmone
November	Kislev	Margasirsa	Nadaw
December	Tevet	Pausa	Pyatho

APPENDIX 4

Phases of the Moon from 2015 to 2030
Given in Eastern Standard Time

Many cultures and religions have attached great importance to the cycles of the moon as visible from their vantage points on Earth. Thus the moon has significantly influenced the development of various calendars around the world throughout history (*see* Appendix 2, **Calendar Systems around the World**). The changing appearance of the moon in its orbit around Earth has inspired peoples to signify events by relating them to phases of the moon and scheduling holy days and festivals accordingly.

The Muslim calendar is strictly based on the moon. Each month begins with the sighting of the new crescent moon in the sky. Thus, the month-long holy fast of Ramadan begins with the new moon and ends with the next new moon when Id al-Fitr celebrates the end of the fast.

In the Christian calendar the most important holiday—Easter—is scheduled after the first full moon after the vernal equinox.

Hindu calendars appoint particular days within the lunar cycle to celebrate numerous holidays. Many are scheduled on particular days counting from the new moon or the full moon of a month. For example, the spring festival of Holi takes place during the waxing phase of the moon in the month of Phalguna—the period of the lunar month during which the moon appears to become fuller. Likewise, many holidays in the Buddhist and Jain calendars—which are based on the Indian calendars—are observed according to the moon's position.

Traditional Chinese holidays are also scheduled according to a calendar that is partly based on the lunar cycle.

Finally, although many Native American tribes observe special occasions according to solar and seasonal changes, some are scheduled with reference to certain phases of the moon, such as the Iroquois Midwinter Festival, which Longhouse followers traditionally hold five days after the first new moon in January.

The table below gives the dates and times of the four major phases of the moon—new, first quarter, half, and full—in U.S. Eastern Standard Time. For ease of reference, an additional table shows civilian equivalents to military time.

Civilian Time – Military Time

12:00 A.M.. – 00:00	08:00 A.M.. – 08:00	04:00 P.M.. – 16:00
01:00 A.M.. – 01:00	09:00 A.M.. – 09:00	05:00 P.M.. – 17:00
02:00 A.M.. – 02:00	10:00 A.M.. – 10:00	06:00 P.M.. – 18:00
03:00 A.M.. – 03:00	11:00 A.M.. – 11:00	07:00 P.M.. – 19:00
04:00 A.M.. – 04:00	12:00 P.M.. – 12:00	08:00 P.M.. – 20:00
05:00 A.M.. – 05:00	01:00 P.M.. – 13:00	09:00 P.M.. – 21:00
06:00 A.M.. – 06:00	02:00 P.M.. – 14:00	10:00 P.M.. – 22:00
07:00 A.M.. – 07:00	03:00 P.M.. – 15:00	11:00 P.M.. – 23:00

Phases of the Moon – 2015			
New Moon ●	**First Quarter ◑**	**Full Moon ○**	**Last Quarter ◐**
	Jan 4 23:53	Jan 13 04:47	Jan 20 08:14
Jan 26 23:48	Feb 3 18:09	Feb 11 22:50	Feb 18 18:47
Feb 25 12:14	Mar 5 13:06	Mar 13 12:48	Mar 20 04:36
Mar 27 02:43	Apr 4 07:06	Apr 11 22:44	Apr 18 13:57
Apr 25 18:55	May 3 22:42	May 11 05:36	May 17 23:13
May 25 12:19	Jun 2 11:19	Jun 9 10:42	Jun 16 09:05
Jun 24 06:03	Jul 1 21:20	Jul 8 15:24	Jul 15 20:24
Jul 23 23:04	Jul 31 05:43	Aug 6 21:03	Aug 14 09:54
Aug 22 14:31	Aug 29 13:35	Sep 5 04:54	Sep 13 01:41
Sep 21 03:59	Sep 27 21:50	Oct 4 16:06	Oct 12 19:06t
Oct 20 15:31	Oct 27 07:05	Nov 3 07:24	Nov 11 12:47
Nov 19 01:27	Nov 25 17:44	Dec 3 02:40	Dec 11 05:29
Dec 18 10:14	Dec 25 06:11		

Phases of the Moon – 2016			
New Moon ●	**First Quarter ◑**	**Full Moon ○**	**Last Quarter ◐**
		Jan 2 00:30	Jan 9 20:30
Jan 16 18:26	Jan 16 18:26	Jan 31 22:28	Feb 8 09:39
Feb 15 02:46	Feb 22 13:20	Mar 1 18:11	Mar 8 20:54
Mar 15 12:03	Mar 23 07:01	Mar 31 10:17	Apr 7 06:24
Apr 13 22:59	Apr 22 00:24	Apr 29 22:29	May 6 14:30
May 13 12:02	May 21 16:15	May 29 07:12	Jun 4 22:00
Jun 12 03:10	Jun 20 06:02	Jun 27 13:19	Jul 4 06:01
Jul 11 19:52	Jul 19 17:57	Jul 26 18:00	Aug 2 15:45
Aug 10 13:21	Aug 18 04:27	Aug 24 22:41	Sep 1 04:03
Sep 9 06:49	Sep 16 14:05	Sep 23 04:56	Sep 30 19:12
Oct 8 23:33	Oct 15 23:23	Oct 22 14:14	Oct 30 12:38
Nov 7 14:51	Nov 14 08:52	Nov 21 03:33	Nov 29 07:18
Dec 7 04:03	Dec 13 19:06	Dec 20 20:56	Dec 29 01:53

Phases of the Moon – 2017

New Moon ●	First Quarter ◗	Full Moon ○	Last Quarter ◖
Jan 5 14:47	Jan 12 06:34	Jan 19 17:14	Jan 27 19:07
Feb 3 23:19	Feb 10 19:33	Feb 18 14:33	Feb 26 09:58
Mar 5 06:32	Mar 12 09:54	Mar 20 10:58	Mar 27 21:57
Apr 3 13:39	Apr 11 01:08	Apr 19 04:57	Apr 26 07:16
May 2 21:47	May 10 16:43	May 18 19:33	May 25 14:44
Jun 1 07:42	Jun 9 08:10	Jun 17 06:33	Jun 23 21:31
Jun 30 19:51	Jul 8 23:07	Jul 16 14:26	Jul 23 04:46
Jul 30 10:23	Aug 7 13:11	Aug 14 20:15	Aug 21 13:30
Aug 29 03:13	Sep 6 02:03	Sep 13 01:25	Sep 20 00:30
Sep 27 21:54	Oct 5 13:40	Oct 12 07:25	Oct 19 14:12
Oct 27 17:22	Nov 4 00:23	Nov 10 15:37	Nov 18 06:42
Nov 26 12:03	Dec 3 10:47	Dec 10 02:51	Dec 18 01:31
Dec 26 04:20			

Phases of the Moon – 2018

New Moon ●	First Quarter ◗	Full Moon ○	Last Quarter ◖
	Jan 1 21:24	Jan 8 17:25	Jan 16 21:17
Jan 24 17:20	Jan 31 08:27	Feb 7 10:54	Feb 15 16:05
Feb 23 03:09	Mar 1 19:51	Mar 9 06:20	Mar 17 08:12
Mar 24 10:35	Mar 31 07:37	Apr 8 02:18	Apr 15 20:57
Apr 22 16:46	Apr 29 19:58	May 7 21:09	May 15 06:48
May 21 22:49	May 29 09:20	Jun 6 13:32	Jun 13 14:43
Jun 20 05:51	Jun 27 23:53	Jul 6 02:51	Jul 12 21:48
Jul 19 14:52	Jul 27 15:20	Aug 4 13:18	Aug 11 04:58
Aug 18 02:49	Aug 26 06:56	Sep 2 21:37	Sep 9 13:01
Sep 16 18:15	Sep 24 21:53	Oct 2 04:45	Oct 8 22:47
Oct 16 13:02	Oct 24 11:45	Oct 31 11:40	Nov 7 11:02
Nov 15 09:54	Nov 23 00:39	Nov 29 19:19	Dec 7 02:20
Dec 15 06:49	Dec 22 12:49	Dec 29 04:34	

Phases of the Moon – 2019			
New Moon ●	**First Quarter ◐**	**Full Moon ○**	**Last Quarter ◑**
			Jan 5 20:28
Jan 14 01:45	Jan 21 00:16	Jan 27 16:10	Feb 4 16:04
Feb 12 17:26	Feb 19 10:53	Feb 26 06:28	Mar 6 11:04
Mar 14 05:27	Mar 20 20:43	Mar 27 23:10	Apr 5 03:50
Apr 12 14:06	Apr 19 06:12	Apr 26 17:18	May 4 17:45
May 11 20:12	May 18 16:11	May 26 11:33	Jun 3 05:02
Jun 10 00:59	Jun 17 03:31	Jun 25 04:46	Jul 2 14:16
Jul 9 05:55	Jul 16 16:38	Jul 24 20:18	Jul 31 22:12
Aug 7 12:31	Aug 15 07:29	Aug 23 09:56	Aug 30 05:37
Sep 5 22:10	Sep 13 23:33	Sep 21 21:41	Sep 28 13:26
Oct 5 11:47	Oct 13 16:08	Oct 21 07:39	Oct 27 22:38
Nov 4 05:23	Nov 12 08:34	Nov 19 16:11	Nov 26 10:06
Dec 4 01:58	Dec 12 00:12	Dec 18 23:57	Dec 26 00:13

Phases of the Moon – 2020			
New Moon ●	**First Quarter ◐**	**Full Moon ○**	**Last Quarter ◑**
Jan 2 23:45	Jan 10 14:21	Jan 17 07:58	Jan 24 16:42
Feb 1 20:42	Feb 9 02:33	Feb 15 17:17	Feb 23 10:32
Mar 2 14:57	Mar 9 12:48	Mar 16 04:34	Mar 24 04:28
Apr 1 05:21	Apr 7 21:35	Apr 14 17:56	Apr 22 21:26
Apr 30 15:38	May 7 05:45	May 14 09:03	May 22 12:39
May 29 22:30	Jun 5 14:12	Jun 13 01:24	Jun 21 01:41
Jun 28 03:16	Jul 4 23:44	Jul 12 18:29	Jul 20 12:33
Jul 27 07:32	Aug 3 10:59	Aug 11 11:45	Aug 18 21:41
Aug 25 12:58	Sep 2 00:22	Sep 10 04:26	Sep 17 06:00
Sep 23 20:55	Oct 1 16:05	Oct 9 19:39	Oct 16 14:31
Oct 23 08:23	Oct 31 09:49	Nov 8 08:46	Nov 15 00:07
Nov 21 23:45	Nov 30 04:30	Dec 7 19:37	Dec 14 11:17
Dec 21 18:41	Dec 29 22:28		

Phases of the Moon – 2021

New Moon ●	First Quarter ◑	Full Moon ○	Last Quarter ◐
			Jan 6 14.37
Jan 13 10.00	Jan 21 02.02	Jan 29 00:16	Feb 4 22.37
Feb 12 00.06	Feb 19 23.47	Feb 27 13:17	Mar 6 06.30
Mar 13 15.21	Mar 21 19.40	Mar 28 23:48	Apr 4 15.02
Apr 12 07.31	Apr 20 11.59	Apr 27 08:31	May 4 00.50
May 12 00.00	May 20 00.13	May 26 16:14	Jun 2 12.24
Jun 10 15.53	Jun 18 08.54	Jun 24 23:40	Jul 2 02.11
Jul 10 06.17	Jul 17 15.11	Jul 24 07:37	Jul 31 18.16
Aug 8 18.50	Aug 15 20.20	Aug 22 17.02	Aug 30 12.13
Sep 7 05.52	Sep 14 01.39	Sep 21 04.55	Sep 29 06.57
Oct 6 16.05	Oct 13 08.25	Oct 20 19.57	Oct 29 01.05
Nov 5 02.15	Nov 11 17.46	Nov 19 13.58	Nov 27 17.28
Dec 4 12.43	Dec 11 06.36	Dec 19 09.36	Dec 27 07.24

Phases of the Moon – 2022

New Moon ●	First Quarter ◑	Full Moon ○	Last Quarter ◐
Jan 02 23.33	Jan 09 23.11	Jan 18 04.49	Jan 25 18.41
Feb 1 10.46	Feb 8 18.50	Feb 16 21.57	Feb 24 03.32
Mar 2 22.35	Mar 10 15.45	Mar 18 12.17	Mar 25 10.37
Apr 1 11.24	Apr 9 11.47	Apr 16 23.55	Apr 23 16.56
May 1 01.28	May 9 05.21	May 16 09.14	May 22 23.43
May 30 16.30	Jun 7 19.48	Jun 14 16.52	Jun 21 08.11
Jun 29 07.52	Jul 7 07.14	July 13 23.37	Jul 20 19.18
Jul 28 22.55	Aug 5 16.06	Aug 12 06.36	Aug 19 09.36
Aug 27 13.17	Sep 3 23.08	Sep 10 14.59	Sep 18 02.52
Sep 26 02.54	Oct 3 05.14	Oct 10 01.55	Oct 17 22.15
Oct 25 15.49	Nov 1 11.37	Nov 8 16.02	Nov 16 18.27
Nov 23 03.57	Nov 30 19.36	Dec 8 09.08	Dec 16 13.56
Dec 23 15.17	Dec 30 06.21		

Phases of the Moon – 2023			
New Moon ●	**First Quarter ◑**	**Full Moon ○**	**Last Quarter ◐**
		Jan 7 04.08	Jan 15 07.10
Jan 22 01.53	Jan 28 20.19	Feb 5 23.29	Feb 13 21.01
Feb 20 12.06	Feb 27 13.06	Mar 7 17.40	Mar 15 07.08
Mar 21 22.23	Mar 29 07.32	Apr 6 09.35	Apr 13 14.11
Apr 20 09.12	Apr 28 02.20	May 5 22.34	May 12 19.28
May 19 20.53	May 27 20.22	Jun 4 08.42	Jun 11 00.31
Jun 18 09.37	Jun 26 12.50	Jul 3 16.39	Jul 10 06.48
Jul 17 23.32	Jul 26 03.07	Aug 1 23.31	Aug 8 15.28
Aug 16 14.38	Aug 24 14.57	Aug 31 06.35	Sep 7 03.21
Sep 15 06.40	Sep 23 00.32	Sep 29 14.57	Oct 6 18.48
Oct 14 22.55	Oct 22 08.29	Oct 29 01.24	Nov 5 13.37
Nov 13 14.27	Nov 20 15.50	Nov 27 14.16	Dec 5 10.49
Dec 13 04.32	Dec 19 23.39	Dec 27 05.33	

Phases of the Moon – 2024			
New Moon ●	**First Quarter ◑**	**Full Moon ○**	**Last Quarter ◐**
			Jan 4 08.30
Jan 11 16.57	Jan 18 08.53	Jan 25 22.54	Feb 3 04.18
Feb 10 03.59	Feb 16 20.01	Feb 24 17.30	Mar 3 20.24
Mar 10 14.00	Mar 17 09.11	Mar 25 12.00	Apr 2 08.15
Apr 8 23.21	Apr 16 00.13	Apr 24 04.49	May 1 16.27
May 8 08.22	May 15 16.48	May 23 18.53	May 30 22.13
Jun 6 17.38	Jun 14 10.18	Jun 22 06.08	Jun 29 02.53
Jul 6 03.57	Jul 14 03.49	Jul 21 15.17	Jul 28 07.51
Aug 4 16.13	Aug 12 20.19	Aug 19 23.26	Aug 26 14.26
Sep 3 06.55	Sep 11 11.06	Sep 18 07.34	Sep 24 23.50
Oct 2 23.49	Oct 10 23.55	Oct 17 16.26	Oct 24 13.03
Nov 1 17.47	Nov 9 10.56	Nov 16 02.29	Nov 23 06.28
Dec 1 11.21	Dec 8 20.27	Dec 15 14.02	Dec 23 03.18
Dec 31 03.27			

Phases of the Moon – 2025			
New Moon ●	**First Quarter ◐**	**Full Moon ○**	**Last Quarter ◑**
	Jan 7 04.56	Jan 14 03.27	Jan 22 01.31
Jan 29 17.36	Feb 5 13.02	Feb 12 18.53	Feb 20 22.33
Feb 28 05.45	Mar 6 21.32	Mar 14 11.55	Mar 22 16.30
Mar 29 15.58	Apr 5 07.15	Apr 13 05.22	Apr 21 06.36
Apr 28 00.31	May 4 18.52	May 12 21.56	May 20 16.59
May 27 08.02	Jun 3 08.41	Jun 11 12.44	Jun 19 00.19
Jun 25 15.31	Jul 3 00.30	Jul 11 01.37	Jul 18 05.38
Jul 25 00.11	Aug 1 17.41	Aug 9 12.55	Aug 16 10.12
Aug 23 11.06	Aug 31 11.25	Sep 7 23.09	Sep 14 15.33
Sep 22 00.54	Sep 30 04.54	Oct 7 08.47	Oct 13 23.13
Oct 21 17.25	Oct 29 21.21	Nov 5 18.19	Nov 12 10.28
Nov 20 11.47	Nov 28 11.59	Dec 5 04.14	Dec 12 01.52
Dec 20 06.43	Dec 28 00.10		

Phases of the Moon – 2026			
New Moon ●	**First Quarter ◐**	**Full Moon ○**	**Last Quarter ◑**
		Jan 3 15.03	Jan 10 20.48
Jan 19 00.52	Jan 26 09.47	Feb 2 03.09	Feb 9 17.43
Feb 17 17.01	Feb 24 17.28	Mar 3 16.38	Mar 11 14.39
Mar 19 06.23	Mar 26 00.18	Apr 2 07.12	Apr 10 09.52
Apr 17 16.52	Apr 24 07.32	May 1 22.23	May 10 02.10
May 17 01.01	May 23 16.11	May 31 13.45	Jun 8 15.00
Jun 15 07.54	Jun 22 02.55	Jun 30 04.57	Jul 8 00.29
Jul 14 14.43	Jul 21 16.06	Jul 29 19.36	Aug 6 07.21
Aug 12 22.37	Aug 20 07.46	Aug 28 09.18	Sep 4 12.51
Sep 11 08.27	Sep 19 01.44	Sep 26 21.49	Oct 3 18.25
Oct 10 20.50	Oct 18 21.13	Oct 26 09.12	Nov 2 01.28
Nov 9 12.02	Nov 17 16.48	Nov 24 19.53	Dec 1 11.09
Dec 9 05.52	Dec 17 10.43	Dec 24 06.28	Dec 30 23.59

Phases of the Moon – 2027			
New Moon ●	**First Quarter ◐**	**Full Moon ○**	**Last Quarter ◑**
Jan 8 01.24	Jan 16 01.34	Jan 22 17.17	Jan 29 15.55
Feb 6 20.56	Feb 14 12.58	Feb 21 04.23	Feb 28 10.16
Mar 8 14.29	Mar 15 21.25	Mar 22 15.44	Mar 30 05.54
Apr 7 04.51	Apr 14 03.57	Apr 21 03.27	Apr 29 01.18
May 6 15.58	May 13 09.44	May 20 15.59	May 28 18.58
Jun 5 00.40	Jun 11 15.56	Jun 19 05.44	Jun 27 09.54
Jul 4 08.02	Jul 10 23.39	Jul 18 20.45	Jul 26 21.55
Aug 2 10.05	Aug 9 09.54	Aug 17 12.29	Aug 25 07.27
Aug 31 22.41	Sep 7 23.31	Sep 16 04.04	Sep 23 15.20
Sep 30 07.36	Oct 7 16.47	Oct 15 18.47	Oct 22 22.29
Oct 29 18.36	Nov 6 13.00	Nov 14 08.26	Nov 21 05.48
Nov 28 08.24	Dec 6 10.22	Dec 13 21.09	Dec 20 14.11
Dec 28 01.12			

Phases of the Moon – 2028			
New Moon ●	**First Quarter ◐**	**Full Moon ○**	**Last Quarter ◑**
	Jan 5 06.40	Jan 12 09.03	Jan 19 00.26
Jan 26 20.12	Feb 4 00.10	Feb 10 20.04	Feb 17 13.08
Feb 25 15.37	Mar 4 14.02	Mar 11 06.06	Mar 18 04.23
Mar 26 09.31	Apr 3 00.15	Apr 9 15.27	Apr 16 21.37
Apr 25 00.47	May 2 07.26	May 9 00.49	May 16 15.43
May 24 13.16	May 31 12.37	Jun 7 11.09	Jun 15 09.27
Jun 22 23.27	Jun 29 17.10	Jul 6 23.11	Jul 15 01.57
Jul 22 08.02	Jul 28 22.40	Aug 5 13.10	Aug 13 16.45
Aug 20 15.44	Aug 27 06.36	Sep 4 04.48	Sep 12 05.46
Sep 18 23.24	Sep 25 18.10	Oct 3 21.25	Oct 11 16.57
Oct 18 07.57	Oct 25 09.53	Nov 2 14.17	Nov 10 02.26
Nov 16 18.18	Nov 24 05.15	Dec 2 06.40	Dec 9 10.39
Dec 16 07.06	Dec 24 02.45	Dec 31 21.48	

Phases of the Moon – 2029

New Moon ●	First Quarter ◐	Full Moon ○	Last Quarter ◑
			Jan 7 18.26
Jan 14 22.24	Jan 23 00.23	Jan 30 11.03	Feb 6 02.52
Feb 13 15.31	Feb 21 20.10	Feb 28 22.10	Mar 7 12.52
Mar 15 09.19	Mar 23 12.33	Mar 30 07.26	Apr 6 00.51
Apr 14 01.40	Apr 22 00.50	Apr 28 15.37	May 5 14.48
May 13 18.42	May 21 09.16	May 27 23.37	Jun 4 06.19
Jun 12 08.51	Jun 19 14.54	Jun 26 08.22	Jul 3 22.58
Jul 11 20.51	Jul 18 19.14	Jul 25 18.36	Aug 2 16.15
Aug 10 06.56	Aug 16 23.55	Aug 24 06.51	Sep 1 09.33
Sep 8 15.44	Sep 15 06.29	Sep 22 21.29	Oct 1 01.57
Oct 8 00.14	Oct 14 16.09	Oct 22 14.28	Oct 30 16.32
Nov 6 09.24	Nov 13 05.35	Nov 21 09.03	Nov 29 04.48
Dec 5 19.52	Dec 12 22.49	Dec 21 03.46	Dec 28 14.49

Phases of the Moon – 2030

New Moon ●	First Quarter ◐	Full Moon ○	Last Quarter ◑
Jan 4 07.49	Jan 11 19.06	Jan 19 20.54	Jan 26 23.14
Feb 2 21.07	Feb 10 16.49	Feb 18 11.20	Feb 25 06.58
Mar 4 11.35	Mar 12 13.48	Mar 19 22.56	Mar 26 14.51
Apr 3 03.02	Apr 11 07.57	Apr 18 08.20	Apr 24 23.39
May 2 19.12	May 10 22.11	May 17 16.19	May 24 09.57
Jun 1 11.21	Jun 9 08.36	Jun 15 23.41	Jun 22 22.19
Jul 1 02.34	Jul 8 16.02	Jul 15 07.12	Jul 22 13.07
Jul 30 16.11	Aug 6 21.43	Aug 13 15.44	Aug 21 06.15
Aug 29 04.07	Sep 5 02.55	Sep 12 02.18	Sep 20 00.56
Sep 27 14.55	Oct 4 08.56	Oct 11 15.47	Oct 19 19.50
Oct 27 01.17	Nov 2 16.56	Nov 10 08.30	Nov 18 13.32
Nov 25 11.46	Dec 2 03.57	Dec 10 03.40	Dec 18 05.01
Dec 24 22.32	Dec 31 18.36		

Source: National Aeronautics and Space Administration, NASA Eclipse Web Site, "Phases of the Moon." Available online at http://eclipse.gsfc.nasa.gov/phase/phase2001gmt.html.

APPENDIX 5

Overview of the World's Major Religions

This section provides basic information about the world's major religions, including when and where they originated; founder(s); theological orientation; major sacred texts; denominations and sects; estimated number of adherents around the world; and a listing of the main holidays in chronological order by the religion's calendar.

Baha'i

When originated: 1844

Where originated: Iran

Founder(s): Mírzá. Husayn-'Ali Núrí (Baha'u'llah); Siyyid 'Alí-Muhammad (the Bab)

Basic orientation: Monotheistic

Major sacred texts: Kitáb-i-Aqdas (The Most Holy Book),Kitáb-i-Ôqán (Book of Certitude), and others written byMírzá Husayn-'Ali Núrí (Baha'u'llah)

Major denominations and sects: none

Approx. number of adherents: 7 million worldwide

Major holidays in order by the religion's calendar:
Mar 21 - Festival of Naw-Rúz
Apr 21 - May 2 - Festival of Ridván
May 23 - Declaration of the Bab
May 29 - Ascension of Baha'u'llah
Jun, second Sun - Race Unity Day
Jul 9 - Martyrdom of the Bab
Oct 20 - Birth of the Bab
Nov 12 - Birth of Baha'u'llah
Nov 26 - Day of the Covenant
Nov 28 - Ascension of 'Abdu'l-Bahá
Jan, third Sun - Ayyám-i-Há
Mar 2-20 - Nineteenth-Month Fast

Buddhism

When originated: Sixth century B.C.E.

Where originated: India

Founder(s): Siddhartha Gautama, the Buddha

Basic orientation: Other: achieving enlightenment by accepting the four noble truths-1. There is suffering; 2. Suffering results from desire; 3. The way to end suffering is to end desire; 4. The Eightfold Path shows the way to end suffering-and the Eightfold Path: 1. Right view or right understanding; 2. Right thoughts and aspirations; 3. Right speech; 4. Right conduct and action; 5. Right way of life; 6. Right effort; 7. Right mindfulness; 8. Right contemplation.

Major sacred texts: The Sutras

Major denominations and sects: Theraveda, Mahayana, Tibetan, Chinese, Japanese, Zen

Approx. number of adherents: 500 million worldwide

Major holidays in order by the religion's calendar:
April 8 or full moon day of Vaisakha - Vesak (birthday of the Buddha)
July 6 - Birthday of the Dalai Lama
July-September - Waso
July-August - Ullambana (Hungry Ghosts Festival)

Christianity - Orthodox

When originated: 30s C.E.

Where originated: Palestine

Founder(s): Jesus of Nazareth

Basic orientation: Monotheistic

Major sacred texts: The Bible

Major denominations and sects: Adherents fall under the Patriarchs of Constantinople, Alexandria, Antioch, and Jerusalem; additional congregations include Russia, Serbia, Romania, Bulgaria, Georgia, Cyprus, Greece, Poland, Albania, Armenia, Slovakia, the Czech Republic, and Ukraine

Approx. number of adherents: 270 million worldwide

Major holidays in order by the religion's calendar:
September 8 - Nativity of the Virgin Mary
September 14 - Elevation of the Life-giving Cross
November 21 - Presentation of the Virgin Mary in the Temple
December 25 or January 7 - Christmas
January 6 or January 19 - Epiphany
February 2 - Presentation of Christ in the Temple
March 25 - The Annunciation
April or May - Palm Sunday
April or May - Easter
40 days after Easter - The Ascension
50 days after Easter - Pentecost
August 6 - The Transfiguration
August 15 - The Repose, or Dormition, of the Virgin Mary

Christianity - Western

When originated: 30s C.E.

Where originated: Palestine

Founder(s): Jesus of Nazareth

Basic orientation: Monotheistic

Major sacred texts: The Bible

Major denominations and sects: Catholicism, Protestantism, Anglican, Episcopalian

Approx. number of adherents: 2 billion worldwide

Major holidays in order by the religion's calendar:
December 25 - Christmas
January 1 - Feast of the Circumcision/Solemnity of Mary
January 6 - Epiphany
Sunday after Epiphany - Feast of the Holy Family
February 2 - Presentation of Jesus in the Temple
February (40 days before Easter) - Ash Wednesday
March 25 - The Annunciation
March or April - Palm Sunday
March or April - Maundy or Holy Thursday
March or April - Good Friday
March or April - Easter
40 days after Easter - The Ascension
50 days after Easter - Pentecost
1st Sunday after Pentecost - Trinity Sunday
Thursday after Trinity Sunday - Corpus Christi
May or July - Feast of the Visitation
August 6 - Feast of the Transfiguration
August 15 - The Assumption of the Blessed Virgin
September 8 - Feast of the Nativity of the Blessed Virgin
November 1 - All Saints' Day
November 2 All Souls' Day
November 21 - Feast of the Presentation of the Virgin Mary

Confucianism

When originated: Fifth century B.C.E.

Where originated: China

Founder(s): Confucius

Basic orientation: Other: philosophical, ethical system

Major sacred texts: The "Four Books," *Lun-yu* (The Analects), *Ta-hsueh* (The Great Learning), *Chung Yung* (The Doctrine of the Mean), *Meng-tzu* (The Book of Mencius), and the Five Classics: *Shu Ching* (The Book of History), *Shih Ching* (The Book of Odes), *I Ching* (The Book of Changes), *Ch-un Ch'ui* (Spring and Autumn Annals), and *Li Chi* (The Book of Rites)

Major denominations and sects: School of Thought, School of the Mind, School of Practical Learning

Approx. number of adherents: 6 million worldwide, most in Asia

Major holidays in order by the religion's calendar:
First Sunday in May - Chongmyo Taeje (Royal Shrine Rite)
September 28 - Confucius's Birthday (Teacher's Day)
During second and eighth Chinese lunar months - Sokjon-Taeje Memorial Rites

Hinduism

When originated: 4000 B.C.E.

Where originated: Indus Valley of the Indian subcontinent

Founder(s): none

Basic orientation: Polytheistic - pantheon includes more than 30 million deities

Major sacred texts: The Vedas and the Epics (*Ramayana, Mahabharata,* and *Bhagavad Gita*)

Major denominations and sects: Vaishnavas, Saivites, Rama cults, and Krishna cults

Approx. number of adherents: 1 billion worldwide

Major holidays in order by the religion's calendar: There are hundreds of holidays, feasts, and fasts observed by the world's Hindus *see index for a listing of those included in this volume*; this list includes only a few of the most widely celebrated.

Vaisakha 1 (April-May) - Vaisakh (Hindu New Year)
2nd day of waxing half of Asadha (June-July) - Rath Yatra full moon day of Sravana (July-August) - Raksha Bandhan
7-10 days during waxing half of Bhadrapada (August-September) - Ganesh Chaturthi
New moon day of Bhadrapada (August-September) - Krishna's Birthday/Janmashtami waxing half of Asvina (September-October) - Durga Purga/ Dussehra/ Navaratri
15th day of waning half of Kartika (October-November) - Dewali
14th day of waxing half of Phalguna (February-March) - Holi
14th day of waning half of Phalguna (February-March) - Shivaratri
9th day of waxing half of Caitra (March-April) - Ramanavami

Islam

When originated: Seventh century C.E.

Where originated: Arabia

Founder(s): Muhammad

Basic orientation: Monotheistic

Major sacred texts: Koran (or Quran)

Major denominations and sects: Sunni, Shia (or Shi'ite), Sufi, Ibadis (or Kharijites)

Approx. number of adherents: 1.5 billion worldwide

Major holidays in order by the religion's calendar:
Muharram 1 - Muharram (New Year)
Muharram 10 - Ashura
Rabi al-Awwal 12 - Mawlid al-Nabi (birthday of Muhammad)
Rajab 27 - Laylat al-Miraj
Ramadan 1-30 - Fast of Ramadan
Ramadan 27 - Laylat al-Qadr
Shawwal 1-3 - Id al-Fitr
Dhu al-Hijjah 8-13 - Hajj (Pilgrimage to Mecca)
Dhu al-Hijjah 10-12 Id al-Adha

Jainism

When originated: Sixth century B.C.E.

Where originated: India

Founder(s): Vardhamana Mahavira

Basic orientation: Polytheistic

Major sacred texts: The angas, the Kalpa Sutra

Major denominations and sects: Digambaras, Svetambaras, Sthanakvasis and Terapanthi

Approx. number of adherents: 5 million worldwide, most in India

Major holidays in order by the religion's calendar:
15th day of waning half of Kartika (October-November) - Dewali
10th day of waning half of Pausa (December-January) - Birthday of Parshva
13th day of waxing half of Caitra (March-April) - Maha vir Jayanti (Birthday of Mahavira)
month of Asadha (June-July) to month of Bhadra pada (August-September) - Caturmas
during waning half of Bhadrapada (August-September) - Paryushana

Judaism

When originated: 1800 B.C.E.

Where originated: Palestine

Founder(s): Abraham

Basic orientation: Monotheistic

Major sacred texts: The Torah, Mishnah, and Talmud

Major denominations and sects: Orthodox, Reform (or Progressive), Conservative, Hasidism, Zionism, Reconstructionist

Approx. number of adherents: 15 million worldwide

Major holidays in order by the religion's calendar:
Nisan 14 - Fast of the First-born
Nisan 15-21 (or 22) - Passover
Nisan 16 - Sivan 5 - Counting of the Omer
Nisan 27 - Yom Hashoah (Holocaust Day)
Iyyar 18 - Lag ba-Omer
Sivan 6 - Shavuot
Tammuz 17 - Fast of the Seventeenth of Tammuz
Tammuz 17 - Av 9 - Three Weeks of Mourning
Av 9 - Tisha be-Av
Tishri 1-2 - Rosh Hashanah (New Year)
Tishri 10 - Yom Kippur
Tishri 15-21 - Sukkot (Fast of Tabernacles)
Tishri 22 - Shemini Atzeret
Tishri 23 - Simhat Torah
Kislev 25 to Tevet 2 - Hanukkah
Tevet 10 - Asarah be-Tevet
Shevat 15 - Tu Bishvat
Adar 13 - Ta-anit Esther (Fast of Esther)
Adar 14 - Purim

Shinto

When originated: Sixth century C.E.

Where originated: Japan

Founder(s): none

Basic orientation: Polytheistic

Major sacred texts: *Kojiki, Nihongi,* and *Engishiki*

Major denominations and sects: Shrine Shinto, Sect Shinto, Confucian Shinto

Approx. number of adherents: 3 million worldwide, most in Japan

Representative holidays included in this volume:
January or February - Hadaka Matsuri
June 17 - Saigusa Matsuri
September 17 - Chinkashiki
October 19 - Bettara-Ichi
Late October to early November - Izumo-taisha Jinzaisai
November - Tori-no-ichi

Sikhism

When originated: Fifteenth century C.E.

Where originated: India

Founder(s): Guru Nanak

Basic orientation: Monotheistic

Major sacred texts: Guru Granth Sahib

Major denominations and sects: Nirankari, Namdhari

Approx. number of adherents: 24 million worldwide, most in India

Major holidays in order by the religion's calendar:
Chait 1 (March-April) - Scriptural New Year
Chait 1 (March-April) - Hola Mohalla
Basakh 1 (April-May) - Baisakhi (Birth of the Khalsa)
Basakh 1 (April-May) - Guru Parab (Guru Nanak's Day)
Har 2 (June-July) - Martyrdom of Guru Arjun
Sawan 8 (July-August) - Birthday of Guru Har Krishan
Bhadro 17 (August-September) - Installation of the Guru Granth Sahib
Asun 25 (September-October) - Birthday of Guru Ram Das
Magar 11 (November-December) - Martyrdom of Guru Teg Bahadur
Poh 23 (December-January) - Guru Gobind Singh's Birthday
During month of Magh (January-February) - Maghi

Taoism

When originated: Fifth century B.C.E.

Where originated: China

Founder(s): Lao Tzu

Basic orientation: Polytheistic

Major sacred texts: *Tao-tsang*

Major denominations and sects: Heavenly Masters, Perfect Truth

Approx. number of adherents: 8 million worldwide, most in Asia

Major holidays in order by the religion's calendar:
23rd day of third Chinese month (March-April) - Matsu Festival
8th day of fourth Chinese month (April-May) - Tam Kung Festival

8th-9th days of fourth Chinese month (April-May) - Birth day of the Third Prince

13th day of sixth Chinese month (June-July) - Birthday of Lu Pan

Full moon day of seventh Chinese month (July-August) - Festival of Hungry Ghosts

First 9 days of ninth Chinese month (September-October) Festival of the Nine Imperial Gods

During ninth Chinese month (September-October) - Monkey God Festival

During 12th Chinese month (December-January) - Ta Chiu

Zoroastrianism

When originated: Before 1500 B.C.E.

Where originated: Iran

Founder(s): Zoroastr (Zarathustra)

Basic orientation: Monotheistic

Major sacred texts: The Avesta

Major denominations and sects: None, though adherents follow one of three calendars: Fasli, Shahanshahi, and Qadimi. Each calendar has the same named months, but their Gregorian equivalents vary.

Approx. number of adherents: 180,000 worldwide

Major holidays in order by the religion's calendar:

Frawardin 1 - Nawruz (New Year)

Frawardin 6 - Khordad Sal

Frawardin 19 - Feast of Frawardin

Ardwahist 3 - Feast of Ardwahist

Ardwahist 11-15 - Maidyozarem

Hordad 6 - Feast of Hordad

Tir 11-15 - Maidyoshahem

Tir 13 - Tiragan

Amurdad 7 - Feast of Amurdad

Shahrewar 4 - Feast of Shahrewar

Shahrewar 26-30 - Paitishahem

Mihr 1 - Feast of Mithra

Mihr 16 - Mihragan

Mihr 26-30 - Ayathrem

Aban 10 - Aban Parab

Adar 9 - Adar Parab

Dae 1, 8, 15, and 23 - Feasts of Dae

Dae 11 - Zarthastno Diso

Dae 16-20 - Maidyarem

Vohuman 2 - Feast of Vohuman

Spendarmad 5 - Feast of Spendarmad

Spendarmad 26-30 - Farvardegan Days

Facts about the U.S. States and Territories

This section lists for each of the 50 states: the date and order of admission to the Union; information about current or past admission day observances, if applicable; state nicknames, mottoes, animals, flowers, and other symbols; and websites and offices to contact for further information. This last item includes governor's offices, secretaries of state, and state libraries. For territories, listed are year of association with the U.S.; nicknames, mottoes, flowers, and other symbols; and websites and offices to contact.

Alabama

Twenty-second state; admitted on December 14, 1819 (seceded from the Union on January 11, 1861, and was readmitted on June 25, 1868)

Alabama does not observe the anniversary of its admission day, but did hold festivities in 1969 in honor of the 150th, or sesquicentennial, anniversary of statehood. There were historical pageants, a boat parade, formal balls, music, fireworks, and the issuance of a commemorative stamp. The state was named for a southern Indian tribe, possibly a subdivision of the Chickasaws.

State capital: Montgomery

Nicknames: The Heart of Dixie; The Yellowhammer State; The Cotton State

State motto: *Audemus jura nostra defendere* (Latin "We dare maintain our rights")

State agricultural museum: Dothan Landmarks Park

State amphibian: Red Hills Salamander (*Phaeognathus hubrichti Highton*)

State barbecue championship: Demopolis Christmas on the River Barbecue Cook-Off

State bible: The Bible

State bird: Yellowhammer or Common Flicker (*Colaptes auratus*)

State butterfly and mascot: Easter tiger swallowtail

State championship horse show: Alabama State Championship Horse Show

State creed: Alabama's Creed

State folk dance: Square dance

State fish: saltwater: Fighting tarpon (*Tarpon atlanticus*); **freshwater**: Largemouth bass (*Micropterus salmoides*)

State flower: Camellia (*Camellia japonica L.*); **wildflower**: Oak-leaf Hydrangea (*Hydrangea quercifolia Bartr*)

State fossil: Basilosaurus cetoides

State fruit: Blackberry

State game bird: Wild turkey

State gemstone: Star blue quartz

State historic theatre: Alabama Theatre for the Performing Arts

State horse: Racking horse

State horseshoe tournament: Stockton Fall Horseshoe Tournament

State insect: Monarch butterfly (*Danaus plexipuss*)

State mammal: Black bear

State mineral: Hematite (red iron ore)

State nut: Pecan

State outdoor drama: *The Miracle Worker*

State outdoor musical drama: *The Incident at Looney's Tavern*

State quilt: Pine Burr Quilt

State Renaissance faire: Florence Renaissance faire

State reptile: Red-bellied turtle (*Pseudemys alabamensis*)

State rock: Marble

State shell: Johnstone's Junonia (*Scaphella junonia johnstoneae*)

State soil: Bama soil series

State song: "Alabama"

State spirit: Conecuh Ridge Alabama Fine Whiskey

State stone: Marble

State tree: Southern Longleaf Pine (*Pinus palustris Miller*)

State tree fruit: Peach

More about state symbols at:
www.archives.state.al.us/kids_emblems/index.html

STATE OFFICES:
State website:
www.alabama.gov

Office of the Governor
State Capitol
600 Dexter Ave.
Montgomery, AL 36130
334-242-7100
fax: 334-353-0004
www.governor.state.al.us

Secretary of State
P.O. Box 5616
Montgomery, AL 36103
334-242-7200
fax: 334-242-4993
www.sos.state.al.us

Alabama Public Library Service
6030 Monticello Dr.
Montgomery, AL 36130
334-213-3900
fax: 334-213-3993
webmini.apls.state.al.us/apls_web/apls/apls

Archives & History Dept
624 Washington Ave
Montgomery, AL 30130
334-242-4435
www.archives.state.al.us

Alaska

Forty-ninth state; admitted on January 3, 1959

SEE ALASKA DAY

State capital: Juneau
Nickname: The Last Frontier
State motto: North to the Future
State bird: Willow ptarmigan (*Lagopus lagopus*)
State fish: Chinook (king) salmon (*Oncorhynchus tshawytscha*)
State flower: Forget-me-not (*Myosotis sylvatica* or *M. scorpioides*)
State fossil: Woolly mammoth (*Mammuthus primigenius*)
State gem: Jade
State insect: Four spot skimmer dragonfly
State land mammal: Moose
State marine mammal: Bowhead whale (*Balaena mysticetus*)
State mineral: Gold
State song: "Alaska's Flag"
State sport: Dogteam racing (mushing)
State tree: Sitka spruce (*Picea sitchensis*)

More about state symbols at:
www.alaska.gov/kids/student.htm

STATE OFFICES:
State website:
www.alaska.gov

Office of the Governor
P.O. Box 110011
Juneau, AK 99811
907-465-3500
fax: 907-465-3532
www.gov.state.ak.us

Alaska State Library
333 Willoughby Ave.

8th Fl.
Juneau, AK 99811
907-465-2920
fax: 907-465-2151
www.library.alaska.gov

Arizona

Forty-eighth state; admitted on February 14, 1912

State capital: Phoenix
Nickname: Grand Canyon State
State motto: *Ditat Deus* (Latin "God Enriches")
State amphibian: Arizona tree frog (*Hyla eximia*)
State bird: Cactus wren (*Campylorhynchus brunneicapillus*)
State butterfly: Two-tailed swallowtail
State colors: Federal blue and old gold
State fish: Apache trout (*Salmo apache*)
State flower: Blossom of the saguaro cactus (*Carnegiea gigantea*)
State fossil: Petrified wood
State gem: Turquoise
State mammal: Ringtail (*Bassariscus astutus*)
State neckwear: Bola tie
State reptile: Arizona ridge-nosed rattlesnake (*Crotalus willardi*)
State songs: "Arizona March Song" and "Arizona"
State tree: Palo Verde (*Cercidium floridum*)

More about state symbols at:
www.azgovernor.gov/governor/arizona-facts
www.azlibrary.gov/state-symbols

STATE OFFICES:
State website:
www.az.gov

Office of the Governor
1700 W. Washington St.
Phoenix, AZ 85007
602-542-4331
www.azgovernor.gov

Secretary of State
1700 W. Washington St.
7th Fl.
Phoenix, AZ 85007
602-542-4285
www.azsos.gov

Arizona State Library
1700 W. Washington St.
Ste. 300
Phoenix, AZ 85007
602-926-3870
fax: 602-256-7984
www.azlibrary.gov

Arkansas

Twenty-fifth state; admitted on June 15, 1836 (seceded from the Union on May 6, 1861, and was readmitted in June 1868)

The state was named for Ohio Valley Indians' name for the Quapaw Indians who lived in northern Arkansas.

State capital: Little Rock
Nickname: The Natural State
State motto: *Regnat populus* (Latin "The people rule")
State beverage: Milk
State bird: Mockingbird (*Mimus polyglottos*)
State flower: Apple blossom (*Malus sylvestris*)
State folk dance: Square dance
State fruit and vegetable: South Arkansas vine-ripe pink tomato
State gem: Diamond
State insect: Honeybee (*Apis mellifera*)
State mammal: White-tail deer
State mineral: Quartz crystal
State musical instrument: Fiddle
State rock: Bauxite
State songs: "Arkansas," "Arkansas (You Run Deep in Me)," "Oh Arkansas," and "The Arkansas Traveler"
State tree: Pine (*Pinus palustris*)

More about state symbols at:
www.sos.arkansas.gov/educational/students/Documents/
Arkansas_State_Symbols.pdf

STATE OFFICES:
State website:
www.arkansas.gov

Office of the Governor
State Capitol Bldg.
500 Woodlane St.
Ste. 250
Little Rock, AR 72201
501-682-2345
www.governor.arkansas.gov

Secretary of State
State Capitol Bldg.
500 Woodlane Ave.
Ste. 256
Little Rock, AR 72201
501-682-1010
www.sos.arkansas.gov

Arkansas State Library
900 W. Capitol
Ste. 100
Little Rock, AR 72201
501-682-2053
www.library.arkansas.gov

California

Thirty-first state; admitted on September 9, 1850

City and state offices, banks, and public schools close in California to mark this legal holiday on the first Monday in September. Two organizations—the Native Sons of the Golden West and the Native Daughters of the Golden West—have sponsored annual programs in different locations throughout the state each year. In addition, many communities hold festivities of their own, including parades, music, food, and dancing.

State capital: Sacramento
Nickname: The Golden State
State motto: *Eureka* (Greek "I Have Found It")
State animal: California grizzly bear (*Ursus (arctos) horribilis*)
State bird: California valley quail (*Callipepla californica*)
State colors: Yale blue and golden yellow
State dance: West Coast swing dance
State fife and drum band: The California Consolidated Drum Band
State fish: South Fork golden trout (*Salmo aguabonita*)
State folk dance: Square dance
State fossil: California saber-toothed cat (*Smilodon californicus*)
State flower: California poppy (*Eschscholtzia californica*)
State gemstone: Benitoite
State gold rush ghost town: Bodie
State grass: Purple needlegrass (*Nassella pulchra*)
State insect: California dog-face butterfly (flying pansy)
State marine fish: Garibaldi
State marine mammal: California gray whale (*Eschrichtius robustus*)
State military museum: The California State Military Museum and Resource Center
State mineral: Native gold
State prehistoric artifact: Chipped stone bear
State reptile: California desert tortoise (*Gopherus agassizii*)
State rock: Serpentine
State silver rush ghost town: Calico
State soil: San Joaquin soil
State song: "I Love You, California"
State tall ship: Californian
State tartan: California State Tartan
State theater: Pasadena Playhouse
State trees: Two species of California redwoods (*Sequoia sempervirens* and *Sequoia gigantea*)

More about state symbols at:
www.library.ca.gov/history/symbols.html

More about the state at:
www.ca.gov/About/Facts.html

CONTACT:
Native Daughters of the Golden West
543 Baker St.
San Francisco, CA 94117
800-994-6349
415-563-9091
fax: 415-563-5230
www.ndgw.org

Native Sons of the Golden West
414 Mason St.
Ste. 300
San Francisco, CA 94102
800-337-1875
415-392-1223
www.nsgwca.com

STATE OFFICES:
State website:
www.ca.gov

Office of the Governor
State Capitol
1st Fl.
Ste. 1173
Sacramento, CA 95814
916-445-2841
fax: 916-558-3160
www.gov.ca.gov

Secretary of State
1500 11th St.
Sacramento, CA 95814
916-653-6814
www.ss.ca.gov

California State Library
P.O. Box 942837
Sacramento, CA 94237
916-654-0261
fax: 916-323-9768
www.library.ca.gov

Colorado

Thirty-eighth state; admitted on August 1, 1876

State capital: Denver
Nickname: Centennial State
State motto: *Nil sine Numine* (Latin "Nothing without the Diety")
State animal: Rocky Mountain bighorn sheep (*Ovis canadensis)*
State bird: Lark bunting (*Calamospiza melanocoryus Stejneger*)
State fish: Greenback cutthroat trout (*Oncorhynchus clarki somias)*
State flower: Columbine (*Aguilegia caerules*)
State folk dance: Square dance
State fossil: Stegosaurus
State gem: Aquamarine
State grass: Blue Grama

State insect: Colorado Hairstreak Butterfly (*Hypaurotis cysalus)*
State mineral: Rhodochrosite
State rock: Yule marble
State song: "Where the Columbines Grow" and "Rocky Mountain High"
State tartan: Colorado State Tartan
State tree: Colorado blue spruce (*Picea pungens*)

More about state symbols at:
www.colorado.gov/pacific/archives/symbols-emblems

STATE OFFICES:
State website:
www.colorado.gov

Office of the Governor
136 State Capitol Bldg.
Denver, CO 80203
303-866-2471
www.colorado.gov

Secretary of State
1700 Broadway
Ste. 200
Denver, CO 80290
303-894-2200
fax: 303-894-4860
www.sos.state.co.us

Colorado State Library
201 E. Colfax Ave.
Rm. 309
Denver, CO 80203
303-866-6900
fax: 303-866-6940
www.cde.state.co.us

Connecticut

Fifth state; adopted the U.S. Constitution on January 9, 1788

State capital: Hartford
Nickname: The Constitution State
State motto: *Qui Transtulit Sustinet* (Latin "He Who Transplanted Still Sustains")
State aircraft: Corsair F4U
State animal: Sperm whale (*Physeter macrocephalus*)
State bird: American robin (*Turdus migratorius*)
State cantata: "The Nutmeg"
State composer: Charles Edward Ives (1874-1954)
State fish: American shad
State flagship: *Schooner Amistad*
State flower: Mountain laurel (*Kalmia latifolia*)
State folk dance: Square dance
State fossil: *Eubrontes giganteus*
State hero: Nathan Hale (1755-1776)
State heroine: Prudence Crandall (1803-1890)

State insect: European (praying) mantis (*Mantis religiosa*)

State mineral: Garnet

State shellfish: Eastern oyster (*Crassostrea virginica*)

State ship: *USS Nautilus* (first nuclear-powered submarine)

State song: "Yankee Doodle"

State tartan: Connecticut State Tartan

State tree: Charter oak or white oak (*Quercus alba*)

More about state symbols at:
www.kids.ct.gov

STATE OFFICES:
State website:
www.ct.gov

Office of the Governor
State Capitol
210 Capitol Ave.
Hartford, CT 06106
800-406-1527
860-566-4840
fax: 860-524-7395
www.governor.ct.gov

Secretary of State
30 Trinity St.
Hartford, CT 06106
860-509-6200
fax: 860-509-6209
www.ct.gov/sots

Connecticut State Library
231 Capitol Ave.
Hartford, CT 06106
866-886-4478
860-757-6500
www.ctstatelibrary.org

Delaware

First state; adopted the U.S. Constitution on December 7, 1787

December 7 is Delaware Day, commemorating the day it became the first state to ratify the Constitution. In 1939, the state legislature decreed that a commission be set up to organize the annual celebration. Since then, the observance has consisted mainly of the singing of patriotic songs, recitations of the Pledge of Allegiance and "Our Heritage," a poem by Herman Hanson, and speeches and readings on the state's history.

State capital: Dover

Nicknames: The First State; The Diamond State; The Blue Hen State

State motto: Liberty and Independence

State beverage: Milk

State bird: Blue Hen

State butterfly: Tiger Swallowtail

State fish: Weakfish (*Cynoscion regalis*)

State flower: Peach blossom (*Prunus persica*)

State fossil: Belemnite

State herb: Sweet golden rod

State insect: Ladybug (*Hippodamia convergens*)

State macroinvertebrate: Stonefly

State marine animal: Horseshoe crab

State mineral: Sillimanite

State soil: Greenwich Loam

State song: "Our Delaware"

State star: Delaware Diamond

State tree: American holly (*Ilex opaca*)

More about state symbols at:
www.delaware.gov/topics/facts/index.shtml

STATE OFFICES:
State website:
www.delaware.gov

Office of the Governor
150 Martin Luther King Jr. Blvd S.
2nd Fl.
Dover, DE 19901
302-744-4101
www.governor.delaware.gov

Secretary of State
401 Federal St.
Ste. 3
Dover, DE 19901
302-739-4111
fax: 302-739-3811
sos.delaware.gov

Delaware Div of Libraries
121 Martin Luther King Jr. Blvd. N.
Dover, DE 19901
800-282-8696
302-739-4748
fax: 302-739-6787
libraries.delware.gov

District of Columbia

Established as a municipal corporation on February 21, 1871

Motto: Justitia omnibus (Latin, "Justice to all")

Flower: American Beauty rose

Tree: Scarlet oak

Bird: Wood thrush

DISTRICT OFFICE:
Government website:
dc.gov

Executive Office of the Mayor
1350 Pennsylvania Ave. NW.
Ste. 316
Washington, DC 20004
mayor.dc.gov

Florida

Twenty-seventh state; admitted on March 3, 1845 (seceded from the Union on January 10, 1861, and was readmitted on June 25, 1868)

Florida does not hold regular admission day celebrations, but a centennial observance did occur in 1945. A three-cent stamp was issued, schools gave presentations, and there were local exhibits and commemorations. The Library of Congress hosted an exhibit on Florida from March 3 through May 31.

SEE ALSO PASCUA FLORIDA DAY

State capital: Tallahassee
Nicknames: The Sunshine State; Alligator State; Everglades State; Southernmost State; Orange State
State motto: In God We Trust
State animal: Florida panther (*Felis concolor*)
State beverage: Orange juice
State bird: Mockingbird (*Mimus polyglottos*)
State butterfly: Zebra longwing
State fish: freshwater: Largemouth bass (*Micropterus salmoides*); **saltwater**: Atlantic sailfish (*Istiophorus platypterus*)
State flower: Orange blossom; **wildflower**: Coreopsis
State gem: Moonstone
State marine mammals: Manatee (*Trichechus manatus*) and porpoise (dolphin) (*Tursiops truncatus*)
State reptile: American alligator (*alligator mississippiensis*)
State shell: Horse conch (*Pleuroploca gigantea*)
State soil: Myakka fine sand
State song: "Old Folks at Home" (also known as "Swanee River")
State stone: Agatized coral
State tree: Sabal palm (*Sabal palmetto*)

More about state symbols at:
www.dos.myflorida.com/florida-facts/florida-state-symbols

STATE OFFICES:
State website:
www.myflorida.com

Office of the Governor
State Capitol
400 S. Monroe St.
Tallahassee, FL 32399
850-717-9337
www.flgov.com

Secretary of State
R A Gray Bldg.
500 S. Bronough St.
Tallahassee, FL 32399
850-245-6500
fax: 850-245-6125
www.dos.myflorida.com

State Library of Florida
R A Gray Bldg.
500 S. Bronough St.

Tallahassee, FL 32399
850-245-6600
fax: 850-245-6735
www.dos.myflorida.com/library-archives

Georgia

Fourth state; adopted the U.S. Constitution on January 2, 1788 (seceded from the Union on January 19, 1861, and was readmitted on July 15, 1870)

State capital: Atlanta
Nicknames: The Empire State of the South; The Peach State; The Goober State; The Peachtree State
State motto: Wisdom, Justice, Moderation
State amphibian: green tree frog
State art museum: Georgia Museum of Art
State atlas: Atlas of Georgia
State ballet: Atlanta Ballet
State beef cook off: Shoot the Bull
State bird: Brown thrasher (*Toxostoma rufum*)
State botanical garden: State Botanical Garden of Georgia
State butterfly: Tiger swallowtail (*Papilio glaucus*)
State creed: Georgian's creed
State crop: Peanut
State fish: Largemouth bass (*Micropterus salmoides*)
State flower: Cherokee rose (*Rosa laevigata*); **wildflower**: Azalea (*Rhododendron*)
State folk dance: Square dance
State folk festival: Georgia Folk Festival
State folk life play: *Swamp Gravy*
State fossil: Shark tooth
State fruit: Peach
State game bird: Bobwhite quail
State gem: Quartz
State historic drama: *The Reach of Song*
State insect: Honeybee (*Apis mellifera*)
State marine mammal: Right whale (*Baleana glacialin*)
State mineral: Staurolite
State musical theater: Jekyll Island Musical Theater Festival
State peanut monument: Turner County Peanut Monument
State pork cook off: Slosheye Trail Big Pig Jig
State 'possum: Pogo 'possum
State poultry: "Poultry Capital of the World"
State prepared food: Grits
State railroad museum: Historic Railroad Shops
State reptile: Gopher tortoise
State seashell: Knobbed whelk (*Busycon carica*)
State school: Plains High School
State song: "Georgia on My Mind"
State tartan: Georgia tartan
State theater: Springer Opera House

State transportation history museum: Southeastern Railway Museum

State tree: Live oak (*Quercus virginiana*)

State vegetable: Vidalia sweet onion

State waltz: "Our Georgia"

More about state symbols at:
www.sos.ga.gov/state_symbols

More about the state at:
georgia.gov/georgia-facts-and-symbols

STATE OFFICES:
State website:
www.georgia.gov

Office of the Governor
State Capitol
206 Washington St.
Rm.111
Atlanta, GA 30334
404-656-1776
fax: 404-657-7332
www.gov.georgia.gov

Secretary of State
State Capitol
Rm. 214
Atlanta, GA 30334
404-656-2881
www.sos.ga.gov

Georgia Public Library Services
1800 Century Pl.
Ste. 150
Atlanta, GA 30345
404-235-7200
www.georgialibraries.org

Hawaii

Fiftieth state; admitted on August 21, 1959

Hawaii's admission day anniversary is observed as a state holiday on the third Friday in August every year.

State capital: Honolulu

Nicknames: Aloha State; Paradise of the Pacific; Pineapple State

State motto: *Ua mau ke ea o ka aina i ka pono* (Hawaiian "The Life of the Land Is Perpetuated in Righteousness")

State bird: Nene (pronounced nay-nay) or Hawaiian goose (*Nesochen sandvicensis*)

State fish: Humuhumunukunukuapua'a (not official; rectangular trigger fish, *Rhinecantus aculeatus*)

State flower: Pua aloalo (Yellow hibiscus, *Hibiscus brackenridgei*)

State gem: Black coral

State language: English and Hawaiian

State mammal: Hawaiian monk seal (ilio-holo-i-ka-uaua; *Monachus schauinslandi*)

State marine mammal: Humpback whale

State song: "Hawaii Ponoi"

State tree: Kukui (Candlenut, *Aleurites moluccana*)

More about state symbols at:
dbedt.hawaii.gov/economic/library/facts/symbols

STATE OFFICES:
State website:
hawaii.gov

Office of the Governor
Executive Chambers State Capitol
Honolulu, HI 96813
808-586-0034
fax: 808-586-0006
www.governor.hawaii.gov

Hawaii State Public Library
478 S King St.
Honolulu, HI 96813
808-586-3617
hawaii.sdp.sirsi.net

Idaho

Forty-third state; admitted on July 3, 1890

In 1963, Idaho held a centennial celebration marking the anniversary of its becoming a territory of the United States. From June 27 to July 6, numerous activities were sponsored by more than 165 organizations in the Boise area, including "Old Fashioned Bargain Days," balls, parades, singing, street dancing, fireworks, a rifle shoot, sports events, an art exhibit, rodeo, picnics, a poetry reading, an air show, and a historical pageant presenting memorable episodes from the state's history.

State capital: Boise

Nickname: Gem State

State motto: *Esto perpetua* (Latin "Let it be perpetual")

State bird: Mountain bluebird (*Sialia arctcia*)

State fish: Cutthroat trout (*Salmo clarki*)

State flower: Syringa (*Philadelphus lewisii*)

State folk dance: Square dance

State fossil: Hagerman horse (*Equus simplicidens*)

State fruit: huckleberry (*Vaccinium membranaceum*)

State gem: Star garnet

State horse: Appaloosa

State insect: Monarch butterfly (*Danaus plexippus*)

State raptor: Peregrine falcon (*falco peregrinus*)

State song: "Here We Have Idaho"

State tree: Western white pine (*Pinus monticola pinaceae*)

State vegetable: Potato

More about state symbols at:
www.sos.idaho.gov/emblems

More about the state at:
www.visitidaho.org/facts-about-idaho

STATE OFFICES:
State website:
www.idaho.gov

Office of the Governor
State Capitol
P.O. Box 83720
Boise, ID 83720
208-334-2100
fax: 208-334-3454
www.gov.idaho.gov

Secretary of State
700 W. Jefferson St.
Rm. E205
Boise, ID 83720
208-334-2300
fax: 208-334-2282
www.sos.idaho.gov

Idaho Commission for Libraries
325 W. State St.
Boise, ID 83702
800-458-3271
208-334-2150
fax: 208-334-4016
www.libraries.idaho.gov

Illinois

Twenty-first state; admitted on December 3, 1818

The 150th, or sesquicentennial, anniversary of Illinois' statehood was celebrated throughout the state during 1968. In December 1967, a year-long exhibit on Illinois history opened at Chicago's Field Museum of Natural History. Miniature replicas of historic rooms—Carl Sandburg's birthplace, Jane Addams's Hull House office, and the Palmer House Hotel's Silver Dollar Barber Shop of 1875—were on display in Carson Pirie Scott department stores. Lincoln's birthday on February 12 was observed with programs commemorating his career in Illinois. On July 4, there was a parade, drama, musical events, fireworks, and speeches at Steeleville. As part of the year-long celebration, the Old State House in Springfield was restored.

State capital: Springfield
Nicknames: Prairie State; Land of Lincoln; Corn State
State motto: State Sovereignty, National Union
State animal: White-tailed deer (*Odocoileus virginianus*)
State amphibian: Eastern tiger salamander
State bird: Cardinal (*Cardinalis cardinalis*)
State dance: Square dance
State fish: Bluegill (*Lepomis macrochirus*)
State flower: Violet (*Viola*)
State fossil: Tully Monster (*Tullimonstrum gregarium*)
State insect: Monarch butterfly (*Danaus plexippus*)

State mineral: Fluorite
State prairie grass: Big bluestem (*Andropogon furcatus*)
State reptile: Painted turtle
State song: "Illinois"
State tree: White oak (*Quercus alba*)

More about state symbols at:
www.illinois.gov/about/Pages/StateSymbols.aspx
www.museum.state.il.us/exhibits/symbols

STATE OFFICES:
State website:
www.illinois.gov

Office of the Governor
207 State House
Springfield, IL 62706
888-261-3336
217-782-0244
TTY: 888-261-3336
www2.illinois.gov/gov

Secretary of State
State Capitol Bldg.
Rm. 213
Springfield, IL 62756
800-252-8980
217-785-3000
TTY: 888-261-2709
www.cyberdriveillinois.com

Illinois State Library
Gwendolyn Brooks Bldg.
300 S. Second St.
Springfield, IL 62701
800-665-5576
217-782-5600
TTY: 888-261-2709
www.cyberdriveillinois.com/departments/library/home.html

Indiana

Nineteenth state; admitted on December 11, 1816

Indiana Day, December 11, is not a legal holiday, but has been observed sporadically since Indiana's General Assembly proclaimed the holiday in February 1925. Schools often hold commemorative programs. The sesquicentennial anniversary in 1966, however, was marked throughout that year with historical pageants and recreations of such notable events as the signing of the state's constitution.

State capital: Indianapolis
Nickname: Hoosier State
State motto: The Crossroads of America
State bird: Cardinal (*Cardinalis cardinalis*)
State flower: Peony (*Paeonia*)
State language: English
State poem: "Indiana"
State river: Wabash

State song: "On the Banks of the Wabash, Far Away"

State stone: Indiana limestone

State tree: Tulip tree (yellow poplar; *Liriodendron tulipfera*)

More about state symbols at:

www.in.gov/history/emblems.htm

www.indianahistory.org/teachers-students/hoosier-facts-fun/fun-facts

More about the state at:

www.in.gov/history/4031.htm

STATE OFFICES:

State website:

www.in.gov

Office of the Governor
State House
200 W. Washington St.
Rm. 206
Indianapolis, IN 46204
800-457-8283
317-232-4567
www.in.gov/gov

Secretary of State
State House
200 W. Washington St.
Rm. 201
Indianapolis, IN 46204
317-232-6531
fax: 317-233-3283
www.in.gov/sos

Indiana State Library
315 W. Ohio St.
Indianapolis, IN 46202
866-683-0008
317-232-3675
www.in.gov/library

Iowa

Twenty-ninth state; admitted on December 28, 1846

State capital: Des Moines

Nicknames: The Hawkeye State; The Corn State

State motto: Our Liberties We Prize, and Our Rights We Will Maintain

State bird: Eastern goldfinch (*Carduelis tristis*)

State flower: Wild rose (*Rosa pratincola*)

State song: "The Song of Iowa"

State stone: Geode

State tree: Oak (*Quercus*)

More about state symbols at:

www.publications.iowa.gov/135/1/profile/8-1.html

www.historycenter.org/2013/10/iowa-state-symbols

More about the state at:

www.iowadatacenter.org/quickfacts

STATE OFFICES:

State website:

www.iowa.gov

Office of the Governor
1007 E. Grand Ave.
Des Moines, IA 50319
515-281-5211
fax: 515-725-3527
www.governor.iowa.gov

Secretary of State
321 E. 12th St.
Lucas Bldg.
1st Fl.
Des Moines, IA 50319
515-281-5204
fax: 515-242-5953
www.sos.iowa.gov

Iowa State Library
1112 E. Grand Ave.
Des Moines, IA 50319
800-248-4483
515-281-4102
www.statelibraryofiowa.org

Kansas

Thirty-fourth state; admitted on January 29, 1861

Kansas Day has been observed since 1877, most often in school programs about the state. The Kansas State Historical Society sponsors celebrations at the Kansas History Center in Topeka.

State capital: Topeka

Nicknames: Sunflower State; Wheat State; Jayhawk State

State motto: *Ad Astra per Aspera* (Latin "To the Stars Through Difficulties")

State amphibian: Barred tiger salamander

State animal: American buffalo or bison (*Bison bison*)

State bird: Western meadowlark (*Sturnella neglecta*)

State flower: Sunflower (*Helianthus annuus*)

State insect: Honeybee (*Apis mellifera*)

State march: "The Kansas March"

State reptile: Ornate box turtle

State song: "Home on the Range"

State tree: Cottonwood (*Populus deltoides*)

More about state symbols at:

www.kshs.org/kansapedia/kansas-symbols/17169

More about the state at:

governor.ks.gov/about-kansas

CONTACT:
Kansas State Historical Society
6425 SW. Sixth Ave.
Topeka, KS 66615
785-272-8681
fax: 785-272-8682
TTY: 785-272-8681
www.kshs.org

STATE OFFICES:
State website:
www.kansas.gov

Office of the Governor
300 SW 10th Ave.
Ste. 241S
Topeka, KS 66612
877-579-6757
785-296-3232
www.governor.ks.gov

Secretary of State
Memorial Hall
120 SW 10th Ave.
1st Fl.
Topeka, KS 66612
785-296-4564
fax: 785-296-4570
TTY: 800-766-3777
www.kssos.org

Kansas State Library
300 SW 10th Ave.
Capitol Bldg.
Rm. 312-N
Topeka, KS 66612
800-432-3919
785-296-3296
www.kslib.info

Kentucky

Fifteenth state; admitted on June 1, 1792

Admission Day is not regularly observed in Kentucky, although festivities were held on the 100th, 150th, and 175th anniversaries of statehood.

State capital: Frankfort
Nicknames: The Bluegrass State; The Hemp State; The Tobacco State; The Dark and Bloody Ground
State motto: United We Stand, Divided We Fall
State bird: Cardinal (*Cardinalis cardinalis*)
State amphitheater: Iroquois Amphitheater
State arboretum: Bernheim Arboretum and Research Forest
State bluegrass song: "Blue Moon of Kentucky"
State botanical garden: University of Kentucky Arboretum
State bourbon festival: Kentucky Bourbon Festival
State butterfly: Viceroy
State center for celebration of African American heritage: Kentucky Center for African American Heritage

State covered bridge: Switzer covered bridge
State dance: Clogging
State drink: Milk
State fish: Kentucky spotted bass
State flower: Goldenrod (*Solidago nemoralis*)
State fossil: Brachiopod
State fruit: blackberry (*Rubus allegheniensis*)
State gemstone: Fresh water pearl
State honey festival: Clarkson Honeyfest
State horse: Thoroughbred
State language: English
State mineral: Coal
State music: Bluegrass
State musical instrument: Appalachian Dulcimer
State outdoor musical: "The Stephen Foster Story"
State pipe band: Louisville Pipe Band
State rock: Kentucky agate
State science center: Louisville Science Center
State silverware pattern: "Old Kentucky Blue Grass, The Georgetown Pattern"
State song: "My Old Kentucky Home"
State soil: Crider soil series
State steam locomotive: *Old 152*
State theatre pipe organ: Kentucky Theatre's Mighty Wurlitzer
State tree: Tulip Poplar (*Lirodendroan tulipifera*)
State tug-o-war championship: The Fordsville Tug-o-War Championship
State wild game animal species: Gray squirrel (*Sciurus carolinensis*)

More about state symbols at:
www.lrc.ky.gov/kidspages/symbols.htm

More about the state at:
www.kentuckytourism.com/explore/kyfacts/facts.aspx

STATE OFFICES:
State website:
www.kentucky.gov

Office of the Governor
State Capitol Bldg.
700 Capitol Ave.
Ste. 100
Frankfort, KY 40601
502-564-2611
fax: 502-564-2517
TTY: 502-564-9551
www.governor.ky.gov

Secretary of State
700 Capitol Ave.
Ste. 152
Frankfort, KY 40601
502-564-3490
fax: 502-564-5687
www.sos.ky.gov

Kentucky Dept for Libraries & Archives
300 Coffee Tree Rd.
P.O. Box 537
Frankfort, KY 40602
502-564-8300
fax: 502-564-5773
www.kdla.ky.gov

Louisiana

Eighteenth state; admitted on April 30, 1812 (seceded in 1861 and was readmitted on June 25, 1868)

State capital: Baton Rouge
Nicknames: The Pelican State; The Bayou State; Fisherman's Paradise; Child of the Mississippi; Sugar State
State motto: Union, Justice, and Confidence
State amphibian: Green tree frog (*Hyla cinerea*)
State bird: Brown pelican (*Pelecanus occidentalis*)
State colors: Blue, white, and gold
State crustacean: Crawfish
State dog: Louisiana Catahoula leopard dog
State drink: Milk
State environmental song: "The Gifts of Earth"
State flower: Magnolia (*Magnolia grandiflora*); **wildflower**: Louisiana iris (*Giganticaerulea*)
State fossil: Petrified palm wood
State freshwater fish: White perch (*pomoxis annularis*)
State gem: Agate
State insect: Honeybee (*Apis mellifera*)
State mammal: Louisiana black bear
State march song: "Louisiana My Home Sweet Home"
State musical instrument: Diatonic ("Cajun") accordion
State painting: "Louisiana"
State reptile: Alligator
State songs: "Give Me Louisiana"; "You Are My Sunshine"
State tree: Bald cypress (*Taxodium distichum*)

More about state symbols at:
www.doa.louisiana.gov/about_emblems.htm

More about the state at:
www.doa.louisiana.gov/about_history.htm
www.louisiana.gov/Explore/About_Louisiana

STATE OFFICES:
State website:
www.louisiana.gov

Office of the Governor
P.O. Box 94004
Baton Rouge, LA 70804
866-366-1121
225-342-7015
fax: 225-342-7099
www.gov.state.la.us

Secretary of State
8585 Archives Ave.

Baton Rouge, LA 70809
225-922-2880
fax: 225-922-2003
www.sos.la.gov

Louisiana State Library
701 N. 4th St.
Baton Rouge, LA 70802
225-342-4913
fax: 225-219-4804
www.state.lib.la.us

Maine

Twenty-third state; admitted on March 15, 1820

State capital: Augusta
Nicknames: The Pine Tree State; The Lumber State; The Border State; The Old Dirigo State
State motto: *Dirigo* (Latin "I lead")
State animal: Moose (*Alces alces*)
State berry: Wild blueberry
State bird: Chickadee (*Parus atricapillus*)
State cat: Maine coon cat
State fish: Landlocked salmon (*Salmo sala Sebago*)
State flower: White pine cone and tassel (*Pinus strobes, Lin-naeus*)
State fossil: *Pertica quadrifaria*
State gemstone: Tourmaline
State herb: Wintergreen (*Gaulthoria procumbens*)
State insect: Honeybee (*Apis mellifera*)
State soil: Chesuncook Soil Series
State soft drink: Moxie
State song: "State of Maine Song"
State tree: Eastern white pine (*Pinus strobus*)
State vessel: *Schooner Bowdoin*

More about state symbols at:
www.maine.gov/sos/kids/about/symbols/symbols.htm

More about the state at:
www.maine.gov/portal/facts_history/facts.html

STATE OFFICES:
State website:
www.maine.gov

Office of the Governor
1 State House Stn.
Augusta, ME 04333
855-721-5203
207-287-3531
fax: 207-287-1034
www.maine.gov/governor

Secretary of State
148 State House Stn.
Augusta, ME 04333

207-626-8400
fax: 207-287-8598
www.maine.gov/sos

Maine State Library
64 State House Stn.
Augusta, ME 04333
207-287-5600
fax: 207-287-5615
www.state.me.us/msl

Maryland

Seventh state; adopted the U.S. Constitution on April 28, 1788

SEE MARYLAND DAY

State capital: Annapolis
Nicknames: The Old Line State; Free State
State motto: *Fatti maschii, parole femine* (Latin "Strong deeds, gentle words")
State bird: Baltimore oriole (*Icterus galbula*)
State boat: Skipjack
State cat: Calico
State crustacean: Maryland blue crab (*Callinectes sapidus*)
State dinosaur: *Astrodon johnstoni*
State dog: Chesapeake Bay retriever
State drink: Milk
State fish: Rockfish (*Morone saxatilis*)
State flower: Black-eyed Susan (*Rudbeckia hirta*)
State folk dance: Square dance
State fossil shell: *Ecphora gardnerae gardnerae*
State gem: Patuxent river stone
State horse: Thoroughbred
State insect: Baltimore checkerspot butterfly (*Euphydryas phaeton*)
State reptile: Diamondback terrapin turtle (*Malaclemys terrapin*)
State song: "Maryland, My Maryland"
State sport: Jousting
State team sport: Lacrosse
State summer theater: Olney Theatre (Montgomery County)
State theater: Center State (Baltimore)
State tree: White oak (*Quercus alba*)

More about state symbols at:
www.mdkidspage.org/StateSymbols.htm

More about the state at:
www.msa.maryland.gov/msa/mdmanual/01glance/html/mdglance.html

STATE OFFICES:
State website:
www.maryland.gov

Office of the Governor State House
100 State Cir.

Annapolis, MD 21401
800-811-8336
410-974-3901
www.governor.maryland.gov

Secretary of State
16 Francis St. Jeffery Bldg.
1st Fl.
Annapolis, MD 21401
888-874-0013
410-974-5521
fax: 410-974-5190
www.sos.state.md.us

State Archives
350 Rowe Blvd.
Dr. Edward C. Papenfuse State Archives Bldg.
Annapolis, MD 21401
800-235-4045
410-260-6400
fax: 410-974-2525
www.msa.maryland.gov

Massachusetts

Sixth state; adopted the U.S. Constitution on February 6, 1788

State capital: Boston
Nicknames: The (Old) Bay State; The Old Colony State; The Puritan State; The Baked Bean State; The Pilgrim State
State motto: *Ense petit placidam sub libertate quietem* (Latin "By the sword we seek peace, but peace only under liberty")
Ode of the Commonwealth: "Ode to Massachusetts"
State artist: Norman Rockwell
State author and illustrator: Theodor Geisel
State bean: Baked navy bean
State berry: Cranberry (*Vaccinium macrocarpon*)
State beverage: Cranberry juice
State bird: Black-capped chickadee (*Penthestes atricapillus*)
State blues artist: Taj Mahal (Henry St. Clair Fredericks)
State building and monument stone: Granite
State cat: Tabby cat (*Felis familiaris*)
State ceremonial march: "The Road to Boston"
State children's book: *Make Way For Ducklings*
State citizenry: Bay Staters
State colors: Blue, green and cranberry
State cookie: Chocolate chip
State designation of citizens: Bay Staters
State dessert: Boston cream pie
State dog: Boston terrier (*Canis familiaris bostenensis*)
State donut: Boston creme doughnut
State explorer rock: Dighton Rock
State fish: Cod (*Gadus morrhua*)
State flower: Mayflower (also called ground laurel or trailing arbutus, *Epigaea regens*)
State folk dance: Square dance

State folk hero: Johnny Appleseed

State folk song: "Massachusetts"

State fossil: Theropod dinosaur tracks

State game bird: Wild turkey (*Meleagris gallopavo*)

State gem: Rhodonite

State glee club song: "The Great State of Massachusetts"

State heroine: Deborah Sampson (1760-1827; while disguised as a man under the name of Robert Shurtleff, she fought with the Continental Army against the British)

State historical rock: Plymouth Rock

State horse: Morgan horse (*Equus cabullus morganensis*)

State insect: Ladybug (*Hippodamia convergens*)

State inventor: Benjamin Franklin

State Korean war memorial: Korean War Memorial (in Shipyard Park)

State marine mammal: Right whale (*Eubabalena glacialis*)

State MIA/POW memorial: MIA/POW Memorial (Bourne)

State mineral: Babingtonite

State muffin: Corn muffin

State patriotic song: "Massachusetts (Because of You Our Land Is Free)"

State peace statue: Orange Peace Statue

State poem: "Blue Hills of Massachusetts"

State polka song: "Say Hello to Someone from Massachusetts"

State reptile: Garter snake

State rock: Roxbury pudding stone (Roxbury conglomerate)

State shell: New England neptune (*Neptuna lyrata decemcostata*)

State soil: Paxton soil series

State song: "All Hail to Massachusetts"

State sport: Basketball

State Southwest Asia war memorial: Southwest Asia War Memorial

State tartan: Bay State Tartan

State tree: American elm (*Ulmus americana*)

State vessel: *Schooner Ernestina*

State Vietnam War memorial: Vietnam War Memorial

More about state symbols at:
www.sec.state.ma.us/cis/cismaf/mf1a.htm
www.mass.gov/portal/articles/massachusetts-fun-facts.html

STATE OFFICES:
State website:
www.mass.gov

Office of the Governor
State House
Rm. 280
Boston, MA 02133
888-870-7770
617-725-4005
fax: 617-727-9725
TTY: 617-727-3666
www.mass.gov/gov

Secretary of the Commonwealth
McCormack Bldg.
1 Ashburton Pl.
Rm. 1611
Boston, MA 02108
800-392-6090
617-727-7030
fax: 617-742-4528
TTY: 617-878-3889
www.sec.state.ma.us

Massachusetts Board of Library Commissioners
98 N. Washington St.
Ste. 401
Boston, MA 02114
800-952-7403
617-725-1860
fax: 617-725-0140
mblc.state.ma.us

Michigan

Twenty-sixth state; admitted on January 26, 1837

The anniversary of Michigan's statehood was previously observed as Michigan Day, but is no longer a holiday.

State capital: Lansing

Nicknames: The Great Lakes State; The Wolverine State; Winter Wonderland; the Upper Peninsula is often referred to as the Land of Hiawatha

State motto: *Si quaeris peninsulam amoenam, circumspice* (Latin "If you seek a pleasant peninsula, look about you")

State bird: Robin (*Turdus migratorius*)

State fish: Brook trout (*Salvelinus fontinalis*)

State flower: Apple blossom (*Malus sylvestris*); **wildflower**: Dwarf lake iris (*Iris lacustris*)

State fossil: Mastadon

State game mammal: Whitetailed deer (*Odocoileus virginianus*)

State gem: Greenstone (chlorastrolite)

State reptile: Painted turtle (*Chysemys picta*)

State soil: Kalkaska sand

State song: "My Michigan" (official); "Michigan, My Michigan" (unofficial)

State stone: Petoskey stone (*Hexagonaria pericarnata*)

State tree: White pine (*Pinus strobus*)

More about state symbols at:
seekingmichigan.org/learn/symbols

More about the state at:
www.legislature.mi.gov/documents/publications/
GettingToKnowMichigan.html
www.michigan.gov/kids/0,4600,7-247-49069-67959--,00.html

STATE OFFICES:
State website:
www.michigan.gov

Office of the Governor
P.O. Box 30013
Lansing, MI 48909
517-373-3400
fax: 517-335-6863
www.michigan.gov/snyder

Secretary of State
430 W Allegan St.
Austin Bldg.
4th Fl.
Lansing, MI 48918
888-767-6424
www.michigan.gov/sos

Library of Michigan
702 W. Kalamazoo St.
P.O. Box 30007
Lansing, MI 48909
877-479-0021
517-373-1580
fax: 517-373-5700
www.michigan.gov/libraryofmichigan

Minnesota

Thirty-second state; admitted on May 11, 1858

State capital: St. Paul

Nicknames: North Star State; Gopher State; Bread and Butter State; The Land of 10,000 Lakes

State motto: *L'Etoile du Nord* (French "The North Star")

State bird: Common loon (*Gavia immer*)

State butterfly: Monarch (*Danaus plexippus*)

State drink: Milk

State fish: Walleye (*Stizostedion vitreum*)

State flower: Pink and white lady's slipper (*Cypripedium reginae)*

State fruit: Honeycrisp apple (*Malus pumila* cultivar Honeycrisp)

State gem: Lake Superior agate

State grain: Wild rice or manomin (*Zizania aquatica* or *Zizania palustris*)

State muffin: Blueberry muffin

State mushroom: Morel or sponge mushroom (*Morchella esculenta*)

State photograph: "Grace"

State song: "Hail! Minnesota"

State tree: Norway (red) pine (*Pinus resinosa*)

More about state symbols at:
www.mn.gov/governor/about-minnesota/state-symbols
www.leg.state.mn.us/leg/symbols.aspx

STATE OFFICES:
State website:
www.mn.gov

Office of the Governor
20 W. 12th St.

116 Veterans Service Bldg.
Saint Paul, MN 55155
800-657-3717
651-201-3400
fax: 651-797-1850
TTY: 800-627-3529
www.mn.gov/governor

Secretary of State
180 State Office Bldg.
100 Rev Dr. Martin Luther King Jr. Blvd.
Saint Paul, MN 55155
651-201-1324
fax: 651-296-9073
www.sos.state.mn.us

Mississippi

Twentieth state; admitted on December 10, 1817 (seceded on January 9, 1861, and was readmitted on February 23, 1870)

No admission day celebrations occur, but in 1917 the state held centennial ceremonies including speeches and music. On the sesquicentennial, or 150th, anniversary in 1967, there were exhibits at the Old Capitol Building museum, and efforts got underway to preserve state historical documents (including appropriating $1,120,000 for building a new archives center).

State capital: Jackson

Nicknames: The Magnolia State; Eagle State; Border-Eagle State; Bayou State; Mud-cat State

State motto: *Virtute et armis* (Latin "By valor and arms")

State beverage: Milk

State bird: Mockingbird (*Mimus polyglottos*)

State butterfly: Spicebush swallowtail (*Papilio troilus*)

State dance: Square dance

State fish: Largemouth or black bass (*Micropterus salmoides*)

State flower: Magnolia blossom (*Magnolia grandiflora*); **wildflower**: Coreopsis

State fossil: Prehistoric whale

State insect: Honeybee (*Apis mellifera*)

State mammal: land: White-tailed deer (*Odocoileus virginianus*); **water**: Bottle-nosed dolphin (*Tursiops truncatus*)

State reptile: Alligator

State shell: Oyster shell (*Crassostrea virginica*)

State song: "Go, Mississippi"

State stone: Petrified wood

State toy: Teddy bear

State tree: Magnolia (*Magnolia grandiflora*)

State waterfowl: Wood duck (*Aix sponsa*)

More about state symbols at:
www.ms.gov/content/Pages/Symbols.aspx

More about the state at:
www.ms.gov/content/pages/about.aspx

STATE OFFICES:
State website:
www.mississippi.gov

Office of the Governor
P.O. Box 139
Jackson, MS 39205
601-359-3150
fax: 601-359-3741
www.governorbryant.com

Secretary of State
401 Mississippi St.
Jackson, MS 39201
601-359-1350
www.sos.ms.gov

Mississippi Library Commission
3881 Eastwood Dr.
Jackson, MS 39211
800-647-7542
601-961-4111
fax: 601-432-4486
TTY: 800-446-0892
www.mlc.lib.ms.us

Mississippi Archives & History Dept
William F Winter Archives & History Bldg.
200 North St.
Jackson, MS 39201
601-576-6850
www.mdah.state.ms.us

Missouri

Twenty-fourth state; admitted on August 10, 1821

State capital: Jefferson City

Nickname: Show Me State

State motto: *Salus populi suprema lex esto* (Latin "Let the welfare of the people be the supreme law")

State amphibian: American Bullfrog (*Rana catesbeiana*)

State bird: Bluebird (*Sialia sialis*)

State day: Missouri Day, third Wednesday in October

State dinosaur: Hadrosaur or duck-billed (*Hypsibema missouriense*)

State fish: Channel catfish (*Ictalurus punctatus*)

State flower: Hawthorn blossom (*Crataegus*)

State folk dance: Square dance

State fossil: Crinoid (*Delocrinus missouriensis*)

State grape: Norton/Cynthiana grape (*Vitis Aestivalis*)

State horse: Missouri fox trotting horse

State insect: Honeybee (*Apis mellifera*)

State land animal: Missouri mule; **aquatic animal**: Paddlefish

State mineral: Galena

State musical instrument: Fiddle

State rock: Mozarkite (chert or flint rock)

State song: "Missouri Waltz"

State tree: Flowering dogwood (*Cornus florida*)

State tree nut: Eastern black walnut (*Juglans nigra*)

More about state symbols at:
www.sos.mo.gov/symbols

STATE OFFICES:
State website:
www.mo.gov

Office of the Governor
P.O. Box 720
Jefferson City, MO 65102
573-751-3222
www.governor.mo.gov

Secretary of State
600 W. Main St.
Jefferson City, MO 65101
573-751-4936
www.sos.mo.gov

Missouri State Library
600 W. Main St.
Jefferson City, MO 65101
800-325-0131
573-522-4036
www.sos.mo.gov/library

Montana

Forty-first state; admitted on November 8, 1889

State capital: Helena

Nicknames: Treasure State; Big Sky Country; Bonanza State; Land of Shining Mountains; Mountain State

State motto: *Oro y Plata* (Spanish "Gold and Silver")

State animal: Grizzly bear (*Ursus (arctos) horribilis*)

State ballad: "Montana Melody"

State bird: Western meadowlark (*Sturnella neglecta*)

State butterfly: Mourning cloak (*Nymphalis antiopa*)

State fish: Black-spotted cutthroat trout (*Salmo clarki*)

State flower: Bitterroot (*Lewisia rediviva*)

State fossil: Duck-billed dinosaur (*Maiasaura peeblesorum*)

State gems: Yogo sapphire; Montana agate

State grass: Bluebunch wheatgrass (*Agropyron spicatum*)

State song: "Montana"

State tree: Ponderosa pine (*Pinus ponderosa*)

More about state symbols at:
www.montanakids.com/facts_and_figures/state_symbols

More about the state at:
www.montanakids.com

STATE OFFICES:
State website:
www.mt.gov

Office of the Governor
P.O. Box 200801
Helena, MT 59620
855-318-1330
406-444-3111
fax: 406-444-5529
www.governor.mt.gov

Secretary of State
State Capitol Bldg.
1301 E. 6th Ave.
Helena, MT 59601
406-444-2034
fax: 406-444-3976
TTY: 406-444-9068
www.sos.mt.gov

Montana State Library
1515 E. 6th Ave.
P.O. Box 201800
Helena, MT 59620
800-338-5087
406-444-3115
fax: 406-444-0266
TTY: 406-444-4799
www.msl.mt.gov

Nebraska

Thirty-seventh state; admitted on March 1, 1867

Nebraska's admission day anniversary is marked as State Day. On March 1 every year, state law requires the governor to issue a proclamation about the anniversary and call on citizens to celebrate. Schools may mark the occasion with programs about the state's history. The centennial celebration was held during much of 1967 with festivals, rodeos, pageants, and exhibits.

State capital: Lincoln
Nicknames: Cornhusker State; Tree Planters' State
State motto: Equality Before the Law
State ballad: "A Place Like Nebraska"
State baseball capital: Wakefield
State beverage: Milk
State bird: Western meadowlark (*Sturnella neglecta*)
State Christmas tree: Colorado blue spruce (planted near the capital in 1876)
State fish: Channel cutfish (*Ictalurus punctatus*)
State flower: Goldenrod (*Solidago serotina*)
State folk dance: Square dance
State fossil: Mammoth
State gem: Blue agate (blue chalcedony)
State grass: Little bluestem (*Schizachyrium scoparium*), also called "bunch grass" or "beard grass"
State historic baseball capital: St. Paul
State insect: Honeybee (*Apis mellifera*)
State mammal: Whitetail deer (*Odocoileus virginianus*)
State poet laureate: John G. Neihardt

State river: Platte River
State rock: Prairie agate
State slogan: "Battle born"
State soil: Holdrege series (*Typic arguistolls*)
State soft drink: Kool-Aid
State song: "Beautiful Nebraska"
State tartan: Nevada Tartan
State tree: Cottonwood (*Populus deltoides*)
State village of lights: Cody

More about state symbols at:
www.sos.ne.gov/ne_symbols.html

More about the state at:
www.nebraskalegislature.gov/about/blue-book.php

STATE OFFICES:
State website:
www.nebraska.gov

Office of the Governor
P.O. Box 94848
Lincoln, NE 68509
402-471-2244
fax: 402-471-6031
www.governor.nebraska.gov

Secretary of State
State Capitol
1445 K St.
Ste. 2300
Lincoln, NE 68509
402-471-2554
fax: 402-471-3237
www.sos.ne.gov

Nebraska State Library
1500 R St.
P.O. Box 82554
Lincoln, NE 68501
800-833-6747
402-471-4745
fax: 402-471-1011
www.nebraskahistory.org

Nevada

Thirty-sixth state; admitted on October 31, 1864

Nevada Day is a legal holiday throughout the state observed the last Friday in October, but the most festive celebrations take place in Carson City, where the Admission Day parade has been held since 1938. There are historical Indian pageants, a costume ball, a Miss Nevada crowning, dancing, picnicking, games, and other events. Students have entered a historical essay contest since 1959, and the winners are awarded during the festivities.

State capital: Carson City
Nicknames: Silver State; Sagebrush State; Battle-Born State

State motto: All for Our Country

State animal: Desert bighorn sheep (*Ovis canadensis*)

State artifact: Tule duck

State bird: Mountain bluebird (*Sialia currucoides*)

State colors: Silver and blue

State fish: Lahontan cutthroat trout (*Salmo clarki henshawi*)

State flower: Sagebrush (*Artemisia tridentata*)

State fossil: Ichthyosaur (*Shonisaurus*)

State grass: Indian ricegrass (*Oryzopsis hymenoides*)

State metal: Silver

State precious gemstone: Virgin Valley Black Fire opal

State reptile: Desert tortoise (*Gopherus agassizii*)

State rock: Sandstone

State semi-precious gemstone: Turquoise

State soil: Orovada series

State song: "Home Means Nevada"

State trees: Single-leaf piñon (*Pinus monophylla*) and Bristle-cone pine (*Pinus aristata*)

More about state symbols at:
www.leg.state.nv.us/General/NVFacts/index.cfm

STATE OFFICES:
State website:
www.nv.gov

Office of the Governor
State Capitol Bldg.
101 N. Carson St.
Carson City, NV 89701
775-684-5670
fax: 775-684-5683
www.gov.nv.gov

Secretary of State
Nevada State Capitol Bldg.
101 N. Carson St.
Ste. 3
Carson City, NV 89701
775-684-5708
fax: 775-684-5725
www.nvsos.gov

Nevada State Library & Archives
100 N. Stewart St.
Carson City, NV 89701
800-922-2880
775-684-3313
fax: 775-684-3311
www.nsla.nv.gov

New Hampshire

Ninth state; adopted the U.S. Constitution on June 21, 1788

State capital: Concord

Nicknames: The Granite State; The Mother of Rivers; Switzerland of America; White Mountain State

State motto: Live Free or Die

State amphibian: Spotted newt (*Notophthalmus viridescens*)

State animal: White-tailed deer (*Odocoileus virginianus*)

State bird: Purple finch (*Carpodacus purpureus*)

State butterfly: Karner blue (*Lycaeides melissa*, subspecies *samuelis*)

State flower: Purple lilac (*Syringa vulgaris*); **wildflower**: Pink lady's slipper (*Cypripedium acaule*)

State freshwater fish: Brook trout (*Salvelinus fontinalis*); **saltwater game fish**: Striped bass (*Roccus saxatilis*)

State fruit: Pumpkin

State gem: Smoky quartz

State insect: Ladybug (*Hippodamia convergens*)

State mineral: Beryl

State rock: Granite

State song: "Old New Hampshire"

State sport: Skiing

State tartan: New Hampshire tartan

State tree: White birch (*Betula papyrifera*)

More about state symbols at:
www.gencourt.state.nh.us/Senate/About_Senate/kids.aspx

More about the state at:
www.nh.gov/nhinfo/fastfact.html

STATE OFFICES:
State website:
www.nh.gov

Office of the Governor
State House
107 N. Main St.
Concord, NH 03301
603-271-2121
fax: 603-271-7640
www.governor.nh.gov

Secretary of State
107 N. Main St.
State House
Rm. 204
Concord, NH 03301
603-271-3242
fax: 603-271-6316
www.sos.nh.gov

New Hampshire State Library
20 Park St.
Concord, NH 03301
603-271-2144
fax: 603-271-2205
TTY: 800-735-2964
www.nh.gov/nhsl

New Jersey

Third state; adopted the U.S. Constitution on December 18, 1787

State capital: Trenton

Nickname: The Garden State

State motto: Liberty and Prosperity

State animal: Horse (*Equus caballus*)

State bird: Eastern goldfinch (*Carduelis tristis*)

State dance: Square dance

State dinosaur: *Hadrosaurus foulki*

State fish: Brook trout (*Salvelinus fontinalis*)

State flower: Purple violet (*Viola sororia*)

State fruit: Blueberry (*Vaccinium corymbosum*)

State insect: Honeybee (*Apis mellifera*)

State memorial tree: Dogwood (*Cornus florida*)

State shell: Knobbed whelk (*Busycon Caricagmelin*)

State ship: *A.J. Meerwald*

State tree: Red oak (*Quercus borealis maxima*)

More about state symbols at:
www.state.nj.us/nj/about/facts/symbols
www.njleg.state.nj.us/kids/1024njsym.asp

STATE OFFICES:
State website:
www.newjersey.gov

Office of the Governor
P.O. Box 001
Trenton, NJ 08625
609-292-6000
www.state.nj.us/governor

Secretary of State
P.O. Box 300
Trenton, NJ 08625
866-534-7789
www.nj.gov/state

New Jersey State Library
185 W. State St.
Trenton, NJ 08608
609-278-2640
fax: 609-278-2652
www.njstatelib.org

New Mexico

Forty-seventh state; admitted on January 6, 1912

New Mexico does not regularly observe the anniversary of its statehood, but in 1972, the 60th anniversary of its admission to the U.S., a commemoration was held in Santa Fe. There was a reception at the Palace of Governors, where members of the Sociedad Folklórica dressed in costumes of the 1910s.

State capital: Santa Fe

Nickname: Land of Enchantment

State motto: *Crescit Eundo* (Latin "It Grows as It Goes")

State aircraft: Hot air balloon

State amphibian: Mexico spadefoot (*Spea multiplicata*)

State ballad: "Land of Enchantment—New Mexico"

State balloon museum: Anderson-Abruzzo International Balloon Museum

State bilingual song: "New Mexico—Mi Lindo Nuevo Mexico"

State bird: Chaparral bird or roadrunner (*Geococcyx californianus*)

State butterfly: Sandia hairstreak (*Callophrys mcfarlandi*)

State cookie: Bizcochito

State fish: Rio Grande cutthroat trout (*Salmo clerki*)

State flower: Yucca flower (*Yucca glauca*)

State fossil: Coelophysis dinosaur

State gem: Turquoise

State grass: Blue grama (*Bouteloua gracillis*)

State insect: Tarantula hawk wasp (*Pepsis formosa*)

State mammal: Black bear (*Ursus americanus*)

State poem: "A Nuevo Mexico" ("To New Mexico")

State question: "Red or Green?" (refers to which chile one prefers)

State reptile: New Mexico whiptail (*Cnemidophorus neomexianus*)

State slogan: *"Everybody is somebody in New Mexico."*

State songs: "O, Fair New Mexico" and "Asi es Nuevo Mejico"

State tie: Bolo tie

State train: Cumbres & Toltec Railroad

State tree: Piñon or nut pine (*Pinus edulis*)

State vegetables: Chile (*Capsicum annum*) and frijol or pinto bean (*Phaseolus vulgaris*)

More about state symbols at:
www.sos.state.nm.us/Kids_Corner/State_Symbols.aspx

More about the state at:
www.newmexicohistory.org

STATE OFFICES:
State website:
www.newmexico.gov

Office of the Governor
490 Santa Fe Trail
Rm. 400
Santa Fe, NM 87501
505-476-2200
fax: 505-476-2226
www.governor.state.nm.us

Secretary of State
New Mexico Capitol Annex N.
325 Don Gaspar Ave.
Ste. 300
Santa Fe, NM 87501
800-477-3632
505-827-3614
fax: 505-827-3611
www.sos.state.nm.us

New Mexico State Library
1209 Camino Carlos Rey
Santa Fe, NM 87507
505-476-9700
www.nmstatelibrary.org

New York

Eleventh state; adopted the U.S. Constitution on July 26, 1788

Capital: Albany
Nickname: The Empire State
State motto: *Excelsior* (Latin "Ever upward")
State animal: Beaver (*Castor canadensis*)
State beverage: Milk
State bird: Bluebird (*Sialia sialis*)
State bush: Lilac
State freshwater fish: Brook or speckled trout (*Salvelinus fontinalis*); **saltwater fish:** Striped bass
State flower: Rose (genus *Rosa*)
State fossil: *Eurypterus remipes* (distant relative of the horseshoe crab)
State fruit: Apple (*Malus sylvestris*)
State gem: Garnet
State insect: Ladybug (*Hippodamia convergens*)
State muffin: Apple muffin
State reptile: Common snapping turtle
State shell: Bay scallop (*Agropecten irradians*)
State tree: Sugar maple (*Acer saccharum*)

More about state symbols at:
www.dos.ny.gov/kids_room/508/symbols2.html
www.dec.ny.gov/education/1887.html

STATE OFFICES:
State website:
www.ny.gov

Office of the Governor
State Capitol
Albany, NY 12224
518-474-8390
www.governor.ny.gov

Secretary of State
123 William St.
New York, NY 10038
518-473-2492
www.dos.ny.gov

New York State Library
222 Madison Ave.
Albany, NY 12230
518-474-5355
fax: 518-474-5786
www.nysl.nysed.gov

North Carolina

Twelfth state; adopted the U.S. Constitution on November 21, 1789 (joined the Confederacy on May 20, 1861, and was readmitted to the Union on June 25, 1868)

State capital: Raleigh
Nicknames: The Tarheel State; Old North State; Turpentine State
State motto: *Esse quam videri* (Latin "To be rather than to seem")
State beverage: Milk
State bird: Cardinal (*Cardinalis cardinalis*)
State birthplace of traditional pottery: Seagrove area
State blue berry: Blueberry; **red berry:** Strawberry
State boat: Shad boat
State carnivorous plant: Venus flytrap
State Christmas tree: Fraser fir
State colors: Red and blue
State folk dance: Clogging; **popular dance:** Shag
State dog: Plott hound (*Canis familiaris*)
State fish: Channel bass (*Sciaenops ocellatus*)
State flower: Dogwood blossom (*Cornus florida*); **wildflower:** Carolina lily (*Lilium michauxii*)
State freshwater trout: Southern Appalachian brook trout
State fruit: Scuppernong grape
State gemstone: Emerald
State historical boat: Shad boat
State insect: Honeybee (*Apis mellifera*)
State mammal: Eastern gray squirrel (*Sciurus carolinensis*)
State reptile: Eastern box turtle (*Terrapene carolina*)
State rock: Granite
State shell: Scotch bonnet (*Phalium granulatum*)
State song: "The Old North State"
State tartan: Carolina tartan
State toast: "Tar Heel Toast"
State tree: Pine (*Pinus palustris*)
State vegetable: Sweet potato (*Ipornoea batatas*)

More about state symbols at:
www.naturalsciences.org/education/learning-resources/nc-state-symbols
www.ncpedia.org/north-carolina-state-symbols-general-statutes

More about the state at:
www.nc.gov/aboutnc.aspx

STATE OFFICES:
State website:
www.nc.gov

Office of the Governor
20301 MSC
Raleigh, NC 27699
919-814-2000
fax: 919-733-2120
www.governor.state.nc.us

Secretary of State
2 S. Salisbury St.
P.O. Box 29622
Raleigh, NC 27601
919-807-2000
www.sosnc.com

North Carolina State Library
109 E. Jones St.
Raleigh, NC 27601
919-807-7400
fax: 919-733-8748
www.statelibrary.dcr.state.nc.us

North Dakota

Thirty-ninth state; admitted on November 2, 1889

State capital: Bismarck
Nicknames: Flickertail State; Peace Garden State; Roughrider State
State motto: Liberty and Union, Now and Forever, One and Inseparable
State beverage: Milk
State bird: Western meadowlark (*Sturnella neglecta*)
State dance: Square dance
State fish: Northern pike (*Esox lucius*)
State flower: Wild prairie rose (*Rosa blanda* or *R. arkansana*)
State fossil: Teredo petrified wood
State fruit: Chokecherry (*Prunus virginiana*)
State grass: Western wheatgrass (*Agropyron smithii*)
State honorary equine: Nokota horse
State language: English
State march: "Flickertail March"
State song: "North Dakota Hymn"
State tree: American elm (*Ulmus americana*)

More about state symbols at:
www.nd.gov/category.htm?id=75

STATE OFFICES:
State website:
www.nd.gov

Office of the Governor
600 E. Boulevard Ave.
Dept. 101
Bismarck, ND 58505
701-328-2200
fax: 701-328-2205
www.governor.nd.gov

Secretary of State
600 E. Boulevard Ave.
Dept. 108
Bismarck, ND 58505
800-352-0867
701-328-2900
fax: 701-328-2992
TTY: 800-366-6888
www.sos.nd.gov

North Dakota State Library
604 E. Boulevard Ave.
Bismarck, ND 58505
800-472-2104
701-328-4622
fax: 701-328-2040
www.library.nd.gov

Ohio

Seventeenth state; admitted on March 1, 1803

State capital: Columbus
Nicknames: Buckeye State; Mother of Presidents; Gateway State
State motto: With God All Things Are Possible
State animal: White-tailed deer (*Odocoileus virginianus*)
State beverage: Tomato juice
State bird: Cardinal (*Cardinalis cardinalis*)
State groundhog: Buckeye Chuck
State flower: Scarlet carnation (*Dianthus caryophyllus*); **wildflower**: Large white trillium (*Trillium grandiflorum*)
State fossil: Trilobite (*Isotelus*)
State gemstone: Ohio flint
State herb capital: Gahanna
State insect: Ladybird beetle (ladybug, *Hippodamia convergens*)
State poetry day: Ohio Poetry Day (third Friday of every October)
State prehistoric monument: Newark earthworks
State reptile: Black racer snake (*Coluber constrictor constrictor*)
State rock song: "Hang on Sloopy"
State song: "Beautiful Ohio"
State tree: Buckeye (*Aesculus glabra*)

More about state symbols at:
www.governorsresidence.ohio.gov/children/symbols.aspx
www.sos.state.oh.us/sos/ProfileOhio/SymbolsofOhio.aspx

More about the state at:
www.ohiohistorycentral.org

STATE OFFICES:
State website:
www.ohio.gov

Office of the Governor
77 S. High St.
Riffe Center
30th Fl.
Columbus, OH 43215
614-466-3555
www.governor.ohio.gov

Secretary of State
180 E. Broad St.
16th Fl.
Columbus, OH 43215

877-767-6446
614-466-2655
TTY: 877-644-6889
www.sos.state.oh.us

State Library of Ohio
274 E. 1st Ave.
Ste. 100
Columbus, OH 43201
800-686-1532
614-644-7061
fax: 614-466-3584
www.library.ohio.gov

Oklahoma

Forty-sixth state; admitted on November 16, 1907

Since 1921, November 16 has been designated Oklahoma Statehood Day. It has also been Oklahoma State Flag Day since 1968. In 1957, in honor of the 50th anniversary of statehood, the state legislature decreed the week of November 11-16 to be Oklahoma Week. In 1965, the lawmakers mandated public schools to conduct programs on the state's history and achievements on November 16. Annual observance of Oklahoma Statehood Day began in 1921 under the sponsorship of the Oklahoma Heritage Association, which continues to hold a dinner at the state capital at which notable Oklahomans are inducted into the Oklahoma Hall of Fame. Oklahoma Statehood Day is also observed annually with a ceremony at the Washington Cathedral in the nation's capital.

SEE ALSO OKLAHOMA DAY

State capital: Oklahoma City
Nickname: The Sooner State
State motto: *Labor omnia vincit* (Latin "Labor conquers all things")
State animal: American buffalo (*Bison bison*)
State amphibian: Bullfrog (*Rana catesbeiana*)
State beverage: Milk
State bird: Scissor-tailed flycatcher (*Muscivora forficatus*)
State butterfly: Black swallowtail (*Papilio polyxenes*)
State cartoon character: Gusty
State children's song: "Oklahoma, My Native Land"
State colors: Green and white
State country and western song: "Faded Love"
State crystal: Hourglass Selenite Crystal
State fish: White (sand) bass (*Morone chrysops*)
State floral emblem: Mistletoe (*Phoradendron serotinum*)
State flower: Oklahoma Rose; **wildflower**: Indian blanket (*Gaillardia pulchella*)
State flying mammal: Mexican free-tailed bat
State folk dance: Square dance
State fossil: Saurophaganax Maximus
State fruit: Strawberry
State furbearer: Raccoon

State game animal: White-tailed deer
State game bird: Wild turkey
State grass: Indiangrass (*Sorghastrum nutans*)
State insect: Honeybee (*Apis mellifera*)
State meal: Fried Okra, Squash, Cornbread, Barbeque Pork, Biscuits, Sausage & Gravy, Grits, Corn, Strawberries, Chicken Fried Steak, Black-eyed Peas, and Pecan Pie
State monument: The Golden Driller
State musical instrument: Fiddle
State percussive musical instrument: Drum
State poem: "Howdy Folks"
State reptile: Collared lizard (mountain boomer, *Crotaphytus collaris*)
State rock: Barite rose (rose rock or Cherokee rose)
State soil: Port Silt Loam (*Cumulic haplustolls*)
State song: "Oklahoma!"
State theater: Lynn Riggs Players of Oklahoma, Inc.
State tree: Redbud (*Cercis canadensis*)
State vegetable: Watermelon (*Citrullus lanatus*)
State waltz: "Oklahoma Wind"

More about state symbols at:
www.okhistory.org/kids/symbols.php
www.ok.gov/osfdocs/stinfo.html

CONTACT:
Oklahoma Heritage Association
1400 Classen Dr.
Oklahoma City, 73106
888-501-2059
405-235-4458
fax: 405-235-2714
www.oklahomahof.com

STATE OFFICES:
State website:
www.ok.gov

Office of the Governor
State Capitol
2300 N. Lincoln Blvd.
Rm. 212
Oklahoma City, OK 73105
405-521-2342
fax: 405-521-3353
www.ok.gov/governor

Secretary of State
2300 N. Lincoln Blvd.
Ste. 101
Oklahoma City, OK 73105
405-521-3912
fax: 405-521-3771
www.sos.ok.gov

Oklahoma Dept of Libraries
200 NE 18th St.
Oklahoma City, OK 73105
405-521-2502
fax: 405-525-7804
www.odl.state.ok.us

Oregon

Thirty-third state; admitted on February 14, 1859

While Admission Day is often commemorated by programs in schools, it is not a legal holiday in Oregon.

State capital: Salem

Nicknames: Beaver State; Pacific Wonderland; Webfoot State

State motto: *Alis volat propiis* (Latin "She flies with her own wings"; motto since 1987); The Union (motto from 1859 to 1987)

State animal: Beaver (*Castor canadensis*)

State beverage: Milk

State bird: Western meadowlark (*Sturnella neglecta*)

State colors: Navy blue and gold

State dance: Square dance

State father: Dr. John McLoughlin (October 19, 1784 – September 3, 1857)

State fish: Chinook salmon (*Oncorhynchus tshawytscha*)

State flower: Oregon grape (*Mahonia aquifolium*)

State fossil: Metasequoia (dawn redwood)

State fruit: Pear (*Pyrus communis*)

State gemstone: Oregon sunstone

State insect: Oregon swallowtail butterfly (*Papilio oregonius*)

State mother: Tabitha Moffatt Brown (May 1, 1780 – May 4, 1858)

State mushroom: Pacific golden chanterelle (*Cantharellus formosus*)

State nut: Hazelnut (*Corylus avellana*)

State rock: Thunderegg (geode)

State seashell: Oregon hairy triton (*Fusitriton oregonensis*)

State song: "Oregon, My Oregon"

State tree: Douglas fir (*Pseudotsuga menziesii*)

More about state symbols at:
www.oregonencyclopedia.org/articles/oregon_state_symbols/#.VORWoN-jnrc
www.oregon.com/attractions/oregon-state-facts

STATE OFFICES:
State website:
www.oregon.gov

Office of the Governor
900 Court St. NE
Ste. 160
Salem, OR 97301
503-378-4582
www.oregon.gov/gov

Secretary of State
900 Court St. NE
Rm. 136
Salem, OR 97301
800-332-2313
503-986-1848
www.oregonlegislature.gov

Oregon State Library
250 Winter St. NE
State Library Bldg.
Salem, OR 97301
503-378-4243
fax: 503-585-8059
www.oregon.gov/OSL

Pennsylvania

Second state; adopted the U.S. Constitution on December 12, 1787

State capital: Harrisburg

Nicknames: Keystone State; Quaker State

State motto: Virtue, Liberty, and Independence

State animal: White-tailed deer (*Odocoileus virginianus*)

State beverage: Milk

State dog: Great Dane

State fish: Brook trout (*Salvelinus fontinalis*)

State flagship: *U.S. Brig Niagara*

State flower: Mountain laurel (*Kalmia latifolia*)

State fossil: *Phacops rana*

State game bird: Ruffed grouse or partridge (*Bonasa umbellus*)

State insect: Firefly (*Poturis pennsylvanica*)

State plant: Penngift crownvetch (*Coronilla varia*)

State song: "Pennsylvania"

State tree: Eastern hemlock (*Tsuga canadensis*)

More about state symbols at:
www.portal.state.pa.us/portal/server.pt/community/things/4280/symbols_of_pennsylvania/478690
sites.state.pa.us/kids/deer.htm

STATE OFFICES:
State website:
www.pa.gov

Office of the Governor
100 State St.
Ste. 205
Erie, PA 16507
814-878-5719
www.governor.pa.gov

Secretary of the Commonwealth
302 N Office Bldg.
Harrisburg, PA 17120
717-787-6458
fax: 717-787-1734
www.dos.pa.gov

Pennsylvania Commonwealth Libraries
607 South Dr.
Forum Bldg.
Harrisburg, PA 17120
717-783-5950
www.portal.state.pa.us

Rhode Island

Thirteenth state; adopted the U.S. Constitution on May 29, 1790

State capital: Providence

Nicknames: The Ocean State; Little Rhody; Plantation State

State motto: Hope

State bird: Rhode Island red hen

State drink: Coffee milk

State flower: Violet (*Viola palmata*)

State folk art: Charles I.D. Looff Carousel (Crescent Park Carousel)

State fruit: Rhode Island greening apple

State mineral: Bowenite

State rock: Cumberlandite

State shell: Quahaug (*Mercenaria mercenaria*)

State song: "Rhode Island, It's for Me"

State tall ship and flagship: *USS Providence* (replica)

State tartan: Rhode Island

State tree: Red maple (*Acer rubrum*)

State yacht: *Courageous*

More about state symbols at:
www.ri.gov/facts/factsfigures.php

More about the state at:
www.visitrhodeisland.com/make-plans/for-students

STATE OFFICES:
State website:
www.ri.gov

Office of the Governor
82 Smith St.
Providence, RI 02903
401-222-2080
fax: 401-222-8096
www.governor.state.ri.us

Secretary of State
82 Smith St.
State House
Rm. 217
Providence, RI 02903
401-222-2357
fax: 401-222-1356
www.sos.ri.gov

Rhode Island Office of Library & Information Services
1 Capitol Hill
4th Fl.
Providence, RI 02908
401-574-9300
fax: 401-574-9320
www.olis.state.ri.us

South Carolina

Eighth state; adopted the U.S. Constitution on May 23, 1788 (seceded from the Union in December 1860, and was readmitted on June 25, 1868)

State capital: Columbia

Nicknames: The Palmetto State; The Rice State; The Swamp State; The Iodine State

State mottoes: *Animis opibusque parati* (Latin "Ready in soul and resource"); *Dum spiro spero* (Latin "While I breathe, I hope")

State American folk dance: Square dance

State amphibian: Spotted salamander (*Ambystomamaculatum*)

State animal: White-tailed deer (*Odocoileus virginianus*)

State beverage: Milk

State bird: Carolina wren (*Thryothorus ludovicianus*)

State botanical garden: Botanical Garden at Clemson University

State butterfly: Eastern tiger swallowtail (*Pterourus glaucus*)

State dance: The shag

State dog: Boykin spaniel

State fish: Striped bass (*Morone saxatilis*)

State flower: Carolina (yellow) jessamine (*Gelsemium sempervirens*)

State fruit: Peach

State gem: Amethyst

State grass: Indian grass (*Sorghastrum nutans*)

State hospitality beverage: South Carolina-grown tea

State insect: Carolina mantid, or praying mantis (*Mantis religiosa*)

State music: The spiritual; **popular music**: Beach music

State opera: *Porgy and Bess*

State railroad museum: South Carolina Railroad Museum in Fairfield County

State reptile: Loggerhead turtle (*Caretta caretta*)

State shell: Lettered olive (*Oliva sayana*)

State songs: "Carolina"; "South Carolina on My Mind"

State spider: Carolina wolf spider (*Hogna carolinensis*)

State stone: Blue granite

State tree: Palmetto

State waltz: Richardson Waltz

State wild game bird: Wild turkey (*Meleagris gallopavo*)

More about state symbols at:
www.scstatehouse.gov/studentpage/coolstuff/symbols.shtml
www.sciway.net/hist/symbols.html

STATE OFFICES:
State website:
www.sc.gov

Office of the Governor
Edgar A. Brown Bldg.
1205 Pendleton St.

Columbia, SC 29201
803-734-0560
www.oepp.sc.gov

Secretary of State
Edgar A. Brown Bldg.
1205 Pendleton St.
Ste. 525
Columbia, SC 29201
803-734-2170
www.scsos.com

South Carolina State Library
1500 Senate St.
P.O. Box 11469
Columbia, SC 29211
888-221-4643
803-734-8666
fax: 803-734-8676
www.statelibrary.sc.gov

South Dakota

Fortieth state; admitted on November 2, 1889

State capital: Pierre
Nickname: Mount Rushmore State
State motto: Under God the People Rule
State animal: Coyote (*Canis latrans*)
State bird: Ring-necked pheasant (*Phasianus colchicus*)
State dessert: Kuchen
State fish: Walleye (*Stizostedion vitreum*)
State flower: American pasque or May Day flower (*Pulsatilla hisutissima*)
State fossil: Triceratops
State gem: Fairburn agate
State insect: Honeybee (*Apis mellifera*)
State jewelry: Black Hills gold
State mineral: Rose quartz
State soil: Houdek soil
State song: "Hail, South Dakota"
State sport: Rodeo
State tree: Black Hills spruce (*Picea glauca densata*)

More about state symbols at:
www.thune.senate.gov/public/index.cfm/state-facts
www.travelsd.com/About-SD/South-Dakota-Facts

STATE OFFICES:
State website:
www.sd.gov

Office of the Governor
500 E. Capitol
Pierre, SD 57501
605-773-3212
www.sd.gov/governor

Secretary of State
Capitol Bldg.

500 E. Capitol
Ste. 204
Pierre, SD 57501
605-773-3537
fax: 605-773-6580
www.sdsos.gov

State Library
MacKay Bldg.
800 Governors Dr.
Pierre, SD 57501
800-423-6665
605-773-3131
fax: 605-773-6962
www.library.sd.gov

Tennessee

Sixteenth state; admitted on June 1, 1796 (seceded on June 8, 1861, and was readmitted on July 24, 1866)

In 1929, the state legislature designated June 1 as Statehood Day in Tennessee.

State capital: Nashville
Nicknames: The Volunteer State; The Big Bend State; The Mother of Southwestern Statesmen
State motto: Agriculture and Commerce
State agricultural insect: Honeybee (*Apis mellifera*)
State amphibian: Tennessee cave salamander (*Gyrinophilu palleucus*)
State animal: Raccoon (*Procyon lotor*)
State aviation hall of fame: Tennessee Aviation Hall of Fame
State bird: Mockingbird (*Mimus polyglottos*)
State butterfly: Zebra swallowtail (*Eurytides marcellus*)
State commercial fish: Channel catfish (*Ictalurus lacustris*); **game fish**: Largemouth bass (*Micropterus salmoides*)
State declamation: "I am Tennessee"
State flower: **cultivated**: Purple iris (Genus *Iridaceae*); **wild**: Passion flower (*Passiflora incarnata*)
State folk dance: Square dance
State fossil: *Pterotrigonia (Scabrotrigonia) thoracica*
State fruit: Tomato (*Lycopersicon lycopersicum*)
State game bird: Bobwhite quail (*Colinus virginianus*)
State gem: Tennessee pearl
State horse: Tennessee Walking Horse
State insects: Ladybug (*Hippodamia convergens*); firefly (*Photinus pyralls*)
State jamboree and crafts festival: Smithville Fiddlers' Jamboree and Crafts Festival
State paintings: *Tennessee Treasures; Tennessee Treasures Too*
State poem: "Oh Tennessee, My Tennessee"
State reptile: Eastern box turtle (*Terrapene carolina*)
State rocks: Limestone; agate
State slogan: Tennessee—America at Its Best

State songs: "When It's Iris Time in Tennessee"; "Tennessee Waltz"; "My Homeland, Tennessee"; "My Tennessee"; "Rocky Top"; "Tennessee"; "The Pride of Tennessee"

State tree: Tulip poplar (*Liriodendron tulipifera*)

State wild animal: Raccoon (*Procyon lotor*)

More about state symbols at:
www.state.tn.us/sos/symbols/symbols.htm
www.tn.gov/state-symbols.shtml

STATE OFFICES:
State website:
www.tennessee.gov

Office of the Governor
State Capitol
1st Fl.
Nashville, TN 37243
615-741-2001
www.tennessee.gov/governor

Secretary of State
State Capitol
Nashville, TN 37243
615-741-2819
www.state.tn.us/sos

Tennessee State Library & Archives
403 7th Ave N.
Nashville, TN 37243
615-741-2764
www.state.tn.us/tsla

Texas

Twenty-eighth state; admitted on December 29, 1845 (seceded from the Union on February 1, 1861, and was readmitted on March 30, 1870)

State capital: Austin

Nickname: The Lone Star State

State motto: Friendship

State air force: Commemorative Air Force (formerly Confederate Air Force)

State bird: Mockingbird (*Mimus polyglottos*)

State bread: Pan de campo

State cooking implement: Cast iron dutch oven

State dinosaurs: Brachiosaur sauropod and pleurocoelus

State dish: Chili

State dog breed: Blue Lacy

State epic poem: "Legend of Old Stone Ranch"

State fiber and fabric: Cotton

State fish: Guadalupe bass

State flower: Bluebonnet (*Lupinus subcarnosus, Lupinus texensis and all other varieties*)

State flower song: "Bluebonnets"

State footwear: Cowboy boot

State flying mammal: Mexican free-tailed bat

State folk dance: Square dance

State fruit: Texas red grapefruit

State gem: Texas blue topaz

State gemstone cut: Lone star cut

State grass: Sideoats Grama

State health nut: Pecan

State insect: Monarch butterfly

State large mammal: Longhorn; **small**: Armadillo

State maritime museum: Texas Maritime Museum

State musical instrument: Guitar

State native pepper: Chiltepin

State native shrub: Texas purple sage

State pastries: Sopaipilla; strudel

State pepper: Jalapeno

State petrified stone: Palmwood

State plant: Prickly pear cactus

State plays: *The Lone Star; Texas; Beyond the Sundown; Fandangle*

State precious metal: Silver

State railroad: Texas State Railroad

State reptile: Texas horned lizard

State rodeo drill team: Ghostriders

State song: "Texas, Our Texas"

State sport: Rodeo

State shell: Lightning whelk

State ship: *USS Texas*

State shrub: Crape myrtle

State snack: Tortilla chips and salsa

State tall ship: *Elissa*

State 10K: Texas Round-up 10K

State tartan: Texas Bluebonnet

State tie: Bolo tie

State tree: Pecan (*Carya illinoensis*)

State vegetable: Sweet onion

State vehicle: Chuck wagon

More about state symbols at:
www.tsl.texas.gov/ref/abouttx/symbols.html
www.senate.state.tx.us/kids/Trivia.htm

More about the state at:
www.tsl.texas.gov/ref/abouttx/index.html

STATE OFFICES:
State website:
www.texas.gov

Office of the Governor
State Insurance Bldg.
1100 San Jacinto Blvd.
Austin, TX 78701
512-463-2000
www.gov.texas.gov

Secretary of State
Capitol Bldg.
1100 Congress

Rm. 1E-8
Austin, TX 78701
512-463-5770
fax: 512-475-2761
www.sos.state.tx.us

Texas State Library
1201 Brazos St.
Austin, TX 78701
512-463-5455
fax: 512-463-5436
www.tsl.texas.gov

Utah

Forty-fifth state; admitted on January 4, 1896

State capital: Salt Lake City

Nicknames: Beehive State; Salt Lake State; Crossroads of the West

State motto: Industry

State animal: Rocky Mountain elk (*Cervus canadensis*)

State bird: California gull (*Larus californicus*)

State cooking pot: Dutch oven

State emblem: Beehive

State fish: Bonneville cutthroat trout (*Salmo clarki*)

State flower: Sego lily (*Calochortus nuttallii*)

State folk dance: Square dance

State fossil: Allosaurus

State fruit: Cherry

State gem: Topaz

State grass: Indian ricegrass (*Oryzopsis hymenoides*)

State historic vegetable: Sugar beet

State hymn: "Utah, We Love Thee"

State insect: Honeybee (*Apis mellifera*)

State mineral: Copper

State rock: Coal

State song: "Utah, This Is The Place"

State Star: Dubhe

State tartan: Utah State Tartan

State vegetable: Spanish sweet onion

State tree: Blue spruce (*Picea pungens*)

More about state symbols at:
www.utah.gov/about/symbols.html
www.pioneer.utah.gov/research/utah_symbols/index.html

More about the state at:
www.utah.gov/about

STATE OFFICES:
State website:
www.utah.gov

Office of the Governor
350 N. State St.
Ste. 200

P.O. Box 142220
Salt Lake City, UT 84114
800-705-2464
801-538-1000
www.utah.gov/governor

Utah State Library
250 N. 1950 W.
Ste. A
Salt Lake City, UT 84116
800-662-9150
801-715-6777
fax: 801-715-6767
www.heritage.utah.gov/library

Vermont

Fourteenth state; admitted on March 4, 1791

Town meetings held all over the state on the first Tuesday in March serve in part to commemorate Vermont's Admission Day (SEE TOWN MEETING DAY).

State capital: Montpelier

Nickname: The Green Mountain State

State motto: Freedom and Unity

State animal: Morgan horse

State beverage: Milk

State bird: Hermit thrush (*Hylocichla guttata*)

State butterfly: Monarch butterfly (*Danaus plexippus*)

State fish: cold water: Brook trout (*Salvelinus fontinalis*); **warm water**: Walleye (*Stizostedion vitreum vitreum*)

State flower: Red clover (*Trifolium pratense*)

State fossil: White whale (*Delphinapterus leucus*)

State fruit and pie: Apple

State gem: Grossular garnet

State insect: Honeybee (*Apis mellifera*)

State mineral: Talc

State rocks: Marble, granite, and slate

State soil: Tunbridge soil series

State song: "These Green Mountains" designated new state song in 2000; old state song was "Hail, Vermont"

State tree: Sugar maple (*Acer saccharum*)

More about state symbols at:
vermonthistory.org/explorer/discover-vermont/facts-figures/state-symbols
www.sec.state.vt.us/kids/symbols.html

More about the state at:
www.sec.state.vt.us/kids/pubs/history_facts_fun.pdf
www.sec.state.vt.us/kids/history.html

STATE OFFICES:
State website:
www.vermont.gov

Office of the Governor
109 State St.

Montpelier, VT 05609
802-828-3333
fax: 802-828-3339
TTY: 800-649-6825
www.governor.vermont.gov

Secretary of State
26 Terrace St.
Montpelier, VT 05663
800-439-8683
802-828-2363
fax: 802-828-2496
www.sec.state.vt.us

Vermont Dept of Libraries
109 State St.
Montpelier, VT 05609
802-828-3265
fax: 802-828-2199
www.libraries.vermont.gov

Virginia

Tenth state; adopted the U.S. Constitution on June 25, 1788 (seceded from the Union in April 1861, and was readmitted on January 26, 1870)

State capital: Richmond

Nicknames: Old Dominion; Mother of Presidents; Mother of Statesmen

State motto: *Sic semper tyrannis* (Latin "Thus ever to tyrants")

State beverage: Milk

State bat: Virginia big-eared bat (*Corynorhinus (= Plecotus) townsendii virginianus*)

State bird: Cardinal (*Cardinalis cardinalis*)

State boat: Chesapeake Bay Deadrise

State dog: American foxhound

State festival: Virginia Covered Bridge Festival.

State fish: Brook trout (*salvelinus fontinalis*)

State flower: American dogwood (*Cornus florida*)

State folk dance: Square dance

State folklore center: Blue Ridge Institute

State fossil: *Chesapecten jeffersonius* (scallop)

State insect: Tiger swallowtail butterfly (*Papilio glaucus Linne*)

State shell: Oyster shell (*Crassostraea virginica*)

State song: "Carry Me Back to Old Virginia" had been state song since 1940; the state held a contest to choose a new song in 1998, but none has been selected (as of April, 2008)

State tree: American dogwood (*Cornus florida*)

More about state symbols at:
capclass.virginiageneralassembly.gov/Emblems
www.virginia.org/statesymbolssealsemblems

STATE OFFICES:
State website:
www.virginia.gov

Office of the Governor
P.O. Box 1475
Richmond, VA 23218
804-786-2211
www.governor.virginia.gov
Secretary of the Commonwealth
1111 E. Broad St.
4th Fl.
Richmond, VA 23219
804-786-2441
fax: 804-371-0017
www.commonwealth.virginia.gov

Library of Virginia
800 E. Broad St.
Richmond, VA 23219
804-692-3500
www.lva.virginia.gov

Washington

Forty-second state; admitted on November 11, 1889

Admission Day is observed in Washington by closing public schools (however, schools are expected to hold special patriotic and historic programs on the preceding Friday). Former significant anniversaries of statehood—the 25th, 50th, and 75th—were commemorated with speeches (by President Franklin D. Roosevelt in 1939) and ceremonies.

State capital: Olympia

Nickname: Evergreen State

State motto: *Alki* (unspecified American Indian language "By and By")

State amphibian: Pacific chorus frog (*Pseudacris regilla*)

State arboretum: Washington Park Arboretum

State bird: Willow goldfinch or wild canary (*Spinus tristis salicamans*)

State colors: Green and gold

State dance: Square dance

State fish: Steelhead trout (*Salmo gairdnerii*)

State flower: Coast or pink rhododendron (*Rhododendron macrophyllum*)

State folk song: "Roll on, Columbia, Roll on"

State fossil: Columbian mammoth (*Mammuthus columbi*)

State fruit: Apple (*Malus sylvestris*)

State gem: Petrified wood

State grass: Bluebunch wheatgrass (*Agropyron spicatum*)

State insect: Green darner dragonfly (*Anax junius Drury*)

State marine mammal: Orca (*Orcinus orca*)

State ship: *Lady Washington*

State song: "Washington, My Home"

State tartan: Washington State Tartan

State tree: Western hemlock (*Tsuga heterophylla*)
State vegetable: Walla Walla sweet onion

More about state symbols at:
www.sos.wa.gov/seal/symbols.aspx
www.leg.wa.gov/Symbols/pages/default.aspx

STATE OFFICES:
State website:
www.access.wa.gov

Office of the Governor
P.O. Box 40002
Olympia, WA 98504
360-902-4111
fax: 360-753-4110
TTY: 800-833-6388
www.governor.wa.gov

Secretary of State
416 Sid Snyder Ave. SW
Legislative Bldg.
Olympia, WA 98504
360-902-4151
www.sos.wa.gov

Washington State Library
Point Plaza E.
6880 Capitol Blvd. SE
Tumwater, WA 98504
360-704-5200
www.sos.wa.gov/library

West Virginia

Thirty-fifth state; admitted on June 20, 1863

The centennial celebration took place throughout the state during the year of 1963 with parades, pageants, sporting events, historical exhibits and reenactments, various arts contests, musical events, fireworks, and, on June 20 at the capitol in Charleston, a speech by President John F. Kennedy.

SEE ALSO WEST VIRGINIA DAY

State capital: Charleston
Nickname: The Mountain State
State motto: *Montani Semper Liberi* (Latin "Mountaineers are always free")
State animal: Black bear (*Ursus (Euarctos) americanus*)
State bird: Cardinal (*Cardinalis cardinalis*)
State butterfly: Monarch
State colors: Old gold and blue
State fish: Brook trout (*Salvelinus fontinalis*)
State flower: Great laurel or Rhodondendron (*Rhododendron maximum*)
State fruit: Golden delicious apple
State gem: Mississippian Fossil Coral (*Lithostrotionella*)
State insect: Honeybee (*Apis mellifera*)
State soil: Monongahela Silt Loam

State songs: "The West Virginia Hills"; "West Virginia, My Home Sweet Home"; "This Is My West Virginia"
State tree: Sugar maple (*Acer saccharum*)

More about state symbols at:
www.legis.state.wv.us/educational/Kids_Page/symbols.cfm
www.wvcommerce.org/travel/requestinformation/statefacts.aspx

More about the state at:
www.wvcommerce.org/travel/wvtravel4kids/funfacts/default.aspx

STATE OFFICES:
State website:
www.wv.gov

Office of the Governor
State Capitol Bldg.
1900 Kanawha Blvd. E.
Charleston, WV 25305
888-438-2731
304-558-2000
www.governor.wv.gov

Secretary of State
1900 Kanawha Blvd. E.
Bldg. 1 Ste. 157K
Charleston, WV 25305
866-767-8683
304-558-6000
fax: 304-558-0900
www.sos.wv.gov

West Virginia Library Commission
1900 Kanawha Blvd. E.
Culture Center,
Bldg. 9
Charleston, WV 25305
800-642-9021
304-558-2041
www.librarycommission.wv.gov

Wisconsin

Thirtieth state; admitted on May 29, 1848

State capital: Madison
Nicknames: Badger State; America's Dairyland; Copper State
State motto: Forward
State animal: Badger (*Taxidea taxus*); **wildlife animal**: White-tailed deer (*Odocoileus virginianus*) **domestic animal**: Dairy cow (*Bos taurus*)
State ballad: "Oh Wisconsin, Land of My Dreams"
State beverage: Milk
State bird: Robin (*Turdus migratorius*)
State dance: Polka
State dog: American water spaniel
State fish: Muskellunge (muskie, *Esox masquinongy Mitchell*)
State flower: Wood violet (*Viola papilionacea*)

State fossil: Trilobite (*Calymene celebra*)

State fruit: Cranberry *(vaccinium macrocarpon)*

State grain: Corn (*Zea mays*)

State insect: Honeybee (*Apis mellifera*)

State mineral: Galena

State rock: Red granite

State soil: Antigo silt loam

State song: "On, Wisconsin!"

State symbol of peace: Mourning dove (*Zenaidura macroura corolinensis linnaus*)

State tree: Sugar maple (*Acer saccharum*)

State waltz: "The Wisconsin Waltz"

More about state symbols at:
www.legis.wisconsin.gov/lrb/bb/13bb/symbols.htm
www.wisconsinhistory.org/Content.aspx?dsNav=N:4294963828-4294963805&dsRecordDetails=R:CS2908

More about the state at:
www.wisconsinhistory.org

STATE OFFICES:
State website:
www.wisconsin.gov

Office of the Governor
115 E. Capitol
Madison, WI 53702
608-266-1212
www.wisgov.state.wi.us

Secretary of State
30 W. Mifflin St.
10th Fl.
P.O. Box 7848
Madison, WI 53703
608-266-8888
fax: 608-266-3159
www.sos.state.wi.us

Wisconsin Dept of Public Instruction
125 S. Webster St.
P.O. Box 7841
Madison, WI 53707
800-441-4563
608-266-3390
www.dpi.wi.gov

Wyoming

Forty-fourth state; admitted on July 10, 1890

State capital: Cheyenne

Nicknames: Equality State; Cowboy State; Big Wyoming

State motto: Equal Rights

State bird: Meadowlark (*Sturnella neglecta*)

State coin: Golden dollar

State dinosaur: Triceratops

State fish: Cutthroat trout (*Salmo clerki*)

State flower: Indian paintbrush (*Castilleja linariaefolia*)

State fossil: Knightia

State gemstone: Jade (nephrite)

State icon: Bucking horse

State mammal: Bison (*Bison bison*)

State reptile: Horned toad (*Douglassi brevirostre*)

State song: "Wyoming"

State sport: Rodeo

State tree: Plains cottonwood (*Populus sargentii*)

More about state symbols at:
www.wyo.gov/about-wyoming/wyoming-facts-and-symbols
soswy.state.wy.us/Information/StateInfo_Symbols.aspx

More about the state at:
www.wyo.gov/about-wyoming/wyoming-history

STATE OFFICES:
State website:
www.wyo.gov

Office of the Governor
State Capitol
200 W. 24th St.
Rm. 124
Cheyenne, WY 82202
307-777-7434
fax: 307-632-3909
governor.wyo.gov

Secretary of State
State Capitol Bldg.
200 W. 24th St.
Rm. 106
Cheyenne, WY 82002
307-777-7378
fax: 307-777-6217
www.soswy.state.wy.us

Wyoming State Library
2301 Capitol Ave.
Cheyenne, WY 82002
307-777-6333
fax: 307-777-6289
www-wsl.state.wy.us

American Samoa

American Samoa has been a U.S. territory since 1899; its inhabitants are considered U.S. nationals.

Capital: Pago Pago

Motto: *Samoa—Muamua le Atua* (Samoan "Samoa—Let God Be First")

Flower: Paogo (ulafala)

Plant: Ava (kava)

Song: "Amerika Samoa"

Tree: Paogo or pandanus

GOVERNMENT OFFICES:
Government website:
www.americansamoa.gov

Office of the Governor
A P Lutali Executive Office Bldg.
Pago Pago, American Samoa 96799
011-684-633-4116
fax: 011-684-633-2269
www.americansamoa.gov

Department of Local Government
011-684-633-5201
fax: 011-684-633-5590
www.americansamoa.gov

Feleti Barstow Public Library
P.O. Box 997687
Pago Pago, American Samoa 96799
011-684-633-5816
fax: 011-684-633-5823
www.fbpl.org

Guam

Guam has been a territory of the U.S. since 1898, but has been allowed autonomy in local affairs since 1950; native inhabitants are citizens of the U.S. but cannot vote in U.S. elections.

Capital: Hagatna (Agana)
Nicknames: Tano I'ManChanorro (Land of the Chamorros); Where America's Day Begins; America's Paradise in the Pacific
Bird: Totot (also known as the Mariana fruit dove or love bird; *Ptilinopus roseicapilla*)
Flower: Puti tai nobio or bougainvillea (*bougainvillea spectabilis*)
Hymn: "Guam Hymn" ("Fanohge Chamorro")
Languages: Chamorro; English
Tree: Ifil or Ifit (Intsia bijuga)

More about the territory at:
www.guam.gov/?pg=guam_history_culture

GOVERNMENT OFFICES:
Government website:
www.guam.gov

Office of the Governor
Ricardo J. Bordallo Governor's Complex
Adelup, Guam 96910
011-671-472-8931
fax: 011-671-477-4826
www.governor.guam.gov

Lieutenant Governor
Ricardo J. Bordallo Governor's Complex
P.O. Box 2950
Hagatna, Guam 96932
011-671-475-9380
fax: 011-671-47-2007
www.lt.guam.gov

Public Library System
254 Martyr St.

Hagatna, Guam 96910
011-671-475-4571
fax: 011-671-477-9777
www.gpls.guam.gov

Northern Mariana Islands

In 1947 the U.N. assigned the Islands to the U.S. to administer; in 1978 the Islands became a self-governing commonwealth under U.S. sovereignty; inhabitants became U.S. citizens in 1986, but cannot vote in U.S. elections.

Capital: Saipan (Capitol Hill)
Bird: Marianas Fruit Dove (*Ptilonopus roseicapilla*)
Flower: Plumeria (*Plumeria rubra forma acutifolia*)
Tree: Flame tree (*Delonix regia*)

GOVERNMENT OFFICES:
Office of the Governor
Juan A Sablan Memorial Bldg.
Caller Box 10007
Capital Hill
Saipan, 96950
670-664-2200
fax: 670-664-2211
www.gov.mp

Northern Mariana Islands State Library
P.O. Box 501092
Saipan, 96950
670-235-7318
fax: 670-235-7550
www.marianaslibrary.org

Puerto Rico

Puerto Rico became a territory of the U.S. in 1917, and, on July 25, 1952, a commonwealth with autonomous local governmental units; inhabitants have been U.S. citizens since 1917.

SEE PUERTO RICO CONSTITUTION DAY

Capital: San Juan
Nickname: Island of Enchantment
Motto: *Joannes est nomen ejus* (Spanish "Juan [John] Is His Name")
Animal: El coquí or tree frog (*Francolinus coqui*)
Bird: Reinita
Flower: Maga or Puerto Rico hibiscus (*Thespesia grandiflora*)
Languages: English; Spanish
Song: "La Borinqueña"
Sport: Beisbol or baseball
Tree: Ceiba or silk-cotton or kapok tree (*Ceiba pentandra*)

More about territory symbols at:
www.topuertorico.org/descrip.shtml

More about the territory at:
www.elboricua.com/FactSheet.html

GOVERNMENT OFFICES:
Government website:
www.gobierno.pr (Spanish only)

Office of the Governor
La Fortaleza
P.O. Box 9020082
San Juan, 00902
787-721-7000
www.fortaleza.gobierno.pr (Spanish only)

State Department
P.O. Box 9023271
San Juan, Puerto Rico 00902
787-722-2121
www.estado.gobierno.pr (Spanish only)

University of Puerto Rico Library System
Rio Piedras Campus
P.O. Box 23302
San Juan, 00931
787-764-0000
fax: 787-772-1479
www.uprrp.edu (Spanish only)

U.S. Virgin Islands

The U.S. Virgin Islands were purchased by the U.S. on March 31, 1917; in 1927 native inhabitants were made U.S. citizens.

SEE TRANSFER DAY

Capital: Charlotte Amalie
Nickname: The American Paradise
Motto: United in Pride and Hope
Bird: Yellow breast (bananaquit; *Coereba flaveola*)
Flower: Yellow cedar or trumpetbush (*Tecoma stans*)
Language (official): English
March: "Virgin Islands March"

More about the territory at:
www.visitusvi.com/culture_history
www.gov.vi/about.html#

GOVERNMENT OFFICES:
Government website:
www.gov.vi

Office of the Governor
Government House
1105 King St.
Christiansted
St. Croix, VI 00820
340-773-1404
fax: 340-713-9806
www.gov.vi

Division of Libraries, Archives and Museums
1122 King St.
Christiansted
St. Croix, 00820
340-773-5715
fax: 340-773-5327
www.virginislandspubliclibraries.org

APPENDIX 7

Legal Holidays by State

The following federal public holidays are observed throughout the United States:

Jan 1	New Year's Day
Jan, third Mon	Martin Luther King Jr. Birthday
Feb, third Mon	Presidents' Day
May, last Mon	Memorial Day
Jul 4	Independence Day
Sep, first Mon	Labor Day
Oct, second Mon	Columbus Day
Nov 11	Veterans Day
Nov, fourth Thurs	Thanksgiving Day
Dec 25	Christmas

Listed below are additional legal holidays observed by the various states, the District of Columbia, the Commonwealth of Puerto Rico, and the territories of American Samoa, Guam, Northern Mariana Islands, and the U.S. Virgin Islands. For Christian movable holidays, the range of months during which the day may fall is provided.

Alabama

Jan, third Mon	Martin Luther King Jr. Birthday and Robert E. Lee's Birthday
Feb, third Mon	Washington and Jefferson's Birthdays
Apr, fourth Mon	Confederate Memorial Day
Jun, first Mon	Jefferson Davis's Birthday
Oct, second Mon	Columbus Day and American Indian Heritage Day

Alaska

Mar, last Mon	Seward's Day
Oct 18	Alaska Day

Arizona

Jan, third Mon	Martin Luther King Jr. Birthday and Civil Rights Day
Sep 17	Constitution Commemoration Day

Arkansas

Jan, third Mon	Martin Luther King Jr. Birthday and Robert E. Lee's Birthday
Feb, third Mon	Washington's Birthday and Daisy Gatson Bates Day
Dec 24	Christmas Eve

California

Feb 12	Lincoln's Birthday
Feb, third Mon	Washington's Birthday
Mar 31 (or next Mon)	Cesar Chavez Day
Nov, Fri after Thanksgiving	Day after Thanksgiving

Colorado

None in addition to the standard holidays

Connecticut

Feb 12	Lincoln Day
Feb, third Mon	Washington's Birthday
Mar-Apr: Fri, before Easter	Good Friday

Delaware

Mar-Apr: Fri, before Easter	Good Friday

917

Nov, Fri after Thanksgiving . . . . Day after Thanks giving
Nov, every two years . . . . General Election Day as it
occurs

District of Columbia

Jan 20   Inauguration Day
(in years when a new president is elected)
April 16 . . . . DC Emancipation Day

Florida

Nov, Fri after Thanksgiving . . . . .Day after Thanksgiving

Georgia

Apr 26 . . . . Confederate Memorial Day
Nov, Fri after Thanksgiving . . . . .Robert E. Lee's
Birthday (traditionally observed Jan 19)
Dec 26 . . . . Presidents' Day
(traditionally observed Feb, third Mon)

Hawaii

Mar 26 . . . . Prince Jonah Kuhio Kalanianaole
Day
Mar-Apr: Fri before Easter . . . . Good Friday
Jun 11 . . . . .King Kamehameha I Day
Aug, third Fri. . . . . .Statehood Day
Nov, first Tues (even years) . . . . Election Day

Idaho

None in addition to the standard holidays

Illinois

Feb 12 . . . . .Lincoln's Birthday
Feb, third Mon . . . . Washington's Birthday
Nov . . . . General Election Day
Nov, Fri after Thanksgiving . . . . .Day after Thanksgiving
Dec 24 . . . . .Christmas Eve

Indiana

Presidents' Day not a legal holiday

Mar-Apr: Fri before Easter . . . . Good Friday
May, first Tues . . . . .Primary Election Day
(except year following presidential election)
Nov, first Tues . . . . General Election Day
(except year following presidential election)
Nov, Fri after Thanksgiving . . . . .Lincoln's Birthday
(traditionally observed Feb 12)
Dec 26 . . . . Washington's Birthday
(traditionally observed Feb, third Mon)

Iowa

Presidents' Day not a legal holiday

Nov, Fri after Thanksgiving . . . . . .Day after Thanksgiving

Kansas

Presidents' Day not observed

Nov, Fri after Thanksgiving . . . . Day After Thanksgiving

Kentucky

Jan, dates vary . . . . .New Year's (2 days)
Mar-Apr, Fri before Easter . . . . . .Good Friday (half day)
Nov . . . . General Presidential
Election
Nov, Fri after Thanksgiving . . . . Day after Thanksgiving
Dec, dates vary. . . . . Christmas (2 days)

Louisiana

**Jan, second Mon every
four years in Baton Rouge** . . . . .Inauguration Day
Feb, day before Ash Wednesday   Mardi Gras Day
Mar-Apr: Fri before Easter . . . . .Good Friday
Nov (even years). . . . . .Election Day

Maine

Apr, third Mon. . . . . .Patriots' Day
Nov, Fri after Thanksgiving . . . . Day after Thanksgiving

Maryland

Nov . . . . Election Day
Nov, Fri after Thanksgiving . . . . Day after Thanksgiving

Massachusetts

Apr, third Mon. . . . . .Patriots' Day

Michigan

Nov, first Tues (even years) . . . . .Election Day
Nov, Fri after Thanksgiving . . . . Day after Thanksgiving
Dec 24 . . . . .Christmas Eve
Dec 31 . . . . New Year's Eve

Minnesota

None in addition to the standard holidays

Mississippi

Jan, third Mon . . . . Martin Luther King Jr.
Birthday and Robert E. Lee's Birthday
Apr, last Mon . . . . Confederate Memorial Day
May, last Mon . . . . .Memorial Day and Jefferson
Davis's Birthday

Missouri

Feb 12 . . . . Lincoln Day
May 8 . . . . .Harry S. Truman Day

Montana

Nov, first Tues . . . . .General Election Day

Nebraska

Apr, last Fri . . . . Arbor Day
Nov, Fri after Thanksgiving . . . . Day after Thanksgiving

Nevada

Oct, last Fri . . . . Nevada Day
Nov, Fri after Thanksgiving . . . . Family Day

New Hampshire

Nov, first Tues (even years) . . . . .Election Day
Nov, Fri after Thanksgiving . . . . Day after Thanksgiving

New Jersey

Feb 12 . . . . Lincoln's Birthday
Feb, third Mon . . . . .Washington's Birthday
Mar-Apr: Fri before Easter . . . . .Good Friday
Nov . . . . .Election Day

New Mexico

None in addition to the standard holidays

New York

Feb 12 . . . . .Lincoln's
Birthday
Feb, third Mon . . . . .Washington's Birthday
Nov . . . . .Election Day

North Carolina

Presidents' Day not a legal holiday

Mar-Apr: Fri before Easter . . . . .Good Friday
Nov, Fri after Thanksgiving . . . . Day After Thanksgiving
Dec 24 . . . . .Christmas Eve

North Dakota

Mar-Apr: Fri before Easter . . . . .Good Friday

Ohio

None in addition to the standard holidays

Oklahoma

Nov, Fri after Thanksgiving . . . . .Day after Thanksgiving

Oregon

None in addition to the standard holidays

Pennsylvania

Nov, Fri after Thanksgiving . . . . .Day after Thanksgiving

Rhode Island

Presidents' Day not a legal holiday

Aug, second Mon . . . . .Victory Day (V-J Day)
Nov . . . . .Election Day

South Carolina

May 10 . . . . Confederate Memorial Day
Nov, Fri after Thanksgiving . . . . .Day after Thanksgiving
Dec 26 . . . . .Day after Christmas

South Dakota

Oct, second Mon . . . . .Native Americans' Day

Tennessee

Mar-Apr: Fri before Easter . . . . .Good Friday

Texas

Jan 19 . . . . Confederate Heroes Day
Mar 2 . . . . .Texas Independence Day
Apr 21 . . . . San Jacinto Day
Jun 19 . . . . Emancipation Day
(Juneteenth)
Aug 27. . . . . .Lyndon Baines Johnson Day
Nov . . . . .Election Day
Nov, Fri after Thanksgiving . . . . .Day after Thanksgiving
Dec 24 . . . . .Christmas Eve
Dec 26 . . . . .Day after Christmas

Utah

Jul 24 . . . . Pioneer Day

Vermont

Mar, first Tues	Town Meeting Day
Aug 16	Bennington Battle Day
Nov, Fri after Thanksgiving	Day after Thanksgiving

Virginia

Jan, Fri before third Mon	Lee-Jackson Day
Oct, second Mon	Columbus Day and Yorktown Victory Day
Nov, Fri after Thanksgiving	Day after Thanksgiving

Washington

Nov, Fri after Thanksgiving	Day after Thanksgiving

West Virginia

Feb, third Mon	Presidents' Day/Washington's Birthday
May, second Tues (even years)	Primary Election Day
Jun 20	West Virginia Day
Nov, first Tues (even years)	Election Day
Nov, Fri after Thanksgiving	Day after Thanksgiving
Dec 24	Christmas Eve (half day)
Dec 31	New Year's Eve (half day)

Wisconsin

Presidents' Day not a legal holiday

Dec 24	Christmas Eve

Wyoming

None in addition to the standard holidays

TERRITORIES

American Samoa

Apr 17	American Samoa Flag Day
Jul 17	Manu'a Day
Dec 31	New Year's Eve

Guam

Presidents' Day and Columbus Day not legal holidays

Jul 21	Liberation Day
Nov 2	All Souls Day
Dec 8	Our Lady of Camarin Day

Northern Mariana Islands

Mar 24	Commonwealth Covenant Day
Mar-Apr: Fri before Easter	Good Friday
Oct, second Mon	Commonwealth Cultural Day
Nov 4	Citizenship Day
Dec 8	Constitution Day

Puerto Rico

Jan 6	Three Kings' Day
Jan, second Mon	Eugenio María de Hostos Day
Mar 22	Emancipation Day
Mar-Apr: Fri before Easter	Good Friday
Apr, third Mon	José de Diego Day
Jul 17	Luis Muñoz Rivera Day
Jul 25	Constitution Day
Jul 27	José Celso Barbosa's Birthday
Nov, first Tuesday	General Election Day
Nov 19	Discovery Day
Dec 24	Christmas Eve (half day)

U.S. Virgin Islands

Jan 6	Three Kings' Day
Mar 31	Transfer Day
Mar-Apr: Thurs before Easter	Holy Thursday
Mar-Apr: Fri before Easter	Good Friday
Mar-Apr: Mon after Easter	Easter Monday
Jul 3	Virgin Islands Emancipation Day
Nov 1	D. Hamilton Jackson Day (Liberty Day)
Dec 26	Christmas Second Day

APPENDIX 8

Tourism Information Sources for the U.S. States and North America

The following includes tourism information sources for the United States, Canada, and Mexico. Within the United States, the list is organized first by state, plus the District of Columbia. Within each state listing, listings are in the following order, although each state may not have all offices:

State-wide tourism office
State-wide chamber of commerce office
Local convention and visitor's bureaus
Local chambers of commerce

UNITED STATES

Alabama

Alabama Tourism & Travel Bureau
401 Adams Ave.
P.O. Box 4927
Montgomery, AL 36103
Phone: 334-242-4169
Toll-free: 800-252-2262
www.alabama.travel

Business Council of Alabama
2 N. Jackson St.
Montgomery, AL 36104
Phone: 334-834-6000 Fax: 334-241-5984
Toll-free: 800-665-9647
www.bcatoday.org

Greater Birmingham Convention & Visitors Bureau
2200 9th Ave. N.
Birmingham, AL 35203
Phone: 205-458-8000 Fax: 205-458-8086
Toll-free: 800-458-8085
www.birminghamal.org

Huntsville/Madison County Convention & Visitor's Bureau
500 Church St. N.W.
Ste. 1
Huntsville, AL 35801
Phone: 256-551-2230 Fax: 256-551-2324
Toll-free: 800-843-0468
www.huntsville.org

Mobile Bay Convention & Visitors Bureau
1 S. Water St.
Mobile, AL 36602
Phone: 251-208-2000 Fax: 251-208-2060
Toll-free: 800-566-2453
www.mobile.org

Montgomery Area Chamber of Commerce Convention & Visitor Bureau
300 Water St.
Montgomery, AL 36104
Phone: 334-261-1100
Toll-free: 800-240-9452
www.visitingmontgomery.com

Tuscaloosa Convention & Visitors Bureau
1900 Jack Warner Pkwy.
P.O. Box 3167
Tuscaloosa, AL 35401
Phone: 205-391-9200 Fax: 205-759-9002
Toll-free: 800-538-8696
www.visittuscaloosa.com

Birmingham Business Alliance
505 20th St. N.
Ste. 200
Birmingham, AL 35203
Phone: 205-324-2100 Fax: 205-324-2560
www.birminghambusinessalliance.com

Chamber of Commerce of Huntsville/Madison County
225 Church St.
Huntsville, AL 35801

Phone: 256-535-2000 Fax: 256-535-2015
www.huntsvillealabamausa.com

Chamber of Commerce of West Alabama
2201 Jack Warner Blvd.
Bldg. C
Tuscaloosa, AL 35401
Phone: 205-758-7588 Fax: 205-391-0565
www.tuscaloosachamber.com

Mobile Area Chamber of Commerce
451 Government St.
Mobile, AL 36602
Phone: 251-433-6951 Fax: 251-432-1143
Toll-free: 800-422-6951
www.mobilechamber.com

Montgomery Area Chamber of Commerce
41 Commerce St.
P.O. Box 79
Montgomery, AL 36101
Phone: 334-834-5200 Fax: 334-265-4745
www.montgomerychamber.com

Alaska

Alaska Tourism Development Office
3032 Vintage Park Blvd.
Ste. 100
Juneau, AK 99801
Phone: 907-465-2510 Fax: 907-465-2103
www.commerce.state.ak.us/dnn/ded/home.aspx

Alaska State Chamber of Commerce
471 W. 36th Ave.
Ste. 201
Anchorage, AK 99503
Phone: 907-278-2727
www.alaskachamber.com

Alaska State Chamber of Commerce
9301 Glacier Hwy.
Ste. 110
Juneau, AK 99801
Phone: 907-586-2323
www.alaskachamber.com

Anchorage Convention & Visitors Bureau
524 W. 4th Ave.
Anchorage, AK 99501
Phone: 907-276-4118 Fax: 907-278-5559
www.anchorage.net

Fairbanks Convention & Visitors Bureau
101 Dunkel St.
Ste. 111
Fairbanks, AK 99701
Phone: 907-457-3282 Fax: 907-459-3787

Toll-free: 877-551-1728
www.explorefairbanks.com

Juneau Convention & Visitors Bureau
800 Glacier Ave.
Ste. 201
Juneau, AK 99801
Phone: 907-586-1737
Toll-free: 800-587-2201
www.traveljuneau.com

Anchorage Chamber of Commerce
1016 W. 6th Ave.
Ste. 303
Anchorage, AK 99501
Phone: 907-272-2401 Fax: 907-272-4117
www.anchoragechamber.org

Fairbanks Chamber of Commerce
100 Cushman St.
Ste. 102
Fairbanks, AK 99701
Phone: 907-452-1105
www.fairbankschamber.org

Juneau Chamber of Commerce
9301 Glacier Hwy.
Ste. 110
Juneau, AK 99801
Phone: 907-463-3488 Fax: 907-463-3489
www.juneauchamber.com

Arizona

Arizona Tourism Office
1110 W. Washington St.
Ste. 155
Phoenix, AZ 85007
Phone: 602-364-3700 Fax: 602-364-3701
www.visitarizona.com

Arizona Chamber of Commerce & Industry
3200 N. Central Ave.
Ste. 1125
Phoenix, AZ 85012
Phone: 602-248-9172 Fax: 602-391-2498
Toll-free: 866-275-5816
www.azchamber.com

Flagstaff Convention & Visitors Bureau
323 W. Aspen Ave.
Flagstaff, AZ 86001
Phone: 928-213-2910 Fax: 928-556-1305
Toll-free: 800-217-2367
www.flagstaffarizona.org

Greater Phoenix Convention & Visitors Bureau
400 E. Van Buren St.

Ste. 600
Phoenix, AZ 85004
Phone: 602-254-6500 Fax: 602-253-4415
Toll-free: 877-225-5749
www.visitphoenix.com

Mesa Convention & Visitors Bureau
120 N. Center St.
Mesa, AZ 85201
Phone: 480-827-4700 Fax: 480-827-4704
Toll-free: 800-283-6372
www.visitmesa.com

Metropolitan Tucson Convention & Visitors Bureau
100 S. Church Ave.
Tucson, AZ 85701
Phone: 520-624-1817 Fax: 520-884-7804
Toll-free: 800-638-8350
www.visittucson.org

Scottsdale Convention & Visitors Bureau
4343 N. Scottsdale Rd.
Ste. 170
Scottsdale, AZ 85251
Phone: 480-421-1004 Fax: 480-421-9733
Toll-free: 800-782-1117
www.experiencescottsdale.com

Tempe Convention & Visitors Bureau
51 W. 3rd St.
Ste. 105
Tempe, AZ 85281
Phone: 480-894-8158 Fax: 480-968-8004
Toll-free: 800-283-6734
www.tempetourism.com

Flagstaff Chamber of Commerce
101 W. Rt.66
Flagstaff, AZ 86001
Phone: 928-774-4505 Fax: 928-779-1209
www.flagstaffchamber.com

Glendale Chamber of Commerce
5800 W. Glenn Dr.
Ste. 275
Glendale, AZ 85301
Phone: 623-937-4754 Fax: 623-937-3333
www.glendaleazchamber.org

Greater Phoenix Chamber of Commerce
201 N. Central Ave.
27th Fl.
Phoenix, AZ 85004
Phone: 602-495-2195 Fax: 602-495-8913
www.phoenixchamber.com

Mesa Chamber of Commerce
40 N. Center St.
Ste. 104
Mesa, AZ 85201

Phone: 480-969-1307 Fax: 480-247-5414
www.mesachamberofcommerce.org

Scottsdale Area Chamber of Commerce
7501 E. McCormick Pkwy
Ste. 202-N
Scottsdale, AZ 85258
Phone: 480-355-2700 Fax: 480-355-2710
www.scottsdalechamber.com

Tempe Chamber of Commerce
909 E. Apache Blvd.
P.O. Box 28500
Tempe, AZ 85285
Phone: 480-967-7891 Fax: 480-966-5365
www.tempechamber.org

Tucson Metropolitan Chamber of Commerce
465 W. St. Mary's Rd.
P.O. Box 991
Tucson, AZ 85702
Phone: 520-792-1212 Fax: 520-882-5704
www.tucsonchamber.org

Arkansas

Arkansas Parks & Tourism Dept
1 Capitol Mall
Little Rock, AR 72201
Phone: 501-682-7777
Toll-free: 800-628-8725
www.arkansas.com

Arkansas State Chamber of Commerce
1200 W. Capitol Ave.
Little Rock, AR 72201
Phone: 501-372-2222
www.arkansasstatechamber.com

Fort Smith Convention & Visitors Bureau
2 N. B St.
Fort Smith, AR 72901
Phone: 479-783-8888 Fax: 479-784-2421
Toll-free: 800-637-1477
www.fortsmith.org

Hot Springs Convention & Visitors Bureau
134 Convention Blvd.
P.O. Box 6000
Hot Springs, AR 71901
Phone: 501-321-2277 Fax: 501-321-2136
Toll-free: 800-543-2284
www.hotsprings.org

Little Rock Convention & Visitors Bureau
426 W. Markham St.
P.O. Box 3232
Little Rock, AR 72203

Phone: 501-376-4781 Fax: 501-376-7833
Toll-free: 800-844-4781
www.littlerock.com

Fort Smith Chamber of Commerce
612 Garrison Ave.
Fort Smith, AR 72901
Phone: 479-783-3111 Fax: 479-783-6110
www.fortsmithchamber.org

Greater Hot Springs Chamber of Commerce
659 Ouachita Ave.
Hot Springs, AR 71901
Phone: 501-321-1700 Fax: 501-321-3551
www.hotspringschamber.com

Greater Little Rock Chamber of Commerce
200 E. Markham St.
Little Rock, AR 72201
Phone: 501-374-2001
www.littlerockchamber.com

California

California Travel & Tourism Commission
P.O. Box 1499
Sacramento, CA 95812
Phone: 916-444-4429
Toll-free: 877-225-4367
www.visitcalifornia.com

California Chamber of Commerce
1215 K St.
Ste. 1400
Sacramento, CA 95814
Phone: 916-444-6670 Fax: 916-325-1272
www.calchamber.com

Anaheim/Orange County Visitor & Convention Bureau
800 W. Katella Ave.
Anaheim, CA 92802
Phone: 714-765-8888
Toll-free: 855-405-5020
www.anaheimoc.org

Chula Vista Convention & Visitors Bureau
233 4th Ave.
Chula Vista, CA 91910
Phone: 619-426-2882 Fax: 619-420-1269
www.chulavistaconvis.com

Fresno City & County Convention & Visitors Bureau
1550 E. Shaw Ave.
Ste. 101
Fresno, CA 93710
Phone: 559-981-5500 Fax: 559-445-0122
Toll-free: 800-788-0836
www.playfresno.org

Garden Grove Visitors Bureau
12866 Main St.
Ste. 102
Garden Grove, CA 92840
Phone: 714-638-7950 Fax: 714-636-6672
Toll-free: 800-959-5560
www.gardengrovechamber.com

Greater Bakersfield Convention & Visitors Bureau
515 Truxtun Ave.
Bakersfield, CA 93301
Phone: 661-852-7282 Fax: 661-325-7074
Toll-free: 866-425-7353
www.visitbakersfield.com

Huntington Beach Conference & Visitors Bureau
301 Main St.
Ste. 212
Huntington Beach, CA 92648
Phone: 714-969-3492
Toll-free: 800-729-6232
www.surfcityusa.com

Long Beach Convention & Visitors Bureau
301 E. Ocean Blvd.
Ste. 1900
Long Beach, CA 90802
Phone: 562-436-3645 Fax: 562-435-5653
Toll-free: 800-452-7829
www.visitlongbeach.com

Los Angeles Convention & Visitors Bureau
333 S Hope St.
Los Angeles, CA 90071
Phone: 213-624-7300 Fax: 213-624-0179
www.discoverlosangeles.com

Modesto Convention & Visitors Bureau
1150 9th St.
Ste. C
Modesto, CA 95354
Phone: 209-526-5588 Fax: 209-526-5586
Toll-free: 888-640-8467
www.visitmodesto.com

Monterey County Convention & Visitors Bureau
P.O. Box 1770
Monterey, CA 93942 Fax: 831-648-5373
Toll-free: 888-221-1010
www.seemonterey.com

Oakland Convention & Visitors Bureau
481 Water St.
Oakland, CA 94607
Phone: 510-839-9000
www.visitoakland.org

Oxnard Convention & Visitors Bureau
1000 Town Center Dr.
Ste. 130

Oxnard, CA 93036
Phone: 805-385-7545 Fax: 805-385-7571
Toll-free: 800-269-6273
www.visitoxnard.com

Palm Springs Desert Resorts Convention & Visitors
  Authority
70-100 Hwy. 111
Rancho Mirage, CA 92270
Phone: 760-770-9000 Fax: 760-770-9001
Toll-free: 800-967-3767
www.visitgreaterpalmsprings.com

Riverside Convention & Visitors Bureau
3637 Fifth St.
Riverside, CA 92501
Phone: 951-222-4700
www.riversidecvb.com

Sacramento Convention & Visitors Bureau
1608 I St.
Sacramento, CA 95814
Phone: 916-808-7777
Toll-free: 800-292-2334
www.visitsacramento.com

San Bernardino Convention & Visitors Bureau
1955 Hunts Ln.
Ste. 102
San Bernardino, CA 92408
Toll-free: 800-867-8366
www.sbcity.org/cityhall/cvb/default.asp

San Diego Convention & Visitors Bureau
750 B St.
Ste. 1500
San Diego, CA 92101
Phone: 619-232-3101 Fax: 619-696-9371
www.sandiego.org

San Francisco Convention & Visitors Bureau
1 Front St.
Ste. 2900
San Francisco, CA 94111
Phone: 415-974-6900 Fax: 415-227-2602
www.sanfrancisco.travel

San Jose Convention & Visitors Bureau
408 Almaden Blvd.
San Jose, CA 95110
Phone: 408-295-9600
Toll-free: 800-726-5673
www.sanjose.org

Santa Barbara Visitors Bureau & Film Commission
500 E. Montecito St.
Santa Barbara, CA 93103
Phone: 805-966-9222 Fax: 805-966-1728
Toll-free: 800-676-1266
www.santabarbaraca.com

Stockton/San Joaquin Convention & Visitors Bureau
125 Bridge Pl.
Stockton, CA 95202
Phone: 209-938-1555 Fax: 209-938-1554
Toll-free: 877-778-6258
www.visitstockton.org

Anaheim Chamber of Commerce
2400 E. Katella Ave.
Ste. 725
Anaheim, CA 92806
Phone: 714-758-0222 Fax: 714-758-0468
www.anaheimchamber.org

Chula Vista Chamber of Commerce
233 4th Ave.
Chula Vista, CA 91910
Phone: 619-420-6603 Fax: 619-420-1269
www.chulavistachamber.org

Fremont Chamber of Commerce
39488 Stevenson Pl.
Ste. 100
Fremont, CA 94539
Phone: 510-795-2244 Fax: 510-795-2240
www.fremontbusiness.com

Fresno Chamber of Commerce
2331 Fresno St.
Fresno, CA 93721
Phone: 559-495-4800 Fax: 559-495-4811
www.fresnochamber.com

Garden Grove Chamber of Commerce
12866 Main St.
Ste. 102
Garden Grove, CA 92840
Phone: 714-638-7950 Fax: 714-636-6672
Toll-free: 800-959-5560
www.gardengrovechamber.com

Glendale Chamber of Commerce
701 N. Brand Blvd.
Ste. 120
Glendale, CA 91203
Phone: 818-240-7870 Fax: 818-240-2872
www.glendalechamber.com

Greater Bakersfield Chamber of Commerce
1725 Eye St.
Bakersfield, CA 93301
Phone: 661-327-4421 Fax: 661-327-8751
www.bakersfieldchamber.org

Greater Riverside Chambers of Commerce
3985 University Ave.
Riverside, CA 92501
Phone: 951-683-7100 Fax: 951-683-2670
www.riverside-chamber.com

Greater Stockton Chamber of Commerce
445 W. Weber Ave.
Ste. 220
Stockton, CA 95203
Phone: 209-547-2770 Fax: 209-466-5271
www.stocktonchamber.org

Huntington Beach Chamber of Commerce
2134 Main St.
Ste. 100
Huntington Beach, CA 92648
Phone: 714-536-8888 Fax: 714-960-7654
www.hbchamber.org

Long Beach Area Chamber of Commerce
1 World Trade Ctr.
Ste. 206
Long Beach, CA 90831
Phone: 562-436-1251 Fax: 562-436-7099
www.lbchamber.com

Los Angeles Area Chamber of Commerce
350 S Bixel St.
Los Angeles, CA 90017
Phone: 213-580-7500 Fax: 213-580-7511
www.lachamber.com

Modesto Chamber of Commerce
1114 J St.
Modesto, CA 95354
Phone: 209-577-5757 Fax: 209-577-2673
www.modchamber.org

Monterey Peninsula Chamber of Commerce
30 Ragsdale Dr.
Ste. 200
Monterey, CA 93940
Phone: 831-648-5360 Fax: 831-649-3502
www.montereychamber.com

Oakland Metropolitan Chamber of Commerce
475 14th St.
Ste. 100
Oakland, CA 94612
Phone: 510-874-4800 Fax: 510-839-8817
www.oaklandchamber.com

Oxnard Chamber of Commerce
400 E. Esplanade Dr.
Ste. 302
Oxnard, CA 93036
Phone: 805-983-6118 Fax: 805-604-7331
www.oxnardchamber.org

Palm Springs Chamber of Commerce
190 W. Amado Rd.
Palm Springs, CA 92262
Phone: 760-325-1577 Fax: 760-325-8549
www.pschamber.org

Sacramento Metro Chamber of Commerce
1 Capital Mall
Ste. 300
Sacramento, CA 95814
Phone: 916-552-6800 Fax: 916-443-2672
www.metrochamber.org

San Bernardino Area Chamber of Commerce
546 W. 6th St.
San Bernardino, CA 92410
Phone: 909-885-7515 Fax: 909-384-9979
www.sbachamber.org

San Diego Regional Chamber of Commerce
402 W. Broadway
Ste. 1000
San Diego, CA 92101
Phone: 619-544-1300
www.sdchamber.org

San Francisco Chamber of Commerce
235 Montgomery St.
Ste. 760
San Francisco, CA 94104
Phone: 415-392-4520 Fax: 415-392-0485
www.sfchamber.com

San Jose Silicon Valley Chamber of Commerce
101 W. Santa Clara St.
San Jose, CA 95113
Phone: 408-291-5250 Fax: 408-286-5019
www.sjchamber.com

Santa Ana Chamber of Commerce
1631 W. Sunflower Ave.
Ste. C-35
Santa Ana, CA 92704
Phone: 714-541-5353 Fax: 714-541-2238
www.santaanachamber.com

Santa Barbara Region Chamber of Commerce
104 W. Anapamu St.
Ste. A
Santa Barbara, CA 93101
Phone: 805-965-3023 Fax: 805-966-5954
www.sbchamber.org

Colorado

Colorado Tourism Office
1625 Broadway
Ste. 2700
Denver, CO 80202
Phone: 303-892-3840
Toll-free: 800-265-6723
www.colorado.com

Colorado Assn of Commerce & Industry
1600 Broadway

Ste. 1000
Denver, CO 80202
Phone: 303-831-7411 Fax: 303-860-1439
www.cochamber.com

Aspen Chamber Resort Assn
425 Rio Grande Pl.
Aspen, CO 81611
Phone: 970-925-1940 Fax: 970-920-1173
Toll-free: 800-670-0792
www.aspenchamber.org

Boulder Convention & Visitors Bureau
2440 Pearl St.
Boulder, CO 80302
Phone: 303-442-2911 Fax: 303-938-2098
Toll-free: 800-444-0447
www.bouldercoloradousa.com

Colorado Springs Convention & Visitors Bureau
515 S. Cascade Ave.
Colorado Springs, CO 80903
Phone: 719-635-7506
Toll-free: 800-888-4748
www.visitcos.com

Denver Metro Convention & Visitors Bureau
1555 California St.
Ste. 300
Denver, CO 80202
Phone: 303-892-1112
Toll-free: 800-233-6837
www.denver.org

Durango Area Tourism Office
802 Main Ave.
Durango, CO 81301
Phone: 970-247-3500
Toll-free: 800-525-8855
www.durango.org

Fort Collins Convention & Visitors Bureau
19 Old Town Sq.
Ste. 137
Fort Collins, CO 80524
Phone: 970-232-3840 Fax: 970-232-3841
Toll-free: 800-274-3678
www.visitftcollins.com

Greater Pueblo Chamber of Commerce & Visitors Council
320 Central Main St.
Pueblo, CO 81003
Phone: 719-542-1100
www.puebloconventioncenter.com

Aurora Chamber of Commerce
14305 E. Alameda Ave.
Ste. 300
Aurora, CO 80012

Phone: 303-344-1500 Fax: 303-344-1564
www.aurorachamber.org

Boulder Chamber of Commerce
2440 Pearl St.
Boulder, CO 80302
Phone: 303-442-1044
www.boulderchamber.com

Colorado Springs Regional Business Alliance
102 S. Tejon St.
Ste. 430
Colorado Springs, CO 8090.
Phone: 719-471-8183 Fax: 719-471-9733
www.coloradospringsbusinessalliance.com

Denver Metro Chamber of Commerce
1445 Market St.
Denver, CO 80202
Phone: 303-534-8500 Fax: 303-534-3200
www.denverchamber.org

Durango Area Chamber of Commerce
111 S. Camino del Rio
P.O. Box 2587
Durango, CO 81302
Phone: 970-247-0312 Fax: 970-385-7884
Toll-free: 888-414-0835
www.durangobusiness.org

Fort Collins Area Chamber of Commerce
225 S. Meldrum St.
Fort Collins, CO 80521
Phone: 970-482-3746
www.fortcollinschamber.com

Greater Pueblo Chamber of Commerce
302 N. Santa Fe Ave.
Pueblo, CO 81003
Phone: 719-542-1704
Toll-free: 800-233-3446
www.pueblochamber.org

Connecticut

Connecticut Commission on Culture & Tourism
1 Constitution Plaza
2nd Fl.
Hartford, CT 06103
Phone: 860-256-2800 Fax: 860-256-2811
www.cultureandtourism.org

Connecticut Tourism Div
1 Constitution Plaza
2nd Fl.
Hartford, CT 06103
Phone: 860-256-2800 Fax: 860-270-8077

Toll-free: 888-288-4748
www.ctvisit.com

Connecticut Business & Industry Assn
350 Church St.
Hartford, CT 06103
Phone: 860-244-1900 Fax: 860-278-8562
www.cbia.com

Greater New Haven Convention & Visitors Bureau
195 Church St.
New Haven, CT 06510
Phone: 203-777-8550
Toll-free: 800-332-7829
www.visitnewhaven.com

Western CT Convention & Visitors Bureau
P.O. Box 968
Litchfield, CT 06759
Phone: 860-567-4506 Fax: 860-567-5214
www.visitfairfieldcountyct.com

Bridgeport Regional Business Council
10 Middle St.
14th Fl.
Bridgeport, CT 06604
Phone: 203-335-3800 Fax: 203-366-0105
www.brbc.org

Greater New Haven Chamber of Commerce
900 Chapel St.
10th Fl.
New Haven, CT 06510
Phone: 203-787-6735 Fax: 203-782-4329
www.gnhcc.com

MetroHartford Alliance
31 Pratt St.
5th Fl.
Hartford, CT 06103
Phone: 860-525-4451 Fax: 860-293-2592
www.metrohartford.com

Stamford Chamber of Commerce
733 Summer St.
Ste. 101
Stamford, CT 06901
Phone: 203-359-4761 Fax: 203-363-5069
www.stamfordchamber.com

Delaware

Delaware Tourism Office
99 Kings Hwy.
Dover, DE 19901
Toll-free: 866-284-7483
www.visitdelaware.com

Delaware State Chamber of Commerce
P.O. Box 671
Wilmington, DE 19899
Phone: 302-655-7221 Fax: 302-654-0691
www.dscc.com

Greater Wilmington Convention & Visitors Bureau
100 W. 10th St.
Ste. 20
Wilmington, DE 19801
Toll-free: 800-489-6664
www.visitwilmingtonde.com

Kent County Tourism Corp
435 N. DuPont Hwy.
Dover, DE 19901
Phone: 302-734-4888 Fax: 302-734-0167
Toll-free: 800-233-5368
www.visitdover.com

Rehoboth Beach Convention Center
229 Rehoboth Ave.
Rehoboth Beach, DE 19971
Phone: 302-227-6181
www.cityofrehoboth.com

Central Delaware Economic Development Council
435 N. DuPont Hwy.
Dover, DE 19901
Phone: 302-734-7513 Fax: 302-678-0189
www.cdcc.net

Rehoboth Beach-Dewey Beach Chamber of Commerce
501 Rehoboth Ave.
P.O. Box 216
Rehoboth Beach, DE 19971
Phone: 302-227-2233 Fax: 302-227-8351
Toll-free: 800-441-1329
www.beach-fun.com

District of Columbia

District of Columbia Convention & Tourism Corp
901 7th St. N.W.
4th Fl.
Washington, DC 20001
Phone: 202-789-7000 Fax: 202-789-7037
Toll-free: 800-422-8644
www.washington.org

District of Columbia Chamber of Commerce
506 9th St. N.W.
Washington, DC 20004
Phone: 202-347-7201
www.dcchamber.org

US Chamber of Commerce
1615 H. St. N.W.

Washington, DC 20062
Phone: 202-659-6000
Toll-free: 800-638-6582
www.uschamber.com

Florida

Florida Tourism Commission
2540 W. Executive Center Cir.
Ste. 200
Tallahassee, FL 32301
Phone: 850-488-5607 Fax: 866-725-5958
Toll-free: 888-735-2872
www.visitflorida.com

Florida Chamber of Commerce
136 S. Bronough St.
P.O. Box 11309
Tallahassee, FL 32301
Phone: 850-521-1200
www.flchamber.com

Alachua County Visitors & Convention Bureau
30 E. University Ave.
Gainesville, FL 32601
Phone: 352-374-5260 Fax: 352-338-3213
Toll-free: 866-778-5002
www.visitgainesville.net

Daytona Beach Area Convention & Visitors Bureau
126 E. Orange Ave.
Daytona Beach, FL 32114
Phone: 386-255-0415 Fax: 386-255-5478
Toll-free: 800-544-0415
www.daytonabeach.com

Greater Fort Lauderdale Convention & Visitors Bureau
101 N.E. 3rd Ave.
Ste. 100
Fort Lauderdale, FL 33301
Phone: 954-765-4466 Fax: 954-765-4467
Toll-free: 800-227-8669
www.sunny.org

Greater Miami Convention & Visitors Bureau
701 Brickell Ave.
Ste. 2700
Miami, FL 33131
Phone: 305-539-3000 Fax: 305-530-5859
Toll-free: 800-933-8448
www.miamiandbeaches.com

Greater Naples Marco Island Everglades Convention &
 Visitors Bureau
2660 N. Horseshoe Dr.
Naples, FL 34104
Phone: 239-403-2384 Fax: 239-403-2404

Toll-free: 800-688-3600
www.paradisecoast.com

Jacksonville & the Beaches Convention & Visitors Bureau
208 N. Laura St.
Ste. 102
Jacksonville, FL 32202
Phone: 800-733-2668 Fax: 904-798-9104
www.visitjacksonville.com

Monroe County Tourist Development Council
1201 White St.
Ste. 102
Key West, FL 33040
Phone: 305-296-1552
Toll-free: 800-352-5397
www.fla-keys.com

Orlando/Orange County Convention & Visitors Bureau
6277 Sea Harbor Dr.
Ste. 400
Orlando, FL 32821
Phone: 407-363-5800
www.visitorlando.com

Palm Beach County Convention & Visitors Bureau
1555 Palm Beach Lakes Blvd.
Ste. 800
West Palm Beach, FL 33401
Phone: 561-233-3000
Toll-free: 800-554-7256
www.palmbeachfl.com

Pensacola Convention & Visitors Bureau
1401 E. Gregory St.
Pensacola, FL 32502
Phone: 800-874-1234
www.visitpensacola.com

Saint Johns County Convention & Visitors Bureau
29 Old Mission Ave.
Saint Augustine, FL 32084
Phone: 904-829-1711
Toll-free: 800-683-0010
www.sapvb.org

Saint Petersburg/Clearwater Area Convention & Visitors
 Bureau
8200 Bryan Dairy Rd.
Ste. 200
Largo, FL 33777
Phone: 727-464-7200
Toll-free: 877-352-3224
www.visitstpeteclearwater.com

Sarasota Convention & Visitors Bureau
1777 Main St.
Ste. 302
Sarasota, FL 34236
Phone: 941-955-0991

Toll-free: 800-348-7250
www.visitsarasota.org

Tallahassee Area Convention & Visitors Bureau
106 E. Jefferson St.
Tallahassee, FL 32301
Phone: 850-606-2305
Toll-free: 800-628-2866
www.visittallahassee.com

Tampa Bay Convention & Visitors Bureau
401 E. Jackson St.
Ste. 2100
Tampa, FL 33602
Phone: 813-223-1111 Fax: 813-229-6616
Toll-free: 800-448-2672
www.visittampabay.com

Chamber of Commerce of the Palm Beaches
401 N. Flagler Dr.
West Palm Beach, FL 33401
Phone: 561-833-3711 Fax: 561-833-5582
www.palmbeaches.org

Daytona Beach-Halifax Area Chamber of Commerce
126 E. Orange Ave.
Daytona Beach, FL 32114
Phone: 386-255-0981 Fax: 386-258-5104
www.daytonachamber.com

Gainesville Area Chamber of Commerce
300 E. University Ave.
Ste. 100
Gainesville, FL 32601
Phone: 352-334-7100 Fax: 352-334-7141
www.gainesvillechamber.com

Greater Fort Lauderdale Chamber of Commerce
512 N.E. 3rd Ave.
Fort Lauderdale, FL 33301
Phone: 954-462-6000
www.ftlchamber.com

Greater Miami Chamber of Commerce
1601 Biscayne Blvd.
Ballroom Level
Miami, FL 33132
Phone: 305-350-7700 Fax: 305-374-6902
Toll-free: 888-660-5955
www.miamichamber.com

Greater Sarasota Chamber of Commerce
1945 Fruitville Rd.
Sarasota, FL 34236
Phone: 941-955-8187 Fax: 941-366-5621
www.sarasotachamber.org

Greater Tampa Chamber of Commerce
201 N. Franklin St.
Ste. 201

Tampa, FL 33602
Phone: 813-228-7777 Fax: 813-223-7899
www.tampachamber.com

Hialeah Chamber of Commerce & Industries
240 E. 1st Ave.
Ste. 217
Hialeah, FL 33010
Phone: 305-888-7780
www.hialeahchamber.org

Jacksonville Chamber of Commerce
3 Independent Dr.
Jacksonville, FL 32202
Phone: 904-366-6600
www.myjaxchamber.com

Key West Chamber of Commerce
510 Greene St.
1St Fl.
Key West, FL 33040
Phone: 305-294-2587
www.keywestchamber.org

Miami Beach Chamber of Commerce
1920 Meridian Ave.
Miami Beach, FL 33139
Phone: 305-674-1300 Fax: 305-538-4336
www.miamibeachchamber.com

Naples Area Chamber of Commerce
2390 Tamiami Trail N.
Ste. 210
Naples, FL 34103
Phone: 239-262-6376 Fax: 239-262-8374
www.napleschamber.org

Orlando Regional Chamber of Commerce
75 S. Ivanhoe Blvd.
P.O. Box 1234
Orlando, FL 32802
Phone: 407-425-1234 Fax: 407-835-2500
www.orlando.org

Pensacola Area Chamber of Commerce
117 W. Garden St.
Pensacola, FL 32502
Phone: 850-438-4081
www.pensacolachamber.com

Saint Augustine & Saint Johns County Chamber of
  Commerce
1 Riberia St.
Saint Augustine, FL 32084
Phone: 904-829-5681 Fax: 904-829-6477
www.stjohnscountychamber.com

Saint Petersburg Area Chamber of Commerce
100 2nd Ave N.
Ste. 150

Saint Petersburg, FL 33701
Phone: 727-821-4069 Fax: 727-895-6326
www.stpete.com

Tallahassee Chamber of Commerce
300 E. Park Ave.
P.O. Box 1639
Tallahassee, FL 32301
Phone: 850-224-8116 Fax: 850-561-3860
www.talchamber.com

Georgia

Georgia Tourism Div
75 5th St. N.W.
Ste. 1200
Atlanta, GA 30308
Phone: 404-962-4000
Toll-free: 800-255-0056
www.georgia.org

Georgia Chamber of Commerce
270 Peachtree St. N.W.
Ste. 2200
Atlanta, GA 30303
Phone: 404-223-2264 Fax: 404-223-2290
Toll-free: 800-241-2286
www.gachamber.com

Atlanta Convention & Visitors Bureau
233 Peachtree St. N.E.
Ste. 1400
Atlanta, GA 30303
Phone: 404-521-6600
Toll-free: 800-285-2682
www.atlanta.net

Augusta Metropolitan Convention & Visitors Bureau
1450 Greene St.
Ste. 110
Augusta, GA 30901
Phone: 706-823-6600 Fax: 706-823-6609
Toll-free: 800-726-0243
www.visitaugusta.com

Columbus Convention & Visitors Bureau
900 Front Ave.
P.O. Box 2768
Columbus, GA 31902
Phone: 706-322-1613 Fax: 706-322-0701
Toll-free: 800-999-1613
www.visitcolumbusga.com

Macon-Bibb County Convention/Visitors Bureau
450 Martin Luther King Jr. Blvd.
Macon, GA 31201
Phone: 478-743-1074 Fax: 478-745-2022

Toll-free: 800-768-3401
www.maconga.org

Savannah Area Convention & Visitors Bureau
101 E. Bay St.
P.O. Box 1628
Savannah, GA 31401
Phone: 912-644-6400
Toll-free: 877-728-2662
www.visitsavannah.com

Augusta Metro Chamber of Commerce
701 Greene St.
Augusta, GA 30901
Phone: 706-821-1300 Fax: 706-821-1330
www.augustametrochamber.com

Greater Columbus Chamber of Commerce
1200 6th Ave.
Columbus, GA 31902
Phone: 706-327-1566 Fax: 706-327-7512
Toll-free: 800-360-8552
www.columbusgachamber.com

Greater Macon Chamber of Commerce
305 Coliseum Dr.
Macon, GA 31217
Phone: 478-621-2000 Fax: 478-621-2021
www.maconchamber.com

Metro Atlanta Chamber of Commerce
235 Andrew Young International Blvd. N.W.
Atlanta, GA 30303
Phone: 404-880-9000
www.metroatlantachamber.com

Savannah Area Chamber of Commerce
101 E. Bay St.
Savannah, GA 31401
Phone: 912-644-6400
www.savannahchamber.com

Hawaii

Hawaii Business Economic Development & Tourism Dept
No. 1 Capitol District Bldg.
250 S. Hotel St.
Honolulu, HI 96813
Phone: 808-586-2355
www.dbedt.hawaii.gov

Hawaii Tourism Authority
1801 Kalakaua Ave.
1st Fl.
Honolulu, HI 96815
Phone: 808-973-2255 Fax: 808-973-2253
www.hawaiitourismauthority.org

Hawaii Chamber of Commerce
1132 Bishop St.
Ste. 2105
Honolulu, HI 96813
Phone: 808-545-4300 Fax: 808-545-4369
www.cochawaii.org

Hawaii Visitors & Convention Bureau
2270 Kalakaua Ave.
Ste. 801
Honolulu, HI 96815
Phone: 808-923-1811 Fax: 808-924-0290
Toll-free: 800-464-2924
www.hvcb.org

Idaho

Idaho Tourism Development Div
700 W. State St.
P.O. Box 83720
Boise, ID 83720
Phone: 208-334-2470 Fax: 208-334-2631
Toll-free: 800-847-4843
www.visitid.org

Idaho Assn of Commerce & Industry
816 W. Bannock St., Ste. 5B
P.O. Box 389
Boise, ID 83701
Phone: 208-343-1849
www.iaci.org

Boise Convention & Visitors Bureau
250 S. 5th St.
Ste. 300
Boise, ID 83702
Phone: 208-472-5205 Fax: 208-472-5201
www.boise.org

Pocatello Convention & Visitors Bureau
324 S. Main St.
Pocatello, ID 83204
Phone: 208-479-7659
www.visitpocatello.com

Boise Metro Chamber of Commerce
250 S. 5th St.
Ste. 300
Boise, ID 83702
Phone: 208-472-5205 Fax: 208-472-5201
www.boisechamber.org

Greater Pocatello Chamber of Commerce
324 S. Main St.
Pocatello, ID 83204
Phone: 208-233-1525
www.pocatelloidaho.com

Illinois

Illinois Tourism Bureau
100 W. Randolph St.
Ste. 3-400
Chicago, IL 60601
Phone: 312-814-4733 Fax: 312-814-6175
Toll-free: 800-226-6632
www.enjoyillinois.com

Illinois State Chamber of Commerce
300 S. Wacker Dr.
Ste. 1600
Chicago, IL 60606
Phone: 312-983-7100
www.ilchamber.org

Abraham Lincoln Tourism Bureau
700 E. Adams St.
Springfield, IL 62701
Phone: 217-525-7980
www.visitlandoflincoln.com

Champaign County Convention & Visitors Bureau
108 S. Neil St.
Champaign, IL 61820
Phone: 217-351-4133
Toll-free: 800-369-6151
www.visitchampaigncounty.org

Chicago Convention & Tourism Bureau
301 E. Cermak Rd.
Chicago, IL 60616
Phone: 312-567-8510 Fax: 312-567-8504
www.choosechicago.com

Chicago Office of Tourism
72 E. Randolph St.
Chicago, IL 60601
www.choosechicago.com

Peoria Area Convention & Visitors Bureau
456 Fulton St.
Ste. 300
Peoria, IL 61602
Phone: 309-676-0303 Fax: 309-676-8470
Toll-free: 800-747-0302
www.peoria.org

Rockford Area Convention & Visitors Bureau
102 N. Main St.
Rockford, IL 61101
Phone: 815-963-8111 Fax: 815-963-4298
Toll-free: 800-521-0849
www.gorockford.com

Springfield Convention & Visitors Bureau
109 N. 7th St.
Springfield, IL 62701
Phone: 217-789-2360 Fax: 217-544-8711

Toll-free: 800-545-7300
www.visitspringfieldillinois.com

Champaign County Chamber of Commerce
303 W. Kirby Ave.
Champaign, IL 61820
Phone: 217-359-1791 Fax: 217-359-1809
www.champaigncounty.org

Chicagoland Chamber of Commerce
410 N. Michigan Ave.
Ste. 900
Chicago, IL 60611
Phone: 312-494-6700 Fax: 312-861-0660
www.chicagolandchamber.org

Greater Springfield Chamber of Commerce
1011 S. 2nd St.
Springfield, IL 62704
Phone: 217-525-1173 Fax: 217-525-8768
www.gscc.org

Peoria Area Chamber of Commerce
100 S.W. Water St.
Peoria, IL 61602
Phone: 309-495-5900
www.peoriachamber.org

Rockford Regional Chamber of Commerce
308 W. State St.
Rockford, IL 61101
Phone: 815-987-8100 Fax: 815-987-8122
www.rockfordchamber.com

Indiana

Indiana Tourism Development Office
1 N. Capitol Ave.
Ste. 600
Indianapolis, IN 46204
Phone: 800-677-9800
www.visitindiana.com

Indiana State Chamber of Commerce
115 W. Washington St.
Ste. 850S
Indianapolis, IN 46204
Phone: 317-264-3110 Fax: 317-264-6855
www.indianachamber.com

Bloomington/Monroe County Convention & Visitors
  Bureau
2855 N. Walnut St.
Bloomington, IN 47404
Phone: 812-334-8900 Fax: 812-334-2344
Toll-free: 800-800-0037
www.visitbloomington.com

Evansville Convention & Visitors Bureau
401 S.E. Riverside Dr.
Evansville, IN 47713
Phone: 812-421-2200 Fax: 812-421-2207
Toll-free: 800-433-3025
www.visitevansville.com

Fort Wayne/Allen County Convention & Visitors Bureau
927 S. Harrison St.
Fort Wayne, IN 46802
Phone: 260-424-3700 Fax: 260-424-3914
Toll-free: 800-767-7752
www.visitfortwayne.com

Indianapolis Convention & Visitors Assn
200 S. Capitol Ave.
Ste. 300
Indianapolis, IN 46225
Phone: 317-262-3000
Toll-free: 800-323-4639
www.visitindy.com

South Bend/Mishawaka Convention & Visitors Bureau
401 E. Colfax Ave.
Ste. 310
South Bend, IN 46617
Phone: 800-519-0577
www.visitsouthbend.com

Chamber of Commerce of Saint Joseph County
401 E. Colfax Ave.
Ste. 310
South Bend, IN 46617
Phone: 574-234-0051
www.sjchamber.org

Greater Bloomington Chamber of Commerce
400 W. 7th St.
Ste. 102
Bloomington, IN 47402
Phone: 812-336-6381 Fax: 812-336-0651
www.chamberbloomington.org

Greater Fort Wayne Chamber of Commerce
200 E. Main St.
Ste. 800
Fort Wayne, IN 46802
Phone: 260-420-6945 Fax: 260-426-0837
www.greaterfortwayneinc.com

Indianapolis Chamber of Commerce
111 Monument Cir.
Ste. 1950
Indianapolis, IN 46204
Phone: 317-464-2222
www.indychamber.com

Metropolitan Evansville Chamber of Commerce
318 Main St.
Ste. 401

Evansville, IN 47708
Phone: 812-425-8147 Fax: 812-421-5883
www.swinchamber.com

Iowa

Iowa Tourism Office
200 E. Grand Ave.
Des Moines, IA 50309
Toll-free: 800-345-4692
www.traveliowa.com

Iowa Assn of Business & Industry
400 E. Court Ave.
Ste. 100
Des Moines, IA 50309
Phone: 515-280-8000 Fax: 515-244-3285
Toll-free: 800-383-4224
www.iowaabi.org

Cedar Rapids Area Convention & Visitors Bureau
87 16th Ave. S.W.
Ste. 200
Cedar Rapids, IA 52404
Phone: 319-398-5009 Fax: 319-398-5089
Toll-free: 800-735-5557
www.cedar-rapids.com

Dubuque Convention & Visitors Bureau
300 Main St.
Ste. 200
Dubuque, IA 52001
Phone: 563-845-7698
Toll-free: 800-798-8844
www.traveldubuque.com

Greater Des Moines Convention & Visitors Bureau
400 Locust St.
Ste. 265
Des Moines, IA 50309 Fax: 515-244-9757
Toll-free: 800-451-2625
www.catchdesmoines.com

Cedar Rapids Area Chamber of Commerce
501 First St. S.E.
Cedar Rapids, IA 52401
Phone: 319-398-5317 Fax: 319-398-5228
www.cedarrapids.org

Dubuque Area Chamber of Commerce
300 Main St.
Ste. 200
Dubuque, IA 52001
Phone: 563-557-9200 Fax: 563-557-1591
Toll-free: 800-798-4748
www.dubuquechamber.com

Greater Des Moines Partnership
601 Locust St.

Ste. 700
Des Moines, IA 50309
Phone: 515-286-4950
www.desmoinesmetro.com

Kansas

Kansas Travel & Tourism Development Div
I - 70 E. Milepost 7
Goodland, KS 67735
Phone: 785-899-6695 Fax: 785-899-2616
www.travelks.com

Kansas Travel & Tourism Development Div
1020 S. Kansas Ave.
Ste. 200
Topeka, KS 66612
Phone: 785-296-1847
Toll-free: 800-684-6966
www.travelks.com

Kansas Chamber of Commerce & Industry
835 S.W. Topeka Blvd.
Topeka, KS 66612
Phone: 785-357-6321 Fax: 785-357-4732
www.kansaschamber.org

Kansas City, Kansas Convention & Visitors Bureau
755 Minnesota Ave.
Kansas City, KS 64105
Phone: 913-321-5800
Toll-free: 800-264-1563
www.visitkansascityks.com

Visit Topeka Inc
618 S. Kansas Ave.
Topeka, KS 66603
Phone: 785-234-1030 Fax: 785-234-8282
Toll-free: 800-235-1030
www.visittopeka.com

Wichita Convention & Visitors Bureau
515 S. Main St.
Ste. 115
Wichita, KS 67202
Phone: 316-265-2800 Fax: 316-265-0162
Toll-free: 800-288-9424
www.visitwichita.com

Greater Topeka Chamber of Commerce
120 S.E. Sixth Ave.
Ste. 110
Topeka, KS 66603
Phone: 785-234-2644 Fax: 785-234-8656
www.topekachamber.org

Kansas City Kansas Area Chamber of Commerce
727 Minnesota Ave.

P.O. Box 171337
Kansas City, KS 66117
Phone: 913-371-3070 Fax: 913-371-3732
www.kckchamber.com

Wichita Area Chamber of Commerce
350 W. Douglas Ave.
Wichita, KS 67202
Phone: 316-265-7771 Fax: 316-265-7502
www.wichitachamber.org

Kentucky

Kentucky Travel Dept
500 Mero St.
Capital Plaza Tower
22nd Fl.
Frankfort, KY 40601
Phone: 502-564-4930 Fax: 502-564-5695
Toll-free: 800-225-8747
www.kentuckytourism.com

Kentucky Chamber of Commerce
464 Chenault Rd.
Frankfort, KY 40601
Phone: 502-695-4700 Fax: 502-695-5051
www.kychamber.com

Frankfort/Franklin County Tourist & Convention
  Commission
100 Capital Ave.
Frankfort, KY 40601
Phone: 502-875-8687
Toll-free: 800-960-7200
www.visitfrankfort.com

Lexington Convention & Visitors Bureau
401 W. Main St.
Ste. 104
Lexington, KY 40507
Phone: 859-233-7299
Toll-free: 800-845-3959
www.visitlex.com

Louisville & Jefferson County Convention & Visitors
  Bureau
1 Riverfront Plaza
401 W. Main St.
Ste. 2300
Louisville, KY 40202
Phone: 502-584-2121 Fax: 502-584-6697
Toll-free: 800-626-5646
www.gotolouisville.com

Frankfort Area Chamber of Commerce
100 Capital Ave.
2nd Fl.
Frankfort, KY 40601

Phone: 502-223-8261 Fax: 502-223-5942
www.frankfortky.info

Greater Lexington Chamber of Commerce
330 E. Main St.
Ste. 100
Lexington, KY 40507
Phone: 859-254-4447 Fax: 859-233-3304
www.commercelexington.com

Greater Louisville Inc
614 W. Main St.
Ste. 6000
Louisville, KY 40202
Phone: 502-625-0000 Fax: 502-625-0010
www.greaterlouisville.com

Louisiana

Louisiana Culture Recreation & Tourism Dept
P.O. Box 94361
Baton Rouge, LA 70804
Phone: 225-342-8115
www.crt.state.la.us

Louisiana Tourism Office
P.O. Box 94291
Baton Rouge, LA 70804
Phone: 225-342-8119
Toll-free: 800-677-4082
www.crt.state.la.us

Louisiana Assn of Business & Industry
3113 Valley Creek Dr.
P.O. Box 80258
Baton Rouge, LA 70898
Phone: 225-928-5388
Toll-free: 888-816-5224
www.labi.org

Baton Rouge Convention & Visitors Bureau
359 Third St.
Baton Rouge, LA 70801
Phone: 225-383-1825 Fax: 225-346-1253
Toll-free: 800-527-6843
www.visitbatonrouge.com

Jefferson Convention & Visitors Bureau
1221 Elmwood Park Blvd.
Ste. 411
New Orleans, LA 70123
Phone: 504-731-7083 Fax: 504-731-7089
Toll-free: 877-572-7474
www.experiencejefferson.com

Lafayette Convention & Visitors Commission
1400 N.W. Evageline Thruway
Lafayette, LA 70501

Phone: 337-232-3737 Fax: 337-232-0161
Toll-free: 800-346-1958
www.lafayettetravel.com

New Orleans Metropolitan Convention & Visitors Bureau
2020 St Charles Ave.
New Orleans, LA 70130
Phone: 504-566-5011 Fax: 504-566-5046
Toll-free: 800-672-6124
www.neworleanscvb.com

Shreveport-Bossier Convention & Tourist Bureau
629 Spring St.
Shreveport, LA 71101
Phone: 318-222-9391 Fax: 318-222-0056
Toll-free: 800-551-8682
www.shreveport-bossier.org

Bossier Chamber of Commerce
710 Benton Rd.
Bossier City, LA 71111
Phone: 318-746-0252 Fax: 318-746-0357
www.bossierchamber.com

Greater Baton Rouge Chamber of Commerce
564 Laurel St.
Baton Rouge, LA 70801
Phone: 225-381-7125
www.brac.org

Greater Shreveport Chamber of Commerce
400 Edwards St.
Shreveport, LA 71101
Phone: 318-677-2500 Fax: 318-677-2541
Toll-free: 800-448-5432
www.shreveportchamber.org

Jefferson Chamber of Commerce
3421 N Causeway Blvd.
Ste. 203
Metairie, LA 70002
Phone: 504-835-3880 Fax: 504-835-3828
www.jeffersonchamber.org

New Orleans Chamber of Commerce
1515 Poydras St.
Ste. 1010
New Orleans, LA 70112
Phone: 504-799-4260 Fax: 504-799-4254
www.neworleanschamber.org

One Acadiana
804 E St Mary Blvd.
P.O. Box 51307
Lafayette, LA 70505
Phone: 337-233-2705 Fax: 337-234-8671
www.oneacadiana.org

Maine

Maine Tourism Office
59 State House Stn.
Augusta, ME 04333
Phone: 207-287-5711 Fax: 207-287-8070
Toll-free: 888-624-6345
www.visitmaine.com

Maine State Chamber of Commerce
125 Community Dr.
Ste. 101
Augusta, ME 04330
Phone: 207-623-4568 Fax: 207-622-7723
www.mainechamber.org

Convention & Visitors Bureau of Greater Portland
94 Commercial St.
Ste. 300
Portland, ME 04101
Phone: 207-772-4994 Fax: 207-874-9043
www.visitportland.com

Greater Bangor Convention & Visitors Bureau
330 Harlow St.
Bangor, ME 04402
Phone: 207-947-5205 Fax: 207-942-2146
Toll-free: 800-916-6673
www.bangorcvb.org

Bangor Region Chamber of Commerce
20 S. St.
Bangor, ME 04401
Phone: 207-947-0307 Fax: 207-990-1427
www.bangorregion.com

Bar Harbor Chamber of Commerce
93 Cottage St.
Ste. 102
Bar Harbor, ME 04609
Phone: 207-288-5103 Fax: 207-667-9080
Toll-free: 888-540-9990
www.barharborinfo.com

Kennebec Valley Chamber of Commerce
21 University Dr.
Augusta, ME 04332
Phone: 207-623-4559 Fax: 207-626-9342
www.augustamaine.com

Portland Regional Chamber
443 Congress St.
Portland, ME 04101
Phone: 207-772-2811 Fax: 207-772-1179
www.portlandregion.com

Maryland

Maryland Tourism Development Office
401 E. Pratt St.
14th Fl.
Baltimore, MD 21202
Phone: 410-767-3400 Fax: 410-333-6643
Toll-free: 800-543-1036
www.visitmaryland.org

Maryland Chamber of Commerce
60 W. St.
Ste. 100
Annapolis, MD 21401
Phone: 410-269-0642 Fax: 410-269-5247
www.mdchamber.org

Annapolis & Anne Arundel County Conference & Visitors
  Bureau
26 W. St.
Annapolis, MD 21401
Phone: 410-280-0445 Fax: 410-263-9591
Toll-free: 888-302-2852
www.visitannapolis.org

Baltimore Area Convention & Visitors Assn
100 Light St.
12th Fl.
Baltimore, MD 21202
Phone: 410-659-7300 Fax: 410-727-2308
Toll-free: 800-343-3468
www.baltimore.org

Ocean City Convention & Visitors Bureau
4001 Coastal Hwy.
Ocean City, MD 21842
Toll-free: 800-626-2326
www.ococean.com

Annapolis & Anne Arundel County Chamber of Commerce
134 Holiday Ct.
Ste. 316
Annapolis, MD 21401
Phone: 410-266-3960 Fax: 410-266-8270
www.annapolischamber.com

Baltimore City Chamber of Commerce
P.O. Box 4483
Baltimore, MD 21223
Phone: 410-837-7101 Fax: 410-837-7104
www.baltimorecitychamber.org

Ocean City Chamber of Commerce
12320 Ocean Gateway
Ocean City, MD 21842
Phone: 410-213-0552
Toll-free: 888-626-3386
www.oceancity.org

Massachusetts

Massachusetts Travel & Tourism Office
10 Park Plaza
Ste. 4510
Boston, MA 02116
Phone: 617-973-8500 Fax: 617-973-8525
Toll-free: 800-227-6277
www.massvacation.com

Massachusetts Chamber of Commerce
60 State St.
Ste. 700, 7th Fl.
Boston, MA 02109
Phone: 413-426-3850 Fax: 413-525-1184
www.massachusettschamberofcommerce.com

New England Council Inc
98 N Washington St.
Ste. 201
Boston, MA 02114
Phone: 617-723-4009 Fax: 617-723-3943
www.newenglandcouncil.com

Greater Boston Convention & Visitors Bureau
2 Copley Pl.
Ste. 105
Boston, MA 02116
Phone: 617-536-4100 Fax: 617-424-7664
Toll-free: 888-733-2678
www.bostonusa.com

Greater Springfield Convention & Visitors Bureau
1441 Main St.
Springfield, MA 01103
Phone: 413-787-1548 Fax: 413-781-4607
Toll-free: 800-723-1548
www.valleyvisitor.com

Worcester County Convention & Visitors Bureau
91 Prescott St.
Worcester, MA 01605
Phone: 508-755-7400 Fax: 508-754-2703
Toll-free: 866-755-7439
www.centralmass.org

Affiliated Chambers of Commerce of Greater Springfield
1441 Main St.
Ste. 136
Springfield, MA 01103
Phone: 413-787-1555 Fax: 413-731-8530
www.myonlinechamber.com

Cape Cod Chamber of Commerce
5 Patti Page Way
Centerville, MA 02632
Phone: 508-362-3225 Fax: 508-362-3698
Toll-free: 888-332-2732
www.capecodchamber.org

Greater Boston Chamber of Commerce
265 Franklin St.
12th. Fl.
Boston, MA 02110
Phone: 617-227-4500 Fax: 617-227-7505
www.bostonchamber.com

Worcester Regional Chamber of Commerce
446 Main St.
Ste. 200
Worcester, MA 01608
Phone: 508-753-2924 Fax: 508-754-8560
www.worcesterchamber.org

Michigan

Michigan Tourism
300 N. Washington Sq.
Lansing, MI 48913
Phone: 517-373-0670 Fax: 517-373-0059
Toll-free: 888-784-7328
www.michigan.org

Michigan Chamber of Commerce
600 S. Walnut St.
Lansing, MI 48933
Phone: 517-371-2100 Fax: 517-371-7224
Toll-free: 800-748-0266
www.michamber.com

Ann Arbor Area Convention & Visitors Bureau
315 W. Huron St.
Ste. 340
Ann Arbor, MI 48104
Phone: 734-995-7281 Fax: 734-995-7283
Toll-free: 800-888-9487
www.visitannarbor.org

Detroit Metropolitan Convention & Visitors Bureau
211 W. Fort St.
Ste. 1000
Detroit, MI 48226
Phone: 313-202-1800
Toll-free: 800-338-7648
www.visitdetroit.com

Grand Rapids/Kent County Convention & Visitors Bureau
171 Monroe Ave. N.W.
Ste. 700
Grand Rapids, MI 49503
Phone: 616-459-8287 Fax: 616-459-7291
Toll-free: 800-678-9859
www.experiencegr.com

Greater Lansing Convention & Visitors Bureau
500 E. Michigan Ave.
Ste. 180
Lansing, MI 48912

Phone: 517-487-6800 Fax: 517-487-5151
Toll-free: 888-252-6746
www.lansing.org

Ann Arbor Area Chamber of Commerce
115 W. Heron
3rd Fl.
Ann Arbor, MI 48104
Phone: 734-665-4433 Fax: 734-665-4191
www.a2ychamber.org

Detroit Regional Chamber
1 Woodward Ave.
Ste. 1900
Detroit, MI 48232
Phone: 313-964-4000 Fax: 313-964-0183
Toll-free: 866-627-5463
www.detroitchamber.com

Flint & Genesee Chamber of Commerce
519 S. Saginaw St.
Ste. 200
Flint, MI 48502
Phone: 810-600-1404 Fax: 810-600-1461
www.flintandgenesee.org

Grand Rapids Area Chamber of Commerce
111 Pearl St. N.W.
Grand Rapids, MI 49503
Phone: 616-771-0300 Fax: 616-771-0318
www.grandrapids.org

Lansing Regional Chamber of Commerce
500 E. Michigan Ave.
Ste. 200
Lansing, MI 48912
Phone: 517-487-6340 Fax: 517-484-6910
www.lansingchamber.org

Minnesota

Minnesota Tourism Office
121 7th Pl. E.
Metro Sq.
Ste. 100
Saint Paul, MN 55101
Phone: 651-296-5029
Toll-free: 888-847-4866
www.exploreminnesota.com

Minnesota Chamber of Commerce
400 Robert St. N.
Ste. 1500
Saint Paul, MN 55101
Phone: 651-292-4650 Fax: 651-292-4656
Toll-free: 800-821-2230
www.mnchamber.com

Duluth Convention & Visitors Bureau
21 W. Superior St.
Duluth, MN 55802
Phone: 218-722-4011 Fax: 218-722-1322
Toll-free: 800-438-5884
www.visitduluth.com

Greater Minneapolis Convention & Visitors Assn
250 Marquette Ave. S.
Minneapolis, MN 55401
Phone: 612-767-8000 Fax: 612-767-8001
Toll-free: 800-445-7412
www.minneapolis.org

Rochester Convention & Visitors Bureau
30 Civic Center Dr. S.E.
Ste. 200
Rochester, MN 55904
Phone: 507-288-4331 Fax: 507-288-9144
Toll-free: 800-634-8277
www.rochestercvb.org

Saint Paul River Centre Convention & Visitors Authority
175 W. Kellogg Blvd.
Ste. 502
Saint Paul, MN 55102
Phone: 651-265-4900
Toll-free: 800-627-6101
www.visitsaintpaul.com

Chamber of Commerce of Fargo Moorhead
202 First Ave. N.
Moorhead, MN 56560
Phone: 218-233-1100 Fax: 218-233-1200
www.fmchamber.com

Duluth Area Chamber of Commerce
5 W. First St.
Ste. 101
Duluth, MN 55802
Phone: 218-722-5501 Fax: 218-722-3223
www.duluthchamber.com

Minneapolis Regional Chamber of Commerce
81 S. Ninth St.
Ste. 200
Minneapolis, MN 55402
Phone: 612-370-9100 Fax: 612-370-9195
www.minneapolischamber.org

Rochester Area Chamber of Commerce
220 S. Broadway
Ste. 100
Rochester, MN 55904
Phone: 507-288-1122 Fax: 507-282-8960
www.rochestermnchamber.com

Saint Paul Area Chamber of Commerce
401 N. Robert St.
Ste. 150

Saint Paul, MN 55101
Phone: 651-223-5000 Fax: 651-223-5119
www.saintpaulchamber.com

Mississippi

Mississippi Tourism Development Div
P.O. Box 849
Jackson, MS 39201
Phone: 601-359-3297 Fax: 601-359-5757
Toll-free: 866-733-6477
www.visitmississippi.org

Mississippi Economic Council
248 E. Capitol St.
Ste. 940
Jackson, MS 39225
Phone: 601-969-0022 Fax: 601-353-0247
Toll-free: 800-748-7626
www.msmec.com

Metro Jackson Convention & Visitors Bureau
111 E. Capitol St.
Ste. 102
Jackson, MS 39201
Phone: 601-960-1891 Fax: 601-960-1827
Toll-free: 800-354-7695
www.visitjackson.com

Mississippi Gulf Coast Convention & Visitors Bureau
P.O. Box 8298
Biloxi, MS 39535
Phone: 228-896-6699 Fax: 228-896-6788
Toll-free: 888-467-4853
www.gulfcoast.org

Tupelo Convention & Visitors Bureau
P.O. Drawer 47
Tupelo, MS 38802
Phone: 662-841-6521 Fax: 662-841-6558
Toll-free: 800-533-0611
www.tupelo.net

Area Development Partnership
1 Convention Center Plaza
Hattiesburg, MS 39401
Phone: 601-296-7500 Fax: 601-296-7505
Toll-free: 800-238-4288
www.theadp.com

Greater Jackson Chamber Partnership
P.O. Box 22548
Jackson, MS 39225
Phone: 601-948-7575 Fax: 601-352-5539
www.greaterjacksonpartnership.com

Mississippi Gulf Coast Chamber of Commerce
11975 E. Seaway Rd.

Gulfport, MS 39503
Phone: 228-604-0014 Fax: 228-604-0105
www.mscoastchamber.com

Missouri

Missouri Tourism Div
P.O. Box 1055
Jefferson City, MO 65102
Phone: 573-751-4133 Fax: 573-751-5160
Toll-free: 800-519-2100
www.visitmo.com

Missouri Chamber of Commerce
428 E. Capitol Ave.
P.O. Box 149
Jefferson City, MO 65102
Phone: 573-634-3511 Fax: 573-634-8855
www.mochamber.com

Branson/Lakes Area Convention & Visitors Bureau
269 State Hwy. 248
P.O. Box 1897
Branson, MO 65616
Phone: 417-334-4084
Toll-free: 800-296-0463
www.bransonchamber.com

Columbia Convention & Visitors Bureau
300 S. Providence Rd.
Columbia, MO 65203
Phone: 573-875-1231 Fax: 573-443-3986
Toll-free: 800-652-0987
www.visitcolumbiamo.com

Convention & Visitors Bureau of Greater Kansas City
1321 Baltimore Ave.
Kansas City, MO 64105
Phone: 816-221-5242
Toll-free: 800-767-7700
www.visitkc.com

Jefferson City Convention & Visitors Bureau
100 E. High St.
Jefferson City, MO 65101
Phone: 573-632-2820 Fax: 573-638-4892
Toll-free: 800-769-4183
www.visitjeffersoncity.com

Saint Louis Convention & Visitors Commission
701 Convention Plaza
Ste. 300
Saint Louis, MO 63101
Phone: 314-421-1023 Fax: 314-421-0039
Toll-free: 800-325-7962
www.explorestlouis.com

Springfield Missouri Convention & Visitors Bureau
815 E. Saint Louis St.

Ste. 100
Springfield, MO 65806
Phone: 417-881-5300 Fax: 417-881-2231
Toll-free: 800-678-8767
www.springfieldmo.org

Branson/Lakes Area Chamber of Commerce
P.O. Box 1897
Branson, MO 65615
Phone: 417-334-4084 Fax: 417-337-5887
www.bransonchamber.com

Columbia Chamber of Commerce
300 S. Providence Rd.
P.O. Box 1016
Columbia, MO 65205
Phone: 573-874-1132 Fax: 573-443-3986
www.columbiamochamber.com

Greater Kansas City Chamber of Commerce
30 W. Pershing Rd.
Ste. 301
Kansas City, MO 64108
Phone: 816-221-2424 Fax: 816-221-7440
www.kcchamber.com

Independence Chamber of Commerce
210 W. Truman Rd.
P.O. Box 1077
Independence, MO 64051
Phone: 816-252-4745 Fax: 816-252-4917
www.ichamber.biz

Jefferson City Area Chamber of Commerce
213 Adams St.
P.O. Box 776
Jefferson City, MO 65101
Phone: 573-634-3616 Fax: 573-634-3805
www.jcchamber.org

Saint Louis Regional Commerce & Growth Assn
1 Metropolitan Sq.
Ste. 1300
Saint Louis, MO 63102
Phone: 314-231-5555
www.stlregionalchamber.com

Springfield Area Chamber of Commerce
202 S. John Q Hammons Pkwy
P.O. Box 1687
Springfield, MO 65806
Phone: 417-862-5567 Fax: 417-862-1611
www.springfieldchamber.com

Montana

Montana Office of Tourism
P.O. Box 200533

Helena, MT 59620
Phone: 406-841-2870
www.visitmt.com

Montana Chamber of Commerce
900 Gibbon St.
P.O. Box 1730
Helena, MT 59624
Phone: 406-442-2405 Fax: 406-442-2409
Toll-free: 888-442-6668
www.montanachamber.com

Billings Convention & Visitors Bureau
815 S 27th St.
P.O. Box 31177
Billings, MT 59107
Phone: 406-245-4111 Fax: 406-245-7333
Toll-free: 800-735-2635
www.visitbillings.com

Helena Convention & Visitors Bureau
225 Cruse Ave.
Helena, MT 59601
Phone: 406-447-1530 Fax: 406-447-1532
Toll-free: 800-743-5362
www.helenamt.com

Billings Area Chamber of Commerce
815 S. 27th St.
Billings, MT 59101
Phone: 406-245-4111 Fax: 406-245-7333
www.billingschamber.com

Great Falls Area Chamber of Commerce
100 1st Ave N.
Great Falls, MT 59401
Phone: 406-761-4434 Fax: 406-761-6129
Toll-free: 800-735-8535
www.greatfallschamber.org

Helena Area Chamber of Commerce
225 Cruse Ave.
Ste. A
Helena, MT 59601
Phone: 406-442-4120 Fax: 406-447-1532
Toll-free: 800-743-5362
www.helenachamber.com

Nebraska

Nebraska Travel & Tourism Div
301 Centennial Mall S.
P.O. Box 98907
Lincoln, NE 68509
Phone: 402-471-3796
www.visitnebraska.com

Nebraska Chamber of Commerce & Industry
1320 Lincoln Mall

Ste. 201
Lincoln, NE 68509
Phone: 402-474-4422 Fax: 402-474-5681
www.nechamber.net

Greater Omaha Convention & Visitors Bureau
1001 Farnam St.
Ste. 200
Omaha, NE 68102
Phone: 402-444-4660 Fax: 402-546-1458
Toll-free: 866-937-6624
www.visitomaha.com

Lincoln Convention & Visitors Bureau
1135 M St.
Ste. 300
Lincoln, NE 68501
Phone: 402-434-5335 Fax: 402-436-2360
Toll-free: 800-423-8212
www.lincoln.org

Greater Omaha Chamber of Commerce
1301 Harney St.
Omaha, NE 68102
Phone: 402-346-5000 Fax: 402-346-7050
Toll-free: 800-852-2622
www.omahachamber.org

Lincoln Chamber of Commerce
1135 M St.
Ste. 200
Lincoln, NE 68508
Phone: 402-436-2350
www.lcoc.com

Nevada

Nevada Tourism Commission
401 N. Carson St.
2nd Fl.
Carson City, NV 89701
Phone: 775-687-4322 Fax: 775-687-6779
Toll-free: 800-638-2328
www.travelnevada.com

Carson City Convention & Visitors Bureau
716 N. Carson St.
Carson City, NV 89701
Phone: 775-687-7410 Fax: 775-687-7416
www.visitcarsoncity.com

Las Vegas Convention & Visitors Authority
3150 Paradise Rd.
Las Vegas, NV 89109
Phone: 702-892-0711
Toll-free: 877-847-4858
www.lvcva.com

Reno-Sparks Convention & Visitors Authority
P.O. Box 837
Reno, NV 89504
Phone: 800-367-7366
www.visitrenotahoe.com

Carson City Area Chamber of Commerce
1900 S. Carson St.
Ste. 200
Carson City, NV 89701
Phone: 775-882-1565 Fax: 775-882-4179
www.carsoncitychamber.com

Las Vegas Chamber of Commerce
575 Symphony Park Ave.
Ste. 100
Las Vegas, NV 89106
Phone: 702-641-5822 Fax: 702-735-0406
www.lvchamber.com

New Hampshire

New Hampshire Div of Travel & Tourism Development
172 Pembroke Rd.
P.O. Box 1856
Concord, NH 03302
Phone: 603-271-2665 Fax: 603-271-6870
Toll-free: 800-262-6660
www.visitnh.gov

New Hampshire Business & Industry Assn
122 N. Main St.
Concord, NH 03301
Phone: 603-224-5388 Fax: 603-224-2872
www.biaofnh.com

Manchester Area Convention & Visitors Bureau
1 City Hall Plaza
Manchester, NH 03101
Phone: 603-624-6505 Fax: 603-624-6308
www.yourmanchesternh.com

Greater Concord Chamber of Commerce
49 S. Main St.
Ste. 104
Concord, NH 03301
Phone: 603-224-2508 Fax: 603-224-8128
www.concordnhchamber.com

Greater Manchester Chamber of Commerce
54 Hanover St.
Manchester, NH 03101
Phone: 603-666-6600 Fax: 603-626-0910
www.manchester-chamber.org

New Jersey

New Jersey Commerce Economic Growth & Tourism
  Commission
36 W. State St.
P.O. Box 990
Trenton, NJ 08625
Phone: 609-858-6700
www.njeda.com

New Jersey Travel & Tourism Div
225 W. State St.
P.O. Box 460
Trenton, NJ 08625
Phone: 609-633-0981
Toll-free: 800-847-4865
www.visitnj.org

New Jersey State Chamber of Commerce
216 W. State St.
Trenton, NJ 08608
Phone: 609-989-7888 Fax: 609-989-9696
www.njchamber.com

Atlantic City Convention & Visitors Authority
2314 Pacific Ave.
Atlantic City, NJ 08401
Phone: 609-348-7100 Fax: 609-345-3685
Toll-free: 888-222-3683
www.atlanticcitynj.com

Capital Region Convention & Visitors Bureau
1A Quakerbridge Plaza Dr.
Ste. 2
Mercerville, NJ 08619
Phone: 609-689-9964
www.go-new-jersey.com

Atlantic City Regional Chamber of Commerce
1125 S Virginia Ave.
Atlantic City, NJ 08401
Phone: 609-345-4524 Fax: 609-345-1666
www.acchamber.com

Greater Paterson Chamber of Commerce
100 Hamilton Plaza
Ste. 1201
Paterson, NJ 07505
Phone: 973-881-7300 Fax: 973-881-8233
www.greaterpatersoncc.org

Hudson County Chamber of Commerce
857 Bergen Ave.
3rd Fl.
Jersey City, NJ 07306
Phone: 201-386-0699 Fax: 201-386-8480
www.hudsonchamber.org

Mercer Regional Chamber of Commerce
1A Quakerbridge Plaza Dr.

Ste. 2
Hamilton, NJ 08619
Phone: 609-689-9960
www.midjerseychamber.org

Newark Regional Business Partnership
60 Park Pl.
Ste. 1800
Newark, NJ 07102
Phone: 973-522-0099 Fax: 973-824-6587
www.newarkrbp.org

New Mexico

New Mexico Tourism Dept
491 Old Santa Fe Trail
Santa Fe, NM 87501
Phone: 505-827-7400 Fax: 505-827-7402
www.newmexico.org

New Mexico Assn of Commerce & Industry
2201 Buena Vista Dr. S.E., Ste. 410
P.O. Box 9706
Albuquerque, NM 87106
Phone: 505-842-0644
www.nmaci.org

Albuquerque Convention & Visitors Bureau
20 First Plaza N.W.
Ste. 601
Albuquerque, NM 87102
Phone: 505-842-9918 Fax: 505-247-9101
Toll-free: 800-733-9918
www.visitalbuquerque.org

Las Cruces Convention & Visitors Bureau
211 N. Water St.
Las Cruces, NM 88001
Phone: 505-541-2444 Fax: 505-541-2164
www.lascrucescvb.org

Santa Fe Convention & Visitors Bureau
201 W. Marcy St.
Santa Fe, NM 87501
Phone: 800-777-2489
www.santafe.org

Greater Albuquerque Chamber of Commerce
115 Gold Ave. S.W.
Ste 201
Albuquerque, NM 87102
Phone: 505-764-3700 Fax: 505-764-3714
www.abqchamber.com

Greater Las Cruces Chamber of Commerce
505 S. Main St.
Ste. 134
Las Cruces, NM 88001

Phone: 505-524-1968 Fax: 505-527-5546
www.lascruces.org

Santa Fe Chamber of Commerce
1644 St. Michael's Dr.
Santa Fe, NM 87505
Phone: 505-988-3279 Fax: 505-984-2205
www.santafechamber.com

New York

New York (State) Tourism Div
30 S. Pearl St.
Albany, NY 12445
Phone: 518-292-5120
Toll-free: 800-225-5697
www.iloveny.com

Business Council of New York State Inc
152 Washington Ave.
Albany, NY 12210
Phone: 518-465-7511 Fax: 518-465-4389
Toll-free: 800-358-1202
www.bcnys.org

Albany County Convention & Visitors Bureau
25 Quackenbush Sq.
Albany, NY 12207
Phone: 518-434-1217 Fax: 518-434-0887
Toll-free: 800-258-3582
www.albany.org

Greater Buffalo Convention & Visitors Bureau
403 Main St.
Ste. 630
Buffalo, NY 14203
Phone: 716-852-0511 Fax: 716-852-0131
Toll-free: 888-228-3369
www.visitbuffaloniagara.com

Greater Rochester Visitors Assn
45 E. Ave.
Ste. 400
Rochester, NY 14604
Phone: 585-279-8300
Toll-free: 800-677-7282
www.visitrochester.com

NYC & Co
810 Seventh Ave.
3rd Fl.
New York, NY 10019
Phone: 212-484-1200 Fax: 212-245-5943
www.nycgo.com

Syracuse Convention & Visitors Bureau
115 W. Fayette St.
Syracuse, NY 13202

Phone: 315-470-1910
Toll-free: 800-234-4797
www.visitsyracuse.org

Westchester County Office of Tourism
148 Martine Ave.
Ste. 104
White Plains, NY 10601
Phone: 914-995-8500 Fax: 914-995-8505
Toll-free: 800-833-9282
www.visitwestchesterny.com

Albany-Colonie Regional Chamber of Commerce
5 Computer Dr. S.
Albany, NY 12205
Phone: 518-431-1400 Fax: 518-431-1402
www.acchamber.org

Buffalo Niagara Partnership
665 Main St.
Ste. 200
Buffalo, NY 14203
Phone: 716-852-7100 Fax: 716-852-2761
www.thepartnership.org

CenterState CEO
115 W. Fayette St.
Syracuse, NY 13202
Phone: 315-470-1800 Fax: 315-471-8545
www.centerstateceo.com

New York City Partnership & Chamber of Commerce Inc
1 Battery Park Plaza
5th Fl.
New York, NY 10004
Phone: 212-493-7400 Fax: 212-344-3344
www.pfnyc.org

Rochester Business Alliance
150 State St.
Ste. 400
Rochester, NY 14614
Phone: 585-244-1800 Fax: 585-263-3679
www.rochesterbusinessalliance.com

Yonkers Chamber of Commerce
55 Main St.
2nd Fl.
Yonkers, NY 10701
Phone: 914-963-0332 Fax: 914-963-0455
www.yonkerschamber.com

North Carolina

North Carolina Tourism Div
301 N. Wilmington St.
Raleigh, NC 27699
Phone: 919-807-3300 Fax: 919-733-8582

Toll-free: 800-847-4862
www.visitnc.com

North Carolina Citizens for Business & Industry
701 Corporate Center Dr.
Ste. 400
Raleigh, NC 27607
Phone: 919-836-1400 Fax: 919-836-1425
www.ncchamber.net

Asheville Area Convention & Visitors Bureau
36 Montford Ave.
Asheville, NC 28801
Phone: 828-258-6101 Fax: 828-254-6054
www.exploreasheville.com

Charlotte Convention & Visitors Bureau
500 S. College St.
Ste. 300
Charlotte, NC 28202
Phone: 704-334-2282 Fax: 704-342-3972
Toll-free: 800-722-1994
www.charlottesgotalot.com

Durham Convention & Visitors Bureau
101 E. Morgan St.
Durham, NC 27701
Phone: 919-687-0288 Fax: 919-683-9555
Toll-free: 800-446-8604
www.durham-nc.com

Greater Raleigh Convention & Visitors Bureau
421 Fayetteville St.
Ste. 1505
Raleigh, NC 27601
Phone: 919-834-5900 Fax: 919-831-2887
Toll-free: 800-849-8499
www.visitraleigh.com

Greensboro Area Convention & Visitors Bureau
2411 High Point Rd.
Greensboro, NC 27403
Phone: 336-274-2282 Fax: 336-230-1183
Toll-free: 800-344-2282
www.visitgreensboronc.com

Winston-Salem Convention & Visitors Bureau
200 Brookstown Ave.
Winston-Salem, NC 27101
Phone: 336-728-4200 Fax: 336-721-2202
Toll-free: 866-728-4200
www.visitwinstonsalem.com

Asheville Area Chamber of Commerce
36 Montford Ave.
P.O. Box 1010
Asheville, NC 28801
Phone: 828-258-6101 Fax: 828-251-0926
www.ashevillechamber.org

Charlotte Chamber of Commerce
330 S. Tryon St.
Charlotte, NC 28202
Phone: 704-378-1300 Fax: 704-374-1903
www.charlottechamber.com

Greater Durham Chamber of Commerce
300 W. Morgan St.
Ste. 1400
Durham, NC 27701
Phone: 919-328-8700 Fax: 919-688-8351
www.durhamchamber.org

Greater Raleigh Chamber of Commerce
800 S. Salisbury St.
P.O. Box 2978
Raleigh, NC 27601
Phone: 919-664-7000 Fax: 919-664-7097
www.raleighchamber.org

Greater Winston-Salem Chamber of Commerce
411 W. Fourth St.
Ste. 211
Winston-Salem, NC 27101
Phone: 336-728-9200 Fax: 336-721-2209
www.winstonsalem.com

Greensboro Area Chamber of Commerce
342 N. Elm St.
Greensboro, NC 27401
Phone: 336-387-8300 Fax: 336-275-9299
www.greensboropartnership.com/chamber-commerce

North Dakota

North Dakota Tourism Div
1600 E. Century Ave., Ste. 2, P.O. Box 2057
Century Center
Bismarck, ND 58502
Phone: 701-328-2525 Fax: 701-328-4878
Toll-free: 800-435-5663
www.ndtourism.com

Greater North Dakota Assn
2000 Schafer St.
P.O. Box 2639
Bismarck, ND 58502
Phone: 701-222-0929 Fax: 701-222-1611
www.ndchamber.com

Bismarck-Mandan Convention & Visitors Bureau
1600 Burnt Boat Dr.
Bismarck, ND 58503
Phone: 701-222-4308 Fax: 701-222-0647
Toll-free: 800-767-3555
www.discoverbismarckmandan.com

Fargo-Moorhead Convention & Visitors Bureau
2001 44th St. S.

Fargo, ND 58103
Phone: 701-282-3653 Fax: 701-282-4366
Toll-free: 800-235-7654
www.fargomoorhead.org

Greater Grand Forks Convention & Visitors Bureau
4251 Gateway Dr.
Grand Forks, ND 58203
Phone: 701-746-0444 Fax: 701-746-0775
Toll-free: 800-866-4566
www.visitgrandforks.com

Bismarck-Mandan Chamber of Commerce
1640 Burnt Boat Dr.
P.O. Box 1675
Bismarck, ND 58502
Phone: 701-223-5660
www.bismarckmandan.com

Grand Forks Chamber of Commerce
202 N. 3rd St.
Grand Forks, ND 58203
Phone: 701-772-7271 Fax: 701-772-9238
www.gochamber.org

Ohio

Ohio Travel & Tourism Div
P.O. Box 1001
Columbus, OH 43216
Toll-free: 800-282-5393
www.consumer.discoverohio.com

Ohio Chamber of Commerce
230 E. Town St.
P.O. Box 15159
Columbus, OH 43215
Phone: 614-228-4201 Fax: 614-228-6403
www.ohiochamber.com

Akron/Summit County Convention & Visitors Bureau
77 E. Mill St.
Akron, OH 44308
Phone: 330-374-7560
Toll-free: 800-245-4254
www.visitakron-summit.org

Convention & Visitors Bureau of Greater Cleveland
334 Euclid Ave.
Cleveland, OH 44114
Phone: 216-875-6680
Toll-free: 800-321-1001
www.thisiscleveland.com

Dayton/Montgomery County Convention & Visitors
  Bureau
1 Chamber Plaza
Ste. A

Dayton, OH 45402
Phone: 937-226-8211 Fax: 937-226-8294
Toll-free: 800-221-8235
www.daytoncvb.com

Greater Cincinnati Convention & Visitors Bureau
525 Vine St.
Ste. 1500
Cincinnati, OH 45202
Phone: 513-621-2142 Fax: 513-621-5020
Toll-free: 800-543-2613
www.cincyusa.com

Greater Columbus Convention & Visitors Bureau
277 W. Nationwide Blvd.
Ste. 125
Columbus, OH 43215
Phone: 614-221-6623 Fax: 614-221-5618
Toll-free: 800-354-2657
www.experiencecolumbus.com

Greater Toledo Convention & Visitors Bureau
401 Jefferson Ave.
Toledo, OH 43604
Phone: 419-321-6404
Toll-free: 800-243-4667
www.dotoledo.org

Youngstown/Mahoning County Convention & Visitors
  Bureau
21 W. Boardman St.
Youngstown, OH 44503
Phone: 330-740-2130 Fax: 330-740-2144
Toll-free: 800-447-8201
www.youngstownlive.com

Cincinnati USA Regional Chamber
3 E. 4th St.
Cincinnati, OH 45202
Phone: 513-579-3100 Fax: 513-579-3101
www.cincinnatichamber.com

Dayton Area Chamber of Commerce
22 E. Fifth St.
Chamber Plaza
Dayton, OH 45402
Phone: 937-226-1444 Fax: 937-226-8254
www.daytonchamber.org

Greater Akron Chamber
1 Cascade Plaza
17th Fl.
Akron, OH 44308
Phone: 330-376-5550 Fax: 330-379-3164
www.greaterakronchamber.org

Greater Cleveland Partnership
1240 Huron Rd. E.
Ste. 300
Cleveland, OH 44115

Phone: 216-621-3300 Fax: 216-621-4617
Toll-free: 888-304-4769
www.gcpartnership.com

Greater Columbus Chamber of Commerce
150 S. Front St.
Ste. 200
Columbus, OH 43215
Phone: 614-221-1321 Fax: 614-221-1408
www.columbus.org

Toledo Regional Chamber of Commerce
300 Madison Ave.
Ste. 200
Toledo, OH 43604
Phone: 419-243-8191 Fax: 419-241-8302
www.toledochamber.com

Youngstown Warren Regional Chamber
197 W. Market St.
Ste. 202
Warren, OH 44481
Phone: 330-392-6140 Fax: 330-746-0330
www.regionalchamber.com

Youngstown Warren Regional Chamber
11 Central Sq.
Ste. 1600
Youngstown, OH 44503
Phone: 330-744-2131 Fax: 330-746-0330
www.regionalchamber.com

Oklahoma

Oklahoma Tourism & Recreation Dept
120 N. Robinson
6th Fl.
Oklahoma City, OK 73102
Phone: 405-230-8312
www.travelok.com

Oklahoma State Chamber
330 NE 10th St.
P.O. Box 53217
Oklahoma City, OK 73104
Phone: 405-235-3669 Fax: 405-235-3670
www.okstatechamber.com

Oklahoma City Convention & Visitors Bureau
123 Park Ave.
Oklahoma City, OK 73102
Phone: 405-297-8912 Fax: 405-297-8888
Toll-free: 800-225-5652
www.visitokc.com

Tulsa Convention & Visitors Bureau
1 W. Third St.
Ste. 100

Tulsa, OK 74103
Toll-free: 800-558-3311
www.visittulsa.com

Greater Oklahoma City Chamber of Commerce
123 Park Ave.
Oklahoma City, OK 73102
Phone: 405-297-8900
www.okcchamber.com

Tulsa Metro Chamber
1 W. Third St.
Ste. 100
Tulsa, OK 74103
Phone: 918-585-1201
www.tulsachamber.com

Oregon

Oregon Tourism Commission
317 S.W. Alder St.
Ste. 200
Portland, OR 97204
Phone: 503-967-1560
www.traveloregon.com

Oregon Tourism Commission
250 Church St. S.E.
Ste. 100
Salem, OR 97301
Phone: 503-967-1560
Toll-free: 800-547-7842
www.traveloregon.com

Oregon State Chamber of Commerce
P.O. Box 3344
Albany, OR 97321
Phone: 888-688-4637
www.oregonchamber.org

Convention & Visitors Assn of Lane County Oregon
754 Olive St.
P.O. Box 10286
Eugene, OR 97440
Phone: 541-484-5307
Toll-free: 800-547-5445
www.visitlanecounty.org

Portland Oregon Visitors Assn
1000 S.W. Broadway
Ste. 2300
Portland, OR 97205
Phone: 503-275-9750
Toll-free: 800-962-3700
www.travelportland.com

Salem Convention & Visitors Assn
181 High St. N.E.

Salem, OR 97301
Phone: 503-581-4325 Fax: 503-581-4540
Toll-free: 800-874-7012
www.travelsalem.com

Eugene Chamber of Commerce
1401 Willamette St.
Eugene, OR 97401
Phone: 541-484-1314 Fax: 541-484-4942
www.eugenechamber.com

Portland Business Alliance
200 S.W. Market St.
Ste. 150
Portland, OR 97201
Phone: 503-224-8684 Fax: 503-323-9186
www.portlandalliance.com

Salem Area Chamber of Commerce
1110 Commercial St. N.E.
Salem, OR 97301
Phone: 503-581-1466 Fax: 503-581-0972
www.salemchamber.org

Pennsylvania

Pennsylvania Tourism Office
Commonwealth Keystone Bldg.
400 N. St.
4th Fl.
Harrisburg, PA 17120
Toll-free: 800-847-4872
www.visitpa.com

Pennsylvania Chamber of Business & Industry
417 Walnut St.
Harrisburg, PA 17101
Phone: 717-255-3252 Fax: 717-255-3298
Toll-free: 800-225-7224
www.pachamber.org

Erie Area Convention & Visitors Bureau
208 E Bayfront Pkwy.
Ste. 103
Erie, PA 16507
Phone: 814-454-7191 Fax: 814-459-0241
Toll-free: 800-524-3743
www.visiteriepa.com

Gettysburg Convention & Visitors Bureau
571 W. Middle St.
Gettysburg, PA 17325
Phone: 717-334-6274 Fax: 717-334-1166
Toll-free: 800-337-5015
www.destinationgettysburg.com

Greater Pittsburgh Convention & Visitors Bureau
120 Fifth Ave.

Ste. 2800
Pittsburgh, PA 15222
Phone: 412-281-7711
Toll-free: 800-359-0758
www.visitpittsburgh.com

Hershey-Capital Region Visitors Bureau
3211 N. Front St.
Ste. 301-A
Harrisburg, PA 17101
Phone: 717-231-7788
Toll-free: 877-727-8573
www.visithersheyharrisburg.org

Lehigh Valley Convention & Visitors Bureau
840 Hamilton St.
Ste. 200
Allentown, PA 18101
Phone: 610-882-9200 Fax: 610-882-0343
Toll-free: 800-747-0561
www.discoverlehighvalley.com

Pennsylvania Dutch Convention & Visitors Bureau
501 Greenfield Rd.
Lancaster, PA 17601
Phone: 717-299-8901 Fax: 717-299-0470
Toll-free: 800-723-8824
www.discoverlancaster.com

Philadelphia Convention & Visitors Bureau
1601 Market St.
Ste. 200
Philadelphia, PA 19103
Phone: 215-636-3300 Fax: 215-636-3327
www.discoverphl.com

Erie Regional Chamber & Growth Partnership
208 E Bayfront Pkwy.
Ste. 100
Erie, PA 16507
Phone: 814-454-7191 Fax: 814-459-0241
www.eriepa.com

Gettysburg-Adams County Area Chamber of Commerce
1382 Biglerville Rd.
Gettysburg, PA 17325
Phone: 717-334-8151
www.gettysburg-chamber.org

Greater Lehigh Valley Chamber of Commerce
840 Hamilton St.
Ste. 205
Allentown, PA 18101
Phone: 610-751-4929 Fax: 610-437-4907
www.lehighvalleychamber.org

Greater Philadelphia Chamber of Commerce
200 S. Broad St.
Ste. 700
Philadelphia, PA 19102

Phone: 215-545-1234 Fax: 215-790-3600
www.greaterphilachamber.com

Greater Pittsburgh Chamber of Commerce
11 Stanwix St.
17th Fl.
Pittsburgh, PA 15222
Phone: 412-281-1890 Fax: 412-281-1896
www.greaterpittsburghchamberofcommerce.com

Greater Scranton Chamber of Commerce
222 Mulberry St.
P.O.Box 431
Scranton, PA 18501
Phone: 570-342-7711 Fax: 570-347-6262
www.scrantonchamber.com

Harrisburg Regional Chamber
3211 N. Front St.
Ste. 201
Harrisburg, PA 17110
Phone: 717-232-4099
Toll-free: 877-883-8339
www.harrisburgregionalchamber.org

Lancaster Chamber of Commerce & Industry
100 S. Queen St.
Lancaster, PA 17603
Phone: 717-397-3531 Fax: 717-293-3159
www.lcci.com

Rhode Island

Rhode Island Tourism Div
315 Iron Horse Way
Ste. 101
Providence, RI 02908
Phone: 401-278-9100 Fax: 401-273-8270
Toll-free: 800-556-2484
www.visitrhodeisland.com

Rhode Island Economic Development Corp
315 Iron Horse Way
Ste. 101
Providence, RI 02908
Phone: 401-278-9100 Fax: 401-273-8270
www.commerceri.com

Newport County Convention & Visitors Bureau
23 America's Cup Ave.
Newport, RI 02840
Phone: 401-849-8048 Fax: 401-849-0291
Toll-free: 800-326-6030
www.discovernewport.org

Providence Warwick Convention & Visitors Bureau
10 Memorial Blvd.
Providence, RI 02903

Phone: 401-456-0200 Fax: 401-351-2090
Toll-free: 800-233-1636
www.goprovidence.com

Greater Providence Chamber of Commerce
30 Exchange Terr.
4th Fl.
Providence, RI 02903
Phone: 401-521-5000 Fax: 401-621-6109
www.providencechamber.com

Newport County Chamber of Commerce
35 Valley Rd.
Middletown, RI 02842
Phone: 401-847-1600 Fax: 401-849-5848
www.newportchamber.com

South Carolina

South Carolina Parks Recreation & Tourism Dept
1205 Pendleton St.
Columbia, SC 29201
Phone: 803-734-0156
www.southcarolinaparks.com

South Carolina Chamber of Commerce
1301 Gervais St.
Ste. 1100
Columbia, SC 29201
Phone: 803-799-4601 Fax: 803-779-6043
Toll-free: 800-799-4601
www.scchamber.net

Charleston Area Convention & Visitors Bureau
423 King St.
Charleston, SC 29403
Phone: 843-853-8000 Fax: 843-853-0444
Toll-free: 800-868-8118
www.charlestoncvb.com

Columbia Metropolitan Convention & Visitors Bureau
1010 Lincoln St.
Columbia, SC 29201
Phone: 803-545-0000 Fax: 803-545-0012
Toll-free: 800-264-4884
www.columbiacvb.com

Greater Greenville Convention & Visitors Bureau
206 S. Main St.
1st Fl.
Greenville, SC 29601
Phone: 864-233-0461
Toll-free: 800-717-0023
www.visitgreenvillesc.com

Hilton Head Island Visitors & Convention Bureau
1 Chamber of Commerce Dr.
Hilton Head Island, SC 29938

Phone: 843-785-3673 Fax: 843-785-7110
Toll-free: 800-523-3373
www.hiltonheadchamber.org

Myrtle Beach Area Convention Bureau
1200 N. Oak St.
P.O. Box 2115
Myrtle Beach, SC 29577
Phone: 843-626-7444 Fax: 843-448-3010
Toll-free: 800-356-3016
www.visitmyrtlebeach.com

Charleston Metro Chamber of Commerce
4500 Leeds Ave.
Ste. 100
North Charleston, SC 29405
Phone: 843-577-2510
www.charlestonchamber.net

Greater Columbia Chamber of Commerce
930 Richland St.
Columbia, SC 29201
Phone: 803-733-1110 Fax: 803-733-1113
www.columbiachamber.com

Greater Greenville Chamber of Commerce
24 Cleveland St.
Greenville, SC 29601
Phone: 864-242-1050 Fax: 864-282-8509
Toll-free: 866-485-5262
www.greenvillechamber.org

Hilton Head Island-Bluffton Chamber of Commerce
1 Chamber Dr.
P.O. Box 5647
Hilton Head Island, SC 29938
Phone: 843-785-3673
Toll-free: 800-523-3373
www.hiltonheadisland.org

Myrtle Beach Area Chamber of Commerce
1200 N. Oak St.
Myrtle Beach, SC 29577
Phone: 843-626-7444 Fax: 843-626-0009
Toll-free: 800-356-3016
www.myrtlebeachareachamber.com

South Dakota

South Dakota Tourism Office
711 E. Wells Ave.
c/o 500 E. Capitol Ave.
Pierre, SD 57501
Phone: 605-773-3301
Toll-free: 800-732-5682
www.travelsouthdakota.com

South Dakota Chamber of Commerce & Industry
222 E. Capitol

Ste. 15
Pierre, SD 57501
Phone: 605-224-6161 Fax: 605-224-7198
www.sdchamber.biz

Rapid City Convention & Visitors Bureau
444 Mt. Rushmore Rd. N.
Rapid City, SD 57701
Phone: 605-718-8484 Fax: 605-348-9217
Toll-free: 800-487-3223
www.visitrapidcity.com

Sioux Falls Convention & Visitors Bureau
200 N. Phillips Ave.
Ste. 102
Sioux Falls, SD 57104
Phone: 605-336-1620
Toll-free: 800-333-2072
www.visitsiouxfalls.com

Pierre Area Chamber of Commerce
800 W. Dakota Ave.
P.O. Box 548
Pierre, SD 57501
Phone: 605-224-7361 Fax: 605-224-6485
Toll-free: 800-962-2034
www.pierre.org

Rapid City Area Chamber of Commerce
444 Mt. Rushmore Rd. N.
P.O. Box 747
Rapid City, SD 57701
Phone: 605-343-1744 Fax: 605-343-6550
www.rapidcitychamber.com

Sioux Falls Area Chamber of Commerce
200 N. Phillips Ave.
Ste. 200
Sioux Falls, SD 57104
Phone: 605-336-1620 Fax: 605-336-6499
www.siouxfallschamber.com

Tennessee

Tennessee Tourist Development Office
312 Rosa L. Parks Ave.
Nashville, TN 37243
Phone: 615-741-2159
www.tnvacation.com

Tennessee Chamber of Commerce & Industry
611 Commerce St.
Ste. 3030
Nashville, TN 37203
Phone: 615-256-5141 Fax: 615-256-6726
www.tnchamber.org

Chattanooga Area Convention & Visitors Bureau
736 Market St.

18th Fl.
Chattanooga, TN 37402
Phone: 423-756-8687 Fax: 423-265-1630
Toll-free: 800-322-3344
www.chattanoogafun.com

Johnson City Convention & Visitors Bureau
601 E Market St.
Johnson City, TN 37601
Phone: 423-434-6000
www.johnsoncitytn.com

Knoxville Tourism & Sports Corp
301 S. Gay St.
Knoxville, TN 37902
Phone: 865-523-7263
Toll-free: 800-727-8045
www.visitknoxville.com

Memphis Convention & Visitors Bureau
47 Union Ave.
Memphis, TN 38103
Phone: 901-543-5300
www.memphistravel.com

Nashville Convention & Visitors Bureau
150 Fourth Ave. N.
Ste. G-250
Nashville, TN 37219
Phone: 615-259-4730 Fax: 615-259-4126
Toll-free: 800-657-6910
www.visitmusiccity.com

Chattanooga Area Chamber of Commerce
811 Broad St.
Chattanooga, TN 37402
Phone: 423-756-2121 Fax: 423-267-7242
www.chattanoogachamber.com

Johnson City/Jonesborough/Washington County Chamber
 of Commerce
603 E. Market St.
Johnson City, TN 37601
Phone: 423-461-8000 Fax: 423-461-8047
Toll-free: 800-852-3392
www.johnsoncitytnchamber.com

Knoxville Area Chamber Partnership
17 Market Sq.
Ste. 201
Knoxville, TN 37902
Phone: 865-637-4550 Fax: 865-523-2071
www.knoxvillechamber.com

Memphis Regional Chamber of Commerce
22 N. Front St.
Ste. 200
Memphis, TN 38103
Phone: 901-543-3500 Fax: 901-543-3510
www.memphischamber.com

Nashville Chamber of Commerce
211 Commerce St.
Ste. 100
Nashville, TN 37201
Phone: 615-743-3000 Fax: 615-256-3002
www.nashvillechamber.com

Texas

Texas Tourism Div
P.O. Box 141009
Austin, TX 78714
Toll-free: 800-452-9292
www.traveltex.com

Texas Assn of Business
1209 Nueces St.
Austin, TX 78701
Phone: 512-477-6721 Fax: 512-477-0836
www.txbiz.org

Abilene Convention & Visitors Bureau
1101 N. 1st St.
Abilene, TX 79601
Phone: 325-676-2556 Fax: 325-676-1630
Toll-free: 800-727-7704
www.abilenevisitors.com

Amarillo Convention & Visitor Council
1000 S. Polk St.
Amarillo, TX 79101
Phone: 806-374-1497
Toll-free: 800-692-1338
www.visitamarillo.com

Arlington Convention & Visitors Bureau
1905 E. Randol Mill Rd.
Arlington, TX 76011
Toll-free: 800-433-5374
www.experiencearlington.org

Austin Convention & Visitors Bureau
301 Congress Ave.
Ste. 200
Austin, TX 78701
Phone: 512-474-5171 Fax: 512-583-7282
Toll-free: 800-926-2282
www.austintexas.org

Brownsville Convention & Visitors Bureau
650 Ruben M. Torres Sr. Blvd.
Brownsville, TX 78521
Phone: 956-546-3721
Toll-free: 800-626-2639
www.brownsville.org

Corpus Christi Convention & Visitors Bureau
101 N. Shoreline Blvd.
Ste. 430

Corpus Christi, TX 78401
Phone: 361-881-1888 Fax: 361-887-9023
Toll-free: 800-678-6232
www.visitcorpuschristitx.org

Dallas Convention & Visitors Bureau
325 N. Saint Paul St.
Ste. 700
Dallas, TX 75201
Phone: 214-571-1000 Fax: 214-571-1008
Toll-free: 800-232-5527
www.visitdallas.com

El Paso Convention & Visitors Bureau
1 Civic Center Plaza
El Paso, TX 79901
Phone: 915-534-0600 Fax: 915-534-0687
Toll-free: 800-351-6024
www.visitelpaso.com

Fort Worth Convention & Visitors Bureau
111 W. 4th St.
Ste. 200
Fort Worth, TX 76102
Toll-free: 800-433-5747
www.fortworth.com

Garland Convention & Visitors Bureau
211 N. 5th St.
Garland, TX 75040
Phone: 972-205-2749
Toll-free: 888-879-0264
www.visitgarlandtx.com

Greater Houston Convention & Visitors Bureau
1331 Lamar St.
Ste. 700
Houston, TX 77010
Phone: 713-437-5200
Toll-free: 800-446-8786
www.visithoustontexas.com

Irving Convention & Visitors Bureau
500 W. Las Colinas Blvd.
Irving, TX 75039
Phone: 972-252-7476 Fax: 972-401-7729
Toll-free: 866-433-2980
www.irvingtexas.com

Lubbock Convention & Visitors Bureau
1500 Broadway
6th Fl.
Lubbock, TX 79401
Phone: 806-747-5232
Toll-free: 800-692-4035
www.visitlubbock.org

Plano Convention & Visitors Bureau
2000 E. Spring Creek Pkwy
Plano, TX 75074

Phone: 972-941-5840 Fax: 972-424-0002
Toll-free: 800-817-5266
www.visitplano.com

San Antonio Convention & Visitors Bureau
203 S. St. Marys St.
Ste. 200
San Antonio, TX 78205
Phone: 210-207-6700 Fax: 210-207-6768
Toll-free: 800-447-3372
www.visitsanantonio.com

South Padre Island Convention & Visitors Bureau
600 Padre Blvd.
South Padre Island, TX 78597
Phone: 956-761-6433
Toll-free: 800-767-2373
www.sopadre.com

Abilene Chamber of Commerce
174 Cypress St., Ste. 200
P.O. Box 2281
Abilene, TX 79601
Phone: 325-677-7241 Fax: 325-677-0622
www.abilenechamber.com

Amarillo Chamber of Commerce
1000 S. Polk St.
P.O. Box 9480
Amarillo, TX 79105
Phone: 806-373-7800 Fax: 806-373-3909
www.amarillo-chamber.org

Arlington Chamber of Commerce
505 E. Border St.
Arlington, TX 76010
Phone: 817-275-2613 Fax: 817-261-7389
www.arlingtontx.com

Brownsville Chamber of Commerce
1600 University Blvd.
Brownsville, TX 78520
Phone: 956-542-4341 Fax: 956-504-3348
www.brownsvillechamber.com

Corpus Christi Chamber of Commerce
1501 N. Chaparral
Corpus Christi, TX 78401
Phone: 361-881-1800
www.corpuschristichamber.org

Fort Worth Chamber of Commerce
777 Taylor St.
Ste. 900
Fort Worth, TX 76102
Phone: 817-336-2491 Fax: 817-877-4034
www.fortworthchamber.com

Garland Chamber of Commerce
520 N. Glenbrook Dr.

Garland, TX 75040
Phone: 972-272-7551 Fax: 972-276-9261
www.garlandchamber.com

Greater Austin Chamber of Commerce
535 E. 5th St.
Austin, TX 78701
Phone: 512-478-9383 Fax: 512-478-9615
www.austinchamber.com

Greater Dallas Chamber of Commerce
500 N. Akard St.
Ste. 2600
Dallas, TX 75201
Phone: 214-746-6600
www.dallaschamber.org

Greater El Paso Chamber of Commerce
10 Civic Center
El Paso, TX 79901
Phone: 915-534-0500 Fax: 915-534-0510
www.elpaso.org

Greater Houston Partnership
1200 Smith St.
Ste. 700
Houston, TX 77002
Phone: 713-844-3600 Fax: 713-844-0200
www.houston.org

Greater Irving & Las Colinas Chamber of Commerce
5201 N. O'Connor Blvd.
Ste. 100
Irving, TX 75039
Phone: 214-217-8484 Fax: 214-389-2513
www.irvingchamber.com

Greater San Antonio Chamber of Commerce
602 E. Commerce
San Antonio, TX 78205
Phone: 210-229-2100 Fax: 210-229-1600
www.sachamber.org

Lubbock Chamber of Commerce
1500 Broadway
Ste. 101
Lubbock, TX 79401
Phone: 806-761-7000 Fax: 806-761-7013
www.lubbockchamber.com

Plano Chamber of Commerce
1200 E. 15th St.
Plano, TX 75074
Phone: 972-424-7547 Fax: 972-422-5182
www.planochamber.org

Utah

Utah Travel Development Div
300 N. State
Salt Lake City, UT 84114
Phone: 801-538-1900
Toll-free: 800-200-1160
www.travel.utah.gov

Utah State Chamber of Commerce
175 E. University Blvd. (400 S.)
Ste. 600
Salt Lake City, UT 84111
Phone: 801-328-5090 Fax: 801-328-5098
www.utahstatechamber.org

Ogden/Weber Convention & Visitors Bureau
2438 Washington Blvd.
Ogden, UT 84401
Phone: 866-867-8824 Fax: 801-399-0783
Toll-free: 800-255-8824
www.visitogden.com

Salt Lake Convention & Visitors Bureau
90 S. W. Temple
Salt Lake City, UT 84101
Phone: 801-534-4900 Fax: 801-534-4927
Toll-free: 800-541-4955
www.visitsaltlake.com

Utah Valley Convention & Visitors Bureau
220 W. Center St.
Ste. 100
Provo, UT 84601
Phone: 801-851-2100
Toll-free: 800-222-8824
www.utahvalley.com

Chamber Ogden/Weber
2484 Washington Blvd.
Ste. 400
Ogden, UT 84401
Phone: 801-621-8300 Fax: 801-392-7609
Toll-free: 866-990-1299
www.ogdenweberchamber.com

Salt Lake City Chamber of Commerce
175 E. University Blvd. (400 S.)
Ste. 600
Salt Lake City, UT 84111
Phone: 801-364-3631
www.slchamber.com

Utah Valley Chamber of Commerce
111 S. University Ave.
Provo, UT 84601
Phone: 801-379-2555
www.thechamber.org

Vermont

Vermont Tourism & Marketing Dept
1 National Life Dr.
6th Fl.
Montpelier, VT 05620
Phone: 802-828-3237
Toll-free: 800-837-6668
www.vermontvacation.com

Vermont Chamber of Commerce
P.O. Box 37
Montpelier, VT 05601
Phone: 802-223-3443 Fax: 802-223-4257
www.vtchamber.com

Central Vermont Chamber of Commerce
33 Stewart Rd.
Berlin, VT 05602
Phone: 802-229-5711 Fax: 802-229-5713
Toll-free: 877-887-3678
www.central-vt.com

Lake Champlain Regional Chamber of Commerce
60 Main St.
Ste. 100
Burlington, VT 05401
Phone: 802-863-3489 Fax: 802-863-1538
Toll-free: 877-686-5253
www.vermont.org

Virginia

Virginia Tourism Corp
901 E. Byrd St.
Richmond, VA 23219
Phone: 804-545-5500 Fax: 804-545-5501
Toll-free: 800-847-4882
www.vatc.org

Virginia Chamber of Commerce
919 E. Main St.
Ste. 900
Richmond, VA 23219
Phone: 804-644-1607 Fax: 804-783-6112
www.vachamber.com

Alexandria Convention & Visitors Assn
221 King St.
Alexandria, VA 22314
Phone: 703-746-3301
Toll-free: 800-388-9119
www.visitalexandriava.com

Arlington Convention & Visitors Service
1100 N. Glebe Rd.
Ste. 1500
Arlington, VA 22201

Phone: 800-296-7996 Fax: 703-228-0806
www.stayarlington.com

Chesapeake Conventions & Tourism Bureau
1224 Progressive Dr.
Chesapeake, VA 23320
Phone: 757-382-6411 Fax: 757-502-8016
Toll-free: 888-889-5551
www.visitchesapeake.com

Newport News Tourism Development Office
700 Town Center Dr.
Ste. 320
Newport News, VA 23606
Phone: 757-926-1400 Fax: 757-926-1441
Toll-free: 888-493-7386
www.newport-news.org

Richmond Metropolitan Convention & Visitors Bureau
401 N. 3rd St.
Richmond, VA 23219
Phone: 804-783-7450
Toll-free: 800-370-9004
www.visitrichmondva.com

Roanoke Valley Convention & Visitors Bureau
101 Shenandoah Ave. N.E.
Roanoke, VA 24016
Phone: 540-342-6025
Toll-free: 800-635-5535
www.visitroanokeva.com

Virginia Beach Convention & Visitor Bureau
2101 Parks Ave.
Ste. 500
Virginia Beach, VA 23451
Toll-free: 800-822-3224
www.visitvirginiabeach.com

Williamsburg Area Convention & Visitors Bureau
421 N. Boundary St.
P.O. Box 3495
Williamsburg, VA 23187
Phone: 757-229-6511
Toll-free: 800-368-6511
www.visitwilliamsburg.com

Alexandria Chamber of Commerce
801 N. Fairfax St.
Ste. 207
Alexandria, VA 22314
Phone: 703-549-1000 Fax: 703-549-1001
www.alexchamber.com

Arlington Chamber of Commerce
611 Massachusetts Ave.
Arlington, VA 02474
Phone: 703-643-4600 Fax: 703-646-5581
www.arlcc.org

Greater Richmond Chamber of Commerce
600 E. Main St.
Ste. 700
Richmond, VA 23219
Phone: 804-648-1234
www.grcc.com

Hampton Roads Chamber of Commerce
500 E. Main St.
Ste. 700
Norfolk, VA 23510
Phone: 757-622-2312 Fax: 757-622-5563
www.hamptonroadschamber.com

Salem/Roanoke County Chamber of Commerce
611 E. Main St.
P.O. Box 832
Salem, VA 24153
Phone: 540-387-0267 Fax: 540-387-4110
www.s-rcchamber.org

Virginia Peninsula Chamber of Commerce
21 Enterprise Pkwy.
Ste. 100
Hampton, VA 23666
Phone: 757-262-2000 Fax: 757-262-2009
www.virginiapeninsulachamber.com

Williamsburg Area Chamber of Commerce
421 N. Boundary St.
Williamsburg, VA 23185
Phone: 757-229-6511 Fax: 757-253-1397
Toll-free: 800-368-6511
www.williamsburgcc.com

Washington

Washington Tourism Alliance
P.O. Box 953
Seattle, WA 98111
Phone: 800-544-1800
www.experiencewa.com

Association of Washington Business
1414 Cherry St. S.E.
Olympia, WA 98501
Phone: 360-943-1600 Fax: 360-943-5811
Toll-free: 800-521-9325
www.awb.org

Olympia/Thurston County Visitor & Convention Bureau
103 Sid Snyder Ave S.W.
Olympia, WA 98501
Phone: 360-704-7544 Fax: 360-704-7533
Toll-free: 877-704-7500
www.visitolympia.com

Seattle's Convention & Visitors Bureau
701 Pike St.

Ste. 800
Seattle, WA 98101
Phone: 206-461-5800 Fax: 206-461-5855
Toll-free: 866-732-2695
www.visitseattle.org

Spokane Convention & Visitors Bureau
801 W. Riverside Ave.
Ste. 301
Spokane, WA 99201
Phone: 509-624-1341 Fax: 509-623-1297
Toll-free: 888-662-0084
www.visitspokane.com

Tacoma Regional Convention & Visitor Bureau
1119 Pacific Ave.
Ste. 1400
Tacoma, WA 98402
Phone: 253-627-2836
Toll-free: 800-272-2662
www.traveltacoma.com

Vancouver Convention & Visitors Bureau
1220 Main St.
Ste. 220
Vancouver, WA 98660
Phone: 360-750-1553
Toll-free: 877-600-0800
www.visitvancouverusa.com

Greater Seattle Chamber of Commerce
1301 5th Ave.
Ste. 1500
Seattle, WA 98101
Phone: 206-389-7200 Fax: 888-392-2795
www.seattlechamber.com

Greater Vancouver Chamber of Commerce
1101 Broadway
Ste. 100
Vancouver, WA 98660
Phone: 360-694-2588
www.vancouverusa.com

Olympia/Thurston County Chamber of Commerce
809 Legion Way S.E.
Olympia, WA 98501
Phone: 360-357-3362
www.thurstonchamber.com

Spokane Regional Chamber of Commerce
801 W. Riverside Ave.
Ste. 100
Spokane, WA 99201
Phone: 509-624-1393 Fax: 509-747-0077
Toll-free: 800-776-5263
www.greaterspokane.org

Tacoma-Pierce County Chamber of Commerce
950 Pacific Ave.

Ste. 300
Tacoma, WA 98401
Phone: 253-627-2175 Fax: 253-597-7305
www.tacomachamber.org

West Virginia

West Virginia Tourism Div
90 MacCorkle Ave. S.W.
South Charleston, WV 25303
Phone: 304-558-2200
Toll-free: 800-225-5982
www.wvtourism.com

West Virginia Chamber of Commerce
1624 Kanawha Blvd. E.
Charleston, WV 25311
Phone: 304-342-1115 Fax: 304-342-1130
www.wvchamber.com

Charleston Convention & Visitors Bureau
601 Morris St.
Ste. 204
Charleston, WV 25301
Phone: 304-344-5075
www.charlestonwv.com

Greater Morgantown Convention & Visitors Bureau
341 Chaplin Rd.
1st Fl.
Morgantown, WV 26501
Phone: 304-292-5081 Fax: 304-291-1354
Toll-free: 800-458-7373
www.tourmorgantown.com

Wheeling Convention & Visitors Bureau
1401 Main St.
Wheeling, WV 26003
Toll-free: 800-828-3097
www.wheelingcvb.com

Charleston Regional Chamber of Commerce
1116 Smith St.
Charleston, WV 25301
Phone: 304-340-4253 Fax: 304-340-4275
Toll-free: 800-792-4326
www.charlestonareaalliance.org

Morgantown Area Chamber of Commerce
1029 University Ave.
Ste. 101
Morgantown, WV 26505
Phone: 304-292-3311 Fax: 304-296-6619
Toll-free: 800-618-2525
www.morgantownchamber.org

Wheeling Area Chamber of Commerce
1310 Market St.

2nd Fl.
Wheeling, WV 26003
Phone: 304-233-2575 Fax: 304-233-1320
www.wheelingchamber.com

Wisconsin

Wisconsin Tourism Dept
P.O. Box 8690
Madison, WI 53708
Phone: 608-266-2161
Toll-free: 800-432-8747
www.travelwisconsin.com

Wisconsin Manufacturers & Commerce
501 E. Washington Ave.
P.O. Box 352
Madison, WI 53703
Phone: 608-258-3400 Fax: 608-258-3413
www.wmc.org

Greater Madison Convention & Visitors Bureau
615 E. Washington Ave.
Madison, WI 53703
Phone: 608-255-2537 Fax: 608-258-4950
Toll-free: 800-373-6376
www.visitmadison.com

Greater Milwaukee Convention & Visitors Bureau
648 N. Plankinton Ave.
Ste. 425
Milwaukee, WI 53203
Phone: 414-273-3950 Fax: 414-273-5596
Toll-free: 800-231-0903
www.milwaukee.org

Packer Country Visitor & Convention Bureau
1901 S. Oneida St.
Green Bay, WI 54304
Phone: 920-494-9507
Toll-free: 888-867-3342
www.greenbay.com

Greater Madison Chamber of Commerce
615 E. Washington Ave.
P.O. Box 71
Madison, WI 53701
Phone: 608-256-8348 Fax: 608-256-0333
www.greatermadisonchamber.com

Green Bay Area Chamber of Commerce
300 N. Broadway
Ste. 3A
Green Bay, WI 54303
Phone: 920-437-8704
www.titletown.org

Metropolitan Milwaukee Assn of Commerce
756 N. Milwaukee St.

Ste. 400
Milwaukee, WI 53202
Phone: 414-287-4100 Fax: 414-271-7753
www.mmac.org

Wyoming

Wyoming Tourism Div
5611 High Plains Rd.
Cheyenne, WY 82007
Phone: 307-777-7777 Fax: 307-777-2877
Toll-free: 800-225-5996
www.wyomingtourism.org

Wyoming State Chamber of Commerce
P.O. Box 418
Laramie, WY 82073
Phone: 307-760-3897
www.wyomingchambers.com

Casper Area Convention & Visitors Bureau
139 W. 2nd St.
Ste. 1B
Casper, WY 82601
Phone: 307-234-5362 Fax: 307-261-9928
Toll-free: 800-852-1889
www.visitcasper.com

Cheyenne Area Convention & Visitors Bureau
121 W. 15th St.
Ste. 202
Cheyenne, WY 82001
Phone: 307-778-3133 Fax: 307-778-3190
Toll-free: 800-426-5009
www.cheyenne.org

Casper Area Chamber of Commerce
500 N. Center St.
Casper, WY 82601
Phone: 307-234-5311
www.casperwyoming.org

Greater Cheyenne Chamber of Commerce
121 W. 15th St.
Ste. 204
Cheyenne, WY 82001
Phone: 307-638-3388 Fax: 307-778-1407
www.cheyennechamber.org

Jackson Hole Chamber of Commerce
112 Center St.
P.O. Box 550
Jackson, WY 83001
Phone: 307-733-3316
www.jacksonholechamber.com

CANADA

Canada Consulate General
1175 Peachtree St. N.E.
100 Colony Sq.
Ste. 1700
Atlanta, GA 30361
Phone: 404-532-2000 Fax: 404-532-2050
www.can-am.gc.ca/atlanta

Canada Consulate General
3 Copley Pl.
Ste. 400
Boston, MA 02116
Phone: 617-247-5100 Fax: 617-247-5190
www.can-am.gc.ca/boston

Canada Consulate General
2 Prudential Plaza
180 N. Stetson Ave.
Ste. 2400
Chicago, IL 60601
Phone: 312-616-1860
www.can-am.gc.ca/chicago

Canada Consulate General
500 N. Akard St.
Ste. 2900
Dallas, TX 75201
Phone: 214-922-9806 Fax: 214-922-9815
www.can-am.gc.ca/dallas

Canada Consulate General
600 Renaissance Ctr.
Ste. 1100
Detroit, MI 48243
Phone: 313-567-2340 Fax: 313-567-2164
www.can-am.gc.ca/detroit

Canada Consulate General
550 S. Hope St.
9th Fl.
Los Angeles, CA 90071
Phone: 213-346-2700 Fax: 213-346-2797
www.can-am.gc.ca/los-angeles

Canada Consulate General
200 S. Biscayne Blvd.
Ste. 1600
Miami, FL 33131
Phone: 305-579-1600 Fax: 305-374-6774
www.can-am.gc.ca/miami

Canada Consulate General
701 Fourth Ave. S.
9th Fl.
Minneapolis, MN 55415
Phone: 612-333-4641 Fax: 612-332-4061
www.can-am.gc.ca/minneapolis

Canada Consulate General
1251 Avenue of the Americas
Concourse Level (between 49th and 50th St., midtown Manhattan)
New York, NY 10020
Phone: 212-596-1628 Fax: 212-596-1790
www.can-am.gc.ca/new-york

Canada Consulate General
1501 4th Ave.
Ste. 600
Seattle, WA 98101
Phone: 206-443-1777 Fax: 206-443-9662
www.can-am.gc.ca/seattle

Canada Embassy
501 Pennsylvania Ave. N.W.
Washington, DC 20001
Phone: 202-682-1740 Fax: 202-682-7726
www.can-am.gc.ca/washington

Canada Permanent Mission to the UN
1 Dag Hammarskjöld Plaza
885 Second Ave.
14th Fl.
New York, NY 10017
Phone: 212-848-1100 Fax: 212-848-1195
www.canadainternational.gc.ca/prmny-mponu

Alberta

Travel Alberta
400-1601 9 Ave. S.E.
Calgary, AB T2G0H4
Phone: 403-648-1000 Fax: 403-648-1111
Toll-free: 800-252-3782
www.travelalberta.com

Alberta Chambers of Commerce
10025 102A Ave.
Ste. 1808
Edmonton, AB T5J2Z2
Phone: 780-425-4180
www.abchamber.ca

Calgary Chamber of Commerce
237 Eighth Ave. S.E.
Ste. 600
Calgary, AB T2G5C3
Phone: 403-750-0400 Fax: 403-266-3413
www.calgarychamber.com

Edmonton Chamber of Commerce
9990 Jasper Ave.
Ste. 600
Edmonton, AB T5J1P7
Phone: 780-426-4620 Fax: 780-424-7946
www.edmontonchamber.com

British Columbia

Canadian Tourism Commission
1055 Dunsmuir St., Ste. 1400
4 Bentall Center
P.O. Box 49220
Vancouver, BC V7X1L2
Phone: 604-638-8300
www.en-corporate.canada.travel

Canadian Tourism Commission
3B 1218 Langley St.
Victoria, BC V8W1W2
Phone: 877-717-9277 Fax: 877-402-7573
www.travel.bc.ca

British Columbia Chamber of Commerce
750 W Pender St.
Ste. 1201
Vancouver, BC V6C2T8
Phone: 604-683-0700 Fax: 604-683-0416
www.bcchamber.org

Greater Victoria Chamber of Commerce
852 Fort St.
Ste. 100
Victoria, BC V8W1H8
Phone: 250-383-7191 Fax: 250-385-3552
www.victoriachamber.ca

North Vancouver Chamber of Commerce
124 W 1st St.
Ste. 102
North Vancouver, BC V7M3N3
Phone: 604-987-4488 Fax: 604-987-8272
Toll-free: 877-880-4699
www.nvchamber.ca

Vancouver Board Of Trade
999 Canada Pl.
Ste. 400
Vancouver, BC V6C3E1
Phone: 604-681-2111 Fax: 604-681-0437
www.boardoftrade.com

West Vancouver Chamber of Commerce
2235 Marine Dr.
West Vancouver, BC V7T1K5
Phone: 604-926-6614 Fax: 604-926-6647
Toll-free: 888-471-9996
www.westvanchamber.com

Manitoba

Travel Manitoba
155 Carlton St.
7th Fl.
Winnipeg, MB R3C3H8

Phone: 204-927-7800 Fax: 204-927-7838
Toll-free: 800-665-0040
www.travelmanitoba.com

Manitoba Chamber of Commerce
227 Portage Ave.
Winnipeg, MB R3B2A6
Phone: 204-948-0100 Fax: 204-948-0110
Toll-free: 877-444-5222
www.mbchamber.mb.ca

Winnipeg Chamber of Commerce
259 Portage Ave.
Ste. 100
Winnipeg, MB R3B2A9
Phone: 204-944-8484 Fax: 204-944-8492
www.winnipeg-chamber.com

New Brunswick

Tourism New Brunswick
P.O. Box 12345
Campbellton, NB E3N3T6
Toll-free: 800-561-0123
www.tourismnewbrunswick.ca

Atlantic Provinces Chamber of Commerce
200-1273 Main St.
Moncton, NB E1C0P4
Phone: 506-866-9260
www.apcc.ca

Fredericton Chamber of Commerce
364 York St., Ste. 200
P.O. Box 275
Fredericton, NB E3B4Y9
Phone: 506-458-8006 Fax: 506-451-1119
www.frederictonchamber.ca

Saint John Board of Trade
40 King St.
Saint John, NB E2L1G3
Phone: 506-634-8111 Fax: 506-632-2008
www.sjboardoftrade.com

Newfoundland & Labrador

Newfoundland & Labrador Tourism
P.O. Box 8700
Saint John's, NL A1B4J6
Phone: 709-729-2830 Fax: 709-729-0870
Toll-free: 800-563-6353
www.newfoundlandlabrador.com

Saint John's Board of Trade
34 Harvey Rd.

Paramount Bldg.
3rd Fl.
Saint John's, NL A1C5V5
Phone: 709-726-2961 Fax: 709-726-2003
www.stjohnsbot.ca

Northwest Territories

NWT Tourism
P.O. Box 610
Yellowknife, NT X1A2N5
Phone: 867-873-7200 Fax: 867-873-4059
Toll-free: 800-661-0788
www.spectacularnwt.com

Northwest Territories Chamber of Commerce
4802-50th Ave.
Unit 13
Yellowknife, NT X1A3S5
Phone: 867-920-9505 Fax: 867-873-4174
www.nwtchamber.com

Nova Scotia

Nova Scotia Dept of Tourism & Culture
8 Water St.
P.O. Box 667
Windsor, NS B0N2T0
Phone: 902-798-6700 Fax: 902-798-6610
www.novascotia.com

Metropolitan Halifax Chamber of Commerce
656 Windmill Rd.
Ste. 200
Dartmouth, NS B3B1B8
Phone: 902-468-7111 Fax: 902-468-7333
www.halifaxchamber.com

Nunavut

Nunavut Tourism
P.O. Box 1450
Iqaluit, NU X0A0H0
Phone: 867-979-6551 Fax: 867-979-1261
Toll-free: 800-491-7910
www.nunavuttourism.com

Ontario

Ontario Tourism Marketing Partnership Corp
10 Dundas St. E.
Ste. 900

Toronto, ON M7A2A1
Toll-free: 800-668-2746
www.ontariotravel.net

York Region Tourism
17250 Yonge St.
Newmarket, ON L3Y6Z1
Phone: 888-967-5426
www.yorkscene.com

Canadian Chamber of Commerce
360 Albert St.
Ste. 420
Ottawa, ON K1R7X7
Phone: 613-238-4000 Fax: 613-238-7643
www.chamber.ca

Canadian Chamber of Commerce Toronto Office
55 University Ave.
Ste. 901
Toronto, ON M5J2H7
Phone: 416-868-6415 Fax: 416-868-0189
www.chamber.ca

Ontario Chamber of Commerce
180 Dundas St. W.
Ste. 1500
Toronto, ON M5G1Z8
Phone: 416-482-5222 Fax: 416-482-5879
www.occ.ca

Ottawa Chamber of Commerce
328 Somerset St. W.
Ottawa, ON K2P0J9
Phone: 613-236-3631 Fax: 613-236-7498
www.ottawachamber.ca

Toronto Board of Trade
1 First Canadian Pl.
P.O. Box 60
Toronto, ON M5X1C1
Phone: 416-366-6811 Fax: 416-366.2444
www.bot.com

Upper Ottawa Valley Chamber of Commerce
224 Pembroke St. W.
Pembroke, ON K8A5N2
Phone: 613-732-1492
www.upperottawavalleychamber.com

Windsor & District Chamber of Commerce
2575 Ouellette Pl.
Windsor, ON N8X1L9
Phone: 519-966-3696 Fax: 519-966-0603
www.windsorchamber.org

Prince Edward Island

Prince Edward Island Tourism
P.O. Box 2000
Charlottetown, PE C1A7N8
Phone: 902-368-4000 Fax: 902-368-5277
www.tourismpei.com

Quebec

Tourism Quebec
1255 Peel St.
Ste. 100
Montreal, QC H3B4V4
Phone: 514-873-7977 Fax: 514-864-3838
Toll-free: 888-883-8801
www.tourisme.gouv.qc.ca

Canadian Chamber of Commerce Montreal Office
999 Blvd de Maisonneuve Ouest
Ste. 560
Montreal, QC H3A3L4
Phone: 514-866-4334 Fax: 514-866-7296
www.chamber.ca

Board of Trade of Metropolitan Montreal
380 St. Antoine St. W.
Ste. 6000
Montreal, QC H2Y3X7
Phone: 514-871-4000 Fax: 514-871-1255
www.btmm.qc.ca

Chambre de Commerce et d'Industrie du Quebec
  Metropolitain
17 St. Louis St.
Quebec, QC G1R3Y8
Phone: 418-692-3853 Fax: 418-694-2286
www.cciquebec.ca

Saskatchewan

Tourism Saskatchewan
189-1621 Albert St.
Regina, SK S4P2S5
Phone: 306-787-9600 Fax: 306-787-6293
Toll-free: 877-237-2273
www.tourismsaskatchewan.com

Yukon

Tourism Yukon
P.O. Box 2703
Whitehorse, YT Y1A2C6
Phone: 867-667-5036 Fax: 867-667-3546

Toll-free: 800-661-0494
www.travelyukon.com

Yukon Chamber of Commerce
2237 Second Ave.
Ste. 205
Whitehorse, YT Y1A0K7
Phone: 867-667-2000 Fax: 867-667-2001
www.yukonchamber.com

Whitehorse Chamber of Commerce
302 Steele St.
Ste. 101
Whitehorse, YT Y1A2C5
Phone: 867-667-7545 Fax: 867-667-4507
www.whitehorsechamber.com

Mexico

Mexico Tourism Board
1700 Chantilly Dr. N.E.
Atlanta, GA 30324
Phone: 303-331-1110 Fax: 303-331-0169
www.visitmexico.com

Mexico Tourism Board
225 N. Michigan Ave.
Ste. 1800
Chicago, IL 60601
Phone: 312-228-0517 Fax: 312-228-0515
www.visitmexico.com

Mexico Tourism Board
4507 San Jacinto
Ste. 308
Houston, TX 77004
Phone: 713-772-2581 Fax: 713-772-6058
www.visitmexico.com

Mexico Tourism Board
2401 W. 6th St.
Los Angeles, CA 90057
Phone: 213-739-6336 Fax: 213-739-6340
www.visitmexico.com

Mexico Tourism Board
1399 S.W. 1st. Ave.
3rd Fl.
Miami, FL 33130
Phone: 786-621-2909 Fax: 786-621-2907
www.visitmexico.com

Mexico Tourism Board
152 Madison Ave.
Ste. 1800
New York, NY 10016
Phone: 212-308-2110 Fax: 212-308-9060
www.visitmexico.com

Mexico Tourism Board
1549 India St.
San Diego, CA 92101
Phone: 619-359-8750 Fax: 619-359-8653
www.visitmexico.com

Mexico Tourism Board
2829 16 St. N.W.
4th Fl.
Washington, DC 20009
Phone: 202-265-9021 Fax: 202-265-9026
www.visitmexico.com

US-Mexico Chamber of Commerce
1300 Pennsylvania Ave. N.W.
Ste. G-0003
Washington, DC 20004
Phone: 202-312-1520 Fax: 202-312-1530
www.usmcoc.org

US-Mexico Chamber of Commerce California Pacific
 Chapter
2450 Colorado Ave.
Ste. 400E
Santa Monica, CA 90404
Phone: 310-586-7901 Fax: 310 586-7800
www.usmcocca.org

US-Mexico Chamber of Commerce Inter-American Chapter
1 Biscayne Tower
2 S. Biscayne Blvd.
Ste. 2100
Miami, FL 33131
Phone: 786-631-4179
www.usmcoc.org

Mexico Consulate
301 Mexico Blvd.
Ste. F-3
Brownsville, TX 78520
Phone: 956-542-4431
www.consulmex.sre.gob.mx/brownsville

Mexico Consulate
408 Heber Ave.
Calexico, CA 92231
Phone: 760-357-3863 Fax: 760-357-6284
www.consulmex.sre.gob.mx/calexico

Mexico Consulate
701 Morrison Knudsen Plaza Dr.
Ste. 102
Boise, ID 83712
Phone: 208-343-6228 Fax: 208-343-6237
www.consulmex.sre.gob.mx/boise

Mexico Consulate
2398 Spur 239
P.O. Box 1275
Del Rio, TX
Phone: 830-775-2352 Fax: 830-774-6497
www.consulmex.sre.gob.mx/delrio

Mexico Consulate
645 Griswold Ave., 8th Fl.
Ste. 830
Detroit, MI 48226
Phone: 313-964-4515 Fax: 313-964-4522
www.consulmex.sre.gob.mx/detroit

Mexico Consulate
1324 G Ave.
Douglas, AZ 85607
Phone: 520-364-3107 Fax: 520-364-1379
www.consulmex.sre.gob.mx/douglas

Mexico Consulate
2252 E. Garrison St.
Eagle Pass, TX 78852
Phone: 830-773-9255 Fax: 830-773-9397
www.consulmex.sre.gob.mx/eaglepass

Mexico Consulate
7435 N. Ingram Ave.
Fresno, CA 93711
Phone: 559-233-3065 Fax: 559-257-4839
www.consulmex.sre.gob.mx/fresno

Mexico Consulate
331 S.E. St.
Indianapolis, IN 46204
Phone: 317-761-7600 Fax: 317-761-7610
www.consulmex.sre.gob.mx/indianapolis

Mexico Consulate
600 S. Broadway St.
McAllen, TX 78501
Phone: 512-686-0243
www.consulmex.sre.gob.mx/mcallen

Mexico Consulate
2550 Technology Dr.
Orlando, FL 32804
Phone: 407-422-0514 Fax: 407-422-9633
www.consulmex.sre.gob.mx/orlando

Mexico Consulate
3151 W. 5th St.
Oxnard, CA 93030
Phone: 805-984-8738 Fax: 805-984-8747
www.consulmex.sre.gob.mx/oxnard

Mexico Consulate
111 S. Independence Mall E.
Ste. 310
Philadelphia, PA 19106

Phone: 215-922-4262 Fax: 215-923-7281
www.consulmex.sre.gob.mx/filadelfia

Mexico Consulate
823 S. 6th. St.
Las Vegas, NV 89101
Phone: 702-477-2700 Fax: 702-477-2727
www.consulmex.sre.gob.mx/lasvegas

Mexico Consulate
1305 S.W. 12th Ave.
Portland, OR 97201
Phone: 503-274-1442 Fax: 503-274-1540
www.consulmex.sre.gob.mx/portland

Mexico Consulate
293 N 'D' St.
San Bernardino, CA 92401
Phone: 909-889-9836 Fax: 909-889-8285
Toll-free: 877-997-9799
www.consulmex.sre.gob.mx/sanbernardino

Mexico Consulate
2132 3rd Ave.
Seattle, WA 98121
Phone: 206-448-3526 Fax: 206-448-4771
www.consulmex.sre.gob.mx/seattle

Mexico Consulate General
11 King St. W.
Ste. 350
Toronto, ON M5H4C7
Phone: 416-368-2875 Fax: 416-368-8342
www.consulmex.sre.gob.mx/toronto

Mexico Consulate General
1549 India St.
San Diego, CA 92101
Phone: 619-231-8414
www.consulmex.sre.gob.mx/sandiego

Mexico Consulate General
532 Folsom St.
San Francisco, CA 94105
Phone: 415-354-1700 Fax: 415-495-3971
www.consulmex.sre.gob.mx/sanfrancisco

Mexico Consulate General
2125 Zanker Rd.
San Jose, CA 95131
Phone: 408-294-3414
www.consulmex.sre.gob.mx/sanjose

Mexico Consulate General
2093 Arena Blvd.
Sacramento, CA 95834
Phone: 916-329-3500 Fax: 916-419-3048
www.consulmex.sre.gob.mx/sacramento

Mexico Consulate General
127 Navarro St.
San Antonio, TX 78205
Phone: 210-227-9145
www.consulmex.sre.gob.mx/sanantonio

Mexico Consulate General
2401 W. 6th St.
Los Angeles, CA 90057
Phone: 213-351-6800
www.consulmex.sre.gob.mx/losangeles

Mexico Consulate General
320 E. McDowell Rd.
Phoenix, AZ 85004
Phone: 602-242-7398 Fax: 602-242-2957
www.consulmex.sre.gob.mx/phoenix

Mexico Consulate General
1399 S.W. 1st. Ave.
Miami, FL 33130
Phone: 786-268-4900 Fax: 786-268-4895
www.consulmex.sre.gob.mx/miami

Mexico Consulate General
27 E. 39th St.
New York, NY 10016
Phone: 212-217-6400
www.consulmex.sre.gob.mx/nuevayork

Mexico Consulate General
135 W. Cardwell St.
Nogales, AZ 85621
Phone: 520-287-2521
www.consulmex.sre.gob.mx/nogales

Mexico Consulate General
1612 Farragut St.
Laredo, TX 78040
Phone: 956-723-6369
www.consulmex.sre.gob.mx/laredo

Mexico Consulate General
4507 San Jacinto St.
Houston, TX 77004
Phone: 713-271-6800
www.consulmex.sre.gob.mx/houston

Mexico Consulate General
910 E. San Antonio Ave.
El Paso, TX 79901
Phone: 915-532-5540 Fax: 915-532-7163
www.consulmex.sre.gob.mx/elpaso

Mexico Consulate General
5350 Leetsdale Dr.
Ste. 100
Denver, CO 80246
Phone: 303-331-1110 Fax: 303-331-0169
www.consulmex.sre.gob.mx/denver

Mexico Consulate General
55 Franklin St Ground Fl.
Boston, MA 02110
Phone: 617-426-4942 Fax: 617-695-1957
Toll-free: 800-601-1289
www.consulmex.sre.gob.mx/boston

Mexico Consulate General
204 S. Ashland Ave.
Chicago, IL 60607
Phone: 312-738-2383 Fax: 312-491-9072
www.consulmex.sre.gob.mx/chicago

Mexico Consulate General
1210 River Bend
Dallas, TX 75247
Phone: 214-932-8670 Fax: 214-932-8673
www.consulmex.sre.gob.mx/dallas

Mexico Consulate General
1610 4th St. N.W.
Albuquerque, NM 87102
Phone: 505-247-2147 Fax: 505-842-9490
www.consulmex.sre.gob.mx/albuquerque

Mexico Consulate General
1700 Chantilly Dr. N.E.
Atlanta, GA 30324
Phone: 404-266-2233 Fax: 404-266-2302
www.consulmex.sre.gob.mx/atlanta

Mexico Consulate General
410 Baylor St.
Austin, TX 78703
Phone: 512-478-2866 Fax: 512-478-8008
www.consulmex.sre.gob.mx/austin

Mexico Embassy
1911 Pennsylvania Ave. N.W.
Washington, DC 20006
Phone: 202-728-1600
www.embamex.sre.gob.mx/eua

Mexico Permanent Mission to the UN
2 United Nations Plaza
28th Fl.
New York, NY 10017
Phone: 212-752-0220 Fax: 212-752-0634
www.mision.sre.gob.mx/onu

APPENDIX 9

Facts about the U.S. Presidents

This section lists all U.S. presidents in the order in which they held office, their birth dates and places, spouses, death dates and places, burial sites, political parties, nicknames, career highlights, and notable landmarks commemorating them. The diamond symbol (◆) indicates that an entry on a festival celebrating the president appears in the main text.

◆ George Washington

First president (1789-97)

Born Feb 22, 1732, Popes Creek (now Wakefield), Westmoreland County, VA

Married Martha Dandridge Custis, 1759

Died Dec 14, 1799, Mt. Vernon, VA

Buried in family vault, Mt. Vernon, VA

Federalist. "Father of His Country." Fought in French and Indian War. Served in Continental Congress. Commander-in-Chief during Revolutionary War. Bill of Rights passed. Laid cornerstone of Capitol in Washington, DC.

LANDMARKS:

Birth site: George Washington Birthplace National Monument, 1732 Popes Creek Rd., Washington's Birthplace, VA, 22443, 804-224-1732; fax: 804-224-2142
www.nps.gov/gewa

Anderson House, 2118 Massachusetts Ave. N.W., Washington, DC, 20008, 202-785-2040
www.societyofthecincinnati.org

Brandywine Battlefield Park, 1491 Baltimore Pike, P.O. Box 202, Chadds Ford, PA, 19317, 610-459-3342 or 610-459-9586
www.ushistory.org/brandywine/index.htm

Deshler-Morris House, 5442 Germantown Ave., Philadelphia, PA, 19144
www.nps.gov/inde/learn/historyculture/places-germantownwhitehouse.htm

Dey Mansion, 199 Totowa Rd., Wayne, NJ, 07470, 973-696-1776
passaiccountynj.org/facilities/facility/details/25

Federal Hall National Memorial, 26 Wall St., New York, NY, 10005, 212-825-6990
www.nps.gov/feha

Gadsby's Tavern Museum, 134 N. Royal St., Alexandria, VA, 22314, 703-746-4242; fax: 703-838-4270
www.alexandriava.gov/GadsbysTavern

George Washington Masonic National Memorial, 101 Callahan Dr., Alexandria, VA, 22301, 703-683-2007; fax: 703-519-9270
www.gwmemorial.org

George Washington's Mount Vernon, 3200 Mount Vernon Memorial Hwy., Mount Vernon, VA, 22121, 703-780-2000
www.mountvernon.org

Mary Washington House, 1200 Charles St., Fredericksburg, VA, 22401, 540-373-1569
preservationvirginia.org/visit/historic-properties/mary-washington-house

Military Office Museum, Corner of Braddock and Cork Streets, Winchester, VA, 22601, 540-662-4412
www.fortedwards.org/cwffa/gw-off.htm

Morristown National Historical Park, 30 Washington Pl., Morristown, NJ, 07960, 973-539-2016; fax: 973-451-9212
www.nps.gov/morr

Rockingham State Historic Site, P.O. Box 496, Kingston, NJ, 08528, 609-683-7132; fax: 609-603-7136
www.state.nj.us/dep/seeds/rokhist.htm

Valley Forge National Historical Park, 1400 N. Louter Line Dr., King of Prussia, PA, 19406, 610-783-1000; fax: 610-783-1053
www.nps.gov/vafo

Washington Monument, 900 Ohio Dr. S.W., Washington, DC, 20024, 202-426-6841
www.nps.gov/wamo

Washington's Headquarters Museum, 30 Washington Pl., Morristown, NY, 07960, 973-539-2016
www.nps.gov/morr

Washington's Headquarters State Historic Site, 84 Liberty St., Newburgh, NY, 12550, 845-562-1195

John Adams

Second president (1797-1801)

Born Oct 30, 1735, Braintree (now Quincy), MA

Married Abigail Smith, 1764

Died Jul 4, 1826, Quincy, MA

Buried at United First Parish Church (Church of the Presidents), 1306 Hancock St., Quincy, MA 02169, 617-773-1290 or 617-773-7499

Federalist. "Father of American Independence." Served in Continental Congress. Helped draft and signed Declaration of Independence. Secretary of War. Minister to Great Britain, Netherlands. Vice President. First occupant of White House. Son was sixth president (see John Quincy Adams).

LANDMARKS:

Birth site: Adams National Historic Park, 135 Adams St., Quincy, MA, 02169, 617-770-1175; fax: 617-472-7562

www.nps.gov/adam

◆ Thomas Jefferson

Third president (1801-09)

Born Apr 13, 1743, Shadwell, Charlottesville, Goochland County (now Albemarle County), VA

Married Martha Wayles Skelton, 1772

Died Jul 4, 1826, Charlottesville, VA

Buried at Monticello, Charlottesville, VA

Democratic-Republican. "Father of the Declaration of Independence." Served in Continental Congress. Drafted Declaration of Independence. Governor of Virginia. Minister to France. Secretary of State. Vice President. Completed Louisiana Purchase.

LANDMARKS:

Birth Site: Shadwell, Charlottesville, VA, 22902

www.monticello.org/site/research-and-collections/shadwell

Jefferson Memorial, 900 Ohio Dr. S.W, Washington, DC, 20024, 202-426-6841

www.nps.gov/thje

Jefferson National Expansion Memorial (Gateway Arch), 11 N. 4th St., St. Louis, MO, 63102, 314-655-1700; fax: 314-655-1641

www.nps.gov/jeff

Monticello, P.O. Box 316, Charlottesville, VA, 22902, 434-984-9800 or 800-243-0743

www.monticello.org

Poplar Forest, P.O. Box 419, Forest, VA, 24551, 434-525-1806; fax: 434-525-7252

www.poplarforest.org

Tuckahoe Plantation, 12601 River Rd., Richmond, VA, 23238, 804-774-1614

www.tuckahoeplantation.com

James Madison

Fourth president (1809-17)

Born Mar 16, 1751, Port Conway, VA

Married Dolley Dandridge Payne Todd, 1794

Died Jun 28, 1836, Orange County, VA

Buried at Montpelier, Orange County, VA

Democratic-Republican. "Father of the Constitution." Served in Continental Congress. Signed Constitution. U.S. Representative. Secretary of State. Participated in War of 1812. Forced to flee White House when British invaded Washington, DC.

LANDMARKS:

Birth Site (Marker): Belle Grove Plantation, 9221 Belle Grove Dr., King George, VA, 22485, 540-621-7340

www.bellegroveplantation.com

James Madison Museum, 129 Caroline St., Orange, VA, 22960, 540-672-1776

www.thejamesmadisonmuseum.org

James Madison's Montpelier, 11407 Constitution Hwy., P.O. Box 911, Montpelier Station, VA, 22957, 540-672-2728

www.nps.gov/nr/travel/presidents/madison_montpelier.html

Octagon House, 1799 New York Ave. N.W., Washington, DC, 20006, 202-626-7439

www.nps.gov/nr/travel/WASH/dc22.htm

James Monroe

Fifth president (1817-25)

Born Apr 28, 1758, Westmoreland County, VA

Married Elizabeth Kortright, 1786

Died Jul 4, 1831, New York, NY

Buried at Marble Cemetery, New York, NY; removed 1858 to Hollywood Cemetery, 412 S. Cherry St., Richmond, VA 23220, 804-648-8501

Democratic-Republican. "Era of Good Feeling President." Fought in Revolutionary War. Served in Continental Congress. Governor of Virginia. U.S. Senator. Secretary of State. Secretary of War. First inauguration held outdoors. Author of the Monroe Doctrine.

LANDMARKS:

Birth Site (Marker): The james monroe birthplace visitors center, 4460 James Monroe Hwy., Colonial Beach, VA, 22443, 804-214-9145

www.monroefoundation.org

Ash Lawn-Highland residence, 2050 James Monroe Pkwy., Charlottesville, VA, 22902, 434-293-8000; fax: 434-979-9181

ashlawnhighland.org

James Monroe Museum and Memorial Library, 908 Charles St., Fredericksburg, VA, 22401, 540-654-1043

jamesmonroemuseum.umw.edu

Oak Hill residence, Loudon County, VA, 22001, (private residence)

www.nps.gov/history/nr/travel/journey/oak.htm

John Quincy Adams

Sixth president (1825-29)

Born Jul 11, 1767, Braintree (now Quincy), MA

Married Louisa Catherine Johnson, 1797

Died Feb 23, 1848, Washington, DC

Buried at United First Parish Church, 1306 Hancock St., Quincy, MA 02269, 617-773-1290

Democratic-Republican. "Old Man Eloquent." Minister to Great Britain, Netherlands, Russia. U.S. Senator. Secretary of State. U.S. Representative. Father was second president (see John Adams).

LANDMARKS:

Birth site: John Quincy Adams Birthsite, 141 Franklin St., Quincy, MA, 02169, 617-773-1177

Adams National Historic Park, 135 Adams St., Quincy, MA, 02169, 617-770-1175; fax: 617-472-7562

www.nps.gov/adam

◆ Andrew Jackson

Seventh president (1829-37)

Born Mar 15, 1767, Waxhaw, SC

Married Rachael Donelson Robards, 1791

Died Jun 8, 1845, Nashville, TN

Buried at the Hermitage Estate, 4580 Rachael's Lane, Hermitage, TN 37076, 615-889-2941; fax: 615-889-9909

Democrat (Democratic-Republican). "Old Hickory." Governor of Florida. U.S. Representative and Senator. Fought against Indians and in War of 1812. First president born in a log cabin.

LANDMARKS:

Birth site (disputed): Andrew Jackson Birthplace Marker, NC 75 (S. Main St.) at Rehobeth Rd., Waxhaw, NC, 28173

Birth site (disputed): Andrew Jackson State Park, 196 Andrew Jackson Park Rd., Lancaster, SC, 29720, 803-285-3344

southcarolinaparks.com/andrewjackson/introduction.aspx

McCamie Cabin site marker, Mecklenburg County, NC

Springfield Plantation, Route 1, Box 201, Fayette, MS, 39069

Martin Van Buren

Eighth president (1837-41)

Born Dec 5, 1782, Kinderhook, NY

Married Hannah Hoes, 1807

Died Jul 24, 1862, Kinderhook, NY

Buried at Kinderhook Cemetery, Albany Ave., Kinderhook, NY

Democrat (Democratic-Republican). "Sage of Kinderhook." U.S. Senator. Governor of New York. Secretary of State. Vice President. First president born a U.S. citizen.

LANDMARKS:

Birth Site (Marker): Martin Van Buren Birthplace, 46 Hudson St., Kinderhook, NY, 12106

www.presidentsusa.net/vanburenbirthplace.html

Martin Van Buren National Historic Site, 1013 Old Post Rd., Kinderhook, NY, 12106, 518-758-9689; fax: 518-758-6986

www.nps.gov/mava

William Henry Harrison

Ninth president (1841)

Born Feb 9, 1773, Berkeley, Charles City County, VA

Married Anna Tuthill Symmes, 1795

Whig. "Old Tippecanoe." Fought against Indians and in War of 1812. U.S. Representative. U.S. Senator. Died in office, serving shortest term of a president. Grandson was twenty-third president (see Benjamin Harrison).

Buried at Harrison Tomb State Memorial, Loop Ave., North Bend, OH, 513-941-3744

LANDMARKS:

Birth Site: Berkeley Plantation, 12602 Harrison Landing Rd., Charles City, VA, 23030, 804-829-6018 or 888-466-6018; fax: 804-829-6757

www.berkeleyplantation.com

Grouseland Foundation, 3 West Scott St., Vincennes, IN, 47591, 812-882-2096

www.grouselandfoundation.org

John Tyler

Tenth president (1841-45)

Born Mar 29, 1790, Greenway, Charles City County, VA

Married Letitia Christian, 1813; Julia Gardiner, 1844

Died Jan 18, 1862, Richmond, VA

Buried at Hollywood Cemetery, 412 S. Cherry St., Richmond, VA 23220, 804-648-8501

Whig. "Accidental president." U.S. Representative. Governor of Virginia. U.S. Senator. Succeeded presidency upon death of William Henry Harrison. Elected representative to Confederate Congress.

LANDMARKS:

Birth Site: John Tyler Memorial Highway, Charles City, VA, 23030, (Private residence)

Sherwood Forest Plantation Foundation, 14501 John Tyler Hwy., Charles City, VA, 23030, 804-829-5377
www.sherwoodforest.org

James Knox Polk

Eleventh president (1845-49)

Born Nov 2, 1795, near Pineville, Mecklenburg County, NC

Married Sarah Childress, 1824

Died Jun 15, 1849, Nashville, TN

Buried at Polk Place, Nashville, TN; removed 1893 to State Capitol Grounds, Nashville, TN 37243, 615-741-0830

Democrat. "Napoleon of the Stump." U.S. Representative. Speaker of the House. Governor of Tennessee. First inauguration ceremony relayed by telegraph. Acquired much of western and southwestern U.S.

LANDMARKS:

Birth Site: President James K. Polk State Historic SiteÂ , Box 475, Pineville, NC, 28134, 704-889-7145
www.nchistoricsites.org/polk/polk.htm

President James K. Polk Home & Museum, 301 W. 7th St., Columbia, TN, 38401, 931-388-2354
www.jameskpolk.com

Zachary Taylor

Twelfth president (1849-50)

Born Nov 24, 1784, Montebello, Gordonsville, VA

Married Margaret Mackall Smith, 1810

Whig. "Old Rough and Ready." Fought against Indians and in War of 1812 and Mexican War. Son-in-law was Jefferson Davis. Died in office.

Buried at Zachary Taylor National Cemetery, 4701 Brownboro Rd., Louisville, KY 40207, 502-893-3852

LANDMARKS:

Birth Site (Marker): Montebello, 7338-7342 Spotswood Trail (US 33 eastbound), Gordonsville, VA, 22942

Springfield, 5608 Apache Rd., Louisville, KY, 40207
www.nps.gov/parkhistory/online_books/presidents/site25.htm

Millard Fillmore

Thirteenth president (1850-53)

Born Jan 7, 1800, Summerhill, Cayuga County, NY

Married Abigail Powers, 1826; Caroline Carmichael McIntosh, 1858

Died Mar 8, 1874, Buffalo, NY

Buried at Forrest Lawn Cemetery, 1411 Delaware Ave., Buffalo, NY 14209, 716-885-1600

Whig. "His Accidency." U.S. Representative. Succeeded presidency upon death of Zachary Taylor.

LANDMARKS:

Birth Site (Marker): Fillmore Rd, Summerhill, NY

Birth Site (Replica): Fillmore Glen State Park, 1686 SR-38, Moravia, NY, 13118, 315-497-0130
www.nystateparkstours.com/fillmoreglen

Childhood home (marker): Carver Rd., New Hope, NY

Millard Fillmore House, 24 Shearer Ave., East Aurora, NY, 14052, 716-652-8875
www.nps.gov/nr/travel/presidents/millard_fillmore_house.html

Franklin Pierce

Fourteenth president (1853-57)

Born Nov 23, 1804, Hillsborough (now Hillsboro), NH

Married Jane Means Appleton, 1834

Died Oct 8, 1869, Concord, NH

Buried at Old North Cemetery, North State St., Concord, NH 03301

Democrat. "Young Hickory of the Granite Hills." U.S. Representative. U.S. Senator. Fought in Mexican War.

LANDMARKS:

Birth Site: Hillsboro, NH

Pierce Homestead, 301 2nd NH Turnpike, P.O. Box 896, Hillsborough, NH, 03244, 603-478-3165
hillsboroughhistory.org/franklin-pierce-homestead-state-historic-site

Pierce House (marker), 52 South Main St., Concord, NH, 03301

Pierce Manse, 14 Horseshoe Pond Ln., Concord, NH, 03301, 603-225-4555
www.piercemanse.org

James Buchanan

Fifteenth president (1857-61)

Born Apr 23, 1791, Cove Gap, PA

Died Jun 1, 1868, Lancaster, PA

Buried at Woodward Hill Cemetery, 538 East Strawberry St., Lancaster, PA 17602, 717-295-7220

Democrat. "Bachelor president." Fought in War of 1812. U.S. Representative. Minister to Russia. U.S. Senator. Secretary of State. Minister to Great Britain.

LANDMARKS:

Birth Site (Cabin): Mercersburg Academy, 300 E. Seminary St., Mercersburg, PA, 17236, 717-328-6173; fax: 717-328-6319

Birth Site (Marker): Buchanan's Birthplace Historical State Park, c/o Cowans Gap, Fort Loudon, PA, 17224, 717-485-3948

www.dcnr.state.pa.us/stateparks/findapark/buchanansbirthplace/index.htm

James Buchanan Hotel (marker), 15 N. Main St., Mercersburg, PA, 17236, 717-328-0011

www.jamesbuchananhotel.com

Wheatland, 1120 Marietta Ave., Lancaster, PA, 17603, 717-392-4633

www.lancasterhistory.org

◆ Abraham Lincoln

Sixteenth president (1861-65)

Born Feb 12, 1809, Hodgenville, Hardin County (now Larue County), KY

Married Mary Todd, 1842

Died Apr 15, 1865, Washington, DC

Buried at Oak Ridge Cemetery, Springfield, IL

Republican. "Honest Abe." Fought in Blackhawk War. U.S. Representative. U.S. divided by Civil War while president. Issued Emancipation Proclamation. Author of Gettysburg Address. First president assassinated.

LANDMARKS:

Birth Site: Abraham Lincoln Birthplace National Historical Park, 2995 Lincoln Farm Rd., Hodgenville, KY, 42748, 270-358-3137; fax: 270-358-3874

www.nps.gov/abli

Childhood home: Knob Creek Farm, 7120 Bardstown Rd., Hodgenville, KY, 42748, 270-358-3137; fax: 270-358-3874

www.nps.gov/abli

Abraham Lincoln Library and Museum, Lincoln Memorial University, 6965 Cumberland Gap Pkwy., Harrogate, TN, 37752, 423-869-3611 or 800-325-0900

www.lmunet.edu/Museum

Abraham Lincoln Presidential Library Foundation, 500 E. Madison St., Ste. 200, Springfield, IL, 62701, 217-557-6250; fax: 217-558-6041

www.alplm.org

Civil War Library and Museum, 1805 Pine St., Philadelphia, PA, 10107, 215-735-8196; fax: 215-735-3812

civilwarmuseumphila.org

Ford's Theatre National Historic Site, 511 10th St. N.W., Washington, DC, 20004, 202-426-6924; fax: 202-426-1845

www.nps.gov/foth

Lincoln Boyhood National Memorial, 2916 E. S. St., P.O. Box 1816, Lincoln City, IN, 47552, 812-937-4541

www.nps.gov/libo

Lincoln Heritage Museum, 1115 Nicholson Rd., Lincoln, IL, 62656, 217-735-7399; fax: 217-732-2815

museum.lincolncollege.edu

Lincoln Home National Historic Site, 413 S. Eighth St., Springfield, IL, 62701-1905, 217-492-4241; fax: 217-492-4673

www.nps.gov/liho

Lincoln Homestead State Park, 5079 Lincoln Park Rd., Springfield, KY, 40069, 859-336-7461

www.parks.ky.gov/parks/recreationparks/lincoln-homestead/default.aspx

Lincoln Log Cabin State Historic Site, 402 S. Lincoln Highway Rd., Lerna, IL, 62440, 217-345-1845

www.lincolnlogcabin.org

Lincoln Memorial, 900 Ohio Dr. S.W., Washington, DC, 20024, 202-426-6841

www.nps.gov/linc

Lincoln Memorial Shrine, 125 W. Vine St., Redlands, CA, 92373, 909-798-7632; fax: 909-798-7566

www.lincolnshrine.org

Lincoln Monument, 339 Lafayette Ave., Council Bluffs, IA, 51503, 712-328-4650 (Council Bluffs Parks, Recreation, and Public Property)

www.councilbluffs-ia.gov/index.aspx?NID=276

Lincoln Museum, 66 Lincoln Sq., Hodgenville, KY, 42748, 270-358-3163

www.lincolnmuseum-ky.org

Lincoln-Herndon Law Offices State Historic Site, 6th & Adams Streets, Springfield, IL, 62701, 217-785-7289

www.illinois.gov/ihpa/Experience/Sites/Central/Pages/Lincoln-Herndon.aspx

Lincoln's New Salem State Historic Site, 15588 History Ln., Petersburg, IL, 62675, 217-632-4000; fax: 217-632-4010

www.lincolnsnewsalem.com

Mount Pulaski Courthouse, 113 S. Washington St., Mount Pulaski, IL, 62548, 217-792-3919

www.illinois.gov/ihpa/Experience/Sites/Central/Pages/Mount-Pulaski.aspx

Oak Ridge Cemetery, 1441 Monument, Springfield, IL, 62702, 217-789-2340; fax: 217-789-2338

www.oakridgecemetery.org

Old State Capitol State Historic Site, Old State Capitol Plaza, 6th & Adams Streets, Springfield, IL, 62701, 217-785-7960

www.illinois.gov/ihpa

Postville Courthouse (replica) State Historic Site, 914 S. 5th St., Lincoln, IL, 62656, 217-732-8687

www.illinois.gov/ihpa/experience/sites/central/pages/postville-courthouse.aspx

Postville Courthouse, Greenfield Village, 20900 Oakwood Blvd., Dearborn, MI, 48124, 313-982-6001
www.thehenryford.org

Andrew Johnson

Seventeenth president (1865-69)

Born Dec 29, 1808, Raleigh, NC

Married Eliza McArdle, 1826

Died Jul 31, 1875, Carter's Station, TN

Buried at Andrew Johnson National Cemetery, Greeneville, TN

Democrat. "Tennessee Tailor." U.S. Representative. Governor of Tennessee. U.S. Senator. Succeeded presidency upon assassination of Abraham Lincoln. First president to be impeached (acquitted).

LANDMARKS:

Andrew Johnson National Site and Cemetery, 121 Monument Ave., Greeneville, TN, 37743, 423-639-3711; fax: 423-798-0754
www.nps.gov/anjo

Mordecai Historic Park, 1 Mimosa St., Raleigh, NC, 27604, 919-996-4364
www.raleigh-nc.org

President Andrew Johnson Museum and Library, Tusculum College, 60 Shiloh Rd., Greeneville, TN, 37743, 423-636-7300 or 800-729-0256
ajmuseum.tusculum.edu

Ulysses Simpson Grant

Eighteenth president (1869-77)

Born Apr 27, 1822, Point Pleasant, OH

Married Julia Boggs Dent, 1848

Died Jul 23, 1885, Mt. McGregor, NY

Buried at General Grant National Memorial, Riverside Dr. and W. 122nd St., New York, NY 10027, 212-666-1640; fax: 212-932-9631

Republican. "United States Grant." Fought in Mexican War. General in Civil War. Fifteenth Amendment (right of suffrage) ratified.

LANDMARKS:

Birth Site: U.S. Grant Birthplace Historic Site, 1551 State Rt. 232, Point Pleasant, OH, 45153, 513-497-0492 or 800-283-8932
www.ohiohistory.org/visit/museum-and-site-locator/us-grant-birthplace

Childhood Home: Ulysses S. Grant Boyhood Home, 219 E. Grant Ave., Georgetown, OH, 45121, 877-372-8177
www.usgrantboyhoodhome.org

City Point Unit Residence, Petersburg National Battlefield, 1539 Hickory Hill Rd., Petersburg, VA, 23803, 804-732-3531; fax: 804-732-3615
www.nps.gov/pete

Grant Cottage State Historic site, P.O. Box 2294, Wilton, NY, 12831, 518-584-4353
www.grantcottage.org

Grant's "Hardscrabble" Farm, 10501 Gravois Rd., St. Louis, MO, 63123, 314-843-1700
www.grantsfarm.com

U.S. Grant Boyhood Public School, 508 S. Water St., Georgetown, OH, 45121, 877-372-8177
www.usgrantboyhoodhome.org

U.S. Grant Home, 500 Bouthillier St., P.O. Box 333, Galena, IL, 61036, 815-777-3310
www.granthome.com

U.S. Grant House, Michigan State Fair Grounds, 234 W. Baraga Ave., Marquette, MI, 49855, 906-228-2850
www.michigan.gov

U.S. Grant National Historic Site, 7400 Grant Rd., St. Louis, MO, 63123, 314-842-1867; fax: 314-842-1659
www.nps.gov/ulsg

Rutherford Birchard Hayes

Nineteenth president (1877-81)

Born Oct 4, 1822, Delaware, OH

Married Lucy Ware Webb, 1852

Died Jan 17, 1893, Fremont, OH

Buried at Spiegel Grove National Historic Landmark, Rutherford B. Hayes Presidential Center, Fremont, OH

Republican. "Dark Horse President." Fought in Civil War. U.S. Representative. Governor of Ohio. Some electoral votes in dispute; election decided by special electoral commission.

LANDMARKS:

Birth Site (Marker): Rutherford B Hayes Birth Place, 17 E. William St., Delaware, OH

Hayes Home, Hayes Museum, and Spiegel Grove National Historic Landmark Rutherford B. Hayes Presidential Center, Spiegel Grove, Fremont, OH, 43420, 419-332-2081; fax: 419-332-4952
www.rbhayes.org

James Abram Garfield

Twentieth president (1881)

Born Nov 19, 1831, Orange (now Moreland Hills), OH

Married Lucretia Rudolph, 1858

Republican. "Martyr President." Fought in Civil War. U.S. Representative. Died of wounds 2 1/2 months after being shot by assassin.

Buried at Lake View Cemetery, 12316 Euclid Ave., Cleveland, OH 44106, 216-421-2665

LANDMARKS:

Birth Site (Marker): James A. Garfield Memorial Cabin, 4350 S.O.M. Center Rd., Moreland Hills, OH, 44022, 440-248-1188; fax: 440-498-9591

morelandhills.com/moreland-hills-historical-society/the-james-a-garfield-memorial-cabin

James A. Garfield National Historic Site, 8095 Mentor Ave., Mentor, OH, 44060, 440-255-8722; fax: 440-205-3849

www.nps.gov/jaga

Chester Alan Arthur

Twenty-first president (1881-85)

Born Oct 5, 1829, Fairfield, VT

Married Ellen Lewis Herndon, 1859

Died Nov 18, 1886, New York, NY

Buried at Albany Rural Cemetery, Cemetery Ave., Menands, NY 12204, 518-463-7017; fax: 518-463-0787

Republican. "Elegant Arthur." Succeeded presidency upon death of James Garfield.

LANDMARKS:

Childhood home (replica): Chester A. Arthur State Historic Site, 4588 Chester Arthur Rd., Fairfield, VT, 05455, 802-933-8362 or 802-828-3051

historicsites.vermont.gov/directory/arthur

Arthur House, 123 Lexington Ave., New York, NY, (private residence; closed to the public)

www.nps.gov/nr/travel/presidents/chester_arthur_house.html

Grover Cleveland

Twenty-second and twenty-fourth president (1885-89; 1893-97)

Born Mar 18, 1837, Caldwell, NJ

Democrat. "Sage of Princeton." Governor of New York. Only president to serve two non-consecutive terms. Only president married in White House.

Died Jun 24, 1908, Princeton, NJ

Buried at Princeton Cemetery, 29 Greenview Ave., Princeton, NJ 08542, 609-924-1369

LANDMARKS:

Birth Site: 207 Bloomfield Ave., Caldwell, NJ, 07006, 973-226-0001; fax: 973-226-1810

www.presidentcleveland.org

Childhood home: 109 Academy St., Fayetteville, NY, (private residence; closed to the public)

Cleveland House, Cleveland Park, Tamworth, NH, (private residence; closed to the public)

Grover Cleveland Cottage, Deer Park Hotel Rd., Deer Park, MD, (private residence; closed to the public)

Westland, 15 Hodge Rd., Princeton, NJ, (private residence; closed to the public)

www.nps.gov/parkhistory/online_books/presidents/site36.htm

Benjamin Harrison

Twenty-third president (1889-93)

Born Aug 20, 1833, North Bend, OH

Married Caroline Lavinia Scott, 1853; Mary Scott Lord Dimmick, 1896

Died Mar 13, 1901, Indianapolis, IN

Buried at Crown Hill Cemetery, 700 W. 38th St., Indianapolis, IN 46208, 317-925-8231

Republican. "Centennial President." Served in Civil War. U.S. Senator. Grandfather was ninth president (see William Henry Harrison).

LANDMARKS:

Birth site (location): William Henry Harrison Tomb, Cliff Road & Bower Rd., North Bend, OH, 45202, 844-288-7709

www.ohiohistory.org/visit/museum-and-site-locator/william-henry-harrison-tomb

Benjamin Harrison Home, 1230 N. Delaware St., Indianapolis, IN, 46202, 317-631-1888; fax: 317-632-5488

www.presidentbenjaminharrison.org

William McKinley

Twenty-fifth president (1897-1901)

Born Jan 29, 1843, Niles, OH

Married Ida Saxton, 1871

Republican. "Idol of Ohio." Served in Civil War. U.S. Representative. Governor of Ohio. Died of wounds almost two weeks after being shot by assassin.

Buried at McKinley National Memorial, Canton, OH

LANDMARKS:

Birth Site: 40 S. Main St., Niles, OH, 44446, 330-652-1774

McKinley National Memorial, Presidential Library & Museum, 800 McKinley Monument Dr. N.W., Canton, OH, 44708, 330-455-7043; fax: 330-455-1137

mckinleymuseum.org

National McKinley Birthplace Memorial Museum and Library, 40 N. Main St., Niles, OH, 44446, 330-652-1704; fax: 330-652-5788

www.mckinley.lib.oh.us

Saxton-McKinley Home, 331 S. Market Ave., Canton, OH, 44702, 330-452-0876

www.firstladies.org/SaxtonMcKinleyHouse.aspx

◆ Theodore Roosevelt

Twenty-sixth president (1901-09)

Born Oct 27, 1858, New York, NY

Married Alice Hathaway Lee, 1880; Edith Kermit Carow, 1886

Died Jan 6, 1919, Oyster Bay, NY

Buried at Youngs Memorial Cemetery, Cove Neck Rd. and East Main St., Oyster Bay, NY

Republican. "Hero of San Juan Hill." Fought in Spanish-American War. Governor of New York. Succeeded presidency upon assassination of William McKinley. Youngest man to become president. Awarded Nobel Peace Prize.

LANDMARKS:

Birth site: Theodore Roosevelt Birthplace National Historic Site, 28 E. 20th St., New York, NY, 10003, 212-260-1616

www.nps.gov/thrb

Sagamore Hill National Historic Site, 20 Sagamore Hill Rd., Oyster Bay, NY, 11771, 516-922-4788; fax: 516-922-4792

www.nps.gov/sahi

Theodore Roosevelt Inaugural National Historic Site, 641 Delaware Ave., Buffalo, NY, 14202, 716-884-0095

www.trsite.org

Theodore Roosevelt Island Park, c/o Turkey Run Park, George Washington Memorial Pkwy., McLean, VA, 22101, 703-289-2500; fax: 703-289-2598

www.nps.gov/this/index.htm

Theodore Roosevelt National Park, 315 Second Ave., P.O. Box 7, Medora, ND, 58645, 701-623-4466; fax: 701-623-4840

www.nps.gov/thro

William Howard Taft

Twenty-seventh president (1909-13)

Born Sep 15, 1857, Cincinnati, OH

Married Helen Herron, 1886

Died Mar 8, 1930, Washington, DC

Buried at Arlington National Cemetery, 214 McNair Rd., Arlington, VA 22211, 703-607-8000

Republican. Solicitor General. Governor-General of Philippines. Secretary of War. First president to throw out baseball on opening day. Sixteenth amendment enacted. Chief Justice of the Supreme Court.

LANDMARKS:

Birth Site: William Howard Taft National Historic Site, 2038 Auburn Ave., Cincinnati, OH, 45219, 513-684-3262; fax: 513-684-3627

www.nps.gov/wiho/index.htm

The Quarry, 1763 E. McMillan St., Cincinnati, OH, (private residence)

Woodrow Wilson

Twenty-eighth president (1913-21)

Born Dec 29, 1856, Staunton, VA

Married Ellen Louise Axson, 1885; Edith Bolling Galt, 1915

Died Feb 3, 1924, Washington, DC

Buried at National Cathedral, Massachusetts and Wisconsin Aves., N.W., Washington, DC 20016, 202-537-6200

Democrat. "Professor." Governor of New Jersey. Held first presidential press conference. Author of Fourteen Points plan. Eighteenth and Nineteenth Amendments enacted. Awarded Nobel Peace Prize.

LANDMARKS:

Birth Site: Woodrow Wilson Birthplace and Museum, 20 N. Coalter St., Staunton, VA, 24401, 540-885-0897

www.woodrowwilson.org

Early Childhood home: Wilson Boyhood Home, P.O. Box 37, Augusta, GA, 30901, 706-722-9828

www.wilsonboyhoodhome.org

Childhood home: 1705 Hampton St., Columbia, SC, 29201, 803-252-7742

www.historiccolumbia.org/woodrow-wilson-family-home

Woodrow Wilson House Museum, 2340 S St., N.W., Washington, DC, 20008, 202-387-4062; fax: 202-483-1466

www.woodrowwilsonhouse.org

Warren Gamaliel Harding

Twenty-ninth president (1921-23)

Born Nov 2, 1865, Blooming Grove (now Corsica), OH

Married Florence Kling De Wolfe, 1891

Republican. U.S. Senator. First presidential election returns broadcast on radio. Teapot Dome Scandal. Died in office.
Buried at Harding Memorial, Vernon Heights Blvd., Marion, OH

LANDMARKS:

Birth site (marker): Corsica, OH

Harding Home and Museum, 380 Mt. Vernon Ave., Marion, OH, 43302, 740-387-9630 or 800-600-6894
www.hardinghome.org

◆ Calvin Coolidge

Thirtieth president (1923-29)
Born Jul 4, 1872, Plymouth Notch, VT
Married Grace Anna Goodhue, 1905
Died Jan 5, 1933, Northampton, MA
Buried at Plymouth Notch Cemetery, Vermont Hwy. 100A, Plymouth Notch, VT 05056, 802-672-3773

Republican. "Silent Cal." Governor of Massachusetts. Succeeded presidency upon death of Warren Harding. First inaugural speech broadcast on radio.

LANDMARKS:

Birth site: Birthplace & Boyhood Home, 3780 Rte. 100A, Plymouth, VT, 802-672-3773
www.nps.gov/nr/travel/presidents/calvin_coolidge_homestead.html
The Beeches, 16 Hampton Terr., Northampton, MA, (private residence; closed to the public)
Calvin Coolidge Memorial Room, Forbes Library, 20 W. St., Northampton, MA, 01060, 413-587-1011
www.forbeslibrary.org/coolidge/coolidge.shtml
Memorial Foundation, P.O. Box 97, Plymouth, VT, 05056, 802-672-3389; fax: 802-672-3289
coolidgefoundation.org
Northampton Home, 21 Massasoit St., Northampton, MA, (private residence; closed to the public)

◆ Herbert Clark Hoover

Thirty-first president (1929-33)
Born Aug 10, 1874, West Branch, IA
Married Lou Henry, 1899
Died Oct 20, 1964, New York, NY
Buried at Herbert Hoover National Historic Site, West Branch, IA

Republican. "Grand Old Man." Involved in Boxer Rebellion in China. Chairman of Commission for Relief in Belgium.

Secretary of Commerce. Wall Street crash (Black Tuesday), 1929.

LANDMARKS:

Birth site: Herbert Hoover National Historic Site, P.O. Box 607, West Branch, IA, 52358, 319-643-2541; fax: 319-643-7864
www.nps.gov/heho
Herbert Hoover Academic Bldg., George Fox University, 414 N. Meridian St., Newberg, OR, 97132, 503-538-8383
www.georgefox.edu
Herbert Hoover Presidential Library and Museum, 210 Parkside Dr., West Branch, IA, 52358, 319-643-5301
hoover.archives.gov
Hoover Institution on War, Revolution and Peace, Stanford University, 434 Galvez Mall, Stanford, CA, 94305-6010, 650-723-1754
www.hoover.org
Hoover Presidential Foundation, 302 Parkside Dr., West Branch, IA, 52358, 319-643-5327; fax: 319-643-2391
www.hooverassociation.org
Hoover-Minthorn House Museum, 115 S. River St., Newberg, OR, 97132, 503-538-6629
www.thehoover-minthornhousemuseum.org
Lou Henry Hoover House, 580 Serra Mall, Stanford, CA, 94304
www.nps.gov/nr/travel/santaclara/hoo.htm
Shenandoah Camp Hoover, Shenandoah National Park, 3655 Hwy 211 E., Luray, VA, 22835, 540-999-3500; fax: 540-999-3601
www.nps.gov/shen

◆ Franklin Delano Roosevelt

Thirty-second president (1933-45)
Born Jan 30, 1882, Hyde Park, NY
Married Eleanor Roosevelt, 1905
Democrat. "F.D.R." Governor of New York. Author of the New Deal. Only four-term president. Died in office.
Buried at Franklin D. Roosevelt National Historic Site, Hyde Park, NY

LANDMARKS:

Birth site: The Roosevelt-Vanderbilt NHS, 4097 Albany Post Rd., Hyde Park, NY, 12538, 845-229-9115
www.nps.gov/hofr
Franklin D. Roosevelt Library and Museum, 4079 Albany Post Rd., Hyde Park, NY, 12538, 845-486-7770
www.fdrlibrary.marist.edu
Franklin Delano Roosevelt Memorial, 900 Ohio Dr. S.W., Washington, DC, 20024, 202-426-6841 or 877-444-6777
www.nps.gov/frde

Roosevelt Campobello International Park, P.O. Box 129, Lubec, ME, 04652, 506-752-2922; fax: 506-752-6000
www.nps.gov/roca

Roosevelt's Little White House Historic Site, 401 Little White House Rd., Warm Springs, GA, 31830, 706-655-5870
www.gastateparks.org/info/littlewhite

◆ Harry S. Truman

Thirty-third president (1945-53)

Born May 10, 1884, Lamar, MO

Married Elizabeth "Bess" Virginia Wallace, 1919

Died Dec 26, 1972, Kansas City, MO

Buried at Harry S. Truman Library and Museum, Independence, MO

Democrat. "Give 'Em Hell Harry." Fought in World War I. U.S. Senator. Succeeded presidency upon death of Franklin D. Roosevelt. Authorized use of atomic bomb against Japan. Implemented the Fair Deal.

LANDMARKS:

Birth site: Harry S. Truman Birthplace State Historic Site, 1009 Truman, Lamar, MO, 64759, 417-682-2279
www.mostateparks.com/park/harry-s-truman-birthplace-state-historic-site

Childhood home: 909 West Waldo St., Independence, MO, (private residence; closed to the public)
www.trumanlibrary.org/places/in2.htm

Harry S. Truman Courtroom and Office, 112 W. Lexington, Independence, MO, 64050, 816-881-3000
www.jacksongov.org

Harry S. Truman Key West Little White House Museum, 111 Front St., Key West, FL, 33040, 305-294-9911; fax: 305-294-9988
www.trumanlittlewhitehouse.com

Harry S. Truman Library and Museum, 500 W. US Hwy. 24, Independence, MO, 64050, 816-268-8200 or 800-833-1225; fax: 816-268-8295
www.trumanlibrary.org

Harry S. Truman National Historic Site, 223 N. Main St., Independence, MO, 64050, 816-254-9929; fax: 816-254-4491
www.nps.gov/hstr

◆ Dwight David Eisenhower

Thirty-fourth president (1953-61)

Born Oct 14, 1890, Denison, TX

Married Marie "Mamie" Geneva Doud, 1916

Died Mar 28, 1969, Washington, DC

Buried at Eisenhower Center, Abilene, KS

Republican. "Ike." General in World War II. Commander of NATO. First televised press conference.

LANDMARKS:

Birth site: Eisenhower Birthplace State Historic Site, 609 S. Lamar Ave., Denison, TX, 75021, 903-465-8908
www.visiteisenhowerbirthplace.com

Eisenhower National Historic Site, 1195 Baltimore Pike, Ste. 100, Gettysburg, PA, 17325, 717-338-9114; fax: 717-338-0821
www.nps.gov/eise

Eisenhower Presidential Library, Museum and Boyhood Home, 200 S.E. 4th St., P.O. Box 339, Abilene, KS, 67410, 785-263-6700 or 877-746-4453
www.eisenhower.archives.gov

◆ John Fitzgerald Kennedy

Thirty-fifth president (1961-63)

Born May 29, 1917, Brookline, MA

Married Jacqueline Lee Bouvier, 1953

Died Nov 22, 1963, Dallas, TX

Buried at Arlington National Cemetery, 214 McNair Rd., Arlington, VA 22211, 703-607-8000

Democrat. "J.F.K." Served in World War II. U.S. Representative. U.S. Senator. First president born in twentieth century. Youngest elected president. Fourth president assassinated.

LANDMARKS:

Birth site: John F. Kennedy National Historic Site, 83 Beals St., Brookline, MA, 02446, 617-566-7937; fax: 617-730-9884
www.nps.gov/jofi

John F. Kennedy Library and Museum, Columbia Point, Boston, MA, 02125, 617-514-1600 or 866-535-1960
www.jfklibrary.org

Kennedy Compound, Hyannis Port, MA, (private residence; closed to the public)

Sixth Floor Museum at Dealey Plaza & Memorial Plaza, 411 Elm St., Dallas, TX, 75202, 214-747-6660; fax: 214-747-6662
www.jfk.org

Lyndon Baines Johnson

Thirty-sixth president (1963-69)

Born Aug 27, 1908, near Stonewall, TX

Married Claudia Alta "Lady Bird" Taylor, 1934

Died Jan 22, 1973, San Antonio, TX

Buried at Johnson Family Cemetery, Lyndon B. Johnson National Historic Park, Johnson City, TX

Democrat. "L.B.J." U.S. Representative. Served in World War II. U.S. Senator. Succeeded presidency upon assassination of John F. Kennedy. Author of the "Great Society."

LANDMARKS:

Birth site: Lyndon B. Johnson National Historical Park, P.O. Box 329, Johnson City, TX, 78636, 830-868-7128 or 830-868-7863

www.nps.gov/lyjo

Childhood home: P.O. Box 329, Johnson City, TX, 78636, 830-868-7128 or 830-868-7863

www.nps.gov/lyjo

Johnson Settlement, P.O. Box 329, Johnson City, TX, 78636, 830-868-7128 or 830-868-7863

www.nps.gov/lyjo/planyourvisit/visitlbjranch.htm

Lyndon B. Johnson State Park & Historic Site, P.O. Box 238, Stonewall, TX, 78671, 830-644-2252

tpwd.texas.gov/state-parks/lyndon-b-johnson

Lyndon Baines Johnson Library and Museum, University of Texas at Austin, 2313 Red River St., Austin, TX, 78705, 512-721-0200

www.lbjlibrary.org

Lyndon Baines Johnson Memorial Grove on the Potomac, C/o Turkey Run Park, George Washington Memorial Pkwy., McLean, VA, 22101, 703-289-2500; fax: 703-289-2598

www.nps.gov/lyba

Richard Milhous Nixon

Thirty-seventh president (1969-74)

Born Jan 9, 1913, Yorba Linda, CA

Married Patricia Ryan, 1940

Died Apr 22, 1994, New York, NY

Buried at Richard Nixon Birthplace, Yorba Linda, CA

Republican. Served in World War II. U.S. Representative. U.S. Senator. Vice President. First president to visit communist China. First and only president to resign (Watergate scandal).

LANDMARKS:

Birth site: Richard Nixon Foundation and Birthplace, 18001 Yorba Linda Blvd., Yorba Linda, CA, 92886, 714-993-5075; fax: 714-528-0544

www.nixonfoundation.org

California White House (La Casa Pacifica), Del Presidente Ave., San Clemente, CA, (private residence; closed to the public)

Nixon Presidential Library and Museum, 18001 Yorba Linda Blvd., Yorba Linda, CA, 92886, 714-983-9120

nixon.archives.gov

Gerald Rudolph Ford

Thirty-eighth president (1974-77)

Born Jul 14, 1913, Omaha, NE

Married Betty Bloomer Warren, 1948

Died Dec 26, 2006, Rancho Mirage, CA

Buried at Gerald R. Ford Museum, Grand Rapids, MI

Republican. Served in World War II. U.S. Representative. First vice president to take office under Twenty-fifth Amendment. Succeeded presidency upon resignation of Richard Nixon. Only president to serve in office without being elected.

LANDMARKS:

Birth site park: Gerald R. Ford Birthsite and Gardens, 3202 Woolworth Ave., Omaha, NE, 68105, 402-444-5955

www.nebraskahistory.org/conserve/brthsite.htm

Childhood home: 649 Union Ave. S.E., Grand Rapids, MI, (private residence; closed to the public)

Family home: 514 Crown View Dr., Alexandria, VA, (private residence; closed to the public)

Gerald R. Ford Conservation Center, 1326 South 32nd St., Omaha, NE, 68105, 402-595-1180

www.nebraskahistory.org/fordcenter

Gerald R. Ford Library, University of Michigan at Ann Arbor, 1000 Beal Ave., Ann Arbor, MI, 48109, 734-205-0555; fax: 734-205-0571

www.fordlibrarymuseum.gov

Gerald R. Ford Museum, 303 Pearl St. N.W., Grand Rapids, MI, 49504, 616-254-0400; fax: 616-254-0386

www.fordlibrarymuseum.gov

Gerald R. Ford Presidential Foundation, 303 Pearl St. N.W., Grand Rapids, MI, 49504, 616-254-0396

www.geraldrfordfoundation.org

Retirement home: Thunderbird Country Club, 40-471 Sand Dune Rd., Rancho Mirage, CA, 92270, (private residence; closed to the public)

James Earl Carter

Thirty-ninth president (1977-81)

Born Oct 1, 1924, Plains, GA

Married Rosalynn Smith, 1946

Democrat. "Jimmy." Governor of Georgia. First president to walk from Capitol to White House after inauguration. Camp David accords signed between Israel and Egypt. U.S. embassy staff held hostage in Tehran, Iran.

LANDMARKS:

Birth site: Plains Nursing Center (now the Lillian G. Carter Nursing Center), 225 Hospital St., Plains, GA, 31780

Childhood home: Jimmy Carter National Historic Site, 300 N. Bond St., Plains, GA, 31780, 229-824-4104; fax: 229-824-3441

www.nps.gov/jica

Carter Center, One Copenhill, 453 Freedom Pkwy., Atlanta, GA, 30307, 404-420-5100 or 800-550-3560

www.cartercenter.org

Jimmy Carter Presidential Library & Museum, 441 Freedom Pkwy., Atlanta, GA, 30307, 404-865-7100; fax: 404-865-7102

www.jimmycarterlibrary.gov

Retirement home: Woodland Dr., Plains, GA, (private residence; closed to the public)

Ronald Wilson Reagan

Fortieth president (1981-89)

Born Feb 6, 1911, Tampico, IL

Married Jane Wyman, 1940, divorced 1949; Nancy Davis, 1952

Died Jun 5, 2004, Los Angeles, CA

Buried at the Ronald Reagan Presidential Library, Simi Valley, CA

Republican. "Great Communicator." Movie actor. Non-combat duty in World War II. Governor of California. Oldest president. Only president to be wounded in assassination attempt and survive. Iran-Contra affair.

LANDMARKS:

Birth Site: 111 Main St., Tampico, IL, 61283, 815-438-2130

www.tampicohistoricalsociety.com/R_Reagan_Birthplace_Museum.html

Childhood home: 816 S. Hennepin Ave., Dixon, IL, 61021, 815-288-5176; fax: 815-288-3642

reaganhome.org

California White House (Rancho del Cielo), 3333 Refugio Canyon, Santa Barbara, CA, (home of Young America's Foundation; closed to the public)

Ronald Reagan Presidential Foundation, 40 Presidential Dr., Simi Valley, CA, 93065, 805-522-2977; fax: 805-520-9702

www.reaganfoundation.org

Ronald Reagan Presidential Library & Museum, 40 Presidential Dr., Simi Valley, CA, 93065, 805-577-4000; fax: 805-577-4074

www.reaganfoundation.org

George Herbert Walker Bush

Forty-first president (1989-93)

Born Jun 12, 1924, Milton, MA

Married Barbara Pierce, 1945

Republican. Served in World War II. U.S. Representative. U.N. Ambassador. C.I.A. Director. Vice President. First acting president under Twenty-fifth amendment. Fall of Berlin Wall. Dissolution of Soviet Union. Persian Gulf War.

LANDMARKS:

Birth Site: 173 Adams St., Milton, MA, 02186, (private residence; closed to the public)

Childhood home: Grove Ln., Greenwich, CT, (private residence; closed to the public)

Family summer home: Walker's Point, Kennebunkport, ME, (private residence; closed to the public)

George Bush Presidential Library & Museum, 1002 George Bush Dr. W., Texas A&M University, College Station, TX, 77845, 979-691-4000; fax: 979-691-4050

www.bush41library.tamu.edu

Bill Clinton

Forty-second president (1993-2001)

Born Aug 19, 1946, Hope, AR

Married Hillary Rodham, 1975

Democrat. Rhodes Scholar. Governor of Arkansas. Proposed national health care plan. North American Free Trade Agreement. Middle East peace accord. Dayton Agreement for peace in Bosnia and Herzegovina. Second president to be impeached (acquitted). First first lady to be elected to the U.S. Senate.

LANDMARKS:

Childhood home (marker): 1011 Park Ave., Hot Springs, AR, (private residence; closed to the public)

Childhood home: 117 S. Hervey St., Hope, AR

Childhood home: 321 E. 13th St., Hope, AR

Clinton Birthplace Foundation, P.O. Box 1925, Hope, AR, 71801, 870-777-4455

www.nps.gov/nr/travel/presidents/bill_clinton_birthplace.html

Clinton Foundation, 1271 Avenue of the Americas, 42nd Fl., New York, NY, 10020, 212-348-8882

www.clintonfoundation.org

William J. Clinton Presidential Center, Library & Museum, 1200 President Clinton Ave., Little Rock, AR, 72201, 501-374-4242; fax: 501-244-2883

www.clintonlibrary.gov

George Walker Bush

Forty-third president (2001-2009)

Born Jul 6, 1946, New Haven, CT

Married Laura Welch, 1977

Republican. "George W." Governor of Texas. Son of forty-first president (see George Herbert Walker Bush). Presided over historic shift in Senate just after first 100 days. War against terrorism in response to the September 11, 2001, attacks in the United States. Invaded Iraq in 2003. Passed "No Child Left Behind" education bill.

LANDMARKS:

Childhood home: 1412 West Ohio Ave., Midland, TX, 79701, 866-684-4380

www.bushchildhoodhome.com

George W. Bush Presidential Center/George W. Bush Foundation, P.O. Box 600610, Dallas, TX, 75360, 214-200-4300; fax: 214-200-4301

www.bushcenter.org

George W. Bush Presidential Library and Museum, 2943 SMU Blvd., Dallas, TX, 75205, 214-346-1650; fax: 214-346-1699

www.georgewbushlibrary.smu.edu

Barack Hussein Obama

Forty-fourth president (2009-)

Born Aug 4, 1961, Honolulu, HI

Married Michelle Robinson, 1992

Democrat. Illinois Senator. U.S. Senator. Passed the American Recovery and Reinvestment Act of 2009 in response to the Great Recession. Passed the Patient Protection and Affordable Care Act health care law, and the Dodd-Frank Wall Street Reform and Consumer Protection Act. Ended the U.S. military involvement in the Iraq War, and U.S. combat operations in Afghanistan. Reestablished U.S. diplomatic relations with Cuba.

LANDMARKS:

Barack Obama Foundation

www.barackobamafoundation.org

Facts about Countries around the World

This section provides basic information about the independent nations of the world: official name (in English); capitalcity; internet count ry code; flag description; national anthem, motto, and symbols (when available); geographical description of location; total area; brief climate description; proper terms for nationality; population numbers; languages spoken; and information on ethnic groups and religions.

Afghanistan

Official name: Islamic Republic of Afghanistan

Capital city: Kabul

Internet country code: .af

Flag description: Three vertical bands of black (hoist), red, and green, with a gold emblem centered on the red band; the emblem features a temple-like structure encircled by a wreath on the left and right and by an inscription above pronouncing the Muslim faith: "There is no God but Allah and Mohammed is his Prophet" and "Allah is Great."

National anthem: "Soroud-e-Melli" (Hymn of the People)

Geographical description: Southern Asia, north and west of Pakistan, east of Iran

Total area: 652,230 sq km

Climate: Arid to semiarid; cold winters and hot summers

Nationality: noun: Afghan(s) *adjective:* Afghan

Population: 31,822,848 (July 2014 CIA est.)

Ethnic groups: Pashtun 42%, Tajik 27%, Hazara 9%, Uzbek 9%, Aimak 4%, Turkmen 3%, Baloch 2%, other 4%

Languages spoken: Afghan Persian or Dari (official) 50%, Pashto (official) 35%, Turkic languages (primarily Uzbek and Turkmen) 11%, 30 minor languages (primarily Balochi and Pashai) 4%, much bilingualism.

Religions: Sunni Muslim 80%, Shi'a Muslim 19%, other 1%

Albania

Official name: Republic of Albania

Capital city: Tirana

Internet country code: .al

Flag description: Red with a black two-headed eagle in the center

National anthem: Himni Flamurit (" The Flag Hymn"; first line in English translation: "United all around the flag")

Geographical description: Southeastern Europe, bordering the Adriatic Sea and Ionian Sea, between Greece in the south and Montenegro and Serbia to the north

Total area: 28,748 sq km

Climate: Mild temperate; cool, cloudy, wet winters; hot, clear, dry summers; interior is cooler and wetter

Nationality: noun: Albanian(s) *adjective:* Albanian

Population: 3,020,209 (July 2014 CIA est.)

Ethnic groups: Albanian 82.6%, Greek 0.9%, other 1% (including Vlach, Roma (Gypsy), Macedonian, Montenegrin, and Egyptian), unspecified 15.5% (2011 CIA est.)

Languages spoken: Albanian 98.8% (official - derived from Tosk dialect), Greek 0.5%, other 0.6% (including Macedonian, Roma, Vlach, Turkish, Italian, and Serbo-Croatian), unspecified 0.1% (2011 CIA est.)

Religions: Muslim 56.7%, Roman Catholic 10%, Orthodox 6.8%, atheist 2.5%, Bektashi (a Sufi order) 2.1%, other 5.7%, unspecified 16.2%

Algeria

Official name: People's Democratic Republic of Algeria

Capital city: Algiers

Internet country code: .dz

Flag description: Two equal vertical bands of green (hoist side) and white; a red, five-pointed star within a red crescent centered over the two-color boundary; the crescent, star, and color green are traditional symbols of Islam (the state religion)

National anthem: "Quassaman," by Moufdi Zakaria

Geographical description: Northern Africa, bordering the Mediterranean Sea, between Morocco and Tunisia

Total area: 2,381,741 sq km

Climate: Arid to semiarid; mild, wet winters with hot, dry summers along coast; drier with cold winters and hot summers on high plateau; sirocco is a hot, dust/sand-laden wind especially common in summer

Nationality: noun: Algerian(s) *adjective:* Algerian

Population: 38,813,722 (July 2014 CIA est.)

Ethnic groups: Arab-Berber 99%, European less than 1%

Languages spoken: Arabic (official), French (lingua franca), Berber dialects: Kabylie Berber (Tamazight), Chaouia Berber (Tachawit), Mzab Berber, Tuareg Berber (Tamahaq)

Religions: Muslim (official; predominantly Sunni) 99%, other (includes Christian and Jewish) <1% (2012 CIA est.)

Andorra

Official name: Principality of Andorra

Capital city: Andorra la Vella

Internet country code: .ad

Flag description: Three equal vertical bands of blue (hoist side), yellow, and red with the national coat of arms centered in the yellow band; the coat of arms features a quartered shield; similar to the flags of Chad and Romania, which do not have a national coat of arms in the center, and the flag of Moldova, which does bear a national emblem

National anthem: "Hymna Andorra" (first line: "El gran Carlemany mon pare dels alarbs me deslliurà"), lyrics by Dr Benlloch, Episcopal Co-Prince of Andorra, music by Father Marfany

National motto: Virtus Unita Fortior

National flower: Grandalla (daffodil family)

Geographical description: Southwestern Europe, between France and Spain

Total area: 468 sq km

Climate: Temperate; snowy, cold winters and warm, dry summers

Nationality: noun: Andorran(s) *adjective:* Andorran

Population: 85,458 (July 2014 CIA est.)

Ethnic groups: Spanish 43%, Andorran 33%, Portuguese 11%, French 7%, other 6% (1998)

Languages spoken: Catalan (official), French, Castilian, Portuguese

Religion: Roman Catholic (predominant)

Angola

Official name: Republic of Angola

Capital city: Luanda

Internet country code: .ao

Flag description: Two equal horizontal bands of red (top) and black with a centered yellow emblem consisting of a five-pointed star within half a cogwheel crossed by a machete (in the style of a hammer and sickle)

Geographical description: Southern Africa, bordering the South Atlantic Ocean, between Namibia and Democratic Republic of the Congo

Total area: 1,246,700 sq km

Climate: Semiarid in south and along coast to Luanda; north has cool, dry season (May to October) and hot, rainy season (November to April)

Nationality: noun: Angolan(s) *adjective:* Angolan

Population: 19,088,106 (July 2014 CIA est.)

Ethnic groups: Ovimbundu 37%, Mbundu 25%, Bakongo 13%, mestico (mixed European and African) 2%, European 1%, other 22%

Languages spoken: Portuguese (official), Bantu and other African languages

Religions: Indigenous religions 47%, Roman Catholic 38%, Protestant 15% (1998 country est.)

Antigua and Barbuda

Official name: Antigua and Barbuda

Capital city: St. John's

Internet country code: .ag

Flag description: Red, with an inverted isosceles triangle based on the top edge of the flag; the triangle contains three horizontal bands of black (top), light blue, and white, with a yellow rising sun in the black band

National anthem: "Fair Antigua and Barbuda / We thy sons and daughters stand" (first lines), lyrics by Novelle Hamilton Richards, music by Walter Garnet Picart Chambers

National motto: "Each Endeavouring, All Achieving"

National animal: European Fallow Deer. (Dama dama dama)

National bird: Frigate Bird, Man-o'-War or Weather Bird. (Fregata magnificens L.)

National flower: Agave, Dagger Log or Batta Log (Barbuda); (Agave karatto Miller)

National fruit: Antigua "Black" Pineapple (Ananas comosus (L.) Merril)

National sea creature: Hawksbill Turtle or 'oxbill. (Eretmochelys imbricata)

National stone: Petrified wood

National tree: Whitewood. (Bucida buceras L.)

Geographical description: Caribbean, islands between the Caribbean Sea and the North Atlantic Ocean, east-southeast of Puerto Rico

Total area: 442.6 sq km (Antigua 280 sq km; Barbuda 161 sq km)

Climate: Tropical maritime; little seasonal temperature variation

Nationality: noun: Antiguan(s), Barbudan(s) *adjective:* Antiguan, Barbudan

Population: 91,295 (July 2014 CIA est.)

Ethnic groups: Black 91%, mixed 4.4%, white 1.7%, other 2.9% (2001 census)

Languages spoken: English (official), local dialects

Religions: Protestant 76.4% (Anglican 25.7%, Seventh-Day Adventist 12.3%, Pentecostal 10.6%, Moravian 10.5%, Methodist 7.9%, Baptist 4.9%, Church of God 4.5%), Roman Catholic 10.4%, other Christian 5.4%, other 2%, none or unspecified 5.8% (2001 census)

Argentina

Official name: Argentine Republic

Capital city: Buenos Aires

Internet country code: .ar

Flag description: Three equal horizontal bands of light blue (top), white, and light blue; centered in the white band is a radiant yellow sun with a human face known as the Sun of May

National anthem: "Himno Nacional Argentino" (first lines: Oíd, mortales, el grito sagrado: "¡libertad, libertad, libertad!"), lyrics by Vicente López y Planes, music by Blas Parera

National flower: flower of the ceibo tree (also called seibo, seíbo or bucaré)

Geographical description: Southern South America, bordering the South Atlantic Ocean, between Chile and Uruguay

Total area: 2,780,400 sq km

Climate: Mostly temperate; arid in southeast; subantarctic in southwest

Nationality: noun: Argentine(s) *adjective:* Argentine

Population: 43,024,374 (July 2014 CIA est.)

Ethnic groups: White (mostly Spanish and Italian) 97%, mestizo (mixed white and Amerindian ancestry), Amerindian, or other non-white groups 3%

Languages spoken: Spanish (official), Italian, English, German, French, indigenous (Mapudungun, Quechua)

Religions: Nominally Roman Catholic 92% (less than 20% practicing), Protestant 2%, Jewish 2%, other 4%

Armenia

Official name: Republic of Armenia

Capital city: Yerevan

Internet country code: .am

Flag description: Three equal horizontal bands of red (top), blue, and orange

National anthem: "Mer Hayrenik" (Our Fatherland), lyrics by Mikael Nalbandian

Geographical description: Southwestern Asia, east of Turkey

Total area: 29,743 sq km

Climate: Highland continental, hot summers, cold winters

Nationality: noun: Armenian(s) *adjective:* Armenian

Population: 3,060,631 (July 2014 CIA est.)

Ethnic groups: Armenian 98.1%, Yezidi (Kurd) 1.1%, other 0.7% (2011 CAI est.)

Languages spoken: Armenian (official) 97.9%, Kurdish (spoken by Yezidi minority) 1%, other 1% (2011 CIA est.)

Religions: Armenian Apostolic 92.6%, Evangelical 1%, other 2.4%, none 1.1%, unspecified 2.9% (2011 CIA est.)

Aruba

Official name: Aruba

Capital city: Oranjestad

Internet country code: .aw

Flag description: Blue, with two narrow, horizontal, yellow stripes across the lower portion and a red four-pointed star outlined in white in the upper hoist-side corner

National anthem: "Aruba Dushi Tera"

Geographical description: Island in the Caribbean Sea, north of Venezuela

Total area: 180 sq km

Climate: Tropical marine; little seasonal temperature variation

Nationality: noun: Aruban(s) *adjective:* Aruban; Dutch

Population: 110,663 (July 2014 CIA est.)

Ethnic groups: Dutch 82.1%, Colombian 6.6%, Venezuelan 2.2%, Dominican 2.2%, Haitian 1.2%, other 5.5%, unspecified 0.1% (2010 CIA est.)

Languages spoken: Papiamento (a Spanish-Portuguese-Dutch-English dialect) 69.4%, Spanish 13.7%, English (widely spoken) 7.1%, Dutch (official) 6.1%, Chinese 1.5%, other 1.7%, unspecified 0.4% (2010 CIA est.)

Religions: Roman Catholic 75.3%, Protestant 4.9% (includes Methodist .9%, Adventist .9%, Anglican .4%, other Protestant 2.7%), Jehovah's Witness 1.7%, other 12%, none 5.5%, unspecified 0.5% (2010 CIA est.)

Australia

Official name: Commonwealth of Australia

Capital city: Canberra

Internet country code: .au

Flag description: Blue with the flag of the United Kingdom in the upper hoist-side quadrant and a large seven-pointed star in the lower hoist-side quadrant known as the Commonwealth or Federation Star, representing the federation of the colonies of Australia in 1901; the star depicts one point for each of the six original states and one representing all of Australia's internal and external territories; on the fly half is a representation of the Southern Cross constellation in white with one small five-pointed star and four larger, seven-pointed stars

National anthem: "Advance Australia Fair" by Peter Dodds McCormick

National flower: Golden wattle (*Acacia pycnantha* Benth.)

Geographical description: Oceania, continent between the Indian Ocean and the South Pacific Ocean

Total area: 7,741,220 sq km

Climate: Generally arid to semiarid; temperate in south and east; tropical in north

Nationality: noun: Australian(s) *adjective:* Australian

Population: 22,507,617 (July 2014 CIA est.)

Ethnic groups: white 92%, Asian 7%, aboriginal and other 1%

Languages spoken: English 76.8%, Mandarin 1.6%, Italian 1.4%, Arabic 1.3%, Greek 1.2%, Cantonese 1.2%, Vietnamese 1.1%, other 10.4%, unspecified 5% (2011 CIA est.)

Religions: Protestant 28.8% (Anglican 17.1%, Uniting Church 5.0%, Presbyterian and Reformed 2.8%, Baptist, 1.6%, Lutheran 1.2%, Pentecostal 1.1%), Catholic 25.3%, Eastern Orthodox 2.6%, other Christian 4.5%, Buddhist

2.5%, Muslim 2.2%, Hindu 1.3%, other 8.4%, unspecified 2.2%, none 22.3%

Austria

Official name: Republic of Austria

Capital city: Vienna

Internet country code: .at

Flag description: Three equal horizontal bands of red (top), white, and red

National anthem: "Land der Berge " (Land of Mountains), lyrics by Paula von Preradovic, composer uncertain

Geographical description: Central Europe, north of Italy and Slovenia

Total area: 83,871 sq km

Climate: Temperate; continental, cloudy; cold winters with frequent rain and some snow in lowlands and snow in mountains; moderate summers with occasional showers

Nationality: noun: Austrian(s) *adjective:* Austrian

Population: 8,223,062 (July 2014 CIA est.)

Ethnic groups: Austrians 91.1%, former Yugoslavs 4% (includes Croatians, Slovenes, Serbs, and Bosniaks), Turks 1.6%, German 0.9%, other or unspecified 2.4% (2001 census)

Languages spoken: German (official nationwide) 88.6%, Turkish 2.3%, Serbian 2.2%, Croatian (official in Burgenland) 1.6%, other (includes Slovene, official in Carinthia, and Hungarian, official in Burgenland) 5.3% (2001 census)

Religions: Roman Catholic 73.6%, Protestant 4.7%, Muslim 4.2%, other 3.5%, unspecified 2%, none 12% (2001 census)

Azerbaijan

Official name: Republic of Azerbaijan

Capital city: Baku

Internet country code: .az

Flag description: Three equal horizontal bands of blue (top), red, and green; a crescent and eight-pointed star in white are centered in the red band

National anthem: "Azerbaijan, Azerbaijan!" lyrics by Ahmed Javad, music by Useyir Hajibeyov

Geographical description: Southwestern Asia, bordering the Caspian Sea, between Iran and Russia, with a small European portion north of the Caucasus range

Total area: 86,600 sq km

Climate: Dry, semiarid steppe

Nationality: noun: Azerbaijani(s) *adjective:* Azerbaijani

Population: 9,686,210 (July 2014 CIA est.)

Ethnic groups: Azerbaijani 91.6%, Lezgian 2%, Russian 1.3%, Armenian 1.3%, Talysh 1.3%, other 2.4%

Languages spoken: Azerbaijani (Azeri) (official) 92.5%, Russian 1.4%, Armenian 1.4%, other 4.7% (2009 CIA est.)

Religions: Muslim 93.4%, Russian Orthodox 2.5%, Armenian Orthodox 2.3%, other 1.8% (1995 CIA est.)

Bahamas

Official name: Commonwealth of The Bahamas

Capital city: Nassau

Internet country code: .bs

Flag description: Three equal horizontal bands of aquamarine (top), gold, and aquamarine, with a black equilateral triangle based on the hoist side

National anthem: "March On Bahamaland" by Timothy Gibson

National motto: "Forward Upward Onward Together"

National bird: Flamingo

National fish: Blue marlin (Makaira nigricans)

National flower: Yellow elder

National song: "God Bless Our Sunny Clime," lyrics by Rev. Philip Rahming, music by Timothy Gibson and Clement Bethel

National tree: Lignum vitae

Geographical description: Caribbean, chain of islands in the North Atlantic Ocean, southeast of Florida, northeast of Cuba

Total area: 13,880 sq km

Climate: Tropical marine; moderated by warm waters of Gulf Stream

Nationality: noun: Bahamian(s) *adjective:* Bahamian

Population: 321,834

Ethnic groups: Black 90.6%, white 4.7%, black and white 2.1%, other 1.9%, unspecified 0.7% (2010 CIA est.)

Languages spoken: English (official), Creole (among Haitian immigrants)

Religions: Protestant 69.9% (includes Baptist 34.9%, Anglican 13.7%, Pentecostal 8.9% Seventh Day Adventist 4.4%, Methodist 3.6%, Church of God 1.9%, Brethren 1.6%), Roman Catholic 12%, other Christian 13% (includes Jehovah's Witness 1.1%), other 0.6%, none 1.9%, unspecified 2.6% (2010 CIA est.)

Bahrain

Official name: Kingdom of Bahrain

Capital city: Manama

Internet country code: .bh

Flag description: Red, the traditional color for flags of Persian Gulf states, with a white serrated band (five white points) on the hoist side; the five points represent the five pillars of Islam

National anthem: "Bahrainona, Maleekuna" (first line; English translation: Our Bahrain, our King)

Geographical description: Middle East, archipelago in the Persian Gulf, east of Saudi Arabia

Total area: 760 sq km

Climate: Arid; mild, pleasant winters; very hot, humid summers

Nationality: noun: Bahraini(s) *adjective:* Bahraini

Population: 1,314,089

Ethnic groups: Bahraini 46%, Asian 45.5%, other Arabs 4.7%, African 1.6%, European 1%, other 1.2% (includes Gulf Co-operative country nationals, North and South Americans, and Oceanians) (2010 CIA est.)

Languages spoken: Arabic (official), English, Farsi, Urdu

Religions: Muslim 70.3%, Christian 14.5%, Hindu 9.8%, Buddhist 2.5%, Jewish 0.6%, folk religion <.1%, unaffiliated 1.9%, other 0.2% (2010 CIA est.)

Bangladesh

Official name: People's Republic of Bangladesh

Capital city: Dhaka

Internet country code: .bd

Flag description: Green field with a large red disk shifted slightly to the hoist side of center; the red disk represents the rising sun and the sacrifice to achieve independence; the green field symbolizes the lush vegetation of Bangladesh

National anthem: "Amar Sonar Bangla" (My Golden Bengal); (first line in English: My Bengal of gold, I love you), lyrics in Bengali by Rabindranath Tagore, translated by Syed Ali Ahsan

National animal: Royal Bengal tiger

National bird: Doel or magpie robin

National flower: Shapla or water lily

National fruit: Jackfruit (Kathal)

Geographical description: Southern Asia, bordering the Bay of Bengal, between Myanmar (Burma) and India

Total area: 143,998 sq km

Climate: Tropical; mild winter (October to March); hot, humid summer (March to June); humid, warm rainy monsoon (June to October)

Nationality: noun: Bangladeshi(s) *adjective:* Bangladeshi

Population: 166,280,712 (July 2014 CIA est.)

Ethnic groups: Bengali 98%, other 2% (includes tribal groups, non-Bengali Muslims) (1998)

Languages spoken: Bangla (official; also known as Bengali), English

Religions: Muslim 89.5%, Hindu 9.6%, other 0.9% (2004)

Barbados

Official name: Barbados

Capital city: Bridgetown

Internet country code: .bb

Flag description: Three equal vertical bands of blue (hoist side), gold, and blue with the head of a black trident centered on the gold band; the trident head represents independence and a break with the past (the colonial coat of arms contained a complete trident)

National anthem: "We loyal sons and daughters all" (first line of chorus), lyrics by Irving Burgie, music by C. Van Roland Edwards

National flower: Pride of Barbados (Dwarf Poinciana or Flower Fence; Poinciana pulcherrima linnaeus)

Geographical description: Caribbean, island in the North Atlantic Ocean, northeast of Venezuela

Total area: 430 sq km

Climate: Tropical; rainy season (June to October)

Nationality: noun: Barbadian(s) or Bajan (colloquial) *adjective:* Barbadian or Bajan (colloquial)

Population: 289,680 (July 2014 CIA est.)

Ethnic groups: Black 92.4%, white 2.7%, mixed 3.1%, East Indian 1.3%, other 0.2%, unspecified 0.2% (2010 CIA est.)

Languages spoken: English (official), Bajan (English-based creole language, widely spoken in informal settings)

Religions: Protestant 66.3% (includes Anglican 23.9%, other Pentecostal 19.5%, Adventist 5.9%, Methodist 4.2%, Wesleyan 3.4%, Nazarene 3.2%, Church of God 2.4%, Baptist 1.8%, Moravian 1.2%, other Protestant .8%), Roman Catholic 3.8%, other Christian 5.4% (includes Jehovah's Witness 2.0%, other 3.4%), Rastafarian 1%, other 1.5%, none 20.6%, unspecified 1.2% (2010 CIA est.)

Belarus

Official name: Republic of Belarus

Capital city: Minsk

Internet country code: .by

Flag description: Red horizontal band (top) and green horizontal band one-half the width of the red band; a white vertical stripe on the hoist side bears Belarusian national ornamentation in red

National anthem: Lyrics by M. Klimkovich and U. Karyzna, music by N. Sakalouski

Geographical description: Eastern Europe, east of Poland

Total area: 207,600 sq km

Climate: Cold winters, cool and moist summers; transitional between continental and maritime

Nationality: noun: Belarusian(s) *adjective:* Belarusian

Population: 9,608,058 (July 2014 CIA est.)

Ethnic groups: Belarusian 83.7%, Russian 8.3%, Polish 3.1%, Ukrainian 1.7%, other 2.4%, unspecified 0.9% (2009 CIA est.)

Languages spoken: Belarusian (official) 23.4%, Russian (official) 70.2%, other 3.1% (includes small Polish- and Ukrainian-speaking minorities), unspecified 3.3% (2009 CIA est.)

Religions: Eastern Orthodox 80%, other (including Roman Catholic, Protestant, Jewish, and Muslim) 20% (1997 CIA est.)

Belgium

Official name: Kingdom of Belgium

Capital city: Brussels

Internet country code: .be

Flag description: Three equal vertical bands of black (hoist side), yellow, and red; the design was based on the flag of France

National anthem: "La Brabançonne"

National motto: French: "L'Union fait la force," Dutch: "Eendracht maakt macht" (Strength lies in unity)

Geographical description: Western Europe, bordering the North Sea, between France and the Netherlands

Total area: 30,528 sq km

Climate: Temperate; mild winters, cool summers; rainy, humid, cloudy

Nationality: noun: Belgian(s) *adjective:* Belgian

Population: 10,449,361 (July 2014 CIA est.)

Ethnic groups: Fleming 58%, Walloon 31%, mixed or other 11%

Languages spoken: Dutch (official) 60%, French (official) 40%, German (official) less than 1%, legally bilingual (Dutch and French)

Religions: Roman Catholic 75%, other (includes Protestant) 25%

Belize

Official name: Belize

Capital city: Belmopan

Internet country code: .bz

Flag description: Blue with a narrow red stripe along the top and the bottom edges; centered is a large white disk bearing the coat of arms; the coat of arms features a shield flanked by two workers in front of a mahogany tree with the national motto *Sub umbra florero* on a scroll at the bottom, all encircled by a green garland

National anthem: "Land of the Free"

National motto: "Sub Umbra Florero" (Under the shade I flourish)

National animal: Tapir or Mountain Cow (Tapirello Bairdii)

National bird: Keel-Billed Toucan (Ramphastos Solfurantus)

National flower: Black Orchid (Encyclia Cochleatum)

National tree: Mahogany tree (Swietenia Macrophilla)

Geographical description: Central America, bordering the Caribbean Sea, between Guatemala and Mexico

Total area: 22,966 sq km

Climate: Tropical; very hot and humid; rainy season (May to November); dry season (February to May)

Nationality: noun: Belizean(s) *adjective:* Belizean

Population: 340,844 (July 2014 CIA est.)

Ethnic groups: Mestizo 48.7%, Creole 24.9%, Maya 10.6%, Garifuna 6.1%, other 9.7% (2000 census)

Languages spoken: Spanish 46%, Creole 32.9%, Mayan dialects 8.9%, English (official) 3.9%, Garifuna (Carib) 3.4%, German 3.3%, other 1.4%, unknown 0.2% (2000 Census)

Religions: Roman Catholic 39.3%, Pentacostal 8.3%, Seventh Day Adventist 5.3%, Anglican 4.5%, Mennonite 3.7%, Baptist 3.5%, Methodist 2.8%, Nazarene 2.8%, Jehovah's Witnesses 1.6%, other 9.9% (includes Baha'i Faith, Buddhism, Hinduism, Islam, and Mormon), other (unknown) 3.1%, none 15.2% (2010 census)

Benin

Official name: Republic of Benin

Capital city: Porto-Novo is official capital city; Cotonou is the seat of government

Internet country code: .bj

Flag description: Two equal horizontal bands of yellow (top) and red (bottom) with a vertical green band on the hoist side

National anthem: "L'Aube Nouvelle" (The New Dawn)

National motto: "Fraternité - Justice - Travail"

Geographical description: Western Africa, bordering the Bight of Benin, between Nigeria and Togo

Total area: 112,622 sq km

Climate: Tropical; hot, humid in south; semiarid in north

Nationality: noun: Beninese (singular and plural) *adjective:* Beninese

Population: 10,160,556

Ethnic groups: Fon and related 39.2%, Adja and related 15.2%, Yoruba and related 12.3%, Bariba and related 9.2%, Peulh and related 7%, Ottamari and related 6.1%, Yoa-Lokpa and related 4%, Dendi and related 2.5%, other 1.6% (includes Europeans), unspecified 2.9% (2002 census)

Languages spoken: French (official), Fon and Yoruba (most common vernaculars in south), tribal languages (at least six major ones in north)

Religions: Catholic 27.1%, Muslim 24.4%, Vodoun 17.3%, Protestant 10.4% (Celestial 5%, Methodist 3.2%, other Protestant 2.2%), other Christian 5.3%, other 15.5% (2002 census)

Bermuda

Official name: Bermuda

Capital city: Hamilton

Internet country code: .bm

Flag description: Red, with the flag of the United Kingdom in the upper hoist-side quadrant and the Bermudian coat of arms (white and green shield with a red lion holding a scrolled shield showing the sinking of the ship *Sea Venture* off Bermuda in 1609) centered on the outer half of the flag

Geographical description: North America, group of islands in the North Atlantic Ocean, east of South Carolina (US)

Total area: 54 sq km

Climate: Subtropical; mild, humid; gales, strong winds common in winter

Nationality: noun: Bermudian(s) *adjective:* Bermudian

Population: 69,839 (July 2014 CIA est.)

Ethnic groups: Black 53.8%, white 31%, mixed 7.5%, other 7.1%, unspecified 0.6% (2010 CIA est.)

Languages spoken: English (official), Portuguese

Religions: Protestant 46.1% (Anglican 15.8%, African Methodist Episcopal 8.6%, Seventh Day Adventist 6.7, Pentecostal 3.5%, Methodist 2.7%, Presbyterian 2.0 %, Church of God 1.6%, Baptist 1.2%, Salvation Army 1.1%, Bretheren 1.0%, other Protestant 2.0%), Roman Catholic 14.5%,

Jehovah's Witness 1.3%, other Christian 9.1%, Muslim 1%, other 3.9%, none 17.8%, unspecified 6.2% (2010 CIA est.)

Bhutan

Official name: Kingdom of Bhutan

Capital city: Thimphu

Internet country code: .bt

Flag description: Divided diagonally from the lower hoist side corner; the upper triangle is yellow and the lower triangle is orange; centered along the dividing line is a large black and white dragon facing away from the hoist side

National anthem: "In the Kingdom of Druk, where cypresses grow" (first line in English translation)

Geographical description: Southern Asia, between China and India

Total area: 38,394 sq km

Climate: Varies; tropical in southern plains; cool winters and hot summers in central valleys; severe winters and cool summers in Himalayas

Nationality: noun: Bhutanese (singular and plural) *adjective:* Bhutanese

Population: 733,643

Ethnic groups: Ngalop (also known as Bhote) 50%, ethnic Nepalese 35% (includes Lhotsampas - one of several Nepalese ethnic groups), indigenous or migrant tribes 15%

Languages spoken: Sharchhopka 28%, Dzongkha (official) 24%, Lhotshamkha 22%, other 26% (includes foreign languages) (2005 CIA est.)

Religions: Lamaistic Buddhist 75.3%, Indian- and Nepalese-influenced Hinduism 22.1%, other 2.6% (2005 CIA est.)

Bolivia

Official name: Republic of Bolivia

Capital city: La Paz

Internet country code: .bo

Flag description: Three equal horizontal bands of red (top), yellow, and green with the coat of arms centered on the yellow band; similar to the flag of Ghana, which has a large black five-pointed star centered in the yellow band

Geographical description: Central South America, southwest of Brazil

Total area: 1,098,581 sq km

Climate: Varies with altitude; humid and tropical to cold and semiarid

Nationality: noun: Bolivian(s) *adjective:* Bolivian

Population: 10,631,486 (July 2014 CIA est.)

Ethnic groups: Quechua 30%, mestizo (mixed white and Amerindian ancestry) 30%, Aymara 25%, white 15%

Languages spoken: Spanish (official) 60.7%, Quechua (official) 21.2%, Aymara (official) 14.6%, Guarani (official), foreign languages 2.4%, other 1.2%

Religions: Roman Catholic 95%, Protestant (Evangelical Methodist) 5%

Bosnia and Herzegovina

Official name: Bosnia and Herzegovina

Capital city: Sarajevo

Internet country code: .ba

Flag description: A wide medium blue vertical band on the fly side with a yellow isosceles triangle abutting the band and the top of the flag; the remainder of the flag is medium blue with seven full five-pointed white stars and two half stars top and bottom along the hypotenuse of the triangle

National anthem: "Intermeco"

Geographical description: Southeastern Europe, bordering the Adriatic Sea and Croatia

Total area: 51,197 sq km

Climate: Hot summers and cold winters; areas of high elevation have short, cool summers and long, severe winters; mild, rainy winters along coast

Nationality: noun: Bosnian(s), Herzegovinian(s) *adjective:* Bosnian, Herzegovinian

Population: 3,871,643 (July 2014 CIA est.)

Ethnic groups: Bosniak 48%, Serb 37.1%, Croat 14.3%, other 0.6% (2000)

Languages spoken: Bosnian (official), Croatian (official), Serbian (official)

Religions: Muslim 40%, Orthodox 31%, Roman Catholic 15%, other 14%

Botswana

Official name: Republic of Botswana

Capital city: Gaborone

Internet country code: .bw

Flag description: Light blue with a horizontal white-edged black stripe in the center

National anthem: "Fatshe La Rona" (Our Land)

Geographical description: Southern Africa, north of South Africa

Total area: 581,730 sq km

Climate: Semiarid; warm winters and hot summers

Nationality: noun: Motswana (singular), Batswana (plural) *adjective:* Motswana (singular), Batswana (plural)

Population: 2,155,784

Ethnic groups: Tswana (or Setswana) 79%, Kalanga 11%, Basarwa 3%, other, including Kgalagadi and white 7%

Languages spoken: Setswana 78.2%, Kalanga 7.9%, Sekgalagadi 2.8%, English (official) 2.1%, other 8.6%, unspecified 0.4% (2001 census)

Religions: Christian 71.6%, Badimo 6%, other 1.4%, unspeficied 0.4%, none 20.6% (2001 census)

Brazil

Official name: Federative Republic of Brazil

Capital city: Brasilia

Internet country code: .br

Flag description: Green with a large yellow diamond in the center bearing a blue celestial globe with 27 white five-pointed stars (one for each state and the Federal District) arranged in the same pattern as the night sky over Brazil; the globe has a white equatorial band with the motto *ordem e progresso* (Order and Progress)

National anthem: "Himno Nacianal Brasileiro," lyrics by Joaquim Osório Duque Estrada, music by Francisco Manuel da Silva

National bird: Sabiá or Thrush (Turdus rufiventris)

National flower: Ipê-amarelo - (Tecoma chrysostricha)

Geographical description: Eastern South America, bordering the Atlantic Ocean

Total area: 8,514,877 sq km

Climate: Mostly tropical, but temperate in south

Nationality: noun: Brazilian(s) *adjective:* Brazilian

Population: 202,656,788 (July 2014 CIA est.)

Ethnic groups: white 47.7%, mulatto (mixed white and black) 43.1%, black 7.6%, Asian 1.1%, indigenous 0.4% (2010 CIA est.)

Languages spoken: Portuguese (official and most widely spoken language)

Religions: Roman Catholic 64.6%, other Catholic 0.4%, Protestant 22.2% (includes Adventist 6.5%, Assembly of God 2.0%, Christian Congregation of Brazil 1.2%, Universal Kingdom of God 1.0%, other Protestant 11.5%), other Christian 0.7%, Spiritist 2.2%, other 1.4%, none 8%, unspecified 0.4% (2010 CIA est.)

Brunei

Official name: Brunei Darussalam

Capital city: Bandar Seri Begawan

Internet country code: .bn

Flag description: Yellow with two diagonal bands of white (top, almost double width) and black starting from the upper hoist side; the national emblem in red is superimposed at the center; the emblem includes a swallow-tailed flag on top of a winged column within an upturned crescent above a scroll and flanked by two upraised hands

National anthem: "Allah Peliharakan Sultan" (God Bless His Majesty), lyrics by Yura Halim, music by Haji Awang Besar Sagap

National motto: "Always Render Service by God's Guidance"

Geographical description: Southeastern Asia, bordering the South China Sea and Malaysia

Total area: 5,765 sq km

Climate: Tropical; hot, humid, rainy

Nationality: noun: Bruneian(s) *adjective:* Bruneian

Population: 422,675 (July 2014 CIA est.)

Ethnic groups: Malay 65.7%, Chinese 10.3%, other indigenous 3.4%, other 20.6% (2011 CIA est.)

Languages spoken: Malay (official), English, Chinese

Religions: Muslim (official) 78.8%, Christian 8.7%, Buddhist 7.8%, other (includes indigenous beliefs) 4.7% (2011 CIA est.)

Bulgaria

Official name: Republic of Bulgaria

Capital city: Sofia

Internet country code: .bg

Flag description: Three equal horizontal bands of white (top), green, and red

National anthem: "Mila Rodino" (O Motherland Most Dear), based on music and lyrics by Tsvetan Radoslavov

National motto: "Unity Makes Strength"

Geographical description: Southeastern Europe, bordering the Black Sea, between Romania and Turkey

Total area: 110,879 sq km

Climate: Temperate; cold, damp winters; hot, dry summers

Nationality: noun: Bulgarian(s) *adjective:* Bulgarian

Population: 6,924,716 (July 2014 CIA est.)

Ethnic groups: Bulgarian 76.9%, Turkish 8%, Roma 4.4%, other 0.7% (including Russian, Armenian, and Vlach), other (unknown) 10% (2011 CIA est.)

Languages spoken: Bulgarian (official) 76.8%, Turkish 8.2%, Roma 3.8%, other 0.7%, unspecified 10.5% (2011 CIA est.)

Religions: Eastern Orthodox 59.4%, Muslim 7.8%, other (including Catholic, Protestant, Armenian Apostolic Orthodox, and Jewish) 1.7%, none 3.7%, unspecified 27.4% (2011 CIA est.)

Burkina Faso

Official name: Burkina Faso

Capital city: Ouagadougou

Internet country code: .bf

Flag description: Two equal horizontal bands of red (top) and green with a yellow five-pointed star in the center; uses the popular pan-African colors of Ethiopia

National anthem: "L' Hymne de la Victoire" / "Ditanyè" (Hymn of Victory)

Geographical description: Western Africa, north of Ghana

Total area: 274,200 sq km

Climate: Tropical; warm, dry winters; hot, wet summers

Nationality: noun: Burkinabe (singular and plural) *adjective:* Burkinabe

Population: 18,365,123

Ethnic groups: Mossi over 40%, other approximately 60% (includes Gurunsi, Senufo, Lobi, Bobo, Mande, and Fulani)

Languages spoken: French (official), native African languages belonging to Sudanic family spoken by 90% of the population

Religions: Muslim 60.5%, Catholic 19%, animist 15.3%, Protestant 4.2%, other 0.6%, none 0.4% (2006 CIA est.)

Burma/Myanmar

Official name: Union of Burma/Myanmar

Capital city: Rangoon

Internet country code: .mm

Flag description: Red with a blue rectangle in the upper hoist-side corner bearing 14 white, five-pointed stars encircling a cogwheel containing a stalk of rice; the 14 stars represent the seven administrative divisions and seven states

National anthem: "Kaba Makye" (Our Free Homeland; first line in English translation: "We shall always love Myanmar, Land of our forefathers") by Y. M. B. Saya Tin

Geographical description: Southeastern Asia, bordering the Andaman Sea and the Bay of Bengal, between Bangladesh and Thailand

Total area: 676,578 sq km

Climate: Tropical monsoon; cloudy, rainy, hot, humid summers (southwest monsoon, June to September); less cloudy, scant rainfall, mild temperatures, lower humidity during winter (northeast monsoon, December to April)

Nationality: noun: Burmese (singular and plural) *adjective:* Burmese

Population: 55,746,253

Ethnic groups: Burman 68%, Shan 9%, Karen 7%, Rakhine 4%, Chinese 3%, Indian 2%, Mon 2%, other 5%

Languages spoken: Burmese (official)

Religions: Buddhist 89%, Christian 4% (Baptist 3%, Roman Catholic 1%), Muslim 4%, Animist 1%, other 2%

Burundi

Official name: Republic of Burundi

Capital city: Bujumbura

Internet country code: .bi

Flag description: Divided by a white diagonal cross into red panels (top and bottom) and green panels (hoist side and fly side) with a white disk superimposed at the center bearing three red six-pointed stars outlined in green arranged in a triangular design (one star above, two stars below)

National anthem: "Burundi Bwacu" (Hymn of Independence)

National motto: Unity-Work-Progress

Geographical description: Central Africa, east of Democratic Republic of the Congo

Total area: 27,830 sq km

Climate: Equatorial; high plateau with considerable altitude variation; two wet seasons (February to May and September to November), and two dry seasons (June to August and December to January)

Nationality: noun: Burundian(s) *adjective:* Burundian

Population: 10,395,931

Ethnic groups: Hutu (Bantu) 85%, Tutsi (Hamitic) 14%, Twa (Pygmy) 1%, Europeans 3,000, South Asians 2,000

Languages spoken: Kirundi 29.7% (official), Kirundi and other language 9.1%, French (official) and French and other language 0.3%, Swahili and Swahili and other language 0.2% (along Lake Tanganyika and in the Bujumbura area), English and English and other language 0.06%, more than 2 languages 3.7%, unspecified 56.9% (2008 CIA est.)

Religions: Catholic 62.1%, Protestant 23.9% (includes Adventist 2.3% and other Protestant 21.6%), Muslim 2.5%, other 3.6%, unspecified 7.9% (2008 CIA est.)

Cambodia

Official name: Kingdom of Cambodia

Capital city: Phnom Penh

Internet country code: .kh

Flag description: Three horizontal bands of blue (top), red (double width), and blue with a white three-towered temple representing Angkor Wat outlined in black in the center of the red band; only national flag to incorporate an actual building in its design

National anthem: "Our Country"

National motto: "Nation, Religion, King"

Geographical description: Southeastern Asia, bordering the Gulf of Thailand, between Thailand, Vietnam, and Laos

Total area: 181,035 sq km

Climate: Tropical; rainy, monsoon season (May to November); dry season (December to April); little seasonal temperature variation

Nationality: noun: Cambodian(s) *adjective:* Cambodian

Population: 15,458,332

Ethnic groups: Khmer 90%, Vietnamese 5%, Chinese 1%, other 4%

Languages spoken: Khmer (official) 96.3%, other 3.7% (2008 CIA est.)

Religions: Buddhist (official) 96.9%, Muslim 1.9%, Christian 0.4%, other 0.8% (2008 CIA est.)

Cameroon

Official name: Republic of Cameroon

Capital city: Yaounde

Internet country code: .cm

Flag description: Three equal vertical bands of green (hoist side), red, and yellow with a yellow five-pointed star centered in the red band; uses the popular pan-African colors of Ethiopia

National anthem: "ô Cameroun, berceau de nos ancêtres" (O Cameroon, Thou Cradle of Our Fathers)

Geographical description: Western Africa, bordering the Bight of Biafra, between Equatorial Guinea and Nigeria

Total area: 475,440 sq km

Climate: Varies with terrain, from tropical along coast to semiarid and hot in north

Nationality: noun: Cameroonian(s) *adjective:* Cameroonian

Population: 23,130,708

Ethnic groups: Cameroon Highlanders 31%, Equatorial Bantu 19%, Kirdi 11%, Fulani 10%, Northwestern Bantu 8%, Eastern Nigritic 7%, other African 13%, non-African less than 1%

Languages spoken: 24 major African language groups, English (official), French (official)

Religions: Indigenous beliefs 40%, Christian 40%, Muslim 20%

Canada

Official name: Canada

Capital city: Ottawa

Internet country code: .ca

Flag description: Two vertical bands of red (hoist and fly side, half width), with white square between them; an 11-pointed red maple leaf is centered in the white square; the official colors of Canada are red and white

National anthem: "O Canada," English lyrics by Justice Robert Stanley Weir, French lyrics by Adolphe-Basile Routhier, music by Calixa Lavallée

National symbols: maple leaf, maple tree, and beaver

Geographical description: Northern North America, bordering the North Atlantic Ocean on the east, North Pacific Ocean on the west, and the Arctic Ocean on the north, north of the conterminous United States

Total area: 9,984,670 sq km

Climate: Varies from temperate in south to subarctic and arctic in north

Nationality: noun: Canadian(s) *adjective:* Canadian

Population: 34,834,841 (July 2014 CIA est.)

Ethnic groups: Canadian 32.2%, English 19.8%, French 15.5%, Scottish 14.4%, Irish 13.8%, German 9.8%, Italian 4.5%, Chinese 4.5%, North American Indian 4.2%, other 50.9%

Languages spoken: English (official) 58.7%, French (official) 22%, Punjabi 1.4%, Italian 1.3%, Spanish 1.3%, German 1.3%, Cantonese 1.2%, Tagalog 1.2%, Arabic 1.1%, other 10.5% (2011 CIA est.)

Religions: Catholic 40.6% (includes Roman Catholic 38.8%, Orthodox 1.6%, other Catholic .2%), Protestant 20.3% (includes United Church 6.1%, Anglican 5%, Baptist 1.9%, Lutheran 1.5%, Pentecostal 1.5%, Presbyterian 1.4%, other Protestant 2.9%), other Christian 6.3%, Muslim 3.2%, Hindu 1.5%, Sikh 1.4%, Buddhist 1.1%, Jewish 1%, other 0.6%, none 23.9% (2011 CIA est.)

Cape Verde/Cabo Verde

Official name: Republic of Cabo Verde

Capital city: Praia

Internet country code: .cv

Flag description: Five unequal horizontal bands; the topmost band of blue - equal to one half the width of the flag - is followed by three bands of white, red, and white, each equal to 1/12 of the width, and a bottom stripe of blue equal to one quarter of the flag width; a circle of 10 yellow five-pointed stars, each representing one of the islands, is centered on the red stripe and positioned 3/8 of the length of the flag from the hoist side

National anthem: "Cântico da Liberdade"

Geographical description: Western Africa, group of islands in the North Atlantic Ocean, west of Senegal

Total area: 4,033 sq km

Climate: Temperate; warm, dry summer; precipitation meager and very erratic

Nationality: noun: Cabo Verdean(s) *adjective:* Cabo Verdean

Population: 538,535 (July 2014 CIA est.)

Ethnic groups: Creole (mulatto) 71%, African 28%, European 1%

Languages spoken: Portuguese (official), Crioulo (a blend of Portuguese and West African words)

Religions: Roman Catholic 77.3%, Protestant 3.7% (includes Church of the Nazarene 1.7%, Adventist 1.5%, Universal Kingdom of God .4%, and God and Love .1%), other Christian 4.3% (includes Christian Rationalism 1.9%, Jehovah's Witness 1%, Assembly of God .9%, and New Apostolic .5%), Muslim 1.8%, other 1.3%, none 10.8%, unspecified 0.7% (2010 CIA est.)

Central African Republic

Official name: Central African Republic

Capital city: Bangui

Internet country code: .cf

Flag description: Four equal horizontal bands of blue (top), white, green, and yellow with a vertical red band in center; there is a yellow five-pointed star on the hoist side of the blue band

National anthem: "Le Renaissance" (Rebirth)

Geographical description: Central Africa, north of Democratic Republic of the Congo

Total area: 622,984 sq km

Climate: Tropical; hot, dry winters; mild to hot, wet summers

Nationality: noun: Central African(s) *adjective:* Central African

Population: 5,277,959

Ethnic groups: Baya 33%, Banda 27%, Mandjia 13%, Sara 10%, Mboum 7%, M'Baka 4%, Yakoma 4%, other 2%

Languages spoken: French (official), Sangho (lingua franca and national language), tribal languages

Religions: Indigenous religions 35%, Roman, Protestant 25%, Catholic 25%, Muslim 15%

Chad

Official name: Republic of Chad

Capital city: N'Djamena

Internet country code: .td

Flag description: Three equal vertical bands of blue (hoist side), yellow, and red; design was based on the flag of France

National anthem: "La Tchadienne" (The Chadian)

Geographical description: Central Africa, south of Libya

Total area: 1.284 million sq km

Climate: Tropical in south, desert in north

Nationality: noun: Chadian(s) *adjective:* Chadian

Population: 11,412,107 (July 2014 CIA est.)

Ethnic groups: Sara 27.7%, Arab 12.3%, Mayo-Kebbi 11.5%, Kanem-Bornou 9%, Ouaddai 8.7%, Hadjarai 6.7%, Tandjile 6.5%, Gorane 6.3%, Fitri-Batha 4.7%, other 6.4%, unknown 0.3% (1993 census)

Languages spoken: French (official), Arabic (official), Sara (in the south), more than 120 other languages and dialects

Religions: Muslim 53.1%, Catholic 20.1%, Protestant 14.2%, animist 7.3%, other 0.5%, unknown 1.7%, atheist 3.1% (1993 census)

Chile

Official name: Republic of Chile

Capital city: Santiago

Internet country code: .cl

Flag description: Two equal horizontal bands of white (top) and red; there is a blue square the same height as the white band at the hoist-side end of the white band; the square bears a white five-pointed star in the center representing a guide to progress and honor; blue symbolizes the sky, white is for the snow-covered Andes, and red stands for the blood spilled to achieve independence; design was influenced by the United States flag

National anthem: "Cancion Nacionale de Chile" (National Song of Chile; first line: "Puro Chile, es tu cielo azulado"), lyrics by Eusebio Lillo, music by Ramón Carnicer

Geographical description: Southern South America, bordering the South Pacific Ocean, between Argentina and Peru

Total area: 756,102 sq km

Climate: Temperate; desert in north; Mediterranean in central region; cool and damp in south

Nationality: noun: Chilean(s) *adjective:* Chilean

Population: 17,363,894 (July 2014 CIA est.)

Ethnic groups: white and non-indigenous 88.9%, Mapuche 9.1%, Aymara 0.7%, other indigenous groups 1% (includes Rapa Nui, Likan Antai, Quechua, Colla, Diaguita, Kawesqar, Yagan or Yamana), unspecified 0.3% (2012 CIA est.)

Languages spoken: Spanish 99.5% (official), English 10.2%, indigenous 1% (includes Mapudungun, Aymara, Quechua, Rapa Nui), other 2.3%, unspecified 0.2%

Religions: Roman Catholic 66.7%, Evangelical or Protestant 16.4%, Jehovah's Witnesses 1%, other 3.4%, none 11.5%, unspecified 1.1% (2012 CIA est.)

China

Official name: People's Republic of China

Capital city: Beijing

Internet country code: .cn

Flag description: Red with a large yellow five-pointed star and four smaller yellow five-pointed stars (arranged in a vertical arc toward the middle of the flag) in the upper hoist-side corner

National anthem: March of the Volunteers, lyrics by Tian Han, music by Nie Er

Geographical description: Eastern Asia, bordering the East China Sea, Korea Bay, Yellow Sea, and South China Sea, between North Korea and Vietnam

Total area: 9,596,960 sq km

Climate: Extremely diverse; tropical in south to subarctic in north

Nationality: noun: Chinese (singular and plural) *adjective:* Chinese

Population: 1,355,692,576 (July 2014 CIA est.)

Ethnic groups: Han Chinese 91.6%, Zhuang 1.3%, other (includes Hui, Manchu, Uighur, Miao, Yi, Tujia, Tibetan, Mongol, Dong, Buyei, Yao, Bai, Korean, Hani, Li, Kazakh, Dai and other nationalities) 7.1%

Languages spoken: Standard Chinese or Mandarin (official; Putonghua, based on the Beijing dialect), Yue (Cantonese), Wu (Shanghainese), Minbei (Fuzhou), Minnan (Hokkien-Taiwanese), Xiang, Gan, Hakka dialects, minority languages (see Ethnic groups entry)

Religions: Buddhist 18.2%, Christian 5.1%, Muslim 1.8%, folk religion 21.9%, Hindu < .1%, Jewish < .1%, other 0.7% (includes Daoist (Taoist)), unaffiliated 52.2%

Colombia

Official name: Republic of Colombia

Capital city: Bogota

Internet country code: .co

Flag description: Three horizontal bands of yellow (top, double-width), blue, and red; similar to the flag of Ecuador, which is longer and bears the Ecuadorian coat of arms superimposed in the center

National bird: Condor

National flower: Orchid (Cattleya trianae)

National tree: Wax palm (Ceroxylon quindiuense)

Geographical description: Northern South America, bordering the Caribbean Sea, between Panama and Venezuela, and bordering the North Pacific Ocean, between Ecuador and Panama

Total area: 1,138,910 sq km

Climate: Tropical along coast and eastern plains; cooler in highlands

Nationality: noun: Colombian(s) *adjective:* Colombian

Population: 46,245,297 (July 2014 CIA est.)

Ethnic groups: mestizo 58%, white 20%, mulatto 14%, black 4%, mixed black-Amerindian 3%, Amerindian 1%

Languages spoken: Spanish (official)

Religions: Roman Catholic 90%, other 10%

Comoros

Official name: Union of the Comoros

Capital city: Moroni

Internet country code: .km

Flag description: Four equal horizontal bands of yellow (top), white, red, and blue with a green isosceles triangle based on the hoist; centered within the triangle is a white crescent with the convex side facing the hoist and four white, five-pointed stars placed vertically in a line between the points of the crescent; the horizontal bands and the four stars represent the four main islands of the archipelago - Mwali, Njazidja, Nzwani, and Mahore (Mayotte - territorial collectivity of France, but claimed by Comoros); the crescent, stars, and color green are traditional symbols of Islam

National anthem: "Udzima Wamasiwa" (Union des îles), lyrics by Said Hachim Sidi Abderemane, music by Kamildine Abdallah et Said Hachim Sidi Abderemane

Geographical description: Southern Africa, group of islands at the northern mouth of the Mozambique Channel, about two-thirds of the way between northern Madagascar and northern Mozambique

Total area: 2,235 sq km

Climate: Tropical marine; rainy season (November to May)

Nationality: noun: Comoran(s) *adjective:* Comoran

Population: 766,865 (July 2014 CIA est.)

Ethnic groups: Antalote, Cafre, Makoa, Oimatsaha, Sakalava

Languages spoken: Arabic (official), French (official), Shikomoro (a blend of Swahili and Arabic)

Religions: Sunni Muslim 98%, Roman Catholic 2%

Congo, Democratic Republic of the

Official name: Democratic Republic of the Congo

Capital city: Kinshasa

Internet country code: .cd

Flag description: Sky blue field divided diagonally from the lower hoist corner to upper fly corner by a red stripe bordered by two narrow yellow stripes; a yellow, five-pointed star appears in the upper hoist corner

National anthem: "Debout Congolaise!" (Arise Congolese!)

National motto: *Justice - Paix - Travail* (Justice, Peace, Work)

Geographical description: Central Africa, northeast of Angola

Total area: 2,344,858 sq km

Climate: Tropical; hot and humid in equatorial river basin; cooler and drier in southern highlands; cooler and wetter in eastern highlands; north of Equator - wet season (April to October), dry season (December to February); south of Equator - wet season (November to March), dry season (April to October)

Nationality: noun: Congolese (singular and plural) *adjective:* Congolese

Population: 77,433,744

Ethnic groups: Over 200 African ethnic groups of which the majority are Bantu; the four largest tribes - Mongo, Luba, Kongo (all Bantu), and the Mangbetu-Azande (Hamitic) make up about 45% of the population

Languages spoken: French (official), Lingala (a lingua franca trade language), Kingwana (a dialect of Kiswahili or Swahili), Kikongo, Tshiluba

Religions: Roman Catholic 50%, Protestant 20%, Kimbanguist 10%, Muslim 10%, other (including indigenous and syncretic faiths) 10%

Congo, Republic of the

Official name: Republic of the Congo

Capital city: Brazzaville

Internet country code: .cg

Flag description: Divided diagonally from the lower hoist side by a yellow band; the upper triangle (hoist side) is green and the lower triangle is red; uses the popular pan-African colors of Ethiopia

National anthem: "La Congolaise"

Geographical description: Western Africa, bordering the South Atlantic Ocean, between Angola and Gabon

Total area: 342,000 sq km

Climate: Tropical; rainy season (March to June); dry season (June to October); persistent high temperatures and humidity; particularly enervating climate astride the Equator

Nationality: noun: Congolese (singular and plural) *adjective:* Congolese or Congo

Population: 4,662,446

Ethnic groups: Kongo 48%, Sangha 20%, M'Bochi 12%, Teke 17%, Europeans and others 3%

Languages spoken: French (official), Lingala and Monokutuba (lingua franca trade languages), many local languages and dialects (of which Kikongo is the most widespread)

Religions: Roman Catholic 33.1%, Awakening Churches/Christian Revival 22.3%, Protestant 19.9%, Salutiste 2.2%, Muslim 1.6%, Kimbanguiste 1.5%, other 8.1%, none 11.3% (2010 CIA est.)

Costa Rica

Official name: Republic of Costa Rica

Capital city: San Jose

Internet country code: .cr

Flag description: Five horizontal bands of blue (top), white, red (double width), white, and blue, with the coat of arms in a white elliptical disk on the hoist side of the red band; above the coat of arms a light blue ribbon contains the words "America Central" and just below it near the top of the coat of arms is a white ribbon with the words, *Republica Costa Rica*

National anthem: "Noble patria, tu hermosa bandera" (first line; Noble Homeland, Your Beautiful Flag), lyrics by José María Zeledón, music by Manuel María Gutiérrez

National bird: Yiguirro (Turdus grayi)

National flower: Guaria Morada (Cattleya skinneri)

National symbol of work: la carreta costarricense (Costa Rican ox-cart)

National tree: Guanacaste Tree (Enterolobium ciclocarpum)

Geographical description: Central America, bordering both the Caribbean Sea and the North Pacific Ocean, between Nicaragua and Panama

Total area: 51,100 sq. km

Climate: Tropical and subtropical; dry season (December to April); rainy season (May to November); cooler in highlands

Nationality: noun: Costa Rican(s) *adjective:* Costa Rican

Population: 4,755,234 (July 2014 CIA est.)

Ethnic groups: White or mestizo 83.6%, mulato 6.7%, indigenous 2.4%, black of African descent 1.1%, other 1.1%, none 2.9%, unspecified 2.2% (2011 CIA est.)

Languages spoken: Spanish (official), English

Religions: Roman Catholic 76.3%, Evangelical 13.7%, Jehovah's Witness 1.3%, other Protestant 0.7%, other 4.8%, none 3.2%

Cote d'Ivoire

Official name: Republic of Cote d'Ivoire

Capital city: Yamoussoukro

Internet country code: .ci

Flag description: Three equal vertical bands of orange (hoist side), white, and green; similar to the flag of Ireland, which is longer and has the colors reversed - green (hoist side), white, and orange; also similar to the flag of Italy, which is green (hoist side), white, and red; design was based on the flag of France

National anthem: "L'Abidjanaise" (Song of Abidjan)

Geographical description: Western Africa, bordering the North Atlantic Ocean, between Ghana and Liberia

Total area: 322,463 sq km

Climate: Tropical along coast, semiarid in far north; three seasons - warm and dry (November to March), hot and dry (March to May), hot and wet (June to October)

Nationality: noun: Ivoirian(s) *adjective:* Ivoirian

Population: 22,848,945

Ethnic groups: Akan 42.1%, Voltaiques or Gur 17.6%, Northern Mandes 16.5%, Krous 11%, Southern Mandes 10%, other 2.8% (includes 130,000 Lebanese and 14,000 French) (1998)

Languages spoken: French (official), 60 native dialects of which Dioula is the most widely spoken

Religions: Muslim 38.6%, Christian 32.8%, indigenous 11.9%, none 16.7%

Croatia

Official name: Republic of Croatia

Capital city: Zagreb

Internet country code: .hr

Flag description: Three equal horizontal bands of red (top), white, and blue superimposed by the Croatian coat of arms (red-and-white checkered)

National anthem: "Lijepa nasa domovino" (Our Beautiful Homeland), lyrics by Antun Mihanović, music by Josip Runjanin

Geographical description: Southeastern Europe, bordering the Adriatic Sea, between Bosnia and Herzegovina and Slovenia

Total area: 56,594 sq km

Climate: Mediterranean and continental; continental climate predominant with hot summers and cold winters; mild winters, dry summers along coast

Nationality: noun: Croat(s), Croatian(s) *adjective:* Croatian

Population: 4,470,534 (July 2014 CIA est.)

Ethnic groups: Croat 90.4%, Serb 4.4%, other 4.4% (including Bosniak, Hungarian, Slovene, Czech, and Roma), unspecified 0.8% (2011 CIA est.)

Languages spoken: Croatian (official) 95.6%, Serbian 1.2%, other 3% (including Hungarian, Czech, Slovak, and Albanian), unspecified 0.2% (2011 CIA est.)

Religions: Roman Catholic 86.3%, Orthodox 4.4%, Muslim 1.5%, other 1.5%, unspecified 2.5%, not religious or atheist 3.8% (2011 CIA est.)

Cuba

Official name: Republic of Cuba

Capital city: Havana

Internet country code: .cu

Flag description: Five equal horizontal bands of blue (top, center, and bottom) alternating with white; a red equilateral triangle based on the hoist side bears a white, five-pointed star in the center

National anthem: "La Bayamesa" (The Bayamo Song) by Pedro Figueredo

Geographical description: Caribbean, island between the Caribbean Sea and the North Atlantic Ocean, 150 km south of Key West, Florida

Total area: 110,860 sq km

Climate: Tropical; moderated by trade winds; dry season (November to April); rainy season (May to October)

Nationality: noun: Cuban(s) *adjective:* Cuban

Population: 11,047,251 (July 2014 CIA est.)

Ethnic groups: white 64.1%, mestizo 26.6%, black 9.3% (2012 CIA est.)

Languages spoken: Spanish (Official)

Religions: Nominally Roman Catholic 85%, Protestant, Jehovah's Witnesses, Jewish, Santeria

Curacao

Official name: Curacao

Capital city: Willemstad

Internet country code: .cw

Flag description: On a blue field a horizontal yellow band somewhat below the center divides the flag into proportions of 5:1:2; two five-pointed white stars - the smaller above and to the left of the larger - appear in the canton; the blue of the upper and lower sections symbolizes the sky and sea respectively; yellow represents the sun; the stars symbolize Curacao and its uninhabited smaller sister island of Klein Curacao; the five star points signify the five continents from which Curacao's people derive

National anthem: Himmo di Korsou; Lyrics by Guillermo ROSARIO, Mae HENRIQUEZ, Enrique MULLER, Betty DORAN/Frater Candidus NOWENS, Errol "El Toro" COLINA

Total area: 444 sq km

Climate: Tropical marine climate, ameliorated by northeast trade winds, results in mild temperatures; semiarid with average rainfall of 600 mm/year

Nationality: noun: Curacaoan *adjective:* Curacaoan; Dutch

Population: 146,836 (July 2013 est.)

Ethnic groups: Afro-Caribbean majority; Dutch, French, Latin American, East Asian, South Asian, Jewish minorities

Languages spoken: Papiamentu (a Spanish-Portuguese-Dutch-English dialect) 81.2%, Dutch (official) 8%, Spanish 4%, English 2.9%, other 3.9% (2001 census)

Religions: Roman Catholic 72.8%, Pentecostal 6.6%, Protestant 3.2%, Adventist 3%, Jehovah's Witness 2%, Evangelical 1.9%, other 3.8%, none 6%, unspecified 0.6% (2011 CIA est.)

Cyprus

Official name: Republic of Cyprus

Capital city: Nicosia

Internet country code: .cy

Flag description: White with a copper-colored silhouette of the island (the name Cyprus is derived from the Greek word for copper) above two green crossed olive branches in the center of the flag; the branches symbolize the hope for peace and reconciliation between the Greek and Turkish communities

National anthem: "Imnos pros tin Eleftherian" (The Hymn to Liberty)

National plant: Cyprus cyclamen

National tree: Golden oak (Quercus alnifolia)

Geographical description: Middle East, island in the Mediterranean Sea, south of Turkey

Total area: 9,251 sq km (of which 3,355 sq km are in north Cyprus)

Climate: Temperate; Mediterranean with hot, dry summers and cool winters

Nationality: noun: Cypriot(s) *adjective:* Cypriot

Population: 1,172,458 (July 2014 CIA est.)

Ethnic groups: Greek 77%, Turkish 18%, other 5% (2001)

Languages spoken: Greek (official) 80.9%, Turkish (official) 0.2%, English 4.1%, Romanian 2.9%, Russian 2.5%, Bulgarian 2.2%, Arabic 1.2%, Filippino 1.1%, other 4.3%, unspecified 0.6% (2011 CIA est.)

Religions: Greek Orthodox 78%, Muslim 18%, other (including Maronite and Armenian Apostolic) 4%

Czech Republic

Official name: Czech Republic

Capital city: Prague

Internet country code: .cz

Flag description: Two equal horizontal bands of white (top) and red with a blue isosceles triangle based on the hoist side (identical to the flag of the former Czechoslovakia)

National anthem: "Kde domov muj?" (Where Is My Home?), lyrics by Josef Kajetán Tyl, music by Frantisek Skroup

National symbols: Lion, eagle, linden tree

Geographical description: Central Europe, southeast of Germany

Total area: 78,867 sq km

Climate: Temperate; cool summers; cold, cloudy, humid winters

Nationality: noun: Czech(s) *adjective:* Czech

Population: 10,627,448 (July 2014 CIA est.)

Ethnic groups: Czech 64.3%, Moravian 5%, Slovak 1.4%, other 1.8%, unspecified 27.5% (2011 CIA est.)

Languages spoken: Czech 95.4%, Slovak 1.6%, other 3% (2011 census)

Religions: Roman Catholic 10.4%, Protestant (includes Czech Brethren and Hussite) 1.1%, other and unspecified 54%, none 34.5% (2011 CIA est.)

Denmark

Official name: Kingdom of Denmark

Capital city: Copenhagen

Internet country code: .dk

Flag description: Red with a white cross that extends to the edges of the flag; the vertical part of the cross is shifted to the hoist side, and that design element of the Dannebrog (Danish flag) was subsequently adopted by the other Nordic countries of Finland, Iceland, Norway, and Sweden

National anthems: Royal anthem: "Kong Christian stod ved højen mast" (King Christian stood by lofty mast), lyrics by Johannes Ewald, original source of melody is unknown; national anthem: "Der er et yndigt land" (There is a lovely land), lyrics by Adam Oehlenschläger, music by Hans Ernst Krøyer

Geographical description: Northern Europe, bordering the Baltic Sea and the North Sea, on a peninsula north of Germany (Jutland); also includes two major islands (Sjaelland and Fyn)

Total area: 43,094 sq km

Climate: Temperate; humid and overcast; mild, windy winters and cool summers

Nationality: noun: Dane(s) *adjective:* Danish

Population: 5,569,077 (July 2014 CIA est.)

Ethnic groups: Scandinavian, Inuit, Faroese, German, Turkish, Iranian, Somali

Languages spoken: Danish, Faroese, Greenlandic (an Inuit dialect), German (small minority)

Religions: Evangelical Lutheran (official) 80%, Muslim 4%, other (denominations of less than 1% each, includes Roman Catholic, Jehovah's Witness, Serbian Orthodox Christian, Jewish, Baptist, and Buddhist) 16% (2012 CIA est.)

Djibouti

Official name: Republic of Djibouti

Capital city: Djibouti

Internet country code: .dj

Flag description: Two equal horizontal bands of light blue (top) and light green with a white isosceles triangle based on the hoist side bearing a red five-pointed star in the center

Geographical description: Eastern Africa, bordering the Gulf of Aden and the Red Sea, between Eritrea and Somalia

Total area: 23,200 sq km

Climate: Desert; torrid, dry

Nationality: noun: Djiboutian(s) *adjective:* Djiboutian

Population: 810,179 (July 2014 CIA est.)

Ethnic groups: Somali 60%, Afar 35%, other (including French, Arab, Ethiopian, and Italian) 5%

Languages spoken: French (official), Arab (official), Somali, Afar

Religions: Muslim 94%, Christian 6%

Dominica

Official name: Commonwealth of Dominica

Capital city: Roseau

Internet country code: .dm

Flag description: Green, with a centered cross of three equal bands - the vertical part is yellow (hoist side), black, and white and the horizontal part is yellow (top), black, and white; superimposed in the center of the cross is a red disk bearing a sisserou parrot encircled by 10 green five-pointed stars edged in yellow; the 10 stars represent the 10 administrative divisions (parishes)

National anthem: "Isle of beauty, isle of splendour" (first line)

National bird: Sisserou parrot

Geographical description: Caribbean, island between the Caribbean Sea and the North Atlantic Ocean, about one-half of the way from Puerto Rico to Trinidad and Tobago

Total area: 751 sq km

Climate: Tropical; moderated by northeast trade winds; heavy rainfall

Nationality: noun: Dominican(s) *adjective:* Dominican

Population: 73,449 (July 2014 CIA est.)

Ethnic groups: Black 86.8%, mixed 8.9%, Carib Amerindian 2.9%, white 0.8%, other 0.7% (2001 census)

Languages spoken: English (official), French patois

Religions: Roman Catholic 61.4%, Protestant 20.6% (Seventh-Day Adventist 6%, Pentecostal 5.6%, Baptist 4.1%, Methodist 3.7%, Church of God 1.2%), Jehovah's Witnesses 1.2%, other Christian 7.7%, Rastafarian 1.3%, other or unspecified 1.6%, none 6.1% (2001 census)

Dominican Republic

Official name: Dominican Republic

Capital city: Santo Domingo

Internet country code: .do

Flag description: A centered white cross that extends to the edges divides the flag into four rectangles - the top ones are blue (hoist side) and red, and the bottom ones are red (hoist side) and blue; a small coat of arms featuring a shield supported by an olive branch (left) and a palm branch (right) is at the center of the cross; above the shield a blue ribbon displays the motto, *Dios, Patria, Libertad* (God, Fatherland, Liberty), and below the shield, *Republica Dominicana* appears on a red ribbon

National bird: "Cigua Palmera"

National flower: Flor de la Caoba

Geographical description: Caribbean, eastern two-thirds of the island of Hispaniola, between the Caribbean Sea and the North Atlantic Ocean, east of Haiti

Total area: 48,670 sq km

Climate: Tropical maritime; little seasonal temperature variation; seasonal variation in rainfall

Nationality: noun: Dominican(s) *adjective:* Dominican

Population: 10,349,741 (July 2014 CIA est.)

Ethnic groups: Mixed 73%, white 16%, black 11%

Languages spoken: Spanish (Official)

Religions: Roman Catholic 95%, other 5%

Ecuador

Official name: Republic of Ecuador

Capital city: Quito

Internet country code: .ec

Flag description: Three horizontal bands of yellow (top, double width), blue, and red with the coat of arms superimposed at the center of the flag

National anthem: info in Spanish at http://www.presidencia.gov.ec/modulos.asp?id=20

Geographical description: Western South America, bordering the Pacific Ocean at the Equator, between Colombia and Peru

Total area: 283,561 sq km

Climate: Tropical along coast, becoming cooler inland at higher elevations; tropical in Amazonian jungle lowlands

Nationality: noun: Ecuadorian(s) *adjective:* Ecuadorian

Population: 15,654,411 (July 2014 CIA est.)

Ethnic groups: Mestizo (mixed Amerindian and white) 71.9%, Montubio 7.4%, Afroecuadorian 7.2%, Amerindian 7%, white 6.1%, other 0.4% (2010 census)

Languages spoken: Spanish (Castillian) 93% (official), Quechua 4.1%, other indigenous 0.7%, foreign 2.2%

Religions: Roman Catholic 95%, other 5%

Egypt

Official name: Arab Republic of Egypt

Capital city: Cairo

Internet country code: .eg

Flag description: Three equal horizontal bands of red (top), white, and black; the national emblem (a gold Eagle of Saladin facing the hoist side with a shield superimposed on its chest above a scroll bearing the name of the country in

Arabic) centered in the white band; design is based on the Arab Liberation

National anthem: "My homeland, my homeland, my hallowed land" (first line in English translation), lyrics by Younis al-Qadi, music by Sayed Darwish

Geographical description: Northern Africa, bordering the Mediterranean Sea, between Libya and the Gaza Strip, and the Red Sea north of Sudan, and includes the Asian Sinai Peninsula

Total area: 1,001,450 sq km

Climate: Desert; hot, dry summers with moderate winters

Nationality: noun: Egyptian(s) *adjective:* Egyptian

Population: 86,895,099 (July 2014 CIA est.)

Ethnic groups: Egyptian 99.6%, other 0.4% (2006 census)

Languages spoken: Arabic (official), English and French widely understood by educated classes

Religions: Muslim (predominantly Sunni) 90%, Christian (majority Coptic Orthodox, other Christians include Armenian Apostolic, Catholic, Maronite, Orthodox, and Anglican) 10% (2012 CIA est.)

El Salvador

Official name: Republic of El Salvador

Capital city: San Salvador

Internet country code: .sv

Flag description: Three equal horizontal bands of blue (top), white, and blue with the national coat of arms centered in the white band; the coat of arms features a round emblem encircled by the words *Republica de El Salvador en la America Central*

National anthem: "Saludemos la patria orgullosos" (first line of chorus), lyrics by Juan José Cañas, music by Juan Aberle

National bird: Torogoz or Talapo

National flower: Izote flower

National tree: Maquilishuat

Geographical description: Central America, bordering the North Pacific Ocean, between Guatemala and Honduras

Total area: 21,041 sq km

Climate: Tropical; rainy season (May to October); dry season (November to April); tropical on coast; temperate in uplands

Nationality: noun: Salvadoran(s) *adjective:* Salvadoran

Population: 6,125,512 (July 2014 CIA est.)

Ethnic groups: Mestizo 86.3%, white 12.7%, Amerindian 1% (2007 census)

Languages spoken: Spanish (official), Nahua (among some Amerindians)

Religions: Roman Catholic 57.1%, Protestant 21.2%, Jehovah's Witnesses 1.9%, Mormon 0.7%, other religions 2.3%, none 16.8% (2003 CIA est.)

Equatorial Guinea

Official name: Republic of Equatorial Guinea

Capital city: Malabo

Internet country code: .gq

Flag description: Three equal horizontal bands of green (top), white, and red with a blue isosceles triangle based on the hoist side and the coat of arms centered in the white band; the coat of arms has six yellow six-pointed stars (representing the mainland and five offshore islands) above a gray shield bearing a silk-cotton tree and below which is a scroll with the motto *Unidad, Paz, Justicia* (Unity, Peace, Justice)

Geographical description: Western Africa, bordering the Bight of Biafra, between Cameroon and Gabon

Total area: 28,051 sq km

Climate: Tropical; always hot, humid

Nationality: noun: Equatorial Guinean(s) or Equatoguinean(s) *adjective:* Equatorial Guinean or Equatoguinean

Population: 722,254 (July 2014 CIA est.)

Ethnic groups: Fang 85.7%, Bubi 6.5%, Mdowe 3.6%, Annobon 1.6%, Bujeba 1.1%, other 1.4% (1994 census)

Languages spoken: Spanish (official) 67.6%, other (includes French (official), Fang, Bubi 32.4% (1994 census)

Religions: Nominally Christian and predominantly Roman Catholic, pagan practices

Eritrea

Official name: State of Eritrea

Capital city: Asmara (Asmera)

Internet country code: .er

Flag description: Red isosceles triangle (based on the hoist side) dividing the flag into two right triangles; the upper triangle is green, the lower one is blue; a gold wreath encircling a gold olive branch is centered on the hoist side of the red triangle

National emblem: Camel

Geographical description: Eastern Africa, bordering the Red Sea, between Djibouti and Sudan

Total area: 117,600 sq km

Climate: Hot, dry desert strip along Red Sea coast; cooler and wetter in the central highlands (heaviest rainfall June to September); semiarid in western hills and lowlands

Nationality: noun: Estonian(s) *adjective:* Estonian

Population: 6,380,803 (July 2014 CIA est.)

Ethnic groups: Nine recognized ethnic groups: Tigrinya 55%, Tigre 30%, Saho 4%, Kunama 2%, Rashaida 2%, Bilen 2%, other (Afar, Beni Amir, Nera) 5% (2010 CIA est.)

Languages spoken: Tigrinya (official), Arabic (official), English (official), Tigre, Kunama, Afar, other Cushitic languages

Religions: Muslim, Coptic Christian, Roman Catholic, Protestant

Estonia

Official name: Republic of Estonia

Capital city: Tallinn

Internet country code: .ee

Flag description: Pre-1940 flag restored by Supreme Soviet in May 1990 - three equal horizontal bands of blue (top), black, and white

National anthem: "My Native Land," lyrics by Johann Voldemar Jannsen, music by Fredrik Pacius

National bird: Swallow

National flower: Cornflower

National stone: Limestone

Geographical description: Eastern Europe, bordering the Baltic Sea and Gulf of Finland, between Latvia and Russia

Total area: 45,228 sq km

Climate: Maritime, wet, moderate winters, cool summers

Nationality: noun:Estonian(s) *adjective:* Estonian

Population: 1,257,921 (July 2014 CIA est.)

Ethnic groups: Estonian 68.7%, Russian 24.8%, Ukrainian 1.7%, Belarusian 1%, Finn 0.6%, other 1.6%, unspecified 1.6% (2011 CIA est.)

Languages spoken: Estonian (official) 68.5%, Russian 29.6%, Ukrainian 0.6%, other 1.2%, unspecified 0.1% (2011 CIA est.)

Religions: Lutheran 9.9%, Orthodox 16.2%, other Christian (including Methodist, Seventh-Day Adventist, Roman Catholic, Pentecostal) 2.2%, other 0.9%, none 54.1%, unspecified 16.7% (2011 CIA est.)

Ethiopia

Official name: Federal Democratic Republic of Ethiopia

Capital city: Addis Ababa

Internet country code: .et

Flag description: Three equal horizontal bands of green (top), yellow, and red with a yellow pentagram and single yellow rays emanating from the angles between the points on a light blue disk centered on the three bands; Ethiopia is the oldest independent country in Africa, and the three main colors of her flag were so often adopted by other African countries upon independence that they became known as the pan-African colors

Geographical description: Eastern Africa, west of Somalia

Total area: 1,104,300 sq km

Climate: Tropical monsoon with wide topographic-induced variation

Nationality: noun: Ethiopian(s) *adjective:* Ethiopian

Population: 96,633,458

Ethnic groups: Oromo 34.4%, Amhara (Amara) 27%, Somali (Somalie) 6.2%, Tigray (Tigrinya) 6.1%, Sidama 4%, Gurage 2.5%, Welaita 2.3%, Hadiya 1.7%, Afar (Affar) 1.7%, Gamo 1.5%, Gedeo 1.3%, Silte 1.3%, Kefficho 1.2%, other 10.5% (2007 CIA est.)

Languages spoken: Oromo (official working language in the State of Oromiya) 33.8%, Amharic (official national language) 29.3%, Somali (official working language of the State of Sumale) 6.2%, Tigrigna (Tigrinya) (official working language of the State of Tigray) 5.9%, Sidamo 4%, Wolaytta 2.2%, Gurage 2%, Afar (official working language of the State of Afar) 1.7%, Hadiyya 1.7%, Gamo 1.5%, Gedeo 1.3%, Opuuo 1.2%, Kafa 1.1%, other 8.1%,

English (major foreign language taught in schools), Arabic (2007 CIA est.)

Religions: Ethiopian Orthodox 43.5%, Muslim 33.9%, Protestant 18.5%, traditional 2.7%, Catholic 0.7%, other 0.6% (2007 CIA est.)

Fiji

Official name: Republic of the Fiji Islands

Capital city: Suva

Internet country code: .fj

Flag description: Light blue with the flag of the United Kingdom in the upper hoist-side quadrant and the Fijian shield centered on the outer half of the flag; the shield depicts a yellow lion above a white field quartered by the cross of Saint George featuring stalks of sugarcane, a palm tree, bananas, and a white dove

National anthem: "Meda Dau Doka" (first line in English: "Blessing grant oh God of nations on the isles of Fiji"), lyrics by Michael Francis Alexander Prescott, music from traditional Fijian song

National symbol: Tabua (whale's tooth)

Geographical description: Oceania, island group in the South Pacific Ocean, about two-thirds of the way from Hawaii to New Zealand

Total area: 18,274 sq km

Climate: Tropical marine; only slight seasonal temperature variation

Nationality: noun: Fiji Islander or Fijian(s) *adjective:* Fiji or Fijian ("Fijian" should only be used to describe a thing or person of indigenous Fijian origin)

Population: 903,207 (July 2014 CIA est.)

Ethnic groups: iTaukei 56.8% (predominantly Melanesian with a Polynesian admixture), Indian 37.5%, Rotuman 1.2%, other 4.5% (European, part European, other Pacific Islanders, Chinese)

Languages spoken: English (official), Fijian (official), Hindustani

Religions: Protestant 45% (Methodist 34.6%, Assembly of God 5.7%, Seventh Day Adventist 3.9%, and Anglican 0.8%), Hindu 27.9%, other Christian 10.4%, Roman Catholic 9.1%, Muslim 6.3%, Sikh 0.3%, other 0.3%, none 0.8% (2007 CIA est.)

Finland

Official name: Republic of Finland

Capital city: Helsinki

Internet country code: .fi

Flag description: White with a blue cross extending to the edges of the flag; the vertical part of the cross is shifted to the hoist side in the style of the Dannebrog (Danish flag)

National anthem: "Maamme" (translated from the Swedish "Vårt land" [Our Land]), lyrics by Johan Ludvig Runeberg, music by Fredrik Pacius

National animal: Brown bear (Ursus arctos)

National bird: Whooper swan (Cygnus Cygnus)

National fish: Perch (Perca fluviatilis)

National flower: Lily-of-the-valley (Convallaria majalis)

National rock anthem: Granite

National tree: Birch (Betula pendula)

Geographical description: Northern Europe, bordering the Baltic Sea, Gulf of Bothnia, and Gulf of Finland, between Sweden and Russia

Total area: 338,145 sq km

Climate: Cold temperate; potentially subarctic but comparatively mild because of moderating influence of the North Atlantic Current, Baltic Sea, and more than 60,000 lakes

Nationality: noun: Finn(s) *adjective:* Finnish

Population: 5,268,799 (July 2014 CIA est.)

Ethnic groups: Finn 93.4%, Swede 5.6%, Russian 0.5%, Estonian 0.3%, Roma (Gypsy) 0.1%, Sami 0.1% (2006)

Languages spoken: Finnish (official) 94.2%, Swedish (official) 5.5%, other (small Sami- and Russian-speaking minorities) 0.2% (2012 CIA est.)

Religions: Lutheran 78.4%, Orthodox 1.1%, other Christian 1.1%, other 0.2%, none 19.2% (2010 CIA est.)

France

Official name: French Republic

Capital city: Paris

Internet country code: .fr (territories' codes are French Guinea .gf, Guadeloupe .gp, Martinique .mq, and Reunion .re)

Flag description: three equal vertical bands of blue (hoist side), white, and red; known as the "Le drapeau tricolore" (French Tricolor), the origin of the flag dates to 1790 and the French Revolution; the official flag for all French dependent areas

National anthem: "La Marseillaise" by Rouget de Lisle

National motto: "Liberté, Egalité, Fraternité" (Liberty, Equality, Fraternity)

National emblem: Gallic rooster

Geographical description: The continental territory is considered "metropolitan France" and is located in western Europe, bordering the Bay of Biscay and English Channel, between Belgium and Spain, southeast of the United Kingdom; bordering the Mediterranean Sea, between Italy and Spain.

Locations of French territories are as follows:

French Guiana: Northern South America, bordering the North Atlantic Ocean, between Brazil and Suriname.

Guadeloupe: Caribbean, islands between the Caribbean Sea and the North Atlantic Ocean, southeast of Puerto Rico.

Martinique: Caribbean, island between the Caribbean Sea and North Atlantic Ocean, north of Trinidad and Tobago.

Reunion: Southern Africa, island in the Indian Ocean, east of Madagascar

Total area: 643,801 sq km; 551,500 sq km (metropolitan France)

Climate: *metropolitan France:* generally cool winters and mild summers, but mild winters and hot summers

along the Mediterranean; occasional strong, cold, dry, north-to-northwesterly wind known as mistral.

French Guiana: tropical; hot, humid; little seasonal temperature variation.

Guadeloupe and Martinique: subtropical tempered by trade winds; moderately high humidity; rainy season (June to October); vulnerable to devastating cyclones (hurricanes) every eight years on average.

Reunion: tropical, but temperature moderates with elevation; cool and dry (May to November), hot and rainy (November to April)

Nationality: noun: Frenchman (men), Frenchwoman (women) *adjective:* French

Population: 66,259,012

Ethnic groups: Celtic and Latin with Teutonic, Slavic, North African, Indochinese, Basque minorities

Languages spoken: French (official) 100%, rapidly declining regional dialects and languages (Provencal, Breton, Alsatian, Corsican, Catalan, Basque, Flemish)

Religions: Metropolitan France: Roman Catholic 83-88%, Muslim 5-10%, Protestant 2%, Jewish 1%, unaffiliated 4%; territories: Roman Catholic, Protestant, Hindu, Muslim, Buddhist, and others

Gabon

Official name: Gabonese Republic

Capital city: Libreville

Internet country code: .ga

Flag description: Three equal horizontal bands of green (top), yellow, and blue

National anthem: "La Concorde"

National motto: "Gouvernement du peuple, par le peuple et pour le peuple"

Geographical description: Western Africa, bordering the Atlantic Ocean at the Equator, between Republic of the Congo and Equatorial Guinea

Total area: 267,667 sq km

Climate: Tropical; always hot, humid

Nationality: noun: Gabonese (singular and plural) *adjective:* Gabonese

Population: 1,672,597

Ethnic groups: Bantu tribes, including four major tribal groupings (Fang, Bapounou, Nzebi, Obamba); other Africans and Europeans, 154,000, including 10,700 French and 11,000 persons of dual nationality

Languages spoken: French (official), Fang, Myene, Nzebi, Bapounou/Eschira, Bandjabi

Religions: Christian 55%-75%, animist, Muslim less than 1%

The Gambia

Official name: Republic of The Gambia

Capital city: Banjul

Internet country code: .gm

Flag description: Three equal horizontal bands of red (top), blue with white edges, and green

National anthem: "For The Gambia, our homeland" (first line), adapted from the traditional Mandinka song "Foday Kaba Dumbuya"

Geographical description: Western Africa, bordering the North Atlantic Ocean and Senegal

Total area: 11,295 sq km

Climate: Tropical; hot, rainy season (June to November); cooler, dry season (November to May)

Nationality: noun: Gambian(s) *adjective:* Gambian

Population: 1,925,527 (July 2014 CIA est.)

Ethnic groups: African 99% (Mandinka 42%, Fula 18%, Wolof 16%, Jola 10%, Serahuli 9%, other 4%), non-African 1% (2003 census)

Languages spoken: English (official), Mandinka, Wolof, Fula, other indigenous vernaculars

Religions: Muslim 90%, Christian 8%, indigenous beliefs 2%

Georgia

Official name: Georgia

Capital city: Tbilisi

Internet country code: .ge

Flag description: White rectangle, in its central portion a red cross connecting all four sides of the flag; in each of the four corners is a small red bolnur-katskhuri cross; the five-cross flag appears to date back to the 14th century

National anthem: "Freedom" (translated by Irakli Charkviani), lyrics by David Magradze, music by Zakaria Paliashvili

Geographical description: Southwestern Asia, bordering the Black Sea, between Turkey and Russia

Total area: 69,700 sq km

Climate: Warm and pleasant; Mediterranean-like on Black Sea coast

Nationality: noun: Georgian(s) *adjective:* Georgian

Population: 4,935,880 (July 2014 CIA est.)

Ethnic groups: Georgian 83.8%, Azeri 6.5%, Armenian 5.7%, Russian 1.5%, other 2.5% (2002 census)

Languages spoken: Georgian (official) 71%, Russian 9%, Armenian 7%, Azeri 6%, other 7%

Religions: Orthodox Christian 83.9%, Muslim 9.9%, Armenian Apostolic 3.9&, Catholic 0.8%, other 0.8%, none 0.7% (2002 Census)

Germany

Official name: Federal Republic of Germany

Capital city: Berlin

Internet country code: .de

Flag description: Three equal horizontal bands of black (top), red, and gold

National anthem: Third verse of "Das Lied der Deutschen" by August Heinrich Hoffmann von Fallersleben, sung to Joseph Haydn's "Kaiserhymne"

Geographical description: Central Europe, bordering the Baltic Sea and the North Sea, between the Netherlands and Poland, south of Denmark

Total area: 357,022 sq km

Climate: Temperate and marine; cool, cloudy, wet winters and summers; occasional warm mountain (foehn) wind

Nationality: noun: German(s) *adjective:* German

Population: 80,996,685 (July 2014 CIA est.)

Ethnic groups: German 91.5%, Turkish 2.4%, other (including Greek, Italian, Polish, Russian, Serbo-Croatian, Spanish) 6.1%

Languages spoken: German

Religions: Protestant 34%, Roman Catholic 34%, Muslim 3.7%, unaffiliated or other 28.3%

Ghana

Official name: Republic of Ghana

Capital city: Accra

Internet country code: .gh

Flag description: Three equal horizontal bands of red (top), yellow, and green with a large black five-pointed star centered in the yellow band; uses the popular pan-African colors of Ethiopia; similar to the flag of Bolivia, which has a coat of arms centered in the yellow band

National anthem: "God bless our homeland Ghana" (first line)

Geographical description: Western Africa, bordering the Gulf of Guinea, between Cote d'Ivoire and Togo

Total area: 238,533 sq km

Climate: Tropical; warm and comparatively dry along southeast coast; hot and humid in southwest; hot and dry in north

Nationality: noun: Ghanaian(s) *adjective:* Ghanaian

Population: 25,758,108

Ethnic groups: Akan 47.5%, Mole-Dagbon 16.6%, Ewe 13.9%, Ga-Dangme 7.4%, Gurma 5.7%, Guan 3.7%, Grusi 2.5%, Mande-Busanga 1.1%, other 1.6% (2010 census)

Languages spoken: Asante 14.8%, Ewe 12.7%, Fante 9.9%, Boron (Brong) 4.6%, Dagomba 4.3%, Dangme 4.3%, Dagarte (Dagaba) 3.7%, Akyem 3.4%, Ga 3.4%, Akuapem 2.9%, other 36.1% (includes English [official]) (2000 Census)

Religions: Christian 71.2% (Pentecostal/Charismatic 28.3%, Protestant 18.4%, Catholic 13.1%, other 11.4%), Muslim 17.6%, traditional 5.2%, other 0.8%, none 5.2% (2010 census)

Greece

Official name: Hellenic Republic

Capital city: Athens

Internet country code: .gr

Flag description: Nine equal horizontal stripes of blue alternating with white; there is a blue square in the upper hoist-side corner bearing a white cross; the cross symbolizes Greek Orthodoxy, the established religion of the country

National anthem: "Hymn to Freedom" (English translation by Rudyard Kipling), first two verses of poem by Dionysios Solomos, music by Nicholas Mantzaros

Geographical description: Southern Europe, bordering the Aegean Sea, Ionian Sea, and the Mediterranean Sea, between Albania and Turkey

Total area: 131,957 sq km

Climate: Temperate; mild, wet winters; hot, dry summers

Nationality: noun: Greek(s) *adjective:* Greek

Population: 10,775,557 (July 2014 CIA est.)

Ethnic groups: Greek 93%, other (foreign citizens) 7% (2001 Census)

Languages spoken: Greek (official) 99%, other (including English, French, Turkish, Albanian) 1%

Religions: Greek Orthodox 98%, Muslim 1.3%, other (including Jewish, Catholic, Protestant and other religions) 0.7%

Grenada

Official name: Grenada

Capital city: Saint George's

Internet country code: .gd

Flag description: A rectangle divided diagonally into yellow triangles (top and bottom) and green triangles (hoist side and outer side), with a red border around the flag; there are seven yellow five-pointed stars with three centered in the top red border, three centered in the bottom red border, and one on a red disk superimposed at the center of the flag; there is also a symbolic nutmeg pod on the hoist-side triangle (Grenada is the world's second-largest producer of nutmeg, after Indonesia); the seven stars represent the seven administrative divisions

National anthem: "Hail! Grenada, land of ours" (first line)

Geographical description: Caribbean, island between the Caribbean Sea and Atlantic Ocean, north of Trinidad and Tobago

Total area: 344 sq km

Climate: Tropical; tempered by northeast trade winds

Nationality: noun: Grenadian(s) *adjective:* Grenadian

Population: 110,152 (July 2014 CIA est.)

Ethnic groups: Black 82%, mixed black and European 13%, European and East Indian 5%, and trace of Arawak/Carib Amerindian

Languages spoken: English (official), French patois

Religions: Roman Catholic 53%, Anglican 13.8%, other Protestant 33.2%

Guatemala

Official name: Republic of Guatemala

Capital city: Guatemala City

Internet country code: .gt

Flag description: Three equal vertical bands of light blue (hoist side), white, and light blue with the coat of arms centered in the white band; the coat of arms includes a green and red quetzal (the national bird) and a scroll bearing the inscription *Libertad 15 de Septiembre de 1821* (the original date of independence from Spain) all superimposed on a pair of crossed rifles and a pair of crossed swords and framed by a wreath

National bird: Quetzal

Geographical description: Central America, bordering the North Pacific Ocean, between El Salvador and Mexico, and bordering the Gulf of Honduras (Caribbean Sea) between Honduras and Belize

Total area: 108,889 sq km

Climate: Tropical; hot, humid in lowlands; cooler in highlands

Nationality: noun: Guatemalan(s) *adjective:* Guatemalan

Population: 14,647,083 (July 2014 CIA est.)

Ethnic groups: Mestizo (mixed Amerindian-Spanish - in local Spanish called *Ladino*) and European 59.4%, K'iche 9.1%, Kaqchikel 8.4%, Mam 7.9%, Q'eqchi 6.3%, other Mayan 8.6%, indigenous non-Mayan 0.2%, other 0.1% (2001 census)

Languages spoken: Spanish 60%, Amerindian languages 40%

Religions: Roman Catholic, Protestant, indigenous Mayan beliefs

Guinea

Official name: Republic of Guinea

Capital city: Conakry

Internet country code: .gn

Flag description: Three equal vertical bands of red (hoist side), yellow, and green; uses the popular pan-African colors of Ethiopia

Geographical description: Western Africa, bordering the North Atlantic Ocean, between Guinea-Bissau and Sierra Leone

Total area: 245,857 sq km

Climate: Generally hot and humid; monsoonal-type rainy season (June to November) with southwesterly winds; dry season (December to May) with northeasterly harmattan winds

Nationality: noun: Guinean(s) *adjective:* Guinean

Population: 11,474,383 (July 2014 CIA est.)

Ethnic groups: Peuhl 40%, Malinke 30%, Soussou 20%, smaller ethnic groups 10%

Languages spoken: French (official), local ethnic languages

Religions: Muslim 85%, Christian 8%, indigenous beliefs 7%

Guinea-Bissau

Official name: Republic of Guinea-Bissau

Capital city: Bissau

Internet country code: .gw

Flag description: Two equal horizontal bands of yellow (top) and green with a vertical red band on the hoist side; there is a black five-pointed star centered in the red band; uses the popular pan-African colors of Ethiopia

National anthem: "Esta é a Nossa Pátria Bem Amada"

National motto: Unidade, Luta, Progress (Union, Fight, Progress)

Geographical description: Western Africa, bordering the North Atlantic Ocean, between Guinea and Senegal

Total area: 36,125 sq km

Climate: Tropical; generally hot and humid; monsoonal-type rainy season (June to November) with southwesterly winds; dry season (December to May) with northeasterly harmattan winds

Nationality: noun: Bissau-Guinean(s) *adjective:* Bissau-Guinean

Population: 1,693,398 (July 2014 CIA est.)

Ethnic groups: African 99% (includes Balanta 30%, Fula 20%, Manjaca 14%, Mandinga 13%, Papel 7%), European and mulatto less than 1%

Languages spoken: Portuguese (official), Crioulo, French, African languages

Religions: Muslim 50%, indigenous beliefs 40%, Christian 10%

Guyana

Official name: Cooperative Republic of Guyana

Capital city: Georgetown

Internet country code: .gy

Flag description: Green, with a red isosceles triangle (based on the hoist side) superimposed on a long, yellow arrowhead; there is a narrow, black border between the red and yellow, and a narrow, white border between the yellow and the green

National anthem: "Dear land of Guyana of rivers and plains" (first line)

Geographical description: Northern South America, bordering the North Atlantic Ocean, between Suriname and Venezuela

Total area: 214,969 sq km

Climate: Tropical; hot, humid, moderated by northeast trade winds; two rainy seasons (May to August, November to January)

Nationality: noun: Guyanese (singular and plural) *adjective:* Guyanese

Population: 735,554

Ethnic groups: East Indian 43.5%, black (African) 30.2%, mixed 16.7%, Amerindian 9.1%, other 0.5% (2002 Census)

Languages spoken: English, Amerindian languages (primarily Carib and Arawak), Guyanese Creole, Caribbean Hindustani (a dialect of Hindi), Urdu

Religions: Protestant 30.5% (Pentecostal 16.9%, Anglican 6.9%, Seventh Day Adventist 5%, Methodist 1.7%), Hindu 28.4%, Roman Catholic 8.1%, Muslim 7.2%, Jehovah's Witnesses 1.1%, other Christian 17.7%, other 1.9%, none 4.3%, unspecified 0.9% (2002 CIA est.)

Haiti

Official name: Republic of Haiti

Capital city: Port-au-Prince

Internet country code: .ht

Flag description: Two equal horizontal bands of blue (top) and red with a centered white rectangle bearing the coat of arms, which contains a palm tree flanked by flags and two cannons above a scroll bearing the motto *L'union fait la force* (Union Makes Strength)

National anthem: "La Dessalinienne," lyrics by Justin Lhérisson, music by Nicolas Geffrard

Geographical description: Caribbean, western one-third of the island of Hispaniola, between the Caribbean Sea and the North Atlantic Ocean, west of the Dominican Republic

Total area: 27,750 sq km

Climate: Tropical; semiarid where mountains in east cut off trade winds

Nationality: noun: Haitian(s) *adjective:* Haitian

Population: 9,996,731

Ethnic groups: Black 95%, mulatto and white 5%

Languages spoken: French (official), Creole (official)

Religions: Roman Catholic 80%, Protestant 16% (Baptist 10%, Pentecostal 4%, Adventist 1%, other 1%), none 1%, other 3%

Honduras

Official name: Republic of Honduras

Capital city: Tegucigalpa

Internet country code: .hn

Flag description: Three equal horizontal bands of blue (top), white, and blue with five blue, five-pointed stars arranged in an X pattern centered in the white band; the stars represent the members of the former Federal Republic of Central America - Costa Rica, El Salvador, Guatemala, Honduras, and Nicaragua

National anthem: "Your flag is a splendor of sky" (first line in English translation); lyrics by Augusto Constancio Coello, music by Carlos Hartling

National flower: Orquid Rhyncholaelya Digviana

Geographical description: Central America, bordering the Caribbean Sea, between Guatemala and Nicaragua and bordering the Gulf of Fonseca (North Pacific Ocean), between El Salvador and Nicaragua

Total area: 112,090 sq km

Climate: Subtropical in lowlands, temperate in mountains

Nationality: noun: Honduran(s) *adjective:* Honduran

Population: 8,598,561

Ethnic groups: Mestizo (mixed Amerindian and European) 90%, Amerindian 7%, African 2%, European 1%

Languages spoken: Spanish (official), Amerindian dialects

Religions: Roman Catholic 97%, Protestant 3%

Hong Kong

Official name: Hong Kong Special Administrative Region [of China]

Internet country code: .hk

Flag description: Red with a stylized, white, five-petal bauhinia flower in the center

Geographical description: Eastern Asia, bordering the South China Sea and China

Total area: 1,104 sq km

Climate: Subtropical monsoon; cool and humid in winter, hot and rainy from spring through summer, warm and sunny in fall

Nationality: noun: Chinese or Hong Konger *adjective:* Chinese or Hong Konger

Population: 7,112,688 (July 2014 CIA est.)

Ethnic groups: Chinese 93.1%, Indonesian 1.9%, Filipino 1.9%, other 3% (2011 CIA est.)

Languages spoken: Cantonese (official) 89.5%, English (official) 3.5%, Putonghua (Mandarin) 1.4%, other Chinese dialects 4%, other 1.6% (2011 CIA est.)

Religions: Eclectic mixture of local religions 90%, Christian 10%

Hungary

Official name: Republic of Hungary

Capital city: Budapest

Internet country code: .hu

Flag description: Three equal horizontal bands of red (top), white, and green

National anthem: "Himnusz" (first line in English translation: O, my God, the Magyar bless), lyrics by Ferenc Kölcsey, music by Ferenc Erkel

Geographical description: Central Europe, northwest of Romania

Total area: 93,028 sq km

Climate: Temperate; cold, cloudy, humid winters; warm summers

Nationality: noun: Hungarian(s) *adjective:* Hungarian

Population: 9,919,128 (July 2014 CIA est.)

Ethnic groups: Hungarian 92.3%, Roma 1.9%, other or unknown 5.8% (2001 Census)

Languages spoken: Hungarian 84.6%, other or unspecified 16.4% (2011 CIA est.)

Religions: Roman Catholic 37.2%, Calvinist 11.6%, Lutheran 2.2%, Greek Catholic 1.8%, other 1.9%, none 18.2%, unspecified 27.2% (2011 CIA est.)

Iceland

Official name: Republic of Iceland

Capital city: Reykjavik

Internet country code: .is

Flag description: Blue with a red cross outlined in white extending to the edges of the flag; the vertical part of the cross is shifted to the hoist side in the style of the Dannebrog (Danish flag)

National anthem: "Ó, Guð vors lands" (O, God of Our Land), lyrics by Matthías Jochumsson, music by Sveinbjörn Sveinbjörnsson

Geographical description: Northern Europe, island between the Greenland Sea and the North Atlantic Ocean, northwest of the United Kingdom

Total area: 103,000 sq km

Climate: Temperate; moderated by North Atlantic Current; mild, windy winters; damp, cool summers

Nationality: noun: Icelander(s) *adjective:* Icelandic

Population: 317,351 (July 2014 CIA est.)

Ethnic groups: Homogeneous mixture of descendants of Norwegians and Celts 94%, population of foreign origin 6%

Languages spoken: Icelandic, English, Nordic languages, German widely spoken

Religions: Evangelical Lutheran Church of Iceland (official) 76.2%, Roman Catholic 3.4%, Reykjavik Free Church 2.9%, Hafnarfjorour Free Church 1.9%, The Independent Congregation 1%, other religions 3.6% (includes Pentecostal and Asatru Association), none 5.2%, other or unspecified 5.9% (2013 CIA est.)

India

Official name: Republic of India

Capital city: New Delhi

Internet country code: .in

Flag description: Three equal horizontal bands of saffron (subdued orange) (top), white, and green with a blue chakra (24-spoked wheel) centered in the white band

National anthem: "Jana-gana-mana" by Rabindranath Tagore ("Thou art the ruler of the minds of all people," Tagore's translation of first line)

National animal: Tiger (Panthera tigris)

National bird: Indian peacock (Pavo cristatus)

National flower: Lotus (Nelumbo Nucipera Gaertn)

National fruit: Mango

National song: "Vande Mataram" by Bankimchandra Chatterji (first line translated by Sri Aurobindo: "I bow to thee, Mother")

National tree: Indian fig tree or banyan tree (Ficus bengalensis)

Geographical description: Southern Asia, bordering the Arabian Sea and the Bay of Bengal, between Burma and Pakistan

Total area: 3,287,263 sq km

Climate: Varies from tropical monsoon in south to temperate in north

Nationality: noun: Indian(s) *adjective:* Indian

Population: 1,236,344,631 (July 2014 CIA est.)

Ethnic groups: Indo-Aryan 72%, Dravidian 25%, Mongoloid and other 3% (2000)

Languages spoken: Hindi 41%, Bengali 8.1%, Telugu 7.2%, Marathi 7%, Tamil 5.9%, Urdu 5%, Gujarati 4.5%, Kannada 3.7%, Malayalam 3.2%, Oriya 3.2%, Punjabi 2.8%, Assamese 1.3%, Maithili 1.2%, other 5.9%

Religions: Hindu 80.5%, Muslim 13.4%, Christian 2.3%, Sikh 1.9%, other (including Buddhist, Jain, Parsi) 1.8%, unspecified 0.1% (2001 Census)

Indonesia

Official name: Republic of Indonesia

Capital city: Jakarta

Internet country code: .id

Flag description: Two equal horizontal bands of red (top) and white; similar to the flag of Monaco, which is shorter; also similar to the flag of Poland, which is white (top) and red

National anthem: "Indonesia Raya" (Great Indonesia) by Wage Rudolf Supratman

Geographical description: Southeastern Asia, archipelago between the Indian Ocean and the Pacific Ocean

Total area: 1,904,569 sq km

Climate: Tropical; hot, humid; more moderate in highlands

Nationality: noun: Indonesian(s) *adjective:* Indonesian

Population: 253,609,643 (July 2014 CIA est.)

Ethnic groups: Javanese 40.1%, Sundanese 15.5%, Malay 3.7%, Batak 3.6%, Madurese 3%, Betawi 2.9%, Minangkabau 2.7%, Buginese 2.7%, Bantenese 2%, Banjarese 1.7%, Balinese 1.7%, Acehnese 1.4%, Dayak 1.4%, Sasak 1.3%, Chinese 1.2%, other 15% (2010 CIA est.)

Languages spoken: Bahasa Indonesia (official, modified form of Malay), English, Dutch, local dialects (the most widely spoken of which is Javanese)

Religions: Muslim 87.2%, Christian 7%, Roman Catholic 2.9%, Hindu 1.7%, other 0.9% (includes Buddhist and Confucian), unspecified 0.4% (2010 CIA est.)

Iran

Official name: Islamic Republic of Iran

Capital city: Tehran

Internet country code: .ir

Flag description: Three equal horizontal bands of green (top), white, and red; the national emblem (a stylized representation of the word Allah in the shape of a tulip, a symbol of martyrdom) in red is centered in the white band; *Allah Akbar* (God Is Great) in white Arabic script is repeated 11 times along the bottom edge of the green band and 11 times along the top edge of the red band

Geographical description: Middle East, bordering the Gulf of Oman, the Persian Gulf, and the Caspian Sea, between Iraq and Pakistan

Total area: 1,648,195 sq km

Climate: Mostly arid or semiarid, subtropical along Caspian coast

Nationality: noun: Iranian(s) *adjective:* Iranian

Population: 80,840,713 (July 2014 CIA est.)

Ethnic groups: Persian 61%, Azeri 16%, Kurd 10%, Lur 6%, Baloch 2%, Arab 2%, Turkmen and Turkic tribes 2%, other 1%

Languages spoken: Persian (official) 53%, Azeri Turkic and Turkic dialects 18%, Kurdish 10%, Gilaki and Mazandarani 7%, Luri 6%, Balochi 2%, Arabic 2%, other 2%

Religions: Muslim (official) 99.4% (Shia 90-95%, Sunni 5-10%), other (includes Zoroastrian, Jewish, and Christian) 0.3%, unspecified 0.4% (2011 CIA est.)

Iraq

Official name: Republic of Iraq

Capital city: Baghdad

Internet country code: .iq

Flag description: Three equal horizontal bands of red (top), white, and black with three green five-pointed stars in a horizontal line centered in the white band; the phrase *Allahu Akbar* (God Is Great) in green Arabic script - *Allahu* to the right of the middle star and *Akbar* to the left of the middle star - was added in January 1991 during the Persian Gulf crisis; similar to the flag of Syria, which has two stars but no script, Yemen, which has a plain white band, and that of Egypt which has a gold Eagle of Saladin centered in the white band; design is based upon the Arab Liberation colors

Geographical description: Middle East, bordering the Persian Gulf, between Iran and Kuwait

Total area: 438,317 sq km

Climate: Mostly desert; mild to cool winters with dry, hot, cloudless summers; northern mountainous regions along Iranian and Turkish borders experience cold winters with occasionally heavy snows that melt in early spring, sometimes causing extensive flooding in central and southern Iraq

Nationality: noun: Iraqi(s) *adjective:* Iraqi

Population: 32,585,692 (July 2014 CIA est.)

Ethnic groups: Arab 75%-80%, Kurdish 15%-20%, Turkoman, Chaldean, Assyrian, or others less than 5%

Languages spoken: Arabic (official), Kurdish (official), Turkmen (a Turkish dialect) and Assyrian (Neo-Aramaic) are official in areas where they constitute a majority of the population), Armenian

Religions: Muslim (official) 99% (Shia 60%-65%, Sunni 32%-37%), Christian 0.8%, Hindu <.1, Buddhist <.1, Jewish <.1, folk religion <.1, unafilliated .1, other <.1

Ireland

Official name: Ireland

Capital city: Dublin

Internet country code: .ie

Flag description: Three equal vertical bands of green (hoist side), white, and orange

National anthem: "The Soldier's Song" by Peadar Kearney

National emblem: Harp

Geographical description: Western Europe, occupying five-sixths of the island of Ireland in the North Atlantic Ocean, west of Great Britain

Total area: 70,273 sq km

Climate: Temperate maritime; modified by North Atlantic Current; mild winters, cool summers; consistently humid; overcast about half the time

Nationality: noun: Irishman(men), Irishwoman(women), Irish (collective plural) *adjective:* Irish

Population: 4,832,765 (July 2014 CIA est.)

Ethnic groups: Irish 84.5%, other white 9.8%, Asian 1.9%, black 1.4%, mixed and other 0.9%, unspecified 1.6% (2011 CIA est.)

Languages spoken: English (official, the language generally used), Irish (Gaelic or Gaeilge) (official, spoken mainly in areas along the western coast)

Religions: Roman Catholic 84.7%, Church of Ireland 2.7%, other Christian 2.7%, Muslim 1.1%, other 1.7%, unspecified 1.5%, none 5.7% (2011 CIA est.)

Israel

Official name: State of Israel

Capital city: Jerusalem

Internet country code: .il

Flag description: White with a blue hexagram (six-pointed linear star) known as the Magen David (Shield of David) centered between two equal horizontal blue bands near the top and bottom edges of the flag

National anthem: "Hatikva"

National emblem: Menorah

Geographical description: Middle East, bordering the Mediterranean Sea, between Egypt and Lebanon

Total area: 20,770 sq km

Climate: Temperate; hot and dry in southern and eastern desert areas

Nationality: noun: Israeli(s) *adjective:* Israeli

Population: 7,821,850

Ethnic groups: Jewish 75.1% (of which Israel-born 73.6%, Europe/America/Oceania-born 17.9%, Africa-born 5.2%, Asia-born 3.2%), non-Jewish 24.9% (mostly Arab) (2012 CIA est.)

Languages spoken: Hebrew (official), Arabic (official for Arab minority), English, Russian

Religions: Jewish 75.1%, Muslim 17.4%, Christian 2%, Druze 1.6%, other 3.9% (2012 CIA est.)

Italy

Official name: Italian Republic

Capital city: Rome

Internet country code: .it

Flag description: Three equal vertical bands of green (hoist side), white, and red; inspired by the French flag brought to Italy by Napoleon in 1797

National anthem: "Fratelli d'Italia" (Brothers of Italy), lyrics by Geoffredo Mameli, music by Michele Novaro

Geographical description: Southern Europe, a peninsula extending into the central Mediterranean Sea, northeast of Tunisia

Total area: 301,340 sq km

Climate: Predominantly Mediterranean; Alpine in far north; hot, dry in south

Nationality: noun: Italian(s) *adjective:* Italian

Population: 61,680,122 (July 2014 CIA est.)

Ethnic groups: Italian (includes small clusters of German-, French-, and Slovene-Italians in the north and Albanian-Italians and Greek-Italians in the south)

Languages spoken: Italian (official), German (parts of Trentino-Alto Adige region are predominantly German speaking), French (small French-speaking minority in Valle d'Aosta region), Slovene (Slovene-speaking minority in the Trieste-Gorizia area)

Religions: Christian 80% (overwhelmingly Roman Catholic with very small groups of Jehovah's Witnesses and Protestants), Muslim (about 800,000 to 1 million), Atheist and Agnostic 20%

Jamaica

Official name: Jamaica

Capital city: Kingston

Internet country code: .jm

Flag description: Diagonal yellow cross divides the flag into four triangles - green (top and bottom) and black (hoist side and outer side)

National anthem: "Eternal Father bless our land" (first line), composed by Hugh Sherlock, Robert Lightbourne, Mapletoft Poulle and Mrs. Poulle

National motto: "Out of Many One People"

National bird: Doctor-Bird (Trochilus polytmus) or Swallow-Tail Hummingbird

National flower: Lignum Vitae (Guiacum officinale)

National fruit: Ackee (Blighia sapida)

National song: "I Pledge My Heart," lyrics by Victor Stafford Reid, sung to tune of "I Vow to Thee My Country"

National tree: Blue Mahoe (Hibiscus elatus)

Geographical description: Caribbean, island in the Caribbean Sea, south of Cuba

Total area: 10,991 sq km

Climate: Tropical; hot, humid; temperate interior

Nationality: noun: Jamaican(s) *adjective:* Jamaican

Population: 2,930,050 (July 2014 CIA est.)

Ethnic groups: Black 92.1%, mixed 6.1%, East Indian 0.8%, other 0.4%, unspecified 0.7% (2011 CIA est.)

Languages spoken: English, patois

Religions: Protestant 64.8% (includes Seventh Day Adventist 12.0%, Pentecostal 11.0%, Other Church of God 9.2%, New Testament Church of God 7.2%, Baptist 6.7%, Church of God in Jamaica 4.8%, Church of God of Prophecy 4.5%, Anglican 2.8%, United Church 2.1%, Methodist 1.6%, Revived 1.4%, Brethren .9%, and Moravian .7%), Roman Catholic 2.2%, Jehovah's Witness 1.9%, Rastafarian 1.1%, other 6.5%, none 21.3%, unspecified 2.3% (2011 CIA est.)

Japan

Official name: Japan

Capital city: Tokyo

Internet country code: .jp

Flag description: White with a large red disk (representing the sun without rays) in the center

National anthem: "Kimigayo," lyrics from traditional poem of unknown authorship, music by Hayashi Hiromori

Geographical description: Eastern Asia, island chain between the North Pacific Ocean and the Sea of Japan, east of the Korean Peninsula

Total area: 377,915 sq km

Climate: Varies from tropical in south to cool temperate in north

Nationality: noun: Japanese (singular and plural) *adjective:* Japanese

Population: 127,103,388 (July 2014 CIA est.)

Ethnic groups: Japanese 98.5%, Koreans 0.5%, Chinese 0.4%, other 0.6%

Languages spoken: Japanese

Religions: Shintoism 83.9%, Buddhism 71.4%, Christianity 2%, other 7.8%

Jordan

Official name: Hashemite Kingdom of Jordan

Capital city: Amman

Internet country code: .jo

Flag description: Three equal horizontal bands of black (top), representing the Abbassid Caliphate; white, representing the Ummayyad Caliphate; and green, representing the Fatimid Caliphate; a red isosceles triangle on the hoist side, representing the Great Arab Revolt of 1916, and bearing a small white seven-pointed star symbolizing the seven verses of the opening Sura (Al-Fatiha) of the Koran; the seven points on the star represent faith in One God, humanity, national spirit, humility, social justice, virtue, and aspirations; design is based on the Arab Revolt flag of World War I

National anthem: "A-Sha-al Maleek"

Geographical description: Middle East, northwest of Saudi Arabia

Total area: 89,342 sq km

Climate: Mostly arid desert; rainy season in west (November to April)

Nationality: noun: Jordanian(s) *adjective:* Jordanian

Population: 7,930,491 (July 2014 CIA est.)

Ethnic groups: Arab 98%, Circassian 1%, Armenian 1%

Languages spoken: Arab (official), English

Religions: Muslim 97.2% (official; predominantly Sunni), Christian 2.2% (majority Greek Orthodox, but some Greek and Roman Catholics, Syrian Orthodox, Coptic Orthodox, Armenian Orthodox, and Protestant denominations), Buddhist 0.4%, Hindu 0.1%, Jewish <.1, folk religion <.1, unaffiliated <.1, other <.1 (2010 CIA est.)

Kazakhstan

Official name: Republic of Kazakhstan

Capital city: Astana

Internet country code: .kz

Flag description: Sky blue background representing the endless sky and a gold sun with 32 rays soaring above a golden steppe eagle in the center; on the hoist side is a national ornamentation in gold

National anthem: "We are a valiant people, sons of honour" (first line in English translation), lyrics by Muzafar Alimbayev, Kadyr Myrzaliyev, Tumanbai Moldagaliyev and Zhadyra Daribayeva, music by Mukan Tulebayev, Eugeny Brusilovsky and Latif Khamidi

Geographical description: Central Asia, northwest of China; a small portion west of the Ural River in eastern-most Europe

Total area: 2,724,900 sq km

Climate: Continental, cold winters and hot summers, arid and semiarid

Nationality: noun: Kazakhstani(s) *adjective:* Kazakhstani

Population: 17,948,816 (July 2014 CIA est.)

Ethnic groups: Kazakh (Qazaq) 63.1%, Russian 23.7%, Uzbek 2.9%, Ukrainian 2.1%, Uighur 1.4%, Tatar 1.3%, German 1.1%, other 4.4% (2009 CIA est.)

Languages spoken: Kazakh (Qazaq, state language) 64.4%, Russian (official, used in everyday business, designated the "language of interethnic communication") 95% (2001 CIA est.)

Religions: Muslim 70.2%, Christian 26.2% (mainly Russian Orthodox), other 0.2%, atheist 2.8%, unspecified 0.5% (2009 CIA est.)

Kenya

Official name: Republic of Kenya

Capital city: Nairobi

Internet country code: .ke

Flag description: Three equal horizontal bands of black (top), red, and green; the red band is edged in white; a large warrior's shield covering crossed spears is superimposed at the center

National anthem: "Ee Mungu nguvu yetu" (first line in English translation: "O God of all creation")

Geographical description: Eastern Africa, bordering the Indian Ocean, between Somalia and Tanzania

Total area: 580,367 sq km

Climate: Varies from tropical along coast to arid in interior

Nationality: noun: Kenyan(s) *adjective:* Kenyan

Population: 45,010,056

Ethnic groups: Kikuyu 22%, Luhya 14%, Luo 13%, Kalenjin 12%, Kamba 11%, Kisii 6%, Meru 6%, other African 15%, non-African (Asian, European, and Arab) 1%

Languages spoken: English (official), Kiswahili (official), numerous indigenous languages

Religions: Christian 82.5% (Protestant 47.4%, Catholic 23.3%, other 11.8%), Muslim 11.1%, Traditionalists 1.6%, other 1.7%, none 2.4%, unspecified 0.7% (2009 census)

Kiribati

Official name: Republic of Kiribati

Capital city: Tarawa

Internet country code: .ki

Flag description: The upper half is red with a yellow frigate bird flying over a yellow rising sun, and the lower half is blue with three horizontal wavy white stripes to represent the ocean

Geographical description: Oceania, group of 33 coral atolls in the Pacific Ocean, straddling the Equator; the capital Tarawa is about one-half of the way from Hawaii to Australia; note - on 1 January 1995, Kiribati proclaimed that all of its territory lies in the same time zone as its Gilbert Islands group (UTC +12) even though the Phoenix Islands and the Line Islands under its jurisdiction lie on the other side of the International Date Line

Total area: 811 sq km

Climate: Tropical; marine, hot and humid, moderated by trade winds

Nationality: noun: I-Kiribati (singular and plural, pronounced ee-keer-ah-bhass) *adjective:* I-Kiribati

Population: 104,488 (July 2014 CIA est.)

Ethnic groups: I-Kiribati 89.5%, I-Kiribati/mixed 9.7%, Tuvaluan 0.1%, other 0.8% (2010 CIA est.)

Languages spoken: English (official), Gilbertese/I-Kiribati

Religions: Roman Catholic 55.8%, Kempsville Presbyterian Church 33.5%, Mormon 4.7%, Baha'i 2.3%, Seventh-Day Adventist 2%, other 1.5%, none 0.2%, unspecified 0.05% (2010 CIA est.)

Korea, North

Official name: Democratic People's Republic of Korea

Capital city: Pyongyang

Internet country code: .kp

Flag description: Three horizontal bands of blue (top), red (triple width), and blue; the red band is edged in white; on the hoist side of the red band is a white disk with a red five-pointed star

Geographical description: Eastern Asia, northern half of the Korean Peninsula bordering the Korea Bay and the Sea of Japan, between China and South Korea

Total area: 120,538 sq km

Climate: Temperate with rainfall concentrated in summer

Nationality: noun: Korean(s) *adjective:* Korean

Population: 24,851,627 (July 2014 CIA est.)

Ethnic groups: Racially homogeneous; there is a small Chinese community and a few ethnic Japanese

Languages spoken: Korean

Religions: Traditionally Buddhist and Confucianist, some Christian and syncretic Chondogyo (Religion of the Heavenly Way)

Korea, South

Official name: Republic of Korea

Capital city: Seoul

Internet country code: .kr

Flag description: White with a red (top) and blue yin-yang symbol in the center; there is a different black trigram

from the ancient *I Ching* (Book of Changes) in each corner of the white field

National anthem: "Aegukga" (Love the Country)

National flower: Rose of Sharon (Hibiscus Syriacus L.)

Geographical description: Eastern Asia, southern half of the Korean Peninsula bordering the Sea of Japan and the Yellow Sea

Total area: 99,720 sq km

Climate: Temperate, with rainfall heavier in summer than winter

Nationality: noun: Korean(s) *adjective:* Korean

Population: 49,039,986 (July 2014 CIA est.)

Ethnic groups: Homogeneous (except for about 20,000 Chinese)

Languages spoken: Korean, English

Religions: Christian 31.6% (Protestant 24%, Roman Catholic 7.6%), Buddhist 24.2%, other or unknown 0.9%, none 43.3% (2010 survey)

Kuwait

Official name: State of Kuwait

Capital city: Kuwait City

Internet country code: .kw

Flag description: Three equal horizontal bands of green (top), white, and red with a black trapezoid based on the hoist side; design, which dates to 1961, based on the Arab revolt flag of World War I

National anthem: "Kuwait, My Country, May you be safe and glorious!" (first line in English translation), lyrics by Meshari Al-Adwani, music by Ibrahim Al-Soula

Geographical description: Middle East, bordering the Persian Gulf, between Iraq and Saudi Arabia

Total area: 17,818 sq km

Climate: Dry desert; intensely hot summers; short, cool winters

Nationality: noun: Kuwaiti(s) *adjective:* Kuwaiti

Population: 2,742,711

Ethnic groups: Kuwaiti 31.3%, other Arab 27.9%, Asian 37.8%, African 1.9%, other 1.1% (includes European, North American, South American, and Australian) (2013 CIA est.)

Languages spoken: Arab (official), English

Religions: Muslim (official) 76.7%, Christian 17.3%, other and unspecified 5.9%

Kyrgyzstan

Official name: Kyrgyz Republic

Capital city: Bishkek

Internet country code: .kg

Flag description: Red field with a yellow sun in the center having 40 rays representing the 40 Kyrgyz tribes; on the obverse side the rays run counterclockwise, on the reverse, clockwise; in the center of the sun is a red ring crossed by two sets of three lines, a stylized representation of the roof of the traditional Kyrgyz yurt

Geographical description: Central Asia, west of China

Total area: 199,951 sq km

Climate: Dry continental to polar in high Tien Shan; subtropical in southwest (Fergana Valley); temperate in northern foothill zone

Nationality: noun: Kyrgyzstani(s) *adjective:* Kyrgyzstani

Population: 5,604,212 (July 2014 CIA est.)

Ethnic groups: Kyrgyz 64.9%, Uzbek 13.8%, Russian 12.5%, Dungan 1.1%, Ukrainian 1%, Uighur 1%, other 5.7% (1999 census)

Languages spoken: Kyrgyz (official) 64.7%, Uzbek 13.6%, Russian (official) 12.5%, Dungun 1%, other 8.2%

Religions: Muslim 75%, Russian Orthodox 20%, other 5%

Laos

Official name: Lao People's Democratic Republic

Capital city: Vientiane

Internet country code: .la

Flag description: Three horizontal bands of red (top), blue (double width), and red with a large white disk centered in the blue band

National anthem: "Xat Lao"

Geographical description: Southeastern Asia, northeast of Thailand, west of Vietnam

Total area: 236,800 sq. km

Climate: Tropical monsoon; rainy season (May to November); dry season (December to April)

Nationality: noun: Lao(s) or Laotian(s) *adjective:* Lao or Laotian

Population: 6,803,699 (July 2014 CIA est.)

Ethnic groups: Lao 55%, Khmou 11%, Hmong 8%, other (over 100 minor ethnic groups) 26% (2005 census)

Languages spoken: Lao (official), French, English, local languages

Religions: Buddhist 67%, Christian 1.5%, other and unspecified 31.5% (2005 census)

Latvia

Official name: Republic of Latvia

Capital city: Riga

Internet country code: .lv

Flag description: Three horizontal bands of maroon (top), white (half-width), and maroon

National anthem: "Dievs, svētī Latviju!" (God bless Latvia!), by Kārlis Baumanis (better known as Baumaņu Kārlis)

National bird: Baltā cielava or white wagtail (Motacilla alba)

National flower: Pīpene or daisy (Leucanthemum vulgare, earlier also known as Chrysanthemum leucanthemum)

National insect: Two-spot ladybird (Adalia bipunctata)

National river: Daugava, the "river of fate" or "mother of rivers"

National stone: Amber

National trees: Linden, or lime tree (Tilia cordata, Latvian: liepa) and the oak (Quercus robur, Latvian: ozols)

Geographical description: Eastern Europe, bordering the Baltic Sea, between Estonia and Lithuania

Total area: 64,589 sq. km

Climate: Maritime; wet, moderate winters

Nationality: noun: Latvian(s) *adjective:* Latvian

Population: 2,165,165 (July 2014 CIA est.)

Ethnic groups: Latvian 61.1%, Russian 26.2%, Belarusian 3.5%, Ukrainian 2.3%, Polish 2.2%, Lithuanian 1.3%, other 3.4% (2013 CIA est.)

Languages spoken: Latvian (official) 56.3%, Russian 33.8%, other 0.6% (includes Polish, Ukrainian, and Belarusian), unspecified 9.4% (2011 CIA est.)

Religions: Lutheran 19.6%, Orthodox 15.3%, other Christian 1%, other 0.4%, unspecified 63.7% (2006)

Lebanon

Official name: Lebanese Republic

Capital city: Beirut

Internet country code: .lb

Flag description: Three horizontal bands consisting of red (top), white (middle, double width), and red (bottom) with a green cedar tree centered in the white band

National anthem: "An-Nashid Al-Watani Al-Lubnani" (All for the country, for the glory, for the flag), lyrics by Rashid Nakhle, music by Wadih Sabra

Geographical description: Middle East, bordering the Mediterranean Sea, between Israel and Syria

Total area: 10,400 sq. km

Climate: Mediterranean; mild to cool, wet winters with hot, dry summers; mountains experience heavy winter snows

Nationality: noun: Lebanese (singular and plural) *adjective:* Lebanese

Population: 5,882,562 (July 2014 CIA est.)

Ethnic groups: Arab 95%, Armenian 4%, other 1%

Languages spoken: Arabic (official), French, English, Armenian

Religions: Muslim 54% (27% Sunni, 27% Shia), Christian 40.5% (includes 21% Maronite Catholic, 8% Greek Orthodox, 5% Greek Catholic, 6.5% other Christian), Druze 5.6%, very small numbers of Jews, Baha'is, Buddhists, Hindus, and Mormons

Lesotho

Official name: Kingdom of Lesotho

Capital city: Maseru

Internet country code: .ls

Flag description: Three horizontal stripes of blue (top), white, and green in the proportions of 3:4:3; the colors represent rain, peace, and prosperity respectively; centered in the white stripe is a black Basotho hat representing the indigenous people; the flag was unfurled in October 2006 to celebrate 40 years of independence

Geographical description: Southern Africa, an enclave of South Africa

Total area: 30,355 sq. km

Climate: Temperate; cool to cold, dry winters; hot, wet summers

Nationality: noun: Mosotho (singular), Basotho (plural) *adjective:* Basotho

Population: 1,942,008

Ethnic groups: Sotho 99.7%, Europeans, Asians, and other 0.3%

Languages spoken: Sesotho (southern Sotho; official), English (official), Zulu, Xhosa

Religions: Christian 80%, indigenous beliefs 20%

Liberia

Official name: Republic of Liberia

Capital city: Monrovia

Internet country code: .lr

Flag description: Eleven equal horizontal stripes of red (top and bottom) alternating with white; there is a white five-pointed star on a blue square in the upper hoist-side corner; the design was based on the United States flag

National anthem: "All Hail, Liberia Hail!", lyrics by Daniel Bashiel Warner, music by Olmstead Luca

National bird: Pepperbird

Geographical description: Western Africa, bordering the North Atlantic Ocean, between Cote d'Ivoire and Sierra Leone

Total area: 111,369 sq.km

Climate: Tropical; hot, humid; dry winters with hot days and cool to cold nights; wet, cloudy summers with frequent heavy showers

Nationality: noun: Liberian(s) *adjective:* Liberian

Population: 4,092,310 (July 2014 CIA est.)

Ethnic groups: Kpelle 20.3%, Bassa 13.4%, Grebo 10%, Gio 8%, Mano 7.9%, Kru 6%, Lorma 5.1%, Kissi 4.8%, Gola 4.4%, other 20.1% (2008 Census

Languages spoken: English 20% (official), some 20 ethnic group languages few of which can be written or used in correspondence

Religions: Christian 85.6%, Muslim 12.2%, Traditional 0.6%, other 0.2%, none 1.4% (2008 Census)

Libya

Official name: Great Socialist People's Libyan Arab Jamahiriya

Capital city: Tripoli

Internet country code: .ly

Flag description: Plain green; green is the traditional color of Islam (the state religion)

Geographical description: Northern Africa, bordering the Mediterranean Sea, between Egypt and Tunisia

Total area: 1,759,540 sq. km

Climate: Mediterranean along coast; dry, extreme desert interior

Nationality: noun: Libyan(s) *adjective:* Libyan

Population: 6,244,174

Ethnic groups: Berber and Arab 97%, other (including Greeks, Maltese, Italians, Egyptians, Pakistanis, Turks, Indians, and Tunisians) 3%

Languages spoken: Arabic (official), Italian, English (all widely understood in the major cities); Berber (Nafusi, Ghadamis, Suknah, Awjilah, Tamasheq)

Religions: Muslim (official; virtually all Sunni) 96.6%, Christian 2.7%, Buddhist 0.3%, Hindu <.1, Jewish <.1, folk religion <.1, unafilliated 0.2%, other <.1

Liechtenstein

Official name: Principality of Liechtenstein

Capital city: Vaduz

Internet country code: .li

Flag description: Two equal horizontal bands of blue (top) and red with a gold crown on the hoist side of the blue band

National anthem: "Oben am jungen Rhein lehnet sich Liechtenstein an Alpenhöhn" (first line), sung to the music of "God Save the King"

Geographical description: Central Europe, between Austria and Switzerland

Total area: 160 sq km

Climate: Continental; cold, cloudy winters with frequent snow or rain; cool to moderately warm, cloudy, humid summers

Nationality: noun: Liechtensteiner(s) *adjective:* Liechtenstein

Population: 37,313 (July 2014 CIA est.)

Ethnic groups: Liechtensteiner 65.6%, other 34.4% (2000 census)

Languages spoken: German 94.5% (official) (Alemannic is the main dialect), Italian 1.1%, other 4.3% (2010 CIA est.)

Religions: Roman Catholic (official) 75.9%, Protestant Reformed 6.5%, Muslim 5.4%, Lutheran 1.3%, other 2.9%, none 5.4%, unspecified 2.6% (2010 CIA est.)

Lithuania

Official name: Republic of Lithuania

Capital city: Vilnius

Internet country code: .lt

Flag description: Three equal horizontal bands of yellow (top), green, and red

Geographical description: Eastern Europe, bordering the Baltic Sea, between Latvia and Russia

Total area: 65,300 sq km

Climate: Transitional, between maritime and continental; wet, moderate winters and summers

Nationality: noun: Lithuanian(s) *adjective:* Lithuanian

Population: 3,505,738

Ethnic groups: Lithuanian 84.1%, Polish 6.6%, Russian 5.8%, Belarusian 1.2%, other 1.1%, unspecified 1.2% (2011 CIA est.)

Languages spoken: Lithuanian (official) 82%, Russian 8%, Polish 5.6%, other 0.9%, unspecified 3.5% (2011 CIA est.)

Religions: Roman Catholic 77.2%, Russian Orthodox 4.1%, Old Believer 0.8%, Evangelical Lutheran 0.6%, Evangelical Reformist 0.2%, other (including Sunni Muslim, Jewish, Greek Catholic, and Karaite) 0.8%, none 6.1%, unspecified 10.1% (2011 CIA est.)

Luxembourg

Official name: Grand Duchy of Luxembourg

Capital city: Luxembourg

Internet country code: .lu

Flag description: Three equal horizontal bands of red (top), white, and light blue; similar to the flag of the Netherlands, which uses a darker blue and is shorter; design was based on the flag of France

National anthem: "Ons Hémécht" (Our Motherland)

National flower: Rose

Geographical description: Western Europe, between France and Germany

Total area: 2,586 sq km

Climate: Modified continental with mild winters, cool summers

Nationality: noun: Luxembourger(s) *adjective:* Luxembourg, Luxembourgian, Luxembourgish

Population: 520,672 (July 2014 CIA est.)

Ethnic groups: Luxembourger 63.1%, Portuguese 13.3%, French 4.5%, Italian 4.3%, German 2.3%, other EU 7.3%, other 5.2% (2000 census)

Languages spoken: Luxembourgish (official administrative language and national language (spoken vernacular)), French (official administrative language), German (official administrative language)

Religions: Roman Catholic 87%, other (includes Protestant, Jewish, and Muslim) 13% (2000)

Macau

Official name: Macau Special Administrative Region [of China]

Capital city: NULL

Internet country code: .mo

Flag description: Light green with a lotus flower above a stylized bridge and water in white, beneath an arc of five gold five-pointed stars: one large in center of arc and four smaller

Geographical description: Eastern Asia, bordering the South China Sea and China

Total area: 28.2 sq. km

Climate: Subtropical; marine with cool winters, warm summers

Nationality: noun: Macanese, Chinese (singular and plural) *adjective:* Macanese, Chinese

Population: 5,87,914

Ethnic groups: Chinese 92.4%, Portuguese 0.6%, mixed 1.1%, other 5.9% (includes Macanese - mixed Portuguese and Asian ancestry) (2011 CIA est.)

Languages spoken: Cantonese 83.3%, Mandarin 5%, Hokkien 3.7%, English 2.3%, other Chinese dialects 2%, Tagalog 1.7%, Portuguese 0.7%, other 1.3%

Religions: Buddhist 50%, Roman Catholic 15%, none or other 35% (1997 CIA est.)

Macedonia

Official name: Republic of Macedonia

Capital city: Skopje

Internet country code: .mk

Flag description: A yellow sun with eight broadening rays extending to the edges of the red field

Geographical description: Southeastern Europe, north of Greece

Total area: 25,713 sq. km

Climate: Warm, dry summers and autumns; relatively cold winters with heavy snowfall

Nationality: noun: Macedonian(s) *adjective:* Macedonian

Population: 2,091,719 (July 2014 CIA est.)

Ethnic groups: Macedonian 64.2%, Albanian 25.2%, Turkish 3.9%, Roma 2.7%, Serb 1.8%, other 2.2% (2002 Census)

Languages spoken: Macedonian 66.5%, Albanian 25.1%, Turkish 3.5%, Roma 1.9%, Serbian 1.2%, other 1.8% (2002 census)

Religions: Macedonian Orthodox 64.7%, Muslim 33.3%, other Christian 0.37%, other and unspecified 1.63% (2002 census)

Madagascar

Official name: Republic of Madagascar

Capital city: Antananarivo

Internet country code: .mg

Flag description: Two equal horizontal bands of red (top) and green with a vertical white band of the same width on hoist side

National anthem: "Ry Tanindraza nay malala ô" (Oh, Our Beloved Fatherland)

National motto: "Tanindrazana, Fahafahana, Fandrosoana" (Fatherland, Liberty, Progress)

Geographical description: Southern Africa, island in the Indian Ocean, east of Mozambique

Total area: 587,041 sq km

Climate: Tropical along coast, temperate inland, arid in south

Nationality: noun: Malagasy (singular and plural) *adjective:* Malagasy

Population: 23,201,926 (July 2014 CIA est.)

Ethnic groups: Malayo-Indonesian (Merina and related Betsileo), Cotiers (mixed African, Malayo-Indonesian, and Arab ancestry - Betsimisaraka, Tsimihety, Antaisaka, Sakalava), French, Indian, Creole, Comoran

Languages spoken: French (official), Malagasy (official), English

Religions: Indigenous religions 52%, Christian 41%, Muslim 7%

Malawi

Official name: Republic of Malawi

Capital city: Lilongwe

Internet country code: .mw

Flag description: Three equal horizontal bands of black (top), red, and green with a radiant, rising, red sun centered in the black band

Geographical description: Southern Africa, east of Zambia

Total area: 118,484 sq km

Climate: Sub-tropical; rainy season (November to May); dry season (May to November)

Nationality: noun: Malian(s) *adjective:* Malian

Population: 17,377,468

Ethnic groups: Chewa 32.6%, Lomwe 17.6%, Yao 13.5%, Ngoni 11.5%, Tumbuka 8.8%, Nyanja 5.8%, Sena 3.6%, Tonga 2.1%, Ngonde 1%, other 3.5%

Languages spoken: English (official), Chichewa (common), Chinyanja, Chiyao, Chitumbuka, Chilomwe, Chinkhonde, Chingoni, Chisena, Chitonga, Chinyakyusa, Chilambya

Religions: Christian 82.6%, Muslim 13%, other 1.9%, none 2.5% (2008 CIA est.)

Malaysia

Official name: Malaysia

Capital city: Kuala Lumpur

Internet country code: .my

Flag description: Fourteen equal horizontal stripes of red (top) alternating with white (bottom); there is a blue rectangle in the upper hoist-side corner bearing a yellow crescent and a yellow 14-pointed star; the crescent and the star are traditional symbols of Islam; the design was based on the flag of the United States

National anthem: "Negaraku" (My Homeland)

National flower: Hibiscus

Geographical description: Southeastern Asia, peninsula bordering Thailand and northern one-third of the island of Borneo, bordering Indonesia, Brunei, and the South China Sea, south of Vietnam

Total area: 329,847 sq km

Climate: Tropical; annual southwest (April to October) and northeast (October to February) monsoons

Nationality: noun: Malaysian(s) *adjective:* Malaysian

Population: 30,073,353 (July 2014 CIA est.)

Ethnic groups: Malay 50.1%, Chinese 22.6%, indigenous 11.8%, Indian 6.7%, other 0.7%, non-citizens 8.2% (2010 CIA est.)

Languages spoken: Bahasa Malaysia (official), English, Chinese (Cantonese, Mandarin, Hokkien, Hakka, Hainan, Foochow), Tamil, Telugu, Malayalam, Panjabi, Thai

Religions: Muslim (official) 61.3%, Buddhist 19.8%, Christian 9.2%, Hindu 6.3%, Confucianism, Taoism, other traditional Chinese religions 1.3%, other 0.4%, none 0.8%, unspecified 1% (2010 CIA est.)

Maldives

Official name: Republic of Maldives

Capital city: Male

Internet country code: .mv

Flag description: Red with a large green rectangle in the center bearing a vertical white crescent; the closed side of the crescent is on the hoist side of the flag

National flower: Finifenmaa (Pink rose)

National tree: Dhivehi Ruh (Coconut palm)

Geographical description: Southern Asia, group of atolls in the Indian Ocean, south-southwest of India

Total area: 298 sq km

Climate: Tropical; hot, humid; dry, northeast monsoon (November to March); rainy, southwest monsoon (June to August)

Nationality: noun: Maldivian(s) *adjective:* Maldivian

Population: 393,595 (July 2014 CIA est.)

Ethnic groups: South Indians, Sinhalese, Arabs

Languages spoken: Dhivehi (official, dialect of Sinhala, script derived from Arabic), English (spoken by most government officials)

Religions: Sunni Muslim (official)

Mali

Official name: Republic of Mali

Capital city: Bamako

Internet country code: .ml

Flag description: Three equal vertical bands of green (hoist side), yellow, and red; uses the popular pan-African colors of Ethiopia

National anthem: "Le Mali"

National motto: "Un Peuple, un But, une Foi" (One Nation, One Goal, One Faith)

Geographical description: Western Africa, southwest of Algeria

Total area: 1,240,192 sq km

Climate: Subtropical to arid; hot and dry (February to June); rainy, humid, and mild (June to November); cool and dry (November to February)

Nationality: noun: Malian(s) *adjective:* Malian

Population: 16,455,903 (July 2014 CIA est.)

Ethnic groups: Mande 50% (Bambara, Malinke, Soninke), Peul 17%, Voltaic 12%, Songhai 6%, Tuareg and Moor 10%, other 5%

Languages spoken: French (official), Bambara 46.3%, Peul/foulfoulbe 9.4%, Dogon 7.2%, Maraka/soninke 6.4%, Malinke 5.6%, Sonrhai/djerma 5.6%, Minianka 4.3%, Tamacheq 3.5%, Senoufo 2.6%, unspecified 0.6%, other 8.5%

Religions: Muslim 94.8%, Christian 2.4%, Animist 2%, none 0.5%, unspecified 0.3% (2009 Census)

Malta

Official name: Republic of Malta

Capital city: Valletta

Internet country code: .mt

Flag description: Two equal vertical bands of white (hoist side) and red; in the upper hoist-side corner is a representation of the St. George Cross, edged in red

National anthem: "L-Innu Malti" (first line in English: Guard her, O Lord, as ever Thou hast guarded!), lyrics by Dun Karm Psaila, music by Robert Samut

Geographical description: Southern Europe, islands in the Mediterranean Sea, south of Sicily (Italy)

Total area: 316 sq. km

Climate: Mediterranean; mild, rainy winters; hot, dry summers

Nationality: noun: Maltese (singular and plural) *adjective:* Maltese

Population: 412,655 (July 2014 CIA est.)

Ethnic groups: Maltese (descendants of ancient Carthaginians and Phoenicians, with strong elements of Italian and other Mediterranean stock)

Languages spoken: Maltese (official) 90.1%, English (official) 6%, multilingual 3%, other 0.9% (2005 CIA est.)

Religions: Roman Catholic (official) more than 90% (2011 CIA est.)

Marshall Islands

Official name: Republic of the Marshall Islands

Capital city: Majuro

Internet country code: .mh

Flag description: Blue with two stripes radiating from the lower hoist-side corner - orange (top) and white; there is a white star with four large rays and 20 small rays on the hoist side above the two stripes

National anthem: "Forever Marshall Islands" by President Amata Kabua

Geographical description: Oceania, two archipelagic island chains of 29 atolls, each made up of many small islets, and five single islands in the North Pacific Ocean, about one-half of the way from Hawaii to Australia

Total area: 181 sq. km

Climate: Tropical; hot and humid; wet season May to November; islands border typhoon belt

Nationality: noun: Marshallese (singular and plural) *adjective:* Marshallese

Population: 70,983 (July 2014 CIA est.)

Ethnic groups: Marshallese 92.1%, mixed Marshallese 5.9%, other 2% (2006)

Languages spoken: Marshallese (official) 98.2%, other languages 1.8% (1999 census)

Religions: Protestant 54.8%, Assembly of God 25.8%, Roman Catholic 8.4%, Bukot nan Jesus 2.8%, Mormon 2.1%, other Christian 3.6%, other 1%, none 1.5% (1999 Census)

Mauritania

Official name: Islamic Republic of Mauritania

Capital city: Nouakchott

Internet country code: .mr

Flag description: Green with a yellow five-pointed star above a yellow horizontal crescent; the closed side of the crescent is down; the crescent, star, and color green are traditional symbols of Islam

National anthem: lyrics taken from poem by Baba Ould Cheikh

Geographical description: Northern Africa, bordering the North Atlantic Ocean, between Senegal and Western Sahara

Total area: 1,030,700 sq km

Climate: Desert; constantly hot, dry, dusty

Nationality: noun: Mauritanian(s) *adjective:* Mauritanian

Population: 3,516,806 (July 2014 CIA est.)

Ethnic groups: Black Moors (Haratines - Arab-speaking slaves, former slaves, and their descendants of African origin, enslaved by white Moors) 40%, white Moors (of Arab-Berber descent, known as Bidhan) 30%, black Africans (non-Arabic speaking, Halpulaar, Soninke, Wolof, and Bamara ethnic groups) 30%

Languages spoken: Arabic (official and national), Pulaar, Soninke, Wolof (all national languages), French, Hassaniya (a variety of Arabic)

Religions: Muslim (Official) 100%

Mauritius

Official name: Republic of Mauritius

Capital city: Port Louis

Internet country code: .mu

Flag description: Four equal horizontal bands of red (top), blue, yellow, and green

National anthem: "Glory to thee, Motherland" (first line), lyrics by Jean Georges Prosper, music by Philippe Gentil

National flower: Trochetia Boutoniana (Boucle d'Oreille)

Geographical description: Southern Africa, island in the Indian Ocean, east of Madagascar

Total area: 2,040 sq km

Climate: Tropical, modified by southeast trade winds; warm, dry winter (May to November); hot, wet, humid summer (November to May)

Nationality: noun: Mauritian(s) *adjective:* Mauritian

Population: 1,331,155 (July 2014 CIA est.)

Ethnic groups: Indo-Mauritian 68%, Creole 27%, Sino-Mauritian 3%, Franco-Mauritian 2%

Languages spoken: Creole 86.5%, Bhojpuri 5.3%, French 4.1%, two languages 1.4%, other 2.6% (includes English, the official language, which is spoken by less than 1% of the population), unspecified 0.1% (2011 CIA est.)

Religions: Hindu 48.5%, Roman Catholic 26.3%, Muslim 17.3%, other Christian 6.4%, other 0.6%, none 0.7%, unspecified 0.1% (2011 CIA est.)

Mexico

Official name: United Mexican States

Capital city: Mexico City

Internet country code: .mx

Flag description: Three equal vertical bands of green (hoist side), white, and red; the coat of arms (an eagle perched on a cactus with a snake in its beak) is centered in the white band

National anthem: "Mexicanos, al grito de Guerra" (Mexicans, at the cry of war - first line of chorus), lyrics by Francisco González Bocanegra, music by Jaime Nunó

Geographical description: Middle America, bordering the Caribbean Sea and the Gulf of Mexico, between Belize and the United States and bordering the North Pacific Ocean, between Guatemala and the United States

Total area: 1,964,375 sq km

Climate: Varies from tropical to desert

Nationality: noun: Mexican(s) *adjective:* Mexican

Population: 120,286,655 (July 2014 CIA est.)

Ethnic groups: Mestizo (Amerindian-Spanish) 60%, Amerindian or predominantly Amerindian 30%, white 9%, other 1%

Languages spoken: Spanish only 92.7%, Spanish and indigenous languages 5.7%, indigenous only 0.8%, unspecified 0.8%

Religions: Roman Catholic 82.7%, Pentecostal 1.6%, Jehovah's Witnesses 1.4%, other Evangelical Churches 5%, other 1.9%, none 4.7%, unspecified 2.7% (2010 CIA est.)

Micronesia

Official name: Federated States of Micronesia

Capital city: Palikir

Internet country code: .fm

Flag description: Light blue with four white five-pointed stars centered; the stars are arranged in a diamond pattern

National anthem: "Tis here we are pledging with heart and with hands" (first line)

Geographical description: Oceania, island group in the North Pacific Ocean, about three-quarters of the way from Hawaii to Indonesia

Total area: 702 sq km

Climate: Tropical; heavy year-round rainfall, especially in the eastern islands; located on southern edge of the typhoon belt with occasionally severe damage

Nationality: noun: Micronesian(s) *adjective:* Micronesian; Chuukese, Kosraen(s), Pohnpeian(s), Yapese

Population: 105,681 (July 2014 CIA est.)

Ethnic groups: Chuukese/Mortlockese 49.3%, Pohnpeian 29.8%, Kosraean 6.3%, Yapese 5.7%, Yap outer islanders 5.1%, Polynesian 1.6%, Asian 1.4%, other 0.8% (2010 CIA est.)

Languages spoken: English (official and common language), Chuukese, Kosrean, Pohnpeian, Yapese, Ulithian, Woleaian, Nukuoro, Kapingamarangi

Religions: Roman Catholic 54.7%, Protestant 41.1% (includes Congregational 38.5%, Baptist 1.1%, Seventh Day Adventist 0.8%, Assembly of God .7%), Mormon 1.5%, other 1.9%, none 0.7%, unspecified 0.1% (2010 CIA est.)

Moldova

Official name: Republic of Moldova

Capital city: Chisinau

Internet country code: .md

Flag description: Same color scheme as Romania - three equal vertical bands of blue (hoist side), yellow, and red; emblem in center of flag is of a Roman eagle of gold outlined in black with a red beak and talons carrying a yellow cross in its beak and a green olive branch in its right talons and a yellow scepter in its left talons; on its breast is a shield divided horizontally red over blue with a stylized ox head, star, rose, and crescent all in black-outlined yellow

National anthem: "Limba noastră-i o comoară" (first line), lyrics by Alexei Mateevici, music by Alexandru Cristea

Geographical description: Eastern Europe, northeast of Romania

Total area: 33,851 sq km

Climate: Moderate winters, warm summers

Nationality: noun: Moldovan(s) *adjective:* Moldovan

Population: 3,583,288 (July 2014 CIA est.)

Ethnic groups: Moldovan 75.8%, Ukrainian 8.4%, Russian 5.9%, Gagauz 4.4%, Romanian 2.2%, Bulgarian 1.9%, other 1%, unspecified 0.4% (2004 CIA est.)

Languages spoken: Moldovan 58.8% (official; virtually the same as the Romanian language), Romanian 16.4%, Russian 16%, Ukrainian 3.8%, Gagauz 3.1% (a Turkish language), Bulgarian 1.1%, other 0.3%, unspecified 0.4%

Religions: Orthodox 93.3%, Baptist 1%, other Christian 1.2%, other 0.9%, atheist 0.4%, none 1%, unspecified 2.2% (2004 CIA est.)

Monaco

Official name: Principality of Monaco

Capital city: Monaco

Internet country code: .mc

Flag description: Two equal horizontal bands of red (top) and white; similar to the flag of Indonesia which is longer and the flag of Poland which is white (top) and red

Geographical description: Western Europe, bordering the Mediterranean Sea on the southern coast of France, near the border with Italy

Total area: 2 sq km

Climate: Mediterranean with mild, wet winters and hot, dry summers

Nationality: noun: Monegasque(s) or Monacan(s) *adjective:* Monegasque or Monacan

Population: 30,508

Ethnic groups: French 47%, Monegasque 16%, Italian 16%, other 21%

Languages spoken: French (official), English, Italian, Monegasque

Religions: Roman Catholic 90%, other 10%

Mongolia

Official name: Mongolia

Capital city: Ulaanbaatar

Internet country code: .mn

Flag description: Three equal, vertical bands of red (hoist side), blue, and red; centered on the hoist-side red band in yellow is the national emblem (*soyombo* - a columnar arrangement of abstract and geometric representation for fire, sun, moon, earth, water, and the yin-yang symbol)

Geographical description: Northern Asia, between China and Russia

Total area: 1,564,116 sq km

Climate: Desert; continental (large daily and seasonal temperature ranges)

Nationality: noun: Mongolian(s) *adjective:* Mongolian

Population: 2,953,190 (July 2014 CIA est.)

Ethnic groups: Khalkh 81.9%, Kazak 3.8%, Dorvod 2.7%, Bayad 2.1%, Buryat-Bouriates 1.7%, Zakhchin 1.2%, Dariganga 1%, Uriankhai 1%, other 4.6% (2010 CIA est.)

Languages spoken: Khalkha Mongol 90% (official), Turkic, Russian (1999)

Religions: Buddhist 53%, Muslim 3%, Christian 2.2%, Shamanist 2.9%, other 0.4%, none 38.6% (2010 CIA est.)

Montenegro

Official name: Republic of Montenegro

Capital city: Podgorica

Internet country code: .me

Flag description: A red field bordered by a narrow golden-yellow stripe with the Montenegrin coat of arms centered

Geographical description: Southeastern Europe, between the Adriatic Sea and Serbia

Total area: 13,812 sq km

Climate: Mediterranean climate, hot dry summers and autumns and relatively cold winters with heavy snowfalls inland

Nationality: noun: Montenegrin(s) *adjective:* Montenegrin

Population: 650,036 (July 2014 CIA est.)

Ethnic groups: Montenegrin 45%, Serbian 28.7%, Bosniak 8.7%, Albanian 4.9%, Muslim 3.3%, Roma 1%, Croat 1%, other 2.6%, unspecified 4.9% (2011 CIA est.)

Languages spoken: Serbian 42.9%, Montenegrin (official) 37%, Bosnian 5.3%, Albanian 5.3%, Serbo-Croat 2%, other 3.5%, unspecified 4% (2011 CIA est.)

Religions: Orthodox 72.1%, Muslim 19.1%, Catholic 3.4%, atheist 1.2%, other 1.5%, unspecified 2.6% (2011 CIA est.)

Morocco

Official name: Kingdom of Morocco

Capital city: Rabat

Internet country code: .ma

Flag description: Red with a green pentacle (five-pointed linear star) known as Sulayman's (Solomon's) seal in the center of the flag; red and green are traditional colors in Arab flags, although the use of red is more commonly associated with the Arab states of the Persian gulf; design dates to 1912

National anthem: "Royaume du Maroc: Garde Royale"

National motto: God, The Country, The King

Geographical description: Northern Africa, bordering the North Atlantic Ocean and the Mediterranean Sea, between Algeria and Western Sahara

Total area: 446,550 sq. km

Climate: Mediterranean, becoming more extreme in the interior

Nationality: noun: Moroccan(s) *adjective:* Moroccan

Population: 32,987,206 (July 2014 CIA est.)

Ethnic groups: Arab-Berber 99%, other 1%

Languages spoken: Arabic (official), Berber languages (Tamazight (official), Tachelhit, Tarifit), French (often the language of business, government, and diplomacy)

Religions: Muslim 99% (official; virtually all Sunni, <.1% Shia), other 1% (includes Christian, Jewish, and Baha'i), Jewish about 6,000 (2010 CIA est.)

Mozambique

Official name: Republic of Mozambique

Capital city: Maputo

Internet country code: .mz

Flag description: Three equal horizontal bands of green (top), black, and yellow with a red isosceles triangle based on the hoist side; the black band is edged in white; centered in the triangle is a yellow five-pointed star bearing a crossed rifle and hoe in black superimposed on an open white book

National anthem: "Moçambique nossa terra gloriosa!" (Mozambique, our Glorious Land - first line of chorus)

Geographical description: Southeastern Africa, bordering the Mozambique Channel, between South Africa and Tanzania

Total area: 799,380 sq km

Climate: Tropical to subtropical

Nationality: noun: Mozambican(s) *adjective:* Mozambican

Population: 24,692,144

Ethnic groups: African 99.66% (Makhuwa, Tsonga, Lomwe, Sena, and others), Europeans 0.06%, Euro-Africans 0.2%, Indians 0.08%

Languages spoken: Emakhuwa 25.3%, Portuguese (official) 10.7%, Xichangana 10.3%, Cisena 7.5%, Elomwe 7%, Echuwabo 5.1%, other Mozambican languages 30.1%, other 4% (1997 census)

Religions: Roman Catholic 28.4%, Muslim 17.9%, Zionist Christian 15.5%, Protestant 12.2% (includes Pentecostal 10.9% and Anglican 1.3%), other 6.7%, none 18.7%, unspecified 0.7% (2007 CIA est.)

Namibia

Official name: Republic of Namibia

Capital city: Windhoek

Internet country code: .na

Flag description: A wide red stripe edged by narrow white stripes divides the flag diagonally from lower hoist corner to upper fly corner; the upper hoist-side triangle is blue and charged with a yellow 12-rayed sunburst; the lower fly-side triangle is green

National anthem: "Namibia Land of the Brave"

National motto: Unity, Liberty, Justice

Geographical description: Southern Africa, bordering the South Atlantic Ocean, between Angola and South Africa

Total area: 824,292 sq km

Climate: Desert; hot, dry; rainfall sparse and erratic

Nationality: noun: Namibian(s) *adjective:* Namibian

Population: 2,198,406

Ethnic groups: Black 87.5%, white 6%, mixed 6.5%

Languages spoken: Oshiwambo languages 48.9%, Nama/Damara 11.3%, Afrikaans 10.4% (common language of most of the population and about 60% of the white population), Otjiherero languages 8.6%, Kavango languages 8.5%, Caprivi languages 4.8%, English (official) 3.4%, other African languages 2.3%, other 1.7%

Religions: Christian 80% to 90% (at least 50% Lutheran 50%), indigenous religions 10% to 20%

Nauru

Official name: Republic of Nauru

Capital city: No official capital; government offices in Yaren District

Internet country code: .nr

Flag description: Blue with a narrow, horizontal yellow stripe across the center and a large white 12-pointed star below the stripe on the hoist side; the star indicates the country's location in relation to the Equator (the yellow stripe) and the 12 points symbolize the 12 original tribes of Nauru

National anthem: "Nauru bwiema" (Nauru Our Homeland)

Geographical description: Oceania, island in the South Pacific Ocean, south of the Marshall Islands

Total area: 21 sq. km

Climate: Tropical with a monsoonal pattern; rainy season (November to February)

Nationality: noun: Nauruan(s) *adjective:* Nauruan

Population: 9,488 (July 2014 CIA est.)

Ethnic groups: Nauruan 58%, other Pacific Islander 26%, Chinese 8%, European 8%

Languages spoken: Nauruan 93% (official, a distinct Pacific Island language), English 2% (widely understood, spoken, and used for most government and commercial purposes), other 5% (includes I-Kiribati 2% and Chinese 2%)

Religions: Protestant 60.4% (includes Nauru Congregational 35.7%, Assembly of God 13%, Nauru Independent Church 9.5%, Baptist 1.5%, and Seventh Day Adventist .7%), Roman Catholic 33%, other 3.7%, none 1.8%, unspecified 1.1% (2011 CIA est.)

Nepal

Official name: Nepal

Capital city: Kathmandu

Internet country code: .np

Flag description: Red with a blue border around the unique shape of two overlapping right triangles; the smaller, upper triangle bears a white stylized moon and the larger, lower triangle bears a white 12-pointed sun

National bird: Impean Pheasant Danfe

National flower: Rhododendron Arboreum (Lali Gurans)

Geographical description: Southern Asia, between China and India

Total area: 147,181 sq km

Climate: Varies from cool summers and severe winters in north to subtropical summers and mild winters in south

Nationality: noun: Nepali (singular and plural) *adjective:* Nepali

Population: 30,986,975 (July 2014 CIA est.)

Ethnic groups: Chhettri 16.6%, Brahman-Hill 12.2%, Magar 7.1%, Tharu 6.6%, Tamang 5.8%, Newar 5%, Kami 4.8%, Muslim 4.4%, Yadav 4%, Rai 2.3%, Gurung 2%, Damai/Dholii 1.8%, Thakuri 1.6%, Limbu 1.5%, Sarki 1.4%, Teli 1.4%, Chamar/Harijan/Ram 1.3%, Koiri/Kushwaha 1.2%, other 19%

Languages spoken: Nepali (official) 44.6%, Maithali 11.7%, Bhojpuri 6%, Tharu 5.8%, Tamang 5.1%, Newar 3.2%, Magar 3%, Bajjika 3%, Urdu 2.6%, Avadhi 1.9%, Limbu 1.3%, Gurung 1.2%, other 10.4%, unspecified 0.2%

Religions: Hindu 81.3%, Buddhist 9%, Muslim 4.4%, Kirant 3.1%, Christian 1.4%, other 0.5%, unspecifed 0.2% (2011 CIA est.)

Netherlands

Official name: Kingdom of the Netherlands

Capital city: Amsterdam

Internet country code: .nl

Flag description: Three equal horizontal bands of red (top), white, and blue; similar to the flag of Luxembourg, which uses a lighter blue and is longer; one of the oldest flags in constant use, originating with William I, Prince of Orange, in the latter half of the 16th century

National anthem: "Wilhelmus"

Geographical description: Western Europe, bordering the North Sea, between Belgium and Germany

Total area: 41,543 sq km

Climate: Temperate; marine; cool summers and mild winters

Nationality: noun: Dutchman(men), Dutchwoman(women) *adjective:* Dutch

Population: 16,877,351 (July 2014 CIA est.)

Ethnic groups: Dutch 80.7%, EU 5%, Indonesian 2.4%, Turkish 2.2%, Surinamese 2%, Moroccan 2%, Caribbean 0.8%, other 4.8% (2008 CIA est.)

Languages spoken: Dutch, Frisian

Religions: Roman Catholic 28%, Protestant 19% (includes Dutch Reformed 9%, Protestant Church of The Netherlands, 7%, Calvinist 3%), other 11% (includes about 5% Muslim and lesser numbers of Hindu, Buddhist, Jehovah's Witness, and Orthodox), none 42% (2009 CIA est.)

New Zealand

Official name: New Zealand

Capital city: Wellington

Internet country code: .nz

Flag description: Blue with the flag of the United Kingdom in the upper hoist-side quadrant with four red five-pointed stars edged in white centered in the outer half of the flag; the stars represent the Southern Cross constellation

National anthems: "God Defend New Zealand" and "God Save the Queen"

Geographical description: Oceania, islands in the South Pacific Ocean, southeast of Australia

Total area: 267,710 sq km

Climate: Temperate with sharp regional contrasts

Nationality: noun: New Zealander(s) *adjective:* New Zealand

Population: 4,401,916 (July 2014 CIA est.)

Ethnic groups: European 71.2%, Maori 14.1%, Asian 11.3%, Pacific peoples 7.6%, Middle Eastern, Latin American, African 1.1%, other 1.6%, not stated or unidentified 5.4%

Languages spoken: English (de facto official) 89.8%, Maori (de jure official) 3.5%, Samoan 2%, Hindi 1.6%, French 1.2%, Northern Chinese 1.2%, Yue 1%, Other or not stated 20.5%, New Zealand Sign Language (de jure official)

Religions: Christian 44.3% (Catholic 11.6%, Anglican 10.8%, Presbyterian and Congregational 7.8%, Methodist, 2.4%, Pentecostal 1.8%, other 9.9%), Hindu 2.1%, Buddhist 1.4%, Maori Christian 1.3%, Islam 1.1%, other religion 1.4% (includes Judaism, Spiritualism and New Age religions, Baha'i, Asian religions other than Buddhism), no religion 38.5%, not stated or unidentified 8.2%, objected to answering 4.1%

Nicaragua

Official name: Republic of Nicaragua

Capital city: Managua

Internet country code: .ni

Flag description: Three equal horizontal bands of blue (top), white, and blue with the national coat of arms centered in the white band; the coat of arms features a triangle encircled by the words *Republica de Nicaragua* on the top and *America Central* on the bottom; similar to the flag of El Salvador, which features a round emblem centered in the white band; also similar to the flag of Honduras, which has five blue stars arranged in an X pattern centered in the white band

Geographical description: Central America, bordering both the Caribbean Sea and the North Pacific Ocean, between Costa Rica and Honduras

Total area: 130,370 sq km

Climate: Tropical in lowlands, cooler in highlands

Nationality: noun: Nicaraguan(s) *adjective:* Nicaraguan

Population: 5,848,641 (July 2014 CIA est.)

Ethnic groups: Mestizo (mixed Amerindian and European) 69%, white 17%, black 9%, Amerindian 5%

Languages spoken: Spanish (official) 95.3%, Miskito 2.2%, Mestizo of the Caribbean coast 2%, other 0.5%

Religions: Roman Catholic 58.5%, Protestant 23.2% (Evangelical 21.6%, Moravian 1.6%), Jehovah's Witnesses 0.9%, other 1.6%, none 15.7% (2005 CIA est.)

Niger

Official name: Republic of Niger

Capital city: Niamey

Internet country code: .ne

Flag description: Three equal horizontal bands of orange (top), white, and green with a small orange disk (representing the sun) centered in the white band

National motto: Fraternity – Work – Progress

Geographical description: Western Africa, southeast of Algeria

Total area: 1.267 million sq km

Climate: Desert; mostly hot, dry, dusty; tropical in extreme south

Nationality: noun: Nigerien(s) *adjective:* Nigerien

Population: 17,466,172 (July 2014 CIA est.)

Ethnic groups: Haoussa 55.4%, Djerma Sonrai 21%, Tuareg 9.3%, Peuhl 8.5%, Kanouri Manga 4.7%, other 1.2% (2001 census)

Languages spoken: French (official), Hausa, Djerma

Religions: Muslim 80%, other (includes indigenous beliefs and Christian) 20%

Nigeria

Official name: Federal Republic of Nigeria

Capital city: Abuja

Internet country code: .ng

Flag description: Three equal vertical bands of green (hoist side), white, and green

National motto: "Unity and Faith, Peace and Progress"

Geographical description: Western Africa, bordering the Gulf of Guinea, between Benin and Cameroon

Total area: 923,768 sq km

Climate: Varies; equatorial in south, tropical in center, arid in north

Nationality: noun: Nigerian(s) *adjective:* Nigerian

Population: 177,155,754

Ethnic groups: Nigeria, Africa's most populous country, is composed of more than 250 ethnic groups; the following are the most populous and politically influential: Hausa and Fulani 29%, Yoruba 21%, Igbo (Ibo) 18%, Ijaw 10%, Kanuri 4%, Ibibio 3.5%, Tiv 2.5%

Languages spoken: English (official), Hausa, Yoruba, Igbo (Ibo), Fulani, over 500 additional indigenous languages

Religions: Muslim 50%, Christian 40%, indigenous beliefs 10%

Niue

Official name: Niue

Capital city: Alofi

Internet country code: .nu

Flag description: Yellow with the flag of the United Kingdom in the upper hoist-side quadrant; the flag of the United Kingdom bears five yellow five-pointed stars - a large one on a blue disk in the center and a smaller one on each arm of the bold red cross

Geographical description: Oceania, island in the South Pacific Ocean, east of Tonga

Total area: 260 sq km

Climate: Tropical; modified by southeast trade winds

Nationality: noun: Niuean(s) *adjective:* Niuean

Population: 1,190 (July 2014 CIA est.)

Ethnic groups: Niuen 66.5%, part-Niuen 13.4%, non-Niuen 20.1% (includes 12% European and Asian and 8% Pacific Islanders) (2011 CIA est.)

Languages spoken: Niuean (official) 46% (a Polynesian language closely related to Tongan and Samoan), Niuean and English 32%, English (official) 11%, Niuean and others 5%, other 6% (2011 CIA est.)

Religions: Ekalesia Niue (Congregational Christian Church of Niue - a Protestant church founded by missionaries from the London Missionary Society) 67%, other Protestant 3% (includes Seventh Day Adventist 1%, Presbyterian 1%, and Methodist 1%), Mormon 10%, Roman Catholic 10%, Jehovah's Witnesses 2%, other 6%, none 2% (2011 CIA est.)

Norway

Official name: Kingdom of Norway

Capital city: Oslo

Internet country code: .no

Flag description: Red with a blue cross outlined in white that extends to the edges of the flag; the vertical part of the cross is shifted to the hoist side in the style of the Dannebrog (Danish flag)

Geographical description: Northern Europe, bordering the North Sea and the North Atlantic Ocean, west of Sweden

Total area: 323,802 sq km

Climate: Temperate along coast, modified by North Atlantic Current; colder interior with increased precipitation and colder summers; rainy year-round on west coast

Nationality: noun: Norwegian(s) *adjective:* Norwegian

Population: 5,147,792 (July 2014 CIA est.)

Ethnic groups: Norwegian 94.4% (includes Sami, about 60,000), other European 3.6%, other 2% (2007 CIA est.)

Languages spoken: Bokmal Norwegian (official), Nynorsk Norwegian (official), small Sami- and Finnish-speaking minorities

Religions: Church of Norway (Evangelical Lutheran - official) 82.1%, other Christian 3.9%, Muslim 2.3%, Roman Catholic 1.8%, other 2.4%, unspecified 7.5% (2011 CIA est.)

Oman

Official name: Sultanate of Oman

Capital city: Muscat

Internet country code: .om

Flag description: Three horizontal bands of white, red, and green of equal width with a broad, vertical red band on the hoist side; the national emblem (a khanjar dagger in its sheath superimposed on two crossed swords in scabbards) in white is centered near the top of the vertical band

Geographical description: Middle East, bordering the Arabian Sea, Gulf of Oman, and Persian Gulf, between Yemen and United Arab Emirates

Total area: 309,500 sq km

Climate: Dry desert; hot, humid along coast; hot, dry interior; strong southwest summer monsoon (May to September) in far south

Nationality: noun: Omani(s) *adjective:* Omani

Population: 3,219,775

Ethnic groups: Arab, Baluchi, South Asian (Indian, Pakistani, Sri Lankan, Bangladeshi), African

Languages spoken: Arabic (official), English, Baluchi, Urdu, Indian dialects

Religions: Muslim (official; majority are Ibadhi, lesser numbers of Sunni and Shia)) 85.9%, Christian 6.5%, Hindu 5.5%, Buddhist 0.8%, Jewish <.1, other 1%, unaffiliated 0.2%

Pakistan

Official name: Islamic Republic of Pakistan

Capital city: Islamabad

Internet country code: .pk

Flag description: Green with a vertical white band (symbolizing the role of religious minorities) on the hoist side; a large white crescent and star are centered in the green field; the crescent, star, and color green are traditional symbols of Islam

National anthem: Blessed be the sacred Land (first line in English translation), lyrics by Abdul Asar Hafeez Jullundhri, music by Ahmed G. Chagla

National animal: Markhor

National bird: Chakor (Red-legged partridge)

National flower: Jasmine

National poet: Allama Muhammad Iqbal (1877-1938)

National tree: Deodar (Cedrus Deodara)

Geographical description: Southern Asia, bordering the Arabian Sea, between India on the east and Iran and Afghanistan on the west and China in the north

Total area: 796,095 sq km

Climate: Mostly hot, dry desert; temperate in northwest; arctic in north

Nationality: noun: Pakistani(s) *adjective:* Pakistani

Population: 196,174,380 (July 2014 CIA est.)

Ethnic groups: Punjabi 44.68%, Pashtun (Pathan) 15.42%, Sindhi 14.1%, Sariaki 8.38%, Muhajirs 7.57%, Balochi 3.57%, other 6.28%

Languages spoken: Punjabi 48%, Sindhi 12%, Saraiki (a Punjabi variant) 10%, Pashto (alternate name, Pashtu) 8%, Urdu (official) 8%, Balochi 3%, Hindko 2%, Brahui 1%, English (official; lingua franca of Pakistani elite and most government ministries), Burushaski, and other 8%

Religions: Muslim (official) 96.4% (Sunni 85-90%, Shia 10-15%), other (includes Christian and Hindu) 3.6% (2010 CIA est.)

Palau

Official name: Republic of Palau

Capital city: Melekeok

Internet country code: .pw

Flag description: Light blue with a large yellow disk (representing the moon) shifted slightly to the hoist side

National anthem: "Belau Rekid" (Our Palau), composed by Ymesei O. Ezekiel

Geographical description: Oceania, group of islands in the North Pacific Ocean, southeast of the Philippines

Total area: 458 sq. km.

Climate: Tropical; hot and humid; wet season May to November

Nationality: noun: Palauan(s) *adjective:* Palauan

Population: 20,842 (July 2007 CIA est.)

Ethnic groups: Palauan (Micronesian with Malayan and Melanesian admixtures) 69.9%, Filipino 15.3%, Chinese 4.9%, other Asian 2.4%, white 1.9%, Carolinian 1.4%, other Micronesian 1.1%, other or unspecified 3.2%

Languages spoken: Palauan 64.7% official in all islands except Sonsoral (Sonsoralese and English are official), Tobi (Tobi and English are official), and Angaur (Angaur, Japanese, and English are official), Filipino 13.5%, English 9.4%, Chinese 5.7%, Carolinian 1.5%, Japanese 1.5%, other Asian 2.3%, other languages 1.5%

Religions: Roman Catholic 41.6%, Protestant 23.3%, Modekngei (indigenous to Palau) 8.8%, Seventh-Day Adventist 5.3%, Jehovah's Witness 0.9%, Latter-Day Saints 0.6%, other 3.1%, unspecified or none 16.4%

Panama

Official name: Republic of Panama

Capital city: Panama City

Internet country code: .pa

Flag description: Divided into four equal rectangles; the top quadrants are white (hoist side) with a blue five-pointed star in the center and plain red; the bottom quadrants are plain blue (hoist side) and white with a red five-pointed star in the center

Geographical description: Central America, bordering both the Caribbean Sea and the North Pacific Ocean, between Colombia and Costa Rica

Total area: 75,420 sq km

Climate: Tropical maritime; hot, humid, cloudy; prolonged rainy season (May to January), short dry season (January to May)

Nationality: noun: Panamanian(s) *adjective:* Panamanian

Population: 3,608,431 (July 2014 CIA est.)

Ethnic groups: Mestizo (mixed African, Amerindian, and European) 70%, Amerindian and mixed (West Indian) 14%, white 10%, Amerindian 6%

Languages spoken: Spanish (official), English 14%

Religions: Roman Catholic 85%, Protestant 15%

Papua New Guinea

Official name: Independent State of Papua New Guinea

Capital city: Port Moresby

Internet country code: .pg

Flag description: Divided diagonally from upper hoist-side corner; the upper triangle is red with a soaring yellow bird of paradise centered; the lower triangle is black with five white five-pointed stars of the Southern Cross constellation centered

National anthem: "O Arise All You Sons"

Geographical description: Oceania, group of islands including the eastern half of the island of New Guinea between the Coral Sea and the South Pacific Ocean, east of Indonesia

Total area: 462,840 sq km

Climate: Tropical; northwest monsoon (December to March), southeast monsoon (May to October); slight seasonal temperature variation

Nationality: noun: Papua New Guinean(s) *adjective:* Papua New Guinean

Population: 6,552,730 (July 2014 CIA est.)

Ethnic groups: Melanesian, Papuan, Negrito, Micronesian, Polynesian

Languages spoken: Tok Pisin (official), English (official), Hiri Motu (official), some 836 indigenous languages spoken (about 12% of the world's total); most languages have fewer than 1,000 speakers

Religions: Roman Catholic 27%, Protestant 69.4% (Evangelical Lutheran 19.5%, United Church 11.5%, Seventh-Day Adventist 10%, Pentecostal 8.6%, Evangelical Alliance 5.2%, Anglican 3.2%, Baptist 2.5%, other Protestant 8.9%), Baha'i 0.3%, indigenous beliefs and other 3.3% (2000 census)

Paraguay

Official name: Republic of Paraguay

Capital city: Asuncion

Internet country code: .py

Flag description: Three equal horizontal bands of red (top), white, and blue with an emblem centered in the white band; unusual flag in that the emblem is different on each side; the obverse (hoist side at the left) bears the national coat of arms (a yellow five-pointed star within a green wreath capped by the words *Republica del Paraguay*, all within two circles); the reverse (hoist side at the right) bears the seal of the treasury (a yellow lion below a red Cap of Liberty and the words *Paz y Justicia* (Peace and Justice) capped by the words *Republica del Paraguay*, all within two circles)

Geographical description: Central South America, northeast of Argentina

Total area: 406,752 sq km

Climate: Subtropical to temperate; substantial rainfall in the eastern portions, becoming semiarid in the far west

Nationality: noun: Paraguayan(s) *adjective:* Paraguayan

Population: 6,703,860 (July 2014 CIA est.)

Ethnic groups: Mestizo (mixed Spanish and Amerindian) 95%, other 5%

Languages spoken: Spanish (official), Guarani (official)

Religions: Roman Catholic 89.6%, Protestant 6.2%, other Christian 1.1%, other or unspecified 1.9%, none 1.1% (2002 census)

Peru

Official name: Republic of Peru

Capital city: Lima

Internet country code: .pe

Flag description: Three equal vertical bands of red (hoist side), white, and red with the coat of arms centered in the white band; the coat of arms features a shield bearing a vicuna, cinchona tree (the source of quinine), and a yellow cornucopia spilling out gold coins, all framed by a green wreath

National anthem: lyrics by Jose de la Torre Ugarte, music by Jose Bernardo Alcedo

Geographical description: Western South America, bordering the South Pacific Ocean, between Chile and Ecuador

Total area: 1,285,216 sq km

Climate: Varies from tropical in east to dry desert in west; temperate to frigid in Andes

Nationality: noun: Peruvian(s) *adjective:* Peruvian

Population: 30,147,935 (July 2014 CIA est.)

Ethnic groups: Amerindian 45%, mestizo (mixed Amerindian and white) 37%, white 15%, black, Japanese, Chinese, and other 3%

Languages spoken: Spanish (official) 84.1%, Quechua (official) 13%, Aymara (official) 1.7%, Ashaninka 0.3%, other native languages (includes a large number of minor Amazonian languages) 0.7%, other (includes foreign languages and sign language) 0.2% (2007 CIA est.)

Religions: Roman Catholic 81.3%, Evangelical 12.5%, other 3.3%, none 2.9% (2007 CIA est.)

Philippines

Official name: Republic of the Philippines

Capital city: Manila

Internet country code: .ph

Flag description: Two equal horizontal bands of blue (top; representing peace and justice) and red (representing courage); a white equilateral triangle based on the hoist side represents equality; the center of the triangle displays a yellow sun with eight primary rays, each representing one of the first eight provinces that sought independence from Spain; each corner of the triangle contains a small yellow five-pointed star representing the three major geographical divisions of the country: Luzon, Visayas, and Mindanao; the design of the flag dates to 1897

National anthem: "Lupang Hinirang," music from "Marcha Nacional Filipina" (Philippine National March) by Julian Felipe; lyrics from poem "Filipinas" by Jose Palma

National motto: "MAKA-DIYOS, MAKA-TAO, MAKAKA-LIKASAN AT MAKABANSA."

Geographical description: Southeastern Asia, archipelago between the Philippine Sea and the South China Sea, east of Vietnam

Total area: 300,000 sq km

Climate: Tropical marine; northeast monsoon (November to April); southwest monsoon (May to October)

Nationality: noun: Filipino(s) *adjective:* Philippine

Population: 107,668,231 (July 2014 CIA est.)

Ethnic groups: Tagalog 28.1%, Cebuano 13.1%, Ilocano 9%, Bisaya/Binisaya 7.6%, Hiligaynon Ilonggo 7.5%, Bikol 6%, Waray 3.4%, other 25.3% (2000 census)

Languages spoken: Filipino (official; based on Tagalog) and English (official); eight major dialects - Tagalog, Cebuano, Ilocano, Hiligaynon or Ilonggo, Bicol, Waray, Pampango, and Pangasinan

Religions: Catholic 82.9% (Roman Catholic 80.9%, Aglipayan 2%), Muslim 5%, Evangelical 2.8%, Iglesia ni Kristo 2.3%, other Christian 4.5%, other 1.8%, unspecified 0.6%, none 0.1% (2000 census)

Poland

Official name: Republic of Poland

Capital city: Warsaw

Internet country code: .pl

Flag description: Two equal horizontal bands of white (top) and red; similar to the flags of Indonesia and Monaco which are red (top) and white

National anthem: "Mazurek Dabrowskiego" (Dombrowski's Mazurka; informally known in English as "Poland Is Not Yet Lost" or "Poland Has Not Yet Perished")

National emblem: White eagle on a red field

Geographical description: Central Europe, east of Germany

Total area: 312,685 sq km

Climate: Temperate with cold, cloudy, moderately severe winters with frequent precipitation; mild summers with frequent showers and thundershowers

Nationality: noun: Pole(s) *adjective:* Polish

Population: 38,346,279 (July 2014 CIA est.)

Ethnic groups: Polish 96.9%, Silesian 1.1%, German 0.2%, Ukrainian 0.1%, other and unspecified 1.7%

Languages spoken: Polish (official) 96.2%, Polish and non-Polish 2%, non-Polish 0.5%, unspecified 1.3%

Religions: Catholic 87.2% (includes Roman Catholic 86.9% and Greek Catholic, Armenian Catholic, and Byzantine-Slavic Catholic .3%), Orthodox 1.3% (almost all are Polish Autocephalous Orthodox), Protestant 0.4% (mainly Augsburg Evangelical and Pentacostal), other 0.4% (includes Jehovah's Witness, Buddhist, Hare Krishna, Gaudiya Vaishnavism, Muslim, Jewish, Mormon), unspecified 10.8% (2012 CIA est.)

Portugal

Official name: Portuguese Republic

Capital city: Lisbon

Internet country code: .pt

Flag description: Two vertical bands of green (hoist side, two-fifths) and red (three-fifths) with the Portuguese coat of arms centered on the dividing line

National anthem: "A Portuguesa"

Geographical description: Southwestern Europe, bordering the North Atlantic Ocean, west of Spain

Total area: 92,090 sq km

Climate: Maritime temperate; cool and rainy in north, warmer and drier in south

Nationality: noun: Portuguese (singular and plural) *adjective:* Portuguese

Population: 10,813,834 (July 2014 CIA est.)

Ethnic groups: Homogeneous Mediterranean stock; citizens of black African descent who immigrated to mainland during decolonization number less than 100,000; since 1990 East Europeans have entered Portugal

Languages spoken: Portuguese (official), Mirandese (official - but locally used)

Religions: Roman Catholic 81%, other Christian 3.3%, other (includes Jewish, Muslim, other) 0.6%, none 6.8%, unspecified 8.3%

Qatar

Official name: State of Qatar

Capital city: Doha

Internet country code: .qa

Flag description: Maroon with a broad white serrated band (nine white points) on the hoist side

National anthem: "Swearing by God who erected the sky" (first line in English translation)

Geographical description: Middle East, peninsula bordering the Persian Gulf and Saudi Arabia

Total area: 11,586 sq km

Climate: Arid; mild, pleasant winters; very hot, humid summers

Nationality: noun: Qatari(s) *adjective:* Qatari

Population: 2,123,160 (July 2014 CIA est.)

Ethnic groups: Arab 40%, Indian 18%, Pakistani 18%, Iranian 10%, other 14%

Languages spoken: Arabic (official), English commonly used as a second language

Religions: Muslim 77.5%, Christian 8.5%, other (includes mainly Hindu and other Indian religions) 14% (2004 CIA est.)

Romania

Official name: Romania

Capital city: Bucharest

Internet country code: .ro

Flag description: Three equal vertical bands of blue (hoist side), yellow, and red; the national coat of arms that used to be centered in the yellow band has been removed

National anthem: "Deşteaptă-te Române!" (Awaken Thee, Romanian!)

Geographical description: Southeastern Europe, bordering the Black Sea, between Bulgaria and Ukraine

Total area: 238,391 sq km

Climate: Temperate; cold, cloudy winters with frequent snow and fog; sunny summers with frequent showers and thunderstorms

Nationality: noun: Romanian(s) *adjective:* Romanian

Population: 21,729,871 (July 2014 CIA est.)

Ethnic groups: Romanian 83.4%, Hungarian 6.1%, Roma 3.1%, Ukrainian 0.3%, German 0.2%, other 0.7%, unspecified 6.1% (2011 CIA est.)

Languages spoken: Romanian (official) 85.4%, Hungarian 6.3%, Romany (Gypsy) 1.2%, other 1%, unspecified 6.1% (2011 CIA est.)

Religions: Eastern Orthodox (including all sub-denominations) 81.9%, Protestant (various denominations including Reformed and Pentecostal) 6.4%, Roman Catholic 4.3%, other (includes Muslim) 0.9%, none or atheist 0.2%, unspecified 6.3% (2011 CIA est.)

Russia

Official name: Russian Federation

Capital city: Moscow

Internet country code: .ru

Flag description: Three equal horizontal bands of white (top), blue, and red

National anthem: lyrics from poem by Sergey Mikhalkov, music by Alexander Alexandrov

National symbol: Two-headed eagle

Geographical description: Northern Asia (the area west of the Urals is considered part of Europe), bordering the Arctic Ocean, between Europe and the North Pacific Ocean

Total area: 17,098,242 sq km

Climate: Ranges from steppes in the south through humid continental in much of European Russia; subarctic in Siberia to tundra climate in the polar north; winters vary from cool along Black Sea coast to frigid in Siberia; summers vary from warm in the steppes to cool along Arctic coast

Nationality: noun: Russian(s) *adjective:* Russian

Population: 142,470,272 (July 2014 CIA est.)

Ethnic groups: Russian 77.7%, Tatar 3.7%, Ukrainian 1.4%, Bashkir 1.1%, Chuvash 1%, Chechen 1%, other 10.2%, unspecified 3.9%

Languages spoken: Russian (official) 96.3%, Dolgang 5.3%, German 1.5%, Chechen 1%, Tatar 3%, other 10.3%

Religions: Russian Orthodox 15-20%, Muslim 10-15%, other Christian 2% (2006 CIA est.)

Rwanda

Official name: Republic of Rwanda

Capital city: Kigali

Internet country code: .rw

Flag description: Three horizontal bands of sky blue (top, double width), yellow, and green, with a golden sun with 24 rays near the fly end of the blue band

National anthem: "Rwanda Nziza"

Geographical description: Central Africa, east of Democratic Republic of the Congo

Total area: 26,338 sq km

Climate: Temperate; two rainy seasons (February to April, November to January); mild in mountains with frost and snow possible

Nationality: noun: Rwandan(s) *adjective:* Rwandan

Population: 12,337,138

Ethnic groups: Hutu (Bantu) 84%, Tutsi (Hamitic) 15%, Twa (Pygmy) 1%

Languages spoken: Kinyarwanda only (official, universal Bantu vernacular) 93.2%, Kinyarwanda and other language(s) 6.2%, French (official) and other language(s) 0.1%, English (official) and other language(s) 0.1%, Swahili

(or Kiswahili, used in commercial centers) 0.02%, other 0.03%, unspecified 0.3% (2002 CIA est.)

Religions: Roman Catholic 49.5%, Protestant 39.4% (includes Adventist 12.2% and other Protestant 27.2%), other Christian 4.5%, Muslim 1.8%, animist 0.1%, other 0.6%, none 3.6% (2001), unspecified 0.5% (2002 CIA est.)

Saint Kitts and Nevis

Official name: Federation of Saint Kitts and Nevis

Capital city: Basseterre

Internet country code: .kn

Flag description: Divided diagonally from the lower hoist side by a broad black band bearing two white five-pointed stars; the black band is edged in yellow; the upper triangle is green, the lower triangle is red

National anthem: "O Land of Beauty!" (first line)

National bird: Brown pelican (Pelecanusoccidentalis)

National flower: Poinciana or flamboyant (Delonix regia)

Geographical description: Caribbean, islands in the Caribbean Sea, about one-third of the way from Puerto Rico to Trinidad and Tobago

Total area: 261 sq km (Saint Kitts 168 sq km; Nevis 93 sq km)

Climate: Tropical, tempered by constant sea breezes; little seasonal temperature variation; rainy season (May to November)

Nationality: noun: Kittitian(s), Nevisian(s) *adjective:* Kittitian, Nevisian

Population: 51,538 (July 2014 CIA est.)

Ethnic groups: Predominantly black; some British, Portuguese, and Lebanese

Languages spoken: English (official)

Religions: Anglican, other Protestant, Roman Catholic

Saint Lucia

Official name: Saint Lucia

Capital city: Castries

Internet country code: .lc

Flag description: Blue, with a gold isosceles triangle below a black arrowhead; the upper edges of the arrowhead have a white border

National anthem: "Sons and daughters of Saint Lucia love the land that gave us birth" (first line)

National motto: "The Land, The People, The Light"

National bird: Saint Lucia parrot (Amazona versicolor)

National flowers: Rose and Marguerite

Geographical description: Caribbean, island between the Caribbean Sea and North Atlantic Ocean, north of Trinidad and Tobago

Total area: 616 sq km

Climate: Tropical, moderated by northeast trade winds; dry season January to April, rainy season May to August

Nationality: noun: Saint Lucian(s) *adjective:* Saint Lucian

Population: 163,362 (July 2014 CIA est.)

Ethnic groups: Black/African descent 85.3%, mixed 10.9%, East Indian 2.2%, other 1.6%, unspecified 0.1% (2010 CIA est.)

Languages spoken: English (official), French patois

Religions: Roman Catholic 61.5%, Protestant 25.5% (includes Seventh Day Adventist 10.4%, Pentecostal 8.9%, Baptist 2.2%, Anglican 1.6%, Church of God 1.5%, other Protestant .9%), other Christian 3.4% (includes Evangelical 2.3% and Jehovah's Witness 1.1%), Rastafarian 1.9%, other 0.4%, none 5.9%, unspecified 1.4% (2010 CIA est.)

Saint Vincent and the Grenadines

Official name: Saint Vincent and the Grenadines

Capital city: Kingstown

Internet country code: .vc

Flag description: Three vertical bands of blue (hoist side), gold (double width), and green; the gold band bears three green diamonds arranged in a V pattern

National anthem: "Saint Vincent, Land so beautiful" (first line)

Geographical description: Caribbean, islands between the Caribbean Sea and North Atlantic Ocean, north of Trinidad and Tobago

Total area: 389 sq km (Saint Vincent 344 sq km)

Climate: Tropical; little seasonal temperature variation; rainy season (May to November)

Nationality: noun: Saint Vincentian(s) or Vincentian(s) *adjective:* Saint Vincentian or Vincentian

Population: 102,918 (July 2014 CIA est.)

Ethnic groups: Black 66%, mixed 19%, East Indian 6%, European 4%, Carib Amerindian 2%, other 3%

Languages spoken: English, French patois

Religions: Protestant 75% (Anglican 47%, Methodist 28%), Roman Catholic 13%, other (includes Hindu, Seventh-Day Adventist, other Protestant) 12%

Samoa

Official name: Independent State of Samoa

Capital city: Apia

Internet country code: .ws

Flag description: Red with a blue rectangle in the upper hoist-side quadrant bearing five white five-pointed stars representing the Southern Cross constellation

National anthem: "O le Fua o le Saolotoga o Samoa" (The Banner of Freedom), lyrics and music by Sauni I. Kuresa

National motto: "Faavae i le Atua Samoa" (God Be the Foundation of Samoa)

Geographical description: Oceania, group of islands in the South Pacific Ocean, about one-half of the way from Hawaii to New Zealand

Total area: 2,831 sq km

Climate: Tropical; rainy season (November to April), dry season (May to October)

Nationality: noun: Samoan(s) *adjective:* Samoan

Population: 196,628

Ethnic groups: Samoan 92.6%, Euronesians (mixed European and Polynesian) 7%, Europeans 0.4% (2001 census)

Languages spoken: Samoan (Polynesian)(official), English

Religions: Protestant 57.4% (Congregationalist 31.8%, Methodist 13.7%, Assembly of God 8%, Seventh-Day Adventist 3.9%), Roman Catholic 19.4%, Mormon 15.2%, Worship Centre 1.7%, other Christian 5.5%, other 0.7%, none 0.1%, unspecified 0.1% (2011 CIA est.)

San Marino

Official name: Republic of San Marino

Capital city: San Marino

Internet country code: .sm

Flag description: Two equal horizontal bands of white (top) and light blue with the national coat of arms superimposed in the center; the coat of arms has a shield (featuring three towers on three peaks) flanked by a wreath, below a crown and above a scroll bearing the word *Libertas* (Liberty)

National anthem: written by Federico Consolo (score only)

Geographical description: Southern Europe, an enclave in central Italy

Total area: 61 sq km

Climate: Mediterranean; mild to cool winters; warm, sunny summers

Nationality: noun: Sammarinese (singular and plural) *adjective:* Sammarinese

Population: 32,742 (July 2014 CIA est.)

Ethnic groups: Sammarinese, Italian

Languages spoken: Italian

Religion: Roman Catholic

São Tomé and Príncipe

Official name: Democratic Republic of São Tomé and Príncipe

Capital city: São Tomé

Internet country code: .st

Flag description: Three horizontal bands of green (top), yellow (double width), and green with two black five-pointed stars placed side by side in the center of the yellow band and a red isosceles triangle based on the hoist side; uses the popular pan-African colors of Ethiopia

Geographical description: Western Africa, islands in the Gulf of Guinea, straddling the Equator, west of Gabon

Total area: 964 sq km

Climate: Tropical; hot, humid; one rainy season (October to May)

Nationality: noun: Sao Tomean (s) *adjective:* Sao Tomean

Population: 190,428 (July 2014 CIA est.)

Ethnic groups: Mestico, angolares (descendants of Angolan slaves), forros (descendants of freed slaves), servicais (contract laborers from Angola, Mozambique, and Cabo Verde), tongas (children of servicais born on the islands), Europeans (primarily Portuguese), Asians (mostly Chinese)

Languages spoken: Portuguese 98.4% (official), Forro 36.2%, Cabo Verdian 8.5%, French 6.8%, Angolar 6.6%, English 4.9%, Lunguie 1%, other (including sign language) 2.4%

Religions: Catholic 55.7%, Adventist 4.1%, Assembly of God 3.4%, New Apostolic 2.9%, Mana 2.3%, Universal Kingdom of God 2%, Jehovah's Witness 1.2%, other 6.2%, none 21.2%, unspecified 1% (2012 CIA est.)

Saudi Arabia

Official name: Kingdom of Saudi Arabia

Capital city: Riyadh

Internet country code: .sa

Flag description: Green, a traditional color in Islamic flags, with the Shahada or Muslim creed in large white Arabic script (translated as "There is no god but God; Muhammad is the Messenger of God") above a white horizontal saber (the tip points to the hoist side); design dates to the early 20th century and is closely associated with the Al Saud family which established the kingdom in 1932

Geographical description: Middle East, bordering the Persian Gulf and the Red Sea, north of Yemen

Total area: 2,149,690 sq km

Climate: Harsh, dry desert with great temperature extremes

Nationality: noun: Saudi(s) *adjective:* Saudi or Saudi Arabian

Population: 27,345,986

Ethnic groups: Arab 90%, Afro-Asian 10%

Languages spoken: Arabic (official)

Religions: Muslim (official; citizens are 85-90% Sunni and 10-15% Shia), other (includes Eastern Orthodox, Protestant, Roman Catholic, Jewish, Hindu, Buddhist, and Sikh) (2012 CIA est.)

Senegal

Official name: Republic of Senegal

Capital city: Dakar

Internet country code: .sn

Flag description: Three equal vertical bands of green (hoist side), yellow, and red with a small green five-pointed star centered in the yellow band; uses the popular pan-African colors of Ethiopia

Geographical description: Western Africa, bordering the North Atlantic Ocean, between Guinea-Bissau and Mauritania

Total area: 196,722 sq km

Climate: Tropical; hot, humid; rainy season (May to November) has strong southeast winds; dry season (December to April) dominated by hot, dry, harmattan wind

Nationality: noun: Senegalese (singular and plural) *adjective:* Senegalese

Population: 13,635,927 (July 2014 CIA est.)

Ethnic groups: Wolof 43.3%, Pular 23.8%, Serer 14.7%, Jola 3.7%, Mandinka 3%, Soninke 1.1%, European and Lebanese 1%, other 9.4%

Languages spoken: French (official), Wolof, Pulaar, Jola, Mandinka

Religions: Muslim 94% (most adhere to one of the four main Sufi brotherhoods), Christian 5% (mostly Roman Catholic), indigenous beliefs 1%

Serbia

Official name: Republic of Serbia

Capital city: Belgrade

Internet country code: .rs

Flag description: Three equal horizontal stripes of red (top), blue, and white; charged with the coat of arms of Serbia shifted slightly to the hoist side

National anthem: "Boze Pravde" (God of Justice), music by Davorin Jenko and lyrics by Jovan Djordjevic

Geographical description: Southeastern Europe, between Macedonia and Hungary

Total area: 77,474 sq km

Climate: In the north, continental climate (cold winters and hot, humid summers with well distributed rainfall); in other parts, continental and Mediterranean climate (relatively cold winters with heavy snowfall and hot, dry summers and autumns)

Nationality: noun: Serb(s) *adjective:* Serbian

Population: 7,209,764

Ethnic groups: Serb 83.3%, Hungarian 3.5%, Romany 2.1%, Bosniak 2%, other 5.7%, undeclared or unknown 3.4% (2011 CIA est.)

Languages spoken: Serbian (official) 88.1%, Hungarian 3.4%, Bosnian 1.9%, Romany 1.4%, other 3.4%, undeclared or unknown 1.8%

Religions: Serbian Orthodox 84.6%, Catholic 5%, Muslim 3.1%, Protestant 1%, atheist 1.1%, other 0.8%, undeclared or unknown 4.5% (2011 CIA est.)

Seychelles

Official name: Republic of Seychelles

Capital city: Victoria

Internet country code: .sc

Flag description: Five oblique bands of blue (hoist side), yellow, red, white, and green (bottom) radiating from the bottom of the hoist side

Geographical description: archipelago in the Indian Ocean, northeast of Madagascar

Total area: 455 sq km

Climate: Tropical marine; humid; cooler season during southeast monsoon (late May to September); warmer season during northwest monsoon (March to May)

Nationality: noun: Seychellois (singular and plural) *adjective:* Seychellois

Population: 91,650 (July 2014 CIA est.)

Ethnic groups: Mixed French, African, Indian, Chinese, and Arab

Languages spoken: Seychellois Creole (official) 89.1%, English (official) 5.1%, French (official) 0.7%, other 3.8%, unspecified 1.4% (2010 CIA est.)

Religions: Roman Catholic 76.2%, Protestant 10.6% (Anglican 6.1%, Pentecoastal Assembly 1.5%, Seventh-Day Adventist 1.2%, other Protestant 1.6), other Christian 2.4%, Hindu 2.4%, Muslim 1.6%, other non-Christian 1.1%, unspecified 4.8%, none 0.9% (2010 CIA est.)

Sierra Leone

Official name: Republic of Sierra Leone

Capital city: Freetown

Internet country code: .sl

Flag description: Three equal horizontal bands of light green (top), white, and light blue

Geographical description: Western Africa, bordering the North Atlantic Ocean, between Guinea and Liberia

Total area: 71,740 sq km

Climate: Tropical; hot, humid; summer rainy season (May to December); winter dry season (December to April)

Nationality: noun: Sierra Leonean(s) *adjective:* Sierra Leonean

Population: 5,743,725 (July 2014 CIA est.)

Ethnic groups: Temne 35%, Mende 31%, Limba 8%, Kono 5%, Kriole 2% (descendants of freed Jamaican slaves who were settled in the Freetown area in the late-18th century; also known as Krio), Mandingo 2%, Loko 2%, other 15% (includes refugees from Liberia's recent civil war, and small numbers of Europeans, Lebanese, Pakistanis, and Indians) (2008 census)

Languages spoken: English (official, regular use limited to literate minority), Mende (principal vernacular in the south), Temne (principal vernacular in the north), Krio (English-based Creole, spoken by the descendants of freed Jamaican slaves who were settled in the Freetown area, a lingua franca and a first language for 10% of the population but understood by 95%)

Religions: Muslim 60%, Christian 10%, indigenous beliefs 30%

Singapore

Official name: Republic of Singapore

Capital city: Singapore

Internet country code: .sg

Flag description: Two equal horizontal bands of red (top) and white; near the hoist side of the red band, there is a vertical, white crescent (closed portion is toward the hoist side) partially enclosing five white five-pointed stars arranged in a circle

National anthem: "Majulah Singapura" (Onward Singapore)

National flower: Vanda Miss Joaquim orchid

National symbol: Lion head

Geographical description: Southeastern Asia, islands between Malaysia and Indonesia

Total area: 697 sq km

Climate: Tropical; hot, humid, rainy; two distinct monsoon seasons - Northeastern monsoon (December to March) and Southwestern monsoon (June to September); inter-monsoon - frequent afternoon and early evening thunderstorms

Nationality: noun: Singaporean(s) *adjective:* Singapore

Population: 5,567,301 (July 2014 CIA est.)

Ethnic groups: Chinese 74.2%, Malay 13.3%, Indian 9.2%, other 3.3% (2013 CIA est.)

Languages spoken: Mandarin (official) 36.3%, English (official) 29.8%, Malay (official) 11.9%, Hokkien 8.1%, Tamil (official) 4.4%, Cantonese 4.1%, Teochew 3.2%, other Indian languages 1.2%, other Chinese dialects 1.1%, other 1.1% (2010 CIA est.)

Religions: Buddhist 33.9%, Muslim 14.3%, Taoist 11.3%, Catholic 7.1%, Hindu 5.2%, other Christian 11%, other 0.7%, none 16.4% (2010 CIA est.)

Sint Maarten

Official name: Country of Sint Maarten

Capital city: Philipsburg

Internet country code: .sx

Flag description: Two equal horizontal bands of red (top) and blue with a white isosceles triangle based on the hoist side; the center of the triangle displays the Sint Maarten coat of arms; the arms consist of an orange-bordered blue shield prominently displaying the white court house in Philipsburg, as well as a bouquet of yellow sage (the national flower) in the upper left, and the silhouette of a Dutch-French friendship monument in the upper right; the shield is surmounted by a yellow rising sun in front of which is a Brown Pelican in flight; a yellow scroll below the shield bears the motto: SEMPER PROGREDIENS (Always Progressing); the three main colors are identical to those on the Dutch flag

National anthem: "O Sweet Saint Martin's Land"; Lyrics by Gerard KEMPS

National motto: SEMPER PROGREDIENS (Always Progressing)

Geographical description: Caribbean, located in the Leeward Islands (northern) group; Dutch part of the island of Saint Martin in the Caribbean Sea; Sint Maarten lies east of the US Virgin Islands

Total area: 34 sq km

Climate: Tropical marine climate, ameliorated by northeast trade winds, results in moderate temperatures; average rainfall of 1500 mm/year; hurricane season stretches from July to November

Population: 39,689 (July 2013 est.)

Languages spoken: English (official) 67.5%, Spanish 12.9%, Creole 8.2%, Dutch (official) 4.2%, Papiamento (a Spanish-Portuguese-Dutch-English dialect) 2.2%, French 1.5%, other 3.5% (2001 census)

Religions: Roman Catholic 39%, Protestant 44.8% (Pentecostal 11.6%, Seventh-Day Adventist 6.2%, other Protestant

27%), none 6.7%, other 5.4%, Jewish 3.4%, not reported 0.7% (2001 census)

Slovakia

Official name: Slovak Republic

Capital city: Bratislava

Internet country code: .sk

Flag description: Three equal horizontal bands of white (top), blue, and red superimposed with the coat of arms of Slovakia (consisting of a red shield bordered in white and bearing a white Cross of Lorraine surmounting three blue hills); the coat of arms is centered vertically and offset slightly to the hoist side

National anthem: "Nad Tatrou sa blýska"

Geographical description: Central Europe, south of Poland

Total area: 49,035 sq km

Climate: Temperate; cool summers; cold, cloudy, humid winters

Nationality: noun: Slovak(s) *adjective:* Slovak

Population: 5,443,583 (July 2014 CIA est.)

Ethnic groups: Slovak 80.7%, Hungarian 8.5%, Roma 2%, other and unspecified 8.8% (2011 CIA est.)

Languages spoken: Slovak (official) 78.6%, Hungarian 9.4%, Roma 2.3%, Ruthenian 1%, other or unspecified 8.8% (2011 CIA est.)

Religions: Roman Catholic 62%, Protestant 8.2%, Greek Catholic 3.8%, other or unspecified 12.5%, none 13.4% (2011 CIA est.)

Slovenia

Official name: Republic of Slovenia

Capital city: Ljubljana

Internet country code: .si

Flag description: Three equal horizontal bands of white (top), blue, and red, with the Slovenian seal (a shield with the image of Triglav, Slovenia's highest peak, in white against a blue background at the center; beneath it are two wavy blue lines depicting seas and rivers, and above it are three six-pointed stars arranged in an inverted triangle, which are taken from the coat of arms of the Counts of Celje, the great Slovene dynastic house of the late 14th and early 15th centuries); the seal is in the upper hoist side of the flag centered in the white and blue bands

National anthem: the seventh stanza of France Preseren's poem "Zdravljica" (A Toast), music by Stanko Premrl

Geographical description: Central Europe, eastern Alps bordering the Adriatic Sea, between Austria and Croatia

Total area: 20,273 sq km

Climate: Mediterranean climate on the coast, continental climate with mild to hot summers and cold winters in the plateaus and valleys to the east

Nationality: noun: Slovene(s) *adjective:* Slovenian

Population: 1,988,292 (July 2014 CIA est.)

Ethnic groups: Slovene 83.1%, Serb 2%, Croat 1.8%, Bosniak 1.1%, other or unspecified 12% (2002 census)

Languages spoken: Slovenian (official) 91.1%, Serbo-Croatian 4.5%, other or unspecified 4.4%, Italian (official, only in municipalities where Italian national communities reside), Hungarian (official, only in municipalities where Hungarian national communities reside) (2002 census)

Religions: Catholic 57.8%, Muslim 2.4%, Orthodox 2.3%, other Christian 0.9%, unaffiliated 3.5%, other or unspecified 23%, none 10.1% (2002 census)

Solomon Islands

Official name: Solomon Islands

Capital city: Honiara

Internet country code: .sb

Flag description: Divided diagonally by a thin yellow stripe from the lower hoist-side corner; the upper triangle (hoist side) is blue with five white five-pointed stars arranged in an X pattern; the lower triangle is green

Geographical description: Oceania, group of islands in the South Pacific Ocean, east of Papua New Guinea

Total area: 28,896 sq km

Climate: Tropical monsoon; few extremes of temperature and weather

Nationality: noun: Solomon Islander(s) *adjective:* Solomon Islander

Population: 609,883 (July 2014 CIA est.)

Ethnic groups: Melanesian 95.3%, Polynesian 3.1%, Micronesian 1.2%, other 0.3% (2009 CIA est.)

Languages spoken: Melanesian pidgin (in much of the country is lingua franca), English (official but spoken by only 1%-2% of the population), 120 indigenous languages

Religions: Protestant 73.4% (Church of Melanesia 31.9%, South Sea Evangelical 17.1%, Seventh Day Adventist 11.7%, United Church 10.1%, Christian Fellowship Church 2.5%), Roman Catholic 19.6%, other Christian 2.9%, other 4%, none 0.03%, unspecified 0.1% (2009 CIA est.)

Somalia

Official name: Somalia

Capital city: Mogadishu

Internet country code: .so

Flag description: Light blue with a large white five-pointed star in the center; blue field influenced by the flag of the United Nations

Geographical description: Eastern Africa, bordering the Gulf of Aden and the Indian Ocean, east of Ethiopia

Total area: 637,657 sq km

Climate: Principally desert; northeast monsoon (December to February), moderate temperatures in north and hot in south; southwest monsoon (May to October), torrid in the north and hot in the south, irregular rainfall, hot and humid periods (tangambili) between monsoons

Nationality: noun: Somali(s) *adjective:* Somali

Population: 10,428,043

Ethnic groups: Somali 85%, Bantu and other non-Somali 15% (including 30,000 Arabs)

Languages spoken: Somali (official), Arabic (official, according to the Transitional Federal Charter), Italian, English

Religions: Sunni Muslim (Islam) (official, according to the Transitional Federal Charter)

South Africa

Official name: Republic of South Africa

Capital city: Pretoria

Internet country code: .za

Flag description: Two equal width horizontal bands of red (top) and blue separated by a central green band which splits into a horizontal Y, the arms of which end at the corners of the hoist side; the Y embraces a black isosceles triangle from which the arms are separated by narrow yellow bands; the red and blue bands are separated from the green band and its arms by narrow white stripes

National anthem: A combination of "Nkosi Sikelel' iAfrika" by Enoch Sontonga and "The Call of South Africa" (Die Stem van Suid-Afrika), lyrics by C. J. Langenhoven, music by M. L. de Villiers

National animal: Springbuck/springbok (Antidorcas marsupialis)

National bird: Blue crane (Anthropoides paradisia)

National fish: Galjoen (Coracinus capensis)

National flower: King Protea (Protea cynaroides)

National tree: Real yellowwood (Podocarpus latifolius)

Geographical description: Southern Africa, at the southern tip of the continent of Africa

Total area: 1,219,090 sq km

Climate: Mostly semiarid; subtropical along east coast; sunny days, cool nights

Nationality: noun: South African(s) *adjective:* South African

Population: 48,375,645

Ethnic groups: Black African 79.2%, white 8.9%, colored 8.9%, Indian/Asian 2.5%, other 0.5% (2011 CIA est.)

Languages spoken: IsiZulu (official) 22.7%, IsiXhosa (official) 16%, Afrikaans (official) 13.5%, English (official) 9.6%, Sepedi (official) 9.1%, Setswana (official) 8%, Sesotho (official) 7.6%, Xitsonga (official) 4.5%, siSwati (official) 2.5%, Tshivenda (official) 2.4%, isiNdebele (official) 2.1%, sign language 0.5%, other 1.6% (2011 CIA est.)

Religions: Protestant 36.6% (Zionist Christian 11.1%, Pentecostal/Charismatic 8.2%, Methodist 6.8%, Dutch Reformed 6.7%, Anglican 3.8%), Catholic 7.1%, Muslim 1.5%, other Christian 36%, other 2.3%, unspecified 1.4%, none 15.1% (2001 census)

South Sudan

Official name: Republic of South Sudan

Capital city: Juba

Internet country code: .ss

Flag description: Three equal horizontal bands of black (top), red, and green; the red band is edged in white; a blue isosceles triangle based on the hoist side contains a gold, five-pointed star; black represents the people of South Sudan, red the blood shed in the struggle for freedom, green the verdant land, and blue the waters of the Nile; the gold star represents the unity of the states making up South Sudan

National anthem: South Sudan Oyee! (Hooray!); Lyrics by collective of 49 poets/Juba University students and teachers

National symbol: African fish eagle

Geographical description: The Sudd is a vast swamp in South Sudan, formed by the White Nile, comprising more than 15% of the total area; it is one of the world's largest wetlands

Total area: 644,329 sq km

Climate: Hot with seasonal rainfall influenced by the annual shift of the Inter-Tropical Convergence Zone; rainfall is heaviest in the upland areas of the south and diminishes to the north

Nationality: noun:South Sudanese (singular and plural) *adjective: adjective:*South Sudanese

Population: 11,562,695 (July 2014 CIA est.)

Languages spoken: English (official), Arabic (includes Juba and Sudanese variants), regional languages include Dinka, Nuer, Bari, Zande, Shilluk

Religions: Animist, Christian

Spain

Official name: Kingdom of Spain

Capital city: Madrid

Internet country code: .es

Flag description: Three horizontal bands of red (top), yellow (double width), and red with the national coat of arms on the hoist side of the yellow band; the coat of arms includes the royal seal framed by the Pillars of Hercules, which are the two promontories (Gibraltar and Ceuta) on either side of the eastern end of the Strait of Gibraltar

National anthem: "Grenadier March" or "Royal Spanish March"

Geographical description: Southwestern Europe, bordering the Bay of Biscay, Mediterranean Sea, North Atlantic Ocean, and Pyrenees Mountains, southwest of France

Total area: 505,370 sq km

Climate: Temperate; clear, hot summers in interior, more moderate and cloudy along coast; cloudy, cold winters in interior, partly cloudy and cool along coast

Nationality: noun: Spaniard(s) *adjective:* Spanish

Population: 47,737,941 (July 2014 CIA est.)

Ethnic groups: Composite of Mediterranean and Nordic types

Languages spoken: Castilian Spanish (official) 74%, Catalan 17%, Galician 7%, and Basque 2%

Religions: Roman Catholic 94%, other 6%

Sri Lanka

Official name: Democratic Socialist Republic of Sri Lanka

Capital city: Colombo

Internet country code: .lk

Flag description: Yellow with two panels; the smaller hoist-side panel has two equal vertical bands of green (hoist side) and orange; the other panel is a large dark red rectangle with a yellow lion holding a sword, and there is a yellow bo leaf in each corner; the yellow field appears as a border around the entire flag and extends between the two panels

National anthem: "Sri Lanka Matha"

National flower: Blue Water Lily (Nymphaea stellata)

Geographical description: Southern Asia, island in the Indian Ocean, south of India

Total area: 65,610 sq km

Climate: Tropical monsoon; northeast monsoon (December to March); southwest monsoon (June to October)

Nationality: noun: Sri Lankan(s) *adjective:* Sri Lankan

Population: 21,866,445 (July 2014 CIA est.)

Ethnic groups: Sinhalese 73.8%, Sri Lankan Moors 7.2%, Indian Tamil 4.6%, Sri Lankan Tamil 3.9%, other 0.5%, unspecified 10% (2001 census provisional data)

Languages spoken: Sinhala (official and national language) 74%, Tamil (national language) 18%, other 8%

Religions: Buddhist (official) 69.1%, Muslim 7.6%, Hindu 7.1%, Christian 6.2%, unspecified 10% (2001 census provisional data)

Sudan

Official name: Republic of the Sudan

Capital city: Khartoum

Internet country code: .sd

Flag description: Three equal horizontal bands of red (top), white, and black with a green isosceles triangle based on the hoist side

Geographical description: Northern Africa, bordering the Red Sea, between Egypt and Eritrea

Total area: 1,861,484 sq km

Climate: tropical in south; arid desert in north; rainy season varies by region (April to November)

Nationality: noun: Sudanese (singular and plural) *adjective:* Sudanese

Population: 35,482,233 (July 2014 CIA est.)

Ethnic groups: Sudanese Arab (approximately 70%), Fur, Beja, Nuba, Fallata

Languages spoken: Arabic (official), English (official), Nubian, Ta Bedawie, Fur

Religions: Sunni Muslim, small Christian minority

Suriname

Official name: Republic of Suriname

Capital city: Paramaribo

Internet country code: .sr

Flag description: Five horizontal bands of green (top, double width), white, red (quadruple width), white, and green (double width); there is a large, yellow, five-pointed star centered in the red band

National anthem: "Rise country men rise" (first line)

National motto: Justitia – Pietas – Fides (Justice-Faith-Loyalty)

National flower: Fajalobi ("passionate love"; orchid)

Geographical description: Northern South America, bordering the North Atlantic Ocean, between French Guiana and Guyana

Total area: 163,820 sq km

Climate: Tropical; moderated by trade winds

Nationality: noun: Surinamer(s) *adjective:* Surinamese

Population: 573,311 (July 2014 CIA est.)

Ethnic groups: Hindustani (also known locally as "East Indians"; their ancestors emigrated from northern India in the latter part of the 19th century) 37%, Creole (mixed white and black) 31%, Javanese 15%, "Maroons" (their African ancestors were brought to the country in the 17th and 18th centuries as slaves and escaped to the interior) 10%, Amerindian 2%, Chinese 2%, white 1%, other 2%

Languages spoken: Dutch (official), English (widely spoken), Sranang Tongo (Surinamese, sometimes called Taki-Taki, is native language of Creoles and much of the younger population and is lingua franca among others), Caribbean Hindustani (a dialect of Hindi), Javanese

Religions: Hindu 27.4%, Protestant 25.2% (predominantly Moravian), Roman Catholic 22.8%, Muslim 19.6%, indigenous beliefs 5%

Swaziland

Official name: Kingdom of Swaziland

Capital city: Mbabane

Internet country code: .sz

Flag description: Three horizontal bands of blue (top), red (triple width), and blue; the red band is edged in yellow; centered in the red band is a large black and white shield covering two spears and a staff decorated with feather tassels, all placed horizontally

Geographical description: Southern Africa, between Mozambique and South Africa

Total area: 17,364 sq km

Climate: Varies from tropical to near temperate

Nationality: noun: Swazi(s) *adjective:* Swazi

Population: 1,419,623

Ethnic groups: African 97%, European 3%

Languages spoken: English (official, used for government business), siSwati (official)

Religions: Zionist 40% (a blend of Christianity and indigenous ancestral worship), Roman Catholic 20%, Muslim 10%, other (includes Anglican, Baha'i, Methodist, Mormon, Jewish) 30%

Sweden

Official name: Kingdom of Sweden

Capital city: Stockholm

Internet country code: .se

Flag description: Blue with a golden yellow cross extending to the edges of the flag; the vertical part of the cross is shifted to the hoist side in the style of the Dannebrog (Danish flag)

National anthem: "Du gamla, Du fria" (Thou ancient, Thou freeborn)

Geographical description: Northern Europe, bordering the Baltic Sea, Gulf of Bothnia, Kattegat, and Skagerrak, between Finland and Norway

Total area: 450,295 sq km

Climate: Temperate in south with cold, cloudy winters and cool, partly cloudy summers; subarctic in north

Nationality: noun: Swede(s) *adjective:* Swedish

Population: 9,723,809 (July 2014 CIA est.)

Ethnic groups: Indigenous population: Swedes with Finnish and Sami minorities; foreign-born or first-generation immigrants: Finns, Yugoslavs, Danes, Norwegians, Greeks, Turks

Languages spoken: Swedish (official), small Sami- and Finnish-speaking minorities

Religions: Lutheran 87%, other (includes Roman Catholic, Orthodox, Baptist, Muslim, Jewish, and Buddhist) 13%

Switzerland

Official name: Swiss Confederation

Capital city: Bern

Internet country code: .ch

Flag description: Red square with a bold, equilateral white cross in the center that does not extend to the edges of the flag

National anthem: "Schweizerpsalm" (Swiss Psalm)

Geographical description: Central Europe, east of France, north of Italy

Total area: 41,277 sq km

Climate: Temperate, but varies with altitude; cold, cloudy, rainy/snowy winters; cool to warm, cloudy, humid summers with occasional showers

Nationality: noun: Swiss (singular and plural) *adjective:* Swiss

Population: 8,061,516 (July 2014 CIA est.)

Ethnic groups: German 65%, French 18%, Italian 10%, Romansch 1%, other 6%

Languages spoken: German (official) 64.9%, French (official) 22.6%, Italian (official) 8.3%, Serbo-Croatian 2.5%, Albanian 2.6%, Portuguese 3.4%, Spanish 2.2%, English 4.6%, Romansch (official) 0.5%, other 5.1%

Religions: Roman Catholic 38.2%, Protestant 26.9%, Muslim 4.9%, other Christian 5.7%, other 1.6%, none 21.4%, unspecified 1.3% (2012 CIA est.)

Syria

Official name: Syrian Arab Republic

Capital city: Damascus

Internet country code: .sy

Flag description: Three equal horizontal bands of red (top), white, and black, colors associated with the Arab Liberation flag; two small green five-pointed stars in a horizontal line centered in the white band; former flag of the United Arab Republic where the two stars represented the constituent states of Syria and Egypt; similar to the flag of Yemen, which has a plain white band, Iraq, which has three green stars (plus an Arabic inscription) in a horizontal line centered in the white band, and that of Egypt, which has a gold Eagle of Saladin centered in the white band; the current design dates to 1980

Geographical description: Middle East, bordering the Mediterranean Sea, between Lebanon and Turkey

Total area: 185,180 sq km

Climate: Mostly desert; hot, dry, sunny summers (June to August) and mild, rainy winters (December to February) along coast; cold weather with snow or sleet periodically in Damascus

Nationality: noun: Syrian(s) *adjective:* Syrian

Population: 17,951,639

Ethnic groups: Arab 90.3%, Kurds, Armenians, and other 9.7%

Languages spoken: Arabic (official), Kurdish, Armenian, Aramaic, Circassian (widely understood); French, English (somewhat understood)

Religions: Muslim 87% (official; includes Sunni 74% and Alawi, Ismaili, and Shia 13%), Christian (includes Orthodox, Uniate, and Nestorian) 10% (includes Orthodox, Uniate, and Nestorian), Druze 3%, Jewish (few remaining in Damascus and Aleppo)

Taiwan

Official name: Taiwan

Capital city: Taipei

Internet country code: .tw

Flag description: Red with a dark blue rectangle in the upper hoist-side corner bearing a white sun with 12 triangular rays

National flower: Plum blossom (prunus mei) [gov website]

Geographical description: Eastern Asia, islands bordering the East China Sea, Philippine Sea, South China Sea, and Taiwan Strait, north of the Philippines, off the southeastern coast of China

Total area: 35,980 sq km

Climate: Tropical; marine; rainy season during southwest monsoon (June to August); cloudiness is persistent and extensive all year

Nationality: noun: Taiwan (singular and plural) *adjective:* Taiwan (or Taiwanese)

Population: 23,359,928 (July 2014 CIA est.)

Ethnic groups: Taiwanese (including Hakka) 84%, mainland Chinese 14%, indigenous 2%

Languages spoken: Mandarin Chinese (official), Taiwanese (Min), Hakka dialects

Religions: Mixture of Buddhist and Taoist 93%, Christian 4.5%, other 2.5%

Tajikistan

Official name: Republic of Tajikistan

Capital city: Dushanbe

Internet country code: .tj

Flag description: Three horizontal stripes of red (top), a wider stripe of white, and green; a gold crown surmounted by seven gold five-pointed stars is located in the center of the white stripe

Geographical description: Central Asia, west of China

Total area: 143,100 sq km

Climate: Mid-latitude continental, hot summers, mild winters; semiarid to polar in Pamir Mountains

Nationality: noun: Tajikistani(s) *adjective:* Tajikistani

Population: 8,051,512 (July 2014 CIA est.)

Ethnic groups: Tajik 79.9%, Uzbek 15.3%, Russian 1.1%, Kyrgyz 1.1%, other 2.6% (2000 census)

Languages spoken: Tajik (official), Russian widely used in government and business

Religions: Sunni Muslim 85%, Shi'a Muslim 5%, other 10% (2003 CIA est.)

Tanzania

Official name: United Republic of Tanzania

Capital city: Dar es Salaam

Internet country code: .tz

Flag description: Divided diagonally by a yellow-edged black band from the lower hoist-side corner; the upper triangle (hoist side) is green and the lower triangle is blue

National anthem: "Wimbo Wa Taifa" (God Bless Africa)

National motto: "Uhuru na Umoja" (Freedom and Unity)

National symbol: Uhuru Torch

Geographical description: Eastern Africa, bordering the Indian Ocean, between Kenya and Mozambique

Total area: 947,300 sq km

Climate: Varies from tropical along coast to temperate in highlands

Nationality: noun: Tanzanian(s) *adjective:* Tanzanian

Population: 49,639,138

Ethnic groups: Mainland - African 99% (of which 95% are Bantu consisting of more than 130 tribes), other 1% (consisting of Asian, European, and Arab); Zanzibar - Arab, African, mixed Arab and African

Languages spoken: Kiswahili or Swahili (official), Kiunguja (name for Swahili in Zanzibar), English (official, primary language of commerce, administration, and higher education), Arabic (widely spoken in Zanzibar), many local languages

Religions: Mainland - Christian 30%, Muslim 35%, indigenous religions 35%; Zanzibar - more than 99% Muslim

Thailand

Official name: Kingdom of Thailand

Capital city: Bangkok

Internet country code: .th

Flag description: Five horizontal bands of red (top), white, blue (double width), white, and red

National animal: Elephant

National architecture: Sala Thai (Thai Pavilion)

National flower: Ratchaphruek (Cassia fistula Linn)

Geographical description: Southeastern Asia, bordering the Andaman Sea and the Gulf of Thailand, southeast of Burma

Total area: 513,120 sq km

Climate: Tropical; rainy, warm, cloudy southwest monsoon (mid-May to September); dry, cool northeast monsoon (November to mid-March); southern isthmus always hot and humid

Nationality: noun: Thai (singular and plural) *adjective:* Thai

Population: 67,741,401

Ethnic groups: Thai 95.9%, Burmese 2%, other 1.3%, unspecified 0.9% (2010 CIA est.)

Languages spoken: Thai (official) 90.7%, Burmese 1.3%, other 8%

Religions: Buddhist (official) 93.6%, Muslim 4.9%, Christian 1.2%, other 0.2%, none 0.1% (2010 CIA est.)

Timor-Leste

Official name: Democratic Republic of Timor-Leste (formerly East Timor)

Capital city: Dili

Internet country code: .tl

Flag description: Red, with a black isosceles triangle (based on the hoist side) superimposed on a slightly longer yellow arrowhead that extends to the center of the flag; there is a white star in the center of the black triangle

National anthem: "Pátria" (Fatherland), lyrics by Francisco Borja da Costa, music by Afonso de Araújo

Geographical description: Southeastern Asia, northwest of Australia in the Lesser Sunda Islands at the eastern end of the Indonesian archipelago; note - Timor-Leste includes the eastern half of the island of Timor, the Oecussi (Ambeno) region on the northwest portion of the island of Timor, and the islands of Pulau Atauro and Pulau Jaco

Total area: 14,874 sq km

Climate: Tropical; hot, humid; distinct rainy and dry seasons

Nationality: noun: Timorese *adjective:* Timorese

Population: 1,201,542

Ethnic groups: Austronesian (Malayo-Polynesian), Papuan, small Chinese minority

Languages spoken: Tetum (official), Portuguese (official), Indonesian, English

Religions: Roman Catholic 96.9%, Protestant / Evangelical 2.2%, Muslim 0.3%, other 0.6% (2005 CIA est.)

Togo

Official name: Togolese Republic

Capital city: Lomé

Internet country code: .tg

Flag description: Five equal horizontal bands of green (top and bottom) alternating with yellow; there is a white five-pointed star on a red square in the upper hoist-side corner; uses the popular pan-African colors of Ethiopia

Geographical description: Western Africa, bordering the Bight of Benin, between Benin and Ghana

Total area: 56,785 sq km

Climate: Tropical; hot, humid in south; semiarid in north

Nationality: noun: Togolese (singular and plural) *adjective:* Togolese

Population: 7,351,374

Ethnic groups: African (37 tribes; largest and most important are Ewe, Mina, and Kabre) 99%, European and Syrian-Lebanese less than 1%

Languages spoken: French (official, the language of commerce), Ewe and Mina (the two major African languages in the south), Kabye (sometimes spelled Kabiye) and Dagomba (the two major African languages in the north)

Religions: Christian 29%, Muslim 20%, indigenous beliefs 51%

Tonga

Official name: Kingdom of Tonga

Capital city: Nuku'alofa

Internet country code: .to

Flag description: Red with a bold red cross on a white rectangle in the upper hoist-side corner

Geographical description: Oceania, archipelago in the South Pacific Ocean, about two-thirds of the way from Hawaii to New Zealand

Total area: 747 sq km

Climate: Tropical; modified by trade winds; warm season (December to May), cool season (May to December)

Nationality: noun: Tongan(s) *adjective:* Tongan

Population: 106,440 (July 2014 CIA est.)

Ethnic groups: Tongan 96.6%, part-Tongan 1.7%, other 1.7%, unspecified 0.03% (2006 CIA est.)

Languages spoken: English and Tongan 87%, Tongan (official) 10.7%, English (official) 1.2%, other 1.1%, uspecified 0.03% (2006 CIA est.)

Religions: Protestant 64.9% (includes Free Wesleyan Church 37.3%, Free Church of Tonga 11.4%, Church of Tonga 7.2%, Tokaikolo Christian Church 2.6%, Assembly of God 2.3% Seventh Day Adventist 2.2%, Constitutional Church of Tonga .9%, Anglican .8% and Full Gospel

Church .2%), Mormon 16.8%, Roman Catholic 15.6%, other 1.1%, none 0.03%, unspecified 1.7% (2006 CIA est.)

Trinidad and Tobago

Official name: Republic of Trinidad and Tobago

Capital city: Port-of-Spain

Internet country code: .tt

Flag description: Red with a white-edged black diagonal band from the upper hoist side to the lower fly side

National anthem: "Forged from the love of liberty" (first line) by Patrick S. Castagne

National motto: "Together We Aspire, Together We Achieve"

National bird: Scarlet Ibis (Tantalus Ruber) and Cocrico (Rufus Tailed Guan)

National flower: Chaconia, called "Wild Poinsettia" or "Pride of Trinidad and Tobago" (of the family Rubianceae)

National watchwords: Discipline, Production, Tolerance

Geographical description: Caribbean, islands between the Caribbean Sea and the North Atlantic Ocean, northeast of Venezuela

Total area: 5,128 sq km

Climate: Tropical; rainy season (June to December)

Nationality: noun: Trinidadian(s), Tobagonian(s) *adjective:* Trinidadian, Tobagonian

Population: 1,223,916 (July 2014 CIA est.)

Ethnic groups: East Indian 35.4%, African 34.2%, mixed - other 15.3%, mixed African/East Indian 7.7%, other 1.3%, unspecified 6.2% (2011 CIA est.)

Languages spoken: English (official), Caribbean Hindustani (a dialect of Hindi), French, Spanish, Chinese

Religions: Protestant 32.1% (Pentecostal/Evangelical/Full Gospel 12%, Baptist 6.9%, Anglican 5.7%, Seventh-Day Adventist 4.1%, Presbyterian/Congretational 2.5, other Protestant .9), Roman Catholic 21.6%, Hindu 18.2%, Muslim 5%, Jehovah's Witness 1.5%, other 8.4%, none 2.2%, unspecified 11.1% (2011 CIA est.)

Tunisia

Official name: Tunisian Republic

Capital city: Tunis

Internet country code: .tn

Flag description: Red with a white disk in the center bearing a red crescent nearly encircling a red five-pointed star; the crescent and star are traditional symbols of Islam

Geographical description: Northern Africa, bordering the Mediterranean Sea, between Algeria and Libya

Total area: 163,610 sq km

Climate: Temperate in north with mild, rainy winters and hot, dry summers; desert in south

Nationality: noun: Tunisian(s) *adjective:* Tunisian

Population: 10,937,521 (July 2014 CIA est.)

Ethnic groups: Arab 98%, European 1%, Jewish and other 1%

Languages spoken: Arabic (official, one of the languages of commerce), French (commerce), Berber (Tamazight)

Religions: Muslim (official; Sunni) 99.1%, other (includes Christian, Jewish, Shia Muslim, and Baha'i) 1%

Turkey

Official name: Republic of Turkey

Capital city: Ankara

Internet country code: .tr

Flag description: Red with a vertical white crescent (the closed portion is toward the hoist side) and white five-pointed star centered just outside the crescent opening

National anthem: "Istiklal Marsi" (The Independence March)

Geographical description: Southeastern Europe and southwestern Asia (that portion of Turkey west of the Bosporus is geographically part of Europe), bordering the Black Sea, between Bulgaria and Georgia, and bordering the Aegean Sea and the Mediterranean Sea, between Greece and Syria

Total area: 783,562 sq km

Climate: Temperate; hot, dry summers with mild, wet winters; harsher in interior

Nationality: noun: Turk(s) *adjective:* Turkish

Population: 81,619,392 (July 2014 CIA est.)

Ethnic groups: Turkish 70-75%, Kurdish 18%, other minorities 7-12% (2008 CIA est.)

Languages spoken: Turkish (official), Kurdish, other minority languages

Religions: Muslim 99.8% (mostly Sunni) , other 0.2% (mostly Christians and Jews)

Turkmenistan

Official name: Turkmenistan

Capital city: Ashgabat (Ashkhabad)

Internet country code: .tm

Flag description: Green field with a vertical red stripe near the hoist side, containing five tribal *guls* (designs used in producing carpets) stacked above two crossed olive branches similar to the olive branches on the United Nations flag; a white crescent moon representing Islam with five white stars representing the regions or *velayats* of Turkmenistan appear in the upper corner of the field just to the fly side of the red stripe

National anthem: "The great creation of Turkmenbashy" (first line in English translation)

Geographical description: Central Asia, bordering the Caspian Sea, between Iran and Kazakhstan

Total area: 488,100 sq km

Climate: Subtropical desert

Nationality: noun: Turkmen(s) *adjective:* Turkmen

Population: 5,171,943 (July 2014 CIA est.)

Ethnic groups: Turkmen 85%, Uzbek 5%, Russian 4%, other 6% (2003)

Languages spoken: Turkmen (offical) 72%, Russian 12%, Uzbek 9%, other 7%

Religions: Muslim 89%, Eastern Orthodox 9%, unknown 2%

Tuvalu

Official name: Tuvalu

Capital city: Funafuti

Internet country code: .tv

Flag description: Light blue with the flag of the United Kingdom in the upper hoist-side quadrant; the outer half of the flag represents a map of the country with nine yellow five-pointed stars symbolizing the nine islands

Geographical description: Oceania, island group consisting of nine coral atolls in the South Pacific Ocean, about one-half of the way from Hawaii to Australia

Total area: 26 sq km

Climate: Tropical; moderated by easterly trade winds (March to November); westerly gales and heavy rain (November to March)

Nationality: noun: Tuvaluan(s) *adjective:* Tuvaluan

Population: 10,782 (July 2014 CIA est.)

Ethnic groups: Polynesian 96%, Micronesian 4%

Languages spoken: Tuvaluan (official), English (official), Samoan, Kiribati (on the island of Nui)

Religions: Protestant 98.4% (Church of Tuvalu (Congregationalist) 97%, Seventh-Day Adventist 1.4%), Baha'i 1%, other 0.6%

Uganda

Official name: Republic of Uganda

Capital city: Kampala

Internet country code: .ug

Flag description: Six equal horizontal bands of black (top), yellow, red, black, yellow, and red; a white disk is superimposed at the center and depicts a red-crested crane (the national symbol) facing the hoist side

National anthem: "Oh, Uganda! may God uphold thee"

National motto: "For God and My Country"

National bird: Crested crane (Regulorum gibbericeps)

Geographical description: Eastern Africa, west of Kenya

Total area: 241,038 sq km

Climate: Tropical; generally rainy with two dry seasons (December to February, June to August); semiarid in northeast

Nationality: noun: Ugandan(s) *adjective:* Ugandan

Population: 35,918,915

Ethnic groups: Baganda 16.9%, Banyankole 9.5%, Basoga 8.4%, Bakiga 6.9%, Iteso 6.4%, Langi 6.1%, Acholi 4.7%, Bagisu 4.6%, Lugbara 4.2%, Bunyoro 2.7%, other 29.6% (2002 census)

Languages spoken: English (official national language, taught in grade schools, used in courts of law and by most newspapers and some radio broadcasts), Ganda or Luganda (most widely used of the Niger-Congo languages, preferred for native language publications in the capital and may be taught in school), other Niger-Congo languages, Nilo-Saharan languages, Swahili, Arabic

Religions: Roman Catholic 41.9%, Protestant 42% (Anglican 35.9%, Pentecostal 4.6%, Seventh-Day Adventist 1.5%), Muslim 12.1%, other 3.1%, none 0.9% (2002 census)

Ukraine

Official name: Ukraine

Capital city: Kyiv (Kiev)

Internet country code: .ua

Flag description: Two equal horizontal bands of azure (top) and golden yellow represent grain fields under a blue sky

National anthem: "Sche ne vmerla Ukrainy i slava i volya" (first line in English translation: The glory and fame of Ukraine are still alive), lyrics by Pavlo Chubynsky, music by Mykhailo Verbytsky

Geographical description: Eastern Europe, bordering the Black Sea, between Poland, Romania, and Moldova in the west and Russia in the east

Total area: 603,550 sq km

Climate: Temperate continental; Mediterranean only on the southern Crimean coast; precipitation disproportionately distributed, highest in west and north, lesser in east and southeast; winters vary from cool along the Black Sea to cold farther inland; summers are warm across the greater part of the country, hot in the south

Nationality: noun: Ukrainian(s) *adjective:* Ukrainian

Population: 44,291,413 (July 2014 CIA est.)

Ethnic groups: Ukrainian 77.8%, Russian 17.3%, Belarusian 0.6%, Moldovan 0.5%, Crimean Tatar 0.5%, Bulgarian 0.4%, Hungarian 0.3%, Romanian 0.3%, Polish 0.3%, Jewish 0.2%, other 1.8% (2001 CIA est.)

Languages spoken: Ukrainian (official) 67%, Russian (regional language) 24%, other (includes small Romanian-, Polish-, and Hungarian-speaking minorities) 9%

Religions: Orthodox (includes Ukrainian Autocephalous Orthodox (UAOC), Ukrainian Orthodox - Kyiv Patriarchate (UOC-KP), Ukrainian Orthodox - Moscow Patriarchate (UOC-MP), Ukrainian Greek Catholic, Roman Catholic, Protestant, Muslim, Jewish

United Arab Emirates

Official name: United Arab Emirates

Capital city: Abu Dhabi

Internet country code: .ae

Flag description: Three equal horizontal bands of green (top), white, and black with a wider vertical red band on the hoist side

Geographical description: Middle East, bordering the Gulf of Oman and the Persian Gulf, between Oman and Saudi Arabia

Total area: 83,600 sq km

Climate: Desert; cooler in eastern mountains

Nationality: noun: Emirati(s) *adjective:* Emirati

Population: 5,628,805

Ethnic groups: Emirati 19%, other Arab and Iranian 23%, South Asian 50%, other expatriates (includes Westerners and East Asians) 8% (1982)

Languages spoken: Arabic (official), Persian, English, Hindi, Urdu

Religions: Muslim (Islam; official) 76%, Christian 9%, other (primarily Hindu and Buddhist, less than 5% of the population consists of Parsi, Baha'i, Druze, Sikh, Ahmadi, Ismaili, Dawoodi Bohra Muslim, and Jewish) 15%

United Kingdom

Official name: United Kingdom of Great Britain and Northern Ireland (note - Great Britain includes England, Scotland, and Wales)

Capital city: London

Internet country code: .uk

Flag description: Blue field with the red cross of Saint George (patron saint of England) edged in white superimposed on the diagonal red cross of Saint Patrick (patron saint of Ireland), which is superimposed on the diagonal white cross of Saint Andrew (patron saint of Scotland); properly known as the Union Flag, but commonly called the Union Jack; the design and colors (especially the Blue Ensign) have been the basis for a number of other flags including other Commonwealth countries and their constituent states or provinces, and British overseas territories

National anthem: "God Save the Queen"

Geographical description: Western Europe, islands including the northern one-sixth of the island of Ireland between the North Atlantic Ocean and the North Sea, northwest of France

Total area: 243,610 sq km

Climate: Temperate; moderated by prevailing southwest winds over the North Atlantic Current; more than one-half of the days are overcast

Nationality: noun: Briton(s), British (collective plural) *adjective:* British

Population: 63,742,977 (July 2014 CIA est.)

Ethnic groups: White 87.2%, black/African/Caribbean/black British 3%, Asian/Asian British: Indian 2.3%, Asian/Asian British: Pakistani 1.9%, mixed 2%, other 3.7% (2011 CIA est.)

Languages spoken: English, Welsh, Irish Gaelic, Scottish Gaelic

Religions: Christian (includes Anglican, Roman Catholic, Presbyterian, Methodist) 59.5%, Muslim 4.4%, Hindu 1.3%, other 2%, none 25.7%, unspecified 7.2% (2011 CIA est.)

United States

Official name: United States of America

Capital city: Washington, D.C.

Internet country code: .us

Flag description: Thirteen equal horizontal stripes of red (top and bottom) alternating with white; there is a blue rectangle in the upper hoist-side corner bearing 50 small white five-pointed stars arranged in nine offset horizontal rows of six stars (top and bottom) alternating with rows of five stars; the 50 stars represent the 50 states, the 13 stripes represent the 13 original colonies; known as Old Glory; the design and colors have been the basis for a number of other flags, including Chile, Liberia, Malaysia, and Puerto Rico

National anthem: "The Star-Spangled Banner"

National mottoes: *E pluribus unum* (Out of Many, One) and "In God We Trust"

National bird: Bald eagle

Geographical description: North America, bordering both the North Atlantic Ocean and the North Pacific Ocean, between Canada and Mexico

Total area: 9,826,675 sq km

Climate: Mostly temperate, but tropical in Hawaii and Florida, arctic in Alaska, semiarid in the Great Plains west of the Mississippi River, and arid in the Great Basin of the southwest; low winter temperatures in the northwest are ameliorated occasionally in January and February by warm chinook winds from the eastern slopes of the Rocky Mountains

Nationality: noun: American(s) *adjective:* American

Population: 318,892,103 (July 2014 CIA est.)

Ethnic groups: White 79.96%, black 12.85%, Asian 4.43%, Amerindian and Alaska native 0.97%, native Hawaiian and other Pacific islander 0.18%, two or more races 1.61% (July 2007 CIA est.)

Languages spoken: English 82.1%, Spanish 10.7%, other Indo-European 3.8%, Asian and Pacific island 2.7%, other 0.7% (2000 census)

Religions: Protestant 51.3%, Roman Catholic 23.9%, Mormon 1.7%, other Christian 1.6%, Jewish 1.7%, Buddhist 0.7%, Muslim 0.6%, other or unspecified 2.5%, unaffiliated 12.1%, none 4% (2007 CIA est.)

Uruguay

Official name: Oriental Republic of Uruguay

Capital city: Montevideo

Internet country code: .uy

Flag description: Nine equal horizontal stripes of white (top and bottom) alternating with blue; there is a white square in the upper hoist-side corner with a yellow sun bearing a human face known as the Sun of May with 16 rays that alternate between triangular and wavy

Geographical description: Southern South America, bordering the South Atlantic Ocean, between Argentina and Brazil

Total area: 176,215 sq km

Climate: Warm temperate; freezing temperatures almost unknown

Nationality: noun: Uruguayan(s) *adjective:* Uruguayan

Population: 3,332,972 (July 2014 CIA est.)

Ethnic groups: White 88%, mestizo 8%, black 4%, Amerindian (practically nonexistent)

Languages spoken: Spanish (official), Portunol, Brazilero (Portuguese-Spanish mix on the Brazilian frontier)

Religions: Roman Catholic 47.1%, non-Catholic Christians 11.1%, nondenominational 23.2%, Jewish 0.3%, atheist or agnostic 17.2%, other 1.1% (2006)

Uzbekistan

Official name: Republic of Uzbekistan

Capital city: Tashkent (Toshkent)

Internet country code: .uz

Flag description: Three equal horizontal bands of blue (top), white, and green separated by red fimbriations with a white crescent moon and 12 white stars in the upper hoist-side quadrant

National anthem: lyrics from poem by A. Aripov, music by M. Burkhanov

Geographical description: Central Asia, north of Afghanistan

Total area: 447,400 sq km

Climate: Mostly mid-latitude desert, long, hot summers, mild winters; semiarid grassland in east

Nationality: noun: Uzbekistani *adjective:* Uzbekistani

Population: 28,929,716 (July 2014 CIA est.)

Ethnic groups: Uzbek 80%, Russian 5.5%, Tajik 5%, Kazakh 3%, Karakalpak 2.5%, Tatar 1.5%, other 2.5% (1996 CIA est.)

Languages spoken: Uzbek 74.3%, Russian 14.2%, Tajik 4.4%, other 7.1%

Religions: Muslim 88% (mostly Sunni), Eastern Orthodox 9%, other 3%

Vanuatu

Official name: Republic of Vanuatu

Capital city: Port-Vila (on Efate)

Internet country code: .vu

Flag description: Two equal horizontal bands of red (top) and green with a black isosceles triangle (based on the hoist side) all separated by a black-edged yellow stripe in the shape of a horizontal Y (the two points of the Y face the hoist side and enclose the triangle); centered in the triangle is a boar's tusk encircling two crossed namele leaves, all in yellow

Geographical description: Oceania, group of islands in the South Pacific Ocean, about three-quarters of the way from Hawaii to Australia

Total area: 12,189 sq km

Climate: Tropical; moderated by southeast trade winds from May to October; moderate rainfall from November to April; may be affected by cyclones from December to April

Nationality: noun: Ni-Vanuatu (singular and plural) *adjective:* Ni-Vanuatu

Population: 266,937 (July 2014 CIA est.)

Ethnic groups: Ni-Vanuatu 97.6%, part Ni-Vanuatu 1.1%, other 1.3% (2009 CIA est.)

Languages spoken: Local languages (more than 100) 63.2%, Bislama (official; creole) 33.7%, English (official) 2%, French (official) 0.6%, other 0.5% (2009 CIA est.)

Religions: Protestant 70% (includes Presbyterian 27.9%, Anglican 15.1%, Seventh Day Adventist 12.5%, Assemblies of God 4.7%, Church of Christ 4.5%, Neil Thomas Ministry 3.1%, and Apostolic 2.2%), Roman Catholic 12.4%, customary beliefs 3.7% (including Jon Frum cargo cult), other 12.6%, none 1.1%, unspecified 0.2% (2009 CIA est.)

Venezuela

Official name: Bolivarian Republic of Venezuela

Capital city: Caracas

Internet country code: .ve

Flag description: Three equal horizontal bands of yellow (top), blue, and red with the coat of arms on the hoist side of the yellow band and an arc of eight white five-pointed stars centered in the blue band

National anthem: "Gloria al Bravo Pueblo"

National bird: Turpial

National flower: Orchid

National tree: Araguaney

Geographical description: Northern South America, bordering the Caribbean Sea and the North Atlantic Ocean, between Colombia and Guyana

Total area: 912,050 sq km

Climate: Tropical; hot, humid; more moderate in highlands

Nationality: noun: Venezuelan(s) *adjective:* Venezuelan

Population: 28,868,486 (July 2014 CIA est.)

Ethnic groups: Spanish, Italian, Portuguese, Arab, German, African, indigenous people

Languages spoken: Spanish (official), numerous indigenous dialects

Religions: Nominally Roman Catholic 96%, Protestant 2%, other 2%

Vietnam

Official name: Socialist Republic of Vietnam

Capital city: Hanoi

Internet country code: .vn

Flag description: Red with a large yellow five-pointed star in the center

National anthem: "Tiến quân ca" (The Song of the Marching Troops) by Văn Cao

Geographical description: Southeastern Asia, bordering the Gulf of Thailand, Gulf of Tonkin, and South China Sea, alongside China, Laos, and Cambodia

Total area: 331,210 sq km

Climate: Tropical in south; monsoonal in north with hot, rainy season (May to September) and warm, dry season (October to March)

Nationality: noun: Vietnamese (singular and plural) *adjective:* Vietnamese

Population: 93,421,835 (July 2014 CIA est.)

Ethnic groups: Kinh (Viet) 85.7%, Tay 1.9%, Thai 1.8%, Muong 1.5%, Khmer 1.5%, Mong 1.2%, Nung 1.1%, others 5.3% (1999 census)

Languages spoken: Vietnamese (official), English (increasingly favored as a second language), some French, Chinese, and Khmer; mountain area languages (Mon-Khmer and Malayo-Polynesian)

Religions: Buddhist 9.3%, Catholic 6.7%, Hoa Hao 1.5%, Cao Dai 1.1%, Protestant 0.5%, Muslim 0.1%, none 80.8% (1999 census)

Yemen

Official name: Republic of Yemen

Capital city: Sanaa

Internet country code: .ye

Flag description: Three equal horizontal bands of red (top), white, and black

Geographical description: Middle East, bordering the Arabian Sea, Gulf of Aden, and Red Sea, between Oman and Saudi Arabia

Total area: 527,968 sq km

Climate: Mostly desert; hot and humid along west coast; temperate in western mountains affected by seasonal monsoon; extraordinarily hot, dry, harsh desert in east

Nationality: noun: Yemeni(s) *adjective:* Yemeni

Population: 26,052,966 (July 2014 CIA est.)

Ethnic groups: Predominantly Arab, but also Afro-Arabs, South Asians, Europeans

Languages spoken: Arabic (official)

Religions: Muslim 99.1% (official; virtually all are citizens, an estimated 65% are Sunni and 35% are Shia), other 0.9% (includes Jewish, Baha'i, Hindu, and Christian; many are refugees or temporary foreign residents) (2010 CIA est.)

Zambia

Official name: Republic of Zambia

Capital city: Lusaka

Internet country code: .zm

Flag description: Green with a panel of three vertical bands of red (hoist side), black, and orange below a soaring orange eagle, on the outer edge of the flag

Geographical description: Southern Africa, east of Angola

Total area: 752,618 sq km

Climate: Tropical; modified by altitude; rainy season (October to April)

Nationality: noun: Zambian(s) *adjective:* Zambian

Population: 14,638,505

Ethnic groups: Bemba 21%, Tonga 13.6%, Chewa 7.4%, Lozi 5.7%, Nsenga 5.3%, Tumbuka 4.4%, Ngoni 4%, Lala 3.1%, Kaonde 2.9%, Namwanga 2.8%, Lunda (north Western)

2.6%, Mambwe 2.5%, Luvale 2.2%, Lamba 2.1%, Ushi 1.9%, Lenje 1.6%, Bisa 1.6%, Mbunda 1.2%, other 13.8%, unspecified 0.4% (2010 CIA est.)

Languages spoken: Bembe 33.4%, Nyanja 14.7%, Tonga 11.4%, Chewa 4.5%, Lozi 5.5%, Nsenga 2.9%, Tumbuka 2.5%, Lunda (North Western) 1.9%, Kaonde 1.8%, Lala 1.8%, Lamba 1.8%, English (official) 1.7%, Luvale 1.5%, Mambwe 1.3%, Namwanga 1.2%, Lenje 1.1%, Bisa 1%, other 9.4%, unspecified 0.4%

Religions: Protestant 75.3%, Roman Catholic 20.2%, other 2.7% (includes Muslim Buddhist, Hindu, and Baha'i), none 1.8% (2010 CIA est.)

Zimbabwe

Official name: Republic of Zimbabwe

Capital city: Harare

Internet country code: .zw

Flag description: Seven equal horizontal bands of green, yellow, red, black, red, yellow, and green with a white isosceles triangle edged in black with its base on the hoist side; a yellow Zimbabwe bird representing the long history of the country is superimposed on a red five-pointed star in the center of the triangle, which symbolizes peace; green symbolizes agriculture, yellow represents mineral wealth, red symbolizes blood shed to achieve independence, and black stands for the native people

Geographical description: Southern Africa, between South Africa and Zambia

Total area: 390,757 sq km

Climate: Tropical; moderated by altitude; rainy season (November to March)

Nationality: noun: Zimbabwean(s) *adjective:* Zimbabwean

Population: 13,771,721

Ethnic groups: African 98% (Shona 82%, Ndebele 14%, other 2%), mixed and Asian 1%, white less than 1%

Languages spoken: English (official), Shona, Sindebele (the language of the Ndebele, sometimes called Ndebele), numerous but minor tribal dialects

Religions: Syncretic (part Christian, part indigenous beliefs) 50%, Christian 25%, indigenous beliefs 24%, Muslim and other 1%

Legal Holidays by Country

Legal holidays in the following countries are listed in Gregorian calendar order. Jewish holidays and Christian movable holidays are listed according to the range of months in which the day may fall. Muslim holidays appear at the bottom of the list for each country, since their dates are determined by the Muslim lunar calendar.

Afghanistan

Feb 15	Liberation Day
Mar	Nauruz
Apr 28	Victory Day
May 1	Labor Day
Aug 19	Independence Day

Muslim holidays:

Muharram	Ashura
Rabi al-Awwa	Mellad Nabi (Mawlid al-Nabi)
1 Ramadan	Ramadan
Shawwal (3 days)	Id al-Fitr
Dhu al-Hijjah (3 days)	Id al-Adha

Albania

Jan 1	New Year's Day
Jan 2	New Year's Holiday
Mar	Nevruz
Mar 14	Summer Day
Mar-Apr	Catholic Easter
Apr-May	Orthodox Easter
May 1	May Day
Oct 19	Mother Teresa Day
Nov 28	Independence Day
Nov 29	National Liberation Day
Dec 8	National Youth Day
Dec 25	Christmas

Muslim holidays:

Shawwal	Lesser Bajram (Id al-Fitr)
Dhu al-Hijjah	Greater Bajram (Id al-Adha)

Algeria

Jan 1	New Year's Day
May 1	Labor Day
Jun 19	Anniversary of June 19
Jul 5	Independence Day
Nov 1	Anniversary of the Revolution (1954)

Muslim holidays:

Muharram	Islamic New Year
Muharram	Achoura (Ashura)
Rabi al-Nabi	Mawlid al-Nabi
Shawwal	Id al-Fitr
Dhu al-Hijjah	Id al-Adha

Andorra

Jan 1	New Year's Day
Jan 6	Twelfth Night
Feb-Mar	Carnival
Mar 14	Day of the Constitution
Mar-Apr: Fri before Easter	Good Friday
Mar-Apr: Mon after Easter	Easter Monday
May-Jun: Mon after Pentecost	Whitsun Monday
May 1	Labour Day
Aug 15	Assumption
Sep 8	National Day (Our Lady of Meritxell)
Nov 1	All Saints' Day
Dec 8	Immaculate Conception
Dec 25	Christmas
Dec 26	St. Etienne's Day (Patron of the Capital)

Angola

Jan 1	New Year's Day
Jan 4	Martyrs of Colonial Repression Day
Feb 4	Day Inicio de Luta Armada (Commencement of Armed Struggle Day)
Feb-Mar	Carnival Day
Mar 8	International Women's Day
Mar-Apr: Fri before Easter	Good Friday
Apr 4	Peace and National Reconciliation Day
May 1	International Workers' Day
May 25	Africa Day
Jun 1	International Children's Day
Sep 17	National Hero's Day (Birthday of President Neto)
Nov 2	All Souls' Day
Nov 11	Independence Day

Dec 10 . . . . . . Foundation of the MPLA Workers' Party Day
Dec 25 . . . . Family Day (Christmas Day)

Antigua and Barbuda

Jan 1 . . . . New Year's Day
Mar-Apr: Fri before Easter . . . . Good Friday
Mar-Apr: Mon after Easter . . . . Easter Monday
May, first Mon . . . . Labour Day
May-Jun: Mon after Pentecost . . . . Whit Monday
Aug, first Mon . . . . J'ouvert (Carnival)
Aug, first Tues . . . . Last Lap (Carnival)
Nov 1 . . . . Independence Day
Dec 9 . . . . National Heroes Day
Dec 25 . . . . Christmas Day
Dec 26 . . . . Boxing Day

Argentina

Jan 1 . . . . New Year's Day
Feb-Mar . . . . Carnival/Shrove Tuesday
Feb-Mar, first Mon of Lent . . . . Carnival
Mar 24 . . . . National Memorial Day (Truth and Justice Day)
Mar-Apr, first and last days . . . . Passover
Mar-Apr: Fri before Easter . . . . Good Friday
Apr 2 . . . . Malvinas Veterans and Memorial Day
May 1 . . . . Labor Day
May 25 . . . . 1810 Revolution Anniversary
Jun 20 . . . . Flag Day
Jul 9 . . . . Independence Day
Aug 17 . . . . San Martín Day
Sep-Oct . . . . Yom Kippur
Oct 12 . . . . Day of Respect for Cultural Diversity
Dec 8 . . . . Immaculate Conception
Dec 25 . . . . Christmas Day

Muslim holidays:
Dhu al-Hijjah . . . . Feast of Sacrifice (Id al-Adha)
Muharram . . . . Islamic New Year
Shawwal . . . . Ending of the Fast (Id al-Fitr)

Armenia

Jan 1-2 . . . . Amanor (New Year's holiday)
Jan 6 . . . . Surb Tsnund (Armenian Christmas Day)
Jan 28 . . . . Army Day
Mar 8 . . . . International Women's Day
Apr 24 . . . . Genocide Memorial Day
May 1 . . . . Labour Day
May 9 . . . . Victory and Peace Day
May 28 . . . . First Republic Day
Jul 5 . . . . Constitution Day
Sep 21 . . . . Independence Day
Dec 31 . . . . New Year's Eve

Australia

Jan 1 . . . . New Year's Day
Jan 26 or following Mon . . . . Australia Day

Mar, second Mon . . . . Labour Day
Mar-Apr: Fri before Easter . . . . Good Friday
Mar-Apr: Sat before Easter . . . . Holy Saturday
Mar-Apr: Mon after Easter . . . . Easter Monday
Apr 25 . . . . Anzac Day
Jun, second Mon . . . . Queen Elizabeth II Birthday
Nov, first Tues . . . . Melbourne Cup Day
Dec 25 . . . . Christmas Day
Dec 26 . . . . Boxing Day

Austria

Jan 1 . . . . New Year's Day
Jan 6 . . . . Epiphany
Mar-Apr: Mon after Easter . . . . Easter Monday
Apr-Jun . . . . Ascension Day
May 1 . . . . Staatsfeiertag (Labour Day)
May-Jun . . . . Corpus Christi
May-Jun: Mon after Pentecost . . . . Whit Monday
Aug 15 . . . . Assumption
Oct 26 . . . . National Day
Nov 1 . . . . All Saints' Day
Dec 8 . . . . Immaculate Conception
Dec 25 . . . . Christtag (Christmas Day)
Dec 26 . . . . Stefanitag (St. Stephen's Day)

Azerbaijan

Jan 1-2 . . . . New Year's Day
Jan 20 . . . . Day of the Martyrs
Mar 8 . . . . International Women's Day
Mar 21 . . . . Novruz Bayrami
May 9 . . . . Victory in World War II Day
May 28 . . . . Republic Day
Jun 15 . . . . National Salvation Day
Jun 26 . . . . Army and Navy Day
Oct 18 . . . . National Independence Day
Nov 9 . . . . State Flag Day
Nov 12 . . . . Constitution Day
Nov 17 . . . . Day of National Revival
Dec 31 . . . . Day of Solidarity of Azerbaijanis throughout the World

Muslim holidays:
Shawwal . . . . Ramazan Bayram (Id al-Fitr)
10 Dhu al-Hijjah . . . . Gurban Bayram (Id al-Adha)

Bahamas

Jan 1 . . . . New Year's Day
Jan 10 . . . . Majority Rule Day
Mar-Apr: Fri before Easter . . . . Good Friday
Mar-Apr: Mon after Easter . . . . Easter Monday
May-Jun: Mon after Pentecost . . . . Whit Monday
Jun, first Fri . . . . Labour Day
Jul 10 . . . . Independence Day
Aug, first Mon . . . . Emancipation Day
Oct, second Mon . . . . National Heroes Day
Dec 25 . . . . Christmas Day
Dec 26 . . . . Boxing Day

Bahrain

Jan 1	New Year's Day
May 1	Labour Day
Dec 17	Accession Day
Dec 16	National Day

Muslim holidays:

1 Muharram	Hijra (Islamic New Year)
10 Muharram	Ashoora
12 Rabi al-Awwal	Prophet's Birthday (Mawlid al-Nabi)
1-3 Shawwal	Eid al Fitr (Id al-Fitr)
10-12 Dhu al-Hijjah	Eid al Adha (Id al-Adha)

Bangladesh

Feb 21	Shahid Dibosh (Mother Language Day)
Mar 17	Birthday of Bangabandhu Sheikh Mujibur Rahman
Mar 26	Independence Day
Apr, mid-	Pahela Baishakh (Bengali New Year)
Apr-May	Buddha Purnima
May 1	May Day
Aug 15	Bangabandhu National Mourning Day
Aug-Sep	Janmashtami
Sep-Oct	Durga Puja
Dec 16	Bijoy Dibosh (Victory Day)
Dec 25	Christmas

Muslim holidays:

Muharram	Ashura
Ramadan, last Fri	Jamat-ul-Wida
Rabi al-Awwal	Mawlid al-Nabi
15 shaban	Shab-e-Barat
Shawwal	Id al-Fitr
Dhu al-Hijjah	Id al-Adha

Barbados

Jan 1	New Year's Day
Jan 21	Errol Barrow Day
Mar-Apr: Fri before Easter	Good Friday
Mar-Apr: Mon after Easter	Easter Monday
Apr 28	National Heroes Day
May 1	Labour Day
May-Jun: Mon after Pentecost	Whit Monday
Aug 1	Emancipation Day
Aug, first Mon	Kadooment Day
Nov 30	Independence Day
Dec 25	Christmas Day
Dec 26	Boxing Day

Belarus

Jan 1-2	New Year's Day holiday
Jan 7	Orthodox Christmas
Mar 8	Women's Day
Apr-May, ninth day after Orthodox Easter	Radunitsa (Ancestors Veneration)
May 1	Labor Day
May 9	Victory Day

Jul 3	Independence Day
Nov 7	October Revolution Day
Dec 25	Catholic Christmas

Belgium

Jan 1	New Year's Day
Mar-Apr: Mon after Easter	Easter Monday
May 1	Labor Day
May-Jun	Ascension Day
May-Jun	Whit Monday
Jul 21	Independence Day
Aug 15	Assumption Day
Nov 1	All Saints' Day
Nov 11	Armistice Day
Dec 25	Christmas Day

Belize

Jan 1	New Year's Day
Mar 9	National Heroes and Benefactors Day
Mar-Apr: Fri before Easter	Good Friday
Mar-Apr: Sat before Easter	Holy Saturday
Mar-Apr: Mon after Easter	Easter Monday
May 1	Labour Day
May 24	Sovereign's Day/Commonwealth Day
Sep 10	St. George's Caye Day (National Day)
Sep 21	Independence Day
Oct 12	Pan American Day
Nov 19	Garifuna Settlement Day
Dec 25	Christmas Day
Dec 26	Boxing Day

Benin

Jan 1	New Year's Day
Jan 10	National Vodoun Day (Traditional Religions Day)
Mar-Apr: Mon after Easter	Easter Monday
May 1	Labor Day
May-Jun	Ascension Day
May-Jun	Whit Monday
Aug 1	Independence Day
Aug 15	Assumption
Nov 1	All Saints' Day
Dec 25	Christmas

Muslim holidays:

Rabi al-Awwal	Maouloud (Prophet's Birthday)
Shawwal	Korite (Id al-Fitr)
Dhu al-Hijjah	Tabaski (Id al-Adha)

Bermuda

Jan 1	New Year's Day
Mar-Apr: Fri before Easter	Good Friday
May 24	Bermuda Day
Jun, second Mon	Queen Elizabeth II Birthday
Jun, third Mon	National Heroes Day

Jul-Aug, Fri before first Mon in Aug . . . Somer's Day (Cup Match)

Jul-Aug, Thurs before first Mon in Aug Emancipation Day (Cup Match)

Sep, first Mon . . . . Labour Day

Oct, second Mon . . Heroes' Day (Dame Lois Browne-Evans)

Nov 11 . . . . Rememberance Day

Dec 25 . . . . Christmas Day

Dec 26 . . . . Boxing Day

Bhutan

Jan . . . . Traditional Day of Offering

Jan-Mar . . . . Losar (Tibetan New Year)

Feb 21 (3 days) . . . . Birthday of King Jigme Khesar Namgyel Wangchuck

Feb 21-23 . . . . Birthday of Fifth Druk Gyalpo

May 2 . . . . Birthday of Third Druk Gyalpo

Aug 8 . . . . Independence Day

Nov 1 . . . . Coronation Anniversary

Nov 11 . . . . . Birthday of HM King Jigme Singye Wangchuck

Dec 17 . . . . National Day

Bolivia

Jan 1 . . . . New Year's Day

Feb-Mar: Mon and Tues before Ash Wednesday . . Carnival

Mar-Apr: Fri before Easter . . . . Good Friday

May 1 . . . . Labor Day

May-Jun . . . . Corpus Christi

Aug 6 . . . . National/Independence Day

Nov 2 . . . . All Souls' Day

Dec 25 . . . . Christmas Day

Bosnia and Herzegovina

Jan 1 . . . . New Year's Day

Jan 7 . . . . Orthodox Christmas

Mar 1 . . . . Independence Day

Mar-Apr, Friday before Easter . . . . Good Friday

Mar-Apr, Monday after Easter . . . . Easter Monday

May 9 . . . . Victory Day

May 1-2 . . . . Labor Day

Nov 25 . . . . Statehood Day

Dec 25 . . . . Christmas Day

Botswana

Jan 1 . . . . New Year's Day

Jan 2 . . . . Public Holiday

Mar-Apr . . . . Good Friday through Easter Monday

May 1 . . . . Labor Day

May-Jun . . . . Ascension Day

Jul 1 . . . . Sir Seretse Khama Day

Jul, third Mon . . . . President's Day

Jul, third Tues . . . . Public Holiday

Sep 30 . . . . Botswana Day

Oct 1 . . . . Public Holiday

Dec 25 . . . . Christmas

Dec 26 . . . . Boxing Day

Brazil

Jan 1 . . . . New Year's Day

Feb-Mar: Mon and Tues before Ash Wednesday . . Carnival

Mar-Apr: Fri before Easter . . . . Good Friday

Apr 21 . . . . Tiradentes Day

Apr 23 . . . . St. George's Day

May 1 . . . . Labor Day

May-Jun . . . . Corpus Christi

Sep 7 . . . . Independence Day

Oct 12 . . . . Our Lady of Aparacida Day

Nov 2 . . . . All Souls' Day

Nov 15 . . . . Proclamation of the Republic

Dec 25 . . . . Christmas Day

Brunei

Jan 1 . . . . New Year's Day

Jan-Feb . . . . Chinese New Year

Feb 23 . . . . National Day

May 31 . . . . Royal Brunei Armed Forces Day

Jul 15 . . . . H.M. the Sultan's Birthday

Dec 25 . . . . Christmas Day

Muslim holidays:

1 Muharram . . . . First Day of Islamic New Year

12 Rabi al-Awwal Muhammad's Birthday (Mawlid al-Nabi)

27 Rajab . . . . Isra Mikraj (Laylat al-Miraj)

1 Ramadan . . . . First Day of fasting month

During Ramadan . . . . Anniversary of the Revelation of the Quran (Laylat al-Qadr)

1 Shawwal . . . . Hari Raya (Id al-Fitr)

10-12 Dhu al-Hijjah . . . . (Id al-Adha)

Bulgaria

Jan 1 . . . . New Year's Day

Mar 3 . . . . National Day/Bulgaria Day

Apr-May: Mon after Easter . . . . Easter Monday

May 1 . . . . Labor Day

May 6 . . . . Day of the Armed Forces

May 24 . . . . Bulgarian Education and Culture Day

Sep 6 . . . . National Unification Day

Sep 22 . . . . Independence Day

Nov 1 . . . . Enlightenment Leaders Day

Dec 24-26 . . . . Christmas

Burkina Faso

Jan 1 . . . . New Year's Day

Jan 3 . . . Revolution Day (Anniversary of the 1966 uprising)

Mar 8 . . . . International Women's Day

Mar-Apr, Monday after Easter . . . . Easter Monday

Apr-Jun . . . . Ascension Day

May 1 . . . . Labor Day

Aug 5 . . . . Independence Day

Aug 15 . . . . Assumption

Nov 1 . . . . All Saints' Day

Dec 11 . . . . . Proclamation of Independence (National Day)

Dec 25 . . . . Christmas Day

Muslim holidays:
Rabi al-Awwal .... Mouloud (Mawlid al-Nabi)
Dhu al-Hijjah .... Tabaski/Aïd El Kebir (Id al-Adha)
Shawwal .... Korite/Aïd El Segheir (Id al-Fitr)

Burma. *See* Myanmar

Burundi

Jan 1 .... New Year's Day
Feb 5 .... Unity Day
Apr 6 .... President Ntaryamira Day
May 1 .... Labor Day
May-Jun .... Ascension Day
Jul 1 .... Independence Day
Aug 15 .... Assumption
Oct 13 .... Prince Rwagasore Day
Oct 21 .... President Ndadaye Day
Nov 1 .... All Saints' Day
Dec 25 .... Christmas

Muslim holidays:
Shawwal .... Aid-El-Fithr (Id al-Fitr)
Dhu al-Hijjah .... Aid-El-Hadj (Id al-Adha)

Cambodia

Jan 1 .... New Year's Day
Jan 7 . Victory Day (Liberation Day over Genocidal Regime)
Feb .... Meak Bochea
Mar 8 .... International Women's Day
Apr 13-15 .... Cambodian New Year
Apr-May . .Visaka Bochea (Birth, Enlightenment, and Death of Buddha)
May 1 .... International Labour Day
May .... Royal Ploughing Ceremony
May 13-15 .... King's Birthday
Jun 1 ...... International and Cambodian Children's Day
Jun 18 .... Former Queen Mother's Birthday
Sep 24 .... Constitution Day
Sep-Oct .... Phchum Ben (Ancestors' Day)
Oct 15 .... King Sihanouk Commemoration Day
Oct 23 .... Paris Peace Agreement Day
Oct 29 ...... King's Coronation Day (Norodom Sihamoni)
Oct-Nov .... Bonn Om Toak (Water Festival)
Nov 9 .... Independence Day
Dec 10 .... International Human Rights' Day (U.N.)
Dec 25 .... Christmas

Cameroon

Jan 1 .... New Year's Day
Feb 11 .... Youth Day
Mar-Apr: Fri before Easter .... Good Friday
May 1 .... Labor Day
May 20 .... National Day
May-Jun .... Ascension Day
Aug 15 .... Assumption
Dec 25 .... Christmas Day

Muslim holidays:
Shawwal .... Djoulde Soumae (Id al-Fitr)
Dhu al-Hijjah .... Tabaski (Id al-Adha)

Canada

Jan 1 .... New Year's Day
Mar-Apr: Fri before Easter .... Good Friday
Mar-Apr: Mon after Easter .... Easter Monday
May 25, Mon before Victoria Day ..... (Queen Elizabeth II Birthday observed)
Jul 1 .... Canada Day
Sep, first Mon .... Labour Day
Oct, second Mon .... Thanksgiving Day
Nov 11 .... Remembrance Day
Dec 25 .... Christmas Day
Dec 26 .... Boxing Day

Cape Verde/Cabo Verde

Jan 1 .... New Year's Day
Jan 13 .... Democracy and Liberty Day
Jan 20 .... National Heroes Day
Feb-Mar .... Ash Wednesday
Mar-Apr: Fri before Easter .... Good Friday
May 1 .... Labor Day
Jun 1 .... Youth Day
Jul 5 .... Independence Day
Aug 15 .... Assumption
Sep 12 .... National Day
Nov 1 .... All Saints' Day
Dec 25 .... Christmas Day

Central African Republic

Jan 1 .... New Year's Day
Mar 29 .... Boganda Day
Mar-Apr: Mon after Easter .... Easter Monday
May 1 .... Labor Day
May-Jun .... Ascension Day
May-Jun .... Whit Monday
Jun 30 .... Prayer Day
Aug 13 .... Independence Day
Aug 15 .... Assumption
Nov 1 .... All Saints' Day
Dec 1 .... National Day (Proclamation of the Republic)
Dec 25 .... Christmas Day

Chad

Jan 1 .... New Year's Day
Mar-Apr: Mon after Easter .... Easter Monday
May 1 .... Labor Day
Aug 11 .... Independence Day
Nov 1 .... All Saints' Day
Nov 28 .... Proclamation of the Republic
Dec 1 .... Freedom and Democracy Day
Dec 25 .... Christmas Day

Muslim holidays:

Rabi al-Awwal ..... Maouloud al Nebi (Mawlid al-Nabi)
Shawwal .... Korite (Aid al-Fitr)
Dhu al-Hijjah .... Tabaski (Id al-Adha)

Chile

Jan 1 .... New Year's Day
Mar-Apr, Fri before Easter .... Good Friday
Mar-Apr, Sat before Easter .... Holy Saturday
May 1 .... Labor Day
May 21 .... Navy Day
June 29 (varies) .... Sts. Peter and Paul Day
Jul 16 .... Lady of Carmen Day
Aug 15 .... Assumption
Sep 18 .... Independence Day
Sep 19 .... Army Day
Oct 12 (varies) .... Dia de la Raza (Columbus Day)
Nov 1 .... All Saints' Day
Dec 8 .... Immaculate Conception
Dec 25 .... Christmas Day

China

Jan 1-3 .... New Year's Day
Jan-Feb (3 days) .... Lunar New Year
April .... Qing Ming Festival
May 1 (3 days) .... Labor Day
June .... Dragon Boat Festival
Sep .... Mid-Autumn Festival
Oct 1 (3 days) .... National Day

Colombia

Jan 1 .... New Year's Day
Jan, first or second Mon .... Epiphany
Mar 19 .... St. Joseph's Day
Mar-Apr: Fri before Easter .... Good Friday
Mar-Apr: Thurs before Easter .... Holy Thursday
Apr-Jun .... Ascension Day
May 1 .... Labor Day
May-Jun .... Corpus Christi
May-Jun: Fri after Corpus Christi .... Sacred Heart of Jesus
Jun 29 (varies) .... Sts. Peter and Paul Day
Jul 20 .... Independence Day
Aug 7 .... Battle of Boyacá Day
Aug 15 .... Assumption
Oct 12 .... Race Day
Nov 1 .... All Saints' Day
Nov 11 .... Cartagena Independence Day
Dec 8 .... Immaculate Conception
Dec 25 .... Christmas Day

Comoros

Jan 1 .... New Year's Day
Mar 18 .... Cheikh Al Maarouf Day

May 1 .... Labor Day
Jul 6 .... Independence Day
Nov 12 .... Journée Nationale Maoré

Muslim holidays:

Muharram .... Islamic New Year
Rabi al-Awwal .... Mouloud (Mawlid al-Nabi)
Rajab .... Laylat Al-Miraj
Shawwal .... Ide El Fitr (Id al-Fitr)
Dhu al-Hijjah .... Ide El Kabir (Id al-Adha)

Congo, Democratic Republic of

Jan 1 .... New Year's Day
Jan 4 .... Day of the Martyrs for Independence
Jan 16 .... Heroes' Day (Laurent Kabila)
Jan 17 .... Heroes' Day (Patrice Lumumba)
May 1 .... Labor Day
May 17 .... Liberation Day
Jun 30 .... Independence Day
Aug 1 .... Parents' Day
Dec 25 .... Christmas Day

Congo, Republic of

Jan 1 .... New Year's Day
Mar-Apr .... Easter Monday
Apr-Jun .... Ascension Day
May 1 .... Labor Day
May-Jun, Mon after Pentecost .... Whit Monday
Jun 10 .... Reconciliation Day
Aug 15 .... Independence Day
Nov 1 .... All Saints' Day
Dec 25 .... Christmas

Costa Rica

Jan 1 .... New Year's Day
Mar-Apr .... Holy Week
Apr 11 .. Anniversary of Rivas Battle (Juan Santamaria Day)
May 1 .... Labor Day
Jul 25 .... Annexation of Guanacaste
Aug 15 .... Assumption (Mother's Day)
Sep 15 .... Independence Day
Oct 12 .... Culture Day/Columbus Day
Dec 25 .... Christmas

Côte d'Ivoire

Jan 1 .... New Year's Day
Mar-Apr: Mon after Easter .... Easter Monday
May 1 .... Labor Day
May-Jun .... Ascension Day
May-Jun .... Whit Monday
Aug 7 .... Independence Day
Nov 1 .... All Saints' Day
Nov 15 .... Peace Day
Dec 25 .... Christmas

Muslim holidays:

Rabi al-Awwal . . . . Mawlid al-Nabi
Shawwal . . . . Korite (Id al-Fitr)
Dhu al-Hijjah . . . . Tabaski (Id al-Adha)

Croatia

Jan 1 . . . . New Year's Day
Jan 6 . . . . Epiphany
Mar-Apr: Mon after Easter . . . . Easter Monday
May 1 . . . . Labor Day
May 30 . . . . Statehood Day (National Day)
May-Jun . . . . Corpus Christi
Jun 22 . . . . Croatian Uprising Day
Jun 25 . . . . Croatian Statehood Day
Aug 5 . . . . Victory and Homeland Gratitude Day
Aug 15 . . . . Assumption
Oct 8 . . . . Croatian Independence Day
Nov 1 . . . . All Saints' Day
Dec 25 . . . . Christmas
Dec 26 . . . . St. Stephen's Day

Cuba

Jan 1 . . . . Liberation Day
Jan 2 . . . . New Year Public Holiday
May 1 . . . . Labor Day
Jul 26 and 27 . . . . National Revolution Day
Oct 10 . . . . Anniversary of the beginning of the War of
Independence (1868)
Dec 25 . . . . Christmas
Dec 31 . . . . End of the Year Public Holiday

Cyprus

Jan 1 . . . . New Year's Day
Jan 6 . . . . Epiphany Day
Feb-Mar: 50 days before Orthodox Easter . Kathara Deftera
(Green Monday)
Mar 25 . . . . Greek Independence Day
Apr 1 . . . . Eoka Day (Greek Cypriot National Day)
Apr 23 . . . . Turkish Independence Day
Apr-May: Fri before Orthodox Easter . . . . Good Friday
Apr-May: Mon after Orthodox Easter . . . . . Easter Monday
May 1 . . . . Labor Day
May 19 . . . . Ataturk Day
May-Jun . . . . Kataklysmos Festival (Pentecost)
Aug 15 . . . . Assumption
Aug 30 . . . . Turkish Victory Day
Oct 1 . . . . Cyprus Independence Day
Oct 28 . . . . Ochi Day (Greek National Holiday)
Oct 29 . . . . Republic of Turkey Day
Dec 24 . . . . Christmas Eve
Dec 25 . . . . Christmas Day
Dec 26 . . . . Boxing Day

Muslim holidays:

12 Rabi al-Awwal . . . . Prophet's Birthday (Mawlid al-Nabi)

1-2 Shawwal . . . . Ramazan Bayrami (Id al-Fitr)
10-12 Dhu al-Hijjah . . . . Kourban Bayrami (Id al-Adha)

Czech Republic

Jan 1 . . . . New Year's Day
Mar-Apr: Mon after Easter . . . . Easter Monday
May 1 . . . . Labor Day
May 8 . . . . Liberation Day
Jul 5 . . . . Sts. Cyril and Methodius Day
Jul 6 . . . . Jan Hus Day
Sep 28 . . . . Czech Statehood Day
Oct 28 . . . . Independence Day
Nov 17 . . . . Freedom and Democracy Day
Dec 24 . . . . Christmas Eve
Dec 25 . . . . Christmas Day
Dec 26 . . . . St. Stephen's Day

Denmark

Jan 1 . . . . New Year's Day
Mar-Apr: Thurs before Easter . . . . Maundy Thursday
Mar-Apr: Fri before Easter . . . . Good Friday
Mar-Apr: Mon after Easter . . . . Easter Monday
Apr-May: fourth Fri after Easter . . . . Store Bededag
(Great Prayer)
Apr-Jun . . . . Ascension Day
May-Jun: Mon after Pentecost . . . . Whit Monday
Jun 5 . . . . Constitution Day
Dec 24 . . . . Christmas Eve
Dec 25 . . . . Christmas Day
Dec 26 . . . . Second Christmas Day

Djibouti

Jan 1 . . . . New Year's Day
May 1 . . . . Labor Day
Jun 27 . . . . Independence Day

Muslim holidays:

1 Muharram . . . . Awal Mouharam (Islamic New Year)
Rabi al-Awwal . . . . Mawlid al-Nabi
Shawwal (two days) . . . . Id al-Fitr
Dhu al-Hijjah (three days) . . . . Id al-Adha

Dominica

Jan 1 . . . . New Year's Day
Feb (two days) . . . . Carnival
Mar-Apr: Fri before Easter . . . . Good Friday
Mar-Apr: Mon after Easter . . . . Easter Monday
May, first Mon . . . . Labor Day
May-Jun . . . . Whit Monday
Aug 5 . . . . Emancipation Day (August Monday)
Nov 3 . . . . Independence Day
Nov 4 . . . . National Day of Community Service
Dec 25 . . . . Christmas
Dec 26 . . . . Boxing Day

Dominican Republic

Mar-Apr: Fri before Easter .... Good Friday
May-Jun .... Corpus Christi

East Timor (Timor-Leste)

Mar-Apr: Fri before Easter .... Good Friday
May-Jun .... Corpus Christi

Muslim holidays:
1 Shawwal .... Idul Fitri (Id al-Fitr)
Dhu al-Hijjah .... Idul Adha (Id al-Adha)

Ecuador

Feb-Mar .... Carnaval
Mar-Apr: Thu before Easter .... Maundy Thursday
Mar-Apr: Fri before Easter .... Good Friday

Egypt

Apr-May: Mon after coptic Easter .... Sham El-Nassem

Muslim holidays:
1 Muharram .... El Hijra (New Year)
12 Rabi al-Awwal .Moulid El Nabi(Muhammad's Birthday)
Shawwal (two days) .... Lesser Bairam (Id al-Fitr)
Dhu al-Hijjah (three days) ..... Great Bairam (Id al-Adha)

El Salvador

Mar-Apr: Thur, Fri, and Sat before Easter ....Maundy
Thursday - Holy Saturday
Jun 17 .... Father's Day
Aug 3 (four days) Festival of El Salvadordel Mundo (Savior
of the World)
Nov 1 (varies) ....Cry of Independence Day

England. *See* United Kingdom

Equatorial Guinea

Mar-Apr ....Easter Sunday
Mar-Apr: Fri before Easter .... Good Friday
Mar-Apr: Sun before Easter ....Palm Sunday
May-Jun .... Corpus Christi

Eritrea

Apr-May .... Tensae (Orthodox Easter)
Apr-May: Fri before Easter .... Orthodox Good Friday

Muslim holidays:
12 Rabi al-Awwal Muhammad's Birthday(Mawlid al-Nabi)
1 Shawwal .... Ed'al Fetir (Id al-Fitr)
10 Dhu al-Hijjah .... Ed'al Adha (Id al-Adha)

Estonia

Mar-Apr .... Easter
Mar-apr: fri before Easter .... Good Friday
May-Jun .... Whit Sunday (Pentecost)

Ethiopia

Jan 19 or 20 .... Timket (Ethiopian Epiphany)
Apr-May .... Fasika (Easter)
Apr-May: Fri before Easter .... Siklet (Good Friday)
Sep 27 or 28 ....Meskel (Finding of the True Cross)

Muslim holidays:
12 Rabi al-Awwal Muhammad's Birthday (Mawlid al-Nabi)
1 Shawwal .... Id al Fetil (Id al-Fitr)
10-12 Dhu al-Hijjah .... Id al Adaha (Id al-Adha)

Fiji

Mar ....Youth Day
Mar-Apr: Fri before Easter .... Good Friday
Mar-Apr: Sat before Easter .... Easter Saturday
Mar-Apr: Mon after Easter ....Easter Monday
Jun, third Mon ....Queen Elizabeth II Birthday
Oct .... Fiji Day
Oct-Nov .... Diwali

Muslim holidays:
12 Rabi al-Awwal Muhammad's Birthday (Mawlid al-Nabi)

Finland

Mar-Apr ....Easter
Mar-Apr, Fri before Easter .... Good Friday
Mar-Apr, Mon after Easter ....Easter Monday
May-Jun .... Ascension Day
May-Jun .... Whitsun (Pentecost)
Jun .... Midsummer
Nov, first Sat .... All Saints' Day

France

Mar-Apr: Mon after Easter ....Easter Monday
May-Jun .... Ascension Day
May-Jun: Mon after pentecost ....Whit Monday

Gabon

Mar 1 .... Renovation Day
Mar-Apr: Mon after Easter ....Easter Monday
May-Jun ....Whit Monday
Aug 16-17 .... Independence Holiday

Muslim holidays:
Shawwal .... Id al-Fitr (Aid El-Fitiry)
Dhu al-Hijjah .... Id al-Adha (Aid El-Kebir)

Gambia

Mar-Apr: Fri before Easter .... Good Friday
Mar-Apr: Mon after Easter ....Easter Monday

Muslim holidays:

Rabi al-Awwal .... Mawlid al-Nabi
Shawwal .... Id al-Fitr
Dhu al-Hijjah .... Tabaski (Id al-Adha)

Georgia, Republic of

Jan 1 .... New Year's Holiday
Apr-May .... Easter
Apr-May: Fri before Easter .... Good Friday
Apr-May: Sat before Easter .... Holy Saturday
Apr-May: Mon after Easter .... Easter Monday

Germany

Mar-Apr .... Easter
Mar-Apr: Fri before Easter .... Good Friday
Mar-Apr: Mon after Easter .... Easter Monday
May-Jun .... Ascension Day
May-Jun .... Pentecost
May-Jun: Mon after pentecost .... Whit Monday

Ghana

Mar-Apr: Fri before Easter .... Good Friday
Mar-Apr: Mon after Easter .... Easter Monday
Dec: first Fri .... Farmers' Day

Muslim holidays:

1 Shawwal .... Eid El Fitr (Id al-Fitr)
10-12 Dhu al-Hijjah .... Eid Ul Adha (Id al-Adha)

Gibraltar

Mar: second Mon .... Commonwealth Day
Mar-Apr: Fri before Easter .... Good Friday
Mar-Apr: Mon after Easter .... Easter Monday
May: first Mon .... May Day
May: last Mon .... Spring Bank Holiday
Jun: third Mon .... Queen Elizabeth II Birthday
Aug: last Mon .... Late Summer Bank Holiday

Greece

Mar-Apr: Mon before Ash Wednesday .... Clean Monday
(Beginning of Lent)
Apr-May: Fri before Easter .... Good Friday
Apr-May: Sat before Easter .... Holy Saturday
Apr-May: Mon after Easter .... Easter Monday
May-Jun: Mon after pentecost .... Whit Monday

Grenada

Mar-Apr: Fri before Easter .... Good Friday
Mar-Apr: Mon after Easter .... Easter Monday
May-Jun .... Corpus Christi
May-Jun: Mon after pentecost .... Whit Monday

Aug (two days) .... Carnival
Aug: first Mon .... Emancipation Day

Guatemala

Apr-May: Wed before Easter .... Holy Wednesday
Apr-May: Thurs before Easter .... Maundy Thursday
Apr-May: Fri before Easter .... Good Friday
Apr-May: Sat before Easter .... Holy Saturday

Guinea

Mar-Apr: Mon after Easter .... Easter Monday

Muslim holidays:

Rabi al-Awwal .... Maoloud (Mawlid al-Nabi)
Shawwal .... End of Ramadan (Id al-Fitr)
Dhu al-Hijjah .... Tabaski (Id al-Adha)

Guinea-Bissau

Jan .... National Heroes' Day

Muslim holidays:

Shawwal .... Id al-Fitr
Dhu al-Hijjah .... Tabaski (Id al-Adha)

Guyana

Mar: full moon day .... Phagwah
Mar-Apr: Fri before Easter .... Good Friday
Mar-Apr: Mon after Easter .... Easter Monday
Jul: first Mon .... Caricom Day
Aug .... Freedom Day
Oct-Nov .... Diwali

Muslim holidays:

12 Rabi al-Awwal .... YouMon-Nabi (Mawlid al-Nabi)
10-12 Dhu al-Hijjah .... Eid-Ul-Azah (Id al-Adha)

Haiti

Feb-Mar: Mon through ash Wednesday .... Carnival
Mar-Apr: Fri before Easter .... Good Friday
May-Jun .... Ascension Day
May-Jun .... Corpus Christi

Honduras

Mar-Apr .... Easter
Apr-May: Thurs before Easter .... Maundy Thursday
Apr-May: Fri before Easter .... Good Friday
Apr-May: Sat before Easter .... Holy Saturday

Hong Kong

Jan-Feb .... Lunar New Year (First three Days)
Mar-Apr .... Ching Ming (Qing Ming)

Mar-Apr: Fri before Easter . . . . Good Friday
Mar-Apr: Sat before Easter . . . . .Holy Saturday
Mar-Apr: Mon after Easter . . . . Easter Monday
Apr-May . . . . .Buddha's Birthday
May-Jun . . . . Tuen Ng Festival (Dragon Boat Festival)
Sep-Oct . . . . .Day Following Mid-Autumn Festival
Sep-Oct . . . . Chung Yeung Festival
Dec 25 and first following weekday . . . . Christmas

Hungary

Mar-Apr: Mon after Easter . . . . Easter Monday
May-Jun . . . . Pentecost
May-Jun: Mon after pentecost . . . . Whit Monday

Iceland

Mar-Apr: Thurs before Easter . . . . .Maundy Thursday
Mar-Apr: Fri before Easter . . . . Good Friday
Mar-Apr: Mon after Easter . . . . Easter Monday
Apr 19-25, Thurs between .Sumardagurinn Fyrsti (First Day of Summer)
May-Jun . . . . Ascension Day
May-Jun: Mon after pentecost . . . . Whit Monday
Aug, first Mon . . . . .Commerce Day

India

Mar-Apr: Fri before Easter . . . . Good Friday
Oct-Nov . . . . .Diwali

Muslim holidays:
1 Muharram . . . . Islamic New Year
12 Rabi al-Awwal . . . . . . .Milad-Un-Nabi (Mawlid al-Nabi)
1 Shawwal . . . . .Id al-Fitr
10-12 Dhu al-Hijjah . . . Id Ul-Zuha (Bakr-Id Or Id al-Adha)

Indonesia

Feb . . . . Chinese New Year
Mar-apr: fri before Easter .Wafat Isa Almasih(Good Friday)
Apr-May . . . . Waisak Day (Vesak or Buddha's Birthday)
May-Jun . . . . Ascension Day

Muslim holidays:
1 Muharram . . . . Islamic New Year
12 Rabi al-Awwal . . . . . . .Milad-Un-Nabi (Mawlid al-Nabi)
27 Rajab . . . . Isra and Miraj of Prophet Muhammad(Laylat Al-Miraj)
1 Shawwal . . . . .Id al-Fitr
10-12 Dhu al-Hijjah . . . Id Ul-Zuha (Bakr-Id Or Id al-Adha)

Iran

Feb . . . . .Victory of Islamic Revolution
Mar 21, around (five days) . . . . .Nowruz (New Year)
Mar . . . . Oil Nationalization Day
Mar-Apr . . . . .Islamic Republic Day
Apr 2, around . . . . .Sizdah Be-Dar (Nature Day)

Jun . . . . .Death of Imam Khomeini
Jun . . . . National Uprising Day (1963)

Muslim holidays:
9 Muharram . . . . Taasou'A
10 Muharram . . . . .Ashura
20 Safar . . . . Arba'In-E Hosseini
28 Safar . . . . Demise of Holy Prophet Andmartyrdom of Imam Hassan
17 Rabi al-Awwal . . . . . .Birth of Prophet Andimam Saadeq (Mawlid al-Nabi)
13 Rajab . . . . Imam Ali's Birthday
27 Rajab . . . . Mission of the Holy Prophet (Laylat al-Miraj)
15 shaban . . . . Birthday of Twelfth Imam
21 Ramadan .Imam Ali's Martyrdom
1 Shawwal . . . . End of Fasting Month (Id al-Fitr)
25 Shawwal . . . . Martyrdom of Imam Saadeq
10 Dhu al-Hijjah Festival of Sacrifices(Qadir Or Id al-Adha)
11 dhu al-qadah . . . . Birthday of Imam Reza

Iraq

Apr 9 . . . . .Baghdad Liberation Day
Oct 3 . . . . National Day

Muslim holidays:
1 Muharram . . . . .Hijra New Year
10 Muharram . . . . Aashuraa Day (Ashura)
12 Rabi al-Awwal Prophet Muhammad's Birthday(Mawlid al-Nabi)
27 Rajab . . . . .Isra'A and Mi'Raj Day (Laylat al-Miraj)
17 Ramadan . . . . .Badder Conquest Day
1-3 Shawwal . . . . .Eid al-Fitr (Id al-Fitr)
10-13 Dhu al-Hijjah . . . . EId al-Adha (Id al-Adha)

Ireland

Mar-Apr: Monday after Easter . . . . .Easter Monday
May, first Mon . . . . May Day Holiday
Jun, first Mon . . . . .June Holiday
Aug, first Mon . . . . August Holiday
Oct, last Mon . . . . October Holiday

Israel

Feb-Mar . . . . .Purim
Mar-Apr . . . . Passover
Apr-May . . . . .Independence Day
May-Jun . . . . Shavuot
Jul-Aug . . . . .Tisha B'Av
Sep-Oct . . . . .Rosh Hashana
Sep-Oct . . . . Yom Kippur
Sep-Oct . . . . Sukkot
Sep-Oct . . . . .Simchat Torah
Oct-Nov . . . . .Ethiopian Sigd Festival
Nov-Dec . . . . .Hanukkah

Italy

Mar-Apr . . . . .Easter
Mar-Apr: Mon after Easter . . . . .Easter Monday
Jun 02 . . . . Republic Day

Jamaica

Feb-Mar	Ash Wednesday
Mar-Apr: Fri before Easter	Good Friday
Mar-Apr: Mon after Easter	Easter Monday
Oct, third Mon	National Heroes' Day

Japan

Jan	Coming-of-Age Day
Mar	Vernal Equinox Day
Jul	Marine Day
Sep	Autumnal Equinox Day
Oct	Health-Sports Day

Jordan

Muslim holidays:

1 Muharram	Hijri New Year
12 Rabi al-Awwal	Prophet Muhammad's Birthday(Mawlid al-Nabi)
27 Rajab	Al-Isra'Wal Mi'Raj (Laylat al-Miraj)
1 Ramadan	Ramadan Begins
1 Shawwal	Eid al-Fitr (Id al-Fitr)
10-12 Dhu al-Hijjah	EId al-Adha (Id al-Adha)

Kazakhstan

Jan 1-2	New Year's Holiday
Mar	Nauryz Meiramy (Spring New Year)

Kenya

1 Shawwal	Id ul-Fitr
Mar-Apr: Fri before Easter	Good Friday
Mar-Apr: Mon after Easter	Easter Monday

Kiribati

Mar-Apr: Fri before Easter	Good Friday
Mar-Apr: Mon after Easter	Easter Monday

Korea, South (Republic of Korea)

Apr-May	Buddha's Birthday

Kosovo, Republic of

Mar-Apr: Mon after Easter	Easter Monday (Catholic)
Mar-Apr: Mon after Easter	Easter Monday (Orthodox)

Muslim holidays:

1 Shawwal	Eid al-Fitr (Id al-Fitr)
10 Dhu al-Hijjah	Eid al-Addha (Id al-Adha)

Kuwait

Muslim holidays:

1 Muharram	Hijri New Year
12 Rabi al-Awwal	Prophet Muhammad's Birthday(Mawlid al-Nabi)
27 Rajab	Ascension of the Prophet (Laylat al-Miraj)
1 Shawwal	Eid al-Fitr (Id al-Fitr)
10-12 Dhu al-Hijjah	EId al-Adha (Id al-Adha)

Kyrgyzstan

Muslim holidays:

1 Shawwal	Orozo Ait (Id al-Fitr)
Dhu al-Hijjah	Kurban Ait (Id al-Adha)

Laos

Apr: three days in mid	Lao New Year (Water Festival)
Oct	Last Day of Buddhist Lent
Oct: day after buddhist lent ends	Boat Racing Festival
Nov	That Luang Festival

Latvia

Mar-Apr	Easter
Mar-Apr: Fri before Easter	Good Friday
Mar-Apr: Mon after Easter	Easter Monday

Lebanon

Jan 1	New Year's Day
Jan 6	Epiphany/Armenian Christmas
Feb 9	St. Maroun's Day
Mar 25	Feast of the Annunciation
Mar-Apr	Catholic Easter
Mar-Apr: Fri before Catholic Easter	Good Friday
Apr-May	Orthodox Easter
Apr-May: Fri before Orthodox Easter	Good Friday
May 1	Labor Day
May 6	Martyr's Day
May 25	Resistance and Liberation Day
Aug 15	Assumption Day
Nov 22	Independence Day
Dec 25	Christmas Day

Muslim holidays:

Muharram 1	Hijra New Year
Muharram 10	Aashuraa Day (Ashura)
Rabi-al-awwal 12	Prophet Muhammad's Birthday(Mawlid al-Nabi)
Shawwal 1	Eid al-Fitr (Id al-Fitr)
Dhu-al-hijjah 10-13	EId al-Adha (Id al-Adha)

Lesotho

Jan 1	New Year's Day
Mar 11	Moshoeshoe's Day

Mar-Apr: Fri before Easter . . . . Good Friday
Mar-Apr: Mon after Easter . . . . Easter Monday
May 1 . . . . Worker's Day
May 25 .Africa Day/Heroe's Day
May-Jun . . . . Ascension Day
Jul 17 . . . . .King's Birthday
Oct 4 . . . . .Independence Day
Dec 25 . . . . Christmas Day

Liberia

Jan 1 . . . . New Year's Day
Feb 11 . . . . Armed Forces Day
Mar 15 . . . . J. J. Robert's Birthday
Mar: Second Wed .Decoration Day
Apr 11 . . . . Fast and Prayer Day
May 14 . . . . National Unification Day
Jul 26 . . . . .Independence Day
Aug 24 . . . . Flag Day
Nov 29 . . . . .President Tubman's Birthday
Nov: First Thurs . . . . Thanksgiving Day
Dec 25 . . . . Christmas Day

Libya

Feb 17 . . . . .Revolution Day
Mar 2 . . . . .Declaration of Jamahiriya Day (1977)
Mar 28 . . . . British Evacuation Day
Jun 11 . . . . Evacuation of Foreign Bases Day
Sep 1 . . . . .Revolution Day
Sep 16 . . . . .Martyr's Day
Oct 7 . . . . Italian Evacuation Day
Oct 23 . . . . Liberation Day
Oct 26 . . . . Day of Mourning
Dec 24 . . . . .Independence Day

Muslim holidays:
Muharram . . . . Islamic New Year
Rabi-al-awwal . . . . Mawlid al-Nabi
Shawwal . . . . .Id al-Fitr
Dhu-al-hijjah . . . . .Id al-Adha

Liechtenstein

Jan 1 . . . . New Year's Day
Jan 6 . . . . .Epiphany
Feb 2 . . . . .Candlemas
Feb-Mar . . . . Shrove Tuesday
Mar 19 . . . . .Feast of St. Joseph
Mar-Apr: Fri before Easter . . . . Good Friday
Mar-Apr: Mon after Easter . . . . Easter Monday
May 1 . . . . Labor Day
May-Jun . . . . Ascension Day
May-Jun . . . . Pentecost
May-Jun . . . . Whit Monday
May-Jun . . . . Corpus Christi Day
Aug 15 . . . . .National Day
Sep 8 . . . . .Nativity of Our Lady
Nov 1 . . . . All Saint's Day
Dec 8 . . . . Immaculate Conception Day

Dec 24 . . . . Christmas Eve
Dec 25 . . . . Christmas Day
Dec 26 . . . . St. Stephen's Day
Dec 31 . . . . .Silvester (New Year's Eve)

Lithuania

Jan 1 . . . . New Year's Day
Feb 16 . . . . .Independence Day
Mar 11 . . . . Restoration of Lithuania's Statehood
Mar-Apr: Mon after Easter . . . . Easter Monday
Mar-Apr: Tue after Easter . . . . Easter Tuesday
May: first Sun . . . . Mother's Day
May 1 . . . . .Labour Day
Jun 24 . . . . St. John's Day
Jul 6 . . . . State Day (Crowning of King Mindaugas)
Aug 15 . . . . Assumption Day
Nov 1 . . . . All Saint's Day
Dec 25-26 . . . . Christmas Day

Luxembourg

Jan 1 . . . . New Year's Day
Mar-Apr: Mon after Easter . . . . Easter Monday
May 1 . . . . May Day
May-Jun . . . . Ascension Day
May-Jun . . . . Whit Monday
June 23 . . . . .National Day (Grand Duke's Birthday)
Aug 15 . . . . Assumption
Nov 1 . . . . All Saint's Day
Dec 25 . . . . Christmas Day
Dec 26 . . . . St. Stephen's Day

Macedonia

Jan 1 . . . . New Year's Day
Jan 6-7 . . . . Orthodox Christmas
May 1 . . . . May Day
May 24 . . . . Sts. Cyril and Methodius Day
Aug 2 . . . . Republic Day
Sep 8 . . . . .Independence Day
Oct 11 . . . . Uprising Against Facism Day
Oct 23 . . . . Day of the Macedonian Revolution
Dec 8 . . . . St. Kliment Ohridski

Madagascar

Jan 1 . . . . New Year's Day
Mar 8 . . . . Women's Day (Women Only)
Mar 29 . . . . Martyr's Day
Mar-Apr: Mon after Easter . . . . Easter Monday
May 1 . . . . Ascension Day/Labor Day
June 26 . . . . .Independence Day
Aug 15 . . . . Assumption Day
Nov 1 . . . . All Saint's Day
Dec 25 . . . . Christmas Day
Dec 30 . . . . Anniversary of the Republic

Malawi

Jan 1	New Year's Day
Jan 15	John Chilembwe Day
Mar 3	Martyr's Day
Mar-Apr: Fri before Easter	Good Friday
Mar-Apr: Mon after Easter	Easter Monday
May 1	Labour Day
May 14	Kamuzu Day
Jun 14	Freedom Day
Jul 6	Republic Day
Oct: Second Mon	Mother's Day
Dec 25	Christmas Day
Dec 26	Boxing Day

Malaysia

Jan-Feb	Chinese New Year
Apr-May	Wesak Day
May 1	Labour Day
Jun	Birthday Celebration of SPB Yang Di Pertuan Agong
Aug 31	National Day
Oct-Nov	Deepavali
Dec 25	Christmas Day

Muslim holidays:

Muharram 1	Maal Hijrah (Hijra New Year)
Rabi-al-awwal 12	Maulidur Rasul (Muhammad's Birthday Or Mawlid al-Nabi)
Shawwal 1	Hari Raya Qurban (Id al-Fitr)
Dhu-al-hijjah 10-12	Hari Raya Aidil Adha (Id al-Adha)

Maldives

Jan 1	New Year's Day
Jan	Maldives Embraced Islam
Jul 26-27	Independence Day Holiday
Nov 3	Victory Day
Nov 11	Republic Day
Dec	National Day

Muslim holidays:

Muharram 1	Islamic New Year
Rabi-al-awwal 12	Muhammad's Birthday(Mawlid al-Nabi)
Ramadan 1	Ramadan Begins
Shawwal 1	Id al-Fitr
Dhu-al-hijjah 10-12	Id al-Adha

Mali

Jan 1	New Year's Day
Jan 20	Armed Forces Day
Mar 26	Day of the Martyrs
May 1	Labor Day
May 25	African Unity Day
Sep 22	Independence Day
Dec 25	Christmas Day

Muslim holidays:

Rabi-al-awwal 12	Mawlud (Mawlid al-Nabi Ormuhammad's Birthday)
Ramadan 1	Ramadan Begins
Shawwal 1	Aïd El-Fitr (Id al-Fitr)
Dhu-al-hijjah 10-12	Tabaski (Aïd El-Kébir; Id al-Adha)

Malta

Jan 1	New Year's Day
Feb 10	Feast of St. Paul's Shipwreck
Mar 19	Feast of St. Joseph
Mar 31	Freedom Day
Mar-Apr: Fri before Easter	Good Friday
May 1	Workers' Day
Jun 7	Commemoration of Uprising of June 7, 1919
Jun 29	Feast of Sts. Peter and Paul (Mnarja)
Aug 15	Assumption
Sep 8	Feast of Our Lady of Victories
Sep 21	Independence Day
Dec 8	Immaculate Conception
Dec 13	Republic Day
Dec 25	Christmas Day

Marshall Islands

Jan 1	New Year's Day
Mar 1	Remembrance Day
Mar-Apr: Fri before Easter	Good Friday
May 1	Constitution Day
Jul 4	Fishermen's Day
Sep 1	Workers' Day
Sep 30	Customs Day
Nov 17	Presidents' Day
Dec 4	Kamolol (Thanksgiving Day)
Dec 25	Christmas Day

Mauritania

Jan 1	New Year's Day
May 1	Labor Day
May 25	Journée De L'Oua (Africa Day)
Nov 28	Independence Day

Muslim holidays:

Muharram 1	Islamic New Year
Rabi-al-awwal 12	Id al Maouloud(Muhammad's Birthday Or Mawlid al-Nabi)
Shawwal 1	Id al-Fitr
Dhu-al-hijjah 10-12	Id al-Adha

Mauritius

Jan 1-2	New Year Holiday
Jan-Feb	Thaipoosam Cavadee
Jan-Feb	Chinese New Year
Feb-Mar	Maha Shivaratree
Mar 12	National Day
Mar-Apr	Ougadi (Telegu New Year)
May 1	Labour Day
Aug 15	Assumption Day
Aug-Sep	Ganesh Chaturti

Oct-Nov . . . . Divali
Nov 1 . . . . All Saints' Day
Dec 25 . . . . Christmas Day

Muslim holidays:
Shawwal 1 . . . . Id al-Fitr

Mexico

Jan 1 . . . . New Year's Day
Feb 5 . . . . Constitution Day
Mar 21 . . . . Birthday of Benito Juarez
Mar-Apr: Thurs before Easter . . . . Holy Thursday
Mar-Apr: Fri before Easter . . . . Good Friday
Apr-May . . . . Easter
May 1 . . . . Labor Day
May 5 . . . . Battle of Puebla (Cinco de Mayo)
Sep 16 . . . . Independence Day
Oct 12 . . . . Día De La Raza
Nov 2 . . . . Día De Los Fieles Difuntos
(Day of the Dead; All Souls' Day)
Nov 20 . . . . Anniversary of the Revolution
Dec 12 . . . . Our Lady of Guadelupe
Dec 25 . . . . Christmas Day

Micronesia

Jan 1 . . . . New Year's Day
May 10 . . . . FSM Day (Constitution Day)
Oct 24 . . . . United Nation's Day
Nov 3 . . . . FSM Independence Day
Nov 11 . . . . Veteran's Day
Dec 25 . . . . Christmas Day

Moldova

Jan 1 . . . . New Year's Day
Jan 7-8 . . . . Orthodox Christmas
Mar 8 . . . . International Women's Day
Apr-May . . . . Easter
Apr-May: Mon one week after Easter . . . . Memorial Easter
May 1 . . . . Labor Day
May 9 . . . . Victory Day
Aug 27 . . . . Independence Day
Aug 31 . . . . Limba Noastra National Language Day

Monaco

Jan 1 . . . . New Year's Day
Jan 27 . . . . St. Dévôte's Day
Mar-Apr: Mon after Easter . . . . Easter Monday
May 1 . . . . Labor Day
May-Jun . . . . Ascension Day
May-Jun . . . . Whit Monday
May-Jun . . . . Fête Dieu (Corpus Christi)
Aug 15 . . . . Assumption Day
Nov 1 . . . . All Saints' Day
Nov 19 . . . . National Day
Dec 8 . . . . Immaculate Conception
Dec 25 . . . . Christmas Day

Mongolia

Jan 1 . . . . New Year's Day
Jan-Feb . . . . Lunar New Year
Mar 8 . . . . International Women's Day
Jun 1 . . . . Mother and Child Day
Jul 11-13 . . . . National Day (Naadam)
Dec 29 . . . . Independence Day

Montenegro

Jan 1-2 . . . . New Year's Holiday
Jan 7 . . . . Orthodox Christmas
Jan 8 . . . . Second Day of Orthodox Christmas
Mar-Apr: Fri before Easter . . . . Orthodox Good Friday
Mar-Apr: Mon after Easter . . . . . . Orthodox Easter Monday
May 1 . . . . May Day
May 21 . . . . Independence Day
Jul 13 . . . . National Day

Morocco

Jan 1 . . . . New Year's Day
Jan 11 . . . . Presentation of Independence Proclamation
May 1 . . . . Labor Day
Jul 30 . . . . Feast of the Throne
Aug 14 . . . . Oued Eddahab Allegiance
Aug 20 . . Anniversary of the revolution of the King and the People
Aug 21 . . . . Youth's Day/King's Birthday
Nov 6 . . . . Green March Day
Nov 18 . . . . Independence Day

Muslim holidays:
Muharram 1 . . . . Islamic New Year
Rabi-al-awwal . . . Muhammad's Birthday(Mawlid al-Nabi)
shawwal . . . . Id al-Fitr
Dhu-al-hijjah . . . . Id al-Adha

Mozambique

Jan 1 . . . . New Year's Day
Feb 3 . . . . Heroes' Day
Apr 7 . . . . Women's Day
May 1 . . . . Workers' Day
Jun 25 . . . . Independence Day
Sep 7 . . . . Victory Day
Sep 25 . . . . Revolution Day
Oct 4 . . . . Day of Peace and Reconciliation
Dec 25 . . . . Family/Christmas Day

Myanmar

Jan 4 . . . . Independence Day
Feb 12 . . . . Union Day
Feb-Mar . . . . Full Moon Day of Tabaung
Mar 2 . . . . Peasants' Day
Mar 27 . . . . Armed Forces Day
Apr: Mid . . . . Thingyan (Water Festival)
Apr: Mid . . . . Myanmar New Year Day

Apr-May	Full Moon Day of Kason
May 1	May Day (Labor Day)
Jun-Jul	Full Moon Day of Waso(Beginning of Buddhist Lent)
Jul 19	Martyrs' Day
Sep-Oct	End of Buddhist Lent (Thadingyut Festival of Lights)
Oct-Nov	Dewali (Depali Festival Day)
Oct-Nov	Tazaungdaing Festival
Nov (movable)	National Day
Dec 25	Christmas Day

Namibia

Jan 1	New Year's Day
Mar 21	Independence Day
Mar-Apr: Fri before Easter	Good Friday
Mar-Apr: Mon after Easter	Easter Monday
May 1	Workers Day
May 4	Cassinga Day
May 25	Africa Day
May-Jun	Ascension Day
Aug 26	Heroes Day
Dec 10	International Human Rights Day
Dec 25	Christmas Day
Dec 26	Family Day

Nauru

Jan 1	New Year's Day
Jan 31	Independence Day
Mar-Apr: Fri before Easter	Good Friday
Mar-Apr: Mon after Easter	Easter Monday
Mar-Apr: Tues after Easter	Easter Tuesday
May 17	Constitution Day
Sep 25	National Youth Day
Oct 26	Angam Day
Dec 25	Christmas Day
Dec 26	Boxing Day

Nepal

Jan 30	Martyrs' Day
Feb 19	Democracy Day
Feb-Mar	Mahashivrati
Mar 8	International Women's Day
Mar-Apr	Fagu Purnima
Mar-Apr	Ramnawami
Mar-Apr	Ghode Jatra
Apr 14	Nepali New Year
Apr-May	Buddha Day
May 1	May Day
May 29	Republic Day
Aug	Janai Purnima
Aug-Sep	Krishnasthami
Sep-Oct	Ghatasthapana
Sep-Oct	Dashain (Six Days)
Oct-Nov	Tihar (Three Days)
Dec 25	Christmas

Netherlands

Jan 1	New Year's Day
Mar-Apr: Fri before Easter	Good Friday
Mar-Apr: Mon after Easter	Easter Monday
Apr 27	King's Birthday
May 5, every 5 years (2005, 2010, etc)	Liberation Day
May-Jun	Ascension Day
May-Jun	Whit Sunday (Pentecost)
May-Jun	Whit Monday
Dec 25	Christmas Day
Dec 26	Second Day of Christmas

New Zealand

Jan 1-2	New Year's Holiday
Feb 6	Waitangi Day
Mar-Apr: Fri before Easter	Good Friday
Mar-Apr: Mon after Easter	Easter Monday
Apr 25	Anzac Day
Jun: first Mon	Queen Elizabeth II Birthday
Oct: first Mon	Labour Day
Dec 25	Christmas Day
Dec 26	Boxing Day

Nicaragua

Jan 1	New Year's Day
Mar-Apr: Thurs before Easter	Holy Thursday
Mar-Apr: Fri before Easter	Good Friday
May 1	Labor Day
Jul 19	Sandinista Revolution Day
Sep 14	Battle of San Jacinto
Sep 15	Independence Day
Dec 8	Immaculate Conception Day
Dec 25	Christmas Day

Niger

Jan 1	New Year's Day
Mar-Apr: Mon after Easter	Easter Monday
Apr 24	Concord Day
May 1	Labor Day
Aug 3	Independence Day
Dec 18	Republic Day
Dec 25	Christmas Day

Muslim holidays:

Rabi-al-awwal	Mouloud (Muhammad's Birthdayor Mawlid al-Nabi)
Ramadan 27	Leilat-Ul-Kadr (Laylat Al-Qadr)
Shawwal	Id al-Fitr
Dhu-al-hijjah	Tabaski (Id al-Adha)

Nigeria

Jan 1	New Year's Day
Mar-Apr: Fri before Easter	Good Friday
Mar-Apr: Mon after Easter	Easter Monday
May 1	Labor Day

May 29	Democracy Day
Oct 1	Independence Day
Dec 25	Christmas Day
Dec 26	Boxing Day

Muslim holidays:

Rabi-al-awwal	The Prophet's Birthday (Id El-Maulud)
Shawwal	Id El-Fitri
Dhu-al-hijjah	Id El-Kabir (Id al-Adha)

Niue

Jan 1	New Year's Day
Feb 6	Waitangi Day
Mar-Apr: Fri before Easter	Good Friday
Mar-Apr: Mon after Easter	Easter Monday
Apr 25	Anzac Day
Jun: first Mon	Queen Elizabeth II Birthday
Oct	Peniamina Gospel Day
Oct	Constitution Day
Dec 25	Christmas Day
Dec 26	Boxing Day
Dec-Jan	Commission Holidaynorth Korea. See Korea,

Northnorthern Ireland. See United Kingdom

Northern Ireland

Jan 1	New Year's Day
Mar: third Mon	St. Patrick's Day
Mar-Apr: Fri before Easter	Good Friday
Mar-Apr: Mon after Easter	Easter Monday
May: First Mon	Early May Bank Holiday
May: Last Mon	Spring Bank Holiday
Jul 12	Battle of the Boyne (Orangemen's Day)
Aug: Last Mon	Summer Bank Holiday
Dec 25	Christmas Day
Dec 26	Boxing Day

Norway

Jan 1	New Year's Day
Mar-Apr	Easter Sunday
Mar-Apr: Sun before Easter	Palm Sunday
Mar-Apr: Thurs before Easter	Maundy Thursday
Mar-Apr: Fri before Easter	Good Friday
Mar-Apr: Mon after Easter	Easter Monday
May 1	Labor Day
May 17	Constitution Day
May-Jun	Ascension Day
May-Jun	Whitsun (Pentecost)
May-Jun	Whit Monday
Dec 25	Christmas Day
Dec 26	Second Day of Christmas

Oman

Jan 1	New Year's Day
Jul 23	Renaissance Day
Nov 18-19	National Day Holiday

Muslim holidays:

1 Muharram	Hijri New Year
Rabi al-Awwal 12	Prophet Muhammad's Birthday(Mawlid al-Nabi)
Rajab 27	Isra and Meiraj (Laylat Al-Miraj)
Shawwal (four days)	Id al-Fitr
Dhu-al-Hijjah (five days)	Id al-Adha

Pakistan

Feb 5	Kashmir Day
Mar 23	Pakistan Day
May 1	Labor Day
Aug 14	Independence Day
Nov 9	Birthday of Muhammad Iqbal
Dec 25	Christmas Day and Birthday of Quaid-E-Azam

Muslim holidays:

Rabi al-Awwal 12	Eid-E-Milad-Un-Nabi(Mawlid al-Nabi)
Shaaban 14	Shab-E-Barat
Shawwal 1	Id al-Fitr
Dhu-al-Hijjah 10	Id-Ul-Azha (Id al-Adha)

Palau

Jan 1	New Year's Day
Mar 15	Youth Day
May 5	Senior Citizens Day
Jun 1	President's Day
Jul 9	Constitution Day
Sep: first Mon	Labor Day
Oct 1	Independence Day
Oct 24	United Nations Day
Nov: last Thurs	Thanksgiving Day
Dec 25	Christmas Day

Panama

Jan 1	New Year's Day
Jan 9	National Mourning Day
Feb	Mardi Gras
Mar-Apr	Easter
Mar-Apr: Fri before Easter	Good Friday
Mar-Apr: Sat before Easter	Holy Saturday
May 1	Labor Day
Nov 3	Independence From Colombia Day
Nov 4	Flag Day
Nov 5	Colon Day
Nov 10	Independence Proclamation/Uprising of Los Santos
Nov 28	Independence From Spain Day
Dec 8	Mother's Day
Dec 25	Christmas Day
Dec 31	New Year's Eve

Papua New Guinea

Jan 1	New Year's Day
Mar-Apr	Easter Sunday
Mar-Apr: Fri before Easter	Good Friday
Mar-Apr: Sat before Easter	Holy Saturday

Mar-Apr: Mon after Easter . . . . .Easter Monday
Jun: second Mon . . . . Queen Elizabeth II Birthday
Jul 23 . . . . Remembrance Day
Aug 26 . . . . National Repentance Day
Sep 16 . . . . Independence Day
Dec 25 . . . . .Christmas Day
Dec 26 . . . . .Boxing Day

Paraguay

Jan 1 . . . . .New Year's Day
Mar 1 . . . . Heroes' Day
Mar-Apr: Thurs before Easter . . . . .Holy Thursday
Mar-Apr: Fri before Easter . . . . .Good Friday
May 1 . . . . .Labor Day
May 15 . . . . Independence Day
Jun 12 . . . . End of the Chaco War
Aug 15 . . . . Founding of Asuncion
Sep 29 . . . . .Victory Day
Dec 8 . . . . Immaculate Conception
Dec 25 . . . . Christmas Day

Peru

Jan 1 . . . . .New Year's Day
Mar-Apr . . . . .Easter
Mar-Apr: Thurs before Easter . . . . .Holy Thursday
Mar-Apr: Fri before Easter . . . . .Good Friday
May 1 . . . . .Labor Day
Jun 29 . . . . Sts. Peter and Paul Day
Jul 28-29 . . . . .Independence Day Holiday
Aug 30 . . . . St. Rose of Lima Day
Oct 8 . . . . Battle of Angamos
Nov 1 . . . . All Saints' Day
Dec 8 . . . . Immaculate Conception
Dec 25 . . . . Christmas Day

Philippines

Jan 1 . . . . .New Year's Day
Feb 24 . . . . Edsa Revolution Day
Mar-Apr: Thurs before Easter . . . . Maundy Thursday
Mar-Apr: Fri before Easter . . . . .Good Friday
Mar-Apr: Sat before Easter . . . . .Black Saturday
Apr 9 . . . . .Araw Ng Kagitingan (Bataan Day)
May 1 . . . . .Labor Day
Jun 12 . . . . Independence Day
Aug: last Sun . . . . National Heroes Day
Nov 1 . . . . All Saints' Day
Nov 30 . . . . .Bonifacio Day
Dec 25 . . . . Christmas Day
Dec 30 . . . . Rizal Day
Dec 31 . . . . New Year's Eve

Poland

Jan 1 . . . . .New Year's Day
Mar-Apr . . . . .Easter
Mar-Apr: Mon after Easter . . . . .Easter Monday
May 1 . . . . .Labor Day

May 3 . . . . Constitution Day
May .Whit Sunday (Pentecost)
May-Jun . . . . Corpus Christi
Aug 15 . . . . .Assumption
Nov 1 . . . . All Saints' Day
Nov 11 . . . . .Independence Day
Dec 25 . . . . Christmas Day
Dec 26 . . . . Second Day of Christmas

Portugal

Jan 1 . . . . .New Year's Day
Feb-Mar . . . . Shrove Tuesday
Mar-Apr . . . . .Easter
Mar-Apr: Fri before Easter . . . . .Good Friday
Apr 25 . . . . .Liberty Day
May 1 . . . . .Labor Day
May-Jun . . . . Corpus Christi
Jun 10 . . . . .National Day
Aug 15 . . . . .Assumption
Oct 5 . . . . Republic Day
Nov 1 . . . . All Saints' Day
Dec 1 . . . . .Independence Day
Dec 8 . . . . Immaculate Conception
Dec 25 . . . . Christmas Day

Qatar

Dec 18 . . . . .National Day (Independence Day)

Muslim holidays:
Shawwal (four days) . . . . .Id al-Fitr
Dhu-al-hijjah . . . . Id al-Adha

Romania

Jan 1-2 . . . . .New Year's Holiday
Apr-May: Mon after Orthodox Easter . . . .Orthodox Easter
Monday
May 1 . . . . .Labor Day
Dec 1 . . . . .National Day
Dec 25-26 . . . . .Christmas Holiday

Russian Federation

Jan 1-5 . . . . .New Year's Holiday
Jan 7 . . . . .Russian Orthodox Christmas
Feb 23 . . . . Protector of Motherland Day
Mar 8 . . . . International Women's Day
May 1 . . . . .Spring and Labor Day
May 9 . . . . . . Victory Day (Over German Nazism in WWII)
Jun 12 . . . . .Independence Day
Nov 4 . . . . Unity Day

Rwanda

Jan 1 . . . . .New Year's Day
Feb 1 . . . . Heroes' Day
Mar-Apr: Fri before Easter . . . . .Good Friday
Mar-Apr: Mon after Easter . . . . .Easter Monday

Apr 7 . . . . .Genocide Memorial Day
May 1 . . . . Labor Day
Jul 1 . . . . .Independence Day
Jul 4 . . . . National Liberation Day
Aug 15 . . . . .Assumption
Oct 1 . . . . Patriotism Day
Dec 25 . . . . Christmas
Dec 26 . . . . Boxing Day

Samoa

Jan 1-2 . . . . .New Year's Holiday
Mar-Apr: Fri before Easter . . . . Good Friday
Mar-Apr: Sat before Easter . . . . Easter Saturday
Mar-Apr: Mon after Easter . . . . Easter Monday
May: second Mon . . . . Mothers' Day
Jun 1-2 . . . . .Independence Day
Aug: second Mon . . . . Fathers' Day
Oct: Mon after second Sun . . . . Lotu-a-Tamaiti
Dec 25 . . . . Christmas
Dec 26 . . . . Boxing Day

San Marino

Jan 1 . . . . New Year's Day
Jan 6 . . . . .Epiphany
Feb 5 . . . . .Anniversary of the Liberation of the
Republic and St. Agatha's Day
Mar 25 . . . . Anniversary of the Arengo (National Assembly)
Mar-Apr: Fri before Easter - Mon after Easter . . . . . . .Good
Friday - Easter Monday
Apr 1 . . . . Investiture of the Regent Captains
May 1 . . . . Labor Day
May-Jun . . . . Corpus Christi
Jul 28 . . . . Anniversary of the Fall of Fascism
Aug 15 . . . . Assumption Day
Sep 3 . . . . San Marino Foundation Day
Oct 1 . . . . Investiture of the Regent Captains
Nov 1 . . . . All Saints' Day
Nov 2 . . . . All Souls' Day
Dec 8 . . . . Immaculate Conception
Dec 24 . . . . .Christmas Eve
Dec 25 . . . . Christmas Day
Dec 26 . . . . St. Stephen's Day/Boxing Day
Dec 31 . . . . New Year's Eve

São Tomé and Príncipe

Jan 1 . . . . New Year's Day
Feb 3 . . . . .Martyrs' Day
May 1 . . . . Labor Day
Jul 12 . . . . .Independence Day
Sep 6 . . . . Armed Forces Day
Sep 30 . . . . Agricultural Reform Day
Dec 21 . . . . .São Tomé Day
Dec 25 . . . . Christmas Day

Saudi Arabia

Sep 23 . . . . .National Day

Muslim holidays:
1 Shawwal . . . . .Id al-Fitr
10 Dhu al-Hijjah . . . . .Id al-Adha

Scotland

Jan 01-02 . . . . New Year's Holiday
Mar-Apr . . . . Good Friday
May: First Mon . . . . Early May Bank Holiday
May: Last Mon . . . . .Spring Bank Holiday
Aug: Last Mon . . . . Summer Bank Holiday
Nov 30 . . . . .St. Andrew's Day
Dec 25 . . . . Christmas Day
Dec 26 . . . . Boxing Day

Senegal

Jan 1 . . . . New Year's Day
Mar-Apr: Mon after Easter . . . . .Easter Monday
Apr 4 . . . . .Independence Day
May 1 . . . . Labor Day
May-Jun . . . . Ascension Day
May-Jun: Mon after Pentecost . . . . Whit Monday
Aug 15 . . . . Assumption Day
Nov 1 . . . . All Saints' Day
Dec 25 . . . . Christmas Day

Muslim holidays:
1 Muharram . . . . .Tamkharit (Islamic New Year)
12 Rabi al-Awwal . . . . . Maulud (Muhammad's Birthday or
Mawlid al-Nabi)
1 Shawwal . . . . Korite (Id al-Fitr)
10 Dhu al-Hijjah . . . . Tabaski (Id al-Adha)

Serbia

Jan 1-2 . . . . New Year's Holiday
Jan 7 . . . . .Orthodox Christmas Day
Feb 15-16 . . . . National Statehood Day
Mar-Apr: Fri before Easter . . . . Great Friday
Mar-Apr: Sat before Easter . . . . . . Orthodox Holy Saturday
Mar-Apr: Mon after Easter . . . . . .Orthodox Easter Monday
Apr 27 . . . . Constitution Day of the Socialist Republic of
Yugoslavia
May 1-2 . . . . May Day
Aug 15 . . . . Assumption
Nov 1 . . . . All Saints' Day
Nov 11 . . . . Armistice Day (Dan primirja)
Dec 25 . . . . Christmas Day

Seychelles

Jan 1-2 . . . . .New Year Holiday
Mar-Apr: Fri before Easter . . . . .Good Friday
Mar-Apr: Sat before Easter . . . . Holy Saturday
May 1 . . . . .Labour Day
May-Jun . . . . Corpus Christi Day
Jun 5 . . . . Liberation Day
Jun 18 . . . . Constitution Day

Jun 29 .... Independence Day
Aug 15 .... Assumption Day
Nov 1 .... All Saints' Day
Dec 8 .... Immaculate Conception Day
Dec 25 .... Christmas Day

Sierra Leone

Jan 1 .... New Year's Day
Mar-Apr: Fri before Easter .... Good Friday
Mar-Apr: Mon after Easter .... Easter Monday
Apr 27 .... Independence Day
Dec 25 .... Christmas Day
Dec 26 .... Boxing Day

Muslim holidays:
Rabi-al-Awwal ...... Maoulid-Un-Nabi (Mawlid al-Nabi)
Shawwal .... Id al-Fitr
Dhu al-Hijjah .... Tabaski (Id al-Adha)

Singapore

Jan 1 .... New Year's Day
Jan-Feb .... Chinese New Year
Mar-Apr: Fri before Easter .... Good Friday
Apr-May .... Vesak Day
May 1 .... Labour Day
Aug 9 .... National Day
Oct-Nov .... Deepavali
Dec 25 .... Christmas Day

Muslim holidays:
1 Shawwal .... Hari Raya Pausa (Id al-Fitr)
10 Dhu al-Hijjah .... Hari Raya Hajj (Id al-Adha)

Slovakia

Jan 1 .... Republic Day/New Year's Day
Jan 6 .... Epiphany
Mar-Apr: Fri before Easter .... Good Friday
Mar-Apr: Mon after Easter .... Easter Monday
May 1 .... May Day
May 8 .... Victory Day
Jul 5 .... Sts. Cyril and Methodius Day
Aug 29 .... Slovak National Uprising Day
Sep 1 .... Constitution Day
Sep 15 .... Lady Mary of Sorrows, Patron of Slovakia
Nov 1 .... All Saints' Day
Nov 17 ...... Day of the Fight for Freedom and Democracy
Dec 24 .... Christmas Eve
Dec 25 .... Christmas Day
Dec 26 .... Second Day of Christmas

Slovenia

Jan 1 .... New Year's Holiday
Feb 8 .... Preseren Day
Mar-Apr .... Easter Sunday
Mar-Apr: Mon after Easter .... Easter Monday
Apr 27 .... Day of Uprising against Nazi Occupation

May 1-2 .... May Day Holiday
May-Jun .... Whit Sunday (Pentecost)
Jun 25 .... National Day
Aug 15 .... Assumption Day
Oct 31 .... Reformation Day
Nov 1 .... All Saints' Day
Dec 25 .... Christmas Day
Dec 26 .... Independence and Unity Day

Solomon Islands

Jan 1 .... New Year's Day
Mar-Apr: Fri before Easter - Mon after Easter ....Good
Friday - Easter Monday
May-Jun .... Whit Monday
Jun .... Queen's Birthday
Jul 7 .... Independence Day
Dec 25 .... Christmas
Dec 26 ....National Day of Thanksgiving

South Africa

Jan 1 .... New Year's Day
Mar 21 .... Human Rights Day
Mar-Apr: Fri before Easter .... Good Friday
Mar-Apr: Mon after Easter .... Family Day
Apr 27 .... Freedom Day
May 1 .... Workers' Day
Jun 16 .... Youth Day
Aug 9 .... National Women's Day
Sep 24 .... Heritage Day
Dec 16 .... Day of Reconciliation
Dec 25 .... Christmas Day
Dec 26 .... Day of Goodwill

South Korea. *See* Korea, South

Spain

Jan 1 .... New Year's Day
Jan 6 .... Epiphany
Mar-Apr .... Easter Sunday
Mar-Apr: Fri before Easter .... Good Friday
May 1 .... Labor Day
Aug 15 .... Assumption Day
Oct 12 .... National Day
Nov 1 .... All Saints' Day
Dec 6 .... Constitution Day
Dec 8 .... Immaculate Conception Day
Dec 25 .... Christmas Day

Sri Lanka

Jan .... Tamil Thai Pongal Day
Feb 4 .... National Day
Feb-Mar .... Maha Sivarathri Day
Mar-Apr: Fri before Easter .... Good Friday
Apr 13 .... Day prior to Sinhala and Tamil New Year
Apr 14 .... Sinhala and Tamil New Year

Apr-May: Day following Vesak Full Moon . . . . . Poya Day
May 1 . . . . May Day
Oct-Nov . . . . Deepavali Festival Day
Dec 25 . . . . Christmas Day

Muslim holidays:
Rabi-al-Awwal . . . . Milad-Un-Nabi (Holy Prophet's
Birthday or Mawlid al-Nabi)
Shawwal . . . Id-Ul-Fitr (Ramazan Festival Day or Id al-Fitr)
Dhu al-Hijjah . . . . Id-Ul-allah
(Hajji Festival Day or Id al-Adha)

St. Kitts and Nevis

Jan 1 . . . . New Year's Day
Jan 2 . . . . Carnival Day
Mar-Apr: Fri before Easter . . . . Good Friday
Mar-Apr: Mon after Easter . . . . Easter Monday
May: first Mon . . . . Labour Day
May-Jun . . . . Whit Monday
Aug . . . . Emancipation Day
Sep 16 . . . . National Heroes' Day
Sep 19 . . . . Independence Day
Dec 25 . . . . Christmas Day
Dec 26 . . . . Boxing Day

St. Lucia

Jan 1-2 . . . . New Year's Holiday
Feb 22 . . . . Independence Day
Mar-Apr: Fri before Easter . . . . Good Friday
Mar-Apr: Mon after Easter . . . . Easter Monday
May 1 . . . . Labor Day
May-Jun . . . . Whit Monday
May-Jun . . . . Corpus Christi
Aug 1 . . . . Emancipation Day
Oct, first Mon . . . . Thanksgiving Day
Dec 13 . . . . National Day
Dec 25 . . . . Christmas Day
Dec 26 . . . . Boxing Day

St. Vincent and the Grenadines

Jan 1 . . . . New Year's Day
Mar 14 . . . . National Heroes' Day
Mar-Apr: Fri before Easter . . . . Good Friday
Mar-Apr: Mon after Easter . . . . Easter Monday
May 1 . . . . Labor Day
May-Jun . . . . Whit Monday
Jul: first Mon . . . . Carnival Monday
Jul: first Tues . . . . Carnival Tuesday
Aug 1 . . . . August Monday (Emancipation Day)
Oct 27 . . . . Independence Day
Dec 25 . . . . Christmas Day
Dec 26 . . . . Boxing Day

Sudan

Jan 1 . . . . Independence Day
Apr 27 . . . . Coptic Easter
Jun 30 . . . . Revolution Day
Dec 25 . . . . Christmas Day

Muslim holidays:
Muharram 1 . . . . Islamic New Year
12 Rabi al-Awwal . . . . Mawlid al-Nabi
1 Shawwal . . . . Id al-Fitr
10 Dhu al-Hijjah . . . . Id al-Adha

Suriname

Jan 1 . . . . New Year's Day
Mar: full moon day . . . . Holi Phagwa
Mar-Apr: Fri before Easter - Mon after Easter . . . . . . Good
Friday - Easter Monday
May 1 . . . . Labor Day
Jul 1 . . . . Emancipation Day (Keti Koti)
Aug 9 . . . . Indigenous People's Day
Oct 10 . . . . Maroons Day
Oct-Nov . . . . Deepavali Festival Day
Nov 25 . . . . Independence Day
Dec 25 . . . . Christmas Day
Dec 26 . . . . Second Day of Christmas

Muslim holidays:
1 Shawwal . . . . Id al-Fitr
Dhu al-Hijjah . . . . Id al-Adha

Swaziland

Jan 1 . . . . New Year's Day
Mar-Apr: Fri before Easter . . . . Good Friday
Mar-Apr: Mon after Easter . . . . Easter Monday
Apr 19 . . . . King's Birthday
Apr 25 . . . . National Flag Day
May 1 . . . . Workers' Day
May-Jun . . . . Ascension Day
Jul 22 . . . . King Father's Birthday
Aug-Sep . . . . Umhlanga Reed Dance
Sep 6 . . . . Somhlolo Day (Independence Day)
Dec 25 . . . . Christmas Day
Dec 26 . . . . Boxing Day
Dec-Jan . . . . Incwala Day

Sweden

Jan 1 . . . . New Year's Day
Jan 6 . . . . Epiphany
Mar-Apr . . . . Easter Sunday
Mar-Apr: Fri before Easter . . . . Good Friday
Mar-Apr: Mon after Easter . . . . Easter Monday
Apr-May . . . . Ascension Day
May 1 . . . . Labor Day
May-Jun . . . . Whit Sunday (Pentecost)
Jun 6 . . . . National Day
Jun . . . . Midsummer's Day
Nov 1 . . . . All Saints' Day
Dec 25 . . . . Christmas Day
Dec 26 . . . . Second Day of Christmas

Switzerland

Jan 1 . . . . New Year's Day
Mar-Apr . . . . Easter Sunday

Mar-Apr: Fri before Easter	Good Friday
Mar-Apr: Mon after Easter	Easter Monday
Apr-May	Ascension Day
May-Jun	Whit Sunday (Pentecost)
May-Jun	Whit Monday
Aug 1	Swiss National Day
Dec 25	Christmas Day

Syria

Jan 1	New Year's Day
Mar 8	Commemoration of the Revolution
Mar 21	Mothers' Day
Mar-Apr	Easter Sunday
Apr 17	Commemoration of the Evacuation
May 1	May Day (Workers' Holiday)
May 6	Martyrs' Day
Oct 6	Tishreen Liberation Day
Dec 25	Christmas Day

Muslim holidays:

1 Shawwal	Id al-Fitr
12 Rabi al-Awwal	Mawlid al-Nabi
10 Dhu al-Hijjah	Id al-Adha

Taiwan (Republic of China)

Jan 1	New Year's Day/Founding Day of the Republic of China
Jan-Feb	Chinese New Year
Feb 28	Peace Memorial Day
Apr 4	Tomb Sweeping Day
May 1	Labor Day
May-Jun	Dragon Boat Festival
Aug-Sep	Mid-Autumn Festival
Oct 10	Double Tenth National Day

Tajikistan

Jan 1	New Year's Day
Mar 8	International Women's Day
Mar 21-24	Nawruz
May 1	Labor Day
May 9	Victory Day
Jun 27	Unity Day
Sep 9	Independence Day
Nov 6	Constitution Day

Muslim holidays:

1 Ramadan	Ramadan
Dhu al-Hijjah	Qurban (Id al-Adha)

Tanzania

Jan 1	New Year's Day
Jan 12	Zanzibar Revolution Day
Mar-Apr: Fri before Easter	Good Friday
Mar-Apr: Mon after Easter	Easter Monday
Apr 7	Karume Day
Apr 26	Union Day

May 1	Labor Day
Jul 7	Saba Saba Day
Aug 8	Farmers' Day
Oct 14	Nyerere Day
Dec 9	Independence Day
Dec 25	Christmas Day
Dec 26	Boxing Day

Muslim holidays:

12 Rabi al-Awwal	Maulid (Mawlid al-Nabi)
1 Shawwal	Idd el Fitr
10 Dhu al-Hijjah	Idd el Hajj (Id al-Adha)

Thailand

Jan 1	New Year's Day
Feb-Mar	Makha Bucha Day
Apr 6	Chakri Day
Apr	Songkran Festival
Apr-May	Wisakha Bucha Day (Buddha's Birthday)
May 1	Labor Day
May 5	Coronation Day
May	Royal Ploughing Ceremony
Jul	Asanha Bucha
Aug 12	Her Majesty the Queen's Birthday
Oct 23	Chulalongkorn Day
Dec 5	His Majesty the King's Birthday
Dec 10	Constitution Day
Dec 31	New Year's Eve

Togo

Jan 1	New Year's Day
Jan 24	Economic Liberation Day
Mar-Apr: Mon after Easter	Easter Monday
Apr 27	Independence Day
May 1	Labor Day
May-Jun	Ascension Day
May-Jun	Whit Monday
Jun 21	Martyrs' Day
Aug 15	Assumption Day
Nov 1	All Saints' Day
Dec 25	Christmas Day

Muslim holidays:

Shawwal	Id al-Fitr
Dhu al-Hijjah	Tabaski (Id al-Adha)

Tonga

Jan 1	New Year's Day
Mar-Apr: Fri before Easter	Good Friday
Mar-Apr: Mon after Easter	Easter Monday
Apr 25	Anzac Day
Jun 4	Emancipation Day
Jul 4	Official Birthday of the Reigning Sovereign of Tonga/Coronation Day
Sep 17	Birthday of the Heir to the Crown of Tonga
Nov 4	National Day
Dec 4	King Tupou I Day
Dec 25	Christmas Day
Dec 26	Boxing Day

Trinidad and Tobago

Jan 1 . . . . New Year's Day
Mar 30 . . . . Spiritual Baptist Liberation Shouter Day
Mar-Apr: Fri before Easter . . . . Good Friday
Mar-Apr: Mon after Easter . . . . Easter Monday
May 30 . . . . Indian Arrival Day
May-Jun . . . . Corpus Christi Day
Jun 19 . . . . Labour Day
Aug 1 . . . . Emancipation Day
Aug 31 . . . . Independence Day
Sep 24 . . . . Republic Day
Oct-Nov . . . . Divali
Dec 25 . . . . Christmas Day
Dec 26 . . . . Boxing Day

Muslim holidays:
1 Shawwal . . . . Id-ul-Fitr

Tunisia

Jan 1 . . . . New Year's Day
Jan 14 . . . . Revolution and Youth Day
Mar 20 . . . . Independence Day
Apr 9 . . . . Martyrs' Day
May 1 . . . . Labor Day
Jul 25 . . . . Republic Day
Aug 13 . . . . Women's Day
Oct 15 . . . . Evacuation Day (Eid El Jalala)

Muslim holidays:
Muharram . . . . Ras el am el Hijra (Islamic New Year)
Rabi-al-Awwal . . . . Mouled (Mawlid al-Nabi)
Shawwal . . . . Aid Esseghir (Id al-Fitr)
Dhu al-Hijjah . . . . Aid el Kebir (Id al-Adha)

Turkey

Jan 1 . . . . New Year's Day
Apr 23 . . . . National Sovereignty and Children's Day
May 1 . . . . Labor Day
May 19 . Atatürk Commemoration and Youth & Sports Day
Aug 30 . . . . Victory Day
Oct 29 . . . . Republic Day

Muslim holidays:
1 Shawwal (three days) . . . . Seker Bayrami (Eid al-Fitr)
10 Dhu al-Hijjah (four days)   Kurban Bayrami (Id al-Adha)

Turkmenistan

Jan 1 . . . . New Year's Day
Jan 12 . . . . Memorial Day
Feb 19 . . . . National Flag Day
Mar 8 . . . . International Women's Day
Mar 21 . . . . Novruz-Bairam
May 9 . . . . Victory Day
May 18 . . . . . Constitution Day and Revival and Unity Day
Oct 6 . . . . Remembrance Day
Oct 27-28 . . . . Independence Day Holiday
Dec 12 . . . . Day of Neutrality

Muslim holidays:
Shawwal . . . . Ramadan-Bairam (Id al-Fitr)
Dhu al-Hijjah . . . . Kurban-Bairam (Id al-Adha)

Tuvalu

Jan 1 . . . . New Year's Day
Mar . . . . Commonwealth Day
Mar-Apr: Fri before Easter - Mon after Easter . . . . . . Good
Friday - Easter Monday
May . . . . Gospel Day (Te Aso o te Tala 'Lei)
Jun: Mon after third Sat . . . . Queen's Birthday
Aug, first Mon . . . . National Children's Day
Oct 1-2 . . . . Independence Day
Dec 25 . . . . Christmas Day
Dec 26 . . . . Boxing Day

Uganda

Jan 1 . . . . New Year's Day
Jan 26 . . . . Liberation Day
Mar 8 . . . . International Women's Day
Mar-Apr: Fri before Easter . . . . Good Friday
Mar-Apr: Mon after Easter . . . . Easter Monday
May 1 . . . . Labor Day
Jun 3 . . . . Martyrs' Day
Jun 9 . . . . National Heroes Day
Oct 9 . . . . Independence Day
Dec 25 . . . . Christmas Day
Dec 26 . . . . Boxing Day

Muslim holidays:
Shawwal . . . . Id al-Fitr
Dhu-Al-Hijjah . . . . Id al-Adha

Ukraine

Jan 1 . . . . New Year's Day
Jan 7 . . . . Orthodox Christmas
Mar 8 . . . . Women's Day
Mar-Apr: Mon after Easter . . . . Easter Monday
Apr-May . . . . Orthodox Easter
May 1 . . . . Labor Day
May 9 . . . . Victory Day
June 28 . . . . Constitution Day
Aug 24 . . . . Independence Day

United Arab Emirates

Jan 1 . . . . New Year's Day
Dec 02-03 . . . . National Day Holiday

Muslim holidays:
Muharram 1 . . . . Islamic New Year
Rabi-al-Awwal . . Muhammad's Birthday (Mawlid al-Nabi)
Shawwal . . . . Id al-Fitr
Dhu-Al-Hijjah . . . . Id al-Adha

United Kingdom England and Wales

Jan 01	New Year's Day
Mar-Apr: Fri before Easter	Good Friday
Mar-Apr: Mon after Easter	Easter Monday
May: First Mon	Early May Bank Holiday
May: Last Mon	Spring Bank Holiday
Aug: Last Mon	Summer Bank Holiday
Dec 25	Christmas Day
Dec 26	Boxing Day

Uruguay

Jan 01	New Year's Day
Jan 6	Epiphany
Feb	Carnival (Two Days)
Mar-Apr: Thurs before Easter	Maundy Thursday
Mar-Apr: Fri before Easter	Good Friday
Apr 19	Desembarco de los 33 Orientales
May 01	Labor Day
May 18	Batalla de las Piedras
Jun 19	Birthday of Artigas
Jul 18	Constitution Day
Aug 25	Independence Day
Oct 12	Día de los Américas
Nov 2	Día de los Difuntos (All Souls' Day)
Dec 25	Christmas Day

Uzbekistan

Jan 01	New Year's Day
Mar 8	Women's Day
Mar 21	Nawruz
May 09	Memorial Day
Sep 01	Independence Day
Oct 1	Teacher's Day
Dec 08	Constitution Day

Muslim holidays:

Shawwal	Id-al Fitr
Dhu al-Hijjah	Id-al Zuha (Id al-Adha)

Vanuatu

Jan 01	New Year's Day
Feb 21	Fr. Walter Lini Day
Mar 06	Custom Chiefs Day
Mar-Apr: Fri before Easter	Good Friday
Mar-Apr: Mon after Easter	Easter Monday
May 01	Labour Day
May-Jun	Ascension Day
Jul 24	Children's Day
Jul 30	Independence Day
Aug 15	Assumption Day
Oct 05	Constitution Day
Nov 29	Unity Day
Dec 25	Christmas Day
Dec 26	Family Day

Venezuela

Jan 01	New Year's Day
Feb-Mar	Carnival Monday and Tuesday
Mar-Apr: Thurs before Easter	Maundy Thursday
Mar-Apr: Fri before Easter	Good Friday
Apr 19	Declaration of Independence Day
May 01	Labor Day
Jun 24	Battle of Carabobo Day
Jul 05	National Day (Independence Day)
Jul 24	Simón Bolívar's Birthday
Oct 12	Day of Indigenous Resistance
Dec 25	Christmas Day

Vietnam

Jan 01	New Year's Day
Jan-Feb (Four Days)	Lunar New Year (Tet Nguyen Dan)
Apr 30	Liberation Day
Apr	Gio to Hung Vuong Day
May 01	International Labor Day
Sep 2	National Day

Wales. *See* United Kingdom | Western Samoa. *See* Samoa

Yemen

May 01	Labor Day
May 22	National Day
Sep 26	Revolution Day
Oct 14	Liberation Day
Nov 30	Independence Day

Muslim holidays:

1 Muharram	Memory of Prophet's Immigration (Islamic New Year)
29 Ramadan-3 Shawwal	Id Al Fitr
9-14 Dhu al-Hijjah	Id Al Adha

Zambia

Jan 01	New Year's Day
Mar 8	International Women's Day
Mar 12	Youth Day
Mar-Apr: Fri before Easter	Good Friday
Mar-Apr: Sat before Easter	Holy Saturday
Mar-Apr: Mon after Easter	Easter Monday
May 01	Labour Day
May 25	African Freedom Day (Anniversary of OAU's Foundation)
Jul: First Mon	Heroes' Day
Jul: First Tues	Unity Day
Aug: First Mon	Farmers' Day
Oct 24	Independence Day
Dec 25	Christmas Day

Zimbabwe

Jan 01	New Year's Day
Mar 29	General Elections Day
Mar-Apr	Easter Sunday
Mar-Apr: Fri before Easter	Good Friday
Mar-Apr: Sat before Easter	Holy Saturday
Mar-Apr: Mon after Easter	Easter Monday
Apr 18	Independence Day
May 01	Labour Day
May 25	Africa Day
Aug 11	Heroes' Day
Aug 12	Defense Forces Day
Dec 22	National Unity Day
Dec 25	Christmas Day
Dec 26	Boxing Day

APPENDIX 12

Tourism Information Sources for Countries around the World

The following list includes tourism information sources for countries around the world, except the United States, Canada, and Mexico (see Appendix 8) The listings are in alphabetical order by name of the country, with cross references where appropriate to other forms of the countries' names. Within each country listing, listings are in the following order, although each country may not have all offices:

National Tourism Office
Chamber of Commerce
Consulate General
Embassy
Permanent Mission to the United Nations

Afghanistan

Afghan Chamber of Commerce
39270 Paseo Padre Pkwy.
Ste. 343
Fremont, CA 94538
Fax: 267-790-8203
www.afghanchamber.com

Afghanistan Consulate General
120 S. Doheny Dr.
Beverly Hills, CA 90211
Phone: 310-288-8334; Fax: 310-288-8355
www.afghanconsulategeneral.org

Afghanistan Consulate General
241-02 Northern Blvd.
Third Fl.
Little Neck, NY 11362
Phone: 212-972-2277; Fax: 718-279-9046
www.afghanconsulate-ny.org

Afghanistan Consulate General
2233 Wisconsin Ave. N.W.
George Town Plaza, Ste. 216
Washington, DC 20007
Phone: 202-298-9125
www.embassyofafghanistan.org

Afghanistan Embassy
2341 Wyoming Ave. N.W.
Washington, DC 20008
Phone: 202-483-6410; Fax: 202-483-6488
www.embassyofafghanistan.org

Afghanistan Permanent Mission to the UN
633 Third Ave.

27A Fl.
New York, NY 10017
Phone: 212-972-1212; Fax: 212-972-1216
www.afghanistan-un.org

Albania

Visit Albania
www.albania.al

Albania Consulate General
156 Fifth Ave.
Ste. 1210
New York, NY 10010
Phone: 212-255-7381; Fax: 212-255-7380
www.ambasadat.gov.al/new-york-consulate/en

Albania Embassy
1312 18th St. N.W.
Washington, DC 20036
Phone: 202-223-4942; Fax: 202-628-7342
www.ambasadat.gov.al/usa/en

Albania Permanent Mission to the UN
320 E. 79th St.
New York, NY 10075
Phone: 212-249-2059; Fax: 212-535-2917
www.ambasadat.gov.al/united-nations/en

Algeria

Algeria Consulate General
866 United Nations Plaza
Ste. 580
New York, NY 10017

Phone: 212-486-6930; Fax: 212-486-6934
algeria-cgny.org

Algeria Embassy
2118 Kalorama Rd N.W.
Washington, DC 20008
Phone: 202-265-2800; Fax: 202-986-5906
www.algerianembassy.org

Algeria Embassy - Consular Section
2137 Wyoming Ave. N.W.
Washington, DC 20008
Fax: 202-265-2848
www.algerianembassy.org

Algeria Permanent Mission to the UN
326 E. 48th St.
New York, NY 10017
Phone: 212-750-1960; Fax: 212-759-5274
www.algeria-un.org

Andorra

Andorra Embassy
2 United Nations Plaza
27th Fl.
New York, NY 10017
Phone: 212-750-8064; Fax: 212-750-6630
www.exteriors.ad/en

Andorra Permanent Mission to the UN
2 United Nations Plaza
27th Fl.
New York, NY 10017
Phone: 212-750-8064; Fax: 212-750-6630
www.mae.ad/en

Angola

US-Angola Chamber of Commerce
1100 17th St. N.W.
Ste. 1000
Washington, DC 20036
Phone: 202-857-0789; Fax: 202-223-0551
www.us-angola.org

Angola Consulate General
3040 Post Oak Blvd.
Ste. 780
Houston, TX 77056
Phone: 713-212-3840; Fax: 713-212-3841
www.angolaconsulate-tx.org

Angola Embassy
2100 - 2108 16th St. N.W.
Washington, DC 20009
Phone: 202-785-1156; Fax: 202-822-9049
www.angola.org

Angola Permanent Mission to the UN
820 2nd Ave.
12th Fl.
New York, NY 10017
Phone: 212-861-5656; Fax: 212-861-9295
www.un.int/angola

Anguilla

Anguilla Tourist Board
246 Central Ave.
White Plains, NY 10606
Phone: 914-287-2400; Fax: 914-287-2404
Toll-free: 877-426-4845
www.ivisitanguilla.com

Antigua and Barbuda

Antigua and Barbuda Dept of Tourism & Trade
25 S.E. 2nd Ave.
Ste. 300
Miami, FL 33131
Phone: 305-381-6762; Fax: 305-381-7908
www.antigua-barbuda.org

Antigua and Barbuda Tourist Office
3 Dag Hammarskjold Plaza
305 E. 47th St.
6th Fl.
New York, NY 10007
Phone: 212-541-4119; Fax: 646-215-6009
Toll-free: 888-268-4227
www.antigua-barbuda.org

Antigua and Barbuda Consulate
25 S.E. 2nd Ave.
Ste. 300
Miami, FL 33131
Phone: 305-381-6762; Fax: 305-381-7908

Antigua and Barbuda Consulate
3 Dag Hammarskjold Plaza
305 E. 47th St.
6th Fl.
New York, NY 10007
Phone: 212-541-4119; Fax: 646-215-6009
www.abconsulateny.org

Antigua and Barbuda Embassy
3216 New Mexico Ave. N.W.
Washington, DC 20016
Phone: 202-362-5122; Fax: 202-362-5225

Antigua and Barbuda Permanent Mission to the UN
305 E. 47th St.
6th Fl.
New York, NY 10017
Phone: 212-541-4117
www.un.org

Argentina

Argentina - National Institute of Tourism Promotion
www.argentina.travel/en

Argentine-American Chamber of Commerce
150 E. 58th St.
New York, NY 10155
Phone: 212-698-2238; Fax: 212-698-1144
www.argentinechamber.org

Argentina Consulate General
245 Peachtree Center Ave. N.E.
Marquis One Bldg.
Ste. 2101
Atlanta, GA 30303
Phone: 404-880-0805; Fax: 404-880-0806
www.catla.cancilleria.gov.ar

Argentina Consulate General
205 N. Michigan Ave.
Ste. 4209
Chicago, IL 60601
Phone: 312-819-2610; Fax: 312-819-2626
www.cchic.mrecic.gov.ar

Argentina Consulate General
2200 - West Loop S.
Ste. 1025
Houston, TX 77027
Phone: 713-871-8935
www.chous.cancilleria.gov.ar

Argentina Consulate General
5055 Wilshire Blvd.
Ste. 210
Los Angeles, CA 90036
Phone: 323-954-9155; Fax: 323-934-9076
www.clang.cancilleria.gov.ar

Argentina Consulate General
1101 Brickell Ave. - N. Tower
Ste.900
Miami, FL 33131
Phone: 305-373-1889; Fax: 305-373-1598
www.consuladoargentinoenmiami.org

Argentina Consulate General
12 W. 56th St.
New York, NY 10019
Phone: 212-603-0400; Fax: 212-541-7746
www.congenargentinany.com

Argentina Embassy
1600 New Hampshire Ave. N.W.
Washington, DC 20009
Phone: 202-238-6400; Fax: 202-332-3171
www.embassyofargentina.us

Argentina Permanent Mission to the UN
1 United Nations Plaza
25 Fl.
New York, NY 10017
Phone: 212-688-6300; Fax: 212-980-8395
www.enaun.mrecic.gov.ar

Armenia

Armenian American Chamber of Commerce
225 E. Broadway
Ste. 313C
Glendale, CA 91205
Phone: 818-247-0196; Fax: 818-247-7668
www.armenianchamber.org

Armenia Consulate General
346 N. Central Ave.

Glendale, CA 91203
Phone: 818-265-5900; Fax: 818-265-3800
www.armeniaconsulatela.org

Armenia Embassy
2225 R St. N.W.
Washington, DC 20008
Phone: 202-319-1976; Fax: 202-319-2982
www.usa.mfa.am

Armenia Permanent Mission to the UN
119 E. 36th St.
New York, NY 10016
Phone: 212-686-9079; Fax: 212-686-3934
www.un.mfa.am

Aruba

Aruba Tourism Authority
1750 Powder Springs St.
Ste. 190
Marietta, GA 30064
Phone: 404-892-7822
www.aruba.com

Australia

Tourism Australia
www.australia.com/en-us

Tourism Australia
2029 Century Park E.
Ste. 3150, Mailbox 358
Los Angeles, CA 90067
Phone: 310-695-3200; Fax: 310-695-3201
www.tourism.australia.com

Australian-American Chamber of Commerce of Hawaii
1000 Bishop St.
Penthouse Ste.
Honolulu, HI 96813
Phone: 808-526-2242; Fax: 808-534-0475
www.usa.embassy.gov.au

Australian American Chamber of Commerce of Houston
134 Gessner Rd.
Houston, TX 77024
Phone: 713-527-9688; Fax: 832-415-0545
aacc-houston.org

Australian-American Chamber of Commerce of San Francisco
P.O. Box 471285
San Francisco, CA 94147
Phone: 415-485-6718
www.sfaussies.com

Australian New Zealand American Chambers of Commerce
c/o Embassy of Australia
1601 Massachusetts Ave. N.W.
Washington, DC 20036
Phone: 202-797-3000; Fax: 202-797-3168
www.usa.embassy.gov.au

Australia Consulate General
123 N. Wacker Dr.
Ste. 1330
Chicago, IL 60606
Phone: 312-419-1480; Fax: 312-419-1499
www.dfat.gov.au

Australia Consulate General
8480 E. Orchad Rd.
Ste. 1100
Greenwood Village, CO 80111
Phone: 303-321-2234; Fax: 303-773-1664
www.dfat.gov.au

Australia Consulate General
1000 Bishop St.
Penthouse
Honolulu, HI 96813
Phone: 808-529-8100; Fax: 808-529-8142
www.dfat.gov.au

Australia Consulate General
2029 Century Park E.
Century City
Los Angeles, CA 90067
Phone: 310-229-2300; Fax: 310-229-2380
www.losangeles.consulate.gov.au

Australia Consulate General
150 E. 42nd St.
34 Fl.
New York, NY 10017
Phone: 212-351-6500; Fax: 212-351-6501
www.newyork.consulate.gov.au

Australia Consulate General
575 Market St.
Ste. 1800 (18th Fl.)
San Francisco, CA 94105
Phone: 415-644-3620; Fax: 415-536-1982
www.dfat.gov.au

Australia Embassy
1601 Massachusetts Ave. N.W.
Washington, DC 20036
Phone: 202-797-3000; Fax: 202-797-3168
www.usa.embassy.gov.au

Australia Permanent Mission to the UN
150 E. 42nd St.
33rd Fl.
New York, NY 10017
Phone: 212-351-6600
www.australia-unsc.gov.au

Austria

Austrian Tourism Board
Phone: 212-944-6880; Fax: 212-730-4568
www.austria.info/us

US-Austrian Chamber of Commerce
c/o RB Interntl Finance
1133 Avenue of the Americas, 16th Fl.
New York, NY 10036

Phone: 212-819-0117
www.usaustrianchamber.org

Austria Consulate General
11859 Wilshire Blvd.
Ste. 501
Los Angeles, CA 90025
Phone: 310-444-9310; Fax: 310-477-9897
www.bmeia.gv.at/en/embassy/los-angeles

Austria Consulate General
31 E. 69th St.
New York, NY 10021
Phone: 212-933-5140; Fax: 212-585-1992
www.bmeia.gv.at/en/embassy/consulate-general-new-york

Austria Embassy
3524 International Ct. N.W.
Washington, DC 20008
Phone: 202-895-6700; Fax: 202-895-6750
www.austria.org

Austria Permanent Mission to the UN
600 3rd Ave.
31st Fl.
New York, NY 10016
Phone: 917-542-8400; Fax: 212-949-1840
www.bmeia.gv.at/oev-new-york

Azerbaijan

Azerbaijan Tourism
azerbaijan.travel/en

US- Azerbaijan Chamber of Commerce
1212 Potomac St. N.W.
Washington, DC 20007
Phone: 202-333-8702; Fax: 202-333-8703
www.usacc.org

Azerbaijan Consulate General
11766 Wilshire Blvd.
Ste. 1410
Los Angeles, CA 90025
Phone: 310-444-9101; Fax: 310-477-4860
www.azconsulatela.org

Azerbaijan Embassy
2741 34th St. N.W.
Washington, DC 20008
Phone: 202-337-3500; Fax: 202-337-5911
www.azembassy.us

Azerbaijan Permanent Mission to the UN
866 United Nations Plaza
Ste. 560
New York, NY 10017
Phone: 212-371-2559; Fax: 212-371-2784
www.un.int/azerbaijan

Bahamas

Bahamas Tourism Office
1200 S. Pine Island Rd.

Plantation, FL 33324
Phone: 954-236-9292; Fax: 954-236-9282
Toll-free: 800-224-2627
www.bahamas.com

Bahamas Consulate General
2970 Clairmont Rd. N.E.
Ste. 290
Atlanta, GA 30329
Phone: 404-214-0492
bahconga.com

Bahamas Consulate General
25 S.E. 2nd Ave.
Ingraham Bldg., Ste. 818
Miami, FL 33131
Phone: 305-373-6295; Fax: 305-373-6312
www.bahamas.gov.bs

Bahamas Consulate General
231 E. 46th St.
New York, NY 10017
Phone: 212-421-6925; Fax: 212-759-2135
www.bahamas.gov.bs

Bahamas Embassy
2220 Massachusetts Ave. N.W.
Washington, DC 20008
Phone: 202-319-2660; Fax: 202-319-2668
www.bahamas.gov.bs

Bahamas Permanent Mission to the UN
231 E. 46th St.
New York, NY 10017
Phone: 212-421-6925
www.un.int/bahamas

Bahrain

Bahrain Consulate General
866 2nd Ave.
14th Fl.
New York, NY 10017
Phone: 212-223-6200; Fax: 212-223-6206
www.mofa.gov.bh/newyork

Bahrain Embassy
3502 International Dr. N.W.
Washington, DC 20008
Phone: 202-342-1111; Fax: 202-362-2192
www.mofa.gov.bh/washington

Bahrain Permanent Mission to the UN
866 2nd Ave.
14th & 15th Floors
New York, NY 10017
Phone: 212-223-6200; Fax: 212-319-6206
www.un.int/bahrai

Bangladesh

Bangladesh America Chamber of Commerce
2761 N.E. 27th Cir.
Boca Raton, FL 33431

Phone: 954-818-2970; Fax: 954-972-1108
www.bangladeshchamber.org

Bangladesh Consulate General
4201 Wilshire Blvd.
Ste. 605
Los Angeles, CA 90010
Phone: 323-932-0100; Fax: 323-932-9703
www.bangladeshconsulatela.com

Bangladesh Consulate General
34-18 Northern Blvd. (Ground Floor)
Long Island City, Queens
New York, NY 11101
Phone: 212-599-6767; Fax: 212-682-9211
www.bdcgny.org

Bangladesh Embassy
3510 International Dr. N.W.
Washington, DC 20008
Phone: 202-244-0183; Fax: 202-244-2771
www.bdembassyusa.org

Bangladesh Permanent Mission to the UN
820 E. 2nd Ave.
Diplomat Centre
4th Fl.
New York, NY 10017
Phone: 212-867-3434; Fax: 212-972-4038
www.un.int/bangladesh

Barbados

Barbados Tourism Authority
820 Second Ave.
5th Fl.
New York, NY 10017
Phone: 212-986-6516; Fax: 212-573-9850
Toll-free: 800-221-9831
www.visitbarbados.org

Barbados Consulate General
2121 Ponce de Leon Blvd.
Ste. 1300 (PH)
Coral Gables, FL 33134
Phone: 786-515-1201; Fax: 305-455-7975

Barbados Consulate General
820 2nd Ave.
Between 43rd & 44th Sts.
5th Fl.
New York, NY 10017
Phone: 212-551-4325; Fax: 212-867-8899

Barbados Embassy
2144 Wyoming Ave. N.W.
Washington, DC 20008
Phone: 202-939-9200; Fax: 202-332-7467

Barbados Permanent Mission to the UN
820 2nd Ave.
9th Fl.
New York, NY 10017
Phone: 212-551-4300; Fax: 212-986-1030
www.un.int/barbados

Belarus

Belarus Consulate General
708 3rd Ave.
20th Fl.
New York, NY 10017
Phone: 212-682-5392; Fax: 212-682-5491
www.usa.mfa.gov.by

Belarus Embassy
1619 New Hampshire Ave. N.W.
Washington, DC 20009
Phone: 202-986-1606; Fax: 202-986-1805
www.usa.mfa.gov.by

Belarus Permanent Mission to the UN
136 E. 67th St.
4th Fl.
New York, NY 10065
Phone: 212-535-3420; Fax: 212-734-4810
www.un.mfa.gov.by

Belgium

Belgian Tourist Office
300 E. 42nd St.
14th Fl.
New York, NY 10017
Phone: 212-758-8130
www.visitbelgium.com

Belgian-American Chamber of Commerce in the US
1177 Ave.
7th Fl.
New York, NY 10036
Phone: 212-541-0771
www.belcham.org

Belgium Consulate General
230 Peachtree St. N.W.
Ste. 2710
Atlanta, GA 30303
Phone: 404-659-2150; Fax: 404-659-8474
countries.diplomatie.belgium.be/en/united_states/embassy_and_consulates

Belgium Consulate General
6100 Wilshire Blvd.
Ste. 1200
Los Angeles, CA 90048
Phone: 323-857-1244; Fax: 323-936-2564
countries.diplomatie.belgium.be/en/united_states/embassy_and_consulates

Belgium Consulate General
1065 Avenue of the Americas
22nd Fl.
New York, NY 10018
Phone: 212-586-5110; Fax: 212-582-9657
countries.diplomatie.belgium.be/en/united_states/embassy_and_consulates

Belgium Embassy
3330 Garfield St. N.W.
Washington, DC 20008

Phone: 202-333-6900; Fax: 202-338-4960
countries.diplomatie.belgium.be/en/united_states/embassy_and_consulates

Belgium Permanent Mission to the UN
885 Second Ave.
One Dag Hammarskjöld Plaza, 41st Fl.
New York, NY 10017
Phone: 212-378-6300; Fax: 212-681-7618
countries.diplomatie.belgium.be/en/newyorkun

Belize

Belize Tourism Board
www.travelbelize.org

Belize Consulate General
4801 Wilshire Blvd.
Ste. 250
Los Angeles, CA 90010
Phone: 323-634-9900; Fax: 323-634-9903
www.consulateofbelizelosangeles.org

Belize Embassy
2535 Massachusetts Ave. N.W.
Washington, DC 20008
Phone: 202-332-9636; Fax: 202-332-6888
www.embassyofbelize.org

Belize Permanent Mission to the UN
675 3rd Ave.
Ste. 1911
New York, NY 10017
Phone: 212-986-1240; Fax: 212-593-0932
www.belizemission.com

Benin

Benin Embassy
2124 Kalorama Rd. N.W.
Washington, DC 20008
Phone: 202-232-6656; Fax: 202-265-1996
www.beninembassy.us

Benin Permanent Mission to the UN
125 E. 38th St.
New York, NY 10016
Phone: 212-684-1339; Fax: 212-684-2058
www.un.int/benin

Bermuda

Bermuda Dept of Tourism
675 3rd Ave.
20th Fl.
New York, NY 10017
Phone: 212-818-9800; Fax: 212-983-5289
Toll-free: 800-223-6106
www.gotobermuda.com

Bhutan

Bhutan Permanent Mission to the UN
343 E. 43rd St.

New York, NY 10017
Phone: 212-682-2268; Fax: 212-661-0551
www.un.int/bhutan

Bolivia

Bolivia Tourism
www.bolivia.travel

Bolivian-American Chamber of Commerce Inc
909 Third Ave.
Ste. 6721
New York, NY 10150
Phone: 212-729-1665; Fax: 917-546-6915
www.bolivia-us.org

Bolivia Consulate General
24001 Fountain View Dr.
Ste. 110
Houston, TX 77057
Phone: 832-916-4200; Fax: 832-916-4201
www.boliviatx.org

Bolivia Consulate General
3701 Wilshire Blvd.
Ste. 1065
Los Angeles, CA 90010
Phone: 213-388-0475; Fax: 213-384-6272
boliviala.org

Bolivia Consulate General
700 S. Royal Poinciana Blvd.
Ste. 505
Miami Springs, FL 33166
Phone: 305-358-6303; Fax: 305-358-6305
consuladoboliviaenmiami.com/eng

Bolivia Consulate General
211 E. 43rd St.
Ste. 1004
New York, NY 10017
Phone: 212-687-0530; Fax: 212-687-0532
www.bolivianyc.com

Bolivia Consulate General
1825 Connecticut Ave. N.W.
Ste. 200C
Washington, DC 20009
Phone: 202-232-4827; Fax: 202-232-8017
www.boliviawdc.org

Bolivia Embassy
3014 Massachusetts Ave. N.W.
Washington, DC 20008
Phone: 202-483-4410; Fax: 202-328-3712
www.bolivia-usa.org

Bolivia Permanent Mission to the UN
801 Second Ave.
4th Fl., Rm. 402
New York, NY 10017
Phone: 212-682-8132
www.un.org/en

Bonaire

Bonaire Government Tourist Office
80 Broad St.
32 Fl., Ste. 3202
New York, NY 10004
Phone: 212-956-5910
www.tourismbonaire.com

Bosnia and Herzegovina

National Tourism Office
www.bhtourism.ba/eng

Bosnia and Herzegovina Consulate General
500 N. Michigan Ave.
Ste. 750
Chicago, IL 60611
Phone: 312-951-1245; Fax: 312-951-1043
www.cgbhchicago.com

Bosnia and Herzegovina Consulate General
2109 E. St. N.W.
Washington, DC 20037
Phone: 202-337-1500; Fax: 202-337-1502
www.bhembassy.org

Bosnia and Herzegovina Embassy
2109 E. St. N.W.
Washington, DC 20037
Phone: 202-337-1500; Fax: 202-337-1502
www.bhembassy.org

Bosnia and Herzegovina Permanent Mission to the UN
420 Lexington Ave.
Stes. 607 & 608
New York, NY 10170
Phone: 212-751-9015; Fax: 212-751-9019
www.bhmissionun.org

Botswana

Botswana Tourism Organization
127 Lubrano Dr.
Ste. 203
Annapolis, MD 21401
Phone: 410-266-8429
Toll-free: 888-675-7660
www.botswanatourism.us

Botswana American Chamber of Commerce
1400 Veteran's Memorial Hwy.
Ste. 134-271
Mableton, GA 30126
Toll-free: 855-444-7852
botswanachamber.org

Botswana Embassy
1531 New Hampshire Ave. N.W.
Washington, DC 20036
Phone: 202-244-4990; Fax: 202-244-4164
www.botswanaembassy.org

Botswana Permanent Mission to the UN
154 E. 46th St.

New York, NY 10017
Phone: 212-889-2277
www.botswanaun.org

Brazil

Brazil Tourism Office
www.visitbrasil.com

Brazilian-American Chamber of Commerce of Georgia
P.O. Box 93411
Atlanta, GA 30377
Phone: 404-880-1551
www.bacc-ga.com/bacc

Brazilian-American Chamber of Commerce of Florida
P.O. Box 310038
Miami, FL 33231
Phone: 305-579-9030; Fax: 305-579-9756
www.brazilchamber.org

Brazilian-American Chamber of Commerce Inc
509 Madison Ave.
Ste. 304
New York, NY 10022
Phone: 212-751-4691; Fax: 212-751-7692
www.brazilcham.com

Brazilian-American Chamber of Commerce of Central
Florida
5950 Lakehurst Dr.
Lakehurst Bldg.
Ste. 205
Orlando, FL 32819
Phone: 407-610-7158
www.cfbacc.com

Brazil Consulate General
8484 Wilshire Blvd.
Ste. 300
Beverly Hills, CA 90211
Phone: 323-651-2664; Fax: 323-651-1274
losangeles.itamaraty.gov.br/en-us

Brazil Consulate General
175 Purchase St.
Boston, MA 02110
Phone: 617-542-4000; Fax: 617-542-4318
boston.itamaraty.gov.br/en-us

Brazil Consulate General
401 N. Michigan Ave.
Ste. 1850
Chicago, IL 60611
Phone: 312-464-0244
chicago.itamaraty.gov.br/en-us

Brazil Consulate General
1233 W. Loop S.
Park Tower N., Ste. 1150
Houston, TX 77027
Phone: 713-961-3063; Fax: 713-961-3070
houston.itamaraty.gov.br/en-us

Brazil Consulate General
3150 S.W. 38th Ave.
Ground Fl.

Miami, FL 33146
Phone: 305-285-6200; Fax: 305-285-6240
miami.itamaraty.gov.br/en-us

Brazil Consulate General
225 E. 41st St.
New York, NY 10017
Phone: 917-777-7777; Fax: 212-827-0225
www.novayork.itamaraty.gov.br

Brazil Consulate General
300 Montgomery St.
Ste. 300
San Francisco, CA 94104
Phone: 415-981-8170; Fax: 415-981-4625
saofrancisco.itamaraty.gov.br/en-us

Brazil Consulate General
1030 15th St. N.W.
Washington, DC 20005
Phone: 202-461-3000; Fax: 202-461-3001
cgwashington.itamaraty.gov.br

Brazil Embassy - Consular Section
3006 Whitehaven St. N.W.
Washington, DC 20008
Phone: 202-238-2700
washington.itamaraty.gov.br/en-us

Brazil Embassy
3006 Massachusetts Ave. N.W.
Washington, DC 20008
Phone: 202-238-2700
washington.itamaraty.gov.br/en-us

Brazil Permanent Mission to the UN
747 3rd Ave.
9th Fl.
New York, NY 10017
Phone: 212-372-2600; Fax: 212-371-5716
www.un.int/brazil

British Virgin Islands

British Virgin Islands Tourist Board
1 W. 34th St.
Ste. 302
New York, NY 10001
Phone: 212-563-3117; Fax: 212-563-2263
Toll-free: 800-835-8530
www.bvitourism.com

Brunei Darussalam

Brunei Tourism
www.bruneitourism.travel

Brunei Darussalam Embassy
3520 International Ct. N.W.
Washington, DC 20008
Phone: 202-237-1838; Fax: 202-885-0560
www.bruneiembassy.org

Brunei Darussalam Permanent Mission to the UN
771 United Nations Plaza
New York, NY 10017
Phone: 212-697-3465; Fax: 212-697-9889
www.un.int/brunei

Bulgaria

Bulgaria Tourism
bulgariatravel.org

North American-Bulgarian Chamber of Commerce (NAB-CC Corp.)
6460 Leona St.
Oakland, CA 94605
Phone: 415-251-2322
www.nabcc.org

Bulgaria Consulate General
737 N. Michigan Ave.
Ste. 2105
Chicago, IL 60611
Phone: 312-867-1904; Fax: 312-867-1906
www.mfa.bg/embassies/usagc3

Bulgaria Consulate General
11766 Wilshire Blvd.
Ste. 440
Los Angeles, CA 90025
Phone: 310-478-6700; Fax: 310-478-6277
www.mfa.bg/embassies/usagc2

Bulgaria Consulate General
121 E. 62nd St.
New York, NY 10065
Phone: 212-935-4646; Fax: 212-319-5955
www.mfa.bg

Bulgaria Embassy
1621 22nd St. N.W.
Dimitar Peshev Plaza
Washington, DC 20008
Phone: 202-387-0174; Fax: 202-234-7973
www.bulgaria-embassy.org

Bulgaria Permanent Mission to the UN
11 E. 84th St.
New York, NY 10028
Phone: 212-737-4790; Fax: 212-472-9865
www.mfa.bg/embassies/usapr

Burkina Faso

Burkina Faso Embassy
2340 Massachusetts Ave. N.W.
Washington, DC 20008
Phone: 202-332-5577; Fax: 202-667-1882
burkina-usa.org

Burkina Faso Permanent Mission to the UN
866 United Nations Plaza
Ste. 326
New York, NY 10017
Phone: 212-308-4720; Fax: 212-308-4690
www.burkina-onu.org

Burma. *See* Myanmar

Burundi

Burundi National Tourism Office
www.burundi-tourism.com

Burundi Embassy
2233 Wisconsin Ave. N.W.
Ste. 408
Washington, DC 20007
Phone: 202-342-2574; Fax: 202-342-2578
www.burundiembassydc-usa.org

Burundi Permanent Mission to the UN
336 E. 45th St.
12th Fl.
New York, NY 10017
Phone: 212-499-0001; Fax: 212-499-0006
www.burundi-un.org

Cambodia

Ministry of Tourism of Cambodia
www.tourismcambodia.org

Cambodian American Chamber of Commerce
Long Beach, CA
www.cambodianuschamber.org

Cambodia Consulate
3448 E. Anaheim St.
Long Beach, CA 90804
Phone: 562-494-3000; Fax: 562-494-3007
www.consulateofcambodiaca.org

Cambodia Embassy
4530 16th St. N.W.
Washington, DC 20011
Phone: 202-726-7742; Fax: 202-726-8381
www.embassyofcambodia.org

Cambodia Permanent Mission to the UN
327 E. 58th St.
New York, NY 10022
Phone: 212-336-0777; Fax: 212-759-7672
www.cambodiaun.org

Cameroon

Cameroon Chamber of Commerce
uscameroonchamber.org

Cameroon Embassy
3400 International Dr. N.W.
Washington, DC 20008
Phone: 202-265-8790; Fax: 202-387-3826
www.cameroonembassyusa.org

Cameroon Permanent Mission to the UN
22 E. 73rd St.
New York, NY 10021
Phone: 212-794-2295
www.delecam.us

Cape Verde/Cabo Verde

Cape Verde Consulate General
300 Congress St.
Ste. 204
Quincy, MA 02169
Phone: 617-353-0014; Fax: 617-859-9798
conscvboston.org

Cape Verde Embassy
3415 Massachusetts Ave. N.W.
Washington, DC 20007
Phone: 202-965-6820; Fax: 202-965-1207
www.embcv-usa.gov.cv

Cape Verde Permanent Mission to the UN
27 E. 69th St.
New York, NY 10021
Phone: 212-472-0333; Fax: 212-794-1398
www.un.int/capeverde

Cayman Islands

Cayman Islands Dept of Tourism
Boston, MA
Phone: 781-431-7771
www.caymanislands.ky

Cayman Islands Dept of Tourism
18 W. 140 Butterfield Rd.
Ste. 920
Chicago, IL 60181
Phone: 630-705-0650; Fax: 630-705-1383
www.caymanislands.ky

Cayman Islands Dept of Tourism
Dallas, TX
Phone: 972-335-3540
www.caymanislands.ky

Cayman Islands Dept of Tourism
820 Gessner Rd.
Ste. 1335
Houston, TX 77024
Phone: 713-461-1317; Fax: 713-461-7409
www.caymanislands.ky

Cayman Islands Dept of Tourism
8300 N.W. 53rd St.
Ste. 103
Miami, FL 33166
Phone: 305-599-9033; Fax: 305-599-3766
www.caymanislands.ky

Cayman Islands Dept of Tourism
350 Fifth Ave.
Empire State Bldg. Ste. 2720
New York, NY 10118
Phone: 212-889-9009; Fax: 212-889-9125
www.caymanislands.ky

Central African Republic

Central African Republic Embassy
2704 Ontario Rd.

Washington, DC 20009
Phone: 202-483-7800; Fax: 202-332-9893
www.rcawashington.org

Central African Republic Permanent Mission to the UN
866 United Nations Plaza
Ste. 444
New York, NY 10017
Phone: 646-415-9122; Fax: 646-415-9149
www.pmcar.org

Chad

Chad Embassy
2002 R. St. N.W.
Washington, DC 20009
Phone: 202-462-4009; Fax: 202-265-1937
chadembassy.com

Chad Embassy
2401 Massachusetts Ave. N.W.
Washington, DC 20008
Phone: 202-652-1312
www.chadembassy.us

Chad Permanent Mission to the UN
211 E. 43rd St.
Ste. 1703
New York, NY 10017
Phone: 212-986-0980; Fax: 212-986-0152
www.un.int/chad

Chile

Chile Tourism
chile.travel/en

Chile-US Chamber of Commerce
8600 N.W. 17th St.
Ste. 110
Doral, FL 33126
Phone: 786-400-1748; Fax: 305-599-2992
www.chileus.org

North American-Chilean Chamber of Commerce
866 United Nations Plaza
Ste. 4019
New York, NY 10017
Phone: 212-317-1959; Fax: 212-758-8598
www.nacchamber.com

Chile Consulate General
1415 N.Dayton St.
2nd Fl.
Chicago, IL 60642
Phone: 312-654-8780; Fax: 312-654-8948
www.chile-usa.org

Chile Consulate General & Trade Office
1415 N. Dayton St.
2nd Fl.
Chicago, IL 60642
Phone: 312-654-8780; Fax: 312-654-8948
www.cgchicago.com

Chile Consulate General
1300 Post Oak Blvd.
Ste. 1130
Houston, TX 77056
Phone: 713-621-5853; Fax: 713-621-8672
www.chile-usa.org

Chile Consulate General
6100 Wilshire Blvd.
Ste. 1240
Los Angeles, CA 90048
Phone: 323-933-3697; Fax: 323-933-3842
www.chile-usa.org

Chile Consulate General
800 Brickell Ave.
Ste. 1200
Miami, FL 33131
Phone: 305-373-8623; Fax: 305-379-6613
www.chile-usa.org

Chile Consulate General
866 United Nations Plaza
Ste. 601
New York, NY 10017
Phone: 212-980-3366; Fax: 212-888-5288
www.chile-usa.org

Chile Consulate General
870 Market St.
Ste. 1058
San Francisco, CA 94102
Phone: 415-982-7662; Fax: 415-982-2384
www.chile-usa.org

Chile Consulate General
1734 Massachusetts Ave. N.W.
Washington, DC 20036
Phone: 202-530-4104; Fax: 202-887-5579
www.chile-usa.org

Chile Embassy
1732 Massachusetts Ave. N.W.
Washington, DC 20036
Phone: 202-785-1746; Fax: 202-887-5579
www.chile-usa.org

Chile Permanent Mission to the UN
885 Second Ave.
40th Fl.
New York, NY 10017
Phone: 917-322-6800; Fax: 917-322-6890
chileabroad.gov.cl/onu/en

China

China National Tourist Office
550 N. Brand Blvd.
Ste. 910
Glendale, CA 91203
Phone: 818-545-7507; Fax: 818-545-7506
Toll-free: 800-670-2228
www.cnto.org

China National Tourist Office
370 Lexington Ave.

Ste. 912
New York, NY 10017
Phone: 212-760-8218; Fax: 212-760-8809
www.cnto.org

USA-China Chamber of Commerce
55 W. Monroe St.
Ste. 630
Chicago, IL 60603
Phone: 312-368-9911; Fax: 312-368-9922
www.usccc.org

Chinese Chamber of Commerce of Hawaii
8 S. King St.
Ste. 201
Honolulu, HI 96813
Phone: 808-533-3181; Fax: 808-537-6767
www.chinesechamber.com

Chinese Chamber of Commerce of Los Angeles
977 N. Broadway
Ground Fl. Ste. E
Los Angeles, CA 90012
Phone: 213-617-0396; Fax: 213-617-2128
www.lachinesechamber.org

Chinese Chamber of Commerce of San Francisco
730 Sacramento St.
San Francisco, CA 94108
Phone: 415-982-3000; Fax: 415-982-4720
sfgsa.org

NJ Chinese-American Chamber of Commerce
28 World's Fair Dr.
Somerset, NJ 08873
Phone: 732-507-7348; Fax: 732-805-0637
www.njcacc.org

China People's Republic of Consulate General
100 W. Erie St.
Chicago, IL 60654
Phone: 312-803-0095; Fax: 312-803-0110
www.chinaconsulatechicago.org/eng

China People's Republic of Consulate General
3417 Montrose Blvd.
Houston, TX 77006
Phone: 713-520-1462; Fax: 713-521-3064
houston.china-consulate.org

China People's Republic of Consulate General
443 Shatto Pl.
Los Angeles, CA 90020
Phone: 213-807-8088; Fax: 213-807-8091
losangeles.china-consulate.org

China People's Republic of Consulate General
520 12th Ave.
New York, NY 10036
Phone: 212-244-9392
newyork.china-consulate.org

China People's Republic of Consulate General
1450 Laguna St.
San Francisco, CA 94115
Phone: 415-852-5900; Fax: 415-852-5920
www.chinaconsulatesf.org

China People's Republic of Embassy
1 E. Erie St.
Ste. 500
Chicago, IL 60611
Phone: 312-453-0210; Fax: 312-453-0211
www.chinaconsulatechicago.org

China People's Republic of Embassy
500 Shatto Pl.
3rd Fl.
Los Angeles, CA 90020
Phone: 213-201-1765
losangeles.china-consulate.org

China People's Republic of Embassy
3505 International Pl. N.W.
Washington, DC 20008
Phone: 202-495-2266; Fax: 202-495-2138
www.china-embassy.org

China People's Republic of Permanent Mission to the UN
350 E. 35th St.
Manhattan, NY 10016
Phone: 212-655-6100; Fax: 212-634-7626
www.china-un.org

Colombia

Colombian American Chamber of Commerce
2305 N.W. 107 Ave.
Ste. 1m14 box 105
Miami, FL 33172
Phone: 305-446-2542
www.colombiachamber.com

Colombia Consulate
270 Carpenter Dr. N.E.
Sandy Springs
Atlanta, GA 30328
Phone: 404-254-3206; Fax: 404-343-4906
Toll-free: 888-764-3326
atlanta.consulado.gov.co

Colombia Consulate General
8383 Wilshire Blvd.
Ste. 420
Beverly Hills, CA 90211
Phone: 323-653-9863; Fax: 323-653-2964
losangeles.consulado.gov.co

Colombia Consulate
31 St James Ave.
Ste. 960 Piso 9
Boston, MA 02116
Phone: 617-536-6222
Toll-free: 888-764-3326
boston.consulado.gov.co

Colombia Consulate General
500 N. Michigan Ave.
Ste. 1960
Chicago, IL 60611
Phone: 312-923-1196
www.colombiaemb.org

Colombia Consulate General
280 Aragon Ave.
Coral Gables, FL 33134
Phone: 305-441-1235; Fax: 305-441-9537
Toll-free: 888-764-3326
miami.consulado.gov.co

Colombia Consulate General
2400 Augusta Dr.
Ste. 400
Houston, TX 77057
Phone: 713-979-0844
Toll-free: 888-764-3326
houston.consulado.gov.co

Colombia Consulate General
10 E. 46th St.
New York, NY 10017
Phone: 212-798-9000; Fax: 212-972-1725
Toll-free: 888-764-3326
nuevayork.consulado.gov.co

Colombia Consulate General
550 Broad St.
15th Fl.
Newark, NJ 07102
Phone: 862-279-7888; Fax: 862-279-7885
Toll-free: 888-764-3326
newark.consulado.gov.co

Colombia Consulate General
201 E. Pine St.
Ste. 470
Orlando, FL 32801
Phone: 407-650-4274; Fax: 407-650-4281
Toll-free: 888-764-3326
orlando.consulado.gov.co

Colombia Consulate General
595 Market St.
Ste. 1190
San Francisco, CA 94105
Phone: 415-495-7195; Fax: 415-777-3731
Toll-free: 888-764-3326
sanfrancisco.consulado.gov.co

Colombia Consulate General
1101 17th St. N.W.
Ste. 1007
Washington, DC 20036
Phone: 202-332-7476
Toll-free: 888-764-3326
washington.consulado.gov.co

Colombia Embassy
2118 Leroy PL. N.W.
Washington, DC 20008
Phone: 202-387-8338
www.colombiaemb.org

Colombia Permanent Mission to the UN
140 E. 57th St.
New York, NY 10022
Phone: 212-355-7776; Fax: 212-371-2813
www.colombiaun.org

Comoros

Comoros Consulate General
2923 N. Milwaukee Ave.
Ste. 106
Chicago, IL 60618
Phone: 312-493-2357; Fax: 315-693-2357
comorosconsulatechicago.org

Comoros Embassy
866 United Nations Plaza
Ste. 418
New York, NY 10017
Phone: 212-750-1637; Fax: 212-750-1657
www.un.int/comoros

Comoros Permanent Mission to the UN
866 United Nations Plaza
Ste. 418
New York, NY 10017
Phone: 212-750-1637; Fax: 212-750-1657
www.un.int/comoros

Congo, Democratic Republic of

Congo Democratic Republic of consulate
1720 16th St. N.W.
Washington, DC 20009
Phone: 202-726-5500
www.ambacongo-us.org

Congo Democratic Republic of Embassy
1726 M St. N.W.
Washington, DC 20036
Phone: 202-234-7690; Fax: 202-234-2609
www.ambardcusa.org

Congo Democratic Republic of Permanent Mission to the UN
866 United Nations Plaza
Ste. 511
New York, NY 10017
Phone: 212-319-8061; Fax: 212-319-8232
www.un.int/drcongo

Congo, Republic of

Congo Republic of Embassy
1720 16th St. N.W.
Washington, DC 20009
Phone: 202-726-5500; Fax: 202-726-1860
www.ambacongo-us.org

Congo Republic of Permanent Mission to the UN
14 E. 65th St.
New York, NY 10065
Phone: 212-744-7840; Fax: 212-744-7975
www.un.int/congo

Costa Rica

Costa Rica Chamber of Commerce
SJO 1576
P.O. Box 025331
Miami, FL 33102
www.amcham.co.cr

Costa Rica Consulate General
1870 The Exchange
Ste. 100
Atlanta, GA 30339
Phone: 770-951-7025; Fax: 770-951-7073

Costa Rica Consulate General
30 N. Michigan Ave.
Ste. 1922
Chicago, IL 60602
Phone: 312-577-4267; Fax: 312-577-4271

Costa Rica Consulate
3100 Wilcrest Dr.
Ste. 260
Houston, TX 77042
Phone: 713-266-0484; Fax: 713-266-1527

Costa Rica Consulate General
1605 W. Olympic Blvd.
Ste. 400
Los Angeles, CA 90015
Phone: 213-380-7915; Fax: 213-380-5639

Costa Rica Consulate General
2730 S.W. 3rd Ave.
Ste. 401
Miami, FL 33131

Costa Rica Consulate General
225 W. 34th St.
Ste. 1105
New York, NY 10122
Phone: 212-509-3066; Fax: 212-509-3068

Costa Rica Consulate General
2112 S. St. N.W.
Washington, DC 20008
Phone: 202-328-6628

Costa Rica Embassy
2114 S. St. N.W.
Washington, DC 20008
Phone: 202-265-4795; Fax: 202-265-4795

Costa Rica Permanent Mission to the UN
211 E. 43rd St.
Rm. 903
New York, NY 10017
Phone: 212-986-6373; Fax: 212-986-6842
www.un.int/costarica

Cote d'Ivoire (Ivory Coast)

Cote d'Ivoire (Ivory Coast) National Tourism office
3421 Massachusetts Ave N.W.
Washington, DC 20007
Phone: 202-797-0300; Fax: 202-387-6381
www.tourismeci.org

Cote d'Ivoire Embassy
2424 Massachusetts Ave. N.W.
Washington, DC 20008
Phone: 202-797-0300
www.ambaciusa.org

Cote d'Ivoire Permanent Mission to the UN
800 2nd Ave.
5th Fl.
New York, NY 10017
Phone: 646-649-5061
www.un.org

Croatia

Croatian National Tourist Office
P.O. Box 2651
New York, NY 10118
www.croatia.hr

Croatia Consulate General
737 N. Michigan Ave.
Ste. 1030
Chicago, IL 60611
Phone: 312-482-9902; Fax: 312-482-9987
www.croatiaemb.org

Croatia Consulate General
11766 Wilshire Blvd.
Ste. 1250
Los Angeles, CA 90025
Phone: 310-477-1009; Fax: 310-477-1866
www.croatiaemb.org

Croatia Consulate General
369 Lexington Ave.
11th Fl.
New York, NY 10017
Phone: 212-599-3066; Fax: 212-599-3106
www.croatiaemb.org

Croatia Embassy
2343 Massachusetts Ave. N.W.
Washington, DC 20008
Phone: 202-588-5899; Fax: 202-588-8936
www.croatiaemb.org

Croatia Permanent Mission to the UN
820 2nd Ave.
19th Fl.
New York, NY 10017
Phone: 212-986-1585; Fax: 212-986-2011
un.mfa.hr

Cuba

Cuba National Tourism Office
www.cubatravel.cu

Cuba Chamber of Commerce
P.O. Box 233
Cuba, NY 14727
Phone: 585-968-5654
www.cubanewyork.us

Cuba Interests Section Embassy of Switzerland
2630 16th St. N.W.
Washington, DC 20009
Phone: 202-797-8518
www.cubadiplomatica.cu

Cuba Permanent Mission to the UN
315 Lexington Ave.
New York, NY 10016
Phone: 212-689-7216; Fax: 212-689-9073
www.cubadiplomatica.cu

Curacao

Curacao Tourist Board
80 S.W. 8th st.
Ste. 2000
Miami, FL 33130
Phone: 305-423-7156
Toll-free: 800-328-7222
www.curacao.com

Cyprus

Cyprus Tourism Organization
13 E. 40th St.
New York, NY 10016
Phone: 212-683-5280; Fax: 212-683-5282
www.cyprustourism.org

Cyprus Chamber of Commerce
805 Third Ave.
10th Fl.
New York, NY 10017
Phone: 201-444-5609; Fax: 201-444-0445
www.cyprususchamber.com

Cyprus Consulate General
13 E. 40th St.
New York, NY 10016
Phone: 212-686-6016; Fax: 212-686-3660
www.cyprusembassy.net

Cyprus Embassy
2211 R St. N.W.
Washington, DC 20008
Phone: 202-462-0632; Fax: 202-462-5091
www.cyprusembassy.net

Cyprus Permanent Mission to the UN
13 E. 40th St.
New York, NY 10016
Phone: 212-481-6023; Fax: 212-685-7316
www.cyprusun.org

Czech Republic

Czech Center & Tourist Authority
321 E. 73rd St.
New York, NY 10021
Phone: 646-422-3399; Fax: 646-422-3383
www.czechcenter.com

Czech Republic Consulate General
10990 Wilshire Blvd.
Ste. 1100
Los Angeles, CA 90024
Phone: 310-473-0889; Fax: 310-473-9813
www.mzv.cz

Czech Republic Consulate General
321 E. 73rd St.
New York, NY 10021
Phone: 646-422-3344; Fax: 646-422-3311
www.mfa.cz

Czech Republic Embassy
3900 Spring of Freedom St. N.W.
Washington, DC 20008
Phone: 202-274-9100; Fax: 202-966-8540
www.mzv.cz

Czech Republic Permanent Mission to the UN
1109-1111 Madison Ave.
New York, NY 10028
Phone: 646-981-4001; Fax: 646-981-4099
www.mzv.cz

Democratic People's Republic of Korea.
See North Korea

Denmark

Danish Tourist Board
655 3rd Ave.
Ste. 1810
New York, NY 10017
Phone: 212-885-9700
www.visitdenmark.com

Danish-American Chamber of Commerce
885 2nd Ave.
18th Fl.
New York, NY 10017
Phone: 646-790-7169
www.daccny.com

Denmark Consulate General
875 N. Michigan Ave.
Ste. 3950
Chicago, IL 60611
Phone: 312-787-8780; Fax: 312-787-8744
usa.um.dk

Denmark Consulate General
1 Dag Hammarskjold Plaza
18th Fl. 885 2nd Ave.
New York, NY 10017
Phone: 212-223-4545; Fax: 212-754-1904
usa.um.dk

Denmark Embassy
3200 Whitehaven St. N.W.
Washington, DC 20008
Phone: 202-234-4300; Fax: 202-328-1470
usa.um.dk

Denmark Permanent Mission to the UN
885 2nd Ave.
18th Fl.
New York, NY 10017
Phone: 212-308-7009; Fax: 212-308-3384
fnnewyork.um.dk

Djibouti

Djibouti National Tourism Office
866 United Nation Plaza
Ste. 4011
New York, NY 10017
Phone: 202-753-3163; Fax: 202-223-1276
www.visitdjibouti.dj

Djibouti Consulate General
866 United Nation Plaza
Ste. 4011
New York, NY 10017
Phone: 202-753-3163; Fax: 202-223-1276
www.visitdjibouti.dj

Djibouti Embassy
1156 15th St. N.W.
Ste. 515
Washington, DC 20005
Phone: 202-331-0270; Fax: 202-331-1988
djibouti.usembassy.gov

Djibouti Permanent Mission to the UN
866 United Nations Plaza
Ste. 4011
New York, NY 10017
Phone: 212-753-3163; Fax: 212-223-1276
www.un.int/djibouti

Dominica

Dominica Consulate General
800 2nd Ave.
Ste. 4oo-H
New York, NY 10017
Phone: 212-599-8478; Fax: 212-661-0979

Dominica Permanent Mission to the UN
800 2nd Ave.
Ste. 400-H
4th Fl.
New York, NY 10017
Phone: 212-949-0853;

Dominican Republic

Dominican Republic Tourist Board
848 Brickell Ave.
Ste. 747
Miami, FL 33131
Phone: 305-358-2899; Fax: 305-358-4185
www.godominicanrepublic.com

Dominican Republic Tourist Board
136 E. 57th St.
Ste. 805
New York, NY 10022
Phone: 212-588-1012; Fax: 212-588-1015
Toll-free: 888-374-6361
www.godominicanrepublic.com

Dominican Republic Consulate General
20 Park Plaza
Ste. 601
Boston, MA 02116
Phone: 617-482-8121; Fax: 617-482-8133
www.domrep.org

Dominican Republic Consulate General
8770 W. Bryn Mawr Ave.
Triangle Plaza
Ste. 1300
Chicago, IL 60631
Phone: 773-714-4924; Fax: 773-714-4926
www.domrep.org

Dominican Republic Consulate General
500 N. Brand Blvd.
Ste. 960
Glendale, CA 91203
Phone: 818-504-6605; Fax: 818-504-6617
www.domrep.org

Dominican Republic Consulate General
1038 Brickell Ave.
Miami, FL 33131
Phone: 305-358-3220; Fax: 305-358-2318
www.domrep.org

Dominican Republic Consulate General
400 Poydras Ave.
Ste. 1520
New Orleans, LA 70130
Phone: 504-522-1843; Fax: 504-522-1007
www.domrep.org

Dominican Republic Consulate General
1501 Broadway Ave.
Ste. 410
New York, NY 10036
Phone: 212-768-2480; Fax: 212-768-2677
www.domrep.org

Dominican Republic Consulate General
1715 22nd St.N.W.
Washington, DC 20008
Phone: 202-332-7670; Fax: 202-265-8057
www.domrep.org

Dominican Republic Embassy
1715 22nd St. N.W.
Washington, DC 20008
Phone: 202-332-7670; Fax: 202-265-8057
www.domrep.org

Dominican Republic Permanent Mission to the UN
144 E. 44th St.
4th Fl.
New York, NY 10017
Phone: 212-867-0833; Fax: 212-986-4694
www.un.int/domrep

Ecuador

Ecuadorian American Chamber of Commerce in Miami

3403 N.W. 82 Ave.
Ste. 310
Miami, FL 33122
Phone: 305-591-0058; Fax: 305-591-0868
www.ecuachamber.com

Ecuador Consulate General
3495 Piedmont Rd. N.E.
Bldg. 12., Ste. 105
Atlanta, GA 30305
Phone: 404-841-2276; Fax: 404-841-2285
atlanta.consulado.gob.ec

Ecuador Consulate General
8484 Wilshire Blvd.
Ste. 540
Beverly Hills, CA 90211
Phone: 323-658-6020; Fax: 323-658-1198
losangeles.consulado.gob.ec

Ecuador Consulate General
30 S. Michigan Ave.
Ste. 700
Chicago, IL 60603
Phone: 312-338-1002; Fax: 312-338-1502
chicago.consulado.gob.ec

Ecuador Consulate General
7510 Acorn Ln.
Frisco, TX 75034
Phone: 972-712-9107; Fax: 928-962-9869
miami.consulado.gob.ec

Ecuador Consulate General
4200 Westheimer Rd.
Ste. 218
Houston, TX 77027
Phone: 713-572-8731; Fax: 713-572-8732
houston.consulado.gob.ec

Ecuador Consulate General
33-25 81st. St.
Apt. 3C
Jackson Heights, NY 11372
Phone: 646-318-4544
miami.consulado.gob.ec

Ecuador Consulate General
117 N.W. 42nd Ave.
Ste. CU-4 & CU-5
Miami, FL 33126
Phone: 305-539-8214; Fax: 305-539-8313
miami.consulado.gob.ec

Ecuador Consulate General
333 E. Hennepin Ave.
Ste. 100
Minneapolis, MN 55414
Phone: 612-721-6468
minneapolis.consulado.gob.ec

Ecuador Consulate General
52 Cranberry Ln.
Needham, MA 02492
Phone: 781-400-1212; Fax: 781-455-9019
miami.consulado.gob.ec

Ecuador Consulate General
1 Church St.
New Haven, CT 06510
Phone: 203-752-1947; Fax: 203-752-1389
miami.consulado.gob.ec

Ecuador Consulate General
800 2nd Ave.
Ste. 600
New York, NY 10017
Phone: 212-808-0170; Fax: 212-808-0188
www.consuladoecuadornewyork.com

Ecuador Consulate General
400 Market St.
4th Fl.
Newark, NJ 07105
Phone: 973-344-8837; Fax: 973-344-0008
www.consuladoecuadornj.com

Ecuador Consulate General
645 E. Missouri Ave.
Ste. 132
Phoenix, AZ 85012
Phone: 602-535-5567; Fax: 602-237-5532
miami.consulado.gob.ec

Ecuador Consulate General
235 Montgomery St.
Ste. 944
San Francisco, CA 94104
Phone: 415-957-5921; Fax: 415-957-5923

Ecuador Consulate General
2535 15th St. N.W.
Washington, DC 20009
Phone: 202-234-7200; Fax: 202-333-2893
www.ecuador.org

Ecuador Embassy
2535 15th St. N.W.
Washington, DC 20009
Phone: 202-234-7200; Fax: 202-333-2893
www.ecuador.org

Ecuador Permanent Mission to the UN
866 United Nations Plaza
Rm. 516
New York, NY 10017
Phone: 212-935-1680; Fax: 212-935-1835
www.un.int/ecuador

Egypt

Egyptian Tourist Authority
45 Rockefeller Plaza
Ste. 2305
New York, NY 10011
Phone: 212-332-2570
www.egypt.travel

American Egyptian Cooperation Foundation
28 E. Jackson Blvd.
Chicago, IL 60604

Phone: 312-427-9368

American Egyptian Cooperation Foundation
1535 W. Loop S.
Ste. 219A
Houston, TX 77027
Phone: 713-993-9650

American Egyptian Cooperation Foundation
733 15th St. N.W.
Ste. 700
Washington, DC 20005
Phone: 202-393-3369

Egypt Consulate General
500 N. Michigan Ave.
Ste. 1900
Chicago, IL 60611
Phone: 312-828-9162; Fax: 312-828-9167
www.egyptchicago.org

Egypt Consulate General
5718 Westheimer St.
Ste. 1350
Houston, TX 77057
Phone: 713-961-4915; Fax: 713-961-3868
www.egyptembassy.net

Egypt Consulate General
4929 Wilshire Blvd.
Ste. 300
Los Angeles, CA 90010
Phone: 323-933-9700; Fax: 323-933-9725
www.egyconsulatela.com

Egypt Consulate General
1110 2nd Ave.
Ste. 201
New York, NY 10022
Phone: 212-759-7120; Fax: 212-308-7643
www.egypt-nyc.com

Egypt Consulate General
Washington, DC
Phone: 202-966-6342; Fax: 202-244-4319
www.egyptembassy.net

Egypt Embassy
3521 International Ct. N.W.
Washington, DC 20008
Phone: 202-895-5400; Fax: 202-244-4319
www.egyptembassy.net

Egypt Permanent Mission to the UN
304 E. 44th St.
New York, NY 10017
Phone: 212-503-0300; Fax: 212-949-5999
www.mfa.gov.eg/english

El Salvador

El Salvador Chamber of Commerce
1717 Pennsylvania Ave.
Ste. 1025
Washington, DC 20006
Phone: 202-370-6955; Fax: 202-747-5622

www.sacocdc.org

El Salvador Consulate General
177 N. State St.
2nd Fl. Mezzanine
Chicago, IL 60601
Phone: 312-332-1393
consuladochicago.rree.gob.sv

El Salvador Consulate General
1250 W. Mockingbird Ln.
Ste. 240
Dallas, TX 75247
Phone: 214-637-1500
consuladodallas.rree.gob.sv

El Salvador Consulate General
8550 N.W. 33rd St.
Ste. 100
Doral, FL 33122
Phone: 305-592-6978
consuladocoralgables.rree.gob.sv

El Salvador Consulate General
10301 Harwin Dr.
Ste. B
Houston, TX 77036
Phone: 713-270-6239
consuladohouston.rree.gob.sv

El Salvador Consulate General
3450 Wilshire Blvd.
Ste. 250
Los Angeles, CA 90020
Phone: 213-383-8580
consuladolosangeles.rree.gob.sv

El Salvador Consulate General
46 Park Ave.
New York, NY 10016
Phone: 212-889-3608
consuladonuevayork.rree.gob.sv

El Salvador Consulate General
507 Polk St.
Ste. 280
San Francisco, CA 94102
Phone: 415-771-8524
consuladosanfrancisco.rree.gob.sv

El Salvador Embassy
1400 16th St. N.W.
Ste. 100
Washington, DC 20036
Phone: 202-595-7500; Fax: 202-232-3763
www.elsalvador.org

El Salvador Permanent Mission to the UN
46 Park Ave.
New York, NY 10016
Phone: 212-679-1616
misiononu.rree.gob.sv

Equatorial Guinea

Equatorial Guinea Embassy
2020 16th St. N.W.
Washington, DC 20009
Phone: 202-518-5700; Fax: 202-518-5252
egembassydc.com

Equatorial Guinea Permanent Mission to the UN
242 E. 51st St.
New York, NY 10022
Phone: 212-223-2324; Fax: 212-223-2366
www.un.int/equatorialguinea

Eritrea

Eritrea Embassy
1708 New Hampshire Ave. N.W.
Washington, DC 20009
Phone: 202-319-1991; Fax: 202-319-1304
www.embassyeritrea.org

Eritrea Permanent Mission to the UN
800 2nd Ave.
Ste. 1801
New York, NY 10017
Phone: 212-687-3390; Fax: 212-687-3138
www.eritrea-unmission.org

Estonia

Estonian American Chamber of Commerce and Industry
157-61 17th Ave.
Whitestone, NY 11357
Phone: 718-747-3805; Fax: 718-767-8825
www.eacci.org

Estonia Consulate General
305 E. 47th St.
3 Dag Hammarskjöld Plaza Ste. 6B
New York, NY 10017
Phone: 212-883-0636; Fax: 212-883-0648
www.nyc.estemb.org

Estonia Embassy
2131 Massachusetts Ave. N.W.
Washington, DC 20008
Phone: 202-588-0101; Fax: 202-588-0108
www.estemb.org

Estonia Permanent Mission to the UN
305 E. 47th St.
6th Fl.
New York, NY 10017
Phone: 212-883-0640; Fax: 646-514-0099
www.un.estemb.org

Ethiopia

Ethiopia Consulate General
3250 Wilshire Blvd.
Ste. 1101
Los Angeles, CA 90010
Phone: 213-365-6651

Ethiopia Embassy
3506 International Dr. N.W.
Washington, DC 20008
Phone: 202-364-1200; Fax: 202-587-0195
www.ethiopianembassy.org

Ethiopia Permanent Mission to the UN
866 2nd Ave.
3rd Fl.
New York, NY 10017
Phone: 212-421-1830
www.un.org

Fiji

Fiji Tourism
5777 W. Century Blvd.
Ste. 220
Los Angeles, CA 90045
Phone: 310-568-1616; Fax: 310-670-2318
Toll-free: 800-932-3454
www.fiji.travel

Fiji Embassy
1707 L St. N.W.
Ste. 200
Washington, DC 20036
Phone: 202-466-8320; Fax: 202-466-8325
www.fijiembassydc.com

Fiji Permanent Mission to the UN
801 Second Ave.
10th Fl.
New York, NY 10017
Phone: 212-687-4130; Fax: 212-687-3963
www.fijiprun.org

Finland

Finnish Tourist Board
www.visitfinland.com

Finnish American Chamber of Commerce Inc
17102 N.E. 37 Pl.
Bellevue, WA 98008
www.facc-usa.com

Finnish American Chamber of Commerce Inc
1511 W. Adams
Ste. 3
Chicago, IL 60607
www.facc-usa.com

Finnish American Chamber of Commerce Inc
1950 Vaughn Rd.
Kennesaw, GA 30144
Phone: 770-436-1542; Fax: 770-436-3432
www.facc-usa.com

Finnish American Chamber of Commerce Inc
523 Lake Ave.
Lake Worth, FL 33460
Phone: 561-582-2335
facc-fl.com

Finnish-American Chamber of Commerce on the Pacific
Coast
1601 Selby Ave.
Los Angeles, CA 92024
www.facc-usa.com

Finnish American Chamber of Commerce Inc
54 W. 40th St.
New York, NY 10018
Phone: 917-214-6465
www.facc-ny.com

Finnish American Chamber of Commerce Inc
5863 Chevy Chase Pkwy. N.W. 44
Washington, DC 20015
Phone: 202-549-4448
www.facc-usa.com

Finland Consulate General
11900 W. Olympic Blvd.
Ste. 580
Los Angeles, CA 90064
Phone: 310-203-9903; Fax: 310-481-8981
www.finland.org

Finland Consulate General
866 United Nations Plaza
Ste. 250
New York, NY 10017
Phone: 212-750-4400; Fax: 212-750-4418
www.finland.org

Finland Embassy
3301 Massachusetts Ave. N.W.
Washington, DC 20008
Phone: 202-298-5800; Fax: 202-298-6030
www.finland.org

Finland Permanent Mission to the UN
866 United Nations Plaza
Ste. 222
New York, NY 10017
Phone: 212-355-2100; Fax: 212-759-6156
www.finlandun.org

France

French Government Tourist Office
825 Third Ave.
New York, NY 10022
Phone: 212-838-7800; Fax: 212-838-7855
int.rendezvousenfrance.com/en

French-American Chamber of Commerce of Atlanta
3399 Peachtree Rd. N.E.
Ste. 500
Atlanta, GA 30326
Phone: 404-997-6800; Fax: 404-997-6810
www.facc-atlanta.com

French-American Chamber of Commerce of Chicago
35 E. Wacker Dr.
Ste. 670
Chicago, IL 60601
Phone: 312-578-0444; Fax: 312-578-0445
www.facc-chicago.com

French-American Chamber of Commerce of Dallas
6060 N. Central Expy.
Ste. 500
Dallas, TX 75206
Phone: 972-241-0111; Fax: 972-241-0901
www.faccdallas.com

French-American Chamber of Commerce of Houston
777 Post Oak Blvd.
Ste. 600
Houston, TX 77056
Phone: 713-985-3280; Fax: 713-572-2911
www.facchouston.com

French-American Chamber of Commerce of Los Angeles
10390 Santa Monica Blvd.
Ste. 410
Los Angeles, CA 90025
Phone: 657-206-7891
www.facclosangeles.org

French-American Chamber of Commerce of Florida
1395 Brickell Ave.
Ste. 900
Miami, FL 33131
Phone: 305-374-5000; Fax: 305-358-8203
www.faccmiami.com

French-American Chamber of Commerce of Louisiana
P.O. Box 57255
New Orleans, LA 70157
Phone: 504-458-3528
www.facc-gc.com

French-American Chamber of Commerce of New York
1375 Broadway
Ste. 504
New York, NY 10018
Phone: 212-867-0123; Fax: 212-867-9050
www.faccnyc.org

French-American Chamber of Commerce of Philadelphia
200 S. Broad St.
Ste. 910
Philadelphia, PA 19102
Phone: 215-716-1996
faccphila.org

French-American Chamber of Commerce of San Francisco
26 O'Farrell St.
Ste. 500
San Francisco, CA 94108
Phone: 415-442-4717; Fax: 415-442-4621
www.faccsf.com

French-American Chamber of Commerce of the Pacific Northwest
2200 Alaskan Way
Ste. 490
Seattle, WA 98121
Phone: 206-443-4703; Fax: 206-448-4218
www.faccpnw.org

France Consulate General
3399 Peachtree Rd. N.E.
Ste. 500

Atlanta, GA 30326
Phone: 404-495-1660; Fax: 404-495-1661
www.consulfrance-atlanta.org

France Consulate General
31 Saint James Ave.
Park Square Bldg. Ste. 750
Boston, MA 02116
Phone: 617-832-4400; Fax: 617-542-8054
www.consulfrance-boston.org

France Consulate General
205 N. Michigan Ave.
Ste. 3700
Chicago, IL 60601
Phone: 312-327-5200; Fax: 312-327-5201
www.consulfrance-chicago.org

France Consulate General
777 Post Oak Blvd.
Ste. 600
Houston, TX 77056
Phone: 713-572-2799
www.consulfrance-houston.org

France Consulate General
10390 Santa Monica Blvd.
Ste. 410
Los Angeles, CA 90025
Phone: 310-235-3200; Fax: 310-479-4813
www.consulfrance-losangeles.org

France Consulate General
1395 Brickell Ave.
Ste. 1050
Miami, FL 33131
Phone: 305-403-4185; Fax: 305-403-4187
www.consulfrance-miami.org

France Consulate General
1340 Poydras St.
Ste. 1710
New Orleans, LA 70112
Phone: 504-569-2870; Fax: 504-569-2871
www.consulfrance-nouvelleorleans.org

France Consulate General
934 Fifth Ave.
New York, NY 10021
Phone: 212-606-3600; Fax: 212-606-3620
www.consulfrance-newyork.org

France Consulate General
88 Kearny St.
Ste. 600
San Francisco, CA 94108
Phone: 415-397-4330
www.consulfrance-sanfrancisco.org

France Embassy
4101 Reservoir Rd. N.W.
Washington, DC 20007
Phone: 202-944-6000
www.ambafrance-us.org

France Permanent Mission to the UN
245 E. 47th St.

44th Fl.
New York, NY 10017
Phone: 212-702-4900; Fax: 212-702-3190
www.franceonu.org

French West Indies. *See* Martinique

Gabon

Gabon Consulate
122 E. 42nd St.
Ste. 519
New York, NY 10168
Phone: 212-683-7371; Fax: 212-686-2427
gabonconsulate-nyc.com/en

Gabon Embassy
2034 20th St. N.W.
Washington, DC 20009
Phone: 202-797-1000; Fax: 202-332-0668
www.gabonembassyusa.org

Gabon Permanent Mission to the UN
18 E. 41st St.
9th Fl.
New York, NY 10017
Phone: 212-686-9720; Fax: 212-689-5769
gabonconsulate-nyc.com/en

Gambia

Gambia Embassy
2233 Wisconsin Ave. N.W.
Georgetown Plaza
Ste. 240
Washington, DC 20007
Phone: 202-785-1399; Fax: 202-342-0240
www.gambiaembassy.us

Gambia Permanent Mission to the UN
800 Second Ave.
Ste. 400F
New York, NY 10017
Phone: 212-949-6640; Fax: 212-856-9820
www.un.int/gambia

Georgia

Georgia Chamber of Commerce
270 Peachtree St. N.W.
Ste. 2200
Atlanta, GA 30303
Phone: 404-223-2264; Fax: 404-223-2290
Toll-free: 800-241-2286
www.gachamber.com

Georgia Consulate General
144 E 44th St.
New York, NY 10017
Phone: 212-922-1722
newyork.con.mfa.gov.ge

Georgia Embassy
1824 R St. N.W.
Washington, DC 20009
Phone: 202-387-2390; Fax: 202-387-0864
usa.mfa.gov.ge

Georgia Permanent Mission to the UN
One United Nations Plaza
26th Fl.
New York, NY 10017
Phone: 212-759-1949; Fax: 212-759-1832
un.mfa.gov.ge

Germany

German National Tourist Office
122 E. 42nd St.
Ste. 2000
New York, NY 10168
Phone: 212-661-4796; Fax: 212-661-7174
www.germany.travel/us

German-American Chamber of Commerce of the Southern US Inc
1170 Howell Mill Rd.
Ste. 300
Atlanta, GA 30318
Phone: 404-586-6800; Fax: 404-586-6820
www.gaccsouth.com/en

German-American Chamber of Commerce of the Midwest Inc
321 N. Clark St.
Ste. 1425
Chicago, IL 60654
Phone: 312-644-2662; Fax: 312-644-0738
www.gaccmidwest.org/en

German-American Chamber of Commerce of the Southern US Inc
1900 W. Loop S.
Ste. 1550
Houston, TX 77027
Phone: 832-384-1200; Fax: 713-715-6599
www.gaccsouth.com/en

German-American Chamber of Commerce Inc
80 Pine St.
24th Fl.
New York, NY 10005
Phone: 212-974-8830; Fax: 212-974-8867
www.gaccny.com/en

German-American Chamber of Commerce Inc - Philadelphia
200 S. Broad St.
Ste. 700
Philadelphia, PA 19103
Phone: 215-665-1585; Fax: 215-864-7288
gaccphiladelphia.com

Representative of German Industry & Trade
1776 I St. N.W.
Ste. 1000
Washington, DC 20006

Phone: 202-659-4777; Fax: 202-659-4779
www.rgit-usa.com

German Consulate General
285 Peachtree Center Ave. N.E.
Marquis Two Tower
Ste. 901
Atlanta, GA 30303
Phone: 404-934-5474
www.germany.info/Atlanta

German Consulate General
Three Copley Pl.
Ste. 500
Boston, MA 02116
Phone: 617-369-4900; Fax: 617-369-4940
www.germany.info/boston

German Consulate General
676 N. Michigan Ave.
Ste. 3200
Chicago, IL 60611
Phone: 312-202-0480; Fax: 312-202-0466
www.germany.info/chicago

German Consulate General
1330 Post Oak Blvd.
Ste. 1850
Houston, TX 77056
Phone: 713-627-7770; Fax: 713-627-0506
www.germany.info/houston

German Consulate General
6222 Wilshire Blvd.
Ste. 500
Los Angeles, CA 90048
Phone: 323-930-2703; Fax: 323-930-2805
www.germany.info/losangeles

German Consulate General
100 N. Biscayne Blvd.
Ste. 2200
Miami, FL 33132
Phone: 305-358-0290; Fax: 305-358-0307
www.germany.info/Miami

German Consulate General
871 United Nations Plaza
New York, NY 10017
Phone: 212-610-9700; Fax: 212-940-0402
www.germany.info/newyork

German Consulate General
1960 Jackson St.
San Francisco, CA 94109
Phone: 415-775-1061; Fax: 415-775-0187
www.germany.info/SanFrancisco

German Embassy
4645 Reservoir Rd. N.W.
Washington, DC 20007
Phone: 202-298-4000
www.germany.info/embassy

Germany Permanent Mission to the UN
871 United Nations Plaza

New York, NY 10017
Phone: 212-940-0400; Fax: 212-940-0402
www.new-york-un.diplo.de

Ghana

Ghana Chamber of Commerce
1100 Peachtree St. N.E.
Ste. 200
Atlanta, GA 30309
Phone: 678-632-2362
www.ghicc.org

Ghana Consulate General
19 E. 47th St.
New York, NY 10017
Phone: 212-832-1300; Fax: 212-751-6743
www.ghanaconsulatenewyork.org

Ghana Embassy
3512 International Dr. N.W.
Washington, DC 20008
Phone: 202-686-4520; Fax: 202-686-4527
www.ghanaembassy.org

Ghana Permanent Mission to the UN
19 E. 47th St.
New York, NY 10017
Phone: 212-832-1300; Fax: 212-751-6743
www.un.int/ghana

Greece

Greek National Tourist Organization
305 E. 47th St.
2nd Fl.
New York, NY 10017
Phone: 212-421-5777; Fax: 212-826-6940
www.visitgreece.gr/en

Greece Consulate
3340 Peachtree Rd. N.E.
Tower Pl. 100
Ste. 1670
Atlanta, GA 30326
Phone: 404-261-3313; Fax: 404-262-2798
www.mfa.gr/usa/en/consulate-in-atlanta

Greece Consulate General
86 Beacon St.
Boston, MA 02108
Phone: 617-523-0100; Fax: 617-523-0511
www.mfa.gr/usa/en/consulate-general-in-boston

Greece Consulate General
650 N. Saint Clair St.
Chicago, IL 60611
Phone: 312-335-3915; Fax: 312-335-3958
www.mfa.gr/usa/en/consulate-general-in-chicago

Greece Consulate
2401 Fountain View Dr.
Ste. 850
Houston, TX 77057

Phone: 713-840-7522; Fax: 713-840-0614
www.mfa.gr/usa/en/consulate-in-houston

Greece Consulate General
12424 Wilshire Blvd.
Ste. 1170
Los Angeles, CA 90025
Phone: 310-826-5555; Fax: 310-826-8670
www.mfa.gr/usa/en/consulate-general-in-los-angeles

Greece Consulate General
69 E. 79th St.
New York, NY 10075
Phone: 212-988-5500; Fax: 212-734-8492
www.mfa.gr/usa/en/consulate-general-in-new-york

Greece Consulate General
2441 Gough St.
San Francisco, CA 94123
Phone: 415-775-2102; Fax: 415-776-6815
www.mfa.gr/usa/en/consulate-general-in-san-francisco

Greece Consulate General
400 N. Tampa St.
Ste. 1160
Tampa, FL 33602
Phone: 813-865-0200; Fax: 813-865-0206
www.mfa.gr/usa/en/consulate-general-in-tampa

Greece Embassy
2217 Massachusetts Ave. N.W.
Washington, DC 20008
Phone: 202-939-1300; Fax: 202-939-1324
www.mfa.gr/usa/en/the-embassy

Greece Embassy - Consular Section
2217 Massachusetts Ave. N.W.
Washington, DC 20008
Phone: 202-939-1306; Fax: 202-234-2803
www.mfa.gr/usa/en

Greece Permanent Mission to the UN
866 Second Ave.
13th Fl.
New York, NY 10017
Phone: 212-888-6900; Fax: 212-888-4440
www.mfa.gr/missionsabroad/en/un-en

Grenada

Grenada Board of Tourism
Phone: 561-948-6925
www.grenadagrenadines.com

Grenada Chamber of Commerce
95 S.W. Frontage Rd.
P.O. BOX 628
Grenada, MS 38902
Phone: 662-226-2571; Fax: 662-226-9745
Toll-free: 800-373-2571
www.grenadamississippi.com

Grenada Consulate General
P.O. Box 1668
Lake Worth, FL 33460

Phone: 561-588-8176; Fax: 561-588-7267
Toll-free: 800-927-9554
www.grenadaconsulate.com

Grenada Embassy
1701 New Hampshire Ave. N.W.
Washington, DC 20009
Phone: 202-265-2561; Fax: 202-265-2468
www.grenadaembassyusa.org

Grenada Permanent Mission to the UN
800 2nd Ave.
Ste. 400K
New York, NY 10017
Phone: 212-599-0301; Fax: 212-599-1540
www.un.int/grenada

Guatemala

Guatemala Consulate General
2750 Buford Hwy N.E.
Ste. 135
Atlanda, GA 30324
Phone: 404-320-8804; Fax: 404-320-8806
www.consatlanta.minex.gob.gt

Guatemala Consulate General
205 N. Michigan Ave.
Ste. 2350
Chicago, IL 60601
Phone: 312-540-0781; Fax: 312-540-0897
www.consulguatechicago.org

Guatemala Consulate General
106 Foster Dr.
Del Rio, TX 78840
Phone: 830-422-2230; Fax: 830-422-2093
www.minex.gob.gt

Guatemala Consulate General
1001 S. Monaco Pkwy.
Ste. 300
Denver, CO 80224
Phone: 303-629-9210; Fax: 303-629-9211
www.consdenver.minex.gob.gt

Guatemala Consulate General
3013 Fountain View
Ste. 210
Houston, TX 77057
Phone: 713-953-9531; Fax: 713-953-9383
www.minex.gob.gt

Guatemala Consulate General
3540 Wilshire Blvd.
Ste. 100
Los Angeles, CA 90010
Phone: 213-365-9251; Fax: 213-365-9245
www.conslosangeles.minex.gob.gt

Guatemala Consulate General
709 S Broadway St
McAllen, TX 78501
Phone: 956-429-3413; Fax: 956-242-0593
www.consmcallen.minex.gob.gt

Guatemala Consulate General
1101 Brickell Ave.
Ste. 603-S
Miami, FL 33131
Phone: 305-679-9945; Fax: 305-679-9983
www.consuladoguatemalamiami.org

Guatemala Consulate General
276 Park Ave. S.
2 Fl.
New York, NY 10010
Phone: 212-686-3837; Fax: 212-271-3503
www.consuladoguatemalanuevayork.org

Guatemala Consulate General
4747 N. 7th. St.
Ste. 410
Phoenix, AZ 85014
Phone: 602-200-3660; Fax: 602-200-3661
www.consphoenix.minex.gob.gt

Guatemala Consulate General
555 Valley St.
Bldg. 321-61
Providence, RI 02908
Phone: 401-270-6345; Fax: 401-270-7039
www.consulguateprovri.org

Guatemala Consulate General
330 N D St.
Ste. 120
San Bernardino, CA 92401
Phone: 909-572-8800
www.minex.gob.gt

Guatemala Consulate General
544 Golden Gate Ave.
Ste. 100
San Francisco, CA 94102
Phone: 415-563-8319; Fax: 415-563-8376
www.minex.gob.gt

Guatemala Consulate General
8124 Georgia Ave.
Silver Spring, MD 20910
Phone: 240-485-5050; Fax: 240-485-5040
www.consmaryland.minex.gob.gt

Guatemala Consulate General
100 N. Stone Ave.
Ste. 704
Tucson, AZ 85701
Phone: 520-798-2217
www.minex.gob.gt

Guatemala Permanent Mission to the UN
57 Park Ave.
New York, NY 10016
Phone: 212-679-4760; Fax: 212-685-8741
www.guatemalaun.org

Guinea

Guinea Chamber of Commerce
1800 JFK Blvd.

Ste. 300
P.O. Box 77
Philadelphia, PA 19103
Phone: 215-248-1701
www.usgncc.org

Guinea Embassy
2112 Leroy Pl. N.W.
Washington, DC 20008
Phone: 202-483-9420; Fax: 202-483-8688
guineaembassyusa.com

Guinea Permanent Mission to the UN
201 E. 42nd St.
Ste. 2411
New York, NY 10017
Phone: 212-557-5001; Fax: 212-557-5009
www.un.int/papuanewguinea

Guyana

Guyana Consulate New York
308 W. 38th St.
New York, NY 10018
Phone: 212-947-5110; Fax: 646-915-0237
guyanaconsulatenewyork.com

Guyana Embassy
2490 Tracy Pl. N.W.
Washington, DC 20008
Phone: 202-265-6900; Fax: 202-232-1297
www.guyana.org

Guyana Permanent Mission to the UN
801 2nd Ave.
5th Fl.
New York, NY 10017
Phone: 212-573-5828; Fax: 212-573-6225
www.un.int/guyana

Haiti

Haiti Chamber of Commerce
1510 N.E. 162nd St.
North Miami Beach, FL 33162
Phone: 305-733-9066
www.haccof.com

Haiti Consulate General
2911 Piedmont Rd. N.E.
Ste. A
Atlanta, GA 30305
Phone: 404-228-5373; Fax: 404-748-1513
consulathaiti-atlanta.org

Haiti Consulate General
545 Boylston St.
Ste. 201
Boston, MA 02116
Phone: 617-266-3660; Fax: 617-778-6898
www.haiti.org

Haiti Consulate General
11 E. Adams St.

Ste. 1400
Chicago, IL 60603
Phone: 312-922-4004; Fax: 312-922-7122
www.haitianconsulate.org

Haiti Consulate General
259 S.W. 13th St.
Ste. 3
Miami, FL 33130
Phone: 305-859-2003; Fax: 305-854-7441
www.haiti.org

Haiti Consulate General
815 2nd Ave.
6th Fl.
New York, NY 10017
Phone: 212-697-9767; Fax: 212-681-6991
www.haiti.org

Haiti Consulate General
1616 E. Colonial Dr.
Orlando, FL 32803
Phone: 407-897-1262; Fax: 407-897-8163
www.haiti.org

Haiti Embassy
2311 Massachusetts Ave. N.W.
Washington, DC 20008
Phone: 202-332-4090; Fax: 202-745-7215
www.haiti.org

Haiti Permanent Mission to the UN
801 2nd Ave.
Ste. 600
New York, NY 10017
Phone: 212-370-4840; Fax: 212-661-8698
www.un.int/haiti

Holy *See* (Vatican City)

Holy See Apostolic Nunciature
3339 Massachusetts Ave. N.W.
Washington, DC 20008
Phone: 203-333-7121; Fax: 202-337-4036
apostolicnunciatureunitedstates.webstarts.com

Holy See Permanent Observer Mission to the UN
25 E. 39th St.
New York, NY 10016
Phone: 212-370-7885; Fax: 212-370-9622
www.holyseemission.org

Honduras

Honduras Chamber of Commerce
10570 N.W.27th St.102
Doral, FL 33172
haccw.org

Honduras Consulate General
2750 Buford Hwy N.E.
Atlanta, GA 30324
Phone: 770-645-8881; Fax: 404-844-4970
consuladohnatl.com

Honduras Consulate General
4439 W. Fullerton Ave.
Chicago, IL 60639
Phone: 773-342-8281; Fax: 773-342-8293
www.hondurasemb.org

Honduras Consulate General
7400 Harwin Dr.
Ste. 200
Houston, TX 77036
Phone: 713-785-5932; Fax: 713-785-5931
www.consuladohondurashouston.org

Honduras Consulate General
3550 Wilshire Blvd.
Ste. 320
Los Angeles, CA 90010
Phone: 213-995-6406; Fax: 213-383-9306
www.hondurasemb.org

Honduras Consulate General
7171 Coral Way
Ste. 311
Miami, FL 33155
Phone: 305-269-3131; Fax: 305-269-9445
www.hondurasemb.org

Honduras Consulate General
One Canal Pl.
365 Canal St.
Ste. 1580
New Orleans, LA 70130
Phone: 504-522-3118; Fax: 504-523-0544
www.hondurasemb.org

Honduras Consulate General
255-2 W. 36 St.
1st Level
New York, NY 10018
Phone: 212-714-9451; Fax: 212-714-9453
www.hondurasemb.org

Honduras Consulate General
4040 E. McDowell Rd.
Ste. 305
Phoenix, AZ 85008
Phone: 602-273-0173; Fax: 602-273-0547
www.hondurasemb.org

Honduras Consulate General
870 Market St.
Ste. 875
San Francisco, CA 94102
Phone: 415-392-0076; Fax: 415-392-6726
www.hondurasemb.org

Honduras Consulate
1014 M St. N.W.
Washington, DC 20001
Phone: 202-506-4995; Fax: 202-525-4004
www.hondurasemb.org

Honduras Embassy
3007 Tilden St. N.W.
Ste. 4M
Washington, DC 20008

Phone: 202-966-7702; Fax: 202-966-9751
www.hondurasemb.org

Honduras Permanent Mission to the UN
866 United Nations Plaza
Ste. 417
New York, NY 10017
Phone: 212-752-3370; Fax: 212-223-0498
www.un.int/honduras

Hong Kong

Hong Kong Tourism Board
5670 Wilshire Blvd.
Ste. 1230
Los Angeles, CA 90036
Phone: 323-938-4582; Fax: 323-938-4583
Toll-free: 800-282-4582
www.discoverhongkong.com

Hong Kong Tourism Board
370 Lexington Ave.
Ste. 1812
New York, NY 10017
Phone: 212-421-3382; Fax: 212-421-8428
Toll-free: 800-282-4582
www.discoverhongkong.com

Hungary

Hungarian National Tourist Office
223 E. 52nd st.
New York, NY 10022
Phone: 212-695-1221
www.gotohungary.com

Hungarian-American Chamber of Commerce in the US Inc
2000 Alameda de Las Pulgas
Ste 250
San Mateo, CA 94403
hacc.us

Hungary Consulate General
11766 Wilshire Blvd.
Ste. 410
Los Angeles, CA 90025
Phone: 310-473-9344; Fax: 310-479-6443
www.mfa.gov.hu

Hungary Consulate General
223 E. 52nd St.
New York, NY 10022
Phone: 212-752-0661; Fax: 212-755-5986
www.mfa.gov.hu

Hungary Consulate General
3910 Shoemaker St. N.W.
Washington, DC 20008
Phone: 202-362-6730; Fax: 202-686-6412

Hungary Embassy
3910 Shoemaker St. N.W.
Washington, DC 20008
Phone: 202-362-6730
washington.kormany.hu

Hungary Permanent Mission to the UN
227 E. 52nd St.
New York, NY 10022
Phone: 212-752-0209; Fax: 212-755-5395
www.mfa.gov.hu

Iceland

Icelandic Tourist Board
www.ferdamalastofa.is

Icelandic-American Chamber of Commerce
amis.is

Iceland Consulate General
800 3rd Ave.
36th Fl.
New York, NY 10022
Phone: 646-282-9360; Fax: 646-282-9369
www.iceland.is

Iceland Embassy
2900 K. St. N.W.
Ste. 509
Washington, DC 20007
Phone: 202-265-6653; Fax: 202-265-6656
www.iceland.is

Iceland Permanent Mission to the UN
800 3rd Ave.
36th Fl.
New York, NY 10022
Phone: 212-593-2700; Fax: 212-593-6269
www.iceland.is

India

India Tourist Office
3550 Wilshire Blvd.
Ste. 204
Los Angeles, CA 90010
Phone: 213-380-8855; Fax: 213-380-6111
tourism.nic.in

India Tourist Office
1270 Avenue of the Americas
Ste. 303
New York, NY 10020
Phone: 212-586-4901; Fax: 212-582-3274
tourism.nic.in

India Chamber of Commerce
12527 Central Ave. N.E.
Ste. 189
Minneapolis, MN 55434
Phone: 612-405-3050
www.indiachamber.org

India Consulate General
5549 Glenridge Dr N.E.
Atlanda, GA 30342
Phone: 404-963-5902; Fax: 678-935-7054
www.indianconsulateatlanta.org

India Consulate General
455 N. City Front Plaza Dr.
NBC Tower Bldg. Ste. 850
Chicago, IL 60611
Phone: 312-595-0405
www.indianconsulate.com

India Consulate General
4300 Scotland St.
Houston, TX 77007
Phone: 713-626-2148; Fax: 713-626-2450
www.cgihouston.org

India Consulate General
3 E. 64th St.
New York, NY 10065
Phone: 212-774-0600; Fax: 212-861-3788
www.indiacgny.org

India Consulate General
540 Arguello Blvd.
San Francisco, CA 94118
Phone: 415-668-0662; Fax: 415-668-9764
www.cgisf.org

India Consulate
2536 Massachusetts Ave. N.W.
Washington, DC 20008
Phone: 202-939-7000; Fax: 202-387-6946
www.indianembassy.org

India Embassy
2107 Massachusetts Ave. N.W.
Washington, DC 20008
Phone: 202-939-7000; Fax: 202-265-4351
www.indianembassy.org

India Permanent Mission to the UN
235 E. 43rd St.
New York, NY 10017
Phone: 212-490-9660; Fax: 212-490-9656
www.pminewyork.org

Indonesia

Indonesia Tourism Board
www.indonesia.travel

American-Indonesian Chamber of Commerce
521 5th Ave.
Ste. 1700
New York, NY 10175
Phone: 212-687-4505
www.aiccusa.org

Indonesia Consulate General
211 W. Wacker Dr.
8th Fl.
Chicago, IL 60606
Phone: 312-920-1880; Fax: 312-920-1881
indonesiachicago.info

Indonesia Consulate General
10900 Richmond Ave.
Houston, TX 77042

Phone: 713-785-1691; Fax: 713-780-9644
www.embassyofindonesia.org

Indonesia Consulate General
3457 Wilshire Blvd.
Los Angeles, CA 90010
Phone: 213-383-5126; Fax: 213-487-3971
www.kemlu.go.id/losangeles

Indonesia Consulate General
5 E. 68th St.
New York, NY 10065
Phone: 212-879-0600; Fax: 212-570-6206
www.indonesianewyork.org

Indonesia Consulate General
1111 Columbus Ave.
San Francisco, CA 94133
Phone: 415-474-9571; Fax: 415-441-4320
www.kemlu.go.id/sanfrancisco

Indonesia Consulate General
2020 Massachusetts Ave. N.W.
Washington, DC 20036
Phone: 202-775-5200
www.embassyofindonesia.org

Indonesia Embassy
2020 Massachusetts Ave. N.W.
Washington, DC 20036
Phone: 202-775-5200
www.embassyofindonesia.org

Indonesia Permanent Mission to the UN
325 E. 38th St.
New York, NY 10016
Phone: 212-972-8333; Fax: 212-972-9780
www.indonesiamission-ny.org

Iran

Iran Interests Section, Embassy of Pakistan
2209 Wisconsin Ave. N.W.
Washington, DC 20007
Phone: 202-965-4990; Fax: 202-965-1073
www.daftar.org/eng

Iran Permanent Mission to the UN
622 3rd Ave.
34th Fl.
New York, NY 10017
Phone: 212-687-2020; Fax: 212-867-7086
iran-un.org

Iraq

Iraq Consulate General
4500 Wilshire Blvd.
Los Angeles, CA 90010
Phone: 213-797-6060; Fax: 213-797-6100
www.iraqiembassy.us

Iraq Consulate General
16445 W. 12 Mile Rd.

Southfield, MI 48076
Phone: 248-423-1250; Fax: 248-423-1259
www.iraqiembassy.us

Iraq Embassy - Consulate Section
1801 P St. N.W.
Washington, DC 20036
Phone: 202-483-7500; Fax: 202-462-8815
www.iraqiembassy.us

Iraq Embassy
3421 Massachusetts Ave. N.W.
Washington, DC 20007
Phone: 202-742-1600; Fax: 202-333-1129
www.iraqiembassy.us

Iraq Permanent Mission to the UN
14 E. 79th St.
New York, NY 10075
Phone: 212-737-4433; Fax: 212-772-1794
iraqmission.us

Ireland

Irish Tourist Board
345 Park Ave.
New York, NY 10154
Phone: 212-418-0800; Fax: 212-371-9052
www.tourismireland.com

Ireland Chamber of Commerce in the US
219 S. St.
Ste. 203
New Providence, NJ 07974
Phone: 908-286-1300; Fax: 908-286-1200
www.iccusa.org

Ireland-US Council for Commerce & Industry
420 Lexington Ave.
Ste. 356
New York, NY 10170
Phone: 212-867-6268; Fax: 212-867-6834
www.irelanduscouncil.com

Ireland Consulate General
3414 Peachtree Rd
Ste. 260 Monarch Plaza
Atlanta, GA 30326
Phone: 404-554-4980; Fax: 678-235-2201
www.dfa.ie/irish-consulate/atlanta

Ireland Consulate General
515 Congress Ave.
Ste. 1720
Austin, TX 78701
Phone: 512-230-5791
www.dfa.ie/irish-consulate/austin

Ireland Consulate General
535 Boylston St.
Boston, MA 02116
Phone: 617-267-9330; Fax: 617-267-6375
www.dfa.ie/irish-consulate/boston

Ireland Consulate General
1 E. Wacker Dr.

Ste. 1820
Chicago, IL 60601
Phone: 312-337-2700; Fax: 312-836-1267
www.dfa.ie/irish-consulate/chicago

Ireland Consulate General
345 Park Ave.
17th Fl.
New York, NY 10154
Phone: 212-319-2555; Fax: 212-980-9475
www.dfa.ie/irish-consulate/newyork

Ireland Consulate General
100 Pine St.
Ste. 3350
San Francisco, CA 94111
Phone: 415-392-4214; Fax: 415-392-0885
www.dfa.ie/irish-consulate/sanfrancisco

Ireland Embassy
2234 Massachusetts Ave. N.W.
Washington, DC 20008
Phone: 202-462-3939
www.dfa.ie/irish-embassy/usa

Ireland Permanent Mission to the UN
885 2nd Ave.
19th Fl.
New York, NY 10017
Phone: 212-421-6934; Fax: 212-752-4726
www.dfa.ie/pmun/newyork

Israel

Israel Government Tourist Office
1349 W. Peachtree St. N.E.
Ste. 1799
Atlanta, GA 30309
Phone: 404-541-2770; Fax: 404-541-2775
www.goisrael.com

Israel Government Tourist Office
205 N. Michigan Ave.
Ste. 2520
Chicago, IL 60601
Phone: 312-803-7080; Fax: 312-803-7079
www.goisrael.com

Israel Government Tourist Office
6380 Wilshire Blvd.
Ste. 1718
Los Angeles, CA 90048
Phone: 323-658-7463; Fax: 323-658-6543
www.goisrael.com

Israel Government Tourist Office
800 2nd Ave.
New York, NY 10017
Phone: 212-499-5650; Fax: 212-499-5655
www.goisrael.com

America-Israel Chamber of Commerce - Chicago
203 N LaSalle St.
Ste. 2100
Chicago, IL 60601

Phone: 312-558-1346; Fax: 312-346-9603
www.americaisrael.org

Ohio-Israel Chamber of Commerce
P.O. Box 39007
Cleveland, OH 44139
Phone: 216-965-4474; Fax: 440-248-4888
www.israeltrade.org

California Israel Chamber of Commerce
20883 Stevens Creek Blvd.
Cupertino, CA 95014
Phone: 408-343-0917; Fax: 408-343-1197
www.israeltrade.org

Texas-Israel Chamber of Commerce Inc
12700 Park Central Dr.
Ste. 101
Dallas, TX 75251
Phone: 855-287-8339; Fax: 214-272-4814
texasisrael.org

American-Israel Chamber of Commerce & Industry of
Minnesota
P.O. Box 5644
Hopkins, MN 55343
www.aiccmn.org

Southern California-Israel Chamber of Commerce
6300 Wilshire Blvd.
Ste. 1010
Los Angeles, CA 90048
Phone: 310-410-2300; Fax: 775-255-6247
www.scicc.biz

America-Israel Chamber of Commerce
3 New York Plaza
10th Fl.
New York, NY 10004
www.israeltrade.org

Philadelphia-Israel Chamber of Commerce
200 S. Broad St.
Ste. 910G
Philadelphia, PA 19102
Phone: 215-703-3135
www.phillyisraelchamber.com

American-Israel Chamber of Commerce Southeast Region
400 Northridge Rd.
Ste. 250
Sandy Springs, GA 30350
Phone: 404-843-9426; Fax: 404-843-1416
www.aiccse.org

Israel Consulate General
1100 Spring St. N.W.
Ste. 440
Atlanta, GA 30309
Phone: 404-487-6500; Fax: 404-487-6555
embassies.gov.il

Israel Consulate General
20 Park Plaza
Boston, MA 02116
Phone: 617-535-0201; Fax: 617-535-0255
embassies.gov.il

Israel Consulate General
500 W. Madison
Ste. 3100
Chicago, IL 60661
Phone: 312-380-8800; Fax: 312-380-8855
embassies.gov.il

Israel Consulate General
24 Greenway Plaza
Ste. 1500
Houston, TX 77046
Phone: 832-301-3500; Fax: 713-627-0149
embassies.gov.il

Israel Consulate General
11766 Wilshire Blvd.
Ste. 1600
Los Angeles, CA 90025
Phone: 323-852-5500; Fax: 323-852-5566
embassies.gov.il

Israel Consulate General
100 N. Biscayne Blvd.
Ste. 1800
Miami, FL 33132
Phone: 305-925-9400; Fax: 305-925-9455
embassies.gov.il

Israel Consulate General in New York
800 2nd Ave.
New York, NY 10017
Phone: 212-499-5000
embassies.gov.il

Israel Consulate
1880 John F. Kennedy Blvd.
Ste. 1818
Philadelphia, PA 19103
Phone: 267-479-5800; Fax: 267-479-5855
embassies.gov.il

Israel Consulate General
456 Montgomery St.
Ste. 2100
San Francisco, CA 94104
Phone: 415-844-7500; Fax: 415-844-7555
embassies.gov.il

Israel Embassy
3514 International Dr. N.W.
Washington, DC 20008
Phone: 202-364-5500
www.israelemb.org

Israel Permanent Mission to the UN
800 2nd Ave.
New York, NY 10017
embassies.gov.il

Italy

Italian Government Tourist Board
10850 Wilshire Blvd.
Ste. 575
Los Angeles, CA 90024

Phone: 310-820-1898; Fax: 310-470-7788
www.italiantourism.com

Italian Government Tourist Board
686 Park Ave.
3rd Fl.
New York, NY 10065
Phone: 212-245-5618; Fax: 212-586-9249
www.italiantourism.com

Italian Government Tourist Board
3800 Division St.
Stone Park, IL 60165
Phone: 312-644-0996; Fax: 312-644-3019
www.italiantourism.com

Italian American Chamber of Commerce of Chicago
500 N. Michigan Ave.
Ste. 506
Chicago, IL 60611
Phone: 312-553-9137; Fax: 312-553-9142
www.iacc-chicago.com

Italian American Chamber of Commerce of Michigan
43843 Romeo Plank Rd.
Clinton Twp, MI 48038
Phone: 586-228-2576; Fax: 586-228-2579
www.iaccm.net

Italy-America Chamber of Commerce of Texas Inc
1800 W. Loop S.
Ste. 1120
Houston, TX 77027
Phone: 713-626-9303; Fax: 713-626-9309
www.iacctexas.com

Italy-America Chamber of Commerce West Inc
10537 Santa Monica Blvd.
Ste. 210
Los Angeles, CA 90025
Phone: 310-557-3017; Fax: 310-470-2200
iaccw.net

Italy-America Chamber of Commerce Southeast Inc
One Biscayne Tower
2 S. Biscayne Blvd.
Ste. 1880
Miami, FL 33131
Phone: 305-577-9868; Fax: 305-577-3956
www.iacc-miami.com

Italy-America Chamber of Commerce Inc
730 5th Ave.
Ste. 502
New York, NY 10019
Phone: 212-459-0044; Fax: 212-459-0090
www.italchamber.org

Italy Consulate General
600 Atlantic Ave.
17th Fl.
Boston, MA 02210
Phone: 617-722-9201; Fax: 617-722-9407
www.consboston.esteri.it

Italy Consulate General
500 N. Michigan Ave.

Ste. 1850
Chicago, IL 60611
Phone: 312-467-1550; Fax: 312-467-1335
www.conschicago.esteri.it

Italy Consulate General
4000 Ponce de Leon
Ste. 590
Coral Gables, FL 33146
Phone: 305-374-6322; Fax: 305-374-7945
www.consmiami.esteri.it

Italy Consulate
535 Griswold St.
Buhl Bldg.
Ste. 1840
Detroit, MI 48226
Phone: 313-963-8560; Fax: 313-963-8180
www.consdetroit.esteri.it

Italy Consulate General
1300 Post Oak Blvd.
Ste. 660
Houston, TX 77056
Phone: 713-850-7520; Fax: 713-850-9113
www.conshouston.esteri.it

Italy Consulate General
1900 Avenue of the Stars
Ste. 1250
Los Angeles, CA 90067
Phone: 310-820-0622; Fax: 310-820-0727
www.conslosangeles.esteri.it

Italy Consulate General
690 Park Ave.
New York, NY 10065
Phone: 212-737-9100; Fax: 212-249-4945
www.consnewyork.esteri.it

Italy Consulate General
150 S. Independence Mall W.
1026 Public Ledger Bldg.
Philadelphia, PA 19106
Phone: 215-592-7329; Fax: 215-592-9808
www.consfiladelfia.esteri.it

Italy Consulate General
2590 Webster St.
San Francisco, CA 94115
Phone: 415-292-9200; Fax: 415-931-7205
www.conssanfrancisco.esteri.it

Italy Embassy
3000 Whitehaven St. N.W.
Washington, DC 20008
Phone: 202-612-4400; Fax: 202-518-2154
www.ambwashingtondc.esteri.it

Italy Permanent Mission to the UN
885 Second Ave.
49th Fl.
New York, NY 10017
Phone: 212-486-9191; Fax: 212-486-1036
www.italyun.esteri.it

Ivory Coast. *See* Cote D'Ivoire

Jamaica

Jamaica Tourist Board
5201 Blue Lagoon Dr.
Ste. 670
Miami, FL 33126
Phone: 800-233-4582
www.visitjamaica.com

Jamaica Consulate General
25 S.E. 2nd Ave.
Ste. 609
Miami, FL 33131
Phone: 305-374-8431; Fax: 305-577-4970
www.jamaicacgmiami.org

Jamaica Consulate General
767 Third Ave.
2nd & 3rd Fl.
New York, NY 10017
Phone: 212-935-9000; Fax: 212-935-7507
www.congenjamaica-ny.org

Jamaica Embassy
1520 New Hampshire Ave. N.W.
Washington, DC 20036
Phone: 202-452-0660; Fax: 202-452-0036
www.embassyofjamaica.org

Jamaica Permanent Mission to the UN
767 3rd Ave.
9th Fl.
New York, NY 10017
Phone: 212-935-7509; Fax: 212-935-7607
www.un.int/jamaica

Japan

Japan National Tourist Organization
340 E. 2nd St.
Little Tokyo Plaza
Ste. 302
Los Angeles, CA 90012
Phone: 213-623-1952; Fax: 213-623-6301
www.jnto.go.jp

Japan National Tourist Organization
One Grand Central Pl.
60 E. 42nd St.
Ste. 448
New York, NY 10165
Phone: 212-757-5640; Fax: 212-307-6754
www.jnto.go.jp

Japanese Chamber of Commerce & Industry of Chicago
541 N. Fairbanks Ct.
Ste. 2050
Chicago, IL 60611
Phone: 312-245-8344; Fax: 312-245-8355
www.jccc-chi.org

Japanese Chamber of Commerce & Industry of Hawaii
714 Kanoelehua Ave.

Hilo, HI 96720
Phone: 808-934-0177; Fax: 808-934-0178
www.jccih.org

Japanese Chamber of Commerce
244 S. San Pedro St.
Ste. 410
Los Angeles, CA 90012
Phone: 213-626-3067; Fax: 213-626-3070
www.jccsc.com

Japanese Chamber of Commerce & Industry of New York
Inc
145 W. 57th St.
New York, NY 10019
Phone: 212-246-8001; Fax: 212-246-8002
www.jcciny.org

Japanese Chamber of Commerce of Northern California
1875 S. Grant St.
Ste. 760
San Mateo, CA 94402
Phone: 650-522-8500; Fax: 650-522-8300
www.jccnc.org

Japan Consulate General
3601 C St.
Ste. 1300
Anchorage, AK 99503
Phone: 907-562-8424; Fax: 907-562-8434
www.anchorage.us.emb-japan.go.jp

Japan Consulate General
3438 Peachtree Rd.
Ste. 850
Atlanta, GA 30326
Phone: 404-240-4300; Fax: 404-240-4311
www.atlanta.us.emb-japan.go.jp

Japan Consulate General
600 Atlantic Ave.
22nd Fl.
Boston, MA 02210
Phone: 617-973-9772; Fax: 617-542-1329
www.boston.us.emb-japan.go.jp

Japan Consulate General
737 N Michigan Ave.
Ste. 1100
Chicago, IL 60611
Phone: 312-280-0400; Fax: 312-280-9568
www.chicago.us.emb-japan.go.jp

Japan Consulate General
1225 17th St.
Ste. 3000
Denver, CO 80202
Phone: 303-534-1151; Fax: 303-534-3393
www.denver.us.emb-japan.go.jp

Japan Consulate General
400 Renaissance Ctr.
Ste. 1600
Detroit, MI 48243
Phone: 313-567-0120; Fax: 313-567-0274
www.detroit.us.emb-japan.go.jp

Japan Consulate General
1742 Nuuanu Ave.
Honolulu, HI 96817
Phone: 808-543-3111; Fax: 808-543-3170
www.honolulu.us.emb-japan.go.jp

Japan Consulate General
900 Fannin St.
Ste 3000
Houston, TX 77010
Phone: 713-652-2977; Fax: 713-651-7822
www.houston.us.emb-japan.go.jp

Japan Consulate General
350 S Grand Ave.
Ste. 1700
Los Angeles, CA 90071
Phone: 213-617-6700; Fax: 213-617-6727
www.la.us.emb-japan.go.jp

Japan Consulate General
80 SW 8th St.
Ste. 3200
Miami, FL 33130
Phone: 305-530-9090; Fax: 305-530-0950
www.miami.us.emb-japan.go.jp

Japan Consulate General
1801 West End Ave.
Ste. 900
Nashville, TN 37203
Phone: 615-340-4300; Fax: 615-340-4311
www.nashville.us.emb-japan.go.jp/en

Japan Consulate General
299 Park Ave.
18th Fl.
New York, NY 10171
Phone: 212-371-8222; Fax: 212-371-1294
www.ny.us.emb-japan.go.jp

Japan Consulate General
Wells Fargo Ctr.
1300 S.W. 5th Ave.
Ste 2700
Portland, OR 97201
Phone: 503-221-1811; Fax: 503-224-8936
www.portland.us.emb-japan.go.jp

Japan Consulate General
275 Battery St.
Ste. 2100
San Francisco, CA 94111
Phone: 415-780-6000; Fax: 415-767-4200
www.sf.us.emb-japan.go.jp

Japan Consulate General
601 Union St.
Ste. 500
Seattle, WA 98101
Phone: 206-682-9107; Fax: 206-624-9097
www.seattle.us.emb-japan.go.jp

Japan Embassy
2520 Massachusetts Ave. N.W.
Washington, DC 20008

Phone: 202-238-6700; Fax: 202-328-2187
www.us.emb-japan.go.jp/english/html

Japan Permanent Mission to the UN
866 United Nations Plaza
2nd Fl.
New York, NY 10017
Phone: 212-223-4300
www.un.emb-japan.go.jp

Jordan

Jordan Tourism Board
1307 Dolley Madison Blvd.
Ste. 2A
McLean, VA 22101
Phone: 703-243-7404; Fax: 703-243-7406
Toll-free: 877-733-5673
www.visitjordan.com

Jordan Embassy
3504 International Dr. N.W.
Washington, DC 20008
Phone: 202-966-2664; Fax: 202-966-3110
www.jordanembassyus.org

Jordan Permanent Mission to the UN
866 Second Ave.
4th Fl.
New York, NY 10017
Phone: 212-832-9553
www.un.org

Kazakhstan

Kazakhstan Tourism Board
visitkazakhstan.kz

Kazakhstan Chamber of Commerce
C/O BMF 45 Rockefeller Pz
Ste. 2000
New York, NY 10111
Phone: 646-461-8105; Fax: 508-448-8105
kazcham.com

Kazakhstan Consulate
535 5th Ave.
19th Fl.
New York, NY 10017
Phone: 646-370-6331; Fax: 646-370-6334
www.kazconsulny.org

Kazakhstan Embassy
1401 16th St. N.W.
Washington, DC 20036
Phone: 202-232-5488
www.kazakhembus.com

Kazakhstan Permanent Mission to the UN
305 E. 47th St.
3rd Fl.
New York, NY 10017
Phone: 212-230-1900; Fax: 212-230-1172
www.kazakhstanun.org

Kenya

Kenya Tourism Board
6033 W. Century Blvd.
Ste. 900
Los Angeles, CA 90045
Phone: 310-649-7718; Fax: 310-649-7713
www.magicalkenya.com

Kenya Embassy
2249 R St. N.W.
Washington, DC 20008
Phone: 202-387-6101; Fax: 202-462-3829
www.kenyaembassy.com

Kenya Permanent Mission to the UN
866 United Nations Plaza
Rm. 304
New York, NY 10017
Phone: 212-421-4741
www.kenyaun.org

Korea, North. *See* North Korea (Democratic People's Republic of Korea

Korea, South. *See* South Korea (Republic of Korea)

Kuwait

Kuwait Embassy
2940 Tilden St. N.W.
Washington, DC 20008
Phone: 202-966-0702; Fax: 202-966-0517
www.kuwaitembassy.us

Kuwait Permanent Mission to the UN
321 E. 44th St.
New York, NY 10017
Phone: 212-973-4300; Fax: 212-370-1733
www.kuwaitmission.com

Kyrgyzstan

Kyrgyzstan Embassy
2360 Massachusetts Ave. N.W.
Washington, DC 20008
Phone: 202-449-9822; Fax: 202-386-7550
www.kgembassy.org

Kyrgyzstan Permanent Mission to the UN
866 United Nations Plaza
Ste. 477
New York, NY 10017
Phone: 212-486-4214; Fax: 212-486-5259
www.un.int/kyrgyzstan

Laos

Lao People's Democratic Republic Embassy
2222 S. St. N.W.
Washington, DC 20008
Phone: 202-332-6416; Fax: 202-332-4923
www.laoembassy.com

Lao People's Democratic Republic Permanent Mission to the UN
317 E. 51st St.
New York, NY 10022
Phone: 212-832-2734; Fax: 212-750-0039
www.un.int/lao

Latvia

Latvia Embassy
2306 Massachusetts Ave. N.W.
Washington, DC 20008
Phone: 202-328-2840; Fax: 202-328-2860
www.mfa.gov.lv

Latvia Permanent Mission to the UN
333 E. 50th St.
New York, NY 10022
Phone: 212-838-8877
www.mfa.gov.lv/en/newyork

Lebanon

Lebanon Ministry of Tourism
www.destinationlebanon.gov.lb/en

Lebanon Consulate General
3031 W. Grand Blvd.
Ste. 560
Detroit, MI 48202
Phone: 313-758-0753; Fax: 313-758-0756
www.lebanonconsulategdetroit.org

Lebanon Consulate General
2400 Augusta Dr.
Ste. 308
Houston, TX 77057
Phone: 713-268-1640; Fax: 713-268-1641
www.ccohouston.org

Lebanon Consulate General
660 S. Figueroa St.
Ste. 1050
Los Angeles, CA 90017
Phone: 213-243-0999; Fax: 213-612-5070
www.lebanonconsulatela.org

Lebanon Consulate General
9 E. 76th St.
New York, NY 10021
Phone: 212-744-7905; Fax: 212-794-1510
www.lebconsny.org

Lebanon Embassy
2560 28th St. N.W.
Washington, DC 20008
Phone: 202-939-6300; Fax: 202-939-6324
www.lebanonembassyus.org

Lebanon Permanent Mission to the UN
866 United Nations Plaza

Rm. 531-533
New York, NY 10017
Phone: 212-355-5460; Fax: 212-838-2819
www.un.int/lebanon

Lesotho

Lesotho Embassy
2511 Massachusetts Ave. N.W.
Washington, DC 20008
Phone: 202-797-5533; Fax: 202-234-6815
www.lesothoemb-usa.gov.ls

Lesotho Permanent Mission to the UN
204 E. 39th St.
New York, NY 10016
Phone: 212-661-1690
www.un.int/lesotho

Liberia

Liberia Consulate General
866 United Nations Plaza
Ste. 249
New York, NY 10017
Phone: 212-687-1025; Fax: 212-599-3189
www.liberianconsulate-ny.com

Liberia Embassy
5201 16th St. N.W.
Washington, DC 20011
Phone: 202-723-0437; Fax: 202-723-0436
www.embassyofliberia.org

Liberia Permanent Mission to the UN
866 United Nations Plaza
Ste. 480
New York, NY 10017
Phone: 212-687-1033; Fax: 212-687-1035
www.liberia-un.org

Libya

Libya Embassy
2600 Virginia Ave. N.W.
Ste. 705
Washington, DC 20037
Phone: 202-944-9601; Fax: 202-944-9606
embassyoflibyadc.org/ar

Libyan Arab Jamahiriya Permanent Mission to the UN
309-315 E. 48th St.
New York, NY 10017
Phone: 212-752-5775; Fax: 212-593-4787
www.libyanmission-un.org

Liechtenstein

Liechtenstein Embassy
2900 K St. N.W.
Ste. 602-B
Washington, DC 20007

Phone: 202-331-0590; Fax: 202-331-3221
www.liechtensteinusa.org

Liechtenstein Permanent Mission to the UN
633 3rd Ave.
27th Fl.
New York, NY 10017
Phone: 212-599-0220
www.un.org

Lithuania

Lithuania Dept of Tourism
www.lithuania.travel

Lithuania Consulate General
211 E. Ontario
Ste. 1500
Chicago, IL 60611
Phone: 312-397-0382; Fax: 312-397-0385
chicago.mfa.lt/cikaga/en

Lithuania Consulate General
420 Fifth Ave.
3rd Fl.
New York, NY 10018
Phone: 212-354-7840; Fax: 212-354-7911
ny.mfa.lt/niujorkas/en

Lithuania Consulate General
2622 16th St. N.W.
Washington, DC 20009
Phone: 202-328-5860; Fax: 202-328-0466
www.ltembassyus.org

Lithuania Embassy
2622 16th St. N.W.
Washington, DC 20009
Phone: 202-234-5860; Fax: 202-328-0466
usa.mfa.lt/usa/en

Lithuania Permanent Mission to the UN
708 3rd Ave.
10th Fl.
New York, NY 10017
Phone: 212-983-9474; Fax: 212-983-9473
mission-un-ny.mfa.lt/missionny/en

Luxembourg

Luxembourg National Tourist Office
www.visitluxembourg.com/en

Luxembourg-American Chamber of Commerce
17 Beekman Pl.
New York, NY 10022
Phone: 212-888-6701; Fax: 212-935-5896
laccnyc.org

Luxembourg Consulate General
17 Beekman Pl.
New York, NY 10022
Phone: 212-888-6664; Fax: 212-888-6116
newyork-cg.mae.lu/en

Luxembourg Consulate General
1 Sansome St.
Ste. 830
San Francisco, CA 94104
Phone: 415-788-0816; Fax: 415-788-0985
sanfrancisco.mae.lu/en

Luxembourg Embassy
2200 Massachusetts Ave. N.W.
Washington, DC 20008
Phone: 202-265-4171; Fax: 202-328-8270
washington.mae.lu/en

Luxembourg Permanent Mission to the UN
17 Beekman Pl.
New York, NY 10022
Phone: 212-935-3589; Fax: 212-935-5896
newyork-un.mae.lu/en

Macau

Macau Government Tourist Office
6033 W. Century Blvd.
Ste. 900
Los Angeles, CA 90045
Phone: 310-545-3464; Fax: 310-545-4221
Toll-free: 866-656-2228
en.macautourism.gov.mo

Macau Government Tourist Office
20 W. 22nd St.
Ste. 603
New York, NY 10010
Phone: 646-227-0690; Fax: 646-366-8170
en.macautourism.gov.mo

Macedonia

Macedonia Tourism
www.tourismmacedonia.gov.mk/en

Macedonia Consulate General
121 W. Wacker Dr.
Ste. 2036
Chicago, IL 60601
Phone: 312-419-8020; Fax: 312-419-8114
www.mfa.gov.mk

Macedonia Consulate General
866 United Nations Plaza
Ste. 522
New York, NY 10017
Phone: 646-524-5750; Fax: 646-524-5752
www.mfa.gov.mk

Macedonia Consulate General
2000 Town Center
Ste. 1130
Southfield, MI 48075
Phone: 248-354-5537; Fax: 248-354-5356
www.mfa.gov.mk

Macedonia Embassy
2129 Wyoming Ave. N.W.

Washington, DC 20008
Phone: 202-667-0501; Fax: 202-667-2131
www.mfa.gov.mk

Macedonia Permanent Mission to the UN
866 United Nations Plaza
Ste. 517
New York, NY 10017
Phone: 212-308-8504; Fax: 212-308-8724
www.mfa.gov.mk

Madagascar

Madagascar Embassy
2374 Massachusetts Ave. N.W.
Washington, DC 20008
Phone: 202-265-5525; Fax: 202-265-3034
www.madagascar-embassy.org

Madagascar Permanent Mission to the UN
820 2nd Ave.
Ste. 800
New York, NY 10017
Phone: 212-986-9491; Fax: 212-986-6271
www.un.int/madagascar

Malawi

Malawi Embassy
2408 Massachusetts Ave. N.W.
Washington, DC 20008
Phone: 202-721-0270; Fax: 202-721-0288
www.malawiembassy-dc.org

Malawi Permanent Mission to the UN
866 United Nations Plaza
Ste. 486
New York, NY 10017
Phone: 212-317-8738; Fax: 212-317-8729
www.un.int/malawi

Malaysia

Malaysia Tourism
818 W. 7th St.
Ste. 970
Los Angeles, CA 90017
Phone: 213-689-9702; Fax: 213-689-1530
Toll-free: 800-336-6842
www.tourismmalaysiausa.com

Malaysia Tourism
120 E. 56th St.
15th Fl.
New York, NY 10022
Phone: 212-754-1113; Fax: 212-754-1116
Toll-free: 800-558-6787
www.tourismmalaysiausa.com

Malaysia Consulate General
550 S. Hope St.
Ste. 400
Los Angeles, CA 90071

Phone: 213-892-1238; Fax: 213-892-9031
www.kln.gov.my/web/usa_los-angeles

Malaysia Consulate General
313 E. 43rd St.
New York, NY 10017
Phone: 212-490-2722; Fax: 212-490-2049
www.kln.gov.my/web/usa_new-york

Malaysia Embassy
3516 International Ct. N.W.
Washington, DC 20008
Phone: 202-572-9700; Fax: 202-572-9882
www.kln.gov.my/web/usa_washington/home

Malaysia Permanent Mission to the UN
313 E. 43rd St.
New York, NY 10017
Phone: 212-986-6310; Fax: 212-490-8576
www.un.int/malaysia

Maldives

Maldives Permanent Mission to the UN
800 2nd Ave.
Ste. 400-E
New York, NY 10017
Phone: 212-599-6194; Fax: 212-661-6405
www.foreign.gov.mv

Mali

Mali Embassy
2130 R St. N.W.
Washington, DC 20008
Phone: 202-332-2249; Fax: 202-332-6603
www.maliembassy.us

Mali Permanent Mission to the UN
111 E 69th St.
New York, NY 10021
Phone: 212-737-4150; Fax: 212-472-3778
www.un.int/mali

Malta

Malta Tourism
www.visitmalta.com

Malta Consulate
56 Lantern Rd.
Belmont, MA 02478
Phone: 617-484-1731; Fax: 617-484-4444
consulatewashington.tripod.com

Malta Embassy
20017 Connecticut Ave. N.W.
Washington, DC 20008
Phone: 202-462-3611; Fax: 202-387-5470
consulatewashington.tripod.com

Malta Permanent Mission to the UN
249 E. 35th St.

New York, NY 10016
Phone: 212-725-2345; Fax: 212-779-7097
www.un.int/malta

Marshall Islands

Marshall Islands Consulate General
1888 Lusitana St.
Ste. 301
Honolulu, HI 96813
Phone: 808-545-7767; Fax: 808-545-7211
www.un.int/marshallislands/marshallislands/embassies

Marshall Islands Embassy
2433 Massachusetts Ave. N.W.
Washington, DC 20008
Phone: 202-234-5414; Fax: 202-232-3236
www.rmiembassyus.org

Marshall Islands Permanent Mission to the UN
800 2nd Ave.
18th Fl.
New York, NY 10017
Phone: 212-983-3040; Fax: 212-983-3202
www.un.int/marshallislands

Martinique

Martinique Promotion Bureau
www.martinique.org

Mauritania

Mauritius Embassy
1709 N. St. N.W.
Washington, DC 20036
Phone: 202-244-1491; Fax: 202-966-0983
www.maurinet.com/embasydc.html

Mauritania Permanent Mission to the UN
116 E. 38th St.
New York, NY 10016
Phone: 212-252-0113; Fax: 212-252-0175
www.un.int/mauritania

Mauritius

Mauritius Permanent Mission to the UN
211 E. 43rd St., 15th Fl.
Ste. 1502
New York, NY 10017
Phone: 212-949-0190; Fax: 212-697-3829
www.un.org

Micronesia

Micronesia Federated States of Consulate
3049 Ualena St.
Ste. 910
Honolulu, HI 96819
Phone: 808-836-4775; Fax: 808-836-6896
www.fsmembassydc.org

Micronesia Federated States of Embassy
1725 N. St. N.W.
Washington, DC 20036
Phone: 202-223-4383; Fax: 202-223-4391
www.fsmembassydc.org

Micronesia Federated States of Permanent Mission to the UN
300 E. 42nd St.
Ste. 1600
New York, NY 10017
Phone: 212-697-8370; Fax: 212-697-8295
www.fsmgov.org/fsmun

Moldova

Moldova Embassy
2101 S. St. N.W.
Washington, DC 20008
Phone: 202-667-1130; Fax: 202-667-1204
www.sua.mfa.md

Moldova Permanent Mission to the UN
35 E. 29th St.
New York, NY 10016
Phone: 212-447-1867; Fax: 212-447-4067
www.onu.mfa.md

Monaco

Monaco Government Tourist Office
565 5th Ave.
23rd Fl.
New York, NY 10017
Phone: 212-286-3330; Fax: 212-286-9890
Toll-free: 800-753-9696
www.visitmonaco.com

Monaco Consulate
565 Fifth Ave.
23rd Fl.
New York, NY 10017
Phone: 212-286-0500; Fax: 212-286-1574
www.monaco-consulate.com

Monaco Embassy
3400 International Dr. N.W.
Ste. 2K - 100
Washington, DC 20008
Phone: 202-234-1530; Fax: 202-244-7656
monacodc.org

Monaco Permanent Mission to the UN
866 United Nations Plaza
Ste. 520
New York, NY 10017
Phone: 212-832-0721; Fax: 212-832-5358
www.monaco-un.org

Mongolia

Mongolia Embassy
2833 M St. N.W.

Washington, DC 20007
Phone: 202-333-7117; Fax: 202-298-9227
www.mongolianembassy.us

Mongolia Permanent Mission to the UN
6 E. 77th St.
New York, NY 10075
Phone: 212-861-9460; Fax: 212-861-9464
www.un.int/mongolia

Montenegro

Montenegro National Tourism
www.montenegro.travel/en

Montenegro Consulate General
801 2nd Ave.
7th Fl.
New York, NY 10022
Phone: 212-661-5400; Fax: 212-661-5466
www.mvpei.gov.me/en

Montenegro Embassy
1610 New Hampshire Ave. N.W.
Washington, DC 20009
Phone: 202-234-6108; Fax: 202-234-6108
www.mvpei.gov.me/en

Montenegro Permanent Mission to the UN
801 Second Ave.
7th Fl.
New York, NY 10017
Phone: 212-661-3700; Fax: 212-661-3755
www.un.org/Montenegro

Morocco

Moroccan National Tourist Office
104 W. 40th St.
Ste. 1820
New York, NY 10018
Phone: 212-221-1583; Fax: 212-221-1887
www.visitmorocco.com

Morocco Consulate General
10 E. 40th St.
New York, NY 10016
Phone: 212-758-2625; Fax: 646-395-8077
www.moroccanconsulate.com

Morocco Embassy
1601 21st St. N.W.
Washington, DC 20009
Phone: 202-462-7980; Fax: 202-462-7643
www.embassyofmorocco.us

Morocco Permanent Mission to the UN
866 2nd Ave.
6th Fl.
New York, NY 10017
Phone: 212-421-1580; Fax: 212-980-1512
www.un.int/morocco

Mozambique

Mozambique Embassy
1525 New Hampshire Ave. N.W.
Washington, DC 20036
Phone: 202-293-7146; Fax: 202-835-0245
www.embamoc-usa.org

Mozambique Permanent Mission to the UN
420 E. 50th St.
New York, NY 10022
Phone: 212-644-6800; Fax: 212-644-5972
www.un.int/mozambique

Myanmar (Burma)

Myanmar Chamber of Commerce
96 Bowery
5th Fl.
New York, NY 10002
Phone: 212-966-6822; Fax: 212-966-6837
www.myanmaruschamber.org

Myanmar Chamber of Commerce
991 Mission St.
San Francisco, CA 94103
Phone: 415-536-5800
usamyanmar.com

Myanmar Consulate General
10 E. 77th St.
New York, NY 10075
Phone: 212-744-1279; Fax: 212-744-1290
www.mmnewyork.org

Myanmar Embassy
2300 S. St. N.W.
Washington, DC 20008
Phone: 202-332-3344; Fax: 202-332-4351
www.mewashingtondc.com

Myanmar Permanent Mission to the UN
10 E. 77th St.
New York, NY 10075
Phone: 212-744-1271; Fax: 212-744-1290
www.mmnewyork.org

Namibia

Namibia Embassy
1605 New Hampshire Ave. N.W.
Washington, DC 20009
Phone: 202-986-0540; Fax: 202-986-0443
www.namibianembassyusa.org

Namibia Permanent Mission to the UN
360 Lexington Ave.
Ste. 1502
New York, NY 10017
Phone: 212-685-2003; Fax: 212-685-1561
www.un.int/namibia

Nauru

Nauru Permanent Mission to the UN

801 Second Ave.
3rd Fl.
New York, NY 10017
Phone: 212-937-0074; Fax: 212-937-0079
www.un.int/nauru

Nepal

Nepal Tourism Board
welcomenepal.com

Nepal Consulate General
820 2nd Ave.
Ste. 17B
New York, NY 10017
Phone: 212-370-3988; Fax: 212-953-2038
www.nepalembassyusa.org

Nepal Embassy
2131 Leroy Pl. N.W.
Washington, DC 20008
Phone: 202-667-4550; Fax: 202-667-5534
www.nepalembassyusa.org

Nepal Permanent Mission to the UN
820 2nd Ave.
Ste. 17B
New York, NY 10017
Phone: 212-370-3988; Fax: 212-953-2038
www.un.int/nepal

Netherlands

Netherlands Board of Tourism & Conventions
215 Park Ave S
Ste 2005
New York, NY 10003
Phone: 212-370-7360; Fax: 212-370-9507
Toll-free: 888-464-6552
www.holland.com

Netherlands Amercian Chamber of Commerce in Texas
410 Pierce St.
Ste. 303
Houston, TX 77002
Phone: 281-895-0038; Fax: 713-895-0039
www.nacctexas.org

Netherlands American Chamber of Commerce, Great Lakes
P.O. Box 691
Hudson, OH 44236
Phone: 330-208-5866
naccgl.org

Netherlands Chamber of Commerce in the US Inc
267 5th Ave.
Ste. 910
New York, NY 10016
Phone: 212-265-6460; Fax: 212-265-6402
www.netherlands.org

Netherlands America Chamber of Commerce for the Washington Metro area
1717 K St. N.W.

Ste. 900
Washington, DC 20006
Phone: 202-780-9422
www.naccwm.org

Netherlands Consulate General
303 E Wacker Dr.
Ste. 2600
Chicago, IL 60601
Phone: 312-856-0110; Fax: 312-856-9218
Toll-free: 877-388-2443
www.the-netherlands.org

Netherlands Consulate General
10777 Westheimer Rd.
Ste. 1055
Houston, TX 77042
Phone: 713-785-2200; Fax: 713-783-1386
www.the-netherlands.org

Netherlands Consulate General
11766 Wilshire Blvd.
Ste. 1150
Los Angeles, CA 90025
Phone: 310-268-1598; Fax: 310-312-0989
www.the-netherlands.org

Netherlands Consulate General
701 Brickell Ave.
Ste. 500
Miami, FL 33131
Phone: 786-866-0480; Fax: 786-866-0497
www.the-netherlands.org

Netherlands Consulate General
666 3rd Ave.
19th Fl.
New York, NY 10017
Phone: 212-246-1429; Fax: 212-333-3603
www.the-netherlands.org

Netherlands Consulate General
120 Kearny St.
Ste. 3100
San Francisco, CA 94104
Phone: 877-388-2443; Fax: 415-291-2049
www.the-netherlands.org

Netherlands Embassy
4200 Linnean Ave. N.W.
Washington, DC 20008
Phone: 202-244-5300; Fax: 202-362-3430
www.the-netherlands.org

Netherlands Permanent Mission to the UN
666 Third Ave.
19th Fl.
Between 42nd and 43rd St
New York, NY 10017
Phone: 212-519-9500
www.netherlandsmission.org

New Zealand

New Zealand Tourism Board
501 Santa Monica Blvd.

Ste. 300
Santa Monica, CA 90401
Phone: 310-395-7480; Fax: 310-395-5453
www.tourismnewzealand.com

Australian New Zealand American Chamber of Commerce
Midwest
P.O. Box 64308
Chicago, IL 60664
Phone: 847-615-9718
www.usa.embassy.gov.au

Australian New Zealand American Chamber of Commerce
28150 N. Alma School Pkwy
Ste. 103-250
Scottsdale, AZ 85262
Phone: 480-784-7377
www.usa.embassy.gov.au

Australian New Zealand American Association
P.O. Box 65010
St Paul, MN 55165
Phone: 763-442-1095
www.usa.embassy.gov.au

MidAtlantic Australian New Zealand American Chamber of
Commerce
1576 Stapler Dr.
Yardley, PA 19067
Phone: 215-321-1662; Fax: 215-321-1666
www.usa.embassy.gov.au

New Zealand Consulate General
222 E. 41st St.
Ste. 2510
New York, NY 10017
Phone: 212-832-4038; Fax: 212-832-7602
www.nzembassy.com

New Zealand Consulate General
2425 Olympic Blvd.
Ste. 600-E
Santa Monica, CA 90404
Phone: 310-566-6555; Fax: 310-566-6556
www.nzembassy.com

New Zealand Embassy
37 Observatory Cir. N.W.
Washington, DC 20008
Phone: 202-328-4800; Fax: 202-667-5227
www.nzembassy.com

New Zealand Permanent Mission to the UN
600 Third Ave.
14th Fl.
New York, NY 10016
Phone: 212-826-1960; Fax: 212-758-0827
www.nzembassy.com

Nicaragua

Nicaragua Tourism Board
visitnicaragua.us

Nicaraguan-American Chamber of Commerce
8370 W. Flagler St.

Ste. 110
Miami, FL 33144
Phone: 786-253-7343
www.naccflorida.com

Nicaragua Consulate General
6300 Hillcrof
Ste. 250
Houston, TX 77081
Phone: 713-272-9628; Fax: 713-272-7131
www.consuladodenicaragua.com

Nicaragua Consulate General
3550 Wilshire Blvd.
Ste. 200
Los Angeles, CA 90010
Phone: 213-252-1170; Fax: 213-252-1177
www.consuladodenicaragua.com

Nicaragua Consulate General
8532 S.W. 8th St.
Ste. 270
Miami, FL 33144
Phone: 305-265-1415; Fax: 305-265-1780
www.consuladodenicaragua.com

Nicaragua Consulate General
820 2nd Ave.
8th Fl. Ste. 802
New York, NY 10017
Phone: 212-983-1981; Fax: 212-989-5528
www.consuladodenicaragua.com

Nicaragua Consulate General
870 Market St.
Ste. 1050
San Francisco, CA 94102
Phone: 415-765-6825; Fax: 415-765-6826
www.consuladodenicaragua.com

Nicaragua Consulate General
1627 New Hampshire Ave. N.W.
Washington, DC 20009
Phone: 202-939-6531; Fax: 202-939-6574
www.consuladodenicaragua.com

Nicaragua Embassy
1627 New Hampshire Ave. N.W.
Washington, DC 20009
Phone: 202-939-6570
www.consuladodenicaragua.com

Nicaragua Permanent Mission to the UN
820 2nd Ave.
8th Fl.
New York, NY 10017
Phone: 212-490-7997; Fax: 212-286-0815
www.un.int/nicaragua

Niger

Niger Embassy
2204 R St. N.W.
Washington, DC 20008
Phone: 202-483-4224; Fax: 202-483-3169
www.embassyofniger.org

Niger Permanent Mission to the UN
417 E. 50th St.
New York, NY 10022
Phone: 212-421-3260; Fax: 212-753-6931
www.un.int/niger

Nigeria

Nigeria Tourism Board
tourism.gov.ng

Nigerian Chamber of Commerce USA
433 N. Camden Dr.
4th Fl.
Beverly Hills, CA 90210
www.ncocusa.com

Nigeria USA Chamber of Commerce
526 Superior Ave.
Ste. 260
Cleveland, OH 44114
Phone: 216-344-0555
www.nusacc.us

American Nigerian International Chamber of Commerce
5855 Jimmy Carter Blvd.
Ste. 190
Norcross, GA 30071
Phone: 404-551-2878; Fax: 679-893-0942
www.anicc-usa.org

Nigeria Consulate General
8060 Roswell Rd.
Atlanta, GA 30350
www.nigeria-consulate-atl.org

Nigeria Consulate General
828 2nd Ave.
New York, NY 10017
Phone: 212-808-0301; Fax: 212-687-1476
www.nigeriahouse.com

Nigeria Embassy
3519 International Ct. N.W.
Washington, DC 20008
Phone: 202-986-8400; Fax: 202-362-6541
www.nigeriaembassyusa.org

Nigeria Permanent Mission to the UN
828 2nd Ave.
New York, NY 10017
Phone: 212-953-9130; Fax: 212-697-1970
redesign.nigeriaunmission.org

North Korea (Democratic People's Republic of Korea)

Korea Permanent Mission to the UN
820 Second Ave.
13th Fl.
New York, NY 10017
Phone: 212-972-3105
www.un.org

Norway

Norway Tourism
www.visitnorway.com

Norwegian-American Chamber of Commerce Southern
California Chapter
3956 Lost Springs Dr.
Calabasas, CA 91301
Phone: 213-761-7090
www.naccsocal.org

Norwegian-American Chamber of Commerce Northern
Chicago
125 South Wacker Dr.
Ste. 1825
Chicago, IL 60606
Phone: 312-377-5050
www.naccchicago.org

Norwegian-American Chamber of Commerce Southwest
Chapter
3410 W. Dallas St.
Ste. 200
Houston, TX 77019
Phone: 281-537-6879; Fax: 281-587-9284
nacchouston.org

Norwegian-American Chamber of Commerce Philadelphia
Chapter Inc
P.O. Box 97
Malvern, PA 19355
Phone: 215-710-0632
www.naccchicago.org

Norwegian-American Chamber of Commerce Florida
P.O.Box 10098
Miami, FL 33101
Phone: 954-850-0474
www.naccchicago.org

Norwegian-American Chamber of Commerce Upper Mid-
west Chapter
P.O. Box 583782
Minneapolis, MN 55458
Phone: 952-210-7168
www.naccminneapolis.org

Norwegian-American Chamber of Commerce Inc
655 Third Ave.
Ste. 1810
New York, NY 10017
Phone: 212-885-9737
www.naccusa.org

Norwegian-American Chamber of Commerce Seattle Chapter
7301 5th Ave. N.E.
Ste. A
Seattle, WA 98115
Phone: 206-445-0606
www.naccchicago.org

Norwegian-American Chamber of Commerce
2720 34th St. N.W.
Washington, DC 20008
www.naccchicago.org

Norway Consulate General
3410 W. Dallas St.
Houston, TX 77019
Phone: 713-620-4200; Fax: 713-620-4290
www.norway.org/embassy

Norway Consulate General
901 Marquette Ave. S.
Ste. 2750
Minneapolis, MN 55402
Phone: 612-332-3338; Fax: 612-332-1386
www.norway.org/embassy

Norway Consulate General
825 3rd Ave.
38th Fl.
New York, NY 10022
Phone: 646-430-7500; Fax: 646-430-7599
www.norway.org/embassy

Norway Consulate General
575 Market St.
Ste. 3950
San Francisco, CA 94105
Phone: 415-882-2000; Fax: 415-882-2001
www.norway.org/embassy

Norway Embassy
2720 34th St. N.W.
Washington, DC 20008
Phone: 202-333-6000; Fax: 202-469-3990
www.norway.org/embassy

Norway Permanent Mission to the UN
825 3rd Ave.
39th Fl.
New York, NY 10022
Phone: 646-430-7510; Fax: 646-430-7591
www.norway-un.org

Oman

National U.S. -ARAB Chamber of Commerce
1023 15th St. N.W.
Ste. 400
Washington, DC 20005
Phone: 202-289-5920; Fax: 202-289-5938
www.nusacc.org

Oman Embassy
2535 Belmont Rd. N.W.
Washington, DC 20008
Phone: 202-387-1980
omani.info

Oman Permanent Mission to the UN
305 E. 47th St.
12th Fl.
New York, NY 10017
Phone: 212-355-3505; Fax: 212-644-0070
www.un.int/oman

Pakistan

Pakistan Chamber of Commerce-USA
11110 Bellaire Blvd.

Ste. 202
Houston, TX 77072
Phone: 832-448-0520
pcc-usa.org

Pakistan Consulate General
333 N. Michigan Ave.
Ste. 728
Chicago, IL 60601
Phone: 312-781-1831; Fax: 312-781-1839
www.cgpkchicago.org

Pakistan Consulate General
11850 Jones Rd.
Houston, TX 77070
Phone: 281-890-2223; Fax: 281-890-1433
www.pakistanconsulatehouston.org

Pakistan Consulate General
10700 Santa Monica Blvd.
Ste. 211
Los Angeles, CA 90025
Phone: 310-441-5114; Fax: 310-441-9256
www.pakconsulatela.org

Pakistan Consulate General
12 E. 65th St.
New York, NY 10065
Phone: 212-879-5800; Fax: 212-517-6987
pakistanconsulateny.org

Pakistan Embassy
3517 International Ct. N.W.
Washington, DC 20008
Phone: 202-243-6500; Fax: 202-686-1534
www.embassyofpakistanusa.org

Pakistan Permanent Mission to the UN
8 E. 65th St.
New York, NY 10065
Phone: 212-879-8600; Fax: 212-744-7348
www.pakun.org

Palau

Palau Visitors Authority
www.visit-palau.com

Palau Embassy
1701 Pennsylvania Ave. N.W.
Ste. 300
Washington, DC 20006
Phone: 202-452-6814; Fax: 202-452-6281
www.palauembassy.com

Palau Permanent Mission to the UN
866 United Nations Plaza
Ste. 575
New York, NY 10017
Phone: 212-813-0310; Fax: 212-813-0317
palauun.org

Panama

Panamanian American Chamber of Commerce

Phone: 786-394-0981
paccmiami.com

Panama Consulate General
24 Greenway Plaza
Ste. 1307
Houston, TX 77046
Phone: 713-622-4451; Fax: 713-622-4468
www.conpahouston.com

Panama Consulate General
5775 Blue Lagoon Dr.
Ste. 200
Miami, FL 33126
Phone: 305-447-3700; Fax: 305-269-7480
www.embassyofpanama.org

Panama Consulate General
1100 Poydras St.
Ste. 2615
New Orleans, LA 70163
Phone: 504-525-3458; Fax: 504-524-8960
www.consulateofpanama.com

Panama Consulate General
1212 Avenue of the Americas
20th Fl.
New York, NY 10036
Phone: 212-840-2450; Fax: 212-840-2469
www.nyconsul.com

Panama Consulate General
124 Chestnut St.
Ste. 1
Philadelphia, PA 19106
Phone: 215-574-2994; Fax: 215-574-4225
www.embassyofpanama.org

Panama Embassy
2862 McGill Terr. N.W.
Washington, DC 20008
Phone: 202-483-1407; Fax: 202-483-8413
www.embassyofpanama.org

Panama Permanent Mission to the UN
866 United Nations Plaza
Ste. 4030
New York, NY 10017
Phone: 212-421-5420; Fax: 212-421-2694
www.panama-un.org

Papua New Guinea

Papua New Guinea Embassy
1779 Massachusetts Ave. N.W.
Ste. 805
Washington, DC 20036
Phone: 202-745-3680; Fax: 202-745-3679
www.pngembassy.org

Papua New Guinea Permanent Mission to the UN
201 E. 42nd St.
Ste. 2411
New York, NY 10017
Phone: 212-557-5001; Fax: 212-557-5009
www.un.int/papuanewguinea

Paraguay

Paraguay Consulate General
25 S.E. 2nd Ave.
Ste. 720
Miami, FL 33131
Phone: 305-374-9090; Fax: 305-374-5522
www.consulparmiami.org

Paraguay Consulate General
801 2nd Ave.
Ste. 600
New York, NY 10017
Phone: 212-682-9441; Fax: 212-682-9443
www.consulparny.com

Paraguay Embassy
2400 Massachusetts Ave. N.W.
Washington, DC 20008
Phone: 202-483-6960; Fax: 202-234-4508
www.mre.gov.py/embaparusa

Paraguay Permanent Mission to the UN
801 Second Ave.
Ste. 702
New York, NY 10017
Phone: 212-687-3490; Fax: 212-818-1282
www.un.int/paraguay

Peru

Peru Tourist Office
www.peru.travel/en-us

Peruvian American Chamber of Commerce
1948 N.W. 82nd Ave.
Doral, FL 33126
Phone: 305-599-1057
www.peruvianchamber.org

Peru Consulate General
20 Park Plaza
Ste. 511
Boston, MA 02116
Phone: 617-338-2227; Fax: 617-338-2742
www.consuladoperu.com

Peru Consulate General
180 N. Michigan Ave.
Ste. 401
Chicago, IL 60601
Phone: 312-782-1599; Fax: 312-704-6969
www.consuladoperu.com

Peru Consulate General
6795 E. Tennessee Ave.
Ste. 550
Denver, CO 80224
Phone: 303-355-8555; Fax: 303-355-8003
www.consuladoperu.com

Peru Consulate General
5177 Richmond Ave.
Ste. 695
Houston, TX 77056

Phone: 713-355-9517; Fax: 713-355-9377
www.consuladoperu.com

Peru Consulate General
3450 Wilshire Blvd.
Ste. 800
Los Angeles, CA 90010
Phone: 213-252-5910; Fax: 213-252-8130
www.consuladoperu.com

Peru Consulate General
444 Brickell Ave.
Ste. M135
Miami, FL 33131
Phone: 786-347-2420; Fax: 305-677-0089
Toll-free: 877-714-7378
www.consulado-peru.com

Peru Consulate General
241 E. 49th St.
New York, NY 10017
Phone: 646-735-3828; Fax: 646-735-3866
www.consuladoperu.com

Peru Consulate General
100 Hamilton Plaza
Ste. 1220 piso 12
Paterson, NJ 07505
Phone: 973-278-3324; Fax: 973-278-0254
www.consuladoperu.com

Peru Consulate General
870 Market St.
Ste. 1075
San Francisco, CA 94102
Phone: 415-362-7136; Fax: 415-362-2836
www.consuladoperu.com

Peru Embassy
1700 Massachusetts Ave. N.W.
Washington, DC 20036
Phone: 202-833-9860; Fax: 202-659-8124
www.embassyofperu.org

Peru Permanent Mission to the UN
820 2nd Ave.
Ste. 1600
New York, NY 10017
Phone: 212-687-3336; Fax: 212-972-6975
www.un.int/peru

Philippines

Philippine Dept of Tourism
556 5th Ave.
New York, NY 10036
Phone: 212-575-7915; Fax: 212-302-6759
www.philippinetourismny.org

Philippine American Chamber of Commerce Inc
556 Fifth Ave.
New York, NY 10036
www.philamchamber.org

Philippine American Chambers of Commerce Inc
447 Sutter St.

Philippine Consulate Bldg.
Ste.700
San Francisco, CA 94108
Phone: 510-541-0964
www.fpachamber.com

Philippines Consulate General
122 S. Michigan Ave.
Ste. 1600
Chicago, IL 60603
Phone: 312-583-0621; Fax: 312-583-0647
www.chicagopcg.com

Philippines Consulate General
2433 Pali Hwy.
Honolulu, HI 96817
Phone: 808-595-6319; Fax: 808-595-2581
www.philippineshonolulu.org

Philippines Consulate General
3435 Wilshire Blvd.
Ste. 550
Los Angeles, CA 90010
Phone: 213-639-0980; Fax: 213-639-0990
www.philippineconsulatela.org

Philippines Consulate General
556 5th Ave.
New York, NY 10036
Phone: 212-764-1330; Fax: 212-764-6010
www.newyorkpcg.org

Philippines Consulate General
447 Sutter St.
6th Fl.
San Francisco, CA 94108
Phone: 415-433-6666; Fax: 415-421-2641
www.philippinessanfrancisco.org

Philippines Embassy
1600 Massachusetts Ave. N.W.
Washington, DC 20036
Phone: 202-467-9300; Fax: 202-467-9417
www.philippineembassy-usa.org

Philippines Permanent Mission to the UN
556 5th Ave.
New York, NY 10036
Phone: 212-764-1300; Fax: 212-840-8602
www.un.int/philippines

Poland

Polish National Tourist Office
5 Marine View Plaza
Ste. 303 B
Hoboken, NJ 07030
Phone: 201-420-9910; Fax: 201-584-9153
www.poland.travel

Polish American Chamber of Commerce, Chicago
5214 W. Lawrence Ave.
Ste. 1
Chicago, IL 60630
Phone: 773-205-1998
www.polishamericanchamber.org

Polish American Chamber of Commerce
8141 S.W. 170 Terr.
Miami, FL 33157
Phone: 305-908-8492; Fax: 305-908-8491
www.polishamericanchamber.com

Polish American Chamber of Commerce Pacific Northwest
1714 18th Ave.
Seattle, WA 98122
www.paccpnw.org

Poland Consulate General
1530 N. Lake Shore Dr.
Chicago, IL 60610
Phone: 312-337-8166; Fax: 312-337-7841
www.polishconsulatechicago.org

Poland Consulate General
12400 Wilshire Blvd.
Ste. 555
Los Angeles, CA 90025
Phone: 310-442-8500; Fax: 310-442-8515
losangeles.msz.gov.pl

Poland Consulate General
233 Madison Ave.
New York, NY 10016
Phone: 646-237-2100
newyork.mfa.gov.pl

Poland Embassy
2640 16th St. N.W.
Washington, DC 20009
Phone: 202-499-1700; Fax: 202-328-6271
www.polandembassy.org

Poland Permanent Mission to the UN
750 Third Ave.
30th Fl.
New York, NY 10017
Phone: 646-559-7552; Fax: 212-517-6771
nowyjorkonz.msz.gov.pl

Portugal

Portuguese Trade & Tourism Office
866 2nd Ave.
8th Fl.
New York, NY 10017
Phone: 646-723-0200; Fax: 212-764-6137
www.visitportugal.com

Portuguese Trade & Tourist Office
88 Kearny St.
Ste. 1770
San Francisco, CA 94108
Phone: 415-391-7080; Fax: 415-391-7147
www.visitportugal.com

Portugal-US Chamber of Commerce
590 5th Ave.
4th Fl.
New York, NY 10036
Phone: 212-354-4627; Fax: 212-575-4737
portugal-us.com

Portugal Consulate General
699 Boylston St.
7th Fl.
Boston, MA 02116
Phone: 617-536-8740; Fax: 617-536-2503

Portugal Consulate
628 Pleasant St.
Rm. 204
New Bedford, MA 02740
Phone: 508-997-6151
www.embassyportugal-us.org

Portugal Consulate General
866 Second Ave.
8th Fl.
New York, NY 10017
Phone: 212-221-3165
www.embassyportugal-us.org

Portugal Consulate General Legal Ctr
1 Riverfront Plaza
Ste. 40
Newark, NJ 07102
Phone: 973-643-4200; Fax: 973-643-3900
www.embassyportugal-us.org

Portugal Consulate
56 Pine St.
Hanley Bldg. 6th Fl.
Providence, RI 02903
Phone: 401-272-2003
www.embassyportugal-us.org

Portugal Consulate General
3298 Washington St.
San Francisco, CA 94115
Phone: 415-346-3400; Fax: 415-346-1440
www.secomunidades.pt/web/saofrancisco

Portugal Consulate
2012 Massachusetts Ave. N.W.
Washington, DC 20036
Phone: 202-332-3007; Fax: 202-223-3926
www.embassyportugal-us.org/Embassy_of_Portugal

Portugal Embassy
2012 Massachusetts Ave. N.W.
Washington, DC 20036
Phone: 202-332-3007; Fax: 202-223-3926
www.embassyportugal-us.org

Portugal Permanent Mission to the UN
866 2nd Ave.
9th Fl.
New York, NY 10017
Phone: 212-759-9444; Fax: 212-355-1124
www.onu.missaoportugal.mne.pt

Puerto Rico

Puerto Rico Tourism Co
Toll-free: 800-866-7827
www.seepuertorico.com

Puerto Rican Chamber of Commerce of South Florida
3550 Biscayne Blvd.
Ste. 306
Miami, FL 33137
Phone: 305-571-8006; Fax: 305-571-8007
www.puertoricanchamber.com

Puerto Rico Chamber of Commerce
100 Tetuan St.
Old San Juan, PR
Phone: 787-721-6060
www.camarapr.org

Qatar

US-Qatar Business Council
1341 Connecticut Ave. N.W.
Ste. 4A
Washington, DC 20036
Phone: 202-457-8555; Fax: 202-457-1919
www.usqbc.org

Qatar Consulate General
9355 Wilshire Blvd.
Ste. 200
Beverly Hills, CA 90210
Phone: 310-246-0005; Fax: 310-246-0023
www.qatarembassy.net

Qatar Consulate General
1990 Post Oak Blvd.
Ste. 900
Houston, TX 77056
Phone: 713-355-8221; Fax: 713-355-8184
www.cgqh.net

Qatar Consulate General
50 Central Park S.
Ste. 1707
New York, NY 10019
Phone: 212-497-2757
www.qatarembassy.net

Qatar Embassy
2555 M St. N.W.
Washington, DC 20037
Phone: 202-274-1600; Fax: 202-237-0061
www.qatarembassy.net

Qatar Permanent Mission to the UN
809 United Nations Plaza
4th Fl.
New York, NY 10017
Phone: 212-486-9335; Fax: 212-758-4952
www.un.org/en

Republic of Korea. *See* South Korea

Romania

Romanian National Tourist Office
355 Lexington Ave.
8th Fl.

New York, NY 10017
Phone: 212-545-8484
www.romaniatourism.com

Romanian-American Chamber of Commerce
2 Wisconsin Cir.
Ste. 700
Chevy Chase, MD 20815
Phone: 240-235-6060; Fax: 240-235-6061
www.racc.ro

Romanian-American Chamber of Commerce
125 Broad St.
New York, NY 01005
Phone: 212-471-8453; Fax: 212-344-3333
www.racc.ro

Romania Consulate General
11766 Wilshire Blvd.
Ste. 200
Los Angeles, CA 90025
Phone: 310-444-0043; Fax: 310-445-0043
losangeles.mae.ro

Romania Consulate General
200 E. 38th St.
New York, NY 10016
Phone: 212-682-9123; Fax: 212-972-8463
newyork.mae.ro

Romania Embassy
1607 23rd St. N.W.
Washington, DC 20008
Phone: 202-332-4846; Fax: 202-232-4748
washington.mae.ro

Romania Permanent Mission to the UN
573-577 3rd Ave.
New York, NY 10016
Phone: 212-682-3274; Fax: 212-682-9746
mpnewyork.mae.ro

Russia

Russian National Tourist Office
224 W. 30th St.
Ste. 701
New York, NY 10001
Phone: 646-473-2233; Fax: 646-473-2205
Toll-free: 877-221-7120
www.russia-travel.com

American-Russian Chamber of Commerce & Industry
200 E. Randolph St.
Ste. 2200
Chicago, IL 60601
Phone: 312-494-6562; Fax: 312-494-9840
www.arcci.org

American-Russian Chamber of Commerce & Industry
1101 Pennsylvania Ave.
6th Fl.
Washington, DC 20004
Phone: 202-756-4943; Fax: 202-362-4634
www.arcci.org

Russian Federation Consulate General
9 E. 91st St.
New York, NY 10128
Phone: 212-348-0926; Fax: 212-831-9162
www.ruscon.org

Russian Federation Consulate General
2790 Green St.
San Francisco, CA 94123
Phone: 415-928-6878; Fax: 415-929-0306
www.consulrussia.org

Russian Federation Consulate General
600 University St., 25th Fl One Union Sq.
Ste. 2510
Seattle, WA 98101
Phone: 206-728-0232; Fax: 206-728-1871
www.netconsul.org

Russian Federation Embassy
2641 Tunlaw Rd. N.W.
Washington, DC 20007
Phone: 202-939-8907; Fax: 202-483-7579
www.russianembassy.org

Russian Federation Embassy
2650 Wisconsin Ave. N.W.
Washington, DC 20007
Phone: 202-298-5700; Fax: 202-298-5735
www.russianembassy.org

Russian Permanent Mission to the UN
136 East 67 St.
New York, NY 10065
Phone: 212-861-4900; Fax: 212-628-0252
russiaun.ru

Rwanda

Rwanda Embassy
1875 Connecticut Ave. N.W.
Ste. 540
Washington, DC 20009
Phone: 202-232-2882; Fax: 202-232-4544
rwandaembassy.org

Rwanda Permanent Mission to the UN
370 Lexington Ave.
Ste. 401
New York, NY 10017
Phone: 212-679-9010; Fax: 212-679-9133
rwandaun.org

Saint Barthelemy

Saint Barthelemy Tourist Office
444 Madison Ave.
16th Fl.
New York, NY 10022
Phone: 212-838-7800; Fax: 212-838-7855
us.franceguide.com

Saint Kitts and Nevis

Saint Kitts Tourism Authority
1001 19th St. N.
Ste. 1200
Arlington, VA 22209
Phone: 571-527-1367; Fax: 202-364-8123
Toll-free: 877-533-1555
www.stkittstourism.kn

Saint Kitts Tourism Authority
350 Fifth Ave.
59th Fl.
New York, NY 10118
Phone: 914-949-2164
Toll-free: 800-582-6208
www.stkittstourism.kn

Saint Kitts Consulate General
412-414 E. 75th St.
5th Fl.
New York, NY 10021
Phone: 212-535-1234; Fax: 212-535-6854
www.stkittsnevis.org

Saint Kitts and Nevis Embassy
3216 New Mexico Ave. N.W.
Washington, DC 20016
Phone: 202-686-2636; Fax: 202-686-5740
www.stkittsnevis.org

Saint Kitts and Nevis Permanent Mission to the UN
414 E. 75th St.
5th Fl.
New York, NY 10021
Phone: 212-535-1234; Fax: 212-535-6854
www.stkittsnevis.org

Saint Lucia

Saint Lucia Tourist Board
800 2nd Ave.
Ste. 5B
New York, NY 10017
Phone: 212-867-2950
www.stlucia.org

Saint Lucia Consulate General
800 2nd Ave.
5th Fl.
New York, NY 10017
Phone: 212-697-9360; Fax: 212-697-4993
saintluciaconsulateny.org

Saint Lucia Embassy
3216 New Mexico Ave N.W.
Washington, DC 20016
Phone: 202-364-6792; Fax: 202-364-6723
stluciaconsulate.ca

Saint Lucia Permanent Mission to the UN
800 2nd Ave.
5th Fl.
New York, NY 10017
Phone: 212-697-9360; Fax: 212-697-4993
saintluciamissionun.org

Saint Martin / Saint Maarten

Saint Martin Tourist Office
825 Third Ave.
29th Fl.
New York, NY 10017
Phone: 212-838-7855
www.stmartinisland.org

Saint Vincent and the Grenadines

Saint Vincent and the Grenadines Tourist Office
801 2nd Ave.
21st Fl.
New York, NY 10017
Phone: 212-687-4981; Fax: 212-949-5946
Toll-free: 800-729-1726
www.visitsvg.com

Saint Vincent and the Grenadines Consulate General
801 2nd Ave.
21st Fl.
New York, NY 10017
Phone: 212-687-4490; Fax: 212-949-5946
www.embsvg.com

Saint Vincent and the Grenadines Embassy
1001 19th St. N.
Arlington, VA 22209
Phone: 202-364-6730
www.embsvg.com

Saint Vincent and the Grenadines Embassy
3216 New Mexico Ave. N.W.
Washington, DC 20016
Phone: 202-364-6730; Fax: 202-364-6736
www.embsvg.com

Saint Vincent and the Grenadines Permanent Mission to the UN
800 2nd Ave.
Ste. 400-G
New York, NY 10017
Phone: 212-599-0950; Fax: 212-599-1020
www.svg-un.org

Samoa

Samoa Tourism Authority
6033 W.Century Blvd.
Ste. 900
Los Angeles, CA 90045
Phone: 310-649-7700; Fax: 310-649-7713
www.samoa.travel

Samoa Embassy
800 2nd Ave.
Ste. 400J
New York, NY 10017
Phone: 212-599-6196; Fax: 212-599-0797
samoa.usembassy.gov

Samoa Permanent Mission to the UN
800 2nd Ave.

Ste. 400J
New York, NY 10017
Phone: 212-599-6196
www.un.int/samoa

San Marino

San Marino Permanent Mission to the UN
327 E 50th St.
New York, NY 10022
Phone: 212-751-1234; Fax: 212-751-1436
www.un.int/sanmarino

Sao Tome and Principe

Sao Tome and Principe Consulate
100 Galleria Pkwy.
Ste. 400
Atlanta, GA 30339
Phone: 770-956-4080; Fax: 770-956-4081
www.saotomeislands.com/embassies.html

Sao Tome and Principe Consulate
1320 Valley Ct.
Libertyville, IL 60048
Phone: 847-362-5615; Fax: 847-362-1637
www.saotomeislands.com/embassies.html

Sao Tome and Principe Embassy
400 Park Ave.
7th Fl.
New York, NY 10022
Phone: 212-317-0644; Fax: 212-317-0624
www.saotomeislands.com/embassies.html

Sao Tome and Principe Permanent Mission to the UN
675 Third Ave.
Ste. 1807
New York, NY 10017
Phone: 212-651-8116; Fax: 212-651-8117
www.un.int/saotomeandprincipe

Saudi Arabia

Saudi Arabia Consulate General
5718 Westheimer Rd.
Ste. 1500
Houston, TX 77057
Phone: 713-785-5577; Fax: 713-785-1163
www.saudiembassy.net

Saudi Arabia Consulate General
2045 Sawtelle Blvd.
Los Angeles, CA 90025
Phone: 310-479-6000; Fax: 310-479-2752
www.saudiembassy.net

Saudi Arabia Consulate General
866 2nd Ave.
5th Fl.
New York, NY 10017
Phone: 212-752-2740; Fax: 212-688-2719
www.saudiembassy.net

Saudi Arabia Embassy
601 New Hampshire Ave. N.W.
Washington, DC 20037
Phone: 202-342-3800; Fax: 202-944-5983
www.saudiembassy.net

Saudi Arabia Permanent Mission to the UN
809 United Nations Plaza
10th Fl.
New York, NY 10017
Phone: 212-557-1525; Fax: 212-983-4895
www.saudimission.org

Senegal

Senagal Consulate
600 Brickell Ave.
Ste. 3800
Miami, FL 33131
Phone: 305-371-4286; Fax: 305-371-4288
senegalconsulatemiami.com

Senegal Embassy
2005 Massachusetts Ave. N.W.
Washington, DC 20036
Phone: 202-234-0540; Fax: 202-332-6315
www.senegalembassy-us.org

Senegal Permanent Mission to the UN
747 Third Ave.
21st Fl.
New York, NY 10021
Phone: 212-517-9030; Fax: 212-517-3032
www.un.int/senegal

Serbia

Serbia National Tourism
www.serbia.travel

Serbia Consulate General
201 E. Ohio St.
Ste. 200
Chicago, IL 60611
Phone: 312-670-6707; Fax: 312-670-6787
www.scgchicago.org

Serbia Embassy
2134 Kalorama Rd. N.W.
Washington, DC 20008
Phone: 202-332-0333; Fax: 202-332-3933
www.washington.mfa.gov.rs

Serbia Permanent Mission to the UN
854 Fifth Ave.
New York, NY 10065
Phone: 646-490-7067; Fax: 212-879-8705
www.un.int/serbia

Seychelles

Seychelles Tourism Board
www.seychelles.travel

Seychelles Consulate
P.O. Box 111909
Anchorage, AK 99511
Phone: 907-244-5375; Fax: 907-646-9872
www.mfa.gov.sc

Seychelles Embassy
800 2nd Ave.
Ste. 400C
New York, NY 10017
Phone: 212-972-1785; Fax: 212-972-1786
www.seychellesembassy.com

Seychelles Permanent Mission to the UN
800 2nd Ave.
Ste. 400C
New York, NY 10017
Phone: 212-972-1785
www.un.int/seychelles

Sierra Leone

Sierra Leone Consulate
5950 Covington Hwy.
Decatur, GA 30035
Phone: 770-884-1633; Fax: 404-920-8991
www.consulateofsierraleoneinatlanta.org

Sierra Leone Embassy
1701 19th St. N.W.
Washington, DC 20009
Phone: 202-939-9261; Fax: 202-483-1793
www.embassyofsierraleone.net

Sierra Leone Permanent Mission to the UN
245 E. 49th St.
New York, NY 10017
Phone: 212-688-1656
www.un.int/sierraleone

Singapore

Singapore Tourism Board
1156 Avenue of the Americas
Ste. 702
New York, NY 10036
Phone: 212-302-4861; Fax: 212-302-4801
www.stb.gov.sg

Singapore Consulate
318 E. 48th St.
New York, NY 10017
Phone: 212-223-3331; Fax: 212-826-5028
www.mfa.gov.sg

Singapore Consulate General
595 Market St.
Ste. 2450
San Francisco, CA 94105
Phone: 415-543-4775; Fax: 415-543-4788
www.mfa.gov.sg

Singapore Embassy
3501 International Pl. N.W.

Washington, DC 20008
Phone: 202-537-3100; Fax: 202-537-0876
www.mfa.gov.sg

Singapore Permanent Mission to the UN
231 E. 51st St., NY 10022
Phone: 212-826-0840; Fax: 212-826-2964
www.mfa.gov.sg

Sint Maarten

Sint Maarten Tourism Bureau
2941 W. Cypress Creek Rd.
2nd Fl.
Fort Lauderdale, FL 33309
Phone: 954-975-2220
www.vacationstmaarten.com

Slovakia

Slovak Tourist Board
18 Florence st.
Edison, NY 08817
www.slovakia.travel

Slovakia Embassy
3523 International Ct. N.W.
Washington, DC 20008
Phone: 202-237-1054; Fax: 202-237-6438
slovakia.usembassy.gov

Slovakia Permanent Mission to the UN
801 2nd Ave.
12th Fl.
New York, NY 10017
Phone: 212-286-8880
www.mzv.sk

Slovenia

Slovenia Tourist Board
www.slovenia.info

Slovenia Consulate
55 Public Sq.
Ste. 945.
Cleveland, OH 44113
Phone: 216-589-9220; Fax: 216-589-9210
cleveland.konzulat.si

Slovenia Embassy
2410 California St. N.W.
Washington, DC 20008
Phone: 202-386-6601; Fax: 202-386-6633
washington.embassy.si

Slovenia Permanent Mission to the UN
600 3rd Ave.
24th Fl.
New York, NY 10016
Phone: 212-370-3007
www.un.org/slovenia

Solomon Islands

Solomon Islands Chamber of Commerce and Industry
www.solomonchamber.com.sb

Solomon Islands Embassy
800 2nd Ave.
Ste. 400L
New York, NY 10017
Phone: 212-599-6192; Fax: 212-661-8925
www.solomons.org.tw

Solomon Islands Permanent Mission to the UN
800 2nd Ave.
Ste. 400L
New York, NY 10017
Phone: 212-599-6192; Fax: 212-661-8925
www.un.int/solomonislands

Somalia

Somali American Chamber of Commerce
5306 Cleveland Ave.
Columbus, OH 43231
Phone: 888-851-5659
www.soamcc.org

Somalia Permanent Mission to the UN
425 E. 61Nd St.
Ste. 702
New York, NY 10021
Phone: 212-688-9410; Fax: 212-759-0651
www.un.int/somalia

South Africa

South African Tourism Board
500 5th Ave.
20th Fl. Ste. 2040
New York, NY 10110
Phone: 212-730-2929; Fax: 212-764-1980
Toll-free: 800-593-1318
www.southafrica.net

South Africa Consulate General
200 S. Michigan Ave.
6th Fl.
Chicago, IL 60604
Phone: 312-939-7929; Fax: 312-939-2588
www.southafricachicago.com

South Africa Consulate General
6300 Wilshire Blvd.
Ste. 600
Los Angeles, CA 90048
Phone: 323-651-0902; Fax: 323-651-5969
www.southafrica-newyork.net

South Africa Consulate General
333 E. 38th St.
9th Fl.
New York, NY 10016

Phone: 212-213-4880; Fax: 212-213-0102
www.southafrica-newyork.net

South Africa Embassy
3051 Massachusetts Ave. N.W.
Washington, DC 20008
Phone: 202-232-4400; Fax: 202-265-1607
www.saembassy.org

South Africa Permanent Mission to the UN
333 E. 38th St.
9th Fl.
New York, NY 10016
Phone: 212-213-5583; Fax: 212-692-2498
www.southafrica-newyork.net

South Korea (Republic of Korea)

Korea National Tourism Organization
737 N Michigan Ave.
Ste. 910
Chicago, IL 60611
Phone: 312-981-1717; Fax: 312-981-1721
Toll-free: 800-868-7567
english.tour2korea.com

Korea National Tourism Organization
2 Executive Dr.
Ste. 750
Fort Lee, NJ 07024
Phone: 201-585-0909; Fax: 201-585-9041
Toll-free: 800-868-7567
english.tour2korea.com

Korea National Tourism Organization
5509 Wilshire Blvd.
Ste. 2010
Los Angeles, CA 90036
Phone: 323-634-0280; Fax: 323-634-0281
Toll-free: 800-868-7567
english.tour2korea.com

Korean Chamber of Commerce
3435 Wilshire Blvd.
Ste. 2450
Los Angeles, CA 90010
Phone: 213-480-1115; Fax: 213-480-7521
www.bizfed.org/members/profile/korean-american-chamber-commerce-los-angeles

Korean Chamber of Commerce & Industry in the USA Inc
460 Park Ave.
Ste. 410
New York, NY 10022
Phone: 212-644-0140; Fax: 212-644-9106
www.kocham.org

Korea Republic Consulate General
229 Peachtree St.
Ste. 2100
Atlanta, GA 30303
Phone: 404-522-1611; Fax: 404-521-3169
usa-atlanta.mofa.go.kr

Korea Republic Consulate General
455 N City Front Plaza Dr.
NBC Tower
Ste. 2700
Chicago, IL 60611
Phone: 312-822-9485; Fax: 312-822-9849
usa-chicago.mofa.go.kr

Korea Republic Consulate General
2756 Pali Hwy.
Honolulu, HI 96817
Phone: 808-595-6109; Fax: 808-595-3046
usa-honolulu.mofa.go.kr

Korea Republic Consulate General
1990 Post Oak Blvd.
Ste. 1250
Houston, TX 77056
Phone: 713-961-0186; Fax: 713-961-3340
usa-houston.mofa.go.kr

Korea Republic Consulate General
3243 Wilshire Blvd.
Los Angeles, CA 90010
Phone: 213-385-9300; Fax: 213-385-1849
usa-losangeles.mofa.go.kr

Korea Republic Consulate General
460 Park Ave.
9th Fl.
Between 57th & 58th St.
New York, NY 10022
Phone: 646-674-6000; Fax: 646-674-6023
Usa-newyork.mofa.go.kr

Korea Republic Consulate General
1 Gateway Ctr.
2nd Fl.
Newton, MA 02458
Phone: 617-641-2830; Fax: 617-641-2831
Usa-newton.mofa.go.kr

Korea Republic Consulate General
3500 Clay St.
San Francisco, CA 94118
Phone: 415-921-2251; Fax: 415-921-5946
Usa-sanfrancisco.mofa.go.kr

Korea Republic Consulate General
2033 6th Ave.
Ste. 1125
Seattle, WA 98121
Phone: 206-441-1011; Fax: 206-441-7912
Usa-seattle.mofa.go.kr

Korea Republic Consulate General
2320 Massachusetts Ave. N.W.
Washington, DC 20008
Phone: 202-939-5661; Fax: 202-342-1597
Usa-seattle.mofa.go.kr

Korea Republic Embassy
2450 Massachusetts Ave. N.W.
Washington, DC 20008
Phone: 202-939-5600; Fax: 202-797-0595
usa.mofa.go.kr

Korea Republic of Permanent Mission to the UN
335 E. 45th St.
New York, NY 10017
Phone: 212-439-4000; Fax: 212-986-1083
www.un.int/korea

South Sudan

South Sudan Embassy
1015 31st St. N.W.
Ste. 300
Washington, DC 20007
Phone: 202-293-7940; Fax: 202-293-7941
www.southsudanembassydc.org

South Sudan Permanent Mission to the UN
336 E. 45th St.
5th Fl.
New York, NY 10017
Phone: 212-937-7977; Fax: 212-867-9242

Spain

Spain Tourist Office
8383 Wilshire Blvd.
Ste. 960
Beverly Hills, CA 90211
Phone: 323-658-7188; Fax: 323-658-1061
www.spain.info

Spain Tourist Office
845 N Michigan Ave.
Ste. 915-E
Chicago, IL 60611
Phone: 312-642-1992; Fax: 312-642-9817
www.spain.info

Spain Tourist Office
1395 Brickell Ave.
Ste. 1130
Miami, FL 33131
Phone: 305-358-1992; Fax: 305-358-8223
www.spain.info

Spain Tourist Office
666 5th Ave.
35th Fl.
New York, NY 10103
Phone: 212-265-8822; Fax: 212-265-8864
www.spain.info

Spain-US Chamber of Commerce
80 Broad St.
Ste. 2103
New York, NY 10004
Phone: 212-967-2170; Fax: 212-564-1415
www.spainuscc.org

Spain Consulate General
31 St. James Ave.
Ste. 905
Boston, MA 02116
Phone: 617-536-2506; Fax: 617-536-8512
www.exteriores.gob.es/Consulados/Boston/en

Spain Consulate General
180 N. Michigan Ave.
Ste. 1500
Chicago, IL 60601
Phone: 312-782-4588; Fax: 312-782-1635
www.exteriores.gob.es/Consulados/CHICAGO/en

Spain Consulate General
1800 Bering Dr.
Ste. 660
Houston, TX 77057
Phone: 713-783-6200; Fax: 713-783-6166
www.exteriores.gob.es/Consulados/houston/en

Spain Consulate General
5055 Wilshire Blvd.
Ste. 860
Los Angeles, CA 90036
Phone: 323-938-0158; Fax: 323-938-2502
www.exteriores.gob.es/Consulados/LosAngeles/en

Spain Consulate General
2655 Le Jeune Rd.
Ste. 203
Miami, FL 33134
Phone: 305-446-5511; Fax: 305-446-0585
www.exteriores.gob.es/Consulados/Miami/en

Spain Consulate General
150 E. 58th St.
30th Fl.
New York, NY 10155
Phone: 212-355-4080; Fax: 212-644-3751
www.exteriores.gob.es/Consulados/NuevaYork/en

Spain Consulate General
1405 Sutter St.
San Francisco, CA 94109
Phone: 415-922-2995; Fax: 415-931-9706
www.exteriores.gob.es/Consulados/SanFrancisco/en

Spain Embassy
2375 Pennsylvania Ave. N.W.
Washington, DC 20037
Phone: 202-452-0100; Fax: 202-833-5670
www.spainemb.org

Spain Permanent Mission to the UN
245 E. 47th St.
36th Fl.
New York, NY 10017
Phone: 212-661-1050; Fax: 212-949-7247
www.spainun.org

Sri Lanka

Sri Lanka Consulate General
3250 Wilshire Blvd.
Ste. 1405
Los Angeles, CA 90010
Phone: 213-387-0210; Fax: 213-387-0216
www.srilankaconsulatela.com

Sri Lanka Consulate General
630 3rd Ave.

20th Fl.
New York, NY 10017
Phone: 212-986-7040; Fax: 212-986-1838

Sri Lanka Embassy
2148 Wyoming Ave. N.W.
Washington, DC 20008
Phone: 202-483-4025; Fax: 202-232-7181
www.slembassyusa.org

Sri Lanka Permanent Mission to the UN
820 2nd Fl.
2nd Ave.
New York, NY 10017
Phone: 212-986-7040; Fax: 212-986-1838
www.slmission.com

Sudan

Sudan Embassy
2210 Massachusetts Ave. N.W.
Washington, DC 20008
Phone: 202-338-8565; Fax: 202-667-2406
www.sudanembassy.org

Sudan Permanent Mission to the UN
305 E. 47th St.
4th Fl.
New York, NY 10017
Phone: 212-573-6033; Fax: 212-573-6160
www.un.int/sudan

Suriname

Suriname Consulate General
7205 Airport Corporate Dr.
Ste. 302
Miami, FL 33126
Phone: 305-463-0694; Fax: 305-463-0715
www.scgmia.com

Suriname Embassy
4301 Connecticut Ave. N.W.
Ste. 460
Washington, DC 20008
Phone: 202-244-7488; Fax: 202-244-5878
www.surinameembassy.org

Suriname Permanent Mission to the UN
866 United Nations Plaza
Ste. 320
New York, NY 10017
Phone: 212-826-0660; Fax: 212-980-7029
www.un.int/suriname

Swaziland

Swaziland Embassy
1712 New Hampshire Ave. N.W.
Washington, DC 20009
Phone: 202-234-5002; Fax: 202-234-8254
swaziland.usembassy.gov

Swaziland Permanent Mission to the UN
408 E. 50th St.
New York, NY 10022
Phone: 212-371-8910; Fax: 212-754-2755
www.un.int/swaziland

Sweden

Swedish Travel & Tourism Council
P.O. Box 4649 Grand Central Station
New York, NY 10163
Phone: 212-885-9700; Fax: 212-885-9710
www.visitsweden.com

Swedish-American Chambers of Commerce USA Inc
1403 King St.
Alexandria, VA 22314
Phone: 703-836-6560; Fax: 703-836-6561
www.sacc-usa.org

Swedish-American Chamber of Commerce Inc Chicago
Chapter
150 N Michigan Ave.
Ste. 2800
Chicago, IL 60601
Phone: 312-863-8592; Fax: 312-624-7701
www.sacc-usa.org/chicago

Swedish-American Chamber of Commerce in Colorado
1720 S. Bellaire St.
Ste. 530
Denver, CO 80110
Phone: 720-515-9421
sacc-co.org

Swedish-American Chamber of Commerce Inc Minnesota
Chapter
American Swedish Institute
2600 Park Ave.
Minneapolis, MN 55407
Phone: 612-991-3001; Fax: 612-333-3914
www.saccmn.org

Swedish-American Chamber of Commerce Inc New England Chapter
2600 Park Ave.
Minneapolis, MA 55407
Phone: 612-424-2496
www.saccmn.org

Swedish-American Chamber of Commerce Inc New York
Chapter
570 Lexington Ave.
20th Fl.
New York, NY 10022
Phone: 212-838-5530; Fax: 212-755-7953
www.saccny.org

Swedish-American Chamber of Commerce Georgia Inc
4775 Peachtree Industrial Blvd.
Bldg 300 Ste. 300
Norcross, GA 30092
Phone: 770-670-2480; Fax: 770-670-2500
www.sacc-georgia.org

Swedish-American Chamber of Commerce San Diego
4475 Mission Blvd.
Ste. 201.
San Diego, CA 92109
Phone: 858-598-4809
www.sacc-sandiego.org

Swedish-American Chamber of Commerce Inc San Francisco Chapter
350 Townsend St.
Ste. 409B
San Francisco, CA 94104
Phone: 415-781-4188; Fax: 415-781-4189
sacc-sf.org

Swedish-American Chamber of Commerce Inc Washington
DC Chapter
2900 K St. N.W.
Ste. 403
Washington, DC 20007
Phone: 202-536-1520; Fax: 202-467-2688
sacc-usa.org

Swedish-American Chamber of Commerce of Greater Los
Angeles Inc
1041 N Formosa Ave.
Formosa Bldg.
Rm. 215
West Hollywood, CA 90046
Phone: 310-622-3616; Fax: 310-622-3617
www.sacc-gla.org

Sweden Consulate General
445 Park Ave.
19th Fl.
New York, NY 10022
Phone: 212-888-3000; Fax: 212-888-3125
www.swedenabroad.com/en-GB/Embassies/New-York

Sweden Consulate General
120 Montgomery St.
Ste. 2175
San Francisco, CA 94104
Phone: 415-788-2631; Fax: 415-788-6841
www.swedishcouncil.org

Sweden Consulate General
505 Sansome St.
Ste. 1010
San Francisco, CA 94111
Phone: 415-788-2631; Fax: 415-788-0141
www.swedenabroad.com

Sweden Embassy
2900 K St. N.W.
Washington, DC 20007
Phone: 202-467-2600; Fax: 202-467-2699
www.swedenabroad.com/en-GB/Embassies/Washington

Sweden Permanent Mission to the UN
885 2nd Ave.
46th Fl.
New York, NY 10017
Phone: 212-583-2500; Fax: 212-832-0389
www.swedenabroad.com

Switzerland

Switzerland Tourism
608 5th Ave.
Ste. 202
New York, NY 10020
Phone: 212-757-5944; Fax: 212-262-6116
Toll-free: 800-794-7795
www.myswitzerland.com

Swiss-American Chamber of Commerce
500 5th Ave.
Rm. 1800
New York, NY 10110
Phone: 212-246-7789; Fax: 212-246-1366
www.amcham.ch

Switzerland Consulate General
1349 W. Peachtree St. N.W.
Ste. 1000
Atlanta, GA 30309
Phone: 404-870-2000; Fax: 404-870-2011
www.eda.admin.ch

Switzerland Consulate General
737 N. Michigan Ave.
Ste. 2301
Chicago, IL 60611
Phone: 312-915-0061; Fax: 312-915-0388

Switzerland Consulate General
11859 Wilshire Blvd.
Ste. 501
Los Angeles, CA 90025
Phone: 310-575-1145; Fax: 310-575-1982
www.eda.admin.ch

Switzerland Consulate General
6920 94th Ave. S.E.
Mercer Island, WA 98040
Phone: 206-228-8110
www.eda.admin.ch

Switzerland Consulate General
633 3rd Ave.
30th Fl.
New York, NY 10017
Phone: 212-599-5700; Fax: 212-599-4266
www.eda.admin.ch

Switzerland Consulate General
456 Montgomery St.
Ste. 1500
San Francisco, CA 94104
Phone: 415-788-2272; Fax: 415-788-1402
www.eda.admin.ch

Switzerland Consulate General
2782 Durban Rd.
Sandy, UT 84093
Phone: 801-804-6727
www.eda.admin.ch

Switzerland Embassy
2900 Cathedral Ave. N.W.
Washington, DC 20008

Phone: 202-745-7900; Fax: 202-387-2564
www.eda.admin.ch

Switzerland Permanent Mission to the UN
633 3rd Ave.
29th Fl.
New York, NY 10011
Phone: 212-286-1540; Fax: 212-286-1555
www.eda.admin.ch

Syria

Syrian Arab Republic Embassy
2215 Wyoming Ave. N.W.
Washington, DC 20008
Phone: 202-232-6313; Fax: 202-234-9548

Syrian Arab Republic Permanent Mission to the UN
820 2nd Ave.
15th Fl.
New York, NY 10017
Phone: 212-661-1313; Fax: 212-983-4439
www.un.int/syria

Tahiti

Tahiti Tourism
300 Continental Blvd.
Ste. 160
El Segundo, CA 90245
Phone: 310-414-8484; Fax: 310-414-8490
www.tahiti-tourisme.com

Taiwan

Taiwan Tourism Bureau
3731 Wilshire Blvd.
Ste. 504
Los Angeles, CA 90010
Phone: 213-389-1158; Fax: 213-389-1094
www.taiwan.net.tw

Taiwan Tourism Bureau
405 Lexington Ave.
New York, NY
Phone: 212-466-0691; Fax: 212-466-6436
www.taiwan.net.tw

Taiwan Tourism Bureau
555 Montgomery St.
Ste. 505
San Francisco, CA 94111
Phone: 415-989-8677; Fax: 415-989-7242
www.taiwan.net.tw

Tajikistan

Tajikistan Embassy
1005 New Hampshire Ave. N.W.
Washington, DC 20037
Phone: 202-223-6090; Fax: 202-223-6091
www.tjus.org

Tajikistan Permanent Mission to the UN
216 E. 49th St.
4th Fl.
New York, NY 10017
Phone: 212-207-3315; Fax: 212-207-3855
www.tajikistan-un.org

Tanzania

Tanzania United Republic of Embassy
1232 22nd St. N.W.
Washington, DC 20037
Phone: 202-884-1080; Fax: 202-797-7408
www.tanzaniaembassy-us.org

Tanzania United Republic of Permanent Mission to the UN
307 E. 53rd St.
4th Fl.
New York, NY 10022
Phone: 212-697-3612; Fax: 212-697-3618
www.tanzania-un.org

Thailand

Thailand Tourism Authority
611 N. Larchmont Blvd.
1st Fl.
Los Angeles, CA 90004
Phone: 323-461-9814
www.tourismthailand.org

Thailand Tourism Authority
61 Broadway
Ste. 2810
New York, NY 10006
Phone: 212-432-0433
www.tourismthailand.org

Thailand Consulate General
700 N. Rush St.
Chicago, IL 60611
Phone: 312-664-3129; Fax: 312-664-3230
www.thaiconsulatechicago.org

Thailand Consulate General
611 N. Larchmont Blvd.
2nd Fl.
Los Angeles, CA 90004
Phone: 323-962-9574; Fax: 323-962-2128
www.thaiconsulatela.org

Thailand Consulate General
351 E. 52nd St.
New York, NY 10022
Phone: 212-754-1770; Fax: 212-754-1907
www.thaicgny.com

Thailand Embassy
1024 Wisconsin Ave. N.W.
Ste. 401
Washington, DC 20007
Phone: 202-944-3600; Fax: 202-944-3611
www.thaiembassydc.org

Thailand Permanent Mission to the UN
351 E. 52nd St.
New York, NY 10022
Phone: 212-754-2230; Fax: 212-688-3029
www.un.int/thailand

Timor-Leste

Timor-Leste Embassy
4201 Connecticut Ave. N.W.
Ste. 504
Washington, DC 20008
Phone: 202-966-3202; Fax: 202-966-3205
www.timorlesteembassy.org

Timor-Leste Permanent Mission to the UN
866 United Nations Plaza
Ste. 441
New York, NY 10017
Phone: 212-759-3675; Fax: 212-759-4196
www.un.org

Togo

Togo Embassy
2208 Massachusetts Ave. N.W.
Washington, DC 20008
Phone: 202-234-4212; Fax: 202-232-3190
www.togoleseembassy.com

Togo Permanent Mission to the UN
112 E. 40th St.
New York, NY 10016
Phone: 212-490-3455; Fax: 212-983-6684
www.togodiplomatie.info

Tonga

Tonga Consulate General
1350 Bayshore Hwy.
Ste. 610
Burlingame, CA 94010
Phone: 650-685-1001; Fax: 650-685-1003
www.tongaconsul.com

Tonga Embassy
250 E. 51St St.
New York, NY 10022
Phone: 917-369-1025; Fax: 917-369-1024

Tonga Permanent Mission to the UN
250 E. 51st St.
New York, NY 10022
Phone: 917-369-1025; Fax: 917-369-1024
www.un.int/tonga

Trinidad and Tobago

Trinidad and Tobago Consulate General
1000 Brickell Ave.
Ste. 800
Miami, FL 33131

Phone: 305-374-2199; Fax: 305-374-3199
www.ttcgmiami.com

Trinidad and Tobago Consulate General
125 Maiden Ln.
Unit 4A, 4th Fl.
New York, NY 10038
Phone: 212-682-7272; Fax: 212-232-0368
www.ttcgnewyork.com

Trinidad and Tobago Embassy
1708 Massachusetts Ave. N.W.
Washington, DC 20036
Phone: 202-467-6490; Fax: 202-785-3130
www.ttembassy.org

Trinidad and Tobago Permanent Mission to the UN
633 3rd Ave.
12th Fl.
New York, NY 10017
Phone: 212-697-7620; Fax: 212-682-3580
www.un.int/trinidadandtobago

Tunisia

Tunisia Embassy
1515 Massachusetts Ave. N.W.
Washington, DC 20005
Phone: 202-862-1850; Fax: 202-862-1858
www.tunconsusa.org

Tunisia Permanent Mission to the UN
31 Beekman Pl.
New York, NY 10022
Phone: 212-751-7503; Fax: 212-751-0569
www.un.int

Turkey

Turkish Culture and Tourism Offices
5055 Wilshire Blvd.
Ste. 850
Los Angeles, CA 90036
Phone: 323-937-8066
www.tourismturkey.org

Turkish Culture and Tourism Offices
825 3rd Ave.
New York, NY 10022
Phone: 212-687-2194; Fax: 212-687-2195
Toll-free: 877-367-8875
www.tourismturkey.org

Turkish American Chamber of Commerce
501 Midway Dr.
Mount Prospect, IL 60056
Phone: 224-333-2088
www.taccusa.org

Turkey Consulate General
455 N. Cityfront Plaza Dr.
NBC Tower
Ste. 2900
Chicago, IL 60611

Phone: 312-263-0644; Fax: 312-263-1449
sikago.bk.mfa.gov.tr

Turkey Consulate General
1990 Post Oak Blvd.
Ste. 1300
Houston, TX 77056
Phone: 713-622-5849; Fax: 713-623-6639
houston.bk.mfa.gov.tr

Turkey Consulate General
6300 Wilshire Blvd.
Ste. 2010
Los Angeles, CA 90048
Phone: 323-655-8832; Fax: 323-655-8681
losangeles.bk.mfa.gov.tr

Turkey Consulate General
825 Third Ave.
28th Fl.
New York, NY 10022
Phone: 646-430-6560; Fax: 212-983-1293
Toll-free: 888-566-7656
newyork.bk.mfa.gov.tr

Turkish Embassy
2525 Massachusetts Ave. N.W.
Washington, DC 20008
Phone: 202-612-6700; Fax: 202-612-6744
www.washington.emb.mfa.gov.tr

Turkey Permanent Mission to the UN
885 Second Ave.
45th Fl.
New York, NY 10017
Phone: 212-949-0150; Fax: 212-949-0086
turkuno.dt.mfa.gov.tr

Turkmenistan

Turkmenistan Embassy
2207 Massachusetts Ave. N.W.
Washington, DC 20008
Phone: 202-588-1500
turkmenistanembassy.org

Turkmenistan Permanent Mission to the UN
866 United Nations Plaza
Ste. 424
New York, NY 10017
Phone: 212-486-8908
www.turkmenistanun.org

Turks and Caicos Islands

Turks and Caicos Islands Tourist Board
80 Broad St.
Ste. 3302
New York, NY 10004
Phone: 646-375-8830; Fax: 646-375-8835
Toll-free: 800-241-0824
www.turksandcaicostourism.com

Tuvalu

Tuvalu Permanent Mission to the UN
800 Second Ave.
Ste. 400-D
New York, NY 10017
Phone: 212-490-0534; Fax: 212-808-4975
www.un.int/tuvalu

Uganda

Uganda Embassy
5911 16th St. N.W.
Washington, DC 20011
Phone: 202-726-7100; Fax: 202-726-1727
washington.mofa.go.ug

Uganda Permanent Mission to the UN
336 E. 45th St.
New York, NY 10017
Phone: 212-949-0110; Fax: 212-687-4517
newyork.mofa.go.ug

Ukraine

Ukrainian-American Chamber of Commerce
3730 Kirby Dr.
Ste. 1200
Houston, TX 77098
Phone: 832-274-5659; Fax: 713-834-1128
www.uacc.us

Ukraine Consulate General
10 E. Huron St.
Chicago, IL 60611
Phone: 312-642-4388; Fax: 312-642-4385
chicago.mfa.gov.ua

Ukraine Embassy
3350 M St. N.W.
Washington, DC 20007
Phone: 202-349-2963; Fax: 202-333-0817
usa.mfa.gov.ua/en

Ukraine Permanent Mission to the UN
220 E. 51st St.
New York, NY 10022
Phone: 212-759-7003; Fax: 212-355-9455
mfa.gov.ua

United Arab Emirates

United Arab Emirates Embassy
3522 International Ct. N.W.
Ste. 400
Washington, DC 20008
Phone: 202-243-2400; Fax: 202-243-2432
www.uae-embassy.org

United Arab Emirates Permanent Mission to the UN
3 Dag Hammarskjöld Plaza 305 E.
47th St.
7th Fl.

New York, NY 10017
Phone: 212-371-0480; Fax: 212-371-4923
www.un.int/uae

United Kingdom

VisitBritain
845 Third Ave.
10th Fl.
New York, NY 10022
Phone: 212-850-0336
www.visitbritain.org

British American Chamber of Commerce, Ohio Region
P.O. Box 372
Hudson, OH 44236
Phone: 216-621-0222; Fax: 330-342-7963
www.babc.org

British American Business Council of Los Angeles
11766 Wilshire Blvd.
Ste. 1230
Los Angeles, CA 90025
Phone: 310-312-1962; Fax: 310-312-1914
www.babc.org

British-American Chamber of Commerce of Miami
333 S.E. 2nd Ave.
Ste. 3200
Miami, FL 33131
Phone: 305-377-0992
babcmiami.org

BritishAmerican Business
52 Vanderbilt Ave.
20th Fl.
New York, NY 10017
Phone: 212-661-4060; Fax: 212-661-4074
www.babc.org

British-American Business Council of Northern California
703 Market St.
Ste. 1214
San Francisco, CA 94103
Phone: 415-296-8645; Fax: 415-296-9649
www.babc.org

British Consulate General
133 Peachtree St. N.E.
Ste. 3400
Atlanta, GA 30303
Phone: 404-954-7700
www.gov.uk/government/world/organisations

British Consulate General
One Broadway
Cambridge, MA 02142
Phone: 617-245-4500
www.gov.uk/government/world/organisations

British Consulate General
625 N. Michigan Ave.
Ste. 2200
Chicago, IL 60611
Phone: 312-970-3800
www.gov.uk/government/world/organisations

British Consulate General
World Trade Centre Tower
1625 Broadway
Ste. 720
Denver, CO 80202
Phone: 303-592-5200
www.gov.uk/government/world/organisations

British Consulate General
1301 Fannin St.
Ste. 2400
Houston, TX 77002
Phone: 713-659-6270
www.gov.uk/government/world/organisations

British Consulate General
2029 Century Park E.
Ste. 1350
Los Angeles, CA 90067
Phone: 310-481-0031
www.gov.uk/government/world/organisations

British Consulate General
1001 Brickell Bay Dr.
Miami, FL 33131
Phone: 305-400-6400
www.gov.uk/government/world/organisations

British Consulate General
845 Third Ave.
New York, NY 10022
Phone: 212-745-0200
www.gov.uk/government/world/organisations

United Kingdom of Great Britain & Northern Ireland Consulate
200 S Orange Ave.
Ste. 2110
Orlando, FL 32801
Phone: 407-254-3300
www.gov.uk/government/world/organisations

British Consulate General
1 Sansome St.
Ste. 850
San Francisco, CA 94104
Phone: 415-617-1300
www.gov.uk/government/world/organisations

British Embassy Washington
3100 Massachusetts Ave. N.W.
Washington, DC 20008
Phone: 202-588-6500
www.gov.uk

UK Mission to the UN
One Dag Hammarskjold Plaza
885 Second Ave.
New York, NY 10017
Phone: 212-745-9200; Fax: 212-745-9316
www.gov.uk

Uruguay

Uruguay Ministry of Tourism
www.turismo.gub.uy

Uruguayan-American Chamber of Commerce
401 E. 88th St.
Ste. 12-A
New York, NY 10128
Phone: 212-722-3306; Fax: 212-996-2580
www.uruguaychamber.com

Uruguay Consulate General
1077 Ponce De Leon Blvd.
Ste. B
Coral Gables, FL 33134
Phone: 305-443-9764; Fax: 305-443-7802
www.uruguaymiami.org

Uruguay Consulate General
420 Madison Ave.
6th Fl.
New York, NY 10017
Phone: 212-753-8581; Fax: 212-753-1603
www.consuladouruguaynewyork.com

Uruguay Consulate General
429 Santa Monica Blvd.
Ste. 400
Santa Monica, CA 90401
Phone: 310-394-5777; Fax: 310-394-5140
www.conurula.org

Uruguay Embassy
1913 I (Eye) St. N.W.
Washington, DC 20006
Phone: 202-331-1313
www.mrree.gub.uy

Uruguay Permanent Mission to the UN
866 United Nations Plaza
Ste. 322
New York, NY 10017
Phone: 212-752-8240
www.un.int/uruguay

US Virgin Islands

US Virgin Islands Dept of Tourism
P.O. Box 6400
Saint Thomas, VI 00804
Phone: 340-774-8784; Fax: 340-774-4390
www.visitusvi.com

Uzbekistan

American-Uzbekistan Chamber of Commerce
Washington, DC
Phone: 202-509-3744
www.aucconline.com

Uzbekistan Consulate General
801 Second Ave.
20th Fl.
New York, NY 10017
Phone: 212-754-7403; Fax: 212-838-9812
www.uzbekconsulny.org

Uzbekistan Embassy
1746 Massachusetts Ave. N.W.

Washington, DC 20036
Phone: 202-887-5300; Fax: 202-293-6804
www.uzbekistan.org

Uzbekistan Permanent Mission to the UN
801 Second Ave.
20th Fl.
New York, NY 10017
Phone: 212-486-4242; Fax: 212-486-7998
www.un.int/uzbekistan

Vanuatu

Vanuatu Permanent Mission to the UN
800 Second Ave.
Ste. 400B
New York, NY 10017
Phone: 212-661-4303; Fax: 212-661-5544
www.un.int/vanuatu

Vatican City. *See* Holy *See*

Venezuela

Vietnam National Tourism
www.vietnamtourism.com

Venezuelan-American Chamber of Commerce of the US
1600 Ponce de Leon Blvd.
10th Fl. Ste. 1033
Coral Gables, FL 33134
Phone: 786-350-1190; Fax: 786-350-1191
venezuelanchamber.org

Venezuela Consulate General
545 Boylston St.
3rd Fl.
Boston, MA 02116
Phone: 617-266-9368; Fax: 617-266-2350
www.embavenez-us.org/_boston

Venezuela Consulate General
20 N. Wacker Dr.
Ste. 1925
Chicago, IL 60606
Phone: 312-324-0907; Fax: 312-580-1010
www.embavenez-us.org/_chicago

Venezuela Consulate General
2401 Fountain View Dr.
Ste. 220
Houston, TX 77057
Phone: 713-974-0028
venezuela-us.org/houston

Venezuela Consulate General
1101 Brickell Ave.
Ste. 300
Miami, FL 33131
Phone: 305-577-4301

Venezuela Consulate General
400 Poydras St.

Ste. 2145
New Orleans, LA 70130
Phone: 504-522-3284
embavenez-us.org/_neworleans

Venezuela Consulate General
7 E. 51st St.
New York, NY 10022
Phone: 212-826-1660; Fax: 212-644-7471
www.embavenez-us.org/_newyork

Venezuela Consulate General
1161 Mission St.
Ste. 300
San Francisco, CA 94103
Phone: 415-294-2252; Fax: 415-296-6479
embavenez-us.org/_sanfrancisco

Venezuela Embassay
1099 30th St. N.W.
Washington, DC 20007
Phone: 202-342-2214; Fax: 202-342-6820
eeuu.embajada.gob.ve

Venezuela Permanent Mission to the UN
335 E. 46th St.
New York, NY 10017
Phone: 212-557-2055; Fax: 212-557-3528
www.un.int/venezuela

Vietnam

Vietnam National Tourism
www.vietnamtourism.com

Vietnamese-American Chamber of Commerce of Hawaii
P.O. Box 240352
Honolulu, HI 96824
Phone: 808-545-1889; Fax: 808-356-1582
www.vacch.org

Vietnam Consulate General
1700 California St.
Ste. 580
San Francisco, CA 94109
Phone: 415-922-1707; Fax: 415-922-1848
www.vietnamconsulate-sf.org

Vietnam Embassy
1233 20th St. N.W.
Ste. 400
Washington, DC 20036
Phone: 202-861-0737; Fax: 202-861-0917
vietnamembassy-usa.org

Viet Nam Permanent Mission to the UN
866 United Nations Plaza
Ste. 435
New York, NY 10017
Phone: 212-644-0594; Fax: 212-644-5732
www.vietnam-un.org

Yemen

Yemen Embassy
2319 Wyoming Ave. N.W.

Washington, DC 20008
Phone: 202-965-4760; Fax: 202-337-2017
www.yemenembassy.org

Yeman Permanent to the UN
413 E. 51st St.
New York, NY 10022
Phone: 212-355-1730; Fax: 212-750-9613
www.un.int/yemen

Zambia

Zambia Embassy
2419 Massachusetts Ave. N.W.
Washington, DC 20008
Phone: 202-265-9717; Fax: 202-332-0826
www.zambiaembassy.org

Zambia Permanent Mission to the UN
237 E. 52nd St.

New York, NY 10022
Phone: 212-888-5770; Fax: 212-888-5213
www.un.int

Zimbabwe

Zimbabwe Embassy
1608 New Hampshire Ave. N.W.
Washington, DC 20009
Phone: 202-332-7100; Fax: 202-483-9326
www.zimbabwe-embassy.us

Zimbabwe Permanent Mission to the UN
128 E. 56th St.
New York, NY 10022
Phone: 212-980-9511; Fax: 212-308-6705
www.un.int/zimbabwe

APPENDIX 13

Bibliography

This annotated bibliography contains sources consulted for *HFCWD*, as well as other sources for further reading. Sources cited in the bibliography are organized under the following categories:

I. Reference and Other Background Works on Holidays

A. *General Works*
B. *Calendars and Time-Reckoning Systems*
C. *Festival Organization*
D. *Philosophy, Theory, and Analysis of Festivity*
E. *Teaching Aids*

II. Holidays of Major Religious Traditions

A. *General Works*
B. *African*
C. *Baha'i*
D. *Buddhism*
E. *Christianity*
F. *Hinduism*
G. *Islam*
H. *Judaism*
I. *Sikhism*
J. *Taoism*
K. *Zoroastrianism*

III. Holidays of Ethnic Groups and Geographic Regions

A. *General Works*
B. *Africa*
C. *Ancient World (Western)*
D. *Asia and the Middle East*
　1. General Works
　2. Bangladesh
　3. China and Honk Kong
　4. India and Sri Lanka
　5. Indonesia
　6. Iran
　7. Japan
　8. Korea
　9. Lebanon
　10. Mongolia
　11. Nepal
　12. Philippines
　13. Saudi Arabia
　14. Thailand
　15. Turkey
　16. Vietnam
E. *Caribbean and Latin America*
　1. General Works
　2. Cuba
　3. Dominican Republic
　4. El Salvador
　5. Haiti
　6. Jamaica
　7. Mexico
　8. Trinidad
F. *South America*
G. *Europe*
　1. General Works
　2. Albania
　3. Bulgaria
　4. Czechoslovakia
　5. France
　6. Germany
　7. Greece
　8. Hungary
　9. Italy
　10. Macedonia
　11. Russia
　12. Scandinavia
　13. Soviet Union (former)
　14. Spain
　15. Ukraine
　16. United Kingdom
H. *North America*
　1. General Works
　2. Canada
　3. Native North America
　4. United States—General Works and Background on Holidays
　5. United States—Works on the Presidents
　6. United States—Works on the States

IV. Individual Holidays

A. *Christmas*
B. *Easter*
C. *Fourth of July*
D. *Halloween*
E. *Mardi Gras*
F. *Memorial Day*
G. *Mother Day*
H. *New Year*

I. REFERENCE AND OTHER BACK-GROUND WORKS ON HOLIDAYS

A. General Works

Augur, Helen. *The Book of Fairs*. Introduction by Hendrik Willem Van Loon. Illustrated by James MacDonald. 1939. Reprint. Detroit: Omnigraphics, Inc., 1992.

> Traces the development of trade, customs, and social life in connection with fairs in history up to the 1939 World's Fair. Includes discussion of fairs and festivals in ancient Tyre, Athens and Rome, the Kinsai Fairs in 13th-century Cathay, festivals in 13th-century France, 15th-century Belgium and Germany, medieval England, Ireland and Scotland, Russia, and the modern expositions.

Blackburn, Bonnie, and Leofranc Holford-Strevens. *The Oxford Companion to the Year: An Exploration of Calendar Customs and Time-Reckoning*. Oxford: Oxford University Press, 2003.

> This day-by-day guide presents idiosyncratic inclusion of mostly English holidays. It claims Chambers's *Book of Days* (see below) as its predecessor and includes much the same kind of material. Part I is arranged by month. Each month opens with a brief history of the month's name, concentrating on ancient Rome and ancient Britain, followed with a brief list of some important holidays around the world. Part I also includes essays on the seasons; Oxford, Cambridge, and law terms; the months; the week; days; the Western Church year and its feasts; the Orthodox Church year and its feasts; and other holidays. Part II provides essays on days and times, calendar systems, and dating.

Chambers, Robert, ed. *The Book of Days: A Miscellany of Popular Antiquities in connection with the Calendar, including Anecdote, Biography, & History, Curiosities of Literature, and Oddities of Human Life and Character*. New introduction by Tristram Potter Coffin. 1862-64. Reprint. Detroit: Omnigraphics, Inc., 1990.

> British tome organized chronologically and covering popular Christian festivals and saints' days; seasonal phenomena; folklore of the British Isles, especially that connected with the passing of time and seasons of the year; "Notable Events, Biographies, and Anecdotes connected with the Days of the Year"; "Articles of Popular Archaeology, of an entertaining character, tending to illustrate the progress of Civilization, Manners, Literature, and Ideas in these kingdoms"; and other miscellaneous items.

Cirlot, J. E. *A Dictionary of Symbols*. 2nd ed. Translated by Jack Sage. Foreword by Herbert Read. New York: Philosophical Library, 1971.

> Hundreds of entries on symbols and their significance. Symbols include animals, objects, natural phenomena, places, and mythological and other characters.

Clynes, Tom. *Wild Planet: 1,001 Extraordinary Events for the Inspired Traveler*. Detroit: Gale Research Inc., 1995.

> Light-hearted look at 1,001 festivals around the world, arranged by geographical region. Entries also provide brief notes on transport, accommodations, and other local festivals, as well as contact information. Festival theme index, chronological index, and festival name index.

Corwin, Judith Hoffman. *Harvest Festivals around the World*. Illustrated by the author. Parsippany, NJ: Silver Burdett Press, 1995.

> Introduction to selected harvest festivals in Barbados, Switzerland, England, Nigeria, Ghana, Israel, Japan, China, India, ancient Egypt, Canada, and among Incans and the Hopi Indians for young readers. Includes craft activities and recipes.

Deems, Edward M., comp. *Holy-Days and Holidays*. 1902. Reprint. Detroit: Gale Research Company, 1968.

> Divided into two major sections—religious and secular holidays—both arranged chronologically. Covers events observed in the United States, Canada, and United Kingdom. For each holiday, the compiler presents an introductory essay, a selection of prose essays, sermons and speeches, an alphabetical list of "suggestive thoughts," and poetry pertaining to the occasion.

Dobler, Lavinia. *Customs and Holidays around the World*. Illustrated and designed by Josephine Little. New York: Fleet Publishing Corporation, 1962.

> Written for children under the supervision of the Rev. Howard V. Harper, this volume describes secular and religious holidays and festivals around the world by season.

Dobler, Lavinia. *National Holidays around the World*. Illustrated and designed by Vivian Browne. New York: Fleet Press Corporation, 1968. 233 pp.

> Covers national and independence days from more than 130 countries. Written for a young audience. Entries are chronologically arranged and provide brief recounting of historical and political circumstances leading up to the observance of the day and a description of the nation's flag.

Dossey, Donald E. *Holiday Folklore, Phobias and Fun: Mythical Origins, Scientific Treatments and Superstitious "Cures."* Los Angeles: Outcomes Unlimited Press, Inc., 1992.

> An expert on phobias and anxiety and stress disorders conducts informal survey of origins of various holiday customs—New Year's, St. Valentine's Day, St. Patrick's Day, Friday the 13th, Easter, April Fools' Day, Halloween, Thanksgiving, Christmas—while offering advice on dealing with holiday stress and anxiety. Appendices include some folklore recipes, tips for cognitive refocusing and keying, and list of phobias and symptoms.

Dunkling, Leslie. *Dictionary of Days*. New York: Facts on File, 1988.

> Alphabetical listing of more than 700 named days: local days, fictional days (such as The Day of the Jackal and Lewis Carroll's "unbirthday"), expressions (such as "hey-day" and "turkey day"), generic (e.g., Friday) and technical terms (e.g., sidereal day) as well as names of holidays and other observed events. Much cross-referencing. Emphasis is on providing general-interest etymological information on the name itself in addition to giving basic definition of the day's significance. Often gives Scottish and northern English dialectical forms. Many entries include relevant literary quotations. A special feature is a calendar that chronologically maps the days discussed.

Frazer, James George. *The Golden Bough: A Study in Magic and Religion*. One volume, abridged ed. New York: Collier Books, 1950.

> Numerous festivals are discussed in this classic work on legends, mythology, and religions throughout the world, abridged in one volume.

Griffin, Robert H., and Ann H. Shurgin, eds. *The Folklore of World Holidays*. 2nd ed. Detroit: Gale Research Inc., 1999.

Chronologically arranged collection of customs, legends, songs, food, superstitions, games, pageants, etc., associated with more than 340 festivals and holidays in over 150 countries. The United States and, for the most part, Canada, are not included. The editor provides a brief explanation of the holiday, followed by excerpts from written material describing actual observances of the event. Bibliographic information for each source follow the excerpts.

Heinberg, Richard. *Celebrate the Solstice: Honoring the Earth's Rhythms Through Festival and Ceremony*. Foreword by Dolores LaChapelle. Wheaton, IL: Quest Books, The Theosophical Publishing House, 1993.

Discusses the celebration of winter and summer solstices and world renewal rites and myths throughout history around the world. Suggests activities for contemporary observance.

Helfman, Elizabeth S. *Celebrating Nature: Rites and Ceremonies Around the World*. Illustrated by Carolyn Cather. New York: The Seabury Press, 1969.

Describes for young readers celebrations associated with the seasons from ancient times among Egyptians, Hebrews, Babylonians, Greeks, Romans, Ashanti, Yoruba, Ga and Kikuyu peoples in Africa, New Guinea peoples, Thai people, Chinese, Japanese, Hindus, Saora people, Muslims, Incans, Mapuche Indians, Aztecs, and North American Indians, as well as observance of Christian holidays throughout the world. Pronunciation guide. Further reading list.

Henderson, Helene, ed. *Holiday Symbols and Customs: A Guide to the Legend and Lore behind the Traditions, Rituals, Foods, Games, Animals, and Other Symbols and Activities Associated with Holidays and Holy Days, Feasts and Fasts, and Other Celebrations Covering Calendar, Religious, Historic, Folkloric, National, Promotional, Sporting and Ancient Events, as Observed in the United States and Around the World*. 4th ed. Detroit: Omnigraphics, 2009.

Provides an introduction to the many ways in which people celebrate and find meaning in their holiday traditions. This revised and expanded edition includes over 300 entries that cover such diverse topics as the Academy Awards, Cinco de Mayo, the Hiroshima Peace Ceremony, the Rose Bowl, and Watch Night. Each entry explains the type of holiday, when and where it is observed, and the related symbols and customs. Additional sections include information on tourism organizations for all U.S. states and for nations around the world; contact information for relevant organizations; explanations of secular and religious calendars; and a bibliography and index.

Hone, William. *The Every-Day Book; or, Everlasting Calendar of Popular Amusements, Sports, Pastimes, Ceremonies, Manners, Customs, and Events, Incident to Each of the Three Hundred and Sixty-Five Days, in Past and Present Times; Forming a Complete History of the Year, Months, & Seasons, and a Perpetual Key to the Almanack; Including Accounts of the Weather, Rules for Health and Conduct, Remarkable and Important Anecdotes, Facts, and Notices, in Chronology, Antiquities, Topography, Biography, Natural History, Art, Science, and General Literature; Derived from the Most Authentic Sources, and Valuable Original Communications, with Poetical Elucidations, for Daily Use and Diversion*. Introduction by Leslie Shepard. 2 vols. 1827. Reprint. Detroit: Omnigraphics, Inc., 1990.

Each volume presents a different collection of miscellany on holy days, festivals, and anniversaries from January 1 through December 31. Indexes of general subjects, Christian saints, poetry, flowers and plants, and engravings are found in both volumes. Bibliography of works by William Hone.

Humphrey, Grace. *Stories of the World's Holidays*. 1924. Reprint. Detroit: Omnigraphics, Inc., 1990.

Twenty stories for young readers describing the origins of commemorated historical events in the United States, England, France, Italy, China, Japan, Poland, Ireland, Czechoslovakia, and South America, arranged in chronological order. Suggested reading list.

Ickis, Marguerite. *The Book of Festivals and Holidays the World Over*. Drawings by Richard E. Howard. New York: Dodd, Mead & Co., 1970.

A selection of "holidays and festivals that are current and give promise of continuing indefinitely," 12 chapters in chronological order cover customs and legends associated with New Year's, Epiphany, Lent, Holy Week, Easter, Advent, and Christmas, as well as more than 80 winter, spring, summer, and fall festivals in nearly 50 countries.

Ingpen, Robert, and Philip Wilkinson. *A Celebration of Customs & Rituals of the World*. New York: Facts on File, 1996.

The first part of the book discusses calendar customs around the world in chronological order by month. Subsequent sections describe life-cycle ceremonies, agricultural customs, social and worship rituals, and art.

James, E. O. *Seasonal Feasts and Festivals*. 1961. Reprint. Detroit: Omnigraphics, Inc., 1993.

Covers more than 100 season-based rituals, dances, plays, and festivals of the Paleolithic era, vegetation cults, Egypt, Mesopotamia, Palestine, Hebrew, Asia Minor and Greece, Rome, Christianity, and medieval to 18th-century Europe. Examines Egyptian, Babylonian, Greek, Roman, Julian, and Christian calendars.

Kindersley, Barnabas, and Annabel Kindersley. *Celebrations! Festivals, Carnivals, and Feast Days from around the World (Children Just Like Me)*. New York: DK Publishing, 1997.

This husband (photographer) and wife (author) traveled around the world collecting photos and stories from children about festivals. Published in association with the United Nations Children's Fund (UNICEF). For young readers.

Leach, Maria, ed. *Funk & Wagnalls Standard Dictionary of Folklore, Mythology & Legend*. San Francisco: HarperSanFrancisco, 1996.

This first one-volume edition contains "a representative sampling," contributions from 34 anthropologists and folklorists of more than 4,500 entries on animals, minerals, vegetables and objects, rituals, festivals and practices, songs, legends and games, and gods, monsters and other entities associated with the folklore and mythology of over 2,000 cultures, peoples, and countries and other geographical regions in the world. More than 50 longer essays surveying the folklore of various cultures and folkloric methodologies, themes and elements conclude with bibliographies. In addition, sources are occasionally inserted throughout in individual entries.

Long, Kim. *The Almanac of Anniversaries*. 2nd ed. Santa Barbara: ABC-CLIO, 1993.

Timeline-like structure provides 25th, 50th, ... 500th anniversaries relating to notable events and people that will take place between 1993 and 2001. Within each year, anniversaries are given chronologically. Calendar Locator chart provides crossreference of years and milestones.

McFarland, Jeanne. *Festivals*. Morristown, NJ: Silver Burdett Company, 1981.

Brief discussion of some major ancient and modern festivals and holidays throughout the world for younger readers.

Merin, Jennifer, with Elizabeth B. Burdick. *International Directory of Theatre, Dance, and Folklore Festivals*. Westport, CT: Greenwood Press, 1979.

More than 850 festivals involving theater, dance or folklore in over 50 countries are covered. The United States is not included. Entries are organized by country and often contain mailing addresses, phone numbers, contact names, and dates of occurrence. Length of festival description varies from a few lines to a few paragraphs. Festival entries are followed by a country-by-country chronological listing of festivals, bibliography, an appendix listing the number of festivals in each country, and index of festivals by festival name.

Nickerson, Betty. *Celebrate the Sun: A Heritage of Festivals Interpreted through the Art of Children from Many Lands*. New York: J. B. Lippincott Company, 1969.

Covers more than 30 holidays worldwide, as well as provides descriptions of such events as spring festivals, weddings, parades, processions, fairs, circuses, and side shows—all accompanied by over 40 paintings by children around the world.

Shemanski, Frances. *A Guide to World Fairs and Festivals*. Westport, CT: Greenwood Press, 1985.

Following the format of *A Guide to Fairs and Festivals in the United States* by the same author, this volume includes entries on more than 280 fairs and festivals held in 75 countries. A country-by-country chronological listing of festivals follows the main text. Appendix lists festivals by type.

Spicer, Dorothy Gladys. *Book of Festivals*. Foreword by John H. Finley. 1937. Reprint. Detroit: Omnigraphics, Inc., 1990.

The main part of the book is broken down into 35 chapters, each covering an ethnic or major religious (Hindu, Jew, and Muslim or Mohammedan) group or nationality. Groups were chosen on the basis of their representation in the United States. Geographic areas covered include Asia, eastern and western Europe, India, the Middle East, and the United States. Within each chapter, holidays and festivals are listed and described in chronological order. Part II of the book is devoted to discussions of the Armenian, Chinese, Gregorian, Hindu, Jewish, Julian, and Mohammedan calendars. Topics include rate of variation between the Julian and Gregorian calendars, dates of Easter computed between 1938 and 1950, and dates of major Jewish holidays computed between 1936 and 1951. The appendix is a glossary of religious and festival terms. The bibliography, with notes, organizes sources by ethnic group or nationality.

Spielgelman, Judith. *UNICEF's Festival Book*. Illustrated by Audrey Preissler. New York: U.S. Committee for UNICEF, 1966.

For young readers. Presents New Year (Enkutatash) in Ethiopia, Divali in India, Now-ruz (Nawruz) in Iran, Hanukkah in Israel, Doll Festival (Hina Matsuri) in Japan, Posadas in Mexico, Sinterklaas (St. Nicholas's Day) in the Netherlands, end of Ramadan ('Id al-Fitr) in Pakistan, Easter in Poland, Lucia Day (St.

Lucy's Day) in Sweden, Songkran in Thailand, and Halloween in Canada and the United States.

Stoll, Dennis Gray. *Music Festivals of the World: A Guide to Leading Festivals of Music, Opera and Ballet*. London: Pergamon Press, Ltd., 1963.

Describes more than 50 music festivals in over 20 countries that run for at least eight days, feature performers known around the world, and show signs of continuing indefinitely. Book is organized into thematic chapters containing essays discussing each event's special features and background and addresses for obtaining tickets. Index of festivals.

Trawicky, Bernard. *Anniversaries and Holidays*. 5th ed. Chicago: American Library Association, 2000.

Organized chronologically, this book offers more than 3,000 short entries on religious and civic holidays and anniversaries marking notable people and events. The first and longest part of the book covers fixed days according to the Gregorian calendar. Months begin with an introductory note covering how the month was named, notable historical events or festivals occurring in the month, and flowers and birthstones associated with it. Entries are grouped together under each date by "Holy Days and Feast Days," "Holidays and Civic Days," and "Anniversaries and Special Events Days." Movable days are listed in the second part of the book and are organized by the Christian, Jewish, Islamic, and Chinese calendars. The annotated bibliography describes more than 400 books and web sites related to primarily U.S. holidays and anniversaries and is broken down by subject.

Van Straalen, Alice. *Book of Holidays around the World*. New York: E. P. Dutton, 1986.

Brief datebook-style entries provide at least one observance or anniversary for each day of the year. Photographs and reproductions of literary illustrations and artwork punctuate nearly every page. Appendices offer brief descriptions of Buddhist, Chinese, Christian, Hindu, Islamic, and Jewish calendars, followed by alphabetical listing of movable festivals and holidays.

Walsh, William S. *Curiosities of Popular Customs and of Rites, Ceremonies, Observances, and Miscellaneous Antiquities*. 1914. Reprint. Detroit: Gale Research Company, 1966.

Dictionary-style coverage of Christian, Jewish, Islamic, Buddhist, Japanese, Chinese, Hindu, ancient, and secular holidays and feasts including entries on people, places, customs, and relics associated with them. Also contains entries on birthdays, the months, and various calendars.

Webster, Hutton. *Rest Days; The Christian Sunday, the Jewish Sabbath, and Their Historical and Anthropological Prototypes*. 1916. Reprint. Detroit: Omnigraphics, Inc., 1992.

The standard work on the origin of holy days and their religious and sociological development. Among topics covered are the tabooed days at critical epochs, the holy days, lunar superstitions and festivals, lunar calendars and the week, market days, unlucky days, the Babylonian "evil days," and the Shabattum.

B. Calendars and Time-Reckoning Systems

Achelis, Elisabeth. *The Calendar for Everybody*. 1943. Reprint. Detroit: Omnigraphics, Inc., 1990.

Traces the calendar from its beginning, relating little-known facts about our present calendar and proposes a new calendar system and presents advantages to be gained by using it. Discusses the earth's time, the Egyptian, Julian, Gregorian, and world calendars.

Asimov, Isaac. *The Clock We Live On*. Revised ed. Illustrated by John Bradford. New York: Abelard-Schuman, 1965.

The scientist-science fiction writer explains the solar and lunar systems by which humans have learned to tell time. Surveys devices for keeping time, from ancient to modern clocks and calendars. Discussion of solar, lunar, Egyptian, Hebrew, Christian, Julian, Gregorian, and French Revolutionary calendars, and chronological eras.

Aveni, Anthony F. *Empires of Time: Calendars, Clocks, and Cultures*. New York: Kodansha International, 1995.

A far-reaching examination of concepts of time and calendar systems across cultures and throughout history. Discusses historical development and workings of various calendar and time-reckoning schemes, pointing out their contribution to cultural systems as well as illustrating the connection between political power and control over the calendar. Explores the evidence for the earliest known calendar systems, including Neolithic time-reckoning systems, calendar systems of the ancient Greeks, and the Stonehenge controversy. Detailed coverage of the Western (Gregorian), Mayan, Aztec, Incan, and Chinese calendars, as well as discussion of the calendar systems of two tribal groups, the Nuer of East Africa, and the Trobriand Islanders of the Pacific.

Coleman, Lesley. *A Book of Time*. Camden, NJ: Thomas Nelson, Inc., 1971.

Survey of Sumerian, Babylonian, Muslim, Christian, Jewish, Egyptian, Roman, Julian, Gregorian, and French Revolutionary calendars and the proposed World Calendar. Includes discussion of timepieces, clockmakers, navigation, and some theories and literature dealing with time.

Couzens, Reginald C. *The Stories of the Months and Days*. 1923. Reprint. Detroit: Omnigraphics, Inc., 1990.

Explains how the months and days were named, telling stories about the Greek, Roman, Anglo and Saxon gods, goddesses, and emperors with whom they are associated.

Irwin, Keith Gordon. *The 365 Days*. Illustrated by Guy Fleming. New York: Thomas Y. Crowell Company, 1963.

Discusses solar, lunar, and astronomical cycles, ancient calendars of Egypt, Babylon, Chaldea, Rome, and the Mayas. Traces origins and development from the Julian to the Gregorian calendars. Note on various calendars proposed in recent history. Section on dating the observance of Easter and Christmas. Discussion of carbon-dating and tree rings.

Krythe, Maymie R. *All About the Months*. New York: Harper & Row, Publishers, 1966.

Discussion, in chronological order, of how each month was named, anniversaries occurring within each month, lore and literature associated with the month, mention of ancient holidays and festivals, and each month's gem and flower.

O'Neil, W. M. *Time and the Calendars*. Sydney, Australia: Sydney University Press, 1975.

Examines Egyptian, Roman, Babylonian, Indian, Chinese, Meso-American, and Gregorian calendars, and the day, week, month, and year. Appendix gives names of the days in various languages.

Parise, Frank, ed. *The Book of Calendars*. 2nd ed. Piscataway, NJ: Gorgias Press, 2002.

Summarizes the history and organization of the Babylonian, Macedonian, Hebrew, Seleucid, Olympiad, Roman, Armenian, Islamic, Fasli, Zoroastrian, Yezdezred, Jelali, Egyptian, Coptic, Ethiopian, Iranian, Afghanistan, Akbar, Fasli Deccan, Parasuram, Burmese and Arakanse, Chinese, Tibetan, Mayan, Julian, Gregorian, and Christian eras and calendars. Tables throughout convert the various ancient and other calendars to Julian or Gregorian dates or years. Dates of Easter provided from the year 1 through 1999. Calendar of Christian saints. Explanations of the French Revolutionary calendar and the Soviet calendar. Table depicts dates various regions in Europe celebrated New Year's Day.

Richard, E. G. *Mapping Time: The Calendar and Its History*. Oxford, England: Oxford University Press, 1998.

Parts I and II present a history of calendar systems from ancient times, including Babylonian and Near Eastern, Egyptian, Chinese and east Asian, Indian, Mayan and Aztec, Greek, Celtic, Teutonic, Icelandic, Roman and Julian, Jewish, Islamic and Baha'i, Gregorian, and French Republican calendars. Part III provides mathematical formulas for calendar conversions. Part IV contains essays giving brief history of Easter and its dating.

Tannenbaum, Beulah, and Myra Stillman. *Understanding Time: The Science of Clocks and Calendars*. Illustrated by William D. Hayes. New York: Whittlesey House, 1958.

Explanation for young readers of time and clocks, calendars, and other measuring systems used throughout history. Each chapter includes suggested experiments.

C. Festival Organization

Goldblatt, Joe Jeff. *Special Events: The Art and Science of Celebration. Foreword by Linda Faulkner, Social Secretary to the White House during the Reagan Administration*. New York: Van Nostrand Reinhold, 1990.

Guide to the special events industry, including social, retail, corporate and government events, meetings, and conventions. Provides techniques for budgeting, planning, and creating events such as theme parties, awards ceremonies, holidays, fairs, festivals, sporting events, and more. Appendices list related books and organizations and provide the text of the Flag Code.

Wilson, Joe, and Lee Udall. *Folk Festivals: A Handbook for Organization and Management*. Knoxville: The University of Tennessee Press, 1982.

Guide for folklore festival organizers covering such topics as administration, programming concepts, planning, publicity, and production. Part Two describes three folk festivals produced in the United States (Tucson Meet Yourself Festivalsissippi Valley Folk Festival, and Open Fiddlers' Contest), including an interview with a festival performer and samples of media releases and public service announcements.

D. Philosophy, Theory, and Analysis of Festivity

Browne, Ray B., and Michael T. Marsden, eds. *The Cultures of Celebrations*. Bowling Green, OH: Bowling Green State University Popular Press, 1994.

Collection of 15 case studies from scholars working in areas relating to popular culture studies. Essays analyze various celebrations and forms of entertainment, including Shi'ite rituals, folk festivals in Australia, Lord Mayor's Procession, Columbus celebrations from the 18th to the 20th centuries, and seasonal festivals in Manitoba.

Cantwell, Robert. *Ethnomimesis: Folklife and the Representation of Culture*. Chapel Hill: The University of North Carolina Press, 1993.

> Describes the Festival of American Folklife, held annually on the Mall in Washington, DC, and discusses it as a cultural artifact that can yield insights on "festivity, identity, and memory."

Cox, Harvey. *The Feast of Fools: A Theological Essay on Festivity and Fantasy*. Cambridge, MA: Harvard University Press, 1969.

> Adapted from the William Belden Noble Lectures given by the author in 1968 at Harvard University. Theological examination of spiritual aspects of festivity and fantasy as practiced in Western cultures. Uses the medieval Feast of Fools and its eventual disappearance as a symbol for thesis that Western civilization needs a rebirth of "the spirit represented by the Feast of Fools."

Falassi, Alessandro, ed. *Time Out of Time: Essays on the Festival*. Albuquerque: University of New Mexico Press, 1987.

> Collection of essays by Goethe, Hemingway and Aldous Huxley, and Victor Turner, Vladimir Propp, and other folklorists describing and analyzing festivals celebrated in Europe, North and South America, Africa, Asia, and Oceania such as the Palio at Siena, the Roman Carnival, bullfighting, Olojo Festival, Carnival at Rio de Janeiro, the Holy Ghost Festival in the Azores, and more.

Handelman, Don. *Models and Mirrors: Towards an Anthropology of Public Events*. Cambridge, England: Cambridge University Press, 1990.

> Analyses of such festivals as the Palio of Siena, Christmas mumming in Newfoundland, observance of Jewish and state holidays in Israel and in Israeli kindergartens, and katchina dancers as well as other forms of public ritual play.

MacAloon, John J., ed. *Rite, Drama, Festival, Spectacle: Rehearsals Toward a Theory of Cultural Performance*. Philadelphia: Institute for the Study of Human Issues, Inc., 1984.

> Papers from 10 scholars in the humanities delivered at the 76th Burg Wartenstein Symposium, sponsored by the Wenner-Gren Foundation for Anthropological Research. Academic essays concerned with various cultural and performative implications of festival and ritual in literature and in actuality: "Liminiality and the Performative Genres," Victor Turner; "Charivari, Honor, and the Community in Seventeenth-Century Lyon and Geneva," Natalie Zemon Davis; "'Rough Music' in The Duchess of Malfi: Webster's Dance of Madmen and Charivari Tradition," Frank W. Wadsworth; "Borges's 'Immortal': Metaritual, Metaliturature, Metaperformance," Sophia S. Morgan; "Arrange Me into Disorder: Fragments and Reflections on Ritual Clowning," Barbara A. Babcock; "The Diviner and the Detective," Hilda Kuper; "A Death in Due Time: Construction of Self and Culture in Ritual Drama," Barbara G. Myerhoff; "The Ritual Process and the Problem of Reflexivity in Sinhalese Demon Exorcisms," Bruce Kapferer; "Carnival in Multiple Planes," Roberto Da Matta; and "Olympic Games and the Theory of Spectacle in Modern Societies," John J. MacAloon.

Pieper, Josef. *In Tune with the World: A Theory of Festivity*. Translated by Richard and Clara Winston. New York: Harcourt, Brace & World, Inc., 1965.

> Philosophical essay discusses what festivity means from a predominantly Western and Christian orientation. Includes consideration of festivity in relation to art, labor, and modern commercialization of history.

Thompson, E. P. *Customs in Common: Studies in Traditional Popular Culture*. New York: The New Press, 1993.

> Scholarly study of English working-class culture in the 18th and early 19th centuries. Includes examination of the historical contexts of such events as beating the bounds, the Horn Fair, and others.

Turner, Victor, ed. *Celebration: Studies in Festivity and Ritual*. Washington, DC: Smithsonian Institution Press, 1982.

> This companion volume to the Smithsonian Institution's exhibition of celebratory objects is a collection of essays exploring such topics as objects used in festivals, celebrations as rites of passage, and political, economic and religious festivals. Events included within the discussions are Juneteenth, Penitentes, Trinidad Carnival, Incwala, Juggernaut (Rath Yatra), Dragon Boat Festival in China, Rama festivals in India, German-American Passion Plays in the United States, and more.

E. Teaching Aids

Bauer, Caroline Feller. *Celebrations: Read-Aloud Holiday and Theme Book Programs*. Drawings by Lynn Gates Bredeson. New York: H. W. Wilson Company, 1985.

> Education specialist offers 16 theme book programs dealing with holidays and such invented celebrations as National Nothing Day and Pigmania for teachers and other professionals working with primarily middle-grade children. Each program includes some prose and poetry selections, ideas for bulletin boards, recipes, activities and jokes, and lists of related books marked for various age groups.

Dupuy, Trevor Nevitt, ed. *Holidays; Days of Significance for All Americans*. New York: Franklin Watts, Inc., 1965.

> Intended for elementary-school teachers. Brief essays from contributors to, and members of, the Historical Evaluation and Research Organization cover 27 patriotic holidays and commemorative days observed in the United States. Further reading list.

Green, Victor J. *Festivals and Saints Days: A Calendar of Festivals for School and Home*. Poole, Dorset, England: Blandford Press Ltd., 1978.

> Beginning with New Year's Day and following the calendar, the book covers more than 30 secular, Christian, Jewish, Hindu and Muslim holidays observed in Britain. Also includes Independence Day and Thanksgiving in the United States. Further reading list.

Hopkins, Lee Bennett, and Misha Arenstein. *Do You Know What Day Tomorrow Is? A Teacher's Almanac*. New York: Citation Press, 1975.

> Guide intended to integrate chronologically presented information about people, places, and events with elementary-school curriculum. Provided for each month are a brief explanation of its name, flower and birthstone, representative poem, and descriptive listings in chronological order of events in history, anniversaries associated with notable people, holidays, admission days, and other events that occur on each day of the year. Appendices include a reference bibliography for teachers and list of sources cited.

II. HOLIDAYS OF MAJOR RELIGIOUS TRADITIONS

A. General Works

Bellenir, Karen. *Religious Holidays and Calendars: An Encyclopedic Handbook*. Foreword by Martin E. Marty. 3rd ed. Detroit: Omnigraphics, Inc., 2004.

This third edition contains more than 100 new entries and is organized into three sections. Part One consists of chapters explaining the history of calendars around the world: Babylonian, Greek, Jewish, Indian, Chinese, Egyptian, Mayan and Aztec, Islamic, Roman, Julian, Gregorian, British, Teutonic, Icelandic, and modern calendar reform movements. Part Two consists of chapters on 17 religious groups. Each chapter provides background of the religion, overview of the religion's calendar, and descriptions of the religion's holidays. Listing of Internet resources. Appendices include: contact information and web sites for sources and organizations offering more information, a bibliography arranged by topic, and a five-year chronological list of holidays. Holiday Index, Calendar Index, and Master Index.

Bowker, John, ed. *The Oxford Dictionary of World Religions*. Oxford: Oxford University Press, 2007.

More than 80 contributors provide over 8,200 cross-referenced entries on major religions, movements, sects, people, texts, sacred sites, customs, festivals, and ethics. Topic index and index of Chinese headwords.

Crim, Keith, ed. *Perennial Dictionary of World Religions* (originally published as *Abingdon Dictionary of Living Religions*). San Francisco: Harper & Row, 1989.

Over 160 scholars contributed more than 1,600 entries on the world's major living systems of faith: deities, saints and other holy figures, religious sites, art and architecture, movements, sects and societies, authors and texts, creeds, prayers, mantras, and spiritual practices. Some bibliography provided throughout in individual entries. Long survey article on each major religion. Good cross-referencing. Guide to abbreviations and pronunciation table. Listing of key entries pertaining to major religions.

Eliade, Mircea, ed. *The Encyclopedia of Religion*. 16 vols. New York: Macmillan, 1987.

A comprehensive collection of articles by leading scholars and religious figures touching on all aspects of religion. Reflects the significant increase in knowledge and changing interpretive frameworks which have marked the study of religion in the last 60 years. Treats religious ideologies and practices, as well as sociological aspects of religions from Paleolithic times to the present. Generates broad view of topics through composite entries joining several articles under a common heading. Articles list works cited and give suggestions for further reading. Ample coverage of non-Western religions. Extensively crossreferenced.

Gross, Ernie. *This Day in Religion*. New York: Neal-Schuman Publishers, Inc., 1990.

Offers a day-by-day listing of significant events in the world of religion from biblical times to the present. Focuses on Christianity, but some coverage of Judaism and Eastern religions. Includes saints' days, the birth or death of religious leaders or notable figures in the world of religion, appointments, canonizations, feast days, founding dates of organizations and associations, and other important events.

Harper, Howard V. *Days and Customs of All Faiths*. 1957. Reprint. Detroit: Omnigraphics, Inc., 1990.

Part One contains more than 300 entries in chronological order that cover Roman, Jewish, and Christian religious festivals, saints' days and major secular holidays observed, especially in the United States. Part Two consists of chapters covering Jewish customs, major Christian holiday customs, including New Year's, words and expressions associated with various lore, and wedding customs.

Hinnells, John R., ed. *The Penguin Dictionary of Religions*. London: Penguin Books, 1997.

More than 1,000 entries contributed by 29 scholars cover deities, beliefs, people, places, texts, institutions, practices, rituals, and festivals associated with the world's religions, past and present. List of contents by subject area and contributor. Maps of Europe, ancient Near East and west Asia, Africa, the Indian sub-continent, Southeast Asia, Japan, China, Southwest Pacific and Australasia, North America, Mesoamerica, and Latin America. Substantial bibliography by subject area, cross-referenced with the entries. Synoptic index. General index.

Jones, Lindsay, ed. *Encyclopedia of Religion*. 2nd ed. Detroit: Macmillan Reference USA, 2005.

A broad encyclopedia that addresses religion through a cross-cultural approach, while emphasizing the role of religion in everyday life. Highlights the major religious events celebrated by the world's different religious groups.

Magida, Arthur J. and Stuart M Maltins. *How to Be a Perfect Stranger: A Guide to Etiquette in Other People's Religious Ceremonies*. Revised and updated. Woodstock, VT: Jewish Lights Pub., 1999.

Provides an overview of the content of and the expected dress and behavior at the services of 20 religious and denominational groups. Covers the Assemblies of God, Baptist, Buddhist, Christian Scientist, Disciples of Christ, Episcopalian, Greek Orthodox, Hindu, Islamic, Jehovah's Witnesses, Jewish, Lutheran, Methodist, Mormon, Presbyterian, Quaker, Catholic, Seventh-day Adventist, and United Church of Christ ceremonies. Lists each group's major religious holidays and their significance. Reviews the calendar systems of the major religions, and furnishes a calendar listing of their holidays for the years 1996 to 1998.

Parrinder, Geoffrey. *A Dictionary of Non-Christian Religions*. Philadelphia: The Westminster Press, 1971.

More than 2,400 entries provide A to Z coverage of people, deities, rites, locations, festivals, texts, philosophies, etc., associated with ancient and living non-Christian religions, including various African religions, Aztec, Baha'i, Buddhism, Confucianism, Hinduism, Islam, Jainism, Judaism, Maori religion, Native American religions, Shinto, Sikhism, Taoism, Theosophy, Yoruba, Zoroastrianism, religions of ancient Rome, Greece, Babylon, and of the Celts, Egyptians, Incans, Mayans, Scandinavians, and others. Cross-referencing. Lists of Egyptian, Chinese, and Islamic dates and dynasties. Further reading list.

Pike, Royston. *Round the Year with the World's Religions*. 1950. Reprint. Detroit: Omnigraphics, Inc., 1993.

Chronologically arranged chapters covering customs, legends, and stories behind religious observances in ancient Rome and Greece, Europe, India, Tibet, China, Japan, and Ceylon (Sri Lanka), and among ancient Romans, Greeks and Egyptians, Jews, Christians, Hindus, Jains, Muslims, Buddhists, Incans, and Aztecs.

Riggs, Thomas, ed. *Worldmark Encyclopedia of Religious Practices*. 2nd ed. Farmington Hills: Gale, Cengage Learning, 2014.

> A three-volume, 1,800-page set that describes current religious practices throughout the world, including festivals and holidays, rituals, rites of passage, dietary practices, modes of dress, and other topics for 13 major religions and 28 religious subgroups.

B. African

King, Noel Q. *Religions of Africa: A Pilgrimage into Traditional Religions*. New York: Harper & Row, Publishers, 1970.

> Discusses Ashanti, Yoruba, and others' religious festivals, ceremonies, and customs, such as the Egungun Festival and ceremonies for Yoruba deities, as well as birth, initiation, marriage, and death customs among various African ethnic groups. Notes on pronunciation. Good further reading list, including many works in English.

Lawson, E. Thomas. *Religions of Africa: Traditions in Transformation*. Religious Traditions of the World Series. San Francisco: Harper & Row, 1984.

> Surveys history and religious traditions of the Zulu and Yoruba peoples. Covers customs, legends, and ceremonies associated with birth, puberty, marriage, and death. Festivals described include the Zulu (or Shembe) Festival, New Year's, and the New Yam Festival. Further reading list.

Murphy, Joseph M. *Working the Spirit: Ceremonies of the African Diaspora*. Boston: Beacon Press, 1994.

> Describes history, significance, and performance of religious ceremonies, practices, music, and dances observed through Voodoo in Haiti, Candomblé in Brazil, Santería in Cuba and among Cuban Americans, Revival Zion in Jamaica, and "the Black Church" in the United States, in attempt to show how all are connected to a common spiritual foundation.

C. Baha'i

Smith, Peter. *A Concise Encyclopedia of the Baha'i Faith*. Oxford: Oneworld, 2008.

> More than 600 entries introduce people, history, places, sacred texts, beliefs, and tenets of the faith. Cross references.

Gaver, Jessyca Russell. *The Baha'i Faith: Dawn of a New Day*. New York: Hawthorn Books, Inc., 1967.

> Surveys the development of the Baha'i faith and its major prophets, beliefs, and laws and obligations. Discussion of observance of the Nineteen-Day Feast, New Year (Nawruz), and the Ridvan Festival.

D. Buddhism

Bechert, Heinz, and Richard Gombrich, eds. *The World of Buddhism: Buddhist Monks and Nuns in Society and Culture*. London: Thames and Hudson, 1984.

> Covers the spread of Buddhism and describes tenets and practices.

Snelling, John. *Buddhist Festivals*. Holidays and Festivals Series. Vero Beach, FL: Rourke Enterprises, Inc., 1987.

> For young readers. Provides historical background on Buddha and discusses Buddhist festivals in Thailand, Sri Lanka, Tibet, and Japan, as well as brief notes on Buddhist observances in Asia, the United States, and Britain. Further reading list.

E. Christianity

Attwater, Donald and Catherine Rachel John. *The Penguin Dictionary of Saints*. 3rd ed. London: Penguin, 1983.

> Covers, in alphabetical order, more than 750 saints. Scope is international. Includes obscure and early, as well as more popular and recent saints. List of emblems associated with saints. Chronological list of feast days.

Bentley, James. *A Calendar of Saints: The Lives of the Principal Saints of the Christian Year*. New York: Facts on File Publications, 1986.

> Brief biographies of more than 300 saints are provided. Inspirational quotes from saints preface each month and also appear throughout. Richly illustrated, over 300 paintings are reproduced.

Brewster, H. Pomeroy. *Saints and Festivals of the Christian Church*. 1904. Reprint. Detroit: Omnigraphics, Inc., 1990.

> Much of the book originally appeared as a series of articles published in the *Union and Advertiser* in Rochester, New York, which the author subsequently revised, adding more material to be published in the form reprinted in 1990. A yearbook of sorts of the Christian calendar, entries are arranged in chronological order, beginning with Advent. At least one saint or church feast is discussed for nearly every day of the year. Chronological list of the bishops and popes of the Christian church since St. Peter. Alphabetical list of canonized saints and others. General Index.

Cowie, L. W., and John Selwyn Gummer. *The Christian Calendar: A Complete Guide to the Seasons of the Christian Year Telling the Story of Christ and the Saints from Advent to Pentecost*. Springfield, MA: G & C Merriam Company, Publishers, 1974.

> Introduction gives historical background on the development of the Christian calendar. Part one discusses each Christian holiday and Sunday of the liturgical year, from Advent to the 24th Sunday after Pentecost, discussing the scripture and/or festival associated with each day covered. Part two provides entries, in chronological order, on saints' days and feasts for every day of the Gregorian year. List of patron saints, in alphabetical order by saint. Glossarial index.

Denis-Boulet, Noële M. *The Christian Calendar*. Vol. 113 of the *Twentieth-Century Encyclopedia of Catholicism*. Translated by P. Hepburne-Scott. New York: Hawthorn Books, 1960.

> Provides historical background on how the Christian calendar evolved from earlier calendars. Discussion of the observance of Sunday, Easter, and other feasts. History of martyrologies. Calendar reforms through history and contemporary reform proposal of a world calendar.

Farmer, David Hugh. *The Oxford Dictionary of Saints*. 5th ed. Oxford, England: Oxford University Press, 2011.

> Covers, in alphabetical order, more than 1,000 saints venerated in the Christian church—mainly in Great Britain, but this edition also includes some Greek and Russian saints from Eastern Orthodoxy. Bibliographical sources conclude the entries. Appendices include a list of English people who have been candidates for canonization and are associated with a popular cult, a list of patronages of saints, iconographical emblems of saints, places in Great Britain and Ireland associated with saints, and a calendar of feast days for saints.

Gwynne, Rev. Walker. *The Christian Year: Its Purpose and Its History.* 1917. Reprint. Detroit: Omnigraphics, Inc., 1990.

> Beginning chapters address the purpose and development of the Christian liturgical year. Discussion of Jewish holidays, as well as early Christians' observance of Jewish feasts and transformation of these into Christian feasts. Church calendar is explained, along with technical terms associated with it. History and description of observances of holidays and saints' days. Appendix includes liturgical colors and questions for review or examination.

Hamilton, Mary. *Greek Saints and Their Festivals.* London: William Blackwood and Sons, 1910.

> Describes the observance of saints' days and other religious, as well as a few secular, holidays as celebrated in Greece, by the Greek Orthodox Church, and in Italy, Sicily, and Sardinia.

Holweck, Frederick George. *A Biographical Dictionary of the Saints, with a General Introduction on Hagiology.* 1924. Reprint. Detroit: Omnigraphics, Inc., 1990.

> Covers thousands of saints—all those venerated in any Christian church, including those not officially canonized but with popular cult following. Brief bibliographical notices.

Metford, J.C.J. *The Christian Year.* London: Thames and Hudson, 1991.

> Explanation of the Christian liturgical year and its feasts, fasts, and other special days.

Monks, James L. *Great Catholic Festivals.* Great Religious Festivals Series. New York: Henry Schuman, 1951.

> Discusses origins and Catholic observance of Christmas, Epiphany, Easter, Pentecost, Corpus Christi, and Assumption.

New Catholic Encyclopedia. 2nd ed. Washington, DC: Catholic University of America Press, 2003.

> Provides information about persons, institutions, religions, philosophies, scientific developments, and social movements related to the Catholic Church.

Rodgers, Edith Cooperrider. *Discussion of Holidays in the Later Middle Ages.* New York: Columbia University Press, 1940. Reprinted by AMS Press, 1967.

> Examines holy days observed (or not observed), the Church's position on feasts, rules of observance, and nature of actual observance of religious holidays between 1200 and the Reformation.

Secretariat, Bishops' Committee on the Liturgy, National Conference of Catholic Bishops [Gurrieri, John A.]. *Holy Days in the United States.* Washington, DC: United States Catholic Conference, 1984.

> Description of history, meaning, and liturgical and popular observance of the six holy days of obligation, as well as saints' days, with discussion of American saints, and other special days for Roman Catholics in the United States. Questions for discussion and suggested reading list conclude each chapter.

Urlin, Ethel L. *Festivals, Holy Days, and Saints' Days: A Study in Origins and Survivals in Church Ceremonies & Secular Customs.* 1915. Reprint. Detroit: Omnigraphics, Inc., 1992.

> Entries cover, in chronological order, major Christian festivals and saints' days in England and Europe. Some mention of ancient Roman and Greek festivals where they figure in the origins of current Christian feasts. Listing of liturgical colors and the festivals during which they are worn by clergy. English calendar of Christian festivals and saints' days.

Wainwright, Geoffrey, and Karen B. Westerfield Tucker, eds. *The Oxford History of Christian Worship.* Oxford: Oxford University Press, 2006.

> Comprehensive history covers the liturgical traditions of Orthodox, Catholic, Protestant, and Pentecostal traditions throughout the world, and includes material on the cultural contexts of those traditions.

Walshchael, ed. *Butler's Lives of the Saints.* Concise ed. Foreword by Cardinal Basil Hume. San Francisco: Harper & Row, Publishers, 1985.

> Abridgement of the four-volume *Lives of the Saints, or The Lives of the Fathers, Martyrs and other Principal Saints: Compiled from Original Monuments and other authentick records: Illustrated with the Remarks of judicious modern criticks and historians,* by Alban Butler, originally published in London between 1756 and 1759. The original contained nearly 1,500 entries. Later editions expanded to include 2,500. This edition provides biographical sketches and legends associated with one saint for each day of the year, in chronological order. List of patron saints.

Weiser, Francis X. *Handbook of Christian Feasts and Customs: The Year of the Lord in Liturgy and Folklore.* New York: Harcourt, Brace & World, Inc., 1958.

> Part I discusses Christian significance of Sunday and other days of the week, ember days, and rogation days. Part II is organized according to the Christian calendar and presents descriptions of major Christian feasts. Part III deals with the veneration of saints and Mary and provides some background on a few of the most popular saints.

F. Hinduism

Gupte, Rai Bahadur B. A. *Hindu Holidays and Ceremonials with Dissertations on Origin, Folklore and Symbols.* Calcutta and Simla, India: Thacker, Spink & Co., 1919.

> The main text contains dictionary-style entries on Hindu festivals, days and places of worship and ceremony, and mythological and historical persons along with constellations associated with them. Brief glossary precedes main text with entries on animals and plants with folkloric significance.

Mitter, Swasti. *Hindu Festivals.* Holidays and Festivals Series. Vero Beach, FL: Rourke Enterprises, Inc., 1989.

> Background for young readers on Hindu beliefs, history, and festivals inside and outside India. Note on the Hindu calendar and chronological table of Hindu holidays by month.

Sivananda, Sri Swami. *Hindu Fasts and Festivals.* India: The Yoga-Vedanta Forest Academy Press, 1983.

> Explains religious significance and customs and observances of 27 popular Hindu festivals. Also discusses folklore surrounding eclipses and special days. Includes some Hindu prayers. Concludes with an essay on the "Philosophy of Idol Worship."

Stutley, Margaret, and James Stutley. *Harper's Dictionary of Hinduism: Its Mythology, Folklore, Philosophy, Literature, and History.* San Francisco: Harper & Row, 1977.

> Contains 2,500 entries on Hindu history, people, deities, texts, rituals, and other subjects.

Thomas, Paul. *Hindu Religion, Customs and Manners, Describing the Customs and Manners, Religious, Social and Domestic*

Life, Arts and Sciences of the Hindus. 4th rev ed. Bombay, India: D. B. Taraporevala Sons & Co., Ltd., 1960.

Covers Hindu history and creation theories, the caste system, religious sects, beliefs and practices, philosophy, social and domestic life, superstitions, etiquette, dress and ornamentation, literature and languages, ceremonies, music, dance, the calendar and holidays, architecture, the fine arts, and courtship and love.

Underhill, M. M. *The Hindu Religious Year.* London: Oxford University Press, 1921.

Discussion of festivals celebrated in India, including one chapter devoted to those in the state of Maharashtra.

G. Islam

Ahsan, M. M. *Muslim Festivals. Holidays and Festivals Series.*

Vero Beach, FL: Rourke Enterprises, Inc., 1987.

Presents Islamic beliefs, holidays, and rites for young readers. Note on Islamic calendar. Chronological table of Muslim holidays by Islamic month. Further reading list.

Feener, R. Michael. *Islam in World Cultures: Comparative Perspectives.* Santa Barbara.: ABC-CLIO, 2004.

Provides an introduction to the issues relating to Islam in the context of globalization. Analyzes differences in Islamic culture and practice by looking at how Islam interacts with local cultures.

Glassé, Cyril. *The Concise Encyclopedia of Islam.* San Francisco: HarperSanFrancisco, 1999.

More than 1,100 entries cover people, places, texts, beliefs, rituals, festivals, and practices associated with the Islamic faith and its branches. Appendices include historical synopsis of the Islamic world, maps of Mecca and description of the Hajj, schematic representation of branches of Islam, genealogical tables, and chronology.

Gulevich, Tanya. *Understanding Islam and Muslim Traditions: An Introduction to the Religious Practices, Celebrations, Festivals, Observances, Beliefs, Folklore, Customs, and Calendar System of the World's Muslim Communities, Including an Overview of Islamic History and Geography.* Detroit: Omnigraphics, 2004.

Introduces readers to Islam through an examination of its religious observances, customs, holidays, calendar system, and folk beliefs, describing how people around the world express their Muslim identity. The book's 43 chapters are organized into three sections: A Brief Introduction to Islam; Religious Customs and Folklore; and Calendar System, Holidays, and Other Days of Observance. Additional resources, relevant web sites, a glossary of terms, a topical bibliography, and an index are also included.

Momen, Moojan. *An Introduction to Shia Islam: The History and Doctrines of Twelver Shiism.* New Haven, CT: Yale University Press, 1985.

A comprehensive treatment of the complex religious movement of Shia Islam.

Musk, Bill A. *Holy War: Why Do Some Muslims Become Fundamentalists?* London: Monarch, 2003.

An informative study of Islamic fundamentalism.

Sanders, Paula. *Ritual, Politics, and the City in Fatimid Cairo.* Albany, NY: State University of New York Press, 1994.

Examines court ritual practices, ceremonial processions, and such festivals as Nawruz, Ramadan, and the Festival of Breaking the Fast ('Id al-Fitr) in fourth- and fifth-century Cairo in terms of social and political culture.

Trimingham, J. Spencer. *Islam in West Africa.* London: Oxford University Press, 1959.

Describes history, beliefs, practices, and observances of Muslim West Africans. Explanation of Islamic calendar, saints, social customs. Glossary-Index of Arabic and African terms. General index.

Von Grunebaum, Gustave E. *Muhammadan Festivals.* Introduction by C. E. Bosworth. New York: Olive Branch Press, 1988.

Provides historical background on Islam, as well as discussion of beliefs, prayers, saints, and worship services. Festivals covered are the pilgrimage to Mecca, Ramadan, Nawruz, Muhammad's birthday (Mawlid al-Nabi), feasts of saints, and the death anniversary of Husain (Ashura).

H. Judaism

Cashman, Greer Fay. *Jewish Days and Holidays.* Illustrated by Alona Frankel. New York: SBS Publishing, Inc., 1979.

Describes for young readers the history of, and traditions and customs associated with, major Jewish holidays, including the Sabbath. Sidebars depict foods and other items used during celebrations. Concludes with quiz on matching sidebar items with appropriate holiday.

Edidin, Ben M. *Jewish Customs and Ceremonies.* Illustrated by Norman Tress. New York: Hebrew Publishing Company, 1941.

A companion to Ben M. Edidin's *Jewish Holidays and Festivals* (see below), intended as an educational supplemental text, describes everyday customs as well as those associated with holidays and other important events, such as birth, bar and bat mitzvah, marriage, burial, and worship.

Edidin, Ben M. *Jewish Holidays and Festivals.* Illustrated by Kyra Markham. 1940. Reprint. Detroit: Omnigraphics, Inc., 1993.

Discusses history, significance, and customs associated with Jewish holidays and anniversaries.

Eisenberg, Azriel. *The Story of the Jewish Calendar.* Wood engravings by Elisabeth Friedlander. New York: Abelard-Schuman, 1958.

A short story of two teenaged boys watching for the new moon prefaces a brief history of the Jewish calendar. Explanation of Jewish holidays and names of months and Sabbaths and their significance. Glossary of Hebrew terms and place-names.

Gaster, Theodor H. *Festivals of the Jewish Year.* New York: William Sloane Associates Publishers, 1953.

Presents origins of Jewish festivals and holy days, draws comparisons to other religious and ethnic holidays, and describes evolving nature of their observance throughout history.

Goldin, Hyman E. *A Treasury of Jewish Holidays: History, Legends, Traditions.* New York: Twayne Publishers, 1952.

Examines Jewish festivals, explaining their meanings, describing customs and traditional beliefs associated with them, and telling the stories of their historical origins. Calendar of Jewish festivals from 1951 to 1971.

Hacohen, Devorah, and Menaham Hacohen. *One People; The Story of the Eastern Jews: Twenty Centuries of Jewish Life in North Africa, Asia and Southeastern Europe*. Introduction by Yigal Allon. Translated by Israel I. Taslitt. New York: Sabra Books, 1969.

> Discusses history, folklore, beliefs and customs, ceremonies, and observance of holidays among Jews in Iraq and Kurdistan, Persia, the Caucasus, Bukhara, Morocco, Algeria, Tunisia and Jreba, Libya, Cyrenaica, Egypt, Syria, Yemen, Hadramaut, Aden, Turkey, Salonika, Bulgaria, and India.

Rockland, Mae Shafter. *The Jewish Party Book: A Contemporary Guide to Customs, Crafts, and Foods*. New York: Schocken Books, 1978.

> Traditional customs, foods, and activities associated with birth, bar and bat mitzvah, marriage, reunions, housewarmings, and holidays. Appendix provides explanation of Jewish calendar and table of holiday dates from 1978 to 2000.

Rosenau, William. *Jewish Ceremonial Institutions*. 3rd rev ed. 1925. Reprint. Detroit: Omnigraphics, Inc., 1992.

> Adapted from a series of lectures given by the author at the Oriental Seminary of the Johns Hopkins University in 1901. Origin and purpose of the synagogue and explanatory commentary on its worship services and customs. Discussion of the Jewish calendar and observance of holidays and festivals at home and at the synagogue. Practices associated with birth, marriage, bar and bat mitzvah, divorce, mourning, and related laws and practices.

Strassfeldchael. *The Jewish Holidays: A Guide and Commentary*. Illustrated by Betsy Platkin Teutsch. New York: Harper & Row, 1985.

> Each of 11 chapters deals with a holiday and its specific practices in depth. Appendices on the Jewish calendar, laws pertaining to holidays, Torah reading list for the holidays, glossary of Hebrew blessings, glossary of Hebrew terms, and dates of holidays to the years 1999-2000.

Trepp, Leo. *The Complete Book of Jewish Observance: A Practical Manuel for the Modern Jew*. New York: Behrman House, Inc./ Simon & Schuster, 1980.

> Covers Jewish prayers, practices, customs, and laws in addition to festivals and fasts.

Turck, Mary. *Jewish Holidays*. New York: Crestwood House, 1990.

> Explanations for young readers of reasons for celebrating the holidays, ways in which they are observed, and food, blessings, and prayers associated with them. Brief further reading list.

Turner, Reuben. *Jewish Festivals*. Holidays and Festivals Series. Vero Beach, FL: Rourke Enterprises, Inc., 1987.

> Presents scriptural background for young readers on the Jewish feasts, along with customs and traditions, recipes and food, and activities associated with them. Sections explaining the Jewish calendar, including a calendar of festivals, and the Hebrew alphabet. Further reading list.

Wigoder, Geoffrey, ed. *The Encyclopedia of Judaism*. New York: Macmillan, 1989.

> Several hundred cross-referenced entries cover religious life and development, from the major and minor prophets to dietary laws, from festivals and ceremonies to definitions of concepts and terms.

I. Sikhism

Cole, William Owen, and Piara Singh Sambhi. *The Sikhs: Their Religious Beliefs and Practices*. Boston: Routledge & Kegan Paul, 1978.

> Covers historical background, beliefs, and practices of the Sikh faith, including discussion of founder Guru Nanak and others, scripture, places and style of worship, ethics, ceremonies, birth, marriage and death rites, and calendar of festivals. Appendices cover the Rehat Maryada, or guide to the Sikh way of life; prayers and meditations; population statistics; and explanation of the structure of the Guru Granth Sahib—the scriptural hymns.

Kapoor, Sukhbir Singh. *Sikh Festivals*. Holidays and Festivals Series. Vero Beach, FL: Rourke Enterprises, Inc., 1989.

> Background for young readers on Sikh religious beliefs, history, and ceremonies and festivals. Chronological table of holidays by Hindu month. List of Sikh gurus. Further reading list.

J. Taoism

Sasochael R. *Taoism and the Rite of Cosmic Renewal*. 2nd ed. Pullman: Washington State University Press, 1990.

> Religious studies professor details his observations of the Chiao Festival at a temple in Taiwan in 1970, and also provides descriptions of other annual events in the Chinese religious calendar.

K. Zoroastrianism

Boyce, Mary. *Zoroastrians: Their Religious Beliefs and Practices*. London: Routledge, 1979.

> Noted Zoroastrian scholar gives history of the religion and describes beliefs and rituals.

III. HOLIDAYS OF ETHNIC GROUPS AND GEOGRAPHIC REGIONS

A. General Works

Countries of the World and Their Leaders Yearbook 2007. Detroit: Gale, 2006.

> Yearbook covering nearly 200 countries based on reports from the U.S. Department of State. Entries typically cover each nation's geography, history, economy, government, political conditions, and state of relations with the United States, as well as detailed travel notes.

Stearns, Peter N., ed. *The Encyclopedia of World History*. Boston: Houghton Mifflin, 2001.

> A broad encyclopedia providing covering of people, nations, and events around the world.

Szajkowski, Bogdan. *Political Parties of the World*. 6th ed. London: John Harper Publishing, 2005.

> Extensive material on politics and major political parties for nations around the world.

World and Its Peoples. 11 vols. New York: Marshall Cavendish, 2007.

> Attempts to go beyond superficial and stereotypical information about people around the world by showing how the nations of the modern world became what they are today.

Worldmark Encyclopedia of the Nations. 12th ed. 5 vols. Detroit: Gale, 2006.

> Information on 193 countries and dependencies, with four country volumes arranged by geographic region and one volume focusing on the United Nations.

B. Africa

Baker, Colin. *State of Emergency: Crisis in Central Africa, Nyasaland 1959-1960*. London: Tauris Academic Studies, 1997.

> Covers a critical period in the history of Central Africa and examines the growth of nationalist violence in Malawi (formerly Nyasaland) and the declaration of the state of emergency.

Beier, Ulli. *Yoruba Myths*. Cambridge, England: Cambridge University Press, 1980.

> The author and contributors present 41 myths from Nigeria about Yoruba deities, including Ogun and Oranmiyan.

Brockman, Norbert C. *An African Biographical Dictionary*. 2nd ed. Millerton, NY: Grey House Publishing, 2006.

> Biographical sketch that describes Chilembwe as "the great hero and martyr of Malawi."

Ellis, Royston, and John R. Jones. *Festivals of the World: Madagascar*. (Festivals of the World Series) Milwaukee: Gareth Stevens Publishing, 1999.

> Provides brief introduction to the country, calendar of selected festivals, description of five festivals, craft activities, further reading, and a recipe for young readers.

Lentakis, Michael B. *Ethiopia: Land of the Lotus Eaters*. London: Janus Publishing, 2005.

> Offers a definitive explanation of modern history in Ethiopia, covering the last century up until 1994. It attempts to describe the changes that have taken place in Ethiopia over the past century.

Levine, Donald N. *Wax & Gold: Tradition and Innovation in Ethiopian Culture*. Chicago: The University of Chicago Press, 1965.

> Social scientist examines history, traditions, lifestyles, literature, art, and religion of Amhara people in Ethiopia. Festivals discussed include Maskal (Exaltation of the Cross), St. Michael's Day and other saints' days, Christmas (Ganna), and Timqat (Epiphany).

Middleton, John, and Joseph C. Miller, eds. *New Encyclopedia of Africa*. 2nd ed. 5 vols. Detroit: Charles Scribner's Sons, 2007.

> Discusses the culture, history, and politics of African nations, from ancient civilizations to the present day.

Miers, Suzanne, and Igor Kopytoff. *Slavery in Africa: Historical and Anthropological*. Madison: University of Wisconsin Press, 1977.

> Uses case studies and an anthropological viewpoint to examine the social effects of slavery in Africa.

Moran, Mary H. *Liberia: The Violence of Democracy*. Philadelphia: University of Pennsylvania Press, 2006.

> An examination of Liberia's democratic origins and violent history.

Opoku, A. A. *Festivals of Ghana*. Accra, Ghana: Ghana Publishing Corporation, 1970.

> Includes 12 chapters that describe traditional festivals in Ghana. The final section presents photographs of additional festivals celebrated in Ghana.

O'Toole, Thomas, and Janice E. Baker. *Historical Dictionary of Guinea*. Lanham, MD: Scarecrow Press, 2005.

> A historical dictionary that provides a range of tools: an introductory narrative covering Guinea's political and economic history; a chronology from the earliest known history to the present day; hundreds of cross-referenced dictionary entries covering people, places, events, institutions, movements, political and social groups, and cultural issues; and an extensive bibliography of current publications.

Townsend, Reginald E., ed. *The Official Papers of William V. S. Tubman, President of Liberia*. London: Longmans, 1968.

> A collection of speeches and written documents by the Liberian president during his years in office, 1944-1971.

Westermarck, Edward. *Ritual and Belief in Morocco*. 2 vols. London: Macmillan and Co., Ltd., 1926.

> Author presents results of on-site research, discussing peoples living in Morocco and their religions, beliefs and practices, saints, charms, and superstitions. Calendar and agricultural rites and festivals are covered in vol. 2. List of tribes and locales.

C. Ancient World (Western)

Adkins, Lesley, and Roy Adkins. *Dictionary of Roman Religion*. Oxford, England: Oxford University Press, 1996.

> More than 1,400 entries discuss Roman mythology, gods, people, temples, and festivals. There is also some coverage of Christianity, Judaismthraism, and ancient Celtic religion. Most entries include bibliographic references.

Avery, Catherine B., ed. *The New Century Classical Handbook*. New York: Appleton-Century-Crofts, Inc., 1962.

> This book has more than 6,000 dictionary-style entries, with pronunciations, covering mythological and historical figures, texts, places, festivals, legends, and artifacts in ancient Greece and Rome. Some cross-referencing.

Brumfield, Allaire Chandor. *The Attic Festivals of Demeter and Their Relation to the Agricultural Year*. Salem, NH: Ayer Company, 1981.

> Scholarly investigation of the various Attic (ancient Greek) festivals of Demeter. Covers Proerosia, Thesmophoria, Haloa, Cloaia, the Lesser Mysteries, various harvest festivals, Skira, and the Eleusinian Mysteries. Argues that these festivals attempted to ritually ensure a good harvest and to consolidate community attention on important moments of the agricultural cycle. List of Athenian months. Appendix provides a glossary of Greek agricultural words. General index and index of Greek words.

Fowler, W. Warde. *The Roman Festivals of the Period of the Republic: An Introduction to the Study of the Religion of the Romans*.

London, England: Macmillan and Co., Ltd., 1899. Reprinted in 1925.

> Describes the Roman calendar and Roman festivals of the Republican era in chronological order, from Mensis Martius, or March, to Mensis Februarius, or February. Chronological table of calendar festivals, according to the Republican calendar. Indexes of subjects, Latin words, Latin authors quoted, and Greek authors quoted.

Grantchael. *A Guide to the Ancient World: A Dictionary of Classical Place Names*. New York: H. W. Wilson Company, 1986.

> Covers place names throughout the Mediterranean world and Europe. Gives location, history of settlement, major historical events, incorporation into states or empires, and current remains. Furnishes 15 maps of various European and Mediterranean regions, with ancient place names marked. Provides a bibliography of sources in the following ancient and modern languages: Greek, Latin, Aramaic, Armenian, Coptic, German, Hebrew, Syriac, and English. Also lists relevant journals and archeological reports.

Hammond, N.G.L., and H. H. Scullard. *The Oxford Classical Dictionary*. 2nd ed. Oxford, England: Clarendon Press, 1970.

> Covers the ancient Greek and Roman worlds. Treats place names, mythological figures, legends, notable individuals, institutions, customs, natural features, political and administrative units, festivals, cults, and more. Entries are substantial; most list sources. Offers bibliography of books in many languages. Index includes people, places, and things mentioned throughout, but not titles of entries.

Lemprière's Classical Dictionary of Proper Names mentioned in Ancient Authors Writ Large. 3rd ed. Introduction by R. Willets. London, England: Routledge & Kegan Paul, 1984.

> More than 10,000 dictionary-style entries cover historical and mythological figures, places, festivals, and other terms relevant to the classical world from the 12th century B.C. to the 15th century A.D. Chronological table of events, from the Trojan War to the fall of Trebizond in 1461, precedes the text of the Dictionary. Originally published in 1788, this source had particular influence on 19th-century English literature.

Parke, H. W. *Festivals of the Athenians*. Ithaca, NY: Cornell University Press, 1977.

> Describes festivals celebrated in ancient Athens. Part one presents, in chronological order, the festivals associated with a specific calendar date. Part two covers local and movable festivals. Gives background information on Athenian religion and daily life. Includes a calendar of Athenian festivals and a map of Athens showing principal sanctuaries.

Scullard, H. H. *Festivals and Ceremonies of the Roman Republic*. Ithaca, NY: Cornell University Press, 1981.

> Describes numerous holidays and ceremonies of the Republic. Part one provides introduction to Roman religion. Part two gives historical background of festivals and identifies (when possible) deity or event celebrated, manner of observance, legends and temple sites associated with the celebration, and references made to the festival in ancient texts. Part three covers other ceremonies, such as those connected with triumphs, ovations, and meetings of the Senate. Provides a map of Rome identifying sites of temples and buildings, a further reading list, a list of Roman calendars and festivals, a complete Roman calendar, and a list of temples and their dates of consecration.

D. Asia and the Middle East

1. General Works

Festivals in Asia. Asian Copublication Programme Series Two. Sponsored by the Asian Cultural Centre for UNESCO. Tokyo: Kodansha International Ltd., 1975.

> For young readers. Describes, in chronological order, the New Year in Singapore, Festival of Fire (New Year) in Iran, Dolls' Day and Boys' Day in Japan, Bengali New Year in Bangladesh, the Water Festival in Burma, New Year in Cambodia, New Year in Laos, Sinhala and Tamil New Year in Sri Lanka, and Maytime in the Philippines, often through storytelling.

Jettmar, Karl, ed. *Cultures of the Hindukush: Selected Papers from the Hindu-Kush Cultural Conference Held at MoesgÅrd 1970*. Wiesbaden, Germany: Franz Steiner Verlag, 1974.

> These papers and notes by more than a dozen scholars were compiled from the conference in 1970 on cultures of peoples in the valley regions of the Hindukush mountain range in Central Asia, including the Kafirs, Kalasha, and Kom. Topics covered include languages, history, festivals, religion, cosmology, mythology, customs, and political organization.

More Festivals in Asia. Asian Copublication Programme Series Two. Sponsored by the Asian Cultural Centre for UNESCO. Tokyo: Kodansha International Ltd., 1975.

> For young readers. Describes, in chronological order, Tano Day in Korea, Eid-ul-Fitr in Pakistan, Lebaran in Indonesia, Hari Raya Puasa in Malaysiad-Autumn Festival in Vietnam, Dasain in Nepal, Diwali Festival of Lights in India, Loy Krathong in Thailand, and the Buzkashi Game in Afghanistan, often through storytelling.

Viesti, Joe, and Diane Hall. *Celebrate! In South Asia*. New York: Lothrop, Lee & Shepard Books, 1996.

> Photos and descriptions of nine festivals in Bangladesh, Bhutan, Burma (Myanmar), India, Nepal, Pakistan, and Sri Lanka.

2. Bangladesh

Anisujjaman, Samsujjaman Khan, and Syed Manzoorul Islam, eds. *Festivals of Bangladesh*. Dhaka, Bangladesh: Nymphea Publication, 2005.

> Covers the celebration of festivals, fasts, and feasts in Bangladesh.

3. China and Hong Kong

Bredon, Juliet, and Igor Mitrophanow. *The Moon Year: A Record of Chinese Customs and Festivals*. Shanghai: Kelly & Walsh, Ltd., 1927.

> Chapters on the Chinese calendar, imperial ceremonies, and the many Chinese gods and cults associated with them, including a discussion of the rise of Confucianism, Taoism, and Buddhism. A chapter is then devoted to each month of the Chinese year, describing the observance of festivals within each month.

Burkhardt, V. R. *Chinese Creeds & Customs*. 2 vols. Hong Kong: The South China Morning Post, Ltd., 1953-55.

> Author describes customs and observance of more than 20 festivals and ceremonies in China, as well as legends, foods, objects, symbols, and fine arts, and discussion of the calendar. Appendices include list of the 24 segments of the Chinese year, the 10 celestial stems and 12 earthly branches, and a table of Chinese

temples that lists each temple's locale, god(s) worshipped, and date founded.

Eberhard, Wolfram. *Chinese Festivals*. Great Religious Festivals Series. New York: Henry Schuman, 1952.

Essays on observance and folklore associated with the New Year, Dragon Boat Festivald-Autumn Festival, Spring Festival, Feast of the Souls, Sending the Winter Dress Festival, and the Weaving Maid and the Cowherd Festival.

Hodous, Lewis. *Folkways in China*. London: Arthur Probsthain, 1929.

Author relates his travels to more than 20 festivals in China, covering history, lore, superstitions, customs, and foods. List of Chinese names.

Latsch, Marie-Luise. *Chinese Traditional Festivals*. Beijing: New World Press, 1984.

Discusses seven major Chinese festivals and their changing significance through history. Festivals covered are New Year Lantern Festival, Pure Brightness Festival (Qing Ming), Dragon Boat Festivald-Autumn Festival, Honoring the Kitchen God, and the Lunar New Year's Eve.

Qi Xing, comp. *Folk Customs at Traditional Chinese Festivals*. Translated by Ren Jiazhen. Illustrated by Yang Guanghua. Beijing: Foreign Languages Press, 1988.

Describes customary festivities for 13 traditional Chinese festivals, including the Spring Festival, Lantern Festival, Spring Dragon Day, Clear and Bright Festival, Dragon Boat Festival, Heaven's Gift Day, Double Seventh Nightddle of the Year Festivald-Autumn Festival, Double Ninth Day, Eighth Day of the Twelfth Month, Kitchen God's Day, and New Year's Eve. Also gives brief descriptions of 10 minor festivals. Covers major festivals of 15 ethnic minority groups, for example Tibetans and Mongolians, as well as 20 minor ethnic festivals. Appendices explain various elements of the traditional Chinese calendar systems, including the 24 solar terms, the 10 heavenly stems and 12 earthly branches, list modern China's commemorative days, and provide a brief chronology of periods in Chinese history.

Stepanchuk, Carol, and Charles Wong. *Mooncakes and Hungry Ghosts: Festivals of China*. San Francisco: China Books & Periodicals, 1991.

Covers legends, history, foods, superstitions, poems, objects, and customs associated with such major Chinese holidays as New Year, Dragon Boat Festivald-Autumn Festival, Clear Brightness Festival, Feast of the Hungry Ghosts, Festival of the Cowherd and the Weaving Maiden, Tian Hou, Protectress of Seafarers, and Double Yang Day, as well as 12 holidays observed by national minorities in China. Appendices include explanation of the Chinese calendar, listing of major festivals by the calendar, table of related symbols, notes on arranging food, pictorial glossary of symbols, Chinese character glossary, and chronology of dynasties.

Tun Li-Ch'en. *Annual Customs and Festivals in Peking*. Translated by Derk Bodde. 2nd rev ed. Hong Kong: Hong Kong University Press, 1965 (1st ed 1936).

Originally written in 1900, this book describes more than 100 annual events in Peking, arranged chronologically by Chinese month. Appendices discuss the Chinese calendar and list units of measure, English equivalents of Chinese names, dynasties and emperors, and concordance of Chinese and Gregorian calendars from 1957-1984.

Ward, Barbara E., and Joan Law. *Chinese Festivals in Hong Kong*. The Guidebook Company, Ltd., 1993.

Presents 30 Chinese festivals and ceremonies as they are observed in contemporary Hong Kong. Explanation of solar calendar and chart. Map of festival locations. Festival calendar, including table converting solar dates from 1992 to 2004.

4. India and Sri Lanka

Bapat, Tara. *Rituals and Festivals of India*. Bombay: Focus Book, 1991.

Covers Hindu holidays, festivals, and rituals.

Gopal, Krishna Dr. and Phal S Girota. *Fairs & Festivals of India*. New Delhi: Gyan Publishing House, 2010.

Provides extensive coverage of various festival and celebrations in India.

Patil, Vimla. *Celebrations: Festive Days of India*. Bombay, India: India Book House Pvt. Ltd., 1994.

Month-by-month discussion of Hindu, Buddhist, Islamic, Christian, and Jain festivals in India, as well as explanation of Hindu, Islamic, and Zoroastrian calendars. Other chapters deal with women's festivals, life-cycle customs, worship, and symbols of religions practiced in India.

Sanon, Arun. *Festive India*. Photographs by Gurmeet Thukral. New Delhi: Frank Bros. & Co., 1987.

Text and photos present a portrait of 26 major festivals celebrated in India. The appendix provides a chronological listing of festivals and their locations within the country.

Welbon, Guy R., and Glenn E. Yocum, eds. *Religious Festivals in South India and Sri Lanka*. New Delhi: Manohar, 1982.

Scholars in anthropology, religious studies, and history of Indian art contribute 12 essays that derive from a workshop at the Conference on Religion in South India. Essays are entitled: "The Hindu Festival Calendar," Karen L. Merrey; "Festivals in Pancaratra Literature," H. Daniel Smith; "The Cycle of Festivals at Parthasarathi Temple," James L. Martin; "The Candala's Song," Guy R. Welbon; "Two Citra Festivals in Madurai," D. Dennis Hudson; "Chronometry, Cosmology, and the Festival Calendar in the Murukan Cult," Fred W. Clothey; "Mahasivaratri: The Saiva Festival of Repentance," J. Bruce Long; "The Festival Interlude: Some Anthropological Observations," Suzanne Hanchett; "The End Is the Beginning: A Festival Chain in Andhra Pradesh," Jane M. Christian; "Kalam Eluttu: Art and Ritual in Kerala," Clifford R. Jones; "The Kataragama and Kandy Asala Peraharas: Juxtaposing Religious Elements in Sri Lanka," Donald K. Swearer; and "An-keliya: A Literary-Historical Approach," Glenn E. Yocum.

5. Indonesia

Berg, Elizabeth. *Festivals of the World: Indonesia*. (Festivals of the World Series) Milwaukee: Gareth Stevens Publishing, 1997. 32 pp. Illustrated. Glossary. Index.

Provides brief introduction to the country, calendar of selected festivals, description of five festivals, craft activities, further reading, and a recipe for young readers.

6. Iran

Aghaie, Kamran Scot. *The Martyrs of Karbala: Shi'i Symbols and Rituals in Modern Iran*. Seattle: University of Washington Press, 2004.

Examines Shi'i symbols and rituals to show the effects of modernization on society, politics and religion in Iran.

Daniel, Elton L., and Ali Akbar Mahdi. *Culture and Customs of Iran.* Westport, CT: Greenwood Publishing, 2006.

Presents an overview of contemporary cultural life in Iran, focusing on such topics as geography, religion, social customs, media, and the arts.

Lorentz, John H. *Historical Dictionary of Iran.* Lanham, MD: Scarecrow Press, 2006.

A historical dictionary that provides a range of tools: an introductory narrative covering Iran's political and economic history; a chronology from the earliest known history to the present day; hundreds of cross-referenced dictionary entries covering people, places, events, institutions, movements, political and social groups, and cultural issues; and an extensive bibliography of current publications.

7. Japan

Ashkenazichael. *Matsuri: Festivals of a Japanese Town.* Honolulu: University of Hawaii Press, 1993.

Scholarly examination of festivals in the town of Yuzawa in Akita Prefecture.

Bauer, Helen, and Sherwin Carlquist. *Japanese Festivals.* Garden City, NY: Doubleday & Company, Inc., 1965.

Essays on 11 major festivals. Chapters on food and flower festivals. Second half of book is a chronological arrangement of Japanese festivals. Back matter includes a pronunciation guide and summary of Japan's history.

Casal, U. A. *The Five Sacred Festivals of Ancient Japan: Their Symbolism & Historical Development.* Tokyo: Charles E. Tuttle Company, Inc., and Sophia University, 1967.

Covers historical background, traditions, legends and myths, food, customs, and current observance of the New Year Festival, the Girls' Festival, the Boys' Festival, the Star Festival, and the Chrysanthemum Festival in Japan.

Epstein, Sam, and Beryl Epstein. *A Year of Japanese Festivals.* Illustrated by Gordon Laite. Champaign, IL: Garrard Publishing Company, 1974.

Descriptions of more than 15 festivals celebrated in Japan. For young readers.

Illustrated Festivals of Japan. Japan Travel Bureau, 1993.

Provides brief information about 271 festivals in Japan and a festival calendar.

Zabilka, Gladys, comp. *Customs and Culture of Okinawa.* Rev ed. Tokyo: Bridgeway Press Books/ Charles E. Tuttle Company, 1959.

Written for American students whose parents lived on the U.S. military base in Okinawa after World War II, the book contains chapters on the geography, people, schools, arts, industry, religions, festivals, customs, health, fairy tales, and songs (including scores) of Okinawa.

8. Korea

Choe Sang-su. *Annual Customs of Korea: Notes on the Rites and Ceremonies of the Year.* Seoul: Seomun-dang Publishing Company, 1983.

Prominent Korean folklorist describes holiday-related customs, games, foods, and celebrations of the year in chronological order by lunar month.

Chun Shin-yong, ed. *Customs and Manners in Korea.* Part of the 10-volume Korean Culture Series. Seoul: International Cultural Foundation and Si-sa-yong-o-sa, Inc., 1982.

Scholars from various academic specialties contribute 10 essays on Korean traditions and values, rituals and rites, mental health, literature and mythology. The essay, "Annual Ceremonies and Rituals," by Choi Gil-sung, discusses the timing, significance, and observance of various festivals throughout Korea. Kim Yol-kyu's "Several Forms of Korean Folk Rituals, Including Shaman Rituals" examines folk dance and festivals.

Ho Siow Yen. *Festivals of the World: South Korea.* (Festivals of the World Series) Milwaukee: Gareth Stevens Publishing, 1998.

Provides brief introduction to the country, calendar of selected festivals, description of five festivals, craft activities, further reading, and a recipe for young readers.

9. Lebanon

AbuKhalil, As'ad. *Historical Dictionary of Lebanon.* Lanham, MD: Scarecrow Press, 1998.

A historical dictionary that provides a range of tools: an introductory narrative covering Lebanon's political and economic history; a chronology from the earliest known history to the present day; hundreds of cross-referenced dictionary entries covering people, places, events, institutions, movements, political and social groups, and cultural issues; and an extensive bibliography of current publications.

10. Mongolia

Fisher, Frederick. *Festivals of the World: Mongolia.* (Festivals of the World Series) Milwaukee: Gareth Stevens Publishing, 1999.

Provides brief introduction to the country, calendar of selected festivals, description of five festivals, craft activities, further reading, and a recipe for young readers.

11. Nepal

Anderson, Mary M. *The Festivals of Nepal.* London: George Allen & Unwin Ltd., 1971.

Describes, in chronological order of occurrence, more than 30 Hindu, Buddhist, and Nepalese festivals attended in Nepal, as well as legends and customs associated with them.

12. Philippines

Mendoza, Lunita. *Festivals of the World: Philippines.* (Festivals of the World Series) Milwaukee: Gareth Stevens Publishing, 1999.

Provides brief introduction to the country, calendar of selected festivals, description of five festivals, craft activities, further reading, and a recipe for young readers.

13. Saudi Arabia

O'Shea, Maria. *Festivals of the World: Saudi Arabia.* (Festivals of the World Series) Milwaukee: Gareth Stevens Publishing, 1999.

Provides brief introduction to the country, calendar of selected festivals, description of five festivals, craft activities, further reading, and a recipe for young readers.

14. Thailand

Whyte, Harlinah. *Festivals of the World: Thailand.* (Festivals of the World Series) Milwaukee: Gareth Stevens Publishing, 1998.

Provides brief introduction to the country, calendar of selected festivals, description of five festivals, craft activities, further reading, and a recipe for young readers.

15. Turkey

O'Shea, Maria. *Festivals of the World: Turkey.* (Festivals of the World Series) Milwaukee: Gareth Stevens Publishing, 1999.

Provides brief introduction to the country, calendar of selected festivals, description of five festivals, craft activities, further reading, and a recipe for young readers.

16. Vietnam

Crawford, Ann Caddell. *Customs and Culture of Vietnam.* Foreword by Henry Cabot Lodge. Illustrations by Hau Dinh Cam. Rutland, VT: Charles E. Tuttle Co., Publishers, 1966.

In addition to providing a calendar and description of festivals and holidays, this book is a survey of mainly South Vietnamese geography, history, culture, religion, education, media, arts, medicine, agriculture, and industry against the backdrop of the Vietnam War. Customs, ceremonies, legends, and points of interest are also included.

McKay, Susan. *Festivals of the World: Vietnam.* (Festivals of the World Series) Milwaukee: Gareth Stevens Publishing, 1997.

Provides brief introduction to the country, calendar of selected festivals, description of five festivals, craft activities, further reading, and a recipe for young readers.

E. Caribbean and Latin America

1. General Works

Houston, Lynn Marie. *Food Culture in the Caribbean.* Westport, CT: Greenwood Publishing, 2005.

Provides insight into the culture of the Caribbean by focusing on its foods. Looks at the region's foods and eating habits, reviewing distinctive social, cultural, linguistic, geographical, political, and economic characteristics. Includes a historical overview, major foods, cooking, typical meals, eating out, special occasions, recipes, and more.

Milne, Jean. *Fiesta Time in Latin America.* Los Angeles: The Ward Ritchie Press, 1965.

Organized chronologically, this book discusses more than 80 festivals celebrated in Mexico and Central and South America. Concludes with list of festivals by country.

2. Cuba

Bettelheim, Judith, ed. *Cuban Festivals: An Illustrated Anthology.* New York: Garland Publishing, Inc., 1993.

Scholars from various academic disciplines present essays on Cuban festivals: "The Afro-Cuban Festival 'Day of the Kings'," Fernando Ortiz; "Annotated Glossary for Fernando Ortiz's The Afro-Cuban Festival 'Day of the Kings'," David H. Brown; "Glossary of Popular Festivals," Rafael Brea and José Millet;

"Carnival in Santiago de Cuba" and "Appendix: The Tumba Francesa and Tajona of Santiago de Cuba," Judith Bettelheim; and "Flashback on Carnival, a Personal Memoir," Pedro Pérez Sarduy.

3. Dominican Republic

Matibag, Eugenio. *Haitian-Dominican Counterpoint: Nation, State, and Race.* New York: Palgrave, 2003.

An analysis of the relationship between Haiti and the Dominican Republic, looking at cultural, economic, social, and political ties across the border.

Zakrewski Brown, Isabel. *Culture and Customs of the Dominican Republic.* Westport, CT: Greenwood Press, 1999.

Presents an overview of contemporary cultural life in the Dominican Republic, focusing on such topics as geography, religion, social customs, media, and the arts.

4. El Salvador

Boyland, Roy. *Culture and Customs of El Salvador.* Westport, CT: Greenwood Publishing, 2001.

Presents an overview of contemporary cultural life in El Salvador, focusing on such topics as geography, religion, social customs, media, and the arts.

5. Haiti

Dunham, Katherine. *Dance of Haiti.* Foreword by Claude Lévi-Strauss. Photographs by Patricia Cummings. Los Angeles: University of California, 1983.

In a revised version of her thesis, the dancer-anthropologist surveys religious, social, and festive uses of dance in Haiti, including some commentary on dance and Lent, Mardi Gras, Holy Week, and Easter.

Matibag, Eugenio. *Haitian-Dominican Counterpoint: Nation, State, and Race.* New York: Palgrave, 2003.

An analysis of the relationship between Haiti and the Dominican Republic, looking at cultural, economic, social, and political ties across the border.

Ngcheong-Lum, Roseline. *Festivals of the World: Haiti.* (Festivals of the World Series) Milwaukee: Gareth Stevens Publishing, 1999.

Provides brief introduction to the country, calendar of selected festivals, description of five festivals, craft activities, further reading, and a recipe for young readers.

Pamphile, Léon Dénius. *Haitians and African Americans: A Heritage of Tragedy.* Gainesville: University Press of Florida, 2001.

Studies the relationship between Haitians and African Americans, from the colonial era to the present day.

Perusse, Roland I. *Historical Dictionary of Haiti.* Lanham, MD: Scarecrow Press, 1977.

A historical dictionary that provides a range of tools: an introductory narrative covering Haiti's political and economic history; a chronology from the earliest known history to the present day; hundreds of cross-referenced dictionary entries covering people, places, events, institutions, movements, political and social groups, and cultural issues; and an extensive bibliography of current publications.

Schiller, Nina Glick, and Georges Eugene Fouron. *Georges Woke Up Laughing: Long-Distance Nationalism.* Durham, NC: Duke University Press, 2001.

Uses history, autobiography, and ethnography to show the Haitian experience of migration to the United States, with insight into the ongoing effects of globalization.

6. Jamaica

Mordecai, Martin, and Pamela Mordecai. *Culture and Customs of Jamaica.* Westport, CT: Greenwood Publishing, 2001.

Presents an overview of contemporary cultural life in Jamaica, focusing on such topics as geography, religion, social customs, media, and the arts.

7. Mexico

Beezley, William H., Cheryl English Martin, and William E. French, eds. *Rituals of Rule, Rituals of Resistance: Public Celebrations and Popular Culture in Mexico.* Wilmington, DE: Scholarly Resources, Inc., 1994.

Presents 15 papers by scholars at the Eighth Conference of Mexican and North American Historians in San Diego, 1990. Essays analyze popular culture, rituals, customs, and festivals in Mexico in the context of political power and colonial domination.

Burland, C. A. *The Gods of Mexico.* New York: G. P. Putnam's Sons, 1967.

Alphabetical listing of Aztec gods. Guide to pronunciation. Covers Aztec, Mayan, Toltec, and Olmec cultures, cities, calendar systems, deities, and religions. Aztec ceremonies and festivals described. Appendices discuss Mayan, Aztec, and other Mexican codices and tlachtli, a ball game.

Fergusson, Erna. *Fiesta in Mexico.* Illustrated by Valentín Vidaurreta. New York: Alfred A. Knopf, 1934.

Account of travel to festivals throughout Mexico, including Pilgrimage to Chalma, Moors and Christians in Tuxpan, La Fiesta de Nuestra Señora de la Soledad in Oaxaca, Passion Play in Tzintzuntzan, Los Voladores in Coxquihui, a Yaqui Indian Pascola, Deer Dance, Coyote Dance, Los Matachines, Holy Week, Good Friday and Holy Saturday in Tlaxcala, Day of the Dead, All Saints' Day and All Souls' Day, Lent, Fiesta of Nuestra Seña de la Santa Vera Cruz, El Viernes de Dolores (fifth Friday in Lent) in Santa Anita, Christmas, and Posadas. Also includes historical discussion of ancient Aztec, Christian, and secular celebrations.

Marcus, Rebecca B., and Judith Marcus. *Fiesta Time in Mexico.* Champaign, IL: Garrard Publishing Company, 1974.

Intended for young readers, this book describes the following holidays and festivals observed in Mexico: Day of the Dead, Our Lady of Guadalupe, Christmas, New Year's, Day of the Three Kings, St. Anthony the Abbot's Day, Holy Week and Easter, St. John's Day, Mexican Independence Day, Fifth of May, and the Twentieth of November. Pronunciation guide.

Miller, Mary, and Karl Taube. *An Illustrated Dictionary of the Gods and Symbols of Ancient Mexico and the Maya.* New York: Thames and Hudson Ltd., 1993.

Nearly 300 entries on religion in ancient Mesoamerica include coverage of gods, symbols, sacred sites, practices, and concepts. Two essays precede the entries: one on Mesoamerican cultural history, the other on Mesoamerican religion.

Toor, Frances. *A Treasury of Mexican Folkways: The Customs, Myths, Folklore, Traditions, Beliefs, Fiestas, Dances, and Songs of the Mexican People.* New York: Bonanza Books, 1985.

Covers agricultural, religious, and folk festivals and ceremonies celebrated by the various peoples in Mexico, including dances, songs, folk arts, legends, riddles, and idiomatic expressions.

8. Trinidad

Hill, Errol. *The Trinidad Carnival: Mandate for a National Theatre.* Austin: University of Texas Press, 1972.

Historical survey of Trinidad and the Carnival, calypso, and masquerades, including descriptions of observances from the 19th century. Argues that elements of the Carnival and its related traditions should be harnessed toward producing a national theater. Appendices provide an example of calypso drama as well as a list of 50 renowned calypsos.

F. South America

Buechler, Hans C. *The Masked Media: Aymara Fiestas and Social Interaction in the Bolivian Highlands.* The Hague, Netherlands: Mouton Publishers, 1980.

Anthropologist presents results of fieldwork on festivals, saints' fiestas, and other rituals among the Aymara people in Bolivia. Appendices offer notes on musical instruments employed during different festivals throughout the year; a description of the Fiesta of the Skulls at the main cemetery in La Paz; comparative table of food and drink expenditures for sponsors of rural and urban festivals during the 1960s and 1970s; a fiesta sponsor's list of participants' contributions to and involvement with a fiesta held in Lamacachi; and a note on recent use of brass bands in Compi fiestas. Index of authors referenced. Index of subjects.

Jermyn, Leslie. *Festivals of the World: Peru.* (Festivals of the World Series) Milwaukee: Gareth Stevens Publishing, 1998.

Provides brief introduction to the country, calendar of selected festivals, description of five festivals, craft activities, further reading, and a recipe for young readers.

Roraff, Susan. *Festivals of the World: Chile.* (Festivals of the World Series) Milwaukee: Gareth Stevens Publishing, 1998.

Provides brief introduction to the country, calendar of selected festivals, description of five festivals, craft activities, further reading, and recipes for young readers.

G. Europe

1. General Works

Cooper, Gordon. *Festivals of Europe.* 1961. Reprint. Detroit: Omnigraphics, Inc., 1994.

Tourist-oriented guide provides brief mentions or descriptions of more than 1,000 festivals in 25 Western and Eastern European countries. Arranged alphabetically by country, festivals are discussed by type of event: agricultural, carnival, cultural, national, religious, sporting, trade, wine and food. Chapter offering travel hints.

Cosman, Madeleine Pelner. *Medieval Holidays and Festivals: A Calendar of Celebrations.* New York: Charles Scribner's Sons, 1981.

Describes customs, activities, food and recipes, music, costume and decoration associated with 12 holidays from the 12th through the 16th centuries, mainly in England, France, Italy, and Germany: Twelfth Night, Valentine's Day, Easter, All Fool's Day, May Daysummer Eve, St. Swithin's Day, Lammaschaelmas, Halloween, St. Catherine's Day, and Christmas. Further reading list.

Crampton, Richard, and Ben Crampton. *Atlas of Eastern Europe in the Twentieth Century*. London: Routledge, 1997.

Draws a definitive picture of the changing shape of Eastern Europe from the beginning of the 20th century to the present.

Hanawalt, Barbara A., and Kathryn L. Reyerson, eds. *City and Spectacle in Medieval Europe*. Minneapolis: University of Minnesota Press, 1994.

Includes 12 papers from a 1991 conference at the University of Minnesota that explore various kinds of ritual and ceremony observed in medieval Europe, including liturgical rites in France, Holy Thursday in Spain, mid-summer in London, accounts of several festivals in medieval Castile, and more.

Johnson, Margaret M. *Festival Europe! Fairs & Celebrations throughout Europe*. Memphis: Mustang Publishing Co., 1992.

Tourist-oriented guide organized by region. Entries on more than 700 festivals in 21 countries are in chronological order, from May to October. Includes descriptions of types of events held in each country. Addresses of tourist boards are provided.

Madden, Daniel M. *A Religious Guide to Europe*. New York: Macmillan Publishing Co., Inc., 1975.

Describes making pilgrimages to hundreds of shrines, sanctuaries, and other holy places in more than 15 European countries, from Ireland to Turkey. Travel and accommodation information, as well as descriptions of secular points of interest are provided.

Perl, Lila. *Foods and Festivals of the Danube Lands: Germany, Austria, Czechoslovakia, Hungary, Yugoslavia, Bulgaria, Romania, Russia*. Illustrated by Leo Glueckselig. Cleveland: The World Publishing Company, 1969.

Discusses foods, festivals, and traditions in countries bordering the Danube River. Provides historical overview on the region and on each country's people and lifestyles, often stretching back to prehistoric times. Heavy coverage of foods prepared and consumed in each country, including recipes.

Rabin, Carol Price. *Music Festivals in Europe and Britain*. Stockbridge, MA: Berkshire Traveller Press, 1980.

More than 90 music festivals in 21 European countries are described, arranged by country. Entries provide historical background, type of music offered, notable features and performers from past festivals, contact names, addresses and phone numbers for obtaining tickets and accommodation, and recommended attire. Listing of addresses and phone numbers of government tourist offices. Suggested reading list.

Spicer, Dorothy Gladys. *Festivals of Western Europe*. 1958. Reprint. Detroit: Omnigraphics, Inc., 1994.

Major festivals in 12 western European countries described in more than 250 entries. Some material duplicates or is revised from that found in the author's *Book of Festivals*. Table of dates for Easter and other Christian movable days from 1958 to 1988. Glossary of festival terms. Suggested reading list. Indexes of festivals by country and by names of festivals.

2. Albania

Jacques, Edwin E. *The Albanians: An Ethnic History from Prehistoric Times to the Present*. Jefferson, NC: McFarland, 1995.

A history of Albania that details the struggle of its people to maintain their cultural and linguistic integrity and their ethnic identity despite foreign influence on the country. Includes Albanian, French, Italian and many other documentary sources.

3. Bulgaria

Crampton, R. J. *A Concise History of Bulgaria*. Cambridge: Cambridge University Press, 2010.

Presents a general introduction to Bulgaria and comments on its historical relationship to Macedonia.

Roudometof, Victor. *Collective Memory, National Identity, and Ethnic Conflict: Greece, Bulgaria, and the Macedonian Question*. Westport, CT: Praeger, 2002.

In-depth analysis of inter-ethnic relations in the southern Balkans. The author examines the evolution of the Macedonian Question and the production of rival national narratives by Greeks, Bulgarians, and Macedonians

4. Czechoslovakia

Martin, Pat, comp. *Czechoslovak Culture: Recipes, History and Folk Arts*. Iowa City, IA: Penfield Press, 1989.

Focus is on Czech-American culture, including traditions and stories carried over from Czechoslovakia. Essays on pioneer experiences, observance of holidays, including lengthy treatment of decorating Easter eggs, folk art, foods and recipes. Profiles of famous Czechs and Czech Americans. A partial list of Czech festivals throughout the United States and tips on planning Czech festivals.

5. France

Janvier, Thomas A. *The Christmas Kalends of Provence*. 1902. Reprint. Detroit: Omnigraphics, Inc., 1990. 262 pp. Illustrated.

Relates tales about rites and celebrations of ancient feasts and festivals practiced in France.

McKay, Susan. *Festivals of the World: France*. (Festivals of the World Series) Milwaukee: Gareth Stevens Publishing, 1998.

Provides brief introduction to the country, calendar of selected festivals, description of five festivals, craft activities, further reading, and a recipe for young readers.

Ozouf, Mona. *Festivals and the French Revolution*. Translated by Alan Sheridan. Cambridge, MA: Harvard University Press, 1988.

Historian examines the Revolutionary festivals observed between 1789 and 1799, and their role in the French Revolution. Discussion of Revolutionary calendar. Brief chronology of the Revolution.

6. Germany

Russ, Jennifer M. *German Festivals & Customs*. London: Oswald Wolff, 1982.

Origins and observance of more than 50 religious, historical, and food festivals, pageants, and social customs and ceremonies. Includes rhymes, food, legends, and songs associated with events. Appendices include list of legal holidays in the Federal Republic of Germany. Subject index. Index of names and places.

7. Greece

Megas, George A. *Greek Calendar Customs*. Athens, Greece: Press and Information Department, 1958.

> Covers customs, beliefs, legends, food, and songs associated with more than 60 saints' days, holidays, festivals, and agricultural activities in Greece (especially rural traditions), according to the seasons of the year.

Roudometof, Victor. *Collective Memory, National Identity, and Ethnic Conflict: Greece, Bulgaria, and the Macedonian Question*. Westport, CT: Praeger, 2002.

> In-depth analysis of inter-ethnic relations in the southern Balkans. The author examines the evolution of the Macedonian Question and the production of rival national narratives by Greeks, Bulgarians, and Macedonians.

Shea, John. *Macedonia and Greece: The Struggle to Define a New Balkan Nation*. Jefferson, NC: McFarland & Company, 1997.

> Details conflict in the Balkans, specifically focusing on the nations of Macedonia and Greece.

8. Hungary

Dömötör, Tekla. *Hungarian Folk Customs*. Translated by Judith Elliott. Corvina, Budapest, Hungary: Corvina Press, 1972.

> Brief survey of folk customs and beliefs, and their study in Hungary. Discussion of history and observance of seasonal, religious, and secular festivals, as well as birth, marriage, and burial practices.

9. Italy

Ashby, Thomas. *Some Italian Scenes and Festivals*. New York: E. P. Dutton and Company, Inc., c1928.

> Describes several religious and folk festivals observed in Italy, while providing impressions of the landscape and peoples, as well as some historical background.

Toor, Frances. *Festivals and Folkways of Italy*. New York: Crown Publishers, Inc., 1953.

> Describes the author's observations of holidays, festivals, and folk customs in Sicily, southern Italy and Sardinia, and Rome and its outskirts. Appendix includes notes on Italian festas, beliefs, folk arts, and folklore bibliography.

10. Macedonia

Crampton, R. J. *A Concise History of Bulgaria*. Cambridge: Cambridge University Press, 2005.

> Presents a general introduction to Bulgaria and comments on its historical relationship to Macedonia.

Poulton, Hugh. *Who Are the Macedonians?* Bloomington: Indiana University Press, 2000.

> Traces the history of Macedonia from antiquity to the present.

Roudometof, Victor. *Collective Memory, National Identity, and Ethnic Conflict: Greece, Bulgaria, and the Macedonian Question*. Westport, CT: Praeger, 2002.

> In-depth analysis of inter-ethnic relations in the southern Balkans. The author examines the evolution of the Macedonian Question and the production of rival national narratives by Greeks, Bulgarians, and Macedonians.

Shea, John. *Macedonia and Greece: The Struggle to Define a New Balkan Nation*. Jefferson, NC: McFarland & Company, 1997.

> Details conflict in the Balkans, specifically focusing on the nations of Macedonia and Greece.

11. Russia

Whyte, Harlinah. *Festivals of the World: Russia*. (Festivals of the World Series) Milwaukee: Gareth Stevens Publishing, 1997. 32 pp. Illustrated. Glossary. Index.

> Provides brief introduction to the country, calendar of selected festivals, description of five festivals, craft activities, further reading, and a recipe for young readers.

12. Scandinavia

Wyndham, Lee. *Holidays in Scandinavia*. Illustrated by Gordon Laite. Champaign, IL: Garrard Publishing Company, 1975.

> Discusses 10 holidays and festivals in Sweden, Norway, and Denmark for young readers. Pronunciation guide.

13. Soviet Union (former)

Petrone, Karen. *Life Has Become More Joyous, Comrades: Celebrations in the Time of Stalin*. Bloomington: Indiana University Press, 2000.

> A social history of such celebrations in the Soviet era as New Year's Day, the anniversary of the 1917 revolution, and other historical and socialist commemorations, and analysis of the role such celebrations played in Soviet life.

Watson, Jane Werner. *A Parade of Soviet Holidays*. Illustrated by Ben Stahl. Champaign, IL: Garrard Publishing Company, 1974.

> Aimed at a young audience, discusses the significance and celebration of more than 20 holidays and festivals observed throughout the former Soviet Union.

14. Spain

Epton, Nina. *Spanish Fiestas (Including Romerías, Excluding Bull-Fights)*. New York: A. S. Barnes and Company, 1968.

> Descriptions of Easter, Corpus Christidsummer, Christmas, New Year's, and Carnival celebrations throughout Spain, as well as Moors and Christians fiestas, and more than 30 other festivals, holy days, and romerías (pilgrimages) observed in Spain.

15. Ukraine

Bassis, Vladimir. *Festivals of the World: Ukraine*. (Festivals of the World Series) Milwaukee: Gareth Stevens Publishing, 1998.

> Provides brief introduction to the country, calendar of selected festivals, description of five festivals, craft activities, further reading, and a recipe for young readers.

16. United Kingdom

Brand, John. *Observations on Popular Antiquities, Chiefly Illustrating the Origin of Our Vulgar Customs, Ceremonies, and Superstitions; with the Additions of Sir Henry Ellis*. London: Chatto and Windus, 1877.

> Chronologically arranged discussion, with historical background, of more than 60 holidays and festivals as observed in western Europe, especially England. Collection of lore on hun-

dreds of items falling under such headings as sports and games, charms and omens, witchcraft and mythology, marriage, child-bearing, death, and drinking customs.

Cameron, David Kerr. *The English Fair*. Thrupp, Stroud, Gloucestershire: Sutton, 1998.

> Beautifully illustrated history of fairs in England from ancient times to the present, based on local sources, interviews, and museum and library archives.

Drake-Carnell, F. J. *Old English Customs and Ceremonies*. New York: Charles Scribner's Sons; London: B. T. Batsford Ltd., 1938.

> Survey of religious, municipal (London), legal, commercialliiary, school, marine, and royal ceremonies, customs and protocol relating to the House of Parliament, and rural festivals and traditions—such as the Furry Dance, Beating the Bounds, and Plough Monday—observed in England.

Hole, Christina. *English Custom & Usage*. 1941-42. Reprint. Detroit: Omnigraphics, Inc., 1990.

> Discusses the celebration of various holidays in England and examines the transformation of pre-Christian observances and rituals into Christian holy days.

Howard, Alexander. *Endless Cavalcade: A Diary of British Festivals and Customs*. London: Arthur Barker Limited, 1964.

> Arranged in chronological order, over 360 entries describe at least one holiday, festival, civic event or custom for every day of the year, as observed in Britain.

Jones, T. Gwynn. *Welsh Folklore and Folk-Custom*. 1930. Reprint. Suffolk, England: D. S. Brewer, 1979.

> Collection of Welsh folklore regarding gods, ghosts, fairies, monsters, caves, lakes, magic, marriage, birth, and death. Recounting of some folk tales. Chapters 9-10 deal with customs concerning such holidays as May Daysummer, Christmas, New Year's, Easter, Mari Lwyd, and others.

Kightly, Charles. *The Customs and Ceremonies of Britain: An Encyclopaedia of Living Traditions*. London: Thames & Hudson Ltd., 1986.

> Book opens with a Calendar of Customs, listing events and holidays in chronological order. Next, in alphabetical order, more than 200 entries describe the observance and historical background of religious holidays, secular festivals, and other elements of social life. Practices associated with other types of events are discussed under such general headings as "Bells and Bellringing Customs," "Birth," "Civic Customs," "Coronations," "Fairs," and "Harvest Customs." Regional listing of events.

Le Vay, Benedict. *Eccentric Britain: The Bradt Guide to Britain's Follies and Foibles*. Guilford, CT: The Globe Pequot Press, 2000.

> Describes quirky events, practices, customs, people, and places in the United Kingdom. Includes travel and contact information.

Long, George. *The Folklore Calendar*. 1930. Reprint. Detroit: Omnigraphics, Inc., 1990.

> Arranged in chronological order, entries provide historical background for, and cover observance of, more than 40 holidays, festivals, ceremonies, and other events in Great Britain.

Owen, Trefor M. *A Pocket Guide: The Customs and Traditions of Wales*. Cardiff: University of Wales Press, 1991.

> Discusses agricultural traditions, customs associated with the home and domestic life, Mari Lwyd, St. Thomas's Day, Twelfth Night, Candlemas, St. David's Day, religious and communal observances and events, and eisteddfod from the 19th century to the present day. Historical survey of the study of folk customs in Wales. Selected reading list by chapter.

Palmer, Geoffrey, and Noel Lloyd. *A Year of Festivals: A Guide to British Calendar Customs*. London: Frederick Warne, 1972.

> Discusses the history and current practice of numerous calendar customs in the United Kingdom in chronological order. Also includes chapters on customs in London and fairs and a list of customs according to county.

Spicer, Dorothy Gladys. *Yearbook of English Festivals*. 1954. Reprint. Detroit: Omnigraphics, Inc., 1993.

> Chronologically arranged descriptions of more than 200 English holidays, ceremonies, anniversaries, and local festivals and traditions. Map of England depicting regions and counties. Explanation of Julian and Gregorian calendars and their coexistence in parts of the country. List of movable Christian feasts dependent upon the date of Easter. List of liturgical colors, what they symbolize and when they are used. Table of dates of Easter for 1954 to 1984. Suggested reading list. Indexes by name of event, county, and region.

Wright, A. R. *British Calendar Customs*. 3 vols. Preface by S. H. Hooke. London: William Glaisher Ltd., 1936.

> Volumes I through III cover popular customs, lore, superstitions, weather omens, and songs associated with holidays and festivals observed in England. Volume I deals with Christian movable holidays from Shrovetide to Corpus Christi, as well as other movable festivals and harvest customs. Volumes II and III survey nearly 100 secular and religious festivals occurring on fixed dates, presented in chronological order.

H. North America

1. General Works

Davis, Alan. *The Fun Also Rises: Travel Guide North America*. San Francisco: Greenline Publications, 1998.

> Travel guide focusing on "the most fun places to be at the right time." For each of 92 events the author provides description of the event, day-by-day plans for attending, travel-related information about accommodations, restaurants, local sights, and nightlife, including contact information. Events and cities are rated for "fun."

2. Canada

Parry, Caroline. *Let's Celebrate! Canada's Special Days*. Toronto, Ontario, Canada: Kids Can Press Ltd., 1987.

> For young readers. Entries cover more than 250 secular and religious holidays and festivals celebrated in Canada, including Muslim, Hindu, Chinese, Jewish, Baha'i, Sikh, Jaina, Buddhist, and Christian holy days. Entries are organized by season of the year and, in addition to discussion of the holiday's background, include riddles, games, poems, crafts, and other activities. Explanation of the calendar, as well as sidebars providing brief background notes on various religious and ethnic groups.

3. Native North America

Eagle/Walking Turtle. *Indian America: A Traveller's Companion*. Santa Fe: John Muir Publications, 1989.

More than 300 Indian tribes in the United States are listed and arranged by geographical region. Entries provide mailing address and location, phone numbers, public ceremony or pow-wow dates, visitor information, and historical background. The appendix offers chronological listing of Indian Moons according to tribe; powwow calendar for North America; Indian arts and crafts shows; Navajo rug auctions; museums with major American Indian collections; Indian-owned and -operated museums and cultural centers, stores, rodeos, and community colleges; populations by state as of April 1980; reservations, rancherias and pueblos with population figures; and urban Indian centers in major metropolitan areas.

Faris, James C. *The Nightway: A History and a History of Documentation of a Navajo Ceremonial.* Albuquerque: University of New Mexico Press, 1990.

Anthropologist presents a study of recordings of the Navajo Nightway Ceremony and its stories, songs, beliefs, prayers and practices, including sandpainting. Charts and figures detail genealogies of medicine men who have led the Nightway, as well as specific elements of Nightways observed over the last 100 years.

Fergusson, Erna. *Dancing Gods: Indian Ceremonials of New Mexico and Arizona.* Foreword by Tony Hillerman. Albuquerque: University of New Mexico Press, 1931. Sixth paperback printing, 1991.

Describes history, meaning, and performance of religious and social dances and ceremonies observed among the Pueblo, Hopi, Navajo, and Apache peoples, including prayers, customs, and some historical background on each.

Fewkes, Jesse Walter. *Hopi Snake Ceremonies; An Eyewitness Account.* Selections from Bureau of American Ethnology, Annual Reports Nos. 16 and 19 for the years 1894-95 and 1897-98. Albuquerque: Avanyu Publishing, Inc., 1986.

Reprint of two papers published in annual reports. Author describes ceremonies performed by the Hopi Snake Society during the 1890s.

Fewkes, Jesse Walter. *Tusayan Katcinas and Hopi Altars.* Introduction by Barton Wright. Albuquerque: Avanyu Publishing, Inc., 1990.

Reprint of two texts by Fewkes, one an article, "The Katcina Altars in Hopi Worship," that appeared in the Annual Report of the Board of Regents of The Smithsonian Institution for 1926. Both represent author's late 19th-century endeavor to describe and analyze katchina ceremonials among the Hopis, including the Powamû ceremony.

Hirschfelder, Arlene, and Paulette Molin. *Encyclopedia of Native American Religions.* Updated ed. Foreword by Walter R. Echo-Hawk. New York: Checkmark Books/Facts on File, 2001.

More than 1,200 cross-referenced entries cover religious beliefs, practices, ceremonies, sacred sites, and symbols of more than 80 North American Indian tribes. There are also entries on Native religion-related court cases and legislation. A subject index and a standard index are provided.

Kavasch, E. Barrie. *Enduring Harvests: Native American Foods and Festivals for Every Season.* Illustrated by Mitzi Rawls. Old Saybrook, CT: The Globe Pequot Press, 1995.

Profiles, in chronological order from September to August, 75 Native festivals in North and South America and provides more than 150 recipes related to the events. Includes a directory of sellers of Native foods.

Tiller, Veronica E., ed. *Discover Indian Reservations USA: A Visitors' Welcome Guide.* Foreword by Ben Nighthorse Campbell. Denver: Council Publications, 1992.

Travel-oriented information provided on more than 350 federal and state Indian reservations in 33 states, listed in alphabetical order by state. Entries include a brief profile on the reservation's land, population, and structure, its location and address, cultural institutes, special events (festivals, powwows, rodeos, etc.), businesses and organizations, accommodations, and special restrictions. Appendix I lists tribes alphabetically and gives their location. Appendix II is a powwow directory by state, then month.

4. United States—General Works and Background on Holidays

Anyike, James C. *African American Holidays: A Historical Research and Resource Guide to Cultural Celebrations.* Chicago: Popular Truth, Inc., 1991.

Covers holidays celebrated by slaves between the 17th and 19th centuries as well as Martin Luther King, Jr. birthday observances, Black History Month, African Liberation Day, Juneteenth, Umoja Karamu (Unity Feast), and Kwanzaa. Appendices include timeline of important dates in history and brief historical background on major holidays observed in the United States. List of related sources and organizations.

Bailey, Carolyn Sherwin. *Stories for Every Holiday.* 1919. Reprint. Detroit: Omnigraphics, Inc., 1990.

Includes 27 stories for young readers about 19 Christian and secular holidays observed in the United States. Arranged in chronological order, beginning with Labor Day.

Coates, Helen R. *The American Festival Guide: A Handbook of More Than 200 Colonial, Homesteading, Western, Spanish, Folk, Rodeo, Sports, Cultural and Other Annual Festivals and Celebrations in the United States and Canada, with a Calendar and a Gazetteer of Festivals for Ready Reference.* 1956. Reprint. Detroit: Omnigraphics, Inc., 1998.

Part One of the book contains detailed descriptions of 10 representative festivals. Part Two covers nearly 200 festivals, arranged by type, in detail. Completing the book are a calendar of festivals, arranged by month, and a gazetteer of festivals, arranged by state.

Coffin, Tristram P., and Hennig Cohen, eds. *Folklore in America: Tales, Songs, Superstitions, Proverbs, Riddles, Games, Folk Drama, and Folk Festivals with 17 Folk Melodies.* 1966. Reprinted by University Press of America, Inc., 1986.

Presents numerous examples of folk tradition among more than 30 ethnic groups in the United States. Index of ethnic groups and geographic locations. Index of titles and first lines of songs. List of tale types and motifs.

Cohen, Hennig, and Tristram Potter Coffin. *America Celebrates! A Patchwork of Weird & Wonderful Holiday Lore.* Detroit: Visible Ink Press, 1991.

Drawing from oral history and newspaper and journal accounts, this book collects more than 200 traditions, legends, beliefs, superstitions, recipes, food, games, dances, poems, riddles, and music associated with over 60 religious, patriotic, commemorative, agricultural, ethnic, and folk holidays and festivals observed among various ethnic, regional, and occupational groups in North America.

Cohen, Hennig, and Tristram Potter Coffin, eds. *The Folklore of American Holidays: A Compilation of More Than 600 Beliefs, Legends, Superstitions, Proverbs, Riddles, Poems, Songs, Dances, Games, Plays, Pageants, Fairs, Foods, and Processions Associated with Over 140 American Calendar Customs and Festivals.* 3rd ed. Detroit: Gale Research Inc., 1999.

Chronologically arranged collection of lore associated with more than 140 holidays and festivals in the United States. Various ethnic, occupational, and religious groups living in the United States are represented. The editors provide brief background information on the event's history, followed by excerpts from written material describing actual observances of the event, as well as accompanying customs, legends, games, recipes, music, etc. Bibliographic information for each source follows the excerpts. Subject Index; Ethnic and Geographic Index; Collectors, Informants, and Translators Index; Song Titles and First Significant Lines Index; and Motif and Tale Types Index.

Le Rouge, Mary. *The American Book of Days.* 5th ed. New York, Dublin: H. W. Wilson Company. Amenia, NY: Grey House Publishing, 2015.

Contains more than 800 entries pertaining to American holidays, festivals, and anniversaries organized by month. Selections reflect events in American history, including entries on each U.S. president and chief justice. There is at least one entry for every day of the year. Entries tend to be lengthy, averaging about 1,300 words. Each month begins with an essay recounting the origin of the month, ancient festivals observed, and the month's birthstone. Nine appendices include essays on "The Calendar," "The Era," "The Days of the Week," "Signs of the Zodiac," a list of "Important Public Holidays and Events," and reprints of the U.S. Constitution, the Declaration of Independence, the Articles of Confederation, and the Mayflower Compact of 1620.

Dillon, Philip Robert. *American Anniversaries; Every Day of the Year; Presenting Seven Hundred and Fifty Events in United States History, from the Discovery of America to the Present Day.* c1918. Reprint. Detroit: Omnigraphics, Inc., 1991.

Opens with a chronology of principal events during World War I and summary of armistice. Book is organized chronologically. At least one anniversary is given for each day of the year. Entries cover anniversaries of historical events and people in politics and legislation, commerce and invention, arts and letters.

Gay, Kathlyn. *African-American Holidays, Festivals, and Celebrations: The History, Customs, and Symbols Associated with Both Traditional and Contemporary Religious and Secular Events Observed by Americans of African Descent.* Detroit: Omnigraphics, 2007.

Presents the history, customs, symbols, and lore of more than 100 diverse African-American holidays and festivals celebrated in the United States. Events covered include contemporary and historical African-American holidays—ranging from slave observances to Kwanzaa. Also covered are holidays and festivals commemorating notable people, historical events, and religious and cultural heritage. Each entry covers the name and date of the holiday or festival; its history and how it was created; when and where it was first celebrated; where and how it is observed today; web sites and contact information for relevant organizations; and suggestions for further reading.

Goring, Ruth. *Latino Life: Holidays and Celebrations.* Vero Beach, FL: Rourke Publications, 1995.

Describes family celebrations, religious and patriotic holidays, and folk festivals observed by Hispanic Americans. Includes a calendar of holidays and festivals. For young readers.

Greif, Martin. *The Holiday Book: America's Festivals and Celebrations.* New York: The Main Street Press, 1978.

Lengthy entries cover, in chronological order, traditions, customs, and poetry associated with 20 major patriotic, religious, and commemorative holidays observed in the United States. Shorter entries discuss background and observance of 20 more special days.

Gutiérrez, Ramón, and Geneviève Fabre, eds. *Feasts and Celebrations in North American Ethnic Communities.* Albuquerque: University of New Mexico Press, 1995.

Includes 12 essays that analyze celebrations and practices surrounding such events as funerals, holidays such as Halloween and Easter, folk festivals, and harvest rites among African Americans, Hispanics, Filipinos, West Indians, urban and rural Americans, and gays throughout North and South America.

Henderson, Helene, ed. *Patriotic Holidays of the United States: An Introduction to the History, Symbols, and Traditions behind the Major Holidays and Days of Observance.* Detroit: Omnigraphics, Inc., 2006.

Provides a wealth of historical material about national patriotic holidays celebrated in the United States. The book also provides an overview of the United States' form of government, national symbols, political parties, and the development of its national identity, as well as 18 important primary sources relating to the holidays. Other features include a chronology of key historical events, a bibliography, a list of web sites, and an index.

Hobbie, Margaret, comp. *Italian American Material Culture: A Directory of Collections, Sites, and Festivals in the United States and Canada.* Westport, CT: Greenwood Press, 1992.

Lists nearly 100 museum collections related to Italian-American culture, more than 40 sites around the U.S. significant in Italian-American history, and more than 100 religious, folk, agricultural, art, music, food, and commemorative festivals associated with Italian-American material culture. Festival entries provide information on event's location, sponsor address and phone number, dates observed, estimated annual attendance and date first observed, and brief description of festival activities. Sponsor name index. Subject index.

Jaynes, Gerald, ed. *Encyclopedia of African American Society.* 2 vols. Thousand Oaks, CA: Sage Reference, 2005.

A two-volume reference set that describes African-American culture, including music, literature, arts, religion, sports, and social issues.

Levinson, David, and Karen Christensen, eds. *Global Perspectives on the United States: A Nation by Nation Survey.* 2 vols. Great Barrington, MA: Berkshire, 2007.

Explores the image of the United States—its government, people, and culture—from the viewpoints of people around the world.

Litwicki, Ellen M. *America's Public Holidays, 1865-1920.* Washington, DC: Smithsonian Institution Press, 2000.

Examines the influence of the end of the Civil War, the wave of immigration, and the labor movement on the creation and observance of public holidays in the U.S. from 1865 to 1920.

Murphy, Joseph M. *Santería: African Spirits in America.* Boston: Beacon Press, 1988.

Traces origins and presents beliefs, rituals, ceremonies, songs, gestures, foods, and herbs associated with the practice of the Santería ("the way of the saints") religion, an Afro-Cuban outgrowth of the Yoruba religion in Nigeria, as observed by African Americans in New York.

Olcott, Frances Jenkins. *Good Stories for Anniversaries.* Illustrated by Hattie Longstreet Price. 1937. Reprint. Detroit: Omnigraphics, Inc., 1990.

More than 120 stories for children relating to holidays and events in the history of the United States, such as Inauguration Day, Bunker Hill Day, and pioneer days. Arranged chronologically by the school year.

Rabin, Carol Price. *The Complete Guide to Music Festivals in America: Classical, Opera, Jazz, Pops, Country, Folk, Bluegrass, Old-Time Fiddlers, Cajun.* 4th ed. Illustrated by Celia Elke. Great Barrington, MA: Berkshire Traveller Press, 1990.

Covers more than 150 music festivals in 40 of the United States and territories, as well as Canada, arranged by type of music. Within each section, festivals are listed by the state in which they take place. Entries include a description of the event and addresses and phone numbers to obtain information on purchasing tickets and finding accommodations. Listing of music festivals by location, with maps. Suggested reading list. Index by name of festival.

Sandak, Cass R. *Patriotic Holidays.* New York: Crestwood House, 1990.

Covers 16 patriotic holidays in the United States, and a handful of others elsewhere, for young readers. Further reading list.

Santino, Jack. *All Around the Year: Holidays and Celebrations in American Life.* Urbana and Chicago: University of Illinois Press, 1994.

Discusses origins and meanings of holidays observed in the United States, and customs, ephemera, and symbols associated with them.

Schaun, George, and Virginia Schaun. *American Holidays and Special Days.* Illustrations by David Wisniewski. Lanham: Maryland Historical Press, 1986.

Alphabetical and chronological listings of holidays. List of dates on which states were admitted to the United States. Part I discusses the various calendars, names of the months and days of the week, movable days, and reasons for observance of special days. Part II consists of more than 60 entries on holidays, festivals, and commemorative days observed in the United States in chronological order.

Schibsby, Marian, and Hanny Cohrsen. *Foreign Festival Customs.* Rev ed. New York: American Council for Nationalities Service, 1974.

Describes Christmas, New Year's, and Easter customs, traditions, and recipes from more than 30 immigrant groups to the United States. Discusses Thanksgiving and harvest traditions from Europe.

Shapiro, Larry. *A Book of Days in American History.* New York: Charles Scribner's Sons, 1987.

Brief entries are arranged in calendar order and cover at least one event in U.S. history. Focus is on European settlement and history from pre-Revolutionary days through the 1970s.

Shemanski, Frances. *A Guide to Fairs and Festivals in the United States.* Westport, CT: Greenwood Press, 1984.

Following the format of *A Guide to World Fairs and Festivals* by the same author, this volume covers more than 260 fairs and festivals in the United States, American Samoa, Puerto Rico, and the U.S. Virgin Islands. Entries are arranged alphabetically by state and city, then by territory. Each entry provides a description of the festival's history, purpose, and idiosyncrasies of observance. A state-by-state chronological listing of festivals follows the main text. Appendix lists festivals by type.

Spicer, Dorothy Gladys. *Folk Festivals and the Foreign Community.* 1923. Reprint. Detroit: Omnigraphics, Inc., 1990.

Offers advice on administration and production gleaned from folk festivals organized during the 1920s that were attempts to bond recent immigrants with those born in the United States by fostering understanding and appreciation of cultural diversity.

Thornton, Willis. *Almanac for Americans.* 1941. Reprint. Detroit: Gale Research Company, 1973.

A "Book of Days of the Republic," arranged chronologically, focuses on patriotic holidays and historical events in the United States.

Tuleja, Tad. *Curious Customs: The Stories Behind 296 Popular American Rituals.* New York: Harmony Books, 1987.

Provides historical information and occasionally tongue-incheek observations on major American holidays as well as customs and superstitions surrounding various social activities including gestures, apparel, etiquette, eating, and courtship.

5. United States—Works on the Presidents

Benbow, Nancy D. Myers, and Christopher H. Benbow. *Cabins, Cottages and Mansions: Homes of the Presidents of the United States.* Gettysburg, PA: Thomas Publications, 1993.

A foreword by Pres. James A. Garfield's great-grandson leads off detailed entries on each president as well as the featured sites. Black-and-white photos and addresses, telephone numbers and traveling directions are included, as is an entry describing the White House.

Haas, Irvin. *Historic Homes of the American Presidents.* New York: Dover Publications, Inc., 1991.

Entries on the homes or birthplaces of 35 U.S. presidents include excellent black-and-white photos (some exterior, some interior) and many detailed descriptions of the residences, though length of the entries varies. Addresses, telephone numbers, and traveling directions are included. The White House is also listed.

Kane, Joseph Nathan. *Facts About the Presidents.* New York: H. W. Wilson Company, 1993.

This is a detailed and exhaustive source for "facts about the presidents." Biographical information on immediate family is included, with selected events of the president's life and administration highlighted. Comparative data (religion, military service and so on) is included along with election information and a section on the vice presidents.

Kern, Ellyn R. *Where the American Presidents Lived, Including a Guide to the Homes that Are Open.* Indianapolis: Cottontail Publications, 1982.

Presidential lives broken down by years, with black-and-white photos and line drawings, followed by brief descriptions and history of sites with addresses, telephone numbers, and locations on line maps organized geographically.

Kochmann, Rachel M. *Presidents' Birthplaces, Homes and Burial Sites*. Osage, MN: Osage Publications, 1999.

Black-and-white photographs accompany the brief text which includes basic facts, dates and a quote from each president. Addresses and traveling directions are listed along with locations on line maps.

Kruh, David, and Louis Kruh. *Presidential Landmarks*. New York: Hippocrene Books, 1992.

Each entry opens with a two- to three-page overview of each president and his administration, followed by descriptions of sites and addresses, telephone numbers, and traveling directions. An entry on "multi-presidential" sites is also included. Photos are black-and-white.

6. United States—Works on the States

Abate, Frank, ed. *American Places Dictionary: A Guide to 45,000 Populated Places, Natural Features, and Other Places in the United States*. Four volumes. Detroit: Omnigraphics, Inc., 1994.

Organized first by state, then by county, this reference work provides coverage of the following places throughout the U.S.: states, counties and county equivalents, incorporated places (cities, towns, etc.), unincorporated places (certain townships, villages, Census Designated Places, etc.), American Indian reservations, major military installations, and geographic features. Place entries for each state are preceded by various geographic and demographic data on the state, including symbols and name origin information, a description of the local government, and an essay on the state's history and boundaries. Place entries provide legal place name and status, latitude and longitude, population, land and water areas, notable background information, and name origin. Miscellany on American Places and American Names—Curiosities and Peculiarities. State indexes. Complete index in volume 4.

Kane, Joseph Nathan, Janet Podell, and Steven Anzovin. *Facts about the States*. 2nd ed. New York: H. W. Wilson Company, 1993.

This reference book presents the following information about each state, organized alphabetically by state: admission date and rank; explanations of state name, nicknames, seal and flag; motto, song, and symbols; geographic and climatic data; national sites; chronology of significant dates in the state's history; demographic data; local government, political history, finances, economy, environment, ethnic groups, educational and cultural facilities; miscellaneous state facts; and bibliography containing fiction and nonfiction works about the state. The District of Columbia and Puerto Rico are also covered. Comparative tables on land areas and shorelines, population, settlement by non-native Americans, geography, finances, transportation, military installations, and educational facilities.

IV. INDIVIDUAL HOLIDAYS

A. Christmas

Auld, William Muir. *Christmas Tidings*. 1933. Reprint. Detroit: Omnigraphics, Inc., 1990.

Describes legends, verse, and such historic liturgies as the Roman Breviary and the Missal.

Auld, William Muir. *Christmas Traditions*. 1931. Reprint. Detroit: Omnigraphics, Inc., 1992.

This history of Christmas surveys origins, antecedents, changes, and developments of the traditions through the ages. Covers ancient English carols, the yule log, the tree, bells, and more. Excerpts from literature, legends, and historical accounts.

Ballam, Harry, and Phyllis Digby Morton, eds. *The Christmas Book*. 1947. Reprint. Detroit: Omnigraphics, Inc., 1990.

Collection of articles and stories by such writers as Charles Dickens, Aldous Huxley, Washington Irving, Bram Stoker, and others on the subject of Christmas. Several holiday quizzes are included, for which the Appendices provide the answers.

Bauer, John E. *Christmas on the American Frontier, 1800-1900*. 1961. Reprint. Detroit: Omnigraphics, Inc., 1993.

Seventeen chapters cover such topics as "A California Festival of Good Will," "Down a Prairie Chimney," "Giving Christmas to the Indians," and more. Contains eyewitness accounts of frontier holidays.

Buday, George. *The History of the Christmas Card*. 1954. Reprint. Detroit: Omnigraphics, Inc., 1992.

Traces the rise of the Christmas card and discusses its forerunners, old Christmas card creators, children's cards, religious cards, and wartime Christmas cards. Appendices list artists and designers, old Christmas card sentiment writers, and Christmas card publishers.

Carucci, Laurence Marshall. *Nuclear Nativity: Rituals of Renewal and Empowerment in the Marshall Islands*. Dekalb: Northern Illinois University Press, 1997.

Anthropologist describes the history, context, and elements of the Kurijmoj festival, the four-month Christmas celebration of the Enewetak people, who, from 1947 to 1980, were forced to live away from their home atoll in the Marshall Islands so the U.S. government could conduct nuclear weapons tests.

Crippen, Thomas G. *Christmas and Christmas Lore*. 1923. Reprint. Detroit: Omnigraphics, Inc., 1990.

Collection of customs, traditions, and legends relating to Christmas, drawn from chapbooks and pamphlets of the 17th and 18th centuries and from various books dealing with antiquities and legends.

Dawson, W. F. *Christmas: Its Origins and Associations*. 1902. Reprint. Detroit: Omnigraphics, Inc., 1990.

Arranged chronologically, this book covers the holiday's origin, its historical events, and festive celebrations during the course of 19 centuries. Considers the evolving tradition in Britain and includes information on the celebration of Christmas in various lands.

Duncan, Edmondstoune. *The Story of the Carol*. 1911. Reprint. Detroit: Omnigraphics, Inc., 1992.

Surveys development of the forms and purposes of carols, as well as the days, feasts, pageants, and religious rites associated with them. Includes words and music to traditional carols. Appendices include brief biographical notes on relevant individuals, glossary, chronological table of development of carols, and list of manuscript carols held in the British Museum.

Foley, Daniel J. *Christmas the World Over: How the Season of Joy and Good Will Is Observed and Enjoyed by Peoples Here and Everywhere*. Illustrated by Charlotte Edwards Bowden. Philadelphia and New York: Chilton Books, 1963.

Customs and traditions associated with Christmas in more than 30 countries around the world. Heavy coverage of Europe and Latin America.

Foley, Daniel J., ed. *Christmas in the Good Old Days: A Victorian Album of Stories, Poems, and Pictures of the Personalities WhoRediscovered Christmas.* 1961. Reprint. Detroit: Omnigraphics, Inc., 1994.

Anthology of stories and poems written during the Victorian era by such authors as Louisa May Alcott, Washington Irving, Bret Harte, O. Henry, Charles Dickens, Hans Christian Andersen, Herman Melville, and others. Includes brief sketches on the authors.

Gulevich, Tanya. *Encyclopedia of Christmas and New Year's Celebrations: Over 240 Alphabetically Arranged Entries Covering Christmas, New Year's, and Related Days of Observance, Including Folk and Religious Customs, History, Legends, and Symbols from Around the World. Supplemented by a Bibliography and Lists of Christmas Web Sites and Associations, as well as an Index.* Illustrated by Mary Ann Stavros-Lanning. Detroit: Omnigraphics, Inc., 2003.

Cross-referenced entries discuss Christmas and New Year's folklore, history, customs, foods, and more. Thirty-nine entries deal with Christmas in Europe, Asia, North Africa, the Middle East, and Latin America. Twenty-one entries treat New Year's Day and Eve. Other holidays discussed include Advent, the Assumption, Candlemas, Epiphany, Feast of the Circumcision, Hanukkah, Holy Innocents' Day, Kwanzaa, and numerous saints' days. Appendices include a bibliography, web sites, and information about associations whose missions relate to the holidays.

Hole, Christina. *Christmas and Its Customs: A Brief Study.* Illustrated by T. Every-Clayton. New York: M. Barrows and Company, Inc., 1957.

Discusses origins of the holiday, as well as garlands, gift giving, carols, food, and legends and superstitions. Also covers Twelfth Night and the New Year.

Hottes, Alfred Carl. *1001 Christmas Facts and Fancies.* 1946. Reprint. Detroit: Omnigraphics, Inc., 1990.

Facts and fancies, stories and legends gathered from author's personal experiences and obscure literature.

Miles, Clement A. *Christmas in Ritual and Tradition; Christian and Pagan.* 1912. Reprint. Detroit: Omnigraphics, Inc., 1990.

Part I deals with the Christian observance, examining Latin and European hymns and poetry, liturgy, popular customs, and dramas, pageants, and plays. Part II covers pre-Christian winter festivals and their surviving customs. Includes discussion of the Christmas tree, gifts, cards, and mumming, as well as more than 20 saints' days and other holidays and festivals observed throughout the year in Europe.

Miller, Daniel, ed. *Unwrapping Christmas.* Oxford, England: Clarendon Press, 1993.

Ten anthropological essays by scholars in various academic fields on contemporary, and international, observance and meaning of Christmas: "A Theory of Christmas" and "Christmas against Materialism in Thailand," Daniel Miller; "Father Christmas Executed," Claude Lévi-Strauss; "The Rituals of Christmas Giving," James Carrier; "Materialism and the Making of the Modern American Christmas," Russell Belk; "Cinderella Christmas: Kitsch, Consumerism, and Youth in Japan," Brian Moeran and Lise Skov; "The English Christmas and the

Family: Time out and Alternative Realities," Adam Kuper; "Christmas Cards and the Construction of Social Relations in Britain Today," Mary Searle-Chatterjee; "Christmas Present: Christmas Public," Barbara Bodenhorn; and "The Great Christmas Quarrel and Other Swedish Traditions," Orvar Löfgren.

Schauffler, Robert, ed. *Christmas: Its Origin, Celebration and Significance as Related in Prose and Verse.* New foreword by Tristram Potter Coffin. 1907. Reprint. Detroit: Omnigraphics, Inc., 1990.

Collection of prose and poetry, hymns and carols divided into sections on origins, celebration, and the significance and spirit of Christmas.

Sechrist, Elizabeth Hough. *Christmas Everywhere: A Book of Christmas Customs of Many Lands.* Rev ed. Philadelphia: Macrae Smith Company, 1962.

For young readers. Stories and customs associated with Christmas in 20 locales around the world.

Silverthorne, Elizabeth. *Christmas in Texas.* College Station: Texas A & M University Press, 1990.

Examines Christmas customs, traditions, including recipes, and folklore of different ethnic groups in Texas, including Hispanic, Chinese, German, French, African American, Scandinavian, Italian, Polish, British, Czech, Wendish, and Orthodox.

Walsh, William S. *The Story of Santa Klaus: Told for Children of All Ages from Six to Sixty.* 1909. Reprint. Detroit: Omnigraphics, Inc., 1991.

Discusses the origin and development of the Klaus legend, mythological concepts absorbed by Christianity, the Three Kings, Twelfth Night customs, Father Christmas, and Christmas traditions and observances in various countries. Illustrations by artists of all times from Fra Angelico to Henry Hutt.

Weiser, Francis X. *The Christmas Book.* Illustrated by Robert Frankenberg. 1952. Reprint. Detroit: Omnigraphics, Inc., 1990.

Relates the story of the celebration of Christmas, from the beginning with its gospel and history, through the festivities of the Middle Ages, to the decline and eventual revival of Christmas customs in Europe and the United States. Ancient and familiar hymns are included, as well as a section on holiday breads and pastries.

Wernecke, Herbert H. *Christmas Customs Around the World.* Philadelphia: The Westminster Press, c1959.

Covers historical background, customs and legends, holiday recipes, and pageants and programs. Describes observance of the holiday in more than 60 countries on all continents.

B. Easter

The Book of Easter. Introduction by William C. Doane. 1910. Reprint. Detroit: Omnigraphics, Inc., 1990.

Collection of Easter poems, stories, hymns, and essays from various sources including the Bible, and by such writers as Elizabeth Barrett Browning, Walter Pater, Robert Browning, Alfred Tennyson, George Herbert, Thomas Hardy, and others. Reproductions of famous paintings relating to Easter by such artists as Rembrandt, Rubens, and Fra Angelico. Provides historic accounts and descriptions of customs and legends associated with Good Friday, Easter, and the Ascension.

Gulevich, Tanya. *Encyclopedia of Easter, Carnival, and Lent: A Guide to This Season's Joyous Celebration and Solemn Worship, Including Folk Customs, Religious Observances, History, Legends, Folklore, Symbols, and Related Days from Europe, the Americas, and Around the World.* Illustrated by Mary Ann Stavros-Lanning. Detroit: Omnigraphics, Inc., 2002.

> More than 150 cross-referenced entries discuss history, religious celebrations, customs, folklore, foods, and symbols related to Easter, Carnival, and Lent in 20 countries around the world. Also includes entries on Ash Wednesday, Pentecost, May Day, Shavuot, Passover, and No Ruz. A bibliography and web sites related to the holiday season are presented in the appendices.

Hazeltine, Alice Isabel, and Elva Sophronia Smith, eds. *The Easter Book of Legends and Stories.* Illustrated by Pamela Bianco. 1947. Reprint. Detroit: Omnigraphics, Inc., 1992.

> Compilation of literature relating to Easter including biblical narrative, poems, plays, legends, and stories by such authors as Robert Frost, Emily Dickinson, A. E. Housman, and others. Indexes of authors and titles.

Lord, Priscilla Sawyer, and Daniel J. Foley. *Easter the World Over.* Philadelphia: Chilton Book Company, 1971.

> Discusses origins of, and traditions, practices, rhymes, songs and music, fine arts, and food associated with, Easter, Holy Week, and Carnival or Mardi Gras in the Middle East, United States, Europe, Bermuda, the Caribbean, and South and Central America. Also covers the spring festivals of Ching-ming (Qing Ming) in China and Setsubun in Japan.

C. Fourth of July

Appelbaum, Diana Karter. *The Glorious Fourth: An American Holiday, an American History.* New York: Facts on File, 1989.

> Covers the history and celebration of Independence Day in the United States, from the beginning until the bicentennial festivities in 1976.

Travers, Len. *Celebrating the Fourth: Independence Day and the Rites of Nationalism in the Early Republic.* Amherst.: University of Massachusetts Press, 1997.

> Discusses the early celebrations of the Fourth of July and their role in fostering a new sense of national identity. Describes celebrations in Boston, Philadelphia, and South Carolina from 1777 to 1826.

D. Halloween

Santino, Jack. *The Hallowed Eve: Dimensions of Culture in a Calendar Festival in Northern Ireland.* Lexington: University Press of Kentucky, 1998.

> Clearly written scholarly examination of Halloween as it is celebrated in Northern Ireland, its history, games, and other traditions, based on the author's fieldwork.

Thompson, Sue Ellen, ed. *Halloween Program Sourcebook: The Story of Halloween, Including Excerpts of Stories and Legends, Strange Happenings, Poems, Plays, Activities, and Recipes Focusing on Halloween from the Eighteenth Century to the Present.* Illustrated by Mary Ann Stavros-Lanning. Detroit: Omnigraphics, 2000.

> Following an introductory essay on the history of the holiday, the book presents a selection of Halloween-related material to be read, spoken, or performed, as well as craft activities, costume ideas, games, and recipes. Works excerpted or reprinted include those by authors such as Washington Irving, Edgar Allan Poe, Robert Burns, and more. Author and Title Index and Index to First Lines of Poetry.

E. Mardi Gras

Mitchell, Reid. *All on a Mardi Gras Day: Episodes in the History of New Orleans Carnival.* Cambridge, MA: Harvard University Press, 1995.

> Retells the story of a number of incidents occurring on or around Mardi Gras, from the early 1800s to the 1990s. Provides a unique window on the history of Mardi Gras, its meaning to various ethnic and social groups across time, and the history and culture of New Orleans. Gives suggested reading list.

F. Memorial Day

Schauffler, Robert, ed. *Memorial Day; Its Celebration, Spirit, and Significance as Related in Prose and Verse, with a Non-sectional Anthology of the Civil War.* 1940. Reprint. Detroit: Omnigraphics, Inc., 1990.

> Compilation of 140 stories and poems relating the significance of Memorial Day in the United States.

G. Mother's Day

Schauffler, Robert, ed. *Mother's Day; Its History, Origin, Celebration, Spirit, and Significance as Related in Prose and Verse.* 1927. Reprint. Detroit: Omnigraphics, Inc., 1990.

> Collection of poetry and stories about mother-worship in pagan times, mother-love antedating Christianity, and some of the ancient customs and rites honoring mothers throughout the centuries. Suggestions for Mother's Day programs for school exercises also included.

H. New Year

Blackwood, Alan. New Year. *Holidays and Festivals Series.* Vero Beach, FL: Rourke Enterprises, Inc., 1987.

> For young readers. Discusses ancient celebrations of the New Year in Egypt, Babylonia, and Rome, and among Celts. Explanation of the Jewish and Chinese calendars, the Muslim and Hindu New Year, the New Year throughout Asia, the New Year in the United States and Britain, and some mentions of customs in various European countries. Entries on St. Sebastian and St. Basil. Further reading list.

Indexes

1. Chronological Index—Fixed Days and Events 1145

The Fixed Days and Events Index organizes holidays according to the month or specific date(s) in which they are observed. For each month, those holidays celebrated within the month are given first, followed by holidays celebrated on specific date(s), then those observed at the same time each year, although not on a fixed date (e.g., the first Monday, the last week, etc.).

2. Chronological Index—Movable Days 1189

The Movable Days Index organizes events according to the dates of non-Gregorian calendars, including the Jewish calendar, Islamic calendar, and the Hindu and Buddhist lunar calendars, or movable Christian holidays that depend on the date of Easter.

3. Special Subject Index 1201

The Special Subject Index divides entries according to eight categories:

Arts 1201
Indexes festivals and events that revolve around the enjoyment, appreciation, and celebration of an art form such as fine and decorative arts, music, dance, film, literary arts, or theater.

Calendar 1204
Indexes festivals and events that deal specifically with the calendar or that are held in celebration of the time of the Year (solstices and equinoxes), the beginning and end of seasons, etc.

Folkloric 1206
Indexes festivals and events deeply rooted in folklore and tradition, as well as those celebrating specific folk tales or myths.

Food 1209
Indexes festivals and events that revolve around the celebration or preparation of foods, the harvest or promotion of a particular crop, or a type of cuisine or style of cooking.

Historic 1209
Indexes festivals and events commemorating specific events from history, such as battles, national independence, the birth dates of famous people, etc.

Promotional 1217
Includes festivals and events that promote everything from city, state, and national pride to agricultural products; from activities (film, quilting, rodeo) to social values (conservation, harmony among people).

Religious 1221
Indexes festivals and events that are part of the customs and practices of a faith tradition, that commemorate events from history of religious significance, or are focused primarily on religious worship services and celebrations.

Sporting 1227
Indexes festivals and events that are based on or revolve around sporting events. It does not include the many fairs and festivals in which games and contents form only a part, although these events can be found in the General Subject Index.

4. General Subject Index 1231
The General Subject Index includes names of main entries in the HFCWD, alternate and foreign names of events, and English translations (when available) of foreign names, by key word. It lists people, places, religions, institutions, and other items of significance (e.g. customs, activities) appearing within the text of the entries.

INDEX 1

Chronological Index
Fixed Days and Events

The Fixed Days and Events Index organizes holidays according to the month or specific date(s) in which they are observed. For each month, those holidays celebrated within the month are given first, followed by holidays celebrated on specific date(s), then those observed at the same time each year, although not on a fixed date (e.g., the first Monday, the last week, etc.).

See also the Chronological Index—Movable Days, the Special Subject Index, and the General Index.

January

Adae-Kese	0015
Australian Open Tennis	0194
Barbados Jazz Festival	0244
Cape Minstrels' Carnival	0492
Doo Dah Parade	0834
Fellsmere Frog Island Festival	0990
Fraternal Order of Real Bearded Santas Reunion and Luncheon	1073
Golden Globe Awards Ceremony	1158
Hadaka Matsuri (Naked Festival)	1252
Iroquois Midwinter Festival	1432
Papa Festival	2206
Peyote Dance (Híkuli Dance)	2248
Sundance Film Festival	2866
Sydney Festival	2893
Usokae	3098

January 01

Bom Jesus dos Navegantes	0359
Christmas (Syria)	0627
Circumcision, Feast of the	0650
Cotton Bowl Game	0703
Cuba Liberation Day	0734
Emancipation Day (United States)	0925
First Foot Day	1020
Haiti Independence Day	1259
Junkanoo Festival	1494
New Year 's Day	2024
New Year 's Day (Denmark) (Nytaarsdag)	2025
New Year 's Day (France)	2026
New Year 's Day (Germany)	2027
New Year 's Day (Lithuania)	2028
New Year 's Day (Malta)	2029
New Year 's Day (Portugal) (Ano Novo)	2031
New Year 's Day (Romania) (Anul Nou)	2032
New Year 's Day (Russia)	2033
New Year 's Day (Switzerland) (Neujahrstag)	2034
New Year 's Day (Netherlands) (Nieuwjaarsdag)	2030
Orange Bowl Game	2147
Oshogatsu (New Year 's Day)	2155
Polar Bear Swim Day	2288
Rose Bowl Game	2429
Slovak Republic Independence Day	2648
St. Basil, Feast of	2706
Sudan Independence Day	2855
Sugar Bowl Classic	2857
Ta'u Fo'ou	2932
Tournament of Roses (Rose Parade)	3015

January 01–02

Sol	2657

January 01–05

Pilgrimage to Chalma	2269

January 01–09

Black Nazarene Fiesta	0332

January 02

Berchtold's Day	0295
Haiti Ancestors' Day	1255

January 02–08 in alternate years

Carnival of the Devil	0535

January 03

Ball–Catching Festival (Tamaseseri)	0231

January 04

Myanmar Independence Day	1959
St. Elizabeth Ann Seton, Feast of	2725

January 04–06

Carnival of Blacks and Whites	0531

Numbers in the index refer to entry numbers, not page numbers

January 05
Befana Festival 0278
Epiphany Eve (Austria) 0942
Epiphany Eve (France) 0943

January 05–06
Día de Negritos and Fiesta de los Blanquitos 0802
Twelfth Night 3064

January 05–February 04
Harbin Ice and Snow Festival 1282

January 06
Día de los Tres Reyes 0801
Epiphany (Germany) (Dreikönigsfest) 0935
Epiphany (Labrador) 0936
Epiphany (Portugal) (Día de Reis) 0937
Epiphany (Spain) (Día de los Reyes Magos) 0939
Epiphany (Sweden) (Trettondag Jul) 0940
Epiphany, Feast of the 0944
Epiphany, Christian Orthodox 0941
Haxey Hood Game 1293
Maroon Festival 1786
New Year 's Parade of Firemen (Dezome–shiki) 2041
Perchtenlauf 2243
Three Kings Day in Indian Pueblos 2976

January 06 or 07
Old Christmas Day 2122

January 06–07
Daruma Ichi (Daruma Doll Fair) 0764

January, Sunday after Epiphany
Baptism of the Lord, Feast of the 0242

January 06, Sunday after
Holy Family, Feast of the 1334

January; first Monday after Epiphany
Plough Monday 2285

January; 7–10 days ending the second Sunday after Epiphany
Bonfim Festival (Festa do Bonfim) 0364

January 07
Cambodia Victory Day (Victory over Genocide Day, Nation Day) 0471
Christmas (Russian Orthodox) 0623
Distaff Day 0813
Ganna (Genna) 1102
Nanakusa Matsuri (Seven Herbs or Grasses Festival) 1973

January 08
Battle of New Orleans Day 0267
Gynaecocratia 1250
St. Gudula's Day 2738

January 09
Agonalia 0035

January 10
Benin National Vodoun Day (Traditional Religions Day) 0292

January 11
Burning the Clavie 0439
Carmentalia 0505
Hostos Day 1371
Juturnalia 1498

January 12
Zanzibar Revolution Day 3309

January 12, first Monday after
Handsel Monday 1277

January 13
Old Silvester 2126
St. Hilary's Day 2741
St. Knut's Day 2766
Togo National Liberation Day 2994

January 13, Sunday nearest
Foster (Stephen) Memorial Day 1061

January 14
Ratification Day 2372
St. Hilary's Day 2741
St. Sava's Day 2808
Tunisia Revolution and Youth Day 3050

January 14, around
Lohri 1692
Magh Sankranti 1733

January 14, every hundred years
Mallard Ceremony 1759

January 15
Black Christ of Esquipulas, Day of the 0326
Carmentalia 0505
Chilembwe (John) Day 0600
King (Martin Luther, Jr.), Birthday 1556
Suminuri Matsuri 2860
Underwater Tug-of-War Festival 3082
Wakakusayama Yaki (Mount Wakakusa Fire Festival) 3171

January 15, Sunday closest to
Toh-shiya 2996

January 17
Franklin's (Benjamin) Birthday 1072
Polish Liberation Day 2291
St. Anthony the Abbot, Feast of 2701

January 17–25
St. Sebastian's Day 2809

January 18
Christmas Eve (Armenia) 0630
Four an' Twenty Day 1063
St. Peter 's Chair, Festival of 2799

Numbers in the index refer to entry numbers, not page numbers

1146

January 18–25
Prayer for Christian Unity, Week of 2311

January 19
Epiphany, Christian Orthodox 0941
Epiphany (Russia) 0938

January 19–20
Timqat (Timkat) 2985

January 20
Azerbaijan Day of the Martyrs 0207
Babin Den 0214
El Pochó Dance-Drama 0902
Guinea–Bissau and Cape Verde National
    Heroes' Day 1234
Inauguration Day 1414
St. Agnes's Eve 2695
St. Sebastian's Day 2809

January 21
Barrow (Errol) Day 0249
St. Sarkis's Day 2807

January 21, week before Sunday nearest
Santa Inés, Fiesta of 2519

January 22
St. Vincent's Day 2825
Ukraine Unification Day (National
    Reunification Day) 3077

January 22–23
San Ildefonso Firelight Dances 2491

January 24
Alasitas Fair 0052

January 24, weekend nearest
California Gold Rush Day 0465

January 25
Burns (Robert) Night 0443
Cow, Festival of the 0707
St. Paul, Feast of the Conversion of 2796

January 26
Australia Day 0193
Duarte Day 0845
India Republic Day 1417
MacArthur (Douglas) Day 1719
St. Polycarp's Day 2803
Uganda Liberation Day 3071

January 26, on or near
Hobart Cup Day 1319

January 27
Holocaust Remembrance Day, International 1332
Mozart (Wolfgang Amadeus), Birthday of 1946

January 28
Albania Republic Day 0056
St. Charlemagne's Day 2713

January 29, Sunday nearest
Paine (Thomas) Day 2183

January 30
Abdullah's (King) Birthday in Jordan 0005
Roosevelt (Franklin D.) Day 2425
St. Charles's Day 2714
Three Archbishops, Day of the 2974

January 31
Nauru Independence Day 1994

January, every other year
Chicago International Puppet Festival 0590

January, in even-numbered years
Dhaka International Film Festival 0795

January, in odd-numbered years
Bocuse D'Or 0350

January, early
Compitalia 0671

January, late
Tunarama Festival 3047

January, a Sunday in late– or early February
Grammy Awards Ceremony 1176

January, a weekend in
Art Deco Weekend 0159

January, first Monday
Handsel Monday 1277

January, first week
Sarasota Circus Festival and Parade 2530

January, second Sunday
Meitlisonntag 1845
Saturnalia Roman Festival 2536

January, second Monday
Seijin-no-Hi (Adults Day; Coming-of-Age Day) 2558

January, second or third weekend, usually
MadFest Juggling Festival 1729

January, mid–
Pongal 2295
Utakai Hajime (Imperial Poem-Reading
    Ceremony) 3100
Western Stock Show, National 3204

January, mid– through mid–February
Edison (Thomas) Festival of Light 0892

January, third Sunday
World Religion Day 3267

January, third Monday
King (Martin Luther, Jr.), Birthday 1556

Numbers in the index refer to entry numbers, not page numbers

King (Martin Luther, Jr.) Drum Major for Justice
   Parade, Battle of the Bands & Drum Line
   Extravaganza, National 1557
Lee (Robert E.) Day 1650

January, third week
Ati-Atihan Festival 0185

January, third weekend
Sinulog Festival 2638

January, third full weekend
Texas Citrus Fiesta............................ 2954

January, two weeks
North American International Auto Show 2086

January, last Sunday
Mount Cameroon Race........................... 1933

January, usually last Sunday
Super Bowl Sunday 2874

January, last Tuesday
Up-Helly-Aa 3091

January, last Thursday
Dicing for the Maid's Money Day 0805
NASA Day of Remembrance 1980

January, last week
Cowboy Poetry Gathering, National 0710
Mozart Week (Mozartwoche) 1948

January, last week, to first week in February
St. Paul Winter Carnival........................ 2797

January, last weekend
Circus Festival of Tomorrow, International.. 0651
Dinagyang 0806
Gasparilla Pirate Festival 1107

January, last two weeks
Southwestern Exposition Livestock Show & Rodeo 2678

January, late, to early February
Hurston (Zora Neale) Festival of the Arts and
   Humanities 1385
Ullr Fest 3080

January or February
Itabashi Suwa Jinja Ta-Asobi.................... 1443

January–February
Dance on Camera 0758
Firecracker Festival 1018
Göteborg International Film Festival.............. 1174
Iyomante Matsuri (Bear Festival) 1449
Lemon Festival 1655
Muscat Festival 1954
Perth International Arts Festival 2245

January–March
Bermuda Festival of the Performing Arts 0303

Sun Pageant Day 2864
Tsagaan Sar (Mongolian New Year)............... 3035

January–October
Macker (Gus) Basketball 1723

January–December, 24th day of each month
Jizo Ennichi 1479

February
Aztec Rain Festival 0209
Hayti Heritage Film Festival.................... 1295
Black History Month........................... 0330
Boston Science Fiction Film Festival 0378
Buena Vista Logging Days 0412
Buffalo's Big Board Surfing Classic 0418
Candelaria (Peru) 0483
Cruft's Dog Show 0733
Dartmouth Winter Carnival 0763
Daytona 500 0773
Hadaka Matsuri (Naked Festival) 1252
Hobart Royal Regatta 1320
Matriculation, Feast of the 1814
Mihr, Festival of 1878
Multicultural Festival, National 1881
Native Islander Gullah Celebration 1989
Pan-African Film Festival 2200
Powamû Ceremony 2308
Premio Lo Nuestro Latin Music Awards 2313
Special Olympics 2681
Thorrablót (Thorri Banquet) 2973
Tohono O'odham Nation Rodeo 2995
Trigo, Fiesta Nacional del (National Wheat Festival) .. 3025
Winterlude................................... 3239
World Championship Crab Races 3252
Yukigassen Festivals 3300

February 01
Cross-Quarter Days 0731
Fire Festivals 1016
Freedom Day, National 1075
Imbolc (Imbolg) 1406
Rwanda National Heroes' Day 2453
St. Bridget's Day 2709

February 01, Saturday nearest
Gable (Clark) Birthday Celebration 1088

February 01 or February 14 (varies)
St. Tryphon's Day (Montenegro and Bulgaria)
(Trifon Zarezan) 2820

February 01–08
Yaya Matsuri (Shouting Festival) 3287

February 01–15
Nombre de Jesús 2081

February 02
Candelaria (Bolivia) 0482

Numbers in the index refer to entry numbers, not page numbers

Candlemas 0485
Cock Festival 0662
Groundhog Day 1222
Yemanjá Festival 3289

February 03
Four Chaplains Day 1064
St. Blaise's Day 2707
San Blas, Fiesta of 2479

February 03 or 04
Setsubun (Bean-Throwing Festival) 2571

February 03–05
St. Agatha Festival. 2694

February 03, Monday after
Hurling the Silver Ball 1383

February 04
Sri Lanka National Day 2693

February 4, Monday following
Parks (Rosa) Day. 2217

February 04 or 05
Li Ch'un 1661

February 05
Runeberg (Johan Ludvig), Birthday of 2446
San Marino Liberation Day (Feast Day of Saint
    Agatha) 2503
Williams (Roger) Day 3228

February 05, Sunday nearest
Igbi 1402

February 06
Sàmi National Holiday. 2474
Waitangi Day 3170

February 06, week of
Marley's (Bob) Birthday 1785

February 07
Grenada Independence Day 1217

February 08
Boy Scouts' Day 0387
Hari-Kuyo (Festival of Broken Needles) 1284

February 09
St. Maron's Day 2775

February 10
Fenkil Day 2217
St. Paul's Shipwreck, Feast of 2798

February 11
Cameroon Youth Day 0476
Edison's (Thomas) Birthday 0893
Iran Victory Day of the Iranian Revolution 1429
Japan National Foundation Day. 1467
Liberia Armed Forces Day. 1663
Our Lady of Lourdes, Feast of 2164

February 12
Amazon & Galapagos Day 0080
Balserías 0233
Georgia Day 1114
Lincoln's (Abraham) Birthday 1680
Myanmar Union Day 1962

February 12, Sunday nearest
Race Relations Sunday 2354

February 12, 13, 14
Borrowed Days 0370

February 13
Faunalia 0987
Parentalia 2212

February 13–15
Namahage Festival 1971

February 14
Allen (Richard), Birthday of 0072
Douglass (Frederick) Day 0837
Valentine's Day 3107
Vinegrower 's Day 3153

February 15
Anthony (Susan B.) Day. 0117
Lupercalia 1715
MaineMemorial Day 1748
Serbia Statehood Day of the Republic 2568

February 15–17
Kamakura Matsuri (Snow Hut Festival) 1510

February 16
Lithuania Independence Day 1684

February 16–17
Bonden Festival (Bonden Matsuri) 0363
Kim Jong-Il, Birthday of 1554

February 17
Fornacalia 1058
Quirinalia 2351

February 17 – 20
Hachinoche Enburi. 1251

February 18
Gambia Independence Day 1096
Kosovo Independence Day 1588
Nepal Democracy Day 2008

February 19
Bombing of Darwin, Anniversary of the 0360

February 21
Feralia 0992
Shaheed Day 2581
Vanuatu Father Walter Lini Day 3114

Numbers in the index refer to entry numbers, not page numbers

February 22
Abu Simbel Festival 0009
St. Lucia Independence Day 2769
Washington's (George) Birthday 3184

February 23
Brunei National Day 0406
Terminalia 2951

February 24
Estonia Independence Day 0958
N'cwala 2001
St. Matthias's Day 2782

February 25
Fiesta sa EDSA (People Power Anniversary) 1005
Kuwait National Day 1601

February 25–March 01
Ayyam-i-Ha 0206

February 26
Kuwait Liberation Day 1600

February 27
Dominican Republic Independence Day 0829
Ecuadoran Civicism & National Unity Day 0888
Equirria 0947

February 28
Arbaeen Pilgrimage 0137
Kalevala Day 1507
Taiwan Peace Memorial Day 2909

February 28–March 01
Marzas 1807

February 29
Leap Year Day 1646
Lee (Ann) Birthday 1649

February, early
Fiesta Day 1004
Quebec Winter Carnival 2344
World Championship Hoop Dance Contest 3253

February, first Friday
Wear Red Day, National 3197

February, first Saturday Sunday
Homstrom 1353

February, begins first Thursday
Great Sami Winter Fair 1202

February, first weekend
Finnish Sliding Festival 1015
Tulsa Indian Arts Festival 3045

February, first full weekend
Ice Worm Festival 1389

February, first week
Beargrease (John) Sled Dog Marathon 0277

February, first half
Washington's (George) Birthday Celebration
(Los Dos Laredos) 3186

February, first new moon
Bianou 0309

February, weekend including second Sunday
Namahage Festival 1971

February, begins second Friday
Anchorage Fur Rendezvous 0097

February, mid
Elephant Festival 0909
Great Backyard Bird Count 1194
Jorvik Viking Festival 1485
Sapporo Snow Festival (Yuki Matsuri) 2529

February, mid, begins
Holetown Festival 1326

February, mid–, weekend in
Battle of Olustee Reenactment 0268

February, mid–late
Hala Festival 1262

February, mid–, to early March
Houston Livestock Show & Rodeo 1374

February, third Monday
Bates (Daisy Gatson) Day 0260
Presidents' Day 2316
Washington's (George) Birthday 3184

February, third Monday and preceding weekend
Washington's (George) Birthday Celebration
(Alexandria, Virginia) 3185

February, third Sunday every two years
Chinchilla Melon Festival 0605

February, third week
Brotherhood/Sisterhood Week 0404
Sundiata, Festival 2873
Viña del Mar International Song Festival 3149

February, last full week
Vaqueros, Fiesta de los 3118

February, last week
Shahi Durbar 2582

February, last weekend
American Birkebeiner 0082

February, late
Nenana Ice Classic 2007

February, late, three-day weekend
Fisher Poets Gathering 1025

Numbers in the index refer to entry numbers, not page numbers

February, late, or March

Golden Shears World Shearing and Wool–handling
Championships 1161

February, late, to first Sunday in March

Vasaloppet 3119

February, late-early March

Sydney Gay and Lesbian Mardi Gras 2895

February, late–early March, even–numbered years

New Zealand Festival. 2047
Tango Festival 2922

February or March

Ku-omboka 1595

February–March

Adelaide Festival 0019
Anthesteria 0116
Argungu Fishing Festival 0145
Carnaval Miami 0506
Casals Festival 0543
Cherry Blossom Festival (Hawaii) 0576
Eleusinian Mysteries. 0911
Hola Mohalla 1325
Hong Kong Arts Festival 1356
Mardi Gras Film Festival 1609
Napa Valley Mustard Festival. 1974
New York International Children's Film Festival 2045
Philadeplphia Flower Show 2252
Phra Buddha Bat Fair 2254

February – March, odd numbered years

Panafrican Film and Television Festival
Of Ouagadougou. 9179

February, 10 days

Berlin International Film Festival. 0300

February–March, two weeks in

Saudi Arabia National Heritage and Folk Culture
Festival (Janadriyah Festival) 2537

February–March, four weeks in

Adelaide Fringe Festival 0020

February–April

Corn-Planting Ceremony 0689
Simadan Festival 2630

February–November, early

Oregon Shakespeare Festival. 2152

February–November, various weekends

Pickett (Bill) Invitational Rodeo 2255

March

Ann Arbor Film Festival 0107
Art Basel (Hong Kong). 0157
Aztec Rain Festival 0209

European Fine Art Fair. 0967
Guadalajara International Film Festival 1223
Nyepi 2101
Sebring 12-Hour Race. 2555
Shishi Odori (Deer Dance) 2609
Spring of Culture 2690
SXSW (South by Southwest) 2891
SXSW (South by southwest) Film. 2892
Tricky Women Festival of Animated Films. 3024
Whale Festivals (California) 3207
Xipe Totec, Festival of 3282
Yukigassen Festivals 3300
Yuma Lettuce Days. 3303

March 01

Chalanda Marz (First of March) 0559
Remembrance Day 2390
Martenitza 1795
Matronalia 1816
Swallow, Procession of the 2881
Samil-jol (Independence Movement Day) 2475
St. David's Day 2719
Whuppity Scoorie 3217

March 01–03

Drymiais 0844

March 01–14

Omizutori Matsuri (Water-Drawing Festival) 2139

March 02

Ethiopia Victory of Adwa Commemoration Day 0963
Libya Declaration of Jamahiriya Day (Declaration
of the People's Authority Day) 1671
Myanmar Peasants' Day 1961
Texas Independence Day 2956

March 2 – 20

Nineteen Day Fast. 2071

March 03

Bulgaria Day of Liberation from Ottoman
Domination 0419
Cambodia National Culture Day 0469
Hina Matsuri (Doll Festival) 1311
Malawi Martyrs' Day 1751

March 03–04

Daruma Ichi (Daruma Doll Fair) 0764

March 04

Fox (George), Death of 1067

March 05

Boston Massacre Day 0376
Vanuatu Custom Chiefs Day. 3113

March 05, about

Excited Insects, Feast of 0971

March 06

Alamo Day 0051
Magellan (Ferdinand) Day 1731

Numbers in the index refer to entry numbers, not page numbers

March 07
Burbank Day 0430

March 07–08
San Juan de Dios, Fiesta of 2498

March 08
Women's Day, International 3244

March 09
Baron Bliss Day 0248
Forty Martyrs' Day 1059
St. Frances of Rome, Feast of 2729

March 11
King's Birthday (Denmark) 1561
Lithuania Restoration of Statehood Day 1685
Moshoeshoe's Day 1926
March 12
Girl Scout Day 1144
Mauritius Independence Day 1821
St. Gregory's Day 2737

March 12–19
St. Joseph's Day 2762

March 13
Kasuga Matsuri 1521

March 14
Equirria 0947
Mamuralia 1764
St. Vincent and the Grenadines National
    Heroes Day 2824

March 15
Anna Parenna Festival 0108
Hungary Revolution and Independence Day 1381
Jackson's (Andrew) Birthday 1452
Quarter Days 2341
Roberts's (Joseph Jenkins) Birthday 2410

March 15, Sunday after
Buzzard Day 0452

March 16
Congo National Days 0678
St. Urho's Day 2821

March 17
Camp Fire Founders' Day 0477
Evacuation Day 0968
Liberalia 1662
St. Patrick's Day. 2792
St. Patrick's Day (Ireland) 2793
St. Patrick's Day Parade (Savannah, Georgia) 2795

March 17, weekend nearest
St. Patrick's Day Encampment 2794

March 18
Sheelah's Day 2594

March 19
San José Day Festival 2496
Swallows of San Juan Capistrano 2882

March 20
Tunisia Independence Day 3048

March 20, on or near
Ibu Afo Festival 1388

March 20 or 21, week including
Higan 1307

March 21
Burning of the Socks 0438
Elimination of Racial Discrimination,
    International Day for the 0915
Shunbun-no-Hi (Vernal Equinox Day) 2621
Vernal Equinox (Chichén Itzá) 3132

March 21, around
Nawruz (Kazakhstan) 1999

March 21, begins about
Nawruz (Naw roz; No Ruz; New Year) 1998

March 21 or 22
Vernal Equinox 3131

March 21 or 22, five days including
Sacaea 2458

March 21, Saturday or Sunday nearest
Marzenna Day 1808

March 22
World Day for Water. 3256

March 22, around
Ostara 2157

March 23
Pakistan Day 2185

March 24
Argentina National Day of Memory for Truth
and Justice 0143

March 25
Annunciation of the Blessed Virgin Mary, Feast of
    the (Belgium) 0114
Annunciation of the Lord 0115
Greece Independence Day 1207
Hilaria 1309
Lady Day 1614
Lady Day among Samis 1615
Maryland Day 1803
San Marino Anniversary of the Arengo 2501
St. Dismas's Day 2722
Tichborne Dole 2979

March 26
Bangladesh Independence Day 0238

Numbers in the index refer to entry numbers, not page numbers

March 26, Monday on or near
Kuhio (Prince) Day 1592

March 27
Myanmar Armed Forces Day 1958

March 28
Teachers' Day in the Czech Republic 2936

March 29
Boganda Day 0353
Madagascar Martyrs' Day (Commemoration Day,
    Insurrection Day) 1726

March 29, 30, 31
Borrowed Days 0370

March 30
Doctors' Day 0817
Spiritual Baptist (Shouters) Liberation Day 2685

March 31
Chavez (Cesar) Day 0568
Malta Freedom Day 1760
Transfer Day 3018

March, usually
Nguillatun 2059

March, early
Iditarod Trail Sled Dog Race 1399
NAACP Image Awards 1965
North Pole Winter Carnival 2089

March, a Wednesday
Budget Day 0411

March, first Sunday
Kyokusui-no-En 1606

March, first Monday
Eight-Hour Day 0898

March, first Tuesday
Town Meeting Day 3016

March, first Saturday
Bal du Rat Mort (Dead Rat's Ball) 0229

March, first Friday
World Day of Prayer 3257

March, first week
Motorcycle Week (Bike Week) 1932

March, first week, five days
Charleston Wine and Food Festival 0565

March, first weekend
Bridge Crossing Jubilee 0397
Jonquil Festival 1482

March, first new moon in
Alahamady Be 0050

March, week including second Sunday
Holmenkollen Day 1330

March, second Monday
Adelaide Cup. 0018
Canberra Day 0481
Commonwealth Day. 0669
Eight-Hour Day 0898

March, second week
Fairbanks Winter Carnival. 0974

March, second weekend
Sweetwater Rattlesnake Round-Up 2889

March, mid–
Macon Cherry Blossom Festival 1724

March, mid–, to mid–April
Houses and Gardens, Festival of 1373

March, third Thursday
Kiplingcotes Derby 1565

March, third Saturday
Bering Sea Ice Golf Classic 0297

March, third week
Dodge National Circuit Finals Rodeo 0820

March, third weekend
Nuuk Snow Festival 2098
Russell (C. M.) Auction 2449

March, last Monday
Seward's Day 2574

March, last Sabbath
Sabbath of Rabbi Isaac Mayer Wise 2457

March, last weekend
Caribou Carnival and Canadian Championship
    Dog Derby 0499

March, late
Academy Awards Ceremony 0010
Los Isleños Fiesta. 1701
Reindeer Driving Competition 2388
Smithsonian Kite Festival 2651
Tok Race of Champions Dog Sled Race 2998
Williams (Tennessee) New Orleans
    Literary Festival. 3229

March, late, or early April
Boat Race Day (Thames River) 0349

March, late, to early April
Cherry Blossom Festival, National 0578
FeatherFest 0989
Ten Days on the Island 2947

March, late to mid–April
Melbourne International Comedy Festival 1848

Numbers in the index refer to entry numbers, not page numbers

March, full moon day
Phagwa 2250

March or April
Costa Rica National Arts Festival 0700
Cow Fights 0708

March–April
Bermuda College Weeks 0301
Brussels International Fantastic Film Festival 0407
Crane Watch 0715
Dipri Festival 0809
Florida Heritage Festival 1047
Hanami 1276
Hong Kong International Film Festival. 1357
Humana Festival of New American Plays 1378
Lac Long Quan Festival 1612
Lord's Evening Meal (Memorial) 1700
Natchez Spring and Fall Pilgrimages 1983
Spoken Word Festival, Calgary International 2687
Spring Break 2689
Thay Pagoda Festival 2966

March–May
Keukenhof Flower Show 1542

March–July
Holy Ghost, Feast of the. 1335

March, or in some areas October
Ngmayem Festival 2056

March–November
Grand Prix 1181

Spring
Daedala 0748
Nyambinyambi 2100
Sabantui 2455
Stickdance 2838
Tangata Manu (Birdman Ceremony) 2920

Spring, early
Cree Walking-Out Ceremony 0718
Eagle Dance 0858
Paro Tsechu 2218

Spring, first Month
Isthmian Games 1442

Spring, during full moon in Sagittarius
World Invocation Day (Festival of Goodwill) 3263

Spring and Fall
Green Festivals 1209

Spring to Summer, every other year
Berlin Biennale. 0298

Vernal Equinox, Sunday following
Marche du Nain Rouge 1773

April
Atlanta Film Festival. 0186
Billboard Latin Music Awards 0316
Birmingham International Center Spotlight 0320
Budapest Spring Festival 0410
Buenos Aires International Festival
    of Independent Cinema 0413
Canes Shopping Festival 0489
Cherry Blossom Festival (Northern California) 0577
Coachella Valley Music and Arts Festival 0660
Confederados Reunion 0674
Dogwood Festival 0824
Geranium Day 1119
Great Moonbuggy Race 1200
Istanbul Festivals, International 1441
Kite Meeting, International 1571
Land Diving 1622
Latin Festival (Feriae Latinae) 1634
Luoyang Peony Cultural Festival (China) 0603
Poetry Month, National 2287
Nashville Film Festival. 1981
Nganja, Feast of 2055
Osaka International Festival 2154
Road Building 2409
Royal Shows 2442
San Francisco Film Festival, International. 2485
Seville Fair 2573
Tako-Age (Kite Flying) 2915
Tribeca Film Festival 3022
Weifang Kite Festival, International. 3200
Winston 500 3235
WorldFest-Houston Film Festival, International 3273

April 01
April Fools' Day 0132
Greek Cypriot National Day 1208

April 01 and October 01
San Marino Investiture of New Captains Regent 2502

April 01 or 02, the 13th day after Nawruz
Sizdah Bedar 2644

April 02
Children's Book Day, International 0596
Pascua Florida Day 2223

April 03
Guinea Second Republic Day 1233

April 04
Megalesia 1842
San Isidro of Seville, Feast of. 2493
Senegal Independence Day 2564
Shellfish Gathering (Shiohi-gari) 2595

April 04–10
Ludi 1710

Numbers in the index refer to entry numbers, not page numbers

April 06
Chakri Day 0558
Latter-Day Saints, Founding of the Church of 1636

April 06, Saturday after
Candle Auction 0484

April 07
Armenia Motherhood and Beauty Day 0153

April 08
Hana Matsuri (Flower Festival) 1274
Vesak (Wesak; Buddha's Birthday) 3134

April 09
Appomattox Day 0131
Bataan Day 0259

April 10
Salvation Army Founder 's Day 2470

April 12
Cosmonauts Day 0697
Halifax Day 1266
Liberia National Redemption Day 1666

April 12–15
Songkran 2662

April 12–19
Ludi 1710

April 13
Jefferson's (Thomas) Birthday. 1471

April 13 or 14
Bisket Jatra 0322
Sinhala Avurudu 2636

April 13–15
Pii Mai. 2261

April 14
Ambedkar Javanti. 0081
Pan American Day 2198

April 14–15
Takayama Matsuri. 2912

April 15
Kim Il-Sung, Birthday of 1553
Robinson (Jackie) Day 2414

April 16
Emancipation Day (Washington, D.C.) 0926
Margrethe's (Queen) Birthday 1778

April 17
Madara Kijinsai (Demon-God Event) 1727
Syria National Day 2897
Verrazano (Giovanni da) Day 3133

April 18
Zimbabwe Independence Day 3313

April 19
Cerealia (Cerialia) 0553
Primrose Day 2318
Venezuela Independence Day. 3126

April 19 and 25, Thursday between
First Day of Summer (Iceland) 1019

April 21
Kartini Day 1518
Parilia (Palilia) 2213
San Jacinto Day 2495

April 21, week including
Inconfidência Week 1415

April 21, 10 days including
San Antonio, Fiesta 2478

April 21–May 02
Ridvan, Feast of 2401

April 22
Arbor Day 0138
Auntie Litter 's Annual Earth Day Parade and
   Celebration 0190
Earth Day 0860
Oklahoma Day 2116

April 22–24
Moors and Christians Fiesta 1915

April 23
Children's Day 0597
Green George Festival 1210
Shakespeare's (William) Birthday 2585
St. George's Day 2733
St. George's Day (Syria) (Id Mar Jurjus) 2735
Turkey National Sovereignty and
   Children's Day 3053
Vinalia 3150

April 23, on or near
Peppercorn Ceremony 2242

April 23, week including
Conch Republic Independence Celebration 0672

April 24
Armenian Martyrs' Day 0154
Children's Day 0597

April 25
Africa Malaria Day 0027
Anzac Day 0123
Italy Liberation Day 1446
Portugal Liberation Day. 2299
River Kwai Bridge Week 2406
Robigalia 2411
Sinai Liberation Day 2633
St. Mark's Day 2773
St. Mark's Day (Hungary) 2774
World Malaria Day 3264

Numbers in the index refer to entry numbers, not page numbers

April 26
Audubon Day 0189
Tanzania Union Day 2926

April 27
King's Day (Koningsdag). 1558
Santo Toribio Fiesta 2525
Sierra Leone Independence Day. 2625
South Africa Freedom Day 2666
Togo Independence Day 2993

April 27–May 03
Floralia 1041
Ludi 1710

April 28
Freedom of Entry Ceremony. 1077

April 29
Kyokusui-no-En 1606

April 29–May 03
Uesugi Matsuri 3069

April 30
May Day Eve (Ireland) 1830
May Day Eve (Italy) 1831
May Day Eve (Switzerland) (MaitagVorabend) 1832
May Day Eve (Czech Republic) 1829
Juliana's (Queen) Birthday 1492
Saigon Liberation Day 2464
St. James's Day. 2745
Walpurgis Night (Walpurgisnacht) 3175

April 30–May 01
Minehead Hobby Horse Parade 1885

April, biennially
Awuru Odo Festival 0202

April, three days
Sandburg Days Festival 2508

April, early
Chinhae Cherry Blossom Festival 0607
Hitachi Furyumono 1316
Sealing the Frost 2552

April, early, Saturday in
Great Falls Ski Club Mannequin Jump 1197

April, early, to mid–May
Ombashira Matsuri 2137

April, first Saturday
Grand National 1180

April, first full week
Masters Golf Tournament 1811

April, first weekend and Monday
Tater Days 2931

April, second Friday
Liberian Fast and Prayer Day 1668

April, mid–
Arctic Circle Race 0139
Chhau Mask-Dance Festival 0583
French Quarter Festival 1081
Kiribati National Health Day 1568
Santamaría (Juan) Day 2523
Thingyan 2970
Water-Splashing Festival (Dai New Year) 3193
Wildlife Film Festival, International 3227

April, mid–, to early May
St. Mark, Fair of (Feria de San Marcos) 2772

April, mid–, to late September
Tivoli Gardens Season 2991

April, third Monday
Boston Marathon 0375
De Diego (Jose) Day 0777
Patriots' Day 2227

April, third Monday, eve of
Annual Lantern Ceremony 0112

April, third Monday and preceding Sunday
Sechseläuten 2556

April, third week
Whistlers Convention, International 3211

April, third weekend
Kewpiesta 1543
New England Folk Festival 2016

April, fourth Monday
Fast Day 0982

April, fourth Thursday
Take Our Daughters to Work Day 2913

April, last Sunday
Landsgemeinde 1624

April, first weekend after last Wednesday
Butter and Egg Days. 0449

April, last Friday
Arbor Day 0138

April, last Saturday
Cynonfardd Eisteddfod 0742
Maryland Hunt Cup 1804

April, begins Sunday before last weekend
University of Pennsylvania Relay Carnival 3090

April, last full week
Administrative Professionals Week 0021
World's Biggest Fish Fry 3274

April, last week
Tucson International Mariachi Conference 3041

Numbers in the index refer to entry numbers, not page numbers

April, last full weekend
Shad Festival 2579

April, last weekend
Landing of d'Iberville 1623
Stockton Asparagus Festival 2841
Vermont Maple Festival 3130
Vidalia Onion Festival 3141

April, last weekend–first weekend in May
Buccaneer Days 0408

April, last two weeks
Carnival (U.S. Virgin Islands) 0526

April, late
Crosses, Festival of the (Fiesta de las Cruces) 0729
Georgia Harmony Jubilee .1115
Jazzkaar Festival 1470

April, late, to early May
New Orleans Jazz and Heritage Festival 2019

April or May
Aboakyer Festival 0007
Diamond Head Crater Celebration 0804
Moro-Moro Play 1923
Spamarama 2680

April–May
Al Hareed Festival 0048
Antigua Sailing Week 0121
Annual Production 2992

April–May, every two years
Dance Festival Birmingham, International 0757

April–May, every 4–6 years
Floralies 1042

April and June, between
Blessing of the Bikes 0341

April–September, every three years
Normandy Impressionist Festival 2083

April–October, every 10 years
Floriade 1046

April and October, two events
Morija Arts and Cultural Festival 1919

April–November
Stratford Festival 2846

May

Brighton Festival 0400
Burning of the Ribbons (Queima das Fitas) 0437
Cannes Film Festival 0488
Ch'un-hyang Festival 0647
Dhungri Fair 0797
Elisabeth (Queen) International Music Competition . . 0916

Fleet Week (New York City) 1033
Geranium Day 1119
Grands Crus, Weekend of the 1185
Jammolpur Ceremony 1461
Land Diving 1622
Lilac Festival 1676
May Festival, International 1833
Mayfest, International 1835
Mayoring Day 1836
Memphis in May International Festival 1852
Mille Miglia 1883
Monaco Grand Prix 1905
Pike Festival, National 2262
Punjabi American Festival 2326
Rodgers Festival, Jimmie 2417
Steinbeck (John) Festival 2834
Tako-Age (Kite Flying) 2915
Tulip Time Festival (Holland Michigan) 3044
Wall Street Rat Race 3173
Washington State Apple Blossom Festival 3183

May 01
Beltane 0290
Bona Dea Festival 0361
Cheese Rolling 0569
Cross-Quarter Days 0731
Fire Festivals 1016
Law Day 1638
Lei Day 1652
Loyalty Day 1707
Marshall Islands Constitution Day 1789
May Day 1824
May Day (France) 1826
May Day (Scandinavia) 1827
May Day (Spain) 1828
May Day (Czech Republic) (Prvého Máje) 1825
Moving Day 1941
New Orleans Wine and Food Experience 2020
Sani Gourmet 2512
St. Evermaire, Game of 2727
St. Joseph the Worker, Feast of 2761
St. Tammany's Day 2816
Vappu 3117

May 01, begins first Thursday after
Calendimaggio 0459

May 01–04
Sant' Efisio, Festival of 2515

May 01–15
San Isidro in Peru, Fiesta of 2492

May 01–31
Flores de Mayo (El Salvador) 1044

May 01–July 31
Wicklow Gardens Festival 3219

May 03
Aymuray (Song of the Harvest) 0205

Numbers in the index refer to entry numbers, not page numbers

Día de la Santa Cruz (Day of the Holy Cross) 0798
Exaltation of the Cross, Feast of the 0970
Polish Constitution Day 2289

May 03–04
Hakata Dontaku 1260

May 03–05
Tako-Age (Kite Flying) 2915

May 04
Cassinga Day 0544
Greenery Day 1213
Kent State Memorial Day 1535
Restoration of Independence of the Republic
    of Latvia 2393
Rhode Island Independence Day 2398

May 04–05
Dutch Liberation Day 0857

May 05
Cinco de Mayo 0649
Ethiopia Patriots' Victory Day 0962
Japan Constitution Memorial Day 1465
Kodomo-no-Hi (Children's Day) 1579
Napoleon's Day 1975
Tango-no-Sekku (Boys' Day Festival) 2923
Thailand Coronation Day 2960
Urini Nal (Children's Day) 3092

May 06
Hidrellez Festival 1306
Martyrs' Day (Lebanon) 1800
St. George's Day (Bulgaria) 2734
Syria Martyrs' Day 2896

May 07
Tagore (Rabindranath), Birthday of 2905

May 07–08
St. Nicholas's Day (Italy) 2790

May 08
Blavatsky (Helena Petrovna), Death of 0339
Helston Flora Day 1298
Nabekamuri Matsuri (Pan-on-Head Festival) 1969

May 09
Lemuralia 1656
St. Christopher 's Day 2715
St. Joan of Arc, Feast Day of 2746
Victory Day (Russia) 3140

May 10
Golden Spike Anniversary 1162

May 11
Lemuralia 1656

May 11–13
Frost Saints' Days 1084

May 12
Garland Day 1105
May 12, week including
Hospital Week, National 1370

May 13
Jamestown Day 1459
Lemuralia 1656
Our Lady of Fátima Day 2161

May 14
Liberia National Unification Day 1667

May 14–15
Carabao Festival 0495
Paraguay Independence Day 2209

May 15
Aoi Matsuri 0124
Race of the Ceri 2353
Restoration of the Aaronic Priesthood
    Commemoration 2394
San Isidro the Farmer, Feast of 2494
St. Dymphna's Day 2724

May 15, Sunday after
St. Gens, Festival of (La Fête de St. Gens) 2732

May 16
St. Brendan's Day 2708

May 17
Mut l-ard 1957
Norway Constitution Day (Syttende Mai) 2092

May 17, weekend nearest
Syttende Mai Fest 2898

May 17–18
Toshogu Haru-No-Taisai (Great Spring Festival of
    the Toshogu Shrine) 3013

May 18
Haiti Flag and University Day 1258

May 18, weekend near
Sanja Matsuri (Three Shrines Festival) 2513

May 19
Atatürk Remembrance (Youth and Sports Day) 0183
Ho Chi Minh's Birthday 1318
Malcolm X's Birthday 1754
St. Dunstan's Day 2723

May 20
Cameroon National Day 0475
East Timor Independence Day 0861
Emancipation Day (Tallahassee, Florida) 0924
Mecklenburg Independence Day 1839

May 21
Chile Battle of Iquique Day (Día de las Glorias
    Navales) 0598

Numbers in the index refer to entry numbers, not page numbers

May 21–23
Anastenaria 0095

May 22
Biological Diversity, International Day for 0319
Maritime Day, National 1783
Milk (Harvey) Day 1881
Santa Rita, Fiesta of 2521
Yemen Independence and National Days 3290

May 22–23
Bab, Declaration of the 0212

May 24
Bermuda Day 0302
Bulgarian Education and Culture Day 0421
Commonwealth Day. 0669
Ecuador Independence Day 0887
Eritrea Independence Day 0950

May 24, Sunday nearest
Aldersgate Experience 0060

May 24, Monday nearest
Bonfire Night 0365

May 24–25
Stes. Maries, Fête des 2835

May 25
African Liberation Day. 0030
Argentine National Day 0144
Jordan Independence Day 1483
Lebanon Resistance and Liberation Day 1648
Moving Day 1941

May 25, week beginning
Week of Solidarity with the Peoples of
Non-Self-Governing Territories 3199

May 26
Georgia Independence Day 1116
Guyana Independence Day 1246

May 27
Children's Day 0597

May 27–June 03
Reconciliation Week, National 2378

May 28
Armenia First Republic Day 0151
Azerbaijan Independence Days 0208
Ethiopia National Day 0961

May 29
Baha'u'llah, Ascension of 0224
Founder's Day 1062
Garland Day 1105
Nepal Republic Day 2009
Shick-Shack Day (Shik-Shak Day, Shicsack Day,
Shig-Shag Day) 2601

May 30
Indian Arrival Day 1418
St. Joan of Arc, Feast Day of 2746

May 30–31
Kaamatan Festival 1504

May 31
Flores de Mayo (Philippines) 1045
Royal Brunei Armed Forces Day 2439
South Africa Republic Day 2669
Visitation, Feast of the 3158

May, biennially
Greenville Treaty Camporee 1215

May, odd-numbered years
Islamic Festival 1434

May, early
Royal Ploughing Ceremony 2441
Shenandoah Apple Blossom Festival 2598

May, three weeks
Prague Spring International Music Festival 2310

May, first Sunday
Chongmyo Taeje (Royal Shrine Rite) 0613
Cosby Ramp Festival 0696
Sunday School Day 2872

May, begins first Sunday
Family Week 0978

May, first Monday
Eight-Hour Day 0898

May, first Thursday
Day of Prayer, National. 0770

May, first Saturday
Kentucky Derby 1536
Prague Kolache Festival 2309
Seagull–Calling Contest 2551

May, first full week
Be Kind to Animals Week 0274

May, first week, through mid–July
Boston Pops 0377

May, first full weekend
Irrigation Festival 1433

May, first weekend
Blessing of the Shrimp Fleet 0343
Crawfish Festival (Breaux Bridge, Louisiana) 0716
Iris Fest (Fete de l'Iris) 1430
Isle of Eight Flags Shrimp Festival 1436
Kelly (Emmett) Clown Festival 1533
Mushroom Festival 1955
Nations, Festival of (Minnesota). 1985

Numbers in the index refer to entry numbers, not page numbers

May, first weekend, biennial
Richmond Fossil Festival 2400

May, second Sunday
Kattestoet (Festival of the Cats) 1525
Mother 's Day 1930

May, second Sunday, to third Sunday in June
Family Month, National. 0977

May, second weekend
Bar-B-Q Festival, International 0245
Bun Bang Fai (Boun Bang Fay; Rocket Festival) 0426
Tulip Time 3043

May, mid–
St. Isidore, Festival of 2744
Tejano Conjunto Festival 2938

May, third Saturday
Armed Forces Day (United States) 0148
Preakness Stakes 2312

May, third Sunday
Bay to Breakers 0270

May, third weekend
Black Ships Festival. 0334
Calaveras County Fair and Frog Jumping Jubilee 0458
Kingsburg Swedish Festival 1564
Magnolia Blossom Festival 1738
Maifest 1745

May, second to last Sunday
Cavalcata Sarda 0548

May, begins last week
Annapolis Valley Apple Blossom Festival 0110

May, a weekend
Festival des Arts de la Rue. 0997

May, Friday after last Monday
Cotswold Olimpik Games

May, last Sunday
Big Singing 0313

May, last Monday
Fiji Ratu Sir Lala Sukuna Day 1011
Memorial Day 1850

May, last weekend
Castroville Artichoke Food and Wine Festival 0546
DC Black Pride Festival 0774
Maytime Festival, International 1837

May, Memorial Day weekend
Alma Highland Festival and Games 0073
Coca-Cola 600 0661
Dakota Cowboy Poetry Gathering. 0752
Movement Electronic Music Festival 1940
General Clinton Canoe Regatta 1113

I Madonnari Italian Street Painting Festival 1387
Italian Festival 1444
Mule Days 1949
Northwest Folklife Festival 2091
Ole Time Fiddlers and Bluegrass Festival 2132
Polka Festival, National 2293
Sasquatch! Music Festival 2532
Tubman (Harriet) Annual Pilgrimage 3040
Ute Bear Dance 3101
Vandalia Gathering 3112

May, Sunday before Memorial Day weekend
Neighbor Day 2004

May, Sunday of Memorial Day weekend
Indianapolis 500 1420

May, late
Chelsea Flower Show 0572
Chestertown Tea Party Festival 0580
Regatta of the Great Maritime Republics 2386

May, late Saturday
Memorial Day Luminaria at Fredericksburg
National Cemetery 1851

May, late, during the week following Victoria Day
Calgary International Children's Festival 0461

May, late, or early June
Bath International Music Festival. 0261
Blackbeard Pirate Festival 0337
Bergen International Festival 0296
Canadian International Military Tattoo 0479
DanceAfrica 0760
Downtown Hoedown. 0839
Gawai Dayak 1109
Hay-on-Wye Festival of Literature 1294
Waila Festival 3169
West Virginia Strawberry Festival 3203

May, late–early July
Barnum Festival. 0247

May or June
Bachok Cultural Festival 0217
Choctaw Trail of Tears Walk 0612

May or June, even–numbered years
Roots Festival 2426

May–June
Alpaufzug 0076
Carnival Memphis 0529
Dance Week Festival. 0759
Documentary Edge Festival 0818
Fes Festival of World Sacred Music 0993
Florence Musical May (Maggio Musicale Fiorentino) 1043
French Open Tennis 1080
Gaspee Days 1108
Gyangzê Horse-Racing Festival 1249

Numbers in the index refer to entry numbers, not page numbers

Israel Festival 1439
Istanbul Festivals, International 1441
Rose Festival 2430
Ruhr Festival 2443
Seattle Film Festival, International............... 2554
Shinran-Shonin Day 2607
Sofia Music Weeks............................. 2655
Spoleto Festival USA 2688
Stuttgart Festival of Animated Film............... 2853
Thargelia 2964
Vienna Festival 3142
Vivid Sydney 3161
Wiener Festwochen............................ 3221

May–June, even–numbered years
Reykjavik Arts Festival (Listaháti íReykjavík) 2397

May–August
Banff Festival of the Arts 0236
Glyndebourne Festival Opera..................... 1149

May–September
Byblos International Festival..................... 0453
Graveyard Cleaning and Decoration Day 1189
Jodlerfests (Yodeling Festivals) 1480
Wolf Trap Summer Festival Season 3242

May–September, Sunday
Pied Piper Open Air Theater...................... 2257

May–October, every 10 years
Oberammergau Passion Play 2104

May–October, full moon nights
Ramayana Ballet 2367

May–November
Flanders Festival 1030

May – November, odd-numbered years
Venice Biennale (La Biennale).................... 3127

May (Main Festival) and December (Winter Weekend Festival)
Jacob's Ladder 1453

June

Aldeburgh Festival of Music and the Arts 0059
Alexandra Rose Day 0061
American Black Film Festival 0083
Anchorage Festival of Music..................... 0096
Annecy Animation Film Festival, International....... .0111
Art Basel.................................... 0156
Aspen Food and Wine Classic.................... 0174
African-American Music Appreciation Month........ 0034
Broadstairs Dickens Festival 0403
Bulu Festival 0423
Bumba-Meu-Boi Folk Drama 0424
Common Ridings Day 0668
Dance Camera West 0756

Dulcimer Days 0851
Edinburgh International film Festival 0891
Egungun Festival 0895
Encaenia Day 0929
Frameline: The San Francisco International
    LGBT Film Festival 1069
Glastonbury Festival of Contemporary
    Performing Arts........................... 1146
Golden Chariot and Battle of the Lumecon,
    Procession of the 1156
Golden Orpheus 1160
Holland Festival 1328
Isle of Wright Festival......................... 1437
Jewish Cultural Festival 1475
Joust of the Saracens 1487
Juvenalia 1500
Le Mans Motor Race 1644
Lewis and Clark Festival 1660
Native American Ceremonies in June at
    Devils Tower 1987
New York Gay Pride March...................... 2044
NXNE (North by Northeast)...................... 2099
Ovoo Worship Festival 2173
Portland Rose Festival 2298
Elizabeth II (Queen) Birthday 0917
San Francisco Ethnic Dance Festival 2483
San Francisco Pride............................ 2486
Sao Paulo Gay Pride Parade 2527
Sanno Matsuri 2514
Seattle International Dance Festival................ 2553
Shanghai International Film Festival............... 2589
Strawberry Festival 2847
Superman Celebration 2875
Sydney Film Festival 2894
Tsunahiki Matsuri 3036
White Nights 3212

June 01
Kenya Madaraka Day........................... 1537
Samoa Independence Day 2476
Young's (Brigham) Birthday 3297

June 02
Malaysia Birthday of SPB Yang di–Pertuan Agong 1753
St. Elmo's Day 2726

June 03
Uganda Martyrs Day 3072

June 04
Tiananmen Square Anniversary 2978
Tonga Emancipation Day........................ 3002

June 05
Congo National Days 0678
Seychelles Liberation Day 2576
World Environment Day 3260

June 06
D-Day 0776

Numbers in the index refer to entry numbers, not page numbers

South Korea Memorial Day 2674
Swedish Flag Day 2886

June 07
Bahamas Labor Day 0223
Malta Sette Guigno (Commemoration of Uprising of June 7, 1919) 1763

June 08
St. Médardus's Day 2783

June 09
Denmark Constitution Day 0786
St. Columba's Day. 2717
Uganda National Heroes Day 3073

June 10
Portugal National Day 2300
Time Observance Day 2981

June 11
Kamehameha (King) Celebration 1511
Matralia 1813
St. Barnabas's Day 2704

June 12
Philippines Independence Day. 2253

June 13
St. Anthony of Padua, Feast of 2700

June 14
Flag Day 1027
Malawi Freedom Day 1750
Rice-Planting Festival at Osaka. 2399
St. Vitus's Day 2826

June 15
Chagu-Chagu Umakko 0557
Magna Carta Day 1737
Valdemar (King) Day 3106

June 16
Bloomsday 0345
South Africa Youth Day 2671

June 17
Bunker Hill Day. 0429
Children's Day 0597
Iceland Independence Day 1390
Saigusa Matsuri 2465
World Day to Combat Desertification and Drought 3258

June 18
Cambodia Queen Sihanouk's Birthday 0470
Seychelles National Day 2577

June 19
Juneteenth 1493
New Church Day 2014

June 19, Saturday nearest
Departure of the Continental Army 0788
Election of the Mayor of Ock Street 0908

June 20
Argentina Flag Day. 0141
Argentine National Day 0144
Eritrean Martyrs' Day. 0951
West Virginia Day 3201

June 20–26, Saturday between
Juhannus (Midsummer Day) 1491

June 21
Aboriginal Day, National 0008
Greenland National Day 1214
Lismore Lantern Parade. 1682
Midnight Sun Festival 1875

June 21, weekend nearest
Fyr-Bål Fest 1087

June 21 or 22, Saturday nearest
Bawming the Thorn Day 0269

June 21–22
Summer Solstice 2862
Winter Solstice 3237
Ysyakh 3298

June 22
St. Alban's Day 2696

June 22, begins
Lily Festival (Festa dei Giglio) 1677

June 22, eight days beginning
Croatia Anti-Fascist Resistance Day (Anti–Fascism Day) 0721
Xilonen, Festival of 3281

June 23
Bonfire Night 0365
Calinda Dance 0466
Druids' Summer Solstice Ceremony 0843
Estonia Victory Day 0960
Luxembourg National Day 1716
So Joo Festival: The Eve of St. John's Feast Day 2654
St. John's Eve (Denmark) 2755
St. John's Eve (France) (La Vielle de la Saint Jean) 2756
St. John's Eve (Germany) (Johannisnacht) 2750
St. John's Eve (Greece) 2757
St. John's Eve (Ireland) 2758
St. John's Eve (Spain) 2759
Wianki Festival of Wreaths 3218

June 23–24
St. John's Eve and Day (Latvia) (JanuVakars) 2760

June 24
Human Towers of Valls 1377
Inti Raymi Fiesta 1424
Kupalo Festival 1596
Ladouvane 1613
Midsummer Day 1877
Quarter Days 2341

Numbers in the index refer to entry numbers, not page numbers

San Juan and San Pedro Festivals 2497
San Juan Pueblo Feast Day 2499
St. Hans Festival 2739
St. John's Day 2751
St. John's Day (Guatemala) 2752
St. John's Day (Portugal) 2753
St. John's Day (Puerto Rico) 2754
Venezuela Battle of Carabobo Day 3125

June 24, Monday nearest
Newfoundland Discovery Day 2049

June 25
Croatia Statehood Day 0723
Mozambique Independence Day 1943
Slovenia National Day 2649

June 25, weekend nearest
Little Big Horn Days 1687

June 26
Madagascar Independence Day 1725

June 27
Djibouti Independence Day 0815
Martyrdom of Joseph and Hyrum Smith 1799
Stonewall Rebellion, Anniversary of the 2842
Tajikistan Day of National Unity 2910

June 28
Ukraine Constitution Day 3075

June 28–29
Palio of the Goose and River Festival 2190

June 29
Haro Wine Festival (Batalla de Vino) 1287
Mnarja (Imnarja; Feast of St. Peter and St. Paul) 1895
San Juan and San Pedro Festivals 2497
Seychelles Independence Day 2575
St. Peter 's Day (Belgium) 2800
Sts. Peter and Paul Day 2850

June 29, weekend nearest
St. Peter 's Fiesta 2801

June 30
Democratic Republic of Congo Independence Day . . . 0785
Guatemala Army Day 1226

June, even–numbered years
Newport to Bermuda Race 2053

June, odd–numbered years
Humor and Satire Festival, International 1379
Moravian Music Festival 1917
Paris Air and Space Show 2214

June, two weeks
Connecticut Early Music Festival 0679

June, early
Crazy Horse Ride and Veterans' Powwow 0717

Derby Day 0789
Miami/Bahamas Goombay Festival 1864
Texas Folklife Festival 2955

June, early, in odd–numbered years
Black and White Ball 0324

June, early, one week in
Lanimer Festival 1626

June, early, weekend
Rock Ness 2416

June, early, three day weekend
Hatfield and McCoy Reunion Festival and
   Marathon 1292

June, early, to mid-July
Festival-Institute at Round Top, International 1000

June, first Sunday
Sjomannadagur (Seaman's Day) 2645

June, first Monday
Davis's (Jefferson) Birthday 0769

June, first Friday
Bahamas Labor Day 0223

June, begins first Friday
Agriculture Fair at Santarém, National 0036

June, first Saturday
Caricom Day 0500
Appleseed (Johnny), Birthday of 0129

June, first full week
Bowlegs (Billy) Festival 0385
Carillon Festival, International 0502

June, first week
Sun Fun Festival 2863

June, a weekend
Ann Arbor Art Fair 0106

June, first weekend
Chicago Gospel Music Festival 0587
Elfreth's Alley Fete Day 0912
Raid on Redding Ridge 2359
Rogers (Roy) Festival 2419
Sea, Festival of the (Seamen's Day, Sjomannadagur) 2546
Yukon International Storytelling Festival 3301

June, usually first weekend
Yale-Harvard Regatta 3283

June, first three weeks
Sitka Summer Music Festival 2643

June, second Sunday
Children's Day 0597
Race Unity Day 2355
Wood (Grant) Art Festival 3245

Numbers in the index refer to entry numbers, not page numbers

June, second week
New Zealand National Agricultural Fieldays 2048
Telluride Hang Gliding Festival 2944

June, second weekend
Dulcimer and Harp Convention 0850
Morris Rattlesnake Roundup 1924
Red Earth Native American Cultural Festival 2379
Sea Music Festival 2548
Spock Days/Galaxyfest 2686

June, second weekend and third week
Frankenmuth Bavarian Festival 1070

June, mid–
Country Music Fan Fair, International 0706
Great American Brass Band Festival 1191
Arab International Festival 0133
Heidi Festival 1296
NEBRASKAland DAYS 2002
Royal Ascot 2438
Schubertiade 2542
Struga Poetry Evenings 2848
Tako-Age (Kite Flying) 2915
Turtle Days 3060
Viking Festival 3148

June, mid Saturday
Vinegar Festival, International 3152

June, mid to late
Jackalope Days 1451

June, mid–, through July
Andersen (Hans Christian) Festival................ 0098

June, mid–, through mid–August
Caramoor International Music Festival 0496

June, a Sunday
Chicago Blues Festival 0585
Flower Communion 1048

June, third Sunday
Father 's Day 0986

June, four days ending third Sunday
United States Open Championship in Golf 3086

June, third Monday
Argentina Flag Day............................. 0141

June, third Saturday
Alabama Blueberry Festival 0049
Jousting Tournament 1489
Bunch (Madam Lou) Day 0427

June, third full week
Oldtime Fiddlers' Contest and Festival, National 2131

June, third week
Five-Petalled Rose Festival 1026

June, third weekend
Kiamichi Owa-Chito (Festival of the Forest) 1548
Okmulgee Pecan Festival......................... 2118

June, Father's Day weekend
Manly Man Festival and Spam Cook–Off, National ... 1769

June, fourth Sunday
Svenskarnas Dag 2879

June; fifth Saturday after first Saturday in May
Belmont Stakes 0289

June, last Sunday
Gioco del Ponte................................ 1142

June, last Tuesday and Wednesday
Windjammer Days 3232

June, last full week
Kiel Week 1550

June, last week, through first week of July, 10 days
Taste of Chicago 2930

June, last full weekend
DC Caribbean Carnival 0775
Watermelon Thump 3191

June, last weekend
Idaho Regatta 1396
Keller (Helen) Festival 1532
Kingdom Days 1559
St. Martha's Day 2777
Verdur Rock 3129

June, last weekend, through first week in July
Montreal Jazz Festival 1910

June, last weekend, to first weekend in July
American Folklife, Festival of 2650

June, late
Gorilla Naming Ceremony (Kwita Izina) 1172
Marbles Tournament, National.................... 1772
Sioux Sun Dance 2639
Utah Arts Festival 3099
Wisconsin Cheese Curd Festival.................. 3240

June, late, including midsummer's eve
Jutajaiset Folklore Festival 1497

June, late, or early July
World's Largest Salmon Barbecue 3276

June, late, to early July
Freedom Festival, International 1076
Wooden Boat Festival 3247

June, late, to early July; begins six weeks before first Monday in August
Wimbledon 3230

June, late, to July
Tartu Hanseatic Days 2929

Numbers in the index refer to entry numbers, not page numbers

June, late, through early July
South Africa National Arts Festival
(Grahamstown Festival) 2668

June, late, to late July, every four years
Landshut Wedding 1625

June, late, to mid–August
Central City Opera Festival 0551

June, late, to late August
Aspen Music Festival 0175

June, late, to early September
Tell (William) Play 2941

June, late, through September; rainy season
Geerewol Celebrations 1112

June, end of
Acadian Festival 0012
Bouphonia (Buphonia) 0384
New Yam Festival 2022

June, end of, through August
Santa Fe Opera Festival 2518

June, end of, through September
Athens Festival 0184

June or July, usually
Hemis Festival 1300

June–July
Istanbul Festivals, International 1441
London, Festival of the City of 1696
Moscow International Film Festival. 1925
Music and Dance Festival, International 1956
Oregon Beach Festival 2149
Poetry Festival of Medellín, International 2286
Special Olympics 2681
Vienna Jazz Festival 3143
Vincy Carnival 3151
Zurich Festival 3315

June–July, every four years
World Cup 3255

June–early July
Mozart Festival (Mozartfest) 1947

June–August
Black Hills Passion Play 0329
Jacob's Pillow Dance Festival 1454
Puccini Festival 2322
Saratoga Festival 2531

June–August, even-numbered years
Biennale of Sydney 0311

June–August, weekends
Mohawk Trail Concerts 1899

June–September
Caturmas 0547
Famadihana 0976
Medora Musical 1840
Nuits de Fourvière 2095
Ravinia Festival 2376

June–September, every five years
Great World Theatre 1205

June–October
Baile de las Turas (Dance of the Flutes) 0228
Charlottetown Festival 0566
Midimu Ceremony 1873

Midsummer
Cronia (Kronia) 0727
Idaho International Summerfest 1395

Summer
Baltic Song Festivals 0234
Route 66 Festival 2437

Summer, varies
Toronto Caribana (Toronto Caribbean Carnival) 3009

Summer, early
Footwashing Day 1055

Summer, mid–
Arapaho Sun Dance 0135

Summer, late
Creek Green Corn Ceremony 0719
Wheat Harvest (Transylvania) 3208

Summer or Fall
Folk Festival, National 1051

Summer, full moon night
Nevis Tea Meeting. 2012

July

Anjou Festival 0105
Avignon Festival 0200
Baltic-Nordic Harmonica Festival 0235
Bascarsija Nights 0251
Bite of Seattle 0323
Boryeong Mud Festival 0371
Calgary Exhibition and Stampede 0460
Camel Market 0474
Caribbean Festival (Feast of Fire) 0498
Common Ridings Day 0668
Curium Festival (Kourion Festival) 0740
Elsie Dairy Festival 0919
Dancing on the Edge. 0761
Dinosaur Days 0807
Dundee International Guitar Festival 0852
Durban International Film Festival 0854
Flagstaff Festival of the Arts 1028

Numbers in the index refer to entry numbers, not page numbers

Hortobágy Bridge Fair and International
    Equestrian Festival 1367
Exit Festival 0972
Festival d'Aix en Provence 0996
Galway International Arts Festival. 1094
Grec Festival de Barcelona. 9115
Istanbul Festivals, International 1441
Jerusalem Film Festival 1473
Jyvaskyla Arts Festival 1503
Lammas Fair 1620
Midnight Sun Intertribal Powwow 1876
Montreux International Jazz Festival 1912
Munich Opera Festival 1952
Niman Festival 2069
American Solar Challenge 0087
Northern Games 2090
Oakley (Annie) Festival 2102
Oath Monday 2103
Potato Blossom Festival 2305
Puppeteers, Festival of 2329
Reggae Sumfest 2387
Royal Shows 2442
Safari Rally 2461
Schützenfest (Marksmen's Festival) 2543
Singapore Food Festival. 2634
Tabuleiros Festival (Festa dos Tabuleiros) 2903
Tour de France 3014
Turkish Wrestling Championships 3056
Twenty-four: Seven Theater Festival 3065
Zanzibar International Film Festival 3308

July 01
Botswana Sir Seretse Khama Day 0380
Burundi Independence Day 0445
Canada Day 0478
Gettysburg Day 1125
Ghana Republic Day. 1127
Hong Kong Special Administrative Region
Establishment Day 1358
Most Precious Blood, Feast of the 1927
Rwanda Independence Day 2451
Somalia Independence Day. 2660

July 01 to last Sunday
Shembe Festival 2596

July 01–15
Hakata Gion Yamagasa 1261

July 02
Bahia Independence Day 0226
Palio, Festival of the 2189

July 03
Belarus Independence Day 0282
St. Thomas's Day 2818

July 03–August 11
Dog Days 0822

July 04
Apache Maidens' Puberty Rites 0125
Caricom Day 0500
Coolidge (Calvin) Birthday Celebration 0683
Esplanade Concerts. 0956
Fourth of July 1065
Fourth of July (Denmark) 1066
Rwanda Liberation Day 2452
Santa Isobel, Fiesta of 2520
Summer Festival 2861
Tupou Vi (King), Birthday of 3051
Turtle Independence Day. 3061

July 04, week including
Kutztown Festival 1599

July 04, week of
Tom Sawyer Days, National 3000
Tonga Heilala Festival 3003

July 04, weekend near
Deep Sea Fishing Rodeo 0781
Fillmore Jazz Festival 1012
Smithville Fiddlers Jamboree and Crafts Festival 2652
Wampanoag Powwow 3176

July 04, begins first Wednesday after
Choctaw Indian Fair 0611

July 04, Thursday after
Vintners' Procession 3155

July 05
Algeria Independence Day 0062
Armenia Constitution Day 0149
Cape Verde Independence Day 0493
Tynwald Ceremony. 3067
Venezuela Independence Day. 3126

July 05, Sunday after
Giants, Festival of the (Fête des Géants) 1133

July 05–31
LaborFest 1611

July 06
Comoros Independence Day. 0670
Dalai Lama, Birthday of the 0753
Hus (Jan) Day 1386
Lithuania State Day (Coronation of King
    Mindaugas) 1686
Malawi Republic Day 1752

July 06–13
Apollonian Games 0126
Ludi 1710

July 06–14
San Fermin Festival. 2482

July 07
Juno Caprotina, Festival of 1495

Saba Saba Day 2454
Solomon Islands Independence Day 2659
Tanabata (Star Festival) 2919

July 09
Argentina Independence Day 0142
Argentine National Day 0144
Bab, Martyrdom of the 0213
South Sudan Independence Day. 2675

July 10
Bahamas Independence Day. 0222
Kiribati Gospel Day (National Church Day) 1566

July 10–12
Kuwana Ishitori Matsuri 1602

July 11
Flemish Community, Feast Day of the 1037
St. Placidus Festival 2802
World Population Day 3266

July 11–13
Naadam 1966

July 12
Kiribati Independence Day 1567
Orange Day (Orangemen's Day) 2148
São Tomé and Principe National Independence Day 2528
Wedding Festivities (Galicnik, Macedonia) 3198

July 13
Night Watch 2067
Tribute of the Three Cows 3023

July 13–15
Obon Festival 2105

July 13 and October 14
Svetitskhovloba 2880

July 14
Bastille Day 0255
Bastille Day (Kaplan, Louisiana) 0256
Tekakwitha (Kateri) Feast Day 2939

July 14, Saturday before
Cape Vincent French Festival 0494

July 14, week of
Guthrie (Woody) Folk Festival 1245

July 14, weekend nearest
Bastille, Festival de la 0257

July 15
Castor and Pollux, Festival of 0545
St. Swithin's Day 2813
St. Vladimir's Day. 2827

July 15, Sunday near
Také-no-Nobori 2914

July 16
Eddy (Mary Baker), Birthday of 0889
La Paz Day 1608
Nuestra Señora de Itatí. 2093
Our Lady of Carmel, Feast of 2160
Pilgrimage of Saut d'Eau 2267

July 16, about two weeks ending
Giglio Feast 1137

July 16, week including
Tirana, La 2988

July 16, two consecutive Mondays after
Guelaguetza, La 1231

July 17
Gion Matsuri 1143
King's Birthday (Lesotho) 1562
Muñoz-Rivera Day 1953
South Korea Constitution Day 2673

July 18
Uruguay Constitution Oath Taking Day 3096

July 19
Myanmar Martyrs' Day 1960

July 20
Colombia Independence Day 0665
Elijah Day 0914
Moon Day 1913

July 20–24
Osorezan Taisai 2156

July 20–26
Naadam 1966

July 21
Belgium Independence Day 0285

July 21, week including
Hemingway (Ernest) Days Festival 1299

July 22
Fasinada 0981
Gambia Revolution Day 1097
Madeleine, Fête de la 1728
Polish Liberation Day 2291

July 22–24
Warei Taisai 3179

July 22–25
Wild Horse Festival (Soma-Nomaioi) 3224

July 23
Egypt Revolution Day 0896
Haile Selassie's Birthday 1253

July 23–25
Nomaoi Matsuri (Horse Festival) 2080

Numbers in the index refer to entry numbers, not page numbers

July 24
Mormon Pioneer Day 1921

July 24, closest weekend
Earhart (Amelia) Festival 0859

July 24–25
Tenjin Matsuri 2948

July 25
Furrinalia 1086
Grotto Day 1221
Jousting the Bear 1488
Puerto Rico Constitution Day 2324
St. Christopher 's Day 2715
St. James's Day.................................. 2745
Tunisia Republic Day 3049

July 25, nearest Monday
Costa Rica Annexation of Guanacaste Day
    (Guanacaste Day, Dia de Guanacaste) 0698

July 25–27
Festivities for the Day of National Rebellion 1001

July 26
Cuba Liberation Day 0734
Liberia Independence Day 1665
Maldives Independence Day....................... 1756
St. Anne's Day 2699

July 27
Korean War Veterans Armistice Day, National 1587
North Korea Victory Day 2088

July 28, and other dates
Buffalo Soldiers Commemorations 0417

July 28–29
Peru Independence Day........................... 2247

July 29
Moreska Sword Dance 1918
St. Martha, Coffin Fiesta of 2776
St. Olav's Day 2791

July 31
Llama Ch'uyay 1690
St. Ignatius Loyola, Feast of....................... 2743
Vanuatu Independence Day 3115

July, usually
British Open 0402
Sandcastle Competition 2509

July, even-numbered years
Holy Queen Isabel, Festival of the 1339
Sound Symposium 2665
York Festival and Mystery Plays 3295

July, every two years
Festival International des Arts de la
    Marionette à Saguenay 0999

July, over three consecutive three-day weekends
Wilder (Laura Ingalls) Pageant 3225

July, early
Lasseters Camel Cup 1632
Cheltenham International Festival of Music 0573
Essence Festival 0957
Roswell UFO Festival 2434
Sata-Häme Accordion Festival 2533
Wife-Carrying World Championships 3222

July, begins early, in odd–numbered years
Transpac Race 3020

July, early, five days in
Henley Royal Regatta 1301

July, early, to early August
Aston Magna Festival 0182
ImPulsTanz: Vienna International Dance Festival 1413
Savonlinna Opera Festival........................ 2539

July, early, to late August
Carthage, International Festival of.................. 0539

July, first Sunday
Clipping the Church Day.......................... 0656

July, first Monday
Zambia Heroes Day 3305

July, first Tuesday
Zambia Unity Day................................ 3307

July, first Thursday and the previous Tuesday
Ommegang 2140

July, first Friday
Marshall Islands Fishermen's Day 1790

July, first Saturday
Cooperatives, International Day of 0684

July, first week
Gettysburg Civil War Heritage Days................ 1124
Great Schooner Race 1203
Pennsylvania Dutch Folk Festival 2239

July, first weekend
Basque Festival, National......................... 0253
Mariposa Folk Festival 1782

July, first or second weekend
Red Waistcoat Festival 2381

July, first week, to second week in August
Baths of Caracalla 0262

July, second Sunday
Schutzengelfest (Festival of the Guardian Angel) 2544

July, second Saturday
Durham Miners' Gala............................. 0856
Wayne Chicken Show............................. 3195

Numbers in the index refer to entry numbers, not page numbers

July, second week
Brady (Captain Samuel) Day 0389
Cherry Festival, National. 0579
North American Indian Days 2085

July, second full weekend
Grandfather Mountain Highland Games and
Gathering of Scottish Clans 1183

July, second weekend
Fur Trade Days 1085
Green River Rendezvous 1212
Lindenfest 1681
Moose Dropping Festival. 1916
Moxie Festival 1942
Stånga Games 2828
Winnipeg Folk Festival. 3234

July, mid–
Chugiak-Eagle River Bear Paw Festival 0644
Great Circus Parade 1196
Marrakech Popular Arts Festival 1787
Newport Music Festival 2052
Pori International Jazz Festival 2297
Ravello Music Festival 2375
Saintes Festival of Ancient Music 2466
South Carolina Peach Festival. 2672
Southern Ute Tribal Sun Dance 2677
World Eskimo-Indian Olympics 3261

July, mid, Friday and Saturday
Robin Hood Festival in Sherwood, Oregon 2413

July, mid, one Saturday
New Deal Festival 2015

July, two weeks in mid– to late
Folkmoot 1053

July, mid, weekend
Denver Black Arts Festival 0787

July, mid, to mid–August
Dubrovnik Summer Games. 0848
Marlboro Music Festival 1784
Quartier d'été 2342
Tailte Fair (Teltown Fair) 2907

July, mid, through early September
Menuhin Festival. 1853

July, a weekend
San Diego Comic-Con International 2480

July, third Sunday
Basset Hound Games 0254
Maidens' Fair on Mount Gaina 1741
Redentore, Festa del 2382

July, third Monday
Japan Marine Day 1466

July, third Saturday
Idlewild Jazz Festival 1400
Mollyockett Day 1904

July, third full week
Kinderzeche (Children's Party) 1555

July, third week
Alpenfest 0077
Golden Days 1157
Kaustinen Folk Music Festival 1526
Rondo Days Celebration 2424
Swan Upping 2883

July, 10 days including third full week
Minneapolis Aquatennial Festival 1886

July, third weekend
Beiderbecke (Bix) Memorial Jazz Festival 0279
Buffalo Days Powwow. 0416
Gold Discovery Days 1154
Dayton Air Show. 0772
Yarmouth Clam Festival. 3286

July, begins third weekend
Hill Cumorah Pageant 1310

July, third–fourth weekends
Michigan Brown Trout Festival 1868

July, fourth Sunday
World Champion Bathtub Race 3251

July, fourth Monday
Hurricane Supplication Day 1384

July, fourth Saturday
Central Maine Egg Festival 0552

July, fourth weekend
Virginia Scottish Games 3158

July, last Sunday
Crom Dubh Sunday 0725
Penitents, Procession of the (Belgium) 2236
Reek Sunday 2384

July, last Thursday, Wednesday before
Chincoteague Pony Roundup and Penning 0606

July, last Saturday
Ghanafest 1128

July, last full week
Cheyenne Frontier Days 0582
Oregon Brewers Festival 2150
RAGBRAI 2358

July, last week
Days of '76 0771

July, last week, to first week in August
Merengue Festival (Festival de Merengue) 1857

Numbers in the index refer to entry numbers, not page numbers

July, last full weekend
Black Ships Festival. 0334
Bologna Festival 0357
Chief Joseph Days 0593
Gilroy Garlic Festival 1138
Nordic Fest 2082

July, last weekend
Antique and Classic Boat Rendezvous 0122
Lumberjack World Championships 1713
Manitoba Sunflower Festival 1768
Nicodemus Emancipation and Homecoming
Celebration 2063
Pardon of Ste. Anne d'Auray 2211

July, last two weekends, and first weekend in August
Song of Hiawatha Pageant 2661

July, late
Just for Laughs Festival 1496
Klondike Days Exposition 1574
World Santa Claus Congress 3269

July, late, in odd–numbered years
Bach Festival 0216

July, late, one full week in
Cornouaille Festival 0688

July, late, to early August
Blessed Sacrament, Feast of the 0340
Carnival (Cuba) 0514
Dodge City Days 0819
Jerash Festival of Culture and Art 1472
Tyre Festival 3068

July, late, to early August. week
Robin Hood Festival in Nottinghamshire, England . . . 2412

July, late, to early August, weekend
Faces Etnofestival 0973

July, late, to first Monday in August
Jamaica Festival 1456

July, late, through August
Bayreuth Festival 0273

July or August
Panathenaea 2202
San Pedro International Costa Maya Festival 2506

July–August
American West, Festival of the 0088
Antigua Carnival 0119
Baalbeck Festival 0210
Beiteddine Festival 0281
Bregenz Festival 0396
Carinthian Summer Music Festival 0503
German-American Volksfest 1122
Grand Haven Coast Guard Festival 1178
Melbourne International Film Festival 1849

Moreska Sword Dance 1918
Rainforest World Music Festival 2360
Salzburg Festival 2471
Santa Fe Chamber Music Festival 2516
Santander International Festival of Music and Dance . . . 2524
Seafair 2550
Tanglewood Music Festival 2921
Trial of Louis Riel 3021
Triple Crown Pack Burro Races 3032

July–first Monday in August
Crop Over 0728

July–August, Friday evenings
'Ksan Celebrations 1591

July–September
Arts and Pageant of the Masters, Festival of 0164
Wood (Henry) Promenade Concerts 3246

July–September, every three years
Echigo-Tsumari Art Triennale 0886

July–September, Sunday
Maverick Sunday Concerts 1822

July–September, weekends
Epidaurus Festival 0934

August
Abbotsford International Air Show 0003
Acadian Day 0011
Belgian-American Days 0284
Busan Sea Festival 0447
Carifest 0501
Chicago Dancing Festival 0586
Clown Festival, International 0658
Damba 0755
Edinburgh International Festival 0890
Floating Lantern Ceremony (Toro Nagashi) 1040
Gaelic Mod 1090
Garma Festival 1106
Great Battle of Hansan Festival (Hansan Daecheop) . . 1195
Harlem Week 1286
Hippokrateia Festival 1312
Homage to Cuauhtemoc (Homenaje a Cuauhtemoc) . . 1350
Hooverfest 1360
Hot Air Balloon Classic 1372
Isle of Wright Garlic Festival 1438
Lollapalooza 1694
Looking Glass Powwow 1698
Maralal Camel Derby 1771
Miramichi Folk Song Festival 1887
Montreal World Film Festival 1911
Mount Isa Rodeo and Mardi Gras 1937
New Jersey Offshore Grand Prix 2018
Newport Fold Festival 2050
Onwasato Festival 2142
Pacific Northwest Festival 2178

Numbers in the index refer to entry numbers, not page numbers

Robots at Play 2415
Royal Shows 2442
Senj International Summer Carnival 2565
St. Rocco's Celebration (Rokovo) 2804
Waratambar 3178
Watts Festival 3194
Whe'wahchee (He'dewachi; Dance of Thanksgiving) ... 3210

August 01
Benin Independence Day........................... 0291
Cross-Quarter Days 0731
Doggett's Coat and Badge Race 0823
Fire Festivals 1016
Lammas 1619
Lughnasadh 1711
Swiss National Day............................. 2890
Trinidad and Tobago Emancipation Day 3027

August 01–02
Forgiveness, Feast of 1057

August 01, or nearest Saturday
Emancipation Day (Canada) 0922

August 02
Macedonian Ilinden (St. Elijah's Uprising Day) 1720
Old Pecos Bull and Corn Dance 2124
Our Lady of the Angels, Feast of 2168
Virgen de Los Angeles Day 3156

August 02–07
Nebuta Matsuri 2003

August 04
San Francisco's Day (Lima, Peru)................... 2488

August 05
Burkina Faso Independence Day 0433
Croatia Victory and Homeland Thanksgiving Day 0724
Grotto Day 1221

August 05–07
Hanagasa Odori 1275

August 06
Bolivia Independence Day......................... 0356
Hiroshima Peace Ceremony 1313
Transfiguration, Feast of the 3019

August 06, Saturday nearest
Rushbearing Festival 2448

August 06–08
Tanabata (Star Festival) 2919

August 07
Colombia Battle of Boyacá Day 0664
Côte d'Ivoire Independence Day 0701
Kiribati Youth Day 1570
Purple Heart Day 2332
Zambia Farmers Day 3304

August 09
Meyboom 1863
Singapore National Day.......................... 2635
South Africa Women's Day 2670
Zimbabwe Heroes' Day 3312

August 09, and two adjoining days
St. Herman Pilgrimage 2740

August 10
Borglum (Gutzon) Day........................... 0369
San Lorenzo, Día de 2500

August 10–12
Perseids 2244
Puck Fair 2323

August 11
Chad Independence Day 0555
St. Clare of Assisi, Feast of 2716

August 12
Glorious Twelfth 1147
Queen's Birthday (Thailand)...................... 2346

August 13
Central African Republic Independence Day 0550
Nemoralia 2006

August 13–15
Congo Independence Day Celebration 0677
Obon Festival 2105

August 14
Pakistan Independence Day 2186
Torta dei Fieschi 3012
V-J Day (Victory over Japan Day) 3162

August 14–15
Mystery Play (Elche)............................ 1963

August 14–16
Pine Battle of Vinuesa 2276

August 15
Assumption of Our Lady (Santa Marija) 0177
Assumption of the Blessed Virgin Mary, Feast of the 0178
Assumption of the Virgin Mary, Feast of the
  (Guatemala) 0179
Assumption of the Virgin Mary, Feast of the (Italy) ... 0181
Bangabandhu National Mourning Day............. 0237
Black Madonna of Jasna Gora, Feast of the 0331
Dozynki Festival 0840
Korea Liberation Day 1585
Prince's Birthday in Liechtenstein 2319
Zimbabwe Defense Forces Day 3311

August 15, Sunday nearest
Blessing of the Grapes (Haghoghy Ortnootyoon) 0342

August 15, Sunday after
Running of the Bulls in Mexico 2447

Numbers in the index refer to entry numbers, not page numbers

August 16
Bennington Battle Day 0293
Daimonji Okuribi (Great Bonfire Event) 0750
Dominican Republic Independence Restoration Day . . 0830
Palio, Festival of the 2189
St. Roch's Day 2805

August 16, every three years
Neri-Kuyo 2010

August 16, week including
Elvis International Tribute Week 0921

August 16–18
Gabon Independence Day 1089

August 17
Indonesia Independence Day 1421

August 17, Monday after
San Martín Day 2504

August 19
Aviation Day 0199
Vinalia 3150

August 20
Estonia Restoration of Independence Day 0959
St. Stephen's Day (Hungary) 2812

August 20, weekend nearest
Our Lady of Sorrows Festival 2167

August 21
Consualia 0682

August 22
Queenship of Mary 2348

August 23
Vulcanalia (Volcanalia) 3168

August 24
Bartholomew Fair 0250
Liberia Flag Day 1664
St. Bartholomew's Day 2705
Ukraine Independence Day 3076

August 24, Sunday of or after
Keaw Yed Wakes Festival 1529

August 24, or following weekend
Schäferlauf 2540

August 24, three weeks beginning
Stourbridge Fair 2845

August 25
Uruguay Independence Day 3097

August 26
Anthony (Susan B.) Day 0117
Namibia Heroes Day 1972

August 26, on or near
Mount Fuji Climbing Season, End of 1935

August 26–27
Chochin Matsuri (Lantern Festival) 0610

August 27
Moldova Independence Day 1901

August 28
St. Augustine of Hippo, Feast of 2702

August 29
St. John the Baptist, Martyrdom of 2748

August 30
Long (Huey P.), Day 1697
St. Rose of Lima's Day 2806
Turkey Victory Day 3055

August 30 and October 17
Flower Festivals of St. Rose and St. Margaret
Mary Alacoque 1049

August 31
Great Montana Sheep Drive 1199
Kyrgyz Independence Day 1607
Merdeka Day 1856
Moldovan Language Day 1903
Polish Solidarity Day 2292
Trinidad and Tobago Independence Day 3029

August, usually
Fairhope Jubilee 0975

August, varies
Emancipation Day Festival 0927

August, probably
Nemean Games 2005

August, every other year
Hopi Snake Dance 1363

August, every four years
Gay Games 1110
Pythian Games 2335

August, every 20–25 years
Vignerons, Fête des (Winegrowers' Festival) 3147

August, Fridays
Pilgrim Progress Pageant 2264

August, early
Cuisinières, Fête des la 0736
Eisteddfod 0899
Grant's (Bill) Bluegrass Festival 1186
Nisei Week 2075
Old Spanish Days 2127
Satchmo SummerFest 2534
Spiedie Fest and Balloon Rally 2683

Numbers in the index refer to entry numbers, not page numbers

August, early, Saturday
World Peace Festival 3265

August, early, week in
Craftsmen's Fair 0711

August, first Sunday
Volksfest 3165

August, begins first Sunday
Gualterianas, Festas 1224

August, first Monday
British Columbia Day 0401
Bahamas Emancipation Day 0221
Jamaica Independence Day 1457
Natal Day in Nova Scotia 1982
New Brunswick Day. 2013

August, first Monday through following Sunday
Sturgis Motorcycle Rally 2852

August, Thursday and Friday before first Monday
Cup Match 0738

August, first Thursday, Friday, and Saturday
Asheville Mountain Dance and Folk Festival 0170

August, first Friday to second Sunday
Interceltique, Festival 1423

August, first Saturday
All-American Soap Box Derby 0071
Hambletonian Harness Racing Classic 1273

August, begins first Saturday
Nations, Festival of (Montana) 1986

August, first week
El Salvador del Mundo, Festival of 0903
Great Wardmote of the Woodmen of Arden 1204
Handy (W. C.) Music Festival 1278
Shambhala Music Festival. 2588

August, a weekend
San Francisco Street Food Festival 2487

August, first full weekend
Czech Festival, National 0744
Gift of the Waters Pageant 1136
Twins Days Festival 3066

August, first weekend
Billy the Kid Pageant 0318
Dublin Irish Festival 0846
Emancipation Day (Hutchinson, Kansas) 0923
Icelandic Festival 1391
Maine Lobster Festival 1747
Marian Days 1779
Sheboygan Bratwurst Days 2593
Sinjska Alka 2637

Telluride Jazz Festival 2946
Thjodhatid 2972

August, second Sunday
Hora at Prislop. 1364
Mount Ceahlau Feast 1934

August, second Thursday
Baby Parade 0215
Bat Flight Breakfast 0258
Battle of Flowers (Jersey, Channel Islands) 0264

August, second Friday
Burry Man Day 0444

August, second Friday and Saturday
Goschenhoppen Historians' Folk Festival 1173

August, second Saturday
Billiken (Bud) Parade and Picnic Day 0317

August, second week
Fox Hill Festival. 1068
Gallup Inter-Tribal Indian Ceremonial 1092
Old Fiddler 's Convention 2123

August, second full weekend
Ste. Genevieve, Jour de Fête à (Days of Celebration) . . 2833

August, second weekend
Hope Watermelon Festival 1361
Omak Stampede and Suicide Race 2135

August, second and third weeks
Marymass Festival 1806

August, mid–
Drachenstich (Spearing the Dragon) 0841
Hobo Convention 1321
JVC Jazz Festival 1501
Kilkenny Arts Festival 1551
Meskwaki Powwow 1859
Sea Islands Black Heritage Festival 2547

August, nine days in mid–
Hopi Flute Ceremony 1362

August, seven days in
Bonneville Speed Week 0367

August, two weeks in
New York International Fringe Festival. 2046

August, ends third Sunday
Iowa State Fair 1425

August, third Monday
Klondike Gold Discovery Day 1575

August, third Friday
God Cup Parade 1153

August, third Saturday
Woodward Dream Cruise 3248

Numbers in the index refer to entry numbers, not page numbers

August, begins third or fourth Sunday
Shepherd's Fair 2599

August, third and fourth Sunday; every seven years
Assumption of the Virgin Mary, Feast of the
(Hasselt, Belgium) 0180

August, third full week
Three Choirs Festival 2975

August, third weekend
Chief Seattle Days 0594
Crow Fair 0732
Daimyo Gyoretsu 0751
Down Home Family Reunion 0838
Indian Market 1419
Mohegan Homecoming 1900
Payson Rodeo 2231
Pickle Festival 2256

August, fourth Sunday
First Fruits of the Alps Sunday 1021

August, fourth weekend
Giants, Festival of the (Belgium) 1134
Great American Duck Race 1192

August, last Sunday
Plague Sunday 2281

August, last Monday
Bog Snorkelling Championship, World 0352

August, last Saturday
African Methodist Quarterly Meeting Day 0031

August, last week
Corn Palace Festival 0687
Mobile Phone Throwing World Championship 1897
Tomatina (Tomato Battle) 3001

August, last full weekend
Rose of Tralee Beauty Contest 2432

August, last weekend
Goombay! 1171
Lochristi Begonia Festival 1691
Parker (Charlie) Jazz Festival 2216
Stiftungsfest 2839
Wheat Harvest Festival (Provins, France) 3209

August, late
Fleadh Cheoil 1031
Grasmere Sports 1188
Jeshn (Afghan Independence Day) 1474
Little League World Series 1688
Mount Hagen Show 1936

August, late, Saturday in
WCSH Sidewalk Art Festival 3196

August, late, one week in
Buskers' Festival 0448

August, late, or early September
Obzinky 2106
Reed Dance 2383

August, late, or September
Pilgrimage to Moulay Idriss 2271

August, late, to early September
Freeing the Insects 1078
Helsinki Festival 1297
Shinju Matsuri Festival 2605

August, late, to Labor Day
Flemington Fair 1036

August, eights days before full moon in
Taungbyon Spirit Festival 2933

August, week beginning day after full moon
Gai Jatra 1091

August–September
Agwunsi Festival 0038
Canadian National Exhibition 0480
Carnea 0507
Homowo 1352
Lucerne International Festival of Music 1709
Michigan Renaissance Festival 1869
Venice Film Festival 3128

August–September, four days preceding Labor Day
Chicago Jazz Festival 0591

August–September, Labor Day weekend
Charleston Sternwheel Regatta 0564

August–September, 11 days ending Saturday before Labor Day
Tennessee Walking Horse National Celebration 2949

August and September, in odd numbered years
Enescu (George) Festival 0930

September

Ak-Sar-Ben Livestock Exposition and Rodeo 0044
Almabtrieb 0074
Amherstburg Heritage Homecoming 0090
Bad Durkheim Wurstmarkt (Sausage Fair) 0218
Ballet Festival of Miami, International 0232
Big Iron Farm Show 0312
Bull Durham Blues Festival 0422
Caruaru Roundup 0541
Dean (James) Festival 0779
Fleet Week (San Diego, California) 1034
Grand Canyon Music Festival 1177
Harlem International Film Festival 1285
Joust of the Saracens 1487
Killing the Pigs, Festival of 1552
Laytown Strand Races 1642
Marriage Fair 1788

Maryland Seafood Festival 1805
Miss America Pageant 1892
Monkey God, Birthday of the 1906
Mothman Festival 1931
Netherlands Military Tattoo 2011
Odwira 2114
Okpesi Festival 2119
Oldenburg International Film Festival 2128
Peace, International Day of 2232
Queer Lisboa: International Queen Film Festival
Royal Shows 2442
Trinidad and Tobago Film Festival. 3028
United States Open Tennis 3087
Warsaw Autumn Festival 3181

September 01
Eritrean Start of the Armed Struggle Day 0952
Evacuation Day 0968
Hermit, Feast of the. 1303
Libya Revolution Day. 1672
Partridge Day 2221
Uzbekistan Independence Day 3103

September 01, Monday–Tuesday after Sunday following
St. Giles Fair 2736

September 01–03
Owara Kaze-no-Bon Festival. 2174

September 01–10
Bosra Festival 0373

September 02
San Estevan, Feast of 2481
Shinbyu 2604
Vietnam National Day 3145
V-J Day (Victory over Japan Day) 3162

September 03
Cromwell's Day 0726
Qatar Independence Day 2336
St. Marinus Day 2771
Taiwan Armed Forces Day 2908

September 04, Monday after first Sunday after
Horn Dance 1366

September 04–19
Ludi 1710
Roman Games (Ludi Romani) 2422

September 05–07
Ginseng Festival 1140

September 05–09
Howl! Festival 1375

September 06
Swaziland Independence Day 2885

September 07
Brazil Independence Day. 0393
Mozambique Lusaka Agreement Day 1944

September 07–09
Piedigrotta, Festival of 2258

September 08
Andorra National Day 0099
Evamelunga 0969
Literacy Day, International 1683
Macedonian Independence Day 1721
Nativity of the Blessed Virgin Mary, Feast of
the (Germany) 1991
Nativity of the Blessed Virgin Mary, Feast of the (Peru) . . 1992
Nativity of the Blessed Virgin Mary, Feast of the 1990
Nativity of the Theotokos 1993
Victory Day (Our Lady of Victories Day) 3139

September 08–15
Serreta, Festa da 2569

September 08–18
Our Lady of Nazaré Festival 2165

September 09
Democratic People's Republic of Korea
Founding Day 0784
Pilgrimage to Shrine of Father Laval 2273
Tajikistan Independence Day 2911

September 10
Belize National Day 0287
Gibraltar National Day. 1135

September 11
Coptic New Year (Feast of El-Nayrouz) 0686
Enkutatash 0931

September 11–13
St. Nichiren's Pardon, Festival of 2787

September 12
Defenders' Day 0782

September 14
Día de los Charros. 0799
Exaltation of the Cross, Feast of the 0970
Nicaragua Battle of San Jacinto Day 2060

September 14–15
Tono Matsuri 3005

September 14–16
Tsurugaoka Hachiman Shrine Matsuri 3037

September 14, Sunday after
Pig's Face Feast 2260

September 14, Wednesday, Friday, and Saturday following
Ember Days 0928

Numbers in the index refer to entry numbers, not page numbers

September 15
Battle of Britain Day 0263
Costa Rica Independence Day 0699
El Salvador Independence Day 0904
Guatemala Independence Day 1227
Honduras Independence Day 1354
Nicaragua Independence Day 2061

September 15, full moon nearest
Mid-Autumn Festival 1870
Mid-Autumn Festival (Singapore) 1871

September 15–16
Mexico Festival of Independence 1862

September 15–October 15
Hispanic Heritage Month 1314

September 16
Cherokee Strip Day 0575
Preservation of the Ozone Layer, International
   Day for the 2315
Papua New Guinea Independence Day 2207
St. Kitts and Nevis National Heroes Day 2765

September 17
Angola National Heroes Day 0104
Chinkashiki (Fire Control Ceremony) 0608
Citizenship Day 0653
Steuben (Baron Friedrich) Day 2836

September 17, beginning week
Constitution Week 0680

September 17, week of
Constitution Week (Mesa, Arizona) 0681

September 18
Apparition of the Infant Jesus 0127

September 18, Saturday after
Johnson (Samuel) Commemoration 1481

September 18–19
Fiestas Patrias 1006

September 19
San Gennaro, Feast of 2489
San José Day Festival 2496
St. Kitts and Nevis Independence Day 2764

September 21
Armenia Independence Day 0152
Belize Independence Day 0286
Malta Independence Day 1761

September 22
Bulgaria Independence Day 0420
Mali Independence Day 1758

September 22 or 23
Mabon 1718

September 22–23
Autumnal Equinox 0197

September 22–24
Aizu Byakko Matsuri 0042

September 23 or 24, week including
Higan 1307

September 23, full moon nearest
Harvest Moon Days 1290

September 24
Cambodia Constitution Day 0467
Erau Festival 0949
Guinea-Bissau Independence Day 1235
Mercè, Festa de la 1854
Schwenkfelder Thanksgiving (Gedaechtnisz Tag) 2545
South Africa Heritage Day 2667
Trinidad and Tobago Republic Day 3030

September 26
Appleseed (Johnny), Birthday of 0129
Yemen Revolution Days 3291

September 26–October 04
San Francisco, Fiesta of 2484

September 27
French Community, Feast Day of the (La fête de la
   Communauté française de Belgique) 1079
Maskal 1810
Sts. Cosmas and Damian Day 2849

September 28
Confucius's Birthday (Teacher 's Day) 0676
Czech Statehood Day (St. Wenceslas Day) 0745
St. Vaclav's Day 2822

September 28, week including
Cabrillo Day and Festival 0454

September 29
Election of the Lord Mayor of London 0907
Michaelmas 1866
Michaelmas (Norway) 1867
Payment of Quit Rent 2230
Quarter Days 2341
San Miguel, Fiesta de 2505
St. Michael's Day 2785
Tura Michele Fair (Augsburg Day) 3052

September 29–30
San Geronimo Feast Day 2490

September 30–October 01
Botswana Independence Day 0379

September, even–numbered years
Dodge (Geraldine R.) Poetry Festival 0821

September, odd–numbered years
Outback Festival 2172

September, early
Kakadu Mahbilil Festival 1505
Limassol Wine Festival 1679
Navajo Nation Fair at Window Rock 1996
Pardon of Nossa Senhora dos Remédios 2210
Zydeco Music Festival (Southwest Louisiana) 3317

September, early over four days
United Tribes International Powwow 3088

September, early Saturday
Dally in the Alley 0754

September, week before Labor Day
Old-Time Country Music Contest and Festival,
National 2130

September, first Sunday
Historical Regatta 1315
Pffiferdaj 2249

September, week beginning first Sunday
San Roque, Fiesta of 2507

September, first Monday
Bread and Roses Heritage Festival 0395
Chile National Unity Day 0599
Labor Day 1610

September, first Saturday
Braemar Highland Gathering 0390

September, beginning first Saturday
Århus Festival 0146

September, first week
Annual Session of the National Baptist
Convention, USA 0113
Toronto International Film Festival 3010
Toronto Veg Food Fest 3011

September, first weekend
Burning Man Festival 0435
Shinnecock Powwow 2606
St. Gens, Festival of (La Fête de St. Gens) 2732

September, Labor Day weekend
Bumbershoot 0425
Cherokee National Holiday 0574
Chuckwagon Races, National Championship 0643
Ellensburg Rodeo 0918
Grape Festival 1187
Hard Crab Derby, National 1283
Hatch Chile Festival 1291
Jubilee Days Festival 1490
Louisiana Shrimp and Petroleum Festival 1704
Mountain Man Rendezvous 1938
Detroit International Jazz Festival 0790
Skipjack Races and Land Festival 2647
Southern 500 2676
Telluride Film Festival 2943

West Virginia Italian Heritage Festival 3202
Tell (Wilhelm) Festival 2940

September, Labor Day weekend, Saturday of
Crandall (Prudence) Day 0714

September, Labor Day weekend, Sunday of
Klondike International Outhouse Race 1576

September, Labor Day, first Sunday after
Grandparents' Day 1184

September, Labor Day, weekend after
Camel and Ostrich Races, International 0473
Ohio River Sternwheel Festival 2115
Santa Fe, Fiesta de 2517
Santa Rosalia Fishermen's Festival 2522

September, second Saturday
Hollerin' Contest, National 1329

September, second Sunday
Bilby Day, National 0314
Watermelon-Eating and Seed-Spitting Contest 3192

September, second Tuesday–Saturday
McClure Bean Soup Festival 1838

September, second week
Vendimia, Fiesta de la 3124

September, second weekend
Joust of the Quintain 1486
Knabenschiessen 1577
Yellow Daisy Festival 3288

**September, second weekend in even–
numbered years**
Living Chess Game (La Partita a Scácchi Viventi) 1689

**September, begins second Friday after
Labor Day**
Eastern States Exposition 0884

**September, four days ending second weekend
after Labor Day**
Air Races and Air Show, National Championship 0039

September, mid–
Pendleton Round-Up and Happy Canyon 2235

September, mid–, to early October
Bruckner Festival, International 0405

September, third Sunday
Walloon Regional Day 3174

September, third Monday
Keiro-no-Hi (Respect-for-the-Aged Day)

September, third Tuesday
Prinsjesdag 2320

Numbers in the index refer to entry numbers, not page numbers

September, third Friday
POW/,IA Recognition Day, National. 2307

September, third week
Idaho Spud Day. 1397
Maafa Commemoration 1717
Nuestra Senora de Peñafrancia, Feast of 2094

September, third weekend
Chilympiad (Republic of Texas Chili Cookoff) 0602
Clearwater County Fair and Lumberjack Days 0655
Appleseed (Johnny) Festival 0130
Wings 'n Water Festival 3233
Wizard of Oz Festival 3241

September, third or fourth weekend
Monterey Jazz Festival 1909

September, fourth Saturday
Kiwanis Kids' Day 1572

September, last Sunday
Gold Star Mother 's Day 1155

September, last Monday or first Monday in

October, weekend nearest
Custer Buffalo Roundup and Arts Festival 0741

September, last Friday
Marshall Islands Manit Day (Marshall Islands
Custom Day) 1793

September, last week
Appleseed (Johnny), Birthday of 0129
Austen (Jane) Festival 0191
Marshall Islands Lutok Kobban Alele 1792

September, last full weekend
Candy Dance Arts and Crafts Faire 0487
Jordbruksdagarna 1484
Marion County Ham Days 1781
Mayberry Days 1834
Valley of the Moon Vintage Festival 3108

September, last weekend
Artcar Fest 0161
Galway Oyster Festival 1095
Kunta Kinte Heritage Festival 1594
Louisiana Sugar Cane Festival 1705

**September, last weekend, to first week in
    October**
Mountain State Forest Festival 1939

September, weekend after fourth Friday
Miwok Acorn Festival 1894

September, late
Eleusinian Mysteries. 0911

September, three days in late
Great American Beer Festival 1190

September, ten days in late
Carthaginians and Romans Fiesta 0540

September, weekend in late
Bayfest 0271

September, late, or early October
Cantaderas, Las 0490

September, late, or early October, to mid–January
Kurijmoj 1597

September, late, or October
Basket Dance 0252

September, late, or early October, two days in
Wide Open Bluegrass Festival. 3220

September, late, to early October
Bratislava Music Festival 0391
Carnival of Flowers. 0532
Middfest International 1872
Oktoberfest 2120
Rumi Festival 2445
State Fair of Texas 2831

**September, last Thursday – October, second
    Saturday**
Dublin Theater Festival 0847

September or October
Cow Fights 0708
Kuta Karnival 1598
Phchum Ben 2251
Rally Day 2362
Yam Festival at Aburi 3284

September–October
Aloha Festivals 0075
ArtPrize 0162
Budapest Music Weeks. 0409
Cure Salée 0739
Ghatasthapana. 1130
New York Film Festival 2043
Thimphu Tsechu 2969

September–November, odd–numbered years
Istanbul Festivals, International 1441

September–December
Ayerye Festival 0204
Paris Autumn Festival (Festival d'Automne) 2215

Autumn
Aztec Rain Festival 0209
Harvest Home Festival 1289
Klo Dance 1573
Min, Festival of 1884
Ngoc Son Temple Festival 2057

Autumn, late
Keretkun Festival 1541

Numbers in the index refer to entry numbers, not page numbers

Autumn, late, or early Winter
Navajo Night Chant 1997

Autumn, every four years
Folklore, National Festival of 1052

Fall and Spring
Green Festivals 1209

October

Acadiens et Creoles, Festivals 0013
BFI London Film Festival. 0305
Busan International Film Festival. 0446
Cafe Budapest 0455
California Avocado Festival 0464
Chicago International Children's Film Festival 0588
Chicago International Film Festival. 0589
CMJ Music Marathon. 0659
Dahlonega Gold Rush Days 0749
Festival Du Nouveau Cinema. 0998
Fleet Week (Hampton Roads, Virginia) 1032
Fleet Week (San Francisco, California) 1035
Foire Internationale d'Art Contemporain 1050
Frieze Art Fair London. 1082
Georgia Peanut Festival 1117
Harvest Festival. 1288
Keene Pumpkin Festival 1530
Latina, Fiesta 1635
Margaret Mead Film Festival 1777
Melbourne Festival. 1847
Mill Valley Film Festival 1882
Misisi Beer Feast 1891
Nagoya City Festival 1970
Natchez Spring and Fall Pilgrimages 1983
Nino Fidencio Festival 2072
North American Wife-Carrying Championship 2087
October Feasts 2108
Our Lady Aparecida, Festival of 2159
Potato Days 2306
Rio de Janeiro International Film Festival
Royal Shows 2442
Shishi Odori (Deer Dance). 2609
Signal: Prague Light Festival. 2626
Tallgrass Film Festival 2916
Telluride Horrow Show 2945
Vancouver Writer's Fest. 3111
Warsaw International Film Festival 3182
World Rock Paper Scissors Championship 3268
World Series 3270

October 01
Cyprus Independence Day 0743
Older Persons, International Day of 2129
Nigeria National Day 2065
Tuvalu Independence Day. 3062

October 01–02
China National Days 0604

October 01 and April 01
San Marino Investiture of New Captains Regent 2502

October 02
Gandhi Jayanti (Mahatma Gandhi's Birthday) 1098
Guardian Angels Day 1225
Guinea Independence Day 1232

October 03
German Unification Day 1120
Honduras Soldiers' Day. 1355
Korea National Foundation Day 1586
Leiden Day 1653
Wolfe (Thomas) Festival. 3243

October 03–04
St. Francis of Assisi, Feast of 2730

October 04
Lesotho Independence Day 1659
Mozambique Peace Day. 1945
Native American Music Awards (Nammys) 1988
San Francisco's Day (Lima, Peru). 2488

October 04–06
Chochin Matsuri (Lantern Festival) 0610

October 04–10
World Space Week. 3271

October 05
Han'gul Day 1279
Portugal Republic Day 2301

October 06
Armed Forces Day (Egypt) 0147
German-American Day 1121
Ivy Day 1448
Kiribati World Teachers' Day 1569
October War of Liberation Anniversary 2110
St. Thomas's Day 2818

October 07–09
Okunchi Matsuri 2121

October 08
Croatia Independence Day 0722
St. Demetrius's Day 2720

October 09
Hanagasa Odori 1275
Leif Erikson Day 1654
St. Denis's Day 2721
Uganda Independence Day. 3070

October 09, week including
Fire Prevention Week, National 1017

October 09–10
Takayama Matsuri. 2912

October 10
Double Tenth Day 0836

Numbers in the index refer to entry numbers, not page numbers

Oklahoma Historical Day 2117
Taiiku-no-Hi 2906

October 10-11
Atlanta Pride Festival

October 10, Monday after
Cuban Anniversary of the Beginning of the Wars of
Independence 0735
Fiji Day 1009
Kenya Moi Day 1539
Pack Monday Fair 2179
Workers' Party of North Korea, Founding of the 3249

October 11
Macedonian National Uprising Day (Day of
Macedonian Uprising in 1941; Macedonian
Revolution Day) 1722
Pulaski Day 2325

October 11–13
Rei-tai-sai 2389

October 12
Columbus Day 0666

October 12, Sunday closest to
Italian Heritage Parade 1445

October, Columbus Day weekend
Cranberry Harvest Festival 0713

October, Columbus Day, first weekend after
Half Moon Bay Art and Pumpkin Festival 1265

October 12
Equatorial Guinea Independence Day 0946
Virgin of the Pillar, Feast of the 3157

October 14
Yemen Revolution Days 3291

October 14 and July 13
Svetitskhovloba 2880

October 14–15
Kenka Matsuri (Roughhouse Festival) 1534

October 14–15, every two years
Kawagoé Matsuri 1527

October 15
October Horse Sacrifice 2109
Sihanouk (King) Commemoration Day 2627
St. Teresa's Day 2817

October 16
World Food Day 3262

October 17
Black Poetry Day 0333
Burgoyne's (John) Surrender Day 0431
Eradication of Poverty, International Day for the 0948

Haiti Anniversary of the Death of Jean-Jacques
Dessalines 1256

October 17 and August 30
Flower Festivals of St. Rose and St. Margaret Mary
Alacoque 1049

October 18
Alaska Day 0053
Azerbaijan Independence Days 0208

October 18–28
Señor de los Milagros 2566

October 19
Bettara-Ichi 0304
Martyrs of North America, Feast of the 1801
Yorktown Day 3296

October 20
Bab, Birth of the 0211
Ebisu Festival 0885
Guatemala Revolution Day 1228
Kenya Mashujaa Day (Heroes Day) 1538

October 21
Black Christ, Festival of the 0325
Trafalgar Day 3017

October 22
Abu Simbel Festival 0009
Hi Matsuri (Fire Festival) 1305
Jidai Matsuri (Festival of the Ages) 1478

October 23
Chulalongkorn Day 0645
Hungary Republic Day 1380
Swallows of San Juan Capistrano 2882

October 24
Pennsylvania Day 2238
United Nations Day 3084
World Development Information Day 3259
Zambia Independence Day 3306

October 24–30
Disarmament Week 0811

October 25
Grenada Thanksgiving Day 1218
St. Crispin's Day 2718

October 26
Angam Day 0100
Austria National Day 0195
St. Demetrius's Day 2720

October 27
St. Vincent and the Grenadines Independence and
Thanksgiving Day 2823

October 27–28
Turkmenistan Independence Day 3057

Numbers in the index refer to entry numbers, not page numbers

October 28
Czechoslovak Independence Day 0746
Oxi Day 2176
St. Jude's Day 2763

October 29
Turkey Republic Day 3054

October 30
Angelitos, Los 0101

October 31
Apple and Candle Night 0128
Halloween 1267
Halloween (Ireland) 1268
Halloween (New Orleans, Louisiana) 1270
Halloween (Scotland) 1271
Halloween (Isle of Man) 1269
Reformation Day 2385

October 31–November 02
All Saints' Day and All Souls' Day (Guatemala) 0067

October, even-numbered years
Shilla (Silla) Cultural Festival 2603

October, Sunday
Our Lady of the Rock, Festival of 2170

October, each Sunday
Pilgrimage of Our Lady of Valme 2266

October, three weeks
Cervantes Festival, International 0554

October, early
Chamizal Festival 0561

October, first Sunday
Agua, La Fiesta de. 0037
Grandparents' Day 1184
Pulaski Day 2325
River to Reef Festival 2407
Rosary, Festival of the 2428
St. Michael's Day 2785

October, first Monday
Eight-Hour Day 0898

October, begins first Thursday
Riley (James Whitcomb) Festival 2402

October, first Friday
Lantern Night at Bryn Mawr College 1629

October, first Saturday
Battle of Germantown, Reenactment of 0266
Black Cowboy Parade. 0327
Red Flannel Festival 2380
Tarantula Fest and Barbecue 2927

October, first full week
Albuquerque International Balloon Fiesta 0058
Boone (Daniel) Festival 0368

October, first full weekend
Paul Bunyan Show 2228
Whole Enchilada Fiesta 3216

October, first weekend
Great Locomotive Chase Festival 1198
Marino Wine Festival 1780
Sonoma Country Harvest Fair. 9212
Storytelling Festival, National. 2844

October, first weekend, usually
Shiprock Navajo Nation Fair. 2608

October, first two weeks
Sibelius Festival 2624

October, first two weekends
Austin City Limits Music Festival 0192

October, second Sunday
Círio de Nazaré 0652
Jousting Tournament 1489
St. Dismas's Day 2722
White Sunday 3214

October, two weeks beginning second Sunday
Festa da Luz (Festival of Light) 0994

October, second Monday
Columbus Day 0666
Thanksgiving 2963

October, second Tuesday
Cranberry Day Festival 0712

October, second Saturday
Eldon Turkey Festival. 0905
Eo e Emalani i Alaka i Festival 0933
World Wristwrestling Championships 3272

October, second week
Frankfurt Book Fair (Buchmesse) 1071
Norsk Høstfest 2084

October, second weekend
Hunters' Moon, Feast of the 1382
Madison County Covered Bridge Festival 1730
Ozark Folk Festival 2177
Shrimp Festival, National 2612
Tucson Meet Yourself Festival. 3042

October, second weekend in odd–numbered years
Swedish Homage Festival 2887

October, mid–
Heritage Holidays 1302
Open Marathon, International 2145
Peanut Festival, National 2233
Ukrainian Harvest Festivals 3078

October, ten days
Berlin Festival of Lights 0299

Numbers in the index refer to entry numbers, not page numbers

October, third Monday
Hurricane Supplication Day 1384
Jamaica National Heroes Day 1458

October, third Saturday
Bridge Day 0398
Sweetest Day 2888

October, third week
Texas Rose Festival 2957

October, third full weekend
Boggy Bayou Mullet Festival 0354
Moore (Billy) Days 1914
St. Mary's County Oyster Festival 2781

October, fourth Sunday
Mother-in-Law Day 1929

October, fourth Friday
Niue Peniamina Gospel Day 2076

October, last Sunday
Saffron Rose Festival 2462

October, last Thursday
Punky (Punkie) Night 2328

October, last Saturday
Guavaween 1229

October, last week
London Bridge Days 1695
Pirates Week 2279

October, last weekend
World Creole Music Festival 3254

October, late
Delaware Big House Ceremony 0783
Impruneta, Festa del 1412
Szüret 2899
Voodoo Music Experience 3167
Wexford Festival Opera 3205

October, late, or November
Reversing Current, Festival of the (Water Festival;
Bonn Om Tuk) 2396

October, late, through early November
Belfast Festival 0283

October, Saturday nearest the full moon
Ironman Triathlon Championships 1431

October–November
Alba White Truffle Fair 0054
American Royal Livestock, Horse Show and Rodeo . . 0086
Art Taipei 0160
Buenos Aires Rojo Sangre 0414
Punkin Chunkin World Championship 2327
Quebec City Festival of Sacred Music 2343
Styrian Autumn (Steirischer Herbst) 2854

Thesmophoria 2967
United Solo Theatre Festival 3085
Warri Festival, National 3180

October–November, every other year
New Vision Arts Festival 2021

October–November, every two years
Arts and Crafts Fair, International 0163

October or November
Gwangiu Kimchi Festival 1247

October–December
Europalia 0966

October and April, two events
Morija Arts and Cultural Festival 1919

November

American Indian Heritage Month 0085
Arabic Music Festival 0134
Black Storytelling Festival and Conference, National . . . 0336
Boston Jewish Film Festival 0374
Columbus International Film and Video Festival 0667
Film Festival of India, International 1013
Golden Horse Film Festival and Awards 1159
Haile Selassie's Coronation Day 1254
Heurigen Parties 1304
Kenya Skydive Boogie 1540
Kolkata International Film Festival 1583
Leeds International Film Festival 1651
Mar del Plata International Film Festival 1770
Mobile International Festival 1896
Tori-no-ichi (Rooster Festival) 3008
Wangala (Hundred Drums Festival) 3177
Wuwuchim 3280

November 01
Algeria National Day 0063
All Saints' Day 0064
All Saints' Day (France) 0065
All Saints' Day (Louisiana) 0066
Antigua and Barbuda Independence Day 0118
Author's Day, National 0196
Cross-Quarter Days 0731
Enlighteners, Day of the (Den na Buditelite) 0932
Fire Festivals 1016
Leaders of the Bulgarian National Revival Day
(National Enlighteners Day) 1645
Samhain (Samain) 2472

November 01–02
All Saints' Day and All Souls' Day (Peru) 0068

November 02
All Souls' Day 0069
All Souls' Day (Cochiti Pueblo) 0070
Balfour Declaration Day 0230
Día de los Muertos 0800

November 02–04
Karatsu Kunchi Festival. 1513

November 03
Bunka-no-Hi (Culture Day). 0428
Dominica Independence Day 0828
Meiji Setsu 1843
Panama Independence Days 2201
St. Hubert de Liège, Feast of 2742

November 04
Mischief Night 1890
Rogers (Will) Day 2420
Tonga National Day 3004

November 04–17
Ludi 1710
Plebeian Games (Ludi Plebeii) 2283

November 05
Bonfire Night 0365
Día del Puno 0803
Fawkes (Guy) Day 0988
Flaming Tar Barrels. 1029

November 05-11
Veterans Homecoming (Branson, Missouri) 3137

November 06
Green March Day 1211
Gustavus Adolphus Day (Gustaf Adolfsdagen) 1244

November 06, or nearest weekend
Leonhardiritt (St. Leonard's Ride) 1658

November 07
Bolshevik Revolution Day 0358

November 08
Michaelmas 1866
Saints, Doctors, Missionaries, and Martyrs Day 2467
St. Michael's Day 2785

November 09
Cambodia Independence Day 0468
Iqbal (Muhammad), Birthday of 1426
St. John Lateran, Feast of the Dedication of 2747

November 09–10
Kristallnacht (Crystal Night) 1589

November 10
St. Martin's Eve (Estonia) (Mardi Päev) 2780

November 10–11
Martinsfest 1798

November 10, Sunday closest to
Edmund Fitzgerald Anniversary 0894

November 11
Angola Independence Day 0103
Concordia Day 0673

Gansabhauet 1103
Martinmas 1796
Martinmas (Ireland) 1797
Polish Independence Day 2290
Quadrilles of San Martin 2340
St. Martin's Day (Portugal) 2779
St. Mennas's Day 2784
Veterans Day 3135
Vietnam Veterans Memorial Anniversary 3146

November 11 and preceding week
Veterans Day (Emporia, Kansas) 3136

November 11 through Shrove Tuesday
Karneval in Cologne 1514

November 12
Baha'u'llah, Birth of 0225
Stanton (Elizabeth Cady) Day. 2829
Sun Yat-sen, Birthday of 2865
Timor Santa Cruz Massacre Day (National
  Youth Day) 2982

November 13
St. Frances Cabrini, Feast of 2728

November 15
Brazil Proclamation of the Republic Day 0394
German-Speaking Community, Feast Day of the 1123
King's Birthday (Belgium) 1560
St. Leopold's Day 2768

November 15 or nearest Sunday
Shichi-Go-San (Seven-Five-Three Festival) 2600

November 15, Sunday nearest, to December 24
Advent 0023

November 17
Marshall Islands President's Day 1794
Polytechneio Day 2294
Queen's Day (England) 2347
Students' Fight for Freedom and Democracy, Day of
  (Struggle for Freedom and Democracy Day, World
  Students' Day) 2851

November 18
Haiti Battle of Vertières' Day 1257
Latvia Independence Day 1637
Morocco Independence Day 1922

November 18–19
Oman National Day 2136

November 19
Discovery Day 0812
Equal Opportunity Day 0945
Garifuna Settlement Day 1104

November 20
Africa Industrialization Day 0026

Numbers in the index refer to entry numbers, not page numbers

November 21
Fast for a World Harvest 0983
Presentation of the Blessed Virgin Mary, Feast of the . . . 2314

November 22
Lebanon National Day 1647
St. Cecilia's Day 2712

November 23
Repudiation Day 2392
St. George's Day 2733

November 23–24
Niisame-sai. 2068

November 23, Wednesday before
Repentance and Prayer Day. 2391

November 25
Bosnia and Herzegovina Statehood Day 0372
Evacuation Day 0968
Manger Yam 1766
St. Catherine's Day 2710
St. Catherine's Day (Estonia). 2711
Suriname Independence Day 2876

November 26
Baha'i Day of the Covenant. 0220

November 28
Abdu'l-Baha, Ascension of 0004
Albania Independence Day 0055
Chad Republic Day 0556
Mauritania Independence Day 1820
Panama Independence Days 2201
Timor-Leste Proclamation of Independence Day 2984

November 29
Liberian President W. V. S.Tubman's Birthday 1669
Solidarity with the Palestinian People, International
    Day of 2658
St. Andrew's Eve (Noc Swietego Andreja) 2698
Vanuatu Unity Day 3116

November 30
Barbados Independence Day 0243
Bonifacio Day. 0366
Eton Wall Game 0965
St. Andrew's Day. 2697
Yemen Independence and National Days 3290

November 30, Sunday nearest, to December 24
Advent 0023
Advent (Germany) 0024

November, usually
Mani Rimdu 1767

November, every four years
Asian Games 0173

November, eight days
GLOW Light Festival 1148

November, early
American Indian Film Festival 0084
An tOireachtas 0093
Sango Festival 2511
State Opening of Parliament 2832
Veterans Pow Wow 3138

November, early, to late January
Winter Festival of Lights 3236

November, first Sunday
New York City Marathon 2042

November, first Monday, begins Friday before
Wurstfest (Sausage Festival) 3279

November, first Tuesday
Melbourne Cup Day 1846

November, Tuesday after first Monday
Election Day 0906

November, Thursday after U.S. Election Day
Return Day 2395

November, first Saturday
Sadie Hawkins Day. 2460

November, first Saturday, on or around
Hogbetsotso Festival. 1323

November, first full weekend
Terlingua Chili Cookoff 2950

November, first weekend
Vintage Computer Festivals 3154

November, second Sunday
Quintaine, La 2350
Stewardship Sunday 2837
Veterans Day 3135

November, second Saturday
Lord Mayor 's Show 1699
Räben-Chilbi 2352

November, mid–
Independence of Cartagena City Day 1416
Jayuya Festival of Indian Lore 1469

November, mid–, to January
Lights, Festival of 1674

November, third Thursday
Great American Smokeout 1193

November, third weekend
Elephant Round-Up 0910
Tellabration 2942
Trois Glorieuses 3033

November, Sunday before Advent
Christ the King, Feast of. 0614

Numbers in the index refer to entry numbers, not page numbers

November, fourth Sunday
Umoja Karamu 3081

November, fourth Monday
Bible Week, National 0310
Zwiebelmarkt (Onion Market) 3316

November, fourth Thursday
Immaculate Conception, Feast of the 1407
Thanksgiving 2963

November; Friday and Saturday after Thanksgiving
Chitlin' Strut 0609

November, Thanksgiving week
World's Championship Duck-Calling Contest and
    Wings Over the Prairie Festival 3275

November, Thanksgiving weekend
Bayou Classic 0272

November, last Thursday
Pilgrim Thanksgiving Day (Plymouth,
    Massachusetts) 2265

November, last week
River Kwai Bridge Week 2406

November, late
Angkor Photography Festival 0102
Bard of Armagh Festival of Humorous Verse 0246
Grey Cup Day 1219

November, late, or early December
Shalako Ceremonial 2586

November, late, through New Year
Natchitoches Christmas Festival 1984

November or December
Sahara National Festival 2463

November–December
Davis Cup 0768
Dom Fair 0827
Jakarta International Film Festival 1455
Monkey Party 1907
Ngondo Festival 2058

November–December; Sunday before Advent
Stir-Up Sunday 2840

November–January
Kwafie Festival 1603

November–February
Bella Coola Midwinter Rites 0288
Kwakiutl Midwinter Ceremony 1604

December

Army-Navy Football Game 0155

Art Basel (Miami Beach) 0158
Capac Raymi 0491
Country Dionysia 0705
Ginem 1139
Itul 1447
Lighting of the National Christmas Tree 1673
Santon Fair 2526

December 01
Central African Republic Independence Day 0550
Seton (Mother) Day 2570
Portugal Restoration of Independence Day 2302
Romania National Day 2423
World AIDS Day 3250

December 02
United Arab Emirates National Day 3083

December 03
Disabled Persons, International Day of 0810

December 04
Siaosi Tupou I (King) Day 2623
St. Barbara's Day 2703

December 05
Discovery Day 0812
Faunalia 0987
Volunteer Day for Economic and
    Social Development, International 3166
King's Birthday (Thailand) 1563
St. Sava's Day 2808

December 06
Finland Independence Day 1014
St. Nicholas's Day 2788
St. Nicholas's Day (Greece) 2789

December 07
Armenia Earthquake Memorial Day 0150
Burning the Devil 0441
Pearl Harbor Day 2234
Timor-Leste Anniversary of the Indonesian Invasion ... 2983

December 08
Bodhi Day (Rohatsu) 0351
Beaches, Day of the (Día de las Playas) 0275
Hari-Kuyo (Festival of Broken Needles) 1284
Immaculate Conception, Feast of the 1407
Immaculate Conception, Feast of the (Argentina) 1408
Immaculate Conception, Feast of the (Malta) 1409
Immaculate Conception, Feast of the (Mexico) 1410
Uzbekistan Constitution Day 3102

December 08, four days around
Fetes des Lumieres 1003

December 09
Antigua National Heroes Day 0120
Tanzania Independence Day 2925

December 10
Human Rights Day, International. 1376
Nobel Prize Ceremony 2078
Thailand Constitution Day 2959

December 11
Burkina Faso Republic Day 0434

December 12
Jamhuri (Kenya Independence Day) 1460
Our Lady of Guadalupe, Feast of (United States) 2162
Our Lady of Guadalupe, Fiesta of 2163
St. Spyridon (Spiridion) Day 2810

December 13
Malta Republic Day 1762
St. Lucy's Day 2770
Susuharai (Soot Sweeping) 2878

December 13, Wednesday, Friday, and Saturday following
Ember Days 0928

December 14
Ako Gishi Sai. 0043
St. Spyridon (Spiridion) Day 2810

December 14–28
Halcyon Days 1264

December 14 to January 06
Christmas Bird Count. 0628

December 15
Bill of Rights Day 0315
Consualia 0682
Dukang Festival. 0849

December 16
Bahrain National Day 0227
Bangladesh Victory Day. 0239
Reconciliation, Day of. 2377

December 16–24
Misa de Gallo 1889
Posadas 2303

December 17
Wright Brothers Day 3278

December 17–23
Newport Harbor Christmas Boat Parade 2051
Saturnalia 2535

December 17, week leading up to
Urs of Jelaluddin al-Rumi (Whirling Dervish
   Festival). 3095

December 18
Closing the Gates Ceremony. 0657
Niger Republic Day 2064
Our Lady of Solitude, Fiesta of. 2166
St. Modesto's Day 2786

December 19
Opalia 2144

December 21
Doleing Day 0826
Dongji (Winter Solstice) 0833
St. Thomas's Day 2818

December 21, on or around
Homeless Persons' Remembrance Day, National 1351

December 21, at least seven days including
Chaomos 0563

December 21 or 22
Forefathers' Day 1056
Juul, Feast of 1499

December 21–22
Burning the Clocks 0440
Summer Solstice 2862
Winter Solstice 3237

December 22
Soyaluna (Hopi Soyal Ceremony) 2679
St. Frances Cabrini, Feast of 2728
Toji (Winter Solstice) 2997
Yule. 3302
Zimbabwe National Unity Day 3314

December 22, 23, and 24
Christmas Eve Bonfires 0639

December 23
Festivus 1002
Japanese Emperor 's Birthday 1468
Larentalia 1631
New Year for Trees 2023
Night of the Radishes 2066
St. Thorlak's Day 2819
Winter Solstice (China) 3238

December 23–24
Giant Lantern Festival 1132

December 24
Christmas Eve 0629
Christmas Eve (Baltics). 0631
Christmas Eve (Bethlehem) 0632
Christmas Eve (Denmark) (Juleaften) 0633
Christmas Eve (Finland) (Jouluaatto) 0634
Christmas Eve (France) (Veille de Noël) 0635
Christmas Eve (Italy) (La Vigilia) 0636
Christmas Eve (Moravian Church) 0637
Christmas Eve (Switzerland) (HeiligerAbend) 0638
Christmas Shooting 0583
"Silent Night, Holy Night" 2629
Tolling the Devil's Knell. 2999
Wigilia 3223

December 24–25
Koledouvane 1582

Numbers in the index refer to entry numbers, not page numbers

December 24-26
Grande, Fiesta 1182

December 25
Christmas 0616
Christmas (Greece) 0617
Christmas (Malta) 0618
Christmas (Marshall Islands) 0619
Christmas (Puerto Rico) 0621
Christmas (Romania) (Craciun) 0622
Christmas (South Africa) 0624
Christmas (Spain) (Pascua de Navidad) 0625
Christmas (Sweden) (Juledagen) 0626
Christmas (Syria) 0627
Crossing of the Delaware 0730
Quarter Days 2341
Yule 3302

December 25, around
Ass, Feast of the 0176

December 25, weekend before Christmas
Carriacou Parang Festival 0538

December 25–26
Christmas (Norway) 0620

December 25–January 05
Russian Winter Festival 2450

December 25–January 06
Christmas Pastorellas (Mexico) 0640
Yancunú, Fiesta del 3285

December 26
Boxing Day 0386
Flight into Egypt 1038
Junkanoo Festival 1494
St. Stephen's Day 2811
Sumamao, Fiesta de 2859

December 26–January 01
Kwanzaa 1605

December 27
Fossey (Dian) Day 1060
St. John the Evangelist's Day 2749
Ta chiu 2900

December 28
Holy Innocents' Day 1336
Holy Innocents' Day (Belgium)
  (Allerkinderendag) 1337

December 28, around
St. Gabriel, Feast of 2731

December 28–January 01
Fools, Feast of 1054

December 29
Black St. Benito, Fiesta of the 0335

December 30
Rizal Day 2408

December 31
Candlewalk 0486
Christmas Shooting 0641
First Night (Boston, Massachusetts) 1023
Hogmanay 1324
Ladouvane 1613
New Year 's Eve 2035
New Years Eve (Australia) 2036
New Year 's Eve (Brazil) 2037
New Year 's Eve (Ecuador) 2038
New Year 's Eve (Germany) (Silvesterabend) 2039
New Year 's Eve (Spain) 2040
Old Silvester 2126
Omisoka 2138
St. Sylvester 's Day 2814
St. Sylvester 's Day (Madeira) 2815
Watch Night (Bolden, Georgia) 3188
Watch Night Service 3189

December, early, through December 24
Christkindlesmarkt 0615

December, early, to January 01
Hong Kong WinterFest 1359

December, early, through January, late
Amsterdam Light Festival 0091

December, first Friday
Ghana Farmers' Day 1126
Marshall Islands Gospel Day 1791

December, begins first Friday
Wrangler National Finals Rodeo 3277

December, first Saturday
Country Christmas Lighted Farm Implement
  Parade 0704
Greenwood (Chester) Day 1216
Noel Night 2079

December, first weekend
Wilderness Woman Competition 3226

December, second Saturday
Old Saybrook Torchlight Parade and Muster 2125

December, mid–
Mevlana, Festival of 1861

December, mid–, weekend in
Escalade (Scaling the Walls) 0955

December; third Sunday before Christmas
Children's Day (former Yugoslavia) 0595

Numbers in the index refer to entry numbers, not page numbers

December, week after Christmas
Turon 3059

December, last week in
Cali Fair (Sugar Cane Fair, Salsa Fair) 0462

December, late, or early January
Haloa 1272

December or January
Ncwala 2000

December, January, or February
Elfstedentocht 0913

December–January
Hmong New Year 1317
Kalakshetra Arts Festival 1506
Rogonadur 2421

December–January; beginning of Advent to Sunday after Epiphany
Blowing the Midwinter Horn 0346

December–February, weekend in
Bishwa Ijtema 0321

December–April
Adam's Peak, Pilgrimage to 0016

December–August, biannually
Odo Festival 2112

December (Winter Weekend Festival) and May (Main Festival)
Jacob's Ladder 1453

Winter, end of
Navajo Mountain Chant 1995

Numbers in the index refer to entry numbers, not page numbers

INDEX 2

Chronological Index
Movable Days

The index below lists entries that are observed according to the dates of non-Gregorian calendars, including the Jewish calendar and Hindu calendar, as well as movable Christian holidays that depend on the date of Easter. Hindu datesare approximate, since some Hindu sects begin reckoning new months at the new moon, while others begin reckon-ing from the full moon.

The listings for each month are followed by listings of other calendar dates, including those of the lunar Chinese andBuddhist calendars, and dates according to the Islamic and Zoroastrian calendars.

See also the Chronological Index—Fixed Days, the Special Subject Index, and the General Index.

GREGORIAN DATES

January–February

January–February; Magh, (Sikh)
Maghi 1736

January–February; Magha
Magh Sankranti 1733

January–February; Magha, three to 12 days
Thaipusam (Thai Poosam) 2961

January–February; Magha, fifth day of waxing half
Vasant Panchami (Basant Panchami) 3120

January–February; Magha, eighth day of waxing half
Bhishma Ashtami 0308

January–February; Magha, night of full moon
Float Festival 1039

January–February; Magha, full moon day
Magha Purnima. 1735

January–February; Magha, fourth day of the waning half
Sakata Chauth 2468

January–February; Magha, 14th and 15th day of waning half
Risabha's Nirvana and Mauni Amavasya. 2404

January–February; Magha, 15th day of waning half
Mauni Amavasya 1819

January–February; Magha, three to 12 days
Thaipusam (Thai Poosam). 2961

January–February, every seven years
Coopers' Dance 0685

January–February; three weekends before Shrove Tuesday
Nice Carnaval 2062

January–March; before Lent
Carnival 0508

January 02 to Ash Wednesday night
Carnival (Martinique and Guadeloupe) 0519

January 06 to Ash Wednesday
Carnival (Hungary) (Farsang). 0517

January, middle; in the Assam month of Magh
 Magh Bihu. 1732

January 16 and February 13, between; Shevat 15
Tu Bishvat (Bi-Shevat; B'Shevat; Hamishah
   Asar Bishevat) 3038

January 26 and March 03, begins between; week before Ash Wednesday
Schemenlauf. 2541

January 29 and March 04, begins between; Thursday before Shrove Tuesday
Carnival Thursday 0537

Numbers in the index refer to entry numbers, not page numbers

January 30 and March 05, begins between; four days before Ash Wednesday
Carnival (Brazil) 0512

January 31 and March 04, begins between
Charro Days Fiesta 0567

January and March, begins between; week before Carnival
Kiddies' Carnival 1549

February–March

February–March
Carnival (Argentina) 0509
Carnival in Bolivia 0511
Carnival (Mexico) 0520
Carnival (Peru) 0522

February–March; Magha, full moon day
Masi Magham 1809

February–March; Phalguna
Shigmo Festival 3121

February–March; Phalguna, 11th day of waxing half
Amalaka Ekadashi 0078

February–March; Phalguna, 14th day of waxing half
Holi 1327
Shivaratri 2610

February–March; Phalguna, full moon day
Dol Purnima 0825

February–March; Monday of seventh week before Orthodox Easter
Clean Monday (Kathara Deftera)

February–March; before Ash Wednesday
Carnival Lamayote 0528
Carnival (Malta) 0518

February–March; four days before Ash Wednesday
Carnival (Panama) 0521

February–March; Friday through Tuesday before Ash Wednesday
Carnival (Colombia) 0513

February–March; Saturday through Tuesday before Ash Wednesday
Carnival (Goa, India) 0515

February–March; two weeks before Ash Wednesday
Mardi Gras 1774

February–March, the week before Ash Wednesday
Butter Week (Russia) 0451
Carnival of Ivrea Orange-Throwing Battle 0533
Carnival of Oruro, Bolivia 0534

February–March; three days before Ash Wednesday
Carnival (Aruba) 0510
Carnival (Haiti) 0516
Carnival (Portugal) 0523
Carnival (Spain) 0524
Carnival (Switzerland) 0525

February–March; Tuesday of Carnival week
St. Martin's Carnival 2778

February 02 and March 08, between; Monday before Ash Wednesday
Fastelavn 0984
Rose Monday 2431
Shrove Monday 2613

February 02 and March 08, between; Monday before Shrove Tuesday
Collop Monday 0663

February 02 and March 08, between; Monday–Tuesday before Ash Wednesday
Trinidad and Tobago Carnival 3026

February 02 and March 08, between; two days before Ash Wednesday
Fasching 0980

February 03 and March 09, between; Tuesday before Ash Wednesday
Brauteln 0392

February 03 and March 09, begins between, and ends on Shrove Tuesday night
Carnival (Venice) 0527

February 03 and March 09, begins between, Tuesday or Thursday before Lent
Paczki Day 2180

February 03 and March 09, between; before Shrove Tuesday
Carnival of Binche 0530
Fastens-een 0985
Kopenfahrt (Barrel Parade) 1584
Mardi Gras (France) 1775
Pancake Day 2203
Shrove Tuesday 2614
Shrove Tuesday (Pennsylvania Dutch) 2619
Shrove Tuesday (Bohemia) 2615
Shrove Tuesday (Estonia) 2616
Shrove Tuesday (Finland) 2617
Shrove Tuesday (Netherlands) 2618

February 03 and March 09, between; Sunday before Ash Wednesday
Shrovetide (Norway) (Fastelavn) 2620

February 04 and March 10, between
Ash Wednesday. 0169
Burial of the Sardine. 0432

February 04 and March 10, begins between
Lent 1657

February 04 and March 10, between; Wednesday, Friday, and Saturday following Ash Wednesday
Ember Days 0928

February 05 and March 11, between; day after Ash Wednesday
Fritter Thursday 1083

February 06 and March 12, between; Friday following Shrove Tuesday
Nippy Lug Day 2073

February 08 and February 28, between; Sunday before Eastern Lent
Cheese Sunday 0570

February 08 and February 28, between; week before Lent
Cheese Week (Sima Sedmitza) 0571

February 08 and March 14, between; first Sunday in Lent
Chalk Sunday 0560
Quadragesima Sunday. 2339
Buergsonndeg 0415

February 25 and March 25, between; Adar 14
Purim 2330

February–April; weekends in Lent
Rara (Ra-Ra). 2369

February–May, Sundays in Eastern Orthodox Lent
Sunday of Orthodoxy. 2867
Sunday of St. Gregory Palamas. 2868
Sunday of the Holy Cross 2871
Sunday of St. John Climacos 2869
Sunday of St. Mary of Egypt 2870

February–May, Saturdays in Eastern Orthodox calendar
Soul Saturdays (Saturday of Souls) 2664

March–April

March–April; Caitra, every 10–15 years
Mahamastakabhishekha (GrandHead-Anointing Ceremony) 1739

March–April; Caitra
Hanuman Jayanti 1281

March–April; Caitra, 10 days
Caitra Purnima 0457

March–April; Caitra, 1st–18th days
Gangaur 1101

March–April; Caitra, waxing half
Vasanth Navaratri. 1818

March–April; Caitra, first day of waxing half
Ghode Jatra 1131
Gudi Padva 1230

March–April; Caitra, eighth day of waxing half
Ashokashtami 0171
Sitala Ashtami 2641

March–April; Caitra, ninth day of waxing half
Ramanavami (Ram Navami). 2366

March–April; Caitra, 13th day of waxing half
Mahavira Jayanti. 1740

March–April; Caitra, eight days before full moon
Caitra Parb 0456

March–April; Caitra, 10 days including full moon day
Panguni Uttiram (Panguni Uthiram) 2205

March – April; Nisan 10
Miriam's Yahrzeit

March–April; Nisan, first Wednesday every 28 years
Blessing the Sun (Birchat Hahamah) 0344

March–April; fourth Sunday in Lent
Mothering Sunday 1928

March–April; Palm Sunday weekend
Calico Pitchin', Cookin', and Spittin' Hullabaloo 0463

March–April; Monday before Easter
Señor de los Temblores Procession. 2567

March–April; Easter eve
Easter Fires. 0881

March–April, Easter weekend
Opal Festival 2143

March–April; one week during the Easter season
Royal Easter Show 2440

March–April; during the Easter season
Rand Show. 2368

March–April; week after Easter
Merrie Monarch Festival 1858

March 01 and April 04, between; Laetare Sunday (three weeks before Easter)
Carnival of the Laetare. 0536
Groppenfasnacht (Fish Carnival) 1220

Numbers in the index refer to entry numbers, not page numbers

March 08 and April 07, between; fourth Sunday in Lent

Mid-Lent (Italy) 1874
Pretzel Sunday 2317

March 08 and April 11, between

Carling Sunday 0504

March 08 and April 11, between; fourth Sunday in Lent

Mi-Carême 1865

March 11 and April 15, begins between; four successive Thursdays before Orthodox Easter

Springtime Festival 2691

March 15 and April 18, between; Sunday before Easter

Fig Sunday 1008
Palm Sunday 2191
Palm Sunday (Austria) 2192
Palm Sunday (Finland) 2193
Palm Sunday (Germany) (Palmsonntag) 2194
Palm Sunday (Italy) (Domenica delle Palme) 2195
Palm Sunday (Netherlands) (PalmZondag) 2196
Palm Sunday (United States) 2197

March 15 and April 18, beginning between, through between March 22 and April 25; Palm Sunday through Easter Monday

Easter Festival (Osterfestspiele) 0880

March 15 and April 18, between

Holy Week 1343
Holy Week (Czech Republic) 1344
Holy Week (Haiti) 1345
Holy Week (Mexico) 1346
Holy Week (Panama) 1347
Holy Week (Portugal) (Semana Santa) 1349
Holy Week (Philippines) 1348
Moriones Festival 1920

March 15 and April 18, between; during Holy Week

Semana Criolla (Gaucho Festival) 2560

March 15 and April 18, between; Palm Sunday to Easter

Semana Santa (Guatemala) 2561

March 15 and April 18, between; Tuesday before Easter

Prisoners, Feast of the 2321

March 19 and April 22, between; Wednesday before Easter

Spy Wednesday 2692

March 19 and April 22, between; Thursday before Easter

Maundy Thursday 1818

March 19 and April 22, between; Thursday and Friday before Easter

Passion Play at Tzintzuntzan 2224

March 19 and April 22, beginning between; Thursday to Saturday before Easter

Silent Days 2628

March 20 and April 23, between; Friday before Easter

Good Friday 1163
Good Friday (Belgium) (Goede Vrijdag) 1164
Good Friday (Bermuda) 1165
Good Friday (England) 1166
Good Friday (Italy) 1167
Good Friday (Mexico) (Viernes Santo) 1168
Good Friday (Poland) (Wielki Piatek) 1169
Good Friday (Spain) 1170
Pleureuses, Ceremony of 2284

March 21 and April 24, between; day before Easter

Carling Sunday 0504
Holy Saturday 1340
Holy Saturday (Mexico) (Sábado de Gloria) 1341

March 22 and April 25, between; Easter

Burning of Judas 0436

March 22 and April 25, between

Easter 0862
Easter (Yaqui Indians) 0878
Easter (Bulgaria) 0863
Easter (Chile) 0864
Easter (Czech Republic) 0866
Easter (Germany) (Ostern) 0868
Easter (Hollywood, California) 0869
Easter (Italy) (La Pasqua) 0870
Easter (Norway) (Paske) 0872
Easter (Poland) (Wielkanoc) 0873
Easter (Spain) 0875
Easter (Sweden) (Påskdagen) 0876
Easter (Netherlands) (Paschen, Paasch Zondag) 0871

March 22 and April 25, between; Easter Sunday and Monday

Vlöggelen 3163

March 23 and April 26, between; Monday after Easter

Bottle Kicking and Hare Pie Scramble, Annual 0381
Easter Egg Roll 0879
Easter Monday 0882
Easter Monday (Netherlands) 0883
Georgiritt (St. George's Parade) 1118
Moldova Memorial Easter (Moldova Grave-Visiting Day) 1902

March 22 and April 25, between; week after Easter

Messiah Festival 1860

Numbers in the index refer to entry numbers, not page numbers

March 26 and April 23, between; Nisan 14
Firstborn, Fast of the 1024

March 26 and Apr 29, between; Thursday after Easter
Khamis al-Amwat 1544

March 27 and April 24, begins between; Nisan 15–21 (or 22)
Passover 2225

March 27 and Apr 30, between; Saturday before Palm Sunday
Lazarus Saturday 1643
St. Lazarus's Day 2767

March 28 and Apr 25, between; day after Passover
Maimona (Maimuna) 1746

March 28 and May 01 in the East, between; Sunday before Easter
Palm Sunday 2191

March 28 and May 01, between
Holy Week 1343

March 29 and May 02, between; Sunday after Easter
Low Sunday 1706

March and May, between; during Caitra or Vaisakha
Meenakshi Kalyanam (Chitrai Festival) 1841

April–May

April–May; Vaisakha
Pooram 2296
Rato (Red) Machhendranath 2373

April–May; Vaisakha, first day
Vaisakh 3104

April–May; Vaisakha, third day of waxing half
Akshya Tritiya 0045
Parshurama Jayanti 2219

April–May; Vaisakha, beginning on third day of waxing half and lasting 42 days
Chandan Yatra 0562

April–May; Vaisakha, ninth day of waxing half
Janaki Navami 1463

April–May; Vaisakha, 14th day of waxing half
Narsimha Jayanti 1979

April–May; Vaisakha, fifth or 10th day of waxing half
Shankaracharya Jayanti 2590

April–May; Vaisakha, full moon day
Bun Bang Fai (Boun Bang Fay; Rocket Festival) 0426
Vesak (Wesak; Buddha's Birthday) 3134

April-May; Vaisakha, last day of waning half
Mata Tirtha Snan (Mother's Day)

April-May; second Monday after Easter
Blajini, Feast of the (Sarbatoarea Blajinilor) 0338

April-May; third through fifth Sundays after Easter
Octave of Our Lady, Consoler of the Afflicted 2107

Apr 01 and May 05, between; Thursday before Easter
Maundy Thursday 1818

Apr 04 and May 08, between
Easter 0862
Easter (Cyprus) 0865
Easter (Egypt) 0867
Easter (Russia) (Paskha) 0874
Easter (Ukraine) 0877

Apr 05 and May 09, between; Monday after Coptic Easter
Sham el-Nessim 2587

Apr 05 and May 09, between; second Monday to Tuesday after Easter
Hocktide 1322

Apr 07 and May 18, between; third Tuesday after Easter
Ropotine (Repotini) 2427

April 08 and May 06, between; Nisan 27
Holocaust Memorial Day 1331

April 13 and May 17, between; 9th day after Eastern Orthodox Easter
Radunitsa 2357

April 15 and May 13, between; Iyyar 4
Yom ha-Zikkaron 3292

April 16 and May 14, between; Iyyar 5
Israel Independence Day 1440

Apr 18 and May 21, between; fourth Friday after Easter
Store Bededag 2843

Apr 27 and May 31, between; Monday before Ascension Thursday
Going to the Fields (Veldgang) 1151

Apr 29 and June 02, between; 25th day after Easter
Rousa, Feast of 2435

Numbers in the index refer to entry numbers, not page numbers

Apr 29 and June 02, between; eve of Ascension Day
Planting the Penny Hedge 2282

Apr 30 and June 03, between; 40 days after Easter
Ascension Day (Portugal) 0168
Ascension Day 0167
Festa del Grillo 0995
Holy Thursday 1342

Apr 30 and June 03, between; Ascension Day
Banntag 0241
Dew Treading 0793
Holy Blood, Procession of the 1333

Apr 30 and June 03, between; Monday to Wednesday before Ascension Day
Rogation Days 2418

May–June

May–June; during the Sikh month of Jaith
Guru Arjan, Martyrdom of 1236

May–June; Jyestha
Ganga Dussehra 1100

May–June; Jyestha, sixth day of waxing half
Sithinakha 2642

May–June; Jyestha, eighth day of waxing half
Jyestha Ashtami 1502

May–June; Jyestha, 11th day of waxing half
Nirjala Ekadashi 2074

May–June; Jyestha, full moon day
Poson 2304
Sanghamita Day 2510
Snan Yatra 2653

May–June; Jyestha, 13th day of waning half
Savitri-Vrata (Savitri Vow) 2538

May–June; seventh Thursday after Easter
Semik 2562

May–June; Friday before Pentecost to Tuesday following
Pilgrimage of the Dew 2268

May–June; around Pentecost (50 days after Easter)
Divine Holy Spirit, Festival of the (Festa do Divino) . . . 0814

May–June; Pentecost or Trinity Sunday, Sunday after Pentecost
Rousalii 2436

May–June; first Sunday after Pentecost
All Saints' Day 0064

May–June; second Saturday after the second Sunday after Pentecost
Immaculate Heart of Mary, Feast of the 1411

May–June
Pilgrimage to Qoyllur Riti 2272

May–June, Whit–Monday week
Walking Days 3172

May 03 and June 06, between; week preceding Pentecost
Penitents, Procession of the (Spain) 2237

May 08 and June 11, between; Pentecost
Meistertrunk Pageant (Master Draught Pageant) 1844

May 09 and June 06, between; Iyyar 28
Yom Yerushalayim 3294

May 09 and June 12, between; Saturday before Pentecost
All Souls' Day 0069
Kallemooi 1509
Luilak 1712

May 10 and June 13, between; 50 days after Easter
Cavalhadas 0549
Kataklysmos, Feast of (Festival of the Flood) 1522
Merchants' Flower Market 1855
Pentecost 2240
Pinkster Day 2278

May 11 and June 14, between; Monday after Pentecost
Cheese Rolling 0569
Matrimonial Tea Party 1815
Whit-Monday (Whitmonday) 3215

May 12 and June 15, between; Whit Tuesday
Dancing Procession 0762
Ram Roasting Fair 2363

May 16 and June 13, between; Sivan 6–7
Shavuot (Shabuoth) 2592

May 17 and June 20, between; Monday after Pentecost in East, Sunday after in West
Trinity Sunday 3031

May 21 and June 24, between; Corpus Christi
Decorated Horse, Procession of the 0780

May 21 and June 24, between; first Thursday after Corpus Christi
Lajkonik 1617

May 21 and June 24, between; Thursday after Trinity Sunday
Corpus Christi 0690
Corpus Christi (England) 0691
Corpus Christi (Germany) (Fronleichnamsfest) 0692
Corpus Christi (Mexico) 0693
Corpus Christi (Switzerland) (Fronleichnamsfest) 0694
Corpus Christi (Venezuela) 0695

Numbers in the index refer to entry numbers, not page numbers

May 22 and June 25, between; Friday after Corpus Christi
Sacred Heart of Jesus, Feast of the 2459

May 24 and June 27, between
Pentecost. 2240

May 24 and June 27, between; 50 days after Easter
Kneeling Sunday 1578

June–July

June–July; Har (Sikh)
Guru Har Krishan, Birthday of 1239

June – July; Asadha
Bonalu. 0362

June–July; Asadha, second day of waxing half
Rath Yatra 2371

June–July; Asadha, 10 days and nights prior to full moon day
Kataragama Festival 1523

June–July; Asadha, full moon day
Guru Purnima 1241

June–July; Asadha, every 20 years on the full moon day of the intercalary month
Kokila Vrata 1581

June–July to October–November; full moon of Asadha to the full moon of Karttika
Vatsa (Ho Khao Slak) 3122

June 17 and July 24, between; Tammuz 17
Tammuz, Fast of the 17th of (Shivah Asar
be-Tammuz) 2918

June 17 and July 24, begins between, and ends between July 17 and August 14; from Tammuz 17 until Av 9
Three Weeks. 2977

June–July; seventh Sunday after Pentecost
Nusardil 2097

July–August

July – August; Sravana
Shravani Mela 2611

July–August; Sravana, seventh day of the waxing half
Tulsidas Jayanti (Birthday of Tulsidas) 3046

July–August; Sravana, 11th day of waxing half
Putrada Ekadashi 2334

July–August; Sravana, waxing half
Naag Panchami 1967

July–August; Sravana, 17 days preceding full moon
Jhulan Yatra 1477

July–August; Sravana, the day before and the full moon day
Devi Dhura. 0792

July–August; Sravana, full moon day
Amarnath Yatra 0079
Nariyal Purnima (Coconut Day). 1978
Raksha Bandhan 2361

July–August; Sravana, third day of waning half
Marya 1802
Teej (Tij; Green Teej) 2937

July–August; Sravana, 14th day of waning half
Ghanta Karna (Gathyamuga) 1129

July 17 and August 14, between; Av 9
Tisha be-Av. 2990

July 23 and August 21, between; Av 15
15th of Av (Tu be-Av; Hamishah Asar b'Av) 1007

August–September

Mid–August; last day of Hindu month of Sravana
Jhapan Festival (Manasa Festival) 1476

August–September; Bhadrapada
Gowri Habba 1175
Paryushana. 2222
Rasa Leela Festival 2370
Samvatsari 2477

August–September; Bhadrapada, during
Avani Mulam. 0198

August–September; Bhadrapada, every 60
Kapila Shashti 1512

August–September; Bhadrapada, four days
Onam. 2141

August–September; Bhadrapada, about nine days during
Tirupati Festival. 2989

August–September; Bhadrapada, three days during
Tarnetar Mela. 2928

August–September; Bhadrapada, fifth to 13th day of the waxing half
Dasa Laksana Parvan (Time of the 10 Characteristics) . 0765

August–September; Bhadrapada, fifth day of waxing half
Rishi Panchami 2405

August–September; Bhadrapada, 12th day
Vaman Dwadashi 3110

Numbers in the index refer to entry numbers, not page numbers

August–September; Bhadrapada, 14th day of waxing half
Anant Chaturdashi 0094

August–September; Bhadrapada, waxing half
Ganesh Chathurthi 1099

August–September; Bhadrapada, new moon day
Janmashtami (Krishnastami; Krishna's Birthday) 1464

August–September; Bhadrapada, waning half
Gokarna Aunsi. 1152

August–September; Bhadrapada, third day of waning half
Panchadaan 2204

August–September; Bhadrapada, sixth day of waning half
Halashashti. 1263

August–September; Bhadrapada, eighth day of waning half
Radha Ashtami 2356

August–September; Bhadrapada, last Thursday
Bera Festival. 0294

August–September; Bhadrapada, end
Visvakarma Puja 3160

August – September; Elul
Elul Selichot 0920

September–October

September–October; Bhadrapada, end of, to early Asvina
Indra Jatra. 1422

September–October; Asun (Sikh), during
Guru Granth Sahib, Installation of the. 1238
Guru Ram Das, Birthday of 1242

September–October; Asvina
Lakshmi Puja 1618

September–October; Asvina, near the 10th day of waxing half
Rama Leela Festival 2364
Durga Puja 0855

September–October; Asvina, waning half
Pitra Visarjana Amavasya 2280

September–October; Asvina, first day of waning half
Ksamavani 1590

September–October; Asvina, full moon day
Kojagara 1580
Sharad Purnima. 2591
Valmiki Jayanti 3109

September–October; Tishri between Rosh Hashanah and Yom Kippur
Teshuvah. 2952

September–October; Tishri 01
Trumpets, Feast of. 3034

September 06 and October 04 between; Tishri 01 and 02
Rosh Hashanah 2433

September 08 and October 06, between; Tishri 03 (first day following Rosh Hashanah)
Gedaliah, Fast of (Tsom Gedalyah, Tzom Gedaliahu) 1111

September 15 and October 13, between; Tishri 10
Yom Kippur 3293

September 20 and October 18, begins between; Tishri 15–21
Sukkot (Sukkoth, Succoth). 2858

September–October; Tishri 22
Last Great Day. 1633

September 20 and October 18, beginning between; night following the first day of Sukkot and each night of the festival thereafter
Water-Drawing Festival 3190

September 27 and October 24, between; Tishri 21
Hoshana Rabbah 1369

September 27 and October 25, between; Tishri 22
Shemini Atzeret. 2597

September 28 and October 26, between; Tishri 22 or 23
Simhat Torah 2632

October–November

October; Kartika, fifth day of waxing half
Gyan Panchami 1248

Mid-October; Kati, Assam month of
Kati Bihu 1524

October–November; Kartika
Kartika Snan. 1517

October–November; Kartika, first day
Annakut Festival. 0109

October – November; Kartika, second day
Bhai dooj. 0306

October–November; Kartika, sixth day of the waxing half
Surya Sashti 2877

October–November; Kartika, 11th day of waxing half
Devathani Ekadashi 0791

October–November; Karitika, full moon day
Guru Parab. 1240
Kartika Purnima 1516
Pushkar Mela. 2333

October–November; Kartika, fourth day of waning half
Karwachoth 1519

October–November; Kartika, 13th day of waning half
Dhan Teras 0796

October–November; Kartika, 14th day of waning half
Narak Chaturdashi 1976

October–November; Kartika, 15th day of waning half
Dewali (Divali, Deepavali, Festival of Lights) 0794

October–November; Kartika, waning half
Tihar 2980

October – November; Heshvan 29
Ethiopian Sigd Festival. 0964

October; ten days after the first new moon of autumn
Atohuna (Friends made Ceremony). 0188

November–December

Mid-November–Mid-December; Karthikai, Tamil month of
Karthikai Deepam. 1515

November–December; Magar, during (Sikh)
Guru Tegh Bahadur, Martyrdom of 1243

November–December; Margasirsa (Agrahayana)
Nabanna. 1968

November–December; Margasirsa, 11th day of waxing
Gita Jayanti. 1145

November–December; Margasirsa, full moon day
Dattatreya Jayanti 0767

November–December; Margasirsa, eighth day of the waning half
Bhairava Ashtami 0307

November–December; Margasirsa, 11th day of the waning half
Vaitarani 3105

November 25 and December 26, between; Kislev 25 to Tevet 2
Hanukkah (Chanukah). 1280

December–January

December–January; Pausa (Poh), during (Sikh)
Guru Gobind Singh, Birthday of. 1237

December – January; Pausa, 10th day
Pausha Dashami 2229

December–January; Pausa, eighth day of waning half
Rukmini Ashtami 2444

December–January; Pausa, 10th day of the waning half (Jain)
Parshva, Birthday of 2220

December – January; Pausa, 12th day of the waning half
Swarupa Dwadashi. 2884

December 13 and January 10, between; Tevet 10
Asarah be-Tevet (Fast of the 10th of Tevet) 0166

CHINESE AND BUDDHIST CALENDAR DATES

First Tibetan lunar month, first day
Losar 1702

First lunar month
Dosmoche. 0835
Pingxi Sky Lantern Festival. 2277

First lunar month, first day
Lunar New Year 1714
Narcissus Festival 1977
Sol 2657

First lunar month, first seven days
Tet 2953

First lunar month, 2nd–15th days
Spirit Burying 2684

First lunar month, fourth day
Lantern Festival (Yuan Hsiao Chieh) 1627

First lunar month, 4th–25th days
Monlam (Prayer Festival) 1908

First lunar month, ninth and 10th days
Making Happiness Festival. 1749

First lunar month, 13th day
Lim Festival 1678

First lunar month, 15th day
Bridge Walking (Dari Balgi). 0399

Numbers in the index refer to entry numbers, not page numbers

Burning the Moon House. 0442
Butter Sculpture Festival 0450
Taeborum (Daeboreum) 2904
Torch Fight 3007

First lunar month, 16th–18th days
Sugar Ball Show (Sugar-Coated Haws Festival) 2856

First lunar month, 18th day
Star Festival 2830

First lunar month, 19th day
Rat's Wedding Day 2374

Second and eighth lunar months
Sokjon-Taeje Memorial Rites 2656

Second lunar month, first day
Wind Festival 3231

Second lunar month, second day
Blue Dragon Festival (Zhonghe Festival)
Bok Kai Festival 0355

Second lunar month, 10th–15th days
Paro Tsechu 2218

Third lunar month, fourth or fifth day
Qing Ming Festival (Ching Ming Festival) 2338

Third lunar month, fifth day
Thanh-Minh. 2962

Third lunar month, 10th day
Gio to Hung Vuong Day 1141
Vietnam Ancestors Death Anniversary 3144

Third lunar month, 15th – 16th day
Sister's Meals Festival 2640

Third lunar month, 19th day
Goddess of Mercy, Birthday of the 1150

Third lunar month, 23rd day
Matsu, Birthday of 1817
Tin Hau Festival 2986

Third lunar month, full moon night
Magha Puja (Maka Buja, Full Moon Day) 1734

**Third lunar month, end of, to 10th day of
fourth lunar month**
Cheung Chau Bun Festival 0581

Fourth lunar month, eighth day
Lantern Festival (Korea). 1628
Tam Kung Festival 2917

Fourth lunar month, eighth and ninth days
Third Prince, Birthday of the. 2971

Fifth lunar month, fifth day
Doan Ngu (Summer Solstice Day) 0816
Dragon Boat Festival 0842

Tano Festival (Dano-nal; Swing Day). 2924
Tuan Wu (Double Fifth) 3039

Fifth lunar month, 14th day
Boat Race Day (Okinawa, Japan) 0348

Fifth lunar month, 14th–16th days
Universal Prayer Day (Dzam Ling Chi Sang). 3089

Sixth lunar month, sixth day
Airing the Classics 0040

Sixth lunar month, 13th day
Lu Pan, Birthday of. 1708

Sixth lunar month, 15th day
Yudu Nal 3299

Sixth lunar month, 24th day
Lotus, Birthday of the. 1703

Sixth lunar month, 24th–26th days
Torch Festival. 3006

Seventh lunar month, seventh day
Chilseog (Seventh Evening). 0601
Seven Sisters Festival 2572

Seventh lunar month, 15th day
Baekjung. 0219

Seventh lunar month, full moon or 15th day
Ullambana (Hungry Ghosts Festival;
All Souls' Feast) 3079

Eighth lunar month, first full moon
Asanha Bucha Day (Asanha Puja Day) 0165

Eighth lunar month, 15th day
Chuseok (Gawi or Hangawi). 0648
Mid-Autumn Festival. 1870

Eighth lunar month, 18th day
Qiantang River Tidal Bore Watching Festival,
International. 2337

Eighth lunar month, 29th day
Seged. 2557

Ninth lunar month, first nine days
Nine Imperial Gods, Festival of the 2070
Vegetarian Festival 3123

Ninth lunar month, ninth day
Chung Yeung. 0646

Ninth lunar month, including ninth day
Chrysanthemum Festival. 0642

10th lunar month
Izumo-taisha Jinzaisai 1450
Ngan Duan Sib (10th Lunar Month Festival) 2054

10th lunar month, first day
Sending the Winter Dress. 2563

Numbers in the index refer to entry numbers, not page numbers

10th lunar month, fifth day
Ta Mo's Day 2901

10th lunar month, 19th day
Goddess of Mercy, Birthday of the 1150

10th lunar month, 25th day
Lights, Festival of (Ganden Ngamcho) 1675

11th lunar month
Dongji (Winter Solstice) 0833

12th lunar month
Boun Phan Vet 0382

12th lunar month, eighth day
Laba Festival 1609
Mochi No Matsuri 1898

12th lunar month, full moon
Loi Krathong 1693

12th lunar month, last day of Tibetan year
Mystery Play (Tibet) 1964

ISLAMIC CALENDAR DATES

Muharram 01
Islamic New Year 1435

Muharram 01–10
Ashura 0172

Muharram 05–06–07
Urs of Baba Farid Shakar Ganj 3094

Muharram 09
Taziyeh 2935

Muharram 10
Hosay Festival 1368

Safar
Mandi Safar 1765

Safar 14–16
Shah Abdul Latif Death Festival 2580

Safar 18
Grand Magal of Shaykh Amadou Bamba 1179

Safar 18–19
Data Ganj Baksh Death Festival 0766
Mawlid al-Nabi (Maulid al-Nabi; Prophet's
    Birthday) 1823

Safar 20
Arbaeen 0136

Safar 28
Holy Prophet and the Martyrdom of Imam Hasan,
Death Anniversary of the 1338

Rabi al–Awwal 01
Maldives National Day 1757

Rabi al–Awwal 12
Lamp Nights (Kandil Geceleri, Candle Feasts) 1621
Seka10 2559

Rajab 01–06
Lamp Nights (Kandil Geceleri, Candle Feasts) 1621
Urs Ajmer Sharif 3093

Rajab 13
Imam Ali's Birthday 1403

Rajab 27
Lamp Nights (Kandil Geceleri, Candle Feasts) 1621
Laylat al-Miraj 1640

Sha'ban 15, eve of
Laylat al-Bara'ah (Shab-Barat) 1639

Sha'ban 15
Lamp Nights (Kandil Geceleri, Candle Feasts) 1621
Shab-Barat 2578
Twelfth Imam, Birthday of the 3063

Ramadan, two weeks before beginning of
Mulid of Shaykh Yusuf Abu el-Haggag (Moulid
    of Abu el-Haggag) 1950

Ramadan
Ramadan 2365

Ramadan, full moon
Boys' Dodo Masquerade 0388

Ramadan 21
Imam Ali's Martyrdom, Anniversary of 1404

Ramadan 27
Lamp Nights (Kandil Geceleri, Candle Feasts) 1621

Ramadan, one of the last 10 days
Laylat al-Qadr 1641

Ramadan, end of
Lanterns Festival 1630

Shawwal 01
Id al-Fitr (Eid) 1393
Id al-Fitr (Nigeria) 1394

Shawwal 25
Imam Sadiq's Martyrdom, Anniversary of 1405

Dhu al–Hijjah 08–13
Pilgrimage to Mecca (Hajj) 2270

Dhu al–Hijjah 09
Libya Day of Arafa 1670

Dhu al–Hijjah 10
Sallah (Salah) Festival 2469

Dhu al–Hijjah 10–12
Id al-Adha (Feast of Sacrifice; Eid) 1392

Numbers in the index refer to entry numbers, not page numbers

Zoroastrian Calendar Dates

Frawardin 01
Jamshed Navaroz (Jamshed Navroz)............... 1462

Frawardin 06
Khordad Sal.. 1547

Frawardin 19
Frawardignan, Feast of........................... 1074

Ardwahist 03
Ardwahist, Feast of.............................. 0140

Ardwahist 11–15
Maidyozarem (Maidhyoizaremaya; Mid-Spring
    Feast)... 1744

Hordad 06
Hordad, Feast of 1365

Tir 11–15
Maidyoshahem (Maidhyoishema; Mid-Summer
    Feast)... 1743

Tir 13
Tiragan 2987

Amurdad 07
Amurdad, Feast of 0092

Shahrewar 04
Shahrewar, Feast of............................. 2583

Shahrewar 26–30
Paitishahem (Patishahya; Feast of Bringing in the
    Harvest)...................................... 2184

Mihr 01
Mithra, Feast of 1893

Mihr 16
Mihragan 1879

Mihr 26–30
Ayathrem (Ayathrima; Bringing Home the Herds) 0203

Aban 10
Aban Parab...................................... 0001

Adar 09
Adar Parab...................................... 0017

Adar 13
Ta'anit Esther (Fast of Esther)..................... 2902

Dae 01, 08, 15, 23
Dae, Feasts of................................... 0747

Dae 11
Zarthastno Diso................................. 3310

Dae 16–20
Maidyarem (Maidhyairya; Mid-Year or
    Winter Feast)................................. 1742

Vohuman 02
Vohuman, Feast of.............................. 3164

Spendarmad 05
Spendarmad, Feast of........................... 2682

Spendarmad 26–30
Farvardegan Days............................... 0979

Miscellaneous Dates

March; Esfand 29
Iran Petroleum Nationalization Anniversary......... 1428

March–April; Farvardin 12
Iran Islamic Republic Day 1427

June; Khordad 14
Khomeini (Ayatollah), Death Anniversary of........ 1545

September–October; full moon of Thadingyut
Thadingyut...................................... 2958

During Mayan month of Xul
Chickaban....................................... 0592

280th day of the Aztec year; end of 14th month
Quecholli 2345

Kasone full moon day
Kasone Festival of Watering the Banyan Tree........ 1520

Tazaungmone full moon day
Tazaungdaing 2934

21st day of the Javanese month of Mulud
Pilgrimage to the Tomb of Sunan Bayat 2275

Numbers in the index refer to entry numbers, not page numbers

INDEX 3

Special Subject Index

This index organizes entries according to eight specific subjects. Many of the entries in HFCWD fall into the following subject categories:

Arts
Calendar
Folkloric
Food
Historic
Promotional
Religious
Sporting

Some events may be listed in more than one category. For instance, St. Patrick's Day is listed under the Historic Index, because it commemorates a historical person, and the Folkloric Index, for all the folk legends and traditions associated with St. Patrick and his feast day.

See also the Chronological Indexes (Fixed Days and Movable Days) and the General Index.

Arts

Indexed below are festivals and events that revolve around the enjoyment, appreciation, and celebration of an art form such as fine and decorative arts, music, dance, film, literary arts, or theater.

Abbey Road on the River	0002
Adelaide Festival	0019
Adelaide Fringe Festival	0020
African American Women in Cinema International Film Festival	0029
African-American Music Appreciation Month	0034
Al Bustan International Festival of Music and the Arts	0047
Aldeburgh Festival of Music and the Arts	0059
American Black Film Festival	0083
American Indian Film Festival	0084
Amsterdam Light Festival	0091
Anchorage Festival of Music	0096
Andersen (Hans Christian) Festival	0098
Angkor Photography Festival	0102
Anjou Festival	0105
Ann Arbor Art Fairs	0106
Ann Arbor Film Festival	0107
Annecy International Animation Film Festival	0111
Arabic Music Festival	0134
Art Basel	0156
Art Basel (Hong Kong)	0157
Art Basel (Miami Beach)	0158
Art Taipei	0160
ArtPrize	0162
Arts and Crafts Fair, International	0163
Arts and Pageant of the Masters, Festival of	0164
Asheville Mountain Dance and Folk Festival	0170
Aspen Music Festival	0175
Aston Magna Festival	0182
Athens Festival	0184
Atlanta Film Festival	0186
Austin City Limits Music Festival	0192
Avignon Festival	0200
Baalbeck Festival	0210
Bach Festival	0216
Bachok Cultural Festival	0217
Ballet Festival of Miami, International	0232
Baltic Song Festivals	0234
Baltic-Nordic Harmonica Festival	0235
Banff Festival of the Arts	0236
Barbados Jazz Festival	0244
Bard of Armagh Festival of Humorous Verse	0246
Bascarsija Nights	0251
Bath International Music Festival	0261
Baths of Caracalla	0262
Bayreuth Festival	0273
Beiderbecke (Bix) Memorial Jazz Festival	0279
Beijing Opera Festival	0280
Beiteddine Festival	0281
Belfast Festival	0283

Numbers in the index refer to entry numbers, not page numbers

Bergen International Festival 0296
Berlin Biennale 0298
Berlin Festival of Lights 0299
Berlin International Film Festival 0300
Bermuda Festival of the Performing Arts 0303
BFI London Film Festival 0305
Biennale of Sydney 0311
Big Singing 0313
Black Poetry Day 0333
Black Storytelling Festival and Conference, National 0336
Bosra Festival 0373
Boston Jewish Film Festival 0374
Boston Pops 0377
Boston Science Fiction Film Festival 0378
Bratislava Music Festival 0391
Bregenz Festival 0396
Brighton Festival 0400
Broadstairs Dickens Festival 0403
Bruckner Festival, International 0405
Brussels International Fantastic Film Festival 0407
Budapest Music Weeks 0409
Budapest Spring Festival 0410
Buenos Aires International Festival of Independent
  Cinema 0413
Buenos Aires Rojo Sangre 0414
Bull Durham Blues Festival 0422
Bumbershoot 0425
Busan International Film Festival 0446
Buskers' Festival 0448
Byblos International Festival 0453
Cafe Budapest 0455
Calgary International Children's Festival 0461
Camp Fire Founders' Day 0477
Cannes Film Festival 0488
Caramoor International Music Festival 0496
Carillon Festival, International 0502
Carinthian Summer Music Festival 0503
Carriacou Parang Festival 0538
Carthage, International Festival of 0539
Casals Festival 0543
Central City Opera Festival 0551
Charlottetown Festival 0566
Cheltenham International Festival of Music 0573
Chhau Mask-Dance Festival 0583
Chicago Blues Festival 0585
Chicago Dancing Festival 0586
Chicago Gospel Music Festival 0587
Chicago International Children's Film Festival 0588
Chicago International Film Festival 0589
Chicago International Puppet Theater Festival 0590
Chicago Jazz Festival 0591
Clown Festival, International 0658
CMJ Music Marathon 0659
Coachella Valley Music and Arts Festival 0660
Columbus International Film and Video Festival 0667
Connecticut Early Music Festival 0679
Costa Rica National Arts Festival 0700
Cow Parade 0709
Cowboy Poetry Gathering, National 0710
Craftsmen's Fair 0711
Cultural Olympiad 0737
Dakota Cowboy Poetry Gathering 0752
Dally in the Alley 0754
Dance Camera West 0756
Dance Festival Birmingham, International 0757
Dance on Camera 0758
Dance Week Festival 0759
DanceAfrica 0760
Dancing on the Edge 0761

Denver Black Arts Festival 0787
Detroit International Jazz Festival 0790
Dhaka International Film Festival 0795
Diamond Head Crater Celebration 0804
Documentary Edge Festival 0818
Dodge (Geraldine R.) Poetry Festival 0821
Drachenstich 0841
Dublin Theatre Festival 0847
Dubrovnik Summer Festival 0848
Dulcimer and Harp Convention 0850
Dulcimer Days 0851
Dundee International Guitar Festival 0852
Durban International Film Festival 0854
Easter Festival 0880
Echigo-Tsumari Art Triennale 0886
Edinburgh International Festival 0890
Edinburgh International Film Festival 0891
Eisteddfod 0899
El Pochó Dance-Drama 0902
Elisabeth (Queen) International Music Competition 0916
Enescu (George) Festival 0930
Epidaurus Festival 0934
Esplanade Concerts 0956
Essence Festival 0957
European Fine Art Fair 0967
Exit Festival 0972
Faces Etnofestival 0973
Fes Festival of World Sacred Music 0993
Festival d'Aix en Provence 0996
Festival des Arts de la Rue (Far de Biarritz) 0997
Festival Du Nouveau Cinema 0998
Festival International des Arts de la Marionette à
  Saguenay 0999
Festival-Institute at Round Top, International 1000
Fetes des Lumieres 1003
Fillmore Jazz Festival 1012
Film Festival of India, International 1013
Fisher Poets Gathering 1025
Flagstaff Festival of the Arts 1028
Flanders Festival 1030
Fleadh Cheoil 1031
Florence Musical May 1043
Foire Internationale d'Art Contemporain 1050
Folk Festival, National 1051
Frameline: The San Francisco International
  LGBT Film Festival 1069
Frieze Art Fair London 1082
Gaelic Mod 1090
Galway International Arts Festival 1094
Glastonbury Festival of Contemporary Performing Arts 1146
GLOW Light Festival 1148
Glyndebourne Festival Opera 1149
Golden Globe Awards Ceremony 1158
Golden Horse Film Festival and Awards 1159
Golden Orpheus 1160
Göteborg International Film Festival 1174
Grammy Awards Ceremony 1176
Grand Canyon Music Festival 1177
Grant's (Bill) Bluegrass Festival 1186
Great American Brass Band Festival 1191
Great World Theatre 1205
Grec Festival de Barcelona 1206
Guadalajara International Film Festival 1223
Guelaguetza, La 1231
Guthrie (Woody) Folk Festival 1245
Handy (W. C.) Music Festival 1278
Harlem International Film Festival 1285
Harlem Week 1286
Hay-on-Wye Festival of Literature 1294

Hayti Heritage Film Festival 1295
Helsinki Festival 1297
Holland Festival 1328
Hong Kong Arts Festival 1356
Hong Kong International Film Festival 1357
Hora at Prislop...1364
Howl! Festival 1375
Humana Festival of New American Plays 1378
Humor and Satire Festival, International 1379
Hurston (Zora Neale) Festival of the Arts and Humanities 1385
I Madonnari Italian Street Painting Festival 1387
Idaho International Summerfest 1395
Idlewild Jazz Festival 1400
ImPulsTanz: Vienna International Dance Festival 1413
Indian Market 1419
Interceltique, Festival 1423
Isle of Wight Festival 1437
Israel Festival 1439
Istanbul Festivals, International 1441
Jacob's Pillow Dance Festival 1454
Jakarta International Film Festival 1455
Jazzkaar Festival 1470
Jerash Festival of Culture and Art 1472
Jerusalem Film Festival 1473
Just for Laughs Festival 1496
Jutajaiset Folklore Festival 1497
JVC Jazz Festival 1501
Jyvaskyla Arts Festival 1503
Kalakshetra Arts Festival 1506
Kaustinen Folk Music Festival 1526
Kelly (Emmett) Clown Festival 1533
Kilkenny Arts Festival 1551
Kolkata International Film Festival 1583
Leeds International Film Festival 1651
Lollapalooza 1694
London, Festival of the City of 1696
Lucerne International Festival of Music 1709
Mar del Plata International Film Festival 1770
Mardi Gras Film Festival 1776
Margaret Mead Film Festival 1777
Mariposa Folk Festival 1782
Marlboro Music Festival 1784
Marrakech Popular Arts Festival 1787
Maverick Sunday Concerts 1822
May Festival, International 1833
Mayfest, International 1835
Maytime Festival, International 1837
Medora Musical...1840
Melbourne Festival 1847
Melbourne International Comedy Festival 1848
Melbourne International Film Festival 1849
Menuhin Festival.......................................1853
Merengue Festival 1857
Messiah Festival 1860
Mill Valley Film Festival 1882
Miramichi Folk Song Festival 1887
Mohawk Trail Concerts 1899
Monterey Jazz Festival 1909
Montreal Jazz Festival 1910
Montreal World Film Festival 1911
Montreux International Jazz Festival 1912
Moravian Music Festival 1917
Moreska Sword Dance 1918
Morija Arts and Cultural Festival 1919
Moscow International Film Festival 1925
Movement Electronic Music Festival 1940
Mozart Festival 1947
Mozart Week 1948
Munich Opera Festival 1952

Music and Dance Festival, International 1956
Nashville Film Festival 1981
Netherlands Military Tattoo 2011
New England Folk Festival 2016
New Orleans Jazz and Heritage Festival 2019
New Vision Arts Festival 2021
New York Film Festival 2043
New York International Children's Film Festival 2045
New York International Fringe Festival 2046
New Zealand Festival 2047
Newport Folk Festival 2050
Newport Music Festival 2052
Normandy Impressionist Festival 2083
Nuits de Fourvière 2095
Nuuk Snow Festival 2098
NXNE (North by Northeast) 2099
Old Fiddler's Convention 2123
Oldenburg International Film Festival 2128
Old-Time Country Music Contest and Festival, National 2130
Oldtime Fiddlers' Contest and Festival, National 2131
Ole Time Fiddlers and Bluegrass Festival 2132
Oregon Bach Festival 2149
Oregon Shakespeare Festival 2152
Osaka International Festival 2154
Ozark Folk Festival 2177
Pacific Northwest Festival 2178
Pafos Aphrodite Festival Cyprus 2181
Panafrican Film and Television Festival of Ouagadougou 2199
Pan-African Film Festival 2200
Paris Autumn Festival 2215
Parker (Charlie) Jazz Festival 2216
Perth International Arts Festival 2245
Poetry Festival of Medellín, International 2286
Poetry Month, National 2287
Pori International Jazz Festival 2297
Prague Spring International Music Festival 2310
Puppeteers, Festival of 2329
Quartier d'été 2342
Quebec City Festival of Sacred Music 2343
Queer Lisboa: International Queer Film Festival 2349
Rainforest World Music Festival 2360
Ramayana Ballet 2367
Ravello Music Festival 2375
Ravinia Festival 2376
Reykjavik Arts Festival (Listahátí í Reykjavík) 2397
Rio de Janeiro International Film Festival 2403
Rock Ness 2416
Rodgers (Jimmie) Festival 2417
Saintes Festival of Ancient Music 2466
Salzburg Festival 2471
San Francisco Ethnic Dance Festival 2483
San Francisco International Film Festival 2485
Santa Fe Chamber Music Festival 2516
Santa Fe Opera Festival 2518
Santander International Festival of Music and Dance 2524
Saratoga Festival 2531
Sasquatch! Music Festival 2532
Satchmo SummerFest 2534
Savonlinna Opera Festival 2539
Schubertiade 2542
Sea Music Festival 2548
Seattle International Dance Festival 2553
Seattle International Film Festival 2554
Shambhala Music Festival 2588
Shanghai International Film Festival 2589
Sibelius Festival 2624
Signal: Prague Light Festival 2626
Sitka Summer Music Festival 2643
Smithville Fiddlers Jamboree and Crafts Festival 2652

Numbers in the index refer to entry numbers, not page numbers

Sofia Music Weeks 2655
Sound Symposium 2665
South Africa National Arts Festival 2668
Spoken Word Festival, Calgary International 2687
Spoleto Festival USA 2688
Spring of Culture 2690
Steinbeck (John) Festival 2834
Storytelling Festival, National 2844
Stratford Festival 2846
Stuttgart Festival of Animated Film 2853
Styrian Autumn 2854
Sundance Film Festival 2866
SXSW (South by Southwest) 2891
SXSW (South by Southwest) Film 2892
Sydney Film Festival 2894
Tallgrass Film Festival 2916
Tanglewood Music Festival 2921
Tango Festival 2922
Tejano Conjunto Festival 2938
Tellabration 2942
Telluride Film Festival 2943
Telluride Horrow Show 2945
Telluride Jazz Festival 2946
Ten Days on the Island 2947
Three Choirs Festival 2975
Tivoli Gardens Season 2991
To Kill a Mockingbird Annual Production 2992
Toronto International Film Festival 3010
Tribeca Film Festival 3022
Tricky Women Festival of Animated Films 3024
Trinidad and Tobago Film Festival 3028
Tucson International Mariachi Conference 3041
Tulsa Indian Arts Festival 3045

Twenty-Four:Seven Theatre Festival 3065
United Solo Theatre Festival 3085
Utah Arts Festival 3099
Utakai Hajime 3100
Vancouver Writer's Fest 3111
Venice Biennale (La Biennale) 3127
Venice Film Festival 3128
Verdur Rock 3129
Vienna Festival 3142
Vienna Jazz Festival (Jazz Fest Wien) .3143
Viña del Mar International Song Festival 3149
Vivid Sydney 3161
Voodoo Music Experience 3167
Waila Festival 3169
Warsaw International Film Festival 3182
WCSH Sidewalk Art Festival 3196
Wexford Festival Opera 3205
Wide Open Bluegrass Festival 3220
Wiener Festwochen 3221
Wildlife Film Festival, International 3227
Williams (Tennessee) New Orleans Literary Festival 3229
Winnipeg Folk Festival 3234
Wolf Trap Summer Festival Season 3242
Wood (Grant) Art Festival 3245
Wood (Henry) Promenade Concerts 3246
World Championship Hoop Dance Contest 3253
World Creole Music Festival 3254
WorldFest-Houston International Film Festival 3273
Yukon International Storytelling Festival 3301
Zanzibar International Film Festival 3308
Zurich Festival 3315
Zydeco Music Festival (Southwest Louisiana) 3317

Calendar

Indexed below are festivals and events that deal specifically with the calendar or that are held in celebration of the time of the year (solstices and equinoxes), the beginning and end of seasons, etc.

Aban Parab 0001
Abu Simbel Festival 0009
Adar Parab 0017
Alahamady Be 0050
Almabtrieb 0074
Alpaufzug 0076
Amurdad, Feast of 0092
Ardwahist, Feast of 0140
Autumnal Equinox 0197
Ayathrem 0203
Aymuray 0205
Ayyam-i-Ha 0206
Baekjung 0219
Baile de las Turas 0228
Beltane 0290
Bianou 0309
Bisket Jatra 0322
Blessing the Sun 0344
Borrowed Days 0370
Bridge Walking 0399
Buergsonndeg 0415
Bulu Festival 0423
Burning of the Socks 0438
Burning the Clavie 0439
Burning the Clocks 0440
Buzzard Day 0452

Cambodian New Year 0472
Candlewalk 0486
Capac Raymi 0491
Caturmas 0547
Chalanda Marz 0559
Chaomos 0563
Chuseok 0648
Coptic New Year 0686
Corn-Planting Ceremony 0689
Cranberry Day Festival 0712
Cranberry Harvest Festival 0713
Crane Watch 0715
Creek Green Corn Ceremony 0719
Cross-Quarter Days 0731
Cure Salée 0739
Dae, Feasts of 0747
Dewali 0794
Doan Ngu 0816
Dog Days 0822
Dongji 0833
Dosmoche 0835
Dozynki Festival 0840
Drymiais 0844
Easter (Czech Republic) 0866
Egyptian Days 0897
Enkutatash 0931

Numbers in the index refer to entry numbers, not page numbers

Excited Insects, Feast of 0971
Firecracker Festival 1018
First Day of Summer (Iceland) 1019
First Fruits of the Alps Sunday 1021
First Night (Boston, Massachusetts) 1023
Four an' Twenty Day 1063
Frawardignan, Feast of 1074
Freeing the Insects 1078
Galungan 1093
Gawai Dayak 1109
Great New Moon Festival (Cheno i-equa) 1201
Gudi Padva 1230
Hachinohe Enburi 1251
Harvest Festival 1288
Harvest Home Festival 1289
Harvest Moon Days 1290
Heurigen Parties 1304
Hidrellez Festival 1306
Higan 1307
Hmong New Year 1317
Holi 1327
Homowo 1352
Homstrom 1353
Hong Kong WinterFest 1359
Hordad, Feast of 1365
Ibu Afo Festival 1388
Ides 1398
Iduna and Summer Finding 1401
Igbi 1402
Imam Sadiq's Martyrdom, Anniversary of 1405
Imbolc 1406
Impruneta, Festa del 1412
Inti Raymi Fiesta 1424
Iroquois Midwinter Festival 1432
Itabashi Suwa Jinja Ta-Asobi 1443
Jamshed Navaroz 1462
Juhannus 1491
Kaamatan Festival 1504
Kallemooi 1509
Kati Bihu 1524
Klo Dance 1573
Ku-omboka 1595
Kupalo Festival 1596
Lammas 1619
Lantern Festival 1627
Leap Year Day 1646
Li Ch'un 1661
Lismore Lantern Parade 1682
Lohri 1692
Losar 1702
Lunar New Year 1714
Mabon 1718
Magh Bihu 1732
Magh Sankranti 1733
Maidyarem 1742
Maidyoshahem 1743
Maidyozarem 1744
Marzas 1807
Marzenna Day 1808
May Day 1824
May Day Eve (Ireland) 1830
Mid-Autumn Festival 1870
Midnight Sun Festival 1875
Midsummer Day 1877
Mihragan 1879
Misisi Beer Feast 1891
Miwok Acorn Festival 1894
Mut l-ard 1957
Narcissus Festival 1977

Native American Ceremonies in June at Devils Tower 1987
Nawruz 1998
Nawruz (Kazakhstan) 1999
N'cwala 2001
New Fire Ceremony 2017
New Year for Trees 2023
New Year's Day 2024
New Year's Day (Denmark) 2025
New Year's Day (France) 2026
New Year's Day (Germany) 2027
New Year's Day (Lithuania) 2028
New Year's Day (Malta) 2029
New Year's Day (Netherlands) 2030
New Year's Day (Portugal) 2031
New Year's Day (Romania) 2032
New Year's Day (Russia) 2033
New Year's Day (Switzerland) 2034
New Year's Eve 2035
New Year's Eve (Australia) 2036
New Year's Eve (Brazil) 2037
New Year's Eve (Ecuador) 2038
New Year's Eve (Germany) 2039
New Year's Eve (Spain) 2040
Nganja, Feast of 2055
Nyambinyambi 2100
Nyepi 2101
Obzinky 2106
Omisoka 2138
Onwasato Festival 2142
Oshogatsu 2155
Paczki Day 2180
Pageant of the Golden Tree 2182
Paitishahem 2184
Perseids 2244
Phagwa 2250
Pii Mai 2261
Pongal 2295
Qiantang River Tidal Bore Watching Festival, International 2337
Quarter Days 2341
Rei-tai-sai 2389
Reversing Current, Festival of the 2396
Rice-Planting Festival at Osaka 2399
Rosh Hashanah 2433
Royal Ploughing Ceremony 2441
Sabantui 2455
Sacaea 2458
Samhain 2472
Saturnalia Roman Festival 2536
Sealing the Frost 2552
Sechseläuten 2556
Setsubun 2571
Shahrewar, Feast of 2583
Shunbun-no-Hi 2621
Simadan Festival 2630
Simbra Oilor 2631
Sinhala Avurudu 2636
Sioux Sun Dance 2639
Sol 2657
Songkran 2662
Soyaluna 2679
Spendarmad, Feast of 2682
Springtime Festival 2691
St. Barnabas's Day 2704
St. Basil, Feast of 2706
St. Demetrius's Day 2720
St. Hans Festival 2739
St. John's Eve (Denmark) 2755
St. John's Eve (France) 2756
Summer Solstice 2862

Numbers in the index refer to entry numbers, not page numbers

Sun Pageant Day 2864
Susuharai 2878
Swallow, Procession of the 2881
Swallows of San Juan Capistrano 2882
Szüret 2899
Tano Festival 2924
Ta'u Fo'ou 2932
Tet 2953
Thingyan 2970
Tiragan 2987
Toji 2997
Trigo, Fiesta Nacional del 3025
Tsagaan Sar 3035
Tsunahiki Matsuri 3036
Twelfth Imam, Birthday of the 3063
Ukrainian Harvest Festivals 3078
Vaisakh 3104

Vasant Panchami 3120
Vernal Equinox 3131
Vernal Equinox 3132
Vinegrower's Day 3153
Vohuman, Feast of 3164
Wangala 3177
Watch Night Service 3189
Wheat Harvest (Transylvania) 3208
Wheat Harvest Festival (Provins, France) 3209
White Nights 3213
Winter Solstice 3237
Winter Solstice (China) 3238
Wuwuchim 3280
Yam Festival at Aburi 3284
Ysyakh 3298
Yule 3302

Folkloric

Indexed below are festivals and events deeply rooted in folklore and tradition, as well as those celebrating specific folk tales or myths.

Agonalia 0035
Anna Parenna Festival 0108
Anthesteria 0116
Aoi Matsuri 0124
Apollonian Games 0126
April Fools' Day 0132
Ascension Day (Portugal) 0168
Assumption of the Virgin Mary, Feast of the
    (Hasselt, Belgium) 0180
Aztec Rain Festival 0209
Babin Den 0214
Baltic Song Festivals 0234
Bawming the Thorn Day 0269
Befana Festival 0278
Bettara-Ichi 0304
Bisket Jatra 0322
Black Christ, Festival of the 0325
Black Storytelling Festival and Conference, National ... 0336
Blajini, Feast of the 0338
Blue Dragon Festival (Zhonghe Festival) 0347
Bona Dea Festival 0361
Borrowed Days 0370
Bottle Kicking and Hare Pie Scramble, Annual 0381
Bouphonia 0384
Boys' Dodo Masquerade 0388
Brauteln 0392
Bumba-Meu-Boi Folk Drama 0424
Burning of Judas 0436
Burning the Clavie 0439
Burning the Moon House 0442
Burry Man Day 0444
Butter Week (Russia) 0451
Candlemas 0485
Carabao Festival 0495
Carberry Day 0497
Carmentalia 0505
Carnea 0507
Carnival 0508
Carnival (Aruba) 0510
Carnival (Goa, India) 0515
Carnival (Hungary) 0517

Carnival (Malta) 0518
Carnival (Martinique and Guadeloupe) 0519
Carnival (Mexico) 0520
Carnival (Portugal) 0523
Carnival (Switzerland) 0525
Carnival (Venice) 0527
Carnival Lamayote 0528
Carnival of Binche 0530
Carnival of Blacks and Whites 0531
Carnival of Oruro, Bolivia 0534
Carnival of the Devil 0535
Castor and Pollux, Festival of 0545
Cerealia 0553
Chalanda Marz 0559
Chilseog 0601
Christmas (Greece) 0617
Christmas (Romania) 0622
Christmas Eve 0629
Christmas Eve (Denmark) 0633
Christmas Eve (Switzerland) 0638
Chung Yeung 0646
Ch'un-hyang Festival 0647
Cock Festival 0662
Compitalia 0671
Consualia 0682
Country Dionysia 0705
Cow, Festival of the 0707
Crom Dubh Sunday 0725
Cronia 0727
Daedala 0748
Decorated Horse, Procession of the 0780
Dew Treading 0793
Dionysia 0808
Dog Days 0822
Dominican Republic Our Lady of Mercedes Day 0832
Down Home Family Reunion 0838
Drachenstich 0841
Drymiais 0844
Easter (Germany) 0868
Easter (Italy) 0870
Easter (Netherlands) 0871

Numbers in the index refer to entry numbers, not page numbers

Easter (Poland) 0873
Easter (Sweden) 0876
Easter Fires 0881
Easter Monday (Netherlands) 0883
Egyptian Days 0897
Eleusinian Mysteries 0911
Epiphany (Germany) 0935
Epiphany (Labrador) 0936
Epiphany (Portugal) 0937
Epiphany Eve (Austria) 0942
Equirria 0947
Faunalia 0987
Feralia 0992
Festa del Grillo 0995
Fifteenth of Av 1007
First Foot Day 1020
Flaming Tar Barrels 1029
Floralia 1041
Folklore, National Festival of 1052
Fornacalia 1058
Forty Martyrs' Day 1059
Frost Saints' Days 1084
Furrinalia 1086
Fyr-Bål Fest 1087
Garland Day 1105
Ghode Jatra 1131
Giants, Festival of the (Belgium) 1134
Good Friday (England) 1166
Grande, Fiesta 1182
Grape Festival 1187
Green George Festival 1210
Groundhog Day 1222
Halcyon Days 1264
Halloween 1267
Halloween (Ireland) 1268
Halloween (Scotland) 1271
Haloa 1272
Helston Flora Day 1298
Hilaria 1309
Hina Matsuri 1311
Hocktide 1322
Holy Innocents' Day 1336
Horn Dance 1366
Hoshana Rabbah 1369
Igbi 1402
Jackalope Days 1451
Junkanoo Festival 1494
Juno Caprotina, Festival of 1495
Jutajaiset Folklore Festival 1497
Juturnalia 1498
Juul, Feast of 1499
Kalakshetra Arts Festival 1506
Kallemooi 1509
Karatsu Kunchi Festival 1513
Karneval in Cologne 1514
Kattestoet 1525
Keaw Yed Wakes Festival 1529
Keretkun Festival 1541
Kopenfahrt 1584
Korea National Foundation Day 1586
Kupalo Festival 1596
Ladouvane 1613
Lag ba-Omer 1616
Lajkonik 1617
Lammas 1619
Lantern Festival 1627
Larentalia 1631
Latin Festival 1634
Lazarus Saturday 1643

Leap Year Day 1646
Lemuralia 1656
Li Ch'un 1661
Liberalia 1662
Loi Krathong 1693
Ludi 1710
Lughnasadh 1711
Luilak 1712
Lunar New Year 1714
Lupercalia 1715
Madeleine, Fête de la 1728
Mamuralia 1764
Marche du Nain Rouge 1773
Martenitza 1795
Martinmas 1796
Martinmas (Ireland) 1797
Marya 1802
Marzenna Day 1808
Mata Tirtha Snan (Mother's Day) 1812
Matralia 1813
Matronalia 1816
Matsu, Birthday of 1817
May Day 1824
May Day (Czech Republic) 1825
May Day (France) 1826
May Day (Scandinavia) 1827
May Day (Spain) 1828
May Day Eve (Czech Republic) .1829
May Day Eve (Ireland) 1830
May Day Eve (Italy) 1831
May Day Eve (Switzerland) 1832
Megalesia 1842
Michaelmas 1866
Mid-Autumn Festival 1870
Mid-Lent (Italy) 1874
Midsummer Day 1877
Mihr, Festival of 1878
Min, Festival of 1884
Minehead Hobby Horse Parade .1885
Mnarja 1895
Mobile International Festival 1896
Moro-Moro Play 1923
Mount Ceahlau Feast 1934
Mut l-ard 1957
Nabanna 1968
Nanakusa Matsuri 1973
Nemean Games 2005
Nemoralia 2006
New Year's Day (Portugal) 2031
New Year's Day (Romania) 2032
New Year's Day (Russia) 2033
New Year's Day (Switzerland) 2034
New Year's Eve 2035
New Year's Eve (Germany) 2039
Ngondo Festival 2058
Octave of Our Lady, Consoler of the Afflicted 2107
October Horse Sacrifice 2109
Ommegang 2140
Opalia 2144
Oshogatsu 2155
Otsa Festival 2158
Our Lady of Nazaré Festival 2165
Owara Kaze-no-Bon Festival 2174
Palm Sunday (Finland) 2193
Palm Sunday (Germany) 2194
Palm Sunday (Netherlands) 2196
Panathenaea 2202
Pardon of Ste. Anne d'Auray 2211
Parentalia 2212

Numbers in the index refer to entry numbers, not page numbers

Parilia 2213
Perchtenlauf 2243
Phagwa 2250
Pied Piper Open Air Theater 2257
Plebeian Games 2283
Punjabi American Festival 2326
Quirinalia 2351
Rainforest World Music Festival 2360
Robigalia 2411
Robin Hood Festival in Nottinghamshire, England 2412
Rogonadur 2421
Roman Games 2422
Ropotine 2427
Rousa, Feast of 2435
Rousalii 2436
Sacaea 2458
Sadie Hawkins Day 2460
San Isidro the Farmer, Feast of 2494
Sanghamita Day 2510
Santa Fe, Fiesta de 2517
Saturnalia 2535
Saudi Arabia National Heritage and Folk Culture Festival . . . 2537
Schemenlauf 2541
Semik 2562
Setsubun 2571
Seven Sisters Festival 2572
Shrove Monday 2613
Shrove Tuesday (Bohemia) 2615
Shrove Tuesday (Finland) 2617
Shrove Tuesday (Netherlands) 2618
Shrove Tuesday (Pennsylvania Dutch) 2619
Shrovetide (Norway) 2620
Sister's Meals Festival 2640
Sizdah Bedar 2644
Smithsonian Folklife Festival 2650
Song of Hiawatha Pageant 2661
Springtime Festival 2691
St. Agnes's Eve 2695
St. Alban's Day 2696
St. Andrew's Day 2697
St. Andrew's Eve 2698
St. Anthony of Padua, Feast of 2700
St. Anthony the Abbot, Feast of 2701
St. Barbara's Day 2703
St. Bartholomew's Day 2705
St. Basil, Feast of 2706
St. Blaise's Day 2707
St. Brendan's Day 2708
St. Catherine's Day 2710
St. Cecilia's Day 2712
St. Christopher's Day 2715
St. Columba's Day 2717
St. Crispin's Day 2718
St. David's Day 2719
St. Denis's Day 2721
St. Elmo's Day 2726
St. Evermaire, Game of 2727
St. Gens, Festival of 2732
St. George's Day 2733
St. George's Day (Bulgaria) 2734
St. George's Day (Syria) 2735
St. Gregory's Day 2737
St. Gudula's Day 2738
St. Hilary's Day 2741
St. John the Evangelist's Day 2749
St. John's Eve (Germany) 2750

St. John's Day 2751
St. John's Day (Portugal) 2753
St. John's Day (Puerto Rico) 2754
St. John's Eve (Denmark) 2755
St. John's Eve (France) 2756
St. John's Eve (Ireland) 2758
St. John's Eve (Spain) 2759
St. John's Eve and Day (Latvia) 2760
St. Jude's Day 2763
St. Lazarus's Day 2767
St. Lucy's Day 2770
St. Marinus Day 2771
St. Mark's Day 2773
St. Martha's Day 2777
St. Martin's Eve (Estonia) 2780
St. Médardus's Day 2783
St. Mennas's Day 2784
St. Michael's Day 2785
St. Modesto's Day 2786
St. Nicholas's Day 2788
St. Nicholas's Day (Italy) 2790
St. Patrick's Day 2792
St. Paul Winter Carnival 2797
St. Paul, Feast of the Conversion of 2796
St. Paul's Shipwreck, Feast of 2798
St. Polycarp's Day 2803
St. Sarkis's Day 2807
St. Stephen's Day 2811
St. Swithin's Day 2813
St. Sylvester's Day 2814
St. Urho's Day 2821
St. Vaclav's Day 2822
St. Vincent's Day 2825
St. Vitus's Day 2826
Stes. Maries, Fête des 2835
Stir-Up Sunday 2840
Storytelling Festival, National 2844
Swallow, Procession of the .2881
Ta Mo's Day 2901
Taeborum 2904
Tailte Fair 2907
Tanabata 2919
Tell (Wilhelm) Festival 2940
Tell (William) Play 2941
Terminalia 2951
Thargelia 2964
Thesmophoria 2967
Tichborne Dole 2979
Tolling the Devil's Knell 2999
Tom Sawyer Days, National 3000
Trinidad and Tobago Carnival 3026
Tuan Wu 3039
Turon 3059
Twelfth Night 3064
Up-Helly-Aa 3091
Usokae 3098
Valdemar (King) Day 3106
Valentine's Day 3107
Vietnam Ancestors Death Anniversary 3144
Vinalia 3150
Vincy Carnival 3151
Vlöggelen 3163
Vulcanalia 3168
Walpurgis Night 3175
Wedding Festivities (Galicnik, Macedonia) 3198
Wianki Festival of Wreaths 3218
Xilonen, Festival of 3281
Xipe Totec, Festival of 3282

Numbers in the index refer to entry numbers, not page numbers

Food

Indexed below are festivals and events that revolve around the celebration or preparation of foods, the harvest or promotion of a particular crop, or a type of cuisine or style of cooking.

Alabama Blueberry Festival 0049
Alba White Truffle Fair 0054
Aspen Food and Wine Classic 0174
Bar-B-Q Festival, International 0245
Bite of Seattle 0323
Bocuse d'Or 0350
Boggy Bayou Mullet Festival 0354
Butter and Egg Days 0449
Castroville Artichoke Food and Wine Festival 0546
Central Maine Egg Festival 0552
Charleston Wine and Food Festival 0565
Cheese Week 0571
Cherry Festival, National 0579
Chilympiad 0602
Chinchilla Melon Festival 0605
Cranberry Day Festival 0712
Cranberry Harvest Festival 0713
Crawfish Festival (Breaux Bridge, Louisiana) 0716
Eldon Turkey Festival 0905
Elsie Dairy Festival 0919
Fellsmere Frog Leg Festival 0990
Galway Oyster Festival 1095
Georgia Peanut Festival 1117
Gilroy Garlic Festival 1138
Ginseng Festival 1140
Grands Crus, Weekend of the 1185
Great American Beer Festival 1190
Gwangiu Kimchi Festival 1247
Haro Wine Festival (Batalla de Vino) 1287
Hatch Chile Festival 1291
Hope Watermelon Festival 1361
Idaho Spud Day 1397
Isle of Eight Flags Shrimp Festival 1436
Isle of Wight Garlic Festival 1438
Killing the Pigs, Festival of 1552
Limassol Wine Festival 1679
Magnolia Blossom Festival 1738
Maine Lobster Festival 1747
Marino Wine Festival 1780

Marion County Ham Days 1781
Maryland Seafood Festival 1805
McClure Bean Soup Festival 1838
Mushroom Festival 1955
Napa Valley Mustard Festival 1974
New Orleans Wine and Food Experience 2020
Niiname-sai 2068
Okmulgee Pecan Festival 2118
Oregon Brewers Festival 2150
Paczki Day 2180
Peanut Festival, National 2233
Pickle Festival 2256
Pig's Face Feast 2260
San Francisco Street Food Festival 2487
Sani Gourmet 2512
Shrimp Festival, National 2612
Singapore Food Festival 2634
Sonoma Country Harvest Fair 2663
South Carolina Peach Festival 2672
Spamarama 2680
Stockton Asparagus Festival 2841
Taste of Chicago 2930
Terlingua Chili Cookoff 2950
Texas Citrus Fiesta 2954
Toronto Veg Food Fest 3011
Tunarama Festival 3047
Vermont Maple Festival 3130
Vidalia Onion Festival 3141
Vinegar Festival, International 3152
Watermelon Thump 3191
West Virginia Strawberry Festival 3203
Whole Enchilada Fiesta 3216
Wisconsin Cheese Curd Festival 3240
World's Biggest Fish Fry 3274
World's Largest Salmon Barbecue 3276
Wurstfest 3279
Yarmouth Clam Festival 3286
Yuma Lettuce Days 3303

Historic

Indexed below are festivals and events commemorating specific events from history, including battles, the birth dates of famous people, national independence, etc.

Abdu'l-Baha, Ascension of 0004
Abdullah's (King) Birthday in Jordan 0005
Acadian Festival 0012
Accession of H.H. Sheikh Zayed as Ruler of Abu Dhabi 0014
African Liberation Day 0030
African Methodist Quarterly Meeting Day 0031
Airing the Classics 0040
Aizu Byakko Matsuri 0042
Alabama Blueberry Festival 0049
Alamo Day 0051
Alaska Day 0053
Albania Independence Day 0055
Albania Republic Day 0056

Aldersgate Experience 0060
Alexandra Rose Day 0061
Algeria Independence Day 0062
Algeria National Day 0063
Allen (Richard), Birthday of 0072
Amazon & Galapagos Day 0080
Ambedkar Jayanti 0081
American West, Festival of the 0088
Amherstburg Heritage Homecoming 0090
Andersen (Hans Christian) Festival 0098
Andorra National Day 0099
Angola Independence Day 0103
Angola National Heroes Day 0104

Numbers in the index refer to entry numbers, not page numbers

Anthony (Susan B.) Day 0117
Antigua and Barbuda Independence Day 0118
Antigua Carnival 0119
Antigua National Heroes Day 0120
Anzac Day 0123
Aoi Matsuri 0124
Appleseed (Johnny) Festival 0130
Appleseed (Johnny), Birthday of 0129
Appomattox Day 0131
Arbaeen 0136
Arbaeen Pilgrimage 0137
Argentina Flag Day 0141
Argentina Independence Day 0142
Argentina National Day of Memory for Truth and Justice 0143
Argentine National Day 0144
Armed Forces Day (Egypt) 0147
Armenia Constitution Day 0149
Armenia Earthquake Memorial Day 0150
Armenia First Republic Day 0151
Armenia Independence Day 0152
Armenian Martyrs' Day 0154
Ataturk Remembrance 0183
Ati-Atihan Festival 0185
Audubon Day 0189
Australia Day 0193
Austria National Day 0195
Aviation Day 0199
Azerbaijan Day of the Martyrs 0207
Azerbaijan Independence Days 0208
Bab, Birth of the 0211
Bab, Declaration of the 0212
Bab, Martyrdom of the 0213
Baha'i Day of the Covenant 0220
Bahamas Emancipation Day 0221
Bahamas Independence Day 0222
Bahamas Labor Day 0223
Baha'u'llah, Ascension of 0224
Baha'u'llah, Birth of 0225
Bahia Independence Day 0226
Bahrain National Day 0227
Balfour Declaration Day 0230
Ball-Catching Festival 0231
Bangabandhu National Mourning Day 0237
Bangladesh Independence Day 0238
Bangladesh Victory Day 0239
Barbados Independence Day 0243
Barnum Festival 0247
Baron Bliss Day 0248
Barrow (Errol) Day 0249
Bastille Day 0255
Bastille Day (Kaplan, Louisiana) 0256
Bastille, Festival de la 0257
Bataan Day 0259
Bates (Daisy Gatson) Day 0260
Battle of Britain Day 0263
Battle of Flowers (Jersey, Channel Islands) 0264
Battle of Germantown, Reenactment of 0266
Battle of New Orleans Day 0267
Battle of Olustee Reenactment 0268
Beargrease (John) Sled Dog Marathon 0277
Beiderbecke (Bix) Memorial Jazz Festival 0279
Belarus Independence Day 0282
Belgium Independence Day 0285
Belize Independence Day 0286
Belize National Day 0287
Benin Independence Day 0291
Benin National Vodoun Day 0292
Bennington Battle Day 0293
Bill of Rights Day 0315

Billy the Kid Pageant 0318
Black Friday 0328
Black History Month 0330
Black Poetry Day 0333
Black St. Benito, Fiesta of the 0335
Blavatsky (Helena Petrovna), Death of 0339
Boganda Day 0353
Bok Kai Festival 0355
Bolivia Independence Day 0356
Bolshevik Revolution Day 0358
Bombing of Darwin, Anniversary of the 0360
Bonfire Night 0365
Bonifacio Day 0366
Boone (Daniel) Festival 0368
Borglum (Gutzon) Day 0369
Bosnia and Herzegovina Statehood Day 0372
Boston Massacre Day 0376
Botswana Independence Day 0379
Botswana Sir Seretse Khama Day 0380
Boun Phan Vet 0382
Boundary Walk 0383
Bowlegs (Billy) Festival 0385
Brady (Captain Samuel) Day 0389
Brazil Independence Day 0393
Brazil Proclamation of the Republic 0394
Bread and Roses Heritage Festival 0395
Bridge Crossing Jubilee 0397
Brunei National Day 0406
Buccaneer Days 0408
Buena Vista Logging Days 0412
Buffalo Soldiers Commemorations 0417
Bulgaria Day of Liberation from Ottoman Domination 0419
Bulgaria Independence Day 0420
Bulgarian Education and Culture Day 0421
Bunch (Madam Lou) Day 0427
Bunker Hill Day 0429
Burbank Day 0430
Burgoyne's (John) Surrender Day 0431
Burkina Faso Independence Day 0433
Burkina Faso Republic Day 0434
Burns (Robert) Night 0443
Burundi Independence Day 0445
Cabrillo Day and Festival 0454
California Gold Rush Day 0465
Cambodia Constitution Day 0467
Cambodia Independence Day 0468
Cambodia Queen Sihanouk's Birthday 0470
Camel and Ostrich Races, International 0473
Cameroon National Day 0475
Cameroon Youth Day 0476
Canada Day 0478
Canadian International Military Tattoo 0479
Canberra Day 0481
Cape Verde Independence Day 0493
Carnival of Blacks and Whites 0531
Carthaginians and Romans Fiesta 0540
Cassinga Day 0544
Cavalcata Sarda 0548
Cavalhadas 0549
Central African Republic Independence Day 0550
Chad Independence Day 0555
Chad Republic Day 0556
Chakri Day 0558
Chamizal Festival 0561
Chavez (Cesar) Day 0568
Cherokee National Holiday 0574
Cherokee Strip Day 0575
Chestertown Tea Party Festival 0580
Cheyenne Frontier Days 0582

Numbers in the index refer to entry numbers, not page numbers

Chief Joseph Days 0593
Chief Seattle Days 0594
Chile Battle of Iquique Day 0598
Chile National Unity Day 0599
Chilembwe (John) Day 0600
China National Days 0604
Chinhae Cherry Blossom Festival 0607
Choctaw Trail of Tears Walk 0612
Chongmyo Taeje 0613
Chulalongkorn Day 0645
Cinco de Mayo 0649
Citizenship Day 0653
Closing the Gates Ceremony 0657
Colombia Battle of Boyacá Day 0664
Colombia Independence Day 0665
Columbus Day 0666
Common Ridings Day 0668
Comoros Independence Day 0670
Concordia Day 0673
Confederados Reunion 0674
Confederate Memorial Day 0675
Confucius's Birthday 0676
Congo Independence Day Celebration 0677
Congo National Days 0678
Constitution Week 0680
Constitution Week (Mesa, Arizona) 0681
Coolidge (Calvin) Birthday Celebration 0683
Cosmonauts Day 0697
Costa Rica Annexation of Guanacaste Day 0698
Costa Rica Independence Day 0699
Côte d'Ivoire Independence Day 0701
Crandall (Prudence) Day 0714
Croatia Anti-Fascist Resistance Day 0721
Croatia Independence Day 0722
Croatia Statehood Day 0723
Croatia Victory and Homeland Thanksgiving Day 0724
Cromwell's Day 0726
Crossing of the Delaware 0730
Cuba Liberation Day 0734
Cuban Anniversary of the Beginning of the Wars
   of Independence 0735
Cup Match 0738
Cyprus Independence Day 0743
Czech Statehood Day 0745
Czechoslovak Independence Day 0746
Dahlonega Gold Rush Days 0749
Daimyo Gyoretsu 0751
Dalai Lama, Birthday of the 0753
Dancing Procession 0762
Data Ganj Baksh Death Festival 0766
Davis's (Jefferson) Birthday 0769
Days of '76 0771
D-Day 0776
De Diego (Jose) Day 0777
Defenders' Day 0782
Democratic People's Republic of Korea Founding Day 0784
Democratic Republic of Congo Independence Day 0785
Denmark Constitution Day 0786
Departure of the Continental Army 0788
Dicing for the Maid's Money Day 0805
Discovery Day 0812
Djibouti Independence Day 0815
Doctors' Day 0817
Doggett's Coat and Badge Race 0823
Dol Purnima 0825
Dominica Independence Day 0828
Dominican Republic Independence Day 0829
Dominican Republic Independence Restoration Day 0830
Dominican Republic Our Lady of Altagracia 0831

Dominican Republic Our Lady of Mercedes Day 0832
Double Tenth Day 0836
Douglass (Frederick) Day 0837
Duarte Day 0845
Durham Miners' Gala 0856
Dutch Liberation Day 0857
Earhart (Amelia) Festival 0859
East Timor Independence Day .0861
Easter (Egypt) 0867
Easter Fires 0881
Ecuador Independence Day 0887
Ecuadoran Civicism & National Unity Day 0888
Eddy (Mary Baker), Birthday of 0889
Edison (Thomas) Festival of Light 0892
Edison's (Thomas) Birthday 0893
Edmund Fitzgerald Anniversary 0894
Egypt Revolution Day 0896
El Salvador Independence Day .0904
Election of the Lord Mayor of London 0907
Election of the Mayor of Ock Street 0908
Elfreth's Alley Fete Day 0912
Elimination of Racial Discrimination, International
   Day for the 0915
Elizabeth II (Queen) Birthday .0917
Elvis International Tribute Week 0921
Emancipation Day (Canada) 0922
Emancipation Day (Hutchinson, Kansas) 0923
Emancipation Day (Tallahassee, Florida) 0924
Emancipation Day (United States) 0925
Emancipation Day (Washington, D.C.) 0926
Emancipation Day Festival 0927
Eo e Emalani i Alaka i Festival 0933
Equal Opportunity Day 0945
Equatorial Guinea Independence Day 0946
Erau Festival 0949
Eritrea Independence Day 0950
Eritrean Martyrs' Day 0951
Eritrean Start of the Armed Struggle Day 0952
Escalade 0955
Estonia Independence Day 0958
Estonia Restoration of Independence Day 0959
Estonia Victory Day 0960
Ethiopia National Day 0961
Ethiopia Patriots' Victory Day .0962
Ethiopia Victory of Adwa Commemoration Day 0963
Evacuation Day 0968
Evamelunga 0969
Exaltation of the Cross, Feast of the 0970
Fawkes (Guy) Day 0988
Fenkil Day 0991
Festivities for the Day of National Rebellion 1001
Fiesta sa EDSA 1005
Fiestas Patrias 1006
Fiji Day 1009
Fiji Ratu Sir Lala Sukuna Day .1011
Finland Independence Day 1014
Firstborn, Fast of the 1024
Flag Day 1027
Flemish Community, Feast Day of the 1037
Float Festival 1039
Floating Lantern Ceremony 1040
Florida Heritage Festival 1047
Forefathers' Day 1056
Forgiveness, Feast of 1057
Forty Martyrs' Day 1059
Fossey (Dian) Day 1060
Foster (Stephen) Memorial Day 1061
Founder's Day 1062
Four an' Twenty Day 1063

Numbers in the index refer to entry numbers, not page numbers

Four Chaplains Day 1064
Fourth of July 1065
Fourth of July (Denmark) 1066
Fox (George), Death of 1067
Fox Hill Festival 1068
Frankenmuth Bavarian Festival 1070
Franklin's (Benjamin) Birthday 1072
Freedom Day, National 1075
Freedom Festival, International 1076
French Community, Feast Day of the 1079
Gable (Clark) Birthday Celebration 1088
Gabon Independence Day 1089
Gambia Independence Day 1096
Gambia Revolution Day 1097
Gandhi Jayanti 1098
Garifuna Settlement Day 1104
Gasparilla Pirate Festival 1107
Gaspee Days 1108
Gedaliah, Fast of 1111
General Clinton Canoe Regatta 1113
Georgia Day 1114
Georgia Harmony Jubilee 1115
Georgia Independence Day 1116
German Unification Day 1120
German-American Day 1121
Gettysburg Civil War Heritage Days 1124
Gettysburg Day 1125
Ghana Republic Day 1127
Giants, Festival of the (Belgium) 1134
Gibraltar National Day 1135
Gift of the Waters Pageant 1136
Gio to Hung Vuong Day 1141
Gion Matsuri 1143
Girl Scout Day 1144
Gold Discovery Days 1154
Golden Days 1157
Golden Spike Anniversary 1162
Goombay! 1171
Grand Haven Coast Guard Festival 1178
Great American Brass Band Festival 1191
Great Battle of Hansan Festival 1195
Great Locomotive Chase Festival 1198
Great Wardmote of the Woodmen of Arden 1204
Greece Independence Day 1207
Greek Cypriot National Day 1208
Green March Day 1211
Green River Rendezvous 1212
Greenery Day 1213
Greenville Treaty Camporee 1215
Greenwood (Chester) Day 1216
Grenada Independence Day 1217
Grenada Thanksgiving Day 1218
Guatemala Army Day 1226
Guatemala Independence Day 1227
Guatemala Revolution Day 1228
Guinea Independence Day 1232
Guinea Second Republic Day 1233
Guinea-Bissau and Cape Verde National Heroes' Day 1234
Guinea-Bissau Independence Day 1235
Guru Parab 1240
Guru Purnima 1241
Gustavus Adolphus Day 1244
Guyana Independence Day 1246
Gyangzê Horse-Racing Festival 1249
Haile Selassie's Birthday 1253
Haile Selassie's Coronation Day 1254
Haiti Ancestors' Day 1255
Haiti Anniversary of the Death of Jean-Jacques Dessalines ... 1256
Haiti Battle of Vertières' Day 1257

Haiti Flag and University Day 1258
Haiti Independence Day 1259
Halifax Day 1266
Handy (W. C.) Music Festival 1278
Han'gul Day 1279
Hanukkah 1280
Harlem Week 1286
Haxey Hood Game 1293
Hemingway (Ernest) Days Festival 1299
Hemis Festival 1300
Heritage Holidays 1302
Hippokrateia Festival 1312
Hiroshima Peace Ceremony 1313
Historical Regatta 1315
Ho Chi Minh's Birthday 1318
Holetown Festival 1326
Holocaust Memorial Day 1331
Holocaust Remembrance Day, International 1332
Holy Blood, Procession of the 1333
Holy Queen Isabel, Festival of the 1339
Holy Thursday 1342
Honduras Independence Day 1354
Honduras Soldiers' Day 1355
Hong Kong Special Administrative Region
    Establishment Day 1358
Hooverfest 1360
Hosay Festival 1368
Hospital Week, National 1370
Hostos Day 1371
Hungary Republic Day 1380
Hungary Revolution and Independence Day 1381
Hunters' Moon, Feast of the 1382
Hus (Jan) Day 1386
Iceland Independence Day 1390
Iditarod Trail Sled Dog Race 1399
Idlewild Jazz Festival 1400
Imam Ali's Birthday 1403
Imam Ali's Martyrdom, Anniversary of 1404
Imam Sadiq's Martyrdom, Anniversary of 1405
Inconfidência Week 1415
Independence of Cartagena City Day 1416
India Republic Day 1417
Indian Arrival Day 1418
Indonesia Independence Day 1421
Iqbal (Muhammad), Birthday of 1426
Iran Islamic Republic Day 1427
Iran Petroleum Nationalization Anniversary 1428
Iran Victory Day of the Iranian Revolution 1429
Irrigation Festival 1433
Israel Independence Day 1440
Isthmian Games 1442
Italian Heritage Parade 1445
Italy Liberation Day 1446
Ivy Day 1448
Jackson's (Andrew) Birthday 1452
Jamaica Independence Day 1457
Jamaica National Heroes Day 1458
Jamestown Day 1459
Jamhuri 1460
Jefferson's (Thomas) Birthday 1471
Jeshn 1474
Jidai Matsuri 1478
Johnson (Samuel) Commemoration 1481
Jordan Independence Day 1483
Jorvik Viking Festival 1485
Joust of the Quintain 1486
Jubilee Days Festival 1490
Juliana's (Queen) Birthday 1492
Juneteenth 1493

Numbers in the index refer to entry numbers, not page numbers

Kalevala Day 1507
Kamehameha (King) Celebration 1511
Kartini Day 1518
Keller (Helen) Festival 1532
Kelly (Emmett) Clown Festival 1533
Kent State Memorial Day 1535
Kenya Madaraka Day 1537
Kenya Mashujaa Day (Heroes Day) 1538
Kenya Moi Day 1539
Kenya Skydive Boogie 1540
Khomeini (Ayatollah), Death Anniversary of 1545
Khordad 15 Revolt, Anniversary of the 1546
Khordad Sal 1547
Kim Il-Sung, Birthday of 1553
Kim Jong-Il, Birthday of 1554
Kinderzeche 1555
King (Martin Luther, Jr.) Drum Major for Justice
    Parade, Battle of the Bands & Drum Line Extravaganza,
    National 1557
King (Martin Luther, Jr.), Birthday 1556
King's Day (Koningsdag) 1558
Kingdom Days 1559
King's Birthday (Belgium) 1560
King's Birthday (Denmark) 1561
King's Birthday (Lesotho) 1562
King's Birthday (Thailand) 1563
Kiribati Independence Day 1567
Klondike Days Exposition 1574
Klondike Gold Discovery Day 1575
Korea Liberation Day 1585
Korean War Veterans Armistice Day, National 1587
Kosovo Independence Day 1588
Kristallnacht 1589
Kuhio (Prince) Day 1592
Kunta Kinte Heritage Festival 1594
Kurijmoj 1597
Kuwait Liberation Day 1600
Kuwait National Day 1601
Kyrgyz Independence Day 1607
La Paz Day 1608
LaborFest 1611
Lag ba-Omer 1616
Lammas Fair 1620
Lamp Nights 1621
Landing of d'Iberville 1623
Landshut Wedding 1625
Lanimer Festival 1626
Latter-Day Saints, Founding of the Church of 1636
Latvia Independence Day 1637
Leaders of the Bulgarian National Revival Day 1645
Lebanon National Day 1647
Lebanon Resistance and Liberation Day 1648
Lee (Ann) Birthday 1649
Lee (Robert E.) Day 1650
Leiden Day 1653
Leif Erikson Day 1654
Lesotho Independence Day 1659
Lewis and Clark Festival 1660
Liberia Flag Day 1664
Liberia Independence Day 1665
Liberia National Redemption Day 1666
Liberia National Unification Day 1667
Liberian President W. V. S. Tubman's Birthday 1669
Libya Declaration of Jamahiriya Day 1671
Libya Revolution Day 1672
Lincoln's (Abraham) Birthday 1680
Lithuania Independence Day 1684
Lithuania Restoration of Statehood Day 1685
Lithuania State Day 1686
Little Big Horn Days 1687

Living Chess Game 1689
Long (Huey P.) Day 1697
Looking Glass Powwow 1698
Lord Mayor's Show 1699
Los Isleños Fiesta 1701
Luxembourg National Day 1716
Maafa Commemoration 1717
MacArthur (Douglas) Day 1719
Macedonian Ilinden 1720
Macedonian Independence Day 1721
Macedonian National Uprising Day 1722
Madagascar Independence Day 1725
Madagascar Martyrs' Day 1726
Magellan (Ferdinand) Day 1731
Maghi 1736
Magna Carta Day 1737
Mahavira Jayanti 1740
Maimona 1746
Maine Memorial Day 1748
Malawi Freedom Day 1750
Malawi Martyrs' Day 1751
Malawi Republic Day 1752
Malcolm X's Birthday 1754
Maldives Independence Day 1756
Mali Independence Day 1758
Mallard Ceremony 1759
Malta Freedom Day 1760
Malta Independence Day 1761
Malta Republic Day 1762
Malta Sette Guigno 1763
Mardi Gras 1774
Maritime Day, National 1783
Maroon Festival 1786
Marshall Islands Constitution Day 1789
Marshall Islands President's Day 1794
Martinmas 1796
Martinmas (Ireland) 1797
Martinsfest 1798
Martyrdom of Joseph and Hyrum Smith 1799
Martyrs' Day (Lebanon) 1800
Martyrs of North America, Feast of the 1801
Maryland Day 1803
Mauritania Independence Day 1820
Mauritius Independence Day 1821
McClure Bean Soup Festival 1838
Mecklenburg Independence Day 1839
Medora Musical 1840
Meiji Setsu 1843
Meistertrunk Pageant 1844
Meitlisonntag 1845
Memorial Day Luminaria at Fredericksburg
    National Cemetery 1851
Merdeka Day 1856
Merrie Monarch Festival 1858
Mexico Festival of Independence 1862
Meyboom 1863
Miami/Bahamas Goombay Festival 1864
Mid-Autumn Festival (Singapore) 1871
Milk (Harvey) Day 1881
Moldova Independence Day 1901
Moldovan Language Day 1903
Mollyockett Day 1904
Moon Day 1913
Moore (Billy) Days 1914
Moors and Christians Fiesta 1915
Moreska Sword Dance 1918
Mormon Pioneer Day 1921
Morocco Independence Day 1922
Moro-Moro Play 1923

Numbers in the index refer to entry numbers, not page numbers

Moshoeshoe's Day 1926
Mountain Man Rendezvous 1938
Mozambique Independence Day 1943
Mozambique Peace Day 1945
Mozart (Wolfgang Amadeus), Birthday of 1946
Muñoz-Rivera Day 1953
Myanmar Armed Forces Day 1958
Myanmar Independence Day 1959
Myanmar Martyrs' Day 1960
Myanmar Union Day 1962
Nabekamuri Matsuri 1969
Namibia Heroes Day 1972
Napoleon's Day 1975
NASA Day of Remembrance 1980
Natal Day in Nova Scotia 1982
Native Islander Gullah Celebration 1989
Nativity of the Blessed Virgin Mary, Feast of the 1990
Nauru Independence Day 1994
NEBRASKAland DAYS 2002
Nebuta Matsuri 2003
Neighbor Day 2004
Nepal Democracy Day 2008
Nepal Republic Day 2009
New Church Day 2014
New Deal Festival 2015
Newfoundland Discovery Day 2049
Ngmayem Festival 2056
Nicaragua Battle of San Jacinto Day 2060
Nicaragua Independence Day 2061
Nicodemus Emancipation and Homecoming Celebration 2063
Niger Republic Day 2064
Nigeria National Day 2065
Night Watch 2067
Nino Fidencio Festival 2072
Niue Peniamina Gospel Day 2076
Nomaoi Matsuri 2080
North Korea Victory Day 2088
Norway Constitution Day 2092
Nunavut Day 2096
Oakley (Annie) Festival 2102
Oath Monday 2103
October War of Liberation Anniversary 2110
Odwira 2114
Ohio River Sternwheel Festival 2115
Oklahoma Day 2116
Oklahoma Historical Day 2117
Oktoberfest 2120
Okunchi Matsuri 2121
Oman National Day 2136
Ommegang 2140
Open Marathon, International 2145
Opening of the Underground Caves Day 2146
Orange Day 2148
Original Gullah Festival 2153
Our Lady of Fátima Day 2161
Oxi Day 2176
Pack Monday Fair 2179
Pageant of the Golden Tree 2182
Paine (Thomas) Day 2183
Pakistan Day 2185
Pakistan Independence Day 2186
Pakistan Kashmir Solidarity Day 2187
Palau Independence Day 2188
Palio of the Goose and River Festival 2190
Pan American Day 2198
Panama Independence Days 2201
Papua New Guinea Independence Day 2207
Paraguay Independence Day 2209
Parks (Rosa) Day 2217

Pascua Florida Day 2223
Passover 2225
Patriot Day 2226
Patriots' Day 2227
Payment of Quit Rent 2230
Pearl Harbor Day 2234
Pennsylvania Day 2238
People's Army of North Korea, Founding of the 2241
Peppercorn Ceremony 2242
Peru Battle of Angamos 2246
Peru Independence Day 2247
Philippines Independence Day 2253
Pig's Face Feast 2260
Pike Festival, National 2262
Pilgrim Progress Pageant 2264
Pilgrim Thanksgiving Day (Plymouth, Massachusetts) 2265
Pilgrimage to Moulay Idriss 2271
Pilgrimage to the Tomb of Sunan Bayat 2275
Pine Battle of Vinuesa 2276
Pirates Week 2279
Plague Sunday 2281
Planting the Penny Hedge 2282
Polish Constitution Day 2289
Polish Independence Day 2290
Polish Liberation Day 2291
Polish Solidarity Day 2292
Polytechneio Day 2294
Portugal Liberation Day 2299
Portugal National Day 2300
Portugal Republic Day 2301
Portugal Restoration of Independence Day 2302
Primrose Day 2318
Prince's Birthday in Liechtenstein 2319
Puerto Rico Constitution Day 2324
Pulaski Day 2325
Purims, Special 2331
Purple Heart Day 2332
Pythian Games 2335
Qatar Independence Day 2336
Quadrilles of San Martin 2340
Queen's Birthday (Thailand) 2346
Queen's Day (England) 2347
Race of the Ceri 2353
Race Relations Sunday 2354
Raid on Redding Ridge 2359
Ratification Day 2372
Reconciliation Week, National 2378
Reconciliation, Day of 2377
Redentore, Festa del 2382
Reformation Day 2385
Regatta of the Great Maritime Republics 2386
Remembrance Day 2390
Repudiation Day 2392
Restoration of Independence of the Republic of Latvia 2393
Return Day 2395
Rhode Island Independence Day 2398
Ridvan, Feast of 2401
Riley (James Whitcomb) Festival 2402
River Kwai Bridge Week 2406
Rizal Day 2408
Roberts's (Joseph Jenkins) Birthday 2410
Robinson (Jackie) Day 2414
Rodgers (Jimmie) Festival 2417
Rogers (Roy) Festival 2419
Rogers (Will) Day 2420
Romania National Day 2423
Roosevelt (Franklin D.) Day 2425
Roots Festival 2426
Rose of Tralee Beauty Contest 2432

Numbers in the index refer to entry numbers, not page numbers

Roswell UFO Festival 2434
Route 66 Festival 2437
Royal Brunei Armed Forces Day 2439
Rumi Festival 2445
Runeberg (Johan Ludvig), Birthday of 2446
Rwanda Independence Day 2451
Rwanda Liberation Day 2452
Rwanda National Heroes' Day 2453
Saba Saba Day 2454
Sabbath of Rabbi Isaac Mayer Wise 2457
Saigon Liberation Day 2464
Salvation Army Founder's Day 2470
Samil-jol 2475
Samoa Independence Day 2476
San Antonio, Fiesta 2478
San Gennaro, Feast of 2489
San Isidro of Seville, Feast of 2493
San Isidro the Farmer, Feast of 2494
San Jacinto Day 2495
San Marino Anniversary of the Arengo 2501
San Marino Liberation Day 2503
San Martín Day 2504
Sandburg Days Festival 2508
Sanghamita Day 2510
Santa Fe, Fiesta de 2517
Santamaría (Juan) Day 2523
São Tomé and Principe National Independence Day 2528
Satchmo SummerFest 2534
Schwenkfelder Thanksgiving 2545
Senegal Independence Day 2564
Serbia Statehood Day of the Republic 2568
Seton (Mother) Day 2570
Seward's Day 2574
Seychelles Independence Day 2575
Seychelles Liberation Day 2576
Seychelles National Day 2577
Shah Abdul Latif Death Festival 2580
Shaheed Day 2581
Shakespeare's (William) Birthday 2585
Shankaracharya Jayanti 2590
Shick-Shack Day 2601
Shilla (Silla) Cultural Festival 2603
Shinju Matsuri Festival 2605
Siaosi Tupou I (King) Day 2623
Sierra Leone Independence Day 2625
Sihanouk (King) Commemoration Day 2627
Silent Night, Holy Night Celebration 2629
Sinai Liberation Day 2633
Singapore National Day 2635
Sinjska Alka 2637
Slovak Republic Independence Day 2648
Slovenia National Day 2649
Solomon Islands Independence Day 2659
Somalia Independence Day 2660
Song of Hiawatha Pageant 2661
South Africa Freedom Day 2666
South Africa Republic Day 2669
South Africa Youth Day 2671
South Korea Constitution Day 2673
South Korea Memorial Day 2674
South Sudan Independence Day 2675
Spiritual Baptist (Shouters) Liberation Day 2685
Sri Lanka National Day 2693
St. Agatha Festival 2694
St. Agnes's Eve 2695
St. Alban's Day 2696
St. Andrew's Day 2697
St. Anthony of Padua, Feast of 2700
St. Anthony the Abbot, Feast of 2701

St. Augustine of Hippo, Feast of 2702
St. Basil, Feast of 2706
St. Blaise's Day 2707
St. Brendan's Day 2708
St. Bridget's Day 2709
St. Charlemagne's Day 2713
St. Charles's Day 2714
St. Christopher's Day 2715
St. Clare of Assisi, Feast of 2716
St. Columba's Day 2717
St. David's Day 2719
St. Demetrius's Day 2720
St. Dunstan's Day 2723
St. Elizabeth Ann Seton, Feast of 2725
St. Elmo's Day 2726
St. Evermaire, Game of 2727
St. Frances Cabrini, Feast of 2728
St. Frances of Rome, Feast of 2729
St. Francis of Assisi, Feast of 2730
St. George's Day 2733
St. Gregory's Day 2737
St. Gudula's Day 2738
St. Herman Pilgrimage 2740
St. Hilary's Day 2741
St. Hubert de Liège, Feast of 2742
St. Ignatius Loyola, Feast of 2743
St. James's Day 2745
St. Joan of Arc, Feast Day of 2746
St. John the Evangelist's Day 2749
St. John's Day 2751
St. Jude's Day 2763
St. Kitts and Nevis Independence Day 2764
St. Knut's Day 2766
St. Leopold's Day 2768
St. Lucia Independence Day 2769
St. Marinus Day 2771
St. Mark's Day 2773
St. Martha's Day 2777
St. Médardus's Day 2783
St. Mennas's Day 2784
St. Modesto's Day 2786
St. Nichiren's Pardon, Festival of 2787
St. Nicholas's Day 2788
St. Nicholas's Day (Italy) 2790
St. Olav's Day 2791
St. Patrick's Day 2792
St. Patrick's Day Encampment 2794
St. Paul, Feast of the Conversion of 2796
St. Paul's Shipwreck, Feast of 2798
St. Placidus Festival 2802
St. Polycarp's Day 2803
St. Roch's Day 2805
St. Rose of Lima's Day 2806
St. Sava's Day 2808
St. Spyridon (Spiridion) Day 2810
St. Stephen's Day 2811
St. Stephen's Day (Hungary) 2812
St. Swithin's Day 2813
St. Sylvester's Day 2814
St. Tammany's Day 2816
St. Teresa's Day 2817
St. Thomas's Day 2818
St. Thorlak's Day 2819
St. Tryphon's Day (Montenegro and Bulgaria) 2820
St. Vaclav's Day 2822
St. Vincent and the Grenadines Independence
    and Thanksgiving Day 2823
St. Vincent and the Grenadines National Heroes Day 2824
St. Vincent's Day 2825

Numbers in the index refer to entry numbers, not page numbers

Stanton (Elizabeth Cady) Day 2829
State Opening of Parliament 2832
Steinbeck (John) Festival 2834
Steuben (Baron Friedrich) Day 2836
Stonewall Rebellion, Anniversary of the 2842
Strawberry Festival 2847
Sts. Cosmas and Damian Day 2849
Students' Fight for Freedom and Democracy, Day of 2851
Sudan Independence Day 2855
Sun Yat-sen, Birthday of 2865
Sunday of Orthodoxy 2867
Sunday of St. Gregory Palamas 2868
Sunday of St. John Climacos 2869
Suriname Independence Day 2876
Swan Upping 2883
Swaziland Independence Day 2885
Swedish Flag Day 2886
Swiss National Day 2890
Syria Martyrs' Day 2896
Syria National Day 2897
Syttende Mai Fest 2898
Ta Mo's Day 2901
Tagore (Rabindranath), Birthday of 2905
Taiiku-no-Hi 2906
Taiwan Armed Forces Day 2908
Taiwan Peace Memorial Day 2909
Tajikistan Day of National Unity 2910
Tajikistan Independence Day 2911
Také-no-Nobori 2914
Tammuz, Fast of the 17th of 2918
Tanzania Independence Day 2925
Tanzania Union Day 2926
Taungbyon Spirit Festival 2933
Teachers' Day in the Czech Republic 2936
Tenjin Matsuri 2948
Texas Independence Day 2956
Thailand Constitution Day 2959
Thailand Coronation Day 2960
Thanksgiving 2963
Thjodhatid 2972
Tiananmen Square Anniversary 2978
Tichborne Dole 2979
Time Observance Day 2981
Timor Santa Cruz Massacre Day 2982
Timor-Leste Anniversary of the Indonesian Invasion 2983
Togo Independence Day 2993
Togo National Liberation Day 2994
Tom Sawyer Days, National 3000
Tonga Emancipation Day 3002
Tonga Heilala Festival 3003
Tonga National Day 3004
Torta dei Fieschi 3012
Toshogu Haru-No-Taisai 3013
Trafalgar Day 3017
Transfer Day 3018
Trial of Louis Riel 3021
Tribute of the Three Cows 3023
Trinidad and Tobago Emancipation Day 3027
Trinidad and Tobago Independence Day 3029
Trinidad and Tobago Republic Day 3030
Tu Bishvat 3038
Tuan Wu 3039
Tulsidas Jayanti 3046
Tunisia Independence Day 3048
Tunisia Republic Day 3049
Tunisia Revolution and Youth Day 3050
Tupou VI (King), Birthday of 3051
Turkey Republic Day 3054
Turkey Victory Day 3055

Turkmenistan Independence Day 3057
Tuvalu Independence Day 3062
Twelfth Imam, Birthday of the 3063
Tynwald Ceremony 3067
Uesugi Matsuri 3069
Uganda Independence Day 3070
Uganda Liberation Day 3071
Uganda Martyrs Day 3072
Uganda National Heroes Day 3073
Ukraine Constitution Day 3075
Ukraine Independence Day 3076
Ukraine Unification Day 3077
United Arab Emirates National Day 3083
United Nations Day 3084
Urs Ajmer Sharif 3093
Urs of Baba Farid Shakar Ganj 3094
Urs of Jelaluddin al-Rumi 3095
Uruguay Constitution Oath Taking Day 3096
Uruguay Independence Day 3097
Uzbekistan Constitution Day 3102
Uzbekistan Independence Day 3103
Vaisakh 3104
Valdemar (King) Day 3106
Valley of the Moon Vintage Festival 3108
Vanuatu Father Walter Lini Day 3114
Vanuatu Independence Day 3115
Vanuatu Unity Day 3116
Venezuela Battle of Carabobo Day 3125
Venezuela Independence Day 3126
Verrazano (Giovanni da) Day 3133
Vesak 3134
Veterans Day 3135
Veterans Day (Emporia, Kansas) 3136
Victory Day 3139
Victory Day (Russia) 3140
Vietnam National Day 3145
Vietnam Veterans Memorial Anniversary 3146
Viking Festival 3148
Vintners' Procession 3155
Virgen de Los Angeles Day 3156
V-J Day 3162
Volksfest 3165
Waitangi Day 3170
Wakakusayama Yaki 3171
Walking Days 3172
Walpurgis Night 3175
Washington's (George) Birthday 3184
Washington's (George) Birthday Celebration
    (Alexandria, Virginia) 3185
Washington's (George) Birthday Celebration
    (Los Dos Laredos) 3186
West Virginia Day 3201
Williams (Roger) Day 3228
Williams (Tennessee) New Orleans Literary Festival 3229
Wolfe (Thomas) Festival 3243
Workers' Party of North Korea, Founding of the 3249
World Space Week 3271
Wright Brothers Day 3278
Wurstfest 3279
Yemen Independence and National Days 3290
Yemen Revolution Days 3291
Yom Yerushalayim 3294
Yorktown Day 3296
Young's Birthday 3297
Zambia Heroes Day 3305
Zambia Independence Day 3306
Zambia Unity Day 3307
Zanzibar Revolution Day 3309
Zimbabwe Heroes' Day 3312
Zimbabwe Independence Day 3313
Zimbabwe National Unity Day 3314

Numbers in the index refer to entry numbers, not page numbers

Promotional

Indexed below are festivals and events that promote everything from city, state, and national pride to agricultural products; from activities (quilting, rodeo) to social values (conservation, harmony among peoples).

Abbotsford International Air Show 0003
Abha Festival 0006
Aboriginal Day, National 0008
Academy Awards Ceremony 0010
Administrative Professionals Week 0021
Africa Industrialization Day 0026
Africa Malaria Day 0027
African American Day Parade 0028
African American Women in Cinema International
    Film Festival 0029
African World Festival 0032
African/Caribbean International Festival of Life 0033
African-American Music Appreciation Month 0034
Agriculture Fair at Santarem, National 0036
AirVenture 0041
Ak-Sar-Ben Livestock Exposition and Rodeo 0044
Al Bustan International Festival of Music and the Arts 0047
Al Hareed Festival 0048
Alabama Blueberry Festival 0049
Alba White Truffle Fair 0054
Alberta Heritage Day 0057
Aloha Festivals 0075
Alpenfest 0077
Amazon & Galapagos Day 0080
American Indian Heritage Month 0085
American Royal Livestock, Horse Show and Rodeo 0086
American Solar Challenge 0087
American West, Festival of the 0088
Angkor Photography Festival 0102
Annapolis Valley Apple Blossom Festival 0110
Annual Session of the National Baptist Convention, USA 0113
Antigua National Heroes Day 0120
Antique and Classic Boat Rendezvous 0122
Arab International Festival 0133
Arabic Music Festival 0134
Arbor Day 0138
Argentina Flag Day 0141
Armed Forces Day (United States) 0148
Armenia Constitution Day 0149
Armenia Motherhood and Beauty Day 0153
Art Deco Weekend 0159
Artcar Fest 0161
Arts and Crafts Fair, International 0163
Asanha Bucha Day 0165
Aspen Food and Wine Classic 0174
Atlanta Pride Festival 0187
Audubon Day 0189
Auntie Litter's Annual Earth Day Parade and Celebration 0190
Austen (Jane) Festival 0191
Author's Day, National 0196
Aviation Day 0199
Baby Parade 0215
Bad Durkheim Wurstmarkt 0218
Bahamas Labor Day 0223
Ballet Festival of Miami, International 0232
Baltic-Nordic Harmonica Festival 0235
Bard of Armagh Festival of Humorous Verse 0246
Barnum Festival 0247
Bascarsija Nights 0251
Basset Hound Games 0254
Bat Flight Breakfast 0258
Battle of Flowers (Vienna, Austria) 0265

Battle of Olustee Reenactment 0268
Be Kind to Animals Week 0274
Beijing Opera Festival 0280
Benin National Vodoun Day 0292
Bermuda Festival of the Performing Arts 0303
Bible Week, National 0310
Big Iron Farm Show 0312
Billboard Latin Music Awards 0316
Biological Diversity, International Day for 0319
Bishwa Ijtema 0321
Bite of Seattle 0323
Black and White Ball 0324
Black Poetry Day 0333
Black Storytelling Festival and Conference,
    National 0336
Blackbeard Pirate Festival 0337
Blessing of the Bikes 0341
Bloomsday 0345
Boggy Bayou Mullet Festival 0354
Bologna Festival 0357
Boryeong Mud Festival 0371
Boy Scouts' Day 0387
Bread and Roses Heritage Festival 0395
British Columbia Day 0401
Broadstairs Dickens Festival 0403
Buffalo Soldiers Commemorations 0417
Bull Durham Blues Festival 0422
Burning of the Ribbons 0437
Busan Sea Festival 0447
Butter and Egg Days 0449
Calgary International Children's Festival 0461
Cali Fair 0462
Calico Pitchin', Cookin', and Spittin' Hullabaloo 0463
California Avocado Festival 0464
Cambodia National Culture Day 0469
Camp Fire Founders' Day 0477
Canadian International Military Tattoo 0479
Canadian National Exhibition 0480
Candy Dance Arts and Crafts Faire 0487
Cannes Film Festival 0488
Cannes Shopping Festival 0489
Caribbean Festival 0498
Carifest 0501
Carinthian Summer Music Festival 0503
Carnival of Flowers 0532
Carnival of the Devil 0535
Carriacou Parang Festival 0538
Casa Grande Cowboy Days & O'odham Tash 0542
Castroville Artichoke Food and Wine Festival 0546
Central Maine Egg Festival 0552
Charleston Wine and Food Festival 0565
Chelsea Flower Show 0572
Cherry Festival, National 0579
Chicago Dancing Festival 0586
Chicago Gospel Music Festival 0587
Children's Book Day, International 0596
Chilympiad 0602
China Luoyang Peony Cultural Festival 0603
Chinchilla Melon Festival 0605
Chitlin' Strut 0609
Christkindlesmarkt 0615
Christmas Bird Count 0628

Numbers in the index refer to entry numbers, not page numbers

Christmas Eve Bonfires 0639
Circus Festival of Tomorrow, International
    (Festival Mondial du Cirque de Demain) 0651
Clown Festival, International 0658
Cooperatives, International Day of 0684
Corn Palace Festival 0687
Costa Rica National Arts Festival 0700
Country Christmas Lighted Farm Implement Parade 0704
Country Music Fan Fair, International 0706
Cow Parade 0709
Cowboy Poetry Gathering, National 0710
Craftsmen's Fair 0711
Cranberry Harvest Festival 0713
Crazy Horse Ride and Veterans' Powwow 0717
Cruft's Dog Show 0733
Czech Festival, National 0744
Dally in the Alley 0754
DanceAfrica 0760
Dayton Air Show 0772
DC Black Pride Festival 0774
DC Caribbean Carnival 0775
Denver Black Arts Festival 0787
Detroit International Jazz Festival 0790
Diamond Head Crater Celebration 0804
Dinosaur Days 0807
Disabled Persons, International Day of 0810
Disarmament Week 0811
Dodge (Geraldine R.) Poetry Festival 0821
Dodge City Days 0819
Dogwood Festival 0824
Doo Dah Parade 0834
Down Home Family Reunion 0838
Downtown Hoedown 0839
Dubrovnik Summer Festival 0848
Dukang Festival 0849
Dundee International Guitar Festival 0852
Durham Miners' Gala 0856
Earth Day 0860
Eastern States Exposition 0884
Ecuadoran Civicism & National Unity Day 0888
El Salvador del Mundo, Festival of 0903
Eldon Turkey Festival 0905
Elephant Festival 0909
Elimination of Racial Discrimination, International
    Day for the 0915
Elsie Dairy Festival 0919
Emancipation Day (Washington, D.C.) 0926
Enescu (George) Festival 0930
Eradication of Poverty, International Day for the 0948
Essence Festival 0957
Faces Etnofestival 0973
Family Month, National 0977
Fast for a World Harvest 0983
Father's Day 0986
FeatherFest 0989
Fes Festival of World Sacred Music 0993
Festival International des Arts de la Marionette à
    Saguenay 0999
Festivus 1002
Fiji Day 1009
Fiji National Youth Day 1010
Fiji Ratu Sir Lala Sukuna Day 1011
Fillmore Jazz Festival 1012
Fire Festivals 1016
Fire Prevention Week, National 1017
Fisher Poets Gathering 1025
Fleet Week (Hampton Roads, Virginia) 1032
Fleet Week (New York City) 1033
Fleet Week (San Diego, California) 1034

Fleet Week (San Francisco, California) 1035
Flemington Fair 1036
Flemish Community, Feast Day of the 1037
Floralies 1042
Floriade 1046
Flower Festivals of St. Rose and St. Margaret Mary
    Alacoque 1049
Fossey (Dian) Day 1060
Frankenmuth Bavarian Festival 1070
Frankfurt Book Fair 1071
Fraternal Order of Real Bearded Santas Reunion and
    Luncheon 1073
French Community, Feast Day of the 1079
Fur Trade Days 1085
Gable (Clark) Birthday Celebration 1088
Galway Oyster Festival 1095
Gambia Revolution Day 1097
Garifuna Settlement Day 1104
Gay Games 1110
Georgia Peanut Festival 1117
Geranium Day 1119
German-American Volksfest 1122
German-Speaking Community, Feast Day of the 1123
Ghana Farmers' Day 1126
Ghanafest 1128
Gibraltar National Day 1135
Gilroy Garlic Festival 1138
Ginseng Festival 1140
Gold Cup Parade 1153
Gold Star Mother's Day 1155
Goombay! 1171
Gorilla Naming Ceremony 1172
Grand Canyon Music Festival 1177
Grand Magal of Shaykh Amadou Bamba 1179
Grandparents' Day 1184
Grands Crus, Weekend of the 1185
Grape Festival 1187
Great American Beer Festival 1190
Great American Smokeout 1193
Great Backyard Bird Count 1194
Great Battle of Hansan Festival 1195
Great Montana Sheep Drive 1199
Great Moonbuggy Race 1200
Green Festivals 1209
Guatemala Army Day 1226
Guatemala Revolution Day 1228
Guinea Second Republic Day 1233
Gwangiu Kimchi Festival 1247
Haiti Flag and University Day 1258
Hala Festival 1262
Half Moon Bay Art and Pumpkin Festival 1265
Hard Crab Derby, National 1283
Harlem Week 1286
Haro Wine Festival (Batalla de Vino) 1287
Hatch Chile Festival 1291
Hatfield and McCoy Reunion Festival and Marathon 1292
Hayti Heritage Film Festival 1295
Hispanic Heritage Month 1314
Holetown Festival 1326
Hollerin' Contest, National 1329
Holy Prophet and the Martyrdom of Imam Hasan,
    Death Anniversary of the 1338
Homeless Persons' Remembrance Day, National 1351
Honduras Soldiers' Day 1355
Hope Watermelon Festival 1361
Hospital Week, National 1370
Howl! Festival 1375
Human Rights Day, International 1376
Hurston (Zora Neale) Festival of the Arts and Humanities 1385

Numbers in the index refer to entry numbers, not page numbers

Idaho Spud Day 1397
Idlewild Jazz Festival 1400
Iowa State Fair 1425
Iran Islamic Republic Day 1427
Iran Petroleum Nationalization Anniversary 1428
Iris Fest 1430
Islamic Festival 1434
Isle of Eight Flags Shrimp Festival 1436
Isle of Wight Garlic Festival 1438
Jacob's Ladder 1453
Jamaica National Heroes Day 1458
Japan Marine Day 1466
Jazzkaar Festival 1470
Jewish Cultural Festival 1475
Jorvik Viking Festival 1485
Jutajaiset Folklore Festival 1497
Keene Pumpkin Festival 1530
Keiro-no-Hi 1531
Kenya Skydive Boogie 1540
Keukenhof Flower Show 1542
Kewpiesta 1543
Khomeini (Ayatollah), Death Anniversary of 1545
Khordad 15 Revolt, Anniversary of the 1546
Kiamichi Owa-Chito 1548
Kilkenny Arts Festival 1551
King (Martin Luther, Jr.) Drum Major for Justice
    Parade, Battle of the Bands & Drum Line
    Extravaganza, National 1557
Kiribati Gospel Day 1566
Kiribati National Health Day 1568
Kiribati World Teachers' Day 1569
Kiribati Youth Day 1570
Kite Meeting, International 1571
Kiwanis Kids' Day 1572
Klondike Days Exposition 1574
Kunta Kinte Heritage Festival 1594
Kuta Karnival 1598
Labor Day 1610
LaborFest 1611
Latina, Fiesta 1635
Laylat al-Bara'ah 1639
Leaders of the Bulgarian National Revival Day 1645
Libya Declaration of Jamahiriya Day 1671
Lilac Festival 1676
Limassol Wine Festival 1679
Literacy Day, International 1683
London Bridge Days 1695
Macon Cherry Blossom Festival 1724
Madison County Covered Bridge Festival 1730
Magnolia Blossom Festival 1738
Maine Lobster Festival 1747
Malaysia Birthday of SPB Yang di-Pertuan Agong 1753
Maldives Embraced Islam Day 1755
Manly Man Festival and Spam Cook-Off, National 1769
Maralal Camel Derby 1771
Mardi Gras Film Festival 1776
Marino Wine Festival 1780
Marion County Ham Days 1781
Marley's (Bob) Birthday 1785
Marrakech Popular Arts Festival 1787
Marshall Islands Gospel Day 1791
Marshall Islands Lutok Kobban Alele 1792
Marshall Islands Manit Day 1793
Memorial Day Luminaria at Fredericksburg
    National Cemetery 1851
Merchants' Flower Market 1855
Meskwaki Powwow 1859
Midnight Sun Intertribal Powwow 1876
Milan Trade Fair 1880

Miss America Pageant 1892
Mobile International Festival 1896
Mobile-Phone Throwing World Championship 1897
Morija Arts and Cultural Festival 1919
Mother-in-Law Day 1929
Mother's Day 1930
Mothman Festival 1931
Mountain State Forest Festival 1939
Movement Electronic Music Festival 1940
Moxie Festival 1942
Mozambique Lusaka Agreement Day 1944
Mule Days 1949
Mulid of Shaykh Yusuf Abu el-Haggag 1950
Multicultural Festival, National 1951
Muscat Festival 1954
Mushroom Festival 1955
Myanmar Peasants' Day 1961
NAACP Image Awards 1965
Nabanna 1968
Napa Valley Mustard Festival 1974
Natal Day in Nova Scotia 1982
Natchez Spring and Fall Pilgrimages 1983
Native American Music Awards 1988
NEBRASKAland DAYS 2002
New Brunswick Day 2013
New Year's Parade of Firemen 2041
New York Gay Pride March 2044
New Zealand National Agricultural Fieldays 2048
Newfoundland Discovery Day 2049
Ngondo Festival 2058
Nicaragua Battle of San Jacinto Day 2060
Nobel Prize Ceremony 2078
Noel Night 2079
North American International Auto Show 2086
Nunavut Day 2096
Oakley (Annie) Festival 2102
Odunde Festival 2113
Okmulgee Pecan Festival 2118
Older Persons, International Day of 2129
Old-Time Country Music Contest and Festival, National ... 2130
Olney White Squirrel Count 2133
Original Gullah Festival 2153
Outback Festival 2172
Paczki Day 2180
Pafos Aphrodite Festival Cyprus 2181
Pageant of the Golden Tree 2182
Parada del Sol 2208
Paris Air and Space Show 2214
Parker (Charlie) Jazz Festival 2216
Paul Bunyan Show 2228
Peace, International Day of 2232
Peanut Festival, National 2233
Philadeplphia Flower Show 2252
Pickle Festival 2256
Pilgrimage to Souvenance 2274
Pirates Week 2279
Poetry Festival of Medellín, International 2286
Poetry Month, National 2287
Portland Rose Festival 2298
Potato Blossom Festival 2305
POW/MIA Recognition Day, National 2307
Prague Kolache Festival 2309
Premio Lo Nuestro Latin Music Awards 2313
Preservation of the Ozone Layer, International Day for the 2315
Puccini Festival 2322
Qiantang River Tidal Bore Watching Festival, International ... 2337
Quebec City Festival of Sacred Music 2343
Räben-Chilbi 2352
Race Relations Sunday 2354

Numbers in the index refer to entry numbers, not page numbers

Race Unity Day 2355
Rainforest World Music Festival 2360
Rand Show 2368
Red Flannel Festival 2380
Richmond Fossil Festival 2400
River to Reef Festival 2407
Robin Hood Festival in Sherwood, Oregon 2413
Robots at Play 2415
Rock Ness 2416
Rondo Days Celebration 2424
Rose Festival 2430
Route 66 Festival 2437
Royal Easter Show 2440
Saffron Rose Festival 2462
Sahara National Festival 2463
Sàmi Easter Festival 2473
Sàmi National Holiday 2474
San Diego Comic-Con International 2480
San Francisco Pride 2486
San Pedro International Costa Maya Festival 2506
Sao Paulo Gay Pride Parade 2527
Satchmo SummerFest 2534
Saturnalia Roman Festival 2536
Saudi Arabia National Heritage and Folk Culture
    Festival 2537
Sea Islands Black Heritage Festival 2547
Sea, Festival of the 2546
Senj International Summer Carnival 2565
Shad Festival 2579
Sheboygan Bratwurst Days 2593
Shenandoah Apple Blossom Festival 2598
Shrimp Festival, National 2612
Smithsonian Folklife Festival 2650
Sofia Music Weeks 2655
Solidarity with the Palestinian People,
    International Day of 2658
South Africa Heritage Day 2667
South Africa National Arts Festival 2668
South Carolina Peach Festival 2672
Southwestern Exposition Livestock Show & Rodeo 2678
Spiedie Fest and Balloon Rally 2683
Spock Days/Galaxyfest 2686
St. Kitts and Nevis National Heroes Day 2765
St. Mary's County Oyster Festival 2781
St. Paul Winter Carnival 2797
St. Rocco's Celebration 2804
State Fair of Texas 2831
Stockton Asparagus Festival 2841
Struga Poetry Evenings 2848
Sun Fun Festival 2863
Sundiata, Festival 2873
Superman Celebration 2875
Sweetest Day 2888
Sydney Festival 2893
Sydney Gay and Lesbian Mardi Gras 2895
Take Our Daughters to Work Day 2913
Tartu Hanseatic Days 2929
Taste of Chicago 2930
Tater Days 2931
Taziyeh 2935
Tellabration 2942
Terlingua Chili Cookoff 2950
Texas Citrus Fiesta 2954
Texas Rose Festival 2957
That Luang Festival 2965
To Kill a Mockingbird Annual Production 2992
Toronto Caribana 3009
Toronto Veg Food Fest 3011
Tribeca Film Festival 3022

Trois Glorieuses 3033
Tucson Meet Yourself Festival 3042
Tulip Time 3043
Tulip Time Festival (Holland Michigan) 3044
Tulsa Indian Arts Festival 3045
Turtle Days 3060
Turtle Independence Day 3061
Tyre Festival 3068
Ullr Fest 3080
United Nations Day 3084
United Tribes International Powwow 3088
Vanuatu Custom Chiefs Day 3113
Vendimia, Fiesta de la 3124
Vermont Maple Festival 3130
Veterans Day (Emporia, Kansas) 3136
Veterans Homecoming (Branson, Missouri) 3137
Veterans Pow Wow 3138
Vidalia Onion Festival 3141
Vietnam Veterans Memorial Anniversary 3146
Viña del Mar International Song Festival 3149
Vinegar Festival, International 3152
Vinegrower's Day 3153
Volunteer Day for Economic and Social
    Development, International 3166
Voodoo Music Experience 3167
Waila Festival 3169
Walloon Regional Day 3174
Washington State Apple Blossom Festival 3183
Watch Night (Bolden, Georgia) 3188
Watermelon Thump 3191
Watermelon-Eating and Seed-Spitting Contest 3192
Watts Festival 3194
Wayne Chicken Show 3195
WCSH Sidewalk Art Festival 3196
Wear Red Day, National 3197
Week of Solidarity with the Peoples of
    Non-Self-Governing Territories 3199
West Virginia Strawberry Festival 3203
Western Stock Show, National 3204
Whole Enchilada Fiesta 3216
Wide Open Bluegrass Festival 3220
Wilder (Laura Ingalls) Pageant 3225
Windjammer Days 3232
Wings 'n Water Festival 3233
Wooden Boat Festival 3247
Woodward Dream Cruise 3248
World AIDS Day 3250
World Champion Bathtub Race 3251
World Championship Hoop Dance Contest 3253
World Creole Music Festival 3254
World Day for Water 3256
World Day of Prayer 3257
World Day to Combat Desertification and Drought 3258
World Development Information Day 3259
World Environment Day 3260
World Food Day 3262
World Malaria Day 3264
World Peace Festival 3265
World Population Day 3266
World Religion Day 3267
World Santa Claus Congress 3269
World Space Week 3271
World's Largest Salmon Barbecue 3276
Wurstfest 3279
Yarmouth Clam Festival 3286
Zambia Farmers Day 3304
Zimbabwe Defense Forces Day 3311
Zwiebelmarkt 3316

Numbers in the index refer to entry numbers, not page numbers

Religious

Indexes festivals and events that are part of the customs and practices of a faith tradition, that commemorate events from history of religious significance, or are focused primarily on religious worship services and celebrations.

Aztec

Xilonen, Festival of 3281
Xipe Totec, Festival of 3282

Baha'i

Abbey Road on the River 0002
Abdu'l-Baha, Ascension of 0004
Admission Day 0022
Bab, Birth of the 0211
Bab, Declaration of the 0212
Bab, Martyrdom of the 0213
Baha'i Day of the Covenant 0220
Nineteen Day Fast 2071
Ridvan, Feast of 2401
World Religion Day 3267

Buddhist

Ako Gishi Sai 0043
Akwambo 0046
Asanha Bucha Day 0165
Baekjung 0219
Bodhi Day (Rohatsu) 0351
Boun Phan Vet 0382
Cambodian New Year 0472
Dosmoche 0835
Esala Perahera 0953
Floating Lantern Ceremony 1040
Goddess of Mercy, Birthday of the 1150
Hana Matsuri 1274
Hari-Kuyo 1284
Hemis Festival 1300
Higan 1307
Jizo Ennichi 1479
Kasone Festival of Watering the Banyan Tree 1520
Kataragama Festival 1523
Laba Festival 1609
Lantern Festival 1627
Lantern Festival (Korea) 1628
Lights, Festival of 1675
Lotus, Birthday of the 1703
Magha Puja 1734
Mani Rimdu 1767
Marya 1802
Monlam 1908
Neri-Kuyo 2010
Ngan Duan Sib 2054
Obon Festival 2105
Omizutori Matsuri 2139
Panchadaan 2204
Paro Tsechu 2218
Phchum Ben 2251
Phra Buddha Bat Fair 2254
Poson 2304
Rato (Red) Machhendranath 2373
Sanghamita Day 2510

Shinbyu 2604
Shinran-Shonin Day 2607
Shwedagon Pagoda Festival 2622
Songkran 2662
Sugar Ball Show 2856
Ta Mo's Day 2901
Tazaungdaing 2934
Thadingyut 2958
That Luang Festival 2965
Thay Pagoda Festival 2966
Thimphu Tsechu 2969
Ullambana 3079
Universal Prayer Day 3089
Vatsa 3122
Vesak 3134
Waso 3187
Water-Splashing Festival 3193

Candomblé

New Year's Eve (Brazil) 2037
Yemanjá Festival 3289

Cherokee

Atohuna (Friends Made Ceremony) 0188
Great New Moon Festival (Cheno i-equa) 1201

Christian

Abdullah's (King) Birthday in Jordan 0005
Aboriginal Day, National 0008
Acadiens et Creoles, Festivals 0013
Accession of H.H. Sheikh Zayed as Ruler of Abu Dhabi 0014
Adae-Kese 0015
Adam's Peak, Pilgrimage to 0016
Advent 0023
Advent (Germany) 0024
AFC Asian Cup 0025
Africa Industrialization Day 0026
African World Festival 0032
African/Caribbean International Festival of Life 0033
Agua, La Fiesta de 0037
Air Races and Air Show, National Championship 0039
AirVenture 0041
Al Bustan International Festival of Music and the Arts 0047
Alexandra Rose Day 0061
Algeria Independence Day 0062
Algeria National Day 0063
All Saints' Day 0064
All Saints' Day (France) 0065
All Saints' Day (Louisiana) 0066
All Saints' Day and All Souls' Day (Guatemala) 0067
All Saints' Day and All Souls' Day (Peru) 0068
All Souls' Day 0069
All Souls' Day (Cochiti Pueblo) 0070
American Indian Heritage Month 0085

Numbers in the index refer to entry numbers, not page numbers

American West, Festival of the 0088
America's Cup 0089
Amherstburg Heritage Homecoming 0090
Anant Chaturdashi 0094
Anastenaria 0095
Apparition of the Infant Jesus 0127
Arctic Circle Race 0139
Ascension Day 0167
Ascension Day (Portugal) 0168
Assumption of Our Lady 0177
Assumption of the Blessed Virgin Mary, Feast of the 0178
Assumption of the Virgin Mary, Feast of the (Guatemala) 0179
Assumption of the Virgin Mary, Feast of the (Italy) 0181
Baptism of the Lord, Feast of the 0242
Bible Week, National 0310
Black Christ of Esquipulas, Day of the 0326
Black Madonna of Jasna Gora, Feast of the 0331
Black Nazarene Fiesta 0332
Burial of the Sardine 0432
Candelaria (Bolivia) 0482
Candlemas 0485
Candlewalk 0486
Carling Sunday 0504
Carnival of the Laetare 0536
Chalk Sunday 0560
Cheese Sunday 0570
Christ the King, Feast of 0614
Christmas 0616
Christmas (Greece) 0617
Christmas (Marshall Islands) 0619
Christmas (Norway) 0620
Christmas (Puerto Rico) 0621
Christmas (Romania) 0622
Christmas (Russian Orthodox) 0623
Christmas (South Africa) 0624
Christmas (Spain) 0625
Christmas (Sweden) 0626
Christmas (Syria) 0627
Christmas Eve 0629
Christmas Eve (Armenia) 0630
Christmas Eve (Baltics) 0631
Christmas Eve (Bethlehem) 0632
Christmas Eve (Denmark) 0633
Christmas Eve (Finland) 0634
Christmas Eve (France) 0635
Christmas Eve (Italy) 0636
Christmas Eve (Moravian Church) 0637
Christmas Eve Bonfires 0639
Christmas Pastorellas (Mexico) 0640
Circumcision, Feast of the 0650
Clean Monday (Kathara Deftera) 0654
Corpus Christi 0690
Corpus Christi (England) 0691
Corpus Christi (Germany) 0692
Corpus Christi (Switzerland) 0694
Corpus Christi (Venezuela) 0695
Día de los Tres Reyes 0801
Divine Holy Spirit, Festival of the 0814
Dominican Republic Our Lady of Altagracia 0831
Dominican Republic Our Lady of Mercedes Day 0832
Easter 0862
Easter (Bulgaria) 0863
Easter (Chile) 0864
Easter (Czech Republic) 0866
Easter (Egypt) 0867
Easter (Germany) 0868
Easter (Hollywood, California) 0869
Easter (Italy) 0870
Easter (Netherlands) 0871

Easter (Norway) 0872
Easter (Poland) 0873
Easter (Russia) 0874
Elijah Day 0914
Ember Days 0928
Epiphany (Germany) 0935
Epiphany (Labrador) 0936
Epiphany (Russia) 0938
Epiphany (Spain) 0939
Epiphany (Sweden) 0940
Epiphany, Christian Orthodox 0941
Epiphany Eve (Austria) 0942
Epiphany Eve (France) 0943
Epiphany, Feast of the 0944
Exaltation of the Cross, Feast of the 0970
Family Week 0978
Fasinada 0981
Flight into Egypt 1038
Flores de Mayo (El Salvador) 1044
Footwashing Day 1055
Forgiveness, Feast of 1057
Forty Martyrs' Day 1059
Frost Saints' Days 1084
Ganna 1102
Giglio Feast 1137
Good Friday 1163
Good Friday (Belgium) 1164
Good Friday (Bermuda) 1165
Good Friday (England) 1166
Good Friday (Italy) 1167
Good Friday (Mexico) 1168
Good Friday (Poland) 1169
Good Friday (Spain) 1170
Guardian Angels Day 1225
Helston Flora Day 1298
Hill Cumorah Pageant 1310
Holy Blood, Procession of the 1333
Holy Family, Feast of the 1334
Holy Ghost, Feast of the 1335
Holy Innocents' Day 1336
Holy Innocents' Day (Belgium) 1337
Holy Queen Isabel, Festival of the 1339
Holy Saturday 1340
Holy Saturday (Mexico) 1341
Holy Thursday 1342
Holy Week 1343
Holy Week (Czech Republic) 1344
Holy Week (Haiti) 1345
Holy Week (Mexico) 1346
Holy Week (Panama) 1347
Holy Week (Philippines) 1348
Holy Week (Portugal) 1349
Hurling the Silver Ball 1383
Immaculate Conception, Feast of the 1407
Immaculate Conception, Feast of the (Argentina) 1408
Immaculate Conception, Feast of the (Malta) 1409
Immaculate Conception, Feast of the (Mexico) 1410
Immaculate Heart of Mary, Feast of the 1411
Kiribati Gospel Day 1566
Kneeling Sunday 1578
Last Great Day 1633
Latter-Day Saints, Founding of the Church of 1636
Lazarus Saturday 1643
Lent 1657
Leonhardiritt 1658
Liberian Fast and Prayer Day 1668
Lord's Evening Meal (Memorial) 1700
Low Sunday 1706
Marian Days 1779

Numbers in the index refer to entry numbers, not page numbers

Marshall Islands Gospel Day 1791
Martinmas 1796
Martinsfest 1798
Martyrdom of Joseph and Hyrum Smith 1799
Maskal 1810
Maundy Thursday 1818
Michaelmas 1866
Misa de Gallo 1889
Moldova Memorial Easter 1902
Moors and Christians Fiesta 1915
Moriones Festival 1920
Most Precious Blood, Feast of the 1927
Mothering Sunday 1928
Nativity of the Blessed Virgin Mary, Feast of the 1990
Nativity of the Blessed Virgin Mary, Feast of the (Germany) . . . 1991
Nativity of the Blessed Virgin Mary, Feast of the (Peru) 1992
Nativity of the Theotokos 1993
New Church Day 2014
Niue Peniamina Gospel Day 2076
Nombre de Jesús 2081
Nusardil 2097
Our Lady Aparecida, Festival of 2159
Our Lady of Carmel, Feast of 2160
Our Lady of Guadalupe, Feast of (United States) 2162
Our Lady of Guadalupe, Fiesta of 2163
Our Lady of Lourdes, Feast of 2164
Our Lady of Solitude, Fiesta of 2166
Our Lady of Sorrows Festival 2167
Our Lady of the Angels, Feast of 2168
Our Lady of the Good Death Festival 2169
Our Lady of the Rock, Festival of 2170
Palm Sunday 2191
Palm Sunday (Austria) 2192
Palm Sunday (Finland) 2193
Palm Sunday (Germany) 2194
Palm Sunday (Italy) 2195
Palm Sunday (Netherlands) 2196
Palm Sunday (United States) 2197
Pancake Day 2203
Pardon of Nossa Senhora dos Remédios 2210
Pardon of Ste. Anne d'Auray 2211
Pentecost 2240
Pilgrimage of Saut d'Eau 2267
Pilgrimage to Qoyllur Riti 2272
Pilgrimage to Shrine of Father Laval 2273
Pinkster Day 2278
Pleureuses, Ceremony of 2284
Prayer for Christian Unity, Week of 2311
Presentation of the Blessed Virgin Mary, Feast of the 2314
Quadragesima Sunday 2339
Quebec City Festival of Sacred Music 2343
Queenship of Mary 2348
Radunitsa 2357
Rally Day 2362
Reek Sunday 2384
Reformation Day 2385
Repentance and Prayer Day 2391
Restoration of the Aaronic Priesthood Commemoration 2394
Rogation Days 2418
Rosary, Festival of the 2428
Sacred Heart of Jesus, Feast of the 2459
San Francisco's Day (Lima, Peru) 2488
San Gennaro, Feast of 2489
San Isidro in Peru, Fiesta of 2492
San José Day Festival 2496
San Juan Pueblo Feast Day 2499
Santa Fe, Fiesta de 2517
Schutzengelfest 2544
Señor de los Milagros 2566

Señor de los Temblores Procession 2567
Seton (Mother) Day 2570
Shrove Monday 2613
Shrove Tuesday 2614
Shrove Tuesday (Bohemia) 2615
Shrove Tuesday (Estonia) 2616
Shrove Tuesday (Finland) 2617
Shrove Tuesday (Pennsylvania Dutch) 2619
Shrovetide (Norway) 2620
Silent Days 2628
Silent Night, Holy Night Celebration 2629
Soul Saturdays 2664
Spy Wednesday 2692
St. Agatha Festival 2694
St. Agnes's Eve 2695
St. Alban's Day 2696
St. Andrew's Day 2697
St. Andrew's Eve 2698
St. Anne's Day 2699
St. Anthony of Padua, Feast of 2700
St. Anthony the Abbot, Feast of 2701
St. Augustine of Hippo, Feast of 2702
St. Barbara's Day 2703
St. Barnabas's Day 2704
St. Basil, Feast of 2706
St. Blaise's Day 2707
St. Brendan's Day 2708
St. Bridget's Day 2709
St. Catherine's Day 2710
St. Catherine's Day (Estonia) 2711
St. Cecilia's Day 2712
St. Charlemagne's Day 2713
St. Charles's Day 2714
St. Christopher's Day 2715
St. Clare of Assisi, Feast of 2716
St. Columba's Day 2717
St. Crispin's Day 2718
St. David's Day 2719
St. Demetrius's Day 2720
St. Denis's Day 2721
St. Dismas's Day 2722
St. Dunstan's Day 2723
St. Dymphna's Day 2724
St. Elizabeth Ann Seton, Feast of 2725
St. Elmo's Day 2726
St. Evermaire, Game of 2727
St. Frances Cabrini, Feast of 2728
St. Frances of Rome, Feast of 2729
St. Francis of Assisi, Feast of 2730
St. Gabriel, Feast of 2731
St. Gens, Festival of 2732
St. George's Day 2733
St. George's Day (Bulgaria) 2734
St. George's Day (Syria) 2735
St. Gregory's Day 2737
St. Gudula's Day 2738
St. Hans Festival 2739
St. Herman Pilgrimage 2740
St. Hilary's Day 2741
St. Hubert de Liège, Feast of 2742
St. Ignatius Loyola, Feast of 2743
St. Isidore, Festival of 2744
St. James's Day 2745
St. Joan of Arc, Feast Day of 2746
St. John Lateran, Feast of the Dedication of 2747
St. John the Baptist, Martyrdom of 2748
St. John the Evangelist's Day 2749
St. John's Eve (Germany) 2750
St. John's Day 2751

Numbers in the index refer to entry numbers, not page numbers

St. John's Day (Puerto Rico) 2754
St. John's Eve (Denmark) 2755
St. John's Eve (France) 2756
St. John's Eve (Ireland) 2758
St. John's Eve (Spain) 2759
St. Joseph the Worker, Feast of 2761
St. Joseph's Day 2762
St. Jude's Day 2763
St. Knut's Day 2766
St. Leopold's Day 2768
St. Lucy's Day 2770
St. Marinus Day 2771
St. Mark's Day 2773
St. Mark's Day (Hungary) 2774
St. Maron's Day 2775
St. Martha, Coffin Fiesta of 2776
St. Martha's Day 2777
St. Martin's Eve (Estonia) 2780
St. Matthias's Day 2782
St. Médardus's Day 2783
St. Mennas's Day 2784
St. Michael's Day 2785
St. Modesto's Day 2786
St. Nichiren's Pardon, Festival of 2787
St. Nicholas's Day 2788
St. Nicholas's Day (Greece) 2789
St. Nicholas's Day (Italy) 2790
St. Olav's Day 2791
St. Patrick's Day 2792
St. Patrick's Day (Ireland) 2793
St. Patrick's Day Encampment 2794
St. Patrick's Day Parade (Savannah, Georgia) 2795
St. Paul, Feast of the Conversion of 2796
St. Paul's Shipwreck, Feast of 2798
St. Peter's Chair, Festival of 2799
St. Peter's Day (Belgium) 2800
St. Peter's Fiesta 2801
St. Placidus Festival 2802
St. Polycarp's Day 2803
St. Rocco's Celebration 2804
St. Roch's Day 2805
St. Rose of Lima's Day 2806
St. Sarkis's Day 2807
St. Sava's Day 2808
St. Sebastian's Day 2809
St. Spyridon (Spiridion) Day 2810
St. Stephen's Day 2811
St. Stephen's Day (Hungary) 2812
St. Swithin's Day 2813
St. Sylvester's Day 2814
St. Sylvester's Day (Madeira) 2815
St. Tammany's Day 2816
St. Teresa's Day 2817
St. Thomas's Day 2818
St. Thorlak's Day 2819
St. Tryphon's Day (Montenegro and Bulgaria) 2820
St. Urho's Day 2821
St. Vaclav's Day 2822
St. Vincent's Day 2825
St. Vitus's Day 2826
St. Vladimir's Day 2827
Sts. Cosmas and Damian Day 2849
Sunday of Orthodoxy 2867
Sunday of St. Gregory Palamas 2868
Sunday of St. John Climacos 2869
Sunday of St. Mary of Egypt 2870
Sunday of the Holy Cross 2871
Tekakwitha (Kateri) Feast Day 2939

Timqat 2985
Transfiguration, Feast of the 3019
Trinity Sunday 3031
Valentine's Day 3107
Virgin of the Pillar, Feast of the 3157
Visitation, Feast of the 3159
Waratambar 3178
Watch Night Service 3189
White Sunday 3214
Wigilia 3223
World Day of Prayer 3257

Effutu

Aboakyer Festival 0007

Ga

Homowo 1352

Hindu

Alasitas Fair 0052
Alaska Day 0053
Alpenfest 0077
Amalaka Ekadashi 0078
Annakut Festival 0109
Ashokashtami 0171
Avani Mulam 0198
Bhai Dooj 0306
Bhairava Ashtami 0307
Bhishma Ashtami 0308
Bonalu 0362
Chandan Yatra 0562
Dattatreya Jayanti 0767
Devi Dhura 0792
Dewali 0794
Dhan Teras 0796
Dhungri Fair 0797
Dol Purnima 0825
Eka Dasa Rudra 0900
Ekadashi 0901
Gai Jatra 1091
Galungan 1093
Ganesh Chathurthi 1099
Ganga Dussehra 1100
Ghanta Karna 1129
Ghatasthapana 1130
Gita Jayanti 1145
Gokarna Aunsi 1152
Gowri Habba 1175
Gudi Padva 1230
Guru Purnima 1241
Halashashti 1263
Hanuman Jayanti 1281
Holi 1327
Indra Jatra 1422
Janaki Navami 1463
Janmashtami 1464
Jhulan Yatra 1477
Jyestha Ashtami 1502
Kali Puja 1508
Kapila Shashti 1512
Karthikai Deepam 1515
Kartika Purnima 1516
Kartika Snan 1517

Numbers in the index refer to entry numbers, not page numbers

Karwachoth 1519
Kojagara 1580
Kokila Vrata 1581
Kumbh Mela 1593
Lakshmi Puja 1618
Magha Purnima 1735
Masi Magham 1809
Mauni Amavasya 1819
Meenakshi Kalyanam 1841
Naag Panchami 1967
Narak Chaturdashi 1976
Nariyal Purnima 1978
Narsimha Jayanti 1979
Nirjala Ekadashi 2074
Odalan 2111
Onam 2141
Panguni Uttiram 2205
Parshurama Jayanti 2219
Phagwa 2250
Pitra Visarjana Amavasya 2280
Pooram 2296
Putrada Ekadashi 2334
Radha Ashtami 2356
Rama Leela Festival 2364
Ramanavami 2366
Rasa Leela Festival 2370
Rath Yatra 2371
Rato (Red) Machhendranath 2373
Rishi Panchami 2405
Rukmini Ashtami 2444
Sakata Chauth 2468
Savitri-Vrata 2538
Shankaracharya Jayanti 2590
Sharad Purnima 2591
Shigmo Festival 2602
Shivaratri 2610
Shravani Mela 2611
Sitala Ashtami 2641
Sithinakha 2642
Skanda Sashti 2646
Smithsonian Folklife Festival 2650
Snan Yatra 2653
Surya Sashti 2877
Swarupa Dwadashi 2884
Thaipusam 2961
Thimithi Fire-Walking Ceremony 2968
Tihar 2980
Tirupati Festival 2989
Vaisakh 3104
Vaitarani 3105
Vaman Dwadashi 3110
Vasant Panchami 3120
Vasanth Navaratri 3121
Visvakarma Puja 3160

Hopi

Argentina National Day of Memory for Truth and Justice 0143
Argentine National Day 0144
Argungu Fishing Festival 0145
Århus Festival 0146
Basket Dance 0252
Hopi Flute Ceremony 1362
Niman Festival 2069
Powamû Ceremony 2308
Soyaluna 2679
Wuwuchim 3280

Igbo

Agwunsi Festival 0038
Okpesi Festival 2119

Iroquois

Amazon & Galapagos Day 0080
Harvest Festival 1288

Jain

Akshya Tritiya 0045
Caturmas 0547
Dasa Laksana Parvan 0765
Gyan Panchami 1248
Ksamavani 1590
Mahamastakabhishekha 1739
Mahavira Jayanti 1740
Parshva, Birthday of 2220
Paryushana 2222
Pausha Dashami 2229
Risabha's Nirvana and Mauni Amavasya 2404
Samvatsari 2477

Jewish

Asarah be-Tevet 0166
Blessing the Sun 0344
Elul Selichot 0920
Ethiopian Sigd Festival 0964
Firstborn, Fast of the 1024
Gedaliah, Fast of 1111
Hanukkah 1280
Hoshana Rabbah 1369
Lag ba-Omer 1616
Miriam's Yahrzeit 1888
Passover 2225
Pilgrim Festivals 2263
Purim 2330
Purims, Special 2331
Rosh Hashanah 2433
Sabbath of Rabbi Isaac Mayer Wise 2457
Seged 2557
Shavuot 2592
Shemini Atzeret 2597
Simhat Torah 2632
Sukkot 2858
Ta'anit Esther 2902
Tammuz, Fast of the 17th of 2918
Teshuvah 2952
Three Weeks 2977
Tisha be-Av 2990
Trumpets, Feast of 3034
Tu Bishvat 3038
Water-Drawing Festival 3190
Yom ha-Zikkaron 3292
Yom Kippur 3293
Yom Yerushalayim 3294

Kwakiuti

Kwakiutl Midwinter Ceremony 1604

Numbers in the index refer to entry numbers, not page numbers

Mayan

Angelitos, Los 0101
Chickaban 0592
Crosses, Festival of the 0729

Muslim

Arbaeen 0136
Arbaeen Pilgrimage 0137
Ashura 0172
Bera Festival 0294
Bianou 0309
Bishwa Ijtema 0321
Damba 0755
Grand Magal of Shaykh Amadou Bamba 1179
Holy Prophet and the Martyrdom of Imam Hasan,
    Death Anniversary of the 1338
Hosay Festival 1368
Id al-Adha 1392
Id al-Fitr 1393
Id al-Fitr (Nigeria) 1394
Imam Ali's Birthday 1403
Imam Ali's Martyrdom, Anniversary of 1404
Imam Sadiq's Martyrdom, Anniversary of 1405
Islamic New Year 1435
Khamis al-Amwat 1544
Lamp Nights 1621
Lanterns Festival 1630
Laylat al-Bara'ah 1639
Laylat al-Miraj 1640
Laylat al-Qadr 1641
Libya Day of Arafa 1670
Maldives Embraced Islam Day 1755
Mandi Safar 1765
Mawlid al-Nabi 1823
Mulid of Shaykh Yusuf Abu el-Haggag 1950
Pilgrimage to Mecca 2270
Pilgrimage to the Tomb of Sunan Bayat 2275
Ramadan 2365
Rumi Festival 2445
Sallah (Salah) Festival 2469
Sekaten 2559
Shab-Barat 2578
St. George's Day (Syria) 2735
Twelfth Imam, Birthday of the 3063
Urs Ajmer Sharif 3093
Urs of Jelaluddin al-Rumi 3095
White Nights 3212

Native American

Arapaho Sun Dance 0135
Arbor Day 0138
Argentina Flag Day 0141
Bear Society Dance 0276
Iroquois Midwinter Festival 1432

Native American (various)

Creek Green Corn Ceremony 0719

Navajo

Navajo Nation Fair at Window Rock 1996
Navajo Night Chant 1997

Neopagan

American Birkebeiner 0082
Cross-Quarter Days 0731
Fire Festivals 1016
Iduna and Summer Finding 1401
Imbolc 1406
Lughnasadh 1711
Mabon 1718
Midsummer Day 1877
Sabbat 2456
Yule 3302

Omaha

Whe'wahchee 3210

Pueblo

Eagle Dance 0858
Old Pecos Bull and Corn Dance 2124
Shalako Ceremonial 2586

Shinto

Aldersgate Experience 0060
Hadaka Matsuri 1252
Hari-Kuyo 1284
Hi Matsuri 1305
Izumo-taisha Jinzaisai 1450
Mochi N o Matsuri 1898
Niiname-sai 2068
Saigusa Matsuri 2465
Sanja Matsuri 2513
Tori-no-ichi 3008

Sikh

Guru Arjan, Martyrdom of 1236
Guru Gobind Singh, Birthday of 1237
Guru Granth Sahib, Installation of the 1238
Guru Har Krishan, Birthday of 1239
Guru Parab 1240
Guru Ram Das, Birthday of 1242
Guru Tegh Bahadur, Martyrdom of 1243
Hola Mohalla 1325
Lohri 1692
Maghi 1736
Vaisakh 3104
Vasant Panchami 3120

Sioux

Sioux Sun Dance 2639

Taoist

Lu Pan, Birthday of 1708
Monkey God, Birthday of the 1906

Numbers in the index refer to entry numbers, not page numbers

Nine Imperial Gods, Festival of the 2070
Ta Chiu 2900
Tam Kung Festival 2917
Third Prince, Birthday of the 2971
Ullambana 3079
Vegetarian Festival 3123

New Yam Festival .... .2022
Odunde Festival .... .2113

Unitarian

Flower Communion 1048

Ute

People's Army of North Korea, Founding of the 2241
Southern Ute Tribal Sun Dance 2677
Ute Bear Dance 3101

Voodoo

Benin National Vodoun Day 0292
Calinda Dance 0466
Manger Yam 1766
Pilgrimage of Saut d'Eau 2267
Pilgrimage to Souvenance 2274
Rara 2369

Yoruba

Egungun Festival 0895

Zoroastrianism

Aban Parab .... .0001
Adar Parab .... .0017
Amurdad, Feast of .... .0092
Ardwahist, Feast of .... .0140
Ayathrem .... .0203
Dae, Feasts of .... .0747
Farvardegan Days .... .0979
Frawardignan, Feast of .... .1074
Hordad, Feast of .... .1365
Jamshed Navaroz .... .1462
Khordad Sal .... .1547
Maidyarem .... .1742
Maidyoshahem .... .1743
Maidyozarem .... .1744
Mihr, Festival of .... .1878
Mihragan .... .1879
Mithra, Feast of .... .1893
Paitishahem .... .2184
Shahrewar, Feast of .... .2583
Spendarmad, Feast of .... .2682
Tiragan .... .2987
Vohuman, Feast of .... .3164
Zarthastno Diso .... .3310

Sporting

Indexed below are festivals and events that are based on or revolve around sporting events. This index does not include the many fairs and festivals in which games and contests form only a part.

Adelaide Cup 0018
AFC Asian Cup 0025
Air Races and Air Show, National Championship 0039
Ak-Sar-Ben Livestock Exposition and Rodeo 0044
Albuquerque International Balloon Fiesta 0058
All-American Soap Box Derby 0071
American Birkebeiner 0082
American Royal Livestock, Horse Show and Rodeo 0086
American Solar Challenge 0087
America's Cup 0089
Anchorage Fur Rendezvous 0097
Antigua Sailing Week 0121
Apollonian Games 0126
Arctic Circle Race 0139
Argungu Fishing Festival 0145
Army-Navy Football Game 0155
Asian Games 0173
Australian Open Tennis 0194
Bay To Breakers 0270
Bayou Classic 0272
Beargrease (John) Sled Dog Marathon 0277
Belgian-American Days 0284
Belmont Stakes 0289
Bering Sea Ice Golf Classic 0297
Boat Race Day (Okinawa, Japan) 0348
Boat Race Day (Thames River) 0349
Bog Snorkelling Championship, World 0352

Bonneville Speed Week 0367
Boston Marathon 0375
Bottle Kicking and Hare Pie Scramble, Annual 0381
Braemar Highland Gathering 0390
British Open 0402
Buffalo's Big Board Surfing Classic 0418
Calaveras County Fair and Frog Jumping Jubilee 0458
Calgary Exhibition and Stampede 0460
Camel and Ostrich Races, International 0473
Caribou Carnival and Canadian Championship Dog Derby ... 0499
Caruaru Roundup 0541
Charleston Sternwheel Regatta 0564
Cheese Rolling 0569
Chuckwagon Races, National Championship 0643
Clearwater County Fair and Lumberjack Days 0655
Coca-Cola 600 0661
Cotswold Olimpick Games 0702
Cotton Bowl Game 0703
Cricket World Cup 0720
Dartmouth Winter Carnival 0763
Davis Cup 0768
Daytona 500 0773
Deep Sea Fishing Rodeo 0781
Derby Day 0789
Día de los Charros 0799
Dodge National Circuit Finals Rodeo 0820
Doggett's Coat and Badge Race 0823

Numbers in the index refer to entry numbers, not page numbers

Elfstedentocht 0913
Ellensburg Rodeo 0918
Eton Wall Game 0965
Finnish Sliding Festival 1015
French Open Tennis 1080
Gay Games 1110
General Clinton Canoe Regatta 1113
Glorious Twelfth 1147
Golden Shears World Shearing and Wool-handling
    Championships 1161
Grand National 1180
Grand Prix 1181
Grandfather Mountain Highland Games and
    Gathering of Scottish Clans 1183
Grasmere Sports 1188
Great Falls Ski Club Mannequin Jump 1197
Great Schooner Race 1203
Great Wardmote of the Woodmen of Arden 1204
Grey Cup Day 1219
Gyangzê Horse-Racing Festival 1249
Hambletonian Harness Racing Classic 1273
Hard Crab Derby, National 1283
Haxey Hood Game 1293
Henley Royal Regatta 1301
Highland Games 1308
Historical Regatta 1315
Hobart Cup Day 1319
Hobart Royal Regatta 1320
Holmenkollen Day 1330
Hortobágy Bridge Fair and International Equestrian Festival . 1367
Hot Air Balloon Classic 1372
Houston Livestock Show & Rodeo 1374
Human Towers of Valls 1377
Hurling the Silver Ball 1383
Idaho Regatta 1396
Iditarod Trail Sled Dog Race 1399
Indianapolis 500 1420
Ironman Triathlon Championships 1431
Isthmian Games 1442
Joust of the Quintain 1486
Joust of the Saracens 1487
Jousting the Bear 1488
Jousting Tournament 1489
Kentucky Derby 1536
Kiel Week 1550
Kiplingcotes Derby 1565
Klondike International Outhouse Race 1576
Knabenschiessen 1577
Lasseters Camel Cup 1632
Laytown Strand Races 1642
Le Mans Motor Race 1644
Little League World Series 1688
Ludi 1710
Lumberjack World Championships 1713
Macker (Gus) Basketball 1723
Maralal Camel Derby 1771
Marbles Tournament, National 1772
Marshall Islands Fishermen's Day 1790
Maryland Hunt Cup 1804
Masters Golf Tournament 1811
Melbourne Cup Day 1846
Michigan Brown Trout Festival 1868
Mille Miglia 1883
Mobile-Phone Throwing World Championship 1897
Monaco Grand Prix 1905
Motorcycle Week 1932
Mount Cameroon Race 1933
Mount Fuji Climbing Season, End of 1935
Mount Isa Rodeo and Mardi Gras 1937

Naadam 1966
Nemean Games 2005
New Jersey Offshore Grand Prix 2018
New York City Marathon 2042
Newport to Bermuda Race 2053
Nomaoi Matsuri 2080
North American Wife-Carrying Championship 2087
Northern Games 2090
Olympic Games 2134
Open Marathon, International 2145
Orange Bowl Game 2147
Oregon Dune Mushers' Mail Run 2151
Ouray Ice Festival 2171
Palio of the Goose and River Festival 2190
Palio, Festival of the 2189
Pancake Day 2203
Partridge Day 2221
Payson Rodeo 2231
Pendleton Round-Up and Happy Canyon 2235
Pickett (Bill) Invitational Rodeo 2255
Plebeian Games 2283
Polar Bear Swim Day 2288
Preakness Stakes 2312
Punkin Chunkin World Championship 2327
Pythian Games 2335
Race of the Ceri 2353
Regatta of the Great Maritime Republics 2386
Reindeer Driving Competition 2388
Robinson (Jackie) Day 2414
Roman Games 2422
Rose Bowl Game 2429
Royal Ascot 2438
Safari Rally 2461
San Fermin Festival 2482
Saturnalia Roman Festival 2536
Schäferlauf 2540
Schützenfest 2543
Seafair 2550
Sebring 12-Hour Race 2555
Semana Criolla 2560
Sinjska Alka 2637
Skipjack Races and Land Festival 2647
Smithsonian Kite Festival 2651
Southern 500 2676
Special Olympics 2681
Stånga Games 2828
Sturgis Motorcycle Rally 2852
Sugar Bowl Classic 2857
Super Bowl Sunday 2874
Tako-Age 2915
Telluride Hang Gliding Festival 2944
Tennessee Walking Horse National Celebration 2949
Tohono O'odham Nation Rodeo 2995
Toh-shiya 2996
Tok Race of Champions Dog Sled Race 2998
Torch Fight 3007
Tour de France 3014
Transpac Race 3020
Triple Crown Pack Burro Races 3032
Turkish Wrestling Championships 3056
United States Open Championship in Golf 3086
United States Open Tennis 3087
University of Pennsylvania Relay Carnival 3090
Vaqueros, Fiesta de los 3118
Vasaloppet 3119
Virginia Scottish Games 3158
Wall Street Rat Race 3173
Weifang International Kite Festival 3200
Western Stock Show, National 3204

Numbers in the index refer to entry numbers, not page numbers

Wife-Carrying World Championships 3222
Wild Horse Festival 3224
Wilderness Woman Competition 3226
Wimbledon 3230
Winston 500 3235
Winterlude 3239
World Champion Bathtub Race 3251
World Championship Crab Races 3252

World Cup 3255
World Eskimo-Indian Olympics 3261
World Rock Paper Scissors Championship 3268
World Series 3270
World Wristwrestling Championships 3272
Wrangler National Finals Rodeo 3277
Yale-Harvard Regatta 3283
Yukigassen Festivals 3300

Numbers in the index refer to entry numbers, not page numbers

General Index

The General Index lists people, places, institutions, religious and ethnic groups, and names of festivals and holidays by keyword. It also lists other items of significance within the entries. For example, foods, animals, music, customs, and activities closely associated with an event are indexed, as are celebratory elements common to various cultures.

See also the Chronological Indexes (Fixed Days and Movable Days) and the Special Subject Index.

A

Aaronic Priesthood, 2394
Aban, 0001
Aban Parab, 0001
Abbas Effendi, 0004
Abbey Road on the River, 0002
Abbotsford International Air Show, 0003
Abdu'l-Baha, 0220
Abdu'l-Baha, Ascension of, 0004
Abdullah's (King) Birthday in Jordan, 0005
Abha Festival, 0006
Abhidhamma Day
        See Thadingyut
Abingdon, England, 0908
Aboakyer Festival, 0007
abolition
        See also emancipation; slavery
        Bahamas, 1068
        New York, 3040
        United States, 0837, 1075
Aboriginal Day, National, 0008
Abu Simbel Festival, 0009
Abu Simbel (temple), 0009
Academy Awards Ceremony, 0010
Acadian Day, 0011
Acadian Festival, 0012
Acadians, 0256, 0257
Acadiens, Festivals, 0013
Accession of H. H. Sheikh Zayed as Ruler of Abu Dhabi, 0014
accordions, 2533
Acorn, Frank, 1153
acorns, 1894
acrobat show, 1377
Adae-Kese, 0015
Adam, 0016
Adam's Peak, Pilgrimage to, 0016
Adar Parab, 0017

Adelaide Cup, 0018
Adelaide Festival, 0019
Adelaide Fringe Festival, 0020
Administrative Professionals Week, 0021
Admission Day, 0022
Adoration of the Cross
        See Exaltation of the Cross, Feast of the
Adults Day
        See Seijin-no-Hi (Adults Day; Coming-of-Age Day)
Advent, 0023
Advent (Germany), 0024
Aeschylus, 0808
AFC Asian Cup, 0025
Afghan Independence Day
        See Jeshn (Afghan Independence Day)
Afghanistan
        independence day, 1474
        spring festival, 1998
Africa
        See also individual countries
        African-American holidays, 1605
        dancing, 0760
        disease awareness, 0027
        family celebrations, 0978
        harvest festival, 1766
        industrialization of, 0026
        liberation, 0030
        Olympic Marathon trial, 0375
Africa Industrialization Day, 0026
Africa Malaria Day, 0027
African folk life celebration, 0838
African Liberation Day, 0030
African Methodist Episcopal (AME) Church, 0072
African Methodist Quarterly Meeting Day, 0031
African music festivals
        Illinois, 0033
        Michigan, 0032
African Union Methodist Protestant Church, 0031
African World Festival, 0032
African-American arts festivals, 0787

Numbers in the index refer to entry numbers, not page numbers

African-American awards, 1965
African-American baseball, 2414
African-American birthday commemorations, 0072, 1754
African-American blues festival, 0422
African-American children, 0317
African-American churches, 0072, 0113
African-American civil rights commemoration, 0397
African-American Day Parade, 0028
African-American events, 1605
    Alabama, 0397
    California, 0327, 1965, 3194
    Colorado, 0787
    Connecticut, 0714
    Florida, 0268
    Georgia, 2547
    Illinois, 0033, 0317
    Louisiana, 0957
    Maryland, 1594
    Michigan, 0032
    Minnesota, 2424
    New York, 0028, 0029, 1286, 2278
    North Carolina, 1295, 0422
    United States, 0072, 0113, 0330, 0034, 0333, 0336, 0417,
        1556, 1605, 1754, 2255, 2354, 2414, 3081, 0083
    Washington (state), 2873
    Washington, D.C., 0774
African-American film festivals, 1295
African-American gays, bisexuals, lesbians, and
  transgenders, 0774
African-American girls education, 0714
African-American history events
    Alabama, 0397
    California, 3194
    Connecticut, 0714
    Delaware, 0031
    Florida, 0268
    Georgia, 2547
    Maryland, 1594
    Minnesota, 2424
    New York, 1286, 2278
    United States, 0072, 0330, 0417, 1556, 1754, 2354, 2414
African-American military commemorations
    Florida, 0268
    United States, 0417
African-American music
    See also blues festivals, jazz festivals
    Black History Month, 0034
    Louisiana, 0957
African-American Music Appreciation Month, 0034
African-American pride festival, 0774
African-American rodeo, 2255
African-American unity festival, 3081
African-American Women in Cinema International Film
  Festival, 0029
African/Caribbean International Festival of Life, 0033
Afro-Brazilian cults, 0364
Agonalia, 0035
Agricola, 1059
agricultural celebrations

ancient Rome, 0671
    Arizona, 3303
    Argentina, 2859
    Australia, 2440, 2442
    England, 2285
    Ghana, 1126
    India, 1461
    Japan, 1251
    Korea, 0219, 2924
    Laos, 0426
    Mexico, 2744
    Nebraska, 0138
    New England, 0884
    New Jersey, 1036
    New Zealand, 2048
    North Dakota, 0312
    Peru, 2492
    Portugal, 0036
    South Africa, 2368
    Tatarstan, 2455
    Thailand, 0426
    United States, 0138
    Zambia, 3304
    Zoroastrian religion, 0203
Agricultural Days
    See Jordbruksdagarna
Agriculture Fair at Santarém, National, 0036
Agua, La Fiesta de, 0037
Aguinaldo, Emilio, 0366
aguinaldos, 0563, 0625
Agwunsi Festival, 0038
Ahura Mazda, 0747
AIDS awareness, 3250
Air Force (U.S.), 0148
Air Races and Air Show, National Championship, 0039
air shows
    Canada, 0003
    England, 0263
    France, 2214
    Kansas, 0859
    Nevada, 0039
    North Carolina, 3278
    Ohio, 0772, 3278
    Washington, D.C., 3278
aircraft conventions, 0041
Airing the Classics, 0040
AirVenture, 0041
Aix en Juin
    See Festival d'Aix en Provence
Aizu Byakko Matsuri, 0042
Akihito, Emperor, 0428
Ako Gishi Sai, 0043
Ak-Sar-Ben Livestock Exposition and Rodeo, 0044
Aksaya Tritiya
    See Akshya Tritiya
Akshya Tritiya, 0045
Akwambo (Path-Clearing Festival), 0046
Al Bustan International Festival of Music and the Arts, 0047
Al Hareed Festival, 0048

Alabama
    African-American civil rights commemoration, 0397
    arts festival, 0320
    blind/deaf/mute commemoration, 1532
    blues festival, 1278
    death commemoration, 0675
    environmental education, 0190
    fishing phenomenon, 0975
    food festivals, 0049, 2233
    international festival, 1896
    literature dramatization, 2992
    moonbuggy race, 1200
    shrimp celebrations, 0343, 2612
    trading bazaar, 1022
Alabama Blueberry Festival, 0049
Alacoque, Margaret Mary, 1049
Alahamady Be, 0050
Alamo Day, 0051
Alasitas Fair, 0052
Alaska
    American Indian ceremonies, 1604, 2838
    American Indian sporting events, 3261
    classical music festival, 0096
    dog racing, 0097, 0974, 1399, 2998
    flag-raising ceremony, 0053
    flower show, 1157
    gold rush festival, 1157
    historic commemoration, 2574
    ice classic, 2007
    moose dropping festival, 1916
    music festival, 2643
    pilgrimages, 2740
    powwow, 1876
    sporting events, 0297, 1399, 3261
    sun festival, 1875
    truck and dog beauty contest, 0644
    unmarried women competition, 3226
    whale festival, 3206
    winter carnivals, 0097, 2089
    worm festival, 1389
Alaska Day, 0053
Alba White Truffle Fair, 0054
Alban Arthan
    See Yule
Albania
    Communist government holiday, 0056
    folklore festival, 1052
    independence day, 0055
Albania Independence Day, 0055
Albania Republic Day, 0056
Alberta
    arts festival, 0236
    Caribbean music festival, 0501
    children's festival, 0461
    cultural heritage celebration, 0057
    Gold Rush festival, 1574
    literature festival, 2687
    powwow, 0416
    rodeo, 0460

Star Trek festival, 2686
Alberta Heritage Day, 0057
Albuquerque International Balloon Fiesta, 0058
Alcântara, Pedro di, 0393
alcohol festival, 0849
Aldeburgh Festival of Music and the Arts, 0059
Aldersgate Experience, 0060
alele, 1644
Alexander II, Czar, 0419
Alexandra Day
    See Alexandra Rose Day
Alexandra, queen of England, 0061
Alexandra Rose Day, 0061
Algeria
    independence day, 0062
    revolution holiday, 0063
Algeria Independence Day, 0062
Algeria National Day, 0063
al-Hussein, Abdullah II bin, 0005
Ali Hujwiri, 0766
Alice Springs Lions Club, 1632
Alice Springs Show
    See Royal Shows
All Fools' Day
    See April Fools' Day
All Hallows' Day
    See All Saints' Day
All Saints' Day, 0064
All Saints' Day and All Souls' Day (Guatemala), 0067
All Saints' Day and All Souls' Day (Peru), 0068
All Saints' Day (France), 0065
All Saints' Day (Louisiana), 0066
All Souls College, 1759
All Souls' Day, 0069
All Souls' Day (Cochiti Pueblo), 0070
All Souls' Day (Guatemala), 0067
All Souls' Day (Peru), 0068
All Souls' Eve
    See All Souls' Day
All Souls' Feast
    See Ullambana (Hungry Ghosts Festival; All Souls' Feast)
All-American Soap Box Derby, 0071
Allen (Richard), Birthday of, 0072
Allende, Salvador, 0599
Allerkinderendag
    See Holy Innocents' Day (Belgium) (Allerkinderendag)
All-Hallomas
    See All Saints' Day
Allied Landing Observances Day
    See D-Day
Allied Tribes of the Northwest Territory, 1215
Alma Highlands Festival and Games, 0073
Alma tree, 0078
Almabtrieb, 0074
almond, hidden, 0634
Alms Giving Festival
    See Panchadaan
Aloha Festivals, 0075

Numbers in the index refer to entry numbers, not page numbers

Alpaufzug, 0076
Alpenfest, 0077
alphabet, Korean
    Korea, 1279
Alpine Cattle Drive
    See Alpaufzug
Altan Khan, 0753
Altar de la Patria, 0756
aluminum pole, 1002
al-Ziyara
    See Khamis al-Amwat
Amalaka Ekadashi, 0078
Amarnath Yatra, 0079
Amazon and Galapagos Day, 0080
Amazon River, 0080
Ambaji, 0855
Ambedkar Jayanti, 0081
Ambedkar, Bhimrao Ramji, 0081
Ambiorix, 1134
Ambohimanga, 0050
Amen Corner, 0691
Amen-Re, 0009
American Birkebeiner, 0082
American Black Film Festival, 0083
American Folklife, Festival of, 2650
American Gold Star Mothers, 1155
American Hinduism, 0339
American Indian awards, 1988
American Indian beatification day, 2939
American Indian events
    See also individual tribe
    Apache, 0125
    Arapaho, 0135
    Athabascan, 2838
    Blackfeet, 2085
    Cherokee, 0574, 0575, 3138, 0188
    Choctaw, 0611, 0612
    Cree, 0718
    Creek, 0719
    Crow, 0732
    Dakota, 2661
    general, 0085, 0088, 0179, 0858, 1092, 1419, 1987, 1988,
        2090, 0542, 2379, 2976, 3045, 3088, 3253, 3261, 0084
    Hopi, 0252, 1362, 1363, 2069, 2308, 2679, 3280
    Inuit, 0008, 2090
    Iroquois, 0276, 0778, 0858, 1432, 2847
    Jemez Pueblo, 2124
    'Ksan, 1591
    Kwakiutl, 1604
    Meskwaki, 1859
    Miwok, 1894
    Mohegan, 1900
    Natchitoches, 1984
    Navajo, 1995, 1996, 1997, 2608
    Nez Perce, 0593, 1698
    Oglala Lakota Sioux, 0717
    Omaha, 3210
    San Ildefonso Pueblo, 2491
    Shinnecock, 2606
    Shoshone, 0135
    Sioux, 0717, 0858, 1154, 2639
    Southern Ute, 2677, 3101
    Suquamish, 0594
    Taino, 1469
    Tohono O'odham, 2995, 3169
    Wampanoag, 3176
    Yaqui, 0878, 2520
    Zuni Pueblo, 2586
American Indian Film Festival, 0084
American Indian Heritage Month, 0085
American Indian treaty, 1215
American Revolution, 0112, 0293, 0389, 0429, 0431, 0968,
    1108, 2372, 2816, 2836
American Royal Livestock, Horse Show and Rodeo, 0086
American Royal Rodeo
    See American Royal Livestock, Horse Show and Rodeo
American Solar Challenge, 0087
American West, Festival of the, 0088
America's Braemar
    See Grandfather Mountain Highland Games and
        Gathering of Scottish Clans
America's Cup, 0089
Amherstburg Heritage Homecoming, 0090
amrita, 0724
Amsterdam Light Festival, 0091
Amurdad, Feast of, 0092
An tOireachtas, 0093
Anant Chaturdashi, 0094
Anastenaria, 0095
ancestor commemoration
    India, 2280
    Nigeria, 2119
    Thailand, 2054
Anchorage Festival of Music, 0096
Anchorage Fur Rendezvous, 0097
ancient Egypt, 1884
ancient Greece
    community guilt festival, 2964
    fertility festivals, 0705, 1272, 2967
    harvest festival, 2967
    religious ceremonies, 0911
    sporting events, 0126, 1442, 2005, 2335
    spring festival, 0116
    theater, 0808, 0934
    tranquillity period, 1264
Ancient Greek Drama Festival
    See Curium Festival (Kourion Festival)
ancient Israelites, 2263
ancient Rome
    agricultural festivals, 0671, 2411
    calendar, 1398
    Cybele holiday, 1842
    death commemorations, 0992, 1631, 2212
    drinking festivals, 0108
    fertility festivals, 1041, 1662, 1715, 2144
    founding holiday, 2351
    horse racing, 0947
    horse sacrifice, 2109

Numbers in the index refer to entry numbers, not page numbers

Latin festival, 1634
marriage festival, 1816
mythological celebrations, 0505, 0545, 0553, 1309, 1764, 1813, 2006, 3150
opera, 0262
property owner ceremony, 2951
rape of the Sabine women, 0682
religious celebrations, 1086, 2213
ridding of spirits, 1656
sacrifice custom, 3168
sporting events, 1710, 2283, 2422
winter solstice festival, 2535
women's festivals, 0361, 1495
Anden Juledag, 0562
Andersen, Hans Christian, 0098, 0596
Andersen (Hans Christian) Festival, 0098
Andes, 0798
Andorra National Day, 0099
"Andy Griffith Show, The," commemoration, 1834
anesthesia, 0817
Angam Day, 0100
Angelitos, Los, 0101
angels, 0472, 1225
Angkor Photography Festival, 0102
Anglican Church
    All Saints' Day, 0064
    All Souls' Day, 0069
    Assumption of the Blessed Virgin Mary, Feast of the, 0178
    Embert Days, 0928
    Exaltation of the Cross, Feast of the, 0970
    Michaelmas, 1866
Anglican Communion, 0023
Angola
    death commemoration, 0104
    harvest festival, 2055
    independence day, 0103
Angola Independence Day, 0103
Angola National Heroes Day, 0104
animal blessing, 2701
animal blood, 1797
animal events, 0274
    Australia, 0314
    California, 1949
    China, 2374
    Illinois, 2133
    India, 2333
    Ireland, 2323
    Mexico, 2447
    Nepal, 2980
    Papua New Guinea, 2259
    Portugal, 2381
    Scandinavia, 2388
    Thailand, 1907, 2175
    Wyoming, 1451
Animal of the Year, 0363
animal sacrifices
    buffaloes, 0792, 0855
    bulls, 0792

goats, 0792, 0855
animal skins, 0505
animals
    See individual animals
animated films, 0111, 2853, 3024
Anjou Festival, 0105
Ann Arbor Art Fair, 0106
Ann Arbor Film Festival, 0107
Anna and the King of Siam (Landon), 0645
Anna Parenna Festival, 0108
Annakut Festival, 0109
Annapolis Valley Apple Blossom Festival, 0110
Anne of Green Gables, 0566
Annecy International Animation Film Festival, 0111
annexation celebration, 0698
Anniversary Day
    See Albania Republic Day; Australia
Annual Lantern Ceremony, 0112
Annual Minstrels' Carnival
    See Cape Minstrels' Carnival
Annual Session of the National Baptist Convention, USA, 0113
Annunciation of the Blessed Virgin Mary
    See Annunciation of the Lord
Annunciation of the Blessed Virgin Mary, Feast of the (Belgium), 0114
Annunciation of the Lord, 0115
Annunciation of the Theotokos
    See Annunciation of the Lord
Ano Novo
    See New Year's Day (Portugal) (Ano Novo)
Antananarivo, Madagascar, 0050
Anthesteria, 0116, 0808
Anthony (Susan B.) Day, 0117
Anti-Fascism Day
    See Croatia Anti-Fascist Resistance Day (Anti-Fascism Day)
Antigua and Barbuda
    board game competition, 3180
    Caribbean community commemoration, 0500
    Carnival celebration, 0119
    heroes celebration, 0120
    independence day, 0118
    music festival, 0119
    sailing festival, 0121
Antigua and Barbuda Independence Day, 0118
Antigua Carnival, 0119
Antigua National Heroes Day, 0120
Antigua Sailing Week, 0121
Antique and Classic Boat Rendezvous, 0122
Anul Nou
    See New Year's Day (Romania) (Anul Nou)
Anusuya, 0767
Anzac Day, 0123
Aoi Matsuri, 0124
Apache Maidens' Puberty Rites, 0125
    See also American Indians
apartheid, 2666
Apollo, 0126

Apollo 11, 1913
Apollo Karneios, 0507
Apollonian Games, 0126
Appalachian music festivals
    North Carolina, 0170
    Tennessee, 0850
    Apparition of the Infant Jesus, 0127
Apple and Candle Night, 0128
apple blossoms, 0110, 2598, 3183
apple fritters, 0633, 1083
apples, 0883
Appleseed (Johnny), Birthday of, 0129
Appleseed (Johnny) Festival, 0130
Appomattox Day, 0131
April Fair
    See Seville Fair
April Fools' Day, 0132, 0553
April (month), 0370
April Noddy Day
    See April Fools' Day
Aquino, Corazon C., 1005
Arab International Festival, 0133
Arab-Americans, 0133
Arabic Music Festival, 0134
Arapaho Sun Dance, 0135
    See also American Indians
Arawng Kagitingan
    See Bataan Day
Arbaeen, 0136
Arbaeen Pilgrimage, 0137
Arbor Day, 0138, 0189
archangels, 1866
archbishops, 2974
archery
    England, 1204
    Japan, 2996
    Mongolia, 1966
    saint's day, 2809
architecture event, 0159
Arctic Circle Race, 0139
Ardwahist, Feast of, 0140
Argentina
    agricultural celebration, 2859
    autumn harvest festival, 2059
    Carnival, 0510
    dancing, 0509, 2922
    death commemorations, 0143, 2504
    flag day, 0141
    independence day, 0142
    military commemoration, 0144
    religious holidays, 1408, 2093
    wheat festival, 3025
Argentina Flag Day, 0141
Argentina Independence Day, 0142
Argentina National Day of Memory and Truth and Justice, 0143
Argentine National Day, 0144
Argungu Fishing Festival, 0145
Århus Festival, 0146

Arizona
    agricultural celebration, 3303
    American Indian ceremonies, 1362, 1995, 1997, 2308, 2679, 3280
    American Indian dancing, 1363, 2069, 3253
    American Indian festivals, 1996, 0542, 2520
    American Indian music festival, 3169
    arts festival, 1028
    bridge festival, 1695
    chamber music festival, 1177
    constitution event, 0681
    Mexican folk music festival, 3041
    Old West festival, 2208
    parades, 3118
    pioneer festival, 1914
    religious holiday, 0878
    road commemoration, 2437
    rodeos, 0542, 2231, 2995, 3118
Arjuna, 1145
Arkansas
    chuckwagon race, 0643
    civil rights commemoration, 0260
    flower festival, 1482
    food festival, 1361, 1738
    music festival, 2177
    sporting event, 3275
Armed Forces Day
    See Haiti Battle of Vertières' Day
Armed Forces Day (Egypt), 0147
Armed Forces Day (United States), 0148
Armenia
    Christmas Eve, 0630
    constitution holiday, 0149
    earthquake commemoration, 0150
    fire festival, 1878
    independence day, 0151, 0152
    memorial day, 0154
    motherhood holiday, 0153
    religious festival, 0342
    saint feast day, 2807
Armenia Constitution Day, 0149
Armenia Earthquake Memorial Day, 0150
Armenia First Republic Day, 0151
Armenia Independence Day, 0152
Armenia Motherhood and Beauty Day, 0153
Armenian Church, 0616
Armenian Martyrs' Day, 0154
Armistice Day
    See Veterans Day
arms race, 0811
Army Day
    See Haiti Battle of Vertières' Day
Army (U.S.), 0148
Army-Navy Football Game, 0155
Arnold, Benedict, 0431
Arrival of the Tooth Relic
    See Esala Perahere (Arrival of the Tooth Relic)
art auction, 2449
Art Basel, 0156

Numbers in the index refer to entry numbers, not page numbers

Art Basel (Hong Kong), 0157
Art Basel (Miami Beach), 0158
Art Deco Weekend, 0159
art exhibition, 0709
Art Taipei, 0160
Artcar Fest, 0161
artichokes, 0546
ArtPrize, 0162
Arts and Crafts Fair, International, 0163
Arts and Pageant of the Masters, Festival of, 0164
arts and sciences awards, 0428
arts festivals
    Alabama, 0320
    Alberta, 0236
    Arizona, 1028
    Australia, 0019, 0020, 2245, 0311, 1847
    Austria, 3221
    Belgium, 0966
    Bermuda, 0303
    California, 0164, 0660
    Canada, 0236, 2665, 2099
    Colorado, 0787
    Costa Rica, 0700
    Croatia, 0848
    England, 0400, 1082, 1146
    Finland, 1503
    Florida, 0158, 0159
    France, 0105, 0966, 2095, 2342, 0997, 1050, 2083
    Germany, 0966
    Hong Kong, 1356, 0157, 2021
    Hungary, 0455
    Iceland, 2397
    Illinois, 2376
    India, 1506
    Iowa, 3245
    Ireland, 1551, 1094
    Israel, 1439
    Jamaica, 1456
    Japan, 0886
    Jordan, 1472
    Lebanon, 0281
    Luxembourg, 0966
    Maine, 3196
    Massachusetts, 1023
    Michigan, 0754, 0106, 0162
    Morocco, 1787
    Netherlands, 0966, 0967
    New Zealand, 2047
    Newfoundland, 2665
    Northern Ireland, 0283
    Oklahoma, 1835
    Ontario, 2099
    Scotland, 0890
    South Africa, 2668
    South Carolina, 2153, 2688
    South Dakota, 0741
    Spain, 1206
    Switzerland, 0156
    Syria, 0373
    Taiwan, 0160, 9016
    Tennessee, 1852
    Utah, 3099
    Washington (state), 0425
Aruba, 0510
Asadha Purnima
    See Guru Purnima
asafo, 0180
Asafo companies, 0007
Asanha Bucha Day (Asanha Puja Day), 0165
Asanha Puja Day
    See Asanha Bucha Day
Asano Naganori, 0043
Asarah be-Tevet (Fast of the Tenth of Tevet), 0166
Asbury, Francis, 0072
Asbury Methodist Church, 0031
Ascension Day, 0167, 0995
Ascension Day (Portugal), 0168
Ascot Gold Cup
    See Royal Ascot
Ash Wednesday, 0169, 0432, 0928
    See also Carnival Ashanti people, 0015
Asheville Mountain Dance and Folk Festival, 0170
Ashokashtami, 0171
Ashura, 0172
ashurer, 0153
Asia
    See also individual countries
    Dewali, 0794
    sporting events, 0173
Asian Film Market, 0446
Asian Football Confederation, 0025
Asian Games, 0173
askoliasmos, 0641
asparagus, 2841
Aspen Music Festival, 0175
Ass, Feast of the, 0176
Assam, India, 1524, 1732
Assateague Island, 0606
Assumption Day
    See Assumption of the Blessed Virgin Mary, Feast of the
Assumption, Feast of the, 0342
Assumption Fiesta
    See Running of the Bulls in Mexico
Assumption of Our Lady (Santa Marija), 0177
Assumption of the Blessed Virgin Mary, Feast of the, 0178
Assumption of the Virgin Mary, Feast of the (Guatemala), 0179
Assumption of the Virgin Mary, Feast of the (Hasselt, Belgium), 0180
Assumption of the Virgin Mary, Feast of the (Italy), 0181
Assyrian Christians, 2097
Aston Magna Festival, 0182
Astrik, 0342
Atash Niyayesh, 0017
Atatürk, Mustafa Kemal, 0183
Atatürk Remembrance (Youth and Sports Day), 0183
Athabascan Indians, 2838
    See also American Indians

Athens Festival, 0184
Ati people, 0185
Ati-Atihan Festival, 0185
Atlanta, Georgia, 0824
Atlanta Film Festival, 0186
Atlanta Pride Festival, 0187
Atohuna (Friends Made Ceremony), 0188
atomic bomb, 1313
Atomic Bomb Day
    See Hiroshima Peace Ceremony
Atri, 0767
Attucks, Crispus, 0376
Atwood, Ellis D., 0713
Audubon Day, 0189
Audubon, John James, 0189
Augsburg Day
    See Tura Michele Fair (Augsburg Day)
Augusta, Maine, 0257
Aung San, 1958, 1960, 1962
Auntie Litter's Annual Earth Day Parade and Celebration, 0190
Auschwitz-Birkenau concentration camp, 1332
Austen (Jane) Festival, 0191
Austin City Limits Music festival, 0192
Australia
    agricultural shows, 2440, 2442
    animal awareness day, 0314
    aquatic carnival, 1320
    arts festivals, 0019, 0020, 2245, 0311, 1847
    British settlement commemoration, 0193
    camel racing, 1632
    Carnival, 0532
    city celebrations, 0481
    comedy festival, 1848
    cultural festivals, 0019, 2407, 1951, 2893
    death commemoration, 0360
    film festivals, 1776, 1849, 2894
    fishing event, 3047
    food festival, 0605
    fossil festival, 2400
    gay rights commemoration, 2895
    horse racing, 1319, 1846
    indigenous commemorations, 1106, 1505, 2378
    lantern parade, 1682
    lights festival, 3161
    military commemoration, 0123
    mining festival, 2143
    music festival, 3161
    national holiday, 0193
    New Year's Eve, 2036
    pearl festival, 2605
    pioneer festival, 2172
    rodeo, 1937
    royal birthday, 0917
    sporting event, 0194, 0018
    tip-collection day, 0386
    trade union celebration, 0898
    winter festival, 1682
Australia Day, 0193

Australian Open Tennis, 0194
Austria
    arts festival, 3221
    autumn festival, 0074
    birthday commemorations, 1946, 1948
    Christmas, 0616, 2629
    classical music festivals, 0405, 0503, 0880, 1948, 2471, 2542
    cultural festivals, 0396, 2541, 2854, 3142
    cultural celebration, 3221
    dance festival, 1413
    film festival, 3024
    flower festival, 0265
    mask ceremonies, 0980, 2243
    national holiday, 0195
    parade, 0265
    procession, 0980
    religious holidays, 0942, 2192
    saint feast day, 2768
    wine feast, 1304
Austria National Day, 0195
Author's Day, National, 0196
automobile blessing, 2715
automobile parades
    California, 0161
    Michigan, 3248
automobile races
    Alabama, 3235
    Florida, 0773, 2555
    France, 1644
    Indiana, 1181, 1420
    Italy, 1883
    Kenya, 2461
    Monaco, 1905
    North Carolina, 0661
    Ohio, 0071
    South Carolina, 2676
    United States, 0087
automobile shows, 2086
automobiles, exploding, 0870
autumn festivals
    Argentina, 2059
    Austria, 0074
    Chile, 2059
    China, 0648
    France, 2215
    Germany, 3052
    Indiana, 0130
    Italy, 1412
    Japan, 0648, 3005, 1513, 2389
    Korea, 0648
    Mexico, 2108
    Vietnam, 0648
Autumnal Equinox, 0197
Avalokitesvara, 1150
Avani Mulam, 0198
Avesta, 0017
Aviation Day, 0199
Avignon Festival, 0200

avocados, 0464
Awa Odori
    See Obon Festival
awards
        California, 1965
        Nobel Prizes, 2078
        United States, 2313
Awate, Idris Hamid, 0952
Awoojah, 0201
Awuru Odo Festival, 0202
axes and trees, 0622
Axum obelisk, 0963
Ayathrem (Ayathrima; Bringing Home the Herds), 0203
Ayathrima
    See Ayathrem (Ayathrima; Bringing Home the Herds)
Ayerye Festival, 0204
Aymará Indians, 0482
Aymuray (Song of the Harvest), 0205, 0798
Ayurveda, 0796
Ayyam-i-Ha, 0206
Azerbaijan
        death commemoration, 0207
        independence day, 0208
Azerbaijan Day of the Martyrs, 0207
Azerbaijan Independence Days, 0208
Aztec festivals, 2345
        Homage to Cuauhtemoc, 1350
        New Fire Ceremony, 2017
        Xilonen, Festival of, 3281
        Xipe Totec, Festival of, 3282
        Aztec Rain Festival, 0209

B

Baal, 0914
Baalbeck Festival, 0210
Bab, Birth of the, 0211
Bab, Declaration of the, 0212
Bab, Martyrdom of the, 0213
Baba, 2106
Babi religion, 0206
babies, 0214
Babin Den, 0214
Baby Parade, 0215
Babylonian new year, 2458
Bacchanalia
    See Dionysia (Bacchanalia)
Bacchus, 0808
Bach Festival, 0216
Bach, Johann Sebastian, 0216, 0502, 0679, 0880
Bacheller, Irving, 0196
Bachelors' Day
    See Leap Year Day
Bach, Johann Sebastian, 2149
Bachok Cultural Festival, 0217
Bachwoche Ansbach
    See Bach Festival
bacon, 0853

Bad Durkheim Wurstmarkt (Sausage Fair), 0218
Bada Dasain
    See Durga Puja
Baden-Powell, Robert S. S., 0387
Baekjung, 0219
Baghdad Purim
    See Purims, Special
Bagnold, Enid, 1180
Bagobo, 1139
bagpipers, 0636
Baha'i Day of the Covenant, 0220
Baha'i events
        Abdu'l-Baha, Ascension of, 0004
        Bab commemorations, the, 0211, 0212, 0213, 0220
        Baha'u'llah commemorations, 0224, 0225
        calendar, 0206
        Nineteen Day Fast, 2071
        Race Unity Day, 2355
        Ridvan, Feast of, 2401
        World Religion Day, 3267
Bahamas
        abolition of slavery, 1068
        Caribbean community commemoration, 0500
        emancipation holiday, 0221
        independence day, 0222
        labor day, 0223
        music festival, 1494
        parade, 0223
Bahamas Emancipation Day, 0221
Bahamas Independence Day, 0222
Bahamas Labor Day, 0223
Bahamian music festival, 1864
Baha'u'llah, Ascension of, 0224
Baha'u'llah, Birth of, 0225
Bahia Independence Day, 0226
Bahrain
        cultural festival, 2690
        national holiday, 0227
Bahrain National Day, 0227
Bahti Meskerem
    See Eritrean Start of the Armed Struggle Day
Bahubali, 1739
Baile de las Turas (Dance of the Flutes), 0228
Baisakh
    See Vaisakh
bajada, la, 0903
Bal du Rat Mort (Dead Rat's Ball), 0229
Balancing Festival
    See Chochin Matsuri (Lantern Festival)
Balarama Shashti
    See Halashashti
Balfour, Arthur J., 0230
Balfour Declaration Day, 0230
Bali
        birthday commemoration, 2111
        religious festival, 1093
Bali, King, 0794
Balinese religion, 0900
Ballad of Baby Doe, The, 0551

Numbers in the index refer to entry numbers, not page numbers

Ball-Catching Festival (Tamaseseri), 0231
ballet, 2367, 0232
Ballet Festival of Miami, International, 0232
balloon festivals
    Iowa, 1372
    New Mexico, 0058
    New York, 2683
Balomain, 0563
balsas, 0803
Balserías, 0233
Balthasar, 0942
Baltic Song Festivals, 0234
Baltic-Nordic Harmonica Festival, 0235
Baltics, 0631
Bamba, Shaykh Amadou, 1179
Bamberger, Leo, 0215
Bamboo Dance, 0495
bamboo pole, 0363
bamboo rockets, 0426
bandes, 0516
Banff Festival of the Arts, 0236
Bangabandhu National Mourning Day, 0237
Bangabandhu Sheikh Mujibur Rahman, 0237
Bangladesh
    death commemoration, 2581
    film festival, 0795
    harvest festivals, 1968, 3104
    independence day, 0238
    military commemoration, 0239
    national holiday, 0237
    raft festival, 0294
    religious celebrations, 0321, 1508
Bangladesh Independence Day, 0238
Bangladesh Victory Day, 0239
Bank Holiday, 0240
Bannock Day
    See Shrove Tuesday
Bannocky Day
    See Shrove Tuesday
Banntag, 0241
banyan tree, 1520
Baoulé people, 1573
baptism, Jesus
    See Epiphany
Baptism of the Lord, Feast of the, 0242
Baptists, 3228
Barbados
    Caribbean community commemoration, 0500
    harvest festival, 0728
    independence day, 0243
    jazz festival, 0244
    political holiday, 0249
    settlement festival, 1326
Barbados Independence Day, 0243
Barbados Jazz Festival, 0244
Bar-B-Q Festival, International, 0245
Barcelona, Spain, 1206
Bard of Armagh Festival of Humorous Verse, 0246
Barnaby Bright

    See St. Barnabas's Day
Barnaby Day
    See St. Barnabas's Day
Barnebirkie, 0082
Barnum Festival, 0247
Barnum, Phineas Taylor (P. T.), 0247
Barók, Bela, 0409
Baron Bliss Day, 0248
baroque music festival, 0182
Barrel Parade
    See Kopenfahrt (Barrel Parade)
barrels, 1029
Barrow (Errol) Day, 0249
Bartholomew Fair, 0250
Basant Panchami
    See Vasant Panchami (Basant Panchami)
Bascarsija Nights, 0251
baseball, 1688, 2414, 3270
Basket Dance, 0252
basket festival, 1792
basketball, 1723
Basotho people, 1926
Basque Festival
    See St. Ignatius Loyola, Feast of
Basque Festival, National, 0253
Basset Hound Games, 0254
Bastille, 2067
Bastille Day, 0255, 0256, 0494
Bastille Day (Kaplan, Louisiana), 0256
Bastille, Festival de la, 0257
Bat Flight Breakfast, 0258
Bataan Day, 0259
Batalia de Vino
    See Haro Wine Festival (Batalia de Vino)
Bates (Daisy Gatson) Day, 0260
Bates, Daisy Gatson, 0260
Bath, England, 0191
Bath International Music Festival, 0261
bathing celebrations
    Caribbean, 2754
    India, 0045, 1517, 1593, 1735, 1809, 1819, 2653
    Malaysia, 1765
Baths of Caracalla, 0262
bathtub race, 3251
Batista, Fulgencio, 0734, 1001
Battalion Day
    See Whit-Monday (Whitmonday)
Battle for the Bridge, 1142
Battle of Adwa, 0963
Battle of Ayacucho, 0356
Battle of Bataan, 0259
Battle of Boyacá, 0664
Battle of Britain Day, 0263
Battle of Cannae, 0553
Battle of Carabobo, 3125
Battle of Cuildremne, 2717
Battle of Flodden, 0668
Battle of Flowers (Colombia), 0513
Battle of Flowers (Jersey, Channel Islands), 0264

Battle of Flowers (Vienna, Austria), 0265
Battle of Germantown, Reenactment of, 0266
Battle of Gettysburg, 1124, 1125
Battle of Golden Spurs, 1037
battle of good over evil, 1156
Battle of Iquique, 0598
Battle of Lake Regillus, 0545
Battle of New Orleans Day, 0267
Battle of North Point, 0782
Battle of Olustee Reenactment, 0268
Battle of Pichincha Day, 0887
Battle of Puebla, 0649
Battle of St. George's Caye, 0287
Battle of Tarqui, 0888
Battle of Vönnu, 0960
Battles of Lexington and Concord Day
    See Patriots' Day
Battleship Day
    See Maine Memorial Day
Bavarian culture, 1070
Bawming the Thorn Day, 0269
Bay to Breakers, 0270
Bayard, 1134
Bayfest, 0271
Bayou Classic, 0272
Bayou Food Festival, 0013
Bayram
    See Id al-Adha (Feast of Sacrifice; Eid)
Bayreuth Festival, 0273
Bazán family, 0142
Be Kind to Animals Week, 0274
beach festival, 2863
Beaches, Day of the (Día de las Playas), 0275
bean soup, 1838
beans, 0069, 0944, 0937, 0942
Bean-Throwing Festival
    See Setsubun (Bean-Throwing Festival)
bear dance, 3101
Bear Festival
    See Iyomante Matsuri (Bear Festival)
Bear Society Dance, 0276
Beard, Dan C., 0387
Beargrease (John) Sled Dog Marathon, 0277
Beatles, 0002
beauty pageants
    Ireland, 2432
    United States, 1892
Bechuanaland, 0380
Beckman, Eric, 2045
beer festivals
    Colorado, 1190
    Germany, 2120
    Oregon, 2150
    Uganda, 1891
Beethoven, Ludwig van, 0096, 0391, 0679, 0880
Befana Festival, 0278
Befana, La
    See Befana Festival
Beggar's Day

    See Martinmas
begging by the poor, 0826
Begging Day
    See Doleing Day
Begin, Menachem, 0147
begonias, 1681
Beiderbecke (Bix) Memorial Jazz Festival, 0279
Beijing Opera Festival, 0280
Beiteddine Festival, 0281
Belarus Independence Day, 0282
Belfast Festival, 0283
Belgian-American Days, 0284
Belgium
    arts festival, 0966
    battle of good over evil, 1156
    Carnival, 0530
    cat festival, 1525
    Christmas, 0616
    classical music competition, 0916
    costumes, 0530
    cultural festivals, 1430, 2182
    film festival, 0407
    flower festival, 1691
    folk festival, 1863
    historic reenactment, 2727
    independence days, 0285, 1079
    laundry festival, 1865
    linguistic heritage, 1079, 1123
    matchmaking party, 1815
    medieval pageant, 2140
    military commemoration, 1037
    music festival, 1030
    processions, 1134
    regional holidays, 3174
    religious celebrations, 0114, 0180, 0536, 0862, 1164, 1333, 1337, 1796, 2236
    rock music festival, 3129
    royal birthdays, 1560
    saint feast days, 2724, 2738, 2742, 2783
    sea commemoration, 2800
    sporting event, 0284
    tree-planting ritual, 1863
Belgium Independence Day, 0285
Belgrano, Manuel, 0141
Belize
    Caribbean community commemoration, 0500
    cultural festival, 2506
    death commemoration, 0248
    independence day, 0286
    military commemoration, 0287
    settlement day, 1104
Belize Independence Day, 0286
Belize National Day, 0287
bell music festival, 0502
bell silence commemoration, 2628
Bella Coola Midwinter Rites, 0288
bell-ringing ceremonies
    England, 2999
    Illinois, 0502

Numbers in the index refer to entry numbers, not page numbers

Scotland, 3217
Switzerland, 0559
Belmont Stakes, 0289
Belo, Carlos, 0861
belsnickers, 0629
Beltane, 0290, 0731, 1016
Beltein
    See Beltane
Beltine
    See Beltane
Belzoni, Giovanni, 0009
Beni, Alejo, 1104
Benihana Grand Prix Power Boat Regatta
    See New Jersey Offshore Grand Prix
Benin
    independence day, 0291
    Vodoun culture, 0292
Benin Independence Day, 0291
Benin National Vodoun Day (Traditional Religions Day),
    0292
Benkowski, Georgi, 0419
Bennington Battle Day, 0293
Bera Festival, 0294
Berchtold's Day, 0295
Berchtoldstag
    See Berchtold's Day
Bergen International Festival, 0296
Bering Sea Ice Golf Classic, 0297
Berlin Biennale, 0298
Berlin Festival of Lights, 0299
Berlin International Film Festival, 0300
berlinda, 0994
Bermuda
    arts festival, 0303
    boat race, 2053
    cultural festival, 0302
    kite-flying, 1165
    political ceremony, 2242
    religious holiday, 1165
    royal birthday, 0917
    rugby, 0301
    sporting event, 0738
    storytelling festival, 2942
Bermuda College Weeks, 0301
Bermuda Day, 0302
Bermuda Festival of the Performing Arts, 0303
Berry, John, 1085
beseda, 0744
Bethlehem (nativity site), 0632
Bethlehem, Pennsylvania, 0637
Bettara-Ichi, 0304
bettera, 0304
BFI London Film Festival, 0305
Bhagavad Gita, 1145
Bhai Dooj, 0306
Bhairava Ashtami, 0307
Bhima, 0797
Bhishma Ashtami, 0308
Bhogali Bihu

See Magh Bihu
Bhumibol Adulyadej, King of Thailand, 1563
Bhutan, 2969
Biandrate, Count Raineri di, 0533
Bianou, 0309
Bible, 0310, 0453, 0970
Bible Week, National, 0310
bicycle races
    France, 3014
    Iowa, 2358
Biennale of Sydney, 0311
Biennale, La
    See Venice Biennale (La Biennale)
biergarten, 1070
Biesenbach, Klaus, 0298
Big August Quarterly, 0031
Big E
    See Eastern States Exposition
Big House Religion, 0783
Big Iron Farm Show, 0312
Big Singing, 0313
Bike Week
    See Motorcycle Week (Bike Week)
Bilby Day, National, 0314
Bill of Rights Day, 0315
Billboard Latin Music Awards, 0316
Billiken (Bud) Parade and Picnic, 0317
Billy the Kid Pageant, 0318
Bin Said, Sultan Qaboos, 2136
Binche, Belgium, 0530
Binding Tuesday
    See Hocktide
Biological Diversity, International Day for, 0319
Birchat Hahamah
    See Blessing the Sun (Birchat Hahamah)
Bird and Arbor Day
    See Arbor Day
bird events, 0628
    California, 2882
    Canada, 1193, 1194
    England, 2883
    Nebraska, 0715
    Texas, 0989
    United States, 0189, 1193, 1194
Bird, Vere Cornwall, 0120
Birdman Ceremony
    See Tangata Manu (Birdman Ceremony)
Birkebeiner Rennet, 0082
Birkie, The
    Birkebeiner Rennet, 0082
Birmingham Hippodrome, 0757
Birmingham International Center Spotlight, 0320
birth goddess, 0505
birthday commemorations
    See also royal birthday commemorations
    African-Americans, 0072
    Alabama, 0769
    Audubon, John James, 0189
    Austria, 1946, 1948

Bali, 2111
Botswana, 0380
California, 0430
Canada, 1982
China, 1150, 1817, 1906, 2865
Christian Science, 0889
Czech Republic, 2936
England, 1481, 2585, 2601
Ethiopia, 1253
Finland, 2446
Florida, 0769, 1557
Honduras, 1355
Hong Kong, 1150, 1708, 2917
India, 0753, 0767, 0825, 1098, 1464, 2905, 3046, 3109
Indonesia, 1518, 2559
Iran, 0211, 3063
Iraq, 1403
Jainism, 2220
Jamaica, 1785
Japan, 0428, 1150, 1213, 1468, 1843, 2558, 2607
Korea, 1150
Liberia, 1669, 2410
Louisiana, 1697
Malaysia, 1150, 1753
Mexico, 3186
Mississippi, 0769
New York, 0837, 2425
Newfoundland, 0443
North Korea, 1553, 1554
Nova Scotia, 1982
Ohio, 1088
Oklahoma, 2420
Oman, 2136
Pakistan, 1426
Pennsylvania, 1072, 2238
Persia, 0211
Peru, 0803
Puerto Rico, 1371, 1953
Scotland, 0443
Sikhs, 1237
Taiwan, 1817
Tennessee, 1452
Texas, 0769, 3186
Tibet, 0753, 1675
United States, 0893, 1556, 1650, 1680, 1719, 1754, 2183, 2836, 3184
Vietnam, 1318
Virginia, 1471, 3185
Washington, D.C., 0837
Birthday of Tulsidas
    See Tulsidas Jayanti (Birthday of Tulsidas)
Bi-Shevat
    See Tu Bishvat (Bi-Shevat; B'Shevat; Hamishah Asar
        Bishevat)
Bishwa Ijtema, 0321
Bisket Jatra, 0322
Bite of Seattle, 0323
black American events
    See African-American events

Black and White Ball, 0324
Black Christ Festival
    See Black Christ, Festival of the
Black Christ, Festival of the, 0325
Black Christ of Esquipulas, Day of the, 0326
black citizens freedom day, 2666
Black Cowboy Parade, 0327
Black Friday, 0328
Black Hills Motorcycle Classic
    See Sturgis Motorcycle Rally
Black Hills Passion Play, 0329
Black History Month, 0330
Black January, 0207
Black Madonna of Jasna Gora, Feast of the, 0331
Black Nazarene Fiesta, 0332
Black Poetry Day, 0333
black robes, 0563
Black Ships Festival, 0334
black shoe polish, 0802
Black St. Benito, Fiesta of the, 0335
Black Storytelling Festival and Conference, National, 0336
Blackbeard Pirate Festival, 0337
Blackfeet Indian Reservation, 2085
Blackfeet Indians, 0085, 2085
    See also American Indians
blaffs, 0736
Blair Thomas & Co., 0590
Blajini, 0338
Blajini, Feast of the (Sarbatoarea Blajinilor), 0338
Blanc-Moussis, 0536
Blank, Harrod, 0161
blanket toss, 3261
Blase
    See St. Blaise's Day
Blasius
    See St. Blaise's Day
Blavatsky (Helena Petrovna), Death of, 0339
Bleak House, 0403
Blessed Sacrament, Feast of the, 0340
Blessing Boat, 0343
Blessing of Horses
    See Nativity of the Blessed Virgin Mary, Feast of the
        (Germany)
Blessing of the Animals
    See St. Anthony the Abbot, Feast of
Blessing of the Bikes, 0341
Blessing of the Cars
    See St. Christopher's Day
Blessing of the Fleet
    See Blessing of the Shrimp Fleet
Blessing of the Grapes (Haghoghy Ortnootyoon), 0341
Blessing of the Sea
    See St. Peter's Day (Belgium)
Blessing of the Shrimp Fleet, 0343
Blessing of the Waters Day
    See Beaches, Day of the (Día de las Playas); Epiphany,
        Christian Orthodox
Blessing of the Wheat
    See St. Mark's Day (Hungary)

Numbers in the index refer to entry numbers, not page numbers

Blessing the Sun (Birchat Hahamah), 0344
blind/deaf/mute commemoration, 1532
bliny, 0451
Bliss, Henry Edward Ernest Victor, 0248
blood, 1797
blood sausage, 0635
Bloody Sunday, 0397
Bloomsday, 0344
Blossom Days
    See Washington State Apple Blossom Festival
Blossom Sunday
    See Palm Sunday
Blowing the Midwinter Horn, 0346
Blue Dragon Festival (Zhonghe Festival), 0347
blueberries, 0049
bluegrass festivals
    Kentucky, 3220
    New Jersey, 2132
    Oklahoma, 1186
    Tennessee, 2652
    Virginia, 2123
blues festivals
    Alabama, 1278
    Illinois, 0585
    North Carolina, 0422
board game competition, 3180
Boat Race Day (Okinawa, Japan), 0348
Boat Race Day (Thames River), 0349
boating events
    Bermuda, 2053
    California, 2051
    China, 0842, 3039
    Connecticut, 0122, 3283
    England, 0349, 1301
    Hong Kong, 0842, 3039
    Idaho, 1396
    Italy, 2386
    Japan, 0348
    Maine, 1203
    Maryland, 2647
    New Jersey, 2018
    Rhode Island, 2053
    Taiwan, 0842, 3039
    Thailand, 3187
    Venice, 1315
    Washington (state), 3247
    West Virginia, 0564
Bob Apple Night
    See Halloween
Bobby Ack Day
    See Shick-Shack Day (Shik-Shak Day; Shicsack Day;
      Shig-Shag Day)
Boccherini, Luigi, 0679
Bocuse, Paul, 0350
Bocuse d'Or, 0350
Bodhi Day (Rohatsu), 0351
Bodhisattva, 1150, 2010
body painting contest, 0407
Bog Snorkelling Championship, World, 0352

Boganda, Barthémy, 0353
Boganda Day, 0353
Boggy Bayou Mullet Festival, 0354
Bohag Bihu
    See Vaisakh
Bohemia, 2615
Bois-Bois, 0519
Bok Eye (Bok I), 0355
Bok Kai Festival, 0355
Bolívar, Simón, 0356, 0664
Bolivia
    Carnival, 0511, 0534
    independence days, 0356, 1608
    llama ritual, 1690
    military commemoration, 0598
    parades, 0534
    religious holidays, 0482
    saint feast days, 2505, 2507
    shopping fair, 0052
Bolivia Independence Day, 0356
Bologna Festival, 0357
bolo-rei, 0937
Bolshevik Revolution Day, 0358
Bom Jesus dos Naveganes, 0359
Bomb Day
    See Bok Kai Festival
Bombing of Darwin, Anniversary of the, 0360
Bon Festival
    See Obon Festival
Bona Dea Festival, 0361
Bonalu, 0362
Bonden Festival (Bonden Matsuri), 0363
Bonden Matsuri
    See Bonden Festival (Bonden Matsuri)
bone-fires, 0365
Bonfiglio, Robert, 1177
Bonfim Festival (Festa do Bonfim), 0364
Bonfire Night, 0365
bonfires
    See also fires
    Brazil, 0365
    Bulgaria, 0571
    Celtic culture, 1016
    Germany, 0868
    Japan, 0750
    Louisiana, 0639
    Luxembourg, 0415
    Neopagan holidays, 1016
    Netherlands, 0871
    Scotland, 0439
    Sweden, 0876
    Texas, 0881
    Wisconsin, 1087
Bonfires of St. Joseph
    See St. Joseph's Day
Boniface IV, Pope, 0064
Bonn Om Tuk
    See Reversing Current, Festival of the (Water Festival;
      Bonn Om Tuk)

Bonifacio Day, 0366
Bonifacio y de Castro, Andres, 0366
Bonneville Speed Week, 0367
Bonney, William (Billy the Kid), 0318
Boogaloo Celebration Parade, 0787
books
    children's, 0596
    China, 0040
    damaged, 0040
    Germany, 1071
Boone (Daniel) Festival, 0368
Bordeaux, France, 1185
Booth, William, 2470
border events
    Scotland, 0668
    Texas-Mexico, 0567
Border Folk Festival
    See Chamizal Festival
Borg, Bjorn, 1080
Borglum (Gutzon) Day, 0369
Borglum, Lincoln, 0369
Borneo, 0949
Borrowed Days, 0370
Borrowing Days
    See Borrowed Days
Boryeong Mud Festival, 0371
Boshin-no-eki, 0042
Bosnia and Herzegovina
    cultural festival, 0251
    national holiday, 0372
Bosnia and Herzegovina Statehood Day, 0372
Bosra Festival, 0373
Boston Jewish Film Festival, 0374
Boston Marathon, 0375
Boston Massacre Day, 0376
Boston Pops, 0377
Boston Science Fiction Film Festival, 0378
Boston Symphony Orchestra, 0377
Boston Tea Party, 0580
Boston's Fourth of July
    See Bunker Hill Day
Botswana
    birthday commemoration, 0380
    independence day, 0379
Botswana Independence Day, 0379
Botswana Sir Seretse Khama Day, 0380
Bottle Kicking and Hare Pie Scramble, Annual, 0381
Bottoni, Stefano, 0448
boudins, 0736
Boun Bang Fay
    See Bun Bang Fai (Boun Bang Fay; Rocket Festival)
Boun Ok Vatsa
    See Thadingyut
Boun Phan Vet, 0382
boundary feasts, 0383
boundary stone festival, 1626
Boundary Walk (Grenzumgang), 0383
Bounds Thursday
    See Ascension Day

Bouphonia (Buphonia), 0384
Bower Award and Prize in Science, 1072
Bowie, James, 0051
Bowing Procession
    See Assumption of the Virgin Mary, Feast of the (Italy)
Bowlegs (Billy) Festival, 0385
bowling, 0173
boxing, 2283, 2422
Boxing Day, 0386
Boy Scout Month
    See Boy Scouts' Day
Boy Scouts' Day, 0387
Boys' Day Festival
    See Tango-no-Sekku (Boys' Day Festival)
Boys' Dodo Masquerade, 0388
Brady (Captain Samuel) Day, 0389
Braemar Highland Gathering, 0390
Brahma, 0767
Brahmans, 2441
Brahms, Johannes, 0880
Braid, Scot James, 0402
Branch Sunday
    See Palm Sunday
branch-striking holiday, 2620
brass band festival, 1191
Bratislava Music Festival, 0391
bratwurst, 2593
Brauteln, 0392
Brazil
    candle procession, 0652
    Carnival, 0512
    cattle roundup, 0541
    church-building feast, 0364
    dancing, 0512
    death commemoration, 2169
    film festival, 2403
    folk drama, 0424
    gay rights commemoration, 2527
    independence days, 0226, 0393, 1415
    military commemoration, 0549
    national holiday, 0394
    New Year's Eve, 2037
    parade, 2527
    procession, 0652
    religious festivals, 0549, 0814, 0994, 3289
    saint feast day, 2849
    Southern United States celebration, 0674
    Virgin Mary celebrations, 2159, 2170
    water festival, 0359
Brazil Independence Day, 0393
Brazil Proclamation of the Republic Day, 0394
bread, 1166
Bread and Roses Heritage Festival, 0395
Bregenz Festival, 0396
Breton festival, 0688
Brewer, Charles, 0717
breweries, 0685
Bride
    See St. Bridget's Day

Numbers in the index refer to entry numbers, not page numbers

bride-wooing ceremony, 0392
bridge celebrations
    Arizona, 1695
    Iowa, 1730
    Thailand, 2406
    West Virginia, 0398
Bridge Crossing Jubilee, 0397
Bridge Day, 0398
Bridge Walking (Dari Balgi), 0399
Brighton, England, 0440
Brighton Festival, 0400
Brightwell, W. T., 0049
Brigid
    See St. Bridget's Day
Bringing Home the Herds
    See Ayathrem (Ayathrima; Bringing Home the Herds)
British Columbia
    air show, 0003
    American Indian dancing, 1591
    bathtub race, 3251
    classical music concert, 0401
    dancing, 0288, 0761
    literary celebration, 3111
    music festival, 2588
    pioneer holiday, 0401
British Columbia Day, 0401
British composers festival, 0573
British Film Institute, 0305
British Honduras, 0286
British Isles, 1485
British Open, 0402
Brittany, 0290
Britten, Benjamin, 0059
Broadstairs Dickens Festival, 0403
Broderick, Jon, 1025
broken crockery, 1166
bronc fanning, 0643
Brotherhood/Sisterhood Week, 0404
Brown, "Tarzan," 0336
Brown University, 0497
Broz, Josip (Tito), 0721
Bruckner, Anton, 0405
Bruckner Festival, International, 0405
Brunei
    military commemoration, 2439
    national holiday, 0406
Brunei National Day, 0406
Brussels International Fantastic Film Festival, 0407
Brussels World Fair, 1030
Bryn Mawr College, 1629
B'Shevat
    See Tu Bishvat (Bi-Shevat; B'Shevat; Hamishah Asar
      Bishevat)
Buc Days
    See Buccaneer Days
Buccaneer Days, 0408
Buchmesse
    See Frankfurt Book Fair (Buchmesse)
Budapest Music Weeks, 0409

Budapest Spring Festival, 0410
Buddha Day
    See Kasone Festival of Watering the Banyan Tree
Buddha Jayanti
    See Vesak (Wesak; Buddha's Birthday)
Buddha Purnima
    See Vesak (Wesak; Buddha's Birthday)
Buddha's Birthday
    See Vesak (Wesak; Buddha's Birthday)
Buddha's tooth celebration, 0953, 3187
Buddhist events, 1150, 2958, 3134
    Adam's Peak, Pilgrimage to, 0065
    Airing the Classics, 0040
    Asanha Bucha Day (Asanha Puja Day), 0165
    Baekjung, 0219
    Bodhi Day (Rohatsu), 0351
    Boun Phan Vet, 0382
    Bun Bang Fai (Boun Bang Fay; Rocket Festival), 0426
    Butter Sculpture Festival, 0450
    Cambodian New Year (Khmer New Year), 0472
    Chrysanthemum Festival, 0642
    Dalai Lama, Birthday of the, 0753
    Dosmoche, 0835
    Esala Perahera (Arrival of the Tooth Relic), 0953
    Floating Lantern Ceremony (Toro Nagashi), 1040
    Hana Matsuri (Flower Festival), 1274
    Hari-Kuyo (Festival of Broken Needles), 1284
    Hemis Festival, 1300
    Higan, 1307
    Jizo Ennichi, 1479
    Kasone Festival of Watering the Banyan Tree, 1520
    Kataragama Festival, 1523
    Laba Festival, 1609
    Lantern Festival (Korea), 1628
    Lantern Festival (Yuan Hsiao Chieh), 1627
    Lights, Festival of (Ganden Ngamcho), 1675
    Lotus, Birthday of the, 1703
    Magha Puja (Maka Buja, Full Moon Day), 1734
    Mani Rimdu, 1767
    Marya, 1802
    Monlam (Prayer Festival), 1908
    Mystery Play (Tibet), 1964
    Neri-Kuyo, 2010
    Ngan Duan Sib (Tenth Lunar Month Festival), 2054
    Obon Festival, 2105
    Omizutori Matsuri (Water-Drawing Festival), 2139
    Panchadaan, 2204
    Paro Tsechu, 2218
    Phra Buddha Bat Fair, 2254
    Poson, 2304
    Raksha Bandhan, 2361
    Rato (Red) Machhendranath, 2382
    Sanghamita Day, 2510
    Shinbyu, 2604
    Shinran-Shonin Day, 2607
    Shunbun-no-Hi (Vernal Equinox Day), 2621
    Shwedagon Pagoda Festival, 2622
    Songkran, 2662
    St. Nichiren's Pardon, Festival of, 2787

Numbers in the index refer to entry numbers, not page numbers

Sugar Ball Show (Sugar-Coated Haws Festival), 2856
Ta Mo's Day, 2901
Tazaungdaing, 2934
That Luang Festival, 2965
Thay Pagoda Festival, 2966
Thimphu Tsechu, 2969
Ullambana (Hungry Ghosts Festival; All Souls' Feast), 3079
Universal Prayer Day (Dzam Ling Chi Sang), 3089
Vatsa (Ho Khao Slak), 3122
Water-Splashing Festival (Dai New Year), 3193
Buddhist Rains Retreat
    See Waso (Buddhist Rains Retreat)
Budget Day, 0411
Buena Vista Logging Days, 0412
Buenos Aires International Festival of Independent Cinema, 0413
Buenos Aires Rojo Sangre, 0414
Buergsonndeg, 0415
Buffalo Days Powwow, 0416
buffalo, 0135, 0794, 0855
buffalo roundup, 0741
Buffalo Soldiers Commemorations, 0417
Buffalo's Big Board Surfing Classic, 0418
Bulgaria
    baby deliveries, 0214
    caroling, 1582
    classical music festival, 2655
    cultural holiday, 1645
    dairy-products celebration, 0571
    dancing, 0863
    educational commemoration, 1645
    fertility rituals, 1613, 1795, 2767
    flower festival, 2430
    humor festival, 1379
    independence days, 0419, 0420
    national holiday, 0932
    popular music competition, 1160
    religious holiday, 0863
    saint feast days, 2734, 2820
    wine festival, 3153
Bulgaria Day of Liberation from Ottoman Domination, 0419
Bulgaria Independence Day, 0420
Bulgarian Education and Culture Day 0421
Bull Durham Blues Festival, 0422
Bull, Ole, 0296
bullfighting
    Colombia, 0462
    New Mexico, 2124
    Paraguay, 2479
    Portugal, 2381
    Spain, 2494
Bullfinch Exchange
    See Usokae (Bullfinch Exchange)
bulls, 0424, 0792, 2980
bulls, running of the, 2447
Bulu Festival, 0423
Bumba-Meu-Boi Folk Drama, 0424

Bumbershoot, 0425
Bun Bang Fai (Boun Bang Fay; Rocket Festival), 0426
Bun Day
    See Shrove Monday
Bunch (Madam Lou) Day, 0427
bunggul, 1106
Bunka-no-Hi (Culture Day), 0428
Bunker Hill Day, 0429
buns, 0581
Bunyan, Paul, 2228
Buphonia
    See Bouphonia (Buphonia)
Burbank Day, 0430
Burbank, Luther, 0430
Burckhardt, Johann, 0009
burgoo, 0245
Burgoyne's (John) Surrender Day, 0431
Burial of the Sardine, 0432
Burkina Faso
    arts and crafts fair, 0163
    children's entertainment festival, 0388
    Christmas, 0616
    film festival, 2199
    independence day, 0433
    national holiday, 0434
    Ramadan, 0388
Burkina Faso Independence Day, 0433
Burkina Faso Republic Day, 0434
Burma
    See Myanmar
Burning Man Festival, 0435
Burning of Judas, 0436
Burning of the Boog, 0077
Burning of the Ribbons (Queima das Fitas), 0437
Burning of the Socks, 0438
Burning the Clavie, 0439
Burning the Clocks, 0440
Burning the Devil, 0441
Burning the Moon House, 0442
Burns (Robert) Night, 0443
burro racing, 3032
Burry Man Day, 0444
Burundi Independence Day, 0445
Busan International Film Festival, 0446
Busan Sea Festival, 0447
Bush, George H. W., 1117
business festival, 0885
Buskers' Festival, 0448
buso, 1139
Butaritari Island, 2146
Butter and Egg Days, 0449
Butter Sculpture Festival, 0450
Butter Week (Russia), 0451
Buza-Szentelo
    See St. Mark's Day (Hungary)
Buzzard Day, 0452
Byakkotai, 0042

Numbers in the index refer to entry numbers, not page numbers

Byblos International Festival, 0453
    Byce, L. C., 0449

C

cabalgata, 0414
caber, 0390
caboclo, 0202
Cabral, Amílcar, 1234
Cabrillo Day and Festival, 0454
Cabrillo, Juan Rodríguez, 0454
Cafe Budapest, 0455
Caitra Parb, 0456
Caitra Purnima, 0457
Cajun culture, Louisiana, 0013, 0639, 0716
Cake Festival
    See Sithinakha
cake of the Kings, 0944
cake-eating festival, 3012
cakes, 0616, 0638, 0874, 0944, 0937, 1059
calabazos, 0487
Calaveras County Fair and Frog Jumping Jubilee, 0458
calendar events, 1646
calendars
    ancient Rome, 1398
    Baha'i faith, 0206
    Julian-to-Gregorian switch, 1063
    Zoroastrian, 0001, 0017
Calendimaggio, 0459
Calgary Exhibition and Stampede, 0460
Calgary International Children's Festival, 0461
Calgary Stampede
    See Calgary Exhibition and Stampede
Cali Fair (Sugar Cane Fair, Salsa Fair), 0462
Calico Pitchin', Cookin', and Spittin' Hullabaloo, 0463
California
    African-American cultural festival, 3194
    American Indian ceremonies, 1604, 1894
    animal festival, 1949
    arts festivals, 0164, 0660
    arts festival, 0164
    award ceremony, 1965
    bird festival, 2882
    birthday commemoration, 0430
    boat parade, 2051
    comic book convention, 2480
    computer festival, 3154
    county fairs, 0458
    crab racing, 3252
    cultural festival, 1611
    dance festivals, 0756, 2483
    egg festival, 0449
    film festivals, 0756, 1069, 1882, 2200, 2485
    fish festival, 3276
    fishermen's festival, 2522
    flooding festival, 0355
    food festivals, 0464, 0546, 1138, 1974, 2841, 2487, 2663
    gay rights commemorations, 1069, 1110, 1881, 2486

    gold rush, 0465
    harvest festival, 1894
    historic celebration, 2217
    Indian festival, 2326
    Japanese cultural celebration, 0577
    Japanese-American festival, 2075
    jazz festivals, 1012, 1909
    labor holiday, 0568
    literature festival, 2834
    Mexican-American celebration, 2127
    military commemorations, 1034, 1035
    music festival, 0660
    musical fundraisers, 0324
    natural resources celebration, 0430
    painting festival, 1387
    parades, 0161, 0327, 0834, 1445, 3015
    Portuguese festival, 0454
    pumpkin festival, 1265
    religious celebrations, 0869, 2569
    running race, 0270
    sandcastle festival, 2509
    Santa Claus event, 1073
    Spanish-American festival, 2127
    spider festival, 2927
    sporting events, 2429, 3272, 9100
    Swedish festival, 1564
    tobacco-spitting contest, 0463
    whale festival, 3207
    wine festival, 3108, 2663
    yacht race, 3020
California Avocado Festival, 0464
California Gold Rush Day, 0465
Calinda Dance, 0466
Calixtus I, Pope, 0928
calypso music
    Antigua and Barbuda, 0119
    U.S. Virgin Islands, 0526
Cambodia
    birthday commemoration, 0470
    constitutional holiday, 0467
    cultural celebration, 0469
    death commemoration, 2251
    historic celebration, 2627
    independence day, 0468
    military commemoration, 0471
    national holiday, 2627
    New Year's celebration, 0472
    photography festival, 0102
    water festival, 2396
Cambodia Constitution Day, 0467
Cambodia Independence Day, 0468
Cambodia National Culture Day, 0469
Cambodia Queen Sihanouk's Birthday, 0470
Cambodia Victory Day, 0471
Cambodian New Year (Khmer New Year), 0472
camel fairs
    India, 2333
    Morocco, 0474
Camel Market, 0474

Numbers in the index refer to entry numbers, not page numbers

Camel and Ostrich Races, International, 0473
camel racing
    Australia, 1632
    Kenya, 1771
    Nevada, 0473
Cameroon
    national holiday, 0475
    religious holiday, 0969
    running race, 1933
    spirits festival, 2058
    youth day, 0476
Cameroon National Day, 0475
Cameroon Youth Day, 0476
Camões, Luis Vas de, 2300
Camões Memorial Day
    See Portugal National Day
Camp David Accords, 0147
Camp Fire Boys and Girls Birthday Sunday
    See Camp Fire Founders' Day
Camp Fire Boys and Girls Birthday Week
    See Camp Fire Founders' Day
Camp Fire Founders' Day, 0477
Campbell, Malcolm, 0773
Canada
    See also individual provinces
    African-American holiday, 1605
    air show, 0003
    American Indian celebration, 0718
    American Indian dancing, 1591
    American Indian festival, 1432
    American Indian sporting event, 2090
    arts festivals, 0236, 2665, 2099
    bathtub race, 3251
    bird counting, 1193, 1194
    birthday commemorations, 0443, 1982
    Caribbean festivals, 0501, 3009
    children's festivals, 0461
    Christmas Eve, 0629
    church funding, 2837
    comedy festival, 1496
    cultural heritage celebration, 0057
    dance festival, 0761
    dog sled race, 0499
    emancipation celebrations, 0922, 0927
    film festival, 3010
    film festivals, 0998, 1911
    flower festival, 1768
    folk festivals, 1782, 3234
    food festival, 0110, 3011
    football championship, 1219
    freedom festival, 1076
    Gold Rush festivals, 1574, 1575
    historic reenactment, 3021
    Icelandic festival, 1391
    indigenous peoples, 0008
    jazz festival, 1910
    literature festivals, 2287, 2687, 3111
    military commemoration, 0479
    music festivals, 0011, 0566, 1887, 2343, 2665, 2588

    national exhibition, 0480
    national holidays, 0478
    parades, 1153
    pioneer holiday, 0401
    poetry celebration, 0443
    powwow, 0416
    provincial holidays, 2013, 2049, 2096
    puppet festival, 0999
    religious holiday, 0936
    rock paper scissors championship, 3268
    rodeo, 0460
    saint feast day, 2699
    Scottish cultural festival, 1090
    Shakespeare festival, 2846
    sporting event, 1576
    Star Trek festival, 2686
    storytelling festivals, 2942, 3301
    tip-collection day, 0386
    winter festivals, 0499, 2344, 3239
Canada Day, 0478, 1076
Canadian Armed Forces, 0003
Canadian International Military Tattoo, 0479
Canadian National Exhibition, 0480
canals, 0037
Canary, "Calamity Jane," 0702
Canary Islands festival, 1701
Canberra Day, 0481
Candelaria
    See Candlemas
Candelaria (Bolivia), 0482
Candelaria (Peru), 0483
Candle Auction, 0484
candle events
    Brazil, 0652
    England, 0484
    Germany, 0024
    Italy, 2353
    Thailand, 0165, 3187
Candle Feasts
    See Lamp Nights (Kandil Geceleri, Candle Feasts)
Candlemas, 0485
Candlewalk, 0486
Candomblé event, 2037, 2169, 3289
Candy Dance Arts and Crafts Faire, 0487
Candy Festival
    See Id al-Fitr (Eid)
Canicular Days
    See Dog Days
Cannes Film Festival, 0488
Cannes Shopping Festival, 0489
Cannon, Hal, 0710
canoe regatta, 1113
Cantaderas, Las, 0490
Cantate Sunday
    See Rogation Days
cantonal meetings, 1624
Capac Raymi, 0491
Cape Minstrels' Carnival, 0492
    Cape Verde death commemoration, 1234

independence day, 0493
Cape Verde Independence Day, 0493
Cape Verde National Heroes' Day
 See Guinea-Bissau and Cape Verde National Heroes'
  Day
Cape Vincent French Festival, 0494
Capek, Norbert, 1048
capitana, 0952
Captain Brady Day
 See Brady (Captain Samuel) Day
Car Festival
 See Rath Yatra
Carabao Festival, 0495
Caramoor International Music Festival, 0496
Carberry Day, 0497
carbonated beverage festival, 1942
Caribbean bathing ritual, 2754
Caribbean community commemoration, 0500
Caribbean Festival (Feast of Fire), 0498
Caribbean festivals
 African American holiday, 1605
 Canada, 3009
 North Carolina, 1171
 Ontario, 3009
 Washington, D.C., 0775
Caribbean music festivals
 Alberta, 0501
 Canada, 0501
Caribou Carnival and Canadian Championship Dog
 Derby, 0499
Caricom Day, 0500
Carifest, 0501
Carillon Festival, International, 0502
Carinthian Summer Music Festival, 0503
Carling Sunday, 0504
Carlsbad Caverns, 0258
Carmenta, 0505
Carmentalia, 0505
Carnaval Miami, 0506
Carnea, 0507
Carneia
 See Carnea
Carnival (Argentina), 0509
Carnival (Aruba), 0510
Carnival (Bolivia), 0511
Carnival (Brazil), 0512
Carnival celebrations
 Antigua and Barbuda, 0119
 Croatia, 2565
 France, 2062
 Germany, 2431
 Haiti, 2369
 Indonesia, 1598
 Italy, 0527
 Russia, 0451
 Spain, 0432
 St. Vincent, 3151
 Trinidad and Tobago, 3026
Carnival (Colombia), 0513

Carnival (Cuba), 0514
Carnival (Goa, India), 0515
Carnival (Haiti), 0516
Carnival (Hungary) (Farsang), 0517
Carnival Lamayote, 0528
Carnival (Malta), 0518
Carnival (Martinique and Guadeloupe), 0519
Carnival Memphis, 0529
Carnival (Mexico), 0520
Carnival of Binche, 0530
Carnival of Blacks and Whites, 0531
Carnival of Flowers, 0532
Carnival of Ivrea Orange-Throwing Batttle, 0533
Carnival of Oruro, Bolivia, 0534
Carnival of the Blanc-Moussis (White Brethren)
 See Carnival of the Laetare
Carnival of the Devil, 0535
Carnival of the Laetare, 0536
Carnival (Panama), 0521
Carnival (Peru), 0522
Carnival (Portugal), 0523
Carnival (Spain), 0524
Carnival (Switzerland), 0525
Carnival Thursday, 0537
Carnival (U.S. Virgin Islands), 0526
Carnival (Venice), 0527
Carnivale du Promenade, 0787
carnivalito, 0461
Carolina blues, 0422
Carriacou, 0538
Carriacou Parang Festival, 0538
cars
 See automobile
Cartegena, 0540
Carter, Jimmy, 0147, 0769
Carthage, International Festival of, 0539
Carthaginians and Romans Fiesta, 0540
Caruaru Roundup, 0541
Casa del Florero, La, 0603
Casa Grande Cowboy Days & O'odham Tash, 0542
Casals Festival, 0543
Casals, Pablo, 0543
Caspar, 0935, 0942
Cassinga Day, 0544
Castañedas family, 0531
Castor and Pollux, Festival of, 0545
Castro, Fidel, 0514, 0734, 1001
Castro, Juan Bautista, 0546
Castroville Artichoke Food and Wine Festival, 0546
cat festival, 1525
Catalina Island, California, 0454
catfish, 3274
cathedral celebration, 2880
Catherine Wheel, 2710
Cathern Day
 See St. Catherine's Day
Catholic events
 See Roman Catholic events
cattle, 0074, 0076, 0541, 1867

Caturmas, 0547
Cavalcata Sarda, 0548
Cavalhadas, 0549
cave festival, 2146
cave pilgrimage, 2269
Cayman Islands, 2279
Cebu, 2638
ceilidh, 0846, 1183
Celebrate Canada, 0008
celestial star tribute, 0601
Celtic celebrations
    Beltane, 0290
    Fire Festivals, 1016
    Interceltique, Festival, 1423
    Samhain, 2472
cenone, 0578
Central African Republic
    death commemoration, 0353
    independence day, 0550
Central African Republic Independence Day, 0550
Central America, 2806
    See also individual countries
Central City Opera Festival, 0551
Central Maine Egg Festival, 0552
Central Pacific Railroad, 1162
cereal, 0505
Cerealia (Cerialia), 0553
Ceremony of the Car, 0870
Ceres, 0553
Cervantes Festival, International, 0554
Cervantes, Miguel de, 0554
Chad
    independence day, 0555
    liberation, 0030
    national holiday, 0556
Chad Independence Day, 0555
Chad Republic Day, 0556
Chagu-Chagu Umakko, 0557
Chaitra Navaratri
    See Vasanth Navaratri
Chakri Day, 0558
Chalanda Marz (First of March), 0559
chalk, 0560, 0935
Chalk Sunday, 0560
Chalma, Mexico, 2269
chamber music festivals
    Arizona, 1177
    England, 3246
    Italy, 1043
    Lebanon, 0453
    Massachusetts, 1899
    New Mexico, 2516
    New York, 1822
    Switzerland, 1853
    Vermont, 1784
Chamberlan, Claude, 0998
Chamizal Festival, 0561
Chamundi, 0855
Chancellor of the Exchequer, 0411

Chandan Yatra, 0562
changing of the seasons, 0438
Channel Islands
    military commemoration, 0264
    parade, 0264
    royal celebration, 0264
chantey, 2548
Chanukah
    See Hanukkah (Chanukah)
Chaomos, 0563
Chapman, John, 0129, 0130
chariot celebrations
    India, 0171, 2371
    Nepal, 2373
Charlemagne, Emperor, 0099, 0970, 1134, 2713
Charles II, 1062, 2601
Charleston Sternwheel Regatta, 0564
Charleston Wine and Food Festival, 0565
Charlottetown, Prince Edward Island, 1153
Charlottetown Festival, 0566
Charro Days Fiesta, 0567
charros, 0727
Chaumont, Le Roy de, 0494
Chavez (Cesar) Day, 0568
cheese commemoration, 1021, 3240
Cheese Rolling, 0569
Cheese Sunday, 0570
Cheese Week (Sima Sedmitza), 0571
Cheesefare Sunday
    See Cheese Sunday
Chelsea Flower Show, 0572
Cheltenham International Festival of Music, 0573
Cheno i-equa
    See Great New Moon Festival (Cheno i-equa)
Cherokee Cane Treaty, 0368
Cherokee Indians, 0368, 0574, 0575, 3138, 1201
    See also American Indians
Cherokee National Holiday, 0574
Cherokee Strip Day, 0575
Cherry Blossom Festival (California), 0577
Cherry Blossom Festival (Hawaii), 0576
Cherry Blossom Festival, National, 0578
cherry blossoms
    California, 0577
    Georgia (state), 1724
    Hawaii, 0576
    Korea, 0607
    Washington, D.C., 0578
Cherry Festival, National, 0579
chess, 0173, 1689
Chestertown Tea Party Festival, 0580
Cheung Chau Bun Festival, 0581
Chew, Benjamin, 0266
Cheyenne Frontier Days, 0582
Chhau Mask-Dance Festival, 0583
Chhit Sek
    See Seven Sisters Festival
Chiao Festival (Rite of Cosmic Renewal), 0584
Chicago Blues Festival, 0585

Numbers in the index refer to entry numbers, not page numbers

Chicago Dancing Festival, 0586
Chicago Gospel Music Festival, 0587
Chicago Jazz Festival, 0591
Chicago International Children's Film Festival, 0588
Chicago International Film Festival, 0589
Chicago International Puppet Theater Festival, 0590
Chichén Itzá
    See Vernal Equinox (Chichén Itzá)
Chickaban, 0592
chicken festival, 3195
Chief Joseph Days, 0593
Chief Looking Glass, 1698
Chief Seattle Days, 0594
Childermas
    See Holy Innocents' Day
Children's Book Day, International, 0596
children's celebrations
    Alberta, 0461
    Burkina Faso, 0388
    Cameroon, 0476
    Canada, 0461
    Fiji, 1010
    Illinois, 0588
    Japan, 1579, 2600, 2923
    Kiribati, 1570
    Missouri, 1745
    Netherlands, 1712
    New York, 2045
    South Africa, 2671
    Trinidad and Tobago, 1549
    Turkey, 3053
    United States, 1572
    Wales, 0128
Children's Day, 0597
    See also Kodomo-no-Hi (Children's Day); Urini Nal
        (Children's Day)
Children's Day (former Yugoslavia), 0595
children's deaths, 0101
Children's Party
    See Kinderzeche (Children's Party)
children's saving of town, 1555
Chile
    autumn harvest festival, 2059
    Christmas, 0616
    independence day, 1006
    kite-flying, 1006
    military commemorations, 0598, 1006
    music festival, 3149
    national holiday, 0599
    religious celebrations, 0864, 1182, 2988
    rodeo, 1006
Chile Battle of Iquique Day (Día de las Glorias Navales),
    0598
Chile National Unity Day, 0599
Chilembwe (John) Day, 0600
chili festivals
    New Mexico, 1291
    Texas, 0602, 2950
Chilseog

    See Seven Sisters Festival
Chilseog (Seventh Evening), 0601
Chilympiad (Republic of Texas Chili Cookoff), 0602
chimbángueles, 0335
China
    alcohol festival, 0849
    autumn harvest festival, 0648
    birthday commemorations, 1150, 1817, 1906, 2865
    boat races, 0842, 3039
    Buddhist holiday, 2901
    Confucius commemorations, 0676, 2656
    death commemorations, 0646, 2338, 2563
    film festival, 2589
    fishermen protection, 1817, 2856
    flower festival, 1703, 0603
    folklore festival, 2640
    herb festival, 1140
    ice festival, 1282
    kite event, 3200
    lantern festivity, 1627
    library collection, 0040
    love legend festival, 2572
    lunar new year, 1714
    moon goddess holiday, 1870
    national holiday, 0604
    new year, 3193
    opera festival, 0280
    religious celebration, 1609
    royal birthday, 2971
    souls festival, 3079
    spring festival, 1661, 0347
    star festival, 2830
    tidal bore festival, 2337
    winter solstice, 3238
    Yi festival, 3006
china doll, 0944
China Luoyang Peony Cultural Festival, 0603
China National Day, 0604
china poblana, 0517
Chinchilla Melon Festival, 0605
Chincoteague Pony Swim and Auction, 0606
Chinese Revolution commemoration, 0836
Ching Che
    See Excited Insects, Feast of
Ching Dynasty, 0836
Ching Ming Festival
    See Qing Ming Festival (Ching Ming Festival)
Chinhae Cherry Blossom Festival, 0607
Chinkashiki (Fire Control Ceremony), 0608
Chiriwano Indians, 0482
Chisholm, Shirley, 0028
Chishti, Moinuddin Muhammad, 3093
Chitlin' Strut, 0609
Chitra Gupta, 0457
Chitrai Festival
    See Meenakshi Kalyanam (Chitrai Festival)
Chochin Matsuri (Lantern Festival), 0610
Choctaw Stickball, 0611
Choctaw Indian Fair, 0611

Choctaw Indians, 0611, 0612
    See also American Indians
Choctaw Trail of Tears Walk, 0612
Choesroes, King, 0970
choir music, 2712, 2975
cholera epidemic, 0325
Chongmyo Taeje (Royal Shrine Rite), 0613
Choro, 0788
Choyo
    See Chrysanthemum Festival
Christ Child images, 2081
Christ the King, Feast of, 0614
Christian events
    See also individual denominations
    Advent, 0023, 0024
    All Saints' Day, 0064, 0065, 0066, 0067, 0068
    All Souls' Day, 0069, 0070
    Annunciation of the Lord, 0115
    Ascension Day, 0167
    Ash Wednesday, 0169
    Assumption of the Blessed Virgin Mary, Feast of the, 0177, 0179, 0180, 0181
    Baptism of the Lord, Feast of the, 0242
    Befana Festival, 0278
    Black Christ, Festival of the, 0325
    Blessed Sacrament, Feast of the, 0340
    Burning of Judas, 0435
    Candlemas, 0485
    Carnival of the Laetare, 0536
    Cavalhadas, 0549
    Chalk Sunday, 0560
    Cheese Sunday, 0570
    Christ the King, Feast of, 0614
    Christkindlesmarkt, 0615
    Christmas, 0616, 0618
    Christmas Eve, 0629, 0632, 0635
    Circumcision, Feast of the, 0650
    Corpus Christi, 0690, 0693
    Dominican Republic Our Lady of Altagracia, 0831
    Easter, 0862, 0864
    Easter Monday, 0882
    Elijah Day, 0914
    Embert Days, 0928
    Epiphany, 0941, 0944
    Exaltation of the Cross, Feast of the, 0970
    Family Week, 0978
    Flight into Egypt, 1038
    Flores de Mayo, 1044
    Forgiveness, Feast of, 1057
    Forty Martyrs' Day, 1059
    Good Friday, 1163, 1164, 1165, 1166
    Holy Family, Feast of the, 1334
    Holy Ghost, Feast of the, 1335
    Holy Innocents' Day, 1336
    Holy Saturday, 1340
    Holy Thursday, 1342
    Holy Week, 1343
    Immaculate Conception, Feast of the, 1407, 1408, 1409, 1410

Immaculate Heart of Mary, Feast of the, 1411
Kneeling Sunday, 1578
Lazarus Saturday, 1643
Lent, 1657
Marian Days, 1779
Martinmas, 1796
Martinsfest, 1798
Martyrdom of Joseph and Hyrum Smith, 1799
Maundy Thursday, 1818
Mercedes Day, 0832
Michaelmas, 1866
Misa de Gallo, 1889
Moldova Memorial Easter (Moldova Grave-Visiting Day), 1902
Most Precious Blood, Feast of the, 1927
Mother's Day, 1930
Nativity of the Blessed Virgin Mary, Feast of the, 1990, 1991, 1992
Nombre de Jesús, 2081
Our Lady of Guadalupe, Feast of (United States), 2162
Our Lady of the Good Death Festival, 2169
Palm Sunday, 2191, 2192, 2194, 2195, 2196
Pardon of Ste. Anne d'Auray, 2211
Pentecost, 2240
Pilgrimage to Shrine of Father Laval, 2273
Prayer for Christian Unity, Week of, 2311
Presentation of the Blessed Virgin Mary, Feast of the, 2314
Queenship of Mary, 2348
Radunitsa, 2357
Rally Day, 2362
Reformation Day, 2385
Rogation Days, 2418
Rosary, Festival of the, 2428
Sacred Heart of Jesus, Feast of the, 2459
San Gennaro, Feast of, 2489
San Jos, Day Festival, 2496
San Juan Pueblo Feast Day, 2499
Señor de los Milagros, 2566
Seton (Mother) Day, 2570, 2725
Shrove Monday, 2613
Shrove Tuesday, 2614
Spy Wednesday, 2692
St. Anthony of Padua, Feast of, 2700
St. Blaise's Day, 2707
St. Catherine's Day, 2710
St. Clare of Assisi, Feast of, 2716
St. Columba's Day, 2717
St. Dismas's Day, 2722
St. Frances Cabrini, Feast of, 2728
St. Gregory's Day, 2737
St. Hilary's Day, 2741
St. Hubert de Liège, Feast of, 2742
St. Ignatius Loyola, Feast of, 2743
St. Isidore, Festival of, 2744
St. John Lateran, Feast of the Dedication of, 2747
St. John the Baptist, Martyrdom of, 2748
St. John the Evangelist's Day, 2749
St. John's Day, 2751

Numbers in the index refer to entry numbers, not page numbers

St. Jude's Day, 2763
St. Mark's Day, 2773
St. Martha's Dy, 2777
St. Matthias's Day, 2782
St. Modesto's Day, 2786
St. Nicholas's Day, 2788
St. Patrick's Day, 2792
St. Paul, Feast of the Conversion of, 2796
St. Peter's Chair, Festival of, 2799
St. Polycarp's Day, 2803
St. Rocco's Celebration (Rokovo), 2804
St. Stephen's Day, 2811
St. Teresa's Day, 2817
St. Thomas's Day, 2818
St. Tryphon's Day (Montenegro and Bulgaria) (Trifon
    Zarezan), 2820
Sts. Peter and Paul Day, 2850
Sunday School Day, 2872
Tekakwitha (Kateri) Feast Day, 2939
Transfiguration, Feast of the, 3019
Trinity Sunday, 3031
Virgin Mary commemoration, 3159
Visitation, Feast of the, 3019
Christian Orthodox Church
    Sunday of Orthodoxy, 2867
    Sunday of St. Gregory Palamas, 2869
    Sunday of St. John Climacos, 2869
    Sunday of St. Mary of Egypt, 2870
    Sunday of the Holy Cross, 2871
Christian Orthodox events
    Advent, 0023
    All Souls' Day, 0069
    Assumption of the Blessed Mary, Feast of the, 0178
    Baptism of the Lord, Feast of the, 0242
    Cheese Sunday, 0570
    Circumcision, Feast of the, 0650
    Elijah Day, 0914
    Epiphany, 0941, 0944
    Exaltation of the Cross, Feast of the, 0970
    Flight into Egypt, 1038
    Forty Martyrs' Day, 1059
    Good Friday, 1163
    Kneeling Sunday, 1578
    Lazarus Saturday, 1643
    Michaelmas, 1866
    Moldova Memorial Easter (Moldova Grave-Visiting
        Day), 1902
    Radunitsa, 2357
    St. John the Baptist, Martyrdom of, 2748
    St. John's Day, 2751
    St. Modesto's Day, 2786
Christian Science, 0813 Christie, George, 1149
Christian X, King, 1066
Christians *vs.* Moors, 0693
Christie, George, 1149
Christie, John, 1149
Christkindlesmarkt, 0615
Christkindli, 0580
Christmas, 0616

Christmas Bird Count, 0628
Christmas cards, 0616
Christmas carols, 1582, 2629
Christmas celebrations
    England, 2122
    Hong Kong, 1359
    Marshall Islands, 1597
    Michigan, 2079
    Norway, 2766
    Poland, 3223
    Scotland, 2122
    Sweden, 2766
Christmas Eve, 0629
Christmas Eve (Armenia), 0630
Christmas Eve (Baltics), 0631
Christmas Eve (Bethlehem), 0632
Christmas Eve Bonfires, 0639
Christmas Eve church services, 0629
Christmas Eve (Denmark) (Juleaften), 0633
Christmas Eve (Finland) (Jouluaatto), 0634
Christmas Eve (France) (Veille de Noël), 0635
Christmas Eve (Italy) (La Vigilia), 0636
Christmas Eve (Moravian Church), 0637
Christmas Eve (Switzerland) (HeiligerAbend), 0637
Christmas (Greece), 0617
Christmas light parade, 0704
Christmas (Malta), 0618
Christmas markets, Germany, 0615, 0827
Christmas (Marshall Islands), 0619
Christmas (Norway), 0620
Christmas parade, 2125
Christmas Pastorellas (Mexico), 0640
Christmas (Puerto Rico), 0621
Christmas (Romania) (Craciun), 0622
Christmas (Russian Orthodox), 0623
Christmas Shooting, 0641
Christmas shopping, 0328, 0616
Christmas (South Africa), 0624
Christmas (Spain) (Pascua de Navidad), 0625
Christmas spirits, 0617
Christmas (Sweden) (Juledagen), 0626
Christmas swinging, 0625
Christmas (Syria), 0627
Christmas tree lighting, 1673
Chrysanthemum Day
    See Chrysanthemum Festival
Chrysanthemum Festival, 0642
Chuckwagon Races, National Championship, 0643
Chugiak-Eagle River Bear Paw Festival, 0644
Chulalongkorn Day, 0645
Ch'un Chieh
    See Lunar New Year
Chung Ch'iu
    See Mid-Autumn Festival
Ch'ung Yang
    See Chung Yeung
Chung Yeung, 0646
Ch'un-hyang Festival, 0647
Ch'un-hyangjon, 0589

Numbers in the index refer to entry numbers, not page numbers

church funding
    Canada, 2837
    England, 1322, 2840
    United States, 2837
Church of Jesus Christ of Latter-Day Saints, 1310, 1799,
    1921, 3297, 2394
Church of the New Jerusalem, 2014
church-building, 0364
Chuseok
    See Mid-Autumn Festival
Chuseok (Gawi or Hangawi), 0648
Chu'ü Yüan, 0842
Cibere, Prince, 0517
cigarettes, 1193
Cigrand, Bernard J., 1027
Cimze, Czar Peter I. Janis, 0234
Cinco de Mayo, 0649
Cinema Arts: An International Film Society
    See WorldFest-Houston International Film Festival
Circumcision, Feast of the, 0650
Circumcision of Jesus
    See Circumcision, Feast of the
circus celebrations
    Florida, 2530
    Wisconsin, 1196
circus celebrations, 0651
Circus Festival of Tomorrow, International (Festival
    Mondial du Cirque de Demain), 0651
Circus Maximus, 2283
Círio de Nazar, 0652
Cithaeron, 0748
Citizenship Day, 0653
citrus industry, 2954
city celebrations, 0481
City Dionysia, 0808
civil new years
    Hindu religion, 1230
    India, 1230
civil rights celebration, 0315, 0397, 1075, 1556, 1754, 1965,
    0260
Civil War bean soup, 1838
Civil War commemorations, 0675, 0769
    African-American military, 0417
    Battle of Gettysburg, 1124, 1125
    Brazil, 0674
    Florida, 0268
    Georgia (state), 1115, 1198, 1302
    Virginia, 0131, 1650
Civil War train chase, 1198
clams, 3286
Clark, John, 1088
Clark, William, 1660
classical music events
    Alaska, 0096
    Austria, 0405, 0503, 0880, 1948, 2471, 2542
    Belgium, 0916
    Bosnia and Herzeovina, 0251
    British Columbia, 0401
    Bulgaria, 2655

    Colorado, 0175
    Connecticut, 0679
    Czech Republic, 2310
    England, 3246
    Finland, 2624
    Germany, 0216, 0273, 1947, 2375
    Hungary, 0409
    Italy, 1043, 2322
    Kansas, 1860
    Lebanon, 0453
    Massachusetts, 0377, 0956
    New Mexico, 2516
    New York, 2531
    Oregon, 2149
    Poland, 3181
    Puerto Rico, 0543
    Rhode Island, 2052
    Romania, 0930
    Scotland, 0852
    Slovak Republic, 0391
    Switzerland, 1709
    Vermont, 1784
    Washington (state), 2178
clavie, 0439
clay figure festival, 2526
Clean Monday
    See Shrove Monday
cleaning rituals
    Nigeria, 3074
    Singapore, 2070
Clean Monday (Kathara Deftera), 0654
Clearwater County Fair annd Lumberjack Days, 0655
Clinton, James, 1113
Clipping the Church Day, 0656
Close Sunday
    See Low Sunday
Closing the Gates Ceremony, 0657
clothing fairs and festivals
    England, 0250
    Michigan, 2380
Clough, Ben C., 0497
clown festival, 0658, 1533
Clown Festival, International, 0658
CMJ Music Marathon, 0659
Coachella Valley Music and Arts Festival, 0660
Coast Guard (U.S.), 1178
Coca-Cola 600, 0661
Cochet, Henri, 1080
Cochiti Pueblo Indians, 0070
Cock Festival, 0662
Cock's Mass
    See Misa de Gallo Coconut Day
    See Nariyal Purnima (Coconut Day)
coffee break, 0077
coffin procession, 2776
coins, 0035, 0864
cojóes, 0825
Cold Food Day
    See Qing Ming Festival (Ching Ming Festival)

Coleman, Mary Jane, 1981
Cole, Sue, 0196
coliva, 0965
College Music Journal, 0659
Collect Stones Festival
    See Kuwana Ishitori Matsuri college events
    England, 1759
    Florida, 2689
    Italy, 1814
    Poland, 1500
    Rhode Island, 0497
College Weeks
    See Bermuda College Weeks
Collop Monday, 0663
Colm Cille
    See St. Columba's Day
Colombia
    bullfighting, 0462
    Carnival, 0513, 0531
    cultural festival, 2484
    good devil celebration, 0535
    independence days, 0665, 1416
    literary festival, 2286
    military commemoration, 0664
    pranks, 0802
    religious celebrations, 2321, 2458
    salsa dancing festival, 0462
    sugar festival, 0462
Colombia Battle of Boyacá Day, 0664
Colombia Independence Day, 0665
colonial commemorations
    Georgia (state), 1114
    Maryland, 1803
Colorado
    African-American arts festival, 0787
    American Indian dances, 2677
    arts festival, 0787
    beer festival, 1190
    burro racing, 3032
    classical music festival, 0175
    dance festival, 3101
    dinosaur festivity, 0807
    film festival, 2943, 2945
    food celebration, 0174
    gliding festival, 2944
    ice festival, 2171
    jazz festival, 2946
    labor holiday, 0568
    livestock exhibition, 3204
    mining festival, 0427
    opera festival, 0551
    winter festival, 3080
Colton, Gardner, 0817
Columbus, Christopher, 0666, 0673, 0812, 0832
Columbus Day, 0666
Columbus Feis, 0846
Columbus International Film and Video Festival, 0667
Columcille
    See St. Columba's Day

Columeille
    See St. Columba's Day
Comanche tribe, 0858
combatting illegal trade of wild plants and animals, 1944
comedy festivals
    Australia, 0020, 1848
    Canada, 1496
    Quebec, 1496
comic book conventions, 2480
comics celebration, 2875
coming-of-age ceremonies, 0125
Coming-of-Age Day
    See Seijin-no-Hi (Adults Day; Coming-of-Age Day)
Commemoration Day
    See Encaenia Day; Madagascar Martyrs' Day
Commemoration of Uprising of June 7, 2088
    See Malta Sette Guigno (Commemoration of Uprising
        of June 7, 2088)
Common Prayer Day
    See Store Bededag
Common Ridings Day, 0668
Common Sense Day
    See Paine (Thomas) Day
Commonwealth Day, 0669
    See also Bermuda Day; Bonfire Night
Communist government holidays, 0056
community festival, 0241
community guilt festival, 2964
Comoros Independence Day, 0670
Compact Day
    See Forefathers' Day
comparsas, 0514
compita, 0608
Compitalia, 0671
computer festival, 3154
Comstock Lode, 0473
Conch Republic Independence Celebration, 0672
Concordia Day, 0673
confections, 0615
Confederados Reunion, 0674
Confederate Heroes Day
    See Confederate Memorial Day; Lee (Robert E.) Day
Confederate Memorial Day, 0675
Confucianism events, 2338
    China, 0676, 2338, 2656
    Korea, 0613
Confucius's Birthday (Teacher's Day), 0676
Congo Independence Day Celebration, 0677
Congo National Days, 0615
conjunto music, 2938
Connecticut
    African-American girls education, 0714
    American Indian festival, 1900
    Barnum, Phineas Taylor (P. T.), 0247
    boating regatta, 3283
    Christmas parade, 2125 classical music festival, 0679
    classical music festival, 0679
    historic reenactment, 2359
    music festival, 2548

Puerto Rican festival, 2754
yachting, 0122
Connecticut Early Music Festival, 0679
Conradh na Gaeilge, 0093
Constantine, Emperor, 0970
Constitution, U.S., 1072
constitution celebrations
Armenia, 0149
Cambodia, 0467
Denmark, 0786
Iceland, 2972
Marshall Islands, 1789
Poland, 2289
Puerto Rico, 2324
South Korea, 2673
Thailand, 2959
Ukraine, 3075
United States, 0680, 0681
Uruguay, 3096
Uzbekistan, 3102
Constitution Day
See Cameroon National Day; Citizenship Day
Constitution Week, 0680
Constitution Week (Mesa, Arizona), 0681
Consualia, 0682
Consus, 0682
Continental Army, 0788
Continental Congress, 1065
Coolidge, Calvin, 0683, 0986
Coolidge (Calvin) Birthday Celebration, 0683
Cooperatives, International Day of, 0684
Coopers' Dance, 0685
Coptic New Year (Feast of El-Nayrouz), 0686
Coptic Orthodox Church, 0867
Corelli, Arcangelo, 0679
corn festival, 0687
corn harvest, 0228
Corn Palace Festival, 0687
Cornouaille Festival, 0688
Corn-Planting Ceremony, 0689
corona di nove, 0795
coronation
celebrations
England, 2347
Ethiopia, 1254
Coronation of King Mindaugas
See Lithuania State Day (Coronation of King Mindaugas)
Coronation Rally
See Safari Rally
Corpus Christi, 0690
Corpus Christi (England), 0691
Corpus Christi (Germany) (Fronleichnamsfest), 0692
Corpus Christi (Italy), 0780
Corpus Christi (Mexico), 0693
Corpus Christi (Switzerland) (Fronleichnamsfest), 0694
Corpus Christi (Venezuela), 0695
Cortés, Hernando, 0209
Cosby Ramp Festival, 0696

Cosmonauts Day, 0697
Costa Rica
annexation celebration, 0698
arts festival, 0700
independence day, 0699
military commemoration, 2523
saint feast day, 3156
Virgin Mary celebration, 2168
Costa Rica Annexation of Guanacaste Day (Guanacaste Day; Día de Guanacaste), 0698
Costa Rica Independence Day, 0699
Costa Rica National Arts Festival, 0700
costumes
Belgium, 0530
Italy, 0527
Korea, 0648
Texas-Mexico border, 0567
Côte d'Ivoire
dancing, 1573
independence day, 0701
spirits celebration, 0809
Côte d'Ivoire Independence Day, 0701
cotton, 0529
Cotton Bowl Game, 0703
Cotton Carnival, 0529
Cotton Maker's Jubilee, 0529
Cotswold Olimpick Games, 0702
counterculture festival, 0435
counting of birds, 0628
Country Christmas Lighted Farm Implement Parade, 0704
Country Dionysia, 0705, 0808
Country Music Fan Fair, International, 0706
country music festivals
Iowa, 2130
Michigan, 0839
Mississippi, 2417
Tennessee, 0706
county fairs, 0458
Couperin, François, 0679
Court Day
See First Monday Trade Days
Court, King, 0120
Court, Margaret Smith, 0194, 1080
courtship rituals
Latvia, 2760
Peru, 0068
Couteau Day
See Oklahoma Historical Day
covered bridge festival, 1730
cow costume, 0648
Cow Festival
See Gai Jatra
Cow, Festival of the, 0707
Cow Fights, 0708
Cow Parade, 0709
cowboy events
California, 0327
Nevada, 0710
North Dakota, 0752

Numbers in the index refer to entry numbers, not page numbers

Uruguay, 2560
Cowboy Poetry Gathering, National, 0710
cows, 0707, 1792, 0709, 2980
cow's head, 1529
Crab Apple Night
    See Halloween
crab festival, 1283
crab racing, 3252
crabes farcis, 0672
Craciun
    See Christmas (Romania) (Craciun)
craft festivals
    Cajun, 0013
    New Hampshire, 0711
Craftsmen's Fair, 0711
Cranberry Day Festival, 0712
Cranberry Harvest Festival, 0713
Crandall (Prudence) Day, 0714
Crane Watch, 0715
Crawfish Festival (Breaux Bridge, Louisiana), 0716
Crawford, Jack, 0194
Crazy Horse Ride and Veterans' Powwow, 0717
crèche, 0616, 0635
Cree Walking-Out Ceremony, 0718
    See also American Indians
Creek Green Corn Ceremony, 0719
    See also American Indians
creole music festival, 3254
cricket, 0738
Cricket Festival
    See Festa del Grillo
Cricket World Cup, 0720
Crispus Attucks Day
    See Boston Massacre Day
Croatia
    arts festival, 0848
    Carnival celebration, 2565
    dancing festival, 1918
    independence days, 0722, 0723
    ousting festival, 2637
    military commemoration, 0724
    national holiday, 0721
    saint feast day, 2804
    theater, 0848
Croatia Anti-Fascist Resistance Day (Anti-Fascism Day), 0721
Croatia Independence Day, 0722
Croatia Statehood Day, 0723
Croatia Victory and Homeland Thanksgiving Day, 0724
Croats, 0372
Crockett, Davy, 0051
Crom Dubh Sunday, 0725
Cromwell's (Oliver) Day, 0726
Cronia (Kronia), 0727
Cronus, 0727
crop ceremonies
    ancient Rome, 2411
    Guatemala, 2552
Crop Over, 0728

cross holiday, 0970
Cross Mass
    See Exaltation of the Cross, Feast of the
cross-country skiing, 3119
crosses, 0619, 0798, 0941, 1810
Crosses, Festival of the (Fiesta de las Cruces), 0729
crossing a home's threshold, 1020
Crossing of the Delaware, 0730
Cross-Quarter Days, 0731, 1016
Crouchmas
    See Exaltation of the Cross, Feast of the
Crow Fair, 0732
Crow Hop, 0732
Crow Indians, 0732
    See also American Indians crows, 2980
Crowsnest Pass Doors Open and Heritage Festival, 0057
Crozier, Eric, 0059
crucifixes
    See crosses
crucifixion, 1163
Cruft, Charles, 0733
Cruft's Dog Show, 0733
Crystal Night
    See Kristallnacht (Crystal Night)
Cuasimodo, 0864
Cuba
    Caribbean festival, 0498
    Carnival, 0514
    dancing, 0514
    floats, 0514
    military commemoration, 0735
    national holiday, 0734, 1001
Cuba Liberation Day, 0734
Cuban Anniversary of the Beginning of the Wars of Independence, 0735
Cuban festival, 1229
Cuchumatan Indians, 2552
cuckoo birds, 0114, 1581, 1827
Cuisinières, Fête des la, 0736
cultural celebrations
    Alabama, 1896
    Alberta, 0057
    American Indians, 0085
    Australia, 2407, 1951, 2893
    Austria, 0396, 2541, 2854, 3142, 3221
    Bahrain, 2690
    Belgium, 1430, 2182
    Belize, 2506
    Bermuda, 0302
    Bosnia and Herzegovina, 0251
    Bulgaria, 1645
    California, 1611
    Cambodia, 0469
    Canada, 0057
    Cebu, 2638
    Colombia, 2484
    Cyprus, 2181
    Denmark, 0146
    Estonia, 2929

Germany, 2443, 3315
Hawaii, 0075
Hungary, 0410
India, 1524
Italy, 3127
Istanbul, 1441
Japan, 1260, 1261, 2154, 2514
Korea, 2603
Lebanon, 3068
Lesotho, 1919
Marshall Islands, 1793
Mexico, 2519
Michigan, 0133
Netherlands, 1328
Nigeria, 2511
Ohio, 1872
Oman, 1954
Pakistan, 2582
Saudi Arabia, 2537
Spain, 2573
Tasmania, 2947
Tennessee, 1852
Texas, 2478
Tunisia, 0539, 2463
Venice, Italy, 3127
Washington, D.C., 2650
Cultural Olympiad, 0737
Culture Day
    See Bunka-no-Hi (Culture Day)
Cup Day
    See Melbourne Cup Day
Cup Match, 0738
cup-and-saucer style house, 0494
Cure Salée, 0739
curiae, 0964
Curium Festival (Kourion Festival), 0740
Custer Buffalo Roundup and Arts Festival, 0741
Custer, George, 1154, 1687
Custer's Last Stand, 1687
customs day, 3113
Cybele holiday, 1842
Cynonfardd Eisteddfod, 0742
Cyprus
    cultural festival, 2181
    drama festival, 0740
    independence day, 0743
    national day, 1208
    religious celebrations, 0865, 1522, 0654
    saint feast day, 2706
    wine festival, 1679
Cyprus Independence Day, 0743
Cyrillic alphabet, 0421
Czarna Madonna, 0297
Czech Festival, National, 0744
Czech festivals
    Nebraska, 0744
    Oklahoma, 2309
Czech Republic
    birthday commemoration, 2936

classical music festival, 2310
    flower celebration, 1048
    harvest festival, 2106
    lights festival, 2626
    maypole rituals, 1825, 1829
    national holidays, 0745, 1386, 2851
    puppet festival, 2329
    religious celebrations, 0866, 1344, 1048
    Renaissance festival, 1026
    saint feast day, 2822
    witch-burning, 1829
Czech Statehood Day (St. Wenceslas Day), 0745
Czechoslovak Independence Day, 0746

D

Dae, Feasts of, 0747
Daecheon, South Korea, 0371
Daedala, 0748
Dahlonega Gold Rush Days, 0749
Dai New Year
    See Water-Splashing Festival (Dai New Year)
Dai people, 3193
Daimonji Okuribi (Great Bonfire Event), 0686
Daimyo Gyoretsu, 0751
Dairy Week
    See Cheese Sunday
dairy-products celebrations, 0570, 0571, 0919
daisies, 0168, 3288
Dakarkari people, 3074
Dakota Cowboy Poetry Gathering, 0752
Dakota Indians, 2661
    See also American Indians
Dalai Lama, Birthday of the, 0753
Dale, Edgar, 0667
Dal-jip-tae-u-gee
    See Burning the Moon House
Dally in the Alley 0691
Dal-ma-ji
    See Burning the Moon House
Damba, 0755
dams, 0198
Dance Camera West, 0756
Dance Festival Birmingham, International, 0757
dance festivals
    See also performing arts events
    Africa, 0760
    American Indians, 0135, 0179, 0276, 0288
    Argentina, 0509, 2922
    Australia, 0019, 0020
    Austria, 1413
    Bella Coola Indians, 0288
    Brazil, 0512
    British Columbia, 0288
    British Columbia, 0761
    Bulgaria, 0863
    Burkina Faso, 0388
    California, 0756, 2483

Canada, 0761
Colombia, 0462
Colorado, 3101
Côte d'Ivoire, 1573
Croatia, 1918, 0759
Cuba, 0514
Democratic Republic of Congo, 1447
Dominican Republic, 1857
England, 0400, 0757
Florida, 0232
French Polynesia, 0255
Germany, 0685
Haiti, 0516
Honduras, 3285
Idaho, 1395
Illinois, 0586
India, 0583, 2218
Indonesia, 2367
Ireland, 1031
Iroquois Indians, 0276
Japan, 1275, 2121, 2609
Kimsquit Indians, 0288
Korea, 0648
Lebanon, 0210
Louisiana, 0466
Luxembourg, 0762
Malaysia, 0217
Massachusetts, 1454
Mexico, 0520, 0693, 0902, 1231, 2248
Michigan, 0032
Montana, 0732
Nevada, 0487
New Mexico, 0858, 2124
New York, 0760, 2531, ~9069
Nigeria, 0895
North Carolina, 0170
Oklahoma, 0719
Philippines, 0806
Portugal, 0523, 0937
Romania, 1364
Spain, 0490, 0524, 1956, 2524
Swaziland, 2383
Tahiti, 0255
Texas, 2293
Turkey, 1861
United States, 2460
Venezuela, 0228, 0695
Washington (state), 2553
Wyoming, 0135
Zambia, 2001
Dance on Camera, 0758
Dance of Thanksgiving
    See Whe'wahchee (He'dewachi; Dance of
        Thanksgiving)
Dance of the Flutes
    See Baile de las Turas (Dance of the Flutes)
Dance of the Jesters, 0179
Dance of the Red-Tiger Devil
    See Mystery Play (Tibet)

Dance Week Festival, 0759
DanceAfrica, 0760
DanceXchange, 0757
Dancing on the Edge, 0761
Dancing Procession, 0762
Danger Night
    See Mischief Night
Dano-nal
    See Tano Festival (Dano-nal; Swing Day)
Danza de los Voladores, 0693
D'Arcy, H. Antoine, 0551
daredevils, 0398
Dari Balgi
    See Bridge Walking (Dari Balgi)
Dartmouth Winter Carnival,
0695 Daruma Doll Fair
    See Daruma Ichi (Dauma Doll Fair)
Daruma Ichi (Dauma Doll Fair
0696 Darwin Show
    See Royal Shows
Dasa Laksana Parvan (Time of the Ten Characteristics), 0765
Dasain
    See Durga Puja
Dashara
    See Durga Puja
Data Ganj Baksh Death Festival, 0766
dates (food), 2463
Dattatreya Jayanti, 0767
daughter encouragement day, 2913
Daughters of the Republic of Texas, 0051
David, Jacques Louis, 0189
Davis, Chuck, 0760
Davis Cup, 0768
Davis, Dwight F., 0768
Davis's (Jefferson) Birthday, 0769
Day of Atonement
    See Yom Kippur
Day of Blowing the Shofar
    See Rosh Hashanah
Day of Good Will
    See Boxing Day
Day of Judgment
    See Yom Kippur
Day of Light
    See Lanterns Festival
Day of Macedonian Uprising in 1941
    See Macedonian National Uprising Day (Day of Mace-
        donian Uprising in 1941; Macedonian Revolution
        Day)
Day of Prayer, National, 0770
Day of Remembrance
    See Rosh Hashanah; Yom ha-Zikkaron
Day of St. Michael and All Angels
    See Michaelmas
Day of the Awakeners
    See Enlighteners, Day of the (Den na Buditelite)
Day of the Black Ones
    See Día de Negritos and Fiesta de los Blanquitos
Day of the Blacks, 0531

Day of the Dead
    See All Souls' Day; Día de los Muertos; Ullambana
        (Hungry Ghosts Festival; All Souls' Feast)
Day of the Founders of the Slavonic Alphabet
    See Bulgarian Education and Culture Day
Day of the Holy Cross
    See Día de la Santa Cruz (Day of the Holy Cross)
Day of the Kings
    See Epiphany, Feast of the
Day of the Midwives
    See Babin Den
Day of the Race
    See Columbus Day
Day of the Vow
    See Reconciliation, Day of
Day of the Whites, 0531
Day of the Wise Men
    See Día de los Tres Reyes
Day of Wreaths
    See Corpus Christi
Days of '76, 0771
Days of Celebration
    See Ste. Genevieve, Jour de Fête à (Days of Celebration)
Days of Ha
    See Ayyam-i-Ha
Dayton Air and Trade Show
    See Dayton Air Show
Dayton Air Fair
    See Dayton Air Show
Dayton Air Show, 0772
Daytona 500, 0773
DC Black Pride Festival, 0774
DC Caribbean Carnival, 0775
D-Day, 0776
De Diego (Jose) Day, 0777
De Niro, Robert, 3022
De Soto Celebration
    See Florida Heritage Festival
Dead, Feast for the, 0778
dead goose festival, 1103
Dead Remembrance Thursday
    See Khamis al-Amwat
dead, visits from the
    Japan, 2105
    Nigeria, 2112
Deadwood, South Dakota, 0771
Dean (James) Festival, 0779
    death commemorations Alabama, 0675
    Alabama, 0675
    ancient Rome, 0992, 1631, 2212
    Angola, 0104
    Argentina, 0143, 2504
    Athens (ancient), 0116
    Australia, 0360
    Azerbaijan, 0207
    Bangladesh, 2581
    Belize, 0248
    Brazil, 2169
    Cambodia, 2251
    Cape Verde, 1234
    Central African Republic, 0353
    China, 0646, 2338, 2563
    Eastern Europe, 2357
    England, 2281, 2318
    Eritrea, 0951
    Florida, 0675
    France, 1728
    Georgia (state), 0675
    Guatemala, 0067
    Guinea-Bissau, 1234
    Haiti, 1255, 1256
    Hong Kong, 0646
    India, 0979, 3093
    Iran, 0213, 0979, 1338, 1405, 1545
    Iraq, 1404
    Ireland, 1448
    Iroquois Indians, 0778
    Israel, 3292
    Italy, 0069
    Japan, 2156
    Kentucky, 1189
    Lebanon, 1800
    Liberia, 1666
    Libya, 1746
    Macau, 0646
    Madagascar, 1726
    Malawi, 1751
    Mayan Indians, 0101
    Mexico, 0069
    Mississippi, 0675
    Morocco, 1746
    Muslim religion, 2578
    Namibia, 0544
    Nepal, 1091, 1129, 1422
    New York, 1801
    Nigeria, 0202
    North Africa, 1746
    Pakistan, 2580, 3094
    Persia, 0213
    Philippines, 2408
    Portugal, 0069, 2300
    Rwanda, 2453
    Sierra Leone, 0201
    South Carolina, 0675
    Sweden, 1244
    Tennessee, 0675, 1189
    Texas, 0675, 1189
    Thailand, 2406
    Theosophical Society, 0339
    Trinidad and Tobago, 1368
    Turkey, 3095
    Uganda, 3073
    United States, 1351, 1370
    Vietnam, 2962, 3144
    Zimbabwe, 3312
    Zoroastrians, 0979
Dechiyi Dan
    See Children's Day (former Yugoslavia)

Numbers in the index refer to entry numbers, not page numbers

Declaration of Independence, 1065, 1072
Declaration of the People's Authority Day
 See Libya Declaration of Jamahiriya Day (Declaration
  of the People's Authority Day)
Decorated Horse, Procession of the, 0780
decoration cake, 0616
Decoration Day
 See Graveyard Cleaning and Decoration Day; Memorial
  Day
Deep Sea Fishing Rodeo, 0781
Deepavali
 See Dewali (Divali, Deepavali, Festival of Lights)
Deer Dance
 See Shishi Odori (Deer Dance)
deer hunt, 0007
deer roasting ceremony, 2363
Deer-Hunting Festival, 0007
Defenders' Day, 0782
Déjeuner Matrimonial
 See Matrimonial Tea Party
 Delaware election day, 2395
 pumpkin festival, 2327
 religious celebration, 0031
Delaware Big House Ceremony, 0783
Delaware River, 0730
Delaware tribe, 0858
Delgado, Fr. José Matías, 0904
Demeter, 0553, 0911
Democratic People's Republic of Korea Founding Day, 0784
Democratic Republic of Congo
 Children's Day, 0597
 dance ritual, 1447
 independence day, 0785
Democratic Republic of Congo Independence Day, 0785
demon events
 India, 2646
 Japan, 1727, 1971
Demon Mask Festival
 See Namahage Festival
Demon-God Event
 See Madara Kijinsai (Demon-God Event)
Den na Buditelite
 See Enlighteners, Day of the (Den na Buditelite)
Denmark
 Christmas Eve, 0633
 clown festival, 0658
 constitution holiday, 0786
 cultural festival, 0146
 fire, 2755
 independence day (United States), 1066
 literary festival, 0098
 new year, 2025
 New Year's Eve, 2035
 prayer day, 2843
 robot festival, 2415
 royal festivities, 1561, 1778, 3106
 saint feast day, 2755
 Santa Claus event, 3269
 Shrovetide buns, 0984

 sporting event, 0146
 summer festival, 2991
Denmark Constitution Day, 0786
Denver Black Arts Festival, 0787
Departure of the Continental Army, 0788
Derby Day, 0789
Descent into Hell
 See Holy Saturday
desertification awareness, 3258
Dessalines, Jean-Jacques, 1256
Detroit, Michigan, 1773
Detroit International Jazz Festival, 0790
Deva Dewali, 0794
Devathani Ekadashi, 0791
Devi Dhura, 0792
devil-dancing play, 1964
devils, 0441, 0534, 0535, 0695
devil's rock commemoration, 1298
Devils Tower, 1987
DeVos, Rick, 0162
devotional painting procession, 2566
Dew Treading, 0793
Dewali (Divali, Deepavali, Festival of Lights), 0794
Dezao, 0563
Dezome-shiki
 See New Year's Parade of Firemen (Dezome-shiki)
Dhaka International Film Festival, 0795
Dhan Teras, 0796
Dhanvantri, 0796
Dhanvantri Trayodashi
 See Dhan Teras
Dhungri Fair, 0797
Día de Corpo de Deus
 See Corpus Christi
Día de Guanacaste
 See Costa Rica Annexation of Guanacaste Day
  (Guanacaste Day; Día de Guanacaste)
Día de la Raza
 See Columbus Day
Día de la Santa Cruz (Day of the Holy Cross), 0798
Día de las Glorias Navales
 See Chile Battle of Iquique Day (Día de las Glorias
  Navales)
Día de las Playas
 See Beaches, Day of the (Día de las Playas)
Día de los Charros, 0799
Día de los Muertos, 0800
 See also All Souls' Day
Día de los Reyes Magos
 See Epiphany (Spain) (Día de los Reyes Magos)
Día de los Tres Reyes, 0801
 See also Epiphany, Feast of the
Día de Negritos and Fiesta de los Blanquitos, 0802
Día de Reis
 See Epiphany (Portugal) (Día de Reis)
Día de San Giuseppe
 See St. Joseph's Day
Día de San Juan
 See St. John's Day

Día de San Pedro y San Pablo
    See Sts. Peter and Paul Day
Día de San Sebastián
    See St. Sebastián's Day
Día del Ejército (Army Day)
    See Guatemala Army Day
Día del Oriente
    See Amazon and Galapagos Day
Día del Puno, 0803
Día dos Finados
    See All Souls' Day
Diablos, 0534
Diamond Head Crater Celebration, 0804
Diary Festival 0919
Diana (goddess) festival, 2006
dice competition, 0805
Dicing for the Maid's Money Day, 0805
Dick, James, 1000
Dickens, Charles, 0403
Digambaras, 0045, 0765
Diipolia
    See Bouphonia (Buphonia)
Dinagyang, 0806
Dingaan's Day
    See Reconciliation, Day of
Dinkins, David, 0028
Dinosaur Days, 0807
dinosaur festivities, 0807
Dionysia (Bacchanalia), 0808
Dionysus, 0116, 0808
Dioscuri, 0545
Dipolia
    See Bouphonia (Buphonia)
Dipri Festival, 0809
Disabled Persons, International Day of, 0810
Disarmament Week, 0811
Discoverers' Day
    See Columbus Day
Discovery Day, 0812
    See also Columbus Day; Klondike Gold Discovery Day;
    Magellan (Ferdinand) Day
Dismal Days
    See Egyptian Days
Disraeli, Benjamin, 2318
Distaff Day, 0813
Divali
    See Dewali (Divali, Deepavali, Festival of Lights)
divination, 0038
Divine Holy Spirit, Festival of the (Festa do Divino), 0814
djellabahs, 0474
Djibouti Independence Day, 0815
Doan Ngu (Summer Solstice Day), 0816
doctor feast days, 0038
Doctors' Day, 0817
Documentary Edge Festival, 0818
Dodd, Sonora Louise Smart, 0986
Dodge City Days, 0819
Dodge (Geraldine R.) Poetry Festival, 0821
Dodge National Circuit Finals Rodeo, 0820

Dodo Masquerad
    See Boys' Dodo Masquerade
Dog Days, 0822
dog games, 0254
dog sled races
    Alaska, 0097, 0974, 1399, 2998
    Canada, 0499
    Minnesota, 0277
    Northwest Territories, 0499
    Oregon, 2151
dog shows
    Alaska, 0644
    France, 0733
Dog Star, 0822
Doggett, Thomas, 0823
Doggett's Coat and Badge Race, 0823
Dogon people, 0423
dogs, 0254, 0644, 0733,, 0822, 2980
Dogwood Festival, 0824
Dol Purnima, 0825
Doleing Day, 0826
Dol-Jatra
    See Holi
doll festivals
    Japan, 0764, 1311
    Missouri, 1543
    Poland, 1808
Dom Fair, 0827
Domenica delle Palme
    See Palm Sunday (Italy) (Domenica delle Palme)
Dominica
    Caribbean community commemoration, 0500
    creole music festival, 3254
    independence day, 0828
Dominica Independence Day, 0828
Dominican Republic
    Christmas, 0621
    dancing festival, 1857
    independence days, 0829, 0830
    national holiday, 0845
    religious holidays, 0831, 0832
Dominican Republic Independence Day, 0829
Dominican Republic Independence Restoration Day, 0830
Dominican Republic Our Lady of Altagracia (Feast of the
    Virgin of Altagracia, Feast of Our Lady of Altagracia),
    0831
Dominican Republic Our Lady of Mercedes Day, 0832
Dominion Day
    See Canada Day
Don Quixote, 0554
donation day, 2204
Dongji (Winter Solstice), 0833
donuts, 2180
Doo Dah Parade, 0834
Dormition of the Most Holy Mother of God
    See Assumption of the Blessed Virgin Mary, Feast of the
Dorsey, Thomas A., 0587
dosmo, 0835
Dosmoche, 0835

Numbers in the index refer to entry numbers, not page numbers

Double Fifth
    See Tuan Wu (Double Fifth)
Double Nine Day
    See Chung Yeung
Double Seventh
    See Seven Sisters Festival
Double Sixth
    See Airing the Classics
Double Tenth Day, 0836
Doudou, 1156
Doughnut Day
    See Shrove Tuesday
Douglass, Frederick, 0330
Douglass (Frederick) Day, 0837
Dover, Robert, 0702
Down Home Family Reunion, 0838
Downtown Hoedown, 0839
Dozynki Festival, 0840
Dozynki Pod Debami
    See Dozynki Festival
Drachenstich (Spearing the Dragon), 0841
Dragon Boat Festival, 0842
dragon boat races, 3039
dragon play, 0841
dragons, 0355, 1118, 1156, 2733
drama
        Cyprus, 0740
        Mexico, 0520
Dreikönigsfest
    See Epiphany (Germany) (Dreikönigsfest)
drinking festivals
        Germany, 1844
        Rome (ancient), 0108
drought, 0198, 3258
Druidic festivals, 0843, 2023
Druids' Summer Solstice Ceremony, 0843
drumming, 0309, 0875, 3177
Drymiais, 0844
Duarte Day, 0845
Duarte, Juan Pablo, 0829, 0845
Dublin Irish Festival, 0846
Dublin Theatre Festival, 0847
Dubrovnik Summer Festival, 0848
duck festivities
        Arkansas, 3275
        New Mexico, 1192
Duck (or Dookie) Apple Night
    See Halloween
Dukang Festival, 0849
Dulcimer and Harp Convention, 0850
Dulcimer Days, 0851
dumplings, 0842
Dundee International Guitar Festival, 0852
Dunmow Flitch Trial, 0853
Durand, Dorothy, 0130
Durban International Film Festival, 0854
Durban Wild Talk Africa Film Festival.
    See Durban International Film Festival
Durbar Festival

    See Sallah (Salah) Festival
Durga, 1130
Durga Puja, 0855
Durham Miners' Gala, 0856
Durham, North Carolina, 1295, 0422
Dussehra
    See Durga Puja
Dussurget, Gabriel, 0996
Dutch festivals
        Japan, 2121
        Pennsylvania, 1599
Dutch Fourth of July
    See Whit-Monday (Whitmonday)
Dutch Liberation Day, 0857
Duwamish tribe, 0594
dyed eggs, 2357
Dynasty Day
    See King's Birthday (Belgium)
Dzam Ling Chi Sang
    See Universal Prayer Day (Dzam Ling Chi Sang)

E

Eagle Dance, 0858
ear commemoration, 2073
Ear of Wheat Thursday
    See Ascension Day (Portugal)
Earhart (Amelia) Festival, 0859
earmuff commemoration, 1216
Earnhardt, Dale, Jr., 0773
Earnhardt, Dale, Sr., 0773
Earp, Wyatt, 0487
Earth Day, 0190, 0860
earthquakes
        Armenia, 0150
        Peru, 2567
East African Safari
    See Safari Rally
East Germany, 1120
East Pakistan, 0238
East Timor Independence Day, 0861
Easter, 0862, 1706, 1902
Easter (Bulgaria), 0863
Easter Bunny, 0862, 0868
Easter (Chile), 0864
Easter (Cyprus), 0865
Easter (Czech Republic), 0866
Easter Egg Roll, 0879
Easter eggs
    See eggs, Easter
Easter (Egypt), 0867
Easter festival, 2473
Easter Festival (Osterfestspiele), 0880
Easter Fires, 0881
Easter (Germany) (Ostern), 0868
Easter (Hollywood, California), 0869
Easter Island, 2920
Easter (Italy) (La Pasqua), 0870

Easter Monday, 0882
Easter Monday (Netherlands), 0883
Easter (Netherlands) (Paschen, Paasch Zondag), 0871
Easter (Norway) (Paske), 0872
Easter (Poland) (Wielkanoc), 0873
Easter (Russia) (Paskha), 0874
Easter smacks, 0868
Easter (Spain), 0875
Easter (Sweden) (Påskdagen), 0876
Easter (Ukraine), 0877
Easter (Yaqui Indians), 0878
Eastern Europe, 2357
Eastern Orthodox events
    See Christians Orthodox events
Eastern States Exposition, 0884
Eastport, Maryland, 0438
Eavis, Michael, 1146
Ebisu, 0304
Ebisu Festival, 0304, 0885
Echigo-Tsumari Art Triennale, 0886
economic development awareness, 3259
Ecuador
    exploration holiday, 0080
    independence day, 0887
    military commemoration, 0888
    New Year's Eve, 2038
Ecuador Independence Day, 0887
Ecuadorian Civicism and National Unity Day, 0888
Eddy (Mary Baker), Birthday of, 0889
Edinburgh International Festival, 0890
Edinburgh International Film Festival, 0891
Edison (Thomas) Festival of Light, 0892
Edison's (Thomas) Birthday, 0893
Edmund Fitzgerald Anniversary, 0894
educational commemorations
    Bulgaria, 1645
    France, 2713
Edward VII, king of England, 0061
Edwards, Thomas C., 0742
effigies, 0436, 0988, 1129
Effutu people, 0007
egg festivals, 0449
egg shells, 0338
egg hunt, 2920
egg-decorating, 1169
eggs, 0552, 0570, 0571
eggs, Easter, 0865, 0868, 0872, 0877, 0883
Egungun Festival, 0895
Egypt
    folk festival, 2587
    martyrs' commemoration, 0686
    military commemorations, 0147, 0896
    music festival, 0134
    national holiday, 2633
    religious holidays, 0867, 1038
    saint feast day, 2784
    shaykh festival, 1950
    sun reaches Abu Simbel, 0009
Egypt, ancient

    See ancient Egypt
Egypt Revolution Day, 0896
Egyptian Days, 0897
Eid
    See Id al-Adha (Feast of Sacrifice; Eid); Id al-Fitr (Eid)
eiergaren, 0808
Eight-Hour Day, 0898
Eipidès, Dimitri, 0998
Eisenhower, Dwight D., 0776, 0879
Eisteddfod, 0742, 0899
Eka Dasa Rudra, 0900
Ekadashi, 0901
Ekeko, 0052
El Chamizal, 0561
El Gran Teatro del Mundo
    See Great World Theatre
El Pochó Dance-Drama, 0902
El Salvador
    Christ Child images, 2081
    independence day, 0904
    procession, 1044
    religious festivals, 0903, 1044
    saint feast day, 2521
El Salvador del Mundo, Festival of, 0903
El Salvador Independence Day, 0904
Elche
    See Mystery Play (Elche)
    elderly commemorations Japan, 1531
    United Nations, 2129
Eldon Turkey Festival, 0905
Eleazer, Eugene, 0256
Election Day, 0906
Election Day (Massachusetts), 2395
Election of the Lord Mayor of London, 0907
Election of the Mayor of Ock Street, 0908
electronic music festivals, 1940
Elegba Folklore Society, 0838
Elephant Festival, 0909
Elephant Round-Up, 0910
elephant-headed god festival, 1099
Eleusinian Mysteries, 0911
Eleven Cities Race
    See Elfstedentocht
Elfreth's Alley Fete Day, 0912
Elfstedentocht, 0913
Elijah Day, 0914
Elimination of Racial Discrimination, International Day for the, 0915
Eliot, T. S., 0890
Elisabeth (Queen) International Music Competition, 0916
Elizabeth II, Queen, 0669
Elizabeth II (Queen) Birthday, 0917
Ellensburg Rodeo, 0918
Ellington, Duke, 0591
Elman, Lee, 0182
Elsie Dairy Festival, 0919
Elul Selichot, 0920
Elvis International Tribute Week, 0921
emancipation

Numbers in the index refer to entry numbers, not page numbers

See also abolition; slavery
Antigua and Barbuda, 0119
Bahamas, 0221
Canada, 0922, 0927
Florida, 0924
Kansas, 0923, 2063
Ontario, 0922, 0927
Texas, 1493
Trinidad and Tobago, 3027
United States, 0925
Washington, D.C., 0926
Emancipation Day (Canada), 0922
Emancipation Day Festival, 0927
Emancipation Day (Hutchinson, Kansas), 0923
Emancipation Day (Tallahassee, Florida), 0924
Emancipation Day (United States), 0925
Emancipation Day (Washington, D.C.), 0926
Emancipation Proclamation, 0923, 0924, 0925, 1075
Ember Days, 0928
embracing churches, 0656
Emeliyanovs, Galina, 0658
Emeliyanovs, Yuri, 0658
Emerson, Roy, 0194
Emma Naea Rooke, Queen, 0933
Emmerson, Michael, 0283
Empire Day
    See Bonfire Night; Commonwealth Day; Japan National
        Foundation Day
Emume Ibo Uzo
    See Road Building
Encaenia Day, 0929
enchiladas, 3216
end of New Year celebration, 2904
end-of-the-year celebration, 1324, 0440
Enescu (George) Festival, 0930
engagements, 0069
England
    See also Great Britain; Scotland; United Kingdom; Wales
    air show, 0263
    arts festivals, 0400, 1082, 1146
    archery contest, 1204
    bank holiday, 0240
    begging by the poor, 0826
    bell silence commemoration, 2628
    bell-ringing ceremonies, 2999, 3217
    bird marking, 2883
    birthday commemorations, 1481, 2585, 2601
    boat races, 0349, 1301
    bonfires, 0365
    calendar switch, 1063
    candle auction, 0484
    charity events, 2470, 2979
    cheese-rolling contest, 0569
    Christmas celebration, 2122
    church payment day, 1322
    clothing fair, 0250
    college founding ceremony, 1759
    coronation holiday, 2347
    crossing a home's threshold, 1020

dance festivals, 0400, 0757
death commemorations, 2281, 2318
deer roasting ceremony, 2363
devil's rock commemoration, 1298
dice competition, 0805
ear commemoration, 2073
elections, 0907, 0908
embracing churches, 0656
end-of-the-year celebration, 1324, 9047
farming holiday, 2285
fig-eating, 1008
film festivals, 0305, 0400, 1651
fishing festival, 1105
flower shows, 0572, 2448
folklore festival, 1029
food celebrations, 1083, 2127, 2203, 2840, 1438
freedom holiday, 1737
fundraiser for the blind, 1119
getting rid of meat, 0663
government budget, 0411
harvest festival, 1289
hawthorn tree commemoration, 0269
hedge-building ceremony, 2282
historic festival, 1696, 2412
hobby horse parade, 1885
honorary degree-awarding, 0929
hood retrieval game, 1293
horse racing, 0789, 1180, 1565, 2438
hospital fundraisers, 0061, 2845
hunting festivities, 1366, 2221
lantern night, 2328
Lenten carnival, 0985
literary festivals, 0191, 0403, 0400
marriage mock trial, 0853
military commemorations, 0263, 0726, 0968, 3017
mining festival, 0856
mischievous children's night, 1890
music festivals, 0059, 0261, 0573, 2712, 2975, 3246, 0400,
    1437
national day of thanksgiving, 0988
noise-making fair, 2179
opera festival, 1149
oyster shell-building, 1221
political ceremonies, 1699, 1836, 2832
processions, 0691, 3155
religious celebrations, 0060, 0115, 0486, 0691, 1166, 1614,
    1928
rent-payment day, 2230, 2341
royal birthdays, 0917, 1062
rushbearing ceremony, 1529
saint feast days, 2467, 2696, 2704, 2705, 2710, 2712, 2714,
    2723, 2733, 2813
sporting events, 0381, 0823, 0965, 1188, 1383, 3230, 0702
summer solstice ceremony, 0843
theater festival, 3295, 0400, 3065
tip-collection day, 0386
trade fairs, 1620, 2736
unlucky day, 0897
walking-only day, 3172

winter solstice festival, 3064
English Opera Group, 0059
Enkutatash, 0931
Enlighteners, Day of the (Den na Buditelite), 0932
Enrile, Juan Ponce, 1005
Entierro de la Sardina
    See Burial of the Sardine
environment celebrations
    Alabama, 0190
    United Nations, 2315, 3260
    United States, 0860, 1209
Eo e Emalani i Alaka i Festival, 0933
Eoff, Dan, 0643
Eostre, 0787
Epidaurus Festival, 0934
epidemics, 0816
epilepsy, 2826
Epiphany, 0801
Epiphany, Christian Orthodox, 0941
Epiphany Eve
    See Twelfth Night
Epiphany Eve (Austria), 0942
Epiphany Eve (France), 0943
Epiphany, Feast of the, 0944
Epiphany (Germany) (Dreikönigsfest), 0935
Epiphany (Labrador), 0936
Epiphany (Portugal) (Día de Reis), 0937
Epiphany (Russia), 0938
Epiphany (Spain) (Día de los Reyes Magos), 0939
Epiphany (Sweden) (Trettondag Jul), 0940
Episcopal Church
    Christ the King, Feast of, 0614
    Circumcision, Feast of the, 0650
Epitaphios, 1056
Equal Opportunity Day, 0945
Equatorial Guinea Independence Day, 0946
equestrian events, 2005, 2335, 2340
    equinox celebrations Autumnal Equinox, 0197
    Vernal Equinox, 1401, 2621, 3131, 3132
Equirria, 0947
Eradication of Poverty, International Day for the, 0948
Erau Festival, 0949
Eritrea
    death commemoration, 0951
    independence day, 0950
    military commemoration, 0952
    national holiday, 0991
Eritrea Independence Day, 0950
Eritrean Martyrs' Day, 0951
Eritrean Start of the Armed Struggle Day, 0952
Ernesaks, Gustav, 0234
Esala Perahere (Arrival of the Tooth Relic), 0953
Esbat, 0954
Escalade (Scaling the Walls), 0955
Eskimo sporting event, 3261
Esplanade Concerts, 0956
Esquipulas, Guatemala, 0326
Essence Festival, 0957
Estonia

Christmas Eve, 0631
    cultural festival, 2929
    folk music festival, 0234
    independence days, 0958, 0959, 0960
    jazz festival, 1470
    military commemoration, 1877
    music festival, 0235
    pig-slaughtering festival, 1552
    saint feast day, 2780
    sledding holiday, 2616
    women's cultural celebration, 2711
Estonia Independence Day, 0958
Estonia Restoration of Independence Day, 0959
Estonia Victory Day, 0960
ether, 0817
Ethiopia
    birthday commemoration, 1253
    coronation anniversary, 1254
    finding of Christ's cross, 1810
    independence day, 0962
    military commemoration, 0963
    national holiday, 0961
    New Year, 0931
    religious celebrations, 0862, 1102, 2557, 2785, 2985, 0964
    saint feast day, 2731
Ethiopia National Day, 0961
Ethiopia Patriots' Victory Day, 0962
Ethiopia Victory of Adwa Commemoration Day, 0963
Ethiopian New Year
    See Enkutatash
ethnic festivals
    Minnesota, 1985
    Montana, 1986
Ethiopian Sigd Festival, 0964
Etnokult, 0973
Eton College, 0965
Eton Wall Game, 0965
Eucharist
    See Corpus Christi
Europalia, 0966
Europe
    See also individual countries African American holiday, 1605
    harvest festival, 1990
    saint feast day, 2703
European Fine Art Fair, 0967
Evacuation Day, 0968
    See also Syria National Day
Evamelunga, 0969
Evert Lloyd, Chris, 1080
evil spirits, 0835
Ewes migration commemoration, 1323
Exaltation of the Cross, 0928
    See also Día de la Santa Cruz (Day of the Holy Cross)
Exaltation of the Cross, Feast of the, 0970
excavation, 0749
Excited Insects, Feast of, 0971
executive assistants, 0021
exhumation of ancestors, 0976

Exit Festival, 0972
Experimental Aircraft Association, 0041
exploration celebrations
    Ecuador, 0080
    Florida, 1047
    Montana, 1660

F

Face on the Barroom Floor, 0551
Faces Etnofestival, 0973
Facets, 0588
Fairbanks Winter Carnival, 0974
Fairhope Jubilee, 0975
fairy fights, 1830
fais-do-do (dance), 0343
Faka Me
    See Sunday School Day
Fall Classic
    See World Series
Famadihana, 0976
Family Day
    See Beaches, Day of the (Día de las Playas); Family
        Week
Family Month, National, 0977
family reunions
    Kentucky, 1292
    West Virginia, 1292
Family Week, 0978
Fante people, 0046
far, 1058
Far de Biarritz
    See Festival des Arts de la Rue (Far de Biarritz)
farm vehicles, 0704
farmers celebrations
    Greece, 2786
    Philippines, 0495
Farmer's Day
    See Nawruz (Naw roz; No Ruz; New Year)
farolitos, 0629
Farrell, Perry, 1694
Farsang
    See Carnival (Hungary) (Farsang)
Farvadin
    See Farvardegan Days
Farvardegan Days 0897
Farvardin
    See Farvardegan Days
Fasching, 0980
fashion shows, 0489
Fasika
    See Easter
Fasinada 0899,
Fasnacht
    See Carnival (Switzerland)
Fasselrutschen
    See St. Leopold's Day
Fast Day, 0982

Fast for a World Harvest, 0983
Fast of Av
    See Tisha be-Av
Fast of Esther
    See Ta'anit Esther (Fast of Esther)
Fast of Ramadan
    See Ramadan
Fast of the Tenth of Tevet
    See Asarah be-Tevet (Fast of the Tenth of Tevet)
Fastelavn, 0984
    See also Shrovetide (Norway) (Fastelawn)
Fastens Tuesday
    See Fastens-een Fastenseen, 0985 Fastens-eve
    See Fastens-een
Fastens-Even
    See Fastens-een
Fastingong
    See Fastens-een; Shrove Tuesday
Fastingong Tuesday
    See Fastens-een
Fastnacht
    See Fasching
Fastnet
    See Fasching
Fat Tuesday
    See Mardi Gras
Father Christmas, 0626
Father Frost, 0623
Fathers commemoration, 1152
Father's Day, 0986
Faunalia, 0987
Faunus, 0361, 0987
Fawkes (Guy) Day, 0988
Feast Monday
    See Hurling the Silver Ball
Feast of Booths
    See Sukkot (Sukkoth, Succoth)
Feast of Bringing in the Harvest
    See Paitishahem (Patishahya; Feast of Bringing in the
        Harvest)
Feast of Dedication
    See Hanukkah (Chanukah)
Feast of Fast-Breaking
    See Id al-Fitr (Eid)
Feast of Fire
    See Caribbean Festival (Feast of Fire)
Feast of Jorday
    See Epiphany, Feast of the
Feast of Mid-Pentecost
    See Rousa, Feast of
Feast of Our Lady of Altagracia
    See Dominican Republic Our Lady of Altagracia (Feast
        of the Virgin of Altagracia, Feast of Our Lady of
        Alta- gracia)
Feast of Our Lady of Czestochowa
    See Black Madonna of Jasna Gora, Feast of the
Feast of Our Lady of the Harvest
    See Assumption of the Blessed Virgin Mary, Feast of the
Feast of Ovens

See Fornacalia

Feast of Pan
See Imbolc (Imbolg)

Feast of Porcingula
See Old Pecos Bull and Corn Dance

Feast of Sacrifice
See Id al-Adha (Feast of Sacrifice; Eid)

Feast of São Martinho
See St. Martin's Day (Portugal)

Feast of St. Isidore the Ploughman
See San Isidro the Farmer, Feast of

Feast of St. Joseph
See St. Joseph's Day

Feast of St. Maron
See St. Maron's Day

Feast of St. Patrick
See St. Patrick's Day

Feast of St. Peter and St. Paul
See Mnarja (Imnarja; Feast of St. Peter and St. Paul)

Feast of the Archangel Michael
See Michaelmas

Feast of the Beheading
See St. John the Baptist, Martyrdom of

Feast of the Birth
See Christmas (Spain) (Pascua de Navidad)

Feast of the Circumcision and the Name of Jesus
See Circumcision, Feast of the

Feast of the Circumcision of Our Lord
See Circumcision, Feast of the

Feast of the Divine Holy Spirit, 0549

Feast of the Exaltation of the Cross, 0205

Feast of the Harvest
See Shavuot (Shabuoth)

Feast of the Holy Ghost
See Divine Holy Spirit, Festival of the (Festa do Divino)

Feast of the Holy Name of Our Lord Jesus Christ
See Circumcision, Feast of the

Feast of the Lanterns
See Vesak (Wesak; Buddha's Birthday)

Feast of the Most Holy Body of Christ
See Corpus Christi

Feast of the Nativity of Our Lady
See Nativity of the Blessed Virgin Mary, Feast of the

Feast of the Nativity of Our Lord
See Christmas

Feast of the Nativity of St. John the Baptist
See St. John's Day

Feast of the North American Martyrs
See Martyrs of North America, Feast of the

Feast of the Presentation of Christ in the Temple
See Candlemas

Feast of the Purification of the Blessed Virgin Mary
See Candlemas

Feast of the Redeemer
See Redentore, Festa del

Feast of the Sun
See Inti Raymi Fiesta

Feast of the Virgin of Altagracia

See Dominican Republic Our Lady of Altagracia (Feast of the Virgin of Altagracia, Feast of Our Lady of Alta- gracia)

Feast of Torches
See Imbolc (Imbolg)

Feast of Unleavened Bread
See Passover

Feast of Waxing Lights
See Imbolc (Imbolg)

Feast of Weeks
See Shavuot (Shabuoth)

FeatherFest, 0989

Federation of Bosnia and Herzegovina, 0372

Feira Nacional de Agricultura
See Agriculture Fair at Santarém, National fell running, 1188

Fellsmere Frog Leg Festival, 0990

female
See women

feminist celebration, 1250

fence-painting competition, 3000

Fenkil Day, 0991

Feralia, 0992

Ferdinand, Archduke, 0372

Ferdinand, King, 0666

Ferdinand, Prince, 0420

Feria de San Marcos
See St. Mark, Fair of (Feria de San Marcos)

Feriae Latinae
See Latin Festival (Feriae Latinae)

Ferrara's Buskers' Festival, 0448

fertility celebrations
ancient Egypt, 1884
ancient Greece, 0705, 1272, 2967
ancient Rome, 1041, 1662, 1715, 2144
Bulgaria, 1613, 1795, 2767
Netherlands, 3163
Nigeria, 2157
Swaziland, 2000
Ukraine, 1596
Vanuatu, 1622

Fes Festival of World Sacred Music, 0993

Fesitval of Young Herbs
See Nanakusa Matsuri (Seven Herbs or Grasses Festival)

Festa Confederada
See Confederados Reunion

Festa da Luz (Festival of Light), 0994

Festival d'Aix en Provence, 0996

Festa dei Giglio
See Lily Festival (Festa dei Giglio)

Festa del Grillo, 0995, 1078

Festa del Perdono
See Forgiveness, Feast of

Festival des Arts de la Rue (Far de Biarritz), 0997

Festa di San Nicola
See St. Nicholas's Day (Italy)

Festa do Bonfim
See Bonfim Festival (Festa do Bonfim)

Festa do Colete Encarnado
  See Red Waistcoat Festival
Festa do Divino
  See Divine Holy Spirit, Festival of the (Festa do Divino)
Festa dos Tabuleiros
  See Tabuleiros Festival (Festa dos Tabuleiros)
Festival d'Automne
  See Paris Autumn Festival (Festival d'Automme)
Festival d'Avignon
  See Avignon Festival
Festival de Merengue
  See Merengue Festival (Festival de Merengue)
Festival du Nouveau Cinéma, 0998
Festival in the City, 0993
Festival International de Jazz de Montréal
  See Montreal Jazz Festival
Festival International des Arts de la Marionette à Saguenay, 0999
Festival Mondial du Cirque de Demain
  See Circus Festival of Tomorrow, International (Festival Mondial du Cirque de Demain)
Festival of Ancient Drama
  See Epidaurus Festival
Festival of Boys
  See Ghanta Karna (Gathyamuga)
Festival of Broken Needles
  See Hari-Kuyo (Festival of Broken Needles)
Festival of Colors
  See Holi
Festival of Goodwill
  See World Invocation Day (Festival of Goodwill)
Festival of Guiseley, 0656
Festival of Hammamet, 0539
Festival of High Places
  See Chung Yeung
Festival of Light
  See Festa da Luz (Festival of Light)
Festival of Lights
  See Dewali (Divali, Deepavali, Festival of Lights)
Festival of Music
  See Fleadh Cheoil
Festival of Sword Dances
  See Moreska Sword Dance
Festival of the Ages
  See Jidai Matsuri (Festival of the Ages)
Festival of the Blessed Sacrament
  See Blessed Sacrament, Feast of the
Festival of the Bonfires, 0639
Festival of the Cats
  See Kattestoet (Festival of the Cats)
Festival of the Christian Home
  See Mother's Day
Festival of the Dead
  See Obon Festival
Festival of the Flood
  See Kataklysmos, Feast of (Festival of the Flood)
Festival of the Forest
  See Kiamichi Owa-Chito (Festival of the Forest)
Festival of the Giving of the Law

  See Shavuot (Shabuoth)
Festival of the Gods of the Sea
  See Boat Race Day (Okinawa, Japan)
Festival of the Guardian Angel
  See Schutzengelfest (Festival of the Guardian Angel)
Festival of the Plow
  See Sabantui
Festival of the Rosary, 1182
Festival of the Waters
  See Thadingyut
Festival of the White Ones
  See Día de Negritos and Fiesta de los Blanquitos
Festival of Tools
  See Visvakarma Puja
Festival of Two Worlds
  See Spoleto Festival USA
Festival Panafricain du Ciné et de la Télévision de Ouagadougou
  See Panafrican Film and Television Festival of Ouagadougou
Festival under the Oaks
  See Dozynki Festival
Festival van Vlaanderen
  See Flanders Festival
Festival-Institute at Round Top, International, 1000
Festivals of St. Walter
  See Gualterianas, Festas
Festivities for the Day of National Rebellion, 1001
Festivus, 1002
Fete Day
  See Elfreth's Alley Fete Day
Fête de Jeanne d'Arc
  See St. Joan of Arc, Feast Day of
fête de la Communauté française de Belgique, La
  See French Community, Feast Day of the (La fête de la Communauté française de Belgique)
Fête de la Dynastie
  See King's Birthday (Belgium)
Fête de l'Independence
  See Morocco Independence Day
Fête de l'Iris
  See Iris Fest (Fête de l'Iris)
Fête de St. Gens, La, 2732
Fête des Bergers, 0635
Fête des Géants
  See Giants, Festival of the (Fête des Géants)
Fête des Rois
  See Epiphany, Feast of the
Fête Nationale
  See Bastille Day
Fête-Dieu
  See Corpus Christi
Fêtes des Lumières, 1003
Fiancé Festival
  See Marriage Fair
fiddling, 2131, 2132, 2249
Fidencio Sintora Constantino, Jose, 2072
Fiedler, Arthur, 0377, 0956
Fiesta Chica, 1182

Fiesta Day, 1004
Fiesta de la Vaca
    See Cow, Festival of the
Fiesta de las Cruces
    See Crosses, Festival of the (Fiesta de las Cruces)
Fiesta de las Golondrinas
    See Swallows of San Juan Capistrano
Fiesta de los Blanquitos, 0802
Fiesta de Santiago Apóstol
    See St. James's Day
Fiesta del Gallo
    See Cock Festival
Fiesta of Alcoy
    See Moors and Christians Fiesta
Fiesta of Las Cantaderas, 0490
Fiesta of Quiapo District
    See Black Nazarene Fiesta
Fiesta of St. James the Apostle
    See St. James's Day
Fiesta Patrias
    See Mexico Festival of Independence
Fiesta sa EDSA (People Power Anniversary), 1005
Fiestas Agostinos
    See El Salvador del Mundo, Festival of
Fiestas Elenas, 0179
Fiestas Patrias, 1006
Fifteenth of Av (Tu be-Av; Hamishah Asar b'Av), 1007
Fifth of May
    See Cinco de Mayo
Fifty-fourth Massachusetts Regiment, 0268
Fig Pudding Day
    See Fig Sunday
Fig Sunday, 1008
Fiji
    independence day, 1009
    national holiday, 1011
    youth activities, 1010
Fiji Day, 1009
Fiji National Youth Day, 1010
Fiji Ratu Sir Lala Sukuna Day, 1011
Fillmore Jazz Festival, 1012
Film Festival of India, International, 1013
film festivals
    Argentina, 0413, 0414, 1770
    Australia, 1776, 1849, 2894
    Austria, 3024
    Bangladesh, 0795
    Belgium, 0407
    Brazil, 2403
    Burkina Faso, 2199
    California, 0084, 0756, 1069, 1882, 2485
    Canada, 3010, 0998, 1911
    China, 2589
    Colorado, 2943, 2945
    England, 0305, 0400, 1651
    France, 0488, 0111
    Georgia, 0186
    Germany, 0300, 2128, 2853
    Hong Kong, 1357

    Hungary, 0455
    Illinois, 0588, 0589
    India, 1013, 1583
    Indonesia, 1455
    Israel, 1473
    Italy, 3128
    Kansas, 2916
    Massachusetts, 0374, 0378
    Mexico, 1223
    Michigan, 0107
    Montana, 3227
    New York, 0029, 3022, 0758, 1285, 1777, 2043, 2045
    New Zealand, 0818
    North Carolina, 1295
    Ohio, 0667
    Ontario, 3010
    Poland, 3182
    Portugal, 2349
    Quebec, 0998, 1911
    Russia, 1925
    Scotland, 0891
    South Africa, 0854
    South Korea, 0446
    Sweden, 1174
    Taiwan, 1159
    Tanzania, 3308
    Tennessee, 1981
    Texas, 2892, 3273
    Trinidad and Tobago, 3028
    United States, 0083, 1158
    Utah, 2866
    Venice, Italy, 3128
    Washington (state), 2554
    Zanzibar, 3308
finding of Christ's cross, 1810
Finland
    arts festival, 1503
    birthday commemoration, 2446
    Christmas Eve, 0634
    classical music festival, 2624
    folk music festival, 1526
    folklore festival, 1497
    harvest festival, 2785
    ice-sliding, 1015
    independence day, 1014
    jazz festival, 2297
    literature commemoration, 1507
    multicultural arts festival, 0973
    music festivals, 1297, 2533
    national holiday, 2474
    opera festival, 2539
    parade, 1014
    phone-throwing contest, 1897
    religious celebrations, 1615, 2193
    sledding holiday, 2617
    snowball fight festival, 3300
    spring festival, 3117
    summer solstice celebration, 1491
    wife-carrying championship, 3222

Numbers in the index refer to entry numbers, not page numbers

winter fair, 1202
Finland Independence Day, 1014
Finnegan, Lillian Virgin, 0487
Finnish joke holiday, 2821
Finnish Sliding Festival, 1015
Fire Control Ceremony
    See Chinkashiki (Fire Control Ceremony) Fire Festival
    See Hi Matsuri (Fire Festival)
Fire Festivals, 1016
Fire Prevention Week, National, 1017
fireball, 3176
Firecracker Festival, 1018
firecrackers, 0355, 1018
firemen, 2041
fires
    See also bonfires
    Armenia, 1878
    Aztecs, 2017
    Beltane, 0290
    Denmark, 2755
    France, 2756
    Ghana, 1603
    Guatemala, 0441
    Illinois, 1017
    Ireland, 2758
    Japan, 1305, 3171
    Mexico, 2017
    Shetland Islands, 3091
    Zoroastrian religious holiday, 0140
fire-taming ceremony, 0608
firewalking ceremonies
    Greece, 0095
    Singapore, 2968
First Day of Summer (Iceland), 1019
First Foot Day, 1020
First Fruits of the Alps Sunday, 1021
First Monday Trade Days, 1022
First Nations peoples, 0008
First Night (Boston, Massachusetts), 1023
First of March
    See Chalanda Marz (First of March)
First of May
    See May Day (France)
Firstborn, Fast of the, 1024
firstborn slaying remembrance, 1024
Fish Carnival
    See Groppenfasnacht (Fish Carnival)
fish (food) festival
    California, 3276
    Louisiana, 0716
    Tennessee, 3274
Fisher Poets Gathering, 1025
fishing events
    Alabama, 0343, 0975
    Australia, 3047
    Brazil, 0814
    California, 2522
    China, 1817, 2856
    England, 1105

    Iceland, 2645
    Japan, 0885, 2787
    Marshall Islands, 1790
    Massachusetts, 2801
    Michigan, 1868
    Mississippi, 0343, 0781
    Netherlands, 1509
    New Jersey, 2579
    Nigeria, 0145
    Oregon, 1025
    Saudi Arabia, 0048
    Switzerland, 1220
Fishkin, Mark, 1882
Fisk, James, 0328
Fitzgerald, Georgia, 1115
Fitzgerald, P. H., 1115
Fitzwater, Robert, 0853
Five-Petalled Rose Festival, 1026
fladbröd, 0620
Flag Day, 1027
    See also Valdemar (King) Day flag events
    Alaska, 0053
    Argentina, 0141
    Denmark, 3106
    England, 0917
    Liberia, 1664
    Sweden, 2886
    United States, 1027
Flagstaff Festival of the Arts, 1028
Flaming Tar Barrels, 1029
Flanders Festival, 1030
flannel, 2380
Fleadh Cheoil, 1031
Fleet Week (Hampton Roads, Virginia), 1032
Fleet Week (New York City), 1033
Fleet Week (San Diego, California), 1034
Fleet Week (San Francisco, California), 1035
Flemington Fair, 1036
Flemish Community, Feast Day of the, 1037
    See also French Community, Feast Day of the (La fête de
        la Communauté française de Belgique)
Fleury, Rohault de, 0970
Flight into Egypt, 1038
flitch, 0853
Flitting Day
    See Moving Day
Float Festival, 1039
float festivals
    Cuba, 0514
    Japan, 1143, 1527, 2912
Floating Lantern Ceremony (Toro Nagashi), 1040
floats, 1513
flooding
    California, 0355
    Cyprus, 1522
    India, 0198
    Zambia, 1595
Flora, 1041
Floralia, 1041

Florence May Festival
    See Florence Musical May (Maggio Musicale Fiorentino)
Florence Musical May (Maggio Musicale Fiorentino), 1043
Flores de Mayo (El Salvador), 1044
Flores de Mayo (Philippines), 1045
Floriade, 1046
Florida
    art festivals, 0158, 0159
    automobile racing, 0773, 2555
    Bahamian music festival, 1864
    ballet festival, 0232
    birthday commemorations, 0769, 1557
    circus festival, 2530
    college student vacations, 2689
    Cuban festival, 1229
    dance festival, 0232
    death commemoration, 0675
    emancipation celebration, 0924
    exploration commemoration, 1047
    food festivals, 0354, 0840, ~9085, 1436
    Hispanic festival, 0506
    historic celebration, 0672, 2223
    lights festival, 0892
    literature festivals, 1299, 1385
    military reenactment, 0268
    motorcycle racing, 1932
    multicultural festival, 1004
    music concert, 1061
    pirate festivals, 0385, 1107
    religious holiday, 0941
    sporting event, 2147
Florida Heritage Festival, 1047
Florida Keys, 0672
Florida State Day
    See Pascua Florida Day
flour, 0522, 1058
flower celebrations
    See also individual flowers
    Alaska, 1157
    Arkansas, 1482
    Australia, 0532
    Austria, 0265
    Belgium, 1691
    Bulgaria, 2430
    California, 3015
    Canada, 1768
    China, 1703, 0603
    Czech Republic, 1048
    England, 0572, 2448
    France, 1826
    Georgia (state), 1724, 3288
    Iowa, 3043
    Italy, 1677
    Japan, 0642, 1274, 1276, 2465
    Korea, 0607
    Manitoba, 1768
    Massachusetts, 1048
    Michigan, 3044
    Nepal, 0855
    Netherlands, 0793, 1046, 1542, 1855
    New York, 1676
    Oregon, 2298
    Pennsylvania, 2252
    St. Lucia, 1049
    Texas, 2957
    Tonga, 3003
    United Kingdom, 0264
    Washington (state), 3183
    Washington, D.C., 0578
Flower Communion, 1048
Flower Festival
    See Hana Matsuri (Flower Festival)
Flower Festivals of St. Rose and St. Margaret Mary
Alacoque, 1049
flowerpot, 0665
flutes, 0228
Flying Pole Dance, 0693
Flyttedag
    See Moving Day
folk dance festival, 2772
Foire Internationale d'Art Contemporain, 1050
folk drama, 0424
Folk Festival, National, 1051
folk festivals
    Belgium, 1863
    Canada, 1782, 3234
    Egypt, 2587
    Manitoba, 3234
    Massachusetts, 2016
    Netherlands Antilles, 2630
    Ontario, 1782
    Pennsylvania, 2239
    Poland, 1617
    Romania, 1741, 1934, 2631
    Texas, 2955
    travelling, 1051
    Washington (state), 2091
    West Virginia, 3112
folk music festivals
    Arizona, 3042
    Arkansas, 2177
    Canada, 1887
    Estonia, 0234
    Finland, 1526
    Idaho, 1395
    Israel, 1453
    Latvia, 0234
    Lithuania, 0234
    North Carolina, 1053
    Ohio, 0851
    Oklahoma, 1245
    Rhode Island, 2050
    Scandinavia, 1526
    Texas, 2938
folklore festivals
    Albania, 1052
    China, 2640
    England, 1029

Finland, 1497
Iran, 2644
Japan, 2174, 3098
Folklore, National Festival of, 1052
Folkmoot, 1053
Fond Pleeaf
    See Plough Monday
Fond Plough
    See Plough Monday
fondas, 1006
food celebrations
    See also individual foods
    Arkansas, 1361, 1738
    Australia, 0605
    California, 0464, 0546, 1138, 1974, 2841, 2487, 2663
    Canada, 0110, 3011
    Colorado, 0174
    England, 1083, 2203, 2260, 2840, 1438
    Florida, 0354, 0990, 1436
    France, 0350
    Georgia (state), 3141
    Germany, 0218
    Ghana, 3284
    Greece, 2512
    Guadeloupe, 0736
    Hungary, 2899
    Iceland, 2973
    Idaho, 1397
    Illinois, 2930
    India, 1978, 1732
    Ireland, 1095
    Japan, 0304, 1898, 2068
    Kentucky, 0245, 1781, 2931
    Louisiana, 1081, 1704, 1705, 2020
    Luxembourg, 2317
    Maine, 0552, 1747, 2305, 3286
    Maryland, 1805, 2781
    Massachusetts, 0712, 0713
    Mexico, 2066
    Michigan, 0357, 0579, 2256
    New Mexico, 3216
    Nigeria, 2022
    Norway, 2306
    Nova Scotia, 0110
    Oklahoma, 2118
    Ontario, 3011
    Pennsylvania, 1838
    Poland, 2180
    Singapore, 1871, 2634
    South Carolina, 0609, 2672, 0565
    South Dakota, 3152
    South Korea, 1247
    Switzerland, 2352, 3316
    Tennessee, 0696
    Texas, 0602, 2680, 2950, 2954, 3191, 3279
    Thailand, 3123
    Tunisia, 2463
    United States, 2180, 2203
    Vermont, 3130

    Virginia, 2598
    Washington (state), 1769, 0323
    West Virginia, 3203
    Wisconsin, 2593, 3240
food fight, 3001
food problem awareness, 3262
Fool Plough
    See Plough Monday
Fooling the April Fish Day
    See April Fools' Day
Fools, Feast of, 1054
Foot, Hugh, 0743
foot problems, 0399
football
    Army-Navy Football Game, 0155
    Bayou Classic, 0272
    Cotton Bowl, 0703
    Grey Cup, 1219
    Orange Bowl, 2147
    Rose Bowl, 2429
    Sugar Bowl, 2857
    Super Bowl, 2874
Football Day
    See Shrove Tuesday
footprint, 0016
Footwashing Day, 1055
Forefathers' Day, 1056
forest festival, 0987
forestry festival, 1548
Forget, Guy, 0768
Forgiveness, Feast of, 1057
Fornacalia, 1058
fornices, 1058
Fornix, 1058
Fort McHenry, 0782, 1027
Forty Martyrs' Day, 1059
Fossey (Dian) Day, 1060
fossil festival, 2400
Foster, Jeanie, 1061
Foster (Stephen) Memorial Day, 1061
Foundation Day
    See Australia
Founders' Day, 1062
Founder 's Day
    See Jefferson's (Thomas) Birthday; Maryland Day
founding celebrations
    ancient Rome, 2351
    Borneo, 0949
    Guam, 1731
    South Africa, 1926
Four an' Twenty Day, 1063
Four Chaplains Day, 1064
Fourth of July, 1065
Fourth of July (Denmark), 1066
fox, 0179
Fox, Rev. George, 1064
Fox (George), Death of, 1067
Fox Hill Festival, 1068
fox hunting, 1188

France
bicycle racing, 3014
Breton festival, 0688
Carnival celebration, 2062
Celtic cultural festival, 1423
Christmas Eve, 0635
circus celebration, 0651
clay figure festival, 2526
death commemoration, 1728
dog show, 0733
educational commemoration, 2713
fashion show, 0489
film festivals, 0488, 0111
fires, 2756
flower festival, 1826
food festival, 0350
friendship commemoration, 3023
fruit festival, 1655
historic commemoration, 1975
independence day, 0255
kite event, 1571
laundry festival, 1865
Lenten holiday, 1775
lights festival, 1003
military commemoration, 2067
mock-religious festival, 1054
music festivals, 2249, 2466, 0996
new year, 2026
prisoner holiday, 2350
processions, 0635, 1133
religious celebrations, 0065, 0176, 0690, 0944, 0943,
    1084, 1796, 2211
saint feast days, 2710, 2713, 2718, 2721, 2732, 2746, 2756,
    2783, 2835
tennis tournament, 1080
theatre festival, 0200
Virgin Mary celebrations, 2164, ~9090
wheat festival, 3209
wine festivals, 3033, 1185
France, William H. G. (Bill), 0773
Franke, Jay, 0586
Frankenmuth Bavarian Festival, 1070
Frankfurt Book Fair (Buchmesse), 1071
Franklin, Benjamin, 0402, 1072
Franklin Institute, 1072
Franklin's (Benjamin) Birthday, 1072
Fraternal Order of the Real Bearded Santas Annual Reunion
    and Luncheon, 1073
Frau Perchta, 0935
fravashis, 0979
Frawardignan, Feast of, 1074
Frederick IX, King of Denmark, 1561
Freedom Day, National, 1075
Freedom Festival, International, 1076
freedom movement, 1098
Freedom of Entry Ceremony, 1077
Freeing the Insects, 1078
freezing water, blessing of, 0938
French Championships

See French Open Tennis
French Community, Feast Day of the (La fête de la
    Communauté française de Belgique), 1079
French festivals
    Louisiana, 0256
    Maine, 0257
    New York, 0494
French impressionism, 2083
French Open Tennis, 1080
French Polynesia, 0255
French Quarter Festival, 1081
French Revolution, 0255
French West Indies, 1865
Friday, Jeff, 0083
Friends Made Ceremony
    See Atohuna (Friends Made Ceremony)
friendship commemorations
    France, 3023
    Hawaii, 1652
    Spain, 3023
Frieze Art Fair London, 1082
Fringe Festival, 0890
FringeNYC
    See New York International Fringe Festival
Fritter Thursday, 1083
frog legs, 0990
frog-jumping contests
    California, 0458
    Missouri, 3000
Fronleichnamsfest
    See Corpus Christi (Germany) (Fronleichnamsfest)
frontier festivals
    Kentucky, 0368
    Nebraska, 1085
Frost Saints' Days, 1084
fruit festival, 1655
full moon, 0954, 2904
Full Moon Day
    See Magha Puja (Maka Buja, Full Moon Day)
Full Moon Day of Thadingyut
    See Waso (Buddhist Rains Retreat)
Full Moon of Kason
    See Vesak (Wesak; Buddha's Birthday)
Fuller, Albert, 0182
Fulpati, 0855
fundraiser for families in need, 1904
fundraiser for the blind, 1119
funerals, 1168
Fur Trade Days, 1085
Furrina, 1086
Furrinalia, 1086
fute-ball and golfe, 0402
    Fyr-Bål Fest, 1087

G

Ga people, 1352
Gable (Clark) Birthday Celebration, 1088

Gable, Kenny, 0034
Gabon Independence Day, 1089
Ga-Dangme Homowo Festival of Thanksgiving, 1128
Gaea, 0727
Gaecheon-jeol
    See Korea National Foundation Day
Gaelic Mod, 1090
Gaense Tag
    See St. Leopold's Day
Gagarin, Yuri, 0697
gahambars, 0179
Gai Jatra, 1091
Galapagos Islands, 0080
galette des rois, 0857
Gallup Inter-Tribal Indian Ceremonial, 1092
Galungan, 1093
Galway International Arts Festival, 1094
Galway Oyster Festival, 1095
Gambia
    independence day, 1096
    national holiday, 1097
    slavery commemoration, 2426
Gambia Independence Day, 1096
Gambia Revolution Day, 1097
Gandhi Jayanti (Mahatma Gandhi's Birthday), 1098
Gandhi, Mohandas Karamchand (Mahatma), 1098
Ganesh Chata
    See Ganesh Chathurthi
Ganesh Chathurthi, 1099
Gang Days
    See Rogation Days
Ganga Dussehra, 1100
Gangaur, 1101
Gange Days
    See Rogation Days
Ganges River, 1100
Ganj, Baba Farid Shakar, 3094
Ganjitsu
    See Oshogatsu (New Year's Day)
Ganna (Genna), 1102
Gansabhauet, 1103
garden festival, 3219
Gareau, Jackie, 0375
Garifuna Settlement Day, 1104
Garland Day, 1105
garlic, 1138, 1438
Garma Festival, 1106
Gaspar, Joeé, 1107
Gasparilla Pirate Festival, 0408, 1107
Gasparilla Pirate Invasion
    See Gasparilla Pirate Festival
Gaspee Days, 1108
Gates, Horatio, 0266, 0431
Gathyamuga
    See Ghanta Karna (Gathyamuga)
Gaucho Festival
    See Semana Criolla (Gaucho Festival)
Gaudete Sunday, 0023
Gauranga, 0825

Gautama, Siddhartha, 3134
Gawai Dayak, 1109
Gawi
    See Chuseok (Gawi or Hangawi)
Gay and Lesbian Mardi Gras
    See Mardi Gras Film Festival
Gay Games, 1110
gay rights commemorations
    Australia, 1776, 2895
    Brazil, 2527
    California, 1069, 1110, 1881, 2486
    Georgia, 0187
    New York, 2842, 2044
    Portugal, 2349
    Washington, D.C., 0774
Gayant, 1133
Gedaechtnisz Tag
    See Schwenkfelder Thanksgiving (Gedaechtnisz Tag)
Gedaliah ben Ahikam, 1111
Gedaliah, Fast of (Tsom Gedalyah, Tzom Gedaliahu),
    1011
Geddes, 0529
Gee Haw Whimmy Diddle World Competition, 0170
geerewol, 1012
Geerewol Celebrations, 1112
geese, 1103, 2190
Gemini, 0545
General Clinton Canoe Regatta, 1113
General Strike, 0328
    See Ganna (Genna)
Genna
Genoa, Nevada, 0487
George I, King, 0823
George III, King, 0917
George V, King, 0917
Georgemas
    See St. George's Day
    Georgia (country)cathedral celebration, 2880
    independence day, 1116
    saint feast day, 2733
Georgia Day, 1114
Georgia Harmony Jubilee, 1115
Georgia Independence Day, 1116
    Georgia (state)African-American cultural festival, 2547
    Civil War commemorations, 1115, 1198, 1302
    colonial founding commemoration, 1114
    death commemoration, 0675
    film festival, 0186
    flower festivals, 1724, 3288
    food festival, 3141
    gay rights commemoration, 0187
    gold festival, 0749
    golf tournament, 1811
    locomotive-chase festival, 1198
    New Year's Eve Watch Night, 3188
    parade, 2795
    peanut festival, 1117
    sporting event, 1811
    tree festival, 0824

Numbers in the index refer to entry numbers, not page numbers

Georgiritt (St. George's Parade), 1118
Geranium Day, 1119
    German festivals Michigan, 1070
    Minnesota, 2839
    Missouri, 1745
    Pennsylvania, 1173
German Luftwaffe, 0263
German Pioneer Day
    See German-American Day
German Settlement Day
    See German-American Day
German Unification Day, 1120
German-American Day, 1121
German-American Volksfest, 1122
German-Speaking Community, Feast Day of the, 1123
    See also French Community, Feast Day of the (La fête de
        la Communauté française de Belgique)
Germantown, Pennsylvania, 0266
Germany
    Advent, 0024
    American cultural festival, 1122
    arts festival, 0966, 0298
    autumn fair, 3052
    beer festival, 2120
    bonfire, 0868
    book fair, 1071
    boundary feast, 0383
    bride-wooing ceremony, 0392
    Carnival celebration, 2431
    Christmas markets, 0615, 0827
    classical music festivals, 0216, 0273, 1947, 2375
    cultural festivals, 2443, 3315
    dancing, 0685
    dragon play, 0841
    drinking feat, 1844
    film festivals, 0300, 2128, 2853
    food celebrations, 0218
    historic reenactments, 1555, 2257
    horse events, 1658, 1991
    lights festival, 0299
    marksmen's festival, 2543
    masks, 0980
    mining festival, 1584
    music festival, 1833
    new year, 2027
    New Year's Eve, 2039
    opera festival, 1952
    parade, 1118
    Passion play, 2104
    political pageant, 2103
    processions, 0692, 0980
    religious celebrations, 0692, 0868, 0935, 1084, 1514,
        1798, 2194, 2391
    reunification day, 1120
    royal wedding reenactment, 1625
    running race, 2540
    sailing regatta, 1550
    saint feast days, 2750, 2826
    sausage fair, 0218

    shooting, 0641
    wine festivals, 0218, 1681
    witches, 3175
Gettysburg Address, 0945
Gettysburg Address Day
    See Equal Opportunity Day
Gettysburg Civil War Heritage Days, 1124
Gettysburg Day, 1125
Ghana
    deer hunt, 0007
    Ewes migration commemoration, 1323
    farmers' day, 1126
    fire festival, 1603
    food festival, 3284
    harvest festivals, 1352, 2056
    independence day, 1127
    military festival, 0204
    Muhammad commemoration, 0755
    path-clearing festival, 0046
    purification festival, 2114
    stool festival, 0015
    tree-planting ceremony, 2206
Ghana Farmers' Day, 1126
Ghana Republic Day, 1127
Ghanafest, 1128
Ghanian festival, 1128
Ghanta Karna (Gathyamuga), 1129
Ghatasthapana, 1130
Ghent, Minnesota, 0284
Ghode Jatra, 1131
Giant Lantern Festival, 1132
Giants, Festival of the (Belgium), 1134
Giants, Festival of the (Fête des Géants, 1133
Gibraltar National Day, 1135
Gift of the Waters Pageant, 1136
Giglio Feast, 1137
Gilles, The, 0530
Gilroy Garlic Festival, 1138
Ginem, 1139
gingerbread, 0615
Ginsberg, Allen, 1375
Ginseng Festival, 1140
Gioco del Ponte, 1142
Gio to Hung Vuong Day, 1141
Gion Matsuri, 1143
Giostra dell' Orso, La
    See Jousting the Bear
Girl Scout Day, 1144
Girl Scouts, 1144, 1851
Gishi Gyoretsu, 0043
Gita Jayanti, 1145
Gjirokastra, Albania, 1052
Glastonbury Festival of Contemporary Performing Arts,
    1146
gliding festival, 2944
Glorious Twelfth, 1147
    See also Orange Day (Orangemen's Day)
GLOW Light Festival, 1148
Gluck, Christoph, 0679

General Index

Glyndebourne Festival Opera, 1149
gnomes, 0633
Goa, India, 0515, 2602
goat ceremonies
    Bohemia, 2615
    India, 0792
    Ireland, 2323
goatskin drum, 1171
Gobelins, 0694
Gobind Singh, 1237
    god and goddess festivals Agonalia, 0035
    Japan, 1450
    Juturnalia, 1498
Goddess of Mercy, Birthday of the, 1150
Goede Vrijdag
    See Good Friday (Belgium) (Goede Vrijdag)
Going Home Ceremony
    See Niman Festival
Going to the Fields (Veldgang), 1151
Gokarna Aunsi, 1152
Gold Cup Parade, 1153
Gold Discovery Days, 1154
gold festivals
    Alaska, 1157
    Alberta, 1574
    California, 0465
    Canada, 1574, 1575
    Colorado, 0427
    Georgia (state), 0749
    South Dakota, 0771, 1154
    Yukon Territory, 1575
Gold Rush of 1859, 0427
Gold Star Mother's Day, 1155
Golden Chariot and Battle of the Lumecon, Procession of
    the, 1156
Golden Days, 1157
Golden Friday
    See Ember Days
Golden Globe Awards, 1158
Golden Horse Film Festival and Awards, 1159
Golden Orpheus, 1160
"golden rule," 0613
Golden Shears World Shearing and Wool-handling
    Championships, 1161
Golden Spike Anniversary, 1162
"golden spurs," 0945
Golden Stool, 0015, 2114
Golden Week
    See Japan Constitution Memorial Day; Kodomo-no-Hi
        (Children's Day)
    Goldenvoice, 0660
Goldman, Michal, 0374
golf events
    Alaska, 0297
    Georgia (state), 1811
    Great Britain, 0402
    Scotland, 0402
    United States, 3086
Goliath, 1134

Gone with the Wind, 0990
good and bad deeds, 0457
Good Friday, 1163
Good Friday (Belgium) (Goede Vrijdag), 1164
Good Friday (Bermuda), 1165
Good Friday England), 1166
Good Friday (Italy), 1167
Good Friday (Mexico) (Viernes Santo), 1168
Good Friday (Poland) (Wielki Piatek), 1169
Good Friday (Spain), 1170
good luck tradition, 1277
good over evil festival, 0855
Good Thief Sunday
    See St. Dismas's Day
Goode, Rabbi Alexander, 1064
Gooding Day
    See Doleing Day Goodwill Day
    See Liberian President W. V. S. Tubman's Birthday
Goombay!, 1171
goombay festival, 1171, 1864
goose, 0635, 2768
Goose Day
    See St. Leopold's Day
Gorilla Naming Ceremony (Kwita Izina), 1172
gorillas, 1060, 1172
Goschenhoppen Historians' Folk Festival, 1173
Gospa od Skrpjela, 0981
gospel music festivals, 0587
Goss, Linda, 0336
Göteborg International Film Festival, 1174
Gould, Jay, 0328
Goûter Matrimonial
    See Matrimonial Tea Party
Govardhan Mountain, 0109
government budget, 0411
Gowkie Day
    See April Fools' Day
Gowri Habba, 1175
Gracchus, Gaius Sempronius, 1086
Graf, Steffi, 1080
Grahamstown Festival
    See South Africa National Arts Festival (Grahamstown
        Festival)
grain, 0505, 0633
Grambling State University, 0272
Grammy Awards Ceremony, 1176
Grand Canyon Music Festival, 1177
Grand Duke Day
    See Luxembourg National Day
Grand Haven Coast Guard Festival, 1178
Grand Head-Anointing Ceremony
    See Mahamastakabhishekha (Grand Head-Anointing
        Grand Magal of Shaykh Amadou Bamba, Ceremony),
        1179
Grand National, 1180
Grand Ole Opry, 0706
Grand Prix, 1181
Grande, Fiesta, 1182
Grandfather Frost, 0623

Grandfather Mountain Highland Games and Gathering of
   Scottish Clans, 1183
Grandmothers' Day
   See All Souls' Day (Cochiti Pueblo)
Grandmother's Day
   See Babin Den
Grandparents' Day, 1184
Grands Crus, Weekend of the, 1185
Granger, Gordon, 0925
Grant, Ulysses S., 0131
Granth Sahib, 1238
Grant's (Bill) Bluegrass Festival, 1186
Grape Festival, 1187
Grape Harvest Festival
   See Vendimia, Fiesta de la
grapefruit, 2954
grapes, 0342, 2040, 2899, 3124
grapevines, 1084
Grasmere Sports, 1188
Grave Day
   See Graveyard Cleaning and Decoration Day
Graveyard Cleaning and Decoration Day, 1189
Great American Beer Festival, 1190
Great American Brass Band Festival, 1191
Great American Duck Race, 1192
Great American Smokeout, 1193
Great Backyard Bird Count, 1194
Great Battle of Hansan Festival (Hansan Daecheop), 1195
Great Bonfire Event
   See Daimonji Okuribi (Great Bonfire Event)
Great Britain
   See also England; Scotland, United Kingdom; Wales
   Druidic festival, 2023
   golf event, 0402
   pagan festival, 1619
   religious commemoration, 0504
   Whitsuntide celebration, 3215
Great Chicago Fire, 1017
Great Circus Parade, 1196
Great Daedala
   See Daedala
Great Dionysia, 0808
Great Falls Ski Club Mannequin Jump, 1197
Great Feast
   See Id al-Adha (Feast of Sacrifice; Eid)
Great Friday
   See Good Friday; Good Friday (Poland) (Wielki Piatek)
Great Hinckley Varmint Hunt, 0452
Great Hoshana
   See Hoshana Rabbah
Great Lent
   See Lent
Great Locomotive Chase Festival, 1198
Great Montana Sheep Drive, 1199
Great Moonbuggy Race, 1200
Great New Moon Festival (Cheno i-equa), 1201
Great Salt Lake, 0367
Great Sami Winter Fair, 1202
Great Schooner Race, 1203

Great Spring Festival of the Toshogu Shrine
   See Toshogu Haru-No-Taisai (Great Spring Festival of
   the Toshogu Shrine)
Great Wardmote of the Woodmen of Arden, 1204
Great World Theatre, 1205
Greater Eleusinia, 0911
Greater Sabbats, 1016
Grec Festival de Barcelona, 1206
Greece
   Christmas, 0617
   dairy-products celebration, 0570
   feminist celebration, 1250
   firewalking ceremony, 0095
   food festivals, 2512
   historic celebrations, 2294
   independence day, 1207
   medical commemoration, 1312
   naked rope-climbing festival, 1252
   national holiday, 2176
   ox-killing ceremony, 0384
   religious celebrations, 0941, 1059, 1578, 1993, 2202,
      2974, 0654
   running race, 2145
   saint feast days, 2706, 2720, 2757, 2784, 2786, 2789, 2810
   scarlet fever curing feast, 2435
   spring celebration, 2881
   summer festival, 0184
   tree imagery, 0748
Greece, ancient
   See ancient Greece
Greece Independence Day, 1207
Greek Cypriot National Day, 1208
Greek mythology, 0727
Greek Orthodox Church, 2664
Greek Orthodox events
   See Christian Orthodox events
Greeley, Horace, 0427
Green Corn Ceremony, 0719
Green Festivals, 1209
Green George Festival, 1210
Green March Day, 1211
Green Mountain Boys, 0293
Green River Rendezvous, 1212
Green Teej
   See Teej (Tij; Green Teej)
Green Thursday
   See Maundy Thursday
Greenery Day, 1213
Greenland
   national day, 1214
   ski race, 0139
   snow-sculpture festival, 2098
Greenland National Day, 1214
Greenville Treaty Camporee, 1215
Greenwood (Chester) Day, 1216
Gregorian calendar, 1063
Gregory I, Pope, 0169
Gregory, John, 0427
Grenada

Caribbean community commemoration, 0500
independence day, 1217
musical competition, 0538
thanksgiving day, 1218
Grenada Independence Day, 1217
Grenada Thanksgiving Day, 1218
Grenzumgang
    See Boundary Walk (Grenzumgang)
Grey Cup Day, 1219
Grieg, Edvard, 0296, 0502
Grierson, John, 0891
Griffith, Andy, 1834
grillo, 0910
Grinnell, George Bird, 0189
Grito de Yara, 0735
Groppenfasnacht (Fish Carnival), 1220
Grotto Day, 1221
Groundhog Day, 0485, 1222
Grouse Day
    See Glorious Twelfth
grouse season, 1147
grove, 1086
Gruver, Timothy, 2916
Guadalajara International Film Festival, 1223
Guadeloupe
    Carnival, 0519
    food festival, 0736
Gualterianas, Festas, 1224
Guam, 1731
Guanacaste Day
    See Costa Rica Annexation of Guanacaste Day
        (Guanacaste Day, Día de Guanacaste)
Guarapo, 0487
Guardian Angels Day, 1225
Guatemala
    corn ceremony, 0689
    crop frost ceremony, 2552
    cross commemoration, 0798
    death commemoration, 0067
    fires, 0441
    independence day, 1227
    military commemorations, 1226, 1228
    pole dance ritual, 2818
    religious celebrations, 0067, 0179, 0326, 2561
    saint feast day, 2752
Guatemala Army Day, 1226
Guatemala Independence Day, 1227
Guatemala Revolution Day, 1228
Guavaween, 1229
Guaymí people, 0233
Gudi Padva, 1230
Guelaguetza, La, 1231
Guinea
    independence day, 1232
    national holiday, 1233
    religious festival, 0172
Guinea Independence Day, 1232
Guinea Second Republic Day, 1233
Guinea-Bissau

death commemoration, 1234
independence day, 1235
Guinea-Bissau and Cape Verde National Heroes' Day,
    1234
Guinea-Bissau Independence Day, 1235
guitars, 0852
Gulch, Gregory, 0427
Gule of August
    See Lammas
Gullah festivals, 1989, 2153
Gunpowder Plot, 0988, 1029
Gunung Agung, 0900
Guru Arjan, Martydom of, 1236
Guru Gobind Singh, Birthday of, 1237
Guru Granth Sahib, Installation of the, 1238
Guru Har Krishan, Birthday of, 1239
guru installation commemoration, 1238
Guru Parab, 1240
Guru Purnima, 1241
Guru Ram Das, Birthday of, 1242
Guru Tegh Bahadur, Martyrdom of, 1243
Gus Macker 3-on-3 Basketball Tournament
    See Macker (Gus) Basketball
Gustaf Adolfsdagen
    See Gustavus Adolphus Day (Gustaf Adolfsdagen)
Gustavus Adolphus Day (Gustaf Adolfsdagen), 1244
Gutek, Roman, 3182
Guthrie (Woody) Folk Festival, 1245
Guy Fawkes Day
    See Bonfire Night
Guyana
    Caribbean community commemoration, 0500
    independence day, 1246
    religious festival, 0172
Guyana Independence Day, 1246
Gwangiu Kimchi Festival, 1247
Gyan Panchami, 1248
Gyangzê Horse-Racing Festival, 1249
Gyatso, Tenzin, 0753
Gyeongchip
    See Excited Insects, Feast of
gymnastics, 1442, 2005
Gymnopaidiai, 0507
Gynaecocratia, 1250
    gypsies, 2835

H

Haakon IV Haakonsson, king of Norway, 0082, 0620
Hachinohe Enburi, 1251
Hadaka Matsuri (Naked Festival), 1252
Hades, 0727
haggis, 0443
Haghoghy Ortnootyoon
    See Blessing of the Grapes (Haghoghy Ortnootyoon)
Haile Selassie, 0961, 0962, 1253, 1254
Haile Selassie's Birthday, 1253
Haile Selassie's Coronation Day, 1254

Haiti
  Caribbean community commemoration, 0500
  Carnival celebrations, 0516, 0528, 2369
  Columbus, Christopher, 0812
  dancing, 0516
  death commemorations, 1255, 1256
  harvest festival, 1766
  independence day, 1259
  military commemoration, 1257
  national holiday, 1258
  religious celebrations, 1345, 2267, 2274
Haiti Ancestors' Day, 1255
Haiti Anniversary of the Death of Jean-Jacques Dessalines, 1256
Haiti Battle of Vertières' Day, 1257
Haiti Flag and University Day, 1258
Haiti Independence Day, 1259
Hajj
  See Pilgrimage to Mecca Hajj)
Hakata Dontaku, 1260
Hakata Gion Yamagasa, 1261
Hala Festival, 1262
Halashashti, 1263
Halcyon Days, 1264
Hale, Mary, 0096
Half Moon Bay Art and Pumpkin Festival, 1265
Half-Vasten
  See Mi-Carême
Halifax Day, 1266
Halifax Independence Day
  See Halifax Day
Halifax Resolutions Day
  See Halifax Day
Halifax Resolutions of Independence Day
  See Halifax Day
Halifax Resolves Day
  See Halifax Day
Halloween, 0128, 1267
Halloween (Ireland), 1268
Halloween (Isle of Man), 1269
Halloween (Louisiana), 1270
Halloween (Scotland), 1271
Haloa, 1272
ham, 1781
Hambletonian Harness Racing Classic, 1273
Hamburger Dom
  See Dom Fair
Hamishah Asar b'Av
  See Fifteenth of Av (Tu be-Av; Hamishah Asar b'Av)
Hamishah Asar Bishevat
  See Tu Bishvat (Bi-Shevat; B'Shevat; Hamishah Asar Bishevat)
Hammon, Jupiter, 0333
Hampton Roads tunnels, 1032
Han Shih
  See Qing Ming Festival (Ching Ming Festival)
Hana Matsuri (Flower Festival), 1274
  See also Vesak (Wesak; Buddha's Birthday)
Hanagasa Odori, 1275

Hanami, 0576, 0577, 1276
Hanbada Festival for the Disabled, 0447
Hancock, John, 1065
Hancox, Bill, 1153
handball, 0173
Handel, Georg Frideric, 0679
Handsel Monday, 1277
Handy (W. C.) Music Festival, 1278
Hangawi
  See Chuseok (Gawi or Hangawi); Mid-Autumn Festival
Han'gul Day, 1279
Hannibal, 0540
Hansan Daecheop
  See Great Battle of Hansan Festival (Hansan Daecheop)
Hanukkah (Chanukah), 1280
Hanuman Jayanti, 1281
happiness festival, 1749
Harbin Ice and Snow Festival, 1282
Hard Crab Derby, National, 1283
Hare Pie, 0381
Hari Raya
  See Id al-Fitr (Eid)
Hari-Kuyo (Festival of Broken Needles), 1284
Harlem International Film Festival, 1285
Harlem Week, 1286
Harlequin, 0527
harmonica music festival, 0235
Haro Wine Festival (Batalia de Vino), 1287
Harvest Festival, 1288
  See Harvest Home Festival
harvest festivals
  Africa, 1766
  ancient Greece, 2967
  Angola, 2055
  Bangladesh, 1968, 3104
  Barbados, 0728
  California, 1894
  Czech Republic, 2106
  England, 1289
  Europe, 1990
  Finland, 2785
  Ghana, 1352, 2056
  Haiti, 1766
  Hopi Indians, 0252
  Illinois, 1490
  Incas, 0205
  India, 1580, 1968, 2141, 2295, 2421, 3104
  Ireland, 1711, 2907
  Iroquois, 1288
  Japan, 1443
  Jewish religion, 1616, 2858
  Lithuania, 2106
  Malaysia, 1504
  Malta, 1895 Netherlands, 1151
  New Mexico, 2481, 2608
  Nigeria, 2142
  Northern Hemisphere, 1290
  Peru, 0205
  Philippines, 1889

Numbers in the index refer to entry numbers, not page numbers

Portugal, 2903
Scotland, 1289
Slovak Republic, 2106
Spain, 0662
Ukraine, 3078
Venezuela, 0228
Zoroastrian religion, 2184
Harvest Home Festival, 1289
Harvest Moon Days, 1290
Harvest Thanksgiving
   See Harvest Home Festival
Harvey, Larry, 0435
Hassan II, King of Morocco, 1211
Hatch Chile Festival, 1291
Hatfield and McCoy Reunion Festival and Marathon, 1292
Hatkoff, Craig, 3022
Havell, Robert, Jr., 0189
Hawaii
   cultural festival, 0075
   friendship day, 1652
   Japanese cultural celebration, 0576
   military commemoration, 2234
   music concert, 0804
   new year festival, 1977
   religious ceremony, 1040
   royal events, 0933, 1511, 1592, 1858
   sporting event, 1431
   surfing contest, 0418
   turtle festival, 3061
   volcano crater music concert, 0804
   yacht race, 3020
hawthorn tree, 0269
Haxey Hood Game, 1293
Haydn, Joseph, 0391, 0409, 0679
Hayes, Rutherford B., 0879
Hay-on-Wye Festival of Literature, 1294
Hayti community, 1295
Hayti Heritage Film Festival, 1295
Head-Smashed-In Buffalo Jump, 0416
healing ceremonies
   Mexico, 2072
   New Mexico, 2608
   Nigeria, 0038
health days, 3197, 3264
Health-Sports Day
   See Taiiku-no-Hi
heart disease, 3197
Heartbreak Hill, 0375
Heaven's Gift Day
   See Airing the Classics
He'dewachi
   See Whe'wahchee (He'dewachi; Dance of
     Thanksgiving)
hedge-building ceremony, 2282
Heidi Festival, 1296
heilala, 3003
HeiligerAbend
   See Christmas Eve (Switzerland) (HeiligerAbend)
Heiva

   See Bastille Day
Helsinki Festival, 1297 Helston Flora Day, 1298
Hemingway (Ernest) Days Festival, 1299
Hemis Festival, 1300
Henius, Max, 1066
Henley Royal Regatta, 1301
Hennessey, Amanda, 3065
Hennessy Grand Prix
   See New Jersey Offshore Grand Prix
Henry, Marguerite, 0606
Henson, Rev. Josiah, 0922
Hera, 0748
Heraclius, Emperor, 0970
herbal festivals
   China, 1140
   Japan, 1973
   Spain, 2462
herding festival, 0076
Herdsman, 0601
Heritage Holidays, 1302
Hermit, Feast of the, 1303
Herod, King, 0176, 0531, 0616, 1038, 1336, 1337
Heroes Day
   See Bataan Day
Heroes' Day
   See Kenya Mashujaa Day (Heroes' Day)
Heurigen Parties, 1304
Hewes, David, 1162
Hi Matsuri (Fire Festival), 1305
Hiawatha, 2661
Hickok, "Wild Bill," 0702
Hidimba, 0797
Hidrellez Festival, 1306
Higan, 1307
Higginson, Henry Lee, 0377
Highland Games, 1308
hikiyama, 1513
Híkuli Dance
   See Peyote Dance (Híkuli Dance)
Hilaria, 1309
Hill Cumorah Pageant, 1310
Himalayas, 1767
Himilce, 0540
Hina Matsuri (Doll Festival), 1311
Hinckley, Ohio, 0452
Hindu events
   Bali, 1093
   Bhai Dooj, 0306
   birthday commemoration, 1145 civil new year, 1230
   death commemoration, 1129
   Dhan Teras, 0796
   disease protection festival, 2641 fasting, 0094, 0901
   fathers commemoration, 1152
   Ganga Dussehra, 1100
   Ghatasthapana, 1130
   Ghode Jatra, 1131
   good over evil, 0855
   Gowri Habba, 1175
   Guru Purnima, 1241

Numbers in the index refer to entry numbers, not page numbers

Gyan Panchami, 1248
Halashashti, 1263
Hali Puja, 1508
Hanuman Jayanti, 1281
Hidimba commemoration, 0797
Holi, 1327
India, 0171, 0198, 0456, 0457, 0562, 1477
Indonesia, 2205
Janaki Navami, 1463
Jyestha Ashtami, 1502
Kapila Shashti, 1512
Kartika Purnima, 1516
Kartika Snan, 1517
Karwachoth, 1519
Kokila Vrata, 1581
Krishna festivals, 0109
Kumbh Mela, 1593
Lakshmi Puja, 1618
Magha Purnima, 1735
mythological celebrations, 0308, 1618, 2219
Naag Panchami, 1967
Narak Chaturdashi, 1976
Nariyal Purnima, 1978
Narsimha Jayanti, 1978
Nirjala Ekadashi, 2074
Phagwa, 2250
purification festival, 2642
Putrada Ekadashi, 2334
Radha Ashtami, 2356
Ramanavami, 2366
Rasa Leela Festival, 2370
Rishi Panchami, 2405
Rukmini Ashtami, 2444
Sakata Chauth, 2468
Savitri-Vrata, 2538
Sharad Purnima, 2591
Shigmo Festival, 2602
Shivaratri, 2610
Shravani Mela, 2611
stone-throwing ritual, 0792
Swarupa Dwadashi, 2884
Thaipusam, 2961
tree worshipping, 0078
Vaitarani, 3105
Vaman Dwadashi, 3110
Vasanth Navaratri, 3121
Vishnu awakening, 0791
women's celebration, 2877
Hippokrateia Festival, 1312
Hirohito, Emperor, 1213
Hiroshima Peace Ceremony, 1313
Hispanic festivals
    Florida, 0506
    Miami, Florida, 0506
    New Jersey, 2754
Hispanic Heritage Month, 1314
Hispanity Day
    See Columbus Day
historic celebrations

Alaska, 2574
California, 2217
Cambodia, 2627
Cayman Islands, 2279
Greece, 2294
England, 1696, 2412
Florida, 2223
France, 1975
Iowa, 1360
Jamaica, 1786
Japan, 1466, 1478, 1970
Jerusalem, 2918
Kenya, 1538
Kosovo, 1588
Maryland, 2372, 2392
Massachusetts, 2227, 2264
Missouri, 2833
Morocco, 1211
Nepal, 2009
Netherlands, 1558
New Mexico, 2517
Oklahoma, 2117
Oregon, 2413
South Sudan, 2675
Tonga, 3051
Tunisia, 3050
United States, 2226, 2316, 2325, 2816, 1064
Vietnam, 1141
Virginia, 1459, 3296
historic reenactments
    Belgium, 2727
    Canada, 3021
    Cartegena, 0540
    Connecticut, 2359
    Germany, 1555, 2257
    Indiana, 1382
    Maryland, 0580
    Massachusetts, 2265
    Mississippi, 1623
    Montana, 1687
    New Jersey, 2794
    New Mexico, 0318
    Pennsylvania, 0730
    Rhode Island, 1108
    San Martin, 2340
    Saskatchewan, 3021
    South Dakota, 0771
    Utah, 1162
    Wyoming, 1136, 1212, 1938
Historical Regatta, 1315
Hitachi Furyumono, 1316
Hitler, Adolf, 0776
Hitler Purim
    See Purims, Special
Hmong New Year, 1317
Ho Chi Minh's Birthday, 1318
Ho Khao Slak
    See Vatsa (Ho Khao Slak)
Hobart Cup Day, 1319

Numbers in the index refer to entry numbers, not page numbers

Hobart Royal Regatta, 1320
Hobart Royal Show
        See Royal Shows
hobby horse parades
        England, 1885
        Wales, 1885
Hobo Convention, 1321
Hock Days
        See Hocktide
Hocktide, 1322
hoe cleaning, 0219
Hoffman, Clare, 1177
hog intestines, 0609
Hogbetsotso Festival, 1323
Hogmanay, 1324
hoko floats, 1143
Hola Mohalla, 1325
Holetown Festival, 1326
Holi, 1327
Holiday of the Three Hierarchs, 2974
Holland
        See Netherlands
Holland Festival, 1328
Holland, Michigan, 3044
Hollerin' Contest, National, 1329 holly, 0616
Hollyhock Festival
        See Aoi Matsuri
hollyhocks, 0124
Hollywood Bowl, 0869
Hollywood, California, 0010, 0869
Holmenkollen Day, 1330
Holocaust Memorial Day, 1331
Holocaust Remembrance Day, International, 1332
Holy Blood, Procession of the, 1333
Holy Cross Day
        See Exaltation of the Cross, Feast of the
Holy Day of Letters
        See Bulgarian Education and Culture Day
Holy Family, 0176
Holy Family, Feast of the, 1334
Holy Ghost Season
        See Holy Ghost, Feast of the
Holy Ghost/Spirit, 0814
Holy Innocents' Day, 1336
Holy Innocents' Day (Belgium) (Allerkinderendag), 1337
Holy Prophet and the Martyrdom of Imam Hasan, Death
    Anniversary of the, 1338
Holy Queen Isabel, Festival of the, 1339
Holy Rood Day
        See Exaltation of the Cross, Feast of the
Holy Saturday, 1340
Holy Saturday (Mexico) (Sábado de Gloria), 1341
Holy Thursday
        See Ascension
Day Holy Week, 1343
Holy Week (Czech Republic), 1344
Holy Week (Haiti), 1345
Holy Week (Mexico), 1346
Holy Week (Panama), 1347

Holy Week (Philippines), 1348
Holy Week (Portugal) (Semana Santa), 1349
Homage to Cuauhtemoc (Homenaje a Cuauhtemoc), 1350
home tours
        Mississippi, 1983
        South Carolina, 1373
Homeless Persons' Remembrance Day, National, 1351
Homenaje a Cuauhtemoc
        See Homage to Cuauhtemoc (Homenaje a Cuauhtemoc)
Homowo, 1352
Homowo, 1352
Homstrom, 1353
Honduras
        birthday commemoration, 1355
        dance festival, 3285
        independence day, 1354
Honduras Independence Day, 1354
Honduras Soldiers' Day, 1355
Hong Kong
        arts festival, 1356, 0157, 2021
        birthday commemorations, 1150, 1708, 2917
        boat races, 0842, 3039
        Christmas celebration, 1359
        Confucius's birthday, 0676
        death commemoration, 0646
        Film festival, 1357
        love legend festival, 2572
        lunar new year, 1714
        massacre commemoration, 2978
        moon goddess holiday, 1870
        political commemoration, 1358
        religious celebration, 2900
        sea festival, 2986
        spirit dedication, 0581
Hong Kong Arts Festival, 1356
Hong Kong International Film Festival, 1357
Hong Kong Special Administrative Region Establishment
    Day, 1358
Hong Kong WinterFest, 1359
honorary degrees, 0929
Honorius III, Pope, 1057
hood retrieval game, 1293
Hoover, Herbert, 1360
Hooverfest, 1360
Hope Watermelon Festival, 1361
hopeless causes, 2763
Hopi Flute Ceremony, 1362
Hopi Indians, 0252, 1362, 1363, 2069, 2308, 2679, 3280
        See also American Indians
Hopi Snake Dance, 1363
Hopi Soyal Ceremony
        See Soyaluna (Hopi Soyal Ceremony)
Hora at Prislop, 1364
Hordad, Feast of, 1365
Horn Dance, 1366
horns, 0346
horror films, 2945
horse events
        Germany, 1658, 1991

Hungary, 1367
Italy, 1486
Japan, 0557, 2080, 3224
Mexico, 0799
Nepal, 1131
Tennessee, 2949
Virginia, 0606
Horse Festival
    See Lajkonik
horse racing
    ancient Rome, 0947
    Australia, 1319, 1846, 0018
    England, 0789, 1180, 1565, 2438
    Guatemala, 0067
    Ireland, 1642
    Italy, 2189
    Kentucky, 1536
    Maryland, 1804, 2312
    Mongolia, 1966
    Nebraska, 0044, 1085
    New Jersey, 1273
    New York, 0289
    Scotland, 1806
    Tibet, 1249
    Washington (state), 2134
horse sacrifice, 2109
horse's head, 1830
Horta, Jose Ramos, 0861
horticultural events
    Massachusetts, 0129
    Netherlands, 1046
    Ohio, 0129
Hortobágy Bridge Fair and International Equestrian
    Festival, 1367
Hosay
    See Ashura
Hosay Festival, 1368
Hoshana Rabbah, 1369
hospital fundraisers, 0061, 2845
Hospital Week, National, 1370
Hostos Day, 1371
Hostos, Eugenio Maria de, 1371
Hot Air Balloon Classic, 1372
hot cross bun, 1166
Hot Springs State Park (Thermopolis, Wyoming), 1136
hot summer days, 0822
hound trailing, 1188
House of Parliament, 0988
house-cleaning, 2878
Houses and Gardens, Festival of, 1373
Houston Livestock Show & Rodeo, 1374
Houston, Sam, 0051, 2956
How, John, 0805
Howe, William, 0968
Howl! Festival, 1375
huasos, 0789, 0916
Huguenots, 0250
Human Rights Day, 0315
Human Rights Day, International, 1376

Human Towers of Valls, 1377
Humana Festival of New American Plays, 1378
Humor and Satire Festival, International, 1379
humor festival, 1379
Humphrey, Hubert, 0030
Hundred Drums Festival
    See Wangala (Hundred Drums Festival)
Hundred Guinea Cup, 0089
Hungary
    Carnival, 0517
    classical music festival, 0409
    cultural celebration, 0410
    film festival, 0455
    food festival, 2899
    horse festival, 1367
    independence day, 1381
    literary celebration, 0455
    music festival, 0410
    national holiday, 1380
    saint feast days, 2774, 2812
    spring festival, 0410
Hungary Republic Day, 1380
Hungary Revolution and Independence Day, 1381
hunger, 0983
Hungry Ghosts Festival
    See Ullambana (Hungry Ghosts Festival; All Souls' Feast)
Hunters' Moon, Feast of the, 1382
Huntigowk Day
    See April Fools' Day
hunting celebrations
    Belgium, 2742
    England, 1366, 2221
Hurling the Silver Ball, 1383
Hurricane Speculation Day, 1384
Hurston (Zora Neale) Festival of the Arts and Humanties,
    1385
Hus (Jan) Day, 1386
Husayn Ali, 0225
Hussein, 0172
Hussein Day
    See Ashura
Hussein Festival
    See Hosay Festival
Hussein, Imam al-, 0136, 0137
Hussein, King, 0005
Hussein, Saddam, 0137
Huston, John, 0473
Hutus, 0445
    Hyacinthia, 0507

I

"I Am an American" Day
    See Citizenship Day
I Madonnari Italian Street Painting Festival, 1387
Ibu Afo Festival, 1388
ice events
    Alaska, 2007

China, 1282
Colorado, 2171
Finland, 1015
Ice Worm Festival, 1389
Iceland
    arts festival, 2397
    Children's Day, 0597
    constitution festival, 2972
    fishermen's holiday, 2645
    food festival, 2973
    independence day, 1390
    New Year's Eve, 2035
    saint feast day, 2819
    sea festival, 2546
    summer festival, 1019
    viking festival, 3148
Iceland Independence Day, 1390
Icelandic Festival, 1391
Icelandic festivals
    Canada, 1391
    Manitoba, 1391
ice-skating race, 0913
icons, 0562
Id al-Adha (Feast of Sacrifice; Eid), 1392
Id al-Arba'in Shahid
    See Forty Martyrs' Day
Id al-Fitr (Eid), 1393
Id al-Fitr (Nigeria), 1394
Id al-Kabir
    See Id al-Adha (Feast of Sacrifice; Eid)
Id Mar Jurjus
    See St. George's Day (Syria) (Id Mar Jurjus)
Idaho
    American Indian ceremony, 1698
    boating regatta, 1396
    dance festival, 1395
    food festival, 1397
    lumberjack festival, 0655
    music festivals, 1395, 2131
    powwow, 1698
    religious festival, 2743
    rodeo, 0820
Idaho International Summerfest, 1395
Idaho Regatta, 1396
Idaho Spud Day, 1397
Idas, 0545
Ides, 1398
Iditarod Trail Sled Dog Race, 1399
Idlewild Jazz Festival, 1400
Iduna and Summer Finding, 1401
Igbi, 1402
Igbo people, 0038, 1388, 2022, 2119, 2142
Iglesia Las Mercedes, 0832
Il Giorno dei Morti
    See All Souls' Day
Illinois
    African-American children, 0317
    animal festival, 2133
    arts festival, 2376

bell music festival, 0502
blues festival, 0585
children's celebration, 0588
comics celebration, 2875
dance festival, 0586
death commemoration, 1799
film festivals, 0588, 0589
fires, 1017
food festival, 2930
Ghanian festival, 1128
gospel music festival, 0587
harvest festival, 1490
jazz festival, 0591
literature festival, 2508
music festivals, 0585, 1694
parade, 0317
puppet festival, 0590
Swedish commemoration, 1484
wine and cheese festival, 1187
Illuminated Water Parade
    See Newport Harbor Christmas Boat Parade
Illyés, Gyula, 0409
Imam Ali's Birthday, 1403
Imam Ali's Martyrdom, Anniversary of, 1404
Imam Sadiq's Martyrdom, Anniversary of, 1405
Imbolc (Imbolg), 0731, 1016, 1406
Imbolg
    See Imbolc (Imbolg)
Immaculate Conception, Feast of the, 1407
Immaculate Conception, Feast of the (Argentina), 1408
Immaculate Conception, Feast of the (Malta), 1409
Immaculate Conception, Feast of the (Mexico), 1410
Immaculate Heart of Mary, Feast of the, 1411
Imnarja
    See Mnarja (Imnarja; Feast of St. Peter and St. Paul)
imperial holiday, 0124
Imperial Poem-Reading Ceremony
    See Utakai Hajime (Imperial Poem-Reading Ceremony)
impressionism, 2083
Impruneta, Festa del, 1412
ImPulsTanz: Vienna International Dance Festival, 1413
Inauguration Day, 1414
Incas
    Día del Puno, 0803
    harvest festival, 0205
    Inti Raymi Fiesta, 1424
    parade, 0534
    solstice festival, 0491
Inconfidência Week, 1415
Independence Day
    See Fourth of July; Lebanon National Day; Nigeria
        National Day; Syria National Day
independence days
    Afghanistan, 1474
    Albania, 0055
    Algeria, 0062
    Antigua and Barbuda, 0118
    Argentina, 0142
    Armenia, 0151, 0152

Azerbaijan, 0208
Bahamas, 0222
Bangladesh, 0238
Barbados, 0243
Belarus, 0282
Belgium, 0285, 1079
Belize, 0286
Benin, 0291
Bolivia, 0356, 1608
Botswana, 0379
Brazil, 0226, 0393, 1415
Bulgaria, 0419, 0420
Burkina Faso, 0433
Burundi, 0445
Cambodia, 0468
Cape Verde, 0493
Central African Republic, 0550
Chad, 0555
Chile, 1006
Colombia, 0665, 1416
Comoros, 0670
Congo, 0677
Costa Rica, 0699
Côte d'Ivoire, 0701
Croatia, 0722, 0723
Cyprus, 0743
Czechoslovakia, 0746
Democratic Republic of Congo, 0785
Djibouti, 0815
Dominica, 0828
Dominican Republic, 0829, 0830
East Timor, 0861
Ecuador, 0887
El Salvador, 0904
Equatorial Guinea, 0946
Eritrea, 0950
Estonia, 0958, 0959, 0960
Ethiopia, 0962
Fiji, 1009
Finland, 1014
France, 0255
Gabon, 1089
Gambia, 1096
Georgia (country), 1116
Ghana, 1127
Greece, 1207
Grenada, 1217
Guatemala, 1227
Guinea, 1232
Guinea-Bissau, 1235
Guyana, 1246
Haiti, 1259
Honduras, 1354
Hungary, 1381
Iceland, 1390
Indonesia, 1421
Israel, 1440
Ivory Coast, 0701
Jamaica, 1457

Jordan, 1483
Kiribati, 1567
Korea, 2475
Kosovo, 1588
Kyrgyzstan, 1607
Latvia, 1637, 2393
Lebanon, 1647
Lesotho, 1659
Liberia, 1665
Lithuania, 1684, 1685
Luxembourg, 1716
Macedonia, 1721
Madagascar, 1725
Malawi, 1752
Malaysia, 1856
Maldives, 1756
Mali, 1758
Malta, 1761
Mauritania, 1820
Mauritius, 1821
Mexico, 1862
Moldova, 1901
Morocco, 1922
Mozambique, 1943
Myanmar, 1959
Nauru, 1994
Nicaragua, 2061
North Carolina, 1266, 1839
Palau, 2188
Panama, 2201
Papua New Guinea, 2207
Paraguay, 2209
Peru, 2247
Philippines, 2253
Poland, 2290
Portugal, 2302
Qatar, 2336
Rhode Island, 2398
Rwanda, 2451
Samoa, 2476
São Tomé and Principe, 2528
Senegal, 2564
Seychelles, 2576
Sierra Leone, 2625
Slovak Republic, 2648
Slovenia, 2649
Solomon Islands, 2659
Somalia, 2660
South Sudan, 2675
St. Kitts and Nevis, 2764
St. Lucia, 2769
St. Vincent and the Grenadines, 2823
Sudan, 2855
Suriname, 2876
Swaziland, 2885
Syria, 2897
Tajikistan, 2911
Tanzania, 2925
Texas, 2956

Numbers in the index refer to entry numbers, not page numbers

Timor-Leste, 2984
Tonga
Trinidad and Tobago, 3029
Tunisia, 3048
Turkmenistan, 3057
Tuvalu, 3062
Uganda, 3070
Ukraine, 3076
United States, 1065, 1066
Uruguay, 3097
Uzbekistan, 3103
Vanuatu, 3115
Venezuela, 3126
Yemen, 3290
Zambia, 3306
Zimbabwe, 3313
Independence Movement Day
    See Samil-jol (Independence Movement Day)
Independence of Cartagena City Day, 1416
India
    agricultural ceremony, 1461
    ancestors commemoration, 2280
    animal fair, 2333
    arts festival, 1506
    bathing festivals, 1517, 1735, 1809, 1819, 2653
    birthday commemorations, 0753, 0767, 0825, 1098, 1464,
        2905, 3046, 3109
    Buddhist celebrations, 1300, 1734
    Carnival, 0515
    chariot festival, 2371
    civil new year, 1230
    cultural celebration, 1524
    dancing, 0583, 2218
    death commemorations, 0979, 3093
    drumming festival, 3177
    elephant-headed god festival, 1099
    film festivals, 1013, 1583
    fire-walking ceremony, 2968
    food festival, 1978, 1732
    good over evil festival, 0855
    harvest festivals, 1580, 1968, 2141, 2295, 2421, 3104
    Hidimba commemoration, 0797
    Hindu celebrations, 0045, 0171, 0198, 0456, 0457, 0562,
        1477, 1175
    Jain festival, 0765
    lights festival, 1515
    literary pageant, 2364
    marriage celebrations, 1101, 1841
    masks, 0583
    military commemoration, 1736
    monsoon festival, 2937
    mythological holiday, 2646
    national holiday, 1417, 0081
    new year, 1462
    parade, 0515
    Passion play, 2935
    pilgrimages, 0079, 2989, 2611
    prospective matrimonial festival, 2928
    purification ceremony, 1100

    raft festival, 0294
    religious ceremonies, 1508, 1547, 1590, 1593, 1739, 1740,
        2610, 0362, 1175, 1515, 2611
    retreat, 0547
    royal festival, 1039
    sacred name day, 0092
    saint feast days, 2590, 2818
    seasonal festival, 1692
    Shi'ite religious festival, 0172
    Shiva, Lord, festival, 2296
    sibling festival, 2361, 0306
    snake festivals, 1476, 1967
    spiritual festival, 2222
    spring festivals, 0078, 1327, 1998, 3120, 2602
    stone-throwing ritual, 0792
    sun holiday, 1733
    tree worshipping, 0078
    water festival, 1325
    women's festival, 1101, 1175
    workers' holiday, 3160
    Zoroastrian religion, 0001, 0017
India Republic Day, 1417
Indian Arrival Day, 1418
Indian festivals
    California, 2326
    Trinidad and Tobago, 1418
Indian Market, 1419
Indiana
    automobile racing, 1181, 1420
    autumn festival, 0130
    Dean, James, tribute, 0779
    historic reenactment, 1382
    literary festival, 2402
    turtle festival, 3060
    Wizard of Oz festival, 3241
Indianapolis 500, 1420
indigenous events (Australia), 1106, 1505, 2378
Indigenous Peoples Day
    See Columbus Day
Indonesia
    ballet, 2367
    birthday commemorations, 1518, 2559
    Carnival festival, 1598
    Children's Day, 0597
    dance event, 2367
    film festival, 1455
    Hindu festival, 2205
    independence day, 1421
    new year, 2101
    religious celebrations, 0900, 2275
Indonesia Independence Day, 1421
Indra, 0109, 0198
Indra Jatra, 1422
Industrial Day
    See Saba Saba Day
Indy 500
    See Indianapolis 500
information specialists, 0021
initiation ceremony, 2604

Innocents' Day
    See Holy Innocents' Day
Insect-Hearing Festival
    See Freeing the Insects
insects, 0547, 0971, 1078
Insurrection Day
    See Madagascar Martyrs' Day
Interceltique, Festival, 1423
intermarriage, 1007
International Animation Film Market, 0111
International Association of Administrative Professionals, 0021
International Bluegrass Music Association, 3220
International Board on Books for Young People (IBBY), 0539
International Centre for Creative Research, 0200
International Cricket Council, 0720
International Festival of Contemporary Music
    See Warsaw Autumn Festival
International Film Festival
    See Cannes Film Festival
International Freedom Festival, 0478
International Istanbul Festival
    See Istanbul Festivals, International
interracial marriage, 0380
Inti Raymi Festival
    See Inti Raymi Fiesta
Inti Raymi Fiesta, 1424
Inti Raymi Pageant
    See Inti Raymi Fiesta
Intruz
    See Carnival (Goa, India)
Inuit Indians, 0008, 2090
    See also American Indians
Inuus, 0987
Invention of the Cross
    See Exaltation of the Cross, Feast of the
Iowa
    American Indian ceremony, 1859
    arts festival, 3245
    balloon festival, 1372
    bicycle racing, 2358
    country music festival, 2130
    covered bridge festival, 1730
    flower festival, 3043
    historic festival, 1360
    hobo convention, 1321
    jazz festival, 0279
    Norwegian festival, 2082
    powwow, 1859
    state fair, 1425
Iowa State Fair, 1425
Iqbal (Muhammad), Birthday of, 1426
Iran
    birthday commemorations, 0211, 3063
    death commemorations, 0213, 0979, 1338, 1405, 1545
    folklore festival, 2644
    national holidays, 1427, 1429, 1546
    oil nationalization commemoration, 1428

    Passion play, 2935
    religious festival, 0212
    sacred name day, 0092
    soccer, 0025
    spring festival, 1998
    Zoroastrian religion, 0001
Iran Islamic Republic Day, 1427
Iran Petroleum Nationalization Anniversary, 1428
Iran Victory Day of the Iranian Revolution, 1429
Iraq
    birthday commemoration, 1403
    death commemoration, 1404
    Islamic history commemorations, 0136, 0137
    Passion play, 2935
    soccer, 0025
Ireland
    animal festival, 2323
    arts festival, 1551, 1094
    beauty contest, 2432
    Celtic holiday, 0290
    cultural celebration, 0093
    dancing, 1031
    death commemoration, 1448
    Druidic festival, 2023
    fairy fight, 1830
    fires, 2758
    food festival, 1095
    garden festival, 3219
    Halloween, 1268
    harvest festivals, 1711, 2907
    horse racing, 1642
    literary holiday, 0345
    marital status, 0560
    military commemoration, 2148
    music festival, 1031
    opera festival, 3205
    pilgrimages, 0725, 2384
    religious holiday, 1797
    saint feast days, 2708, 2709, 2717, 2758, 2792, 2793
    singing competition, 0093
    theater festival, 1837, 0847
    whiskey commemoration, 2594
Iris Fest (Fête de l'Iris), 1430
    See also French Community, Feast Day of the (La fête de la Communauté française de Belgique)
Ireland, Dan, 2554
Irish festival, 0846
iron rings, 1129
Ironman Triathlon Championships, 1431
Iroquois Indians, 0276, 0778, 0858, 1432, 2847, 1288
    See also American Indians
Iroquois Midwinter Festival, 1432
Irrigation Festival, 1433
Irwin, Kenny, 0773
Isabel, Queen, 0549
Isabella, Queen, 0666
Islamic events
    Adam's Peak, Pilgrimage to, 0016
    Arbaeen, 0136

Arbaeen Pilgrimage, 0137
Ashura, 0172
Bera Festival, 0294
Bishwa Ijtema, 0321
Damba, 0755
Grand Magal of Shaykh Amadou Bamba, 1179
Holy Prophet and the Martyrdom of Imam Hasan, Death Anniversary of the, 1338
Id al-Adha, 1392
Id al-Fitr, 1393
Imam Ali's Birthday, 1403
Imam Ali's Martyrdom, Anniversary of, 1404
Imam Sadiq's Martyrdom, Anniversary of, 1405
Islamic New Year, 1435
Khamis al-Amwat, 1544
Khomeini (Ayatollah), Death Anniversary of, 1545
Lamp Nights, 1621
Lanterns Festival, 1630
Laylat al-Miraj, 1640
Laylat al-Qadr, 1641
Libya Day of Arafa, 1670
Maldives, 1755
Mandi Safar, 1765
Muhammad commemorations, 0755
Muhammad's birthday, 1823
Mulid of Shaykh Yusuf Abu el-Haggag (Moulid of Abu el-Haggag), 1950
Portugal, 1434
Pakistan Day, 2185
Pilgrimage to Mecca (Hajj), 2270
Pilgrimage to the Tomb of Sunan Bayat, 2275
Ramadan, 2365
Rumi Festival, 2445
Sallah (Salah) Festival, 2469
Sekaten, 2559
Shab-Barat, 2578
Springtime Festival, 2691
St. George's Day (Syria) (Id Mar Jurjus), 2735
summer twilight festival, 3213
Twelfth Imam, Birthday of the, 3063
Urs Ajmer Sharif, 3093
Urs of Jelaluddin al-Rumi (Whirling Dervish Festival), 3095
Yugoslavia, 0372
Islamic Festival, 1434
Islamic New Year, 1435
Isle of Eight Flags Shrimp Festival, 1436
Isle of Man
    Celtic holiday, 0290
    Halloween, 1269
    political ceremony, 3067
Isle of Wight Festival, 1437
Isle of Wight Garlic Festival, 1438
Islendingadagurinn
    See Icelandic Festival
Islentildeos Fiesta, Los, 1701
Israel
    cultural festival, 1439
    death commemoration, 3292

film festival, 1473
Holocaust commemoration, 1331
independence day, 1440
military commemoration, 3294
music festival, 1453
national holiday, 0230
relationship with Egypt, 0147
Israel Festival, 1439
Israel Independence Day, 1440
Istanbul, 1441
Istanbul Festivals, International, 1441
Isthmian Games, 1442
Itabashi Suwa Jinja Ta-Asobi, 1443
Italian Festival, 1444
Italian festivals
    California, 1445
    Oklahoma, 1444
    West Virginia, 3202
Italian Heritage Parade, 1445
Italy
    automobile racing, 1883
    autumn harvest festival, 1412
    boat racing, 2386
    cake-eating festival, 3012
    Carnival, 0527
    chess living game, 1689
    Christmas, 0616
    Christmas Eve, 0636
    classical music festival, 2322
    college feast, 1814
    Corpus Christi, 0780
    costumes, 0527
    cultural celebration, 3127
    death commemoration, 0069
    film festival, 3128
    flower festival, 1677
    food festival, 0054
    gift-giving festival, 0278
    horse event, 1486
    horse racing, 2189
    jazz festivals, 3143
    jousting festivals, 1486, 1487, 1488
    Lenten festival, 1874
    music festivals, 0448, 1043, 3143
    national holiday, 1446
    operas, 0262, 1043
    orange-throwing contest, 0533
    pagan destruction ceremony, 2258
    papal festival, 2799
    processions, 0548, 1167
    religious celebrations, 0069, 0181, 0870, 1057, 1167, 2195, 2382, 2694
    running race, 2353
    saint feast days, 2515, 2726, 2729, 2730, 2762, 2790, 2805
    serenading night, 1831
    singing contest, 0459
    sporting events, 1142, 2190
    spring festival, 0995
    trade fair, 1880

Numbers in the index refer to entry numbers, not page numbers

Virgin Mary festival, 2160
wine festival, 1780
Italy Liberation Day, 1446
Itensi
    See Okpesi Festival
Itul, 1447
Ivan Kupalo
    See Kupalo Festival
Ivory Coast
    See Côte d'Ivoire
ivy, 0616
Ivy Day, 1448
Iyomante Matsuri (Bear Festival), 1449
Izumo-taisha Jinzaisai, 1450

J

J. J. Roberts Day
    See Roberts's (Joseph Jenkins) Birthday
Jaanipäev, 0960
Jackalope Days, 1451
Jackson, Andrew, 0267
Jackson, Charles, 0817
Jackson Day
    See Battle of New Orleans Day
Jackson's (Andrew) Birthday, 1452
Jacob's Ladder, 1453
Jacob's Pillow Dance Festival, 1454
Jagannath, 2371
Jagannath Festival
    See Rath Yatra
Jagannatha, Lord, 0562
jaguar, 0535
Jain events
    Akshya Tritiya, 0045
    Caturmas, 0547
    Dasa Laksana Parvan, 0765
    Dewali, 0794
    Gyan Panchami, 1248
    Ksamavani, 1590
    Mahamastakabhishekha, 1739
    Mahavira Jayanti, 1740
    Parshva, Birthday of, 2220
    Paryushana, 2222
    Pausha Dashami, 2229
    Risabha's Nirvana and Mauni Amavasya, 2404
    Samvatsari, 2477
Jakarta International Film Festival, 1455
Jamaica
    arts festival, 1456
    birthday commemoration, 1785
    Caribbean community commemoration, 0500
    historic festival, 1786
    national holidays, 1457, 1458
    reggae music festival, 2387
    religious festival, 0172
Jamaica Festival, 1456
Jamaica Independence Day, 1457

Jamaica National Heroes Day, 1458
James I, King, 0988, 0702
James II, King, 0402, 0657
James IV, King, 0668
James, Red Fox, 0085
Jamestown Day, 1459
Jamhuri (Kenya Independence Day), 1460
Jammeh, Yahya, 1097
Jammolpur Ceremony, 1461
Jamshed Navaroz (Jamshed Navroz), 1462
Jamshed Navroz
    See Jamshed Navaroz (Jamshed Navroz)
Janadriyah Festival
    See Saudi Arabia National Heritage and Folk Culture
        Festival (Janadriyah Festival)
Janaki Navami, 1463
Janmashtami (Krishnastami; Krishna's Birthday), 1463
Jannsen, J. V., 0234
Jans vakars
    See St. John's Eve and Day (Latvia) (Jans vakars)
Janus, 0035
Japan
    agricultural celebration, 1251
    archery contest, 2996
    arts and sciences award, 0428
    arts festival, 0886
    autumn festivals, 0648, 3005, 1513, 2389
    bean-throwing festival, 2571
    bear festival, 1449
    birthday commemorations, 0428, 1150, 1213, 1468, 1843,
        2558, 2607
    boat races, 0348
    Bodhisattva ceremony, 2010
    bonfires and souls, 0750
    Buddhist holidays, 1479, 2787, 2901, 0351
    business festival, 0885
    castle commemoration, 0042
    children's days, 0597, 1579
    Christmas, 0616
    Christmas Eve, 0629
    cultural festivals, 1260, 1261, 2154, 2514
    dance festivals, 1275, 2609
    dead, visits from the, 2105
    death commemoration, 2156
    demon commemorations, 1727, 1971
    doll festivals, 0764, 1311
    Dutch and Chinese dancing festival, 2121
    elderly commemoration, 1531
    fire festivals, 1305, 3171
    fire-taming ceremony, 0608
    fishing festival, 0885, 2787
    float festivals, 1143, 1527, 2912
    flower festivals, 0642, 1274, 1276, 2465
    folklore festivals, 2174, 3098
    food festivals, 0304, 1898, 2068
    god festival, 1450
    harvest festivals, 1443
    herbal festival, 1973
    historic festivals, 1466, 1478, 1970

horse festivals, 2080, 3224
house-cleaning, 2878
imperial holiday, 0124
insect freedom, 1078
kite festival, 2915
lantern festival, 0610
literary events, 1606, 2948, 3100
military commemoration, 3069
moon goddess holiday, 1870
mountain climbing, 1935
national holidays, 0197, 1465, 1467
needle festival, 1284
new year, 2155, 2860
New Year's Eve celebration, 2138
pan-on-head festival, 1969
papier-mâché festival, 2003
parades, 0751, 2041
peace ceremony, 1313
pole-carrying contest, 0363
procession, 0042
puppet festival, 1316
rain festival, 2914
rake festival, 3008
religious celebrations, 0348, 2513
rice-planting festival, 2399
samurai festival, 3013, 0043
shellfish festival, 2595
shrine commemorations, 1521, 2137, 3037, 3287
shrine-jostling festival, 1534
snake festival, 3082
snow festivals, 1510, 2529
snowball fight festivals, 3300
soccer, 0025
sporting event, 0025, 0231, 2906
spring equinox, 1307
star festival, 2919
stone festival, 1602
summer festival, 3179
time-keeping custom, 2981
tug-of-wars, 3036, 3082
vernal equinox celebration, 2621
water festival, 2139
winter equinox, 1307
winter solstice celebration, 2997
youth celebrations, 2600, 2923
Japan Constitution Memorial Day, 1465
Japan Marine Day, 1466
Japan National Foundation Day, 1467
Japan-America Society of Rhode Island, 0334
Japanese celebrations
California, 0577, 2075
Hawaii, 0576
Rhode Island, 0334
Japanese Emperor's Birthday, 1468
jaripeo, 0799
Jashgawronsky Brothers, 0658
Java, 2549
Jawara, Dawda, 1097
Jayuya Festival of Indian Lore, 1469

Jayuya Indian Festival
    See Jayuya Festival of Indian Lore
Jazan, Saudi Arabia, 0048
Jazz Fest Wien
    See Venice Jazz Festival (Jazz Fest Wien)
jazz festivals
    Barbados, 0244
    California, 1012, 1909
    Canada, 1910
    Colorado, 2946
    Estonia, 1470
    Finland, 2297
    Illinois, 0591
    Iowa, 0279
    Italy, 3143
    Lebanon, 0453
    Louisiana, 2019, 2534
    Michigan, 0790, 1400
    New York, 2216
    Quebec, 1910
    Rhode Island, 1501
    Spain, 2524
    Switzerland, 1912
    Venice, Italy, 3143
Jazzkaar Festival, 1470
"Jeanie auditions," 0967
Jeffers, Susan, 0594
Jefferson, Thomas, 0369
Jefferson's (Thomas) Birthday, 1471
Jehovah's Witnesses events, 1700
Jerash Festival of Culture and Art, 1472
Jersey Battle of Flowers
    See Battle of Flowers (Jersey, Channel Islands)
Jerusalem
    folk festival, 1007
    historical commemoration, 2918
Jerusalem Day
    See Yom Yerushalayim
Jerusalem Film Festival, 1473
Jeshn (Afghan Independence Day), 1474
Je-sok
    See Lunar New Year
Jesus
    See also individual religious celebration entries
    apparation, 0127
    ascension, 0167
    baptism of (*See* Epiphany)
    birth of (*See* Christmas)
    birthplace of, 0632
    blood of, 1927
    Candlemas, 0485
    footwashing, 1055
    Last Supper, 1700
    religious plays, 0329
    resurrection of (*See* Easter)
    statue, 0326, 0332
Jewish Cultural Festival, 1475
Jewish festival, 0230
    Balfour Declaration Day, 0230

Boston Jewish Film Festival, 0374
cultural event, 1475
Ehiopian Sigd Festival, 0964
Elul Selichot, 0920
family celebrations, 0978
fasting holidays, 0166, 1111
firstborn slaying remembrance, 1024
folk festival, 1007
Hanukkah, 1280
harvest festivals, 1616, 2858
history, 0230, 1331, 1589
Hoshana Rabbah, 1369
Lag ba-Omer, 1616
Miriam's Yahrzeit, 1888
Nazis, 1589
new year, 2433
Passover, 2225
Purim, 2330
Purim, Special, 2331
Rosh Hashanah, 2433
Seged, 2557
Shavuot, 2592
Shemini Atzeret, 2597
Simhat Torah, 2632
Sukkot, 2858
sun ceremony, 0344
Ta'anit Esther, 2902
Tammuz, Fast of the 17th of, 2918
Teshuvah, 2952
Three Weeks, 2977
Tisha be-Av, 2990
Trumpets, Feast of, 3034
Tu Bishvat, 3038
Water-Drawing Festival, 3190
Yom ha-Zikkaron, 2226
Yom Kippur, 3293
Yom Yerushalayim, 2228
Jewish New Year
     See Rosh Hashanah
Je-ya
     See Lunar New Year
Jhapan Festival (Manasa Festival), 1476
Jharkhand, India, 2611
Jhulan Latra
     See Jhulan Yatra
Jhulan Yatra, 1477
Jiao Festival
     See Chiao Festival (Rite of Cosmic Renewal)
Jidai Matsuri (Festival of the Ages), 1478
jinas, 0547
Jin-jitsu Man Day
     See Nanakusa Matsuri (Seven Herbs or Grasses Festival)
Jizo Ennichi, 1479
Jockey Day
     See First Monday Trade Days
Jodlerfests (Yodeling Festivals), 1480
Johannisnacht
     See St. John's Eve (Germany) (Johannisnacht)
John Paul II, Pope, 0831

John the Baptist, 0242
Johnny Appleseed Civic Day
     See Appleseed (Johnny), Birthday of
Johnson (Samuel) Commemoration, 1481
Jones, Bobby, 0402
Jonquil Festival, 1482
Jordan
     arts festival, 1472
     independence day, 1483
     royal birthday commemoration, 0005
Jordan Independence Day, 1483
Jordbruksdagarna, 1484
Jorvik Viking Festival, 1485
Joseph (husband of the Virgin Mary), 1038
Jouluaatto
     See Christmas Eve (Finland) (Jouluaatto)
Jour de l'An, Le
     See New Year's Day (France)
Jour des Aïeux (Ancestors' Day)
     See Haiti Ancestors' Day
Jour des Étrennes, Le
     See New Year's Day (France)
Jour des Rois, Le
     See Epiphany Eve (France); Epiphany, Feast of the
Joust of the Quintain, 1486
Joust of the Saracens, 1487
jousting festivals
     Croatia, 2637
     Italy, 1486, 1487, 1488
     Virginia, 1489
Jousting the Bear, 1488
Jousting Tournament, 1489
Joyce, James, 0345
Jubayl (Jubeil), Lebanon, 0453
Jubilee Days Festival, 1490
Judas Iscariot, 0436, 0864, 0865, 0871, 1166, 1167, 2692
Juggernaut
     See Rath Yatra
juggling festival, 1729
Juhannus (Midsummer Day), 1491
Juleaften
     See Christmas Eve (Denmark) (Juleaften)
Juledag
     See Christmas (Norway)
Juledagen
     See Christmas (Sweden) (Juledagen)
Julenisse, 0633
Julian calendar, 1063
Juliana's (Queen) Birthday, 1492
Julius I, Pope, 0616
Julotta, 0626
jultomte, 0626
July Festival
     See Shembe Festival
Juneteenth, 1075, 1493
Junior, Celso, 2349
Junkanoo Festival, 1494
Juno, 1816
Juno Caprotina, Festival of, 1495

Just for Laughs Festival, 1496
Juste pour rire
    See Just for Laughs Festival
Jutajaiset Folklore Festival, 1497
Juturnalia, 1498
Juul, Feast of, 1499
Juvenalia, 1500
JVC Jazz Festival, 1501
Jyestha Ashtami, 1502
Jyvaskyla Arts Festival, 1503

K

Kaamatan Festival, 1504
Kadooment
    See Crop Over
Kakadu Mahbilil Festival, 1505
Kalakaua, King David, 1858
Kalakshetra Arts Festival, 1506
kalash, 0855
Kalasha, 0563
Kalevala Day, 1507
Kali Puja, 1508
Kalinitsa, 2757
Kallemooi, 1509
kallikantzari, 0617, 0941
Kalratri, 0855
Kaluahi, 0933
Kamakura Matsuri (Snow Hut Festival), 1510
Kambutsu-e
    See Hana Matsuri (Flower Festival); Vesak (Wesak;
      Bud-dha's Birthday)
Kamehameha (King) Celebration, 1511
Kandil Geceleri
    See Lamp Nights (Kandil Geceleri, Candle Feasts)
Kandy, Sri Lanka, 0953
Kansas
    air show, 0859
    American Indian dancing, 3138
    emancipation celebrations, 0923, 2063
    emancipation celebrations, 0923, 2063
    film festival, 2916
    motorcycles, 0341
    music festival, 1860
    Old West celebration, 0819
    powwow, 3138
    Swedish festival, 2887
    Veterans Day, 3136, 3138
kanto, 0610
Kapila Shashti, 1512
Kaplan, Louisiana, 0256
Karajan, Herbert von, 0880
karate, 0173
Karneia
    See Carnea
Karneval
    See Fasching
Karneval in Cologne, 1514

Karthikai Deepam, 1515
Kartika Purnima, 1516
Kartika Snan, 1517
Kartini Day, 1518
Karwachoth, 1519
Kashmir, 1998
Kasone Festival of Watering the Banyan Tree, 1520
Kasone Full Moon Day
    See Kasone Festival of Watering the Banyan Tree
Kasuga Matsuri, 1521
Kataklysmos, Feast of (Festival of the Flood), 1522
Kataragama Festival, 1523
Katatsu Kunchi Festival, 1513
Kathara Deftera
    See Clean Monday (Kathara Deftera)
Katherine Show
    See Royal Shows
Kati Bihu, 1524
Kathin
    See Waso (Buddhist Rains Retreat)
Kattestoet (Festival of the Cats), 1525
Katipunan, 0366
Kaustinen Folk Music Festival, 1526
kavadee, 2961
Kawagoé Matsuri, 1527
Kazakhstan
    national holiday, 1528
    new year, 1999
Kazakhstan National Days, 1528
Keaulana, "Buffalo," 0373
Keaw Yed Wakes Festival, 1529
Keene Pumpkin Festival, 1530
Keiro-no-Hi (Respect-for-the-Aged Day), 1531
Keith's (Alexander) Natal Day, 1982
Kekekou, Mathieu, 0292
Kekri
    See St. Michael's Day
Keller (Helen) Festival, 1532
Kelley, John J. ("young"), 0375
Kelley, John ("old"), 0375
Kelly (Emmett) Clown Festival, 1533
Kempo Kinen-Bi
    See Japan Constitution Memorial Day
Kenka Matsuri (Roughhouse Festival), 1534
Kenkoku Kinen-no-Hi
    See Japan National Foundation Day
Kennedy, John F., 0030
Kent State Memorial Day, 1535
kenti, 1127
Kentucky
    bluegrass festival, 3220
    brass band festival, 1191
    death commemoration, 1189
    family reunion, 1292
    food festivals, 0245, 1781, 2931
    footwashing, 1055
    frontier festival, 0368
    horse racing, 1536
    religious festival, 2584

Numbers in the index refer to entry numbers, not page numbers

shape-note singing, 0313
theater festival, 1378
water vehicle festival, 2861
Kentucky Derby, 1536
Kentucky Fried Chicken, 0629
Kenya
    automobile racing, 2461
    camel racing, 1771
    historic celebration, 1538
    independence day, 1460
    national holidays, 1537, 1539
    skydiving festival, 1540
Kenya Independence Day
    See Jamhuri (Kenya Independence Day) Kenya
        Madaraka Day, 1537
Kenya Mashujaa Day (Heroes' Day), 1538
Kenya Moi Day, 1539
Kenya Skydive Boogie, 1540
Kenyatta, Jomo, 1538
Keretkun Festival, 1541
Keukenhof Flower Show, 1542
Kewpie doll, 1543
Kewpiesta, 1543
Key, Francis Scott, 0782, 1027
Khama, Sir Seretse, 0380
Khamis al-Amwat, 1544
Khmer New Year
    See Cambodian New Year (Khmer New Year)
Khmer Rouge, 0471
Khomeini (Ayatollah), Death Anniversary of, 1545
Khomeini, Ayatollah Ruhollah, 1429, 1546
Khordad 15 Revolt, Anniversary of the, 1546
Khordad Sal, 1547
Kiamichi Owa-Chito (Festival of the Forest), 1548
Kiddies' Carnival, 1549
Kids Day, National, 0977
KidsPeace, 0977
Kiel Week, 1550
Kilkenny Arts Festival, 1551
Killing the Pigs, Festival of, 1552
Kim Il-Sung, 0784
Kim Il-Sung, Birthday of, 1553
Kim Jong-Il, Birthday of, 1554
kimchi, 1247
Kimsquit tribe, 0288
Kinderzeche (Children's Party), 1555
King Herod play, 0616
King, Martin Luther, Jr., 0397, 1556, 1557
King (Martin Luther, Jr.), Birthday, 1556
King (Martin Luther, Jr.) Drum Major for Justice Parade,
    Battle of the Bands & Drum Line Extravaganza,
    National, 1557
King Sihamoni Coronation Day
    See Sihanouk's (King) Birthday (Former King's
        Birthday and King Sihamoni Coronation Day)
Kingdom Days, 1559
King's Birthday (Belgium), 1560
King's Birthday (Denmark), 1561
King's Birthday (Lesotho), 1562

King's Birthday (Thailand), 1563
King's Day (Koningsdag), 1558
Kingsburg Swedish Festival, 1564
Kinro Kansha-no-Hi
    See Labor Day
kiping, 0970
Kipling, Rudyard, 0710
Kiplingcotes Derby, 1565
Kipnis, Igor, 0679
Kirchner, Nestor, 0143
Kiribati
    children day, 1570
    health day, 1568
    independence day, 1567
    military commemoration, 2146
    religious celebration, 1566
    teacher appreciation day, 1569
Kiribati Gospel Day (National Church Day), 1566
Kiribati Independence Day, 1567
Kiribati National Health Day, 1568
Kiribati World Teachers' Day, 1569
Kiribati Youth Day, 1570
Kirn
    See Harvest Home Festival
kisielius, 0631
Kissing Day
    See Hocktide
kite events
    Bermuda, 1165
    Chile, 1006
    China, 0646, 3200
    Cyprus, 0654
    France, 1571
    Greece, 0654
    France, 1571
    Greece, 0654
    Guatemala, 0067
    Japan, 2915
    Washington, D.C., 2651
Kite Meeting, International, 1571
kiva, 0252
Kiwanis Kids' Day, 1572
Klo Dance, 1573
Klondike Days Exposition, 1574
Klondike Gold Discovery Day, 1575
Klondike International Outhouse Race, 1576
Knabenschiessen, 1577
Knapp, Pascal, 0709
Kneeling Sunday, 1578
Knight, Gary, 0102
Knudsen, Eric, 0933
Kocharian, Robert, 0150
Kodály, Zoltan, 0409
Kodomo-no-Hi (Children's Day), 1579
Kohl, Helmut, 1120
Koidula, Lydia, 0234
Kojagara, 1580
Kokila Vrata, 1581
kokoretsi, 0865

Numbers in the index refer to entry numbers, not page numbers

kola nuts, 0201
kolaches, 0744
Koledouvane, 1582
Kolkata International Film Festival, 1583
Komensky Day
    See Teachers' Day in the Czech Republic
Komensky, Jan Amos, 2936
Kongali Bihu
    See Kati Bihu
Kope Festival
    See Kopenfahrt (Barrel Parade)
Kope Procession
    See Kopenfahrt (Barrel Parade)
Kopenfahrt (Barrel Parade), 1584
Korea
    See also North Korea; South Korea agricultural festivals,
        0219, 2924
    alphabet commemoration, 1279
    birthday commemoration, 1150
    bridge walking, 0399
    Buddha's birthday, 1628
    celestial star tribute, 0601
    cherry blossoms, 0607
    Confucian memorial ceremony, 0613
    costumes, 0648
    cultural festival, 2603
    dancing, 0648
    end of New Year celebration, 2904
    female virtue celebration, 0647
    flower festival, 0607
    foot problems, 0399
    independence day, 2475
    love legend festival, 2572
    lunar new year, 1714, 2657
    moon goddess holiday, 1870 moon tribute, 0442
    national holiday, 1585, 1586, 2088
    picnic, 3299
    spirit festival, 2684
    spring feast, 0971
    torch fights, 3007
    wind festival, 3231
    winter solstice, 0833
Korea Liberation Day, 1585
Korea National Foundation Day, 1586
Korean War, 2088
Korean War Veterans Armistice Day, National, 1587
Kortelopet, 0082
Kosovo
    historic celebration, 1588
    independence day, 1588
Kosovo Independence Day, 1588
koulich, 0874
Kourion Festival
    See Curium Festival (Kourion Festival)
Krack, Paul, 0762
kraslice, 0866
krewes, 0529
Krishna, Lord, 0109, 0562, 1145
Krishna's Birthday

    See Janmashtami (Krishnastami; Krishna's Birthday)
Krishnastami
    See Janmashtami (Krishnastami; Krishna's Birthday)
Kristallnacht (Crystal Night), 1589
Kronia
    See Cronia (Kronia)
Kronos, 0727
Ksamavani, 1590
'Ksan Celebrations, 1591
Kshitigarba Jizo, 1479
Kuan Yin, 1150
kucios, 0631
Kuhio (Prince) Day, 1592
Kuhkämpfe
    See Cow Fights
Kukulcán, 0592
Kumbh Mela (Pitcher Fair), 1593
K'ung-fu-tzu, 0676
Kunta Kinte Heritage Festival, 1594
Ku-omboka, 1595
Kupalo Festival, 1596
Kurijmoj, 1597
Kurofune, 0334
Kuse Aunsi
    See Gokarna Aunsi
kusiotem dances, 0288
kusiut, 0288
Kuta Karnival, 1598
Kutza, Michael, 0589
Kutztown Festival, 1599
Kuwait
    national holidays, 1600, 1601
    spring festival, 1262
Kuwait Liberation Day, 1600
Kuwait National Day, 1601
Kuwana Ishitori Matsuri, 1602
KW Institute for Contemporary Art, 0298
Kwafie Festival, 1603
Kwakiutl Midwinter Ceremony, 1604
    See also American Indians
Kwanzaa, 1605
Kwita Izina
    See Gorilla Naming Ceremony (Kwita Izina)
Kyokusui-no-En, 1606
Kyongchip
    See Excited Insects, Feast of
    Kyrgyz Independence Day, 1607

L

La Paz Day, 1608
Laba Festival, 1609
Labor Day, 1610
Labor Day (Bahamas), 0223
labor holiday, 0568
labor strike commemoration, 0395
Labor Thanksgiving Day
    See Labor Day

LaborFest, 1611
Labour Day
    See Labor Day
Labrador, 0936
Lac Long Quan Festival, 1612
lacrosse, 0611
ladders, 0939
Ladies' Day
    See Leap Year Day
Ladouvane, 1613
Lady Day, 0484, 1614
    See also Annunciation of the Lord
Lady Day among Samis, 1615
Laetare Sunday
    See Mothering Sunday
Lag ba-Omer, 1616
Lai-Lai-Tu-Gadri
    See Lanterns Festival
Lajkonik, 1617
Lakshmi, 0045, 0794, 0855
Lakshmi Puja, 1618
lamayotes, 0480
lambropsomo, 0790
Lammas, 0731, 1016, 1619
Lammas Fair, 1620
Lamp Nights (Kandil Geceleri, Candle Feasts), 1621
Land Diving, 1622
land runs, 0575, 2116
Landing Day
    See Columbus Day
Landing of d'Iberville, 1623
Landon, Margaret, 0645
Landsgemeinde, 1624
Landshut Wedding, 1625
Langfredag
    See Good Friday
language day, 1903
Lanimer Festival, 1626
Lantern Festival
    See Chochin Matsuri (Lantern Festival)
Lantern Festival (Korea), 1628
Lantern Festival (Yuan Hsiao Chieh), 1627
lantern festivities
    Australia, 1682
    China, 1627
    England, 2328
    Korea, 1628
    Pennsylvania, 1629
    Philippines, 1132
    Sierra Leone, 1630
Lantern Night at Bryn Mawr College, 1629
Lanterns Festival, 1630
Laos
    agriculture festival, 0426
    Buddhist festivities, 1734, 3122
    elephant festival, 0909
    monk festival, 2965
    national holiday, 0382
    new year, 1317

Lapps, 1202
Larentalia, 1631
lares, 0608
Laskiainen
    See Finnish Sliding Festival
Laskiaispäivä
    See Shrove Tuesday (Finland)
Lasseters Camel Cup, 1632
Last Great Day, 1633
Last Supper, 0690, 1055, 1818, 1700
Late May Bank Holiday
    See Whit-Monday (Whitmonday)
Latif, Shah Abdul, 2580
Latin Festival (Feriae Latinae), 1634
Latin Music Awards, 0316, 2313
Latina, Fiesta, 1635
Latino festival, 1635
Latter-Day Saints, Founding of the Church of, 1636
Latvia
    Christmas Eve, 0631
    courtship ritual, 2760
    folk music festival, 0234
    independence day, 1637, 2393
    saint feast day, 2760
Latvia Independence Day, 1637
Laulupidu, 0210
laundry festivals
    Belgium, 1865
    France, 1865
    French West Indies, 1865
Laval, Père Jacques Désiré, 2273
Laveau, Marie, 0466
Laver, Rod, 0194
law commemoration, 1638
Law Day, 1638
lawn bowling, 0284
Lawn Tennis Championships
    See Wimbledon
Lawrence, Massachusetts, 0395
Laylat al-Bara'ah (Shab-Barat), 1639
    See also Shab-Barat
Laylat al-Miraj, 1640
Laylat al-Qadr, 1641
Laytown Strand Races, 1642
Lazarouvane
    See St. Lazarus's Day
Lazarovden
    See St. Lazarus's Day
Lazarus Saturday, 1643
Lazybones Day
    See Luilak
Le Mans 24-Hour Grand Prix d'Endurance
    See Le Mans Motor Race
Le Mans Motor Race, 1644
Le Moyne d'Iberville, Pierre, 1623
le part Dieu, 0857
Leaders of the Bulgarian National Revival Day (National Enlighteners Day), 1645
League off New Hampshire Craftsmen's Fair

Numbers in the index refer to entry numbers, not page numbers

See Craftsmen's Fair
Leap Year Day, 1646
Lebanon
    arts festival, 0281
    cultural festival, 3068
    dance festival, 0210
    death commemoration, 1800
    independence day, 1647
    music festivals, 0047, 0210, 0453
    national holiday, 1648
    religious festival, 2690
    saint feast day, 2775
    theater performance, 0210
Lebanon National Day, 1647
Lebanon Resistance and Liberation Day, 1648
Lebaran
    See Id al-Fitr (Eid)
Lebkuchen, 0557
Leconte, Henri, 0768
Leda, 0545
Leddat
    See Ganna (Genna)
Lee (Ann) Birthday, 1649
Lee, Robert E., 0131, 0675, 1124, 1125, 1650
Lee (Robert E.) Day, 1650
Lee, Spike, 0028
Leeds International Film Festival, 1651
Lee-Jackson-King Day
    See King (Martin Luther Jr.), Birthday
lefse, 0562
Lei Day, 1652
Leiden Day, 1653
Leif Erikson Day, 1654
Lemon Festival, 1655
Lemuralia, 1656
Lemuria
    See Lemuralia
Lenaea, 0808
Lenape Indians, 0783
Lent, 1657
    See also Carnival
Lenten birches, 0984
Lenten celebrations
    England, 0985
    Fastens-een, 0985
    France, 1775
    Italy, 1874
    Louisiana, 1774
    pre-Lenten festivals, 0507, 2339
    Russian Orthodox Christians, 0451
    Scotland, 0985
Leonhardifahrt
    See Leonhardiritt (St. Leonard's Ride)
Leonhardiritt (St. Leonard's Ride), 1658
Leonowens, Anna, 0645
Leopold I, King, 0285, 1123
Leopold I, King of Belgium, 1560
Les Vêpres de Gouyasse, 1134
lesbian, gay, bisexual, and transgender (LGBT)

See gay rights commemorations
Lesotho
    arts and cultural festival, 1919
    independence day, 1659
    royal birthday, 1562
Lesotho Independence Day, 1659
Lesser Eleusinia, 0911
Lesser Feast
    See Id al-Fitr (Eid)
Letsie III, King of Lesotho, 1562
lettuce, 3303
Leutze, Emanual, 0730
Levin, Irving "Bud," 9196
Lewis and Clark Festival, 1660
Lewis, Meriwether, 1660
Lexington Day
    See Patriots' Day
LGBT
    See gay rights commemorations
Li Ch'un, 1661
Liber, 0553
Libera, 0553
Liberalia, 1662
liberation, 0030
Liberation Day
    See Dutch Liberation Day
Liberia
    birthday commemorations, 1669, 2410
    death commemoration, 1666
    flag day, 1664
    independence day, 1665
    military commemoration, 1663
    national holiday, 1667
    prayer day, 1668
Liberia Armed Forces Day, 1663
Liberia Flag Day, 1664
Liberia Independence Day, 1665
Liberia National Redemption Day, 1666
Liberia National Unification Day, 1667
Liberian Fast and Prayer Day, 1668
Liberian President W. V. S. Tubman's Birthday, 1669
Liberty Day
    See Portugal Liberation Day
libraries
    Alabama, 1532
    China, 0040
    Colombia, 2286
    United States, 0330, 2287
Libya
    death commemoration, 1746
    national holiday, 1671
    religious holiday, 1670
    revolutionary holiday, 1672
Libya Day of Arafa, 1670
Libya Declaration of Jamahiriya Day (Declaration of the People's Authority Day), 1671
Libya Revolution Day, 1672
Licinius, Emperor, 1059
Liechtenstein, 2319

"lifting" (Easter Monday), 0882
lighted boat festival, 1693
Lighting of the National Christmas Tree, 1673
Lights, Festival of, 1674
Lights, Festival of (Ganden Ngamcho), 1675
lights festivals
    Australia, 3161
    Czech Republic, 2626
    Florida, 0892
    France, 1003
    Germany, 0299
    India, 1515
    Myanmar, 3187
    Netherlands, 0091, 1148
    New York, 1674
    West Virginia, 3236
Ligo Svetki
    See St. John's Eve and Day (Latvia) (JanuVakars)
Lilac Festival, 1676
lilies, 1137, 2465
lilies-of-the-valley, 1826
Lily Festival
    See Saigusa Matsuri
Lily Festival (Festa dei Giglio), 1677
Lim Festival, 1678
Limassol Wine Festival, 1679
    Lincoln, Abraham birthday, 0330
    District of Columbia Emancipation Act, 0926
    Emancipation Proclamation, 0923, 0924, 0925, 1493
    Fourth of July (Denmark), 1066
    Freedom Day, National, 1075
    Gettysburg Address, 0945
    Mount Rushmore, 0369
Lincoln's (Abraham) Birthday, 1680
Lind, Jenny, 0247
Linden Tree Festival
    See Lindenfest
Lindenfest, 1681
lingams, 0079
Lingaraj, Lord, 0171
linguistics, Belgium, 1079, 1123
Lini, Father Walter, 3114
lion strangling, 2005
lipeäkala, 0576
Lismore Lantern Parade, 1682
Listahátí í Reykjavik
    See Reykjavik Arts Festival (Listahátí í Reykjavik)
Liszt, Franz, 0391, 0409
Literacy Day, International, 1683
literary celebrations
    Alabama, 2992
    Alberta, 2687
    British Columbia, 3111
    California, 2834
    Canada, 2287, 2687, 3111
    Colombia, 2286
    Denmark, 0098
    England, 0191, 0403, 0400
    Finland, 1507
    Florida, 1299, 1385
    Hungary, 0455
    Illinois, 2508
    India, 2364
    Indiana, 2402
    Ireland, 0345
    Japan, 1606, 2948, 3100
    Louisiana, 3229
    Mexico, 0554
    Missouri, 3000
    New York, 0333, 1375
    North Carolina, 3243
    Oregon, 0333
    South Dakota, 3225
    United States, 0196, 2287
    Wales, 0899, 1294
litham, 0426
Lithuania
    Christmas Eve, 0631
    folk music festival, 0234
    harvest festival, 2106
    independence days, 1684, 1685
    new year, 2028
    royal holiday, 1686
Lithuania Independence Day, 1684
Lithuania Restoration of Statehood Day, 1685
Lithuania State Day (Coronation of King Mindaugas), 1686
Little Big Horn Days, 1687
Little Daedala
    See Daedala
Little House on the Prairie (Wilder), 3225
Little League World Series, 1688
Little Rock (Arkansas) Central High School, 0260
livestock shows
    Colorado, 3204
    Missouri, 0086
    Nebraska, 0044
    New England, 0884
    Texas, 1374, 2678
Living Chess Game (La Partita a Scácchi Viventi), 1689
Llama Ch'uyay, 1690
llamas, 0534, 1690
Lloyd, Henry, 0333
Lloyd, John, 0333
Lloyd, Joseph, 0333
lobster festival, 1747
Lochristi Begonia Festival, 1691
Lockhart, Keith, 0377
locomotive-chase festival, 1198
Loeung Sack, 0424
log-throwing contest, 0233
Lohri, 1692
Loi Krathong, 1693
Lollapalooza, 1694
Lon Nol, 0467
London Bridge Days, 1695
London, England, 0907
London, Festival of the City of, 1696
Londonderry, Northern Ireland, 0657

Numbers in the index refer to entry numbers, not page numbers

Long, Crawford W., 0817
Long Friday
    See Good Friday
Long (Huey P.), Day, 1697
Longfellow, Henry Wadsworth, 0110
Longhouse religion, 2847
longhouses, 1109
Looking Glass Powwow, 1698
Lord Jesus of Seafarers
    See Bom Jesus dos Naveganes
Lord Mayor's Day
    See Lord Mayor's Show
Lord Mayor's Show, 1699
Lord's Evening Meal (Memorial), 1700
Lord's Prayer, 0691
Los Angelitos
    See Angelitos, Los
Losar, 1702
Lottrup, Lars, 0658
Lotus, Birthday of the, 1703
Lotus Sutra, 1046
Louis IX, King, 0780
Louisiana
    Acadian festival, 0013
    African-American music festival, 0957
    American Indian Christmas festival, 1984
    birthday commemoration, 1697
    bonfire, 0639
    Canary Islands festival, 1701
    dancing, 0466
    fish festival, 0716
    food festivals, 1081, 1704, 1705, 2020
    football game celebration, 0272
    French independence commemoration, 0256
    French Quarter Festival, 1081
    Halloween, 1270
    jazz festivals, 2019, 2534
    Lenten holiday, 1774
    literary festival, 3229
    Mardi Gras, 1774
    military holiday, 0267
    music festivals, 1081, 3167
    religious holidayss, 0066
    sporting event, 2857
    Voodoo ritual, 0466
    wine festival, 2020
    Zydeco music festival, 3317
Louisiana Shrimp and Petroleum Festival, 1704
Louisiana Sugar Cane Festival, 1705
love legend festival, 2572
lovers holiday, 3107
Loviny, Christophe, 0102
Low Easterday
    See Low Sunday
Low, Juliette Gordon, 1144
Low Sunday, 1706
Lowman, Bill, 0752
low-oxygen water, 0975
Loyalty Day, 1707

Lu Pan, Birthday of, 1708
Lubovitch, Lar, 0586
Lucerne Festival
    See Lucerne International Festival of Music
Lucerne International Festival of Music, 1709
Luciadagen
    See St. Lucy's Day
luck, 0442
Ludi, 1710
Ludi Apollinares
    See Apollonian Games; Ludi
Ludi Megalenses
    See Ludi
Ludi Plebei
    See Ludi
Ludi Plebeii
    See Plebeian Games (Ludi Plebeii)
Ludi Romani
    See Ludi; Roman Games (Ludi Romani)
Lughnasadh, 0725, 1711
Luilak, 1712
Lumarhi Devi, 1131
lumber camps, 1887
    lumberjack festivals Idaho, 0655
    Minnesota, 0412
    Ohio, 2228
Lumberjack World Championships, 1713
lumecon, 1051
luminarias, 0571
Lunar New Year, 1714, 2657
Lundy, Colonel, 0657
Lunes del Cerro, Los
    See Guelaguetza, La
Lupercalia, 1715
Lupercus, 0987
lutefisk, 0562
Luther, Martin, 0060, 2385
Lutheran Church, 0650
Luther's Theses Day
    See Reformation Day
Luxembourg
    arts festival, 0966
    bonfire, 0415
    dancing, 0762
    food festival, 2317
    independence day, 1716
    procession, 0762
    religious celebration, 2107
    shepherd's fair, 2599
Luxembourg National Day, 1716
Lynceus, 0545
Lynn, William, 1180
    Lyon, France, 0350

M

Maafa Commemoration, 1717
Mabon, 1718

Numbers in the index refer to entry numbers, not page numbers

Macao, 1817
MacArthur (Douglas) Day, 1719 Macau, 0646
MacDonald, Darryl, 2554
Macedonia
    dairy-products celebration, 0570
    independence day, 1721
    military commemorations, 1720, 1722
    poetry festival, 2848
    superstitious beliefs, 0844
    wedding ceremony, 3198
Macedonian Ilinden (St. Elijah's Uprising Day), 1720
Macedonian Independence Day, 1721
Macedonian National Uprising Day (Day of Macedonian
    Uprising in 1941; Macedonian Revolution Day), 1722
Macedonian Revolution Day
    See Macedonian National Uprising Day (Day of
        Macedonian Uprising in 1941; Macedonian
        Revolution Day)
Machhendranath, 2373
Macker (Gus) Basketball, 1723
Macon Cherry Blossom Festival, 1724
Mad Thursday
    See Carnival Thursday
Madagascar
    death commemoration, 1726
    exhumation of ancestors, 0976
    independence day, 1725
    New Year's celebration, 0050
Madagascar Independence Day, 1725
Madagascar Martyrs' Day (Commemoration Day,
    Insurrection Day), 1726
Madara Kijinsai (Demon-God Event), 1727
Madawaska Territory, 0012
Madeira, 2815
Madeleine, Fête de la, 1728
MadFest Juggling Festival, 1729
Madison County Covered Bridge Festival, 1730
Madonna de la Mercè, 1854
Madurai, India, 0198
Magdalene Festival
    See Madeleine, Fête de la
Magellan (Ferdinand) Day, 1731
Maggio Musicale Fiorentino
    See Florence Musical May (Maggio Musicale Fiorentino)
Magh Sankranti, 1733
Magh Bihu, 1732
Magha Puja (Maka Buja, Full Moon Day), 1734
Magha Purnima, 1735
Maghi, 1736
Magi, 0278, 0627
    See also Epiphany
Magna Carta Day, 1737
Magnolia Blossom Festival, 1738
Mahabharata, 0583, 1145
Mahakali, 0362
Mahamastakabhishekha (Grand Head-Anointing
    Ceremony), 1739
Mahandeu, 0563
Mahaprabhu, Chaitanya, 0825

Mahatma Gandhi's Birthday
    See Gandhi Jayanti (Mahatma Gandhi's Birthday)
Mahavira, 0547, 0794
Mahavira Jayanti, 1740
Mahisasura, 0855
Mahler, Gustav, 0880
Maia Maiesta Festival
    See Bona Dea Festival
Maidens' Fair on Mount Gaina, 1741
Maiden's Festival
    See Seven Sisters Festival
Maidhyairya
    See Maidyarem (Maidhyairya; Mid-Year or Winter Fest)
Maidhyoishema
    See Maidyoshahem (Maidhyoishema; Mid-Summer
        Feast)
Maidhyoizremaya
    See Maidyozarem (Maidhyoizaremaya; Mid-Spring
        Feast)
maids, 0805
Maidyarem (Maidhyairya; Mid-Year or Winter Fest), 1742
Maidyoshahem (Maidhyoishema; Mid-Summer Feast), 1743
Maidyozarem (Maidhyoizaremaya; Mid-Spring Feast), 1744
Maifest, 1745
Maimona (Maimuna), 1746
Maimuna
    See Maimona (Maimuna)
Maine
    Acadian celebrations, 0011, 0012
    arts festival, 3196
    boat race, 1203
    carbonated beverage festival, 1942
    earmuff commemoration, 1216
    food festivals, 0552, 1747, 2305, 3286
    French independence commemoration, 0257
    fundraiser for families in need, 1904
    historic celebration, 2227
    lobster festival, 1747
    military ceremony, 0112
    ship festival, 3232
    wife-carrying championship, 2087
Maine Lobster Festival, 1747
Maine Memorial Day, 1748
Maitag Vorabend
    See May Day Eve (Switzerland) (Maitag Vorabend)
Maka Buja
    See Magha Puja (Maka Buja, Full Moon Day)
Makar Sankranti
    See Magh Sankranti
Makara Sankranti
    See Pongal
Makarios III, Archbishop, 0743
Makha Bouxa
    See Magha Puja (Maka Buja, Full Moon Day)
Making Happiness Festival, 1749
Makonde, 1873
Maksoutsoff, Dmitri, 0053
malaria, 0027, 3264
Malaria Day

Numbers in the index refer to entry numbers, not page numbers

See World Malaria Day
Malawi
    death commemoration, 1751
    freedom day, 1750
    independence day, 1752
    masked dancing, 1873
    national holiday, 0600
Malawi Freedom Day, 1750
Malawi Martyrs' Day, 1751
Malawi Republic Day, 1752
Malaysia
    bathing festival, 1765
    birthday commemorations, 1150, 1753
    dance performance, 0217
    harvest festival, 1504
    independence day, 1856
    military commemoration, 1077
    rice harvest festival, 1109
    royal birthday, 1753
    world music festival, 2360
Malaysia Birthday of SPB Yang di-Pertuan Agong, 1753
Malcolm III, King, 0444
Malcolm X, 0030, 1754
Malcolm X's Birthday, 1754
Maldives
    independence day, 1756
    Islam acceptance holiday, 1755
    national holiday, 1757
Maldives Embraced Islam Day, 1755
Maldives Independence Day, 1756
Maldives National Day, 1757
male beauty contest, 1112
Mali
    independence day, 1758
    planting festival, 0423
Mali Independence Day, 1758
Mallard Ceremony, 1759
Mallard Day
    See Mallard Ceremony
Mallard Feast
    See Mallard Ceremony
malowanki, 1169
Malta
    Carnival, 0518
    Christmas, 0618
    harvest festival, 1895
    independence day, 1761
    military commemorations, 0177, 1760, 1990, 3139
    national holiday, 1762
    new year, 2029
    religious celebrations, 0177, 1409
    riot, 1763
    saint feast days, 2761, 2798
Malta Freedom Day, 1760
Malta Independence Day, 1761
Malta Republic Day, 1762
Malta Sette Guigno (Commemoration of Uprising of June 7, 2088), 1763
Mama Ocllo, 0803

Mamuralia, 1764
Man from Snowy River, The 0585
Manasa Festival
    See Jhapan Festival (Manasa Festival)
Manco Capac, 0803
Mandi Safar, 1765
manes, 0992
manger, 0616, 0632, 0636
Manger Yam, 1766
mangos, 0456
Mani Rimdu, 1767
Manitoba
    flower festival, 1768
    folk festival, 3234
    Icelandic festival, 1391
Manitoba Sunflower Festival, 1768
man-lion, 1978
Manly Man Festival and Spam Cook-off, National, 1769
mannequin jumping, 1197
maple, 3130
Mara, Ratu Sir Kamisese, 1011
Maralal Camel Derby, 1771
marathons, 0375
Marbles Tournament, National, 1772
March (month), 0370
marchandes, 0516
Marcos, Ferdinand, 1005
Mar del Plata International Film Festival, 1770
Marche du Nain Rouge, 1773
Mardi Gras, 1774
Mardi Gras Film Festival, 1776
Mardi Gras (France), 1775
Mardi Gras of the North
    See Anchorage Fur Rendezvous
    Mardi Gras, Sydney Gay and Lesbian
    See Sydney Gay and Lesbian Mardi Gras
Mardi Päev
    See St. Martin's Eve (Estonia) (Mardi Päev)
Margaret Mead Film Festival, 1777
Margrethe's (Queen) Brithday, 1778
Marian Days, 1779
Marine Corps (U.S.), 0148
Mariners' Church (Detroit, Michigan), 0894
Marino Wine Festival, 1780
Marion County Ham Days, 1781
Mariposa Folk Festival, 1782
marital status, 0560
Maritime Day, National, 1783
Maritime Provinces, 0011
Mark (apostle), 0867
marksmen's events, 1577, 2543
Marlboro Music Festival, 1784
Marley's (Bob) Birthday, 1785
Maroon Festival, 1786
Marrakech Popular Arts Festival, 1787
marriage celebrations
    ancient Rome, 1816
    Illinois, 1187
    India, 1101, 1841

Morocco, 1788
Marriage Fair, 1788
marriage mock trial, 0853
"Marriage of the Giants," 1032
Marrow Bone, King, 0517
Mars, 0947
Marshall Gold Discovery State Historic Park, 0465
Marshall Islands
    basket festival, 1792
    Christmas, 0619
    constitution day, 1789
    cultural holiday, 1793
    fishermen's holiday, 1790
    memorial day, 2390
    nuclear fallout, 2390
    president's day, 1794
    religious holiday, 1597
    thanksgiving day, 1791
Marshall Islands Constitution Day, 1789
Marshall Islands Custom Day
    See Marshall Islands Manit Day (Marshall Islands
        Custom Day
Marshall Islands Fishermen's Day, 1790
Marshall Islands Gospel Day, 1791
Marshall Islands Lutok Kobban Alele, 1792
Marshall Islands Manit Day (Marshall Islands Custom
    Day), 1793
Marshall Islands President's Day, 1794
Marshall, James W., 0465
Marten Gas
    See Martinmas
Martenitza, 1795
Martin Luther King and Robert E. Lee's Birthday
    See King (Martin Luther Jr.), Birthday
Martin, Sterling, 0773
Martinique, 0519
Martinmas, 1796
Martinmas (Ireland), 1797
Martin's Festival
    See Martinsfest
Martin's Goose Day
    See Martinmas
Martinsfest, 1798
martyr commemorations
    Egypt, 0686
    Forty Martyrs' Day, 1059
    Sikhs, 1236
    Syria, 2896
Martyrdom of Joseph and Hyrum Smith, 1799
Martyrs' Day
    See Eritrean Martyrs' Day
Martyrs' Day (Lebanon), 1800
Martyrs of North America, Feast of the, 1801
Mary Magdalene, 0862, 1728
Mary of Hungary, 0530
Marya, 1802
Maryland
    African American festival, 1594
    boat racing, 2647

changing of the seasons, 0438
colonist commemoration, 1803
crab festival, 1283
food festivals, 1805, 2781
historic commemorations, 2372, 2392
historic reenactments, 0580
horse racing, 1804, 2312
military commemoration, 0782
tea party festival, 0580
Maryland Day, 1803
Maryland Hunt Cup, 1804
Maryland Preakness Celebration
    See Preakness Stakes
Maryland Seafood Festival, 1805
Marymass Festival, 1806
Marzas, 1807
Marzenna Day, 1808
Masi Magham, 1809
Maskal, 1810
masked ceremonies
    Austria, 0980, 2243
    Germany, 0980
    Hungary, 0517
    India, 0583
    Malawi, 1873
    Malta, 0518
    Martinique and Guadeloupe, 0519
    Mozambique, 1873
    Nigeria, 0202, 0895
    Switzerland, 0525
    Tanzania, 1873
    Zambia, 1873
    Zimbabwe, 1873
Maslyanitsa
    See Butter Week (Russia)
masquerade plays, 2158
Mass of the Cock, 0640
Massachusetts
    American Indian festivities, 3176
    arts festival, 1023
    baroque music festival, 0182
    chamber music festival, 1899
    civil rights celebrations, 0315
    classical music concerts, 0377, 0956
    dance festival, 1454
    film festivals, 0374, 0378
    fishermen's festival, 2801
    flower celebration, 1048
    folk festival, 2016
    food festivals, 0712, 0713
    historic celebrations, 2227, 2264
    historic reenactment, 2265
    horticultural commemoration, 0129
    labor strike commemoration, 0395
    military commemorations, 0112, 0376, 0429
    music festival, 2921
    Pilgrims' anniversary, 1056
    Portuguese immigration, 0340
    powwow, 3176

Numbers in the index refer to entry numbers, not page numbers

religious celebration, 1048
running race, 0375
tennis tournament, 0768
Massachusetts Cranberry Festival
    See Cranberry Harvest Festival
massacre commemorations
    Hong Kong, 2978
    Timor-Leste, 2982
    Uganda, 3072
Massing of the Flags, 0769
Massy, Arnaud, 0402
Master Draught Pageant
    See Meistertrunk Pageant (Master Draught Pageant)
master liar's contest, 0336
Masters, The
    See Masters Golf Tournament
Masters Golf Tournament, 1811
matchmaking party, 1815
Mata Tirtha Aunsi
    See Mata Tirtha Snan (Mother's Day)
Mata Tirtha Snan (Mother's Day), 1812
Mater Matuta, 1813
Matralia, 1813
Matriculation, Feast of the, 1814
Matrimonial Tea Party, 1815
Matronales Feriae
    See Matronalia
Matronalia, 1816
Matsu, Birthday of, 1817
Matsu Festival
    See Matsu, Birthday of
Maulid al-Nabi
    See Mawlid al-Nabi (Maulid al-Nabi; Prophet's
        Birthday)
Maundy Thursday, 1818
Mauni Amavasya, 1819
Mauritania Independence Day, 1820
Mauritius
    independence day, 1821
    religious pilgrimage, 2273
Mauritius Independence Day, 1821
Maverick Sunday Concerts, 1822
Mawlid al-Nabi (Maulid al-Nabi; Prophet's Birthday), 1823
Mawlid-al-Nabi, 0755, 1823
May Day, 1824
May Day (Czech Republic) (Prvého Máje), 1825
May Day Eve (Czech Republic), 1829
May Day Eve (Ireland), 1830
May Day Eve (Italy), 1831
May Day Eve (Switzerland) (Maitag Vorabend), 1832
May Day (France), 1826
May Day (Scandinavia), 1827
May Day (Spain), 1828
May Festival, International, 1833
Mayans, 0101, 0592, 0729
Mayberry Days, 1834
Mayfest, International, 1835
mayoral introduction, 1836
Mayoring Day, 1836

Mayor's Sunday
    See Mayoring Day
maypole rituals
    Czech Republic, 1825, 1829
    Haiti, 0516
    Spain, 1828
Maytime Festival, International, 1837
Mayurbhanj Chhau Dance, 0583
mazanec, 0866
McCabe, Robert, 0790
McCall, Jack, 0771
McCanless, Allen, 0710
McClure Bean Soup Festival, 1838
McCook, Edward M., 0924
McElwee, Fr. Robert, 0341
McPherson, Nellie Verne Burt, 0196
McQuade, Marion, 1184
Mead, Margaret, 1777
Meade, George G., 1124, 1125
Mecca, 1392, 1435, 1670, 1754, 1823, 2270
Mecklenburg Independence Day, 1839
medialuna, 1006
medical commemoration, 1312
medieval celebrations
    Belgium, 2140
    Russia, 2077
Medora Musical, 1840
Meenakshi, 1039
Meenakshi Kalyanam (Chitrai Festival), 1841
Megalensian Games
    See Ludi
Megalesia, 1842
Meier, Josef, 0329
Meiji, Emperor, 0428, 1843
Meiji Setsu, 1843
Meistertrunk Pageant (Master Draught Pageant), 1844
Meitlisonntag, 1845
Melbourne Cup Day, 1846
Melbourne Festival, 1847
Melbourne International Comedy Festival, 1848
Melbourne International Film Festival, 1849
Melchior, 0935, 0942
Mella, Ramón, 0829, 0845
melons, 0605
Memorial
    See Lord's Evening Meal (Memorial)
Memorial Day, 1850
    See also Graveyard Cleaning and Decoration Day
Memorial Day Luminaria at Fredericksburg National
    Cemetery, 1851
memorial days
    Armenia, 0154
    Marshall Islands, 2390
    Myanmar, 1960
    South Korea, 2674
    United States, 1748
    Virginia, 1851
Memory Day
    See Graveyard Cleaning and Decoration Day

Numbers in the index refer to entry numbers, not page numbers

Memphis in May International Festival, 1852
Memphis, Tennessee, 0529, 0921
Menelik II, Emperor, 0963
Menuhin Festival, 1853
Menuhin, Yehudi, 0261, 0303
Mercè, Festa de la, 1854
Merchants' Flower Market, 1855
Merdeka Day, 1856
Merengue Festival (Festival de Merengue), 1857
Meritxell, Jungfrau von, 0099
Merrie Monarch Festival, 1858
Mesa, Arizona, 0681
Mescalero Apache Tribe, 0125
Meskwaki Powwow, 1859
    See also American Indians
Messiah Festival, 1860
meteors, 2244
Methodist Church, 0486
Métis, 0008
Mevlana, Festival of, 1861
Mexican folk music festival, 3041
Mexican-American celebration, 2127
Mexico
    agricultural festival, 2744
    American Indian festival, 2520
    animal event, 2447
    autumn feast, 2108
    Aztec commemoration, 1350
    birthday commemoration, 3186
    border festival, 0567
    Carnival, 0520
    Christmas celebration, 0640
    cross commemoration, 0798
    cultural festival, 2519
    dancing, 0520, 0693, 0902, 1231, 2248
    death commemoration, 0069
    drama, 0520
    film festival, 1223
    fire ceremony, 2017
    folk dance festival, 2772
    ood festival, 2066
    healing festival, 2072
    horsemen event, 0799
    independence day, 1862
    literary festival, 0554
    Mayan feasts, 0592, 0729
    military commemoration, 0649
    mock church battle, 2778
    Passion play, 2224
    processions, 0693, 1168
    rain festival, 0209
    religious celebrations, 0069, 0693, 0801, 1168, 1341,
        1346, 1410
    religious pilgrimages, 2269
    religious reenactment, 2303
    rodeo, 0799
    saint feast days, 2500, 2701, 2744, 2751, 2809
    spirits, return of the, 0800
    Vernal Equinox, 3132

    Virgin Mary celebrations, 2163, 2166
Mexico Festival of Independence, 1862
Meyboom, 1863
Mezza Quaresima
    See Mid-Lent (Italy)
Miami, Florida, 0506
Miami/Bahamas Goombay Festival, 1864
Miami Beach, Florida, 0158
Miami, Florida, 0159
Miami Hispanic Ballet Company, 0232
Mi-Carême, 1865
Michaelmas, 1866
Michaelmas (Norway), 1867
Michigan
    African cultural festival, 0032
    Arab cultural festival, 0133
    arts fair, 0754, 0106, 0162
    automobile parade, 3248
    automobile show, 2086
    basketball tournament, 1723
    Christmas festivities, 2079
    clothing festival, 2380
    country music festival, 0839
    dairy festival, 0919
    electronic music festival, 1940
    fish festival, 1868
    flower celebration, 3044
    food festivals, 0357, 0579, 2256
    freedom festival, 1076
    German festival, 1070
    jazz festivals, 0790, 1400
    military commemoration, 1178
    parade, 3248, 1773
    Renaissance festival, 1869
    Scottish Highlands festival, 0073
    ship-sinking remembrance, 0894
    sporting event, 1723
    summer festival, 0077
Michigan Brown Trout Festival, 1868
Michigan Renaissance Festival, 1869
Michizane, Sugawara, 2948
Mid-Autumn Festival, 1870
Mid-Autumn Festival (Singapore), 1871
Middfest International, 1872
Mid-Eastern Regional Dulcimer Championships
    See Dulcimer Days
Midimu Ceremony, 1873
Mid-Lent
    See Mi-Carême
Mid-Lent (Italy), 1874
Mid-Lent Sunday
    See Mothering Sunday
Midnight Sun Festival, 1875
midnight sun festival
    Alaska, 1875
    Russia, 3298
Midnight Sun Intertribal Powwow, 1876
Midori-no-Hi
    See Greenery Day

Midsommar
>> *See* Midsummer Day

Mid-Spring Feast
>> *See* Maidyozarem (Maidhyoizaremaya; Mid-Spring Feast)

Midwinterhoorn Blazen
>> *See* Blowing the Midwinter Horn

midwives, 0505

Mid-Year or Winter Feast
>> *See* Maidyarem (Maidhyairya; Mid-Year or Winter Fest)

Mihr, Festival of, 1878

Mihragan, 1879

Mikkelin Paiva
>> *See* St. Michael's Day

mikoshi, 0751

Milan Trade Fair, 1880

Mildmay, Audrey, 1149

military aircraft, 0199

military commemorations
>> Argentina, 0144
>> Australia, 0123
>> Bangladesh, 0239
>> Belgium, 1037
>> Belize, 0287
>> Brazil, 0549
>> Brunei, 2439
>> California, 1034, 1035
>> Cambodia, 0471
>> Canada, 0479
>> Channel Islands, 0264
>> Chile, 0598, 1006
>> Colombia, 0664
>> Costa Rica, 2523
>> Croatia, 0724
>> Cuba, 0735
>> D-Day, 0776
>> Ecuador, 0888
>> Egypt, 0147, 0896
>> England, 0263, 0726, 0968, 3017
>> Eritrea, 0952
>> Estonia, 1877
>> Ethiopia, 0963
>> France, 2067
>> Ghana, 0204
>> Guatemala, 1226, 1228
>> Haiti, 1257
>> Hawaii, 2234
>> India, 1736
>> Ireland, 2148
>> Israel, 3294
>> Japan, 3069
>> Kiribati, 2146
>> Liberia, 1663
>> Louisiana, 0267
>> Macedonia, 1720, 1722
>> Maine, 0112
>> Malaysia, 1077
>> Malta, 0177, 1760, 1990, 3139
>> Maryland, 0782

Massachusetts, 0112, 0376, 0429
Mexico, 0649
Michigan, 1178
Myanmar, 1958
Namibia, 1972
Netherlands, 2011
New York, 0431, 1033
New Zealand, 0123
Nicaragua, 2060
North Korea, 2088, 2241
Northern Ireland, 0657
Ontario, 0479
Peru, 2246
Philippines, 0259
Portugal, 2299
Russia, 1824, 3140
South Africa, 2377
South Korea, 1195
Spain, 1915
Switzerland, 0955
Taiwan, 2908
Texas, 0051, 2495
Timor-Leste, 2983
Turkey, 0183, 3055
Uganda, 3071
United States, 0148, 0968, 1587, 2332, 3162, 2307
Venezuela, 3125
Vermont, 0293
Virginia, 0131, 1032
Zimbabwe, 3311

military reenactments
>> Florida, 0268
>> Missouri, 1559
>> Ohio, 0389
>> Pennsylvania, 0266, 0788, 1124, 1125
>> Switzerland, 1845

Military Tattoo, 0890
milk cartons, 1886
Milk (Harvey) Day, 1881
Milk, Harvey, 1881
Mill Valley Film Festival, 1882
Mille Miglia, 1883
Milwaukee Air Pageant, 0041
Min, Festival of, 1884
Mindaugas, King, 1686
Minehead Hobby Horse Parade, 1885

mining festivals
>> Australia, 2143
>> Colorado, 0427
>> England, 0856
>> Germany, 1584, 2443

Minneapolis Aquatennial Festival, 1886

Minnesota
>> African-American festival, 2424
>> American Indian pageant, 2661
>> dog-sledding festival, 0277
>> ethnic festival, 1985
>> Finnish joke holiday, 2821
>> German music festival, 2839

lumberjack festival, 0412
Norwegian festival, 2898
sporting event, 0284
summer festival, 1886
Swedish festival, 2879
winter carnival, 2797
Minnie, T. J., 0357
miracles, 0331
Miramichi Folk Song Festival, 1887
Miriam's Yahrzeit, 1888
Mirza Ali Mohammad, 0206, 0211, 0212
Mirza Husayn Ali, 0004, 0224, 0225
Misa de Gallo, 0640, 1889
mischief commemoration, 1890, 2436
Mischief Night, 1890
Mischievous Night
    See Mischief Night
Misers Sunday
    See Mothering Sunday
Misisi Beer Feast, 1891
Miss America Pageant, 1892
Miss Sepia Pageant, 0927
Mississippi
    American Indian festival, 0611
    birthday commemoration, 0769
    country music festival, 2417
    death commemoration, 0675
    fishing festivals, 0343, 0781
    historic reenactment, 1623
    home tour, 1983
Missouri
    children's festival, 1745
    clown festival, 1533
    doll festival, 1543
    fence-painting competition, 3000
    frog-jumping contest, 3000
    German festival, 1745
    historic festival, 2833
    literature commemoration, 3000
    livestock show, 0086
    military reenactment, 1559
    mushroom festival, 1955
    rodeo, 0086
    turkey festival, 0905
    Veterans Day, 3137
    Vietnamese commemoration of the Virgin Mary, 1779
mistletoe, 0616
Mithra, Feast of, 1893
Miwok Acorn Festival, 1894
    See also American Indians
Mnarja (Imnarja; Feast of St. Peter and St. Paul), 1895
Mobile International Festival, 1896
Mobile Phone Throwing World Championship, 1897
Mochi No Matsuri, 1898
mock religion
    France, 1054
    Mexico, 2778
Moha Sangkran, 0472
Mohawk Trail Concerts, 1899

Mohegan Homecoming, 1900
    See also American Indians
Moi, Daniel arap, 1539
Moldova
    independence day, 1901
    language day, 1903
    religious holiday, 1902
Moldova Grave-Visiting Day
    See Moldova Memorial Easter (Moldova Grave-Visiting Day)
Moldova Independence Day, 1901
Moldova Memorial Easter (Moldova Grave-Visiting Day), 1902
Moldovan Language Day, 1903
Molera, Andrew J., 0546
Mollyockett Day, 1904
Momo, King, 0515
Momus, King, 0521
mona, 0875
Monaco Grand Prix, 1905
Mondays of the Hill
    See Guelaguetza, La
Mongolia
    new year, 3035
    religious celebration, 2173
    sporting event, 1966
Mongolian New Year
    See Tsagaan Sar (Mongolian New Year)
monk festival, 2965
Monkey God, Birthday of the, 1906
Monkey Party, 1907
Monlam, 0450, 1908
Monlam (Prayer Festival), 1908
Monroe, Bill, 3220
Monroe, James, 0730
Monroe, Marilyn, look-alike contest, 0512
monsoon festivals
    India, 2937
    Nepal, 2937
monsters, 0528
    American Indian celebrations, 0732, 2085
Montana
    art auction, 2449
    dancing, 0732
    ethnic festival, 1986
    exploration festival, 1660
    film festival, 3227
    historic reenactment, 1687
    mannequin jumping, 1197
    sheep drives, 1199
    sporting event, 1197
Montenegro
    saint feast day, 2820
    shipwrecked sailor's church, 0981
Monterey Jazz Festival, 1909
Monteverdi, Claudio, 0679
Montgomery, Lucy Maud, 0566
Montreal International Comedy Festival
    See Just for Laughs Festival

Montreal Jazz Festival, 1910
Montreal World Film Festival, 1911
Montreux International Jazz Festival, 1912
Montserrat, 0500
    Moon Cake Festival *See* Mid-Autumn Festival
Moon Day, 1913
moon festival, 0442, 2591
moon goddess holidays
    China, 1870
    Hong Kong, 1870
    Japan, 1870
    Korea, 1870
    Taiwan, 1870
    Vietnam, 1870
moonbuggy race, 1200
Mooncake Festival
    See Mid-Autumn Festival (Singapore)
Moore (Billy) Days, 1914
Moore, Clement, 0629
Moors, 0490, 0693, 1915
Moors and Christians Fiesta, 1915
Moose Dropping Festival, 1916
Moravia, 0637
Moravian Church, 0637
Moravian Music Festival, 1917
Morazán, Francisco, 1355
morel mushrooms, 1955
Moreska Sword Dance, 1918
Móricz, Zsigmond, 0409
Morija Arts and Cultural Festival, 1919
Moriones Festival, 1920
Mormon Pioneer Day, 1921
Mormons, 1799, 2394
Morocco
    arts festival, 1787
    camel-trading fair, 0474
    death commemoration, 1746
    historic celebration, 1211
    independence day, 1922
    marriage fair, 1788
    national holidays, 1211
    religious music festival, 0993
    religious pilgrimage, 2271
    summer ritual, 1957
Morocco Independence Day, 1922
Moro-Moro Play, 1923
Morris dancers, 0908
Morris Rattlesnake Roundup, 1924
Morton, Julius Sterling, 0138
Morton, William Thomas, 0817
Moscow International Film Festival, 1925
Moses, 1888
Moses Maimonides, 1746
Moshesh
    See Moshoeshoe's Day
Moshoeshoe's Day, 1926
Most Precious Blood, Feast of the, 1927
Mota, Rosa, 0375
mother commemorations

Armenia, 0153
    United States, 1155, 1930
    Yugoslavia, 0595
Mother Goddess, 0855
mother-godmother ritual, 0509
Mothering Sunday, 1928
Mother-in-Law Day, 1929
Mother-in-Law's Day
    See Mother-in-Law Day
Mother's Day, 1930
    See also Mata Tirtha Snan (Mother's Day)
Mothman Festival, 1931
motorcycle activities
    Florida, 1932
    Kansas, 0341
    South Dakota, 2852
    Virginia, 1032
Motorcycle Week (Bike Week), 1932
Mott, Lucretia, 0117
Moulay Idriss I, 2271
Moulid of Abu el-Haggag
    See Mulid of Shaykh Yusuf Abu el-Haggag (Moulid of
        Abu el-Haggag)
Mount Brandon, 0725
Mount Cameroon Race, 1933
Mount Ceahlau Feast, 1934
Mount Fuji Climbing Season, End of, 1935
Mount Hagen Show, 1936
Mount Isa Rodeo and Mardi Gras, 1937
Mount Rushmore, 0369
Mount Wakakusa Fire Festiva
    See Wakakusayama Yaki (Mount Wakakusa Fire
        Festival)
mountain activities
    Ireland, 0725, 2384
    Japan, 1935
Mountain Man Rendezvous, 1938
mountain men, 1212, 1938
Mountain State Forest Festival, 1939
Mouride Brotherhood, 1179
mouriscadas, 0937
Movement Electronic Music Festival, 1940
movie awards, 0010
Moving Day, 1941
Moxie Festival, 1942
Moyers, Bill, 0821
Mozambique
    combatting illegal trade of wild plants and animals,
        1944
    independence day, 1943
    masked dancing, 1873
    peace commemoration, 1945
Mozambique Independence Day, 1943
Mozambique Lusaka Agreement Day, 1944
Mozambique Peace Day, 1945
Mozart Festival
    See Salzburg Festival
Mozart Festival (Mozartfest), 1947
Mozart Week (Mozartwoche), 1948

Mozart, Wolfgang Amadeus, 0096, 0391, 0502, 0679, 0880, 1149, 2471
Mozart (Wolfgang Amadeus), Birthday of, 1946
Mshweshwe
    See Moshoeshoe's Day
Mt. Wakakusa Dead Grass-Burning Event
    See Wakakusayama Yaki (Mount Wakakusa Fire Festival)
Mtskhetoba (Day of Mtskheta)
    See Svetitskhovloba
mud festival, 0371
Muhammad commemorations, 0755, 1823
Mule Days, 1949
Mulid of Shaykh Yusuf Abu el-Haggag (Moulid of Abu el-Haggag), 1950
mullet dogs, 0354
multicultural celebrations
    Finland, 0973
    Florida, 1004
    Texas, 0271
Multicultural Festival, 1951
mummers, 0629
Mumping Day
    See Doleing Day
Munich Opera Festival, 1952
Muñoz-Rivera Day, 1953
Muñoz-Rivera, Luis, 1953
Muscat Festival, 1954
Museum Days/Remembering James Dean
    See Dean (James) Festival
Mushroom Festival, 1955
Music and Dance Festival, International, 1956
music awards, 0316, 1176
music commemoration
    Austria, 2629
music competition, 0538
music festivals
    See also specific music genres; performing arts events
    Acadian, 0011
    Alaska, 2643
    Antigua and Barbuda, 0119
    Arkansas, 2177
    Aruba, 0510
    Australia, 0019, 0020, 3161
    Bahamas, 1494
    Belgium, 1030
    British Columbia, 2588
    Bulgaria, 1160
    California, 0660
    Canada, 0011, 0566, 1887, 2343, 2665, 2588
    Chile, 3149
    Connecticut, 2548
    Egypt, 0134
    England, 0059, 0261, 0573, 2712, 2975, 3246, 0400, 1437
    Finland, 1297, 2533
    Florida, 1061
    France, 2249, 2466, 0996
    French Polynesia, 0255
    Germany, 1833
    Hawaii, 0804
    Hungary, 0410
    Idaho, 1395, 2131
    Illinois, 0585, 1694
    Ireland, 1031
    Israel, 1453
    Italy, 0448, 1043, 3143
    Kansas, 1860
    Lebanon, 0047, 0210, 0453
    Louisiana, 1081, 3167
    Massachusetts, 2921
    Michigan, 1940, 0790
    New Brunswick, 1887
    New Mexico, 2516
    New York, 0496, 0659
    Newfoundland, 2665
    Norway, 0296
    Oregon, 2149
    Portugal, 0437
    Prince Edward Island, 0566
    Quebec, 2343
    Rhode Island, 2050
    Saudi Arabia, 0006
    Scotland, 2416
    Serbia, 0972
    South Africa, 0492
    Spain, 1956, 2482, 2524
    Switzerland, 1480
    Tahiti, 0255
    Texas, 1000, 0192, 2891
    United States, 1917
    Venice, Italy, 3143
    Vermont, 1784
    Vietnam, 1678
    Wales, 0899
music fundraiser, 0324
Muskogee, State of, 0385
Muskogee-Creek Indians, 0719
Muslim events
    See Islamic events
mustard, 1974
Mut I-ard, 1957
Myanmar
    Buddha's birthday, 1520
    Buddhist festival, 2934
    independence day, 1959
    light festival, 3187
    memorial day, 1960
    military commemoration, 1958
    national holiday, 1962
    new year, 2970
    peasants holiday, 1961
    spirit festival, 2933
    temple celebration, 2622
Myanmar Armed Forces Day, 1958
Myanmar Independence Day, 1959
Myanmar Martyrs' Day, 1960
Myanmar Peasants' Day, 1961
Myanmar Union Day, 1962

Numbers in the index refer to entry numbers, not page numbers

Mysteries
  See Eleusinian Mysteries
Mystery Play (Elche), 1963
Mystery Play (Tibet), 1964
mythological celebrations
  ancient Rome, 0505, 0545, 0553, 1309, 1764, 1813
  forest festival, 0987
  Hindu religion, 0308, 1618
  India, 2646

N

Naa Damba, 0755
NAACP Image Awards, 1965
Naadam, 1966
Naag Panchami, 1967
Nabanna, 1968
Nabekamuri Matsuri (Pan-on-Head Festival), 1969
nacimiento, 0621
Nada Festival
  See Kenka Matsuri (Roughhouse Festival)
Nadaam
  See Naadam
Nagoya City Festival, 1970
Nain Rouge, 1773
Naked Festival
  See Hadaka Matsuri (Naked Festival)
naked rope-climbing festival, 1252
naluyuks, 0936
Namahage Festival, 1971
Namahage Sedo Matsuri
  See Namahage Festival
Namibia
  death commemoration, 0544
  military commemoration, 1972
  planting festival, 2100
Namibia Heroes Day, 1972
Nammys
  See Native American Music Awards (Nammys)
Nanakusa Matsuri (Seven Herbs or Grasses Festival), 1973
Napa Valley Mustard Festival, 1974
Napoleon I, 0494
Napoleon III, 0649
Napoleon's Day, 1975
Narak Chaturdashi, 1976
Narcissus Festival, 1977
Nariyal Purnima (Coconut Day), 1978
Narsimha Jayanti, 1979
NASA Day of Remembrance, 1980
NASCAR Winston Cup circuit, 0661, 0773
Nashville Film Festival, 1981
Nashville, Tennessee, 0706
Nast, Thomas, 0629
Natal Day in Nova Scotia, 1982
Natchez Spring and Fall Pilgrimages, 1983
Natchitoches Christmas Festival, 1984
  See also American Indians
Nation Day

  See Cambodia Victory Day
National Academy of Recording Arts and Sciences, 1176
National Anthem Day
  See Defenders' Day
National Association for the Advancement of Colored
    People (NAACP), 1965
National Association of Black Storytellers, 0336
National Audubon Society, 0189, 0628
National Aviation Day
  See Aviation Day
National Balloon Classic
  See Hot Air Balloon Classic
National Baptist Convention, USA, 0113
National Conference for Community and Justice, 0404
National Constitution Center, 0680
National Council for the Traditional Arts, 1051
National Day
  See Belgium Independence Day; Dutch Liberation Day;
    Ecuador Independence Day; Iceland Independence
    Day; Iran Islamic Republic Day; Malawi Republic
    Day
National Day of Oil
  See Iran Petroleum Nationalization Anniversary
National Enlighteners Day
  See Leaders of the Bulgarian National Revival Day
    (National Enlighteners Day)
national exhibitions, 0480
National Family Week
  See Family Week
national holidays
  See also specific national holiday, e.g., independence
    days
  Andorra, 0099
  Antigua and Barbuda, 0120
  Australia, 0193
  Austria, 0195
  Bahrain, 0227
  Bangladesh, 0237
  Bosnia and Herzegovina, 0372
  Brazil, 0394
  Brunei, 0406
  Bulgaria, 0932
  Burkina Faso, 0434
  Cambodia, 2627
  Cameroon, 0475
  Canada, 0478, 2013, 2049, 2096
  Chad, 0556
  Chile, 0599
  China, 0604
  Congo, 0678
  Croatia, 0721
  Cuba, 0734, 1001
  Cyprus, 1208
  Czech Republic, 0745, 1386, 2851
  Dominican Republic, 0845
  Egypt, 2633
  England, 0988, 1737
  Eritrea, 0991
  Ethiopia, 0961

Fiji, 1011
Finland, 2474
Gambia, 1097
Greece, 2176
Greenland, 1214
Guinea, 1233
Haiti, 1258
Hungary, 1380
India, 1417, 0081
Iran, 1427, 1429, 1546
Israel, 0230
Italy, 1446
Jamaica, 1458
Japan, 0197, 1465, 1467
Kazakhstan, 1528
Kenya, 1537, 1539
Korea, 1585
Kuwait, 1600, 1601
Laos, 0382
Lebanon, 1648
Liberia, 1667
Libya, 1671
Malawi, 0600, 1750
Maldives, 1757
Malta, 1762
Marshall Islands, 1794
Morocco, 1211
Myanmar, 1962
Nepal, 2009
Netherlands, 0857
New Brunswick, 2013
New Zealand, 3170
Newfoundland, 2049
Nigeria, 2065
North Korea, 0784, 1585
Norway, 2474
Nunavut, 2096
Pakistan, 2186, 2187
Philippines, 0366
Poland, 2291, 2292
Portugal, 2301
Puerto Rico, 0777
Romania, 2423
Russia, 2474
Rwanda, 2452
San Marino, 2501, 2503, 2771
Serbia, 2568
Seychelles, 2577
South Africa, 2667, 2669
South Korea, 1585, 1586, 3092
Soviet Union, 0358
Sri Lanka, 2693
St. Kitts and Nevis, 2765
St. Maarten, 0673
St. Vincent and the Grenadines, 2824
Sweden, 2474
Switzerland, 2890
Tajikistan, 2910
Tanzania, 2454, 2926
Thailand, 0645
Togo, 2994
Tonga, 3004
Trinidad and Tobago, 3030
Tunisia, 3049
Turkey, 3054
Turkmenistan, 3058
Ukraine, 3077
United Arab Emirates, 3083
United Kingdom, 0669
United States, 0315, 1027, 1707
Vanuatu, 3114, 3116
Vietnam, 2464, 3145
Virgin Islands (U.S.), 3018
Zambia, 3305, 3307
Zimbabwe, 3314
National Reunification Day
    See Ukraine Unification Day (National Reunification Day)
National Velvet, 1070
National Wheat Festival, 3025
National Youth Day
    See Timor Santa Cruz Massacre Day (National Youth Day)
Nations, Festival of (Minnesota), 1985
Nations, Festival of (Montana), 1986
Native American Ceremonies in June at Devils Tower, 1987
Native American Music Awards (Nammys), 1988
Native Americans
    See American Indians;
    See also individual tribes
Native Islander Gullah Celebration, 1989
Nativity of Our Most Holy Lady, the Theotokos
    See Nativity of the Theotokos
Nativity of the Blessed Virgin Mary, Feast of the, 1990
Nativity of the Blessed Virgin Mary, Feast of the (Germany), 1991
Nativity of the Blessed Virgin Mary, Feast of the (Peru), 1992
Nativity of the Theotokos, 1993
nativity scene, 0621
natural resources celebration, 0430
nature appreciation, 3178
Nauru
    independence day, 1994
    population concern, 0100
Nauru Independence Day, 1994
Nauruz
    See Nawruz (Naw roz; No Ruz; New Year)
Nav Roz
    See Nawruz (Naw roz; No Ruz; New Year)
Nava Varsa
    See Bisket Jatra
Navabarsha
    See Bisket Jatra
Navajo Indians, 1995, 1996, 1997, 2608
    See also American Indians
Navajo Mountain Chant, 1995
Navajo Nation Fair at Window Rock, 1996

Numbers in the index refer to entry numbers, not page numbers

Navajo Night Chant, 1997
Navanna
     See Nabanna
Navaratri
     See Durga Puja
Navel, Jean-Yves, 0102
Navy (U.S.), 0148
Naw roz
     See Nawruz (Naw roz; No Ruz; New Year)
Nawruz (Kazakhstan), 1999
Nawruz (Naw roz; No Ruz; New Year), 1998
Nayak, Tirumala, 1039
Nazis
     Croatia, 0721
     Czech Republic, 2851
     Germany, 1589
     Israel, 1331
     Netherlands, 0857
     Poland, 2291
     Russia, 3140
Ncwala, 2000
N'cwala, 2001
Nebraska
     agricultural holiday, 0138
     American Indian dance festival, 3210
     bird event, 0715
     chicken festival, 3195
     Czech festival, 0744
     frontier days, 1085
     horse racing, 1085
     livestock exposition, 0044
     rodeo, 0044
     western heritage festival, 2002
NEBRASKAland DAYS, 2002
Nebuchadnezzar, King, 0166, 1111
Nebuta Matsuri, 2003
Nedele velikonocnní, 0791
needle festival, 1284
Nefertiti, 0009
Negro History Week
     See Black History Month
Neighbor Day, 2004
Nelson Day
     See Trafalgar Day
Nemean Games, 2005
Nemoralia, 2006
Nenana Ice Classic, 2007
Neopagan events
     bonfires, 1016
     Celtic festivals, 0731
     harvest festivals, 1718
     Imbolc, 1406
     Sabbat, 2456
     summer solstice, 0843
     vernal equinox, 1401
Nepal
     animal festival, 2980
     animal sacrifice, 0855
     Buddha holiday, 1802

chariot procession, 2373
     death commemorations, 1091, 1129, 1422
     donation day, 2204
     fathers commemoration, 1152
     flower festival, 0855
     good over evil festival, 0855
     Hindu events, 1130, 1131
     historic celebrations, 2009
     horse events, 1131
     monsoon festival, 2937
     Mother's Day, 1812
     national holiday, 2008, 2009
     pole ceremony, 0322
     religious holiday, 2610, 1130, 1131
     sibling festival, 2361
     snake festival, 1967
     sun holiday, 1733
Nepal Democracy Day, 2008
Nepal Republic Day, 2009
Neri-Kuyo, 2010
Netherlands
     arts festival, 0966, 0967
     bonfire, 0871
     children's festival, 1712
     cultural festival, 1328
     fertility ceremony, 3163
     fishermen's holiday, 1509
     flower festivals, 1046, 1542, 1855
     flower-gathering, 0793
     golf, 0402
     harvest procession, 1151
     heroism commemoration, 1653
     historic celebration, 1558
     horticultural exhibition, 1046
     ice-skating race, 0913
     lights festivals, 0091, 1148
     military event, 2011
     national holiday, 0857
     new year, 2029
     political ceremony, 2320
     religious holidays, 0871, 0883, 1796, 2196, 2618
     royal birthday, 1492
     winter festival, 0346
Netherlands Antilles, 2630
Netherlands Military Tattoo, 2011
Neto, Antonio Agostinho, 0104
Nettle Day
     See Shick-Shack Day (Shik-Shak Day, Shicsack Day,
        Shig-Shag Day)
Neujahr
     See New Year's Day (Germany)
Neujahrstag
     See New Year's Day (Switzerland) (Neujahrstag)
Nevada
     air show, 0039
     Basque festival, 0253
     camel racing, 0473
     counterculture festival, 0435
     dancing, 0487

Numbers in the index refer to entry numbers, not page numbers

poetry celebration, 0710
rodeo, 3277
Nevis, 2012
Nevis Tea Meeting, 2012
New Brunswick
    Acadian celebrations, 0011, 0012
    music festival, 1887
    provincial holiday, 2013
New Brunswick Day, 2013
New Church Day, 2014
New Deal Festival, 2015
New England, 0884
New England Folk Festival, 2016
New Fire Ceremony, 2017
New Granada, 0664
New Hampshire
    craft fair, 0711
    outdoor recreation and spring chores, 0982
    pumpkin festival, 1530
    winter carnival, 0763
New Jersey
    agricultural fair, 1036
    bluegrass music festival, 2132
    boat racing, 2018
    fish festival, 2579
    Hispanic festival, 2754
    historic reenactment, 2794
    horse racing, 1273
    parade, 0215
    poetry festival, 0821
    sporting event, 1772
    state fair, 1036
    water festival, 3233
New Jersey Offshore Grand Prix, 2018
New Jersey State Agricultural Fair
    See Flemington Fair
New Mexico
    American Indian celebrations, 0125, 0858, 1092, 1419,
        2124, 2491, 2586, 2976
    balloon festival, 0058
    bats, 0258
    bullfight, 2124
    chili festival, 1291
    Christmas Eve fires, 0629
    dancing, 0858, 2124
    duck racing, 1192
    food festivals, 1291, 3216
    harvest festivals, 2481, 2608
    healing ceremony, 2608
    historic festival, 2517
    historical reenactment, 0318
    music festival, 2516
    opera festival, 2518
    religious celebrations, 0070, 1057, 2517
    road commemoration, 2437
    saint feast days, 1303, 2481, 2490, 2496, 2499, 2745
    UFO festival, 2434
New Orleans Jazz and Heritage Festival, 2019
New Orleans Wine and Food Experience, 2020

New Vision Arts Festival, 2021
New World, 0666
New Yam Festival, 2022
New Year for Trees, 2023
    See also Tu Bishvat (Bi-Shevat; B'Shevat; Hamishah
        Asar Bishevat)
New Year Archery
    See Toh-shiya
New Year's Day, 2024
    See also Oshogatsu (New Year's Day)
    Babylonians, 2458
    Cambodia, 0472
    China, 3193
    Denmark, 2025
    Ethiopia, 0931
    France, 2026
    Germany, 2027
    Hawaii, 1977
    India, 1462
    Indonesia, 2101
    Japan, 2155, 2860
    Kazakhstan, 1999
    Laos, 1317
    Lithuania, 2028
    lunar, 1714
    Madagascar, 0050
    Malta, 2029
    Mongolia, 3035
    Myanmar, 2970
    Netherlands, 2029
    Portugal, 2031
    Romania, 2032
    Russia, 2033
    Sri Lanka, 2636
    Switzerland, 2034
    Taiwan, 2277
    Thailand, 2662, 2261
    Tibet, 1702
    Tonga, 2932
    United States, 2024
    Vietnam, 2953
New Year's Day (Denmark) (Nytaarsdag), 2025
New Year's Day (France), 2026
New Year's Day (Germany), 2027
New Year's Day (Lithuania), 2028
New Year's Day (Malta), 2029
New Year's Day (Netherlands) (Nieuwjaarsdag), 2030
New Year's Day (Portugal) (Ano Novo), 2031
New Year's Day (Romania) (Anul Nou), 2032
New Year's Day (Russia), 2033
New Year's Day (Switzerland) (Neujahrstag), 2034
New Year's Eve, 2035
    Australia, 2036
    Brazil, 2037
    Candlewalk, 0486
    Denmark, 2035
    Ecuador, 2038
    Germany, 2039
    Iceland, 2035

Numbers in the index refer to entry numbers, not page numbers

Japan, 2138
Nigeria, 1388
Romania, 2035
Scotland, 2035
Spain, 2040
United States, 2035, 3188, 3189
New Year's Eve (Australia), 2036
New Year's Eve (Brazil), 2037
New Year's Eve (Ecuador), 2038
New Year's Eve (Germany) (Silvesterabend), 2039
New Year's Eve (Japan)
    See Omisoka
New Year's Eve (Spain), 2040
New Year's Eve Watch Night
    Georgia (state), 3188
    Pennsylvania, 3189
New Year's Parade of Firemen (Dezome-shiki), 2041
New York
    abolition movement, 3040
    African-American festivals, 1286, 2278
    American Indian festival, 2847
    balloon festival, 2683
    birthday commemorations, 0837, 2425
    canoe regatta, 1113
    chamber music festival, 1822
    classical music festival, 2531
    dance festivals, 0760, 2531, 0758
    death commemoration, 1801
    discovery day, 3133
    film festival, 3022, 0758, 1285, 1777, 2043, 2045
    flower festival, 1676
    French festival, 0494
    gay rights commemoration, 2842, 2044
    horse racing, 0289
    jazz festival, 2216
    lights festival, 1674
    literary celebrations, 0333, 1375
    military commemorations, 0431, 1033
    music concert, 0496
    music festival, 0659
    onion festival, 0840
    parade, 0028
    peace festival, 3265
    procession, 1137
    religious festival, 1310
    running races, 2042, 3173
    saint feast day, 2489
    slavery commemoration, 1717
    theater festivals, 2046, 3085
    women's rights celebration, 2829
New York City Fire Department, 1033
New York City Marathon, 2042
New York City Police Department, 1033
New York Film Festival, 2043
New York Gay Pride March, 2044
New York International Children's Film Festival, 2045
New York International Fringe Festival, 2046
New Zealand
    agricultural show, 2048

arts festival, 2047
film festival, 0818
military commemoration, 0123
national holiday, 3170
shearing competition, 1161
yacht race, 0089
New Zealand Day
    See Waitangi Day
New Zealand Festival, 2047
New Zealand National Agricultural Fieldays, 2048
Newfoundland
    arts festivals, 2665
    birthday commemoration, 0443
    Christmas Eve, 0629
    music festivals, 2665
    poetry celebration, 0443
    provincial holiday, 2049
Newfoundland Discovery Day, 2049
Newman, Robert, 0112
Newport Folk Festival, 2050
Newport Harbor Christmas Boat Parade, 2051
Newport Jazz Festival
    See JVC Jazz Festival
Newport Music Festival, 2052
Newport to Bermuda Race, 2053
Nez Perce Indians, 0593, 1698
    See also American Indians
Ngan Duan Sib (Tenth Lunar Month Festival), 2054
Nganja, Feast of, 2055
Ngmayem Festival, 2056
Ngoc Son Temple Festival, 2057
Ngondo Festival, 2058
Ngoni tribe, 2001
Ngouabi, Marien, 0678
Nguillatun, 2059
Niagara Falls, 1674
Nicaragua
    independence day, 2061
    military commemoration, 2060
Nicaragua Battle of San Jacinto Day, 2060
Nicaragua Independence Day, 2061
Nice Carnaval, 2062
Nicklaus, Jack, 0402
Nicodemus Emancipation and Homecoming Celebration, 2063
Nicolaus Esterházy, Prince, 0409
Niemeyer, Oscar, 0512
Nieuwjaarsdag
    See New Year's Day (Netherlands) (Nieuwjaarsdag)
Niger
    male beauty contest, 1112
    national holiday, 2064
    rain celebration, 0739
    seasonal celebration, 0309
Niger Republic Day, 2064
Nigeria
    ancestor commemoration, 2119
    Children's Day, 0597
    cleaning festival, 3074

cultural festival, 2511
dead, honoring the, 0202
dead, visits from the, 2112
doctor feast day, 0038
fishing festival, 0145
food festival, 2022
harvest festival, 2142
masked dancing, 0895
masquerade plays, 2158
national holiday, 2065
New Year's Eve, 1388
Ramadan feast, 1394
religious festival, 2469
road maintenance, 2409
theatre festival, 0202
Nigeria National Day, 2065
Nigerian festival, 2113
Night Journey
    See Laylat al-Miraj
Night of Destiny
    See Laylat al-Qadr
Night of Forgiveness
    See Laylat al-Bara'ah (Shab-Barat); Shab-Barat
Night of the Broken Glass
    See Kristallnacht (Crystal Night)
Night of the Radishes, 2066
Night of the Three Holy Kings
    See Epiphany (Sweden) (Trettondag Jul)
Night Watch, 2067
Nightingale, Florence, 1370
Nilsson, Birgit, 1149
Niman Festival, 2069
Niname-sai, 2068
Nine Imperial Gods, Festival of the, 2070
Nineteen Day Fast, 2071
Nino Fidencio Festival, 2072
Nippy Lug Day, 2073
Nirjala Ekadashi, 2074
Nisei Week, 2075
Niue Peniamina Gospel Day, 2076
Nizhni Novgorod, 2077
No Ruz
    See Nawruz (Naw roz; No Ruz; New Year)
Noah, 0172
Noah, Yannick, 0768
Nobel Prize Ceremony, 2078
Noble, Richard, 0367
Noc Swietego Andreja
    See St. Andrew's Eve (Noc Swietego Andreja)
Noel Night, 2079
noise-making fair, 2179
Nomaoi Matsuri (Horse Festival), 2080
Nombre de Jesuacutes, 2081
Nonae Caprotinae
    See Juno Caprotina, Festival of
non-self-governing territories, 3199
Nordic Fest, 2082
Normandy, France, 0776
Normandy Impressionist Festival, 2083

Norodom Monineath Sihanouk, 0470
Norodom Sihamoni, King, 0470
Norodom Sihanouk, King, 0467
Norris, William Hutchinson, 0674
Norsk Høstfest, 2084
North Africa
    death commemoration, 1746
    saint feast day, 2702
North America
    See individual countries
North American Indian Days, 2085
North American International Auto Show, 2086
North American Wife-Carrying Championship, 2087
North Atlantic Festival
    See Reykjavik Arts Festival (Listahátí í Reykjavik)
North Carolina
    air show, 3278
    "Andy Griffith Show, The" commemoration, 1834
    Appalachian music festival, 0170
    automobile racing, 0661
    blues festival, 0422
    Caribbean festival, 1171
    Christmas Eve, 0637
    dance festival, 0170
    film festival, 1295
    folk music festival, 1053
    hollering contest, 1329
    independence days, 1266, 1839
    Latino festival, 1635
    literature festival, 3243
    religious observance, 0486
    Scottish festival, 1183
    Sufi Muslim festival, 2445
    whistler's convention, 3211
    North by Northeast.
        See NXNE (North by Northeast)
North Dakota
    agricultural fair, 0312
    American Indian festival, 3088
    cowboy poetry festival, 0752
    poetry festival, 0752
    powwow, 3088
    Roosevelt, Theodore, 1840
    Scandinavian festival, 2084
North Korea
    See also Korea
    birthday commemorations, 1553, 1554
    founding day, 0784
    military commemorations, 2088, 2241
    national holiday, 1585
    political commemoration, 3249
North Korea Victory Day, 2088
North Pole Winter Carnival, 2089
Northern Games, 2090
Northern Hemisphere, 1290, 3131
Northern Ireland
    See also United Kingdom
    arts festival, 0283
    military commemoration, 0657

Numbers in the index refer to entry numbers, not page numbers

poetry festival, 0246
rent-payment day, 2341
Northern Navajo Fair
    See Shiprock Navajo Nation Fair
Northrup, Philo, 0161
Northwest Folklife Festival, 2091
Northwest Territories
    American Indian sporting event, 2090
    dog sled race, 0499
    winter sports festival, 0499
Norway
    branch-striking holiday, 2620
    cattle herding, 1867
    Christmas celebrations, 0620, 2766
    cuckoo superstition, 1827
    Easter festival, 2473
    food festival, 2306
    moving day, 1941
    music festival, 0296
    national holiday, 2474
    religious celebrations, 0872, 2739
    saint feast day, 2791
    skiing, 0082, 1330
    sporting event, 1330
    spring festival, 2092
    sun festival, 2864
    winter fair, 1202
    winter sports, 0872
Norway Constitution Day (Syttende Mai), 2092
Norway's Liberation Day
    See Norway Constitution Day (Syttende Mai)
Norway's National Day
    See Norway Constitution Day (Syttende Mai)
Norwegian festivals
    Iowa, 2082
    Minnesota, 2898
Norwegian spruce tree, 0620
Nosa Senhora dos Navegantes
    See Assumption of the Blessed Virgin Mary, Feast of the
Nossa Senhora da Agonia
    See Our Lady of Sorrows Festival
Nossa Señora da Penha
    See Our Lady of the Rock, Festival of
Notre Dame de la Prospérité
    See Annunciation of the Blessed Virgin Mary, Feast of the (Belgium)
Notre Dame la Consolatrice des Affligés
    See Octave of Our Lady, Consoler of the Afflicted
Nova Scotia
    Acadian celebration, 0011
    birthday commemoration, 1982
    Christmas Eve, 0629
    food festival, 0110
    Scottish cultural festival, 1090
Novena, 0636
Novrus Bairam
    See Nawruz (Naw roz; No Ruz; New Year)
Nubaigai
    See Obzinky

nuclear fallout, 2390
Nuestra Señora de Guadalupe
    See Our Lady of Guadalupe, Fiesta of
Nuestra Señora de Itatí, 2093
Nuestra Señora de los Angeles
    See Our Lady of the Angels, Feast of
Nuestra Señora de Mercedes, 0832
Nuestra Senora de Peñafrancia, Feast of, 2094
Nuits de Fourvière, 2095
Numa Pompilius, 0035
number 13, 2644
Nunavut Day, 2096
Nusardil, 2097
Nutcrack Night
    See Halloween; Halloween (Ireland)
nuts, 0295
Nuuk Snow Festival, 2098
NXNE (North by Northeast), 2099
Nyambinyambi, 2100
Nyepi, 2101
Nytaarsdag
    See New Year's Day (Denmark) (Nytaarsdag)

O

Oak Apple Day
    See Shick-Shack Day (Shik-Shak Day, Shicsack Day, Shig-Shag Day)
Oak Ball Day
    See Shick-Shack Day (Shik-Shak Day, Shicsack Day, Shig-Shag Day)
Oakley (Annie) Festival, 2102
Oath Monday, 2103
Ober, Randy, 0463
Oberammergau Passion Play, 2104
Obon Festival, 2105
Oburata Kofi, 0046
Obzinky, 2106
Ocevi, 0595
Ochichi, 0595
Octave of Our Lady, Consoler of the Afflicted, 2107
Octave of the Birth of Our Lord
    See Circumcision, Feast of the
October Feasts, 2108
October Horse Sacrifice, 2109
October Revolution of 1917, 0358
October War of 1973, 0147
October War of Liberation Anniversary, 2110
Odalan (Temple's Birthday), 2111
Odo Festival, 2112
Odunde Festival, 2113
Odwira, 2114
office managers, 0021
ofrendas, 0800
Oglala Lakota Sioux Indians, 0717
    See also American Indians;
    See also Sioux Indians
Oglethorpe Day

See Georgia Day
Oglethorpe, James Edward, 1114
Ohgiwe
    See Dead, Feast for the
Ohio
    air shows, 0772, 3278
    American Indian treaty, 1215
    automobile race, 0071
    birthday commemoration, 1088
    boating festival, 2115
    film festival, 0667
    folk music festival, 0851
    horticultural commemoration, 0129
    international culture festival, 1872
    Irish festival, 0846
    lumberjack festival, 2228
    military reenactment, 0389
    Old West festival, 2102
    student-shooting memorial, 1535
    transportation festival, 2262
    turkey buzzards, 0452
    twins festival, 3066
    Western commemoration, 2419
Ohio River Sternwheel Festival, 2115
oil festival, 1704
oil nationalization commemoration, 1428
Oimelc
    See Imbolc (Imbolg)
Ok-Barnsa
    See Waso (Buddhist Rains Retreat)
Oklahoma
    American Indian celebrations, 0574, 0575, 0719, 2379,
        3045
    American Indian reenactments, 0612
    arts festival, 1835
    birthday commemoration, 2420
    bluegrass festival, 1186
    Czech festival, 2309
    dancing, 0719
    folk music festival, 1245
    food festival, 2118
    forestry festival, 1548
    historic celebration, 2117
    Italian festival, 1444
    "land run" commemoration, 2116
Oklahoma Day, 2116
Oklahoma 89ers Day
    See Oklahoma Day
Oklahoma Historical Day, 2117
Okmulgee Pecan Festival, 2118
okoztah-pol, 0729
Okpesi Festival, 2119
Oktoberfest, 2120
Okunchi Matsuri, 2121
Olavsoka
    See St. Olav's Day
Olcott, Henry, 0339
Old Christmas Day, 2122
    See also Epiphany, Feast of the

Old Fiddler's Convention, 2123
Old Hickory's Day
    See Battle of New Orleans Day
Old Inauguration Day
    See Inauguration Day
Old May Day
    See Garland Day
Old New Year's Eve, 0439
Old Pecos Bull and Corn Dance, 2124
Old Saybrook Torchlight Parade and Muster, 2125
Old Silvester, 2126
Old Spanish Days, 2127
Old Twelfth Day
    See Four an' Twenty Day
Old West celebrations
    Arizona, 2208
    Kansas, 0819
    Ohio, 2102
    Utah, 0088
Old Year's Night
    See New Year's Eve
Oldenburg International Film Festival, 2128
Older Persons, International Day of, 2129
Oldfield, Barney, 0773
Old-Time Country Music Contest and Festival, National, 2130
Oldtime Fiddlers' Contest and Festival, National, 2131
Ole Time Fiddlers and Bluegrass Festival, 2132
olive branches, 0168
Olney White Squirrel Count, 2133
Olsok
    See St. Olav's Day
Olympic Arts Festival
    See Cultural Olympiad
Olympic Games, 0737, 2134, 0702
Omaha Indians, 3210
    See also American Indians
Omak Stampede and Suicide Race, 2135
Oman
    arts and cultural festival, 1954
    birthday commemoration, 2136
Oman National Day, 2136
Ombashira Matsuri, 2137
Omisoka, 2138
Omizutori Matsuri (Water-Drawing Festival), 2139
Ommegang, 2140
Onam, 2141
onion festivals
    Florida, 0840
    Georgia (state), 3141
    New York, 0840
Onion Market
    See Zwiebelmarkt (Onion Market)
Ontario
    arts festival, 2099
    Caribbean festival, 3009
    emancipation celebrations, 0922, 0927
    film festival, 3010
    folk festival, 1782
    food celebrations, 3011

General Index

freedom festival, 1076
military commemoration, 0479
rock paper scissors championship, 3268
Shakespeare festival, 2846
slavery remembrances, 0090
winter festival, 3239
Onwasato Festival, 2142
Opal Festival, 2143
Opalia, 2144
Open
   See British Open
Open Championship of the British Isles
   See British Open
Open Marathon, International, 2145
open-house day, 0912
Opening of the Underground Caves Day (Te Kauki
   Nanganga'), 2146
opera music
   Australia, 0019
   China, 0280
   Colorado, 0551
   England, 1149, 3246
   Finland, 2539
   Germany, 1952
   Ireland, 3205
   Italy, 0262, 1043
   New Mexico, 2518
Opera Festival
   See Central City Opera Festival
Operation Fenkil, 0991
Operation Pedestal, 0177
Operation Storm, 0724
Orange Bowl Game, 2147
Orange Day (Orangemen's Day), 2148
Orangemen's Day
   See Orange Day (Orangemen's Day)
orange-throwing contest, 0533
Orchestra of Linz, 0405
ordinations, 0928
Oregon
   American Indian celebration, 0593
   beer festival, 2150
   dog events, 0254, 2151
   flower festival, 2298
   historic festival, 2413
   literary holiday, 0333
   music festival, 2149
   poetry and fishing, 1025
   rodeo, 2235
   Shakespeare festival, 2152
   theater festivals, 2152
Oregon Bach Festival, 2149
Oregon Basset Hound Rescue, 0254
Oregon Brewers Festival, 2150
Oregon Dune Mushers' Mail Run, 2151
Oregon Shakespeare Festival, 2152
Organization of African Unity, 0030
Organization of American States, 2198

orgies, 0466
Original Gullah Festival, 2153
orphanages, 2728
Orpheus, 1160
Orthodox Christian events
   See Christian Orthodox events
Osaka International Festival, 2154
Oschophoria, 0808
Osei Tutu, King, 0015
Oshogatsu (New Year's Day), 2155
Osorezan Taisai, 2156
Ossiach Abbey, 0503
Ostara, 0862, 2157
Osterfestspiele
   See Easter Festival (Osterfestspiele)
Ostern
   See Easter (Germany) (Ostern)
Otsa Festival, 2158
Ottoman Turks, 0419, 3139
Ouiatenon Indians, 1382
Ouidah, Benin, 0292
Our Friends, the Enemy, 1115
Our Lady Aparecida, Festival of, 2159
Our Lady Day
   See Lady Day
Our Lady of Carmel, Feast of, 2160
Our Lady of Fátima Day, 2161
Our Lady of Guadalupe, Feast of (United States), 2162
Our Lady of Guadalupe, Fiesta of, 2163
Our Lady of Lourdes, Feast of, 2164
Our Lady of Luxembourg
   See Octave of Our Lady, Consoler of the Afflicted
Our Lady of Mercedes Day, 0832
Our Lady of Mount Carmel, 1137
Our Lady of Nazaré Festival, 2165
Our Lady of Nazareth, 0994
Our Lady of Peñafrancia, 2094
Our Lady of Solitude, Fiesta of, 2166
Our Lady of Sorrows Festival, 2167
Our Lady of the Angels, Feast of, 2168
Our Lady of the Chisels, 0981
Our Lady of the Good Death Festival, 2169
Our Lady of the Happy Ending, 0364
Our Lady of the Rock, Festival of, 2170
Our Lady of Victories Day
   See Victory Day (Our Lady of Victories Day)
Ouray Ice Festival, 2171
Outback Festival, 2172
outhouses, 1576
ovens, 1058
Ovid, 1058
Ovoo Worship Festival, 2173
Owara Kaze-no-Bon Festival, 2174
Ox Cart Festival, 2175
oxen, 0384, 0648, 0908, 2980
Oxi Day 2176
Oyo people, 2511
oysters, 1095, 1221, 2781

Numbers in the index refer to entry numbers, not page numbers

Ozark Folk Festival, 2177
    ozone layer, 2315

P

Paasch Maandag
    See Easter Monday (Netherlands)
Paasch Zondag
    See Easter (Netherlands) (Paschen, Paasch Zondag)
Pachamama, 0486
Pacific Northwest Festival, 2178
Pack Monday Fair, 2179
Paczki Day, 2180
Padua Purim
    See Purims, Special
Paepcke, Walter, 0175
Pafos Aphrodite Festival Cyprus, 2181
pagan events
    Great Britain, 1619
    Italy, 2258
    North aCarolina, 0486
    Scotland, 1619
Pageant of Peace
    See Lighting of the National Christmas Tree
Pageant of the Golden Tree, 2182
Pageant of the Lamas
    See Mystery Play (Tibet)
Paha Sapa, 1049
Paine (Thomas) Day, 2183
painting festival, 1387
Paitishahem (Patishahya; Feast of Bringing in the Harvest), 2184
Pak Tai, 0581
Pakistan
    birthday commemoration, 1426
    cultural festival, 2582
    death commemorations, 2580, 3094
    national holidays, 2185, 2186, 2187
    Passion play, 2935
    pilgrimage, 0766
    saint feast day, 2818
    winter festival, 0563
Pakistan Day, 2185
Pakistan Independence Day, 2186
Pakistan Kashmir Solidarity Day, 2187
Palau Independence Day, 2188
Palestine, 2658
Palio, Festival of the, 2189
Palio of the Contrade
    See Palio, Festival of the
Palio of the Goose and River Festival, 2190
Palm Sunday, 1008, 2191
Palm Sunday (Austria), 2192
Palm Sunday (Finland), 2193
Palm Sunday (Germany) (Palmsonntag), 2194
Palm Sunday (Italy) (Domenica delle Palme), 2195
Palm Sunday (Netherlands) (PalmZondag), 2196

Palm Sunday (United States), 2197
Palmsonntag
    See Palm Sunday (Germany) (Palmsonntag)
PalmZondag
    See Palm Sunday (Netherlands) (PalmZondag)
palo sebo, 0447
Pan-African Film Festival, 2200
Panafrican Film and Television Festival of Ouagadougou, 2199
Pan American Day, 2024
Panama
    Carnival, 0521
    independence day, 2201
    log-throwing contest, 0233
    parade, 0521
    religious celebrations, 0325, 1347
Panama Independence Days, 2201
Panathenaea, 2202
Pancake Day, 2203
Panchadaan, 2204
Panguni Uthiram
    See Panguni Uttiram (Panguni Uthiram)
Panguni Uttiram (Panguni Uthiram), 2205
Panic of 1873, 0328
Pan-on-Head Festival
    See Nabekamuri Matsuri (Pan-on-Head Festival)
pantomimes, 0624
Panza, Sancho, 0554
Papa Festival, 2206
Papa Noel, 0639
papal festival, 2799
papier-mâché dolls, 0764
papier-mâché festival, 2003
Papua New Guinea
    animal festival, 2259
    independence day, 2207
    nature appreciation, 3178
    tribal culture festival, 1936
Papua New Guinea Independence Day, 2207
papyrus, 0453
parachutists, 0398
Parada del Sol, 2208
Parade of Nations, 1053
parades
    See also processions
    African American, 0028
    Arizona, 3118
    Austria, 0265
    Brazil, 2527
    baby, 0215
    Bahamas, 0223
    Bolivia, 0534
    California, 0161, 0327, 0834, 1445, 3015
    Canada, 1153
    Channel Islands, 0264
    Finland, 1014
    Georgia (state), 2795
    Germany, 1118

Illinois, 0317
India, 0515
Japan, 0557, 0751, 2041
Marinique and Guadeloupe, 0519
Michigan, 3248, 1773
New Jersey, 0215
Panama, 0521
pirate, 0385
Prince Edward Island, 1153
Spain, 0490
Switzerland, 0525
United Arab Emirates (UAE), 0014
Virgin Islands (U.S.), 0526
Wisconsin, 1196
Paraguay
    independence day, 2209
    saint feast days, 2479, 2497
Paraguay Independence Day, 2209
paralysis, 0762
paranormal festival, 1931
Pardon of Nossa Senhora dos Remédios, 2210
Pardon of Our Lady of Sorrows
    See Our Lady of Sorrows Festival
Pardon of Ste. Anne d'Auray, 2211
Parentalia, 0992, 1189, 2036
parenting, 2334
Pariapunko, 0037
Parilia (Palilia), 2213
Paris Air and Space Show, 2214
Paris Autumn Festival (Festival d'Automme), 2215
Park, Willie, 0402
Parker, Charlie, 0591, 2216
Parker (Charlie) Jazz Festival, 2216
Parks, Rosa, 2217
Parks (Rosa) Day, 2217
Parnell, Charles Stewart, 1448
Paro Tsechu, 2218
Parshurama Jayanti, 2219
Parshva, Birthday of, 2220
Parsis, 0017
Parsons, John, 0805
Parton, Dolly, 0706
Partridge Day, 2221
Parvati, 1099, 1101
Paryushana, 0765, 2222
Pasch Monday
    See Easter Monday
Paschal Thursday
    See Maundy Thursday
Paschen
    See Easter (Netherlands) (Paschen, Paasch Zondag)
Pascua de Navidad
    See Christmas (Spain) (Pascua de Navidad)
Pascua Florida Day, 2223
Påskdagen
    See Easter (Sweden) (Påskdagen)
Paske
    See Easter (Norway) (Paske)

Paskha
    See Easter (Russia) (Paskha)
pasos, 0800, 1170
Pasqua, La
    See Easter (Italy) (La Pasqua)
Passion Play at Tzintzuntzan, 2224
Passion Plays
    Germany, 2104
    India, 2935
    Iran, 2935
    Iraq, 2935
    Mexico, 2224
    Pakistan, 2935
    Philippines, 1920
    South Dakota, 0329
Passion Sunday
    See Carling Sunday
Passion Thursday
    See Maundy Thursday
Passion Week
    See Holy Week
Passover, 2225
pastries, 0870, 0875
Paternoster Row, 0691
path-clearing festivals, 0046
Patishahya
    See Paitishahem (Patishahya; Feast of Bringing in the Harvest)
Patriot Day (September 11 Day), 2226
Patriots' Day, 0112, 0375, 2227
Paul Bunyan Festival
    See Paul Bunyan Show
Paul Bunyan Show, 2228
paulitos, 0860
Pausha Dashami, 2229
Pavarotti, Luciano, 1149
Pawnee tribe, 0858
Payment of Quit Rent, 2230
Payson Rodeo, 2231
peace celebrations
    Japan, 1313
    Mozambique, 1945
    New York, 3265
    Organization of American States, 2198
    Taiwan, 2909
    United Nations, 2232
Peace, International Day of, 2232
Peace Treaty of San Stefano, 0419
peaches, 2672
peanut festival, 1117
Peanut Festival, National, 2233
pearl festival, 2605
Pearl Harbor Day, 2234
"Pearl Harbor of Australia," 0325
Pearl Jam, 0660
Pears, Peter, 0059
peas, 0504
peasant holidays

Myanmar, 1961
Poland, 3059
peat bogs, 0352
pecans, 2118
Pecos Pueblo, 2124
Pedro, Felix, 1157
Pedro I, 0393
Pedro II, 0394
Pendleton Round-Up and Happy Canyon, 2235
Penitents, Procession of the (Belgium), 2236
Penitents, Procession of the (Spain), 2237
Penkye Otu, 0007
Penn Day
    See Pennsylvania Day
Penn Relays
    See University of Pennsylvania Relay Carnival
Penn, William, 1067, 2238
Pennsylvania
    automobile blessing, 2715
    birthday commemorations, 1072, 2238
    Christmas Eve, 0637
    constitution event, 0680
    Dutch festival, 1599
    flower celebrations, 2252
    folk festival, 2239
    food festival, 1838
    German folk festival, 1173
    historic reenactment, 0730
    lantern festivity, 1629
    military reenactments, 0266, 0788, 1124, 1125
    New Year's Eve Watch Night, 3189
    Nigerian festival, 2113
    open-house day, 0912
    political commemoration, 0945
    religious holiday, 2545
    running race, 3090
    snake roundup, 1924
    sporting events, 1688, 3090
    transportation festival, 2262
    TV-invented holiday, 1002
    weather prognostication, 1222
    Welsh recitation, 0742
Pennsylvania Day, 2238
Pennsylvania Dutch
    folk festival, 1173
    religious holiday, 2619
    Whitsuntide celebrations, 3215
Pennsylvania Dutch Folk Festival, 2239
    See also Kutztown Festival
Pennsylvania Week
    See Pennsylvania Day
penny, 2282
"Penny for the Guy," 0905
Pentagon, 2226
pentathlons, 0253
Pentecost, 0928, 2240
peony, 0603
People Power Anniversary

    See Fiesta sa EDSA (People Power Anniversary)
People's Army of North Korea, Founding of the, 2241
People's Republic of China
    See China
pepinos, 0463
Peppercorn Ceremony, 2242
Perahära
    See Kataragama Festival
Perchta, 0935
Perchtenlauf, 2243
Perchtennacht
    See Epiphany (Germany) (Dreikönigsfest)
performing arts events
    See also arts festivals; dance festivals; music festivals;
        theater festivals
    Alabama, 0320
    Arizona, 1028
    Australia, 2245
    Austria, 0503
    Bermuda, 0303
    Canada, 1910
    Colorado, 0787
    Czech Republic, 2310, 2329
    France, 0105
    Japan, 1316
    Iceland, 2397
    Jordan, 1472
    Michigan, 0754, 1940, 0790
    New York, 2531
    Oklahoma, 1835
    Switzerland, 1912
    Syria, 0373
    Tennessee, 1852
    Texas, 2938
    Virginia, 2173
    Washington (state), 2178, 2532
Perry, Matthew C., 0334
Perry, Ted, 0594
Perry, Walter, 0927
Persai (Aeschylus), 0808
Perseids, 2244
Persephone, 0911
Persia
    birthday commemoration, 0211
    death commemoration, 0213
    religious festival, 0212
Perth International Arts Festival, 2245
Perth Royal Show
    See Royal Shows
Peru
    agricultural celebration, 2492
    birthday commemoration, 0803
    Carnival, 0522
    cross commemoration, 0798
    devotional painting procession, 2566
    earthquake commemoration, 2567
    harvest festival, 0205
    independence day, 2247

military commemoration, 2246
processions, 0127
religious celebrations, 0068, 0127, 0483, 1992
religious pilgrimages, 2272
saint feast days, 2488, 2498, 2525
War of the Pacific, 0598
water festival, 0037
winter solstice festival, 1424
Peru Battle of Angamos, 2246
Peru Independence Day, 2247
Pesah
    See Passover
pesebre, 0558
Petaluma, California, 0449
Petit Martinique, 0538
Petty, Adam, 0773
Petty, Richard, 0773
Peyote Dance (Híkuli Dance), 2248
Pferdeweihe
    See Nativity of the Blessed Virgin Mary, Feast of the
       (Germany)
Pffiferdaj, 2249
Pfingsten
    See Pentecost
Pfingstrosen
    See Pentecost
Phagwa, 2250
phallic symbols, 0079
Phansa
    See Waso (Buddhist Rains Retreat)
Phat Dan Day
    See Vesak (Wesak; Buddha's Birthday)
Phchum Ben, 2251
Philadelphia Flower Show, 2252
Philadelphia, Pennsylvania, 0912
Philip II of Spain, 0530
Philippines
    dancing, 0806
    death commemoration, 2408
    farming festival, 0495
    harvest festival, 1889
    independence day, 2253
    lantern festival, 1132
    military commemoration, 0259
    national holiday, 0366
    religious celebrations, 0185, 0332, 0970, 1045, 1348, 2094
    revolution commemoration, 1005
    saint feast day, 2806
    spirit ceremony, 1139
    theater festivals, 1920, 1923
Philippines Independence Day, 2253
Phillip, Arthur, 0193
phone-throwing contest, 1897
photography festivals, 0102
Phra Buddha Bat Fair, 2254
physically disabled, 2736
Pickett (Bill) Invitational Rodeo, 2255
Pickett's Charge, 1125
Pickle Festival, 2256

Pickle Market
    See Bettara-Ichi
pickled radishes, 0304
picnics, 3299
Pied Piper of Hamelin, 1070
Pied Piper Open Air Theater, 2257
Piedigrotta, Festival of, 2258
Piedmont blues, 0422
pierced ears, 0491
Pierrot, 0527
Pig Festivals, 2259
Pig's Face Feast, 2260
pig's head, 0729
Pii Mai, 2261
pig-slaughtering festival, 1552
Pike Festival, National, 2262
Pilgrim celebrations
    Forefather's Day, 1056
    Pilgrim Progress Pageant, 2264
    Thanksgiving, 2265, 2963
Pilgrim Festivals, 2263
Pilgrim Progress Pageant, 2264
Pilgrim Thanksgiving Day (Plymouth, Massachusetts), 2265
Pilgrimage of Our Lady of Valme, 2266
Pilgrimage of Saut d'Eau, 2267
Pilgrimage of the Dew, 2268
Pilgrimage to Chalma, 2269
Pilgrimage to Mecca (Hajj), 2270
Pilgrimage to Moulay Idriss, 2271
Pilgrimage to Qoyllur Riti, 2272
Pilgrimage to Shrine of Father Laval, 2273
Pilgrimage to Souvenance, 2274
Pilgrimage to the Tomb of Sunan Bayat, 2275
pilgrimages
    Alaska, 2740
    Haiti, 2267, 2274
    India, 0079, 2989
    Indonesia, 2275
    Mauritius, 2273
    Mexico, 2269
    Morocco, 2271
    Pakistan, 0766
    Peru, 2272
    Saudi Arabia, 2270
    Senegal, 1179
    Shi'ite Muslims, 0136, 0137
    Spain, 2266, 2268
    Sri Lanka, 0016
Pilula, 0658
Pine Battle of Vinuesa, 2276
Pineda, Alonzo Alvarez, 0408
Pingxi Sky Lantern Festival, 2277
Pinkster Day, 2278
Pinochet, Augusto, 0599
pinole, 0729
pioneer celebrations
    Arizona, 1914
    Australia, 2172
    British Columbia, 0401

Numbers in the index refer to entry numbers, not page numbers

Canada, 0401
Utah, 0088
Pioneer Day
    See Mormon Pioneer Day
piradzini, 0573
pirate festivals
    Florida, 0385, 1107
    Texas, 0408
    Virginia, 0337
Pirates Week, 2279
pisanki, 1169
Pitcher Fair
    See Kumbh Mela (Pitcher Fair)
Pitkäperjantai
    See Good Friday
Pitra Visarjana Amavasya, 2280
Pius XI, Pope, 0614
Pius XII, Pope, 0178
Plague Sunday, 2281
planned town festival, 2015
planting festivals
    Mali, 0423
    Namibia, 2100
Planting the Penny Hedge, 2282
Plataea, 0748
Plebeian Games (Ludi Plebeii), 2283
Pleureuses, Ceremony of, 2284
plotkeles, 0631
Plough Monday, 0671, 2285
Plumley, Gary, 0174
Pluto, 0911
Plymouth, Massachusetts, 1056
pochoveras, 0825
poetry celebrations
    Colombia, 2286
    Japan, 3100
    Macedonia, 2848
    Nevada, 0710
    New Jersey, 0821
    North Dakota, 0752
    Northern Ireland, 0246
    Oregon, 1025
    Scotland, 0443
    United States, 2287
Poetry Festival of Medellín, International, 2286
Poetry Month, National, 2287
poison, 2749
Pol Pot, 0471
Poland
    Christmas celebrations, 0616, 3223
    classical music festival, 3181
    college festival, 1500
    constitution holiday, 2289
    doll festival, 1808
    film festival, 3182
    folk festival, 1617
    food festival, 2180
    independence day, 2290
    Jewish cultural festival, 1475

national holidays, 2291, 2292
    peasant holiday, 3059
    religious holidays, 0873, 1169
    religious pilgrimage, 0331
    saint feast day, 2698
    spring ritual, 1808
    wheat harvest festival, 0840
    wreath festival, 3218
Polar Bear Swim Day, 2288
poles, 0322, 0363, 0390, 0495, 0835, 2818
Poling, Rev. Clark, 1064
Polish Constitution Day, 2289
Polish Independence Day, 2290
Polish Liberation Day, 2291
Polish Solidarity Day, 2292
political commemorations
    Bangladesh, 0237
    Barbados, 0249
    Bermuda, 2242
    England, 1699, 2832
    Germany, 2103
    Hong Kong, 1358
    Isle of Man, 3067
    Netherlands, 2320
    North Korea, 3249
    Pennsylvania, 0945
    San Marino, 2502
    Sweden, 1827
    United States, 1414
    Vermont, 3016
Polk County Ramp Festival, 0696
Polka Festival, National, 2293
Pollera Day, 0521
Pollux, 0545
Polytechneio Day, 2294
Pongal, 2295
poor people, 0944, 0943, 0948, 2716
Poor Richard's Almanac, 0976
Pooram, 2296
poppies, 0168
Poppy Day
    See Veterans Day
Pops, Boston, 0377
population awareness, 0100, 3266
Porciúncula, 0963
Pori International Jazz Festival, 2297
porridge, 0633
Portland Rose Festival, 2298
Portobelo, Panama, 0325
Portugal
    agricultural fair, 0036
    animal festival, 2381
    Carnival, 0523
    charity for poor, 2903
    dancing, 0523, 0937
    death commemorations, 0069, 2300
    film festival, 2349
    full moon celebration, 2904
    gay rights commemorations, 2349

Numbers in the index refer to entry numbers, not page numbers

harvest festival, 2903
independence day, 2302
Islamic festival, 1434
military commemoration, 2299
music festival, 0437
national holiday, 2301
new year, 2031
religious celebrations, 0069, 0168, 0690, 0937, 1224,
    1349, 2161, 2210
saint feast days, 1339, 2654, 2753, 2779, 2825
Virgin Mary celebrations, 2161, 2165, 2167
Portugal Day
    See Portugal National Day
Portugal Liberation Day, 2299
Portugal National Day, 2300
Portugal Republic Day, 2301
Portugal Restoration of Independence Day, 2302
Portuguese celebrations
    California, 0454
    Massachusetts, 0340
Posadas, 0640, 2303
Poseidon, 0727
Poson, 2304
Posviceni
    See Obzinky
Potato Blossom Festival, 2305
Potato Days, 2306
potatoes, 1397
pots and pans, 0178
poverty, 0944, 0943, 0948, 2716, 0983
Powamû Ceremony, 2308
Powell, Colin, 0417
POW-MIA Recognition Day, National, 2307
powwows
    Alaska, 1876
    Alberta, 0416
    Canada, 0416
    Idaho, 1698
    Iowa, 1859
    Massachusetts, 3176
    North Dakota, 3088
    South Dakota, 0717
Prachum-Ben
    See Phchum Ben
practical jokes, 0132
Prague Kolache Festival, 2309
Prague Light Festival
    See Signal: Prague Light Festival
Prague Spring International Music Festival, 2310
pranks, 0132, 0531
prayer days
    Denmark, 2843
    Germany, 2391
    Liberia, 1668
    United States, 0770
    Tibet, 1908
    worldwide, 2311, 3257, 3263
Prayer Festival
    See Monlam (Prayer Festival)

Prayer for Christian Unity, Week of, 2311
Preakness Festival
    See Preakness Stakes
pre-Lenten festivals, 0507
prémices des Alpes, 1021
Premio Lo Nuestro Latin Music Awards, 2313
Prescott, William, 0429
Presentation of the Blessed Virgin Mary, Feast of the, 2314
presépio, 0616, 0636
Preservation of the Ozone Layer, International Day for the,
    2315
Presidents' Day, 2316
Presley, Elvis, 0921
Pretzel Sunday, 2317
    Pride Week
    See New York Gay Pride March
"Priedka tat-Tifel," 0560
Primrose Day, 2318
Prince Edward Island, 0011, 0566, 1153
Prince's Birthday in Liechtenstein, 2319
Prinsjesdag, 2320
prisoner holidays, 2350, 2307
Prisoners, Feast of the, 2321
Procession of 1,000 People
    See Toshogu Haru-No-Taisai (Great Spring Festival of
        the Toshogu Shrine)
Procession of the Caparisoned Horse, 0780
processions
    See also parades
    Austria, 0980
    Belgium, 1134
    Brazil, 0652
    El Salvador, 1044
    England, 0691, 3155
    France, 0635, 1133
    Germany, 0692, 0980
    Ghana, 0046
    Hussein funeral reenactment, 0172
    India, 0171
    Italy, 0548, 1167
    Japan, 0042
    Luxembourg, 0762
    Mexico, 0693, 1168
    New York, 1137
    Panama, 0325
    Peru, 0127
    Scotland, 0439
    Venezuela, 0695
Proms, The
    See Wood (Henry) Promenade Concerts
property owner ceremony, 2951
Prophet's Birthday
    See Mawlid al-Nabi (Maulid al-Nabi; Prophet's
        Birthday)
Proserpine, 0553
prospective matrimonial festival, 2928
Protestant events
    All Saints' Day, 0064
    Ascension Day, 0167

Epiphany, 0944
Family Week, 0978
Good Friday, 1163
Martinsfest, 1798
Mother's Day, 1930
Rally Day, 2362
Reformation Day, 2385
Rogation Days, 2418
Sunday School Day, 2872
Transfiguration, Feast of the, 3019
Prvého Máje
    See May Day (Czech Republic) (Prvého Máje)
Ptah, 0009
Pterandon Ptrot, 0807
public servants, 0625
Puccini Festival, 2322
Puccini, Giacomo, 2322
Puck Fair, 2323
pudding, 2840
Pueblo Indians, 2586
Puerto Rico
    birthday commemorations, 1371, 1953
    Christmas, 0621
    classical music festival, 0543
    Columbus, Christopher, 0812
    constitution day, 2324
    Indian festival, 1469
    national holiday, 0777
    saint feast days, 2745, 2754
Puerto Rico Constitution Day, 2324
Pukllay, 0509
Pulaski, Casimir, 2325
Pulaski Day, 2325
pumpkin festivals
    California, 1265
    Delaware, 2327
    New Hampshire, 1530
Punchinello, 0527
Punjabi American Festival, 2326
Punkin Chunkin World Championship, 2327
Punky (Punkie) Night, 2328
Punxsutawney Phil, 1222
puppet festivals
    Canada, 0999
    Czech Republic, 2329
    Illinois, 0590
    Japan, 1316
    Quebec, 0999
    Vietnam, 2966
Puppeteers, Festival of, 2329
puppets, 0217
puppy-dog pie, 0656
Pura Besakih, 0900
Purcell, Henry, 0679
purification ceremonies
    China, 0584
    Ghana, 2114
    India, 1100
    Japan, 2948

    Pakistan, 0563
Purim, 2330
Purims, Special, 2331
purnima, 0456
Purple Heart Day, 2332
Pushkar Mela, 2333
pussy willows, 0866
Putrada Ekadashi, 2334
putz, 0637
pysanky, 0877
Pythian Games, 2335

Q

Qatar Independence Day, 2336
Qiantang River Tidal Bore Watching Festival, International, 2337
Qing Dynasty, 0836
Qing Ming Festival (Ching Ming Festival), 2338
Qoyllur Riti, Peru, 2272
Quadragesima Sunday, 2339
Quadrilles of San Martin, 2340
Quakers, 1067
Quarter Days, 2341
Quartier d'été, 2342
Quasimodo Sunday
    See Low Sunday
Quebec
    Acadian festival, 0011
    comedy festival, 1496
    film festivals, 0998, 1911
    music festivals, 1910, 2343
    puppet festival, 0999
    saint feast day, 2699
    winter carnival, 2344
Quebec City Festival of Sacred Music, 2343
Quebec Winter Carnival, 2344
Quecholli, 2345
Quechua Indians, 0205, 0482
Queen Elizabeth's Day
    See Queen's Day (England)
Queen's Birthday (Thailand), 2346
Queen's Day (England), 2347
Queen's Day (Netherlands)
    See King's Day (Koningsdag)
Queenship of Mary, 2348
Queer Film Festival, International. Queer Lisboa: International Queer Film Festival, 2349
Queima das Fitas
    See Burning of the Ribbons (Queima das Fitas)
Quema de Judas, La
    See Burning of Judas
Quema del Diablo, La
    See Burning the Devil
Quiché Indians, 0326, 0689
Quinta Feira da Espiga
    See Ascension Day (Portugal)
Quintaine, La, 2350

Numbers in the index refer to entry numbers, not page numbers

Quirinalia, 2351
Quirinalia festival, 1058
Quirinus, 1058
Quist, Adrian, 0194
Qur'an, 1641, 2365

R

rabbit
        See Easter Bunny
Räben-Chilbi, 2352
Race of the Ceri, 2353
Race of the Cow, 0707
Race Relations Sunday, 2354
Race Unity Day, 2355
racial discrimination elimination day, 0915
Radha Ashtami, 2356
radishes, 0304, 2066
Radunitsa, 2357
raft festival, 0294
RAGBRAI, 2358
Raghunathji, 0855
Raid on Redding Ridge, 2359
Rain Dance
        See Nyambinyambi
rain events
        England, 2813
        Japan, 2914
        Mexico, 0209
        Namibia, 2100
        Niger, 0739
Rain-Calling Ceremony
        See Nyambinyambi
Rainforest World Music Festival, 2360
Rains Retreat, 0165
rake festival, 3008
Raksha Bandhan, 2361
Rally Day, 2362
Ram Roasting Fair, 2363
Rama Leela Festival, 2364
Rama, Lord, 0562, 0794, 0855
Rama V, King, 0645
Ramadan, 2365
Ramanavami (Ram Navami), 2366
Ramayana, 0583, 0855
Ramayana Ballet, 2367
Rameaux
        See Palm Sunday
Ramírez, Juan Sánchez, 0829, 0845
Ramos, Fidel, 1005
Ramos, Thomas Vincent, 1104
ramp (plant), 0696
rams, 0172
Ramses, 0009
Rand Easter Show
        See Rand Show
Rand Show, 2368
Ransom, Stanley A., 0333

Rara (Ra-Ra), 2369
Ras al-Am
        See Nawruz (Naw roz; No Ruz; New Year)
Rasa Leela Festival, 2370
Rashtriya Prajatantra Divas
        See Nepal Democracy Day
Rath Yatra, 2371
Ratification Day, 2372
Rato (Red) Machhendranath, 2373
Rat's Wedding Day, 2374
Rattlesnake Roundup
        See Morris Rattlesnake Roundup
rattlesnake round-ups
        Pennsylvania, 1924
        Texas, 2889
Ravana, 0794, 0855
Ravello Music Festival, 2375
Reagan, Ronald, 0680, 0770
Ravinia Festival, 2376
Reagan, Ronald, 0680, 0770
Reconciliation, Day of, 2377
Reconciliation Week, National, 2378
Recovery
        See Exaltation of the Cross, Feast of the red bean stew,
        0833
red clothes, 3197
Red Earth Native American Cultural Festival, 2379
Red Festival Day
        See Red Flannel Festival
Red Flannel Festival, 2380
Red Rum, 1180
Red Sea, 0048
Red Waistcoat Festival, 2381
Redentore, Festa del, 2382
Reed Dance, 2383
Reek Sunday, 2384
Rees, Thomas, 0502
Reform Judaism commemoration, 2457
Reformation Day, 2385
Reformation Sunday
        See Reformation Day
Refreshment Sunday
        See Mothering Sunday
Regatta of the Great Maritime Republics, 2386
Regency era, 0191
reggae music celebrations (Jamaica), 1785, 2387
Reggae Sumfest, 2387
Register's Annual Great Bicycle Ride Across Iowa
        See RAGBRAI
Re-Horakhty, 0009
reinado, 0600
reindeer, 0616, 2388
Reindeer Driving Competition, 2388
Rei-tai-sai, 2389
relationship festival, 0188
religious celebrations
        See also individual religions
        ancient Greece, 0911
        ancient Israelites, 2263

Numbers in the index refer to entry numbers, not page numbers

ancient Rome, 1086, 2213
Argentina, 1408, 2093
Arizona, 0878
Armenia, 0342
Austria, 0942, 2192
Baha'i religion, 0220
Bali, 1093
Bangladesh, 0321, 1508
Belgium, 0114, 0180, 0536, 0862, 1164, 1333, 1337, 1796, 2236
Bermuda, 1165
Bhutan, 2969
Bolivia, 0482
Brazil, 0549, 0814, 3289
Bulgaria, 0863
California, 0869, 2569
Cameroon, 0969
Canada, 0936
Cherokee, 1201
Chile, 0864, 1182, 2988
China, 1609
Colombia, 2321, 2458
Cyprus, 0865, 1522, 0654
Czech Republic, 0866, 1344, 1048
Delaware, 0031
Dominican Republic, 0831, 0832
Egypt, 0867, 1038
El Salvador, 0903, 1044
England, 0060, 0486, 0691, 1166, 1614, 1928
Ethiopia, 0862, 1102, 2557, 2785, 2985, 0964
Finland, 1615, 2193
Florida, 0941
France, 0065, 0176, 0690, 0944, 0943, 1084, 1796, 2211
Germany, 0692, 0868, 0935, 1084, 1514, 1798, 2194, 2391
Great Britain, 0504
Greece, 0941, 1059, 1578, 1993, 2202, 2974, 0654
Guatemala, 0067, 0179, 0326, 2561
Guinea, 0172
Guyana, 0172
Haiti, 1345
Hawaii, 1040
Hindus, 0045, 0307
Hong Kong, 2900
Idaho, 2743
India, 0172, 1547, 1590, 1593, 1739, 1740, 2610, 0362, 1175, 1515, 2611
Indonesia, 0900
Iran, 0212
Ireland, 1797
Italy, 0069, 0181, 0870, 1057, 1167, 2195, 2382, 2694
Jamaica, 0172
Japan, 0348, 2513
Jewish faith, 2225
Kentucky, 2584
Kiribati, 1566
Labrador, 0936
Lebanon, 2690
Libya, 1670
Louisiana, 0066

Luxembourg, 2107
Malta, 0177, 1409
Marshall Islands, 1597
Massachusetts, 1048
Mexico, 0069, 0693, 0801, 1168, 1341, 1346, 1410, 2303
Moldova, 1902
Mongolia, 2173
Morocco, 0993
Muslims, 0321
National Bible Week, 0310
Nepal, 2610, 1130, 1131
Netherlands, 0871, 0883, 1796, 2196, 2618
New Mexico, 0070, 1057, 2517
New York, 1310
Nigeria, 2469
Niue, 2076
North Carolina, 0486
Norway, 0872, 2739
Orthodox Church, 0242
Panama, 0325, 1347
Pennsylvania, 2545
Pennsylvania Dutch, 2619
Persia, 0212
Peru, 0068, 0127, 0483, 1992
Philippines, 0185, 0332, 0970, 1045, 1348, 2094
Poland, 0873, 1169
Portugal, 0069, 0168, 0690, 0937, 1224, 1349, 2210
Roman Catholic Church, 0115, 0242
Romania, 1059
Russia, 0874, 0941, 0938, 1643
Samoa, 3214
Senegal, 0172
Shi'ite Muslims, 0172
Sierra Leone, 0172
South Africa, 2596
South Dakota, 0329
Spain, 0875, 1170, 1225, 1854, 1963, 2237
Sparta, 0507
Sri Lanka, 1523, 2510
Sweden, 0876, 0940, 1796
Switzerland, 0694, 1205, 2284, 2544
Syria, 1059
Trinidad, 0172
Turkey, 0172, 1621
Ukraine, 0877, 2827
United States, 1636, 2197, 3228, 0770, 1064
Utah, 1921
Venezuela, 0335, 0695, 0801
West Africa, 0172
religious diversity celebration, 0404
religious education, 2872
religious pilgrimages
Guatemala, 0326
Haiti, 2267, 2274
Indonesia, 2275
Mauritius, 2273
Mexico, 2269
Morocco, 2271
Peru, 2272

Numbers in the index refer to entry numbers, not page numbers

Poland, 0331
Saudi Arabia, 2270
Spain, 2266, 2268
Remembrance Day, 2390
See Veterans Day
Remembrance of the Departed
See Farvardegan Days
Remuria
See Lemuralia
Renaissance festivals
Czech Republic, 1026
Michigan, 1869
Renaissance music, 2466
rent-payment days
England, 2230
United Kingdom, 2341
repentance, 2952
Repentance and Prayer Day, 2391
reposiar, 0693
Repotini
See Ropotine (Repotini)
Republic Day
See Madagascar Independence Day; Mali Independence
Day; Pakistan Day
Republic of Korea
See North Korea
Republic of Texas Chili Cookoff
See Chilympiad (Republic of Texas Chili Cookoff)
Repudiation Day, 2392
Restoration Day
See Shick-Shack Day (Shik-Shak Day, Shicsack Day,
Shig-Shag Day)
Restoration of Independence of the Republic of Latvia, 2393
Restoration of the Aaronic Priesthood Commemoration,
2394
Retraite aux Flambeaux, La
See Night Watch
retreat, 0547
Return Day, 2395
Return from the Mountain Pasture
See Almabtrieb
reunification day, 1120
réveillon, 0635
Revere, Paul, 0112
Reversing Current, Festival of the (Water Festival; Bonn Om
Tuk), 2396
revolution commemorations
Algeria, 0063
Libya, 1672
Philippines, 1005
Tunisia, 3050
Yemen, 3291
Zanzibar, 3309
Revolution Day
See Algeria National Day; Guatemala Army Day
Revolutionary War
See American Revolution
Reykjavik Arts Festival (Listahátí í Reykjavik), 2397
Rhode Island

boat racing, 2053
classical music festival, 2052
college pranks, 0497
folk music festivals, 2050
historic reenactment, 1108
independence days, 2398
Japanese cultural festival, 0334
jazz festival, 1501
music festivals, 2050
neighbor day, 2004
Rhode Island Independence Day, 2398
Ribatejo Fair
See Agriculture Fair at Santarém, National ribbon
burning, 0437
rice, 0901, 2640
Rice Cake Festival
See Mochi No Matsuri
rice dumplings, 0842
rice harvest festival, 1109, 2068
rice paddies, 1443
rice-planting ceremony, 2399, 2441
Rice-Planting Festival at Osaka, 2399
Rich, Robert, 0713
Richards, Vivian, 0120
Richmond Fossil Festival, 2400
ridding of spirits, 1656
Riding the Marches
See Common Ridings Day
rice dumplings, 0842
rice harvest festival, 1109
rice paddies, 1443
rice-planting ceremony, 2399, 2441
Rice-Planting Festival at Osaka, 2399
Rich, Robert, 0713
Richards, Vivian, 0120
Richmond Fossil Festival, 2400
ridding of spirits, 1656
Riding the Marches
See Common Ridings Day
Ridvan, Feast of, 2401
Riley, (James Whitcomb) Festival, 2402
Rilling, Helmuth, 2149
Rio de Janeiro International Film Festival, 2403
Rio Grande, 0561
riots, 1763
Risabha, 0045, 2404
Risabha's Nirvana and Mauni Amavasya, 2404
risengrød, 0633
Rishi Panchami, 2405
Rite of Cosmic Renewal
See Chiao Festival (Rite of Cosmic Renewal)
River Kwai Bridge Week, 2406
River to Reef Festival, 2407
riverboats, 2115
Rizal Day, 2408
Rizal, José, 2408
Road Building, 2409
road commemorations
Arizona, 2437

Numbers in the index refer to entry numbers, not page numbers

New Mexico, 2437
Nigeria, 2409
road maintenance, 2409
Roatán Island, Honduras, 1104
Robe Offering Month
    See Thadingyut
Roberts's (Joseph Jenkins) Birthday, 2410
robes, 0474
Robigalia, 1151, 2411
Robin Hood Festival in Nottinghamshire, England, 2412
Robin Hood Festival in Sherwood, Oregon, 2413
robins, 2717
Robinson, Ellen Georgian Nellie, 0120
Robinson (Jackie) Day, 2414
Robots at Play, 2415
Rochambeau
    See World Rock Paper Scissors Championship
Rock Day
    See Distaff Day
rock music festivals
    Belgium, 3129
    Kentucky, 0002
    Tennessee, 0921
    United States, 0002
    Washington (state), 2532
Rock Ness, 2416
Rock of Gibraltar, 1135
rock paper scissors championship, 3268
Rocket Festival
    See Bun Bang Fai (Boun Bang Fay; Rocket Festival)
rockets, 0426
rodeos
    Alberta, 0460
    Arizona, 0542, 2231, 2995, 3118
    Australia, 1937
    Canada, 0460
    Chile, 1006
    Idaho, 0820
    Mexico, 0799
    Missouri, 0086
    Nebraska, 0044
    Nevada, 3277
    Oregon, 2235
    Tennessee, 2255
    Texas, 2678
    Washington (state), 0918, 2135
    Wyoming, 0582
Rodgers (Jimmie) Festival, 2417
Rodriguez, Santiago, 0830
Roe, Teddy, 2179
Rogation Days, 2418
Rogation Sunday
    See Rogation Days
Rogationtide procession, 1151
Rogers (Roy) Festival, 2419
Rogers, Will, 1138
Rogers (Will) Day, 2420
Rogonadur, 2421
Rohatsu
    See Bodhi Day (Rohatsu)
Rokoku Festival
    See Time Observance Day
rokovo
    See St. Rocco's Celebration (Rokovo)
Roldós Aguilera, Jaime, 0080
Roll Back Malaria, 0027
rolle bolle, 0284
roller skating, 0629
Roman Catholic events
    Advent, 0023, 0024
    All Saints' Day, 0064, 0065, 0066, 0067, 0068
    All Souls' Day, 0069, 0070
    Annunciation of the Lord, 0115
    Assumption of the Blessed Virgin Mary, Feast of the, 0177, 0179, 0180, 0181
    Baptism of the Lord, Feast of the, 0242
    Befana Festival, 0278
    Black Christ, Festival of the, 0325
    Blessed Sacrament, Feast of the, 0340
    Burning of Judas, 0435
    Candlemas, 0485
    Carnival of the Laetare, 0536
    Cavalhadas, 0549
    Chalk Sunday, 0560
    Christ the King, Feast of, 0614
    Christkindlesmarkt, 0615
    Christmas Eve, 0629, 0632, 0635
    Christmas, 0616, 0618
    Circumcision, Feast of the, 0650
    Corpus Christi, 0690, 0693
    Dominican Republic Our Lady of Altagracia, 0831
    Easter, 0862, 0864
    Elijah Day, 0914
    Embert Days, 0928
    Epiphany, 0944
    Exaltation of the Cross, Feast of the, 0970
    Family Week, 0978
    Flores de Mayo, 1044
    Forgiveness, Feast of, 1057
    Good Friday, 1163, 1164, 1165, 1166
    Holy Family, Feast of the, 1334
    Holy Ghost, Feast of the, 1335
    Holy Week, 1343
    Immaculate Conception, Feast of the, 1407, 1408, 1409, 1410
    Immaculate Heart of Mary, Feast of the, 1411
    Marian Days, 1779
    Martinmas, 1796
    Martinsfest, 1798
    Martyrdom of Joseph and Hyrum Smith, 1799
    Maundy Thursday, 1818
    Mercedes Day, 0832
    Michaelmas, 1866
    Misa de Gallo, 1889
    Most Precious Blood, Feast of the, 1927
    Nativity of the Blessed Virgin Mary, Feast of the, 1990, 1991, 1992
    Nombre de Jesús, 2081

Our Lady of Guadalupe, Feast of (United States),
  1990
Our Lady of the Good Death Festival, 2169
Palm Sunday, 2191, 2192, 2194, 2195, 2196
Pardon of Ste. Anne d'Auray, 2211
Pilgrimage to Shrine of Father Laval, 2273
Presentation of the Blessed Virgin Mary, Feast of the,
  2314
Queenship of Mary, 2348
Rogation Days, 2418
Rosary, Festival of the, 2428
Sacred Heart of Jesus, Feast of the, 2459
San Gennaro, Feast of, 2489
San Jos, Day Festival, 2496
San Juan Pueblo Feast Day, 2499
Señor de los Milagros, 2566
Seton (Mother) Day, 2570, 2725
St. Anthony of Padua, Feast of, 2700
St. Blaise's Day, 2707
St. Catherine's Day, 2710
St. Clare of Assisi, Feast of, 2716
St. Columba's Day, 2717
St. Dismas's Day, 2722
St. Frances Cabrini, Feast of, 2728
St. Hubert de Liège, Feast of, 2742
St. Ignatius Loyola, Feast of, 2743
St. Isidore, Festival of, 2744
St. John Lateran, Feast of the Dedication of, 2747
St. Jude's Day, 2763
St. Mark's Day, 2773
St. Patrick's Day, 2792
St. Peter's Chair, Festival of, 2799
St. Rocco's Celebration (Rokovo), 2804
St. Teresa's Day, 2817
St. Thomas's Day, 2818
St. Tryphon's Day (Montenegro and Bulgaria) (Trifon
  Zarezan), 2820
Tekakwitha (Kateri) Feast Day, 2939
Transfiguration, Feast of the, 3019
Visitation, Feast of the, 3019
Roman Games (Ludi Romani), 2422
Roman mythology
  Agonalia, 0035
  Anna Parenna Festival, 0108
Romania
  Christmas, 0622
  classical music festival, 0930
  dancing festival, 1364
  Easter feast, 0338
  folk festivals, 1741, 1934, 2631
  mischief commemoration, 2436
  national holiday, 2423
  new year, 2032
  New Year's Eve, 2035
  religious holiday, 1059
  wheat festival, 3208
  women's festival, 2427
Romania National Day, 2423
romazava, 0050

Rome
  See ancient Rome
Romería del Rocío
  See Pilgrimage of the Dew
Romulus, 0682, 0947
Ron blanco, 0513
Rondo Days Celebration, 2424
Rondy
  See Anchorage Fur Rendezvous
Roodmas
  See Exaltation of the Cross, Feast of the
Rooney, Mickey, 1180
Roosevelt, Franklin D., 0315, 0879, 2425
Roosevelt (Franklin D.) Day, 2425
Roosevelt, Theodore, 0369, 0593, 1840
Rooster Festival
  See Tori-no-ichi (Rooster Festival)
Roots Festival, 2426
Roper, Tony, 0773
Ropotine (Repotini), 2427
Roquefort cheese, 1187
Rosary, Festival of the, 2428
Rose Bowl Game, 2429
Rose Bowl parade, 0834
Rose Day
  See Alexandra Rose Day
Rose Festival, 2430
Rose Monday, 0980, 2431
Rose of Lima, 1049
Rose of Tralee Beauty Contest, 2432
Rose Sunday
  See Mothering Sunday
Rosen, Walter and Lucie, 0496
Rosenmontag
  See Rose Monday
Rosenthal, Jane, 3022
roses, 0061, 0430, 2298, 2957
Rosewall, Ken, 0194
Rosh Hashanah, 2433
Rosie the Ribiter (frog), 0458
Ross, Betsy, 1027
Rossini, Gioacchino, 0096
Roswell UFO Festival, 2434
Roud, Richard, 2043
Roughhouse Festival
  See Kenka Matsuri (Roughhouse Festival)
Rousa, Feast of, 2435
Rousalii, 2436
Route 66 Festival, 2437
rowing
  Asia, 0173
  England, 0823
  Italy, 2190
Royal, The
  See American Royal Livestock, Horse Show and Rodeo
Royal Adelaide Show
  See Royal Shows
Royal Air Force, 0003, 0263
Royal Ascot, 2438

royal birthday commemorations
    See also birthday commemorations
    Australia, 0917
    Belgium, 1560
    Bermuda, 0917
    China, 2971
    Denmark, 1561, 1778
    England, 0917, 1062
    Jordan, 0005
    Lesotho, 1562
    Liechtenstein, 2319
    Malaysia, 1753
    Netherlands, 1492
    Singapore, 2971
    Thailand, 1563, 2346
Royal Brunei Armed Forces Day, 2439
royal celebrations
    Channel Islands, 0264
    Denmark, 3106
    Germany, 1625
    Hawaii, 0933, 1511, 1592, 1858
    India, 1039
    Lithuania, 1686
    Nevis, 2012
    Thailand, 0558, 2960
    Tonga, 2623
    Vietnam, 1612
Royal Easter Show, 2440
Royal Hobart Regatta
    See Hobart Royal Regatta
Royal Malaysian Navy, 1077
Royal Meeting
    See Royal Ascot
Royal Melbourne Show
    See Royal Shows
Royal National Eisteddfod of Wales
    See Eisteddfod
Royal Oak Day, 1062
Royal Ploughing Ceremony, 2441
Royal Queensland Show
    See Royal Shows
Royal Shows, 2442
Royal Shrine Rite
    See Chongmyo Taeje (Royal Shrine Rite)
Royals
    See Royal Shows
Royaume, Mère, 0955
Rubinstein, Anton, 0391
rugby
    Bermuda, 0301
    England, 0965
Rugby Weeks
    See Bermuda College Weeks
Ruhr Festival, 2443
Ruiz, Rosie, 0375
Rukmini Ashtami, 2444
rum, 0513
Rumi Festival, 2445
Rumi, Jelaluddin al-, 3095

Run for the Roses
    See Kentucky Derby
Runeberg (Johan Ludvig), Birthday of, 2446
Rung Khelna
    See Holi
Running of the Bulls in Mexico, 2447
Running of the Spectres
    See Schemenlauf
running races
    ancient Rome, 2283, 2422
    California, 0270
    Cameroon, 1933
    Germany, 2540
    Greece, 2145
    Italy, 2353
    Massachusetts, 0375
    New York, 2042, 3173
    Pennsylvania, 3090
    Sweden, 2828
    Switzerland, 0955
Rural Life Sunday
    See Rogation Days
rushbearing ceremony, 1529
Rushbearing Festival, 2448
Russell (C. M.) Auction, 2449
Russia
    butter celebration, 0451
    Carnival celebration, 0451
    Christmas, 0623
    cosmonaut commemoration, 0697
    film festival, 1925
    medieval fair, 2077
    midnight sun festival, 3298
    military commemorations, 1824, 3140
    national holiday, 2474
    new year, 2033
    religious holidays, 0874, 0941, 0938, 1643
    summer twilight festival, 3212
    transgression festival, 1402
    winter festival, 2450
    woods ceremony, 2562
Russian Orthodox Christians
    Christmas, 0623
    Lent, 0451
Russian Winter Festival, 2450
Rwanda
    death commemoration, 2453
    gorilla commemorations, 1060, 1172
    independence day, 2451
    national holiday, 2452
Rwanda Independence Day, 2451
Rwanda Liberation Day, 2452
Rwanda National Heroes' Day, 2453

S

Saarinen, Eero, 0175
Saba Saba Day, 2454

Saba Saba Peasants' Day
    See Saba Saba Day
Sábado de Gloria
    See Holy Saturday (Mexico) (Sábado de Gloria)
Sabantui, 2455
Sabbat, 2456
Sabbath of Rabbi Isaac Mayer Wise, 2457
Sabine women, 0682
Sabzeh, 2644
Sacaea, 2458
Sacred Heart of Jesus, Feast of the, 2459
sacred music, 2343
sacred name days, 0092, 1074
Sadat, Anwar, 0147
Sadie Hawkins Day, 2460
Safari Rally, 2461
Saffron Rose Festival, 2462
Sagra di Sant' Efisio
    See Sant' Efisio, Festival of
Sahara National Festival, 2463
Saigon Liberation Day, 2464
Saigusa Matsuri, 2465
sailing events
    Antigua and Barbuda, 0121
    Germany, 1550
saint feast days
    Armenia, 2807
    Austria, 2768
    Belgium, 2724, 2738, 2742, 2783
    Bolivia, 2505, 2507
    Brazil, 2849
    Bulgaria, 2734, 2820
    Canada, 2699
    Central America, 2806
    Christian Orthodox Church, 2868, 2869, 2870
    Costa Rica, 3156
    Croatia, 2804
    Cyprus, 2706
    Czech Republic, 2822
    Denmark, 2755
    Egypt, 2784
    El Salvador, 2521
    England, 2467, 2696, 2704, 2705, 2710, 2712, 2714, 2723,
        2733, 2813
    Estonia, 2780
    Ethiopia, 2731
    Europe, 2703
    France, 0065, 2710, 2713, 2718, 2721, 2732, 2746, 2756,
        2783, 2835
    Georgia (country), 2733
    Germany, 2750, 2826
    Greece, 2706, 2720, 2757, 2784, 2786, 2787, 2810
    Guatemala, 2752
    Hungary, 2774, 2812
    Iceland, 2819
    India, 2590, 2818
    Ireland, 2708, 2709, 2717, 2758, 2792, 2793
    Italy, 2515, 2726, 2729, 2730, 2762, 2790, 2805
    Latvia, 2760

    Lebanon, 2775
    Louisiana, 0066
    Madeira, 2815
    Malta, 2761, 2798
    Mexico, 2500, 2701, 2744, 2751, 2809
    Montenegro, 2820
    New Mexico, 1303, 2481, 2490, 2496, 2499, 2745
    New York, 2489
    North Africa, 2702
    Norway, 2791
    Pakistan, 2818
    Paraguay, 2479, 2497
    Peru, 2488, 2498, 2525
    Philippines, 2806
    Poland, 2698
    Portugal, 1339, 2654, 2753, 2779, 2825
    Puerto Rico, 2745, 2754
    Quebec, 2699
    San Marino, 2503
    Scotland, 2697
    South America, 2806
    Spain, 2493, 2745, 2759, 2762, 2817
    Sweden, 2770
    Switzerland, 2814
    Syria, 2735
    United States, 2570, 2715, 2719, 2725, 2728
    Vietnam, 2057
    Wales, 2719
    worldwide, 0064, 2695, 2700
    Yugoslavia, 2808
Saintes Festival of Ancient Music, 2466
Saints Cyril and Methodius's Day
    See Bulgarian Education and Culture Day
Saints, Doctors, Missionaries, and Martyrs Day, 2467
Sajigor, 0563
Sakata Chauth, 2468
Salieri, Antonio, 0679
Sallah (Salah) Festival, 2469
Salley, Dempsey Hammond, 0609
salmon, 3275
Salon International de l'Artisanat de Ouagadougou, 0163
Salons Internationaux de l'Aéronautique et de l'Espace
    See Paris Air and Space Show
salsa dancing festival, 0462
Salsa Fair
    See Cali Fair (Sugar Cane Fair, Salsa Fair)
salt, 0367, 0739, 0935
Salt Festival
    See Cure Salée
salt flats, 0367
salt mines, 1584
salted cod, 1165
Saltzman, Royce, 2149
Salvation Army Founders' Day, 2470
Salzburg Festival, 2471
Sam Houston Day
    See Texas Independence Day
Samain
    See Samhain (Samain)

samba schools, 0512
Samhain (Samain), 0731, 1016, 2472
Sami Easter Festival, 2473
Sàmi National Holiday, 2474
Samil-jol (Independence Movement Day), 2475
Samis, 1202
Samoa
    independence day, 2476
    religious commemoration, 3214
Samoa Independence Day, 2476
Sample, Junior, 0706
Samson, 1134
samurai festivals, 3013, 0043
Samvatsari, 2477
San Antonio, Fiesta, 2478
San Antonio's Day
    See St. Anthony of Padua, Feast of
San Blas, Fiesta of, 2479
San Clemente Island, California, 0454
San Diego, California, 0454, 1035
San Diego Comic-Con International, 2480
San Estevan, Feast of, 2481
San Fermin Festival, 2482
San Francisco, California, 0161, 1035, 0270
San Francisco Ethnic Dance Festival, 2483
San Francisco, Fiesta of, 2484
San Francisco International Film Festival, 2485
San Francisco International LGBT Film Festival
    See Frameline: The San Francisco International LGBT
        Film Festival
San Francisco Lesbian, Gay, Bisexual, and Transgender
    (LGBT) Pride Celebration
    See San Francisco Pride
San Francisco Pride, 2486
San Francisco Street Food Festival, 2487
San Francisco Symphony, 0324
San Francisco's Day (Lima, Peru), 2488
San Gennaro, Feast of, 2489
San Geronimo Feast Day, 2490
San Ildefonso Firelight Dances, 2491
San Isidro in Peru, Fiesta of, 2492
San Isidro Labrador, 0495
San Isidro of Seville, Feast of, 2493
San Isidro the Farmer, Feast of, 2494
San Jacinto, 0051, 2495
San Jacinto Day, 2495
San José Day Festival, 2496
San Juan and San Pedro Festivals, 2497
San Juan Day
    See St. John's Day (Puerto Rico)
San Juan de Dios, Fiesta of, 2498
San Juan Fiesta
    See St. John's Day
San Juan Pueblo Feast Day, 2499
San Lorenzo, Día de, 2500
San Marino
    national holidays, 2501, 2503, 2771
    political ceremony, 2502
    saint feast day, 2503

San Marino Anniversary of the Arengo, 2501
San Marino Investiture of New Captains Regent, 2502
San Marino Liberation Day (Feast Day of Saint Agatha),
    2503
San Martin, 2340
San Martín Day, 2504
San Martín, Francisco de, 2504
San Martín, José, 0356
San Miguel, Fiesta de, 2505
San Paolino, 1677
San Pedro International Costa Maya Festival, 2506
San Roque, Fiesta of, 2507
sand, 0472
Sandburg, Carl, 2508
Sandburg Days Festival, 2508
Sandcastle Competition, 2509
Sanders, Colonel, 0629
Sangare, Omar, 3085
Sanghamita Day, 2510
Sango Festival, 2511
Sang-Sin
    See Lunar New Year
Sani Gourmet, 2512
Sanja Matsuri (Three Shrines Festival), 2513
Sankt Hans Aften
    See St. John's Eve (Denmark)
Sankt Hans Dag
    See St. Hans Festival
Sankt Placidusfest
    See St. Placidus Festival
Sanno Matsuri, 2514
Sant' Efisio, Festival of, 2515
Santa Anna, Antonio López de, 0051
Santa Claus, 0629, 3269, 1073
Santa Fe Chamber Music Festival, 2516
Santa Fe, Fiesta de, 2517
Santa Fe Opera Festival, 2518
Santa Inés, Fiesta of, 2519
Santa Isobel, Fiesta of, 2520
Santa Maria de los Angeles, 2124
Santa Marija
    See Assumption of Our Lady (Santa Marija)
Santa Rita, Fiesta of, 2521
Santa Rosalia Fishermen's Festival, 2522
Santacruzan
    See Exaltation of the Cross, Feast of the
Santamaría (Juan) Day, 2523
Santander International Festival of Music and Dance, 2524
Santo Niño, 0806
Santo Toribio Fiesta, 2525
Santon Fair, 0635, 2526
São Paulo Gay Pride Parade, 2527
São Tomé and Principe National Independence Day, 2528
São Vicente
    See St. Vincent's Day
Saora people, 2421
Sapporo Snow Festival (Yuki Matsuri), 2529
Sarajevo Symphony Orchestra, 0251
Sarasota Circus Festival and Parade, 2530

Sarasvati, 0855
Saratoga Festival, 2531
Sarazen, Gene, 0402
Sarbatoarea Blajinilor
     See Blajini, Feast of the (Sarbatoarea Blajinilor)
Sardinia, 0548
Saskatchewan, 3021
Sasquatch! Music Festival, 2532
Sassou-Nguesso, Denis, 0678
Sata-Häme Accordion Festival, 2533
Satchmo SummerFest, 2534
Saturday of Souls
     See Soul Saturdays (Saturday of Souls)
Saturn festival, 2536
Saturnalia, 0616, 2535
Saturnalia Roman Festival, 2536
Satyavati, 0308
Saudi Arabia
     cultural festivals, 2537, 0048
     religious pilgrimage, 2270
     soccer, 0025
     summer festival, 0006
Saudi Arabia National Heritage and Folk Culture
     Festival(Janadriyah Festival), 2537
sausage, 0218
Sausage Fair
     See Bad Durkheim Wurstmarkt (Sausage Fair)
Sausage Festival
     See Wurstfest (Sausage Festival)
Saut d'Eau, 2267
Savannah, Georgia, 1114
Savitri Vow
     See Savitri-Vrata (Savitri Vow)
Savitri-Vrata (Savitri Vow), 2538
Savonlinna Opera Festival, 2539
Saxony, 2391
Scaling the Walls
     See Escalade (Scaling the Walls)
Scandinavia
     animal roundup, 2388
     folk music festival, 1526
     summer-winter mock battle, 1827
     sun festival, 1877
     Yule log ceremony, 1499
Scandinavian festivals
     North Dakota, 2084
     Wisconsin, 1087
scarlet fever curing feast, 2435
Schäferlauf, 2540
Schemenlauf, 2541
Schilling, Jean and Lee, 0850
Schmeckostern, 0868
schoolchildren, 2737
Schoppen, 0218
science fiction, 0378
Schubert, Franz, 0502, 0679, 2542
Schubertiade, 2542
Schuddig Fools, 0980
Schueberfouer

     See Shepherd's Fair
Schuebermesse
     See Shepherd's Fair
Schumann, Benny, 0658
Schützenfest (Marksmen's Festival), 2543
Schutzengelfest (Festival of the Guardian Angel), 2544
Schuyler, Philip, 0431
Schwenkfelder Thanksgiving (Gedaechtnisz Tag), 2545
Scoppio del Carro, 0870
Scotland
     See also England; Great Britain; United Kingdom;
          Wales appearance of man wearing flowered headdress,
          0444
     arts festival, 0890
     birthday commemoration, 0443
     bonfires, 0365, 0439
     border commemoration, 0668
     boundary stone festival, 1626
     calendar event, 0290, 1063
     Christmas celebration, 2122
     classical guitar festival, 0852
     crossing a home's threshold, 1020
     ear commemoration, 2073
     end-of-the-year celebration, 1324
     film festival, 0891
     good luck tradition, 1277
     grouse season, 1147
     Halloween, 1271
     harvest festival, 1289
     horse racing, 1806
     Lenten carnival, 0985
     moving day, 1941
     music festival, 2416
     New Year's Eve, 2035
     pagan festival, 1619
     poetry celebration, 0443
     procession, 0439
     saint feast day, 2697
     sporting events, 0390, 0402, 1308
     weather festival, 0370
Scott, Myron, 0071
Scottish croquet, 0402
Scottish festivals
     Canada, 1090
     Michigan, 0073
     North Carolina, 1183
     Nova Scotia, 1090
     Virginia, 3158
Scottish Highlands, 0290
Scottish Highlands festival (Michigan), 0073
scouting celebrations (United States), 0387, 1144
scribe of the gods, 0457
sea animal festival, 1541
Sea, Festival of the (Seamen's Day, Sjomannadagur), 2546
sea festivals
     Belgium, 2800
     Hong Kong, 2986
     Iceland, 2546
     Java, 2549

Macao, 1817
South Korea, 0447
Sea Islands Black Heritage Festival, 2547
Sea Music Festival, 2548
Sea Offering Ceremonies, 2549
Seafair, 2550
Seagull-Calling Contest, 2551
Seal Festival
    See Keretkun Festival
Sealing the Frost, 2552
Seaman's Day
    See Sjomannadagur (Seaman's Day)
Seamen's Day
    See Sea, Festival of the (Seamen's Day, Sjomannadagur)
sean-nós, 0093
Seattle International Dance Festival, 2553
Seattle International Film Festival, 2554
Seattle, Washington, 0425, 0594, 0323
Sebring 12-Hour Race, 2555
Sechseläuten, 2556
Second Christmas Day, 0620
Second Temple, 1007
secretaries, 0021
Seged, 2557
Segrave, Henry, 0773
Seijin-no-Hi (Adults Day; Coming-of-Age Day), 2558
"Seinfeld," 0913
seises, los, 0524
Sekaten, 2559
Seker Bayrami
    See Id al-Fitr (Eid)
sékés, 0809
Selassie, Haile
    See Haile Selassie
Seles, Monica, 1080
Selma, Alabama, 0397
Semana Criolla (Gaucho Festival), 2560
Semana Santa, 0864
    See also Holy Week (Portugal) (Semana Santa)
Semana Santa (Guatemala), 2561
Semik, 2562
Seminole tribe, 0719
Sen, Aloke, 0855
Sending the Winter Dress, 2563
Senegal
    independence day, 2564
    pilgrimage, 1179
    religious festival, 0172
Senegal Independence Day, 2564
Senj International Summer Carnival, 2565
Sennin Gyoretsu
    See Toshogu Haru-No-Taisai (Great Spring Festival of the Toshogu Shrine)
Señor de los Milagros, 2566
Señor de Temblores Procession, 2567
Seraikella Chhau dance, 0583
Serbia
    historic commemoration, 2808
    music festivals, 0972

statehood day, 2568
Serbia Statehood Day of the Republic, 2568
Serbs, 0372
serenading nights
    Italy, 1831
    Spain, 1807
Serpent Parade, 0498
serpents, 0581
Serreta, Festa da, 2569
Servius Tullius, 0671
Seton, Elizabeth Ann, 2725
Seton, Ernest Thompson, 0387
Seton (Mother) Day, 2570
Setsubun (Bean-Throwing Festival), 2571
settlement celebrations
    Barbados, 1326
    Belize, 1104
Seven Herbs or Grasses Festival
    See Nanakusa Matsuri (Seven Herbs or Grasses Festival)
Seven Sisters Festival, 2572
Seven-Five-Three Festival
    See Shichi-Go-San (Seven-Five-Three Festival)
Seventh Evening
    See Chilseog (Seventh Evening)
Seventh-Day Adventists, 3034
Seville Fair, 2573
Seward, William Henry, 2574
Seward's Day, 2574
sewing, 0601
Seychelles
    independence day, 2575
    national holidays, 2576, 2577
Seychelles Independence Day, 2575
Seychelles Liberation Day, 2576
Seychelles National Day, 2577
sfintisori, 1059
Shaaban
    See Shab-Barat
Shab-Barat, 2578
    See also Laylat al-Bara'ah (Shab-Barat)
Shab-i-Barat
    See Shab-Barat
Shad Festival, 2579
shadow plays, 0217
Shah Abdul Latif Death Festival, 2580
Shaheed Day, 2581
Shahi Durbar, 2582
Shahid Day
    See Shaheed Day
Shahrewar, Feast of, 2583
Shaker Festivals, 2584
Shakers, 1649, 2584
Shakespeare festival, 2846, 2152
Shakespeare's (William) Birthday, 2585
Shakti, 3121
Shalako Ceremonial, 2586
Sham el-Nessim, 2587
Shambhala Music Festival, 2588
Shanghai International Film Festival, 2589

Shankaracharya Jayanti, 2590
Shanksville, Pennsylvania, 2226
Shantanu, 0308
shape-note singing, 0313
Sharad Purnima, 2591
Sharpton, Al, 0028
Shavuot (Shabuoth), 2592
Shaw, Robert, 0096
shaykh festival, 1950
shearing competition, 1161
Sheboygan Bratwurst Days, 2593
Sheelah's Day, 2594
Sheep Counting
    See Simbra Oiler
sheep events
    Germany, 2540
    Iowa, 1425
    Montana, 1199
    Morocco, 1788
    Romania, 2631
    New Zealand, 1161
Sheer Thursday
    See Maundy Thursday
Sheikh Shakhbut Bin-Sultan Al Nahyan, 0014
Sheikh Zayed bin Sultan Al Nahyan, 0014
shellfish festival, 2595
Shellfish Gathering (Shiohi-gari), 2595
shelves, 0616
Shembe Festival, 2596
Shembe, Isaiah, 2596
Shemini Atzeret, 2597
Shenandoah Apple Blossom Festival, 2598
shepherds, 1102, 2784
Shepherd's Fair, 2599
Shepherds' Festival/Mass, 0635
Shere
    See Maundy Thursday
Shetland Islands, 3091
Shichi-Go-San (Seven-Five-Three Festival), 2600
Shick-Shack Day, 1105
Shick-Shack Day (Shik-Shak Day; Shicsack Day; Shig-Shag Day), 2601
Shicsack Day, Shick–Shack Day (Shik–Shak Day; Shicsack Day; Shig–Shag Day)
Shigmo Festival, 2602
Shigmotsav
    See Shigmo Festival
Shig-Shag Day,
    Shick–Shack Day (Shik–Shak Day; Shicsack Day; Shig–Shag Day)
Shi'ite Muslims
    See also Islamic events; Sunni Muslims Imam Ali commemorations, 1403, 1404
    Islamic history commemorations, 0136, 0137
    Laylat al-Bara'ah (Shab-Barat), 1639
    religious festival, 0172
Shik-Shak Day
    See Shick-Shack Day (Shik-Shak Day; Shicsack Day; Shig-Shag Day)

Shilla (Silla) Cultural Festival, 2603
Shinbyu, 2604
Shinju Matsuri Festival, 2605
Shinnecock Powwow, 2606
    See also American Indians
Shinran-Shonin Day, 2607
Shinto events
    Japan, 0304, 0608, 1252, 1305, 1450, 2465, 3008, 2389
Shiohi-gari
    See Shellfish Gathering (Shiohi-gari)
ship festival, 3232
shipping holiday, 1783
Shiprock Navajo Nation Fair, 2608
ships, 2787
shipwrecked sailor's church, 0981
Shishi Odori (Deer Dance), 2609
Shiva, Lord, 0016, 0079, 0171, 0307, 0767, 1099, 1101, 1152, 2296
Shivah Asar be-Tammuz
    See Tammuz, Fast of the 17th of (Shivah Asar be-Tammuz); Three Weeks
Shivaratri, 2610
Shluh, 0474
shoes, 0625, 0635
Shogatsu
    See Lunar New Year
Shoghi Effendi, 0004
shooting, 0641, 1577
shooting stars, 2244
shopping fair, 0052, 0489
Shoshone Indians, 0135
    See also American Indians
Shouting Festival
    See Yaya Matsuri (Shouting Festival)
Shravani Mela, 2611
shrimp events
    Alabama, 0343, 2612
    Florida, 1436
    Louisiana, 1704
Shrimp Festival and Blessing of the Fleet
    See Louisiana Shrimp and Petroleum Festival
Shrimp Festival, National, 2612
shrine celebrations
    Japan, 1521, 1534, 2137, 3037, 3287
    Mongolia, 2173
Shrove Monday, 2613
Shrove Sunday
    See Shrovetide (Norway) (Fastelawn)
Shrove Tuesday, 0392, 0980, 2614
Shrove Tuesday (Bohemia), 2615
Shrove Tuesday (Estonia), 2616
Shrove Tuesday (Finland), 2617
Shrove Tuesday (Netherlands), 2618
Shrove Tuesday (Pennsylvania Dutch), 2619
Shrovetide buns, 0984
Shrovetide (Norway) (Fastelawn), 2620
Shunbun-no-Hi (Vernal Equinox Day), 2621
Shuni-e
    See Omizutori Matsuri (Water-Drawing Festival)

Numbers in the index refer to entry numbers, not page numbers

Shuttlecock Day
    See Shrove Tuesday
Shwedagon Pagoda Festival, 2622
Siam, 0645
Siaosi Tupou I (King) Day, 2623
Sibelius Festival, 2624
Sibelius, Jean, 2624
Siberia, 1541
sibling festivals
    India, 2361, 0306
    Nepal, 2361
Siddhartha Guatama, 0351
Siebold, George, 1155
Siebold, Grace Darling, 1155
Sierra Leone
    death commemoration, 0201
    independence day, 2625
    lantern festivity, 1630
    religious festival, 0172
Sierra Leone Independence Day, 2625
Sigd, 0964
Sigmaringen, Germany, 0392
Signal: Prague Light Festival, 2626
Sihanouk (King) Commemoration Day, 2627
Sihanouk, Norodom, King of Cambodia, 2627
Sikh events
    birthday commemorations, 1237, 1239, 1242
    guru commemorations, 1236, 1237, 1238, 1239, 1240, 1242, 1243
    Hola Mohalla, 1325
    Lohri, 1692
    Maghi, 1736
    martyr commemoration, 1236, 1243
    Vaisakh, 3104
Silent Days, 2628
"Silent Night, Holy Night" Celebration, 2629
Silent Week
    See Holy Week
Silvesterabend
    See New Year's Eve (Germany) (Silvesterabend)
Silvesterklausen
    See Old Silvester
Simadan Festival, 2630
Simbang Gabi
    See Misa de Gallo
Simbra Oilor (Sheep Counting), 2631
Simeon, 0485
Simhat Tbet ha-Sho'evah
    See Water-Drawing Festival
Simhat Torah, 2632
Sinai Liberation Day, 2633
Singapore
    cleansing ritual, 2070
    food festival, 1871, 2634
    national holiday, 2635
    royal birthday, 2971
    Singapore Food Festival, 2634
Singapore National Day, 2635
singing competitions

Ireland, 0093
    Italy, 0459
Singing to Rings
    See Ladouvane
Sinhala Avurudu, 2636
Sinjska Alka, 2637
Sinking Creek Film Celebration
    See Nashville Film Festival
Sint Maartens Dag
    See Martinmas
Sinterklass, 0629
Sinulog Festival, 2638
Sioux Sun Dance, 2639
Sioux Indians, 0717, 0858, 1154, 2639
    See also American Indians
Sirius, 0686, 0822
Sisters' Meals Festival, 2640
Sita, 0855
Sitala Ashtami, 2641
Sithinakha, 2642
Sitka Summer Music Festival, 2643
siyyum, 1024
Sizdah Bedar, 2644
Sjomannadagur (Seaman's Day), 2645
    See also Sea, Festival of the (Seamen's Day, Sjoman-nadagur)
Skanda Sashti, 2646
Skanderbeg, 0055
skiing events
    Greenland, 0139
    Montana, 1197
    Norway, 1330
    Sweden, 3119
    Wisconsin, 0082
skillets, 0552
Skipjack Races and Land Festival, 2647
skrobanki, 1169
skulls, 1139
skydiving festival, 1540
Slack, David, 3065
slavery
    See also abolition; emancipation
    Benin, 0292
    Gambia, 2426
    New York, 1717
    Ontario, 0090
Slavonic alphabet, 0421
sledding holidays
    Estonia, 2616
    Finland, 2617
sled dog races
    Alaska, 0097, 0974, 1399, 2998
    Canada, 0499
    Minnesota, 0277
    Northwest Territories, 0499
    Oregon, 2151
Slide of the Great Cask
    See St. Leopold's Day
Slovak Republic

Numbers in the index refer to entry numbers, not page numbers

classical music festival, 0391
harvest festival, 2106
independence day, 2648
Slovak Republic Independence Day, 2648
Slovenia National Day, 2649
smigus, 0873
Smiley, Jim, 0458
Smith, Brendan, 0847
Smith, Harvy, 0594
Smith, Henry Weston "Preacher," 0702
Smith, Hyrum, 1799
Smith, Joseph, 1799
Smith, Mary Carter, 0336
Smithsonian Kite Festival, 2651
Smithville Fiddlers Jamboree and Crafts Festival, 2652
smoke detectors, 1017
Smoke Nights, 0942
smoking cessation/discouragement day, 1193
Snake Dance, 0179
snake dances, 0179, 1363
snake festivals
    India, 1476, 1967
    Japan, 3082
    Nepal, 1967
snake roundup, 1924
Snan Yatra, 2653
snorkeling, 0352
snow events
    Finland, 3300
    Greenland, 2098
    Japan, 1510, 2529, 3300
Snow Hut Festival
    See Kamakura Matsuri (Snow Hut Festival)
Snow Purim
    See Purims, Special
Snowbirds Jet Team, 0003
Snowy River Race, 0643
So Joo Festival: The Eve of St. John's Feast Day, 2654
Soap Box Derby, 0071
Sobhuza Day
    See Swaziland Independence Day
soccer, 3255
Society of Friends, 1067
Society of Jesus, 2743
socks, 0438
Sofia Music Weeks, 2655
Soil Stewardship Sunday
    See Rogation Days
Sokjon-Taeje Memorial Rites, 2656
Sol, 2657
Solday
    See Sun Pageant Day
Solemnity of Mary, the Mother of God
    See Circumcision, Feast of the
solidarity events
    non-self-governing territories, 3199
    Palestine, 2658
Solidarity (Poland), 2292

Solidarity with the Palestinian People, International Day of, 2658
Solomon Islands Independence Day, 2659
Solomon, Izler, 1028
solstice festivals
    ancient Rome, 2535
    China, 3238
    England, 0843, 3064
    Finland, 1491
    Inca empire, 0491
    Japan, 2997
    Korea, 0833
    Peru, 1424
    Vietnam, 0816
    worldwide, 2862, 3237
Solum, John, 0679
Somalia Independence Day, 2660
Soma-Nomaioi
    See Wild Horse Festival (Soma-Nomaioi)
Somba Damba, 0755
Somhlolo Day
    See Swaziland Independence Day
"Song Celestial," 1043
Song of Hiawatha Pageant, 2661
Song of the Harvest
    See Aymuray (Song of the Harvest)
Songkran, 2662
Sonoma County Harvest Fair, 2663
Sons of Daniel Boone, 0387
Soot Sweeping
    See Susuharai (Soot Sweeping)
Sopatrus, 0384
sorghum, 2630
Sorrowful Friday
    See Good Friday
sotadera, 0490
Soto, Hernando de, 1047
Soul Saturdays (Saturday of Souls), 2664
Soulé, John Babsone, 0427
souls festivals
    China, 3079
    Vietnam, 3079
Sound Symposium, 2665
South Africa
    agricultural festival, 2368
    arts festival, 2668
    black citizens freedom day, 2666
    Botswana interracial marriage, 0380
    Christmas, 0624
    film festivals, 0854
    founder's day, 1926
    military commemoration, 2377
    music festival, 0492
    national holidays, 2667, 2669
    racial discrimination elimination day, 0915
    religious festival, 2596
    tip-collection day, 0386
    women's day, 2670
    youth day, 2671

Numbers in the index refer to entry numbers, not page numbers

South Africa Freedom Day, 2666
South Africa Heritage Day, 2667
South Africa National Arts Festival (Grahamstown Festival), 2668
South Africa Republic Day, 2669
South Africa Women's Day, 2670
South Africa Youth Day, 2671
South America, 2806
    See also individual countries
South Australian Jockey Club, 0018
South by Southwest
    See SXSW (South by Southwest)
South by Southwest Film
    See SXSW (South by Southwest) Film
South Carolina
    arts festivals, 2153, 2688
    automobile race, 2676
    beach festival, 2863
    death commemoration, 0675
    food festivals, 0609, 2672, 0565
    Gullah festival, 1989
    home tours, 1373
    wine festival, 0565
South Carolina Peach Festival, 2672
South Dakota
    American Indian celebration, 0717
    buffalo roundup, 0741
    corn festival, 0687
    food festival, 3152
    gold festivals, 0771, 1154
    historical reenactment, 0771
    literature pageant, 3225
    motorcycle racing, 2852
    Mount Rushmore commemoration, 0369
    religious play, 0329
South Korea
    See also Korea constitution day, 2673
    film festival, 0446
    food festival, 1247
    memorial day, 2674
    military commemorations, 1195
    mud festival, 0371
    national holidays, 1585, 1586, 3092
    sea festival, 0447
    soccer, 0025
South Korea Constitution Day, 2673
South Korea Memorial Day, 2674
South Sudan
    historic celebrations, 2675
    independence day, 2675
South Sudan Independence Day, 2675
South West Africa People's Organization (SWAPO), 0544
Southern 500, 2676
Southern Harmony singing, 0313
Southern Hemisphere, 3131
Southern United States, 0674, 0675
Southern University, 0272
Southern Ute Indians, 2677, 3101
    See also American Indians

Southern Ute Tribal Sun Dance, 2677
Southwestern Exposition Livestock Show & Rodeo, 2678
Souvenance, Haiti, 2274
Soviet Union
    Christmas, 0623
    collapse of, 0207
    Estonia, 0958
    national holiday, 0358
    rule of, 0208
Soweto Day
    See South Africa Youth Day
Soyaluna (Hopi Soyal Ceremony), 2679
space commemorations
    United Nations, 3271
    United States, 1913, 1980
Spain
    acrobat show, 1377
    arts festival, 1206
    bullfighting festival, 2494
    Carnival celebrations, 0432, 0524
    Christmas, 0625
    coffin procession, 2776
    cow racing, 0707
    cultural festival, 2573
    dance events, 0490, 0524, 1956, 2524
    food fight, 3001
    friendship commemoration, 3023
    harvest renewal, 0662
    herbal festival, 2462
    maypole ritual, 1828
    military commemoration, 1915
    music festivals, 1956, 2482, 2524
    New Year's Eve, 2040
    religious celebrations, 0875, 1170, 1225, 1854, 2237, 2493
    religious pilgrimages, 2266, 2268
    religious play, 1963
    Rock of Gibraltar, 1135
    saint feast days, 2493, 2745, 2759, 2762, 2817
    serenading night, 1807
    tree-planting ceremony, 2276
    Virgin Mary commemoration, 3157
    wine festivals, 3124, 1287
Spam, 1769, 2680
Spamarama, 2680
Spanish-American festival, 2127
Spanish-American War Memorial Day
    See Maine Memorial Day
Sparta, 0507
Spearing the Dragon
    See Drachenstich (Spearing the Dragon)
spears, 1143
Special Olympics, 2681
speed records, 0367
Speight, George, 1011
Spel van Sint Evermarus
    See St. Evermaire, Game of
Spencer, Baldwin, 0120
Spencer, Peter, 0031
Spendarmad, Feast of, 2682

spider festival, 2927
Spiedie Fest and Balloon Rally, 2683
spikes, 1162
spinach, 0630
Spinning Maiden, 0601
Spirit Burying, 2684
spirit ceremonies
    ancient Rome, 0992
    Cameroon, 2058
    Côte d'Ivoire, 0809
    Hong Kong, 0581
    India, 2222
    Korea, 2684
    Mexico, 0800
    Myanmar, 2933
    Philippines, 1139
Spiritual Baptist (Shouters) Liberation Day, 2685
spiritual music, 2343
Spock Days/Galaxyfest, 2686
Spoken Word Festival, Calgary International, 2687
Spoleto Festival USA, 2688
sponges, 0941
sporting events
    See also individual sports
    Alaska, 1399, 3261
    ancient Greece, 0126, 1442, 2005, 2335
    ancient Rome, 1710, 2283, 2422
    Arkansas, 3275
    Asia, 0173
    Australia, 0194
    Bermuda, 0738
    California, 2429, 3272, 1110
    Canada, 1576
    cricket, 0720
    Denmark, 0146
    England, 0381, 0823, 0965, 1188, 1383, 3230, 0702
    Florida, 2147
    Georgia, 1811
    Greenland, 0139
    Hawaii, 1431
    Iroquois, 1288
    Italy, 1142, 2190
    Japan, 0231, 2906
    Louisiana, 2857
    Michigan, 1723
    Minnesota, 0284
    Mongolia, 1966
    Montana, 1197
    Netherlands, 0913
    New Jersey, 1772
    Norway, 1330
    Olympic Games, 2134
    Pennsylvania, 1688, 3090
    Scotland, 0390, 1308
    Special Olympics, 2681
    Sweden, 2828, 3119
    Switzerland, 1577
    Turkey, 3056
    United States, 1688, 2414, 2874, 3086, 3087, 3270, 0155

    Wales, 0352
    Wisconsin, 2288
    World Cup, 3255
    Yukon Territory, 1576
Sprangprocession
    See Dancing Procession
Spreckles, Joan, 1088
Spring Break, 2689
spring celebrations
    Afghanistan, 1998
    ancient Greece, 0116
    China, 1661, 0347
    Finland, 3117
    Greece, 2881
    Hungary, 0410
    India, 0078, 1327, 1998, 3120, 2602
    Iran, 1998
    Italy, 0995
    Japan, 1307
    Kashmir, 1998
    Korea, 0971
    Kuwait, 1262
    Poland, 1808
    Switzerland, 2556
    Turkey, 1306
    Turkmenistan, 1998
spring chores, 0982
Spring Festival
    See Lunar New Year
Spring of Culture, 2690
Spring Racing Carnival
    See Melbourne Cup Day
Springtime Festival, 2691
Spy Wednesday, 2693
Spyan-ras gzigs, 1046
squirrels, 2133
Sri Lanka
    Buddha's tooth celebration, 0953
    Buddhism holiday, 2304
    mountain climbing, 0016
    national holiday, 2693
    new year, 2636
    religious festivals, 1523, 2510
Sri Lanka National Day, 2693
St. Agatha Festival, 2694
St. Agnes' Eve, 2695
St. Alban's Day, 2696
St. All-Fools' Morn
    See April Fools' Day
St. Andrew's Day, 0965, 2697
St. Andrew's Eve (Noc Swietego Andreja), 2698
St. Andrews golf course, 0402
St. Anne's Day, 2699
St. Anthony of Padua, Feast of, 2700
St. Anthony the Abbot, Feast of, 2701
St. Augustine of Hippo, Feast of, 2702
St. Barbara's Day, 2703
St. Barnabas's Day, 2704
St. Bartholomew's Day, 0250, 2705

Numbers in the index refer to entry numbers, not page numbers

St. Basil, Feast of, 2706
St. Benedict's Rule of Life, 0898
St. Benito, 0335
St. Blaise's Day, 2707
St. Brendan, 0725
St. Brendan's Day, 2708
St. Bridget's Day, 2709
St. Catherine's Day, 2710
St. Catherine's Day (Estonia), 2711
St. Cecilia's Day, 2712
St. Charlemagne's Day, 2713
St. Charles's Day, 2714
St. Christopher's Day, 2715
St. Clare of Assisi, Feast of, 2716
St. Columba's Day, 2717
St. Crispin's Day, 2718
St. Cyril, 0421
St. David's Day, 2719
St. Demetrius's Day, 2720
St. Denis's Day, 2721
St. Dismas's Day, 2722
St. Distaff's Day
    See Distaff Day
St. Dunstan's Day, 2723
St. Dymphna's Day, 2724
St. Edmund of Abingdon's Feast Day, 0908
St. Elijah's Uprising Day
    See Macedonian Ilinden (St. Elijah's Uprising Day)
St. Elizabeth Ann Seton, Feast of, 2725
St. Elmo's Day, 2726
St. Erasmus, 2726
St. Evermaire, Game of, 2727
St. Frances Cabrini, Feast of, 2728
St. Frances of Rome, Feast of, 2729
St. Francis of Assisi, 0459, 0636, 1057
St. Francis of Assisi, Feast of, 2730
St. Gabriel, Feast of, 2731
St. Gens, Festival of (La Fête de St. Gens), 2732
St. George, 1156
St. George's Caye Day
    See Belize National Day
St. George's Day, 2733
St. George's Day (Bulgaria), 2734
St. George's Day (Syria) (Id Mar Jurjus), 2735
St. George's Parade
    See Georgiritt (St. George's Parade)
St. Giles Fair, 2736
St. Gregory Palamas, 2868
St. Gregory's Day, 2737
St. Gudula's Day, 2738
St. Hans Festival, 2739
St. Helena, 0970
St. Herman Pilgrimage, 2740
St. Hilary's Day, 2741
St. Hubert de Liège, Feast of, 2742
St. Ignatius Loyola, Feast of, 2743
St. Ignatius Loyola Picnic
    See St. Ignatius Loyola, Feast of
St. Isidore, Festival of, 2744

St. Isidore the Farmer, 0495
St. James's Day, 2745
St. Joan of Arc, Feast Day of, 2746
St. Joan's Day
    See St. Joan of Arc, Feast Day of
St. John Climacos, 2869
St. John Lateran, Feast of the Dedication of, 2747
St. John the Baptist, 2654
St. John the Baptist, Martyrdom of, 2748
St. John the Divine
    See St. John the Evangelist's Day
St. John the Evangelist's Day, 2749
St. John's Day, 0960, 2751
    See also St. Hans Festival
St. John's Day (Guatemala), 2752
St. John's Day (Portugal), 2753
St. John's Day (Puerto Rico), 2754
St. John's Eve and Day (Latvia) (Jans vakars), 2760
St. John's Eve (Denmark), 2755
St. John's Eve (France) (La Vielle de la Saint Jean), 2756
St. John's Eve (Germany) (Johannisnacht), 2750
St. John's Eve (Greece), 2757
St. John's Eve (Ireland), 2758
St. John's Eve (Spain), 2759
St. Joseph the Worker, Feast of, 2761
St. Joseph's Day, 2762
St. Joseph's Historic Foundation, 0422
St. Jude's Day, 2763
St. Kitts and Nevis
    Caribbean community commemoration, 0500
    independence day, 2764
    national holiday, 2765
St. Kitts and Nevis Independence Day, 2764
St. Kitts and Nevis National Heroes Day, 2765
St. Knut's Day, 2766
St. Lazarus's Day, 2767
St. Leonard, 2350
St. Leonard's Ride
    See Leonhardiritt (St. Leonard's Ride)
St. Leopold's Day, 2768
St. Lucia
    Caribbean community commemoration, 0500
    flower festival, 1049
    independence day, 2769
St. Lucia Independence Day, 2769
St. Lucy's Day, 0928, 2770
St. Maarten, 0673
St. Mammertus, 1084
St. Marinus Day, 2771
St. Mark, Fair of (Feria de San Marcos), 2772
St. Mark's Day, 2773
St. Mark's Day (Hungary), 2774
St. Maron's Day, 2775
St. Martha, Coffin Fiesta of, 2776
St. Martha's Day, 2777
St. Martin, 0673
St. Martin of Tours, 1796, 1797, 1798
St. Martin's Carnival, 2778
St. Martin's Day

See Martinmas (Ireland)
St. Martin's Day (Portugal), 2779
St. Martin's Eve (Estonia) (Mardi Päev), 2780
St. Mary of Egypt, 2870
St. Mary's County Oyster Festival, 2781
St. Matthias's Day, 2782
St. Médardus's Day, 2783
St. Mennas's Day, 2784
St. Methodius, 0421
St. Michael's Day, 2785
St. Modesto's Day, 2786
St. Nichiren's Pardon, Festival of, 2787
St. Nicholas of Metz, 0629
St. Nicholas's Day, 2788
St. Nicholas's Day (Greece), 2789
St. Nicholas's Day (Italy), 2790
St. Odilo, 0069
St. Olav's Day, 2791
St. Oswald's Day, 0656
    See also Leap Year Day
St. Pancras, 1084
St. Patrick's Day, 0968, 2792
St. Patrick's Day Encampment, 2794
St. Patrick's Day (Ireland), 2793
St. Patrick's Day Parade (Savannah, Georgia), 2795
St. Paul, Feast of the Conversion of, 2796
St. Paul Winter Carnival, 2797
St. Paulinus, 1137
St. Paul's Shipwreck, Feast of, 2798
St. Peter's Chair, Festival of, 2799
St. Peter's Day
    See St. Peter's Fiesta
St. Peter's Day (Belgium), 2800
St. Peter's Fiesta, 2801
St. Placidus Festival, 2802
St. Polycarp's Day, 2803
St. Rocco's Celebration (Rokovo), 2804
St. Roch's Day, 2805
St. Rose of Lima's Day, 2806
St. Sarkis's Day, 2807
St. Sava's Day, 2808
St. Sebastian's Day, 2809
St. Servatus, 1084
St. Sigisbert, 2802
St. Spyridon (Spiridion) Day, 2810
St. Stephen's Day, 2811
St. Stephen's Day (Hungary), 2812
St. Swithin's Day, 2813
St. Sylvester's Day, 2814
St. Sylvester's Day (Madeira), 2815
St. Tammany's Day, 2816
St. Teresa's Day, 2817
St. Thomas, 0016
St. Thomas's Day, 0826, 2818
St. Thorlak's Day, 2819
St. Tryphon's Day (Montenegro and Bulgaria) (Trifon
    Zarezan), 2820
St. Urho's Day, 2821
St. Vaclav's Day, 2822

St. Valentine's Day
    See Valentine's Day
St. Vincent, 3151
St. Vincent and the Grenadines
    Caribbean community commemoration, 0500
    independence day, 2823
    national holiday, 2824
St. Vincent and the Grenadines Independence and
    Thanksgiving Day, 2823
St. Vincent and the Grenadines National Heroes Day, 2824
St. Vincent's Day, 2825
St. Vitus's Day, 2826
St. Vladimir's Day, 2827
St. Walter, 1224
St. Waudru, 1156
St. Wenceslas, 0745
    See also St. Vaclav's Day
St. Wilfred, 0762
St. Willibrord, 0762
Stalin, Joseph, 0623
Stanford, Leland, 1162
Stånga Games, 2828
Stanton, Elizabeth Cady, 0117, 2829
Stanton (Elizabeth Cady) Day, 2829
Star Boys, 0940
star celebration, 2244
Star Festival, 2830
star festivals
    China, 2830
    Japan, 2919
Star Trek festival, 2686
Starsingers, 0935
"Star-Spangled Banner, The," 0936
State Fair of Texas, 2831
state fairs
    Iowa, 1425
    New Jersey, 1036
    Texas, 2831
State Opening of Parliament, 2832
Stations of the Cross, 1164
Ste. Anne d'Auray, 2211
Ste. Geneviève, Jour de Fête à (Days of Celebration), 2833
steak, 1738
steaua, 0622
steeplechase, 1180
Stegosaurus Stomp, 0807
Steinbeck (John) Festival, 2834
Steirischer Herbst
    See Styrian Autumn (Steirischer Herbst)
Sternsinger, 0935
sternwheeler, 2115
Stes. Maries, Fête des, 2835
Steuben (Baron Friedrich) Day, 2836
Steuben, Baron Friedrich von, 0788, 2836
Stevens, Isaac, 0594
Stevens, J. C., 0089
Stewardship Sunday, 2837
stickball, 0611
Stickdance, 2838

Sticky-Sticky Fair
  See Bettara-Ichi
Stiftungsfest, 2839
Still Days
  See Silent Days
Still Week
  See Holy Week
Stillman, William O., 0274
Stir-Up Sunday, 2840
Stjärngossar, 0940
St.-John's-wort, 2751
Stockton Asparagus Festival, 2841
stone festival, 1602
Stonehenge, 0843
stone-throwing ritual, 0792
Stonewall Rebellion, Anniversary of the, 2842
Stonewall Riots, 2044
stool festival, 0015
Store Bededag, 2843
Storytelling Festival, National, 2844
storytelling festivals
  Bermuda, 2942
  Canada, 2942, 3301
  Tennessee, 2844
  United States, 0336, 2942
  Yukon Territory, 3301
Stourbridge Fair, 2845
Stowe, Harriet Beecher, 0922
Stratford Festival, 2846
Stratton, Charles Sherwood, 0247
strawberries, 0629, 2847, 3203
Strawberry Festival, 2847
strawberry shortcake, 0629
Struga Poetry Evenings, 2848
Struggle for Freedom and Democracy Day
  See Students' Fight for Freedom and Democracy, Day
    of (Struggle for Freedom and Democracy; World
    Students' Day)
Sts. Cosmas and Damian Day, 2849
Sts. Peter and Paul Day, 2850
Students' Fight for Freedom and Democracy, Day of
  (Struggle for Freedom and Democracy; World Students'
  Day), 2851
student-shooting memorial, 1535
Sturgis Motorcycle Rally, 2852
Stuttgart Festival of Animated Film, 2853
Styrian Autumn (Steirischer Herbst), 2854
success, 1099
Sucre, Antonio José de, 0888
Sudan Independence Day, 2855
Sufi Muslim festival, 2445
Sufism, 0766, 2445
Sugar Ball Show (Sugar-Coated Haws Festival), 2856
Sugar Bowl Classic, 2857
sugar cane
  Barbados, 0728
  Colombia, 0462
  Louisiana, 1705
Sugar Cane Fair

  See Cali Fair (Sugar Cane Fair, Salsa Fair)
Sugar-Coated Haws Festival
  See Sugar Ball Show (Sugar-Coated Haws Festival)
Sugawara no Michizane, 3098
Sukkot (Sukkoth, Succoth), 2858
Sukuna, Rau Sir Lala, 1011
Sumamao, Fiesta de, 2859
Suminuri Matsuri, 2860
Summer Festival, 2861
summer festivals
  Denmark, 2991
  Greece, 0184
  Iceland, 1019
  Islam, 3213
  Japan, 3179
  Michigan, 0077
  Minnesota, 1886
  Morocco, 1957
  Russia, 3212
  Virginia, 3242
Summer Solstice, 2862
summer solstice celebrations
  England, 0843
  Finland, 1491
  Vietnam, 0816
  worldwide, 2862
Summer Solstice Day
  See Doan Ngu (Summer Solstice Day)
summer temperatures, 0822
summer-day cakes, 1019
summer-winter mock battle, 1827
sun celebrations
  Alaska, 1875
  India, 1733
  Israel, 0344
  Nepal, 1733
  Norway, 2864
  Peru, 1424
  Scandinavia, 1877
  South America, 2863
  Sweden, 1877
  Wyoming, 0135
Sun Dance, 0135
Sun Day
  See Sun Pageant Day
Sun Festival
  See Inti Raymi Fiesta
Sun Fun Festival, 2863
Sun Pageant Day, 2864
Sun Yat-sen, 0836
Sun Yat-sen, Birthday of, 2865
Sunan Bayat, 2275
Sundance Film Festival, 2866
Sundara, 0198
Sunday of Orthodoxy, 2867
Sunday of St. Gregory Palamas, 2868
Sunday of St. John Climacos, 2869
Sunday of St. Mary of Egypt, 2870
Sunday of the Holy Cross, 2871

Numbers in the index refer to entry numbers, not page numbers

Sunday School Day, 2872
Sundiata, Festival, 2873
sunflowers, 1768
Sunni Muslims
    See also Islamic events; Shi'ite Muslims
    Imam Ali's Birthday, 1403
    Laylat al-Bara'ah (Shab-Barat), 1639
Super Bowl Sunday, 2874
Superman Celebration, 2875
Suquamish Indians, 0594
    See also American Indians
surfing contests, 0418
Suriname
    Caribbean community commemoration, 0500
    independence day, 2876
Suriname Independence Day, 2876
Surisan, 0563
Surya Sashti, 2877
Susuharai (Soot Sweeping), 2878
Sutherland, Joan, 1149
Sutter, John A., 0465
Suwa Shrine, 0610
Svensk Hyllningsfest
    See Swedish Homage Festival
Svenskarnas Dag, 2879
Svetambaras Jains, 0045
Svetitskhovloba, 2880
Svetla Nedelya, 0863
Swallow, Procession of the, 2881
Swallows of San Juan Capistrano, 2882
Swan, Joseph Wilson, 0893
Swan Upping, 2883
Swarupa Dwadashi, 2884
Swaziland
    dance ceremony, 2383
    fertility festival, 2000
    independence celebration, 2885
Swaziland Independence Day, 2885
Sweden
    bonfires, 0876
    Christmas celebrations, 0626, 2766
    death commemoration, 1244
    film festival, 1174
    flag and constitution commemoration, 2886
    national holiday, 2474
    political speeches, 1827
    religious holidays, 0115, 0876, 0940, 1796
    saint feast day, 2770
    ski race, 3119
    sporting events, 2828, 3119
    sun festival, 1877
    winter fair, 1202
    winter sports, 0876
Swedenborg, Emanuel, 2014
Swedish festivals
    California, 1564
    Illinois, 1484
    Kansas, 2887
    Minnesota, 2879

Swedish Flag Day, 2886
Swedish Homage Festival, 2887
sweet potatoes, 2931
Sweetest Day, 2888
Sweetwater Rattlesnake Round-Up, 2889
Swidges
    See Silent Days
Swieto Trzeciego Maja
    See Polish Constitution Day
swimming
    Asia, 0173
    Canada, 2288
    Italy, 2190
    Olympic Games, 2134
    Wisconsin, 2288
Swing Day
    See Tano Festival (Dano-nal; Swing Day)
Swing Festival
    See Holi
Swiss festivals (Wisconsin), 1296, 2940, 3165
Swiss National Day, 2890
Switzerland
    art festival, 0156
    bell celebrations, 0525, 0559
    cantonal meeting, 1624
    Carnival, 0525
    chamber music festival, 1853
    cheese commemoration, 1021
    Christmas Eve, 0637
    classical music festival, 1709
    community festival, 0241
    cow fight, 0708
    dead goose festival, 1103
    fishing celebration, 1220
    food festivals, 2352, 3316
    herding festival, 0076
    jazz festival, 1912
    masks, 0525
    military commemoration, 0955
    military reenactment, 1845
    music festival, 1480
    national holiday, 2890
    new year, 2034
    nut activity, 0295
    parade, 0525
    religious celebrations, 0694, 2284, 2544, 2802
    religious drama, 1205
    running race, 0955
    saint feast day, 2814
    sporting event, 1577
    spring festival, 2556
    theater, 2941
    tree-planting ritual, 1832
    winegrowers festival, 3147
    winter festival, 1353
    yodeling ritual, 2126
SXSW (South by Southwest), 2891
SXSW (South by Southwest) Film, 2892
Sydney Festival, 2893

Numbers in the index refer to entry numbers, not page numbers

Sydney Film Festival, 2894
Sydney Gay and Lesbian Mardi Gras, 2895
Sydney, Australia, 0311
swords, 1918
Symphony Splash, 0401
Syria
    arts festival, 0373
    Christmas, 0627
    independence celebration, 2897
    martyrs' commemoration, 2896
    military commemoration, 2110
    religious holiday, 1059
    saint feast day, 2735
Syria Martyrs' Day, 2896
Syria National Day, 2897
syrup, 3130
Syttende Mai
    See Norway Constitution Day (Syttende Mai)
Syttende Mai Fest, 2898
Szüret, 2899

T

Ta Chiu, 2900
Ta Mo's Day, 2901
Ta'anit Esther (Fast of Esther), 2902
Tabaski
    See Id al-Adha (Feast of Sacrifice; Eid)
tableaux vivants, 0145
tabot, 2985
Tabuleiros Festival (Festa dos Tabuleiros), 2903
Tadja
    See Ashura
Taeborum (Daeboreum), 2904
taffy, 0571
Taggart, Glen L., 0088
Tagore (Rabindranath), Birthday of, 2905
Tahiti
    dance festival, 0255
    music festival, 0255
Taiiku-no-Hi, 2906
Tailte Fair (Teltown Fair), 2907
Taino Indians, 1469
    See also American Indians
Taipei Golden Horse Film Festival
    See Golden Horse Film Festival and Awards
Taiwan
    art festival, 0160
    birthday commemoration, 1817
    boat races, 0842, 3039
    Chinese Revolution commemoration, 0836
    Confucius's birthday, 0676
    film festival, 1159
    happiness festival, 1749
    love legend festival, 2572
    lunar new year, 1714
    military commemoration, 2908
    moon goddess holiday, 1870

    New Year, 2277
    peace celebration, 2909
    temple rededication festival, 0584
Taiwan Armed Forces Day, 2908
Taiwan Peace Memorial Day, 2909
Tajikistan
    independence day, 2911
    unity celebration, 2910
Tajikistan Day of National Unity, 2910
Tajikistan Independence Day, 2911
Takayama Matsuri, 2912
Take Our Daughters to Work Day, 2913
Také-no-Nobori, 2914
Taking Away of the Burden of Sin, The
    See Evamelunga
Tako-Age (Kite Flying), 2915
talcum powder pranks, 0802
talking animals, 0638
Tallgrass Film Festival, 2916
tall ships, 0337
Tam Kung Festival, 2917
Tamaseseri
    See Ball-Catching Festival (Tamaseseri)
tamborada, 0800
Tamil Nadu, 1515
Tammuz, Fast of the 17th of (Shivah Asar be-Tammuz), 2918
Tanabata (Star Festival), 2919
Tanekert
    See Cure Salée
Tangata Manu (Birdman Ceremony), 2920
Tanglewood Music Festival, 2921
Tango Festival, 2922
Tango-no-Sekku (Boys' Day Festival), 2923
Tangun Day
    See Korea National Foundation Day
Tano Festival (Dano-nal; Swing Day), 2924
Tanovic, Sejfudin, 0251
Tanzania
    film festival, 3308
    independence celebration, 2925
    masked dancing, 1873
    national holidays, 2454, 2926
Tanzania Independence Day, 2925
Tanzania Union Day, 2926
Taoist events, 1708, 1906, 2070, 2917, 2971, 3079, 3123, 2900
tapestries, 0694
Tarantula Fest and Barbecue, 2927
Tarnetar Mela, 2928
Tarpon Springs, Florida, 0941
Tarquin the Proud, 0671
Tartar invasion, 1617
Tartu Hanseatic Days, 2929
Tasmania, 2947
Tassaung Daing
    See Waso (Buddhist Rains Retreat)
Taste of Chicago, 2930
Tatarstan, 2455
Tater Days, 2931
Ta'u Fo'ou, 2932

Taungbyon Spirit Festival, 2933
Taylor, Elizabeth, 1180
Taylor, John Henry, 0402
Tazaungdaing, 2934
Taziyeh, 2935
Te Kauki Nanganga'.
    See Opening of the Underground Caves Day (Te Kauki
        Nanganga')
Tea Meeting
    See Nevis Tea Meeting
tea party festival, 0580
teacher appreciation day, 1569
Teacher's Day
    See Confucius's Birthday (Teacher's Day)
Teachers' Day in the Czech Republic, 2936
Teej (Tij; Green Teej), 2937
Tejano Conjunto Festival, 2938
Tekakwitha (Kateri) Feast Day, 2939
Telemann, Georg, 0679
Telengana, India, 0362
Tell (Wilhelm) Festival, 2940
Tell (William) Play, 2941
Tellabration, 2942
Telluride Film Festival, 2943
Telluride Hang Gliding Festival, 2944
Telluride Horror Show, 2945
Telluride Jazz Festival, 2946
Teltown Fair
    See Tailte Fair (Teltown Fair)
temple celebrations
    Myanmar, 2622
    Taiwan, 0584
Ten Days on the Island, 2947
Ten Years' War, 0735
Tenekert
    See Cure Salée
Tenjin Matsuri, 2948
Tennant Creek Show
    See Royal Shows
Tennessee
    Appalachian folk festival, 0850
    birthday commemoration, 1452
    bluegrass festival, 2652
    Carnival, 0529
    country music festival, 0706
    cultural festival, 1852
    death commemorations, 0675, 1189
    film festival, 1981
    fish festival, 3274
    food festival, 0696
    horse show, 2949
    Presley, Elvis, tribute, 0921
    rodeo, 2255
    storytelling festival, 2844
Tennessee Walking Horse National Celebration, 2949
tennis tournaments
    Australia, 0194
    England, 3230
    France, 1080

New York, 3087
    worldwide, 0768
Tenth Lunar Month Festival
    See Ngan Duan Sib (Tenth Lunar Month Festival)
Terlingua Chili Cookoff, 2950
Term Day
    See Moving Day
Terminalia, 2951
Terrell, St. John, 0730
Teshuvah, 2952
"Testament of Judas," 0391
Tet, 1018, 2953
Tet Nguyen Dan
    See Tet
Tetzlaff, Teddy, 0367
Texas
    bird festival, 0989
    birthday commemorations, 0769, 3186
    bonfires, 0881
    border events, 0561, 0567
    chili festivals, 0602, 2950
    cultural festival, 2478
    dance festival, 2293
    death commemorations, 0675, 1189
    emancipation celebrations, 0925, 1493
    film festivals, 2892, 3273
    flower show, 2957
    folk music festival, 2938
    folklife festival, 2955
    food festivals, 0602, 2680, 2950, 2954, 3191, 3279
    independence day, 2956
    labor holiday, 0568
    livestock shows, 1374, 2678
    military commemorations, 0051, 2495
    multicultural celebration, 0271
    music festivals, 0271, 1000, 0192, 2891
    pirate festival, 0408
    rattlesnake round-up, 2889
    rodeo, 2678
    state fair, 2831
    trading bazaar, 1022
    watermelon festival, 3191
Texas Citrus Fiesta, 2954
Texas Flag Day
    See Texas Independence Day
Texas Folklife Festival, 2955
Texas Heroes' Day
    See Alamo Day
Texas Independence Day, 2956
Texas Rose Festival, 2957
textile workers, 0395
Thadingyut, 2958
Thai Poosam
    See Thaipusam (Thai Poosam)
Thailand
    agriculture festival, 0426
    ancestors' ghosts festival, 2054
    animal festivals, 0910, 1907, 2175
    boat race, 3187

Numbers in the index refer to entry numbers, not page numbers

bridge commemoration, 2406
Buddhist celebrations, 0165, 1734, 2254
candle festival, 3187
constitution day, 2959
death commemoration, 2406
food festival, 3123
lighted boat festival, 1693
national holiday, 0645
new year, 2662, 2261
rice-planting ceremony, 2441
royal celebrations, 0558, 1563, 2346, 2960
Thailand Constitution Day, 2959
Thailand Coronation Day, 2960
Thaipusam (Thai Poosam), 2961
thangkas, 3089
Thanh-Minh, 2962
Thanksgiving, 2963
thanksgiving days
Grenada, 1218
Marshall Islands, 1791
Thargelia, 2964
That Luang Festival, 2965
Thay Pagoda Festival, 2966
theater festivals
See also performing arts events
ancient Greece, 0808, 0934
Australia, 0019, 0020
Croatia, 0848
England, 3295, 0400, 3065
Germany, 0841
Ireland, 1837, 0847
Kentucky, 1378
Lebanon, 0210
New York, 2046, 3085
Nigeria, 0202
Oregon, 2152
Philippines, 1920, 1923
Switzerland, 2941
"Their Grandfathers Arrive from the West Feast."
See All Souls' Day (Cochiti Pueblo)
Theosophical Society, 0339
theosophy, 0339
Theotokos, 1993
Thesmophoria, 2967
Thimithi Fire-Walking Ceremony, 2968
Thimphu Tsechu, 2969
Thingyan, 2970
Third Prince, Birthday of the, 2971
Thirteenth Amendment, 1075
Thjodhatid, 2972
Thorrablót (Thorri Banquet), 2973
Thorri Banquet
See Thorrablót (Thorri Banquet)
Thousand Miles
See Mille Miglia
Three Archbishops, Day of the, 2974
Three Choirs Festival, 2975
Three Glorious Days

See Congo Independence Day Celebration; Trois Glorieuses
Three Kings, 0935
See also Epiphany
Three Kings Day
See Día de los Tres Reyes; Epiphany, Feast of the
Three Kings Day in Indian Pueblos, 2976
Three Shrines Festival
See Sanja Matsuri (Three Shrines Festival)
Three Weeks, 2977
Three Wise Men, 0278, 0616
throats, 2707, 2770
Throwing the Hood
See Haxey Hood Game
Thumb, Tom, 0247
Thump-the-door Night
See Halloween; Halloween (Isle of Man)
Tiananmen Square Anniversary, 2978
Tiankuang Jie
See Airing the Classics
Tibet
birthday commemorations, 0753, 1675
Buddhist events, 1767, 1908, 3089
butter sculptures, 0450
devil-dancing play, 1964
evil spirits, 0835
horse racing, 1249
new year, 1702
Tichborne Dole, 2979
tidal bore festival, 2337
tigres, 0825
Tihar, 0794, 2980
Tij
See Teej (Tij; Green Teej)
Tilden, William T., 0768
timber industry festival, 1939
Time Observance Day, 2981
Time of the Ten Characteristics
See Dasa Laksana Parvan (Time of the Ten Characteristics)
time-keeping custom, 2981
Timkat
See Timqat (Timkat)
Timor Santa Cruz Massacre Day (National Youth Day), 2982
Timor-Leste
independence day, 2984
massacre commemoration, 2982
military commemoration, 2983
Timor-Leste Anniversary of the Indonesian Invasion, 2983
Timor-Leste Proclamation of Independence Day, 2984
Timqat (Timkat), 2985
Tin Hau Festival, 2986
tincunaco, 0461
Tiong-chhiu Choeh
See Mid-Autumn Festival
tip-collection day, 0386
Tiradentes
See Inconfidência Week
Tiragan, 2987

Tirana, La, 2988
Tirggel, 0580
tiropita, 0790
Tirupati Festival, 2989
Tisha be-Av, 2990
Tishrin
    See October War of Liberation Anniversary
Tito, Josip Broz, 0721
Tiurai
    See Bastille Day
Tivoli Gardens Season, 2991
Tjugondag Knut
    See St. Knut's Day
Tlaloc, 0209
To Kill a Mockingbird Annual Production, 2992
tobacco-spitting contest, 0463
Tobas, 0534
Tod Kathin
    See Thadingyut
toddlers' first walk, 0718
Togo
    independence day, 2993
    national holiday, 2994
Togo Independence Day, 2993
Togo National Liberation Day, 2994
Tohono O'odham Nation Rodeo, 2995, 3169
    See also American Indians
Toh-shiya, 2996
Toji (Winter Solstice), 2997
Tok Race of Champions Dog Sled Race, 2998
Tola, Carlos Julio Arosemena, 0888
Tollet, Paul, 0660
Tolling the Devil's Knell, 2999
Tom Sawyer Days, National, 3000
Tomatina (Tomato Battle), 3001
Tomato Battle
    See Tomatina (Tomato Battle)
tomte, 0568
Tonga
    flower festival, 3003
    historic celebrations, 3051
    independence day, 3002
    national holiday, 3004
    new year, 2932
    religious education, 2872
    royal commemoration, 2623
Tonga Constitution Day
    See Tonga National Day
Tonga Emancipation Day, 3002
Tonga Heilala Festival, 3003
Tonga National Day, 3004
Tongji
    See Dongji (Winter Solstice)
Tono Matsuri, 3005
Toowoomba Carnival of Flowers
    See Carnival of Flowers
Torah, 2632
Torch Festival, 3006
Torch Fight, 3007

Tori-no-ichi (Rooster Festival), 3008
Toro Nagashi
    See Floating Lantern Ceremony (Toro Nagashi)
Toronto Caribana (Toronto Caribbean Carnival), 3009
Toronto Caribbean Carnival
    See Toronto Caribana (Toronto Caribbean Carnival)
Toronto Industrial Exhibition
    See Canadian National Exhibition
Toronto International Film Festival, 3010
Toronto Veg Food Fest, 3011
Torta dei Fieschi, 3012
tortoises, 0581
torttuja, 0576
Toshogu Haru-No-Taisai (Great Spring Festival of the Toshogu Shrine), 3013
Tour de France, 3014
Tournament of Roses (Rose Parade), 3015
Toussaint, La
    See All Saints' Day (France)
tower jumping, 1622
Town Meeting Day, 3016
Townshend Acts, 1108
track and field
    Highland Games, 1308
    Penn Relays, 3090
    Olympic Games, 2134
    Stanga Games, 2828
trade fairs
    Alabama, 1022
    England, 1620, 2736
    Italy, 1880
    Texas, 1022
    Virginia, 1022
trade union celebration, 0898
Traditional Religions Day
    See Benin National Vodoun Day (Traditional Religions Day)
Trafalgar Day, 3017
Trail of Tears, 0612
tranquillity period, 1264
transcontinental railroad, 1162
Transfer Day, 3018
Transfiguration, Feast of the, 3019
transgression festival, 1402
Transpac Race, 3020
transportation festivals
    Ohio, 2262
    Pennsylvania, 2262
    West Virginia, 2262
Transylvania, 1210
Traunstein, Germany, 1118
travelers, 2715
Travis, William Barret, 0051
Tre Ore, 1056
tree celebrations
    Belgium, 1863
    England, 0269
    Georgia (state), 0824
    Ghana, 2206

Greece, 0748
Macedonia, 0844
Spain, 2276
Switzerland, 1832
Transylvania, 1210
United States, 0138
worshipping, 0078
Trettondag Jul
  See Epiphany (Sweden) (Trettondag Jul)
Trial of Louis Riel, 3021
triathlon, 1431
tribes, Indian.
  See American Indians
Tribeca Film Festival, 3022
Tribute of the Three Cows, 3023
Trick or Treat Night
  See Halloween
Tricky Women Festival of Animated Films, 3024
Trifon Zarezan
  See St. Tryphon's Day (Montenegro and Bulgaria)
    (Trifon Zarezan); Vinegrower's Day
Trigo, Fiesta Nacional del (National Wheat Festival), 3025
Trinidad, 0172
Trinidad and Tobago
  Caribbean community commemoration, 0500
  Carnival celebration, 3026
  children's Carnival, 1549
  Columbus, Christopher, 0812
  death commemoration, 1368
  emancipation day, 3027
  film festival, 3028
  independence day, 3029
  Indian festival, 1418
  national holiday, 3030
  religious holiday, 2685
Trinidad and Tobago Carnival, 3026
Trinidad and Tobago Emancipation Day, 0812, 3027
Trinidad and Tobago Film Festival, 3028
Trinidad and Tobago Independence Day, 3029
Trinidad and Tobago Republic Day, 3030
Trinity Sunday, 3031
Triple Crown, 0289
Triple Crown Pack Burro Races, 3032
Triumph of the Cross
  See Exaltation of the Cross, Feast of the
Trois Glorieuses, 3033
  See also Congo Independence Day Celebration
Trooping the Colour, 0917
trout, 1868
truck beauty contest, 0644
truffles, 0054
Truman, Harry S., 0148, 1075, 0770
Trumpets, Feast of, 3034
Trung Nguyen
  See Ullambana (Hungry Ghosts Festival; All Souls'
    Feast)
Trung Thursday
  See Mid-Autumn Festival
Tsagaan Sar (Mongolian New Year), 3035

Tso-Fu
  See Making Happiness Festival
Tsom Gedalyah
  See Gedaliah, Fast of (Tsom Gedalyah, Tzom
    Gedaliahu)
Tsongkhapa, 1675
Tsunahiki Matsuri, 3036
Tsurugaoka Hachiman Shrine Matsure, 3037
Tu be-Av
  See Fifteenth of Av (Tu be-Av; Hamishah Asar b'Av)
Tu Bishvat (Bi-Shevat; B'Shevat; Hamishah Asar Bishevat),
  3038
Tuan Wu (Double Fifth), 3039
Tuareg nomads, 0309, 0474, 0739
Tubman (Harriet) Annual Pilgrimage, 3040
Tucson International Mariachi Conference, 3041
Tucson Meet Yourself Festival, 3042
tug-of-wars
  Italy, 1142
  Japan, 3036, 3082
Tulip Time, 3043
Tulip Time Festival (Holland, MI), 3044
Tulsa Indian Arts Festival, 3045
Tulsidas Jayanti (Birthday of Tulsidas), 3046
Tunarama Festival, 3047
Tunisia
  cultural festivals, 0539, 2463
  food festival, 2463
  historic celebration, 3050
  independence day, 3048
  national holiday, 3049
  revolution commemoration, 3050
Tunisia Independence Day, 3048
Tunisia Republic Day, 3049
Tunisia Revolution and Youth Day, 3050
Tupou VI (King), Birthday of, 3051
Tupou VI, King of Tonga, 3051
Tura Michele Fair (Augsburg Day), 3052
Turkey
  children's days, 0597, 3053
  dancing festivals, 1861
  death commemoration, 3095
  military commemorations, 0183, 3055
  national holiday, 3054
  religious festivals, 0172, 1621
  sporting event, 3056
  spring festival, 1306
turkey buzzards, 0452
turkey festival, 0905
Turkey National Sovereignty and Children's Day, 3053
Turkey Republic Day, 3054
Turkey Victory Day, 3055
Turkish Wrestling Championships, 3056
Turkmenistan
  independence day, 3057
  national holiday, 3058
  spring festival, 1998
Turkmenistan Independence Day, 3057
Turkmenistan National Days, 3058

Numbers in the index refer to entry numbers, not page numbers

Turner, Bob, 0438
turnips, 2352
Turon, 3059
turte, 0564
Turtle Days, 3060
turtle festivals
    Hawaii, 3061
    Indiana, 3060
Turtle Independence Day, 3061
Tutsis, 0445
Tuvalu, 3062
Tuvalu Independence Day, 3062
TV-invented holiday, 1002
Twain, Mark, 0458
Twelfth, The
    See Orange Day (Orangemen's Day)
Twelfth Day
    See Epiphany, Feast of the; Twelfth Night
Twelfth Imam, Birthday of the, 3063
Twelfth Night, 3064
Twelfthtide
    See Twelfth Night
Twentieth Day
    See St. Knut's Day
Twenty-Four: Seven Theatre Festival, 3065
twigs, 0153
twins, 0545, 3066
Twins Days Festival, 3066
Tyndareus, 0545
Tynwald Ceremony, 3067
Tyre Festival, 3068
Tyvendedagen
    See St. Knut's Day
Tzom Gedaliahu
    See Gedaliah, Fast of (Tsom Gedalyah, Tzom
        Gedaliahu)

U

Uesugi Matsuri, 3069
UFO festival, 2434
Uganda
    beer festival, 1891
    death commemoration, 3073
    independence day, 3070
    massacre commemoration, 3072
    military commemoration, 3071
Uganda Independence Day, 3070
Uganda Liberation Day, 3071
Uganda Martyrs Day, 3072
Uganda National Heroes Day, 3073
Ugly Truck and Dog Contest, 0644
Uhola Festival, 3074
Ukraine
    constitution day, 3075
    fertility festival, 1596
    harvest festival, 3078
    independence day, 3076

    national holiday, 3077
    religious holiday, 0877, 2827
Ukraine Constitution Day, 3075
Ukraine Independence Day, 3076
Ukraine Unification Day (National Reunification Day), 3077
Ukrainian Harvest Festivals, 3078
Ullambana (Hungry Ghosts Festival; All Souls' Feast), 3079
Ullortuneq, 1214
Ullr Fest, 3080
Ulysses (Joyce), 0345
umbrella, 0425, 0520
Umoja Karamu, 3081
Uncle Chimney, 0629
Uncle Tom's Cabin (Stowe), 0922
Underground Railroad, 0090, 0922, 2816
Underwater Tug-of-War Festival, 3082
Unification Day, 0420
Union, admission to, 0022
Union Pacific Railroad, 1162
United Arab Emirates National Day, 3083
    United Arab Emirates (UAE) national holiday, 3083
    royal celebration, 0014
United Church of Christ (Marshall Islands), 0619
United Church of God
    Last Great Day, 1633
    Trumpets, Feast of, 3034
United Kingdom, 0669
    See also England; Great Britain; Scotland; Wales
United Nations
    biological diversity, 0319
    cooperatives commemoration, 0684
    desertification awareness, 3258
    drought awareness, 3258
    economic development awareness, 3259
    elderly commemoration, 2129
    environment celebration, 3260
    food problem awareness, 3262
    human rights, 0315
    peace celebration, 2232
    poor recognition, 0948
    population awareness, 3266
    space week, 3271
    volunteer day, 3166
    water resource commemoration, 3256
United Nations Day, 3084
United Nations Decade of Disabled Persons, 0810
United Nations Disarmament Week, 0811
United Nations Educational, Scientific and Cultural
    Organization (UNESCO), 1683
United Nations General Assembly, 1376
United Nations Week
    See United Nations Day
United Solo Theatre Festival, 3085
United States
    See also individual states abolition, 0837, 1075
    African American celebrations, 0417, 1605, 1754, 2354,
        3081
    agricultural holiday, 0138
    AIDS awareness, 3250

American Indian events, 0085, 0858, 1432, 1996, 2085, 2379, 2606, 2639, 3088
automobile racing, 0087
award ceremony, 2313
awards, 1158
bank holiday, 0240
beauty pageant, 1892
bird counting events, 1193, 1194
birthday commemorations, 1556, 1650, 1680, 1719, 1754, 2183, 2836, 3184
children's days, 0597, 1572
Christmas tree lighting, 1673
church funding, 2837
citizenship celebration, 0653
Columbus Day, 0666
constitution event, 0680
dance ceremony, 2460
daughter encouragement day, 2913
death commemorations, 1351, 1370
Election Day, 0906
emancipation celebration, 0925
environment celebrations, 0860, 1209
fathers commemoration, 0986
film festival, 1158
fire awareness, 1017
food festivals, 2180, 2203
German-American commemoration, 1121
gift-giving holiday, 2888
golf championship, 3086
grandparents commemoration, 1184
Halloween, 1267
Hispanic Heritage Month, 1314
historic celebrations, 2226, 2316, 2325, 2816, 1064
independence days, 1065, 1066
law commemoration, 1638
literary event, 2287
memorial days, 1748, 1850
military commemorations, 0148, 0968, 1587, 2332, 3162
mother-in-law day, 1929
mothers commemorations, 1155, 1930
music awards, 1176
music festival, 1917
national holidays, 0315, 1027
new year, 2024
New Year's Eve, 2035
patriotic holiday, 1707
political holiday, 1414
Reform Judaism commemoration, 2457
religious celebrations, 1636, 2162, 2197, 3228, 1064
saint feast days, 2570, 2715, 2719, 2725, 2728
scouting celebrations, 0387, 1144
shipping holiday, 1783
smoking cessation/discouragement, 1193
space commemorations, 1913, 1980
sporting events, 1688, 2414, 2874, 3086, 3087, 3270
storytelling festival, 2942
tennis tournament, 3087
Viking commemoration, 1654
women's day, 3244

workers' holidays, 1610
yacht race, 0089
United States Open Championship in Golf, 3086
United States Open Tennis, 3087
United Tribes International Powwow, 3088
Unity Day
   See German Unification Day
Universal Declaration of Human Rights, 1376
Universal Prayer Day (Dzam Ling Chi Sang), 3089
University of Coimbra, 0437
University of Pennsylvania Relay Carnival, 3090
unlucky days, 0897
unmarried women competition, 3226
Uphaliday
   See Up-Helly-Aa
Uphalie Day
   See Up-Helly-Aa
Uphalimass
   See Up-Helly-Aa
Up-Helly-Aa, 3091
Up-Helly-Day
   See Up-Helly-Aa
Uphelya
   See Up-Helly-Aa
Upper Volta
   See Burkina Faso
Uranus, 0727
urban Dionysia, 0808
urine, 0068
Urini Nal (Children's Day), 3092
Urs Ajmer Sharif, 3093
Urs of Baba Farid Shakar Ganj, 3094
Urs of Jelaluddin al-Rumi (Whirling Dervish Festival), 3095
Uruguay
   constitution day, 3096
   cowboy festival, 2560
   independence day, 3097
   water festivity, 0275
Uruguay Constitution Oath Taking Day, 3096
Uruguay Independence Day, 3097
U.S. Air Force, 1032
U.S. Air Force Thunderbirds, 0003
U.S. Army, 1032
U.S. Championships
   See United States Open Tennis
U.S. Coast Guard, 1033, 1035
U.S. Constitution, 0315
U.S. Marine Corps, 1032, 1033, 1035
U.S. Navy, 1032, 1033, 1035
U.S. Open
   See United States Open Championship in Golf; United States Open Tennis
Usokae (Bullfinch Exchange), 3098
Utah
   arts festival, 3099
   car speed records, 0367
   film festival, 2866
   historic reenactment, 1162
   Indian festival, 0088

General Index

pioneer festival, 0088
religious holiday, 1921
Utah Arts Festival, 3099
Utakai Hajime (Imperial Poem-Reading Ceremony), 3100
Ute Bear Dance, 3101
Uzbekistan
constitution day, 3102
independence day, 3103
Uzbekistan Constitution Day, 3102
Uzbekistan Independence Day, 3103

V

vaca, 0707
vagabond musicians, 0448
Vaisakh, 3104
Vaisakha, 0562
Vaitarani, 3105
Valade, Gretchen Carhartt, 0790
Valdemar (King) Day, 3106
Valentine's Day, 3107
Valle del Cauca, Colombia, 0462
Valley Forge, 0788
Valley of the Moon Vintage Festival, 3108
Valmiki Jayanti, 3109
Vaman Dwadashi, 3110
Vana Bat, 0472
Vancouver Writer's Fest, 3111
Vandalia Gathering, 3112
Vanuatu
customs day, 3113
fertility ritual, 1622
independence day, 3115
national holiday, 3114
tower jumping, 1622
unity day, 3116
Vanuatu Custom Chiefs Day, 3113
Vanuatu Father Walter Lini Day, 3114
Vanuatu Independence Day, 3115
Vanuatu Unity Day, 3116
Vappu, 3117
Vaqueros, Fiesta de los, 3118
Varahi Devi, 0792
Vardon, Harry, 0402
Varfrudagen
See Annunciation of the Lord
Vasaloppet, 3119
Vasant Panchami (Basant Panchami), 3120
Vasanth Navaratri, 3121
Vassa, 0165
See also Waso (Buddhist Rains Retreat)
Vastenavond
See Shrove Tuesday (Netherlands)
Vastla Päev
See Shrove Tuesday (Estonia)
Vatsa (Ho Khao Slak), 3122
Vaval, King, 0519
Vegetarian Festival, 3123

vegetarianism, 3011
Veille de Noël
See Christmas Eve (France) (Veille de Noël)
veils, 0474
Veldgang
See Going to the Fields (Veldgang)
Velikden
See Easter (Bulgaria)
Velikonoce, 0866
Velorio de Cruz
See Día de la Santa Cruz (Day of the Holy Cross)
Vendimia, Fiesta de la, 3124
Venezuela
Christmas Eve, 0629
cross commemoration, 0798
dancing, 0228, 0695
effigy burning, 0436
harvest festival, 0228
independence day, 3126
military commemoration, 3125
procession, 0695
religious celebrations, 0335, 0695, 0801
Venezuela Battle of Carabobo Day, 3125
Venezuela Independence Day, 3126
Venice Biennale (La Biennale), 3127
Venice Film Festival, 3128
Venice, Italy
boating regatta, 1315
Carnival, 0527
cultural celebration, 3127
film festival, 3128
jazz festival, 3143
music festival, 3143
Venice Jazz Festival (Jazz Fest Wien), 3143
Venus festival, 3150
Verdi, Giuseppe, 0880
Verdur Rock, 3129
Vermont
food festival, 3130
military commemoration, 0293
music festival, 1784
political holiday, 3016
presidential birthday, 0683
Vermont Maple Festival, 3130
Vernal Equinox, 3131
Japan, 2621
Mexico, 3132
Neopagans, 1401
Wiccans, 1401
Vernal Equinox (Chichén Itzá), 3132
Vernal Equinox Day
See Shunbun-no-Hi (Vernal Equinox Day)
Verrazano (Giovanni da) Day, 3133
Vesak (Wesak; Buddha's Birthday), 3134
Vesakha Puja, 0426
Vessantara, Prince, 0382
Veterans Day, 3135
Veterans Day (Emporia, Kansas), 3136
Veterans Homecoming (Branson, Missouri), 3137

Numbers in the index refer to entry numbers, not page numbers

Veterans Memorial anniversary (Vietnam War), 3146
Veterans Pow Wow, 3138
Victoria Day
    See Commonwealth Day
Victoria, Queen, 0669, 0733
Victory Day
    See Midsummer Day
Victory Day (Our Lady of Victories Day), 3139
Victory Day (Russia), 3140
Victory over Genocide Day
    See Cambodia Victory Day
Victory over Japan Day
    See V-J Day (Victory over Japan Day)
Vidalia Onion Festival, 3141
Vielle de la Saint Jean, La
    See St. John's Eve (France) (La Vielle de la Saint Jean)
Vienna Festival, 3142
Viernes Santo
    See Good Friday (Mexico) (Viernes Santo)
Vietnam
    autumn harvest festival, 0648
    birthday commemoration, 1318
    death commemorations, 2962, 3144
    firecrackers, 1018
    historic celebrations, 1141
    lunar new year, 1714
    military action, 2953
    moon goddess holiday, 1870
    music festival, 1678
    national holidays, 2464, 3145
    new year, 2953
    puppet festival, 2966
    royal holiday, 1612
    saint festival, 2057
    souls festival, 3079
    summer solstice, 0816
    Veterans Memorial anniversary, 3146
Vietnam Ancestors Death Anniversary, 3144
Vietnam National Day, 3145
Vietnam Veterans Memorial Anniversary, 3146
Vietnam War, 2953
Vietnamese commemoration of the Virgin Mary, 1779
Vieux Carré, 1081
Vighnesa/Vighneswara, 1099
Vigil of Easter
    See Holy Saturday
Vigil of Epiphany
    See Epiphany Eve (Austria)
Vignerons, Fête des (Winegrowers' Festival), 3147
Viking celebrations
    British Isles, 1485
    Iceland, 3148
    United States, 1654
Viking chieftain, 1087
Viking Festival, 3148
Viligia, La
    See Christmas Eve (Italy) (La Vigilia)
Viña del Mar International Song Festival, 3149
Vinalia, 3150

Vinalia Priora
    See Vinalia
Vinalia Rustica
    See Vinalia
Vincy Carnival, 3151
Vinegar Festival, International, 3152
Vinegrower's Day, 3153
Vintage Computer Festivals, 3154
Vintners' Procession, 3155
vipukelka, 1015
Virgen de Candelaria, 0482
Virgen de la Soledad
    See Our Lady of Solitude, Fiesta of
Virgen de Los Angeles Day, 3156
Virgen del Rosario, 1182
Virgen del Socavón, 0534
    Virgin Islands (U.S.)Carnival, 0526
    national holiday, 3018
    weather safety day, 1384
Virgin Mary celebrations
    Belgium, 0114, 0180
    Bolivia, 0482
    Brazil, 2159, 2170
    Costa Rica, 2168
    Dominican Republic, 0831, 0832
    El Salvador, 1044
    England, 1614
    France, 2164, 1003
    Guatemala, 0179
    Italy, 0181, 2160
    Luxembourg, 2107
    Mexico, 2163, 2166
    Missouri, 1779
    Peru, 0483, 1992
    Poland, 0331
    Portugal, 2161, 2165, 2167
    Spain, 1963, 2266, 3157
    United States (southwestern), 2162
    worldwide, 0178, 1993
Virgin of the Pillar, Feast of the, 3157
Virgin of the Rosary, 1182
Virginia
    African folk life celebration, 0838
    birthday commemorations, 1471, 3185
    bluegrass festival, 2123
    food festival, 2598
    historic commemorations, 1459, 3296
    horse-corralling festival, 0606
    jousting festival, 1489
    memorial day, 1851
    military commemorations, 0131, 1032
    pirate festival, 0337
    Scottish festival, 3158
    summer festival, 3242
Virginia Scottish Games, 3158
Vishnu, 0045, 0078, 0094, 0767, 0791, 1129, 1978, 2884
Vishu
    See Vaisakh
"Visit from St. Nicholas, A" (Moore), 0629

Numbers in the index refer to entry numbers, not page numbers

Visitation, Feast of the, 3159
Víspera de San Juan, La
    See St. John's Eve (Spain)
visual arts festivals
    See arts festivals
Visvakarma Puja, 3160
Vivaldi, Antonio, 0679
Vivid Sydney, 3161
Vixakha Bouxa
    See Vesak (Wesak; Buddha's Birthday)
V-J Day (Victory over Japan Day), 3162
Vlöggelen, 3163
Vodoun
    See Voodoo events
Vogel, Anne, 2043
Voidupuha
    See Midsummer Day
Volcanalia
    See Vulcanalia (Volcanalia)
volcano crater music concert, 0804
Volkfest, 3165
Volunteer Day for Economic and Social Development,
    International, 3166
Voodoo events
    Benin, 0292
    Haiti, 1766, 2267, 2274, 2369
    Louisiana, 0466
Voodoo Music Experience, 3167
Vossa
    See Waso (Buddhist Rains Retreat)
Voting Rights Act, 0397
Vu Lan Day
    See Ullambana (Hungry Ghosts Festival; All Souls'
        Feast)
Vulcanalia (Volcanalia), 3168
Vuzkresenie
    See Easter (Bulgaria)
Vyasa Purnima
    See Guru Purnima

W

Wadell, Tom, 1110
wafers, 0862
Wagner, Richard, 0273, 0880, 2375
Waila Festival, 3169
Waisak
    See Vesak (Wesak; Buddha's Birthday)
Waitangi Day, 3170
Wakakusayama Yaki (Mount Wakakusa Fire Festival), 3171
Wakana-setsu
    See Nanakusa Matsuri (Seven Herbs or Grasses
        Festival)
Wakes Monday
    See Horn Dance
Wales
    See also England; Great Britain; Scotland; United
        Kingdom
    Celtic holiday, 0290
    children's games, 0128
    Eisteddfod, 0742
    hobby horse parade, 1885
    literary festivals, 0899, 1294
    music festival, 0899
    rent-payment day, 2341
    saint feast day, 2719
    Saturn festival, 2536
    sporting event, 0352
Walking Day, 3172
Wall Street Panic, 0328
Wall Street Rat Race, 3173
Wall, the (Vietnam Veterans Memorial), 3146
Walloon Regional Day, 3174
    See also French Community, Feast Day of the (La fête de
        la Communauté française de Belgique)
Walpurgis Night (Walpurgisnacht), 3175
Walpurgisnacht
    See Walpurgis Night (Walpurgisnacht)
Waltrip, Michael, 0773
Wampanoag Powwow, 3176
    See also American Indians
Wanabot, 0472
Wangala (Hundred Drums Festival), 3177
War of the Restoration, 0830
Waratambar, 3178
Ward, Holcombe, 0768
Wardlow, Dennis, 0672
Warei Taisai, 3179
Warner, Seth, 0293
Warren, Lavinia, 0247
Warri Festival, National, 3180
Warsaw Autumn Festival, 3181
Warsaw International Film Festival, 3182
Wasa
    See Waso (Buddhist Rains Retreat)
Washington, Fr. John, 1064
Washakie, Chief, 1136
    Washington (state)African-American cultural festival,
        2873
    American Indian celebration, 0594
    arts festival, 0425
    boat festival, 3247
    Christmas light parade, 0704
    classical music festival, 2178
    dance festival, 2553
    film festival, 2554
    flower festival, 3183
    folk festival, 2091
    food festival, 1769, 0323
    irrigation festival, 1433
    rock music festival, 2532
    rodeos, 0918, 2135
    seagull-calling festival, 2551
    water festival, 2550
Washington, Booker T., 1295
    Washington, D.C.
    African-American pride festival, 0774

air show, 3278
    birthday commemoration, 0837
    Caribbean cultural festival, 0775
    cultural festival, 2650
    Easter egg roll, 0879
    emancipation celebration, 0926
    flower festival, 0578
    kite festival, 2651
Washington, Denzel, 0028
Washington, George, 0266, 0369, 0404, 0730, 0788, 0968, 1027
Washington State Apple Blossom Festival, 3183
Washington's Crossing of the Delaware
    See Crossing of the Delaware
Washington's (George) Birthday, 3184
Washington's (George) Birthday Celebration
    (Alexandria, Virginia), 3185
Washington's (George) Birthday Celebration (Los Dos
    Laredos), 3186
Waso (Buddhist Rains Retreat), 3187
Watch Night, 0486, 3188, 3189
Watch Night (Bolden, Georgia), 3188
Watch Night Service, 3189
water buffalo, 0495
Water Clock Festival
    See Time Observance Day
water, Easter, 0868
Water Festival
    See Agua, La Fiesta de; Reversing Current, Festival of
        the (Water Festival; Bonn Om Tuk); Thingyan
water festivals
    Australia, 1320
    Brazil, 0359
    Cambodia, 2396
    India, 1325
    Japan, 2139
    New Jersey, 3233
    Peru, 0037
    Uruguay, 0275
    Washington (state), 2550
water resource commemoration, 3256
water, thrown, 0522
water vehicle festival, 2861
Water-Drawing Festival, 3190
    See also Omizutori Matsuri (Water-Drawing Festival)
Waterer, Gladys, 0403
Waterman's Derby
    See Doggett's Coat and Badge Race
watermelon festivals
    Arkansas, 1361
    Texas, 3191
    Wisconsin, 3192
Watermelon Thump, 3191
Watermelon-Eating and Seed-Spitting Contest, 3192
Waters, Muddy, 0585
Water-Splashing Festival (Dai New Year), 3193
water-throwing, 0873
Watson, Tom, 0402
Watts Festival, 3194
Wavescape Surf Film Festival.

    See Durban International Film Festival
Wayne Chicken Show, 3195
Wazo Full Moon Day
    See Waso (Buddhist Rains Retreat)
WCSH Sidewalk Art Festival, 3196
Weadick, Guy, 0460
Weadickville, Alberta, Canada, 0460
Wear Red Day, National, 3197
weather events
    Pennsylvania, 1222
    Scotland, 0370
    Virgin Islands (U.S.), 1384
wedding ceremonies, 3198
Wedding Festivities (Galicnik, Macedonia), 3198
Wedding of the Wine and Cheese
    See Grape Festival
weeding party, 0219
Week of Solidarity with the Peoples of Non-Self-Governing
    Territories, 3199
Weifang International Kite Festival, 3200
Wein, George, 2050
Wells, Horace, 0817
Welsh recitations, 0742
Wenatchee Apple Blossom Festival
    See Washington State Apple Blossom Festival
Wesak
    See Vesak (Wesak; Buddha's Birthday)
Wesley, John, 0060, 0486
West Africa, 0172
West Bengal, India, 1583
West Germany, 1120
West Virginia
    boating festival, 0564
    bridges, 0398
    family reunions, 1292
    folk festival, 3112
    food festival, 3203
    Italian cultural festival, 3202
    lights festival, 3236
    paranormal festival, 1931
    planned town festival, 2015
    state holiday, 3201
    timber industry festival, 1939
    transportation festival, 2262
West Virginia Day, 3201
West Virginia Italian Heritage Festival, 3202
West Virginia Strawberry Festival, 3203
Western Stock Show, National, 3204
Weston, Randy, 0591
Wexford Festival Opera, 3205
Whale Festivals (Alaska), 3206
Whale Festivals (California), 3207
wheat festivals
    Argentina, 3025
    France, 3209
    Hungary, 2774
    Poland, 0840
    Romania, 3208
Wheat Harvest Festival (Provins, France), 3209

Numbers in the index refer to entry numbers, not page numbers

Wheat Harvest (Transylvania), 3208
Wheel of the Year, 0731, 1016
Whe'wahchee (He'dewachi; Dance of Thanksgiving), 3210
whimmy diddle, 0170
Whirling Dervish Festival
    See Urs of Jelaluddin al-Rumi (Whirling Dervish
      Festival)
whirling dervishes, 1861, 3095
whiskey commemoration, 2594
Whistlers Convention, International, 3211
white horse, 0780
White Nights, 3212, 3213
White Painted Woman, 0125
White Sunday, 3214
    See also Pentecost
White Tiger Band, 0042
Whit-Monday (Whitmonday), 3215
Whitsun
    See Pentecost
Whitsunday
    See Pentecost
Whitsuntide
    See Pentecost
Whole Enchilada Fiesta, 3216
Whuppity Scoorie, 3217
Wianki Festival of Wreaths, 3218
Wiccan celebrations
    Imbolc, 1406
    Mabon, 1718
    Vernal Equinox, 1401
    Yule, 3302
Wiccan covens, 0954
Wicklow Gardens Festival, 3219
Wide Open Bluegrass Festival, 3220
widows, 2729
Wielkanoc
    See Easter (Poland) (Wielkanoc)
Wielki Piatek
    See Good Friday (Poland) (Wielki Piatek)
Wiener Festwochen, 3221
Wiesbaden May Festival
    See May Festival, International
wife-carrying championships
    Finland, 3222
    Maine, 2087
Wife-Carrying World Championships, 3222
Wigilia, 3223
Wilander, Mats, 0194
Wild Horse Festival (Soma-Nomaioi), 3224
Wilderness Woman Competition, 3226
Wildlife Film Festival, International, 3227
William I, King, 1079
William Penn Commemoration Day
    See Pennsylvania Day
Williams, John, 0377
Williams (Roger) Day, 3228
Williams (Tennessee) New Orleans Literary Festival, 3229
willow branches, 0167, 1643
Willow Sunday

    See Palm Sunday
Willowswitch Saturday
    See Palm Sunday (Finland)
Willowswitch Sunday
    See Palm Sunday (Finland)
Wilson, Woodrow, 0746, 1027
Wimbledon, 3230
Wind Festival, 3231
    See also Kakadu Mahbilil Festival
Windjammer Days, 3232
Window Rock, Arizona, 1996
wine country, 1084
wine festivals
    Austria, 1304
    Bulgaria, 3153
    California, 3108, 2663
    Colorado, 0174
    Cyprus, 1679
    France, 3033, 1185
    Germany, 0218, 1681
    Italy, 1780
    Louisiana, 2020
    South Carolina, 0565
    Spain, 3124, 1287
    Switzerland, 3147
winemakers' procession, 3155
Winging Ceremony
    See Vlöggelen
Wings 'n Water Festival, 3233
Wings Over the Platte
    See Crane Watch
Winnipeg Folk Festival, 3234
Winston 500, 3235
winter clothes, 2563
Winter Feast
    See Maidyarem (Maidhyairya; Mid-Year or Winter Fest)
Winter Festival of Lights, 3236
winter festivals
    Alaska, 0097, 2089
    Australia, 1682
    Canada, 2344, 3239
    Colorado, 3080
    Finland, 1202
    India, 1692
    Minnesota, 2797
    Netherlands, 0346
    New Hampshire, 0763
    Niger, 0309
    Norway, 1202
    Ontario, 3239
    Pakistan, 0563
    Quebec, 2344
    Russia, 2450
    Sweden, 1202
    Switzerland, 1353
Winter Solstice, 3237
    ancient Rome, 2535
    China, 3238
    England, 3064

Japan, 2997
Korea, 0833
Peru, 1424
worldwide, 3237
Winter Solstice (China), 3238
winter sports
Canada, 0499
Northwest Territories, 0499
Norway, 0872
Sweden, 0876
Winterlude, 3239
Wisakha Bucha
See Vesak (Wesak; Buddha's Birthday)
Wisconsin
aircraft convention, 0041
bonfires, 1087
cheese festival, 3240
circus, 1196
food festival, 2593
juggling festival, 1729
lumberjack festival, 1713
parade, 1196
Scandinavian festival, 1087
ski race, 0082
sporting event, 2288
Swiss festivals, 1296, 2940, 3165
watermelon-eating/spitting contest, 3192
Wisconsin Cheese Curd Festival, 3240
wisdom, 1099
Wise, Isaac Mayer, 2457
witch doctors, 0534
witches
Czech Republic, 1829
Germany, 0935, 3175
Italy, 0278
Sweden, 0876
Wizard of Oz Festival, 3241
Wolf Trap Summer Festival Season, 3242
Wolfe (Thomas) Festival, 3243
Women Cooks' Festival
See Cuisinières, Fête des la
women filmmakers, 0029
women's celebrations
Estonia, 2711
Hindu religion, 2877
Women's Day, International, 3244
women's festivals
ancient Rome, 1495
India, 1101, 1175
Romania, 2427
Rome, 0361
women's military reenactment, 1845
women's rights events
South Africa, 2670
United States, 0117, 2829
women's suffrage movement, 0117, 2829
women's virtue celebration, 0647
Wood (Grant) Art Festival, 3245
Wood (Henry) Promenade Concerts, 3246

Wood, Pat, 0194
Woodcraft Indians, 0387
Wooden Boat Festival, 3247
wooden boxes, 0528
woods ceremony, 2562
Woodson, Carter G., 0330
Woodward Dream Cruise, 3248
Wooing a Bride Ceremony
See Brauteln
wool, 1161
workers' holidays
India, 3160
United States, 1610
Workers' Party of North Korea, Founding of the, 3249
World AIDS Day, 3250
World Champion Bathtub Race, 3251
World Championship Crab Races, 3252
World Championship Flat Water Endurance Race
See General Clinton Canoe Regatta
World Championship Hoop Dance Contest, 3253
World Championship Steak Cookoff.
See Magnolia Blossom Festival
World Creole Music Festival, 3254
World Cup, 3255
World Day for Water, 3256
World Day of Prayer, 3257
World Day to Combat Desertification and Drought, 3258
World Development Information Day, 3259
World Environment Day, 3260
World Eskimo-Indian Olympics, 3261
World Food Day, 3262
World Invocation Day (Festival of Goodwill), 3263
World Malaria Day, 3264
world music festival, 2360
World of Speed
See Bonneville Speed Week
World Peace Festival, 3265
World Population Day, 3266
World Religion Day, 3267
World Rock Paper Scissors Championship, 3268
World Santa Claus Congress, 3269
World Series, 3270
World Space Week, 3271
World Students' Day
See Students' Fight for Freedom and Democracy, Day of (Struggle for Freedom and Democracy; World Students' Day)
World Trade Center, 2226
World War I, 0177, 3135
World War II
Allies, 3162
Arkansas, 1719
Australia, 0360
England, 0968
Hawaii, 1040, 2234
Japan, 1313
Kiribati, 2146
Malta, 0177, 3139
Philippines, 0259

Russia, 3140
Taiwan, 2908
Thailand, 2406
World Wristwrestling Championships, 3272
WorldFest-Houston International Film Festival, 3273
Worldloppet, 0082
World's Biggest Fish Fry, 3274
World's Championship Duck-Calling Contest and Wings
    Over the Prairie Festival, 3275
World's Largest Salmon Barbecue, 3276
worm festival, 1389
Wrangler National Finals Rodeo, 3277
Wren, Christopher, 0929
wrestling
    ancient Rome, 2283, 2422
    England, 1188
    Mongolia, 1966
    Sweden, 2828
    Turkey, 3056
Wright Brothers Day, 3278
Wright, Ed, 0034
Wright, Orville, 0199
Wright, Richard Robert, Sr., 1075
wristwrestling, 3272
Wurstfest (Sausage Festival), 3279
Wuwuchim, 3280
Wyoming
    American Indian religious ceremony, 1987
    animal festival, 1451
    dancing, 0135
    historic reenactments, 1136, 1212, 1938
    rodeo, 0582

X

Xilonen, Festival of, 3281
Xipe Totec, Festival of, 3282
Xiquets de Valls
    See Human Towers of Valls

Y

yaake, 1112
yachting events
    California, 3020
    Connecticut, 0122
    Hawaii, 3020
    New Zealand, 0089
    United States, 0089
Yack Bob Day
    See Shick-Shack Day (Shik-Shak Day, Shicsack Day,
        Shig-Shag Day)
Yakima Indians, 0918
Yakut region, 3298
Yale Bologna, 0357
Yale-Harvard Regatta, 3283

Yam Festival at Aburi, 3284
Yama, 1976
yama floats, 1143
yams, 1766, 2022
Yancunú, Fiesta del, 3285
Yaqui Indians, 0878, 2520
    See also American Indians
Yarmouth Clam Festival, 3286
yaselko, 0616
Yaya Matsuri (Shouting Festival), 3287
yazata, 0001, 0017, 1074
Ybor City, Florida, 1004
Ye Mystic Krewe, 1107
Yellow Daisy Festival, 3288
Yemanjá Festival, 3289
Yemen
    independence day, 3290
    revolution commemoration, 3291
Yemen Independence and National Days, 3290
Yemen Revolution Days, 3291
Yenaandi
    See Nyambinyambi
Yevmi Ashurer
    See Ashura
Yi Dynasty, 0613
Yi festival, 3006
Yi Mongnyong, 0647
Yi Sun-shin, 0607, 1195
yodeling, 1480, 2126
Yodeling Festivals
    See Jodlerfests (Yodeling Festivals)
Yolngu, 1106
Yom ha-Atzma'ut
    See Israel Independence Day
Yom ha-Din
    See Yom Kippur
Yom ha-Shoah
    See Holocaust Memorial Day
Yom ha-Zikkaron, 3292
Yom Kippur, 3293
Yom Kippur War, 0147
Yom Yerushalayim, 3294
York Festival and Mystery Plays, 3295
Yorktown Day, 3296
Yoruba people, 2022, 2113
Young's (Brigham) Birthday, 3297
Youth and Sports Day
    See Atatürk Remembrance (Youth and Sports Day)
Ysaÿe, Eugène, 0916
Ysyakh, 3298
Yuan Hsiao Chieh
    See Lantern Festival (Yuan Hsiao Chieh)
Yuan Tan
    See Lunar New Year
Yuchi tribe, 0719, 0858
Yudu Nal, 3299
Yue Lan
    See Ullambana (Hungry Ghosts Festival; All Souls'
        Feast)

Numbers in the index refer to entry numbers, not page numbers

Yugoslavia
 See also Bosnia and Herzegovina
 Children's Day, 0595
 saint feast day, 2808
Yuki Matsuri
 See Sapporo Snow Festival (Yuki Matsuri)
Yukigassen Festival, 3300
Yukon International Storytelling Festival, 3301
Yukon Territory
 Gold Rush festival, 1575
 sporting event, 1576
 storytelling festival, 3301
Yule, 3302
Yule Day
 See Yule
Yule log, 0616, 0636, 1499
Yuma Lettuce Days, 3303

Z

Zagar, Mirna, 0759
Zagreb, Croatia, 0759
Zaire, 0785
Zambia
 agricultural commemoration, 3304
 dancing festival, 2001
 flooding festival, 1595
 independence day, 3306
 Liberation, 0030
 masked dancing, 1873
 national holiday, 3305
 unity day, 3307
Zambia Farmers Day, 3304
Zambia Heroes Day, 3305
Zambia Independence Day, 3306
Zambia Unity Day, 3307
zampognari, 0636
Zanzibar Revolution Day, 3309
Zaragoza, Ignacio, 0649
Zarathushtra, 0001, 0017
Zarthastno Diso, 3310
Zeus, 0384, 0545, 0727, 0748, 0808
Zhonghe Festival.

 See Blue Dragon Festival (Zhonghe Festival)
ziarats, 0136
Zimbabwe
 death commemoration, 3312
 independence day, 3313
 masked dancing, 1873
 military commemoration, 3311
 unity day, 3314
Zimbabwe Defense Forces Day, 3311
Zimbabwe Heroes' Day, 3312
Zimbabwe Independence Day, 3313
Zimbabwe National Unity Day, 3314
Zora! Festival
 See Hurston (Zora Neale) Festival of the Arts and
  Humanities
Zoroastrian New Year
 See Jamshed Navaroz (Jamshed Navroz)
Zoroastrian religion
 Aban Parab, 0001
 Abar Parab, 0017
 Amurdad, Feast of, 0092
 Ardwahist, Feast of, 0140
 Ayathrem, 0203
 Dae, Feasts of, 0747
 Farvardegan Days, 0979
 Frawardignan, 1074
 Hordad, Feast of, 1365
 Khordad Sal, 1547
 Maidyarem, 1742
 Maidyoshahem, 1743
 Maidyozarem, 1744
 Mihragan, 1879
 Mithra, Feast of, 1893
 Paitishahem, 2184
 Shahrewar, Feast of, 2583
 Sizdah Bedar, 2644
 Spendarmad, Feast of, 2682
 Tiragan, 2987
 Vohuman, Feast of, 3164
 Zarthastno Diso, 3310
Zurich Festival, 3315
Zwetschgenmannlein, 0557
Zwiebelmarkt (Onion Market), 3316
Zydeco Music Festival (Southwest Louisiana), 3317